with MyEconLab®

- **Learning Catalytics**—Generates classroom discussion, guides lectures, and promotes peer-to-peer learning with real-time analytics. Students can use any device to interact in the classroom, engage with content, and even draw and share graphs.

- **Real-Time Data Analysis Exercises**—Using current macro data to help students understand the impact of changes in economic variables, Real-Time Data Analysis Exercises communicate directly with the Federal Reserve Bank of St. Louis's FRED® site and update as new data are available.

- **Current News Exercises**—Every week, current microeconomic and macroeconomic news stories, with accompanying exercises, are posted to MyEconLab. Assignable and auto-graded, these multi-part exercises ask students to recognize and apply economic concepts to real-world events.

- **Experiments**—Flexible, easy-to-assign, auto-graded, and available in Single and Multiplayer versions, Experiments in MyEconLab make learning fun and engaging.

- **Reporting Dashboard**—View, analyze, and report learning outcomes clearly and easily. Available via the Gradebook and fully mobile-ready, the Reporting Dashboard presents student performance data at the class, section, and program levels in an accessible, visual manner.

- **LMS Integration**—Link from any LMS platform to access assignments, rosters, and resources, and synchronize MyLab grades with your LMS gradebook. For students, new direct, single sign-on provides access to all the personalized learning MyLab resources that make studying more efficient and effective.

- **Mobile Ready**—Students and instructors can access multimedia resources and complete assessments right at their fingertips, on any mobile device.

PEARSON

Economics

The Pearson Series in Economics

Abel/Bernanke/Croushore
*Macroeconomics**

Acemoglu/Laibson/List
*Economics**

Bade/Parkin
*Foundations of Economics**

Berck/Helfand
The Economics of the Environment

Bierman/Fernandez
Game Theory with Economic Applications

Blanchard
*Macroeconomics**

Blau/Ferber/Winkler
The Economics of Women, Men, and Work

Boardman/Greenberg/Vining/Weimer
Cost-Benefit Analysis

Boyer
Principles of Transportation Economics

Branson
Macroeconomic Theory and Policy

Bruce
Public Finance and the American Economy

Carlton/Perloff
Modern Industrial Organization

Case/Fair/Oster
*Principles of Economics**

Chapman
Environmental Economics: Theory, Application, and Policy

Cooter/Ulen
Law & Economics

Daniels/VanHoose
International Monetary & Financial Economics

Downs
An Economic Theory of Democracy

Ehrenberg/Smith
Modern Labor Economics

Farnham
Economics for Managers

Folland/Goodman/Stano
The Economics of Health and Health Care

Fort
Sports Economics

Froyen
Macroeconomics

Fusfeld
The Age of the Economist

Gerber
*International Economics**

González-Rivera
Forecasting for Economics and Business

Gordon
*Macroeconomics**

Greene
Econometric Analysis

Gregory
Essentials of Economics

Gregory/Stuart
Russian and Soviet Economic Performance and Structure

Hartwick/Olewiler
The Economics of Natural Resource Use

Heilbroner/Milberg
The Making of the Economic Society

Heyne/Boettke/Prychitko
The Economic Way of Thinking

Holt
Markets, Games, and Strategic Behavior

Hubbard/O'Brien
*Economics**

*Money, Banking, and the Financial System**

Hubbard/O'Brien/Rafferty
*Macroeconomics**

Hughes/Cain
American Economic History

Husted/Melvin
International Economics

Jehle/Reny
Advanced Microeconomic Theory

Johnson-Lans
A Health Economics Primer

Keat/Young/Erfle
Managerial Economics

Klein
Mathematical Methods for Economics

Krugman/Obstfeld/Melitz
*International Economics: Theory & Policy**

Laidler
The Demand for Money

Leeds/von Allmen
The Economics of Sports

Leeds/von Allmen/Schiming
*Economics**

Lynn
Economic Development: Theory and Practice for a Divided World

Miller
*Economics Today**

Understanding Modern Economics

Miller/Benjamin
The Economics of Macro Issues

Miller/Benjamin/North
The Economics of Public Issues

Mills/Hamilton
Urban Economics

Mishkin
*The Economics of Money, Banking, and Financial Markets**

*The Economics of Money, Banking, and Financial Markets, Business School Edition**

*Macroeconomics: Policy and Practice**

Murray
Econometrics: A Modern Introduction

O'Sullivan/Sheffrin/Perez
*Economics: Principles, Applications and Tools**

Parkin
*Economics**

Perloff
*Microeconomics**

*Microeconomics: Theory and Applications with Calculus**

Perloff/Brander
*Managerial Economics and Strategy**

Phelps
Health Economics

Pindyck/Rubinfeld
*Microeconomics**

Riddell/Shackelford/Stamos/Schneider
Economics: A Tool for Critically Understanding Society

Roberts
The Choice: A Fable of Free Trade and Protection

Rohlf
Introduction to Economic Reasoning

Roland
Development Economics

Scherer
Industry Structure, Strategy, and Public Policy

Schiller
The Economics of Poverty and Discrimination

Sherman
Market Regulation

Stock/Watson
Introduction to Econometrics

Studenmund
Using Econometrics: A Practical Guide

Tietenberg/Lewis
Environmental and Natural Resource Economics
Environmental Economics and Policy

Todaro/Smith
Economic Development

Waldman/Jensen
Industrial Organization: Theory and Practice

Walters/Walters/Appel/Callahan/Centanni/Maex/O'Neill
Econversations: Today's Students Discuss Today's Issues

Weil
Economic Growth

Williamson
Macroeconomics

*denotes MyEconLab titles   Visit www.myeconlab.com to learn more.

Economics

Sixth Edition

R. Glenn Hubbard
Columbia University

Anthony Patrick O'Brien
Lehigh University

PEARSON

Boston Columbus Indianapolis New York San Francisco
Amsterdam Cape Town Dubai London Madrid Milan Munich Paris Montréal Toronto
Delhi Mexico City São Paulo Sydney Hong Kong Seoul Singapore Taipei Tokyo

Vice President, Business Publishing: Donna Battista
Executive Editor: David Alexander
Executive Development Editor: Lena Buonanno
Editorial Assistant: Michelle Zeng
Vice President, Product Marketing: Maggie Moylan
Director of Marketing, Digital Services and Products: Jeanette Koskinas
Senior Product Marketing Manager: Alison Haskins
Field Marketing Manager: Ramona Elmer
Product Marketing Assistant: Jessica Quazza
Team Lead, Program Management: Ashley Santora
Program Manager: Lindsey Sloan
Team Lead, Project Management: Jeff Holcomb
Project Manager: Carla Thompson
Operations Specialist: Carol Melville
Creative Director: Blair Brown
Art Director: Jon Boylan
Vice President, Director of Digital Strategy and Assessment: Paul Gentile
Manager of Learning Applications: Paul DeLuca
Digital Editor: Denise Clinton
Director, Digital Studio: Sacha Laustsen
Digital Studio Manager: Diane Lombardo
Digital Studio Project Manager: Melissa Honig
Digital Studio Project Manager: Robin Lazrus
Digital Content Team Lead: Noel Lotz
Digital Content Project Lead: Courtney Kamauf
Full-Service Project Management and Composition: Cenveo® Publisher Services
Interior Designer: Cenveo Publisher Services
Cover Designer: Jon Boylan
Cover Art: © Oleksiy Mark/Fotolia
Printer/Binder: RR Donnelley / Willard
Cover Printer: Phoenix Color / Hagerstown

Library of Congress Cataloging-in-Publication Data

Names: Hubbard, R. Glenn, author. | O'Brien, Anthony Patrick, author.
Title: Economics / R. Glenn Hubbard, Columbia University, Anthony Patrick O'Brien, Lehigh University.
Description: Sixth Edition. | Boston : Pearson, 2015. | Revised edition of the authors' Economics. | Includes bibliographical references and index.
Identifiers: LCCN 2015043546| ISBN 9780134105840 | ISBN 0134105842
Subjects: LCSH: Economics—Textbooks.
Classification: LCC HB171.5 .H79 2015 | DDC 330—dc23
LC record available at http://lccn.loc.gov/2015043546

10 9 8 7 6 5 4 3 2 1

PEARSON

ISBN 10: 0-13-410584-2
ISBN 13: 978-0-13-410584-0

For Constance, Raph, and Will

—R. Glenn Hubbard

For Cindy, Matthew, Andrew, and Daniel

—Anthony Patrick O'Brien

ABOUT THE **AUTHORS**

Glenn Hubbard, policymaker, professor, and researcher. R. Glenn Hubbard is the dean and Russell L. Carson Professor of Finance and Economics in the Graduate School of Business at Columbia University and professor of economics in Columbia's Faculty of Arts and Sciences. He is also a research associate of the National Bureau of Economic Research and a director of Automatic Data Processing, Black Rock Closed-End Funds, and MetLife. He received his Ph.D. in economics from Harvard University in 1983. From 2001 to 2003, he served as chairman of the White House Council of Economic Advisers and chairman of the OECD Economic Policy Committee, and from 1991 to 1993, he was deputy assistant secretary of the U.S. Treasury Department. He currently serves as co-chair of the nonpartisan Committee on Capital Markets Regulation. Hubbard's fields of specialization are public economics, financial markets and institutions, corporate finance, macroeconomics, industrial organization, and public policy. He is the author of more than 100 articles in leading journals, including *American Economic Review, Brookings Papers on Economic Activity, Journal of Finance, Journal of Financial Economics, Journal of Money, Credit, and Banking, Journal of Political Economy, Journal of Public Economics, Quarterly Journal of Economics, RAND Journal of Economics*, and *Review of Economics and Statistics*. His research has been supported by grants from the National Science Foundation, the National Bureau of Economic Research, and numerous private foundations.

Tony O'Brien, award-winning professor and researcher. Anthony Patrick O'Brien is a professor of economics at Lehigh University. He received his Ph.D. from the University of California, Berkeley, in 1987. He has taught principles of economics for more than 20 years, in both large sections and small honors classes. He received the Lehigh University Award for Distinguished Teaching. He was formerly the director of the Diamond Center for Economic Education and was named a Dana Foundation Faculty Fellow and Lehigh Class of 1961 Professor of Economics. He has been a visiting professor at the University of California, Santa Barbara, and the Graduate School of Industrial Administration at Carnegie Mellon University. O'Brien's research has dealt with issues such as the evolution of the U.S. automobile industry, the sources of U.S. economic competitiveness, the development of U.S. trade policy, the causes of the Great Depression, and the causes of black–white income differences. His research has been published in leading journals, including *American Economic Review, Quarterly Journal of Economics, Journal of Money, Credit, and Banking, Industrial Relations, Journal of Economic History*, and *Explorations in Economic History*. His research has been supported by grants from government agencies and private foundations.

BRIEF CONTENTS

CONTENTS

*These end-of-chapter resource materials repeat in all chapters. Select chapters also include Real-Time Data Exercises.

FLEXIBILITY CHART

The following chart helps you organize your syllabus based on your teaching preferences and objectives:

Core	Optional	Policy
Chapter 1: Economics: Foundations and Models	**Chapter 1 Appendix:** Using Graphs and Formulas	
Chapter 2: Trade-offs, Comparative Advantage, and the Market System		
Chapter 3: Where Prices Come From: The Interaction of Demand and Supply		
	Chapter 4 Appendix: Quantitative Demand and Supply Analysis	**Chapter 4:** Economic Efficiency, Government Price Setting, and Taxes
		Chapter 5: Externalities, Environmental Policy, and Public Goods
Chapter 6: Elasticity: The Responsiveness of Demand and Supply		
		Chapter 7: The Economics of Health Care
	Chapter 8: Firms, the Stock Market, and Corporate Governance	
	Chapter 8 Appendix: Tools to Analyze Firms' Financial Information	
Chapter 9: Comparative Advantage and the Gains from International Trade		
	Chapter 10: Consumer Choice and Behavioral Economics	
	Chapter 10 Appendix: Using Indifference Curves and Budget Lines to Understand Consumer Behavior	
Chapter 11: Technology, Production, and Costs	**Chapter 11 Appendix:** Using Isoquants and Isocost Lines to Understand Production and Cost	
Chapter 12: Firms in Perfectly Competitive Markets		
Chapter 13: Monopolistic Competition: The Competitive Model in a More Realistic Setting		
Chapter 14: Oligopoly: Firms in Less Competitive Markets		
Chapter 15: Monopoly and Antitrust Policy		
	Chapter 16: Pricing Strategy	

Core	Optional	Policy
Chapter 17: The Markets for Labor and Other Factors of Production		
		Chapter 18: Public Choice, Taxes, and the Distribution of Income
Chapter 19: GDP: Measuring Total Production and Income		
Chapter 20: Unemployment and Inflation		
Chapter 21: Economic Growth, the Financial System, and Business Cycles		
Chapter 22: Long-Run Economic Growth: Sources and Policies		
	Chapter 23: Aggregate Expenditure and Output in the Short Run	
	Chapter 23 Appendix: The Algebra of Macroeconomic Equilibrium	
Chapter 24: Aggregate Demand and Aggregate Supply Analysis		
	Chapter 24 Appendix: Macroeconomic Schools of Thought	
Chapter 25: Money, Banks, and the Federal Reserve System		
		Chapter 26: Monetary Policy
	Chapter 27 Appendix: A Closer Look at the Multiplier	**Chapter 27:** Fiscal Policy
		Chapter 28: Inflation, Unemployment, and Federal Reserve Policy
	Chapter 29: Macroeconomics in an Open Economy	
	Chapter 30: The International Financial System	
	Chapter 30 Appendix: The Gold Standard and the Bretton Woods System	

PREFACE

Our approach in this new edition remains what it was in the first edition, published more than 10 years ago: To provide students and instructors with an economics text that delivers complete economics coverage with many real-world business examples. Our goal has been to teach economics in a "widget-free" way by using real-world business and policy examples. We are gratified by the enthusiastic response from students and instructors who have used the first five editions of this book and who have made it one of the best-selling economics textbooks on the market.

Much has happened in the U.S. and world economies since we prepared the previous edition. We have incorporated many of these developments in the new real-world examples in this edition and also in the digital resources.

Digital Resources

While our basic approach of placing applications in the forefront of the discussion remains the same, this new edition has been thoroughly revised. We have a wide array of digital resources for students and instructors to use with either the eText version of the book or the MyEconLab supplement to the printed text. Below is an overview. Please see Preface pages 15–19 for more details.

Digital Features Located in MyEconLab

MyEconLab is a unique online course management, testing, and tutorial resource. It is included with the eText version of the book or as a supplement to the print book. Students and instructors will find the following online resources to accompany the sixth edition:

- **Videos.** There are more than 100 *Making the Connection* features in the book that provide real-world reinforcement of key concepts. Each feature is accompanied by a two- or three-minute video of the author explaining the key point of that *Making the Connection*. Related assessment is included with each video, so students can test their understanding. The goal of these videos is to summarize key content and bring the applications to life. In our experience, many students benefit from this type of online learning and assessment.
- **Concept Checks.** Each section of each learning objective concludes with an online Concept Check that contains one or two multiple-choice, true/false, or fill-in questions. These checks act as "speed bumps" that encourage students to stop and check their understanding of fundamental terms and concepts before moving on to the next section. The goal of this digital resource is to help students assess their progress on a section-by-section basis, so they can be better prepared for homework, quizzes, and exams.
- **Animations.** Graphs are the backbone of introductory economics, but many students struggle to understand and work with them. Each of the 267 numbered figures in the text has a supporting animated version online. The goal of this digital resource is to help students understand shifts in curves, movements along curves, and changes in equilibrium values. Having an animated version of a graph helps students who have difficulty interpreting the static version in the printed text. Graded practice exercises are included with the animations. In our experience, many students benefit from this type of online learning.
- **Interactive *Solved Problems*.** Many students have difficulty applying economic concepts to solving problems. The goal of this digital resource is to help students overcome this hurdle by giving them a model of how to solve an economic problem by breaking it down step by step. Each of the 60 *Solved Problems* in the printed text is accompanied by a similar problem online, so students can have more practice and build their

problem-solving skills. These interactive tutorials help students learn to think like economists and apply basic problem-solving skills to homework, quizzes, and exams. The goal is for students to build skills they can use to analyze real-world economic issues they hear and read about in the news. Each *Solved Problem* in MyEconLab and the digital eText also includes at least one additional graded practice exercise for students.

- **Graphs Updated with Real-Time Data from FRED.** Approximately 25 graphs are continuously updated online with the latest available data from FRED (Federal Reserve Economic Data), which is a comprehensive, up-to-date data set maintained by the Federal Reserve Bank of St. Louis. Students can display a pop-up graph that shows new data plotted in the graph. The goal of this digital feature is to help students understand how to work with data and understand how including new data affects graphs.
- **Interactive Problems and Exercises Updated with Real-Time Data from FRED.** The end-of-chapter problems in select chapters include *Real-Time Data Exercises* that use the latest data from FRED. The book contains more than 50 of these exercises. The goals of this digital feature are to help students become familiar with this key data source, learn how to locate data, and develop skills in interpreting data.

New to the Sixth Edition Chapters

- All companies in the chapter openers have been either replaced with new companies or updated with current information.
- Chapters 1–4 include new *An Inside Look* news articles and analyses to help students apply economic thinking to current events and policy debates. Additional news articles and analyses are updated weekly on MyEconLab.
- There are 38 new *Making the Connection* features to help students tie economic concepts to current events and policy issues.
- There are 16 new *Solved Problems*. This feature helps students break down and answer economic problems step by step.

New Chapter Openers, *Making the Connections*, *Solved Problems*, and *Inside Looks*

Here are the new or heavily revised chapter-opening business cases and accompanying *Inside Look* news articles. The business or issue introduced in the chapter opener is revisited within the chapter in either a *Making the Connection* or a *Solved Problem*. The following are new to this edition. Please see the detailed table of contents for the list of features for all chapters.

Chapter 1, "Economics: Foundations and Models," opens with a new discussion of whether smart devices will revolutionize health care and closes with *An Inside Look* newspaper article and analysis of how Google is adding to its growing list of technological innovations by partnering with Swiss pharmaceutical company Novartis to develop smart contact lenses to help patients manage diabetes. New *Solved Problem 1.1* examines how managers at medical technology firm OraSure use marginal analysis to make an advertising decision. A new *Making the Connection* examines how opportunity costs can help us understand why many students have stopped attending college football games.

Chapter 2, "Trade-offs, Comparative Advantage, and the Market System," opens with a new discussion of the manufacturing decisions managers at Tesla Motors face and closes with *An Inside Look* that discusses the resources Apple has assembled to meet an aggressive plan to develop and produce an electric vehicle as early as 2020. A new *Making the Connection* uses Sir Arthur Conan Doyle's legendary character Sherlock Holmes to illustrate copyright laws for books and movies.

Chapter 3, "Where Prices Come From: The Interaction of Demand and Supply," opens with a new discussion of the market for smartwatches and closes with *An Inside Look* that examines how the Apple smartwatch is inspiring the development of other wearable devices. There are three new *Making the Connections*: "Are Smartwatches Substitutes for Smartphones?"; "Tough Times for Big Macs and Golf"; and "Demand and Supply Trashes Plastic Recycling."

Chapter 4, "Economic Efficiency, Government Price Setting, and Taxes," opens with an updated discussion of how Airbnb and the sharing economy affects rent control policy in San Francisco and closes with *An Inside Look* that examines why government officials in Malibu, California, imposed a tax on short-term rentals of apartments booked through Airbnb. A new *Making the Connection* examines why investors expect Uber to be very profitable.

Chapter 5, "Externalities, Environmental Policy, and Public Goods," opens with a new discussion of President Obama's Clean Power Plan. A new *Making the Connection* uses the frequent conflicts between passengers over reclining airline seats to illustrate property rights.

Chapter 6, "Elasticity: The Responsiveness of Demand and Supply," opens with a revised and updated discussion of the price elasticity of gasoline. A new *Making the Connection* discusses why Amazon cares about price elasticity.

Chapter 7, "The Economics of Health Care," opens with a new discussion of how the Patient Protection and Affordable Care Act of 2010 could affect the health care plan at T. Cain Grocery, which operates five Piggly Wiggly supermarkets in Alabama and Florida. New *Solved Problem 7.4* shows students how to use the demand and supply model to explain changes in health care spending. A new *Making the Connection* discusses the increasing importance of health care in the U.S. economy.

Chapter 8, "Firms, the Stock Market, and Corporate Governance," opens with a new discussion of Twitter and the benefits and costs of becoming a publicly owned firm. New *Solved Problem 8.2* analyzes why Warren Buffett likes mutual funds, and new *Solved Problem 8.4* discusses whether Dodd-Frank will improve corporate governance. There are two new *Making the Connections*: "Why Are Fewer Young People Starting Businesses?" and "Why Are Many People Poor Stock Market Investors?"

Chapter 9, "Comparative Advantage and the Gains from International Trade," opens with a new discussion of President Obama, Nike, and the Trans-Pacific Partnership (TPP). There are three new *Making the Connections*: "Would New Balance Be Helped or Hurt by the Trans-Pacific Partnership?"; "Smoot-Hawley, the Politics of Tariffs, and Protecting a Vanishing Industry"; and "Protecting Consumer Health or Protecting U.S. Firms from Competition?"

Chapter 10, "Consumer Choice and Behavioral Economics," opens with an updated discussion of a failed pricing strategy at J. C. Penney. A new *Making the Connection* discusses whether Uber is price gouging by charging more when demand for rides is high.

Chapter 11, "Technology, Production, and Costs," opens with a new discussion of MOOCs (massive open online courses). A new *Making the Connection* explains how UPS adopted new technology to deliver more packages with the same number of workers and planes. A new *Solved Problem* in the appendix discusses how firms respond to differences in input price ratios.

Chapter 12, "Firms in Perfectly Competitive Markets," opens with a new discussion of cage-free eggs. New *Solved Problem 12.4* examines when managers should shut down an oil well.

Chapter 13, "Monopolistic Competition: The Competitive Model in a More Realistic Setting," opens with a new discussion of the sources of Chipotle Mexican Grill's success. There are two new *Making the Connections*: "Is the Trend toward Healthy Eating a Threat to Chipotle's Market Niche?" and "Are All Cupcakes the Same?" New *Solved Problem 13.3* examines Buffalo Wild Wings' strategy to differentiate its restaurants.

Chapter 14, "Oligopoly: Firms in Less Competitive Markets," opens with a new discussion of Apple, Spotify, and the music streaming revolution. The chapter includes two new *Making the Connections*: "Hard Times in Atlantic City" and "Do Airlines Collude on Capacity to Keep Prices High?"

Chapter 15, "Monopoly and Antitrust Policy," includes a new *Making the Connection* that examines whether the National Collegiate Athletic Association (NCAA) should be considered a monopoly. New *Solved Problem 15.5* shows students how to determine a pricing strategy for a MOOC (massive open online course).

Chapter 16, "Pricing Strategy," opens with new coverage of Walt Disney's MagicBands and how the company uses "big data" to help determine pricing. A new *Making the Connection* illustrates how clothing manufacturers can segment their sales by using outlet stores.

Chapter 17, "The Markets for Labor and Other Factors of Production," opens with a new discussion of how Rio Tinto Mines has used robots to replace some workers. There are three new *Making the Connections*: "Is Investing in a College Education a Good Idea?"; "Should You Fear the Effect of Robots on the Labor Market?"; and "Technology and the Earnings of 'Superstars.'"

Chapter 18, "Public Choice, Taxes, and the Distribution of Income," opens with updated coverage of the debate about tax policy among the 2016 presidential candidates and includes new *Solved Problem 18.4* about income mobility.

Chapter 19, "GDP: Measuring Total Production and Income," opens with updated coverage of how the business cycle affects Ford Motor Company and includes a new *Making the Connection* about how calculating GDP changes the way the standard of living in Nigeria is measured.

Chapter 20, "Unemployment and Inflation," opens with a new discussion of JPMorgan's 2015 decision to lay off workers. There are two new *Making the Connections*: "Eight Million Workers Are Missing!" and "How Should We Categorize Unemployment at JPMorgan Chase?" New *Solved Problem 20.5* shows students how to use data to calculate real hourly wages.

Chapter 21, "Economic Growth, the Financial System, and Business Cycles," opens with a new discussion of how Corning has experienced long-run growth while experiencing the ups and downs of the business cycle. New *Solved Problem 21.1* focuses on the connection between productivity and prosperity, and new *Solved Problem 21.2* shows students how to apply the loanable funds model to analyze the effect of budget deficits.

Chapter 22, "Long-Run Economic Growth: Sources and Policies," opens with a new discussion of whether economic reforms will help to increase Mexico's growth rate and includes a new *Making the Connection* that compares economic growth in Mexico and China.

Chapter 23, "Aggregate Expenditure and Output in the Short Run," opens with an updated opener on the effects of fluctuations in aggregate expenditure on Intel and includes a new *Making the Connection* about the link between student loans and the number of young people purchasing homes.

Chapter 24, "Aggregate Demand and Aggregate Supply Analysis," opens with a new discussion of the effect of the business cycle on Delta Airlines and includes a new *Making the Connection* that discusses how unusually long it took following the 2007–2009 recession for real GDP and employment to return to the levels achieved at the business cycle peak.

Chapter 25, "Money, Banks, and the Federal Reserve System," opens with a new discussion of the 2015 banking crisis in Greece and includes a new *Making the Connection* on peer-to-peer lending.

Chapter 26, "Monetary Policy," opens with a new discussion of the connection between monetary policy and borrowers in Europe paying negative nominal interest rates on bank loans. Two new *Making the Connections* examine the connection between central bank policies of quantitative easing and negative interest rates, and why the Federal Reserve usually ignores fluctuations in food and energy prices.

Chapter 27, "Fiscal Policy," opens with a new discussion of the effects of federal government spending to rebuild a highway leading to the Golden Gate Bridge. A new *Making the Connection* discusses whether macroeconomic policy is too dependent on the Federal Reserve. New *Solved Problem 27.6* analyzes the effects of the Greek government attempting to balance its budget during a recession.

Chapter 28, "Inflation, Unemployment, and Federal Reserve Policy," opens with a new discussion of why a company like Goodyear is concerned about monetary policy. A new *Making the Connection* examines whether it is important for the Fed to provide the public with accurate guidance on the future of monetary policy.

Chapter 29, "Macroeconomics in an Open Economy," opens with a new discussion on how fluctuations in the exchange rate affect IBM's profits. A new *Making the Connection* examines whether a strong dollar is a good for the U.S. economy. New *Solved Problem 29.2* analyzes how Subaru is affected by fluctuations in the value of the yen.

Chapter 30, "The International Financial System," opens with a new discussion about how Bayer deals with fluctuating exchange rates. There are two new *Making the Connections*: "Greece and Germany: Diverse Economies, Common Currency" and "The Chinese Yuan: The World's Most Controversial Currency."

Other Changes to Chapters

- In Chapter 18, Section 18.4, "Income Distribution and Policy," has been reorganized and includes the new subsection "Policies to Reduce Income Inequality."
- Chapter 21 includes a new section that discusses why firms like Corning are particularly vulnerable to fluctuations in demand during the business cycle.
- Chapter 28 includes a new final section that covers the debate over the future of the Fed.
- We have added the following five new tables to present information in an easy-to-read format: Table 1.1, "Issues in Microeconomics and Macroeconomics"; Table 15.2, "Federal Government Standards for Horizontal Mergers"; Table 17.3, "Differences in Education among Ethnic Groups," which presents data on the education levels for three ethnic groups; Table 18.8, "The Effect of Taxes and Transfers on the Distribution of Household Income in the United States"; and Table 26.3, "Treasury and Fed Actions at the Beginning of the Financial Crisis."
- To make room for the new content described earlier, we have cut approximately 35 *Making the Connections* and 10 *Solved Problems* from the previous edition and transferred some of them to the book's *Instructor's Manual*, where they are available for instructors who wish to continue using them.
- Figures and tables have been updated with the latest data available.
- Many of the end-of-chapter problems have been either replaced or updated. To most chapters, we have added one or two new problems that include graphs for students to analyze. Select chapters have a category called *Real-Time Data Exercises*. Some of these exercises have been updated for this new edition.
- Finally, we have gone over the text literally line by line, tightening the discussion, rewriting unclear points, and making many small changes. We are grateful to the many instructors and students who made suggestions for improvements in the previous edition. We have done our best to incorporate as many of those suggestions as possible.

The Foundation:

Contextual Learning and Modern Organization

We believe a course is a success if students can apply what they have learned to both their personal lives and their careers, and if they have developed the analytical skills to understand what they read in the media. That's why we explain economic concepts by using many real-world business examples and applications in the chapter openers, graphs, *Making the Connection* features, *An Inside Look* features, and end-of-chapter problems. This approach helps both business majors and liberal arts majors become educated consumers, voters, and citizens. In addition to our widget-free approach, we have a modern organization and place interesting policy topics early in the book to pique student interest.

Microeconomics

We are convinced that students learn to apply economic principles best if they are taught in a familiar context. Whether they become artists, social workers, bankers, or government employees, students benefit from understanding economics. Though business students will have many opportunities to see economic principles in action in various courses, liberal arts students may not. We therefore use many diverse real-world business and policy examples to illustrate economic concepts and develop educated consumers, voters, and citizens. Here are a few highlights of our approach to microeconomics:

- **A strong set of introductory chapters.** The introductory chapters provide students with a solid foundation in the basics. We emphasize the key ideas of marginal analysis and economic efficiency. In Chapter 4, "Economic Efficiency, Government Price Setting, and Taxes," we use the concepts of consumer and producer surplus to measure the economic effects of price ceilings and price floors as they relate to the familiar examples of rental properties and the minimum wage. (We revisit consumer and producer surplus in Chapter 9, "Comparative Advantage and the Gains from International Trade," where we discuss outsourcing and analyze government policies that affect trade; in Chapter 15, "Monopoly and Antitrust Policy," where we examine the effect of market power on economic efficiency; and in Chapter 16, "Pricing Strategy," where we examine the effect of firm pricing policy on economic efficiency.) In Chapter 8, "Firms, the Stock Market, and Corporate Governance," we provide students with a basic understanding of how firms are organized, raise funds, and provide information to investors. We also illustrate how in a market system entrepreneurs meet consumer wants and efficiently organize production.
- **Early coverage of policy issues.** To expose students to policy issues early in the course, we discuss health care policy in Chapter 1, "Economics: Foundations and Models"; rent control and the minimum wage in Chapter 4, "Economic Efficiency, Government Price Setting, and Taxes"; air pollution, global warming, and public goods in Chapter 5, "Externalities, Environmental Policy, and Public Goods"; government policy toward illegal drugs in Chapter 6, "Elasticity: The Responsiveness of Demand and Supply"; and health care policy in Chapter 7, "The Economics of Health Care."
- **Complete coverage of monopolistic competition.** We devote a full chapter, Chapter 13, "Monopolistic Competition: The Competitive Model in a More Realistic Setting," to monopolistic competition prior to covering oligopoly and monopoly in Chapter 14, "Oligopoly: Firms in Less Competitive Markets," and Chapter 15, "Monopoly and Antitrust Policy." Although many instructors cover monopolistic competition very briefly or dispense with it entirely, we think it is an overlooked tool for reinforcing the basic message of how markets work in a context that is much more familiar to students than are the agricultural examples that dominate other discussions of perfect competition. We use the monopolistic competition model to introduce the

downward-sloping demand curve material usually introduced in a monopoly chapter. This approach helps students grasp the important point that nearly all firms—not just monopolies—face downward-sloping demand curves. Covering monopolistic competition directly after perfect competition also allows for early discussion of topics such as brand management and sources of competitive success. Nevertheless, we wrote the chapter so that instructors who prefer to cover monopoly (Chapter 15, "Monopoly and Antitrust Policy") directly after perfect competition (Chapter 12, "Firms in Perfectly Competitive Markets") can do so without loss of continuity.

- **Extensive, realistic game theory coverage.** In Chapter 14, "Oligopoly: Firms in Less Competitive Markets," we use game theory to analyze competition among oligopolists. Game theory helps students understand how companies with market power make strategic decisions in many competitive situations. We use familiar companies such as Apple, Amazon, Dell, Spotify, and Walmart in our game theory applications.
- **Unique coverage of pricing strategy.** In Chapter 16, "Pricing Strategy," we explore how firms use pricing strategies to increase profits. Students encounter pricing strategies everywhere—when they buy a movie ticket, book a flight for spring break, or research book prices online. We use these relevant, familiar examples to illustrate how companies use strategies such as price discrimination, cost-plus pricing, and two-part tariffs.

Macroeconomics

Students come to study macroeconomics with a strong interest in understanding events and developments in the economy. We try to capture that interest and develop students' economic intuition and understanding. We present macroeconomics in a way that is modern and based in the real world of business and economic policy. And we believe we achieve this presentation without making the analysis more difficult. We avoid the recent trend of using simplified versions of intermediate models, which are often more detailed and complex than what students need to understand the basic macroeconomic issues. Instead, we use a more realistic version of the familiar aggregate demand and aggregate supply model to analyze short-run fluctuations and monetary and fiscal policy. We also avoid the "dueling schools of thought" approach often used to teach macroeconomics at the principles level. We emphasize the many areas of macroeconomics where most economists agree. And we present throughout real business and policy situations to develop students' intuition. Here are a few highlights of our approach to macroeconomics:

- **A broad discussion of macro statistics.** Many students pay at least some attention to the financial news and know that the release of statistics by federal agencies can cause movements in stock and bond prices. A background in macroeconomic statistics helps clarify some of the policy issues encountered in later chapters. In Chapter 19, "GDP: Measuring Total Production and Income," and Chapter 20, "Unemployment and Inflation," we provide students with an understanding of the uses and potential shortcomings of the key macroeconomic statistics, without getting bogged down in the minutiae of how the statistics are constructed. So, for instance, we discuss the important differences between the payroll survey and the household survey for understanding conditions in the labor market. We explain why financial markets react more strongly to news from the payroll survey. We provide a discussion of the employment–population ratio, which is not covered in some other books but which many economists regard as a key measure of labor market performance. Chapter 26, "Monetary Policy," discusses why the Federal Reserve prefers to measure inflation using the core personal consumption expenditures price index rather than the consumer price index.
- **Early coverage of long-run topics.** We place key macroeconomic issues in their long-run context in Chapter 21, "Economic Growth, the Financial System, and Business Cycles," and Chapter 22, "Long-Run Economic Growth: Sources and Policies."

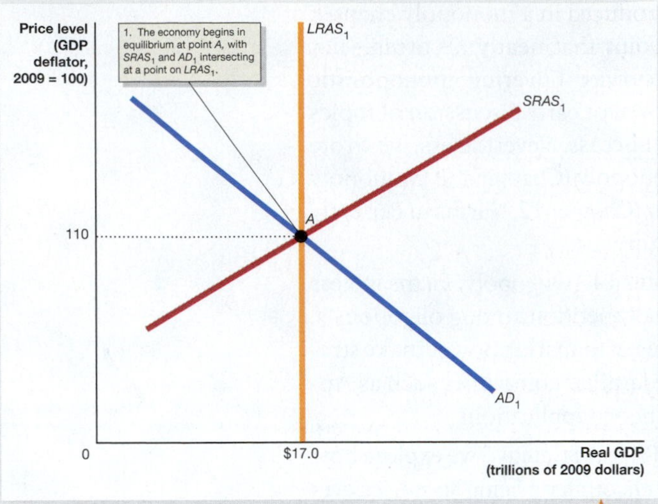

The first acetate overlay adds the shifts in the long- and short-run aggregate supply curves.

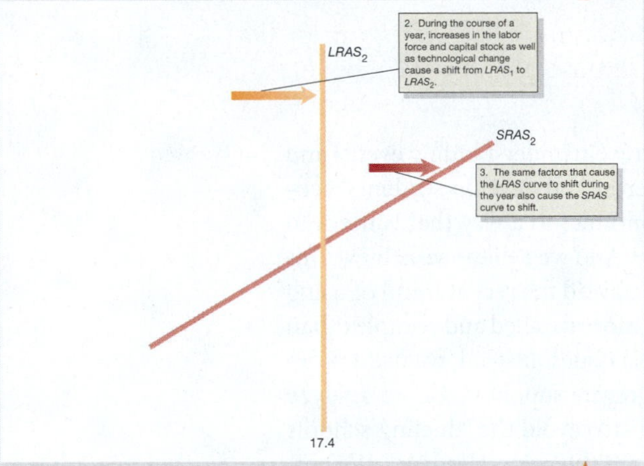

The second acetate overlay adds the shifts in the aggregate demand curve to complete the dynamic model.

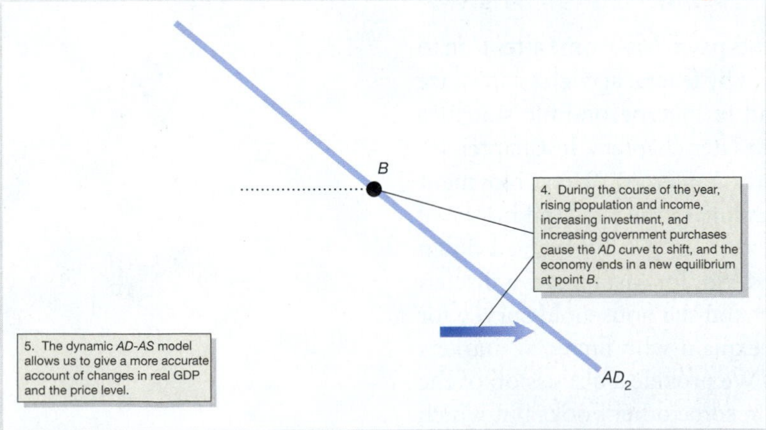

Chapter 21 puts the business cycle in the context of underlying long-run growth and discusses what actually happens during the phases of the business cycle. We believe this material is important if students are to have the understanding of business cycles they will need to interpret economic events; this material is often discussed only briefly or omitted entirely in other books. We know that many instructors prefer to have a short-run orientation to their macro courses, with a strong emphasis on policy. Accordingly, we have structured Chapter 21 so that its discussion of long-run growth is sufficient for instructors who want to move quickly to short-run analysis. Chapter 22 uses a simple neoclassical growth model to explain important growth issues. We apply the model to topics such as the decline of the Soviet economy, the long-run prospects for growth in China, the implications of the slowdown in productivity growth for the U.S. economy, and the failure of many developing countries to sustain high growth rates. *And* we challenge students with the discussion "Why Isn't the Whole World Rich?"

- **A dynamic model of aggregate demand and aggregate supply.** We take a fresh approach to the standard aggregate demand and aggregate supply (*AD–AS*) model. We realize there is no good, simple alternative to using the *AD–AS* model when explaining movements in the price level and in real GDP. But we know that more instructors are dissatisfied with the *AD–AS* model than with any other aspect of the macro principles course. The key problem, of course, is that *AD–AS* is a static model that attempts to account for dynamic changes in real GDP and the price level. Our approach retains the basics of the *AD–AS* model but makes it more accurate and useful by making it more dynamic. We emphasize two points: (1) Changes in the position of the short-run (upward-sloping) aggregate supply curve depend mainly on the state of expectations of the inflation rate and (2) the existence of growth in the economy means that the long-run (vertical) aggregate supply curve shifts to the right every year. This "dynamic" *AD–AS* model provides students with a more accurate understanding of the causes and consequences of fluctuations in real GDP and the price level. Chapter 24, "Aggregate Demand and Aggregate Supply Analysis," includes a three-layer, full-color acetate for the key introductory dynamic *AD–AS* graph (Figure 24.8, "A Dynamic Aggregate Demand and Aggregate Supply Model," on page 838 and reproduced on the left). We created this acetate to help students see how the graph builds step by step and to help make the graph easier for instructors to present. The acetate will help instructors who want to use dynamic *AD–AS* in class but believe the model needs to be developed carefully. We introduce this model in Chapter 24 and use it to discuss monetary policy in Chapter 26, "Monetary Policy," and

Economics

The Pearson Series in Economics

Abel/Bernanke/Croushore
*Macroeconomics**

Acemoglu/Laibson/List
*Economics**

Bade/Parkin
*Foundations of Economics**

Berck/Helfand
The Economics of the Environment

Bierman/Fernandez
Game Theory with Economic Applications

Blanchard
*Macroeconomics**

Blau/Ferber/Winkler
The Economics of Women, Men, and Work

Boardman/Greenberg/Vining/Weimer
Cost-Benefit Analysis

Boyer
Principles of Transportation Economics

Branson
Macroeconomic Theory and Policy

Bruce
Public Finance and the American Economy

Carlton/Perloff
Modern Industrial Organization

Case/Fair/Oster
*Principles of Economics**

Chapman
Environmental Economics: Theory, Application, and Policy

Cooter/Ulen
Law & Economics

Daniels/VanHoose
International Monetary & Financial Economics

Downs
An Economic Theory of Democracy

Ehrenberg/Smith
Modern Labor Economics

Farnham
Economics for Managers

Folland/Goodman/Stano
The Economics of Health and Health Care

Fort
Sports Economics

Froyen
Macroeconomics

Fusfeld
The Age of the Economist

Gerber
*International Economics**

González-Rivera
Forecasting for Economics and Business

Gordon
*Macroeconomics**

Greene
Econometric Analysis

Gregory
Essentials of Economics

Gregory/Stuart
Russian and Soviet Economic Performance and Structure

Hartwick/Olewiler
The Economics of Natural Resource Use

Heilbroner/Milberg
The Making of the Economic Society

Heyne/Boettke/Prychitko
The Economic Way of Thinking

Holt
Markets, Games, and Strategic Behavior

Hubbard/O'Brien
*Economics**
*Money, Banking, and the Financial System**

Hubbard/O'Brien/Rafferty
*Macroeconomics**

Hughes/Cain
American Economic History

Husted/Melvin
International Economics

Jehle/Reny
Advanced Microeconomic Theory

Johnson-Lans
A Health Economics Primer

Keat/Young/Erfle
Managerial Economics

Klein
Mathematical Methods for Economics

Krugman/Obstfeld/Melitz
*International Economics: Theory & Policy**

Laidler
The Demand for Money

Leeds/von Allmen
The Economics of Sports

Leeds/von Allmen/Schiming
*Economics**

Lynn
Economic Development: Theory and Practice for a Divided World

Miller
*Economics Today**
Understanding Modern Economics

Miller/Benjamin
The Economics of Macro Issues

Miller/Benjamin/North
The Economics of Public Issues

Mills/Hamilton
Urban Economics

Mishkin
*The Economics of Money, Banking, and Financial Markets**
*The Economics of Money, Banking, and Financial Markets, Business School Edition**
*Macroeconomics: Policy and Practice**

Murray
Econometrics: A Modern Introduction

O'Sullivan/Sheffrin/Perez
*Economics: Principles, Applications and Tools**

Parkin
*Economics**

Perloff
*Microeconomics**
*Microeconomics: Theory and Applications with Calculus**

Perloff/Brander
*Managerial Economics and Strategy**

Phelps
Health Economics

Pindyck/Rubinfeld
*Microeconomics**

Riddell/Shackelford/Stamos/Schneider
Economics: A Tool for Critically Understanding Society

Roberts
The Choice: A Fable of Free Trade and Protection

Rohlf
Introduction to Economic Reasoning

Roland
Development Economics

Scherer
Industry Structure, Strategy, and Public Policy

Schiller
The Economics of Poverty and Discrimination

Sherman
Market Regulation

Stock/Watson
Introduction to Econometrics

Studenmund
Using Econometrics: A Practical Guide

Tietenberg/Lewis
Environmental and Natural Resource Economics
Environmental Economics and Policy

Todaro/Smith
Economic Development

Waldman/Jensen
Industrial Organization: Theory and Practice

Walters/Walters/Appel/Callahan/Centanni/Maex/O'Neill
Econversations: Today's Students Discuss Today's Issues

Weil
Economic Growth

Williamson
Macroeconomics

*denotes MyEconLab titles   Visit www.myeconlab.com to learn more.

fiscal policy in Chapter 27, "Fiscal Policy." The material on dynamic *AD–AS* is presented in self-contained sections in Chapters 24, 26, and 27, so instructors may safely omit the sections on the dynamic *AD–AS* model without any loss in continuity to the discussion of macroeconomic theory and policy.

- **Extensive coverage of monetary policy.** Because of the central role monetary policy plays in the economy and in students' curiosity about business and financial news, we devote two chapters—Chapter 26, "Monetary Policy," and Chapter 28, "Inflation, Unemployment, and Federal Reserve Policy"—to the topic. We emphasize the issues involved in the Fed's choice of monetary policy targets, and we include coverage of the Taylor rule. We also cover the debate over the Fed's policies, including recent proposals in Congress to reduce the Fed's independence.
- **Coverage of both the demand-side and supply-side effects of fiscal policy.** Our discussion of fiscal policy in Chapter 27, "Fiscal Policy," carefully distinguishes between automatic stabilizers and discretionary fiscal policy. We also provide significant coverage of the supply-side effects of fiscal policy.
- **A self-contained but thorough discussion of the Keynesian income–expenditure approach.** The Keynesian income–expenditure approach (the "45°-line diagram," or "Keynesian cross") is useful for introducing students to the short-run relationship between spending and production. Many instructors, however, prefer to omit this material. Therefore, we use the 45°-line diagram only in Chapter 23, "Aggregate Expenditure and Output in the Short Run." The discussions of monetary and fiscal policy in Chapter 26, "Monetary Policy," and Chapter 27, "Fiscal Policy," respectively, uses only the *AD–AS* model, making it possible to omit Chapter 23.
- **Extensive international coverage.** We include three chapters devoted to international topics: Chapter 9, "Comparative Advantage and the Gains from International Trade," Chapter 29, "Macroeconomics in an Open Economy," and Chapter 30, "The International Financial System." Having a good understanding of the international trading and financial systems is essential to understanding the macroeconomy and to satisfying students' curiosity about the economic world around them. In addition to the material in our three international chapters, we weave international comparisons into the narratives of several other chapters, including our discussion of labor market policies in Chapter 28, "Inflation, Unemployment, and Federal Reserve Policy," and central banking in Chapter 25, "Money, Banks, and the Federal Reserve System."
- **Flexible chapter organization.** Because we realize that there are a variety of approaches to teaching principles of macroeconomics, we have structured our chapters for maximum flexibility. For example, our discussion of long-run economic growth in Chapter 21, "Economic Growth, the Financial System, and Business Cycles," makes it possible for instructors to omit the more thorough discussion of these issues in Chapter 22, "Long-Run Economic Growth: Sources and Policies." Our discussion of the Keynesian 45°-line diagram is confined to Chapter 23, "Aggregate Expenditure and Output in the Short Run," so that instructors who do not use this approach can proceed directly to aggregate demand and aggregate supply analysis in Chapter 24, "Aggregate Demand and Aggregate Supply Analysis." While we devote two chapters to monetary policy, the first of these—Chapter 26, "Monetary Policy"—is a self-contained discussion, so instructors may safely omit the material in Chapter 28, "Inflation, Unemployment, and Federal Reserve Policy," if they choose to. Finally, instructors may choose to omit all three of the international chapters (Chapter 9, "Comparative Advantage and the Gains from International Trade," Chapter 29, "Macroeconomics in an Open Economy," and Chapter 30, "The International Financial System"), cover just Chapter 9 on international trade, cover just Chapter 29, or cover Chapters 29 and 30 while omitting Chapter 9. Please refer to the flexibility chart on pages xxvi–xxvii to help select the chapters and order best suited to your classroom needs.

Special Features:

A Real-World, Hands-on Approach to Learning Economics

Business Cases and *An Inside Look* News Articles

Each chapter-opening case provides a real-world context for learning, sparks students' interest in economics, and helps unify the chapter. The case describes an actual company facing a real situation. The company is integrated in the narrative, graphs, and pedagogical features of the chapter. Some of the chapter openers focus on the role of entrepreneurs in developing new products and bringing them to market. For example, Chapter 1 discusses Walter De Brouwer, the founder of Scanadu, which develops smart devices for health care; Chapter 2 discusses Elon Musk of Tesla Motors; and Chapter 13 discusses Steve Ells of Chipotle Mexican Grill. Here are a few examples of companies we discuss in the chapter openers:

- Tesla Motors (Chapter 2, "Trade-offs, Comparative Advantage, and the Market System")
- Apple (Chapter 3, "Where Prices Come From: The Interaction of Demand and Supply")
- Twitter (Chapter 8, "Firms, the Stock Market, and Corporate Governance")
- Delta Airlines (Chapter 24, "Aggregate Demand and Aggregate Supply Analysis")

CHAPTER 3

Where Prices Come From: The Interaction of Demand and Supply

Chapter Outline and Learning Objectives

3.1 **The Demand Side of the Market,** page 74
List and describe the variables that influence demand.

3.2 **The Supply Side of the Market,** page 82
List and describe the variables that influence supply.

3.3 **Market Equilibrium: Putting Demand and Supply Together,** page 86
Use a graph to illustrate market equilibrium.

3.4 **The Effect of Demand and Supply Shifts on Equilibrium,** page 90
Use demand and supply graphs to predict changes in prices and quantities.

How Smart Is Your Watch?

Fashions can change quickly. For many years, most people wore wristwatches. With the popularity of cellphones in the 2000s, many people stopped wearing wristwatches—which was bad news for the watch industry. Once a product falls out of fashion, its sales are unlikely to return to past levels. Will watches prove an exception?

Until recently attempts to have watches do more than tell the time have not been successful. For instance, during the 1980s Texas Instruments and several other firms added small calculators to watches, but sales were limited. In 2004, Microsoft introduced the SPOT watch, which enabled users to receive instant messages, weather reports, and news headlines. But few consumers purchased it so the company stopped production of the watch in 2008. By 2013, several firms had introduced "smartwatches" that enabled users to make phone calls, text, take photos or videos, monitor their heart rates, and calculate calories burned while exercising.

In 2015, Apple introduced the Apple Watch, which combined most of the capabilities of the smartwatches from competing firms with popular features from Apple's iPhone and iPad, such as access to the iTunes music store and Siri, the voice-activated personal assistant. The Apple Watch was immediately popular, with more than 2.5 million being sold during the first five weeks. These sales were higher than initial sales of Apple's previous products—the iPod, iPhone, or iPad. More than 25 other firms entered the smartwatch market, hoping to participate in the rapid growth of a hot product.

But there are no guarantees in a market system. Would the Apple Watch and its competitors succeed in bringing the wristwatch back into style, or would they fail like the Texas Instruments calculator watch and the Microsoft SPOT watch? Smartwatches have relatively high prices, are somewhat complicated to use, and have small screens that make it difficult to display photos or maps. Ultimately, the success of the smartwatch is likely to depend on whether consumers like the applications, or "apps," on these watches and are willing to wear wristwatches again.

The intense competition among firms selling smartwatches is a striking example of how the market responds to changes in technology and consumer tastes. Although competition is not always good news for firms trying to sell products, it is great news for consumers because it increases the available choice of products and lowers the prices consumers pay for those products.

AN INSIDE LOOK on **page 98** discusses how the Apple smartwatch is inspiring firms to develop other wearable devices.

Sources: Daniel Matte and Kevin McCullagh, "Will Smartwatches Be a Hit?" *Wall Street Journal*, May 10, 2015; and Mitchel Broussard, "Apple Watch Orders Estimated to Average 30,000 per Day in U.S. after Initial Surge," macrumors.com, May 22, 2015.

Economics in Your Life

Will You Buy a Smartphone or a Smartwatch?

You use your smartphone mainly to text, read e-mail, and keep track of your appointments. Your smartphone is old, though, and you are thinking of buying a new one ... or should you buy a smartwatch? What factors are most important in your decision: the features of a smartwatch versus a smartphone, or the relative prices of these products? If you know that you are soon going to get a raise at your job, would you be more likely to buy a smartwatch? As you read this chapter, try to answer these questions. You can check your answers against those we provide on **page 97** at the end of this chapter.

73

An Inside Look is a two-page feature that shows students how to apply the concepts from the chapter to the analysis of a news article. The feature appears at the end of Chapters 1–4. *An Inside Look* feature presents an excerpt from an article, analysis of the article, a graph(s), and critical thinking questions. Additional articles are located on MyEconLab, where they are continuously updated.

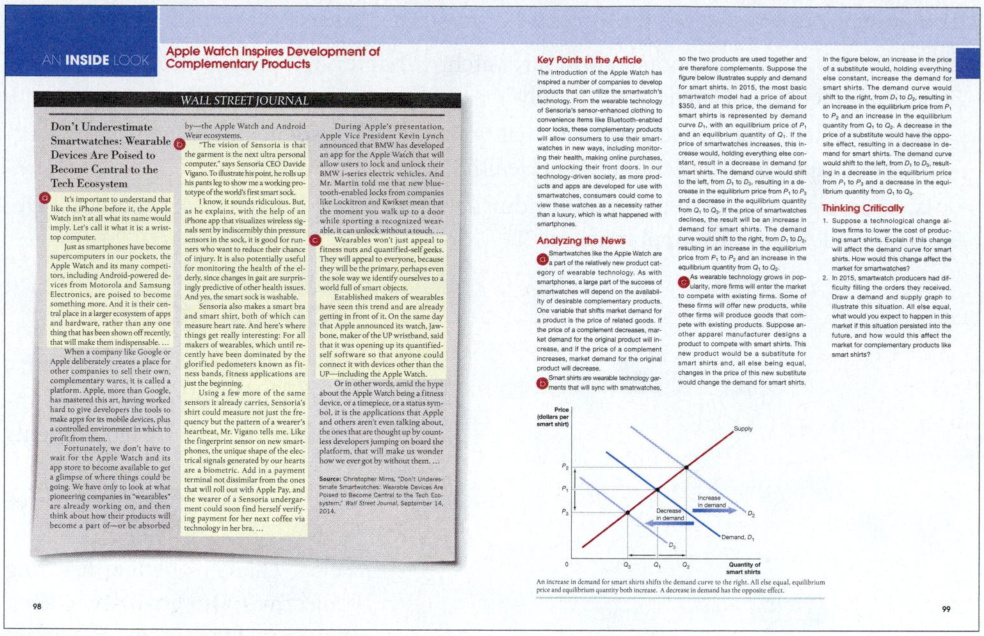

AN **INSIDE** LOOK

Apple Watch Inspires Development of Complementary Products

WALL STREET JOURNAL

Don't Underestimate Smartwatches: Wearable Devices Are Poised to Become Central to the Tech Ecosystem

a It's important to understand that like the iPhone before it, the Apple Watch isn't at all what its name would imply. Let's call it what it is: a wrist-top computer.

Just as smartphones have become supercomputers in our pockets, the Apple Watch and its many competitors, including Android-powered devices from Motorola and Samsung Electronics, are poised to become something more. And it is their central place in a larger ecosystem of apps and hardware, rather than any one thing that has been shown off recently, that will make them indispensable. …

When a company like Google or Apple deliberately creates a place for other companies to sell their own, complementary wares, it is called a platform. Apple, more than Google, has mastered this art, having worked hard to give developers the tools to make apps for its mobile devices, plus a controlled environment in which to profit from them.

Fortunately, we don't have to wait for the Apple Watch and its app store to become available to get a glimpse of where things could be going. We have only to look at what pioneering companies in "wearables" are already working on, and then think about how their products will become a part of—or be absorbed by—the Apple Watch and Android Wear ecosystems.

b "The vision of Sensoria is that the garment is the next ultra personal computer," says Sensoria CEO Davide Vigano. To illustrate his point, he rolls up his pants leg to show me a working prototype of the world's first smart sock.

I know, it sounds ridiculous. But, as he explains, with the help of an iPhone app that visualizes wireless signals sent by indiscernibly thin pressure sensors in the sock, it is good for runners who want to reduce their chance of injury. It is also potentially useful for monitoring the health of the elderly, since changes in gait are surprisingly predictive of other health issues. And yes, the smart sock is washable.

Sensoria also makes a smart bra and smart shirt, both of which can measure heart rate. And here's where things get really interesting: For all makers of wearables, which until recently have been dominated by the glorified pedometers known as fitness bands, fitness applications are just the beginning.

Using a few more of the same sensors it already carries, Sensoria's shirt could measure not just the frequency but the pattern of a wearer's heartbeat, Mr. Vigano tells me. Like the fingerprint sensor on new smartphones, the unique shape of the electrical signals generated by our hearts are a biometric. Add in a payment terminal not dissimilar from the ones that will roll out with Apple Pay, and the wearer of a Sensoria undergarment could soon find herself verifying payment for her next coffee via technology in her bra. …

During Apple's presentation, Apple Vice President Kevin Lynch announced that BMW has developed an app for the Apple Watch that will allow users to lock and unlock their BMW i-series electric vehicles. And Mr. Martin told me that new bluetooth-enabled locks from companies like Lockitron and Kwikset mean that the moment you walk up to a door while sporting a recognized wearable, it can unlock without a touch. …

c Wearables won't just appeal to fitness nuts and quantified-self geeks. They will appeal to everyone, because they will be the primary, perhaps even the sole way we identify ourselves to a world full of smart objects.

Established makers of wearables have seen this trend and are already getting in front of it. On the same day that Apple announced its watch, Jawbone, maker of the UP wristband, said that it was opening up its quantified-self software so that anyone could connect it with devices other than the UP—including the Apple Watch.

Or in other words, amid the hype about the Apple Watch being a fitness device, or a timepiece, or a status symbol, it is the applications that Apple and others aren't even talking about, the ones that are thought up by countless developers jumping on board the platform, that will make us wonder how we ever got by without them. …

Source: Christopher Mims, "Don't Underestimate Smartwatches: Wearable Devices Are Poised to Become Central to the Tech Ecosystem," *Wall Street Journal*, September 14, 2014.

98

Key Points in the Article

The introduction of the Apple Watch has inspired a number of companies to develop products that can utilize the smartwatch's technology. From the wearable technology of Sensoria's sensor-enhanced clothing to convenience items like Bluetooth-enabled door locks, these complementary products will allow consumers to use their smartwatches in new ways, including monitoring their health, making online purchases, and unlocking their front doors. In our technology-driven society, as more products and apps are developed for use with smartwatches, consumers could come to view these watches as a necessity rather than a luxury, which is what happened with smartphones.

Analyzing the News

a Smartwatches like the Apple Watch are a part of the relatively new product category of wearable technology. As with smartphones, a large part of the success of smartwatches will depend on the availability of desirable complementary products. One variable that shifts market demand for a product is the price of related goods. If the price of a complement decreases, market demand for the original product will increase, and if the price of a complement increases, market demand for the original product will decrease.

b Smart shirts are wearable technology garments that will sync with smatrwatches, so the two products are used together and are therefore complements. Suppose the figure below illustrates supply and demand for smart shirts. In 2015, the most basic smartwatch model had a price of about \$350, and at this price, the demand for smart shirts is represented by demand curve D_1, with an equilibrium price of P_1 and an equilibrium quantity of Q_1. If the price of smartwatches increases, this increase would, holding everything else constant, result in a decrease in demand for smart shirts. The demand curve would shift to the left, from D_1 to D_3, resulting in a decrease in the equilibrium price from P_1 to P_3 and a decrease in the equilibrium quantity from Q_1 to Q_3. If the price of smartwatches declines, the result will be an increase in demand for smart shirts. The demand curve would shift to the right, from D_1 to D_2, resulting in an increase in the equilibrium price from P_1 to P_2 and an increase in the equilibrium quantity from Q_1 to Q_2.

c As wearable technology grows in popularity, more firms will enter the market to compete with existing firms. Some of these firms will offer new products, while other firms will produce goods that compete with existing products. Suppose another apparel manufacturer designs a product to compete with smart shirts. This new product would be a substitute for smart shirts and, all else being equal, changes in the price of this new substitute would change the demand for smart shirts. In the figure below, an increase in the price of a substitute would, holding everything else constant, increase the demand for smart shirts. The demand curve would shift to the right, from D_1 to D_2, resulting in an increase in the equilibrium price from P_1 to P_2 and an increase in the equilibrium quantity from Q_1 to Q_2. A decrease in the price of a substitute would have the opposite effect, resulting in a decrease in demand for smart shirts. The demand curve would shift to the left, from D_1 to D_3, resulting in a decrease in the equilibrium price from P_1 to P_3 and a decrease in the equilibrium quantity from Q_1 to Q_3.

Thinking Critically

1. Suppose a technological change allows firms to lower the cost of producing smart shirts. Explain if this change will affect the demand curve for smart shirts. How would this change affect the market for smartwatches?
2. In 2015, smartwatch producers had difficulty filling the orders they received. Draw a demand and supply graph to illustrate this situation. All else equal, what would you expect to happen in this market if this situation persisted into the future, and how would this affect the market for complementary products like smart shirts?

An increase in demand for smart shirts shifts the demand curve to the right. All else equal, equilibrium price and equilibrium quantity both increase. A decrease in demand has the opposite effect.

99

Economics in Your Life

After the chapter-opening real-world business case, we have added a personal dimension to the chapter opener with a feature titled *Economics in Your Life,* which asks students to consider how economics affects their lives. The feature piques the interest of students and emphasizes the connection between the material they are learning and their experiences.

Economics in Your Life

Will You Buy a Smartphone or a Smartwatch?

You use your smartphone mainly to text, read e-mail, and keep track of your appointments. Your smartphone is old, though, and you are thinking of buying a new one … or should you buy a smartwatch? What factors are most important in your decision: the features of a smartwatch versus a smartphone, or the relative prices of these products? If you know that you are soon going to get a raise at your job, would you be more likely to buy a smartwatch? As you read this chapter, try to answer these questions. You can check your answers against those we provide on **page 97** at the end of this chapter.

At the end of the chapter, we use the chapter concepts to answer the questions asked at the beginning of the chapter.

Continued from page 73

Economics in Your Life

Will You Buy a Smartphone or a Smartwatch?

At the beginning of this chapter, we asked you to consider how you might choose between buying a smartwatch and buying a smartphone. There are certain activities, such as watching YouTube or Netflix, that you can do on a smartphone but not on a smartwatch. There are other activities, such as tracking calories burned during a workout, that are probably easier to do on a smartwatch. If you can engage in the activities you like most on either device, then you probably consider the two devices to be close substitutes, and you are likely to buy the one with the lower price. Suppose that you are currently leaning toward buying a smartphone because its price is lower than the price of a comparable smartwatch. If an increase in your income would cause you to change your decision and buy the smartwatch, then the smartphone is an inferior good for you.

The following are examples of the topics we cover in the *Economics in Your Life* feature:

- Will you buy a smartphone or a smartwatch? (Chapter 3, "Where Prices Come From: The Interaction of Demand and Supply")
- Is your take-home pay affected by what your employer spends on your health insurance? (Chapter 7, "The Economics of Health Care")
- Is an employer likely to cut your pay during a recession? (Chapter 24, "Aggregate Demand and Aggregate Supply Analysis")

Solved Problems

Many students have great difficulty handling applied economics problems. We help students overcome this hurdle by including in each chapter two or three worked-out problems tied to select chapter-opening learning objectives. Our goals are to keep students focused on the main ideas of each chapter and give them a model of how to solve an economic problem by breaking it down step by step. Additional exercises in the end-of-chapter *Problems and Applications* section are tied to every *Solved Problem.* Additional *Solved Problems* appear in the *Instructor's Manuals.* In addition, the Test Item Files include problems tied to the *Solved Problems* in the main book.

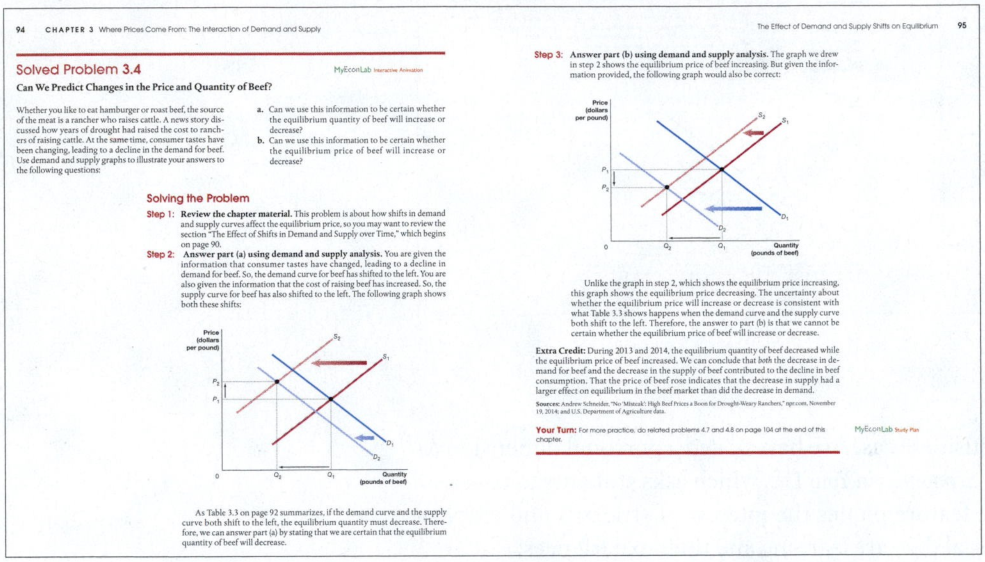
94 CHAPTER 3 Where Prices Come From: The Interaction of Demand and Supply

Solved Problem 3.4 MyEconLab Interactive Animation

Can We Predict Changes in the Price and Quantity of Beef?

Whether you like to eat hamburger or roast beef, the source of the meat is a rancher who raises cattle. A news story discussed how years of drought had raised the cost to ranchers of raising cattle. At the same time, consumer tastes have been changing, leading to a decline in the demand for beef. Use demand and supply graphs to illustrate your answers to the following questions:

a. Can we use this information to be certain whether the equilibrium quantity of beef will increase or decrease?
b. Can we use this information to be certain whether the equilibrium price of beef will increase or decrease?

Solving the Problem

Step 1: **Review the chapter material.** This problem is about how shifts in demand and supply curves affect the equilibrium price, so you may want to review the section "The Effect of Shifts in Demand and Supply over Time," which begins on page 90.

Step 2: **Answer part (a) using demand and supply analysis.** You are given the information that consumer tastes have changed, leading to a decline in demand for beef. So, the demand curve for beef has shifted to the left. You are also given the information that the cost of raising beef has increased. So, the supply curve for beef has also shifted to the left. The following graph shows both these shifts:

As Table 3.3 on page 92 summarizes, if the demand curve and the supply curve both shift to the left, the equilibrium quantity must decrease. Therefore, we can answer part (a) by stating that we are certain that the equilibrium quantity of beef will decrease.

The Effect of Demand and Supply Shifts on Equilibrium 95

Step 3: **Answer part (b) using demand and supply analysis.** The graph we drew in step 2 shows the equilibrium price of beef increasing. But given the information provided, the following graph would also be correct:

Unlike the graph in step 2, which shows the equilibrium price increasing, this graph shows the equilibrium price decreasing. The uncertainty about whether the equilibrium price will increase or decrease is consistent with what Table 3.3 shows happens when the demand curve and the supply curve both shift to the left. Therefore, the answer to part (b) is that we cannot be certain whether the equilibrium price of beef will increase or decrease.

Extra Credit: During 2013 and 2014, the equilibrium quantity of beef decreased while the equilibrium price of beef increased. We can conclude that *both* the decrease in demand for beef and the decrease in the supply of beef contributed to the decline in beef consumption. That the price of beef rose indicates that the decrease in supply had a larger effect on equilibrium in the beef market than did the decrease in demand.

Sources: Andrew Schneider, "No 'Misteak': High Beef Prices a Boon for Drought-Weary Ranchers," npr.com, November 19, 2014; and U.S. Department of Agriculture data.

Your Turn: For more practice, do related problems 4.7 and 4.8 on page 104 at the end of this chapter. MyEconLab Study Plan

Don't Let This Happen to You

Don't Let This Happen to You

Remember: A Change in a Good's Price Does *Not* Cause the Demand or Supply Curve to Shift

Suppose a student is asked to draw a demand and supply graph to illustrate how an increase in the price of oranges would affect the market for apples, with other variables being constant. He draws the graph on the left and explains it as follows: "Because apples and oranges are substitutes, an increase in the price of oranges will cause an initial shift to the right in the demand curve for apples, from D_1 to D_2. However, because this initial shift in the demand curve for apples results in a higher price for apples, P_2, consumers will find apples less desirable, and the demand curve will shift to the left, from D_2 to D_3, resulting in a final equilibrium price of P_3." Do you agree or disagree with the student's analysis? MyEconLab Study Plan

You should disagree. The student has correctly understood that an increase in the price of oranges will cause the demand curve for apples to shift to the right. But, the second demand curve shift the student describes, from D_2 to D_3, will not take place. Changes in the price of a product do not result in shifts in the product's demand curve. Changes in the price of a product result only in movements along a demand curve.

The graph on the right shows the correct analysis. The increase in the price of oranges causes the demand curve for apples to increase from D_1 to D_2. At the original price, P_1, the increase in demand initially results in a shortage of apples equal to $Q_3 - Q_1$. But, as we have seen, a shortage causes the price to increase until the shortage is eliminated. In this case, the price will rise to P_2, where both the quantity demanded and the quantity supplied are equal to Q_2. Notice that the increase in price causes a decrease in the *quantity demanded,* from Q_3 to Q_2, but does *not* cause a decrease in demand.

Your Turn: Test your understanding by doing related problems 4.13 and 4.14 on page 105 at the end of this chapter.

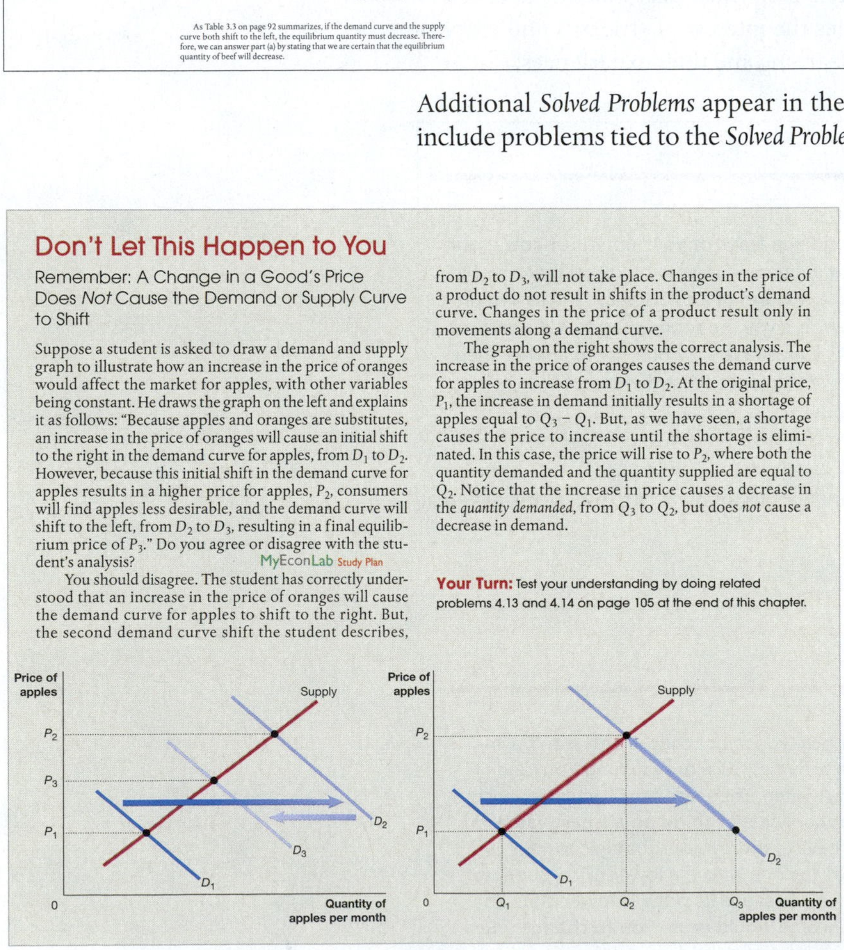

We know from many years of teaching which concepts students find most difficult. Each chapter contains a box feature called *Don't Let This Happen to You* that alerts students to the most common pitfalls in that chapter's material. We follow up with a related question in the end-of-chapter *Problems and Applications* section.

Making the Connection

Each chapter includes two to four *Making the Connection* features that provide real-world reinforcement of key concepts and help students learn how to interpret what they read on the Web and in newspapers. Most *Making the Connection* features use relevant, stimulating, and provocative news stories focused on businesses and policy issues. One-third of them are new to this edition, and most others have been updated. Several discuss health care, which remains a pressing policy issue. Each *Making the Connection* has at least one supporting end-of-chapter problem to allow students to test their understanding of the topic discussed.

Making the Connection MyEconLab Video

Are Smartwatches Substitutes for Smartphones?

Is the smartwatch a hot new must-have gadget, even for people who already own a smartphone?

Two products are rarely perfect substitutes because consumers may find them more or less useful for some purposes. As Apple and other firms began selling smartwatches, a key question they needed to answer was whether consumers considered smartwatches close substitutes for smartphones. You can use either a smartwatch or a smartphone to check the time, send a text, keep a list of appointments, or use a GPS map. But you need a smartphone if you want to surf the Web or watch a movie, while you are better off buying a smartwatch if you want to monitor your heartbeat or keep track of how many calories you are burning while exercising.

So smartwatches and smartphones are substitutes—but they aren't *perfect* substitutes. To correctly forecast sales and produce the correct quantity of smartwatches, firms that sell them need to evaluate how close substitutes consumers consider smartwatches and smartphones to be. Many people who might consider buying a smartwatch already own a smartphone. So the closer consumers consider the two products to be as substitutes, the less likely they are to buy a smartwatch in addition to a smartphone.

When Apple introduced the Apple Watch in 2015, sales were initially very strong, which would seem to indicate that many consumers believed that the unique features of the smartwatch made it worth buying, even if they owned a smartphone. Some analysts, though, wondered how large future sales would be after people who buy each new electronic device soon after it hits the market—early adopters—had made their purchases. One early reviewer of the Apple Watch noted that he was unsure "that I need this thing on my wrist every day." Similarly, the *Economist* magazine offered the opinion, "Apple seems unlikely to turn its watch into the next big must-have gadget. … People are unlikely to want to shell out … $350 … for something with so few extra functions."

Other industry observers were more optimistic about the size of the market for smartwatches. Writing in the *Wall Street Journal*, one analyst argued that smartwatches performed several functions faster or more conveniently than smartphones. He concluded, "Billions of consumers who own a smartphone are likely to consider purchasing a smartwatch." Given these different evaluations, it wasn't surprising that forecasts of sales of the Apple Watch during its first year varied widely from 8 million to 41 million.

In the end, as with most new products, the success of smartwatches depends on whether consumers see them as filling a need that other products don't meet. In other words, the less close a substitute consumers believe smartwatches to be for smartphones, the more likely they are to buy a smartwatch.

Sources: Joshua Topolsky, "Apple Watch Review: You'll Want One, but You Don't Need One," bloomberg.com, April 8, 2015; "The Time Machine," *Economist*, March 9, 2015; and Daniel Matte and Kevin McCullagh, "Will Smartwatches Be a Hit?" *Wall Street Journal*, May 10, 2015.

Your Turn: Test your understanding by doing related problem 1.12 on page 101 at the end of this chapter.

MyEconLab Study Plan

Graphs and Summary Tables

Graphs are an indispensable part of a principles of economics course but are a major stumbling block for many students. Every chapter except Chapter 1 includes end-of-chapter problems that require students to draw, read, and interpret graphs. Interactive graphing exercises appear on the book's supporting Web site. We use four devices to help students read and interpret graphs:

1. Detailed captions
2. Boxed notes
3. Color-coded curves
4. Summary tables with graphs (see pages 80, 85, and 830 for examples)

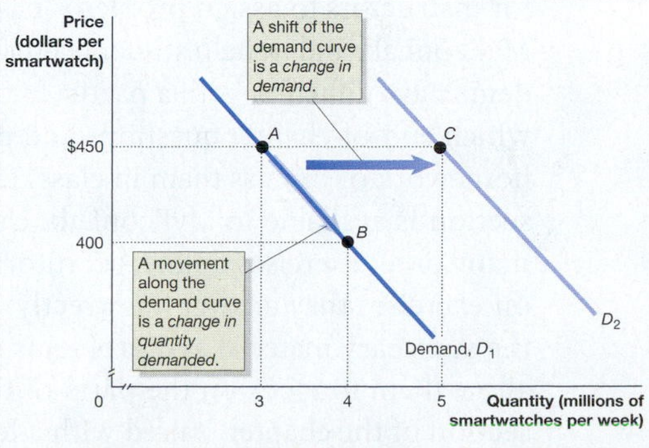

MyEconLab Animation

Figure 3.3

A Change in Demand versus a Change in Quantity Demanded

If the price of smartwatches falls from $450 to $400, the result will be a movement along the demand curve from point *A* to point *B*—an increase in quantity demanded from 3 million to 4 million. If consumers' incomes increase, or if another factor changes that makes consumers want more of the product at every price, the demand curve will shift to the right—an increase in demand. In this case, the increase in demand from D_1 to D_2 causes the quantity of smartwatches demanded at a price of $450 to increase from 3 million at point *A* to 5 million at point *C*.

Table 3.1

Variables That Shift Market Demand Curves

An increase in ...	shifts the demand curve ...	because ...
income (and the good is normal)	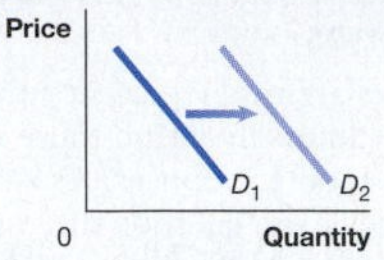	consumers spend more of their higher incomes on the good.
income (and the good is inferior)	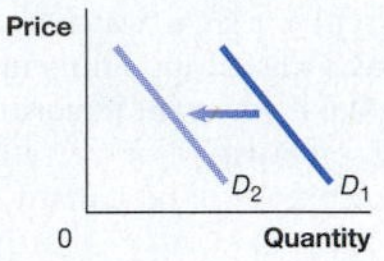	consumers spend less of their higher incomes on the good.
the price of a substitute good	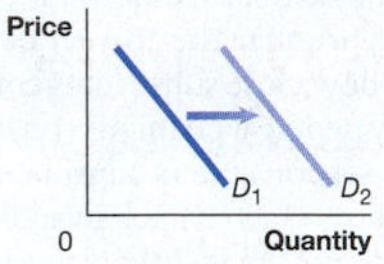	consumers buy less of the substitute good and more of this good.
the price of a complementary good	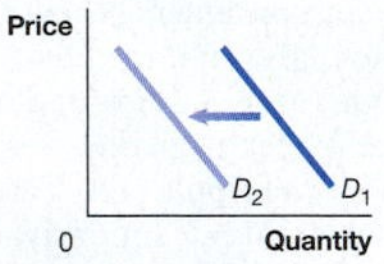	consumers buy less of the complementary good and less of this good.
taste for the good	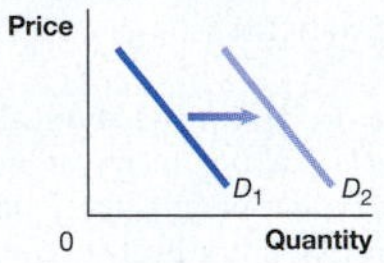	consumers are willing to buy a larger quantity of the good at every price.
population	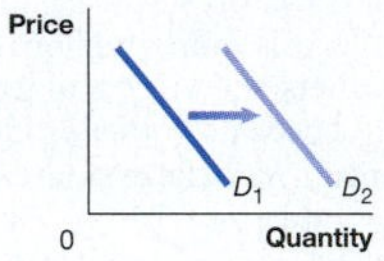	additional consumers result in a greater quantity demanded at every price.
the expected price of the good in the future	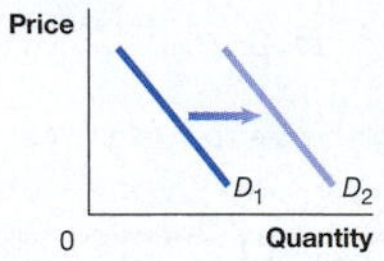	consumers buy more of the good today to avoid the higher price in the future.

Review Questions and *Problems and Applications*—Grouped by Learning Objective to Improve Assessment

All end-of-chapter material—*Summary, Review Questions,* and *Problems and Applications*—is grouped under learning objectives. The goals of this organization are to make it easier for instructors to assign problems based on learning objectives, both in the book and in MyEconLab, and to help students efficiently review material that they find difficult. If students have difficulty with a particular learning objective, an instructor can easily identify which end-of-chapter questions and problems support that objective and assign them as homework or discuss them in class. Every exercise in a chapter's *Problems and Applications* section is available in MyEconLab. Using MyEconLab, students can complete these and many other exercises online, get tutorial help, and receive instant feedback and assistance on exercises they answer incorrectly. Also, student learning will be enhanced by having the summary material and problems grouped together by learning objective, which will allow them to focus on the parts of the chapter they find most challenging. Each major section of the chapter, paired with a learning objective, has at least two review questions and three problems.

As in the previous editions, we include one or more end-of-chapter problems that test students' understanding of the content presented in the *Solved Problem, Making the Connection,* and *Don't Let This Happen to You* special features in the chapter. Instructors can cover a feature in class and assign the corresponding problem for homework. The Test Item Files also include test questions that pertain to these special features.

Real-Time Data Exercises

Select chapters end with at least two *Real-Time Data Exercises* that help students become familiar with a key data source, learn how to locate data, and develop skills in interpreting data. *Real-Time Data Analysis (RTDA) Exercises,* marked with , allow students and instructors to use the very latest data from FRED.

Integrated Supplements

The authors and Pearson Education/Prentice Hall have worked together to integrate the text, print, and media resources to make teaching and learning easier.

MyEconLab

MyEconLab is a unique online course management, testing, and tutorial resource.

For the Instructor

Instructors can choose how much or how little time to spend setting up and using MyEconLab. Here is a snapshot of what instructors are saying about MyEconLab:

> MyEconLab offers [students] a way to practice every week. They receive immediate feedback and a feeling of personal attention. As a result, my teaching has become more targeted and efficient.—Kelly Blanchard, Purdue University
>
> Students tell me that offering them MyEconLab is almost like offering them individual tutors.—Jefferson Edwards, Cypress Fairbanks College
>
> MyEconLab's eText is great—particularly in that it helps offset the skyrocketing cost of textbooks. Naturally, students love that.—Doug Gehrke, Moraine Valley Community College

Each chapter contains two preloaded exercise sets that can be used to build an individualized study plan for each student. These study plan exercises contain tutorial resources, including instant feedback, links to the appropriate learning objective in the eText, pop-up definitions from the text, and step-by-step guided solutions, where appropriate. After the initial setup of the course by the instructor, student use of these materials requires no further instructor setup. The online grade book records each student's performance and time spent on the tests and study plan and generates reports by student or chapter.

Alternatively, instructors can fully customize MyEconLab to match their course exactly, including reading assignments, homework assignments, video assignments, current news assignments, and quizzes and tests. Assignable resources include:

- Preloaded exercise assignments sets for each chapter include the student tutorial resources mentioned earlier.
- Preloaded quizzes for each chapter are unique to the text and not repeated in the study plan or homework exercise sets.
- Study plan problems are similar to the end-of-chapter problems and numbered exactly as in the book to make assigning homework easier.
- *Real-Time Data Analysis Exercises,* marked with , allow students and instructors to use the very latest data from FRED. By completing the exercises, students become familiar

with a key data source, learn how to locate data, and develop skills in interpreting data. In the eText available in MyEconLab, select figures labeled MyEconLab Real-Time Data allow students to display a pop-up graph updated with real-time data from FRED.

- *Current News Exercises* provide a turnkey way to assign gradable news-based exercises in MyEconLab. Each week, Pearson scours the news, finds a current microeconomics article and a current macroeconomics article, creates exercises around these news articles, and adds them to MyEconLab. Assigning and grading current news-based exercises that deal with the latest micro and macro events and policy issues has never been more convenient.
- *Experiments in MyEconLab* provide a fun and engaging way to promote active learning and mastery of important economic concepts. Pearson's Experiments program is flexible, easy-to-assign, auto-graded, and available in Single and Multiplayer versions. Single-player experiments allow your students to play against virtual players from anywhere at any time, as long as they have an Internet connection. Multiplayer experiments allow you to assign and manage a real-time experiment with your class. Pre- and post-questions for each experiment are available for assignment in MyEconLab. For a complete list of available experiments, visit **www.myeconlab.com**.
- Test Item File questions allow you to assign quizzes or homework that look just like your exams.
- *Econ Exercise Builder* allows you to build customized exercises. Exercises include multiple-choice, graph drawing, and free-response items, many of which are generated algorithmically so that each time a student works them, a different variation is presented. MyEconLab grades every problem type except essays—even problems with graphs. When working homework exercises, students receive immediate feedback, with links to additional learning tools.

Customization and Communication

MyEconLab in MyLab/Mastering provides additional optional customization and communication tools. Instructors who teach distance-learning courses or very large lecture sections find the MyLab/Mastering format useful because they can upload course documents and assignments, customize the order of chapters, and use communication features such as Document Sharing, Chat, ClassLive, and Discussion Board.

For the Student

MyEconLab puts students in control of their learning through a collection of testing, practice, and study tools tied to the online, interactive version of the textbook and other media resources. Here is a snapshot of what students are saying about MyEconLab:

> It was very useful because it had EVERYTHING, from practice exams to exercises to reading. Very helpful.—student, Northern Illinois University
>
> I would recommend taking the quizzes on MyEconLab because it gives you a true account of whether or not you understand the material.—student, Montana Tech
>
> It made me look through the book to find answers, so I did more reading.—student, Northern Illinois University

Students can study on their own or can complete assignments created by their instructor. In MyEconLab's structured environment, students practice what they learn, test their understanding, and pursue a personalized study plan generated from their performance on sample tests and from quizzes created by their instructors. In Homework or Study Plan mode, students have access to a wealth of tutorial features, including:

- Instant feedback on exercises that helps students understand and apply the concepts
- Links to the eText to promote reading of the text just when the student needs to revisit a concept or an explanation

- Step-by-step guided solutions that force students to break down a problem in much the same way an instructor would do during office hours
- Pop-up key term definitions from the eText to help students master the vocabulary of economics
- A graphing tool that is integrated into the various exercises to enable students to build and manipulate graphs to better understand how concepts, numbers, and graphs connect

Additional MyEconLab Tools

MyEconLab includes the following additional features:

- **Enhanced eText.** Students actively read and learn, and with more engagement than ever before, through embedded and auto-graded practice, real-time data-graph updates, animations, author videos, and more.
- **Print upgrade.** For students who wish to complete assignments in MyEconLab but read in print, Pearson offers registered MyEconLab users a loose-leaf version of the print text at a significant discount.
- **Glossary flashcards.** Every key term is available as a flashcard, allowing students to quiz themselves on vocabulary from one or more chapters at a time.

MyEconLab content has been created through the efforts of Chris Annala, State University of New York–Geneseo; Charles Baum, Middle Tennessee State University; Peggy Dalton, Frostburg State University; Carol Dole, Jacksonville University; David Foti, Lone Star College; Sarah Ghosh, University of Scranton; Satyajit Ghosh, University of Scranton; Melissa Honig, Pearson Education; Woo Jung, University of Colorado; Courtney Kamauf, Pearson Education; Chris Kauffman, University of Tennessee–Knoxville; Russell Kellogg, University of Colorado–Denver; Noel Lotz, Pearson Education; Katherine McCann, University of Delaware; Daniel Mizak, Frostburg State University; Christine Polek, University of Massachusetts–Boston; Mark Scanlan, Stephen F. Austin State University; Leonie L. Stone, State University of New York–Geneseo; and Bert G. Wheeler, Cedarville University.

Other Resources for the Instructor

Instructor's Manuals

Edward Scahill of the University of Scranton prepared the *Instructor's Manual* for *Microeconomics* and for *Macroeconomics*. The *Instructor's Manuals* include chapter-by-chapter summaries, learning objectives, extended examples and class exercises, teaching outlines incorporating key terms and definitions, teaching tips, topics for class discussion, new *Solved Problems*, new *Making the Connection* features, and solutions to all review questions, problems, and real-time data exercises in the book. The *Instructor's Manuals* are available in print and for download from the Instructor's Resource Center (**www.pearsonhighered.com/hubbard**). The solutions to the end-of-chapter review questions and problems were prepared by the authors and Edward Scahill of the University of Scranton.

Two Test Item Files

Randy Methenitis of Richland College prepared Test Item Files for *Microeconomics* and for *Macroeconomics*. Each Test Item File includes 4,000 multiple-choice, true/false, short-answer, and graphing questions. There are questions to support each key feature in the book. The Test Item Files are available in print and for download from the Instructor's Resource Center (**www.pearsonhighered.com/hubbard**). Test questions are annotated with the following information:

- **Difficulty**—1 for straight recall, 2 for some analysis, 3 for complex analysis
- **Type**—multiple-choice, true/false, short-answer, essay

- **Topic**—the term or concept the question supports
- **Learning outcome**
- **AACSB** (see the description that follows)
- **Page number** in the text
- **Special feature in the main book**—chapter-opening business example, *Economics in Your Life, Solved Problem, Making the Connection,* and *Don't Let This Happen to You*

The Association to Advance Collegiate Schools of Business (AACSB)

The Test Item File author has connected select questions to the general knowledge and skill guidelines found in the AACSB Assurance of Learning Standards.

What Is the AACSB?

The AACSB is a not-for-profit corporation of educational institutions, corporations, and other organizations devoted to the promotion and improvement of higher education in business administration and accounting. A collegiate institution offering degrees in business administration or accounting may volunteer for AACSB accreditation review. The AACSB makes initial accreditation decisions and conducts periodic reviews to promote continuous quality improvement in management education. Pearson Education is a proud member of the AACSB and is pleased to provide advice to help you apply AACSB Assurance of Learning Standards.

What Are AACSB Assurance of Learning Standards?

One of the criteria for AACSB accreditation is the quality of curricula. Although no specific courses are required, the AACSB expects a curriculum to include learning experiences in the following categories of Assurance of Learning Standards:

- Written and Oral Communication
- Ethical Understanding and Reasoning
- Analytical Thinking Skills
- Information Technology
- Diverse and Multicultural Work
- Reflective Thinking
- Application of Knowledge

Questions that test skills relevant to these standards are tagged with the appropriate standard. For example, a question testing the moral questions associated with externalities would receive the Ethical Understanding and Reasoning tag.

How Can Instructors Use the AACSB Tags?

Tagged questions help you measure whether students are grasping the course content that aligns with the AACSB guidelines noted earlier. This in turn may suggest enrichment activities or other educational experiences to help students achieve these skills.

TestGen

The computerized TestGen package allows instructors to customize, save, and generate classroom tests. The test program permits instructors to edit, add, or delete questions from the Test Item Files; analyze test results; and organize a database of tests and student results. This software allows for extensive flexibility and ease of use. It provides many options for organizing and displaying tests, along with search and sort features. The software and the Test Item Files can be downloaded from the Instructor's Resource Center (**www.pearsonhighered.com/hubbard**).

PowerPoint Lecture Presentation

Three sets of PowerPoint slides, prepared by Paul Holmes of Ashland University, are available:

1. A comprehensive set of PowerPoint slides can be used by instructors for class presentations or by students for lecture preview or review. These slides include all the graphs, tables, and equations in the textbook. Two versions are available—step-by-step mode, in which you can build graphs as you would on a blackboard, and automated mode, in which you use a single click per slide.
2. A comprehensive set of PowerPoint slides have Classroom Response Systems (CRS) questions built in so that instructors can incorporate CRS "clickers" into their classroom lectures. Instructors can download these PowerPoint presentations from the Instructor's Resource Center (**www.pearsonhighered.com/hubbard**).
3. A student version of the PowerPoint slides is available as .pdf files. This version allows students to print the slides and bring them to class for note taking. Instructors can download these PowerPoint presentations from the Instructor's Resource Center (**www.pearsonhighered.com/hubbard**).

Learning Catalytics

Learning Catalytics is a "bring your own device" Web-based student engagement, assessment, and classroom intelligence system. This system generates classroom discussion, guides lectures, and promotes peer-to-peer learning with real-time analytics. Students can use any device to interact in the classroom, engage with content, and even draw and share graphs.

To learn more, ask your local Pearson representative or visit **www.learningcatalytics.com**.

Digital Interactives

Focused on a single core topic and organized in progressive levels, each interactive immerses students in an assignable and auto-graded activity. Digital Interactives are also engaging lecture tools for traditional, online, and hybrid courses, many incorporating real-time data, data displays, and analysis tools for rich classroom discussions.

Other Resources for the Student

In addition to MyEconLab, Pearson provides the following resources.

Dynamic Study Modules

With a focus on key topics, these modules work by continuously assessing student performance and activity in real time and, using data and analytics, provide personalized content to reinforce concepts that target each student's particular strengths and weaknesses.

PowerPoint Slides

For student use as a study aid or note-taking guide, PowerPoint slides, prepared by Paul Holmes of Ashland University, can be downloaded from MyEconLab or the Instructor's Resource Center and made available to students. The slides include:

- All graphs, tables, and equations in the text
- Figures in step-by-step mode and automated modes, using a single click per graph curve
- End-of-chapter key terms with hyperlinks to relevant slides

Accuracy Review Board and Reviewers

The guidance and recommendations of the following instructors helped us develop the revision plans for the sixth edition and the supplements package. While we could not incorporate every suggestion from every consultant board member, reviewer, or accuracy checker, we do thank each and every one of you and acknowledge that your feedback was indispensable in developing this text. We greatly appreciate your assistance in making this the best text it could be; you have helped teach a whole new generation of students about the exciting world of economics.

Accuracy Review Board

Our accuracy checkers did a particularly painstaking and thorough job of helping us proof the graphs, equations, and features of the text and supplements. We are grateful for their time and commitment:

Fatma Abdel-Raouf, Goldey-Beacom College
Clare Battista, California Polytechnic State University
Doris Bennett, Jacksonville State University
Harry Ellis, University of North Texas
Robert Gillette, University of Kentucky
Edward T. Gullason, formerly, Dowling College
Anthony Gyapong, Pennsylvania State University—Abington
Randy Methenitis, Richland College
Brian Rosario, University of California–Davis
Edward Scahill, University of Scranton

Reviewers

The guidance and thoughtful recommendations of many instructors helped us develop and implement a revision plan that improved the book's content, enhanced the figures, and strengthened the assessment features. We extend special thanks to Edward Scahill of the University of Scranton for helping us revise the chapter openers and the solutions to the end-of-chapter questions and problems, to Randy Methenitis of Richland College for helping us revise the *An Inside Look* feature in Chapters 1–4, and to Fernando Quijano for creating all the figures in the book and supplements. We are grateful for the comments and many helpful suggestions received from the following reviewers:

Sindy Abadie, Southwest Tennessee Community College
Olugbenga Ajilore, The University of Toledo
Robert Berman, American University
Benjamin Blair, Columbus State University
William Browning, Florida Gulf Coast University
Eliane P. Catilina, Graduate School USA
Lisa Citron, Cascadia College
Erik Craft, University of Richmond
Eva Dziadula, University of Notre Dame
Christi Esquivel, Navarro College
Mary Flannery, University of Notre Dame
Alan S. Fudge, Linn-Benton Community College
Ward Hooker, Central Community College
Michael Jones, University of Cincinnati
Janice Kinghorn, Miami University
Tom Lehman, Indiana Wesleyan University
Svitlana Maksymenko, University of Pittsburgh
Robin S. McCutcheon, Marshall University College of Business
Charles Meyrick, Housatonic Community College
Victoria Willis-Miller, Piedmont Technical College
Fola Odebunmi, Cypress College
Sheri Perez, College of Southern Nevada
Mehul Rangwala, University of Phoenix
Nicole L. Cornell Sadowski, York College of Pennsylvania
Edward Scahill, University of Scranton
Richard Lee Slotkin, Pasadena City College
Ralph Sonenshine, American University
Laura Storino, Rowan University
John Tommasi, University of Massachusetts–Lowell
Christopher Westley, Jacksonville State University
Mark Witte, Northwestern University

Previous Edition Class Testers, Accuracy Reviewers, and Consultants

Class Testers

We are grateful to both the instructors who class-tested manuscript of the first edition and their students for providing useful recommendations on how to make chapters more interesting, relevant, and comprehensive:

Charles A. Bennett, Gannon University
Anne E. Bresnock, University of California–Los Angeles, and California State Polytechnic University–Pomona
Linda Childs-Leatherbury, Lincoln University, Pennsylvania
John Eastwood, Northern Arizona University
David Eaton, Murray State University
Paul Elgatian, St. Ambrose University
Patricia A. Freeman, Jackson State University
Robert Godby, University of Wyoming
Frank Gunter, Lehigh University
Ahmed Ispahani, University of LaVerne
Brendan Kennelly, Lehigh University and National University of Ireland–Galway
Ernest Massie, Franklin University
Carol McDonough, University of Massachusetts–Lowell
Shah Mehrabi, Montgomery College
Sharon Ryan, University of Missouri–Columbia
Bruce G. Webb, Gordon College
Madelyn Young, Converse College
Susan Zumas, Lehigh University

Accuracy Review Boards

We are grateful to the following accuracy checkers of the previous editions for their hard work on the book and supplements:

Fatma Abdel-Raouf, Goldey-Beacom College
Anne Alexander, University of Wyoming
Mohammad Bajwa, Northampton Community College
Cynthia Bansak, St. Lawrence University
Hamid Bastin, Shippensburg University
Kelly Hunt Blanchard, Purdue University
Don Bumpass, Sam Houston State University
Charles Callahan III, State University of New York–Brockport
Mark S. Chester, Reading Area Community College
Kenny Christianson, Binghamton University
Ishita Edwards, Oxnard College
Harold Elder, University of Alabama
Harry Ellis, University of North Texas
Can Erbil, Brandeis University
Marc Fusaro, Arkansas Tech University
Sarah Ghosh, University of Scranton
Robert Gillette, University of Kentucky
Maria Giuili, Diablo Valley College
Mark Gius, Quinnipiac University
Robert Godby, University of Wyoming
William L. Goffe, Pennsylvania State University
Anthony Gyapong, Pennsylvania State University—Abington
Travis Hayes, University of Tennessee–Chattanooga
Carol Hogan, University of Michigan–Dearborn
Anisul M. Islam, University of Houston–Downtown
Aaron Jackson, Bentley College
Nancy Jianakoplos, Colorado State University
Thomas C. Kinnaman, Bucknell University
Mary K. Knudson, University of Iowa
Faik A. Koray, Louisiana State University
Stephan Kroll, California State University–Sacramento
Tony Lima, California State University–East Bay
Randy Methenitis, Richland College
Normal C. Miller, Miami University
David Mitch, University of Maryland–Baltimore County
James A. Moreno, Blinn College
Michael Potepan, San Francisco State University
Mary L. Pranzo, California State University–Fresno
Fernando Quijano, Dickinson State University
Matthew Rafferty, Quinnipiac University
Ratha Ramoo, Diablo Valley College
Jeff Reynolds, Northern Illinois University
Brian Rosario, University of California–Davis
Joseph M. Santos, South Dakota State University
Edward Scahill, University of Scranton
Mark V. Siegler, California State University–Sacramento
Rachel Small, University of Colorado–Boulder
Stephen Smith, Bakersfield College
Rajeev Sooreea, Pennsylvania State University–Altoona
Rebecca Stein, University of Pennsylvania
Ed Steinberg, New York University
Michael Stone, Quinnipiac University
Arlena Sullivan, Jones County Junior College
Wendine Thompson–Dawson, University of Utah
Julianne Treme, University of North Carolina–Wilmington
Robert Whaples, Wake Forest University

Consultant Boards

We received guidance from a dedicated consultant board during the development of the previous editions at several critical junctures. We relied on the board for input on content, figure treatment, and design:

Kate Antonovics, University of California–San Diego
Robert Beekman, University of Tampa
Valerie Bencivenga, University of Texas–Austin
Kelly Blanchard, Purdue University
Susan Dadres, Southern Methodist University
Harry Ellis, Jr., University of North Texas
Sherman T. Folland, Oakland University
Robert Gillette, University of Kentucky
Robert Godby, University of Wyoming
William L. Goffe, Pennsylvania State University
Jane S. Himarios, University of Texas–Arlington
Donn M. Johnson, Quinnipiac University
Mark Karscig, Central Missouri State University
Jenny Minier, University of Kentucky
David Mitch, University of Maryland–Baltimore County
Nicholas Noble, Miami University
Michael Potepan, San Francisco State University
Matthew Rafferty, Quinnipiac University
Helen Roberts, University of Illinois–Chicago
Robert Rosenman, Washington State University
Joseph M. Santos, South Dakota State University
Stephen Snyder, University of Pittsburgh
Martin C. Spechler, Indiana University–Purdue University Indianapolis
Robert Whaples, Wake Forest University
Jonathan B. Wight, University of Richmond

Reviewers

The guidance and recommendations of the following instructors helped us shape the previous editions.

ALABAMA

William P. Aldridge, University of Alabama
Doris Bennett, Jacksonville State University
Harold W. Elder, University of Alabama–Tuscaloosa
Wanda Hudson, Alabama Southern Community College
Keith D. Malone, University of North Alabama
Edward Merkel, Troy University
James L. Swofford, University of Southern Alabama

ARIZONA

Doug Conway, Mesa Community College
John Eastwood, Northern Arizona University
Price Fishback, University of Arizona
Anne Williams, Gateway Community College

ARKANSAS

Jerry Crawford, Arkansas State University
Marc Fusaro, Arkansas Tech University
Randall Kesselring, Arkansas State University
Dan Marburger, Arkansas State University

CALIFORNIA

Shawn Abbott, College of the Siskiyous
Renatte Adler, San Diego State University
Ercument Aksoy, Los Angeles Valley College
Maneeza Aminy, Golden Gate University
Kate Antonovics, University of California–San Diego
Becca Arnold, Mesa College
Asatar Bair, City College of San Francisco
Diana Bajrami, College of Alameda
Robert Bise, Orange Coast Community College
Victor Brajer, California State University–Fullerton
Anne E. Bresnock, University of California–Los Angeles, and California State Polytechnic University–Pomona
David Brownstone, University of California–Irvine
Maureen Burton, California State Polytechnic University–Pomona
Annette Chamberlin, National College
Anoshua Chaudhuri, San Francisco State University
James G. Devine, Loyola Marymount University
Jose Esteban, Palomar College
Roger Frantz, San Diego State University
Craig Gallet, California State University–Sacramento
Andrew Gill, California State University–Fullerton
Maria Giuili, Diablo Valley College
Julie Gonzalez, University of California–Santa Cruz
Lisa Grobar, California State University–Long Beach
Steve Hamilton, California State University–Fullerton
Dewey Heinsma, Mt. San Jacinto Community College
Jessica Howell, California State University–Sacramento
Greg Hunter, California State University–Pomona
John Ifcher, Santa Clara University
Ahmed Ispahani, University of LaVerne
George A. Jouganatos, California State University–Sacramento
Jonathan Kaplan, California State University–Sacramento
Leland Kempe, California State University–Fresno
Philip King, San Francisco State University
Lori Kletzer, University of California, Santa Cruz
Stephan Kroll, California State University–Sacramento
David Lang, California State University–Sacramento
Carsten Lange, California State Polytechnic University–Pomona
Don Leet, California State University–Fresno
Rose LeMont, Modesto Junior College
Tony Lima, California State University–East Bay
Solina Lindahl, California Polytechnic State University–San Luis Obispo
Roger Mack, DeAnza College
Michael Marlow, California Polytechnic State University
Kristen Monaco, California State University–Long Beach
W. Douglas Morgan, University of California, Santa Barbara
Nivedita Mukherji, Oakland University
Solomon Namala, Cerritos College
Andrew Narwold, University of San Diego
Hanna Paulson, West Los Angeles College
Joseph M. Pogodzinksi, San Jose State University

Michael J. Potepan, San Francisco State University
Mary L. Pranzo, California State University–Fresno
Sasha Radisich, Glendale Community College
Ratha Ramoo, Diablo Valley College
Scott J. Sambucci, California State University–East Bay
Ariane Schauer, Marymount College
Frederica Shockley, California State University–Chico
Mark Siegler, California State University–Sacramento
Jonathan Silberman, Oakland University
Lisa Simon, California Polytechnic State University–San Luis Obispo
Stephen Smith, Bakersfield College
Rodney B. Swanson, University of California–Los Angeles
Martha Stuffler, Irvine Valley College
Lea Templer, College of the Canyons
Kristin A. Van Gaasbeck, California State University–Sacramento
Va Nee Van Vleck, California State University–Fresno
Michael Visser, Sonoma State University
Steven Yamarik, California State University–Long Beach
Guy Yamashiro, California State University–Long Beach
Kevin Young, Diablo Valley College
Anthony Zambelli, Cuyamaca College

COLORADO

Mohammed Akacem, Metropolitan State College of Denver
Rhonda Corman, University of Northern Colorado
Dale DeBoer, University of Colorado–Colorado Springs
Debbie Evercloud, University of Colorado–Denver
Karen Gebhardt, Colorado State University
Scott Houser, Colorado School of Mines
Murat Iyigun, University of Colorado at Boulder
Nancy Jianakoplos, Colorado State University
Jay Kaplan, University of Colorado–Boulder
William G. Mertens, University of Colorado–Boulder
Rachael Small, University of Colorado–Boulder
Stephen Weiler, Colorado State University

CONNECTICUT

Christopher P. Ball, Quinnipiac University
Mark Gius, Quinnipiac University
Mark Jablonowski, University of Hartford
Donn M. Johnson, Quinnipiac University
Robert Martel, University of Connecticut
Judith Mills, Southern Connecticut State University
Matthew Rafferty, Quinnipiac University
Christian Zimmermann, University of Connecticut

DELAWARE

Fatma Abdel-Raouf, Goldey-Beacom College
Ali Ataiifar, Delaware County Community College
Andrew T. Hill, University of Delaware

FLORIDA

Frank Albritton, Seminole State College
Herman Baine, Broward Community College
Robert L. Beekman, University of Tampa
Eric P. Chiang, Florida Atlantic University
Martine Duchatelet, Barry University
Hadley Hartman, Santa Fe Community College
Richard Hawkins, University of West Florida
Brad Kamp, University of South Florida
Brian Kench, University of Tampa
Carrie B. Kerekes, Florida Gulf Coast University
Thomas McCaleb, Florida State University
Barbara A. Moore, University of Central Florida
Augustine Nelson, University of Miami
Jamie Ortiz, Florida Atlantic University
Deborah Paige, Santa Fe Community College
Robert Pennington, University of Central Florida
Bob Potter, University of Central Florida
Jerry Schwartz, Broward Community College–North
William Stronge, Florida Atlantic University
Nora Underwood, University of Central Florida
Zhiguang Wang, Florida International University
Joan Wiggenhorn, Barry University

GEORGIA

Greg Brock, Georgia Southern University
Donna Fisher, Georgia Southern University
Shelby Frost, Georgia State University
John King, Georgia Southern University
Constantin Ogloblin, Georgia Southern University
Dr. Greg Okoro, Georgia Perimeter College–Clarkston
Michael Reksulak, Georgia Southern University
Bill Yang, Georgia Southern University

IDAHO

Cynthia Hill, Idaho State University
Don Holley, Boise State University
Tesa Stegner, Idaho State University

ILLINOIS

Teshome Abebe, Eastern Illinois University
Ali Akarca, University of Illinois–Chicago
Zsolt Becsi, Southern Illinois University–Carbondale
James Bruehler, Eastern Illinois University
Louis Cain, Loyola University and Northwestern University
Rosa Lea Danielson, College of DuPage
Kevin Dunagan, Oakton Community College
Scott Gilbert, Southern Illinois University
Rajeev K. Goel, Illinois State University
David Gordon, Illinois Valley Community College
Alan Grant, Eastern Illinois University
Rik Hafer, Southern Illinois University–Edwardsville
Alice Melkumian, Western Illinois University
Christopher Mushrush, Illinois State University
Jeff Reynolds, Northern Illinois University
Helen Roberts, University of Illinois–Chicago
Thomas R. Sadler, Western Illinois University
Eric Schulz, Northwestern University
Dennis Shannon, Southwestern Illinois College

Charles Sicotte, Rock Valley Community College
Neil T. Skaggs, Illinois State University
Kevin Sylwester, Southern Illinois University–Carbondale
Wendine Thompson-Dawson, Monmouth College
Tara Westerhold, Western Illinois University
Mark Witte, Northwestern University
Laurie Wolff, Southern Illinois University–Carbondale
Paula Worthington, Northwestern University

INDIANA

Kelly Blanchard, Purdue University
Cecil Bohanon, Ball State University
Kirk Doran, University of Notre Dame
Thomas Gresik, University of Notre Dame
Robert B. Harris, Indiana University–Purdue University Indianapolis
Fred Herschede, Indiana University–South Bend
Abraham Mathew, Indiana University–Purdue University Indianapolis
John Pomery, Purdue University
Curtis Price, University of Southern Indiana
Rob Rude, Ivy Tech Community College
James K. Self, Indiana University–Bloomington
Esther-Mirjam Sent, University of Notre Dame
Virginia Shingleton, Valparaiso University
Martin C. Spechler, Indiana University–Purdue University Indianapolis
Arun K. Srinivasan, Indiana University–Southeast Campus
Geetha Suresh, Purdue University

IOWA

Terry Alexander, Iowa State University
Paul Elgatian, St. Ambrose University
Jennifer Fuhrman, University of Iowa
Ken McCormick, University of Northern Iowa
Andy Schuchart, Iowa Central Community College
John Solow, University of Iowa
Jonathan Warner, Dordt College

KANSAS

Guatam Bhattacharya, University of Kansas
Amanda Freeman, Kansas State University
Dipak Ghosh, Emporia State University
Alan Grant, Baker University
Wayne Oberle, St. Ambrose University
Jodi Messer Pelkowski, Wichita State University
Martin Perline, Wichita State University
Joel Potter, Kansas State University
Joshua Rosenbloom, University of Kansas
Shane Sanders, Kansas State University
Dosse Toulaboe, Fort Hays State University
Bhavneet Walia, Kansas State University

KENTUCKY

Tom Cate, Northern Kentucky University
Nan-Ting Chou, University of Louisville
David Eaton, Murray State University
Ann Eike, University of Kentucky
Robert Gillette, University of Kentucky
Barry Haworth, University of Louisville
Gail Hoyt, University of Kentucky
Donna Ingram, Eastern Kentucky University
Waithaka Iraki, Kentucky State University
Hak Youn Kim, Western Kentucky University
Martin Milkman, Murray State University
Jenny Minier, University of Kentucky
David Shideler, Murray State University
John Vahaly, University of Louisville

LOUISIANA

Lara Gardner, Southeastern Louisiana University
Jay Johnson, Southeastern Louisiana University
Faik Koray, Louisiana State University
Paul Nelson, University of Louisiana–Monroe
Sung Chul No, Southern University and A&M College
Tammy Parker, University of Louisiana–Monroe
Wesley A. Payne, Delgado Community College
Nancy Rumore, University of Louisiana at Lafayette

MARYLAND

Carey Borkoski, Anne Arundel Community College
Kathleen A. Carroll, University of Maryland–Baltimore County
Jill Caviglia-Harris, Salisbury University
Dustin Chambers, Salisbury University
Karl Einolf, Mount Saint Mary's University
Marsha Goldfarb, University of Maryland–Baltimore City
Bruce Madariaga, Montgomery College
Shah Mehrabi, Montgomery College
Gretchen Mester, Anne Arundel Community College
David Mitch, University of Maryland–Baltimore County
John Neri, University of Maryland
Henry Terrell, University of Maryland

MASSACHUSETTS

William L. Casey, Jr., Babson College
Arthur Schiller Casimir, Western New England College
Michael Enz, Western New England College
Can Erbil, Brandeis University
Lou Foglia, Suffolk University
Gerald Friedman, University of Massachusetts
Todd Idson, Boston University
Aaron Jackson, Bentley College
Russell A. Janis, University of Massachusetts–Amherst
Anthony Laramie, Merrimack College
Carol McDonough, University of Massachusetts–Lowell
William O'Brien, Worcester State College
Ahmad Saranjam, Bridgewater State College
Howard Shore, Bentley College
Janet Thomas, Bentley College
Gregory H. Wassall, Northeastern University
Bruce G. Webb, Gordon College
Gilbert Wolpe, Newbury College
Jay Zagorsky, Boston University

MICHIGAN
Eric Beckman, Delta College
Jared Boyd, Henry Ford Community College
Victor Claar, Hope College
Dr. Sonia Dalmia, Grand Valley State University
Daniel Giedeman, Grand Valley State University
Allen C. Goodman, Wayne State University
Steven Hayworth, Eastern Michigan University
Gregg Heidebrink, Washtenaw Community College
Carol Hogan, University of Michigan–Dearborn
Marek Kolar, Delta College
Susan J. Linz, Michigan State University
James Luke, Lansing Community College
Ilir Miteza, University of Michigan–Dearborn
John Nader, Grand Valley State University
Norman P. Obst, Michigan State University
Laudo M. Ogura, Grand Valley State University
Robert J. Rossana, Wayne State University
Michael J. Ryan, Western Michigan University
Charles A. Stull, Kalamazoo College
Michael J. Twomey, University of Michigan–Dearborn
Mark Wheeler, Western Michigan University
Wendy Wysocki, Monroe County Community College

MINNESOTA
Mary Edwards, Saint Cloud State University
Phillip J. Grossman, Saint Cloud State University
Monica Hartman, University of St. Thomas
Matthew Hyle, Winona State University
David J. O'Hara, Metropolitan State University–Minneapolis
Kwang Woo (Ken) Park, Minnesota State University–Mankato
Artatrana Ratha, Saint Cloud State University
Ken Rebeck, Saint Cloud State University
Katherine Schmeiser, University of Minnesota

MISSISSIPPI
Becky Campbell, Mississippi State University
Randall Campbell, Mississippi State University
Patricia A. Freeman, Jackson State University
Arlena Sullivan, Jones County Junior College

MISSOURI
Chris Azevedo, University of Central Missouri
Ariel Belasen, Saint Louis University
Catherine Chambers, University of Central Missouri
Paul Chambers, University of Central Missouri
Kermit Clay, Ozarks Technical Community College
Ben Collier, Northwest Missouri State University
John R. Crooker, University of Central Missouri
Jo Durr, Southwest Missouri State University
Julie H. Gallaway, Southwest Missouri State University
Terrel Gallaway, Southwest Missouri State University
Mark Karscig, Central Missouri State University
Nicholas D. Peppes, Saint Louis Community College–Forest Park
Steven T. Petty, College of the Ozarks
Sharon Ryan, University of Missouri–Columbia
Ben Young, University of Missouri–Kansas City

MONTANA
Agnieszka Bielinska-Kwapisz, Montana State University–Bozeman
Jeff Bookwalter, University of Montana–Missoula

NEBRASKA
John Dogbey, University of Nebraska–Omaha
Allan Jenkins, University of Nebraska–Kearney
James Knudsen, Creighton University
Craig MacPhee, University of Nebraska–Lincoln
Kim Sosin, University of Nebraska–Omaha
Mark E. Wohar, University of Nebraska–Omaha

NEVADA
Michael H. Lampert, Truckee Meadows Community College
Bernard Malamud, University of Nevada–Las Vegas
Bill Robinson, University of Nevada–Las Vegas

NEW HAMPSHIRE
Evelyn Gick, Dartmouth College
Neil Niman, University of New Hampshire

NEW JERSEY
Len Anyanwu, Union County College
Maharuk Bhiladwalla, Rutgers University–New Brunswick
Giuliana Campanelli-Andreopoulos, William Paterson University
Gary Gigliotti, Rutgers University–New Brunswick
John Graham, Rutgers University–Newark
Berch Haroian, William Paterson University
Paul Harris, Camden County College
Jeff Rubin, Rutgers University
Henry Ryder, Gloucester County College
Donna Thompson, Brookdale Community College

NEW MEXICO
Donald Coes, University of New Mexico
Kate Krause, University of New Mexico
Curt Shepherd, University of New Mexico

NEW YORK
Seemi Ahmad, Dutchess Community College
Chris Annala, State University of New York–Geneseo
Erol Balkan, Hamilton College
John Bockino, Suffolk County Community College–Ammerman
Charles Callahan III, State University of New York–Brockport
Michael Carew, Baruch College
Sean Corcoran, New York University
Ranjit S. Dighe, City University of New York–Bronx Community College
Debra Dwyer, Stony Brook University
Glenn Gerstner, Saint John's University–Queens
Susan Glanz, Saint John's University–Queens

Wayne A. Grove, LeMoyne College
Nancy Howe, Hudson Valley Community College
Christopher Inya, Monroe Community College
Ghassan Karam, Pace University
Clifford Kern, State University of New York–Binghamton
Mary Lesser, Iona College
Anna Musatti, Columbia University
Theodore Muzio, St. John's University, New York
Emre Ozsoz, Fashion Institute of Technology
Howard Ross, Baruch College
Ed Steinberg, New York University
Leonie Stone, State University of New York–Geneseo
Ganti Subrahmanyam, University of Buffalo
Jogindar S. Uppal, State University of New York–Albany
Susan Wolcott, Binghamton University

NORTH CAROLINA

Rita Balaban, University of North Carolina
Otilia Boldea, North Carolina State University
Robert Burrus, University of North Carolina–Wilmington
Lee A. Craig, North Carolina State University
Alexander Deshkovski, North Carolina Central University
Kathleen Dorsainvil, Winston–Salem State University
Lydia Gan, School of Business, University of North Carolina–Pembroke
Michael Goode, Central Piedmont Community College
Salih Hakeem, North Carolina Central University
Melissa Hendrickson, North Carolina State University
Haiyong Liu, East Carolina University
Kosmas Marinakis, North Carolina State University
Todd McFall, Wake Forest University
Shahriar Mostashari, Campbell University
Jonathan Phillips, North Carolina State University
Bobby Puryear, North Carolina State University
Jeff Sarbaum, University of North Carolina–Greensboro
Peter Schuhmann, University of North Carolina–Wilmington
Robert Shoffner, Central Piedmont Community College
Catherine Skura, Sandhills Community College
Carol Stivender, University of North Carolina–Charlotte
Vera Tabakova, East Carolina University
Eric Taylor, Central Piedmont Community College
Julianne Treme, University of North Carolina–Wilmington
Hui-Kuan Tseng, University of North Carolina at Charlotte
Robert Whaples, Wake Forest University
John Whitehead, Appalachian State University
Gary W. Zinn, East Carolina University
Rick Zuber, University of North Carolina at Charlotte

OHIO

John P. Blair, Wright State University
Bolong Cao, Ohio University–Athens
Kyongwook Choi, Ohio University
James D'Angelo, University of Cincinnati
Darlene DeVera, Miami University
Rudy Fichtenbaum, Wright State University
Tim Fuerst, Bowling Green University
Harley Gill, Ohio State University
Leroy Gill, Ohio State University
Steven Heubeck, Ohio State University
Daniel Horton, Cleveland State University
Kristen Keith, University of Toledo
Jean Kujawa, Lourdes College
Ernest Massie, Franklin University
Ida A. Mirzaie, Ohio State University
Jay Mutter, University of Akron
Mike Nelson, University of Akron
Nicholas Noble, Miami University
Dennis C. O'Neill, University of Cincinnati
Joseph Palardy, Youngstown State University
Charles Reichheld, Cuyahoga Community College
Teresa Riley, Youngstown State University
Rochelle Ruffer, Youngstown State University
Kate Sheppard, University of Akron
Richard Stratton, University of Akron
Albert Sumell, Youngstown State University
Steve Szheghi, Wilmington College
Melissa Thomasson, Miami University
Yaqin Wang, Youngstown State University
Bert Wheeler, Cedarville University
Kathryn Wilson, Kent State University
Sourushe Zandvakili, University of Cincinnati

OKLAHOMA

David Hudgins, University of Oklahoma
Bill McLean, Oklahoma State University
Denny Myers, Oklahoma City Community College
Ed Price, Oklahoma State University
Abdulhamid Sukar, Cameron University
Zhen Zhu, University of Central Oklahoma

OREGON

Bill Burrows, Lane Community College
Tom Carroll, Central Oregon Community College
Tim Duy, University of Oregon
B. Starr McMullen, Oregon State University
Ted Scheinman, Mount Hood Community College
Larry Singell, University of Oregon
Ayca Tekin-Koru, Oregon State University

PENNSYLVANIA

Bradley Andrew, Juniata College
Mohammad Bajwa, Northampton Community College
Gustavo Barboza, Mercyhurst College
Charles A. Bennett, Gannon University
Cynthia Benzing, West Chester University
Howard Bodenhorn, Lafayette College
Milica Bookman, St. Joseph's University
Robert Brooker, Gannon University

Eric Brucker, Widener University
Shirley Cassing, University of Pittsburgh
Linda Childs-Leatherbury, Lincoln University
Scott J. Dressler, Villanova University
Satyajit Ghosh, University of Scranton
William L. Goffe, Pennsylvania State University
Anthony Gyapong, Pennsylvania State University–Abington
Mehdi Haririan, Bloomsburg University
Andrew Hill, Federal Reserve Bank of Philadelphia
Steven Husted, University of Pittsburgh
James Jozefowicz, Indiana University of Pennsylvania
Stephanie Jozefowicz, Indiana University of Pennsylvania
Nicholas Karatjas, Indiana University of Pennsylvania
Mary Kelly, Villanova University
Brendan Kennelly, Lehigh University
Thomas C. Kinnaman, Bucknell University
Christopher Magee, Bucknell University
Katherine McCann, Penn State
Judy McDonald, Lehigh University
Ranganath Murthy, Bucknell University
Hong V. Nguyen, University of Scranton
Cristian Pardo, Saint Joseph's University
Iordanis Petsas, University of Scranton
Denis Raihall, West Chester University
Adam Renhoff, Drexel University
Nicole Sadowski, York College of Pennsylvania
Edward Scahill, University of Scranton
Ken Slaysman, York College of Pennsylvania
Rajeev Sooreea, Pennsylvania State University–Altoona
Rebecca Stein, University of Pennsylvania
Sandra Trejos, Clarion University
Peter Zaleski, Villanova University
Ann Zech, Saint Joseph's University
Lei Zhu, West Chester University
Susan Zumas, Lehigh University

RHODE ISLAND

Jongsung Kim, Bryant University
Leonard Lardaro, University of Rhode Island
Nazma Latif-Zaman, Providence College

SOUTH CAROLINA

Calvin Blackwell, College of Charleston
Ward Hooker, Orangeburg–Calhoun Technical College
Woodrow W. Hughes, Jr., Converse College
John McArthur, Wofford College
Chad Turner, Clemson University
Madelyn Young, Converse College

SOUTH DAKOTA

Joseph M. Santos, South Dakota State University
Jason Zimmerman, South Dakota State University

TENNESSEE

Sindy Abadie, Southwest Tennessee Community College
Charles Baum, Middle Tennessee State University
John Brassel, Southwest Tennessee Community College
Bichaka Fayissa, Middle Tennessee State University
Michael J. Gootzeit, University of Memphis
Travis Hayes, University of Tennessee–Chattanooga
Christopher C. Klein, Middle Tennessee State University
Leila Pratt, University of Tennessee at Chattanooga
Millicent Sites, Carson-Newman College

TEXAS

Carlos Aguilar, El Paso Community College
Rashid Al-Hmoud, Texas Tech University
William Beaty, Tarleton State University
Klaus Becker, Texas Tech University
Alex Brown, Texas A&M University
Jack A. Bucco, Austin Community College–Northridge and Saint Edward's University
Don Bumpass, Sam Houston State University
Marilyn M. Butler, Sam Houston State University
Mike Cohick, Collin County Community College
Cesar Corredor, Texas A&M University
Steven Craig, University of Houston
Patrick Crowley, Texas A&M University–Corpus Christi
Richard Croxdale, Austin Community College
Susan Dadres, Southern Methodist University
David Davenport, McLennan Community College
Harry Ellis, Jr., University of North Texas
Paul Emberton, Texas State University
Diego Escobari, Texas A&M University
Nicholas Feltovich, University of Houston–Main
Charles Harold Fifield, Baylor University
Jamal G. Husein, Angelo State University
Mark Frank, Sam Houston State University
Alejandro Gelves, Midwestern State University
Edgar Ghossoub, University of Texas–San Antonio
Richard Gosselin, Houston Community College–Central
Sheila Amin Gutierrez de Pineres, University of Texas–Dallas
Tina J. Harvell, Blinn College–Bryan Campus
James W. Henderson, Baylor University
Jane S. Himarios, University of Texas–Arlington
James Holcomb, University of Texas–El Paso
Jamal Husein, Angelo State University
Ansul Islam, University of Houston–Downtown
Karen Johnson, Baylor University
Kathy Kelly, University of Texas–Arlington
Thomas Kemp, Tarrant County College–Northwest
Jim Lee, Texas A&M University–Corpus Christi
Ronnie W. Liggett, University of Texas–Arlington
Akbar Marvasti, University of Houston–Downtown
James Mbata, Houston Community College
Kimberly Mencken, Baylor University
Randy Methenitis, Richland College
Carl Montano, Lamar University
James Moreno, Blinn College
Camille Nelson, Texas A&M University
Michael Nelson, Texas A&M University

Charles Newton, Houston Community College–Southwest College
John Pisciotta, Baylor University
Shofiqur Rahman, University of Texas–El Paso
Sara Saderion, Houston Community College–Southwest College
George E. Samuels, Sam Houston State University
David Schutte, Mountain View College
Ivan Tasic, Texas A&M University
David Torres, University of Texas–El Paso
Ross vanWassenhove, University of Houston
Roger Wehr, University of Texas–Arlington
Jim Wollscheid, Texas A&M University–Kingsville
J. Christopher Wreh, North Central Texas College
David W. Yoskowitz, Texas A&M University–Corpus Christi
Inske Zandvliet, Brookhaven College

UTAH

Chris Fawson, Utah State University
Lowell Glenn, Utah Valley State College
Aric Krause, Westminster College
Arden Pope, Brigham Young University

VERMONT

Nancy Brooks, University of Vermont

VIRGINIA

Lee Badgett, Virginia Military Institute
Lee A. Coppock, University of Virginia
Janelle Davenport, Hampton University
Philip Heap, James Madison University
George E. Hoffer, Virginia Commonwealth University
Oleg Korenok, Virginia Commonwealth University
Larry Landrum, Virginia Western Community College
Frances Lea, Germanna Community College
Carrie Meyer, George Mason University
John Min, Northern Virginia Community College
Eugene Bempong Nyantakyi, West Virginia University
James Roberts, Tidewater Community College–Virginia Beach
Robert Rycroft, University of Mary Washington
Araine A. Schauer, Mary Mount College
Sarah Stafford, The College of William & Mary
Bob Subrick, James Madison University
Susanne Toney, Hampton University
Michelle Vachris, Christopher Newport University
James Wetzel, Virginia Commonwealth University
George Zestos, Christopher Newport University

WASHINGTON

Genevieve Briand, Washington State University
Andrew Ewing, University of Washington
Stacey Jones, Seattle University
Dean Peterson, Seattle University
Robert Rosenman, Washington State University

WEST VIRGINIA

Jacqueline Agesa, Marshall University
Richard Agesa, Marshall University

WISCONSIN

Peng Huang, Ripon College
Marina Karabelas, Milwaukee Area Technical College
Elizabeth Sawyer Kelly, University of Wisconsin–Madison
Pascal Ngoboka, University of Wisconsin–River Falls
Kevin Quinn, St. Norbert College
John R. Stoll, University of Wisconsin–Green Bay

WYOMING

Robert Godby, University of Wyoming

DISTRICT OF COLUMBIA

Leon Battista, American Enterprise Institute
Michael Bradley, George Washington University
Colleen M. Callahan, American University
Robert Feinberg, American University
Walter Park, American University

INTERNATIONAL

Minh Quang Dao, Carleton University–Ottawa, Canada

A Word of Thanks

Once again, we benefited greatly from the dedication and professionalism of the Pearson Economics team. Executive Editor David Alexander's energy and support were indispensable. David helped mold the presentation and provided words of encouragement whenever our energy flagged. Executive Development Editor Lena Buonanno worked tirelessly to ensure that this text was as good as it could be and to coordinate the many moving parts involved in a project of this magnitude. This new edition posed particular challenges, and we remain astonished at the amount of time, energy, and unfailing good humor she brings to this project. As we worked on the first edition, former Director of Key Markets David Theisen provided invaluable insight into how best to structure a principles text. His advice helped shape nearly every chapter. Lindsey Sloan managed all aspects of the media resources and helped keep both them and the print book on schedule. Carla Thompson managed the entire production process, and Sarah Dumouchelle managed the extensive supplement package that accompanies the book. Carla Thompson and Jonathan Boylan turned our manuscript pages into a beautiful published book. Editorial Assistant Michelle Zeng assisted the team in completing several tasks to help produce both the media resources and the book. We received excellent research assistance on this and previous editions from Dante DeAntonio, Ed Timmons, Matthew Saboe, David Van Der Goes, and Jason Hockenberry. We thank Elisa Adams, Pam Smith, Elena Zeller, Jennifer Brailsford, Lindsay K. Clark, Deborah Crowell, Ellen Vandevort Wolf, and Cindy O'Brien for their careful proofreading of first- and second-round page proofs. Over all editions of our books, we received helpful feedback and recommendations from Lehigh University faculty colleagues Frank R. Gunter, Thomas J. Hyclak, and Robert J. Thornton.

As instructors, we recognize how important it is for students to view graphs that are clear and accessible. We are fortunate to have Fernando Quijano render all the figures in our books and also our supplements. Market feedback on the figures continues to be positive. We extend our thanks to Fernando not only for collaborating with us and creating the best figures possible but also for his patience with our demanding schedule.

This sixth edition has several media components, which required skilled and patient creators and developers. We extend special thanks to Andy Taylor of Hodja Media for preparing the video clips and to Paul Graf of the University of Indiana–Bloomington for preparing the graph animations. These videos and animations are an important part of our revision.

A good part of the burden of a project of this magnitude is borne by our families. We appreciate the patience, support, and encouragement of our wives and children.

Economics

CHAPTER

1

Economics: Foundations and Models

Chapter Outline and Learning Objectives

Will Smart Devices Revolutionize Health Care?

If you get sick, your doctor may send you to a hospital or clinic for a series of tests. You'll need to schedule an appointment, travel to the clinic, and spend time in a waiting room. Depending on your medical insurance, you'll also need to pay for the tests. But what if you had an inexpensive smart device that would allow you to test yourself at home and send the results to your doctor? Walter De Brouwer is a Belgian-born entrepreneur who worked in various industries, including telecommunications and publishing. When his son was badly injured in a fall, De Brouwer was inspired to create such a smart device. His California-based firm, Scanadu, developed the Scout, a small disk that when pressed against the side of your head can record your blood pressure, heart rate, and temperature. According to the firm's advertising, the Scout allows you to "Check your health as easily as your e-mail." Some people have compared the Scout to the Tricorder medical device from the *Star Trek* TV series.

Scanadu is not alone in developing new consumer medical devices. The Apple Watch monitors your heart rate, as well as how much exercise you've performed and how many calories you've burned; OraSure sells a home HIV test; and Alivecor sells a device that can be attached to a smartphone and allows people with heart problems to perform their own electrocardiograms.

These firms are reacting to several trends: Many people have become more health conscious; as the population ages, more people are experiencing medical problems; and technological progress has made it possible for small electronic devices, including smartwatches and smartphones, to monitor blood pressure and perform other tasks. These firms are responding to changing *economic incentives*. As we will see, the *market system* provides firms with the incentive and the resources to both create new goods and services and improve existing goods and services. The result is an ever-increasing standard of living for the average person.

Over time, as technology, consumer demand, and government policies change, the market system enables the flow of resources out of some industries and into others. For instance, in the United States resources have been flowing out of the production of manufactured goods such as steel, shoes, and furniture and into the production of services, including medical services. In fact, health care has been the most rapidly expanding sector of the U.S. economy.

AN INSIDE LOOK on **page 20** explores how Google is adding to its growing list of technological innovations by developing smart contact lenses to help patients manage diabetes.

Sources: Timothy Hay, "Gadgets Bring Diagnostics into the Home," *Wall Street Journal*, April 27, 2015; Jacopo Prisco, "Scanadu: The Medical Tricorder from *Star Trek* Is Here," cnn.com, February 11, 2015; and Peter Andrey Smith, "Zombies, Workout Music and Baby Trackers: Health Tech for Everyone," *New York Times*, March 10, 2014.

Economics in Your Life

Will There Be Plenty of Jobs Available in the Health Care Industry?

The U.S. Health Resources and Services Administration (HRSA) forecasts that there will be 866,400 doctors in the United States in 2020. The HRSA also forecasts that by 2020 the country will need 922,000 doctors. In other words, this federal government agency forecasts that there will be a *shortage* of about 55,600 doctors in 2020. The U.S. Bureau of Labor Statistics forecasts that 13 of the 20 fastest-growing occupations over the next 10 years will be in the medical field. But the availability of these jobs depends on the reliability of the forecasts. What is the basis for these forecasts and how reliable are they? As you read this chapter, try to answer this question. You can check your answer against the one we provide on **page 19** at the end of this chapter.

In this book, we use economics to answer questions such as the following:

- What determines the prices of smartwatches?
- Why have health care costs risen so rapidly?
- Why do firms engage in international trade, and how do government policies affect international trade?
- Why does the government control the prices of some goods and services, and what are the effects of those controls?

Economists do not always agree on the answers to every question, and there are lively debates on some issues. Because new problems and issues are constantly arising, economists are always developing new methods to analyze economic questions.

All the topics we discuss in this book illustrate a basic fact of life: To attain our goals, we must make choices. We must make choices because we live in a world of **scarcity**, which means that although our wants are *unlimited*, the resources available to fulfill those wants are *limited*. You might want to own a BMW and spend each summer vacationing at five-star European hotels, but unless Bill Gates is a close and generous relative, you probably lack the funds to fulfill these wants. Every day, you make choices as you spend your limited income on the many goods and services available. The finite amount of time you have also limits your ability to attain your goals. If you spend an hour studying for your economics midterm, you have one hour less to study for your history midterm. Firms and the government are in the same situation as you: They must also attain their goals with limited resources. **Economics** is the study of the choices consumers, business managers, and government officials make to attain their goals, given their scarce resources.

Scarcity A situation in which unlimited wants exceed the limited resources available to fulfill those wants.

Economics The study of the choices people make to attain their goals, given their scarce resources.

We begin this chapter by discussing three important economic ideas that we will return to many times in the following chapters: *People are rational, people respond to economic incentives,* and *optimal decisions are made at the margin*. Then, we consider the three fundamental questions that any economy must answer: *What* goods and services will be produced? *How* will the goods and services be produced? and *Who* will receive the goods and services produced? Next, we consider the role of *economic models* in analyzing economic issues. **Economic models** are simplified versions of reality used to analyze real-world economic situations. We will explore why economists use models and how they construct them. Finally, we will discuss the difference between microeconomics and macroeconomics, and we will preview some important economic terms.

Economic model A simplified version of reality used to analyze real-world economic situations.

1.1 Three Key Economic Ideas

LEARNING OBJECTIVE: Explain these three key economic ideas: People are rational; people respond to economic incentives; and optimal decisions are made at the margin.

Whether your goal is to buy a smartwatch or find a part-time job, you will interact with other people in *markets*. A **market** is a group of buyers and sellers of a good or service and the institution or arrangement by which they come together to trade. Examples of markets are the markets for smartwatches, houses, haircuts, stocks and bonds, and labor. Most of economics involves analyzing how people make choices and interact in markets. Here are the three important ideas about markets that we'll return to frequently:

Market A group of buyers and sellers of a good or service and the institution or arrangement by which they come together to trade.

1. People are rational.
2. People respond to economic incentives.
3. Optimal decisions are made at the margin.

People Are Rational

Economists generally assume that people are rational. This assumption does *not* mean that economists believe everyone knows everything or always makes the "best" decision. It means that economists assume that consumers and firms use all available information as they act to achieve their goals. Rational individuals weigh the benefits and costs of each action, and they choose an action only if the benefits outweigh the costs. For example, if Apple charges a price of $349 for the basic model of its smartwatch, economists assume that the managers at Apple have estimated that this price will earn the company the most profit. Even though the managers may be wrong—maybe a price of $325 or $375 would be more profitable—economists assume that the managers at Apple have acted rationally, on the basis of the information available to them, in choosing the price of $349. Although not everyone behaves rationally all the time, the assumption of rational behavior is very useful in explaining most of the choices that people make.

MyEconLab Concept Check

People Respond to Economic Incentives

Human beings act from a variety of motives, including envy, compassion, and religious belief. While not ignoring other motives, economists emphasize that consumers and firms consistently respond to *economic incentives*. This point may seem obvious, but it is often overlooked. For example, according to an article in the *Wall Street Journal*, the FBI couldn't understand why banks were not taking steps to improve security in the face of an increase in robberies: "FBI officials suggest that banks place uniformed, armed guards outside their doors and install bullet-resistant plastic, known as a 'bandit barrier,' in front of teller windows." FBI officials were surprised that few banks took their advice. But the article also reported that installing bullet-resistant plastic costs $10,000 to $20,000, and a well-trained security guard receives $50,000 per year in salary and benefits. The average loss in a bank robbery is only about $1,200. The economic incentive to banks is clear: It is less costly to put up with bank robberies than to take additional security measures. FBI agents may be surprised by how banks respond to the threat of robberies—but economists are not.

In each chapter, the *Making the Connection* feature discusses a news story or another application related to the chapter material. Read this *Making the Connection* for a discussion of whether people respond to economic incentives even when deciding how much to eat and how much to exercise.

MyEconLab Concept Check

Making the Connection
MyEconLab Video

Does Health Insurance Give People an Incentive to Become Obese?

Obesity is a significant health problem in the United States. Body mass index (BMI) is a measurement of a person's weight relative to the person's height. The U.S. Centers for Disease Control and Prevention (CDC) defines *obesity* for an adult as having a body mass index (BMI) of 30 or greater. For example, a 5'4" adult with a BMI of 30 is 30 pounds overweight. Obesity is a factor in a variety of diseases, including heart disease, stroke, diabetes, and hypertension.

The two maps on the next page show the dramatic increase in obesity between 1994 and 2013. In 1994, in a majority of states, only between 10 percent and 14 percent of the adult population was obese, and in no state was more than 20 percent of the adult population obese. By 2013, in every state, at least 20 percent of the adult population was obese, and in 43 states, at least 25 percent of the adult population was obese.

Many people who suffer from obesity have underlying medical conditions. For these people, obesity is a medical problem that they cannot control. The fact that obesity has increased, though, indicates that for some people obesity is the result of

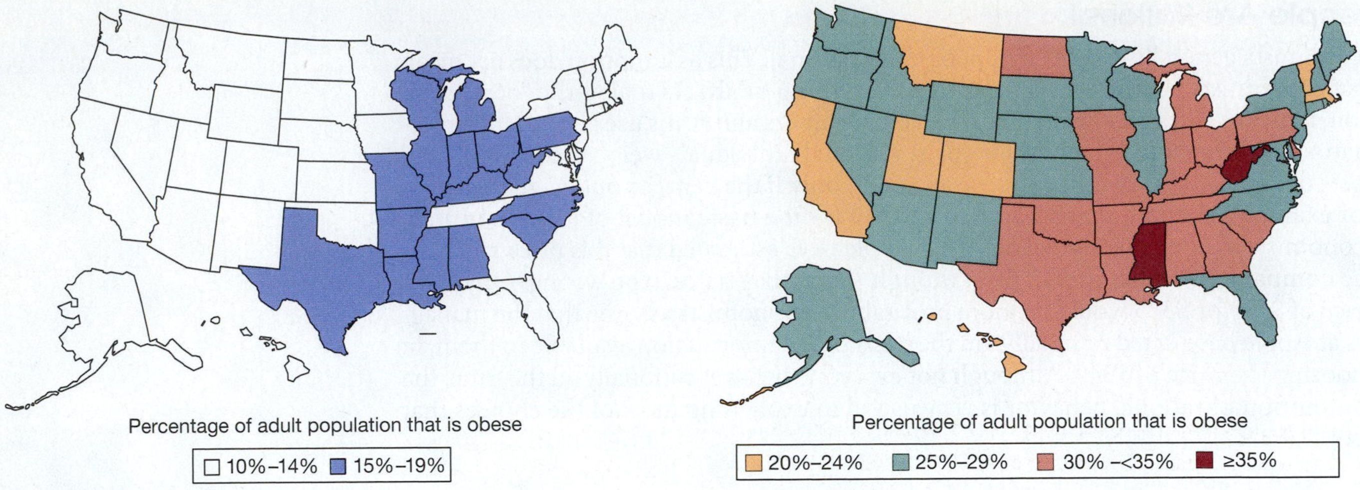

(a) Obesity rates in 1994

(b) Obesity rates in 2013

Source: Centers for Disease Control and Prevention, "Prevalence of Self-Reported Obesity among U.S. Adults."

diet and lifestyle choices. Potential explanations for the increase in obesity include greater intake of high-calorie fast foods, insufficient exercise, and a decline in the physical activity associated with many jobs. The CDC recommends that teenagers get a minimum of 60 minutes of aerobic exercise per day, a standard that only 15 percent of high school students meet. In 1960, 50 percent of jobs in the United States required at least moderate physical activity. Today, only 20 percent of jobs do. As a result, a typical worker today who may work at a computer is burning off about 130 *fewer* calories per workday than a worker in the 1960s who may have walked frequently in a manufacturing plant.

In addition to eating too much and not exercising enough, could having health insurance be a cause of obesity? Obese people tend to suffer more medical problems and so incur higher medical costs. Obese people with health insurance that will reimburse them for only part of their medical bills, or who have no health insurance, must pay some or all of these higher medical bills themselves. People with health insurance that covers most of their medical bills will not suffer as large a monetary cost from being obese. In other words, by reducing some of the costs of obesity, health insurance may give people an economic incentive to gain weight.

At first glance, this argument may seem implausible. Some people suffer from medical conditions that can make physical activity difficult or that can cause weight gain even with moderate eating, so they may become obese whether they have health insurance or not. Some people are obese because of poor eating habits or lack of exercise, and they probably don't consider health insurance when deciding whether to have another slice of chocolate cake or to watch Netflix instead of going to the gym. But if economists are correct about the importance of economic incentives, then we would expect that if we hold all other personal characteristics—such as age, gender, and income—constant, people with health insurance will be more likely to be overweight than people without health insurance.

Jay Bhattacharya and Kate Bundorf of Stanford University, Noemi Pace of the University of Venice, and Neeraj Sood of the University of Southern California, have analyzed the effects of health insurance on weight. Using a sample that followed nearly 80,000 people from 1989 to 2004, they found that after controlling for factors including age, gender, income, education, and race, people with health insurance were significantly more likely to be overweight than people without health insurance. Having private health insurance increased BMI by 1.3 points. Having public health insurance, such as Medicaid, which is a program under which the government provides health care to low-income people, increased BMI by 2.3 points. These findings suggest that people respond to economic incentives even when making decisions about what they eat and how much they exercise.

Note: The exact formula for the body mass index is BMI = (Weight in pounds/Height in inches^2) × 703.

Sources: Centers for Disease Control and Prevention, "Prevalence of Self-Reported Obesity among U.S. Adults," www.cdc.gov; Katherine M. Flegal, Margaret D. Caroll, Cynthia L. Ogden, and Lester R. Curtin, "Prevalence and Trends in Obesity among U.S. Adults, 1999–2008," *Journal of the American Medical Association*, Vol. 303, No. 3, January 20, 2010, pp. 235–241; Jay Bhattacharya, Kate Bundorf, Noemi Pace, and Neeraj Sood, "Does Health Insurance Make You Fat?" in Michael Grossman and Naci H. Mocan, eds., *Economic Aspects of Obesity*, Chicago: University of Chicago Press, 2011; and Tara Parker-Pope, "Less Active at Work, Americans Have Packed on Pounds," *New York Times*, May 25, 2011.

Your Turn: Test your understanding by doing related problems 1.7 and 1.8 on page 23 at the end of this chapter.

MyEconLab Study Plan

Optimal Decisions Are Made at the Margin

Some decisions are "all or nothing." For instance, when an entrepreneur decides whether to open a new restaurant, she starts the new restaurant or she doesn't. When you decide whether to attend graduate school, you either enter graduate school or you don't. But rather than being all or nothing, most decisions in life involve doing a little more or a little less. If you are trying to decrease your spending and increase your saving, the decision is not really between saving all the money you earn or spending it all. Rather, many small choices are involved, such as whether to buy a caffè mocha at Starbucks every day or just once a week.

Economists use the word *marginal* to mean "extra" or "additional." Should you watch another hour of television or spend that hour studying? The *marginal benefit* (*MB*) of watching more television is the additional enjoyment you receive. The *marginal cost* (*MC*) is the reduction in your test score from having studied a little less. Should Apple produce an additional 300,000 smartwatches? Firms receive *revenue* from selling goods. Apple's marginal benefit is the additional revenue it receives from selling 300,000 more smartwatches. Apple's marginal cost is the additional cost—for wages, parts, and so forth—of producing 300,000 more smartwatches. *Economists reason that the optimal decision is to continue any activity up to the point where the marginal benefit equals the marginal cost—that is, to the point where* MB = MC. Often we apply this rule without consciously thinking about it. Usually you will know whether the additional enjoyment from watching a television program is worth the additional cost you pay by not spending that hour studying, without giving the decision a lot of thought. In business situations, however, firms often have to make careful calculations to determine, for example, whether the additional revenue received from increasing production is greater or less than the additional cost of the production. Economists refer to analysis that involves comparing marginal benefits and marginal costs as **marginal analysis.**

Marginal analysis Analysis that involves comparing marginal benefits and marginal costs.

In each chapter, you will see the feature *Solved Problem*. This feature will increase your understanding of the material by leading you through the steps of solving an applied economic problem. After reading the problem, test your understanding by doing the related problems that appear at the end of the chapter. You can also complete Solved Problems on **www.myeconlab.com** and receive tutorial help. MyEconLab Concept Check

Solved Problem 1.1

MyEconLab Interactive Animation

OraSure Makes a Decision at the Margin

OraSure is a medical technology firm based in Pennsylvania that produces, among other products, a device that allows consumers to test for HIV (human immunodeficiency virus) at home. In 2015, OraSure decided to reduce advertising for this device. The firm's chief executive officer (CEO) stated that the advertising had not been as effective as he had hoped in increasing sales of the device. A news story quoted him as saying, "Consequently, we had to adjust our [spending on advertising to] make it more proportional to revenue." Assuming that reducing advertising will reduce OraSure's sales of the device, how should the firm determine by what amount to reduce its advertising? Is it possible that OraSure is making a mistake by reducing its advertising? Briefly explain.

Solving the Problem

Step 1: Review the chapter material. This problem is about making decisions, so you may want to review the section "Optimal Decisions Are Made at the Margin," which begins on page 7.

Step 2: Explain how OraSure should determine by what amount to reduce its advertising. We have seen that any activity should be continued to the point where the marginal benefit is equal to the marginal cost. In this case, OraSure apparently believes it is violating this rule because the additional cost from advertising is greater than the additional revenue it receives from the increased sales that result from the advertising. Therefore, OraSure will be better off reducing its advertising because the decline in cost will be greater than the decline in revenue. The company's goal should be to reduce advertising spending to the amount where the additional revenue resulting from the last dollar of advertising equals the additional cost of the advertising.

Step 3: Explain whether it is possible that OraSure's decision to reduce advertising is a mistake. OraSure's CEO was disappointed in the extent to which advertising was increasing sales of the device. But the firm might still be spending the optimal amount on advertising even though the CEO hoped the effect of the advertising would be greater than it was. If the marginal revenue from the last dollar of advertising were equal to its marginal cost, reducing advertising spending would make the firm worse off. The only way to ensure a correct decision is for the firm to analyze the effect of changes in advertising spending on the firm's revenues and costs.

Source: Scott Krause, "OraSure's Ebola Test Moving Forward in Africa," (Allentown, PA) *Morning Call*, May 6, 2015.

MyEconLab Study Plan

Your Turn: For more practice, do related problems 1.9 and 1.10 on page 23 at the end of this chapter.

1.2 The Economic Problem That Every Society Must Solve

LEARNING OBJECTIVE: Discuss how an economy answers these questions: What goods and services will be produced? How will the goods and services be produced? Who will receive the goods and services produced?

Trade-off The idea that, because of scarcity, producing more of one good or service means producing less of another good or service.

Opportunity cost The highest-valued alternative that must be given up to engage in an activity.

Because we live in a world of scarcity, any society faces the *economic problem* that it has only a limited amount of economic resources—such as workers, machines, and raw materials—and so can produce only a limited amount of goods and services. Therefore, every society faces **trade-offs**: Producing more of one good or service means producing less of another good or service. The best measure of the cost of producing a good or service is the value of what has to be given up to produce it. The **opportunity cost** of any activity—such as producing a good or service—is the highest-valued alternative that must be given up to engage in that activity. The concept of opportunity cost is very important in economics and applies to individuals, firms, and society as a whole. For instance, suppose that you earn a salary of $100,000 per year working for Scanadu, the medical technology firm discussed at the beginning of the chapter. You decide to open your own firm to create and sell medical devices. In this case, the opportunity cost of the services you supply to your own firm is the $100,000 you give up by not working for Scanadu, *even if you do not explicitly pay yourself a salary*. As in this example, opportunity costs often do not involve actual payments of money.

Making the Connection MyEconLab Video

It's Saturday Afternoon; Why Aren't You at the Game?

For many students, attending college football games is an enjoyable way to spend Saturday afternoons in the fall. However, some colleges have experienced a decline in the number of students attending their games. In 2014, average attendance at the 127 larger schools that make up the Football Bowl Subdivision declined to the lowest level in 14 years. In the past few years, nearly 40 percent of the tickets allocated to students at the University of Georgia have gone unsold. Even coach Nick Saban, whose University of Alabama team has won several national championships in recent years, has publically voiced concern about low student attendance at the team's games.

There are more empty seats at college football stadiums because the opportunity cost of attending games has increased.

What explains the decrease in the number of students willing to attend football games? In some schools, rising ticket prices help explain the decline. One student at the University of Michigan was quoted as saying: "People are looking to trim costs, and for a lot of folks, football is an easy thing to cut. It's not essential to going to college."

Remember that the opportunity cost of engaging in an activity is the value of the best alternative that must be given up to engage in that activity. The opportunity cost of attending a college football game is *not* just the price of a ticket. If the price of a ticket to a game is $50, your opportunity cost is the ticket price *plus* the value you place on what else you could do if you don't attend the game. At one time, relatively few college football games were televised, but today multiple cable networks broadcast games. If you attend your college's games, you miss the opportunity to watch the games being broadcast at the same time—in high-definition with replays shown from multiple camera angles and expert commentary to clarify what is happening. When watching games in your room or at a sports restaurant, you can also post to Facebook, Instagram, or Twitter, read e-mail, surf the Web, and take or receive phone calls. Wi-Fi and cellular reception is often poor in college stadiums, making these activities difficult.

So the opportunity cost of attending college football games has increased in recent years, not just because ticket prices have risen but because the number of alternative activities that students value highly has also increased. We expect that when the opportunity cost of engaging in an activity increases, people will engage in that activity less, as we've seen with student attendance at college football games.

Colleges have responded to declining student attendance by reducing ticket prices, improving Wi-Fi and cellular service, and installing high-definition video boards that show replays as they appear on television. Whether these attempts to lower the opportunity cost of attending college football games will succeed remains to be seen.

Sources: Jon Solomon, "College Football Attendance: Home Crowds Drop to Lowest in 14 Years," cbssports.com, December 15, 2014; Adam Rittenberg, "Attendance Challenges Big Deal for B1G," espn.com, February 14, 2014; and Ben Cohen, "At College Football Games, Student Sections Likely to Have Empty Seats," *Wall Street Journal*, August 27, 2014.

Your Turn: Test your understanding by doing related problem 2.7 on page 24 at the end of this chapter.

Trade-offs force society to make choices when answering the following three fundamental questions:

1. *What* goods and services will be produced?
2. *How* will the goods and services be produced?
3. *Who* will receive the goods and services produced?

Throughout this book, we will return to these questions many times. For now, we briefly introduce each question.

What Goods and Services Will Be Produced?

How will society decide whether to produce more economics textbooks or more Blu-ray players? More daycare facilities or more football stadiums? Of course, "society" does not make decisions; only individuals make decisions. The answer to the question of what will be produced is determined by the choices that consumers and people working for firms or the government make. Every day, you help decide which goods and services firms will produce when you choose to buy an iPhone instead of a Samsung Galaxy or a caffè mocha rather than a chai tea. Similarly, managers at Apple must choose whether to devote the company's scarce resources to making more iPhones or more smartwatches. Members of Congress and the president must choose whether to spend more of the federal government's limited budget on breast cancer research or on repairing highways. In each case, consumers, managers of firms, and government policymakers face the problem of scarcity by trading off one good or service for another. And each choice made comes with an opportunity cost, measured by the value of the best alternative given up. MyEconLab Concept Check

How Will the Goods and Services Be Produced?

Firms choose how to produce the goods and services they sell. In many cases, firms face a trade-off between using more workers or using more machines. For example, a local service station has to choose whether to provide car repair services using more diagnostic computers and fewer auto mechanics or fewer diagnostic computers and more auto mechanics. Similarly, movie studios have to choose whether to produce animated films using highly skilled animators to draw them by hand or fewer animators and more computers. In deciding whether to move production offshore to China, firms may need to choose between a production method in the United States that uses fewer workers and more machines and a production method in China that uses more workers and fewer machines. MyEconLab Concept Check

Who Will Receive the Goods and Services Produced?

In the United States, who receives the goods and services produced depends largely on how income is distributed. The higher a person's income, the more goods and services he or she can buy. Often, people are willing to give up some of their income—and, therefore, some of their ability to purchase goods and services—by donating to charities to increase the incomes of poorer people. Each year, Americans donate more than $325 billion to charity, or an average donation of $2,800 for each household in the country. An important policy question, however, is whether the government should intervene to make the distribution of income more equal. Such intervention already occurs in the United States because people with higher incomes pay a larger fraction of their incomes in taxes and because the government makes payments to people with low incomes. There is disagreement over whether the current attempts to redistribute income are sufficient or whether there should be more or less redistribution. MyEconLab Concept Check

Centrally Planned Economies versus Market Economies

Centrally planned economy An economy in which the government decides how economic resources will be allocated.

Market economy An economy in which the decisions of households and firms interacting in markets allocate economic resources.

To answer the three questions—what, how, and who—societies organize their economies in two main ways. A society can have a **centrally planned economy** in which the government decides how economic resources will be allocated. Or a society can have a **market economy** in which the decisions of households and firms interacting in markets allocate economic resources.

From 1917 to 1991, the most important centrally planned economy in the world was that of the Soviet Union, which was established when Vladimir Lenin and the Communist Party staged a revolution and took control of the Russian Empire. In the Soviet Union, the government decided what goods to produce, how the goods would be produced, and who would receive the goods. Government employees managed factories and stores. The objective of these managers was to follow the government's orders rather than to satisfy the wants of consumers.

Centrally planned economies like that of the Soviet Union have not been successful in producing low-cost, high-quality goods and services. As a result, the standard of living of the average person in a centrally planned economy tends to be low. All centrally planned economies have also been political dictatorships. Dissatisfaction with low living standards and political repression finally led to the collapse of the Soviet Union in 1991. Today, only North Korea still has a completely centrally planned economy.

All high-income democracies, including the United States, Canada, Japan, and the countries of Western Europe, have market economies. Market economies rely primarily on privately owned firms to produce goods and services and to decide how to produce them. Markets, rather than the government, determine who receives the goods and services produced. In a market economy, firms must produce goods and services that meet the wants of consumers, or the firms will go out of business. In that sense, it is ultimately consumers who decide what goods and services will be produced. Because firms in a market economy compete to offer the highest-quality products at the lowest price, they are under pressure to use the lowest-cost methods of production. For example, in the past 10 years, some U.S. firms have been under pressure to reduce their costs to meet competition from Chinese firms.

In a market economy, the income of an individual is determined by the payments he receives for what he has to sell. If you become a civil engineer, and firms are willing to pay a salary of $85,000 per year for someone with your training and skills, you will have this amount of income to purchase goods and services. If you also buy a house that you rent out, your income will be even higher. One of the attractive features of markets is that they reward hard work. Generally, the more extensive the training you have received and the longer the hours you work, the higher your income will be. Of course, luck—both good and bad—also plays a role here. Someone might have a high income because she won the state lottery, while someone else might have a low income because he has severe medical problems. We can conclude that market economies respond to the question, "Who receives the goods and services produced?" with the answer, "Those who are most willing and able to buy them." MyEconLab Concept Check

The Modern "Mixed" Economy

In the 1800s and early 1900s, the U.S. government engaged in relatively little regulation of markets for goods and services. Beginning in the mid-1900s, government intervention in the economy dramatically increased in the United States and other market economies. This increase was primarily caused by the high rates of unemployment and business bankruptcies during the Great Depression of the 1930s. Some government intervention was also intended to raise the incomes of the elderly, the sick, and people with limited skills. For example, in the 1930s, the United States established the *Social Security system*, which provides government payments to retired and disabled workers, and minimum wage legislation, which sets a floor on the wages employers can pay workers in many occupations. In more recent years, government intervention in the economy has also expanded to meet goals such as protecting the environment, promoting civil rights, and providing medical care to low-income people and the elderly.

Some economists argue that the extent of government intervention makes it no longer accurate to refer to the economies of the United States, Canada, Japan, and Western Europe as pure market economies. Instead, they should be referred to as *mixed economies*. A **mixed economy** is still primarily a market economy because most economic decisions result from the interaction of buyers and sellers in markets. However, the government plays a significant role in the allocation of resources. As we will see in later chapters, economists continue to debate the role government should play in a market economy.

Mixed economy An economy in which most economic decisions result from the interaction of buyers and sellers in markets but in which the government plays a significant role in the allocation of resources.

One of the most important developments in the international economy in recent years has been the movement of China from being a centrally planned economy to being a more mixed economy. The Chinese economy suffered decades of economic stagnation following the takeover of the government in 1949 by Mao Zedong and the Communist Party. Although China remains a political dictatorship, the production of most goods and services is now determined in the market rather than by the government. The result has been rapid economic growth that has lifted more than a billion people in China out of poverty. MyEconLab Concept Check

Efficiency and Equity

Productive efficiency A situation in which a good or service is produced at the lowest possible cost.

Allocative efficiency A state of the economy in which production is in accordance with consumer preferences; in particular, every good or service is produced up to the point where the last unit provides a marginal benefit to society equal to the marginal cost of producing it.

Voluntary exchange A situation that occurs in markets when both the buyer and the seller of a product are made better off by the transaction.

Market economies tend to be more efficient than centrally planned economies. There are two types of efficiency. **Productive efficiency** occurs when a good or service is produced at the lowest possible cost. **Allocative efficiency** occurs when production is in accordance with consumer preferences. Markets tend to be efficient because they promote competition and facilitate voluntary exchange. With **voluntary exchange**, both the buyer and the seller of a product are made better off by the transaction. We know that they are both made better off because, otherwise, the buyer would not have agreed to buy the product or the seller would not have agreed to sell it. Productive efficiency is achieved when competition among firms forces them to produce goods and services at the lowest cost. Allocative efficiency is achieved when the combination of competition among firms and voluntary exchange between firms and consumers results in firms producing the mix of goods and services that consumers prefer the most. Competition will result in firms continuing to produce and sell goods and services as long as the additional benefit to consumers is greater than the additional cost of production. In this way, the mix of goods and services produced will match consumer preferences.

Although markets promote efficiency, they don't guarantee it. Inefficiency can arise from various sources. For instance, it may take some time for firms to learn how to efficiently produce a good or service. When Blu-ray players were introduced, firms did not instantly achieve productive efficiency because it took several years to discover the lowest-cost method of producing this good. As we will discuss in later chapters, inefficiency can also arise if governments interfere with voluntary exchange in markets. For example, many governments limit the imports of some goods from foreign countries. This limitation reduces efficiency by keeping goods from being produced at the lowest cost. The production of some goods damages the environment. In this case, government intervention can increase efficiency because without such intervention, firms may ignore the costs of environmental damage and thereby fail to produce the goods at the lowest possible cost.

Equity The fair distribution of economic benefits.

An economically efficient outcome is not necessarily desirable. Many people prefer economic outcomes that they consider fair or equitable, even if those outcomes are less efficient. **Equity** is harder to define than efficiency because there isn't an agreed-upon definition of fairness. For some people, equity means a more equal distribution of economic benefits than would result from an emphasis on efficiency alone. For example, some people support raising taxes on people with higher incomes to provide the funds for programs that aid the poor. Although governments may increase equity by reducing the incomes of high-income people and increasing the incomes of the poor, efficiency may be reduced. People have less incentive to open new businesses, work hard, and save if the government takes a significant amount of the income they earn from working or saving. The result is that fewer goods and services are produced, and less saving takes place. As this example illustrates, *there is often a trade-off between efficiency and equity*. Government policymakers frequently confront this trade-off. MyEconLab Concept Check

MyEconLab Study Plan

1.3 Economic Models

LEARNING OBJECTIVE: Describe the role of models in economic analysis.

As mentioned at the start of the chapter, economic models are simplified versions of reality. Many professions rely on models: An engineer may use a computer model of a bridge to help test whether it will withstand high winds, or a biologist may make a physical model of a nucleic acid to better understand its properties. Economists rely on economic models, or theories, to analyze real-world issues ranging from the role of government in monitoring smart devices to whether a society should redistribute income. (This book uses the words *model* and *theory* interchangeably.) One purpose of economic models is to make economic ideas sufficiently explicit and concrete so that individuals, firms, or the government can use them to make decisions. For example, we will see in Chapter 3 that the model of demand and supply is a simplified version of how the prices of products are determined by the interactions among buyers and sellers in markets.

Economists use economic models to answer questions such as, "Will the United States have a sufficient number of doctors in 2020?" Economists at the U.S. Bureau of Labor Statistics (BLS) build models that allow them to forecast future employment in different occupations. These models enable the BLS to forecast how many doctors there are likely to be at a future date. Economists also use models to forecast the demand for medical services. By separately forecasting the number of doctors and the demand for medical services, these models provide a forecast of whether there will be a sufficient number of doctors in 2020. As mentioned at the beginning of the chapter, economists at the U.S. Health Resources and Services Administration (HRSA) have used models to forecast that there will be a shortage of 55,600 doctors in 2020.

Sometimes economists use an existing model to analyze a real-world problem or issue, but in other cases, they have to develop a new model. To develop a model, economists generally follow these steps:

1. Decide on the assumptions to use in developing the model.
2. Formulate a testable hypothesis.
3. Use economic data to test the hypothesis.
4. Revise the model if it fails to explain the economic data well.
5. Retain the revised model to help answer similar economic questions in the future.

The Role of Assumptions in Economic Models

Any model is based on making assumptions because models have to be simplified to be useful. For example, economic models make *behavioral assumptions* about the motives of consumers and firms. Economists assume that consumers will buy the goods and services that will maximize their well-being or their satisfaction. Similarly, economists assume that firms act to maximize their profits. These assumptions are simplifications because they do not describe the motives of every consumer and every firm. How can we know whether the assumptions in a model are too simplified or too limiting? We can determine the usefulness of assumptions by forming hypotheses based on the assumptions and then testing the hypotheses using real-world information. MyEconLab Concept Check

Forming and Testing Hypotheses in Economic Models

An **economic variable** is something measurable that can have different values, such as the incomes of doctors. In an economic model, a hypothesis is a statement that may be either correct or incorrect about an economic variable. An example of a hypothesis in an economic model is the statement that the falling incomes earned by primary care physicians—often referred to as *family doctors*—will result in a decline in the number of physicians choosing to enter primary care in the United States in 2020. An economic hypothesis is usually about a *causal relationship*; in this case, the hypothesis states that lower incomes cause, or lead to, fewer doctors entering primary care.

Economic variable Something measurable that can have different values, such as the incomes of doctors.

Before we can accept a hypothesis, we have to test it by analyzing statistics on the relevant economic variables. In our example, we would gather statistics on the incomes of family doctors, the number of family doctors, and perhaps other variables. Testing a hypothesis can be tricky. For example, showing that the number of family doctors declined at a time when the average income of these doctors declined would not be enough to demonstrate that the decline in income *caused* the decline in the number of family doctors. Just because two things are correlated—that is, they happen at the same time—does not mean that one caused the other. For example, before entering practice, a doctor spends time in a teaching hospital as a resident in his or her field. Teaching hospitals determine how many residencies they will offer in a particular field. Suppose that teaching hospitals decreased the number of residencies in primary care at the same time that the incomes of family doctors were declining. In that case, the declining number of residencies, rather than the declining incomes, might have caused the decline in the number of family doctors. Over a period of time, many economic variables change, which complicates the testing of hypotheses. In fact, when economists disagree about a hypothesis, such as the effect of falling incomes on the number of family doctors, it is often because of disagreements over interpreting the statistical analysis used to test the hypothesis.

Note that hypotheses must be statements that could, in principle, turn out to be incorrect. Statements such as "Increasing the number of family doctors is good" or "Increasing the number of family doctors is bad" are value judgments rather than hypotheses because it is not possible to disprove them.

Economists accept and use an economic model if it leads to hypotheses that are confirmed by statistical analysis. In many cases, the acceptance is tentative, however, pending the gathering of new data or further statistical analysis. In fact, economists often refer to a hypothesis having been "not rejected," rather than having been "accepted," by statistical analysis. But what if statistical analysis clearly rejects a hypothesis? For example, what if a model leads to a hypothesis that declining incomes of family doctors will cause a decline in the number of these doctors, but the data reject this hypothesis? In this case, the model must be reconsidered. It may be that an assumption used in the model was too simplified or too limiting. For example, perhaps the model ignored the fact that family doctors were moving from owning their own practices to becoming salaried employees of hospitals, where their incomes would be lower but they would be freed from the responsibilities involved in running their own businesses. This change in how primary care physicians are employed might explain why the data rejected the hypothesis.

The BLS has analyzed the accuracy of the projections it had made in 1996 of employment levels in 2006. Some projections were quite accurate, while others were less so. For instance, the BLS had projected that 677,917 physicians and surgeons would be employed in 2006, but actual employment was only 633,292, or about 7 percent less than projected. The error with respect to physician's assistants was much larger, with the projection being that 93,485 physician's assistants would be employed in 2006, but actual employment was only 65,628, or about 30 percent fewer than expected. Analyzing the errors in these projections helps the BLS to improve the models it uses to make projections of occupational employment.

The process of developing models, testing hypotheses, and revising models occurs not just in economics but also in disciplines such as physics, chemistry, and biology. This process is often referred to as the *scientific method*. Economics is a *social science* because it applies the scientific method to the study of the interactions among individuals.

MyEconLab Concept Check

Positive and Normative Analysis

Positive analysis Analysis concerned with what is.

Normative analysis Analysis concerned with what ought to be.

Throughout this book, as we build economic models and use them to answer questions, bear in mind the following important distinction: **Positive analysis** is concerned with *what is*, and **normative analysis** is concerned with *what ought to be*. Economics is about positive analysis, which measures the costs and benefits of different courses of action.

We can use the federal government's minimum wage law to compare positive and normative analysis. In 2015, under this law, it was illegal for an employer to hire a worker at a wage less than $7.25 per hour. Without the minimum wage law, some firms and workers would voluntarily agree to a lower wage. Because of the minimum wage law, some workers have difficulty finding jobs, and some firms end up paying more for labor than they otherwise would have. A positive analysis of the federal minimum wage law uses an economic model to estimate how many workers have lost their jobs because of the law, its effect on the costs and profits of businesses, and the gains to workers receiving the minimum wage. After economists complete this positive analysis, the decision as to whether the minimum wage law is a good or a bad idea is a normative one and depends on how people evaluate the trade-off involved. Supporters of the law believe that the losses to employers and workers who are unemployed as a result of the law are more than offset by the gains to workers who receive higher wages than they would without the law. Opponents of the law believe the losses are greater than the gains. The assessment by any individual depends, in part, on that person's values and political views. The positive analysis an economist provides would play a role in the decision but can't by itself decide the issue one way or the other.

In each chapter, you will see a *Don't Let This Happen to You* box like the one below. These boxes alert you to common pitfalls in thinking about economic ideas. After reading this box, test your understanding by working the related problem that appears at the end of the chapter.

MyEconLab Concept Check

Don't Let This Happen to You

Don't Confuse Positive Analysis with Normative Analysis

"Economic analysis has shown that the minimum wage law is a bad idea because it causes unemployment." Is this statement accurate? As of 2015, the federal minimum wage law prevents employers from hiring workers at a wage of less than $7.25 per hour. This wage is higher than some employers are willing to pay some workers. If there were no minimum wage law, some workers who currently cannot find any firm willing to hire them at $7.25 per hour would be able to find employment at a lower wage. Therefore, positive economic analysis indicates that the minimum wage law causes unemployment. (In Chapter 4, we'll explore why economists disagree about *how much* unemployment the minimum wage law causes.) But, some workers who have jobs benefit from the minimum wage law because they are paid a higher wage than they otherwise would be. In other words, the minimum wage law creates both losers—the workers who become unemployed and the firms that have to pay higher wages—and winners—the workers who receive higher wages.

Should we value the gains to the winners more than we value the losses to the losers? The answer involves normative analysis. Positive economic analysis can show the consequences of a particular policy, but it cannot tell us whether the policy is "good" or "bad." So, the statement at the beginning of this box is inaccurate.

MyEconLab Study Plan

Your Turn: Test your understanding by doing related problems 3.6 and 3.7 on page 25 at the end of this chapter.

Economics as a Social Science

Because economics studies the actions of individuals, it is a social science. Economics is therefore similar to other social science disciplines, such as psychology, political science, and sociology. As a social science, economics considers human behavior—particularly decision-making behavior—in every context, not just in the context of business. Economists have studied issues such as how families decide on the number of children to have, why people have difficulty losing weight or attaining other goals, and why people often ignore relevant information when making decisions. Economics also has much to contribute to questions of government policy. As we will see throughout this book, economists have played an important role in formulating government policies in areas such as the environment, health care, and poverty.

MyEconLab Concept Check

Making the Connection
MyEconLab Video

Should Medical School Be Free?

The U.S. population continues to increase, which by itself would increase the demand for medical services. In addition, the average age of the population is rising, and older people need more medical care than do younger people. So, over time, the number of doctors needs to increase. As mentioned at the beginning of this chapter, the U.S. Health Resources and Services Administration (HRSA) estimates that the number of doctors needed to provide patient care will rise to 922,000 in 2020.

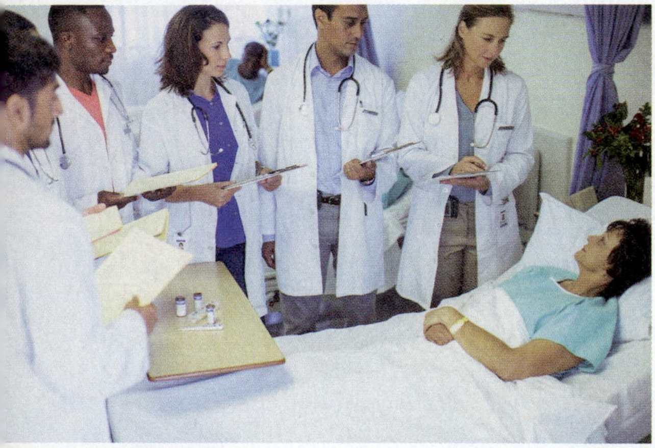

Should these medical students have to pay tuition?

Can we be sure that these additional doctors will be available in 2020? The HRSA forecasts that, in fact, there will be a shortage of 55,600 doctors in 2020. The bulk of that shortage is likely to be in primary care physicians, or family doctors. As we will discuss in later chapters, ordinarily we expect that when consumers want more of a product, higher wages and salaries and more job openings will attract workers to that industry. For example, during the U.S. housing boom of the mid-2000s, the number of workers in the building trades—carpenters, plumbers, roofers, and others—increased rapidly. But producing more doctors is a long process. After completing an undergraduate education, a doctor spends four years in medical school and then three to five years at a teaching hospital, pursuing a residency in a particular field of medicine. Apparently convinced that hospitals will not train enough doctors unless they get help, Congress contributes $10 billion per year to teaching hospitals, based on the number of residents they train.

Peter Bach of the Sloan-Kettering Cancer Center and Robert Kocher of the Brookings Institution have proposed that medical schools should charge no tuition. They argue that nearly all students graduate from medical school owing money on student loans, with the average student owing more than $160,000. We might expect that these debts, although large, would *not* deter students from applying to medical school, because in 2015, the average income of physicians was more than $250,000 per year. Bach and Kocher argue, however, that the high cost of medical school has two bad outcomes: (1) Some good students do not apply because they either do not want to be saddled with such large debts or are unable to borrow sufficient money, and (2) many students avoid going into primary care—where average incomes are $190,000—in favor of specialties such as plastic surgery or anesthesiology—where average incomes are $325,000. Teaching hospitals pay doctors a salary of about $50,000 per year during their residencies. Bach and Kocher propose that hospitals continue to pay residents who pursue primary care but not pay residents who specialize. The money that hospitals would otherwise pay to these residents would be paid to medical schools instead to finance the free tuition. The plan would give residents an incentive to pursue primary care rather than to specialize. Critics of the Bach and Kocher proposal have questioned whether many students capable of being admitted to medical school actually are deterred by medical school tuition. They also question whether many residents who intend to specialize would choose primary care instead, even if specializing means they have to borrow to meet living expenses rather than pay for them with a hospital salary.

Like many other policy debates, the debate over whether changes should be made in how medical school is paid for has positive and normative elements. By gathering data and using economic models, we can assess some of the quantitative claims made by each side in the debate: What role does tuition play in a student's decision about whether to attend medical school? Have tuition increases had a large effect or a small effect on the number of applications to medical school? How do changes in expected future incomes affect the decisions of medical students about which specialty to choose? These are all positive questions, so it is possible to formulate quantitative answers. Ultimately, though, this debate also has a normative element. For instance, some doctors, economists, and policymakers argue that it is important that people living in low-income or rural areas have improved access to health care, so they are willing to support policies that would redirect medical students away from specialized fields and toward primary care. Other doctors, economists, and policymakers believe that medical students who enter specialized fields make a larger contribution to society than do students who enter primary care. A disagreement of this type is unlikely to be resolved by building models and analyzing data because the issue involved is essentially normative.

In 2010, President Obama and Congress enacted the Patient Protection and Affordable Care Act, which made major changes to the U.S. health care system. Most of the changes were in effect by 2015. Additional changes are likely as policymakers grapple with the increasing costs of health care. Whether Congress and the president will enact policies intended to increase the number of family doctors remains to be seen.

Sources: Uwe E. Reinhardt, "Producing More Primary-Care Doctors," *New York Times*, June 10, 2011; Uwe E. Reinhardt, "The Debt of Medical Students," *New York Times*, September 14, 2012; and Peter B. Bach and Robert Kocher, "Why Medical School Should Be Free," *New York Times*, May 28, 2011.

Your Turn: Test your understanding by doing related problem 3.8 on page 25 at the end of this chapter.

MyEconLab Study Plan

1.4 Microeconomics and Macroeconomics

LEARNING OBJECTIVE: Distinguish between microeconomics and macroeconomics.

Economic models can be used to analyze decision making in many areas. We group some of these areas together as *microeconomics* and others as *macroeconomics*. **Microeconomics** is the study of how households and firms make choices, how they interact in markets, and how the government attempts to influence their choices. **Macroeconomics** is the study of the economy as a whole, including topics such as inflation, unemployment, and economic growth. Table 1.1 gives examples of microeconomic and macroeconomic issues.

Microeconomics The study of how households and firms make choices, how they interact in markets, and how the government attempts to influence their choices.

Macroeconomics The study of the economy as a whole, including topics such as inflation, unemployment, and economic growth.

The division between microeconomics and macroeconomics is not a bright line. Many economic situations have *both* a microeconomic aspect and a macroeconomic aspect. For example, the level of total investment by firms in new machinery and equipment helps to determine how rapidly the economy grows—which is a macroeconomic issue. But to understand how much new machinery and equipment firms decide to purchase, we have to analyze the incentives individual firms face—which is a microeconomic issue.

MyEconLab Concept Check

MyEconLab Study Plan

Table 1.1

Issues in Microeconomics and Macroeconomics

Examples of microeconomic issues	Examples of macroeconomic issues
• How consumers react to changes in product prices • How firms decide what prices to charge for the products they sell • Which government policy would most efficiently reduce teenage smoking • What are the costs and benefits of approving the sale of a new prescription drug • What is the most efficient way to reduce air pollution	• Why economies experience periods of recession and increasing unemployment • Why, over the long run, some economies have grown much faster than others • What determines the inflation rate • What determines the value of the U.S. dollar • Whether government intervention can reduce the severity of recessions

1.5 A Preview of Important Economic Terms

LEARNING OBJECTIVE: Define important economic terms.

In the following chapters, you will encounter certain important terms again and again. Becoming familiar with these terms is a necessary step in learning economics. Here we provide only a brief introduction to some of these terms. We will discuss them all in greater depth in later chapters:

- *Firm, company, or business.* A *firm* is an organization that produces a good or service. Most firms produce goods or services to earn profits, but there are also nonprofit firms, such as universities and some hospitals. Economists use the terms *firm*, *company*, and *business* interchangeably.

- *Entrepreneur.* An *entrepreneur* is someone who operates a business. In a market system, entrepreneurs decide what goods and services to produce and how to produce them. An entrepreneur starting a new business puts his or her own funds at risk. If an entrepreneur is wrong about what consumers want or about the best way to produce goods and services, his or her funds can be lost. Losing money in a failed business is not unusual: In the United States, about half of new businesses close within four years. Without entrepreneurs willing to assume the risk of starting and operating businesses, economic progress would be impossible in a market system.
- *Innovation.* There is a distinction between an *invention* and an *innovation*. An *invention* is a new good or a new process for making a good. An *innovation* is the practical application of an invention. (*Innovation* may also be used more broadly to refer to any significant improvement in a good or in the means of producing a good.) Much time often passes between the appearance of a new idea and its development for widespread use. For example, the Wright brothers first achieved self-propelled flight at Kitty Hawk, North Carolina, in 1903, but the Wright brothers' plane was very crude, and it wasn't until the introduction of the DC-3 by Douglas Aircraft in 1936 that regularly scheduled intercity airline flights became common in the United States. Similarly, the first digital electronic computer—the ENIAC—was developed in 1945, but the first IBM personal computer was not introduced until 1981, and widespread use of computers did not have a significant effect on the productivity of U.S. business until the 1990s.
- *Technology.* A firm's *technology* is the processes it uses to produce goods and services. In the economic sense, a firm's technology depends on many factors, such as the skill of its managers, the training of its workers, and the speed and efficiency of its machinery and equipment.
- *Goods. Goods* are tangible merchandise, such as books, computers, or Blu-ray players.
- *Services. Services* are activities done for others, such as providing haircuts or investment advice.
- *Revenue.* A firm's *revenue* is the total amount received for selling a good or service. We calculate it by multiplying the price per unit by the number of units sold.
- *Profit.* A firm's *profit* is the difference between its revenue and its costs. Economists distinguish between *accounting profit* and *economic profit*. In calculating accounting profit, we exclude the costs of some economic resources that the firm does not pay for explicitly. In calculating economic profit, we include the opportunity costs of all resources used by the firm. When we refer to *profit* in this book, we mean economic profit. It is important not to confuse *profit* with *revenue*.
- *Household.* A *household* consists of all persons occupying a home. Households are suppliers of factors of production—particularly labor—used by firms to make goods and services. Households also demand goods and services produced by firms and governments.
- *Factors of production, economic resources, or inputs.* Firms use *factors of production* to produce goods and services. The main factors of production are labor, capital, natural resources—including land—and entrepreneurial ability. Households earn income by supplying the factors of production to firms. Economists use the terms *factors of production, economic resources,* and *inputs* interchangeably.
- *Capital.* In everyday speech, the word *capital* can refer to *financial capital* or to *physical capital*. Financial capital includes stocks and bonds issued by firms, bank accounts, and holdings of money. In economics, though, *capital* refers to physical capital, which includes manufactured goods that are used to produce other goods and

services. Examples of physical capital are computers, factory buildings, machine tools, warehouses, and trucks. The total amount of physical capital available in a country is referred to as the country's *capital stock*.

- *Human capital. Human capital* refers to the accumulated training and skills that workers possess. For example, college-educated workers generally have more skills and are more productive than workers who have only high school degrees; therefore, college-educated workers have more human capital. MyEconLab Concept Check

MyEconLab Study Plan

Continued from page 3

Economics in Your Life

Will There Be Plenty of Jobs Available in the Health Care Industry?

At the beginning of this chapter, we posed the question: "What is the basis for the forecasts on the availability of jobs in health care, and how reliable are the forecasts?" As the U.S. population increases and as the average age of the population rises, it seems likely that there will be an increase in the number of doctors, nurses, physician's assistants, and other health care workers. The U.S. Bureau of Labor Statistics (BLS) publishes the most widely used occupational forecasts. Economists at the BLS base these forecasts on economic models. The forecasts can be inaccurate, however. For example, in 1996, the BLS forecast that 93,485 physician's assistants would be employed in 2006, when in fact only 65,628 were. The BLS analyzes errors like these in attempting to improve its forecasts. So, it is likely that the BLS's forecasts will become more accurate over time, but it would be a mistake to expect the forecasts to be exact.

Conclusion

Economics is a group of useful ideas about how individuals make choices. Economists have put these ideas into practice by developing economic models. Consumers, business managers, and government policymakers use these models every day to help make choices. In this book, we explore many key economic models and give examples of how to apply them in the real world.

Reading the news is an important part of understanding the current business climate and learning how to apply economic concepts to a variety of real-world events. At the end of each of the first four chapters, you will see a two-page feature titled *An Inside Look*. This feature consists of an excerpt from an article that relates to the company or economic issue introduced at the start of the chapter and also to the concepts discussed in the chapter. A summary and an analysis with a supporting table or graph highlight the key economic points of the article. Read *An Inside Look* for a discussion of how technological change, such as the development of smart medical devices, affects the way doctors provide health care. Test your understanding by answering the *Thinking Critically* questions.

Smart Medical Devices—Right Before Your Very Eyes

FORBES

Google Smart Contact Lens Focuses On Healthcare Billions

a Google is developing a smart contact lens, with pharmaceutical giant Novartis, to help patients manage diabetes—in one of a number of moves focused squarely on billions of dollars of potential revenue available across the total digital healthcare market.

As technology moves further into treatment with remote consultations, monitoring and operations, robotic treatments, and advanced digital diagnosis, Google has seen the opportunity to apply its own eyewear technology (up until now limited as glasses called Google Glass) to the healthcare field.

Google's 3D mobile technology and its offering around health record digitization form potential other strands of its expansion in the health market. Last month, it released the Google Fit platform to track exercise and sleep, among other health factors—but it is far from alone, as Apple and Samsung offer similar systems in that area.

b Today, under a new development and licensing deal between Google and the Alcon eyewear division at Novartis, the two companies said they will create a smart contact lens that contains a low power microchip and an almost invisible, hair-thin electronic circuit. The lens can measure diabetics' blood sugar levels directly from tear fluid on the surface of the eyeball. The system sends data to a mobile device to keep the individual informed.

Google co-founder Sergey Brin said the company wanted to use "the latest technology in 'minituarisation' of electronics" in order to improve people's "quality of life".

Novartis chief executive Joe Jimenez added that technology as a whole, starting with smart eyewear, could be used to "manage human diseases," and indicated that diseases will be mapped in the body using a range of other devices in the future—many of which are in development across universities and research laboratories.

An official timescale for the product's development and commercialization has not been made public, though Jimenez said in *Reuters* and *WSJ* interviews respectively that the company "would hope to be able to commercialize it within about five years", adding that it was expected to create a "large revenue stream".

c The combination of Google's technology background and Novartis' pharmaceutical knowledge would help meet "unmet medical needs," Jimenez claimed.

The pharmaceutical firm is also looking into how to enable the contact lens technology to assess long sighted people's vision and autofocus it on what they are looking at, working rather like an automatic camera lens when taking a picture. Such technology would help them avoid the need for glasses when reading or looking at other nearby objects.

The Google team involved in the contact lens development is called Google[x], and it focuses on "finding new solutions to big global problems" in healthcare and beyond, according to the companies.

The secretive Google[x] facility operates in Mountain View, California, and one of its most high profile projects has been a self driving car. It is also working closely on speech recognition, balloon powered internet access for rural areas, wind power, and technology for the Internet of Things—in which internet connected home, personal and city objects communicate with each other and take automatic action when different events take place.

Source: Leo King, "Google Smart Contact Lens Focuses On Healthcare Billions," *Forbes*, July 15, 2014.

Key Points in the Article

Google is adding to its growing list of technological innovations by partnering with Swiss pharmaceutical company Novartis to develop smart contact lenses to help patients manage diabetes. A microchip and electronic circuit in the contact lenses will measure blood sugar levels from tear fluids on the surface of the eye and transmit the data to a mobile device. Novartis is also exploring ways to incorporate autofocus technology in the contact lens, which could eliminate the need for reading glasses. The smart contact lens is just one of a growing number of products being developed in the multibillion-dollar, rapidly expanding digital health care market. Novartis chief executive Joe Jiminez hopes to see the smart contact lens available in the market within five years.

Analyzing the News

a Advances in technology are having a profound effect on many sectors of the economy, and one of the fastest-growing sectors is the digital health care market. Rapid improvements in smartphone technology have played a large role in expanding the use of smart medical devices. The future of health care may be greatly affected by partnerships between high-tech firms like Google and health industry firms like Novartis. These partnerships can lead to the development of smart devices designed to facilitate and improve medical diagnoses and conditions.

b According to the Centers for Disease Control and Prevention (CDC), diabetes ranks seventh among the leading causes of death in the United States, with more than 75,000 deaths in 2012 attributed to the disease. The total estimated cost of diabetes that year was $245 billion, which included the costs of direct medical care as well as the costs associated with disability, work loss, and premature death. In 2012, the CDC estimated that 28.9 million people in the United States age 20 or older had diabetes, and almost 28 percent of those cases were undiagnosed. The table below shows these data as well as data on the number of new, diagnosed cases of diabetes. Given the number of people suffering from diabetes, the development of the smart contact lens has the potential to help patients manage their disease. For example, being able to monitor blood sugar levels via the contact lens and a smartphone could be more convenient and less painful than the common finger-prick testing method and might therefore encourage more people to regularly monitor their diabetes. An effective and relatively inexpensive smart contact lens could end up saving not only time and money but also lives.

c The health care industry is growing as well as changing, and technology is fueling a large part of the change. Smart medical devices are still in their infancy, but rapid technological advancement has led many new firms to enter this industry, introducing innovative new products. As the average age of the U.S. population continues to increase, and as people spend more time and resources on maintaining good health, smart medical devices may revolutionize the way health care is administered. This revolution will benefit not only those companies involved with the development of new products but also health care professionals and their patients.

Thinking Critically

1. One key economic idea is that people respond to economic incentives. What economic incentives are Google and Novartis responding to?
2. Some diabetic patients need to monitor their condition by pricking their finger for blood to check blood sugar levels. If these patients could instead use the smart contact lens, it could improve the effectiveness of monitoring and, therefore, treatment. Develop an economic model to analyze the relationship between using the smart contact lens or the finger-prick method of monitoring blood sugar levels and the number of diabetes-related deaths in the United States. Use information from the article to explain the steps you would take to develop this model.

Total cases of diabetes (diagnosed and undiagnosed), and new cases of diagnosed diabetes among people aged 20 years or older, United States, 2012

	Total Number in Age Group with Diabetes	Percentage of Age Group with Diabetes	Number of New Diabetes Cases	Rate of New Diabetes Cases Per 1,000 People
20 years or older	28.9 million	12.3%	1,663,000	7.8
20–44	4.3 million	4.1	371,000	3.6
45–64	13.4 million	16.2	892,000	12.0
65 years or older	11.2 million	25.9	400,000	11.5

Sources: 2010–2012 National Health Interview Survey, 2009–2012 National Health and Nutrition Examination Survey; and 2012 U.S. Census data.

CHAPTER SUMMARY AND PROBLEMS

Key Terms

Allocative efficiency, p. 12	Economics, p. 4	Market economy, p. 10	Positive analysis, p. 14
Centrally planned economy, p. 10	Equity, p. 12	Microeconomics, p. 17	Productive efficiency, p. 12
Economic model, p. 4	Macroeconomics, p. 17	Mixed economy, p. 11	Scarcity, p. 4
Economic variable, p. 13	Marginal analysis, p. 7	Normative analysis, p. 14	Trade-off, p. 8
	Market, p. 4	Opportunity cost, p. 8	Voluntary exchange, p. 12

1.1 Three Key Economic Ideas, pages 4–8

LEARNING OBJECTIVE: Explain these three key economic ideas: People are rational; people respond to economic incentives; and optimal decisions are made at the margin.

Summary

Economics is the study of the choices consumers, business managers, and government officials make to attain their goals, given their scarce resources. We must make choices because of **scarcity**, which means that although our wants are unlimited, the resources available to fulfill those wants are limited. Economists assume that people are rational in the sense that consumers and firms use all available information as they take actions intended to achieve their goals. Rational individuals weigh the benefits and costs of each action and choose an action only if the benefits outweigh the costs. Although people act from a variety of motives, ample evidence indicates that they respond to economic incentives. Economists use the word **marginal** to mean extra or additional. The optimal decision is to continue any activity up to the point where the marginal benefit equals the marginal cost.

MyEconLab Visit www.myeconlab.com to complete these exercises online and get instant feedback.

Review Questions

1.1 Briefly discuss each of the following economic ideas: People are rational, people respond to economic incentives, and optimal decisions are made at the margin.

1.2 What is scarcity? Why is scarcity central to the study of economics?

Problems and Applications

1.3 Do you agree with the following statement: "The problem with economics is that it assumes that consumers and firms always make the correct decisions. But we know that everyone makes mistakes."

1.4 According to the FBI Bank Crime Statistics, there were nearly 4,000 bank robberies in the United States in 2014. The FBI claims that banks have made themselves easy targets by refusing to install clear acrylic partitions, called *bandit barriers*, that separate bank tellers from the public. According to a special agent with the FBI, "Bandit barriers are a great deterrent. We've talked to guys who rob banks, and as soon as they see a bandit barrier, they go find another bank." Despite this finding, many banks have been reluctant to install these barriers. Wouldn't banks have a strong incentive to install bandit barriers to deter robberies? Why, then, do so many banks not do so?

Sources: U.S. Department of Justice, Federal Bureau of Investigation, "Bank Crime Statistics (BCS) Federally Insured Financial Institutions, January 1, 2014–December 31, 2014," www.fbi.gov; and Richard Cowen, "FBI Says Banks Are to Blame for Rise in Robberies," NorthJersey.com, March 10, 2009.

1.5 The grading system plays an important role in student learning. In their book *Effective Grading: A Tool for Learning and Assessment in College*, Barbara Walvoord and Virginia Anderson state that "grading infuses everything that happens in the classroom." They also argue that grading "needs to be acknowledged and managed from the first moment that an instructor begins planning a class."

a. How could the grading system a teacher uses affect the incentives of students to learn the course material?

b. If teachers put too little weight in the grading scale on a certain part of the course, such as readings outside the textbook, how might students respond?

c. Teachers often wish that students came to class prepared, having read the upcoming material. How could a teacher design the grading system to motivate students to come to class prepared?

Source: Barbara E. Walvoord and Virginia Johnson Anderson, *Effective Grading: A Tool for Learning and Assessment in College*, 2nd ed., San Francisco: Jossey-Bass, 2010, p. 1.

1.6 The federal government subsidizes some loans to college students. Typically, the more students who participate in these programs and the more they borrow, the higher the cost to the federal government. In 2011, President Barack Obama convinced Congress to pass these changes to the federal student loan programs: (1) Payments were capped at 10 percent of a borrower's discretionary income; (2) any unpaid balances for people working for government or in the nonprofit sector were forgiven after 10 years; and (3) people working in the private sector had their loans forgiven after 20 years.

a. As a result of these changes in the federal student loan program, would you predict that the total amount that students borrowed under these programs increased or decreased? Briefly explain.

b. As part of his 2016 federal budget proposals, President Obama recommended significant changes to the federal student loan programs. Given your answer to part (a), do you think President Obama was likely to have recommended changes that would increase or changes that would decrease the payments that borrowers would have to make? Briefly explain.

c. How might President Obama and his advisers have failed to correctly forecast the effects of the 2011 changes to the loan programs?

Sources: Allesandra Lanza, "What Obama's 2016 Budget Proposal Means for Student Borrowers," usnews.com, February 11, 2015; and Josh Mitchell, "Student-Debt Forgiveness Plans Skyrocket, Raising Fears over Costs, Higher Tuition," *Wall Street Journal*, April 22, 2014.

1.7 (Related to the Making the Connection on page 5) Many universities and corporations offer a health and wellness program that helps their employees improve or maintain their health and get paid (a relatively small amount) for doing so. The programs vary but typically consist of employees completing a health assessment, receiving a program for healthy living, and monitoring their monthly health activities.

a. Why would universities and corporations pay employees to improve or maintain their health?

b. How does health insurance affect the incentive of employees to improve or maintain their health?

c. Would a wellness program increase or decrease the health insurance premiums that an insurance company would charge the university or corporation to provide insurance coverage? Briefly explain.

1.8 (Related to the Making the Connection on page 5) Jay Bhattacharya and Kate Bundorf of Stanford University have found evidence that people who are obese and who work for firms that provide health insurance receive lower wages than workers at those firms who are not obese. At firms that do not provide health insurance, obese workers do not receive lower wages than workers who are not obese.

a. Why might firms that provide workers with health insurance pay a lower wage to obese workers than to workers who are not obese?

b. Is Bhattacharya and Bundorf's finding relevant to the question of whether health insurance provides people with an incentive to become obese? Briefly explain.

Source: Jay Bhattacharya and M. Kate Bundorf, "The Incidence of the Health Care Costs of Obesity," *Journal of Health Economics*, Vol. 28, No. 3, May 2009, pp. 649–658.

1.9 (Related to Solved Problem 1.1 on page 7) McDonald's typically serves breakfast until only 10:30 A.M. on weekdays and 11:00 A.M. on weekends. In 2015, the company began to experiment with serving breakfast all day at various locations in San Diego. Several owners of McDonald's restaurants, however, point out that offering breakfast 24 hours a day presents two logistical problems: (1) Burgers and other meats need to be cooked at a higher temperature than eggs, so it would be difficult for employees to set the grill at the right temperature for both foods, and (2) scrambled eggs require employees to continually stir, while hamburgers don't require this attention. In addition, some customers might buy the cheaper breakfast rather than the more expensive lunch or dinner meals. If McDonald's made you responsible for making this decision, discuss how you would go about analyzing whether to serve breakfast all day. Would your decision have to be all or nothing—either serve breakfast up to 10:30 A.M. or serve breakfast all day? Would you have to serve the entire breakfast menu all day?

Sources: Associated Press, "McDonald's Gives All-Day Breakfast a Test Try," usatoday.com, March 30, 2015; and Susan Berfield and Leslie Patton, "What's So Hard About a 24/7 McMuffin?" *Bloomberg BusinessWeek*, May 6–12, 2013.

1.10 (Related to Solved Problem 1.1 on page 7) Late in the semester, a friend tells you, "I was going to drop my psychology course so I could concentrate on my other courses, but I had already put so much time into the course that I decided not to drop it." What do you think of your friend's reasoning? Would it make a difference to your answer if your friend has to pass the psychology course at some point to graduate? Briefly explain.

1.11 In a paper written by Bentley College economists Patricia M. Flynn and Michael A. Quinn, the authors state:

> We find evidence that Economics is a good choice of major for those aspiring to become a CEO [chief executive officer]. When adjusting for size of the pool of graduates, those with undergraduate degrees in Economics are shown to have had a greater likelihood of becoming an S&P 500 CEO than any other major.

A list of famous economics majors published by Marietta College includes business leaders Elon Musk, Warren Buffett, Donald Trump, David Rockefeller, Ted Turner, Bill Belichick, Diane von Furstenberg, and Sam Walton, as well as Presidents George H.W. Bush, Gerald Ford, and Ronald Reagan and Supreme Court Justice Sandra Day O'Connor. Why might studying economics be particularly good preparation for being the top manager of a corporation or a leader in government?

Sources: Patricia M. Flynn and Michael A. Quinn, "Economics: A Good Choice of Major for Future CEOs," *Social Science Research Network*, November 28, 2006; and *Famous Economics Majors*, Marietta College, Marietta, Ohio, November 21, 2014.

1.2 The Economic Problem That Every Society Must Solve, pages 8–12

LEARNING OBJECTIVE: Discuss how an economy answers these questions: What goods and services will be produced? How will the goods and services be produced? Who will receive the goods and services produced?

Summary

Society faces **trade-offs**: Producing more of one good or service means producing less of another good or service. The **opportunity cost** of any activity—such as producing a good or service—is the highest-valued alternative that must be given up to engage in that activity. The choices of consumers, firms, and governments determine what goods and services will be produced. Firms choose how to produce the goods and services they sell. In the United States, who receives the goods and services produced depends largely on how income is distributed in the marketplace. In a **centrally planned economy**, most economic decisions are made by the government. In a **market economy**, most economic decisions are made by consumers and firms. Most economies, including that of the United States, are **mixed economies** in which most economic decisions are made by consumers and firms but in which the government also plays a significant role. There are two types of efficiency: productive efficiency and allocative efficiency. **Productive efficiency** occurs when a good or service is produced at the lowest possible cost. **Allocative efficiency** occurs when production corresponds with consumer preferences. **Voluntary exchange** is a situation that occurs in markets when both the buyer and the seller of a product are made better off by the transaction. **Equity** is more difficult to define than efficiency, but it usually involves a fair distribution of economic benefits. Government policymakers often face a trade-off between equity and efficiency.

MyEconLab Visit **www.myeconlab.com** to complete these exercises online and get instant feedback.

Review Questions

2.1 Why does scarcity imply that every society and every individual face trade-offs?

2.2 What are the three economic questions that every society must answer? Briefly discuss the differences in the way centrally planned, market, and mixed economies answer these questions.

2.3 What is the difference between productive efficiency and allocative efficiency?

2.4 What is the difference between efficiency and equity? Why do government policymakers often face a trade-off between efficiency and equity?

Problems and Applications

2.5 According to Forbes magazine, in 2015 Bill Gates was the world's richest person, with wealth of $79.2 billion. Does Bill Gates face scarcity? Does everyone? Are there any exceptions?

Source: "The World's Billionaires," forbes.com, March 2, 2015.

2.6 Consider an organization that exists to help the poor. The members of the organization are discussing alternative methods of aiding the poor, when a proponent of one particular method asserts, "If even one poor person is helped with this method, then all our time and money would have been worth it." If you were a member of the organization, how would you reply to this assertion?

2.7 **(Related to the Making the Connection on page 9)** An article on espn.com about declining attendance at college football games noted that schools in the central time zone had particular problems with attendance at games that started at 11 A.M. The athletic director at the University of Illinois was quoted as saying, "I'm a big fan of evening games." How would playing games in the late afternoon or evening rather than in the morning affect the opportunity cost of a student attending a game?

Source: Adam Rittenberg, "Attendance Challenges Big Deal for B1G," espn.com, February 14, 2014.

2.8 In a market economy, why does a firm have a strong incentive to be productively efficient and allocatively efficient? What does the firm earn if it is productively and allocatively efficient, and what happens if it is not?

2.9 Alberto Chong of the University of Ottawa and several colleagues conducted an experiment to test the efficiency of government postal services around the world. They mailed letters to nonexistent businesses in 159 countries and kept track of how many of the letters were returned. Was this test most relevant to evaluating the productive efficiency or the allocative efficiency of these postal services? Briefly explain.

Source: Alberto Chong, Rafael La Porta, Florencio Lopez-de-Silanes, and Andrei Shleifer, "Letter Grading Government Efficiency," *Journal of the European Economic Association*, Vol. 12, No. 2, April 2014, pp. 277–299.

2.10 The Food and Drug Administration (FDA) is part of the federal government's Department of Health and Human Services. Among its other functions, the FDA evaluates the safety and effectiveness of drugs and medical devices. FDA approval had to be granted before OraSure was allowed to market its home HIV test. In a centrally planned economy, the government decides how resources will be allocated. In a market economy, the decisions of households and firms interacting in markets allocate resources. Briefly explain which statement is more accurate: (a) The regulation of the production and sale of drugs and medical devices in the United States is an example of how resources are allocated in a centrally planned economy, or (b) the regulation of the production and sale of drugs and medical devices in the United States is an example of how resources are allocated in a market economy.

2.11 Would you expect a centrally planned economy to be better at productive efficiency or allocative efficiency? Be sure to define productive efficiency and allocative efficiency in your answer.

2.12 Leonard Fleck, a philosophy professor at Michigan State University, has written:

> When it comes to health care in America, we have limited resources for unlimited health care needs. We want everything contemporary medical technology can offer that will improve the length or quality of our lives as we age. But as presently healthy taxpayers, we want costs controlled.

Why is it necessary for all economic systems to limit services such as health care? How does a market system prevent people from getting as many goods and services as they want?

Source: Leonard Fleck, *Just Caring: Health Care Rationing and Democratic Deliberation*, New York: Oxford University Press, 2009.

2.13 Suppose that your college decides to give away 1,000 tickets to the football game against your school's biggest rival. The athletic department elects to distribute the tickets by giving them away to the first 1,000 students who show up at the department's office at 10 A.M. the following Monday.

a. Which groups of students will be most likely to try to get the tickets? Think of specific examples and then generalize.

b. What is the opportunity cost of distributing the tickets this way?

c. Productive efficiency occurs when a good or service (such as the distribution of tickets) is produced at the lowest possible cost. Is this an efficient way to distribute the tickets? If possible, think of a more efficient method of distributing the tickets.

d. Is this an equitable way to distribute the tickets? Briefly explain.

1.3 Economic Models, pages 12–17

LEARNING OBJECTIVE: Describe the role of models in economic analysis.

Summary

An **economic variable** is something measurable that can have different values, such as the wages of software programmers. Economists rely on economic models when they apply economic ideas to real-world problems. **Economic models** are simplified versions of reality used to analyze real-world economic situations. Economists accept and use an economic model if it leads to hypotheses that are confirmed by statistical analysis. In many cases, the acceptance is tentative, however, pending the gathering of new data or further statistical analysis. Economics is a *social science* because it applies the scientific method to the study of the interactions among individuals. Economics is concerned with positive analysis rather than normative analysis. **Positive analysis** is concerned with what is. **Normative analysis** is concerned with what ought to be. As a social science, economics considers human behavior in every context of decision making, not just in business.

MyEconLab Visit **www.myeconlab.com** to complete these exercises online and get instant feedback.

Review Questions

3.1 Why do economists use models? How are economic data used to test models?

3.2 Describe the five steps economists follow to arrive at a useful economic model.

3.3 What is the difference between normative analysis and positive analysis? Is economics concerned mainly with normative analysis or positive analysis? Briefly explain.

Problems and Applications

3.4 Suppose an economist develops an economic model and finds that "it works great in theory, but it fails in practice." What should the economist do next?

3.5 Dr. Strangelove's theory is that the price of mushrooms is determined by the activity of subatomic particles that exist in another universe parallel to ours. When the subatomic particles are emitted in profusion, the price of mushrooms is high. When subatomic particle emissions are low, the price of mushrooms is also low. How would you go about testing Dr. Strangelove's theory? Discuss whether this theory is useful.

3.6 **(Related to the Don't Let This Happen to You on page 15)** Briefly explain which of the following statements represent positive analysis and which represent normative analysis.

a. A 50-cent-per-pack tax on cigarettes will lead to a 12 percent reduction in smoking by teenagers.
b. The federal government should spend more on AIDS research.
c. Rising wheat prices will increase bread prices.
d. The price of coffee at Starbucks is too high.

3.7 **(Related to the Don't Let This Happen to You on page 15)** Warren Buffet is the chief executive officer of the investment firm Berkshire Hathaway and one of the wealthiest people in the world. In an editorial in the *Wall Street Journal*, Buffet argued that economic policies in the United States should be designed so that people who are willing to work receive enough income to live a "decent lifestyle." He argued that an expansion of the Earned Income Tax Credit (EITC) would be superior to an increase in the minimum wage as a means to reach this goal. The EITC is a program under which the federal government makes payments to low-income workers. Is Buffet correct that it is the role of the federal government to make sure people who work will have enough income to live a "decent lifestyle"?

Source: Warren Buffet, "Better Than Raising the Minimum Wage," *Wall Street Journal*, May 21, 2015.

3.8 **(Related to the Making the Connection on page 16)** The *Making the Connection* feature explains that there are both positive and normative elements to the debate over whether medical schools should charge tuition and whether hospitals should continue to pay residents who pursue primary care but not residents who specialize. What economic statistics would be most useful in evaluating the positive elements in this debate? Assuming that these statistics are available or could be gathered, are they likely to resolve the normative issues in this debate?

3.9 **(Related to the Chapter Opener on page 3)** An article in the *Wall Street Journal* discussing Sanadu's prospects for successfully selling its home medical devices observes, "Another challenge will be getting doctors on board with the idea of patients bringing them information from home." What economic incentives do doctors have to accept this information? What economic incentives do they have not to accept it?

Source: Timothy Hay, "Gadgets Bring Diagnostics into the Home," *Wall Street Journal*, April 27, 2015.

3.10 Suppose you were building an economic model to forecast the number of physicians and physician's assistants likely to be needed in 2020. Should your model take into account the growth of the home medical device industry? Briefly explain.

3.11 To receive a medical license in the United States, a doctor must complete a residency program at a hospital. Hospitals are not free to expand their residency programs in a particular medical specialty without approval from a residency review committee (RRC), which is made up of physicians in that specialty. A hospital that does not abide by the rulings of the RRC runs the risk of losing its accreditation from the Accreditation Council for Graduate Medical Education (ACGME). The RRCs and ACGME argue that this system ensures that residency programs do not expand to the point where they are not providing residents with high-quality training.

a. How does this system help protect consumers?
b. How might this system protect the financial interests of doctors more than the well-being of consumers?
c. Briefly explain whether you consider this system to be good or bad. Is your conclusion an example of normative economics or of positive economics? Briefly explain.

Sources: Brian Palmer, "We Need More Doctors, Stat!" *Slate*, June 27, 2011; and Sean Nicholson, "Barriers to Entering Medical Specialties," Wharton School, September 2003.

1.4 Microeconomics and Macroeconomics, page 17

LEARNING OBJECTIVE: Distinguish between microeconomics and macroeconomics.

Summary

Microeconomics is the study of how households and firms make choices, how they interact in markets, and how the government attempts to influence their choices. **Macroeconomics** is the study of the economy as a whole, including topics such as inflation, unemployment, and economic growth.

MyEconLab Visit **www.myeconlab.com** to complete these exercises online and get instant feedback.

Review Question

4.1 Briefly discuss the difference between microeconomics and macroeconomics.

4.2 Is every economic issue either strictly microeconomic or strictly macroeconomic? Briefly explain.

Problems and Applications

4.3 Briefly explain whether each of the following is primarily a microeconomic issue or a macroeconomic issue.

a. The effect of higher cigarette taxes on the quantity of cigarettes sold

b. The effect of higher income taxes on the total amount of consumer spending

c. The reasons the economies of East Asian countries grow faster than the economies of sub-Saharan African countries

d. The reasons for low rates of profit in the airline industry

4.4 Briefly explain whether you agree with the following assertion: "Microeconomics is concerned with things that happen in one particular place, such as the unemployment rate in one city. In contrast, macroeconomics is concerned with things that affect the country as a whole, such as how the rate of teenage smoking in the United States would be affected by an increase in the tax on cigarettes."

1.5 A Preview of Important Economic Terms, pages 17–19

LEARNING OBJECTIVE: Define important economic terms.

Summary

Becoming familiar with important terms is a necessary step in learning economics. These important economic terms include *capital, entrepreneur, factors of production, firm, goods, household, human capital, innovation, profit, revenue, services,* and *technology.*

Appendix

Using Graphs and Formulas

LEARNING OBJECTIVE: Use graphs and formulas to analyze economic situations.

Graphs are used to illustrate key economic ideas. Graphs appear not just in economics textbooks but also on Web sites and in newspaper and magazine articles that discuss events in business and economics. Graphs serve two useful purposes: (1) They simplify economic ideas, and (2) they make the ideas more concrete so they can be applied to real-world problems. Economic and business issues can be complicated, but a graph can help cut through complications and highlight the key relationships needed to understand the issue. In that sense, a graph can be like a street map.

Suppose you take a bus to New York City to see the Empire State Building. After arriving at the Port Authority Bus Terminal, you will probably use a map similar to this one to find your way to the Empire State Building.

Maps are simplified versions of reality. This map shows the streets in this part of New York City and some of the most important buildings. The map does not show stores, most buildings, or the names, addresses, and telephone numbers of the people who live and work in the area. In fact, the map shows almost nothing about the messy reality of life in this section of New York City, except how the streets are laid out, which is the essential information you need to get from the Port Authority Bus Terminal to the Empire State Building.

Street map of New York City. Copyright © 2011 City Maps Inc. Reprinted by permission.

Think about someone who says, "I know how to get around in the city, but I just can't figure out how to read a map." It certainly is possible to find your destination in a city without a map, but it's a lot easier with one. The same is true of using graphs in economics. It is possible to arrive at a solution to a real-world problem in economics and business without using graphs, but it is usually a lot easier if you use them.

With practice, you will become familiar with the graphs and formulas in this text, and you will know how to use them to analyze problems that would otherwise seem very difficult. What follows is a brief review of how graphs and formulas are used.

Graphs of One Variable

Figure 1A.1 displays values for *market shares* in the U.S. automobile market, using two common types of graphs. Market shares show the percentage of industry sales accounted for by different firms. In this case, the information is for groups of firms: the "Big Three"—Ford, General Motors, and Chrysler—as well as Japanese, European, and Korean firms. Panel (a) displays the information about market shares as a *bar graph*, where the market share of each group of firms is represented by the height of its bar. Panel (b) displays the same information as a *pie chart*, where the market share of each group of firms is represented by the size of its slice of the pie.

Information about an economic variable is also often displayed in a *time-series graph*, which shows on a coordinate grid how the values of a variable change over time. In a coordinate grid, we can measure the value of one variable along the vertical axis (or *y*-axis) and the value of another variable along the horizontal axis (or *x*-axis). The point where the vertical axis intersects the horizontal axis is called the *origin*. At the origin, the value of both variables is zero. The points on a coordinate grid represent values of the two variables.

In Figure 1A.2, we measure the number of automobiles and trucks sold worldwide by Ford Motor Company on the vertical axis, and we measure time on the horizontal axis. In time-series graphs, the height of the line at each date shows the value of the

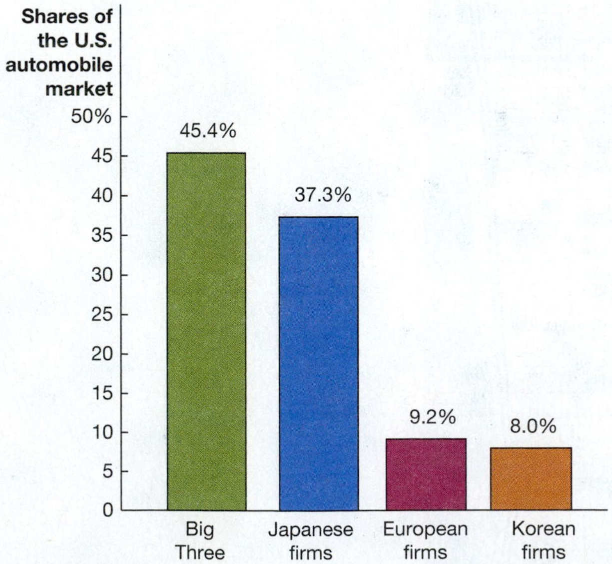

(a) Bar Graphs

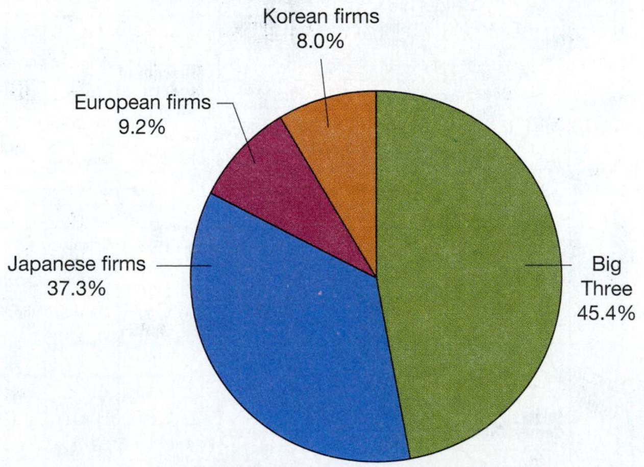

(b) Pie Chart

Figure 1A.1 Bar Graphs and Pie Charts

Values for an economic variable are often displayed as a bar graph or a pie chart. In this case, panel (a) shows market share data for the U.S. automobile industry as a bar graph, where the market share of each group of firms is represented by the height of its bar. Panel (b) displays the same information as a pie chart, where the market share of each group of firms is represented by the size of its slice of the pie.

Source: "Auto Sales," *Wall Street Journal*, May 21, 2015.

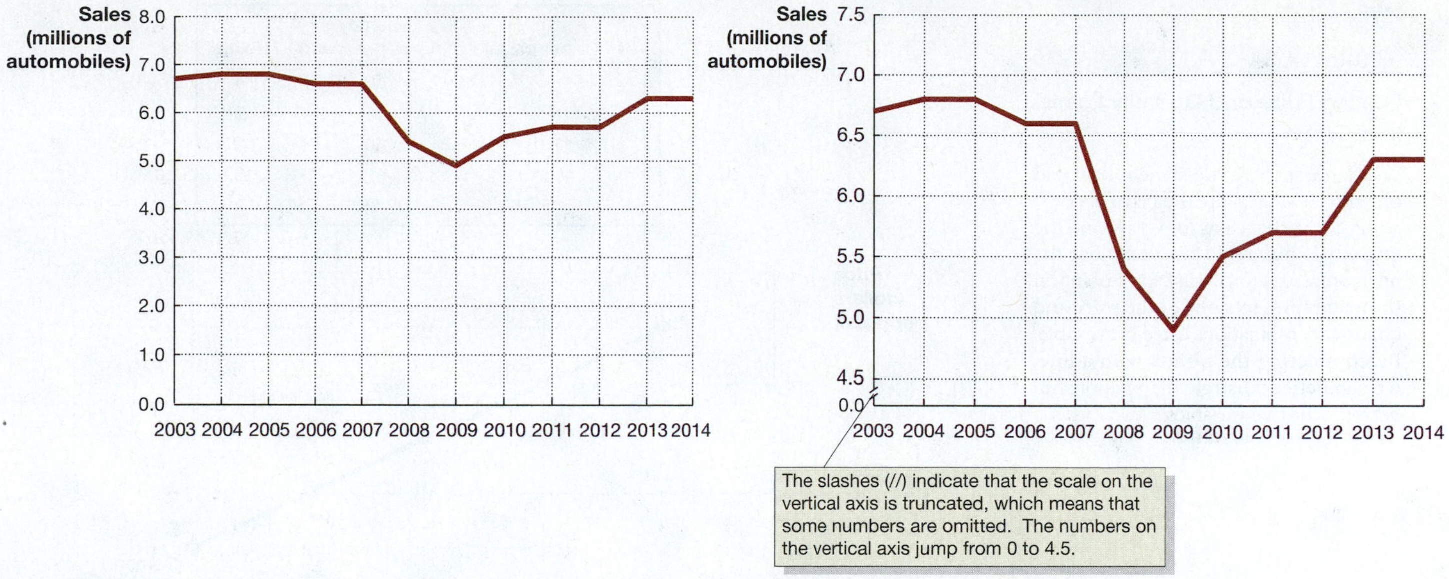

(a) Time-series graph where the scale is not truncated

(b) Time-series graph with truncated scale

MyEconLab Animation

Figure 1A.2 Time-Series Graphs

Both panels present time-series graphs of Ford Motor Company's worldwide sales during each year from 2003 to 2014. In panel (a), the vertical axis starts at 0, and the distance between each pair of values shown is the same. In panel (b), the scale on the vertical axis is truncated, which means that although it starts at 0, it then jumps to 4.5 million. As a result, the fluctuations in Ford's sales appear smaller in panel (a) than in panel (b).

Source: Ford Motor Company, *Annual Report*, various years.

variable measured on the vertical axis. Both panels of Figure 1A.2 show Ford's worldwide sales during each year from 2003 to 2014. The difference between panel (a) and panel (b) illustrates the importance of the scale used in a time-series graph. In panel (a), the vertical axis starts at 0, and the distance between each pair of values shown is the same. In this panel, the decline in Ford's sales during 2008 and 2009 appears relatively small. In panel (b), the scale on the vertical axis is truncated, which means that although it starts at zero, it jumps to 4.5 million. As a result, the distance on the vertical axis from 0 to 4.5 million is much smaller than the distance from 4.5 million to 5.0 million. The slashes (//) near the bottom of the axis indicate that the scale is truncated. In panel (b), the decline in Ford's sales during 2008 and 2009 appears much larger than in panel (a). (Technically, the horizontal axis in both panels is also truncated because we start with 2003, not 0.) MyEconLab Concept Check

Graphs of Two Variables

We often use graphs to show the relationship between two variables. Suppose you are interested in the relationship between the price of a cheese pizza and the quantity of pizzas sold per week in the town of Statesboro, Georgia. A graph showing the relationship between the price of a good and the quantity of the good demanded at each price is called a *demand curve*. (As we will discuss later, in drawing a demand curve for a good, we have to hold constant any variables other than price that might affect the willingness of consumers to buy the good.) Figure 1A.3 shows the data collected on price and quantity. The figure shows a two-dimensional grid on which we measure the price of pizza along the *y*-axis and the quantity of pizza sold per week along the *x*-axis. Each point on the grid represents one of the price and quantity combinations listed in the table. We can connect the points to form the demand curve for pizza in Statesboro, Georgia. Notice that the scales on both axes in the graph are truncated. In this case, truncating the axes allows the graph to illustrate more clearly the relationship between price and quantity by excluding low prices and quantities.

MyEconLab Concept Animation

Figure 1A.3

Plotting Price and Quantity Points in a Graph

The figure shows a two-dimensional grid on which we measure the price of pizza along the vertical axis (or *y*-axis) and the quantity of pizza sold per week along the horizontal axis (or *x*-axis). Each point on the grid represents one of the price and quantity combinations listed in the table. By connecting the points with a line, we can better illustrate the relationship between the two variables.

Price (dollars per pizza)	Quantity (pizzas per week)	Points
$15	50	*A*
14	55	*B*
13	60	*C*
12	65	*D*
11	70	*E*

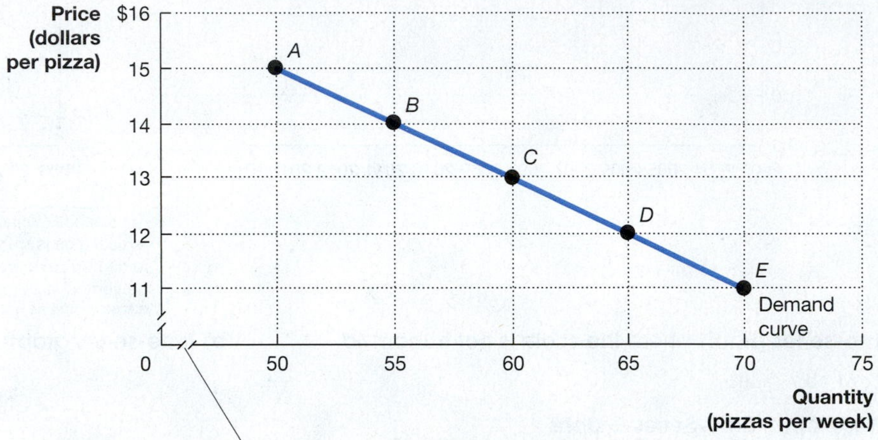

As we saw in Figure 1A.2, the slashes (//) indicate that the scales on the axes are truncated, which means that numbers are omitted: On the horizontal axis numbers jump from 0 to 50, and on the vertical axis numbers jump from 0 to 11.

Slopes of Lines

Once you have plotted the data in Figure 1A.3, you may be interested in how much the quantity of pizza sold increases as the price decreases. The *slope* of a line tells us how much the variable we are measuring on the *y*-axis changes as the variable we are measuring on the *x*-axis changes. We can use the Greek letter delta (Δ) to stand for the change in a variable. The slope is sometimes referred to as the rise over the run. So, we have several ways of expressing slope:

$$\text{Slope} = \frac{\text{Change in value on the vertical axis}}{\text{Change in value on the horizontal axis}} = \frac{\Delta y}{\Delta x} = \frac{\text{Rise}}{\text{Run}}.$$

Figure 1A.4 reproduces the graph from Figure 1A.3. Because the slope of a straight line is the same at any point, we can use any two points in the figure to calculate the slope of the line. For example, when the price of pizza decreases from $14 to $12, the quantity of pizza sold increases from 55 per week to 65 per week. Therefore, the slope is:

$$\text{Slope} = \frac{\Delta\text{Price of pizza}}{\Delta\text{Quantity of pizza}} = \frac{(\$12 - \$14)}{(65 - 55)} = \frac{-2}{10} = -0.2.$$

The slope of this line shows us how responsive consumers in Statesboro, Georgia, are to changes in the price of pizza. The larger the value of the slope (ignoring the negative sign), the steeper the line will be, which indicates that not many additional pizzas are sold when the price falls. The smaller the value of the slope, the flatter the line will be, which indicates a greater increase in pizzas sold when the price falls. MyEconLab Concept Check

Taking into Account More Than Two Variables on a Graph

The demand curve graph in Figure 1A.4 shows the relationship between the price of pizza and the quantity of pizza demanded, but we know that the quantity of any good demanded depends on more than just the price of the good. For example, the quantity of pizza demanded in a given week in Statesboro, Georgia, can be affected by other

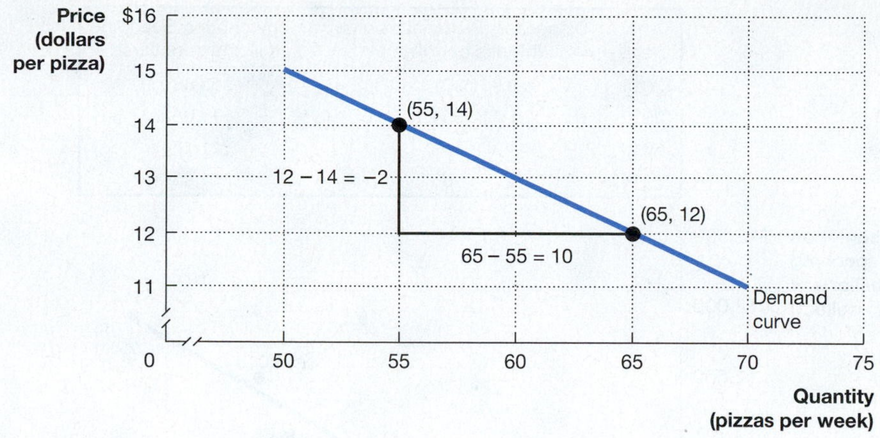

MyEconLab Animation

Figure 1A.4

Calculating the Slope of a Line

We can calculate the slope of a line as the change in the value of the variable on the *y*-axis divided by the change in the value of the variable on the *x*-axis. Because the slope of a straight line is constant, we can use any two points in the figure to calculate the slope of the line. For example, when the price of pizza decreases from \$14 to \$12, the quantity of pizza demanded increases from 55 per week to 65 per week. So, the slope of this line equals −2 divided by 10, or −0.2.

variables—the price of hamburgers, whether an advertising campaign by local pizza parlors has begun that week, and so on. Allowing the values of any other variables to change will cause the position of the demand curve in the graph to change.

Suppose that the demand curve in Figure 1A.4 were drawn holding the price of hamburgers constant, at \$1.50. If the price of hamburgers rises to \$2.00, some consumers will switch from buying hamburgers to buying pizza, and more pizzas will be demanded at every price. The result on the graph will be to shift the line representing the demand curve to the right. Similarly, if the price of hamburgers falls from \$1.50 to \$1.00, some consumers will switch from buying pizza to buying hamburgers, and fewer pizzas will be demanded at every price. The result on the graph will be to shift the line representing the demand curve to the left.

The table in Figure 1A.5 shows the effect of a change in the price of hamburgers on the quantity of pizza demanded. On the graph, suppose that at first we are on the line labeled Demand curve_1. If the price of pizza is \$14 (point *A*), an increase in the price of

	Quantity (pizzas per week)		
Price (dollars per pizza)	When the Price of Hamburgers = \$1.00	When the Price of Hamburgers = \$1.50	When the Price of Hamburgers = \$2.00
\$15	45	50	55
14	50	55	60
13	55	60	65
12	60	65	70
11	65	70	75

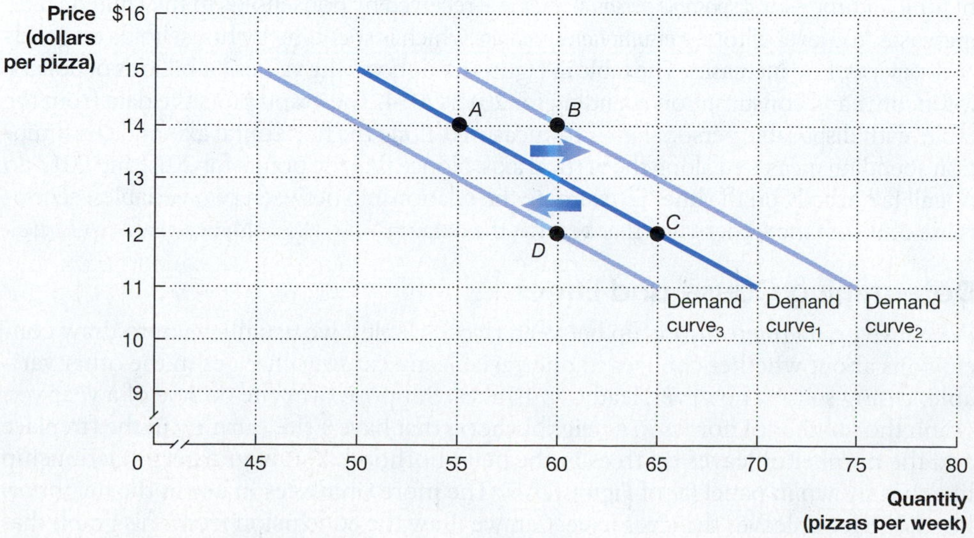

MyEconLab Animation

Figure 1A.5

Showing Three Variables on a Graph

The demand curve for pizza shows the relationship between the price of pizzas and the quantity of pizzas demanded, *holding constant other factors that might affect the willingness of consumers to buy pizza.* If the price of pizza is \$14 (point *A*), an increase in the price of hamburgers from \$1.50 to \$2.00 increases the quantity of pizzas demanded from 55 to 60 per week (point *B*) and shifts us to Demand curve_2. Or, if we start on Demand curve_1 and the price of pizza is \$12 (point *C*), a decrease in the price of hamburgers from \$1.50 to \$1.00 decreases the quantity of pizza demanded from 65 to 60 per week (point *D*) and shifts us to Demand curve_3.

MyEconLab Animation

Figure 1A.6

Graphing the Positive Relationship between Income and Consumption

In a positive relationship between two economic variables, as one variable increases, the other variable also increases. This figure shows the positive relationship between disposable personal income and consumption spending. As disposable personal income in the United States has increased, so has consumption spending.

Source: U.S. Department of Commerce, Bureau of Economic Analysis.

Year	Disposable Personal Income (billions of dollars)	Consumption Spending (billions of dollars)
2011	$11,801	$10,689
2012	12,384	11,083
2013	12,505	11,484
2014	12,986	11,930

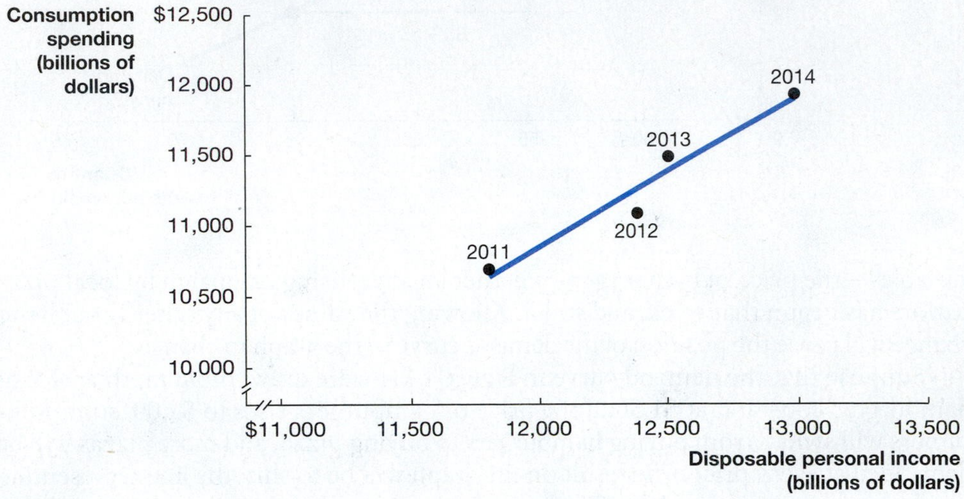

hamburgers from \$1.50 to \$2.00 increases the quantity of pizzas demanded from 55 to 60 per week (point *B*) and shifts us to Demand curve$_2$. Or, if we start on Demand curve$_1$ and the price of pizza is \$12 (point *C*), a decrease in the price of hamburgers from \$1.50 to \$1.00 decreases the quantity of pizzas demanded from 65 to 60 per week (point *D*) and shifts us to Demand curve$_3$. By shifting the demand curve, we have taken into account the effect of changes in the value of a third variable—the price of hamburgers. We will use this technique of shifting curves to allow for the effects of additional variables many times in this book. MyEconLab Concept Check

Positive and Negative Relationships

We can use graphs to show the relationships between any two variables. Sometimes the relationship between the variables is *negative,* meaning that as one variable increases in value, the other variable decreases in value. This was the case with the price of pizza and the quantity of pizzas demanded. The relationship between two variables can also be *positive,* meaning that the values of both variables increase or decrease together. For example, when the level of total income—or *disposable personal income*—received by households in the United States increases, the level of total *consumption spending,* which is spending by households on goods and services, also increases. The table in Figure 1A.6 shows the values (in billions of dollars) for income and consumption spending for 2011–2014. The graph plots the data from the table, with disposable personal income measured along the horizontal axis and consumption spending measured along the vertical axis. Notice that the points for 2012 and 2013 do not all fall exactly on the line. To examine the relationship between two variables, economists often use the straight line that best fits the data. MyEconLab Concept Check

Determining Cause and Effect

When we graph the relationship between two variables, we usually want to draw conclusions about whether changes in one variable are causing changes in the other variable. Doing so can, however, lead to mistakes. Suppose over the course of a year you graph the number of homes in a neighborhood that have a fire burning in the fireplace and the number of leaves on trees in the neighborhood. You would get a relationship like that shown in panel (a) of Figure 1A.7: The more fireplaces in use in the neighborhood, the fewer leaves the trees have. Can we draw the conclusion from this graph that

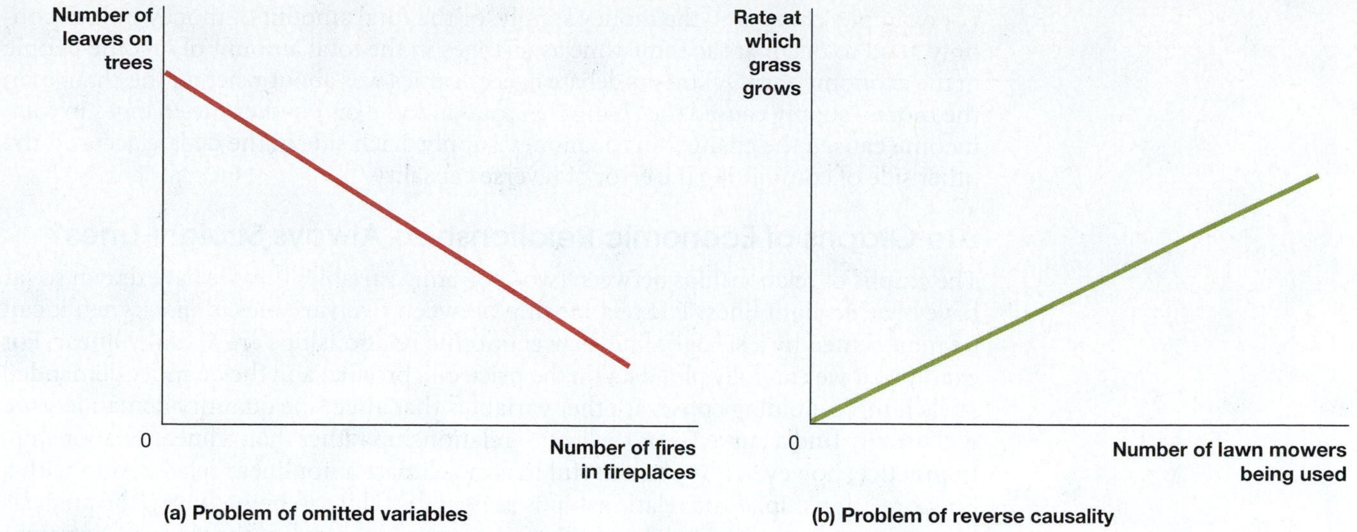

MyEconLab Animation

Figure 1A.7 Determining Cause and Effect

Using graphs to draw conclusions about cause and effect can be hazardous. In panel (a), we see that there are fewer leaves on the trees in a neighborhood when many homes have fires burning in their fireplaces. We cannot draw the conclusion that using fireplaces causes the leaves to fall because we have an *omitted variable*—the season of the year. In panel (b), we see that more lawn mowers are used in a neighborhood during times when the grass grows rapidly and fewer lawn mowers are used when the grass grows slowly. Concluding that using lawn mowers *causes* the grass to grow faster would be making the error of *reverse causality*.

using a fireplace causes trees to lose their leaves? We know, of course, that such a conclusion is incorrect. In spring and summer, there are relatively few fireplaces being used, and the trees are full of leaves. In the fall, as trees begin to lose their leaves, fireplaces are used more frequently. And in winter, many fireplaces are being used and many trees have lost all their leaves. The reason that the graph in Figure 1A.7 is misleading about cause and effect is that there is obviously an *omitted variable* in the analysis—the season of the year. An omitted variable is one that affects other variables, and its omission can lead to false conclusions about cause and effect.

Although in our example the omitted variable is obvious, there are many debates about cause and effect where the existence of an omitted variable has not been clear. For instance, it has been known for many years that people who smoke cigarettes suffer from higher rates of lung cancer than do nonsmokers. For some time, tobacco companies and some scientists argued that there was an omitted variable—perhaps failure to exercise or poor diet—that made some people more likely to smoke and more likely to develop lung cancer. If this omitted variable existed, then the finding that smokers were more likely to develop lung cancer would not have been evidence that smoking *caused* lung cancer. In this case, however, nearly all scientists eventually concluded that the omitted variable did not exist and that, in fact, smoking does cause lung cancer.

A related problem in determining cause and effect is known as *reverse causality*. The error of reverse causality occurs when we conclude that changes in variable *X* cause changes in variable *Y* when, in fact, it is actually changes in variable *Y* that cause changes in variable X. For example, panel (b) of Figure 1A.7 plots the number of lawn mowers being used in a neighborhood against the rate at which grass on lawns in the neighborhood is growing. We could conclude from this graph that using lawn mowers *causes* the grass to grow faster. We know, however, that in reality, the causality is in the other direction. Rapidly growing grass during the spring and summer causes the increased use of lawn mowers. Slowly growing grass in the fall or winter or during periods of low rainfall causes the decreased use of lawn mowers.

Once again, in our example, the potential error of reverse causality is obvious. In many economic debates, however, cause and effect can be more difficult to determine.

For example, changes in the money supply, or the total amount of money in the economy, tend to occur at the same time as changes in the total amount of income people in the economy earn. A famous debate in economics was about whether the changes in the money supply caused the changes in total income or whether the changes in total income caused the changes in the money supply. Each side in the debate accused the other side of committing the error of reverse causality. MyEconLab Concept Check

Are Graphs of Economic Relationships Always Straight Lines?

The graphs of relationships between two economic variables that we have drawn so far have been straight lines. The relationship between two variables is *linear* when it can be represented by a straight line. Few economic relationships are actually linear. For example, if we carefully plot data on the price of a product and the quantity demanded at each price, holding constant other variables that affect the quantity demanded, we will usually find a curved—or *nonlinear*—relationship rather than a linear relationship. In practice, however, it is often useful to approximate a nonlinear relationship with a linear relationship. If the relationship is reasonably close to being linear, the analysis is not significantly affected. In addition, it is easier to calculate the slope of a straight line, and it is also easier to calculate the area under a straight line. So, in this textbook, we often assume that the relationship between two economic variables is linear, even when we know that this assumption is not precisely correct. MyEconLab Concept Check

Slopes of Nonlinear Curves

In some situations, we need to take into account the nonlinear nature of an economic relationship. For example, panel (a) of Figure 1A.8 shows the hypothetical relationship between Apple's total cost of producing smartwatches and the quantity of smartwatches produced. The relationship is curved rather than linear. In this case, the cost of production is increasing at an increasing rate, which often happens in manufacturing. In other words, as we move up the curve, its slope becomes larger. (Remember that with a straight line, the slope is always constant.) To see why, first remember that we calculate the slope of a curve by dividing the change in the variable on the *y*-axis by the change in the variable on the *x*-axis. As we move from point *A* to point *B*, the quantity produced increases by 1 million smartwatches, while the total cost of production increases by $50 million. Farther up the curve, as we move from point *C* to point *D*, the change in quantity is the same—1 million smartwatches—but the change in the total cost of production is now much larger—$250 million. Because the change in the *y* variable has increased, while the change in the *x* variable has remained the same, we know that the slope has increased.

To measure the slope of a nonlinear curve at a particular point, we measure the slope of the line that is tangent to that curve at that point. This tangent line will touch the curve only at that point. We can measure the slope of the tangent line just as we would measure the slope of any other straight line. In panel (b), the tangent line at point *B* has a slope equal to:

$$\frac{\Delta\,\text{Cost}}{\Delta\,\text{Quantity}} = \frac{75}{1} = 75.$$

The tangent line at point *C* has a slope equal to:

$$\frac{\Delta\,\text{Cost}}{\Delta\,\text{Quantity}} = \frac{150}{1} = 150.$$

Once again, we see that the slope of the curve is larger at point *C* than at point *B*.

MyEconLab Concept Check

Formulas

We have just seen that graphs are an important economic tool. In this section, we will review several useful formulas and show how to use them to summarize data and calculate important relationships.

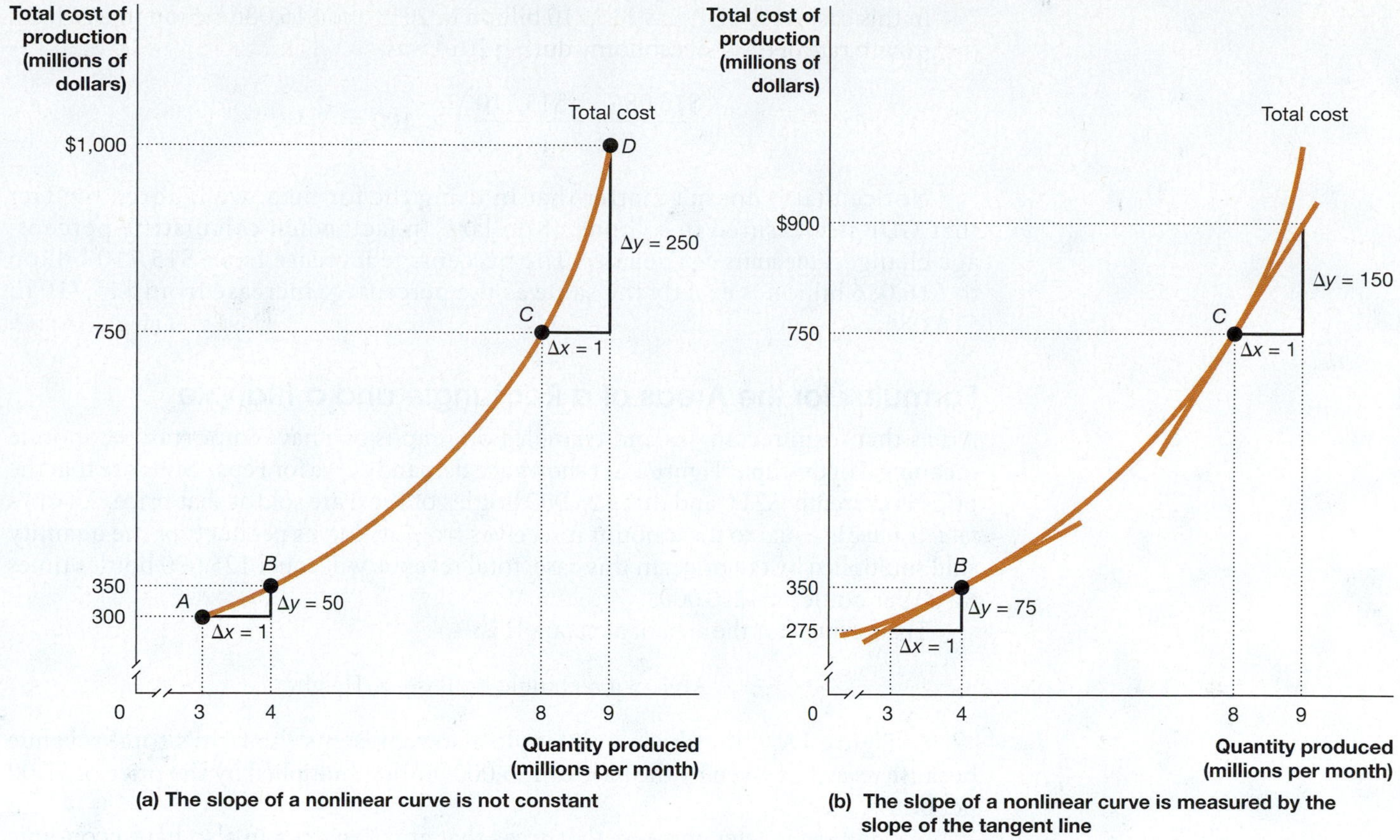

MyEconLab Animation

Figure 1A.8 The Slope of a Nonlinear Curve

The relationship between the quantity of Apple Watches produced and the total cost of production is curved rather than linear. In panel (a), when we move from point *A* to point *B*, the quantity produced increases by 1 million Apple Watches, while the total cost of production increases by $50 million. Farther up the curve, as we move from point *C* to point *D*, the change in quantity is the same—1 million Apple Watches—but the change in the total cost of production is now much larger—$250 million.

Because the change in the *y* variable has increased, while the change in the *x* variable has remained the same, we know that the slope has increased. In panel (b), we measure the slope of the curve at a particular point by calculating the slope of the tangent line at that point. The slope of the tangent line at point *B* is 75, and the slope of the tangent line at point *C* is 150.

Formula for a Percentage Change

The *percentage change* is the change in some economic variable, usually from one period to the next, expressed as a percentage. A key macroeconomic measure is the real gross domestic product (GDP). GDP is the value of all the final goods and services produced in a country during a year. "Real" GDP is corrected for the effects of inflation. When economists say that the U.S. economy grew 2.4 percent during 2014, they mean that real GDP was 2.4 percent higher in 2014 than it was in 2013. The formula for making this calculation is:

$$\left(\frac{\text{GDP}_{2014} - \text{GDP}_{2013}}{\text{GDP}_{2013}}\right) \times 100$$

or, more generally, for any two periods:

$$\text{Percentage change} = \left(\frac{\text{Value in the second period} - \text{Value in the first period}}{\text{Value in the first period}}\right) \times 100.$$

In this case, real GDP was $15,710 billion in 2013 and $16,086 billion in 2014. So, the growth rate of the U.S. economy during 2014 was:

$$\left(\frac{\$16{,}086 - \$15{,}710}{\$15{,}710}\right) \times 100 = 2.4\%.$$

Notice that it doesn't matter that in using the formula, we ignored the fact that GDP is measured in billions of dollars. In fact, when calculating percentage changes, *the units don't matter*. The percentage increase from $15,710 billion to $16,086 billion is exactly the same as the percentage increase from $15,710 to $16,086. MyEconLab Concept Check

Formulas for the Areas of a Rectangle and a Triangle

Areas that form rectangles and triangles on graphs can have important economic meaning. For example, Figure 1A.9 shows the demand curve for Pepsi. Suppose that the price is currently $2.00 and that 125,000 bottles of Pepsi are sold at that price. A firm's *total revenue* is equal to the amount it receives from selling its product, or the quantity sold multiplied by the price. In this case, total revenue will equal 125,000 bottles times $2.00 per bottle, or $250,000.

The formula for the area of a rectangle is:

$$\text{Area of a rectangle} = \text{Base} \times \text{Height}.$$

In Figure 1A.9, the shaded rectangle also represents the firm's total revenue because its area is given by the base of 125,000 bottles multiplied by the price of $2.00 per bottle.

We will see in later chapters that areas that are triangles can also have economic significance. The formula for the area of a triangle is:

$$\text{Area of a triangle} = \frac{1}{2} \times \text{Base} \times \text{Height}.$$

The shaded area in Figure 1A.10 is a triangle. The base equals 150,000 − 125,000, or 25,000. Its height equals $2.00 − $1.50, or $0.50. Therefore, its area equals 1/2 × 25,000 × $0.50, or $6,250. Notice that the shaded area is a triangle only if the demand curve is a straight line, or linear. Not all demand curves are linear. However, the formula for the area of a triangle will usually still give a good approximation, even if the demand curve is not linear. MyEconLab Concept Check

MyEconLab Study Plan

MyEconLab Animation

Figure 1A.9

Showing a Firm's Total Revenue on a Graph

The area of a rectangle is equal to its base multiplied by its height. Total revenue is equal to quantity multiplied by price. Here, total revenue is equal to the quantity of 125,000 bottles times the price of $2.00 per bottle, or $250,000. The area of the shaded rectangle shows the firm's total revenue.

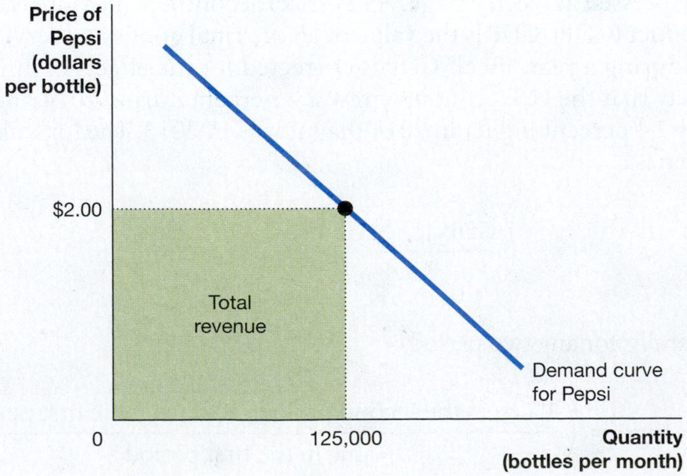

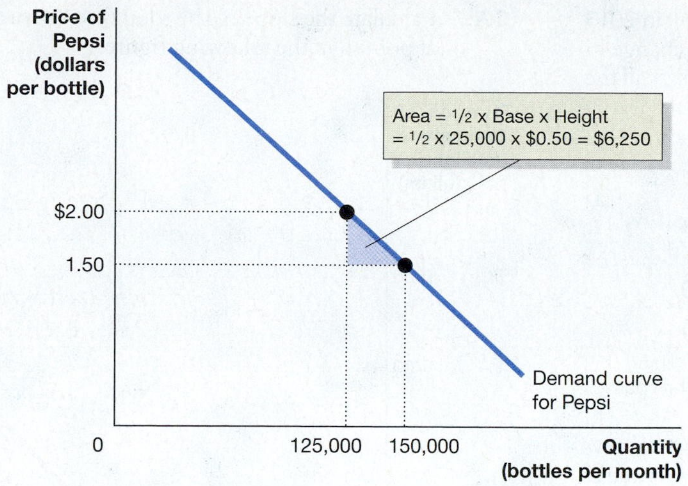

MyEconLab Animation

Figure 1A.10

The Area of a Triangle

The area of a triangle is equal to 1/2 multiplied by its base multiplied by its height. The area of the shaded triangle has a base equal to 150,000 − 125,000, or 25,000, and a height equal to $2.00 − $1.50, or $0.50. Therefore, its area is equal to 1/2 × 25,000 × $0.50, or $6,250.

Summary of Using Formulas

You will encounter several other formulas in this book. Whenever you use a formula, you should follow these steps:

1. Make sure you understand the economic concept the formula represents.
2. Make sure you are using the correct formula for the problem you are solving.
3. Make sure the number you calculate using the formula is economically reasonable. For example, if you are using a formula to calculate a firm's revenue and your answer is a negative number, you know you made a mistake somewhere. MyEconLab Concept Check

MyEconLab Study Plan

1A Using Graphs and Formulas, pages 27–37

LEARNING OBJECTIVE: Use graphs and formulas to analyze economic situations.

MyEconLab Visit www.myeconlab.com to complete these exercises online and get instant feedback.

Problems and Applications

1A.1 The following table shows the relationship between the price of custard pies and the number of pies Jacob buys per week:

Price (dollars per pie)	Quantity of pies	Week
$3.00	6	July 2
2.00	7	July 9
5.00	4	July 16
6.00	3	July 23
1.00	8	July 30
4.00	5	August 6

a. Is the relationship between the price of pies and the number of pies Jacob buys a positive relationship or a negative relationship?

b. Plot the data from the table on a graph similar to Figure 1A.3 on page 30. Draw a straight line that best fits the points.

c. Calculate the slope of the line.

1A.2 The following table gives information about the quantity of glasses of lemonade demanded on sunny and overcast days:

Price (dollars per glass)	Quantity (glasses of lemonade per day)	Weather
$0.80	30	Sunny
0.80	10	Overcast
0.70	40	Sunny
0.70	20	Overcast
0.60	50	Sunny
0.60	30	Overcast
0.50	60	Sunny
0.50	40	Overcast

Plot the data from the table on a graph similar to Figure 1A.5 on page 31. Draw two straight lines representing the two demand curves—one for sunny days and one for overcast days.

1A.3 Using the information in Figure 1A.2 on page 29, calculate the percentage change in Ford's auto sales from one year to the next. During which year did sales fall at the highest rate?

1A.4 Real GDP in 2012 was $15,369 billion. Real GDP in 2013 was $15,710 billion. What was the percentage change in real GDP from 2012 to 2013? What do economists call the percentage change in real GDP from one year to the next?

1A.5 Assume that the demand curve for Pepsi passes through the following two points:

Price per bottle of Pepsi (in dollars)	Number of bottles demanded
$2.50	100,000
1.25	200,000

a. Draw a graph with a linear demand curve that passes through these two points.

b. Show on the graph the areas representing total revenue at each price. Give the value for total revenue at each price.

1A.6 What is the area of the triangle shown in the following figure?

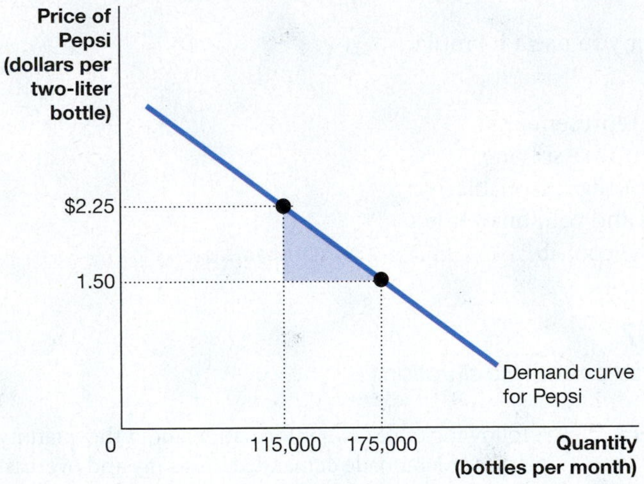

1A.7 Calculate the slope of the total cost curve at point A and at point B in the following figure.

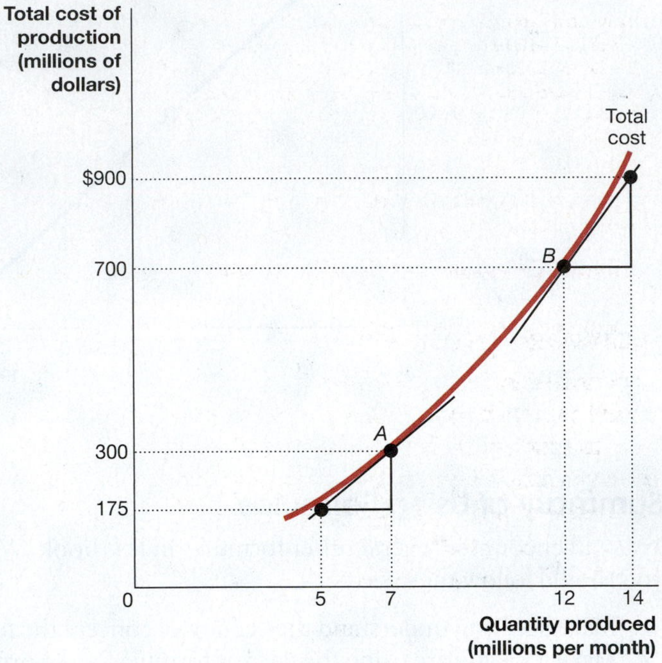

CHAPTER

2

Trade-offs, Comparative Advantage, and the Market System

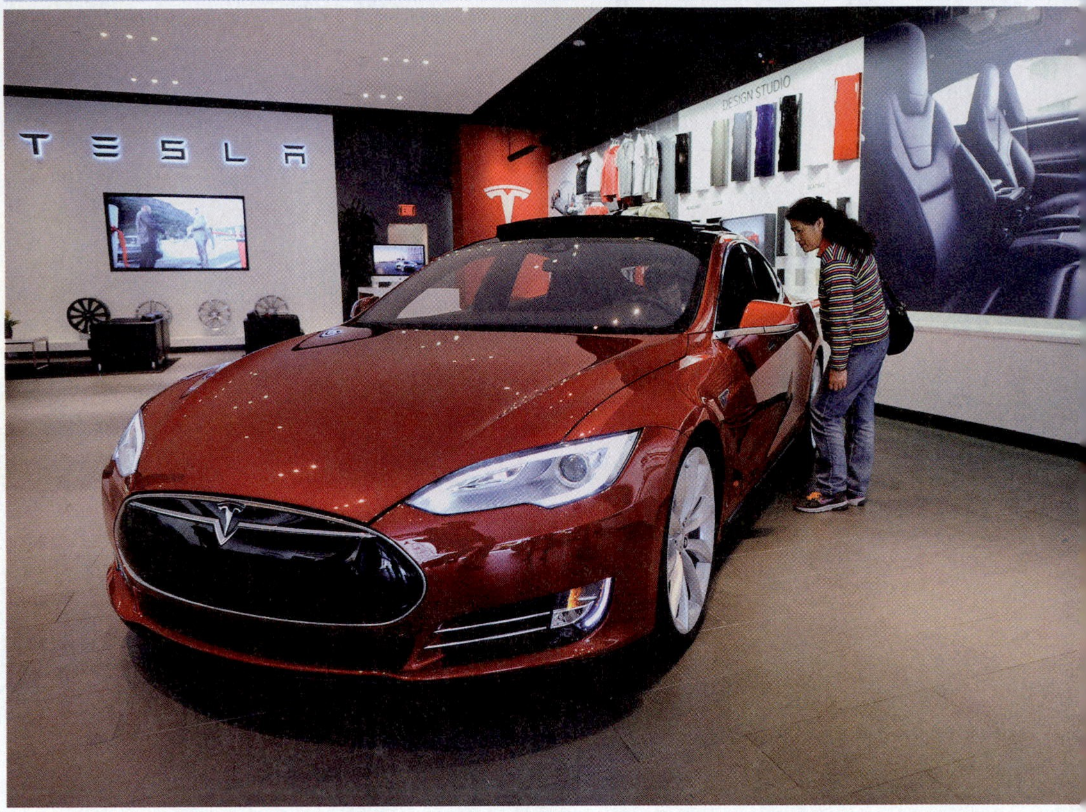

Chapter Outline and Learning Objectives

Managers at Tesla Motors Face Trade-offs

Are all-electric cars the wave of the future? If you're like most drivers, you probably like the idea of skipping the gas station in favor of powering up your car by plugging it into an electric outlet. Yet, all-electric cars have struggled to succeed in the marketplace for two key reasons: (1) The lithium batteries that power electric cars are costly, forcing up the prices of the cars, and (2) available batteries need to be recharged every 100 to 300 miles, making the cars impractical for long trips.

Tesla Motors is an American-based automobile manufacturer founded in 2003 by billionaire Elon Musk, who also started the online payment system PayPal and the private space firm SpaceX. Although in 2015 the firm held only a tiny 0.1 percent share of the U.S. car market, it had the goal of becoming the first firm to sell large numbers of all-electric cars. Tesla is building a nationwide network of fast-charging stations to make it easier for drivers to make longer trips. In 2015, its current models had high prices, but it intended to introduce a lower-priced model that would appeal to people who had been buying gasoline-powered cars such as the Toyota Camry or Honda Accord.

Tesla manufactures its cars in Fremont, California. To compete in the automobile market, Tesla's managers must make many strategic decisions, such as whether to introduce new car models. Tesla initially sold only the Model S sedan, with a base price of $75,000. In late 2015, Tesla introduced a second model, the Model X, a cross between a sport utility vehicle (SUV) and a minivan. The Model X was designed for families who would otherwise buy traditional gasoline-powered SUVs or minivans. But it also had a very high base price. Ultimately, Tesla's plan to gain a significant share of the automobile market required that it allocate resources to producing an all-electric car priced at about $35,000.

Tesla's managers must also decide how to sell and service its cars. Tesla has no dealerships. Instead, the company sells its cars only online and relies on company-owned service centers to provide maintenance and repair services. Some economists have questioned whether Tesla will be able to meet its future sales goals without selling cars through dealerships.

Managers also make smaller-scale decisions. For instance, in scheduling production at its Fremont plant, each month Tesla's managers must decide the quantity of Model S sedans and Model X SUVs to manufacture. Like other decisions managers make, this one involves a trade-off: Producing more of one of these two models means producing fewer of the other.

Apple is among a growing list of companies exploring the electric vehicle market. **AN INSIDE LOOK** on page 64 discusses the resources Apple has assembled to produce an electric vehicle as early as 2020.

Sources: Mike Ramsey and Anne Steele, "Tesla Loss Widens as Spending Jumps," *Wall Street Journal*, May 6, 2015; and Charles Fleming, "Tesla Introduces Lower Priced AWD Electric Model S," *Los Angeles Times*, April 8, 2015.

Economics in Your Life

The Trade-offs When You Buy a Car

When you buy a gasoline-powered car, you probably consider factors such as safety and fuel efficiency. To increase fuel efficiency, automobile manufacturers make some cars that are small and light. Large cars absorb more of the impact of an accident than do small cars, so people are usually safer driving large cars. What do these facts tell us about the relationship between safety and fuel efficiency? Under what circumstances would it be possible for automobile manufacturers to make cars that are both safer and more fuel efficient? As you read the chapter, try to answer these questions. You can check your answers against those provided on **page 62** at the end of this chapter.

In a market system, managers are always making decisions like those made by Tesla's managers. These decisions reflect a key fact of economic life: *Scarcity requires trade-offs.* **Scarcity** exists because we have unlimited wants but only limited resources available to fulfill those wants. Goods and services are scarce. So, too, are the economic resources, or *factors of production*—workers, capital, natural resources, and entrepreneurial ability—used to make goods and services. Your time is scarce, which means you face trade-offs: If you spend an hour studying for an economics exam, you have one less hour to spend studying for a psychology exam or going to the movies. If your university decides to use some of its scarce budget to buy new computers for the computer labs, those funds will not be available to buy new books for the library or to resurface the student parking lots. If Tesla decides to devote some of the scarce workers and machinery in its Fremont assembly plant to producing more Model X SUVs, those resources will not be available to produce more Model S sedans.

Scarcity A situation in which unlimited wants exceed the limited resources available to fulfill those wants.

Households and firms make many of their decisions in markets. Trade is a key activity that takes place in markets. Trade results from the decisions of millions of households and firms around the world. By engaging in trade, people can raise their incomes. In this chapter, we provide an overview of how the market system coordinates the independent decisions of these millions of households and firms. We begin our analysis of the economic consequences of scarcity and how a market system works by introducing an important economic model: the *production possibilities frontier.*

2.1 Production Possibilities Frontiers and Opportunity Costs

LEARNING OBJECTIVE: Use a production possibilities frontier to analyze opportunity costs and trade-offs.

As we saw in the chapter opener, Tesla operates an automobile factory in Fremont, California, where it assembles two car models. Because the firm's resources—workers, machinery, materials, and entrepreneurial ability—are limited, Tesla faces a trade-off: Resources devoted to producing one model are not available for producing the other model. Chapter 1 explained that economic models can be useful in analyzing many questions. We can use a simple model called the *production possibilities frontier* to analyze the trade-offs Tesla faces in its Fremont plant. A **production possibilities frontier (*PPF*)** is a curve showing the maximum attainable combinations of two goods that can be produced with available resources and current technology. In Tesla's case, the company produces only Model S sedans and Model X SUVs at the Fremont plant, using workers, materials, robots, and other machinery.

Production possibilities frontier (*PPF*) A curve showing the maximum attainable combinations of two goods that can be produced with available resources and current technology.

Graphing the Production Possibilities Frontier

Figure 2.1 uses a production possibilities frontier to illustrate the trade-offs that Tesla faces. The numbers from the table are plotted in the graph. The line in the graph represents Tesla's production possibilities frontier. If Tesla uses all its resources to produce Model S sedans, it can produce 80 per day—point *A* at one end of the production possibilities frontier. If Tesla uses all its resources to produce Model X SUVs, it can produce 80 per day—point *E* at the other end of the production possibilities frontier. If Tesla devotes resources to producing both vehicles, it could be at a point like *B*, where it produces 60 sedans and 20 SUVs.

All the combinations either on the frontier—like points *A*, *B*, *C*, *D*, and *E*—or inside the frontier—like point *F*—are *attainable* with the resources available. Combinations on the frontier are *efficient* because all available resources are being fully

Tesla's Production Choices at Its Fremont Plant		
Choice	Quantity of Sedans Produced	Quantity of SUVs Produced
A	80	0
B	60	20
C	40	40
D	20	60
E	0	80

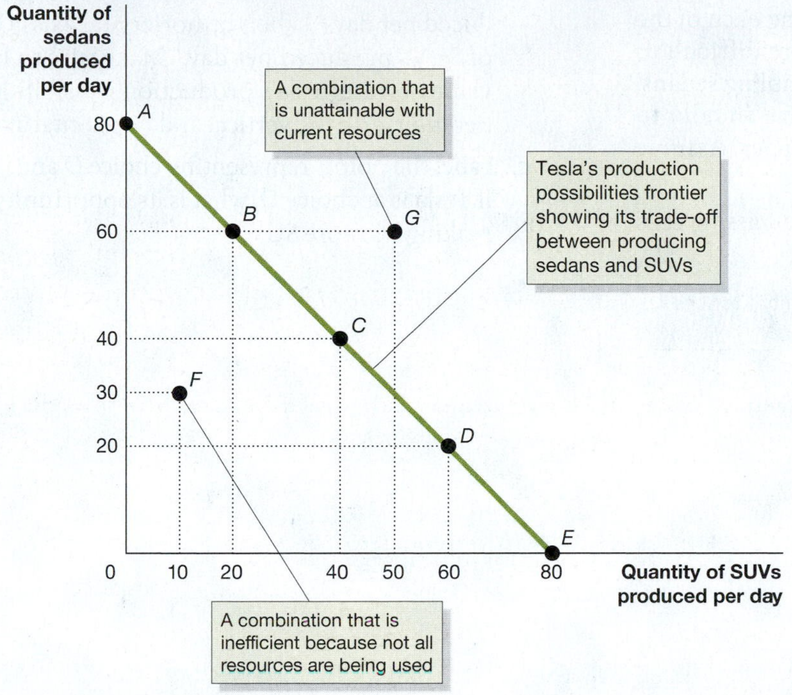

MyEconLab Animation

Figure 2.1

Tesla's Production Possibilities Frontier

Tesla faces a trade-off: To build one more sedan, it must build one fewer SUV. The production possibilities frontier illustrates the trade-off Tesla faces. Combinations on the production possibilities frontier—like points *A*, *B*, *C*, *D*, and *E*—are *efficient* because the maximum output is being obtained from the available resources. Combinations inside the frontier—like point *F*—are *inefficient* because some resources are not being used. Combinations outside the frontier—like point *G*—are *unattainable* with current resources.

utilized, and the fewest possible resources are being used to produce a given amount of output. Combinations inside the frontier—like point *F*—are *inefficient* because maximum output is not being obtained from the available resources—perhaps because the assembly line is not operating at its capacity. Tesla might like to be beyond the frontier—at a point like *G*, where it would be producing 60 sedans and 50 SUVs per day—but points beyond the production possibilities frontier are *unattainable*, given the firm's current resources. To produce the combination at *G*, Tesla would need more machines and more workers.

Notice that if Tesla is producing efficiently and is on the production possibilities frontier, the only way to produce more of one vehicle is to produce fewer of the other vehicle. Recall from Chapter 1 that the **opportunity cost** of any activity is the highest-valued alternative that must be given up to engage in that activity. For Tesla, the opportunity cost of producing one more SUV is the number of sedans the company will not be able to produce because it has shifted those resources to producing the SUV. For example, if Tesla moves from point *B* to point *C*, the opportunity cost of producing 20 more SUVs per day is the 20 fewer sedans that it can produce.

Opportunity cost The highest-valued alternative that must be given up to engage in an activity.

What point on the production possibilities frontier is best? We can't tell without further information. If consumer demand for SUVs is greater than the demand for sedans, the company is likely to choose a point closer to *E*. If demand for sedans is greater than the demand for SUVs, the company is likely to choose a point closer to *A*.

MyEconLab Concept Check

Solved Problem 2.1

MyEconLab Interactive Animation

Drawing a Production Possibilities Frontier for Tesla Motors

Suppose, for simplicity, that during any given week, the machinery and number of workers at Tesla Motors's Fremont plant cannot be increased. So the number of sedans or SUVs the company can produce during the week depends on how many hours are devoted to assembling each of the different models. Assume that SUVs are more difficult to assemble, so if Tesla devotes an hour to assembling sedans, it will produce 15 vehicles, but if Tesla devotes an hour to producing SUVs, it will produce only 10 vehicles. Assume that the plant can run for 8 hours per day.

a. Use the information given to fill in the missing cells in the following table:

	Hours Spent Making		Quantity Produced per Day	
Choice	Sedans	SUVs	Sedans	SUVs
A	8	0		
B	7	1		
C	6	2		
D	5	3		
E	4	4		
F	3	5		
G	2	6		
H	1	7		
I	0	8		

b. Use the data in the table to draw a production possibilities frontier graph illustrating Tesla's trade-off between assembling sedans and assembling SUVs. Label the vertical axis "Quantity of sedans produced per day." Label the horizontal axis "Quantity of SUVs produced per day." Make sure to label the values where Tesla's production possibilities frontier intersects the vertical and horizontal axes.

c. Label the points representing choice *D* and choice *E*. If Tesla is at choice *D*, what is its opportunity cost of making 10 more SUVs?

Solving the Problem

Step 1: Review the chapter material. This problem is about using production possibilities frontiers to analyze trade-offs, so you may want to review the section "Graphing the Production Possibilities Frontier," which begins on page 42.

Step 2: Answer part (a) by filling in the table. If Tesla can assemble 15 sedans in 1 hour, then with choice A, it can assemble 120 sedans and 0 SUVs. Because Tesla can assemble 10 SUVs in 1 hour, with choice B, it will produce 105 sedans and 10 SUVs. Using similar reasoning, you can fill in the remaining cells in the table as follows:

	Hours Spent Making		Quantity Produced per Day	
Choice	Sedans	SUVs	Sedans	SUVs
A	8	0	120	0
B	7	1	105	10
C	6	2	90	20
D	5	3	75	30
E	4	4	60	40
F	3	5	45	50
G	2	6	30	60
H	1	7	15	70
I	0	8	0	80

Step 3: Answer part (b) by drawing the production possibilities frontier graph. Using the data in the table in step 2, you should draw a graph that looks like this:

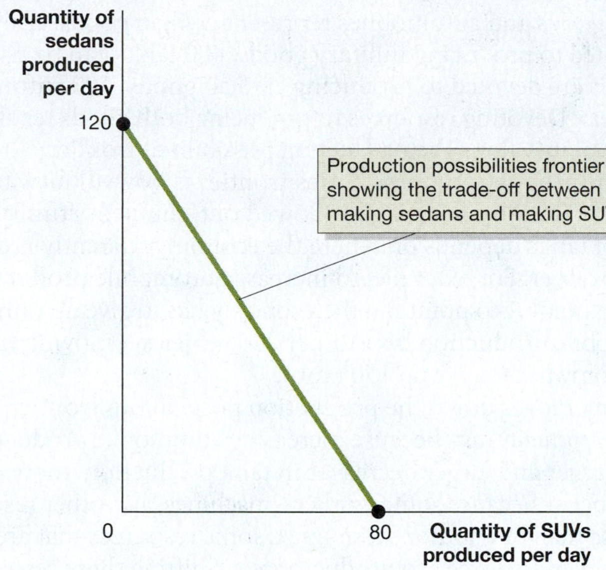

If Tesla devotes all 8 hours to assembling sedans, it will produce 120 sedans. Therefore, Tesla's production possibilities frontier will intersect the vertical axis at 120 sedans produced. If Tesla devotes all 8 hours to assembling SUVs, it will produce 80 SUVs. Therefore, Tesla's production possibilities frontier will intersect the horizontal axis at 80 SUVs produced.

Step 4: Answer part (c) by labeling choices *D* and *E* on your graph. The points for choices *D* and *E* can be plotted using the information from the table:

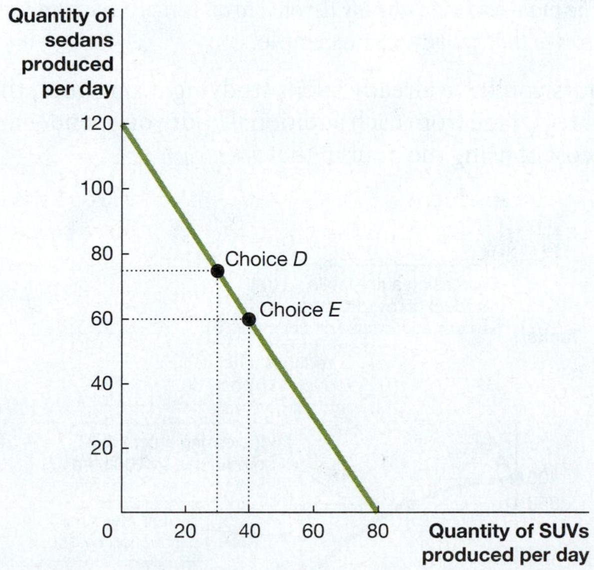

Moving from choice *D* to choice *E* increases Tesla's production of SUVs by 10 but lowers its production of sedans by 15. Therefore, Tesla's opportunity cost of producing 10 more SUVs is making 15 fewer sedans.

Your Turn: For more practice, do related problem 1.10 on page 67 at the end of this chapter.

MyEconLab Study Plan

Increasing Marginal Opportunity Costs

We can use the production possibilities frontier to explore issues concerning the economy as a whole. Suppose we divide all the goods and services produced in the economy into just two types: military goods and civilian goods. In Figure 2.2, we let tanks represent military goods and automobiles represent civilian goods. If all the country's resources are devoted to producing military goods, 400 tanks can be produced in one year. If all resources are devoted to producing civilian goods, 500 automobiles can be produced in one year. Devoting resources to producing both goods results in the economy being at other points along the production possibilities frontier.

Notice that this production possibilities frontier is bowed outward rather than being a straight line. Because the curve is bowed out, the opportunity cost of automobiles in terms of tanks depends on where the economy currently is on the production possibilities frontier. For example, to increase automobile production from 0 to 200—moving from point *A* to point *B*—the economy has to give up only 50 tanks. But to increase automobile production by another 200 vehicles—moving from point *B* to point *C*—the economy has to give up 150 tanks.

As the economy moves down the production possibilities frontier, it experiences *increasing marginal opportunity costs* because increasing automobile production by a given quantity requires larger and larger decreases in tank production. Increasing marginal opportunity costs occur because some workers, machines, and other resources are better suited to one use than to another. At point *A*, some resources that are well suited to producing automobiles are forced to produce tanks. Shifting these resources into producing automobiles by moving from point *A* to point *B* allows a substantial increase in automobile production, without much loss of tank production. But as the economy moves down the production possibilities frontier, more and more resources that are better suited to tank production are switched to automobile production. As a result, the increases in automobile production become increasingly smaller, while the decreases in tank production become increasingly larger. We would expect in most situations that production possibilities frontiers will be bowed outward rather than linear, as in the Tesla example discussed earlier.

The idea of increasing marginal opportunity costs illustrates an important economic concept: *The more resources already devoted to an activity, the smaller the payoff to devoting additional resources to that activity.* For example:

- The more hours you have already spent studying economics, the smaller the increase in your test grade from each additional hour you spend—and the greater the opportunity cost of using the hour in that way.

MyEconLab Animation

Figure 2.2

Increasing Marginal Opportunity Costs

As the economy moves down the production possibilities frontier, it experiences *increasing marginal opportunity costs* because increasing automobile production by a given quantity requires larger and larger decreases in tank production. For example, to increase automobile production from 0 to 200—moving from point *A* to point *B*—the economy has to give up only 50 tanks. But to increase automobile production by another 200 vehicles—moving from point *B* to point *C*—the economy has to give up 150 tanks.

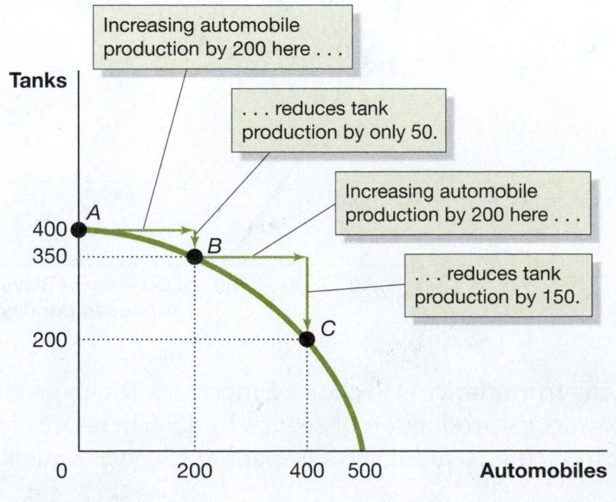

- The more funds a firm has devoted to research and development during a given year, the smaller the amount of useful knowledge it receives from each additional dollar spent—and the greater the opportunity cost of using the funds in that way.
- The more funds the federal government spends cleaning up the environment during a given year, the smaller the reduction in pollution from each additional dollar spent—and, once again, the greater the opportunity cost of using the funds in that way.

MyEconLab Concept Check

Economic Growth

At any given time, the total resources available to any economy are fixed. So, for example, if the United States produces more automobiles, it must produce less of something else—tanks in our example. The capital stock is the amount of machinery and other physical capital available in an economy. Over time, the resources available to an economy may increase because both the labor force and the capital stock increase. When the amount of resources increases, the economy's production possibilities frontier shifts outward, making it possible to produce both more automobiles and more tanks. Panel (a) of Figure 2.3 shows that over time the economy can move from point A to point B, producing more tanks and more automobiles.

Similarly, technological change makes it possible to produce more goods with the same number of workers and the same amount of machinery, which also shifts the production possibilities frontier outward. Technological change need not affect all sectors equally. Panel (b) of Figure 2.3 shows the results of technological change in the automobile industry that increases the quantity of automobiles workers can produce per year while leaving unchanged the quantity of tanks they can produce.

Outward shifts in the production possibilities frontier represent **economic growth** because they allow the economy to increase the production of goods and services, which ultimately raises the standard of living. In the United States and other high-income countries, the market system has aided the process of economic growth, which over the past 200 years has greatly increased the well-being of the average person.

MyEconLab Concept Check

Economic growth The ability of the economy to increase the production of goods and services.

MyEconLab Study Plan

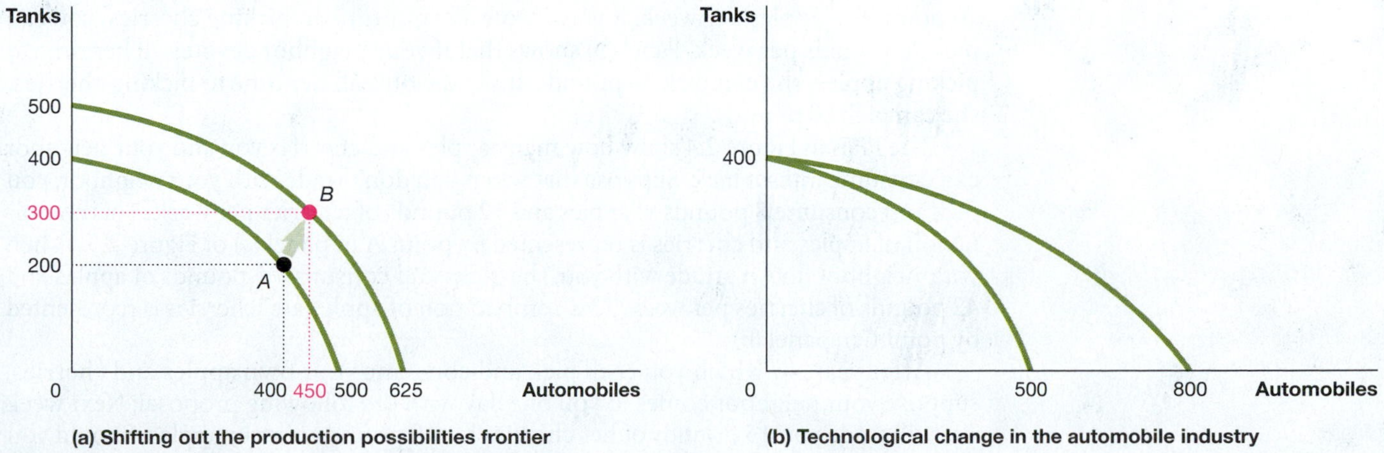

MyEconLab Animation

Figure 2.3 Economic Growth

Panel (a) shows that as more economic resources become available and technological change occurs, the economy can move from point A to point B, producing more tanks and more automobiles. Panel (b) shows the results of technological change in the automobile industry that increases the quantity of vehicles workers can produce per year while leaving unchanged the maximum quantity of tanks they can produce. Outward shifts in the production possibilities frontier represent *economic growth*.

2.2 Comparative Advantage and Trade

LEARNING OBJECTIVE: Describe comparative advantage and explain how it serves as the basis for trade.

Trade The act of buying and selling.

We can use the concepts of the production possibilities frontier and opportunity cost to understand the basic economic activity of *trade*. Markets are fundamentally about **trade**, which is the act of buying and selling. Sometimes we trade directly, as when children trade one baseball card for another baseball card. But often we trade indirectly: We sell our labor services as, say, an accountant, a salesperson, or a nurse for money, and then we use the money earned to buy goods and services. Although in these cases trade takes place indirectly, ultimately the accountant, salesperson, or nurse is trading his or her services for food, clothing, and other goods and services. One of the great benefits of trade is that it makes it possible for people to become better off by increasing both their production and their consumption.

Specialization and Gains from Trade

Consider the following situation: You and your neighbor both have fruit trees on your properties. Initially, suppose you have only apple trees and your neighbor has only cherry trees. In this situation, if you both like apples and cherries, there is an obvious opportunity for both of you to gain from trade: You trade some of your apples for some of your neighbor's cherries, making you both better off. But what if there are apple and cherry trees growing on both of your properties? In that case, there can still be gains from trade. For example, your neighbor might be very good at picking apples, and you might be very good at picking cherries. It would make sense for your neighbor to concentrate on picking apples and for you to concentrate on picking cherries. You can then trade some of the cherries you pick for some of the apples your neighbor picks. But what if your neighbor is actually better at picking both apples and cherries than you are?

We can use production possibilities frontiers (*PPFs*) to show how your neighbor can benefit from trading with you *even though she is better than you are at picking both apples and cherries.* (For simplicity, and because it will not have any effect on the conclusions we draw, we will assume that the *PPFs* in this example are straight lines.) The table in Figure 2.4 shows how many apples and how many cherries you and your neighbor can pick in one week. The graph in the figure uses the data from the table to construct *PPFs*. Panel (a) shows your *PPF*. If you devote all your time to picking apples, you can pick 20 pounds of apples per week. If you devote all your time to picking cherries, you can pick 20 pounds per week. Panel (b) shows that if your neighbor devotes all her time to picking apples, she can pick 30 pounds. If she devotes all her time to picking cherries, she can pick 60 pounds.

The *PPFs* in Figure 2.4 show how many apples and cherries you and your neighbor can consume *without trade.* Suppose that when you don't trade with your neighbor, you pick and consume 8 pounds of apples and 12 pounds of cherries per week. This combination of apples and cherries is represented by point *A* in panel (a) of Figure 2.5. When your neighbor doesn't trade with you, she picks and consumes 9 pounds of apples and 42 pounds of cherries per week. This combination of apples and cherries is represented by point *C* in panel (b).

After years in which you each pick and consume your own apples and cherries, suppose your neighbor comes to you one day with the following proposal: Next week she will trade you 15 pounds of her cherries for 10 pounds of your apples. Should you accept this proposal? As we can show in Figure 2.5, you should accept because you will end up with more apples and more cherries to consume. To take advantage of her proposal, you should specialize in picking only apples rather than splitting your time between picking apples and picking cherries. We know specializing will allow you to pick 20 pounds of apples. You can trade 10 pounds of apples to your neighbor for 15 pounds of her cherries. The result is that you will be able to consume 10 pounds of

	You		Your Neighbor	
	Apples	Cherries	Apples	Cherries
Devote all time to picking apples	20 pounds	0 pounds	30 pounds	0 pounds
Devote all time to picking cherries	0 pounds	20 pounds	0 pounds	60 pounds

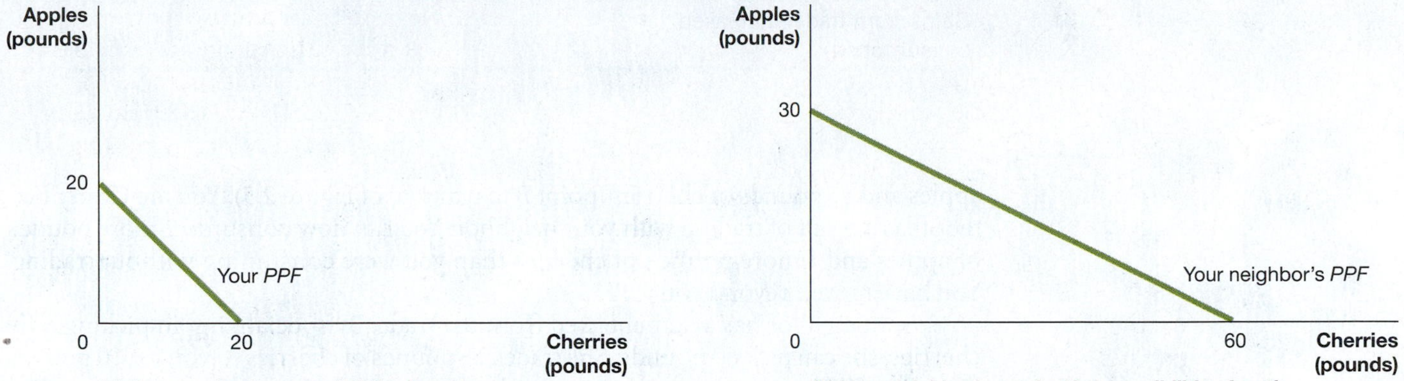

(a) Your production possibilities frontier **(b) Your neighbor's production possibilities frontier**

MyEconLab Animation

Figure 2.4 Production Possibilities for You and Your Neighbor, without Trade

The table shows how many pounds of apples and how many pounds of cherries you and your neighbor can each pick in one week. The graphs use the data from the table to construct *PPF*s for you and your neighbor. Panel (a) shows your *PPF*. If you devote all your time to picking apples and none to picking cherries, you can pick 20 pounds. If you devote all your time to picking cherries, you can pick 20 pounds. Panel (b) shows that if your neighbor devotes all her time to picking apples, she can pick 30 pounds. If she devotes all her time to picking cherries, she can pick 60 pounds.

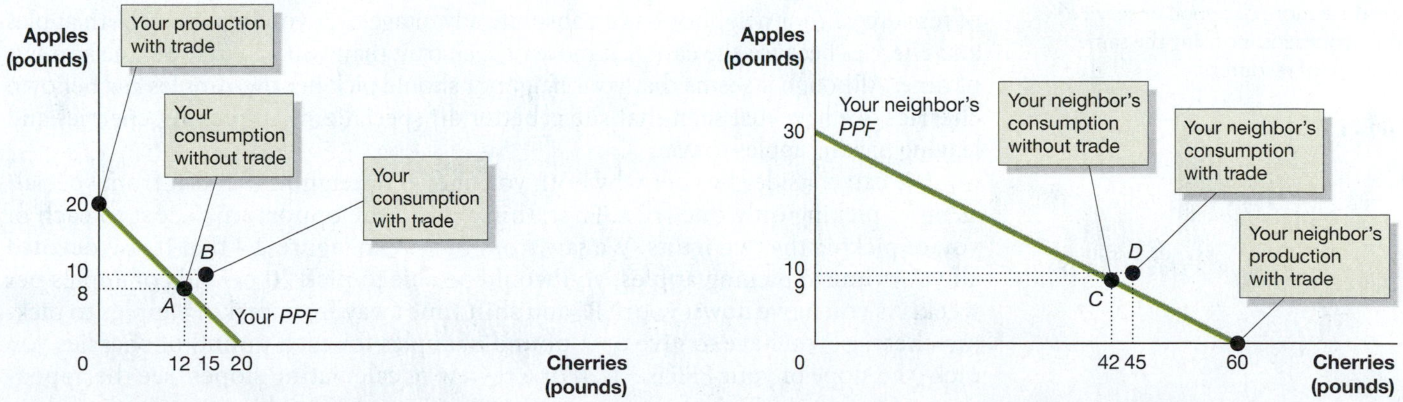

(a) Your production and consumption with trade **(b) Your neighbor's production and consumption with trade**

MyEconLab Animation

Figure 2.5 Gains from Trade

When you don't trade with your neighbor, you pick and consume 8 pounds of apples and 12 pounds of cherries per week—point *A* in panel (a). When your neighbor doesn't trade with you, she picks and consumes 9 pounds of apples and 42 pounds of cherries per week—point *C* in panel (b). If you specialize in picking apples, you can pick 20 pounds. If your neighbor specializes in picking cherries, she can pick 60 pounds. If you trade 10 pounds of your apples for 15 pounds of your neighbor's cherries, you will be able to consume 10 pounds of apples and 15 pounds of cherries—point *B* in panel (a). Your neighbor can now consume 10 pounds of apples and 45 pounds of cherries—point *D* in panel (b). You and your neighbor are both better off as a result of the trade.

Table 2.1

A Summary of the Gains from Trade

	You		Your Neighbor	
	Apples (in pounds)	Cherries (in pounds)	Apples (in pounds)	Cherries (in pounds)
Production *and* consumption *without* trade	8	12	9	42
Production *with* trade	20	0	0	60
Consumption *with* trade	10	15	10	45
Gains from trade (increased consumption)	2	3	1	3

apples and 15 pounds of cherries (point *B* in panel (a) of Figure 2.5). You are clearly better off as a result of trading with your neighbor: You can now consume 2 more pounds of apples and 3 more pounds of cherries than you were consuming without trading. You have moved beyond your *PPF*!

Your neighbor has also benefited from the trade. By specializing in picking only cherries, she can pick 60 pounds. She trades 15 pounds of cherries to you for 10 pounds of apples. She can then consume 10 pounds of apples and 45 pounds of cherries (point *D* in panel (b) of Figure 2.5). This combination is 1 more pound of apples and 3 more pounds of cherries than she was consuming before trading with you. She also has moved beyond her *PPF*. Table 2.1 summarizes the changes in production and consumption that result from your trade with your neighbor. (In this example, we chose one specific rate of trading cherries for apples—15 pounds of cherries for 10 pounds of apples. There are, however, many other rates of trading cherries for apples that would also make you and your neighbor better off.) MyEconLab Concept Check

Absolute Advantage versus Comparative Advantage

Absolute advantage The ability of an individual, a firm, or a country to produce more of a good or service than competitors, using the same amount of resources.

Perhaps the most remarkable aspect of the preceding example is that your neighbor benefits from trading with you even though she is better than you at picking both apples and cherries. **Absolute advantage** is the ability of an individual, a firm, or a country to produce more of a good or service than competitors, using the same amount of resources. Your neighbor has an absolute advantage over you in picking both apples and cherries because she can pick more of each fruit than you can in the same amount of time. Although it seems that your neighbor should pick her own apples *and* her own cherries, we have just seen that she is better off specializing in picking cherries and leaving picking apples to you.

We can consider further why both you and your neighbor benefit from specializing in picking only one fruit. First, think about the opportunity cost to each of you of picking the two fruits. We saw from the *PPF* in Figure 2.4 that if you devoted all your time to picking apples, you would be able to pick 20 pounds of apples per week. As you move down your *PPF* and shift time away from picking apples to picking cherries, you have to give up 1 pound of apples for each pound of cherries you pick (the slope of your *PPF* is −1). (For a review of calculating slopes, see the appendix to Chapter 1.) Therefore, your opportunity cost of picking 1 pound of cherries is 1 pound of apples. By the same reasoning, your opportunity cost of picking 1 pound of apples is 1 pound of cherries. Your neighbor's *PPF* has a different slope, so she faces a different trade-off: As she shifts time from picking apples to picking cherries, she has to give up 0.5 pound of apples for every 1 pound of cherries she picks (the slope of your neighbor's *PPF* is −0.5). As she shifts time from picking cherries to picking apples, she gives up 2 pounds of cherries for every 1 pound of apples she picks. Therefore, her opportunity cost of picking 1 pound of apples is 2 pounds of cherries, and her opportunity cost of picking 1 pound of cherries is 0.5 pound of apples.

MyEconLab Study Plan

Table 2.2

Opportunity Costs of Picking Apples and Cherries

	Opportunity Cost of Picking 1 Pound of Apples	Opportunity Cost of Picking 1 Pound of Cherries
You	1 pound of cherries	1 pound of apples
Your Neighbor	2 pounds of cherries	0.5 pound of apples

Table 2.2 summarizes the opportunity costs for you and your neighbor of picking apples and cherries. Note that even though your neighbor can pick more apples in a week than you can, the *opportunity cost* of picking apples is higher for her than for you because when she picks apples, she gives up more cherries than you do. So, even though she has an absolute advantage over you in picking apples, it is more costly for her to pick apples than it is for you. The table also shows that her opportunity cost of picking cherries is lower than yours. **Comparative advantage** is the ability of an individual, a firm, or a country to produce a good or service at a lower opportunity cost than competitors. In picking apples, your neighbor has an *absolute advantage* over you, while you have a *comparative advantage* over her. Your neighbor has both an absolute advantage and a comparative advantage over you in picking cherries. As we have seen, you are better off specializing in picking apples, and your neighbor is better off specializing in picking cherries.

Comparative advantage The ability of an individual, a firm, or a country to produce a good or service at a lower opportunity cost than competitors.

MyEconLab Concept Check

Comparative Advantage and the Gains from Trade

We have just arrived at an important economic principle: *The basis for trade is comparative advantage, not absolute advantage.* The fastest apple pickers do not necessarily do much apple picking. If the fastest apple pickers have a comparative advantage in some other activity—picking cherries, playing Major League Baseball, or being industrial engineers—they are better off specializing in that activity. Individuals, firms, and countries are better off if they specialize in producing goods and services for which they have a comparative advantage and obtain the other goods and services they need by trading. We will return to the important concept of comparative advantage in Chapter 9, which is devoted to the subject of international trade.

MyEconLab Concept Check

Don't Let This Happen to You

Don't Confuse Absolute Advantage and Comparative Advantage

First, make sure you know the definitions:

- **Absolute advantage.** The ability of an individual, a firm, or a country to produce more of a good or service than competitors, using the same amount of resources. In our example, your neighbor has an absolute advantage over you in both picking apples and picking cherries.
- **Comparative advantage.** The ability of an individual, a firm, or a country to produce a good or service at a lower opportunity cost than competitors. In our example, your neighbor has a comparative advantage in picking cherries, but you have a comparative advantage in picking apples.

Keep these two key points in mind:

1. It is possible to have an absolute advantage in producing a good or service without having a comparative advantage. This is the case with your neighbor picking apples.
2. It is possible to have a comparative advantage in producing a good or service without having an absolute advantage. This is the case with your picking apples.

MyEconLab Study Plan

Your Turn: Test your understanding by doing related problem 2.5 on page 68 at the end of this chapter.

Solved Problem 2.2

MyEconLab Interactive Animation

Comparative Advantage and the Gains from Trade

Suppose that Canada and the United States both produce maple syrup and honey, which are sold for the same price in both countries. These are the combinations of the two goods that each country can produce in one day, using the same amounts of capital and labor:

Canada		United States	
Honey (in tons)	Maple Syrup (in tons)	Honey (in tons)	Maple Syrup (in tons)
0	60	0	50
10	45	10	40
20	30	20	30
30	15	30	20
40	0	40	10
		50	0

a. Which country has a comparative advantage in producing maple syrup? Which country has a comparative advantage in producing honey?

b. Suppose that Canada is currently producing 30 tons of honey and 15 tons of maple syrup, and the United States is currently producing 10 tons of honey and 40 tons of maple syrup. Demonstrate that Canada and the United States can both be better off if they specialize in producing only one good and trade for the other.

c. Illustrate your answer to part (b) by drawing a *PPF* for the United States and a *PPF* for Canada. Show on your *PPFs* the combinations of honey and maple syrup produced and consumed in each country before and after trade.

Solving the Problem

Step 1: Review the chapter material. This problem is about comparative advantage, so you may want to review the section "Absolute Advantage versus Comparative Advantage," which begins on page 50.

Step 2: Answer part (a) by calculating which country has a comparative advantage in each activity. Remember that a country has a comparative advantage in producing a good if it can produce the good at the lowest opportunity cost. When Canada produces 1 more ton of honey, it produces 1.5 tons less of maple syrup. When the United States produces 1 more ton of honey, it produces 1 ton less of maple syrup. Therefore, for the United States, the opportunity cost of producing honey—1 ton of maple syrup—is lower than for Canada—1.5 tons of maple syrup. When Canada produces 1 more ton of maple syrup, it produces 0.67 ton less of honey. When the United States produces 1 more ton of maple syrup, it produces 1 ton less of honey. Therefore, Canada's opportunity cost of producing maple syrup—0.67 ton of honey—is lower than that of the United States—1 ton of honey. We can conclude that the United States has a comparative advantage in the production of honey and Canada has a comparative advantage in the production of maple syrup.

Step 3: Answer part (b) by showing that specialization makes Canada and the United States better off. We know that Canada and the United States should each specialize where it has a comparative advantage. If both countries specialize, Canada will produce 60 tons of maple syrup and 0 tons of honey, and the United States will produce 0 tons of maple syrup and 50 tons of honey. After both countries specialize, the United States could then trade 30 tons of honey to Canada for 40 tons of maple syrup. (Other mutually beneficial trades are possible as well.) We can summarize the results in a table:

	Before Trade		After Trade	
	Honey (in tons)	Maple Syrup (in tons)	Honey (in tons)	Maple Syrup (in tons)
Canada	30	15	30	20
United States	10	40	20	40

The United States is better off after trade because it can consume the same amount of maple syrup and 10 more tons of honey. Canada is better off after trade because it can consume the same amount of honey and 5 more tons of maple syrup.

Step 4: Answer part (c) by drawing the *PPFs*.

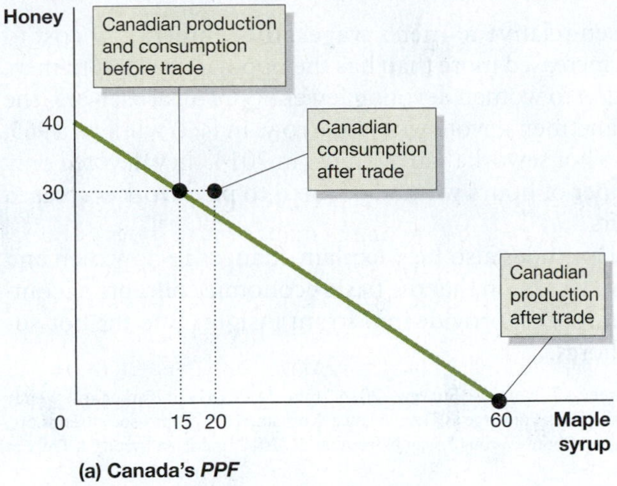

(a) Canada's *PPF*

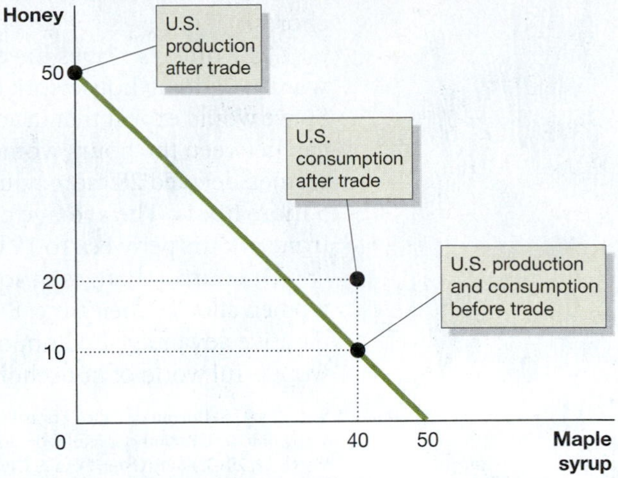

(b) The United States's *PPF*

Your Turn: For more practice, do related problems 2.6 and 2.7 on pages 68–69 at the end of this chapter.

Making the Connection
MyEconLab Video

Comparative Advantage, Opportunity Cost, and Housework

Among roommates, married couples, and other people living together, dividing up the household chores can be a source of stress. Traditionally among married couples, women did most of the housework, such as preparing meals, cleaning, and doing laundry. In 1965, married women with children averaged about 32 hours of housework per week, while married men averaged only 4 hours. Today, women average about 15 hours of housework, while men average about 10 hours.

Housework doesn't seem to be part of buying, selling, and the usual topics of business and economics. In fact, we can use basic economic concepts to analyze housework. Consider first the most efficient way to divide up household chores. Suppose Jack and Jill need to decide how they will get the cooking and laundry done. Assume that Jack has an absolute advantage over Jill in both chores, but he has a big advantage over Jill in cooking—he takes much less time to prepare very tasty meals—but is only a little faster than Jill in doing laundry. In other words, assuming that they have the same amount of time available to do housework, Jack has a comparative advantage in cooking, while Jill has a comparative advantage in doing laundry. So rather than Jack and Jill both doing some of the cooking and some of the laundry, they would be better off if Jack follows his comparative advantage and does all the cooking, while Jill follows her comparative advantage and does all the laundry.

What's the most efficient way to divide up household chores?

Economics can also provide some insight into the decline in the number of hours spent on housework since the 1960s. Combined, men and women now spend more than 30 percent fewer hours on housework. This decline has been partly driven by technology, particularly improvements in household appliances, such as dishwashers and microwave ovens. The decline in the number of hours women devote to housework also reflects the greater job opportunities available to women today compared with the 1960s. The opportunity cost to a woman of spending time on housework and childcare is the wage she gives up by not spending that time in paid work. If a woman could work for an hour at a wage of $20 but spends that hour doing household chores, the opportunity cost of the time spent on chores is $20. As job opportunities for women and the wages those jobs pay have increased, so has the opportunity cost of doing housework. So in addition to taking advantage of improved appliances, many families have found that the cost of hiring specialists in household chores, such as cleaning services and lawn care services, is lower than the cost of the wife (or husband) performing those chores.

As women's wages have risen relative to men's wages, the opportunity cost to women of doing housework has increased more than has the opportunity cost to men. So we would expect that in addition to women devoting fewer hours to housework, the gap between the hours women and men devote would narrow. In fact, while in 1965, women devoted 28 more hours to housework than did men, in 2014, they devoted only 5 more hours. The average number of hours women devoted to paid work increased from 8 hours per week to 19 hours.

Of course, changes in social attitudes also help explain changes in how men and women allocate their time. But we have seen that the basic economic concepts of comparative advantage and opportunity cost provide important insights into the not-so-wonderful world of household chores.

Sources: U.S. Bureau of Labor Statistics, "American Time Use Survey—2014," June 24, 2015; Kim Parker and Wendy Wang, "Modern Parenthood: Roles of Moms and Dads Converge as They Balance Work and Family," pewsocialtrends.org, March 14, 2013; Emily Oster, "You're Dividing the Chores Wrong," *Slate*, November 21, 2012; and Ellen Byron, "A Truce in the Chore Wars," *New York Times*, December 4, 2012.

MyEconLab Study Plan

Your Turn: Test your understanding by doing related problems 2.14 and 2.15 on page 69 at the end of this chapter.

2.3 The Market System

LEARNING OBJECTIVE: Explain the basics of how a market system works.

We have seen that households, firms, and the government face trade-offs and incur opportunity costs because resources are scarce. We have also seen that trade allows people to specialize according to their comparative advantage. By engaging in trade, people can raise their incomes and their standard of living. Of course, trade in the modern world is much more complex than the examples we have considered so far. Trade today involves the decisions of millions of people around the world. How are the decisions of these millions of people coordinated? In the United States and most other countries, trade is carried out in markets. Markets also determine the answers to the three fundamental questions discussed in Chapter 1:

1. What goods and services will be produced?
2. How will the goods and services be produced?
3. Who will receive the goods and services produced?

Market A group of buyers and sellers of a good or service and the institution or arrangement by which they come together to trade.

Product market A market for goods—such as computers—or services—such as medical treatment.

Factor market A market for the factors of production, such as labor, capital, natural resources, and entrepreneurial ability.

Factors of production Labor, capital, natural resources, and other inputs used to make goods and services.

Recall that a **market** is a group of buyers and sellers of a good or service and the institution or arrangement by which they come together to trade. Markets take many forms: They can be physical places, such as the pizza parlors in your city or the New York Stock Exchange, or virtual places, such as eBay. In a market, the buyers are demanders of goods or services, and the sellers are suppliers of goods or services. Households and firms interact in two types of markets: *product markets* and *factor markets*. **Product markets** are markets for goods—such as computers—and services—such as medical treatment. In product markets, households are demanders and firms are suppliers. **Factor markets** are markets for the *factors of production*. **Factors of production** are the inputs used to make goods and services. Factors of production are divided into four broad categories:

1. *Labor* includes all types of work, from the part-time labor of teenagers working at McDonald's to the work of senior managers in large corporations.
2. *Capital* refers to physical capital, such as computers and machine tools, that is used to produce other goods.
3. *Natural resources* include land, water, oil, iron ore, and other raw materials (or "gifts of nature") that are used in producing goods.

4. An *entrepreneur* is someone who operates a business. *Entrepreneurial ability* is the ability to bring together the other factors of production to successfully produce and sell goods and services.

The Circular Flow of Income

Two key groups participate in markets:

1. *Households* are all the individuals in a home. Households are suppliers of factors of production—particularly labor—employed by firms to make goods and services. Households use the income they receive from selling the factors of production to purchase the goods and services supplied by firms. We are familiar with households as suppliers of labor because most people earn most of their income by going to work, meaning they are selling their labor services to firms in the labor market. But households own the other factors of production as well, either directly or indirectly, by owning the firms that own these resources. All firms are owned by households. Small firms, like a neighborhood restaurant, might be owned by one person. Large firms, like Apple, are owned by millions of households that buy shares of stock in them. When firms pay profits to the people who own them, the firms are paying for using the capital and natural resources that are supplied to them by those owners. So, we can generalize by saying that in factor markets, households are suppliers and firms are demanders.
2. *Firms* are suppliers of goods and services. Firms use the funds they receive from selling goods and services to buy or hire the factors of production needed to make the goods and services.

We can use a simple economic model called the **circular-flow diagram** to see how participants in markets are linked. Figure 2.6 shows that in factor markets, households supply labor and other factors of production in exchange for wages and other

Circular-flow diagram A model that illustrates how participants in markets are linked.

MyEconLab Animation

Figure 2.6

The Circular-Flow Diagram

Households and firms are linked together in a circular flow of production, income, and spending. The blue arrows show the flow of the factors of production. In factor markets, households supply labor, entrepreneurial ability, and other factors of production to firms. Firms use these factors of production to make goods and services that they supply to households in product markets. The red arrows show the flow of goods and services from firms to households. The green arrows show the flow of funds. In factor markets, households receive wages and other payments from firms in exchange for supplying the factors of production. Households use these wages and other payments to purchase goods and services from firms in product markets. Firms sell goods and services to households in product markets, and they use the funds to purchase the factors of production from households in factor markets.

payments from firms. In product markets, households use the payments they earn in factor markets to purchase the goods and services supplied by firms. Firms produce these goods and services using the factors of production supplied by households. In the figure, the blue arrows show the flow of factors of production from households through factor markets to firms. The red arrows show the flow of goods and services from firms through product markets to households. The green arrows show the flow of funds from firms through factor markets to households and the flow of spending from households through product markets to firms.

Like all economic models, the circular-flow diagram is a simplified version of reality. Figure 2.6 leaves out the important role of government in buying goods from firms and in making payments, such as Social Security or unemployment insurance payments, to households. The figure also leaves out the roles played by banks, the stock and bond markets, and other parts of the *financial system* in aiding the flow of funds from lenders to borrowers. Finally, the figure does not show that some goods and services purchased by domestic households are produced in foreign countries and some goods and services produced by domestic firms are sold to foreign households. (We explore the government, the financial system, and the international sector further in later chapters.) Despite these simplifications, the circular-flow diagram in Figure 2.6 is useful for seeing how product markets, factor markets, and their participants are linked together. One of the great wonders of the market system is that it manages to successfully coordinate the independent activities of so many households and firms. MyEconLab Concept Check

The Gains from Free Markets

Free market A market with few government restrictions on how a good or service can be produced or sold or on how a factor of production can be employed.

A **free market** exists when the government places few restrictions on how goods and services can be produced or sold or on how factors of production can be employed. Governments in all modern economies intervene more than is consistent with a fully free market. In that sense, we can think of the free market as being a benchmark against which we can judge actual economies. There are relatively few government restrictions on economic activities in the United States, Canada, Western Europe, Hong Kong, Singapore, and Estonia. So these countries come close to the free market benchmark. In countries such as Cuba and North Korea, the free market system has been rejected in favor of centrally planned economies with extensive government control over product and factor markets. Countries that come closest to the free market benchmark have been more successful than countries with centrally planned economies in providing their people with rising living standards.

The Scottish philosopher Adam Smith is considered the father of modern economics because his book, *An Inquiry into the Nature and Causes of the Wealth of Nations*, published in 1776, was an early and very influential argument for the free market system. Smith was writing at a time when extensive government restrictions on markets were common. In many parts of Europe, the *guild system* prevailed. Under this system, governments would give guilds, or organizations of producers, the authority to control the production of a good. For example, the shoemakers' guild controlled who was allowed to produce shoes, how many shoes they could produce, and what price they could charge. In France, the cloth makers' guild even dictated the number of threads in the weave of the cloth.

Smith argued that such restrictions reduced the income and wealth of a country and its people by restricting the quantity of goods produced. Some people at the time supported the restrictions of the guild system because it was in their financial interest to do so. If you were a member of a guild, the restrictions served to reduce the competition you faced. But other people sincerely believed that the alternative to the guild system was economic disorder. Smith argued that these people were wrong and that a country could enjoy a smoothly functioning economic system if firms were freed from guild restrictions. MyEconLab Concept Check

The Market Mechanism

In Smith's day, defenders of the guild system argued that if the shoemakers' guild did not control shoe production, either too many or too few shoes would be produced.

In contrast, Smith maintained that prices would do a better job of coordinating the activities of buyers and sellers than the guilds could. A key to understanding Smith's argument is the assumption that *individuals usually act in a rational, self-interested way*. In particular, individuals take those actions that are most likely to make themselves better off financially. This assumption of rational, self-interested behavior underlies nearly all economic analysis. In fact, economics can be distinguished from other disciplines that study human behavior—such as sociology and psychology—by its emphasis on the assumption of self-interested behavior. Adam Smith understood—as economists today understand—that people's motives can be complex. But when we analyze people in the act of buying and selling, the motivation of financial reward usually provides the best explanation for the actions people take.

For example, suppose that a significant number of consumers switch from buying regular gasoline-powered cars to buying gasoline/electric-powered hybrid cars, such as the Toyota Prius, or all-electric cars, such as the Tesla Model S. Firms will find that they can charge relatively higher prices for hybrid cars and electric cars than they can for gasoline-powered cars. The self-interest of these firms will lead them to respond to consumers' wishes by producing more hybrid and electric cars and fewer gasoline-powered cars. Or suppose that consumers decide that they want to eat less bread, pasta, and other foods that are high in carbohydrates. Then the prices firms can charge for bread and pasta will fall. The self-interest of firms will lead them to produce less bread and pasta, which, in fact, is what has happened over the past 10 years.

Note that for the market mechanism to work in response to changes in consumers' wants, *prices must be flexible*. The *relative price* is the price of one good or service relative to the prices of other goods or services. Changes in relative prices provide information, or a signal, to both consumers and firms. For example, consumers worldwide have increased their demand for cattle and poultry. Because corn is fed to cattle and poultry, prices for corn have increased relative to prices for other crops. Many farmers in the United States received this price signal and responded by increasing the amount of corn they planted and decreasing the amount of soybeans and wheat. One Kansas farmer was quoted as saying, "It seemed to me there was $100 to $150 per acre more money in the corn than there was in the beans. That's the kind of math that a lot of guys were using." In recent years, the United States has experienced record corn crops. Similarly, falling prices for DVDs and music CDs in the 2000s were a signal to movie studios and record companies to devote fewer resources to these products and more resources to making movies and music available online.

In the United States today, governments at the federal, state, and local levels set or regulate the prices of only about 10 to 20 percent of goods and services. The prices of other goods and services are free to change as consumer wants change and as costs of production change.

In the case where consumers want more of a product, and in the case where they want less of a product, the market system responds without a guild or the government giving orders about how much to produce or what price to charge. Economists have used Adam Smith's metaphor of the *invisible hand* to describe how the market leads firms to provide consumers with the goods they want. Firms respond *individually* to changes in prices by making decisions that *collectively* end up satisfying the wants of consumers. MyEconLab Concept Check

Making the Connection MyEconLab Video

A Story of the Market System in Action: How Do You Make an iPad?

Apple produces the iPad. Because Apple's headquarters is in Cupertino, California, it seems reasonable to assume that iPads are also manufactured in that state. A poll by the *New York Times* showed that, in fact, a majority of people interviewed believed that iPads were manufactured in the United States, if not specifically in California. Although engineers at Apple designed the iPad, the company produces none of the components of the iPad, nor does it assemble the

The market coordinates the activities of many people spread around the world who contribute to making an iPad.

components into a finished product. Far from being produced entirely by one company in one country, the iPad requires the coordinated activities of thousands of workers and dozens of firms spread around the world.

Foxconn, which is based in Taiwan, assembles the iPad in factories in Shenzhen and Chengdu, China, and Jundiai, São Paulo, Brazil, and ships them to Apple for sale in the United States. Although Foxconn does final assembly, it doesn't make any of the components and, in fact, charges Apple only about $6 for assembling each iPad.

The following table lists just some of the suppliers of iPad components.

Firm	Location of the firm	The iPad component the firm supplies
AKM	Japan	Motion sensor
AU Optronics	Taiwan	Display
Avago Technologies	United States (Pennsylvania)	Wireless technology
Bosch Sensortec	Germany	Accelerometer
Broadcom	United States (California)	Touchscreen controller and wireless chip
Cirrus Logic	United States (Texas)	Audio chip
Corning	United States (New York)	Glass screen cover
Dialog Semiconductor	Germany	Power management chip
Elpida	United States (Idaho)	System memory
Infineon Technologies	Germany	Semiconductors
LG Electronics	South Korea	Display
Quicomm	United Kingdom	Wireless section
Samsung	South Korea	Display, flash memory, and applications processor
Sharp	Japan	Display
SK Hynix	South Korea	Flash memory
Skyworks Solutions	United States (Massachusetts)	Wireless technology
STMicroelectronics	France/Italy	Motion sensors
Texas Instruments	United States (Texas)	Touchscreen controller
Toshiba	Japan	Flash memory
TriQuint Semiconductor	United States (Oregon)	Wireless technology

Each of these suppliers in turn relies on its own suppliers. For example, Broadcom designs the touchscreen controller for the iPad and supplies it to Apple, but it does not manufacture the components of the controller or assemble them. To manufacture the components, Broadcom relies on SilTerra, based in Malaysia; SMIC, based in mainland China; and Taiwan Semiconductor Manufacturing Corporation (TSMC) and UMC, based in Taiwan. TSMC's factories are for the most part not in Taiwan but in mainland China and Eastern Europe. To assemble the components, Broadcom uses several companies, including Amkor Technology, based in Chandler, Arizona, and STATS ChipPAC, based in Singapore.

All told, an iPad contains hundreds of parts that are designed, manufactured, and assembled by firms around the world. Many of these firms are not even aware of which other firms are also producing components for the iPad. Few of the managers of these firms have met managers of the other firms or shared knowledge of how their particular components are produced. In fact, no one person from Tim Cook, the chief executive officer of Apple, on down possesses the knowledge of how to produce all the components that are assembled into an iPad. Instead, the invisible hand of the market has led these firms to contribute their knowledge and resources to the process that ultimately results in an iPad available for sale in a store in the United States. Apple has so efficiently organized the process of producing the iPad that you can order a custom iPad with a personal engraving and have it delivered from an assembly plant in China or Brazil to your doorstep in the United States in as little as three days.

Sources: Marjorie Connelly, "Poll Finds Consumer Confusion on Where Apple Devices Are Made," *New York Times*, January 25, 2012; "New iPad Air Costs Less to Make Than Third-Generation iPad Model, IHS Teardown Reveals," technology.ihs.com, November 5, 2013; and Arik Hesseldahl, "iPad Air Has Spendier Display, Costs Less to Make Than Earlier Models," allthingsd.com, November 5, 2013.

Your Turn: Test your understanding by doing related problems 3.8 and 3.9 on page 70 at the end of this chapter.

MyEconLab Study Plan

The Role of the Entrepreneur in the Market System

Entrepreneur Someone who operates a business, bringing together the factors of production—labor, capital, and natural resources—to produce goods and services.

Entrepreneurs are central to the working of the market system. An **entrepreneur** is someone who operates a business. Entrepreneurs first determine what goods and services they believe consumers want and then decide how to produce those goods and services most profitably, using the available factors of production—labor, capital, and natural resources. Successful entrepreneurs are able to search out opportunities to provide new goods and services. Frequently these opportunities are created by new technology. Consumers and existing businesses often do not at first realize that the new technology makes new products feasible. For example, even after the development of the internal combustion engine had made automobiles practicable, Henry Ford remarked, "If I had asked my customers what they wanted, they would have said a faster horse." Because consumers often cannot evaluate a new product before it exists, some of the most successful entrepreneurs, such as the late Steve Jobs of Apple, rarely use *focus groups*, or meetings with consumers in which the consumers are asked what new products they would like to see. Instead, entrepreneurs think of products that consumers may not even realize they need, such as, in Jobs's case, an MP3 player— the iPod— or a tablet computer— the iPad. Entrepreneurs are important to the economy because they are often responsible for making new products widely available to consumers, as Henry Ford did with the automobile and Steve Jobs did with the iPod.

The firms that entrepreneurs found are typically small at first, as Apple and Ford were. Table 2.3 lists some of the important products entrepreneurs at small firms introduced during the twentieth century.

Entrepreneurs put their own funds at risk when they start businesses. If they are wrong about what consumers want or about the best way to produce goods and services, they can lose those funds. In fact, it is not unusual for entrepreneurs who eventually achieve great success to fail at first. For instance, early in their careers, both Henry Ford and Sakichi Toyoda, who eventually founded the Toyota Motor Corporation, started companies that quickly failed. Research by Richard Freeman of Harvard University has shown that a typical entrepreneur earns less than an employee at a large firm who has the same education and other characteristics. Few entrepreneurs make the fortunes earned by Mark Zuckerberg (Facebook), Steve Jobs (Apple), or Bill Gates (Microsoft).

Entrepreneurs make a vital contribution to economic growth through their roles in responding to consumer demand and introducing new products. Government policies that encourage entrepreneurship are also likely to increase economic growth and raise the standard of living. In the next section, we consider the legal framework required for a successful market in which entrepreneurs can succeed. MyEconLab Concept Check

The Legal Basis of a Successful Market System

In a free market, government does not restrict how firms produce and sell goods and services or how they employ factors of production. But the absence of government intervention is not enough for the market system to work well. Government has to take active steps to provide a *legal environment* that will allow markets to operate efficiently.

Table 2.3

Important Products Introduced by Entrepreneurs at Small Firms

Product	Inventor
Air conditioning	William Haviland Carrier
Airplane	Orville and Wilbur Wright
Automobile, mass produced	Henry Ford
Automobile windshield wiper	Mary Anderson
Biomagnetic imaging	Raymond Damadian
Biosynthetic insulin	Herbert Boyer
Disposable diaper	Marion Donovan
DNA fingerprinting	Alec Jeffries
FM radio	Edwin Howard Armstrong
Helicopter	Igor Sikorsky
High-resolution CAT scanner	Robert Ledley
Hydraulic brake	Malcolm Lockheed
Integrated circuit	Jack Kilby
Microprocessor	Ted Hoff
Optical scanner	Everett Franklin Lindquist
Oral contraceptives	Carl Djerassi
Overnight delivery service	Fred Smith
Personal computer	Steve Jobs and Steve Wozniak
Quick-frozen foods	Clarence Birdseye
Safety razor	King Gillette
Soft contact lens	Kevin Tuohy
Solid fuel rocket engine	Robert Goddard
Supercomputer	Seymour Cray
Vacuum tube (television)	Philo Farnsworth
Zipper	Gideon Sundback

Sources: William J. Baumol, *The Microtheory of Innovative Entrepreneurship*, Princeton, NJ: Princeton University Press, 2010; Lemelson-MIT Program (http://lemelson.mit.edu); and various other sources. Note that historians sometimes dispute the identity of the person who first commercially developed a particular product.

Protection of Private Property For the market system to work well, individuals must be willing to take risks. Someone with $250,000 can be cautious and keep it safely in a bank—or even in cash, if the person doesn't trust banks. But the market system won't work unless a significant number of people are willing to risk their funds by investing them in businesses. Investing in businesses is risky in any country. Many businesses fail every year in the United States and other high-income countries. But in high-income countries, someone who starts a new business or invests in an existing business doesn't have to worry that the government, the military, or criminal gangs might decide to seize the business or demand payments for not destroying it. Unfortunately, in many poor countries, business owners are not well protected from having their businesses seized by the government or from having their profits taken by criminals. Where these problems exist, opening a business can be extremely risky. Cash can be concealed easily, but a business is difficult to conceal or move.

Property rights The rights individuals or firms have to the exclusive use of their property, including the right to buy or sell it.

Property rights are the rights individuals or firms have to the exclusive use of their property, including the right to buy or sell it. Property can be physical property, such as a store or factory. Property can also be intangible, such as the right to an idea. Two amendments to the U.S. Constitution guarantee property rights: The Fifth Amendment states that the federal government shall not deprive any person "of life, liberty, or property, without due process of law." The Fourteenth Amendment extends this guarantee to the actions of state governments: "No state . . . shall deprive any person of life, liberty, or property, without due process of law." Similar guarantees exist in every high-income country. Unfortunately, in many developing countries, such guarantees do not exist or are poorly enforced.

In any modern economy, *intellectual property rights* are very important. Intellectual property includes books, films, software, and ideas for new products or new ways of producing products. To protect intellectual property, the federal government grants a *patent* that gives an inventor—often a firm—the exclusive right to produce and sell a new product for a period of 20 years from the date the patent was filed. For instance, because Microsoft has a patent on the Windows operating system, other firms cannot sell their own versions of Windows. The government grants patents to encourage firms to spend money on the research and development necessary to create new products. If other companies could freely copy Windows, Microsoft would not have spent the funds necessary to develop it. Just as a new product or a new method of making a product receives patent protection, new books, films, and software receive *copyright* protection. Under U.S. law, the creator of a book, film, or piece of music has the exclusive right to use the creation during the creator's lifetime. The creator's heirs retain this exclusive right for 70 years after the death of the creator.

In providing copyright protection for only a limited time, Congress provides economic incentives to creators while eventually—after the period of copyright has ended—allowing the creators' works to be freely available to others. The longer the period of copyright, the longer the creator (or the creators' family) can restrict others from using the work.

Making the Connection
MyEconLab Video

An Elementary Case of Copyright

The U.S. Congress provides copyright protection to authors to give them an economic incentive to invest the time and effort required to write a book. While a book is under copyright, only the author—or whoever the author sells the copyright to—can legally publish a paper or digital copy of the book. Once the copyright expires, however, the book enters the *public domain*, and anyone is free to publish the book. Copies of classic books written in the 1800s, such as Mark Twain's *Huckleberry Finn* and Charles Dickens's *Oliver Twist*, are available from many publishers that do not have to pay a fee to the authors' heirs.

Who owns the classic character Sherlock Holmes?

Arthur Conan Doyle was a doctor in England when he published his first story featuring the detective Sherlock Holmes in 1887. Anyone who wants to publish any of the Sherlock Holmes stories that Doyle wrote from 1887 through the end of 1922 is free do so. But the last 10 Sherlock Holmes stories that Doyle wrote from 1923 to 1927 remain under copyright protection. Doyle's heirs argue that because the author continued to develop the personalities of Sherlock Holmes and his companion Dr. John Watson in the 10 stories that remain under copyright protection, the characters cannot be used in new books, films, or television shows without payment. Doyle's heirs have asked anyone who wants to include Holmes in a new work to pay them a fee of $5,000 per use.

The producers of two recent Sherlock Holmes films starring Robert Downey, Jr., and the producers of the television series *Sherlock*, starring Benedict Cumberbatch, and *Elementary*, starring Jonny Lee Miller, agreed to pay the fee, as have most authors of books using Holmes as a character. In 2011, when Leslie S. Klinger published *A Study in Sherlock*, a collection of new stories involving Sherlock Holmes, his publisher insisted that he pay the usual fee to Doyle's descendants. But two years later, when Klinger decided to publish another collection, *In the Company of Sherlock Holmes*, he decided that rather than pay the fee he would sue Doyle's descendants, hoping the federal courts would rule against their copyright claims.

Federal Appeals Judge Richard Posner—who is also an economist—eventually ruled in favor of Klinger. He argued that copyright law did not allow authors or their heirs to require fees for the use of characters from stories in the public domain. He also noted that, "the longer the copyright term is, the less public-domain material there will be and so the greater will be the cost of authorship, because authors will have to obtain licenses from copyright holders for more material." As a result of this ruling, for the first time since 1887, anyone can use Sherlock Holmes as a character in a book, television show, or movie without having to pay a fee.

Sources: Jennifer Schuessler, "Appeals Court Affirms Sherlock Holmes Is in Public Domain," *New York Times*, June 17, 2014; Jennifer Schuessler, "Conan Doyle Estate Told to Pay Legal Fees," *New York Times*, August 5, 2014; Eriq Gardner, "Conan Doyle Estate Loses Appeal Over 'Sherlock Holmes' Rights," *Hollywood Reporter*, June 16, 2014; and *Leslie S. Kling v. Conan Doyle Estate, Ltd.* (7th Cir. 2014), media.ca7.uscourts.gov.

MyEconLab Study Plan

Your Turn: Test your understanding by doing related problems 3.15 and 3.16 on page 71 at the end of this chapter.

Enforcement of Contracts and Property Rights Business activity often involves someone agreeing to carry out some action in the future. For example, you may borrow $20,000 to buy a car and promise the bank—by signing a loan contract—that you will pay back the money over the next five years. Or Facebook may sign a licensing agreement with a small technology company, agreeing to use that company's technology for a period of several years in return for a fee. Usually these agreements take the form of legal contracts. For the market system to work, businesses and individuals have to rely on these contracts being carried out. If one party to a legal contract does not fulfill its obligations—perhaps the small company had promised Facebook exclusive use of its technology but then begins licensing it to other companies—the other party can go to court to have the agreement enforced. Similarly, if you believe that the federal or state government has violated your property rights under the Fifth or Fourteenth Amendments, you can go to court to have your rights enforced.

But going to court to enforce a contract or property rights will be successful only if the court system is independent and judges are able to make impartial decisions on the basis of the law. In the United States and other high-income countries, the court systems have enough independence from other parts of the government and enough protection from intimidation by outside forces—such as criminal gangs—that they are able to make their decisions based on the law. In many developing countries, the court systems lack this independence and will not provide a remedy if the government violates property rights, or if a person with powerful political connections decides to violate a business contract.

If property rights are not well enforced, fewer goods and services will be produced. This reduces economic efficiency, leaving the economy inside its production possibilities frontier.

MyEconLab Study Plan

MyEconLab Concept Check

Continued from page 41

Economics in Your Life

The Trade-offs When You Buy a Car

At the beginning of the chapter, we asked you to think about two questions: What is the relationship between safety and fuel efficiency for gasoline-powered cars? and, Under what circumstances would it be possible for automobile manufacturers to make cars that are both safer and more fuel efficient? To answer the first question, you have to recognize that there is a trade-off between safety and fuel efficiency. With the technology available at any particular time, an automobile manufacturer can increase fuel efficiency by making a car smaller and lighter. But driving a lighter car increases your chances of being injured if you have an accident. The trade-off between safety and fuel efficiency would look much like the relationship in Figure 2.1 on page 43. To get more of both safety and gas mileage, automobile makers would have to discover new technologies that allow them to make cars lighter and safer at the same time. Such new technologies would make points like *G* in Figure 2.1 attainable.

Conclusion

We have seen that by trading in markets, people are able to specialize and pursue their comparative advantage. Trading on the basis of comparative advantage makes all participants in trade better off. The key role of markets is to facilitate trade. In fact, the market system is a very effective means of coordinating the decisions of millions of consumers, workers, and firms. At the center of the market system is the consumer. To be successful, firms must respond to the desires of consumers. These desires are communicated to firms through prices. To explore how markets work, we must study the behavior of consumers and firms. We continue this exploration of markets in Chapter 3, when we develop the model of demand and supply.

Before moving on to Chapter 3, read *An Inside Look* on the next page for a discussion of Apple's plans to produce an electric car.

AN INSIDE LOOK

You're Going to Need a MUCH Bigger Charging Station

BLOOMBERG

Apple Wants to Start Producing Cars as Soon as 2020

a Apple Inc., which has been working secretly on a car, is pushing its team to begin production of an electric vehicle as early as 2020, people with knowledge of the matter said.

The timeframe—automakers typically spend five to seven years developing a car—underscores the project's aggressive goals and could set the stage for a battle for customers with Tesla Motors Inc. and General Motors Co. Both automakers are targeting a 2017 release of an electric vehicle that can go more than 200 miles on a single charge and cost less than $40,000. . . .

Apple, which posted record profit of $18 billion during the past quarter, has $178 billion in cash with few avenues to spend it. The Cupertino, California-based company's research and development costs were $6.04 billion in the past year, and Chief Executive Officer Tim Cook is facing increased pressure to return cash to shareholders. . . .

Car Team

Tesla's success in creating a startup car company has shown that the traditional barriers of entry into the auto industry aren't as difficult to overcome as originally thought, said one person, who asked not to be identified because the matter is private. At the same time, automakers have struggled to bring technical leaps to car development, something that Silicon Valley is also seeking to accomplish. For example, Google Inc. has invested in developing an autonomous vehicle since 2010.

b "Apple would have some advantages as a new entrant to the auto industry," including its cash, ability to connect with its own devices and the infancy of the electric-vehicle market, Barclays analysts Ben Reitzes and Brian Johnson wrote in a note to investors. "Finally, Apple's brand—arguably the most important advantage—is a big attraction for the next generation of car customers."

Apple may decide to scrap its car effort or delay it if executives are unhappy with progress, as they've done before with other secret projects, the people said. The car team, which already has about 200 people, began ramping up hiring within the past couple of months as the company sought out experts in technologies for batteries and robotics, said one of the people.

Battery Lawsuit

An experienced automaker typically spends five to seven years developing a new vehicle before bringing it to market, according to Dennis Virag, president of Automotive Consulting Group.

"If you're starting from scratch, you're probably talking more like 10 years," Virag said. "A car is a very complex technological machine."

A lawsuit filed this month gives a window into Apple's efforts to create an automotive team for the project. Apple began around June an "aggressive campaign to poach" employees from A123 Systems LLC, the Waltham, Massachusetts-based battery maker said in the lawsuit.

Apple hired five people from A123 and has tried to hire battery experts from LG Chem Ltd., Samsung Electronics Co., Panasonic Corp., Toshiba Corp. and Johnson Controls Inc., according to the lawsuit. . . .

Tesla CEO Elon Musk told Bloomberg Businessweek this month that Apple was seeking to hire away his workers, offering $250,000 signing bonuses and 60 percent salary increases.

Bricks and Mortar

c "Apple is good at developing technology but car making is, and will continue to be, a bricks-and-mortar proposition," Matt DeLorenzo, an analyst at Kelley Blue Book, wrote in an e-mail. "Apple will need a partner, perhaps a Chinese manufacturer, with an infrastructure if it's going to hit the five-year goal."

Some parts of the automotive industry seem unfazed by Silicon Valley's increasing interest in the market. Last month, before Apple's efforts were revealed, Volkswagen AG Chief Executive Officer Martin Winterkorn brushed off the increasing competition.

"We're not afraid of these new competitors," Winterkorn said at a reception outside Stuttgart, Germany, according to a transcript obtained by Bloomberg. "The opposite is true: they encourage us to look more intensively into the chances of the digital world."

Source: Tim Higgins, "Apple Wants to Start Producing Cars as Soon as 2020," *Bloomberg*, February 19, 2015.

Key Points in the Article

Apple is on a growing list of companies exploring the electric vehicle market and has assembled a team of managers to develop and produce an electric vehicle as early as 2020. To meet this aggressive five-year timeframe, Apple has been aggressive in hiring away experts from a number of companies, including Samsung, Panasonic, Toshiba, battery maker A123 Systems, and electric car manufacturer Tesla. By taking advantage of its available cash, communications technology, and extensive and loyal customer base, Apple has developed the potential to produce a successful product that can effectively compete with electric vehicles manufactured by companies like Tesla and General Motors.

Analyzing the News

a With \$178 billion in cash, Apple tops the list of the world's most cash-rich companies. Apple has a history of developing innovative technology for its computers and smartphones, and it has the resources to continue developing these technological innovations while branching out into new markets. Apple also wants to keep the investors who bought its stock happy because they are the legal owners of the company. So Apple has to carefully choose new projects that help it remain successful and profitable. Once Apple decides which products to make, its managers must choose the quantities of these products to make. The managers face trade-offs when choosing which products to make and how to make them.

Suppose that Apple does begin selling electric cars in 2020; that it produces two models, a two-door convertible and a four-door sedan; and that it has the capability of producing a total of 100,000 vehicles per month. This capacity is represented by PPF_{2020} in the figure below. This curve shows that Apple would have to sacrifice production (and therefore sales) of one type of vehicle to produce more of the other. If these vehicles are successful and the market grows, Apple will need to produce a larger number of these electric automobiles, which is represented by PPF_{2025} in the figure.

b Not only do companies have decisions to make when choosing which projects to pursue, but once a decision is made, a company may choose to delay or even kill a project if it proves difficult to develop or if the market for the product changes. Apple has a brand and an image to protect, and moving forward with projects that may not be successful, even after the company has invested substantial funds in developing them, could harm its reputation. Not mentioned in the article is that Apple has had its share of failed products, from computers like the \$10,000 Lisa in 1983 and the 16-pound Macintosh Portable in 1989 to the Pippin game console in 1995, which retailed for two to three times the price of the PlayStation and Nintendo consoles. In some instances, a failed product can do more damage to a company than scrapping the development of the product even after millions of dollars have been invested.

c Automobile manufacturing is not part of Apple's core consumer electronics business, so the company needs a completely different set of manufacturing, service, and distribution skills. With such a tight timeline to bring its car to market, Apple will face a trade-off when deciding on the production of its electric vehicle. As Kelly Blue Book's Matt DeLorenzo stated, "Apple will need a partner, perhaps a Chinese manufacturer, with an infrastructure if it's going to hit the five-year goal." Should Apple decide to work with an outside firm in the production of its automobile rather than attempt to build the vehicle completely in-house, it will give up some level of control in exchange for a greater chance at producing a successful product in a short period of time.

Thinking Critically

1. Suppose that from 2020 to 2025, the resources Apple uses to produce its automobiles remain constant, while improvements in technology in 2025 allow Apple to produce the additional quantity of two-door convertibles shown in the figure below, but no additional four-door sedans. Draw a graph that illustrates this technology change. Be sure to show both the 2020 and the new 2025 *PPF*s. What is the opportunity cost to Apple of producing one four-door sedan in 2020? Briefly explain whether the opportunity cost will be the same in 2025.
2. Assume that the figure below accurately represents Apple's *PPF*s for 2020 and 2025 and that in 2025 it has customer orders for 110,000 four-door sedans and 65,000 two-door convertibles. Explain whether Apple can fill all of these orders.

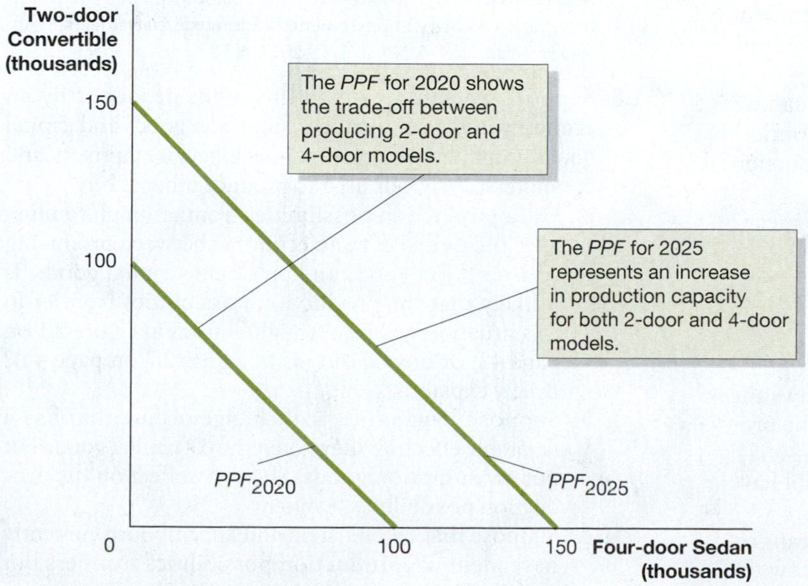

These *PPFs* show the trade-off Apple's managers face between producing different types of cars, and how that trade-off may change over time.

CHAPTER SUMMARY AND PROBLEMS

Key Terms

2.1 Production Possibilities Frontiers and Opportunity Costs, pages 42–47

LEARNING OBJECTIVE: Use a production possibilities frontier to analyze opportunity costs and trade-offs.

Summary

The **production possibilities frontier** (***PPF***) is a curve that shows the maximum attainable combinations of two goods that can be produced with available resources. The *PPF* is used to illustrate the trade-offs that arise from **scarcity**. Points on the *PPF* are technically efficient. Points inside the *PPF* are inefficient, and points outside the *PPF* are unattainable. The **opportunity cost** of any activity is the highest-valued alternative that must be given up to engage in that activity. Because of increasing marginal opportunity costs, production possibilities frontiers are usually bowed out rather than straight lines. This illustrates the important economic concept that the more resources that are already devoted to any activity, the smaller the payoff from devoting additional resources to that activity is likely to be. **Economic growth** is illustrated by an outward shift in the production possibilities frontier.

MyEconLab Visit **www.myeconlab.com** to complete these exercises online and get instant feedback.

Review Questions

1.1 What do economists mean by *scarcity*? Can you think of anything that is not scarce according to the economic definition?

1.2 What is a production possibilities frontier? How can we show efficiency on a production possibilities frontier? How can we show inefficiency? What causes a production possibilities frontier to shift outward?

1.3 What does increasing marginal opportunity costs mean? What are the implications of this idea for the shape of the production possibilities frontier?

Problems and Applications

1.4 Draw a production possibilities frontier that shows the trade-off between the production of cotton and the production of soybeans.

a. Show the effect that a prolonged drought would have on the initial production possibilities frontier.

b. Suppose that genetic modification makes soybeans resistant to insects, allowing yields to double. Show the effect of this technological change on the initial production possibilities frontier.

1.5 **(Related to the Chapter Opener on page 41)** One of the trade-offs Tesla faces is between safety and the maximum range someone can drive an all-electric car before having to recharge it. For example, adding steel to a car makes it safer but also heavier, which results in fewer miles between recharges. Draw a hypothetical production possibilities frontier that Tesla engineers face that shows this trade-off.

1.6 **(Related to the Chapter Opener on page 41)** In addition to making cars, Tesla planned to open a new factory in Nevada in 2016 to make batteries, including home storage battery packs. What is the opportunity cost to Tesla of investing in a battery factory?

Source: Mike Ramsey and Anne Steele, "Tesla Loss Widens as Spending Jumps," *Wall Street Journal*, May 6, 2015.

1.7 An economist remarks that "the cost of consuming a book is the combination of the retail price and the opportunity cost of the time spent reading." Isn't the cost of consuming a book just the price you pay to buy the book? Why include the cost of the time spent reading the book in the cost of consuming the book?

Source: Craig L. Garthwaite, "Demand Spillovers, Combative Advertising, and Celebrity Endorsements," *American Economic Journal: Applied Economics*, Vol. 6, No. 2, April 2014, p. 78.

1.8 Suppose we can divide all the goods produced by an economy into two types: consumption goods and capital goods. Capital goods, such as machinery, equipment, and computers, are goods used to produce other goods.

a. Use a production possibilities frontier graph to illustrate the trade-off to an economy between producing consumption goods and producing capital goods. Is it likely that the production possibilities frontier in this situation will be a straight line (as in Figure 2.1 on page 43) or bowed out (as in Figure 2.2 on page 46)? Briefly explain.

b. Suppose a technological change occurs that has a favorable effect on the production of capital goods but not consumption goods. Show the effect on the production possibilities frontier.

c. Suppose that Lichtenstein and Luxembourg currently have identical production possibilities frontiers but that Lichtenstein devotes only 5 percent of its resources to producing capital goods over each of the next 10 years, while Luxembourg devotes 30 percent. Which country is likely to experience more rapid economic growth in the future? Illustrate using a production possibilities frontier graph. Your graph should include production possibilities frontiers for Liechtenstein and Luxembourg today and in 10 years.

1.9 Use the following production possibilities frontier for a country to answer the questions.

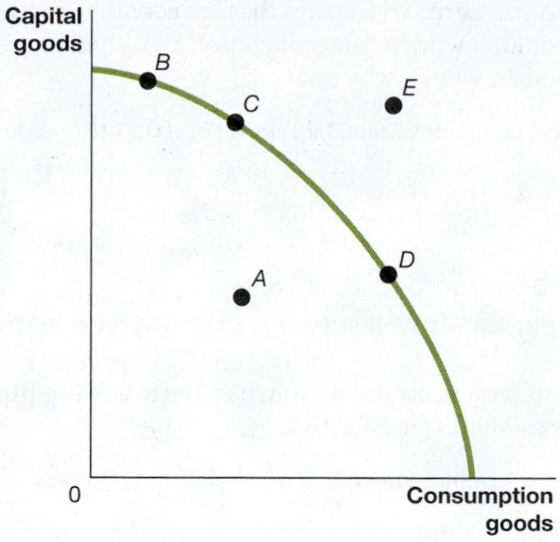

a. Which point or points are unattainable? Briefly explain why.
b. Which point or points are efficient? Briefly explain why.
c. Which point or points are inefficient? Briefly explain why.
d At which point is the country's future growth rate likely to be the highest? Briefly explain why.

1.10 **(Related to Solved Problem 2.1 on page 44)** You have exams in economics and chemistry coming up, and you have 5 hours available for studying. The following table shows the trade-offs you face in allocating the time you will spend studying each subject:

	Hours Spent Studying		Midterm Score	
Choice	Economics	Chemistry	Economics	Chemistry
A	5	0	95	70
B	4	1	93	78
C	3	2	90	84
D	2	3	86	88
E	1	4	81	90
F	0	5	75	91

a. Use the data in the table to draw a production possibilities frontier graph. Label the vertical axis "Score on economics exam," and label the horizontal axis "Score on chemistry exam." Make sure to label the values where your production possibilities frontier intersects the vertical and horizontal axes.
b. Label the points representing choice *C* and choice *D*. If you are at choice *C*, what is your opportunity cost of increasing your chemistry score by 4 points?
c. Under what circumstances would choice *A* be a sensible choice?

1.11 Suppose the U.S. president is attempting to decide whether the federal government should spend more on research to find a cure for heart disease. Imagine that you are the president's economic advisor and need to prepare a report discussing the relevant factors the president should consider. Use the concepts of opportunity cost and trade-offs to discuss some of the main issues you would deal with in your report.

1.12 State government Medicaid programs provide medical insurance to poor and disabled people. Under federal law, the programs must provide reimbursements to people who use any prescription drug that has been approved as effective by the U.S. Food and Drug Administration (FDA). In recent years, pharmaceutical firms have developed new prescription drugs that cost as much as $1,000 per pill to treat hepatitis C, a liver disease. A news story notes, "State Medicaid programs are particularly sensitive to annual cost increases . . . [because] coverage is paid for, in part, out of state budgets, which have to be balanced every year." What trade-offs do state governments face when new prescription drugs are introduced with much higher prices than existing drugs? Do you agree with the federal law requiring that Medicaid programs must cover every drug that has FDA approval? Briefly explain.

Sources: Joseph Walker, "Expensive Hepatitis C Medications Drive Prescription-Drug Spending," *Wall Street Journal*, March, 10, 2015; and Margot Sanger-Katz, "$1,000 Hepatitis Pill Shows Why Fixing Health Costs Is So Hard," *New York Times*, August 2, 2014.

1.13 Lawrence Summers served as secretary of the Treasury in the Clinton administration and as director of the National Economic Council in the Obama administration. He has been quoted as giving the following defense of the economic approach:

> There is nothing morally unattractive about saying: We need to analyze which way of spending money on health care will produce more benefit and which less, and using our money as efficiently as we can. I don't think there is anything immoral about seeking to achieve environmental benefits at the lowest possible costs.

Would it be more ethical to reduce pollution without worrying about the cost or by taking the cost into account? Briefly explain.

Source: David Wessel, "Precepts from Professor Summers," *Wall Street Journal*, October 17, 2002.

1.14 In *The Wonderful Wizard of Oz* and his other books about the Land of Oz, L. Frank Baum observed that if people's wants were limited enough, most goods would not be scarce. According to Baum, this was the case in Oz:

> There were no poor people in the Land of Oz, because there was no such thing as money. . . . Each person was given freely by his neighbors whatever he required for his use, which is as much as anyone may reasonably desire. Some tilled the lands and raised great crops of grain, which was divided equally among the whole population, so that

all had enough. There were many tailors and dressmakers and shoemakers and the like, who made things that any who desired them might wear. Likewise there were jewelers who made ornaments for the person, which pleased and beautified the people, and these ornaments also were free to those who asked for them. Each man and woman, no matter what he or she produced for the good of the community, was supplied by the neighbors with food and clothing and a house and furniture and ornaments and games. If by chance the supply ever ran short, more was taken from the great storehouses of the Ruler, which were afterward filled up again when there was more of any article than people needed. . . .

You will know, by what I have told you here, that the Land of Oz was a remarkable country. I do not suppose such an arrangement would be practical with us.

Do you agree with Baum that the economic system in Oz wouldn't work in the contemporary United States? Briefly explain why or why not.

Source: L. Frank Baum, *The Emerald City of Oz*, 1910, pp. 30–31.

2.2 Comparative Advantage and Trade, pages 48–54

LEARNING OBJECTIVE: Describe comparative advantage and explain how it serves as the basis for trade.

Summary

Fundamentally, markets are about **trade**, which is the act of buying and selling. People trade on the basis of comparative advantage. An individual, a firm, or a country has a **comparative advantage** in producing a good or service if it can produce the good or service at the lowest opportunity cost. People are usually better off specializing in the activity for which they have a comparative advantage and trading for the other goods and services they need. It is important not to confuse comparative advantage with absolute advantage. An individual, a firm, or a country has an **absolute advantage** in producing a good or service if it can produce more of that good or service using the same amount of resources. It is possible to have an absolute advantage in producing a good or service without having a comparative advantage.

MyEconLab Visit **www.myeconlab.com** to complete these exercises online and get instant feedback.

Review Questions

2.1 What is absolute advantage? What is comparative advantage? Is it possible for a country to have a comparative advantage in producing a good without also having an absolute advantage? Briefly explain.

2.2 What is the basis for trade: absolute advantage or comparative advantage? How can an individual or a country gain from specialization and trade?

Problems and Applications

2.3 Look again at the information in Figure 2.4 on page 49. Choose a rate of trading cherries for apples different from the rate used in the text (15 pounds of cherries for 10 pounds of apples) that will allow you and your neighbor to benefit from trading. Prepare a table like Table 2.1 on page 50 to illustrate your answer.

2.4 Using the same amount of resources, the United States and Canada can both produce lumberjack shirts and lumberjack boots, as shown in the following production possibilities frontiers:

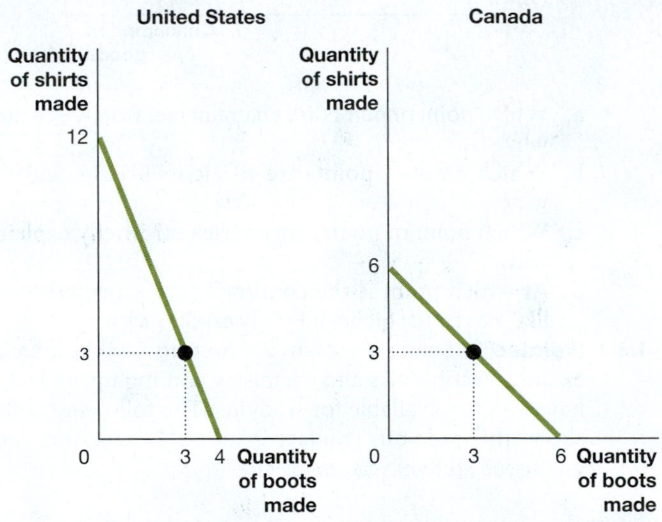

a. Who has a comparative advantage in producing lumberjack boots? Who has a comparative advantage in producing lumberjack shirts? Explain your reasoning.
b. Does either country have an absolute advantage in producing both goods? Briefly explain.
c. Suppose that both countries are currently producing three pairs of boots and three shirts. Show that both can be better off if they each specialize in producing one good and then trade for the other.

2.5 **(Related to the Don't Let This Happen to You on page 51)** In the 1950s, the economist Bela Balassa compared 28 manufacturing industries in the United States and Britain. In every one of the 28 industries, Balassa found that the United States had an absolute advantage. In these circumstances, would there have been any gain to the United States from importing any of these products from Britain? Explain.

2.6 **(Related to Solved Problem 2.2 on page 52)** Suppose the United Kingdom and Norway both produce oil and fish oil, which are sold for the same prices in both countries.

The following table shows the combinations of both goods that each country can produce in a day, measured in thousands of barrels, using the same amounts of capital and labor:

United Kingdom		Norway	
Oil	Fish oil	Oil	Fish Oil
0	8	0	4
2	6	1	3
4	4	2	2
6	2	3	1
8	0	4	0

a. Who has the comparative advantage in producing oil? Explain.
b. Can these two countries gain from trading oil and fish oil? Explain.

2.7 **(Related to** Solved Problem 2.2 **on page 52)** Suppose that France and Germany both produce schnitzel and wine. The following table shows combinations of the goods that each country can produce in a day:

France		Germany	
Wine (bottles)	Schnitzel (pounds)	Wine (bottles)	Schnitzel (pounds)
0	8	0	15
1	6	1	12
2	4	2	9
3	2	3	6
4	0	4	3
		5	0

a. Who has a comparative advantage in producing wine? Who has a comparative advantage in producing schnitzel?
b. Suppose that France is currently producing 1 bottle of wine and 6 pounds of schnitzel, and Germany is currently producing 3 bottles of wine and 6 pounds of schnitzel. Demonstrate that France and Germany can both be better off if they specialize in producing only one good and then trade for the other.

2.8 Can an individual or a country produce beyond its production possibilities frontier? Can an individual or a country consume beyond its production possibilities frontier? Explain.

2.9 If Nicaragua can produce with the same amount of resources twice as much coffee as Colombia, explain how Colombia could have a comparative advantage in producing coffee.

2.10 Imagine that the next time the Indianapolis Colts play the New England Patriots at Lucas Oil Stadium in Indianapolis, Colts star quarterback Andrew Luck has a temporary lack of judgment and plans to sell Colts memorabilia during the game because he realizes that he can sell five times more Colts products than any other player. Likewise, imagine that you are a creative and effective manager at work and that you tell your employees that during the next six months, you plan to clean the offices because you can clean five times better than the cleaning staff. What error in judgment are both you and Andrew making? Why shouldn't you and Andrew do what you are better than anyone else at doing?

2.11 After Russia seized what had formerly been the Ukrainian territory of Crimea in February 2014, the United States and many other countries imposed economic sanctions that reduced the ability of Russia to engage in international trade. A columnist writing in the *New York Times* noted, "If sanctions push Russia onto a path of greater self-reliance, its manufacturing and service industries will surely grow faster. . . ." If the columnist is correct about the effect of the sanctions, are the sanctions likely to improve the economic well-being of the average Russian in the long run? Briefly explain.

Source: Anatole Kaletsky, "Reasons to Welcome a Ukraine Deal," *New York Times*, September 18, 2014.

2.12 In colonial America, the population was spread thinly over a large area, and transportation costs were very high because it was difficult to ship products by road for more than short distances. As a result, most of the free population lived on small farms, where they not only grew their own food but also usually made their own clothes and very rarely bought or sold anything for money. Explain why the incomes of these farmers were likely to rise as transportation costs fell. Use the concept of comparative advantage in your answer.

2.13 During the 1928 U.S. presidential election campaign, Herbert Hoover, the Republican candidate, argued that the United States should import only products that could not be produced here. Do you believe that this would be a good policy? Explain.

2.14 **(Related to the** Making the Connection **on page 53)** In discussing dividing up household chores, Emily Oster, an economist at the University of Chicago, advises, "No, you shouldn't always unload the dishwasher because you're better at it." If you are better at unloading the dishwasher, why shouldn't you be the one to unload it?

Source: Emily Oster, "You're Dividing the Chores Wrong," *Slate*, November 21, 2012.

2.15 **(Related to the** Making the Connection **on page 53)** The chapter mentions that in 1965, married women with children did an average of 32 hours of housework per week, while men did an average of only 4 hours of housework—a total of 36 hours of housework. In 2014, the estimated average weekly hours of housework for women declined to 15, while the hours worked by men increased to 10—a total of 25 hours of housework. Does the decrease in the total number of hours of housework—from 36 to 25—mean that families are willing to live in messier homes? Briefly explain.

Source: U.S. Bureau of Labor Statistics, "American Time Use—2014," June 24, 2015.

2.3 The Market System, pages 54–63

LEARNING OBJECTIVE: Explain the basics of how a market system works.

Summary

A **market** is a group of buyers and sellers of a good or service and the institution or arrangement by which they come together to trade. **Product markets** are markets for goods and services, such as computers and medical treatment. **Factor markets** are markets for the **factors of production**, such as labor, capital, natural resources, and entrepreneurial ability. A **circular-flow diagram** shows how participants in product markets and factor markets are linked. Adam Smith argued in his 1776 book *The Wealth of Nations* that in a **free market**, where the government does not control the production of goods and services, changes in prices lead firms to produce the goods and services most desired by consumers. If consumers demand more of a good, its price will rise. Firms respond to rising prices by increasing production. If consumers demand less of a good, its price will fall. Firms respond to falling prices by producing less of a good. An **entrepreneur** is someone who operates a business. In the market system, entrepreneurs are responsible for organizing the production of goods and services. The market system will work well only if there is protection for **property rights**, which are the rights of individuals and firms to use their property.

Review Questions

3.1 What is a circular-flow diagram, and what does it demonstrate?

3.2 What are the two main categories of participants in markets? Which participants are of greatest importance in determining what goods and services are produced?

3.3 What is a free market? In what ways does a free market economy differ from a centrally planned economy?

3.4 What is an entrepreneur? Why do entrepreneurs play a key role in a market system?

3.5 Under what circumstances are firms likely to produce more of a good or service? Under what circumstances are firms likely to produce less of a good or service?

3.6 What are property rights? What role do they play in the working of a market system? Why are independent courts important for a well-functioning economy?

Problems and Applications

3.7 Identify whether each of the following transactions will take place in the factor market or in the product market and whether households or firms are supplying the good or service or demanding the good or service.

a. George buys a Tesla Model S.
b. Tesla increases employment at its Fremont plant.
c. George works 20 hours per week at McDonald's.
d. George sells the land he owns to McDonald's so that it can build a new restaurant.

3.8 **(Related to the Making the Connection on page 57)** Nobel Prize–winning economist Kenneth Arrow of Stanford University once wrote that the argument that the outcomes in a market system "may be very different from, and even opposed to, intentions is surely the most important intellectual contribution that economic thought has made." Briefly explain how it is possible for the outcomes in a market system to be different from what firms and consumers intended them to be. Why is this idea such an important intellectual contribution?

Sources: Kenneth J. Arrow, "Economic Equilibrium," *Encyclopedia of the Social Sciences*, 1968; and Encyclopedia.com.

3.9 **(Related to the Making the Connection on page 57)** In a famous essay on the market system, the economist Leonard Read discussed how a pencil sold by the U.S. firm Eberhard Faber Pencil Company (now owned by Paper Mate) was made. He noted that logging companies in California and Oregon grew the cedar wood used in the pencil. The wood was milled into pencil-width slats at a factory in San Leandro, California. The graphite for the pencil was mined in Sri Lanka and mixed with clay purchased from a firm in Mississippi and wax from a firm in Mexico. The rubber was purchased from a firm in Indonesia. Was it necessary for the managers of all these firms to know how the components they produced were assembled into a pencil? Was it necessary for the chief executive officer (CEO) of the Eberhard Faber Company to know this information? Briefly explain.

Source: Leonard E. Read, *I, Pencil: My Family Tree as told to Leonard E. Read*, Irvington-on-Hudson, NY: The Foundation for Economic Education, Inc., December 1958.

3.10 Evaluate the following argument: "Adam Smith's analysis of the market system is based on a fundamental flaw: He assumes that people are motivated by self-interest. But this isn't true. I'm not selfish, and most people I know aren't selfish."

3.11 Writing in the *New York Times*, Michael Lewis argued that "a market economy is premised on a system of incentives designed to encourage an ignoble human trait: self-interest." Do you agree that self-interest is an "ignoble human trait"? What incentives does a market system provide to encourage self-interest?

Source: Michael Lewis, "In Defense of the Boom," *New York Times*, October 27, 2002.

3.12 Some economists have been puzzled that although entrepreneurs take on the risk of losing money by starting new businesses, on average their incomes are lower than those of people with similar characteristics who go to work at large firms. Economist William Baumol believes part of the explanation for this puzzle may be that entrepreneurs are like people who buy lottery tickets. On average, people who don't buy lottery tickets are left with more money than people who buy tickets because lotteries take in more money than they give out. Baumol argues that "the masses of purchasers who grab up the [lottery] tickets are not irrational if they receive an adequate payment in another currency: psychic rewards."

a. What are "psychic rewards"?
b. What psychic rewards might an entrepreneur receive?

c. Do you agree with Baumol that an entrepreneur is like someone buying a lottery ticket? Briefly explain.

Source: William J. Baumol, *The Microtheory of Innovative Entrepreneurship*, Princeton, NJ: Princeton University Press, 2010.

3.13 In a report on property rights around the world, Peruvian economist Hernando De Soto noted the increasing evidence of a strong relationship between "economic successes and countries that include protective policy measures over property rights." Why would the protection of property rights be likely to increase economic growth in a developing, or low-income, country?

Source: Hernando De Soto, "Introduction," *International Property Rights Index, 2014*, internationalpropertyrightsindex.org.

3.14 According to an article on Phillyburbs.com, some farmers in rural Pennsylvania are causing a "stink" by using pig manure for fertilizer. The farmers purchase the pig manure, which is an organic fertilizer, from a nearby pork processing plant and spread it across the fields where they grow corn and soybeans. The article asserts that the farmers switched to pig manure because of the skyrocketing price of chemical fertilizers. Some of the residents of the town of Milford, however, have complained about the smell, but the "farmers are likely protected under Pennsylvania's Right to Farm Act, which allows farmers to engage in practices that are common to agriculture."

a. What price signal did the farmers respond to in their switch to the organic pig manure fertilizer?

b. According to the Pennsylvania Right to Farm Act, do the farmers or the townspeople have the property right to the smell of the air around the farms? (Some of the residents did ask the township to urge the farmers to plow under the manure to reduce its stench.)

Source: Amanda Cregan, "Milford Farmers Switch to Pig Manure Causing a Stink for Neighbors," Phillyburbs.com, March 6, 2013.

3.15 **(Related to the Making the Connection on page 61)** The British historian Thomas Macaulay once remarked that copyrights are "a tax on readers." In what sense are copyrights a tax on readers? If copyrights are a tax on readers, why do governments enact them?

3.16 **(Related to the Making the Connection on page 61)** In the court case over whether anyone could use Conan Doyle's character Sherlock Holmes without paying a fee, Judge Posner argued that the first Sherlock Holmes story was written in 1887, so allowing the author's descendants to continue to claim a copyright to the character raised the possibility of "perpetual, or at least nearly perpetual, copyright." The judge also noted that the U.S. Constitution had given Congress the authority to grant copyright for only a limited time. What would be the disadvantages to the economy of allowing an author and his or her descendants to have a copyright forever on a book or character? Would there be any advantages? Briefly explain.

Source: *Leslie S. Kling v. Conan Doyle Estate, Ltd.* (7th Cir. 2014), media.ca7.uscourts.gov.

CHAPTER

3

Where Prices Come From: The Interaction of Demand and Supply

Chapter Outline and Learning Objectives

How Smart Is Your Watch?

Fashions can change quickly. For many years, most people wore wristwatches. With the popularity of cellphones in the 2000s, many people stopped wearing wristwatches—which was bad news for the watch industry. Once a product falls out of fashion, its sales are unlikely to return to past levels. Will watches prove an exception?

Until recently attempts to have watches do more than tell the time have not been successful. For instance, during the 1980s Texas Instruments and several other firms added small calculators to watches, but sales were limited. In 2004, Microsoft introduced the SPOT watch, which enabled users to receive instant messages, weather reports, and news headlines. But few consumers purchased it so the company stopped production of the watch in 2008. By 2013, several firms had introduced "smartwatches" that enabled users to make phone calls, text, take photos or videos, monitor their heart rates, and calculate calories burned while exercising.

In 2015, Apple introduced the Apple Watch, which combined most of the capabilities of the smartwatches from competing firms with popular features from Apple's iPhone and iPad, such as access to the iTunes music store and Siri, the voice-activated personal assistant. The Apple Watch was immediately popular, with more than 2.5 million being sold during the first five weeks. These sales were higher than initial sales of Apple's previous products—the iPod, iPhone, or iPad. More than 25 other firms entered the smartwatch market, hoping to participate in the rapid growth of a hot product.

But there are no guarantees in a market system. Would the Apple Watch and its competitors succeed in bringing the wristwatch back into style, or would they fail like the Texas Instruments calculator watch and the Microsoft SPOT watch? Smartwatches have relatively high prices, are somewhat complicated to use, and have small screens that make it difficult to display photos or maps. Ultimately, the success of the smartwatch is likely to depend on whether consumers like the applications, or "apps," on these watches and are willing to wear wristwatches again.

The intense competition among firms selling smartwatches is a striking example of how the market responds to changes in technology and consumer tastes. Although competition is not always good news for firms trying to sell products, it is great news for consumers because it increases the available choice of products and lowers the prices consumers pay for those products.

AN INSIDE LOOK on **page 98** discusses how the Apple smartwatch is inspiring firms to develop other wearable devices.

Sources: Daniel Matte and Kevin McCullagh, "Will Smartwatches Be a Hit?" *Wall Street Journal*, May 10, 2015; and Mitchel Broussard, "Apple Watch Orders Estimated to Average 30,000 per Day in U.S. after Initial Surge," macrumors.com, May 22, 2015.

Economics in Your Life

Will You Buy a Smartphone or a Smartwatch?

You use your smartphone mainly to text, read e-mail, and keep track of your appointments. Your smartphone is old, though, and you are thinking of buying a new one … or should you buy a smartwatch? What factors are most important in your decision: the features of a smartwatch versus a smartphone, or the relative prices of these products? If you know that you are soon going to get a raise at your job, would you be more likely to buy a smartwatch? As you read this chapter, try to answer these questions. You can check your answers against those we provide on **page 97** at the end of this chapter.

In Chapter 1, we explored how economists use models to predict human behavior. In Chapter 2, we used the production possibilities frontiers (*PPF*) model to analyze scarcity and trade-offs. In this chapter and the next, we explore the model of demand and supply, which is the most powerful tool in economics, and use the model to explain how prices are determined.

Economic models are simplified versions of reality that are based on assumptions. In some cases, the assumptions of a model may not describe exactly the economic situation we are analyzing. For example, the model of demand and supply assumes that we are analyzing a **perfectly competitive market**, which is a market where there are many buyers and sellers, all the products sold are identical, and there are no barriers to new firms entering the market. These assumptions are very restrictive and apply exactly to only a few markets, such as the markets for wheat and other agricultural products. Experience has shown, however, that the model of demand and supply can be very useful in analyzing markets where competition among sellers is intense, even if there are relatively few sellers and the products being sold are not identical. In fact, in recent studies, the model of demand and supply has been successful in analyzing markets with as few as four buyers and four sellers. As we will see in this chapter, this model is often successful in predicting changes in quantities and prices in many markets.

Perfectly competitive market A market that meets the conditions of having (1) many buyers and sellers, (2) all firms selling identical products, and (3) no barriers to new firms entering the market.

We begin studying the model of demand and supply by discussing consumers and the demand side of the market, and then we turn to firms and the supply side. Throughout this text, we will apply this model to understand business, the economy, and economic policy.

3.1 The Demand Side of the Market

LEARNING OBJECTIVE: List and describe the variables that influence demand.

We saw in Chapter 2 that in a market system, consumers ultimately determine which goods and services will be produced. The most successful businesses are the ones that respond best to consumer demand. But what determines consumer demand for a product? Certainly, many factors influence the willingness of consumers to buy a particular product. For example, consumers who are considering buying a smartwatch, such as an Apple Watch or a Samsung Gear S, will make their decisions based on, among other factors, the income they have available to spend and the effectiveness of the advertising campaigns of the companies that sell smartwatches. For most consumers, the primary factor in their buying decision is the price of the product. So, we focus on this factor first. As we discuss demand, keep in mind that we are considering not what a consumer *wants* to buy but what the consumer is both willing and *able* to buy.

Demand Schedules and Demand Curves

Tables that show the relationship between the price of a product and the quantity of the product demanded are called **demand schedules**. The table in Figure 3.1 shows the number of smartwatches consumers would be willing and able to buy over the course of a week at five different prices. The amount of a good or service that a consumer is willing and able to purchase at a given price is called the **quantity demanded**. The graph in Figure 3.1 plots the numbers from the table as a **demand curve**, which shows the relationship between the price of a product and the quantity of the product demanded. (Note that, for convenience, we made the demand curve in Figure 3.1 a straight line, or linear. There is no reason that all demand curves need to be straight lines.) The demand curve in Figure 3.1 shows the **market demand**, which is the demand by all the consumers of a given good or service. The market for a product, such as restaurant meals, that is sold locally would include all the consumers in a city or a relatively small area. The market for a product, such as smartwatches, that is sold internationally would include all the consumers in the world.

Demand schedule A table that shows the relationship between the price of a product and the quantity of the product demanded.

Quantity demanded The amount of a good or service that a consumer is willing and able to purchase at a given price.

Demand curve A curve that shows the relationship between the price of a product and the quantity of the product demanded.

Market demand The demand by all the consumers of a given good or service.

Demand Schedule	
Price (dollars per smartwatch)	Quantity (millions of smartwatches per week)
$450	3
400	4
350	5
300	6
250	7

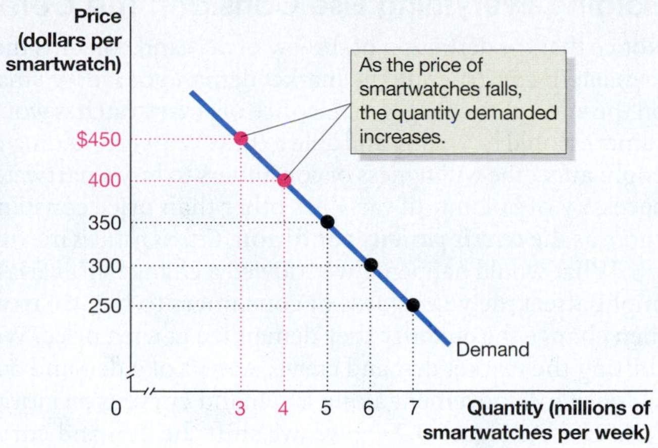

MyEconLab Animation

Figure 3.1

A Demand Schedule and Demand Curve

As the price changes, consumers change the quantity of smartwatches they are willing and able to buy. We can show this as a *demand schedule* in a table or as a *demand curve* on a graph. The table and graph both show that as the price of smartwatches falls, the quantity demanded increases. When the price of smartwatches is $450, consumers buy 3 million smartwatches per week. When the price falls to $400, consumers buy 4 million. Therefore, the demand curve for smartwatches is downward sloping.

The demand curve in Figure 3.1 slopes downward because consumers will buy more smartwatches as the price falls. When the price of smartwatches is $450, consumers buy 3 million smartwatches per week. When the price falls to $400, consumers buy 4 million. Buyers demand a larger quantity of a product as the price falls because the product becomes less expensive relative to other products and because they can afford to buy more at a lower price. MyEconLab Concept Check

The Law of Demand

The inverse relationship between the price of a product and the quantity of the product demanded is called the **law of demand**: Holding everything else constant, when the price of a product falls, the quantity demanded of the product will increase, and when the price of a product rises, the quantity demanded of the product will decrease. The law of demand holds for any market demand curve. Economists have found only a very few exceptions to this law. MyEconLab Concept Check

Law of demand A rule that states that, holding everything else constant, when the price of a product falls, the quantity demanded of the product will increase, and when the price of a product rises, the quantity demanded of the product will decrease.

What Explains the Law of Demand?

It makes sense that consumers will buy more of a good when its price falls and less of a good when its price rises, but let's look more closely at why this result holds. When the price of a product falls, consumers buy a larger quantity because of two effects, the *substitution effect* and the *income effect*:

1. The **substitution effect** refers to the change in the quantity demanded of a good that results because a change in price makes the good more or less expensive *relative* to other goods that are *substitutes*. When the price of smartwatches falls, people will substitute buying smartwatches for other goods, such as regular wristwatches or smartphones, such as the iPhone.
2. The **income effect** of a price change refers to the change in the quantity demanded of a good that results because a change in the good's price increases or decreases consumers' purchasing power. *Purchasing power* is the quantity of goods a consumer can buy with a fixed amount of income. When the price of a good falls, the increased purchasing power of consumers' incomes will usually lead them to purchase a larger quantity of the good. When the price of a good rises, the decreased purchasing power of consumers' incomes will usually lead them to purchase a smaller quantity of the good.

Substitution effect The change in the quantity demanded of a good that results from a change in price, making the good more or less expensive relative to other goods that are substitutes.

Income effect The change in the quantity demanded of a good that results from the effect of a change in the good's price on consumers' purchasing power.

Although we can analyze them separately, the substitution effect and the income effect occur simultaneously whenever a price changes. So, a fall in the price of smartwatches leads consumers to buy more smartwatches both because the smartwatches are now less expensive relative to substitute products and because the purchasing power of consumers' incomes has increased. MyEconLab Concept Check

Holding Everything Else Constant: The *Ceteris Paribus* Condition

Notice that the definition of the law of demand contains the phrase *holding everything else constant*. In constructing the market demand curve for smartwatches, we focused only on the effect that changes in the price of smartwatches would have on the quantity consumers would be willing and able to buy. We were holding constant other variables that might affect the willingness of consumers to buy smartwatches. Economists refer to the necessity of holding all variables other than price constant in constructing a demand curve as the ***ceteris paribus* condition**. *Ceteris paribus* means "all else equal" in Latin.

***Ceteris paribus* ("all else equal") condition** The requirement that when analyzing the relationship between two variables—such as price and quantity demanded—other variables must be held constant.

What would happen if we allowed a change in a variable—other than price—that might affect the willingness of consumers to buy smartwatches? Consumers would then change the quantity they demanded at each price. We can illustrate this effect by shifting the market demand curve. A shift of a demand curve is *an increase or a decrease in demand*. A movement along a demand curve is *an increase or a decrease in the quantity demanded*. As Figure 3.2 shows, we shift the demand curve to the right if consumers decide to buy more smartwatches at each price, and we shift the demand curve to the left if consumers decide to buy less at each price.

Variables That Shift Market Demand

Many variables other than price can influence market demand. These five are the most important:

- Income
- Prices of related goods
- Tastes
- Population and demographics
- Expected future prices

We next discuss how changes in each of these variables affect the market demand curve.

Income The income that consumers have available to spend affects their willingness and ability to buy a good. Suppose that the market demand curve in Figure 3.1 on page 75 represents the willingness of consumers to buy smartwatches when average household income is $50,000. If average household income rises to $52,000, the demand for smartwatches will increase, which we show by shifting the demand curve to the right. A good is a **normal good** when the demand for the good increases following a rise in income and decreases following a fall in income. Most goods are

Normal good A good for which the demand increases as income rises and decreases as income falls.

MyEconLab Animation

Figure 3.2

Shifting the Demand Curve

When consumers increase the quantity of a product they want to buy at a given price, the demand curve shifts to the right, from D_1 to D_2. When consumers decrease the quantity of a product they want to buy at a given price, the demand curve shifts to the left, from D_1 to D_3.

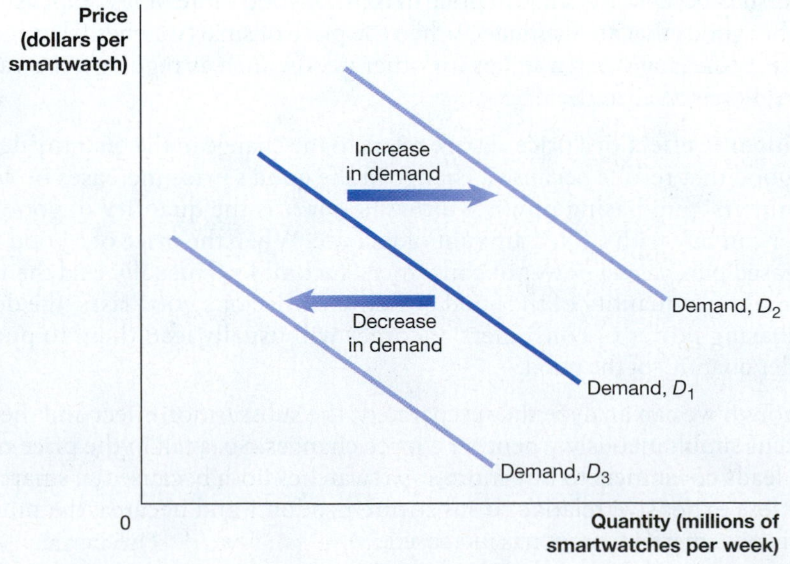

normal goods, but some goods are *inferior goods.* A good is an **inferior good** when the demand for it decreases following a rise income and increases following a fall in income. For instance, as your income rises, you might buy fewer cans of tuna or packages of instant noodles, and buy more shrimp or whole grain pasta. So, for you, canned tuna and instant noodles would be examples of inferior goods—not because they are of low quality but because you buy less of them as your income increases.

Inferior good A good for which the demand increases as income falls and decreases as income rises.

Prices of Related Goods The prices of other goods can also affect consumers' demand for a product. Consumers who would use a smartwatch primarily for checking the time, making phone calls, and keeping track of their appointments could use a smartphone instead. Goods and services that can be used for the same purpose are called **substitutes.** When two goods are substitutes, the more you buy of one, the less you will buy of the other. A decrease in the price of a substitute causes the demand curve for a good to shift to the left. An increase in the price of a substitute causes the demand curve for a good to shift to the right.

Substitutes Goods and services that can be used for the same purpose.

Suppose that the market demand curve in Figure 3.1 on page 75 represents the willingness and ability of consumers to buy smartwatches during a week when the average price of smartphones is $400. If the average price of smartphones falls to $300, consumers will demand fewer smartwatches at every price. We show this change by shifting the demand curve for smartwatches to the left.

Making the Connection
MyEconLab Video

Are Smartwatches Substitutes for Smartphones?

Two products are rarely perfect substitutes because consumers may find them more or less useful for some purposes. As Apple and other firms began selling smartwatches, a key question they needed to answer was whether consumers considered smartwatches close substitutes for smartphones. You can use either a smartwatch or a smartphone to check the time, send a text, keep a list of appointments, or use a GPS map. But you need a smartphone if you want to surf the Web or watch a movie, while you are better off buying a smartwatch if you want to monitor your heartbeat or keep track of how many calories you are burning while exercising.

Is the smartwatch a hot new must-have gadget, even for people who already own a smartphone?

So smartwatches and smartphones are substitutes—but they aren't *perfect* substitutes. To correctly forecast sales and produce the correct quantity of smartwatches, firms that sell them need to evaluate how close substitutes consumers consider smartwatches and smartphones to be. Many people who might consider buying a smartwatch already own a smartphone. So the closer consumers consider the two products to be as substitutes, the less likely they are to buy a smartwatch in addition to a smartphone.

When Apple introduced the Apple Watch in 2015, sales were initially very strong, which would seem to indicate that many consumers believed that the unique features of the smartwatch made it worth buying, even if they owned a smartphone. Some analysts, though, wondered how large future sales would be after people who buy each new electronic device soon after it hits the market—early adopters—had made their purchases. One early reviewer of the Apple Watch noted that he was unsure "that I need this thing on my wrist every day." Similarly, the *Economist* magazine offered the opinion, "Apple seems unlikely to turn its watch into the next big must-have gadget. … People are unlikely to want to shell out … $350 … for something with so few extra functions."

Other industry observers were more optimistic about the size of the market for smartwatches. Writing in the *Wall Street Journal*, one analyst argued that smartwatches performed several functions faster or more conveniently than smartphones. He concluded, "Billions of consumers who own a smartphone are likely to consider purchasing a smartwatch." Given these different evaluations, it wasn't surprising that forecasts of sales of the Apple Watch during its first year varied widely from 8 million to 41 million.

In the end, as with most new products, the success of smartwatches depends on whether consumers see them as filling a need that other products don't meet. In other words, the less close a substitute consumers believe smartwatches to be for smartphones, the more likely they are to buy a smartwatch.

Sources: Joshua Topolsky, "Apple Watch Review: You'll Want One, but You Don't Need One," bloomberg.com, April 8, 2015; "The Time Machine," *Economist*, March 9, 2015; and Daniel Matte and Kevin McCullagh, "Will Smartwatches Be a Hit?" *Wall Street Journal*, May 10, 2015.

MyEconLab Study Plan

Your Turn: Test your understanding by doing related problem 1.12 on page 101 at the end of this chapter.

Complements Goods and services that are used together.

Goods and services that are used together—such as hot dogs and hot dog buns—are called **complements**. When two goods are complements, the more consumers buy of one, the more they will buy of the other. A decrease in the price of a complement causes the demand curve for a good to shift to the right. An increase in the price of a complement causes the demand curve for a good to shift to the left.

People use applications, or "apps," on their smartwatches. So, smartwatches and apps are complements. Suppose the market demand curve in Figure 3.1 represents the willingness of consumers to buy smartwatches at a time when the average price of an app is $1.99. If the average price of apps falls to $0.99, consumers will buy more apps *and* more smartwatches, and the demand curve for smartwatches will shift to the right.

Tastes An advertising campaign for a product can influence consumer demand. If Apple, Samsung, LG, and other firms making smartwatches begin to advertise heavily, consumers are likely to buy more smartwatches at every price, and the demand curve will shift to the right. An economist would say that the advertising campaign has affected consumers' *taste* for smartwatches. Taste is a catchall category that refers to the many subjective elements that can enter into a consumer's decision to buy a product. A consumer's taste for a product can change for many reasons. Sometimes trends play a substantial role. For example, the popularity of low-carbohydrate diets caused a decline in demand for some goods, such as bread and donuts, and an increase in demand for fish. In general, when consumers' taste for a product increases, the demand curve will shift to the right, and when consumers' taste decreases, the demand curve will shift to the left.

Demographics The characteristics of a population with respect to age, race, and gender.

Population and Demographics As the population of a country increases, the number of consumers and the demand for most products will increase. The **demographics** of a population refers to its characteristics, with respect to age, race, and gender. As the demographics of a country or region change, the demand for particular goods will increase or decrease because different categories of people tend to have different preferences for those goods. For instance, the U.S. Census Bureau forecasts that Hispanics will increase from 18 percent of the U.S. population in 2015 to 26 percent in 2050. This increase will expand demand for Spanish-language books, Web sites, and cable television channels, among other goods and services.

McDonalds introduced new products to appeal to millennials as sales of Big Macs declined.

Making the Connection
MyEconLab Video

Tough Times for Big Macs and Golf

Changing demographics can affect the demand for products. Clearly, the usefulness of products may vary with age. For example, when birth rates are high, the demand for formula, diapers, and other baby products increases. Similarly, when there are more older people, the demand for nursing homes increases. Some retail analysts believe, though, that tastes for products may also differ across generations, so that some products may remain popular with older generations while declining in popularity with younger generations. There are no exact definitions of generations, but the chart on the next page shows common labels.

Years Born	Generation Label	Age Range in 2015	Number of People in the Generation in 2015
1946–1964	Baby boom generation	51–69	79 million
1965–1984	Generation X	31–50	83 million
1985–2004	Millennials, or Generation Y	11–30	87 million

The millennials outnumber the two generations that preceded them, but the size of each generation doesn't tell the whole story for retailers. Market research indicates that consumers between the ages of 18 and 49 account for a large fraction of all retail sales. This fact helps explain why firms are willing to pay high prices to run commercials on television programs, such as NBC's *The Voice*, that this "prime demographic" watches. Note that the whole of the baby boom generation is now older than this age group. Members of generation X are also beginning to age out of this group, and over time millennials will begin to make up the bulk of this demographic.

Because of their importance as consumers, firms become concerned if millennials don't have a strong demand for their products. Consider problems that McDonald's and Dick's Sporting Goods were facing in 2015. Millennials were shifting from buying Big Macs to visiting "fast casual" restaurants, such as Chipotle Mexican Grill and Panera Bread. In 2014, the revenue and profits of McDonald's both declined for the first time in more than 30 years. McDonald's was suffering particular problems with college-age consumers. The number of consumers aged 19 to 21 who visit McDonald's at least once per month declined 15 percent between 2011 and 2015.

Dick's Sporting Goods faced a similar problem with demand for golf clubs and other golf equipment. The average age of people who regularly play golf has increased over time and was 56 in 2015. During the past five years, the number of people aged 18 to 34 who played at least one round of golf during the year has been continually declining. As fewer young people play golf, sales of golf equipment, rounds of golf at golf courses, and ratings of golf tournaments on television have all declined. Sales of golf equipment at Dick's declined by more than 15 percent between 2013 and 2015.

How should a business respond if the demand for its products is decreasing among younger consumers? The answer depends partly on whether offering different products or changing existing products might increase demand from these consumers. McDonald's tried this strategy by introducing McWrap sandwiches—tortillas stuffed with chicken or vegetables— and other new meals to appeal to millennials. It also planned to use healthier ingredients by, for example, reducing the use of chicken that had been fed antibiotics while being raised. Dick's decided that it probably could not revive demand for its golf equipment. The chain laid off most of the golf pros who had been working in its stores, and reduced the number of golf clubs and golf balls and the amount of golf clothing it offered for sale.

As firms make plans for the long run, they have to take into account how changing demographics may affect demand for their products.

Sources: Annie Gasparro, "McDonald's Puts Its Plan on Display," *Wall Street Journal*, May 3, 2015; Julie Jargon, "McDonald's Faces 'Millennial' Challenge," *Wall Street Journal*, August 24, 2014; Sara Germano, "A Game of Golf? Not for Many Millennials," *Wall Street Journal*, August 1, 2014; Lisa Beilfuss, "Dick's Sporting Goods Profit Falls 10%," *Wall Street Journal*, May 19, 2015; and "Dick's Sporting Goods Lays Off 478 PGA Golf Pros," Associated Press, July 24, 2014.

Your Turn: Test your understanding by doing related problem 1.13 on page 101 at the end of this chapter.

MyEconLab Study Plan

Expected Future Prices Consumers choose not only which products to buy but also when to buy them. For instance, if enough consumers become convinced that houses will be selling for lower prices in three months, the demand for houses will decrease now, as some consumers postpone their purchases to wait for the expected price decrease. Alternatively, if enough consumers become convinced that the price of houses will be higher in three months, the demand for houses will increase now, as some consumers try to beat the expected price increase.

Table 3.1 summarizes the most important variables that cause market demand curves to shift. Note that the table shows the shift in the demand curve that results from an *increase* in each of the variables. A *decrease* in these variables would cause the demand curve to shift in the opposite direction. MyEconLab Concept Check

Table 3.1

Variables That Shift Market Demand Curves

An increase in ...	shifts the demand curve ...	because ...
income (and the good is normal)	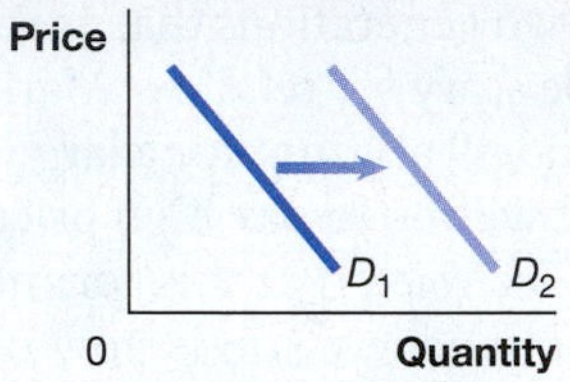	consumers spend more of their higher incomes on the good.
income (and the good is inferior)	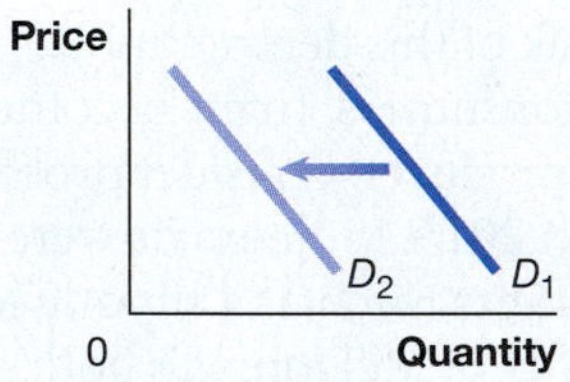	consumers spend less of their higher incomes on the good.
the price of a substitute good	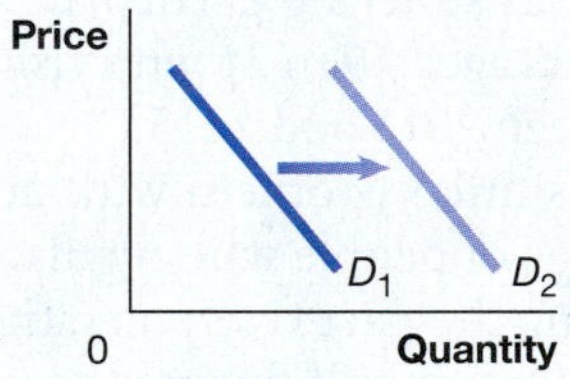	consumers buy less of the substitute good and more of this good.
the price of a complementary good	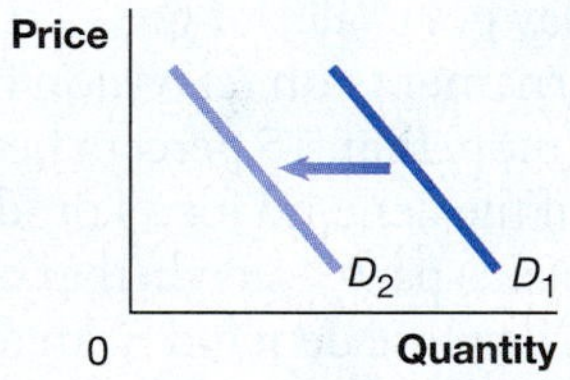	consumers buy less of the complementary good and less of this good.
taste for the good	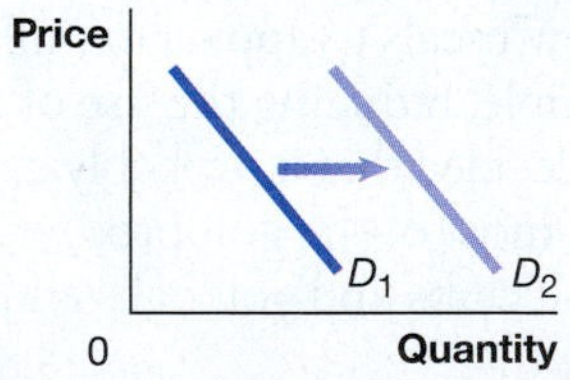	consumers are willing to buy a larger quantity of the good at every price.
population	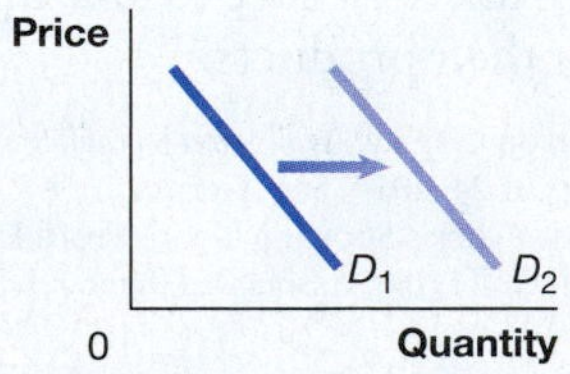	additional consumers result in a greater quantity demanded at every price.
the expected price of the good in the future	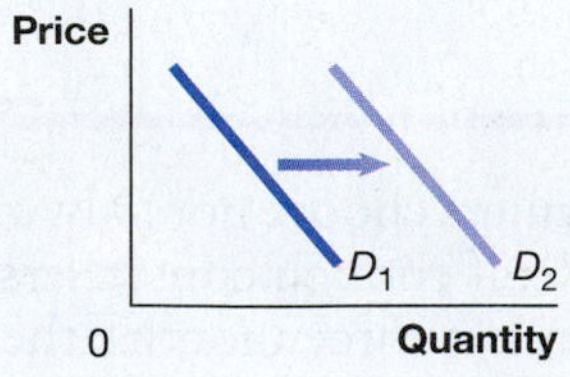	consumers buy more of the good today to avoid the higher price in the future.

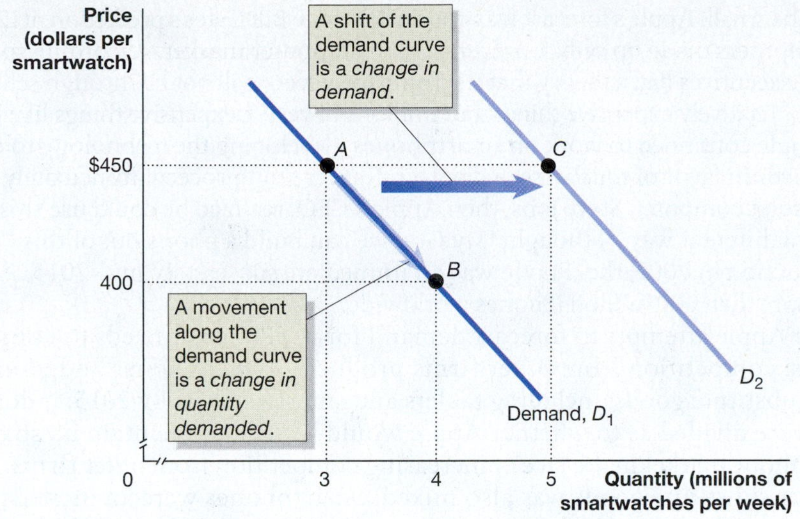

MyEconLab Animation

Figure 3.3

A Change in Demand versus a Change in Quantity Demanded

If the price of smartwatches falls from \$450 to \$400, the result will be a movement along the demand curve from point A to point *B*—an increase in quantity demanded from 3 million to 4 million. If consumers' incomes increase, or if another factor changes that makes consumers want more of the product at every price, the demand curve will shift to the right—an increase in demand. In this case, the increase in demand from D_1 to D_2 causes the quantity of smartwatches demanded at a price of \$450 to increase from 3 million at point *A* to 5 million at point C.

A Change in Demand versus a Change in Quantity Demanded

It is important to understand the difference between a *change in demand* and a *change in quantity demanded*. A change in demand refers to a shift of the demand curve. A shift occurs if there is a change in one of the variables—*other than the price of the product*—that affects the willingness of consumers to buy the product. A change in quantity demanded refers to a movement along the demand curve as a result of a change in the product's price. Figure 3.3 illustrates this important distinction. If the price of smartwatches falls from \$450 to \$400, the result will be a movement along the demand curve from point A to point *B*—an increase in quantity demanded from 3 million to 4 million. If consumers' incomes increase, or if another factor changes that makes consumers want more of the product at every price, the demand curve will shift to the right—an increase in demand. In this case, the increase in demand from D_1 to D_2 causes the quantity of smartwatches demanded at a price of \$450 to increase from 3 million at point A to 5 million at point C.

Making the Connection
MyEconLab Video

Forecasting the Demand for iPhones

One of the most important decisions that managers of any large firm face is choosing which new products to develop. A firm must devote people, time, and money to design a new product, negotiate with suppliers, create a marketing campaign, and perform many other tasks. But any firm has only limited resources and so faces a trade-off: Resources used to develop one product will not be available to develop another product. Ultimately, the products a firm chooses to develop will be those that it believes will be the most profitable. So, to decide which products to develop, firms need to forecast the demand for those products.

Will demand for iPhones continue to grow despite increasing competition?

David Sobotta, who worked at Apple for 20 years and eventually became its national sales manager, has described discussions at Apple during 2002 about whether to develop a tablet computer. According to Sobotta, representatives of the U.S. National Institutes of Health urged Apple to develop a tablet computer, arguing that it would be particularly useful to doctors, nurses, and hospitals. In 2001, Bill Gates, chairman of Microsoft, had predicted that "within five years … [tablet PCs] will be the most popular form of PC sold in America." Apple's managers decided not to develop a tablet computer, however, because they believed the technology available at that time was too complex for an average computer user, and they also believed that the demand from doctors and nurses would be small. Apple's forecast was correct. Despite Bill Gates's prediction, in 2006, tablet computers made up only 1 percent of the computer market. According to Sobotta, "Apple executives had a theory that the route to success will not be through selling thousands of relatively expensive things, but millions of very inexpensive things like iPods."

Apple continued to work on smartphones, developing the technology to eliminate keyboards in favor of touchscreen displays. Rather than proceed immediately to building a tablet computer, Steve Jobs, then Apple's CEO, realized he could use this technology in a different way: "I thought 'My God we can build a phone out of this.'" From its introduction in 2007, the iPhone was an immediate success. By mid-2015, Apple had sold more than 600 million iPhones worldwide.

As Apple attempts to forecast demand for its iPhone, it needs to consider two factors: competition from other firms producing smartphones and competition from substitute goods, including tablets and smartwatches. By 2015, industry analysts were divided as to whether Apple would be able to maintain its share of the smartphone market in the face of increasing competition from other firms. The outlook for substitute goods was also mixed. Smartphones were an increasing share of the overall worldwide cellphone market, so there are relatively few consumers left to switch to smartphones from basic cellphones. The increasing availability of apps, including mobile payment apps like Apple Pay that can be used in place of credit cards, was increasing the usefulness of smartphones. But some consumers preferred to use tablets, with their larger screens, for checking e-mail and surfing the Web. With apps like FaceTime or Skype, a tablet can be used to make phone calls. Another unknown was the extent to which sales of smartwatches might eventually cut into smartphone sales.

As any firm does in forecasting demand, Apple faced a trade-off: If it was too cautious in expanding capacity or buying components for smartphones, other firms might seize a large share of the market. But, if Apple was too optimistic, it ran the risk of spending on capacity to produce more units than it could actually sell—an outcome that might turn potential profits into losses. Apple has spent billions of dollars buying large quantities of motion sensors, screens, and other components from suppliers. That will be money well spent ... if the forecast of demand turns out to be accurate. Time will tell whether the future demand for smartphones will be as large as Apple and other firms were forecasting.

Sources: Daisuke Wakabayashi, "Apple Earnings Surge 33% on iPhone Sales," *Wall Street Journal*, April 27, 2015; David Sobotta, "What Jobs Told Me on the iPhone," (London) *Guardian*, January 3, 2007; "Jobs Says iPad Idea Came before iPhone," Associated Press, January 2, 2010; and "More Smartphones Were Shipped in Q1 2013 Than Feature Phones, an Industry First According to IDC," www.idc.com, April 25, 2013.

MyEconLab Study Plan

Your Turn: Test your understanding by doing related problem 1.17 on page 101 at the end of this chapter.

3.2 The Supply Side of the Market

LEARNING OBJECTIVE: List and describe the variables that influence supply.

Quantity supplied The amount of a good or service that a firm is willing and able to supply at a given price.

Just as many variables influence the willingness and ability of consumers to buy a particular good or service, many variables influence the willingness and ability of firms to supply a good or service. The most important of these variables is price. The amount of a good or service that a firm is willing and able to supply at a given price is the **quantity supplied**. Holding other variables constant, when the price of a good rises, producing the good is more profitable, and the quantity supplied will increase. When the price of a good falls, selling the good is less profitable, and the quantity supplied will decrease. In addition, as we saw in Chapter 2, devoting more and more resources to the production of a good results in increasing marginal costs. For example, if Apple, Samsung, LG, and other firms increase production of smartwatches during a given time period, they are likely to find that the cost of producing additional smartwatches increases as their suppliers run existing factories for longer hours and pay higher prices for components

Supply Schedule	
Price (dollars per smartwatch)	Quantity (millions of smartwatches per week)
$450	7
400	6
350	5
300	4
250	3

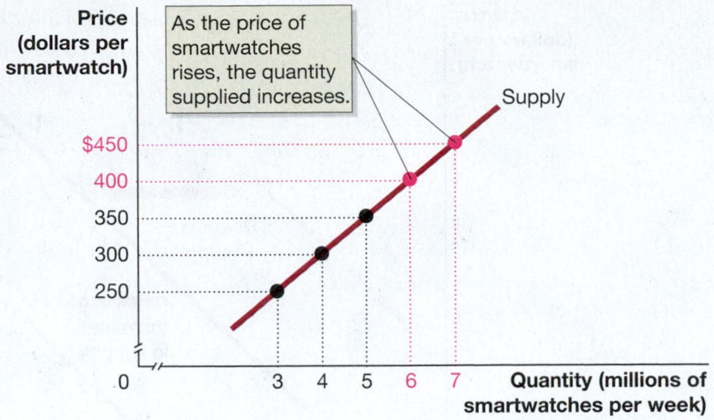

MyEconLab Animation

Figure 3.4

A Supply Schedule and Supply Curve

As the price changes, Apple, Samsung, LG, and other firms producing smartwatches change the quantity they are willing to supply. We can show this as a *supply schedule* in a table or as a *supply curve* on a graph. The supply schedule and supply curve both show that as the price of smartwatches rises, firms will increase the quantity they supply. At a price of $400 per smartwatch, firms will supply 6 million smartwatches per week. At a price of $450, firms will supply 7 million.

and higher wages for workers. With higher marginal costs, firms will supply a larger quantity only if the price is higher.

Supply Schedules and Supply Curves

A **supply schedule** is a table that shows the relationship between the price of a product and the quantity of the product supplied. The table in Figure 3.4 is a supply schedule showing the quantity of smartwatches that firms would be willing to supply per month at different prices. The graph in Figure 3.4 plots the numbers from the table as a **supply curve**, which shows the relationship between the price of a product and the quantity of the product supplied. The supply schedule and supply curve both show that as the price of smartwatches rises, firms will increase the quantity they supply. At a price of $400 per smartwatch, firms will supply 6 million smartwatches per week. At a higher price of $450, firms will supply 7 million. (Once again, we are assuming for convenience that the supply curve is a straight line, even though not all supply curves are actually straight lines.) MyEconLab Concept Check

Supply schedule A table that shows the relationship between the price of a product and the quantity of the product supplied.

Supply curve A curve that shows the relationship between the price of a product and the quantity of the product supplied.

The Law of Supply

The *market supply curve* in Figure 3.4 is upward sloping. We expect most supply curves to be upward sloping, according to the **law of supply**, which states that, holding everything else constant, increases in price cause increases in the quantity supplied, and decreases in price cause decreases in the quantity supplied. Notice that the definition of the law of supply—like the definition of the law of demand—contains the phrase *holding everything else constant*. If only the price of the product changes, there is a movement along the supply curve, which is *an increase or a decrease in the quantity supplied*. As Figure 3.5 shows, if any other variable that affects the willingness of firms to supply a good changes, the supply curve will shift, which is *an increase or a decrease in supply*. When firms increase the quantity of a product they want to sell at a given price, the supply curve shifts to the right. The shift from S_1 to S_3 represents *an increase in supply*. When firms decrease the quantity of a product they want to sell at a given price, the supply curve shifts to the left. The shift from S_1 to S_2 represents *a decrease in supply*. MyEconLab Concept Check

Law of supply A rule that states that, holding everything else constant, increases in price cause increases in the quantity supplied, and decreases in price cause decreases in the quantity supplied.

Variables That Shift Market Supply

The following are the five most important variables that shift market supply:

- Prices of inputs
- Technological change
- Prices of related goods in production
- Number of firms in the market
- Expected future prices

We next discuss how changes in each of these variables affect the market supply curve.

MyEconLab Animation

Figure 3.5

Shifting the Supply Curve

When firms increase the quantity of a product they want to sell at a given price, the supply curve shifts to the right. The shift from S_1 to S_3 represents an *increase in supply*. When firms decrease the quantity of a product they want to sell at a given price, the supply curve shifts to the left. The shift from S_1 to S_2 represents a *decrease in supply*.

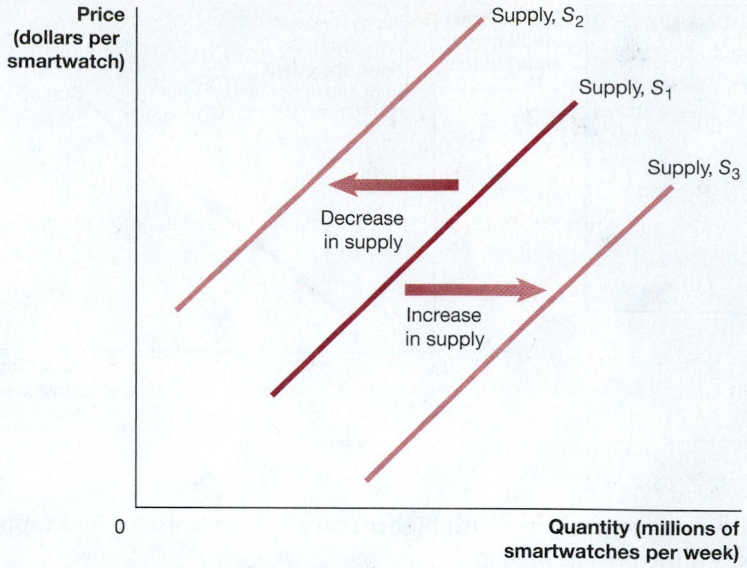

Prices of Inputs The factor most likely to cause the supply curve for a product to shift is a change in the price of an *input*. An input is anything used in the production of a good or service. For instance, if the price of a component of smartwatches, such as memory chips, rises, the cost of producing smartwatches will increase, and smartwatches will be less profitable at every price. The supply of smartwatches will decline, and the market supply curve for smartwatches will shift to the left. Similarly, if the price of an input declines, the supply of smartwatches will increase, and the market supply curve will shift to the right.

Technological change A positive or negative change in the ability of a firm to produce a given level of output with a given quantity of inputs.

Technological Change A second factor that causes a change in supply is **technological change**, which is a positive or negative change in the ability of a firm to produce a given level of output with a given quantity of inputs. Positive technological change occurs whenever a firm is able to produce more output using the same amount of inputs. In other words, the *productivity* of the firm's workers or machines has increased. If a firm can produce more output with the same amount of inputs, its costs will be lower, and the good will be more profitable to produce at any given price. As a result, when positive technological change occurs, the firm will increase the quantity supplied at every price, and its supply curve will shift to the right.

Negative technological change is relatively rare, although it could result from an earthquake or another natural disaster or from a war that reduces the ability of firms to supply as much output with a given amount of inputs. Negative technological change will raise firms' costs, and firms will earn lower profits from producing the good. Therefore, negative technological change will cause the market supply curve to shift to the left.

Prices of Related Goods in Production Firms often choose which good or service they will produce. Alternative goods that a firm could produce are called *substitutes in production*. Many of the firms that produce smartwatches also produce other consumer electronics. For example, Apple produces the iPhone and the iPad, and Samsung produces the Galaxy S smartphone and Galaxy Tab. These products typically use similar components and are often assembled in the same factories. If the price of smartphones increases relative to the price of smartwatches, smartphones will become more profitable, and Apple, Samsung, and other firms making smartwatches will shift some of their productive capacity away from smartwatches and toward smartphones. The firms will offer fewer smartwatches for sale at every price, so the supply curve for smartwatches will shift to the left.

Goods that are produced together are called *complements in production*. For example, the same geological formations that contain oil usually also contain natural gas. If the price of oil rises, oil companies that begin pumping more oil from these formations will also produce more natural gas. As a result, an increase in the price of oil will cause the supply curve for natural gas—a complement in production—to shift to the right.

Number of Firms in the Market A change in the number of firms in the market will change supply. When new firms *enter* a market, the supply curve shifts to the right, and when existing firms leave, or *exit*, a market, the supply curve shifts to the left. In 2015, for instance, Apple entered the market for smartwatches, which shifted the market supply curve to the right.

Expected Future Prices If a firm expects that the price of its product will be higher in the future, it has an incentive to decrease supply now and increase it in the future. For instance, if Apple believes that prices for smartwatches are temporarily low—perhaps because of a recession—it may store some of its production today to sell later on, when it expects prices to be higher.

Table 3.2 summarizes the most important variables that cause market supply curves to shift. Note that the table shows the shift in the supply curve that results from an *increase* in each of the variables. A *decrease* in these variables would cause the supply curve to shift in the opposite direction. MyEconLab Concept Check

Table 3.2

Variables That Shift Market Supply Curves

An increase in ...	shifts the supply curve ...	because ...
the price of an input	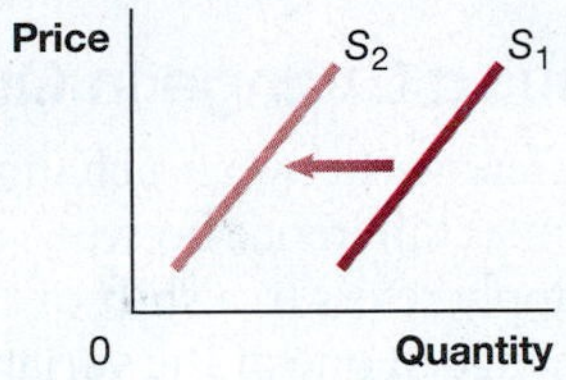	the costs of producing the good rise.
productivity	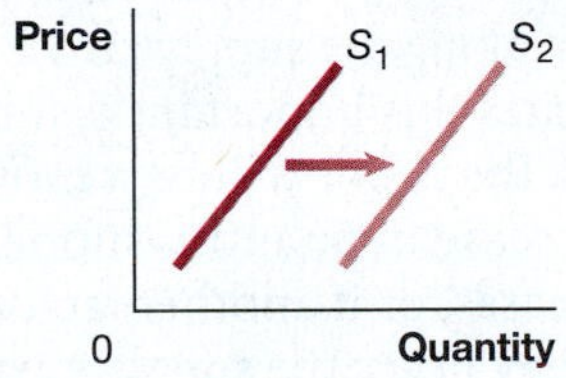	the costs of producing the good fall.
the price of a substitute in production	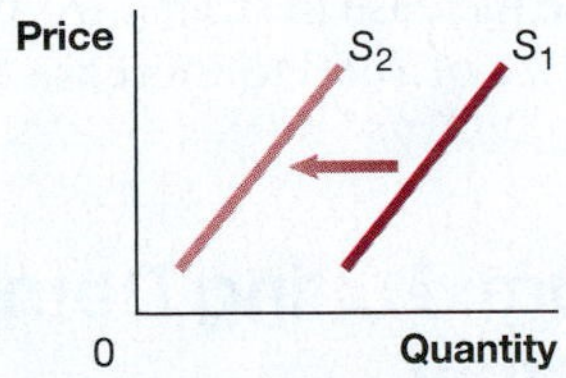	more of the substitute is produced and less of the good is produced.
the price of a complement in production	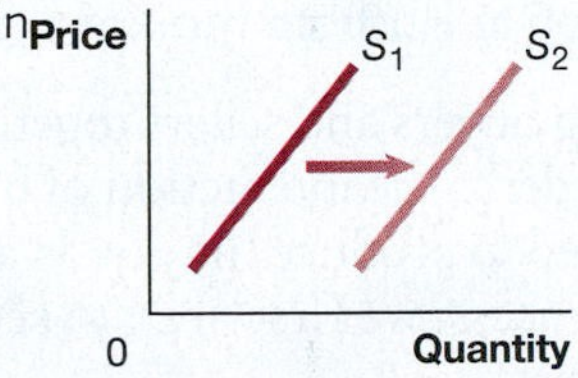	more of the good and the complementary good are produced.
the number of firms in the market	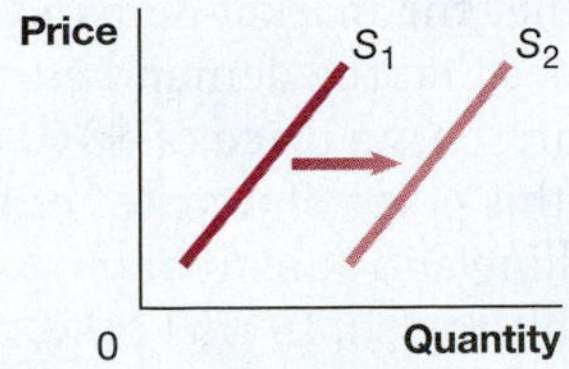	additional firms result in a greater quantity supplied at every price.
the expected future price of the product	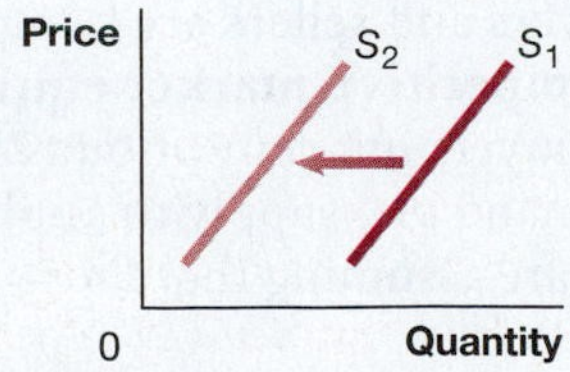	less of the good will be offered for sale today to take advantage of the higher price in the future.

MyEconLab Animation

Figure 3.6

A Change in Supply versus a Change in Quantity Supplied

If the price of smartwatches rises from \$400 to \$450, the result will be a movement up the supply curve from point *A* to point *B*—an increase in the quantity supplied by Apple, Samsung, Nokia, and other firms from 6 million to 7 million. If the price of an input decreases, or if another factor changes that causes sellers to supply more of the product at every price, the supply curve will shift to the right—an increase in supply. In this case, the increase in supply from S_1 to S_2 causes the quantity of smartwatches supplied at a price of \$450 to increase from 7 million at point *B* to 9 million at point *C*.

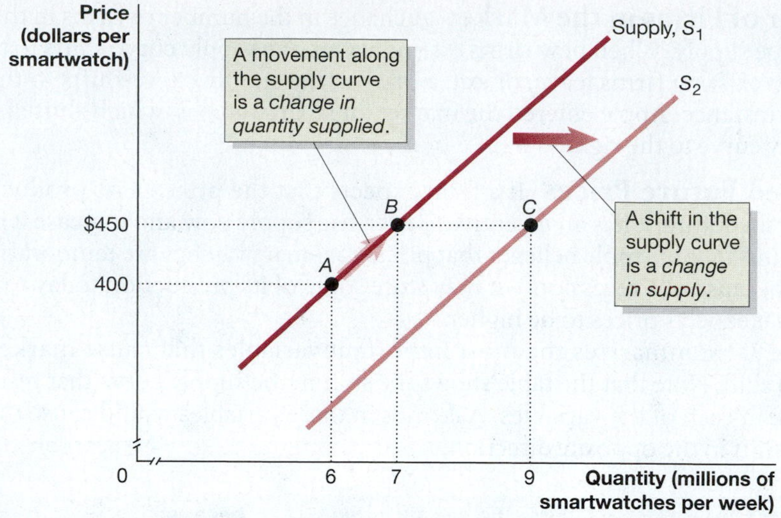

A Change in Supply versus a Change in Quantity Supplied

We noted earlier the important difference between a change in demand and a change in quantity demanded. There is a similar difference between a *change in supply* and a *change in quantity supplied*. A change in supply refers to a shift of the supply curve. The supply curve will shift when there is a change in one of the variables—*other than the price of the product*—that affects the willingness of suppliers to sell the product. A change in quantity supplied refers to a movement along the supply curve as a result of a change in the product's price. Figure 3.6 illustrates this important distinction. If the price of smartwatches rises from \$400 to \$450, the result will be a movement up the supply curve from point *A* to point *B*—an increase in quantity supplied from 6 million to 7 million. If the price of an input decreases, or if another factor changes that causes sellers to supply more of a product at every price, the supply curve will shift to the right—an increase in supply. In this case, the increase in supply from S_1 to S_2 causes the quantity of smartwatches supplied at a price of \$450 to increase from 7 million at point *B* to 9 million at point *C*.

MyEconLab Concept Check

MyEconLab Study Plan

3.3 Market Equilibrium: Putting Demand and Supply Together

LEARNING OBJECTIVE: Use a graph to illustrate market equilibrium.

The purpose of markets is to bring buyers and sellers together. As we saw in Chapter 2, instead of being chaotic and disorderly, the interaction of buyers and sellers in markets ultimately results in firms being led to produce the goods and services that consumers want most. To understand this process, we first need to see how markets work to reconcile the plans of buyers and sellers.

In Figure 3.7, we bring together the market demand curve and the market supply curve for smartwatches. Notice that the demand curve crosses the supply curve at only one point. This point represents a price of \$350 and a quantity of 5 million smartwatches per week. Only at this point of **market equilibrium** is the quantity of smartwatches consumers are willing and able to buy equal to the quantity of smartwatches firms are willing and able to sell. In this case, the *equilibrium price* is \$350, and the *equilibrium quantity* is 5 million. As we noted at the beginning of the chapter, markets that have many buyers and sellers are competitive markets, and equilibrium in these markets is a **competitive market equilibrium**. In the market for smartwatches, there are many buyers but only about 25 firms. Whether 25 firms are enough for our model of demand and supply to apply to this market is a matter of judgment. In this chapter, we are assuming that the market for smartwatches has enough sellers to be competitive.

Market equilibrium A situation in which quantity demanded equals quantity supplied.

Competitive market equilibrium A market equilibrium with many buyers and sellers.

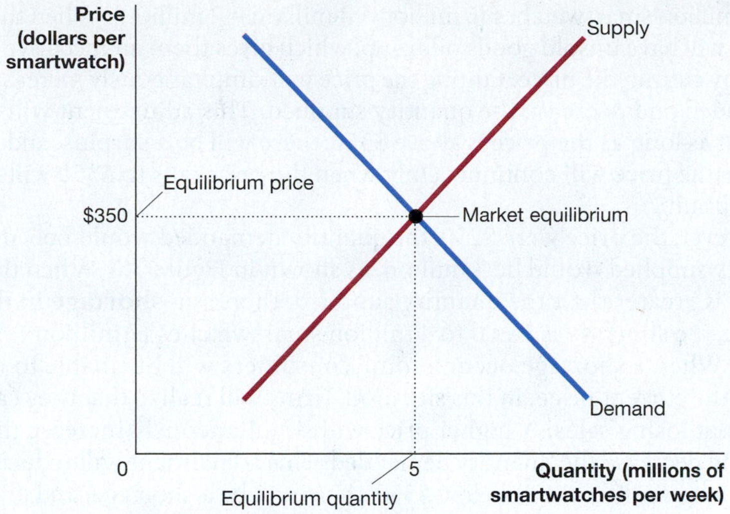

MyEconLab Animation

Figure 3.7

Market Equilibrium

Where the demand curve crosses the supply curve determines market equilibrium. In this case, the demand curve for smartwatches crosses the supply curve at a price of $350 and a quantity of 5 million smartwatches. Only at this point is the quantity of smartwatches consumers are willing to buy equal to the quantity that Apple, Samsung, LG, and other firms are willing to sell: The quantity demanded is equal to the quantity supplied.

How Markets Eliminate Surpluses and Shortages

A market that is not in equilibrium moves toward equilibrium. Once a market is in equilibrium, it remains in equilibrium. To see why, consider what happens if a market is not in equilibrium. Suppose that the price in the market for smartwatches was $400 rather than the equilibrium price of $350. As Figure 3.8 shows, at a price of $400, the quantity of smartwatches supplied would be 6 million, and the quantity of smartwatches demanded would be 4 million. When the quantity supplied is greater than the quantity demanded, there is a **surplus** in the market. In this case, the surplus is

Surplus A situation in which the quantity supplied is greater than the quantity demanded.

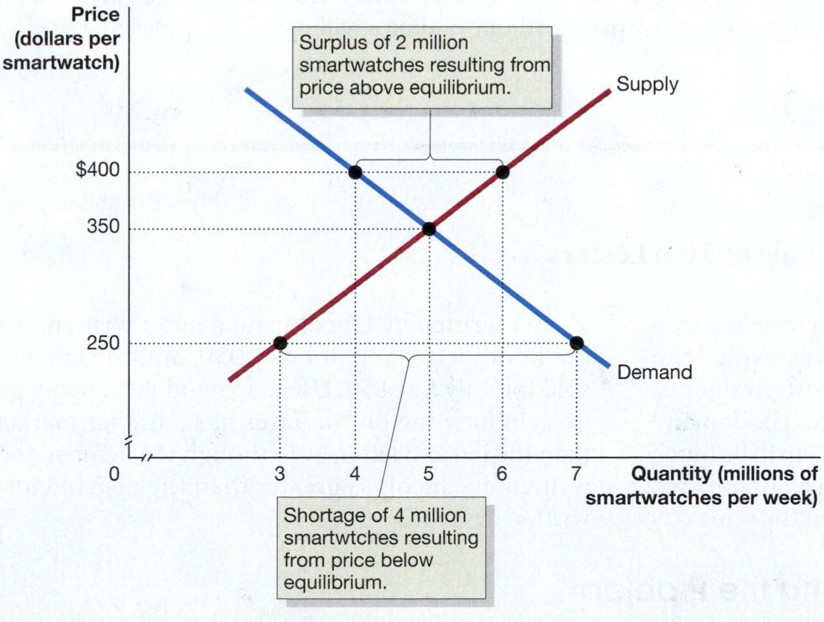

MyEconLab Animation

Figure 3.8 The Effect of Surpluses and Shortages on the Market Price

When the market price is above equilibrium, there will be a *surplus*. A price of $400 for smartwatches results in 6 million smartwatches being supplied but only 4 million being demanded, or a surplus of 2 million. As Apple, Nokia, LG, and other firms cut the price to dispose of the surplus, the price will fall to the equilibrium price of $350. When the market price is below equilibrium, there will be a *shortage*. A price of $250 results in 7 million smartwatches being demanded but only 3 million being supplied, or a shortage of 4 million. As firms find that consumers who are unable to find smartwatches available for sale are willing to pay higher prices to get them, the price will rise to the equilibrium price of $350.

equal to 2 million smartwatches (6 million − 4 million = 2 million). When there is a surplus, firms will have unsold goods piling up, which gives them an incentive to increase their sales by cutting the price. Cutting the price will simultaneously increase the quantity demanded and decrease the quantity supplied. This adjustment will reduce the surplus, but as long as the price is above $350, there will be a surplus, and downward pressure on the price will continue. Only when the price falls to $350 will the market be in equilibrium.

Shortage A situation in which the quantity demanded is greater than the quantity supplied.

If, however, the price were $250, the quantity demanded would be 7 million, and the quantity supplied would be 3 million, as shown in Figure 3.8. When the quantity demanded is greater than the quantity supplied, there is a **shortage** in the market. In this case, the shortage is equal to 4 million smartwatches (7 million − 3 million = 4 million). When a shortage occurs, some consumers will be unable to buy smartwatches at the current price. In this situation, firms will realize that they can raise the price without losing sales. A higher price will simultaneously increase the quantity supplied and decrease the quantity demanded. This adjustment will reduce the shortage, but as long as the price is below $350, there will be a shortage, and upward pressure on the price will continue. Only when the price rises to $350 will the market be in equilibrium.

At a competitive market equilibrium, all consumers willing to pay the market price will be able to buy as much of the product as they want, and all firms willing to accept the market price will be able to sell as much of the product as they want. As a result, there will be no reason for the price to change unless either the demand curve or the supply curve shifts. MyEconLab Concept Check

Demand and Supply Both Count

Keep in mind that the interaction of demand and supply determines the equilibrium price. Neither consumers nor firms can dictate what the equilibrium price will be. No firm can sell anything at any price unless it can find a willing buyer, and no consumer can buy anything at any price without finding a willing seller. MyEconLab Concept Check

Solved Problem 3.3

MyEconLab Interactive Animation

Demand and Supply Both Count: A Tale of Two Letters

Which letter is likely to be worth more: one written by Abraham Lincoln or one written by his assassin, John Wilkes Booth? Lincoln is one of the greatest presidents, and many people collect anything he wrote. The demand for letters written by Lincoln surely would seem to be much greater than the demand for letters written by Booth. Yet, when R.M. Smythe and Co. auctioned off on the same day a letter written by Lincoln and a letter written by Booth, the Booth letter sold for $31,050, and the Lincoln letter sold for only $21,850. Use a demand and supply graph to explain how the Booth letter has a higher market price than the Lincoln letter, even though the demand for letters written by Lincoln is greater than the demand for letters written by Booth.

Solving the Problem

Step 1: Review the chapter material. This problem is about prices being determined at market equilibrium, so you may want to review the section "Market Equilibrium: Putting Demand and Supply Together," which begins on page 86.

Step 2: Draw demand curves that illustrate the greater demand for Lincoln's letters. Begin by drawing two demand curves. Label one "Demand for Lincoln's letters" and the other "Demand for Booth's letters." Make sure that the Lincoln demand curve is much farther to the right than the Booth demand curve.

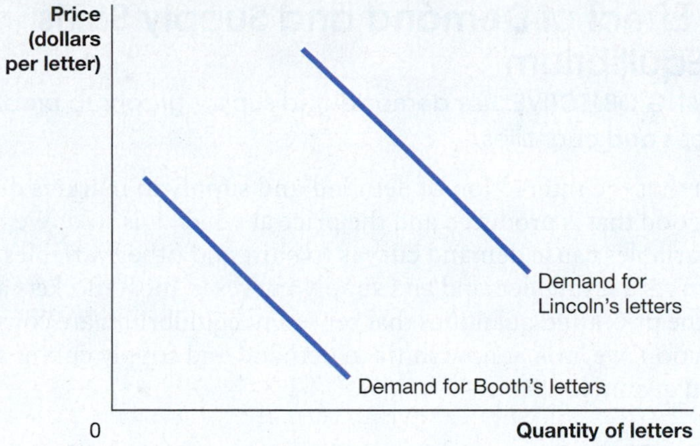

Step 3: Draw supply curves that illustrate the equilibrium price of Booth's letters being higher than the equilibrium price of Lincoln's letters. Based on the demand curves you have just drawn, think about how it might be possible for the market price of Lincoln's letters to be lower than the market price of Booth's letters. This outcome can occur only if the supply of Lincoln's letters is much greater than the supply of Booth's letters. Draw on your graph a supply curve for Lincoln's letters and a supply curve for Booth's letters that will result in an equilibrium price of Booth's letters of \$31,050 and an equilibrium price of Lincoln's letters of \$21,850. You have now solved the problem.

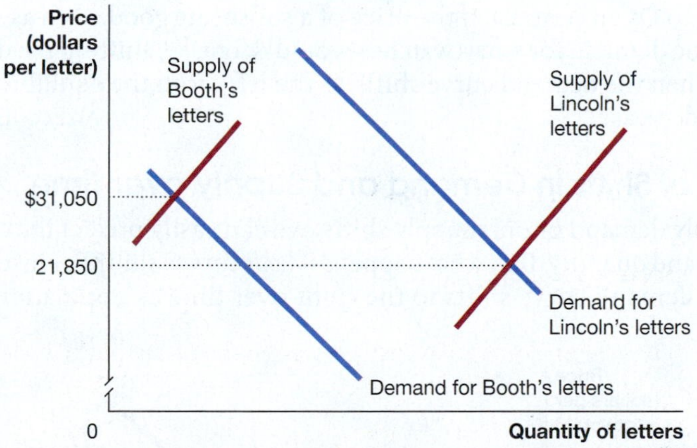

Extra Credit: The explanation for this puzzle is that both demand and supply count when determining market price. The demand for Lincoln's letters is much greater than the demand for Booth's letters, but the supply of Booth's letters is very small. Historians believe that only eight letters written by Booth exist today. (Note that the supply curves for letters written by Booth and by Lincoln are upward sloping, even though only a fixed number of each of these letters is available and, obviously, no more can be produced. The upward slope of the supply curves occurs because the higher the price, the larger the quantity of letters that will be offered for sale by people who currently own them.)

Your Turn: For more practice, do related problems 3.5, 3.6, and 3.7 on page 103 at the end of this chapter.

MyEconLab Study Plan

3.4 The Effect of Demand and Supply Shifts on Equilibrium

LEARNING OBJECTIVE: Use demand and supply graphs to predict changes in prices and quantities.

We have seen that the interaction of demand and supply in markets determines the quantity of a good that is produced and the price at which it is sold. We have also seen that several variables cause demand curves to shift and other variables cause supply curves to shift. As a result, demand and supply curves in most markets are constantly shifting, and the prices and quantities that represent equilibrium are constantly changing. In this section, we look at how shifts in demand and supply curves affect equilibrium price and quantity.

The Effect of Shifts in Supply on Equilibrium

When Apple entered the market for smartwatches, the market supply curve for smartwatches shifted to the right. Figure 3.9 shows the supply curve shifting from S_1 to S_2. When the supply curve shifts to the right, there will be a surplus at the original equilibrium price, P_1. The surplus is eliminated as the equilibrium price falls to P_2 and the equilibrium quantity rises from Q_1 to Q_2. If an existing firm exits the market, the supply curve will shift to the left, causing the equilibrium price to rise and the equilibrium quantity to fall. MyEconLab Concept Check

The Effect of Shifts in Demand on Equilibrium

Because smartwatches are a normal good, when incomes increase, the market demand curve shifts to the right. Figure 3.10 shows the effect of a demand curve shifting to the right, from D_1 to D_2. This shift causes a shortage at the original equilibrium price, P_1. To eliminate the shortage, the equilibrium price rises to P_2, and the equilibrium quantity rises from Q_1 to Q_2. In contrast, if the price of a substitute good, such as smartphones, were to fall, the demand for smartwatches would decrease, shifting the demand curve to the left. When the demand curve shifts to the left, both the equilibrium price and quantity will decrease. MyEconLab Concept Check

The Effect of Shifts in Demand and Supply over Time

Whenever only demand or only supply shifts, we can easily predict the effect on equilibrium price and quantity. But, what happens if *both* curves shift? For instance, in many markets, the demand curve shifts to the right over time as population and income

MyEconLab Animation

Figure 3.9

The Effect of an Increase in Supply on Equilibrium

If a firm enters a market, as Apple entered the market for smartwatches, the equilibrium price will fall, and the equilibrium quantity will rise:

1. As Apple enters the market for smartwatches, a larger quantity of smartwatches will be supplied at every price, so the market supply curve shifts to the right, from S_1 to S_2, which causes a surplus of smartwatches at the original price, P_1.
2. The equilibrium price falls from P_1 to P_2.
3. The equilibrium quantity rises from Q_1 to Q_2.

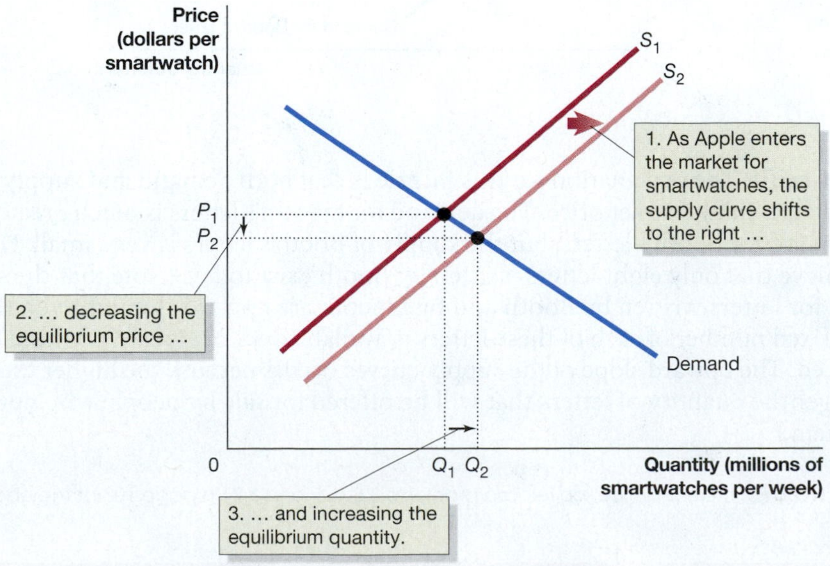

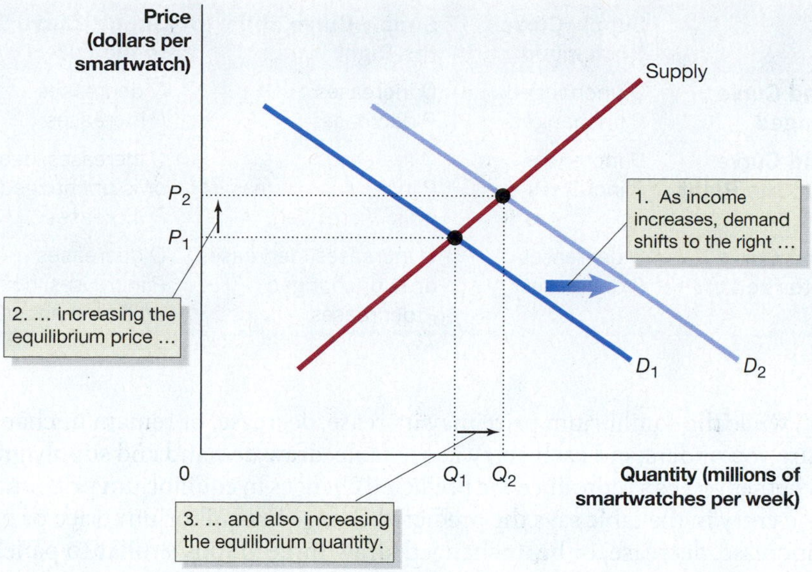

MyEconLab Animation

Figure 3.10

The Effect of an Increase in Demand on Equilibrium

Increases in income will cause the equilibrium price and quantity to rise:

1. Because smartwatches are a normal good, as income increases, the quantity demanded increases at every price, and the market demand curve shifts to the right, from D_1 to D_2, which causes a shortage of smartwatches at the original price, P_1.
2. The equilibrium price rises from P_1 to P_2.
3. The equilibrium quantity rises from Q_1 to Q_2.

increase. The supply curve also often shifts to the right as new firms enter the market and positive technological change occurs. Whether the equilibrium price in a market rises or falls over time depends on whether demand shifts to the right more than does supply. Panel (a) of Figure 3.11 shows that when demand shifts to the right more than supply, the equilibrium price rises, while panel (b) shows that when supply shifts to the right more than demand, the equilibrium price falls.

Table 3.3 on page 92 summarizes all possible combinations of shifts in demand and supply over time and the effects of the shifts on equilibrium price (*P*) and quantity (*Q*). For example, the entry in red in the table shows that if the demand curve shifts to the right and the supply curve also shifts to the right, the equilibrium quantity will

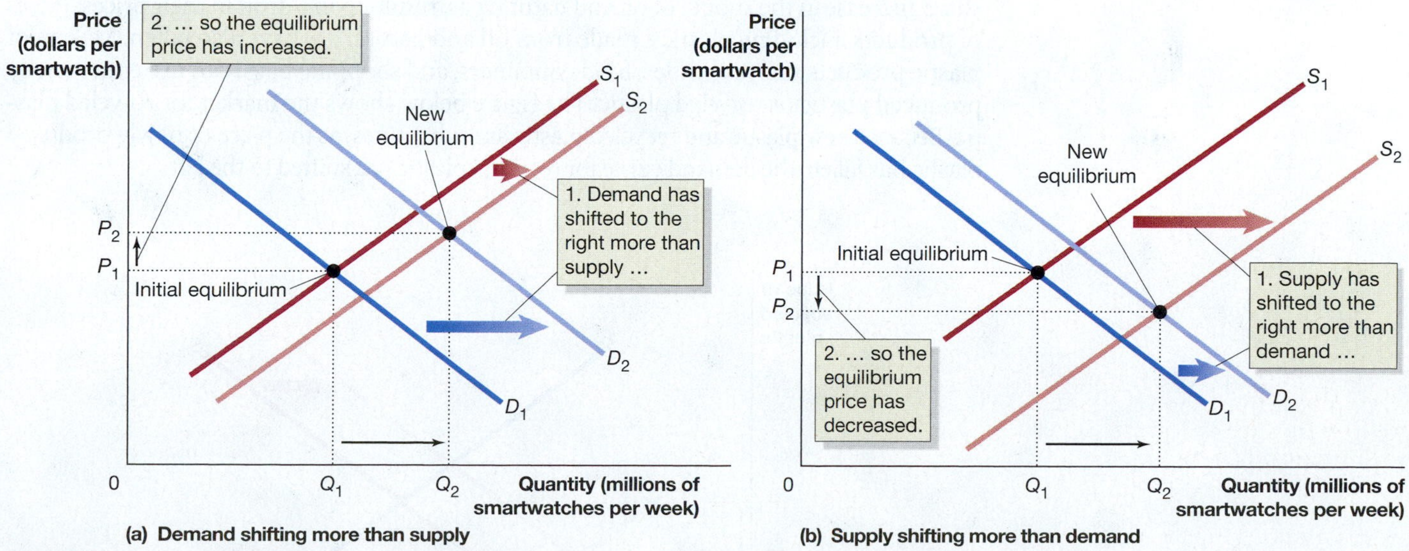

Figure 3.11 Shifts in Demand and Supply over Time

Whether the price of a product rises or falls over time depends on whether demand shifts to the right more than supply.

In panel (a), demand shifts to the right more than supply, and the equilibrium price rises:
1. Demand shifts to the right more than supply.
2. The equilibrium price rises from P_1 to P_2.

In panel (b), supply shifts to the right more than demand, and the equilibrium price falls:
1. Supply shifts to the right more than demand.
2. The equilibrium price falls from P_1 to P_2.

Table 3.3

How Shifts in Demand and Supply Affect Equilibrium Price (*P*) and Quantity (*Q*)

The entry in red shows that if the demand curve shifts to the right and the supply curve also shifts to the right, the equilibrium quantity will increase, while the equilibrium price may increase, decrease, or remain unchanged.

	Supply Curve Unchanged	Supply Curve Shifts to the Right	Supply Curve Shifts to the Left
Demand Curve Unchanged	*Q* unchanged *P* unchanged	*Q* increases *P* decreases	*Q* decreases *P* increases
Demand Curve Shifts to the Right	*Q* increases *P* increases	*Q* increases *P* increases, decreases, or is unchanged	*Q* increases, decreases, or is unchanged *P* increases
Demand Curve Shifts to the Left	*Q* decreases *P* decreases	*Q* increases, decreases, or is unchanged *P* decreases	*Q* decreases *P* increases, decreases, or is unchanged

increase, while the equilibrium price may increase, decrease, or remain unchanged. To make sure you understand each entry in the table, draw demand and supply graphs to check whether you can reproduce the predicted changes in equilibrium price and quantity. If the entry in the table says the predicted change in equilibrium price or quantity can be increase, decrease, or be unchanged, draw three graphs similar to panels (a) or (b) of Figure 3.11, one showing the equilibrium price or quantity increasing, one showing it decreasing, and one showing it unchanged. MyEconLab Concept Check

Making the Connection

MyEconLab Video

Demand and Supply Trashes Plastic Recycling

Cities hire private firms to collect plastic bottles and containers for recycling. Until recently, recycling was profitable for these firms. The profits attracted thieves who would steal the used bottles and containers from recycling bins before the firms could pick them up. By 2015, though, firms no longer had to worry about thieves because they had bigger problems: Falling oil prices were decreasing the demand for recycled plastic at the same time that costs were rising as cities began requiring recycling firms to recycle many more types of plastic.

The development in the United States of hydraulic fracturing ("fracking") has led to a sharp increase in the supply of oil and natural gas, resulting in a drop in their prices. Prices of products, including plastics, made from oil and natural gas have also fallen. Makers of plastic products such as bottles, food containers, and shopping bags, can use either newly produced plastic or recycled plastic. The figure below shows the market for recycled plastic. Because new plastic and recycled plastic are substitutes, as the price of newly produced plastic has fallen, the demand curve for recycled plastic has shifted to the left.

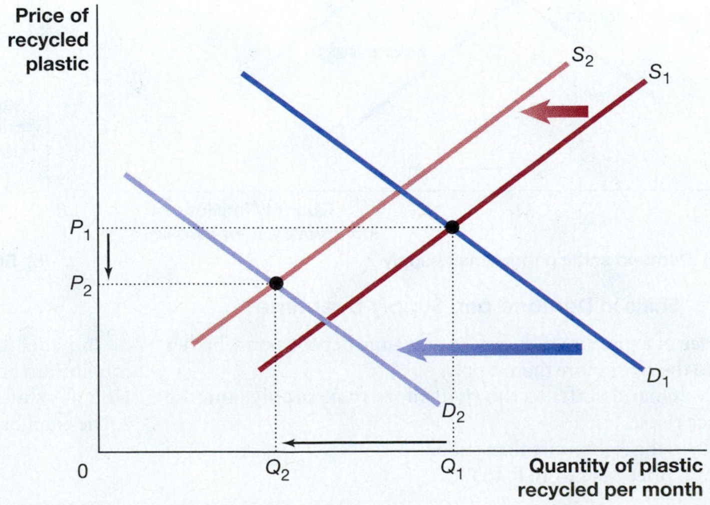

Many cities began plastic recycling by focusing on soda and milk bottles. But as recycling plans have become more ambitious, cities have required recycling firms to pick up nearly all plastics, including products like shopping bags and fast-food containers that are made of lower-quality plastic. It's costly for firms to separate different types of plastic before they can be processed and resold. This increase in cost shifts the supply curve for recycled plastic to the left. The figure shows that the equilibrium price of recycled plastic fell from P_1 to P_2, and the equilibrium quantity fell from Q_1 to Q_2. (Note that if the shift in the supply curve had been greater than the shift in the demand curve, the equilibrium price would have increased.)

As the quantity of recycled plastic declined, a number of recycling firms went out of business. Other firms stored plastic recyclables in the hopes that oil prices would eventually rise, increasing the demand for recyclable plastic.

The effects of these shifts in demand and supply were not good news for the recycling programs in many cities. Plastic recycling had been a steady source of revenue for local governments, but now they faced losing money by having to pay recycling companies to haul away some plastic the companies could no longer sell for a profit. Unless cities were willing to suffer losses or scale back their recycling programs, they would have to hope that higher oil prices might eventually increase the demand for recycled plastic.

The decline in demand for recycled plastic has left some recycling firms stuck with mountains of plastic bottles.

Sources: Georgi Kantchev and Serena Ng, "Recycling Becomes a Tougher Sell as Oil Prices Drop," *Wall Street Journal*, April 5, 2015; Stacey Vanek Smith, "How the Price of Oil Caused a Downturn in the Recycling Business," npr.org, April 3, 2015; and Aaron Elstein, "City's Recycling Is Trashed as Cheap Oil Sinks Plastic," crainsnewyork.com, May 10, 2015.

Your Turn: Test your understanding by doing related problem 4.6 on page 104 at the end of this chapter.

MyEconLab Study Plan

Solved Problem 3.4

MyEconLab Interactive Animation

Can We Predict Changes in the Price and Quantity of Beef?

Whether you like to eat hamburger or roast beef, the source of the meat is a rancher who raises cattle. A news story discussed how years of drought had raised the cost to ranchers of raising cattle. At the same time, consumer tastes have been changing, leading to a decline in the demand for beef. Use demand and supply graphs to illustrate your answers to the following questions:

a. Can we use this information to be certain whether the equilibrium quantity of beef will increase or decrease?

b. Can we use this information to be certain whether the equilibrium price of beef will increase or decrease?

Solving the Problem

Step 1: Review the chapter material. This problem is about how shifts in demand and supply curves affect the equilibrium price, so you may want to review the section "The Effect of Shifts in Demand and Supply over Time," which begins on page 90.

Step 2: Answer part (a) using demand and supply analysis. You are given the information that consumer tastes have changed, leading to a decline in demand for beef. So, the demand curve for beef has shifted to the left. You are also given the information that the cost of raising beef has increased. So, the supply curve for beef has also shifted to the left. The following graph shows both these shifts:

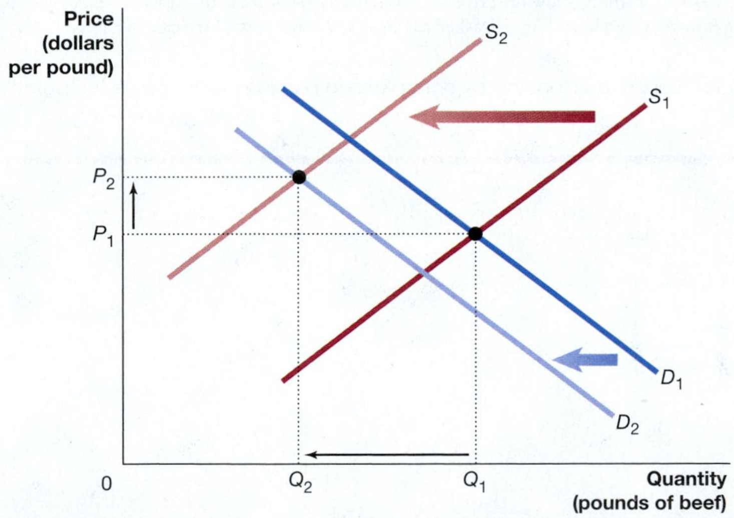

As Table 3.3 on page 92 summarizes, if the demand curve and the supply curve both shift to the left, the equilibrium quantity must decrease. Therefore, we can answer part (a) by stating that we are certain that the equilibrium quantity of beef will decrease.

Step 3: Answer part (b) using demand and supply analysis. The graph we drew in step 2 shows the equilibrium price of beef increasing. But given the information provided, the following graph would also be correct:

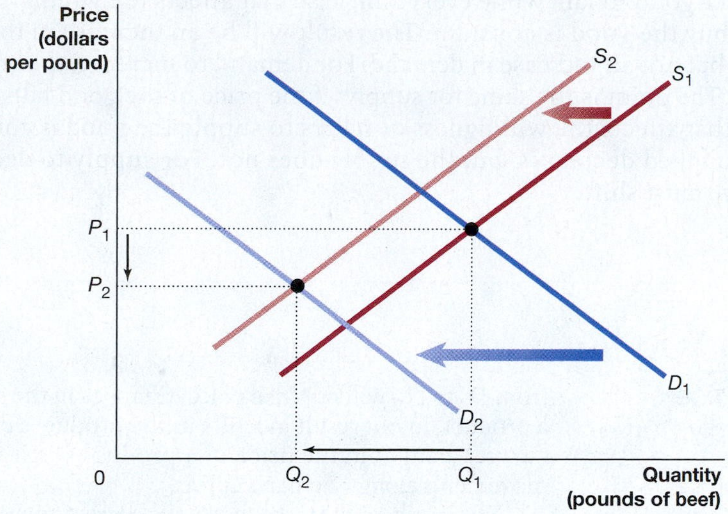

Unlike the graph in step 2, which shows the equilibrium price increasing, this graph shows the equilibrium price decreasing. The uncertainty about whether the equilibrium price will increase or decrease is consistent with what Table 3.3 shows happens when the demand curve and the supply curve both shift to the left. Therefore, the answer to part (b) is that we cannot be certain whether the equilibrium price of beef will increase or decrease.

Extra Credit: During 2013 and 2014, the equilibrium quantity of beef decreased while the equilibrium price of beef increased. We can conclude that *both* the decrease in demand for beef and the decrease in the supply of beef contributed to the decline in beef consumption. That the price of beef rose indicates that the decrease in supply had a larger effect on equilibrium in the beef market than did the decrease in demand.

Sources: Andrew Schneider, "No 'Misteak': High Beef Prices a Boon for Drought-Weary Ranchers," npr.com, November 19, 2014; and U.S. Department of Agriculture data.

Your Turn: For more practice, do related problems 4.7 and 4.8 on page 104 at the end of this chapter.

MyEconLab Study Plan

Shifts in a Curve versus Movements along a Curve

When analyzing markets using demand and supply curves, remember that *when a shift in a demand or supply curve causes a change in equilibrium price, the change in price does not cause a further shift in demand or supply*. Suppose an increase in supply causes the price of a good to fall, while everything else that affects the willingness of consumers to buy the good is constant. The result will be an increase in the quantity demanded but not an increase in demand. For demand to increase, the whole curve must shift. The point is the same for supply: If the price of the good falls but everything else that affects the willingness of sellers to supply the good is constant, the quantity supplied decreases, but the supply does not. For supply to decrease, the whole curve must shift.

MyEconLab Study Plan

MyEconLab Concept Check

Don't Let This Happen to You

Remember: A Change in a Good's Price Does *Not* Cause the Demand or Supply Curve to Shift

Suppose a student is asked to draw a demand and supply graph to illustrate how an increase in the price of oranges would affect the market for apples, with other variables being constant. He draws the graph on the left and explains it as follows: "Because apples and oranges are substitutes, an increase in the price of oranges will cause an initial shift to the right in the demand curve for apples, from D_1 to D_2. However, because this initial shift in the demand curve for apples results in a higher price for apples, P_2, consumers will find apples less desirable, and the demand curve will shift to the left, from D_2 to D_3, resulting in a final equilibrium price of P_3." Do you agree or disagree with the student's analysis?

MyEconLab Study Plan

You should disagree. The student has correctly understood that an increase in the price of oranges will cause the demand curve for apples to shift to the right. But, the second demand curve shift the student describes, from D_2 to D_3, will not take place. Changes in the price of a product do not result in shifts in the product's demand curve. Changes in the price of a product result only in movements along a demand curve.

The graph on the right shows the correct analysis. The increase in the price of oranges causes the demand curve for apples to increase from D_1 to D_2. At the original price, P_1, the increase in demand initially results in a shortage of apples equal to $Q_3 - Q_1$. But, as we have seen, a shortage causes the price to increase until the shortage is eliminated. In this case, the price will rise to P_2, where both the quantity demanded and the quantity supplied are equal to Q_2. Notice that the increase in price causes a decrease in the *quantity demanded*, from Q_3 to Q_2, but does *not* cause a decrease in demand.

Your Turn: Test your understanding by doing related problems 4.13 and 4.14 on page 105 at the end of this chapter.

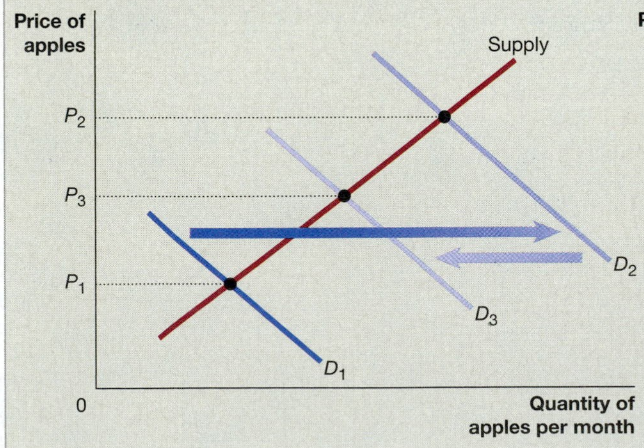

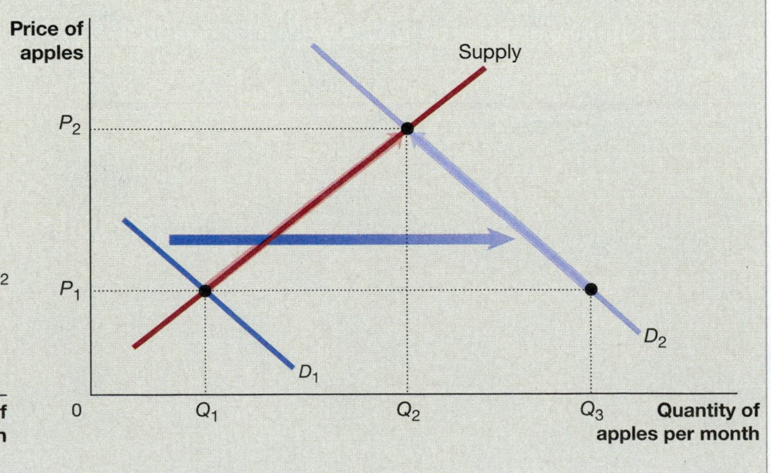

Continued from page 73

Economics in Your Life

Will You Buy a Smartphone or a Smartwatch?

At the beginning of this chapter, we asked you to consider how you might choose between buying a smartwatch and buying a smartphone. There are certain activities, such as watching YouTube or Netflix, that you can do on a smartphone but not on a smartwatch. There are other activities, such as tracking calories burned during a workout, that are probably easier to do on a smartwatch. If you can engage in the activities you like most on either device, then you probably consider the two devices to be close substitutes, and you are likely to buy the one with the lower price. Suppose that you are currently leaning toward buying a smartphone because its price is lower than the price of a comparable smartwatch. If an increase in your income would cause you to change your decision and buy the smartwatch, then the smartphone is an inferior good for you.

Conclusion

The interaction of demand and supply determines market equilibrium. The model of demand and supply is a powerful tool for predicting how changes in the actions of consumers and firms will cause changes in equilibrium prices and quantities. As we have seen in this chapter, we can use the model to analyze markets that do not meet all the requirements for being perfectly competitive. As long as there is intense competition among sellers, the model of demand and supply can often successfully predict changes in prices and quantities. We will use this model in the next chapter to analyze economic efficiency and the results of government-imposed price floors and price ceilings.

Before moving on to Chapter 4, read *An Inside Look* on the next page for a discussion of how the Apple watch has inspired companies to develop complementary products.

AN **INSIDE** LOOK

Apple Watch Inspires Development of Complementary Products

WALL STREET JOURNAL

Don't Underestimate Smartwatches: Wearable Devices Are Poised to Become Central to the Tech Ecosystem

a It's important to understand that like the iPhone before it, the Apple Watch isn't at all what its name would imply. Let's call it what it is: a wrist-top computer.

Just as smartphones have become supercomputers in our pockets, the Apple Watch and its many competitors, including Android-powered devices from Motorola and Samsung Electronics, are poised to become something more. And it is their central place in a larger ecosystem of apps and hardware, rather than any one thing that has been shown off recently, that will make them indispensable. ...

When a company like Google or Apple deliberately creates a place for other companies to sell their own, complementary wares, it is called a platform. Apple, more than Google, has mastered this art, having worked hard to give developers the tools to make apps for its mobile devices, plus a controlled environment in which to profit from them.

Fortunately, we don't have to wait for the Apple Watch and its app store to become available to get a glimpse of where things could be going. We have only to look at what pioneering companies in "wearables" are already working on, and then think about how their products will become a part of—or be absorbed by—the Apple Watch and Android Wear ecosystems.

b "The vision of Sensoria is that the garment is the next ultra personal computer," says Sensoria CEO Davide Vigano. To illustrate his point, he rolls up his pants leg to show me a working prototype of the world's first smart sock.

I know, it sounds ridiculous. But, as he explains, with the help of an iPhone app that visualizes wireless signals sent by indiscernibly thin pressure sensors in the sock, it is good for runners who want to reduce their chance of injury. It is also potentially useful for monitoring the health of the elderly, since changes in gait are surprisingly predictive of other health issues. And yes, the smart sock is washable.

Sensoria also makes a smart bra and smart shirt, both of which can measure heart rate. And here's where things get really interesting: For all makers of wearables, which until recently have been dominated by the glorified pedometers known as fitness bands, fitness applications are just the beginning.

Using a few more of the same sensors it already carries, Sensoria's shirt could measure not just the frequency but the pattern of a wearer's heartbeat, Mr. Vigano tells me. Like the fingerprint sensor on new smartphones, the unique shape of the electrical signals generated by our hearts are a biometric. Add in a payment terminal not dissimilar from the ones that will roll out with Apple Pay, and the wearer of a Sensoria undergarment could soon find herself verifying payment for her next coffee via technology in her bra. ...

During Apple's presentation, Apple Vice President Kevin Lynch announced that BMW has developed an app for the Apple Watch that will allow users to lock and unlock their BMW i-series electric vehicles. And Mr. Martin told me that new bluetooth-enabled locks from companies like Lockitron and Kwikset mean that the moment you walk up to a door while sporting a recognized wearable, it can unlock without a touch. ...

c Wearables won't just appeal to fitness nuts and quantified-self geeks. They will appeal to everyone, because they will be the primary, perhaps even the sole way we identify ourselves to a world full of smart objects.

Established makers of wearables have seen this trend and are already getting in front of it. On the same day that Apple announced its watch, Jawbone, maker of the UP wristband, said that it was opening up its quantified-self software so that anyone could connect it with devices other than the UP—including the Apple Watch.

Or in other words, amid the hype about the Apple Watch being a fitness device, or a timepiece, or a status symbol, it is the applications that Apple and others aren't even talking about, the ones that are thought up by countless developers jumping on board the platform, that will make us wonder how we ever got by without them. ...

Source: Christopher Mims, "Don't Underestimate Smartwatches: Wearable Devices Are Poised to Become Central to the Tech Ecosystem," *Wall Street Journal*, September 14, 2014.

Key Points in the Article

The introduction of the Apple Watch has inspired a number of companies to develop products that can utilize the smartwatch's technology. From the wearable technology of Sensoria's sensor-enhanced clothing to convenience items like Bluetooth-enabled door locks, these complementary products will allow consumers to use their smartwatches in new ways, including monitoring their health, making online purchases, and unlocking their front doors. In our technology-driven society, as more products and apps are developed for use with smartwatches, consumers could come to view these watches as a necessity rather than a luxury, which is what happened with smartphones.

Analyzing the News

(a) Smartwatches like the Apple Watch are a part of the relatively new product category of wearable technology. As with smartphones, a large part of the success of smartwatches will depend on the availability of desirable complementary products. One variable that shifts market demand for a product is the price of related goods. If the price of a complement decreases, market demand for the original product will increase, and if the price of a complement increases, market demand for the original product will decrease.

(b) Smart shirts are wearable technology garments that will sync with smatrwatches, so the two products are used together and are therefore complements. Suppose the figure below illustrates supply and demand for smart shirts. In 2015, the most basic smartwatch model had a price of about $350, and at this price, the demand for smart shirts is represented by demand curve D_1, with an equilibrium price of P_1 and an equilibrium quantity of Q_1. If the price of smartwatches increases, this increase would, holding everything else constant, result in a decrease in demand for smart shirts. The demand curve would shift to the left, from D_1 to D_3, resulting in a decrease in the equilibrium price from P_1 to P_3 and a decrease in the equilibrium quantity from Q_1 to Q_3. If the price of smartwatches declines, the result will be an increase in demand for smart shirts. The demand curve would shift to the right, from D_1 to D_2, resulting in an increase in the equilibrium price from P_1 to P_2 and an increase in the equilibrium quantity from Q_1 to Q_2.

(c) As wearable technology grows in popularity, more firms will enter the market to compete with existing firms. Some of these firms will offer new products, while other firms will produce goods that compete with existing products. Suppose another apparel manufacturer designs a product to compete with smart shirts. This new product would be a substitute for smart shirts and, all else being equal, changes in the price of this new substitute would change the demand for smart shirts. In the figure below, an increase in the price of a substitute would, holding everything else constant, increase the demand for smart shirts. The demand curve would shift to the right, from D_1 to D_2, resulting in an increase in the equilibrium price from P_1 to P_2 and an increase in the equilibrium quantity from Q_1 to Q_2. A decrease in the price of a substitute would have the opposite effect, resulting in a decrease in demand for smart shirts. The demand curve would shift to the left, from D_1 to D_3, resulting in a decrease in the equilibrium price from P_1 to P_3 and a decrease in the equilibrium quantity from Q_1 to Q_3.

Thinking Critically

1. Suppose a technological change allows firms to lower the cost of producing smart shirts. Explain if this change will affect the demand curve for smart shirts. How would this change affect the market for smartwatches?
2. In 2015, smartwatch producers had difficulty filling the orders they received. Draw a demand and supply graph to illustrate this situation. All else equal, what would you expect to happen in this market if this situation persisted into the future, and how would this affect the market for complementary products like smart shirts?

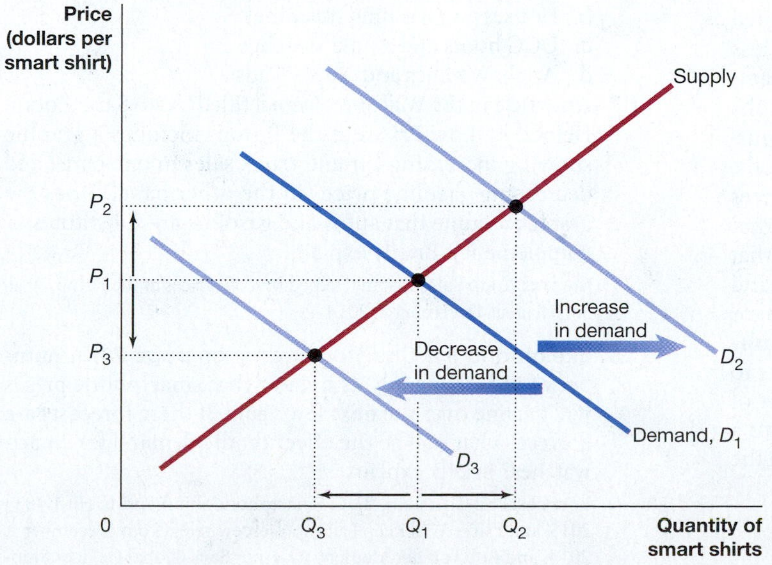

An increase in demand for smart shirts shifts the demand curve to the right. All else equal, equilibrium price and equilibrium quantity both increase. A decrease in demand has the opposite effect.

CHAPTER SUMMARY AND PROBLEMS

Key Terms

Ceteris paribus ("all else equal") condition, p. 76
Competitive market equilibrium, p. 87
Complements, p. 78
Demand curve, p. 74
Demand schedule, p. 74
Demographics, p. 78
Income effect, p. 75
Inferior good, p. 77
Law of demand, p. 75
Law of supply, p. 83
Market demand, p. 74
Market equilibrium, p. 86
Normal good, p. 76
Perfectly competitive market, p. 74
Quantity demanded, p. 74
Quantity supplied, p. 82
Shortage, p. 88
Substitutes, p. 77
Substitution effect, p. 75
Supply curve, p. 83
Supply schedule, p. 83
Surplus, p. 87
Technological change, p. 84

3.1 The Demand Side of the Market, pages 74–82

LEARNING OBJECTIVE: List and describe the variables that influence demand.

Summary

The model of demand and supply is the most powerful tool in economics. The model applies exactly only to **perfectly competitive markets**, where there are many buyers and sellers, all the products sold are identical, and there are no barriers to new sellers entering the market. But the model can also be useful in analyzing markets that don't meet all these requirements. The **quantity demanded** is the amount of a good or service that a consumer is willing and able to purchase at a given price. A **demand schedule** is a table that shows the relationship between the price of a product and the quantity of the product demanded. A **demand curve** is a graph that shows the relationship between the price of a product and the quantity of the product demanded. **Market demand** is the demand by all consumers of a given good or service. The **law of demand** states that ***ceteris paribus***—holding everything else constant—the quantity of a product demanded increases when the price falls and decreases when the price rises. Demand curves slope downward because of the **substitution effect**, which is the change in quantity demanded that results from a price change making one good more or less expensive relative to another good, and the **income effect**, which is the change in quantity demanded of a good that results from the effect of a change in the good's price on consumer purchasing power. Changes in income, the prices of related goods, tastes, population and demographics, and expected future prices all cause the demand curve to shift. **Substitutes** are goods that can be used for the same purpose. **Complements** are goods that are used together. A **normal good** is a good for which demand increases as income increases. An **inferior good** is a good for which demand decreases as income increases. **Demographics** refers to the characteristics of a population with respect to age, race, and gender. A change in demand refers to a shift of the demand curve. A change in quantity demanded refers to a movement along the demand curve as a result of a change in the product's price.

MyEconLab Visit **www.myeconlab.com** to complete these exercises online and get instant feedback.

Review Questions

1.1 What is a demand schedule? What is a demand curve?

1.2 What do economists mean when they use the Latin expression *ceteris paribus*?

1.3 What is the difference between a change in demand and a change in quantity demanded?

1.4 What is the law of demand? Use the substitution effect and the income effect to explain why an increase in the price of a product causes a decrease in the quantity demanded.

1.5 What are the main variables that will cause the demand curve to shift? Give an example of each.

Problems and Applications

1.6 For each of the following pairs of products, briefly explain which are complements, which are substitutes, and which are unrelated.

a. New cars and used cars
b. Houses and washing machines
c. UGG boots and Apple Watches
d. Apple Watches and Apple iPads

1.7 An article in the *Wall Street Journal* titled "Auto Sales Zoom, Helped by Low Prices at the Pump" includes a graphic showing increasing car and truck sales in one panel and decreasing gasoline prices in the other panel. Does the graphic assume that autos and gasoline are substitutes or complements? Briefly explain.

Source: "Auto Sales Zoom, Helped by Low Prices at the Pump," *Wall Street Journal*, December 3, 2014.

1.8 **(Related to the Chapter Opener on page 73)** A number of industry analysts believe that smartphone prices will decline over the next few years. If these forecasts are correct, what will be the effect on the demand for smartwatches? Briefly explain.

Sources: Phil Goldstein, "IDC: Smartphone Shipments to Hit 1.4B in 2015, and Prices Will Keep Falling," fiercewireless.com, December 2, 2014; and Rob van der Meulen, "Gartner Says Global Devices Shipments to Grow 2.8 Percent in 2015," gartner.com, March 19, 2015.

1.9 State whether each of the following events will result in a movement along the demand curve for McDonald's Big Mac hamburgers or whether it will cause the curve to shift. If the demand curve shifts, indicate whether it will shift to the left or to the right and draw a graph to illustrate the shift.

a. The price of Burger King's Whopper hamburger declines.
b. McDonald's distributes coupons for $1.00 off the purchase of a Big Mac.
c. Because of a shortage of potatoes, the price of French fries increases.
d. Fast-food restaurants post nutrition warning labels.
e. The U.S. economy enters a period of rapid growth in incomes.

1.10 Suppose that the following table shows the quantity demanded of UGG boots at five different prices in 2016 and 2017:

	Quantity Demanded (thousands of pairs of boots)	
Price	**2016**	**2017**
$160	5,000	4,000
170	4,500	3,500
180	4,000	3,000
190	3,500	2,500
200	3,000	2,000

Name two different variables that if their values were to change would cause the quantity demanded of UGG boots to change from 2016 to 2017, as indicated in the table.

1.11 Suppose that the curves in the following graph represent two demand curves for traditional chicken wings (basket of six) at Buffalo Wild Wings. What would cause a movement from point *A* to point *B* on D_1? Name two variables that if their values were to change would cause a movement from point *A* to point C.

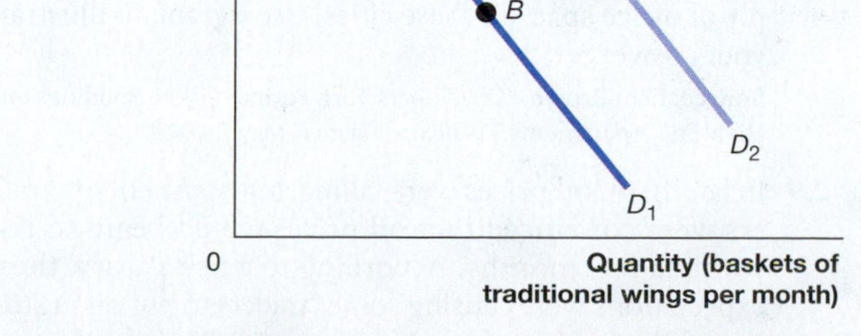

1.12 **(Related to the Making the Connection on page 77)** Both smartwatches and smartphones use applications, or "apps," which are software that consumers can download and use to play games, check stock market prices, and read news stories, among many other activities. Particularly useful apps are called "killer apps." One industry analyst remarked, "There is no one killer app for smartwatches." If the analyst's observation is correct, does it make smartwatches closer or less close substitutes for smartphones? Briefly explain.

Source: Daniel Matte and Kevin McCullagh, "Will Smartwatches Be a Hit?" *Wall Street Journal*, May 10, 2015

1.13 **(Related to the Making the Connection on page 78)** Since 1979, China has had a policy that allows couples to have only one child. This policy has caused a change in the demographics of China. Between 1980 and 2013, the share of the population under age 14 decreased from 36 percent to 18 percent. And, as parents attempt to ensure that the lone child is a son, the number of newborn males relative to females has increased. Choose three goods and explain how the demand for them has been affected by China's one-child policy.

Sources: World Bank, *World Development Indicators*, April 2015; and "China's Family Planning: Illegal Children Will Be Confiscated" and "China's Population: Only and Lonely," *Economist*, July 21, 2011.

1.14 Suppose the following table shows the price of a base model Toyota Prius hybrid and the quantity of Priuses sold for three years. Do these data indicate that the demand curve for Priuses is upward sloping? Briefly explain.

Year	Price	Quantity
2014	$31,880	35,265
2015	30,550	33,250
2016	33,250	36,466

1.15 An article in the *Wall Street Journal* noted that an "increase in the price of oil quickly reduces demand for oil." Do you agree with this statement? Briefly explain.

Source: Josh Zumbrun, "Oil's Plunge Could Help Send Its Price Back Up," *Wall Street Journal*, February 22, 2015.

1.16 A journalist wrote the following about the effects of falling gasoline prices: "With lower prices, demand rises and people consume more." Briefly explain whether you agree with the journalist's analysis.

Source: Jeff Sommer, "Cheaper Oil, Fatter Wallets and a National Opportunity," *New York Times*, December 20, 2014.

1.17 **(Related to the Making the Connection on page 81)** According to an article in the *Wall Street Journal* in 2015, "Apple Inc.'s surging smartphone sales in China may have busted a myth: that many Chinese consumers couldn't, or wouldn't, shell out for an iPhone." The article noted that iPhone sales were growing faster in China than in the United States, Europe, or other high-income countries.

a. Why would sales of iPhones be likely to be growing faster in China than in the United States and in other high-income countries?
b. Why were many industry analysts surprised by Apple's strong sales in China? Would forecasting sales in the United States be easier or harder than forecasting sales in countries such as China? Briefly explain.

Source: Juro Osawan, "China's Middle-Class Propels Apple's iPhone Sales," *Wall Street Journal*, April 28, 2015.

3.2 The Supply Side of the Market, pages 82–86

LEARNING OBJECTIVE: List and describe the variables that influence supply.

Summary

The **quantity supplied** is the amount of a good that a firm is willing and able to supply at a given price. A **supply schedule** is a table that shows the relationship between the price of a product and the quantity of the product supplied. A **supply curve** is a curve that shows the relationship between the price of a product and the quantity of the product supplied. When the price of a product rises, producing the product is more profitable, and a greater amount will be supplied. The **law of supply** states that, holding everything else constant, the quantity of a product supplied increases when the price rises and decreases when the price falls. Changes in the prices of inputs, technology, the prices of related goods in production, the number of firms in a market, and expected future prices all cause the supply curve to shift. **Technological change** is a positive or negative change in the ability of a firm to produce a given level of output with a given quantity of inputs. A change in supply refers to a shift of the supply curve. A change in quantity supplied refers to a movement along the supply curve as a result of a change in the product's price.

MyEconLab Visit **www.myeconlab.com** to complete these exercises online and get instant feedback.

Review Questions

2.1 What is a supply schedule? What is a supply curve?

2.2 What is the difference between a change in supply and a change in the quantity supplied?

2.3 What is the law of supply? What are the main variables that cause a supply curve to shift? Give an example of each.

Problems and Applications

2.4 Briefly explain whether each of the following statements describes a change in supply or a change in quantity supplied.

a. To take advantage of high prices for snow shovels during a snowy winter, Alexander Shovels, Inc., decides to increase output.

b. The success of the Apple Watch leads more firms to begin producing smartwatches.

c. In the six months following the Japanese earthquake and tsunami in 2011, production of automobiles in Japan declined by 20 percent.

2.5 According to a news story about the International Energy Agency, the agency forecast that "the current slide in [oil] prices won't [reduce] global supply." Would a decline in oil prices ever cause a reduction in the supply of oil? Briefly explain.

Source: Sarah Kent, "Plunging Oil Prices Won't Dent Supply in Short Term," *Wall Street Journal*, December 12, 2014.

2.6 Suppose that the curves in the following graph represent two supply curves for traditional chicken wings (basket of six) at Buffalo Wild Wings. What would cause a movement from point *A* to point *B* on S_1? Name two variables that if their values were to change would cause a movement from point *A* to point *C*.

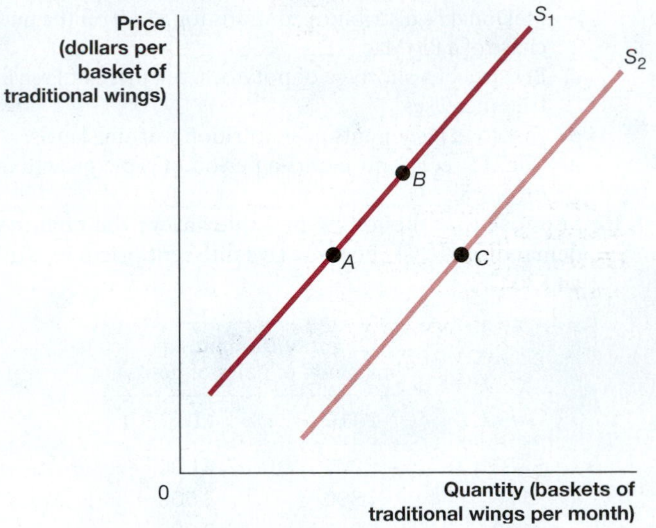

2.7 Suppose that the following table shows the quantity supplied of UGG boots at five different prices in 2016 and 2017:

Price	Quantity Supplied (thousands of pairs of boots) 2016	2017
$160	3,000	2,000
170	3,500	2,500
180	4,000	3,000
190	4,500	3,500
200	5,000	4,500

Name two different variables that if their values were to change would cause the quantity supplied of UGG boots to change from 2016 to 2017, as indicated in the table.

2.8 In most cities, firms that own office buildings can renovate them for use as residential apartments. According to a news story, in many cities "residential rents are surpassing office rents." Predict the effect of this trend on the supply of office space in these cities. Use a graph to illustrate your answer.

Source: Eliot Brown, "Developers Turn Former Office Buildings into High-End Apartments," *Wall Street Journal*, May 7, 2014.

2.9 In late 2014, oil prices were falling, but some energy traders were convinced that oil prices would begin to rise within a few months. According to a news story, these expectations were causing some "traders to put oil in storage while they wait for prices to rise." Predict the effect of this strategy for the supply of oil. Use a graph to illustrate your answer.

Source: Nicole Friedman, "Saudi Arabia's Surprise Move Spurs Quirk for U.S. Oil Futures," *Wall Street Journal*, November 4, 2014.

3.3 Market Equilibrium: Putting Demand and Supply Together, pages 86–89

LEARNING OBJECTIVE: Use a graph to illustrate market equilibrium.

Summary

Market equilibrium occurs where the demand curve intersects the supply curve. A **competitive market equilibrium** has a market equilibrium with many buyers and sellers. Only at this point is the quantity demanded equal to the quantity supplied. Prices above equilibrium result in **surpluses**, with the quantity supplied being greater than the quantity demanded. Surpluses cause the market price to fall. Prices below equilibrium result in **shortages**, with the quantity demanded being greater than the quantity supplied. Shortages cause the market price to rise.

MyEconLab Visit **www.myeconlab.com** to complete these exercises online and get instant feedback.

Review Questions

3.1 What do economists mean by *market equilibrium*?

3.2 What do economists mean by *shortage*? By *surplus*?

3.3 What happens in a market if the current price is above the equilibrium price? What happens if the current price is below the equilibrium price?

Problems and Applications

3.4 Briefly explain whether you agree with the following statement: "When there is a shortage of a good, consumers eventually give up trying to buy it, so the demand for the good declines, and the price falls until the market is finally in equilibrium."

3.5 **(Related to Solved Problem 3.3 on page 88)** In *The Wealth of Nations*, Adam Smith discussed what has come to be known as the "diamond and water paradox":

> Nothing is more useful than water: but it will purchase scarce anything; scarce anything can be had in exchange for it. A diamond, on the contrary, has scarce any value in use; but a very great quantity of other goods may frequently be had in exchange for it.

Graph the market for diamonds and the market for water. Show how it is possible for the price of water to be much lower than the price of diamonds, even though the demand for water is much greater than the demand for diamonds.

Source: Adam Smith, *An Inquiry into the Nature and Causes of the Wealth of Nations*, Vol. I, Oxford, UK: Oxford University Press, 1976; original edition, 1776.

3.6 **(Related to Solved Problem 3.3 on page 88)** An article discusses the market for autographs by Mickey Mantle, the superstar center fielder for the New York Yankees during the 1950s and 1960s: "At card shows, golf outings, charity dinners, Mr. Mantle signed his name over and over." One expert on sport autographs is quoted as saying, "He was a real good signer. … He is not rare." Yet the article quotes another expert as saying, "Mr. Mantle's autograph ranks No. 3 of most-popular autographs, behind Babe Ruth and Muhammad Ali." A baseball signed by Mantle is likely to sell for the relatively high price of $250 to $400. By contrast, baseballs signed by Whitey Ford, a teammate of Mantle's on the Yankees, typically sell for less than $150. Use one graph to show both the demand and supply for autographs by Whitey Ford and the demand and supply for autographs by Mickey Mantle. Show how it is possible for the price of Mantle's autographs to be higher than the price of Ford's autographs, even though the supply of Mantle autographs is larger than the supply of Ford autographs.

Source: Beth DeCarbo, "Mantle Autographs Not Rare, but Collectors Don't Care," *Wall Street Journal*, August 4, 2008.

3.7 **(Related to Solved Problem 3.3 on page 88)** Comic book fans eagerly compete to buy copies of *Amazing Fantasy* No. 15, which contains the first appearance of the superhero Spider-Man. At the same time the publisher printed copies of the comic for the U.S. market, with the price printed on the cover in cents, it printed copies for the U.K. market, with the price printed on the cover in British pence. About 10 times as many U.S. copies of *Amazing Fantasy* No. 15 have survived as U.K. copies. Yet in auctions that occurred at about the same time, a U.S. copy sold for $29,000, while a U.K. copy in the same condition sold for only $10,755. Use a demand and supply graph to explain how the U.S. version of the comic has a higher price than the U.K. version, even though the supply of the U.S. version is so much greater than the supply of the U.K. version.

Source: Auction price data from *GPA Analysis for CGC Comics*, www.comics.gpanalysis.com.

3.8 If a market is in equilibrium, is it necessarily true that all buyers and sellers are satisfied with the market price? Briefly explain.

3.9 A news story from 2015 about the oil market stated, "the global glut of crude that has hit [oil] prices is starting to shrink."

a. What does the article mean by a "glut"? What does a glut imply about the quantity demanded of oil relative to the quantity supplied?

b. What would be the effect of the glut on oil prices?

c. Briefly explain what would make the glut start to shrink.

Source: Christopher Harder, "Investors Take Closer Look at Output," *Wall Street Journal*, May 18, 2015.

3.4 The Effect of Demand and Supply Shifts on Equilibrium, pages 90–96

LEARNING OBJECTIVE: Use demand and supply graphs to predict changes in prices and quantities.

Summary

In most markets, demand and supply curves shift frequently, causing changes in equilibrium prices and quantities. Over time, if demand increases more than supply, equilibrium price will rise. If supply increases more than demand, equilibrium price will fall.

MyEconLab Visit **www.myeconlab.com** to complete these exercises online and get instant feedback.

Review Questions

4.1 Draw a demand and supply graph to show the effect on the equilibrium price in a market in the following situations.
  a. The demand curve shifts to the right.
  b. The supply curve shifts to the left.

4.2 If, over time, the demand curve for a product shifts to the right more than the supply curve does, what will happen to the equilibrium price? What will happen to the equilibrium price if the supply curve shifts to the right more than the demand curve? For each case, draw a demand and supply graph to illustrate your answer.

Problems and Applications

4.3 **(Related to the Chapter Opener on page 73)** Suppose the demand for smartwatches increases rapidly during 2016. At the same time, six more firms begin producing smartwatches. A student remarks that, because of these events, we can't know for certain whether the price of smartwatches will rise or fall. Briefly explain whether you agree. Be sure to include a demand and supply graph of the market for smartwatches to illustrate your answer.

4.4 According to an article in the *Wall Street Journal*, a decline in demand for ethanol, which is made from corn, has reduced the demand for corn. Many U.S. farmers can use the same acreage to grow either corn or soybeans. Use a demand and supply graph to analyze the effect on the equilibrium price of soybeans resulting from a fall in the demand for corn.

Source: Jesse Newman, "Soybeans and Corn Locked in Food Fight," *Wall Street Journal*, March 29, 2015.

4.5 According to an article in the *Wall Street Journal*, the demand for orange juice is declining in the United States "as newer entrants in the beverage aisle, including more-exotic fruit juices, such as pomegranate, energy drinks and ready-to-drink coffee, have grabbed a greater share of the market." At the same time, orange juice production has been declining as bacterial infections reduce the quantity of fruit that orange trees can produce. The article notes that despite the decline in the demand for orange juice, the price of orange juice might increase. Use a demand and supply graph of the orange juice market to illustrate how the price of orange juice might increase as a result of these events. Be sure that all curves on your graphs are properly labeled, that you show any shifts in those curves, and that you indicate the initial and final equilibrium points.

Source: Alexandra Wexler, "U.S. Orange-Juice Sales Fall to Record Low," *Wall Street Journal*, August 18, 2014.

4.6 **(Related to the Making the Connection on page 92)** Suppose that oil prices sharply increase, while more cities pass laws banning the use of plastic bags at stores. Use a demand and supply graph to illustrate your answers to the following questions.
  a. Can we use this information to be certain whether the equilibrium price of recycled plastic will increase or decrease?
  b. Can we use this information to be certain whether the equilibrium quantity of recycled plastic will increase or decrease?

4.7 **(Related to Solved Problem 3.4 on page 93)** The demand for watermelons is highest during summer and lowest during winter. Yet watermelon prices are normally lower in summer than in winter. Use a demand and supply graph to demonstrate how this is possible. Be sure to carefully label the curves in your graph and to clearly indicate the equilibrium summer price and the equilibrium winter price.

4.8 **(Related to Solved Problem 3.4 on page 93)** According to one observer of the lobster market: "After Labor Day, when the vacationers have gone home, the lobstermen usually have a month or more of good fishing conditions, except for the occasional hurricane." Use a demand and supply graph to explain whether lobster prices are likely to be higher or lower during the fall than during the summer.

Source: Jay Harlow, "Lobster: An Affordable Luxury," www.Sallybernstein.com.

4.9 Years ago, an apple producer argued that the United States should enact a tariff, or a tax, on imports of bananas. His reasoning was that "the enormous imports of cheap bananas into the United States tend to curtail the domestic consumption of fresh fruits produced in the United States."
  a. Was the apple producer assuming that apples and bananas are substitutes or complements? Briefly explain.
  b. If a tariff on bananas acts as an increase in the cost of supplying bananas in the United States, use two demand and supply graphs to show the effects of the apple producer's proposal. One graph should show the effect on the banana market in the United States, and the other graph should show the effect on the apple market in the United States. Be sure to label the change in equilibrium price and quantity in each market and any shifts in the demand and supply curves.

Source: Douglas A. Irwin, *Peddling Protectionism: Smoot-Hawley and the Great Depression*, Princeton, NJ: Princeton University Press, 2011, p. 22.

4.10 According to one news story, the cost of producing 4K televisions has been declining. According to a second story, many people have switched from watching programs on television sets to watching them on smartphones, tablets, or laptops. After reading these news stories, a student argues: "From this information, we know that the price of 4K televisions will fall, but we don't know whether the quantity of television sets sold will increase or decrease." Is the student's analysis correct? Illustrate your answer with a demand and supply graph.

Sources: Geoffrey A. Fowler, "Vizio Fixes Flaw in Cheap 4K TV ... as Competition Heats Up," *Wall Street Journal*, January 13, 2015; and Suzanne Vranica and Shalini Ramachandran, "Streaming Services Hammer Cable TV Ratings," *Wall Street Journal*, March 10, 2015.

4.11 Historically, the production of many perishable foods, such as dairy products, was highly seasonal. As the supply of those products fluctuated, prices tended to fluctuate tremendously—typically by 25 to 50 percent or more—over the course of the year. One effect of mechanical refrigeration, which was commercialized on a large scale in the last decade of the nineteenth century, was that suppliers could store perishable foods from one season to the next. Economists have estimated that as a result of refrigerated storage, wholesale prices rose by roughly 10 percent during peak supply periods, while they fell by almost the same amount during the off season. Use a demand and supply graph for each season to illustrate how refrigeration affected the market for perishable food.

Source: Lee A. Craig, Barry Goodwin, and Thomas Grennes, "The Effect of Mechanical Refrigeration on Nutrition in the U.S.," *Social Science History*, Vol. 28, No. 2, Summer 2004, pp. 327–328.

4.12 If the equilibrium price and quantity of a product were \$100 and 1,000 units per month in 2015 and \$150 and 800 units per month in 2016, did this product experience a larger shift in its demand curve or in its supply curve from 2015 to 2016? Briefly explain.

4.13 **(Related to the Don't Let This Happen to You on page 95)** A student writes the following: "Increased production leads to a lower price, which in turn increases demand." Do you agree with his reasoning? Briefly explain.

4.14 **(Related to the Don't Let This Happen to You on page 95)** A student was asked to draw a demand and supply graph to illustrate the effect on the market for smartwatches of a fall in the price of displays used in smartwatches, holding everything else constant. She drew the following graph and explained it as follows:

> Displays are an input to smartwatches, so a fall in the price of displays will cause the supply curve for smartwatches to shift to the right

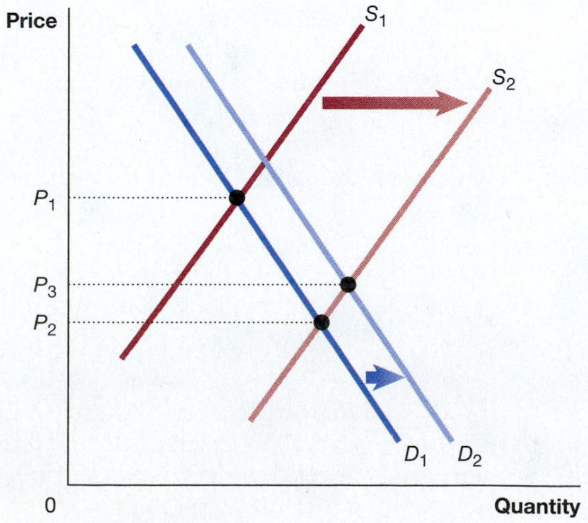

> (from S_1 to S_2). Because this shift in the supply curve results in a lower price (P_2), consumers will want to buy more smartwatches, and the demand curve will shift to the right (from D_1 to D_2). We know that more smartwatches will be sold, but we can't be sure whether the price of smartwatches will rise or fall. That depends on whether the supply curve or the demand curve has shifted farther to the right. I assume that the effect on supply is greater than the effect on demand, so I show the final equilibrium price (P_3) as being lower than the initial equilibrium price (P_1).

Explain whether you agree with the student's analysis. Be careful to explain exactly what—if anything—you find wrong with her analysis.

4.15 The following four graphs represent four market scenarios, each of which would cause either a movement along the supply curve for Pepsi or a shift of the supply curve. Match each scenario with the appropriate graph.

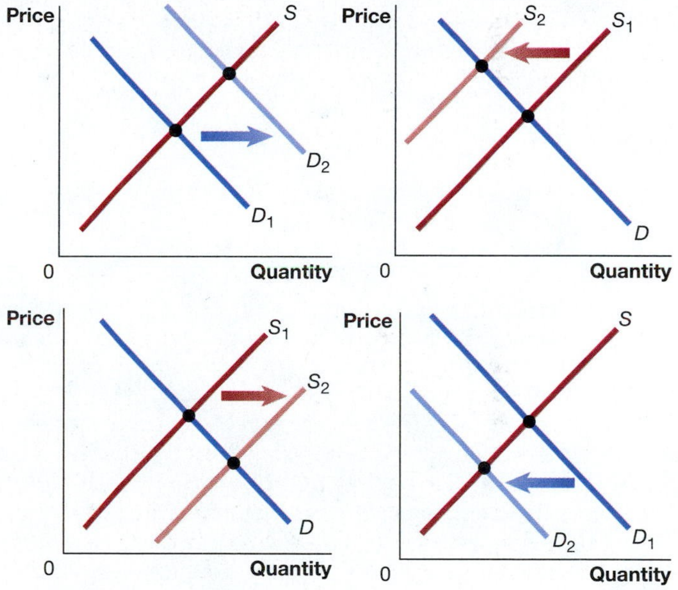

a. A decrease in the supply of Coke
b. A drop in the average household income in the United States from \$52,000 to \$50,000
c. An improvement in soft drink bottling technology
d. An increase in the prices of sugar and high-fructose corn syrup

4.16 Proposals have been made to increase government regulation of firms providing childcare services by, for instance, setting education requirements for childcare workers. Suppose that these regulations increase the quality of childcare and cause the demand for childcare services to increase. At the same time, assume that complying with the new government regulations increases the costs of firms providing childcare services. Draw a demand and supply graph to illustrate the effects of these changes in the market for childcare services. Briefly explain whether the total quantity of childcare services purchased will increase or decrease as a result of the regulations.

4.17 Which of the following graphs best represents what happens in the market for hotel rooms at a ski resort during the winter? Briefly explain. From the graph that you picked, what would be the result during the winter if hotel rates stayed at their summer level?

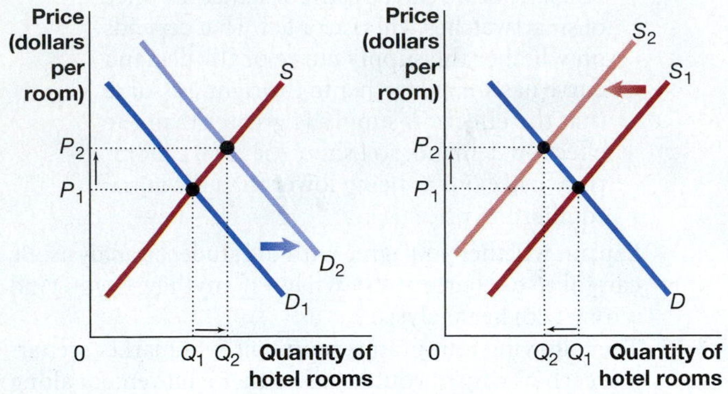

4.18 The following graphs show the supply and demand curves for two markets. One of the markets is for Tesla automobiles, and the other is for a cancer-fighting drug, without which lung cancer patients will die. Briefly explain which graph most likely represents which market.

CHAPTER

4

Economic Efficiency, Government Price Setting, and Taxes

Chapter Outline and Learning Objectives

The Sharing Economy, Phone Apps, and Rent Control

The role of markets is to bring together buyers and sellers. A market can be a physical place, like a retail mall, or a virtual place, like eBay. What if you need to rent an apartment or a bicycle for only a day or a week? Internet startup companies have created rental markets for short-term use of products including apartments, cars, boats, and bicycles. For example, people who download the Airbnb app can search for short-term room rentals in 30,000 cities in 192 countries. The suppliers in this market are typically people who want to earn extra money by renting their house, apartment, or sometimes just a single room for a few days. The *Economist* magazine has referred to the rapid increase in the number of people using peer-to-peer rental sites as the rise of the "sharing economy."

More than 25 million people had rented rooms on Airbnb by 2015. Despite this success, Airbnb has run into problems, particularly in cities that have rent control regulations. In New York, San Francisco, Los Angeles, and nearly 200 smaller cities in the United States, apartments are subject to rent control by the local government. Rent control puts a legal limit on the rent that landlords can charge for an apartment. Supporters of rent control argue that it is necessary to preserve affordable apartments in cities where equilibrium market rents would be above what middle- and lower-income people are willing and able to pay. But, as we will see in this chapter, rent controls cause a shortage of apartments and give people an incentive to list their apartments on sites like Airbnb at rents far above the controlled rents. In San Francisco, landlords complain that some high-income renters have moved out of the city but have kept their rent-controlled apartments in order to rent them using the apartment-sharing sites. In New York, where it is against the law to rent a room in an apartment for less than 30 days, officials struggled with how to enforce the rules despite Airbnb's great popularity.

Some observers argue that the difficulty governments face regulating peer-to-peer rental sites will make it impossible to enforce rent control rules. In San Francisco, where an estimated 1,300 people a night were renting rooms through Airbnb, supporters and opponents were battling over attempts to further regulate the site, including imposing fines of $1,000 a day on anyone violating existing rental regulations.

AN INSIDE LOOK AT POLICY on **page 132** explores why government officials in Malibu, California, imposed a tax on short-term rentals of apartments booked through Airbnb.

Sources: "The Rise of the Sharing Economy," *Economist*, March 9, 2013; Ronda Kaysen, "What's Up Next in New York?" *New York Times*, December 26, 2014; Carolyn Said, "Airbnb Fights Back as Pending Laws Seek to Curtail Home Stays," sfgate.com, April 19, 2015; and C.W. Nevius, "Rent Control Sometimes Benefitting the Rich," *San Francisco Chronicle*, June 16, 2012.

Economics in Your Life

Does Rent Control Make It Easier for You to Find an Affordable Apartment?

Suppose you have job offers in two cities. One factor in deciding which job to accept is whether you can find an affordable apartment. If one city has rent control, are you more likely to find an affordable apartment in that city, or would you be better off looking for an apartment in a city without rent control? As you read the chapter, try to answer this question. You can check your answer against the one we provide on **page 131** at the end of this chapter.

In a competitive market, the price adjusts to ensure that the quantity demanded equals the quantity supplied. Stated another way, in equilibrium, every consumer willing to pay the market price is able to buy as much of the product as the consumer wants, and every firm willing to accept the market price can sell as much as it wants. Consumers would naturally prefer to pay a lower price, and sellers would prefer to receive a higher price. Normally, consumers and firms have no choice but to accept the equilibrium price if they wish to participate in the market.

Occasionally, however, consumers or firms persuade the government to intervene to try to lower or raise the market price of a good or service:

Price ceiling A legally determined maximum price that sellers may charge.

Price floor A legally determined minimum price that sellers may receive.

- Consumers sometimes succeed in having the government impose a **price ceiling**, which is a legally determined maximum price that sellers may charge. Rent control is an example of a price ceiling.
- Firms sometimes succeed in having the government impose a **price floor**, which is a legally determined minimum price that sellers may receive. In markets for farm products such as milk, the government has been setting price floors that are above the equilibrium market price since the 1930s.

Another way the government intervenes in markets is by imposing taxes. The government relies on the revenue raised from taxes to finance its operations. But taxes also affect the decisions that consumers and firms make.

Each of these government interventions has predictable negative consequences for economic efficiency. Economists have developed the concepts of *consumer surplus, producer surplus,* and *deadweight loss* to help policymakers and voters analyze the economic effects of price ceilings, price floors, and taxes.

4.1 Consumer Surplus and Producer Surplus

LEARNING OBJECTIVE: Distinguish between the concepts of consumer surplus and producer surplus.

Consumer surplus measures the dollar benefit consumers receive from buying goods or services in a particular market. Producer surplus measures the dollar benefit firms receive from selling goods or services in a particular market. Economic surplus in a market is the sum of consumer surplus and producer surplus. As we will see, *when the government imposes a price ceiling or a price floor, the amount of economic surplus in a market is reduced*; in other words, price ceilings and price floors reduce the total benefit to consumers and firms from buying and selling in a market. To understand why this is true, we need to understand how consumer surplus and producer surplus are determined.

Consumer Surplus

Consumer surplus The difference between the highest price a consumer is willing to pay for a good or service and the actual price the consumer pays.

Consumer surplus is the difference between the highest price a consumer is willing to pay for a good or service and the actual price the consumer pays. Suppose you are in Walmart, and you see a DVD of *Star Wars: The Force Awakens* on the shelf. The DVD doesn't have a price sticker, so you take it to the register to check the price. As you walk to the register, you think to yourself that $18 is the highest price you would be willing to pay. At the register, you find out that the price is actually $12, so you buy the DVD. Your consumer surplus in this example is $6: the difference between the $18 you were willing to pay and the $12 you actually paid.

Marginal benefit The additional benefit to a consumer from consuming one more unit of a good or service.

We can use the demand curve to measure the total consumer surplus in a market. Demand curves show the willingness of consumers to purchase a product at different prices. Consumers are willing to purchase a product up to the point where the marginal benefit of consuming a product is equal to its price. The **marginal benefit** is the additional benefit to a consumer from consuming one more unit of a good or service. As a simple example, suppose there are only four consumers in the market for chai tea: Theresa, Tom, Terri, and Tim. Because these four consumers have different tastes for

Consumer	Highest Price Willing to Pay
Theresa	$6
Tom	5
Terri	4
Tim	3

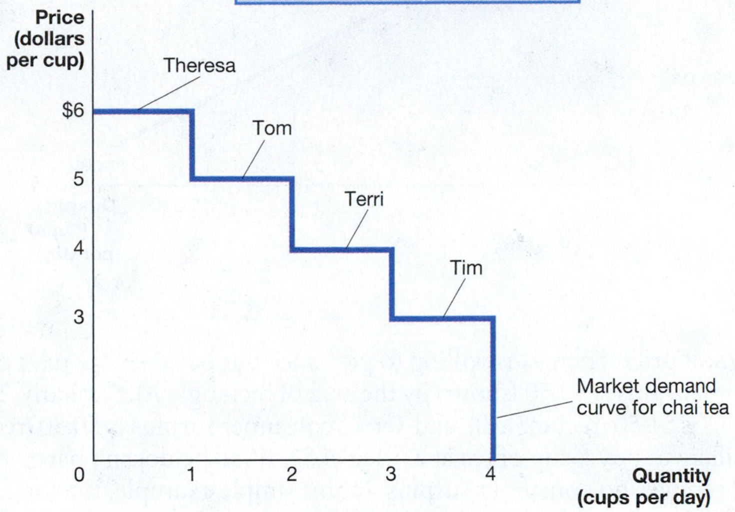

MyEconLab Animation

Figure 4.1

Deriving the Demand Curve for Chai Tea

With four consumers in the market for chai tea, the demand curve is determined by the highest price each consumer is willing to pay. At prices above $6, no tea is sold because $6 is the highest price any consumer is willing to pay. At prices of $3 and below, each of the four consumers is willing to buy a cup of tea.

tea and different incomes, the marginal benefit each of them receives from consuming a cup of tea will be different. Therefore, the highest price each is willing to pay for a cup of tea is also different. In Figure 4.1, the information from the table is used to construct a demand curve for chai tea. At prices above $6 per cup, no tea is sold because $6 is the highest price any of the consumers is willing to pay. At a price of $5, both Theresa and Tom are willing to buy tea, so two cups are sold. At prices of $3 and below, all four consumers are willing to buy tea, and four cups are sold.

Suppose the market price of tea is $3.50 per cup. As Figure 4.2 shows, the demand curve allows us to calculate the total consumer surplus in this market. Panel (a) shows

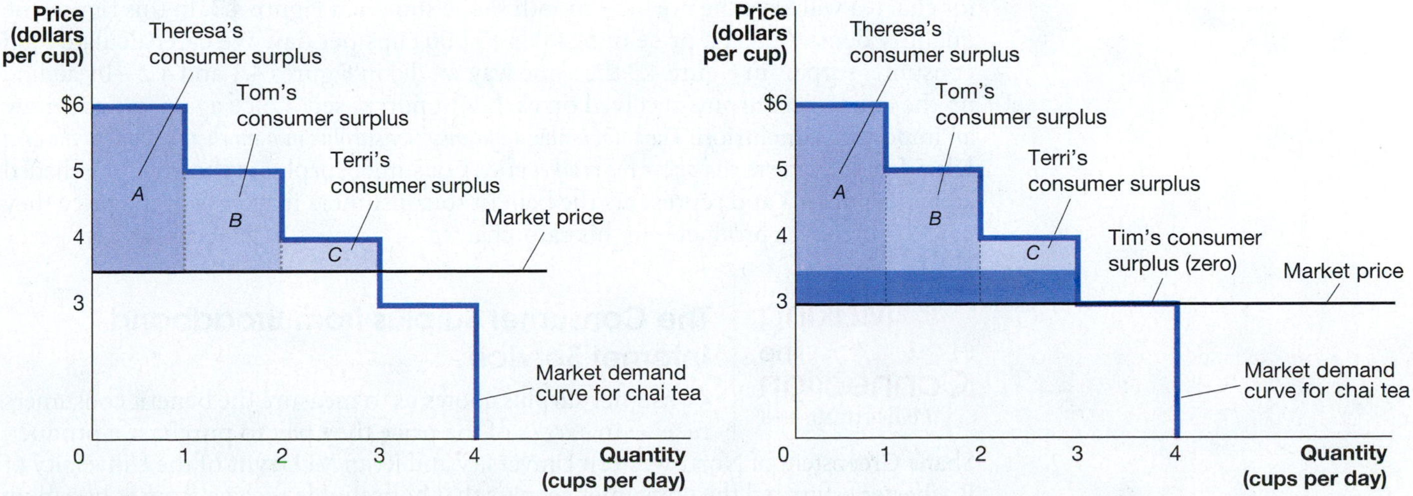

(a) Consumer surplus with a market price of $3.50

(b) Consumer surplus with a market price of $3.00

MyEconLab Animation

Figure 4.2 Measuring Consumer Surplus

Panel (a) shows the consumer surplus for Theresa, Tom, and Terri when the price of tea is $3.50 per cup. Theresa's consumer surplus is equal to the area of rectangle *A* and is the difference between the highest price she would pay—which is $6—and the market price of $3.50. Tom's consumer surplus is equal to the area of rectangle *B*, and Terri's consumer surplus is equal to the area of rectangle *C*. Total consumer surplus in this market is equal to the sum of the areas of rectangles *A*, *B*, and *C*, or the total area below the demand curve and above the market price. In panel (b), consumer surplus increases by the dark blue area as the market price declines from $3.50 to $3.00.

MyEconLab Animation

Figure 4.3

Total Consumer Surplus in the Market for Chai Tea

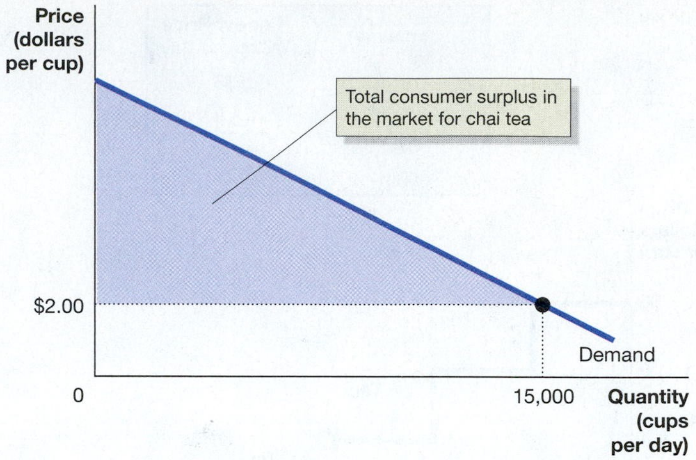

The demand curve shows that most buyers of chai tea would have been willing to pay more than the market price of $2.00. For each buyer, consumer surplus is equal to the difference between the highest price he or she is willing to pay and the market price actually paid. Therefore, the total amount of consumer surplus in the market for chai tea is equal to the area below the demand curve and above the market price. Consumer surplus represents the benefit to consumers in excess of the price they paid to purchase a product.

that the highest price Theresa is willing to pay is $6, but because she pays only $3.50, her consumer surplus is $2.50 (shown by the area of rectangle *A*). Similarly, Tom's consumer surplus is $1.50 (rectangle *B*), and Terri's consumer surplus is $0.50 (rectangle *C*). Tim is unwilling to buy a cup of tea at a price of $3.50, so he doesn't participate in this market and receives no consumer surplus. In this simple example, the total consumer surplus is equal to $2.50 + $1.50 + $0.50 = $4.50 (or the sum of the areas of rectangles *A*, *B*, and *C*). Panel (b) shows that a lower price will increase consumer surplus. If the price of tea falls from $3.50 per cup to $3.00, Theresa, Tom, and Terri each receive $0.50 more in consumer surplus (shown by the dark blue areas), so the total consumer surplus in the market rises to $6.00. Tim now buys a cup of tea but doesn't receive any consumer surplus because the price is equal to the highest price he is willing to pay. In fact, Tim is indifferent between buying the cup or not—his well-being is the same either way.

The market demand curves shown in Figures 4.1 and 4.2 do not look like the typical smooth demand curve because in this case we have only a small number of consumers, each consuming a single cup of tea. With many consumers, the market demand curve for chai tea will have the normal smooth shape shown in Figure 4.3. In this figure, the quantity demanded at a price of $2.00 is 15,000 cups per day. We can calculate total consumer surplus in Figure 4.3 the same way we did in Figures 4.1 and 4.2—by adding up the consumer surplus received on each unit purchased. Once again, we can draw an important conclusion: *The total amount of consumer surplus in a market is equal to the area below the demand curve and above the market price.* Consumer surplus is shown as the shaded area in Figure 4.3 and represents the benefit to consumers in excess of the price they paid to purchase a product—in this case, chai tea. MyEconLab Concept Check

Making the Connection

MyEconLab Video

The Consumer Surplus from Broadband Internet Service

Consumer surplus allows us to measure the benefit consumers receive in excess of the price they pay to purchase a product. Shane Greenstein of Northwestern University and Ryan McDevitt of the University of Rochester estimated the consumer surplus that households receive from subscribing to broadband Internet service. To carry out the analysis, they estimated the demand curve for broadband Internet service and then computed the shaded area shown in the following graph.

In the year they analyzed, 47 million consumers paid an average price of $36 per month to subscribe to a broadband Internet service. The demand curve shows the marginal benefit consumers receive from subscribing to a broadband Internet service rather than using dialup or doing without access to the Internet. The area below the demand curve and above the $36 price line represents the difference between the price consumers

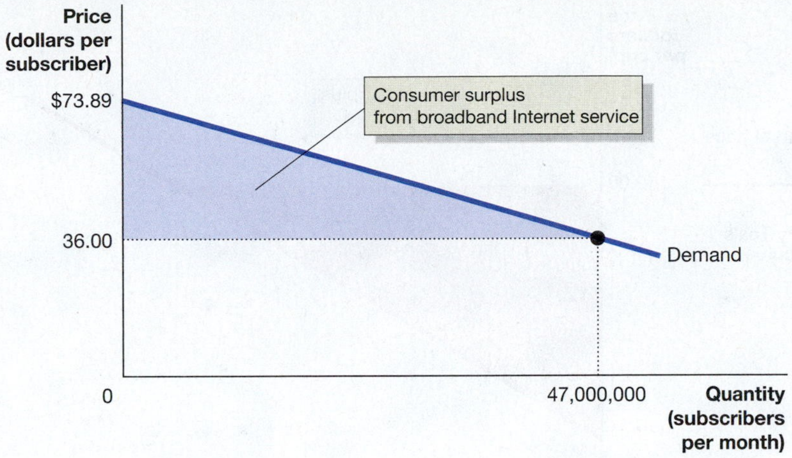

would have paid rather than do without broadband service and the $36 they did pay. The shaded area on the graph represents the total consumer surplus in the market for broadband Internet service. Greenstein and McDevitt estimate that the value of this area is $890.4 million. This value is one month's benefit to the consumers who subscribe to a broadband Internet service.

Sources: Shane Greenstein and Ryan C. McDevitt, "The Broadband Bonus: Estimating Broadband Internet's Economic Value," *Telecommunications Policy*, Vol. 35, No. 7, August 2011, pp. 617–632; and Shane Greenstein, "Measuring Consumer Surplus Online," *Economist*, March 11, 2013.

Your Turn: For more practice do related problem 1.13 on page 135 at the end of this chapter.

MyEconLab Study Plan

Producer Surplus

Just as demand curves show the willingness of consumers to buy a product at different prices, supply curves show the willingness of firms to supply a product at different prices. The willingness to supply a product depends on the cost of producing it. Firms will supply an additional unit of a product only if they receive a price equal to the additional cost of producing that unit. **Marginal cost** is the additional cost to a firm of producing one more unit of a good or service. Consider the marginal cost to the firm Heavenly Tea of producing one more cup of tea: In this case, the marginal cost includes the ingredients to make the tea and the wages paid to the worker preparing the tea. Often, the marginal cost of producing a good increases as more of the good is produced during a given period of time. Increasing marginal cost is the key reason that supply curves are upward sloping.

Marginal cost The additional cost to a firm of producing one more unit of a good or service.

Panel (a) of Figure 4.4 shows Heavenly Tea's producer surplus. For simplicity, we show Heavenly producing only a small quantity of tea. The figure shows that Heavenly's marginal cost of producing the first cup of tea is $1.25, its marginal cost of producing the second cup is $1.50, and so on. The marginal cost of each cup of tea is the lowest price Heavenly is willing to accept to supply that cup. The supply curve, then, is also a marginal cost curve. Suppose the market price of tea is $2.00 per cup. On the first cup of tea, the price is $0.75 higher than the lowest price that Heavenly is willing to accept. **Producer surplus** is the difference between the lowest price a firm would be willing to accept for a good or service and the price it actually receives. Therefore, Heavenly's producer surplus on the first cup is $0.75 (shown by the area of rectangle *A*), its producer surplus on the second cup is $0.50 (rectangle *B*), and its producer surplus on the third cup is $0.25 (rectangle *C*). Heavenly will not be willing to supply the fourth cup because the marginal cost of producing it is greater than the market price. Heavenly Tea's total producer surplus is equal to $0.75 + $0.50 + $0.25 = $1.50 (or the sum of the areas of rectangles *A*, *B*, and *C*). A higher price will increase producer surplus. For example, if the market price of chai tea rises from $2.00 to $2.25, Heavenly Tea's producer surplus

Producer surplus The difference between the lowest price a firm would be willing to accept for a good or service and the price it actually receives.

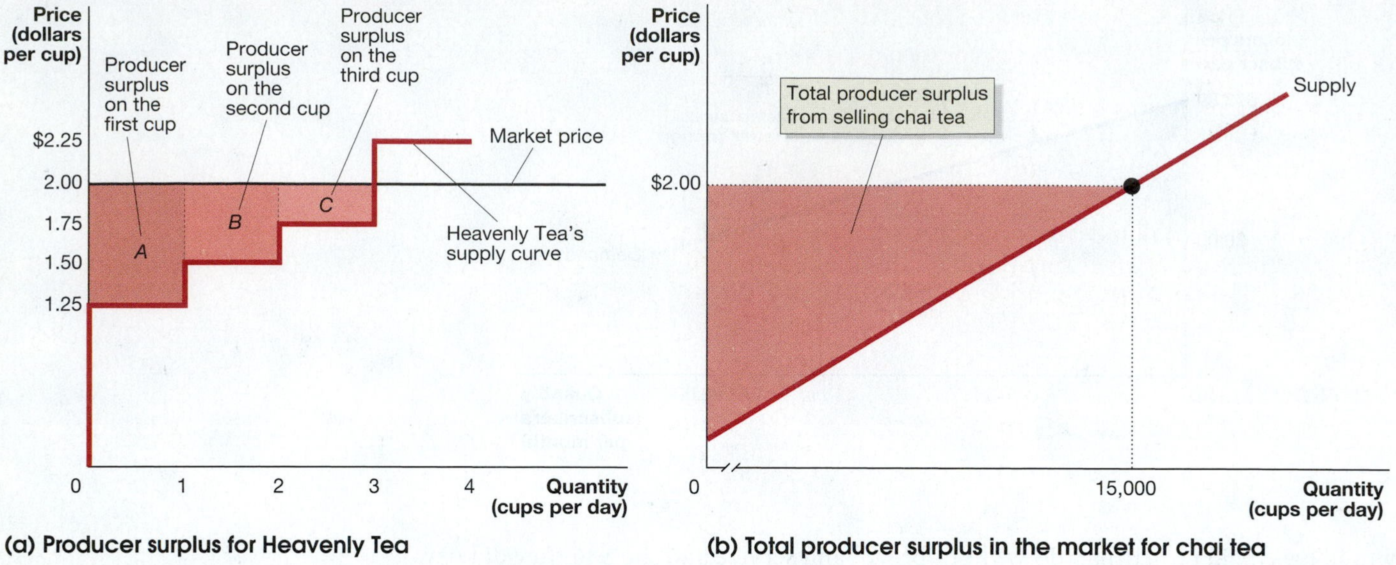

MyEconLab Animation

Figure 4.4 Measuring Producer Surplus

Panel (a) shows Heavenly Tea's producer surplus. The lowest price Heavenly Tea is willing to accept to supply a cup of tea is equal to its marginal cost of producing that cup. When the market price of tea is $2.00, Heavenly receives producer surplus of $0.75 on the first cup (the area of rectangle *A*), $0.50 on the second cup (rectangle *B*), and $0.25 on the third cup (rectangle *C*). In panel (b), the total amount of producer surplus tea sellers receive from selling chai tea can be calculated by adding up for the entire market the producer surplus received on each cup sold. In the figure, total producer surplus is equal to the shaded area above the supply curve and below the market price.

will increase from $1.50 to $2.25. (Make sure you understand how the new level of producer surplus was calculated.)

The supply curve shown in panel (a) of Figure 4.4 does not look like the typical smooth supply curve because we are looking at a single firm producing only a small quantity of tea. With many firms, the market supply curve for chai tea will have the normal smooth shape shown in panel (b) of Figure 4.4. In panel (b), the quantity supplied at a price of $2.00 is 15,000 cups per day. We can calculate total producer surplus in panel (b) the same way we did in panel (a): by adding up the producer surplus received on each cup sold. Therefore, *the total amount of producer surplus in a market is equal to the area above the market supply curve and below the market price*. The total producer surplus tea sellers receive from selling chai tea is shown as the shaded area in panel (b) of Figure 4.4.

MyEconLab Concept Check

What Consumer Surplus and Producer Surplus Measure

We have seen that consumer surplus measures the benefit to consumers from participating in a market, and producer surplus measures the benefit to producers from participating in a market. It is important to be clear about what these concepts are measuring. In a sense, consumer surplus measures the *net* benefit to consumers from participating in a market rather than the *total* benefit. That is, if the price of a product were zero, the consumer surplus in a market would be all of the area under the demand curve. When the price is not zero, consumer surplus is the area below the demand curve and above the market price. So, consumer surplus in a market is equal to the total benefit consumers receive minus the total amount they must pay to buy the good or service.

Similarly, producer surplus measures the *net* benefit received by producers from participating in a market. If producers could supply a good or service at zero cost, the producer surplus in a market would be all of the area below the market price. When cost is not zero, producer surplus is the area below the market price and above the supply curve. So, producer surplus in a market is equal to the total dollar amount firms receive from consumers minus the cost of producing the good or service.

MyEconLab Concept Check

MyEconLab Study Plan

4.2 The Efficiency of Competitive Markets

LEARNING OBJECTIVE: Explain the concept of economic efficiency.

Recall that a *competitive market* is a market with many buyers and many sellers. An important advantage of the market system is that it results in efficient economic outcomes. But what does *economic efficiency* mean? The concepts we have developed so far in this chapter give us two ways to think about the economic efficiency of competitive markets. We can think in terms of marginal benefit and marginal cost. We can also think in terms of consumer surplus and producer surplus. As we will see, these two approaches lead to the same outcome, but using both can increase our understanding of economic efficiency.

Marginal Benefit Equals Marginal Cost in Competitive Equilibrium

Figure 4.5 again shows the market for chai tea. Recall that the demand curve shows the marginal benefit received by consumers, and the supply curve shows the marginal cost of production. For this market to achieve economic efficiency, the marginal benefit from the last unit sold should equal the marginal cost of production. The figure shows that this equality occurs at competitive equilibrium where 15,000 cups per day are produced and marginal benefit and marginal cost are both equal to $2.00. This outcome is economically efficient because every cup of chai tea has been produced where the marginal benefit to buyers is greater than or equal to the marginal cost to producers.

To further understand why the level of output at competitive equilibrium is efficient, consider what the situation would be if output were at a different level. Suppose that output of chai tea were 14,000 cups per day. Figure 4.5 shows that at this level of output, the marginal benefit from the last cup sold is $2.20, while the marginal cost is only $1.80. This level of output is not efficient because 1,000 more cups could be produced for which the additional benefit to consumers would be greater than the additional cost of production. Consumers would willingly purchase those cups, and tea sellers would willingly supply them, making both consumers and sellers better off. Similarly, if the output of chai tea were 16,000 cups per day, the marginal cost of the 16,000th cup is $2.20, while the marginal benefit is only $1.80. Tea sellers would only be willing to supply this cup at a price of $2.20, which is $0.40 higher than consumers would be willing to pay. In fact, consumers would not be willing to pay the price tea sellers would need to receive for any cup beyond the 15,000th.

To summarize: *Equilibrium in a competitive market results in the economically efficient level of output, at which marginal benefit equals marginal cost.* MyEconLab Concept Check

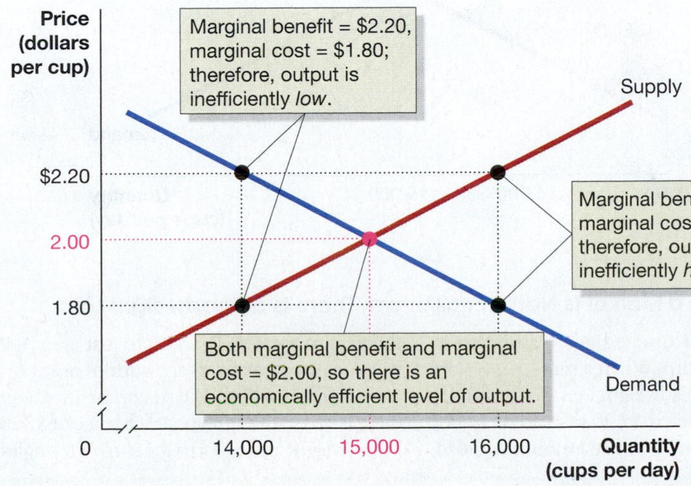

MyEconLab Animation

Figure 4.5

Marginal Benefit Equals Marginal Cost Only at Competitive Equilibrium

In a competitive market, equilibrium occurs at a quantity of 15,000 cups and a price of $2.00 per cup, where marginal benefit equals marginal cost. This level of output is economically efficient because every cup has been produced for which the marginal benefit to buyers is greater than or equal to the marginal cost to producers.

MyEconLab Animation

Figure 4.6

Economic Surplus Equals the Sum of Consumer Surplus and Producer Surplus

The economic surplus in a market is the sum of the blue area, representing consumer surplus, and the red area, representing producer surplus.

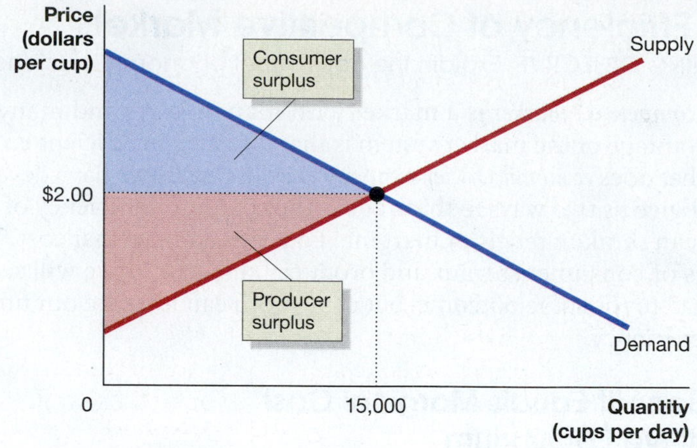

Economic surplus The sum of consumer surplus and producer surplus.

Economic Surplus

Economic surplus in a market is the sum of consumer surplus and producer surplus. In a competitive market, with many buyers and sellers and no government restrictions, economic surplus is at a maximum when the market is in equilibrium. To see this point, let's look at the market for chai tea shown again in Figure 4.6. The consumer surplus in this market is the blue area below the demand curve and above the line indicating the equilibrium price of $2.00. The producer surplus is the red area above the supply curve and below the price line. MyEconLab Concept Check

Deadweight Loss

To show that economic surplus is maximized at equilibrium, consider a situation in which the price of chai tea is *above* the equilibrium price, as shown in Figure 4.7. At a

	At Competitive Equilibrium	At a Price of $2.20
Consumer Surplus	*A* + *B* + *C*	*A*
Producer Surplus	*D* + *E*	*B* + *D*
Deadweight Loss	None	*C* + *E*

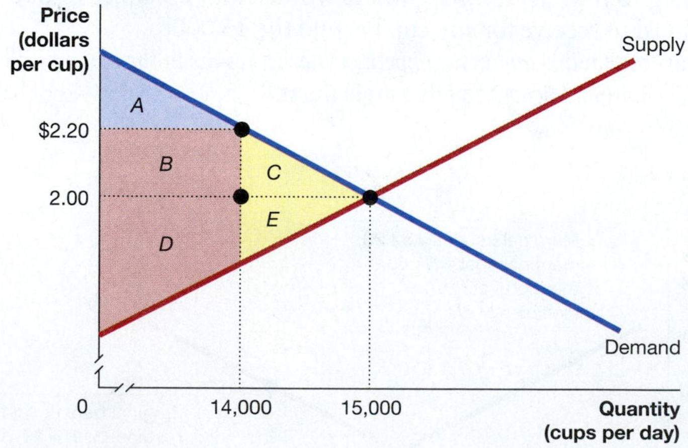

MyEconLab Animation

Figure 4.7 When a Market Is Not in Equilibrium, There Is a Deadweight Loss

Economic surplus is maximized when a market is in competitive equilibrium. When a market is not in equilibrium, there is a deadweight loss. For example, when the price of chai tea is $2.20 instead of $2.00, consumer surplus declines from an amount equal to the sum of areas *A*, *B*, and *C* to just area *A*. Producer surplus increases from the sum of areas *D* and *E* to the sum of areas *B* and *D*. At competitive equilibrium, there is no deadweight loss. At a price of $2.20, there is a deadweight loss equal to the sum of triangles *C* and *E*.

price of $2.20 per cup, the number of cups consumers are willing to buy per day falls from 15,000 to 14,000. At competitive equilibrium, consumer surplus is equal to the sum of areas *A*, *B*, and *C*. At a price of $2.20, fewer cups are sold at a higher price, so consumer surplus declines to just the area of *A*. At competitive equilibrium, producer surplus is equal to the sum of areas *D* and *E*. At the higher price of $2.20, producer surplus changes to be equal to the sum of areas *B* and *D*. The sum of consumer and producer surplus—economic surplus—has been reduced to the sum of areas *A*, *B*, and *D*. Notice that this sum is less than the original economic surplus by an amount equal to the sum of triangles *C* and *E*. Economic surplus has declined because at a price of $2.20, all the cups between the 14,000th and the 15,000th, which would have been produced in competitive equilibrium, are not being produced. These "missing" cups are not providing any consumer or producer surplus, so economic surplus has declined. The reduction in economic surplus resulting from a market not being in competitive equilibrium is called the **deadweight loss**. In the figure, deadweight loss is equal to the sum of the triangles *C* and *E*.

MyEconLab Concept Check

Deadweight loss The reduction in economic surplus resulting from a market not being in competitive equilibrium.

Economic Surplus and Economic Efficiency

Consumer surplus measures the benefit to consumers from buying a particular product, such as chai tea. Producer surplus measures the benefit to firms from selling a particular product. Therefore, economic surplus—which is the sum of the benefit to firms plus the benefit to consumers—is the best measure we have of the benefit to society from the production of a particular good or service. Economic surplus gives us a second way of characterizing the economic efficiency of a competitive market: *Equilibrium in a competitive market results in the greatest amount of economic surplus, or total net benefit to society, from the production of a good or service.* Anything that causes the market for a good or service not to be in competitive equilibrium reduces the total benefit to society from the production of that good or service.

Now we can give a more general definition of *economic efficiency* in terms of our two approaches: **Economic efficiency** is a market outcome in which the marginal benefit to consumers of the last unit produced is equal to its marginal cost of production and in which the sum of consumer surplus and producer surplus is at a maximum.

MyEconLab Concept Check

Economic efficiency A market outcome in which the marginal benefit to consumers of the last unit produced is equal to its marginal cost of production and in which the sum of consumer surplus and producer surplus is at a maximum.

4.3 Government Intervention in the Market: Price Floors and Price Ceilings

LEARNING OBJECTIVE: Explain the economic effect of government-imposed price floors and price ceilings.

Notice that we have *not* concluded that every *individual* is better off if a market is at competitive equilibrium. We have concluded only that economic surplus, or the *total* net benefit to society, is greatest at competitive equilibrium. Any individual producer would rather receive a higher price, and any individual consumer would rather pay a lower price, but usually producers can sell and consumers can buy only at the competitive equilibrium price.

Producers or consumers who are dissatisfied with the competitive equilibrium price can lobby the government to legally require that a different price be charged. In the United States, the government only occasionally overrides the market outcome by setting prices. When the government does intervene, it can attempt to aid either sellers by requiring that a price be above equilibrium—a price floor—or buyers by requiring that a price be below equilibrium—a price ceiling. To affect the market outcome, the government must set a legal price floor that is above the equilibrium price or set a legal price ceiling that is below the equilibrium price. Otherwise, the price ceiling or price floor will not be *binding* on buyers and sellers. We can use the concepts of consumer surplus, producer surplus, and deadweight loss to understand more clearly why price floors and price ceilings reduce economic efficiency.

Price Floors: Government Policy in Agricultural Markets

The Great Depression of the 1930s was the worst economic disaster in U.S. history, affecting every sector of the economy. Many farmers could sell their products only at very low prices, so they convinced the federal government to set price floors for many agricultural products, such as wheat and corn. Government intervention in agriculture—often referred to as the *farm program*—has continued ever since. To understand how a price floor in an agricultural market works, suppose that the equilibrium price in the wheat market is $6.50 per bushel, but the government decides to set a price floor of $8.00 per bushel. As Figure 4.8 shows, the price of wheat rises from $6.50 to $8.00, and the quantity of wheat sold falls from 2.0 billion bushels per year to 1.8 billion. Initially, suppose that production of wheat also falls to 1.8 billion bushels.

The producer surplus received by wheat farmers increases by an amount equal to the area of rectangle *A* and decreases by an amount equal to the area of triangle *C*. (This is the same result we saw in the market for chai tea in Figure 4.7.) The area of rectangle *A* represents a transfer from consumer surplus to producer surplus. The total fall in consumer surplus is equal to the sum of the areas of rectangle *A* and triangle *B*. Wheat farmers benefit from this program, but consumers lose. There is also a deadweight loss equal to the areas of triangles *B* and *C* because economic efficiency declines as the price floor reduces the amount of economic surplus in the market for wheat. In other words, the price floor has caused the marginal benefit of the last bushel of wheat to be greater than the marginal cost of producing it. We can conclude that a price floor reduces economic efficiency.

We assumed initially that farmers reduce their production of wheat to the amount consumers are willing to buy. In fact, as Figure 4.8 shows, a price floor will cause the quantity of wheat that farmers want to supply to increase from 2.0 billion to 2.2 billion bushels. Because the higher price also reduces the amount of wheat consumers want to buy, the result is a surplus of 0.4 billion bushels of wheat (the 2.2 billion bushels supplied minus the 1.8 billion demanded).

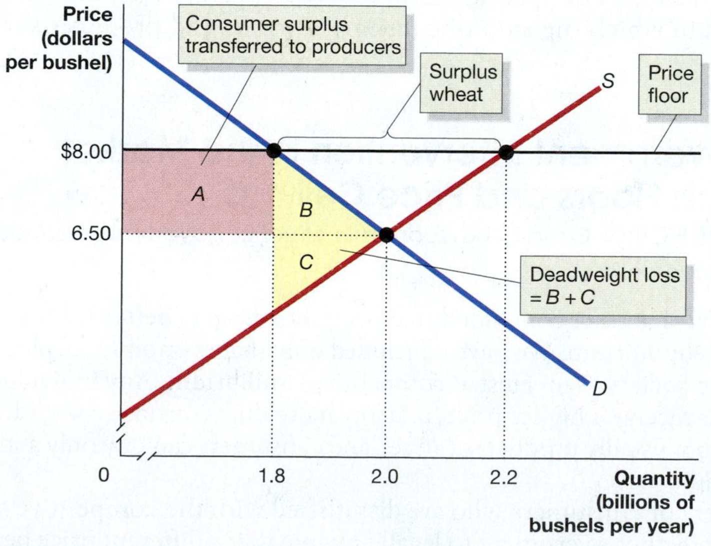

MyEconLab Animation

Figure 4.8 The Economic Effect of a Price Floor in the Wheat Market

If wheat farmers convince the government to impose a price floor of $8.00 per bushel, the amount of wheat sold will fall from 2.0 billion bushels per year to 1.8 billion. If we assume that farmers produce 1.8 billion bushels, producer surplus then increases by rectangle *A*—which is transferred from consumer surplus—and falls by triangle *C*. Consumer surplus declines by rectangle *A* plus triangle *B*. There is a deadweight loss equal to triangles *B* and *C*, representing the decline in economic efficiency due to the price floor. In reality, a price floor of $8.00 per bushel will cause farmers to expand their production from 2.0 billion to 2.2 billion bushels, resulting in a surplus of wheat.

The federal government's farm programs have often resulted in large surpluses of wheat and other agricultural products. In response, the government has usually either bought the surplus food or paid farmers to restrict supply by taking some land out of cultivation. Because both of these options are expensive, Congress passed the Freedom to Farm Act of 1996. The intent of the act was to phase out price floors and government purchases of surpluses and return to a free market in agriculture. To allow farmers time to adjust, the federal government began paying farmers *subsidies*, or cash payments based on the number of acres planted. Although the subsidies were originally scheduled to be phased out, Congress has passed additional farm bills that have resulted in the continuation of subsidies requiring substantial federal government spending. In 2015, the Congressional Budget Office estimated that the farm program would result in federal spending of more than $145 billion over the following 10 years.

MyEconLab Concept Check

Making the Connection

MyEconLab Video

Price Floors in Labor Markets: The Debate over Minimum Wage Policy

The minimum wage may be the most controversial "price floor." Supporters see the minimum wage as a way of raising the incomes of low-skilled workers. Opponents argue that it results in fewer jobs and imposes large costs on small businesses.

Since 2009, the national minimum wage as set by Congress has been $7.25 per hour for most occupations. It is illegal for an employer to pay less than this wage in these occupations. Although only about 4 percent of workers in the United States earn the minimum wage or less, many people are concerned that workers who receive the minimum wage or a wage a little above the minimum are not earning a "living wage" that would allow them to escape from poverty. In 2015, President Barack Obama proposed raising the minimum wage in a series of steps to $10.10 per hour. Some members of Congress introduced legislation to raise it to $12 per hour. Several cities and states are increasing their minimum wage to as high as $15 per hour. Protests in a number of cities were intended to pressure fast-food restaurants and other employers to voluntarily raise the minimum wage they paid to $15 per hour.

For many workers, the legal minimum wage is irrelevant because it is well below the wage employers are voluntarily willing to pay them. But for some low-skilled workers—such as restaurant workers—the minimum wage is above the wage they would otherwise receive. The following figure shows the effect of the minimum wage on employment in the market for low-skilled labor.

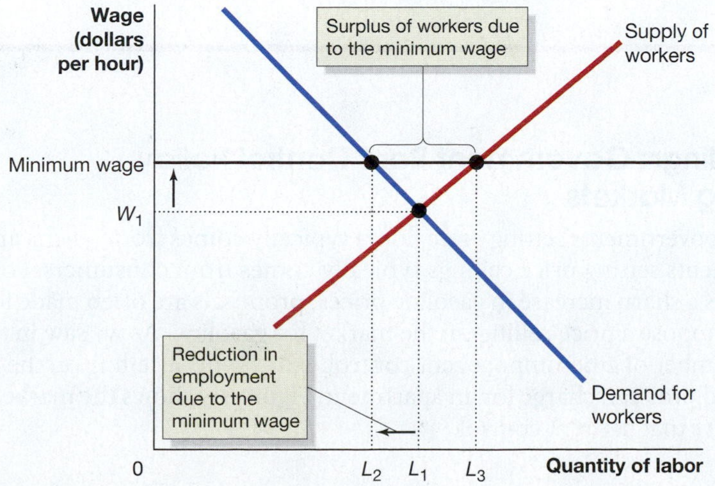

Without a minimum wage, the equilibrium wage would be W_1 and the number of workers hired would be L_1. With a minimum wage set above the equilibrium wage, the number of workers employers demand declines from L_1 to L_2, and the quantity of labor supplied increases to L_3, leading to a surplus of workers unable to find jobs equal to $L_3 - L_2$. The quantity of labor supplied increases because the higher wage attracts more people to work. For instance, some teenagers may decide that working after school is worthwhile at the minimum wage of $7.25 per hour but would not be worthwhile at a lower wage.

This analysis is very similar to our analysis of the wheat market in Figure 4.8. Just as a price floor in the wheat market leads to less wheat being consumed, a price floor in the labor market should lead to fewer workers being hired. Views differ sharply among economists, however, concerning how large a reduction in employment the minimum wage causes. The U.S. Congressional Budget Office (CBO) estimates that raising the minimum wage to $10.10 per hour would result in a decline in employment of 500,000 workers. Some economists believe that the effects of the minimum wage on employment are far smaller, however. For instance, David Card of the University of California, Berkeley, and Alan Krueger of Princeton University conducted a study of fast-food restaurants in New Jersey and Pennsylvania. Their study indicated that the effect of past minimum wage increases on employment has been very small. This study has been controversial, and other economists have examined similar data and come to the different conclusion that the minimum wage leads to a significant decrease in employment.

Whatever the extent of employment losses from the minimum wage, because it is a price floor, it will cause a deadweight loss, just as a price floor in the wheat market does. Therefore, many economists favor alternative policies for attaining the goal of raising the incomes of low-skilled workers. One policy many economists support is the *earned income tax credit*, which reduces the amount of tax that low-income wage earners would otherwise pay to the federal government. Workers with very low incomes who do not owe any tax receive a payment from the government. Unlike with the minimum wage, the earned income tax credit can increase the incomes of low-skilled workers without reducing employment. The earned income tax credit also places a lesser burden on the small businesses that employ many low-skilled workers and may cause a smaller loss of economic efficiency.

Sources: Noam Scheiber, "Democrats Are Rallying around $12 Minimum Wage," *New York Times*, April 22, 2015; U.S. Bureau of Labor Statistics, "Characteristics of Minimum Wage Workers, 2014," BLS Reports 1054, April 2015; U.S. Congressional Budget Office, "The Effects of a Minimum-Wage Increase on Employment and Family Income," February 2014; David Card and Alan B. Krueger, *Myth and Measurement: The New Economics of the Minimum Wage*, Princeton, NJ: Princeton University Press, 1995; and David Neumark and William Wascher, "Minimum Wages and Employment: A Case Study of the Fast-Food Industry in New Jersey and Pennsylvania: Comment," *American Economic Review*, Vol. 90, No. 5, December 2000, pp. 1362–1396.

MyEconLab Study Plan

Your Turn: Test your understanding by doing related problem 3.10 on page 138 at the end of this chapter.

Price Ceilings: Government Rent Control Policy in Housing Markets

Support for governments setting price floors typically comes from sellers, and support for governments setting price ceilings typically comes from consumers. For example, when there is a sharp increase in gasoline prices, proposals are often made for the government to impose a price ceiling on the market for gasoline. As we saw in the chapter opener, a number of cities impose rent control, which puts a ceiling on the maximum rent that landlords can charge for an apartment. Figure 4.9 shows the market for apartments in a city that has rent control.

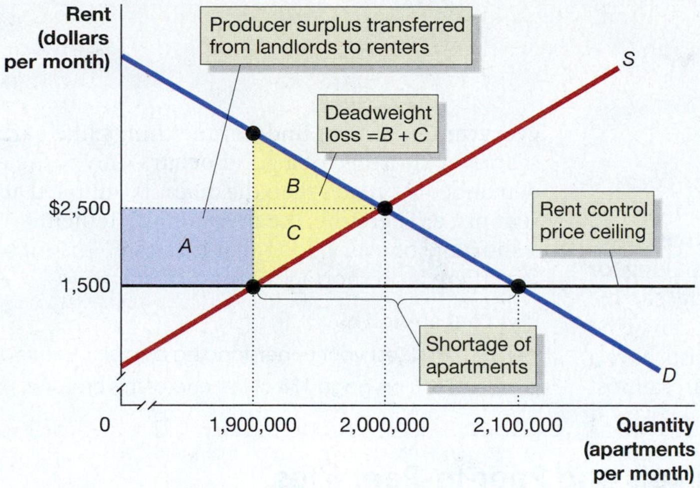

MyEconLab Animation

Figure 4.9 The Economic Effect of a Rent Ceiling

Without rent control, the equilibrium rent is $2,500 per month. At that price, 2,000,000 apartments would be rented. If the government imposes a rent ceiling of $1,500 per month, the quantity of apartments supplied decreases to 1,900,000, and the quantity of apartments demanded increases to 2,100,000, resulting in a shortage of 200,000 apartments. Producer surplus equal to the area of rectangle A is transferred from landlords to renters, and there is a deadweight loss equal to the areas of triangles B and C.

Without rent control, the equilibrium rent would be $2,500 per month, and 2,000,000 apartments would be rented. With a maximum legal rent of $1,500 per month, landlords reduce the quantity of apartments supplied to 1,900,000. The fall in the quantity of apartments supplied can be the result of landlords converting some apartments into offices, selling some off as condominiums, or converting some small apartment buildings into single-family homes. Over time, landlords may even abandon some apartment buildings. At one time in New York City, rent control resulted in landlords abandoning whole city blocks because they were unable to cover their costs with the rents the government allowed them to charge. In London, when rent controls were applied to rooms and apartments located in a landlord's own home, the quantity of these apartments supplied decreased by 75 percent.

In Figure 4.9, with the rent ceiling of $1,500 per month, the quantity of apartments demanded rises to 2,100,000, resulting in a shortage of 200,000 apartments. Consumer surplus increases by rectangle *A* and falls by triangle *B*. Rectangle *A* would have been part of producer surplus if rent control were not in place. With rent control, it is part of consumer surplus. Rent control causes the producer surplus landlords receive to fall by rectangle *A* plus triangle *C*. Triangles *B* and *C* represent the deadweight loss, which results from rent control reducing the amount of economic surplus in the market for apartments. Rent control has caused the marginal benefit of the last apartment rented to be greater than the marginal cost of supplying it. We can conclude that a price ceiling, such as rent control, reduces economic efficiency. The appendix to this chapter shows how we can make quantitative estimates of the deadweight loss and provides an example of the changes in consumer surplus and producer surplus that can result from rent control.

Renters as a group benefit from rent controls—total consumer surplus is larger—but landlords lose. Because of the deadweight loss, the total loss to landlords is greater than the gain to renters. Notice also that although renters as a group benefit, the number of renters is reduced, so some renters are made worse off by rent controls because they are unable to find an apartment at the legal rent. MyEconLab Concept Check

Don't Let This Happen to You

Don't Confuse "Scarcity" with "Shortage"

At first glance, the following statement seems correct: "There is a shortage of every good that is scarce." In everyday conversation, we describe a good as "scarce" if we have trouble finding it. For instance, if you are looking for a gift for a child, you might call the latest hot toy "scarce" if you are willing to buy it at its listed price but can't find it online or in any store. But recall that economists have a broader definition of *scarce*. In the economic sense, almost everything—except undesirable things like garbage—is scarce. A shortage of a good occurs only if the quantity demanded is greater than the quantity supplied at the current price. Therefore, the preceding statement—"There is a shortage of every good that is scarce"—is incorrect. In fact, there is no shortage of most scarce goods.

MyEconLab Study Plan

Your Turn: Test your understanding by doing related problem 3.13 on page 138 at the end of this chapter.

Black Markets and Peer-to-Peer Sites

When governments regulate prices by enacting price ceilings or price floors, buyers and sellers often find a way around the regulations. As a result, renters may be worse off and landlords may be better off than Figure 4.9 makes it seem. We have assumed that renters and landlords actually abide by the price ceiling, but sometimes they don't. Because rent control leads to a shortage of apartments, renters who would otherwise not be able to find apartments have an incentive to offer landlords rents *above* the legal maximum. The result is a **black market** in which buying and selling take place at prices that violate government price regulations.

Black market A market in which buying and selling take place at prices that violate government price regulations.

Online peer-to-peer rental sites like Airbnb have provided landlords and tenants another way to avoid rent controls. Landlords can use these sites to convert a regular yearly rental into a series of short-term rentals for which they can charge above the legal maximum rent. Tenants can also use the sites to make a profit from rent controls. As we saw in the chapter opener, in San Francisco, some tenants moved out of the city but kept their rent-controlled apartments and rented them using peer-to-peer rental sites. Both San Francisco and New York have taken actions against peer-to-peer rental sites because some government officials believe the sites undermine rent control. Both cities have laws that prohibit landlords from renting apartments for less than 30 days. San Francisco also announced that anyone renting rooms through Airbnb and similar sites must pay the city's 14 percent hotel tax.

Some government officials in both cities, however, were reluctant to take actions that might limit the growth of the sharing economy of peer-to-peer rental sites. The sharing economy has the potential to improve economic efficiency and make available to consumers goods, such as cars, bikes, boats, and apartments, at lower prices. When cities have rent control laws, though, peer-to-peer sites perform a somewhat different function, making apartments available at rents higher than the legal price ceiling—apartments that renters might otherwise have difficulty finding because of the shortage caused by rent control. It remains to be seen whether local policymakers can resolve the conflict between putting legal ceilings on rents and encouraging peer-to-peer sites to operate in their cities.

MyEconLab Concept Check

Solved Problem 4.3

MyEconLab Interactive Animation

What's the Economic Effect of a Black Market in Renting Apartments?

In many cities that have rent controls, such as New York and San Francisco, the actual rents paid can be much higher than the legal maximum. Because rent controls cause a shortage of apartments, desperate tenants are often willing to pay landlords rents that are higher than the law allows, perhaps by writing a check for the legally allowed rent and paying an additional amount in cash. Look again at Figure 4.9 on page 121. Suppose that competition among tenants results in the black market rent rising to $3,500 per month. At this rent, tenants demand 1,900,000 apartments. Draw a graph showing the market for apartments and compare this situation with the one shown in Figure 4.9. Be sure to note any differences in consumer surplus, producer surplus, and deadweight loss.

Solving the Problem

Step 1: Review the chapter material. This problem is about price controls in the market for apartments, so you may want to review the section "Price Ceilings: Government Rent Control Policy in Housing Markets," which begins on page 120.

Step 2: Draw a graph similar to Figure 4.9, with the addition of the black market price.

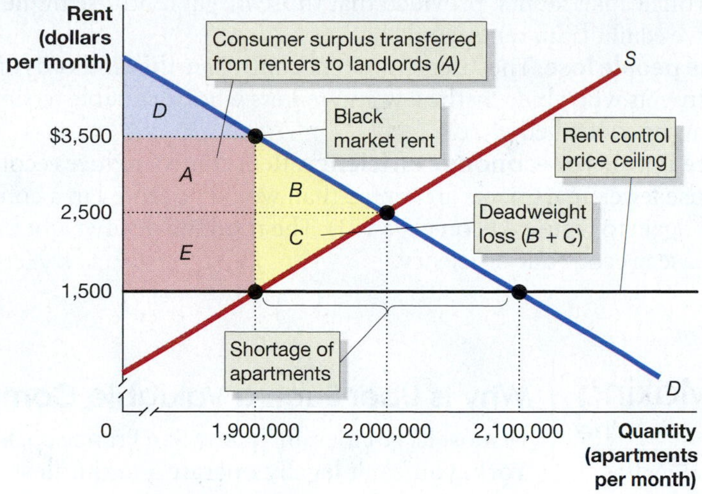

Step 3: Analyze the changes from Figure 4.9. The black market rent is now $3,500 per month—even higher than the original competitive equilibrium rent shown in Figure 4.9. So, consumer surplus declines by an amount equal to the sum of the areas of rectangle *A* and rectangle *E*. The remaining consumer surplus is triangle *D*. Note that rectangle *A*, which would have been part of consumer surplus without rent control, represents a transfer from renters to landlords. Compared with the situation shown in Figure 4.9, producer surplus has increased by an amount equal to the sum of the areas of rectangles *A* and *E*, and consumer surplus has declined by the same amount. Deadweight loss is equal to the sum of the areas of triangles *B* and *C*, the same as in Figure 4.9.

Extra Credit: This analysis leads to a surprising result: With an active black market in apartments, rent control may leave renters as a group worse off—with less consumer surplus—than if there were no rent control. There is one more possibility to consider, however. If enough landlords become convinced that they can get away with charging rents above the legal ceiling, the quantity of apartments supplied will increase. Eventually, the market could even end up at the competitive equilibrium, with an equilibrium rent of $2,500 and equilibrium quantity of 2,000,000 apartments. In that case, the rent control price ceiling becomes nonbinding, not because it was set below the equilibrium price but because it was not legally enforced.

Your Turn: For more practice, do related problem 3.14 on page 138 at the end of this chapter.

MyEconLab Study Plan

Rent controls can also lead to an increase in racial and other types of discrimination. With rent controls, more renters are looking for apartments than there are apartments to rent. Landlords can afford to indulge their prejudices by refusing to rent to people from groups they don't like. In cities without rent controls, landlords face more competition, which makes it more difficult to reject tenants on the basis of irrelevant characteristics, such as race.

The Results of Government Price Controls: Winners, Losers, and Inefficiency

When the government imposes price floors or price ceilings, three important results occur:

1. **Some people win.** The winners from rent control are the people who are paying less for rent because they live in rent-controlled apartments. Landlords may also gain if they break the law by charging rents above the legal maximum for their rent-controlled apartments, provided that those illegal rents are higher than the competitive equilibrium rents would be.
2. **Some people lose.** The losers from rent control are the landlords of rent-controlled apartments who abide by the law and renters who are unable to find apartments to rent at the controlled price.
3. **There is a loss of economic efficiency.** Rent control reduces economic efficiency because fewer apartments are rented than would be rented in a competitive market (refer again to Figure 4.9, on page 121). The resulting deadweight loss measures the decrease in economic efficiency. MyEconLab Concept Check

Making the Connection
MyEconLab Video

Why Is Uber Such a Valuable Company?

In most large cities, including San Francisco, Boston, and New York, you can't legally operate a taxi unless you have a permit from the city government. For example, New York City requires taxi drivers to purchase a medallion issued by the city government. The number of medallions issued is limited, and in recent years, the price of a medallion has sometimes exceeded $1 *million*. Clearly, it is very expensive to enter the taxi business in most large cities. City governments also typically regulate the price of taxi rides. Because the price of taxi rides in these cities is usually above its equilibrium level, we know that there is a loss of consumer surplus.

Some people would rather use their smartphone to order a ride from Uber than use a taxi.

Entrepreneur Travis Kalanick of California founded Uber Technologies in 2009 as an alternative to conventional taxis. The firm's slogan is "Choice is a beautiful thing." Uber is a mobile app that allows users to quickly summon a car—often a luxury car such as a BMW or Cadillac—owned by a driver who signs up with Uber and agrees to meet certain requirements. Anyone in a big city who wants to enter the business of offering rides would find it much easier to sign up with Uber than to obtain the permit necessary to operate a conventional taxi. Uber believes that local regulations governing taxis do not apply to its services.

Uber claims to be adding as many as 20,000 new drivers per month worldwide. Taxi drivers in many cities have protested against Uber because they believe competition from Uber drivers will reduce the profitability of driving a taxi. In New York City, in 2015, the price of taxi medallions had fallen by more than 20 percent. Some New York City taxi drivers predicted that the industry would collapse unless the city government more closely regulated Uber.

Investors have estimated that Uber could have a value of $50 billion—or more than three times the values of auto rental firms Hertz and Avis combined. A much smaller rival ride-sharing service, Lyft, was valued at $2.5 billion. Investors expect that Uber and Lyft will be very profitable because they offer consumers lower-priced or more convenient car rides than are available from taxis. Uber and Lyft's high profits depend on the large gap between the regulated price of taxi rides and the equilibrium price.

In other words, the high profits show that government regulation of the taxi industry has greatly reduced consumer surplus.

Sources: Douglas MacMillan and Telis Demosu, "Uber Eyes $50 Billion Valuation in New Funding," *Wall Street Journal*, May 9, 2015; Douglas MacMillan, "Carl Icahn Takes $100 Million Stake in Lyft," *Wall Street Journal*, May 15, 2015; and Andrew J. Hawkins, "Taxi Interests Sue City, Predicting Collapse of Their Industry," crainsnewyork.com, May 27, 2015.

Your Turn: Test your understanding by doing related problem 3.15 on page 138 at the end of this chapter.

MyEconLab Study Plan

Positive and Normative Analysis of Price Ceilings and Price Floors

Are rent controls, government farm programs, and other price ceilings and price floors bad? As we saw in Chapter 1, questions of this type do not have right or wrong answers. Economists are generally skeptical of government attempts to interfere with competitive market equilibrium. Economists know the role competitive markets have played in raising the average person's standard of living. They also know that too much government intervention has the potential to reduce the ability of the market system to produce similar increases in living standards in the future.

But recall the difference between positive and normative analysis. Positive analysis is concerned with *what is*, and normative analysis is concerned with *what should be*. Our analysis of rent control and the federal farm programs in this chapter is positive analysis. We discussed the economic results of these programs. Whether these programs are desirable or undesirable is a normative question. Whether the gains to the winners more than make up for the losses to the losers and for the decline in economic efficiency is a matter of judgment and not strictly an economic question. Price ceilings and price floors continue to exist partly because people who understand their downside still believe they are good policies and therefore support them. The policies also persist because many people who support them do not understand the economic analysis in this chapter and so do not understand the drawbacks to these policies. MyEconLab Concept Check

MyEconLab Study Plan

4.4 The Economic Effect of Taxes

LEARNING OBJECTIVE: Analyze the economic effect of taxes.

Supreme Court Justice Oliver Wendell Holmes once remarked: "Taxes are what we pay for a civilized society." When the government taxes a good or service, however, it affects the market equilibrium for that good or service. Just as with a price ceiling or price floor, one result of a tax is a decline in economic efficiency. Analyzing taxes is an important part of the field of economics known as *public finance*. In this section, we will use the model of demand and supply and the concepts of consumer surplus, producer surplus, and deadweight loss to analyze the economic effect of taxes.

The Effect of Taxes on Economic Efficiency

Whenever a government taxes a good or service, less of that good or service will be produced and consumed. For example, a tax on cigarettes will raise the cost of smoking and reduce the amount of smoking that takes place. We can use a demand and supply graph to illustrate this point. Figure 4.10 shows the market for cigarettes.

Without the tax, the equilibrium price of cigarettes would be $5.00 per pack, and 4 billion packs of cigarettes would be sold per year (point A). If the federal government requires sellers of cigarettes to pay a $1.00-per-pack tax, then their cost of selling cigarettes will increase by $1.00 per pack. This increase in cost causes the supply curve for cigarettes to shift up by $1.00 because sellers will now require a price that is $1.00 greater to supply the same quantity of cigarettes. In Figure 4.10, the supply curve shifts up by $1.00 to show the effect of the tax, and there is a new equilibrium price of $5.90 and a new equilibrium quantity of 3.7 billion packs (point B).

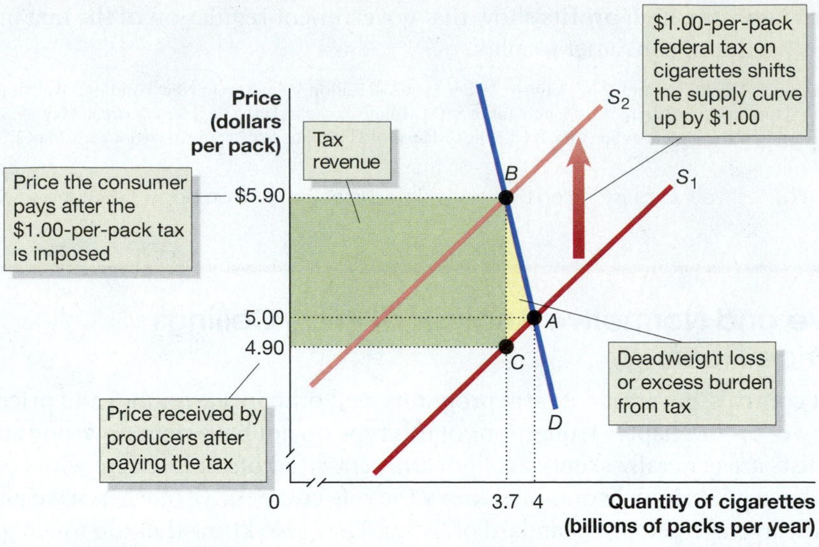

MyEconLab Animation

Figure 4.10 The Effect of a Tax on the Market for Cigarettes

Without the tax, market equilibrium occurs at point A. The equilibrium price of cigarettes is $5.00 per pack, and 4 billion packs of cigarettes are sold per year. A $1.00-per-pack tax on cigarettes will cause the supply curve for cigarettes to shift up by $1.00, from S_1 to S_2. The new equilibrium occurs at point B. The price of cigarettes will increase by $0.90, to $5.90 per pack, and the quantity sold will fall to 3.7 billion packs. The tax on cigarettes has increased the price paid by consumers from $5.00 to $5.90 per pack. Producers receive a price of $5.90 per pack (point B), but after paying the $1.00 tax, they are left with $4.90 (point C). The government will receive tax revenue equal to the green-shaded box. Some consumer surplus and some producer surplus will become tax revenue for the government, and some will become deadweight loss, shown by the yellow-shaded area.

The federal government will collect tax revenue equal to the tax per pack multiplied by the number of packs sold, or $3.7 billion. The area shaded in green in Figure 4.10 represents the government's tax revenue. Consumers will pay a higher price of $5.90 per pack. Although sellers appear to be receiving a higher price per pack, once they have paid the tax, the price they receive falls from $5.00 per pack to $4.90 per pack. There is a loss of consumer surplus because consumers are paying a higher price. The price producers receive falls, so there is also a loss of producer surplus. Therefore, the tax on cigarettes has reduced *both* consumer surplus and producer surplus. Some of the reduction in consumer and producer surplus becomes tax revenue for the government. The rest of the reduction in consumer and producer surplus is equal to the deadweight loss from the tax, shown by the yellow-shaded triangle in the figure.

We can conclude that the true burden of a tax is not just the amount consumers and producers pay the government but also includes the deadweight loss. The deadweight loss from a tax is referred to as the *excess burden* of the tax. *A tax is efficient if it imposes a small excess burden relative to the tax revenue it raises.* One contribution economists make to government tax policy is to advise policymakers on which taxes are most efficient.

MyEconLab Concept Check

Tax Incidence: Who Actually Pays a Tax?

Tax incidence The actual division of the burden of a tax between buyers and sellers in a market.

The answer to the question "Who pays a tax?" seems obvious: Whoever is legally required to send a tax payment to the government pays the tax. But there can be an important difference between who is legally required to pay the tax and who actually *bears the burden* of the tax. The actual division of the burden of a tax between buyers and sellers is referred to as **tax incidence**. For example, the federal government currently levies an excise tax of 18.4 cents per gallon of gasoline sold. Gas station owners collect this tax and forward it to the federal government, but who actually bears the burden of the tax?

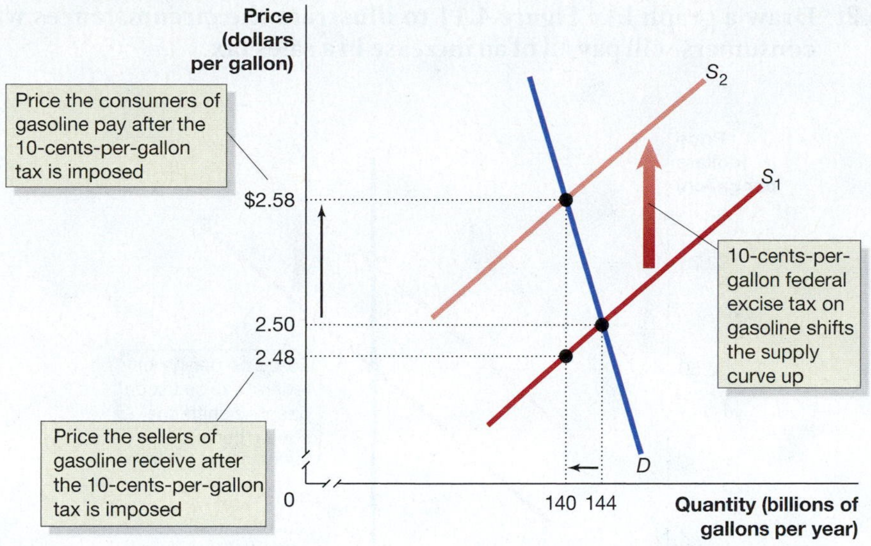

MyEconLab Animation

Figure 4.11

The Incidence of a Tax on Gasoline

With no tax on gasoline, the price would be $2.50 per gallon, and 144 billion gallons of gasoline would be sold each year. A 10-cents-per-gallon excise tax shifts up the supply curve from S_1 to S_2, raises the price consumers pay from $2.50 to $2.58, and lowers the price sellers receive from $2.50 to $2.48. Therefore, consumers pay 8 cents of the 10-cents-per-gallon tax on gasoline, and sellers pay 2 cents.

Determining Tax Incidence on a Demand and Supply Graph Suppose that currently the federal government does not impose a tax on gasoline. In Figure 4.11, equilibrium in the retail market for gasoline occurs at the intersection of the demand curve and supply curve, S_1. The equilibrium price is $2.50 per gallon, and the equilibrium quantity is 144 billion gallons per year. Now suppose that the federal government imposes a 10-cents-per-gallon tax. As a result of the tax, the supply curve for gasoline will shift up by 10 cents per gallon. At the new equilibrium, where the demand curve intersects the supply curve, S_2, the price has risen by 8 cents per gallon, from $2.50 to $2.58. Notice that only in the extremely unlikely case that demand is a vertical line will the market price rise by the full amount of the tax. Consumers are paying 8 cents more per gallon. Sellers of gasoline receive a new higher price of $2.58 per gallon, but after paying the 10-cents-per-gallon tax, they are left with $2.48 per gallon, or 2 cents less than they were receiving in the old equilibrium.

Although the sellers of gasoline are responsible for collecting the tax and sending the tax receipts to the government, they do not bear most of the burden of the tax. In this case, consumers pay 8 cents of the tax because the market price has risen by 8 cents, and sellers pay 2 cents of the tax because after sending the tax to the government, they are receiving 2 cents less per gallon of gasoline sold. Expressed in percentage terms, consumers pay 80 percent of the tax, and sellers pay 20 percent of the tax.

Solved Problem 4.4

MyEconLab Interactive Animation

When Do Consumers Pay All of a Sales Tax Increase?

A student makes the following statement: "If the federal government raises the sales tax on gasoline by $0.25, then the price of gasoline will rise by $0.25. Consumers can't get by without gasoline, so they have to pay the whole amount of any increase in the sales tax." Under what circumstances will the student's statement be true? Use a graph of the market for gasoline to illustrate your answer.

Solving the Problem

Step 1: Review the chapter material. This problem is about tax incidence, so you may want to review the section "Tax Incidence: Who Actually Pays a Tax?" which begins on page 126.

Step 2: Draw a graph like Figure 4.11 to illustrate the circumstances when consumers will pay all of an increase in a sales tax.

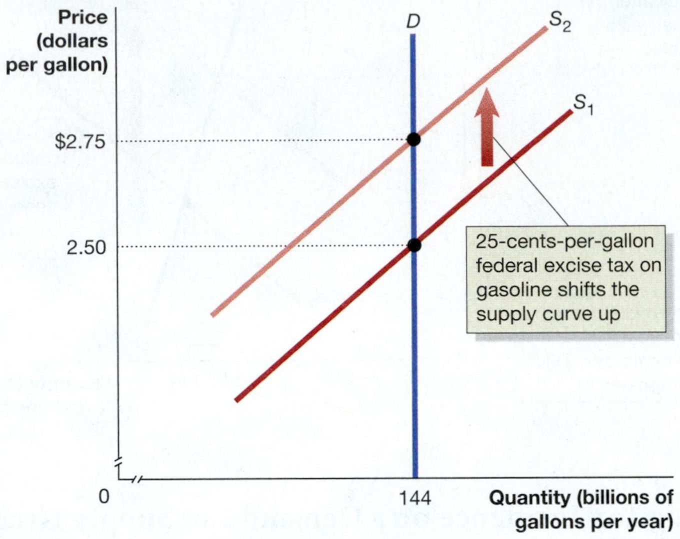

Step 3: Use the graph to evaluate the statement. The graph shows that consumers will pay all of an increase in a sales tax only if the demand curve is a vertical line. It is very unlikely that the demand for gasoline would look like this because we expect that for every good, an increase in price will cause a decrease in the quantity demanded. Because the demand curve for gasoline is not a vertical line, the statement is incorrect.

MyEconLab Study Plan

Your Turn: For more practice, do related problem 4.8 on page 140 at the end of the chapter.

Does It Make a Difference Whether the Government Collects a Tax from Buyers or Sellers? We have already seen the important distinction between who is legally required to pay a tax and who actually bears the burden of a tax. We can reinforce this point by noting explicitly that the incidence of a tax does *not* depend on whether the government collects a tax from the buyers of a good or from the sellers. Figure 4.12 illustrates this point by showing the effect on equilibrium in the market for gasoline if a 10-cents-per-gallon tax is imposed on buyers rather than on sellers. That is, we are now assuming that instead of sellers having to collect the 10-cents-per-gallon tax at the pump, buyers are responsible for keeping track of how many gallons of gasoline they purchase and sending the tax to the government. (Of course, it would be very difficult for buyers to keep track of their purchases or for the government to check whether they were paying all of the taxes they owe. That is why the government collects the tax on gasoline from sellers.)

Figure 4.12 is similar to Figure 4.11 except that it shows the gasoline tax being imposed on buyers rather than on sellers. In Figure 4.12, the supply curve does not shift because nothing has happened to change the quantity of gasoline sellers are willing to supply at any given price. The demand curve has shifted, however, because consumers now have to pay a 10-cent tax on every gallon of gasoline they buy. Therefore, at every quantity, they are willing to pay a price 10 cents lower than they would have without the tax. In the figure, we indicate the effect of the tax by shifting the demand curve down by 10 cents, from D_1 to D_2. Once the tax has been imposed and the demand curve has shifted down, the new equilibrium quantity of gasoline is 140 billion gallons, which is exactly the same as in Figure 4.11.

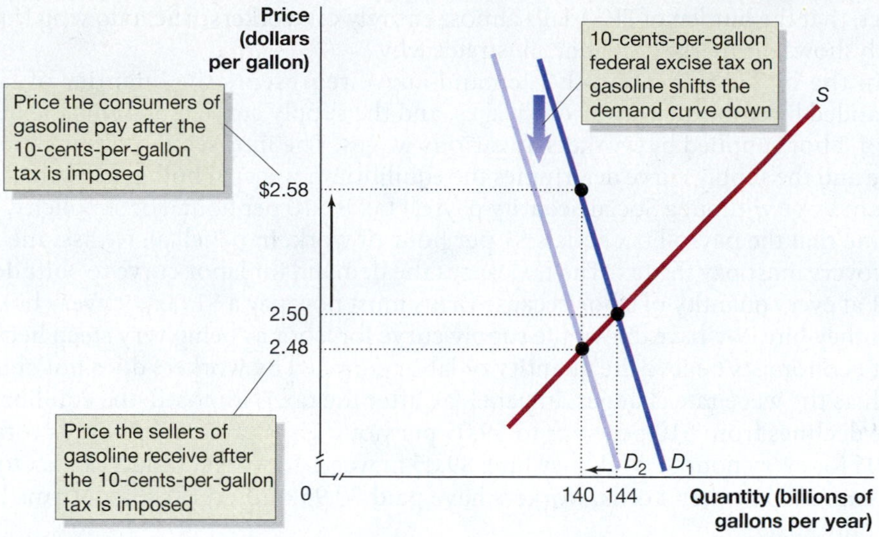

MyEconLab Animation

Figure 4.12 The Incidence of a Tax on Gasoline Paid by Buyers

With no tax on gasoline, the demand curve is D_1. If a 10-cents-per-gallon tax is imposed that consumers are responsible for paying, the demand curve shifts down by the amount of the tax, from D_1 to D_2. In the new equilibrium, consumers pay a price of $2.58 per gallon, including the tax. Producers receive $2.48 per gallon. The result is the same as when producers were responsible for paying the tax.

The new equilibrium price after the tax is imposed appears to be different in Figure 4.12 than in Figure 4.11, but if we include the tax, buyers will pay the same price and sellers will receive the same price in both figures. To see this point, notice that in Figure 4.11, buyers pay sellers a price of $2.58 per gallon. In Figure 4.12, they pay sellers only $2.48, but they must also pay the government a tax of 10 cents per gallon. So, the total price buyers pay remains $2.58 per gallon. In Figure 4.11, sellers receive $2.58 per gallon from buyers, but after they pay the tax of 10 cents per gallon, they are left with $2.48, which is the same amount they receive in Figure 4.12. MyEconLab Concept Check

Making the Connection

MyEconLab Video

Is the Burden of the Social Security Tax Really Shared Equally between Workers and Firms?

Most people who receive paychecks have several different taxes withheld by their employers, who forward the taxes directly to the government. In fact, after getting their first job, many people are shocked when they discover the gap between their gross pay and their net pay after taxes have been deducted. The largest tax many people of low or moderate income pay is FICA, which stands for the Federal Insurance Contributions Act. FICA funds the Social Security and Medicare programs, which provide income and health care to the elderly and disabled. FICA is sometimes referred to as the *payroll tax*. When Congress passed the act, it wanted employers and workers to equally share the burden of the tax. Currently, FICA is 15.3 percent of wages, with workers paying 7.65 percent, which is withheld from their paychecks, and employers paying the other 7.65 percent.

But does requiring workers and employers to each pay half the tax mean that the burden of the tax is also shared equally? Our discussion in this chapter shows that the answer is "no." In the labor market, employers are buyers, and workers are sellers. As we saw in the example of the federal tax on gasoline, whether the tax is collected from buyers or from sellers does not affect the incidence of the tax. Most economists believe, in fact, that the burden of FICA falls almost entirely on workers. The following figure, which shows the market for labor, illustrates why.

In the market for labor, the demand curve represents the quantity of labor demanded by employers at various wages, and the supply curve represents the quantity of labor supplied by workers at various wages. The intersection of the demand curve and the supply curve determines the equilibrium wage. In both panels, the equilibrium wage without a Social Security payroll tax is $10 per hour. For simplicity, let's assume that the payroll tax equals $1 per hour of work. In panel (a), we assume that employers must pay the tax. The tax causes the demand for labor curve to shift down by $1 at every quantity of labor because firms must now pay a $1 tax for every hour of labor they hire. We have drawn the supply curve for labor as being very steep because most economists believe the quantity of labor supplied by workers does not change much as the wage rate changes. In panel (a), after the tax is imposed, the equilibrium wage declines from $10 per hour to $9.05 per hour. Firms are now paying a total of $10.05 for every hour of work they hire: $9.05 in wages to workers and $1 in tax to the government. In other words, workers have paid $0.95 of the $1 tax, and firms have paid only $0.05.

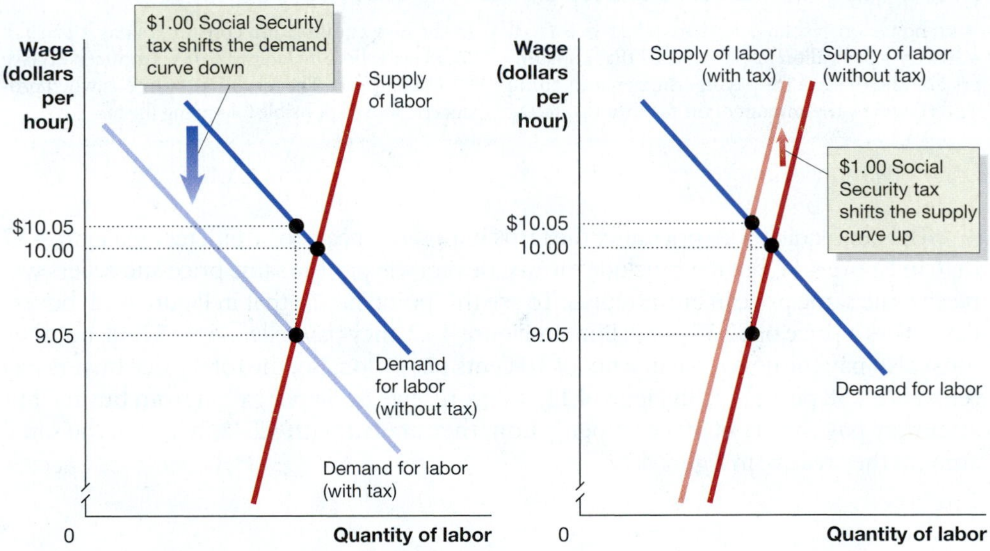

(a) The Social Security tax paid by employers

(b) The Social Security tax paid by workers

Panel (b) shows that this result is exactly the same when the tax is imposed on workers rather than on firms. In this case, the tax causes the supply curve for labor to shift up by $1 at every quantity of labor because workers must now pay a tax of $1 for every hour they work. After the tax is imposed, the equilibrium wage increases to $10.05 per hour. But workers receive only $9.05 after they have paid the $1.00 tax. Once again, workers have paid $0.95 of the $1 tax, and firms have paid only $0.05.

Although the figure presents a simplified analysis, it reflects the conclusion of most economists who have studied the incidence of FICA: Even though Congress requires employers to pay half the tax and workers to pay the other half, in fact, the burden of the tax falls almost entirely on workers. This conclusion would not be changed even if Congress revised the law to require either employers or workers to pay all of the tax. The forces of demand and supply working in the labor market, and not Congress, determine the incidence of the tax.

MyEconLab Study Plan

Your Turn: Test your understanding by doing related problems 4.9 and 4.10 on page 140 at the end of this chapter.

Continued from page 109

Economics in Your Life

Does Rent Control Make It Easier for You to Find an Affordable Apartment?

At the beginning of the chapter, we posed the following question: If you have job offers in two different cities, one with rent control and one without, are you more likely to find an affordable apartment in the city with rent control, or would you be better off looking for an apartment in a city without rent control? This chapter has shown that although rent control can keep rents lower than they might otherwise be, it can also lead to a permanent shortage of apartments. You may have to search for a long time to find a suitable apartment, and landlords may even ask you to give them additional payments in violation of the rent control law, which would make your actual rent higher than the controlled rent. Finding an apartment in a city without rent control should be much easier, although the rent may be higher.

Conclusion

Our discussion of the model of demand and supply shows that markets free from government intervention eliminate surpluses and shortages and do a good job of responding to the wants of consumers. We have seen that both consumers and firms sometimes try to use the government to change market outcomes in their favor. The concepts of consumer surplus, producer surplus, and deadweight loss allow us to measure the benefits consumers and producers receive from competitive market equilibrium. These concepts also allow us to measure the effects of government price floors and price ceilings and the economic effect of taxes.

Read *An Inside Look at Policy* on the next page for an example of regulatory and legal challenges that Airbnb faced in Malibu, California.

AN INSIDE LOOK AT POLICY

Airbnb Customers to Pay Hotel Taxes

MALIBU TIMES

Airbnb to Begin Collecting Taxes for City: Nearly a Year after Subpoenas Were Sent, Airbnb and Malibu Have Come to an Agreement

Those who rent out their homes or guest houses during busy weekends or keep a rental property by the beach to make extra cash will soon be kicking a few bucks back to Malibu [California] since Airbnb, one of the last holdouts against Malibu's demand for taxes, has finally come to an agreement with the City.

(a) City Council's May 2014 decision to subpoena vacation rental sites for info so they could collect transient occupancy "hotel" tax (TOT) from individuals leasing out private homes raised a few eyebrows around town, but nearly a year later, Airbnb has finally responded and, beginning on April 20, four out of the five sites they requested will now be handing the City its 12%.

"We are pleased to add Malibu to the growing list of cities where Airbnb is able to collect and remit occupancy taxes on behalf of our hosts, and where local rules embrace home sharing and the peer to peer economy," reads the official Airbnb announcement, authored by regional head of public policy David Owen.

City Attorney Christi Hogin explained that Airbnb is essentially agreeing to provide a service to those who rent out houses and apartments on its site, who are the ones legally responsible for collecting the tax.

"Airbnb is going to make it easy on the hosts by collecting the tax on their behalf and remitting it to the City, which the City is thrilled with," Hogin said.

"We think that Airbnb is totally doing the right thing here," Hogin added.

(b) The story began 11 months ago, when Assistant City Manager Reva Feldman prepared a staff report for City Council suggesting they go after rental sites, including Airbnb, HomeAway (owners of VRBO and FlipKey) and YBYC.

According to Feldman, the City was missing out on hundreds of thousands of dollars in tax revenue.

Now, Feldman says, though numbers from Airbnb aren't finalized, the city expects a bump from TOT.

"I can tell you that we expect for this fiscal year to get $450,000," Feldman said, "That's what we expect [now]. But I don't know until Airbnb provides me with data, what we can expect."

Hogin added that the tax money goes back to renters and hosts. "The money that we can use from those taxes is basically used for police, fire, roads, clean water: all of those things that both the residents and visitors employ," Hogin said.

As for the other sites issued subpoenas, only HomeAway is holding out. According to Feldman, there doesn't seem to be much hope for the City to collect the TOT from them, since they are not under legal obligation.

Since HomeAway does not have an L.A. County office, the subpoena from the City does not put any pressure on them, and, in addition, unlike some of the other sites, VRBO and FlipKey do not collect rental fees themselves.

"They're just an advertising site; they don't collect revenue through the site," Feldman said. "Unless they willingly comply, there's nothing we can do further with that."

(c) The City is making its money, but there has been little word about whether the tax will help cut down on vacation rentals, which was listed as a primary reason to issue the subpoenas in spring 2014.

"This is not a revenue-generating item. The reason we're doing this, the genesis of this, was we've been getting a tremendous amount of complaints from residents throughout all areas of the city," said Councilman Lou La Monte during a May 2014 council meeting.

Airbnb seems to have taken its agreement with the City to mean it's more welcome than ever to operate in Malibu neighborhoods.

"Our community in Malibu already brings significant economic and cultural benefits to the city, and this is another way we can make it even stronger," reads the Airbnb statement.

Source: Emily Sawicki, "Airbnb to Begin Collecting Taxes for City: Nearly a Year after Subpoenas Were Sent, Airbnb and Malibu Have Come to an Agreement," *Malibu Times*, April 8, 2015.

Key Points in the Article

The affluent beach community of Malibu, California, has reached an agreement with Airbnb that will require the company to collect hotel taxes on behalf of its customers who rent their homes through the Internet site. Beginning in April 2015, the city's 12 percent transient occupancy tax (TOT) will apply to anyone leasing out private homes via Airbnb. The city's initial estimate of first-year tax revenues collected from Airbnb was $450,000, which City Attorney David Hogin said will go toward services such as police and fire protection. While the collection of the TOT will generate revenue for the city, the primary motivation for collecting the tax was to cut down on vacation rentals in the community.

Analyzing the News

a Airbnb is an Internet site that matches homeowners who want to rent out rooms or their entire homes for a short period with travelers looking for short-term rentals. Since the company's inception in 2008, Airbnb has been criticized by hotel companies and some local government officials for not collecting local hotel taxes from its customers. Over the past few years, Airbnb has made an effort to appease the cities and hotel companies by agreeing to collect these taxes, as was demonstrated by the company's agreement with the city of Malibu to collect the 12 percent TOT. The figure below shows a hypothetical example of the effect of this tax on the market for vacation rental homes in Malibu. Without the tax, the equilibrium rent is $1,000 per week, with a quantity of 400 homes being rented each month. With a 12 percent tax ($120), the supply curve shifts up by $120, increasing the price the consumer pays to $1,060, decreasing the price the homeowner receives to $940, and decreasing the quantity of homes being rented to 320. The tax revenue is equal to $38,400 per month ($120 per rental × 320 rentals).

b The imposition of the 12 percent tax on Airbnb rentals will generate revenue for the city of Malibu, but it will also affect economic efficiency by reducing consumer and producer surplus. The renters (consumers), will pay a higher price for their vacation home rentals, which reduces consumer surplus, and the homeowners, or suppliers, will receive a lower price for renting their homes, which reduces producer surplus. Some of the reduction in consumer and producer surplus will become tax revenue for the city of Malibu, which the assistant city manager estimates at $450,000 for the first fiscal year the tax is in effect, but the rest of the loss in consumer and producer surplus is deadweight loss from the tax, a result of the decrease in the number of rentals due to the imposition of the tax.

c Although the imposition of a tax does generate revenue for Malibu, additional revenue is not necessarily the reason certain taxes are imposed. While the city pledged that the tax will be used to help pay for city services, the primary motivation for this tax is to discourage vacation home rentals. The city council cited complaints from residents about the number of homes in the community being used as short-term rental properties and proposed charging this tax as a way to reduce the number of rentals. As the figure below illustrates, when a tax is imposed, supply decreases, as does the equilibrium quantity of the product or service.

Thinking Critically about Policy

1. The figure below shows the market for vacation rental homes before and after the imposition of a 12 percent tax. How can we use the figure to measure the effect the tax has on economic efficiency? Redraw the graph and show the area representing the excess burden created by the implementation of the tax.
2. Airbnb has begun collecting hotel taxes in a number of cities. The figure below shows a hypothetical example of the effects of this tax on the market for vacation rental homes in Malibu. Redraw the graph to show what happens if renters, instead of Airbnb, were responsible for directly paying the tax to the city. Explain any differences in price, quantity, and tax incidence.

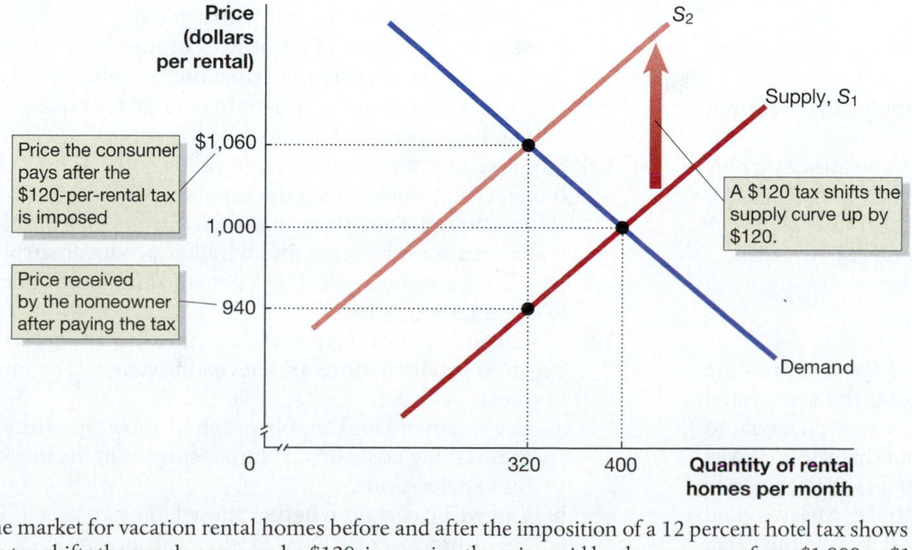

The market for vacation rental homes before and after the imposition of a 12 percent hotel tax shows that the tax shifts the supply curve up by $120, increasing the price paid by the consumer from $1,000 to $1,060 and decreasing the price received by the homeowner from $1,000 to $940.

CHAPTER SUMMARY AND PROBLEMS

Key Terms

Black market, p. 122
Consumer surplus, p. 110
Deadweight loss, p. 117
Economic efficiency, p. 117
Economic surplus, p. 116
Marginal benefit, p. 110
Marginal cost, p. 113
Price ceiling, p. 110
Price floor, p. 110
Producer surplus, p. 113
Tax incidence, p. 126

4.1 Consumer Surplus and Producer Surplus, pages 110–114

LEARNING OBJECTIVE: Distinguish between the concepts of consumer surplus and producer surplus.

Summary

Although most prices are determined by demand and supply in markets, the government sometimes imposes *price ceilings* and *price floors*. A **price ceiling** is a legally determined maximum price that sellers may charge. A **price floor** is a legally determined minimum price that sellers may receive. Economists analyze the effects of price ceilings and price floors by using the concepts of *consumer surplus*, *producer surplus*, and *deadweight loss*. **Marginal benefit** is the additional benefit to a consumer from consuming one more unit of a good or service. The demand curve is also a marginal benefit curve. **Consumer surplus** is the difference between the highest price a consumer is willing to pay for a good or service and the actual price the consumer pays. The total amount of consumer surplus in a market is equal to the area below the demand curve and above the market price. **Marginal cost** is the additional cost to a firm of producing one more unit of a good or service. The supply curve is also a marginal cost curve. **Producer surplus** is the difference between the lowest price a firm is willing to accept for a good or service and the price it actually receives. The total amount of producer surplus in a market is equal to the area above the supply curve and below the market price.

MyEconLab Visit **www.myeconlab.com** to complete these exercises online and get instant feedback.

Review Questions

1.1 What is marginal benefit? Why is the demand curve referred to as a marginal benefit curve?

1.2 What is marginal cost? Why is the supply curve referred to as a marginal cost curve?

1.3 What is consumer surplus? How does consumer surplus change as the equilibrium price of a good rises or falls?

1.4 What is producer surplus? How does producer surplus change as the equilibrium price of a good rises or falls?

Problems and Applications

1.5 On a shopping trip, Melanie decided to buy a light blue coat made from woven fabric. A tag on the coat stated that the price was $79.95. When she brought the coat to the store's sales clerk, Melanie was told that the coat was on sale, and she would pay 20 percent less than the price on the tag. After the discount was applied, Melanie paid $63.96, $15.99 less than the original price. Was the value of Melanie's consumer surplus from this purchase $79.95? $63.96? $15.99? Or some other amount? Briefly explain.

1.6 Uber is a company that offers people transportation by drivers who use their own cars for this purpose. Customers pay for their rides with their smartphone apps. Uber's prices fluctuate with the demand for the service. This "surge pricing" can result in different prices for the same distance traveled at different times of day or days of the week. Annie Lowrey, a writer for the *New York Times*, explained that she paid $13 for a 10 P.M. two-mile trip in downtown Washington, DC, on New Year's Eve. Three hours later she paid $47 for the return trip to her home. Did she receive negative consumer surplus on her return trip? Briefly explain.

Source: Annie Lowrey, "Is Uber's Surge-Pricing an Example of High Tech Gouging?" *New York Times*, January 10, 2014.

1.7 Consider the information given in the table on four consumers in the market for orange juice.

Consumer	Highest Price Willing to Pay
Jill	$4
Jose	3
Josh	2
Jordan	1

a. If the price of a bottle of orange juice is $0.75, what is the total consumer surplus received by these consumers? Illustrate your answer with a graph.

b. Suppose the price of a bottle of orange juice rises to $1.50. Now what is the consumer surplus received by these consumers? Illustrate your answer using the graph you prepared in part (a).

1.8 Suppose that a frost in Florida reduces the size of the orange crop, which causes the supply curve for oranges to shift to the left. Briefly explain whether consumer surplus will increase or decrease and whether producer surplus will increase or decrease. Use a demand and supply graph to illustrate your answers.

1.9 A *Wall Street Journal* article noted that as manufacturers began to produce more 4K television sets, their production costs declined.

a. Use a demand and supply graph to show the effect of these falling costs on consumer surplus in the marker for 4K televisions.

b. Can we be certain whether these falling costs will increase producer surplus? Briefly explain.

Source: Jack Wetherill and Brett Sappington, "Is Now the Time to Buy a 4K TV Set?" *Wall Street Journal*, May 11, 2014.

1.10 A student makes the following argument: "When a market is in equilibrium, there is no consumer surplus. We know this because in equilibrium, the market price is equal to the price consumers are willing to pay for the good." Briefly explain whether you agree with the student's argument.

1.11 In the following graph, is the consumer surplus larger with demand curve D_1 or demand curve D_2? Briefly explain. Compare the producer surplus with demand curve D_1 and with demand curve D_2.

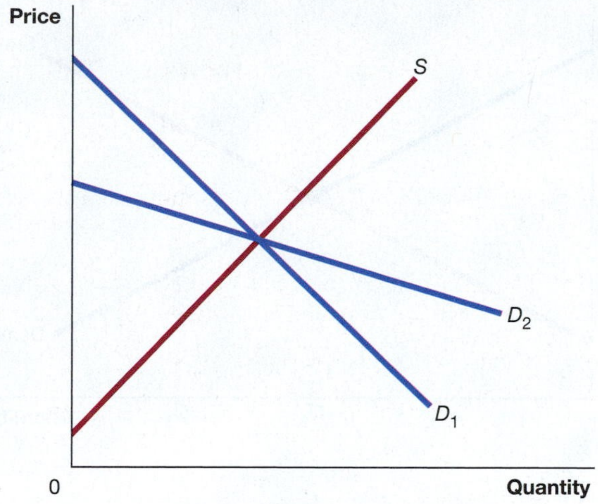

1.12 Assume that the following graph illustrates the market for a breast cancer–fighting drug, without which breast cancer patients cannot survive. What is the consumer surplus in this market? How does it differ from the consumer surplus in the markets you have studied up to this point?

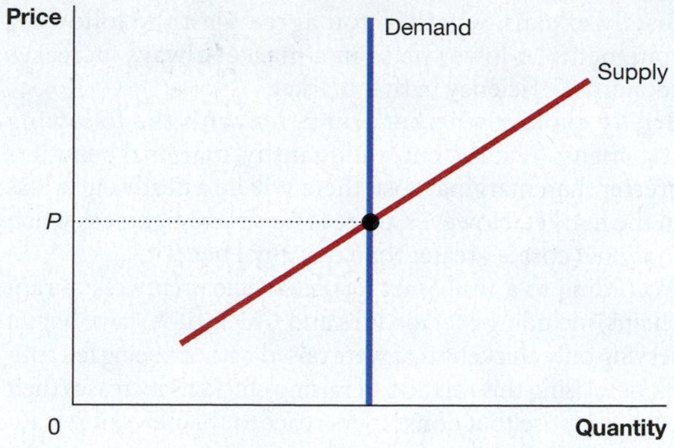

1.13 **(Related to the Making the Connection on page 112)** The *Making the Connection* states that the value of the area representing consumer surplus from broadband Internet service is $890.4 million. Use the information from the graph in the *Making the Connection* to show how this value was calculated. (For a review of how to calculate the area of a triangle, see the appendix to Chapter 1.)

1.14 The following graph shows the market for tickets to a concert that will be held in a local arena that seats 15,000 people. What is the producer surplus in this market? How does it differ from the producer surplus in the markets you have studied up to this point?

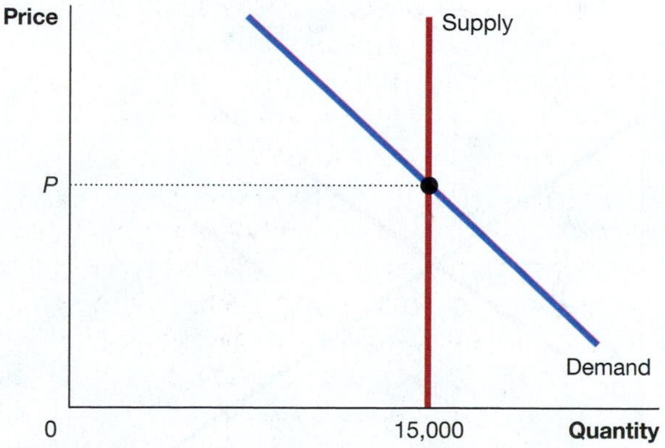

4.2 The Efficiency of Competitive Markets, pages 115–117

LEARNING OBJECTIVE: Explain the concept of economic efficiency.

Summary

Equilibrium in a competitive market is economically efficient. **Economic surplus** is the sum of consumer surplus and producer surplus. **Economic efficiency** is a market outcome in which the marginal benefit to consumers from the last unit produced is equal to the marginal cost of production and in which the sum of consumer surplus and producer surplus is at a maximum. When the market price is above or below the equilibrium price, there is a reduction in economic surplus. The reduction in economic surplus resulting from a market not being in competitive equilibrium is called the **deadweight loss**.

MyEconLab Visit **www.myeconlab.com** to complete these exercises online and get instant feedback.

Review Questions

2.1 Define *economic surplus* and *deadweight loss*.

2.2 What is economic efficiency? Why do economists define efficiency in this way?

Problems and Applications

2.3 A *Wall Street Journal* article about a drought in California indicated that one result would be a smaller tomato crop. Use a demand and supply graph of the tomato market to illustrate the effect of the drought. Is economic efficiency affected? Briefly explain.

Source: Jim Carlton, "California Farmers Face Another Year without Federal Water," *Wall Street Journal*, February 27, 2015.

2.4 Briefly explain whether you agree with the following statement: "A lower price in a market always increases economic efficiency in that market."

2.5 Briefly explain whether you agree with the following statement: "If at the current quantity, marginal benefit is greater than marginal cost, there will be a deadweight loss in the market. However, there is no deadweight loss when marginal cost is greater than marginal benefit."

2.6 According to a *Wall Street Journal* article, many restaurant chains, including McDonald's and Chick-fil-A, have begun serving only chickens that were raised without being fed antibiotics. Using this method of raising chickens increases their cost. Suppose that consumers react to the news of restaurants selling antibiotic-free chicken sandwiches by increasing their demand for the sandwiches. Can you tell whether economic surplus will increase in the market for chicken sandwiches? Use a graph of the market for chicken sandwiches to illustrate your answer.

Source: David Kesmodel, Jacob Bunge, and Annie Gasparro, "McDonald's to Curb Antibiotics in Chicken," *Wall Street Journal*, March 4, 2015.

2.7 Briefly explain whether you agree with the following statement: "If consumer surplus in a market increases, producer surplus must decrease."

2.8 Using the following graph, show the effects on consumer surplus and producer surplus of an increase in supply from S_1 to S_2. By how much does economic surplus increase?

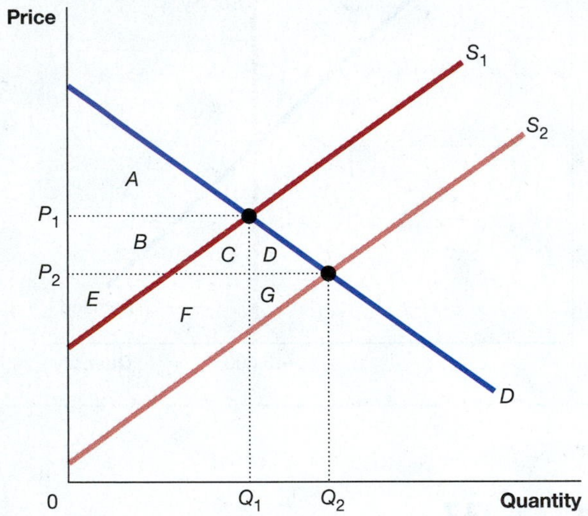

2.9 A student argues: "Economic surplus is greatest at the level of output where the difference between marginal benefit and marginal cost is largest." Do you agree? Briefly explain.

2.10 Using the following graph, explain why economic surplus would be smaller if Q_1 or Q_3 were the quantity produced than if Q_2 is the quantity produced.

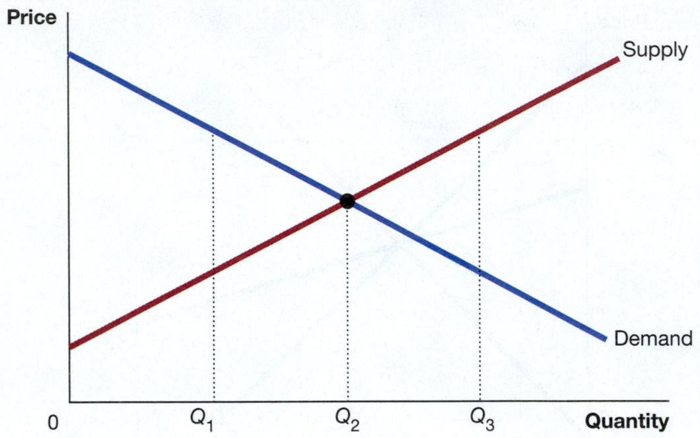

4.3 Government Intervention in the Market: Price Floors and Price Ceilings, pages 117–125

LEARNING OBJECTIVE: Explain the economic effect of government-imposed price floors and price ceilings.

Summary

Producers or consumers who are dissatisfied with the equilibrium in a market can attempt to convince the government to impose a price floor or a price ceiling. Price floors usually increase producer surplus, decrease consumer surplus, and cause a deadweight loss. Price ceilings usually increase consumer surplus, reduce producer surplus, and cause a deadweight loss. The results of the government imposing price ceilings and price floors are that some people win, some people lose, and a loss of economic efficiency occurs. Price ceilings and price floors can lead to a **black market**, in which buying and selling take place at prices that violate government price regulations. Positive analysis is concerned with *what is*, and normative analysis is concerned with *what should be*. Positive analysis shows that price ceilings and price floors cause deadweight losses. Whether these policies are desirable or undesirable, though, is a normative question.

MyEconLab Visit **www.myeconlab.com** to complete these exercises online and get instant feedback.

Review Questions

3.1 Why do some consumers tend to favor price controls while others tend to oppose them?

3.2 Do producers tend to favor price floors or price ceilings? Briefly explain.

3.3 What is a black market? Under what circumstances do black markets arise?

3.4 Can economic analysis provide a final answer to the question of whether the government should intervene in markets by imposing price ceilings and price floors? Briefly explain.

Problems and Applications

3.5 The following graph shows the market for apples. Assume that the government has imposed a price floor of $10 per crate.

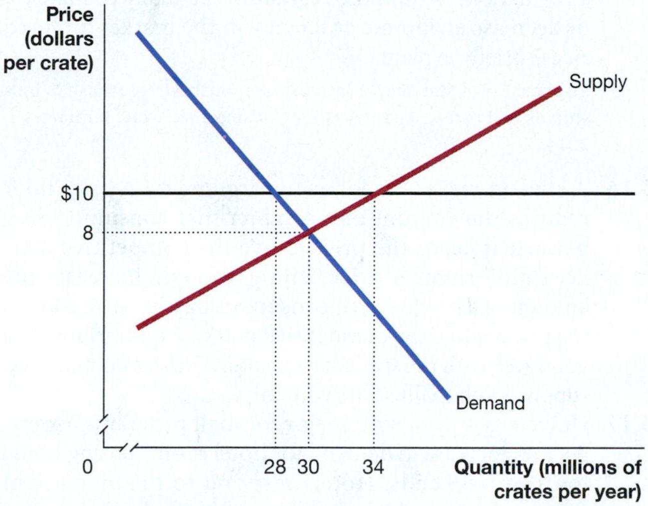

a. How many crates of apples will be sold to consumers after the price floor has been imposed?
b. Will there be a shortage or a surplus of apples? If there is a shortage or a surplus, how large will it be?
c. Will apple producers benefit from the price floor? If so, explain how they will benefit.

3.6 Use the information on the kumquat market in the table to answer the following questions:

Price (per Crate)	Quantity Demanded (Millions of Crates per Year)	Quantity Supplied (Millions of Crates per Year)
$10	120	20
15	110	60
20	100	100
25	90	140
30	80	180
35	70	220

a. What are the equilibrium price and quantity? How much revenue do kumquat producers receive when the market is in equilibrium? Draw a graph showing the market equilibrium and the area representing the revenue kumquat producers receive.
b. Suppose the federal government decides to impose a price floor of $30 per crate. Now how many crates of kumquats will consumers purchase? How much revenue will kumquat producers receive? Assume that the government does not purchase any surplus kumquats. On your graph from part (a), show the price floor, the change in the quantity of kumquats purchased, and the revenue kumquat producers receive after the price floor is imposed.
c. Suppose the government imposes a price floor of $30 per crate and purchases any surplus kumquats from producers. Now how much revenue will kumquat producers receive? How much will the government spend on purchasing surplus kumquats? On your graph from part (a), show the area representing the amount the government spends to purchase the surplus kumquats.

3.7 Suppose that the government sets a price floor for milk that is above the competitive equilibrium price and that the government does not purchase any surplus milk.
a. Draw a graph showing this situation. Be sure your graph shows the competitive equilibrium price, the price floor, the quantity that would be sold in competitive equilibrium, and the quantity that would be sold with the price floor.
b. Compare the economic surplus in this market when there is a price floor and when there is not.

3.8 In Allentown, Pennsylvania, in the summer of 2014, the average price of a gallon of gasoline was $3.68—a 22-cent increase from the year before. Many consumers were upset by the increase. One consumer was quoted in a local newspaper as saying, "It's crazy. The government should step in." Suppose the government had stepped in and imposed a price ceiling equal to the old price of $3.46 per gallon.
a. Draw a graph showing the effect of the price ceiling on the market for gasoline. Be sure that your graph shows:
   i. The price and quantity of gasoline before and after the price ceiling is imposed
   ii. The areas representing consumer surplus and producer surplus before and after the price ceiling is imposed
   iii. The area of deadweight loss
b. Will the consumer who was complaining about the increase in the price of gasoline definitely be made better off by the price ceiling? Briefly explain.

Source: Sam Kennedy, "Valley Feeling Pain at the Pump," (Allentown, PA) *Morning Call*, June 21, 2014.

3.9 According to a *New York Times* article, the Venezuelan government "imposes strict price controls that are intended to make a range of foods and other goods more affordable for the poor. They are often the very products that are the hardest to find."
a. Why would imposing price controls on goods make them hard to find?
b. One of the goods subject to price controls was toothpaste. Draw a graph to illustrate this situation. On your graph, be sure to indicate the areas representing consumer surplus, producer surplus, and deadweight loss.

Source: William Neuman, "With Venezuelan Cupboards Bare, Some Blame Price Controls," *New York Times*, April 20, 2012.

3.10 **(Related to the Making the Connection on page 119)** A *Wall Street Journal* article noted that a study by the U.S. Congressional Budget Office "estimated raising the minimum wage to $10.10 an hour would reduce U.S. employment by 500,000 but lift 900,000 Americans out of poverty." Why might raising the minimum wage reduce employment? How would it raise some people out of poverty? What effect might these estimates have on a *normative* analysis of the minimum wage?

Source: Julie Jargon and Eric Morath, "As Wage Debate Rages, Some Have Made the Shift," *Wall Street Journal*, April 8, 2014.

3.11 **(Related to the Chapter Opener on page 109)** If San Francisco were to repeal its rent control law, would the prices for short-term rentals in the city listed on Airbnb and other peer-to-peer sites be likely to rise or fall? Briefly explain.

3.12 **(Related to the Chapter Opener on page 109)** The competitive equilibrium rent in the city of Lowell is currently $1,000 per month. The government decides to enact rent control and establish a price ceiling of $750 per month for apartments. Briefly explain whether rent control is likely to make each of the following people better or worse off.

a. Someone currently renting an apartment in Lowell
b. Someone who will be moving to Lowell next year and who intends to rent an apartment
c. A landlord who intends to abide by the rent control law
d. A landlord who intends to ignore the law and illegally charge the highest rent possible for his apartments

3.13 **(Related to the Don't Let This Happen to You on page 121)** Briefly explain whether you agree with the following statement: "If there is a shortage of a good, it must be scarce, but there is not a shortage of every scarce good."

3.14 **(Related to Solved Problem 4.3 on page 122)** Use the information on the market for apartments in Bay City in the table to answer the following questions:

Rent	Quantity Demanded	Quantity Supplied
$500	375,000	225,000
600	350,000	250,000
700	325,000	275,000
800	300,000	300,000
900	275,000	325,000
1,000	250,000	350,000

a. In the absence of rent control, what is the equilibrium rent, and what is the equilibrium quantity of apartments rented? Draw a demand and supply graph of the market for apartments to illustrate your answer. In equilibrium, will there be any renters who are unable to find an apartment to rent or any landlords who are unable to find a renter for an apartment?
b. Suppose the government sets a ceiling of $600 per month on rents. What is the quantity of apartments demanded, and what is the quantity of apartments supplied?
c. Assume that all landlords abide by the law in part (b). Use a demand and supply graph to illustrate the effect of this price ceiling on the market for apartments. Be sure to indicate on your graph each of the following: (i) the area representing consumer surplus after the price ceiling has been imposed, (ii) the area representing producer surplus after the price ceiling has been imposed, and (iii) the area representing the deadweight loss after the price ceiling has been imposed.
d. Assume that the quantity of apartments supplied is the same as you determined in (b), but now assume that landlords ignore the law and rent this quantity of apartments for the highest rent they can get. Briefly explain what this rent will be.

3.15 **(Related to the Making the Connection on page 124)** According to a news story, after taxi drivers in Paris protested against Uber, the government passed a new regulation "requiring a minimum 15-minute wait between the time a car is booked and the passenger is picked up." Why would taxi drivers believe they benefit from such a regulation? Would the regulation be likely to increase or decrease economic efficiency in the market for hired rides? Briefly explain.

Source: Carol Matlack, "Paris Cabbies Slash Tires, Smash Windshields in Protest Against Uber," *businessweek.com*, January 13, 2014.

3.16 A student makes the following argument: "A price floor reduces the amount of a product that consumers buy because it keeps the price above the competitive market equilibrium. A price ceiling, though, increases the amount of a product that consumers buy because it keeps the price below the competitive market equilibrium." Do you agree with the student's reasoning? Use a demand and supply graph to illustrate your answer.

3.17 University towns with major football programs experience an increase in demand for hotel rooms during home football weekends. Hotels respond to the increase in demand by increasing the prices they charge for rooms. Periodically, there is an outcry against the higher prices and accusations of "price gouging."

a. Draw a demand and supply graph of the market for hotel rooms in Boostertown for weekends with home football games and another graph for weekends without home football games. If the Boostertown city council passes a law stating that prices for rooms are not allowed to rise, what would happen to the market for hotel rooms during home football game weekends? Show your answer on your graph.
b. If the prices of hotel rooms are not allowed to increase, what will be the effect on out-of-town football fans?
c. How might the city council's law affect the supply of hotel rooms over time? Briefly explain.
d. University towns are not the only places that face peak and nonpeak "seasons." Can you think of other locations that face a large increase in demand for hotel rooms during particular times of the year? Why do we typically not see laws limiting the prices hotels can charge during peak seasons?

3.18 Suppose that initially the gasoline market is in equilibrium, at a price of $2.50 per gallon and a quantity of 45 million gallons per month. Then a war in the Middle East disrupts imports of oil into the United States, shifting the supply curve for gasoline from S_1 to S_2. The price of gasoline begins to rise, and consumers protest. The federal government responds by setting a price ceiling of $2.50 per gallon. Use the graph to answer the following questions.

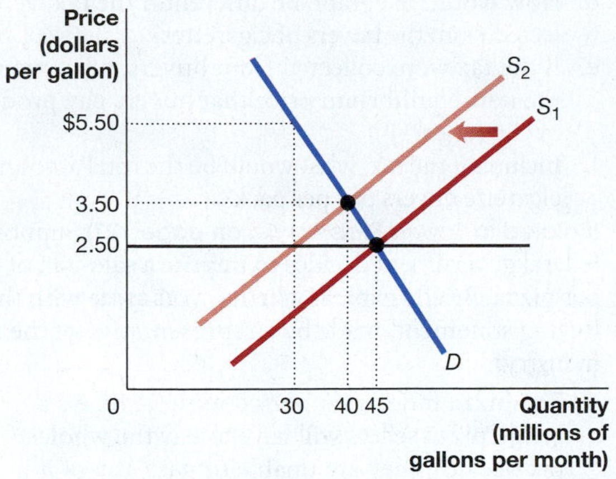

a. If there were no price ceiling, what would be the equilibrium price of gasoline, the quantity of gasoline demanded, and the quantity of gasoline supplied? Now assume that the price ceiling is imposed and that there is no black market in gasoline. What are the price of gasoline, the quantity of gasoline demanded, and the quantity of gasoline supplied? How large is the shortage of gasoline?

b. Assume that the price ceiling is imposed, and there is no black market in gasoline. Show on the graph the areas representing consumer surplus, producer surplus, and deadweight loss.

c. Now assume that there is a black market, and the price of gasoline rises to the maximum that consumers are willing to pay for the amount supplied by producers, at $2.50 per gallon. Show on the graph the areas representing producer surplus, consumer surplus, and deadweight loss.

d. Are consumers made better off with the price ceiling than without it? Briefly explain.

3.19 An editorial in the *Economist* magazine discusses the fact that in most countries—including the United States—it is illegal for individuals to buy or sell body parts, such as kidneys.

a. Draw a demand and supply graph for the market for kidneys. Show on your graph the legal maximum price of zero and indicate the quantity of kidneys supplied at this price. (*Hint:* Because we know that some kidneys are donated, the quantity supplied will not be zero.)

b. The editorial argues that buying and selling kidneys should be legalized:

> With proper regulation, a kidney market would be a big improvement over the current sorry state of affairs. Sellers could be checked for disease and drug use, and cared for after operations. ... Buyers would get better kidneys, faster. Both sellers and buyers would do better than in the illegal market, where much of the money goes to middlemen.

Do you agree with this argument? Should the government treat kidneys like other goods and allow the market to determine the price?

Source: "Psst, Wanna Buy a Kidney?" *Economist*, November 18, 2006.

4.4 The Economic Effect of Taxes, pages 125–130

LEARNING OBJECTIVE: Analyze the economic effect of taxes.

Summary

Most taxes result in a loss of consumer surplus, a loss of producer surplus, and a deadweight loss. The true burden of a tax is not just the amount consumers and producers pay to the government but also includes the deadweight loss. The deadweight loss from a tax is called the excess burden of the tax. **Tax incidence** is the actual division of the burden of a tax. In most cases, consumers and firms share the burden of a tax levied on a good or service.

MyEconLab Visit **www.myeconlab.com** to complete these exercises online and get instant feedback.

Review Questions

4.1 What is meant by *tax incidence?*

4.2 What do economists mean by an *efficient tax?*

4.3 Does who is legally responsible for paying a tax—buyers or sellers—make a difference in the amount of tax each pays? Briefly explain.

4.4 As explained in the chapter, economic efficiency is a market outcome in which the marginal benefit to consumers of the last unit produced is equal to its marginal cost of production. Using this explanation of economic efficiency, explain why a tax creates a deadweight loss.

Problems and Applications

4.5 Suppose the current equilibrium price of a quarter-pound hamburger is $5, and 10 million quarter-pound hamburgers are sold per month. After the federal government imposes a tax of $0.50 per hamburger, the equilibrium price of hamburgers rises to $5.20, and the equilibrium quantity falls to 9 million. Illustrate this situation with a demand and supply graph. Be sure your graph shows the equilibrium price before and after the tax; the equilibrium quantity before and after the tax; and the areas representing consumer surplus after the tax, producer surplus after the tax, tax revenue collected by the government, and deadweight loss.

4.6 The following graph shows the effect of a tax imposed on soft drinks. Use this graph to answer the questions.

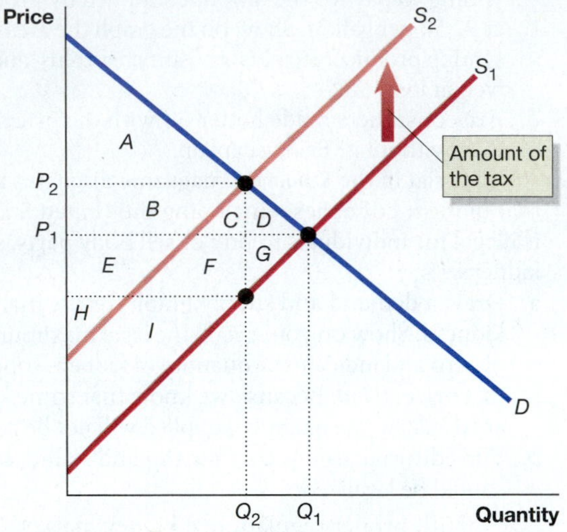

a. Which areas in the graph represent the excess burden (deadweight loss) of the tax?
b. Which areas represent the revenues collected by the government from the tax?
c. Would this tax on soft drinks be considered efficient? Briefly explain.

4.7 Use the following graph of the market for cigarettes to answer the questions.

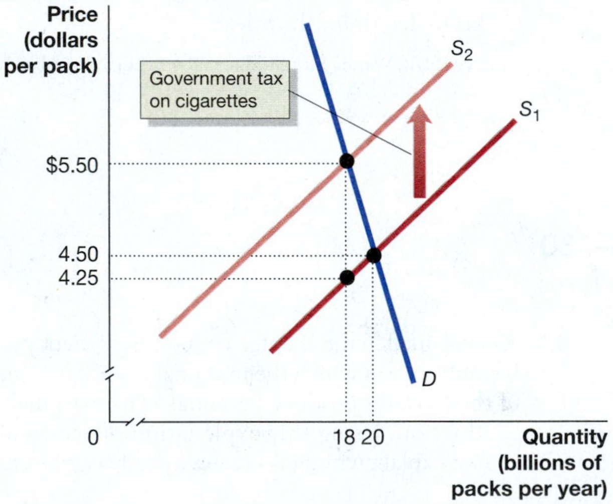

a. According to the graph, how much is the government tax on cigarettes?
b. What price do producers receive after paying the tax?
c. How much tax revenue does the government collect?
d. How would the graph be different if the tax were collected from the buyers of cigarettes?
e. If the tax were collected from buyers, what would be the new equilibrium price that buyers pay producers of cigarettes?
f. Including the tax, what would be the total amount that cigarette buyers pay per pack?

4.8 **(Related to Solved Problem 4.4 on page 127)** Suppose the federal government decides to impose a sales tax of $1.00 per pizza. Briefly explain whether you agree with the following statement, made by a representative of the pizza industry:

> The pizza industry is very competitive. As a result, pizza sellers will have to pay the whole tax because they are unable to pass any of it on to consumers in the form of higher prices. Therefore, a sales tax of $1.00 per pizza will result in pizza sellers receiving $1.00 less on each pizza sold, after paying the tax.

Illustrate your answer with a graph.

4.9 **(Related to the Making the Connection on page 129)** According to a news story, Pennsylvania's liquor tax is "paid by the seller—the restaurant or bar owner—when the seller buys liquor from state-run wine and spirit stores." Briefly explain the effect of how liquor taxes in Pennsylvania are collected has on the price of a glass of wine purchased by a consumer in a restaurant in the state.

Source: Matt Assad, "How Booze Brings Heady Development," (Allentown, PA) *Morning Call*, February 22, 2015.

4.10 **(Related to the Making the Connection on page 129)** Suppose the government imposes a payroll tax of $1 per hour of work and collects the tax from employers. Use a graph for the market for labor to show the effect of the payroll tax, assuming the special case of a vertical supply curve of labor. By how much does the new equilibrium wage that employers pay workers fall?

Appendix

Quantitative Demand and Supply Analysis

LEARNING OBJECTIVE: Use quantitative demand and supply analysis.

Graphs help us understand economic change *qualitatively*. For instance, a demand and supply graph can tell us that if household incomes rise, the demand curve for a normal good will shift to the right, and the price of the good will rise. Often, though, economists, business managers, and policymakers want to know more than the qualitative direction of change; they want a *quantitative estimate* of the size of the change.

In this chapter, we carried out a qualitative analysis of rent controls. We saw that imposing rent controls involves a trade-off: Renters as a group gain, but landlords lose, and the market for apartments becomes less efficient, as shown by the deadweight loss. To better evaluate rent controls, we need to know more than just that these gains and losses exist; we need to know how large they are. A quantitative analysis of rent controls will tell us how large the gains and losses are.

Demand and Supply Equations

The first step in a quantitative analysis is to supplement our use of demand and supply curves with demand and supply *equations*. Economists use data on prices, quantities, and other economic variables to statistically estimate equations for demand and supply curves. For example, suppose that economists have estimated that the demand for apartments in New York City is:

$$Q^D = 4{,}750{,}000 - 1{,}000P,$$

and the supply of apartments is:

$$Q^S = -1{,}000{,}000 + 1{,}300P.$$

We have used Q^D for the quantity of apartments demanded per month, Q^S for the quantity of apartments supplied per month, and P for the apartment rent, in dollars per month. In reality, both the quantity of apartments demanded and the quantity of apartments supplied will depend on more than just the rental price of apartments in New York City. The demand for apartments in New York City will also depend, for instance, on the average incomes of families in the New York area and on the rents of apartments in the surrounding cities. For simplicity, we will ignore these other factors.

With no government intervention, we know that at competitive market equilibrium, the quantity demanded must equal the quantity supplied, or:

$$Q^D = Q^S.$$

We can use this equation, which is called an *equilibrium condition*, to solve for the equilibrium monthly apartment rent by setting the quantity demanded from the demand equation equal to the quantity supplied from the supply equation:

$$4{,}750{,}000 - 1{,}000P = -1{,}000{,}000 + 1{,}300P$$

$$5{,}750{,}000 = 2{,}300P$$

$$P = \frac{5{,}750{,}000}{2{,}300} = \$2{,}500.$$

We can then substitute this price back into either the supply equation or the demand equation to find the equilibrium quantity of apartments rented:

$$Q^D = 4{,}750{,}000 - 1{,}000P = 4{,}750{,}000 - 1{,}000(2{,}500) = 2{,}250{,}000,$$

or:

$$Q^S = -1{,}000{,}000 + 1{,}300P = -1{,}000{,}000 + 1{,}300(2{,}500) = 2{,}250{,}000.$$

Figure 4A.1 illustrates the information from these equations in a graph. The figure shows the values for rent when both the quantity supplied and the quantity demanded are zero. These values can be calculated from the demand and supply equations by setting Q^D and Q^S equal to zero and solving for price:

$$Q^D = 0 = 4{,}750{,}000 - 1{,}000P$$

$$P = \frac{4{,}750{,}000}{1{,}000} = \$4{,}750$$

and:

$$Q^S = 0 = -1{,}000{,}000 + 1{,}300P$$

$$P = \frac{-1{,}000{,}000}{-1{,}300} = \$769.23.$$

MyEconLab Concept Check

Calculating Consumer Surplus and Producer Surplus

Figure 4A.1 shows consumer surplus and producer surplus in this market.

Recall that the sum of consumer surplus and producer surplus equals the net benefit that renters and landlords receive from participating in the market for apartments. We can use the values from the demand and supply equations to calculate the value of consumer surplus and producer surplus. Remember that consumer surplus is the area below the demand curve and above the line representing market price. Notice that this area forms a right triangle because the demand curve is a straight line—it is *linear*. As we noted in the appendix to Chapter 1, the area of a triangle is equal to ½ × Base × Height. In this case, the area is:

$$\frac{1}{2} \times (2{,}250{,}000) \times (4{,}750 - 2{,}500) = \$2{,}531{,}250{,}000.$$

So, this calculation tells us that the consumer surplus in the market for rental apartments in New York City is about \$2.5 billion per month.

MyEconLab Animation

Figure 4A.1

Graphing Supply and Demand Equations

After statistically estimating supply and demand equations, we can use the equations to draw supply and demand curves. In this case, the equilibrium rent for apartments is \$2,500 per month, and the equilibrium quantity of apartments rented is 2,250,000. The supply equation tells us that at a rent of \$769, the quantity of apartments supplied will be zero. The demand equation tells us that at a rent of \$4,750, the quantity of apartments demanded will be zero. The areas representing consumer surplus and producer surplus are also indicated on the graph.

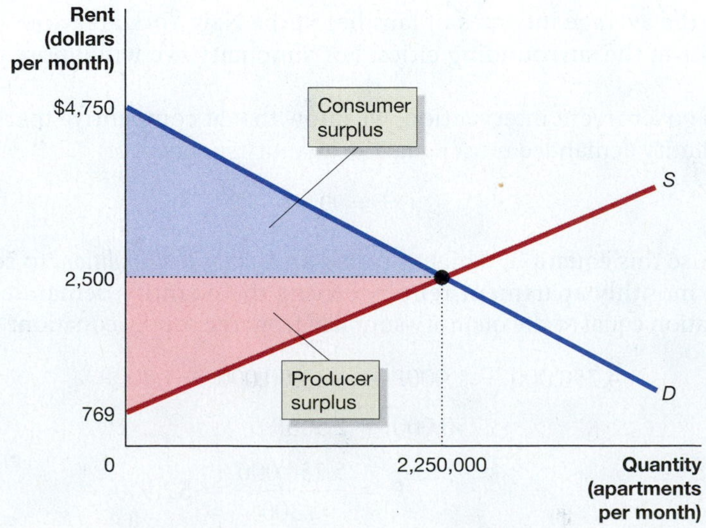

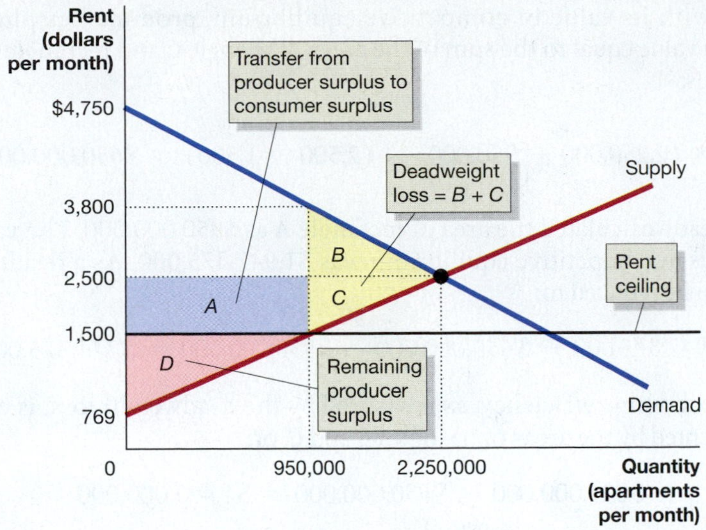

MyEconLab Animation

Figure 4A.2

Calculating the Economic Effect of Rent Controls

Once we have estimated equations for the demand and supply of rental housing, a diagram can guide our numerical estimates of the economic effects of rent control. Consumer surplus falls by an amount equal to the area of triangle *B* and increases by an amount equal to the area of rectangle *A*. Producer surplus falls by an amount equal to the sum of the areas of rectangle *A* and triangle *C*. The remaining producer surplus is equal to the area of triangle *D*. Deadweight loss is equal to the sum of the areas of triangles *B* and *C*.

We can calculate producer surplus in a similar way. Remember that producer surplus is the area above the supply curve and below the line representing market price. Because the supply curve is also a straight line, producer surplus in the figure is equal to the area of the triangle:

$$\frac{1}{2} \times 2{,}250{,}000 \times (2{,}500 - 769) = \$1{,}947{,}375{,}000.$$

This calculation tells us that the producer surplus in the market for rental apartments in New York City is about $1.9 billion per month.

We can use the same type of analysis to measure the effect of rent control on consumer surplus, producer surplus, and economic efficiency. For instance, suppose the city imposes a rent ceiling of $1,500 per month. Figure 4A.2 can help guide us as we measure the effect.

First, we can calculate the quantity of apartments that will actually be rented by substituting the rent ceiling of $1,500 into the supply equation:

$$Q^S = -1{,}000{,}000 + (1{,}300 \times 1{,}500) = 950{,}000.$$

We also need to know the price on the demand curve when the quantity of apartments is 950,000. We can do this by substituting 950,000 for quantity in the demand equation and solving for price:

$$950{,}000 = 4{,}750{,}000 - 1{,}000P$$

$$P = \frac{-3{,}8000{,}000}{-1{,}000} = \$3{,}800.$$

Compared with its value in competitive equilibrium, consumer surplus has been reduced by a value equal to the area of triangle *B* but increased by a value equal to the area of rectangle A. The area of triangle *B* is:

$$\frac{1}{2} \times (2{,}250{,}000 - 950{,}000) \times (3{,}800 - 2{,}500) = \$845{,}000{,}000,$$

and the area of rectangle *A* is Base × Height, or:

$$(\$2{,}500 - \$1{,}500) \times (950{,}000) = \$950{,}000{,}000.$$

The value of consumer surplus in competitive equilibrium was $2,531,250,000. As a result of the rent ceiling, it will be increased to:

$$(\$2{,}531{,}250{,}000 + 950{,}000{,}000) - \$845{,}000{,}000 = \$2{,}636{,}250{,}000.$$

Compared with its value in competitive equilibrium, producer surplus has been reduced by a value equal to the sum of the areas of triangle C and rectangle A. The area of triangle C is:

$$\frac{1}{2} \times (2{,}250{,}000 - 950{,}000) \times (2{,}500 - 1{,}500) = \$650{,}000{,}000.$$

We have already calculated the area of rectangle A as $950,000,000. The value of producer surplus in competitive equilibrium was $1,947,375,000. As a result of the rent ceiling, it will be reduced to:

$$\$1{,}947{,}375{,}000 - \$650{,}000{,}000 - \$950{,}000{,}000 = \$347{,}375{,}000.$$

The loss of economic efficiency, as measured by the deadweight loss, is equal to the value represented by the areas of triangles B and C, or:

$$\$845{,}000{,}000 + \$650{,}000{,}000 = \$1{,}495{,}000{,}000$$

The following table summarizes the results of the analysis (the values are in millions of dollars):

Consumer Surplus		Producer Surplus		Deadweight Loss	
Competitive Equilibrium	Rent Control	Competitive Equilibrium	Rent Control	Competitive Equilibrium	Rent Control
$2,531	$2,636	$1,947	$347	$0	$1,495

Qualitatively, we know that imposing rent control will make consumers better off, make landlords worse off, and decrease economic efficiency. The advantage of the analysis we have just gone through is that it puts dollar values on the qualitative results. We can now see how much consumers have gained, how much landlords have lost, and how great the decline in economic efficiency has been. Sometimes the quantitative results can be surprising. Notice, for instance, that after the imposition of rent control, the deadweight loss is actually much greater than the remaining producer surplus. Of course, these results are dependent on the numbers we chose for the demand and supply curve equations. Choosing different numbers would have changed the results.

Economists often study issues where the qualitative results of actions are apparent, even to non-economists. You don't have to be an economist to understand who wins and who loses from rent control or that if a company cuts the price of its product, its sales will increase. Business managers, policymakers, and the general public do, however, need economists to measure quantitatively the effects of different actions—including policies such as rent control—so that they can better assess the results of these actions.

MyEconLab Study Plan

4A Quantitative Demand and Supply Analysis, pages 141–144

LEARNING OBJECTIVE: Use quantitative demand and supply analysis.

MyEconLab Visit www.myeconlab.com to complete these exercises online and get instant feedback.

Review Questions

4A.1 In a linear demand equation, what economic information is conveyed by the intercept on the price axis? Similarly, what economic information is conveyed by the intercept on the price axis in a linear supply equation?

4A.2 Suppose you were assigned the task of choosing a price that maximizes economic surplus in a market. What price would you choose? Why?

4A.3 Consumer surplus is used as a measure of a consumer's net benefit from purchasing a good or service. Explain why consumer surplus is a measure of net benefit.

4A.4 Why would economists use the term *deadweight loss* to describe the effect on consumer surplus and producer surplus from a price control?

Problems and Applications

4A.5 Suppose that you have been hired to analyze the effect on employment from the imposition of a minimum wage in the labor market. Further suppose that you estimate the demand and supply functions for labor, where L stands for the quantity of labor (measured in thousands of workers) and W stands for the wage rate (measured in dollars per hour):

$$\text{Demand: } L^D = 100 - 4W$$

$$\text{Supply: } L^S = 6W$$

First, calculate the free market equilibrium wage and quantity of labor. Now suppose the proposed minimum wage is \$12. How large will the surplus of labor in this market be?

4A.6 The following graphs illustrate the markets for two different types of labor. Suppose an identical minimum wage is imposed in both markets. In which market will the minimum wage have the largest impact on employment? Why?

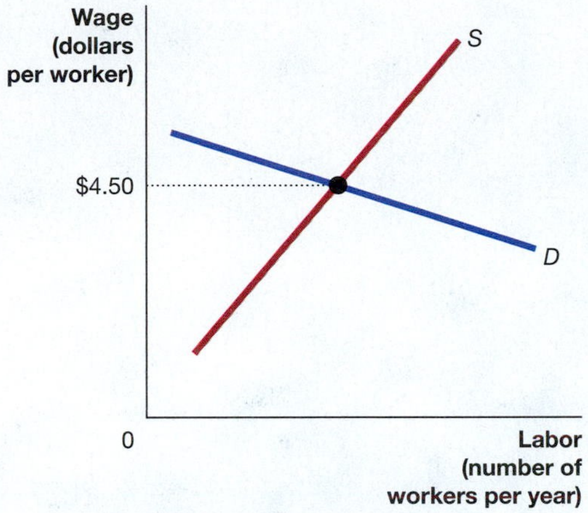

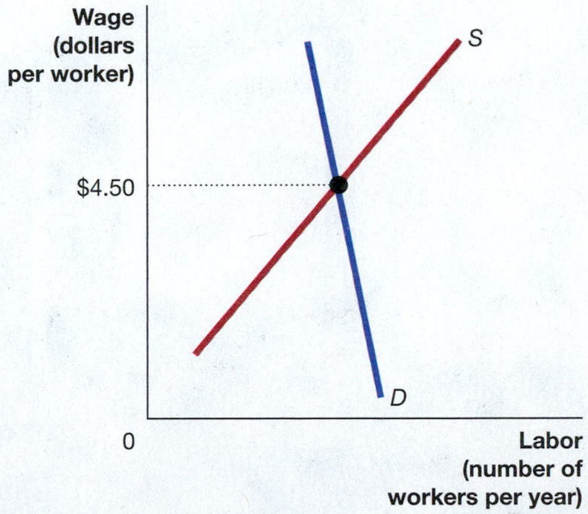

4A.7 Suppose that you are the vice president of operations of a manufacturing firm that sells an industrial lubricant in a competitive market. Further suppose that your economist gives you the following demand and supply functions:

$$\text{Demand: } Q^D = 45 - 2P$$

$$\text{Supply: } Q^S = -15 + P$$

What is the consumer surplus in this market? What is the producer surplus?

4A.8 The following graph shows a market in which a price floor of \$3.00 per unit has been imposed. Calculate the values of each of the following.

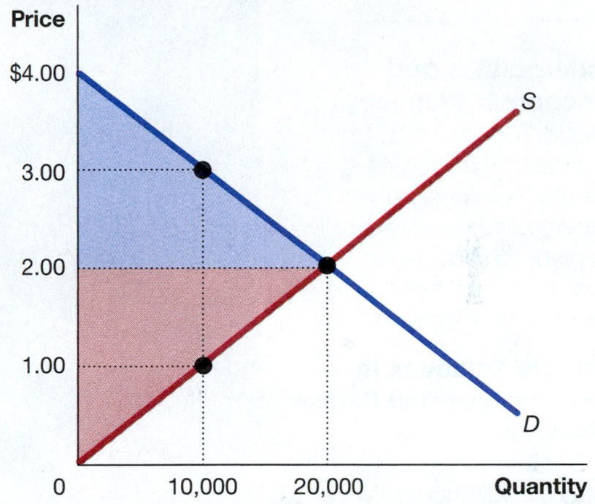

a. The deadweight loss
b. The transfer of producer surplus to consumers or the transfer of consumer surplus to producers
c. Producer surplus after the price floor is imposed
d. Consumer surplus after the price floor is imposed

4A.9 Construct a table like the one in this appendix on page 144 but assume that the rent ceiling is \$2,000 rather than \$1,500.

CHAPTER

5

Externalities, Environmental Policy, and Public Goods

Chapter Outline and Learning Objectives

Can Economic Policy Help Protect the Environment?

Suppose you work as a manager at a utility firm like We Energies, based in Milwaukee, Wisconsin. Your main job is to provide electric power to homes and businesses in your area. But unlike many other businesses, you must follow government regulation to determine *how* you produce your service. We Energies generates the electricity it sells mainly by burning coal. Most scientists believe that burning fossil fuels like coal generates carbon dioxide and other greenhouse gases that can increase global warming and cause potentially costly changes in climate.

In 2015, the Environmental Protection Agency (EPA) in President Barack Obama's administration announced the Clean Power Plan, which requires states to reduce power plant emissions to 32 percent below 2005 levels by 2030. Public opinion polls show that a large majority of people believe that the government should regulate greenhouse gases. Most economists agree that government policy should attempt to reduce these gases, but they disagree with the public about which government policies would be best. The public tends to support government rules that require firms to use particular methods to reduce pollution—for example, by requiring that automobile companies produce cars with better gas mileage. Many economists believe that using these *command-and-control policies* is a less economically efficient way to reduce pollution than is using *market-based policies* that rely on economic incentives rather than on administrative rules.

A carbon tax is an example of a market-based policy. If the government taxes oil, coal, and other carbon-based fuels that generate carbon dioxide when burned, households and firms will have an economic incentive to reduce their use of those fuels. Government policies to reduce pollution, including the carbon tax, have been controversial, however. Some businesses oppose the carbon tax because they believe it will raise their costs of production. Other businesses view the carbon tax favorably, particularly in comparison with command-and-control policies that they see as more costly and less effective. The Pacific Gas and Electric Company, a utility based in California, has noted "the flexibility and power of market incentives to promote a cleaner environment and more sustainable economy."

As we will see in this chapter, economic analysis plays an important role in the debate over environmental policies.

Sources: Coral Davenport, "A Challenge From Climate Change Regulations," *New York Times*, April 22, 2015; Thomas Content, "We Energies Seeks to Modify Oak Creek Power Plant," *Milwaukee Journal Sentinel*," July 8, 2014; Jonathan Marshall, "California's Cap-and-Trade Program: In Good Company," *Currents: News and Perspectives from Pacific Gas and Electric Company*, November 20, 2012; and Paola Sapienza and Luigi Zingales, "Economic Experts vs. Average Americans," *American Economic Review, Papers and Proceedings*, Vol. 103, No. 3, May 2013, pp. 636–642.

Economics in Your Life

What's the "Best" Level of Pollution?

Policymakers debate alternative approaches for achieving the goal of reducing carbon dioxide emissions. But how do we know the "best" level of carbon emissions? If carbon dioxide emissions hurt the environment, should the government take action to eliminate them completely? As you read this chapter, try to answer these questions. You can check your answers against those we provide on **page 173** at the end of this chapter.

Pollution is a part of economic life. Consumers create air pollution by burning gasoline to power their cars and natural gas to heat their homes. Firms create air pollution when they produce electricity, pesticides, or plastics, among other products. Utilities such as electric power plants produce sulfur dioxide when they burn coal to generate electricity. Sulfur dioxide contributes to acid rain, which can damage trees, crops, and buildings. The burning of fossil fuels generates carbon dioxide and other greenhouse gases that can increase global warming.

Externality A benefit or cost that affects someone who is not directly involved in the production or consumption of a good or service.

Pollution is just one example of an *externality*. An **externality** is a benefit or cost that affects someone who is not directly involved in the production or consumption of a good or service. In the case of air pollution, there is a *negative externality* because, for example, people with asthma may bear a cost even though they were not involved in the buying or selling of the electricity that caused the pollution. *Positive externalities* are also possible. For instance, medical research can provide a positive externality because people who are not directly involved in producing it or paying for it can benefit.

A competitive market usually does a good job of producing the economically efficient quantity of a good or service, but not when there is an externality in the market. When there is a negative externality, the market may produce a quantity of the good that is greater than the efficient amount. When there is a positive externality, the market may produce a quantity that is less than the efficient amount. Government interventions in the economy—such as the price floors on agricultural products or price ceilings on rents we discussed in Chapter 4—can reduce economic efficiency. But, when there are externalities, government intervention may actually *increase* economic efficiency and enhance the well-being of society. The way in which government intervenes is important, however. Economists can help policymakers ensure that government programs are as efficient as possible.

In this chapter, we explore how best to deal with the problem of pollution and other externalities. We also look at *public goods*, such as national defense, which may not be produced at all unless the government produces them.

5.1 Externalities and Economic Efficiency

LEARNING OBJECTIVE: Identify examples of positive and negative externalities and use graphs to show how externalities affect economic efficiency.

When you consume a Big Mac, only you benefit, but when you consume a college education, other people also benefit. College-educated people are less likely to commit crimes, and by being better-informed voters, they are more likely to contribute to better government policies. So, although you capture most of the benefits of your college education, you do not capture all of them.

When you buy a Big Mac, the price you pay covers all of the cost McDonald's incurs in producing the Big Mac. When you buy electricity from a utility that burns coal and generates carbon dioxide, though, the price you pay covers some of the costs the utility incurs, but does not cover the cost of the damage carbon dioxide does to the environment.

So, there is a *positive externality* in the production of college educations because people who do not pay for them will nonetheless benefit from them. There is a *negative externality* in the generation of electricity. For example, if fish and wildlife have disappeared from a lake because of acid rain generated by a utility, people who live near the lake incur a cost—even though they may not purchase electricity from that utility.

The Effect of Externalities

Externalities interfere with the *economic efficiency* of a market equilibrium. A competitive market achieves economic efficiency by maximizing the sum of consumer surplus and producer surplus (see Chapter 4). *But that result holds only if there are no externalities in production or consumption*. An externality can cause a difference between the *private cost* of production and the *social cost*.

- The **private cost** is the cost borne by the producer of a good or service.
- The **social cost** is the total cost of producing a good or service, and it is equal to the private cost plus any external cost, such as the cost of pollution.

Private cost The cost borne by the producer of a good or service.

Social cost The total cost of producing a good or service, including both the private cost and any external cost.

Unless there is an externality, the private cost and the social cost are equal.

An externality can also cause a difference between the *private benefit* from consumption and the *social benefit*.

- The **private benefit** is the benefit received by the consumer of a good or service.
- The **social benefit** is the total benefit from consuming a good or service, and it is equal to the private benefit plus any external benefit, such as the benefit to others resulting from your college education.

Private benefit The benefit received by the consumer of a good or service.

Social benefit The total benefit from consuming a good or service, including both the private benefit and any external benefit.

Unless there is an externality, the private benefit and the social benefit are equal.

How a Negative Externality in Production Reduces Economic Efficiency Typically, economists assume that the producer of a good or service must bear all the costs of production. But we now know that this assumption is not always true. In the production of electricity, private costs are borne by the utility, but some external costs of pollution are borne by people who are not customers of the utility. The social cost of producing electricity is the sum of the private cost plus the external cost. Figure 5.1 shows the effect on the market for electricity of a negative externality in production.

S_1 is the market supply curve and represents only the private costs that utilities have to bear in generating electricity. Firms will supply an additional unit of a good or service only if they receive a price equal to the additional cost of producing that unit, so a supply curve represents the *marginal cost* of producing a good or service (see Chapter 4). If utilities also had to bear the cost of pollution, the supply curve would be S_2, which represents the true marginal social cost of generating electricity. The equilibrium with price $P_{Efficient}$ and quantity $Q_{Efficient}$ is efficient. The equilibrium with price P_{Market} and quantity Q_{Market} is not efficient.

To see why, remember that an equilibrium is economically efficient if economic surplus—which is the sum of consumer surplus plus producer surplus—is at a

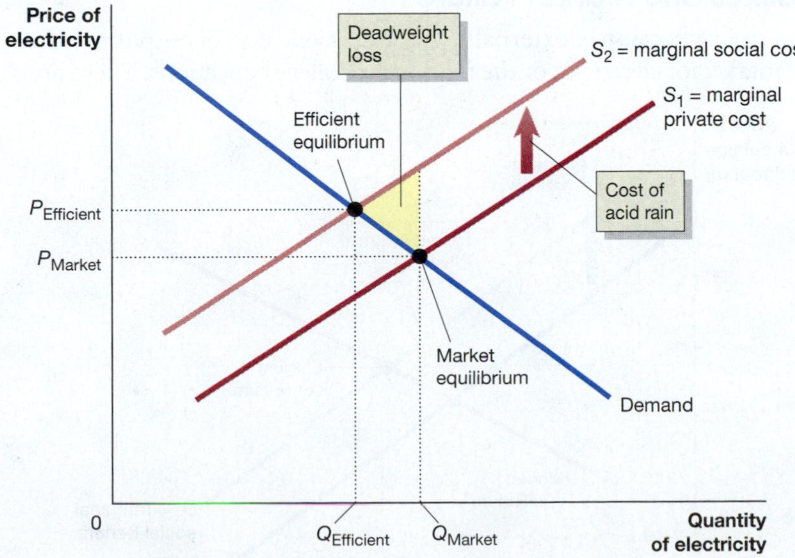

MyEconLab Animation

Figure 5.1

The Effect of Pollution on Economic Efficiency

Because utilities do not bear the cost of acid rain, they produce electricity beyond the economically efficient level. Supply curve S_1 represents just the marginal private cost that the utility has to pay. Supply curve S_2 represents the marginal social cost, which includes the costs to those affected by acid rain. If the supply curve were S_2 rather than S_1, market equilibrium would occur at price $P_{Efficient}$ and quantity $Q_{Efficient}$, the economically efficient level of output. But, when the supply curve is S_1, the market equilibrium occurs at price P_{Market} and quantity Q_{Market} where there is a deadweight loss equal to the area of the yellow triangle. Because of the deadweight loss, this equilibrium is not efficient.

maximum (see Chapter 4). When economic surplus is at a maximum, the net benefit to society from the production of the good or service is at a maximum. With an equilibrium quantity of $Q_{Efficient}$, economic surplus is at a maximum, and the equilibrium is efficient. But, with an equilibrium quantity of Q_{Market}, economic surplus is reduced by the deadweight loss—equal to the yellow triangle in Figure 5.1—and the equilibrium is not efficient. The deadweight loss occurs because the supply curve is above the demand curve for the production of the units of electricity between $Q_{Efficient}$ and Q_{Market}. That is, the additional cost—including the external cost—of producing these units is greater than the marginal benefit to consumers, as represented by the demand curve. In other words, because of the cost of the pollution, economic efficiency would be improved if less electricity were produced.

We can conclude the following: *When there is a negative externality in producing a good or service, too much of the good or service will be produced at market equilibrium.*

How a Positive Externality in Consumption Reduces Economic Efficiency We have seen that a negative externality interferes with achieving economic efficiency. The same holds true for a positive externality. In earlier chapters, we assumed that the demand curve represents all the benefits that come from consuming a good. But a college education generates benefits that are not captured by the student receiving the education and so are not included in the market demand curve for college educations. Figure 5.2 shows the effect of a positive externality in consumption on the market for college educations.

If students receiving a college education could capture all its benefits, the demand curve would be D_2, which represents the marginal social benefits. The actual demand curve is D_1, however, which represents only the marginal private benefits received by students. The efficient equilibrium would occur at price $P_{Efficient}$ and quantity $Q_{Efficient}$. At this equilibrium, economic surplus is maximized. The market equilibrium, at price P_{Market} and quantity Q_{Market}, will not be efficient because the demand curve is above the supply curve for production of the units between Q_{Market} and $Q_{Efficient}$. That is, the marginal benefit—including the external benefit—of producing these units is greater than the marginal cost. As a result, there is a deadweight loss equal to the area of the yellow triangle. Because of the positive externality, economic efficiency would be improved if more college educations were produced.

We can conclude the following: *When there is a positive externality in consuming a good or service, too little of the good or service will be produced at market equilibrium.* MyEconLab Concept Check

Externalities and Market Failure

We have seen that because of externalities, the efficient level of output may not occur in either the market for electricity or the market for college educations. These are examples

MyEconLab Animation

Figure 5.2

The Effect of a Positive Externality on Economic Efficiency

People who do not consume college educations can still benefit from them. As a result, the marginal social benefit from a college education is greater than the marginal private benefit to college students. Because only the marginal private benefit is represented in the market demand curve D_1, the quantity of college educations produced, Q_{Market}, is too low. If the market demand curve were D_2 instead of D_1, the level of college educations produced would be $Q_{Efficient}$, which is the efficient level. At the market equilibrium of Q_{Market}, there is a deadweight loss equal to the area of the yellow triangle.

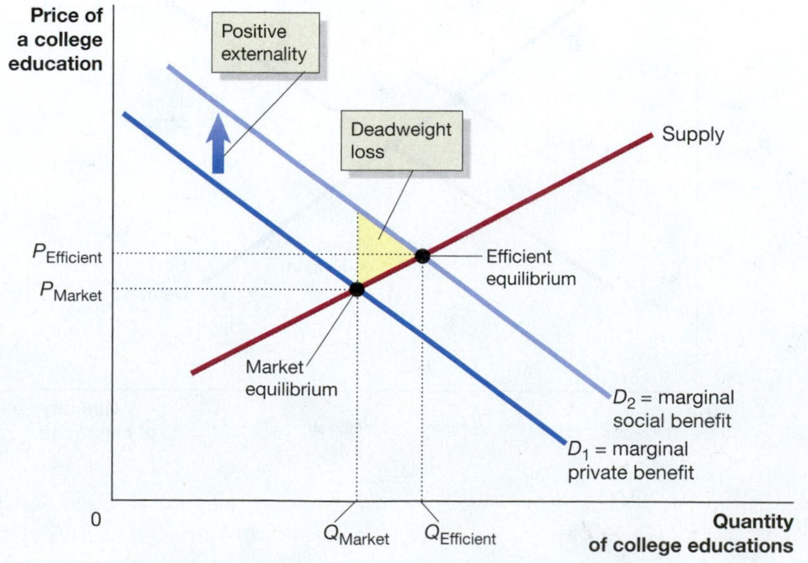

of **market failure**—situations in which the market fails to produce the efficient level of output. In Section 5.3, we will discuss possible solutions to problems of externalities. But, first, we need to consider why externalities occur. MyEconLab Concept Check

Market failure A situation in which the market fails to produce the efficient level of output.

What Causes Externalities?

Governments need to guarantee *property rights* in order for a market system to function well (see Chapter 2). **Property rights** refer to the rights individuals or businesses have to the exclusive use of their property, including the right to buy or sell it. Property can be tangible or physical, such as a store or factory. Property can also be intangible, such as the right to an idea. Most of the time, the governments of the United States and other high-income countries do a good job of enforcing property rights, but in certain situations, property rights do not exist or cannot be legally enforced.

Property rights The rights individuals or businesses have to the exclusive use of their property, including the right to buy or sell it.

Consider the following situation: Lee owns land that includes a lake. A paper company wants to lease some of Lee's land to build a paper mill. The paper mill will discharge pollutants into Lee's lake. Because Lee owns the lake, he can charge the paper company the cost of cleaning up the pollutants. The result is that the cost of the pollution is a private cost to the paper company and is included in the price of the paper it sells. There is no externality, the efficient level of paper is produced, and there is no market failure.

Now suppose that the paper company again builds its paper mill on privately owned land but discharges its pollutants into a lake that is owned by the state government rather than by an individual. In the absence of any government regulations, the company can discharge pollutants into the lake without having to pay a fee. The cost of the pollution will be external to the company because it doesn't have to pay the cost of cleaning it up. The paper mill will produce a quantity of paper that is greater than the economically efficient level, and a market failure will occur. Or, suppose that Lee owns the lake, but the pollution is caused by acid rain generated by an electric utility hundreds of miles away. The law does not allow Lee to charge the electric utility for the damage caused by the acid rain. Even though someone is damaging Lee's property, he cannot enforce his property rights in this situation. Once again, there is an externality, and the market failure will result in too much electricity being produced.

If you buy a house, the government will protect your right to exclusive use of that house. No one else can use the house without your permission. Because of your property rights in the house, your private benefit from the house and the social benefit are the same. When you buy a college education, however, other people are able to benefit from it. You have no property right that will enable you to prevent them from benefiting or to charge them for the benefits they receive. As a result, there is a positive externality, and the market failure will result in too few college educations being supplied.

We can conclude the following: *Externalities and market failures result from incomplete property rights or from the difficulty of enforcing property rights in certain situations.* MyEconLab Concept Check

5.2 Private Solutions to Externalities: The Coase Theorem

LEARNING OBJECTIVE: Discuss the Coase theorem and explain how private bargaining can lead to economic efficiency in a market with an externality.

As noted at the beginning of this chapter, government intervention may actually increase economic efficiency and enhance the well-being of society when externalities are present. It is also possible, however, for people to find private solutions to the problem of externalities.

Can the market cure market failure? In an influential article written in 1960, Ronald Coase formerly of the University of Chicago, winner of the 1991 Nobel Prize in Economics, argued that under some circumstances, private solutions to the problem of externalities will occur. To understand Coase's argument, we need to recognize that completely eliminating an externality usually is not economically efficient. Consider pollution, for example. There is, in fact, an *economically efficient level of pollution reduction.*

At first, this seems paradoxical. Pollution is bad, and you might think the efficient amount of a bad thing is zero. But it isn't zero.

The Economically Efficient Level of Pollution Reduction

Chapter 1 introduced the important idea that the optimal decision is to continue any activity up to the point where the marginal benefit equals the marginal cost. This idea applies to reducing pollution just as much as it does to other activities. Sulfur dioxide emissions contribute to smog and acid rain. As sulfur dioxide emissions—or any other type of pollution—decline, society benefits: Fewer trees die, fewer buildings are damaged, and fewer people suffer breathing problems. But, a key point is that the additional benefit—that is, the *marginal benefit*—received from eliminating another ton of sulfur dioxide *declines* as sulfur dioxide emissions are reduced. To see why, consider what happens if utilities generate electricity without attempting to reduce sulfur dioxide emissions. In this situation, many smoggy days will occur in the cities of the Midwest and Northeast. Even healthy people may experience breathing problems. As sulfur dioxide emissions are reduced, the number of smoggy days will fall, and healthy people will no longer experience breathing problems. Eventually, if sulfur dioxide emissions fall to low levels, people with asthma will no longer be affected. Further reductions in sulfur dioxide emissions will have little additional benefit. The same will be true of the other benefits from reducing sulfur dioxide emissions: As the reductions increase, the additional benefits from fewer buildings and trees being damaged and lakes polluted will decline.

Making the Connection
MyEconLab Video

The Clean Air Act: How a Government Policy Reduced Infant Mortality

The following bar graphs show that the United States has made tremendous progress in reducing air pollution since Congress passed the Clean Air Act in 1970: By 2013, total emissions of the six main air pollutants had fallen dramatically. Over the same period, real U.S. gross domestic product (GDP)—which measures the value, corrected for inflation, of all the final goods and services produced in the country—more than tripled, energy consumption increased by half, and the number of miles traveled by all vehicles doubled.

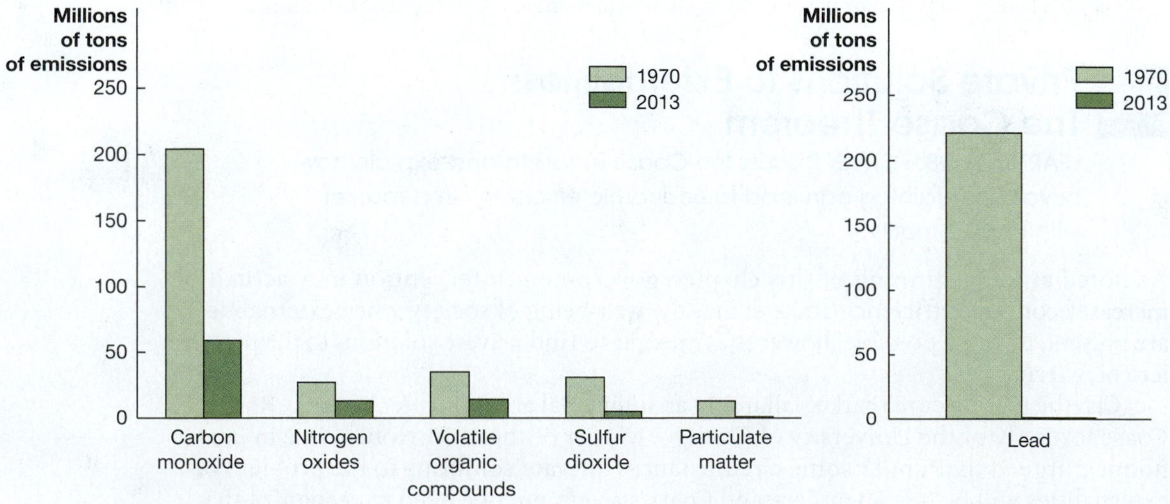

Source: U.S. Environmental Protection Agency, "Air Quality Trends," www.epa.gov/airtrends/aqtrends.html.

As we have seen, when levels of pollution are high, the marginal benefit of reducing pollution is also high. We would expect, then, that the benefit of reducing air pollution in 1970 was much higher than the benefit from a proportional reduction in air pollution would be today, when the level of pollution is much lower. Kenneth Y. Chay of Brown University and Michael Greenstone of the University of Chicago have shown that the benefits from the reductions in air pollution that occurred in the period immediately after passage of the Clean Air Act were indeed large. Chay and Greenstone argue that the exposure of pregnant women to high levels of air pollution can be damaging to their unborn children, possibly by reducing lung functioning. This damage would increase the chance that the infant would die in the first weeks after being born. In the two years following passage of the Clean Air Act, there was a sharp reduction in air pollution and also in infant mortality. The decline was mainly due to a reduction in deaths within one month of birth. Of course, other factors may also have contributed to the decline in infant mortality, but Chay and Greenstone use statistical analysis to isolate the effect of the decline in air pollution. They conclude that "1,300 fewer infants died in 1972 than would have in the absence of the Clean Air Act."

Further research by economists Adam Isen, of the U.S. Department of the Treasury, Maya Rossin-Slater, of the University of California, Santa Barbara, and W. Reed Walker, of the University of California, Berkeley, indicates that a reduction in exposure to pollution had a lasting effect on people who were small children at the time the act was passed. They estimate that as a result of improved health, the 1.5 million children born each year into the counties that had been the most polluted earn about $4,300 more as adults than they would have if pollution had not been reduced.

Sources: Kenneth Y. Chay and Michael Greenstone, "Air Quality, Infant Mortality, and the Clean Air Act of 1970," National Bureau of Economic Research Working Paper 10053, October 2003; and Adam Isen, Maya Rossin-Slater, and W. Reed Walker, "Every Breath You Take—Every Dollar You'll Make: The Long-Term Consequences of the Clean Air Act of 1970," National Bureau of Economic Research Working Paper 19858, January 2014.

Your Turn: Test your understanding by doing related problem 2.8 on page 176 at the end of this chapter.

What about the marginal cost to electric utilities of reducing pollution? To reduce sulfur dioxide emissions, utilities have to switch from burning high-sulfur coal to burning more costly fuel, or they have to install pollution control devices, such as scrubbers. As the level of pollution falls, further reductions become increasingly costly. Reducing emissions or other types of pollution to very low levels can require complex and expensive new technologies. For example, Arthur Fraas, formerly of the federal Office of Management and Budget, and Vincent Munley, of Lehigh University, have shown that the marginal cost of removing 97 percent of pollutants from municipal wastewater is more than twice as high as the marginal cost of removing 95 percent.

The *net benefit* to society from reducing pollution is equal to the difference between the benefit of reducing pollution and the cost. For us to maximize the net benefit to society, sulfur dioxide emissions—or any other type of pollution—should be reduced up to the point where the marginal benefit from another ton of reduction is equal to the marginal cost. Figure 5.3 illustrates this point.

In Figure 5.3, we measure *reductions* in sulfur dioxide emissions on the horizontal axis. We measure the marginal benefit and marginal cost in dollars from eliminating another ton of sulfur dioxide emissions on the vertical axis. As reductions in pollution increase, the marginal benefit declines and the marginal cost increases. The economically efficient amount of pollution reduction occurs where the marginal benefit equals the marginal cost. The figure shows that, in this case, the economically efficient reduction of sulfur dioxide emissions is 8.5 million tons per year. In a program begun in 1990, this is the amount of reduction Congress decided should occur by 2010. At that level of emission reduction, the marginal benefit and the marginal cost of the last ton of sulfur dioxide emissions eliminated are both $200 per ton. Suppose instead that the

MyEconLab Concept Animation

Figure 5.3

The Marginal Benefit from Pollution Reduction Should Equal the Marginal Cost

If the reduction of sulfur dioxide emissions is 7.0 million tons per year, the marginal benefit of $300 per ton is greater than the marginal cost of $140 per ton. Further reductions in emissions will increase the net benefit to society. If the reduction of sulfur dioxide emissions is 10.0 million tons, the marginal cost of $260 per ton is greater than the marginal benefit of $100 per ton. An increase in sulfur dioxide emissions will increase the net benefit to society. Only when the reduction is 8.5 million tons is the marginal benefit equal to the marginal cost. This level is the economically efficient level of pollution reduction.

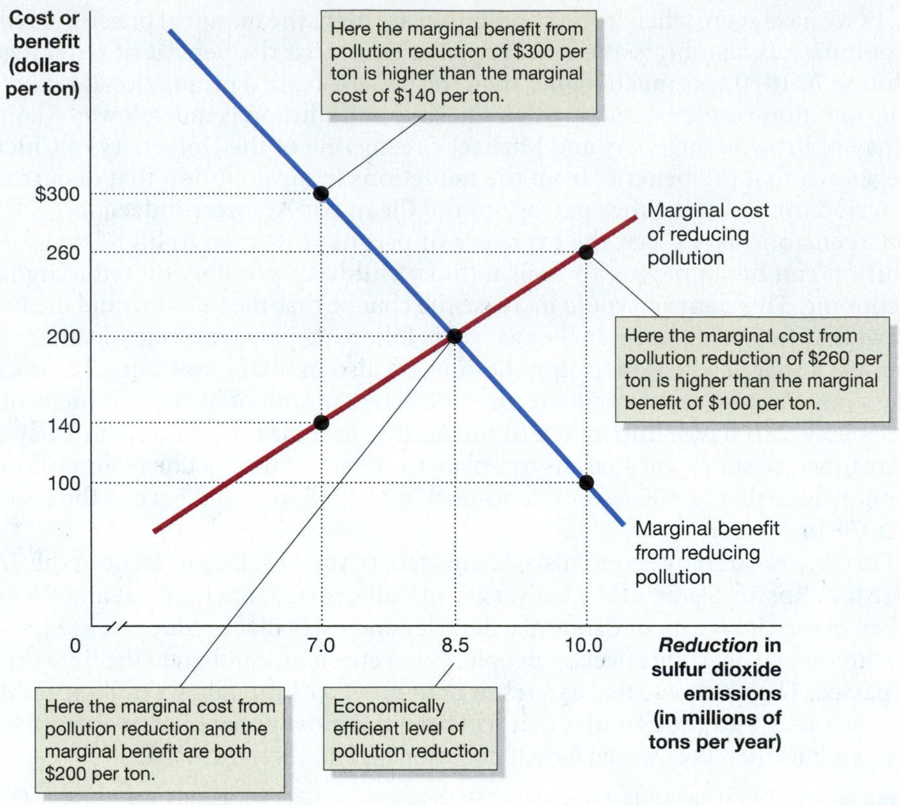

emissions target was only 7.0 million tons. The figure shows that, at that level of reduction, the last ton of reduction has added $300 to the benefits received by society, but it has added only $140 to the costs of utilities. There has been a net benefit to society of $160 from this ton of pollution reduction. In fact, the figure shows a net benefit to society from pollution reduction for every ton from 7.0 million to 8.5 million. Only when sulfur dioxide emissions are reduced by 8.5 million tons per year will marginal benefit fall enough and marginal cost rise enough that the two are equal.

Now suppose Congress had set the target for sulfur dioxide emissions reduction at 10 million tons per year. Figure 5.3 shows that the marginal benefit at that level of reduction falls to only $100 per ton and the marginal cost rises to $260 per ton. The last ton of reduction actually *reduces* the net benefit to society by $160 per ton. In fact, every ton of reduction beyond 8.5 million reduces the net benefit to society.

To summarize:

- If the marginal benefit of reducing pollution is greater than the marginal cost, further reductions will make society better off.
- If the marginal cost of reducing pollution is greater than the marginal benefit, further reductions will actually make society worse off.

MyEconLab Concept Check

The Basis for Private Solutions to Externalities

In arguing that private solutions to the problem of externalities were possible, Ronald Coase emphasized that when more than the optimal level of pollution is occurring, the benefits from reducing the pollution to the optimal level are greater than the costs. Figure 5.4 illustrates this point using the example of sulfur dioxide pollution.

The marginal benefit curve shows the additional benefit from each reduction in a ton of sulfur dioxide emissions. The area under the marginal benefit curve between the two emission levels is the *total* benefit received from reducing emissions from one level to another. For instance, in Figure 5.4, the total benefit from increasing the reduction in sulfur dioxide emissions from 7.0 million tons to 8.5 million tons is the sum of the areas

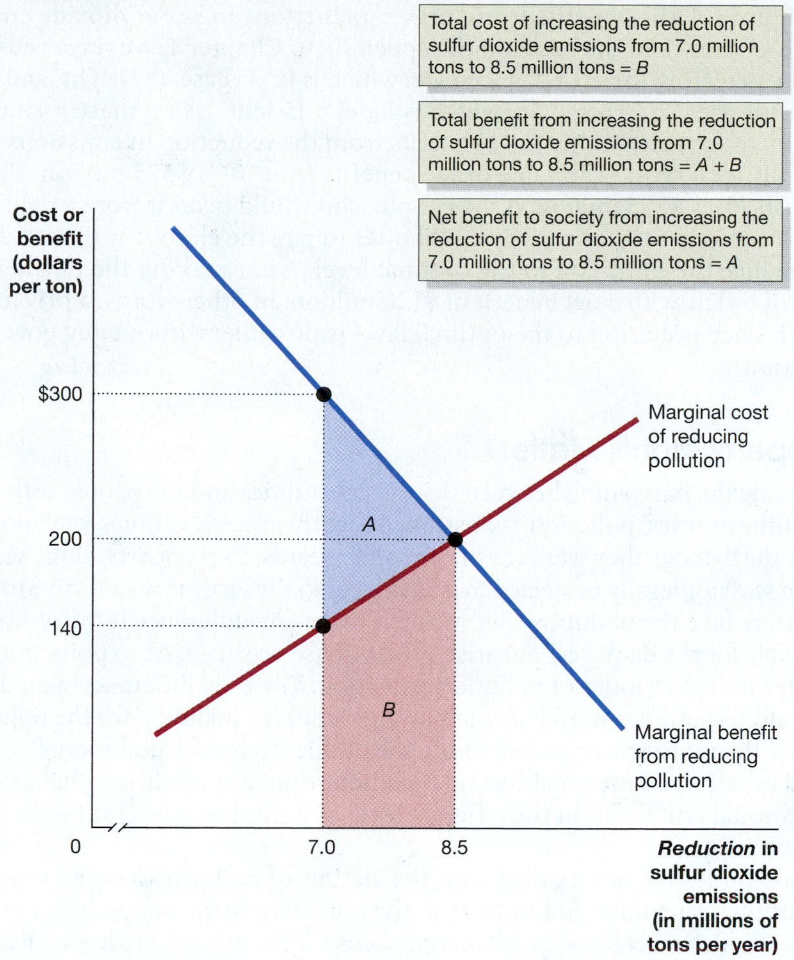

MyEconLab Concept Animation

Figure 5.4

The Benefits of Reducing Pollution to the Optimal Level Are Greater Than the Costs

Increasing the reduction in sulfur dioxide emissions from 7.0 million tons to 8.5 million tons results in total benefits equal to the sum of the areas of *A* and *B* under the marginal benefit curve. The total cost of this decrease in pollution is equal to the area of *B* under the marginal cost curve. The total benefits are greater than the total costs by an amount equal to the area of *A*. Because the total benefits from reducing pollution are greater than the total costs, it is possible for those receiving the benefits to arrive at a private agreement with polluters to pay them to reduce pollution.

of *A* and *B*. The marginal cost curve shows the additional cost from each reduction in a ton of emissions. The *total* cost of reducing emissions from one level to another is the area under the marginal cost curve between the two emission levels. The total cost from increasing the reduction in emissions from 7.0 million tons to 8.5 million tons is the area of *B*. The net benefit from reducing emissions is the difference between the total cost and the total benefit, which is equal to the area of *A*.

Don't Let This Happen to You

Remember That It's the *Net* Benefit That Counts

Why not *completely* eliminate anything unpleasant? As long as any person suffers any unpleasant consequences from air pollution, the marginal benefit of reducing air pollution will be positive. Therefore, removing every particle of air pollution will result in the largest *total* benefit to society. But removing every particle of air pollution is not optimal for the same reason that it is not optimal to remove every particle of dirt or dust from a room when cleaning it. The cost of cleaning your room is not just the price of the cleaning products but also the opportunity cost of your time. The more time you devote to cleaning your room, the less time you have for other activities. As you devote more and more additional hours to cleaning your room, the alternative activities you have to give up are likely to increase in value, raising the opportunity cost of cleaning: Cleaning instead of watching television may not be too costly, but cleaning instead of eating any meals or getting any sleep is very costly. Optimally, you should eliminate dust and dirt in your room up to the point where the marginal benefit of the last dirt removed equals the marginal cost of removing it. Society should take the same approach to air pollution. The result is the largest *net* benefit to society.

MyEconLab Study Plan

Your Turn: Test your understanding by doing related problem 2.9 on page 176 at the end of this chapter.

In Figure 5.4, the benefits from further reductions in sulfur dioxide emissions are much greater than the costs. In the appendix to Chapter 1, we reviewed the formula for calculating the area of a triangle, which is ½ × Base × Height, and the formula for the area of a rectangle, which is Base × Height. Using these formulas, we can calculate the value of the total benefits from the reduction in emissions and the value of the total costs. The value of the benefits ($A + B$) is $375 million. The value of the costs (B) is $255 million. If the people who would benefit from a reduction in pollution could get together, they could offer to pay the electric utilities $255 million to reduce the pollution to the optimal level. After making the payment, they would still be left with a net benefit of $120 million. In other words, a private agreement to reduce pollution to the optimal level is possible, without any government intervention. MyEconLab Concept Check

Do Property Rights Matter?

In discussing the bargaining between the electric utilities and the people suffering the effects of the utilities' pollution, we assumed that the electric utilities were not legally liable for the damage they were causing. In other words, the property of the victims of pollution was not legally protected from damage, so the victims would have to pay the utilities to reduce the pollution. But would it make any difference if the utilities were legally liable for the damages? Surprisingly, as Coase was the first to point out, it does not matter for the amount of pollution reduction. The only difference would be that now the electric utilities would have to pay the victims of pollution for the right to pollute rather than the victims having to pay the utilities to reduce pollution. Because the marginal benefits and marginal costs of pollution reduction would not change, the bargaining should still result in the efficient level of pollution reduction—in this case, 8.5 million tons.

If the utilities are not legally liable, the victims of pollution have an incentive to pay the utilities to reduce pollution up to the point where the marginal benefit of the last ton of reduction is equal to the marginal cost. If the utilities are legally liable, they have an incentive to pay the victims of pollution to allow them to pollute up to the same point. MyEconLab Concept Check

The Problem of Transactions Costs

Unfortunately, often polluters and the victims of pollution have difficulty arriving at a private solution to the problem of externalities. One important reason is that there are often both many polluters and many people suffering from the negative effects of pollution. Negotiating an agreement between the people suffering from pollution and the firms causing the pollution often fails because of the *transactions costs* involved. **Transactions costs** are the costs in time and other resources that parties incur in the process of agreeing to and carrying out an exchange of goods or services. In this case, the transactions costs would include the time and other costs of negotiating an agreement, drawing up a binding contract, and monitoring the agreement. Unfortunately, when many people are involved, the transactions costs are often higher than the net benefits from reducing the externality. In that case, the cost of transacting ends up exceeding the gain from the transaction, and a private solution to an externality problem is not feasible. MyEconLab Concept Check

Transactions costs The costs in time and other resources that parties incur in the process of agreeing to and carrying out an exchange of goods or services.

The Coase Theorem

Coase's argument that private solutions to the problem of externalities are possible is summed up in the **Coase theorem**: *If transactions costs are low, private bargaining will result in an efficient solution to the problem of externalities.* We have seen the basis for the Coase theorem in the preceding example of pollution by electric utilities: Because the benefits from reducing an externality are often greater than the costs, private bargaining can lead to an efficient outcome. But we have also seen that this outcome will occur only if

Coase theorem The argument of economist Ronald Coase that if transactions costs are low, private bargaining will result in an efficient solution to the problem of externalities.

transactions costs are low, and in the case of pollution, they usually are not. In general, private bargaining is most likely to reach an efficient outcome if the number of parties bargaining is small.

In practice, we must add a couple of other qualifications to the Coase theorem. In addition to low transactions costs, private solutions to the problem of externalities will occur only if all parties to the agreement have full information about the costs and benefits associated with the externality, and all parties must be willing to accept a reasonable agreement. For example, if those suffering from the effects of pollution do not have information on the costs of reducing pollution, it is unlikely that the parties can reach an agreement. Unreasonable demands can also hinder an agreement. For instance, in the example of pollution by electric utilities, we saw that the total benefit of reducing sulfur dioxide emissions was $375 million. Even if transactions costs are very low, if the utilities insist on being paid more than $375 million to reduce emissions, no agreement will be reached because the amount paid exceeds the value of the reduction to those suffering from the emissions.

MyEconLab Concept Check

MyEconLab Study Plan

Making the Connection
MyEconLab Video

How Can You Defend Your Knees on a Plane Flight?

Imagine that you are on a plane peacefully using your laptop on the tray table. Then, with no warning, the person in front of you forcefully reclines her seat, banging your knees and—much worse!—cracking the screen of your laptop. Unfortunately, this problem has become common. Until a few years ago, most seats in the coach section of airplanes had 32 inches of space from the front of one seat to the back of the seat in the next row. But airlines have been reconfiguring their planes to fit more seats. Today, many coach seats have only 29 inches of space, and those missing 3 inches can make a big difference, particularly if you have long legs!

If you were on a plane, would you be willing to pay the passenger in front of you to not recline her seat?

Clearly there is an externality involved when someone reclines a seat. The person reclining gets the benefit of a more comfortable position, but as the person in the seat behind, you have to bear the cost of a seat reclining into your space. But is it your space? If you had a property right to the space, you could choose to make the person in front of you pay a fee to recline her chair. But the airlines own the space, and their policy is to allow people to recline their seats. The airlines' views became clear following incidents involving the Knee Defender, a device invented by Ira Goldman. When you slip Goldman's gadget over the bars on your tray table, it prevents the seat in front of you from being reclined. When fights broke out over the use of the gadget, most major U.S. airlines banned its use.

So, with the airlines having given passengers the right to recline their seats, what can you do if the person in front of you is squeezing your knees or making it impossible for you to use your laptop on your tray table? If the cost to you from these problems is greater than the benefit to the person in front of you from reclining, then there should be a payment that you can make to that person in exchange for not reclining. That's the solution that Josh Barro, a frequent flier and *New York Times* columnist, suggested: "If my reclining bothers you, you can pay me to stop." He was skeptical that many people really are bothered by having the seat in front of them reclined: "If they really cared that much, someone would have opened his wallet and paid me by now."

Applying Coase's theorem, Barro's analysis seems to be correct: If the cost to you from having the seat in front of yours reclined is greater than the benefit to the recliner, you should make a payment to the recliner. Because this outcome rarely occurs, people reclining must get a larger benefit than the cost imposed on people behind them. But economist Donald Marron of the Urban Institute argues that this analysis holds only if we assume that the transactions costs of negotiating an agreement are low. If many people don't like the idea of negotiating with a stranger about a payment for not reclining a seat, then the transactions costs might be too high for the efficient outcome to occur.

Ronald Coase passed away in 2013, so we may never know how he dealt with the issue of someone in front of him reclining his or her seat.

Sources: Scott McCartney, "Airline Seat Battles: Be Kind, Don't Recline?" *Wall Street Journal*, September 3, 2014; Josh Barro, "Don't Want Me to Recline My Airline Seat? You Can Pay Me," *New York Times*, August 27, 2014; Donald Marron, "Who Owns the Right to Recline? Property Rights in the Sky," dmarron.com, August 26, 2014; and Adam Levine-Weinberg, "It's No Surprise Airlines Have Banned the 'Knee Defender,'" fool.com, September 7, 2014.

MyEconLab Study Plan

Your Turn: Test your understanding by doing related problems 2.10 and 2.11 on page 176 at the end of this chapter.

5.3 Government Policies to Deal with Externalities

LEARNING OBJECTIVE: Analyze government policies to achieve economic efficiency in a market with an externality.

When private solutions to externalities are not feasible, how should the government intervene? British economist A. C. Pigou of Cambridge University was the first to analyze market failure systematically.

Imposing a Tax When There Is a Negative Externality

Pigou argued that to deal with a negative externality in production, the government should impose a tax equal to the cost of the externality. The effect of such a tax is shown in Figure 5.5, which reproduces the negative externality from acid rain shown in Figure 5.1 on page 149.

By imposing a tax on the production of electricity equal to the cost of acid rain, the government will cause electric utilities to *internalize* the externality. As a consequence, the cost of the acid rain will become a private cost borne by the utilities, and the supply curve for electricity will shift from S_1 to S_2. The result will be a decrease in the equilibrium output of electricity from Q_{Market} to the efficient level, $Q_{Efficient}$. The price consumers pay for electricity will rise from P_{Market}—which does not include the cost of acid

MyEconLab Animation

Figure 5.5

When There Is a Negative Externality, a Tax Can Lead to the Efficient Level of Output

Because utilities do not bear the cost of acid rain, they produce electricity beyond the economically efficient level. If the government imposes a tax equal to the cost of acid rain, the utilities will internalize the externality. As a consequence, the supply curve will shift up, from S_1 to S_2. The market equilibrium quantity changes from Q_{Market}, where an inefficiently high level of electricity is produced, to $Q_{Efficient}$, the economically efficient equilibrium quantity. The price of electricity will rise from P_{Market}—which does not include the cost of acid rain—to $P_{Efficient}$—which does include the cost. Consumers pay the price $P_{Efficient}$, while producers receive the price P, which is equal to $P_{Efficient}$ minus the amount of the tax.

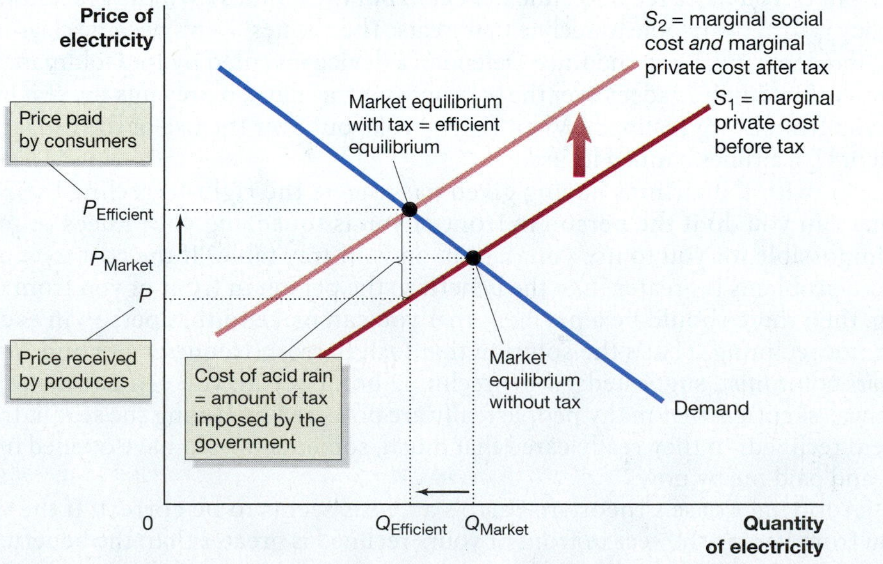

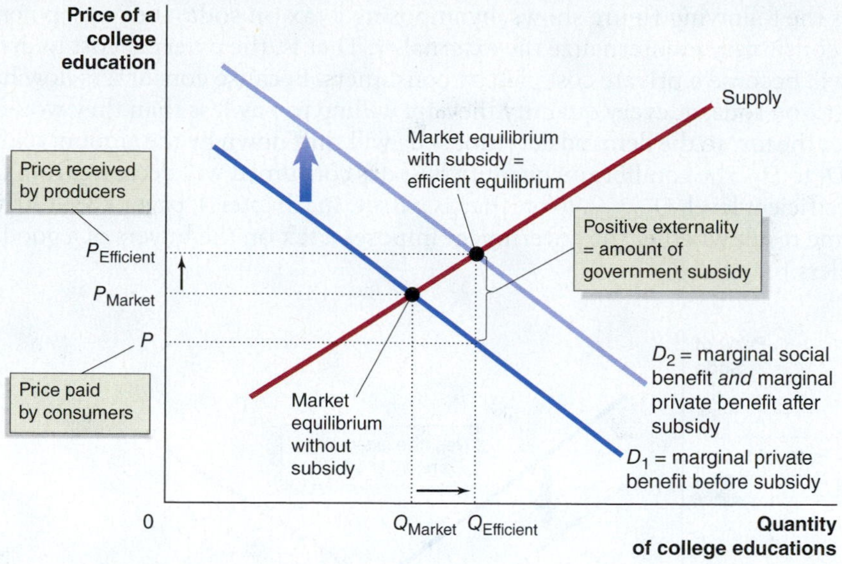

MyEconLab Animation

Figure 5.6

When There Is a Positive Externality, a Subsidy Can Bring about the Efficient Level of Output

People who do not consume college educations can benefit from them. As a result, the social benefit from a college education is greater than the private benefit to college students. If the government pays a subsidy equal to the external benefit, students will internalize the externality. The subsidy will cause the demand curve to shift up, from D_1 to D_2. As a result, the market equilibrium quantity will shift from Q_{Market}, where an inefficiently low level of college educations is supplied, to $Q_{Efficient}$, the economically efficient equilibrium quantity. Producers receive the price $P_{Efficient}$, while consumers pay the price P, which is equal to $P_{Efficient}$ minus the amount of the subsidy.

rain—to $P_{Efficient}$—which does include the cost. Producers will receive a price P, which is equal to $P_{Efficient}$ minus the amount of the tax.

Providing a Subsidy When There Is a Positive Externality

Pigou also reasoned that the government can deal with a positive externality in consumption by giving consumers a subsidy, or payment, equal to the value of the externality. The effect of such a subsidy is shown in Figure 5.6, which reproduces the positive externality from college education shown in Figure 5.2 on page 150.

By paying college students a subsidy equal to the external benefit from a college education, the government will cause students to *internalize* the externality. That is, the external benefit from a college education will become a private benefit received by college students, and the demand curve for college educations will shift from D_1 to D_2. The equilibrium number of college educations supplied will increase from Q_{Market} to the efficient level, $Q_{Efficient}$. Producers receive the price $P_{Efficient}$, while consumers pay the price P, which is equal to $P_{Efficient}$ minus the amount of the subsidy. In fact, the government does heavily subsidize college educations. All states have government-operated universities that charge tuitions well below the cost of providing the education. The state and federal governments also provide students with grants and low-interest loans that subsidize college educations. The economic justification for these programs is that college educations provide an external benefit to society.

Making the Connection
MyEconLab Video

Should the Government Tax Cigarettes and Soda?

Generally, governments use Pigovian taxes to deal with negative externalities in *production*. Governments also impose taxes—sometimes called *sin taxes*—on products such as cigarettes and alcohol. Some policymakers have argued that these products generate negative externalities in *consumption*, so a tax on them can increase economic efficiency. Recently, several cities have considered taxing sweetened soda, on the grounds that they cause a negative externality by raising medical costs. Just as governments can deal with a positive externality in consumption by giving consumers a subsidy, they can deal with a negative externality by imposing a tax.

As the following figure shows, by imposing a tax on soda, the government will cause consumers to internalize the externality. That is, the external cost to drinking soda will become a private cost paid by consumers. Because consumers now have to pay a tax on soda, at every quantity they are willing to pay less than they would have without the tax, so the demand curve for soda will shift down by the amount of the tax, from D_1 to D_2. The equilibrium quantity of sodas consumed will decrease from Q_{Market} to the efficient level, $Q_{Efficient}$. (Note that as we saw in Chapter 4, pages 128–130, we get the same result whether the government imposes a tax on the buyers of a good or on the sellers.)

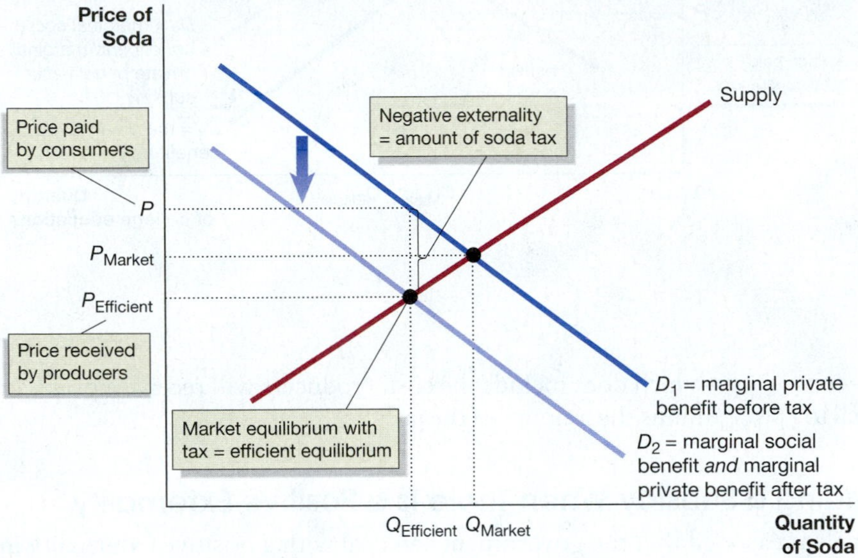

But do people actually cause a negative externality by smoking and drinking sweetened sodas? It might seem that they don't, because consumers of cigarettes and sodas bear the costs of any health problems they experience. In fact, though, the higher medical expenses from treating the complications of cigarette smoking or obesity are not paid entirely by the smokers or soda drinkers. A smoker who receives health insurance through his employer may increase the costs of that insurance, which all the workers at the firm will pay. Similarly, taxpayers partly pay for the health care of someone who is over age 65 and is enrolled in the federal government's Medicare program. The costs of medical care that smokers or soda drinkers do not pay themselves represent a negative externality.

There is a complication to this conclusion, however: Smokers and people who are obese tend to die early. This tragic outcome means that smokers and the obese may have been paying taxes to help pay for Social Security and Medicare benefits that they will never receive. They may also have made payments into company and public employee pension plans and purchased long-term care insurance, but they may not have lived long enough to receive many pension payments or to have spent time in a nursing home. So, there are offsetting effects: While alive, smokers and obese people may impose costs on others who bear the expense of their higher medical costs, but because they are likely to die early, they provide a financial gain to recipients of Social Security, Medicare, company and public employee pension plans, and purchasers of long-term care insurance.

W. Kip Viscusi of Vanderbilt University has studied the case of tobacco smoking and concluded that the external costs and benefits roughly offset each other, meaning that there doesn't appear to be a significant negative externality from smoking. Studies of obesity have arrived at somewhat conflicting results: A study of obesity in the Netherlands found that the cost savings from premature death offset the additional lifetime medical costs of obese people. But another study using U.S. data found that obesity did lead to a net increase in lifetime medical costs, even taking into account the shorter average life spans of obese people.

There may also be costs to smoking and obesity beyond additional medical costs. Smokers may inflict costs on others because of secondhand smoke or because smoking during pregnancy can lead to low birth weights and other health problems for babies. Airlines have noted that they spend more on fuel costs because of the increasing weight of passengers.

Economists and policymakers continue to debate whether the government should use taxes to deal with negative externalities in consumption.

Sources: Stephanie Strom, "Election Day Entailed Casting Votes for Soda Taxes and Food Issues Too," *New York Times*, November 5, 2014; W. Kip Viscusi, "Cigarette Taxation and the Social Consequences of Smoking," in James Poterba, ed., *Tax Policy and the Economy*, Vol. 9, Cambridge: MIT Press, 1995; Pieter H. M. van Baal, et al., "Lifetime Medical Costs of Obesity: Prevention No Cure for Increasing Health Expenditure," *PLoS Medicine*, Vol. 5, No. 2, February 2008, pp. 242–249; Pierre-Carl Michaud, "Understanding the Economic Consequences of Shifting Trends in Population Health," National Bureau of Economic Research Working Paper 15231, August 2009; and "Feds Say Obesity Epidemic Hurts Airlines by Increasing Fuel Costs," Associated Press, November 5, 2004.

Your Turn: Test your understanding by doing related problem 3.9 on pages 177–178 at the end of this chapter.

Solved Problem 5.3

MyEconLab Interactive Animation

Dealing with the Externalities of Car Driving

When you drive a car, you generate several negative externalities: You cause some additional air pollution, you increase the chances that other drivers will have an accident, and you cause some additional congestion on roads, causing other drivers to spend more time in traffic. Ian Parry of the International Monetary Fund and Kenneth Small of the University of California, Irvine, have estimated that these external costs amount to about $1.00 per gallon of gasoline. Taxes on gasoline vary by state and currently average about $0.50 per gallon.

a. Draw a graph showing the gasoline market. Indicate the efficient equilibrium quantity and the market equilibrium quantity.

b. Given the information in this problem, if the government wanted to bring about the efficient level of gasoline production, how large a tax should the government impose on gasoline? Will the price consumers pay for gasoline rise by the full amount of the tax? Briefly explain using your graph from part (a).

Solving the Problem

Step 1: Review the chapter material. This problem is about the government using a tax to deal with a negative externality, so you may want to review the section "Government Policies to Deal with Externalities," which begins on page 158.

Step 2: Answer part (a) by drawing a graph of the gasoline market. In this case, the tax is levied on the consumption of gasoline rather than on its production, so your graph should show the demand curve representing marginal social benefit being below the demand curve showing marginal private benefit. (Of course, the government actually collects the tax from sellers rather than from consumers, but we get the same result whether the government imposes a tax on the buyers of a good or on the sellers.) Your graph should also show the market equilibrium quantity of gasoline, Q_{Market}, being greater than the efficient equilibrium quantity, $Q_{Efficient}$.

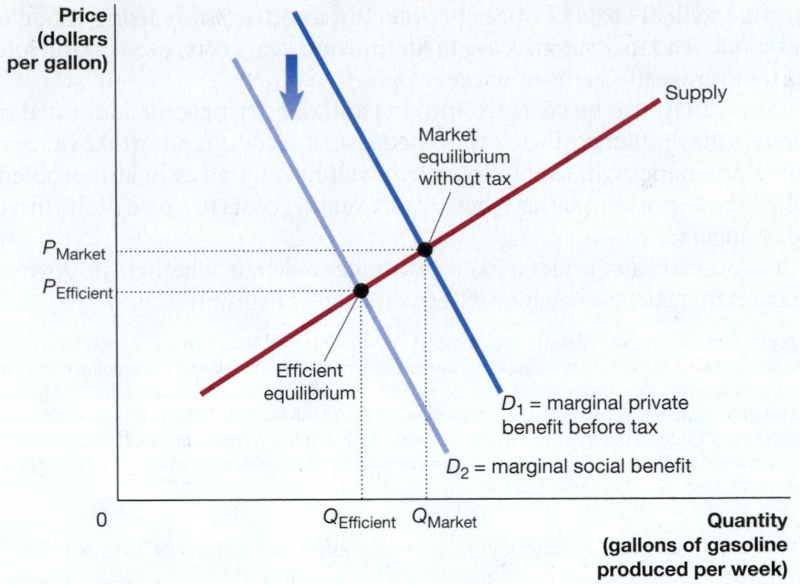

Step 3: Answer part (b) by explaining the size of the necessary tax, indicating the tax on your graph from part (a), and explaining the effect of the tax on the equilibrium price. If Parry and Small are correct that the external cost from consuming gasoline is $1.00 per gallon, then the tax per gallon should be raised from $0.50 to $1.00 per gallon. You should show the effect of the increase in the tax on your graph.

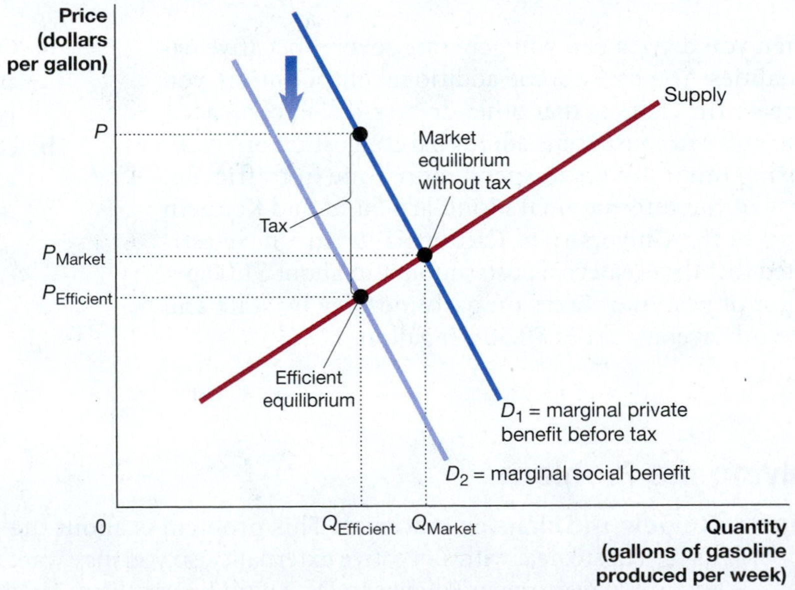

The graph shows that although the tax shifts down the demand curve for gasoline, the price consumers pay increases by less than the amount of the tax. To see this, note that the price consumers pay rises from P_{Market} to P, which is smaller than the per gallon tax, which equals the vertical distance between $P_{Efficient}$ and P.

Source: Ian W. H. Parry and Kenneth A. Small, "Does Britain or the United States Have the Right Gasoline Tax?" American Economic Review, Vol. 95, No. 4, September 2005, pp. 1276–1289.

MyEconLab Study Plan

Your Turn: For more practice, do related problems 3.10, 3.11, and 3.12 on page 178 at the end of this chapter.

Because Pigou was the first economist to propose using government taxes and subsidies to deal with externalities, they are sometimes referred to as **Pigovian taxes and subsidies**. Note that a Pigovian tax eliminates deadweight loss and improves economic efficiency, unlike most taxes, which are intended simply to raise revenue and can reduce consumer surplus and producer surplus and create a deadweight loss (see Chapter 4). In fact, one reason that economists support Pigovian taxes as a way to deal with negative externalities is that the government can use the revenues raised by Pigovian taxes to lower other taxes that reduce economic efficiency. For instance, the Canadian province of British Columbia has enacted a Pigovian tax on carbon dioxide emissions and uses the revenue raised to reduce personal income taxes.

Pigovian taxes and subsidies Government taxes and subsidies intended to bring about an efficient level of output in the presence of externalities.

Command-and-Control versus Market-Based Approaches

Although the federal government has sometimes used taxes and subsidies to deal with externalities, it has more frequently used a *command-and-control approach* to deal with pollution. A **command-and-control approach** to reducing pollution involves the government imposing quantitative limits on the amount of pollution firms are allowed to emit or requiring firms to install specific pollution control devices. For example, in the 1980s, the federal government required auto manufacturers such as Ford and General Motors to install catalytic converters to reduce auto emissions on all new automobiles.

Command-and-control approach A policy that involves the government imposing quantitative limits on the amount of pollution firms are allowed to emit or requiring firms to install specific pollution control devices.

Congress could have used a command-and-control approach to achieve its goal of reducing sulfur dioxide emissions by 8.5 million tons per year by 2010. However, this approach would not have been an economically efficient solution to the problem because utilities can have very different costs of reducing sulfur dioxide emissions. Some utilities that already used low-sulfur coal could reduce emissions further only at a high cost. Other utilities, particularly those in the Midwest, were able to reduce emissions at a lower cost.

Congress decided to use a market-based approach to reducing sulfur dioxide emissions by setting up a *cap-and-trade system* of tradable emission allowances. The federal government gave allowances to utilities equal to the total target amount of sulfur dioxide emissions. The utilities were then free to buy and sell the allowances. An active market where the allowances could be bought and sold was conducted on the Chicago Mercantile Exchange. Utilities that could reduce emissions at low cost did so and sold their allowances. Utilities that could only reduce emissions at high cost bought allowances.

Using tradable emission allowances to reduce acid rain was a success in that it made it possible for utilities to meet Congress's emissions goal at a much lower cost than expected. Just before Congress enacted the allowances program in 1990, the Edison Electric Institute estimated that the cost to utilities of complying with the program would be $7.4 billion by 2010. By 1994, the federal government's General Accounting Office estimated that the cost would be less than $2 billion. In practice, the cost was almost 90 percent less than the initial estimate, or only about $870 *million*. MyEconLab Concept Check

The End of the Sulfur Dioxide Cap-and-Trade System

The dollar value of the total benefits of reducing sulfur dioxide emissions turned out to be at least 25 times as large as the costs. Despite its successes, however, the sulfur dioxide cap-and-trade system had effectively ended by 2013. Over the years, research showed that the amount of illnesses caused by sulfur dioxide emissions was greater than had been thought. In response to these findings, President George W. Bush proposed legislation lowering the cap on sulfur dioxide emissions, but Congress did not pass the legislation. Court rulings kept the Environmental Protection Agency (EPA) from using regulations to set up a new trading system for sulfur dioxide allowances with a lower cap. As a result, the EPA reverted to the previous system of setting limits on sulfur dioxide emissions at the state or individual power plant level.

Because nationwide trading of emission allowances was no longer possible, the allowances lost their value. Many economists continue to believe that using market-based policies, such as the sulfur dioxide cap-and-trade system, is an efficient way to deal with the externalities of pollution. But in the end, any policy requires substantial political support to be enacted and maintained. MyEconLab Concept Check

Are Tradable Emission Allowances Licenses to Pollute?

Tradable emission allowances face a political problem because some environmentalists have criticized them for being "licenses to pollute." These environmentalists argue that just as the government does not issue licenses to rob banks or drive drunk, it should not issue licenses to pollute. But, this criticism ignores one of the central lessons of economics: Because resources are scarce, trade-offs exist. Resources that are spent on reducing one type of pollution are not available to reduce other types of pollution or for any other use. Because reducing acid rain using tradable emission allowances cost utilities $870 million per year, rather than $7.4 billion, as originally estimated, society saved more than $6.5 billion per year.

MyEconLab Concept Check

Making the Connection MyEconLab Video

Can a Carbon Tax Reduce Global Warming?

In the past 35 years, the global temperature has increased about 0.75 degree Fahrenheit (or 0.40 degree Celsius) compared with the average for the period between 1951 and 1980. The following graph shows changes in temperature in the years since 1880.

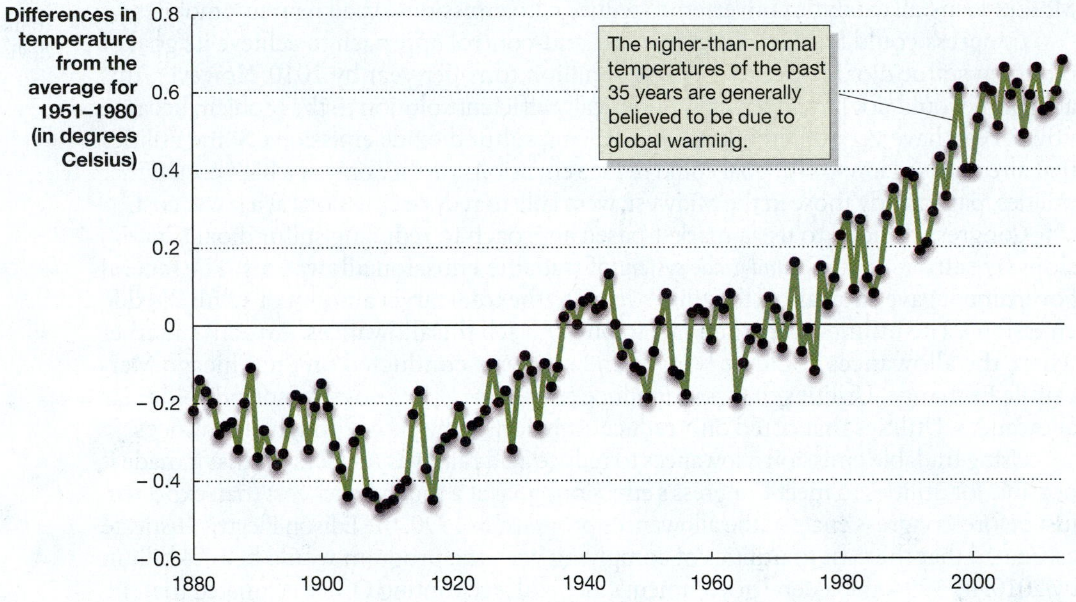

Source: NASA, Goddard Institute for Space Studies, data.giss.nasa.gov/gistemp/tabledata_v3/GLB.Ts.txt.

Over the centuries, global temperatures have gone through many long periods of warming and cooling. Nevertheless, many scientists are convinced that the recent warming trend is not part of the natural fluctuations in temperature but is primarily caused by the burning of fossil fuels, such as coal, natural gas, and petroleum. Burning these fuels releases carbon dioxide, which accumulates in the atmosphere as a "greenhouse gas." Greenhouse gases cause some of the heat released from the earth to be reflected back, increasing temperatures. Annual carbon dioxide emissions increased from about 50 million metric tons of carbon in 1850 to 1,600 million metric tons in 1950 and to nearly 9,900 million metric tons in 2013.

If greenhouse gases continue to accumulate in the atmosphere, according to some estimates, global temperatures could increase by 3 degrees Fahrenheit or more during the next 100 years. Such an increase in temperature could lead to significant changes in climate, which might result in more hurricanes and other violent weather conditions, disrupt farming in many parts of the world, and lead to increases in sea levels, which could result in flooding in coastal areas.

Although most economists and policymakers agree that emitting carbon dioxide results in a significant negative externality, there has been extensive debate over which policies should be adopted. Part of the debate arises from disagreements about how rapidly global warming is likely to occur and what the economic cost will be. In addition, carbon dioxide emissions are a worldwide problem; sharp reductions in carbon dioxide emissions only in the United States and Europe, for instance, would not be enough to stop global warming. But coordinating policy across countries has proven difficult. Finally, policymakers and economists debate the relative effectiveness of different policies.

Governments have used several approaches to reducing carbon dioxide emissions. The European Union has established a cap-and-trade system under which each country issues emission allowances that can be freely traded among firms in different countries. The European Parliament, though, has been unwilling to reduce the number of allowances available over time, making it unclear how the system could be used to further reduce carbon dioxide emissions.

As mentioned in the chapter opener, in 2015, the Obama administration introduced the Clean Power Plan, which requires states to reduce power plant emissions to 32 percent below 2005 levels by 2030. To meet the goals, utilities, such as We Energies in Wisconsin, need to close coal-burning electric power plants and replace them with plants burning natural gas or powered by alternative energy sources, such as wind or solar. Some economists and policymakers are unsure whether the plan's goals can be met without disrupting the country's power supply.

Many economists favor a carbon tax as a market-based policy to reduce carbon dioxide emissions. Economists working at federal government agencies have estimated that the marginal social cost of carbon dioxide emissions is about $21 per ton. The Congressional Budget Office estimates that a Pigovian tax equal to that amount would reduce carbon dioxide emissions in the United States by about 8 percent over 10 years. The federal government would collect about $1.2 trillion in revenues from the tax over the same period. One government study indicates that 87 percent of a carbon tax would be borne by consumers in the form of higher prices for gasoline, electricity, natural gas, and other goods. For example, a $21 per ton carbon tax would increase the price of gasoline by about $0.18 to $0.20 per gallon. Because lower-income households spend a larger fraction of their incomes on gasoline than do higher-income households, they would bear a proportionally larger share of the tax. Most proposals for a carbon tax include a way of refunding to lower-income households some part of their higher tax payments.

As of late 2015, it seemed doubtful that Congress would pass a carbon tax. The debate over policies to deal with global warming is likely to continue for many years.

Sources: Coral Davenport, "A Challenge from Climate Change Regulations," *New York Times*, April 22, 2015; "ETS, RIP?" *The Economist*, April 20, 2013; Congressional Budget Office, "Effects of a Carbon Tax on the Economy and the Environment," May 2013, www.cbo.gov/publication/44223; and Daniel F. Morris and Clayton Munnings, "Progressing to a Fair Carbon Tax," April 2013, www.rff.org/RFF/Documents/RFF-IB-13-03.pdf.

Your Turn: Test your understanding by doing related problems 3.15 and 3.16 on page 179 at the end of this chapter.

MyEconLab Study Plan

5.4 Four Categories of Goods

LEARNING OBJECTIVE: Explain how goods can be categorized on the basis of whether they are rival or excludable and use graphs to illustrate the efficient quantities of public goods and common resources.

We can explore further the question of when the market is likely to succeed in supplying the efficient quantity of a good by understanding that goods differ on the basis of whether their consumption is *rival* and *excludable*:

- **Rivalry** occurs when one person's consumption of a unit of a good means no one else can consume it. If you consume a Big Mac, for example, no one else can consume it.
- **Excludability** means that anyone who does not pay for a good cannot consume it. If you don't pay for a Big Mac, McDonald's can exclude you from consuming it. The consumption of a Big Mac is therefore rival and excludable.

Rivalry The situation that occurs when one person's consumption of a unit of a good means no one else can consume it.

Excludability The situation in which anyone who does not pay for a good cannot consume it.

MyEconLab Animation

Figure 5.7

Four Categories of Goods

Goods and services can be divided into four categories on the basis of whether people can be excluded from consuming them and whether they are rival in consumption. A good or service is rival in consumption if one person consuming a unit of the good means that another person cannot consume that unit.

	Excludable	Nonexcludable
Rival	**Private Goods** *Examples:* *Big Macs* *Running shoes*	**Common Resources** *Examples:* *Tuna in the ocean* *Public pasture land*
Nonrival	**Quasi-Public Goods** *Examples:* *Cable TV* *Toll road*	**Public Goods** *Examples:* *National defense* *Court system*

The consumption of some goods, however, can be either *nonrival* or *nonexcludable*:

- Nonrival means that one person's consumption does not interfere with another person's consumption.
- Nonexcludable means that it is impossible to exclude others from consuming the good, whether they have paid for it or not.

Figure 5.7 shows four possible categories into which goods can fall. We next consider each of the four categories:

Private good A good that is both rival and excludable.

1. A **private good** is both rival and excludable. Food, clothing, haircuts, and many other goods and services fall into this category. One person's consuming a unit of these goods keeps other people from consuming that unit, and no one can consume these goods without buying them. Although we didn't state it explicitly, when we analyzed the demand and supply for goods and services in earlier chapters, we assumed that the goods and services were all private goods.

Public good A good that is both nonrival and nonexcludable.

Free riding Benefiting from a good without paying for it.

2. A **public good** is both nonrival and nonexcludable. Public goods are often, although not always, supplied by a government rather than by private firms. The classic example of a public good is national defense. Your consuming national defense does not interfere with your neighbor consuming it, so consumption is nonrival. You also cannot be excluded from consuming it, whether you pay for it or not. No private firm would be willing to supply national defense because everyone can consume national defense whether they pay for it or not. The behavior of consumers in this situation is called **free riding** because individuals benefit from a good—in this case, national defense—without paying for it.
3. A *quasi-public good* is excludable but not rival. An example is cable television. People who do not pay for cable television do not receive it, but one person watching it doesn't prevent other people from watching it. Another example is a toll road. Anyone who doesn't pay the toll doesn't get on the highway, but one person using the highway doesn't interfere with someone else using the highway (unless so many people are using the highway that it becomes congested). Goods that fall into this category are called *quasi-public goods*.

Common resource A good that is rival but not excludable.

4. A **common resource** is rival but not excludable. Forest land in many poor countries is a common resource. If one person cuts down a tree, no one else can use that tree. But if no one has a property right to the forest, no one can be excluded from using it. As we will discuss in more detail later, people often overuse common resources.

We analyzed the demand and supply for private goods in earlier chapters. For the remainder of this chapter, we focus on the categories of public goods and common resources. To determine the optimal quantity of a public good, we have to modify our usual demand and supply analysis to take into account that a public good is both nonrival and nonexcludable.

The Demand for a Public Good

We can determine the market demand curve for a good or service by adding up the quantity of the good demanded by each consumer at each price. To keep things simple, let's consider the case of a market with only two consumers. Figure 5.8 shows that the market demand curve for hamburgers depends on the individual demand curves of Jill and Joe.

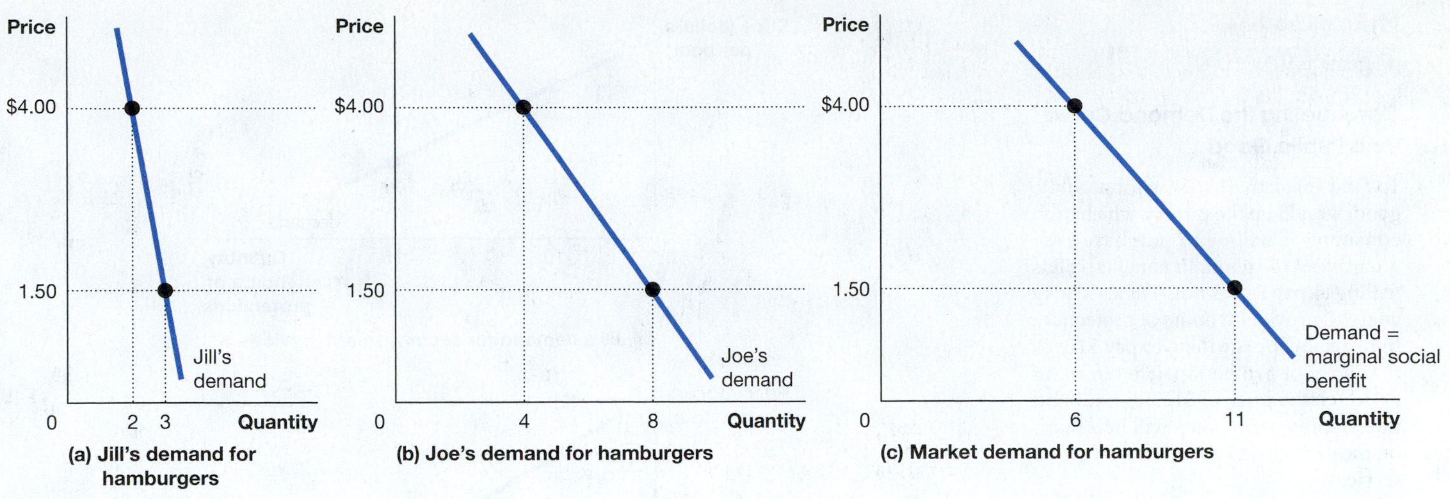

MyEconLab Animation

Figure 5.8 Constructing the Market Demand Curve for a Private Good

The market demand curve for private goods is determined by adding horizontally the quantity of the good demanded at each price by each consumer. For instance, in panel (a), Jill demands 2 hamburgers when the price is $4.00, and in panel (b), Joe demands 4 hamburgers when the price is $4.00. So, a quantity of 6 hamburgers and a price of $4.00 is a point on the market demand curve in panel (c).

At a price of $4.00, Jill demands 2 hamburgers per week and Joe demands 4. Adding horizontally, the combination of a price of $4.00 per hamburger and a quantity demanded of 6 hamburgers will be a point on the market demand curve for hamburgers. Similarly, adding horizontally at a price of $1.50, we have a price of $1.50 and a quantity demanded of 11 as another point on the market demand curve. A consumer's demand curve for a good represents the marginal benefit the consumer receives from the good, so when we add together the consumers' demand curves, we have not only the market demand curve but also the marginal social benefit curve for this good, assuming that there is no externality in consumption.

How can we find the demand curve or marginal social benefit curve for a public good? Once again, for simplicity, assume that Jill and Joe are the only consumers. Unlike with a private good, where Jill and Joe can end up consuming different quantities, with a public good, they will consume *the same quantity*. Suppose that Jill owns a service station on an isolated rural road, and Joe owns a car dealership next door. These are the only two businesses around for miles. Both Jill and Joe are afraid that unless they hire a security guard at night, their businesses may be burgled. Like national defense, the services of a security guard are in this case a public good: Once hired, the guard will be able to protect both businesses, so the good is nonrival. It also will not be possible to exclude either business from being protected, so the good is nonexcludable.

To arrive at a demand curve for a public good, we don't add quantities at each price, as with a private good. Instead, we add the price each consumer is willing to pay for each quantity of the public good. This value represents the total dollar amount consumers as a group would be willing to pay for that quantity of the public good. In other words, to find the demand curve, or marginal social benefit curve, for a private good, we add the demand curves of individual consumers horizontally; for public goods, we add individual demand curves vertically. Figure 5.9 shows how the marginal social benefit curve for security guard services depends on the individual demand curves of Jill and Joe.

The figure shows that Jill is willing to pay $8 per hour for the guard to provide 10 hours of protection per night. Joe would suffer a greater loss from a burglary, so he is willing to pay $10 per hour for the same amount of protection. Adding the dollar amount that each is willing to pay gives us a price of $18 per hour and a quantity of 10 hours as a point on the marginal social benefit curve for security guard services. The figure also shows that because Jill is willing to spend $4 per hour for 15 hours of guard services and Joe is willing to pay $5, a price of $9 per hour and a quantity of 15 hours is another point on the marginal social benefit curve for security guard services.

MyEconLab Concept Check

MyEconLab Animation

Figure 5.9

Constructing the Demand Curve for a Public Good

To find the demand curve for a public good, we add up the price at which each consumer is willing to purchase each quantity of the good. In panel (a), Jill is willing to pay $8 per hour for a security guard to provide 10 hours of protection. In panel (b), Joe is willing to pay $10 for that level of protection. Therefore, in panel (c), the price of $18 per hour and the quantity of 10 hours will be a point on the demand curve for security guard services.

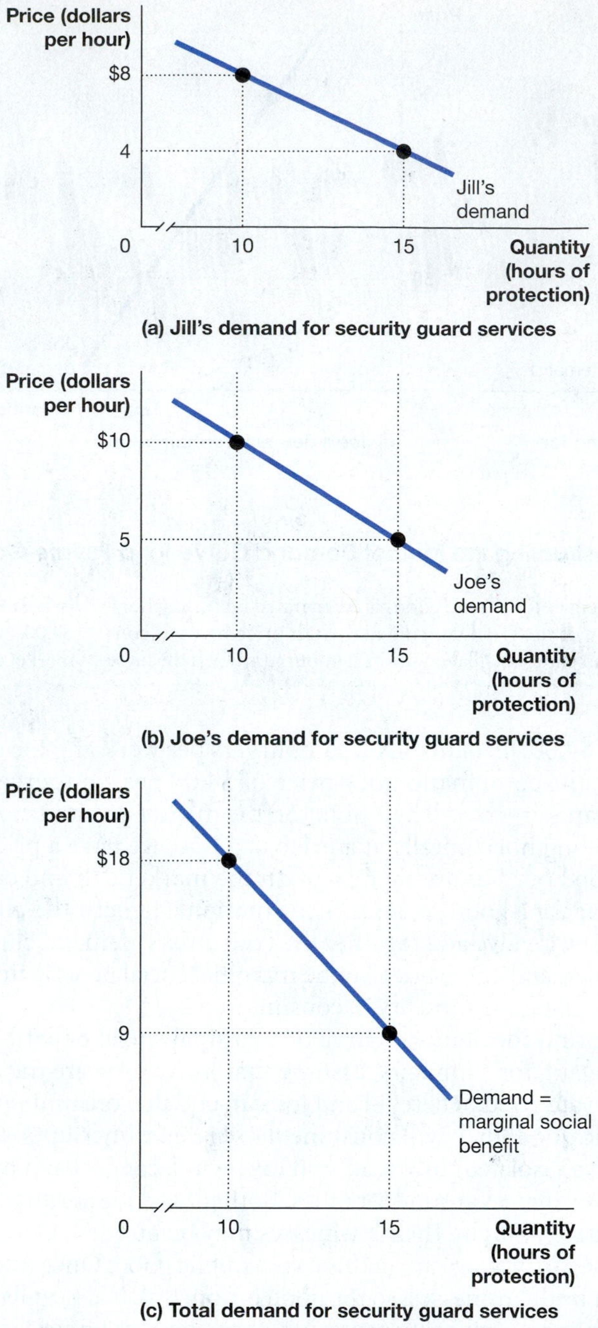

The Optimal Quantity of a Public Good

We know that to achieve economic efficiency, a good or service should be produced up to the point where the sum of consumer surplus and producer surplus is maximized, or, alternatively, where the marginal social cost equals the marginal social benefit. Therefore, the optimal quantity of security guard services—or any other public good—will occur where the marginal social benefit curve intersects the supply curve. As with private goods, in the absence of an externality in production, the supply curve represents the marginal social cost of supplying the good. Figure 5.10 shows that the optimal quantity of security guard services supplied is 15 hours, at a price of $9 per hour.

Will the market provide the economically efficient quantity of security guard services? One difficulty is that the individual preferences of consumers, as shown by their demand curves, are not revealed in this market. This difficulty does not arise with private goods because consumers must reveal their preferences in order to purchase private goods. If the market price of Big Macs is $4.00, Joe either reveals that he is willing to pay that much by

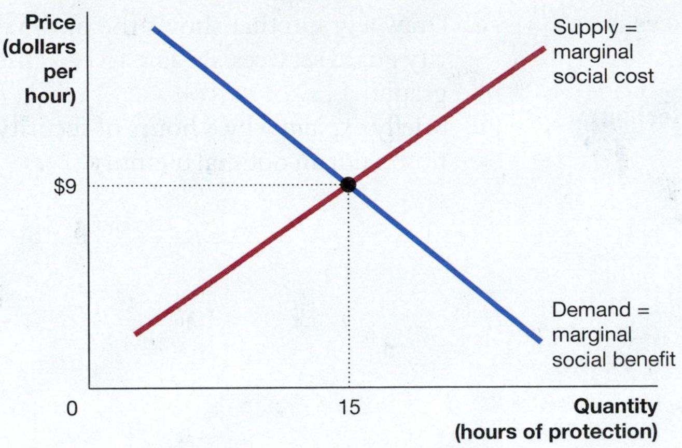

MyEconLab Animation

Figure 5.10

The Optimal Quantity of a Public Good

The optimal quantity of a public good is produced where the sum of consumer surplus and producer surplus is maximized, which occurs where the demand curve intersects the supply curve. In this case, the optimal quantity of security guard services is 15 hours, at a price of $9 per hour.

buying it or he does without it. In our example, neither Jill nor Joe can be excluded from consuming the services provided by a security guard once either hires one, and, therefore, neither has an incentive to reveal her or his preferences. In this case, though, with only two consumers, it is likely that private bargaining will result in an efficient quantity of the public good. This outcome is not likely for a public good—such as national defense—that is supplied by the government to millions of consumers.

Governments sometimes use *cost–benefit analysis* to determine what quantity of a public good should be supplied. For example, before building a dam on a river, the federal government will attempt to weigh the costs against the benefits. The costs include the opportunity cost of other projects the government cannot carry out if it builds the dam. The benefits include improved flood control or new recreational opportunities on the lake formed by the dam. However, for many public goods, including national defense, the government does not use a formal cost–benefit analysis. Instead, the quantity of national defense supplied is determined by a political process involving Congress and the president. Even here, of course, Congress and the president realize that trade-offs are involved: The more resources used for national defense, the fewer resources are available for other public or private goods.

MyEconLab Concept Check

Solved Problem 5.4

MyEconLab Interactive Animation

Determining the Optimal Level of Public Goods

Suppose, once again, that Jill and Joe run businesses that are next door to each other on an isolated road, and both need a security guard. Their demand schedules for security guard services are as follows:

Joe		Jill	
Price (dollars per hour)	**Quantity (hours of protection)**	**Price (dollars per hour)**	**Quantity (hours of protection)**
$20	0	$20	1
18	1	18	2
16	2	16	3
14	3	14	4
12	4	12	5
10	5	10	6
8	6	8	7
6	7	6	8
4	8	4	9
2	9	2	10

The supply schedule for security guard services is as follows:

Price (dollars per hour)	Quantity (hours of protection)
$8	1
10	2
12	3
14	4
16	5
18	6
20	7
22	8
24	9

a. Draw a graph that shows the optimal level of security guard services. Be sure to label the curves on the graph.

b. Briefly explain why 8 hours of security guard protection is not an optimal quantity.

Solving the Problem

Step 1: Review the chapter material. This problem is about determining the optimal level of public goods, so you may want to review the section "The Optimal Quantity of a Public Good," which begins on page 168.

Step 2: Begin by deriving the demand curve or marginal social benefit curve for security guard services. To calculate the marginal social benefit of guard services, we need to add the prices that Jill and Joe are willing to pay at each quantity:

Demand or Marginal Social Benefit	
Price (dollars per hour)	**Quantity (hours of protection)**
$38	1
34	2
30	3
26	4
22	5
18	6
14	7
10	8
6	9

Step 3: Answer part (a) by plotting the demand (marginal social benefit) and supply (marginal social cost) curves. The graph shows that the optimal level of security guard services is 6 hours.

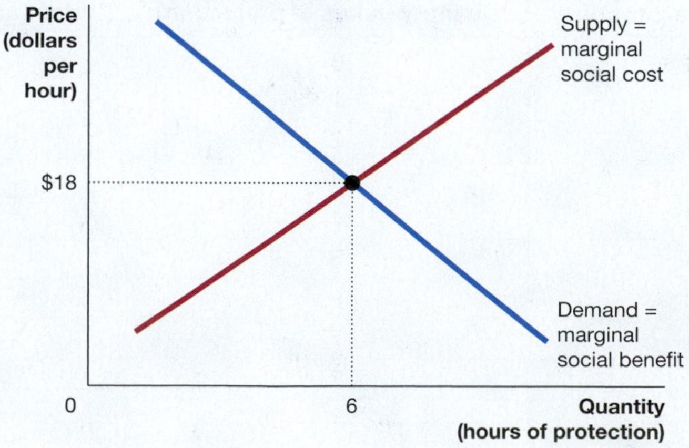

Step 4: Answer part (b) by explaining why 8 hours of security guard protection is not an optimal quantity. For each hour beyond 6, the supply curve is above the demand curve. Therefore, the marginal social benefit received will be less than the marginal social cost of supplying these hours. This results in a deadweight loss and a reduction in economic surplus.

Your Turn: For more practice, do related problem 4.5 on pages 179–180 at the end of this chapter.

MyEconLab Study Plan

Common Resources

In England during the Middle Ages, each village had an area of pasture, known as a *commons*, on which any family in the village was allowed to graze its cows or sheep without charge. Of course, the grass one family's cow ate was not available for another family's cow, so consumption was rival. But every family in the village had the right to use the commons, so it was nonexcludable. Without some type of restraint on usage, the commons would be overgrazed. To see why, consider the economic incentives facing a family that was thinking of buying another cow and grazing it on the commons. The family would gain the benefits from increased milk production, but adding another cow to the commons would create a negative externality by reducing the amount of grass available for the cows of other families. Because this family—and the other families in the village—did not take this negative externality into account when deciding whether to add another cow to the commons, too many cows would be added. The grass on the commons would eventually be depleted, and no family's cow would get enough to eat.

The Tragedy of the Commons

The tendency for a common resource to be overused is called the **tragedy of the commons**. The forests in many poor countries are a modern example. When a family chops down a tree in a public forest, it takes into account the benefits of gaining firewood or wood for building, but it does not take into account the costs of deforestation. Haiti, for example, was once heavily forested. Today, 80 percent of the country's forests have been cut down, primarily to be burned to create charcoal for heating and cooking. Because the mountains no longer have tree roots to hold the soil, heavy rains now often lead to devastating floods.

Tragedy of the commons The tendency for a common resource to be overused.

Figure 5.11 shows that with a common resource such as wood from a forest, the efficient level of use, $Q_{Efficient}$, is determined by the intersection of the demand curve, which represents the marginal social benefit received by consumers, and S_2, which

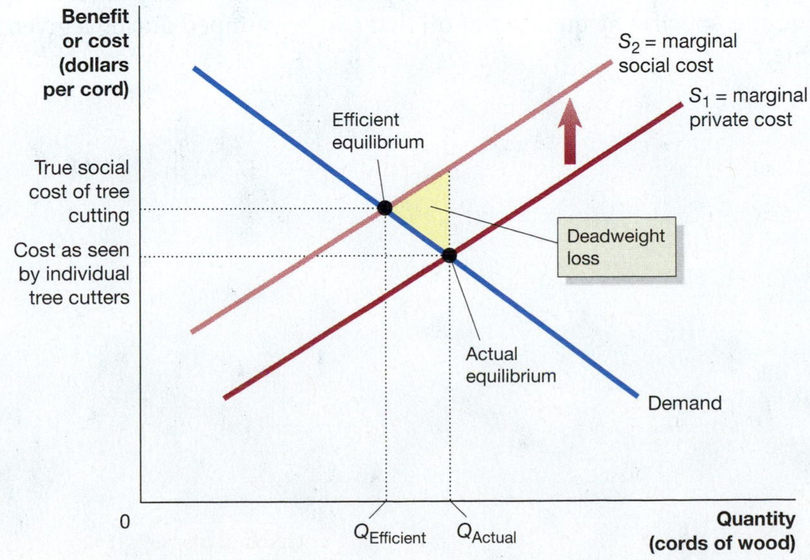

MyEconLab Animation

Figure 5.11

Overuse of a Common Resource

For a common resource such as wood from a forest, the efficient level of use, $Q_{Efficient}$, is determined by the intersection of the demand curve, which represents the marginal social benefit received by consumers, and S_2, which represents the marginal social cost of cutting the wood. Because each individual tree cutter ignores the external cost, the equilibrium quantity of wood cut is Q_{Actual}, which is greater than the efficient quantity. At the actual equilibrium level of output, there is a deadweight loss, equal to the area of the yellow triangle.

represents the marginal social cost of cutting the wood. As in our discussion of negative externalities, the social cost is equal to the private cost of cutting the wood plus the external cost. In this case, the external cost represents the fact that the more wood each person cuts, the less wood there is available for others and the greater the deforestation, which increases the chances of floods. Because each individual tree cutter ignores the external cost, the equilibrium quantity of wood cut is Q_{Actual}, which is greater than the efficient quantity. At the actual equilibrium level of output, there is a deadweight loss, equal to the area of the yellow triangle in Figure 5.11.

Is There a Way out of the Tragedy of the Commons? Notice that our discussion of the tragedy of the commons is very similar to our earlier discussion of negative externalities. The source of the tragedy of the commons is the same as the source of negative externalities: lack of clearly defined and enforced property rights. For instance, suppose that instead of being held as a collective resource, a piece of pastureland is owned by one person. That person will take into account the effect of adding another cow on the grass available to cows already using the pasture. As a result, the optimal number of cows will be placed on the pasture. Over the years, most of the commons lands in England were converted to private property. Most of the forestland in Haiti and other developing countries is actually the property of the government. The failure of the government to protect the forests against trespassers or convert them to private property is the key reason those forests are overused.

In some situations, though, enforcing property rights is *not* feasible. An example is the oceans. Because no country owns the oceans beyond its own coastal waters, the fish and other resources of the ocean will remain a common resource. In situations in which enforcing property rights is not feasible, two types of solutions to the tragedy of the commons are possible:

1. If the geographic area involved is limited and the number of people involved is small, access to the commons can be restricted through community norms and laws. If the geographic area or the number of people involved is large, legal restrictions on access to the commons are required. For instance, the tragedy of the commons was avoided in the Middle Ages by traditional limits on the number of animals each family was allowed to put on the common pasture. Although these traditions were not formal laws, they were usually enforced adequately by social pressure.
2. If the geographic area or the number of people involved is large, legal restrictions on access to the commons are required. These restrictions can take several different forms, including taxes, quotas, and tradable permits. By setting a tax equal to the external cost, governments can ensure that the efficient quantity of a resource is used. In the United States, the government has used quotas to limit access to pools of oil that are beneath property owned by many different persons. The quotas specify the quantity of oil that can be pumped during a given period of time.

MyEconLab Study Plan

MyEconLab Concept Check

Continued from page 147

Economics in Your Life

What's the "Best" Level of Pollution?

At the beginning of this chapter, we asked you to think about what is the "best" level of carbon emissions. Conceptually, this is a straightforward question to answer: The efficient level of carbon emissions is the level for which the marginal benefit of reducing carbon emissions exactly equals the marginal cost of reducing carbon emissions. In practice, however, this question is very difficult to answer. For example, scientists disagree about how much carbon emissions are contributing to climate change and what the damage from climate change will be. In addition, the cost of reducing carbon emissions depends on the method of reduction used. As a result, neither the marginal cost curve nor the marginal benefit curve for reducing carbon emissions is known with certainty. This uncertainty makes it difficult for policymakers to determine the economically efficient level of carbon emissions and is the source of much of the current debate. In any case, economists agree that the total cost of *completely* eliminating carbon emissions is much greater than the total benefit.

Conclusion

Government interventions in the economy, such as imposing price ceilings and price floors, can reduce economic efficiency. But in this chapter, we have seen that the government plays an important role in the economy when the absence of well-defined and enforceable property rights keeps the market from operating efficiently. For instance, because no one has a property right to clean air, in the absence of government intervention, firms will produce too great a quantity of products that generate air pollution. We have also seen that public goods are nonrival and nonexcludable, so the government often supplies them.

Visit MyEconLab for a news article and analysis related to the concepts in this chapter.

CHAPTER SUMMARY AND PROBLEMS

Key Terms

Coase theorem, p. 156
Command-and-control approach, p. 163
Common resource, p. 166
Excludability, p. 165
Externality, p. 148
Free riding, p. 166
Market failure, p. 151
Pigovian taxes and subsidies, p. 163
Private benefit, p. 149
Private cost, p. 149
Private good, p. 166
Property rights, p. 151
Public good, p. 166
Rivalry, p. 165
Social benefit, p. 149
Social cost, p. 149
Tragedy of the commons, p. 171
Transactions costs, p. 156

5.1 Externalities and Economic Efficiency, pages 148–151

LEARNING OBJECTIVE: Identify examples of positive and negative externalities and use graphs to show how externalities affect economic efficiency.

Summary

An **externality** is a benefit or cost to parties who are not involved in a transaction. Pollution and other externalities in production cause a difference between the **private cost** borne by the producer of a good or service and the **social cost**, which includes any external cost, such as the cost of pollution. An externality in consumption causes a difference between the **private benefit** received by the consumer and the **social benefit**, which includes any external benefit. If externalities exist in production or consumption, the market will not produce the optimal level of a good or service. This outcome is referred to as **market failure**. Externalities arise when property rights do not exist or cannot be legally enforced. **Property rights** are the rights individuals or businesses have to the exclusive use of their property, including the right to buy or sell it.

MyEconLab Visit **www.myeconlab.com** to complete these exercises online and get instant feedback.

Review Questions

1.1 What is an externality? Give an example of a positive externality, and give an example of a negative externality.

1.2 When will the private cost of producing a good differ from the social cost? Give an example. When will the private benefit from consuming a good differ from the social benefit? Give an example.

1.3 What is economic efficiency? How do externalities affect the economic efficiency of a market equilibrium?

1.4 What is market failure? When is market failure likely to arise?

1.5 Briefly explain the relationship between property rights and the existence of externalities.

Problems and Applications

1.6 A neighbor's barking dog can be both a positive externality and a negative externality. Under what circumstances would a dog's bark be a positive externality? Under what circumstances would a dog's bark be a negative externality?

1.7 Yellowstone National Park is in bear country. The National Park Service, at its Yellowstone Web site, states the following about camping and hiking in bear country:

> Do not leave packs containing food unattended, even for a few minutes. Allowing a bear to obtain human food even once often results in the bear becoming aggressive about obtaining such food in the future. Aggressive bears present a threat to human safety and eventually must be destroyed or removed from the park. Please obey the law and do not allow bears or other wildlife to obtain human food.

What negative externality does obtaining human food pose for bears? What negative externality do bears obtaining human food pose for future campers and hikers?

Source: National Park Service, Yellowstone National Park, "Backcountry Camping and Hiking," www.nps.gov/yell/planyourvisit/backcountryhiking.htm.

1.8 Every year at the beginning of flu season, many people, including the elderly, get a flu shot to reduce their chances of contracting the flu. One result is that people who do *not* get a flu shot are less likely to contract the flu.

a. What type of externality (negative or positive) arises from getting a flu shot?

b. On the graph that follows, show the effects of this externality by drawing in and labeling any additional curves that are needed and by labeling the efficient quantity and the efficient price of flu shots. Label the area representing deadweight loss in this market.

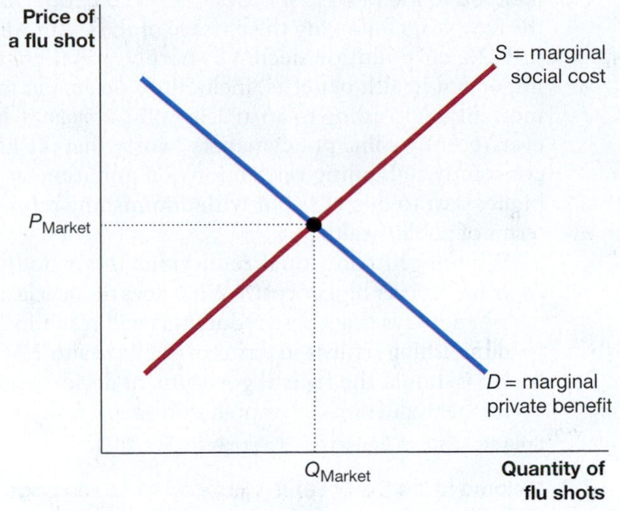

1.9 John Cassidy, a writer for the *New Yorker*, wrote a blog post arguing against New York City's having installed bike lanes. Cassidy complained that the bike lanes had eliminated traffic lanes on some streets as well as some on-street parking. A writer for the *Economist* disputed Cassidy's argument with the following comment: "I hate to belabour the point, but driving, as it turns out, is associated with a number of negative externalities." What externalities are associated with driving? How do these externalities affect the debate over whether big cities should install more bike lanes?

Sources: John Cassidy, "Battle of the Bike Lanes," *New Yorker*, March 8, 2011; and "The World Is His Parking Spot," *Economist*, March 9, 2011.

1.10 In a study at a large state university, students were randomly assigned roommates. Researchers found that, on average, males assigned to roommates who reported drinking alcohol in the year before entering college earned GPAs one-quarter point lower than those assigned to nondrinking roommates. For males who drank frequently before college, being assigned to a roommate who also drank frequently before college reduced their GPAs by two-thirds of a point. Draw a graph showing the price of alcohol and the quantity of alcohol consumption on college campuses. Include in the graph the demand for drinking and the private and social costs of drinking. Label any deadweight loss that arises in this market.

Source: Michael Kremer and Dan M. Levy, "Peer Effects and Alcohol Use among College Students," *Journal of Economic Perspectives*, Vol. 22, No. 3, Summer 2008, pp. 189–206.

1.11 Tom and Jacob are college students. Each of them will probably get married later and have two or three children. Each knows that if he studies more in college, he'll get a better job and earn more money. Earning more will enable them to spend more on their future families for things such as orthodontia, nice clothes, admission to expensive colleges, and travel. Tom thinks about the benefits to his potential children when he decides how much studying to do. Jacob doesn't.

a. What type of externality arises from studying?
b. Draw a graph showing this externality, contrasting the responses of Tom and Jacob. Who studies more? Who acts more efficiently? Briefly explain.

1.12 In recent years, companies have used fracking, or hydraulic fracturing, in drilling for oil and natural gas that previously could not be profitably recovered. According to an article in the *New York Times*, "horizontal drilling has enabled engineers to inject millions of gallons of high-pressure water directly into layers of shale to create the fractures that release the gas. Chemicals added to the water dissolve minerals, kill bacteria that might plug up the well, and insert sand to prop open the fractures." Experts are divided about whether fracking results in significant pollution, but some people worry that chemicals used in fracking might lead to pollution of underground supplies of water used by households and farms.

a. First, assume that fracking causes no significant pollution. Use a demand and supply graph to show the effect of fracking on the market for natural gas.
b. Now assume that fracking does result in pollution. On your graph from part (a), show the effect of fracking. Be sure to carefully label all curves and all equilibrium points.
c. In your graph in part (b), what has happened to the efficient level of output and the efficient price in the market for natural gas compared with the situation before fracking? Can you be certain that the efficient level of output and the efficient price have risen or fallen as a result of fracking? Briefly explain.

Source: Susan L. Brantley and Anna Meyendorff, "The Facts on Fracking," New York Times, March 13, 2013.

1.13 In an article in the agriculture magazine *Choices*, Oregon State University economist JunJie Wu made the following observation about the conversion of farmland to urban development:

> Land use provides many economic and social benefits, but often comes at a substantial cost to the environment. Although most economic costs are figured into land use decisions, most environmental externalities are not. These environmental "externalities" cause a divergence between private and social costs for some land uses, leading to an inefficient land allocation. For example, developers may not bear all the environmental and infrastructural costs generated by their projects. Such "market failures" provide a justification for private conservation efforts and public land use planning and regulation.

What does the author mean by *market failures* and *inefficient land allocation*? Explain why the author describes inefficient land allocation as a market failure. Illustrate your argument with a graph showing the market for land to be used for urban development.

Source: JunJie Wu, "Land Use Changes: Economic, Social, and Environmental Impacts," *Choices*, Vol. 23, No. 4, Fourth Quarter 2008, pp. 6–10.

5.2 Private Solutions to Externalities: The Coase Theorem, pages 151–158

LEARNING OBJECTIVE: Discuss the Coase theorem and explain how private bargaining can lead to economic efficiency in a market with an externality.

Summary

Externalities and market failures result from incomplete property rights or from the difficulty of enforcing property rights in certain situations. When an externality exists and the efficient quantity of a good is not being produced, the total cost of reducing the externality is usually less than the total benefit. **Transactions costs** are the costs in time and other resources that parties incur in the process of agreeing to and carrying out an exchange of goods or services. According to the **Coase theorem**, if these costs are low, private bargaining will result in an efficient solution to the problem of externalities.

MyEconLab Visit **www.myeconlab.com** to complete these exercises online and get instant feedback.

Review Questions

2.1 What do economists mean by "an economically efficient level of pollution"?

2.2 What is the Coase theorem? Why do the parties involved in an externality have an incentive to reach an efficient solution?

2.3 What are transactions costs? When are we likely to see private solutions to the problem of externalities?

Problems and Applications

2.4 Is it ever possible for an *increase* in pollution to make society better off? Briefly explain, using a graph like Figure 5.3 on page 154.

2.5 If the marginal cost of reducing a certain type of pollution is zero, should all that type of pollution be eliminated? Briefly explain.

2.6 Discuss the factors that determine the marginal cost of reducing crime. Discuss the factors that determine the marginal benefit of reducing crime. Would it be economically efficient to reduce the amount of crime to zero? Briefly explain.

2.7 In discussing the reduction of air pollution in the developing world, Richard Fuller of the Blacksmith Institute, an environmental organization, observed, "It's the 90/10 rule. To do 90 percent of the work only costs 10 percent of the money. It's the last 10 percent of the cleanup that costs 90 percent of the money." Why should it be any more costly to clean up the last 10 percent of polluted air than to clean up the first 90 percent? What trade-offs would be involved in cleaning up the final 10 percent?

Source: Tiffany M. Luck, "The World's Dirtiest Cities," *Forbes*, February 28, 2008.

2.8 **(Related to the Making the Connection on page 152)** In the first years following the passage of the Clean Air Act in 1970, air pollution declined sharply, and there were important health benefits, including a decline in infant mortality. According to an article in the *Economist*, however, recently some policymakers "worry that the EPA is constantly tightening restrictions on pollution, at ever higher cost to business but with diminishing returns in terms of public health."

a. Why might additional reductions in air pollution come at "ever higher cost"? What does the article mean when it says that these reductions will result in "ever diminishing returns in terms of public health"?

b. How should the federal government decide whether further reductions in air pollution are needed?

Source: "Soaring Emissions," *Economist*, June 2, 2011.

2.9 **(Related to the Don't Let This Happen to You on page 155)** Mabel is an advocate for a "zero tolerance" policy regarding all illegal street drugs, including cocaine, marijuana, and heroin. Mabel has witnessed high crime and violence in her neighborhood and believes that only if police arrest and prosecute anyone who sells or uses illegal drugs will she and her neighbors and their children live without fear. Is the policy that Mabel endorses economically efficient? Briefly explain.

2.10 **(Related to the Making the Connection on page 157)** Ira Goldman invented the Knee Defender, which keeps the airline seat in front of you from reclining. He argues that airlines have sold the space between two seats to the person occupying the seat but also to the person in the seat in front of that seat by allowing the occupant of that seat to recline it. Assume that Goldman is correct. According to the Coase theorem, does this airline policy make it impossible for passengers to achieve an economically efficient outcome with respect to the issue of reclining seats? Briefly explain.

Source: Damon Darlin, "In Defense of the Knee Defender," *New York Times*, August 28, 2014.

2.11 **(Related to the Making the Connection on page 157)** An article in the *Economist* discussing the struggle among airline passengers over reclining seats offered the following observation: "Given that airlines are unlikely to increase the [distance between] their seats any time soon, better that all planes come with fixed, non-reclining chairs in the first place." Would the change proposed result in an economically efficient outcome? Briefly explain.

Source: "Upright and Uptight," *Economist*, June 7, 2014.

5.3 Government Policies to Deal with Externalities, pages 158–165

LEARNING OBJECTIVE: Analyze government policies to achieve economic efficiency in a market with an externality.

Summary

When private solutions to externalities are unworkable, the government sometimes intervenes. One way to deal with a negative externality in production is to impose a tax equal to the cost of the externality. The tax causes the producer of the good to internalize the externality. The government can deal with a positive externality in consumption by giving consumers a subsidy, or payment, equal to the value of the externality. Government taxes and subsidies intended to bring about an efficient level of output in the presence of externalities are called **Pigovian taxes and subsidies**. Although the federal government has sometimes used subsidies and taxes to deal with externalities, in dealing with pollution it has more often used a command-and-control approach. A **command-and-control approach** involves the government imposing quantitative limits on the amount of pollution allowed or requiring firms to install specific pollution control devices. Direct pollution controls of this type are not economically efficient, however. As a result, economists generally prefer reducing pollution by using market-based policies.

MyEconLab Visit **www.myeconlab.com** to complete these exercises online and get instant feedback.

Review Questions

3.1 What is a Pigovian tax? How large should a Pigovian tax be to achieve efficiency?

3.2 What does it mean for a producer or consumer to internalize an externality? What would cause a producer or consumer to internalize an externality?

3.3 Why do most economists prefer tradable emission allowances to the command-and-control approach to pollution?

Problems and Applications

3.4 Some coal is mined by private companies on land owned by the federal government. Two economists writing in an opinion column argue, "The federal government should also take into account the economic consequences of burning coal when pricing this fuel. The price for taxpayer-owned coal should reflect, in some measure, the added costs associated with the impacts of greenhouse gas emissions."

a. What do these economists mean by "the added costs associated with the impacts of greenhouse gas emissions"?

b. Do you agree that the price the federal government charges the coal companies should include this cost? Briefly explain.

Source: David J. Hayes and James H. Stock, "The Real Cost of Coal," *New York Times*, March 24, 2015.

3.5 A column in the *New York Times* notes that many economists "support Pigovian taxes because, in some sense, we are already paying them." In what sense might consumers in a market be "paying" a Pigovian tax even if the government hasn't imposed an explicit tax?

Source: Adam Davidson, "Should We Tax People for Being Annoying?" *New York Times*, January 8, 2013.

3.6 Many antibiotics are no longer effective in eliminating infections because bacteria have evolved to become resistant to them. Some bacteria are now resistant to all but one or two existing antibiotics. In 2015, the Obama administration proposed subsidizing research aimed at developing new antibiotics.

a. Are there externalities involved in the market for antibiotics that would require a government subsidy to achieve an economically efficient outcome? Briefly explain.

b. Many people have health insurance that covers the majority of the cost of their prescription drugs, including antibiotics. Does that fact make the case for a government subsidy of the production of antibiotics stronger or weaker? Briefly explain.

Source: Sabrina Tavernise and Michael D. Shear, "Obama Seeks to Double Funding to Fight Antibiotic Resistance," *New York Times*, March 27, 2015.

3.7 A column in the *New York Times* has the headline, "Should We Tax People for Being Annoying?"

a. Do annoying people cause a negative externality? Should they be taxed? Do crying babies on a bus or plane cause a negative externality? Should the babies (or their parents) be taxed?

b. Do people who plant flowers and otherwise have beautiful gardens visible from the street cause a positive externality? Should these people receive a government subsidy?

c. Should every negative externality be taxed? Should every positive externality be subsidized? How might the government decide whether using Pigovian taxes and subsidies is appropriate?

Source: Adam Davison, "Should We Tax People for Being Annoying?" *New York Times*, January 8, 2013.

3.8 Writing in the *New York Times*, Michael Lewis argued, "Good new technologies are a bit like good new roads: Their social benefits far exceed what any one person or company can get paid for creating them." Does this observation justify the government subsidizing the production of new technologies? If so, how might the government do this?

Source: Michael Lewis, "In Defense of the Boom," *New York Times*, October 27, 2002.

3.9 **(Related to the Making the Connection on page 159)** Eric Finklestein, an economist at Duke University, has argued that the external costs from being obese are larger than the external costs from smoking because "the mortality effect for obesity is much smaller than it is for smoking and the costs start much earlier in life."

a. What does Finklestein mean by the "mortality effect"? Why would the mortality effect of obesity being smaller than the mortality effect of smoking result in obesity having a larger external cost?

b. Tobacco taxes have been more politically popular than taxes on soda. Why might the general public be more willing to support cigarette taxes than soda taxes?

Source: David Leonhardt, "Obama Likes Some Sin Taxes More Than Others," *New York Times*, April 10, 2013.

3.10 **(Related to Solved Problem 5.3 on page 161)** Solved Problem 5.3 contains the statement "Of course, the government actually collects the tax from sellers rather than from consumers, but we get the same result whether the government imposes a tax on the buyers of a good or on the sellers." Demonstrate that this statement is correct by solving the problem, assuming that the increase in the tax on gasoline shifts the supply curve rather than the demand curve.

3.11 **(Related to Solved Problem 5.3 on page 161)** The fumes from dry cleaners can contribute to air pollution. Suppose the following graph illustrates the situation in the dry cleaning market.

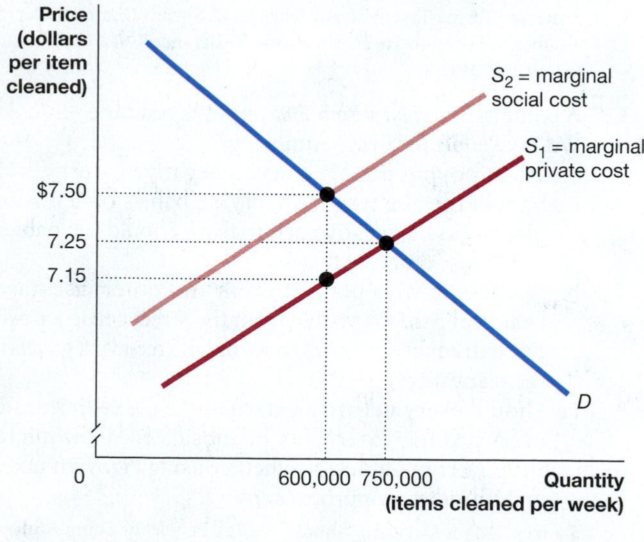

a. Explain how a government can use a tax on dry cleaning to bring about the efficient level of production. What should the value of the tax be?

b. How large is the deadweight loss (in dollars) from excessive dry cleaning, according to the figure?

3.12 **(Related to Solved Problem 5.3 on page 161)** Companies that produce toilet paper bleach the paper to make it white. Some paper plants discharge the bleach into rivers and lakes, causing substantial environmental damage. Suppose the following graph illustrates the situation in the toilet paper market.

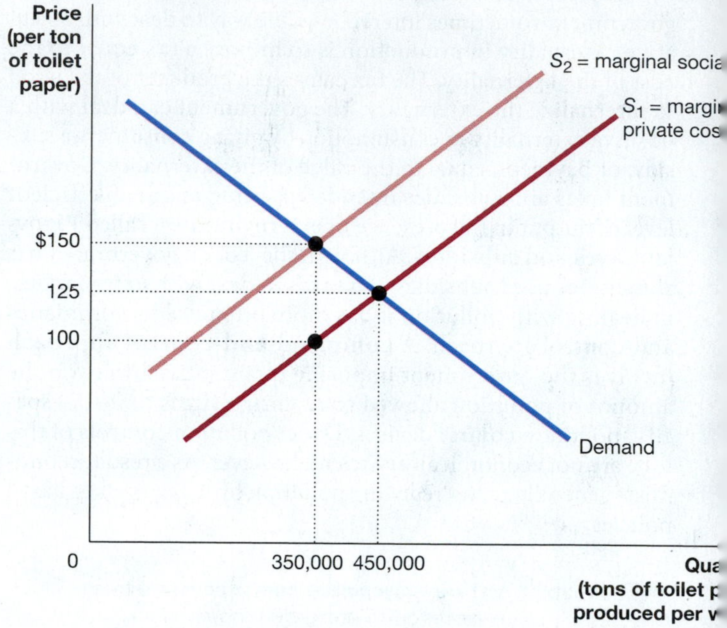

Explain how the federal government can use a tax on toilet paper to bring about the efficient level of production. What should be the value of the tax?

3.13 Former Massachusetts Governor Deval Patrick once proposed that criminals would have to pay a "safety fee" to the government. The size of the fee would be based on the seriousness of the crime (that is, the fee would be larger for more serious crimes).

a. Is there an economically efficient amount of crime? Briefly explain.

b. Briefly explain whether the "safety fee" is a Pigovian tax of the type discussed in this chapter.

Source: Michael Levenson, "Patrick Proposes New Fee on Criminals," *Boston Globe*, January 14, 2007.

3.14 The graph on the next page illustrates the situation in the dry cleaning market, assuming that the marginal social cost of the pollution *increases* as the quantity of items cleaned per week increases. The graph includes two demand curves: one for a smaller city, D_S, and the other for a larger city, D_L.

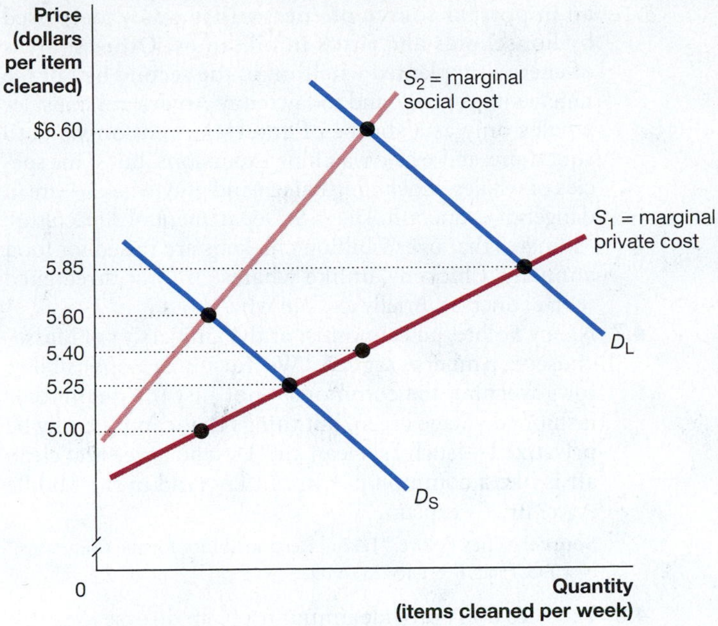

a. Explain why the marginal social cost curve has a different slope than the marginal private cost curve.
b. What tax per item cleaned will achieve economic efficiency in the smaller city? In the larger city? Explain why the efficient tax is different in the two cities.

3.15 **(Related to the Making the Connection on page 164)** An economist discussing the Obama administration's Clean Power Plan argued, "The best solutions would involve replacing EPA-centered regulation with better-suited tools, including a carbon tax."
a. Why might implementing a carbon tax be a better approach to reducing carbon dioxide emissions than an approach that relies on directly regulating how power plants in each state generate electricity?
b. Why might a command-and-control approach to pollution control be more politically popular than an approach that relies on taxes? Include in your answer a brief discussion of the difference between the normative analysis and positive analysis of this policy issue.

Source: Phillip A. Wallach, "Debating the EPA's Clean Power Plan Proposal—The Big Picture for the EPA's Clean Power Plan," brookings.edu, August 27, 2014.

3.16 **(Related to the Making the Connection on page 164]** According to a Congressional Budget Office report, the burden of a carbon tax would fall disproportionately on low-income households.
a. What does the report mean by the "burden" of the tax?
b. Why would the burden of a carbon tax fall disproportionately on low-income households? What actions might the government take to reduce the burden on these households?

Source: Congressional Budget Office, "Effects of a Carbon Tax on the Economy and the Environment," May 2013, p. 8.

5.4 Four Categories of Goods, pages 165–172

LEARNING OBJECTIVE: Explain how goods can be categorized on the basis of whether they are rival or excludable and use graphs to illustrate the efficient quantities of public goods and common resources.

Summary

There are four categories of goods: private goods, public goods, quasi-public goods, and common resources. **Private goods** are both rival and excludable. **Rivalry** means that when one person consumes a unit of a good, no one else can consume that unit. **Excludability** means that anyone who does not pay for a good cannot consume it. **Public goods** are both nonrival and nonexcludable. Private firms are usually not willing to supply public goods because of free riding. **Free riding** involves benefiting from a good without paying for it. *Quasi-public goods* are excludable but not rival. **Common resources** are rival but not excludable. The **tragedy of the commons** refers to the tendency for a common resource to be overused. The tragedy of the commons results from a lack of clearly defined and enforced property rights. We find the market demand curve for a private good by adding the quantity of the good demanded by each consumer at each price. We find the demand curve for a public good by adding vertically the price each consumer would be willing to pay for each quantity of the good. The optimal quantity of a public good occurs where the demand curve intersects the curve representing the marginal cost of supplying the good.

MyEconLab Visit **www.myeconlab.com** to complete these exercises online and get instant feedback.

Review Questions

4.1 Define *rivalry* and *excludability* and use these terms to discuss the four categories of goods.
4.2 What is free riding? How is free riding related to the need for public goods?
4.3 What is the tragedy of the commons? How can it be avoided?

Problems and Applications

4.4 The merry-go-round in Ross Park, a public park in Binghamton, New York, was first installed in 1920 and has been periodically refurbished by the city in the years since. There is no entry fee to visit the park or to ride the merry-go-round. Is the merry-go-round a public good? Briefly explain.

Source: http://www.visitbinghamton.org/ebrochures/carousels.pdf.

4.5 **(Related to Solved Problem 5.4 on page 169)** Suppose that Jill and Joe are the only two people in the small town of Andover. Andover has land available to build a park of no more than 9 acres. Jill and Joe's demand schedules for the park are as follows:

Joe	
Price per Acre	**Number of Acres**
$10	0
9	1
8	2
7	3
6	4
5	5
4	6
3	7
2	8
1	9

Jill	
Price per Acre	**Number of Acres**
$15	0
14	1
13	2
12	3
11	4
10	5
9	6
8	7
7	8
6	9

The supply curve is as follows:

Price per Acre	Number of Acres
$11	1
13	2
15	3
17	4
19	5
21	6
23	7
25	8
27	9

a. Draw a graph showing the optimal size of the park. Be sure to label the curves on the graph.
b. Briefly explain why a park of 2 acres is not optimal.

4.6 As readers of Herman Melville's 1851 novel *Moby Dick* know, at one time oil made from whale blubber was an important source of energy that was widely used by households and firms in oil lamps. Other sources of energy supplanted whale oil in the second half of the nineteenth century, and today many Americans consider whales only as a source of entertainment on visits to aquariums and whale watching excursions. But some species of whales—including baleen and gray whales—are in danger of extinction. The U.S. Department of Agriculture estimates that over 9 billion chickens are raised for food annually. Chickens, unlike whales, are not threatened with extinction. Briefly explain why.

4.7 Nancy Folbre, an economist at the University of Massachusetts, Amherst, argued, "We must take responsibility for governing the commons—not just the quaint old-fashioned village green, but things that cannot easily be privatized—[such as] clean air." Do you agree that clean air is like a common pasture in England in the Middle Ages? Briefly explain.

Source: Nancy Folbre, "Taking Responsibility for the Commons," *New York Times*, February 26, 2009.

4.8 Vaccines don't provide immunity from disease for some people. But if most people get vaccinated against a disease, such as measles, then the population achieves "herd immunity," which means that there are so few cases of the disease that even people for whom vaccinations are ineffective are unlikely to contract the disease. An article in the *Economist* argues that "herd immunity is a classic public good."

a. Do you agree with this statement?
b. The same article argues that there is an incentive to "'free ride' off the contributions of others" by not getting vaccinated. What does the author mean by "free ride"? If the author is correct, what will be the effect of this free riding?
c. Given your answer to part (b), why do most people vaccinate their children against childhood diseases, and why do many adults get vaccinated against influenza?

Source: "Resorting to Freedom," *Economist*, February 4, 2015.

4.9 Put each of the following goods or services into one of the categories shown in Figure 5.7 on page 166. That is, categorize them as private goods, public goods, quasi-public goods, or common resources.

a. A television broadcast of baseball's World Series
b. Home mail delivery
c. Education in a public school
d. Education in a private school
e. Hiking in a park surrounded by a fence
f. Hiking in a park not surrounded by a fence
g. An apple

4.10 Barney subscribes to the NFL Sunday Ticket, a program package offered by DirecTV that allows Barney to watch every regular season NFL game played on Sundays. The subscription price for the Sunday Ticket is in addition to the fee paid for Barney's DirecTV package. Barney invites two friends who work with him to watch football on Sundays at his home. Is Barney a free rider because he can watch any football game broadcast on Sundays, including those games not shown on his local television stations? Are Barney's friends free riders?

4.11 Jeff and James have different opinions regarding the amount the U.S. government should spend on national defense. Jeff believes that more should be spent in order to ensure that the country's enemies will not challenge the United States militarily. James believes that a lot of defense spending is wasted on overpriced military equipment and that the United States "should not be the world's policeman." Suppose that instead of the U.S. Congress and the president having the authority to determine the amount the military has to spend, this authority is turned over to the private sector. A privately owned firm conducts a survey to determine the willingness of people to pay for national defense. In response to the survey, both Jeff and James state that they are not willing to pay anything for national defense. Explain why they would both give this response.

4.12 William Easterly in *The White Man's Burden* shares the following account by New York University Professor Leonard Wantchekon of how Professor Wantchekon's village in Benin, Africa, managed the local fishing pond when he was growing up:

> To open the fishing season, elders performed ritual tests at Amlé, a lake fifteen kilometers from the village. If the fish were large enough, fishing was allowed for two or three days. If they were too small, all fishing was forbidden, and anyone who secretly fished the lake at this time was outcast, excluded from the formal and informal groups that formed the village's social structure. Those who committed this breach of trust were often shunned by the whole community; no one would speak to the offender, or even acknowledge his existence for a year or more.

What economic problem were the village elders trying to prevent? Do you think their solution was effective?

Source: William Easterly, *The White Man's Burden: Why the West's Efforts to Aid the Rest Have Done So Much Ill and So Little Good*, New York: Penguin Books, 2006, p. 94.

CHAPTER

6

Elasticity: The Responsiveness of Demand and Supply

Chapter Outline and Learning Objectives

Do People Respond to Changes in the Price of Gasoline?

When you drive into a Shell or an Exxon service station to buy gas, you may think you are dealing with an outlet owned by a gigantic multinational oil company. Most likely, though, the service station is actually owned by a local businessperson who buys oil from a large oil company but is responsible for running the business. In fact, in the United States more than half the owners of service stations or convenience stores that sell gas own just one store. These local businesspeople have experienced a bumpy ride over the past few years, as gasoline prices have been on a roller coaster.

In the summer of 2008, the average price of a gallon of gasoline was $4.00. By the end of the year, it had fallen to around $1.50. It rose back to nearly $4.00 by 2011 before falling to below $2.00 at the beginning of 2015 and then rising again. Service station and convenience store owners usually gain from falling gasoline prices because the price the oil companies charge them—the wholesale price of gasoline—falls faster than the price they charge to their customers—the retail price. For instance, as gasoline prices fell in late 2014, the gap between the wholesale and retail prices of gasoline increased from about 26 cents per gallon to about 37 cents. This gain was only temporary, however, because competition among service stations eventually forced down the retail price.

But do fluctuations in gas prices have much effect on sales of gasoline? Some people argue that consumers don't vary the quantity of gas they buy as the price fluctuates because the number of miles they need to drive to get to work or school or to run errands is roughly constant. An article in the *Wall Street Journal* quoted a spokesperson for the American Automobile Association (AAA) as saying, "Falling gasoline prices haven't historically led to more driving." Actual consumer behavior contradicts this observation. For example, in December 2014, when the average price of gasoline was $2.50 per gallon, U.S. consumers bought about 7 percent more gasoline than they did during April 2014, when the average price of gasoline was $3.60 per gallon.

All businesses have a financial incentive to determine how much their sales will increase as prices fall. Governments also have an incentive to determine how consumers will react if the price of a product such as gasoline rises following a tax increase. In this chapter, we will explore what determines the responsiveness of the quantity demanded and the quantity supplied to changes in the market price.

Sources: John D. Stoll and Jeff Bennett, "U.S. Auto Buyers Spend to Trade Up," *Wall Street Journal*, May 1, 2015; Nicole Friedman, "Why Gas Stations Are Cleaning Up Even As Prices Plummet," *Wall Street Journal*, October 23, 2014; "US Transit Rides at 58-Year High While Gas Prices Fall," boston.com, March 9, 2015; and data on gasoline prices and gasoline consumption from the U.S. Energy Information Administration.

Economics in Your Life

How Much Do Gas Prices Matter to You?

What factors would make you more or less responsive to price when purchasing gasoline? Have you responded differently to price changes during different periods of your life? Why do consumers seem to respond more to changes in gas prices at a particular service station but seem less sensitive when gas prices rise or fall at all service stations? As you read this chapter, try to answer these questions. You can check your answers against those we provide on **page 207** at the end of this chapter.

Whether you manage a service station, a restaurant, or a coffee shop, you need to know how an increase or a decrease in the price of your products will affect the quantity consumers are willing to buy. We know that cutting the price of a good increases the quantity demanded and that raising the price reduces the quantity demanded. But the critical question is: *How much* will the quantity demanded change as a result of a price increase or decrease? Economists use the concept of **elasticity** to measure how one economic variable—such as the quantity demanded—responds to changes in another economic variable—such as the price. For example, the responsiveness of the quantity demanded of a good to changes in its price is called the *price elasticity of demand*. Knowing the price elasticity of demand allows you to compute the effect of a price change on the quantity demanded. This knowledge is important to a business in determining the price that will maximize profit

Elasticity A measure of how much one economic variable responds to changes in another economic variable.

In addition to a good's price, consumer income and the prices of related goods also affect the quantity of the good that consumers demand. As a manager, you can also apply the concept of elasticity to measure the responsiveness of demand to these other variables. There are many economic issues where we are also interested in the responsiveness of the quantity supplied of a good to changes in its price, which is called the *price elasticity of supply*.

In this chapter, we will see that elasticity is an important concept not just for business managers but for policymakers as well. For example, if the government wants to discourage teenage smoking, it can raise the price of cigarettes by increasing the tax on them. If policymakers know the price elasticity of demand for cigarettes, they can calculate how many fewer packs of cigarettes teenagers will demand at a higher price.

6.1 The Price Elasticity of Demand and Its Measurement

LEARNING OBJECTIVE: Define price elasticity of demand and understand how to measure it.

We know from the law of demand that when the price of a product falls, the quantity demanded of the product increases. But the law of demand tells firms only that the demand curves for their products slope downward. It is more useful to have a measure of the responsiveness of the quantity demanded to a change in price. This measure is called the **price elasticity of demand**.

Price elasticity of demand The responsiveness of the quantity demanded to a change in price, measured by dividing the percentage change in the quantity demanded of a product by the percentage change in the product's price.

Measuring the Price Elasticity of Demand

We might measure the price elasticity of demand by using the slope of the demand curve because the slope tells us how much quantity changes as price changes, but this approach has a drawback: The measurement of slope is sensitive to the units chosen for quantity and price. For example, suppose a \$1 per gallon decrease in the price of gasoline leads to an increase in the quantity demanded from 10.1 million gallons to 10.2 million gallons per day. The change in quantity is 0.1 million gallons, and the change in price is $-\$1$, so the slope is $0.1/-1 = -0.1$. But:

- If we measure price in cents, rather than in dollars, the slope is $0.1/-100 = -0.001$.
- If we measure price in dollars and gallons in thousands, instead of millions, the slope is $100/-1 = -100$.
- If we measure price in cents and gallons in thousands, the slope is $100/-100 = -1$.

Clearly, the value we compute for the slope can change dramatically, depending on the units we use for quantity and price.

To avoid this confusion over units, economists use *percentage changes* when measuring the price elasticity of demand. Percentage changes are not dependent on units of measurement. (For a review of calculating percentage changes, see the appendix to Chapter 1.) No matter what units we use to measure the quantity of gasoline, 10 percent more gasoline is 10 percent more gasoline. Therefore, the price elasticity of demand is measured by dividing the percentage change in the quantity demanded by the percentage change in the product's price. Or:

$$\text{Price elasticity of demand} = \frac{\text{Percentage in quantity demanded}}{\text{Percentage change in price}}.$$

It's important to remember that *the price elasticity of demand is not the same as the slope of the demand curve.*

If we calculate the price elasticity of demand for a price cut, the percentage change in price will be negative, and the percentage change in quantity demanded will be positive. Similarly, if we calculate the price elasticity of demand for a price increase, the percentage change in price will be positive, and the percentage change in quantity demanded will be negative. Therefore, the price elasticity of demand is always negative. In comparing elasticities, though, we are usually interested in their relative size. So, we often drop the minus sign and compare their *absolute values.* For example, although -3 is actually a smaller number than -2, we say that a price elasticity of -3 is larger than a price elasticity of -2. MyEconLab Concept Check

Elastic Demand and Inelastic Demand

If the quantity demanded is very responsive to changes in price, the percentage change in quantity demanded will be *greater* than the percentage change in price, and the price elasticity of demand will be greater than 1 in absolute value. In this case, demand is **elastic**. For example, if a 10 percent decrease in the price of bagels results in a 20 percent increase in the quantity of bagels demanded, then:

Elastic demand Demand is elastic when the percentage change in the quantity demanded is *greater* than the percentage change in price, so the price elasticity is *greater* than 1 in absolute value.

$$\text{Price elasticity of demand} = \frac{20\%}{-10\%} = -2,$$

and we can conclude that the demand for bagels is elastic.

When the quantity demanded is not very responsive to price, however, the percentage change in quantity demanded will be *less* than the percentage change in price, and the price elasticity of demand will be less than 1 in absolute value. In this case, demand is **inelastic**. For example, if a 10 percent decrease in the price of wheat results in a 5 percent increase in the quantity of wheat demanded, then:

Inelastic demand Demand is inelastic when the percentage change in quantity demanded is *less* than the percentage change in price, so the price elasticity is *less* than 1 in absolute value.

$$\text{Price elasticity of demand} = \frac{5\%}{-10\%} = -0.5,$$

and we can conclude that the demand for wheat is inelastic.

In the special case where the percentage change in quantity demanded is equal to the percentage change in price, the price elasticity of demand equals -1 (or 1 in absolute value). In this case, demand is **unit elastic**. MyEconLab Concept Check

Unit-elastic demand Demand is unit elastic when the percentage change in quantity demanded is *equal to* the percentage change in price, so the price elasticity is equal to 1 in absolute value.

An Example of Computing Price Elasticities

Suppose you own a service station, and you are trying to decide whether to cut the price you are charging for a gallon of gas. You are currently at point A in Figure 6.1, selling 1,000 gallons per day at a price of \$3.00 per gallon. How many more gallons you will sell by cutting the price to \$2.70 depends on the price elasticity of demand for gasoline

MyEconLab Animation

Figure 6.1

Elastic and Inelastic Demand

Along D_1, cutting the price from \$3.00 to \$2.70 increases the number of gallons demanded from 1,000 to 1,200 per day. Because the percentage change in quantity demanded is greater than the percentage change in price (in absolute value), demand is elastic between point A and point B. Along D_2, cutting the price from \$3.00 to \$2.70 increases the number of gallons demanded only from 1,000 to 1,050 per day. Because the percentage change in quantity demanded is smaller than the percentage change in price (in absolute value), demand is inelastic between point A and point C.

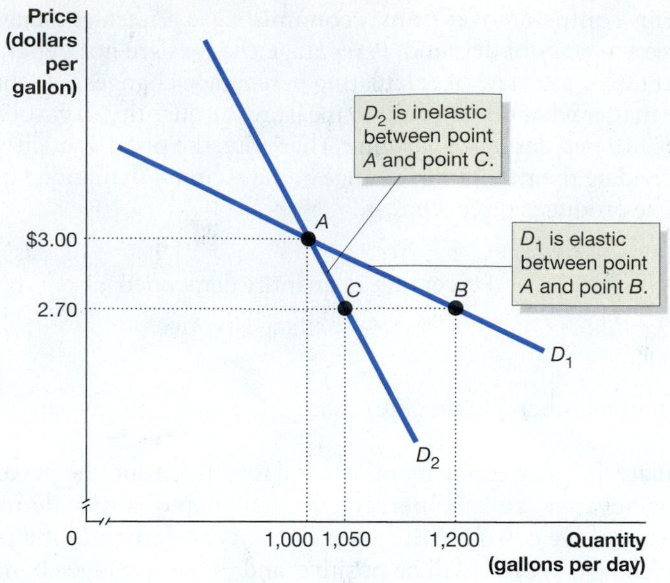

at your service station. Let's consider two possibilities: If D_1 is the demand curve for gasoline at your station, your sales will increase to 1,200 gallons per day, point B. But if D_2 is your demand curve, your sales will increase only to 1,050 gallons per day, point C. We might expect—correctly, as we will see—that between these points, demand curve D_1 is *elastic* and demand curve D_2 is *inelastic*.

To confirm that D_1 is elastic between these points and that D_2 is inelastic, we need to calculate the price elasticity of demand for each curve. In calculating price elasticity between two points on a demand curve, though, we face a problem because we get a different value for price increases than for price decreases. Suppose we calculate the price elasticity for D_1 as the price is cut from \$3.00 to \$2.70. This 10 percent price cut increases the quantity demanded from 1,000 gallons to 1,200 gallons, or by 20 percent. Therefore, the price elasticity of demand between points A and B is $20\%/-10\% = -2.0$. Now let's calculate the price elasticity for D_1 as the price is *increased* from \$2.70 to \$3.00. This 11.1 percent price increase causes a decrease in the quantity demanded from 1,200 gallons to 1,000 gallons, or by 16.7 percent. So, now our measure of the price elasticity of demand between points A and B is $-16.7\%/11.1\% = -1.5$. It can be confusing to have different values for the price elasticity of demand between the same two points on the same demand curve. As we will see in the next section, economists use a formula that allows them to avoid this confusion when calculating elasticities.

MyEconLab Concept Check

The Midpoint Formula

We can use the *midpoint formula* to ensure that we have only one value of the price elasticity of demand between the same two points on a demand curve. The midpoint formula uses the *average* of the initial and final quantities and the initial and final prices. If Q_1 and P_1 are the initial quantity and price, and Q_2 and P_2 are the final quantity and price, the midpoint formula is:

$$\text{Price elasticity of demand} = \frac{(Q_2 - Q_1)}{\left(\frac{Q_1 + Q_2}{2}\right)} \div \frac{(P_2 - P_1)}{\left(\frac{P_1 + P_2}{2}\right)}.$$

The midpoint formula may seem challenging at first, but the numerator is just the change in quantity divided by the average of the initial and final quantities, and the denominator is just the change in price divided by the average of the initial and final prices.

Let's apply the formula to calculating the price elasticity of D_1 in Figure 6.1. Between point A and point B on D_1, the change in quantity is 200, and the average of the two quantities is 1,100. Therefore, there is an 18.2 percent change in quantity demanded. The change in price is −\$0.30, and the average of the two prices is \$2.85. Therefore, there is a −10.5 percent change in price. So, the price elasticity of demand is 18.2%/−10.5% = −1.7. Notice these three results from calculating the price elasticity of demand using the midpoint formula:

1. As we suspected from examining Figure 6.1, demand curve D_1 is elastic between points A and B.
2. The value for the price elasticity calculated using the midpoint formula is between the two values we calculated earlier.
3. The midpoint formula will give us the same value whether we are moving from the higher price to the lower price or from the lower price to the higher price.

We can also use the midpoint formula to calculate the elasticity of demand between point A and point C on D_2. In this case, there is a 4.9 percent change in quantity and a −10.5 percent change in price. So, the elasticity of demand is 4.9%/−10.5% = −0.5. Once again, as we suspected, demand curve D_2 is price inelastic between points A and C.

MyEconLab Concept Check

Solved Problem 6.1

Calculating the Price Elasticity of Demand

Suppose you own a service station, and you are currently selling gasoline for \$2.50 per gallon. At this price, you can sell 2,000 gallons per day. You are considering cutting the price to \$2.30 to attract drivers who have been buying their gas at competing stations. The following graph shows two possible increases in the quantity of gasoline sold as a result of your price cut. Use the information in the graph to calculate the price elasticity between these two prices on each of the demand curves. Use the midpoint formula in your calculations. State whether each demand curve is elastic or inelastic between these two prices.

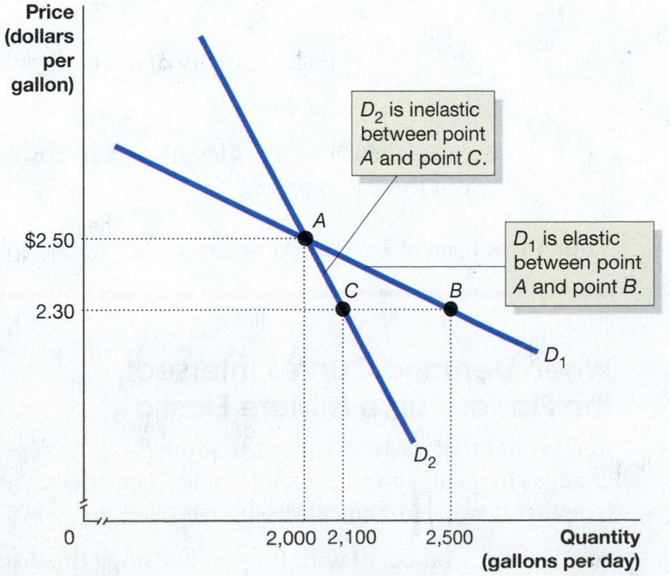

Solving the Problem

Step 1: Review the chapter material. This problem requires calculating the price elasticity of demand, so you may want to review the material in the section "The Midpoint Formula," which begins on page 186.

Step 2: To begin using the midpoint formula, calculate the average quantity and the average price for demand curve D_1.

$$\text{Average quantity} = \frac{2{,}000 + 2{,}500}{2} = 2{,}250$$

$$\text{Average price} = \frac{\$2.50 + \$2.30}{2} = \$2.40$$

Step 3: Now calculate the percentage change in the quantity demanded and the percentage change in price for demand curve D_1.

$$\text{Percentage change in quantity demanded} = \frac{2{,}500 - 2{,}000}{2{,}250} \times 100 = 22.2\%$$

$$\text{Percentage change in price} = \frac{\$2.30 - \$2.50}{\$2.40} \times 100 = -8.3\%$$

Step 4: Divide the percentage change in the quantity demanded by the percentage change in price to arrive at the price elasticity for demand curve D_1.

$$\text{Price elasticity of demand} = \frac{22.2\%}{-8.3\%} = -2.7$$

Because the elasticity is greater than 1 in absolute value, D_1 is price *elastic* between these two prices.

Step 5: Calculate the price elasticity of demand curve D_2 between these two prices.

$$\text{Percentage change in quantity demanded} = \frac{2{,}100 - 2{,}000}{2{,}050} \times 100 = 4.9\%$$

$$\text{Percentage change in price} = \frac{\$2.30 - \$2.50}{\$2.40} \times 100 = -8.3\%$$

$$\text{Price elasticity of demand} = \frac{4.9\%}{-8.3\%} = -0.6$$

Because the elasticity is less than 1 in absolute value, D_2 is price *inelastic* between these two prices.

MyEconLab Study Plan

Your Turn: For more practice, do related problem 1.7 on pages 209–210 at the end of this chapter.

When Demand Curves Intersect, the Flatter Curve Is More Elastic

Remember that *elasticity* is not the same thing as *slope*. While slope is calculated using changes in quantity and price, elasticity is calculated using percentage changes. But it *is* true that if two demand curves intersect:

- The demand curve with the smaller slope (in absolute value)—the flatter demand curve—is more elastic.
- The demand curve with the larger slope (in absolute value)—the steeper demand curve—is less elastic.

In Figure 6.1, for a given change in price, demand curve D_1 is more elastic than demand curve D_2.

MyEconLab Concept Check

Polar Cases of Perfectly Elastic and Perfectly Inelastic Demand

Although they do not occur frequently, you should be aware of the extreme, or *polar*, cases of price elasticity. If a demand curve is a vertical line, it is **perfectly inelastic**. In this case, the quantity demanded is completely unresponsive to price, and the price elasticity of demand equals zero. No matter how much price may increase or decrease, the quantity remains the same. For only a very few products will the quantity demanded be completely unresponsive to the price, making the demand curve a vertical line. The drug insulin is an example. Some diabetics must take a certain amount of insulin each day. If the price of insulin declines, it will not affect the required dose and therefore will not increase the quantity demanded. Similarly, a price increase will not affect the required dose or decrease the quantity demanded. (Of course, some diabetics may not be able to afford insulin at a higher price. If so, even in this case the demand curve may not be completely vertical and, therefore, not perfectly inelastic.)

Perfectly inelastic demand The case where the quantity demanded is completely unresponsive to price and the price elasticity of demand equals zero.

If a demand curve is a horizontal line, it is **perfectly elastic**. In this case, the quantity demanded is infinitely responsive to price, and the price elasticity of demand equals infinity. If a demand curve is perfectly elastic, an increase in price causes the quantity demanded to fall to zero. Once again, perfectly elastic demand curves are rare, and it is important not to confuse *elastic* with *perfectly elastic*. Table 6.1 on the next page summarizes the different price elasticities of demand. MyEconLab Concept Check

Perfectly elastic demand The case where the quantity demanded is infinitely responsive to price and the price elasticity of demand equals infinity.

Don't Let This Happen to You

Don't Confuse Inelastic with Perfectly Inelastic

You may be tempted to simplify the concept of elasticity by assuming that any demand curve described as being inelastic is *perfectly* inelastic. You should never make this assumption because perfectly inelastic demand curves are rare. For example, consider the following problem: "Use a demand and supply graph to show how a decrease in supply affects the equilibrium quantity of gasoline. Assume that the demand for gasoline is inelastic." The following graph would be an *incorrect* answer to this problem:

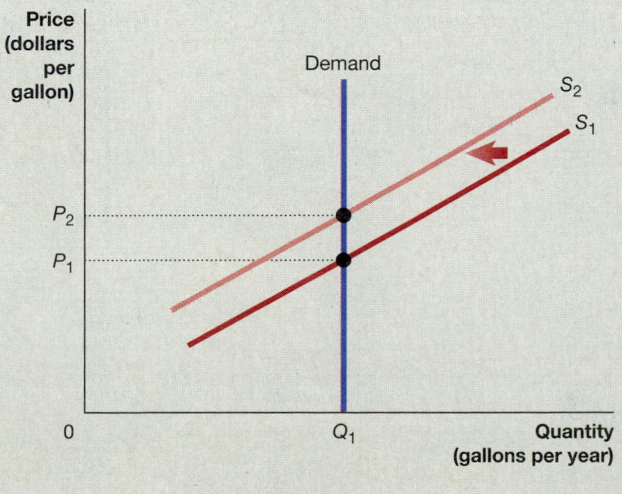

The demand for gasoline is inelastic, but it is not *perfectly* inelastic. When the price of gasoline rises, the quantity demanded falls. So, the correct answer to this problem would use a graph showing a typical downward-sloping demand curve rather than a vertical demand curve:

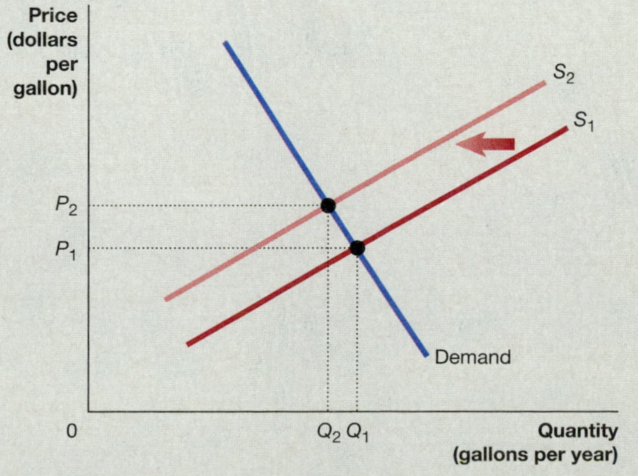

MyEconLab Study Plan

Your Turn: Test your understanding by doing related problem 1.10 on page 210 at the end of this chapter.

Table 6.1

Summary of the Price Elasticity of Demand

If demand is ...	then the absolute value of price elasticity is ...	
elastic	greater than 1	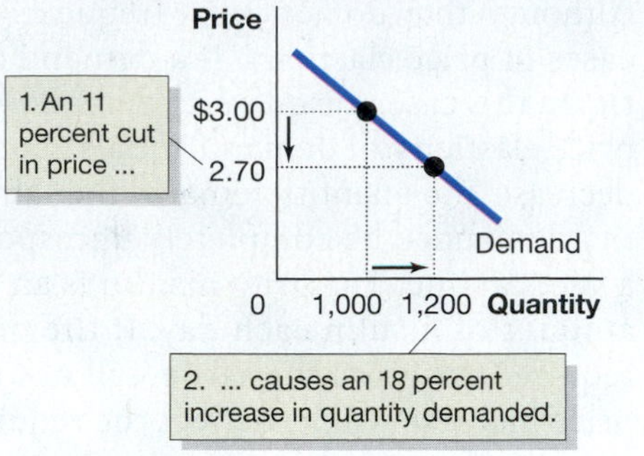
inelastic	less than 1	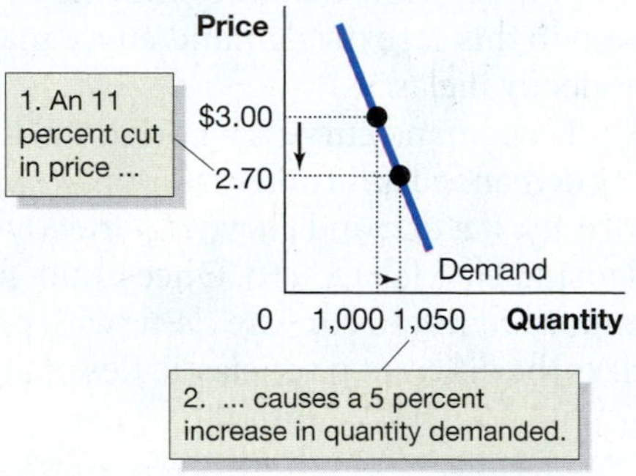
unit elastic	equal to 1	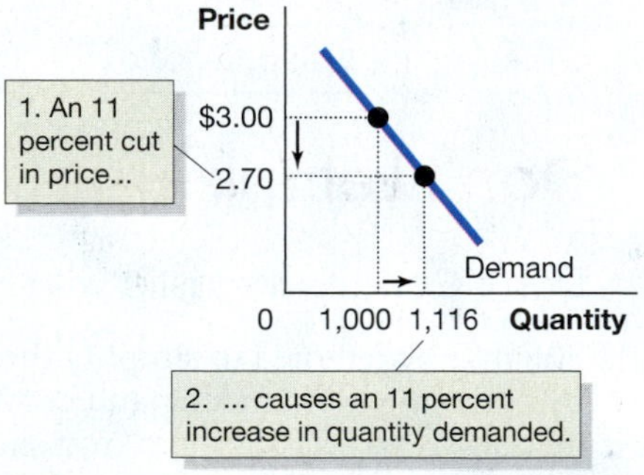
perfectly elastic	equal to infinity	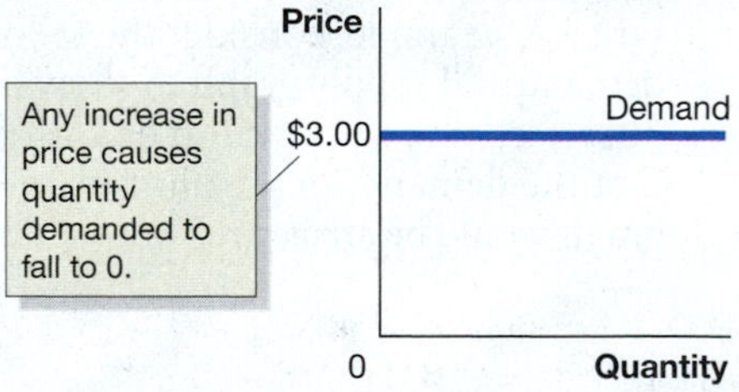
perfectly inelastic	equal to 0	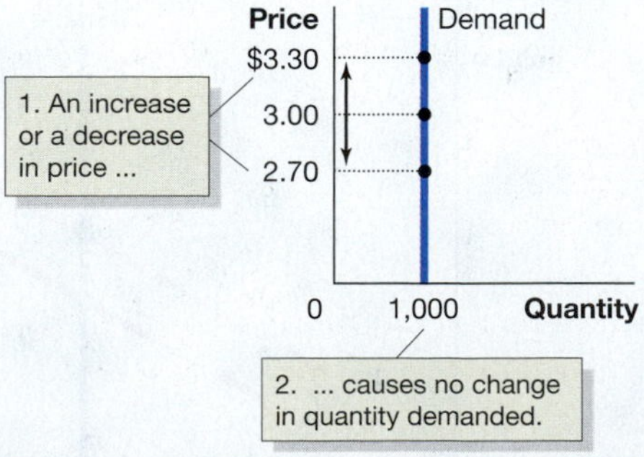

MyEconLab Study Plan

Note: The percentage changes shown in the boxes in the graphs were calculated using the midpoint formula, given on page 186, and are rounded to the nearest whole number.

6.2 The Determinants of the Price Elasticity of Demand

LEARNING OBJECTIVE: List and explain the determinants of the price elasticity of demand.

We have seen that the demand for some products may be elastic, while the demand for other products may be inelastic. In this section, we examine why price elasticities differ among products. The key determinants of the price elasticity of demand are:

- The availability of close substitutes to the good
- The passage of time
- Whether the good is a luxury or a necessity
- The definition of the market
- The share of the good in the consumer's budget

Availability of Close Substitutes

How consumers react to a change in the price of a product depends on whether there are alternative products. So the availability of substitutes is the most important determinant of price elasticity of demand. For example, when the price of gasoline rises, consumers have few alternatives, so the quantity demanded falls only a little. But if the price of pizza rises, consumers have many alternative foods they can eat, so the quantity demanded is likely to fall substantially. In fact, a key constraint on a firm's pricing policies is how many close substitutes exist for its product. In general, *if a product has more substitutes available, it will have a more elastic demand. If a product has fewer substitutes available, it will have a less elastic demand.*

MyEconLab Concept Check

Passage of Time

It usually takes consumers some time to adjust their buying habits when prices change. If the price of chicken falls, for example, it takes a while before consumers decide to change from eating chicken for dinner once a week to eating it twice a week. If the price of gasoline increases, it also takes a while for consumers to decide to begin taking public transportation, to buy more fuel-efficient cars, or to find new jobs closer to where they live. *The more time that passes, the more elastic the demand for a product becomes.*

MyEconLab Concept Check

Luxuries versus Necessities

Goods that are luxuries usually have more elastic demand curves than goods that are necessities. For example, the demand for bread is inelastic because bread is a necessity, and the quantity that people buy is not very dependent on its price. Tickets to a concert are a luxury, so the demand for concert tickets is much more elastic than the demand for bread. *The demand curve for a luxury is more elastic than the demand curve for a necessity.*

MyEconLab Concept Check

Definition of the Market

In a narrowly defined market, consumers have more substitutes available. For example, if you own a service station and raise the price you charge for gasoline, many of your customers will switch to buying from a competitor. So, the demand for gasoline at one particular station is likely to be elastic. The demand for gasoline as a product, on the other hand, is inelastic because consumers have few alternatives (in the short run) to buying it. *The more narrowly we define a market, the more elastic demand will be.*

MyEconLab Concept Check

Share of a Good in a Consumer's Budget

Goods that take only a small fraction of a consumer's budget tend to have less elastic demand than goods that take a large fraction. For example, most people buy table salt infrequently and in relatively small quantities. The share of an average consumer's budget that is spent on salt is very low. As a result, even a doubling of the price of salt is likely to result in only a small decline in the quantity of salt demanded. "Big-ticket items," such as houses, cars, and furniture, take up a larger share in the average consumer's budget. Increases in the prices of these goods are likely to result in significant declines in the quantity demanded. In general, *the demand for a good will be more elastic the larger the share of the good in the average consumer's budget.*

MyEconLab Concept Check

Some Estimated Price Elasticities of Demand

Table 6.2 shows some estimated short-run price elasticities of demand. It's important to remember that estimates of the price elasticities of different goods can vary, depending on the data used and the time period over which the estimates were made. The results given in the table are consistent with our discussion of the determinants of price elasticity. Goods for which there are few substitutes, such as cigarettes, gasoline, and health insurance, are price inelastic, as are broadly defined goods, such as bread and beer. Particular brands of products such as Coca-Cola, Tide, and Post Raisin Bran are price elastic.

Table 6.2 also shows that:

- The demand for books or DVDs bought from a particular retailer is typically price elastic. Note, though, that the demand for books from Amazon is inelastic, which indicates that consumers do not consider ordering from other online sites to be good substitutes for ordering from Amazon.
- An increase in the price of grapes will lead some consumers to substitute other fruits, so demand for grapes is price elastic.
- Similarly, an increase in the price of new automobiles will lead some consumers to buy used automobiles or to continue driving their current cars, so demand for automobiles is also price elastic.
- The demand for necessities, such as natural gas and water, is price inelastic.

MyEconLab Concept Check

Table 6.2

Estimated Real-World Price Elasticities of Demand

Product	Estimated Elasticity	Product	Estimated Elasticity
Books (Barnes & Noble)	−4.00	Water (residential use)	−0.38
Books (Amazon)	−0.60	Chicken	−0.37
DVDs (Amazon)	−3.10	Cocaine	−0.28
Post Raisin Bran	−2.50	Cigarettes	−0.25
Automobiles	−1.95	Beer	−0.29
Tide (liquid detergent)	−3.92	Catholic school attendance	−0.19
Coca-Cola	−1.22	Residential natural gas	−0.09
Grapes	−1.18	Gasoline	−0.06
Restaurant meals	−0.67	Milk	−0.04
Health insurance (low-income households)	−0.65	Sugar	−0.04
Bread	−0.40		

Source: See Text Credits at the back of the book for complete source list.

6.3 The Relationship between Price Elasticity of Demand and Total Revenue

LEARNING OBJECTIVE: Explain the relationship between the price elasticity of demand and total revenue.

Knowing the price elasticity of demand allows a firm to calculate how changes in price will affect its **total revenue**, which is the total amount of funds it receives from selling a good or service. Total revenue is calculated by multiplying price per unit by the number of units sold:

Total revenue The total amount of funds a seller receives from selling a good or service, calculated by multiplying price per unit by the number of units sold.

- When demand is inelastic, price and total revenue move in the same direction: An increase in price raises total revenue, and a decrease in price reduces total revenue.
- When demand is elastic, price and total revenue move inversely: An increase in price reduces total revenue, and a decrease in price raises total revenue.

To understand the relationship between price elasticity and total revenue, consider Figure 6.2. Panel (a) shows a demand curve for gasoline that is inelastic between point A and point B. (It was demand curve D_2 in Figure 6.1 on page 186.) The total revenue received by the service station owner at point A equals the price of \$3.00 multiplied by the 1,000 gallons sold, or \$3,000. This amount equals the areas of rectangles C and D in the figure because together the rectangles have a height of \$3.00 and a base of 1,000 gallons. Because this demand curve is inelastic between point A and point B, cutting the price to \$2.70 (point B) reduces total revenue. The new total revenue is shown by the areas of rectangles D and E and is equal to \$2.70 multiplied by 1,050 gallons, or \$2,835. Total revenue falls because the increase in the quantity demanded is not large enough to make up for the decrease in price. As a result, the \$135 increase in revenue gained as a result of the price cut—rectangle E—is less than the \$300 in revenue lost—rectangle C.

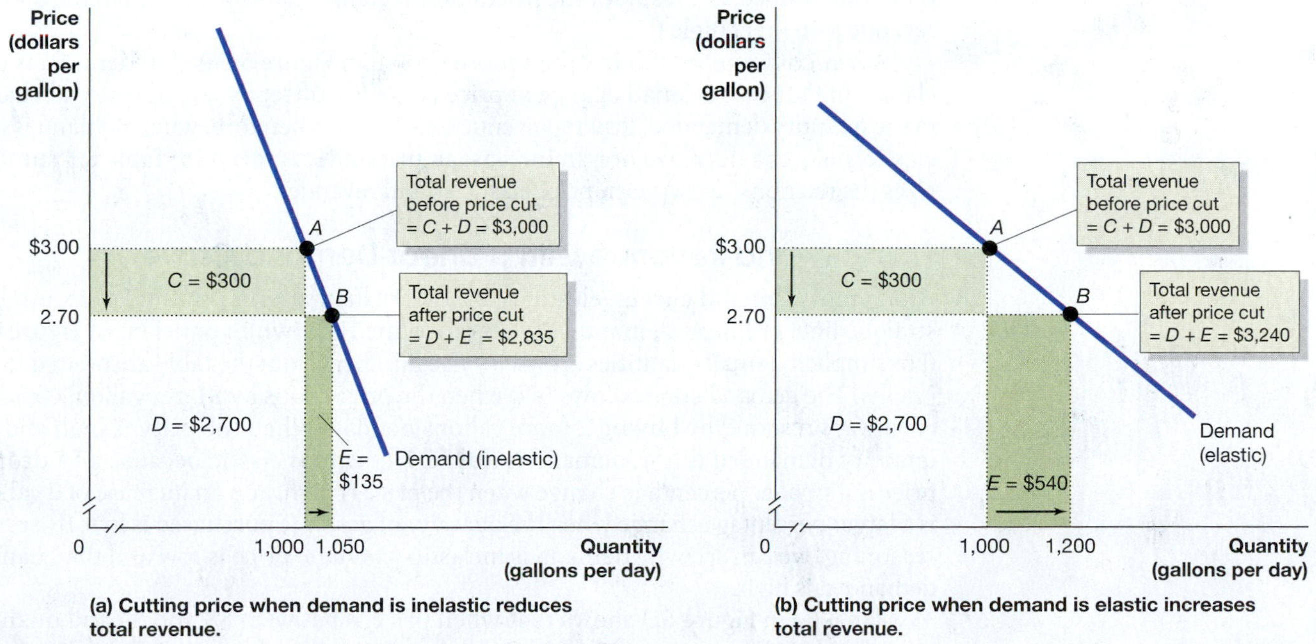

MyEconLab Animation

Figure 6.2 The Relationship between Price Elasticity and Total Revenue

When demand is inelastic, a cut in price will decrease total revenue. In panel (a), at point A, the price is \$3.00, 1,000 gallons are sold, and total revenue received by the service station equals \$3.00 × 1,000 gallons, or \$3,000. At point B, cutting the price to \$2.70 increases the quantity demanded to 1,050 gallons, but the fall in price more than offsets the increase in quantity. As a result, revenue falls to \$2.70 × 1,050 gallons, or \$2,835. When demand is elastic, a cut in the price will increase total revenue. In panel (b), at point A, the areas of rectangles C and D are still equal to \$3,000. But at point B, the areas of rectangles D and E are equal to \$2.70 × 1,200 gallons, or \$3,240. In this case, the increase in the quantity demanded is large enough to offset the fall in price, so total revenue increases.

Table 6.3

The Relationship between Price Elasticity and Revenue

If demand is ...	then ...	because ...
elastic	an increase in price reduces revenue	the decrease in quantity demanded is proportionally *greater* than the increase in price.
elastic	a decrease in price increases revenue	the increase in quantity demanded is proportionally *greater* than the decrease in price.
inelastic	an increase in price increases revenue	the decrease in quantity demanded is proportionally *smaller* than the increase in price.
inelastic	a decrease in price reduces revenue	the increase in quantity demanded is proportionally *smaller* than the decrease in price.
unit elastic	an increase in price does not affect revenue	the decrease in quantity demanded is proportionally *the same as* the increase in price.
unit elastic	a decrease in price does not affect revenue	the increase in quantity demanded is proportionally *the same as* the decrease in price.

Panel (b) of Figure 6.2 shows a demand curve that is elastic between point *A* and point *B*. (It was demand curve D_1 in Figure 6.1.) With this demand curve, cutting the price increases total revenue. At point *A*, the areas of rectangles *C* and *D* are still equal to \$3,000, but at point *B*, the areas of rectangles *D* and *E* are equal to \$2.70 multiplied by 1,200 gallons, or \$3,240. Here, total revenue rises because the increase in the quantity demanded is large enough to offset the lower price. As a result, the \$540 increase in revenue gained as a result of the price cut—rectangle *E*—is greater than the \$300 in revenue lost—rectangle *C*.

A less common possibility than those shown in Figure 6.2 is that demand is unit elastic. In that case, a small change in price is exactly offset by a proportional change in the quantity demanded, leaving revenue unaffected. Therefore, when demand is unit elastic, neither a decrease nor an increase in price affects revenue. Table 6.3 summarizes the relationship between price elasticity and revenue.

Elasticity and Revenue with a Linear Demand Curve

Along most demand curves, elasticity is not constant at every point. For example, a straight-line, or linear, demand curve for gasoline is shown in panel (a) of Figure 6.3. (For simplicity, small quantities are used.) The numbers from the table are plotted in the graphs. The demand curve shows that when the price drops by \$1 per gallon, consumers always respond by buying 2 more gallons per day. When the price is high and the quantity demanded is low, demand is elastic. Demand is elastic because a \$1 drop in price is a smaller percentage change when the price is high, and an increase of 2 gallons is a larger percentage change when the quantity of gasoline purchased is low. By similar reasoning, we can see why demand is inelastic when the price is low and the quantity demanded is high.

Panel (a) in Figure 6.3 shows that when price is between \$8 and \$4 and quantity demanded is between 0 gallons and 8 gallons, demand is elastic. Panel (b) shows that over this same range, total revenue will increase as price falls. For example, in panel (a), as price falls from \$7 to \$6, the quantity demanded increases from 2 to 4, and in panel (b), total revenue increases from \$14 to \$24. Similarly, when price is between \$4 and \$0 and the quantity demanded is between 8 and 16, demand is inelastic. Over this same range, total revenue will decrease as price falls. For example, as price falls from \$3 to \$2 and the quantity demanded increases from 10 to 12, total revenue decreases from \$30 to \$24.

MyEconLab Concept Check

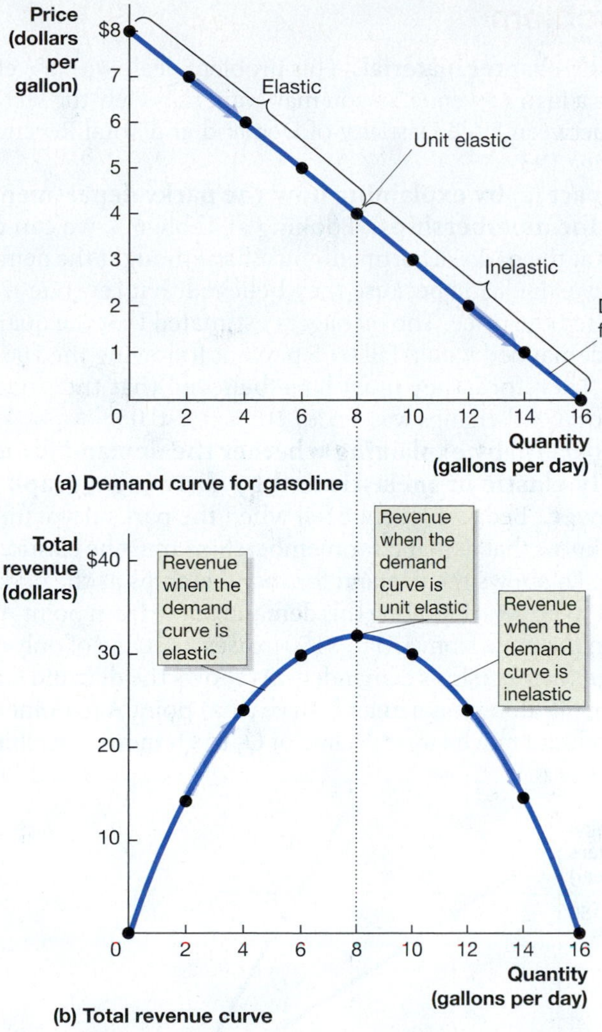

Price	Quantity Demanded	Total Revenue
$8	0	$0
7	2	14
6	4	24
5	6	30
4	8	32
3	10	30
2	12	24
1	14	14
0	16	0

MyEconLab Animation

Figure 6.3 Elasticity Is Not Constant along a Linear Demand Curve

The data from the table are plotted in the graphs. Panel (a) shows that as we move down the demand curve for gasoline, the price elasticity of demand declines. In other words, at higher prices, demand is elastic, and at lower prices, demand is inelastic. Panel (b) shows that as the quantity of gasoline purchased increases from 0, revenue will increase until it reaches a maximum of $32 when 8 gallons are purchased. As purchases increase beyond 8 gallons, revenue falls because demand is inelastic on this portion of the demand curve.

Solved Problem 6.3

MyEconLab Interactive Animation

Price and Revenue Don't Always Move in the Same Direction

New York City officials believed they needed more revenue to maintain 35 city-owned recreation centers. To raise the additional revenue, the city's parks department increased the annual membership fee to use the centers from $75 to $150. According to an article in the *New York Times*, "the department had hoped to realize $4 million in new revenue, but in fact, it lost about $200,000." The article also explains that the parks department had expected a 5 percent decline in memberships due to the price increase.

a. What did the parks department believe about the price elasticity of demand for memberships in its recreation centers?

b. Is demand for memberships actually elastic or inelastic? Briefly explain. Illustrate your answer with a graph showing the demand curve for memberships as the parks department believed it to be and as it actually is.

Solving the Problem

Step 1: Review the chapter material. This problem deals with the effect of a price change on a firm's revenue, so you may want to review the section "The Relationship between Price Elasticity of Demand and Total Revenue," which begins on page 193.

Step 2: Answer part (a) by explaining how the parks department viewed the demand for memberships. Looking at Table 6.3, we can conclude that managers at the parks department must have thought the demand for memberships was inelastic because they believed that revenue would increase if they raised the price. The managers estimated that the quantity of memberships demanded would fall by 5 percent following the 100 percent price increase. Therefore, they must have believed that the price elasticity of demand for memberships was $-5\% / 100\% = -0.05$.

Step 3: Answer part (b) by explaining whether the demand for memberships is actually elastic or inelastic and by drawing a graph to illustrate your answer. Because revenue fell when the parks department raised the price, we know that demand for memberships must be elastic. In the following graph, D_1 shows the demand for memberships as the parks department believed it to be. Moving along this demand curve from point A to point B, an increase in the price from \$75 to \$150 causes a decline of only Q_1 to Q_2 in the quantity of memberships demanded. D_2 shows the demand curve as it actually is. Moving along this demand curve from point A to point C, the increase in price causes a much larger decline of Q_1 to Q_3 in memberships demanded.

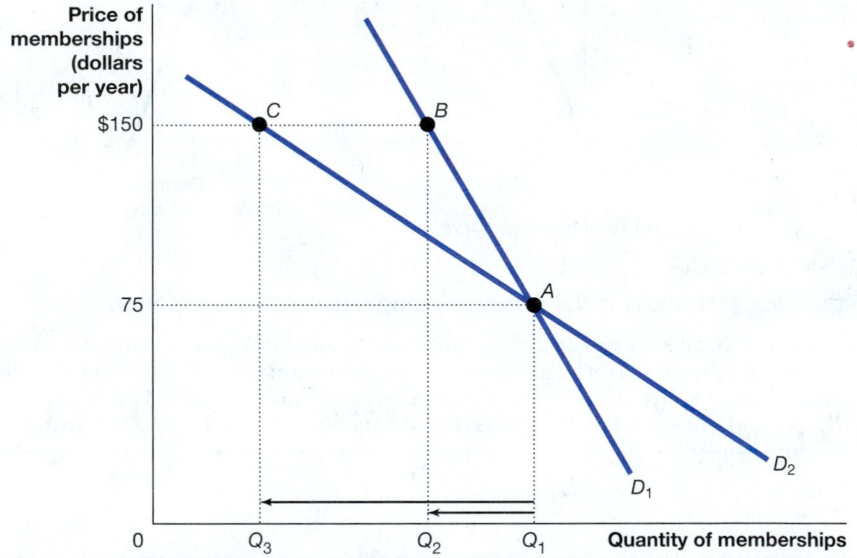

Source: Lisa W. Foderaro, "Public Recreation Centers Looking to Stem Exodus," *New York Times*, February 15, 2013.

MyEconLab Study Plan

Your Turn: For more practice, do related problems 3.8 and 3.9 on page 212 at the end of this chapter.

Making the Connection
MyEconLab Video

Why Does Amazon Care about Price Elasticity?

In 2014, Amazon was in a dispute with a large book publisher called Hachette whose authors include James Patterson, J.K. Rowling, and J.D. Salinger. Hachette was charging between \$14.99 and \$19.99 for its e-books, but Amazon wanted the publisher to lower the price to only \$9.99. Amazon's tactics included reducing discounts on Hachette's hardcover books, not allowing preorders of the publisher's books, and delaying shipping some of its books by two to three weeks.

But why did Amazon want Hachette to lower the price of e-books? In a posting on its Web site, Amazon asserted, "We've quantified the price elasticity of e-books from repeated measurements across many titles." Amazon estimated that the price elasticity of demand for e-books is −1.74. The following table uses Amazon's estimate to show how sales revenue would change in response to a decrease in the price of e-books.

Price of Book	Copies Sold at That Price	Total Revenue at That Price
$14.99	100,000	$1,499,000
$9.99	174,000	$1,738,260

Amazon concluded, "At $9.99, even though the customer is paying less, the total pie is bigger and there is more to share amongst [Amazon, Hachette, and the author of the book]."

If Amazon's analysis is correct, why would Hachette resist cutting the prices of e-books? Hachette believed that while the demand for bestsellers by authors such as James Patterson and J.K. Rowling might be price elastic, the demand for other e-books it published by less-well-known authors or on obscure subjects was price inelastic. For those books, cutting the price would reduce Hachette's revenue. In addition, Hachette believed that lower prices on e-books might come at the expense of sales of hardcover copies of those books, on which the publisher made higher profits. Eventually, Amazon and Hachette reached an agreement that allowed Hachette to determine the prices its e-books would sell for on Amazon's site.

With a relatively new product, such as e-books, businesses often have to experiment with different prices as they attempt to determine the price elasticity of demand. Knowing the price elasticity is important to a business in determining the price that will maximize profit.

In 2014, Amazon and book publishers debated the benefit of lowering e-book prices.

Sources: The Amazon Books Team, "Announcement Update re: Amazon/Hachette Business Interruption," Amazon.com, July 29, 2014; Farhad Manjoo, "Amazon Wants Cheaper E-books. But Should It Get to Enforce Prices?" *New York Times*, August 1, 2014; Tom Ryan, "Amazon Explains Digital Pricing Elasticity," retailwire.com, August 4, 2014; David Streitfeld, "Amazon and Hachette Resolve Dispute," *New York Times*, November 13, 2014; and Vauhini Vara, "Amazon's Failed Pitch to Authors," *New Yorker*, July 31, 2014.

Your Turn: Test your understanding by doing related problems 3.10 and 3.11 on page 212 at the end of this chapter.

MyEconLab Study Plan

6.4 Other Demand Elasticities

LEARNING OBJECTIVE: Define cross-price elasticity of demand and income elasticity of demand and understand their determinants and how they are measured.

Elasticity is an important concept in economics because it allows us to quantify the responsiveness of one economic variable to changes in another economic variable. In addition to price elasticity, two other demand elasticities are important:

1. Cross-price elasticity of demand
2. Income elasticity of demand

Cross-Price Elasticity of Demand

Suppose you work at Apple, and you need to predict the effect of an increase in the price of Samsung's Galaxy Gear smartwatch on the quantity of Apple Watches demanded, holding other factors constant. You can do this by calculating the **cross-price elasticity of demand**, which is the percentage change in the quantity of Apple

Cross-price elasticity of demand The percentage change in the quantity demanded of one good divided by the percentage change in the price of another good.

Table 6.4

Summary of Cross-Price Elasticity of Demand

If the products are ...	then the cross-price elasticity of demand will be ...	Example
substitutes	positive.	Two brands of smartwatches
complements	negative.	Smartwatches and applications downloaded from online stores
unrelated	zero.	Smartwatches and peanut butter

Watches demanded divided by the percentage change in the price of Galaxy Gears—or, in general:

$$\text{Cross-price elasticity of demand} = \frac{\text{Percentage change in quantity demanded of one good}}{\text{Percentage change in price of another good}}.$$

The cross-price elasticity of demand is positive or negative, depending on whether the two products are substitutes or complements. Recall that substitutes are products that can be used for the same purpose, such as two brands of smartwatches. Complements are products that are used together, such as smartwatches and applications that can be downloaded from online stores. An increase in the price of a substitute will lead to an increase in the quantity demanded, so the cross-price elasticity of demand will be positive. An increase in the price of a complement will lead to a decrease in the quantity demanded, so the cross-price elasticity of demand will be negative. Of course, if the two products are unrelated—such as smartwatches and peanut butter—the cross-price elasticity of demand will be zero. Table 6.4 summarizes the key points about the cross-price elasticity of demand.

Cross-price elasticity of demand is important to firm managers because it allows them to measure whether products sold by other firms are close substitutes for their products. For example, Pepsi-Cola and Coca-Cola both spend heavily on advertising, each hoping to convince consumers that its cola tastes better than its rival's. How can these firms tell whether their advertising campaigns have been effective? One way is by seeing whether the cross-price elasticity of demand has changed. If, for instance, Coca-Cola has a successful advertising campaign, when it increases the price of Coke, the percentage increase in sales of Pepsi should be smaller. In other words, the value of the cross-price elasticity of demand should have declined. MyEconLab Concept Check

Income Elasticity of Demand

Income elasticity of demand A measure of the responsiveness of the quantity demanded to changes in income, measured by the percentage change in the quantity demanded divided by the percentage change in income.

The **income elasticity of demand** measures the responsiveness of the quantity demanded to changes in income. It is calculated as follows:

$$\text{Income elasticity of demand} = \frac{\text{Percentage change in quantity demanded}}{\text{Percentage change in income}}.$$

We know that if the quantity demanded of a good increases as income increases, then the good is a *normal good* (see Chapter 3). Normal goods are often further subdivided into *luxuries* and *necessities.* A good is a luxury if the quantity demanded is very responsive to changes in income so that a 10 percent increase in income results in more than a 10 percent increase in the quantity demanded. Expensive jewelry and vacation homes are examples of luxuries. A good is a necessity if the quantity demanded is not very responsive to changes in income so that a 10 percent increase in income results in less than a 10 percent increase in the quantity demanded. Food and clothing are examples of necessities. A good is *inferior* if the quantity demanded falls when income increases. Ground beef with a high fat content is an example of an inferior good. We should note that *normal good, inferior good, necessity,* and *luxury* are just labels economists use for goods with different income elasticities; the labels are not intended to be value judgments about the worth of these goods.

Table 6.5

Summary of Income Elasticity of Demand

If the income elasticity of demand is ...	then the good is ...	Example
positive but less than 1	normal and a necessity.	Bread
positive and greater than 1	normal and a luxury.	Caviar
negative	inferior.	High-fat meat

Because most goods are normal goods, during periods of economic expansion when consumer income is rising, most firms can expect—holding other factors constant—that the quantity demanded of their products will increase. Sellers of luxuries can expect particularly large increases. During recessions, falling consumer income can cause firms to experience increases in demand for inferior goods. For example, the demand for bus trips increases as consumers cut back on air travel, and supermarkets find that the demand for canned tuna increases relative to the demand for fresh salmon. Table 6.5 summarizes the key points about the income elasticity of demand.

MyEconLab Concept Check

Making the Connection

MyEconLab Video

Price Elasticity, Cross-Price Elasticity, and Income Elasticity in the Market for Alcoholic Beverages

Many public policy issues are related to the consumption of alcoholic beverages. These issues include underage drinking, drunk driving, and the possible beneficial effects of red wine in lowering the risk of heart disease. Knowing how responsive the demand for alcohol is to changes in price provides insight into these policy issues. Christopher Ruhm of the University of Virginia and colleagues have estimated statistically the following elasticities. (*Spirits* refers to all beverages, other than beer and wine, that contain alcohol.)

Price elasticity of demand for beer	−0.30
Cross-price elasticity of demand between beer and wine	−0.83
Cross-price elasticity of demand between beer and spirits	−0.50
Income elasticity of demand for beer	0.09

These results indicate that the demand for beer is inelastic. A 10 percent increase in the price of beer will result in a 3 percent decline in the quantity of beer demanded. Somewhat surprisingly, both wine and spirits are complements for beer rather than substitutes. A 10 percent increase in the price of wine will result in an 8.3 percent *decrease* in the quantity of beer demanded. Previous studies of the price elasticity of beer had found that beer was a substitute for other alcoholic drinks. Ruhm and his colleagues argue that their results are more reliable because they use Uniform Product Code (UPC) scanner data on prices and quantities sold in grocery stores. They argue that these price data are more accurate than the data used in many previous studies that included the prices of only one brand each of beer, wine, and whiskey.

The results in the table also show that a 10 percent increase in income will result in a 0.9 percent *increase* in the quantity of beer demanded. So, beer is a normal good. According to the definitions given earlier, beer would be classified as a necessity because it has an income elasticity that is positive but less than 1.

Source: Christopher J. Ruhm, et al., "What U.S. Data Should Be Used to Measure the Price Elasticity of Demand for Alcohol," *Journal of Health Economics*, Vol. 31, No. 6, December 2012.

Your Turn: Test your understanding by doing related problem 4.8 on page 213 at the end of this chapter.

MyEconLab Study Plan

6.5 Using Elasticity to Analyze the Disappearing Family Farm

LEARNING OBJECTIVE: Use price elasticity and income elasticity to analyze economic issues.

The concepts of price elasticity and income elasticity can help us understand many economic issues. For example, some people are concerned that the family farm is becoming an endangered species in the United States. Although food production has been growing steadily, the number of farms and farmers continue to dwindle. In 1950, the United States had more than 5 million farms, and more than 23 million people lived on farms. By 2015, only about 2 million farms remained, and fewer than 3 million people lived on them. The federal government has several programs that are intended to aid farmers (see Chapter 4). Many of these programs have been aimed at helping small, family-operated farms, but growth in farm production, combined with low price and income elasticities for most food products, have made it difficult for owners of family farms to earn a profit.

Productivity measures the ability of firms to produce goods and services with a given amount of economic inputs, such as workers, machines, and land. Productivity has grown very rapidly in U.S. agriculture. In 1950, the average U.S. wheat farmer harvested about 17 bushels from each acre of wheat planted. By 2015, because of the development of superior strains of wheat and improvements in farming techniques, the average American wheat farmer harvested 44 bushels per acre. So, even though the total number of acres devoted to growing wheat declined from about 62 million to about 48 million, total wheat production rose from about 1.0 billion bushels to about 2.1 billion.

Unfortunately for U.S. farmers, this increase in wheat production resulted in a substantial decline in wheat prices. Two key factors explain this decline: (1) The demand for wheat is inelastic, and (2) the income elasticity of demand for wheat is low. Even though the U.S. population has increased greatly since 1950 and the income of the average American is much higher than it was in 1950, the demand for wheat has increased only moderately. For all of the additional wheat to be sold, the price has had to decline. Because the demand for wheat is inelastic, the price decline has been substantial. Figure 6.4 illustrates these points.

A large shift in supply, a small shift in demand, and an inelastic demand curve combined to drive down the price of wheat from $19.53 per bushel in 1950 to $5.00 in

MyEconLab Animation

Figure 6.4

Elasticity and the Disappearing Family Farm

In 1950, U.S. farmers produced 1.0 billion bushels of wheat at a price of $19.53 per bushel. Over the next 65 years, rapid increases in farm productivity caused a large shift to the right in the supply curve for wheat. The income elasticity of demand for wheat is low, so the demand for wheat increased relatively little over this period. Because the demand for wheat is also inelastic, the large shift in the supply curve and the small shift in the demand curve resulted in a sharp decline in the price of wheat, from $19.53 per bushel in 1950 to $5.00 in 2015.
Source: U.S. Department of Agriculture, *Wheat Yearbook Tables*, May 21, 2015.

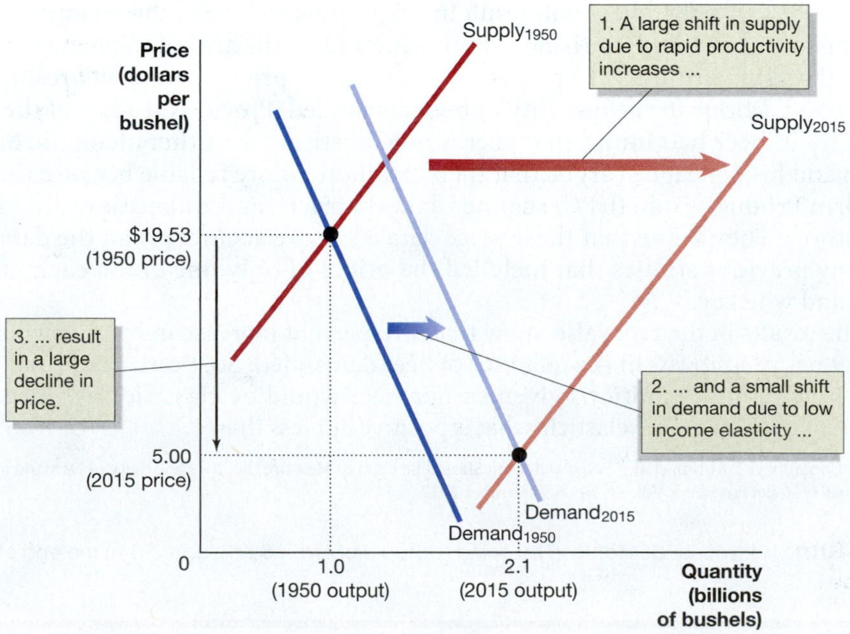

2015. (We measure the price in 1950 in terms of prices in 2015, to adjust for the general increase in prices since 1950.) With low prices, only the most efficiently run farms have been able to remain profitable. Small family-run farms have found it difficult to survive, and many of these farms have disappeared. The markets for most other food products are similar to the market for wheat. They are characterized by output growth and low income and price elasticities. The result is the paradox of U.S. farming: ever more abundant and cheaper food, supplied by fewer and fewer farms. U.S. consumers have benefited, but most family farmers have not.

Solved Problem 6.5

MyEconLab Interactive Animation

Using Price Elasticity to Analyze a Policy of Taxing Gasoline

If the consumption of a product results in a negative externality, taxing the product may improve economic efficiency (see Chapter 5). Some economists and policymakers argue that driving cars and trucks causes an externality because they: (1) burn gasoline, which increases emissions of greenhouse gases; (2) contribute to the congestion that clogs many highways in and around big cities; and (3) cause accidents that take more than 30,000 lives per year. Some economists have suggested substantially increasing the federal excise tax on gasoline, which in 2015 was 18.4 cents per gallon. How much the tax would cause consumption to fall and how much revenue the tax would raise depend on the price elasticity of demand. Suppose that the price of gasoline is currently $3.00 per gallon, the quantity of gasoline demanded is 140 billion gallons per year, the price elasticity of demand for gasoline is −0.06, and the federal government decides to increase the excise tax on gasoline by $1.00 per gallon. The price of a product will not rise by the full amount of a tax increase unless the demand for the product is perfectly inelastic (see Chapter 4). In this case, suppose that the price of gasoline increases by $0.80 per gallon after the $1.00 excise tax is imposed.

a. What is the new quantity of gasoline demanded after the tax is imposed? How effective would a gas tax be in reducing consumption of gasoline in the short run?

b. How much revenue does the federal government receive from the tax?

Solving the Problem

Step 1: Review the chapter material. This problem deals with applications of the price elasticity of demand formula, so you may want to review the section "Measuring the Price Elasticity of Demand," which begins on page 184.

Step 2: Answer the first question in part (a) using the formula for the price elasticity of demand to calculate the new quantity demanded.

$$\text{Price elasticity of demand} = \frac{\text{Percentage change in quantity demanded}}{\text{Percentage change in price}}.$$

We can plug into the midpoint formula the values given for the price elasticity, the original price of $3.00, and the new price of $3.80 (= $3.00 + $0.80).

$$-0.06 = \frac{\text{Percentage change in quantity demanded}}{\dfrac{(\$3.80 - \$3.00)}{\left(\dfrac{\$3.00 + \$3.80}{2}\right)}}.$$

Or, rearranging and writing out the expression for the percentage change in the quantity demanded:

$$-0.014 = \frac{(Q_2 - 140\text{ billion})}{\left(\dfrac{140\text{ billion} + Q_2}{2}\right)}.$$

Solving for Q_2, the new quantity demanded is:

$$Q_2 = 138.1\text{ billion gallons}.$$

Step 3: Answer the second question in part (a). Because the price elasticity of demand for gasoline is only −0.06, even a substantial increase in the gasoline tax of $1.00 per gallon would reduce gasoline consumption by only a small amount: from 140 billion gallons of gasoline per year to 138.1 billion gallons. Note, though, that price elasticities typically increase over time. Economists estimate that the long-run price elasticity of gasoline is in the range of −0.40 to −0.60, so in the long run, the decline in the consumption of gasoline would be larger.

Step 4: Calculate the revenue earned by the federal government to answer part (b). The federal government would collect an amount equal to the tax per gallon multiplied by the number of gallons sold: $1 per gallon × 138.1 billion gallons = $138.1 billion.

Extra Credit: The tax of $138.1 billion calculated in step 4 is substantial: It is equivalent to about 10 percent of all the revenue the federal government raised from the personal income tax in 2014. It is also much larger than the roughly $25 billion the federal government receives each year from the existing 18.4-cents-per-gallon gasoline tax. We can conclude that raising the federal excise tax on gasoline would be a good way to raise revenue for the federal government. But, at least in the short run, increasing the tax would not greatly reduce the quantity of gasoline consumed. Notice that if the demand for gasoline were elastic, this result would be reversed: The quantity of gasoline consumed would decline much more, but so would the revenue that the federal government would receive from the tax increase.

MyEconLab Study Plan

Your Turn: For more practice, do related problems 5.2 and 5.3 on pages 213–214 at the end of this chapter.

6.6 The Price Elasticity of Supply and Its Measurement

LEARNING OBJECTIVE: Define price elasticity of supply and understand its determinants and how it is measured.

We can use the concept of elasticity to measure the responsiveness of firms to a change in price, just as we used it to measure the responsiveness of consumers. We know from the law of supply that when the price of a product increases, the quantity supplied increases. To measure how much the quantity supplied increases when price increases, we use the *price elasticity of supply*.

Measuring the Price Elasticity of Supply

Price elasticity of supply The responsiveness of the quantity supplied to a change in price, measured by dividing the percentage change in the quantity supplied of a product by the percentage change in the product's price.

As we did with the price elasticity of demand, we calculate the **price elasticity of supply** by using percentage changes:

$$\text{Price elasticity of supply} = \frac{\text{Percentage change in quantity supplied}}{\text{Percentage change in price}}.$$

Notice that because supply curves are upward sloping, the price elasticity of supply will be a positive number. We categorize the price elasticity of supply the same way we categorized the price elasticity of demand:

- If the price elasticity of supply is less than 1, then supply is *inelastic*. For example, economists have estimated that over a period of a year, the price elasticity of supply of gasoline from U.S. oil refineries is about 0.20. So, gasoline supply is inelastic: A 10 percent increase in the price of gasoline will result in only a 2 percent increase in the quantity supplied.
- If the price elasticity of supply is greater than 1, then supply is *elastic*. For example, if the price of wheat increases by 10 percent and the quantity of wheat that farmers supply increases by 15 percent, the price elasticity of supply is 1.5. So wheat supply is elastic.
- If the price elasticity of supply is equal to 1, the supply is *unit elastic*. For example, if the price of bottled water increases by 10 percent and the quantity of bottled

water that firms supply increases by 10 percent, the price elasticity of supply equals 1. So bottled water supply is unit elastic.

As with other elasticity calculations, when we calculate the price elasticity of supply, we hold constant the values of other variables. MyEconLab Concept Check

Determinants of the Price Elasticity of Supply

Whether supply is elastic or inelastic depends on the ability and willingness of firms to alter the quantity they produce as price increases. Often, firms have difficulty increasing the quantity of the product they supply during any short period of time. For example, a pizza parlor cannot produce more pizzas on any one night than is possible using the ingredients in the kitchen. Within a day or two, it can buy more ingredients, and within a few months, it can hire more cooks and install additional ovens. As a result, the supply curve for pizza and most other products will be inelastic if we measure it over a short period of time, but the supply curve will be increasingly elastic the longer the period of time over which we measure it. Products that require resources that are themselves in fixed supply are an exception to this rule. For example, a French winery may rely on a particular variety of grape. If all the land on which that grape can be grown is already planted in vineyards, then the supply of that wine will be inelastic even over a long period. MyEconLab Concept Check

Making the Connection
MyEconLab Video

Why Are Oil Prices So Unstable?

Bringing oil to market is a long process. Oil companies hire geologists to locate fields for exploratory oil well drilling. If significant amounts of oil are present, the company begins full-scale development of the field. From exploration to pumping significant amounts of oil can take years. This long process is the reason for the low short-run price elasticity of supply for oil. Because there are no close substitutes for oil, the short-run price elasticity of demand for oil is also low.

As the world economy recovered from the effects of the deep recession of 2007–2009, the demand for oil increased rapidly in a number of countries, particularly China, India, Russia, and Brazil. As the following graph shows, when supply is inelastic, an increase in demand can cause a large increase in price. The shift in the demand curve from D_1 to D_2 causes the equilibrium quantity of oil to increase by less than 5 percent, from 85 million barrels per day in 2009 to 89 million in 2011, but the equilibrium price to increase 175 percent, from $40 to $110 per barrel.

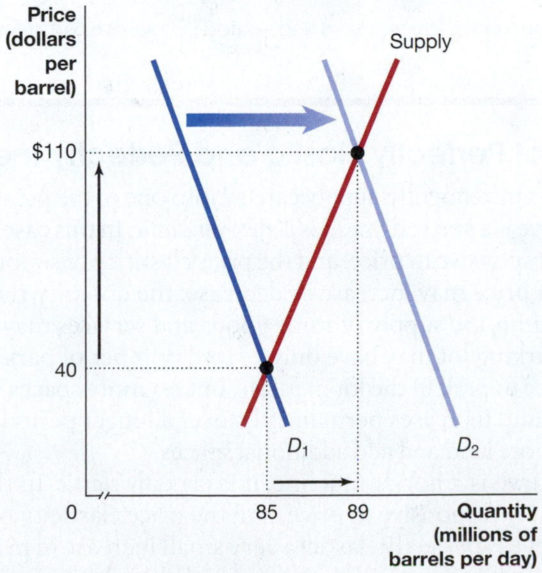

Since the 1970s, the world oil market has been heavily influenced by the Organization of the Petroleum Exporting Countries (OPEC). OPEC has 11 members, including Saudi Arabia, Kuwait, Iran, Venezuela, and Nigeria. Together, OPEC members own 75 percent

of the world's proven oil reserves. In recent years, though, production of oil in the United States has increased rapidly as a result of widespread adoption of a new technology called hydraulic fracturing, or *fracking*. Fracking involves injecting a mixture of water, sand, and chemicals into a rock formation at high pressure to release oil and natural gas that could not have been recovered using traditional methods. Largely due to fracking, oil production in the United States rose from 5.6 million barrels per day in 2011 to 8.7 million in 2014.

As the following graph shows, this expansion in U.S. production combined with greater production from some OPEC member countries caused a significant increase in the world supply of oil. (Production in some other regions, such as the North Sea, has been declining.) The price of oil declined from $110 in 2011 to $47 in early 2015. The extent of the price change reflected not only the size of the increase in supply but also the low short-run price elasticity of demand for oil.

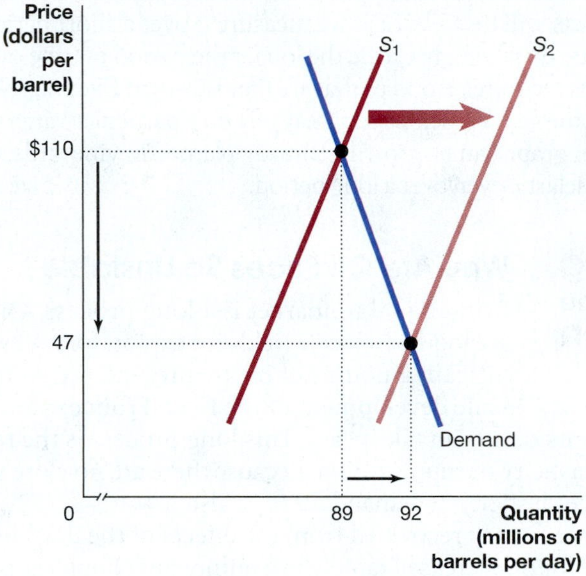

The combination of a low price elasticity of demand and a low price elasticity of supply means that even relatively small increases or decreases in the demand or supply of oil can result in large swings in its equilibrium price. Over the past 40 years, the price has been as low as $10 per barrel and as high as $140. These price swings are likely to continue in the future.

MyEconLab Study Plan

Your Turn: Test your understanding by doing related problems 6.5 and 6.6 on page 215 at the end of this chapter.

Polar Cases of Perfectly Elastic and Perfectly Inelastic Supply

Although it occurs infrequently, supply can fall into one of the polar cases of price elasticity. If a supply curve is a vertical line, it is *perfectly inelastic*. In this case, the quantity supplied is completely unresponsive to price, and the price elasticity of supply equals zero. Regardless of how much price may increase or decrease, the quantity remains the same. Over a brief period of time, the supply of some goods and services may be perfectly inelastic. For example, a parking lot may have only a fixed number of parking spaces. If demand increases, the price to park in the lot may rise, but no more spaces will become available. Of course, if demand increases permanently, over a longer period of time, the owner of the lot may buy more land and add additional spaces.

If a supply curve is a horizontal line, it is *perfectly elastic*. In this case, the quantity supplied is infinitely responsive to price, and the price elasticity of supply equals infinity. If a supply curve is perfectly elastic, a very small increase in price causes a very large increase in the quantity supplied. Just as with demand curves, it is important not to confuse a supply curve being elastic with its being perfectly elastic and not to confuse a supply curve being inelastic with its being perfectly inelastic. Table 6.6 summarizes the different price elasticities of supply.

MyEconLab Concept Check

Table 6.6

Summary of the Price Elasticity of Supply

If supply is...	then the value of price elasticity is ...	
elastic	greater than 1	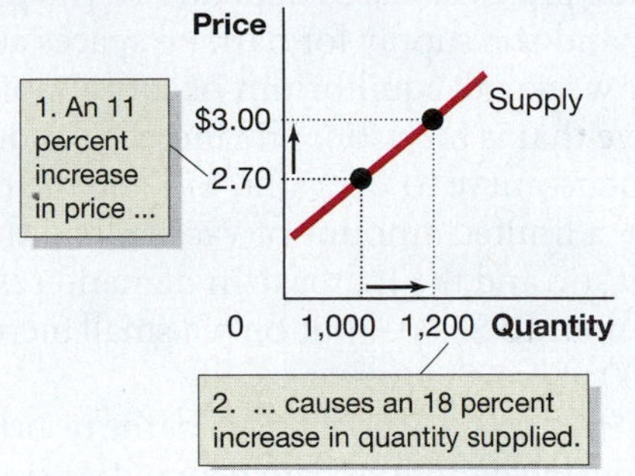
inelastic	less than 1	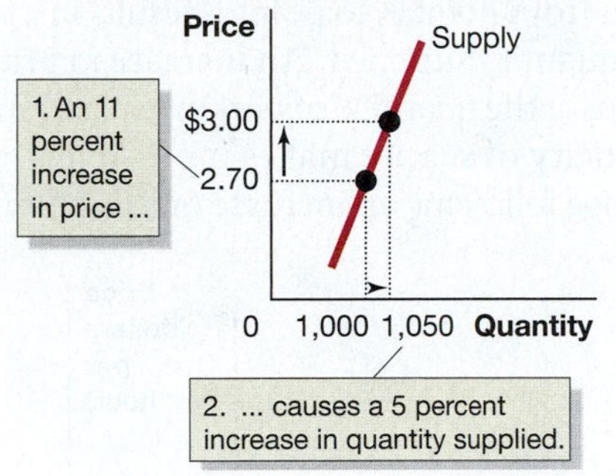
unit elastic	equal to 1	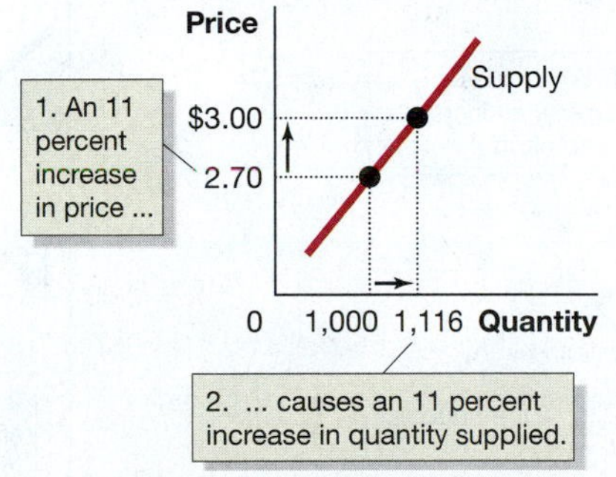
perfectly elastic	equal to infinity	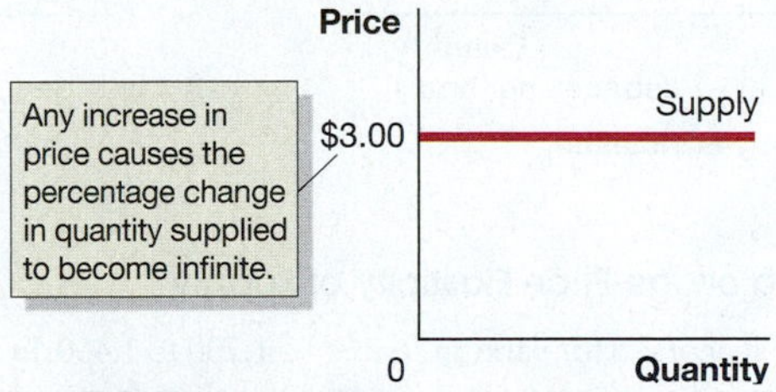
perfectly inelastic	equal to 0	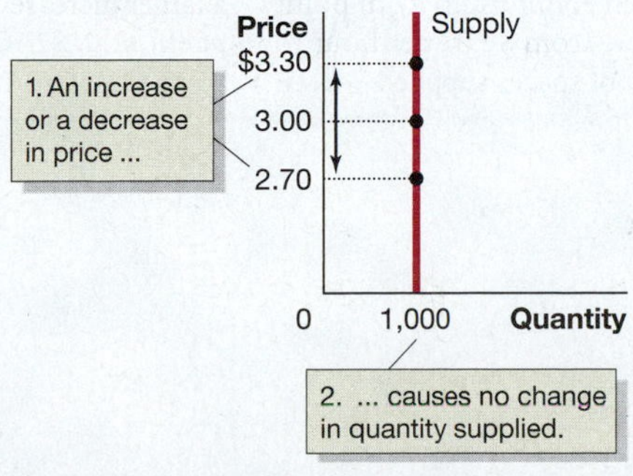

Note: The percentage increases shown in the boxes in the graphs were calculated using the midpoint formula, given on page 186, and are rounded to the nearest whole number.

Using Price Elasticity of Supply to Predict Changes in Price

Figure 6.5 illustrates the important point that when demand increases, the amount by which price increases depends on the price elasticity of supply. The figure shows the demand and supply for parking spaces at a beach resort. In panel (a), on a typical summer weekend, equilibrium occurs at point *A*, where $\text{Demand}_{\text{Typical}}$ intersects a supply curve that is inelastic. The increase in demand for parking spaces on July 4 shifts the demand curve to the right, moving the equilibrium to point *B*. Because the resort has only a limited amount of vacant land that it can use for parking, the supply curve is inelastic and the increase in demand results in a large increase in price—from $2.00 per hour to $4.00—but only a small increase in the quantity of spaces supplied—from 1,200 to 1,400.

In panel (b), we assume that the resort has a lot of vacant land that it can use for parking during periods of high demand, so supply is elastic. As a result, the change in equilibrium from point *A* to point *B* results in a smaller increase in price and a larger increase in the quantity supplied. An increase in price from $2.00 per hour to $2.50 is sufficient to increase the quantity of parking spaces supplied from 1,200 to 2,100. Knowing the price elasticity of supply makes it possible to predict more accurately how much price will change following an increase or a decrease in demand.

MyEconLab Study Plan

MyEconLab Concept Check

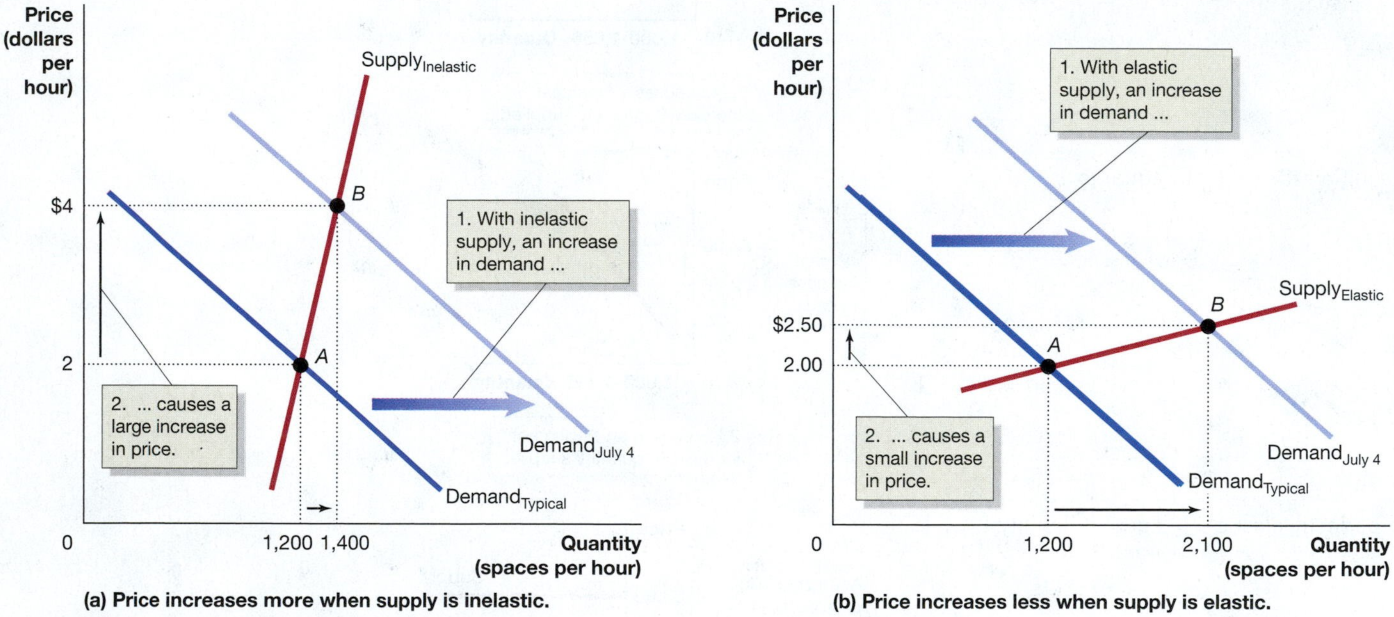

MyEconLab Animation

Figure 6.5 Changes in Price Depend on the Price Elasticity of Supply

In panel (a), $\text{Demand}_{\text{Typical}}$ represents the typical demand for parking spaces on a summer weekend at a beach resort. $\text{Demand}_{\text{July4}}$ represents demand on July 4. Because supply is inelastic, the shift in equilibrium from point *A* to point *B* results in a large increase in price—from $2.00 per hour to $4.00—but only a small increase in the quantity of spaces supplied—from 1,200 to 1,400. In panel (b), supply is elastic. As a result, the change in equilibrium from point *A* to point *B* results in a smaller increase in price and a larger increase in the quantity supplied. An increase in price from $2.00 per hour to $2.50 is sufficient to increase the quantity of parking supplied from 1,200 to 2,100.

Continued from page 183

Economics in Your Life

How Much Do Gas Prices Matter to You?

At the beginning of the chapter, we asked you to think about three questions: What factors would make you more or less responsive to price when purchasing gasoline? Have you responded differently to price changes during different periods of your life? and Why do consumers seem to respond more to changes in gas prices at a particular service station but seem less sensitive when gas prices rise or fall at all service stations?

A number of factors are likely to affect your sensitivity to changes in gas prices, including: (1) how high your income is (and, therefore, how large a share of your budget is taken up by gasoline purchases), (2) whether you live in an area with good public transportation (which can be a substitute for having to use your own car), and (3) whether you live within walking distance of your school or job. Each of these factors may change over the course of your life, making you more or less sensitive to changes in gas prices. Finally, consumers respond to changes in the price of gas at a particular service station because gas at other service stations is a good substitute. But there are presently few good substitutes for gasoline as a product, so consumers respond much less to changes in prices at all service stations.

Conclusion

In this chapter, we have explored the important concept of elasticity. Table 6.7 summarizes the various elasticities we discussed. Computing elasticities is important in economics because it allows us to measure how one variable changes in response to changes in another variable. For example, by calculating the price elasticity of demand for its product, a firm can make a quantitative estimate of the effect of a price change on the revenue it receives. Similarly, by calculating the price elasticity of demand for cigarettes, the government can better estimate the effect of an increase in cigarette taxes on smoking.

Before going further in analyzing how firms decide on the prices to charge and the quantities to produce, we need to look at how firms are organized. We discuss this topic in the next chapter.

Visit MyEconLab for a news article and analysis related to the concepts in this chapter.

Table 6.7

Summary of Elasticities

PRICE ELASTICITY OF DEMAND

$$\text{Formula: } \frac{\text{Percentage change in quantity demanded}}{\text{Percentage change in price}}$$

$$\text{Midpoint formula: } \frac{(Q_2 - Q_1)}{\left(\frac{Q_1 + Q_2}{2}\right)} \div \frac{(P_2 - P_1)}{\left(\frac{P_1 + P_2}{2}\right)}$$

	Absolute Value of Price Elasticity	Effect on Total Revenue of an Increase in Price
Elastic	Greater than 1	Total revenue falls
Inelastic	Less than 1	Total revenue rises
Unit elastic	Equal to 1	Total revenue unchanged

CROSS-PRICE ELASTICITY OF DEMAND

$$\text{Formula: } \frac{\text{Percentage change in quantity demanded of one good}}{\text{Percentage change in price of another good}}$$

Types of Products	Value of Cross-Price Elasticity
Substitutes	Positive
Complements	Negative
Unrelated	Zero

INCOME ELASTICITY OF DEMAND

$$\text{Formula: } \frac{\text{Percentage change in quantity demanded}}{\text{Percentage change in income}}$$

Types of Products	Value of Income Elasticity
Normal and a necessity	Positive but less than 1
Normal and a luxury	Positive and greater than 1
Inferior	Negative

PRICE ELASTICITY OF SUPPLY

$$\text{Formula: } \frac{\text{Percentage change in quantity supplied}}{\text{Percentage change in price}}$$

	Value of Price Elasticity
Elastic	Greater than 1
Inelastic	Less than 1
Unit elastic	Equal to 1

CHAPTER SUMMARY AND PROBLEMS

Key Terms

Cross-price elasticity of demand, p. 197
Elastic demand, p. 185
Elasticity, p. 184
Income elasticity of demand, p. 198
Inelastic demand, p. 185
Perfectly elastic demand, p. 189
Perfectly inelastic demand, p. 189
Price elasticity of demand, p. 184
Price elasticity of supply, p. 202
Total revenue, p. 193
Unit-elastic demand, p. 185

6.1 The Price Elasticity of Demand and Its Measurement, pages 184–190

LEARNING OBJECTIVE: Define *price elasticity of demand* and understand how to measure it.

Summary

Elasticity measures how much one economic variable responds to changes in another economic variable. The **price elasticity of demand** measures how responsive the quantity demanded is to changes in price. The price elasticity of demand is equal to the percentage change in the quantity demanded divided by the percentage change in price. If the quantity demanded changes more than proportionally when price changes, the price elasticity of demand is greater than 1 in absolute value, and demand is **elastic**. If the quantity demanded changes less than proportionally when price changes, the price elasticity of demand is less than 1 in absolute value, and demand is **inelastic**. If the quantity demanded changes proportionally when price changes, the price elasticity of demand is equal to 1 in absolute value, and demand is **unit elastic**. **Perfectly inelastic demand** curves are vertical lines, and **perfectly elastic demand** curves are horizontal lines. Relatively few products have perfectly elastic or perfectly inelastic demand curves.

MyEconLab Visit **www.myeconlab.com** to complete these exercises online and get instant feedback.

Review Questions

1.1 Write the formula for the price elasticity of demand. Why isn't elasticity just measured by the slope of the demand curve?

1.2 If a 10 percent increase in the price of Cheerios causes a 25 percent reduction in the number of boxes of Cheerios demanded, what is the price elasticity of demand for Cheerios? Is the demand for Cheerios elastic or inelastic?

1.3 What is the midpoint formula for calculating price elasticity of demand? How else can you calculate the price elasticity of demand? What is the advantage of using the midpoint formula?

1.4 Draw a graph of a perfectly inelastic demand curve. Think of a product that would have a perfectly inelastic demand curve. Explain why demand for this product would be perfectly inelastic.

Problems and Applications

1.5 **(Related to the Chapter Opener on page 183)** According to a news story, during the summer of 2015, gasoline prices were expected to decline by 32 percent, while "U.S. drivers are expected to consume slightly more gasoline, a 1.6 percent increase, during the summer." Given this information, calculate the price elasticity of demand for gasoline. Is demand price elastic or price inelastic? Briefly explain.

Source: Damian J. Troise, "Summer Gas Prices Expected to Be 32 Percent Lower This Year," Associated Press, April 7, 2015.

1.6 Suppose that the following table gives data on the price of rye and the number of bushels of rye sold in 2015 and 2016:

Year	Price (dollars per bushel)	Quantity (bushels)
2015	$3.00	8 million
2016	2.00	12 million

a. Calculate the change in the quantity of rye demanded divided by the change in the price of rye. Measure the quantity of rye in bushels.

b. Calculate the change in the quantity of rye demanded divided by the change in the price of rye, but this time measure the quantity of rye in millions of bushels. Compare your answer to the one you computed in (a).

c. Assuming that the demand curve for rye did not shift between 2015 and 2016, use the information in the table to calculate the price elasticity of demand for rye. Use the midpoint formula in your calculation. Compare the value for the price elasticity of demand to the values you calculated in (a) and (b).

1.7 **(Related to Solved Problem 6.1 on page 187)** You own a hot dog stand that you set up outside the student union every day at lunchtime. Currently, you are selling hot dogs for a price of $3 each, and you sell 30 hot dogs a day. You are considering cutting the price to $2. The graph on the next page shows two possible increases in the quantity sold as a result of your price cut. Use the information in the graph to calculate the price elasticity of demand between these two prices on each of the demand curves. Use the midpoint formula to calculate the price elasticities.

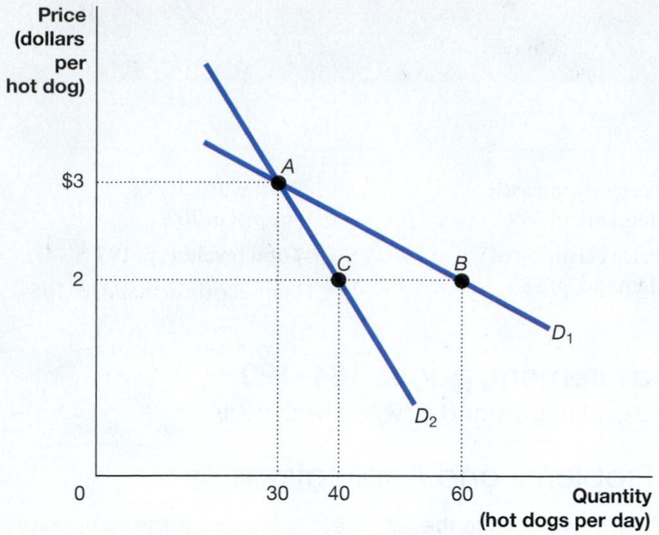

1.8 In the fall of 2006, Pace University in New York raised its annual tuition from $24,751 to $29,454. Freshman enrollment declined from 1,469 in the fall of 2005 to 1,131 in the fall of 2006. Assuming that the demand curve for places in the freshman class at Pace did not shift between 2005 and 2006, calculate the price elasticity of demand. Use the midpoint formula in your calculation. Is the demand for places in Pace's freshman class elastic or inelastic? Did the total amount of tuition Pace received from its freshman class rise or fall in 2006 compared with 2005?

Source: Karen W. Arenson, "At Universities, Plum Post at Top Is Now Shaky," *New York Times*, January 9, 2007.

1.9 In 1916, the Ford Motor Company sold 500,000 Model T Fords at a price of $440 each. Henry Ford believed that he could increase sales of the Model T by 1,000 cars for every dollar he cut the price. Use this information to calculate the price elasticity of demand for Model T Fords. Use the midpoint formula in your calculation.

1.10 **(Related to the Don't Let This Happen to You on page 189)** The publisher of a magazine gives his staff the following information:

Current price	$2.00 per issue
Current sales	150,000 copies per month
Current total costs	$450,000 per month

The publisher tells the staff, "Our costs are currently $150,000 more than our revenues each month. I propose to eliminate this problem by raising the price of the magazine to $3.00 per issue. This will result in our revenue being exactly equal to our cost." Do you agree with the publisher's analysis? Explain. (*Hint:* Remember that a firm's revenue is calculated by multiplying the price of the product by the quantity sold.)

6.2 The Determinants of the Price Elasticity of Demand, pages 191–192

LEARNING OBJECTIVE: List and explain the determinants of the price elasticity of demand.

Summary

The main determinants of the price elasticity of demand for a good are the availability of close substitutes, the passage of time, whether the good is a necessity or a luxury, how narrowly the market for the good is defined, and the share of the good in the consumer's budget.

MyEconLab Visit **www.myeconlab.com** to complete these exercises online and get instant feedback.

Review Questions

2.1 What are the key determinants of the price elasticity of demand for a product? Which determinant is the most important?

2.2 Is the demand for most agricultural products elastic or inelastic? Briefly explain.

Problems and Applications

2.3 Briefly explain whether the demand for each of the following products is likely to be elastic or inelastic:

a. Milk
b. Frozen cheese pizza
c. Cola
d. Prescription medicine

2.4 According to a news story about the bus system in the Lehigh Valley in Pennsylvania, "Ridership fell 14 percent in 2012 after a 33 percent increase" in bus fares. Based on this information, is the demand for bus trips price elastic or price inelastic? Explain your answer in terms of the five determinants of price elasticity.

Source: Dan Hartzell, "Rebounding from a 2012 Rate Hike, LANTA's Ridership Was up Last Year," (Allentown, PA) *Morning Call*, March 13, 2014.

2.5 One study found that the price elasticity of demand for soda is −0.78, while the price elasticity of demand for Coca-Cola is −1.22. Coca-Cola is a type of soda, so why isn't its price elasticity the same as the price elasticity for soda as a product?

Source: Kelly D. Brownell and Thomas R. Frieden, "Ounces of Prevention—The Public Policy Case for Taxes on Sugared Beverages," *New England Journal of Medicine*, April 30, 2009, pp. 1805–1808.

2.6 The price elasticity of demand for crude oil in the United States has been estimated to be −0.06 in the short run and −0.45 in the long run. Why would the demand for crude oil be more price elastic in the long run than in the short run?

Source: John C. B. Cooper, "Price Elasticity of Demand for Crude Oil: Estimate for 23 Countries," *OPEC Review*, March 2003, pp. 1–8.

2.7 The entrance fee into Yellowstone National Park in northwestern Wyoming is "$50 for a private, noncommercial vehicle; $40 for a motorcycle; or $20 for each visitor 16 and older entering by foot, bike, ski, etc." The fee provides the visitor with a seven-day entrance permit into Yellowstone and nearby Grand Teton National Park.

a. Would you expect the demand for entry into Yellowstone National Park for visitors in private, noncommercial vehicles to be elastic or inelastic? Briefly explain.

b. There are three general ways to enter the park: in a private, noncommercial vehicle; on a motorcycle; and by foot, bike, or ski. Which way would you expect to have the largest price elasticity of demand, and which would you expect to have the smallest price elasticity of demand? Briefly explain.

Source: National Park Service, Yellowstone National Park, "Fees, Reservations, and Permits," http://www.nps.gov/yell/planyourvisit/feesandreservations.htm, 2015.

6.3 The Relationship between Price Elasticity of Demand and Total Revenue, pages 193–197

LEARNING OBJECTIVE: Explain the relationship between the price elasticity of demand and total revenue.

Summary

Total revenue is the total amount of funds received by a seller of a good or service. When demand is inelastic, a decrease in price reduces total revenue, and an increase in price raises total revenue. When demand is elastic, a decrease in price increases total revenue, and an increase in price decreases total revenue. When demand is unit elastic, an increase or a decrease in price leaves total revenue unchanged.

MyEconLab Visit **www.myeconlab.com** to complete these exercises online and get instant feedback.

Review Questions

3.1 If the demand for orange juice is inelastic, will an increase in the price of orange juice increase or decrease the revenue that orange juice sellers receive?

3.2 The price of organic apples falls, and apple growers find that their revenue increases. Is the demand for organic apples elastic or inelastic?

Problems and Applications

3.3 A sportswriter writing about the Cleveland Indians baseball team made the following observation: "If the Indians suddenly slashed all tickets to $10, would their attendance actually increase? Not all that much and revenue would drop dramatically." What is the sportswriter assuming about the price elasticity of demand for Indians tickets?

Source: David Schoenfield, "Chat with David Schoenfield," espn.com, November 27, 2012.

3.4 An article in the *Wall Street Journal* about the financial problems of the New York Metropolitan Opera contained the observation that "a ticket-price increase in 2012 backfired."

a. What does the author mean that the increase in ticket prices to the opera "backfired"?

b. Based on this information, is it likely that demand for tickets to the Metropolitan Opera are price elastic or price inelastic? Briefly explain.

Source: Jennifer Maloney, "A Mixed Bill at the Metropolitan Opera," *Wall Street Journal*, July 1, 2014.

3.5 Economists' estimates of price elasticities can differ somewhat, depending on the time period and on the markets in which the price and quantity data used in the estimates were gathered. An article in the *New York Times* contained the following statement from the Centers for Disease Control and Prevention: "A 10 percent increase in the price of cigarettes reduces consumption by 3 percent to 5 percent." Given this information, compute the range of the price elasticity of demand for cigarettes. Explain whether the demand for cigarettes is elastic, inelastic, or unit elastic. If cigarette manufacturers raise prices, will their revenue increase or decrease? Briefly explain.

Source: Shaila Dewan, "States Look at Tobacco to Balance the Budget," *New York Times*, March 20, 2009.

3.6 Coca-Cola has been focusing on selling more 7.5-ounce cans in displays near supermarket checkout lines. Previously, Coke had relied more heavily on 20-ounce bottles displayed in the beverage sections of supermarkets. An article in the *Wall Street Journal* noted that, "The smaller 7.5 ounce mini-cans are typically priced at five to seven cents an ounce, compared with three or four cents an ounce for 12-ounce cans." It quoted a Coca-Cola executive as arguing that consumers "don't care about the price. They will pick it up if you put Coke within arm's reach."

a. What is the Coca-Cola executive assuming about the price elasticity of demand for Coke? Briefly explain.

b. If the executive is correct, what will the effect of this marketing strategy be on the firm's revenues from selling Coke? Briefly explain.

c. Why did the executive believe that having the cans "within arm's reach" in the checkout line was important? Could this positioning have an effect on the price elasticity of demand? Briefly explain.

Source: Mike Esterl, "Coke under Pressure as Sales Abroad Weaken," *Wall Street Journal*, July 30, 2014.

3.7 Use the following graph for Yolanda's Frozen Yogurt Stand to answer the questions on the next page.

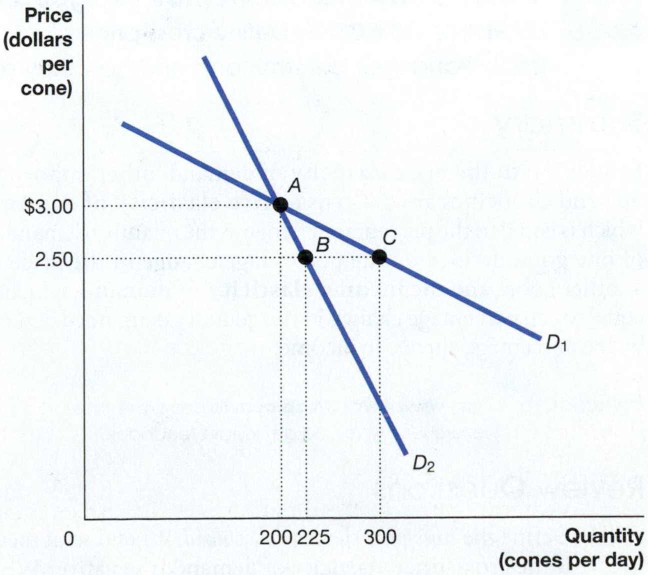

a. Use the midpoint formula to calculate the price elasticity of demand for D_1 between point A and point C and the price elasticity of demand for D_2 between point A and point B. Which demand curve is more elastic, D_1 or D_2? Briefly explain.

b. Suppose Yolanda is initially selling 200 cones per day at a price of $3.00 per cone. If she cuts her price to $2.50 per cone and her demand curve is D_1, what will be the change in her revenue? What will be the change in her revenue if her demand curve is D_2?

3.8 **(Related to Solved Problem 6.3 on page 195)** Briefly explain whether you agree with Manager 2's reasoning:

Manager 1: "The only way we can increase the revenue we receive from selling our frozen pizzas is by cutting the price."

Manager 2: "Cutting the price of a product never increases the amount of revenue you receive. If we want to increase revenue, we have to increase the price."

3.9 **(Related to Solved Problem 6.3 on page 195)** According to a company news release, during the third quarter of 2014, the Coca-Cola Company sold 1 percent less soda in North America while earning more revenue.

a. Did Coke increase or decrease its soda prices during this period? Briefly explain.

b. Based on this information, is the demand for the soda Coke sells price elastic or price inelastic? Briefly explain.

Source: The Coca-Cola Company, "The Coca-Cola Company Reports Third Quarter and Year-to-Date 2014 Results," October 21, 2014.

3.10 **(Related to the Making the Connection on page 196)** According to an article in the *New York Times*, some small publishers have argued that Amazon has been increasing the prices it charges for their books on its Web site. Amazon was increasing the prices by reducing the discount it offered consumers on the retail prices of the books. One small nonfiction publisher said that Amazon had reduced the discount on its books from about 30 percent to about 16 percent. According to the author of the article, "For this publisher, that means less revenue and less profit as some buyers reject the more expensive books."

a. Does the fact that some buyers will no longer buy the publisher's books at a higher price necessarily mean the publisher will earn less revenue? Briefly explain.

b. What must be true about the price elasticity of demand for the publisher's books for the author's statement to be correct?

Source: David Streitfeld, "As Competition Wanes, Amazon Cuts Back Its Discounts," *New York Times*, July 4, 2013.

3.11 **(Related to the Making the Connection on page 196)** Amazon allows authors who self-publish their e-books to set the prices they charge. One author was quoted as saying: "I am able to drop prices and, by sheer volume of sales, increase my income." Was the demand for her books price elastic or price inelastic? Briefly explain.

Source: David Streitfeld, "For the Indie Writers of Amazon, It's Publish or Perish," *New York Times*, January 4, 2015.

3.12 The Delaware River Joint Toll Bridge Commission increased the toll from $0.50 to $1.00 on the bridges on Route 22 and Interstate 78 from New Jersey to Pennsylvania. Use the information in the following table to answer the questions. (Assume that besides the toll change, nothing occurred during these months that would affect consumer demand.)

Number of Vehicles Crossing the Bridge

Month	Toll	Route 22 Bridge	Interstate 78 Bridge
November	$0.50	519,337	728,022
December	$1.00	433,691	656,257

a. Calculate the price elasticity of demand for each bridge, using the midpoint formula.

b. How much total revenue did the commission collect from these bridges in November? How much did it collect in December? Relate your answer to your answer in (a).

Source: Garrett Therolf, "Frugal Drivers Flood Free Bridge," (Allentown, PA) *Morning Call*, January 20, 2003.

6.4 Other Demand Elasticities, pages 197–199

LEARNING OBJECTIVE: Define cross-price elasticity of demand and income elasticity of demand and understand their determinants and how they are measured.

Summary

In addition to the price elasticity of demand, other important demand elasticities are the **cross-price elasticity of demand**, which is equal to the percentage change in the quantity demanded of one good divided by the percentage change in the price of another good, and the **income elasticity of demand**, which is equal to the percentage change in the quantity demanded divided by the percentage change in income.

MyEconLab Visit **www.myeconlab.com** to complete these exercises online and get instant feedback.

Review Questions

4.1 Define the *cross-price elasticity of demand*. What does it mean if the cross-price elasticity of demand is negative? What does it mean if the cross-price elasticity of demand is positive?

4.2 Define the *income elasticity of demand*. How does the income elasticity of a normal good differ from the income elasticity of an inferior good. Is it possible to tell from the income elasticity of demand whether a product is a luxury good or a necessity good?

Problems and Applications

4.3 When lettuce prices doubled, from about $1.50 per head to about $3.00, the reaction of one consumer was quoted in a newspaper article: "I will not buy [lettuce] when it's $3 a head," she said, adding that other green vegetables can fill in for lettuce. "If bread were $5 a loaf we'd still have to buy it. But lettuce is not that important in our family."

a. For this consumer's household, which product has the higher price elasticity of demand: bread or lettuce? Briefly explain.
b. Is the cross-price elasticity of demand between lettuce and other green vegetables positive or negative for this consumer? Briefly explain.

Source: Justin Bachman, "Sorry, Romaine Only," Associated Press, March 29, 2002.

4.4 In the following graph, the demand for hot dog buns has shifted to the right because the price of hot dogs has fallen from \$2.20 to \$1.80 per package. Calculate the cross-price elasticity of demand between hot dogs and hot dog buns.

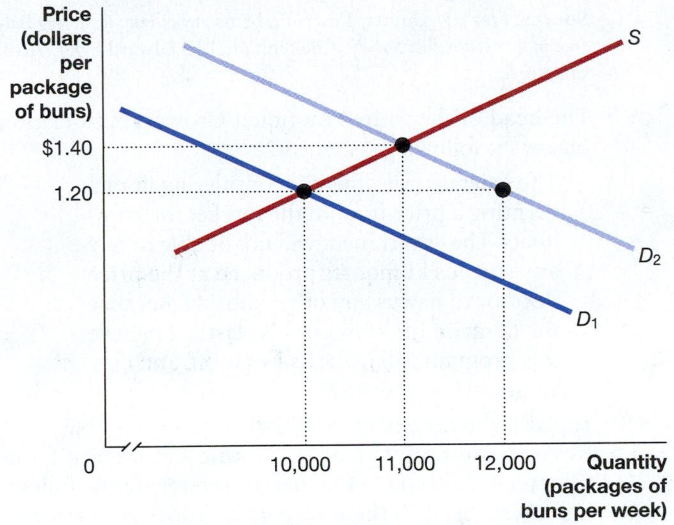

4.5 Are the cross-price elasticities of demand between the following pairs of products likely to be positive or negative? Briefly explain.
a. Iced coffee and iced tea
b. French fries and ketchup
c. Steak and chicken
d. Blu-ray players and Blu-ray discs

4.6 **(Related to the Chapter Opener on page 183)** According to an article on the *Boston Globe's* Web site, during the last three months of 2014, gasoline prices dropped 33 percent at the same time as ridership on mass transit, such as subways and trains, increased by 1 percent. According to a spokesperson for the American Public Transportation Association, a group that lobbies Congress on behalf of public transit systems, "Even with gas prices dropping like a rock, the public is still demanding more transit options."
a. On the basis of this information, is the cross-price elasticity of demand between gasoline and rides on mass transit positive or negative? Would you conclude that gasoline and rides on mass transit are substitutes or complements? Briefly explain.
b. During this period unemployment was declining, and the news story also included the observation, "An improving economy means more people need to get to work." Does this observation cause you to modify your answer to part (a)? Briefly explain.

Source: "US Transit Rides at 58-year High While Gas Prices Fall," bostonglobe.com, March 9, 2015.

4.7 Rank the following four goods from lowest income elasticity of demand to highest income elasticity of demand. Briefly explain your ranking.
a. Bread
b. Pepsi
c. Mercedes-Benz automobiles
d. Laptop computers

4.8 **(Related to the Making the Connection on page 199)** The elasticities reported in this *Making the Connection* were calculated using price data for many brands of beer. Why might price elasticity estimates be less reliable if they use data for only one brand of beer?

4.9 Consider firms selling three goods: One firm sells a good with an income elasticity of demand less than zero, one firm sells a good with an income elasticity of demand greater than zero but less than one, and one firm sells a good with an income elasticity of demand greater than one. In a recession when incomes fall, which firm is likely to see its sales decline the most? Which firm is likely to see its sales increase the most? Briefly explain.

6.5 Using Elasticity to Analyze the Disappearing Family Farm, pages 200–202

LEARNING OBJECTIVE: Use price elasticity and income elasticity to analyze economic issues.

Summary

Price elasticity and income elasticity can be used to analyze many economic issues. One example is the disappearance of the family farm in the United States. Because the income elasticity of demand for food is low, the demand for food has not increased proportionally as incomes in the United States have grown. As farmers have become more productive, they have increased the supply of most foods. Because the price elasticity of demand for food is low, increasing supply has resulted in continually falling food prices.

MyEconLab Visit **www.myeconlab.com** to complete these exercises online and get instant feedback.

Review Questions

5.1 The demand for agricultural products is inelastic, and the income elasticity of demand for agricultural products is low. How do these facts help explain the decline of the family farm in the United States?

Problems and Applications

5.2 **(Related to Solved Problem 6.5 on page 201)** According to a study by the U.S. Centers for Disease Control and Prevention, the price elasticity of demand for cigarettes is −0.25. Americans purchase about 360 billion cigarettes each year.

a. If the federal tax on cigarettes were increased enough to cause a 50 percent increase in the price of cigarettes, what would be the effect on the quantity of cigarettes demanded?
b. Is raising the tax on cigarettes a more effective way to reduce smoking if the demand for cigarettes is elastic or if it is inelastic? Briefly explain.

Source: "Response to Increases in Cigarette Prices by Race/Ethnicity, Income, and Age Groups—United States, 1976–1993," *Morbidity and Mortality Weekly Report*, July 31, 1998.

5.3 **(Related to Solved Problem 6.5 on page 201)** Suppose that the long-run price elasticity of demand for gasoline is −0.55. Assume that the price of gasoline is currently $3.00 per gallon, the equilibrium quantity of gasoline is 140 billion gallons per year, and the federal government decides to increase the excise tax on gasoline by $1.00 per gallon. Suppose that in the long run, the price of gasoline increases by $0.70 per gallon after the $1.00 excise tax is imposed.
a. What is the new quantity of gasoline demanded after the tax is imposed? How effective would a gas tax be in reducing consumption of gasoline in the long run?
b. How much does the federal government receive from the tax?
c. Compare your answers to those in Solved Problem 6.5 on page 201.

5.4 Corruption has been a significant problem in Iraq. Opening and running a business in Iraq usually requires paying multiple bribes to government officials. We can think of there being a demand and supply for bribes, with the curves having the usual shapes: The demand for bribes will be downward sloping because the smaller the bribe, the more business owners will be willing to pay it. The supply of bribes will be upward sloping because the larger the bribe, the more government officials will be willing to run the risk of breaking the law by accepting the bribe. Suppose that the Iraqi government introduces a new policy to reduce corruption that raises the cost to officials of accepting bribes—perhaps by increasing the jail term for accepting a bribe. As a result, the supply curve for bribes will shift to the left. If we measure the burden on the economy from corruption by the total value of the bribes paid, what must be true of the demand for bribes if the government policy is to be effective? Illustrate your answer with a demand and supply graph. Be sure to show on your graph the areas representing the burden of corruption before and after the government policy is enacted.

Source: Frank R. Gunter, *The Political Economy of Iraq: Restoring Balance in a Post-Conflict Society*, Cheltenham, UK: Edward Elgar, 2013, Chapter 4.

5.5 The head of the United Kumquat Growers Association makes the following statement:

> The federal government is considering implementing a price floor in the market for kumquats. The government will not be able to buy any surplus kumquats produced at the price floor or to pay us any other subsidy. Because the demand for kumquats is elastic, I believe this program will make us worse off, and I say we should oppose it.

Explain whether you agree with this reasoning.

5.6 Review the concept of economic efficiency from Chapter 4, pages 115–117, before answering the following question: Will there be a greater loss of economic efficiency from a price ceiling when demand is elastic or inelastic? Illustrate your answer with a demand and supply graph.

6.6 The Price Elasticity of Supply and Its Measurement, pages 202–206

LEARNING OBJECTIVE: Define *price elasticity of supply* and understand its determinants and how it is measured.

Summary

The **price elasticity of supply** is equal to the percentage change in quantity supplied divided by the percentage change in price. The supply curves for most goods are inelastic over a short period of time, but they become increasingly elastic over longer periods of time. Perfectly inelastic supply curves are vertical lines, and perfectly elastic supply curves are horizontal lines. Relatively few products have perfectly elastic or perfectly inelastic supply curves.

MyEconLab Visit **www.myeconlab.com** to complete these exercises online and get instant feedback.

Review Questions

6.1 Write the formula for the price elasticity of supply. If an increase of 10 percent in the price of frozen pizzas results in a 9 percent increase in the quantity of frozen pizzas supplied, what is the price elasticity of supply for frozen pizzas? Is the supply of pizzas elastic or inelastic?

6.2 What is the main determinant of the price elasticity of supply?

Problems and Applications

6.3 Globe Life Park in Arlington is the home ball park of the Texas Rangers, a Major League Baseball team. The seating capacity of Globe Life Park is 49,170. Among the home games played by the Rangers in 2015 were these four:

Date	Opponent	Attendance
April 10	Houston Astros	48,085
April 11	Houston Astros	36,833
May 11	Kansas City Royals	21,206
May 12	Kansas City Royals	23,659

Can we use this information to calculate the price elasticity of supply of Rangers tickets? Briefly explain.

6.4 To legally operate a taxi in New York City, a driver must have a medallion issued by the New York City Taxi and

Limousine Commission, an agency of the city's government. In 2015 the number of medallions was 13,605. In recent years the taxi industry in New York and other large cities has encountered competition from companies such as Uber, an app-based service that offers rides from drivers who own their own cars. Uber varies the prices it charges based on the demand for rides, with rides during busier periods, such as Saturday nights, having higher prices.

a. What does the limitation on their number imply about the price elasticity of supply of taxi medallions?
b. Is the supply of Uber rides more or less elastic than the supply of taxi rides in New York City? Briefly explain.

Source: Annie Lowrey, "Is Uber's Surge-Pricing an Example of High-Tech Gouging?" *New York Times*, January 10, 2014.

6.5 **(Related to the Making the Connection on page 203)** An article in the *Wall Street Journal* notes that although U.S. oil production has increased rapidly in recent years, the increase has still amounted to only 5 percent of world production. Still, that increase has been "enough to help trigger a price collapse." Briefly explain under what circumstances a small increase in supply can lead to a large decline in equilibrium price.

Source: Georgi Kantchev and Bill Spindle, "Shale-Oil Producers Ready to Raise Output," *Wall Street Journal*, May 13, 2015.

6.6 **(Related to the Making the Connection on page 203)** Suppose that instead of being highly inelastic, the demand for oil is highly elastic.

a. Given the situation illustrated by the first graph in the *Making the Connection* on page 203, would the resulting price change be larger, smaller, or the same as the actual price change shown in the graph? Briefly explain.
b. Given the situation illustrated by the second graph in the *Making the Connection* on page 204, would the resulting price change be larger, smaller, or the same as the actual price change shown in the graph? Briefly explain.

6.7 Use the midpoint formula for calculating elasticity to calculate the price elasticity of supply between point *A* and point *B* for each panel of Figure 6.5 on page 206.

6.8 Like many other cities, Denver experienced a sharp decline in construction of new homes in the years following 2006. Many carpenters, roofers, and other skilled workers left the area or found jobs in other industries. In addition, builders stopped buying and preparing home lots for construction. According to an article in the *Wall Street Journal*, by 2014, as consumers increased their demand for new homes in Denver, "New-home prices have surged over the past two years … amid a shortage of home lots and skilled construction workers." Predict what is likely to happen to the price of new homes in Denver in the future. Use a graph to illustrate your answer.

Source: Kris Hudson, "Labor Shortage Besets Home Builders," *Wall Street Journal*, May 1, 2014.

6.9 On most days, the price of a rose is $1, and 8,000 roses are purchased. On Valentine's Day, the price of a rose jumps to $2, and 30,000 roses are purchased.

a. Draw a demand and supply graph that shows why the price jumps.
b. Based on this information, what do we know about the price elasticity of demand for roses? What do we know about the price elasticity of supply for roses? Calculate values for the price elasticity of demand and the price elasticity of supply or explain why you can't calculate these values.

6.10 Use the following graph of the market for basketball tickets at State University to answer the questions.

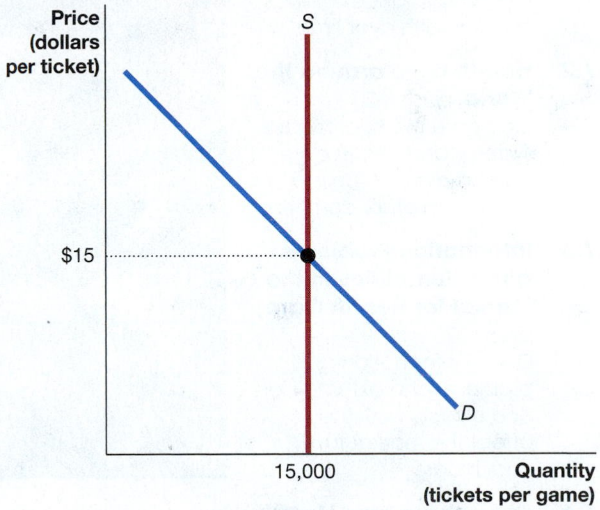

a. What is the price elasticity of supply?
b. Suppose the basketball team at State University goes undefeated in the first half of the season, and the demand for basketball tickets increases. Show the effects of this increase in demand on the graph. What happens to the equilibrium price and quantity of tickets? Briefly explain.
c. If the State University basketball team continues to do very well in future years, what is likely to happen to the price elasticity of supply of tickets to its games? Briefly explain.

CHAPTER

7

The Economics of Health Care

Chapter Outline and Learning Objectives

How Much Will You Pay for Health Insurance?

In 2010, President Barack Obama and Congress enacted the Patient Protection and Affordable Care Act (ACA), which made major changes to the U.S. health care system. If you are young and healthy, you may rarely go to the doctor and may not think much about health insurance. Under the ACA, however, you must have health insurance or pay a fine. In 2016, the fine was $695 or 2.5 percent of your income, whichever was higher.

Many people receive health insurance through their employers. If you take a full-time job, how much will you pay for health insurance? T. Cain Grocery operates five Piggly Wiggly supermarkets in Alabama and Florida. In 2015, Cain deducted $2,800 per year from each employee's paycheck in exchange for providing health insurance. The insurance would pay most of an employee's medical bills—but only *after* the employee had paid for the first $4,500 in bills. Some of the state and federal taxes withheld from the employee's paycheck would be used to support two federal programs: *Medicare*, which provides health insurance to people aged 65 and older, and *Medicaid*, which provides health insurance to low-income people. When they take their first job, many college students are surprised at the big bite that health care costs take out of their paychecks.

For many small firms like Cain's, providing health insurance for workers represents their most rapidly increasing cost. Included in the ACA was a provision that businesses with 50 or more full-time employees (those working 30 or more hours per week) must provide health insurance to all full-time employees or face fines. Under the act, states have also set up health insurance marketplaces with the goal of making health insurance less expensive for small businesses and individuals by allowing them to enter an insurance pool where both healthy and sick people will be in the same insurance plan and pay the same insurance premium.

The increasing health care costs faced by small businesses are reflected in trends in the overall economy. Health care spending increased from about 5 percent of gross domestic product (GDP) in 1960 to about 18 percent in 2015, an upward trend that is expected to continue.

It remains to be seen what the full effects of the ACA will be on health care spending and on health care outcomes.

Sources: Angus Loten, "Small Business Owners Scramble to Prepare for New Tax Form," *Wall Street Journal*, March 4, 2015; Sarah E. Needleman and Angus Loten, "Small Businesses Find Benefits, Costs as They Navigate Affordable Care Act," *Wall Street Journal*, April 23, 2014; U.S. Centers for Medicare & Medicaid Studies, "National Health Expenditure Data," www.cms.gov; and "Employment," cainspigglywiggly.com.

Economics in Your Life

Is Your Take-Home Pay Affected by What Your Employer Spends on Your Health Insurance?

If you work for a firm that offers you health insurance, the firm will withhold some amount from each of your paychecks to pay for the insurance. Typically, firms pay the majority of the cost of health insurance for their employees. In 2014, employees paid only 18 percent of the cost of coverage for themselves or 29 percent of the cost of coverage for their family. Your paycheck probably doesn't show the amount your employer pays on your behalf for health insurance, but does that amount affect your take-home pay? As you read this chapter, try to answer this question. You can check your answer against the one we provide on **page 243** at the end of this chapter.

Source: The Kaiser Family Foundation and Health Research and Educational Trust, *Employer Health Benefits, 2014 Annual Survey*, September 10, 2014.

Health care Goods and services, such as prescription drugs, consultations with a doctor, and surgeries, that are intended to maintain or improve a person's health.

Health care refers to goods and services, such as prescription drugs, consultations with a doctor, and surgeries, that are intended to maintain or improve a person's health. Health care makes up more than one-sixth of the U.S. economy—about the size of the entire economy of France. Improvements in health care are an important part of the tremendous increase in living standards people in the United States and other high-income countries have experienced over the past 100 years. Health care has seen rapid technological change with new products, such as MRI units and other diagnostic equipment; prescription drugs to treat cancer, high blood pressure, and AIDS; vaccinations for meningitis; and new surgical techniques, such as cardiac catheterizations for treatment of heart disease.

Health care is provided through markets, just as are most other goods and services, such as smartphones and haircuts. So, we can apply to health care the tools of economic analysis we used in previous chapters. But the market for health care is different from other markets. In the United States, doctors and hospitals that supply most health care are primarily private firms, but the government also provides some health care services directly through the Veterans Health Administration, which is part of the U.S. Department of Veterans Affairs, and indirectly through the Medicare and Medicaid programs.

In addition to having a large role for government, the market for health care differs from most markets in other ways. Most importantly, a typical consumer of health care doesn't pay full price for that care. Most people have private health insurance, either provided through their employers or purchased on the government-run health insurance marketplaces, or they are enrolled in the Medicare or Medicaid programs. Consumers who have insurance make different decisions about the quantity of health care they wish to consume than they would if they were paying the full cost of the services. So, to analyze the market for health care, we will need to use economic tools beyond those introduced in previous chapters. We begin our analysis of health care with an overview of health care around the world.

7.1 The Improving Health of People in the United States

LEARNING OBJECTIVE: Use data to discuss trends in U.S. health over time.

Two hundred years ago, the whole world was very poor by modern standards. Today, an average person in a high-income country has a standard of living well beyond what even the richest people in the past could have imagined. One aspect of this higher standard of living is the improved health the average person enjoys. For example, in the late 1700s, England had the highest level of income per person of any large country. But the average person in England had a short life span and many people suffered from diseases—such as cholera, yellow fever, dysentery, and smallpox—that have disappeared from high-income countries today. The average life expectancy at birth was only 38 years, and 30 percent of the population died before reaching age 30. Even people who survived to age 20 could expect to live only an average of 34 more years. Today, the average life expectancy at birth in the United Kingdom and other high-income countries is around 80 years. People in eighteenth-century England were also short by modern standards. The average height of an adult male was 5 feet, 5 inches compared with 5 feet, 9 inches today.

In this section, we discuss the health of people in the United States. In Section 7.2, we discuss health care in other countries.

Table 7.1

Health in the United States, 1850 and 2015

Variable	1850	2015
Life expectancy at birth	38.3 years	79.6 years
Average height (adult males)	5′7″	5′9.5″
Infant mortality (death of a child aged 1 year or less)	228.9 per 1,000 live births	6.2 per 1,000 live births

Note: The data on heights for 1850 include only native-born white and black male citizens. The data on height for 2015 were gathered in 2007–2010 and represent the median height of adult males 20 years and older.

Sources: Susan B. Carter et al., eds., *Historical Statistics of the United States: Millennium Edition*; U.S. National Center for Health Statistics, *Anthropometric Reference Data for Children and Adults: United States, 2007–2010*, October 2012; and U.S. Central Intelligence Agency, *World Factbook*.

Changes over Time in U.S. Health

When economists measure changes over time in the standard of living in a country, they usually look first at increases in income per person. However, changes in health are also important because health is an essential part of a person's well-being and, therefore, of his or her standard of living. The health of the average person in the United States improved significantly during the nineteenth and twentieth centuries, and by and large, it continues to improve today.

Table 7.1 compares three indicators of health in the United States in 1850 and 2015. Individuals in the United States today are taller, live much longer, and are much less likely to die in the first months of life than was true 165 years ago. Economists often use height as a measure of long-run changes in the average well-being of a population. A person's height depends partly on genetics—that is, tall parents tend to have tall children—but also on a person's *net nutritional status*. Net nutritional status depends on a person's food intake relative to the work the person has to perform, whether the person is able to remain warm in cold weather, and the diseases to which the person is exposed. Over time, people in the United States and other high-income countries have, on average, become taller, which is an indication that their nutritional status has improved. MyEconLab Concept Check

Reasons for Long-Run Improvements in U.S. Health

For most of the country's history, the health of people in the United States has steadily improved, with life expectancies increasing and death rates decreasing. Panel (a) of Figure 7.1 shows for the years 1900–2013 the increase in life expectancy and the decline in the mortality rate, or death rate, measured as deaths per 100,000 people. Note that the mortality rate is "age adjusted," which means that it is not affected by changes in the number of people in each age group. Life expectancy at birth in the United States increased from 47.3 years in 1900 to 79.6 years in 2015. Panel (b) shows for recent years the change in the overall mortality rate of the U.S. population, measured as deaths per 100,000 people, and the age-adjusted mortality rates for several diseases. The overall mortality rate decreased by more than 25 percent between 1981 and 2013. Over this same period, deaths from cancer, cardiovascular disease, such as heart attacks and strokes, and diseases of the liver all declined significantly. For example, cancer deaths were 20 percent lower in 2013 than they were in 1981, while deaths from cardiovascular disease declined by more than half during this time. Deaths from diabetes and kidney disease both increased slightly during this period, largely due to the effects of increasing obesity. The overall decline in death rates in the United States since 1981 was due to changes in lifestyle, particularly a decline in smoking, and advances in new diagnostic equipment, prescription drugs, and surgical techniques.

What explains increases in life expectancy and declines in death rates in the years since 1850? Improvements in sanitation and in the distribution of food during the late 1800s and early 1900s led to better health during that period. More generally, the late Nobel Laureate Robert Fogel of the University of Chicago and Roderick Floud of Gresham College, along

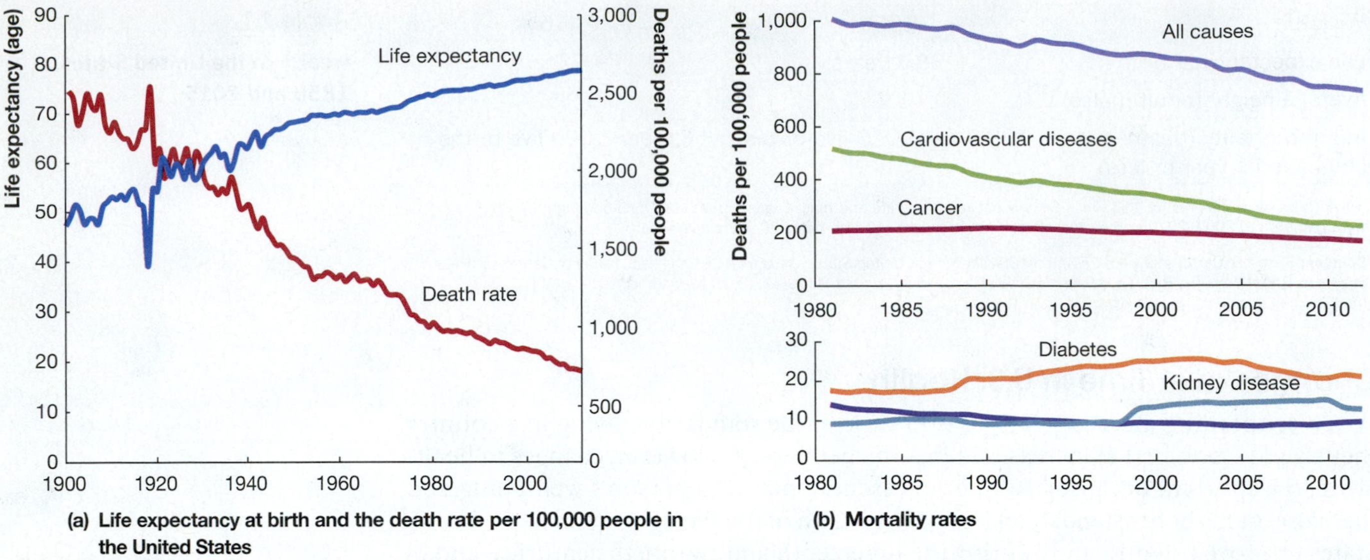

MyEconLab Animation

Figure 7.1 The Improving Health of the U.S. Population

Since 1900, life expectancy has increased and mortality rates have decreased in the United States. Since 1981, there have been significant decreases in rates of death due to cancer, cardiovascular diseases, and diseases of the liver. Rates of death due to kidney disease and diabetes increased slightly because of an increase in obesity. Note that in panel (a), the increase in mortality and decrease in life expectancy in 1918 are due to the severe influenza epidemic of that year.

Sources: For panel (a): Susan B. Carter et al., eds., *Historical Statistics of the United States: Millennium Edition*, Series Ab644; and Centers for Disease Control and Prevention, *National Vital Statistics Reports*, various issues; for panel (b): Centers for Disease Control and Prevention, National Center for Health Statistics, *National Vital Statistics Reports*, Vol. 63, No. 9: Deaths Final Data for 2012. (2015), http://www.cdc.gov/nchs/data/nvsr/nvsr63/nvsr63_09.pdf.

with coauthors, have described a process by which better health makes it possible for people to work harder as they become taller, stronger, and more resistant to disease. Working harder raises a country's total income, making it possible for the country to afford better sanitation, more food, and a better system for distributing the food. In effect, improving health shifts out a country's production possibilities frontier. Higher incomes also allow the country to devote more resources to research and development, including medical research. The United States has been a pioneer in the development of medical technology, new surgical techniques, and new pharmaceuticals, which have played important roles in lengthening life spans and reducing the death toll from diseases. MyEconLab Concept Check

MyEconLab Study Plan

7.2 Health Care around the World

LEARNING OBJECTIVE: Compare the health care systems and health care outcomes in the United States and other countries.

In the United States, private firms provide most health care, through either doctors' practices or hospitals. The main exception is the care the government provides through the network of hospitals operated by the federal government's Veterans Administration, although some cities also own and operate hospitals. Governments in most countries outside the United States have a more substantial direct role in paying for or providing health care. Policymakers and economists debate the effects of greater government involvement in the health care system on health outcomes such as life expectancy, infant mortality, and successful treatment of diseases.

The U.S. Health Care System

Health insurance A contract under which a buyer agrees to make payments, or *premiums*, in exchange for the provider's agreeing to pay some or all of the buyer's medical bills.

One important difference among health care systems in different countries is the way people pay for their health care. Most people in the United States have *health insurance* that helps them to pay their medical bills. **Health insurance** is a contract

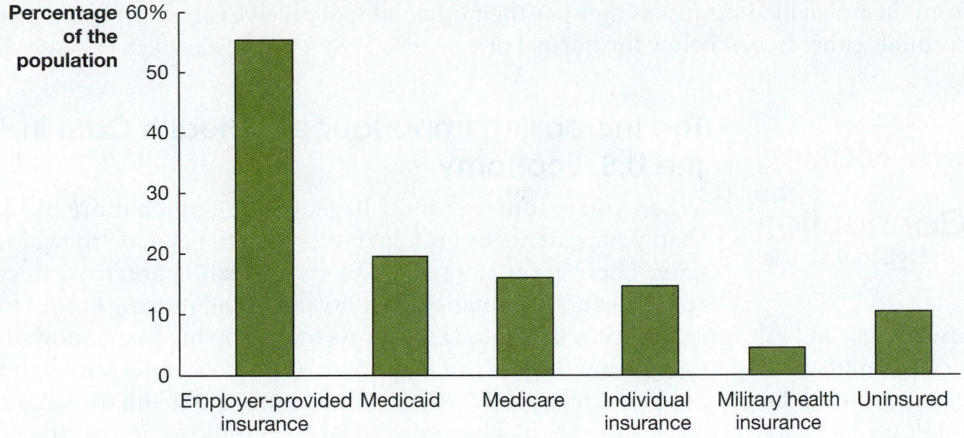

Figure 7.2

Sources of Health Insurance in the United States, 2014

In 2014, about 55 percent of people received health insurance through their employer and about 15 percent directly purchased an individual or family health insurance policy from an insurance company. About 36 percent of people received health insurance through a government program including Medicaid, Medicare, and the program run by the Department of Veteran Affairs. About 10 percent of people were uninsured.

Note: Because some people have more than one type of health insurance, the sum of the values for each category shown is greater than 100 percent.

Source: Jessica Smith and Carla Medalia, *Health Insurance Coverage in the United States: 2014*, U.S. Census Bureau, Current Population Reports, P60–253, Washington, DC: U.S. Government Printing Office, September 2015, Table 1.

under which a buyer agrees to make payments, or *premiums*, in exchange for the provider's agreeing to pay some or all of the buyer's medical bills. Figure 7.2 shows the sources of health insurance in the United States in 2014. Some people have insurance of more than one type by, for example, participating in a government insurance program such as Medicare as well as having a private insurance policy. About 55 percent of people received health insurance through their employer, and about 15 percent directly purchased an individual or family health insurance policy from an insurance company. About 36 percent of people received health insurance through a government program including Medicaid, Medicare, and the program run by the Department of Veterans Affairs.

Most people who have private health insurance receive it through their employer. In 2014, about 98 percent of firms employing more than 200 workers and about 54 percent of firms employing between 3 and 199 workers offered health insurance as a fringe benefit (that is, a type of non-wage compensation) to their employees. Private health insurance companies can be either not-for-profit firms, such as some of the Blue Cross and Blue Shield organizations, or for-profit firms, such as Aetna and John Hancock, which typically also sell other types of insurance. Private health insurance companies sell *group plans* to employers to cover all of their employees and individual plans directly to the public. Some health insurance plans reimburse doctors and hospitals on a **fee-for-service** basis, which means that doctors and hospitals receive a payment for each service they provide. Other health insurance plans are organized as *health maintenance organizations* (HMOs), which typically reimburse doctors mainly by paying a flat fee per patient rather than paying a fee for each individual office visit or other service provided.

Fee-for-service A system under which doctors and hospitals receive a payment for each service they provide.

About 10 percent of people were not covered by health insurance in 2014. This percentage was lower than in previous years, partly as a result of passage of the Affordable Care Act in 2010, but still represented millions of uninsured people. Many people lack health insurance because their incomes are low, and they believe they cannot afford to buy private health insurance even with government subsidies. Some low-income people either do not qualify for Medicaid or choose not to participate in that program. About 70 percent of uninsured people live in families in which at least one member has a job. These individuals either were not offered health insurance through their employers or chose not to purchase it. Some young people opt out of employer-provided health insurance because they are healthy and do not believe that the cost of the premium their employer charges for the insurance is worth the benefit of having the insurance. More than half the uninsured were younger than age 35. Although most large firms offer their employees health insurance, fewer than two-thirds accept it. The remaining employees are covered by a spouse's policy, are not eligible for coverage, or have decided to go uninsured because they do not want to pay the premium for the insurance. The uninsured must pay for their own medical bills *out of pocket*, with money from their own income, just as they pay their other bills, or receive care from doctors or hospitals either free or below the normal price. MyEconLab Concept Check

Making the Connection MyEconLab Video

The Increasing Importance of Health Care in the U.S. Economy

When you graduate from college, you are much more likely than your parents or grandparents were to get a job in health care. There are many types of jobs in health care, from doctors and nurses to managers at hospitals and nursing homes to researchers and salespeople at pharmaceutical firms. As the following maps show, in 1990, manufacturing was the largest source of employment in most states, and in no state was health care the largest employer. By 2000, manufacturing was still the largest employer in 27 states, but health care had become the largest employer in two states. The results for 2014 are strikingly different, with manufacturing the largest employer in only 7 states and health care the largest employer in 34 states.

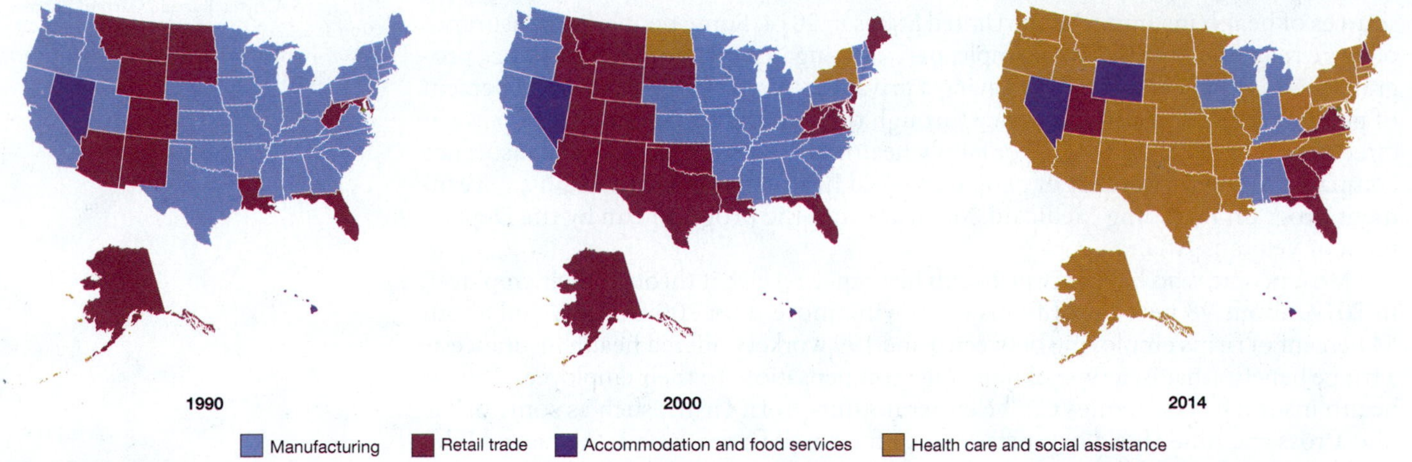

(a) In 1990, manufacturing was the largest source of employment in most states.

(b) In 2000, manufacturing was still the largest employer in 27 states, but health care had become the largest employer in 2 states.

(c) In 2014, manufacturing was the largest employer in only 7 states, and health care was the largest employer in 34 states.

In 1990, almost twice as many people in the United States worked in manufacturing as worked in health care. Today, employment in health care has doubled, while employment in manufacturing has declined by more than 30 percent. And these trends are likely to continue. The U.S. Bureau of Labor Statistics forecasts that 13 of the 20 fastest-growing occupations over the next 10 years will be in health care.

What explains these trends? We discuss explanations for rising health care spending in the United States in Section 7.4. For now, note that the growth of employment in health care is similar to that in other service industries, such as retail stores and restaurants, and that the growth of employment in the health care and service industries is much faster than that in goods-producing industries, such as manufacturing. In addition, there is evidence that as people's incomes grow, their demand for health care grows faster than their demand for most other goods and services. The average age of the U.S. population is also increasing, and older people have a greater demand for health care. Finally, the Affordable Care Act has increased the demand for health care among low-income people in two ways: by providing subsidies to buy health insurance for people whose incomes fall below a certain level and by expanding the Medicaid system.

It seems likely that health care will continue to be a booming sector of the economy and an important source of new jobs in the coming decades.

Sources: U.S. Bureau of Labor Statistics; U.S. Census Bureau; Rani Molla, "How America's Top Industries Have Changed," *Wall Street Journal*, July 28, 2014; and "Why Nurses Are the New Auto Workers," *Economist*, July 25, 2014.

Your Turn: Test your understanding by doing related problem 2.9 on page 245 at the end of this chapter.

The Health Care Systems of Canada, Japan, and the United Kingdom

In many countries, such as Canada, Japan, and the United Kingdom, the government either supplies health care directly by operating hospitals and employing doctors and nurses or pays for most health care expenses, even if hospitals are not government owned and doctors are not government employees. In this section, we look briefly at the health care systems in three countries.

Canada Canada has a **single-payer health care system**, in which the government provides *national health insurance* to all Canadian residents. Each of the 10 Canadian provinces has its own system, although each system must meet the federal government's requirement of covering 100 percent of the cost of all medically necessary procedures. Individuals pay nothing for doctor's visits or hospital stays; instead, they pay for medical care indirectly through the taxes they pay to the provincial and federal governments. As in the United States, most doctors and hospitals are private businesses, but unlike in the United States, doctors and hospitals are required to accept the fees that are set by the government. Also as in the United States, doctors and hospitals are typically reimbursed on a fee-for-service basis.

Single-payer health care system A system, such as the one in Canada, in which the government provides health insurance to all of the country's residents.

Japan Japan has a system of *universal health insurance* under which every resident of the country is required to enroll either in one of the many nonprofit health insurance societies that are organized by industries or professions or in the health insurance program provided by the national government. The system is funded by a combination of premiums paid by employees and firms and a payroll tax similar to the tax that funds the Medicare program in the United States. Unlike the Canadian system, the Japanese system requires substantial *copayments*, under which patients pay as much as 30 percent of their medical bills, while health insurance pays for the rest. Japanese health insurance does not pay for most preventive care, such as annual physical exams, or for medical expenses connected with pregnancies, unless complications result. Health insurance in the United States and Canada typically does cover these expenses. As in the United States, most doctors in Japan do not work for the government, and there are many privately owned hospitals. The number of government-run hospitals, though, is greater than in the United States.

The United Kingdom In the United Kingdom, the government, through the National Health Service (NHS), owns nearly all hospitals and directly employs nearly all doctors. This system contrasts with those in the United States, Canada, and Japan, where the government employs relatively few doctors and owns relatively few hospitals. Because there are few private insurance plans and private hospitals in the United Kingdom, its health care system is often called **socialized medicine**. With 1.7 million employees, the NHS is the largest government-run health care system in the world. Apart from a small copayment for prescriptions, the NHS supplies health care services without charge to patients because it receives its funding from income taxes. The NHS concentrates on preventive care and care for acute conditions. Nonemergency care, also called elective care—such as hip replacements, knee surgery following a sports injury, or reconstructive surgery following a mastectomy—is a low priority. The NHS's goals result in waiting lists for elective procedures that can be very long, with patients sometimes waiting a year or more for a procedure that would be available in a few weeks or less in the United States. To avoid the waiting lists, more than 10 percent of the population also has private health insurance, frequently provided by employers, which the insured use to pay for elective procedures.

Socialized medicine A health care system under which the government owns most of the hospitals and employs most of the doctors.

The NHS essentially trades off broader coverage for longer waiting times and performing fewer procedures, particularly nonemergency surgeries. MyEconLab Concept Check

Comparing Health Care Outcomes around the World

We have seen that the way health care systems are organized varies significantly across countries. Health care outcomes and the amounts countries spend on health care are also quite different. As Figure 7.3 shows, typically, the higher the level of income per person in a country, the higher the level of spending per person on health care. This result is not surprising because health care is a *normal good*. We know that as income increases, so does spending on normal goods (see Chapter 3, Section 3.1). The line in the figure shows the average relationship between income per person and health care spending per person. The dots for most countries are fairly close to the line, but note that the dot representing the United States is significantly above the line. Being well above the line indicates that health care spending per person in the United States is higher than in other countries, even taking into account the relatively high income levels in the United States. In Section 7.4, we will discuss explanations for the high level of health care spending in the United States.

Has the high level of health care spending in the United States resulted in better health outcomes? Are people in the United States healthier, and do they have their medical problems addressed more rapidly than do people in other countries? Table 7.2 compares several health outcomes for the countries that are members of the Organization for Economic Co-operation and Development (OECD), a group of 34 high-income countries. The table shows that the United States does relatively poorly with respect to infant mortality, while it does about average with respect to life expectancy. People in the United States are more likely to be obese than are people in other countries, which can lead to developing diabetes and other health problems.

The United States rates well in the availability of medical equipment that can be used in diagnosing and treating illness. Table 7.2 shows that the United States has nearly three times as many MRI units and over 50 percent more CT scanners than the average of European countries, although the United States has relatively fewer of these machines than does Japan. The United States also appears to do well in cancer treatment with a lower rate of cancer deaths and a relatively low mortality ratio from cancer. The mortality ratio measures the rate at which people die from cancer relative to the rate at which they are diagnosed with cancer. A low cancer mortality ratio indicates that the U.S. health care system does a relatively good job of reducing the death rate among people diagnosed with cancer.

MyEconLab Animation

Figure 7.3

Levels of Income per Person and Spending per Person on Health Care

The United States is well above the line showing the average relationship between income per person and health care spending per person, which indicates that the United States spends more on health care per person than do other countries, even taking into account the relatively high levels of income in the United States.

Note: Income per person is measured as real GDP per person.

Source: Organization for Economic Co-operation and Development, *OECD Health Data 2014*, November 2014.

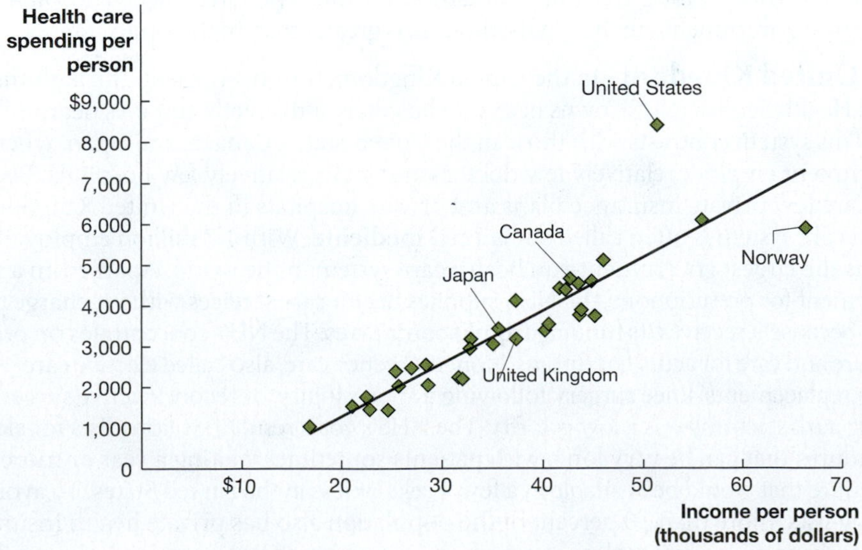

Table 7.2 Health Outcomes in High-Income Countries

Health Care Outcome	United States	Canada	Japan	United Kingdom	OECD Average
Life Expectancy					
Life expectancy at birth	79.6 years	81.0 years	82.7 years	81.1 years	80.1 years
Male life expectancy at age 65	17.8 years	18.8 years	18.9 years	18.5 years	17.6 years
Female life expectancy at age 65	20.4 years	21.7 years	23.8 years	20.9 years	20.9 years
Infant mortality (deaths per 1,000 live births)	6.1	4.9	2.3	4.3	4.1
Health Problems					
Obesity (percentage of the population with BMI > 30)	33.7%	28.0%	3.3%	28.1%	23.4%
Diagnostic Equipment					
MRI units per 1,000,000 population	34.5	8.8	46.9	6.8	12.3
CT scanners per 1,000,000 population	40.9	14.6	101.3	8.7	23.1
Cancer					
Deaths from cancer per 100,000 population	105.8	103.2	93.8	110.0	109.5
Risk of dying of cancer before age 75	11.2%	10.8%	9.3%	11.3%	11.5%
Mortality ratio for cancer	33.3%	34.9%	43.2%	40.3%	40.4%

Sources: Organization for Economic Co-operation and Development, *OECD Health Statistics*, most recent data available, typically 2012; World Health Organization, *Global Health Observatory Data Repository*, 2014; and World Health Organization, Agency for Research on Cancer, "Globocan 2012: Estimated Cancer Incidence, Mortality, and Prevalence Worldwide in 2012." For cancer data, the final column uses the average for European Union countries rather than for OECD countries.

How useful are cross-country comparisons of health outcomes in measuring the effectiveness of different health care systems? Health economists and other researchers disagree strongly about the answer to this question. Here are some factors that make cross-country comparisons in health outcomes difficult:

- **Data problems.** Countries do not always collect data on diseases and other health problems in the same way. So, there are not enough consistent data available to compare health outcomes for more than a few diseases.
- **Problems with measuring health care delivery.** The easiest outcomes to measure are deaths because a specific event has occurred. So, measures of life expectancy, infant mortality, and mortality rates from some diseases, such as cancer, are available across countries. But much of health care involves treatment for injuries, simple surgical procedures, writing of pharmaceutical prescriptions, and other activities for which outcomes are difficult to measure. For example, although the United Kingdom does well in many of the measures shown in Table 7.2, patients have long waiting times for elective surgical procedures that can be arranged much more quickly in some other countries, including the United States. Economists have difficulty measuring the cost to patients of these waiting times.
- **Problems with distinguishing health care effectiveness from lifestyle choices.** Health outcomes depend partly on the effectiveness of doctors and hospitals in delivering medical services. But they also depend on the choices of individuals. For example, in the United States, the high rates of obesity and hospitalizations for diabetes—which can be a complication of obesity—may be caused more by the decisions individuals make about diet and exercise than by the effectiveness of the U.S. health care system.
- **Problems with determining consumer preferences.** In most markets, we can assume that the quantities and prices we observe reflect the interactions of the

preferences of consumers (demand) with the costs to firms of producing goods and services (supply). Given their incomes and preferences, consumers compare the prices of different goods and services when making their buying decisions. The prices firms charge represent the costs of providing the good or service. In the market for health care, however, the government plays the dominant role in supplying the service in most countries other than the United States, so the cost of the service is not fully represented in its price, which in some countries is zero. Even in countries where consumers must pay for medical services, the prices they pay usually do not represent the cost of providing the service. In the United States, for instance, consumers with private health insurance typically pay only 10 to 20 percent of the price as a copayment. For these reasons, it is difficult to determine whether some countries do a better job than others in providing health care services whose cost and effectiveness are consistent with consumer preferences.

MyEconLab Study Plan

MyEconLab Concept Check

7.3 Information Problems and Externalities in the Market for Health Care

LEARNING OBJECTIVE: Define information problems and externalities, and explain how they affect the market for health care.

Asymmetric information A situation in which one party to an economic transaction has less information than the other party.

The market for health care is significantly affected by the problem of **asymmetric information**, which occurs when one party to an economic transaction has less information than the other party. Understanding the concept of asymmetric information can help us analyze the actions of buyers and sellers of health care and health insurance and the actions of the government in the health care market. The consequences of asymmetric information may be easier to understand if we first consider its effect on the market for used automobiles, which is the market in which economists first began to carefully study this problem.

Adverse Selection and the Market for "Lemons"

Nobel Laureate George Akerlof of Georgetown University pointed out that the seller of a used car will always have more information on the true condition of the car than will potential buyers. For example, a car that has not had its oil changed regularly may have damage that even a trained mechanic may have difficulty detecting.

If potential buyers of used cars know that they will have difficulty distinguishing good used cars from bad used cars, or "lemons," they will take this into account in the prices they are willing to pay. Consider the following simple example: Suppose that half of the 2013 Volkswagen Jettas offered for sale have been well maintained and are good, reliable used cars. The other half have been poorly maintained and are lemons that will be unreliable. Suppose that potential buyers of 2013 Jettas would be willing to pay $10,000 for a reliable one but only $5,000 for an unreliable one. The sellers know how well they have maintained their cars and whether they are reliable, but the buyers do not have this information and so have no way of distinguishing the reliable used cars from the unreliable ones.

In this situation, buyers will generally offer a price somewhere between the price they would be willing to pay for a good car and the price they would be willing to pay for a lemon. With a 50–50 chance of buying a good car or a lemon, buyers might offer $7,500, which is halfway between the price they would pay if they knew for certain the car was a good one and the price they would pay if they knew it was a lemon.

Unfortunately for used car buyers, a major glitch arises at this point. From the buyers' perspective, given that they don't know whether any particular car offered for sale is a good car or a lemon, an offer of $7,500 seems reasonable. But the sellers do know whether the cars they are offering are good cars or lemons. To a seller of a good car, an offer of $7,500 is $2,500 below the true value of the car, and the seller will be reluctant to sell. But to a seller of a lemon, an offer of $7,500 is $2,500 above the true value of the car, and the seller will be quite happy to sell. As sellers of lemons take advantage of knowing more about the cars they are selling than buyers do, buyers in the used car market will fall victim to **adverse selection**: Most used cars offered for sale will be lemons. In other words, because of asymmetric information, the market has selected adversely the cars that will be offered for sale. Notice as well that the problem of adverse selection reduces the total quantity of used cars bought and sold in the market because few good cars are offered for sale. MyEconLab Concept Check

Adverse selection The situation in which one party to a transaction takes advantage of knowing more than the other party to the transaction.

Asymmetric Information in the Market for Health Insurance

Asymmetric information problems are particularly severe in the markets for all types of insurance, including health insurance. To understand this point, first consider how insurance works. Insurance companies provide the service of *risk pooling* when they sell policies to households. For example, if you own a $150,000 house but do not have a fire insurance policy, a fire that destroys your house can be a financial catastrophe. But an insurance company can pool the financial risk of your house burning down by selling fire insurance policies to you and thousands of other homeowners. Homeowners are willing to accept the certain cost represented by the premium they pay for insurance in return for eliminating the uncertain—but potentially very large—cost should their house burn down.

Notice that for the insurance company to cover all of its costs, the total amount it receives in premiums must be greater than the amount it pays out in claims to policyholders. To survive, insurance companies have to predict accurately the amount they are likely to pay out to policyholders. For instance, if an insurance company predicts that the houses of only 2 percent of policyholders will burn down during a year when 5 percent of houses actually burn down, the company will suffer losses. However, if the company predicts that 8 percent of houses will burn down when only 5 percent actually do, the company will have charged premiums that are too high. A company that charges premiums that are too high will lose customers to other companies and may eventually be driven out of business.

Adverse Selection in the Market for Health Insurance One obstacle to health insurance companies accurately predicting the number of claims policyholders will make is that buyers of health insurance policies always know more about the state of their health—and, therefore, how likely they are to submit medical bills for payment—than will the insurance companies. In other words, insurance companies face an adverse selection problem because sick people are more likely to want health insurance than are healthy people. If insurance companies have trouble determining who is healthy and who is sick, they are likely to sell policies to more sick people than they had expected, with the result that the premiums they charge will be too low to cover their costs.

An insurance company faces a financial problem if the premiums it is charging are too low to cover the costs of the claims being submitted. The company might try to increase the premiums it charges, but this may make the adverse selection problem worse. If premiums rise, then younger, healthier people who rarely visit the doctor may respond to the increase in premiums by dropping their insurance. The higher premiums have made the adverse selection problem worse for the insurance company because it will have fewer healthy policyholders than it had before the premium increase. The situation is similar to that facing a used car buyer who knows that adverse selection is a problem in the used car market and decides to compensate for it by lowering the price he is willing to pay for a car. The lower price will reduce the number of sellers of good cars willing to sell to him, making his adverse selection problem worse.

One way to deal with the problem of adverse selection is for the government to require every person to buy insurance. Most states require all drivers to buy automobile insurance so that both high-risk and low-risk drivers will carry insurance. The Patient Protection and Affordable Care Act (ACA) passed in 2010 requires that residents of the United States must buy health insurance or pay a fine. This provision of the law is known as the *individual mandate* and has been controversial. We discuss it further in Section 7.4.

Moral hazard The actions people take after they have entered into a transaction that make the other party to the transaction worse off.

Moral Hazard in the Market for Health Insurance The insurance market is subject to a second consequence of asymmetric information. **Moral hazard** refers to actions people take after they have entered into a transaction that make the other party to the transaction worse off. Moral hazard in the insurance market occurs when people change their behavior after becoming insured. For example, once a firm has taken out a fire insurance policy on a warehouse, its managers might be reluctant to install an expensive sprinkler system. Similarly, someone with health insurance may visit the doctor for treatment of a cold or other minor illness, which he would not do if he lacked insurance. Or someone with health insurance might engage in risky activities, such as riding a motorcycle, which she would not do if she lacked insurance.

One way to think about the basic moral hazard problem with insurance is to note that normally there are two parties to an economic transaction: the buyer and the seller. The insurance company becomes a third party to the purchase of medical services because the insurance company, rather than the patient, pays for some or all of the service. For this reason, economists refer to traditional health insurance as a *third-party payer* system. Because of this system, consumers of health care do not pay a price that reflects the full cost of providing the service. This lower price leads consumers to use more health care than they otherwise would.

Don't Let This Happen to You

Don't Confuse Adverse Selection with Moral Hazard

The two key consequences of asymmetric information are adverse selection and moral hazard. It is easy to mix up these concepts. One way to keep the concepts straight is to remember that adverse selection refers to what happens at the time of entering into a transaction. An example would be an insurance company selling a life insurance policy to a terminally ill person because the company lacks full information on the person's health. Moral hazard refers to what happens after entering into a transaction, such as a nonsmoker buying a life insurance policy and then starting to smoke four packs of cigarettes a day. (It may help to remember that *a* comes before *m* alphabetically, just as *a*dverse selection comes before *m*oral hazard.)

MyEconLab Study Plan

Your Turn: Test your understanding by doing related problems 3.9 and 3.10 on page 246 at the end of this chapter.

Third-party payer health insurance can also lead to another consequence of moral hazard, known as the *principal–agent problem*, because doctors may be led to take actions that are not necessarily in the best interests of their patients, such as increasing their incomes by prescribing unnecessary tests or other treatments for which the doctors receive payment. The **principal–agent problem** results from agents—in this case, doctors—pursuing their own interests rather than the interests of the principals—in this case, patients—who hired them. If patients had to pay the full price of lab tests, MRI scans, and other procedures, they would be more likely to question whether the procedures were really necessary. Because health insurance pays most of the bill for these procedures, patients are more likely to accept them. Note that the fee-for-service aspect of most health insurance in the United States can make the principal–agent problem worse because doctors and hospitals are paid for each service performed, whether or not the service was necessary or effective.

Principal–agent problem A problem caused by agents pursuing their own interests rather than the interests of the principals who hired them.

The number of medical procedures performed in the United States has been continually increasing. Many doctors argue that the increasing number of medical procedures is not the result of third-party payer health insurance. Instead, the increase is due to the improved effectiveness of the procedures in diagnosing illness and the tendency of some doctors to practice "defensive medicine" because they fear that if they fail to correctly diagnose an illness, a patient may file a malpractice lawsuit against them.

How Insurance Companies Deal with Adverse Selection and Moral Hazard Insurance companies can take steps to reduce adverse selection and moral hazard problems. For example, insurance companies can use deductibles and coinsurance (or copayments) to reduce moral hazard. A deductible requires the policyholder to pay a certain dollar amount before the insurance begins paying claims. With coinsurance, the insurance company pays only a percentage of any claim. Suppose you have a health insurance policy with a $200 deductible and 20 percent coinsurance, and you receive a medical bill for $1,000. You must pay the first $200 of the bill and 20 percent of the remaining $800. Deductibles and coinsurance make the policies less attractive to people who intend to file many claims, thereby reducing the adverse selection problem. Deductibles and coinsurance also provide policyholders with an incentive to avoid filing claims, thereby reducing the moral hazard problem. Notice, though, that deductibles and coinsurance reduce, but do not eliminate, adverse selection and moral hazard. People who anticipate having large medical bills will still have a greater incentive than healthy people to buy insurance, and people with health insurance are still more likely to visit the doctor even for a minor illness than are people without health insurance.

To reduce the problem of adverse selection, someone applying for an individual health insurance policy is usually required to submit his or her medical records to the insurance company. Insurance companies often also carry out their own medical examinations. Prior to the passage of the ACA in 2010, companies typically limited coverage of *preexisting conditions,* which are medical problems, such as heart disease or cancer, that the buyer already has before purchasing insurance. Health insurance companies typically would not cover preexisting conditions for a year or two after a consumer purchased insurance, and sometimes they would permanently decline to cover these conditions. Limits on coverage of preexisting conditions were very common in health insurance policies for individuals but were also sometimes included in *group policies,* such as the policy T. Cain Grocery purchased to cover its employees, as described in the chapter opener. Exclusions and limits on coverage of preexisting conditions have been controversial.

Critics argue that by excluding coverage of preexisting conditions, insurance companies were forcing people with serious illnesses to pay the entire amount of what might be very large medical bills or to go without medical care. Some people with chronic or terminal illnesses found it impossible to buy an individual health insurance policy. The insurance companies argued that if they did not exclude coverage of preexisting conditions, they might have been unable to offer any health insurance policies or might have been forced to charge premiums that were so high as to cause relatively healthy people to not renew their policies, which would have made adverse selection problems worse. To some extent, the debate over coverage of preexisting conditions is a normative one. Ordinarily, in a market system, people who cannot afford a good or service must do without it. However, many people do not want others to be without health insurance because they cannot afford it. As we will discuss in the next section, Congress included significant restrictions on the ability of insurance companies to limit coverage of preexisting conditions when it passed the ACA. MyEconLab Concept Check

Externalities in the Market for Health Care

For most goods and services, we assume that the consumer receives all the benefits from consuming the good and that the firm producing the good bears all of the costs of production. Some goods or services, though, involve an *externality,* which is a benefit or cost that affects someone who is not directly involved in the production or consumption of a good or service. For example, if a utility burns coal to produce electricity, the result will be air pollution, which causes a *negative externality* because people with asthma or other breathing problems may bear a cost even though they were not involved in buying or selling the electricity that caused the pollution. College education may result in a *positive externality* because college-educated people are less likely to commit crimes and, by being better-informed voters, more likely to contribute to better government policies. So, although you receive most of the benefits of your college education, other people also receive some of the benefits.

Externalities interfere with the economic efficiency of a market equilibrium. A competitive market achieves economic efficiency by maximizing the sum of consumer surplus and producer surplus (see Chapter 4, Section 4.1). But when there is a negative externality in production, as with air pollution, the market will produce more than the efficient quantity. When there is a positive externality in consumption, as with college educations, the market will produce less than the efficient quantity. (A more complete discussion of externalities appears in Chapter 5, "Externalities, Environmental Policy, and Public Goods.")

Many economists believe several aspects of health care involve externalities. For example, anyone vaccinated against a communicable disease not only protects herself or himself but also reduces the chances that people who have not been vaccinated will contract the disease. The positive externality from vaccinations causes a difference between the *private benefit* from being vaccinated and the *social benefit*. The *private benefit* is the benefit received by the consumer of a good or service. The *social benefit* is the total benefit from consuming a good or service, and it is equal to the private benefit plus any external benefit, such as the benefit to others from a reduced chance of getting a disease for which you have been vaccinated. Because of the positive externality, the social benefit of vaccinations is greater than the private benefit.

Figure 7.4 shows the market for vaccinations. If people receiving vaccinations could capture all the benefits, the demand curve would be D_2, which represents the marginal social benefit. The actual demand curve is D_1, however, which represents only the marginal private benefit received by people getting vaccinations. The efficient equilibrium would occur at price $P_{Efficient}$ and quantity $Q_{Efficient}$. At this equilibrium, economic surplus is maximized (see Chapter 4). The market equilibrium, at price P_{Market} and quantity Q_{Market}, will not be efficient because the demand curve is above the supply curve for production of the vaccinations between Q_{Market} and $Q_{Efficient}$. That is, the marginal benefit—including the external benefit—for producing these vaccinations is greater than the marginal cost. As a result, there is a deadweight loss equal to the area of the yellow triangle. Because of the positive externality, economic efficiency would be improved if more people were vaccinated.

Figure 7.4 assumes that the market for vaccinations is like the market for goods such as hamburgers, with consumers paying the full price of the vaccinations. In practice, people with health insurance pay a reduced price for vaccinations, and the government often provides further subsidies to the firms that produce vaccines. One reason for the government subsidies is to overcome the effects of the positive externality.

Externalities are important in health care markets, though economists and policymakers continue to debate the extent to which they require significant government involvement in health care. MyEconLab Concept Check

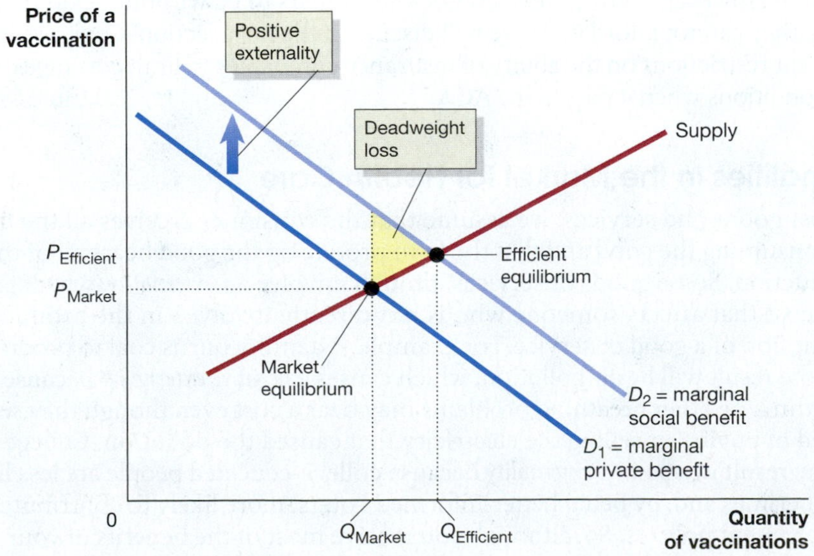

MyEconLab

Figure 7.4

The Effect of a Positive Externality on the Market for Vaccinations

People who do not get vaccinated still benefit from other people being vaccinated. As a result, the marginal social benefit from vaccinations is greater than the marginal private benefit to people being vaccinated. Because only the marginal private benefit is represented in the market demand curve D_1, the quantity of vaccinations produced, Q_{Market}, is too low. If the market demand curve were D_2 instead of D_1, the level of vaccinations would be $Q_{Efficient}$, which is the efficient level. At the market equilibrium of Q_{Market}, there is a deadweight loss equal to the area of the yellow triangle.

Should the Government Run the Health Care System?

Some members of Congress have proposed expanding the federal government's role in health care by adopting a system similar to the single-payer system used in Canada, under which the government would provide health care to all residents of the United States. What role the federal government should play in health care is a controversial public policy issue.

Economists categorize goods on the basis of whether they are *rival* and *excludable*. Rivalry occurs when one person consuming a unit of a good means no one else can consume it. If you consume a burrito from Chipotle Mexican Grill, for example, no one else can consume it. Excludability means that anyone who does not pay for a good cannot consume it. If you don't pay for a burrito, for example, Chipotle can exclude you from consuming it. A *public good* is both nonrival and nonexcludable. Public goods are often, although not always, supplied by a government rather than by private firms. The classic example of a public good is national defense. Your consuming national defense does not interfere with your neighbor consuming it, so consumption is nonrival. You also cannot be excluded from consuming it, whether you pay for it or not. No private firm would be willing to supply national defense because everyone can consume national defense without paying for it.

Is health care a public good that government should supply—or, at least, pay for? Is it a private good, like furniture, clothing, or computers, that private firms should supply and consumers should pay for without government aid? Should private firms supply most health care, subject to some government regulation? Economists differ in their answers to these questions because the delivery of health care involves a number of complex issues, but we can consider briefly some of the most important points. Because public goods must be both nonrival and nonexcludable, health care does not qualify as a public good under the usual definition. More than one person cannot simultaneously "consume" the same surgical operation performed by a particular doctor in a particular hospital. And someone who will not pay for an operation can be excluded from consuming it. (Most states require hospitals to treat patients who are too poor to pay for treatment, and many doctors will treat poor people at a reduced price. But health care does not fit the definition of a public good because there is nothing about health care that keeps people who do not pay for it from being excluded from consuming.)

However, there are aspects of the delivery of health care that have convinced some economists that government intervention is justified. For example, consuming certain types of health care generates positive externalities. Being vaccinated against a communicable disease, such as influenza or meningitis, reduces not only the chance that the person vaccinated will catch the disease but also the probability that an epidemic of the disease will occur. Therefore, the market may supply an inefficiently small quantity of vaccinations unless vaccinations receive a government subsidy.

Information problems can also be important in the market for private health insurance. Consumers who buy health insurance often know much more about the state of their health than do the companies selling health insurance. This information problem may raise costs to insurance companies when the pool of people being insured is small, making insurance companies less willing to offer health insurance to consumers the companies suspect may file too many claims. Economists debate how important information problems are in health care markets and whether government intervention is required to reduce them.

Many economists believe that market-based solutions are the best approach to improving the health care system. As we saw in Table 7.2 on page 225, the United States has a mixed record on health outcomes. The United States is, however, a world leader in innovation in medical technology and prescription drugs. The market-oriented approach to reforming health care starts with the goal of improving health care outcomes while preserving incentives for U.S. firms to continue with innovations in medical screening equipment, surgical procedures, and prescription drugs. Presently, markets are delivering inaccurate signals to consumers because when buying health care, unlike when buying most other goods and services, consumers pay a price well below the true cost of providing the service. Under current tax laws, people do not pay taxes on health insurance benefits they receive from their employers, and this benefit encourages them to want generous coverage that reduces incentives to control costs. As we will discuss later in the chapter, market-based approaches to health care reform attempt to address these issues.

It remains an open question whether the U.S. health care system will continue to move toward greater government intervention, which is the approach adopted in most other countries, or whether market-based reforms will be implemented. Because health care is so important to consumers and because health care is an increasingly large part of the U.S. economy, the role of the government in the health care system is likely to be the subject of intense debate for some time to come. MyEconLab Concept Check

7.4 The Debate over Health Care Policy in the United States

LEARNING OBJECTIVE: Explain the major issues involved in the debate over health care policy in the United States.

Shortly after taking office in January 2009, President Barack Obama proposed far-reaching changes in the U.S. health care system. The result was the Patient Protection and Affordable Care Act (ACA), which Congress passed in March 2010. The act was controversial, with every Republican member of Congress and 34 Democratic members voting against it. Since passage of the ACA, economists have vigorously debated its effects on health care and the economy. Next we explore the issue of rising health care costs, which played an important role in the health care debate, before discussing the details of the ACA and the debate over the legislation's effect.

The Rising Cost of Health Care

Figure 7.5 illustrates a key fact underlying the debate over health care policy in the United States: Health care's share of gross domestic product (GDP), which is the total value of output in the economy, is increasing. Panel (a) shows that spending on health care was less than 6 percent of GDP in 1965 but had risen to nearly 18 percent in 2015 and is projected to continue rising in future years. In other words, an increasing percentage of total production in the United States is being devoted to health care. Panel (b) shows increases in health care spending per person in the United States and 10 other high-income countries. Spending on health care has grown faster in the United States than in other countries.

Does it matter that spending on health care is an increasing share of total spending and output in the U.S. economy? The shares of different products in total spending change frequently. For instance, in the United States, the shares of spending on smartphones or 4K televisions were much greater in 2015 than in 2010. Spending on food as a share of total spending has been declining for decades. Economists interpret these changes as reflecting in part consumers' preferences: Consumers choose to spend relatively more of their incomes on smartphones and relatively less on food. As we have seen, though, most people pay for health care by relying on third-party payers, such as employer-provided health insurance or government-provided Medicare or Medicaid. Out-of-pocket spending, spending on health care that consumers pay out of their own incomes rather than through health insurance, has been declining.

Figure 7.6 shows that out-of-pocket spending on health care as a percentage of all spending on health care has fallen steadily since 1960. In 1960, 48 percent of all health care spending was out of pocket, while today only about 12 percent is. As a result, in recent years, consumers of health care have been directly paying for only a small fraction of the true cost of providing health care, with third-party payers picking up the remainder. As average incomes rise, consumers might be expected to spend a rising share of the increase on health care. But because consumers do not pay the full cost of increases in health care spending, they may not be willing to buy as much health care as they currently receive if they had to pay the full price.

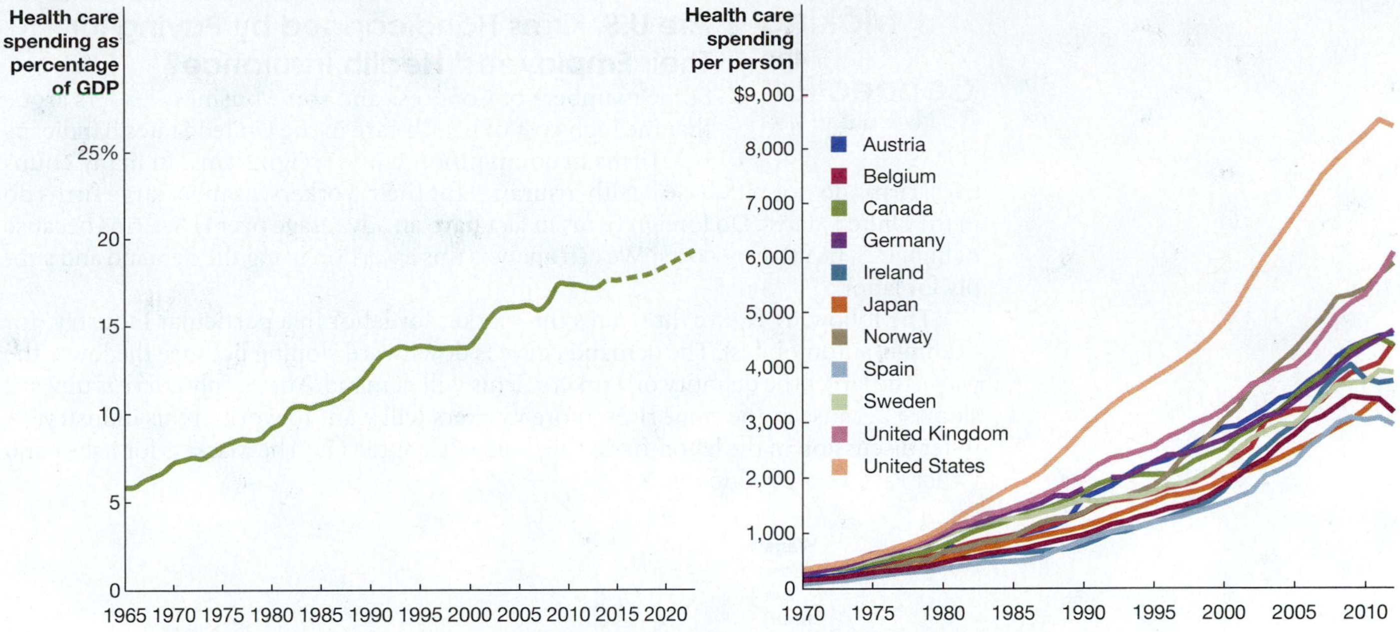

(a) Spending on health care in the United States as a percentage of GDP, 1965–2023

(b) Health care spending per person, 1970–2012

MyEconLab Real-time data

Figure 7.5 Spending on Health Care around the World

Panel (a) shows that health care spending has been a rising percentage of GDP in the United States. Health care spending rose from less than 6 percent of GDP in 1965 to nearly 18 percent in 2015, and it is projected to rise to further in future years. (The projected increases are shown by the dotted line.) Panel (b) shows that health care spending per person has been growing faster in the United States than in other high-income countries.

Sources: For panel (a): U.S. Department of Health and Human Services, Centers for Medicare & Medicaid Services; for panel (b): Organization for Economic Co-operation and Development, *OECD Health Data 2014*, November 2014.

Because the federal and state governments in the United States pay for just over half of health care spending through Medicare, Medicaid, and other programs, increases in health care spending can cause problems for government budgets. The Medicare and Medicaid programs began in 1965. By 2015, spending on these programs had grown to 6 percent of GDP. That percentage is expected to double over the next 40 years unless health care costs begin to grow at a slower rate. Congress and the president have been struggling to find ways to pay for the projected increases in Medicare and Medicaid without severely cutting other federal spending or sharply raising taxes. MyEconLab Concept Check

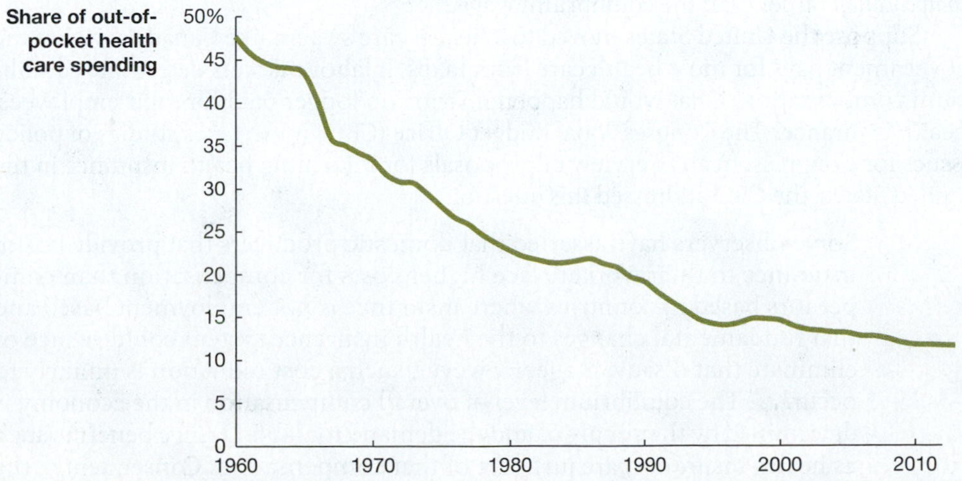

MyEconLab Animation

Figure 7.6

The Declining Share of U.S. Out-of-Pocket Health Care Spending

Out-of-pocket spending on health care has declined sharply as a fraction of all health care spending, while the fraction of spending accounted for by third-party payers, such as firms or the government, has increased.

Source: U.S. Department of Health and Human Services, Centers for Medicare & Medicaid Services.

Making the Connection

MyEconLab Video

Are U.S. Firms Handicapped by Paying for Their Employees' Health Insurance?

Some members of Congress and some business leaders argue that the high cost of health care in the United States handicaps U.S. firms in competition with foreign firms. In many countries, firms do not purchase health insurance for their workers, as most large firms do in the United States. Do foreign firms in fact have an advantage over U.S. firms because of high U.S. health care costs? We can analyze this assertion using the demand and supply for labor.

The following figure illustrates the market for labor in a particular industry (for example, automobiles). The demand curve is downward sloping because the lower the wage, the larger the quantity of workers firms will demand. The supply curve is upward sloping because as the wage rises, more workers will want to work in this industry. (A fuller discussion of the labor market appears in Chapter 17, "The Markets for Labor and Other Factors of Production.")

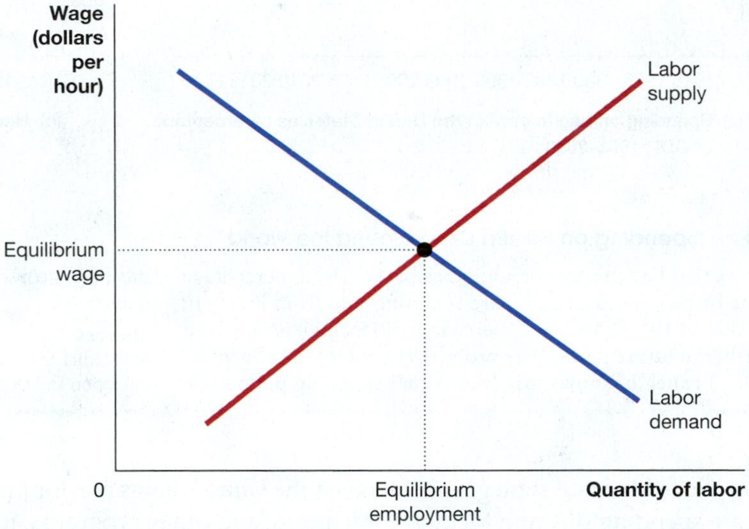

Equilibrium in this labor market occurs where the quantity of labor demanded equals the quantity of labor supplied. On the vertical axis, we measure the wage, so the graph shows the determination of the equilibrium wage. When choosing among jobs, however, workers don't just consider the wages firms offer; they also take into account *fringe benefits,* such as employer contributions to retirement accounts or employer-provided health insurance. It would therefore be more accurate to describe the intersection of the labor demand and labor supply curves as determining *the equilibrium compensation* rather than the equilibrium wage.

Suppose the United States moved to a health care system like Canada's, where the government pays for most health care from taxes. If labor markets determine equilibrium compensation, what would happen if firms no longer paid for their employees' health insurance? The Congressional Budget Office (CBO) undertakes studies of policy issues for Congress. In an overview of proposals for reforming health insurance in the United States, the CBO addressed this question:

> Some observers have asserted that domestic producers that provide health insurance to their workers face higher costs for compensation than competitors based in countries where insurance is not employment based and that fundamental changes to the health insurance system could reduce or eliminate that disadvantage. However, such a cost reduction is unlikely to occur. . . . The equilibrium level of overall compensation in the economy is determined by the supply of and the demand for labor. Fringe benefits (such as health insurance) are just part of that compensation. Consequently, the

costs of fringe benefits are borne by workers largely in the form of lower cash wages than they would receive if no such benefits were provided by their employer. Replacing employment-based health care with a government-run system could reduce employers' payments for their workers' insurance, but the amount that they would have to pay in overall compensation would remain essentially unchanged.

To give an example, suppose a firm was paying its workers $50,000 in wages and paying $10,000 per worker for health insurance, thereby providing total compensation of $60,000. If the government began paying all health care expenses, it might appear that the firm's labor costs would drop by $10,000 per worker. But if the firm offered its employees only $50,000 in wages as their total compensation, many would leave to work for other firms. The firm would have to pay its employees an additional $10,000 in wages so that the total compensation it offered would be at the equilibrium level of $60,000 for the industry. In other words, basic demand and supply analysis indicates that having firms rather than the government provide health insurance to workers changes the *composition* of the compensation the firms pay but does not change its level.

Source: Congressional Budget Office, "Key Issues in Analyzing Major Health Insurance Proposals," December 2008, p. 167.

Your Turn: Test your understanding by doing related problem 4.11 on page 248 at the end of this chapter.

MyEconLab Study Plan

Explaining Increases in Health Care Spending

In this section, we briefly discuss some explanations for why health care's share of the U.S. economy has been continually increasing. We start by reviewing explanations that are sometimes offered by policymakers and journalists but that are unlikely to account for most of the increases in health care costs.

Factors That Do *Not* Explain Sustained Increases in Health Care Spending The two panels of Figure 7.5 on page 233 show that spending on health care has been growing faster than the economy as a whole for at least the past several decades. Explaining the rapid growth of health care spending requires identifying factors that have more than a one-time effect. For example, because the U.S. health care system relies on many independent hospitals, medical practices, and insurance companies, some observers argue that it generates more paperwork, duplication, and waste than systems in other countries. Even if this observation is correct, it cannot account for health care's rising share of GDP unless paperwork and waste are *increasing* year after year, which seems unlikely.

Unlike in most countries, it is relatively easy in the United States for patients who have been injured by medical errors to sue doctors and hospitals for damages. The Congressional Budget Office (CBO) estimates, though, that the payments to settle malpractice lawsuits plus the premiums doctors pay for malpractice insurance amount to less than 1 percent of health care costs. Other economists believe the CBO estimate is too low and that the costs of malpractice lawsuits, including the costs of unnecessary tests and procedures doctors order to avoid being sued, are as much as 7 percent of total health care costs. Still, these costs have not been significantly increasing over time.

Somewhere between 1 and 4 percent of health care costs are due to uninsured patients receiving treatments at hospital emergency rooms that could have been provided less expensively in doctors' offices. But once again, this cost has not been increasing rapidly enough to account for much of the increase in health care costs as a percentage of GDP.

"Cost Disease" in the Health Care Sector Some economists argue that health care suffers from a problem often encountered in service industries. In the sectors of the economy that produce goods, such as the manufacturing sector, *productivity*, or the amount of output each worker can produce in a given period, increases steadily. These increases in productivity occur because over time firms provide workers with more machinery and equipment, including computers, with which to work, and because technological progress results in improvements in machinery and equipment and in other parts of the production process. As workers produce more goods, firms are able to pay them higher wages. In service-producing industries, increasing output per worker is more difficult. In medicine, MRI units, CT scanners, and other medical technology have improved diagnosis and treatment, but most medicine still requires a face-to-face meeting between a doctor and a patient. As wages rise in industries in which productivity is increasing rapidly, service industries in which productivity is increasing less rapidly must match these wage increases or lose workers. Because increases in wages are not offset by increases in productivity in service industries, the cost to firms of supplying services increases.

William Baumol of New York University has labeled the tendency for low productivity in service industries to lead to higher costs in those industries as "the cost disease of the service sector." There is good reason to think that health care suffers from this cost disease because growth in labor productivity in health care has been less than half as fast as labor productivity growth in the economy as a whole. This slow growth in productivity can help explain why the cost of health care has been rising rapidly, thereby increasing health care's share of total spending and output.

The Aging of the Population and Advances in Medical Technology As people age, they increase their spending on health care. Firms continue to develop new prescription drugs and medical equipment that typically have higher costs than the drugs and equipment they replace. The aging of the U.S. population and the introduction of higher-cost drugs and medical equipment interact to drive up spending on the federal government's Medicare program and on health care generally. Many newly introduced drugs and diagnostic tools are used disproportionately by people over age 65. Partly as a result, health care spending on people over age 65 is six times greater than spending on people aged 18 to 24 and four times greater than on people aged 25 to 44. In 2015, more than 54 million people were enrolled in Medicare, and that number is expected to grow to 74 million by 2025. As we have seen, even in the absence of the development of new drugs and other medical technology, low rates of productivity in the health care sector could be expected to drive up costs. In fact, as Figure 7.7 illustrates, the CBO estimates that most of the increase in federal spending on Medicare and Medicaid benefits will be due to increases in the cost of providing health care rather than to the aging of the population. In the figure, "effect of excess cost growth" refers to the extent to which health care costs

MyEconLab Animation

Figure 7.7

Reasons for Rising Federal Spending on Medicare and Medicaid

Although the aging of the U.S. population will increase federal government spending on the Medicare and Medicaid programs, increases in the cost of providing health care will have a larger effect on government spending on these programs.

Source: U.S. Congressional Budget Office.

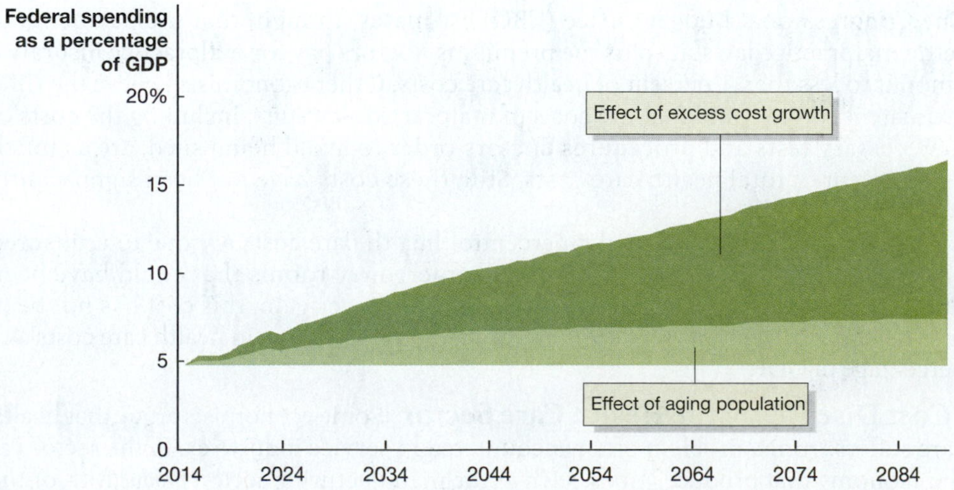

per person grow faster than GDP per person. An aging population and increases in the cost of providing health care are key reasons why health care spending is an increasing percentage of GDP.

Distorted Economic Incentives As we noted earlier, some part of the increase in health care spending over the years represents consumers choosing to allocate more of their incomes to health care as their incomes rise. But as we have also seen, consumers usually pay less than the true cost of medical treatment because a third party—typically an insurance company or the government—often pays most of the bill. For example, consumers who have health insurance provided by their employers usually pay only a small amount—perhaps $20—for a visit to a doctor's office, when the true cost of the visit might be $80 or $90. The result is that consumers demand a larger quantity of health care services than they would if they paid a price that better represented the cost of providing the services.

Figure 7.8 illustrates this situation. If consumers paid the full price of medical services, their demand would be D_1. The marginal benefit to consumers from medical services would equal the marginal cost of producing the services, and the equilibrium quantity would be at the efficient level $Q_{Efficient}$. However, because consumers pay only a fraction of the true cost of medical services, their demand increases to D_2. In this equilibrium, the quantity of medical services produced increases to Q_{Market}, which is beyond the efficient level. The marginal cost of producing these additional units is greater than the marginal benefit consumers receive from them. As a result, there is a deadweight loss equal to the area of the yellow triangle. Doctors and other suppliers of medical services receive a price, P_{Market}, that is well above the price, P, paid by consumers. Note that the effect of a third-party payer is common to nearly all health care systems, whether the government provides health care directly, as is done in the United Kingdom, or whether many people have private health insurance, as in the United States.

In important ways, health insurance is different from other types of insurance. As we discussed earlier, the basic idea of insurance is that the financial risk of an unpredictable, high-cost event—a house fire or a serious car accident—is pooled among the many consumers who buy insurance. Health insurance, though, also typically covers many planned expenses, such as routine health checkups, annual physicals, and other low-cost events, such as treatment for minor illnesses. By disguising the true cost of these routine expenses, health insurance encourages overuse of health care services.

We discuss the role of economic incentives in health care further in the next section.

MyEconLab Concept Check

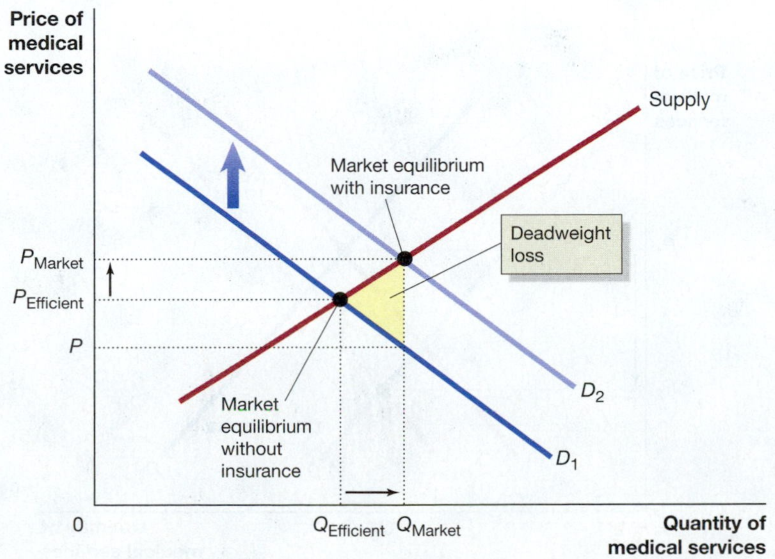

MyEconLab Animation

Figure 7.8

The Effect of the Third-Party Payer System on the Demand for Medical Services

If consumers paid the full price of medical services, their demand would be D_1, and the equilibrium quantity would be at the efficient level $Q_{Efficient}$. Because consumers pay only a fraction of the true cost of medical services, their demand is D_2, and the equilibrium quantity of medical services produced increases to Q_{Market}, which is beyond the efficient level. There is a deadweight loss equal to the yellow triangle. Doctors and other suppliers of medical services receive a price, P_{Market}, that is well above the price, P, paid by consumers.

Solved Problem 7.4

MyEconLab Interactive Animation

Recent Trends in Health Care

An article in the *New York Times* about recent trends in health care mentioned several developments:

1. An increase in the size of deductibles in employer-provided health care plans. For instance, the health plan at T. Cain Grocery supermarket chain mentioned in the chapter opener changed from having a premium of $950 per month and a yearly deductible of $500 to having a premium of $400 per month and a yearly deductible of $4,500.
2. An increase in the availability of lower-cost generic drugs.
3. A decline in patients being readmitted to hospitals after the Patient Protection and Affordable Care Act (ACA) imposed penalties on hospitals that readmit too many patients.

a. Use a graph of the market for medical services to show the effect of these trends. Be sure to explain any shifts in the demand curve or supply curve.

b. Assuming that these are the only changes happening in the market for medical services, can we be certain whether they will result in an increase or decrease in the equilibrium price of medical services? In the equilibrium quantity of medical services? Briefly explain.

Solving the Problem

Step 1: Review the chapter material. This problem is about explaining changes in health care spending, so you may want to review the section "Explaining Increases in Health Care Spending," which begins on page 235.

Step 2: Answer part (a) by drawing a graph of the market for medical services that shows the effect of the three trends and by explaining shifts in the curves. The first trend—higher deductibles—reduces moral hazard and adverse selection problems by increasing the quantity of medical services that employees purchase out-of-pocket. Employees are likely to visits doctors less frequently for minor illnesses such as colds. So, the demand curve for medical services will shift to the left. The second trend—greater availability of lower-cost drugs—reduces the cost of providing this type of medical service, which will shift the supply curve for medical services to the right. The third trend—a decline in the number of patients being readmitted to hospitals—should reduce the cost of hospitalizations because more patients are being successfully treated in a single stay. This trend will also cause the supply curve for medical services to shift to the right.

Your graph should look like the one below.

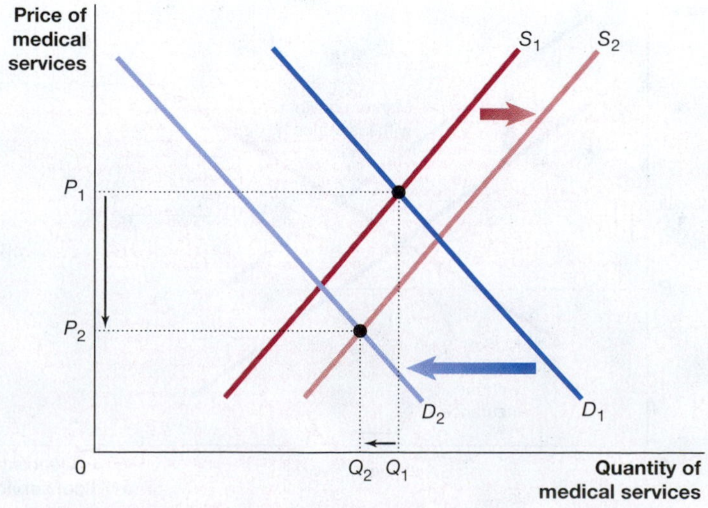

Step 3: Answer part (b) by explaining whether these trends will increase or decrease the equilibrium price and quantity of medical services. The graph in part (a) shows both the equilibrium price and the equilibrium quantity declining. We can be certain that the equilibrium price will decline because the shift of the demand curve to the left and the shift of the supply curve to the right both cause the equilibrium price to decline. However, we can't be certain that the equilibrium quantity will decline because the effect of the supply curve shifting to the right is to make the equilibrium quantity *increase*. Whether the equilibrium quantity declines depends on whether demand shifts more or less than supply shifts. Although two of the trends listed affect supply and only one affects demand, we do not know the size of the shift that results from any of the trends, so we can't tell with certainty what the effect will be on the equilibrium quantity.

Extra Credit: The cost of medical care has continued to increase. In 2015, however, economists were analyzing the reasons for a slowdown in the *rate* of that increase. The trends mentioned in this problem were among the likely factors. The quantity of medical services continued to increase, at least partly as a result of the effects of the Affordable Care Act. The act provides subsidies to buy health insurance for people whose incomes fall below a certain level and has expanded the Medicaid system, thereby increasing the demand for health care among low-income people.

Source: Margot Sanger-Katz, "Has the Law Contributed to a Slowdown in Health Care Spending?" *New York Times*, October 26, 2014.

Your Turn: For more practice, do related problems 4.12 on page 248 at the end of this chapter.

MyEconLab Study Plan

The Continuing Debate over Health Care Policy

As we have seen, the United States has been unusual among high-income countries in relying on private health insurance, usually purchased through employers or the new health insurance marketplaces, to provide health care coverage to the majority of the population. Most other high-income countries either provide health care directly, as the United Kingdom does, through government-owned hospitals and government-employed doctors, or provide health insurance to all residents, as Canada does, without directly employing doctors or owning hospitals. There have been several attempts to reorganize the U.S. health care system to make it more like the systems in other countries. In 1945, President Harry Truman proposed a plan for *national health insurance* under which anyone could purchase health insurance from the federal government. The health insurance would have covered treatment received from doctors and hospitals that agreed to enroll in the system. Congress declined to enact the plan. In 1993, President Bill Clinton proposed a health care plan intended to provide universal coverage. While somewhat complex, the plan was based on requiring most businesses to provide health insurance to their employees and new government-sponsored health alliances that would ensure coverage for anyone who otherwise would not have health insurance. After a prolonged political debate, Congress chose not to enact President Clinton's plan.

The Patient Protection and Affordable Care Act

In 2009, President Barack Obama proposed health care legislation that after much debate and significant changes was signed into law as the **Patient Protection and Affordable Care Act (ACA)** in March 2010. The act was long and complex, taking up over 20,000 pages and touching nearly every aspect of health care in the United States. Here is a summary of only the main provisions of the act:

Patient Protection and Affordable Care Act (ACA) Health care reform legislation passed by Congress and signed by President Barack Obama in 2010.

- **Individual mandate.** The act requires that, with limited exceptions, every resident of the United States have health insurance that meets certain basic requirements. Individuals who do not acquire health insurance are subject to a fine. In 2016 the fine was $695 or 2.5 percent of income, whichever was greater. (The fine will rise with inflation in future years). For example, in 2016 an adult with an income of $40,000 per year paid a fine of $1,000 if he or she did not buy health insurance.

- **State health insurance marketplaces.** Each state must establish a marketplace called an Affordable Insurance Exchange. Separate marketplaces were established for individuals and small businesses with fewer than 50 employees. The marketplaces offer health insurance policies that meet certain specified requirements. Although the marketplaces were intended to be run by a state government agency or a nonprofit firm, a number of states decided to allow the federal government to run the marketplace in their state. Private insurance companies compete by offering policies on the marketplaces to individuals and small businesses. Low-income individuals and small businesses with 25 or fewer employees are eligible for tax credits to offset the costs of buying health insurance. The purpose of the marketplaces is to allow greater risk pooling and lower administrative costs than had existed in the market for health insurance policies sold to individuals or small businesses. If successful, greater risk pooling and lower administrative costs will make it possible for individuals and small businesses to buy polices with lower premiums than had been available.
- **Employer mandate.** Every firm with more than 200 full-time employees must offer health insurance to its employees and must automatically enroll them in the plan. Firms with 50 or more full-time employees must offer health insurance or pay a fee of $3,000 to the federal government for every employee who receives a tax credit from the federal government for obtaining health insurance through a health insurance marketplace. A worker is a full-time employee if he or she works at least 30 hours per week.
- **Regulation of health insurance.** Insurance companies are required to participate in a high-risk pool that will insure individuals with preexisting medical conditions who have been unable to buy health insurance for at least six months. All individual and group policies must provide coverage for dependent children up to age 26. Lifetime dollar maximums on coverage are prohibited. Limits are also placed on the size of deductibles and on the waiting period before coverage becomes effective.
- **Changes to Medicare and Medicaid.** Eligibility for Medicaid was originally expanded to persons with incomes up to 138 percent of the federal poverty line, although a 2012 Supreme Court decision resulted in the states being allowed to opt out of this requirement. In an attempt to control increases in health care costs, the Independent Payment Advisory Board (IPAB) was established and given the power to reduce Medicare payments for prescription drugs and the use of diagnostic equipment and other technology if Medicare spending exceeds certain levels. Some Medicare reimbursements to hospitals and doctors were reduced.
- **Taxes.** Several new taxes help fund the program. Workers earning more than $200,000 pay higher Medicare payroll taxes, and people who earn more than $200,000 pay a new 3.8 percent tax on their investment income. Beginning in 2018, a tax is scheduled to be imposed on employer-provided health insurance plans that have a value above $10,200 for an individual or $27,500 for a family—so-called Cadillac plans. Pharmaceutical firms, health insurance firms, and firms producing medical devices also pay new taxes.

The ACA is scheduled to be fully implemented by 2019, at which point more than 30 million additional individuals are expected to have health care coverage. The CBO estimates that the law will increase federal government spending by about $2.0 trillion over the period 2016 to 2025. Increases in taxes and fees will reduce the net increase in federal spending resulting from the act to about $1.4 trillion.

The Debate over the ACA Any law as far-reaching and complex as the ACA is bound to draw criticism. The congressional debate over the law was highly partisan, with every Republican ultimately voting against it and most Democrats voting in favor of it. Critics of the act can be divided into two broad groups: those who argue that health care reform should involve a greater movement toward a system similar to the British, Canadian, and Japanese systems and those who argue that health care reform should include more market-based changes.

As we discussed in the previous section, some economists and policymakers believe that information problems and externalities in the market for health care are sufficiently large that the government should either provide health care directly through government-owned hospitals and government-employed doctors or pay for health care through national health insurance, sometimes called a *single-payer system*. Although the ACA significantly increased the federal government's involvement in the health care system, it stopped short of the degree of government involvement that exists in Canada, Japan, or the United Kingdom. Those in favor of moving toward greater government involvement typically argue that doing so would reduce the paperwork and waste caused by the current system. They argue that the current Medicare system—which is essentially a single-payer system for people over age 65—has proved to have lower administrative costs than have private health insurance companies. Supporters of greater government involvement in the health care system have also argued that the Canadian and British systems have had lower levels of health care spending per person and lower rates of increase in total health care spending, while providing good health outcomes.

Market-based reforms involve changing the market for health care so that it becomes more like the markets for other goods and services. As in other markets, the prices consumers pay and suppliers receive would do a better job of conveying information on consumer demand and supplier costs. The expectation is that increased competition among doctors, hospitals, pharmaceutical companies, and other providers of health care would reduce costs and increase economic efficiency. Economists who support market-based reforms as the best way to improve the health care system were disappointed that the ACA did not adopt this approach. Currently, markets are delivering inaccurate signals to consumers because when buying health care, unlike when buying most other goods and services, consumers pay a price well below the true cost of providing the service.

MyEconLab Concept Check

Market-based reforms Changes in the market for health care that would make it more like the markets for other goods and services.

Making the Connection
MyEconLab Video

How Much Is That MRI Scan?

Magnetic resonance imaging (MRI) units play an important role in modern medicine. First introduced in the early 1980s, they allow doctors to see inside the body's soft tissues to identify tumors, torn muscles, and other medical problems. As we noted in Section 7.2, MRI units are more widely available in the United States than in most other countries. We would normally expect that when a product is widely available, competition among firms results in the price of the product being about the same everywhere. Customers would not buy a best-selling book from Amazon.com if the price was 50 percent higher there than on BarnesandNoble.com.

Does competition equalize the prices of medical services? The evidence indicates that it doesn't. The exact services each hospital or clinic offers are difficult to discover, which makes it difficult for consumers to compare prices. The data in the table below indicate that the prices of abdominal MRI scans vary widely. In most cities in the United States, the most expensive MRI scan has a price that is more than double the least expensive scan. And prices for MRI scans also vary widely across cities. Two reporters looking at prices for shoulder MRI scans in Pensacola, Florida, found that Sacred Heart Hospital was charging $800 for a shoulder MRI scan, while Pensacola Open MRI & Imaging, a private firm located less than one mile away, was charging $450 for the same scan. Pensacola Open MRI & Imaging was actually using newer MRI units that give higher-resolution images, so it was charging less for a better service.

City	Highest Price	Lowest Price	Difference
Houston, Texas	$4,800	$675	$4,125
Baton Rouge, Louisiana	4,400	600	3,800
Chicago, Illinois	4,200	450	3,750
Atlanta, Georgia	4,400	700	3,700
Omaha, Nebraska	4,100	600	3,500
Lexington, Kentucky	4,000	550	3,450
Charlotte, North Carolina	3,500	600	2,900
Orlando, Florida	2,475	650	1,825
San Francisco, California	2,400	650	1,750
New York, New York	2,175	800	1,375

How can some providers of medical services charge hundreds or thousands of dollars more than competitors and remain in business? The answer is that most patients are not concerned about prices because they either do not pay them or they pay only a small fraction of them. Patients typically rely on doctors to refer them to a facility for an MRI scan or other procedure and make little or no effort to determine the price the facility charges. A goal of market-based reforms of the health care system is to give patients an incentive to pay more attention to the prices of medical services.

Sources: Caitlin Kenney, "Shopping for an MRI," www.npr.org, November 6, 2009; MRI prices from newchoicehealth.com, June 3, 2015.

MyEconLab Study Plan

Your Turn: Test your understanding by doing related problem 4.13 on page 248 at the end of this chapter.

Supporters of market-based reforms note that employees have to pay federal income and payroll taxes on the wages their employers pay them, but in most circumstances they do not pay taxes on the value of the health insurance their employers provide them. This feature of the tax laws encourages employees to want generous health care coverage; in fact, if offered the choice between a $1,000 salary increase or increased health care coverage that was worth $1,000, many people would choose the increased health care coverage because it would be tax free (although someone who was young and healthy and did not expect to have medical bills would probably choose the increase in salary). The size of this tax break is quite substantial—more than $250 billion in 2015. But individuals typically get no tax break when buying an individual health insurance policy or when they spend money on health care out of pocket.[1]

Some economists have proposed making the tax treatment of employer-provided health insurance the same as the tax treatment of individually purchased health insurance and out-of-pocket health care spending. They argue that this change could, potentially, significantly reduce spending on health care without reducing the effectiveness of the health care received. Such tax law changes would make it more likely that employer-provided health insurance would focus on large medical bills—such as those resulting from hospitalizations—while consumers would pay prices closer to the costs of providing routine medical care. John Cogan of the Hoover Institution, Glenn Hubbard of Columbia University, and Daniel Kessler of Stanford University estimate that repealing the tax preference for employer-provided health insurance would reduce spending by people enrolled in these programs by 33 percent.

[1] Individuals receive a deduction on their federal income tax only if their medical expenses are greater than 10 percent of their income. Only a relatively small number of individuals have expenses high enough to use that deduction.

Currently, the U.S. health care system is a world leader in innovation in medical technology and prescription drugs. About two-thirds of pharmaceutical patents are issued to U.S. firms and about two-thirds of research on new medicines is carried out in the United States. One goal of market-based reforms would be to ensure that U.S. firms continue with innovations in medical screening equipment, surgical procedures, and prescription drugs. Executives of U.S. pharmaceutical firms have voiced concern over whether aspects of the ACA will affect their ability to profitably bring new prescription drugs to market. In particular, managers at these firms worry that the new Independent Payment Advisory Board (IPAB) might reduce the payments Medicare would make for new prescription drugs.

Both critics of the ACA who favor greater government involvement in health care and those who favor market reforms raise questions about the act's individual mandate. The individual mandate requires every U.S. resident to have health insurance. The mandate was considered necessary because otherwise healthy people might avoid buying insurance until they become ill. Because insurance companies would not be allowed to deny coverage for preexisting conditions, they would end up paying large medical bills for people who had not been paying premiums to support the system while they were healthy. People who do not buy insurance are subject to fines under the act, but there were questions about how effective the fines would be in pushing people to buy insurance. In 2015, several million people paid the fine rather than buy insurance.

MyEconLab Study Plan

Continued from page 217

Economics in Your Life

Is Your Take-Home Pay Affected by What Your Employer Spends on Your Health Insurance?

At the beginning of this chapter, we asked you to think about this question: Your paycheck doesn't show the amount your employer pays on your behalf for health insurance, but does that amount affect your take-home pay? The *Making the Connection* on page 234 shows that the equilibrium compensation that workers receive in labor markets is made up partly of wages and partly of fringe benefits such as health insurance. So, while the amount that a firm pays on your behalf for health insurance may not affect your total compensation, it will affect the amount of your take-home pay. For a given level of compensation, the more a firm pays for your health insurance, the less it will pay you in wages. A related question is why a firm would buy health insurance for you rather than increase your wages by the same amount and let you buy your own insurance. We have seen that there are two important reasons so many people receive health insurance from their employers: (1) The wage an employer pays you is taxable income to you, but the money an employer spends to buy health insurance for you is not taxable; and (2) insurance companies are typically willing to charge lower premiums for group insurance, particularly to large employers, because risk pooling is improved and adverse selection and moral hazard problems are lower than with individual policies.

Conclusion

In this chapter, we have seen that economic analysis can provide important insights into the market for health care. As with many other policy issues, though, economic analysis can help inform the debate but cannot resolve it. Because health care is so important to consumers and health care services are such a large part of the U.S. economy, the role of the government in the health care system is likely to be the subject of intense debate for years to come.

Visit MyEconLab for a news article and analysis related to the concepts in this chapter.

CHAPTER SUMMARY AND PROBLEMS

Key Terms

Adverse selection, p. 227
Asymmetric information, p. 226
Fee-for-service, p. 221
Health care, p. 218
Health insurance, p. 220
Market-based reforms, p. 241
Moral hazard, p. 228
Patient Protection and Affordable Care Act (ACA), p. 239
Principal–agent problem, p. 228
Single-payer health care system, p. 223
Socialized medicine, p. 223

7.1 The Improving Health of People in the United States, pages 218–220

LEARNING OBJECTIVE: Discuss trends in U.S. health over time.

Summary

Health care refers to goods and services, such as prescription drugs and consultations with a doctor, that are intended to maintain or improve health. Over time, the health of people in most countries has improved. In the United States, as a result of improving health, life expectancy has increased, death rates have decreased, infant mortality has decreased, and the average person has become taller.

MyEconLab Visit **www.myeconlab.com** to complete these exercises online and get instant feedback.

Review Questions

1.1 Briefly discuss the most important differences between the market for health care and the markets for other goods and services.

1.2 Briefly describe changes over time in the health of the average person in the United States.

1.3 How can improvements in health increase a country's total income? How can increases in a country's total income improve health?

Problems and Applications

1.4 In what sense have improvements in the health of the average American caused the U.S. production possibilities frontier to shift out? Panel (a) in Figure 7.1 on page 220 indicates that life expectancy in the United States declined in 1918. What effect did this decline in life expectancy likely have on the U.S. production possibilities frontier? Briefly explain.

1.5 The widespread realization in the late nineteenth century that bacteria causes diseases helped lead to a public health movement. This movement eventually brought sewers, clean drinking water, and garbage removal to all U.S. cities. What effect did the public health movement in the United States in the late nineteenth and early twentieth centuries have on the country's production possibilities frontier?

1.6 Between 1830 and 1890, the height of the average adult male in the United States declined by about 2 inches at the same time that average incomes more than tripled. Did the standard of living in the United States increase during this period? What insight into the health and well-being of the U.S. population might the decline in height provide? Briefly explain.

7.2 Health Care around the World, pages 220–226

LEARNING OBJECTIVE: Compare the health care systems and health care outcomes in the United States and other countries.

Summary

Health insurance is a contract under which a buyer agrees to make payments, or premiums, in exchange for the provider agreeing to pay some or all of the buyer's medical bills. A majority of people in the United States live in households that have private health insurance, which they typically obtain through an employer. Other people have health insurance through the Veteran's Administration or the Medicare and Medicaid programs. In 2014, about 10 percent of people in the United States lacked health insurance. Many health insurance plans operate on a **fee-for-service** basis, under which doctors and hospitals receive a payment for each service they provide. Most countries outside the United States have greater government involvement in their health care systems. Canada has a **single-payer health care system**, in which the government provides national health insurance to all Canadian residents. In the United Kingdom, the government owns most hospitals and employs most doctors, so the health care system is referred to as **socialized medicine**. The United States spends more per person on health care than do other high-income countries. The United States has lower life expectancy, higher infant mortality, and a greater incidence of obesity than do other high-income countries. The United States has more medical technology per person and has lower mortality rates for people diagnosed with cancer than do other high-income countries. Data and other problems make it difficult to compare health care outcomes across countries.

MyEconLab Visit **www.myeconlab.com** to complete these exercises online and get instant feedback.

Review Questions

2.1 Define the following terms:
a. Health insurance
b. Fee-for-service
c. Single-payer health care system
d. Socialized medicine

2.2 What are the main sources of health insurance in the United States?

2.3 Briefly compare the health care systems in Canada, Japan, and the United Kingdom with the health care system in the United States.

2.4 What is meant by the phrase "health outcome"? How do health outcomes in the United States compare with those of other high-income countries? What problems arise in attempting to compare health outcomes across countries?

Problems and Applications

2.5 According to an article in the *Economist* about the health care system in the United Kingdom: "A defining principle of the National Health Service is that it is 'free at the point of delivery.'" What does "free at the point of delivery" mean? Is health care actually free to residents of the United Kingdom? Briefly explain.

Source: "Free-for-All," *Economist*, June 1, 2013.

2.6 In an opinion column about improving the performance of doctors in the United States, a health economist observed that "it's very hard to measure the things we really care about, like quality of life and improvements in functioning." Why is it difficult to measure outcomes like these? Does the economist's observation have relevance to comparisons in health outcomes across countries? Briefly explain.

Source: Aaron E. Carroll, "The Problem With 'Pay for Performance' in Medicine," *New York Times*, July 28, 2014.

2.7 An article in the *Economist* on evaluating health outcomes is subtitled "To Improve Health Care, Governments Need to Use the Right Data." Among the data not currently being collected in most countries, the article mentions "how soon after surgery patients get back to work." Why don't governments currently collect such data? Why might such data be important in evaluating the effectiveness of a country's health care system?

Source: "Measuring Health Care," *Economist*, February 1, 2014.

2.8 Two health care analysts argue that in the United States, "we have arrived at a moment where we are making little headway in defeating various kinds of diseases. Instead, our main achievements today consist of devising ways to marginally extend the lives of the very sick."
a. Should "marginally extend[ing] the lives of the very sick" be an important goal of a health care system? What other goals should have a higher priority? (*Note:* This question is basically a normative one without a definitive correct or incorrect answer. You are being asked to consider what the goals of a health care system *should be.*)
b. Would it be possible to measure how successful the health care systems of different countries are in extending the lives of the very sick? If so, how might it be done?

Source: David Brooks, "Death and Budgets," *New York Times*, July 14, 2011.

2.9 **(Related to the Making the Connection on page 222)** An article in the *Economist* notes that about 10 percent of people in the United States work in health care and that "these workers have the crucial job of making American health care more efficient, probably the country's top domestic challenge."
a. How might we measure the efficiency of a country's health care sector? Is there evidence that the U.S. health care sector is more or less efficient than the health care sectors in other countries? Briefly explain.
b. If the efficiency of the U.S. health care sector improves, will it be likely to employ more workers or fewer workers than if its efficiency does not improve? Briefly explain.

Source: "Why Nurses Are the New Auto Workers," *Economist*, July 25, 2014.

7.3 Information Problems and Externalities in the Market for Health Care, pages 226–232

LEARNING OBJECTIVE: Discuss how information problems and externalities affect the market for health care.

Summary

The market for health care is affected by the problem of **asymmetric information**, which occurs when one party to an economic transaction has less information than the other party. **Adverse selection**, the situation in which one party to a transaction takes advantage of knowing more than the other party to the transaction, is a problem for firms selling health insurance policies because it results in people who are less healthy being more likely to buy insurance than people who are healthier. **Moral hazard**, actions people take after they have entered into a transaction that make the other party to the transaction worse off, is also a problem for insurance companies because once people have health insurance, they are likely to make more visits to their doctors and in other ways increase their use of medical services. Moral hazard can also involve a **principal–agent problem**, in which doctors may order more lab tests, MRI scans, and other procedures than they would if their patients lacked health insurance. Insurance companies use deductibles and copayments to reduce the problems of adverse selection and moral hazard. There may be externalities involved with medicine and health care because, for example, people who are vaccinated against influenza or other diseases may not receive all of the benefits from having been vaccinated, and people who become obese may not bear all of the costs from their obesity.

MyEconLab Visit **www.myeconlab.com** to complete these exercises online and get instant feedback.

Review Questions

3.1 Define the following terms:
a. Asymmetric information
b. Adverse selection
c. Moral hazard
d. Principal–agent problem

3.2 What are the asymmetric information problems in the market for health insurance?

3.3 How do health insurance companies deal with asymmetric information problems?

3.4 What is an externality? Are there externalities in the market for health care? Briefly explain.

Problems and Applications

3.5 Suppose you see a 2013 Volkswagen Jetta GLS Turbo Sedan advertised in the campus newspaper for $9,000. If you knew the car was reliable, you would be willing to pay $10,000 for it. If you knew the car was unreliable, you would be willing to pay $5,000 for it. Under what circumstances should you buy the car?

3.6 What is the *lemons problem*? Is there a lemons problem in the market for health insurance? Briefly explain.

3.7 Michael Kinsley, a political columnist, observes: "The idea of insurance is to share the risks of bad outcomes." In what sense does insurance involve sharing risks? How does the problem of adverse selection affect the ability of insurance to provide the benefit of sharing risk?

Source: Michael Kinsley, "Congress on Drugs," *Slate*, August 1, 2002.

3.8 Under the Social Security retirement system, the federal government collects a tax on most people's wage income and makes payments to retired workers above a certain age who are covered by the system. (The age to receive full Social Security retirement benefits varies based on the year the worker was born.) The Social Security retirement system is sometimes referred to as a program of social insurance. Is Social Security an insurance program in the same sense as a health insurance policy that a company provides to its workers? Briefly explain.

3.9 **(Related to the Don't Let This Happen to You on page 228)** Briefly explain whether you agree with the following statement: "The reluctance of healthy young adults to buy health insurance creates a moral hazard problem for insurance companies."

3.10 **(Related to the Don't Let This Happen to You on page 228)** While teaching the concepts of asymmetric information, a professor asked his students for examples of adverse selection or moral hazard in marriage. One of the students, who happened to be married, replied: "Your spouse doesn't bring you flowers anymore!" Would the student's reply be an example of adverse selection or moral hazard? Briefly explain.

3.11 A news story notes that some features of the U.S. health care system contribute "to the high cost of medical care by encouraging hospitals and doctors to perform tests and procedures regardless of the value to a patient." What features is the article referring to? Why would hospitals and doctors perform tests that may not be of any value to patients?

Source: Reed Abelson, "Industry Group to Back Results-Focused Care," *New York Times*, January 28, 2015.

3.12 An opinion column in the *Wall Street Journal* observes about "defensive medicine" that "many physicians maintain that fear of lawsuits significantly affects the practice of medicine, and that reform of the malpractice system is crucial for containing costs." Is there another economic explanation—apart from fear of lawsuits—for why doctors may end up ordering unnecessary tests and other medical procedures? Briefly explain.

Source: Amitabh Chandra, Anupam B. Jena, and Seth A. Seabury, "Defensive Medicine May Be Costlier Than It Seems," *Wall Street Journal*, February 7, 2013.

3.13 An article in the *Economist* argues that the real problem with health insurance is:

> The healthy people who decide not to buy insurance out of rational self-interest, and who turn out to be right. By not buying insurance, those (largely young) healthy people will be failing to subsidize the people insurance is meant for: the ones who end up getting sick.

a. Why is it rational for healthy people not to buy health insurance?
b. Do you agree that health insurance is meant for people who end up getting sick?
c. Why is the situation described here a problem for a system of health insurance? If it is a problem, suggest possible solutions.

Source: "Romney on Health Care: To Boldly Go Where He Had Already Been Before," *Economist*, May 13, 2011.

3.14 An article in the *Los Angeles Times* describes a healthy 23-year-old woman who has decided not to buy health insurance as "exactly the type of person insurance plans, states and the federal government are counting on to make health reform work." Why are healthy 23-year-olds needed to make health reform work?

Source: Anna Gorman, "Affordable Care Act's Challenge: Getting Young Adults Enrolled," *Los Angeles Times*, June 2, 2013.

3.15 Explain whether you agree with the following statement:

> Providing health care is obviously a public good. If one person becomes ill and doesn't receive treatment, that person may infect many other people. If many people become ill, then the output of the economy will be negatively affected. Therefore, providing health care is a public good that should be supplied by the government.

7.4 The Debate over Health Care Policy in the United States, pages 232–243

LEARNING OBJECTIVE: Explain the major issues involved in the debate over health care policy in the United States.

Summary

In 2010, Congress passed the **Patient Protection and Affordable Care Act (ACA)**, which significantly reorganized the U.S. health care system. Spending on health care in the United States has been growing rapidly as a percentage of GDP, and spending per person on health care has been growing more rapidly than in other high-income countries. Third-party payers, such as employer-provided health insurance and the Medicare and Medicaid programs, have financed an increasing fraction of health care spending, while out-of-pocket payments have sharply declined as a fraction of total health care spending. Several explanations have been offered for the rapid increase in health care spending in the United States: Slow rates of growth of labor productivity in health care may be driving up costs, the U.S. population is becoming older, medical technology and new prescription drugs have higher costs, and the tax system and the reliance on third-party payers have distorted the economic incentives of consumers and suppliers of health care. The ACA has several important provisions: (1) an individual mandate that requires every resident of the United States to obtain health insurance or be fined; (2) the establishment of health exchanges that will be run by the state or federal governments and provide a means for individuals and small businesses to purchase health insurance; (3) an employer mandate that requires every firm with more than 200 employees to offer health insurance to them; (4) increased regulation of health insurance companies; (5) expansion of eligibility for Medicaid and the establishment of the Independent Payment Advisory Board (IPAB), which has the power to reduce Medicare payments for prescription drugs and for the use of diagnostic equipment and other technology if Medicare spending exceeds certain levels; and (6) increased taxes on people with incomes above $200,000. Some critics of the ACA argue that it does not go far enough in increasing government involvement in the health care system, while other critics argue that health care reform should rely more heavily on **market-based reforms**, which involve changing the market for health care so that it becomes more like the markets for other goods and services.

MyEconLab Visit **www.myeconlab.com** to complete these exercises online and get instant feedback.

Review Questions

4.1 What is the Patient Protection and Affordable Care Act (ACA)? Briefly list its major provisions.

4.2 In the United States, what has been the trend in health care spending as a percentage of GDP? Compare the increases in health care spending per person in the United States with the increases in health care spending per person in other high-income countries. What implications do current trends in health care spending have for the growth of federal government spending in the United States?

4.3 Briefly discuss how economists explain the rapid increases in health care spending.

4.4 What arguments do economists and policymakers who believe that the federal government should have a larger role in the health care system make in criticizing the ACA?

4.5 What arguments do economists and policymakers who believe that market-based reforms are the key to improving the health care system make in criticizing the ACA?

Problems and Applications

4.6 Figure 7.7 on page 236 shows that the Congressional Budget Office forecasts that only about 10 percent of future increases in spending on Medicare as a percentage of GDP will be due to the aging of the population. What factors explain the other 90 percent of the increase?

4.7 Improvements in technology usually result in lower costs of production or new and improved consumer goods and services. Assume that an improvement in medical technology results in an increase in life expectancy for people 65 years of age and older. How would this technological advance be likely to affect expenditures on health care?

4.8 Some economists and policymakers have argued that one way to control federal government spending on Medicare is to have a board of experts decide whether new medical technologies are worth their higher costs. If the board decides that they are *not* worth the costs, Medicare would not pay for them. Other economists and policymakers argue that the costs to beneficiaries should more closely represent the costs of providing medical services. This result might be attained by raising premiums, deductibles, and copayments or by "means testing," which would limit the Medicare benefits that high-income individuals receive. Political columnist David Brooks has summarized these two ways to restrain the growth of spending on Medicare: "From the top, a body of experts can be empowered to make rationing decisions. … Alternatively, at the bottom, costs can be shifted to beneficiaries with premium supports to help them handle the burden."

a. What are "rationing decisions"? How would these decisions restrain the growth of Medicare spending?

b. How would shifting the costs of Medicare to beneficiaries restrain the growth of Medicare spending? What does Brooks mean by "premium supports"?

c. Should Congress and the president be concerned about the growth of Medicare spending? If so, which of these approaches should they adopt, or is there a third approach that might be better? (*Note:* This last question is normative and has no definitive answer. It is intended to lead you to consider possible approaches to the Medicare program.)

Source: David Brooks, "The Missing Fifth," *New York Times*, May 9, 2011.

4.9 The text refers to health care as a normal good. Briefly explain why. In the future, is it possible that health care in the United States could become an inferior good? Briefly explain how it would be possible to tell if this change had occurred.

4.10 The late Nobel Laureate Robert Fogel of the University of Chicago argued, "Expenditures on health care are driven by demand, which is spurred by income and by advances in biotechnology that make health interventions increasingly effective."

a. If Fogel was correct, should policymakers be concerned by projected increases in health care spending as a percentage of GDP?
b. What objections do some economists raise to Fogel's analysis of what is driving increases in spending on health care?

Source: Robert Fogel, "Forecasting the Cost of U.S. Healthcare," *The American*, September 3, 2009.

4.11 **(Related to the Making the Connection on page 234)** Employees in most circumstances do not pay taxes on the value of the health insurance provided by their employers. If employees were taxed on the value of the employer-provided health insurance, what would you expect to happen to the overall compensation employers pay employees? To the value of health insurance provided by employers? To the wages paid to employees? Briefly explain.

4.12 **(Related to Solved Problem 7.4 on page 238)** Suppose consumers pay less than the true cost of medical services because a third party, such as an insurance company or the government, pays most of the bill. In the following graph, D_1 represents the demand for medical services if consumers paid the full price of medical services; D_2 represents the demand for medical services when consumers pay only a fraction of the true cost of medical services; and S represents the supply of medical services. Use the graph to answer the following questions. Briefly explain your answers.

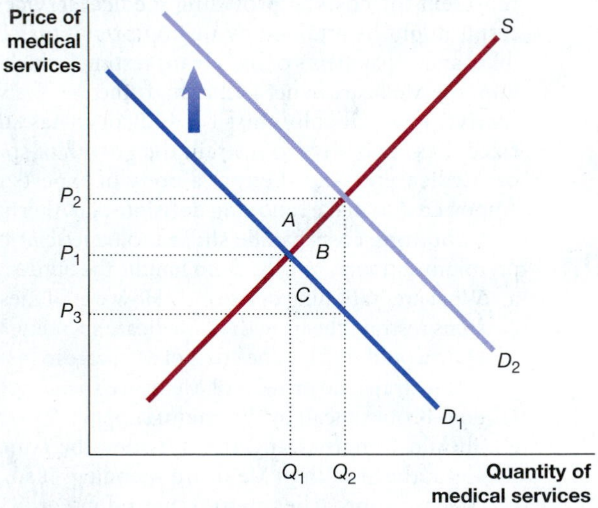

a. What is the equilibrium market price received by doctors and other suppliers of medical services?
b. What is the efficient quantity of medical services?
c. What is the price paid by consumers of medical services?
d. Which area represents the deadweight loss resulting from consumers not paying the full price of medical services?

4.13 **(Related to the Making the Connection on page 241)** A column in the *Wall Street Journal* observes, "Independent websites like Edmunds.com, AutoTrader.com and Kelley Blue Book publish detailed pricing information [on automobiles] for consumers and do so for free. Consumers want such information and businesses see opportunity in providing it, even for free, in order to attract eyeballs for advertising. ... Such information doesn't exist in health care." Why aren't there Web sites that offer pricing data on health care and make a profit from selling advertisements?

Source: Holman W, Jenkins, Jr., "The Young Won't Buy ObamaCare," *Wall Street Journal*, June 18, 2013.

4.14 **(Related to the Chapter Opener on page 217)** We saw in the chapter opener that the T. Cain Grocery offers its employees a health care plan with a high deductible of $4,500 per year. What effect do high-deductible plans have on how often employees visit doctors or otherwise use health care services? If the federal government were to require that employer health care plans have deductibles that were no greater than $200 per year, would the employees in these plans be better off? Would the employers offering these plans be worse off? Briefly explain.

CHAPTER

8

Firms, the Stock Market, and Corporate Governance

Chapter Outline and Learning Objectives

Is Twitter the Next Facebook?

Most people today have trouble imagining a world without Facebook, Twitter, Snapchat, and Instagram. All four of these social networking applications ("apps") are businesses that started small but have since grown rapidly. To finance that growth, they needed to raise funds. Some businesses raise funds by borrowing from banks. Once firms grow large enough, they can become *public firms* and sell stocks and bonds to investors in financial markets, such as the New York Stock Exchange. Firms that do not sell stock are called *private firms.* Both Facebook and Twitter have made the transition to being public firms. The founders of Snapchat, the mobile photo-sharing app, took a different approach: In 2012, they sold their company to Facebook for $1 billion. In the summer of 2015, Instagram, which allows people to share photos and 15-second videos, was still a private company. It was relying on investments from venture capital firms, which provide funds to private companies in exchange for part ownership.

A major decision for a successful social media startup is whether to remain a private firm, to become a public firm, or to sell itself to a larger firm as Snapchat did. Becoming a public firm provides access to greater financing but can also have drawbacks. From the time Mark Zuckerberg started Facebook in 2004 as a sophomore in college until the company went public in 2012, he was the unquestioned leader of the company. But buyers of Facebook's stock have partial ownership of the firm and a claim on its profits and can question Zuckerberg's decisions. Twitter became a public firm in 2013.

Stockholders want to invest in companies that can earn a profit. During its first year as a public company, Facebook struggled to meet the expectations of its investors. Eventually, Facebook was able to find a better way to target advertising on its app, and its stock more than doubled from its initial price in 2012 of $38 per share.

Twitter, however, found life as a public company to be more challenging. By 2015, it had more than 300 million active users and had become an important part of many people's lives. But advertisers who provided most of the company's revenue weren't convinced that advertising on the site was actually effective.

As we will see in this chapter, the ability of firms such as Twitter and Facebook to raise funds in financial markets is crucial to the health of the economy. Financial markets are also an important source of investment opportunities to households as they accumulate savings to buy houses, pay for college, and prepare for retirement.

Sources: Jack Marshall and Yoree Koh, "The Problem with Twitter Ads," *Wall Street Journal*, April 30, 2015; Douglas MacMillan, "Snapchat Raises Another $500 Million From Investors," *Wall Street Journal*, May 29, 2015; and Vindu Goel, "An Early Twitter Investor Calls for Change," *New York Times*, June 3, 2015.

Economics in Your Life

Would You Pay to Use Facebook or Twitter?

You can use Facebook or Twitter for free—or can you? Social media apps don't charge you directly; instead they earn their revenue primarily by displaying ads as you use the app. Most sites collect data about your Web searches and browsing habits and then display ads for products they think you might buy. But many people see targeted ads as an invasion of their privacy. Some of these people would be willing to pay to use these apps if they could do so without having to see advertisements. Would you be willing to pay to use social media apps? Do you think other users would be willing to pay enough that firms could rely on that source of revenue? As you read this chapter, try to answer these questions. You can check your answers against those we provide on **page 269** at the end of this chapter.

In this chapter, we look at firms: how they are organized, how they raise funds, and the information they provide to investors. As we have discussed in earlier chapters, firms in a market system are responsible for organizing the factors of production to produce goods and services. Entrepreneurs start firms to earn a profit by offering a good or service. To succeed, entrepreneurs must meet consumers' wants by producing new or better goods and services or by finding ways to produce existing goods and services at a lower cost so that they can be sold at a lower price. Entrepreneurs also need access to sufficient funds, and they must be able to efficiently organize production. As the typical firm in many industries has become larger over the past 100 years, the task of efficiently organizing production has become more difficult. In the final section of this chapter, we look at problems of *corporate governance* that have occurred in recent years. We also look at the steps firms and the government have taken to avoid similar problems in the future.

8.1 Types of Firms

LEARNING OBJECTIVE: Categorize the major types of firms in the United States.

In studying a market economy, it is important to understand the basics of how firms operate. In the United States, there are three main categories of firms:

Sole proprietorship A firm owned by a single individual and not organized as a corporation.

Partnership A firm owned jointly by two or more persons and not organized as a corporation.

Corporation A legal form of business that provides owners with protection from losing more than their investment should the business fail.

1. A **sole proprietorship** is a firm owned by a single individual. Although most sole proprietorships are small, some employ many workers and earn large profits.
2. A **partnership** is a firm owned jointly by two or more—sometimes many—persons. Most law and accounting firms are partnerships. Some of them can be quite large. For instance, in 2015, the Baker & McKenzie law firm based in Chicago had 1,400 partners.
3. A **corporation** is a legal form of business that provides owners with protection from losing more than their investment in the firm should the business fail. Most large firms are organized as corporations.

Who Is Liable? Limited and Unlimited Liability

Asset Anything of value owned by a person or a firm.

A key distinction among the three types of firms is that the owners of sole proprietorships and partnerships have unlimited liability, which means that there is no legal distinction between the personal assets of the owners of the firm and the assets of the firm. An **asset** is anything of value owned by a person or a firm. If a sole proprietorship or a partnership owes a lot of money to the firm's suppliers or employees, the suppliers and employees have a legal right to sue the firm for payment, even if in order to pay their debts, the firm's owners have to sell some of their personal assets, such as stocks or bonds. In other words, with sole proprietorships and partnerships, the owners are not legally distinct from the firms they own.

It may only seem fair that the owners of a firm be responsible for the firm's debts. But in the early 1800s, many state legislatures in the United States realized that unlimited liability was a significant problem for any firm that was attempting to raise funds from large numbers of investors. An investor might be interested in making a relatively small investment in a firm but be unwilling to become a partner in the firm for fear of placing at risk all of his or her personal assets if the firm were to fail. To get around this problem, state legislatures began to pass *general incorporation laws,* which allowed firms to more easily be organized as corporations. Under the corporate form of business, the owners of a firm have **limited liability**, which means that if the firm fails, the owners can never lose more than the amount they have invested in the firm. The personal assets of the owners of the firm are not affected by the failure of the firm. In fact, in the eyes of the law, a corporation is a legal "person," separate from its owners. Limited liability has made it possible for corporations to raise funds by issuing shares of stock to large numbers of investors. For example, if you buy a share of Twitter stock, you are a part owner of the firm, but if Twitter were to go bankrupt, you would not be

Limited liability A legal provision that shields owners of a corporation from losing more than they have invested in the firm.

Table 8.1

Differences among Business Organizations

	Sole Proprietorship	Partnership	Corporation
Advantages	• Control by owner • No layers of management	• Ability to share work • Ability to share risks	• Limited personal liability • Greater ability to raise funds
Disadvantages	• Unlimited personal liability • Limited ability to raise funds	• Unlimited personal liability • Limited ability to raise funds	• Costly to organize • Possible double taxation of income

personally responsible for any of Twitter's debts. Therefore, you could not lose more than the amount you paid for the stock.

Organizing a firm as a corporation also has some disadvantages. In the United States, corporate profits are taxed twice—once at the corporate level and again when investors in the firm receive a share of the firm's profits. Corporations generally are larger than sole proprietorships and partnerships and are therefore more difficult to organize and run. Table 8.1 reviews the advantages and disadvantages of the three types of business organizations. MyEconLab Concept Check

Corporations Earn the Majority of Revenue and Profits

Figure 8.1 gives basic statistics on the three types of business organizations. Panel (a) shows that almost three-quarters of all firms are sole proprietorships. Panels (b) and (c) show that although only 18 percent of all firms are corporations, they account for a majority of the revenue and profits earned by all firms. *Profit* is the difference between revenue and the total cost to a firm of producing the goods and services it offers for sale.

There are more than 5.8 million corporations in the United States, but only 37,000 have annual revenues of more than $50 million. We can think of these 37,000 firms—including Apple, McDonald's, and Facebook—as representing "big business." These large firms earn more than 80 percent of the total profits of all corporations in the United States. MyEconLab Concept Check

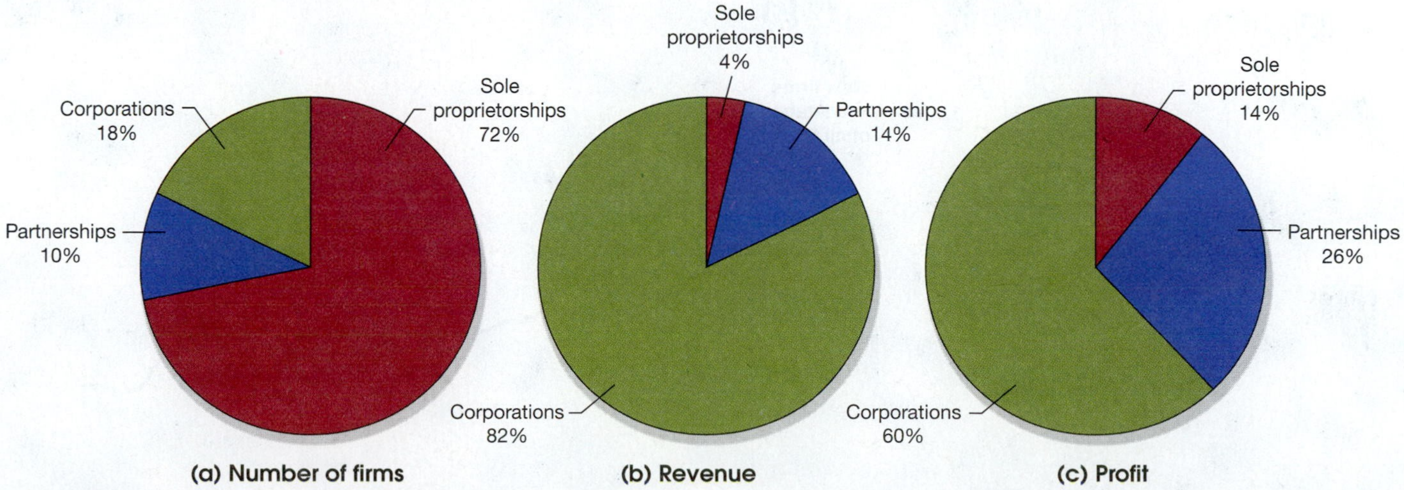

MyEconLab Animation

Figure 8.1 **Business Organizations: Sole Proprietorships, Partnerships, and Corporations**

The three types of firms in the United States are sole proprietorships, partnerships, and corporations. Panel (a) shows that only 18 percent of all firms are corporations. Yet, as panels (b) and (c) show, corporations account for a majority of the revenue and profit earned by all firms.

Source: Internal Revenue Service, *Statistics on Income*, April 27, 2015.

Making the Connection
MyEconLab Video

Why Are Fewer Young People Starting Businesses?

We have seen that although a large majority of all firms are sole proprietorships, they account for only a small fraction of the total revenue and profit earned by all firms. In fact, more than 70 percent of people work at firms that have 50 or more employees. Does this mean that small businesses are not important to the U.S. economy?

On the contrary, most economists would argue that small businesses are vital to the health of the economy. Starting a small firm provides an entrepreneur with a vehicle for bringing a new product or process to market. During the late nineteenth and early twentieth centuries, Thomas Edison, Henry Ford, and the Wright Brothers were all responsible for introducing important products shortly after starting what were initially very small firms. In more recent years, Bill Gates, Steve Jobs, Michael Dell, and Mark Zuckerberg decided that the best way to develop their ideas was by founding Microsoft, Apple, Dell Computer, and Facebook rather than by choosing to work for large corporations.

In most years, more than 400,000 new firms open in the United States, and, of these, more than 95 percent employ fewer than 20 workers. In a typical year, new small firms create 3.3 million jobs. Forty percent of all new jobs are created by small firms, and in some years more than half are. Looking just at newly started firms, more than 85 percent of jobs created are created by small firms.

Because of the importance of small firms, some economists and policymakers have been concerned by a slowdown in recent years in the number of firms started. As the graph below shows, in the late 1970s, more than 15 percent of all firms were less than a year old. In recent years, only about 8 percent were. In absolute numbers, in recent years business startups have been running about 25 percent below the levels of just 10 years ago. The decline in starting new businesses is not concentrated in one industry or geographic area but has occurred across industries, including the information and high-tech sectors, and in most states and cities.

The decline in starting new firms has been particularly large among people under the age of 35. At first, this trend may seem surprising because of the publicity received by high-tech startups such as Twitter, Facebook, Uber, and Airbnb, all of which were started by young entrepreneurs. But while in the 1990s about one-third of all new firms were started by people younger than 35, today fewer than one-quarter are.

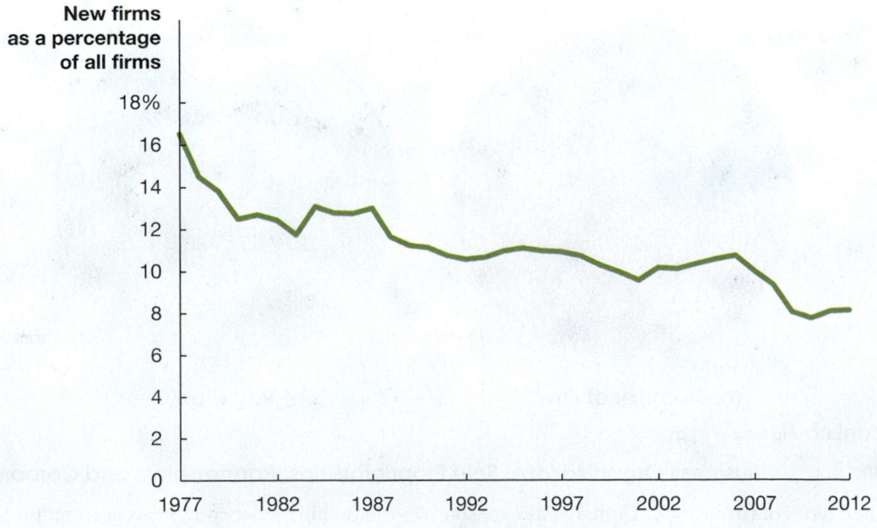

Source: U.S. Census Bureau, "Business Dynamics Statistics, Firm Characteristics Data Tables," June 2015.

Economists have not come to a consensus on the reasons for the decline in business startups. Some economists believe that despite the publicity received by innovative high-tech firms, the overall U.S. economy is experiencing a slowdown in technological progress. With fewer new technologies being introduced, there are fewer opportunities to start new firms selling new goods and services. Some economists believe that an increase in government regulations has raised the costs of starting and running a small business. For example, state and local governments have imposed licensing requirements on many occupations. According to one study, while at one time only 5 percent of workers were in an occupation that required a license, today more than 20 percent are. Slowing population growth may also have reduced the opportunities to start new businesses.

Whatever the explanation, many economists and policymakers worry that without an increase in young entrepreneurs starting new firms, the U.S. economy will become less dynamic and less able to sustain high rates of economic growth.

Sources: Asma Ghribi, "Why It's Worrying That U.S. Companies Are Getting Older," *Wall Street Journal*, August 4, 2014; Ian Hathaway and Robert E. Litan, "What's Driving the Decline in the Firm Formation Rate? A Partial Explanation," *Brookings Economic Studies*, November 20, 2014; Morris M. Kleiner and Alan B. Krueger, "Analyzing the Extent and Influence of Occupational Licensing on the Labor Market," *Journal of Labor Economics*, Vol. 31, No. 2, April 2013, pp. S173–S202; David Neumark, Brandon Wall, and Junfu Zhang, "Do Small Businesses Create More Jobs? New Evidence for the United States from the National Establishment Time Series," *Review of Economics and Statistics*, Vol. 93, No. 1, February 2011, pp. 16–29.

Your Turn: Test your understanding by doing related problems 1.10 and 1.11 on page 271 at the end of this chapter.

MyEconLab Study Plan

The Structure of Corporations and the Principal–Agent Problem

Large corporations account for a majority of sales and profits in the economy, so it is important to know how they are managed. Most large corporations have a similar management structure. The way in which a corporation is structured and the effect that structure has on the corporation's behavior is referred to as **corporate governance**.

Corporate governance The way in which a corporation is structured and the effect that structure has on the corporation's behavior.

Corporations are legally owned by their *shareholders*, the owners of the corporation's stock. Unlike with a sole proprietorship, a corporation's shareholders own the firm but don't directly manage it. Instead, they elect a *board of directors* to represent their interests. The board of directors appoints a *chief executive officer* (CEO) to run the day-to-day operations of the corporation. Sometimes the board of directors also appoints other members of *top management*, such as the *chief financial officer* (CFO). At other times, the CEO appoints other members of top management. Members of top management—sometimes called C-suite executives—including the CEO and CFO, often serve on the board of directors. They are called *inside directors*. Members of the board of directors who do not have a direct management role in the firm are called *outside directors*. The outside directors are intended to act as a check on the decisions of top managers.

Unlike the owners of family businesses, the top management of a large corporation does not generally own a large share of the firm's stock, so large corporations have a **separation of ownership from control**. Although the shareholders actually own the firm, the top management controls the firm's day-to-day operations. Because top managers own only a small percentage of the firm's stock, they may decrease the firm's profits by spending money to purchase private jets or schedule management meetings at luxurious resorts. Economists refer to the conflict between the interests of shareholders and the interests of the top management as a **principal–agent problem**.[1] This problem occurs when agents—in this case, a firm's top management—pursue their own interests rather than the interests of the principal who hired them—in this case, the shareholders of the corporation. Because the outside directors are not involved with the daily operations of the firm, they may have difficulty deciding whether the actions taken by

Separation of ownership from control A situation in a corporation in which the top management, rather than the shareholders, controls day-to-day operations.

Principal–agent problem A problem caused by an agent pursuing his own interests rather than the interests of the principal who hired him.

[1] In Chapter 7, we saw that the principal–agent problem arises from moral hazard that can occur because of asymmetric information. In this case, the asymmetric information involves top managers knowing more about how the firm is actually run than do the firm's shareholders.

top managers really are in the best interests of shareholders. To reduce the effect of the principal–agent problem, many boards of directors in the 1990s began to tie the salaries of top managers to the profits of the firm or to the price of the firm's stock. They hoped this step would give top managers an incentive to make the firm as profitable as possible, thereby benefiting its shareholders. Sometimes, though, top managers act in ways that increase the profits of the firm in the short run—and the salaries and bonuses of the top managers—but actually reduce the profits of the firm in the long run.

MyEconLab Concept Check

8.2 How Firms Raise Funds

LEARNING OBJECTIVE: Explain how firms raise the funds they need to operate and expand.

Owners and managers of firms try to earn a profit. To succeed, a firm must raise funds to pay for its operations, including paying its employees and buying or renting computers and other machinery and equipment. In fact, a central challenge for anyone running a firm, whether that person is a sole proprietor or a top manager of a large corporation, is raising the funds needed to operate and expand the business. Suppose you develop a new social networking app, and you decide to start a business using $100,000 you have saved in a bank. You use the $100,000 to rent an office for your firm, buy computers, and pay other startup expenses. Your firm is a great success, and you decide to expand it by moving to a larger office and buying more computers. As the owner of a small business, you can raise the funds for this expansion in three ways:

1. If you are making a profit, you could reinvest the profits back into your firm. Profits that are reinvested in a firm rather than taken out of the firm and paid to the firm's owners are called *retained earnings*.
2. You could raise funds by recruiting additional owners to invest in the firm. This arrangement would increase the firm's *financial capital*.
3. Finally, you could borrow the funds from relatives, friends, or a bank.

The managers of a large public firm have some additional ways to raise funds, as we will see in the next section.

Sources of External Funds

Unless firms rely on retained earnings, they have to raise the *external funds* they need from those who have funds available to invest. It is the role of an economy's *financial system* to transfer funds from savers to borrowers.

Indirect finance A flow of funds from savers to borrowers through financial intermediaries such as banks. Intermediaries raise funds from savers to lend to firms (and other borrowers).

Most firms raise external funds in two ways. The first way, called **indirect finance**, relies on financial intermediaries such as banks. If you put $1,000 in a checking account or in a certificate of deposit (CD), the bank will loan most of those funds to borrowers. The bank will combine your funds with those of other depositors and, for example, make a $100,000 loan to a local business. Small businesses rely heavily on bank loans as their primary source of external funds.

Direct finance A flow of funds from savers to firms through financial markets, such as the New York Stock Exchange.

A second way for firms to acquire external funds is through *financial markets*. Raising funds in these markets, such as the New York Stock Exchange on Wall Street in New York City, is called **direct finance**. Direct finance usually takes the form of the borrower selling the lender a *financial security*. A financial security is a document—sometimes in electronic form—that states the terms under which the funds are passed from the buyer of the security (who is lending funds) to the borrower. *Bonds* and *stocks* are the two main types of financial securities. Typically, only large corporations are able to sell bonds and stocks on financial markets. Investors are generally unwilling to buy securities issued by small and medium-sized firms because the investors lack sufficient information on the financial health of smaller firms.

Bond A financial security that represents a promise to repay a fixed amount of funds.

Bonds **Bonds** are financial securities that represent promises to repay a fixed amount of funds. When Apple sells a bond to raise funds, it promises to pay the purchaser of the bond an interest payment each year for the term of the bond, as well as a payment of the loan amount, or the *principal*, at the end of the term. Apple may need to raise many millions of dollars to build new offices, but each individual bond has a principal, or *face value*, of $1,000, which is the amount each bond purchaser is lending Apple. So, Apple must sell many bonds to raise all the funds it needs. Suppose Apple promises it will pay interest of $40 per year to anyone who buys one of its bonds. The interest payments on a bond are called **coupon payments**. The **interest rate** is the cost of borrowing funds, usually expressed as a percentage of the amount borrowed. We can calculate the interest rate on the bond, called the *coupon rate*, by dividing the coupon by the face value of the bond. In this case, the coupon rate is:

Coupon payment An interest payment on a bond.

Interest rate The cost of borrowing funds, usually expressed as a percentage of the amount borrowed.

$$\frac{\$40}{\$1{,}000} = 0.04, \text{ or } 4\%.$$

Many bonds that corporations issue have terms, or *maturities*, of 30 years. In this example, if you bought a bond from Apple, Apple would pay you $40 per year for 30 years, and at the end of the thirtieth year, Apple would repay the $1,000 principal to you.

The interest rate that a corporation selling a bond has to pay depends on how likely bond buyers—investors—think that the corporation is to default, or not make the promised coupon or principal payments. The higher the *default risk* on a bond, the higher the interest rate will be. For example, investors see the federal government as being very unlikely to default on its bonds, so federal government bonds pay a lower interest rate than do bonds of a firm such as Apple. In turn, Apple pays a lower interest rate on its bonds than does a corporation that investors believe is not as likely to make its bond payments.

Making the Connection

MyEconLab Video

The Rating Game: Is the U.S. Treasury Likely to Default on Its Bonds?

Federal regulations require that before they can sell bonds to investors, firms and governments must first have bonds rated by one of the credit-rating agencies. The three largest rating agencies are Moody's Investors Service, Standard & Poor's Corporation, and Fitch Ratings. These private firms rate bonds by giving them letter grades—AAA or Aaa being the highest—that reflect the likelihood that the firm or government will be able to make the payments on the bond. The following table shows the ratings:

	Moody's Investors Service	Standard & Poor's (S&P)	Fitch Ratings	Meaning of the Ratings
Investment-grade bonds	Aaa	AAA	AAA	Highest credit quality
	Aa	AA	AA	Very high credit quality
	A	A	A	High credit quality
	Baa	BBB	BBB	Good credit quality
Non-investment-grade bonds	Ba	BB	BB	Speculative
	B	B	B	Highly speculative
	Caa	CCC	CCC	Substantial default risk
	Ca	CC	CC	Very high levels of default risk
	C	C	C	Exceptionally high levels of default risk
	—	D	D	Default

Note: The entries in the "Meaning of the Ratings" column are slightly modified from those that Fitch uses. The other two rating agencies have similar descriptions. For each rating from Aa to Caa, Moody's adds a numerical modifier of 1, 2, or 3. The rating Aa1 is higher than the rating Aa2, and the rating Aa2 is higher than the rating Aa3. Similarly, Standard & Poor's and Fitch Ratings add a plus (+) or minus (−) sign. The rating AA+ is higher than the rating AA, and the rating AA is higher than the rating AA-.

Source: *Money, Banking, and the Financial System*, 2nd edition, by R. Glenn Hubbard and Anthony P. O'Brien. Copyright © 2014 by Pearson Education, Inc. Reprinted and electronically reproduced by permission of Pearson Education, Inc., Upper Saddle River, New Jersey.

Investors can use the ratings in deciding how much risk they are willing to accept when buying a bond. Generally, the lower the rating, the higher the interest rate an investor will receive but also the higher the risk that the issuer of the bond will default.

The rating agencies charge firms and governments—rather than investors—for their services. This arrangement raises the question of whether rating agencies face a conflict of interest. Because firms issuing bonds can choose which of the agencies to hire to rate their bonds, the agencies may have an incentive to give higher ratings than might be justified in order to keep the firms' business. During the housing boom of the mid-2000s, some financial firms issued *mortgage-backed bonds*. These bonds were similar to regular corporate bonds except that the interest payments came from mortgage loans people had taken out to buy houses. The money from those mortgage payments was passed along to investors who had bought the mortgage-backed bonds. The rating agencies gave many of these bonds AAA ratings, even though when housing prices began to decline in 2006, many homeowners stopped making their mortgage payments and the value of the bonds declined sharply. Some economists and policymakers believe the rating agencies provided the high ratings primarily to ensure that the firms that issued the bonds would continue to hire them.

Some investors worry that the U.S. government might someday default on the bonds that it has sold. Over the past 15 years, the federal government has been spending more than it has been collecting in taxes. The result is a federal budget deficit, which forces the Treasury to sell bonds equal to the amount of the deficit. The budget deficit was particularly large during and immediately after the 2007–2009 recession, which resulted in sharp declines in tax receipts and increases in government spending. Forecasts from the U.S. Congressional Budget Office indicate that large budget deficits will continue indefinitely because spending on Social Security, Medicare, Medicaid, and other government programs is expected to increase faster than tax revenues.

In 2011, Standard & Poor's (S&P) decided that because of these continuing deficits, it would downgrade U.S. Treasury bonds from AAA to AA+. Never before had a rating agency given Treasury bonds less than an AAA rating.

Is it likely that the U.S. Treasury will default on its bonds? S&P argued that while a default is still unlikely, the continuing large deficits increased the chance that someday the Treasury might not make the interest payments on its bonds. Most investors, though, appear confident that the Treasury will not default and are willing to buy Treasury bonds despite the historically low interest rates on the bonds. Like the Ghost of Christmas Yet to Come in Charles Dickens's *A Christmas Carol*, S&P was giving a warning of something that might happen rather than something that necessarily must happen.

Sources: Mary Williams Walsh, "Credit Ratings Services Give Mixed Reviews to Tax Deal," *New York Times*, January 3, 2013; and Cyrus Sanati, "S.E.C. Urges Changes to Ratings-Agency Rules," *New York Times*, August 28, 2009.

MyEconLab Study Plan

Your Turn: Test your understanding by doing related problems 2.8 and 2.9 on page 272 at the end of this chapter.

Stock A financial security that represents partial ownership of a firm.

Stocks When you buy a newly issued bond from a firm, you are lending funds to that firm. When you buy **stock** issued by a firm, you are actually buying part ownership of the firm. When a corporation sells stock, it is doing the same thing the owner of a small business does when he or she takes on a partner: The firm is increasing its financial capital by bringing additional owners into the firm. Any one shareholder usually owns only a small fraction of the total shares of stock issued by a corporation.

Many small investors buy shares of *mutual funds* rather than directly buying stocks issued by individual companies. Mutual funds, such as Fidelity Investment's Magellan Fund, sell shares to investors and use the funds to invest in a portfolio of financial assets, such as stocks and bonds. By buying shares in a mutual fund, small investors reduce the costs they would pay to buy many individual stocks and bonds. Small savers who have only enough money to buy a few individual stocks and bonds can use mutual funds to *diversify*, which lowers their investment risk because most mutual funds hold a large number of stocks and bonds. If a firm issuing a stock or bond declares bankruptcy, causing the stock or bond to lose all of its value, the effect on a mutual fund's portfolio is likely to be small. The effect might be devastating, though, to a small investor who invested most of his or her savings in the stock or bond. Because mutual funds are willing to buy back their shares at any time, they also provide savers with easy access to their money.

Exchange-traded funds (ETFs) are similar to mutual funds in that when you buy shares in an ETF, you are buying a claim to a portfolio of stocks or bonds. But mutual funds can only be bought from or sold back to the firm that issues them. ETFs can be bought and sold to other investors in financial markets, just as individual stocks or bonds can.

A shareholder is entitled to a portion of the corporation's profits, if there are any. Corporations generally keep some of their profits as retained earnings to finance future expansion. The remaining profits are paid to shareholders as **dividends**. If a firm uses its retained earnings to grow and earn economic profits, its share price rises, which provides a *capital gain* for investors. If a corporation is unable to make a profit, it usually does not pay a dividend. Under the law, corporations must make payments on any debt they have before making payments to their owners. That is, a corporation must make promised payments to bondholders before it can make any dividend payments to shareholders. Unlike bonds, stocks do not have a maturity date, so the firm is not obliged to return the investor's funds at any particular date. MyEconLab Concept Check

Dividends Payments by a corporation to its shareholders.

Stock and Bond Markets Provide Capital—and Information

The original purchasers of stocks and bonds may resell them to other investors. In fact, most of the buying and selling of stocks and bonds that takes place each day involves investors reselling existing stocks and bonds to each other rather than corporations selling new stocks and bonds to investors. The buyers and sellers of stocks and bonds together make up the *stock and bond markets.* There is no single place where stocks and bonds are bought and sold. Some trading of stocks and bonds takes place in buildings known as *exchanges,* such as the New York Stock Exchange or the Tokyo Stock Exchange. In the United States, the stocks and bonds of the largest corporations are traded on the New York Stock Exchange. The development of computer technology has spread the trading of stocks and bonds outside exchanges to *securities dealers* linked by computers. These dealers comprise the *over-the-counter market.* The stocks of many high-technology firms—including Apple, Twitter, and Facebook—are traded in the most important of the over-the-counter markets, the *National Association of Securities Dealers Automated Quotations* system, which is referred to by its acronym, NASDAQ.

Shares of stock represent claims on the profits of the firms that issue them. Therefore, as the fortunes of the firms change and they earn more or less profit, the prices of the stock the firms have issued should also change. Similarly, bonds represent claims to receive coupon payments and one final payment of the principal. Therefore, a particular bond that was issued in the past may have its price go up or down, depending on whether the coupon payments being offered on newly issued bonds are higher or lower than those on existing bonds. If you hold a bond with a coupon of $30 per year, and similar newly issued bonds have coupons of $40 per year, the price of your bond will fall because it is less attractive to investors. The price of a bond will also be affected by changes in *default risk,* which reflects investors' expectations of the issuing firm's ability to make the coupon payments. For example, if investors begin to believe that a firm may soon go out of business and stop making coupon payments to its bondholders, the price of the firm's bonds will fall to very low levels.

Changes in the value of a firm's stocks and bonds provide important information for a firm's managers, as well as for investors. An increase in the stock price means that investors are more optimistic about the firm's profit prospects, and the firm's managers might want to expand the firm's operations as a result. By contrast, a decrease in the firm's stock price indicates that investors are less optimistic about the firm's profit prospects, so management may want to shrink the firm's operations. Similarly, changes in the value of the firm's bonds imply changes in the cost of external funds to finance the firm's investment in research and development or in new factories. A higher bond price indicates a lower cost of new external funds, while a lower bond price indicates a higher cost of new external funds. MyEconLab Concept Check

Don't Let This Happen to You

When Twitter Shares Are Sold, Twitter Doesn't Get the Money

Twitter is a popular investment, with investors buying and selling shares often as their views about the value of the firm shift. That's great for Twitter, right? Think of Twitter collecting all that money as shares change hands and the stock price goes up. *Wrong.* Twitter raises funds in a primary market, but its shares trade in a secondary market. Those trades don't put money into Twitter's hands, but they do give important information to the firm's managers. Let's see why.

Primary markets are markets in which firms sell newly issued stocks and bonds to initial buyers. Businesses can raise funds in a primary financial market in two ways—by borrowing (selling bonds) or selling shares of stock—which result in different types of claims on the borrowing firm's future income. Although you may hear about the stock market fluctuations every day in news updates, bonds actually account for more of the funds raised by borrowers. The total value of bonds in the United States is typically about twice the value of stocks.

In *secondary markets*, stocks and bonds that have already been issued are sold by one investor to another. If Twitter sells shares to the public, it is turning to a primary market for new funds. Once Twitter shares are issued, investors trade the shares in the secondary market. Twitter does not receive any new funds when its shares are traded. The initial seller of a stock or bond raises funds from an investor only in the primary market. Secondary markets convey information to firms' managers and investors by determining the price of stocks and bonds. For example, a major increase in Twitter's stock price conveys the market's optimism about the firm, and Twitter may decide to raise funds to expand. So, secondary markets are valuable sources of information for corporations that are considering raising funds.

Primary and secondary markets are both important, but they play different roles. As an investor, you principally trade stocks and bonds in a secondary market. As a corporate manager, you may help decide how to raise new funds to expand the firm where you work.

MyEconLab Study Plan

Your Turn: Test your understanding by doing related problem 2.11 on page 272 at the end of this chapter.

The Fluctuating Stock Market

The performance of the U.S. stock market is often measured using *stock market indexes*. Stock market indexes are averages of stock prices, with the value of the index set equal to 100 in a particular year, called the *base year*. Because the stock indexes are intended to show movements in prices from one year to the next, rather than the actual dollar values of the underlying stocks, the year chosen for the base year is unimportant. Figure 8.2 shows movements from January 1998 to June 2015 in the three most widely followed stock indexes (the shaded areas represent months in which the U.S. economy was in a business cycle recession when the production and profits of many firms are falling):

- The Dow Jones Industrial Average, which is an index of the stock prices of 30 large U.S. corporations.
- The S&P 500, which is an index prepared by Standard & Poor's Corporation and includes the stock prices of 500 large U.S. firms.
- The NASDAQ Composite Index, which includes the stock prices of more than 4,000 firms whose shares are traded in the NASDAQ stock market. NASDAQ is an over-the-counter market, meaning that buying and selling on NASDAQ is carried out between dealers who are linked together by computer. The listings on NASDAQ are dominated by high-tech firms such as Apple, Facebook, and Twitter.

As we have seen, ownership of a firm's stock represents a claim on the firm's profits. So, the larger the firm's profits are, the higher its stock price will be. When the overall economy is expanding, incomes, employment, and spending will all increase, as will corporate profits. When the economy is in a recession, incomes, employment, and spending will fall, as will corporate profits. Therefore, we would expect that stock prices will rise when the economy is expanding and fall when the economy is in recession. We see this pattern reflected in the three stock market indexes shown in Figure 8.2. All three

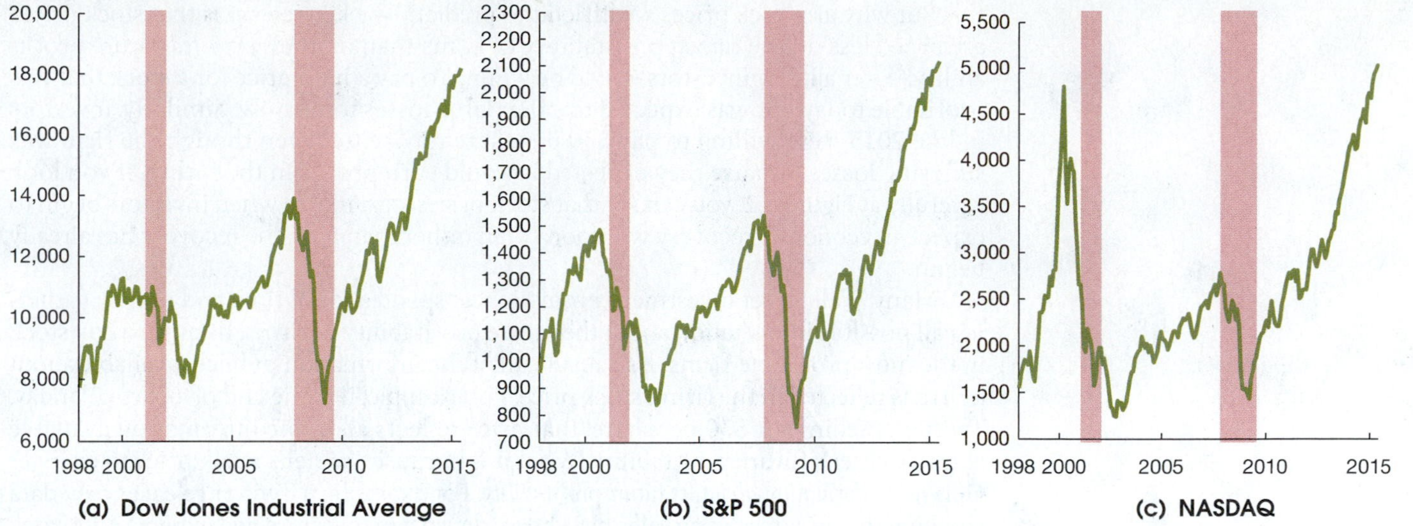

MyEconLab Real-time data

Figure 8.2 Movements in Stock Market Indexes, January 1998 to June 2015

The performance of the U.S. stock market is often measured by market indexes, which are averages of stock prices. The three most important indexes are the Dow Jones Industrial Average, the S&P 500, and the NASDAQ. During the period from 1998 to 2015, the three indexes followed similar patterns, rising when the U.S. economy was expanding and falling when the economy was in recession. Note that in all three panels, the vertical axis does not start at zero.

indexes follow a roughly similar pattern: increases in stock prices during the economic expansion of the late 1990s, declines after the "dot-com crash" of 2000 and the recession of 2001, increases from late 2001 to late 2007, declines as the U.S. economy entered a recession at the end of 2007, and then increases beginning in early 2009.

The stock prices of many early Internet companies soared in the late 1990s, as some analysts made what turned out to be overly optimistic predictions about how rapidly online retailing would grow. In 2000, when investors realized that many dot-coms would never be profitable, their stock prices crashed. Because the NASDAQ is dominated by high-tech stocks, it experienced greater swings during the dot-com boom and bust of the late 1990s and early 2000s than did the other two indexes. The sharp declines in all three indexes beginning in late 2007 reflected the severity of the recession that began in December of that year. The severity of the recession was due in part to problems with financial firms, which we will discuss in Section 8.4. By 2015, as recovery from the recession continued, all three indexes had reached their highest values ever.

MyEconLab Concept Check

Making the Connection MyEconLab Video

Why Are Many People Poor Stock Market Investors?

New information about Twitter's future profitability would cause the price of its stock to change.

You've probably heard this standard advice about investing: "Buy low and sell high." That is, you should buy shares of stocks and other financial assets when their prices are low and sell them when their prices are high. Unfortunately, many people do the opposite. For instance, many people bought shares of Apple stock when it was selling for more than $700 per share in September 2012 and sold when it was below $400 per share in April 2013.

Stock prices are difficult to predict, but many people convince themselves that a stock whose price has been rising will continue to rise and that a stock whose price has been falling will continual to fall. As a result, people end up buying high and selling low rather than the reverse. Studies have shown that individual investors consistently earn lower returns on their investments when they frequently buy and sell stock hoping to predict changes in stock prices.

But why are stock prices so difficult to predict? The key reason is that stock prices are based less on the *current* profitability of firms than on their *expected* future profitability. After all, few investors would be willing to pay a high price for a stock that was profitable today but was expected to suffer large losses tomorrow. Similarly, investors in late 2015 were willing to pay $30 per share for Twitter even though the firm was suffering losses because they expected it would earn profits in the future. If you look carefully at Figure 8.2, you can see that stock prices start to rise when investors begin to expect an economic recovery will soon begin rather than after the recovery has already begun.

Many Wall Street investment professionals spend a lot of time and money gathering all possible information about the future profitability of firms, hoping to buy stock in the most profitable firms. As a result, all of the information publicly available about a firm is reflected in the firm's stock price. For example, if at the end of a particular day, Twitter is selling for $30 per share, that price reflects all of the information available about Twitter's future profitability. What might cause Twitter's stock price to change? *Only new information about its future profitability.* For example, if Twitter releases new data showing that its advertising sales have been lower than investors had expected, its stock price will fall.

Even highly paid professional investors cannot consistently predict stock prices. The managers of mutual funds who try to earn high returns by frequently buying and selling stocks are rarely able to beat the stock market averages, such as the S&P 500. One study found that, in a typical year, only one-third of mutual fund managers were able to earn their investors a higher return than a small investor could earn by investing in an index mutual that buys only the stocks in the S&P 500. Only 10 percent of mutual fund managers earned a higher return than an index fund for two consecutive years.

Whichever way you—or Wall Street professionals—predict stock prices will move in the future, you are as likely to be wrong as you are to be right.

Sources: Morgan Housel, "Three Mistakes Investors Keep Making Again and Again," *Wall Street Journal*, September 12, 2014; Joe Light, "How to Find a Fund Manager Who Can Beat the Market," *Wall Street Journal*, January 11, 2013; and Howard Gold, "Almost No One Can Beat the Market," marketwatch.com, October 25, 2013.

MyEconLab Study Plan

Your Turn: Test your understanding by doing related problem 2.12 on page 272 at the end of this chapter.

Solved Problem 8.2

MyEconLab Interactive Animation

Why Does Warren Buffett Like Mutual Funds?

Warren Buffett is considered one of the greatest investors who has ever lived. His ability to predict which firms' stocks are likely to rise in price helped make him one of the richest people in the world. Yet Buffett advises that individual investors not try to pick individual stocks but instead use 90 percent of their savings to buy shares in mutual funds that charge low fees, such as those offered by the Vanguard Group. Is it likely that anyone investing mostly in mutual funds will become as wealthy as Buffett? Why would Buffett give this advice?

Solving the Problem

Step 1: Review the chapter material. This problem is about investing in the stock market, so you may want to review the section "The Fluctuating Stock Market" on page 260 and the *Making the Connection*, "Why Are Many People Poor Stock Market Investors?" which begins on page 261.

Step 2: Answer the first question by discussing whether investing in low-cost mutual funds is a way to become as wealthy as Warren Buffett. Most investors who have become wealthy have done so by making large investments in just a few firms. Mutual funds typically hold large numbers of stocks and bonds, so even if one or two of the stocks do extremely well, the total investment return from the fund will be held back by the smaller increases (or losses) in the other stocks in the fund. By investing in mutual funds, you can accumulate significant amounts to pay for a house, a college education, or retirement. Many people who have earned only middle-class incomes have accumulated a million dollars or more by retirement age by investing in low-cost mutual funds. But no one is known to have become fabulously wealthy with this approach to saving.

Step 3: Answer the second question by explaining why Warren Buffett would advise most people to put their savings in mutual funds, even though they are unlikely to become wealthy by doing so. Mutual funds give individual investors a low-cost way to diversify. Although it's possible to earn a high return investing in the stocks of individual firms, it's also easy for a small investor to lose all of his or her money if those firms run into financial problems.

Extra Credit: Warren Buffett may have become a billionaire by being better than other investors at predicting the future profits of the firms he invests in. Or he may have become a billionaire because he was lucky that the firms he invested in did particularly well—in which case he may not be better at forecasting the future profitability of firms than are other investors. Given that nearly all other equally intelligent and hardworking professional investors have been unable to consistently "beat the market" by earning higher returns than those earned by the typical low-cost, well-diversified mutual fund, it is impossible to know with certainty the true reasons for Buffett's success.

Source: Warren Buffett, *Letter to Berkshire Shareholders*, March 1, 2014, p. 20.

Your Turn: For more practice, do related problem 2.13 on page 272 at the end of this chapter.

MyEconLab Study Plan

8.3 Using Financial Statements to Evaluate a Corporation

LEARNING OBJECTIVE: Understand the information corporations include in their financial statements.

To raise funds, a firm's managers must persuade potential lenders or investors that the firm will be profitable. Before a firm can sell new issues of stocks or bonds, it must first provide investors and financial regulators with information about its finances. To borrow from a bank, a firm must also provide the bank with financial information.

In most high-income countries, government agencies require firms to disclose specific financial information to the public before they are allowed to sell securities such as stocks or bonds in financial markets. In the United States, the Securities and Exchange Commission (SEC) requires publicly owned firms to report their performance in financial statements prepared using standard accounting methods, often referred to as *generally accepted accounting principles*. Such disclosure reduces the cost to investors of gathering information about firms, but it doesn't eliminate these costs—for two reasons. First, some firms may be too young to have much information for potential investors to evaluate. Second, managers may try to present the required information in the most favorable way so that investors will overvalue their securities.

Private firms also collect information on business borrowers and sell the information to lenders and investors. If the information-gathering firms do a good job, lenders and investors purchasing the information will be better able to judge the quality of borrowing firms. Some firms—including Moody's Investors Service, Standard & Poor's Corporation, Value Line, and Dun & Bradstreet—collect information from businesses and sell it to subscribers. Buyers include individual investors, libraries, and financial intermediaries. You can find some of these publications in your college library or through online information services.

What kind of information do investors and firm managers need? A firm must answer three basic questions: What to produce? How to produce it? What price to charge? To answer these questions, a firm's managers need two pieces of information: The first is the firm's revenues and costs, and the second is the value of the property and other assets the firm owns and the firm's debts, or other **liabilities**, that it owes to households and other firms. Potential investors in the firm also need this information to decide whether to buy the firm's stocks or bonds. The information can be found in the firm's *financial statements*, principally its income statement and balance sheet, which we discuss next. MyEconLab Concept Check

Liability Anything owed by a person or a firm.

The Income Statement

A firm's **income statement** shows its revenues, costs, and profit over a period of time. Corporations issue annual income statements, although the 12-month *fiscal year* covered may be different from the calendar year to better represent the seasonal pattern of the business. We explore income statements in greater detail in the appendix to this chapter.

Income statement A financial statement that shows a firm's revenues, costs, and profit over a period of time.

Accounting Profit An income statement shows a firm's revenue, costs, and profit for the firm's fiscal year. To determine profitability, the income statement starts with the firm's revenue and subtracts its operating expenses and taxes paid. The remainder, *net income*, is the **accounting profit** of the firm.

Accounting profit A firm's net income, measured as revenue minus operating expenses and taxes paid.

Economic Profit Accounting profit provides information on a firm's current net income, measured according to accepted accounting standards. Accounting profit is not, however, the ideal measure of a firm's profits because it neglects some of the firm's costs. *Economic profit* provides a better indication than accounting profit of how successful a firm is because economic profit is calculated using all of a firm's costs. Firms making an economic profit will remain in business and may even expand. Firms making an *economic loss* are unlikely to remain in business in the long run. To understand how economic profit is calculated, remember that economists always measure cost as *opportunity cost*. The **opportunity cost** of any activity is the highest-valued alternative that must be given up to engage in that activity. Costs are either *explicit* or *implicit*. When a firm spends money, an **explicit cost** results. If a firm incurs an opportunity cost but does not spend money, an **implicit cost** results. For example, firms incur an explicit labor cost when they pay wages to employees. Firms have many other explicit costs as well, such as the cost of the electricity used to light their buildings or the costs of advertising or insurance.

Opportunity cost The highest-valued alternative that must be given up to engage in an activity.

Explicit cost A cost that involves spending money.

Implicit cost A nonmonetary opportunity cost.

Some costs are implicit, however. The most important of these is the opportunity cost to investors of the funds they have invested in the firm. Economists use the term *normal rate of return* to refer to the minimum amount that investors must earn on the funds they invest in a firm, expressed as a percentage of the amount invested. If a firm fails to provide investors with at least a normal rate of return, it will not be able to remain in business over the long run because investors will not continue to invest their funds in the firm. For example, Borders was once the second-largest bookstore chain in the United States and a very profitable firm, with stock that sold for more than $40 per share. By 2010, investors became convinced that the firm's difficulty competing with Amazon and other online booksellers and its loss of sales to e-books meant that the firm would never be able to provide investors with a normal rate of return. Many investors expected that the firm would eventually have to declare bankruptcy, and as a result, the price of Borders stock plummeted to less than $1 per share. Within a year, the firm declared bankruptcy, and its remaining assets were sold off. The return (in dollars) that investors require to continue investing in a firm is a true cost to the firm and should be subtracted from the firm's revenues to calculate its profits.

The rate of return that investors require to continue investing in a firm varies from firm to firm. If the investment is risky—as would be the case with a biotechnology startup—investors may require a high rate of return to compensate them for the risk. Investors in firms in more established industries, such as electric utilities, may require lower rates of return. The exact rate of return investors require to invest in any particular firm is difficult to calculate, which also makes it difficult for an accountant to include the return as a cost on an income statement. Firms have other implicit costs, besides the return investors require, that can also be difficult to calculate. As a result, the rules of accounting generally require that only explicit costs be included in the firm's financial records. *Economic costs* include both explicit costs *and* implicit costs. **Economic profit** is equal to a firm's revenues minus its economic costs. Because accounting profit excludes some implicit costs, it is larger than economic profit.

Economic profit A firm's revenues minus all of its implicit and explicit costs.

MyEconLab Concept Check

The Balance Sheet

A firm's **balance sheet** shows its financial position on a particular day, usually the end of a quarter or year. Recall that an asset is anything of value that a firm owns, and a liability is a debt or an obligation owed by a firm. Subtracting the value of a firm's liabilities from the value of its assets leaves its *net worth*. We can think of the net worth as what the firm's owners would be left with if the firm were closed, its assets were sold, and its liabilities were paid off. Investors can determine a firm's net worth by inspecting its balance sheet. We analyze a balance sheet in more detail in the appendix to this chapter.

Balance sheet A financial statement that sums up a firm's financial position on a particular day, usually the end of a quarter or year.

MyEconLab Concept Check

MyEconLab Study Plan

8.4 Corporate Governance Policy and the Financial Crisis of 2007–2009

LEARNING OBJECTIVE: Explain the role that corporate governance problems may have played in the financial crisis of 2007–2009.

Accurate and easy-to-understand financial statements help the firm's managers make decisions and provide information to investors who are considering buying the firm's stock or bonds. In fact, the information in financial statements helps guide resource allocation in the economy.

Firms disclose financial statements in periodic filings to the federal government and in *annual reports* to shareholders. An investor is more likely to buy a firm's stock if the firm's income statement shows a large after-tax profit and if its balance sheet shows a large net worth. The top management of a firm has at least two reasons to attract investors and keep the firm's stock price high. First, a higher stock price increases the funds the firm can raise when it sells a given amount of stock. Second, to reduce the principal–agent problem, boards of directors often tie the salaries of top managers to the firm's stock price or to the profitability of the firm.

Top managers clearly have an incentive to maximize the profits reported on the income statement and the net worth reported on the balance sheet. If top managers make good decisions, the firm's profits will be high, and the firm's assets will be large relative to its liabilities. Problems that surfaced during the early 2000s, however, revealed that some top managers have inflated profits and hidden liabilities that should have been listed on their balance sheets. At other firms, managers took on more risk than they disclosed to investors. We will explore problems with corporate governance and the government's reaction to these problems by discussing the accounting scandals of the early 2000s and problems that many financial firms encountered during 2007–2009.

The Accounting Scandals of the Early 2000s

In the early 2000s, the top managers of several well-known firms, including Enron, an energy trading firm, and WorldCom, a telecommunications firm, falsified their firms' financial statements in order to mislead investors about how profitable the firms actually were. Several top managers were sentenced to long prison terms, and some of the firms, including Enron, went out of business.

How was it possible for corporations such as Enron and WorldCom to falsify their financial statements? The federal government regulates how financial statements are prepared, but this regulation cannot by itself guarantee the accuracy of the statements. All firms that issue stock to the public have certified public accountants working for outside firms *audit* their financial statements. Unfortunately, as the Enron and WorldCom scandals revealed, top managers who are determined to deceive investors about the true financial condition of their firms can also deceive outside auditors.

To guard against future scandals, new federal legislation was enacted in 2002. The landmark *Sarbanes-Oxley Act* of 2002 requires that CEOs personally certify the accuracy of financial statements. The Sarbanes-Oxley Act also requires that financial analysts and auditors disclose whether any conflicts of interest might exist that would limit their independence in evaluating a firm's financial condition. On balance, most observers acknowledge that the Sarbanes-Oxley Act increased confidence in the U.S. corporate governance system. However, as we will discuss in the next section, problems during 2007–2009 at financial firms again raised questions about whether corporations were adequately disclosing information to investors. MyEconLab Concept Check

The Financial Crisis of 2007–2009

Beginning in 2007 and lasting into 2009, the U.S. economy suffered the worst financial crisis since the Great Depression of the 1930s. At the heart of the crisis was a problem in the market for home mortgages. When people buy houses, they typically borrow the money by taking out a mortgage loan from a bank or another financial institution. The house they are buying is pledged as collateral for the loan, meaning that the bank can take possession of the house and sell it if the borrower defaults by failing to make the payments on the loan.

Securitizing Home Mortgages For many years, a bank or other financial institution granting a mortgage would keep the loan until the borrower had paid it off. Beginning in the 1970s, financial institutions began *securitizing* some mortgage loans, which means that groups of mortgages were bundled together and sold to investors. These *mortgage-backed securities* are very similar to bonds in that the investor who buys one receives regular interest payments, which in this case come from the payments being made on the original mortgage loans. At first, the securitization process was carried out by the Federal National Mortgage Association ("Fannie Mae") and the Federal Home Loan Mortgage Corporation ("Freddie Mac"), which Congress had established to help increase the volume of lending in the home mortgage market. Fannie Mae and Freddie Mac would buy mortgages granted to creditworthy borrowers and bundle them into securities that were then sold to investors.

Looser Lending Standards Fuel a Housing Bubble Beginning in the 1990s, private financial firms, primarily investment banks, started to securitize mortgages. By the early 2000s, banks and other financial institutions were loosening the standards for granting mortgages. Lenders began granting mortgages to "subprime" borrowers, whose credit histories included failing to pay all of their bills on time, and "Alt-A" borrowers, who failed to document that their incomes were high enough to afford their mortgage payments. The ease of obtaining a mortgage increased demand for housing, and caused prices to soar. This housing bubble began to deflate in mid-2006, with prices in many cities beginning a sharp downturn. By 2007, many borrowers—particularly subprime and Alt-A borrowers—began to default on their mortgages. These defaults were bad news for anyone owning mortgage-backed securities because the value of these securities depended on steady payments being made on the underlying mortgages. As prices of these securities plunged, the result was a financial crisis as many financial institutions suffered heavy losses, and some of the largest of them remained in business only because they received aid from the federal government. Some economists argue that the firms did a poor job of correctly assessing the risk of the investments they made in these securities. This failure may be an indication of poor corporate governance if top managers were unable to effectively monitor the employees who were deciding to invest in risky securities.

Government Regulation in Response to the Financial Crisis During the financial crisis, many investors complained that they weren't aware of the riskiness of some of the assets—particularly mortgage-backed securities—on the balance sheets of financial firms. Some observers believed that the managers of many financial firms had intentionally misled investors about the riskiness of these assets. Others argued that the managers themselves had not understood how risky the assets were. In the fall of 2008, Fannie Mae and Freddie Mac were brought under direct control of the government. As the crisis passed, in July 2010, Congress overhauled the regulation of the financial system with the passage of the **Wall Street Reform and Consumer Protection Act**, referred to as the **Dodd-Frank Act**. Among its provisions, the act created the Consumer Financial Protection Bureau, housed in the Federal Reserve—the central bank of the United States—to write rules intended to protect consumers in their borrowing and investing activities. The act also established the Financial Stability Oversight Council, which includes representatives from all the major federal financial regulatory bodies, including the SEC and the Federal Reserve. The council is intended to identify and act on risks to the financial system. Economists are divided in their opinions about whether the Dodd-Frank Act will significantly reduce the risk of future financial crises. MyEconLab Concept Check

Wall Street Reform and Consumer Protection Act (Dodd-Frank Act) Legislation passed during 2010 that was intended to reform regulation of the financial system.

Did Principal-Agent Problems Help Cause the 2007–2009 Financial Crisis?

As we have seen, the process of securitizing mortgages played an important role in the financial crisis of 2007–2009. Beginning in the 1990s, private investment banks began to securitize mortgages. Unlike commercial banks, whose main activities are accepting deposits and making loans, investment banks had traditionally concentrated on providing advice to corporations on selling new stocks and bonds and on *underwriting* the issuance of stocks and bonds by guaranteeing a price to the firm selling them. Investment banking is considered riskier than commercial banking because investment banks can suffer substantial losses on underwriting. To address this greater risk, Congress passed the *Glass-Steagall Act* in 1933. The act prevented financial firms from being both commercial banks and investment banks.

Some economists and policymakers argued that Glass-Steagall reduced competition for investment banking services by prohibiting commercial banks from offering these services. Congress repealed the Glass-Steagall Act in 1999, after which some commercial banks began engaging in investment banking. Many of the largest, best-known investment banks, such as Lehman Brothers, Bear Stearns, Goldman Sachs, Merrill Lynch, and Morgan Stanley, remained exclusively investment banks. The mortgage-backed securities originated by the investment banks were mostly sold to investors, but some were retained as investments by these firms. As a result, when the prices of these securities declined beginning in 2007, the investment banks suffered heavy losses. Lehman Brothers was forced to declare bankruptcy; Merrill Lynch and Bear Stearns were sold to commercial banks in deals arranged by the U.S. government; and Goldman Sachs and Morgan Stanley became bank holding companies, which allowed them to engage in commercial banking activity.

Why did investment banks take on so much risk by originating securities backed by mortgages granted to borrowers who had a significant likelihood of defaulting on the loans? Michael Lewis, a financial journalist and former Wall Street bond salesman, has argued that a key reason was a change in how the investment banks were organized. Traditionally, large Wall Street investment banks had been organized as partnerships, but by 2000 they had all converted to being publicly traded corporations. As we have seen, in a partnership, the funds of the relatively small group of owners are put directly at risk, and the principal–agent problem is reduced because there is little separation of ownership from control. With a publicly traded corporation, on the other hand, the principal–agent problem can be severe. Lewis argues:

> No investment bank owned by its employees would have ... bought and held $50 billion in [exotic mortgage-backed securities] ... or even allow [these securities] to be sold to its customers. The hoped-for short-term gain would not have justified the long-term hit.

Issues of corporate governance will clearly continue to be a concern for economists, policymakers, and investors.

MyEconLab Concept Check

Solved Problem 8.4

MyEconLab Interactive Animation

Will Dodd-Frank Improve Corporate Governance?

Commercial and investment banks, mutual funds, and brokerage firms are often called *financial service firms*. A review of the effects of the Dodd-Frank Act by an accountant included the opinion that, "Clearly, the drive for improved governance in financial services will continue for years to come." What does the author mean by "improved governance"? Why has improved governance at financial service firms been a significant policy issue?

Solving the Problem

Step 1: Review the chapter material. This problem is about whether government regulation can reduce the principal–agent problem in financial firms, so you may want to review the section "Government Regulation in Response to the Financial Crisis" and the section "Did Principal–Agent Problems Help Cause the 2007–2009 Financial Crisis?" which are both on page 267.

Step 2: Answer the first question by explaining what "improved governance" means. Some economists argue that one factor that caused the financial crisis of 2007–2009 was top managers of large financial services firms making riskier investments than were in the best interests of the firms' shareholders. Some economists also argue that financial service firms should have done a better job of assessing the risk involved in investing in mortgage-backed securities. Better governance in this context refers to improvements in aligning the actions of top managers with the preferences of shareholders and in improving the assessment and monitoring of investments.

Step 3: Answer the second question by explaining why improved governance at financial service firms has become a political issue. Policymakers recognize that poor corporate governance may have played a role in the financial crisis. Given its severity, they have been looking for ways to increase the stability of the financial system.

Extra Credit: Many economists and policymakers are hopeful that the Dodd-Frank Act has improved governance at financial service firms. Some economists, though, believe that the administrative costs the act imposes on firms may be greater than any benefits from improved governance. Some economists have also criticized other provisions of the act that restrict the monetary policy actions the Federal Reserve may take in a financial crisis.

Source: David Wright. "Dodd-Frank Four Years Later," *Wall Street Journal*, January 28, 2015.

MyEconLab Study Plan

Your Turn: Test your understanding by doing related problem 4.6 on page 273 at the end of this chapter.

Continued from page 251

Economics in Your Life

Would You Pay to Use Facebook or Twitter?

At the beginning of the chapter, we asked you to consider two questions: Would you be willing to pay to use social media apps such as Facebook and Twitter if the apps no longer targeted you with ads? and Do you think other users would be willing to pay enough that firms could rely on that source of revenue? The answer to the first question is likely to depend on what price the apps would charge, what your income is, and how annoyed you are by targeted ads. Of course, some people find the information in targeted ads useful and would prefer to see the ads rather than pay any fee.

In practice, people have become increasingly reluctant to pay anything to download and use an app. Some free apps are downloaded millions of times, while very similar apps that charge a small fee have significantly fewer downloads. In a given year, only about one-third of smartphone or tablet owners will pay for any apps. App developers have mostly adopted the business model of allowing their apps to be downloaded and used for free, while trying to still earn money from users. For instance, the popular games *Clash of Clans* and *Candy Crush Saga* can be downloaded and played for free. The developers earn a profit from people who pay to play the game faster, get extra turns, or otherwise receive benefits not available to those who play for free. The usefulness of social media apps increases as more people use them. If only a few people were on Facebook or used Twitter, these apps wouldn't be much fun. So, these apps can't afford the significant decline in users that would likely occur if they began to charge a fee. The remaining users who were paying would likely find the apps less fun because fewer people would be on them, and they might gradually stop using them.

So, whether you like targeted ads or hate them, it seems likely that you will have to continue putting up with them on social media apps.

Conclusion

In a market system, firms make independent decisions about which goods and services to produce, how to produce them, and what prices to charge. In modern high-income countries, such as the United States, large corporations account for a majority of the sales and profits earned by firms. Generally, the managers of these corporations do a good job of representing the interests of stockholders while providing the goods and services demanded by consumers. As the business scandals of the early 2000s and the problems with financial firms in 2007–2009 showed, however, the principal–agent problem can sometimes become severe. Economists debate the costs and benefits of regulations proposed to address these problems.

Visit MyEconLab for a news article and analysis related to the concepts in this chapter.

CHAPTER SUMMARY AND PROBLEMS

Key Terms

Accounting profit, p. 264	Direct finance, p. 256	Interest rate, p. 257	Separation of ownership from control, p. 255
Asset, p. 252	Dividends, p. 259	Liability, p. 264	Sole proprietorship, p. 252
Balance sheet, p. 265	Economic profit, p. 265	Limited liability, p. 252	Stock, p. 258
Bond, p. 256	Explicit cost, p. 264	Opportunity cost, p. 264	Wall Street Reform and Consumer Protection Act (Dodd-Frank Act), p. 267
Corporate governance, p. 255	Implicit cost, p. 264	Partnership, p. 252	
Corporation, p. 252	Income statement, p. 264	Principal–agent problem, p. 255	
Coupon payment, p. 257	Indirect finance, p. 256		

8.1 Types of Firms, pages 252–256

LEARNING OBJECTIVE: Categorize the major types of firms in the United States.

Summary

There are three types of firms: A **sole proprietorship** is a firm owned by a single individual and not organized as a corporation; a **partnership** is a firm owned jointly by two or more persons and not organized as a corporation; and a **corporation** is a legal form of business that provides its owners with limited liability. An **asset** is anything of value owned by a person or a firm. The owners of sole proprietorships and partnerships have unlimited liability, which means there is no legal distinction between the personal assets of the owners of the business and the assets of the business. The owners of corporations have **limited liability**, which means they can never lose more than their investment in the firm. Although only 18 percent of firms are corporations, they account for the majority of revenue and profits earned by all firms. **Corporate governance** refers to the way in which a corporation is structured and the effect a corporation's structure has on the firm's behavior. Most corporations have a similar management structure: The shareholders elect a board of directors that appoints the corporation's top managers, such as the chief executive officer (CEO). Because top managers often do not own a large fraction of the stock in the corporation, large corporations have a **separation of ownership from control**. When top managers have less incentive to increase the corporation's profits than to increase their own salaries and their own enjoyment, corporations can suffer from the **principal–agent problem**. The principal–agent problem exists when the principals—in this case, the shareholders of the corporation—have difficulty getting the agent—the corporation's top management—to carry out their wishes.

MyEconLab Visit **www.myeconlab.com** to complete these exercises online and get instant feedback.

Review Questions

1.1 What are the three major types of firms in the United States? Briefly discuss the most important characteristics of each type.

1.2 What is limited liability? Why does the government grant limited liability to the owners of corporations?

1.3 Why is limited liability more important for firms trying to raise funds from a large number of investors than for firms trying to raise funds from a small number of investors?

1.4 What does it mean to say that there is a separation of ownership from control in large corporations?

1.5 How is the separation of ownership from control related to the principal–agent problem?

Problems and Applications

1.6 Suppose that shortly after graduating from college, you decide to start your own business. Will you be likely to organize the business as a sole proprietorship, a partnership, or a corporation? Explain your reasoning.

1.7 An article discussing the reasons that the Connecticut state legislature passed a general incorporation law observes that prior to the passage of the law, investors were afraid that large businesses "were not a safe bet for their money." Briefly explain the author's reasoning.

Source: Anne Rajotte, "Connecticut's General Incorporation Law Was the First of Its Kind," ctstatelibrary.org, June 10, 2014.

1.8 Evaluate the following argument:

> I would like to invest in the stock market, but I think that buying shares of stock in a corporation is too risky. Suppose I buy $10,000 of Twitter stock, and the company ends up going bankrupt. Because as a stockholder I'm part owner of the company, I might be responsible for paying hundreds of thousands of dollars of the company's debts.

1.9 According to an article in the *Economist*, historian David Faure has argued that the Chinese economy failed to grow rapidly during the nineteenth century because "family-run companies ... could not raise sufficient capital to exploit the large-scale opportunities tied to the rise of the steam engine, notably railways and (with limited exceptions) global shipping and automated manufacturing." How did the United States solve the problem of firms raising enough funds to operate railroads and other large-scale businesses?

Source: "The PCCW Buy-Out in Court," *Economist*, April 21, 2009.

1.10 **(Related to the Making the Connection on page 254)** Two economists at the Brookings Institution argue that "new firms rather than existing ones have accounted for a disproportionate share of disruptive and thus highly productivity enhancing innovations in the past—the automobile, the airplane, the computer and personal computer, air conditioning, and Internet search, to name just a few."

a. Why might new firms be more likely than older firms to introduce "disruptive" innovations?

b. Assuming these economists are correct about the most important source of productivity enhancing innovations, what are the implications for the future of the U.S. economy of recent trends in the formation of new businesses?

Source: Ian Hathaway and Robert E. Litan, "What's Driving the Decline in the Firm Formation Rate? A Partial Explanation," *Brookings Economic Studies*, November 20, 2014.

1.11 **(Related to the Making the Connection on page 254)** An Associated Press article noted that some groups have filed law suits over what the groups describe as "overzealous licensing schemes, in occupations such as hair braiders, yoga teachers and casket makers."

a. What effect might such government licensing requirements have on the rate of new businesses being formed?

b. Given your answer to part (a), why might state and local governments pass such licensing requirements?

Source: Associated Press, "High Court Asked to Rule on Tour-Guide Licensing," *New York Times*, November 18, 2014.

1.12 The principal–agent problem arises almost everywhere in the business world, and it also crops up even closer to home. Discuss the principal–agent problem that exists in the college classroom. Who is the principal? Who is the agent? What potential conflicts in objectives exist between this principal and this agent?

1.13 In a public corporation, the principal–agent problem between ownership and top management results from asymmetric information. What information, if known, would prevent this principal–agent problem?

1.14 Salespeople, whether selling life insurance, automobiles, or pharmaceuticals, typically get paid on commission instead of a straight hourly wage. How does paying a commission help solve the principal–agent problem between the owners of a business and their salespeople?

1.15 Private equity firms, such as Blackstone and Kohlberg Kravis Roberts & Co., search for firms where the managers appear not to be maximizing profits. A private equity firm can buy stock in these firms and have its employees elected to the firms' boards of directors and may even acquire control of the targeted firm and replace the top management. Does the existence of private equity firms reduce any problems in corporate governance? Briefly explain.

8.2 How Firms Raise Funds, pages 256–263

LEARNING OBJECTIVE: Explain how firms raise the funds they need to operate and expand.

Summary

Firms rely on retained earnings—which are profits kept by the firm and not paid out to the firm's owners—or on using the savings of households for the funds they need to operate and expand. With **direct finance**, the savings of households flow directly to businesses when investors buy **stocks** and **bonds** in financial markets. With **indirect finance**, savings flow indirectly to businesses when households deposit money in savings and checking accounts in banks and the banks lend these funds to businesses. Federal, state, and local governments also sell bonds in financial markets, and households also borrow funds from banks. When a firm sells a bond, it is borrowing money from the buyer of the bond. Firms make **coupon payments** to buyers of bonds. The **interest rate** is the cost of borrowing funds, usually expressed as a percentage of the amount borrowed. When a firm sells stock, it is selling part ownership of the firm to the buyer of the stock. **Dividends** are payments by a corporation to its shareholders. The original purchasers of stocks and bonds may resell them in stock and bond markets, such as the New York Stock Exchange. The performance of the U.S. stock market is often measured using stock market indexes. The three most widely followed stock indexes are the Dow Jones Industrial Average, the S&P 500, and the NASDAQ Composite Index.

MyEconLab Visit www.myeconlab.com to complete these exercises online and get instant feedback.

Review Questions

2.1 What is the difference between direct finance and indirect finance? If you borrow money from a bank to buy a new car, are you using direct finance or indirect finance?

2.2 Why is a bond considered to be a loan but a share of stock is not? Why do corporations issue both bonds and shares of stock?

2.3 How do the stock and bond markets provide information to businesses? Why do stock and bond prices change over time?

Problems and Applications

2.4 Suppose that a firm in which you have invested is losing money. Would you rather own the firm's stock or the firm's bonds? Briefly explain.

2.5 Suppose you originally invested in a firm when it was small and unprofitable. Now the firm has grown to be large and profitable. Would you be better off if you had bought the firm's stock or the firm's bonds? Briefly explain.

2.6 If you deposit $20,000 in a savings account at a bank, you might earn 1 percent interest per year. Someone who borrows $20,000 from a bank to buy a new car might have to pay an interest rate of 6 percent per year on the loan. Knowing this, why don't you just lend your money directly to the car buyer and cut out the bank?

2.7 **(Related to the Chapter Opener on page 251)** Were the shares of stock issued as a result of Twitter's initial public offering (IPO) sold in a primary market or a secondary market? Was the IPO an example of direct finance or indirect finance?

2.8 **(Related to the Making the Connection on page 257)** According to an article in the *Wall Street Journal*, in May 2015, Moody's Investors Service cut its rating on McDonald's bonds from A3 to A2.

a. What is Moody's top bond rating? Under what circumstances would Moody's, or the other bond rating agencies, be likely to cut the rating on a firm's bonds?

b. What will be the likely result of this rating's cut for the interest rate McDonald's will have to pay when it sells new bonds? Briefly explain.

Source: Chelsey Dulaney, "Moody's Downgrades McDonald's, Following S&P and Fitch," *Wall Street Journal*, May 15, 2015.

2.9 **(Related to the Making the Connection on page 257)** Investors use the bond ratings from Moody's, S&P, and Fitch to determine which bonds they will buy and the prices they are willing to pay for them. The rating services charge the firms and governments that issue bonds, rather than investors, for their services. Critics argue that the rating agencies may give higher ratings than are justified in order to continue to sell their services to bond issuing firms. To avoid this impression, why don't Moody's, S&P, and Fitch sell their services directly to investors?

2.10 What effect would the following events be likely to have on the price of Google's stock?

a. A competitor launches a search engine that is better than Google's.

b. The corporate income tax is abolished.

c. Google's board of directors becomes dominated by close friends and relatives of its top management.

d. The price of wireless Internet connections in developing countries unexpectedly drops, so more and more people worldwide use the Internet.

e. Google announces a profit of $10 billion, but investors anticipated that Google would earn a profit of $11 billion.

2.11 **(Related to the Don't Let This Happen to You on page 260)** Briefly explain whether you agree with the following statement: "The total value of the shares of Microsoft stock traded on the NASDAQ last week was $250 million, so the firm actually received more revenue from stock sales than from selling software."

2.12 **(Related to the Making the Connection on page 261)** A column in the *Wall Street Journal* listed "trying to forecast what stocks will do next" as one of the three mistakes investors make repeatedly. Briefly explain why trying to forecast stock prices would be a mistake for the average investor.

Source: Morgan Housel, "Three Mistakes Investors Keep Making Again and Again," *Wall Street Journal*, September 12, 2014.

2.13 **(Related to Solved Problem 8.2 on page 262)** In a letter to his company's stockholders, Warren Buffett offered the following opinion: "Most investors, of course, have not made the study of business prospects a priority in their lives. . . . I have good news for these non-professionals: The typical investor doesn't need this skill." Briefly explain Buffett's reasoning.

Source: Warren Buffett, *Letter to Berkshire Shareholders*, March 1, 2014, p. 20.

8.3 Using Financial Statements to Evaluate a Corporation, pages 263–265

LEARNING OBJECTIVE: Understand the information corporations include in their financial statements.

Summary

A firm's **income statement** shows its revenues, costs, and profit over a period of time. A firm's **balance sheet** shows its financial position on a particular day, usually the end of a quarter or year. A balance sheet records a firm's assets and liabilities. A **liability** is anything owed by a person or a firm. Firms report their **accounting profit** on their income statements. Accounting profit does not always include all of a firm's **opportunity cost**. **Explicit cost** is a cost that involves spending money. **Implicit cost** is a nonmonetary opportunity cost. Because accounting profit excludes some implicit costs, it is larger than **economic profit**.

MyEconLab Visit **www.myeconlab.com** to complete these exercises online and get instant feedback.

Review Questions

3.1 What is the difference between a firm's assets and its liabilities? Give an example of an asset and an example of a liability.

3.2 What is the difference between a firm's balance sheet and its income statement?

3.3 Distinguish between a firm's explicit costs and its implicit costs and between a firm's accounting profit and its economic profit.

3.4 Would a business be expected to survive in the long run if it earned a positive accounting profit but a negative economic profit? Briefly explain.

Problems and Applications

3.5 Paolo currently has $100,000 invested in bonds that earn him 10 percent interest per year. He wants to open a pizza restaurant and is considering either selling the bonds and using the $100,000 to start his restaurant or borrowing $100,000 from a bank, which would charge him an annual interest rate of 7 percent. He finally decides to sell the bonds and not take out the bank loan. He reasons, "Because I already have the $100,000 invested in the bonds, I don't have to pay anything to use the money. If I take out the bank loan, I have to pay interest, so my costs of producing pizza will be higher if I take out the loan than if I sell the bonds." Evaluate Paolo's reasoning.

3.6 Paolo and Alfredo are twins who both want to open pizza restaurants. Their parents have always liked Alfredo best, and they buy two pizza ovens and give both to him. Unfortunately, Paolo must buy his own pizza ovens. Does Alfredo have a lower cost of producing pizza than Paolo does because Alfredo received his pizza ovens as a gift, while Paolo had to pay for his? Briefly explain.

3.7 Dane decides to give up a job earning $200,000 per year as a corporate lawyer and converts the duplex that he owns into a UFO museum. (He had been renting out the duplex for $20,000 a year.) His explict costs are $75,000 per year paid to his assistants and $10,000 per year for utilities. Fans flock to the museum to see his collection of extraterrestrial paraphernalia, which he could easily sell on eBay for $1,000,000. Over the course of the year, the museum brings in revenues of $200,000.

a. How much is Dane's accounting profit for the year?
b. Is Dane earning an economic profit? Explain.

3.8 Twitter was founded in 2006, but it wasn't until 2013 that Twitter filed its first annual report with the Securities and Exchange Commission (SEC). Briefly explain why.

3.9 Jay Ritter, a professor at the University of Florida, was quoted in the *Wall Street Journal* as saying about Facebook: "It's entirely possible for a company to have solid growth prospects while its stock is overvalued."

a. What does it mean to say that a stock is "overvalued"?
b. Why might a firm's stock be overvalued despite the firm having "solid growth prospects"?

Source: Mark Hulbert, "A Year after Its Debut, Facebook Still Looks Overpriced," *Wall Street Journal*, May 17, 2013.

8.4 Corporate Governance Policy and the Financial Crisis of 2007–2009, pages 265–268

LEARNING OBJECTIVE: Explain the role that corporate governance problems may have played in the financial crisis of 2007–2009.

Summary

Because their compensation often rises with the profitability of the corporation that employs them, top managers have an incentive to overstate the profits reported on their firm's income statements. During the early 2000s, it became clear that the top managers of several large corporations had done this, even though intentionally falsifying financial statements is illegal. The *Sarbanes-Oxley Act* of 2002 took several steps intended to increase the accuracy of financial statements and increase the penalties for falsifying them. The financial crisis of 2007–2009 revealed that many financial firms held assets that were far riskier than investors had realized. Congress passed the **Wall Street Reform and Consumer Protection Act (Dodd-Frank Act)** in July 2010 to address some of the issues raised by the financial crisis of 2007–2009.

MyEconLab Visit **www.myeconlab.com** to complete these exercises online and get instant feedback.

Review Questions

4.1 What is the Sarbanes-Oxley Act? Why was it passed?

4.2 What was the source of the problems encountered by many financial firms during the crisis of 2007–2009?

Problems and Applications

4.3 The following is from an article in *USA Today*:

> In what some call a worldwide corporate-governance movement, shareholders are pushing for stronger corporate-governance laws, teaming with investors from different countries and negotiating behind the scenes with businesses.

What is corporate governance? Why would shareholders push for stronger corporate governance laws?

Sources: Edward Iwata, "Corporate Governance Gets More Transparent Worldwide," *USA Today*, February 17, 2008.

4.4 According to an article in the *Wall Street Journal*, "Companies in Standard & Poor's 500 stock index elected the smallest number of new directors last year in 10 years." Is having members of boards of directors serve for longer periods likely to be good news or bad news for corporate governance? Briefly explain.

Source: Joann S. Lublin, "The 40-Year Club: America's Longest-Serving Directors," *Wall Street Journal*, July 16, 2013.

4.5 Michael Dell founded PCs Limited in 1984. The firm had an initial public offering (IPO) in 1988, under the name Dell Computer Corporation, which enabled the company to raise money it used for expansion. In 2013, Michael Dell and a private equity firm bought back ownership of the company from its shareholders. Dell is now a privately owned firm. What would motivate Michael Dell to make this change?

Source: Michael Dell, "Going Private Is Paying Off for Dell," *Wall Street Journal*, November 24, 2014.

4.6 **(Related to Solved Problem 8.4 on page 268)** An article on forbes.com about corporate fraud stated that "misleading accounting and disclosure practices weaken the integrity of capital markets." The article noted that using incentive contracts for top managers can create a "'perverse' incentive to manipulate stock prices because their (executive) total package is based on stock price appreciation."

a. Why do financial markets depend on accurate accounting and disclosure practices? Why can misleading accounting and disclosure practices weaken the integrity of financial markets?
b. Why do corporate boards of directors sometimes link top managers' compensation to the corporations' stock prices? Briefly explain how tying compensation too closely to stock prices might create an incentive for corporate fraud.

Source: John Wasik, "How Corporate Fraud Costs You Money: Four Red Flags," forbes.com, June 17, 2013.

Real-Time Data Exercises

D8.1 **(Exploring stock data)** On June 19, 2015 the closing price of a share of Facebook stock was $82.51. About 21.5 million shares of stock were traded on this date. Go to wsj.com for a recent trading day and use Facebook's stock symbol (FB) to find the following.
a. The closing price of Facebook stock
b. The market value of the shares traded
c. The number of shares (volume) traded
d. The total number of shares outstanding
e. The number of shares traded relative to the number of shares outstanding

D8.2 **(The stock market and recessions)** Go to the Web site of the Federal Reserve Bank of St. Louis (FRED) (research.stlouisfed.org/fred2/) and download and graph the data series for the Nasdaq Composite Index from February 1971 until the most recent day available. Go to the Web site of the National Bureau of Economic Research (nber.org) and find the dates for business cycle peaks and troughs (the period between a business cycle peak and trough is a recession). Describe how stock prices move just before, during, and just after a recession. Is the pattern the same across recessions?

D8.3 **(Exploring dividends)** Go to wsj.com and find the dividend per share for each of the following firms.
a. Microsoft
b. Apple
c. Coca-Cola
d. Facebook

To find the dividend per share, enter the company's name in the search box on the home page. Which pays the highest dividend? Which has the highest dividend yield? Which does not pay a dividend? Why might a firm not pay a dividend? Why would investors buy the stock of a firm that does not pay a dividend?

D8.4 **(Using stock data)** The following table lists the closing stock prices for three financial firms—Morgan Stanley, Citigroup Inc. and PNC Bank—for Friday, June 19, 2015. The table also includes the most recent dividends paid to shareholders by these firms.

	Morgan Stanley	Citigroup Inc.	PNC
Stock symbol	MS	C	PNC
Closing price	$39.37	$56.23	$97.13
Latest dividend	$0.15	$0.05	$0.51
Number of shares	100	100	100
Value of shares			
Total dividend			
Stock price increase	5 percent	5 percent	5 percent
New stock price			
Value of shares			
Capital gain			

Fill in the blank cells in the table by computing (a) the value of 100 shares of each company's stock, (b) total dividend payments for 100 shares of stock, and (c) assuming that each company's stock price increases by 5 percent, the new stock prices, the value of shares, and the increase in the value of each company's stock (capital gains). How will the price increases affect the total amount of dividends paid for each company's stock?

Appendix

Tools to Analyze Firms' Financial Information

LEARNING OBJECTIVE: Understand the concept of present value and the information contained on a firm's income statement and balance sheet.

As we saw in the chapter, modern firms are not just "black boxes" transforming inputs into output. The majority of business revenues and profits are earned by large corporations. Unlike founder-dominated firms, the typical large corporation is run by managers who generally do not own a controlling interest in the firm. Large firms raise funds from outside investors, and outside investors seek information on firms and the assurance that the managers of firms will act in the interests of the investors.

This chapter shows how corporations raise funds by issuing stocks and bonds. This appendix provides more detail to support that discussion. We begin by analyzing *present value* as a key concept in determining the prices of financial securities. We then provide greater information on *financial statements* issued by corporations, using Twitter as an example.

Using Present Value to Make Investment Decisions

Firms raise funds by selling equity (stock) and debt (bonds and loans) to investors and lenders. If you own shares of stock or a bond, you will receive payments in the form of dividends or coupons over a number of years. Most people value funds they already have more highly than funds they will receive some time in the future. For example, you would probably not trade $1,000 you already have for $1,000 you will not receive for one year. The longer you have to wait to receive a payment, the less value it will have for you. One thousand dollars you will not receive for two years is worth less to you than $1,000 you will receive after one year. The value you give today to money you will receive in the future is called the future payment's **present value**. The present value of $1,000 you will receive in one year will be less than $1,000.

Present value The value in today's dollars of funds to be paid or received in the future.

Why is the $1,000 you will not receive for one year less valuable to you than the $1,000 you already have? The most important reason is that if you have $1,000 today, you can use that $1,000 today. You can buy goods and services with the money and receive enjoyment from them. The $1,000 you receive in one year does not have direct use to you now.

Also, prices will likely rise during the year you are waiting to receive your $1,000. So, when you finally do receive the $1,000 in one year, you will not be able to buy as much with it as you could with $1,000 today. Finally, there is some risk that you will not receive the $1,000 in one year. The risk may be very great if an unreliable friend borrows $1,000 from you and vaguely promises to pay you back in one year. The risk may be very small if you lend money to the federal government by buying a U.S. Treasury bond. In either case, though, there is at least some risk that you will not receive the funds promised.

When someone lends money, the lender expects to be paid back both the amount of the loan and some additional interest. Say you are willing to lend $1,000 today if you are paid back $1,100 one year from now. In this case, you are charging $\$100/\$1{,}000 = 0.10$, or 10 percent interest on the funds you have loaned. Economists would say that you value $1,000 today as equivalent to the $1,100 to be received one year in the future.

Notice that $1,100 can be written as $\$1{,}000(1 + 0.10)$. That is, the value of money received in the future is equal to the value of money in the present multiplied by 1 plus the interest rate, with the interest rate expressed as a decimal. Or:

$$\$1{,}100 = \$1{,}000(1 + 0.10).$$

Notice, also, that if we divide both sides by (1 + 0.10), we can rewrite this formula as:

$$\$1{,}000 = \frac{\$1{,}100}{(1 + 0.10)}.$$

The rewritten formula states that the present value is equal to the future value to be received in one year divided by 1 plus the interest rate. This formula is important because you can use it to convert any amount to be received in one year into its present value. Writing the formula generally, we have:

$$\text{Present value} = \frac{\text{Future value}_1}{(1 + i)}.$$

The present value of funds to be received in one year—Future value$_1$—can be calculated by dividing the amount of those funds to be received by 1 plus the interest rate. With an interest rate of 10 percent, the present value of \$1,000,000 to be received one year from now is:

$$\frac{\$1{,}000{,}000}{(1 + 0.10)} = \$909{,}090.91.$$

This formula allows us to calculate the value today of funds that will be received in one year. But financial securities such as stocks and bonds involve promises to pay funds over many years. Therefore, it would be useful if we could expand this formula to calculate the present value of funds to be received more than one year in the future.

Go back to the original example, where we assumed you were willing to loan out your \$1,000 for one year, provided that you received 10 percent interest. Suppose you are asked to lend the funds for two years and that you are promised 10 percent interest per year for each year of the loan. That is, you are lending \$1,000, which at 10 percent interest will grow to \$1,100 after one year, and you are agreeing to loan that \$1,100 for a second year at 10 percent interest. So, after two years, you will be paid back \$1,100(1 + 0.10), or \$1,210. Or:

$$\$1{,}210 = \$1{,}000(1 + 0.10)\,(1 + 0.10),$$

or:

$$\$1{,}210 = \$1{,}000(1 + 0.10)^2.$$

This formula can also be rewritten as:

$$\$1{,}000 = \frac{\$1.210}{(1 + 0.10)^2}.$$

To put this formula in words, the \$1,210 you receive two years from now has a present value equal to \$1,210 divided by the quantity 1 plus the interest rate squared. If you agree to lend out your \$1,000 for three years at 10 percent interest, you will receive:

$$\$1{,}331 = \$1{,}000(1 + 0.10)^3.$$

Notice, again, that:

$$\$1{,}000 = \frac{\$1{,}331}{(1 + 0.10)^3}.$$

You can probably see a pattern here. We can generalize the concept to say that the present value of funds to be received *n* years in the future—whether *n* is 1, 20, or 85 does not matter—equals the amount of the funds to be received divided by the quantity 1 plus the interest rate raised to the *n*th power. For instance, with an interest rate of 10 percent, the value of \$1,000,000 to be received 25 years in the future is:

$$\text{Present value} = \frac{\$1{,}000{,}000}{(1 + 0.10)^{25}} = \$92{,}296.$$

Or, more generally:

$$\text{Present value} = \frac{\text{Future value}_n}{(1 + i)^n},$$

where Future value$_n$ represents funds that will be received in n years.

Solved Problem 8A.1

MyEconLab Interactive Animation

How to Receive Your Contest Winnings

Suppose you win a contest and are given the choice of the following prizes:

Prize 1: \$50,000 to be received right away, with four additional payments of \$50,000 to be received each year for the next four years

Prize 2: \$175,000 to be received right away

Explain which prize you would choose and the basis for your decision.

Solving the Problem

Step 1: Review the material. This problem involves applying the concept of present value, so you may want to review the section "Using Present Value to Make Investment Decisions," which begins on page 275.

Step 2: Explain the basis for choosing the prize. Unless you need cash immediately, you should choose the prize with the highest present value.

Step 3: Calculate the present value of each prize. Prize 2 consists of one payment of \$175,000 received right away, so its present value is \$175,000. Prize 1 consists of five payments spread out over time. To find the present value of the prize, we must find the present value of each of these payments and add them together. To calculate present value, we must use an interest rate. Let's assume an interest rate of 10 percent. In that case, the present value of Prize 1 is:

$$\$50{,}000 + \frac{\$50{,}000}{(1 + 0.10)} + \frac{\$50{,}000}{(1 + 0.10)^2} + \frac{\$50{,}000}{(1 + 0.10)^3} + \frac{\$50{,}000}{(1 + 0.10)^4}$$

$$= \$50{,}000 + \$45{,}454.55 + \$41{,}322.31 + \$37{,}565.74 + \$34{,}150.67$$

$$= \$208{,}493.27$$

Step 4: State your conclusion. Prize 1 has the greater present value, so you should choose it rather than Prize 2.

Your Turn: For more practice, do related problems 8A.6, 8A.7, 8A.8, and 8A.9 on page 282 at the end of this appendix.

MyEconLab Study Plan

Using Present Value to Calculate Bond Prices

Anyone who buys stocks or bonds is really buying a promise to receive certain payments—dividends in the case of stocks or coupons in the case of bonds. The price investors are willing to pay for a financial asset should be equal to the value of the payments they will receive as a result of owning the asset. Because most of the coupon or dividend payments will be received in the future, it is their present value that matters. We therefore have the following important idea: *The price of a financial asset should be equal to the present value of the payments to be received from owning that asset.*

Let's look at an example. Suppose that in 1988, General Electric issued a bond with an \$80 coupon that will mature in 2018. It is now 2016, and that bond has been bought and sold by investors many times. You are considering buying it. If you buy the bond, you will receive two years of coupon payments plus a final payment of the bond's principal, or face value, of \$1,000. Suppose, once again, that you need an interest rate of 10 percent to invest your funds. If the bond has a coupon of \$80, the present value of the payments you receive from owning the bond—and, therefore, the present value of the bond—will be:

$$\text{Present value} = \frac{\$80}{(1+0.10)} + \frac{\$80}{(1+0.10)^2} + \frac{\$1{,}000}{(1+0.10)^2} = \$965.29.$$

That is, the present value of the bond will equal the present value of the three payments you will receive during the two years you own the bond. You should, therefore, be willing to pay \$965.29 to own this bond and have the right to receive these payments from GE. This process of calculating present values of future payments is used to determine bond prices, with one qualification: The relevant interest rate used by investors in the bond market to calculate the present value and, therefore, the price of an existing bond is usually the coupon rate on comparable newly issued bonds. Therefore, the general formula for the price of a bond is:

$$\text{Bond price} = \frac{\text{Coupon}_1}{(1+i)} + \frac{\text{Coupon}_2}{(1+i)^2} + \cdots + \frac{\text{Coupon}_n}{(1+i)^n} + \frac{\text{Face value}}{(1+i)^n},$$

where:

- Coupon_1 is the coupon payment to be received after one year.
- Coupon_2 is the coupon payment to be received after two years.
- Coupon_n, is the coupon payment received in the year the bond matures.
- The ellipsis takes the place of the coupon payments—if any—received between the second year and the year when the bond matures.
- Face value is the amount that will be received when the bond matures.
- i is the interest rate on comparable newly issued bonds.

MyEconLab Concept Check

Using Present Value to Calculate Stock Prices

When you own a firm's stock, you are legally entitled to your share of the firm's profits. Remember that the profits a firm pays out to its shareholders are called *dividends*. The price of a share of stock should equal the present value of the dividends investors expect to receive as a result of owning that stock. Therefore, the general formula for the price of a stock is:

$$\text{Stock price} = \frac{\text{Dividend}_1}{(1+i)} + \frac{\text{Dividend}_2}{(1+i)^2} + \ldots$$

Notice that this formula looks very similar to the one we used to calculate the price of a bond, with a couple of important differences:

- First, unlike a bond, a share of stock has no maturity date, so we have to calculate the present value of an infinite number of dividend payments. It may seem that the stock's price must be infinite as well, but remember that dollars you don't receive for many years are worth very little today. For instance, a dividend payment of \$10 that will be received 40 years in the future is worth only a little more than \$0.20 today at a 10 percent interest rate.
- Second, you know with certainty the coupon payments you will receive from owning the bond because they are set when the bond is issued and cannot be changed. However, you don't know for sure what the dividend payments from owning a stock will be. How large a dividend payment you will receive depends on how profitable the company will be in the future.

Although it is possible to forecast the future profitability of a company, this cannot be done with perfect accuracy. To emphasize this point, some economists rewrite the basic stock price formula by adding a superscript *e* to each dividend term to emphasize that these are *expected* dividend payments. Because the future profitability of companies is often very difficult to forecast, it is not surprising that differences of opinion exist over what the price of a particular stock should be. Some investors will be optimistic about the future profitability of a company and will, therefore, believe that the company's stock should have a high price. Other investors might be pessimistic and believe that the company's stock should have a low price. MyEconLab Concept Check

A Simple Formula for Calculating Stock Prices

It is possible to simplify the formula for determining the price of a stock. If we assume that dividends will grow at a constant rate, we get the following equation:

$$\text{Stock price} = \frac{\text{Dividend}}{(i - \text{Growth rate})}.$$

In this equation, Dividend is the dividend expected to be received one year from now, and Growth rate is the rate at which those dividends are expected to grow. If a company pays a dividend of \$1 per share to be received one year from now and Growth rate is 10 percent, the company is expected to pay a dividend of \$1.10 the following year, \$1.21 the year after that, and so on.

Now suppose that IBM will pay a dividend of \$5 per share at the end of year, the consensus of investors is that these dividends will increase at a rate of 5 percent per year for the indefinite future, and the interest rate is 10 percent. Then the price of IBM's stock should be:

$$\text{Stock price} = \frac{\$5.00}{(0.10 - 0.05)} = \$100.00.$$

In recent years, investors have debated whether the high prices of the stocks of many high-tech firms, including Twitter, were justified, given that many of these companies had not made any profit yet and so had not paid any dividends. Is there any way that a rational investor would pay a high price for the stock of a company currently not earning profits? The formula for determining stock prices shows that it is possible, provided that the investor's assumptions are optimistic enough! For example, during 2015, one stock analyst predicted that Twitter would soon be earning \$1 per share of stock. That is, Twitter's total earnings divided by the number of shares of its stock outstanding would be \$1. Suppose Twitter pays out that \$1 in dividends and that the \$1 will grow rapidly over the years, by, say, 7 percent per year. Then the formula indicates that the price of Twitter's stock should be:

$$\text{Stock price} = \frac{\$1.00}{(0.10 - 0.07)} = \$33.33.$$

If you are sufficiently optimistic about the future prospects of a company, a high stock price can be justified even if the company is not currently earning a profit. But investors in stocks must be careful. Suppose investors decide that growth prospects for Twitter are only 4 percent per year instead of 7 percent because the firm turns out not to be as profitable as initially believed. Then our formula indicates that the price of Twitter's stock should be:

$$\text{Stock price} = \frac{\$1.00}{(0.10 - 0.04)} = \$16.67.$$

This price is only half the price determined assuming a more optimistic growth rate. We can conclude that investors use information about a firm's profitability and growth prospects to determine what the firm is worth. MyEconLab Concept Check

Going Deeper into Financial Statements

Corporations disclose substantial information about their business operations and financial position to actual and potential investors. Some of this information meets the demands of participants in financial markets and of information-collection agencies, such as Moody's Investors Service, which develops credit ratings that help investors judge how risky corporate bonds are. Other information meets the reporting requirements of the U.S. Securities and Exchange Commission.

Key sources of information about a corporation's profitability and financial position are its principal financial statements—the *income statement* and the *balance sheet*. These important information sources were first introduced in the chapter. In the following section we go into more detail, using recent data for Twitter as an example.

Analyzing Income Statements

As discussed in the chapter, a firm's income statement summarizes its revenues, costs, and profit over a period of time. Figure 8A.1 shows Twitter's income statement for 2014.

Twitter's income statement presents the results of the company's operations during the year. Listed first are the revenues it earned, largely from selling advertising on its app, from January 1, 2014, to December 31, 2014: $1,403 million. Listed next are Twitter's operating expenses, the most important of which is its *cost of revenue*—which is commonly known as *cost of sales* or *cost of goods sold*: $446 million. Cost of revenue is the direct cost of producing the products sold, including in this case the salaries of the computer programmers Twitter hires to write the software for its app. Twitter also has substantial costs for researching and developing its products ($692 million) and for advertising and marketing them ($614 million). General and administrative expenses ($190 million) include costs such as the salaries of top managers.

The difference between a firm's revenue and its costs is its *profit*. Profit shows up in several forms on an income statement. A firm's *operating income* is the difference between its revenue and its operating expenses. Most corporations, including Twitter, also have interest expenses and income from investments, such as government and corporate bonds. In this case, Twitter paid $39 million more in interest expenses than it earned on its investments. Because its costs were greater than its revenue, Twitter's *income before taxes* was a loss (a loss in financial statements is indicated by the use of parenthesis) of $578 million. The federal government taxes the profits of corporations, but because Twitter experienced a

Revenue	$1,403	Revenue from sales
Operating expenses		
Cost of revenues	446	Categories of costs
Research and development	692	
Sales and marketing	614	
General and administrative	190	
Total operating expenses	1,942	Total cost
Operating income	(539)	Operating income = Revenue − Operating expenses
Investment income	(39)	
Income before income taxes	(578)	Before-tax accounting profit
Income taxes	0	
Net income (accounting loss)	(578)	After-tax accounting loss

Note: All numbers are in millions of dollars.

Figure 8A.1 Twitter's Income Statement for 2014

Twitter's income statement shows the company's revenue, costs, and profit for 2014. The difference between its revenue ($1,403 million) and its operating expenses ($1,942 million) is its operating income (a loss of $539 million). Most corporations also have interest expenses and income from investments, such as government and corporate bonds. In this case, Twitter paid $39 million more in interest expenses than it earned on its investments, so its *income before taxes* was a loss of $578 million. Twitter had a net loss, or accounting loss, of $578 million for the year.

Note: Negative values in the figure are shown in parentheses.

Source: Twitter, *Annual Report, 2014*.

loss in 2014, it paid no taxes. Therefore, Twitter's *net income* after taxes was also a loss of $578 million. The fact that Twitter could experience a loss while still having a high stock price is an indication that investors were expecting Twitter to earn significant profits in the future. The net income that firms report on their income statements is referred to as their after-tax *accounting profit*.

MyEconLab Concept Check

Analyzing Balance Sheets

As discussed in the chapter, while a firm's income statement reports the firm's activities for a period of time, a firm's balance sheet summarizes its financial position on a particular day, usually the end of a quarter or year. To understand how a balance sheet is organized, first recall that an asset is anything of value that the firm owns, and a liability is a debt or an obligation that the firm owes. Subtracting the value of a firm's liabilities from the value of its assets leaves its *net worth*. Because a corporation's stockholders are its owners, net worth is often listed as **stockholders' equity** on a balance sheet. Using these definitions, we can state the balance sheet equation (also called the basic accounting equation) as follows:

Stockholders' equity The difference between the value of a corporation's assets and the value of its liabilities; also known as *net worth*.

$$\text{Assets} - \text{Liabilities} = \text{Stockholders' Equity},$$

or:

$$\text{Assets} = \text{Liabilities} + \text{Stockholders' Equity}.$$

This equation tells us that the value of a firm's assets must equal the value of its liabilities plus the value of stockholders' equity. An important accounting convention dating back to the beginning of modern bookkeeping in fifteenth-century Italy holds that balance sheets should list assets on the left side and liabilities and net worth, or stockholders' equity, on the right side. Notice that this means that *the value of the left side of the balance sheet must always equal the value of the right side*. Figure 8A.2 shows Twitter's balance sheet as of December 31, 2014.

A couple of the entries on the asset side of the balance sheet may be unfamiliar: *Current assets* are assets that the firm could convert into cash quickly, such as the balance in its checking account or its accounts receivable, which is money currently owed to the firm for products that have been delivered but not yet paid for. *Goodwill* represents the difference between the purchase price of a company and the market value of its assets. It represents the ability of a business to earn an economic profit from its assets. For example, if you buy a restaurant that is located on a busy intersection and you employ a chef with a reputation for preparing delicious food, you may pay more than the market value of the tables, chairs, ovens, and other assets. This additional amount you pay will be entered on the asset side of your balance sheet as goodwill.

Current liabilities are short-term debts such as accounts payable, which is money owed to suppliers for goods received but not yet paid for, or bank loans that will be paid back in less than one year. Long-term bank loans, the value of outstanding corporate bonds, and other long-term debts are *long-term liabilities*.

MyEconLab Study Plan

Assets		Liabilities and Stockholders' Equity	
Current assets	$4,256	Current liabilities	$ 394
Property and equipment	557	Long-term liabilities	1,563
Goodwill	623	Total liabilities	1,957
Other assets	147	Stockholders' equity	3,626
Total assets	$5,583	Total liabilities and stockholders' equity	$5,583

Note: All values are in millions of dollars.

Figure 8A.2

Twitter's Balance Sheet as of December 31, 2014

Corporations list their assets on the left of their balance sheets and their liabilities on the right. The difference between the value of a firm's assets and the value of its liabilities equals the net worth of the firm, or stockholders' equity. Stockholders' equity is listed on the right side of the balance sheet. Therefore, the value of the left side of the balance sheet must always equal the value of the right side.
Source: Twitter, *Annual Report, 2014*.

Key Terms

Present value, p. 275

Stockholders' equity, p. 281

8A Tools to Analyze Firms' Financial Information, pages 275–281

LEARNING OBJECTIVE: Understand the concept of present value and the information contained on a firm's income statement and balance sheet.

MyEconLab Visit **www.myeconlab.com** to complete these exercises online and get instant feedback.

Review Questions

8A.1 Why is money you receive at some future date worth less to you than money you receive today? If the interest rate rises, what effect does this have on the present value of payments you receive in the future?

8A.2 Give the formula for calculating the present value of a bond that will pay a coupon of $100 per year for 10 years and that has a face value of $1,000.

8A.3 Compare the formula for calculating the present value of the payments you will receive from owning a bond to the formula for calculating the present value of the payments you will receive from owning a stock. What are the key similarities? What are the key differences?

8A.4 How is operating income calculated? How does operating income differ from net income? How does net income differ from accounting profit?

8A.5 What is the key difference between a firm's income statement and its balance sheet? What is listed on the left side of a balance sheet? What is listed on the right side?

Problems and Applications

8A.6 **(Related to Solved Problem 8A.1 on page 277)** If the interest rate is 10 percent, what is the present value of a bond that matures in two years, pays $85 one year from now, and pays $1,085 two years from now?

8A.7 **(Related to Solved Problem 8A.1 on page 277)** Before the 2013 season, the Los Angeles Angels signed outfielder Josh Hamilton to a contract that would pay him an immediate $10 million signing bonus and the following amounts: $15 million for the 2013 season, $15 million for the 2014 season, $23 million for the 2015 season, $30 million for the 2016 season, and $30 million for the 2017 season. The contract also specified that $2 million would be given to a charity. Assume that Hamilton receives each of his five seasonal salaries as a lump-sum payment at the end of the season.

a. Some newspaper reports described Hamilton as having signed a $125 million contract with the Angels. Do you agree that $125 million was the value of this contract? Briefly explain.

b. What was the present value of Hamilton's contract at the time he signed it (assuming an interest rate of 10 percent)? For simplicity, you can ignore the $2 million given to charity.

c. If you use an interest rate of 5 percent, what was the present value of Hamilton's contract?

Source: Drew Silva, "Breaking Down Josh Hamilton's Five-Year, $125M Contract," hardballtalk.nbcsports.com, December 15, 2012.

8A.8 **(Related to Solved Problem 8A.1 on page 277)** A winner of the Pennsylvania Lottery was given the choice of receiving $18 million at once or $1,440,000 per year for 25 years.

a. If the winner had opted for the 25 annual payments, how much in total would she have received?

b. At an interest rate of 10 percent, what would be the present value of the 25 payments?

c. At an interest rate of 5 percent, what would be the present value of the 25 payments?

d. What interest rate would make the present value of the 25 payments equal to the one payment of $18 million? (This question is difficult and requires the use of a financial calculator or a spreadsheet. *Hint:* If you are familiar with the Excel spreadsheet program, use the RATE function. You can answer parts (b) and (c) by using the Excel PV [Present Value] function.)

8A.9 **(Related to Solved Problem 8A.1 on page 277)** Before the start of the 2000 baseball season, the New York Mets decided that they didn't want Bobby Bonilla playing for them any longer. But Bonilla had a contract with the Mets for the 2000 season that would have obliged the Mets to pay him $5.9 million. When the Mets released Bonilla, he agreed to take the following payments in lieu of the $5.9 million the Mets would have paid him in the year 2000: He would receive 25 equal payments of $1,193,248.20 each July 1 from 2011 to 2035. If you were Bobby Bonilla, which would you rather have had, the lump-sum $5.9 million in 2000 or the 25 payments beginning in 2011? Explain the basis for your decision.

Source: Mike Sielski, "There's No Accounting for This," *Wall Street Journal*, July 1, 2010.

8A.10 Suppose that eLake, an online auction site, is paying a dividend of $2 per share. You expect this dividend to grow 2 percent per year, and the interest rate is 10 percent. What is the most you would be willing to pay for a share of stock in eLake? If the interest rate is 5 percent, what is the most you would be willing to pay? When interest rates in the economy decline, would you expect stock prices in general to rise or fall? Briefly explain.

8A.11 Suppose you buy the bond of a large corporation at a time when the inflation rate is very low. If the inflation rate increases during the time you hold the bond, what is likely to happen to the price of the bond?

8A.12 Use the information in the following table for calendar year 2014 to prepare an income statement for McDonald's Corporation. Be sure to include entries for operating income and net income.

Revenue from company restaurants	$18,169 million
Revenue from franchised restaurants	9,272 million
Cost of operating company-owned restaurants	15,288 million
Income taxes	2,614 million
Interest expense	577 million
General and administrative cost	2,507 million
Cost of restaurant leases	1,697 million

Source: McDonalds Corp., *Annual Report, 2014.*

8A.13 Use the information in the following table on the financial situation of Starbucks Corporation as of September 28, 2014 (the end of the firm's financial year), to prepare a balance sheet for the firm. Be sure to include an entry for stockholders' equity.

Current assets	$4,169 million
Current liabilities	3,039 million
Property and equipment	3,519 million
Long-term liabilities	2,441 million
Goodwill	856 million
Other assets	2,209 million

Source: Starbucks Corp., *Annual Report, 2014.*

8A.14 The *current ratio* is equal to a firm's current assets divided by its current liabilities. Use the information in Figure 8A.2 on page 281 to calculate Twitter's current ratio on December 31, 2014. Investors generally prefer that a firm's current ratio be greater than 1.5. What problems might a firm encounter if the value of its current assets is low relative to the value of its current liabilities?

CHAPTER

9

Comparative Advantage and the Gains from International Trade

Chapter Outline and Learning Objectives

President Obama, Nike, and Free Trade

Where were your shoes made? If you answer either China or Vietnam, you are likely to be correct. But if you lived in the United States during the 1930s, you would have answered "right here." At that time, there were nearly 2,000 shoe factories in the United States, employing more than 275,000 workers. Today, 99 percent of shoes sold in the United States are made overseas, and U.S. shoe factories employ fewer than 15,000 workers. Nike illustrates the evolution of today's U.S. shoe industry. Headquartered in Beaverton, Oregon, Nike employs about 26,000 people in the United States, but most work in administration, sales, and research and development. Nike has contracts with foreign shoe firms that employ nearly 1 million workers to manufacture Nike shoes in factories in China, Vietnam, and Indonesia.

Would U.S. consumers and workers be better off if the federal government banned imports of shoes, so all shoes bought in the United States were made here? President Barack Obama would answer "no." In 2015, he visited Nike's headquarters to push for Congressional passage of the *Trans-Pacific Partnership (TPP)*, an agreement between the United States and 11 other countries, including Canada, Japan, Mexico, and Vietnam. The TPP is meant to reduce trade barriers among these countries. The Obama administration argued that the TPP will "unlock opportunities for American manufacturers, workers, service providers, farmers, and ranchers—to support job creation and wage growth."

Critics argued that the TPP will further expose U.S. firms and workers to competition from foreign firms where the average wage is less than $5 per day. Although the TPP includes provisions to enforce environmental standards in foreign factories, some environmentalists are skeptical that the provisions will be enforced. The AFL-CIO, a labor union organization, argued, "Unfortunately, it is becoming clear the TPP will not create jobs, protect the environment and ensure safe imports."

Does eliminating restrictions on international trade help workers and consumers in the United States, or does it hurt them? In this chapter, we will analyze this and other important questions related to international trade.

Sources: Peter Baker, "Obama Scolds Democrats on Trade Pact Stance," *Wall Street Journal*, May 8, 2015; Office of the United States Trade Representative, "TPP Issue-by-Issue Information Center," ustr.gov; "Trans-Pacific Partnership Free Trade Agreement (TPP)," aflcio.org; and U.S. Department of Commerce, Bureau of the Census, *Fifteenth Census of the United States, Manufactures: 1929*, Vol. III, Washington, DC: Government Printing Office, 1933.

Economics in Your Life

Did You Know There Is a Tariff on Running Shoes?

Politicians often support polices that restrict imports from foreign countries because they want to convince people to vote for them. The workers in the industries these restrictions protect are likely to vote for the politicians because they believe the restrictions will save their jobs. But most people do *not* work in industries that are protected from foreign competition by trade restrictions. The federal government imposes a tariff, or tax, on imports of most shoes into the United States. As a result, U.S. consumers pay higher prices for shoes. But very few people in the United States today are employed in shoe factories. Why, then, does the federal government have a tariff on shoes, and why are so few people aware that it exists? As you read this chapter, try to answer these questions. You can check your answers against those we provide on **page 309** at the end of this chapter.

Trade is simply the act of buying or selling. Is there a difference between trade that takes place within a country and international trade? Within the United States, domestic trade makes it possible for consumers in Ohio to eat salmon caught in Alaska and for consumers in Montana to drive cars built in Michigan or Kentucky. Similarly, international trade makes it possible for consumers in the United States to drink wine from France and use Blu-ray players from Japan. One significant difference between domestic trade and international trade is that international trade is more controversial. At one time, nearly all the televisions, shoes, clothing, and toys bought in the United States were also produced here. Today, firms in other countries produce most of these goods. This shift has benefited U.S. consumers because foreign-made goods have lower prices or higher quality than the U.S.-made goods they have replaced. At the same time, though, many U.S. firms that produced these goods have gone out of business, and their workers have had to find other jobs. Not surprisingly, opinion polls show that many Americans favor reducing international trade because they believe doing so will preserve jobs in the United States. But is this belief accurate?

We can use the tools of demand and supply to analyze markets for internationally traded goods and services. We have seen that trade in general—whether within a country or between countries—is based on the principle of comparative advantage (see Chapter 2). In this chapter, we look more closely at the role of comparative advantage in international trade. We also use the concepts of consumer surplus, producer surplus, and deadweight loss (see Chapter 4) to analyze government policies that interfere with trade. With this background, we can return to the political debate over whether the United States benefits from international trade. We begin by looking at how large a role international trade plays in the U.S. economy.

9.1 The United States in the International Economy

LEARNING OBJECTIVE: Discuss the role of international trade in the U.S. economy.

International trade has grown tremendously over the past 50 years due primarily to these three factors: The decreasing costs of shipping products around the world, the spread of inexpensive and reliable communications, and changes in government policies. Firms can use large container ships to send their products across oceans at low cost. Businesspeople today can travel to Europe or Asia, using fast, inexpensive, and reliable air transportation. The Internet, cellphones, and text messaging allow managers to communicate instantaneously and at a very low cost with customers and suppliers around the world. These and other improvements in transportation and communication have created an integrated global marketplace that earlier generations of businesspeople could only dream of.

Tariff A tax imposed by a government on imports.

Imports Goods and services bought domestically but produced in other countries.

Exports Goods and services produced domestically but sold in other countries.

Over the past 50 years, many governments have changed policies to facilitate international trade. For example, tariff rates have fallen. A **tariff** is a tax imposed by a government on *imports* into a country. **Imports** are goods and services bought domestically but produced in other countries. In the 1930s, the United States charged an average tariff rate above 50 percent. Today, the rate is less than 1.5 percent. In North America, most tariffs between Canada, Mexico, and the United States were eliminated following the passage of the North American Free Trade Agreement (NAFTA) in 1994. In Europe, 29 countries have formed the European Union, which has eliminated all tariffs among member countries, greatly increasing both imports and **exports**, which are goods and services produced domestically but sold in other countries. In 2015, the Obama administration concluded negotiating the Trans-Pacific Partnership (TPP), which is an agreement between the United States and 11 other countries around the Pacific Ocean, including Canada, Japan, Mexico, and Vietnam. The TPP will eliminate most tariffs between these countries, which together account for nearly 40 percent of world production of goods and services.

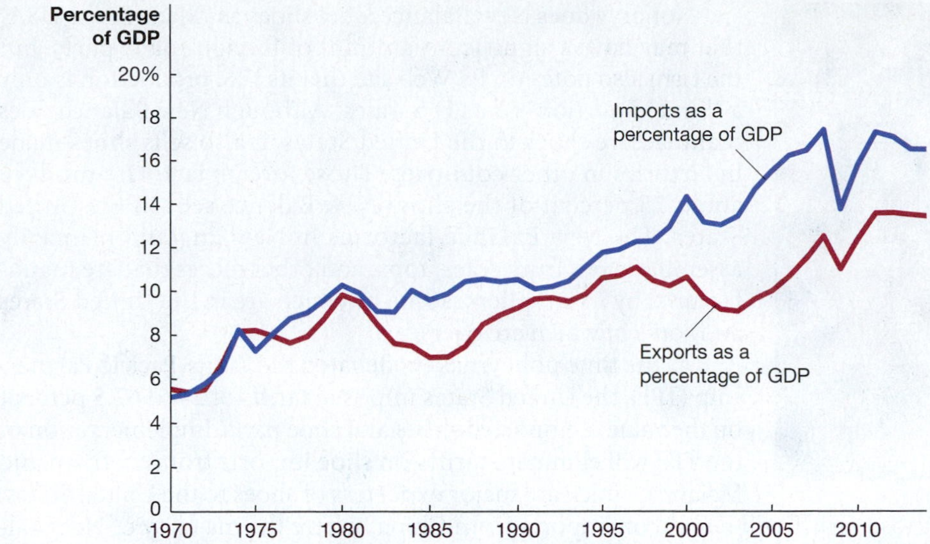

MyEconLab Real-time data

Figure 9.1

International Trade Is of Increasing Importance to the United States

Exports and imports of goods and services as a percentage of total production—measured by GDP—show the importance of international trade to an economy. Since 1970, both imports and exports have been steadily rising as a fraction of U.S. GDP.

Source: U.S. Department of Commerce, Bureau of Economic Analysis.

The Importance of Trade to the U.S. Economy

U.S. consumers buy increasing quantities of goods and services produced in other countries. At the same time, U.S. businesses sell increasing quantities of goods and services to consumers in other countries. Figure 9.1 shows that since 1970, with the exception of the period of the severe recession of 2007–2009, both exports and imports have been increasing as a fraction of U.S. gross domestic product (GDP). Recall that GDP is the value of all the final goods and services produced in a country during a year. In 1970, exports and imports were both less than 6 percent of U.S. GDP. In 2014, exports were about 13 percent of GDP, and imports were about 17 percent.

Not all sectors of the U.S. economy are affected equally by international trade. For example, although it's difficult to import or export some services, such as haircuts and appendectomies, a large percentage of U.S. agricultural production is exported. Each year, the United States exports about 50 percent of its wheat and rice crops and 20 percent of its corn crop.

Many U.S. manufacturing industries also depend on trade. About 20 percent of U.S. manufacturing jobs depend directly or indirectly on exports. In some industries, such as pharmaceutical drugs, the products are directly exported. In other industries, such as steel, the products are used to make other products, such as bulldozers or machine tools, that are then exported. In all, about two-thirds of U.S. manufacturing industries depend on exports for at least 10 percent of jobs. MyEconLab Concept Check

Making the Connection
MyEconLab Video

Would New Balance Be Helped or Hurt By the Trans-Pacific Partnership?

Founded in 1906, New Balance Athletic Shoe, which is headquartered in Boston, Massachusetts, seems to have bucked the long-run trend of shoe production leaving the United States. New Balance operates two factories in Massachusetts and three in Maine, employing about 1,400 workers to manufacture shoes. Many people think of New Balance as the "Made in America" shoe company, and it is the only company making significant quantities of shoes in the United States. It labels its shoes as "Made in the USA" when they contain at least 70 percent U.S.-made parts.

New Balance Athletic Shoe assembles more than 4 million pairs of athletic shoes a year in its Massachusetts and Maine factories.

Not only does New Balance label shoes as "Made in the USA" that may have a significant amount of foreign-made parts, but the firm also notes on its Web site that its U.S. production is only a "limited portion" of its U.S. sales. Although New Balance does manufacture shoes in the United States, it also sells shoes made in factories in other countries. Those foreign factories produce about 75 percent of the shoes New Balance sells in the United States. The New Balance factories in New England primarily assemble shoes from soles, tops, and other pieces that are manufactured by its suppliers, some of which are in the United States and some of which are overseas.

At the time policymakers debated the Trans-Pacific Partnership (TPP), the United States imposed tariffs of 25 to 67.5 percent on the value of imported shoes and shoe parts. Implementation of the TPP will eliminate tariffs on shoe imports from Vietnam and Malaysia, which are major exporters of shoes to the United States, but those tariffs will remain on imports from China, where the majority of New Balance shoes sold in the United States are made. Nike, New Balance's key competitor, imports the majority of its shoes from Vietnam, so it will receive a larger benefit from the passage of the TPP than New Balance will.

New Balance, then, was in a somewhat complicated situation as the debate over the TPP took place. Eliminating the tariff on shoes imported from TPP countries will hurt New Balance by lowering the prices on some of the imported shoes sold by other companies that compete with New Balance's U.S.-produced shoes. But New Balance will benefit because it will be able to sell the shoes it imports from TPP countries at a lower price, and because the cost of the shoe parts it imports from TPP countries for use in its U.S. factories will also decline. Not surprisingly, the company did not voice a strong position either for or against the TPP. A spokesperson for the company was quoted as saying, "We've had productive discussions with the Obama administration regarding TPP, and we're hopeful that the final agreement will reflect those discussions and will allow us to continue to thrive as a domestic producer."

Today, few U.S.-based manufacturing firms make their products exclusively in the United States out of entirely U.S.-made parts. As a result, the positions of these firms on reducing barriers to international trade can be difficult to predict.

Sources: William Mauldin and Sara Germano, "Obama Visits Importer Nike, Defends Pacific Trade Agreement," *Wall Street Journal*, May 8, 2015; Eric Bradner, "Obama Steps in with Outsourcer at Nike," cnn.com, May 8, 2015; and New Balance, *New Balance Responsible Leadership Report*, newbalance.com.

MyEconLab Study Plan

Your Turn: Test your understanding by doing related problem 1.7 on page 310 at the end of this chapter.

U.S. International Trade in a World Context

The United States is the second-largest exporter in the world, just behind China, as Figure 9.2 illustrates. Six of the other seven leading exporting countries are also high-income countries. Although China is still a relatively low-income country, the rapid growth of the Chinese economy over the past 35 years has resulted in its becoming the largest exporter. Three of the top exporting countries are in East Asia, four are in Western Europe, and one is in North America.

Figure 9.3 shows that international trade is less important to the United States than it is to many other countries, with imports and exports being lower percentages of GDP. In some smaller countries, such as Belgium and the Netherlands, imports and exports make up more than half of GDP. In the larger European economies, imports and exports make up one-quarter to one-half of GDP.

MyEconLab Study Plan

MyEconLab Concept Check

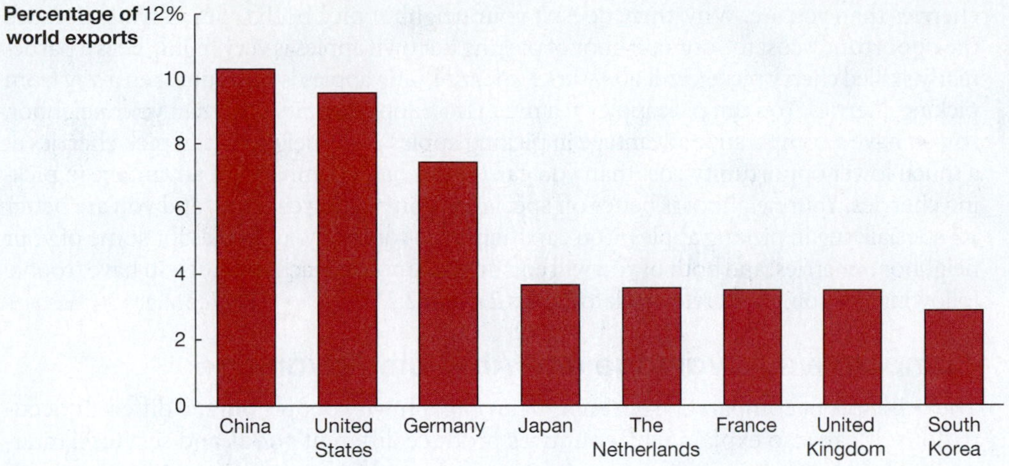

MyEconLab Animation

Figure 9.2

The Eight Leading Exporting Countries, 2014

China is the leading exporting country, accounting for 10.3 percent of total world exports. The United States is second, with a 9.6 percent share. The values are the shares of total world exports of merchandise and commercial services.

Source: World Trade Organization, *International Trade Statistics*, 2014.

9.2 Comparative Advantage in International Trade

LEARNING OBJECTIVE: Explain the difference between comparative advantage and absolute advantage in international trade.

Why have businesses around the world increasingly looked for markets in other countries? Why have consumers increasingly purchased goods and services made in other countries? People trade for one reason: Trade makes them better off. Whenever a buyer and seller agree to a sale, they must both believe they are better off; otherwise, there would be no sale. This outcome must hold whether the buyer and seller live in the same city or in different countries. As we will see, governments are more likely to interfere with international trade than they are with domestic trade, but the reasons for the interference are more political than economic.

A Brief Review of Comparative Advantage

Recall that **comparative advantage** is the ability of an individual, a firm, or a country to produce a good or service at a lower opportunity cost than competitors. **Opportunity cost** is the highest-valued alternative that must be given up to engage in an activity. People, firms, and countries specialize in economic activities in which they have a comparative advantage. In trading, we benefit from the comparative advantage of other people (or firms or countries), and they benefit from our comparative advantage.

A good way to think of comparative advantage is to recall the example of you and your neighbor picking fruit (see Chapter 2). Your neighbor is better at picking both apples and

Comparative advantage The ability of an individual, a firm, or a country to produce a good or service at a lower opportunity cost than competitors.

Opportunity cost The highest-valued alternative that must be given up to engage in an activity.

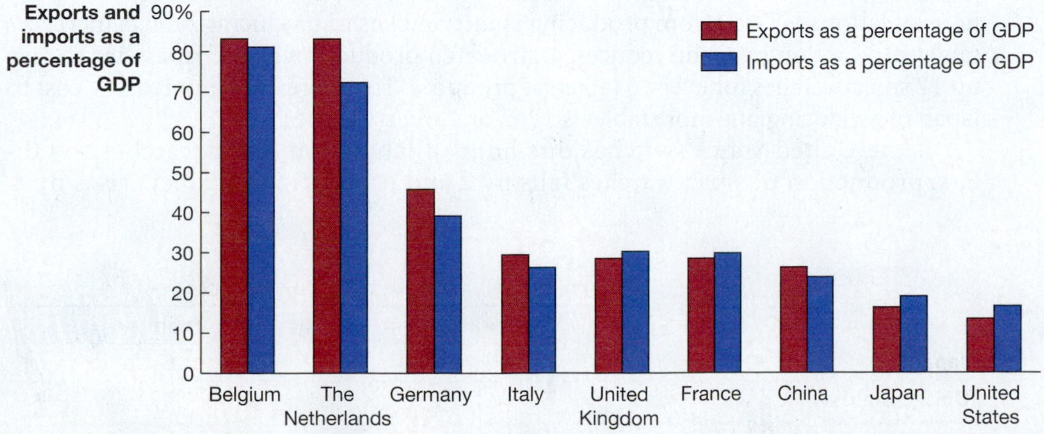

MyEconLab Real-time data

Figure 9.3

International Trade as a Percentage of GDP, 2014

International trade is still less important to the United States than it is to most other countries.

Source: Organization for Economic Co-operation and Development, *Country Statistical Profiles*.

cherries than you are. Why, then, doesn't your neighbor pick both types of fruit? Because the opportunity cost to your neighbor of picking her own apples is very high: She is a particularly skilled cherry picker, and every hour spent picking apples is an hour taken away from picking cherries. You can pick apples at a much lower opportunity cost than your neighbor, so you have a comparative advantage in picking apples. Your neighbor can pick cherries at a much lower opportunity cost than you can, so she has a comparative advantage in picking cherries. Your neighbor is better off specializing in picking cherries, and you are better off specializing in picking apples. You can then trade some of your apples for some of your neighbor's cherries, and both of you will end up with more of each fruit. (If you have trouble following the point here, refer back to Tables 2.1 and 2.2.) MyEconLab Concept Check

Comparative Advantage and Absolute Advantage

The principle of comparative advantage can explain why people pursue different occupations. It can also explain why countries produce different goods and services. International trade involves many countries importing and exporting many different goods and services. Countries are better off if they specialize in producing the goods for which they have a comparative advantage. They can then trade for the goods for which other countries have a comparative advantage.

We can illustrate why specializing on the basis of comparative advantage makes countries better off with a simple example involving just two countries and two products. Suppose the United States and Japan produce only smartwatches and tablet computers, like Apple's iPad or Samsung's Galaxy Tab. Assume that each country uses only labor to produce each good and that Japanese and U.S. smartwatches and tablets are exactly the same. Table 9.1 shows how much each country can produce of each good with one hour of labor.

Notice that Japanese workers are more productive than U.S. workers in making both goods. In one hour, Japanese workers can make six times as many smartwatches and one and one-half times as many tablets as U.S. workers. Japan has an *absolute advantage* over the United States in producing both goods. **Absolute advantage** is the ability to produce more of a good or service than competitors when using the same amount of resources. In this case, Japan can produce more of both goods using the same amount of labor as the United States.

Absolute advantage The ability to produce more of a good or service than competitors when using the same amount of resources.

It might seem at first that Japan has nothing to gain from trading with the United States because it has an absolute advantage in producing both goods. However, Japan should specialize and produce only smartwatches and obtain the tablets it needs by exporting smartwatches to the United States in exchange for tablets. The reason Japan benefits from trade is that although it has an *absolute advantage* in the production of both goods, it has a *comparative advantage* only in the production of smartwatches. The United States has a comparative advantage in the production of tablets.

If it seems contrary to common sense that Japan should import tablets from the United States even though Japan can produce more of them per hour of labor, think about the opportunity cost to each country of producing each good. If Japan wants to produce more tablets, it has to switch labor away from smartwatch production. Every hour of labor switched from producing smartwatches to producing tablets increases tablet production by 6 and reduces smartwatch production by 12. Japan has to give up 12 smartwatches for every 6 tablets it produces. Therefore, the opportunity cost to Japan of producing one more tablet is 12/6, or 2 smartwatches.

If the United States switches one hour of labor from smartwatches to tablets, production of smartwatches falls by 2 and production of tablets rises by 4.

Table 9.1

An Example of Japanese Workers Being More Productive Than American Workers

	Output per Hour of Work	
	Smartwatches	Tablets
Japan	12	6
United States	2	4

	Opportunity Costs	
	Smartwatches	Tablets
Japan	0.5 tablet	2 smartwatches
United States	2 tablets	0.5 smartwatch

Table 9.2

The Opportunity Costs of Producing Smartwatches and Tablets
The table shows the opportunity cost each country faces in producing smartwatches and tablets. For example, the entry in the first row and second column shows that Japan must give up 2 smartwatches for every tablet it produces.

Therefore, the opportunity cost to the United States of producing one more tablet is 2/4, or 0.5 smartwatch. The United States has a lower opportunity cost of producing tablets and, therefore, has a comparative advantage in making this product. By similar reasoning, we can see that Japan has a comparative advantage in producing smartwatches. Table 9.2 summarizes the opportunity cost each country faces in producing these goods. MyEconLab Concept Check

9.3 How Countries Gain from International Trade

LEARNING OBJECTIVE: Explain how countries gain from international trade.

Can Japan really gain from producing only smartwatches and trading with the United States for tablets? To see that it can, assume at first that Japan and the United States do not trade with each other. A situation in which a country does not trade with other countries is called **autarky**. Assume that in autarky, each country has 1,000 hours of labor available to produce the two goods, and each country produces the quantities of the two goods shown in Table 9.3. Because there is no trade, these quantities also represent consumption of the two goods in each country.

Autarky A situation in which a country does not trade with other countries.

Increasing Consumption through Trade

Suppose now that Japan and the United States begin to trade with each other. The **terms of trade** is the ratio at which a country can trade its exports for imports from other countries. For simplicity, let's assume that the terms of trade end up with Japan and the United States being willing to trade one smartwatch for one tablet.

Terms of trade The ratio at which a country can trade its exports for imports from other countries.

Once trade has begun, the United States and Japan can exchange tablets for smartwatches or smartwatches for tablets. For example, if Japan specializes by using all 1,000 available hours of labor to produce smartwatches, it will be able to produce 12,000 smartwatches. It then could export 1,500 smartwatches to the United States in exchange for 1,500 tablets. (Remember that we are assuming the terms of trade are 1 smartwatch for 1 tablet.) Japan ends up with 10,500 smartwatches and 1,500 tablets. Compared with the situation before trade, Japan has the same number of tablets but 1,500 more smartwatches. If the United States specializes in producing tablets, it will be able to produce 4,000 tablets. It could then export 1,500 tablets to Japan in exchange for 1,500 smartwatches. The United States ends up with 2,500 tablets and 1,500 smartwatches. Compared with the situation before trade, the United States has the same number of smartwatches but 1,500 more tablets. Trade has allowed both countries to increase the quantities of goods consumed. Table 9.4 summarizes the gains from trade for the United States and Japan.

By trading, Japan and the United States are able to consume more than they could without trade. This outcome is possible because world production of both goods increases after trade. (In this example, our "world" consists of just the United States and Japan.)

Why does total production of smartwatches and tablets increase when the United States specializes in producing tablets and Japan specializes in producing smartwatches?

	Production and Consumption	
	Smartwatches	Tablets
Japan	9,000	1,500
United States	1,500	1,000

Table 9.3

Production without Trade

Table 9.4

Gains from Trade for Japan and the United States

Without Trade

	Production and Consumption	
	Smartwatches	Tablets
Japan	9,000	1,500
United States	1,500	1,000

With Trade

	Production with Trade		Trade		Consumption with Trade	
	Smartwatches	Tablets	Smartwatches	Tablets	Smartwatches	Tablets
Japan	12,000	0	Export 1,500	Import 1,500	10,500	1,500
United States	0	4,000	Import 1,500	Export 1,500	1,500	2,500

With trade, the United States and Japan specialize in the good they have a comparative advantage in producing . . .

. . . and export some of that good in exchange for the good the other country has a comparative advantage in producing.

Gains from Trade

	Increased Consumption
Japan	1,500 Smartwatches
United States	1,500 Tablets

The increased consumption made possible by trade represents the gains from trade.

A domestic analogy helps to answer this question: If a company shifts production from an old factory to a more efficient modern factory, its output will increase. The same thing happens in our example. Producing tablets in Japan and smartwatches in the United States is inefficient. Shifting production to the more efficient country—the one with the comparative advantage—increases total production. The key point is: *Countries gain from specializing in producing goods in which they have a comparative advantage and trading for goods in which other countries have a comparative advantage.* MyEconLab Concept Check

Solved Problem 9.3

MyEconLab Interactive Animation

The Gains from Trade

The first discussion of comparative advantage appears in *On the Principles of Political Economy and Taxation*, a book written by the British economist David Ricardo in 1817. Ricardo provided a famous example of the gains from trade, using wine and cloth production in Portugal and England. The following table is adapted from Ricardo's example, with cloth measured in sheets and wine measured in kegs:

	Output per Year of Labor	
	Cloth	Wine
Portugal	100	150
England	90	60

a. Explain which country has an absolute advantage in the production of each good.

b. Explain which country has a comparative advantage in the production of each good.

c. Suppose that Portugal and England currently do not trade with each other. Each country has 1,000 workers, so each has 1,000 years of labor time to use in producing cloth and wine, and the countries are currently producing the amounts of each good shown in the following table:

	Cloth	Wine
Portugal	18,000	123,000
England	63,000	18,000

Show that Portugal and England can both gain from trade. Assume that the terms of trade are that one sheet of cloth can be traded for one keg of wine.

Solving the Problem

Step 1: Review the chapter material. This problem is about absolute and comparative advantage and the gains from trade, so you may want to review the sections "Comparative Advantage in International Trade," which begins on page 289, and "How Countries Gain from International Trade," which begins on page 291.

Step 2: Answer part (a) by determining which country has an absolute advantage. Remember that a country has an absolute advantage over another country when it can produce more of a good using the same resources. The first table in the problem shows that Portugal can produce more cloth *and* more wine with one year's worth of labor than can England. Therefore, Portugal has an absolute advantage in the production of both goods, and England does not have an absolute advantage in the production of either good.

Step 3: Answer part (b) by determining which country has a comparative advantage. A country has a comparative advantage when it can produce a good at a lower opportunity cost. To produce 100 sheets of cloth, Portugal must give up producing 150 kegs of wine. Therefore, Portugal's opportunity cost of producing 1 sheet of cloth is 150/100, or 1.5 kegs of wine. England has to give up producing 60 kegs of wine to produce 90 sheets of cloth, so its opportunity cost of producing 1 sheet of cloth is 60/90, or 0.67 keg of wine. The opportunity costs of producing wine can be calculated in the same way. The following table shows the opportunity cost to Portugal and England of producing each good.

	Opportunity Costs	
	Cloth	Wine
Portugal	1.5 kegs of wine	0.67 sheet of cloth
England	0.67 keg of wine	1.5 sheets of cloth

Portugal has a comparative advantage in wine because its opportunity cost is lower. England has a comparative advantage in cloth because its opportunity cost is lower.

Step 4: Answer part (c) by showing that both countries can benefit from trade. By now it should be clear that both countries will be better off if they specialize in producing the good for which they have a comparative advantage and trade for the other good. The following table is very similar to Table 9.4 and shows one example of trade making both countries better off. (To test your understanding, construct another example.)

Without Trade

	Production and Consumption	
	Cloth	Wine
Portugal	18,000	123,000
England	63,000	18,000

With Trade

	Production with Trade		Trade		Consumption with Trade	
	Cloth	Wine	Cloth	Wine	Cloth	Wine
Portugal	0	150,000	Import 18,000	Export 18,000	18,000	132,000
England	90,000	0	Export 18,000	Import 18,000	72,000	18,000

Gains from Trade

	Increased Consumption
Portugal	9,000 wine
England	9,000 cloth

MyEconLab Study Plan

Your Turn: For more practice, do related problems 3.5 and 3.6 on page 312 at the end of this chapter.

Why Don't We See Complete Specialization?

In our example of two countries producing only two products, each country specializes in producing one of the goods. In the real world, many goods and services are produced in more than one country. For example, the United States, Japan, Germany, Canada, Mexico, India, China, and other countries produce automobiles. We do not see complete specialization in the real world for three main reasons:

- **Not all goods and services are traded internationally.** For example, even if Japan had a comparative advantage in the production of medical services, it would be difficult for Japan to specialize in producing medical services and then export them. There is no easy way for U.S. patients who need appendectomies to receive them from surgeons in Japan.
- **Production of most goods involves increasing opportunity costs.** Recall that production of most goods involves increasing opportunity costs (see Chapter 2). In our example, if the United States devotes more workers to producing tablets, the opportunity cost of producing more tablets will increase. At some point, the opportunity cost of producing tablets in the United States may rise to the level of the opportunity cost of producing tablets in Japan. When that happens, international trade will no longer push the United States further toward specialization. The same will be true of Japan: The increasing opportunity cost of producing smartwatches will cause Japan to stop short of complete specialization.
- **Tastes for products differ.** Most products are *differentiated*. Smartwatches, tablets, cars, and televisions—to name just a few products—come with a wide variety of features. When buying automobiles, some people look for reliability and fuel efficiency, others look for room to carry seven passengers, and still others want styling and high performance. So, some car buyers prefer Toyota Prius hybrids, and some prefer Chevy Suburbans, and others prefer BMWs. As a result, Japan, the United States, and Germany may each have a comparative advantage in producing different types of automobiles.

MyEconLab Concept Check

Does Anyone Lose as a Result of International Trade?

In our smartwatch and tablet example, consumption increases in both the United States and Japan as a result of trade. Everyone gains, and no one loses. Or do they? In our example, we referred repeatedly to "Japan" or the "United States" producing smartwatches or tablets. But countries do not produce goods—firms do. In a world without trade, there would be smartwatch and tablet firms in both Japan and the United States. In a world with trade, there would be only Japanese smartwatch firms and U.S. tablet firms. Japanese tablet firms and U.S. smartwatch firms would close. Overall, total employment would not change, and production would increase as a result of trade. Nevertheless, the owners of Japanese tablet firms, the owners of U.S. smartwatch firms, and the people who work for them are worse off as a result of trade. The losers from trade are likely to do their best to convince the Japanese and U.S. governments to interfere with trade by barring imports of the competing products from the other country or by imposing high tariffs on them.

MyEconLab Concept Check

Don't Let This Happen to You

Remember That Trade Creates Both Winners and Losers

The following statement is from a Federal Reserve publication: "Trade is a win–win situation for all countries that participate." People sometimes interpret statements like this to mean that there are no losers from international trade. But notice that the statement refers to *countries,* not individuals. When countries participate in trade, they make their consumers better off by increasing the quantity of goods and services available to them. As we have seen, however, expanding trade eliminates the jobs of workers employed at companies that are less efficient than foreign companies. Trade also creates new jobs at companies that export products to foreign markets. It may be difficult, though, for workers who lose their jobs because of trade to easily find others. That is why in the United States the federal government uses the Trade Adjustment Assistance program to provide funds for workers who have lost their jobs due to international trade. Qualified unemployed workers can use these funds to pay for retraining, searching for new jobs, or relocating to areas where new jobs are available. This program—and similar programs in other countries—recognizes that there are losers from international trade as well as winners.

Source: Federal Reserve Bank of Dallas, "International Trade and the Economy," www.dallasfed.org/educate/everyday/ev7.html.

MyEconLab Study Plan

Your Turn: Test your understanding by doing related problem 3.12 on page 313 at the end of this chapter.

Where Does Comparative Advantage Come From?

Among the main sources of comparative advantage are the following:

- **Climate and natural resources.** This source of comparative advantage is the most obvious. Because of geology, Saudi Arabia has a comparative advantage in the production of oil. Because of climate and soil conditions, Costa Rica has a comparative advantage in the production of bananas, and the United States has a comparative advantage in the production of wheat.
- **Relative abundance of labor and capital.** Some countries, such as the United States, have many highly skilled workers and a great deal of machinery. Other countries, such as China, have many unskilled workers and relatively little machinery. As a result, the United States has a comparative advantage in the production of goods that require highly skilled workers or sophisticated machinery, such as aircraft and computer software. China has a comparative advantage in the production of goods, such as tools, clothing, and children's toys, that require unskilled workers and small amounts of simple machinery.
- **Technology.** Broadly defined, *technology* is the process firms use to turn inputs into goods and services. At any given time, firms in different countries do not all have access to the same technologies. In part, this difference is a result of past investments countries have made in higher education or in supporting research and development. Some countries are strong in *product technologies,* which involve the ability to develop new products. For example, firms in the United States have pioneered the development of such products as radios, televisions, digital computers, airliners, medical equipment, and many prescription drugs. Other countries are strong in *process technologies,* which involve the ability to improve the processes used to make existing products. For example, Japanese-based firms, such as Toyota and Honda, have succeeded by greatly improving the processes for designing and manufacturing automobiles.
- **External economies.** It is difficult to explain the location of some industries on the basis of climate, natural resources, the relative abundance of labor and capital, or technology. For example, why does southern California have a comparative advantage in making movies or Switzerland in making watches or New York in providing financial services? The answer is that once an industry becomes established in an area, firms located in that area gain advantages over firms located elsewhere.

The advantages include the availability of skilled workers, the opportunity to interact with other firms in the same industry, and proximity to suppliers. These advantages result in lower costs to firms located in the area. Because these lower costs result from increases in the size of the industry in an area, economists refer to them as **external economies**. MyEconLab Concept Check

External economies Reductions in a firm's costs that result from an increase in the size of an industry.

Comparative Advantage over Time: The Rise and Fall—and Rise—of the U.S. Consumer Electronics Industry

A country may develop a comparative advantage in the production of a good, and then, as time passes and circumstances change, the country may lose its comparative advantage in producing that good and develop a comparative advantage in producing other goods. For several decades, the United States had a comparative advantage in the production of consumer electronic goods, such as televisions, radios, and stereos. The comparative advantage of the United States in these products was based on having developed most of the underlying technology, having the most modern factories, and having a skilled and experienced workforce. Gradually, however, other countries, particularly Japan, gained access to the technology, built modern factories, and developed skilled workforces. As mentioned earlier, Japanese firms have excelled in process technologies, which involve the ability to improve the processes used to make existing products. By the 1970s and 1980s, Japanese firms were able to produce many consumer electronic goods more cheaply and with higher quality than could U.S. firms. Japanese firms Sony, Panasonic, and Pioneer replaced U.S. firms Magnavox, Zenith, and RCA as world leaders in consumer electronics.

By the mid-2000s, however, as the technology underlying consumer electronics had evolved, comparative advantage had shifted again, and several U.S. firms had surged ahead of their Japanese competitors. For example, Apple had developed the iPod, iPhone, iPad, and Apple Watch; Linksys, a division of Cisco Systems, took the lead in home wireless networking technology; and TiVo pioneered the digital video recorder (DVR). As pictures and music converted to digital data, process technologies became less important than the ability to design and develop new products. These new consumer electronic products required skills similar to those in computer design and software writing, where the United States had long maintained a comparative advantage. Although for the most part these firms did not manufacture within the United States the products they designed and marketed, even that may be changing. Apple has begun assembling its Mac Pro computer in the United States. Foxconn, a Taiwanese electronics manufacturer, also announced plans to build factories in the United States that will produce robots and displays for electronic devices.

Once a country has lost its comparative advantage in producing a good, its income will be higher and its economy will be more efficient if it switches from producing the good to importing it, as the United States did when it switched from producing televisions to importing them. As we will see in the next section, however, there is often political pressure on governments to attempt to preserve industries that have lost their comparative advantage. MyEconLab Concept Check

MyEconLab Study Plan

9.4 Government Policies That Restrict International Trade

LEARNING OBJECTIVE: Analyze the economic effects of government policies that restrict international trade.

Free trade Trade between countries that is without government restrictions.

Free trade, or trade between countries without government restrictions, makes consumers better off. We can expand on this idea by using the concepts of consumer surplus and producer surplus (see Chapter 4, Section 4.1). Figure 9.4 shows the market in the United States for the biofuel ethanol, which can be used as a substitute for gasoline. The figure shows the situation of autarky, where the United States does not trade with other countries. The equilibrium price of ethanol is $2.00 per gallon, and the

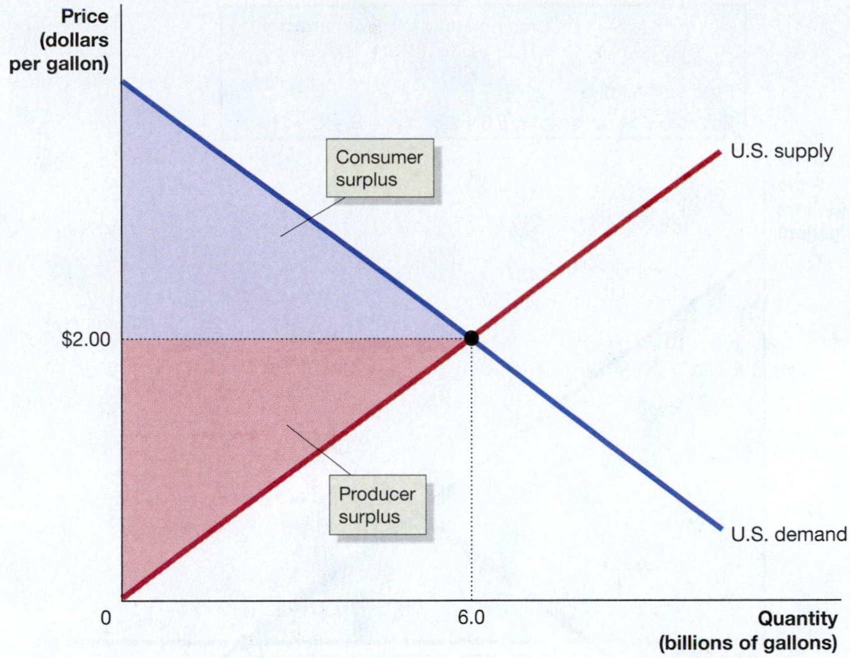

MyEconLab Animation

Figure 9.4

The U.S. Market for Ethanol under Autarky

This figure shows the market for ethanol in the United States, assuming autarky, where the United States does not trade with other countries. The equilibrium price of ethanol is $2.00 per gallon, and the equilibrium quantity is 6.0 billion gallons per year. The blue area represents consumer surplus, and the red area represents producer surplus.

equilibrium quantity is 6.0 billion gallons per year. The blue area represents consumer surplus, and the red area represents producer surplus.

Now suppose that the United States begins importing ethanol from Brazil and other countries that produce ethanol for $1.00 per gallon. Because the world market for ethanol is large, we will assume that the United States can buy as much ethanol as it wants without causing the *world price* of $1.00 per gallon to rise. Therefore, once imports of ethanol are allowed into the United States, U.S. firms will not be able to sell ethanol at prices higher than the world price of $1.00, and the U.S. price will become equal to the world price.

Figure 9.5 shows the result of allowing imports of ethanol into the United States. With the price lowered from $2.00 to $1.00, U.S. consumers increase their purchases from 6.0 billion gallons to 9.0 billion gallons. Equilibrium moves from point *F* to point *G*. In the new equilibrium, U.S. producers have reduced the quantity of ethanol they supply from 6.0 billion gallons to 3.0 billion gallons. Imports will equal 6.0 billion gallons, which is the difference between U.S. consumption and U.S. production.

Under autarky, consumer surplus would be area *A* in Figure 9.5. With imports, the reduction in price increases consumer surplus, so it is now equal to the sum of areas *A*, *B*, *C*, and *D*. Although the lower price increases consumer surplus, it reduces producer surplus. Under autarky, producer surplus was equal to the sum of areas *B* and *E*. With imports, it is equal to only area *E*. Recall that economic surplus equals the sum of consumer surplus and producer surplus. Moving from autarky to allowing imports increases economic surplus in the United States by an amount equal to the sum of areas *C* and *D*.

We can conclude that international trade helps consumers but hurts firms that are less efficient than foreign competitors. As a result, these firms and their workers are often strong supporters of government policies that restrict trade. These policies usually take one of two forms: (1) *tariffs*, and (2) *quotas* and *voluntary export restraints*.

Tariffs

The most common interferences with trade are *tariffs*, which are taxes imposed by a government on goods imported into the country. Like any other tax, a tariff increases the cost of selling a good. Figure 9.6 shows the effect of a tariff of $0.50 per gallon on ethanol imports into the United States. The $0.50 tariff raises the price of ethanol in the United States from the world price of $1.00 per gallon to $1.50 per gallon. At this

MyEconLab Animation

Figure 9.5

The Effect of Imports on the U.S. Ethanol Market

When imports are allowed into the United States, the price of ethanol falls from \$2.00 to \$1.00. U.S. consumers increase their purchases from 6.0 billion gallons to 9.0 billion gallons. Equilibrium moves from point *F* to point *G*. U.S. producers reduce the quantity of ethanol they supply from 6.0 billion gallons to 3.0 billion gallons. Imports equal 6.0 billion gallons, which is the difference between U.S. consumption and U.S. production. Consumer surplus equals the sum of areas *A*, *B*, *C*, and *D*. Producer surplus equals the area *E*.

	Under Autarky	With Imports
Consumer Surplus	*A*	*A* + *B* + *C* + *D*
Producer Surplus	*B* + *E*	*E*
Economic Surplus	*A* + *B* + *E*	*A* + *B* + *C* + *D* + *E*

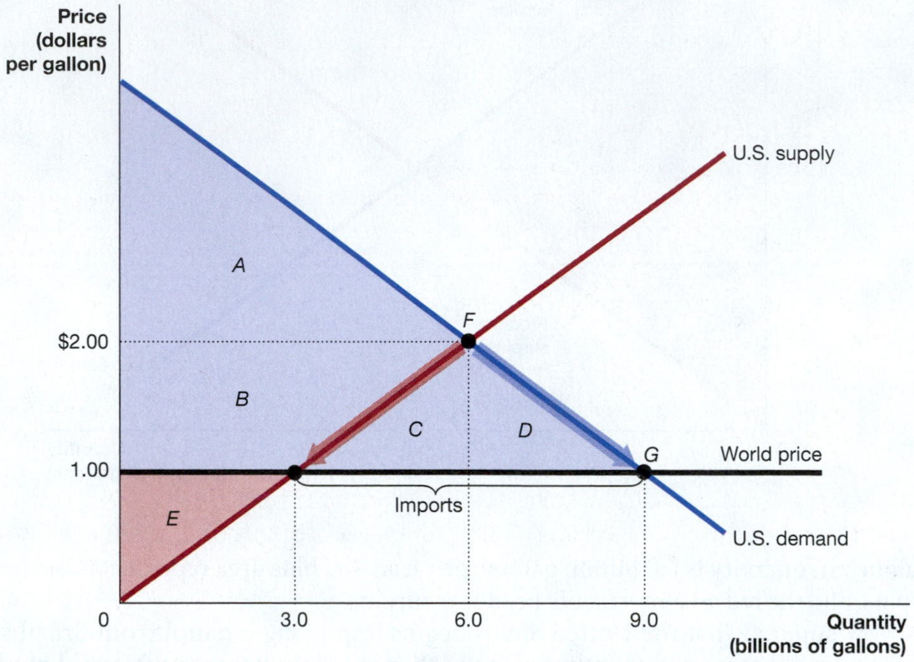

higher price, U.S. ethanol producers increase the quantity they supply from 3.0 billion gallons to 4.5 billion gallons. U.S. consumers, though, cut back their purchases of ethanol from 9.0 billion gallons to 7.5 billion gallons. Imports decline from 6.0 billion gallons (9.0 billion − 3.0 billion) to 3.0 billion gallons (7.5 billion − 4.5 billion). Equilibrium moves from point *G* to point *H*.

MyEconLab Animation

Figure 9.6

The Effects of a Tariff on Ethanol

Without a tariff on ethanol, U.S. producers will sell 3.0 billion gallons of ethanol, U.S. consumers will purchase 9.0 billion gallons, and imports will be 6.0 billion gallons. The U.S. price will equal the world price of \$1.00 per gallon. The \$0.50-per-gallon tariff raises the price of ethanol in the United States to \$1.50 per gallon, and U.S. producers increase the quantity they supply to 4.5 billion gallons. U.S. consumers reduce their purchases to 7.5 billion gallons. Equilibrium moves from point *G* to point *H*. The ethanol tariff causes a loss of consumer surplus equal to the area *A* + *C* + *T* + *D*. The area *A* is the increase in producer surplus due to the higher price. The area *T* is the government's tariff revenue. The areas *C* and *D* represent deadweight loss.

Loss of Consumer Surplus	=	Increase in Producer Surplus	+	Government Tariff Revenue	+	Deadweight Loss
A + *C* + *T* + *D*		*A*		*T*		*C* + *D*

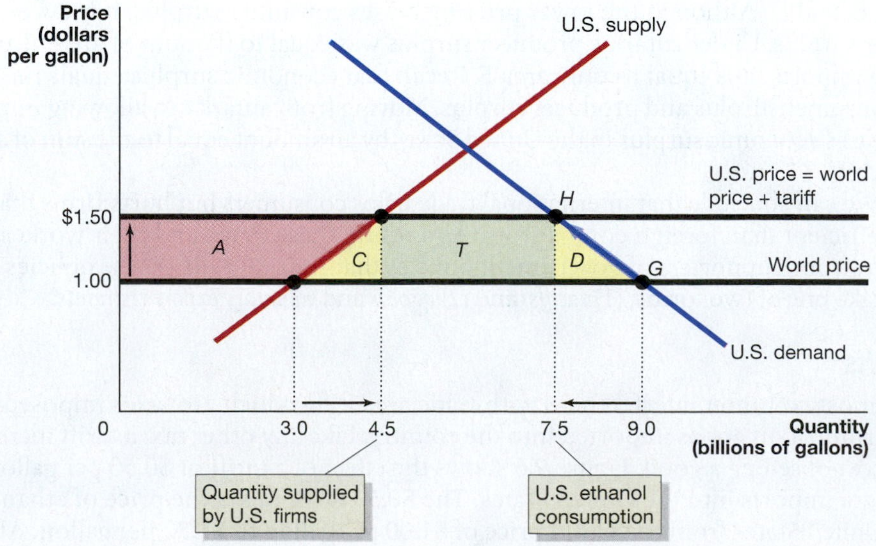

By raising the price of ethanol from $1.00 to $1.50, the tariff reduces consumer surplus by the sum of areas *A*, *T*, *C*, and *D*. Area *A* is the increase in producer surplus from the higher price. The government collects tariff revenue equal to the tariff of $0.50 per gallon multiplied by the 3.0 billion gallons imported. Area *T* represents the government's tariff revenue. Areas *C* and *D* represent losses to U.S. consumers that are not captured by anyone. These areas are deadweight loss and represent the decline in economic efficiency resulting from the ethanol tariff. Area *C* shows the effect of U.S. consumers being forced to buy from U.S. producers that are less efficient than foreign producers, and area *D* shows the effect of U.S. consumers buying less ethanol than they would have at the world price. As a result of the tariff, economic surplus has been reduced by the sum of areas *C* and *D*.

We can conclude that the tariff succeeds in helping U.S. ethanol producers but hurts U.S. consumers and the efficiency of the U.S. economy. MyEconLab Concept Check

Quotas and Voluntary Export Restraints

A **quota** is a numerical limit on the quantity of a good that can be imported, and it has an effect similar to that of a tariff. A quota is imposed by the government of the importing country. A **voluntary export restraint (VER)** is an agreement negotiated between two countries that places a numerical limit on the quantity of a good that can be imported by one country from the other country. In the 1980s, the United States and Japan negotiated a VER that limited the quantity of automobiles the United States would import from Japan. The Japanese government agreed to the VER primarily because it was afraid that if it did not, the United States would impose a tariff or quota on imports of Japanese automobiles. Quotas and VERs have similar economic effects.

Quota A numerical limit a government imposes on the quantity of a good that can be imported into the country.

Voluntary export restraint (VER) An agreement negotiated between two countries that places a numerical limit on the quantity of a good that can be imported by one country from the other country.

The main purpose of most tariffs and quotas is to reduce the foreign competition that domestic firms face. For many years, Congress has imposed a quota on sugar imports to protect U.S. sugar producers. Figure 9.7 shows the actual statistics for the

Loss of Consumer Surplus	=	Gain to U.S. Sugar Producers	+	Gain to Foreign Sugar Producers	+	Deadweight Loss
A + *C* + *B* + *D*		*A*		*B*		*C* + *D*
$3.26 billion	=	$1.71 billion	+	$0.90 billion	+	$0.65 billion

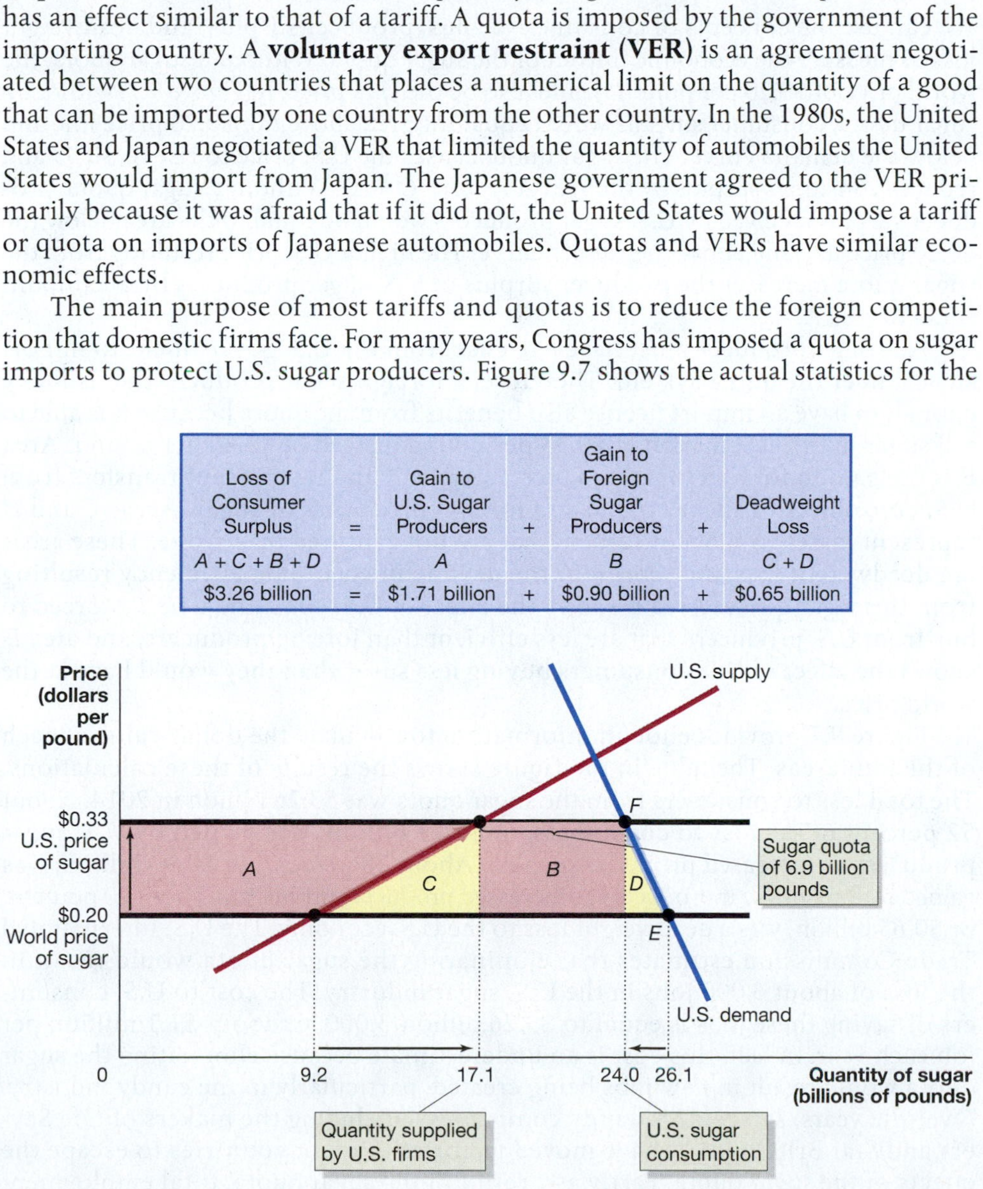

MyEconLab Animation

Figure 9.7

The Economic Effect of the U.S. Sugar Quota

Without a sugar quota, U.S. sugar producers would have sold 9.2 billion pounds of sugar, U.S. consumers would have purchased 26.1 billion pounds of sugar, and imports would have been 16.9 billion pounds. The U.S. price would have equaled the world price of $0.20 per pound. Because the sugar quota limits imports to 6.9 billion pounds (the bracket in the graph), the price of sugar in the United States rises to $0.33 per pound, and U.S. producers supply 17.1 billion pounds. U.S. consumers purchase 24.0 billion pounds rather than the 26.1 billion pounds they would purchase at the world price. Without the import quota, equilibrium would be at point *E*; with the quota, equilibrium is at point *F*. The sugar quota causes a loss of consumer surplus equal to the area *A* + *B* + *C* + *D*. The area *A* is the gain to U.S. sugar producers. The area *B* is the gain to foreign sugar producers. The areas *C* and *D* represent deadweight loss. The total loss to U.S. consumers in 2014 was $3.26 billion.

U.S. sugar market in 2014. The effect of a quota is very similar to the effect of a tariff. By limiting imports, a quota forces the domestic price of a good above the world price. In this case, the sugar quota limits sugar imports to 6.9 billion pounds per year (shown by the bracket in Figure 9.7), forcing the U.S. price of sugar up to $0.33 per pound, or $0.13 higher than the world price of $0.20 per pound. The U.S. price is above the world price because the quota keeps foreign sugar producers from selling the additional sugar in the United States that would drive the U.S. price down to the world price. At a price of $0.33 per pound, U.S. producers increase the quantity of sugar they supply from the 9.2 billion pounds they would supply at the world price to 17.1 billion pounds, and U.S. consumers cut back their purchases of sugar from the 26.1 billion pounds they would purchase at the world price to the 24.0 billion pounds they are willing to purchase at the higher U.S. price. If there were no import quota, equilibrium would be at the world price (point *E*), but with the quota, equilibrium is at the U.S. price (point *F*).

MyEconLab Concept Check

Measuring the Economic Effect of the Sugar Quota

We can use the concepts of consumer surplus, producer surplus, and deadweight loss to measure the economic impact of the sugar quota. Without a sugar quota, the world price of $0.20 per pound would also be the U.S. price. In Figure 9.7, without a sugar quota, consumer surplus would equal the area above the $0.20 price line and below the demand curve. The sugar quota causes the U.S. price to rise to $0.33 and reduces consumer surplus by the area $A + B + C + D$. Without a sugar quota, producer surplus received by U.S. sugar producers would be equal to the area below the $0.20 price line and above the supply curve. The higher U.S. price resulting from the sugar quota increases the producer surplus of U.S. sugar producers by an amount equal to area *A*.

A foreign producer must have a license from the U.S. government to import sugar under the quota system. Therefore, a foreign sugar producer that is lucky enough to have an import license also benefits from the quota because it is able to sell sugar in the U.S. market at $0.33 per pound instead of $0.20 per pound. Area *B* is the gain to foreign sugar producers. Areas *A* and *B* represent transfers from U.S. consumers of sugar to U.S. and foreign producers of sugar. Areas *C* and *D* represent losses to U.S. consumers that are not captured by anyone. These areas are deadweight loss and represent the decline in economic efficiency resulting from the sugar quota. Area *C* shows the effect of U.S. consumers being forced to buy from U.S. producers that are less efficient than foreign producers, and area *D* shows the effect of U.S. consumers buying less sugar than they would have at the world price.

Figure 9.7 provides enough information to calculate the dollar value of each of the four areas. The table in the figure shows the results of these calculations. The total loss to consumers from the sugar quota was $3.26 billion in 2014. About 52 percent of the loss to consumers, or $1.71 billion, was gained by U.S. sugar producers as increased producer surplus. About 28 percent, or $0.90 billion, was gained by foreign sugar producers as increased producer surplus, and about 20 percent, or $0.65 billion, was a deadweight loss to the U.S. economy. The U.S. International Trade Commission estimates that eliminating the sugar quota would result in the loss of about 3,000 jobs in the U.S. sugar industry. The cost to U.S. consumers of saving these jobs is equal to $3.26 billion/3,000, or about $1.1 million per job each year. In fact, this cost is an underestimate because eliminating the sugar quota would result in new jobs being created, particularly in the candy industry. Over the years, several U.S. candy companies—including the makers of Life Savers and Star Brite mints—have moved factories to other countries to escape the effects of the sugar quota. Partly as a result of the sugar quota, total employment in U.S. chocolate and candy firms that use sugar as an input declined by one-third between 1996 and 2014.

MyEconLab Concept Check

Solved Problem 9.4

MyEconLab Interactive Animation

Measuring the Economic Effect of a Quota

Suppose that the United States currently both produces and imports apples. The U.S. government then decides to restrict international trade in apples by imposing a quota that allows imports of only 4 million boxes of apples into the United States each year. The figure shows the results of imposing the quota.

Fill in the following table, using the prices, quantities, and letters in the figure:

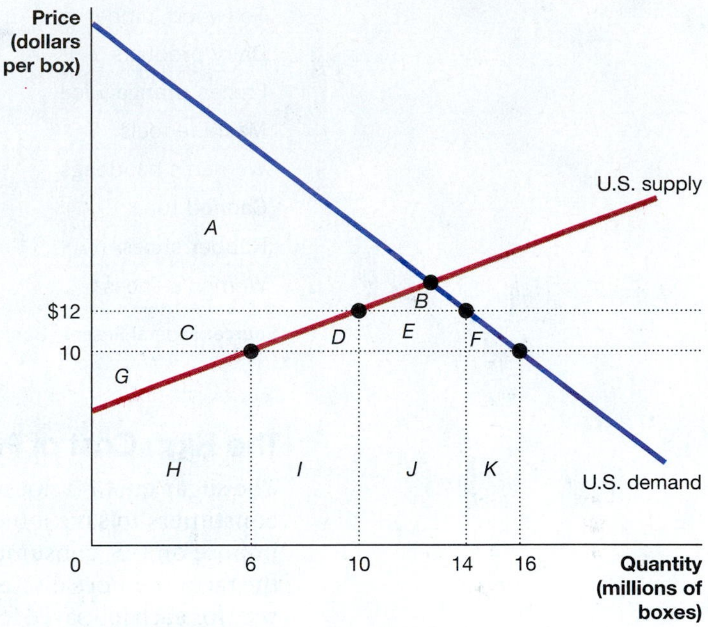

	Without Quota	With Quota
World price of apples		
U.S. price of apples		
Quantity supplied by U.S. firms		
Quantity demanded by U.S. consumers		
Quantity imported		
Area of consumer surplus		
Area of domestic producer surplus		
Area of deadweight loss		

Solving the Problem

Step 1: Review the chapter material. This problem is about measuring the economic effects of a quota, so you may want to review the sections "Quotas and Voluntary Export Restraints," which begins on page 299, and "Measuring the Economic Effect of the Sugar Quota," which begins on page 300.

Step 2: Fill in the table. After studying Figure 9.7, you should be able to fill in the table. Remember that consumer surplus is the area below the demand curve and above the market price.

	Without Quota	With Quota
World price of apples	$10	$10
U.S. price of apples	$10	$12
Quantity supplied by U.S. firms	6 million boxes	10 million boxes
Quantity demanded by U.S. consumers	16 million boxes	14 million boxes
Quantity imported	10 million boxes	4 million boxes
Area of consumer surplus	$A + B + C + D + E + F$	$A + B$
Area of domestic producer surplus	G	$G + C$
Area of deadweight loss	No deadweight loss	$D + F$

Your Turn: For more practice, do related problem 4.12 on pages 314–315 at the end of this chapter.

MyEconLab Study Plan

Table 9.5

Preserving U.S. Jobs with Tariffs and Quotas Is Expensive

Product	Number of Jobs Saved	Cost to Consumers per Year for Each Job Saved
Benzenoid chemicals	216	$1,376,435
Luggage	226	1,285,078
Softwood lumber	605	1,044,271
Dairy products	2,378	685,323
Frozen orange juice	609	635,103
Machine tools	1,556	479,452
Women's handbags	773	263,535
Canned tuna	390	257,640
Rubber shoes	1,701	168,312
Women's shoes	3,702	132,870

Source: Federal Reserve Bank of Dallas, 2002 *Annual Report*, Exhibit 11.

The High Cost of Preserving Jobs with Tariffs and Quotas

The sugar quota is not the only government policy that imposes a high cost on U.S. consumers to save jobs at U.S. firms. Table 9.5 shows the costs tariffs and quotas impose on U.S. consumers per year for each job saved in several industries. Note that the tariff on shoes discussed in the chapter opener costs U.S. consumers $300,000 per year for each job saved for just the two types of shoes listed.

Just as the sugar quota costs jobs in the candy industry, other tariffs and quotas cost jobs outside the industries immediately affected. For example, in 1991, the United States imposed tariffs on flat-panel displays used in laptop computers. The tariff was good news for U.S. producers of these displays but bad news for companies producing laptop computers. Toshiba, Sharp, and Apple all closed their U.S. laptop production facilities and moved production overseas. In fact, whenever one industry receives tariff or quota protection, other domestic industries lose jobs. MyEconLab Concept Check

Making the Connection
MyEconLab Video

Smoot-Hawley, the Politics of Tariffs, and the Cost of Protecting a Vanishing Industry

How does the Smoot-Hawley Tariff Act of 1930 affect what you pay for your shoes today?

In the 1920s, U.S. farmers faced severe financial hardship. Congress and the president responded to that hardship. As a result of that response, in 2015 many U.S. businesses that import foreign-made shoes into the United States paid tariffs of 35 percent or more on the value of the shoes. Sound illogical? The politics of tariffs can certainly seem to be.

Here is the connection between farmers in the 1920s and shoes today: The 1920s were a period of rapid economic progress in the United States, with the mass production of automobiles, the expansion of electricity use in homes and businesses, improvements in public health, a boom in housing construction, and the development of network radio and talking films. But the incomes of many farmers declined, partly because of increasing agricultural production from foreign competitors. During the 1928 presidential election, Herbert Hoover, the Republican Party candidate, promised that if elected, he would aid farmers by raising tariffs on agriculture goods imported into the United States.

After Hoover won the election, Congress in 1929 considered a new tariff bill. During Congressional negotiations, the number of products on which tariffs would be raised quickly expanded beyond agricultural products, in a process known as *logrolling*.

Logrolling refers to members of Congress promising to support each other's legislation. In this case, a member of Congress from a district with a lot of dairy farms who wanted the tariff on milk increased would seek out a member of Congress from a district with shoe factories and negotiate along these lines: "If you vote to increase tariffs on milk, I'll vote to increase tariffs on shoes." The law Congress finally passed in 1930 is called the *Smoot-Hawley Tariff Act* and raised tariffs to the highest level in U.S. history. As a percentage of the value of imports covered by the law, tariffs reached nearly 60 percent.

The process of logrolling can lead to very detailed and complex tariffs as members of Congress attempt to protect specific firms in their districts from competition from foreign producers. For example, the 2015 tariff on shoes contains hundreds of entries, many aimed at very specific types of shoes. Here are *just a few* of those entries:

Type of Shoe	Tariff
Footwear designed to be worn over, or in lieu of, other footwear as a protection against water, oil, grease, or chemicals or cold or inclement weather	37.5%
Parts of footwear (including uppers whether or not attached to soles other than outer soles); removable insoles, heel cushions and similar articles; gaiters, leggings and similar articles, and parts thereof: Valued not over $3/pair	33.6%
Parts of footwear (including uppers whether or not attached to soles other than outer soles); removable insoles, heel cushions and similar articles; gaiters, leggings and similar articles, and parts thereof: Valued over $3/pair but not over $6.50	63 cents per pair plus 26.2%
Tennis shoes, basketball shoes, gym shoes, training shoes and the like, costing more than $12 per pair	20.0%
Footwear having uppers of which over 90 percent of the external surface area (including any accessories or reinforcements such as those mentioned in note 4(a) to this chapter) is rubber or plastics (except footwear having a foxing or a foxing-like band applied or made on a base or platform of cork)	12.5%
Footwear with open toes or open heels; footwear of the slip-on type, that is held to the foot without the use of laces or buckles or other fasteners, the foregoing except footwear of subheading 6402.99.20 and except footwear having a foxing or a foxing-having outer sole with textile materials having the greatest surface area in contact with the ground, but not taken into account under the terms of additional U.S. note 5 to this chapter	12.5%
House slippers valued not over $3 per pair having outer soles with textile materials having the greatest surface area in contact with the ground, but not taken into account under the terms of additional U.S. note 5 to this chapter	12.5%
Footwear having uppers of which over 90 percent of the external surface area (including any accessories or reinforcements such as those mentioned in note 4(a) to this chapter) is rubber or plastics (except footwear having a foxing or a foxing-like band applied or made on a base or platform of wood)	8.0%
Footwear with outer soles of rubber, plastics, leather or composition leather and uppers of textile materials: Having soles (or mid-soles, if any) of rubber or plastics which are affixed to the upper exclusively with an adhesive (any mid-soles also being affixed exclusively to one another and to the sole with an adhesive); the foregoing except footwear having uppers of vegetable fibers and having outer soles with textile materials having the greatest surface area in contact with the ground, but not taken into account under the terms of additional U.S. note 5 to this chapter	7.5%
Sandals and similar footwear of plastics, produced in one piece by molding	3.0%

Are you having trouble understanding the entries in the table? Imagine being the owner of a small business in 2015 who wants to import shoes. You will have a lot of difficulty just determining what tariff to pay, given the complexity of the law.

Canada, the largest trading partner of the United States, reacted to passage of the Smoot-Hawley Tariff by enacting large increases in tariffs on U.S. imports. Other countries raised tariffs as well, resulting in a *trade war* that led to a sharp decrease in global trade and helped increase the severity of the Great Depression of the 1930s.

Since the end of World War II in 1945, the United States and most other countries have engaged in rounds of negotiations that have greatly reduced tariffs on most goods. But the United States continues to impose high tariffs on shoes 85 years after the passage of Smoot-Hawley. During that time, employment in the U.S. shoe industry has fallen from 275,000 workers to fewer than 15,000, as more than 98 percent of the shoes sold in the United States are imported. As Table 9.5 on page 302 shows, the cost to U.S. consumers of preserving those remaining jobs is very high. The total cost to U.S. consumers from higher shoe prices due to the tariff is more than $2 billion per year. The fact that high tariffs on shoes have survived despite few shoes being manufactured in the United States anymore demonstrates how difficult it can sometimes be to remove government protection for an industry once the protection has been enacted.

One way to avoid logrolling when passing tariff laws is for Congress to give the president *fast-track authority* when negotiating trade agreements with other countries. Under fast-track authority, once the president has finished negotiating an agreement with other countries, Congress can either pass or reject the agreement but cannot change any of its provisions. With fast-track authority, the vote trading that occurred during the Congressional deliberations over Smoot-Hawley would not be possible. In 2015, only after a long political struggle was President Obama able to get Congress to grant him the fast-track authority he needed to finish negotiating the Trans-Pacific Partnership trade agreement.

Sources: U.S. International Trade Commission, *Harmonized Tariff Schedule of the United States (2015)*, http://hts.usitc.gov; Carl Hulse and Gardiner Harris, "House Republicans and White House Try to Revive Trade Bill Stalled by Democrats," *New York Times*, June 15, 2015; and Blake W. Krueger, "A Shoe Tariff With a Big Footprint," *Wall Street Journal*, November 22, 2012.

MyEconLab Study Plan

Your Turn: Test your understanding by doing related problems 4.14 and 4.15 on page 315 at the end of this chapter.

Gains from Unilateral Elimination of Tariffs and Quotas

Some politicians argue that eliminating U.S. tariffs and quotas would help the U.S. economy only if other countries eliminated their tariffs and quotas in exchange. It is easier to gain political support for reducing or eliminating tariffs or quotas if it is done as part of an agreement with other countries that involves their eliminating some of their tariffs or quotas. But as the example of the sugar quota shows, *the U.S. economy would experience a gain in economic surplus from the elimination of tariffs and quotas even if other countries did not reduce their tariffs and quotas.*

MyEconLab Concept Check

Other Barriers to Trade

In addition to tariffs and quotas, governments sometimes erect other barriers to trade. For example, all governments require that imports meet certain health and safety requirements. Sometimes, however, governments use these requirements to shield domestic firms from foreign competition. For example, a government may impose stricter health and safety requirements on imported goods than on goods produced by domestic firms.

Many governments also restrict imports of certain products on national security grounds. The argument is that in time of war, a country should not be dependent on imports of critical war materials. Once again, these restrictions are sometimes used more to protect domestic companies from competition than to protect national security. For example, for years, the U.S. government would buy military uniforms only from U.S. manufacturers, even though uniforms are not a critical war material. The Defense Department gives each army recruit a voucher to purchase a pair of athletic shoes for training. New Balance has attempted to force the Defense Department to require the vouchers be used only to purchase U.S.-made shoes. Many officials in the Defense Department didn't see soldiers training in foreign-made running shoes as a threat to national security. MyEconLab Concept Check

MyEconLab Study Plan

9.5 The Arguments over Trade Policies and Globalization

LEARNING OBJECTIVE: Evaluate the arguments over trade policies and globalization.

The argument over whether the U.S. government should regulate international trade has continued since the founding of the country. One particularly controversial attempt to restrict trade took place during the Great Depression of the 1930s. At that time, the United States and other countries attempted to help domestic firms by raising tariffs on imports. The United States started the process by passing the Smoot-Hawley Tariff in 1930, which raised average tariff rates to nearly 60 percent. As other countries retaliated by raising their tariffs, international trade collapsed.

By the end of World War II in 1945, government officials in the United States and Europe were looking for a way to reduce tariffs and revive international trade. To help achieve this goal, they set up the General Agreement on Tariffs and Trade (GATT) in 1948. Countries that joined the GATT agreed not to impose new tariffs or import quotas. In addition, a series of *multilateral negotiations,* called *trade rounds,* took place, in which countries agreed to reduce tariffs from the very high levels of the 1930s.

In the 1940s, most international trade was in goods, and the GATT agreement covered only goods. In the following decades, trade in services and products incorporating *intellectual property,* such as software programs and movies, grew in importance. Many GATT members pressed for a new agreement that would cover services and intellectual property, as well as goods. A new agreement was negotiated, and in January 1995, the GATT was replaced by the **World Trade Organization (WTO)**, headquartered in Geneva, Switzerland. More than 150 countries are currently members of the WTO.

World Trade Organization (WTO) An international organization that oversees international trade agreements.

Why Do Some People Oppose the World Trade Organization?

During the years immediately after World War II, many low-income, or developing, countries enacted high tariffs and restricted investment by foreign companies. When these policies failed to produce much economic growth, many of these countries decided during the 1980s to become more open to foreign trade and investment. This process became known as **globalization**. Most developing countries joined the WTO and began to follow its policies.

Globalization The process of countries becoming more open to foreign trade and investment.

During the 1990s, opposition to globalization began to increase. Over the years, protests, which have sometimes turned violent, have occurred in cities hosting WTO meetings. Why would attempts to reduce trade barriers with the objective of increasing income around the world cause such a furious reaction? The opposition to the WTO comes from three sources. First, some opponents are specifically against the globalization process that began in the 1980s and became widespread in the 1990s. Second, other opponents have the same motivation as the supporters of tariffs in the 1930s—to erect trade barriers to protect domestic firms from foreign competition. Third, some critics of the WTO support globalization in principle but believe that the WTO favors the interests of the high-income countries at the expense of the low-income countries. Let's look more closely at the sources of opposition to the WTO.

Anti-Globalization Many of those who protest at WTO meetings distrust globalization. Some believe that free trade and foreign investment destroy the distinctive cultures of many countries. As developing countries began to open their economies to imports from the United States and other high-income countries, the imports of food, clothing, movies, and other goods began to replace the equivalent local products. So, a teenager in Thailand might be sitting in a McDonald's restaurant, wearing Levi's jeans and a Ralph Lauren shirt, listening to a song by Lady Gaga on his iPhone, before downloading *Star Wars: The Force Awakens* to his iPad. Globalization has increased the variety of products available to consumers in developing countries, but some people argue that this is too high a price to pay for what they see as damage to local cultures.

Globalization has also allowed multinational corporations to relocate factories from high-income countries to low-income countries. These new factories in Indonesia, Malaysia, Pakistan, and other countries pay much lower wages than are paid in the United States, Europe, and Japan and often do not meet the environmental or safety regulations that are imposed in high-income countries. Some factories use child labor, which is illegal in high-income countries. Some people have argued that firms with factories in developing countries should pay workers wages as high as those paid in high-income countries. They also believe these firms should abide by the health, safety, and environmental regulations that exist in the high-income countries.

The governments of most developing countries have resisted these proposals. They argue that when the currently rich countries were poor, they also lacked environmental or safety standards, and their workers were paid low wages. They argue that it is easier for rich countries to afford high wages and environmental and safety regulations than it is for poor countries. They also point out that many jobs that seem to have very low wages based on the standards of high-income countries are often better than the alternatives available to workers in low-income countries.

Protectionism The use of trade barriers to shield domestic firms from foreign competition.

"Old-Fashioned" Protectionism The anti-globalization argument against free trade and the WTO is relatively new. Another argument against free trade, called *protectionism*, has been around for centuries. **Protectionism** is the use of trade barriers to shield domestic firms from foreign competition. For as long as international trade has existed, governments have attempted to restrict it to protect domestic firms. As we saw with the analysis of the sugar quota, protectionism causes losses to consumers and eliminates jobs in the domestic industries that buy the protected product. In addition, by reducing the ability of countries to produce according to comparative advantage, protectionism reduces incomes.

Why, then, does protectionism attract support? Protectionism is usually justified on the basis of one of the following arguments:

- **Saving jobs.** Supporters of protectionism argue that free trade reduces employment by driving domestic firms out of business. It is true that when more-efficient foreign firms drive less-efficient domestic firms out of business, jobs are lost, but jobs are also lost when more-efficient domestic firms drive less-efficient domestic firms out of business. These job losses are rarely permanent. In the U.S. economy, jobs are lost and new jobs are created continually. No economic study has ever found a long-term connection between the total number of jobs available and the level of tariff protection for domestic industries. In addition, trade restrictions destroy jobs in some industries at the same time that they preserve jobs in others. The U.S. sugar quota may have saved jobs in the U.S. sugar industry, but it has also destroyed jobs in the U.S. candy industry.
- **Protecting high wages.** Some people worry that firms in high-income countries will have to start paying much lower wages to compete with firms in developing countries. This fear is misplaced, however, because free trade actually raises living standards by increasing economic efficiency. When a country practices protectionism and produces goods and services it could obtain more inexpensively from other countries, it reduces its standard of living. The United States could ban imports of coffee and begin growing it domestically. But doing so would entail a very high opportunity cost because coffee could only be grown in the continental United States in greenhouses and would require large amounts of labor and equipment. The coffee would have to sell for a very high price to cover these costs. Suppose the United States did ban coffee imports: Eliminating the ban at some

future time would eliminate the jobs of U.S. coffee workers, but the standard of living in the United States would rise as coffee prices declined and labor, machinery, and other resources were moved out of coffee production and into production of goods and services for which the United States has a comparative advantage.

- **Protecting infant industries.** It is possible that firms in a country may have a comparative advantage in producing a good, but because the country begins production of the good later than other countries, its firms initially have higher costs. In producing some goods and services, substantial "learning by doing" occurs. As workers and firms produce more of the good or service, they gain experience and become more productive. Over time, these firms will have lower costs and can charge lower prices. As the firms in the "infant industry" gain experience, they will be able to compete successfully with foreign producers. Under free trade, however, they may not get a chance. The established foreign producers can sell the product at a lower price and drive domestic producers out of business before they gain enough experience to compete. To economists, the infant industry argument is the most persuasive of the protectionist arguments. It has a significant drawback, however. Tariffs eliminate the need for firms in an infant industry to become productive enough to compete with foreign firms. After World War II, the governments of many developing countries used the infant industry argument to justify high tariff rates. Unfortunately, most of their infant industries never grew up, and they continued for years as inefficient drains on their economies.
- **Protecting national security.** A country will typically not want to rely on other countries for goods that are critical to its military defense. For example, the United States would probably not want to import all its jet fighter engines from China. The definition of which goods are critical to military defense is a slippery one, however. In fact, it is rare for an industry to ask for protection without raising the issue of national security, even if its products have mainly nonmilitary uses.

MyEconLab Concept Check

Making the Connection
MyEconLab Video

Protecting Consumer Health or Protecting U.S. Firms from Competition?

The World Trade Organization and other international agreements limit the use of tariffs and quotas. So to protect firms from foreign competition, governments sometimes regulate imports by claiming that they pose a threat to consumer health or safety.

Is imported catfish safe for U.S. consumers to eat, or does it contain bacteria and dangerous chemicals? The U.S. states that produce the most catfish are Alabama, Arkansas, Mississippi, and Texas. In 2008, members of Congress from those states pushed through legislation setting up a catfish inspection office in the U.S. Department of Agriculture. By 2014, the office had spent $20 million but had not actually inspected any imported catfish. The money had been spent on just setting up offices and paying administrators' salaries. That year, Congress set a deadline for the inspection program to begin.

Vietnam and other countries that export catfish to the United States objected that the real purpose of the inspections was to erect a barrier to trade. Those governments argued that the inspections would violate the commitments of the United States under the World Trade Organization not to erect barriers to trade. Further complicating the situation for the U.S. government was the fact that these countries were in talks with the United States about the Trans-Pacific Partnership, an agreement to reduce trade barriers among countries in the Pacific that we discussed earlier in this chapter. A trade war over catfish could interfere with completing those talks.

Are restrictions on catfish imports protecting the health of U.S. consumers or the interests of U.S. producers?

A study by the U.S. Government Accountability Office indicated that the health risk to U.S. consumers from imported catfish was very low, even without the proposed inspections. Some members of Congress from states that do not produce catfish also argued that new inspections of imported catfish were unnecessary and would result in U.S. consumers paying higher prices.

Congress and the president are often caught in a policy dilemma over imports. Firms want to reduce or eliminate sales lost to imports, but imposing trade barriers reduces economic efficiency, lowers incomes, and invites retaliation from foreign governments. Although some imported goods can, in fact, pose threats to the health and safety of U.S. consumers, some health and safety regulations are intended to protect the U.S. firms involved rather than U.S. consumers.

Sources: Ron Nixon, "U.S. Catfish Program Could Stymie Pacific Trade Pact, 10 Nations Say," *New York Times*, June 27, 2014; Bruce Einhorn and Chau Mai, "The Catfish Wars Could Derail U.S.–Asia Trade," businessweek.com, June 30, 2014; and U.S. Government Accountability Office, *Seafood Safety: Responsibility for Inspecting Catfish Should Not Be Assigned to USDA*, GAO 12-411, May 2012.

MyEconLab Study Plan

Your Turn: Test your understanding by doing related problem 5.10 on page 317 at the end of this chapter.

Dumping

Dumping Selling a product for a price below its cost of production.

In recent years, the United States has extended protection to some domestic industries by using a provision in the WTO agreement that allows governments to impose tariffs in the case of *dumping*. **Dumping** is selling a product for a price below its cost of production. Using tariffs to offset the effects of dumping is controversial despite being allowed under the WTO agreement.

In practice, it is difficult to determine whether foreign companies are dumping goods because the true production costs of a good are not easy for governments to calculate. As a result, the WTO allows countries to determine that dumping has occurred if a product is exported for a lower price than it sells for on the home market. There is a problem with this approach, however. Often there are good business reasons for a firm to sell a product for different prices to different consumers. For example, the airlines charge business travelers higher ticket prices than leisure travelers. Firms also use "loss leaders"—products that are sold below cost, or even given away free—when introducing a new product or, in the case of retailing, to attract customers who will also buy full-price products. For example, during the holiday season, Walmart sometimes offers toys at prices below what it pays to buy them from manufacturers. It's unclear why these normal business practices should be unacceptable when used in international trade.

MyEconLab Concept Check

Positive versus Normative Analysis (Once Again)

Economists emphasize the burden on the economy imposed by tariffs, quotas, and other government restrictions on free trade. Does it follow that these interferences are bad? Remember that positive analysis concerns what *is*, while normative analysis concerns what *ought to be*. Measuring the effect of the sugar quota on the U.S. economy is an example of positive analysis. Asserting that the sugar quota is bad public policy and should be eliminated is normative analysis. The sugar quota—like all other interferences with trade—makes some people better off and some people worse off, and it reduces total income and consumption. Whether increasing the profits of U.S. sugar companies and the number of workers they employ justifies the costs imposed on consumers and the reduction in economic efficiency is a normative question.

Most economists do not support interferences with trade, such as the sugar quota. Few people become economists if they don't believe that markets should be as free as possible. But the opposite view is certainly intellectually respectable. It is possible for someone to understand the costs of tariffs and quotas but still believe that tariffs and quotas are a good idea, perhaps because he or she believes unrestricted free trade would cause too much disruption to the economy.

The success of industries in getting the government to erect barriers to foreign competition depends partly on some members of the public knowing the costs of trade barriers but supporting them anyway. However, two other factors are also at work:

1. The costs tariffs and quotas impose on consumers are large in total but relatively small per person. For example, the sugar quota imposes a total burden of $3.26 billion per year on consumers. Spread across 320 million Americans, the burden is only about $10 per person—too little for most people to worry about, even if they know the burden exists.
2. The jobs lost to foreign competition are easy to identify, but the jobs created by foreign trade are less easy to identify.

In other words, the industries that benefit from tariffs and quotas benefit a lot—for example, the sugar quota increases the profits of U.S. sugar producers by $1.71 billion per year—while each consumer loses relatively little. This concentration of benefits and widely spread burdens makes it easy to understand why members of Congress receive strong pressure from some industries to enact tariffs and quotas and relatively little pressure from the general public to reduce them. MyEconLab Concept Check

MyEconLab Study Plan

Continued from page 285

Economics in Your Life

Did You Know There Is a Tariff on Running Shoes?

At the beginning of the chapter, we asked you to consider why the federal government has imposed a tariff on shoes, even though there are very few shoe factories remaining in the United States. We also asked why relatively few people have heard of this tariff. In the chapter, we saw that trade restrictions tend to preserve relatively few jobs in the protected industries, while they lead to job losses in other industries and cost consumers billions of dollars per year in higher prices. However, we have also seen that *per person*, the burden of specific trade restrictions can be small. For example, the tariff on shoes might cause you to pay $20 dollars more for a $100 pair of running shoes. The average person buys only one pair of running shoes per year, and few people will take the trouble of writing a letter to their member of Congress or otherwise express their views to try to save $20 per year. In fact, few people will even spend the time to become aware that a specific trade restriction exists. So, if you had never heard of the shoe tariff before you read this chapter, you are certainly not alone.

Conclusion

There are few issues economists agree upon more than the economic benefits of free trade. However, there are few political issues as controversial as government policy toward trade. Many people who would be reluctant to see the government interfere with domestic trade are quite willing to see it interfere with international trade. The damage high tariffs inflicted on the world economy during the 1930s shows what can happen when governments around the world abandon free trade. Whether future episodes of that type can be avoided is by no means certain.

Visit MyEconLab for a news article and analysis related to the concepts in this chapter.

CHAPTER SUMMARY AND PROBLEMS

Key Terms

Absolute advantage, p. 290
Autarky, p. 291
Comparative advantage, p. 289
Dumping, p. 308
Exports, p. 286
External economies, p. 296
Free trade, p. 296
Globalization, p. 305
Imports, p. 286
Opportunity cost, p. 289
Protectionism, p. 306
Quota, p. 299
Tariff, p. 286
Terms of trade, p. 291
Voluntary export restraint (VER), p. 299
World Trade Organization (WTO), p. 305

9.1 The United States in the International Economy, pages 286–289

LEARNING OBJECTIVE: Discuss the role of international trade in the U.S. economy.

Summary

International trade has been increasing in recent decades, in part because of reductions in *tariffs* and other barriers to trade. A **tariff** is a tax imposed by a government on imports. The quantity of goods and services the United States imports and exports has been continually increasing. **Imports** are goods and services bought domestically but produced in other countries. **Exports** are goods and services produced domestically and sold to other countries. Today, the United States is the second-leading exporting country in the world behind China, and about 20 percent of U.S. manufacturing jobs depend on exports.

MyEconLab Visit **www.myeconlab.com** to complete these exercises online and get instant feedback.

Review Questions

1.1 Briefly explain whether the value of U.S. exports is typically larger or smaller than the value of U.S. imports.

1.2 Are imports and exports now a smaller or larger fraction of GDP than they were 40 years ago?

1.3 Briefly explain whether you agree with the following statement: "International trade is more important to the U.S. economy than it is to most other economies."

Problems and Applications

1.4 If the United States were to stop trading goods and services with other countries, which U.S. industries would be likely to see their sales decline the most? Briefly explain.

1.5 Briefly explain whether you agree with the following statement: "Japan has always been much more heavily involved in international trade than are most other nations. In fact, today Japan exports a larger fraction of its GDP than Germany, Great Britain, or the United States."

1.6 Why might a smaller country, such as the Netherlands, be more likely to import and export larger fractions of its GDP than would a larger country, such as China or the United States?

1.7 **(Related to the Chapter Opener on page 285 and the Making the Connection on page 287)** New Balance manufactures shoes in the United States, so you might expect that the firm would benefit from a tariff on shoes. Yet New Balance did not actively oppose the Obama administration's attempts to eliminate the shoe tariff imposed on countries that would be part of the Trans-Pacific Partnership. Briefly explain New Balance's position.

9.2 Comparative Advantage in International Trade, pages 289–291

LEARNING OBJECTIVE: Explain the difference between comparative advantage and absolute advantage in international trade.

Summary

Comparative advantage is the ability of an individual, a firm, or a country to produce a good or service at the lowest **opportunity cost**. **Absolute advantage** is the ability to produce more of a good or service than competitors when using the same amount of resources. Countries trade on the basis of comparative advantage, not on the basis of absolute advantage.

MyEconLab Visit **www.myeconlab.com** to complete these exercises online and get instant feedback.

Review Questions

2.1 What is the difference between absolute advantage and comparative advantage? Will a country always be an exporter of a good in the production of which it has an absolute advantage? Briefly explain.

2.2 A World Trade Organization (WTO) publication calls comparative advantage "arguably the single most powerful insight in economics." What is comparative advantage? What makes it such a powerful insight?

Source: World Trade Organization, "Understanding the WTO," www.wto.org/english/thewto_e/whatis_e/tif_e/fact3_e.htm.

Problems and Applications

2.3 In the 2012 Summer Olympic Games, Ashton Eaton (from the United States) won a gold medal in the decathlon, which requires athletes to compete in 10 different track and field events. In one of these events Eaton ran a 100-meter race in 10.35 seconds. In a separate event, Usain Bolt (from Jamaica) won a gold medal and set a world record by running 100 meters in 9.58 seconds.

a. Which performance—Eaton's or Bolt's—is better explained by the concept of comparative advantage? Briefly explain.

b. Based on their performance at the 2012 Olympic Games, can we say whether Eaton or Bolt was the better athlete? Briefly explain.

2.4 An article in the *New York Times* quoted an economist as arguing that "global free trade and the European single market ... encourage countries to specialize in sectors where they enjoy comparative advantage. Germany's [comparative advantage] is in cars and machine tools." For the author's observation to be correct, must Germany be able to produce more cars and machine tools per hour worked than do France, Italy, the United Kingdom, and Germany's other trading partners? Briefly explain.

Source: Anatole Kaletsky, "In Disguise, a Budget That Britain Needs," *New York Times*, March 24, 2014.

2.5 Briefly explain whether you agree with the following argument: "Unfortunately, Bolivia does not have a comparative advantage with respect to the United States in the production of any good or service." (*Hint:* You do not need any specific information about the economies of Bolivia or the United States to be able to answer this question.)

2.6 The following table shows the hourly output per worker for Greece and Italy measured as quarts of olive oil and pounds of pasta.

	Output per Hour of Work	
	Olive Oil	**Pasta**
Greece	4	2
Italy	4	8

Calculate the opportunity cost of producing olive oil and pasta in both Greece and Italy.

2.7 Using the numbers in the table, explain which country has a comparative advantage in producing smartwatches.

	Output per Hour of Work	
	Smartwatches	**Fitness Bracelets**
Switzerland	8	10
Canada	5	3

2.8 Patrick J. Buchanan, a former presidential candidate, argued in his book on the global economy that there is a flaw in David Ricardo's theory of comparative advantage:

> Classical free trade theory fails the test of common sense. According to Ricardo's law of comparative advantage ... if America makes better computers and textiles than China does, but our advantage in computers is greater than our advantage in textiles, we should (1) focus on computers, (2) let China make textiles, and (3) trade U.S. computers for Chinese textiles... . The doctrine begs a question. If Americans are more efficient than Chinese in making clothes ... why surrender the more efficient American industry? Why shift to a reliance on a Chinese textile industry that will take years to catch up to where American factories are today?

Do you agree with Buchanan's argument? Briefly explain.

Source: Patrick J. Buchanan, *The Great Betrayal: How American Sovereignty and Social Justice Are Being Sacrificed to the Gods of the Global Economy*, Boston: Little, Brown & Company, 1998, p. 66.

2.9 While running for president, Barack Obama made the following statement: "Well, look, people don't want a cheaper T-shirt if they're losing a job in the process." What did Obama mean by the phrase "losing a job in the process"? Using the economic concept of comparative advantage, explain under what circumstances it would make sense for the United States to produce all of the T-shirts purchased in the United States. Do you agree with President Obama's statement? Briefly explain.

Source: James Pethokoukis, "Democratic Debate Spawns Weird Economics," *U.S. News & World Report*, August 8, 2007.

9.3 How Countries Gain from International Trade, pages 291–296

LEARNING OBJECTIVE: Explain how countries gain from international trade.

Summary

Autarky is a situation in which a country does not trade with other countries. The **terms of trade** is the ratio at which a country can trade its exports for imports from other countries. When a country specializes in producing goods for which it has a comparative advantage and trades for the other goods it needs, the country will have a higher level of income and consumption. We do not see complete specialization in production for three reasons: (1) Not all goods and services are traded internationally, (2) production of most goods involves increasing opportunity costs, and (3) tastes for products differ across countries. Although the population of a country as a whole benefits from trade, firms—and their workers—that are unable to compete with lower-cost foreign producers lose. Among the main sources of comparative advantage are climate and natural resources, relative abundance of labor and capital, technology, and external economies. **External economies** are reductions in a firm's costs that result from an increase in the size of an industry. A country may develop a comparative advantage in the production of a good, and then as time passes and circumstances change, the country may lose its comparative advantage in producing that good and develop a comparative advantage in producing other goods.

MyEconLab Visit **www.myeconlab.com** to complete these exercises online and get instant feedback.

Review Questions

3.1 Briefly explain how international trade increases a country's consumption.

3.2 What is meant by a country specializing in the production of a good? Is it typical for countries to be completely specialized? Briefly explain.

3.3 What are the main sources of comparative advantage?

3.4 Does everyone gain from international trade? If not, explain which groups lose.

Problems and Applications

3.5 **(Related to** Solved Problem 9.3 **on page 292)** The following table shows the hourly output per worker in two industries in Chile and Argentina.

	Output per Hour of Work	
	Hats	**Beer**
Chile	8	6
Argentina	1	2

a. Explain which country has an absolute advantage in the production of hats and which country has an absolute advantage in the production of beer.

b. Explain which country has a comparative advantage in the production of hats and which country has a comparative advantage in the production of beer.

c. Suppose that Chile and Argentina currently do not trade with each other. Each has 1,000 hours of labor to use producing hats and beer, and the countries are currently producing the amounts of each good shown in the following table.

	Hats	**Beer**
Chile	7,200	600
Argentina	600	800

Using this information, give a numerical example of how Chile and Argentina can both gain from trade. Assume that after trading begins, one hat can be exchanged for one barrel of beer.

3.6 **(Related to** Solved Problem 9.3 **on page 292)** A political commentator makes the following statement:

> The idea that international trade should be based on the comparative advantage of each country is fine for rich countries like the United States and Japan. Rich countries have educated workers and large quantities of machinery and equipment. These advantages allow them to produce every product more efficiently than poor countries can. Poor countries like Kenya and Bolivia have nothing to gain from international trade based on comparative advantage.

Do you agree with this argument? Briefly explain.

3.7 The following data summarize the trade between Canada and the United States in 2013 and 2014.

	Exports from the United States to Canada (billions of U.S. dollars)	**Exports from Canada to the United States (billions of U.S. dollars)**
2013	$300.8	$332.6
2014	312.4	347.8

In each year, the value of Canada's exports to the United States exceeded the value of U.S. exports to Canada. Can we conclude that foreign trade between the two countries benefited Canada more than it benefited the United States? Briefly explain.

Source: U.S. Department of Commerce, Census Bureau, Economic Indicators Division.

3.8 Is free trade likely to benefit a large, populous country more than a small country with fewer people? Briefly explain.

3.9 An article in the *New Yorker* states, "the main burden of trade-related job losses and wage declines has fallen on middle- and lower-income Americans. But … the very people who suffer most from free trade are often, paradoxically, among its biggest beneficiaries." Explain how it is possible that middle- and lower-income Americans are both the biggest losers and at the same time the biggest winners from free trade.

Source: James Surowiecki, "The Free-Trade Paradox," *New Yorker*, May 26, 2008.

3.10 Hal Varian, chief economist at Google, has made the following two observations about international trade.

a. Trade allows a country "to produce more with less."

b. "There is little doubt who wins [from trade] in the long run: consumers."

Briefly explain whether you agree with either or both of these observations.

Source: Hal R. Varian, "The Mixed Bag of Productivity," *New York Times*, October 23, 2003.

3.11 Suppose the graph on the next page shows Tanzania's production possibilities frontier for cashew nuts and mangoes. Assume that the output per hour of work is 8 bushels of cashew nuts or 2 bushels of mangoes and that Tanzania has 1,000 hours of labor. Without trade, Tanzania evenly splits its labor hours between cashews and mangoes and produces and consumes at point A.

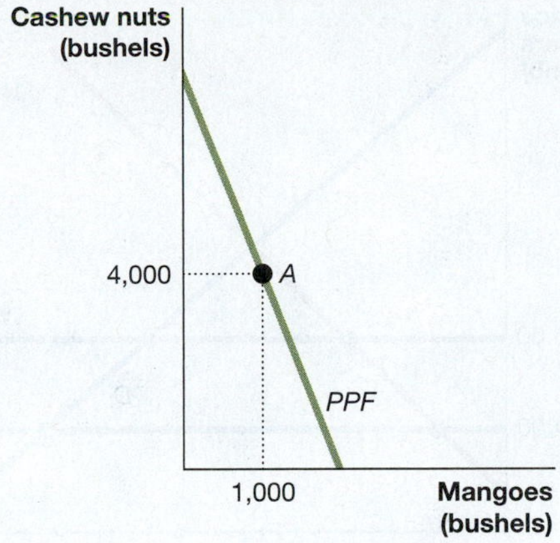

a. Suppose Tanzania opens trade with Kenya, and Kenya's output per hour of work is 1 bushel of cashew nuts or 1 bushel of mangoes. Having the comparative advantage, Tanzania completely specializes in cashew nuts. How many bushels of cashew nuts can Tanzania produce? Denote this point on the graph as point *B*.

b. Suppose Tanzania keeps 5,000 bushels of cashew nuts and exports the remaining 3,000 bushels. If the terms of trade are 1 bushel of mangoes for 2 bushels of cashew nuts, how many bushels of mangoes will Tanzania get in exchange? Denote on the graph the quantity of cashew nuts and mangoes that Tanzania consumes with trade and label this point as point *C*. How does point *C* with trade compare to point *A* without trade?

c. With trade, is Tanzania producing on its production possibilities frontier? With trade, is Tanzania consuming on its production possibilities frontier?

3.12 **(Related to the Don't Let This Happen to You on page 295)** President Barack Obama described a trade agreement reached with the government of Colombia as a "'win–win' for both our countries." Is everyone in both countries likely to win from the agreement? Briefly explain.

Source: Kent Klein, "Obama: Free Trade Agreement a 'Win–Win' for US, Colombia," voanews.com.

3.13 Instagram is a smartphone app that Facebook now owns. According to an article that discusses the climate for software firms in the San Francisco Bay Area, the success of Instagram "is a tale about the culture of the Bay Area tech scene, driven by a tightly woven web of entrepreneurs and investors who nurture one another's projects with money, advice and introductions to the right people." What advantages does being located in the Bay Area give to startup software firms? In what circumstances can software firms located elsewhere overcome these advantages? Are the advantages the Bay Area has likely to persist over time?

Source: Somini Sengupta, Nicole Perlroth, and Jenna Wortham, "Behind Instagram's Success, Networking the Old Way," *New York Times*, April 13, 2012.

9.4 Government Policies That Restrict International Trade, pages 296–305

LEARNING OBJECTIVE: Analyze the economic effects of government policies that restrict international trade.

Summary

Free trade is trade between countries without government restrictions. Government policies that interfere with trade usually take the form of *tariffs, quotas,* or *voluntary export restraints*. A tariff is a tax imposed by a government on imports. A **quota** is a numerical limit imposed by a government on the quantity of a good that can be imported into the country. A **voluntary export restraint (VER)** is an agreement negotiated between two countries that places a numerical limit on the quantity of a good that can be imported by one country from the other country. The federal government's sugar quota costs U.S. consumers $3.26 billion per year, or about $1.1 million per year for each job saved in the sugar industry. Saving jobs by using tariffs and quotas is often very expensive.

MyEconLab Visit **www.myeconlab.com** to complete these exercises online and get instant feedback.

Review Questions

4.1 What is a tariff? What is a quota? Give an example, other than a quota, of a nontariff barrier to trade.

4.2 Who gains and who loses when a country imposes a tariff or a quota on imports of a good?

Problems and Applications

4.3 Political commentator B. Bruce-Briggs once wrote the following in the *Wall Street Journal*: "This is not to say that the case for international free trade is invalid; it is just irrelevant. It is an 'if only everybody … argument… . In the real world almost everybody sees benefits in economic nationalism." What do you think he means by "economic nationalism"? Do you agree that a country benefits from free trade only if every other country also practices free trade? Briefly explain.

Source: B. Bruce-Biggs, "The Coming Overthrow of Free Trade," *Wall Street Journal*, February 24, 1983.

4.4 **(Related to the Chapter Opener on page 285)** While running for the 2016 Democratic nomination for president, Vermont Senator Bernie Sanders opposed the Trans-Pacific Partnership in part because he believed that as a result of the agreement, "the U.S. will lose more than 130,000 jobs to Vietnam and Japan alone." Do you agree that reducing barriers to trade reduces the number of jobs available to workers in the United States? Briefly explain.

Source: Bernie Sanders, "Senator Bernie Sanders: The Trans-Pacific Trade (TPP) Agreement Must Be Defeated," http://www.sanders.senate.gov/download/the-trans-pacific-trade-tpp-agreement-must-be-defeated?inline=file.

4.5 The United States produces beef and also imports beef from other countries.

a. Draw a graph showing the demand and supply of beef in the United States. Assume that the United States can import as much as it wants at the world price of beef without causing the world price of beef to increase. Be sure to indicate on your graph the quantity of beef imported.

b. Now show on your graph the effect of the United States imposing a tariff on beef. Be sure to indicate on your graph the quantity of beef sold by U.S. producers before and after the tariff is imposed, the quantity of beef imported before and after the tariff, and the price of beef in the United States before and after the tariff.

c. Discuss who benefits and who loses when the United States imposes a tariff on beef.

4.6 When Congress was considering a bill to impose quotas on imports of textiles, shoes, and other products, the late Milton Friedman, a Nobel Prize–winning economist, made the following comment: "The consumer will be forced to spend several extra dollars to subsidize the producers [of these goods] by one dollar. A straight handout would be far cheaper."

a. Why would a quota result in consumers paying much more than domestic producers receive? Where do the other dollars go?

b. What does Friedman mean by a "straight handout"? Why would a straight handout be cheaper than a quota?

Source: Milton Friedman, "Free Trade," *Newsweek Magazine*, August 27, 1970.

4.7 A student makes the following argument:

> Tariffs on imports of foreign goods into the United States will cause the foreign companies to add the amount of the tariff to the prices they charge in the United States for those goods. Instead of putting a tariff on imported goods, we should ban importing them. Banning imported goods is better than putting tariffs on them because U.S. producers benefit from the reduced competition, and U.S. consumers don't have to pay the higher prices caused by tariffs.

Briefly explain whether you agree with the student's reasoning.

4.8 Suppose China decides to pay large subsidies to any Chinese company that exports goods or services to the United States. As a result, these companies are able to sell products in the United States at far below their cost of production. In addition, China decides to bar all imports from the United States. The dollars that the United States pays to import Chinese goods are left in banks in China. Will this strategy raise or lower the standard of living in China? Will it raise or lower the standard of living in the United States? Briefly explain. Be sure to provide a definition of "standard of living" in your answer.

4.9 The following graph shows the effect on consumer surplus, producer surplus, government tariff revenue, and economic surplus of a tariff of $1 per unit on imports of plastic combs into the United States. Use the areas denoted in the graph to answer the following questions.

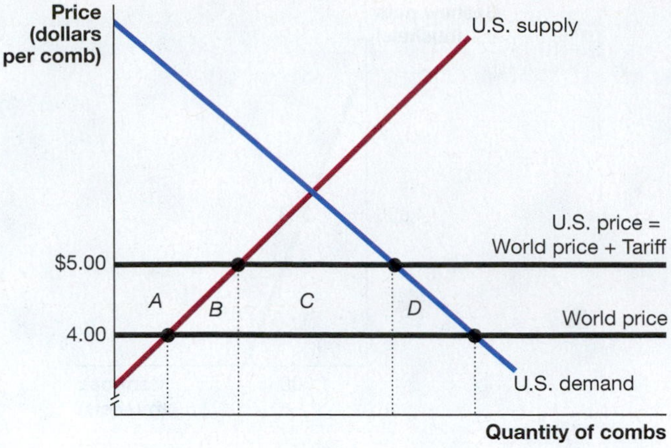

a. Which area shows the losses to U.S. consumers of buying a smaller quantity of combs than they would have if they could have purchased them at the world price?

b. Which area shows the losses to U.S. consumers of having to buy combs from U.S. producers who are less efficient than foreign producers?

c. Which areas show the deadweight loss to the U.S. economy as a result of the tariff on combs?

4.10 The following graph shows the situation after the U.S. government removes a tariff on imports of canned tuna.

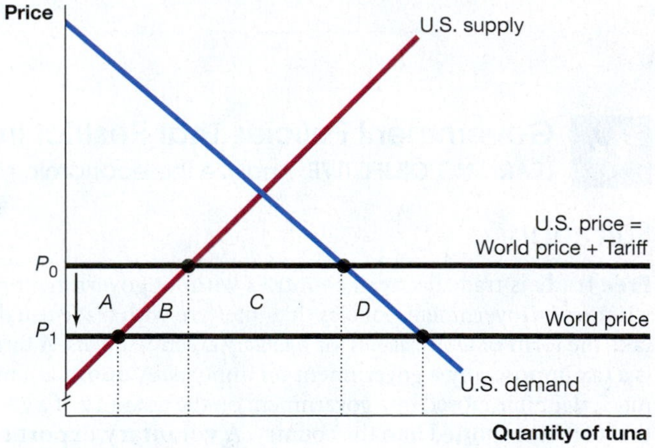

a. Which areas show the gain in consumer surplus?

b. Which area shows the loss in producer surplus?

c. Which area shows the loss in government tariff revenue?

d. Which areas show the gain in economic surplus?

4.11 According to an editorial in the *Washington Post*, "Sugar protectionism is a burden on consumers and a job-killer."

a. In what sense does the United States practice "sugar protectionism"?

b. In what way is sugar protectionism a burden on consumers? In what way is it a job-killer?

c. If sugar protectionism has the bad effects stated in the editorial, why don't Congress and the president eliminate it?

Source: "Sourball," *Washington Post*, March 22, 2010.

4.12 **(Related to Solved Problem 9.4 on page 301)** Suppose that the United States currently both produces kumquats and imports them. The U.S. government then decides to restrict international trade in kumquats by imposing a quota that allows imports of only 6 million pounds of kumquats into the United States each year. The figure shows the results of imposing the quota.

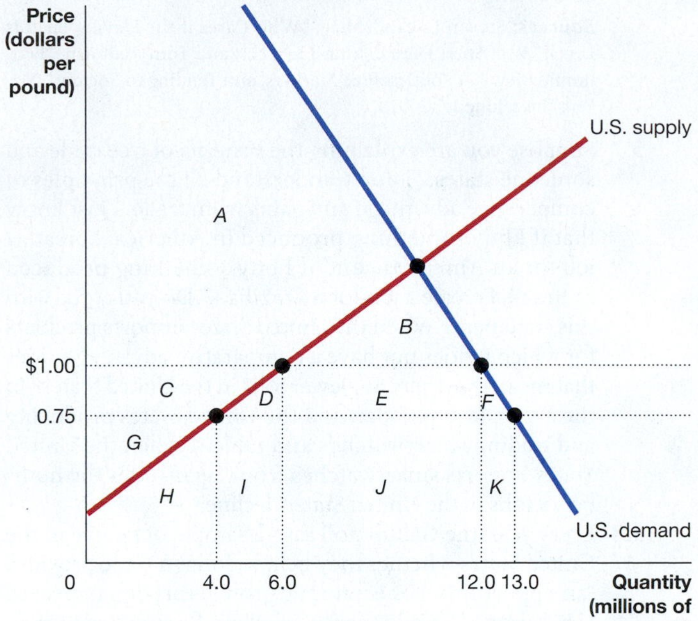

Fill in the table below using the letters in the figure:

	Without Quota	With Quota
World price of kumquats		
U.S. price of kumquats		
Quantity supplied by U.S. firms		
Quantity demanded		
Quantity imported		
Area of consumer surplus		
Area of domestic producer surplus		
Area of deadweight loss		

4.13 Suppose the government is considering imposing either a tariff or a quota on canned peaches. Assume that the proposed quota has the same effect on the U.S. price of canned peaches as the proposed tariff. Use the graph to answer the following questions.

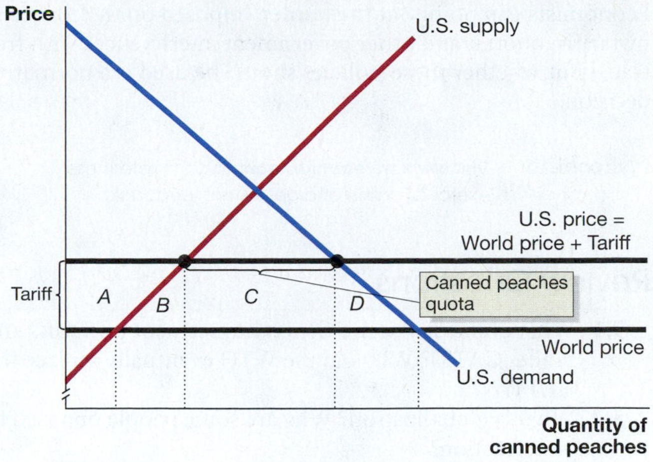

a. If the government imposes a tariff, which area shows the government tariff revenue?
b. If the government imposes a quota, which area shows the gain to foreign producers of canned peaches?
c. As a consumer of peaches, would you prefer the government impose the tariff or the quota? Briefly explain.

4.14 **(Related to the Making the Connection on page 302)** An economic analysis of a proposal to impose a quota on steel imports into the United States indicated that the quota would save 3,700 jobs in the steel industry but cost about 35,000 jobs in other U.S. industries. Why would a quota on steel imports cause employment to decline in other industries? Which other industries is a steel quota likely to affect?

Source: Douglas A. Irwin, *Free Trade Under Fire*, Princeton, NJ: Princeton University Press, 2002, p. 82.

4.15 **(Related to the Making the Connection on page 302)** For several years, the United States imposed a tariff on tire imports. According to an analysis by economists Gary Clyde Hufbauer and Sean Lowry of the Petersen Institute, of the additional $1.1 billion consumers spent on tires as a result of the tariff on Chinese tires, the workers whose jobs were saved in the U.S. tire industry received only about $48 million in wages. Wouldn't it have been cheaper for the federal government to have raised taxes on U.S. consumers and given the money to tire workers rather than to have imposed a tariff? If so, why didn't the federal government adopt this alternative policy?

Source: Gary Clyde Hufbauer and Sean Lowry, "US Tire Tariffs: Saving Few Jobs at High Cost," Peterson Institute for International Economics, Policy Brief Number PB12-9, April 2012.

9.5 The Arguments over Trade Policies and Globalization, pages 305–309

LEARNING OBJECTIVE: Evaluate the arguments over trade policies and globalization.

Summary

The **World Trade Organization (WTO)** is an international organization that enforces trade agreements among members. The WTO has promoted **globalization**, the process of countries becoming more open to foreign trade and investment. Some critics of the WTO argue that globalization has damaged local cultures around the world. Other critics oppose the WTO because they believe in **protectionism**, which is the use of trade barriers to shield domestic firms from foreign competition. The WTO allows countries to use tariffs in cases of **dumping**, when an imported product is sold for a price below its cost of production.

Economists can point out the burden imposed on the economy by tariffs, quotas, and other government interferences with free trade. But whether these policies should be used is a normative decision.

MyEconLab Visit **www.myeconlab.com** to complete these exercises online and get instant feedback.

Review Questions

5.1 What events led to the General Agreement on Tariffs and Trade (GATT)? Why did the WTO eventually replace the GATT?

5.2 What is globalization? Why are some people opposed to globalization?

5.3 What is protectionism? Who benefits and who loses from protectionist policies? What are the main arguments people use to justify protectionism?

5.4 What is dumping? Who benefits and who loses from dumping? What problems arise when anti-dumping laws are implemented?

Problems and Applications

5.5 In 2015, several U.S. paper manufacturers asked the federal government to impose tariffs on paper imported from China, Indonesia, Brazil, Portugal, and Australia. According to an article in the *Wall Street Journal*, firms in these countries were accused of "dumping certain types of uncoated paper on the U.S. market, including that used for such things as computer printers, book publishing, junk mail and envelopes." What is "dumping"? If the U.S. firms succeed in having tariffs imposed on imports of paper, briefly explain who will gain and who will lose.

Source: James R. Hagerty, "The Next Trade Fight: Office Paper," *Wall Street Journal*, January 21, 2015.

5.6 Steven Landsburg, an economist at the University of Rochester, wrote the following in an article in the *Wall Street Journal*:

> Free trade is not only about the right of American consumers to buy at the cheapest possible price; it's also about the right of foreign producers to earn a living. Steelworkers in West Virginia struggle hard to make ends meet. So do steelworkers in South Korea. To protect one at the expense of the other, solely because of where they happened to be born, is a moral outrage.

How does the U.S. government protect steelworkers in West Virginia at the expense of steelworkers in South Korea? Is Landsburg making a positive statement or a normative statement? A few days later, Tom Redburn published an article disagreeing with Landsburg. Redburn argued that caring about the welfare of people in the United States more than about the welfare of people in other countries isn't "some evil character flaw." According to Redburn, "A society that ignores the consequences of economic disruption on those among its citizens who come out at the short end of the stick is not only heartless,it also undermines its own cohesion and adaptability."

Which of the two arguments do you find most convincing?

Sources: Steven E. Landsburg, "Who Cares if the Playing Field Is Level?" *Wall Street Journal*, June 13, 2001; and Tom Redburn, "Economic View: Of Politics, Free Markets, and Tending to Society," *New York Times*, June 17, 2001.

5.7 Suppose you are explaining the benefits of free trade and someone states, "I don't understand all the principles of comparative advantage and gains from trade. I just know that if I buy something produced in America, I create a job for an American, and if I buy something produced in Brazil, I create a job for a Brazilian." Do you agree with this statement? When the United States imports products for which it does not have a comparative advantage, does that mean that there are fewer jobs in the United States? In the example with Japan and the United States producing and trading smartwatches and tablets, when the United States imports smartwatches from Japan, does the number of jobs in the United States decline?

5.8 Every year, the Gallup poll asks a sample of people in the United States whether they believe foreign trade provides "an opportunity for economic growth through increased U.S. exports," or whether they believe foreign trade represents "a threat to the economy from foreign imports." The table shows the responses for two years:

	View of Foreign Trade		
Year	Favorable to Foreign Trade	Unfavorable	State of the U.S. Economy
2008	41%	52%	Deep economic recession
2015	58%	33%	Economic expansion

a. Do you believe that foreign trade helps or hurts the economy? (Be sure to define what you mean by "helps" or "hurts.")

b. Why might the general public's opinion of foreign trade be substantially different during an economic recession, when production and employment are falling, than during an economic expansion, when production and employment are increasing?

c. Typically polls show that people in the United States under 30 years of age have a more favorable opinion of foreign trade than do people age 65 and over. Why might younger people have a more favorable view of foreign trade than older people?

Source: Gallup Poll, February 8–11, 2015, http://www.gallup.com/poll/181886/majority-opportunity-foreign-trade.aspx.

5.9 At one time, Eastman Kodak was the world's largest producer of photographic film, employing nearly 145,000 workers worldwide, including thousands at its headquarters in Rochester, New York. The firm eventually laid off most of those workers because its sales declined as it failed to adjust to digital photography as quickly as many of its foreign competitors. A member of Congress from Rochester described the many new firms that were now located in buildings that were formerly owned by Kodak.

A *New York Times* columnist concluded, "Which, of course, is precisely the way globalization is supposed to work." Briefly explain what the columnist meant. Do you agree with his conclusion? Does the outcome in Rochester show that globalization is good? Briefly explain.

Source: Joe Nocera, "Don't Blame Nafta," *New York Times*, January 23, 2015.

5.10 **(Related to the Making the Connection on page 307)** According to an opinion column in the *New York Times*, because of attempts to make it more difficult to import catfish into the United States, during 2015 many Vietnamese businesses that export catfish shifted from exporting to the United States to exporting to China. Briefly explain who gained and who lost as a result of this adjustment by Vietnamese businesses resulting from U.S. trade restrictions.

Source: Roger Cohen, "Of Catfish Wars and Shooting Wars," *New York Times*, March 26, 2015.

CHAPTER

10

Consumer Choice and Behavioral Economics

Chapter Outline and Learning Objectives

J.C. Penney Customers Didn't Buy into "Everyday Low Prices"

In 2010, the J.C. Penney department store chain had nearly 600 "sales," and it sold almost three-quarters of its products at prices marked down by at least 50 percent. However, these sales were illusions because Penney had raised prices before discounting them. The company also often required customers to clip coupons to get the sale price. Soon after being named chief executive officer (CEO) of Penney in 2011, Ron Johnson, who had had a successful career as head of Apple's retail stores, decided to try a new pricing strategy of "everyday low prices" that eliminated most sales and coupons. But the new pricing policy backfired. Penney's sales plunged 25 percent in 2012, and the company fired Johnson after only 17 months. By 2015, Penney was still struggling, with its revenue and profits remaining well below 2010 levels.

What was wrong with Johnson's pricing policy? First, the everyday low prices ended up being higher than the sale prices under the previous pricing policy. Some customers noticed and switched to shopping at Walmart and other department stores. Some economists, though, believe that Johnson ran into an even bigger problem: Although economists generally assume that people have enough information to make optimal buying decisions, this assumption may not always be accurate. For example, many consumers have only a rough idea of the typical price of a pair of jeans or a shirt. These consumers have difficulty knowing whether everyday low prices really are low. Instead, they wait for sales and use coupons because they believe doing so allows them to buy at lower-than-normal prices. As Alexander Chernev of Northwestern University put it, "J.C. Penney might say it's a fair price, but why should consumers trust J.C. Penney?" He argued that consumers "want a great deal," which they believe they get only if a store is having a sale or if they use coupons.

We can better understand the failure of Penney's pricing strategy by using insights from *behavioral economics,* which is the study of situations in which people make choices that do not appear to be economically rational. Firms must understand consumer behavior to determine what strategies are likely to be most effective in selling their products. In this chapter, we will examine how consumers make decisions about which products to buy.

Sources: Brett Arends, "Why You Want to Buy the Most Hated Stocks on Wall Street," marketwatch.com, June 19, 2015; Stephanie Clifford and Catherine Rampell, "Sometimes, We Want Prices to Fool Us," *New York Times*, April 13, 2013; Wendy Liebmann, "What Will We Learn from Ron Johnson's Mistake?" *Forbes*, May 8, 2013; and Brad Tuttle, "The 5 Big Mistakes That Led to Ron Johnson's Ouster at JC Penney," *Time*, April 9, 2013.

Economics in Your Life

Do You Make Rational Decisions?

Economists generally assume that people make decisions in a rational, consistent way. But are people actually as rational as economists assume? Consider the following situation: You bought a concert ticket for $75, which is the most you were willing to pay. While you are in line to enter the concert hall, someone offers you $90 for the ticket. Would you sell the ticket? Would an economist think it is rational to sell the ticket? As you read this chapter, try to answer these questions. You can check your answers against those we provide on **page 342** at the end of this chapter.

We begin this chapter by exploring how consumers make decisions. We have seen that economists usually assume that people act in a rational, self-interested way. In explaining consumer behavior, economists believe people make choices that will leave them as satisfied as possible, given their *tastes*, their *incomes*, and the *prices* of the goods and services available to them. We will see how downward-sloping demand curves result from the economic model of consumer behavior. We will also explore how in certain situations, knowing which decision is the best one can be difficult. In these cases, economic reasoning provides a powerful tool for consumers to improve their decision making. Finally, we will see that *experimental economics* has shown that factors such as social pressure and notions of fairness can affect consumer behavior. We will look at how businesses take these factors into account when setting prices. In the appendix to this chapter, we extend the analysis by using indifference curves and budget lines to understand consumer behavior.

10.1 Utility and Consumer Decision Making

LEARNING OBJECTIVE: Define utility and explain how consumers choose goods and services to maximize their utility.

We have seen that the model of demand and supply is a powerful tool for analyzing how prices and quantities are determined. We have also seen that, according to the *law of demand*, whenever the price of a good falls, the quantity demanded increases. In this section, we will show how the economic model of consumer behavior leads to the law of demand.

An Overview of the Economic Model of Consumer Behavior

Imagine walking through a shopping mall, trying to decide how to spend your clothing budget. If you had an unlimited budget, your decision would be easy: Just buy as much of everything as you want. Given that you have a limited budget, what do you do? Economists assume that consumers act so as to make themselves as well off as possible. Therefore, you should choose the one combination of clothes that makes you as well off as possible from among those combinations that you can afford. Stated more generally, the economic model of consumer behavior predicts that consumers will choose to buy the combination of goods and services that makes them as well off as possible from among all the combinations that their budgets allow them to buy.

Although this prediction may seem obvious and not particularly useful, we will see that it leads to conclusions that are useful—but not obvious. MyEconLab Concept Check

Utility

Utility The enjoyment or satisfaction people receive from consuming goods and services.

The amount of satisfaction you receive from consuming a particular combination of goods and services depends on your tastes or preferences. There is an old saying—"There's no accounting for taste"—and economists don't try to. If you buy a can of Red Bull energy drink instead of a can of Monster Energy, even though Monster Energy has a lower price, you must receive more enjoyment or satisfaction from drinking Red Bull. Economists refer to the enjoyment or satisfaction people receive from consuming goods and services as **utility**. So we can say that the goal of a consumer is to spend available income so as to maximize utility. But utility is a difficult concept to measure because there is no way of knowing exactly how much enjoyment or satisfaction someone receives from consuming a product. Similarly, it is not possible to compare utility across consumers. There is no way of knowing for sure whether Jill receives more or less satisfaction than Jack from drinking a can of Red Bull.

Two hundred years ago, economists hoped to measure utility in units called *utils*. The util would be an objective measure in the same way that temperature is: If it is 75 degrees in New York and 75 degrees in Los Angeles, it is just as warm in both cities. These economists wanted to say that if Jack's utility from drinking a can of Red Bull is

10 utils and Jill's utility is 5 utils, then Jack receives exactly twice the satisfaction from drinking a can of Red Bull as Jill does. In fact, it is *not* possible to measure utility across people. It turns out that none of the important conclusions of the economic model of consumer behavior depend on utility being directly measurable (a point we demonstrate in the appendix to this chapter). Nevertheless, the economic model of consumer behavior is easier to understand if we assume that utility is something directly measurable, like temperature. MyEconLab Concept Check

The Principle of Diminishing Marginal Utility

To make the model of consumer behavior more concrete, let's see how a consumer makes decisions in a case involving just two products: pizza and Coke. To begin, consider how the utility you receive from consuming a good changes with the quantity of the good you consume. Suppose that you have just arrived at a Super Bowl party where the hosts are serving pizza and you are very hungry. In this situation, you are likely to receive quite a lot of enjoyment, or utility, from consuming the first slice of pizza. Suppose this satisfaction is measurable and is equal to 20 units of utility, or utils. After eating the first slice, you decide to have a second slice. Because you are no longer as hungry, the satisfaction you receive from eating the second slice of pizza is less than the satisfaction you received from eating the first slice. Consuming the second slice increases your utility by only an *additional* 16 utils, which raises your *total* utility from eating the 2 slices to 36 utils. If you continue eating slices, each additional slice gives you less and less additional satisfaction.

The table in Figure 10.1 shows the relationship between the number of slices of pizza you consume while watching the Super Bowl and the amount of utility you receive. The second column in the table shows the total utility you receive from eating a particular number of slices. The third column shows the additional utility, or **marginal utility (*MU*)**, you receive from consuming one additional slice. (Remember that in economics, *marginal* means *additional*.) For example, as you increase your consumption from 2 slices to 3 slices, your total utility increases from 36 to 46, so your marginal utility from consuming the third slice is 10 utils. As the table shows, by the time you eat the fifth slice of pizza that evening, your marginal utility is very low: only 2 utils. If you were to eat a sixth slice, you would become slightly ill, and your marginal utility would actually be a *negative* 3 utils.

Marginal utility (*MU*) The change in total utility a person receives from consuming one additional unit of a good or service.

Figure 10.1 also plots the numbers from the table as graphs. Panel (a) shows how your total utility rises as you eat the first 5 slices of pizza and then falls as you eat the sixth slice. Panel (b) shows how your marginal utility declines with each additional slice you eat and finally becomes negative when you eat the sixth slice. The height of the marginal utility line at any quantity of pizza in panel (b) represents the change in utility as a result of consuming that additional slice. For example, the change in utility as a result of consuming 4 slices instead of 3 is 6 utils, so the height of the marginal utility line in panel (b) for the fourth slice is 6 utils.

The relationship illustrated in Figure 10.1 between consuming additional units of a product during a period of time and the marginal utility received from consuming each additional unit is called the **law of diminishing marginal utility**. For nearly every good or service, the more you consume during a period of time, the less you increase your total satisfaction from each additional unit you consume. MyEconLab Concept Check

Law of diminishing marginal utility The principle that consumers experience diminishing additional satisfaction as they consume more of a good or service during a given period of time.

The Rule of Equal Marginal Utility per Dollar Spent

The key challenge for consumers is to decide how to allocate their limited incomes among all the products they want to buy. Every consumer has to make trade-offs: If you have $100 to spend on entertainment for the month, then the more movies you rent or buy online, the fewer movies you can see in the theater. Economists refer to the limited amount of income you have available to spend on goods and services as your **budget constraint**. The principle of diminishing marginal utility helps us understand how consumers can best spend their limited incomes on the products available to them.

Budget constraint The limited amount of income available to consumers to spend on goods and services.

MyEconLab Animation

Figure 10.1

Total and Marginal Utility from Eating Pizza on Super Bowl Sunday

The table shows that for the first 5 slices of pizza, the more you eat, the more your total satisfaction, or utility, increases. If you eat a sixth slice, you start to feel ill from eating too much pizza, and your total utility falls. Each additional slice increases your utility by less than the previous slice, so your marginal utility from each slice is less than the one before. Panel (a) shows your total utility rising as you eat the first 5 slices and falling with the sixth slice. Panel (b) shows your marginal utility falling with each additional slice you eat and becoming negative with the sixth slice. The height of the marginal utility line at any quantity of pizza in panel (b) represents the change in utility as a result of consuming that additional slice. For example, the change in utility as a result of consuming 4 slices instead of 3 is 6 utils, so the height of the marginal utility line in panel (b) for the fourth slice is 6 utils.

Number of Slices	Total Utility from Eating Pizza	Marginal Utility from the Last Slice Eaten
0	0	—
1	20	20
2	36	16
3	46	10
4	52	6
5	54	2
6	51	–3

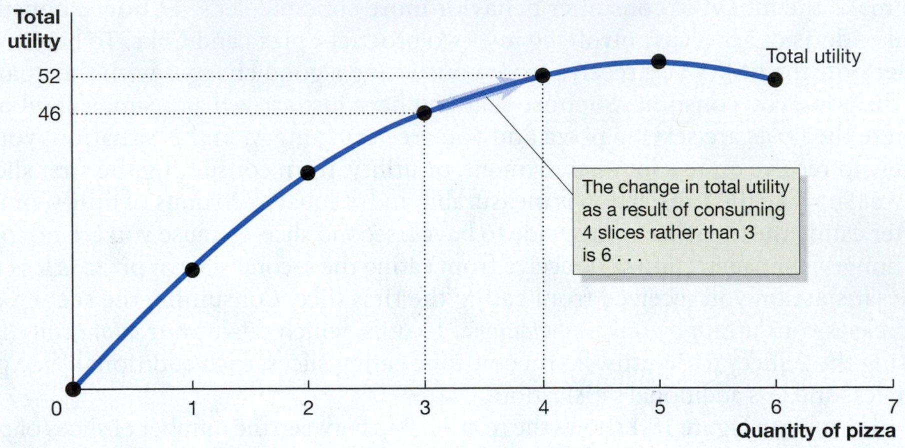

(a) Total utility

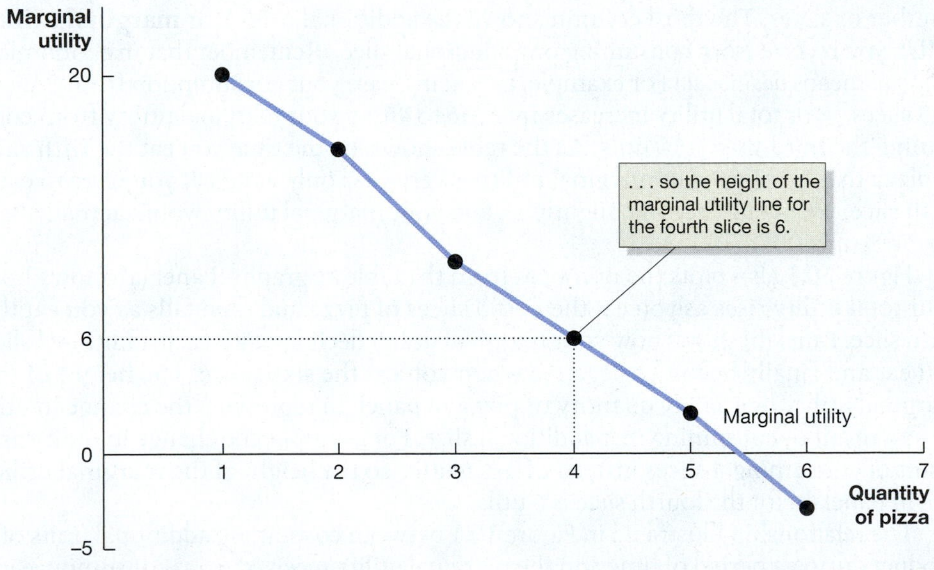

(b) Marginal utility

Suppose you attend a Super Bowl party at a restaurant, and you have $10 to spend on refreshments. Pizza is selling for $2 per slice, and Coke is selling for $1 per cup. Table 10.1 shows the relationship between the amount of pizza you eat, the amount of Coke you drink, and the amount of satisfaction, or utility, you receive. The values for pizza are repeated from the table in Figure 10.1. The values for Coke also follow the principle of diminishing marginal utility.

How many slices of pizza and how many cups of Coke should you buy if you want to maximize your utility? If you did not have a budget constraint, you would buy 5 slices of pizza and 5 cups of Coke because that would give you total utility of 107 (=54 + 53), which is the maximum utility you can achieve. Eating another slice of pizza or drinking another cup of Coke during the evening would lower your utility. Unfortunately, you do

Number of Slices of Pizza	Total Utility from Eating Pizza	Marginal Utility from the Last Slice	Number of Cups of Coke	Total Utility from Drinking Coke	Marginal Utility from the Last Cup
0	0	—	0	0	—
1	20	20	1	20	20
2	36	16	2	35	15
3	46	10	3	45	10
4	52	6	4	50	5
5	54	2	5	53	3
6	51	−3	6	52	−1

Table 10.1

Total Utility and Marginal Utility from Eating Pizza and Drinking Coke

have a budget constraint: You have only $10 to spend. To buy 5 slices of pizza (at $2 per slice) and 5 cups of Coke (at $1 per cup), you would need $15.

To select the best way to spend your $10, remember this key economic principle: *Optimal decisions are made at the margin*. That is, most of the time economic decision makers—consumers, firms, and the government—are faced with decisions about whether to do a little more of one thing or a little more of an alternative. In this case, you are choosing to consume a little more pizza or a little more Coke. Tesla chooses whether to manufacture more sedans or more SUVs in its California factory. Congress and the president choose whether to spend more for research on heart disease or more to repair highways. Everyone faces a budget constraint, and everyone faces trade-offs.

The key to making the best consumption decision is to maximize utility by following the *rule of equal marginal utility per dollar spent*. As you decide how to spend your income, you should buy pizza and Coke up to the point where the last slice of pizza and the last cup of Coke purchased give you equal increases in utility *per dollar*. By using this apporach, you will have maximized your total utility, given your budget constraint.

It is important to remember that to follow this rule, you must equalize your marginal utility per dollar spent, *not* your marginal utility from each good. Buying season tickets for your favorite National Football League (NFL) team or for the symphony or buying a BMW may give you a lot more satisfaction than drinking a cup of Coke, but the NFL tickets may well give you less satisfaction *per dollar spent*. To decide how many slices of pizza and cups of Coke to buy, you must convert the values for marginal utility in Table 10.1 into marginal utility per dollar. You can do this by dividing marginal utility by the price of each good, as shown in Table 10.2.

In column (3), we calculate marginal utility per dollar spent on pizza. Because the price of pizza is $2 per slice, the marginal utility per dollar from eating 1 slice of pizza

(1) Slices of Pizza	(2) Marginal Utility (MU_{Pizza})	(3) Marginal Utility per Dollar $\left(\frac{MU_{Pizza}}{P_{Pizza}}\right)$	(4) Cups of Coke	(5) Marginal Utility (MU_{Coke})	(6) Marginal Utility per Dollar $\left(\frac{MU_{Coke}}{P_{Coke}}\right)$
1	20	10	1	20	20
2	16	8	2	15	15
3	10	5	3	10	10
4	6	3	4	5	5
5	2	1	5	3	3
6	−3	−1.5	6	−1	−1

Table 10.2

Converting Marginal Utility to Marginal Utility per Dollar

Table 10.3

Equalizing Marginal Utility per Dollar Spent

Combinations of Pizza and Coke with Equal Marginal Utilities per Dollar	Marginal Utility per Dollar (*MU/P*)	Total Spending	Total Utility
1 slice of pizza and 3 cups of Coke	10	\$2 + \$3 = \$5	20 + 45 = 65
3 slices of pizza and 4 cups of Coke	5	\$6 + \$4 = \$10	46 + 50 = 96
4 slices of pizza and 5 cups of Coke	3	\$8 + \$5 = \$13	52 + 53 = 105

equals 20 divided by \$2, or 10 utils per dollar. Similarly, we show in column (6) that because the price of Coke is \$1 per cup, the marginal utility per dollar from drinking 1 cup of Coke equals 20 divided by \$1, or 20 utils per dollar. To maximize the total utility you receive, you must make sure that the utility per dollar of pizza for the last slice of pizza is equal to the utility per dollar of Coke for the last cup of Coke. Table 10.2 shows that there are three combinations of slices of pizza and cups of Coke where marginal utility per dollar is equalized. Table 10.3 lists the combinations, the total amount of money needed to buy each combination, and the total utility received from consuming each combination.

Looking at the bottom row of the table, if you buy 4 slices of pizza, the last slice gives you 3 utils per dollar. If you buy 5 cups of Coke, the last cup also gives you 3 utils per dollar, so you have equalized your marginal utility per dollar. Unfortunately, as the third column in the table shows, to buy 4 slices and 5 cups, you would need \$13, and you have only \$10. The top row of the table shows that you could also equalize your marginal utility per dollar by buying 1 slice and 3 cups, but that would cost just \$5, leaving you with \$5 not spent. As the middle row shows, only when you buy 3 slices and 4 cups have you equalized your marginal utility per dollar and spent neither more nor less than the \$10 available.

We can summarize the two conditions for maximizing utility:

1. $\frac{MU_{Pizza}}{P_{Pizza}} = \frac{MU_{Coke}}{P_{Coke}}$

   This condition states that the marginal utility per dollar spent must be the same for both goods.

2. Spending on pizza + Spending on Coke = Amount available to be spent

   This condition is the budget constraint, which states that total spending on both goods must equal the amount available to be spent.

Of course, these conditions for maximizing utility apply not just to pizza and Coke but to any pairs of goods. MyEconLab Concept Check

Solved Problem 10.1

MyEconLab Interactive Animation

Finding the Optimal Level of Consumption

The following table shows Lee's utility from consuming ice cream cones and cans of Lime Fizz soda:

Number of Ice Cream Cones	Total Utility from Ice Cream Cones	Marginal Utility from Last Cone	Number of Cans of Lime Fizz	Total Utility from Cans of Lime Fizz	Marginal Utility from Last Can
0	0	—	0	0	—
1	30	30	1	40	40
2	55	25	2	75	35
3	75	20	3	101	26
4	90	15	4	119	18
5	100	10	5	134	15
6	105	5	6	141	7

a. Ed inspects this table and concludes, "Lee's optimal choice would be to consume 4 ice cream cones and 5 cans of Lime Fizz because with that combination, his marginal utility from ice cream cones is equal to his marginal utility from Lime Fizz." Do you agree with Ed's reasoning? Briefly explain.

b. Suppose that Lee has an unlimited budget to spend on ice cream cones and cans of Lime Fizz. Under these circumstances, how many ice cream cones and how many cans of Lime Fizz will he consume? (Assume that Lee cannot consume more than 6 ice cream cones or 6 cans of Lime Fizz.)

c. Suppose that Lee has $7 per week to spend on ice cream cones and cans of Lime Fizz. The price of an ice cream cone is $2, and the price of a can of Lime Fizz is $1. If Lee wants to maximize his utility, how many ice cream cones and how many cans of Lime Fizz should he buy?

Solving the Problem

Step 1: Review the chapter material. This problem involves finding the optimal consumption of two goods, so you may want to review the section "The Rule of Equal Marginal Utility per Dollar Spent," which begins on page 321.

Step 2: Answer part (a) by analyzing Ed's reasoning. Ed's reasoning is incorrect. To maximize utility, Lee needs to equalize marginal utility *per dollar* for the two goods.

Step 3: Answer part (b) by determining how Lee would maximize utility with an unlimited budget. With an unlimited budget, consumers maximize utility by continuing to buy each good as long as their utility is increasing. In this case, Lee will maximize utility by buying 6 ice cream cones and 6 cans of Lime Fizz, given that we are assuming he cannot buy more than 6 units of either good.

Step 4: Answer part (c) by determining Lee's optimal combination of ice cream cones and cans of Lime Fizz. Lee will maximize his utility if he spends his $7 per week so that the marginal utility of ice cream cones divided by the price of ice cream cones is equal to the marginal utility of Lime Fizz divided by the price of Lime Fizz. We can use the following table to solve this part of the problem:

	Ice Cream Cones		Cans of Lime Fizz	
Quantity	*MU*	$\frac{MU}{P}$	*MU*	$\frac{MU}{P}$
1	30	15	40	40
2	25	12.5	35	35
3	20	10	26	26
4	15	7.5	18	18
5	10	5	15	15
6	5	2.5	7	7

Lee will maximize his utility by buying 1 ice cream cone and 5 cans of Lime Fizz. At this combination, the marginal utility of each good divided by its price equals 15. He has also spent all of his $7.

Your Turn: For more practice, do related problems 1.8 and 1.9 on page 345 at the end of this chapter. MyEconLab Study Plan

What if the Rule of Equal Marginal Utility per Dollar Does Not Hold?

The idea of getting the maximum utility by equalizing the ratio of marginal utility to price for the goods you are buying can be difficult to grasp, so it is worth thinking about in another way. Suppose that instead of buying 3 slices of pizza and 4 cups of Coke, you buy 4 slices and 2 cups. This combination costs $10, so you would meet your

Don't Let This Happen to You

Equalize Marginal Utilities *per Dollar*

Harry likes to read e-books and watch movies on his tablet. The following table gives Harry's utility from buying books and movies:

Harry's Utility from Buying Books and Movies

Quantity of Books	Total Utility from Books	Marginal Utility from Last Book	Quantity of Movies	Total Utility from Movies	Marginal Utility from Last Movie
0	0	—	0	0	—
1	50	50	1	60	60
2	85	35	2	105	45
3	110	25	3	145	40
4	130	20	4	175	30
5	140	10	5	195	20
6	145	5	6	210	15

Can you determine from this table the optimal combination of books and movies for Harry? It is very tempting to say that Harry should buy 4 books and 5 movies because his marginal utility from books is equal to his marginal utility from movies with that combination. In fact, we can't be sure this is the best combination because we are lacking some critical information: Harry's budget constraint—how much he has available to spend on books and movies—and the prices of books and movies.

Let's say that Harry has $100 to spend this month, the price of an e-book is $10, and the price of an online movie is $20. Using the information from the first table, we can now calculate Harry's marginal utility per dollar for both goods, as shown in the following table:

Harry's Marginal Utility and Marginal Utility per Dollar from Buying Books and Movies

Quantity of Books	Marginal Utility from Last Book (MU_{Books})	Marginal Utility per Dollar $\left(\frac{MU_{Books}}{P_{Books}}\right)$	Quantity of Movies	Marginal Utility from Last Movie (MU_{Movies})	Marginal Utility per Dollar $\left(\frac{MU_{Movies}}{P_{Movies}}\right)$
1	50	5	1	60	3
2	35	3.5	2	45	2.25
3	25	2.5	3	40	2
4	20	2	4	30	1.5
5	10	1	5	20	1
6	5	0.5	6	15	0.75

Harry's marginal utility per dollar is the same for two combinations of books and movies, as shown in the following table:

Combinations of Books and Movies with Equal Marginal Utilities per Dollar	Marginal Utility per Dollar (MU/P)	Total Spending	Total Utility
5 books and 5 movies	1	$50 + $100 = $150	140 + 195 = 335
4 books and 3 movies	2	$40 + $60 = $100	130 + 145 = 275

Unfortunately, 5 books and 5 movies would cost Harry $150, and he has only $100. The best Harry can do is to buy 4 books and 3 movies. This combination provides him with the maximum amount of utility attainable, given his budget constraint.

The key point is the same as in Solved Problem 10.1 on page 324: Consumers maximize their utility when they equalize marginal utility *per dollar* for every good they buy, *not* when they equalize marginal utility.

MyEconLab Study Plan

Your Turn: Test your understanding by doing related problem 1.11 on page 345 at the end of this chapter.

budget constraint by spending all the money available to you, but would you have gotten the maximum amount of utility? No, you wouldn't have. From the information in Table 10.2 on page 323, we can list the additional utility per dollar you are getting from the last slice and the last cup and the total utility from consuming 4 slices and 2 cups:

Marginal utility per dollar for the fourth slice of pizza = 3 utils per dollar
Marginal utility per dollar for the second cup of Coke = 15 utils per dollar
Total utility from 4 slices of pizza and 2 cups of Coke = 87 utils

Obviously, the marginal utilities per dollar are not equal. The last cup of Coke gave you considerably more satisfaction per dollar than did the last slice of pizza. You could raise your total utility by buying less pizza and more Coke. Buying 1 less slice of pizza frees up \$2 that will allow you to buy 2 more cups of Coke. Eating 1 less slice of pizza reduces your utility by 6 utils, but drinking 2 additional cups of Coke raises your utility by 15 utils (make sure you see this), for a net increase of 9. You end up equalizing your marginal utility per dollar (5 utils per dollar for both the last slice and the last cup) and raising your total utility from 87 to 96 utils. MyEconLab Concept Check

The Income Effect and Substitution Effect of a Price Change

We can use the rule of equal marginal utility per dollar to analyze how consumers adjust their buying decisions when a price changes. Suppose you are back at the restaurant for the Super Bowl party, but this time the price of pizza is \$1.50 per slice, rather than \$2. You still have \$10 to spend on pizza and Coke.

When the price of pizza was \$2 per slice and the price of Coke was \$1 per cup, your optimal choice was to consume 3 slices of pizza and 4 cups of Coke. The fall in the price of pizza to \$1.50 per slice has two effects on the quantity of pizza you consume.

The Income Effect When the price of a good falls, you have more purchasing power. In our example, 3 slices of pizza and 4 cups of Coke now cost a total of only \$8.50 instead of \$10.00. An increase in purchasing power is essentially the same thing as an increase in income. The change in the quantity of pizza you will demand because of this increase in purchasing power—holding all other factors constant—is the **income effect** of the price change. Recall that if a product is a *normal good,* a consumer increases the quantity demanded as the consumer's income rises, but if a product is an *inferior good,* a consumer decreases the quantity demanded as the consumer's income rises (see Chapter 3). So, if we assume that pizza is a normal good for you, the income effect of a fall in price causes you to consume more pizza. If pizza were an inferior good for you, the income effect of a fall in the price would have caused you to consume less pizza.

Income effect The change in the quantity demanded of a good that results from the effect of a change in price on consumer purchasing power, holding all other factors constant.

The Substitution Effect When the price of pizza falls, pizza becomes cheaper *relative* to Coke, and the marginal utility per dollar for each slice of pizza you consume increases. If we hold constant the effect of the price change on your purchasing power and just focus on the effect of the price being lower relative to the price of the other good, we have isolated the **substitution effect** of the price change. The lower price of pizza relative to the price of Coke has lowered the *opportunity cost* to you of consuming pizza because now you have to give up less Coke to consume the same quantity of pizza. Therefore, the substitution effect from the fall in the price of pizza relative to the price of Coke causes you to eat more pizza and drink less Coke. In this case, both the income effect and the substitution effect of the fall in price cause you to eat more pizza. If the price of pizza had risen, both the income effect and the substitution effect would have caused you to eat less pizza. Table 10.4 summarizes the effect of a price change on the quantity demanded.

Substitution effect The change in the quantity demanded of a good that results from a change in price making the good more or less expensive relative to other goods, holding constant the effect of the price change on consumer purchasing power.

We can use Table 10.5 to determine the effect of the fall in the price of pizza on your optimal consumption. Table 10.5 has the same information as Table 10.2, with one change: The marginal utility per dollar from eating pizza has been changed to

Table 10.4

Income Effect and Substitution Effect of a Price Change

When price ...	consumer purchasing power ...	The income effect causes quantity demanded to ...	The substitution effect causes the opportunity cost of consuming a good to ...
decreases,	increases.	increase, for a normal good, and decrease, for an inferior good.	decrease when the price decreases, which causes the quantity of the good demanded to increase.
increases,	decreases.	decrease, for a normal good, and increase, for an inferior good.	increase when the price increases, which causes the quantity of the good demanded to decrease.

reflect the new lower price of $1.50 per slice. Examining the table, we can see that the fall in the price of pizza will result in you eating 1 more slice of pizza, so your optimal consumption now becomes 4 slices of pizza and 4 cups of Coke. You will be spending all of your $10, and the last dollar you spend on pizza will provide you with about the same marginal utility per dollar as the last dollar you spend on Coke. You will not be receiving exactly the same marginal utility per dollar spent on the two products. As Table 10.5 shows, the last slice of pizza gives you 4 utils per dollar, and the last cup of Coke gives you 5 utils per dollar. But this is as close as you can come to equalizing marginal utility per dollar for the two products, unless you can buy a fraction of a slice of pizza or a fraction of a cup of Coke.

MyEconLab Study Plan

MyEconLab Concept Check

10.2 Where Demand Curves Come From

LEARNING OBJECTIVE: Use the concept of utility to explain the law of demand.

According to the *law of demand*, whenever the price of a product falls, the quantity demanded increases (see Chapter 3). Now that we have covered the concepts of total utility, marginal utility, and the budget constraint, we can look more closely at why the law of demand holds.

In our example of optimal consumption of pizza and Coke at the Super Bowl party, we found the following:

$$\text{Price of pizza} = \$2 \text{ per slice} \rightarrow \text{Quantity of pizza demanded} = 3 \text{ slices}$$

$$\text{Price of pizza} = \$1.50 \text{ per slice} \rightarrow \text{Quantity of pizza demanded} = 4 \text{ slices}$$

Table 10.5

Adjusting Optimal Consumption to a Lower Price of Pizza

Number of Slices of Pizza	Marginal Utility from Last Slice (MU_{Pizza})	Marginal Utility per Dollar $\left(\frac{MU_{Pizza}}{P_{Pizza}}\right)$	Number of Cups of Coke	Marginal Utility from Last Cup (MU_{Coke})	Marginal Utility per Dollar $\left(\frac{MU_{Coke}}{P_{Coke}}\right)$
1	20	13.33	1	20	20
2	16	10.67	2	15	15
3	10	6.67	3	10	10
4	6	4	4	5	5
5	2	1.33	5	3	3
6	−3	—	6	−1	—

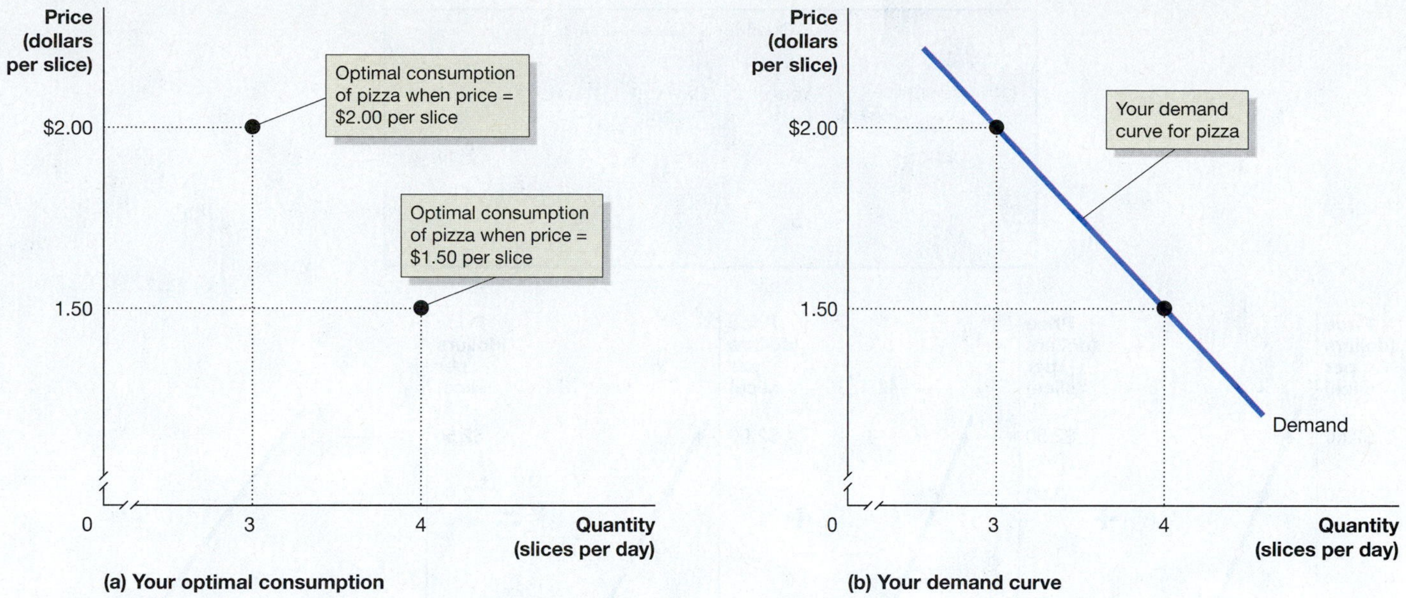

MyEconLab Animation

Figure 10.2 Deriving the Demand Curve for Pizza

A consumer responds optimally to a fall in the price of a product by consuming more of that product. In panel (a), the price of pizza falls from $2 per slice to $1.50, and the optimal quantity of slices consumed rises from 3 to 4. When we graph this result in panel (b), we have the consumer's demand curve.

In panel (a) of Figure 10.2, we plot the two points showing the optimal number of slices of pizza you choose to consume at each price. In panel (b), we draw a line connecting the two points. This downward-sloping line represents your demand curve for pizza. We could find more points on the line by changing the price of pizza and using the information in Table 10.2 to find the new optimal number of slices of pizza you would demand at each price.

To this point in the chapter, we have been looking at an individual demand curve. Economists, though, are typically interested in market demand curves. We can construct the market demand curve from the individual demand curves for all the consumers in the market. To keep things simple, let's assume that there are only three consumers in the market for pizza: you, David, and Lori. The table in Figure 10.3 shows the individual demand schedules for the three consumers. Because consumers differ in their incomes and their preferences for products, we would not expect every consumer to demand the same quantity of a given product at each price. The final column gives the market demand, which is simply the sum of the quantities demanded by each of the three consumers at each price. For example, at a price of $1.50 per slice, your quantity demanded is 4 slices, David's is 6 slices, and Lori's is 5 slices. So, at a price of $1.50, a quantity of 15 slices is demanded in the market. The graphs in the figure show that we can obtain the market demand curve by adding horizontally the individual demand curves.

Remember that according to the law of demand, market demand curves always slope downward. We now know that this result holds because the income and substitution effects of a decrease in price cause consumers to increase the quantity of the good they demand. There is a complicating factor, however. As we discussed earlier, only for a normal good will the income effect lead consumers to increase the quantity of the good they demand when the price falls. For an inferior good, the income effect leads consumers to *decrease* the quantity of the good they demand. The substitution effect, on the other hand, results in consumers increasing the quantity they demand of both normal and inferior goods when the price falls. So, when the price of an inferior good falls, the income effect and substitution effect work in opposite directions: The income effect causes consumers to decrease the quantity of the good they demand, while the substitution effect causes consumers to increase the quantity of the good they demand. Is it possible, then, that consumers might actually buy less of a good when the price falls? If they did, the demand curve would be upward sloping. MyEconLab Concept Check

Price (dollars per slice)	Quantity (slices per day) You	David	Lori	Market
$2.50	2	4	1	7
2.00	3	5	3	11
1.50	4	6	5	15
1.00	5	7	7	19
0.50	6	8	9	23

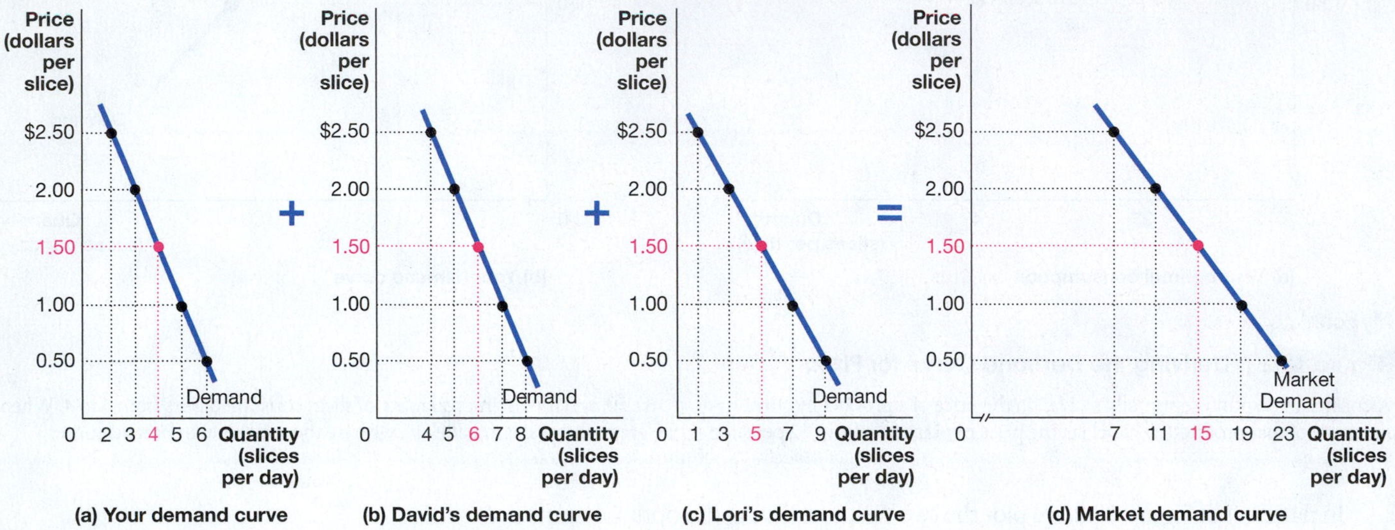

MyEconLab Animation

Figure 10.3 Deriving the Market Demand Curve from Individual Demand Curves

The table shows that the total quantity demanded in a market is the sum of the quantities demanded by each buyer. We can find the market demand curve by adding horizontally the individual demand curves in panels (a), (b), and (c). For instance, at a price of $1.50, your quantity demanded is 4 slices, David's is 6 slices, and Lori's is 5 slices. Therefore, panel (d) shows that a price of $1.50 and a quantity demanded of 15 is a point on the market demand curve.

Making the Connection — Are There Any Upward-Sloping Demand Curves in the Real World?

MyEconLab Video

Rice is a Giffen good in poor parts of China.

For a demand curve to be upward sloping, the good would have to be an inferior good, and the income effect would have to be larger than the substitution effect. Economists have understood the conditions for an upward-sloping demand curve since the possibility was first discussed by the British economist Alfred Marshall in the 1890s. Marshall wrote that his friend, Sir Robert Giffen, had told him that when the price of bread rose, very poor people in British cities would actually buy more bread rather than less. Since that time, goods with upward-sloping demand curves have been referred to as *Giffen goods*.

For more than a century, finding an actual Giffen good proved impossible. A close examination of the data showed that Giffen had been mistaken and that poor people in British cities bought less bread when prices rose, so their demand curves were downward sloping. Other possible candidates for being Giffen goods were also found to actually have downward-sloping demand curves. Finally, in 2006, Robert Jensen of Brown University and Nolan Miller of Harvard discovered two Giffen goods. They reasoned that to be a Giffen good, with an income effect larger than its substitution effect, a good must be inferior and make up a very large portion of consumers' budgets. Jensen and Miller knew that very poor people in the Hunan region of China spent most of their incomes on rice, while in the Gansu province, very poor people spent most of their income on wheat-based foods, such as buns and noodles. In both places, poor people ate meat when their incomes made it possible because they preferred the taste of meat, even though it did not supply as many calories as the rice or wheat they could purchase for the same price.

Jensen and Miller carried out the following experiment: In Hunan, for a five-month period, they gave a selected number of poor families coupons that would allow them to buy rice at a lower price. Families could not use the coupons for any other purpose. In Gansu, they gave a selected number of poor families coupons to buy wheat at a lower price. Jensen and Miller then observed the purchases of the families during the time they received the coupons and during the period immediately thereafter. In Hunan, during the months they received the coupons, the families bought less rice and more meat, and in Gansu, they bought less wheat and more meat. Because in Hunan, families bought less rice when the price was lower, their demand curves for rice were upward sloping. Similarly, in Gansu, families bought less wheat when the price was lower, so their demand curves for wheat were upward sloping. After more than a century of searching, economists had finally discovered examples of a Giffen good.

Source: Robert T. Jensen and Nolan H. Miller, "Giffen Behavior and Subsistence Consumption," *American Economic Review*, Vol. 98, No. 4, September 2008, pp. 1553–1577.

Your Turn: Test your understanding by doing related problem 2.9 on page 346 at the end of this chapter.

MyEconLab Study Plan

10.3 Social Influences on Decision Making

LEARNING OBJECTIVE: Explain how social influences can affect consumption choices.

Sociologists and anthropologists have argued that social factors such as culture, customs, and religion are very important in explaining the choices people make. Economists have traditionally seen such factors as being relatively unimportant, if they take them into consideration at all. Recently, however, some economists have begun to study how social factors influence consumer choice.

For example, people seem to receive more utility from consuming goods they believe are popular. As the economists Gary Becker, a Nobel Prize winner in economics, and Kevin Murphy put it:

> The utility from drugs, crime, going bowling, owning a Rolex watch, voting Democratic, dressing informally at work, or keeping a neat lawn depends on whether friends and neighbors take drugs, commit crimes, go bowling, own Rolex watches, vote Democratic, dress informally, or keep their lawns neat.

This reasoning can help explain why one restaurant is packed, while another restaurant that serves essentially the same food and has similar decor has many fewer customers. Consumers decide which restaurant to go to not only on the basis of food and decor but also on the basis of the restaurant's popularity. People receive utility from being seen eating at a popular restaurant because they believe it makes them appear knowledgeable and fashionable. Whenever consumption takes place publicly, some consumers base their purchasing decisions on what other consumers are buying. Examples of public consumption include eating in restaurants, attending sporting events, wearing clothes or jewelry, and driving cars. In all these cases, the decision to buy a product depends partly on the characteristics of the product and partly on how many other people are buying the product.

The Effects of Celebrity Endorsements

In many cases, it is not just the number of people who use a product that makes it desirable but the types of people who use it. If consumers believe that media stars or professional athletes use a product, demand for the product will often increase. For example, New England Patriots quarterback Tom Brady is one of the biggest stars in the National Football League, so it may not be surprising that companies including

Glaceau Smartwater, Movado watches, Under Armour sportswear, and UGG footwear have lined up to have him endorse their products. Brady makes around $7 million per year from his endorsements.

Tom Brady is a great football player, but why do consumers care what products he uses? They may believe Brady has better information than they do about the products he endorses. The average football fan might believe that if Brady endorses Under Armour sportswear, maybe Under Armour makes better sportswear. It seems more likely, however, that people buy products associated with Tom Brady or other celebrities because using these products makes them feel closer to the celebrity endorser or because it makes them appear to be fashionable. MyEconLab Concept Check

Network Externalities

Network externality A situation in which the usefulness of a product increases with the number of consumers who use it.

Technology can play a role in explaining why consumers buy products that many other consumers are already buying. There is a **network externality** in the consumption of a product if the usefulness of the product increases with the number of consumers who use it.

There's Strength in Numbers If you owned the only phone in the world, it would not be very useful. The usefulness of phones increases as the number of people who own them increases. Similarly, your willingness to buy an Apple iPad depends in part on the number of other people who own iPads. The more people who own iPads, the more applications, or "apps," other firms will produce for the iPad, and the more novels, textbooks, newspapers, and magazines publishers will make available for downloading to the iPad, and, therefore, the more useful an iPad is to you.

Do Switching Costs Cause Inferior Technologies to Survive? Some economists have suggested the possibility that network externalities may have a significant downside because they might result in consumers buying products that contain inferior technologies. This outcome could occur because network externalities can create significant *switching costs* related to changing products: When a product becomes established, consumers may find switching to a new product that contains a better technology too costly. The selection of products may be *path dependent*: Because of switching costs, the technology that was first available may have advantages over better technologies that were developed later. In other words, the path along which the economy has developed in the past is important.

One possible example of path dependence and the use of an inferior technology is the QWERTY order of the letters along the top row of most computer keyboards. This order became widely used when manual typewriters were developed in the late nineteenth century. The metal keys on manual typewriters would stick together if a user typed too fast, so the QWERTY keyboard was designed to slow down typists and minimize the problem of the keys sticking together. With computers, the problem that QWERTY was developed to solve no longer exists, so keyboards could be changed to have letters in a more efficient layout. But because the overwhelming majority of people have learned to use keyboards with the QWERTY layout, there might be significant costs to them if they had to switch, even if a new layout ultimately made them faster typists.

Other products that supposedly embodied inferior technologies are VHS video recorders—supposedly inferior to Sony Betamax recorders—and the Windows computer operating system—supposedly inferior to the Macintosh operating system.

Do Network Externalities Result in Market Failures? Some economists have argued that because of path dependence and switching costs, network externalities can result in *market failures*, which are situations in which the market fails to produce the efficient level of output (see Chapter 5). If network externalities result in market failure, government intervention in these markets might improve economic efficiency. Many economists are skeptical, however, that network externalities really do lead to consumers being locked into products with inferior technologies. In particular, economists Stan Leibowitz of the University of Texas, Dallas, and Stephen Margolis of

North Carolina State University have argued that, in practice, the gains from using a superior technology are larger than the losses due to switching costs. After carefully studying the cases of the QWERTY keyboard, VHS video recorders, and the Windows computer operating system, they have concluded that there is no good evidence that the alternative technologies were actually superior. The implications of network externalities for economic efficiency remain controversial among economists. MyEconLab Concept Check

Does Fairness Matter?

If people were only interested in making themselves as well off as possible in a material sense, they would not be concerned with fairness. There is a great deal of evidence, however, that people like to be treated fairly and that they usually attempt to treat others fairly, even if doing so makes them worse off financially. Tipping servers in restaurants is an example. In the United States, diners in restaurants typically add 15 to 20 percent to their food bills as tips to their servers. Tips are not *required*, but most people consider not tipping to be very unfair, unless the service has been exceptionally bad. You could argue that people leave tips not to be fair but because they are afraid that if they don't leave a tip, the next time they visit the restaurant, they will receive poor service. Studies have shown, however, that most people leave tips at restaurants even while on vacation or in other circumstances where they are unlikely to visit the restaurant again.

There are many other examples where people willingly part with money when they are not required to do so and when they receive nothing material in return. The most obvious example is making donations to charity. Apparently, donating money to charity or leaving tips in restaurants that they will never visit again gives people more utility than they would receive from keeping the money and spending it on themselves.

A Test of Fairness in the Economic Laboratory: The Ultimatum Game Experiment Economists have used experiments to understand the role that fairness plays in consumer decision making. *Experimental economics* has been widely used during the past two decades, and a number of experimental economics laboratories exist in the United States and Europe. Economists Maurice Allais, Reinhard Selten, and Vernon Smith were awarded the Nobel Prize in Economics in part because of their contributions to experimental economics. Experiments make it possible to focus on a single aspect of consumer behavior. The *ultimatum game,* first popularized by Werner Güth of the Max Planck Institute of Economics in Germany, is an experiment that tests whether fairness is important in consumer decision making. Various economists have conducted the ultimatum game experiment under slightly different conditions but with generally the same result.

Figure 10.4 illustrates the ultimatum game. A group of volunteers—often college students—are divided into pairs. One member of each pair is the "allocator," and the other member of the pair is the "recipient." Each pair is given an amount of money, say \$20. The allocator decides how much of the \$20 each member of the pair will get. There are no restrictions on how the allocator divides up the money. The allocator could keep it all, give it all to the recipient, or anything in between. The recipient must then decide whether to accept the allocation or reject it. If the recipient decides to accept the

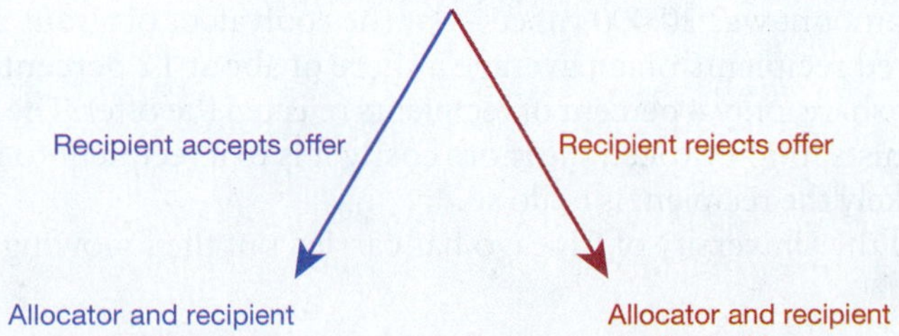

MyEconLab Animation

Figure 10.4

The Ultimatum Game

In the ultimatum game, an allocator divides an amount of money between himself or herself and the recipient. If the recipient rejects the division of money, neither player receives anything. In experiments, most recipients would rather receive nothing than receive what they believe to be an unfair division of the money.

allocation, each member of the pair gets to keep his or her share. If the recipient decides to reject the allocation, both members of the pair receive nothing.

If neither the allocator nor the recipient cares about fairness, optimal play in the ultimatum game is straightforward: The allocator should propose a division of the money in which the allocator receives $19.99 and the recipient receives $0.01. The allocator has maximized his or her gain. The recipient should accept the division because the alternative is to reject it and receive nothing at all: Even a penny is better than nothing. In fact, when the ultimatum game experiment is carried out, both allocators and recipients act as if fairness is important. Allocators usually offer recipients at least a 40 percent share of the money, and recipients almost always reject offers of less than a 10 percent share.

Why do allocators offer recipients more than a negligible amount? It might be that allocators do not care about fairness but fear that recipients do care and will reject offers they consider unfair. This possibility was tested in an experiment known as the *dictator game* carried out by Daniel Kahneman (a psychologist who shared the Nobel Prize in Economics), Jack Knetsch, and Richard Thaler, using students at Cornell University. In this experiment, the allocators were given only two possible divisions of $20: either $18 for themselves and $2 for the recipient or an even division of $10 for themselves and $10 for the recipient. One important difference from the ultimatum game was that *the recipient was not allowed to reject the division.* Of the 161 allocators, 122 chose the even division of the $20. Because there was no possibility of the $18/$2 split being rejected, the allocators must have chosen the even split because they valued acting fairly.

Why would recipients in the ultimatum game ever reject any division of the money in which they receive even a very small amount, given that even a small amount of money is better than nothing? Apparently, most people value fairness enough that they will refuse to participate in transactions they consider unfair, even if they are worse off financially as a result.

Are the Results of Economic Experiments Reliable? Economists have conducted the ultimatum game and the dictator game many times in different countries using different groups of people. Therefore, most economists believe that the results of the game provide strong evidence that people value fairness. Recently, however, some economists have begun to question this conclusion. They argue that the experimental situation is artificial, so results may not hold up in the real world. Although allocators in the dictatorship game give money to the other player, whose identity is not known to the allocator, in the real world, people rarely just hand money to strangers. So, it is possible that the fairness observed in the experiments may be the result of people wanting to avoid appearing selfish rather than people valuing fairness. For instance, in the ultimatum game, anyone who kept $19.99 and gave the other person only $0.01 might be afraid of appearing selfish in the eyes of the economist conducting the experiment. Particularly because the dollar amounts in the experiment are small, wanting to please the person conducting the experiment may be the main motive behind the choices made.

There is some experimental evidence that when the amount being divided is large, recipients in ultimatum games will accept even very uneven divisions. Steffen Andersen of the Copenhagen Business School and colleagues conducted the dictator game with poor villagers in India, whose average daily wage was about 100 rupees. In their experiments, the amounts to be divided varied from 20 rupees to 20,000 rupees. They found that the larger the amount at stake, the smaller the share the allocator offered the recipient. When the amount was 20,000 rupees—or the equivalent of about 200 days' pay—allocators offered recipients on an average a share of about 12 percent. Despite being offered this low share, only 4 percent of recipients rejected the offer. The results indicate that, as economists might expect, the more costly it is to a recipient to reject an unfair offer, the less likely the recipient is to do so.

John List of the University of Chicago has carried out the following versions of the dictator game:

Version 1: When List gave every player $5 and followed the usual procedure of having half the players act as dictators in dividing up the $5, he found the usual result, with 71 percent of dictators allocating some money to the other player.

Version 2: When List gave the dictator the choice of either giving money to the other player or *taking* up to $5 from the other player, only 10 percent of dictators gave the other player any money, and more than half the dictators took money from the other player.

Version 3: When List asked players to work for 30 minutes at a simple task to earn the $5 before playing the game, two-thirds of the dictators neither gave anything to nor took anything from the other player. This last result may indicate that the source of the money being allocated matters.

This recent research does not completely reverse the usual interpretation of the results of the ultimatum and dictator games. However, the research does show that the results of the games are not as clear-cut as many economists had thought. It also shows that adjusting one detail of an economic experiment can have a significant effect on its results.

Business Implications of Fairness If consumers value fairness, how does this affect firms? One consequence is that firms will sometimes not raise prices of goods and services, even when there is a large increase in demand, because they are afraid their customers will consider the price increases unfair and may buy elsewhere.

Consider three examples where it seems that businesses could increase their profits by raising prices:

- When the dance rock band LCD played a concert at New York's Madison Square Garden, the tickets were priced at $50 each. But, demand for the tickets was so high that tickets sold online for as much as $2,500 each. Why didn't the band or the concert promoter charge more than $50 for the tickets?
- Each year, many more people would like to buy tickets to see the Super Bowl than there are tickets for them to buy at the price the National Football League (NFL) charges. Why doesn't the NFL raise prices?
- When the restaurant Next opened in Chicago, it used a unique approach to pricing. The restaurant sold tickets that entitled the buyer to a dinner, including drinks and tip. The restaurant sold the tickets for $45 to $75, depending on the dinner chosen. The tickets were resold online for prices from $500 to $3,000. Why didn't Next increase its ticket prices?

In each of these cases, it appears that a firm could increase its profits by raising prices. The seller would be selling the same quantity—of seats at a concert or in a football stadium, or meals in a restaurant—at a higher price, so profits should increase. Economists have provided two explanations for why firms sometimes do not raise prices in these situations. Gary Becker has suggested that the products involved—concerts, football games, or restaurant meals—are all products that buyers consume together with other buyers. In those situations, the amount consumers wish to buy may be related to how much of the product other people are consuming. People like to consume, and be seen consuming, a popular product—ones where the quantity demanded appears to be much greater than the quantity supplied. If rock bands, the NFL, and popular restaurants increased their prices enough to equate the quantity of tickets demanded with the quantity supplied, they might find that they had also eliminated their popularity.

Daniel Kahneman, Jack Knetsch, and Richard Thaler have offered another explanation for why firms don't always raise prices when doing so would seem to increase their profits. In surveys of consumers, these researchers found that most people considered it fair for firms to raise their prices following an increase in costs but unfair to raise prices following an increase in demand. For example, Kahneman, Knetsch, and Thaler conducted a survey in which people were asked their opinion of the following situation: "A hardware store has been selling snow shovels for $15. The morning after a large snowstorm, the store raises the price to $20." Eighty-two percent of respondents said that they considered the hardware store's actions to be unfair. Kahneman, Knetsch, and Thaler have concluded that firms may sometimes not raise their prices even when the quantity demanded of their product is greater than the quantity supplied out of fear that, in the long run, they will lose customers who believe the price increases were unfair.

In analyzing the pricing of Super Bowl tickets, economist Alan Krueger of Princeton University provided some support for Kahneman, Knetsch, and Thaler's explanation of why companies do not always raise prices when the quantity demanded is greater than the quantity supplied. In 2015, the NFL charged $2,000 for the best seats at the Super Bowl and at least $800 for the other seats. Many of these tickets were resold online for as much as $10,000 each. Krueger surveyed football fans attending the game to see if their views could help explain why the NFL didn't charge higher prices for the tickets. In the year he conducted the survey, the face value of Super Bowl tickets was $325 to $400. When asked whether it would "be fair for the NFL to raise the [price of tickets] to $1,500 if that is still less than the amount most people are willing to pay for tickets," 92 percent of the fans surveyed answered "no." Even 83 percent of the fans who had paid more than $1,500 for their tickets answered "no." Krueger concluded that whatever the NFL might gain in the short run from raising ticket prices, it would more than lose in the long run by alienating football fans.

These explanations for why firms don't always raise prices to a level that would equate the quantity demanded with the quantity supplied share the same basic idea: Sometimes firms will give up some profits in the short run to keep their customers happy and increase their profits in the long run. MyEconLab Concept Check

Making the Connection
MyEconLab Video

Is Uber Price Gouging?

Is it "fair" for Uber to charge more when demand for rides is high?

The Uber mobile app has become very popular. Rather than call or flag down a taxi for a ride home after a party or a football game, many people use the app to summon a driver who uses his or her own car to provide rides. Many consumers prefer Uber because they believe Uber drivers are more reliable in responding and arrive faster than taxis, particularly in smaller cities where taxi service is not always dependable. In addition, some consumers find Uber's payment system to be convenient. Because the user's credit card information is loaded into the app, the price of a trip is automatically billed to the card, and the driver does not have to be tipped. Business travelers also use Uber. In 2015, business travelers were making about 33 percent as many trips using Uber as using a taxi, up from only 11 percent one year earlier.

Travis Kalanick and Garrett Camp founded Uber in San Francisco in 2009. They believed that the restrictions many local governments placed on taxi services meant that an inefficiently small quantity of taxi rides were being supplied in many markets. Because Uber relies on individuals driving their own cars, it is not legally a taxi service, and so it is not subject to government regulations on taxis. Taxi companies in many cities, though, have protested against Uber because it usually charges prices lower than the local governments allow the taxi companies to charge.

Typically, Uber charges lower prices than taxi companies charge—but not always. Uber sets prices based on the number of people who request rides at a given time in a given area, and it raises prices as demand increases. This "surge pricing" can more than triple normal prices when demand is very high. One rider used Uber to call for a ride on New Year's Eve only to find that instead of the expected price of $35, the charge would be $262. Kalanick argues that consumers should think of Uber prices the same way they think of airline ticket prices: "You know that if you buy a flight on the day before Christmas, it's probably 10 times more expensive than two weeks after Christmas." In addition, he argues that increasing prices when demand increases gives drivers—whose pay increases with prices—an incentive to provide rides at busy times, such as New Year's Eve or at a stadium at the end of a football game.

But as the research of Kahneman, Knetsch, and Thaler has shown, consumers see it as more fair for firms to raise prices after an increase in costs than as a result of an increase in demand. Not surprisingly, Uber has come under criticism on Facebook and other social networking sites as a result of its surge pricing. Financial writer James Surowiecki suggests that firms such as Uber can avoid this criticism that surge pricing is unfair if they label the surge price the normal price and the lower non-surge price as a discount price. Just as movie theaters label the price they charge for tickets in the evening—when demand is high—the normal ticket price and the price they charge in the afternoon—when demand is low—as a discount from the normal price.

It remains to be seen whether the resentment of some consumers over what they see as Uber's unfair surge pricing will limit the growth of the service.

Sources: "Uber Uber Alles," *Economist*, March 11, 2015; "Pricing the Surge," *Economist*, March 19, 2014; Douglas MacMillan, "Uber CEO: Surge Pricing Is Here to Stay," *Wall Street Journal*, January 7, 2014; James Surowiecki, "In Praise of Efficient Price Gouging," technologyreview.com, August 19, 2014; and Daniel Kahneman, Jack Knetsch, and Richard Thaler, "Fairness as a Constraint on Profit Seeking: Entitlements in the Market," *American Economic Review*, Vol. 76, No. 4, September 1986, pp. 728–741.

Your Turn: Test your understanding by doing related problems 3.8 and 3.9 on page 347 at the end of this chapter.

MyEconLab Study Plan

10.4 Behavioral Economics: Do People Make Their Choices Rationally?

LEARNING OBJECTIVE: Describe the behavioral economics approach to understanding decision making.

When economists say that consumers and firms are behaving "rationally," they mean that consumers and firms are taking actions that are appropriate to reach their goals, given the information available to them. In recent years, some economists have begun studying situations in which people do not appear to be making choices that are economically rational. This new area of economics is called **behavioral economics**. Why might consumers or businesses not act rationally? The most obvious reason is that they do not realize that their actions are inconsistent with their goals. One of the objectives of economics is to suggest ways to make better decisions. In this section, we discuss ways in which people can improve their decisions by avoiding some common pitfalls. We also use ideas from behavioral economics to analyze how consumers make decisions when shopping.

Behavioral economics The study of situations in which people make choices that do not appear to be economically rational.

Pitfalls in Decision Making

Consumers commonly commit the following three mistakes when making decisions:

1. They take into account monetary costs but ignore nonmonetary opportunity costs that don't involve explicitly spending money.
2. They fail to ignore sunk costs.
3. They are unrealistic about their future behavior.

Ignoring Nonmonetary Opportunity Costs Remember that the **opportunity cost** of any activity is the highest-valued alternative that must be given up to engage in that activity. For example, if you own something you could sell, you incur an opportunity cost if you use it yourself. It is often difficult for people to think of opportunity costs in these terms.

Opportunity cost The highest-valued alternative that must be given up to engage in an activity.

Consider the following example: The NFL ran a lottery that allowed the winners to purchase Super Bowl tickets at their face value, which was either $325 or $400, depending on where in the stadium the seats were located. Economist Alan Krueger of Princeton surveyed the lottery winners, asking them two questions:

Question 1: If you had not won the lottery, would you have been willing to pay $3,000 for your ticket?
Answer 1: Ninety-four percent answered that they would not have paid $3,000 for a ticket.

Question 2: If after winning your ticket (and before arriving in Florida for the Super Bowl) someone had offered you $3,000 for your ticket, would you have sold it?
Answer 2: Ninety-two percent answered that they would not have sold their ticket for $3,000.

But these answers are contradictory! If someone offers you $3,000 for your ticket, then by using the ticket rather than selling it, you incur an opportunity cost of $3,000. There really is a $3,000 cost involved in using that ticket, even though you do not pay $3,000 in cash. The two alternatives—either paying $3,000 or not receiving $3,000—amount to exactly the same thing.

If the ticket is really *not* worth $3,000 to you, you should sell it. If it is worth $3,000 to you, you should be willing to pay $3,000 in cash to buy it. Not being willing to sell a ticket you already own for $3,000 while at the same time not being willing to buy a ticket for $3,000 if you didn't already own one is inconsistent behavior. The inconsistency comes from a failure to take into account nonmonetary opportunity costs. Behavioral economists believe this inconsistency is caused by the **endowment effect**, which is the tendency of people to be unwilling to sell a good they already own even if they are offered a price that is greater than the price they would be willing to pay to buy the good if they didn't already own it.

Endowment effect The tendency of people to be unwilling to sell a good they already own even if they are offered a price that is greater than the price they would be willing to pay to buy the good if they didn't already own it.

The failure to take into account opportunity costs is a very common error in decision making. Suppose, for example, that a friend is in a hurry to have his room cleaned—it's the Friday before parents' weekend—and he offers you $50 to do it for him. You turn him down and spend the time cleaning your own room, even though you know somebody down the hall who would be willing to clean your room for $20. Leave aside complicating details—the guy who asked you to clean his room is a real slob, or you don't want the person who offered to clean your room for $20 to go through your stuff—and you should see the point we are making. The opportunity cost of cleaning your own room is $50—the amount your friend offered to pay you to clean his room. It is inconsistent to turn down an offer from someone else to clean your room for $20 when you are doing it for yourself at a cost of $50. The key point here is this: *Nonmonetary opportunity costs are just as real as monetary costs, and people should take them into account when making decisions.*

There are many examples of businesses taking advantage of the tendency of consumers to ignore nonmonetary costs. For example, some firms sell products with mail-in rebates. Rather than have a mail-in rebate of $10, why not just cut the price by $10? Companies are relying on the fact that failing to mail in a rebate form once you have already paid for a product is a nonmonetary opportunity cost rather than a direct monetary cost. In fact, only a small percentage of customers actually mail in rebates.

Failing to Ignore Sunk Costs A **sunk cost** is a cost that has already been paid and cannot be recovered. Once you have paid money and can't get it back, you should ignore that money in any later decisions you make. Consider the following two situations:

Sunk cost A cost that has already been paid and cannot be recovered.

Situation 1: You bought a ticket to a play for $75. The ticket is nonrefundable and must be used on Tuesday night, which is the only night the play will be performed. On Monday, a friend calls and invites you to a local comedy club to see a comedian you both like who is appearing only on Tuesday night. Your friend offers to pay the cost of going to the club.

Situation 2: It's Monday night, and you are about to buy a ticket for the Tuesday night performance of the same play as in situation 1. As you are leaving to buy the ticket, your friend calls and invites you to the comedy club.

Would your decision to go to the play or the comedy club be different in situation 1 than in situation 2? Most people would say that in situation 1, they would go to the play because otherwise they would lose the $75 they had paid for the ticket. In fact, the $75 is "lost" no matter what you do because the ticket is nonrefundable. The only real issue for you to decide is whether you would prefer to see the play or prefer to go with your friend to the comedy club. If you would prefer to go to the club, the fact that you have already paid $75 for the ticket to the play is irrelevant. Your decision should be the same in situation 1 as in situation 2.

Psychologists Daniel Kahneman and Amos Tversky explored the tendency of consumers to *not* ignore sunk costs by asking two samples of people the following questions:

Question 1: One sample of people was asked: "Imagine that you have decided to see a play and have paid the admission price of $10 per ticket. As you enter the theater, you discover that you have lost the ticket. The seat was not marked, and the ticket cannot be recovered. Would you pay $10 for another ticket?" Of those asked, 46 percent answered "yes," and 54 percent answered "no."

Question 2: A different sample of people was asked: "Imagine that you have decided to see a play where admission is $10 per ticket. As you enter the theater, you discover that you have lost a $10 bill. Would you still pay $10 for a ticket to the play?" Of those asked, 88 percent answered "yes," and 12 percent answered "no."

The situations presented in the two questions are actually the same and should have received the same fraction of yes and no responses. Many people, though, have trouble seeing that in question 1, when deciding whether to see the play, they should ignore the $10 already paid for a ticket because it is a sunk cost.

Making the Connection
MyEconLab Video

A Blogger Who Understands the Importance of Ignoring Sunk Costs

In recent years, many people have started blogs—or "Web logs"—where they record their thoughts on politics, sports, their favorite hobbies, or anything else that interests them. Some bloggers can spend hours a day writing up their latest ideas and providing links to relevant material on the Web. A few blogs become so successful that they attract paid advertising and earn their owners a good income. Arnold Kim began blogging about Apple products in 2000 during his fourth year of medical school. He continued blogging on his site, MacRumors.com, over the next eight years, while pursuing a medical career as a nephrologist—a doctor who treats kidney problems.

Arnold Kim, founder of MacRumors.com, gave up a medical career to blog full time.

By 2008, Kim's site had become very successful, attracting 4.4 million people and more than 40 million page views each month. He was earning more than $100,000 per year from paid advertising by companies such as Verizon, Audible.com, and CDW. But the tasks of compiling rumors about new Apple products, keeping an Apple buying guide up to date, and monitoring multiple discussion boards on the site became more than he could handle as a part-time job. Kim enjoyed working on the Web site and believed that ultimately it could earn him more than he was earning as a doctor. Still, he hesitated to abandon his medical career because he had invested nearly $200,000 in his education.

But the $200,000, as well as the years he had spent in medical school, completing a residency in internal medicine, and completing a fellowship in nephrology, were sunk costs. Kim realized that he needed to ignore these sunk costs in order to make a rational decision about whether to continue in medicine or to become a full-time blogger. After calculating that he would make more from his Web site than from his medical career—and taking into account that by working from home he could spend more time with his young daughter—he decided to blog full time. He was quoted as saying that, "on paper it was an easy decision." Despite competition from new blogs, MacRumors continued to do well, being viewed by 10 million people per month in mid-2015, and Kim's income had risen above what he would have made as a doctor.

Knowing that it is rational to ignore sunk costs can be important in making key decisions in life.

Sources: Brian X. Chen, "Arnold Kim Celebrates 10 Years as Apple Rumor King," www.wired.com, February 23, 2010; Brian Stelter, "My Son, the Blogger: An M.D. Trades Medicine for Apple Rumors," *New York Times*, July 21, 2008; Dan Frommer, "Nephrologist to Mac Blogger: The Unlikely Career Path of MacRumors' Arnold Kim," www.businessinsider.com, July 13, 2008; and "Macrumors Traffic," www.quantcast.com, June 23, 2015.

Your Turn: Test your understanding by doing related problems 4.9, 4.10, and 4.11 on page 348 at the end of this chapter.

MyEconLab Study Plan

Being Unrealistic about Future Behavior Studies have shown that a majority of adults in the United States are overweight. Why do many people choose to eat too much? One possibility is that they receive more utility from eating high-calorie foods than they would from being thin. A more likely explanation, however, is that many people eat a lot today because they expect to eat less tomorrow. But they never do eat less, and so they end up overweight. (Of course, some people also suffer from medical problems that lead to weight gain.) Similarly, some people continue smoking today because they expect to be able to give it up sometime in the future. Unfortunately, for many people that time never comes, and they suffer the health consequences of years of smoking. In both these cases, people are overvaluing the utility from current choices—eating chocolate cake or smoking—and undervaluing the utility to be received in the future from being thin or not getting lung cancer.

Economists who have studied this question argue that many people have preferences that are not consistent over time. In the long run, you would like to be thin or give up smoking or achieve some other goal, but each day, you make decisions (such as to eat too much or smoke) that are not consistent with this long-run goal. If you are unrealistic about your future behavior, you underestimate the costs of choices—such as overeating or smoking—that you make today. A key way of avoiding this problem is to be realistic about your future behavior.

Taking into account nonmonetary opportunity costs, ignoring sunk costs, and being more realistic about future behavior are three ways in which consumers are able to improve the decisions they make. MyEconLab Concept Check

The Behavioral Economics of Shopping

In Section 10.1, we analyzed how consumers can choose the products they buy so as to maximize utility. In this section, we briefly consider problems consumers may encounter that keep them from making optimal consumption choices.

In discussing how consumers maximize utility, we used simple examples where people were choosing the optimal quantity of two goods subject to a budget constraint. Consider, though, a typical trip to the supermarket. Someone shopping for a family of four might end up buying 25 or more products. A consumer in that situation is unlikely to equate the ratios of the marginal utilities to the prices for all these products when deciding the quantities to buy. Does it matter that consumers often do not make optimal consumption choices? Economists are divided in their answers to this question. Many economists make these two points in arguing that the answer to the question is "no":

1. The assumptions in most scientific models, including economic models, are not literally correct. In the model of consumer choice, for example, unrealistic assumptions are necessary to simplify a complex reality by focusing on the most important factors involved in decision making.
2. Models are best judged by the success of their predictions rather than by the realism of their assumptions. Predictions based on the model of consumer choice have been successful in predicting many types of consumer behavior.

Rules of Thumb Behavioral economists argue that it *does* matter that consumers usually do not make optimal consumption choices. These economists believe that there are benefits to analyzing *how* consumers actually make decisions. The model we have used in this chapter assumes that:

- When people shop, they have full information on the prices of products, including information on differences in prices across stores.
- People can make complicated calculations such as computing the ratios of marginal utilities to prices across many products.

In fact, people often make choices on the basis of only limited information and without the time or capacity to calculate their optimal choices. As a result, rather than making optimal choices, people often use *rules of thumb*, which are guides to decision making that may not produce optimal choices. For example, a consumer may decide that a particular supermarket has the lowest prices for the products he or she buys, without continually checking whether this assumption is correct. If a new supermarket with lower prices opens, the consumer, at least for a period, may continue shopping at the old supermarket, even though doing so is no longer optimal.

Anchoring How do shoppers decide whether the price of a product is high or low? Behavioral economists use the word *anchoring* to describe one aspect of how consumers evaluate prices. If people are uncertain about a value, such as a price, they often relate—or anchor—that value to some other known value, even if the second value is irrelevant. Psychologists Amos Tversky and Daniel Kahnemann carried out an experiment to illustrate the effects of anchoring. They constructed a wheel that when spun always stopped on a value of either 10 or 65. They spun the wheel for different participants in the experiment and then asked them: "What is your best guess of the percentage of African nations in the United Nations?" When the wheel stopped on a value of 10, the average answer of the participants was 25 percent. When the wheel stopped on 65, the average answer was 45 percent. Even though the value from the spin of the wheel had no relevance to the question being asked, the value anchored the participants' responses. In another experiment, conducted by Brian Wansink of Cornell University, Robert Kent of the University of Delaware, and Stephen Hoch of the University of Pennsylvania, three supermarkets offered cans of Campbell's soup for sale at a 12-percent reduction in price. On one day during the sale, a display sign said "Limit of 12 per person"; on another day, a display sign said "No limit per person." On the day when the sign limited sales, the supermarkets sold an average of 7 cans per person. On the day when the sign said there was no limit on sales, the supermarkets sold 3.3 cans per person. The number 12 on the sign had anchored the shoppers' decisions on how many cans to buy.

Consumers often lack the information to evaluate whether the price of a good is "high" or "low." Stores can take advantage of this lack of information to anchor consumers' estimates by marking a high "regular price" on a product, which makes the discounted "sale price" appear to be a bargain even if the product is very rarely offered for sale at the regular price.

MyEconLab Concept Check

Making the Connection

MyEconLab Video

J.C. Penney Meets Behavioral Economics

We saw at the beginning of this chapter that Ron Johnson, after a very successful career as the head of Apple's retail stores, was recruited to become the CEO of the J.C. Penney department store chain. Johnson instituted a new pricing strategy of offering goods at "everyday low prices" and rarely discounting prices below those levels. The new strategy turned out to be a failure, as Penney's revenue declined. Johnson was fired as CEO after only 17 months.

Consumers generally respond strongly to sales that offer discounted prices, so a strategy that replaces sales with low fixed prices is not likely to be effective.

Ideas from behavioral economics can help explain what went wrong. First, Johnson assumed that consumers would understand that the everyday low prices really were low, at least compared with the very high regular prices that Penney had previously used when calculating the discounts it advertised when having a sale. However, there is substantial evidence that some consumers are not well aware of prices even for goods they buy regularly. One study of supermarket shoppers asked people the prices of goods they had just placed in their shopping carts. Fewer than half the shoppers could accurately recall the prices, and one-quarter couldn't even offer a guess, even though they had placed the goods in their carts less than a minute earlier. Another study asked people who were about to enter a department store questions about the prices of goods they frequently purchased. Only about one-third could give accurate answers. When asked to evaluate whether a specific price of a good they frequently purchased was high or low, about 15 percent of people identified prices that were actually high as being good deals and prices that were actually low as being bad deals.

Studies of retail sales show that consumers purchase a significant fraction of goods at discount prices. For example, a study of checkout scanner data from nine supermarkets showed that while liquid laundry detergent was offered at discount prices only about one-quarter of the time, nearly half of detergent was purchased at the sale prices. Because consumers respond so strongly to sales that offer discounted prices, a strategy that replaces sales with low fixed prices is not likely to be effective.

Why do consumers respond to sales? Why wasn't Penney able to convince consumers that everyday low prices really were low? One possibility is that by displaying both a high "regular price" and a low "sale price," sales provide consumers with an "anchor," or reference point, to interpret the prices being offered. A sale price seems low if offered as a markdown from a higher regular price even if—because of sales and the use of coupons—few people ever buy the good at the regular price. Without the anchor of the regular price, consumers can have difficulty deciding whether an everyday low price is actually low, particularly because some consumers enter a store with little idea of what typical prices are. As the Northwestern professor quoted in the chapter opener put it, "J.C. Penney might say it's a fair price, but why should consumers trust J.C. Penney?"

By largely eliminating sales, Johnson disregarded some of the insights of behavioral economics. As a result, Penney suffered losses, and Johnson lost his job.

Sources: Stephanie Clifford and Catherine Rampell, "Sometimes, We Want Prices to Fool Us," *New York Times*, April 13, 2013; Daniel Kahneman, *Thinking, Fast and Slow*, New York: Farrar, Strauss and Giroux, 2011; Julio Rotemberg, "Behavioral Aspects of Price Setting, and Their Policy Implications," National Bureau of Economic Research, Working Paper 13754, January 2008; Marc Vanhuele and Xavier Drèze, "Measuring the Price Knowledge Shoppers Bring to the Store," *Journal of Marketing*, Vol. 66, No. 4, October 2002, pp. 72–85; Peter R. Dickson and Alan G. Sawyer, "The Price Knowledge and Search of Supermarket Shoppers," *Journal of Marketing*, Vol. 54, No. 3, July 1990, pp. 42–53; and Igal Hendel and Aviv Nevo, "Measuring the Implications of Sales and Consumer Inventory Behavior," *Econometrica*, Vol. 74, No. 6, November 2006, pp. 1637–1673.

MyEconLab Study Plan

Your Turn: Test your understanding by doing related problem 4.15 on page 349 at the end of this chapter.

Continued from page 319

Economics in Your Life

Do You Make Rational Decisions?

At the beginning of this chapter, we asked you to consider a situation in which you had paid $75 for a concert ticket, which is the most you would be willing to pay. Just before you enter the concert hall, someone offers you $90 for the ticket. We posed two questions: Would you sell the ticket? and Would an economist think it is rational to sell the ticket? If you answered that you would sell, then your answer is rational in the sense in which economists use the term. The cost of going to see the concert is what you have to give up for the ticket. Initially, the cost was just $75—the dollar price of the ticket. This amount was also the most you were willing to pay. However, once someone offers you $90 for the ticket, the cost of seeing the concert rises to $90. The reason the cost of the concert is now $90 is that once you turn down an offer of $90 for the ticket, you have incurred a nonmonetary opportunity cost of $90 if you use the ticket yourself. The endowment effect explains why some people would not sell the ticket. People seem to value something that they own more than something that they do not own. Therefore, a concert ticket you already own may be worth more to you than a concert ticket you have yet to purchase. Behavioral economists study situations like this where people make choices that do not appear to be economically rational.

Conclusion

In a market system, consumers are in the driver's seat. Goods are produced only if consumers want them to be. Therefore, how consumers make their decisions is an important area for economists to study. Economists expect that consumers will spend their incomes so that the last dollar spent on each good provides them with equal additional amounts of satisfaction, or utility. In practice, there are significant social influences on consumer decision making, particularly when a good or service is consumed in public. Fairness also seems to be an important consideration for most consumers. Finally, many consumers could improve the decisions they make if they would take into account nonmonetary opportunity costs, ignore sunk costs, and be more realistic about their future behavior.

In this chapter, we studied consumers' choices. In the next several chapters, we will study firms' choices.

Visit MyEconLab for a news article and analysis related to the concepts in this chapter.

CHAPTER SUMMARY AND PROBLEMS

Key Terms

10.1 Utility and Consumer Decision Making, pages 320–328

LEARNING OBJECTIVE: Define utility and explain how consumers choose goods and services to maximize their utility.

Summary

Utility is the enjoyment or satisfaction that people receive from consuming goods and services. The goal of a consumer is to spend available income so as to maximize utility. **Marginal utility** is the change in total utility a person receives from consuming one additional unit of a good or service. The **law of diminishing marginal utility** states that consumers receive diminishing additional satisfaction as they consume more of a good or service during a given period of time. The **budget constraint** is the amount of income consumers have available to spend on goods and services. To maximize utility, consumers should make sure they spend their income so that the last dollar spent on each product gives them the same marginal utility. The **income effect** is the change in the quantity demanded of a good that results from the effect of a change in the price on consumer purchasing power. The **substitution effect** is the change in the quantity demanded of a good that results from a change in price making the good more or less expensive relative to other goods, holding constant the effect of the price change on consumer purchasing power.

MyEconLab Visit **www.myeconlab.com** to complete these exercises online and get instant feedback.

Review Questions

1.1 What is the economic definition of *utility*? Is it possible to measure utility?

1.2 What is the definition of *marginal utility*? What is the law of diminishing marginal utility? Why is marginal utility more useful than total utility in consumer decision making?

1.3 What is meant by a consumer's *budget constraint*? What is the rule of equal marginal utility per dollar spent?

1.4 How does a change in the price of a product cause both a substitution effect and an income effect?

Problems and Applications

1.5 Does the law of diminishing marginal utility hold true in every situation? Is it possible to think of goods for which consuming additional units, at least initially, will result in increasing marginal utility?

1.6 If consumers should allocate their income so that the last dollar spent on every product gives them the same amount of additional utility, how should they decide the amount of their income to save?

1.7 You have six hours to study for two exams tomorrow. The following table shows the relationship between hours of study and test scores:

Economics		Psychology	
Hours	Score	Hours	Score
0	54	0	54
1	62	1	60
2	69	2	65
3	75	3	69
4	80	4	72
5	84	5	74
6	87	6	75

a. Use the rule for determining optimal purchases to decide how many hours you should study each subject. Treat each point on an exam as 1 unit of utility and assume that you consider an extra point on an economics exam to have the same value as an extra point on a psychology exam.

b. Now suppose that you are a psychology major and that you value each point you earn on a psychology exam as being worth three times as much as each point you earn on an economics exam. Now how many hours should you study each subject?

1.8 **(Related to Solved Problem 10.1 on page 324)** Joe has $16 to spend on Twinkies and Ho-Hos. Twinkies have a price of $1 per pack, and Ho-Hos have a price of $2 per pack. Use the information in these graphs to determine the number of Twinkies and Ho-Hos packs Joe should buy to maximize his utility. Briefly explain your reasoning.

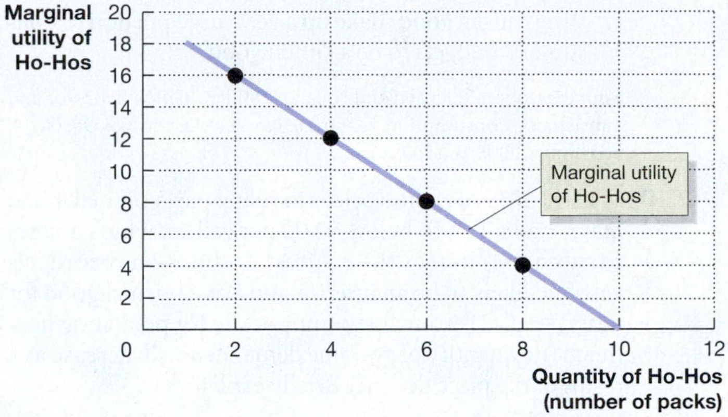

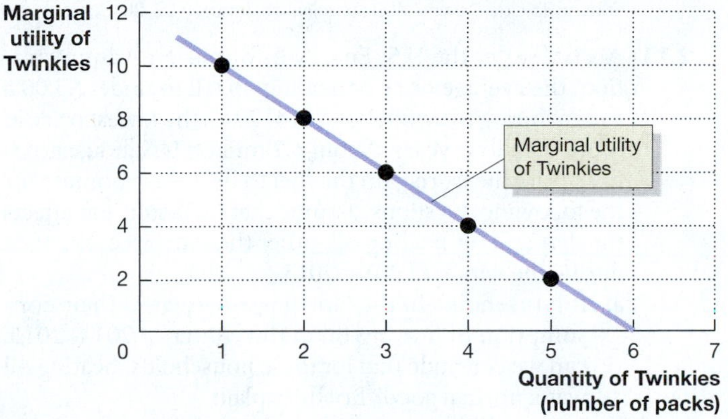

1.9 **(Related to Solved Problem 10.1 on page 324)** Joe has $55 to spend on apples and oranges. Given the information in the following table, is Joe maximizing utility? Briefly explain.

	Price	Quantity	Total Utility	Marginal Utility of Last Unit
Apples	$0.50	50	1,000	20
Oranges	$0.75	40	500	30

1.10 Maya spends her $50 budget on two goods, cans of tuna and bottles of ginger ale. Initially, the marginal utility per dollar she spends on tuna is equal to the marginal utility per dollar she spends on ginger ale. Then the price of ginger ale decreases, while her income and the price of tuna do not change. Briefly explain whether each of the following statements about what happens as a result of the decrease in the price of ginger ale is true or false.

a. Her marginal utility from consuming ginger ale increases.
b. The marginal utility per dollar she spends on ginger ale increases.
c. Because of the substitution effect, Maya will buy more ginger ale. Therefore, we can conclude that ginger ale is a normal good.
d. As Maya adjusts to the change in the price of ginger ale, her marginal utility per dollar spent on tuna will increase.

1.11 **(Related to the Don't Let This Happen to You on page 326)** LaToya is buying corn chips and soda. She has 4 bags of corn chips and 5 bottles of soda in her shopping cart. The marginal utility of the fourth bag of corn chips is 10, and the marginal utility of the fifth bottle of soda is also 10. Is LaToya maximizing utility? Briefly explain.

1.12 When the price of pizza falls in the Super Bowl example on pages 327–328, both the income effect and the substitution effect cause you to want to consume more pizza. If pizza were an inferior good, how would the analysis be changed? In this case, is it possible that a lower price for pizza might lead you to buy less pizza? Briefly explain.

10.2 Where Demand Curves Come From, pages 328–331

LEARNING OBJECTIVE: Use the concept of utility to explain the law of demand.

Summary

When the price of a good falls, the ratio of the marginal utility to price rises. This change leads consumers to buy more of that good. As a result, whenever the price of a product falls, the quantity demanded increases. We saw in Chapter 3, Section 3.1 that this relationship is known as the *law of demand*. The market demand curve can be constructed from the individual demand curves for all the consumers in the market.

MyEconLab Visit **www.myeconlab.com** to complete these exercises online and get instant feedback.

Review Questions

2.1 Explain how a downward-sloping demand curve results from consumers adjusting their consumption choices to changes in price.

2.2 How is the market demand curve derived from consumers' individual demand curves?

2.3 What would need to be true for a demand curve to be upward sloping?

Problems and Applications

2.4 Considering only the income effect, if the price of an inferior good declines, would a consumer want to buy a larger quantity or a smaller quantity of the good? Does your answer mean that the demand curves for inferior goods should slope upward? Briefly explain.

2.5 The chapter states that "when the price of an inferior good falls, the income effect and substitution effect work in opposite directions." Explain what this statement means.

2.6 Suppose the market for ice cream cones is made up of three consumers: Tiago, Terrell, and Tim. Use the information in the following table to construct the market demand curve for ice cream cones. Show the information in a table and in a graph.

	Tiago	Terrell	Tim
Price	Quantity Demanded (cones per week)	Quantity Demanded (cones per week)	Quantity Demanded (cones per week)
$1.75	2	1	0
1.50	4	3	2
1.25	6	4	3
1.00	7	6	4
0.75	9	7	5

2.7 Marty and Ann discussed the rule of equal marginal utility per dollar spent, a topic that was recently covered in the economics course they were both taking:

Marty: "When I use my calculator to divide the marginal utility of pizza by a price of zero, I don't get an answer. This result must mean that if pizza were being sold for a price of zero, the quantity demanded would be infinite."

Ann: "Marty, that can't be true. No producer would be willing to 'sell' pizza, or any other product, for a zero price. Quantity demanded cannot be infinite, so zero prices cannot appear on demand curves and demand schedules."

Assume that Marty and Ann ask you for advice. Which of their statements is correct?

2.8 Consider two goods: pizza and Coke. Along an individual's demand curve for pizza, as the price of pizza falls, does the marginal utility per dollar spent on pizza always equal the marginal utility per dollar spent on Coke? In other words, does the rule of equal marginal utility per dollar spent hold as the price changes and you move up or down the demand curve? How can the rule hold, given that the price of pizza changes along the demand curve? If you need help to answer this problem, look back at the discussion of Figure 10.2 on deriving the demand curve for pizza.

2.9 **(Related to Making the Connection on page 330)** In studying the consumption of very poor families in China, Robert Jensen and Nolan Miller found that in both Hunan and Gansu, "Giffen behavior is most likely to be found among a range of households that are poor (but not too poor or too rich)."

a. What do Jensen and Miller mean by "Giffen behavior"?
b. Why would the poorest of the poor be less likely than people with slightly higher incomes to exhibit this behavior?
c. Why must a good make up a very large portion of consumers' budgets to be a Giffen good?

Source: Robert T. Jensen and Nolan H. Miller, "Giffen Behavior and Subsistence Consumption," *American Economic Review*, Vol. 98, No. 4, September 2008, p. 1569.

2.10 In early 2015, gasoline prices in many parts of the United States had fallen to below $2.00 per gallon, which a news story called "one of the swiftest declines on record." Is gasoline likely to be an inferior good or a normal good for most people? Is your answer important for predicting how much the quantity of gasoline demanded will increase as a result of the price decline? Briefly explain.

Source: Nick Timiraos, "As Gasoline Heads Toward $2, the Benefits Start to Trickle Down," *Wall Street Journal*, January 22, 2015.

2.11 According to the U.S. Energy Information Administration, the average price of heating oil fell to under $3.00 a gallon during the winter of 2014–2015, the lowest price in more than four years. About 6.2 million U.S. households in the Northeast rely on the fuel to heat their homes. For the following questions, assume that no factor that affects the demand for heating oil, other than its price, changed during the winter of 2014–2015.

a. If households in the Northeast increased their consumption of heating oil in the winter of 2014–2015, can we conclude that for these households, heating oil was a normal good? Briefly explain.
b. If households in the Northeast decreased their consumption of heating oil in the winter of 2014–2015, can we conclude that for these households heating oil is an inferior good? Briefly explain.
c. If households in the Northeast decreased their consumption of heating oil in the winter of 2014–2015, can we conclude that for these households heating oil is a Giffen good? Briefly explain.

Source: Jon Kamp, "Cheaper Hearing Oil Fuels Billions in Savings in Northeast," *Wall Street Journal*, January 16, 2015.

10.3 Social Influences on Decision Making, pages 331–337

LEARNING OBJECTIVE: Explain how social influences can affect consumption choices.

Summary

Social factors can have an effect on consumption. For example, the amount of utility people receive from consuming a good often depends on how many other people they know who also consume the good. There is a **network externality** in the consumption of a product if the usefulness of the product increases with the number of consumers who use it. There is evidence that people like to be treated fairly and that they usually attempt to treat others fairly, even if doing so makes them worse off financially. This result has been demonstrated in laboratory experiments such as the ultimatum game. When firms set prices, they take into account consumers' preference for fairness. For example, hardware stores often do not increase the price of snow shovels to take advantage of a temporary increase in demand following a snowstorm.

MyEconLab Visit www.myeconlab.com to complete these exercises online and get instant feedback.

Review Questions

3.1 In which of the following situations are social influences on consumer decision making likely to be greater: choosing a restaurant for dinner or choosing which brand of toothpaste to buy? Briefly explain.

3.2 What are network externalities? For what types of products are network externalities likely to be important? What is path dependence?

3.3 How does the fact that consumers apparently value fairness affect the pricing decisions that businesses make?

Problems and Applications

3.4 Which of the following products are most likely to have significant network externalities? Briefly explain.
a. Smartwatches
b. Dog food
c. Board games
d. LCD televisions
e. 3D televisions

3.5 Writing about a trip to Switzerland in an article in the *New York Times*, economist Daniel Hamermesh noted that electrical outlets in Switzerland use an unusual three-prong plug. Adapters for that type of plug are not typically included in adapter sets, so he and his wife weren't able to plug their computers into their hotel's outlets. Hamermesh wondered: "Why does Switzerland renounce the network externalities that would come with using standard European plugs with their standard 220-volt electricity?" How is Switzerland "renouncing network externalities" by not using standard European plugs?
Source: Daniel Hamermesh, "If Switzerland Would Only Change Its Plugs," *New York Times*, September 23, 2008.

3.6 According to an opinion survey, Snoopy is the most appealing celebrity endorser. The beagle from the popular *Peanuts* comic strip appears in commercials for the insurance company MetLife. What advantages and disadvantages are there in using Snoopy, rather than a real person, to endorse a product?
Source: Jeff Berçovici, "America's Most Loved Spokescharacters," *Forbes*, March 14, 2011.

3.7 Las Vegas is one of the most popular tourist destinations in the United States. Several years ago, the Rio Hotel and Casino in Las Vegas dropped the price of its breakfast buffet to $5.99 for local residents, while keeping the regular price of $14.99 for nonlocals. When setting the price for a meal, why would it matter to the restaurant if the customer is a local resident?
Source: *Las Vegas Advisor*, November 2008.

3.8 **(Related to Making the Connection on page 336)** An article in the *New York Times* notes that classic rock star Tom Petty likes to perform in smaller venues that don't have as many seats as large venues such as Madison Square Garden in New York. According to the article, Petty insists that tickets to his concert be sold "below market price." The author of the article wondered why "Petty and his promoter would price tickets so low when there were clearly people willing to pay much, much more."
a. How does the author know that the prices for Petty's concert tickets are below the market price?
b. Why might Petty and his manager want tickets to have prices below the market price?
Source: Adam Davidson, "How Much Is Michael Bolton Worth to You?" *New York Times*, June 4, 2013.

3.9 **(Related to Making the Connection on page 336)** Suppose that Uber decides that its strategy of using surge pricing during times of high demand is causing the company to receive too much bad publicity. It decides that it will maintain its regular prices even during periods of high demand.
a. If you are trying to get a ride through Uber at the end of a football game or on New Year's Eve, will you benefit from Uber's change in policy? Briefly explain.
b. Uber received criticism for using surge pricing following a severe snowstorm in Boston. Why might some people be more critical of Uber's using surge pricing after a snowstorm than using this pricing strategy on New Year's Eve? Would consumers benefit if Uber decided not to use surge pricing during snowstorms or other weather-related situations? Briefly explain.

10.4 Behavioral Economics: Do People Make Their Choices Rationally? pages 337–342

LEARNING OBJECTIVE: Describe the behavioral economics approach to understanding decision making.

Summary

Behavioral economics is the study of situations in which people act in ways that are not economically rational. **Opportunity cost** is the highest-valued alternative that must be given up to engage in an activity. People would improve their decision making if they took into account nonmonetary opportunity costs. People sometimes ignore nonmonetary opportunity costs because of the **endowment effect**—the tendency of people to be unwilling to sell something they already own even if they are offered a price that is greater than the price they would be willing to pay to buy the good if they didn't already own it. People would also improve their decision making if they ignored *sunk costs*. A **sunk cost** is a cost that has already been paid and cannot be recovered. Finally, people would improve their decision making if they were more realistic about their future behavior. Behavioral economics gives insights into consumer behavior that can guide business strategies.

MyEconLab Visit www.myeconlab.com to complete these exercises online and get instant feedback.

Review Questions

4.1 What does it mean to be economically rational?

4.2 Define *behavioral economics*. What are the three common mistakes that consumers often make? Give an example of each mistake.

4.3 Does using rules of thumb increase or decrease the likelihood of a consumer making an optimal choice? Briefly explain.

4.4 What is anchoring? How might a firm use anchoring to influence consumer choices so as to increase sales?

Problems and Applications

4.5 Marvin visits his aunt and uncle who live in Milwaukee. The Milwaukee Bucks basketball team is scheduled to play a home game against the Golden State Warriors during Marvin's visit. An online broker has a ticket for sale in Section 212 of the arena where the game will be played but the price, $75, is more than Marvin is willing to pay. From another online ticket broker he buys a ticket for $50 for a seat in Section 212 of the arena. On the day of the game, a friend of Marvin's uncle offers to pay Marvin $75 for his ticket. He declines the offer. How can Marvin's refusal to sell his ticket be explained?

4.6 Richard Thaler, an economist at the University of Chicago, is the person who first used the term *endowment effect* to describe placing a higher value on something already owned than would be placed on the object if not currently owned. According to an article in the *Economist*:

> Dr. Thaler, who recently had some expensive bottles of wine stolen, observes that he is "now confronted with precisely one of my own experiments: these are bottles I wasn't planning to sell and now I'm going to get a cheque from an insurance company and most of these bottles I will not buy. I'm a good enough economist to know there's a bit of an inconsistency there."

Based on Thaler's statement, how do his stolen bottles of wine illustrate the endowment effect, and why does he make the statement: "I'm a good enough economist to know there's a bit of an inconsistency there"?

Source: "It's Mine, I Tell You," *Economist*, June 19, 2008.

4.7 Suppose that you are a big fan of the Harry Potter books. You would love to own a copy of the very first printing of the first book, but unfortunately you can't find it for sale for less than $5,000. You are willing to pay at most $200 for a copy but can't find one at that price until one day in a used bookstore you see a copy selling for $10, which you immediately buy. Are you being irrational if you keep the copy rather than sell it?

4.8 Someone who owns a townhouse wrote to a real estate advice columnist to ask whether he should sell his townhouse or wait and sell it in the future, when he hoped that prices would be higher. The columnist replied: "Ask yourself: Would you buy this townhouse today as an investment? Because every day you don't sell it, you're buying it." Do you agree with the columnist? In what sense are you buying something if you don't sell it? Should the owner's decision about whether to sell depend on what price he originally paid for the townhouse?

Source: Edith Lane, "Contract Exclusion OK?" (Allentown, PA) *Morning Call*, May 22, 2011.

4.9 **(Related to Making the Connection on page 339)** Rob Neyer is a baseball writer for sbnation.com. He has described attending a Red Sox game at Fenway Park in Boston and having a seat in the sun on a hot, humid day: "Granted, I could have moved under the overhang and enjoyed today's contest from a nice, cool, shady seat. But when you paid forty-five dollars for a ticket in the fourth row, it's tough to move back to the twenty-fourth [row]." Briefly evaluate Neyer's reasoning.

Source: Rob Neyer, *Feeding the Green Monster*, New York: iPublish.com, 2001, p. 50.

4.10 **(Related to Making the Connection on page 339)** The Washington National Football League team paid a very high price to select Baylor quarterback Robert Griffin III in the 2012 player draft. In addition to paying Griffin a high salary, the team made a trade with the St. Louis team in which they had to give up the rights to select several other highly ranked players. According to a news story, by 2014, the team's coaches seemed to view the team's backup quarterback as a better player than Griffin "but had to go with Griffin because the organization was so committed to him." The story described the price the team had paid "the highest price ever to draft an N.F.L. player." Should the price the team paid matter to its decision as to whether Griffin or his backup should start for the team? Briefly explain.

Source: Neil Irwin, "Robert Griffin III and the Sunk Cost Fallacy," *New York Times*, September 15, 2014.

4.11 **(Related to Making the Connection on page 339)** The following excerpt is from a letter sent to a financial advice columnist: "My wife and I are trying to decide how to invest a $250,000 windfall. She wants to pay off our $114,000 mortgage, but I'm not eager to do that because we refinanced only nine months ago, paying $3,000 in fees and costs." Briefly discuss what effect the $3,000 refinancing cost should have on this couple's investment decision.

Source: Liz Pulliam, *Los Angeles Times* advice column, March 24, 2004.

4.12 Andrea grew up enjoying her Italian grandmother's home-cooked meals. Chicken and pasta with meatballs were her favorite foods. But after Andrea graduated from college, found a job, and got married, she became a vegetarian and no longer ate chicken or meatballs. Briefly explain which of the following statements provides the most likely explanation of Andrea's decision to become a vegetarian:

- When Andrea was young, she was unrealistic about her future behavior. Therefore, she did not act rationally.
- Andrea was not working when she was young. After she graduated from college and became employed, her income rose. We can conclude that for Andrea, chicken, meatballs, and other meat products are inferior goods.
- Social influences explain Andrea's decision to become a vegetarian. More people, including celebrities from the entertainment field, have become vegetarians. Andrea became a vegetarian because she now feels a kinship with these celebrities, and being a vegetarian makes her appear to be fashionable.

4.13 In an article in the *Quarterly Journal of Economics*, Ted O'Donoghue and Matthew Rabin make the following observation: "People have self-control problems caused by a tendency to pursue immediate gratification in a way that their 'long-run selves' do not appreciate." What do they mean by a person's "long-run self"? Give two examples of people pursuing immediate gratification that their long-run selves would not appreciate.

Source: Ted O'Donoghue and Matthew Rabin, "Choice and Procrastination," *Quarterly Journal of Economics*, Vol. 116, No. 1, February 2001, pp. 125–126.

4.14 According to an article in the *New York Times*, the Web site Stickk offers a service where you give them money that they will donate to charity if you fail to go to the gym as often as you promise to. (You can even have the money donated to an anti-charity—a cause you disapprove of.) Why would anyone use this service?

Source: Josh Barro, "How to Make Yourself Go to the Gym," *New York Times*, January 10, 2015.

4.15 **(Related to Making the Connection on page 341)** The *Economist* offered the following two options for subscribing:

1. $56 per year for an online-only subscription
2. $125 per year for print plus online access subscription

A large majority of subscribers chose option 1. But the magazine would have preferred to sell more $125 subscriptions because it can charge higher rates to advertisers in the print magazine than it can online. The magazine decided to rely on insights from behavioral economics to try to increase the number of people choosing the $125 subscriptions. It began offering the following three options:

1. $56 per year for an online-only subscription
2. $125 print plus online access subscription
3. $125 print-only subscription

A large majority of subscribers now chose option 2 rather than option 1. What insights from behavioral economics that were discussed in this chapter can help explain this result?

Source: Mukul Patki, "5 Behavioral Economics Principles Marketers Can't Afford to Ignore," *Forbes*, March 1, 2013.

4.16 **(Related to the Chapter Opener on page 319)** An article in the *New York Times* about J.C. Penney's pricing strategy under former CEO Ron Johnson observes, "Penney had pulled up the anchor, only to see many of its customers sail away."

a. In behavioral economics, what is an "anchor"?
b. In what sense did Penney "pull up the anchor"?
c. Why did Penney follow this strategy, and what was the result?

Source: Stephanie Clifford and Katherine Rampell, "Sometimes We Want Prices to Fool Us," *New York Times*, April 13, 2013.

Appendix

Using Indifference Curves and Budget Lines to Understand Consumer Behavior

LEARNING OBJECTIVE: Use indifference curves and budget lines to understand consumer behavior.

Consumer Preferences

In this chapter, we analyzed consumer behavior using the assumption that satisfaction, or *utility*, is measurable in utils. Although this assumption made our analysis easier to understand, it is unrealistic. In this appendix, we use the more realistic assumption that consumers are able to *rank* different combinations of goods and services in terms of how much utility they provide. For example, a consumer is able to determine whether he or she prefers 2 slices of pizza and 1 can of Coke or 1 slice of pizza and 2 cans of Coke, even if the consumer is unsure exactly how much utility he or she would receive from consuming these goods. This approach has the advantage of allowing us to actually draw a map of a consumer's preferences.

To begin with, suppose that a consumer is presented with the following alternatives, or *consumption bundles*:

Consumption Bundle A	Consumption Bundle B
2 slices of pizza and 1 can of Coke	1 slice of pizza and 2 cans of Coke

We assume that the consumer will always be able to decide which of the following is true:

- The consumer prefers bundle A to bundle B.
- The consumer prefers bundle B to bundle A.
- The consumer is indifferent between bundle A and bundle B. That is, the consumer would be equally happy to receive either bundle, so we can say the consumer receives equal utility from the two bundles.

For consistency, we also assume that the consumer's preferences are *transitive*. For example, if a consumer prefers pepperoni pizza to mushroom pizza and prefers mushroom pizza to anchovy pizza, the consumer must prefer pepperoni pizza to anchovy pizza.

Indifference Curves

Indifference curve A curve that shows the combinations of consumption bundles that give the consumer the same utility.

Given the assumptions in the preceding section, we can draw a map of a consumer's preferences by using indifference curves. An **indifference curve** shows combinations of consumption bundles that give the consumer the same utility. In reality, consumers choose among consumption bundles containing many goods and services, but to make the discussion easier to follow, we will assume that only two goods are involved. Nothing important would change if we expanded the discussion to include many goods instead of just two.

The table in Figure 10A.1 gives Dave's preferences for pizza and Coke. The graph plots the information from the table. Every possible combination of pizza and Coke will have an indifference curve passing through it, although in the figure we have shown only four of Dave's indifference curves. Dave is indifferent among all the consumption bundles that are on the same indifference curve. So, he is indifferent among bundles *E*, *B*, and *F* because they all lie on indifference curve I_3. Even though Dave has 4 fewer cans of Coke with bundle *B* than with bundle *E*, the additional slice of pizza he has in bundle *B* results in his having the same amount of utility at both points.

Consumption Bundle	Slices of Pizza	Cans of Coke
A	1	2
B	3	4
C	4	5
D	1	6
E	2	8
F	5	2

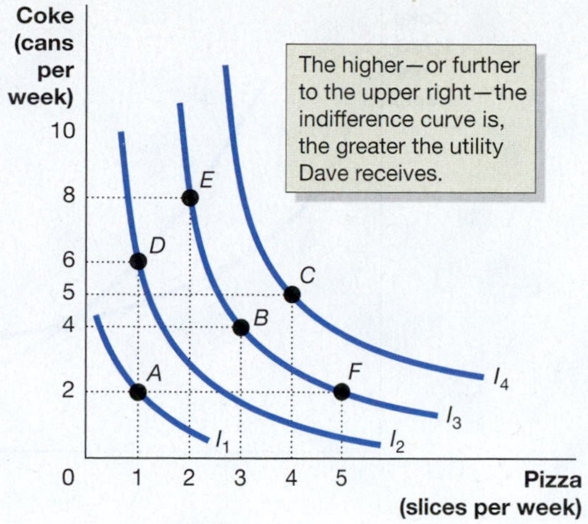

MyEconLab Animation

Figure 10A.1

Plotting Dave's Preferences for Pizza and Coke

Every possible combination of pizza and Coke will have an indifference curve passing through it, although in the graph we show just four of Dave's indifference curves. Dave is indifferent among all the consumption bundles that are on the same indifference curve. So, he is indifferent among bundles *E*, *B*, and *F* because they all lie on indifference curve I_3. Moving to the upper right in the graph increases the quantities of both goods available for Dave to consume. Therefore, the further to the upper right the indifference curve is, the greater the utility Dave receives.

Even without looking at Dave's indifference curves, we know he will prefer consumption bundle *D* to consumption bundle *A* because in *D* he receives the same quantity of pizza as in *A* but 4 additional cans of Coke. But we need to know Dave's preferences, as shown by his indifference curves, to know how he will rank bundle *B* and bundle *D*. Bundle *D* contains more Coke but less pizza than bundle *B*, so Dave's ranking will depend on how much pizza he would be willing to give up to receive more Coke. The higher the indifference curve—that is, the further to the upper right on the graph—the greater the amounts of both goods that are available for Dave to consume and the greater his utility. In other words, Dave receives more utility from the consumption bundles on indifference curve I_2 than from the consumption bundles on indifference curve I_1, more utility from the bundles on I_3 than from the bundles on I_2, and so on. MyEconLab Concept Check

The Slope of an Indifference Curve

Remember that the slope of a curve is the ratio of the change in the variable on the vertical axis to the change in the variable on the horizontal axis. Along an indifference curve, the slope tells us the rate at which the consumer is willing to trade off one product for another while keeping the consumer's utility constant. Economists call this rate the **marginal rate of substitution (*MRS*)**.

Marginal rate of substitution (*MRS*) The rate at which a consumer would be willing to trade off one good for another.

We expect that the *MRS* will change as we move down an indifference curve. In Figure 10A.1, at a point like *E* on indifference curve I_3, Dave's indifference curve is relatively steep. As we move down the curve, it becomes less steep, until it becomes relatively flat at a point like *F*. This is the usual shape of indifference curves: They are bowed in, or convex. A consumption bundle like *E* contains a lot of Coke and not much pizza. We would expect that Dave could give up a significant quantity of Coke for a smaller quantity of additional pizza and still have the same level of utility. Therefore, the *MRS* will be high. As we move down the indifference curve, Dave moves to bundles, like *B* and *F*, that have more pizza and less Coke. At those points, Dave is willing to trade less Coke for pizza, and the *MRS* declines. MyEconLab Concept Check

Can Indifference Curves Ever Cross?

Remember that we assume that consumers have transitive preferences. That is, if Dave prefers consumption bundle *X* to consumption bundle *Y* and prefers consumption bundle *Y* to consumption bundle *Z*, he must prefer bundle *X* to bundle *Z*. If indifference curves cross, this assumption is violated. To understand why, look at Figure 10A.2, which shows two of Dave's indifference curves crossing.

Because bundle *X* and bundle *Z* are both on indifference curve I_1, Dave must be indifferent between them. Similarly, because bundle *X* and bundle *Y* are on indifference curve I_2, Dave must be indifferent between them. The assumption of transitivity means that Dave should also be indifferent between bundle *Z* and bundle *Y*. We know he won't be,

MyEconLab Animation

Figure 10A.2

Indifference Curves Cannot Cross

Because bundle *X* and bundle *Z* are both on indifference curve I_1, Dave must be indifferent between them. Similarly, because bundle *X* and bundle *Y* are on indifference curve I_2, Dave must be indifferent between them. The assumption of transitivity means that Dave should also be indifferent between bundle *Z* and bundle *Y*. We know he won't be, however, because bundle *Y* contains more pizza and more Coke than bundle *Z*. So, Dave will definitely prefer bundle *Y* to bundle *Z*, which violates the assumption of transitivity. Therefore, none of Dave's indifference curves can cross.

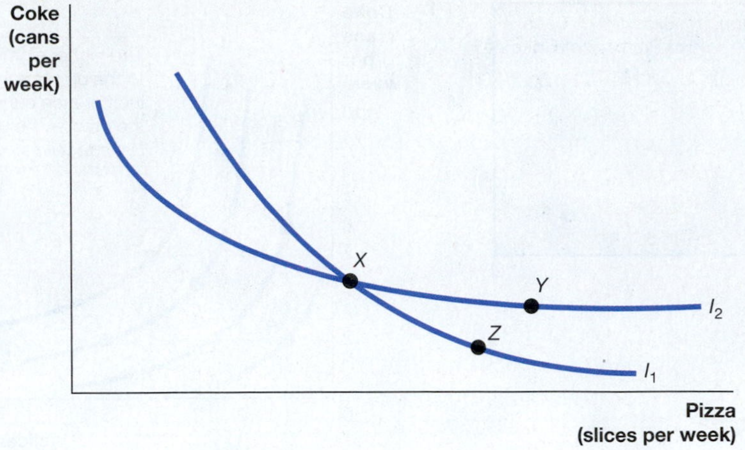

however, because bundle *Y* contains more pizza and more Coke than bundle *Z*. So, Dave will definitely prefer bundle *Y* to bundle *Z*, which violates the assumption of transitivity. Therefore, none of Dave's indifference curves can cross. MyEconLab Concept Check

The Budget Constraint

Remember that a consumer's *budget constraint* is the amount of income he or she has available to spend on goods and services. Suppose that Dave has $10 per week to spend on pizza and Coke. The table in Figure 10A.3 shows the combinations that he can afford

MyEconLab Animation

Figure 10A.3

Dave's Budget Constraint

Dave's budget constraint shows the combinations of slices of pizza and cans of Coke he can buy with $10. The price of Coke is $1 per can, so if he spends all of his $10 on Coke, he can buy 10 cans (bundle *G*). The price of pizza is $2 per slice, so if he spends all of his $10 on pizza, he can buy 5 slices (bundle *L*). As he moves down his budget constraint from bundle *G*, he gives up 2 cans of Coke for every slice of pizza he buys. Any consumption bundles along the line or inside the line are affordable. Any bundles that lie outside the line are unaffordable.

Combinations of Pizza and Coke Dave Can Buy with $10

Consumption Bundle	Slices of Pizza	Cans of Coke	Total Spending
G	0	10	$10.00
H	1	8	10.00
I	2	6	10.00
J	3	4	10.00
K	4	2	10.00
L	5	0	10.00

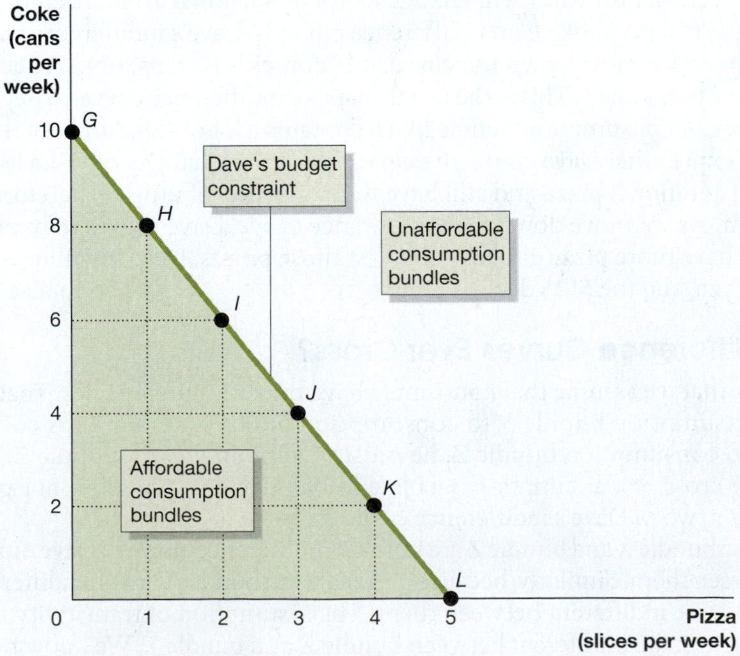

to buy if the price of pizza is $2 per slice and the price of Coke is $1 per can. As you can see, all the points lie on a straight line. This line represents Dave's budget constraint. The line intersects the vertical axis at the maximum number of cans of Coke Dave can afford to buy with $10, which is consumption bundle *G*. The line intersects the horizontal axis at the maximum number of slices of pizza Dave can afford to buy with $10, which is consumption bundle *L*. As he moves down his budget constraint from bundle *G*, he gives up 2 cans of Coke for every slice of pizza he buys.

Any consumption bundle along the line or inside the line is *affordable* for Dave because he has the income to buy those combinations of pizza and Coke. Any bundle that lies outside the line is *unaffordable* because those bundles cost more than the income Dave has available to spend.

The slope of the budget constraint is constant because the budget constraint is a straight line. The slope of the line equals the change in the number of cans of Coke divided by the change in the number of slices of pizza. In this case, moving down the budget constraint from one point to another point, the change in the number of cans of Coke equals −2, and the change in the number of slices of pizza equals 1, so the slope equals −2/1, or −2. Notice that with the price of pizza equal to $2 per slice and the price of Coke equal to $1 per can, the slope of the budget constraint is equal to the ratio of the price of pizza to the price of Coke (multiplied by −1). In fact, this result will always hold: *The slope of the budget constraint is equal to the ratio of the price of the good on the horizontal axis divided by the price of the good on the vertical axis multiplied by −1.*

MyEconLab Concept Check

Choosing the Optimal Consumption of Pizza and Coke

Dave would like to be on the highest possible indifference curve because higher indifference curves represent more pizza and more Coke. But Dave can only buy the bundles that lie on or inside his budget constraint. In other words, *to maximize utility, a consumer needs to be on the highest indifference curve, given his budget constraint.*

Figure 10A.4 plots the consumption bundles from Figure 10A.1 along with the budget constraint from Figure 10A.3. The figure also shows the indifference curves that pass through each consumption bundle. In Figure 10A.4, the highest indifference curve

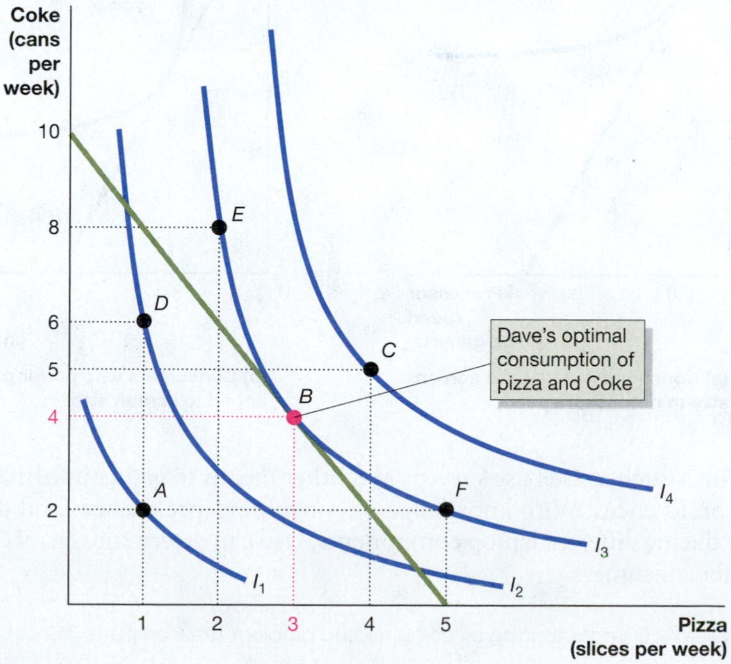

MyEconLab Animation

Figure 10A.4

Finding Optimal Consumption

Dave would like to be on the highest possible indifference curve, but he cannot reach indifference curves such as I_4 that are outside his budget constraint. Dave's optimal combination of slices of pizza and cans of Coke is at point *B*, where his budget constraint just touches—or is *tangent* to—the highest indifference curve he can reach. At point *B*, he buys 3 slices of pizza and 4 cans of Coke.

shown is I_4. Unfortunately, Dave lacks the income to purchase consumption bundles—such as *C*—that lie on I_4. He has the income to purchase bundles such as *A* and *D*, but he can do better. If he consumes bundle *B*, he will be on the highest indifference curve he can reach, given his budget constraint of $10. The resulting combination of 3 slices of pizza and 4 cans of Coke represents Dave's optimal consumption of pizza and Coke, given his preferences and his budget constraint. Notice that at point *B*, Dave's budget constraint just touches—or is *tangent* to—I_3. In fact, bundle *B* is the only bundle on I_3 that Dave is able to purchase for $10.

Making the Connection
MyEconLab Video

Dell Determines the Optimal Mix of Products

Consumers have different preferences, which helps explain why many firms offer products with a variety of characteristics. For example, Dell sells laptop computers with different screen sizes, processor speeds, hard drive sizes, graphics cards, and so on. We can use the model of consumer choice to analyze a simplified version of the situation Dell faces in deciding which features to offer consumers.

Assume that consumers have $500 each to spend on a Dell laptop and that they are concerned with only two laptop characteristics: screen size and processor speed. Because larger screens and faster processors increase Dell's cost of producing laptops, consumers face a trade-off: The larger the screen, the slower the processor speed. Consumers in panel (a) of the figure prefer screen size to processor speed. For this group, the point of tangency between a typical consumer's indifference curve and the budget constraint shows an optimal choice of a 17-inch screen and a 2.0-gigahertz processor. Consumers in panel (b) prefer processor speed to screen size. For this group, the point of tangency between a typical consumer's indifference curve and the budget constraint shows an optimal choice of a 13-inch screen and 3.4-gigahertz processor.

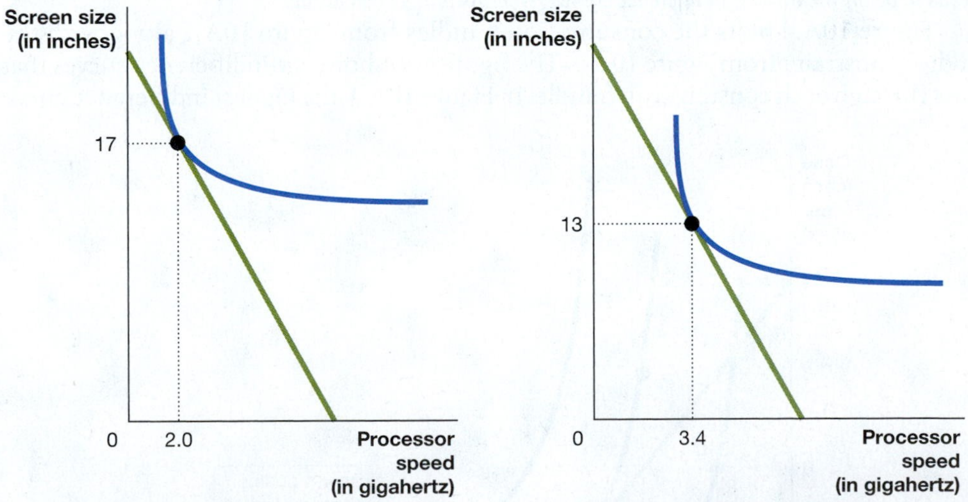

(a) Consumers who prefer screen size to processor speed

(b) Consumers who prefer processor speed to screen size

Companies such as Dell use surveys and other means to gather information about consumer preferences. With knowledge of consumers' preferences and data on the costs of producing different laptop components, Dell can determine the mix of components to offer consumers.

MyEconLab Study Plan

Your Turn: Test your understanding by doing related problem 10A.8 on page 362 at the end of this appendix.

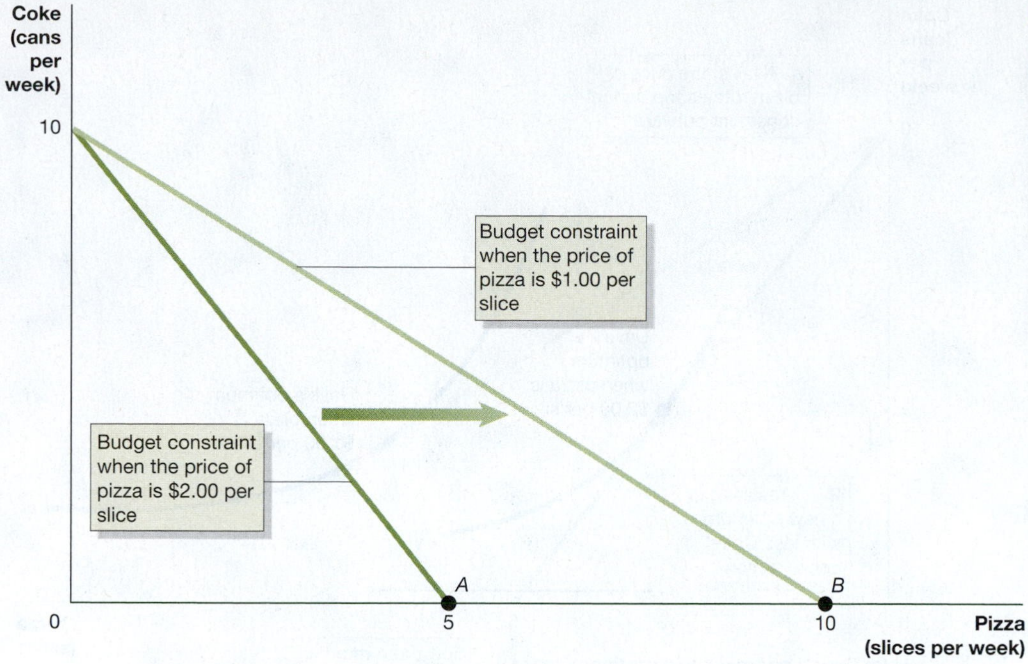

MyEconLab Animation

Figure 10A.5

How a Price Decrease Affects the Budget Constraint

A fall in the price of pizza from $2 per slice to $1 per slice increases the maximum number of slices Dave can buy with $10 from 5 to 10. The budget constraint rotates outward from point *A* to point *B* to show the effect of the price decrease.

Deriving the Demand Curve

Suppose the price of pizza falls from $2 per slice to $1 per slice. How will this change affect Dave's decision about which combination of pizza and Coke is optimal? First, notice what happens to Dave's budget constraint when the price of pizza falls. As Figure 10A.5 shows, when the price of pizza is $2 per slice, the maximum number of slices Dave can buy is 5. After the price of pizza falls to $1 per slice, Dave can buy a maximum of 10 slices. His budget constraint rotates outward from point A to point B to represent this. (Notice that the fall in the price of pizza does not affect the maximum number of cans of Coke Dave can buy with his $10.)

When his budget constraint rotates outward, Dave is able to purchase consumption bundles that were previously unaffordable. Panel (a) of Figure 10A.6 shows that the combination of 3 slices of pizza and 4 cans of Coke was optimal when the price of pizza was $2 per slice, but the combination of 7 slices of pizza and 3 cans of Coke is optimal when the price of pizza falls to $1. The lower price of pizza causes Dave to consume more pizza and less Coke and to end up on a higher indifference curve.

The change in Dave's optimal consumption of pizza as the price changes explains why demand curves slope downward. Dave adjusted his consumption of pizza as follows:

Price of pizza = $2 per slice → Quantity of pizza demanded = 3 slices

Price of pizza = $1 per slice → Quantity of pizza demanded = 7 slices

In panel (b) of Figure 10A.6, we plot the two points of optimal consumption and draw a line to connect the points. This downward-sloping line is Dave's demand curve for pizza. We could find more points on the demand curve by changing the price of pizza and finding the new optimal number of slices of pizza Dave would demand.

Remember that according to the law of demand, demand curves always slope downward. We have just shown that the law of demand results from the optimal adjustment by consumers to changes in prices. A fall in the price of a good will rotate *outward* the budget constraint and make it possible for a consumer to reach higher indifference curves. As a result, the consumer will increase the quantity of the good demanded. An increase in price will rotate *inward* the budget constraint and force the consumer to a lower indifference curve. As a result, the consumer will decrease the quantity of the good demanded.

MyEconLab Concept Check

MyEconLab Animation

Figure 10A.6

How a Price Change Affects Optimal Consumption

In panel (a), a fall in the price of pizza results in Dave's consuming less Coke and more pizza:

1. A fall in the price of pizza rotates the budget constraint outward because Dave can now buy more pizza with his $10.
2. In the new optimum on indifference curve I_2, Dave changes the quantities he consumes of both goods. His consumption of Coke falls from 4 cans to 3 cans.
3. In the new optimum, Dave's consumption of pizza increases from 3 slices to 7 slices.

In panel (b), Dave responds optimally to the fall in the price of pizza from $2 per slice to $1 per slice by increasing the quantity of slices he consumes from 3 slices to 7 slices. When we graph this result, we have Dave's demand curve for pizza.

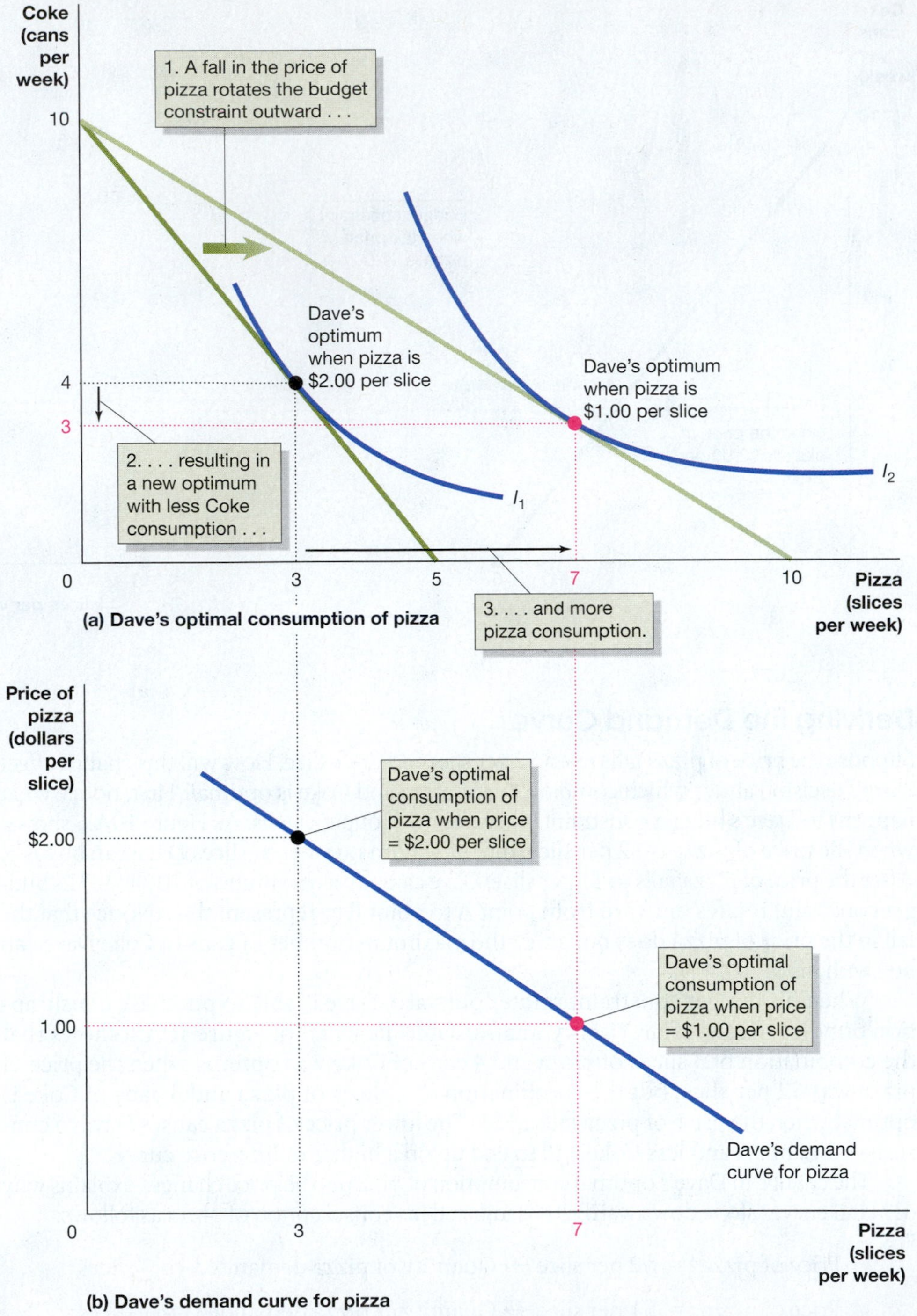

Solved Problem 10A.1

MyEconLab Interactive Animation

When Does a Price Change Make a Consumer Better Off?

Dave has $300 to spend each month on pizzas and downloads of movies. Pizzas and movie downloads have a price of $10, and Dave is maximizing his utility by buying 20 pizzas and 10 movies. Suppose Dave still has $300 to spend, but the price of movies rises to $20, while the price of pizzas drops to $5. Is Dave better or worse off than he was before the price change? Use a budget constraint–indifference curve graph to illustrate your answer.

Solving the Problem

Step 1: Review the chapter material. This problem concerns the effect of price changes on optimal consumption, so you may want to review the section "Deriving the Demand Curve," which begins on page 355.

Step 2: Solve the problem by drawing the appropriate graph. We begin by drawing the budget constraint, indifference curve, and point of optimal consumption for the original prices:

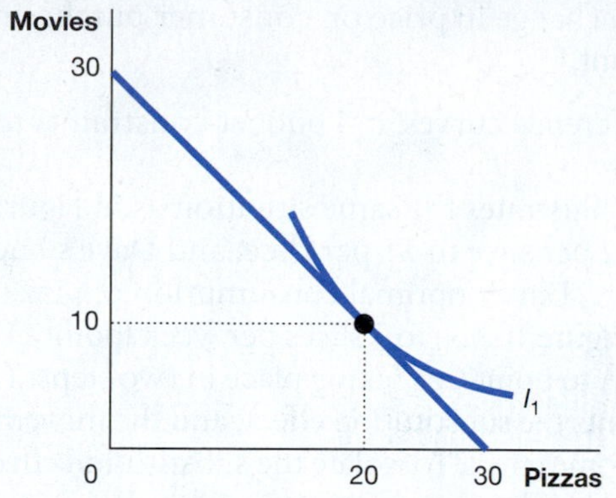

Now draw a graph that shows the results of the price changes. Notice that in this problem, the prices of *both* goods change. You can determine the position of the new budget constraint by calculating the maximum quantity of pizzas and movies Dave can buy after the price changes. You should also note that after the price changes, Dave can still buy his original optimal consumption bundle—20 pizzas and 10 movies—by spending all his $300, so his new budget constraint must pass through this point.

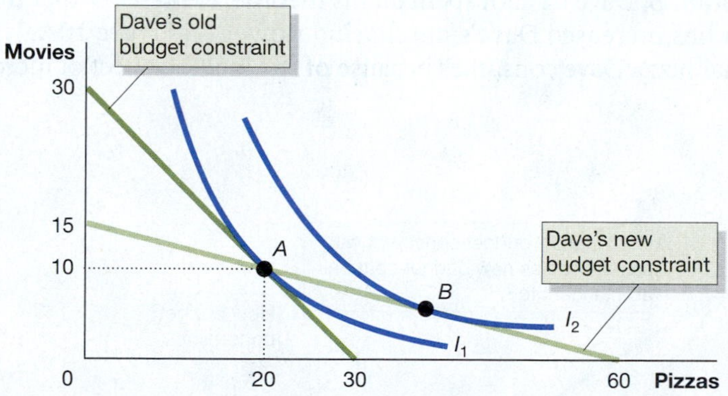

At the new prices, Dave can buy a maximum of 60 pizzas or 15 movies. Both his old and new budget constraints pass through the consumption bundle at point *A*. This consumption bundle is no longer optimal, however, because with the new prices, it is possible for him to reach an indifference curve that is higher than I_1. We can draw in the new highest indifference curve he can reach—I_2—and show the new optimal consumption bundle—point *B*.

Because Dave can now reach a higher indifference curve, we can conclude that he is better off as a result of the price change.

Your Turn: For more practice, do related problem 10A.10 on page 362 at the end of this appendix.

MyEconLab Study Plan

The Income Effect and the Substitution Effect of a Price Change

We saw in this chapter that a price change has these two effects on the quantity of a good consumed:

1. The *substitution effect* is the change in the quantity demanded of a good that results from a change in price making the good more or less expensive relative to other goods, holding constant the effect of the price change on consumer purchasing power.
2. The *income effect* is the change in the quantity demanded of a good that results from the effect of a change in price on consumer purchasing power, holding all other factors constant.

We can use indifference curves and budget constraints to analyze these two effects more precisely.

Figure 10A.7 illustrates the same situation as in Figure 10A.6: The price of pizza has fallen from $2 per slice to $1 per slice, and Dave's budget constraint has rotated outward. As before, Dave's optimal consumption of pizza increases from 3 slices per week (point A in Figure 10A.7) to 7 slices per week (point C). We can think of this movement from point A to point C as taking place in two steps: The movement from point A to point B represents the substitution effect, and the movement from point B to point C represents the income effect. To isolate the substitution effect, we have to hold constant the effect of the price change on Dave's income. We do this by changing the price of pizza relative to the price of Coke *but at the same time holding his utility constant by keeping Dave on the same indifference curve*. In Figure 10A.7, in moving from point A to point B, Dave remains on indifference curve I_1. Point A is a point of tangency between I_1 and Dave's original budget constraint. Point B is a point of tangency between I_1 and a new, *hypothetical* budget constraint that has a slope equal to the new ratio of the price of pizza to the price of Coke. At point B, Dave has increased his consumption of pizza from 3 slices to 5 slices. Because we are still on indifference curve I_1, we know that this increase is Dave's response only to the change in the relative price of pizza and, therefore, that the increase represents the substitution effect of the fall in the price of pizza.

At point B, Dave has not spent all his income. Remember that the fall in the price of pizza has increased Dave's purchasing power. In Figure 10A.7, we illustrate the additional pizza Dave consumes because of the income effect of increased purchasing

MyEconLab Animation

Figure 10A.7

Income and Substitution Effects of a Price Change

Following a decline in the price of pizza, Dave's optimal consumption of pizza increases from 3 slices per week (point A) to 7 slices per week (point C). We can think of this movement from point A to point C as taking place in two steps: The movement from point A to point B along indifference curve I_1 represents the substitution effect, and the movement from point B to point C represents the income effect. Dave increases his consumption of pizza from 3 slices per week to 5 slices per week because of the substitution effect of a fall in the price of pizza and from 5 slices per week to 7 slices per week because of the income effect.

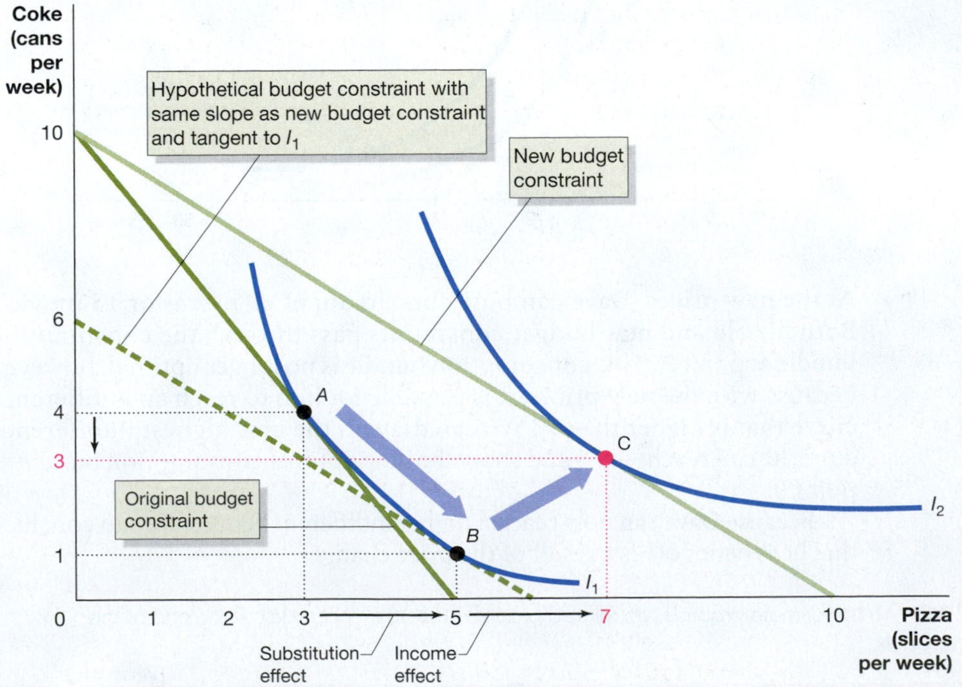

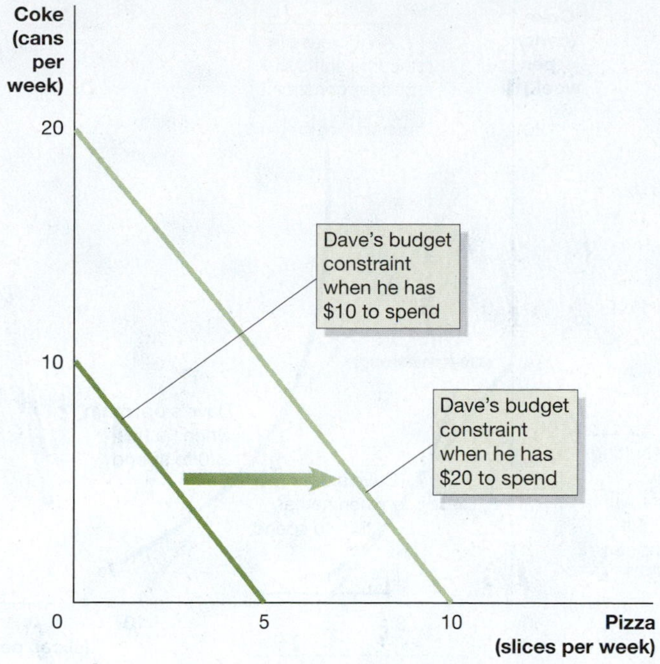

MyEconLab Animation

Figure 10A.8

How a Change in Income Affects the Budget Constraint

When the income Dave has to spend on pizza and Coke increases from $10 to $20, his budget constraint shifts outward. With $10, Dave could buy a maximum of 5 slices of pizza or 10 cans of Coke. With $20, he can buy a maximum of 10 slices of pizza or 20 cans of Coke.

power by the movement from point *B* to point *C*. Notice that in moving from point *B* to point *C*, the price of pizza relative to the price of Coke is constant because the slope of the new budget constraint is the same as the slope of the hypothetical budget constraint that is tangent to I_1 at point *B*.

We can conclude that Dave increases his consumption of pizza from 3 slices per week to 5 slices per week because of the substitution effect of a fall in the price of pizza and from 5 slices per week to 7 slices per week because of the income effect. Recall from our discussion of income and substitution effects in this chapter that the income effect of a price decline causes consumers to buy more of a normal good and less of an inferior good. Because the income effect causes Dave to increase his consumption of pizza, pizza must be a normal good for him. MyEconLab Concept Check

How a Change in Income Affects Optimal Consumption

Suppose that the price of pizza remains at $2 per slice, but the income Dave has to spend on pizza and Coke increases from $10 to $20. Figure 10A.8 shows how this change affects his budget constraint. With an income of $10, Dave could buy a maximum of 5 slices of pizza or 10 cans of Coke. With an income of $20, he can buy 10 slices of pizza or 20 cans of Coke. The additional income allows Dave to increase his consumption of both pizza and Coke and to move to a higher indifference curve.

Figure 10A.9 shows Dave's new optimum. Dave is able to increase his consumption of pizza from 3 to 7 slices per week and his consumption of Coke from 4 to 6 cans per week. MyEconLab Concept Check

The Slope of the Indifference Curve, the Slope of the Budget Line, and the Rule of Equal Marginal Utility per Dollar Spent

In this chapter, we saw that consumers maximize utility when they consume each good up to the point where the marginal utility per dollar spent is the same for every good. This condition seems different from the one we stated earlier in this appendix that to maximize utility, a consumer needs to be on the highest indifference curve, given his budget constraint. In fact, the two conditions are equivalent. To see this, begin by looking at Figure 10A.10, which again combines Dave's indifference curve and budget constraint. Remember that at the point of optimal consumption, the indifference curve and

MyEconLab Animation

Figure 10A.9

How a Change in Income Affects Optimal Consumption

An increase in income leads Dave to consume more Coke and more pizza:

1. An increase in income shifts Dave's budget constraint outward because he can now buy more of both goods.
2. In the new optimum on indifference curve I_2, Dave changes the quantities he consumes of both goods. His consumption of Coke increases from 4 to 6 cans.
3. In the new optimum, Dave's consumption of pizza increases from 3 to 7 slices.

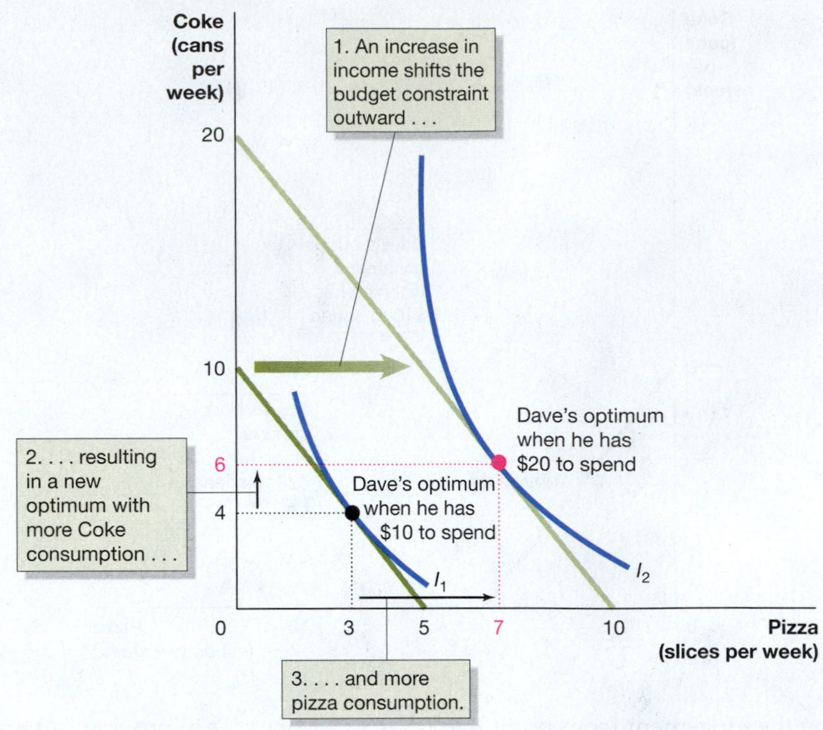

the budget constraint are tangent, so they have the same slope. Therefore, *at the point of optimal consumption, the marginal rate of substitution* (MRS) *is equal to the ratio of the price of the product on the horizontal axis to the price of the product on the vertical axis.*

The slope of the indifference curve tells us the rate at which a consumer is *willing* to trade off one good for the other. The slope of the budget constraint tells us the rate at which a consumer is *able* to trade off one good for the other. Only at the point of optimal consumption is the rate at which a consumer is willing to trade off one good for the other equal to the rate at which the consumer can trade off one good for the other.

The Rule of Equal Marginal Utility per Dollar Spent Revisited

Recall from this chapter the *rule of equal marginal utility per dollar,* which states that to maximize utility, consumers should spend their income so that the last dollar spent on

MyEconLab Animation

Figure 10A.10

At the Optimum Point, the Slopes of the Indifference Curve and Budget Constraint Are the Same

At the point of optimal consumption, the marginal rate of substitution is equal to the ratio of the price of the product on the horizontal axis to the price of the product on the vertical axis.

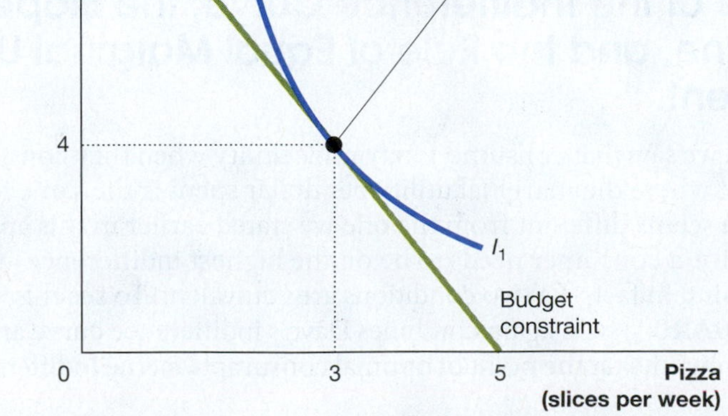

each product gives them the same marginal utility. We can use our indifference curve and budget constraint analysis to see why this rule holds. When we move from one point on an indifference curve to another, we end up with more of one product and less of the other product but the same amount of utility. For example, as Dave moves down an indifference curve, he consumes less Coke and more pizza, but he has the same amount of utility.

Remember that marginal utility (*MU*) tells us how much additional utility a consumer gains (or loses) from consuming more (or less) of a good. So when Dave consumes less Coke by moving down an indifference curve, he loses utility equal to:

$$-\text{Change in the quantity of Coke} \times MU_{Coke}$$

but he consumes more pizza, so he gains utility equal to:

$$\text{Change in the quantity of Pizza} \times MU_{Pizza}.$$

We know that the gain in utility from the additional pizza is equal to the loss from the smaller quantity of Coke because Dave's total utility remains the same along an indifference curve. Therefore, we can write:

$$-(\text{Change in the quantity of Coke} \times MU_{Coke}) = (\text{Change in the quantity of pizza} \times MU_{Pizza}).$$

Loss in utility from consuming less Coke

Gain in utility from consuming more pizza

If we rearrange terms, we have:

$$\frac{-\text{Change in the quantity of Coke}}{\text{Change in the quantity of Pizza}} = \frac{MU_{Pizza}}{MU_{Coke}}.$$

Because the expression:

$$\frac{-\text{Change in the quantity of Coke}}{\text{Change in the quantity of Pizza}}$$

is the slope of the indifference curve, it is equal to the *MRS* (multiplied by −1). So, we can write:

$$\frac{-\text{Change in the quantity of Coke}}{\text{Change in the quantity of Pizza}} = MRS = \frac{MU_{Pizza}}{MU_{Coke}}.$$

The slope of Dave's budget constraint equals the price of pizza divided by the price of Coke (multiplied by −1). We saw earlier in this appendix that at the point of optimal consumption, the *MRS* equals the ratio of the prices of the two goods. Therefore:

$$\frac{MU_{Pizza}}{MU_{Coke}} = \frac{P_{Pizza}}{P_{Coke}}.$$

We can rewrite this to show that at the point of optimal consumption:

$$\frac{MU_{Pizza}}{P_{Pizza}} = \frac{MU_{Coke}}{P_{Coke}}.$$

This last expression is the rule of equal marginal utility per dollar that we first developed in this chapter. So we have shown how this rule follows from the indifference curve and budget constraint approach to analyzing consumer choice. MyEconLab Concept Check MyEconLab Study Plan

Key Terms

Indifference curve, p. 350

Marginal rate of substitution (*MRS*), p. 351

10.A Using Indifference Curves and Budget Lines to Understand Consumer Behavior, pages 350–361

LEARNING OBJECTIVE: Use indifference curves and budget lines to understand consumer behavior.

MyEconLab Visit **www.myeconlab.com** to complete these exercises online and get instant feedback.

Review Questions

10A.1 What are the two assumptions economists make about consumer preferences?

10A.2 What is an indifference curve? What is a budget constraint?

10A.3 How do consumers choose the optimal consumption bundle?

Problems and Applications

10A.4 Jacob receives an allowance of $5 per week. He spends all his allowance on ice cream cones and cans of Lemon Fizz soda.

a. If the price of ice cream cones is $0.50 per cone and the price of cans of Lemon Fizz is $1 per can, draw a graph showing Jacob's budget constraint. Be sure to indicate on the graph the maximum number of ice cream cones and the maximum number of cans of Lemon Fizz that Jacob can buy.

b. Jacob buys 8 ice cream cones and 1 can of Lemon Fizz. Draw an indifference curve representing Jacob's choice, assuming that he has chosen the optimal combination.

c. Suppose that the price of ice cream cones rises to $1 per cone. Draw Jacob's new budget constraint and his new optimal consumption of ice cream cones and cans of Lemon Fizz.

10A.5 Suppose that Jacob's allowance in problem 10A.4 climbs from $5 to $10 per week.

a. Show how the increased allowance alters Jacob's budget constraint.

b. Draw a set of indifference curves showing how Jacob's choice of ice cream cones and cans of Lemon Fizz changes when his allowance increases. Assume that both goods are normal.

c. Draw a set of indifference curves showing how Jacob's choice of ice cream cones and cans of Lemon Fizz changes when his allowance increases. Assume that Lemon Fizz is a normal good but ice cream is an inferior good.

10A.6 Suppose that Calvin considers Pepsi and Coke to be perfect substitutes. They taste the same to him, and he gets exactly the same amount of enjoyment from drinking a can of Pepsi or a can of Coke.

a. Will Calvin's indifference curves showing his trade-off between Pepsi and Coke have the same curvature as the indifference curves drawn in the figures in this appendix? Briefly explain.

b. How will Calvin decide whether to buy Pepsi or Coke?

10A.7 In the following budget constraint–indifference curve graph, Nikki has $200 to spend on blouses and skirts.

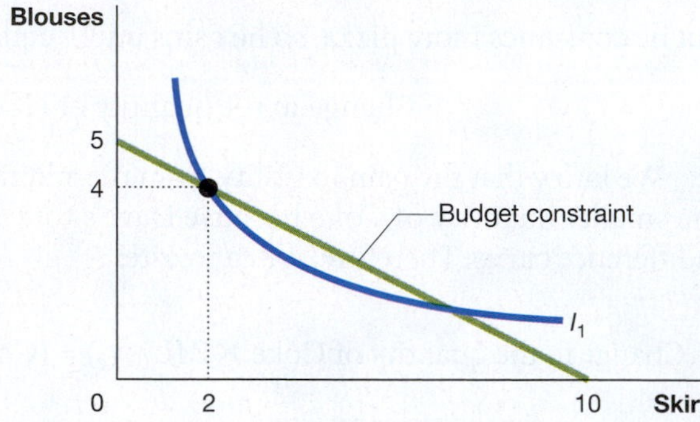

a. What is the price of blouses? What is the price of skirts?

b. Is Nikki making the optimum choice if she buys 4 blouses and 2 skirts? Explain how you know this.

10A.8 **(Related to** Making the Connection **on page 354)** Marilou and Hunter both purchase milk and doughnuts at the same Quik Mart. They have different tastes for milk and doughnuts and different incomes. They both buy some milk and some doughnuts, but they buy considerably different quantities of the two goods. Can we conclude that their marginal rate of substitution between milk and doughnuts is the same? Draw a graph showing their budget constraints and indifference curves and explain.

10A.9 Sunsweet decides that prune juice has a bad image, so it launches a slick advertising campaign to convince young people that prune juice is very hip. The company hires Taylor Swift, Jay-Z, and Trick Daddy to endorse its product. The campaign works! Prune juice sales soar, even though Sunsweet hasn't cut the price. Draw a budget constraint and indifference curve diagram with Sunsweet prune juice on one axis and other drinks on the other axis and show how the celebrity endorsements have changed things.

10A.10 **(Related to** Solved Problem 10A.1 **on page 356)** Dave has $300 to spend each month on DVDs and CDs. DVDs and CDs both currently have a price of $10, and Dave is maximizing his utility by buying 20 DVDs and 10 CDs. Suppose Dave still has $300 to spend, but the price of a DVD rises to $12, while the price of a CD drops to $6. Is Dave better or worse off than he was before the price change? Use a budget constraint–indifference curve graph to illustrate your answer.

10A.11 The following graph illustrates the combination of apples and oranges (point *A*) that maximizes Yolanda's total utility, given her budget. Suppose the price of oranges doubles, while the price of apples and Yolanda's income both stay the same.

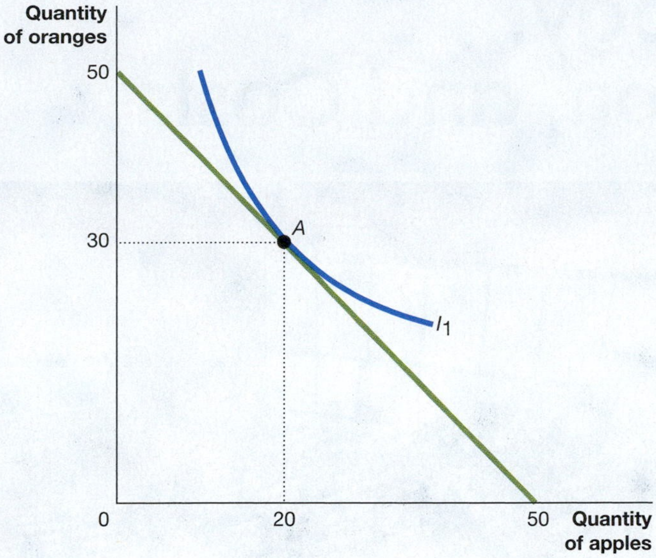

a. Draw a new budget constraint to reflect the increase in the price of oranges.

b. Based on the assumptions regarding consumer preferences listed at the beginning of this appendix, sketch in a new indifference curve to reflect the new optimal combination of apples and oranges now that the price of oranges has doubled.

c. Are there any circumstances in which the new optimal combination of apples and oranges will include a larger quantity of oranges (compared to the original combination)? Briefly explain.

10A.12 An article in the *Wall Street Journal* noted that as a result of lower gasoline prices, sales "improved notably over the last two months at Back Yard Burgers, a dining chain based in Nashville, Tenn." A student is asked to use an indifference curve and budget constraint graph to show the effect on a consumer of lower gasoline prices, making the following assumptions:

1. The consumer has $120 per month to spend on gasoline and burgers.
2. The price of gasoline falls from $3.00 per gallon to $2.00 per gallon.
3. The price of burgers is unchanged at $6.

The student draws the following graph.

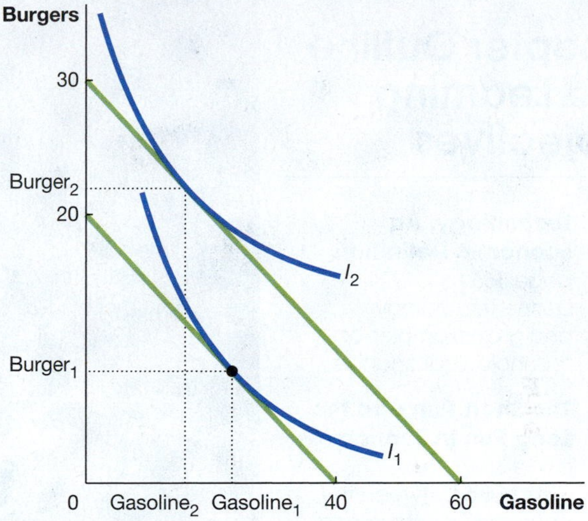

Comment on whether the student has correctly drawn each of the following.

a. The consumer's original budget constraint before the decline in the price of gasoline

b. The consumer's budget constraint after the decline in the price of gasoline

c. The change in the quantity of gasoline the consumer buys after the decline in the price of gasoline

Source: Nick Timiraos, "Pump Prices Prime Economy for Growth," *Wall Street Journal*, December 11, 2014.

CHAPTER
11

Technology, Production, and Costs

Chapter Outline and Learning Objectives

Will the Cost of MOOCs Revolutionize Higher Education?

For hundreds of years, college education has typically taken place in lecture halls where instructors and students interact. A large part of the total cost of supplying college educations is the expense of constructing and maintaining buildings and paying the salaries of instructors and administrators. Economists refer to these costs as *fixed costs* because they remain the same regardless of the number of students enrolled. The *marginal cost* of higher education, the cost of instructing one additional student, is very low as long as there are empty seats in classrooms. But once classrooms are full, the marginal cost rises significantly because a school would need to build more classrooms and hire more instructors.

New technology has started changing colleges' costs. For example, some colleges now offer massive open online courses (MOOCs). The fixed cost of an online course is relatively high because instructors must develop new syllabi, exams, and teaching notes, as well as determine when and how to interact with their students. But after the courses are placed online, the cost of providing instruction to an additional student is close to zero because instruction is not limited by the size of a classroom. Because the marginal cost is low, after the fixed costs are covered, colleges can earn substantial revenues from MOOCs, even if they charge students low prices for these courses. In 2015, Arizona State announced that it would offer all its freshman year courses as MOOCs. Students will pay $200 per credit but will be charged only after they have passed a course.

Early results for MOOCs have been mixed. Although some students do well in online courses, dropout rates tend to be higher than for traditional courses. In MOOCs with large enrollments, instructors cannot interact with individual students. And not all instructors are comfortable with the new technology. A major challenge that universities need to meet is determining how to evaluate student learning when traditional testing methods can't be used. But the cost advantages of online instruction suggest that it will not be a passing fad.

In this chapter, we will analyze the types of costs involved in the production of a good or service and see how those costs affect how firms operate.

Sources: Tamar Lewin, "Promising Full College Credit, Arizona State University Offers Online Freshman Program," *New York Times*, April 22, 2015; "Massive Open Online Forces," *Economist*, February 8, 2014; and "The Digital Degree," *Economist*," June 28, 2014.

Economics in Your Life

Using Cost Concepts in Your Online Business

Suppose you are considering starting a Web site to sell iPhone cases online. You locate a Taiwanese manufacturer who will sell you the cases for $10 each. Your friend José already is running such a site, and you plan to buy the same computers and software that José uses. Like José, you intend to rent a small building in an industrial park where you can have an office and storage space for your inventory. You plan to sell the cases for $15. You find out that José is selling more cases per month than you expect to sell and that he is selling them for only $13. You wonder how José makes a profit at the lower price. As José sells more cases per month, will his firm's costs be lower than your firm's costs? As you read the chapter, see if you can answer this question. You can check your answers against those we provide on **page 384** at the end of this chapter.

In Chapter 10, we looked behind the demand curve to better understand consumer decision making. In this chapter, we look behind the supply curve to better understand firm decision making. Earlier chapters showed that supply curves are upward sloping because marginal cost increases as firms increase the quantity of a good that they supply. In this chapter, we look more closely at why this is true. In the appendix to this chapter, we extend the analysis by using isoquants and isocost lines to understand the relationship between production and costs. Once we have a good understanding of production and cost, we can proceed in the following chapters to understand how firms decide what level of output to produce and what price to charge.

11.1 Technology: An Economic Definition

LEARNING OBJECTIVE: Define technology and give examples of technological change.

Technology The processes a firm uses to turn inputs into outputs of goods and services.

Technological change A change in the ability of a firm to produce a given level of output with a given quantity of inputs.

The basic activity of a firm is to use *inputs*, such as workers, machines, and natural resources, to produce *outputs* of goods and services. A pizza parlor, for example, uses inputs such as pizza dough, pizza sauce, cooks, and ovens to produce pizza. A firm's **technology** is the processes it uses to turn inputs into outputs of goods and services. Notice that this economic definition of technology is broader than the everyday definition. When we use the word *technology* in everyday language, we usually refer only to the development of new products. In the economic sense, a firm's technology depends on many factors, such as the skills of its managers, the training of its workers, and the speed and efficiency of its machinery and equipment. A pizza parlor's technology of pizza production, for example, includes not only the capacity of its pizza ovens and how quickly they bake the pizza but also how quickly the cooks can prepare the pizza for baking and how well the firm's manager motivates the workers and arranges the facilities to allow the cooks to quickly prepare the pizzas and get them in the ovens.

Whenever a firm experiences positive **technological change**, it is able to produce more output using the same inputs or the same output using fewer inputs. Positive technological change can come from many sources. A firm's managers may rearrange the factory floor or the layout of a retail store in order to increase production and sales. The firm's workers may go through a training program. The firm may install faster or more reliable machinery or equipment. It is also possible for a firm to experience negative technological change. If a firm, for example, hires less-skilled workers or if a hurricane damages its facilities, the quantity of output it can produce from a given quantity of inputs may decline.

MyEconLab Concept Check

Making the Connection

MyEconLab Video

UPS Uses Technology to Deal with a Surge in Holiday Packages

After struggling with a high volume of packages, UPS adopted new technology to deliver more packages with the same number of workers and planes.

Christmas 2013 was not the season of joy at United Parcel Services (UPS). For decades, most of the company's business was shipping packages from one company to another. But with the rise of e-commerce sites such as Amazon starting in the late 1990s, the volume of packages being shipped to homes has greatly increased. Most shipments to homes consist of a single package, which makes delivery more costly than to businesses, where each shipment typically consists of multiple packages. During the holiday season, competition among Internet sellers, including Amazon, Walmart, and Target, has led them to guarantee deliveries by Christmas Eve, even on orders received as late as December 23. Although UPS—like its rival, FedEx—promised the sellers that it would be able to make the deliveries, in fact it failed to deliver millions of packages until Christmas morning or later. Parents had some explaining to do to their disappointed children … and UPS managers had some explaining to do to Amazon and other Internet sellers.

To ensure that they met their commitments during the next holiday season, UPS managers could have hired more workers and purchased more airplanes. Although UPS does temporarily increase its hiring each December, doing so raises its costs. If the company bought more planes, they would sit unused during most of the year because fewer than half as many packages are delivered in other months as are delivered in December. UPS delivers more than 30 million packages on December 22 alone. Instead of continually increasing the number of workers and planes, UPS decided to use technology to allow it to deliver more packages with the same number of workers and planes.

Some of the new technology took the form of new equipment. Previously, employees in UPS sorting facilities needed to memorize more than 100 zip codes in order to know which chute to send a package down on its way to being deposited in a truck or plane. The new equipment scans a package and instantly tells the worker in which color-coded chute to place the package. This equipment allows UPS workers to process 15 percent more packages per day.

Other changes at UPS involved no new equipment but were instead improvements in the way packages were routed. The firm started using more detailed maps to plan the routes for packages. As a result, the typical delivery driver could travel fewer miles per day while delivering more packages. UPS also began taking better account of weather forecasts to avoid delays in flying packages. These improvements in handling packages meet the economic definition of positive technological change because they allow the firm to produce a larger output—more packages delivered—with the same amount of inputs—workers, planes, and other equipment.

Harnessing technological change can allow firms to reduce costs and better compete against other firms in their industry. In this case, UPS is using technology to make profitable the large volume of e-commerce packages the company delivers to homes.

Sources: Laura Stevens, "UPS Reports Higher Earnings," *Wall Street Journal*, April 28, 2015; Laura Stevens, "A Test for UPS: One Day, 34 Million Packages," *Wall Street Journal*, December 21, 2014; and Elizabeth A. Harris and Vindu Goel, "After Carriers Falter, Questions for Web Shopping," *New York Times*, December 26, 2013.

Your Turn: Test your understanding by doing related problem 1.5 on page 386 at the end of this chapter.

MyEconLab Study Plan

11.2 The Short Run and the Long Run in Economics

LEARNING OBJECTIVE: Distinguish between the economic short run and the economic long run.

When firms analyze the relationship between their level of production and their costs, they separate the time period involved into the short run and the long run. In the **short run**, at least one of the firm's inputs is fixed. In particular, in the short run, the firm's technology and the size of its physical plant—its factory, store, or office—are both fixed, while the number of workers the firm hires is variable. In the **long run**, the firm is able to vary all its inputs and can adopt new technology and increase or decrease the size of its physical plant.

Short run The period of time during which at least one of a firm's inputs is fixed.

Long run The period of time in which a firm can vary all its inputs, adopt new technology, and increase or decrease the size of its physical plant.

The actual length of calendar time before the short run becomes the long run differs from firm to firm. A pizza parlor may have a short run of just a few weeks before it is able to increase its physical plant by adding another pizza oven and some tables and chairs. General Motors, in contrast, may have a short run of a year or more before it can increase the capacity of one of its automobile assembly plants by installing new equipment.

The Difference between Fixed Costs and Variable Costs

Total cost is the cost of all the inputs a firm uses in production. We have just seen that in the short run, some inputs are fixed and others are variable. The costs of the fixed inputs are called *fixed costs*, and the costs of the variable inputs are called *variable costs*. We can also think of **variable costs** as the costs that change as output changes. Similarly, **fixed costs** are costs that remain constant as output changes. A typical firm's variable costs include its labor costs, raw material costs, and costs of electricity and other utilities. Typical fixed costs include lease payments for factory or retail space, payments for

Total cost The cost of all the inputs a firm uses in production.

Variable costs Costs that change as output changes.

Fixed costs Costs that remain constant as output changes.

fire insurance, and payments for online and television advertising. All of a firm's costs are either fixed or variable, so we can state the following:

$$\text{Total cost} = \text{Fixed cost} + \text{Variable cost}$$

or, using symbols:

$$TC = FC + VC.$$

MyEconLab Concept Check

Making the Connection

MyEconLab Video

The wages of this worker are a variable cost to the printer who employs him.

Fixed Costs in the Publishing Industry

An editor at Cambridge University Press gives the following estimates of the annual fixed cost for a medium-size academic book publisher:

Cost	Amount
Salaries and benefits	$625,000
Rent	75,000
Utilities	20,000
Supplies	6,000
Postage	5,000
Travel	9,000
Subscriptions, etc.	5,000
Miscellaneous	5,000
Total	$750,000

Academic book publishers hire editors, designers, and production and marketing managers who help prepare books for publication. Because these employees work on several books simultaneously, the number of people the company hires does not go up and down with the quantity of books the company publishes during any particular year. Publishing companies therefore consider the salaries and benefits of people in these job categories to be fixed costs.

In contrast, for a company that *prints* books, the quantity of workers varies with the quantity of books printed. The wages and benefits of the workers operating the printing presses, for example, would be a variable cost.

The other costs listed in the table are typical of fixed costs at many firms.

Source: *Handbook for Academic Authors*, 5th edition, by Beth Lucy. Copyright © 2010 by Cambridge University Press. Reprinted by permission.

MyEconLab Study Plan

Your Turn: Test your understanding by doing related problems 2.6, 2.7, and 2.8 on page 387 at the end of this chapter.

Implicit Costs versus Explicit Costs

Opportunity cost The highest-valued alternative that must be given up to engage in an activity.

Explicit cost A cost that involves spending money.

Implicit cost A nonmonetary opportunity cost.

Remember that economists always measure cost as **opportunity cost**, which is the highest-valued alternative that must be given up to engage in an activity. As we saw in Chapter 8, costs are either *explicit* or *implicit*. When a firm spends money, it incurs an **explicit cost**. When a firm experiences a nonmonetary opportunity cost, it incurs an **implicit cost**.

For example, suppose that Jill Johnson owns a pizza restaurant. Her explicit costs include the wages she pays her workers and the payments she makes for rent and electricity. But some of Jill's most important costs are implicit. Before opening her own restaurant, Jill earned a salary of $30,000 per year managing a restaurant for someone else. To start her restaurant, Jill quit her job, withdrew $50,000 from her bank account—where it earned her interest of $3,000 per year—and used the funds to equip her restaurant with tables, chairs, a cash register, and other equipment. To open her own business, Jill had to give up the $30,000 salary and the $3,000 in interest. This $33,000 is an implicit cost because it does not represent payments that Jill has to make. Nevertheless, giving up this $33,000 per year is a real cost to Jill.

Table 11.1

Jill Johnson's Costs per Year

Jill's Costs	Amount
Pizza dough, tomato sauce, and other ingredients	$20,000
Wages	48,000
Interest payments on loan to buy pizza ovens	10,000
Electricity	6,000
Lease payment for store	24,000
Forgone salary	30,000
Forgone interest	3,000
Economic depreciation	10,000
Total	**$151,000**

In addition, during the course of the year, the $50,000 worth of tables, chairs, and other physical capital in Jill's store will lose some of its value partly due to wear and tear and partly due to better furniture, cash registers, and so forth, becoming available. *Economic depreciation* is the difference between what Jill paid for her capital at the beginning of the year and what she would receive if she sold the capital at the end of the year. If Jill could sell the capital for $40,000 at the end of the year, the $10,000 in economic depreciation represents another implicit cost. (Note that the whole $50,000 she spent on the capital is not a cost because she still has the equipment at the end of the year, although it is now worth only $40,000.)

Table 11.1 lists Jill's costs. The entries in red are explicit costs, and the entries in blue are implicit costs. The rules of accounting generally require that only explicit costs be used for purposes of keeping the company's financial records and for paying taxes (see Chapter 8). Therefore, explicit costs are sometimes called *accounting costs*. *Economic costs* include both accounting costs and implicit costs. MyEconLab Concept Check

The Production Function

Let's look at the relationship in the short run between Jill Johnson's level of production and her costs. We can simplify the situation in Table 11.1 by assuming that Jill uses only labor—workers—and one type of capital—pizza ovens—to produce a single good: pizzas. Many firms use more than two inputs and produce more than one good, but it is easier to understand the relationship between output and cost by focusing on the case of a firm using only two inputs and producing only one good. In the short run, Jill doesn't have time to build a larger restaurant, install additional pizza ovens, or redesign the layout of her restaurant. So, in the short run, she can increase or decrease the quantity of pizzas she produces only by increasing or decreasing the number of workers she employs.

The first three columns of Table 11.2 show the relationship between the quantity of workers and ovens Jill uses per week and the quantity of pizzas she can produce.

Table 11.2

Short-Run Production and Cost at Jill Johnson's Restaurant

Quantity of Workers	Quantity of Pizza Ovens	Quantity of Pizzas per Week	Cost of Pizza Ovens (Fixed Cost)	Cost of Workers (Variable Cost)	Total Cost of Pizzas per Week	Cost per Pizza (Average Total Cost)
0	2	0	$800	$0	$800	—
1	2	200	800	650	1,450	$7.25
2	2	450	800	1,300	2,100	4.67
3	2	550	800	1,950	2,750	5.00
4	2	600	800	2,600	3,400	5.67
5	2	625	800	3,250	4,050	6.48
6	2	640	800	3,900	4,700	7.34

Production function The relationship between the inputs employed by a firm and the maximum output it can produce with those inputs.

The relationship between the inputs employed by a firm and the maximum output it can produce with those inputs is called the firm's **production function**. Because a firm's technology is the processes it uses to turn inputs into output, the production function represents the firm's technology. The first three columns of Table 11.2 show Jill's *short-run* production function because we are assuming that the time period is too short for Jill to increase or decrease the quantity of ovens she is using. MyEconLab Concept Check

A First Look at the Relationship between Production and Cost

Average total cost Total cost divided by the quantity of output produced.

Table 11.2 shows Jill Johnson's costs. We can determine the total cost of producing a given quantity of pizzas if we know how many workers and ovens are required to produce that quantity and how much Jill has to pay for those workers and ovens. Suppose Jill has taken out a bank loan to buy two pizza ovens. The cost of the loan is $800 per week. Therefore, her fixed costs are $800 per week. If Jill pays $650 per week to each worker, her variable costs depend on how many workers she hires. In the short run, Jill can increase the quantity of pizzas she produces only by hiring more workers. Table 11.2 shows that if she hires 1 worker, she produces 200 pizzas during the week; if she hires 2 workers, she produces 450 pizzas; and so on. For a particular week, Jill's total cost of producing pizzas is equal to the $800 she pays on the loan for the ovens plus the amount she pays to hire workers. If Jill decides to hire 4 workers and produce 600 pizzas, her total cost is $3,400: $800 to lease the ovens and $2,600 to hire the workers. Her cost per pizza is equal to her total cost of producing pizzas divided by the quantity of pizzas produced. If she produces 600 pizzas at a total cost of $3,400, her cost per pizza, or *average total cost*, is $3,400/600 = $5.67. A firm's **average total cost** is always equal to its total cost divided by the quantity of output produced.

Panel (a) of Figure 11.1 uses the numbers in the next-to-last column of Table 11.2 to graph Jill's total cost. Panel (b) uses the numbers in the last column to graph her average

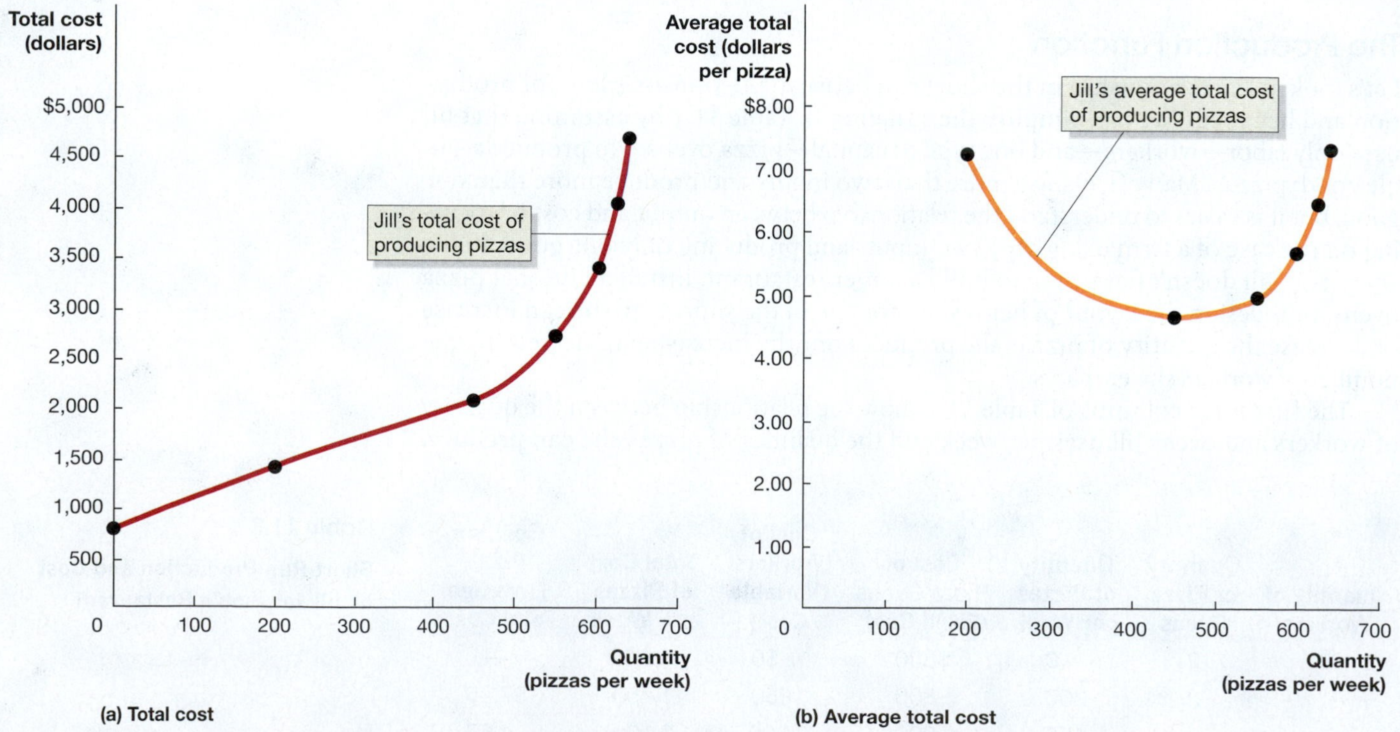

MyEconLab Animation

Figure 11.1 Graphing Total Cost and Average Total Cost at Jill Johnson's Restaurant

We can use the information from Table 11.2 to graph the relationship between the quantity of pizzas Jill produces and her total cost and average total cost. Panel (a) shows that total cost increases as the level of production increases. Panel (b) shows that her average total cost is roughly U shaped: As production increases from low levels, average total cost falls, before rising at higher levels of production.

total cost. Notice in panel (b) that Jill's average cost curve has a roughly U shape. As production increases from low levels, average total cost falls. Average total cost then becomes fairly flat, before rising at higher levels of production. To understand why average total cost curve has this U shape, we first need to look more closely at the technology of producing pizzas, as shown by the production function for Jill's restaurant. Then we need to look at how this technology determines the relationship between production and cost. MyEconLab Concept Check

MyEconLab Study Plan

11.3 The Marginal Product of Labor and the Average Product of Labor

LEARNING OBJECTIVE: Understand the relationship between the marginal product of labor and the average product of labor.

To better understand the choices Jill faces, given the technology available to her, think first about what happens if she hires only one worker. That one worker will have to perform several different activities, including taking orders from customers, baking the pizzas, bringing the pizzas to the customers' tables, and ringing up sales on the cash register. If Jill hires two workers, some of these activities can be divided up: One worker could take the orders and ring up the sales, and one worker could bake the pizzas. With such a division of tasks, Jill will find that hiring two workers actually allows her to produce more than twice as many pizzas as she could produce with just one worker.

The additional output a firm produces as a result of hiring one more worker is called the **marginal product of labor**. We can calculate the marginal product of labor by determining how much total output increases as each additional worker is hired, which we do for Jill's restaurant in Table 11.3.

Marginal product of labor The additional output a firm produces as a result of hiring one more worker.

When Jill hires only one worker, she increases output from 0 pizzas to 200 pizzas per week. So, the marginal product of labor for the first worker is 200 pizzas. When she hires two workers, she produces 450 pizzas per week. Hiring the second worker increases her output by 250 pizzas per week. For the second worker, the marginal product of labor rises to 250 pizzas. This increase in marginal product results from the *division of labor* and from *specialization*. By dividing the tasks to be performed—the division of labor—Jill reduces the time workers lose moving from one activity to the next. She also allows them to become more specialized at their tasks. For example, a worker who concentrates on baking pizzas will become skilled at doing so quickly and efficiently.

The Law of Diminishing Returns

In the short run, the quantity of pizza ovens Jill leases is fixed, so as she hires more workers, the marginal product of labor eventually begins to decline. At some point, Jill uses up all the gains from the division of labor and from specialization and starts to experience the effects of the **law of diminishing returns**. This law states that adding more of a variable input, such as labor, to the same amount of a fixed input, such as capital, will eventually cause the marginal product of the variable input to decline. For Jill, the marginal product of labor begins to decline when she hires the third worker.

Law of diminishing returns The principle that, at some point, adding more of a variable input, such as labor, to the same amount of a fixed input, such as capital, will cause the marginal product of the variable input to decline.

Table 11.3

The Marginal Product of Labor at Jill Johnson's Restaurant

Quantity of Workers	Quantity of Pizza Ovens	Quantity of Pizzas	Marginal Product of Labor
0	2	0	—
1	2	200	200
2	2	450	250
3	2	550	100
4	2	600	50
5	2	625	25
6	2	640	15

Hiring three workers raises the quantity of pizzas she produces from 450 per week to 550. But the increase in the quantity of pizzas—100—is less than the increase when she hired the second worker—250—so the marginal product of labor has declined.

If Jill kept adding more and more workers to the same quantity of pizza ovens, workers would eventually begin to get in each other's way, and the marginal product of labor would actually become negative. When the marginal product is negative, the level of total output declines. No firm would actually hire so many workers as to experience a negative marginal product of labor and falling total output. MyEconLab Concept Check

Graphing Production

Panel (a) in Figure 11.2 graphs the relationship between the quantity of workers Jill hires and her total output of pizzas, using the numbers from Table 11.3. Panel (b) graphs the marginal product of labor. In panel (a), output increases as more workers are hired, but

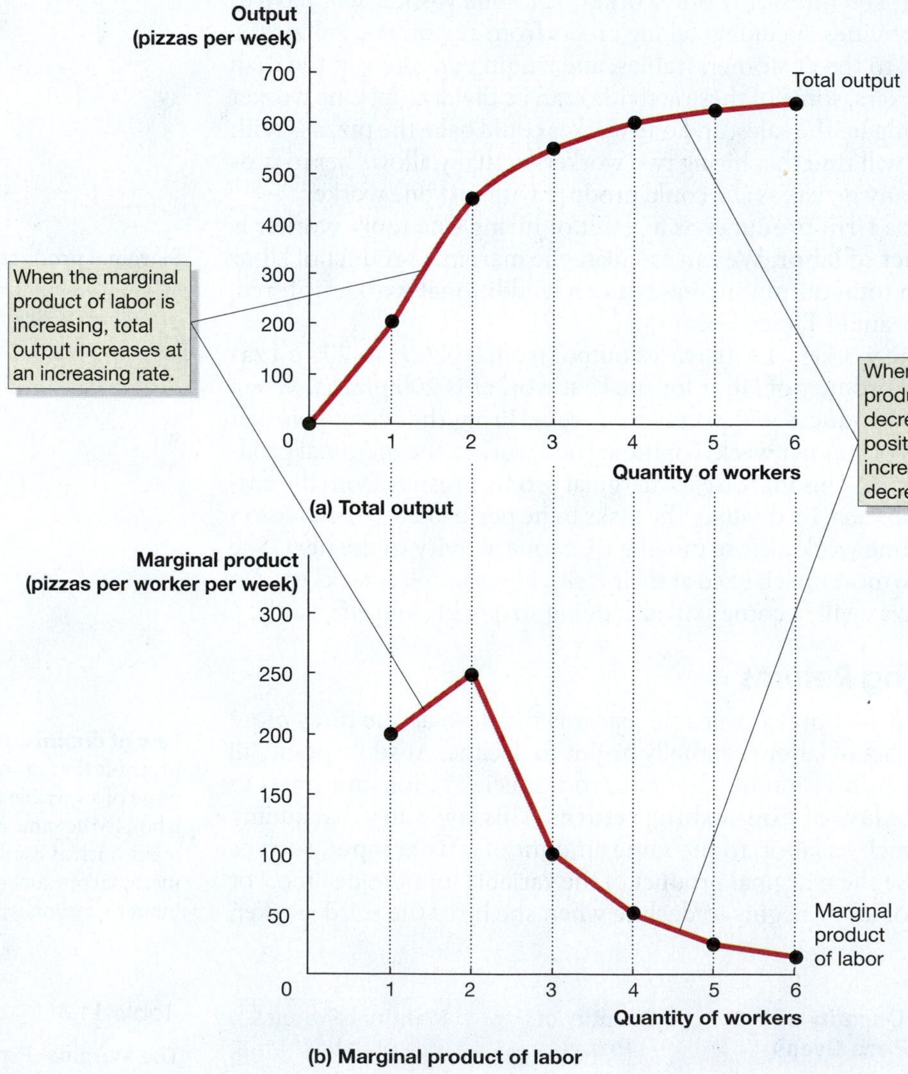

MyEconLab Animation

Figure 11.2 Total Output and the Marginal Product of Labor

In panel (a), output increases as more workers are hired, but the increase in output does not occur at a constant rate. Because of specialization and the division of labor, output at first increases at an increasing rate, with each additional worker hired causing production to increase by a *greater* amount than did the hiring of the previous worker. When the point of diminishing returns is reached, production increases at a decreasing rate. Each additional worker Jill hires after the second worker causes production to increase by a *smaller* amount than did the hiring of the previous worker. In panel (b), the *marginal product of labor* is the additional output produced as a result of hiring one more worker. The marginal product of labor rises initially because of the effects of specialization and division of labor, and then it falls because of the effects of diminishing returns.

the increase in output does not occur at a constant rate. Because of specialization and the division of labor, output at first increases at an increasing rate, with each additional worker hired causing production to increase by a *larger* amount than did the hiring of the previous worker. But after the second worker has been hired, hiring more workers while keeping the quantity of ovens constant results in diminishing returns. When the point of diminishing returns is reached, production increases at a decreasing rate. Each additional worker Jill hires after the second worker causes production to increase by a *smaller* amount than did the hiring of the previous worker. In panel (b), the marginal product of labor curve rises initially because of the effects of specialization and the division of labor, and then it falls because of the effects of diminishing returns. MyEconLab Concept Check

Making the Connection
MyEconLab Video

Adam Smith's Famous Account of the Division of Labor in a Pin Factory

The Wealth of Nations, written in Scotland by Adam Smith in 1776, is the first book to have discussed some of the key ideas of economics. Smith considered the concept of the division of labor important enough to discuss in the first chapter of the book. He illustrated the concept by using an example of a pin factory. The following is an excerpt from his account of how pin making was divided into a series of tasks:

> One man draws out the wire, another straightens it, a third cuts it, a fourth points it, a fifth grinds it at the top for receiving the head; to make the head requires two or three distinct operations; to put it on is a … [distinct operation], to whiten the pins is another; it is even a trade by itself to put them into the paper; and the important business of making a pin is, in this manner, divided into eighteen distinct operations.

Because the labor of pin making was divided up in this way, an average worker was able to produce about 4,800 pins per day. Smith estimated that a single worker using the pin-making machinery by himself would make only about 20 pins per day. This lesson from 240 years ago, showing the tremendous gains from the division of labor and specialization, remains relevant to most business situations today.

Source: Adam Smith, *An Inquiry into the Nature and Causes of the Wealth of Nations*, Vol. I, Oxford, UK: Oxford University Press, 1976 (originally published 1776), pp. 14–15.

The gains from division of labor and specialization are as important to firms today as they were in the eighteenth century, when Adam Smith first discussed them.

Your Turn: Test your understanding by doing related problem 3.7 on page 388 at the end of this chapter.

MyEconLab Study Plan

The Relationship between Marginal Product and Average Product

The marginal product of labor tells us how much total output changes as the quantity of workers hired changes. We can also calculate the average quantity of pizzas workers produce. The **average product of labor** is the total output produced by a firm divided by the quantity of workers. For example, using the numbers in Table 11.3, if Jill hires 4 workers to produce 600 pizzas, the average product of labor is 600/4 = 150.

Average product of labor The total output produced by a firm divided by the quantity of workers.

We can state the relationship between the marginal and average products of labor this way: *The average product of labor is the average of the marginal products of labor.* For example, the numbers from Table 11.3 show that the marginal product of the first worker Jill hires is 200, the marginal product of the second worker is 250, and the marginal product of the third worker is 100. Therefore, the average product of labor for three workers is 183.3:

$$183.3 = (200 + 250 + 100) / 3$$

- 183.3: Average product of labor for three workers
- 200: Marginal product of labor of first worker
- 250: Marginal product of labor of second worker
- 100: Marginal product of labor of third worker

By taking the average of the marginal products of the first three workers, we have the average product of the three workers.

Whenever the marginal product of labor is greater than the average product of labor, the average product of labor must be increasing. This statement is true for the same reason that a person 6 feet, 2 inches tall entering a room where the average height is 5 feet, 9 inches raises the average height of people in the room. Whenever the marginal product of labor is less than the average product of labor, the average product of labor must be decreasing. The marginal product of labor equals the average product of labor at the quantity of workers for which the average product of labor is at its maximum. MyEconLab Concept Check

An Example of Marginal and Average Values: College Grades

The relationship between the marginal product of labor and the average product of labor is the same as the relationship between the marginal and average values of any variable. To see this point more clearly, think about the familiar relationship between a student's grade point average (GPA) in one semester and his overall, or cumulative, GPA. The table in Figure 11.3 shows Paul's college grades for each semester, beginning

MyEconLab Animation

Figure 11.3

Marginal and Average GPAs

The relationship between marginal and average values for a variable can be illustrated using GPAs. We can calculate the GPA Paul earns in a particular semester (his "marginal GPA"), and we can calculate his cumulative GPA for all the semesters he has completed so far (his "average GPA"). Paul's GPA is only 1.50 in the fall semester of his first year. In each following semester through the fall of his junior year, his GPA for the semester increases—raising his cumulative GPA. In Paul's junior year, even though his semester GPA declines from fall to spring, his cumulative GPA rises. Only in the fall of his senior year, when his semester GPA drops below his cumulative GPA, does his cumulative GPA decline.

	Semester GPA (marginal GPA)	Cumulative GPA (average GPA)
First year		
Fall	1.50	1.50
Spring	2.00	1.75
Sophomore year		
Fall	2.20	1.90
Spring	3.00	2.18
Junior year		
Fall	3.20	2.38
Spring	3.00	2.48
Senior year		
Fall	2.40	2.47
Spring	2.00	2.41

Average GPA continues to rise, although marginal GPA falls.

With the marginal GPA below the average, the average GPA falls.

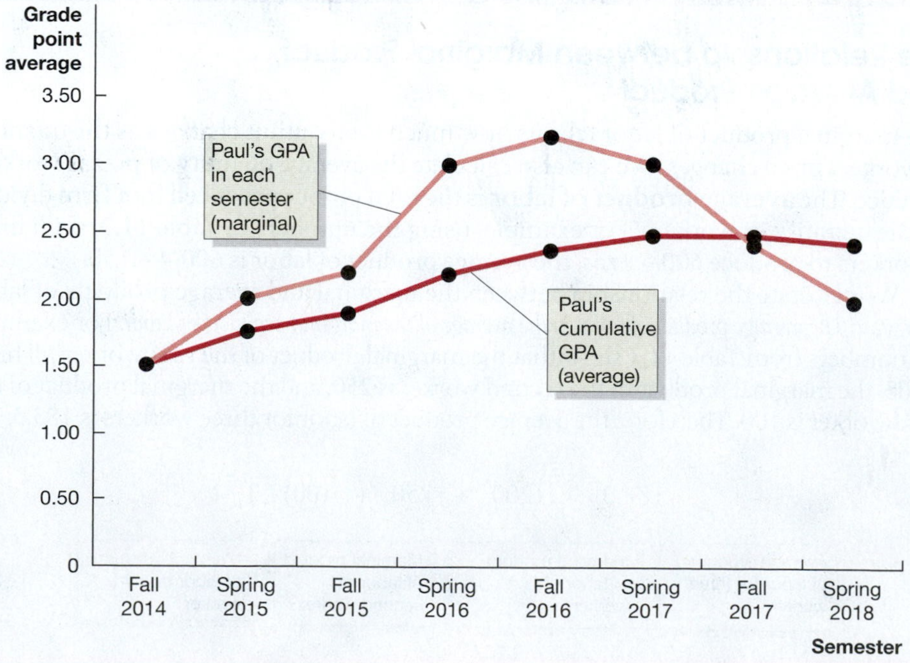

with fall of his first year. The graph in Figure 11.3 plots the grades from the table. Just as each additional worker hired adds to a firm's total production, each additional semester adds to Paul's total grade points. We can calculate what hiring each individual worker adds to total production (marginal product), and we can calculate the average production of the workers hired so far (average product).

Similarly, we can calculate the GPA Paul earns in a particular semester (his "marginal GPA"), and we can calculate his cumulative GPA for all the semesters he has completed so far (his "average GPA"). As the table shows, Paul gets off to a weak start in the fall semester of his first year, earning only a 1.50 GPA. In each subsequent semester through the fall of his junior year, his GPA for the semester increases from the previous semester—raising his cumulative GPA. As the graph shows, however, his cumulative GPA does not increase as rapidly as his semester-by-semester GPA because his cumulative GPA is held back by the low GPAs of his first few semesters. Notice that in Paul's junior year, even though his semester GPA declines from fall to spring, his cumulative GPA rises. Only in the fall of his senior year, when his semester GPA drops below his cumulative GPA, does his cumulative GPA decline. MyEconLab Concept Check

MyEconLab Study Plan

11.4 The Relationship between Short-Run Production and Short-Run Cost

LEARNING OBJECTIVE: Explain and illustrate the relationship between marginal cost and average total cost.

We have seen that technology determines the values of the marginal product of labor and the average product of labor. In turn, the marginal and average products of labor affect the firm's costs. Keep in mind that the relationships we are discussing are *short-run* relationships: We are assuming that the time period is too short for the firm to change its technology or the size of its physical plant.

The average total cost curve in panel (b) of Figure 11.1 on page 370 for Jill Johnson's restaurant has a U shape. As we will soon see, the U shape of the average total cost curve is determined by the shape of the curve that shows the relationship between *marginal cost* and the level of production.

Marginal Cost

One of the key ideas in economics is that optimal decisions are made at the margin (see Chapter 1). Consumers, firms, and government officials usually make decisions about doing a little more or a little less. As Jill Johnson considers whether to hire additional workers to produce additional pizzas, she needs to consider how much she will add to her total cost by producing the additional pizzas. **Marginal cost** is the change in a firm's total cost from producing one more unit of a good or service. We can calculate marginal cost for a particular increase in output by dividing the change in total cost by the change in output. We can express this idea mathematically (remember that the Greek letter delta, Δ, means, "change in"):

Marginal cost The change in a firm's total cost from producing one more unit of a good or service.

$$MC = \frac{\Delta TC}{\Delta Q}.$$

In the table in Figure 11.4, we use this equation to calculate Jill's marginal cost of producing pizzas. The other values in the table are from Table 11.2 and Table 11.3.

MyEconLab Concept Check

Why Are the Marginal and Average Cost Curves U Shaped?

Notice in the graph in Figure 11.4 that Jill's marginal cost of producing pizzas declines at first and then increases, giving the marginal cost curve a U shape. The table in Figure 11.4 also shows the marginal product of labor. This table helps us understand the important relationship between the marginal product of labor and the marginal cost of production:

- The marginal product of labor is *rising* for the first two workers, but the marginal cost of the pizzas produced by these workers is *falling*.

MyEconLab Animation

Figure 11.4

Jill Johnson's Marginal Cost and Average Total Cost of Producing Pizzas

We can use the information in the table to calculate Jill's marginal cost and average total cost of producing pizzas. For the first two workers hired, the marginal product of labor is increasing, which causes the marginal cost of production to fall. For the last four workers hired, the marginal product of labor is falling, which causes the marginal cost of production to increase. Therefore, the marginal cost curve falls and then rises—that is, has a U shape—because the marginal product of labor rises and then falls. As long as marginal cost is below average total cost, average total cost will be falling. When marginal cost is above average total cost, average total cost will be rising. The relationship between marginal cost and average total cost explains why the average total cost curve also has a U shape.

Quantity of Workers	Quantity of Pizzas	Marginal Product of Labor	Total Cost of Pizzas	Marginal Cost of Pizzas	Average Total Cost of Pizzas
0	0	–	$800	–	–
1	200	200	1,450	$3.25	$7.25
2	450	250	2,100	2.60	4.67
3	550	100	2,750	6.50	5.00
4	600	50	3,400	13.00	5.67
5	625	25	4,050	26.00	6.48
6	640	15	4,700	43.33	7.34

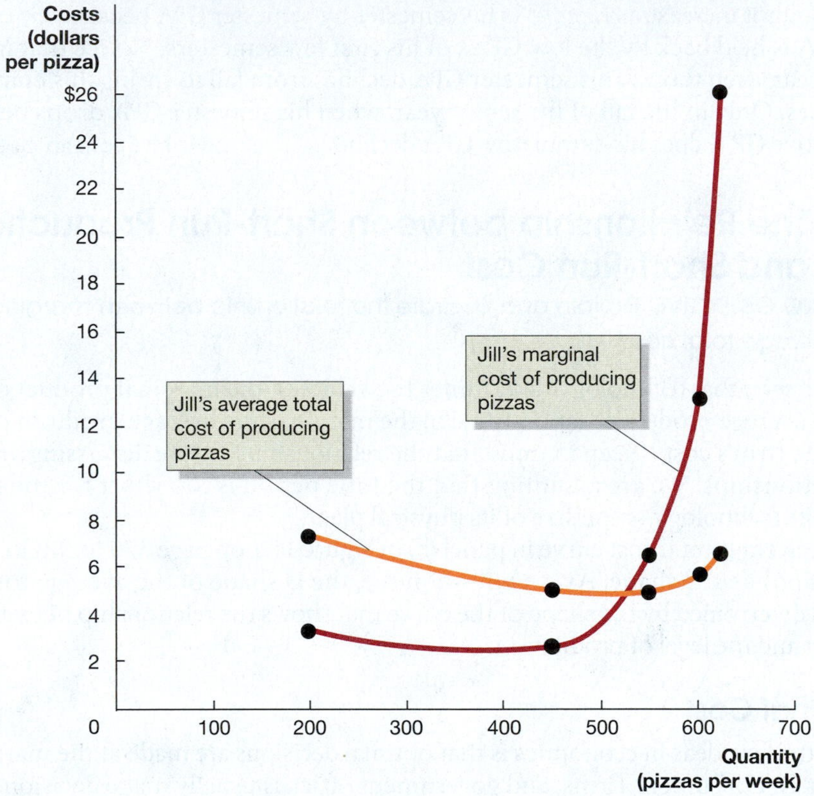

- The marginal product of labor is *falling* for the last four workers, but the marginal cost of pizzas produced by these workers is *rising*.

We can generalize what the table shows us: *When the marginal product of labor is rising, the marginal cost of output is falling. When the marginal product of labor is falling, the marginal cost of output is rising.*

One way to understand the relationship between the marginal product of labor and the marginal cost of output is to notice that the only additional cost to Jill from producing more pizzas is the additional wages she pays to hire more workers. She pays each new worker the same $650 per week. So the marginal cost of the additional pizzas each worker makes depends on that worker's additional output, or marginal product. As long as the additional output from each new worker is rising, the marginal cost of that output is falling. When the additional output from each new worker is falling, the marginal cost of that output is rising. *We can conclude that the marginal cost of output falls and then rises—forming a U shape—because the marginal product of labor rises and then falls.*

The relationship between marginal cost and average total cost follows the usual relationship between marginal and average values. As long as marginal cost is below average total cost, average total cost falls. When marginal cost is above average total cost, average total cost rises. Marginal cost equals average total cost when average total cost is at its lowest point. Therefore, the average total cost curve has a U shape because the marginal cost curve has a U shape. MyEconLab Concept Check

Solved Problem 11.4

MyEconLab Interactive Animation

Calculating Marginal Cost and Average Cost

Santiago Delgado owns a copier store. He leases two copy machines for which he pays $12.50 each per day. He cannot increase the number of machines he leases without giving the office machine company six weeks' notice. He can hire as many workers as he wants, at a cost of $50 per day per worker. These are the only two inputs he uses to produce copies.

a. Fill in the remaining columns in the table by using the definitions of costs.

b. Draw the average total cost curve and marginal cost curve for Santiago's store. Do these curves have the expected shape? Briefly explain.

Quantity of Workers	Quantity of Copies per Day	Fixed Cost	Variable Cost	Total Cost	Average Total Cost	Marginal Cost
0	0					
1	625					
2	1,325					
3	2,200					
4	2,600					
5	2,900					
6	3,100					

Solving the Problem

Step 1: Review the chapter material. This problem requires you to understand definitions of costs, so you may want to review the section "The Difference between Fixed Costs and Variable Costs," which begins on page 367, and the section "Why Are the Marginal and Average Cost Curves U Shaped?" which begins on page 375.

Step 2: Answer part (a) by using the definitions of costs. Santiago's fixed cost is the amount he pays to lease the copy machines. He uses two copy machines and pays $12.50 each to lease them, so his fixed cost is $25. Santiago's variable cost is the amount he pays to hire workers. He pays $50 per worker per day. His total cost is the sum of his fixed cost and his variable cost. His average total cost is his total cost divided by the quantity of copies he produces that day. His marginal cost is the change in total cost divided by the change in output. For example, his marginal cost of producing 1,325 copies per day, rather than 625 copies, is:

$$MC = (\$125 - \$75)/(1{,}325 - 625) = \$0.07.$$

Quantity of Workers	Quantity of Copies per Day	Fixed Cost	Variable Cost	Total Cost	Average Total Cost	Marginal Cost
0	0	$25	$0	$25	—	—
1	625	25	50	75	$0.12	$0.08
2	1,325	25	100	125	0.09	0.07
3	2,200	25	150	175	0.08	0.06
4	2,600	25	200	225	0.09	0.13
5	2,900	25	250	275	0.09	0.17
6	3,100	25	300	325	0.10	0.25

Step 3: Answer part (b) by drawing the average total cost and marginal cost curves for Santiago's store and by explaining whether they have the usual shape. Use the numbers from the table to draw your graph:

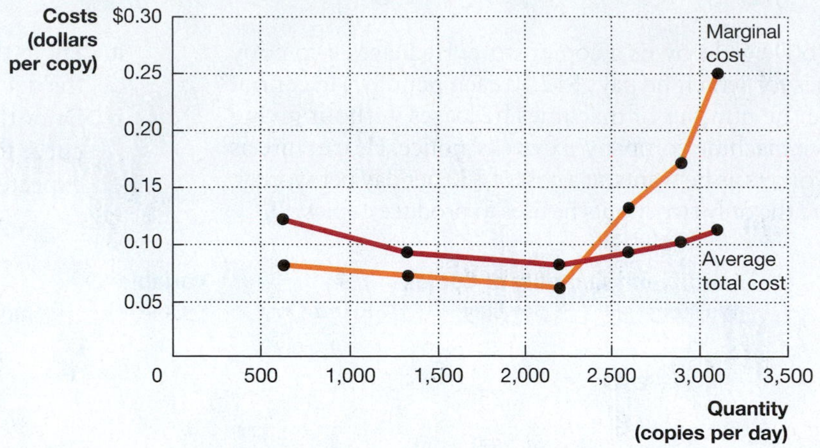

We expect average total cost and marginal cost curves to have a U shape, which Santiago's cost curves do. Both cost curves fall and then rise in the same way as the cost curves in Figure 11.4 on page 376.

MyEconLab Study Plan

Your Turn: For more practice, do related problem 4.7 on page 389 at the end of this chapter.

11.5 Graphing Cost Curves

LEARNING OBJECTIVE: Graph average total cost, average variable cost, average fixed cost, and marginal cost.

Average fixed cost Fixed cost divided by the quantity of output produced.

Average variable cost Variable cost divided by the quantity of output produced.

We have seen that we calculate average total cost by dividing total cost by the quantity of output produced. Similarly, we can calculate **average fixed cost** by dividing fixed cost by the quantity of output produced. And we can calculate **average variable cost** by dividing variable cost by the quantity of output produced. We can present these three measures of cost mathematically (with Q representing the level of output) as:

$$\text{Average total cost} = ATC = \frac{TC}{Q}$$

$$\text{Average fixed cost} = AFC = \frac{FC}{Q}$$

$$\text{Average variable cost} = AVC = \frac{VC}{Q}$$

Finally, notice that average total cost is the sum of average fixed cost plus average variable cost:

$$ATC = AFC + AVC.$$

The only fixed cost Jill incurs in operating her restaurant is the $800 per week she pays on the bank loan for her pizza ovens. Her variable costs are the wages she pays her workers. The table and graph in Figure 11.5 show Jill's costs.

We will use graphs like the one in Figure 11.5 in the next several chapters to analyze how firms decide the level of output to produce and the price to charge. Before going further, be sure you understand the following three key facts about Figure 11.5:

1. The marginal cost (*MC*), average total cost (*ATC*), and average variable cost (*AVC*) curves are all U shaped, and the marginal cost curve intersects both the average

Quantity of Workers	Quantity of Ovens	Quantity of Pizzas	Cost of Ovens (fixed cost)	Cost of Workers (variable cost)	Total Cost of Pizzas	*ATC*	*AFC*	*AVC*	*MC*
0	2	0	$800	$0	$800	–	–	–	–
1	2	200	800	650	1,450	$7.25	$4.00	$3.25	$3.25
2	2	450	800	1,300	2,100	4.67	1.78	2.89	2.60
3	2	550	800	1,950	2,750	5.00	1.45	3.54	6.50
4	2	600	800	2,600	3,400	5.67	1.33	4.33	13.00
5	2	625	800	3,250	4,050	6.48	1.28	5.20	26.00
6	2	640	800	3,900	4,700	7.34	1.25	6.09	43.33

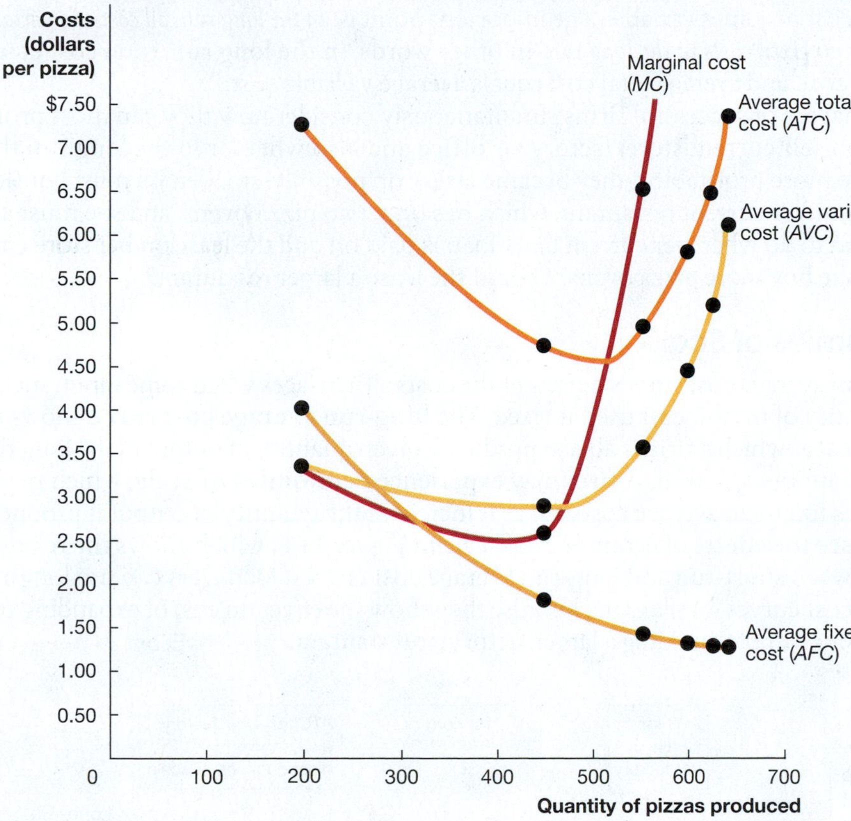

MyEconLab Animation

Figure 11.5

Costs at Jill Johnson's Restaurant

Jill's costs of making pizzas are shown in the table and plotted in the graph. Notice three important facts about the graph: (1) The marginal cost (*MC*), average total cost (*ATC*), and average variable cost (*AVC*) curves are all U shaped, and the marginal cost curve intersects both the average variable cost curve and the average total cost curve at their minimum points. (2) As output increases, average fixed cost (*AFC*) gets smaller and smaller. (3) As output increases, the difference between average total cost and average variable cost decreases. Make sure you can explain why each of these three facts is true. You should spend time becoming familiar with this graph because it is one of the most important graphs in microeconomics.

variable cost curve and the average total cost curve at their minimum points. When marginal cost is below either average variable cost or average total cost, it causes them to decrease. When marginal cost is above average variable cost or average total cost, it causes them to increase. Therefore, when marginal cost equals average variable cost or average total cost, they must be at their minimum points.

2. As output increases, average fixed cost gets smaller and smaller. This result occurs because in calculating average fixed cost, we are dividing something that gets larger and larger—output—into something that remains constant—fixed cost. Firms often refer to this process of lowering average fixed cost by selling more output as "spreading the overhead" (where "overhead" refers to fixed costs).
3. As output increases, the difference between average total cost and average variable cost decreases. This result occurs because the difference between average total cost and average variable cost is average fixed cost, which gets smaller as output increases.

MyEconLab Concept Check

MyEconLab Study Plan

11.6 Costs in the Long Run

LEARNING OBJECTIVE: Understand how firms use the long-run average cost curve in their planning.

The distinction between fixed cost and variable cost that we just discussed applies to the short run but *not* to the long run. For example, in the short run, Jill Johnson has fixed costs of $800 per week because she signed a loan agreement with a bank when she bought her pizza ovens. But in the long run, the cost of buying more pizza ovens becomes variable because Jill can choose whether to expand her business by buying more of them. The same would be true of any other fixed costs a company like Jill's might have. Once a company has purchased a fire insurance policy, the cost of the policy is fixed. But when the policy expires, the company must decide whether to renew it, and the cost becomes variable. The important point is: *In the long run, all costs are variable. There are no fixed costs in the long run.* In other words, in the long run, total cost equals variable cost, and average total cost equals average variable cost.

Managers of successful firms simultaneously consider how they can most profitably run their current store, factory, or office and also whether in the long run they would be more profitable if they became larger or, possibly, smaller. Jill must consider how to run her current restaurant, which has only two pizza ovens, and she must also plan what to do when her current bank loan is paid off and the lease on her store ends. Should she buy more pizza ovens? Should she lease a larger restaurant?

Economies of Scale

Long-run average cost curve A curve that shows the lowest cost at which a firm is able to produce a given quantity of output in the long run, when no inputs are fixed.

Economies of scale The situation when a firm's long-run average costs fall as it increases the quantity of output it produces.

Short-run average cost curves represent the costs a firm faces when some input, such as the quantity of machines it uses, is fixed. The **long-run average cost curve** shows the lowest cost at which a firm is able to produce a given quantity of output in the long run, when no inputs are fixed. A firm may experience **economies of scale**, which means the firm's long-run average costs fall as it increases the quantity of output it produces. We can see the effects of economies of scale in Figure 11.6, which shows the relationship between short-run and long-run average cost curves. Managers can use long-run average cost curves for planning because they show the effect on cost of expanding output by, for example, building a larger factory or restaurant. MyEconLab Concept Check

MyEconLab Animation

Figure 11.6

The Relationship between Short-Run Average Cost and Long-Run Average Cost

If a small car company expects to sell only 20,000 cars per year, it will be able to produce cars at the lowest average cost of $52,000 per car if it builds the small factory represented by the *ATC* curve on the left of the figure. A larger factory will be able to produce 200,000 cars per year at a lower cost of $27,000 per car. An automobile factory producing 200,000 cars per year and a factory producing 400,000 cars per year will experience constant returns to scale and have the same average cost. An automobile factory assembling 200,000 cars per year will have reached minimum efficient scale. Very large automobile factories will experience diseconomies of scale, and their average costs will rise as production increases beyond 400,000 cars per year.

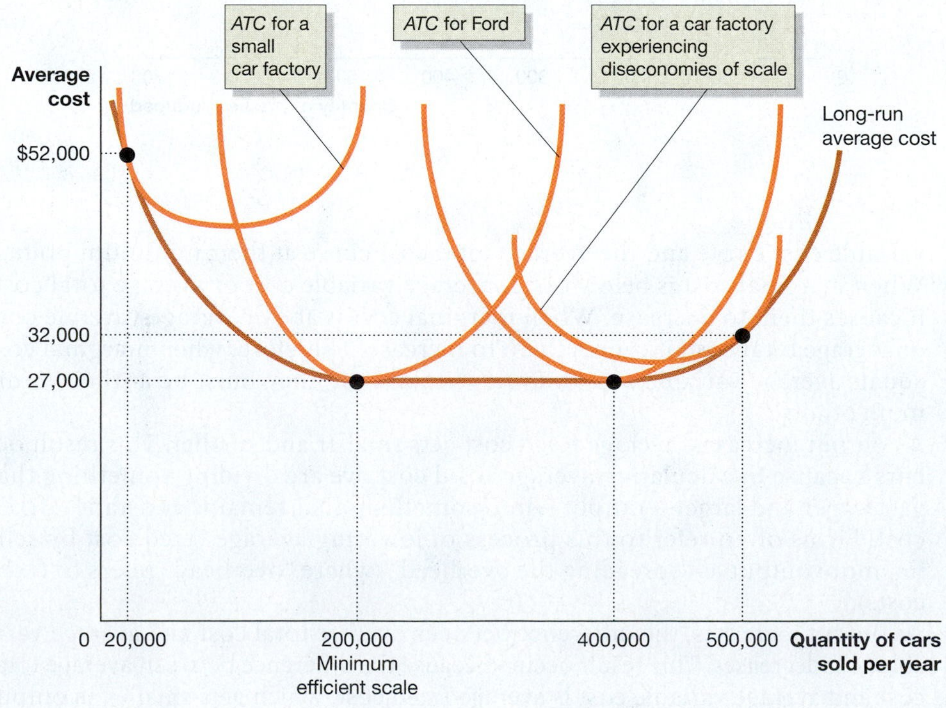

Long-Run Average Cost Curves for Automobile Factories

Figure 11.6 shows long-run average cost in the automobile industry. If a small company, such as Tesla Motors, expects to sell only 20,000 cars per year, then it will be able to assemble cars at the lowest average cost of $52,000 per car if it builds a small factory, as represented by the *ATC* curve on the left of the figure. A much larger factory, such as those operated by Ford, General Motors, and Toyota, will be able to produce 200,000 cars per year at a lower average cost of $27,000 per car. This decline in average cost from $52,000 to $27,000 represents the economies of scale that exist in manufacturing automobiles. Why would the larger automobile factory have lower average costs? One important reason is that a company like Ford is producing 10 times as many cars per year in one of its factories as Tesla produces in its factory but might need only 6 times as many workers. This saving in labor cost would reduce Ford's average cost of selling cars.

In general, firms may experience economies of scale for a number of reasons, with these being the most important:

1. As in the case of automobile production, the firm's technology may make it possible to increase production with a smaller proportional increase in at least one input.
2. Both workers and managers can become more specialized, enabling them to become more productive, as output expands.
3. Large firms, like Ford, Walmart, or Apple, may be able to purchase inputs at lower costs than smaller competitors. In fact, as Apple and Walmart expanded, their bargaining power with their suppliers increased, and their average costs fell.
4. As a firm expands, it may be able to borrow money at a lower interest rate, thereby lowering its costs.

Economies of scale do not continue indefinitely as the firm increases its output. The long-run average cost curve in most industries has a flat segment that often stretches over a substantial range of output. As Figure 11.6 shows, an automobile factory producing 200,000 cars per year and a factory producing 400,000 cars per year have the same average cost. Over this range of output, firms in the industry experience **constant returns to scale**. As these firms increase their output, they increase their inputs, such as the size of the factory and the quantity of workers, proportionally. The level of output at which all economies of scale are exhausted is known as **minimum efficient scale**. An automobile factory producing 200,000 cars per year has reached minimum efficient scale. Firms that produce at less than minimum efficient scale may have difficulty surviving because they will be producing output at higher cost than competitors.

Constant returns to scale The situation in which a firm's long-run average costs remain unchanged as it increases output.

Minimum efficient scale The level of output at which all economies of scale are exhausted.

Very large automobile factories experience increasing average costs as managers begin to have difficulty coordinating the operation of the factory. Figure 11.6 shows that for production above 400,000 cars per year, firms in the industry experience **diseconomies of scale**. For instance, Toyota found that as it expanded production at its Georgetown, Kentucky, plant and its plants in China, its managers had difficulty keeping average cost from rising. According to the president of Toyota's Georgetown plant: "Demand for … high volumes saps your energy. Over a period of time, it eroded our focus … [and] thinned out the expertise and knowledge we painstakingly built up over the years." One analysis of the problems Toyota faced in expanding production concluded: "It is the kind of paradox many highly successful companies face: Getting bigger doesn't always mean getting better." MyEconLab Concept Check

Diseconomies of scale The situation in which a firm's long-run average costs rise as the firm increases output.

Solved Problem 11.6

MyEconLab Interactive Animation

Using Long-Run Average Cost Curves to Understand Business Strategy

Medium trucks are larger than pickup trucks and are primarily purchased by construction firms and other businesses. Ford has a successful line of F-series pickup trucks. In 2015, Ford announced plans to start building medium trucks in its factory in Avon Lake, Ohio. According to an article in the *Wall Street Journal*, Ford's new medium trucks "would share engines, transmissions and cab components with its other F-series vehicles to build economies of scale." According to the same article, Ford's new medium truck would have costs that were $5,000 less per vehicle than the similar trucks produced by competing firms.

a. Explain what the article means by saying Ford intends "to build economies of scale" means.

b. Use a long-run average cost curve to illustrate Ford's strategy.

c. What does the article allow us to conclude about the operations of Ford's competitors?

Solving the Problem

Step 1: Review the chapter material. This problem is about the long-run average cost curve, so you may want to review the material in the section "Costs in the Long Run," which begins on page 380.

Step 2: Answer part (a) by explaining what the article means by saying that Ford intends "to build economies of scale." By producing many of the components of its new medium trucks in the same factory where it produces its F-series trucks, Ford intends to lower its average cost by increasing its output. In other words, by expanding its factory, Ford is taking advantage of economies of scale in truck production.

Step 3: Answer part (b) by drawing a long-run average cost graph for Ford's truck factory. For Ford's strategy to be successful, its factory must not currently be at minimum efficient scale. In the following graph, we assume that Ford is currently producing at point A on its long-average cost curve, where truck output equals Q_1 and average total cost equals Average cost_1. Ford's strategy is to expand production to point B, where truck output equals Q_2 and average total cost equals Average cost_2.

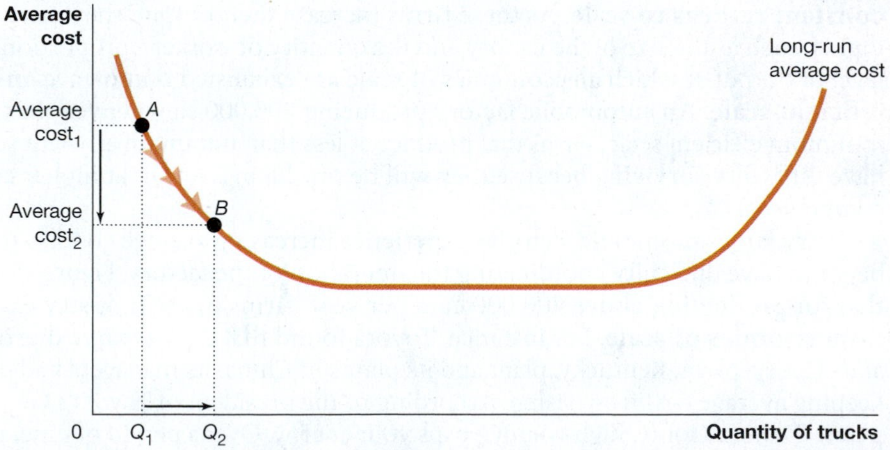

Step 4: Answer part (c) by explaining what we can conclude about the operations of Ford's competitors. After expanding its truck factory, Ford's average cost of producing trucks will be $5,000 less per vehicle than its competitors. We can conclude that Ford's competitors are failing to take advantage of economies of scale in truck production. The competitors' factories are apparently operating below minimum efficient scale.

Source: Bob Tita, "Navistar Steels Itself for Ford Business Loss," *Wall Street Journal*, May 12, 2014.

MyEconLab Study Plan

Your Turn: For more practice, do related problems 6.7, 6.8, and 6.9 on pages 391–392 at the end of this chapter.

Over time, most firms in an industry will build factories or stores that are at least as large as the minimum efficient scale but not so large that diseconomies of scale occur. For example, in the automobile industry, most factories will produce between 200,000 and 400,000 cars per year. However, firms often do not know the exact shape of their long-run average cost curves. As a result, they may mistakenly build factories or stores that are either too large or too small.

Making the Connection

MyEconLab Video

The Colossal River Rouge: Diseconomies of Scale at Ford Motor Company

When Henry Ford started the Ford Motor Company in 1903, automobile companies produced cars in small workshops, using highly skilled workers. Ford introduced two new ideas to the automobile industry that allowed him to take advantage of economies of scale. First, Ford used identical—or, interchangeable—parts so that unskilled workers could assemble the cars. Second, instead of having groups of workers moving from one stationary automobile to the next, he had the workers remain stationary, while the automobiles moved along an assembly line. Ford built a large factory at Highland Park, outside Detroit, where he used these ideas to produce the famous Model T at an average cost well below what his competitors could match using older production methods in smaller factories.

Was Ford's River Rouge plant too big?

Ford believed that he could produce automobiles at an even lower average cost by building a still larger plant along the River Rouge in Dearborn, Michigan. Unfortunately, Ford's River Rouge plant was too large and suffered from diseconomies of scale. Ford's managers had great difficulty coordinating the production of automobiles in such a large plant. The following description of the River Rouge plant comes from a biography of Ford by Allan Nevins and Frank Ernest Hill:

> A total of 93 separate structures stood on the [River Rouge] site . . . . Railroad trackage covered 93 miles, conveyors 27 [miles]. About 75,000 men worked in the great plant. A force of 5000 did nothing but keep it clean, wearing out 5000 mops and 3000 brooms a month, and using 86 tons of soap on the floors, walls, and 330 acres of windows. The Rouge was an industrial city, immense, concentrated, packed with power . . . . By its very massiveness and complexity, it denied men at the top contact with and understanding of those beneath, and gave those beneath a sense of being lost in inexorable immensity and power.

Beginning in 1927, Ford produced the Model A—its only car model at that time—at the River Rouge plant. Ford failed to achieve economies of scale and actually *lost money* on each of the four Model A body styles.

Ford could not raise the price of the Model A to make it profitable because at a higher price, the car could not compete with similar models produced by competitors such as General Motors and Chrysler. Ford eventually reduced the cost of making the Model A by constructing smaller factories spread out across the country. These smaller factories produced the Model A at a lower average cost than was possible at the River Rouge plant.

Source: Allan Nevins and Frank Ernest Hill, *Ford: Expansion and Challenge, 1915–1933*, New York: Scribner, 1957, pp. 293, 295.

Your Turn: Test your understanding by doing related problem 6.10 on page 392 at the end of this chapter.

MyEconLab Study Plan

Don't Let This Happen to You

Don't Confuse Diminishing Returns with Diseconomies of Scale

The concepts of diminishing returns and diseconomies of scale may seem similar, but they are actually unrelated. Diminishing returns applies only to the short run, when at least one of the firm's inputs, such as the quantity of machinery it uses, is fixed. The law of diminishing returns tells us that in the short run, hiring more workers will, at some point, result in less additional output. Diminishing returns explains why marginal cost curves eventually slope upward. Diseconomies of scale apply only in the long run, when the firm is free to vary all its inputs, can adopt new technology, and can vary the amount of machinery it uses and the size of its facility. Diseconomies of scale explain why long-run average cost curves eventually slope upward.

MyEconLab Study Plan

Your Turn: Test your understanding by doing related problem 6.12 on page 392 at the end of this chapter.

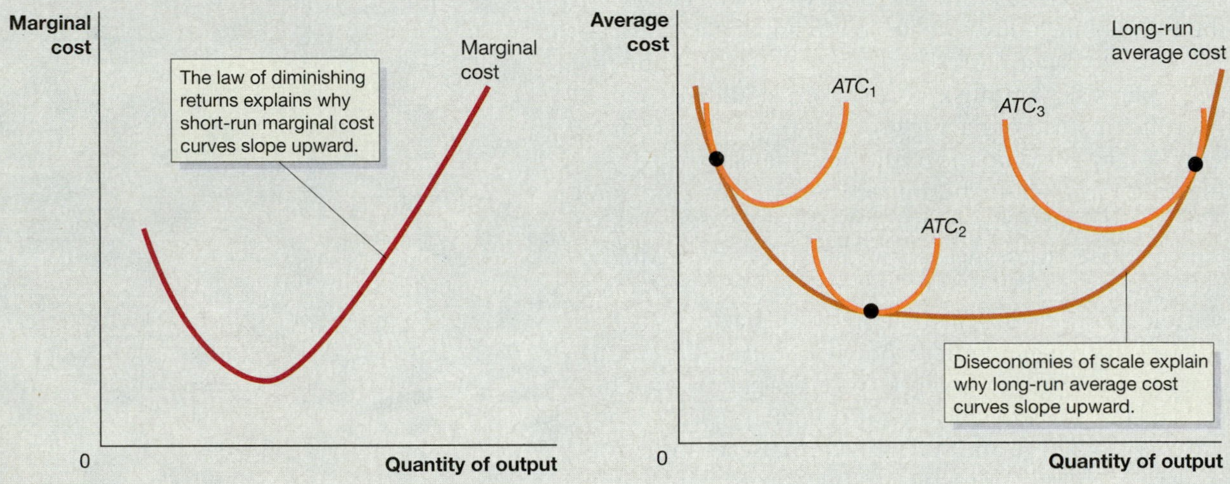

Continued from page 365

Economics in Your Life

Using Cost Concepts in Your Online Business

At the beginning of the chapter, we asked you to suppose that you are about to start a Web site to sell iPhone cases. Both you and your friend José can buy cases from the manufacturer for $10 each. But because José sells more cases per month than you expect to be able to sell, his costs per case are lower than yours. We asked you to think about why this might be true.

In this chapter, we have seen that firms often experience declining average costs as the quantity they sell increases. A key reason José's average costs might be lower than yours has to do with fixed costs. Because you will have the same computers and software and rent an office similar to José's, you may be paying about the same amount for equipment and an office lease. You may also be paying about the same amounts for utilities, insurance, and advertising. All these are fixed costs because they do not change as the quantity of cases you sell changes. Because José's fixed costs are the same as yours, but he is selling more cases, his average fixed costs are lower than yours, and, therefore, so are his average total costs. With lower average total costs, he can sell his cases for a lower price than you do and still make a profit.

Conclusion

In this chapter, we discussed the relationship between a firm's technology, production, and costs. We encountered a number of definitions of costs. Because we will use these definitions in later chapters, it is useful to bring them together in Table 11.4 for you to review.

We have seen the important relationship between a firm's level of production and its costs. This information is vital to all firms as they attempt to decide the optimal level of production and the optimal prices to charge for their products. We will explore this point further in the next chapter.

Visit MyEconLab for a news article and analysis related to the concepts in this chapter.

Table 11.4

A Summary of Definitions of Cost

Term	Definition	Symbols and Equations
Total cost	The cost of all the inputs used by a firm, or fixed cost plus variable cost	TC
Fixed costs	Costs that remain constant as a firm's level of output changes	FC
Variable costs	Costs that change as a firm's level of output changes	VC
Marginal cost	An increase in total cost resulting from producing another unit of output	$MC = \frac{\Delta TC}{\Delta Q}$
Average total cost	Total cost divided by the quantity of output produced	$ATC = \frac{TC}{Q}$
Average fixed cost	Fixed cost divided by the quantity of output produced	$AFC = \frac{FC}{Q}$
Average variable cost	Variable cost divided by the quantity of output produced	$AVC = \frac{VC}{Q}$
Implicit cost	A nonmonetary opportunity cost	—
Explicit cost	A cost that involves spending money	—

CHAPTER SUMMARY AND PROBLEMS

Key Terms

Average fixed cost, p. 378
Average product of labor, p. 373
Average total cost, p. 370
Average variable cost, p. 378
Constant returns to scale, p. 381
Diseconomies of scale, p. 381
Economies of scale, p. 380
Explicit cost, p. 368
Fixed costs, p. 367
Implicit cost, p. 368
Law of diminishing returns, p. 371
Long run, p. 367
Long-run average cost curve, p. 380
Marginal cost, p. 375
Marginal product of labor, p. 371
Minimum efficient scale, p. 381
Opportunity cost, p. 368
Production function, p. 370
Short run, p. 367
Technological change, p. 366
Technology, p. 366
Total cost, p. 367
Variable costs, p. 367

11.1 Technology: An Economic Definition, pages 366–367

LEARNING OBJECTIVE: Define technology and give examples of technological change.

Summary

The basic activity of a firm is to use inputs, such as workers, machines, and natural resources, to produce goods and services. The firm's **technology** is the processes it uses to turn inputs into goods and services. **Technological change** refers to a change in the ability of a firm to produce a given level of output with a given quantity of inputs.

MyEconLab Visit **www.myeconlab.com** to complete these exercises online and get instant feedback.

Review Questions

1.1 What is the difference between technology and technological change?

1.2 Is it possible for technological change to be negative? If so, give an example.

Problems and Applications

1.3 Briefly explain whether you agree with the following observation: "Technological change refers only to the introduction of new products, so it is not relevant to the operations of most firms."

1.4 Which of the following are examples of a firm experiencing positive technological change?

a. A fall in the wages it pays its mechanics leads United Airlines to lower its ticket prices.
b. A training program makes a firm's workers more productive.
c. An exercise program makes a firm's workers healthier and more productive.
d. A firm cuts its workforce and is able to maintain its initial level of output.
e. A firm rearranges the layout of its factory and finds that by using its initial set of inputs, it can produce exactly as much as before.

1.5 (Related to the Making the Connection on page 366) UPS has reorganized the routes its drivers take to deliver packages to homes. According to an article in the *Wall Street Journal*, "The company can save $50 million a year by reducing by one mile the average aggregated daily travel of its drivers."

a. Briefly explain whether this cost saving is due to technological change at the firm.
b. Suppose that UPS saves $50 million per year because of lower gasoline prices. Would that cost saving be due to technological change at the firm? Briefly explain.

Source: Steven Rosenbush and Laura Stevens, "At UPS, the Algorithm Is the Driver," *Wall Street Journal*, February 16, 2015.

11.2 The Short Run and the Long Run in Economics, pages 367–371

LEARNING OBJECTIVE: Distinguish between the economic short run and the economic long run.

Summary

In the **short run**, a firm's technology and the size of its factory, store, or office are fixed. In the **long run**, a firm is able to adopt new technology and increase or decrease the size of its physical plant. **Total cost** is the cost of all the inputs a firm uses in production. **Variable costs** are costs that change as output changes. **Fixed costs** are costs that remain constant as output changes. **Opportunity cost** is the highest-valued alternative that must be given up to engage in an activity. An **explicit cost** is a cost that involves spending money. An **implicit cost** is a nonmonetary opportunity cost. The relationship between the inputs employed by a firm and the maximum output it can produce with those inputs is called the firm's **production function**.

MyEconLab Visit **www.myeconlab.com** to complete these exercises online and get instant feedback.

Review Questions

2.1 What is the difference between the short run and the long run? Is the amount of time that separates the short run from the long run the same for every firm?

2.2 Distinguish between a firm's fixed costs and variable costs and give an example of each.

2.3 What are implicit costs? How are they different from explicit costs?

2.4 What is the production function? What does the short-run production function hold constant?

Problems and Applications

2.5 According to an article in *Forbes*, the cost of materials in Apple's iPhone 6 with 16 gigabytes of memory was estimated to be $227. Apple was selling the iPhone 6 for $650. Most phone carriers, like AT&T and Verizon, made payments to Apple that reduced the price to consumers to $200. Can we conclude from this information that Apple is making a profit of about $423 per iPhone? Briefly explain.

Source: Chuck Jones, "Apple's iPhone 6 Teardown and Other Costs Analysis," *Forbes*, September 24, 2014.

2.6 (Related to the Making the Connection on page 368) Small business owner Jay Goltz described several decisions he made to reduce the fixed costs of his businesses, including replacing halogen lamps with LED lamps. Goltz noted, "I'm guessing that many business owners could save a lot more than pennies on their fixed costs, and those savings ... fall right to the bottom line."

a. Why are the costs of electricity used to power the lights used in Mr. Goltz's businesses fixed costs?
b. Explain why Goltz wrote that reducing fixed costs results in savings that "fall right to the bottom line."

Source: Jay Goltz, "Not All Fixed Costs Are Truly Fixed," *New York Times*, May 25, 2011.

2.7 (Related to the Making the Connection on page 368) For Jill Johnson's pizza restaurant, explain whether each of the following is a fixed cost or a variable cost:

a. The payment she makes on her fire insurance policy
b. The payment she makes to buy pizza dough
c. The wages she pays her workers
d. The lease payment she makes to the landlord who owns the building where her store is located
e. The $300-per-month payment she makes to her local newspaper for running her weekly advertisements

2.8 (Related to the Making the Connection on page 368) The *Statistical Abstract of the United States* was published for many years by the U.S. Census Bureau. The *Abstract* provided a summary of business, economic, social, and political statistics. It was available for free online, and a printed copy could also be purchased from the U.S. Government Printing Office for $39. Because government documents are not copyrighted, anyone could print and sell copies of the *Statistical Abstract*. Each year, typically one or two companies would print and sell copies for a significantly lower price than the Government Printing Office did. The copies of the *Statistical Abstract* that these companies sold were usually identical to those sold by the government, except for having different covers. How could these companies have sold the same book for a lower price than the government did and still have covered their costs?

2.9 Suppose that Bill owns an automobile collision repair shop. The following table shows how the quantity of cars Bill can repair per month depends on the number of workers he hires. Assume that he pays each worker $4,000 per month and his fixed cost is $6,000 per month. Using the information provided, complete the following table.

Quantity of Workers	Quantity of Cars per Month	Fixed Cost	Variable Cost	Total Cost	Average Total Cost
0	0	$6,000			—
1	20				
2	30				
3	40				
4	50				
5	55				

2.10 A study analyzed the costs to a pharmaceutical firm of developing a prescription drug and receiving government approval. An article in the *Wall Street Journal* noted that included in the firm's costs was "the return that could be gained if the money [used to develop the drug] were invested elsewhere." Briefly explain whether you agree that this return should be included in the firm's costs.

Source: Ed Silverman, "Can It Really Cost $2.6 Billion to Develop a Drug?" *Wall Street Journal*, November 21, 2014.

2.11 Suppose Jill Johnson operates her pizza restaurant in a building she owns in the center of the city. Similar buildings in the neighborhood rent for $4,000 per month. Jill is considering selling her building and renting space in the suburbs for $3,000 per month, but she decides not to make the move. She reasons: "I would like to have a restaurant in the suburbs, but I pay no rent for my restaurant now, and I don't want to see my costs rise by $3,000 per month." Evaluate Jill's reasoning.

2.12 When the DuPont chemical company first attempted to enter the paint business, it was not successful. According to a company report, in one year it "lost nearly $500,000 in actual cash in addition to an expected return on investment of nearly $500,000, which made a total loss of income to the company of nearly a million." Why did this report include as part of the company's loss the amount it had expected to earn—but didn't—on its investment in manufacturing paint?

Source: Alfred D. Chandler, Jr., Thomas K. McCraw, and Richard Tedlow, *Management Past and Present*, Cincinnati, OH: South-Western, 2000.

11.3 The Marginal Product of Labor and the Average Product of Labor, pages 371–375

LEARNING OBJECTIVE: Understand the relationship between the marginal product of labor and the average product of labor.

Summary

The **marginal product of labor** is the additional output produced by a firm as a result of hiring one more worker. Specialization and division of labor cause the marginal product of labor to rise for the first few workers hired. Eventually, the **law of diminishing returns** causes the marginal product of labor to decline. The **average product of labor** is the total amount of output produced by a firm divided by the quantity of workers hired. When the marginal product of labor is greater than the average product of labor, the average product of labor increases. When the marginal product of labor is less than the average product of labor, the average product of labor decreases.

MyEconLab Visit **www.myeconlab.com** to complete these exercises online and get instant feedback.

Review Questions

3.1 Draw a graph that shows the usual relationship between the marginal product of labor and the average product of labor. Why do the marginal product of labor and the average product of labor curves have the shapes you drew?

3.2 How do specialization and division of labor typically affect the marginal product of labor?

3.3 What is the law of diminishing returns? Does it apply in the long run?

Problems and Applications

3.4 Fill in the missing values in the following table.

Quantity of Workers	Total Output	Marginal Product of Labor	Average Product of Labor
0	0		
1	400		
2	900		
3	1,500		
4	1,900		
5	2,200		
6	2,400		
7	2,300		

3.5 Use the numbers from problem 3.4 to draw one graph that shows how total output increases with the quantity of workers hired and a second graph that shows the marginal product of labor and the average product of labor.

3.6 A student looks at the numbers in Table 11.3 on page 371 and draws this conclusion:

> The marginal product of labor is increasing for the first two workers hired, and then it declines for the next four workers. I guess each of the first two workers must have been hard workers. Then Jill must have had to settle for increasingly bad workers.

Do you agree with the student's analysis? Briefly explain.

3.7 **(Related to the Making the Connection on page 373)** Briefly explain whether you agree with the following argument:

> Adam Smith's idea of the gains to firms from the division of labor makes a lot of sense when the good being manufactured is something complex like automobiles or computers, but it doesn't apply in the manufacturing of less complex goods or in other sectors of the economy, such as retail sales.

3.8 Sally looks at her college transcript and asks you, "How is this possible? My grade point average for this semester's courses is higher than my grade point average for last semester's courses, but my cumulative grade point average still went down from last semester to this semester." Explain to Sally how this is possible.

3.9 Is it possible for a firm to experience a technological change that would increase the marginal product of labor while leaving the average product of labor unchanged? Explain.

3.10 The following table shows the quantity of workers and total output for a local pizza parlor. Answer the following questions based on this table:

Quantity of Workers	Total Output
0	0
1	5
2	—
3	19
4	24
5	28
6	26

a. When the owner hires 4 workers, what is average product of labor?

b. What is the marginal product of the fifth worker?

c. If the marginal product of the second worker is 6, what is the total number of pizzas produced when 2 workers are hired?

d. Assuming that the marginal product of the second worker is 6, with which worker hired does the law of diminishing returns set in?

11.4 The Relationship between Short-Run Production and Short-Run Cost, pages 375–378

LEARNING OBJECTIVE: Explain and illustrate the relationship between marginal cost and average total cost.

Summary

The **marginal cost** of production is the increase in total cost that results from producing another unit of output. The marginal cost curve has a U shape because when the marginal product of labor is rising, the marginal cost of output is falling, and when the marginal product of labor is falling, the marginal cost of output is rising. When marginal cost is less than average total cost, average total cost falls. When marginal cost is greater than average total cost, average total cost rises. Therefore, the average total cost curve also has a U shape.

MyEconLab Visit **www.myeconlab.com** to complete these exercises online and get instant feedback.

Review Questions

4.1 What is the difference between the average cost of production and the marginal cost of production?

4.2 If the marginal product of labor is rising, is the marginal cost of production rising or falling? Briefly explain.

4.3 Explain why the marginal cost curve intersects the average total cost curve at the level of output where average total cost is at a minimum.

Problems and Applications

4.4 Older oil wells that produce fewer than 10 barrels of oil a day are called "stripper" wells. Suppose that you and a partner own a stripper well that can produce 8 barrels of oil per day, and you estimate that the marginal cost of producing another barrel of oil is $80. In making your calculation, you take into account the cost of labor, materials, and other inputs that increase when you produce more oil. Your partner looks over your calculation of marginal cost and says: "You forgot about that bank loan we received two years ago. If we take into account the amount we pay on that loan, it adds $10 per barrel to our marginal cost of production." Briefly explain whether you agree with your partner's analysis.

4.5 Is it possible for average total cost to be decreasing over a range of output where marginal cost is increasing? Briefly explain.

4.6 Suppose a firm has no fixed costs, so all its costs are variable, even in the short run.

a. If the firm's marginal costs are continually increasing (that is, marginal cost is increasing from the first unit of output produced), will the firm's average total cost curve have a U shape?

b. If the firm's marginal costs are $5 at every level of output, what shape will the firm's average total cost have?

4.7 **(Related to** Solved Problem 11.4 **on page 377)** Santiago Delgado owns a copier store. He leases two copy machines for which he pays $20 each per day. He cannot increase the number of machines he leases without giving the office machine company six weeks' notice. He can hire as many workers as he wants, at a cost of $40 per day per worker. These are the only two inputs he uses to produce copies.

a. Fill in the remaining columns in the following table.

b. Draw the average total cost curve and marginal cost curve for Santiago's store. Do these curves have the expected shape? Briefly explain.

Quantity of Workers	Quantity of Copies per Day	Fixed Cost	Variable Cost	Total Cost	Average Total Cost	Marginal Cost
0	0					
1	600					
2	1,100					
3	1,500					
4	1,800					
5	2,000					
6	2,100					

4.8 Is Jill Johnson correct when she states the following: "I am currently producing 10,000 pizzas per month at a total cost of $50,000.00. If I produce 10,001 pizzas, my total cost will rise to $50,011.00. Therefore, my marginal cost of producing pizzas must be increasing." Draw a graph to illustrate your answer.

4.9 Is Jill Johnson correct when she states the following: "I am currently producing 20,000 pizzas per month at a total cost of $75,000. If I produce 20,001 pizzas, my total cost will rise to $75,002. Therefore, my marginal cost of producing pizzas must be increasing." Illustrate your answer with a graph.

4.10 (This problem is somewhat advanced.) Using symbols, we can write that the marginal product of labor is equal to $\Delta Q/\Delta L$. Marginal cost is equal to $\Delta TC/\Delta Q$. Because fixed costs by definition don't change, marginal cost is also equal to $\Delta VC/\Delta Q$. If Jill Johnson's only variable cost (VC) is labor cost, then her variable cost equals the wage multiplied by the quantity of workers hired, or wL.

a. If the wage Jill pays is constant, then what is ΔVC in terms of w and L?

b. Use your answer to part (a) and the expressions given for the marginal product of labor and the marginal cost of output to find an expression for marginal cost, $\Delta TC/\Delta Q$, in terms of the wage, w, and the marginal product of labor, $\Delta Q/\Delta L$.

c. Use your answer to part (b) to determine Jill's marginal cost of producing pizzas if the wage is $750 per week and the marginal product of labor is 150 pizzas. If the wage falls to $600 per week and the marginal product of labor is unchanged, what happens to Jill's marginal cost? If the wage is unchanged at $750 per week and the marginal product of labor rises to 250 pizzas, what happens to Jill's marginal cost?

11.5 Graphing Cost Curves, pages 378–379

LEARNING OBJECTIVE: Graph average total cost, average variable cost, average fixed cost, and marginal cost.

Summary

Average fixed cost is equal to fixed cost divided by the level of output. **Average variable cost** is equal to variable cost divided by the level of output. Figure 11.5 on page 379 shows the relationship among marginal cost, average total cost, average variable cost, and average fixed cost. It is one of the most important graphs in microeconomics.

Review Questions

5.1 Where does the marginal cost curve intersect the average variable cost curve and the average total cost curve?

5.2 As the level of output increases, what happens to the difference between the value of average total cost and the value of average variable cost?

Problems and Applications

5.3 Suppose the total cost of producing 10,000 tennis balls is $30,000 and the fixed cost is $10,000.
a. What is the variable cost?
b. When output is 10,000, what are the average variable cost and the average fixed cost?
c. Assume that the cost curves have the usual shape. Is the dollar difference between the average total cost and the average variable cost greater when the output is 10,000 tennis balls or when the output is 30,000 tennis balls? Explain.

5.4 One description of the costs of operating a railroad makes the following observation: "The fixed ... expenses which attach to the operation of railroads ... are in the nature of a tax upon the business of the road; the smaller the [amount of] business, the larger the tax." Briefly explain why fixed costs are like a tax. In what sense is this tax smaller when the amount of business is larger?

Source: Alfred D. Chandler, Jr., Thomas K. McCraw, and Richard Tedlow, *Management Past and Present*, Cincinnati, OH: South-Western, 2000, pp. 2–27.

5.5 In the ancient world, a book could be produced either on a scroll or as a codex, which was made of folded sheets glued together, something like a modern book. One scholar has estimated the following variable costs (in Greek drachmas) of the two methods:

	Scroll	Codex
Cost of writing (wage of a scribe)	11.33 drachmas	11.33 drachmas
Cost of paper	16.50 drachmas	9.25 drachmas

Another scholar points out that a significant fixed cost was involved in producing a codex:

> In order to copy a codex ... the amount of text and the layout of each page had to be carefully calculated in advance to determine the exact number of sheets ... needed. No doubt, this is more time-consuming and calls for more experimentation than the production of a scroll would. But for the next copy, these calculations would be used again.

a. Suppose that the fixed cost of preparing a codex was 58 drachmas and that there was no similar fixed cost for a scroll. Would an ancient book publisher who intended to sell 5 copies of a book be likely to publish it as a scroll or as a codex? What if he intended to sell 10 copies? Briefly explain.
b. Although most books were published as scrolls in the first century A.D., by the third century, most were published as codices. Considering only the factors mentioned in this problem, explain why this change may have taken place.

Sources: T. C. Skeat, "The Length of the Standard Papyrus Roll and the Cost-Advantage of the Codex," *Zeitschrift fur Pspyrologie and Epigraphik*, Germany: Rudolph Habelt, 1982, p. 175; and David Trobisch, *The First Edition of the New Testament*, New York: Oxford University Press, 2000, p. 73.

5.6 **(Related to the Chapter Opener on page 365)** We saw in the chapter opener that some colleges and private companies have launched online courses that anyone with an Internet connection can take. The most successful of these massive open online courses (MOOCs) have attracted tens of thousands of students. Suppose that your college offers a MOOC and spends a total of $200,000 on one-time costs to have instructors prepare the course material and to buy additional server capacity. The college administration estimates that the variable cost of offering the course will be $20 per student per course. This variable cost is the same, regardless of how many students enroll in the course.
a. Use this information to fill in the missing values in the table:

Number of Students Taking the Course	Average Total Cost	Average Variable Cost	Average Fixed Cost	Marginal Cost
1,000				
10,000				
20,000				

b. Use your answer to part (a) to draw a cost curve graph to illustrate your college's costs of offering this course. Your graph should measure cost on the vertical axis and the quantity of students taking the course on the horizontal axis. Be sure your graph contains the following curves: average total cost, average variable cost, average fixed cost, and marginal cost.

5.7 Use the information in the graph to find the values for the following at an output level of 1,000.

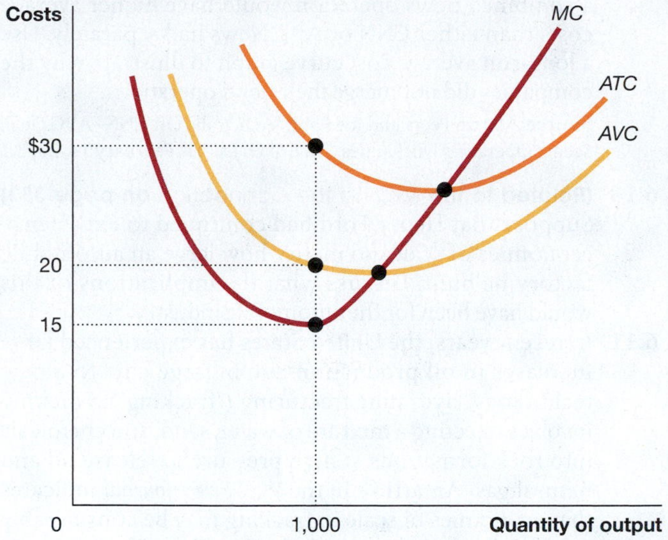

a. Marginal cost
b. Total cost
c. Variable cost
d. Fixed cost

5.8 List the errors in the following graph. Carefully explain why the curves drawn this way are incorrect. In other words, why can't these curves be as they are shown in the graph?

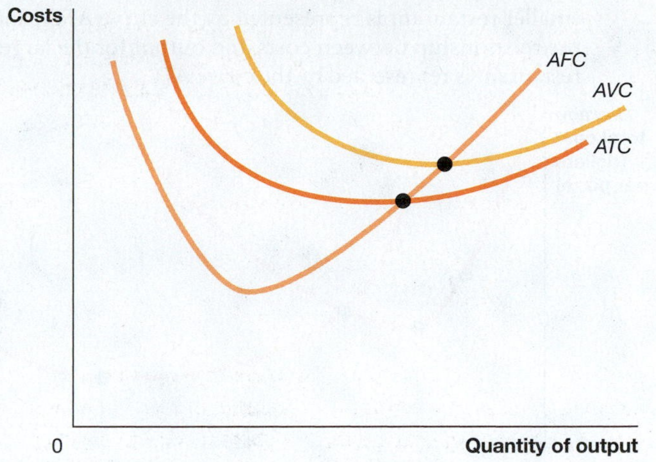

5.9 Explain how the events listed in (a) through (d) would affect the following costs at Southwest Airlines:
1. Marginal cost
2. Average variable cost
3. Average fixed cost
4. Average total cost
   a. Southwest signs a new contract with the Transport Workers Union that requires the airline to increase wages for its flight attendants.
   b. The federal government starts to levy a $20-per-passenger carbon emissions tax on all commercial air travel.
   c. Southwest decides on an across-the-board 10 percent cut in executive salaries.
   d. Southwest decides to double its television advertising budget.

11.6 Costs in the Long Run, pages 380–384

LEARNING OBJECTIVE: Understand how firms use the long-run average cost curve in their planning.

Summary

The **long-run average cost curve** shows the lowest cost at which a firm is able to produce a given level of output in the long run. For many firms, the long-run average cost curve falls as output expands because of **economies of scale**. **Minimum efficient scale** is the level of output at which all economies of scale have been exhausted. After economies of scale have been exhausted, firms experience **constant returns to scale**, where their long-run average cost curve is flat. At high levels of output, the long-run average cost curve turns up as the firm experiences **diseconomies of scale**.

MyEconLab Visit **www.myeconlab.com** to complete these exercises online and get instant feedback.

Review Questions

6.1 What is the difference between total cost and variable cost in the long run?

6.2 What is minimum efficient scale? What is likely to happen in the long run to firms that do not reach minimum efficient scale?

6.3 What are economies of scale? What are four reasons that firms may experience economies of scale?

6.4 What are diseconomies of scale? What is the main reason that a firm eventually encounters diseconomies of scale as it keeps increasing the size of its store or factory?

6.5 Why can short-run average cost never be less than long-run average cost for a given level of output?

Problems and Applications

6.6 An article in the *Wall Street Journal* described the Chinese automobile industry as "a hodgepodge of companies," most of which produce fewer than 100,000 cars per year. Ford Chief Executive Alan Mulally commented on the situation by saying, "If you don't have scale, you just won't be able to be competitive."
a. Briefly explain what Mulally meant.
b. How would you predict the structure of the Chinese automobile industry (in terms of the number of firms and the size of firms) will change over the next 10 years?

Source: Colum Murphy, "Chinese Car Makers Struggle to Lure Buyers," *Wall Street Journal*, April 19, 2014.

6.7 **(Related to Solved Problem 11.6 on page 381)** Suppose that Jill Johnson has to choose between building a smaller restaurant and a larger restaurant. In the graph on the next page, the relationship between costs and output for the smaller restaurant is represented by the curve ATC_1, and the relationship between costs and output for the larger restaurant is represented by the curve ATC_2.

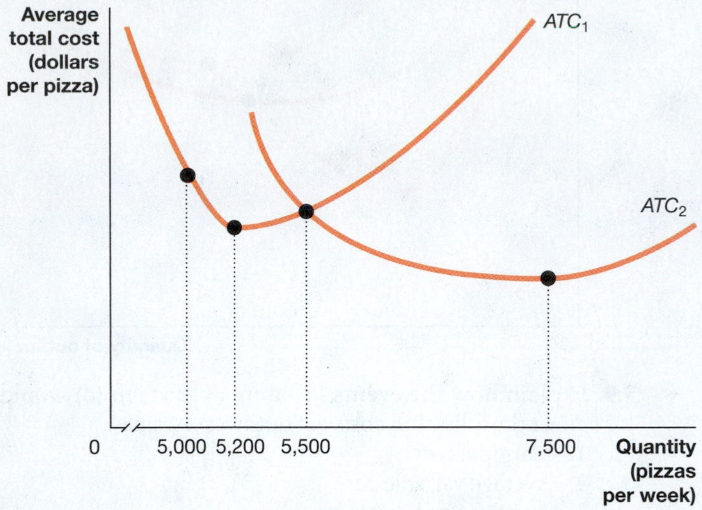

a. If Jill expects to produce 5,100 pizzas per week, should she build a smaller restaurant or a larger restaurant? Briefly explain.
b. If Jill expects to produce 6,000 pizzas per week, should she build a smaller restaurant or a larger restaurant? Briefly explain.
c. A student asks, "If the average cost of producing pizzas is lower in the larger restaurant when Jill produces 7,500 pizzas per week, why isn't it also lower when Jill produces 5,200 pizzas per week?" Give a brief answer to the student's question.

6.8 **(Related to** Solved Problem 11.6 **on page 381)** An article in the *Wall Street Journal* discussed the purchase of the small Zipcar rental car firm by the much larger Avis. The article predicted that the purchase would be successful because of the "efficiencies gained by putting the two companies together." The article also observed: "On its own, Zipcar is too small to achieve economies of scale."
a. What economies of scale may exist in the rental car industry? Why would a rental car firm that is too small be unable to achieve these economies of scale?
b. What does the article mean by "efficiencies" that might be gained by putting the two companies together?
c. If Avis had already achieved minimum efficient scale before buying Zipcar, would the combined companies still be more efficient than if they operated separately? Briefly explain.

Source: Rolfe Winkler, "Avis Puts Some Zip in Its Weekend," *Wall Street Journal*, January 2, 2013.

6.9 **(Related to** Solved Problem 11.6 **on page 381)** At one point, Time Warner and the Walt Disney Company discussed merging their news operations. Time Warner owns Cable News Network (CNN), and Disney owns ABC News. After analyzing the situation, the companies decided that a combined news operation would have higher average costs than either CNN or ABC News had separately. Use a long-run average cost curve graph to illustrate why the companies did not merge their news operations.

Source: Martin Peers and Joe Flint, "AOL Calls Off CNN–ABC Deal, Seeing Operating Difficulties," *Wall Street Journal*, February 14, 2003.

6.10 **(Related to the** Making the Connection **on page 383)** Suppose that Henry Ford had continued to experience economies of scale, no matter how large an automobile factory he built. Discuss what the implications of this would have been for the automobile industry.

6.11 In recent years, the United States has experienced large increases in oil production due in large part to a new technology, hydraulic fracturing ("fracking"). Fracking involves injecting a mixture of water, sand, and chemicals into rock formations at high pressure to release oil and natural gas. An article in the *Wall Street Journal* indicates that economies of scale in fracking may be considerably smaller than in conventional oil drilling. If this view is correct, what would the likely consequences be for the number of firms drilling for oil in the United States?

Source: Russell Gold and Theo Francis, "The New Winners and Losers in America's Shale Boom," *Wall Street Journal*, April 20, 2014.

6.12 **(Related to the** Don't Let This Happen to You **on page 384)** In his autobiography, T. Boone Pickens, a geologist, entrepreneur, and oil company executive, wrote:

> It's unusual to find a large corporation that's efficient. . . . When you get an inside look, it's easy to see how inefficient big business really is. Most corporate bureaucracies have more people than they have work.

Was Pickens describing diminishing returns or diseconomies of scale? Briefly explain.

Source: T. Boone Pickens, *The Luckiest Man in the World*, Washington, DC: Beard Books, 2000, p. 275.

6.13 In 2012, then Barnes & Noble CEO William Lynch predicted that although the firm was suffering losses in selling its Nook tablet, "the Nook business will scale in fiscal 2013, reducing losses from last year."
a. What did Lynch mean that "the Nook business will scale"?
b. Why would the Nook business scaling reduce the firm's losses?
c. In 2013, Barnes & Noble's losses from selling the Nook increased, and Lynch resigned as CEO. Can we conclude that the Nook business didn't scale? Briefly explain.

Source: Jeffrey A. Trachtenberg, "Nook Loses Ground in Tablet War," *Wall Street Journal*, January 3, 2013.

Appendix

Using Isoquants and Isocost Lines to Understand Production and Cost

LEARNING OBJECTIVE: Use isoquants and isocost lines to understand production and cost.

Isoquants

In this chapter, we studied the important relationship between a firm's level of production and its costs. In this appendix, we look more closely at how firms choose the combination of inputs to produce a given level of output. Firms usually have a choice about how they will produce their output. For example, Jill Johnson is able to produce 5,000 pizzas per week by using 10 workers and 2 ovens or by using 6 workers and 3 ovens. We will see that firms search for the *cost-minimizing* combination of inputs that will allow them to produce a given level of output. The cost-minimizing combination of inputs depends on two factors: technology—which determines how much output a firm receives from employing a given quantity of inputs—and input prices—which determine the total cost of each combination of inputs.

An Isoquant Graph

We begin by graphing the levels of output that Jill can produce using different combinations of two inputs: labor—the quantity of workers she hires per week—and capital—the quantity of ovens she uses per week. In reality, of course, Jill uses more than just these two inputs to produce pizzas, but nothing important would change if we expanded the discussion to include many inputs instead of just two. Figure 11A.1 measures the quantity of capital along the vertical axis and the quantity of labor along the horizontal axis. The curves in the graph are **isoquants**, which show all the combinations of two inputs—in this case capital and labor—that will produce the same level of output.

Isoquant A curve that shows all the combinations of two inputs, such as capital and labor, that will produce the same level of output.

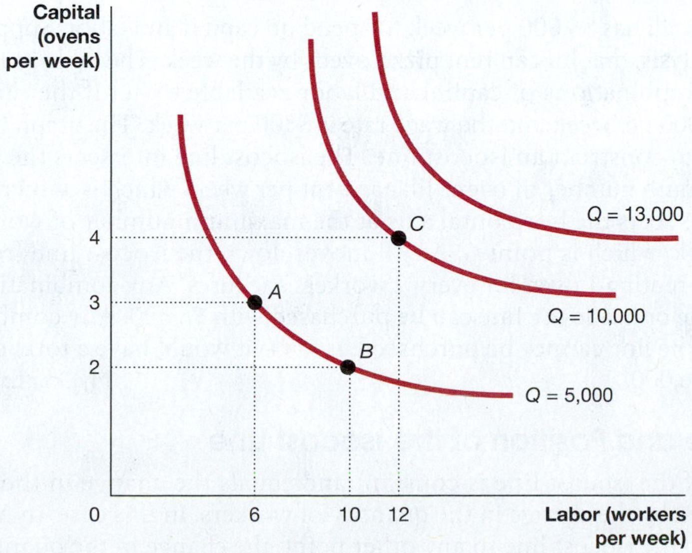

MyEconLab Animation

Figure 11A.1

Isoquants

Isoquants show all the combinations of two inputs—in this case capital and labor—that will produce the same level of output. For example, the isoquant labeled Q = 5,000 shows all the combinations of ovens and workers that enable Jill to produce that quantity of pizzas per week. At point *A*, she produces 5,000 pizzas using 3 ovens and 6 workers, and at point *B*, she produces the same output using 2 ovens and 10 workers. With more ovens and workers, she can move to a higher isoquant. For example, with 4 ovens and 12 workers, she can produce at point *C* on the isoquant Q = 10,000. With even more ovens and workers, she could move to the isoquant Q = 13,000.

The isoquant labeled $Q = 5{,}000$ shows all the combinations of workers and ovens that enable Jill to produce that quantity of pizzas per week. For example, at point *A*, she produces 5,000 pizzas using 6 workers and 3 ovens, and at point *B*, she produces the same output using 10 workers and 2 ovens. With more workers and ovens, she can move to a higher isoquant. For example, with 12 workers and 4 ovens, she can produce at point *C* on the isoquant $Q = 10{,}000$. With even more workers and ovens, she could move to the isoquant $Q = 13{,}000$. The higher the isoquant—that is, the further to the upper right on the graph—the more output the firm produces. Although we have shown only three isoquants in this graph, there is, in fact, an isoquant for every level of output. MyEconLab Concept Check

The Slope of an Isoquant

Marginal rate of technical substitution (*MRTS*) The rate at which a firm is able to substitute one input for another while keeping the level of output constant.

Remember that the slope of a curve is the ratio of the change in the variable on the vertical axis to the change in the variable on the horizontal axis. Along an isoquant, the slope tells us the rate at which a firm is able to substitute one input for another while keeping the level of output constant. This rate is called the **marginal rate of technical substitution (*MRTS*)**.

We expect that the *MRTS* will change as we move down an isoquant. In Figure 11A.1, at a point like *A* on isoquant $Q = 5{,}000$, the isoquant is relatively steep. As we move down the curve, it becomes less steep at a point like *B*. This shape is the usual one for isoquants: They are bowed in, or convex. The reason isoquants have this shape is that as we move down the curve, we continue to substitute labor for capital. As the firm produces the same quantity of output using less capital, the additional labor it needs increases because of diminishing returns. Remember from the chapter that, as a consequence of diminishing returns, for a given decline in capital, increasing amounts of labor are necessary to produce the same level of output. Because the *MRTS* is equal to the change in capital divided by the change in labor, it will become smaller (in absolute value) as we move down an isoquant. MyEconLab Concept Check

Isocost Lines

Isocost line All the combinations of two inputs, such as capital and labor, that have the same total cost.

A firm wants to produce a given quantity of output at the lowest possible cost. We can show the relationship between the quantity of inputs used and the firm's total cost by using an *isocost* line. An **isocost line** shows all the combinations of two inputs, such as capital and labor, that have the same total cost.

Graphing the Isocost Line

Suppose that Jill has $6,000 per week to spend on capital and labor. Suppose, to simplify the analysis, that Jill can rent pizza ovens by the week. The table in Figure 11A.2 shows the combinations of capital and labor available to her if the rental price of ovens is $1,000 per week and the wage rate is $500 per week. The graph uses the data in the table to construct an isocost line. The isocost line intersects the vertical axis at the maximum number of ovens Jill can rent per week, which is shown by point *A*. The line intersects the horizontal axis at the maximum number of workers Jill can hire per week, which is point *G*. As Jill moves down the isocost line from point *A*, she gives up renting 1 oven for every 2 workers she hires. Any combination of inputs along the line or inside the line can be purchased with $6,000. Any combination that lies outside the line cannot be purchased because it would have a total cost to Jill of more than $6,000. MyEconLab Concept Check

The Slope and Position of the Isocost Line

The slope of the isocost line is constant and equals the change in the quantity of ovens divided by the change in the quantity of workers. In this case, in moving from any point on the isocost line to any other point, the change in the quantity of ovens equals -1, and the change in the quantity of workers equals 2, so the slope equals $-1/2$. Notice that with a rental price of ovens of $1,000 per week and a wage rate for labor of

Combinations of Workers and Ovens with a Total Cost of $6,000			
Point	Ovens	Workers	Total Cost
A	6	0	(6 x $1,000) + (0 x $500) = $6,000
B	5	2	(5 x $1,000) + (2 x $500) = $6,000
C	4	4	(4 x $1,000) + (4 x $500) = $6,000
D	3	6	(3 x $1,000) + (6 x $500) = $6,000
E	2	8	(2 x $1,000) + (8 x $500) = $6,000
F	1	10	(1 x $1,000) + (10 x $500) = $6,000
G	0	12	(0 x $1,000) + (12 x $500) = $6,000

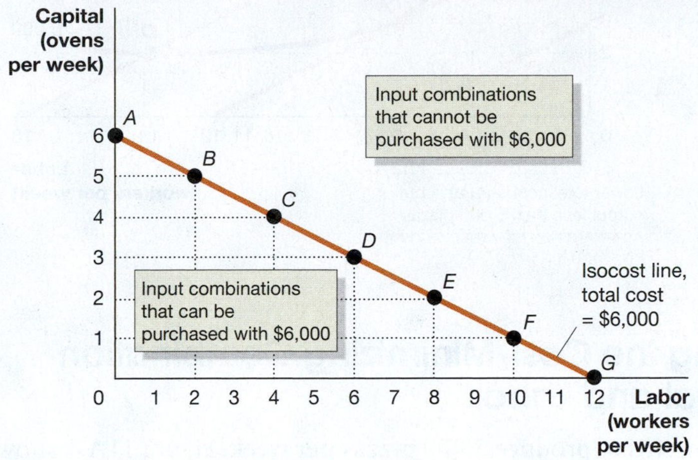

MyEconLab Animation

Figure 11A.2

An Isocost Line

The isocost line shows the combinations of inputs with a total cost of $6,000. The rental price of ovens is $1,000 per week, so if Jill spends the whole $6,000 on ovens, she can rent 6 ovens (point A). The wage rate is $500 per week, so if Jill spends the whole $6,000 on workers, she can hire 12 workers (point G). As she moves down the isocost line, she gives up renting 1 oven for every 2 workers she hires. Any combination of inputs along the line or inside the line can be purchased with $6,000. Any combination that lies outside the line cannot be purchased with $6,000.

$500 per week, the slope of the isocost line is equal to the ratio of the wage rate divided by the rental price of capital, multiplied by −1, or −$500/$1,000 = −1/2. In fact, this result will always hold, whatever inputs are involved and whatever their prices may be: *The slope of the isocost line is equal to the ratio of the price of the input on the horizontal axis divided by the price of the input on the vertical axis multiplied by* −1.

The position of the isocost line depends on the level of total cost. Higher levels of total cost shift the isocost line outward, and lower levels of total cost shift the isocost line inward. This can be seen in Figure 11A.3, which shows isocost lines for total costs of $3,000, $6,000, and $9,000. We have shown only three isocost lines in the graph, but there is, in fact, a different isocost line for each level of total cost. MyEconLab Concept Check

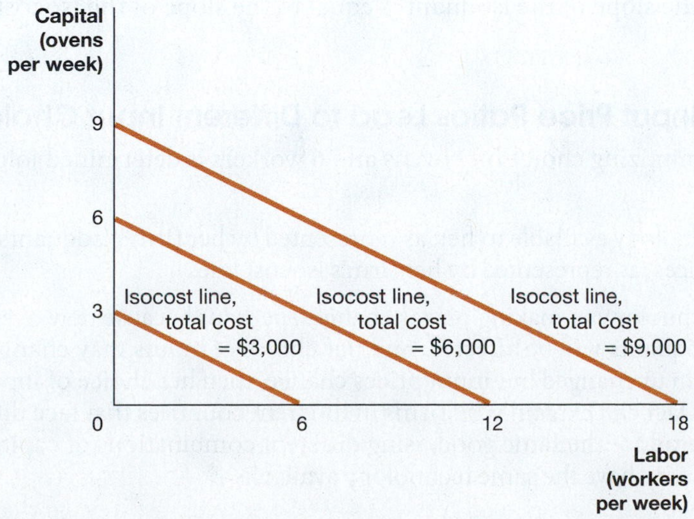

MyEconLab Animation

Figure 11A.3

The Position of the Isocost Line

The position of the isocost line depends on the level of total cost. As total cost increases from $3,000 to $6,000 to $9,000 per week, the isocost line shifts outward. For each isocost line shown, the rental price of ovens is $1,000 per week, and the wage rate is $500 per week.

MyEconLab Animation

Figure 11A.4

Choosing Capital and Labor to Minimize Total Cost

Jill wants to produce 5,000 pizzas per week at the lowest total cost. Point *B* is the lowest-cost combination of inputs shown in the graph, but this combination of 1 oven and 4 workers will produce fewer than the 5,000 pizzas needed. Points *C* and *D* are combinations of ovens and workers that will produce 5,000 pizzas, but their total cost is $9,000. The combination of 3 ovens and 6 workers at point *A* produces 5,000 pizzas at the lowest total cost of $6,000.

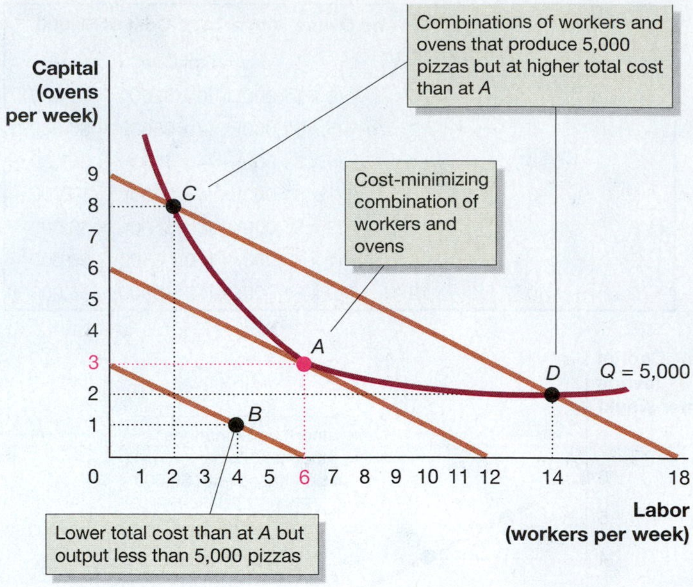

Choosing the Cost-Minimizing Combination of Capital and Labor

Suppose Jill wants to produce 5,000 pizzas per week. Figure 11A.1 shows that there are many combinations of ovens and workers that will allow Jill to produce this level of output. There is only one combination of ovens and workers, however, that will allow her to produce 5,000 pizzas *at the lowest total cost*. Figure 11A.4 shows the isoquant $Q = 5{,}000$ along with three isocost lines. Point *B* is the lowest-cost combination of inputs shown in the graph, but this combination of 1 oven and 4 workers will produce fewer than the 5,000 pizzas needed. Points *C* and *D* are combinations of ovens and workers that will produce 5,000 pizzas, but their total cost is $9,000. The combination of 3 ovens and 6 workers at point *A* produces 5,000 pizzas at the lowest total cost of $6,000.

Figure 11A.4 shows that moving to an isocost line with a total cost of less than $6,000 would mean producing fewer than 5,000 pizzas. Being at any point along the isoquant $Q = 5{,}000$ other than point *A* would increase total cost above $6,000. In fact, the combination of inputs at point *A* is the only one on isoquant $Q = 5{,}000$ that has a total cost of $6,000. All other input combinations on this isoquant have higher total costs. Notice also that at point *A*, the isoquant and the isocost lines are tangent, so the slope of the isoquant is equal to the slope of the isocost line at that point.

Different Input Price Ratios Lead to Different Input Choices

Jill's cost-minimizing choice of 3 ovens and 6 workers is determined jointly by these two factors:

1. The technology available to her, as represented by her firm's isoquants
2. Input prices, as represented by her firm's isocost lines

If the technology of making pizzas changes, perhaps because new ovens are developed, her isoquants will be affected, and her choice of inputs may change. If her isoquants remain unchanged but input prices change, then her choice of inputs may also change. This fact can explain why firms in different countries that face different input prices may produce the same good using different combinations of capital and labor, even though they have the same technology available.

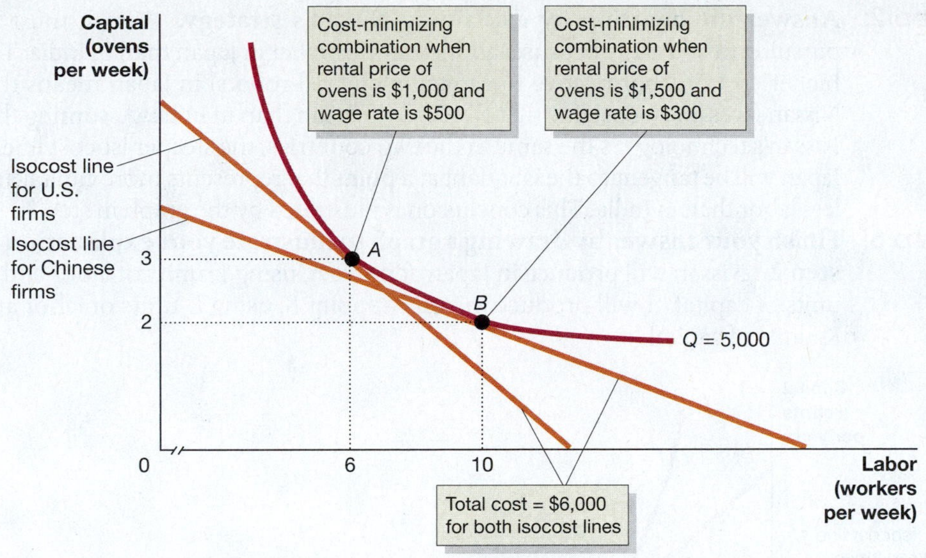

MyEconLab Animation

Figure 11A.5

Changing Input Prices Affects the Cost-Minimizing Input Choice

As the graph shows, the input combination at point *A*, which was optimal for Jill, is not optimal for a businessperson in China. Using the input combination at point *A* would cost businesspeople in China more than $6,000. Instead, the Chinese isocost line is tangent to the isoquant at point *B*, where the input combination is 2 ovens and 10 workers. Because ovens cost more in China but workers cost less, a Chinese firm will use fewer ovens and more workers than a U.S. firm, even if it has the same technology as the U.S. firm.

For example, suppose that in China, pizza ovens are higher priced and labor is lower priced than in the United States. In our example, Jill Johnson pays $1,000 per week to rent pizza ovens and $500 per week to hire workers. Suppose a businessperson in China must pay a price of $1,500 per week to rent the identical pizza ovens but can hire Chinese workers who are as productive as U.S. workers at a wage of $300 per week. Figure 11A.5 shows how the cost-minimizing input combination for the businessperson in China differs from Jill's.

Remember that the slope of the isocost line equals the wage rate divided by the rental price of capital multiplied by -1. The slope of the isocost line that Jill and other U.S. firms face is $-\$500/\$1{,}000$, or $-1/2$. Firms in China, however, face an isocost line with a slope of $-\$300/\$1{,}500$, or $-1/5$. As Figure 11A.5 shows, the input combination at point A, which was optimal for Jill, is not optimal for a firm in China. Using the input combination at point A would cost a firm in China more than $6,000. Instead, the Chinese isocost line is tangent to the isoquant at point *B*, where the input combination is 2 ovens and 10 workers. This result makes sense: Because ovens cost more in China but workers cost less, a Chinese firm will use fewer ovens and more workers than a U.S. firm, even if it has the same technology as the U.S. firm. MyEconLab Concept Check

Solved Problem 11A.1

MyEconLab Interactive Animation

Firms Responding to Differences in Input Price Ratios

David Autor, an economist at MIT, has written that, "When Nissan Motor Company builds cars in Japan, it makes extensive use of industrial robots to reduce labor costs. When it assembles cars in India, it uses robots far more sparingly."

Explain why Nissan uses this strategy. Illustrate your answer with an isoquant–isocost line graph.

Source: David Autor, "The 'Task' Approach to Labor Markets: An Overview," *Journal of Labor Market Research*, Vol. 46, No. 3 (February 2013), pp. 185–199.

Solving the Problem

Step 1: **Review the chapter material.** This problem is about determining the optimal choice of inputs when input price ratios differ, so you may want to review the section "Different Input Price Ratios Lead to Different Input Choices," which begins on page 396.

Step 2: **Answer the question by explaining Nissan's strategy.** Nissan must be pursuing this strategy because labor costs are higher in Japan than in India. The higher cost of labor relative to capital (industrial robots) in Japan means that Nissan faces an isocost line that is steeper in Japan than in India. Assuming that Nissan's technology is the same in the two countries, the steeper isocost line in Japan will be tangent to the isoquant at a point that represents more capital and less labor than in India. This conclusion is illustrated by the graph in step 3.

Step 3: **Finish your answer by drawing a graph to illustrate your explanation in step 2.** Nissan will produce in Japan at point *A*, using L_J units of labor and K_J units of capital. It will produce in India at point *B*, using L_I units of labor and K_I units of capital.

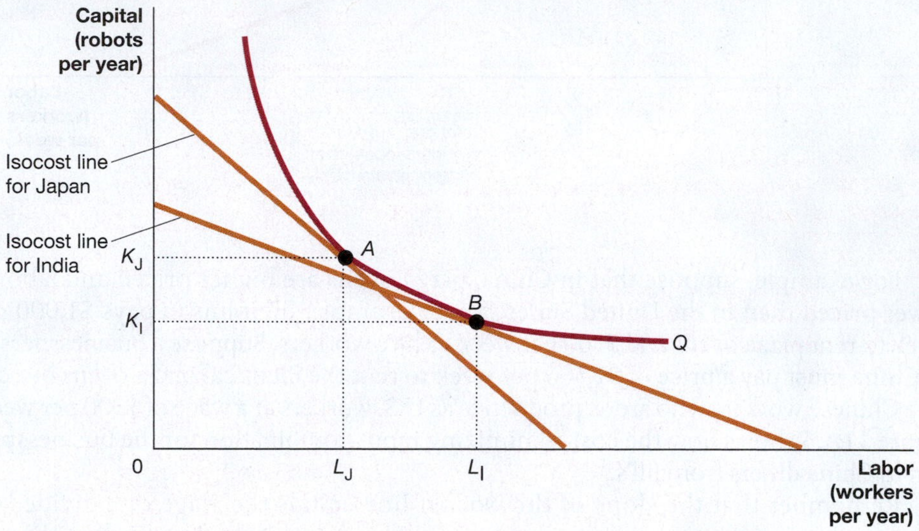

MyEconLab Study Plan

Your Turn: For more practice, do related problem 11A.6 on page 403 at the end of this appendix.

Another Look at Cost Minimization

We know that consumers maximize utility when they consume each good up to the point where the marginal utility per dollar spent is the same for every good. We can derive a very similar cost-minimization rule for firms. Remember that at the point of cost minimization, the isoquant and the isocost line are tangent, so they have the same slope. Therefore, *at the point of cost minimization, the marginal rate of technical substitution (MRTS) is equal to the wage rate divided by the rental price of capital.*

The slope of the isoquant tells us the rate at which a firm is able to substitute labor for capital, *keeping the level of output constant*. The slope of the isocost line tells us the rate at which a firm is able to substitute labor for capital, *given current input prices*. Only at the point of cost minimization are these two rates the same.

When we move from one point on an isoquant to another, we end up using more of one input and less of the other input, but the level of output remains the same. For example, as Jill moves down an isoquant, she uses fewer ovens and more workers but produces the same quantity of pizzas. In this chapter, we defined the *marginal product of labor* (MP_L) as the additional output produced by a firm as a result of hiring one more worker. Similarly, we can define the *marginal product of capital* (MP_K) as the additional output produced by a firm as a result of using one more machine. So, when Jill uses fewer ovens by moving down an isoquant, she loses output equal to:

$$-\text{Change in the quantity of ovens} \times MP_K.$$

But she uses more workers, so she gains output equal to:

$$\text{Change in the quantity of workers} \times MP_L.$$

We know that the gain in output from the additional workers is equal to the loss from the smaller quantity of ovens because total output remains the same along an isoquant. Therefore, we can write:

$$-\text{Change in the quantity of ovens} \times MP_K = \text{Change in the quantity of workers} \times MP_L.$$

Loss in output from using fewer ovens — Gain in output from using more workers

If we rearrange terms, we have the following:

$$\frac{-\text{Change in the quantity of ovens}}{\text{Change in the quantity of workers}} = \frac{MP_L}{MP_K}.$$

Because:

$$\frac{-\text{Change in the quantity of ovens}}{\text{Change in the quantity of workers}}$$

is the slope of the isoquant, it is equal to the marginal rate of technical substitution (multiplied by negative 1). So, we can write:

$$\frac{-\text{Change in the quantity of ovens}}{\text{Change in the quantity of workers}} = MRTS = \frac{MP_L}{MP_K}.$$

The slope of the isocost line equals the wage rate (w) divided by the rental price of capital (r). We saw earlier in this appendix that at the point of cost minimization, the *MRTS* equals the ratio of the prices of the two inputs. Therefore:

$$\frac{MP_L}{MP_K} = \frac{w}{r}.$$

We can rewrite this to show that at the point of cost minimization:

$$\frac{MP_L}{w} = \frac{MP_K}{r}.$$

This last expression tells us that to minimize cost for a given level of output, a firm should hire inputs up to the point where the last dollar spent on each input results in the same increase in output. If this equality did not hold, a firm could lower its costs by using more of one input and less of the other. For example, if the left side of the equation were greater than the right side, a firm could rent fewer ovens, hire more workers, and produce the same output at lower cost. MyEconLab Concept Check

Solved Problem 11A.2

MyEconLab Interactive Animation

Determining the Optimal Combination of Inputs

Consider the information in the following table for Jill Johnson's restaurant:

Marginal product of capital	3,000 pizzas per oven
Marginal product of labor	1,200 pizzas per worker
Wage rate	$300 per week
Rental price of ovens	$600 per week

Briefly explain whether Jill is minimizing costs. If she is not minimizing costs, explain whether she should rent more ovens and hire fewer workers or rent fewer ovens and hire more workers.

Solving the Problem

Step 1: Review the chapter material. This problem is about determining the optimal choice of inputs by comparing the ratios of the marginal products of inputs to their prices, so you may want to review the section "Another Look at Cost Minimization," which begins on page 398.

Step 2: Compute the ratios of marginal product to input price to determine whether Jill is minimizing costs. If Jill is minimizing costs, the following relationship should hold:

$$\frac{MP_L}{w} = \frac{MP_K}{r}.$$

In this case, we have:

$$MP_L = 1{,}200$$
$$MP_K = 3{,}000$$
$$w = \$300$$
$$r = \$600.$$

So:

$$\frac{MP_L}{w} = \frac{1{,}200}{\$300} = 4 \text{ pizzas per dollar, and } \frac{MP_K}{r} = \frac{3{,}000}{\$600} = 5 \text{ pizzas per dollar.}$$

Because the two ratios are not equal, Jill is not minimizing cost.

Step 3: Determine how Jill should change the mix of inputs she uses. Jill produces more pizzas per dollar from the last oven than from the last worker. This indicates that she has too many workers and too few ovens. Therefore, to minimize cost, Jill should use more ovens and hire fewer workers.

MyEconLab Study Plan

Your Turn: For more practice, do related problems 11A.7 and 11A.8 on page 403 at the end of this appendix.

Making the Connection

MyEconLab Video

Do National Football League Teams Behave Efficiently?

Did a rule change keep Tampa Bay from paying Jameis Winston too much?

In the National Football League (NFL), the "salary cap" is the maximum amount each team can spend in a year on salaries for football players. Each year's salary cap results from negotiations between the league and the union representing the players. To achieve efficiency, an NFL team should distribute salaries among players so as to maximize the level of output—in this case, winning football games—given the constant level of cost represented by the salary cap. (Notice that maximizing the level of output for a given level of cost is equivalent to minimizing cost for a given level of output. To see why, think about the situation in which an isocost line is tangent to an isoquant. At the point of tangency, the firm has simultaneously minimized the cost of producing the level of output represented by the isoquant and maximized the output produced at the level of cost represented by the isocost line.)

In distributing the fixed amount of salary payments available, teams should equalize the ratios of the marginal productivity of players, as represented by their contribution to winning games, to the salaries players receive. Just as a firm may not use a machine that has a very high marginal product if its rental price is very high, a football team may not want to hire a superstar player if the salary the team would need to pay is too high.

Economists Cade Massey, of the University of Pennsylvania, and Richard Thaler, of the University of Chicago, have analyzed whether NFL teams distribute their salaries efficiently. NFL teams obtain their players either by signing free agents—who are players whose contracts with other teams have expired—or by signing players chosen in the annual draft of eligible college players. The college draft consists of seven rounds, with the teams with the worst records the previous year choosing first. Massey and Thaler find that, in fact, NFL teams do not allocate salaries efficiently. In particular, the players chosen with the first few picks of the first round of the draft tend to be paid salaries that are much higher relative to their marginal products than are players taken later in the first round. A typical team with a high draft pick would increase its ability to win football games at the constant cost represented by the salary cap if it traded for lower draft picks, providing it could find another team willing to make the trade. Why do NFL teams apparently make the error of not efficiently distributing salaries? Massey and Thaler argue that general managers of NFL teams tend to be overconfident in their ability to forecast how well a college player is likely to perform in the NFL.

General managers of NFL teams are not alone in suffering from overconfidence. Studies have shown that, in general, people tend to overestimate their ability to forecast an uncertain outcome. Because NFL teams tend to overestimate the future marginal productivity of high draft picks, they pay them salaries that are inefficiently high compared to salaries other draft picks receive. NFL teams were aware that they were probably overpaying high draft picks. In 2011, they negotiated a new contract with the NFL Players Union that limited the salaries that drafted players could receive.

This example shows that the concepts developed in this chapter provide powerful tools for analyzing whether firms are operating efficiently.

Source: Cade Massey and Richard Thaler, "The Loser's Curse: Decision Making and Market Efficiency in the National Football League Draft," *Management Science*, Vol. 59, No. 7, (July 2013), pp. 1479–1495.

Your Turn: Test your understanding by doing related problem 11A.14 on page 404 at the end of this appendix.

MyEconLab Study Plan

The Expansion Path

We can use isoquants and isocost lines to examine what happens as a firm expands its level of output. Figure 11A.6 shows three isoquants for a firm that produces bookcases. The isocost lines are drawn under the assumption that the machines used in producing bookcases can be rented for $100 per day and the wage rate is $25 per day. The point where each isoquant is tangent to an isocost line determines the cost-minimizing combination of capital and labor for producing that level of output. For example, 10 machines and 40 workers is the cost-minimizing combination of inputs for producing 50 bookcases per day. The cost-minimizing points *A*, *B*, and *C* lie along the firm's **expansion path**, which is a curve that shows the cost-minimizing combination of inputs for every level of output.

Expansion path A curve that shows a firm's cost-minimizing combination of inputs for every level of output.

An important point to note is that the expansion path represents the least-cost combination of inputs to produce a given level of output *in the long run*, when the firm is able to vary the levels of all of its inputs. We know, though, that in the short run, at least one input is fixed. We can use Figure 11A.6 to show that as the firm expands in the short run, its costs will be higher than in the long run. Suppose that the firm is currently at point *B*, using 15 machines and 60 workers to produce 75 bookcases per day. The firm wants to expand its output to 100 bookcases per day, but in the short run, it is unable to increase the quantity of machines it uses. Therefore, to expand output, it must hire more workers. The figure shows that in the short run, to produce 100 bookcases per day using 15 machines, the lowest costs it can attain are at point *D*, where it employs 110 workers. With a rental price of machines of $100 per day and a wage rate of $25 per day, in the short run, the firm will have total costs

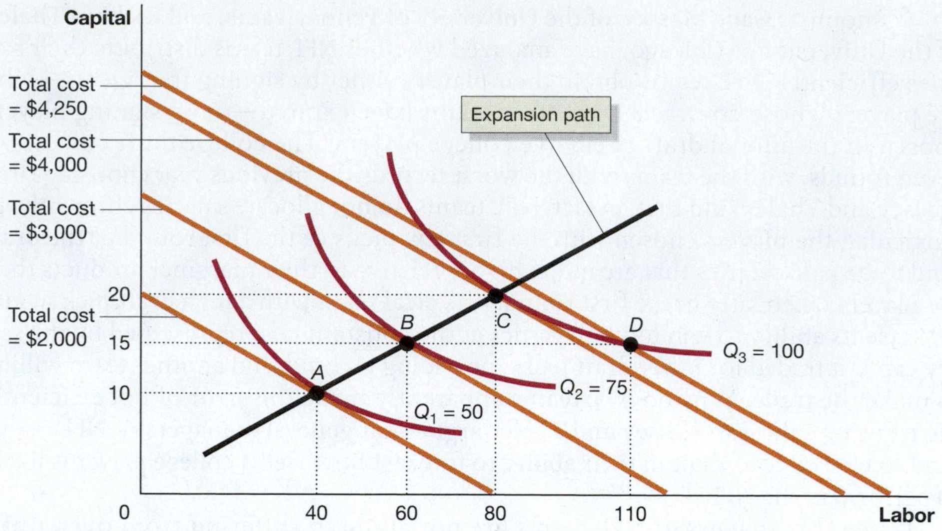

MyEconLab Animation

Figure 11A.6 The Expansion Path

The tangency points *A*, *B*, and *C* lie along the firm's expansion path, which is a curve that shows the cost-minimizing combination of inputs for every level of output. In the short run, when the quantity of machines is fixed, the firm can expand output from 75 bookcases per day to 100 bookcases per day at the lowest cost only by moving from point *B* to point *D* and increasing the number of workers from 60 to 110. In the long run, when it can increase the quantity of machines it uses, the firm can move from point *D* to point *C*, thereby reducing its total costs of producing 100 bookcases per day from $4,250 to $4,000.

of $4,250 to produce 100 bookcases per day. In the long run, though, the firm can increase the number of machines it uses from 15 to 20 and reduce the number of workers from 110 to 80. This change allows it to move from point *D* to point *C* on its expansion path and to lower its total costs of producing 100 bookcases per day from $4,250 to $4,000. The firm's minimum total costs of production are lower in the long run than in the short run.

MyEconLab Study Plan

MyEconLab Concept Check

Key Terms

Expansion path, p. 401

Isocost line, p. 394

Isoquant, p. 393

Marginal rate of technical substitution (*MRTS*), p. 394

11A Using Isoquants and Isocost Lines to Understand Production and Cost, pages 393–402

LEARNING OBJECTIVE: Use isoquants and isocost lines to understand production and cost.

MyEconLab Visit **www.myeconlab.com** to complete these exercises online and get instant feedback.

Review Questions

11A.1 What is an isoquant? What is the slope of an isoquant?

11A.2 What is an isocost line? What is the slope of an isocost line?

11A.3 How do firms choose the optimal combination of inputs?

Problems and Applications

11A.4 Draw an isoquant–isocost line graph to illustrate the following situation: Jill Johnson can rent pizza ovens for $400 per week and hire workers for $200 per week. She is currently using 5 ovens and 10 workers to produce 20,000 pizzas per week and has total costs of $4,000. Make sure to label your graph to show the cost-minimizing input combination and the maximum quantity of labor and capital she can use with total costs of $4,000.

11A.5 Use the following graph to answer the questions.

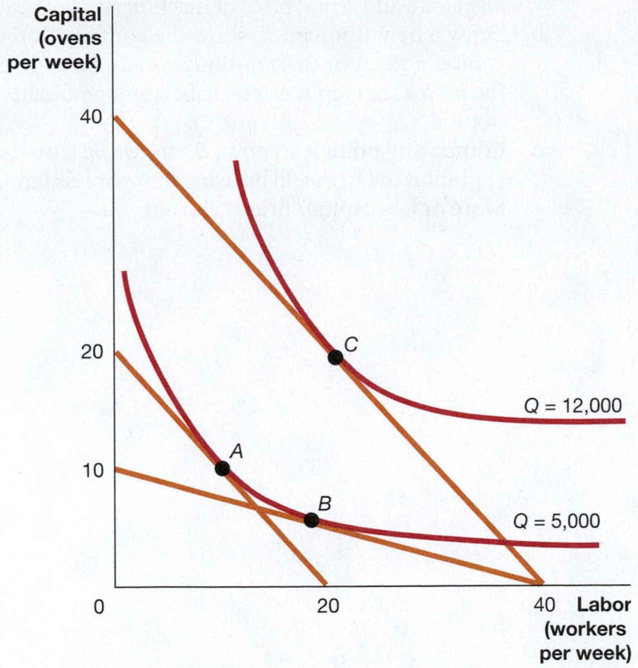

a. If the wage rate and the rental price of ovens are both $100 and total cost is $2,000, is the cost-minimizing point *A*, *B*, or *C*? Briefly explain.

b. If the wage rate is $25, the rental price of ovens is $100, and total cost is $1,000, is the cost-minimizing point *A*, *B*, or *C*? Briefly explain.

c. If the wage rate and the rental price of ovens are both $100 and total cost is $4,000, is the cost-minimizing point *A*, *B*, or *C*? Briefly explain.

11A.6 **(Related to Solved Problem 11A.1 on page 397)** During the eighteenth century, the American colonies had much more land per farmer than did Europe. As a result, the price of labor in the colonies was much higher relative to the price of land than it was in Europe. Assume that Europe and the colonies had access to the same technology for producing food. Use an isoquant–isocost line graph to illustrate why the combination of land and labor used in producing food in the colonies would have been different from the combination used to produce food in Europe.

11A.7 **(Related to Solved Problem 11A.2 on page 399)** Consider the information in the following table for Jill Johnson's restaurant:

Marginal product of capital	4,000
Marginal product of labor	100
Wage rate	$10
Rental price of pizza ovens	$500

Briefly explain whether Jill is minimizing costs. If she is not minimizing costs, explain whether she should rent more ovens and hire fewer workers or rent fewer ovens and hire more workers.

11A.8 **(Related to Solved Problem 11A.2 on page 399)** Draw an isoquant–isocost line graph to illustrate the following situation: Jill Johnson can rent pizza ovens for $200 per week and hire workers for $100 per week. Currently, she is using 5 ovens and 10 workers to produce 20,000 pizzas per week and has total costs of $2,000. Jill's marginal rate of technical substitution (*MRTS*) equals -1. Explain why this means that she's not minimizing costs and what she could do to minimize costs.

11A.9 Draw an isoquant–isocost line graph to illustrate the following situation and the change that occurs: Jill Johnson can rent pizza ovens for $2,000 per week and hire workers for $1,000 per week. Currently, she is using 5 ovens and 10 workers to produce 20,000 pizzas per week and has total costs of $20,000. Then Jill reorganizes the way things are done in her business and achieves positive technological change.

11A.10 Use the following graph to answer the following questions about Jill Johnson's isoquant curve.

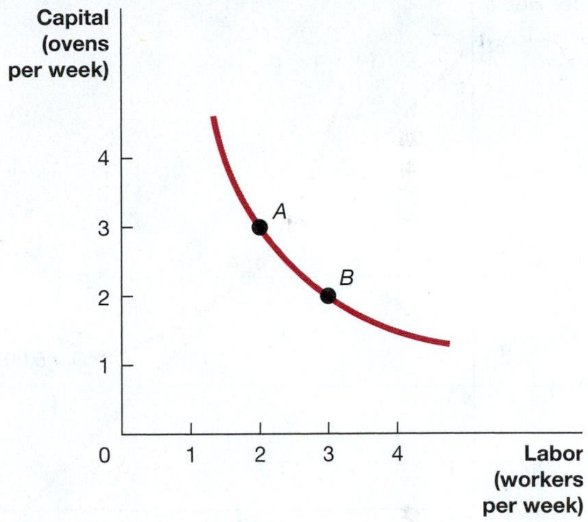

a. Which combination of inputs yields more output: combination *A* (3 ovens and 2 workers) or combination *B* (2 ovens and 3 workers)?

b. What will determine whether Jill selects *A*, *B*, or some other point along this isoquant curve?

c. Is the marginal rate of technical substitution (*MRTS*) greater at point *A* or point *B*?

11A.11 Draw an isoquant–isocost line graph to illustrate the following situation: Jill Johnson can rent pizza ovens for $2,000 per week and hire workers for $1,000 per week. She can minimize the cost of producing 20,000 pizzas per week by using 5 ovens and 10 workers, at a total cost of $20,000. She can minimize the cost of producing 45,000 pizzas per week by using 10 ovens and 20 workers, at a total cost of $40,000. She can minimize the cost of producing 60,000 pizzas per week by using 15 ovens and 30 workers, at a total cost of $60,000. Draw Jill's long-run average cost curve and discuss its economies of scale and diseconomies of scale.

11A.12 In Brazil, a grove of oranges is picked using 20 workers, ladders, and baskets. In Florida, a grove of oranges is picked using 1 worker and a machine that shakes the oranges off the trees and scoops up the fallen oranges. Using an isoquant–isocost line graph, illustrate why these two different methods are used to pick the same number of oranges per day in these two locations.

11A.13 Jill Johnson is minimizing the costs of producing pizzas. The rental price of one of her ovens is $2,000 per week, and the wage rate is $600 per week. The marginal product of capital in her business is 12,000 pizzas. What must be the marginal product of her workers?

11A.14 **(Related to the Making the Connection on page 400)** If Cade Massey and Richard Thaler are correct, should the team that has the first pick in the draft keep the pick or trade it to another team for a lower pick? Briefly explain. Does the 2011 agreement that limits the salaries of drafted players affect your answer?

11A.15 Swift Ellis, Inc., manufactures running shoes. The following graph illustrates the combination of capital and labor (point *A*) that minimizes the firm's cost of producing 5,000 pairs of shoes. Suppose both the wage rate and the rental price of machinery doubles.

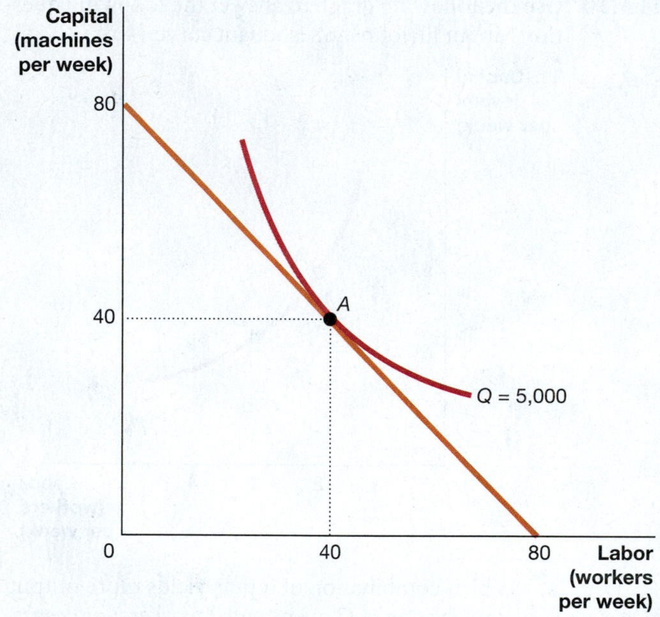

a. Draw a new isocost line to reflect this change in the wage rate and rental price of machinery.
b. Draw a new isoquant to show the combination of capital and labor that minimizes total cost, given the increase in input prices. Label this combination point *B*.
c. Comparing point *A* to point *B*, can we be sure that at point *B* the firm will be using more or less labor? More or less capital? Briefly explain.

CHAPTER

12

Firms in Perfectly Competitive Markets

Chapter Outline and Learning Objectives

Are Cage-Free Eggs the Road to Riches?

In recent years, the demand for healthier foods has increased. In addition, many people are concerned that some animals being raised for food are not being treated humanely. There are more than 65,000 poultry farms in the United States that specialize in producing eggs. Most farmers raise chickens in cages that restrict their movement. Some farmers, though, have begun selling eggs produced using "cage-free" or "free-range" methods. Although the U.S. Department of Agriculture has not developed official definitions of these terms, chickens raised this way have significant room to move around, and some are raised outdoors.

Some consumers are willing to pay more for eggs produced by cage-free chickens. An article in the *Wall Street Journal* quoted one consumer's reason for buying cage-free eggs: "I like my chickens able to eat bugs and scratch." Costs of raising chickens this way are higher because fewer chickens can be raised in an area of a given size, the chickens eat more because they are moving around, and some chickens die from being pecked by other chickens. Some farmers, though, can sell cage-free eggs for as much as double the price of eggs produced using conventional methods. Overall, farmers have been earning higher profits on cage-free eggs than on conventionally produced eggs.

As of 2015, only about 6 percent of eggs were produced by cage-free chickens. But many farmers were switching to this method. One farmer gave this explanation, "Farming is about making a profit, and if someone is willing to pay us extra, we're going to do that." But how much longer would these profits continue? Although the share of cage-free eggs was small, it was growing rapidly, and as more farmers switched to these methods, there was already an indication that the premium over the prices of conventional eggs was shrinking.

The process of new firms entering a profitable market and driving down prices and profits is not found only in agriculture. Throughout the economy, entrepreneurs are continually introducing new products or new ways of selling products, which—when successful—enable them to earn economic profits in the short run. But in the long run, competition among firms forces prices to the level where they just cover the costs of production. This process of competition is at the heart of the market system and is the focus of this chapter.

Sources: David Kesmodel, "Latest Flap on Egg Farms: Whether to Go 'Cage-Free,'" *Wall Street Journal*, March 11, 2015; David Kesmodel, "Free-Range? Cage-Free? Organic?" *Wall Street Journal*, March 11, 2015; "Dunkin' Donuts Eyes Shift to All Cage-Free Eggs Globally," Associated Press, March 30, 2015; and U.S. Department of Agriculture data.

Economics in Your Life

Are You an Entrepreneur?

Were you an entrepreneur during high school? You may have worked as a babysitter or mowed lawns for your neighbors. While you may not think of these jobs as being small businesses, that is exactly what they are. How did you decide what price to charge for your services? You may have wanted to charge $25 per hour for babysitting or mowing lawns, but you probably charged much less. As you read the chapter, think about the competitive situation you faced as a teenage entrepreneur and try to determine why the prices received by most people who babysit and mow lawns are so low. You can check your answers against those we provide on **page 432** at the end of this chapter.

An *industry* refers to all the firms selling a particular good or service—for instance, eggs, automobiles, or life insurance. Poultry farming is an example of a *perfectly competitive* industry. Firms in these industries are unable to control the prices of the products they sell and are unable to earn an economic profit in the long run for two main reasons:

1. Firms in these industries sell identical products.
2. It is easy for new firms to enter these industries.

Studying how perfectly competitive industries operate is the best way to understand how markets answer the fundamental economic questions discussed in Chapter 1:

- What goods and services will be produced?
- How will the goods and services be produced?
- Who will receive the goods and services produced?

Most industries, though, are not perfectly competitive. In most industries, firms do *not* produce identical products. And in some industries, it may be difficult for new firms to enter. There are thousands of industries in the United States. Although in some ways each industry is unique, industries share enough similarities that economists can group them into four market structures. In particular, any industry has three key characteristics:

1. The number of firms in the industry
2. The similarity of the good or service produced by the firms in the industry
3. The ease with which new firms can enter the industry

Economists use these characteristics to classify industries into the four market structures listed in Table 12.1.

Many industries, including restaurants, clothing stores, and other retailers, have a large number of firms selling products that are differentiated, rather than identical, and fall into the category of *monopolistic competition*. Some industries, such as computers and automobiles, have only a few firms and are *oligopolies*. Finally, a few industries, such as the delivery of first-class mail by the U.S. Postal Service, have only one firm and are *monopolies*. After discussing perfect competition in this chapter, we will devote a chapter to each of these other market structures.

Table 12.1

The Four Market Structures

	Market Structure			
Characteristic	**Perfect Competition**	**Monopolistic Competition**	**Oligopoly**	**Monopoly**
Number of firms	Many	Many	Few	One
Type of product	Identical	Differentiated	Identical or differentiated	Unique
Ease of entry	High	High	Low	Entry blocked
Examples of industries	• Growing wheat • Poultry farming	• Clothing stores • Restaurants	• Manufacturing computers • Manufacturing automobiles	• First-class mail delivery • Providing tap water

12.1 Perfectly Competitive Markets

LEARNING OBJECTIVE: Explain what a perfectly competitive market is and why a perfect competitor faces a horizontal demand curve.

Why are firms in a **perfectly competitive market** unable to control the prices of the goods they sell, and why are the owners of these firms unable to earn economic profits in the long run? We can begin our analysis by listing the three conditions that make a market perfectly competitive:

Perfectly competitive market A market that meets the conditions of (1) many buyers and sellers, (2) all firms selling identical products, and (3) no barriers to new firms entering the market.

1. There must be many buyers and many firms, all of which are small relative to the market.
2. All firms in the market must sell identical products.
3. There must be no barriers to new firms entering the market.

All three of these conditions hold in markets for agricultural products. For example, no single consumer or producer of apples buys or sells more than a tiny fraction of the total apple crop. The apples sold by each apple grower are identical, and there are no barriers to a new firm entering this market by purchasing land and planting apple trees. As we will see, it is the existence of many firms, all selling the same good, that keeps any single apple farmer from affecting the price of apples.

Although the market for apples meets the conditions for perfect competition, the markets for most goods and services do not. In particular, the second and third conditions are very restrictive. In most markets that have many buyers and sellers, firms do not sell identical products. For example, not all restaurant meals are the same, nor is all women's clothing the same. In later chapters, we will explore the common situation of monopolistic competition where many firms are selling similar but not identical products, and we will analyze industries that are oligopolies, where entry of new firms is difficult, and industries that are monopolies, where entry of new firms is impossible. In this chapter, we concentrate on perfectly competitive markets so we can use them as a benchmark to analyze how firms behave when they face the maximum possible competition.

A Perfectly Competitive Firm Cannot Affect the Market Price

Prices in perfectly competitive markets are determined by the interaction of demand and supply for the good or service. The actions of any single consumer or any single firm have no effect on the market price. Consumers and firms have to accept the market price if they want to buy and sell in a perfectly competitive market.

Because a firm in a perfectly competitive market is very small relative to the market and because it is selling exactly the same product as every other firm, it can sell as much as it wants without having to lower its price. If a perfectly competitive firm tries to raise its price, it won't sell anything at all because consumers will switch to buying the product from the firm's competitors. Therefore, the firm will be a **price taker** and will have to charge the same price as every other firm in the market. Although we don't usually think of firms as being too small to affect the market price, consumers are often in the position of being price takers. For instance, suppose your local supermarket is selling bread for $2.50 per loaf. You can load up your shopping cart with 20 loaves of bread, and the supermarket will gladly sell them all to you for $2.50 per loaf. But if you go to the cashier and offer to buy the bread for $2.49 per loaf, he or she will not sell it to you at that price. As a buyer, you are too small relative to the bread market to have any effect on the equilibrium price. Whether you leave the supermarket and buy no bread or you buy 20 loaves, you are unable to change the market price of bread by even one cent.

Price taker A buyer or seller that is unable to affect the market price.

The situation you face as a bread buyer is the same one a wheat farmer faces as a wheat seller. There are about 150,000 farmers growing wheat in the United States. The market price of wheat is determined not by any individual wheat farmer but by the interaction of all the buyers and all the sellers in the wheat market. If any one wheat farmer has the best crop the farmer has ever had, or if any one wheat farmer stops growing wheat altogether, the market price of wheat will not be affected *because the market supply curve for wheat will not shift enough to change the equilibrium price by even one cent.*

MyEconLab Concept Check

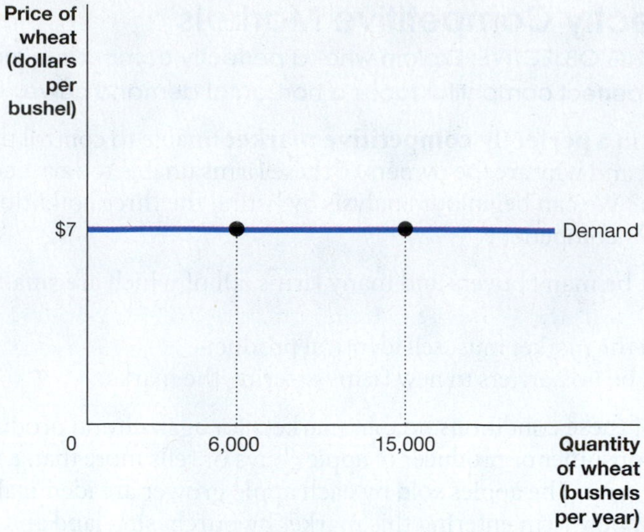

MyEconLab Animation

Figure 12.1 A Perfectly Competitive Firm Faces a Horizontal Demand Curve

A firm in a perfectly competitive market is selling exactly the same product as all of the other firms in the market. Therefore, it can sell as much as it wants at the current market price, but it cannot sell anything at all if it raises the price by even 1 cent. As a result, the demand curve for a perfectly competitive firm's output is a horizontal line. In the figure, whether the wheat farmer sells 6,000 bushels or 15,000 bushels per year has no effect on the market price of $7.

The Demand Curve for the Output of a Perfectly Competitive Firm

Suppose Bill Parker grows wheat on a 250-acre farm in Washington State. Farmer Parker is selling wheat in a perfectly competitive market, so he is a price taker. Because he can sell as much wheat as he chooses at the market price—but can't sell any wheat at all at a higher price—the demand curve for his wheat has an unusual shape: It is horizontal, as shown in Figure 12.1. With a horizontal demand curve, Farmer Parker must accept the market price, which in this case is $7 per bushel. Whether Farmer Parker sells 6,000 bushels per year or 15,000 has no effect on the market price.

Don't Let This Happen to You

Don't Confuse the Demand Curve for Farmer Parker's Wheat with the Market Demand Curve for Wheat

The demand curve for wheat has the normal downward-sloping shape. If the price of wheat goes up, the quantity of wheat demanded goes down, and if the price of wheat goes down, the quantity of wheat demanded goes up. But the demand curve for the output of a single wheat farmer is *not* downward sloping: It is a horizontal line. If an individual wheat farmer tries to increase the price he charges for his wheat, the quantity demanded falls to zero because buyers will purchase from one of the other 150,000 wheat farmers. But any one farmer can sell as much wheat as the farmer can produce without needing to cut the price. Both of these features of this market hold because each wheat farmer is very small relative to the overall market for wheat.

When we draw graphs of the wheat market, we usually show the market equilibrium quantity in millions or billions of bushels. When we draw graphs of the demand for wheat produced by one farmer, we usually show the quantity produced in smaller units, such as thousands of bushels. It is important to remember this difference in scale when interpreting these graphs.

Finally, it is not just wheat farmers who have horizontal demand curves for their products; any firm in a perfectly competitive market faces a horizontal demand curve.

MyEconLab Study Plan

Your Turn: Test your understanding by doing related problem 1.6 on page 434 at the end of this chapter.

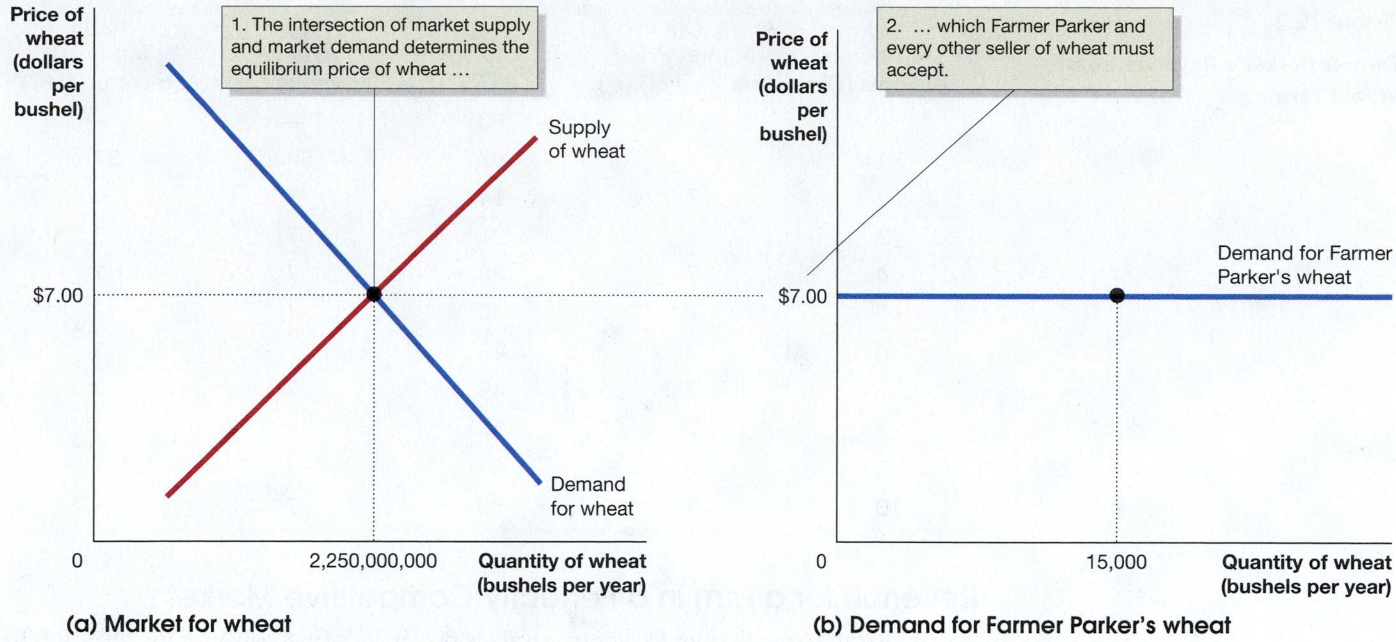

MyEconLab Animation

Figure 12.2 The Market Demand for Wheat versus the Demand for One Farmer's Wheat

In a perfectly competitive market, price is determined by the intersection of market demand and market supply. In panel (a), the demand and supply curves for wheat intersect at a price of $7 per bushel. An individual wheat farmer like Farmer Parker cannot affect the market price for wheat. Therefore, as panel (b) shows, the demand curve for Farmer Parker's wheat is a horizontal line. To understand this figure, it is important to notice that the scales on the horizontal axes in the two panels are very different. In panel (a), the equilibrium quantity of wheat is 2.25 *billion* bushels, and in panel (b), Farmer Parker is producing only 15,000 bushels of wheat.

The demand curve for Farmer Parker's wheat is very different from the market demand curve for wheat. Panel (a) of Figure 12.2 shows the market for wheat. The demand curve in panel (a) is the *market demand curve for wheat* and has the normal downward slope we are familiar with from the market demand curves in Chapter 3. Panel (b) of Figure 12.2 shows the demand curve for Farmer Parker's wheat, which is a horizontal line. By viewing these graphs side by side, you can see that the price Farmer Parker receives for his wheat in panel (b) is determined by the interaction of all sellers and all buyers of wheat in the wheat market in panel (a). Notice, however, that the scales on the horizontal axes in the two panels are very different. In panel (a), the equilibrium quantity of wheat is 2.25 *billion* bushels. In panel (b), Farmer Parker is producing only 15,000 bushels, or less than 0.001 percent of market output. We need to use different scales in the two panels so we can display both of them on one page. Keep in mind this key point: Farmer Parker's output of wheat is very small relative to the total market output. MyEconLab Concept Check

MyEconLab Study Plan

12.2 How a Firm Maximizes Profit in a Perfectly Competitive Market

LEARNING OBJECTIVE: Explain how a firm maximizes profit in a perfectly competitive market.

We have seen that Farmer Parker cannot control the price of his wheat. In this situation, how does he decide how much wheat to produce? We assume that Farmer Parker's objective is to maximize profit. This assumption is reasonable for most firms, most of the time. Remember that **profit** is the difference between total revenue (*TR*) and total cost (*TC*):

Profit Total revenue minus total cost.

$$\text{Profit} = TR - TC.$$

To maximize his profit, Farmer Parker should produce the quantity of wheat where the difference between the total revenue he receives and his total cost is as large as possible.

Table 12.2

Farmer Parker's Revenue from Wheat Farming

(1) Number of Bushels (*Q*)	(2) Market Price (per bushel) (*P*)	(3) Total Revenue (*TR*)	(4) Average Revenue (*AR*)	(5) Marginal Revenue (*MR*)
0	$7	$0	—	—
1	7	7	$7	$7
2	7	14	7	7
3	7	21	7	7
4	7	28	7	7
5	7	35	7	7
6	7	42	7	7
7	7	49	7	7
8	7	56	7	7
9	7	63	7	7
10	7	70	7	7

Revenue for a Firm in a Perfectly Competitive Market

To understand how Farmer Parker maximizes profit, let's first consider his revenue. To keep the numbers simple, we will assume that he owns a very small farm and produces at most 10 bushels of wheat per year. Table 12.2 shows the revenue Farmer Parker will earn from selling various quantities of wheat if the market price for wheat is $7.

The third column in Table 12.2 shows that Farmer Parker's *total revenue* rises by $7 for every additional bushel he sells because he can sell as many bushels as he wants at the market price of $7 per bushel. The fourth and fifth columns in the table show Farmer Parker's *average revenue* and *marginal revenue* from selling wheat. His **average revenue (AR)** equals his total revenue divided by the quantity of bushels he sells. For example, if he sells 5 bushels for a total of $35, his average revenue is $35/5 = $7. Notice that his average revenue is also equal to the market price of $7. In fact, for any level of output, a firm's average revenue is always equal to the market price. This equality holds because total revenue equals price times quantity ($TR = P \times Q$), and average revenue equals total revenue divided by quantity ($AR = TR/Q$). So, $AR = TR/Q = (P \times Q)/Q = P$.

Average revenue (AR) Total revenue divided by the quantity of the product sold.

Farmer Parker's **marginal revenue (MR)** is the change in his total revenue from selling one more bushel:

Marginal revenue (MR) The change in total revenue from selling one more unit of a product.

$$\text{Marginal revenue} = \frac{\text{Change in total revenue}}{\text{Change in quantity}}, \text{ or } MR = \frac{\Delta TR}{\Delta Q}.$$

Each additional bushel Farmer Parker sells always adds $7 to his total revenue, so his marginal revenue is $7. Farmer Parker's marginal revenue is $7 per bushel because he is selling wheat in a perfectly competitive market and can sell as much as he wants at the market price. In fact, Farmer Parker's marginal revenue and average revenue are both equal to the market price. This is an important point: *For a firm in a perfectly competitive market, price is equal to both average revenue and marginal revenue.* MyEconLab Concept Check

Determining the Profit-Maximizing Level of Output

To determine how Farmer Parker can maximize profit, we have to consider his costs as well as his revenue. A wheat farmer has many costs, including the costs of seed and fertilizer, as well as the wages of farm workers. In Table 12.3, we bring together the revenue data from Table 12.2 with cost data for Farmer Parker's farm. Recall that a firm's *marginal cost* is the increase in total cost resulting from producing another unit of output.

We calculate profit in the fourth column by subtracting total cost in the third column from total revenue in the second column. The fourth column shows that as long as Farmer Parker produces between 3 and 9 bushels of wheat, he will earn a profit.

Table 12.3

Farmer Parker's Profit from Wheat Farming

(1) Quantity (bushels) (*Q*)	(2) Total Revenue (*TR*)	(3) Total Cost (*TC*)	(4) Profit (*TR* − *TC*)	(5) Marginal Revenue (*MR*)	(6) Marginal Cost (*MC*)
0	$0.00	$10.00	−$10.00	—	—
1	7.00	14.00	−7.00	$7.00	$4.00
2	14.00	16.50	−2.50	7.00	2.50
3	21.00	18.50	2.50	7.00	2.00
4	28.00	21.00	7.00	7.00	2.50
5	35.00	24.50	10.50	7.00	3.50
6	42.00	29.00	13.00	7.00	4.50
7	49.00	35.50	13.50	7.00	6.50
8	56.00	44.50	11.50	7.00	9.00
9	63.00	56.50	6.50	7.00	12.00
10	70.00	72.00	−2.00	7.00	15.50

His maximum profit is $13.50, which he will earn by producing 7 bushels of wheat. Because Farmer Parker wants to maximize his profit, we would expect him to produce 7 bushels of wheat. Producing more than 7 bushels reduces his profit. For example, if he produces 8 bushels of wheat, his profit will decline from $13.50 to $11.50. The values for marginal cost given in the last column of the table help us understand why Farmer Parker's profits will decline if he produces more than 7 bushels of wheat: After the seventh bushel of wheat, rising marginal cost causes Farmer Parker's profits to decline.

In fact, comparing the marginal cost and marginal revenue at each level of output is an alternative method of calculating Farmer Parker's profit. We illustrate the two methods of calculating profit in Figure 12.3. We show the total revenue and total cost

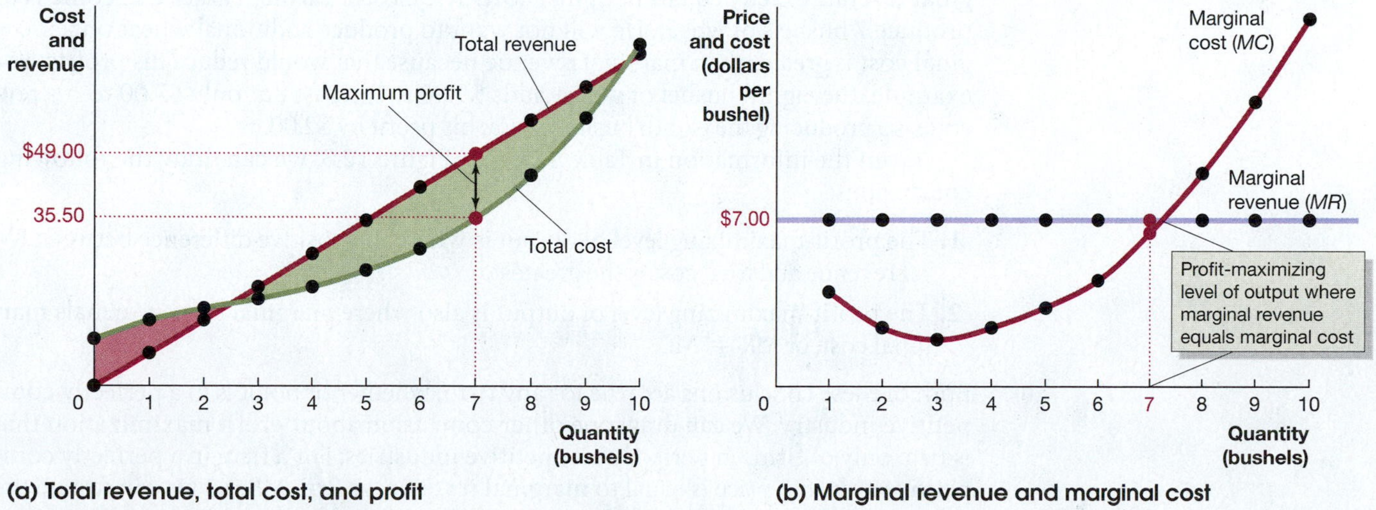

MyEconLab Animation

Figure 12.3 The Profit-Maximizing Level of Output

In panel (a), Farmer Parker maximizes his profit where the positive vertical distance between total revenue and total cost is the largest, which occurs at an output of 7 bushels. Panel (b) shows that Farmer Parker's marginal revenue (*MR*) is equal to a constant $7 per bushel. He maximizes profit by producing wheat up to the point where the marginal revenue of the last bushel produced is equal to its marginal cost, or *MR* = *MC*. In this case, at no level of output does marginal revenue exactly equal marginal cost. The closest Farmer Parker can come is to produce 7 bushels of wheat. He will not want to continue to produce once marginal cost is greater than marginal revenue because that would reduce his profits. Panels (a) and (b) show alternative ways of thinking about how Farmer Parker can determine the profit-maximizing quantity of wheat to produce.

approach in panel (a) and the marginal revenue and marginal cost approach in panel (b). Total revenue is a straight line on the graph in panel (a) because total revenue increases at a constant rate of $7 for each additional bushel sold. Farmer Parker's profit is maximized when the vertical distance between the line representing total revenue and the total cost curve is as large as possible. Just as we saw in Table 12.3, his maximum profit occurs at an output of 7 bushels.

The last two columns of Table 12.3 show the marginal revenue (*MR*) Farmer Parker receives from selling another bushel of wheat and his marginal cost (*MC*) of producing another bushel of wheat. Panel (b) of Figure 12.3 shows Farmer Parker's marginal revenue and marginal cost. Because marginal revenue is always equal to $7, it is a horizontal line at the market price. We have already seen that the demand curve for a perfectly competitive firm is also a horizontal line at the market price. *Therefore, the marginal revenue curve for a perfectly competitive firm is the same as its demand curve.* Farmer Parker's marginal cost of producing wheat first falls and then rises, following the usual pattern we discussed in the previous chapter.

We know from panel (a) that profit is at a maximum at 7 bushels of wheat. In panel (b), profit is also at a maximum at 7 bushels of wheat. To understand why profit is maximized at the level of output where marginal revenue equals marginal cost, remember a key economic principle: *Optimal decisions are made at the margin.* Firms use this principle to decide the quantity of a good to produce. For example, in deciding how much wheat to produce, Farmer Parker needs to compare the marginal revenue he earns from selling another bushel of wheat to the marginal cost of producing that bushel. The difference between the marginal revenue and the marginal cost is the additional profit (or loss) from producing one more bushel. As long as marginal revenue is greater than marginal cost, Farmer Parker's profits are increasing, and he will want to expand production. For example, he will not stop producing at 6 bushels of wheat because producing and selling the seventh bushel adds $7.00 to his revenue but only $6.50 to his cost, so his profit increases by $0.50. He wants to continue producing until the marginal revenue he receives from selling another bushel is equal to the marginal cost of producing it. At that level of output, he will make no *additional* profit by selling another bushel, so he will have maximized his profit.

By inspecting Table 12.3, we can see that there is no level of output at which marginal revenue exactly equals marginal cost. The closest Farmer Parker can come is to produce 7 bushels of wheat. He will not want to produce additional wheat once marginal cost is greater than marginal revenue because that would reduce his profits. For example, the eighth bushel of wheat adds $9.00 to his cost but only $7.00 to his revenue, so producing the eighth bushel *reduces* his profit by $2.00.

From the information in Table 12.3 and Figure 12.3, we can draw the following conclusions:

1. The profit-maximizing level of output is where the positive difference between total revenue and total cost is the greatest.
2. The profit-maximizing level of output is also where marginal revenue equals marginal cost, or $MR = MC$.

Both of these conclusions are true for any firm, whether or not it is in a perfectly competitive industry. We can draw one other conclusion about profit maximization that is true only of firms in perfectly competitive industries: For a firm in a perfectly competitive industry, price is equal to marginal revenue, or $P = MR$. So we can restate the $MR = MC$ condition as $P = MC$.

MyEconLab Study Plan

MyEconLab Concept Check

12.3 Illustrating Profit or Loss on the Cost Curve Graph

LEARNING OBJECTIVE: Use graphs to show a firm's profit or loss.

We have seen that profit is the difference between total revenue and total cost. We can also express profit in terms of *average total cost* (*ATC*). This approach allows us to show profit on the cost curve graph we developed in the last chapter.

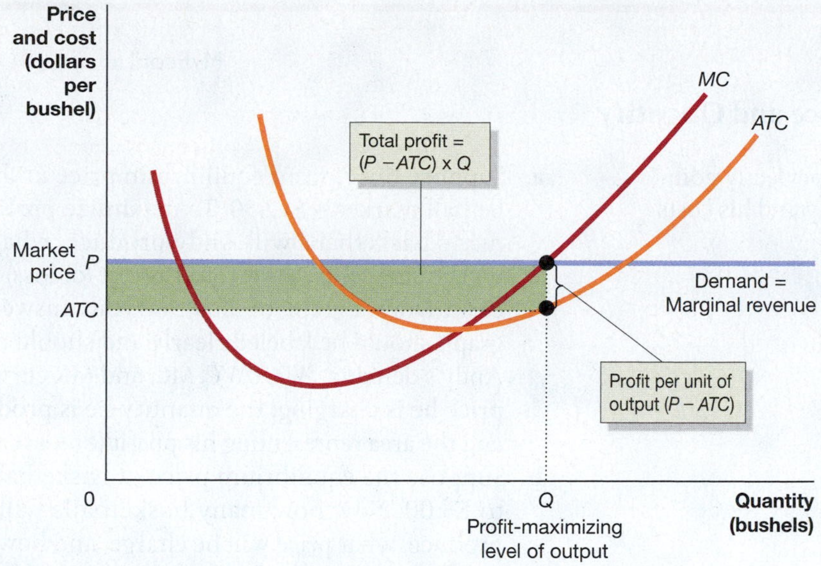

MyEconLab Animation

Figure 12.4 The Area of Maximum Profit

A firm maximizes profit at the level of output at which marginal revenue equals marginal cost. The difference between price and average total cost equals profit per unit of output. Total profit equals profit per unit multiplied by the number of units produced. Total profit is represented by the area of the green-shaded rectangle, which has a height equal to ($P - ATC$) and a width equal to Q.

To begin, we need to work through several steps to determine the relationship between profit and average total cost. Because profit is equal to total revenue (TR) minus total cost (TC) and total revenue is price times quantity, we can write the following:

$$\text{Profit} = (P \times Q) - TC.$$

If we divide both sides of this equation by Q, we have:

$$\frac{\text{Profit}}{Q} = \frac{(P \times Q)}{Q} - \frac{TC}{Q},$$

or:

$$\frac{\text{Profit}}{Q} = P - ATC,$$

because TC/Q equals ATC. This equation tells us that profit per unit (or average profit) equals price minus average total cost. Finally, we obtain the equation for the relationship between total profit and average total cost by multiplying by Q:

$$\text{Profit} = (P - ATC) \times Q.$$

This equation tells us that a firm's total profit is equal to the difference between price and average total cost multiplied by the quantity produced.

Showing Profit on a Graph

Figure 12.4 shows the relationship between a firm's average total cost and its marginal cost that we discussed in the last chapter. In this figure, we also show the firm's marginal revenue curve (which is the same as its demand curve) and the area representing total profit. Using the relationship between profit and average total cost that we just determined, we can say that the area representing total profit has a height equal to ($P - ATC$) and a base equal to Q. This area is shown by the green-shaded rectangle.

Solved Problem 12.3

MyEconLab Interactive Animation

Determining Profit-Maximizing Price and Quantity

Suppose that Andy sells basketballs in the perfectly competitive basketball market. His output per day and his costs are as follows:

Output per Day	Total Cost
0	$10.00
1	20.50
2	24.50
3	28.00
4	34.00
5	43.00
6	55.50
7	72.00
8	93.00
9	119.00

a. Suppose the current equilibrium price in the basketball market is $12.50. To maximize profit, how many basketballs will Andy produce, what price will he charge, and how much profit (or loss) will he earn? Draw a graph to illustrate your answer. Your graph should be labeled clearly and should include Andy's demand, *ATC*, *AVC*, *MC*, and *MR* curves; the price he is charging; the quantity he is producing; and the area representing his profit (or loss).

b. Suppose the equilibrium price of basketballs falls to $6.00. Now how many basketballs will Andy produce, what price will he charge, and how much profit (or loss) will he make? Draw a graph to illustrate this situation, using the instructions in part (a).

Solving the Problem

Step 1: Review the chapter material. This problem is about using cost curve graphs to analyze perfectly competitive firms, so you may want to review the section "Illustrating Profit or Loss on the Cost Curve Graph," which begins on page 414.

Step 2: Calculate Andy's marginal cost, average total cost, and average variable cost. To maximize profit, Andy will produce the level of output where marginal revenue is equal to marginal cost. We can calculate marginal cost from the information given in the following table. We can also calculate average total cost and average variable cost in order to draw the required graph. Average total cost (*ATC*) equals total cost (*TC*) divided by the level of output (*Q*). Average variable cost (*AVC*) equals variable cost (*VC*) divided by output (*Q*). To calculate variable cost, recall that total cost equals variable cost plus fixed cost. When output equals zero, total cost equals fixed cost. In this case, fixed cost equals $10.00.

Output per Day (*Q*)	Total Cost (*TC*)	Fixed Cost (*FC*)	Variable Cost (*VC*)	Average Total Cost (*ATC*)	Average Variable Cost (*AVC*)	Marginal Cost (*MC*)
0	$10.00	$10.00	$0.00	—	—	—
1	20.50	10.00	10.50	$20.50	$10.50	$10.50
2	24.50	10.00	14.50	12.25	7.25	4.00
3	28.00	10.00	18.00	9.33	6.00	3.50
4	34.00	10.00	24.00	8.50	6.00	6.00
5	43.00	10.00	33.00	8.60	6.60	9.00
6	55.50	10.00	45.50	9.25	7.58	12.50
7	72.00	10.00	62.00	10.29	8.86	16.50
8	93.00	10.00	83.00	11.63	10.38	21.00
9	119.00	10.00	109.00	13.22	12.11	26.00

Step 3: Use the information from the table in step 2 to calculate how many basketballs Andy will produce, what price he will charge, and how much profit he will earn if the market price of basketballs is $12.50. Andy's marginal revenue is equal to the market price of $12.50. Marginal revenue equals marginal cost when Andy produces 6 basketballs per day. So, Andy will produce 6 basketballs per day and charge a price of $12.50 per basketball. Andy's profit is equal to his total revenue minus his total costs. His total revenue equals the 6 basketballs he sells multiplied by the $12.50 price, or $75.00. So, his profit equals $75.00 − $55.50 = $19.50.

Step 4: Use the information from the table in step 2 to illustrate your answer to part (a) with a graph.

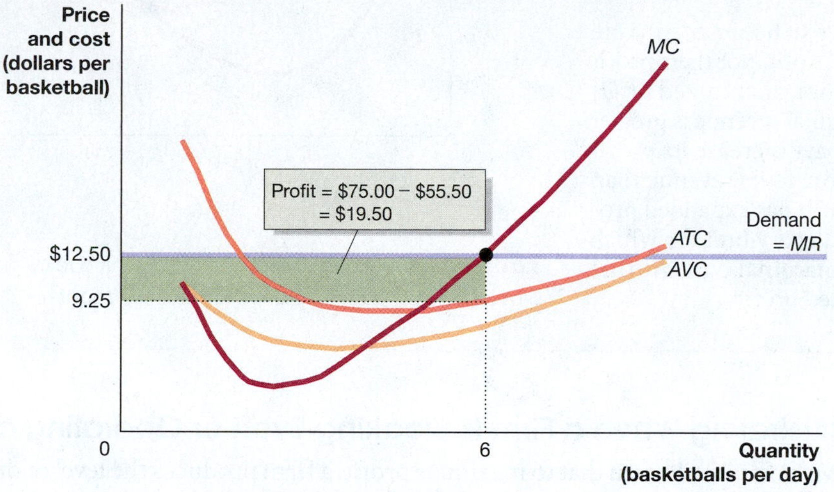

Step 5: Calculate how many basketballs Andy will produce, what price he will charge, and how much profit he will earn when the market price of basketballs is $6.00. Referring to the table in step 2, we can see that marginal revenue equals marginal cost when Andy produces 4 basketballs per day. He charges the market price of $6.00 per basketball. His total revenue is only $24.00, while his total costs are $34.00, so he will have a loss of $10.00. (Can we be sure that Andy will continue to produce even though he is operating at a loss? We answer this question in the next section.)

Step 6: Illustrate your answer to part (b) with a graph.

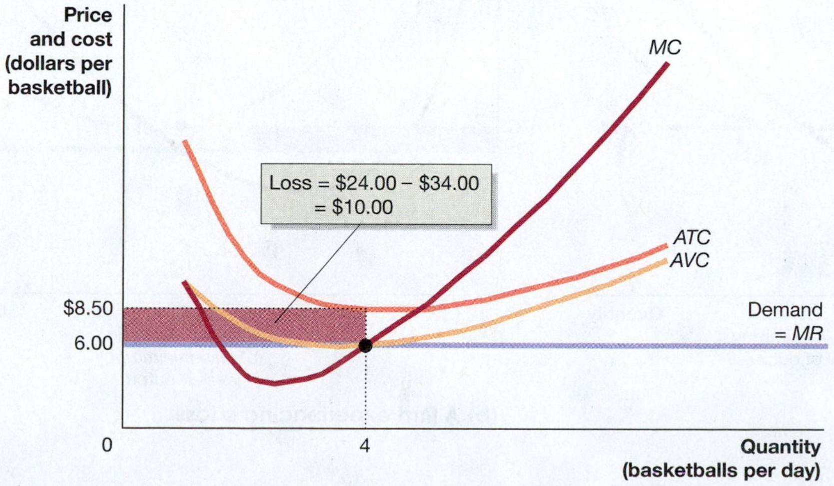

Your Turn: For more practice, do related problems 3.3 and 3.4 on pages 435–436 at the end of this chapter. MyEconLab Study Plan

Don't Let This Happen to You

Remember That Firms Maximize Their Total Profit, Not Their Profit per Unit

A student examines the following graph and argues: "I think that a firm will want to produce at Q_1, not Q_2. At Q_1, the distance between price and average total cost is the greatest. So at Q_1, the firm will be maximizing its profit per unit." Briefly explain whether you agree with the student's argument.

The student's argument is incorrect because firms are interested in maximizing their *total* profit, not their profit per unit. We know that profit is not maximized at Q_1 because at that level of output, marginal revenue is greater than marginal cost. A firm can always increase its profit by producing any unit that adds more to its revenue than it does to its costs. Only when the firm has expanded production to Q_2 will it have produced every unit for which marginal revenue is greater than marginal cost. At that level of output, it will have maximized profit.

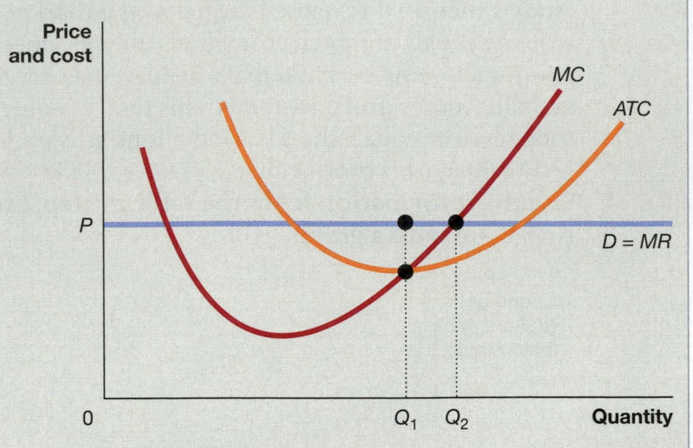

MyEconLab Study Plan

Your Turn: Test your understanding by doing related problem 3.5 on page 436 at the end of this chapter.

Illustrating When a Firm Is Breaking Even or Operating at a Loss

We have already seen that to maximize profit, a firm produces the level of output where marginal revenue equals marginal cost. But will the firm actually make a profit at that level of output? It depends on the relationship of price to average total cost. There are three possibilities:

1. $P > ATC$, which means the firm makes a profit.
2. $P = ATC$, which means the firm *breaks even* (its total cost equals its total revenue).
3. $P < ATC$, which means the firm experiences a loss.

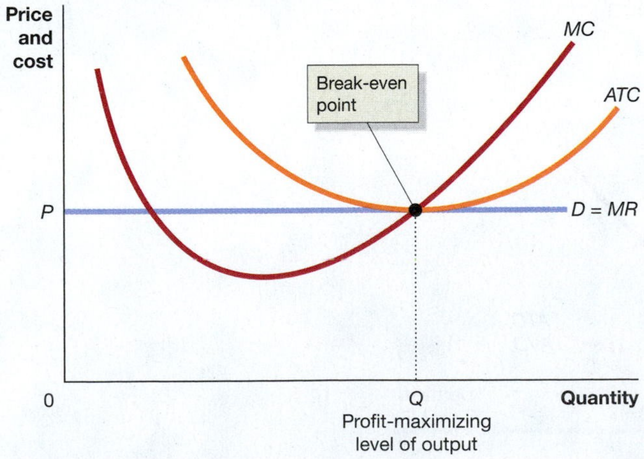

(a) A firm breaking even

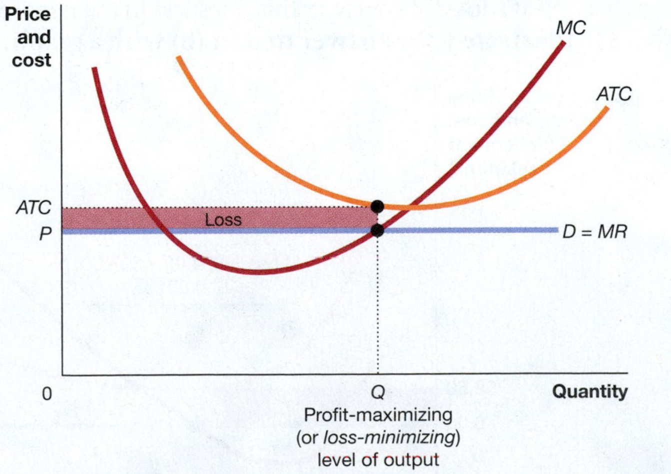

(b) A firm experiencing a loss

MyEconLab Animation

Figure 12.5 A Firm Breaking Even and a Firm Experiencing a Loss

In panel (a), price equals average total cost, and the firm breaks even because its total revenue will be equal to its total cost. In this situation, the firm makes zero economic profit. In panel (b), price is below average total cost, and the firm experiences a loss. The loss is represented by the area of the red-shaded rectangle, which has a height equal to $(ATC - P)$ and a width equal to Q.

Figure 12.4 on page 415 shows the first possibility, where the firm makes a profit. Panels (a) and (b) of Figure 12.5 show the situations where a firm breaks even or suffers a loss. In panel (a) of Figure 12.5, at the level of output at which $MR = MC$, price is equal to average total cost. Therefore, total revenue is equal to total cost, and the firm will break even, making zero economic profit. In panel (b), at the level of output at which $MR = MC$, price is less than average total cost. Therefore, total revenue is less than total cost, and the firm suffers a loss. In this case, maximizing profit amounts to *minimizing* loss.

MyEconLab Concept Check

Making the Connection

MyEconLab Video

Losing Money in the Solar Panel Industry

In a market system, a good or service becomes available to consumers only if an entrepreneur brings the product to market. Thousands of new businesses open every week in the United States. Each new business represents an entrepreneur risking his or her funds to earn a profit. Of course, there are no guarantees of success, and many new businesses experience losses rather than earn the profits their owners hoped for.

By the mid-2000s, high oil prices and concern over the pollution caused by burning fossil fuels led more people to become interested in solar energy. Technological advances reduced the cost of solar photovoltaic cells used in solar panels. In addition, households installing a solar energy system could receive a federal tax credit equal to 30 percent of the cost of the system. For several years, falling production costs and increased demand led entrepreneurs in the United States to start new firms manufacturing solar panels. By 2009, though, large imports of solar panels produced by Chinese firms were driving down the market price. As panel (a) in the following figure shows, the price of solar panels, measured as dollars per watt of power produced, declined by three-quarters, from $2.00 per watt in 2009 to $0.36 per watt in 2014.

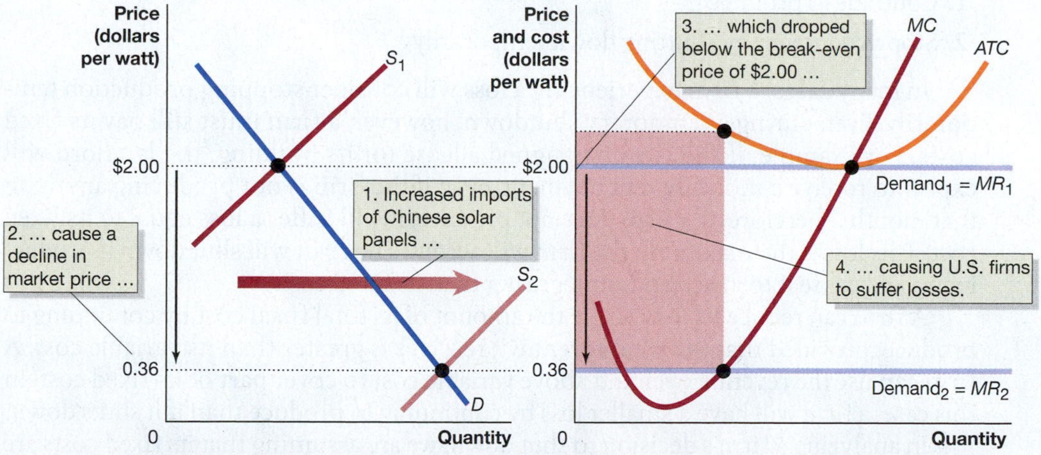

(a) Market for solar panels

(b) Losses for a U.S. solar panel firm

Panel (b) shows the situation a typical U.S. firm producing solar panels faced. The price of $0.36 was below these firms' average total cost of producing solar panels, so the firms began to suffer losses. U.S. firms argued that Chinese firms were able to sell at low prices because they were receiving subsidies from the Chinese government, which are not allowed under international trade agreements. By 2014, the tariff the U.S. government imposed on imports of solar panels from China was as high as 78 percent. Most environmentalists opposed the tariff, arguing that if it resulted in higher prices for solar panels, fewer people would convert their homes to use solar power to generate electricity. Some U.S. firms also opposed the tariff because they use solar panels in products they export, which meant the tariff would raise their production costs.

The tariff, though, did not seem to be having much effect on the U.S. market in part because Chinese imports were being replaced by imports from Malaysia.

Why didn't the U.S. firms producing solar panels just raise the price they charged to the level they needed to break even? We have already seen that any firm that tries to raise the price of its product above the market price loses customers to competing firms. What will happen to the U.S. solar panel industry in the long run is unclear. In 2015, some U.S. firms were optimistic about the effects of an announcement from Tesla Motors that the company would be introducing home batteries. The home batteries would allow someone who had installed solar panels to store energy produced on sunny days for use on cloudy days or at night. By reducing reliance on buying electricity, the batteries had the potential to increase the demand for solar panels, raising the price enough for U.S firms to at least break even. That development was coming too late, though, for a number of U.S. solar panel firms that had already gone out of business. The entrepreneurs who had started those businesses lost most of their investments.

Sources: Diane Cardwell, "U.S. Imposes Steep Tariffs on Chinese Solar Panels," *New York Times*, December 16, 2014; Kate Galbraith, "With Tesla Entering Market, Hopes for Home Batteries Grow," *New York Times*, May 13, 2015; and Peter Diamandis, "Solar Energy Revolution: A Massive Opportunity," forbes.com, September 2, 2014.

MyEconLab Study Plan

Your Turn: Test your understanding by doing related problem 3.7 on page 436 at the end of this chapter.

12.4 Deciding Whether to Produce or to Shut Down in the Short Run

LEARNING OBJECTIVE: Explain why firms may shut down temporarily.

In panel (b) of Figure 12.5, we assumed that the firm would continue to produce even though it was operating at a loss. In the short run, a firm experiencing a loss has two choices:

1. Continue to produce
2. Stop production by shutting down temporarily

In many cases, a firm experiencing a loss will consider stopping production temporarily. Even during a temporary shutdown, however, a firm must still pay its fixed costs. For example, if the firm has signed a lease for its building, the landlord will expect to receive a monthly rent payment, even if the firm is not producing anything that month. Therefore, if a firm does not produce, it will suffer a loss equal to its fixed cost. This loss is the maximum the firm will accept. The firm will shut down if producing would cause it to lose an amount greater than its fixed cost.

A firm can reduce its loss below the amount of its total fixed cost by continuing to produce, provided that the total revenue it receives is greater than its variable cost. A firm can use the revenue over and above variable cost to cover part of its fixed cost. In this case, a firm will have a smaller loss by continuing to produce than if it shuts down.

Sunk cost A cost that has already been paid and cannot be recovered.

In analyzing a firm's decision to shut down, we are assuming that its fixed costs are *sunk costs*. Remember that a **sunk cost** is a cost that has already been paid and cannot be recovered. We assume, as is usually the case, that the firm cannot recover its fixed costs by shutting down. For example, if a farmer has taken out a loan to buy land, the farmer is legally required to make the monthly loan payment whether he grows any wheat that season or not. The farmer has to spend those funds and cannot get them back, *so the farmer should treat his sunk costs as irrelevant to his short-run decision making*. For any firm, whether total revenue is greater or less than *variable cost* is the key to deciding whether to shut down or to continue producing in the short run. As long as a firm's total revenue is greater than its variable cost, it should continue to produce no matter how large or small its fixed cost is.

One option not available to a firm with losses in a perfectly competitive market is to raise its price. If the firm did raise its price, it would lose all its customers, and its sales would drop to zero. For example, during the past 20 years, the price of wheat has usually been high enough for a typical wheat farmer in the United States to at least break even. But in 2015, the price of wheat fell to about $5 per bushel from more than $7.50 per bushel three years earlier. Some wheat farmers found the $5 per bushel price was below their break-even point. But any wheat farmer who tried to raise his price to $7.50 per bushel would have seen his sales quickly disappear because buyers could purchase all the wheat they wanted at $5 per bushel from the thousands of other wheat farmers.

The Supply Curve of a Firm in the Short Run

Remember that the supply curve for a firm tells us how many units of a product the firm is willing to sell at any given price. Notice that the marginal cost curve for a firm in a perfectly competitive market tells us the same thing. The firm will produce at the level of output where $MR = MC$. Because price equals marginal revenue for a firm in a perfectly competitive market, the firm will produce where $P = MC$. For any given price, we can determine from the marginal cost curve the quantity of output the firm will supply. *Therefore, a perfectly competitive firm's marginal cost curve is also its supply curve.* There is, however, an important qualification to this fact. We have seen that if a firm is experiencing a loss, it will shut down if its total revenue is less than its variable cost:

$$\text{Total revenue} < \text{Variable cost},$$

or, in symbols:

$$(P \times Q) < VC.$$

If we divide both sides by Q, we have the result that the firm will shut down if:

$$P < AVC.$$

If the price drops below average variable cost, the firm will have a smaller loss if it shuts down and produces no output. *So, the firm's marginal cost curve is its supply curve only for prices at or above average variable cost.*

Recall that the marginal cost curve intersects the average variable cost where the average variable cost curve is at its minimum point. Therefore, as shown in Figure 12.6, the firm's supply curve is its marginal cost curve above the minimum point of the average variable cost curve. For prices below minimum average

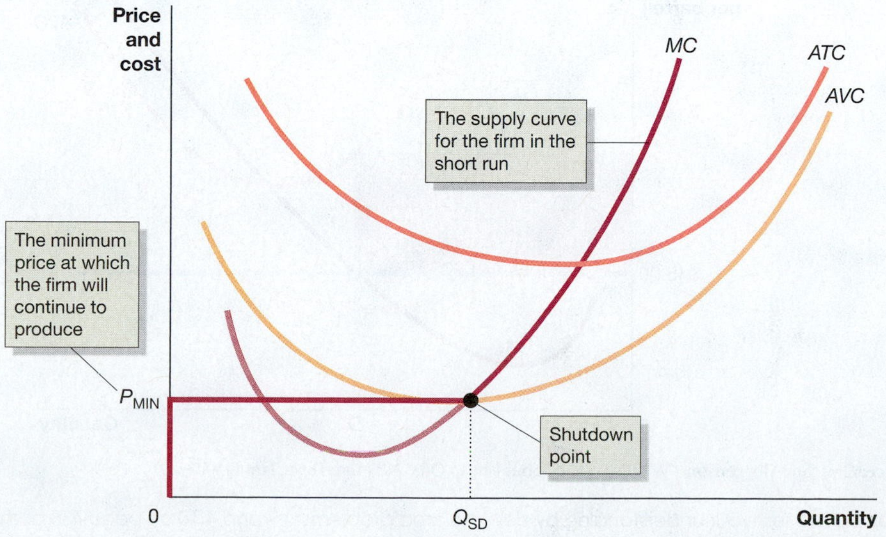

MyEconLab Animation

Figure 12.6

The Firm's Short-Run Supply Curve

Because price equals marginal revenue for a firm in a perfectly competitive market, the firm will produce where $P = MC$. For any given price, we can determine the quantity of output the firm will supply from the marginal cost curve, so the marginal cost curve is the firm's supply curve. But the firm will shut down if the price falls below average variable cost. The marginal cost curve crosses the average variable cost at the firm's shutdown point at the output level Q_{SD}. For prices below P_{MIN}, the supply curve is a vertical line along the price axis, which shows that the firm will supply zero output at those prices. The red line is the firm's short-run supply curve.

Shutdown point The minimum point on a firm's average variable cost curve; if the price falls below this point, the firm shuts down production in the short run.

variable cost (P_{MIN}), the firm will shut down, and its output will drop to zero. The minimum point on the average variable cost curve is called the **shutdown point**, and it occurs at the output level Q_{SD}. The dark red line in Figure 12.6 shows the supply curve for the firm in the short run. MyEconLab Concept Check

Solved Problem 12.4

MyEconLab Interactive Animation

When to Shut Down an Oil Well

In 2015, as oil prices declined, an industry analyst commented that many wells pumping shale oil had variable production costs of only $20 per barrel. He argued that as a result, the wells would not stop producing "just because oil prices have fallen to $45 a barrel." Briefly explain why the analyst thought the variable cost of producing oil from these wells, rather than the total cost, was the key to determining whether the wells would stop operating. Illustrate your answer with a graph.

Solving the Problem

Step 1: Review the chapter material. This problem is about firms deciding whether to produce when price is below average total cost, so you may want to review the section "Deciding Whether to Produce or to Shut Down in the Short Run," which begins on page 420.

Step 2: Answer the problem by discussing the roles of variable costs and total costs in the decision of firms to continue producing in the short run. When a firm is deciding whether to produce in the short run, the difference between variable cost and total cost is important if price has fallen below average total cost. Because the analyst makes the distinction between variable cost and total cost, we know that the owners of these wells must be suffering a loss when the price of oil is $45 per barrel. In other words, this price must be below their average total cost. However, because the price is above average variable cost, the analyst concluded that the firms would continue to operate the wells.

Step 3: Finish answering the problem by drawing a graph to illustrate your answer from step 2. Your graph should look like this one. Note that the price is shown as being above average variable cost but below average total cost.

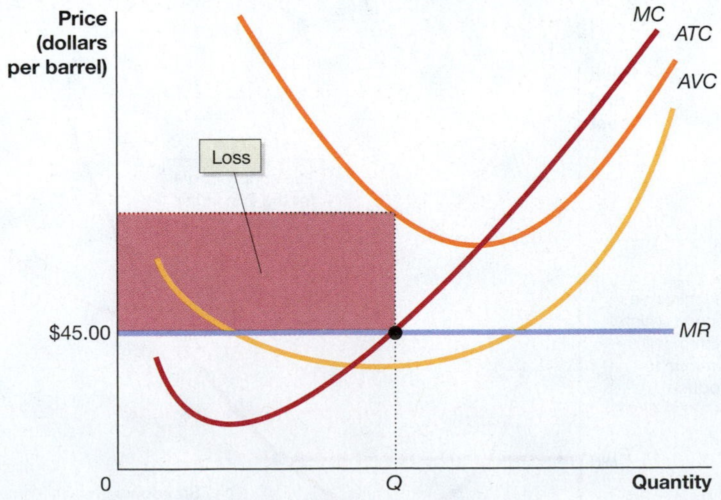

Source: Gretchen Morgenson, "What's So Bad about Cheap Oil?" *New York Times*, January 17, 2015.

MyEconLab Study Plan

Your Turn: Test your understanding by doing related problems 4.9 and 4.10 on page 438 at the end of this chapter.

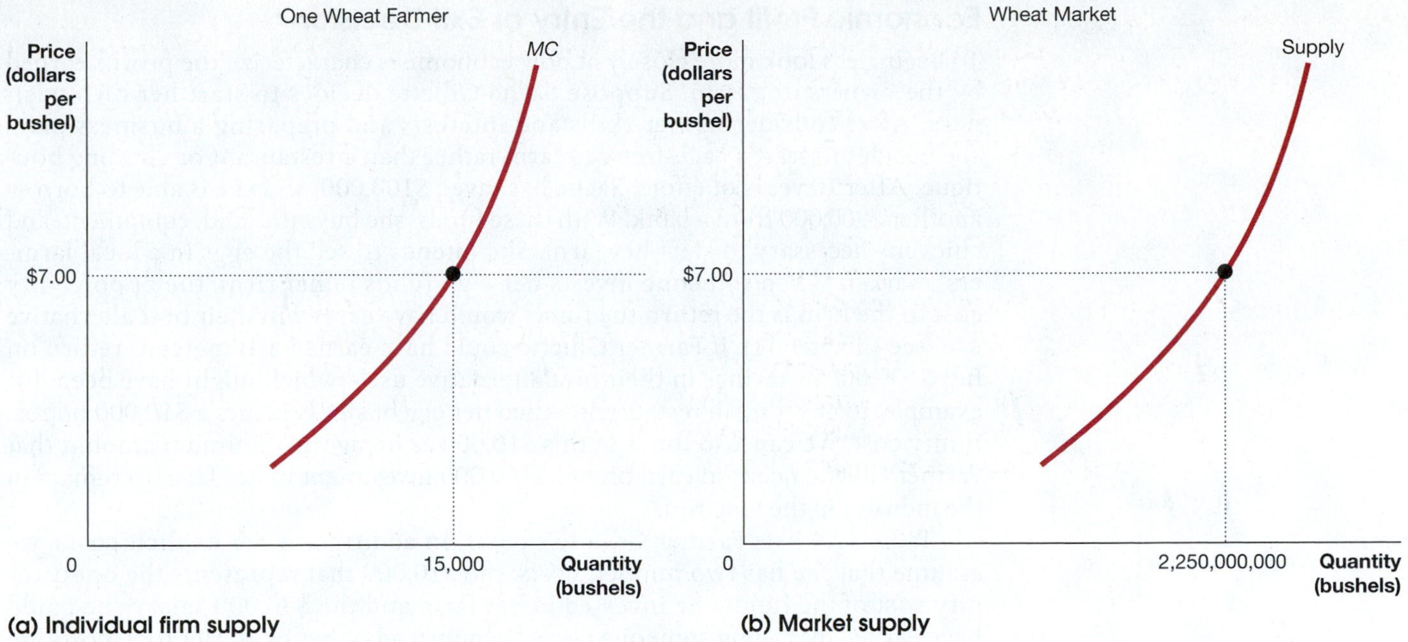

MyEconLab Animation

Figure 12.7 Firm Supply and Market Supply

We can derive the market supply curve by adding up the quantity that each firm in the market is willing to supply at each price. In panel (a), one wheat farmer is willing to supply 15,000 bushels of wheat at a price of $7 per bushel. If every wheat farmer supplies the same amount of wheat at this price and if there are 150,000 wheat farmers, the total amount of wheat supplied at a price of $7 will equal 15,000 bushels per farmer × 150,000 farmers = 2.25 billion bushels of wheat. This amount is one point on the market supply curve for wheat shown in panel (b). We can find the other points on the market supply curve by determining how much wheat each farmer is willing to supply at each price.

The Market Supply Curve in a Perfectly Competitive Industry

The market demand curve is determined by adding up the quantity demanded by each consumer in the market at each price (see Chapter 10). Similarly, the market supply curve is determined by adding up the quantity supplied by each firm in the market at each price. Each firm's marginal cost curve tells us how much that firm will supply at each price. So, the market supply curve can be derived directly from the marginal cost curves of the firms in the market. Panel (a) of Figure 12.7 shows the marginal cost curve for one wheat farmer. At a price of $7, this wheat farmer supplies 15,000 bushels of wheat. If every wheat farmer supplies the same amount of wheat at this price and if there are 150,000 wheat farmers, the total amount of wheat supplied at a price of $7 will be:

15,000 bushels per farmer × 150,000 farms = 2.25 billion bushels of wheat.

Panel (b) shows a price of $7 and a quantity of 2.25 billion bushels as a point on the market supply curve for wheat. In reality, of course, not all wheat farms are alike. Some wheat farms supply more at the market price than the typical farm; other wheat farms supply less. The key point is that we can derive the market supply curve by adding up the quantity that each firm in the market is willing and able to supply at each price. MyEconLab Concept Check

MyEconLab Study Plan

12.5 "If Everyone Can Do It, You Can't Make Money at It": The Entry and Exit of Firms in the Long Run

LEARNING OBJECTIVE: Explain how entry and exit ensure that perfectly competitive firms earn zero economic profit in the long run.

In the long run, unless a firm can cover all its costs, it will shut down and exit the industry. In a market system, firms continually enter and exit industries. In this section, we will see how profits and losses provide signals to firms that lead to entry and exit.

Economic Profit and the Entry or Exit Decision

To begin, let's look more closely at how economists characterize the profits earned by the owners of a firm. Suppose Sacha Gillette decides to start her own business. After considering her skills and interests and preparing a business plan, she decides to start a cage-free egg farm rather than a restaurant or clothing boutique. After 10 years of effort, Sacha has saved $100,000, and she is able to borrow another $900,000 from a bank. With these funds, she buys the land, equipment, and chickens necessary to start her farm. She intends to sell the eggs in a local farmers' market. When someone invests her own funds in her firm, the opportunity cost to the firm is the return the funds would have earned in their best alternative use (see Chapter 11). If Farmer Gillette could have earned a 10 percent return on her $100,000 in savings in their best alternative use—which might have been, for example, to buy a small restaurant—then her egg business incurs a $10,000 opportunity cost. We can also think of this $10,000 as being the minimum amount that Farmer Gillette needs to earn on her $100,000 investment in her farm to remain in the industry in the long run.

Table 12.4 lists Farmer Gillette's costs. In addition to her explicit costs, we assume that she has two implicit costs: the $10,000 that represents the opportunity cost of the funds she invested in her farm and the $30,000 salary she could have earned managing someone else's farm instead of her own. Her total costs are $125,000. If the market price of cage-free eggs is $3 per dozen and Farmer Gillette sells 50,000 dozen, her total revenue will be $150,000, and her economic profit will be $25,000 (total revenue of $150,000 minus total costs of $125,000). Recall that **economic profit** equals a firm's revenues minus all its costs, implicit and explicit.

Economic profit A firm's revenues minus all its costs, implicit and explicit.

Economic Profit Leads to Entry of New Firms Unfortunately, Farmer Gillette is unlikely to earn an economic profit for very long. Suppose other farmers are just breaking even by selling regular eggs. In that case, they will have an incentive to switch to selling cage-free eggs so they can begin earning an economic profit. As we saw in the chapter opener, in recent years more farmers have been switching from producing eggs using older methods to using cage-free methods, in the hope of earning a higher profit. Remember that the more firms there are in an industry, the farther to the right the market supply curve is. Panel (a) of Figure 12.8 shows that as more farmers begin selling cage-free eggs, the market supply curve shifts to the right. Farmers will continue entering the market until the market supply curve has shifted from S_1 to S_2.

With the supply curve at S_2, the market price will fall to $2 per dozen. Panel (b) shows the effect on Farmer Gillette, whom we assume has the same costs as other egg farmers. As the market price falls from $3 to $2 per dozen, Farmer Gillette's demand curve shifts down, from D_1 to D_2. In the new equilibrium, Farmer Gillette is selling 40,000 dozen eggs, at a price of $2 per dozen. She and the other egg farmers are no

Table 12.4

Farmer Gillette's Costs per Year

Explicit Costs	
Water	$15,000
Wages	$25,000
Fertilizer	$20,000
Electricity	$10,000
Payment on bank loan	$15,000
Implicit Costs	
Forgone salary	$30,000
Opportunity cost of the $100,000 she has invested in her farm	$10,000
Total cost	**$125,000**

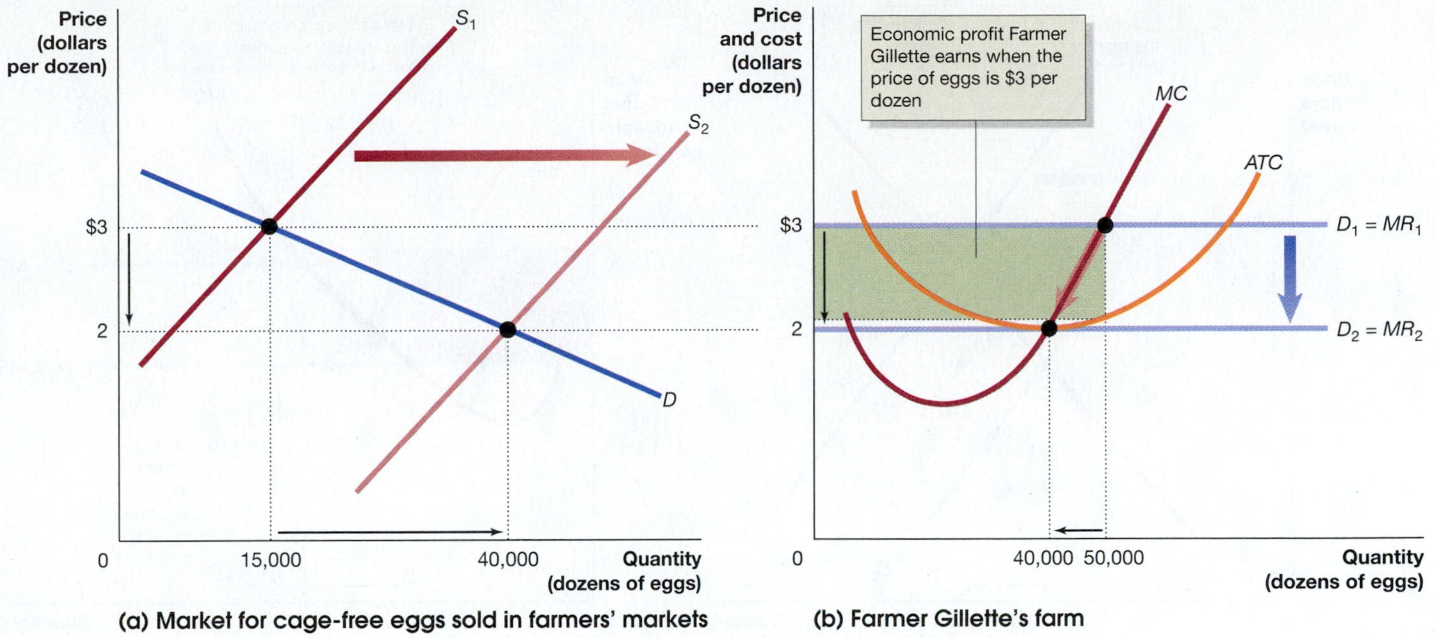

MyEconLab Animation

Figure 12.8 The Effect of Entry on Economic Profit

Initially, Farmer Gillette and other farmers selling cage-free eggs are able to charge $3 per dozen and earn an economic profit. Farmer Gillette's economic profit is represented by the area of the green box in panel (b). Panel (a) shows that as other farmers begin to sell cage-free eggs, the market supply curve shifts to the right, from S_1 to S_2, and the market price drops to $2 per dozen. Panel (b) shows that the falling price causes Farmer Gillette's demand curve to shift down from D_1 to D_2, and she reduces her output from 50,000 dozen eggs to 40,000. At the new market price of $2 per dozen, cage-free egg farmers are just breaking even: Their total revenue is equal to their total cost, and their economic profit is zero. Notice the difference in scale between the graphs in panels (a) and (b).

longer earning any economic profit. They are just breaking even, and the return on their investment is just covering the opportunity cost of these funds. New farmers will stop entering the market because the rate of return from selling cage-free eggs is now no better than they can earn by selling regular eggs.

Will Farmer Gillette continue to sell cage-free eggs even though she is just breaking even? She will because she earns as high a return on her investment as she could earn elsewhere. It may seem strange that new firms will continue to enter a market until all economic profit is eliminated and that established firms remain in a market despite not earning any economic profit. But it seems strange only because we are used to thinking in terms of accounting profit rather than *economic* profit. Remember that accounting rules generally require that only explicit costs be included on a firm's financial statements. The opportunity cost of the funds Farmer Gillette invested in her farm—$10,000—and her forgone salary—$30,000—are economic costs, but neither of them is an accounting cost. So, although an accountant would see Farmer Gillette as earning a profit of $40,000, an economist would see her as just breaking even. Farmer Gillette must pay attention to her accounting profit when preparing her financial statements and when paying her income tax. But because economic profit takes into account all her costs, it gives a more accurate indication of the financial health of her farm.

Economic Losses Lead to Exit of Firms Suppose some consumers decide that they no longer want to eat eggs, whether cage-free or not. Panel (a) of Figure 12.9 shows that the demand curve for cage-free eggs will shift to the left, from D_1 to D_2, and the market price will fall from $2 per dozen to $1.75. Panel (b) shows that as the price falls, a farmer like Sacha Gillette will move down her marginal cost curve to a lower level of output. At the lower level of output and lower price, she will be suffering

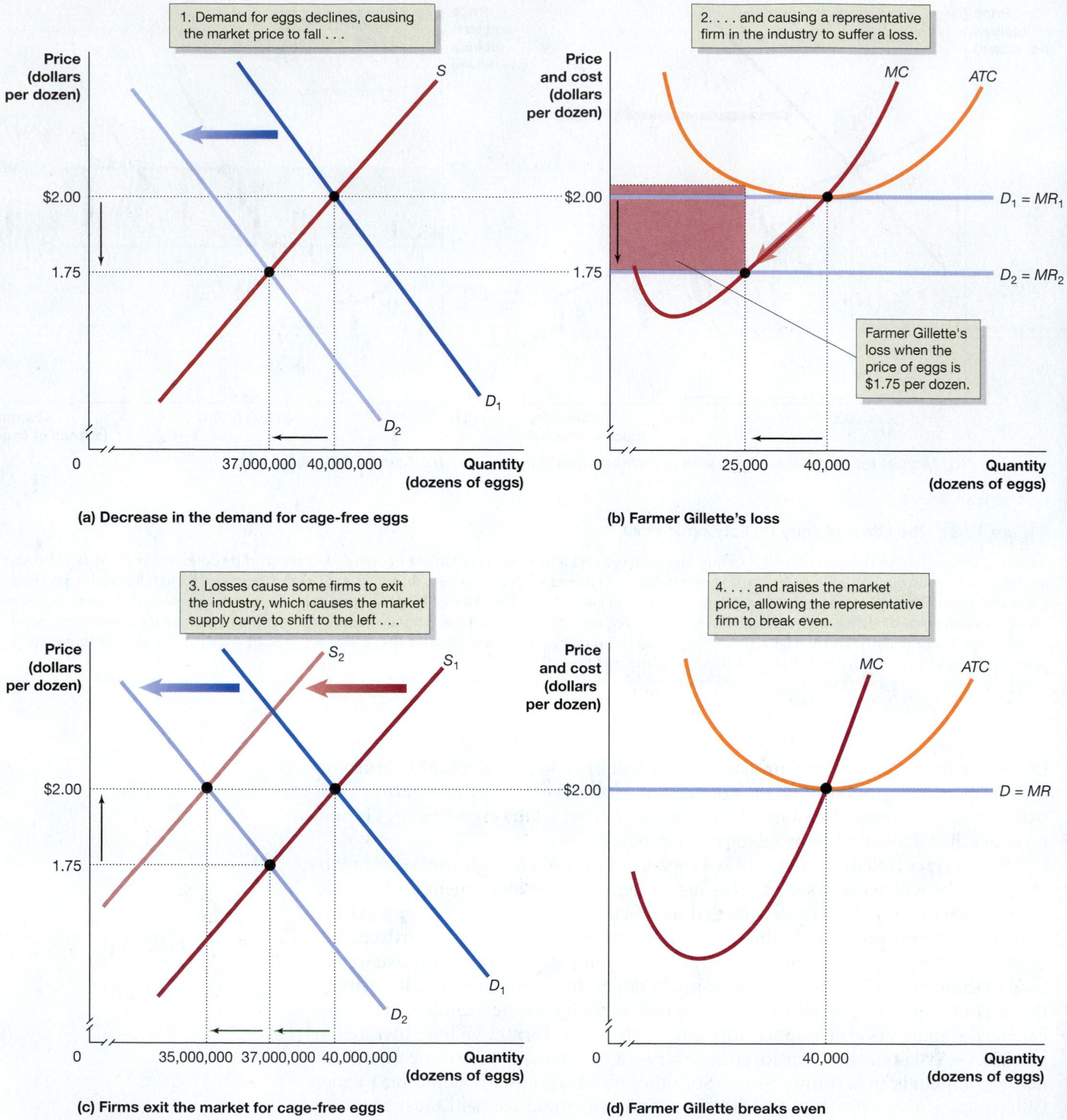

MyEconLab Animation

Figure 12.9 The Effect of Exit on Economic Losses

When the price of cage-free eggs is $2 per dozen, Farmer Gillette and other farmers are breaking even. A total quantity of 40,000,000 dozen eggs is sold in the market. Farmer Gillette sells 40,000 dozen. Panel (a) shows a decline in the demand for cage-free eggs from D_1 to D_2 that reduces the market price to $1.75 per dozen. Panel (b) shows that the falling price causes Farmer Gillette's demand curve to shift down from D_1 to D_2 and her output to fall from 40,000 to 25,000 dozen. At a market price of $1.75 per dozen, farmers have losses, represented by the area of the red box. As a result, some farmers will exit the market, which shifts the market supply curve to the left. Panel (c) shows that exit continues until the supply curve has shifted from S_1 to S_2 and the market price has risen from $1.75 back to $2.00. Panel (d) shows that with the price back at $2.00, Farmer Gillette will break even. In the new market equilibrium in panel (c), total sales of cage-free eggs have fallen from 40,000,000 to 35,000,000 dozen.

an **economic loss** because she will not cover all her costs. As long as price is above average variable cost, she will continue to produce in the short run, even when suffering losses. But in the long run, firms will exit an industry if they are unable to cover all their costs. In this case, some farmers will switch from producing eggs to producing other agricultural products or will leave farming.

Economic loss The situation in which a firm's total revenue is less than its total cost, including all implicit costs.

Panel (c) of Figure 12.9 shows that as firms exit from selling cage-free eggs, the market supply curve shifts to the left. Firms will continue to exit, and the supply curve will continue to shift to the left until the price has risen back to \$2 and the market supply curve is at S_2. Panel (d) shows that when the price is back to \$2, the remaining firms in the industry will be breaking even. MyEconLab Concept Check

Long-Run Equilibrium in a Perfectly Competitive Market

We have seen that economic profits attract firms to enter an industry. The entry of firms forces down the market price until a typical firm is breaking even. Economic losses cause firms to exit an industry. The exit of firms forces up the equilibrium market price until the typical firm is breaking even. In **long-run competitive equilibrium**, entry and exit have resulted in the typical firm breaking even. In the long run, firms can also vary their scale by becoming larger or smaller (see Chapter 11). The *long-run average cost curve* shows the lowest cost at which a firm is able to produce a given quantity of output in the long run. So, we would expect that in the long run, competition drives the market price to the minimum point on the typical firm's long-run average cost curve.

Long-run competitive equilibrium The situation in which the entry and exit of firms has resulted in the typical firm breaking even.

The long run in selling cage-free eggs appears to be several years, which is the amount of time it takes farmers to convert from using traditional methods of producing eggs to cage-free methods. As we discussed in the chapter opener, the number of farmers producing cage-free eggs has been rapidly increasing, but cage-free eggs are still more profitable than eggs produced using conventional methods. So we can predict that in the coming years more farmers will begin producing eggs using cage-free methods.

Firms in perfectly competitive markets are in a constant struggle to stay one step ahead of their competitors. They are always looking for new ways to provide a product, such as selling cage-free eggs. It is possible for firms to find ways to earn an economic profit for a while, but competition typically eliminates that profit in just a few years. This observation is not restricted to agriculture. In any perfectly competitive market, an opportunity to make an economic profit never lasts long. As Sharon Oster, an economist at Yale University, has put it: "If everyone can do it, you can't make money at it." MyEconLab Concept Check

The Long-Run Supply Curve in a Perfectly Competitive Market

If a typical poultry farmer selling cage-free eggs breaks even at a price of \$2 per dozen, in the long run, the market price will always return to this level. If an increase in demand causes the market price to rise above \$2, farmers will be earning an economic profit. That profit will attract additional farmers into the market, and the market supply curve will shift to the right until the price is back to \$2. Panel (a) in Figure 12.10 illustrates the long-run effect of an increase in demand. An increase in demand from D_1 to D_2 causes the market price to rise temporarily from \$2 per dozen to \$3. At this price, farmers are making an economic profit selling cage-free eggs, but the profit attracts the entry of new farmers. The result is an increase in supply from S_1 to S_2, which forces the price back down to \$2 per dozen and eliminates the economic profit.

Similarly, if a decrease in demand causes the market price to fall below \$2, farmers will experience an economic loss. The loss will cause some farmers to exit the market, the supply curve will shift to the left, and the price will return to \$2. Panel (b)

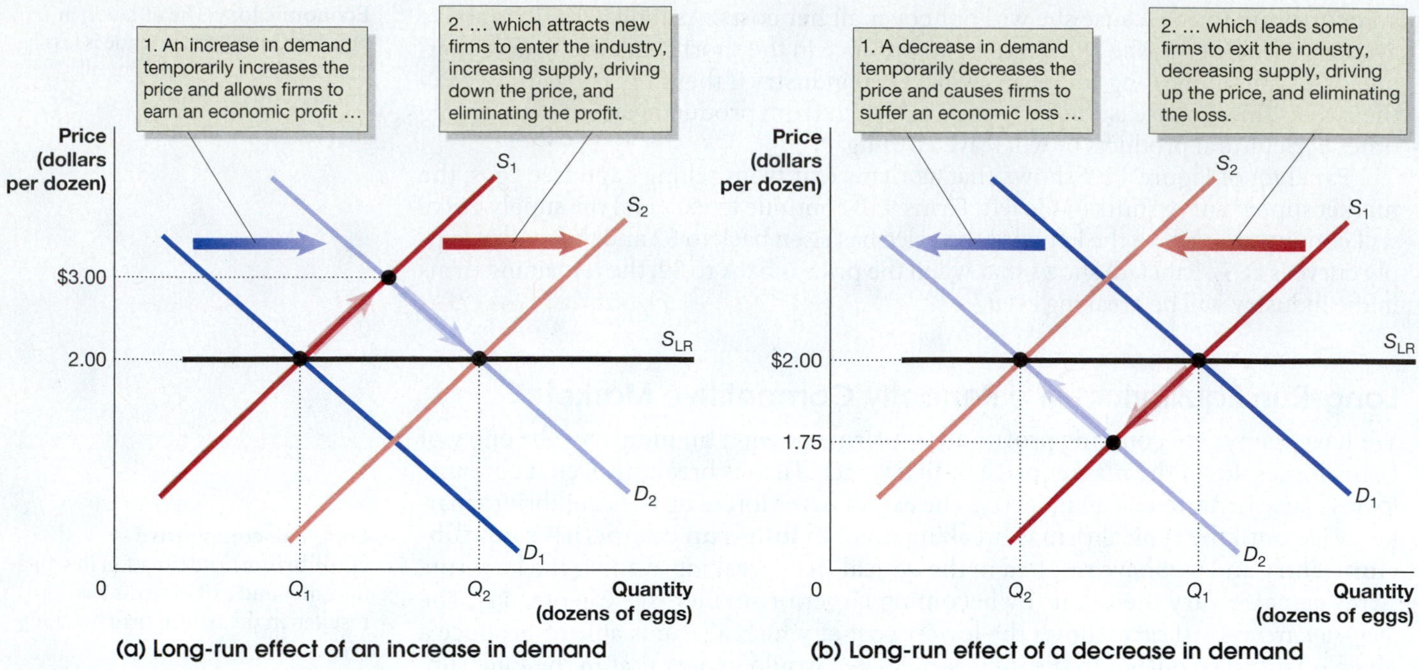

MyEconLab Animation

Figure 12.10 The Long-Run Supply Curve in a Perfectly Competitive Industry

Panel (a) shows that an increase in demand for cage-free eggs will lead to a temporary increase in price from \$2.00 to \$3.00 per dozen, as the market demand curve shifts to the right, from D_1 to D_2. The entry of new firms shifts the market supply curve to the right, from S_1 to S_2, which will cause the price to fall back to its long-run level of \$2.00. Panel (b) shows that a decrease in demand will lead to a temporary decrease in price from \$2.00 to \$1.75 per dozen, as the market demand curve shifts to the left, from D_1 to D_2. The exit of firms shifts the market supply curve to the left, from S_1 to S_2, which causes the price to rise back to its long-run level of \$2.00. The long-run supply curve (S_{LR}) shows the relationship between market price and the quantity supplied in the long run. In this case, the long-run supply curve is a horizontal line.

in Figure 12.10 illustrates the long-run effect of a decrease in demand. A decrease in demand from D_1 to D_2 causes the market price to fall temporarily from \$2 per dozen to \$1.75. At this price, farmers are suffering an economic loss, but the loss causes some farmers to exit the market for selling cage-free eggs. The result is a decrease in supply from S_1 to S_2, which forces the price back up to \$2 per dozen and eliminates the loss.

Long-run supply curve A curve that shows the relationship in the long run between market price and the quantity supplied.

The **long-run supply curve** shows the relationship in the long run between market price and the quantity supplied. In the long run, the price will be \$2 per dozen, no matter how many eggs are produced. So, as Figure 12.10 shows, the long-run supply curve (S_{LR}) is a horizontal line at a price of \$2. Remember that the price returns to \$2 in the long run because at this price a typical firm in the industry just breaks even. The typical firm breaks even because \$2 is at the minimum point on the firm's average total cost curve. We can draw the important conclusion that *in the long run, a perfectly competitive market will supply whatever amount of a good consumers demand at a price determined by the minimum point on the typical firm's average total cost curve.*

Because the position of the long-run supply curve is determined by the minimum point on the typical firm's average total cost curve, anything that raises or lowers the costs of the typical firm in the long run will cause the long-run supply curve to shift. For example, if the cost of the feed for chickens increases and the cost of the feed adds \$0.25 per dozen to every farmer's cost of producing cage-free eggs, the long-run supply curve will shift up by \$0.25.

MyEconLab Concept Check

Making the Connection
MyEconLab Video

In the Apple Apps Store, Easy Entry Makes the Long Run Pretty Short

Economic profit is rapidly competed away in the iTunes App Store.

One reason for the popularity of Apple's iPhones and iPads is the section of Apple's iTunes music and video store devoted to applications (or "apps"). Independent software programmers write apps that Apple makes available in the store in exchange for receiving 30 percent of the revenue the app generates. Major software companies, as well as individuals writing their first software programs, have posted games, calendars, dictionaries, and many other types of apps to the App Store.

At first, app developers were able to earn significant amounts by charging for downloads. For example, Hogrocket, a three-person company, developed the game Tiny Invaders and began selling it in the App Store in 2011. Initially, the company was successful in selling the app for $2.99. As we have seen, though, when firms earn an economic profit in a market, other firms have a strong economic incentive to enter that market. By 2015, about 750 new games were being added to the App Store *per day*. This flood of games forced Hogrocket to lower the price of its game to $0.99. At that price, though, the company was unable to sell enough downloads to break even, and the firm had to shut down.

The competiton in the App Store is so intense that by 2015, many people were unwilling to download games unless they were free. According to one estimate, fewer than one-third of smartphone and tablet users will purchase an app during the year. Some app designers have tried the strategy of allowing apps to be downloaded for free while attempting to earn revenue by forcing users to see advertisements before the app opens or while it runs. Many people find these advertisements annoying, though, so developers have begun offering free apps that lack advertisements but where the developers earn revenue from users making in-app purchases. For instance, in the popular game Candy Crush Saga, users are given free turns. After they have used them up, they can wait 30 minutes for another free turn or they can pay a small amount to immediately receive five more turns. Similarly, in the Clash of Clans game, players can slowly build up their villages' defenses and their armies for free or they can make an in-app purchase of "gems" to speed up the process.

Still, only about 3 percent of people who play these games make any in-app purchases. That leaves developers dependent on "whales" who make $50 to $100 per month in in-app game purchases. Only the best games can attract whale players and survive the intense competition of the App Store. And even these games have to constantly add new features if they hope to keep users from switching to playing newly released games. Yet, the incentive to develop new games remains substantial, with U.S. players of app games spending nearly $2 billion per year on them.

In a competitive market, earning an economic profit in the long run is extremely difficult. And the ease of entering the market for smartphone and tablet apps has made the long run pretty short.

Sources: Sarah E. Needleman, "Mobile-Game Makers Try to Catch More 'Whales' Who Pay for Free Games," *Wall Street Journal*, May 10, 2015; Jens Hansegard, "The Drama behind 'Candy Crush Soda Saga': Creating New Levels," *Wall Street Journal*, April 7, 2015; and Jussi Rosendahl, "Less Is More? 'Clash of Clans' Maker Banks on Handful of Games," Reuters, May 20, 2015.

Your Turn: Test your understanding by doing related problem 5.10 on page 439 at the end of this chapter.

MyEconLab Study Plan

Increasing-Cost and Decreasing-Cost Industries

Any industry in which the typical firm's average costs do not change as the industry expands production will have a horizontal long-run supply curve, like the one in Figure 12.10. These industries, including the egg industry, are called *constant-cost industries*. It's possible, however, for the typical firm's average costs to change as an industry expands.

For example, if an input used in producing a good is available in only limited quantities, the cost of the input will rise as the industry expands. If only a limited amount of land is available on which to grow the grapes to make a certain variety of wine, an increase in demand for wine made from these grapes will result in competition for the land and will drive up its price. As a result, more of the wine will be produced in the long run only if the price rises to cover the typical firm's higher average cost. In this case, the long-run supply curve will slope upward. Industries with upward-sloping long-run supply curves are called *increasing-cost industries*.

Finally, in some cases, the typical firm's costs may fall as the industry expands. Suppose that someone invents a new smartwatch that uses as an input a specialized memory chip that is currently produced only in small quantities. If demand for the smartwatch increases, firms that produce smartwatches will increase their orders for the memory chip. If there are *economies of scale* in producing a good, the average cost of producing it will decline as output increases (see Chapter 11). If there are economies of scale in producing this memory chip, the average cost of producing it will fall, and competition will result in its price falling as well. This price decline, in turn, will lower the average cost of producing the new smartwatch. In the long run, competition will force the price of the smartwatch to fall to the level of the typical firm's new lower average cost. In this case, the long-run supply curve will slope downward. Industries with downward-sloping long-run supply curves are called *decreasing-cost industries*.

MyEconLab Study Plan

MyEconLab Concept Check

12.6 Perfect Competition and Efficiency

LEARNING OBJECTIVE: Explain how perfect competition leads to economic efficiency.

Notice how powerful consumers are in a market system. If consumers want more cage-free eggs, the market will supply them. More cage-free eggs are supplied not because a government bureaucrat in Washington, DC, or an official in a farmers' association gives orders. The additional eggs are produced because an increase in demand results in higher prices and a larger profit from selling cage-free eggs. Farmers, trying to get the highest possible return on their investments, begin to switch from producing eggs the old way to producing eggs using cage-free methods. If consumers lose their taste for these eggs and demand falls, the process works in reverse.

Productive Efficiency

Productive efficiency The situation in which a good or service is produced at the lowest possible cost.

In a market system, consumers get as many cage-free eggs as they want, produced at the lowest average cost possible. The forces of competition will drive the market price to the typical firm's minimum average cost. **Productive efficiency** refers to the situation in which a good or service is produced at the lowest possible cost. As we have seen, perfect competition results in productive efficiency.

The managers of every firm strive to earn an economic profit by reducing costs. But in a perfectly competitive market, other firms quickly copy ways of reducing costs. Therefore, in the long run, only the consumer benefits from cost reductions.

MyEconLab Concept Check

Solved Problem 12.6

MyEconLab Interactive Animation

How Productive Efficiency Benefits Consumers

Financial writer Michael Lewis once remarked, "The sad truth, for investors, seems to be that most of the benefits of new technologies are passed right through to consumers free of charge."

a. What do you think Lewis means by the benefits of new technology being "passed right through to consumers free of charge"? Use a graph like Figure 12.8 on page 425 to illustrate your answer.

b. Explain why this result is a "sad truth" for investors.

Solving the Problem

Step 1: Review the chapter material. This problem is about perfect competition and efficiency, so you may want to review the section "Perfect Competition and Efficiency," which begins on page 430.

Step 2: Use the concepts from this chapter to explain what Lewis means. By "new technologies," Lewis means new products—such as smartwatches or 4K television sets—or lower-cost ways of producing existing products. In either case, new technologies will allow firms to earn an economic profit for a while, but the profit will lead new firms to enter the market in the long run.

Step 3: Use a graph like Figure 12.8 on page 425 to illustrate why the benefits of new technologies are "passed right through to consumers free of charge." Figure 12.8 shows the situation in which a firm is making an economic profit in the short run but the profit is eliminated by entry in the long run. We can draw a similar graph to analyze what happens in the long run in the market for 4K televisions.

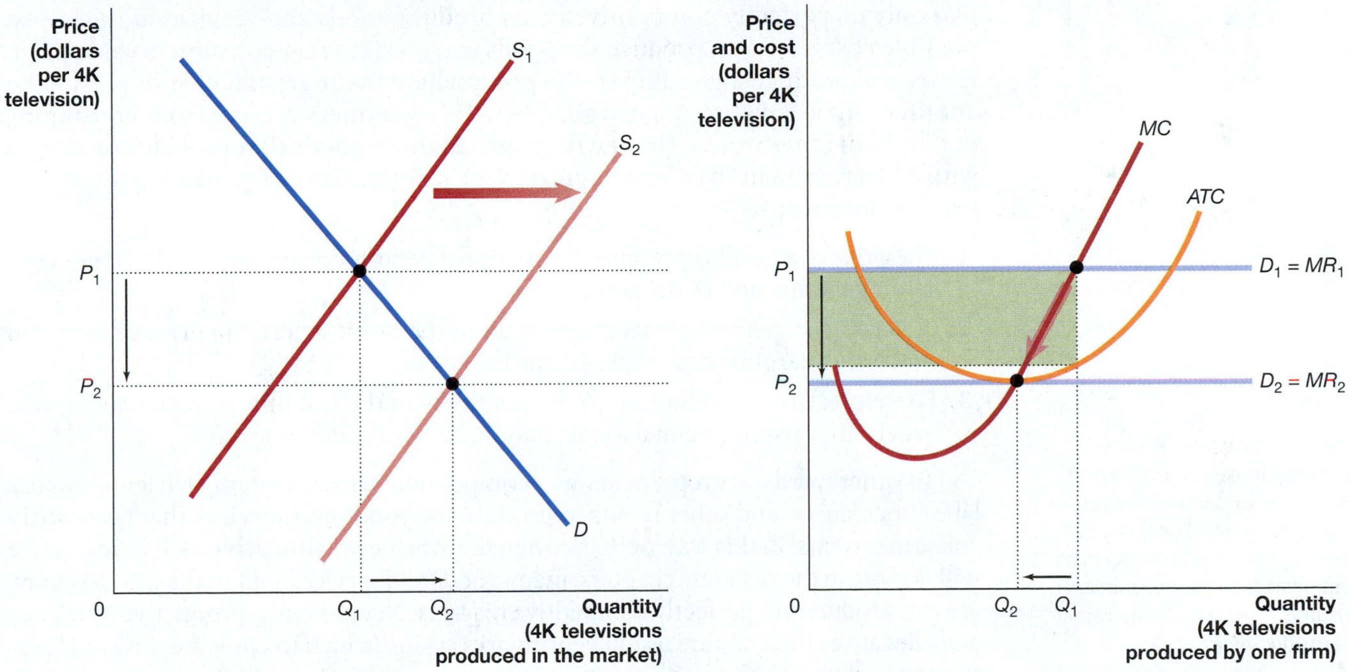

(a) Market for 4K televisions

(b) One firm selling 4K televisions

When 4K televisions were first introduced, prices were high, and only a few firms were in the market. Panel (a) shows that the initial equilibrium price in the market for 4K televisions is P_1. Panel (b) shows that at this price, the typical firm in the industry is earning an economic profit, which is shown by the green-shaded box. The economic profit attracts new firms into the industry. This entry shifts the market supply curve from S_1 to S_2 in panel (a) and lowers the equilibrium price from P_1 to P_2. Panel (b) shows that at the new market price, P_2, the typical firm is breaking even. Therefore, 4K televisions are being produced at the lowest possible cost, and productive efficiency is achieved. Consumers receive the new technology "free of charge" in the sense that they only have to pay a price equal to the lowest possible cost of production.

Step 4: Answer part (b) by explaining why the result in part (a) is a "sad truth" for investors. We have seen in answering part (a) that in the long run, firms only break even on their investment in producing high-technology goods. That result implies that investors in these firms are also unlikely to earn an economic profit in the long run.

Extra Credit: Lewis is using a key result from this chapter: In the long run, the entry of new firms competes away economic profit. Notice that, strictly speaking, the high-technology industries Lewis is discussing are not perfectly competitive. Smartwatches and 4K televisions, for instance, are not identical, and each smartphone company produces a quantity large enough to affect the market price. However, as we will see in the next chapter, these deviations from perfect competition do not change the important conclusion that the entry of new firms benefits consumers by forcing prices down to the level of average cost. In fact, the price of 4K televisions dropped by more than 50 percent within three years of their first becoming widely available.

Source: Michael Lewis, "In Defense of the Boom," *New York Times*, October 27, 2002.

MyEconLab Study Plan

Your Turn: For more practice, do related problems 6.6, 6.7, and 6.8 on page 440 at the end of this chapter.

Allocative Efficiency

Not only do perfectly competitive firms produce goods and services at the lowest possible cost, they also produce the goods and services that consumers value most. Firms will produce a good up to the point where the marginal cost of producing another unit is equal to the marginal benefit consumers receive from consuming that unit. In other words, firms will supply all those goods that provide consumers with a marginal benefit at least as great as the marginal cost of producing them. This result holds because:

1. The price of a good represents the marginal benefit consumers receive from consuming the last unit of the good sold.
2. Perfectly competitive firms produce up to the point where the price of the good equals the marginal cost of producing the last unit.
3. Therefore, firms produce up to the point where the last unit provides a marginal benefit to consumers equal to the marginal cost of producing it.

Allocative efficiency A state of the economy in which production represents consumer preferences; in particular, every good or service is produced up to the point where the last unit provides a marginal benefit to consumers equal to the marginal cost of producing it.

In other words, entrepreneurs in a competitive market system efficiently *allocate* labor, machinery, and other inputs to produce the goods and services that best satisfy consumer wants. In this way, perfect competition achieves **allocative efficiency**. As we will explore in the next few chapters, many goods and services sold in the U.S. economy are not produced in perfectly competitive markets. Nevertheless, productive efficiency and allocative efficiency are useful benchmarks against which to compare the actual performance of the economy.

MyEconLab Concept Check

MyEconLab Study Plan

Continued from page 407

Economics in Your Life

Are You an Entrepreneur?

At the beginning of the chapter, we asked you to think about why you can charge only a relatively low price for babysitting or mowing lawns. In the chapter, we saw that firms selling products in competitive markets can't charge prices higher than those being charged by competing firms. The market for babysitting and mowing lawns is very competitive because in most neighborhoods, there are many teenagers willing to supply these services. The price you can charge for babysitting may not be worth your time when you are 20 but is enough to cover the opportunity cost of a 14-year-old eager to enter the market. In other words, the ease of entry into babysitting and mowing lawns is high. So, in your career as a teenage entrepreneur, you may have become familiar with one of the lessons of this chapter: A firm in a competitive market has no control over price.

Conclusion

The competitive forces of the market impose relentless pressure on firms to produce new and better goods and services at the lowest possible cost. Firms that fail to adequately anticipate changes in consumer tastes or that fail to adopt the latest and most efficient technology do not survive in the long run. In the nineteenth century, the biologist Charles Darwin developed a theory of evolution based on the idea of the "survival of the fittest." Only those plants and animals that are best able to adapt to the demands of their environment are able to survive. Darwin first realized the important role that the struggle for existence plays in the natural world after reading early nineteenth-century economists' descriptions of the role it plays in the economic world. Just as "survival of the fittest" is the rule in nature, so it is in the economy.

At the start of this chapter, we saw that there are four market structures: perfect competition, monopolistic competition, oligopoly, and monopoly. Now that we have studied perfect competition, in the following chapters we move on to the other three market structures.

Visit MyEconLab for a news article and analysis related to the concepts in this chapter.

CHAPTER SUMMARY AND PROBLEMS

Key Terms

12.1 Perfectly Competitive Markets, pages 409–411

LEARNING OBJECTIVE: Explain what a perfectly competitive market is and why a perfect competitor faces a horizontal demand curve.

Summary

A **perfectly competitive market** must have many buyers and sellers, firms must be producing identical products, and there must be no barriers to new firms entering the market. The demand curve for a good or service produced in a perfectly competitive market is downward sloping, but the demand curve for the output of one firm in a perfectly competitive market is a horizontal line at the market price. Firms in perfectly competitive markets are **price takers**, and their sales drop to zero if they attempt to charge more than the market price.

MyEconLab Visit **www.myeconlab.com** to complete these exercises online and get instant feedback.

Review Questions

1.1 What are the three conditions for a market to be perfectly competitive?

1.2 What is a price taker? When are firms likely to be price takers?

1.3 Draw a graph showing the market demand and supply curves for corn and the demand curve for the corn produced by one corn farmer. Be sure to indicate the market price and the price the corn farmer receives.

Problems and Applications

1.4 Explain whether each of the following is a perfectly competitive market. For each market that is not perfectly competitive, explain why it is not.

a. Corn farming
b. Coffee shops
c. Automobile manufacturing
d. New home construction

1.5 The late Nobel Prize–winning economist George Stigler once wrote, "the most common and most important criticism of perfect competition ... [is] that it is unrealistic." Since few firms sell identical products in markets where there are no barriers to entry, why do economists believe that the model of perfect competition is important?

Source: George Stigler, "Perfect Competition, Historically Contemplated," *Journal of Political Economy*, Vol. 65, No. 1, February 1957, pp. 1–17.

1.6 **(Related to the Don't Let This Happen to You on page 410)** Explain whether you agree with the following remark:

> According to the model of perfectly competitive markets, the demand curve for wheat should be a horizontal line. But this can't be true: When the price of wheat rises, the quantity of wheat demanded falls, and when the price of wheat falls, the quantity of wheat demanded rises. Therefore, the demand curve for wheat is not a horizontal line.

1.7 The financial writer Andrew Tobias described an incident that occurred when he was a student at the Harvard Business School: Each student in the class was given large amounts of information about a particular firm and asked to determine a pricing strategy for the firm. Most of the students spent hours preparing their answers and came to class carrying many sheets of paper with their calculations. Tobias came up with the correct answer after just a few minutes and without having made any calculations. When his professor called on him in class for an answer, Tobias stated: "The case said the XYZ Company was in a very competitive industry ... and the case said that the company had all the business it could handle." Given this information, what price do you think Tobias argued the company should charge? Briefly explain. (Tobias says the class greeted his answer with "thunderous applause.")

Source: Andrew Tobias, *The Only Investment Guide You'll Ever Need*, Boston: Houghton Mifflin Harcourt, 2010, pp. 7–8.

1.8 In 2015, some beer drinkers filed a lawsuit against Anheuser-Busch, the brewer of Beck's beer. The beer drinkers claimed that Beck's was marketed as an authentic German beer but was actually brewed in St. Louis. Other breweries have established facilities in Canada so they can truthfully claim that their beers are "imported." If the market for beer were perfectly competitive, would the location of breweries matter to consumers? Briefly explain.

Source: Jacob Gershman and Tripp Mickle, "Trouble Brews for 'Imported' Beers Made in America," *Wall Street Journal*, June 24, 2015.

12.2 How a Firm Maximizes Profit in a Perfectly Competitive Market, pages 411–414

LEARNING OBJECTIVE: Explain how a firm maximizes profit in a perfectly competitive market.

Summary

Profit is the difference between total revenue (*TR*) and total cost (*TC*). **Average revenue (*AR*)** is total revenue divided by the quantity of the product sold. A firm maximizes profit by producing the level of output where the difference between revenue and cost is the greatest. This is the same level of output where marginal revenue is equal to marginal cost. **Marginal revenue (*MR*)** is the change in total revenue from selling one more unit.

MyEconLab Visit **www.myeconlab.com** to complete these exercises online and get instant feedback.

Review Questions

2.1 Explain why it is true that for a firm in a perfectly competitive market, $P = MR = AR$.

2.2 Explain why at the level of output where the difference between *TR* and *TC* is at its maximum positive value, *MR* must equal *MC*.

2.3 Explain why it is true that for a firm in a perfectly competitive market, the profit-maximizing condition $MR = MC$ is equivalent to the condition $P = MC$.

Problems and Applications

2.4 A student argues: "To maximize profit, a firm should produce the quantity where the difference between marginal revenue and marginal cost is the greatest. If a firm produces more than this quantity, then the profit made on each additional unit will be falling." Briefly explain whether you agree with this reasoning.

2.5 Why don't firms maximize revenue rather than profit? Briefly explain whether a firm that maximized revenue would be likely to produce a smaller or larger quantity than if it were maximizing profit.

2.6 Refer to Table 12.3 on page 413. Suppose the price of wheat falls to $5.50 per bushel. How many bushels of wheat will Farmer Parker produce, and how much profit will he make? Briefly explain.

2.7 Refer to Table 12.3 on page 413. Suppose that the marginal cost of wheat is $0.50 higher for every bushel of wheat produced. For example, the marginal cost of producing the eighth bushel of wheat is now $9.50. Assume that the price of wheat remains $7 per bushel. Will this increase in marginal cost change the profit-maximizing level of production for Farmer Parker? Briefly explain. How much profit will Farmer Parker make now?

2.8 In Table 12.3 on page 413, what are Farmer Parker's fixed costs? Suppose that his fixed costs increase by $10. Will this increase change the profit-maximizing level of production for Farmer Parker? Briefly explain. How much profit will Farmer Parker make now?

12.3 Illustrating Profit or Loss on the Cost Curve Graph, pages 414–420

LEARNING OBJECTIVE: Use graphs to show a firm's profit or loss.

Summary

From the definitions of profit and average total cost, we can develop the following expression for the relationship between total profit and average total cost: Profit $= (P - ATC) \times Q$. Using this expression, we can determine the area showing profit or loss on a cost curve graph: The area of profit or loss is a rectangle with a height equal to price minus average total cost (for profit) or average total cost minus price (for loss) and a base equal to the quantity of output.

MyEconLab Visit **www.myeconlab.com** to complete these exercises online and get instant feedback.

Review Questions

3.1 Draw a graph showing a firm that is making a profit in a perfectly competitive market. Be sure your graph includes the firm's demand curve, marginal revenue curve, marginal cost curve, average total cost curve, and average variable cost curve and make sure to indicate the area representing the firm's profit.

3.2 Draw a graph showing a firm that is operating at a loss in a perfectly competitive market. Be sure your graph includes the firm's demand curve, marginal revenue curve, marginal cost curve, average total cost curve, and average variable cost curve and make sure to indicate the area representing the firm's loss.

Problems and Applications

3.3 **(Related to Solved Problem 12.3 on page 416)** Frances sells pencils in the perfectly competitive pencil market. Her output per day and her costs are as follows:

Output per Day	Total Cost
0	$1.00
1	2.50
2	3.50
3	4.20
4	4.50
5	5.20
6	6.80
7	8.70
8	10.70
9	13.00

a. If the current equilibrium price in the pencil market is \$1.80, how many pencils will Frances produce, what price will she charge, and how much profit (or loss) will she make? Draw a graph to illustrate your answer. Your graph should be clearly labeled and should include Frances's demand, *ATC*, *AVC*, *MC*, and *MR* curves; the price she is charging; the quantity she is producing; and the area representing her profit (or loss).

b. Suppose the equilibrium price of pencils falls to \$1.00 per pair. Now how many pencils will Frances produce, what price will she charge, and how much profit (or loss) will she make? Show your work. Draw a graph to illustrate this situation, using the instructions in part (a).

c. Suppose the equilibrium price of pencils falls to \$0.25. Now how many pencils will Frances produce, what price will she charge, and how much profit (or loss) will she make?

3.4 **(Related to Solved Problem 12.3 on page 416)** Review Solved Problem 12.3 and then answer the following: Suppose the equilibrium price of basketballs falls to \$2.50. Now how many basketballs will Andy produce? What price will he charge? How much profit (or loss) will he make?

3.5 **(Related to the Don't Let This Happen to You on page 418)** A student examines the following graph and argues: "I believe that a firm will want to produce at Q_1, not at Q_2. At Q_1, the distance between price and marginal cost is the greatest. Therefore, at Q_1, the firm will be maximizing its profit." Briefly explain whether you agree with the student's argument.

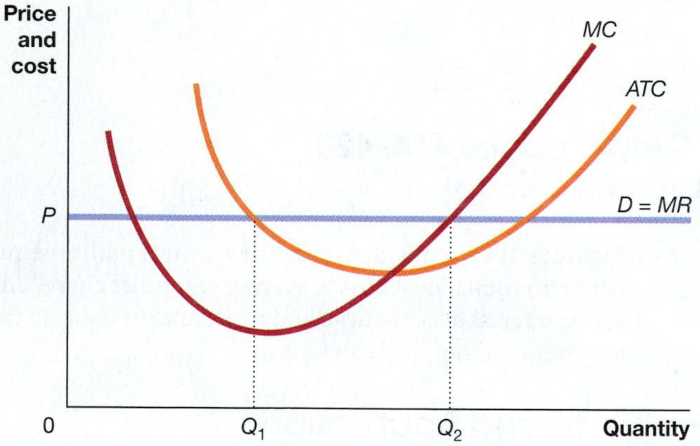

3.6 An article in the *Wall Street Journal* discussed the financial results for BlackBerry, the smartphone and software company: "Revenue tumbled 32% from a year earlier to \$658 million in the quarter ended May 30 from \$966 million a year earlier.... BlackBerry posted profit of \$68 million ... up from \$23 million a year earlier." How is it possible for BlackBerry's revenue to decrease but its profit to increase? Doesn't BlackBerry have to maximize its revenue to maximize its profit? Briefly explain.

Source: Ben Dummett, "BlackBerry Results Miss Expectations," *Wall Street Journal*, June 23, 2015.

3.7 **(Related to the Making the Connection on page 419)** Suppose that the price of oil doubles, raising the cost of home-heating oil and electricity. What effect would this development have on U.S. firms manufacturing solar panels? Illustrate your answer with two graphs: one showing the situation in the market for solar panels and another graph showing the situation for a representative firm in the industry. Be sure your graph for the industry shows any shifts in the market demand and supply curve and any changes in the equilibrium market price. Be sure that your graph for the representative firm includes its demand curve, marginal revenue curve, marginal cost curve, and average total cost curve.

3.8 The following graph represents the situation of Marguerite's Caps, a firm selling caps in the perfectly competitive cap industry:

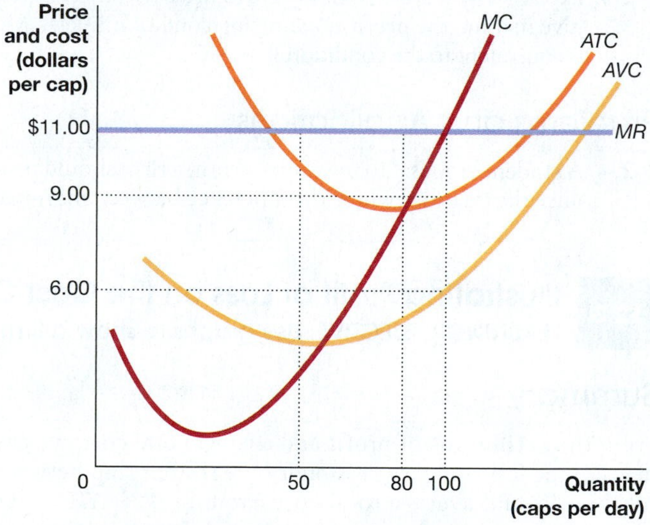

a. How much output should Marguerite produce to maximize her profits?

b. How much profit will she earn?

c. Suppose Marguerite decides to shut down. What would her loss be?

12.4 Deciding Whether to Produce or to Shut Down in the Short Run, pages 420–423

LEARNING OBJECTIVE: Explain why firms may shut down temporarily.

Summary

In deciding whether to shut down or produce in the short run, a firm should ignore its *sunk costs*. A **sunk cost** is a cost that has already been paid and that cannot be recovered. In the short run, a firm continues to produce as long as its price is at least equal to its average variable cost. A perfectly competitive firm's **shutdown point** is the minimum point on the firm's average variable cost curve. If price falls below average variable cost, the firm shuts down in the short run. For prices above the shutdown point, a perfectly competitive firm's marginal cost curve is also its supply curve.

MyEconLab Visit www.myeconlab.com to complete these exercises online and get instant feedback.

Review Questions

4.1 What is the difference between a firm's shutdown point in the short run and in the long run? Why are firms willing to accept losses in the short run but not in the long run?

4.2 What is the relationship between a perfectly competitive firm's marginal cost curve and its supply curve?

4.3 How is the market supply curve derived from the supply curves of individual firms?

Problems and Applications

4.4 Consider a firm in each of the following three situations. For each situation, carefully explain whether the firm will produce in the short run or shut down in the short run.

	Situation 1	Situation 2	Situation 3
Price	$10	$10	$10
Quantity	1,000	1,000	1,000
Variable cost	$5,000	$5,000	$11,000
Fixed cost	$5,000	$6,000	$5,000
Marginal cost of 1,000th unit	$10	$10	$10

4.5 Ed Scahill produces table lamps in the perfectly competitive desk lamp market.

a. Fill in the missing values in the following table.

Output per Week	Total Cost	*AFC*	*AVC*	*ATC*	*MC*
0	$100				
1	150				
2	175				
3	190				
4	210				
5	240				
6	280				
7	330				
8	390				
9	460				
10	540				

b. Suppose the equilibrium price in the desk lamp market is $50. How many table lamps should Ed produce, and how much profit will he make?

c. If next week the equilibrium price of desk lamps drops to $30, should Ed shut down? Explain.

4.6 Matt Rafferty produces hiking boots in the perfectly competitive hiking boots market.

a. Fill in the missing values in the following table.

Output per Week	Total Cost	*AFC*	*AVC*	*ATC*	*MC*
0	$100.00				
1	155.70				
2	205.60				
3	253.90				
4	304.80				
5	362.50				
6	431.20				
7	515.10				
8	618.40				
9	745.30				
10	900.00				

b. Suppose the equilibrium price in the hiking boots market is $100. How many pairs of boots should Matt produce, what price should he charge, and how much profit will he make?

c. If next week the equilibrium price of boots drops to $65, how many pairs of boots should Matt produce, what price should he charge, and how much profit (or loss) will he make?

d. If the equilibrium price of boots falls to $50, how many pairs of boots should Matt produce, what price should he charge, and how much profit (or loss) will he make?

4.7 The following graph represents the situation of a perfectly competitive firm. Indicate on the graph the areas that represent the following:

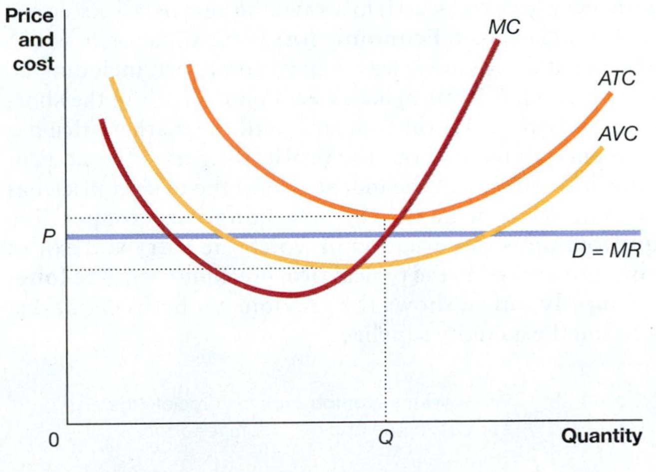

a. Total cost

b. Total revenue

c. Variable cost

d. Profit or loss

Briefly explain whether the firm will continue to produce in the short run.

4.8 According to an article in the *New York Times*, interest payments on bank loans make up more than half the costs of a typical solar panel manufacturer. The owner of a firm that imports solar panels made this observation about solar panel manufacturers: "So as long as companies can cover their variable costs and earn at least some revenue to put toward interest payments, they will continue to operate even at a loss."
  a. Are the interest payments these firms make a variable cost or a fixed cost? Briefly explain.
  b. Does the quotation accurately describe the behavior of solar panel manufacturers in the short run? Does it accurately describe their behavior in the long run? Briefly explain.

Source: Diane Cardwell, "Solar Tariffs Upheld, but May Not Help in U.S.," *New York Times*, November 7, 2012.

4.9 **(Related to Solved Problem 12.4 on page 422)** Suppose you decide to open a copy store. You rent store space (signing a one-year lease to do so), and you take out a loan at a local bank and use the money to purchase 10 copiers. Six months later, a large chain opens a copy store two blocks away from yours. As a result, the revenue you receive from your copy store, while sufficient to cover the wages of your employees and the costs of paper and utilities, doesn't cover all your rent and the interest and repayment costs on the loan you took out to purchase the copiers. Briefly explain whether you should continue operating your business.

4.10 **(Related to Solved Problem 12.4 on page 422)** According to an article in the *Wall Street Journal*, in 2007 the insurance company AXA Equitable signed a long-term lease on 2 million square feet of office space in a skyscraper on Sixth Avenue in Manhattan in New York City. In 2013, AXA decided that it only needed 1.7 million square feet of office space, so it subleased 300,000 square feet of space to several other firms. Although AXA is paying a rent of $88 per square foot on all 2 million square feet it is leasing, it is only receiving $40 per square foot from the firms it is subleasing the 300,000 square feet to. Briefly explain why AXA's actions might make economic sense in the short run. Would these actions make sense in the long run? Briefly explain.

Source: Molly Hensley-Clancy, "A Slump on Sixth Avenue," *Wall Street Journal*, June 16, 2013.

12.5 "If Everyone Can Do It, You Can't Make Money at It": The Entry and Exit of Firms in the Long Run, pages 423–430

LEARNING OBJECTIVE: Explain how entry and exit ensure that perfectly competitive firms earn zero economic profit in the long run.

Summary

Economic profit is a firm's revenue minus all its costs, implicit and explicit. **Economic loss** is the situation in which a firm's total revenue is less than its total cost, including all implicit costs. If firms make an economic profit in the short run, new firms enter the industry until the market price has fallen enough to wipe out the profit. If firms suffer an economic loss, firms exit the industry until the market price has risen enough to wipe out the loss. **Long-run competitive equilibrium** is the situation in which the entry and exit of firms has resulted in the typical firm breaking even. The **long-run supply curve** shows the relationship between market price and the quantity supplied.

Review Questions

5.1 When are firms likely to enter an industry? When are they likely to exit an industry?

5.2 Would a firm earning zero economic profit continue to produce, even in the long run?

5.3 Discuss the shape of the long-run supply curve in a perfectly competitive market. Suppose that a perfectly competitive market is initially at long-run equilibrium and then there is a permanent decrease in the demand for the product. Draw a graph showing how the market adjusts in the long run.

Problems and Applications

5.4 Suppose an assistant professor of economics is earning a salary of $75,000 per year. One day she quits her job, sells $100,000 worth of bonds that had been earning 3 percent per year, and uses the funds to open a bookstore. At the end of the year, she shows an accounting profit of $80,000 on her income tax return. What is her economic profit?

5.5 A study analyzed a pharmaceutical firm's costs to develop a prescription drug and receive government approval. An article in the *Wall Street Journal* describing the study noted that included in the firm's costs was "the return that could be gained if the money [used to develop the drug] were invested elsewhere." Briefly explain whether you agree that this return should be included in the firm's costs.

Source: Jason Millman, "Does It Really Cost $2.6 Billion to Develop a Drug?" *Wall Street Journal*, November 18, 2014.

5.6 **(Related to the Chapter Opener on page 407)** The following questions are about long-run equilibrium in the market for cage-free eggs.
  a. As described in the chapter opener, was the market for cage-free eggs in 2015 in long run equilibrium? Briefly explain.
  b. What would we expect to happen to the price of cage-free eggs and the quantity of cage-free eggs produced in the long run? Briefly explain.
  c. In January 2015, California began requiring that all eggs sold in the state be cage-free. Dunkin' Donuts also announced that it would eventually use only cage-free

eggs in its breakfast sandwiches nationwide. Other firms made similar announcements. What effect will this increased demand have on the long-run price of cage-free eggs? Briefly explain.

Source: John Kell, "Dunkin' Donuts Considers Using Only Cage-Free Eggs," fortune.com, March 30, 2015.

5.7 In panel (b) of Figure 12.9 on page 426, Sacha Gillette reduces her output from 40,000 to 25,000 dozen eggs when the price falls to \$1.75. At this price and this output level, she is operating at a loss. Why doesn't she just continue charging the original \$2.00 and continue producing 40,000 dozen eggs?

5.8 According to an article in the *Wall Street Journal*, rapid growth in consumer demand for natural and organic food helped make the Whole Foods supermarket chain very profitable. But according to that same story, "its accomplishment drew broad new competition, from mainstream retailers like Kroger and Safeway Inc. and upstarts like Sprouts Farmers Market Inc. and Fresh Market Inc." As a result, the prices of the organic food sold by Whole Foods and these other stores has declined, and so have the stores' profits. Illustrate what happened to Whole Foods and to the market for organic food sold in supermarkets using two graphs: One graph should illustrate the situation for Whole Foods, and the other graph should show what happened in the market for organic foods. Be sure that all curves in your graphs are correctly labeled and that you show any shifts in the curves as a result of increased competition in the market for organic foods.

Source: Annie Gasparro, "Slow to Cut Prices, Whole Foods Is Punished," *Wall Street Journal*, May 7, 2014.

5.9 A student in a principles of economics course makes the following remark:

> The economic model of perfectly competitive markets is fine in theory but not very realistic. It predicts that in the long run, a firm in a perfectly competitive market will earn no profits. No firm in the real world would stay in business if it earned zero profits.

Briefly explain whether you agree with this remark.

5.10 **(Related to the Making the Connection on page 429)** According to a news story, the Boston-based game company Proletariat launched its first mobile game, World Zombination, after having "spent nearly 18 months and \$2 million to develop it." In the first three months following the game's release in February 2015, it was downloaded more than 3 million times. Yet the firm was just breaking even on the game. If game companies can only break even on the mobile games they develop, would we expect them to continue developing such games in the long run? Briefly explain.

Source: Sarah E. Needleman, "Mobile-Game Makers Try to Catch More 'Whales' Who Pay for Free Games," *Wall Street Journal*, May 10, 2015.

5.11 Suppose that currently the market for gluten-free spaghetti is in long-run equilibrium at a price of \$3.50 per box and a quantity of 4 million boxes sold per year. If the demand for gluten-free spaghetti permanently increases, which of the following combinations of equilibrium price and equilibrium quantity would you expect to see in the long run? Carefully explain why you chose the answer you did.

a. A price of \$3.50 per box and a quantity of 4 million boxes
b. A price of \$3.50 per box and a quantity of more than 4 million boxes
c. A price of more than \$3.50 per box and a quantity of more than 4 million boxes
d. A price of less than \$3.50 per box and a quantity of less than 4 million boxes

5.12 Suppose that each of the following is true: (1) The laptop computer industry is perfectly competitive and that the firms that assemble laptops do not also make the displays, or screens; (2) the laptop display industry is also perfectly competitive; and (3) because the demand for laptop displays is currently relatively small, firms in the laptop display industry have not been able to take advantage of all the economies of scale in laptop display production. Use a graph of the laptop computer market to illustrate the long-run effects on equilibrium price and quantity in the laptop computer market of a substantial and sustained increase in the demand for laptop computers. Use another graph to show the effect on the cost curves of a typical firm in the laptop computer industry. Briefly explain your graphs. Do your graphs indicate that the laptop computer industry is a constant-cost industry, an increasing-cost industry, or a decreasing-cost industry?

5.13 According to an article in the *Wall Street Journal*, as a result of U.S. consumers increasing their demand for beef, in 2015 world beef prices increased. For example, according to the article, "Australian beef prices are up 40% this year, while New Zealand prices are 17% higher." The article observed, "The gains show no signs of stopping, given the [increasing] U.S. demand…." If U.S. demand for beef continues to increase, will beef prices also continue to increase in the long run? Briefly explain.

Source: Lucy Craymer, "Beef Prices Sizzle With U.S. Demand," *Wall Street Journal*, September 10, 2015.

5.14 Suppose that at the beginning of a year, the price of corn is \$3.80 per bushel and 14 billion bushels are harvested. There are approximately 400,000 corn farmers, so the average output per farmer is about 350,000 bushels. The following graphs assume that the market for corn is initially in long-run equilibrium. Favorable weather during the year increases the total corn harvest to 16 billion bushels. Assume that no other factors affect the market for corn.

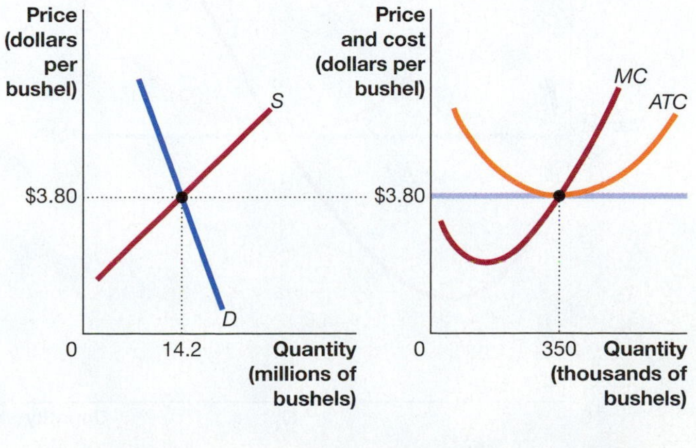

a. What percentage of the total corn output did the average corn farmer produce at the beginning of the year?
b. Show on the graph for the total market for corn and the graph for the typical farm any changes that occur in the short run as a result of the increase in the corn harvest. Be sure to note whether any curves shift and whether there are any changes in the equilibrium price or the equilibrium quantities.
c. Show on the graph for the total market for corn and the graph for the typical farm any changes that occur in the long run as a result of the increase in the corn harvest. Be sure to note whether any curves shift and whether there are any changes in the equilibrium price or the equilibrium quantities.

12.6 Perfect Competition and Efficiency, pages 430–432

LEARNING OBJECTIVE: Explain how perfect competition leads to economic efficiency.

Summary

Perfect competition results in **productive efficiency**, which means that goods and services are produced at the lowest possible cost. Perfect competition also results in **allocative efficiency**, which means the goods and services are produced up to the point where the last unit provides a marginal benefit to consumers equal to the marginal cost of producing it.

MyEconLab Visit **www.myeconlab.com** to complete these exercises online and get instant feedback.

Review Questions

6.1 Why are consumers so powerful in a market system?

6.2 What is meant by allocative efficiency? What is meant by productive efficiency? Briefly discuss the difference between these two concepts.

6.3 How does perfect competition lead to allocative and productive efficiency?

Problems and Applications

6.4 The chapter states, "Firms will supply all those goods that provide consumers with a marginal benefit at least as great as the marginal cost of producing them." A student objects to this statement, arguing, "I doubt that firms will really do this. After all, firms are in business to make a profit; they don't care about what is best for consumers." Evaluate the student's argument.

6.5 The following graph represents the situation of Karl's Kumquats, a kumquat grower.

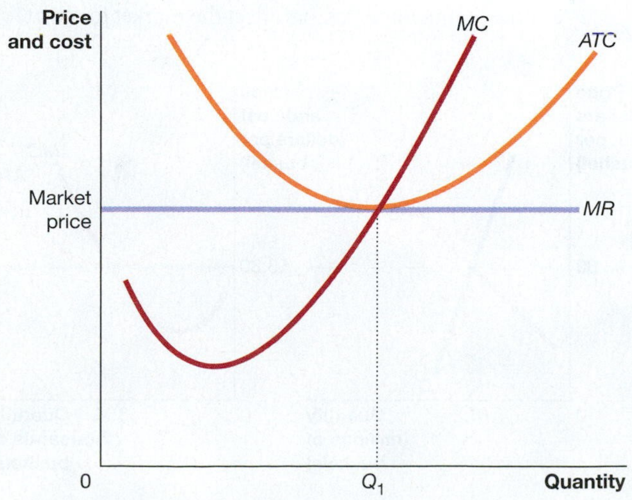

a. How much profit is Karl earning?
b. Does the current situation of Karl's firm illustrate productive efficiency or allocative efficiency? If so, briefly explain how.

6.6 **(Related to Solved Problem 12.6 on page 430)** Discuss the following statement: "In a perfectly competitive market, in the long run consumers benefit from reductions in costs, but firms don't." Don't firms also benefit from cost reductions because they are able to earn larger profits?

6.7 **(Related to Solved Problem 12.6 on page 430)** Suppose you read the following item in a newspaper article, under the headline "Price Gouging Alleged in Pencil Market":

> Consumer advocacy groups charged at a press conference yesterday that there is widespread price gouging in the sale of pencils. They released a study showing that whereas the average retail price of pencils was $1.00, the average cost of producing pencils was only $0.50. "Pencils can be produced without complicated machinery or highly skilled workers, so there is no justification for companies charging a price that is twice what it costs them to produce the product. Pencils are too important in the life of every American for us to tolerate this sort of price gouging any longer," said George Grommet, chief spokesperson for the consumer groups. The consumer groups advocate passage of a law that would allow companies selling pencils to charge a price no more than 20 percent greater than their average cost of production.

Do you believe such a law would be advisable in a situation like this? Explain.

6.8 **(Related to Solved Problem 12.6 on page 430)** Sony suffered losses for a decade selling televisions before finally earning a profit in 2014. Given the strong consumer demand for plasma, LCD, and LED television sets, shouldn't Sony have been able to raise prices to earn a profit during that decade of losses? Briefly explain.

Source: Eric Pfanner and Takashi Mochizuki, "Sony's TV Business Mends, but Will It Be Enough?" *Wall Street Journal*, December 12, 2014.

6.9 An article in the *Wall Street Journal* discusses the visual effects industry, which is made up of firms that provide visual effects for films and television programs. The article notes: "Blockbusters ... often have thousands of visual effects shots. Even dramas and comedies today can include hundreds of them." But the article also notes that the firms producing the effects have not been very profitable. Some firms have declared bankruptcy, and the former general manager of one firm was quoted as saying, "A good year for us was a 5% return." If demand for visual effects is so strong, why is it difficult for the firms that supply them to make an economic profit?

Source: Ben Fritz, "Visual Effects Industry Does a Disappearing Act," *Wall Street Journal*, February 22, 2013.

6.10 Although New York State is second only to Washington State in production of apples, its production has been declining during the past 20 years. The decline has been particularly steep in counties close to New York City. In 1985, there were more than 11,000 acres of apple orchards in Ulster County, which is 75 miles north of New York City. Today, only about 6,000 acres remain. As it became difficult for apple growers in the county to compete with lower-cost producers elsewhere, the resources these entrepreneurs were using to produce apples—particularly land—became more valuable in other uses. Many farmers sold their land to housing developers. Suppose a nutritionist develops a revolutionary new diet that involves eating 10 apples per day. The new diet becomes wildly popular. What effect is the new diet likely to have on the number of apple orchards within 100 miles of New York City? What effect is the diet likely to have on housing prices in New York City?

CHAPTER 13

Monopolistic Competition: The Competitive Model in a More Realistic Setting

Chapter Outline and Learning Objectives

Is Chipotle the New McDonald's?

Steve Ells majored in art history at the University of Colorado before attending the Culinary Institute of America and working as a chef in San Francisco. In 1993, he opened Chipotle Mexican Grill in a small storefront in Denver. Although many other restaurants in the area served Mexican food, Ells took a somewhat different approach: The food was made entirely from locally grown fresh ingredients prepared in an "open kitchen" visible to his customers, and the menu was streamlined to focus on varieties of just two items, burritos and tacos. Ells's approach has proven very successful. By 2015, the company had revenue of more than $4 billion from its more than 1,800 restaurants, and it employed more than 50,000 workers. In fact, Chipotle is credited with having started a new category of restaurant—"fast casual." Like Chipotle, fast-casual restaurants prepare fresh food quickly but do not offer table service. These restaurants offer food that many customers consider healthier because it is made with higher-quality ingredients than the food at Taco Bell and McDonald's.

When we discussed the situation of firms in perfectly competitive markets in Chapter 12, we saw that these markets share three key characteristics:

1. There are many firms.
2. All firms sell identical products.
3. There are no barriers to new firms entering the industry.

The market Chipotle competes in shares two of these characteristics: There are many restaurants serving Mexican food, and the barriers to entering the market are very low. But the products that Chipotle and its competitors sell are *differentiated* rather than identical. So, the market for Mexican food is *monopolistically competitive* rather than perfectly competitive.

Can Chipotle continue to succeed? In 2015, the firm's growth slowed more than expected and competitors, such as Qdoba and Moe's Southwest Grill, that had adopted similar approaches to preparing and selling Mexican food were attracting some of Chipotle's customers. As we will see, most monopolistically competitive firms are unable to earn an economic profit in the long run.

Sources: Ilan Brat and Tess Stynes, "Chipotle Raises Concerns Its Growth May Be Cooling," *Wall Street Journal*, February 3, 2015; Charles Passy, "10 Things Chipotle Won't Tell You," marketwatch.com, June 16, 2015; and Jay Cheshes, "The Chipotle Effect: How Chefs Are Reinventing Fast Food," *Wall Street Journal*, February 6, 2015.

Economics in Your Life

Can You Operate a Successful Restaurant?

After you graduate, you plan to realize your dream of opening an Italian restaurant. You have many decisions to make in operating your restaurant. Will it be "family style," with sturdy but inexpensive furniture, or will it be more elegant, with nice furniture, tablecloths, and candles? Will you offer a full menu or concentrate on pasta dishes that use your grandmother's secret sauce? These and other decisions you make will distinguish your restaurant from competitors. What's likely to happen in the restaurant market in your hometown after you open your restaurant? How successful are you likely to be? Try to answer these questions as you read this chapter. You can check your answers against those we provide on **page 461** at the end of this chapter.

Many markets in the U.S. economy are similar to the restaurant market: They have many buyers and sellers, and the barriers to entry are low, but the goods and services offered for sale are differentiated rather than identical. Examples of these markets include coffee houses, movie theaters, supermarkets, and clothing manufacturing. In fact, the majority of the firms you buy from are competing in **monopolistically competitive** markets.

Monopolistic competition A market structure in which barriers to entry are low and many firms compete by selling similar, but not identical, products.

We have seen how perfect competition benefits consumers and results in economic efficiency. Will these same desirable outcomes also hold for monopolistically competitive markets? This question is important because monopolistically competitive markets are common.

13.1 Demand and Marginal Revenue for a Firm in a Monopolistically Competitive Market

LEARNING OBJECTIVE: Explain why a monopolistically competitive firm has downward-sloping demand and marginal revenue curves.

If the Chipotle restaurant located a mile from where you live raises the price of a veggie burrito from $7.00 to $7.50, it will lose some, but not all, of its customers. Some customers will switch to buying their burritos at another restaurant, but other customers will be willing to pay the higher price for a variety of reasons: This restaurant may be closer to them, or they may prefer Chipotle's burritos to similar burritos at competing restaurants. So, a Chipotle restaurant will face a downward-sloping demand curve, unlike a wheat farmer who will sell no wheat if he raises his price and, therefore, faces a horizontal demand curve.

The Demand Curve for a Monopolistically Competitive Firm

Figure 13.1 shows how a change in price affects the quantity of burritos Chipotle sells. The increase in the price from $7.00 to $7.50 decreases the quantity of burritos sold from 3,000 per week to 2,400 per week. MyEconLab Concept Check

Marginal Revenue for a Firm with a Downward-Sloping Demand Curve

For a firm in a perfectly competitive market, the demand curve and the marginal revenue curve are the same (see Chapter 12). A perfectly competitive firm faces a horizontal demand curve and does not have to cut the price to sell a larger quantity. A monopolistically competitive firm, however, must cut the price to sell more, so its marginal revenue curve will slope downward and will be below its demand curve.

The data in Table 13.1 illustrate this point. To keep the numbers simple, let's assume that your local Chipotle restaurant is very small and sells at most 11 burritos per week. If this Chipotle charges a price of $10.00 or more, all of its potential customers will buy

MyEconLab Animation

Figure 13.1

The Downward-Sloping Demand Curve for Burritos at Chipotle

If a Chipotle restaurant increases the price of its burritos, it will lose some, but not all, of its customers. In this case, raising the price from $7.00 to $7.50 reduces the quantity of burritos sold from 3,000 to 2,400. Therefore, unlike a perfect competitor, a Chipotle restaurant faces a downward-sloping demand curve.

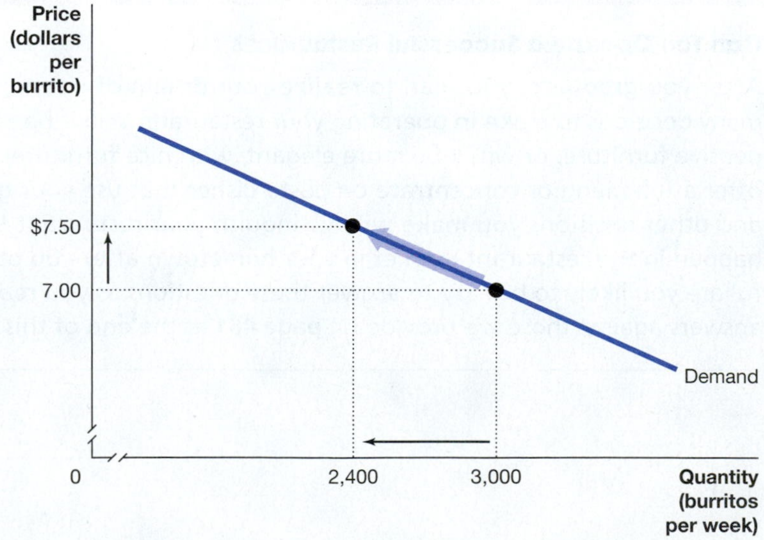

Table 13.1

Demand and Marginal Revenue at a Chipotle

Burritos Sold per Week (Q)	Price (P)	Total Revenue ($TR = P \times Q$)	Average Revenue $\left(AR = \frac{TR}{Q}\right)$	Marginal Revenue $\left(MR = \frac{\Delta TR}{\Delta Q}\right)$
0	$10.00	$0.00	—	—
1	9.50	9.50	$9.50	$9.50
2	9.00	18.00	9.00	8.50
3	8.50	25.50	8.50	7.50
4	8.00	32.00	8.00	6.50
5	7.50	37.50	7.50	5.50
6	7.00	42.00	7.00	4.50
7	6.50	45.50	6.50	3.50
8	6.00	48.00	6.00	2.50
9	5.50	49.50	5.50	1.50
10	5.00	50.00	5.00	0.50
11	4.50	49.50	4.50	−0.50

their burritos somewhere else. If it charges $9.50, it will sell 1 burrito per week. For each additional $0.50 this Chipotle reduces the price, it increases the number of burritos it sells by 1. The third column in the table shows how the firm's *total revenue* changes as it sells more burritos. The fourth column shows the firm's revenue per unit, or its *average revenue*. Average revenue is equal to total revenue divided by quantity. Because total revenue equals price multiplied by quantity, dividing by quantity leaves just price. Therefore, *average revenue is always equal to price*. This result will be true for firms selling in any of the four market structures (see Chapter 12).

The last column in Table 13.1 shows the firm's marginal revenue, or the change in total revenue as the firm sells 1 more burrito. For a perfectly competitive firm, the additional revenue received from selling 1 more unit is just equal to the price. That will *not* be true for this Chipotle because to sell another burrito, it has to reduce the price. When the firm cuts the price by $0.50, one good thing happens, and one bad thing happens:

- ***The good thing.*** It sells 1 more burrito; we can call this the *output effect*.
- ***The bad thing.*** It receives $0.50 less for each burrito that it could have sold at the higher price; we can call this the *price effect*.

Figure 13.2 illustrates what happens when the firm cuts the price from $7.50 to $7.00. Selling the sixth burrito adds the $7.00 price to the firm's revenue; this is the

MyEconLab Animation

Figure 13.2

How a Price Cut Affects a Firm's Revenue

If a local Chipotle reduces the price of a burrito from $7.50 to $7.00, the number of burritos it sells per week will increase from 5 to 6. Its marginal revenue from selling the sixth burrito will be $4.50, which is equal to the $7.00 additional revenue from selling 1 more burrito (the area of the green rectangle) minus the $2.50 loss in revenue from selling the first 5 burritos for $0.50 less each (the area of the red rectangle).

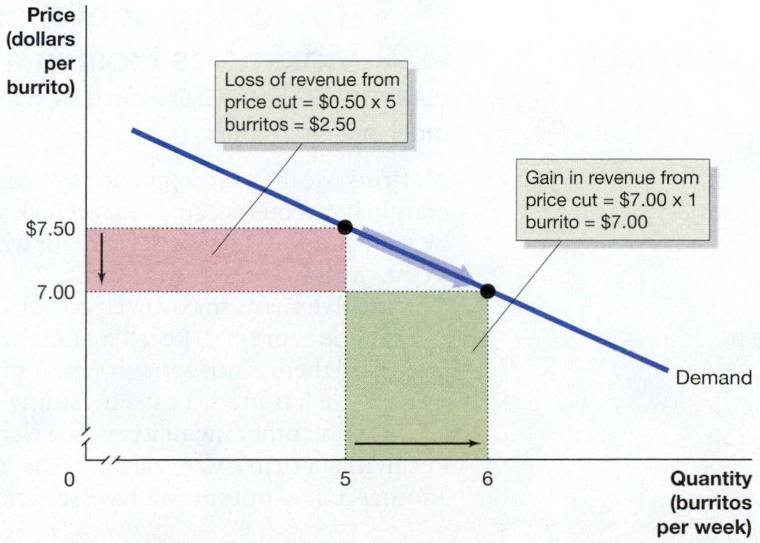

MyEconLab Animation

Figure 13.3

The Demand and Marginal Revenue Curves for a Monopolistically Competitive Firm

Any firm that has the ability to affect the price of the product it sells will have a marginal revenue curve that is below its demand curve. We plot the data from Table 13.1 to create the demand and marginal revenue curves. After the tenth burrito, marginal revenue becomes negative because the additional revenue received from selling 1 more burrito is smaller than the revenue lost from receiving a lower price on the burrito that could have been sold at the original price.

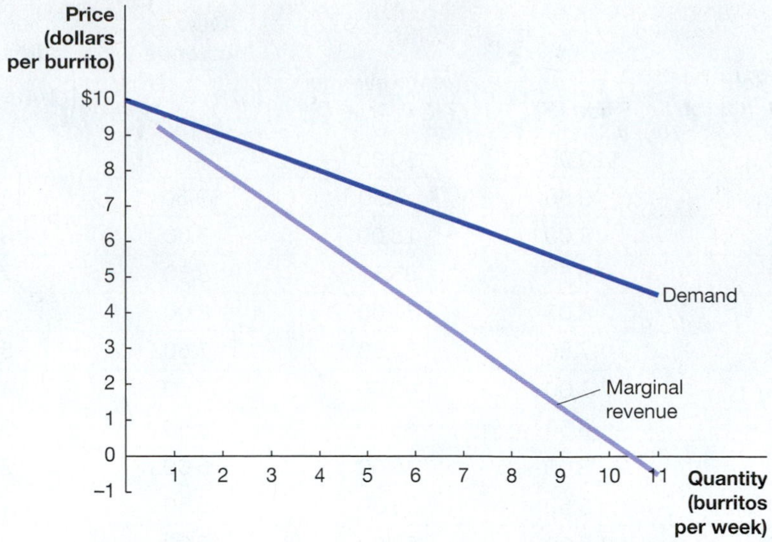

output effect. But this Chipotle now receives a price of $7.00, rather than $7.50, on the first 5 burritos sold; this is the price effect. As a result of the price effect, the firm's revenue on these 5 burritos is $2.50 less than it would have been if the price had remained at $7.50. So, the firm has gained $7.00 in revenue on the sixth burrito and lost $2.50 in revenue on the first 5 burritos, for a net change in revenue of $4.50. Marginal revenue is the change in total revenue from selling 1 more unit. Therefore, the marginal revenue of the sixth burrito is $4.50. Notice that the marginal revenue of the sixth burrito is far below its price of $7.00. In fact, for each additional burrito this Chipotle sells, marginal revenue will be less than price. There is an important general point: *Every firm that has the ability to affect the price of the good or service it sells will have a marginal revenue curve that is below its demand curve.* Only firms in perfectly competitive markets, which can sell as many units as they want at the market price, have marginal revenue curves that are the same as their demand curves.

Figure 13.3 shows the relationship between the demand curve and the marginal revenue curve for the local Chipotle. Notice that after the tenth burrito, marginal revenue becomes negative. This occurs because the additional revenue received from selling 1 more burrito is smaller than the revenue lost from receiving a lower price on the burritos that could have been sold at the original price. MyEconLab Concept Check

MyEconLab Study Plan

13.2 How a Monopolistically Competitive Firm Maximizes Profit in the Short Run

LEARNING OBJECTIVE: Explain how a monopolistically competitive firm maximizes profit in the short run.

All firms use the same approach to maximize profit: They produce the quantity where marginal revenue is equal to marginal cost. So the local Chipotle will maximize profit by selling the quantity of burritos for which the last burrito sold adds the same amount to the firm's revenue as to its costs. Let's look more carefully at how monopolistically competitive firms maximize profit by considering the situation the local Chipotle faces in the short run. Recall that in the short run, at least one factor of production is fixed, and there is not enough time for new firms to enter the market (see Chapter 11). A Chipotle has many costs, including the cost of purchasing the ingredients for its burritos and other menu items, the electricity it uses, and the wages of its employees. Recall that a firm's *marginal cost* is the increase in total cost resulting from producing another unit of output. We have seen that for many firms, the marginal cost curve has a U shape. We will assume that the marginal cost curve for this Chipotle has the usual shape.

We combine the revenue data for this Chipotle from Table 13.1 with cost data to create the table in Figure 13.4. The graphs in Figure 13.4 plot the data from the table. In panel (a), we see how this Chipotle can determine its profit-maximizing quantity and price. As long as the marginal cost of selling 1 more burrito is less than the marginal revenue, the firm should sell additional burritos. For example, increasing the quantity of burritos sold from 3 per week to 4 per week increases cost by $5.00 but increases revenue by $6.50. So, the firm's profits are increased by $1.50 as a result of selling the fourth burrito.

As this Chipotle sells more burritos, rising marginal cost eventually equals marginal revenue, and the firm sells the profit-maximizing quantity of burritos. Marginal

Burritos Sold per Week (*Q*)	Price (*P*)	Total Revenue (*TR*)	Marginal Revenue (*MR*)	Total Cost (*TC*)	Marginal Cost (*MC*)	Average Total Cost (*ATC*)	Profit
0	$10.00	$0.00	—	$6.00	—	—	–$6.00
1	9.50	9.50	$9.50	11.00	$5.00	$11.00	–1.50
2	9.00	18.00	8.50	15.50	4.50	7.75	2.50
3	8.50	25.50	7.50	19.50	4.00	6.50	6.00
4	8.00	32.00	6.50	24.50	5.00	6.13	7.50
5	7.50	37.50	5.50	30.00	5.50	6.00	7.50
6	7.00	42.00	4.50	36.00	6.00	6.00	6.00
7	6.50	45.50	3.50	42.50	6.50	6.07	3.00
8	6.00	48.00	2.50	49.50	7.00	6.19	–1.50
9	5.50	49.50	1.50	57.00	7.50	6.33	–7.50
10	5.00	50.00	0.50	65.00	8.00	6.50	–15.00
11	4.50	49.50	–0.50	73.50	8.50	6.68	–24.00

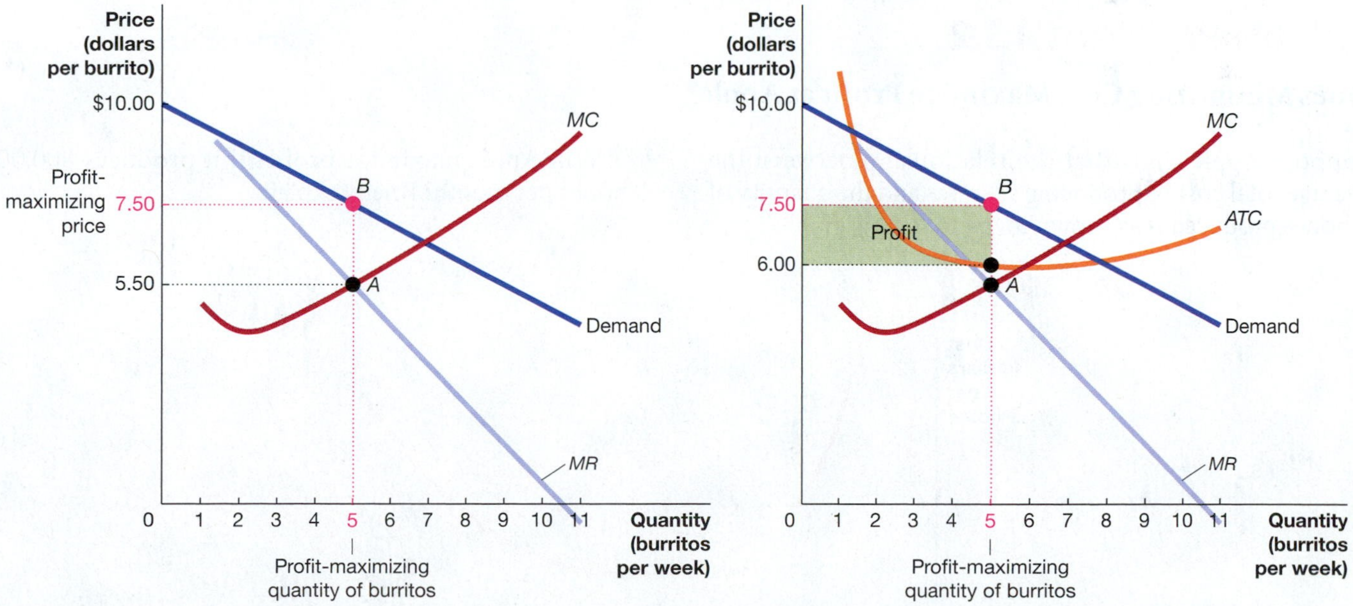

MyEconLab Animation

Figure 13.4 Maximizing Profit in a Monopolistically Competitive Market

To maximize profit, a Chipotle restaurant wants to sell burritos up to the point where the marginal revenue from selling the last burrito is just equal to the marginal cost. As the table shows, selling the fifth burrito—point *A* in panel (a)—adds $5.50 to the firm's costs and $5.50 to its revenues. The firm then uses the demand curve to find the price that will lead consumers to buy this quantity of burritos (point *B*). In panel (b), the green rectangle represents the firm's profits. The rectangle has a height equal to $1.50, which is the $7.50 price minus the average total cost of $6.00, and it has a base equal to the quantity of 5 burritos. So, for this Chipotle profit equals $1.50 × 5 = $7.50.

cost equals marginal revenue with the fifth burrito, which adds \$5.50 to the firm's costs and \$5.50 to its revenues—point *A* in panel (a) of Figure 13.4. The demand curve tells us the price at which the firm is able to sell 5 burritos per week. In Figure 13.4, if we draw a vertical line from 5 burritos up to the demand curve, we can see that the price at which the firm can sell 5 burritos per week is \$7.50 (point *B*). We can conclude that for this Chipotle, the profit-maximizing quantity is 5 burritos, and the profit-maximizing price is \$7.50. If the firm sells more than 5 burritos per week, its profit will fall. For example, selling a sixth burrito adds \$6.00 to its costs and only \$4.50 to its revenues. So, its profit will fall from \$7.50 to \$6.00.

Panel (b) adds the average total cost curve for Chipotle. The panel shows that the average total cost of selling 5 burritos is \$6.00. Recall from Chapter 12 that:

$$\text{Profit} = (P - ATC) \times Q.$$

In this case, profit = (\$7.50 − \$6.00) × 5 = \$7.50. The green rectangle in panel (b) shows the amount of profit. The rectangle has a base equal to Q and a height equal to $(P - ATC)$, so its area equals profit.

Notice that, unlike a perfectly competitive firm, which produces where $P = MC$, a monopolistically competitive firm produces where $P > MC$. In this case, this Chipotle is charging a price of \$7.50, although marginal cost is \$5.50. For a perfectly competitive firm, price equals marginal revenue, $P = MR$. Therefore, to fulfill the $MR = MC$ condition for profit maximization, a perfectly competitive firm will produce where $P = MC$. $P > MR$ for a monopolistically competitive firm because the firm's marginal revenue curve is below its demand curve. Therefore, a monopolistically competitive firm will maximize profits by producing where $P > MC$.

Solved Problem 13.2

MyEconLab Interactive Animation

Does Minimizing Cost Maximize Profit at Apple?

Suppose Apple finds that the relationship between the average total cost of producing iPhones and the quantity of iPhones produced is as shown in the following graph.

Will Apple maximize profits if it produces 800,000 iPhones per month? Briefly explain.

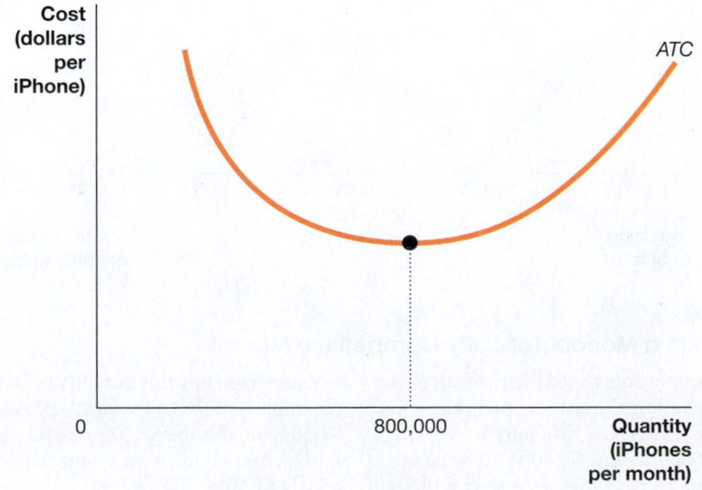

Solving the Problem

Step 1: Review the chapter material. This problem is about how monopolistically competitive firms maximize profit, so you may want to review the section "How a Monopolistically Competitive Firm Maximizes Profit in the Short Run," which begins on page 446.

Step 2: Discuss the relationship between minimizing costs and maximizing profits. Firms often talk about the steps they take to reduce costs. The graph shows that by producing 800,000 iPhones per month, Apple will minimize its average cost of production. But remember that minimizing cost is not the firm's ultimate goal; the firm's ultimate goal is to maximize profit. Depending on demand, a firm may maximize profit by producing a quantity that is either larger or smaller than the quantity that would minimize average total cost.

Step 3: Draw a graph that shows Apple maximizing profit at a quantity where average cost is not minimized. Note that in the graph, average total cost reaches a minimum at a quantity of 800,000, but profit is maximized at a quantity of 600,000.

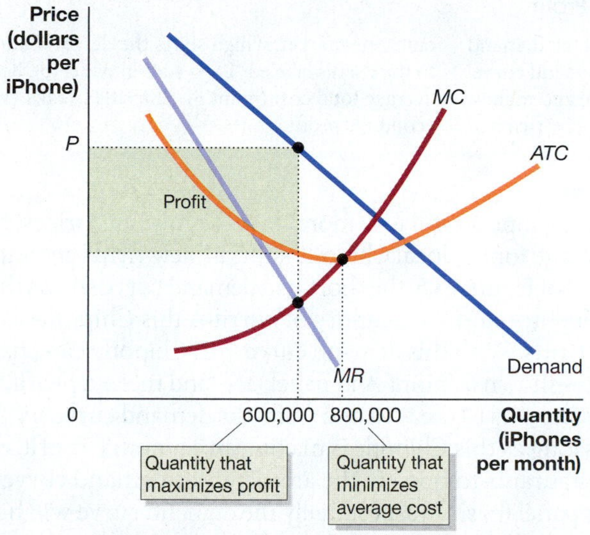

Your Turn: For more practice, do related problem 2.5 on pages 463–464 at the end of this chapter. MyEconLab Study Plan

13.3 What Happens to Profits in the Long Run?

LEARNING OBJECTIVE: Analyze the situation of a monopolistically competitive firm in the long run.

Remember that a firm makes an economic profit when its total revenue is greater than all of its costs, including the opportunity cost of the funds invested in the firm by its owners. Because cost curves include the owners' opportunity costs, the Chipotle restaurant represented in Figure 13.4 on page 447 is making an economic profit. This economic profit gives entrepreneurs an incentive to enter this market and establish new firms. If a Chipotle is earning an economic profit selling burritos, new restaurants serving similar food are likely to open in the same area.

How Does the Entry of New Firms Affect the Profits of Existing Firms?

As new restaurants open near a local Chipotle, the firm's demand curve will shift to the left. The demand curve will shift because the Chipotle will sell fewer burritos at each price when there are additional restaurants in the area selling food. The demand curve will also become more elastic because consumers have additional restaurants from which to buy

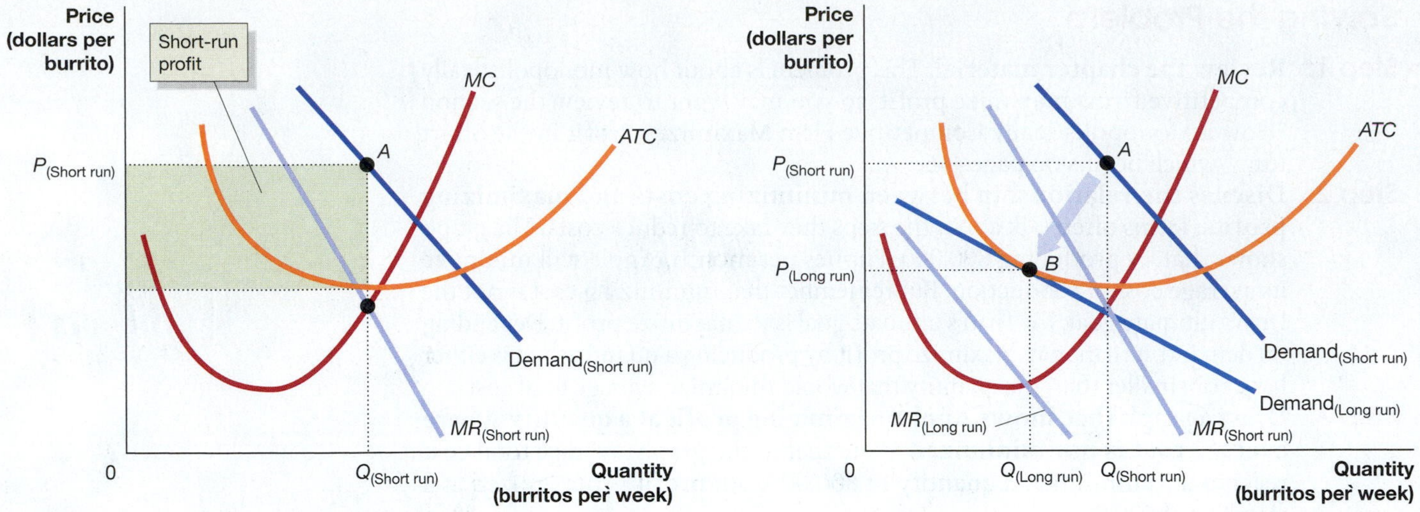

MyEconLab Animation

Figure 13.5 How Entry of New Firms Eliminates Profit

Panel (a) shows that in the short run, the local Chipotle faces the demand and marginal revenue curves labeled "Short run." With this demand curve, Chipotle can charge a price above average total cost (point A) and make a profit, shown by the green rectangle. But this profit attracts new firms to enter the market, which shifts the demand and marginal revenue curves to the curves labeled "Long run" in panel (b). Because price is now equal to average total cost (point B), Chipotle breaks even and no longer earns an economic profit.

burritos, so the Chipotle will lose more sales if it raises its prices. Figure 13.5 shows how the demand curve for the local Chipotle shifts as new firms enter its market.

In panel (a) of Figure 13.5, the short-run demand curve shows the relationship between the price of burritos and the quantity of burritos this Chipotle sells per week before the entry of new firms. With this demand curve, this Chipotle can charge a price above average total cost—shown as point A in panel (a)—and make a profit. But this profit attracts additional restaurants to the area and shifts the demand curve for this Chipotle's burritos to the left. As long as this Chipotle is making an economic profit, there is an incentive for additional restaurants to open in the area, and the demand curve will continue shifting to the left. As panel (b) shows, eventually the demand curve will have shifted to the point where it is just touching—or tangent to—the average total cost curve.

In the long run, at the point where the demand curve is tangent to the average total cost curve, price is equal to average total cost (point B), the firm is breaking even, and it no longer earns an economic profit. In the long run, the demand curve is also more elastic because the more restaurants there are in the area, the more sales this Chipotle will lose to other restaurants if it raises its price.

Don't Let This Happen to You

Don't Confuse Zero Economic Profit with Zero Accounting Profit

Remember that economists count the opportunity cost of the owner's investment in a firm as a cost. Suppose you invest $200,000 opening a pizza parlor, and the return you could earn on those funds each year in a similar investment—such as opening a sandwich shop—is 10 percent. Therefore, the annual opportunity cost of investing the funds in your own business is 10 percent of $200,000, or $20,000. This $20,000 is part of your profit in the accounting sense, and you would have to pay taxes on it. But in an economic sense, the $20,000 is a cost. In long-run equilibrium, we would expect that entry of new firms would keep you from earning more than 10 percent on your investment. So, you would end up breaking even and earning zero economic profit, even though you were earning an accounting profit of $20,000.

MyEconLab Study Plan

Your Turn: Test your understanding by doing related problem 3.7 on page 465 at the end of this chapter.

Of course, it is possible that a monopolistically competitive firm will suffer an economic loss in the short run. As a consequence, the owners of the firm will not be covering the opportunity cost of their investment. We expect that, in the long run, firms will exit an industry if they are suffering an economic loss. If firms exit, the demand curve for the output of a remaining firm will shift to the right. This process will continue until the representative firm in the industry is able to charge a price equal to its average total cost and break even. Therefore, in the long run, monopolistically competitive firms will experience neither an economic profit nor an economic loss. Table 13.2 summarizes the short run and the long run for a monopolistically competitive firm.

MyEconLab Concept Check

Table 13.2 **The Short Run and the Long Run for a Monopolistically Competitive Firm**

Relationship between Price and Marginal Cost	Relationship between Price and Average Total Cost	Profit and Loss	Elasticity of Demand Curve
Short Run *P* > *MC*	**Short Run** *P* > *ATC*	**Short Run** Economic profit	**Short Run** Less elastic demand curve
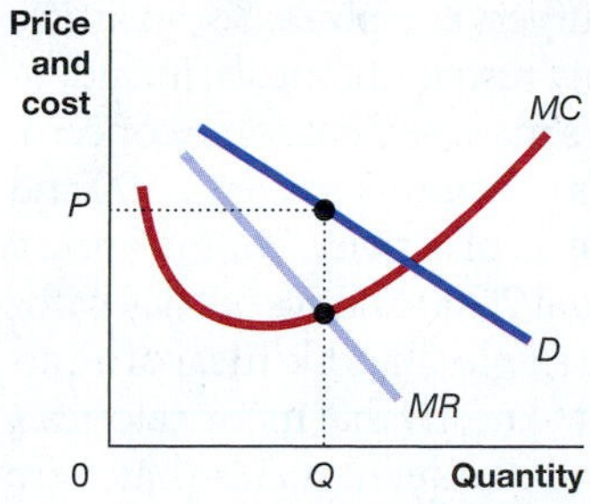	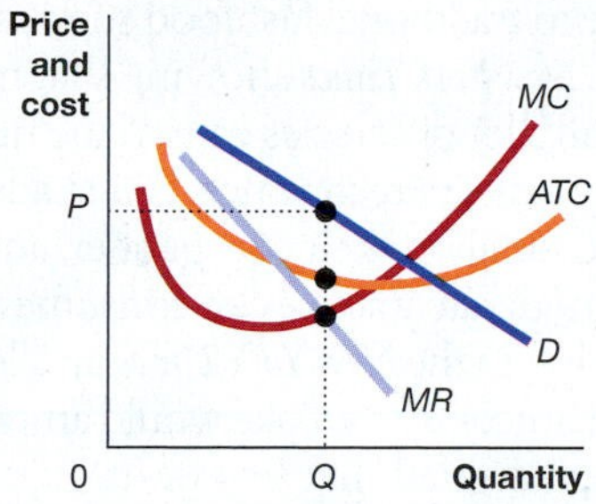	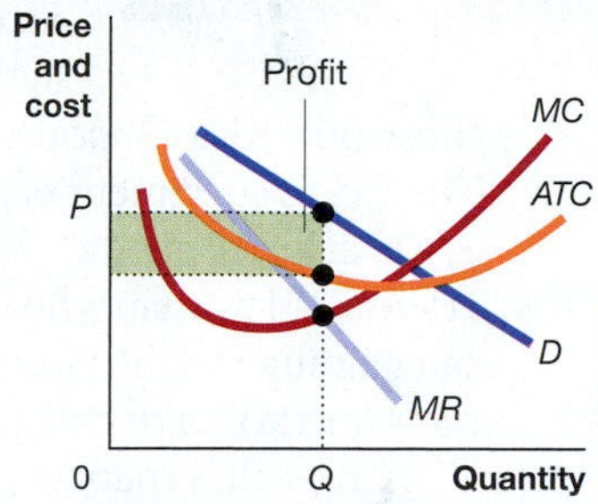	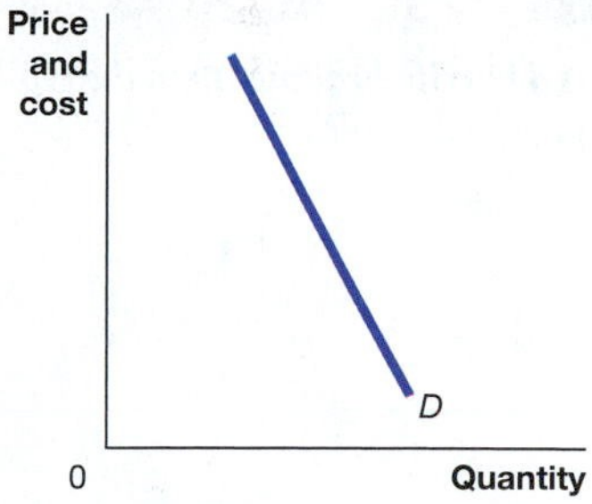
	or P < *ATC*	*or* Economic loss	
	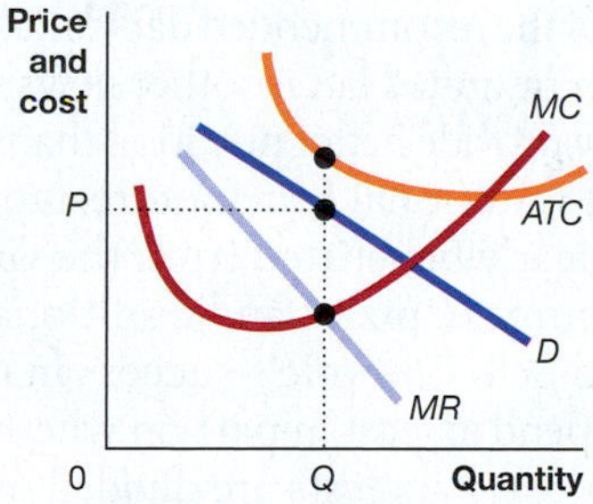	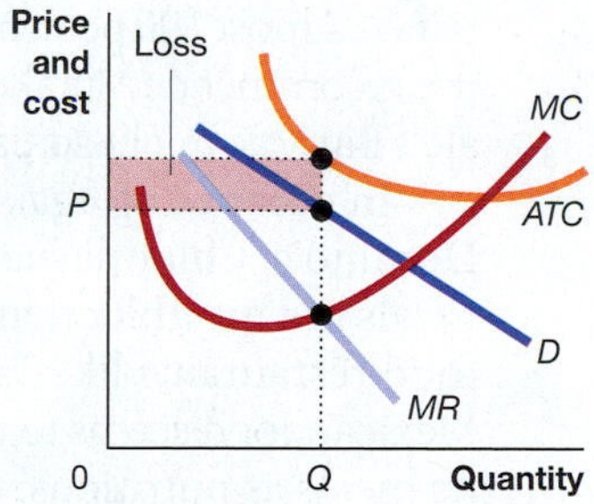	
Long Run *P* > *MC*	**Long Run** *P* = *ATC*	**Long Run** Zero economic profit	**Long Run** More elastic demand curve
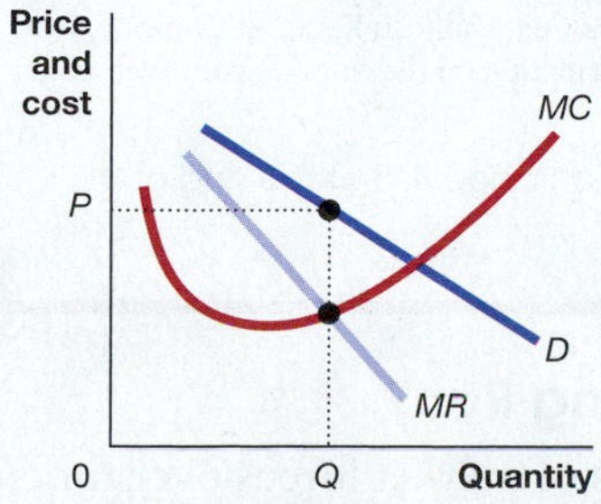	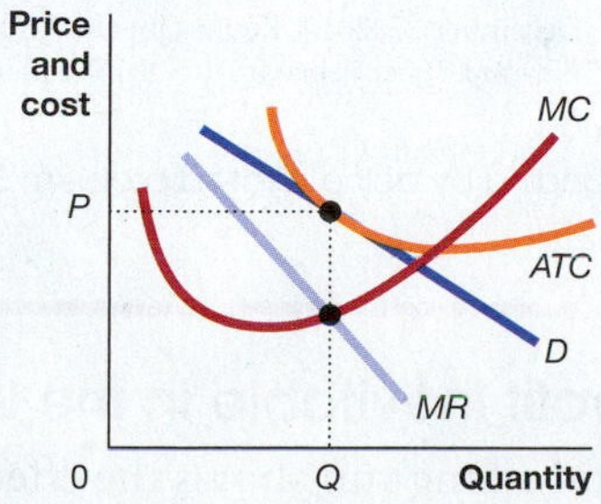	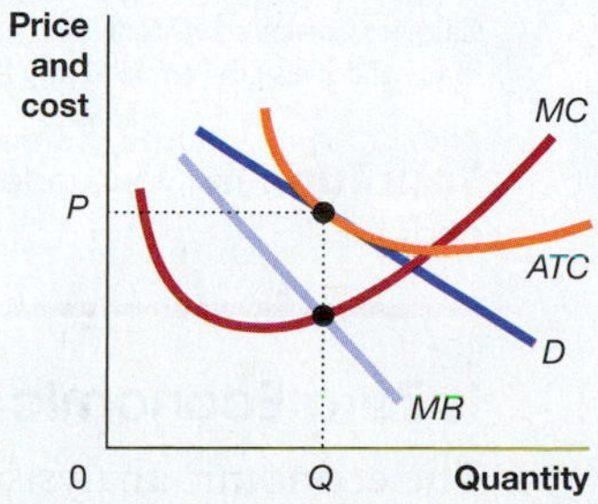	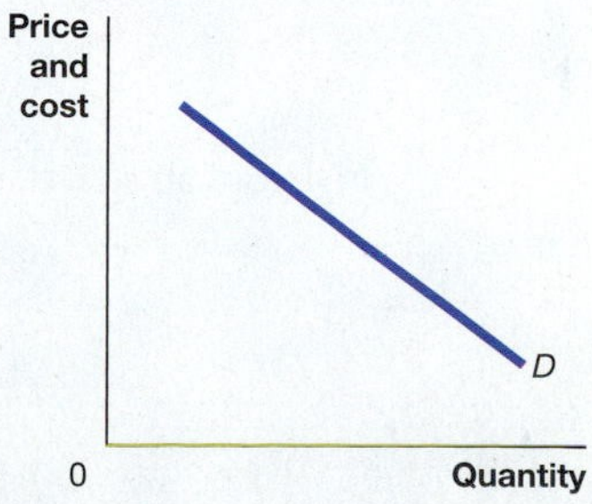

Making the Connection
MyEconLab Video

Is the Trend toward Healthy Eating a Threat to Chipotle's Market Niche?

Is a burrito healthier than the typical fast-food meal?

A burger, French fries, and a soft drink. Or a pepperoni pizza with extra cheese. For generations, these were typical meals for many teenagers and young adults. Today, however, some people view these traditional fast-food meals as unhealthy. "Fast-casual" restaurants such as Chipotle have benefitted from that view. Chipotle advertises that it is committed "to sourcing the very best ingredients we can find and preparing them by hand." The restaurant chain also notes that it prepares its food only with "vegetables grown in healthy soil, and pork from pigs allowed to freely root and roam outdoors or in deeply bedded barns." Here's how one news story summarized the appeal of fast-casual restaurants like Chipotle: They offer "food that's fresh, wholesome and designed to move." In an interview, Chipotle CEO Steve Ells said, "People understand that as a country, we are not as healthy as we should be, that a lot of our health issues are probably related to diet, and that we could be a lot healthier and happier if we just ate the right foods."

Clearly, part of Chipotle's appeal is that it offers a healthier alternative to traditional fast food such as burgers and pizza. So, an article in the *New York Times* showing that many restaurant meals, including those offered at Chipotle, had a lot of calories caused the firm's management some concern. The U.S. Department of Agriculture recommends that adults consume between 1,600 and 2,400 calories per day, depending on their age, gender, and level of activity. For instance, a 20-year old woman who is moderately active can consume about 2,200 calories per day without gaining weight. According to the *New York Times* article, a single Chipotle meal of a carnitas burrito, chips and guacamole, and a Coke would amount to nearly that many calories.

Chipotle's management argued that few of its customers ordered meals that were that high in calories. A followup *New York Times* article noted that data on online ordering gathered from the GrubHub Web site indicated that the typical meal ordered at Chipotle contained only 1,070 calories. But the data also showed that the typical Chipotle meal contained almost 100 percent of the recommended daily intake of salt and nearly 75 percent of the recommended intake of saturated fat. Another news story pointed out that a McDonald's Big Mac might actually provide better nutrition than many of Chipotle's burritos.

In competing against traditional fast-food restaurants such as McDonald's and Domino's, Chipotle has clearly benefitted from the view of many consumers that its meals are healthier than burgers, pizza, and traditional Mexican food served by fast-food restaurants like Taco Bell. Chipotle's success in the market niche of fast-casual Mexican food seems to depend at least in part on whether consumers continue to view its meals as nutritious. Industry analysts are divided over whether these issues pose a significant threat to Chipotle's continued success in its market niche.

Sources: Jay Cheshes, "The Chipotle Effect: How Chefs Are Reinventing Fast Food," *Wall Street Journal*, February 6, 2015; "Chipotle: Fast Food with 'Integrity,'" bloomberg.com, February 16, 2007; Charles Passy, "10 Things Chipotle Won't Tell You," marketwatch.com, June 16, 2015; Josh Barro, Troy Griggs, David Leonhardt, and Claire Cain Miller, "What 2,000 Calories Looks Like," *New York Times*, December 22, 2014; Kevin Quealy, Amanda Cox, and Josh Katz, "At Chipotle, How Many Calories Do People Really Eat?" *New York Times*, February 17, 2015; and information on the chipotle.com Web site.

MyEconLab Study Plan

Your Turn: Test your understanding by doing related problem 3.9 on page 465 at the end of this chapter.

Is Zero Economic Profit Inevitable in the Long Run?

The economic analysis of the long run shows the effects of market forces over time. Owners of monopolistically competitive firms, of course, do not have to passively accept this long-run result. The key to earning an economic profit is either to sell a differentiated product or to find a way of producing an existing product at a lower cost.

If a monopolistically competitive firm selling a differentiated product is earning a profit, the profit will attract the entry of additional firms, and the entry of those firms will eventually eliminate the firm's profit. If a firm introduces new technology that allows it to sell a good or service at a lower cost, competing firms will eventually duplicate that technology and eliminate the firm's profit. *But this result holds only if the firm stands still and fails to find new ways of differentiating its product or fails to find new ways of lowering the cost of producing its product.*

In 2015, Chipotle's growth began to slow as new competitors such as Qdoba and Moe's Southwest Grill entered its market and existing firms such as Taco Bell began to adopt similar menu items. In response, Chipotle's management took steps to increase its image as a healthier, more socially responsible alternative to its competitors. For instance, it announced that it was the first major restaurant chain to stop using genetically modified ingredients. It also publicized its buying more ingredients from local farms than any other restaurant chain. Firms continually struggle to find new ways of differentiating their products as they try to stay one step ahead of other firms that are attempting to copy their success.

The owner of a competitive firm is in a position like that of Ebenezer Scrooge in Charles Dickens's *A Christmas Carol*. When the Ghost of Christmas Yet to Come shows Scrooge visions of his own death, he asks the ghost, "Are these the shadows of the things that Will be, or are they shadows of things that May be, only?" The shadow of the end of their profits haunts owners of every firm. Firms try to continue earning a profit by reducing costs, by improving their products, by providing exceptional customer service, or by convincing consumers that their products are indeed different from what competitors offer. To stay one step ahead of its competitors, a firm has to offer consumers goods or services that they perceive to have greater *value* than those competing firms offer. Value can take the form of product differentiation that makes the good or service more suited to consumers' preferences, or it can take the form of a lower price.

MyEconLab Concept Check

Solved Problem 13.3

MyEconLab Interactive Animation

Buffalo Wild Wings Increases Costs to Increase Demand

In recent years, Buffalo Wild Wings has been very successful serving chicken wings and other inexpensive food in restaurants that feature large-screen televisions showing sporting events. Based in Minneapolis, the chain has in the past 10 years grown from 300 restaurants to more than 1,000. But competitors can easily copy this format, so CEO Sally Smith has adopted a strategy of spending heavily on a new layout for the restaurants aimed at attracting more lunch customers and more families. The layout has more natural light, larger televisions, and more of a sports stadium look than the previous layout. To renovate the restaurants, the firm will incur a one-time cost of more than $200 million. But increasing cost in the hope of increasing demand—and profit—is always risky.

Suppose that Smith's strategy fails to increase demand at her restaurants. What will be the effect on each of the following for a typical Buffalo Wild Wings restaurant: average total cost, average variable cost, average fixed cost, marginal cost, demand, and economic profit? Use a graph to illustrate your answer. Your graph should show the situation of the typical restaurant before and after the new strategy is implemented.

Solving the Problem

Step 1: Review the chapter material. This problem is about how a monopolistically competitive firm maximizes profit and how firms attempt to earn an economic profit in the long run, so you may want to review the section "How a Monopolistically Competitive Firm Maximizes Profit in the Short Run," which begins on page 446, and the section "Is Zero Economic Profit Inevitable in the Long Run?" which begins on page 452.

Step 2: Explain the effect of Smith's strategy on a Buffalo Wild Wings restaurant's costs, demand, and profit. If Smith's strategy fails to increase demand at her restaurants, then the demand curve for the typical Buffalo

Wild Wings restaurant will remain unchanged (rather than shifting to the right, as she hopes it will) because consumers will not view the restaurant any more favorably, and it will not be able to sell more chicken wings and other food at every price. Because the cost of the new layout is a one-time charge, it is an addition to the restaurant's fixed cost, so there is no effect on the restaurant's marginal cost or average variable cost, but the restaurant's average fixed cost and average total cost will both increase. Because the restaurant's cost will be increasing, while the demand for its chicken wings is unchanged, the restaurant's profit will decrease.

Step 3: **Draw a graph to illustrate your argument.** For simplicity, the graph assumes that chicken wings are the only item the restaurant sells. The demand curve and marginal revenue curves are unchanged, the average fixed cost curve shifts up from AFC_1 to AFC_2, and the average total cost curve shifts up from ATC_1 to ATC_2. The graph shows that the restaurant's profits are lower after the new strategy is implemented.

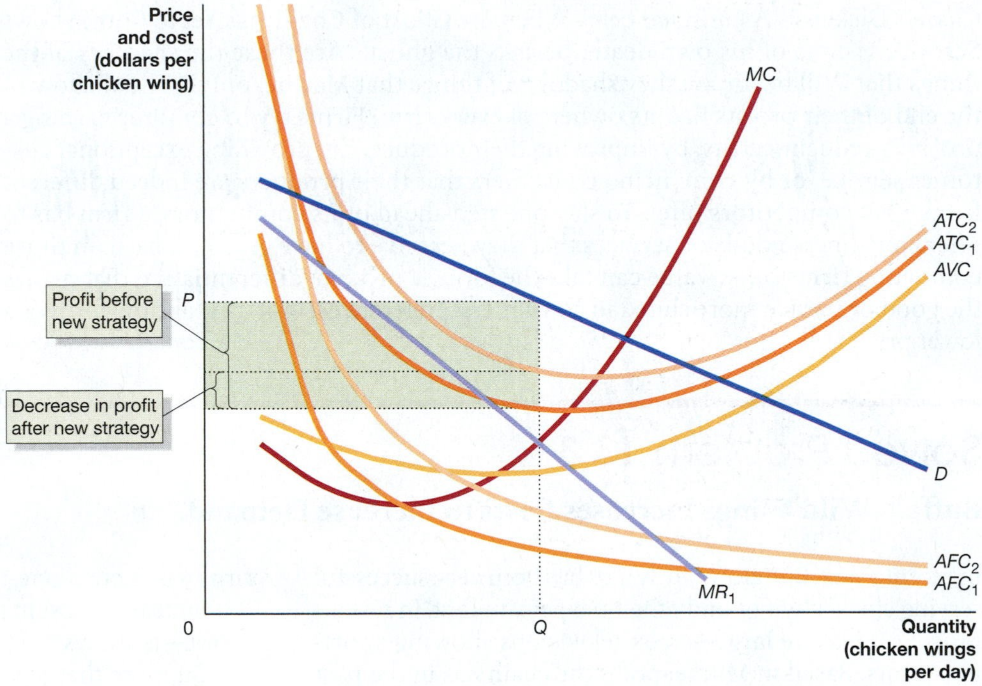

Extra Credit: As we have seen, firms constantly search for means of differentiating themselves from their competitors. Often, differentiation works for a while but then breaks down as competitors copy the strategy. In 2015, as Smith was implementing her new strategy, she was attempting to offset the effects of similar restaurants entering into the market. There were questions, though, as to whether the new approach featuring much larger televisions would necessarily appeal to families, one of Smith's key targets. Like CEOs of other monopolistically competitive firms, Smith knew that without innovating, her firm's profit would eventually be competed away by other firms, so she was willing to take the risk that increased spending on renovating her restaurants would increase demand enough to increase profit, despite the increase in cost. This problem shows that it was possible for her strategy to actually result in a lower profit.

Source: Bryan Gruley, "The Secret Sauce," bloomberg.com, April 6, 2015.

Your Turn: For more practice, do related problem 3.10 on page 466 at the end of this chapter.

13.4 Comparing Monopolistic Competition and Perfect Competition

LEARNING OBJECTIVE: Compare the efficiency of monopolistic competition and perfect competition.

We have seen that monopolistic competition and perfect competition share the characteristic that in long-run equilibrium, firms earn zero economic profit. As Figure 13.6 shows, however, there are two important differences between long-run equilibrium in the two markets:

- Monopolistically competitive firms charge a price greater than marginal cost.
- Monopolistically competitive firms do not produce at minimum average total cost.

Excess Capacity under Monopolistic Competition

Recall that a firm in a perfectly competitive market faces a perfectly elastic demand curve that is also its marginal revenue curve. Therefore, the firm maximizes profit by producing the quantity where price equals marginal cost. As panel (a) of Figure 13.6 shows, in long-run equilibrium, a perfectly competitive firm produces at the minimum point of its average total cost curve.

Panel (b) of Figure 13.6 shows that the profit-maximizing level of output for a monopolistically competitive firm comes at a level of output where price is greater than marginal cost, and the firm is not at the minimum point of its average total cost curve. A monopolistically competitive firm has *excess capacity*: If it increased its output, it could produce at a lower average total cost. MyEconLab Concept Check

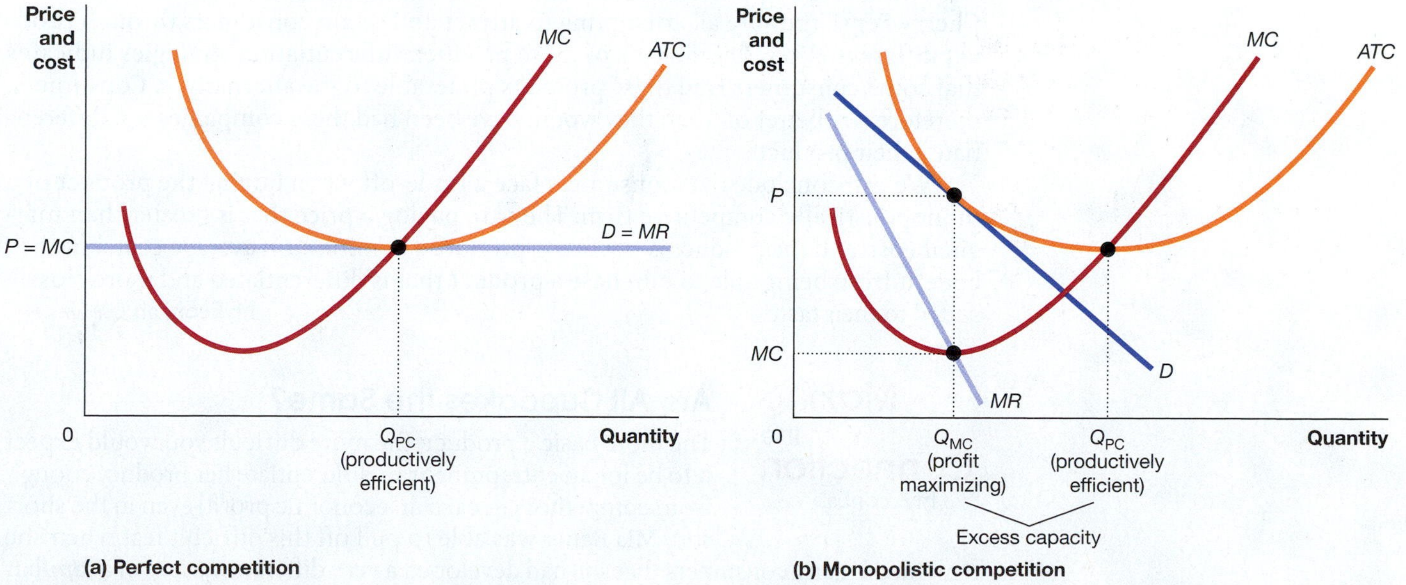

MyEconLab Animation

Figure 13.6 Comparing Long-Run Equilibrium under Perfect Competition and Monopolistic Competition

In panel (a), a perfectly competitive firm in long-run equilibrium produces at Q_{PC}, where price equals marginal cost, and average total cost is at a minimum. The perfectly competitive firm is both allocatively efficient and productively efficient. In panel (b), a monopolistically competitive firm produces at Q_{MC}, where price is greater than marginal cost, and average total cost is not at a minimum. As a result, the monopolistically competitive firm is neither allocatively efficient nor productively efficient. The monopolistically competitive firm has excess capacity equal to the difference between its profit-maximizing level of output and the productively efficient level of output.

Is Monopolistic Competition Inefficient?

We previously discussed the difference between productive efficiency and allocative efficiency (see Chapter 12).

- *Productive efficiency* refers to the situation where a good is produced at the lowest possible cost. For productive efficiency to hold, firms must produce at the minimum point of the average total cost curve.
- *Allocative efficiency* refers to the situation where every good or service is produced up to the point where the last unit provides a marginal benefit to consumers equal to the marginal cost of producing it. For allocative efficiency to hold, firms must charge a price equal to marginal cost.

In a perfectly competitive market, both productive efficiency and allocative efficiency are achieved, but in a monopolistically competitive market, neither is achieved. Does it matter? Economists have debated whether monopolistically competitive markets being neither productively nor allocatively efficient results in a significant loss of well-being to society in these markets compared with perfectly competitive markets.

MyEconLab Concept Check

How Consumers Benefit from Monopolistic Competition

Looking again at Figure 13.6, you can see that the key difference between the monopolistically competitive firm and the perfectly competitive firm is that the demand curve for the monopolistically competitive firm slopes downward, while the demand curve for the perfectly competitive firm is a horizontal line. The demand curve for the monopolistically competitive firm slopes downward because the good or service the firm is selling is differentiated from those being sold by competing firms. The perfectly competitive firm is selling a good or service identical to those being sold by its competitors. Remember that *firms differentiate their products to appeal to consumers.* For example, when Chipotle restaurants begin offering chicken and pork chorizo burritos, when Apple begins selling smartphones with larger screens, when General Mills introduces Apple-Cinnamon Cheerios, or when PepsiCo introduces Diet Wild Cherry Pepsi, they are all attempting to attract and retain consumers through product differentiation. The success of these product differentiation strategies indicates that some consumers find these products preferable to the alternatives. Consumers, therefore, are better off than they would have been had these companies not differentiated their products.

We can conclude that consumers face a trade-off when buying the product of a monopolistically competitive firm: They are paying a price that is greater than marginal cost, and the product is not being produced at minimum average cost, but they benefit from being able to purchase a product that is differentiated and more closely suited to their tastes.

MyEconLab Concept Check

Making the Connection
MyEconLab Video

Are All Cupcakes the Same?

The more basic a product, the more difficult you would expect it to be for an entrepreneur to differentiate her product enough from competitors to earn an economic profit, even in the short run. Mia Bauer was able to pull off this difficult feat when she convinced many consumers that she had developed a very different variety of a familiar product—the cupcake.

In 2002, Mia Bauer could find cupcakes only in basic flavors—strawberry, vanilla, and chocolate—in most bakeries and supermarkets. She thought that consumers might prefer the more elaborate cupcakes she baked; cupcakes such as Caramel Macchiato, which is a chocolate cupcake filled with caramel and topped with a frosting of coffee cream cheese. Rather than sell the cupcakes to bakeries or supermarkets, Mia and her husband Jason decided to open their own gourmet cupcake store, Crumbs Bake Shop, in New York City. At the time, there were only three other stores in the United States devoted exclusively to selling cupcakes. The Bauers believed that their cupcakes were so much tastier than other cupcakes that consumers would be willing to pay the relatively high price of $3.75 for a single cupcake. Initially, the Bauers' gamble paid off, and their store was profitable. They eventually expanded by opening 63 cupcake stores in 10 states.

But an entrepreneur can easily open a new cupcake store, which makes the barriers to entering the retail cupcake industry low. By 2013, many entrepreneurs had opened cupcake stores to compete with the Bauers. Many of these stores offered gourmet cupcakes very similar to the Bauers' cupcakes—but at lower prices. When asked how he could compete with these new entrants, John Bauer said, "Everybody sells cupcakes and will continue to do so, [but] we're building a nationally recognizable brand."

Can you make a profit selling gourmet cupcakes?

A nationally recognizable brand wasn't enough, however, and by late 2013, falling sales led the Bauers to close 10 stores. Sales continued to fall, and in July 2014, the Bauers closed all of their remaining stores and declared bankruptcy. A few months later, new owners assumed control of the firm and reopened some of the stores—with a new menu much less focused on cupcakes. The head of a market research firm commented that to succeed, the new owners "need to ... convince people that the new products are going to be different in some way."

Unfortunately for the Bauers, while consumers may not believe that all cupcakes are the same, they apparently didn't believe that cupcakes from Crumbs Bake Shop were significantly different from other cupcakes.

Sources: Sara Randazzo, "Crumbs Bake Shop Closing Its Doors," *Wall Street Journal*, July 7, 2014; Julie Halpert, "Crumbs Bake Shop about to Get Bigger," newsweek.com, February 3, 2011; Hilary Stout, "For Crumbs, Growth May Have Come Too Fast," *New York Times*, July 8, 2014; and Phyllis Furman, "Crumbs Bake Shop Set to Reopen First of 16 NYC-Area Stores," *New York Daily News*, October 14, 2014.

Your Turn: Test your understanding by doing related problem 4.7 on page 467 at the end of this chapter.

MyEconLab Study Plan

13.5 How Marketing Differentiates Products

LEARNING OBJECTIVE: Define marketing and explain how firms use marketing to differentiate their products.

Firms can differentiate their products through **marketing**, which refers to all the activities necessary for a firm to sell a product to a consumer. Marketing includes activities such as determining which product to sell, designing the product, advertising the product, deciding how to distribute the product—for example, in retail stores or through a Web site—and monitoring how changes in consumer tastes are affecting the market for the product. Peter F. Drucker, a leading business strategist, described marketing as follows: "It is the whole business seen from the point of view of its final result, that is, from the consumer's point of view. . . . True marketing . . . does not ask, 'What do we want to sell?' It asks, 'What does the consumer want to buy?'"

Marketing All the activities necessary for a firm to sell a product to a consumer.

For monopolistically competitive firms to earn an economic profit and defend the profit from competitors, they must differentiate their products. Firms use two marketing tools to differentiate their products: brand management and advertising.

Brand Management

Once a firm has succeeded in differentiating its product, it must try to maintain that differentiation over time through **brand management**. As we have seen, whenever a firm successfully introduces a new product or a significantly different version of an old

Brand management The actions of a firm intended to maintain the differentiation of a product over time.

product, it earns an economic profit in the short run. But the success of the firm inspires competitors to copy the new or improved product, and, in the long run, the firm's economic profit will be competed away. Firms use brand management to postpone the time when they will no longer be able to earn an economic profit. MyEconLab Concept Check

Advertising

An innovative advertising campaign can make even long-established and familiar products, such as Coke or McDonald's Big Mac hamburgers, seem more desirable than competing products. When a firm advertises a product, it is trying to shift the demand curve for the product to the right and to make it more inelastic. If the firm is successful, it will sell more of the product at every price, and it will be able to increase the price it charges without losing as many customers. Of course, advertising also increases a firm's costs. If the increase in revenue that results from the advertising is greater than the increase in costs, the firm's profit will increase. MyEconLab Concept Check

Defending a Brand Name

Once a firm has established a successful brand name, it has a strong incentive to defend it. A firm can apply for a *trademark*, which grants legal protection against other firms using its product's name.

One threat to a trademarked name is the possibility that it will become so widely used for a type of product that it will no longer be associated with the product of a specific company. Courts in the United States have ruled that when this happens, a firm is no longer entitled to legal protection of the brand name. For example, "aspirin," "escalator," and "thermos" were originally all brand names of the products of particular firms, but each became so widely used to refer to a type of product that none remains a legally protected brand name. Firms spend substantial amounts of money trying to prevent this from happening. Coca-Cola, for example, employs people to travel to restaurants around the country and order a "Coke" with their meal. If the restaurant serves Pepsi or some other cola, rather than Coke, Coca-Cola's legal department sends the restaurant a letter reminding the owner that "Coke" is a trademarked name and not a generic name for any cola. Similarly, Xerox Corporation spends money on advertising to remind the public that "Xerox" is not a generic term for making photocopies.

Legally enforcing trademarks can be difficult. Estimates are that each year, U.S. firms lose hundreds of billions of dollars in sales worldwide as a result of unauthorized use of their trademarked brand names. U.S. firms often find it difficult to enforce their trademarks in the courts of some foreign countries, although recent international agreements have increased the legal protections for trademarks.

Firms that sell their products through franchises rather than through company-owned stores encounter the problem that if a franchisee does not run his or her business well, the firm's brand may be damaged. Firms can take steps to keep such damage from happening. For example, automobile firms send "roadmen" to visit their dealers to make sure the dealerships are clean and well maintained and that the service departments employ competent mechanics and are well equipped with spare parts. Similarly, McDonald's sends employees from corporate headquarters to visit McDonald's franchises to make sure the bathrooms are clean and the French fries are hot. MyEconLab Concept Check

MyEconLab Study Plan

13.6 What Makes a Firm Successful?

LEARNING OBJECTIVE: Identify the key factors that determine a firm's success.

A firm's owners and managers control some of the factors that make a firm successful and allow it to earn economic profits. The most important of these is the firm's ability to differentiate its product or to produce it at a lower average cost than competing firms. A firm that successfully does one or both of these things creates *value* for its

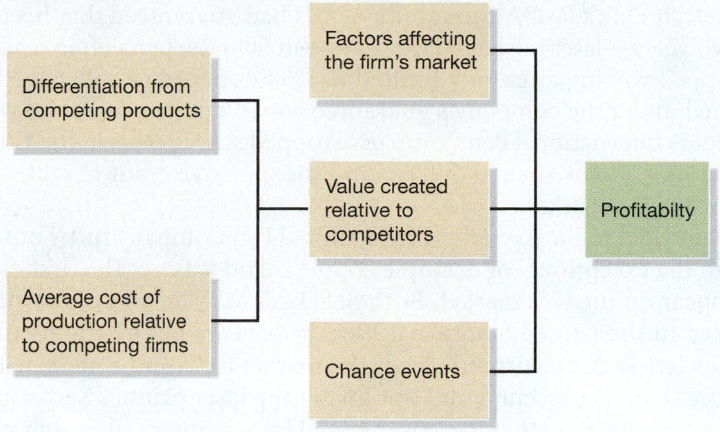

MyEconLab Animation

Figure 13.7 What Makes a Firm Successful?

The factors under a firm's control—the ability to differentiate its product and the ability to produce it at lower cost—combine with the factors beyond its control to determine the firm's profitability.

Source: Adapted from Figure 9.2 in David Besanko, David Dranove, Mark Shanley, and Scott Schaefer, *The Economics of Strategy*, 6th edition, New York: John Wiley & Sons, Inc., 2012, p. 295.

customers. Consumers will buy a product if they believe it meets a need not met by competing products or if its price is below that of competitors.

Some factors that affect a firm's profitability are not directly under the firm's control. Certain factors will affect all the firms in a market. For example, rising prices for jet fuel will reduce the profitability of all airlines. When many consumers decided that rather than buy DVDs, they preferred to download or stream movies from Netflix, iTunes, or Amazon, the profitability of all stores selling DVDs was reduced.

Sheer chance also plays a role in business, as it does in all other aspects of life. A struggling McDonald's franchise may see profits increase dramatically after the county unexpectedly decides to build a new road nearby. Many businesses in New York City, including restaurants, hotels, and theaters, experienced a marked drop in customers and profits as a result of the effects of Hurricane Sandy in October 2012. Figure 13.7 illustrates the important point that factors within the firm's control and factors outside the firm's control interact to determine the firm's profitability.

Making the Connection

MyEconLab Video

Is Being the First Firm in the Market a Key to Success?

Some business analysts argue that the first firm to enter a market can have important *first-mover advantages*. By being the first to sell a particular good, a firm may find its name closely associated with the good in the public's mind, as, for instance, Amazon is closely associated with ordering books online or eBay is associated with online auctions. This close association may make it more difficult for new firms to enter the market and compete against the first mover.

Surprisingly, though, recent research has shown that the first firm to enter a market often does *not* have a long-lived advantage over later entrants. Consider, for instance, the market for pens. Until the 1940s, the only pens available were fountain pens that had to be refilled frequently from an ink bottle and used ink that dried slowly and smeared easily. In October 1945, entrepreneur Milton Reynolds introduced the first ballpoint pen, which did not need to be refilled. When it went on sale at Gimbel's department store in New York City, it was an instant success. Although the pen had a price of $12.00—the equivalent of about $155.00 at today's prices—hundreds of thousands were sold, and Milton Reynolds became a millionaire.

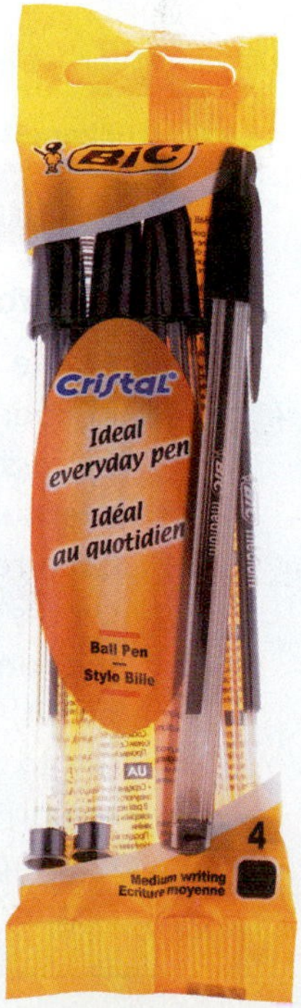

Although not first to market, Bic ultimately was more successful than the firm that pioneered ballpoint pens.

Unfortunately, it didn't last. Although Reynolds had guaranteed that his pens would write for two years—later raised to five years—in fact, the pens often leaked and frequently stopped writing after only limited use. Sales began to collapse, the flood of pens returned under the company's guarantee wiped out its profit, and within a few years, Reynolds International Pen Company stopped selling pens in the United States. By the late 1960s, firms such as Bic, selling inexpensive—but reliable—ballpoint pens, dominated the market.

What happened to the Reynolds International Pen Company turns out to be more the rule than the exception. For example, Apple's iPod was not the first digital music player to appear on the U.S. market. Both SeaHan's MPMan and Diamond's PMP300 were released in the United States in 1998, three years before the iPod. Similarly, although Hewlett-Packard currently leads the market for laser printers, with a market share of more than 35 percent, it did not invent the laser printer. Xerox invented the laser printer, and IBM sold the first commercial laser printers, although neither firm is important in the market today. As another example, Procter & Gamble was not the first firm to sell disposable diapers when it introduced Pampers in 1961. Microsoft's Internet Explorer was not the first Web browser: Before Internet Explorer, there was Netscape; before Netscape, there was Mosaic; and before Mosaic, there were several other Web browsers that for a time looked as if they might dominate the market. As we saw in Chapter 3, in 2004 Microsoft introduced the SPOT smartwatch, but the company discontinued it in 2008 when it failed to find many buyers. In all these cases, the firms that were first to introduce a product ultimately lost out to other companies that arrived on the scene later but did a better job of providing consumers with products that were more reliable, less expensive, more convenient or that otherwise provided greater value.

Sources: Steven P. Schnaars, *Managing Imitation Strategies: How Late Entrants Seize Markets from Pioneers*, New York: The Free Press, 1994; and Gerard J. Tellis and Peter N. Golder, *Will and Vision: How Latecomers Grow to Dominate Markets*, Los Angeles: Figueroa Press, 2002.

MyEconLab Study Plan

Your Turn: Test your understanding by doing related problem 6.5 on page 468 at the end of this chapter.

Continued from page 443

Economics in Your Life

Can You Operate a Successful Restaurant?

At the beginning of the chapter, we asked you to think about how successful you are likely to be in opening an Italian restaurant in your hometown. As you saw in this chapter, if your restaurant is successful, other people are likely to open competing restaurants, and all your economic profit will eventually disappear. Your new competitors will sell Italian food, but it won't be exactly like yours. Each restaurant will have its own ideas on how best to appeal to people who like Italian food. Unless your food is very different from your competitors' food—or your service is much better—in the long run, you will be unable to charge prices high enough to allow you to earn an economic profit.

In a monopolistically competitive market, free entry will reduce prices and lead to zero economic profit in the long run. In addition to lowering prices, competition benefits consumers by leading firms to offer somewhat different versions of the same product; for example, two Italian restaurants will rarely be exactly alike.

Conclusion

In this chapter, we applied to the more common market structure of monopolistic competition many of the ideas about competition we developed in discussing perfect competition. At the end of Chapter 12, we concluded: "The competitive forces of the market impose relentless pressure on firms to produce new and better goods and services at the lowest possible cost. Firms that fail to adequately anticipate changes in consumer tastes or that fail to adopt the latest and most efficient production technology do not survive in the long run." These conclusions are as true for fast-casual restaurants and firms in other monopolistically competitive markets as they are for wheat farmers and cage-free egg farmers in perfectly competitive markets.

In next two chapters, we discuss the remaining market structures: oligopoly and monopoly.

Visit MyEconLab for a news article and analysis related to the concepts in this chapter.

CHAPTER SUMMARY AND PROBLEMS

Key Terms

Brand management, p. 457

Marketing, p. 457

Monopolistic competition, p. 444

13.1 Demand and Marginal Revenue for a Firm in a Monopolistically Competitive Market, pages 444–446

LEARNING OBJECTIVE: Explain why a monopolistically competitive firm has downward-sloping demand and marginal revenue curves.

Summary

A firm competing in a **monopolistically competitive** market sells a differentiated product. Therefore, unlike a firm in a perfectly competitive market, it faces a downward-sloping demand curve. When a monopolistically competitive firm cuts the price of its product, it sells more units but must accept a lower price on the units it could have sold at the higher price. As a result, its marginal revenue curve is downward sloping. Every firm that has the ability to affect the price of the good or service it sells will have a marginal revenue curve that is below its demand curve.

MyEconLab Visit **www.myeconlab.com** to complete these exercises online and get instant feedback.

Review Questions

1.1 What are the most important differences between perfectly competitive markets and monopolistically competitive markets? Give two examples of products sold in perfectly competitive markets and two examples of products sold in monopolistically competitive markets.

1.2 Why does a local McDonald's face a downward-sloping demand curve for its Quarter Pounders? If McDonald's raises the price of Quarter Pounders above the prices other fast-food restaurants charge for hamburgers, won't it lose all its customers?

1.3 With a downward-sloping demand curve, why is average revenue equal to price? Why is marginal revenue less than price?

Problems and Applications

1.4 There are about 400 wineries in California's Napa Valley. Describe the reaction of consumers if the owner of one of the wineries—Jerry's Wine Emporium—raises the price of his wine by \$5.00 per bottle, assuming the following:

a. The industry is perfectly competitive.

b. The industry is monopolistically competitive.

1.5 Purell announced that the new chemical formula for its hand sanitizer was so effective that "just 1 squirt of Purell Advanced Hand Sanitizer kills as many germs as two squirts of any other national brand." If Purell succeeds in convincing consumers that its claim is correct, would its demand curve become more elastic or less elastic? Briefly explain.

Source: http://www.purell.com/purell-advanced.aspx.

1.6 Complete the following table, which shows the demand for snow skiing lessons per day:

Snow Skiing Lessons per Day (Q)	Price (P)	Total Revenue ($TR = P \times Q$)	Average Revenue $\left(AR = \frac{TR}{Q}\right)$	Marginal Revenue $\left(MR = \frac{\Delta TR}{\Delta Q}\right)$
0	\$80.00			
1	75.00			
2	70.00			
3	65.00			
4	60.00			
5	55.00			
6	50.00			
7	45.00			
8	40.00			

1.7 There are many wheat farms in the United States, and there are also more than 1,800 Chipotle restaurants. Why, then, does a Chipotle restaurant face a downward-sloping demand curve, while a wheat farmer faces a horizontal demand curve?

1.8 Is it possible for marginal revenue to be negative for a firm selling in a perfectly competitive market? Is it possible for marginal revenue to be negative for a firm selling in a monopolistically competitive market? Briefly explain.

1.9 In the graph on the following page, consider the marginal revenue of the eleventh unit sold. When the firm cuts the price from \$5.00 to \$4.75 to sell the eleventh unit, what area in the graph denotes the output effect, and what is the dollar value of the output effect? What area in the graph denotes the price effect, and what is the dollar value of the price effect? What is the marginal revenue of the eleventh unit?

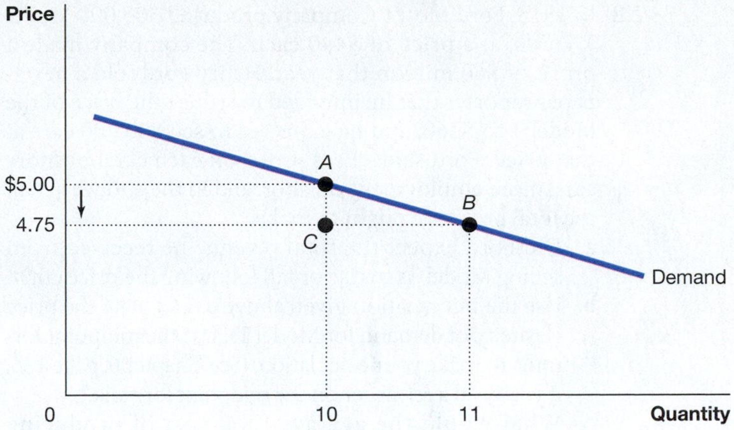

1.10 Sally runs a vegetable stand. The following table shows two points on the demand curve for the heirloom tomatoes she sells:

Price	Quantity Demanded per Week
$5.00	100,000
$3.25	200,000

a. What would Sally's marginal revenue be from lowering the price of tomatoes from $5.00 to $3.25?
b. Calculate the output effect and the price effect from lowering the price to $3.25.

13.2 How a Monopolistically Competitive Firm Maximizes Profit in the Short Run, pages 446–449

LEARNING OBJECTIVE: Explain how a monopolistically competitive firm maximizes profit in the short run.

Summary

A monopolistically competitive firm maximizes profit at the level of output where marginal revenue equals marginal cost. Price equals marginal revenue for a perfectly competitive firm, but price is greater than marginal revenue for a monopolistically competitive firm. Therefore, unlike a perfectly competitive firm, which produces where $P = MC$, a monopolistically competitive firm produces where $P > MC$.

MyEconLab Visit **www.myeconlab.com** to complete these exercises online and get instant feedback.

Review Questions

2.1 Why doesn't a monopolistically competitive firm produce where $P = MC$, as a perfectly competitive firm does?

2.2 Stephen runs a pet salon. He is currently grooming 125 dogs per week. If instead of grooming 125 dogs, he grooms 126 dogs, he will add $68.50 to his costs and $60.00 to his revenues. What will be the effect on his profit of grooming 126 dogs instead of 125 dogs?

2.3 If Daniel sells 350 Big Macs at a price of $3.25 each, and his average cost of producing 350 Big Macs is $3.00 each, what is his profit?

Problems and Applications

2.4 Maria manages a bakery that specializes in ciabatta bread, and she has the following information on the bakery's demand and costs:

Ciabatta Bread Sold per Hour (Q)	Price (P)	Total Cost (TC)
0	$6.00	$3.00
1	5.50	7.00
2	5.00	10.00
3	4.50	12.50
4	4.00	14.50
5	3.50	16.00
6	3.00	17.00
7	2.50	18.50
8	2.00	21.00

a. To maximize profit, how many loaves of ciabatta bread should Maria sell per hour, what price should she charge, and how much profit will she make?
b. What is the marginal revenue Maria receives from selling the profit-maximizing quantity of ciabatta bread? What is the marginal cost of producing the profit-maximizing quantity of ciabatta bread?

2.5 **(Related to Solved Problem 13.2 on page 448)** Suppose a firm producing table lamps has the following costs:

Quantity	Average Total Cost
1,000	$15.00
2,000	9.75
3,000	8.25
4,000	7.50
5,000	7.75
6,000	8.50
7,000	9.75
8,000	10.50
9,000	12.00

Ben and Jerry are managers at the company, and they have this discussion:

Ben: We should produce 4,000 lamps per month because that will minimize our average cost.
Jerry: But shouldn't we maximize profit rather than minimize cost? To maximize profit, don't we need to take demand into account?
Ben: Don't worry. By minimizing average cost, we will be maximizing profit. Demand will determine how high the price we can charge will be, but it won't affect our profit-maximizing quantity.

Evaluate the discussion between the two managers.

2.6 **(Related to the Chapter Opener on page 443)** According to an article in the *New York Times*, in 2014 Chipotle Mexican Grill experienced an increase in the cost of the beef used in its beef burritos. Draw a graph showing the effect of this increase on the price of Chipotle's burritos and on the quantity of burritos Chipotle sells. Be sure that your graph includes Chipotle's demand, marginal revenue, marginal cost, and average total cost curves. Your graph should show changes in any of the curves.

Source: Stephanie Strom, "Shares Fall at Chipotle although Sales Rise," *New York Times*, February 3, 2015.

2.7 William Germano previously served as the vice president and publishing director at the Routledge publishing company. He once gave the following description of how a publisher might deal with an unexpected increase in the cost of publishing a book:

> It's often asked why the publisher can't simply raise the price [if costs increase]. . . . It's likely that the editor [is already] . . . charging as much as the market will bear. . . . In other words, you might be willing to pay $50.00 for a . . . book on the Brooklyn Bridge, but if . . . production costs [increase] by 25 percent, you might think $62.50 is too much to pay, though that would be what the publisher needs to charge. And indeed the publisher may determine that $50.00 is this book's ceiling—the most you would pay before deciding to rent a movie instead.

a. According to what you have learned in this chapter, how do firms adjust the price of a good when there is an increase in cost? Use a graph to illustrate your answer.
b. Does the model of monopolistic competition seem to fit Germano's description? If a publisher does not raise the price of a book following an increase in its production cost, what will be the result?
c. How would the elasticity of demand for published books affect the ability of the publishing company to raise book prices when costs increase?

Source: William Germano, *Getting It Published: A Guide to Scholars and Anyone Else Serious about Serious Books*, 2nd edition, Chicago: University of Chicago Press, 2008, p. 107.

2.8 In 1916, Ford Motor Company produced 500,000 Model T Fords, at a price of $440 each. The company made a profit of $60 million that year. Henry Ford told a newspaper reporter that he intended to reduce the price of the Model T to $360, and he expected to sell 800,000 cars at that price. Ford said, "Less profit on each car, but more cars, more employment of labor, and in the end we get all the total profit we ought to make."

a. Did Ford expect the total revenue he received from selling Model Ts to rise or fall following the price cut?
b. Use the information given above to calculate the price elasticity of demand for Model Ts. Use the midpoint formula to make your calculation. (See Chapter 6, page 186, if you need a refresher on the midpoint formula.)
c. What would the average total cost of producing 800,000 Model Ts have to be for Ford to make as much profit selling 800,000 Model Ts as it made selling 500,000 Model Ts? Is this smaller or larger than the average total cost of producing 500,000 Model Ts?
d. Assume that Ford would make the same total profit when selling 800,000 cars as when selling 500,000 cars. Was Henry Ford correct in saying he would make less profit per car when selling 800,000 cars than when selling 500,000 cars?

2.9 Use the following graph for Elijah's Burgers to answer the questions.

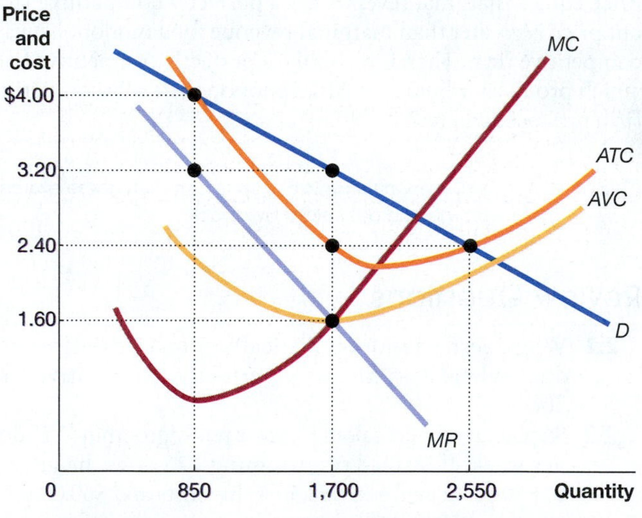

a. If Elijah produces at the profit-maximizing level of output, how much is his total revenue? How much is his total cost? Briefly explain your calculations.
a. How much economic profit is Elijah earning? Briefly explain your calculation.

13.3 What Happens to Profits in the Long Run? pages 449–454

LEARNING OBJECTIVE: Analyze the situation of a monopolistically competitive firm in the long run.

Summary

If a monopolistically competitive firm earns an economic profit in the short run, entry of new firms will eliminate the profit in the long run. If a monopolistically competitive firm is suffering an economic loss in the short run, exit of existing firms will eliminate the loss in the long run. Monopolistically competitive firms continually struggle to find new ways of differentiating their products as they try to stay one step ahead of other firms that are attempting to copy their success.

MyEconLab Visit **www.myeconlab.com** to complete these exercises online and get instant feedback.

Review Questions

3.1 What effect does the entry of new firms have on the economic profit of existing firms?

3.2 Why does the entry of new firms cause the demand curve of an existing firm in a monopolistically competitive market to shift to the left and to become more elastic?

3.3 What is the difference between zero accounting profit and zero economic profit?

3.4 Is it possible for a monopolistically competitive firm to continue to earn an economic profit as new firms enter the market?

Problems and Applications

3.5 **(Related to the Chapter Opener on page 443)** Chipotle Mexican Grill restaurants have been a very popular "fast-casual" dining option—with better food choices than fast-food restaurants like McDonald's and faster service and lower prices than traditional restaurants. Chipotle's profit per restaurant is much greater than McDonald's. Ten years from now, would you expect Chipotle's economic profit per restaurant to be higher, lower, or about the same as they are today? Briefly explain.

3.6 Suppose Angelica opens a small store near campus, selling beef brisket sandwiches. Use the graph below, which shows the demand and cost for Angelica's beef brisket sandwiches, to answer the following questions.

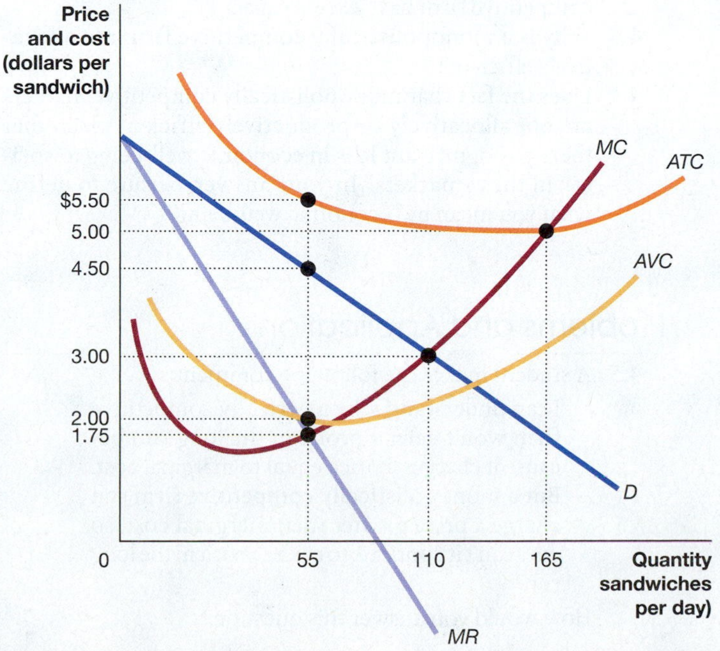

a. If Angelica wants to maximize profit, how many beef brisket sandwiches should she sell per day, and what price should she charge? Briefly explain your answer.

b. How much economic profit (or loss) is Angelica earning? Briefly explain.

c. Is Angelica likely to continue selling this number of beef brisket sandwiches in the long run? Briefly explain.

3.7 **(Related to the Don't Let This Happen to You on page 450)** A student remarks:

> If firms in a monopolistically competitive industry are earning an economic profit, new firms will enter the industry. Eventually, a representative firm will find that its demand curve has shifted to the left, until it is just tangent to its average total cost curve and it is earning zero profit. Because firms are earning zero profit at that point, some firms will leave the industry, and the representative firm will find that its demand curve will shift to the right. In long-run equilibrium, price will be above average total cost by just enough so that each firm is just breaking even.

Briefly explain whether you agree with this analysis.

3.8 Competition from Amazon and other online booksellers has resulted in some brick-and-mortar bookstores suffering losses. According to an article in the *New York Times*, over the past 15 years, the number of bookstores in the borough of Manhattan in New York City has declined by 30 percent. Draw a graph showing the effect on a remaining bookstore of the exit of many competitors from this industry. Be sure that your graph includes the bookstore's demand, marginal revenue, marginal cost, and average total cost curves. Your graph should show changes in any of the curves. It should also show any changes in the area representing the store's economic profit (or loss). Be sure to explain any assumptions you are making.

Source: Julie Bosman, "Literary City, Bookstore Desert," *New York Times*, March 25, 2014.

3.9 **(Related to the Making the Connection on page 452)** An article in the *New York Times* describes Chipotle as "the restaurant chain that has come to symbolize the tastes of the millennial generation" and lists the sources of Chipotle's success as including the restaurant's allowing "their customers to tailor their meals, and still have them ready in a flash … playing to consumer tastes for customization, speed and ingredients from sources that adhere to animal welfare, organic and other standards." Are these attributes likely to ensure that Chipotle will earn an economic profit in the long run? Briefly explain.

Source: Stephanie Strom, "Chipotle Posts Another Quarter of Billion-Dollar Sales," *New York Times*, April 21, 2015.

3.10 **(Related to Solved Problem 13.3 on page 453)** In 2015, analysts at the Goldman Sachs investment bank were optimistic that Buffalo Wild Wings would increase its profit over the next few years. They cited two factors as favorable to the chain's profitability: The chain's "greater pricing power allows them to easily implement menu changes to take advantage of [changes in] consumer preferences" and "the opportunity for the chain to grow as a lunch destination."

a. What do the analysts mean by the chain's greater pricing power? Is Buffalo Wild Wings likely to be able to sustain this greater pricing power in the long run? Briefly explain.
b. Why might doing additional business at lunchtime be particularly likely to add to the profit that Buffalo Wild Wings earns? Would this additional lunchtime business result in the chain's earning an economic profit in the long run? Briefly explain.

Source: Kathleen Burke, "Goldman Upbeat on Casual Dining amid Changing Consumer Tastes," marketwatch.com, July 1, 2015.

3.11 Michael Korda was, for many years, editor-in-chief at the Simon & Schuster book publishing company. He has written about the many books that have become bestsellers by promising to give readers financial advice that will make them wealthy, by, for example, buying and selling real estate. Korda is skeptical about the usefulness of the advice in these books because "I have yet to meet anybody who got rich by buying a book, though quite a few people got rich by writing one." On the basis of the analysis in this chapter, discuss why it may be very difficult to become rich by following the advice found in a book.

Source: Michael Korda, *Making the List: A Cultural History of the American Bestseller, 1900–1999*, New York: Barnes & Noble Books, 2001, p. 168.

3.12 An article in the *Wall Street Journal* reported that Western European brewers such as Heineken, Carlsberg, and Anheuser-Busch InBev are increasing their production and marketing of nonalcoholic beer. The article quotes a Carlsberg executive for new-product development as saying:

> Nonalcoholic beer is a largely unexploited opportunity for big brewers. It is quite a natural move when you see that the overall beer market [in Western Europe is] going down. So, of course, we're battling for market share.

The article further states that "brewers are hoping to capitalize on health consciousness" and that "recent brewing advances are helping improve the taste of nonalcoholic beers."

a. In what sense is nonalcoholic beer an "unexploited opportunity" for big brewers?
b. Are the brewers responding to consumer desires, or are brewers exploiting consumers? Briefly explain.
c. How will the "recent brewing advances" that improve taste affect the market for nonalcoholic beer?

Source: Ilan Brat, "Taking the Buzz out of the Beer," *Wall Street Journal*, August 30, 2011.

13.4 Comparing Monopolistic Competition and Perfect Competition, pages 455–457

LEARNING OBJECTIVE: Compare the efficiency of monopolistic competition and perfect competition.

Summary

Perfectly competitive firms produce at a quantity where price equals marginal cost and at minimum average total cost. Perfectly competitive firms achieve both allocative and productive efficiency. Monopolistically competitive firms produce at a quantity where price is greater than marginal cost and above minimum average total cost. Monopolistically competitive firms do not achieve either allocative or productive efficiency. Consumers face a trade-off when buying the product of a monopolistically competitive firm: They are paying a price that is greater than marginal cost, and the product is not being produced at minimum average total cost, but they benefit from being able to purchase a product that is differentiated and more closely suited to their tastes.

MyEconLab Visit **www.myeconlab.com** to complete these exercises online and get instant feedback.

Review Questions

4.1 What are the differences between the long-run equilibrium of a perfectly competitive firm and the long-run equilibrium of a monopolistically competitive firm?

4.2 Why is a monopolistically competitive firm not productively efficient? In what sense does a monopolistically competitive firm have excess capacity?

4.3 Why is a monopolistically competitive firm not allocatively efficient?

4.4 Does the fact that monopolistically competitive markets are not allocatively or productively efficient mean that there is a significant loss in economic well-being to society in these markets? In your answer, be sure to define what you mean by "economic well-being."

Problems and Applications

4.5 A student makes the following comment:

> I can understand why a perfectly competitive firm won't earn a profit in the long run because it charges a price equal to marginal cost. But a monopolistically competitive firm can charge a price greater than marginal cost, so why can't it continue to earn a profit in the long run?

How would you answer this question?

4.6 Consider the following graph:

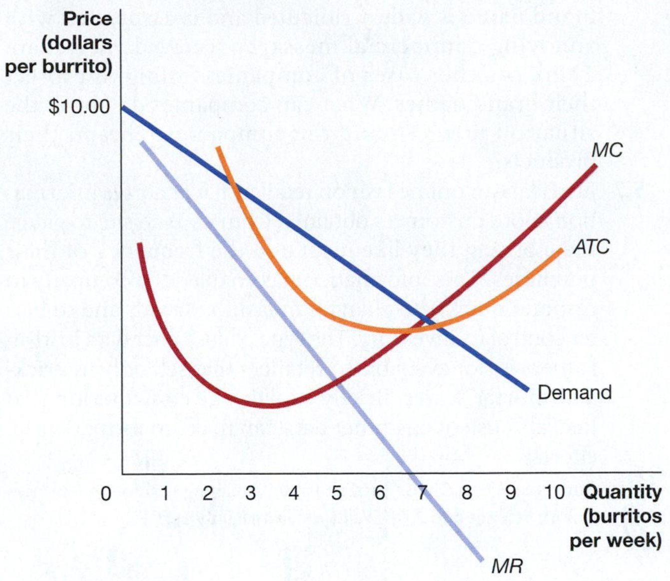

a. Is it possible to say whether this firm is a perfectly competitive firm or a monopolistically competitive firm? If so, explain how you are able to make this determination.

b. Does the graph show a short-run equilibrium or a long-run equilibrium? Briefly explain.

c. What quantity on the graph represents long-run equilibrium if the firm is perfectly competitive?

4.7 **(Related to the Making the Connection on page 456)** In describing what happened to Crumbs Bakery, an analyst of the food industry noted the entry of competitors such as Sprinkles and Georgetown Cupcake. He concluded, "It got to the level where there were too many cupcakes and not enough people who wanted to or could afford to eat them."

a. Briefly explain what the analyst meant by there being too many cupcakes and not enough people who wanted to eat them.

b. Could the Bauers, who founded Crumbs, have anticipated this outcome? Is it possible that they might still have started the company if they had? Briefly explain.

Source: Sydney Ember, "As the Cupcake Declines, Crumbs Shuts Its Doors," *New York Times*, July 8, 2014.

4.8 Consider the following graph:

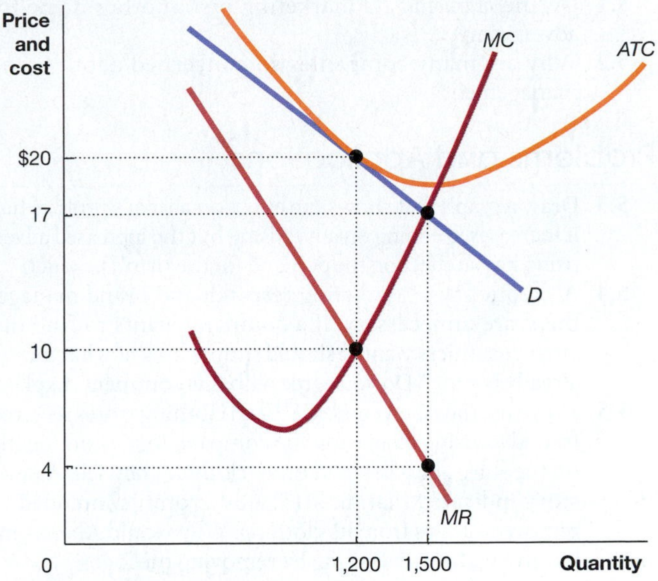

a. At the profit-maximizing level of output, how much economic profit is this firm earning? Briefly explain.

b. Is this firm allocatively efficient? Is it productively efficient? Briefly explain.

4.9 In recent years, consumers have been less willing to buy packaged foods that contain gluten or high levels of fat and salt or soft drinks containing sugar. Firms such as General Mills, Kellogg, and Coca-Cola have responded by modifying many of their products by, for example, making them gluten-free and eliminating or reducing salt, sugar, and artificial flavors and colors. General Mills Chief Executive Officer Ken Powell explained, "The reality of the changing food values of our consumers is central to what we're doing." Monopolistically competitive firms do not achieve productive efficiency or allocative efficiency, but economists argue that consumers benefit when these firms differentiate their products to appeal to consumers. Briefly explain how the actions taken by General Mills and other food and beverage firms may benefit their consumers.

Source: Chelsey Dulaney and Julie Jargon, "Changing Consumer Tastes Continue to Weigh on General Mills," *Wall Street Journal*, July 1, 2015.

13.5 How Marketing Differentiates Products, pages 457–458

LEARNING OBJECTIVE: Define marketing and explain how firms use marketing to differentiate their products.

Summary

Marketing refers to all the activities necessary for a firm to sell a product to a consumer. Firms use two marketing tools to differentiate their products: brand management and advertising. **Brand management** refers to the actions of a firm intended to maintain the differentiation of a product over time. When a firm has established a successful brand name, it has a strong incentive to defend it. A firm can apply for a *trademark*, which grants legal protection against other firms using its product's name.

MyEconLab Visit www.myeconlab.com to complete these exercises online and get instant feedback.

Review Questions

5.1 Define *marketing*. Is marketing just another name for advertising?

5.2 Why are many companies so concerned about brand management?

Problems and Applications

5.3 Draw a graph that shows the effect on a firm's profit when it increases spending on advertising but the increased advertising has *no* effect on the demand for the firm's product.

5.4 A skeptic says: "Marketing research and brand management are unnecessary. If a company wants to find out what customers want, it should simply look at what they're already buying." Do you agree with this comment? Explain.

5.5 For years, the Abercrombie & Fitch clothing stores received free advertising by placing the company logo prominently on the shirts, hoodies, and other clothing they sell. A news story indicated that in 2015, Abercrombie intended to remove its logos from its clothing. Why would Abercrombie give up free advertising by removing the logos?

Source: Suzanne Kapner and Erin McCarthy, "Abercrombie to Remove Logos from Most Clothing," *Wall Street Journal*, August 29, 2014.

5.6 Some companies have done a poor job protecting the images of their products. For example, Hormel's Spam brand name is widely ridiculed and is associated with annoying commercial messages received via e-mail. Think of other cases of companies failing to protect their brand names. What can companies do about the situation now? Should the companies rebrand their products?

5.7 JustFab is an online fashion retailer that analyzes information about customers obtained from its Web site to gauge the clothing they like most and the frequency of their purchases. This information has enabled the company to respond quickly to changes in fashion trends and to better control its inventory. The type of customer data JustFab gathers is not available to retailers that sell only in brick-and-mortar stores. Briefly explain the contribution that JustFab's use of customer data can make to its marketing efforts.

Source: Loretta Chao, "JustFab Finds Managing Fashion Inventories Is Both Science and Art," *Wall Street Journal*, July 1, 2015.

13.6 What Makes a Firm Successful? pages 458–460

LEARNING OBJECTIVE: Identify the key factors that determine a firm's success.

Summary

A firm's owners and managers control some of the factors that determine the profitability of the firm. Other factors affect all the firms in the market or result from chance, so they are not under the control of the firm's owners. The interactions between factors the firm controls and factors it does not control determine its profitability.

MyEconLab Visit **www.myeconlab.com** to complete these exercises online and get instant feedback.

Review Questions

6.1 What are the key factors that determine the profitability of a firm in a monopolistically competitive market?

6.2 How might a monopolistically competitive firm continually earn an economic profit?

Problems and Applications

6.3 According to an article in the *Wall Street Journal*:

> In early January last year, after a disappointing Christmas season and amid worries about competition from discount retailers, Zale Corp. decided to shake things up: The self-proclaimed jeweler to Middle America was going to chase upscale customers. . . . The move was a disaster. The Irving, Texas, retailer lost many of its traditional customers without winning the new ones it coveted.

Why would a firm like Zale abandon one market niche for another market niche? We know that in this case, the move was not successful. Can you think of other cases where such a move has been successful?

Source: Ann Zimmerman and Kris Hudson, "Chasing Upscale Customers Tarnishes Mass-Market Jeweler," *Wall Street Journal*, June 26, 2006.

6.4 7-Eleven, Inc., operates more than 20,000 convenience stores worldwide. Edward Moneypenny, 7-Eleven's chief financial officer, was asked to name the biggest risk the company faced. He replied, "I would say that the biggest risk that 7-Eleven faces, like all retailers, is competition ... because that is something that you've got to be aware of in this business." In what sense is competition a "risk" to a business? Why would a company in the retail business need to be particularly aware of competition?

Source: Company Report, "CEO Interview: Edward Moneypenny—7-Eleven, Inc.," The Wall Street Transcript Corporation, February 24, 2003.

6.5 **(Related to the Making the Connection on page 459)** A firm that is first to market with a new product frequently discovers that there are design flaws or problems with the product that were not anticipated. For example, the ballpoint pens made by the Reynolds International Pen Company often leaked. What effect do such problems cause for the innovating firm, and how do these unexpected problems create possibilities for other firms to enter the market?

6.6 Wealthy investors often invest in hedge funds. Hedge fund managers use investors' money to buy stocks, bonds, and other investments with the intention of earning high returns. But an article in the *New York Times* notes, "Even professionals have a problem in evaluating hedge fund performance, because distinguishing skill from luck … is extremely difficult." Is it ever easy to determine whether a firm making an economic profit is doing so because of the skills of the firm's managers or because of luck? Briefly explain.

Source: Jesse Eisinger, "Pruning Hedge Fund Regulation without Cultivating Better Rules," *New York Times*, September 5, 2012.

CHAPTER

14

Oligopoly: Firms in Less Competitive Markets

Chapter Outline and Learning Objectives

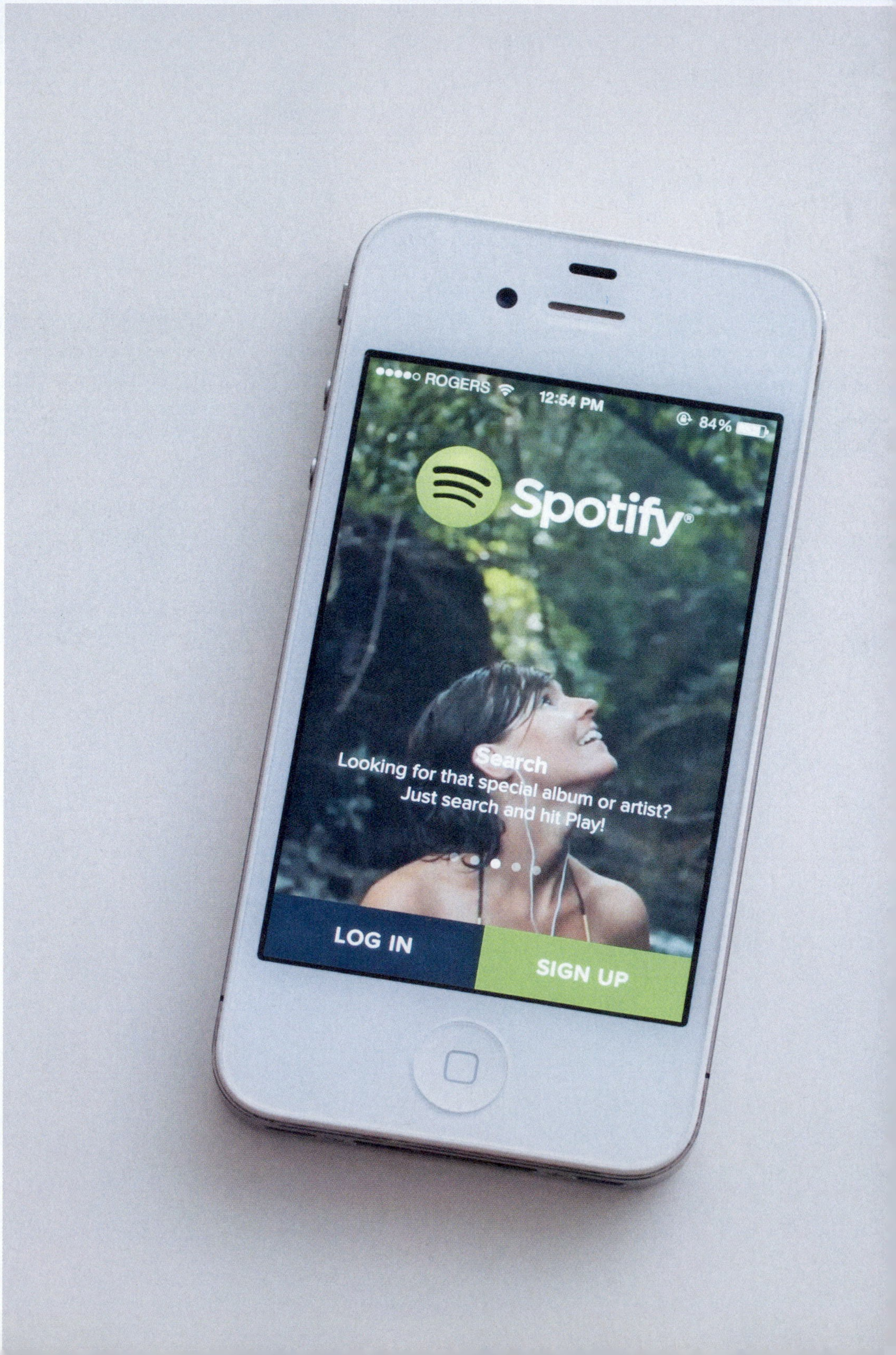

Apple, Spotify, and the Music Streaming Revolution

Few industries have experienced the disruptive force of technology the way the music industry has. For decades prior to the 1990s, large recording companies such as Universal Music Group, EMI, Warner Music, and Columbia dominated the music industry.

By the mid-1990s, though, the music industry faced a serious threat as people started to download songs from the Internet. MP3 files compressed standard music files to be small enough to make downloading songs from the Internet feasible. Many people were buying CDs, converting the songs on them to MP3 files, and posting the songs to the Internet, where they were available for anyone to download for free, in violation of the copyright laws.

In 2001, Apple introduced the iPod, the first successful portable MP3 player. As CD sales declined sharply, most record companies became willing to sell music in Apple's iTunes store, which opened in 2003 and allowed people to legally download millions of songs for $0.99 each. Although Apple gave the record companies a 70 percent share of the revenue from downloads, that didn't come close to replacing what the record companies and musicians were losing from the collapse of CD sales.

Apple's iTunes was tremendously successful, but it did not put an end to digital piracy. By 2015, many consumers were switching from buying individual songs to streaming songs from YouTube or other sites without purchasing them. Several companies offered plans that allowed people to stream for free, although with advertisements similar to those on commercial radio stations. Spotify, a music streaming service based in Sweden, offered a subscription plan that allowed unlimited streaming for $9.99 per month without advertisements. In 2015, Apple began offering Apple Music, in direct competition with Spotify.

An industry like music streaming that includes only a few firms is an *oligopoly*. In an oligopoly, a firm's profitability depends on its interactions with other firms. In these industries, firms must develop *business strategies*, which involve not just deciding what price to charge and how many units to produce but also how much to advertise, which new technologies to adopt, how to manage relations with suppliers, and which new markets to enter.

Because there are relatively few firms competing in an oligopolistic industry, each firm must continually react to other firms' actions or risk a substantial decline in sales. In this chapter, we focus on strategic interactions among firms.

Sources: Brian X. Chen, "Taylor Swift Scuffle Aside, Apple's New Music Service Is Expected to Thrive," *New York Times*, June 28, 2015; and Hannah Karp, "Apple iTunes Sees Big Drop in Music Sales," *Wall Street Journal*, October 24, 2014.

Economics in Your Life

Why Can't You Find a Cheap PlayStation 4?

You and your roommates have just moved into a great apartment and decide to treat yourselves to a PlayStation 4 game system—provided that you can find one at a relatively low price. You check Amazon, Best Buy, and Target and find a price of $399.99 at all three. Finally, you check Walmart, and you find a lower price: $399.00, a whopping discount of $0.99. Why isn't one of these big retailers willing to charge a lower price? What happened to price competition? As you read this chapter, try to answer these questions. You can check your answers against those we provide on **page 491** at the end of this chapter.

In studying perfectly competitive and monopolistically competitive industries, our analysis focused on how to determine a firm's profit-maximizing price and quantity. We concluded that firms maximize profit by producing where marginal revenue equals marginal cost. To determine marginal revenue and marginal cost, we used graphs that included the firm's demand, marginal revenue, and marginal cost curves. In this chapter, we will study oligopoly, a market structure in which a small number of interdependent firms compete. In analyzing oligopoly, we cannot rely on the same types of graphs we use in analyzing perfect competition and monopolistic competition—for two reasons:

1. We need to use economic models that allow us to analyze the more complex business strategies of large oligopoly firms. These strategies involve more than choosing the profit-maximizing price and output.
2. Even in determining the profit-maximizing price and output for an oligopoly firm, demand curves and cost curves are not as useful as in the cases of perfect competition and monopolistic competition. We are able to draw the demand curves for competitive firms by assuming that the prices these firms charge have no effect on the prices other firms in their industries charge. This assumption is realistic when each firm is small relative to the market. It is not a realistic assumption, however, for firms that are as large relative to their markets as Microsoft, General Motors, or Walmart.

When large firms cut their prices, their rivals in the industry often—but not always—respond by also cutting their prices. Because we don't know for sure how other firms will respond to a price change, we don't know the quantity an oligopolist will sell at a particular price. In other words, it is difficult to know what an oligopolist's demand curve will look like. As we have seen, a firm's marginal revenue curve depends on its demand curve. If we don't know what an oligopolist's demand curve looks like, we also don't know what its marginal revenue curve looks like. Because we don't know marginal revenue, we can't calculate the profit-maximizing level of output and the profit-maximizing price the way we do for competitive firms.

The approach we use in this chapter to analyze competition among oligopolists is called *game theory*. Game theory can be used to analyze any situation in which groups or individuals interact. In the context of economic analysis, game theory is the study of the decisions of firms in industries where the profit of each firm depends on its interactions with other firms. It has also been applied to strategies for nuclear war, international trade negotiations, and political campaigns, among many other examples.

14.1 Oligopoly and Barriers to Entry

LEARNING OBJECTIVE: Show how barriers to entry explain the existence of oligopolies.

Oligopoly A market structure in which a small number of interdependent firms compete.

An **oligopoly** is an industry with only a few firms. This market structure lies between competitive industries, which have many firms, and monopolies, which have only a single firm. One measure of the extent of competition in an industry is the *concentration ratio*. Every five years, the U.S. Bureau of the Census publishes four-firm concentration ratios that measure the fraction of each industry's sales accounted for by its four largest firms. Most economists believe that a four-firm concentration ratio greater than 40 percent indicates that an industry is an oligopoly.

However, concentration ratios have the following flaws as measures of the extent of competition in an industry:

1. They do not include the goods and services that foreign firms export to the United States.

Table 14.1

Examples of Oligopolies in Retail Trade and Manufacturing

Retail Trade		Manufacturing	
Industry	**Four-Firm Concentration Ratio**	**Industry**	**Four-Firm Concentration Ratio**
Discount department stores (Walmart and Target)	97%	Cigarettes (Phillip Morris and R.J. Reynolds)	98%
Warehouse clubs and supercenters (Sam's Club and BJ's Wholesale Club)	94%	Beer (Anheuser-Busch and MillerCoors)	90%
College bookstores (Barnes & Noble and Follett)	75%	Computers (Hewlett-Packard and Dell)	87%
Hobby, toy, and game stores (Toys"R"Us and Michael's)	72%	Aircraft (Boeing and Lockheed Martin)	81%
Radio, television, and other electronic stores (Best Buy and Apple)	70%	Breakfast cereal (Kellogg's and General Mills)	80%
Athletic footwear stores (Footlocker and Champs)	68%	Dog and cat food (Mars and Procter & Gamble)	71%
Pharmacies and drugstores (Walgreens and CVS Caremark)	63%	Automobiles (General Motors and Ford)	68%

Source: U.S. Census Bureau, *Concentration Ratios*, 2007.

2. They are calculated for the national market, even though the competition in some industries, such as restaurants or college bookstores, is mainly local.
3. They do not account for competition that sometimes exists between firms in different industries. For example, Walmart is included in the discount department store industry but also competes with firms in the supermarket industry and the retail toy store industry.

Some economists prefer another measure of competition, known as the *Herfindahl-Hirschman Index* (see Chapter 15). Despite their shortcomings, concentration ratios can provide a general idea of the extent of competition in an industry.

Table 14.1 lists examples of oligopolies in manufacturing and retail trade (along with representative firms from each industry). The Bureau of the Census does not track the streaming music industry separately, but in 2015, just a few firms—including Apple, Spotify, Google, and Rdio—accounted for more than 90 percent of paid music streaming subscriptions, making the industry an oligopoly.

Barriers to Entry

Why do oligopolies exist? Why aren't there many more firms in the computer, discount department store, beer, or video game console industries? Recall that new firms will enter industries when existing firms are earning an economic profit. But new firms often have difficulty entering an oligopoly. Anything that keeps new firms from entering an industry in which firms are earning an economic profit is called a **barrier to entry**. Three important barriers to entry are economies of scale, ownership of a key input, and government-imposed barriers.

Barrier to entry Anything that keeps new firms from entering an industry in which firms are earning economic profits.

Economies of Scale The most important barrier to entry is **economies of scale**, which exist when a firm's long-run average costs fall as the firm increases output (see Chapter 11). The greater the economies of scale, the smaller the number of firms that will be in the industry. Figure 14.1 illustrates this point.

Economies of scale The situation when a firm's long-run average costs fall as the firm increases output.

MyEconLab Animation

Figure 14.1

Economies of Scale Help Determine the Extent of Competition in an Industry

An industry will be competitive if the minimum point on the typical firm's long-run average cost curve ($LRAC_1$) occurs at a level of output that is a small fraction of total industry sales, such as Q_1. The industry will be an oligopoly if the minimum point comes at a level of output that is a large fraction of industry sales, such as Q_2.

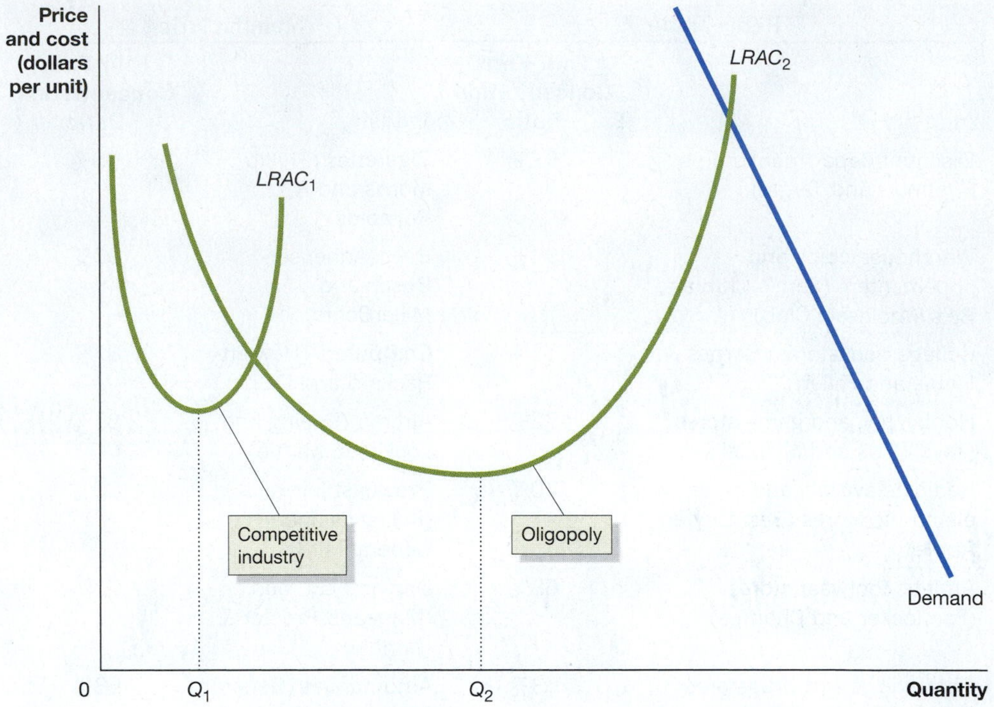

If economies of scale are relatively unimportant in the industry, the typical firm's long-run average cost curve (*LRAC*) will reach a minimum at a level of output (Q_1 in Figure 14.1) that is a small fraction of total industry sales. The industry will have room for a large number of firms and will be competitive. If economies of scale are significant, the typical firm will not reach the minimum point on its long-run average cost curve (Q_2 in Figure 14.1) until it has produced a large fraction of industry sales. In that case, the industry will have room for only a few firms and will be an oligopoly.

Economies of scale can explain why there is much more competition in the restaurant industry than in the music streaming industry. Because very large restaurants do not have significantly lower average costs than smaller restaurants, the restaurant industry has room for many firms. In contrast, a large music streaming firm such as Spotify has much lower average costs than would a small music streaming firm, partly because a large firm can spread the high fixed costs of streaming music—including very large server capacity, large research and development costs for its app, and the costs of the complex accounting necessary to keep track of the payments to the musicians and other copyright holders whose songs are being streamed—over a much larger quantity of subscriptions sold.

Ownership of a Key Input If production of a good requires a particular input, then control of that input can be a barrier to entry. For many years, the Aluminum Company of America (Alcoa) controlled most of the world's supply of high-quality bauxite, the mineral needed to produce aluminum. The only way other companies could enter the industry to compete with Alcoa was to recycle aluminum. The De Beers Company of South Africa was able to block competition in the diamond market by controlling the output of most of the world's diamond mines. Until the 1990s, Ocean Spray had very little competition in the market for fresh and frozen cranberries because it controlled almost the entire supply of cranberries. Even today, Ocean Spray controls about 65 percent of the cranberry crop through agreements with 650 cranberry growers.

Government-Imposed Barriers Firms sometimes try to convince the government to impose barriers to entry. Many large firms employ *lobbyists* to persuade state legislators and members of Congress to pass laws that are favorable to the economic interests of the firms. There are tens of thousands of lobbyists in Washington,

DC, alone. Top lobbyists command annual salaries of $300,000 or more, which indicates the value firms place on their activities. Three important government-imposed barriers to entry are patents, licensing requirements, and restrictions on international trade.

A **patent** gives a firm the exclusive right to a new product for a period of 20 years from the date the patent application is filed with the government. Governments use patents to encourage firms to carry out research and development of new and better products and better ways of producing existing products. Output and living standards increase faster when firms devote resources to research and development, but a firm that spends money to develop a new product may not earn much profit if other firms can copy the product. For example, the pharmaceutical company Merck spends more than $5 billion per year on developing new prescription drugs. If rival companies could freely produce these new drugs as soon as Merck developed them, most of the firm's investment would be wasted. Because Merck can patent a new drug, the firm can charge higher prices during the years the patent is in force and make an economic profit on its successful innovation.

Patent The exclusive right to a product for a period of 20 years from the date the patent application is filed with the government.

Governments also restrict competition through *occupational licensing*. For example, doctors and dentists in every state need licenses to practice. Licensing has expanded in recent years, though, to include occupations such as teeth whitening, irrigation contracting, and art therapy. Nearly one-third of professions in the United States currently require a license. The justification for the laws is to protect the public from incompetent practitioners, but by restricting the number of people who can enter the licensed professions, the laws also raise prices. Studies have shown that states that make it harder to earn a dentist's license have prices for dental services that are about 15 percent higher than in other states. Similarly, states that require a license for out-of-state firms to sell contact lenses have higher prices for contact lenses. When state licenses are required for occupations such as hair braiding or yoga instruction, restricting competition is the main result.

Governments also impose barriers to entering some industries by imposing tariffs and quotas on foreign competition. A *tariff* is a tax on imports, and a *quota* limits the quantity of a good that can be imported into a country (see Chapter 9). A quota on foreign sugar imports severely limits competition in the U.S. sugar market. As a result, U.S. sugar companies can charge prices that are much higher than the prices companies outside the United States charge.

Making the Connection
MyEconLab Video

Hard Times in Atlantic City

In the early twentieth century, Atlantic City, New Jersey, was a booming resort town and vacation destination with many hotels being built along the city's famed boardwalk. (The properties in the Monopoly board game are named after streets in Atlantic City.) By the 1950s, Atlantic City was in economic decline because low-priced airline travel made it possible for people in northeastern states to travel to vacation destinations such as Miami and the Caribbean. At that time, casino gambling was illegal in the United States everywhere outside of Nevada.

New competition from nearby states that established casinos contributed to Atlantic City closing 4 of its 12 casinos, including the Trump Plaza.

In an attempt to attract visitors back to Atlantic City, in 1976 New Jersey voters passed a referendum to legalize gambling. Several gambling casinos opened in Atlantic City beginning in 1978 and were initially very profitable, attracting people from the Mid-Atlantic and Northeastern states. Entrepreneurs in these states were unable to compete with the Atlantic City casinos because casino gambling was illegal in their states. In effect, the government had imposed legal barriers to entry into the casino gambling industry.

Eventually, though, some other eastern states repealed their laws against casino gambling, and entrepreneurs opened new casinos in those states. By 2014, casino gambling was legal in Pennsylvania, New York, Connecticut, Delaware, and Maryland. The entry of these new casinos caused a sharp decline in the demand for Atlantic City casinos. In particular, gamblers in the large New York City market now had several casinos that were closer than those in Atlantic City. By 2014, the revenues of Atlantic City casinos, which had peaked at $5.2 billion in 2006, had fallen to $2.5 billion.

In 2014, 4 of the city's 12 gambling casinos announced that they would be closing. Most shockingly, 1 of the 4 was the Revel Casino Hotel, which had opened only two years before, at a cost of $2.4 billion. Several other casinos were also in danger of failing.

The casino industry in Atlantic City prospered when government regulations limited the competition they faced. As governments began to remove these legal barriers to entry, the profitability of the casinos sharply declined.

Sources: Emily Brennan, "In Time for Memorial Day, Atlantic City Attempts a Turnaround," *New York Times*, May 8, 2015; Charles V. Bagli, "Owner of Revel Casino in Atlantic City Files for Bankruptcy Protection," *New York Times*, June 19, 2014; Josh Dawsey and Heather Haddon, "Revel Casino, Still Shiny and New, Teeters on the Edge," *Wall Street Journal*, July 10, 2014; and Daniel Kelley, "Atlantic City Casino Workers Fear Bleak Future," (Allentown) *Morning Call*, July 14, 2014.

MyEconLab Study Plan

Your Turn: Test your understanding by doing related problem 1.10 on page 493 at the end of this chapter.

In summary, to earn an economic profit, all firms would like to charge a price well above average cost, but earning an economic profit attracts new firms to enter the industry. Eventually, the increased competition forces price down to average total cost, and firms just break even. In an oligopoly, barriers to entry prevent—or at least slow down—entry, which allows firms to earn an economic profit over a longer period.

MyEconLab Study Plan

MyEconLab Concept Check

14.2 Game Theory and Oligopoly

LEARNING OBJECTIVE: Use game theory to analyze the strategies of oligopolistic firms.

Game theory The study of how people make decisions in situations in which attaining their goals depends on their interactions with others; in economics, the study of the decisions of firms in industries where the profits of a firm depend on its interactions with other firms.

As we noted at the beginning of the chapter, economists analyze oligopolies by using *game theory*, which was developed during the 1940s by the mathematician John von Neumann and the economist Oskar Morgenstern. **Game theory** is the study of how people make decisions in situations in which attaining their goals depends on their interactions with others. In oligopolies, the interactions among firms are crucial in determining profitability because the firms are large relative to the market.

In all games—whether poker, chess, or Monopoly—the interactions among the players are crucial in determining the outcome. In addition, games share three key characteristics:

1. *Rules* that determine what actions are allowable
2. *Strategies* that players employ to attain their objectives in the game
3. *Payoffs* that are the results of the interactions among the players' strategies

Business strategy Actions that a firm takes to achieve a goal, such as maximizing profits.

In business situations, the rules of the "game" include not just laws that a firm must obey but also other factors beyond a firm's control—at least in the short run—such as its production function. A **business strategy** is a set of actions that a firm takes to achieve a goal, such as maximizing profit. The *payoff* is the profit a firm earns as a result of how its strategies interact with the strategies of other firms. The best way to understand the game theory approach is to look at an example.

A Duopoly Game: Price Competition between Two Firms

In this simple example, we use game theory to analyze price competition in a *duopoly*—an oligopoly with two firms. We assume that Apple and Spotify are the only two firms selling subscriptions for music streaming. In 2015, both firms were charging $9.99 per month in exchange for allowing consumers to choose from 30 million songs

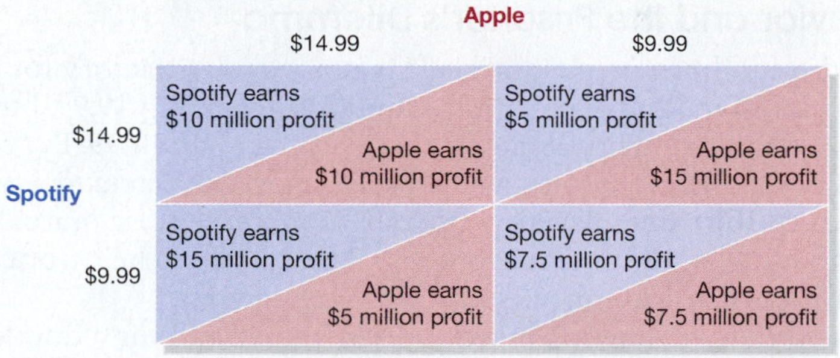

MyEconLab Animation

Figure 14.2

A Duopoly Game

Spotify's profit is shown in blue, and Apple's profit is shown in red. Spotify and Apple would each make a profit of $10 million per month on sales of streaming music subscriptions if they both charge $14.99. However, each firm has an incentive to undercut the other by charging a lower price. If both firms charge $9.99, they would each make a profit of only $7.5 million per month.

available for streaming. Some industry analysts thought that the services might have difficulty becoming consistently profitable unless the companies charged a monthly price of $14.99. Let's focus on the pricing decisions Apple and Spotify face. We assume that the managers of the two firms have to decide whether to charge $9.99 or $14.99 for subscriptions. Which price will be more profitable depends on the price the other firm charges. Choosing a price is an example of a business strategy. In Figure 14.2, we organize the possible outcomes that result from the actions of the two firms into a **payoff matrix**, which is a table that shows the payoffs that each firm earns from every combination of strategies by the firms.

Payoff matrix A table that shows the payoffs that each firm earns from every combination of strategies by the firms.

Apple's profit is shown in red, and Spotify's profit is shown in blue. Each of the four quadrants of the payoff matrix shows the results of different combinations of strategies the two firms use. For example, if Apple and Spotify both charge $14.99 per month for unlimited music streaming, we are in the upper-left quadrant, which shows that each firm will make a profit of $10 million per month. If Apple charges the lower price of $9.99 while Spotify charges $14.99, Apple will gain many of Spotify's customers. Apple's profit will be $15 million, and Spotify's profit will be only $5 million. Similarly, if Spotify charges $9.99 while Apple charges $14.99, Apple's profit will be only $5 million while Spotify's profit will be $15 million. If both firms charge $9.99, each will earn a profit of $7.5 million per month.

Clearly, the firms will be better off if they both charge $14.99 per month. But will they both charge this price? One possibility is that Apple's managers and Spotify's managers will get together and *collude* by agreeing to charge the higher price. **Collusion** is an agreement among firms to charge the same price or otherwise not to compete. Unfortunately for Apple and Spotify—but fortunately for their customers—collusion is against the law in the United States and Europe. The government can fine companies that collude and send the managers involved to prison.

Collusion An agreement among firms to charge the same price or otherwise not to compete.

Apple's managers can't legally discuss their pricing decision with Spotify's managers, so they have to predict what the other managers will do. Suppose Apple's managers are convinced that Spotify's managers will charge $14.99. In this case, Apple's managers will definitely charge $9.99 because doing so will increase Apple's profit from $10 million to $15 million. But suppose that, instead, Apple's managers are convinced that Spotify's managers will charge $9.99. Then Apple's managers also will definitely charge $9.99 because that will increase their profit from $5 million to $7.5 million. In fact, regardless of which price Spotify's managers decide to charge, Apple's managers are better off charging $9.99. So, we know that Apple's managers will choose a price of $9.99 per month.

Now consider the situation from the point of view of Spotify's managers. They are in the same position as Apple's managers, so we can expect them to make the same decision to charge $9.99 per month. In this situation, both firms have a *dominant strategy*. A **dominant strategy** is the best strategy for a firm, no matter what strategies other firms use. The result is an equilibrium where both firms charge $9.99 per month. This situation is an equilibrium because each firm is maximizing profit, *given the price chosen by the other firm*. In other words, neither firm can increase its profit by changing its price, given the price chosen by the other firm. An equilibrium in which each firm chooses the best strategy, given the strategies chosen by other firms, is called a **Nash equilibrium**, named after the late Nobel Laureate John Nash of Princeton University, a pioneer in the development of game theory. MyEconLab Concept Check

Dominant strategy A strategy that is the best for a firm, no matter what strategies other firms use.

Nash equilibrium A situation in which each firm chooses the best strategy, given the strategies chosen by other firms.

Firm Behavior and the Prisoner's Dilemma

Cooperative equilibrium An equilibrium in a game in which players cooperate to increase their mutual payoff.

Noncooperative equilibrium An equilibrium in a game in which players do not cooperate but pursue their own self-interest.

Prisoner's dilemma A game in which pursuing dominant strategies results in noncooperation that leaves everyone worse off.

Notice that the equilibrium in Figure 14.2 is not very satisfactory for either firm. The firms earn $7.5 million in profit each month by charging $9.99, but they could have earned $10 million in profit if they both had charged $14.99. By "cooperating" and charging the higher price, they would have achieved a *cooperative equilibrium*. In a **cooperative equilibrium**, players cooperate to increase their mutual payoff. We have seen, though, that the outcome of this game is likely to be a **noncooperative equilibrium**, in which each firm pursues its own self-interest.

A situation like the one in Figure 14.2, in which pursuing dominant strategies results in noncooperation that leaves everyone worse off, is called a **prisoner's dilemma**. The game gets its name from the problem two suspects face when arrested for a crime. If the police lack other evidence, they may separate the suspects and offer each a reduced prison sentence in exchange for confessing to the crime and testifying against the other suspect. Because each suspect has a dominant strategy to confess to the crime, they both will confess and serve a jail term, even though they would have gone free if they both had remained silent. MyEconLab Concept Check

Don't Let This Happen to You

Don't Misunderstand Why Each Firm Ends Up Charging a Price of $9.99

It is tempting to think that Apple and Spotify would each charge $9.99 rather than $14.99 for a month of unlimited music streaming because each is afraid that the other firm will charge $9.99. In fact, fear of being undercut by the other firm charging a lower price is not the key to understanding each firm's pricing strategy. Notice that charging $9.99 is the most profitable strategy for each firm, regardless of which price the other firm decides to charge. For example, even if Apple's managers somehow knew for sure that Spotify's managers intended to charge $14.99, Apple would still charge $9.99 because its profits would be $15 million instead of $10 million. Spotify's managers are in the same situation. That is why charging $9.99 is a dominant strategy for both firms.

MyEconLab Study Plan

Your Turn: Test your understanding by doing related problem 2.9 on page 494 at the end of the chapter.

Solved Problem 14.2

Is Same-Day Delivery a Prisoner's Dilemma for Walmart and Amazon?

Online shopping has increased dramatically in the past 15 years. One drawback consumers face when shopping online, though, is the wait to receive a good compared with going to a store and buying it off the shelf. Amazon has been a pioneer in reducing delivery times, including offering a same-day delivery service in several cities. To avoid losing customers to Amazon, several other firms, including Walmart, eBay, and Google, have begun offering same-day delivery in some cities. Firms typically hire people to go to retail stores, buy the products customers have ordered, and deliver the products directly to them. Some retail analysts ague that this process is so costly that the firms are actually losing money on most same-day delivery orders. Failing to offer the service, though, might cause customers to take all of their business—including their profitable orders—to firms that did offer the service.

Suppose Amazon and Walmart are competing with same-day delivery in a particular city. Construct a payoff matrix using the following hypothetical information:

- If neither firm offers same-day delivery, Amazon and Walmart each earn a profit of $7 million per month.
- If both firms offer same-day delivery, Amazon and Walmart each earn a profit of $5 million per month.
- If Amazon offers same-day delivery and Walmart doesn't, Amazon earns a profit of $9 million, and Walmart earns a profit of $4 million.
- If Walmart offers same-day delivery and Amazon doesn't, Walmart earns a profit of $9 million, and Amazon earns a profit of $4 million.

a. If Amazon wants to maximize profit, will it offer same-day delivery? Briefly explain.
b. If Walmart wants to maximize profit, will it offer same-day delivery? Briefly explain.
c. Is there a Nash equilibrium to this game? If so, what is it?

Solving the Problem

Step 1: **Review the chapter material.** This problem uses payoff matrixes to analyze a business situation, so you may want to review the section "A Duopoly Game: Price Competition between Two Firms," which begins on page 476.

Step 2: **Construct the payoff matrix.**

		Walmart: Don't Offer	Walmart: Offer
Amazon	Don't Offer	Amazon earns $7 million profit / Walmart earns $7 million profit	Amazon earns $4 million profit / Walmart earns $9 million profit
	Offer	Amazon earns $9 million profit / Walmart earns $4 million profit	Amazon earns $5 million profit / Walmart earns $5 million profit

Step 3: **Answer part (a) by showing that Amazon has a dominant strategy of offering same-day delivery.** If Walmart doesn't offer the service, Amazon will make $9 million if it offers the service but only $7 million if it doesn't. If Walmart offers the service, Amazon will make $5 million if it offers the service but only $4 million if it doesn't. Therefore, offering the service is a dominant strategy for Amazon.

Step 4: **Answer part (b) by showing that Walmart has a dominant strategy of offering same-day delivery.** Walmart is in the same position as Amazon, so it also has a dominant strategy of offering the service.

Step 5: **Answer part (c) by showing that there is a Nash equilibrium for this game.** Both firms offering same-day delivery is a Nash equilibrium. Given that Amazon is offering the service, Walmart's best strategy is to offer the service. Given that Walmart is offering the service, Amazon's best strategy is to offer it. Therefore, offering same-day delivery is the optimal decision for both firms, *given the decision by the other firm*.

Extra Credit: This game is another example of the prisoner's dilemma. Amazon and Walmart would be more profitable if neither offered same-day delivery, thereby saving the high cost of hiring people to deliver individual packages in a short amount of time. Each firm's dominant strategy is to offer the service, however, so they end up in an equilibrium where both offer the service, and their profits are reduced.

Your Turn: For more practice, do related problems 2.10 and 2.11 on page 494 at the end of this chapter.

MyEconLab Study Plan

Can Firms Escape the Prisoner's Dilemma?

Although the prisoner's dilemma game seems to show that cooperative behavior always breaks down, we know that people often cooperate to achieve their goals, and firms find ways to cooperate by not competing on price. The reason the basic prisoner's dilemma story is not always applicable in the real world is that it assumes the game will be played *only once*. Most business situations, however, are repeated over and over. For example, consider the following situation: Suppose that in a small town, the

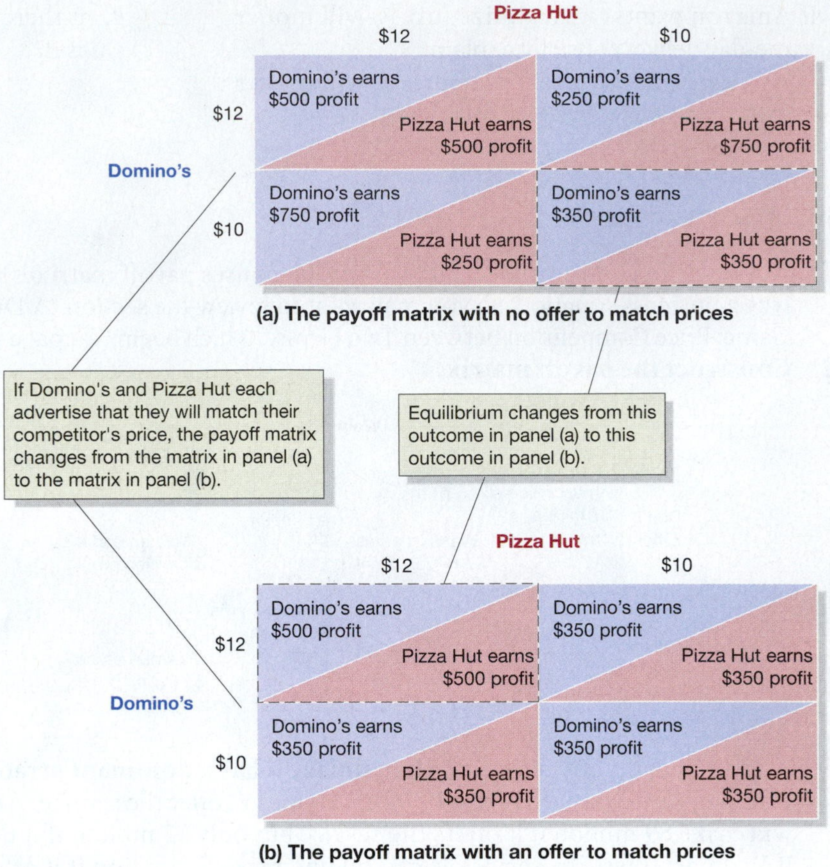

MyEconLab Animation

Figure 14.3 Changing the Payoff Matrix in a Repeated Game

Domino's and Pizza Hut can change the payoff matrix for selling pepperoni pizzas by advertising that each will match its competitor's price. This retaliation strategy provides a signal that one restaurant charging a lower price will be met automatically by the other restaurant charging a lower price. In the payoff matrix in panel (a), there is no advertisement about matching prices, and each restaurant benefits if it charges $10 when the other charges $12. In the payoff matrix in panel (b), after advertising that they will match prices, the managers have only two choices: They can charge $12 and receive a profit of $500 per day, or they can charge $10 and receive a profit of $350 per day. The equilibrium shifts from the prisoner's dilemma result of both restaurants charging the low price and receiving low profits to both restaurants charging the high price and receiving high profits.

only places to buy a pizza are Domino's and Pizza Hut. Assume that the managers will charge either $12 or $10 for a large pepperoni pizza. Panel (a) of Figure 14.3 gives the payoff matrix. Notice that each manager has an incentive to charge the lower price. Once again, the firms appear to be caught in a prisoner's dilemma. But the managers will not play this game only once; each day they will decide again what price to charge for a pizza. In the language of game theory, the managers are playing a *repeated game*, where the losses from not cooperating are greater than in a game played only once, and players can employ *retaliation strategies* against other players who don't cooperate. As a result, firms have a greater incentive to cooperate.

Panel (a) of Figure 14.3 shows that Domino's and Pizza Hut are earning $150 less per day by both charging $10 instead of $12 for the pizza. Every day that passes with both stores charging $10 increases the total amount lost: A year of charging $10 will cause each store to lose more than $50,000 in profit. This lost profit increases the incentive for the store managers to cooperate by *implicitly* colluding. Remember that *explicit* collusion—such as the managers meeting and agreeing to charge $12—is illegal. But if the managers can find a way to signal each other that they will charge $12, they may be within the law.

Suppose that Domino's and Pizza Hut both advertise that they will match the lowest price offered by any competitor—in our simple example, they are each other's only competitor. These advertisements are signals to each other that they intend to charge $12 for a pizza. The signal is clear because each restaurant knows that if it charges $10, the other restaurant will automatically retaliate by also lowering its price to $10. The offer to match prices is a good *enforcement mechanism* because it guarantees that if either restaurant fails to cooperate and charges the lower price, the competing restaurant will automatically punish that restaurant by also charging the lower price. As Figure 14.3 shows, the restaurants have changed the payoff matrix they face.

With the original payoff matrix in panel (a), there are no advertisements about matching prices, and each restaurant makes more profit if it charges $10 when the other charges $12. The advertisements about matching prices change the payoff matrix to the one shown in panel (b). Now the managers can charge $12 and receive a profit of $500 per day, or they can charge $10 and receive a profit of $350 per day. The equilibrium shifts from the prisoner's dilemma result of both managers charging the low price and receiving low profits to a result where both charge the high price and receive the high profits. An advertisement offering to match competitors' prices might seem to benefit consumers, but game theory shows that it actually may hurt consumers by helping to keep prices high.

One form of implicit collusion occurs as a result of **price leadership**, where one firm takes the lead in announcing a price change that other firms in the industry then match. For example, through the 1970s, General Motors (GM) would announce a price change in the fall at the beginning of a model year, and Ford and Chrysler would match GM's price change. In some cases, such as in the airline industry, firms have attempted to act as price leaders but failed when other firms in the industry have refused to cooperate.

MyEconLab Concept Check

Price leadership A form of implicit collusion in which one firm in an oligopoly announces a price change and the other firms in the industry match the change.

Making the Connection
MyEconLab Video

Do Airlines Collude on Capacity to Keep Prices High?

Coordinating prices is easier in some industries than in others. Fixed costs in the airline industry are very large, and marginal costs are very small. The marginal cost of flying one more passenger from Chicago to New York is no more than a few dollars: the cost of another snack served and a little additional jet fuel. As a result, airlines often engage in last-minute price cutting to fill the remaining empty seats on a flight. Even a low-price ticket will increase marginal revenue more than marginal cost. As with other oligopolies, if all airlines cut prices, industry profits will decline. Airlines therefore continually adjust their prices while at the same time monitoring their rivals' prices and retaliating against them for either cutting prices or failing to go along with price increases.

Airlines saved a lot of money due to low fuel costs in 2014, but they used very little of that savings to expand capacity.

In recent years, mergers in the airline industry have increased the possibility of implicit collusion. In 2015, just four airlines—American, Delta Airlines, United, and Southwest—flew 80 percent of all passengers. Smaller airlines, such as JetBlue, Spirit Airlines, and Allegiant Air, provided competition on some routes, but the four big airlines were the only ones offering service between many pairs of cities.

A 40 percent decline in jet fuel costs during 2014 saved the airlines billions of dollars and allowed them to earn record profits. During previous periods of high profits, the airlines had often invested in expanding their capacity by buying additional planes or flying more routes. Adding more capacity, though, means having more tickets to sell and increases the likelihood of price cutting to fill the seats. Investment analysts attempt to predict the future profitability of firms because the firms' stock prices depend on their profitability. Some analysts predicted that the airlines' future profitability would decline because the analysts expected the airlines to add capacity. As a result, the prices of the airlines' stocks fell. Top managers don't like to see declines in their firms' stock prices in part because their own compensation is often tied to the stock price and also because a lower stock price means the firm receives a smaller amount if it raises funds by selling stock. As a result, in an attempt to reassure analysts and stock investors that the airlines' profits would remain high, top managers of all four major airlines publicly stated that they intended to undertake only modest increases in capacity.

Were these executives just responding to the concerns of investment analysts, or were they engaging in implicit collusion? If the four major airlines all declined to increase capacity, then the quantity of tickets to be sold would not increase as much, and it would be easier for them to avoid cutting prices. As we will discuss in Chapter 15, the U.S. Department of Justice is responsible for enforcing the laws against collusion. In July 2015, the Department of Justice began investigating the airlines to see if the managers' statements about not expanding capacity amounted to illegal collusion. As one airline industry analyst put it, "If you're listening as a Justice Department attorney, you'd say, 'Wait a minute, these guys are all saying the same thing, and that can't just happen naturally, can it?'"

The airlines denied that they were colluding and argued that they were slowly expanding capacity not by adding new planes on new routes but by adding more seats to existing planes. One manager for Delta stated, "We're making the planes we have more efficient. Without building any infrastructure, we can transport more people." The Department of Justice's investigation would help determine whether the airlines were colluding ... and whether consumers could look forward to lower airline ticket prices in the future.

Sources: Christopher Drew, "Airlines under Justice Dept. Investigation over Possible Collusion," *New York Times*, July 1, 2015; Jack Nicas, Brent Kendall, and Susan Carey, "Justice Department Probes Airlines for Collusion," *Wall Street Journal*, July 1, 2015; and Susan Carey and Jack Nicas, "Airlines' New Normal: More Seats, Fewer Flights," *Wall Street Journal*, July 2, 2015.

MyEconLab Study Plan

Your Turn: Test your understanding by doing related problems 2.15, 2.16, and 2.17 on page 495 at the end of this chapter.

Cartels: The Case of OPEC

In the United States, firms cannot legally meet to agree on what prices to charge and how much to produce. But suppose they could. Would this be enough to guarantee that their collusion would be successful? The example of the Organization of the Petroleum Exporting Countries (OPEC) indicates that the answer to this question is "no." OPEC has 12 members, including Saudi Arabia, Kuwait, and other Arab countries, as well as Iran, Venezuela, and Nigeria. Together, these countries own more than 75 percent of the world's proven crude oil reserves, although they supply only about 35 percent of the total oil sold each year. OPEC operates as a **cartel**, which is a group of firms that collude by agreeing to restrict output to increase prices and profits. The members of OPEC meet periodically and agree on quotas, which are quantities of oil that each country agrees to produce. The quotas are intended to reduce oil production well below the competitive level to force up the price of oil and increase the profits of member countries.

Cartel A group of firms that collude by agreeing to restrict output to increase prices and profits.

Figure 14.4 shows oil prices from 1972 to mid-2015. The blue line shows the price of a barrel of oil in each year. Prices in general have risen since 1972, which has reduced the amount of goods and services that consumers can purchase with a dollar. The red line corrects for general price increases by measuring oil prices in terms of the dollar's purchasing power in 2015. The figure shows that OPEC succeeded in raising the price of oil during the mid-1970s and early 1980s, although political unrest in the Middle East and other factors also affected the price of oil during these years. Oil prices had been below $3 per barrel in 1972 but rose to more

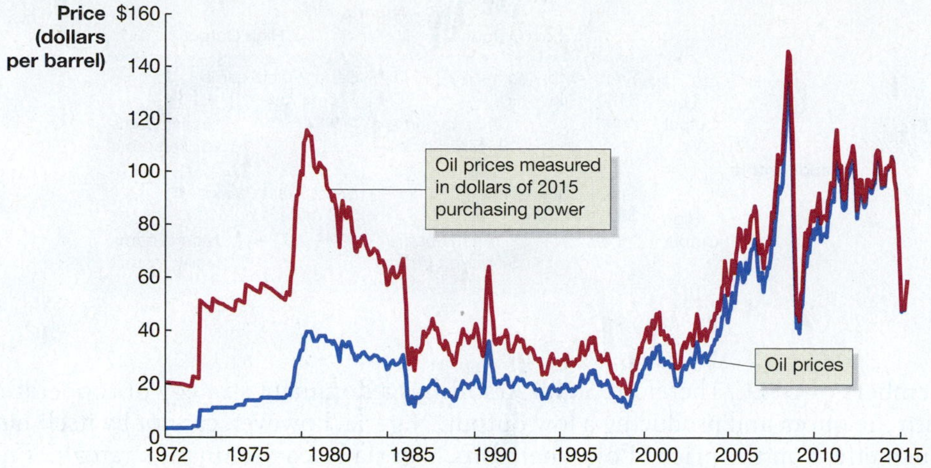

MyEconLab Animation

Figure 14.4 Oil Prices, 1972 to mid-2015

The blue line shows the price of a barrel of oil in each year. The red line measures the price of a barrel of oil in terms of the purchasing power of the dollar in 2015. By reducing oil production, OPEC was able to raise the world price of oil in the mid-1970s and early 1980s. Sustaining high prices has been difficult over the long run, however, because OPEC members often exceed their output quotas.

Source: Federal Reserve Bank of St. Louis.

than $39 per barrel in 1980, which was more than $115 measured in dollars of 2015 purchasing power. The figure also shows that OPEC has had difficulty sustaining the high prices of 1980 in later years, although oil prices rose sharply between 2004 and mid-2008, in part due to increasing demand from China and India. In the past few years, OPEC has also had difficulty maintaining oil prices because of a surge in U.S. production as oil companies have used "fracking" techniques to recover oil from shale deposits.

Game theory helps us understand why oil prices have fluctuated. If every member of OPEC cooperates and produces the low output level dictated by its quota, prices will be high, and the cartel will earn large profits. (Even though OPEC cannot raise prices as high as it did before U.S. production increased, it can still increase world oil prices if all of its members agree to restrict production.) Once the price has been driven up, however, each member has an incentive to stop cooperating and to earn even higher profits by increasing output beyond its quota. But if no country sticks to its quota, total oil output will increase, and profits will decline. In other words, OPEC is caught in a prisoner's dilemma.

If the members of OPEC always exceeded their production quotas, the cartel would have no effect on world oil prices. In fact, the members of OPEC periodically meet and assign new quotas that, at least for a while, enable them to restrict output enough to raise prices. Two factors explain OPEC's occasional success at behaving as a cartel. First, the members of OPEC are participating in a repeated game. As we have seen, being in a repeated game increases the likelihood of a cooperative outcome. Second, Saudi Arabia has far larger oil reserves than any other member of OPEC. Therefore, it has the most to gain from high oil prices and a greater incentive to cooperate. To see this, consider the payoff matrix shown in Figure 14.5. To keep things simple, let's assume that OPEC has only two members: Saudi Arabia and Nigeria. In Figure 14.5, "Low Output" corresponds to cooperating with the OPEC-assigned output quota, and "High Output" corresponds to producing at maximum capacity. The payoff matrix shows the profits received per day by each country.

We can see that Saudi Arabia has a strong incentive to cooperate and maintain its low output quota. By keeping output low, Saudi Arabia can by itself significantly raise the world price of oil, increasing its own profits as well as those of other

MyEconLab Animation

Figure 14.5

The OPEC Cartel with Unequal Members

Because Saudi Arabia can produce much more oil than Nigeria, its output decisions have a larger effect on the price of oil. In the figure, Low Output corresponds to cooperating with the OPEC-assigned output quota, and High Output corresponds to producing at maximum capacity. Saudi Arabia has a dominant strategy to cooperate and produce a low output. Nigeria, however, has a dominant strategy not to cooperate and instead produce a high output. Therefore, the equilibrium of this game will occur with Saudi Arabia producing a low output and Nigeria producing a high output.

Saudi Arabia \ Nigeria	Nigeria: Low Output	Nigeria: High Output
Low Output	Saudi Arabia earns $100 million profit; Nigeria earns $10 million profit	Saudi Arabia earns $75 million profit; Nigeria earns $15 million profit
High Output	Saudi Arabia earns $80 million profit; Nigeria earns $7 million profit	Saudi Arabia earns $60 million profit; Nigeria earns $10 million profit

members of OPEC. Therefore, Saudi Arabia has a dominant strategy of cooperating with the quota and producing a low output. Nigeria, however, cannot by itself have much effect on the price of oil. Therefore, Nigeria has a dominant strategy of not cooperating and instead producing a high output. The equilibrium of this game will occur with Saudi Arabia producing a low output and Nigeria producing a high output. In fact, OPEC often operates in just this way. Saudi Arabia will cooperate with the quota, while the other 11 members produce at capacity. Because this is a repeated game, however, Saudi Arabia will occasionally produce more oil than its quota to intentionally drive down the price and retaliate against the other members for not cooperating.

MyEconLab Study Plan

MyEconLab Concept Check

14.3 Sequential Games and Business Strategy

LEARNING OBJECTIVE: Use sequential games to analyze business strategies.

We have been analyzing games in which both players move simultaneously. In many business situations, however, one firm will act first, and then other firms will respond. These situations can be analyzed using *sequential games*. We will use sequential games to analyze two business strategies: deterring entry and bargaining between firms. To keep things simple, we consider situations that involve only two firms.

Deterring Entry

In Section 14.1, we saw that barriers to entry are a key to firms continuing to earn an economic profit. Can firms create barriers to deter new firms from entering an industry? Some recent research in game theory has focused on this question. Suppose that Apple and Dell are the only makers of very thin, light laptop computers. One factor firms consider in pricing a new product is the effect different prices have on the likelihood that competitors will enter the market. A high price might lead to a large profit if other firms do not enter the market, but if a high price attracts entry from other firms, it might actually result in a smaller profit. A low price, by deterring entry, might lead to a larger profit. Assume that managers at Apple have developed a very thin, light laptop before Dell has and are considering what price to charge. To break even by covering the opportunity cost of the funds used, laptops must provide a minimum rate of return of 15 percent on Apple's investment. If Apple has the market for this type of laptop to itself and charges a price of $800, it will earn an economic profit by receiving a return of 20 percent. If Apple charges a price of $1,000 and has the market to itself, it will receive a higher return of 30 percent.

It seems clear that Apple should charge $1,000 for its laptops, but the managers are worried that Dell might also begin selling this type of laptop. If Apple charges $800 and Dell enters the market, Apple and Dell will divide up the market, and both will earn only 5 percent on their investments, which is below the 15 percent return each firm needs to break even. If Apple charges $1,000 and Dell enters, although the market will still be divided, the higher price means that each firm will earn 16 percent on its investment.

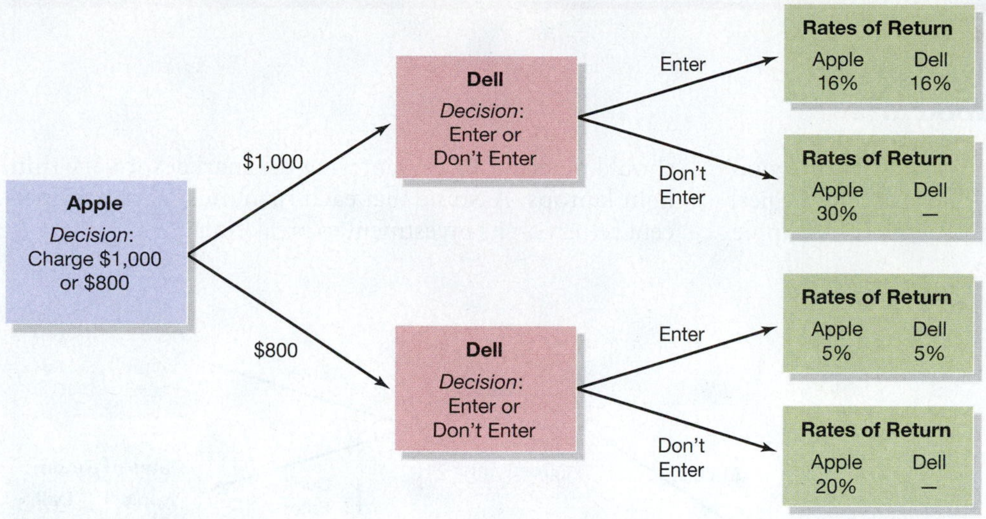

MyEconLab Animation

Figure 14.6 The Decision Tree for an Entry Game

Apple earns its highest return if it charges $1,000 for its very thin, light laptop and Dell does not enter the market. But at that price, Dell will enter the market, and Apple will earn only 16 percent. If Apple charges $800, Dell will not enter because Dell will suffer an economic loss by receiving only a 5 percent return on its investment. Therefore, Apple's best decision is to deter Dell's entry by charging $800. Apple will earn an economic profit by receiving a 20 percent return on its investment. Note that the dashes (—) indicate the situation where Dell does not enter the market and so makes no investment and receives no return.

Apple and Dell are playing a sequential game because Apple makes the first move—deciding what price to charge—and Dell responds. We can analyze a sequential game by using a *decision tree*, like the one shown in Figure 14.6. The boxes in the figure represent *decision nodes*, which are points where the firms must make the decisions contained in the boxes. At the left, Apple makes the initial decision of what price to charge, and then Dell responds by either entering the market or not. The decisions made are shown beside the arrows. The *terminal nodes*, in green at the right side of the figure, show the resulting rates of return.

Let's start with Apple's initial decision. If Apple charges $1,000, then the arrow directs us to the upper red decision node for Dell. If Dell decides to enter, it will earn a 16 percent rate of return on its investment, which represents an economic profit because it is above the opportunity cost of the funds involved. If Dell doesn't enter, Apple will earn 30 percent, and Dell will not earn anything in this market (indicated by the dash). Apple's managers can conclude that if they charge $1,000 for their laptops, Dell will enter the very thin, light laptop market, and both firms will earn 16 percent on their investments.

If Apple decides to charge $800, then the arrow directs us to the lower red decision node for Dell. If Dell decides to enter, it will earn only a 5 percent rate of return. If it doesn't enter, Apple will earn 20 percent, and Dell will not earn anything in this market. Apple's managers can conclude that if they charge $800, Dell will not enter, and Apple will earn 20 percent on its investment.

This analysis should lead Apple's managers to conclude that they can charge $1,000 and earn 16 percent—because Dell will enter—or they can charge $800 and earn 20 percent by deterring Dell's entry. Using a decision tree helps Apple's managers make the correct choice and charge $800 to deter Dell's entry into this market. Note that our discussion is simplified because we are ignoring other characteristics, apart from price, on which the firms also compete. In practice, Apple charged a relatively high price for its lightweight laptop, the MacBook Air, which caused Dell to enter the market with the lower-priced XPS 15z Ultrabook. Apple's managers believed that the MacBook Air's features would remain attractive to consumers, despite the XPS 15z Ultrabook having a lower price. Time will tell whether Apple made the correct decision by not charging a low enough price to deter Dell's entry. MyEconLab Concept Check

Solved Problem 14.3

Is Deterring Entry Always a Good Idea?

Like any other business strategy, deterring entry is a good idea only if it has a higher payoff than alternative strategies. Use the following decision tree to decide whether Apple should deter Dell from entering the market for very thin, light laptops. Assume that each firm must earn a 15 percent return on its investment to break even.

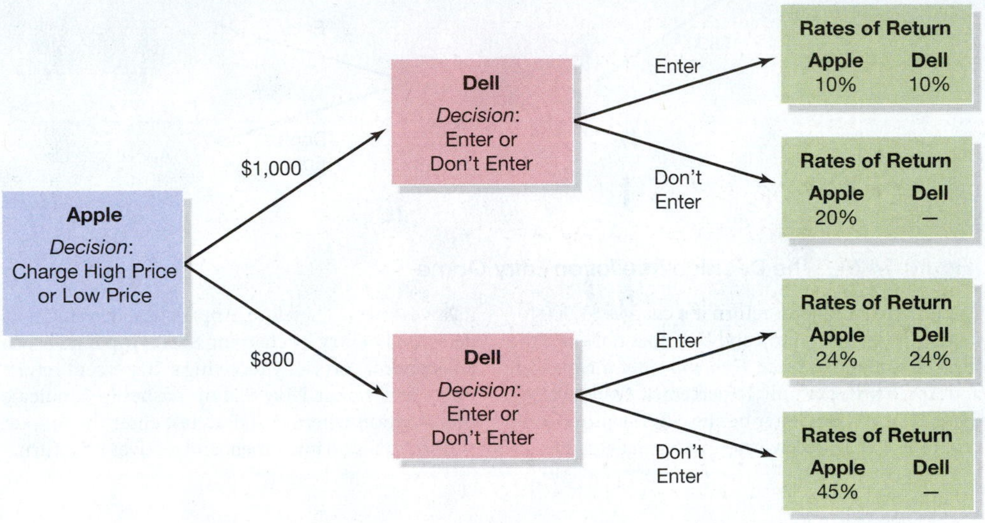

Solving the Problem

Step 1: Review the chapter material. This problem is about sequential games, so you may want to review the section "Deterring Entry," which begins on page 484.

Step 2: Determine how Dell will respond to Apple's decision. If Apple charges $1,000 for its very thin, light laptops, Dell will not enter the market because the return on its investment represents an economic loss. If Apple charges $800, Dell will enter because it will earn a return that represents an economic profit.

Step 3: Given how Dell will react, determine which strategy maximizes profits for Apple. If Apple charges $1,000, it will deter Dell's entry, and the rate of return on its investment will be 20 percent. If Apple charges $800, Dell will enter, but because these low prices will substantially increase the market for these laptops, Apple will actually earn a higher return of 24 percent. By splitting the market with Dell at a lower price, Apple earns a higher return than it would have if it had the whole market to itself at a high price.

Step 4: State your conclusion. Like any other business strategy, deterrence is worth pursuing only if the payoff is higher than for other strategies. In this case, expanding the market for very thin, light laptops by charging a lower price has a higher payoff for Apple, even given that Dell will enter the market.

MyEconLab Study Plan

Your Turn: For more practice, do related problem 3.3 on page 496 at the end of this chapter.

Bargaining

The success of many firms depends on how well they bargain with other firms. For example, firms often must bargain with their suppliers over the prices they pay for inputs. Suppose that TruImage is a small firm that has developed software that

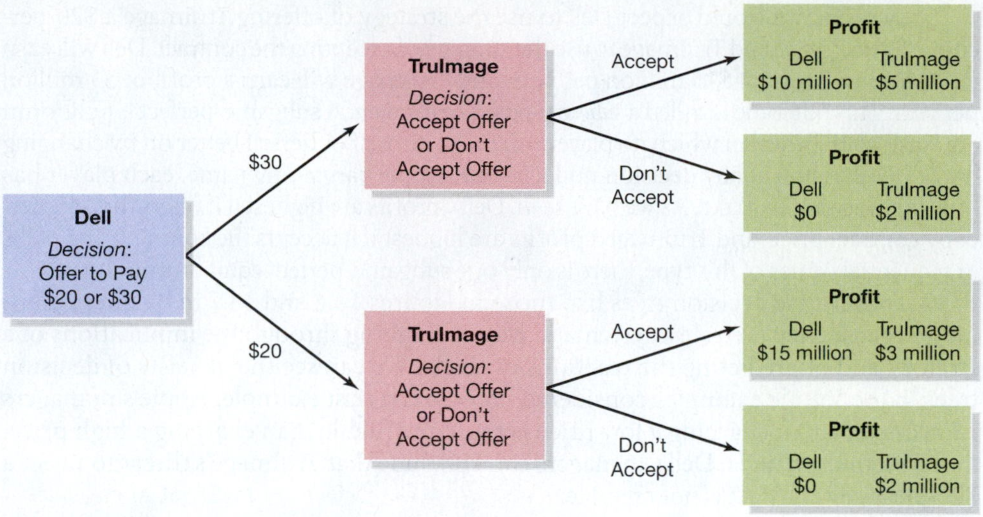

MyEconLab Animation

Figure 14.7 The Decision Tree for a Bargaining Game

Dell earns the highest profit if it offers a contract price of $20 per copy and TruImage accepts the contract. TruImage earns the highest profit if Dell offers it a contract of $30 per copy and it accepts the contract. TruImage may attempt to bargain by threatening to reject a $20-per-copy contract. But Dell knows this threat is not credible because once Dell has offered a $20-per-copy contract, TruImage's profits are higher if it accepts the contract than if it rejects it.

improves how pictures from digital cameras or smartphones are displayed on computer screens. TruImage currently sells its software only on its Web site and earns a profit of $2 million per year. Dell informs TruImage that it is considering installing the software on every new computer Dell sells. Dell expects to sell more computers at a higher price if it can install TruImage's software on its computers. The two firms begin bargaining over what price Dell will pay TruImage for its software.

The decision tree in Figure 14.7 illustrates this bargaining game. At the left, Dell makes the initial decision about what price to offer TruImage for its software, and then TruImage responds by either accepting or rejecting the contract offer. Suppose that Dell offers TruImage a contract price of $30 per copy for its software. If TruImage accepts this contract, its profit will be $5 million per year, and Dell will earn $10 million in additional profit. If TruImage rejects the contract, its profit will be the $2 million per year it earns selling its software on its Web site, and Dell will earn zero additional profit.

Now, suppose Dell offers TruImage a contract price of $20 per copy. If TruImage accepts this contract, its profit will be $3 million per year, and Dell will earn $15 million in additional profit. If TruImage rejects this contract, its profit will be the $2 million it earns selling its software on its Web site, and Dell will earn zero additional profit. Clearly, for Dell, a contract price of $20 per copy is more profitable, while for TruImage, a contract price of $30 per copy is more profitable.

Suppose TruImage attempts to obtain a favorable outcome from the bargaining by telling Dell that it will reject a $20-per-copy contract price. If Dell believes this threat, then it will offer TruImage a $30-per-copy contract price because Dell is better off with the $10 million additional profit that will result from TruImage accepting the contract than with the zero additional profit Dell will earn if TruImage rejects the $20-per-copy contract price. This result is a Nash equilibrium because neither firm can increase its profit by changing its choice—*provided that Dell believes TruImage's threat.* But is TruImage's threat credible? Once Dell has offered TruImage the $20 contract price, TruImage's choices are to accept the contract and earn $3 million or reject the contract and earn only $2 million. Because rejecting the contract reduces TruImage's profit, TruImage's threat to reject the contract is not credible, and Dell should ignore it.

As a result, we would expect Dell to use the strategy of offering TruImage a $20-per-copy contract price and TruImage to use the strategy of accepting the contract. Dell will earn an additional profit of $15 million per year, and TruImage will earn a profit of $3 million per year. This outcome is called a *subgame-perfect equilibrium*. A subgame-perfect equilibrium is a Nash equilibrium in which no player can make himself or herself better off by changing his or her decision at any decision node. In our simple bargaining game, each player has only one decision to make. As we have seen, Dell's profits are highest if it offers the $20-per-copy contract price, and TruImage's profits are highest if it accepts the contract. Typically, in sequential games of this type, there is only one subgame-perfect equilibrium.

Managers use decision trees like those in Figures 14.6 and 14.7 in business planning because they provide a systematic way of thinking through the implications of a strategy and of predicting the reactions of rivals. We can see the benefits of decision trees in the simple examples considered here. In the first example, Apple's managers can conclude that charging a low price is more profitable than charging a high price. In the second example, Dell's managers can conclude that TruImage's threat to reject a $20-per-copy contract is not credible.

MyEconLab Study Plan

MyEconLab Concept Check

14.4 The Five Competitive Forces Model

LEARNING OBJECTIVE: Use the five competitive forces model to analyze competition in an industry.

We have seen that the number of competitors in an industry affects a firm's ability to charge a price above average cost and earn an economic profit. The number of firms is not the only determinant of the level of competition in an industry, however. Michael Porter of the Harvard Business School has developed a model that shows how five competitive forces determine the overall level of competition in an industry.

In this section, we briefly discuss each of the five competitive forces: (1) competition from existing firms, (2) the threat from potential entrants, (3) competition from substitute goods or services, (4) the bargaining power of buyers, and (5) the bargaining power of suppliers.

Competition from Existing Firms

We have already seen that competition among firms in an industry can lower prices and profits. Consider another example: Educational Testing Service (ETS) produces the Scholastic Aptitude Test (SAT) and the Graduate Record Exam (GRE). High school students applying to college take the SAT, and college students applying to graduate school take the GRE. In 2015, ETS charged a price of $52.50 to take the SAT, and it charged $195 to take the GRE. Part of the explanation for this large price difference is that ETS faces competition in the market for tests given to high school students applying to college, where the SAT competes with the ACT Assessment, produced by ACT, Inc. But there is no competition for the GRE. As we saw in Section 14.2, when there are only a few firms in a market, it is easier for them to implicitly collude and to charge a price close to the monopoly price. In this case, however, competition from a single firm was enough to cause ETS to keep the price of the SAT near the competitive level.

Competition in the form of advertising, better customer service, or longer warranties can also reduce profits by raising costs. For example, online booksellers Amazon.com and BarnesandNoble.com have competed by offering low-cost—or free—shipping, by increasing their customer service staffs, and by building more warehouses to provide faster deliveries. These activities have raised the booksellers' costs and reduced their profits.

MyEconLab Concept Check

The Threat from Potential Entrants

Firms face competition from companies that currently are not in the market but might enter. We have already seen how actions taken to deter entry can reduce profits. In our hypothetical example in the previous section, Apple charged a lower price and earned less profit to deter Dell's entry. Business managers often take actions aimed at deterring entry. Some of these actions include advertising to create product loyalty, introducing new products—such as slightly different cereals or toothpastes—to fill market niches, and setting lower prices to keep profits at a level that makes entry less attractive. As we saw in the chapter opener, Apple entered the market for streaming music in 2015. Spotify had hoped to deter Apple's entry by keeping its monthly subscription charge at $9.99—a price at which it struggled to earn a profit. Apple, however, was willing to match that price and appeared confident that it would be able to earn a profit on its service. MyEconLab Concept Check

Competition from Substitute Goods or Services

Firms are always vulnerable to competitors introducing a new product that fills a consumer need better than their current product does. Consider the encyclopedia business. For decades, many parents bought expensive and bulky encyclopedias for their children attending high school or college. By the 1990s, computer software companies such as Microsoft were offering electronic encyclopedias that sold for a small fraction of the price of printed encyclopedias. Encyclopedia Britannica and the other encyclopedia publishers responded by cutting prices and launching advertising campaigns aimed at showing the superiority of printed encyclopedias. Still, profits continued to decline, and by the end of the 1990s, most printed encyclopedias had disappeared. Eventually, the free Web site Wikipedia made it difficult for firms to sell even low-priced electronic encyclopedias, and Microsoft and most other firms discontinued producing them. MyEconLab Concept Check

The Bargaining Power of Buyers

If buyers have enough bargaining power, they can insist on lower prices, higher-quality products, or additional services. Automobile companies, for example, have significant bargaining power in the tire market, which tends to lower tire prices and limit the profitability of tire manufacturers. Some retailers have significant buying power over their suppliers. For instance, Walmart has required many of its suppliers to alter their distribution systems because it wants to reduce the inventories it holds in its warehouses. MyEconLab Concept Check

The Bargaining Power of Suppliers

If many firms can supply an input and the input is not specialized, the suppliers are unlikely to have the bargaining power to limit a firm's profit. For instance, suppliers of paper napkins to McDonald's restaurants have very little bargaining power. With only a single or a few suppliers of an input, however, the purchasing firm may face a high price. During the 1930s and 1940s, for example, the Technicolor Company was the only producer of the cameras and film that studios needed to produce color movies. Technicolor charged the studios high prices to use its cameras, and it had the power to insist that only its technicians could operate the cameras. The only alternative for the studios was to make black-and-white movies.

As with other competitive forces, the bargaining power of suppliers can change over time. For instance, when IBM chose Microsoft to supply the operating system for its personal computers, Microsoft was a small company with very limited bargaining power. As Microsoft's Windows operating system became standard in more than 90 percent of personal computers, this large market share increased Microsoft's bargaining power. MyEconLab Concept Check

Making the Connection
MyEconLab Video

Can We Predict Which Firms Will Continue to Be Successful?

For years, economists and business strategists believed that market structure was the most important factor in explaining the ability of some firms to continue earning economic profits. For example, most economists argued that during the first few decades after World War II, steel

Although Circuit City's business strategy had once been widely admired, the company declared bankruptcy in 2009.

companies in the United States earned an economic profit because barriers to entry were high, there were few firms in the industry, and competition among firms was low. In contrast, restaurants were seen as less profitable because barriers to entry were low, and the industry was intensely competitive. One problem with this approach to analyzing the profitability of firms is that it does not explain how firms in the same industry can have very different levels of profit.

Today, economists and business strategists put greater emphasis on the characteristics of individual firms and the strategies their managers use to continue to earn economic profits. This approach helps explain why Nucor continues to be a profitable steel company while Bethlehem Steel, at one time the second-largest steel producer in the United States, was forced into bankruptcy. It also explains why Amazon, which began as a small company Jeff Bezos started in Seattle, Washington, with a handful of employees, became the leading online retailer, while many other online retailers that were also started in the 1990s have long since disappeared.

Is it possible to draw general conclusions about which business strategies are likely to be successful in the future? A number of business analysts have tried to identify strategies that have made firms successful and have recommended those strategies to other firms. Although books with these recommendations are often bestsellers, they have a mixed record in identifying winning strategies. For instance, in 1982, Thomas J. Peters and Robert H. Waterman, Jr., published *In Search of Excellence: Lessons from America's Best-Run Companies*. The book was favorably reviewed by business magazines and sold more than 3 million copies. Peters and Waterman identified 43 companies that were the best at using eight key strategies to "stay on top of the heap." But just two years after the book was published, an article in *BusinessWeek* pointed out that 14 of the 43 companies were experiencing significant financial difficulties. The article noted, "It comes as a shock that so many companies have fallen from grace so quickly—and it also raises some questions. Were these companies so excellent in the first place?"

In 2002, Jim Collins published *Good to Great: Why Some Companies Make the Leap … and Others Don't*, with the goal of determining how companies can "achieve enduring greatness." Although this book also sold 3 million copies, not all of the 11 "great companies" it identified were able to remain successful. For instance, Circuit City was forced to file for bankruptcy in 2009, and the Federal National Mortgage Association ("Fannie Mae") avoided bankruptcy only after the federal government largely took it over in 2008.

These two books, and many others like them, provide useful analyses of the business strategies of successful firms. That many of the firms highlighted in these books are unable to sustain their success should not be surprising. Many successful strategies can be copied—and often improved on—by competitors. Even in oligopolies, competition can quickly erode profits and even turn a successful firm into an unsuccessful one. It remains difficult to predict which currently successful firms will maintain their success.

Sources: Thomas J. Peters and Robert H. Waterman, Jr., *In Search of Excellence: Lessons from America's Best-Run Companies*, New York: HarperCollins Publishers, 1982; Jim Collins, *Good to Great: Why Some Companies Make the Leap … and Others Don't*, New York: HarperCollins Publishers, 2001; "Oops. Who's Excellent Now?" *BusinessWeek*, November 5, 1984; and Steven D. Levitt, "From Good to Great … to Below Average," *New York Times*, July 28, 2008.

MyEconLab Study Plan

Your Turn: Test your understanding by doing related problem 4.6 on page 497 at the end of this chapter.

Continued from page 471

Economics in Your Life

Why Can't You Find a Cheap PlayStation 4?

At the beginning of this chapter, we asked you to consider why the price of the PlayStation 4 game console is almost the same at every large retailer, from Amazon to Walmart. Why don't these retailers seem to compete on price for this type of product? In this chapter, we have seen that when large firms are engaged in a one-time game of pricing, they are in a prisoner's dilemma and will probably all charge a low price. However, pricing PlayStations is actually a repeated game because the retailers involved will be selling the game system in competition over a long period of time. In this situation, it is more likely that the retailers will arrive at a cooperative equilibrium, in which they will all charge a high price—a result that is good news for the profits of the retailers but bad news for consumers! This analysis is one of many insights that game theory provides into the business strategies of oligopolists.

Conclusion

Firms are locked in a never-ending struggle to earn an economic profit. As we have noted several times, competition erodes economic profits. Even in the oligopolies discussed in this chapter, firms have difficulty earning an economic profit in the long run. We have seen that firms attempt to avoid the effects of competition in various ways. For example, they can occupy a secure niche in the market, they can engage in implicit collusion with competing firms, or they can try to persuade the government impose barriers to entry.

Visit MyEconLab for a news article and analysis related to the concepts in this chapter.

CHAPTER SUMMARY AND PROBLEMS

Key Terms

14.1 Oligopoly and Barriers to Entry, pages 472–476

LEARNING OBJECTIVE: Show how barriers to entry explain the existence of oligopolies.

Summary

An **oligopoly** is a market structure in which a small number of interdependent firms compete. **Barriers to entry** keep new firms from entering an industry. The three most important barriers to entry are economies of scale, ownership of a key input, and government barriers. Economies of scale are the most important barrier to entry. **Economies of scale** exist when a firm's long-run average costs fall as it increases output. Government barriers include patents, licensing, and barriers to international trade. A **patent** is the exclusive right to a product for a period of 20 years from the date the patent application is filed with the government.

MyEconLab Visit **www.myeconlab.com** to complete these exercises online and get instant feedback.

Review Questions

1.1 What is an oligopoly? Give three examples of oligopolistic industries in the United States.

1.2 In his review of a book, business writer Nick Schultz cited the following passage that refers to the market for high-speed Internet access: "There are two enormous monopoly submarkets—one for wireless and one for wired transmission. Both are dominated by two or three large companies." Schultz commented on this passage that, "The claim is by definition nonsense." Briefly explain his criticism.

Source: Nick Schulz, "The Joys Of Oligopoly," *Wall Street Journal*, January 10, 2013.

1.3 What do barriers to entry have to do with the extent of competition in an industry? What is the most important reason that some industries, such as music streaming, are dominated by just a few firms?

1.4 Give an example of a government-imposed barrier to entry. Why would a government be willing to erect barriers to firms entering an industry?

Problems and Applications

1.5 Michael Porter has argued that "the intensity of competition in an industry is neither a matter of coincidence nor bad luck. Rather, competition in an industry is rooted in its underlying economic structure." What does Porter mean by "economic structure"? What factors besides economic structure might be expected to determine the intensity of competition in an industry?

Source: Michael Porter, *Competitive Strategy: Techniques for Analyzing Industries and Competitors*, New York: The Free Press, 1980, p. 3.

1.6 An article in the *Wall Street Journal* noted that Google was planning on entering the market to provide wireless data services. According to the article, "Google has said it isn't looking to supplant the big carriers, and Verizon's and AT&T's enormous scale means they can't easily be dislodged."

a. What does Google mean that it was not trying to "supplant" the big wireless carriers?
b. What does Verizon and AT&T's enormous scale have to do with the difficulty that Google, or another entrant, would have in supplanting them?

Source: Drew Fitzgerald, "Google Wants to Make Wireless Airwaves Less Exclusive, Cheaper," *Wall Street Journal*, March 3, 2015.

1.7 While a professor at the Harvard Business School, the late Thomas McCraw wrote: "Throughout American history, entrepreneurs have tried, sometimes desperately, to create big businesses out of naturally small-scale operations. It has not worked." What advantage would entrepreneurs expect to gain from creating "big businesses"? Why would entrepreneurs fail to create big businesses with "naturally small-scale operations"? Illustrate your answer with a graph showing long-run average costs.

Source: Thomas K. McCraw, ed., *Creating Modern Capitalism*, Cambridge, MA: Harvard University Press, 1997, p. 323.

1.8 The graph on the next page illustrates the average total cost curves for two automobile manufacturing firms: Little Auto and Big Auto. Under which of the following conditions would you expect to see the market composed of firms like Little Auto, and under which conditions would you expect to see the market dominated by firms like Big Auto?

a. When the market demand curve intersects the quantity axis at fewer than 1,000 units
b. When the market demand curve intersects the quantity axis at more than 1,000 units but fewer than 10,000 units

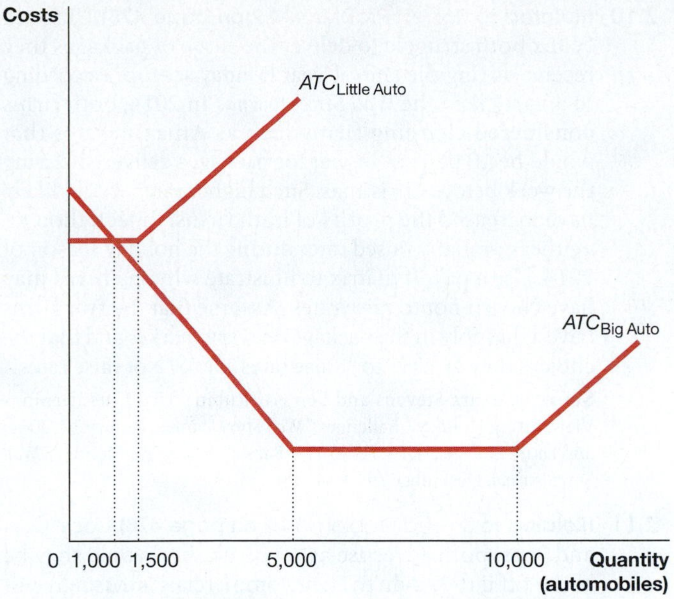

c. When the market demand curve intersects the quantity axis at more than 10,000 units

1.9 Alfred Chandler, who was a professor at the Harvard Business School, once observed: "Imagine the diseconomies of scale—the great increase in unit costs—that would result from placing close to one-fourth of the world's production of shoes, or textiles, or lumber into three factories or mills!" The shoe, textile, and lumber industries are very competitive, with many firms producing each of these products. Briefly explain how Chandler's observation helps explain why these industries are competitive.

Source: Alfred D. Chandler, Jr., "The Emergence of Managerial Capitalism," in Alfred D. Chandler, Jr., and Richard S. Tedlow, *The Coming of Managerial Capitalism*, New York: Irwin, 1985, p. 406.

1.10 (Related to the Making the Connection on page 475) The North Carolina State Board of Dental Examiners had been requiring that only licensed dentists be allowed to sell teeth-whitening services. The board brought legal action against hair salons and spas that also offered these services, arguing that only licensed dentists had the training to ensure that consumers weren't injured in the teeth-whitening process. In 2015, the U.S. Supreme Court ruled that a federal government agency had the authority to stop the board from preventing non-dentists from offering teeth-whitening services. According to a news report, the federal agency argued that "the dental board was motivated by financial self-interest, not health concerns."

a. Predict the effect of the Supreme Court ruling on the price and quantity of teeth-whitening services offered in North Carolina.
b. Can we be sure that the result of the decision will be to increase the well-being of consumers of teeth-whitening services in the state? Briefly explain.

Source: Brent Kendall, "Supreme Court Affirms FTC Antitrust Authority over Licensing Boards," *Wall Street Journal*, February 25, 2015.

14.2 Game Theory and Oligopoly, pages 476–484

LEARNING OBJECTIVE: Use game theory to analyze the strategies of oligopolistic firms.

Summary

Because an oligopoly has only a few firms, interactions among those firms are particularly important. **Game theory** is the study of how people make decisions in situations in which attaining their goals depends on their interactions with others; in economics, it is the study of the decisions of firms in industries where the profits of each firm depend on its interactions with other firms. A **business strategy** refers to actions taken by a firm to achieve a goal, such as maximizing profit. Oligopoly games can be illustrated with a **payoff matrix**, which is a table that shows the payoffs that each firm earns from every combination of strategies by the firms. One possible outcome in oligopoly is **collusion**, which is an agreement among firms to charge the same price or otherwise not to compete. A **cartel** is a group of firms that collude by agreeing to restrict output to increase prices and profits. In a **cooperative equilibrium**, firms cooperate to increase their mutual payoff. In a **noncooperative equilibrium**, firms do not cooperate but pursue their own self-interest. A **dominant strategy** is a strategy that is the best for a firm, no matter what strategies other firms choose. A **Nash equilibrium** is a situation in which each firm chooses the best strategy, given the strategies chosen by other firms. A situation in which pursuing dominant strategies results in noncooperation that leaves everyone worse off is called a **prisoner's dilemma**. Because many business situations are repeated games, firms may end up implicitly colluding to keep prices high. With **price leadership**, one firm takes the lead in announcing a price change, which is then matched by the other firms in the industry.

MyEconLab Visit **www.myeconlab.com** to complete these exercises online and get instant feedback.

Review Questions

2.1 Give brief definitions of the following concepts.
a. Game theory
b. Cooperative equilibrium
c. Noncooperative equilibrium
d. Dominant strategy
e. Nash equilibrium
f. Price leadership

2.2 Why do economists refer to the methodology for analyzing oligopolies as game theory?

2.3 What is the difference between explicit collusion and implicit collusion? Give an example of each.

2.4 What is a prisoner's dilemma game? Is the outcome of the game likely to be different in a repeated game? Briefly explain.

Problems and Applications

2.5 Bob and Tom are two criminals who have been arrested for burglary. The police put Tom and Bob in separate cells. They offer to let Bob go free if he confesses to the crime and testifies against Tom. Bob also is told that he will serve a 15-year sentence if he remains silent while Tom confesses. If Bob confesses and Tom also confesses, they will each serve a 10-year sentence. Separately, the police make the same offer to Tom. Assume that Bob and Tom know that if they both remain silent, the police have only enough evidence to convict them of a lesser crime, and they will both serve 3-year sentences.

a. Use the information provided to write a payoff matrix for Bob and Tom.
b. Does Bob have a dominant strategy? If so, what is it?
c. Does Tom have a dominant strategy? If so, what is it?
d. What sentences do Bob and Tom serve? How might they have avoided this outcome?

2.6 Explain how collusion makes firms better off. Given the incentives to collude, briefly explain why every industry doesn't become a cartel.

2.7 Under "early decision" college admission plans, students apply to a college in the fall and, if they are accepted, they must enroll in that college. Some critics of early decision plans, including some college presidents, argue that the plans put too much pressure on students to decide early in their senior year in high school which college to attend. Some college administrators have proposed abolishing early decision plans, but as a headline in the *New York Times* put it: "Applicants Continue to Flock to Early Admission Programs." If many college administrators believe that early decision plans should be abolished, why do their schools continue to use them? Can game theory help analyze this situation?

Source: Jacques Steinberg and Tanya Abrams, "Applicants Continue to Flock to Early Admission Programs," *New York Times*, December 20, 2012.

2.8 For several years, a professor at Johns Hopkins University had been using the following grading scheme for his final exam: He would give an A to the student with the highest score. The grades of the remaining students were then based on what percentage their scores were of the top student's score. In the fall of 2012, the students in the class came up with the idea of boycotting the final exam. They stood in the hallway outside the classroom but did not enter the room to take the exam. After waiting for a time, the professor cancelled the exam and, applying his grading scale, gave everyone in the class an A on the exam. An article in the *New York Times* about this incident observes: "This is an amazing game theory outcome, and not one that economists would likely predict." Do you agree with this observation that game theory indicates the students' strategy was unlikely to work? Briefly explain.

Source: Catherine Rampell, "Gaming the System," *New York Times*, February 14, 2013.

2.9 **(Related to the Don't Let This Happen to You on page 478)** A student argues: "The prisoner's dilemma game is unrealistic. Each player's strategy is based on the assumption that the other player won't cooperate. But if each player assumes that the other player *will* cooperate, the 'dilemma' disappears." Briefly explain whether you agree with this argument.

2.10 **(Related to Solved Problem 14.2 on page 478)** UPS and FedEx both struggle to deliver the surge of packages they receive during the end-of-year holiday season. According to an article in the *Wall Street Journal*, in 2014, both firms considered charging firms such as Amazon rates that would be 10 percent higher for packages delivered during the week before Christmas. Such higher rates would likely have increased the profits of both firms. In fact, though, neither company raised rates during the holiday season of 2014. Use a payoff matrix to illustrate why the firms may have chosen not to raise rates. Assume that the two firms have a duopoly in the package delivery market and that the choices they face are to "Raise rates" or to "Not raise rates."

Sources: Laura Stevens and Ben Fox Rubin, "UPS Cuts Earnings View, Citing Holiday Challenges," *Wall Street Journal*, January 17, 2014; and Laura Stevens, "UPS, FedEx Got Back on Time This Holiday," *Wall Street Journal*, December 29, 2014.

2.11 **(Related to Solved Problem 14.2 on page 478)** Coca-Cola and Pepsi both advertise aggressively, but would they be better off if they didn't? Their commercials are usually not designed to convey new information about their products. Instead, they are designed to capture each other's customers. Construct a payoff matrix using the following hypothetical information:

- If neither firm advertises, Coca-Cola and Pepsi each earn a profit of $750 million per year.
- If both firms advertise, Coca-Cola and Pepsi each earn a profit of $500 million per year.
- If Coca-Cola advertises and Pepsi doesn't, Coca-Cola earns a profit of $900 million, and Pepsi earns a profit of $400 million.
- If Pepsi advertises and Coca-Cola doesn't, Pepsi earns a profit of $900 million, and Coca-Cola earns a profit of $400 million.

a. If Coca-Cola wants to maximize profit, will it advertise? Briefly explain.
b. If Pepsi wants to maximize profit, will it advertise? Briefly explain.
c. Is there a Nash equilibrium to this advertising game? If so, what is it?

2.12 An economist argues that with respect to advertising in some industries, "gains to advertising firms are matched by losses to competitors" in the industry. Briefly explain the economist's reasoning. If his reasoning is correct, why do firms in these industries advertise?

Source: Craig L. Garthwaite, "Demand Spillovers, Combative Advertising, and Celebrity Endorsements," *American Economic Journal: Applied Economics*, Vol. 6, No. 2, April 2014, p. 76.

2.13 World War I began in August 1914 and on the Western Front quickly bogged down into trench warfare. In Belgium and northern France, British and French troops were dug into trenches facing German troops a few hundred yards away. The troops continued firing back and forth until a remarkable event occurred, which historians have labeled "The Christmas Truce." On Christmas Eve, along several sectors of the front, British and German troops stopped firing and eventually came out into the area between the trenches to sing Christmas carols and exchange small gifts. The truce lasted until Christmas night in most areas of the front, although it continued until New Year's Day in a few areas. Most of the troops' commanding officers were unhappy with the truce—they would have preferred the troops to keep fighting through Christmas—and in the future they often used a policy of rotating troops around the front so that the same British and German troops did not face each other for more than relatively brief periods. Can game theory explain why the Christmas Truce occurred? Can game theory help explain why the commanding officers' strategy was successful in reducing future unauthorized truces?

Source: Robert M. Sapolsky, "The Spirit of the 1914 Christmas Truce," *Wall Street Journal*, December 19, 2014.

2.14 In 2014, Walmart decided that it would begin a new policy in which its stores would match prices being charged by large Web retailers such as Amazon. For example, if it was selling a 4K television for $899 and Amazon was selling it for $799, Walmart would match Amazon's price. An economist comments that this new policy was more likely to end up raising the prices Walmart and Amazon charged than lowering them. Briefly explain the economist's reasoning.

Source: Shelly Banjo, "Wal-Mart Weighs Matching Online Prices," *Wall Street Journal*, October 30, 2014.

2.15 **(Related to the Making the Connection on page 481)** In 2015, the U.S. Department of Justice was investigating whether the four major U.S. airlines were colluding by restraining increases in capacity with the goal of avoiding price cutting. An airline industry analyst commented on the investigation, "I don't sense that the executives talk to each other. They actually hate each other, truth be told. But with so few of them left, there's almost a natural oligopoly."

a. What does the analyst mean by "a natural oligopoly"?
b. Would it be necessary for the airline executives to talk to each other to collude? Briefly explain.

Source: Christopher Drew, "Airlines under Justice Dept. Investigation over Possible Collusion," *New York Times*, July 1, 2015.

2.16 **(Related to the Making the Connection on page 481)** Airlines sometimes find themselves in price wars. Consider the following game: Delta and United are the only two airlines flying the route from Houston to Omaha. Each firm has two strategies: charge a high price or charge a low price.

		United: High	United: Low
Delta	High	Delta earns $20,000; United earns $20,000	Delta earns −$10,000; United earns $30,000
	Low	Delta earns $30,000; United earns −$10,000	Delta earns $0; United earns $0

a. What (if any) is the dominant strategy for each firm?
b. Is this game a prisoner's dilemma?
c. How could repeated playing of the game change the strategy each firm uses?

2.17 **(Related to the Making the Connection on page 481)** For many years, airlines would post proposed changes in ticket prices on computer reservation systems several days before the new ticket prices went into effect. Eventually, the federal government took action to end this practice. Now airlines can post prices on their reservation systems only for tickets that are immediately available for sale. Why would the federal government object to the old system of posting prices before they went into effect?

Source: Scott McCartney, "Airfare Wars Show Why Deals Arrive and Depart," *Wall Street Journal*, March 19, 2002.

2.18 Finding dominant strategies is often a very effective way of analyzing a game. Consider the following game: Microsoft and Apple are the two firms in the market for operating systems. Each firm has two strategies: charge a high price or charge a low price.

		Apple: High	Apple: Low
Microsoft	High	Microsoft earns $1 billion; Apple earns $6 billion	Microsoft earns $10 billion; Apple earns $6 billion
	Low	Microsoft earns $8 billion; Apple earns $2 billion	Microsoft earns $4 billion; Apple earns $3 billion

a. What (if any) is the dominant strategy for each firm?
b. Is there a Nash equilibrium? Briefly explain.

2.19 Suppose there are four large manufacturers of toilet tissue. The largest of these manufacturers announces that it will raise its prices by 15 percent due to higher paper costs. Within three days, the other three large toilet tissue manufacturers announce similar price hikes. Would this decision to raise prices be evidence of explicit collusion among the four companies? Briefly explain.

2.20 Anheuser-Busch InBev is the Belgian company that produces Budweiser, which has a large market share in the U.S. beer industry. According to an article in the *New York Times*, "Anheuser-Busch (InBev) signals to its competitors that if they lower prices, it will start a vicious retail war."

a. What does the article mean by a "retail war"?
b. Why would Anheuser-Busch threaten to start a retail war?

Source: Adam Davidson, "Are We in Danger of a Beer Monopoly?" *New York Times*, February 26, 2013.

14.3 Sequential Games and Business Strategy, pages 484–488

LEARNING OBJECTIVE: Use sequential games to analyze business strategies.

Summary

Recent work in game theory has focused on actions firms can take to deter the entry of new firms into an industry. Deterring entry can be analyzed using a sequential game, where first one firm makes a decision and then another firm reacts to that decision. Sequential games can be illustrated using decision trees.

MyEconLab Visit www.myeconlab.com to complete these exercises online and get instant feedback.

Review Questions

3.1 What is a sequential game?

3.2 How are decision trees used to analyze sequential games?

Problems and Applications

3.3 **(Related to Solved Problem 14.3 on page 486)** Bradford is a small town that currently has no fast-food restaurants. McDonald's and Burger King both are considering entering this market. Burger King will wait until McDonald's has made its decision before deciding whether to enter. McDonald's will choose between building a large store and building a small store. Once McDonald's has made its decision about the size of the store it will build, Burger King will decide whether to enter this market. Use the following decision tree to decide the optimal strategy for each company. Does your answer depend on the rate of return that owners of fast-food restaurants must earn on their investments to break even? Briefly explain.

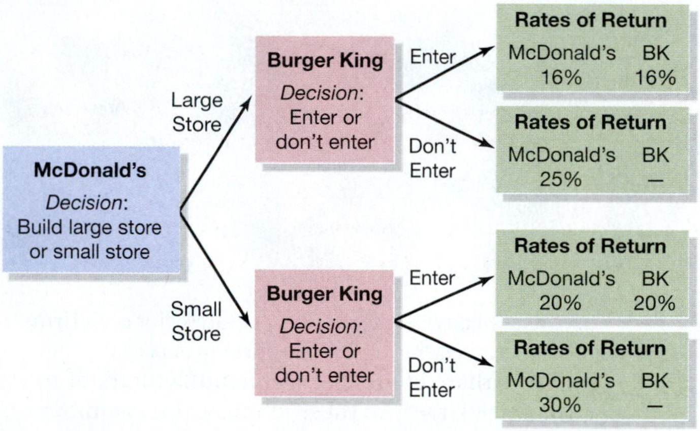

3.4 In June 2013, Microsoft announced that its new Xbox One video game console would have a price of $499. Sony then announced that its new PlayStation 4 video game console would have a price of $399. An article on the event where Microsoft introduced the new console noted that the Microsoft spokesperson "started by showing off features like live-television technology and the ability to video-chat through its Skype service." The article goes on to say that not until nearly halfway through the presentation did the Microsoft spokesperson mention the new games the console could play.

a. Why in announcing a new video game console would Microsoft focus its presentation on features of the console other than its ability to play games?

b. Was it an advantage to Sony that Microsoft announced the price of the Xbox One before Sony announced the price of the PlayStation 4? Briefly explain.

Source: Ian Sherr and Daisuke Wakabayashi, "Xbox One to Launch at $499, PlayStation 4 at $399," *Wall Street Journal*, June 10, 2013.

3.5 Suppose that in the situation shown in Figure 14.7 on page 487, TruImage's profit is $1.5 million if the firm accepts Dell's contract offer of $20 per copy. Now will Dell offer TruImage a contract for $20 per copy or a contract for $30 per copy? Briefly explain.

3.6 Refer to Figure 14.5 on page 484. Consider the entries in the row of the payoff matrix that correspond to Saudi Arabia choosing "Low Output." Suppose the numbers change so that Nigeria's profit is $15 million when Nigeria chooses "Low Output" and $10 million when it chooses "High Output."

a. Create the payoff matrix for this new situation, assuming that Saudi Arabia and Nigeria choose their output levels simultaneously. Is there a Nash equilibrium to this game? If so, what is it?

b. Draw the decision tree for this situation (using the values from the payoff matrix you created in part (a), assuming that Saudi Arabia and Nigeria make their decisions sequentially: First, Saudi Arabia chooses its output level, and then Nigeria responds by choosing its output level. Is there a Nash equilibrium in this game? If so, what is it?

c. Compare your answers to parts (a) and (b). Briefly explain the reason for any differences in the outcomes of these two games.

14.4 The Five Competitive Forces Model, pages 484–491

LEARNING OBJECTIVE: Use the five competitive forces model to analyze competition in an industry.

Summary

Michael Porter of the Harvard Business School argues that the state of competition in an industry is determined by five competitive forces: competition from existing firms, the threat from new entrants, competition from substitute goods or services, the bargaining power of buyers, and the bargaining power of suppliers.

MyEconLab Visit **www.myeconlab.com** to complete these exercises online and get instant feedback.

Review Questions

4.1 Describe the five competitive forces model.

4.2 Does the strength of each of the five competitive forces remain constant over time? Briefly explain.

Problems and Applications

4.3 Briefly explain which of the five competitive forces is involved in each of these business developments.

a. The effect on Samsung, maker of the Galaxy large-screen smartphone, as Apple introduces the iPhone 6 with a larger screen.

b. The effect on McDonald's as White Castle and Taco Bell consider starting to sell breakfast food.
c. The effect on cable television firms as Apple plans a Web TV service that will include programs from 25 to 30 cable networks.
d. The effect on the publishing firm Hachette when Amazon bargains to lower the prices of the books Hachette sells on Amazon's site.
e. The effect on the Carmike movie theater chain of IMAX increasing the fees it charges to theaters to use its technology.

4.4 Michael Porter argued that in many industries, "strategies converge and competition becomes a series of races down identical paths that no one can win." Briefly explain whether firms in these industries will likely earn economic profits.

Source: Michael E. Porter, "What Is Strategy?" *Harvard Business Review*, November–December 1996, p. 64.

4.5 **(Related to the Chapter Opener on page 471)** When Apple first launched Apple Music, singer Taylor Swift refused to allow her album *1989*, which had been the best-selling album of 2014, to be made available for the service because Apple did not intend to pay royalties on songs it streamed during an initial three-month period when the service would be free to subscribers. In response, Apple changed its policy and agreed to pay royalties during those three months, even though doing so reduced its profit. Do singers typically have substantial bargaining power with Apple, Spotify, and the other streaming services? Briefly explain.

Source: Mike Ayers and Ethan Smith, "Taylor Swift Is Now Making '1989' Available on Apple Music," *Wall Street Journal*, June 25, 2015.

4.6 **(Related to the Making the Connection on page 489)** In the preface to the 2004 reprint of *In Search of Excellence*, Thomas Peters and Robert Waterman wrote: "Our main detractors point to the decline of some of the companies we featured. They miss the point.... We weren't writing *Forever Excellent*, just as it would be absurd to expect any great athlete not to age." Is the analogy the authors make between great firms and great athletes accurate? Should we expect firms to become less successful as they age, just as athletes do?

Source: Thomas Peters and Robert H. Waterman, Jr., "Authors' Note: Excellence 2003," in *In Search of Excellence: Lessons from America's Best-Run Companies*, New York: HarperCollins, 2004 (original edition 1982).

4.7 Under Armour, Inc., was founded in 1996 by Kevin Plank, a 23-year-old former University of Maryland football player. The company specializes in manufacturing and selling athletic and casual apparel made from synthetic material that repels moisture. The company does not have patents on the fabric it uses or on its manufacturing process. Use Michael Porter's five competitive forces model to analyze the competition Under Armour faces in the athletic and casual apparel industry.

Source: Katherine Arline, "Porter's Five Forces: Analyzing the Competition," *Business News Daily*, February 18, 2015.

4.8 Movie studios split ticket revenues with the owners of the movie theaters that show their films. An article in the *Wall Street Journal* in 2015 discussed how the Disney studio was attempting to negotiate a larger share of the ticket revenue because it had a string of movies about to open that appeared likely to be very successful, including *Avengers: Age of Ultron* and *Star Wars: The Force Awakens*. Typically, would you expect that the profits of movie studios are more at risk from the bargaining power of theaters or are the profits of theaters more at risk from the bargaining power of movie studios? Briefly explain your reasoning.

Source: Erich Schwartzel and Ben Fritz, "Disney, Theater Operators Battle over New 'Avengers,'" *Wall Street Journal*, May 4, 2015.

CHAPTER

15

Monopoly and Antitrust Policy

Chapter Outline and Learning Objectives

A Monopoly on Lobster Dinners in Maine?

A *New York Times* article written from Stonington, Maine, explained, "Lobsters are flooding the market here." The reporter observed that the huge lobster harvest was not good news for fishermen because "the law of supply and demand has forced the price down to a 40-year low" of $1.35 per pound. Yet shortly after this article appeared, a columnist for *Slate*, an online magazine, had dinner with his father at the only lobster restaurant in Stonington, The Fisherman's Friend. He was surprised that the restaurant charged $20.99 for each dinner.

How could The Fisherman's Friend charge so much for a lobster dinner when the price of lobsters was so low? The answer is that The Fisherman's Friend is the *only* seafood restaurant in Stonington. The *Slate* reporter and his father couldn't eat at "the competitor next door" because there wasn't one. To eat lobster while staying in Stonington, they had to eat at that restaurant or buy lobsters in a supermarket and cook them. In other words, The Fisherman's Friend has a *monopoly* on selling seafood dinners in that town.

Few firms in the United States are monopolies because in a market system whenever a firm earns an economic profit, typically other firms will enter that market. Therefore, it is very difficult for a firm to remain the only provider of a good or service. Only if the gap between the price of lobsters and the price of lobster dinners in Stonington fails to attract a competitor would The Fisherman's Friend be able to maintain its monopoly. Although not common, monopolies are worth studying because they provide a benchmark for how firms behave when they face little or no competition. In this chapter, we will build a model to analyze monopolies.

Sources: Katharine Q. Seelye, "In Maine, More Lobsters Than They Know What to Do With," *New York Times*, July 28, 2012; and Matthew Yglesias, "The Mystery of the Market Price" www.slate.com, August 21, 2012.

Economics in Your Life

Can a Business Run from Your Dorm Be a Monopoly?

You and your roommate Fatma hear students complaining about the lack of food services on campus on Saturday and Sunday evenings, so you come up with an idea for a business: You will buy rolls, lunch meat, lettuce, and tomatoes and become the sole seller of submarine sandwiches in your school's dormitories on those evenings. You believe that there will be many hungry customers when students return to campus from the library and off-campus events. What price will you charge for the subs?

Fatma argues that because your business is a monopoly, you can charge prices much higher than what local shops charge for subs during the day; hungry students will have to buy your subs or stay hungry until the following day. You want to make a profit from your business but are not sure whether Fatma is right. Is your business a monopoly? Should you charge high prices for your subs? As you read this chapter, try to answer these questions. You can check your answers against those we provide on **page 523** at the end of this chapter.

Although few firms are monopolies, the economic model of monopoly can be quite useful. As we have seen, even though perfectly competitive markets are rare, the competitive market model provides a benchmark for how a firm acts in the most competitive situation possible: when it is in an industry, such as farming, with many firms that all supply the same product. Monopoly provides a benchmark for the other extreme, where a firm is the only one in its market and, therefore, faces no competition from other firms supplying its product. The monopoly model is also useful in analyzing situations in which firms agree to *collude*, or not compete, and act together as if they were a monopoly. As we will discuss in this chapter, collusion is illegal in the United States, but it occasionally happens.

Monopolies pose a dilemma for the government. Should the government allow monopolies to exist? Are there circumstances in which the government should actually promote the existence of monopolies? Should the government regulate the prices monopolies charge? If so, will such price regulation increase economic efficiency? In this chapter, we will explore these public policy issues.

15.1 Is Any Firm Ever Really a Monopoly?

LEARNING OBJECTIVE: Define monopoly.

Monopoly A firm that is the only seller of a good or service that does not have a close substitute.

A **monopoly** is a firm that is the only seller of a good or service that does not have a close substitute. Because substitutes of some kind exist for just about every product, are there actually any monopolies? The answer is "yes," provided that the substitutes are not "close" substitutes. But how do we decide whether a substitute is a close substitute? A narrow definition of monopoly that some economists use is that a firm has a monopoly if it can ignore the actions of all other firms. In other words, if a firm can ignore the prices other firms charge, it has a monopoly because other firms must not be producing close substitutes. For example, candles are a substitute for electric lights, but your local electric company can ignore candle prices because however low the price of candles becomes, almost no customers will give up using electric lights and switch to candles. Therefore, your local electric company is clearly a monopoly.

Many economists, however, use a broader definition of *monopoly*. For example, consider again The Fisherman's Friend seafood restaurant in Stonington, Maine, that we discussed in the chapter opener. Does this restaurant have a monopoly? Substitutes for lobster dinners certainly exist. If the price of lobster dinners is too high, people will switch to steak dinners or spaghetti dinners or some other food. People do not have to eat at The Fisherman's Friend or starve. The restaurant is in competition with several other local restaurants. So, The Fisherman's Friend does not meet the narrow definition of a monopoly. Many economists, however, would still argue that it is useful to think of the restaurant as having a monopoly.

Although steak and spaghetti are substitutes for lobster, competition from firms selling them is not enough to keep The Fisherman's Friend from earning an economic profit. We have seen that when firms earn an economic profit, we can expect new firms to enter the industry, and in the long run, the economic profit is competed away (see Chapter 12). The Fisherman's Friend's profit will not be competed away as long as it is the *only* seller of lobster dinners. The reporter mentioned in the chapter opener noted, "Stonington is a great place to visit. But it's also a very small town." So it's possible that no other seafood restaurants will choose to open in the town. In that case, using the broader definition of monopoly, The Fisherman's Friend has a monopoly because there are no other firms selling a substitute close enough that its economic profit will be competed away in the long run. MyEconLab Concept Check

Making the Connection
MyEconLab Video

Is the NCAA a Monopoly?

In 1905, President Theodore Roosevelt was disturbed by the 18 deaths and many injuries college football players had suffered during the previous season. A meeting took place at the White House between Roosevelt and several college presidents to discuss rule changes that would make the game safer. This meeting eventually led to the establishment of the National Collegiate Athletic Association (NCAA) in 1910. NCAA rules now govern men's and women's athletics at more than 1,200 institutions. On its Web site, the NCAA states, "The National Collegiate Athletic Association is a membership-driven organization dedicated to safeguarding the well-being of student-athletes and equipping them with the skills to succeed on the playing field, in the classroom and throughout life." Some economists wonder whether the NCAA's rules might also have other goals.

Do NCAA rules preserve the ideal of amateurism in college sports, or are they violations of federal antitrust laws?

Harvard University economist Robert Barro claims that the NCAA is effectively a monopoly. Nearly all colleges want their teams to participate in NCAA tournaments and other events. Those colleges therefore have to agree to the NCAA's rules. Included in those rules are limits on the number of scholarships that a college can award student athletes and a prohibition on paying salaries to athletes. These restrictions reduce the cost to colleges of running their athletic programs. Noting that very few college athletes go on to careers in professional sports, Barro argues that "many college basketball players come from poor families… . Absent the NCAA, such a student would be able to amass significant cash during a college career. With the NCAA in charge, this student remains poor." The NCAA defends its restrictions on scholarships and its prohibition on paying salaries to athletes as a way of preserving the amateur status of collegiate sports.

Because the NCAA does not directly control the operations of the athletic departments of the member colleges, some economists argue that it is better to think of the organization as a cartel than as a monopoly. As we saw in Chapter 13, when discussing the Organization of the Petroleum Exporting Countries (OPEC), a cartel is a group of firms that collude by agreeing to restrict output to increase prices and profits. The NCAA restricts the number of games the member schools' teams can play, effectively restricting output. For decades, the NCAA also restricted the number of college football and basketball games that could be televised. Some larger schools did not support these restrictions, however, and in 1982, the University of Georgia and the University of Oklahoma sued the NCAA under the federal antitrust laws. As we will see in Section 15.5, the antitrust laws are aimed at eliminating collusion and promoting competition among firms. In 1984, the Supreme Court decided the case against the NCAA, noting that "good motives alone will not validate an otherwise anticompetitive practice." Following the decision, college football and basketball broadcasts have greatly increased.

In 2014, the NCAA was the subject of two antitrust lawsuits related to video games. The NCAA reached a settlement in which it agreed to pay a total of $20 million to 100,000 current and former athletes whose names or images had been used in NCAA-branded videogames. In a separate lawsuit, a federal court judge ruled in favor of former University of California, Los Angeles, basketball player Ed O'Bannon, who argued that he should have received compensation after his image was used in an NCAA-branded video game. The judge handed down a broad ruling that, if upheld by the U.S. Supreme Court, would allow colleges to compensate current athletes for their appearances both in video games and on television. The NCAA also agreed to allow the five most successful conferences—the Southeastern Conference, the Atlantic Coast Conference, the Pacific-12, the Big Ten, and the Big 12—more freedom to determine the compensation they would give athletes.

The NCAA's defenders argue that its rules and restrictions are necessary to preserve the ideal of amateurism in college sports, and to make it possible for colleges to offer students the opportunity to participate in sports that do not generate much revenue from ticket sales and broadcasting rights, while preserving the ability of smaller schools to compete with larger schools. The organization's critics believe that many of the NCAA's regulations and restrictions are inconsistent with federal antitrust laws and argue that they should be removed.

Sources: Mar Tracy, "N.C.A.A. Votes to Give Richest Conferences More Autonomy," *New York Times*, August 7, 2014; Sharon Terlep, "NCAA Reaches $20 Million Settlement with Ex-Players over Videogames," *Wall Street Journal*, June 9, 2014; Gary Becker, "The NCAA as a Powerful Cartel," becker-posnerlog.com, April 4, 2011; Robert Barro, "The Best Little Monopoly in America," bloomberg.com, December 8, 2002; "Who We Are," ncaa.org; and Michael A. Leeds and Peter von Allmen, *The Economics of Sports*, 5th edition, Boston: Pearson, 2014.

MyEconLab Study Plan

Your Turn: Test your understanding by doing related problem 1.6 on page 524 at the end of this chapter.

15.2 Where Do Monopolies Come From?

LEARNING OBJECTIVE: Explain the four main reasons monopolies arise.

Because monopolies do not face competition, every firm would like to have a monopoly. But to have a monopoly, barriers to entering the market must be so high that no other firms can enter. *Barriers to entry* may be high enough to keep out competing firms for four main reasons:

1. Government action blocks the entry of more than one firm into a market.
2. One firm has control of a key resource necessary to produce a good.
3. There are important *network externalities* in supplying the good or service.
4. Economies of scale are so large that one firm has a *natural monopoly*.

Government Action Blocks Entry

As we will discuss in Section 15.5, governments ordinarily try to promote competition in markets, but sometimes governments take action to block entry into a market. In the United States, governments block entry in two main ways:

1. By granting a *patent, copyright,* or *trademark* to an individual or a firm, giving it the exclusive right to produce a product
2. By granting a firm a *public franchise,* making it the exclusive legal provider of a good or service

Patent The exclusive right to a product for a period of 20 years from the date the patent application is filed with the government.

Patents, Copyrights, and Trademarks The U.S. government grants patents to firms that develop new products or new ways of making existing products. A **patent** gives a firm the exclusive right to a new product for a period of 20 years from the date the patent application is filed with the government. Because Apple has a patent on the iOS operating system for smartphones and other mobile devices, other firms can't sell their versions of iOS. The government grants patents to encourage firms to spend money on the research and development necessary to create new products. If other firms could freely copy iOS, Apple would have been unlikely to spend the money necessary to develop it. Sometimes a firm is able to maintain a monopoly in the production of a good without patent protection, provided that it can keep secret how the product is made.

Patent protection is critical to pharmaceutical firms because they start research and development work on a new prescription drug an average of 12 years before the drug is available for sale. A firm applies for a patent about 10 years before it begins to sell the product. The average 10-year delay between the government granting a patent and the firm actually selling the drug is due to the federal Food and Drug Administration's requirements that the firm demonstrate that the drug is both safe and effective. Therefore, during the period before the drug can be sold, the firm will have significant costs to develop and test it. If the drug does not successfully make it to market, the firm will have a substantial loss.

Once a drug is available for sale, the profits the firm earns from the drug will increase throughout the period of patent protection—which is usually about 10 years—as the drug becomes more widely known to doctors and patients. After the patent has expired, other firms are free to legally produce chemically identical drugs called *generic drugs*. Gradually, competition from generic drugs will eliminate the profit the original firm had been earning. For example, when patent protection expired for Glucophage, a diabetes drug manufactured by Bristol-Myers Squibb, revenue from the drug declined by more than $1.5 billion in the first year due to competition from 12 generic versions of the drug produced by other firms. When the patent expired on Prozac, an antidepressant drug manufactured by Eli Lilly, revenue dropped by more than 80 percent. Most economic profit from selling a prescription drug is eliminated 20 years after the drug is first offered for sale.

A *trademark* grants a firm legal protection against other firms using its product's name. Trademarks are also referred to as *brand names*. The U.S. Patent and Trademark Office defines a trademark as "any word, name, symbol, device, or any combination, used or intended to be used to identify and distinguish the goods/services of one seller or provider from those of others, and to indicate the source of the goods/services." Firms often vigorously defend their trademarks, including by filing lawsuits against other firms for selling goods that infringe on their trademarks. For example, Christian Louboutin filed a lawsuit against Yves Saint Laurent, claiming that Yves Saint Laurent had infringed on Louboutin's trademark on women's shoes with red soles.

Making the Connection
MyEconLab Video

Does Hasbro Have a Monopoly on Monopoly?

To receive a copyright, patent, or trademark, a work has to be substantially new. Once a work no longer has legal protection, it is in the *public domain* and available to be freely used. It wouldn't be possible, for example, to make small changes to Mark Twain's novel *Huckleberry Finn* and then claim copyright on the book because it has been in the public domain for decades. (If you drew new illustrations for the book, however, it would be possible to copyright those illustrations independently of the text of the book.)

Hasbro's trademark on its Monopoly game prevents other companies from creating and selling similar games using the same title.

Hasbro is the multinational U.S. company that owns Monopoly, one of the world's most popular board games. The company estimates that more than 275 million copies of the game have been sold, and it is available in 43 languages. According to Hasbro, Charles Darrow invented the game in the 1930s. After selling many homemade copies, Darrow sold the game to Parker Brothers. In 1935, the U.S. Patent and Trademark Office issued Parker Brothers a trademark on the use of the name Monopoly for a board game. Hasbro bought Parker Brothers in 1991. Trademarks, unlike patents and copyrights, never expire, so Hasbro continues to have a trademark on the name Monopoly.

Economics professor Ralph Anspach of California State University, San Francisco, received an unexpected lesson in the law of trademarks when he decided in the 1970s to sell a game about competition that he titled Anti-Monopoly. The game was a hit, selling 200,000 copies the first year. Parker Brothers sued Anspach, though, on the grounds that his game infringed on its Monopoly trademark. In the course of defending the lawsuit, Anspach believed he had uncovered evidence that in 1904, a woman named Elizabeth Magie had developed The Landlord's Game, which was very similar to Monopoly. The game was never trademarked and was played for years on the East Coast. According to Anspach, Darrow became aware of The Landlord's Game in the mid-1930s, made a few changes to it, and sold it to Parker Brothers in 1935. A federal appeals court largely agreed with Anspach that given the history of the game, the name Monopoly was in the public domain and so couldn't be trademarked. Congress later amended the law, though, in a way that reinstated the Parker Brothers trademark. Eventually, Anspach and Hasbro worked out a settlement under which Anspach was allowed to sell his Anti-Monopoly game under a license from Hasbro.

Losing the trademark on its Monopoly game would have cost Hasbro millions of dollars per year because other companies could have begun to market similar games using the same title. The long legal fight the company had with Professor Anspach illustrates that companies consider it critical to retain exclusive control over their products.

Sources: Mary Pilon, "How a Fight Over a Board Game Monopolized an Economist's Life," *Wall Street Journal*, October 20, 2009; Ralph Anspach, *The Billion Dollar Monopoly® Swindle*, 2nd edition, Bloomington, IN: Xlibris, 2007; and Rachel Doepker, "Monopoly Patented," Business Reference Services, Library of Congress, www.loc.gov/rr/business/businesshistory/December/monopoly.html.

MyEconLab Study Plan

Your Turn: Test your understanding by doing related problem 2.9 on page 525 at the end of this chapter.

Copyright A government-granted exclusive right to produce and sell a creation.

Just as the government grants a new product patent or trademark protection, it grants books, films, and pieces of music **copyright** protection. U.S. law grants the creator of a book, film, or piece of music the exclusive right to use the creation during the creator's lifetime. The creator's heirs retain this exclusive right for 70 years after the creator's death. In effect, copyrights create monopolies for the copyrighted items. Without copyrights, individuals and firms would be less likely to invest in creating new books, films, and software.

Public franchise A government designation that a firm is the only legal provider of a good or service.

Public Franchises In some cases, the government grants a firm a **public franchise** that allows it to be the only legal provider of a good or service. For example, state and local governments often designate one company as the sole provider of electricity, natural gas, or water.

Occasionally, a government may decide to provide certain services directly to consumers through a *public enterprise*. This is much more common in Europe than in the United States. For example, the governments in most European countries own the railroad systems. In the United States, many city governments provide water and sewage service rather than rely on private firms. Congress has given the U.S. Postal Service the exclusive right to deliver first-class mail. No other company can legally deliver a letter to your mailbox.

MyEconLab Concept Check

Control of a Key Resource

Another way for a firm to become a monopoly is by controlling a key resource. Firms rarely gain this control because most resources, including raw materials such as oil or iron ore, are widely available from a variety of suppliers. There are, however, a few prominent examples of monopolies based on control of a key resource, such as the Aluminum Company of America (Alcoa) and the International Nickel Company of Canada.

For many years, until the 1940s, Alcoa either owned or had long-term contracts to buy nearly all of the available bauxite, the mineral needed to produce aluminum. Without access to bauxite, competing firms had to use recycled aluminum, which limited the amount of aluminum they could produce. Similarly, the International Nickel Company of Canada controlled more than 90 percent of available nickel supplies. Competition in the nickel market increased when the Petsamo nickel fields in northern Russia were developed after World War II.

In the United States, a key resource for a professional sports team is a large stadium. The teams that make up the major professional sports leagues—Major League Baseball, the National Football League, the National Hockey League, and the National Basketball Association—usually either own or have long-term leases with the stadiums in major cities. Control of these stadiums is a major barrier to new professional baseball, football, hockey, or basketball leagues forming.

MyEconLab Concept Check

Making the Connection MyEconLab Video

Are Diamond Profits Forever? The De Beers Diamond Monopoly

The most famous monopoly based on control of a raw material is the De Beers diamond mining and marketing company of South Africa. Before the 1860s, diamonds were extremely rare. Only a few pounds of diamonds were produced each year, primarily from Brazil and India. Then in 1870, enormous deposits of diamonds were discovered along the Orange River in South Africa. It became possible to produce thousands of pounds of diamonds per year, and the owners of the new mines feared that the price of diamonds would plummet. To avoid financial disaster, the mine owners decided in 1888 to merge and form De Beers Consolidated Mines, Ltd.

De Beers promotes the sentimental value of diamonds as a way to maintain its position in the diamond market.

De Beers became one of the most profitable and longest-lived monopolies in history. The company carefully controlled the supply of diamonds to keep prices high. As new diamond deposits were discovered in Russia and Zaire, De Beers was able to maintain prices by buying most of the new supplies.

Because diamonds are rarely destroyed, De Beers has always worried about competition from the resale of stones. Heavily promoting diamond engagement and wedding rings with the slogan "A Diamond Is Forever" was a way around this problem. Because engagement and wedding rings have great sentimental value, they are seldom resold, even by the heirs of the original recipients. De Beers advertising has been successful even in some countries, such as Japan, that have had no custom of giving diamond engagement rings. As the populations in De Beers's key markets age, its advertising in recent years has focused on middle-aged men presenting diamond rings to their wives as symbols of financial success and continuing love, and on women buying "right-hand rings" for themselves.

Over the years, competition has gradually increased in the diamond business. By 2000, De Beers directly controlled only about 40 percent of world diamond production. The company became concerned about how much it was spending to buy diamonds from other sources to keep them off the market. It decided to abandon its strategy of attempting to control the worldwide supply of diamonds and to concentrate instead on differentiating its diamonds by relying on its name recognition. Each De Beers diamond is now marked with a microscopic brand—a "Forevermark"—to reassure consumers of its high quality. Other firms, such as BHP Billiton, which owns mines in northern Canada, have followed suit by branding their diamonds. Whether consumers will pay attention to brands on diamonds remains to be seen, although through 2015, the branding strategy had helped De Beers to maintain about a 35 to 40 percent share of the diamond market.

Sources: Alex MacDonald, "De Beers Brings Oppenheimer Era to End," *Wall Street Journal*, October 3, 2012; William J. Holstein, "De Beers Reworks Its Image as Rivals Multiply," *New York Times*, December 12, 2008; Edward Jay Epstein, "Have You Ever Tried to Sell a Diamond?" *Atlantic Monthly*, February 1982; and Donna J. Bergenstock, Mary E. Deily, and Larry W. Taylor, "A Cartel's Response to Cheating: An Empirical Investigation of the De Beers Diamond Empire," *Southern Economic Journal*, Vol. 73, No. 1, July 2006, pp. 173–189.

Your Turn: Test your understanding by doing related problem 2.10 on page 525 at the end of this chapter.

MyEconLab Study Plan

Network Externalities

There are **network externalities** in the consumption of a product if its usefulness increases with the number of people who use it. If you owned the only HD television in the world, for example, it would not be very valuable because firms would not have an incentive to develop HD programming. The more HD televisions there are in use, the more valuable they become to consumers.

Network externalities A characteristic of a product in which its usefulness increases with the number of consumers who use it.

Some economists argue that network externalities can serve as barriers to entry. For example, in the early 1980s, Microsoft gained an advantage over other software companies by developing MS-DOS, the operating system for the first IBM personal computers. Because IBM sold more computers than any other company, software developers wrote many application programs for MS-DOS. The more people who used MS-DOS–based programs, the greater the value to a consumer of using an MS-DOS–based program. By the 1990s, Microsoft had replaced MS-DOS with Windows. Today, Windows has an 85 percent share in the market for personal computer operating systems, with Apple's operating system having a 10 percent share, and other operating systems, including the open-source Linux system, having shares of about 1 percent or less. If another firm introduced a new operating system, some economists argue that relatively few people would use it initially, and few applications would run on it, which would limit the operating system's value to other consumers.

eBay was the first Internet site to attract a significant number of people to its online auctions. Once many people began to use eBay to buy and sell collectibles, antiques, and many other products, it became a more valuable place to buy and sell. Yahoo.com, Amazon.com, and other Internet sites eventually started online auctions, but they had difficulty attracting buyers and sellers. On eBay, a buyer expects to find more sellers, and a seller expects to find more potential buyers than on Amazon or other auction sites.

As these examples show, from a firm's point of view, network externalities can set off a *virtuous cycle*: If a firm can attract enough customers initially, it can attract additional customers because the value of its product has been increased by more people using it, which attracts even more customers, and so on. With products such as computer operating systems and online auctions, it might be difficult for new firms to enter the market and compete away the profit being earned by the first firm in the market.

Economists debate, however, the extent to which network externalities are important barriers to entry in the business world. Some economists argue that Microsoft and eBay have dominant positions primarily because they are efficient in offering products that satisfy consumer preferences rather than because of the effects of network externalities. In this view, the advantages firms gain from network externalities would not be enough to protect them from competing firms offering better products. For example, many people have switched from computers to tablets and smartphones that run on Apple's iOS or Google's Android operating system, making Microsoft's domination of computer operating systems less important. MyEconLab Concept Check

Natural Monopoly

Natural monopoly A situation in which economies of scale are so large that one firm can supply the entire market at a lower average total cost than can two or more firms.

Economies of scale exist when a firm's long-run average cost falls as it increases the quantity of output it produces (see Chapter 11). A **natural monopoly** occurs when economies of scale are so large that one firm can supply the entire market at a lower average total cost than can two or more firms. In that case, there is "room" in the market for only one firm.

Figure 15.1 shows the average total cost curve for a firm producing electricity and the total demand for electricity in the firm's market. Notice that the average total

MyEconLab Animation

Figure 15.1

Average Total Cost Curve for a Natural Monopoly

With a natural monopoly, the average total cost curve is still falling when it crosses the demand curve (point *A*). If only one firm is producing electric power in the market, and it produces where the average cost curve intersects the demand curve, average total cost will equal $0.04 per kilowatt-hour of electricity produced. If the market is divided between two firms, each producing 15 billion kilowatt-hours, the average cost of producing electricity rises to $0.06 per kilowatt-hour (point *B*). In this case, if one firm expands production, it can move down the average total cost curve, lower its price, and drive the other firm out of business.

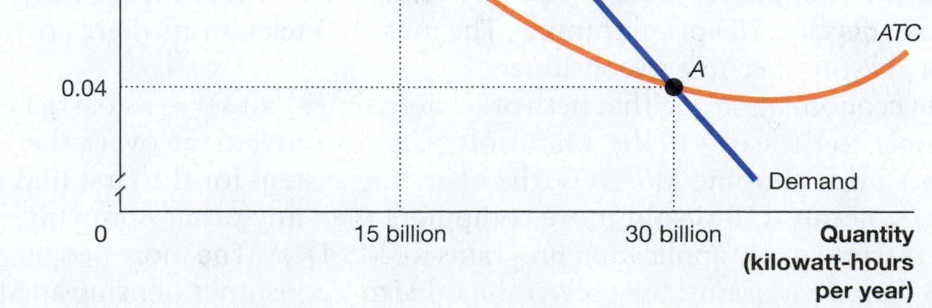

cost curve is still falling when it crosses the demand curve at point A. If the firm is a monopoly and produces 30 billion kilowatt-hours of electricity per year, its average total cost of production will be $0.04 per kilowatt-hour. Suppose instead that two firms are in the market, each producing half the market output, or 15 billion kilowatt-hours per year. Assume that each firm has the same average total cost curve. The figure shows that producing 15 billion kilowatt-hours would move each firm back up its average cost curve so that the average cost of producing electricity would rise to $0.06 per kilowatt-hour (point *B*). In this case, if one of the firms expands production, it will move down the average total cost curve. With lower average costs, it will be able to offer electricity at a lower price than the other firm can offer. Eventually, the other firm will be driven out of business, and the remaining firm will have a monopoly. Because a monopoly would develop automatically—or *naturally*—in this market, it is a natural monopoly.

Natural monopolies are most likely to occur in markets where fixed costs are very large relative to variable costs. For example, a firm that produces electricity must make a substantial investment in machinery and equipment necessary to generate the electricity and in the wires and cables necessary to distribute it. Once the firm makes the initial investment, however, the marginal cost of producing another kilowatt-hour of electricity is relatively small.

MyEconLab Concept Check

15.3 How Does a Monopoly Choose Price and Output?

LEARNING OBJECTIVE: Explain how a monopoly chooses price and output.

Like every other firm, a monopoly maximizes profit by producing where marginal revenue equals marginal cost. A monopoly differs from other firms in that *a monopoly's demand curve is the same as the market demand curve for the product*. When discussing perfect competition, we emphasized that the market demand curve for wheat was very different from the demand curve for the wheat produced by any one farmer (see Chapter 12). If, however, one farmer had a monopoly on wheat production, the two demand curves would be exactly the same.

Marginal Revenue Once Again

Recall that firms in perfectly competitive markets—such as a farmer in the wheat market—face horizontal demand curves. These firms are *price takers*. All other firms, including monopolies, are *price makers*. If price makers raise their prices, they will lose some, but not all, of their customers. Therefore, they face both a downward-sloping demand curve and a downward-sloping marginal revenue curve. Let's review why a firm's marginal revenue curve slopes downward if its demand curve slopes downward.

Remember that when a firm cuts the price of a product:

- **One good thing happens.** The firm sells more units of the product.
- **One bad thing happens.** The firm receives less revenue from each unit than it would have received at the higher price.

For example, consider the table in Figure 15.2, which shows information on the market for Comcast's basic cable package. To operate a cable system in a city, firms typically need a license from the city government. Comcast is the only cable television available in some cities. For simplicity, we assume that a particular market has only 10 potential subscribers. If Comcast charges a price of $60 per month, it won't have any subscribers. If it charges a price of $57, it sells 1 subscription. At $54, it sells 2 subscriptions, and so on. Comcast's total revenue is equal to the number of subscriptions sold per month multiplied by the price. The firm's average revenue—or revenue per subscription sold—is equal to its total revenue divided by the quantity of subscriptions sold. Comcast is particularly interested in marginal revenue because marginal revenue tells the firm how much its revenue will increase if it cuts the price to sell one more subscription.

Subscribers per Month (*Q*)	Price (*P*)	Total Revenue (*TR* = *P* x *Q*)	Average Revenue (*AR* = *TR*/*Q*)	Marginal Revenue (*MR* = Δ*TR*/Δ*Q*)
0	$60	$0	–	–
1	57	57	$57	$57
2	54	108	54	51
3	51	153	51	45
4	48	192	48	39
5	45	225	45	33
6	42	252	42	27
7	39	273	39	21
8	36	288	36	15
9	33	297	33	9
10	30	300	30	3

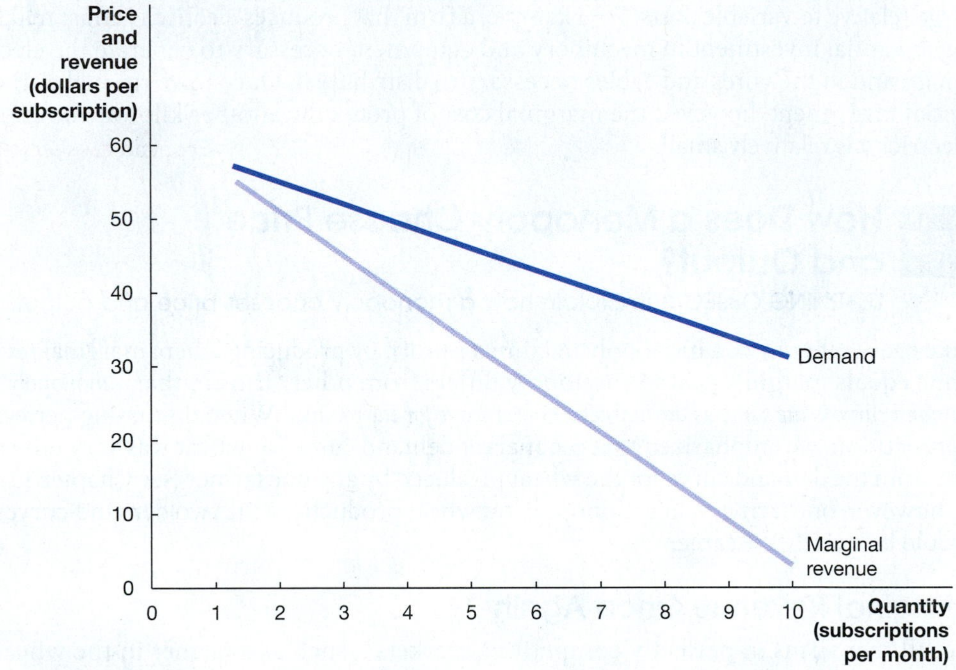

MyEconLab Animation

Figure 15.2

Calculating a Monopoly's Revenue

Comcast Cable faces a downward-sloping demand curve for subscriptions to basic cable. To sell more subscriptions, it must cut the price. When this happens, it gains revenue from selling more subscriptions but loses revenue from selling at a lower price the subscriptions that it could have sold at a higher price. The firm's marginal revenue is the change in revenue from selling another subscription. We can calculate marginal revenue by subtracting the revenue lost as a result of a price cut from the revenue gained. The table shows that Comcast's marginal revenue is less than the price for every subscription sold after the first subscription. Therefore, Comcast's marginal revenue curve will be below its demand curve.

Notice that Comcast's marginal revenue is less than the price for every subscription sold after the first subscription. To see why, think about what happens if Comcast cuts the price of its basic cable package from $42 to $39, which increases its subscriptions sold from 6 to 7. Comcast increases its revenue by the $39 it receives for the seventh subscription. But it also loses revenue of $3 per subscription on the first 6 subscriptions because it could have sold them at the old price of $42. So, its marginal revenue on the seventh subscription is $39 − $18 = $21, which is the value shown in the table. The graph in Figure 15.2 plots Comcast's demand and marginal revenue curves, based on the information in the table.

MyEconLab Concept Check

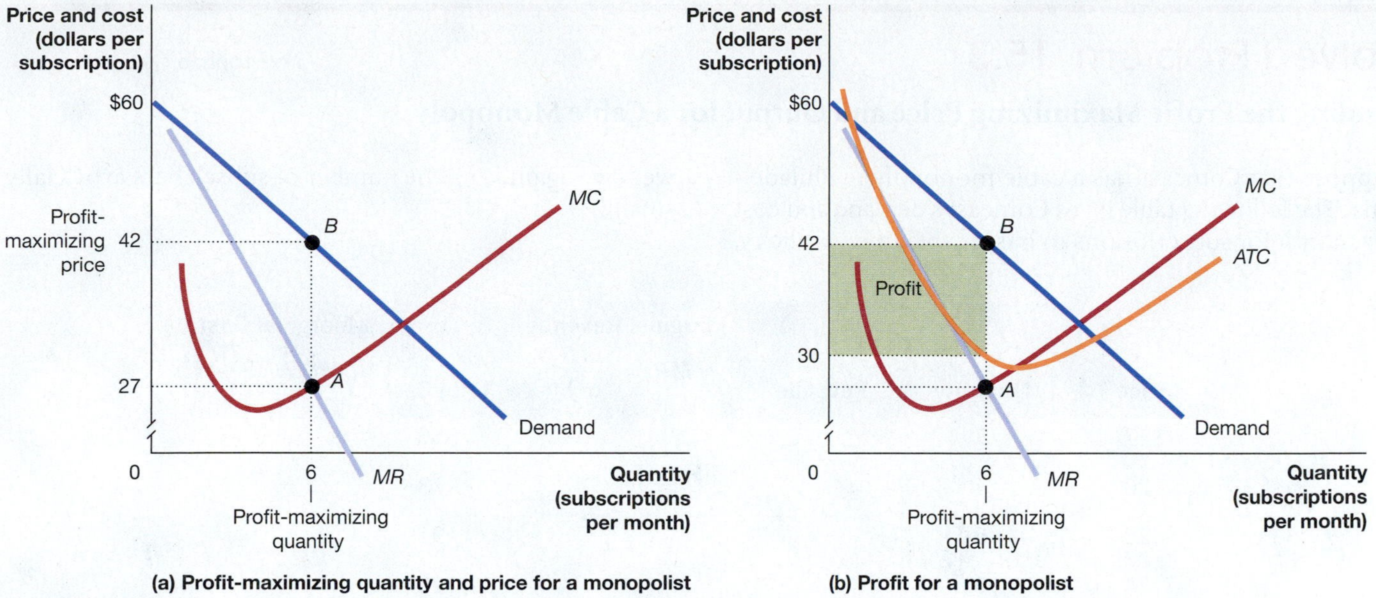

MyEconLab Animation

Figure 15.3 Profit-Maximizing Price and Output for a Monopoly

Panel (a) shows that to maximize profit, Comcast should sell subscriptions up to the point where the marginal revenue from selling the last subscription equals its marginal cost (point *A*). In this case, both the marginal revenue from selling the sixth subscription and the marginal cost are $27. Comcast maximizes profit by selling 6 subscriptions per month and charging a price of $42 (point *B*). In panel (b), the green rectangle represents Comcast's profit. The rectangle has a height equal to $12, which is the price of $42 minus the average total cost of $30, and a base equal to the quantity of 6 cable subscriptions. Comcast's profit therefore equals $12 × 6 = $72.

Profit Maximization for a Monopolist

Figure 15.3 shows how Comcast combines the information on demand and marginal revenue with information on average and marginal costs to decide how many subscriptions to sell and what price to charge. We assume that the firm's marginal cost and average total cost curves have the usual U shapes we encountered in previous chapters (see Chapters 11 and 12). In panel (a), we see how Comcast can calculate its profit-maximizing quantity and price. As long as the marginal cost of selling one more subscription is less than the marginal revenue, the firm should sell additional subscriptions because it is adding to its profit. As Comcast sells more cable subscriptions, rising marginal cost will eventually equal marginal revenue, and the firm will be selling the profit-maximizing quantity of subscriptions. Comcast maximizes profit with the sixth subscription, which adds $27 to the firm's costs and $27 to its revenues—point A in panel (a) of Figure 15.3. The demand curve indicates that Comcast can sell 6 subscriptions for a price of $42 per month. We can conclude that Comcast's profit-maximizing quantity of subscriptions is 6, and its profit-maximizing price is $42.

Panel (b) shows that the average total cost of 6 subscriptions is $30 and that Comcast can sell 6 subscriptions at a price of $42 per month (point *B* on the demand curve). Comcast is making a profit of $12 per subscription—the price of $42 minus the average cost of $30. Its total profit is $72 (= 6 subscriptions × $12 profit per subscription), which is shown by the area of the green-shaded rectangle in the figure. We could also have calculated Comcast's total profit as the difference between its total revenue and its total cost. Its total revenue from selling 6 subscriptions is $252. Its total cost equals its average total cost multiplied by the number of subscriptions sold, or $30 × 6 = $180. So, its profit is $252 − $180 = $72.

Note that even though Comcast is earning an economic profit, new firms will *not* enter the market unless they can obtain licenses from the city. If it holds the only license, Comcast has a monopoly and will not face competition from other cable operators. Therefore, if other factors remain unchanged, Comcast will be able to continue to earn an economic profit, even in the long run. MyEconLab Concept Check

Solved Problem 15.3

MyEconLab Interactive Animation

Finding the Profit-Maximizing Price and Output for a Cable Monopoly

Suppose that Comcast has a cable monopoly in Philadelphia. The following table gives Comcast's demand and cost per month for subscriptions to basic cable (for simplicity, we once again keep the number of subscribers artificially small):

Price	Quantity	Total Revenue	Marginal Revenue $\left(MR = \frac{\Delta TR}{\Delta Q}\right)$	Total Cost	Marginal Cost $\left(MC = \frac{\Delta TR}{\Delta Q}\right)$
$27	3			$56	
26	4			73	
25	5			91	
24	6			110	
23	7			130	
22	8			151	

a. Fill in the missing values in the table.

b. If Comcast wants to maximize profit, what price should it charge, and how many cable subscriptions per month should it sell? How much profit will Comcast make? Briefly explain.

c. Suppose the local government imposes a $25-per-month tax on Comcast. Now what price should Comcast charge, how many subscriptions should it sell, and what will its profit be?

Solving the Problem

Step 1: Review the chapter material. This problem is about finding the profit-maximizing quantity and price for a monopolist, so you may want to review the section "Profit Maximization for a Monopolist," which begins on page 509.

Step 2: Answer part (a) by filling in the missing values in the table. Remember that to calculate marginal revenue and marginal cost, you divide the change in total revenue or total cost by the change in quantity.

We don't have enough information from the table to fill in the values for marginal revenue and marginal cost in the first row.

Price	Quantity	Total Revenue	Marginal Revenue $\left(MR = \frac{\Delta TR}{\Delta Q}\right)$	Total Cost	Marginal Cost $\left(MC = \frac{\Delta TR}{\Delta Q}\right)$
$27	3	$81	—	$56	—
26	4	104	$23	73	$17
25	5	125	21	91	18
24	6	144	19	110	19
23	7	161	17	130	20
22	8	176	15	151	21

Step 3: Answer part (b) by determining the profit-maximizing quantity and price. We know that Comcast will maximize profit by selling subscriptions up to the point where marginal cost equals marginal revenue. In this case, that means selling 6 subscriptions per month. From the information in the

first two columns, we know Comcast can sell 6 subscriptions at a price of $24 each. Comcast's profit is equal to the difference between its total revenue and its total cost: Profit = $144 − $110 = $34 per month.

Step 4: Answer part (c) by analyzing the effect of the tax. The tax is a fixed cost to Comcast because it is a flat $25 no matter how many subscriptions it sells. Because the tax doesn't affect Comcast's marginal revenue or marginal cost, the profit-maximizing level of output has not changed. So, Comcast will still sell 6 subscriptions per month at a price of $24, but its profit will fall by the amount of the tax, from $34 per month to $9 per month.

Your Turn: For more practice, do related problems 3.4 and 3.5 on page 526 at the end of this chapter.

MyEconLab Study Plan

Don't Let This Happen to You

Don't Assume That Charging a Higher Price Is Always More Profitable for a Monopolist

In answering part (c) of Solved Problem 15.3, it's tempting to argue that Comcast should increase its price to make up for the tax. After all, Comcast is a monopolist, so why can't it just pass along the tax to its customers? The reason it can't is that Comcast, like any other monopolist, must pay attention to demand. Comcast is not interested in charging high prices for the sake of charging high prices; it is interested in maximizing profit. Charging a price of $1,000 per month for a basic cable subscription sounds nice, but if no one will buy at that price, Comcast would hardly be maximizing profit.

To look at it another way, before the tax is imposed, Comcast has already determined that $24 per month is the price that will maximize its profit. After the tax is imposed, it must determine whether $24 is still the profit-maximizing price. Because the tax has not affected Comcast's marginal revenue or marginal cost (or had any effect on consumer demand), $24 is still the profit-maximizing price, and Comcast should continue to charge it. The tax reduces Comcast's profit but doesn't cause it to increase the price of cable subscriptions.

MyEconLab Study Plan

Your Turn: Test your understanding by doing related problem 3.8 on page 526 at the end of this chapter.

15.4 Does Monopoly Reduce Economic Efficiency?

LEARNING OBJECTIVE: Use a graph to illustrate how a monopoly affects economic efficiency.

We have seen that a perfectly competitive market is economically efficient (see Chapter 12). How would economic efficiency be affected if instead of being perfectly competitive, a market were a monopoly? *Economic surplus* provides a way of characterizing the economic efficiency in a market. *Equilibrium in a perfectly competitive market results in the greatest amount of economic surplus, or total benefit to society, from the production of a good or service* (see Chapter 4). What happens to economic surplus under a monopoly? We can begin the analysis by considering the hypothetical case of what would happen if the market for smartphones begins as perfectly competitive and then becomes a monopoly.

Comparing Monopoly and Perfect Competition

Panel (a) in Figure 15.4 illustrates the situation if the market for smartphones is perfectly competitive. Price and quantity are determined by the intersection of the demand and supply curves. Remember that none of the individual firms in a perfectly competitive industry has any control over price. Each firm must accept the price determined by the market. Panel (b) shows what happens if the smartphone market becomes a monopoly. We know that the monopoly will maximize profit by producing where marginal revenue equals marginal cost. To do this, the monopoly reduces the quantity

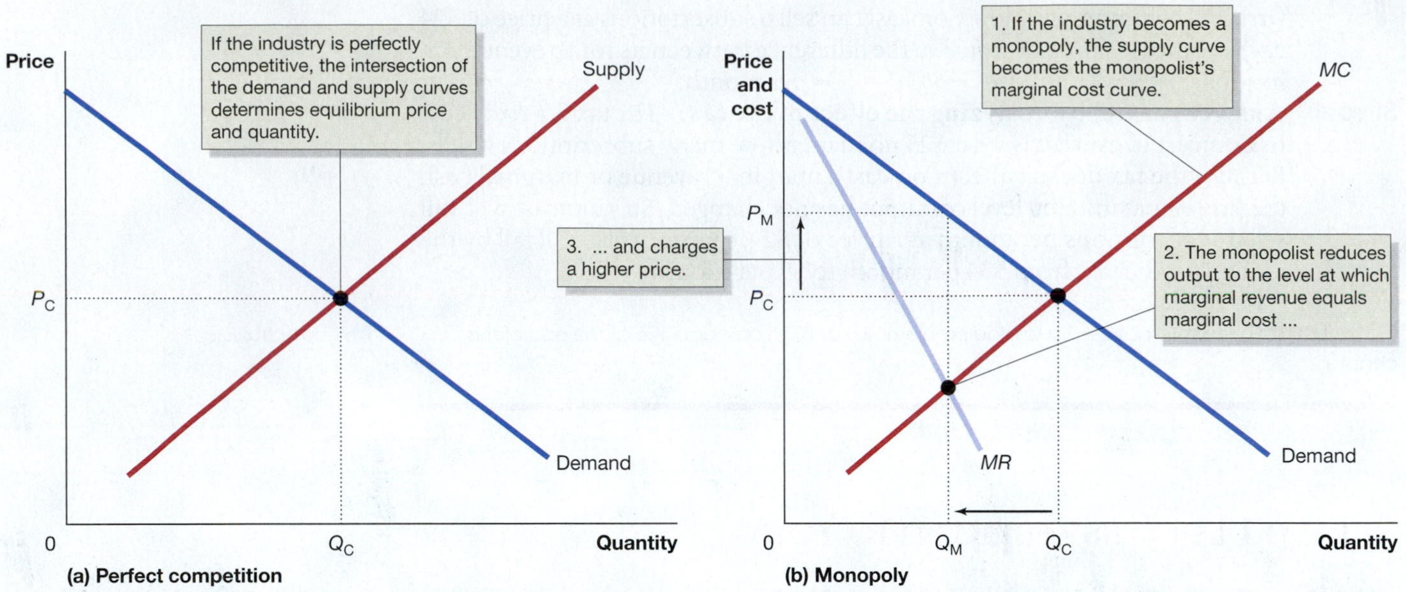

MyEconLab Animation

Figure 15.4 What Happens if a Perfectly Competitive Industry Becomes a Monopoly?

In panel (a), the market for smartphones is perfectly competitive, and price and quantity are determined by the intersection of the demand and supply curves. In panel (b), the perfectly competitive smartphone market becomes a monopoly. As a result, we have the following:

1. The industry supply curve becomes the monopolist's marginal cost curve.
2. The monopolist reduces output to where marginal revenue equals marginal cost, Q_M.
3. The monopolist raises the price from P_C to P_M.

of smartphones that would have been produced if the industry were perfectly competitive and increases the price. Panel (b) illustrates an important conclusion: *A monopoly will produce less and charge a higher price than would a perfectly competitive industry producing the same good.*

MyEconLab Concept Check

Measuring the Efficiency Losses from Monopoly

Figure 15.5 uses panel (b) from Figure 15.4 to illustrate how monopoly affects consumers, producers, and the efficiency of the economy. Recall that *consumer surplus*

MyEconLab Animation

Figure 15.5

The Inefficiency of Monopoly

A monopoly charges a higher price, P_M, and produces a smaller quantity, Q_M, than a perfectly competitive industry, which charges price P_C and produces Q_C. The higher price reduces consumer surplus by the area equal to the rectangle *A* and the triangle *B*. Some of the reduction in consumer surplus is captured by the monopoly as producer surplus, and some becomes deadweight loss, which is the area equal to triangles *B* and *C*.

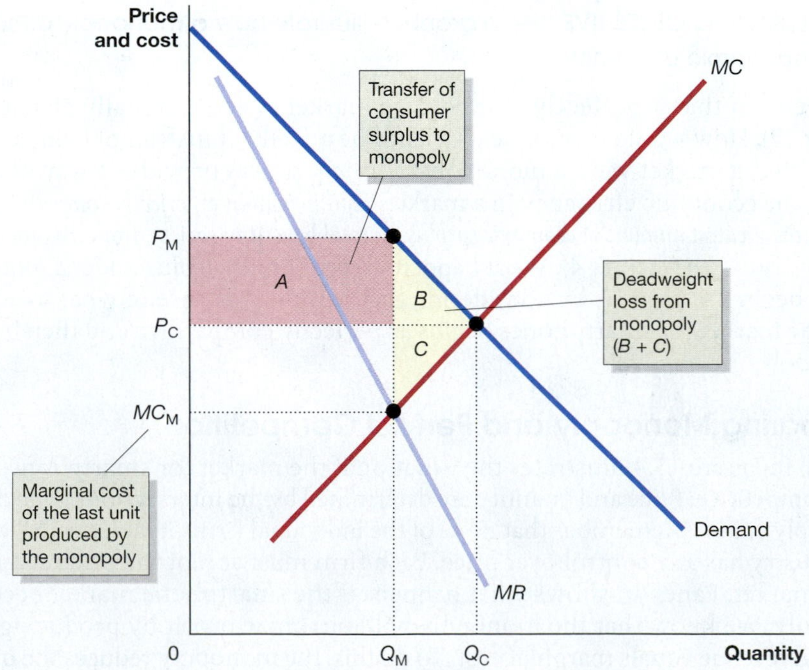

measures the net benefit received by consumers from purchasing a good or service (see Chapter 4). We measure consumer surplus as the area below the demand curve and above the market price. The higher the price, the smaller the consumer surplus. Because a monopoly raises the market price, it reduces consumer surplus. In Figure 15.5, the loss of consumer surplus is equal to rectangle *A* plus triangle *B*. Remember that *producer surplus* measures the net benefit to producers from selling a good or service. We measure producer surplus as the area above the supply curve and below the market price. The increase in price due to monopoly increases producer surplus by an amount equal to rectangle *A* and reduces it by an amount equal to triangle *C*. Because rectangle *A* is larger than triangle *C*, we know that a monopoly increases producer surplus compared with perfect competition.

Economic surplus is equal to the sum of consumer surplus and producer surplus. By increasing price and reducing the quantity produced, the monopolist has reduced economic surplus by an amount equal to the areas of triangles *B* and *C*. This reduction in economic surplus is called *deadweight loss* and represents the loss of economic efficiency due to monopoly.

The best way to understand how a monopoly causes a loss of economic efficiency is to recall that price is equal to marginal cost in a perfectly competitive market. As a result, a consumer in a perfectly competitive market is always able to buy a good if she is willing to pay a price equal to the marginal cost of producing it. As Figure 15.5 shows, the monopolist stops producing smartphones at a point where the price is well above marginal cost. Consumers are unable to buy some smartphones for which they would be willing to pay a price greater than the marginal cost of producing them. Why doesn't the monopolist produce these additional smartphones? Because the monopolist's profit is greater if it restricts output and forces up the price. A monopoly produces the profit-maximizing level of output but fails to produce the efficient level of output from the point of view of society.

We can summarize the effects of monopoly as follows:

1. Monopoly causes a reduction in consumer surplus.
2. Monopoly causes an increase in producer surplus.
3. Monopoly causes a deadweight loss, which represents a reduction in economic efficiency.

MyEconLab Concept Check

How Large Are the Efficiency Losses Due to Monopoly?

We know that there are relatively few monopolies, so the loss of economic efficiency due to monopoly must be small. Many firms, though, have **market power**, which is the ability of a firm to charge a price greater than marginal cost. The analysis we just completed shows that some loss of economic efficiency will occur whenever a firm has market power and can charge a price greater than marginal cost, even if the firm is not a monopoly. The only firms that do *not* have market power are firms in perfectly competitive markets, which must charge a price equal to marginal cost. Because few markets are perfectly competitive, *some loss of economic efficiency occurs in the market for nearly every good or service.*

Market power The ability of a firm to charge a price greater than marginal cost.

Is the total loss of economic efficiency due to market power large or small? It is possible to put a dollar value on the loss of economic efficiency by estimating for every industry the size of the deadweight loss triangle, as in Figure 15.5. The first economist to do this was Arnold Harberger of the University of California, Los Angeles. His estimates—largely confirmed by later researchers—indicated that the total loss of economic efficiency in the U.S. economy due to market power is relatively small. According to his estimates, if every industry in the economy were perfectly competitive, so that price were equal to marginal cost in every market, the gain in economic efficiency would equal less than 1 percent of the value of total production in the United States, or less than $600 per person.

The loss of economic efficiency is this small primarily because true monopolies are very rare. In most industries, competition keeps price much closer to marginal cost than would be the case in a monopoly. The closer price is to marginal cost, the smaller the size of the deadweight loss.

MyEconLab Concept Check

Market Power and Technological Change

Some economists argue that the economy may actually benefit from firms having market power. This argument is most closely identified with Joseph Schumpeter, an Austrian economist who spent many years as a professor of economics at Harvard. Schumpeter argued that economic progress depends on technological change in the form of new products. For example, the replacement of horse-drawn carriages by automobiles, the replacement of ice boxes by refrigerators, and the replacement of mechanical calculators by electronic computers all represent technological change that significantly raised living standards. In Schumpeter's view, new products unleash a "gale of creative destruction" that drives older products—and, often, the firms that produce them—out of the market. Schumpeter was not concerned that firms with market power would charge higher prices than perfectly competitive firms:

> It is not that kind of [price] competition which counts but the competition from the new commodity, the new technology, the new source of supply, the new type of organization ... competition which commands a decisive cost or quality advantage and which strikes not at the margins of the profits and outputs of the existing firms but at their foundations and their very lives.

Economists who support Schumpeter's view argue that the introduction of new products requires firms to spend funds on research and development. It is possible for firms to raise this money by borrowing from investors or banks. But investors and banks are usually skeptical of ideas for new products that have not yet passed the test of consumer acceptance in the market. As a result, firms are often forced to rely on their profits to finance the research and development needed for new products. Because firms with market power are more likely to earn an economic profit than are perfectly competitive firms, they are also more likely to carry out research and development and introduce new products. In this view, the higher prices firms with market power charge are unimportant compared with the benefits from the new products these firms introduce to the market.

Some economists disagree with Schumpeter's views. These economists point to the number of new products developed by smaller firms, including, for example, Steve Jobs and Steve Wozniak inventing the first Apple computer in Jobs's garage, and Larry Page and Sergey Brin inventing the Google search engine as graduate students at Stanford. As we will see in the next section, government policymakers continue to struggle with the issue of whether, on balance, large firms with market power are good or bad for the economy.

MyEconLab Study Plan

MyEconLab Concept Check

15.5 Government Policy toward Monopoly

LEARNING OBJECTIVE: Discuss government policies toward monopoly.

Collusion An agreement among firms to charge the same price or otherwise not to compete.

Because monopolies reduce consumer surplus and economic efficiency, most governments have policies that regulate their behavior. **Collusion** refers to an agreement among firms to charge the same price or otherwise not to compete (see Chapter 14). In the United States, *antitrust laws* are designed to prevent monopolies and collusion. Governments also regulate firms that are natural monopolies, often by controlling the prices they charge.

Antitrust Laws and Antitrust Enforcement

The first important law regulating monopolies in the United States was the Sherman Act, which Congress passed in 1890 to promote competition and prevent the formation of monopolies. Section 1 of the Sherman Act outlaws "every contract, combination in the form of trust or otherwise, or conspiracy in restraint of trade." Section 2 states that "every person who shall monopolize, or attempt to monopolize, or combine or conspire with any other person or persons, to monopolize any part of the trade or commerce ... shall be deemed guilty of a felony."

Table 15.1

Important U.S. Antitrust Laws

Law	Date Enacted by Congress	Purpose
Sherman Act	1890	Prohibited "restraint of trade," including price fixing and collusion. Also outlawed monopolization.
Clayton Act	1914	Prohibited firms from buying stock in competitors and from having directors serve on the boards of competing firms.
Federal Trade Commission Act	1914	Established the Federal Trade Commission (FTC) to help administer antitrust laws.
Robinson–Patman Act	1936	Prohibited firms from charging buyers different prices if the result would reduce competition.
Cellar–Kefauver Act	1950	Toughened restrictions on mergers by prohibiting any mergers that would reduce competition.

The Sherman Act targeted firms in several industries that had combined during the 1870s and 1880s to form "trusts." In a trust, the firms were operated independently but gave voting control to a board of trustees. The board enforced collusive agreements for the firms to charge the same price and not to compete for each other's customers. The most notorious of the trusts was the Standard Oil Trust, organized by John D. Rockefeller. In the years following passage of the Sherman Act, business trusts disappeared, but the term **antitrust laws** has lived on to refer to the laws aimed at eliminating collusion and promoting competition among firms.

Antitrust laws Laws aimed at eliminating collusion and promoting competition among firms.

The Sherman Act prohibited trusts and collusive agreements, but it left several loopholes. For example, it was not clear whether it would be legal for two or more firms to merge to form a new, larger firm that would have substantial market power. A series of Supreme Court decisions interpreted the Sherman Act narrowly, and the result was a wave of mergers at the turn of the twentieth century. Included in these mergers was U.S. Steel Corporation, which was formed from dozens of smaller companies. U.S. Steel, organized by J. P. Morgan, was the first billion-dollar corporation, and it controlled two-thirds of steel production in the United States. The Sherman Act also left unclear whether any business practices short of outright collusion were illegal.

To address the loopholes in the Sherman Act, in 1914, Congress passed the Clayton Act and the Federal Trade Commission Act. Under the Clayton Act, a merger was illegal if its effect was "substantially to lessen competition, or to tend to create a monopoly." The Federal Trade Commission Act set up the Federal Trade Commission (FTC), which was given the power to police unfair business practices. The FTC has brought lawsuits against firms employing a variety of business practices, including deceptive advertising. In setting up the FTC, Congress divided the authority to police mergers. Currently, both the Antitrust Division of the U.S. Department of Justice and the FTC are responsible for merger policy. Table 15.1 lists the most important U.S. antitrust laws and the purpose of each.

MyEconLab Concept Check

Making the Connection
MyEconLab Video

Did Apple Violate the Law in Pricing e-Books?

People who buy e-books got some bad news in 2010 when Apple introduced the iPad: The prices of new books and best sellers increased from $9.99 to $12.99 or $14.99. The price increases were not just for books sold in Apple's iBooks Store but also for books Amazon was selling for its Kindle. Why did this big jump in prices happen? The U.S. Justice Department had a straightforward answer: Apple had organized an agreement

Did Apple illegally restrict competition to raise the prices of e-books?

with five large book publishers to raise the prices of e-books. As one Justice Department lawyer put it, Apple had directed "an old-fashioned, straight-forward price-fixing agreement." Accordingly, the Justice Department sued Apple for violating the antitrust laws. The lawsuit was a civil action, meaning that the Justice Department was not pursuing criminal charges against Apple executives.

When Amazon introduced its Kindle e-reader in 2007, it priced most new books and best sellers at $9.99, even though this price was less than the price the publishers were charging Amazon for the books. Amazon believed that by selling e-books at a loss, it would increase sales of the Kindle. Most publishers were unhappy with Amazon's low e-book prices, however, because they believed the prices reduced sales of hardcover copies of best sellers on which the publishers made a larger profit. According to the Justice Department, Apple took advantage of the publishers' unhappiness to propose an "agency pricing model." Under this model, the publishers would set the retail price of e-books, and Apple would keep 30 percent of the price of every e-book it sold.

In addition, Apple negotiated a clause in its contracts with the publishers that allowed Apple to match the retail prices of other e-book sellers. By invoking this clause, Apple would be able to sell e-books for $9.99 if Amazon continued to do so. The publishers then insisted that Amazon switch to an agency pricing model. If Amazon failed to switch, the publishers said they would not allow Amazon to sell electronic versions of their books until months after the hardcover editions were first published, which would give Apple a huge advantage in the e-book market. Faced with this situation, Amazon also adopted the agency pricing model, and the publishers were able to raise the prices of most new books to $12.99 or $14.99.

At the trial, Apple argued that it had not attempted to organize a price-fixing agreement with the publishers. Instead, Apple had simply proposed a pricing model similar to the one it was already using for songs in its iTunes store. As Apple's executive in charge of negotiating with the publishers put it, "I didn't raise prices. The publishers set the prices." Representatives of the publishers also testified during the trial that they had not conspired with Apple or with each other to fix the prices of e-books.

In the end, a judge ruled that Apple had conspired with the publishers to raise e-book prices. Following the decision, the Justice Department proposed that the judge bar Apple from entering agency pricing contracts with publishers for a period of five years. Apple appealed the judge's decision, and in 2015 an appeals court agreed that Apple had violated the law. One of the justices dissented, though, arguing, "Apple took steps to compete with a monopolist and open the market to more entrants, generating only minor competitive restraints in the process." The Justice Department disagreed with this analysis and welcomed the decision, asserting, "Because Apple and the defendant publishers sought to eliminate price competition in the sale of e-books, consumers were forced to pay higher prices for many e-book titles." Apple appealed the decision to the U.S. Supreme Court.

The lawsuit the Justice Department brought against Apple is an example of attempts by the government to keep firms from artificially restricting competition to raise prices. As we have seen, higher prices reduce consumer surplus and economic efficiency.

Sources: Larry Neumeister, "US Court Agrees Apple Violated Antitrust Law in e-Book Entry," Associated Press, June 30, 2015; Chad Bray, "Apple's e-Book Damages Trial Set to Begin in May," *Wall Street Journal*, August 15, 2013; Bob Van Voris, "Apple Awaits e-Book Decision with State, Private Suits in Wings," *Bloomberg BusinessWeek*, June 22, 2013; Joe Palazzolo and Chad Bray, "Apple's Civil Antitrust Trial: The Highlights," *Wall Street Journal*, June 20, 2013; and Julie Bosman, "Publishers Tell of Disputes with Apple on e-Book Prices," *New York Times*, June 5, 2013.

MyEconLab Study Plan

Your Turn: Test your understanding by doing related problems 5.6 and 5.7 on page 528 at the end of this chapter.

Mergers: The Trade-off between Market Power and Efficiency

The federal government regulates business mergers because if firms gain market power by merging, they may use that market power to raise prices and reduce output. As a result, the government is most concerned with **horizontal mergers**, or mergers between firms in the same industry. Two airlines or two candy manufacturers merging are examples of a horizontal merger. Horizontal mergers are more likely to increase market power than **vertical mergers**, which are mergers between firms at different stages of the production of a good. An example of a vertical merger would be a merger between a company making soft drinks and a company making plastic bottles.

Horizontal merger A merger between firms in the same industry.

Vertical merger A merger between firms at different stages of production of a good.

Federal regulators deal with two factors that can complicate evaluating horizontal mergers:

1. **The extent of the market.** The "market" that firms are in is not always clear. For example, if Hershey Foods wants to merge with Mars, Inc., maker of M&Ms, Snickers, and other candies, what is the relevant market?
   - If the government looks just at the candy market, the newly merged company would have more than 70 percent of the market, a level at which the government would likely oppose the merger.
   - If the government looks at the broader market for snacks, Hershey and Mars compete with makers of potato chips, pretzels, and peanuts—and perhaps even producers of fresh fruit. With this broader definition of the market, the market shares of Hershey and Mars would likely be too low for federal regulators to oppose their merger.
   - If the government looked at the very broad market for food, then both Hershey and Mars have very small market shares, and there would be no reason for federal regulators to oppose their merger.

   In practice, the government defines the relevant market on the basis of whether there are close substitutes for the products being made by the merging firms. In this case, potato chips and the other snack foods mentioned are not close substitutes for candy. So, the government would consider the candy market to be the relevant market and would oppose the merger, on the grounds that the new firm would have too much market power.

2. **Possible increases in economic efficiency.** The second factor that complicates merger policy is the possibility that the newly merged firm might be more efficient than the merging firms were individually. For example, one firm might have an excellent product but a poor distribution system for getting the product into the hands of consumers. A competing firm might have built a great distribution system but have an inferior product. Allowing these firms to merge might be good for both the firms and consumers. Or, two competing firms might each have an extensive system of warehouses that are only half full, but if the firms merged, they could consolidate their warehouses and significantly reduce their average costs.

Most of the mergers that come under the scrutiny of the Department of Justice and the FTC are between large firms. For simplicity, though, let's consider a case in which all the firms in a perfectly competitive industry want to merge to form a monopoly. As we saw in Figure 15.5 on page 512, as a result of this merger, prices will rise and output will fall, leading to a decline in consumer surplus and economic efficiency. But what if the larger, newly merged firm actually is more efficient than the smaller firms were? Figure 15.6 shows a possible result.

If the merger doesn't affect costs, we have the same result as in Figure 15.5: Price rises from P_C to P_M, quantity falls from Q_C to Q_M, consumer surplus declines, and there is a loss of economic efficiency. If the monopoly has lower costs than the competitive firms, it is possible for price to decline and quantity to increase. In Figure 15.6, note that after the merger *MR* crosses *MC* at the new profit-maximizing quantity, Q_{Merge}. The demand curve shows that the monopolist can sell this quantity of the good at a price of P_{Merge}. Therefore, the price declines after the merger from P_C to P_{Merge}, and the quantity

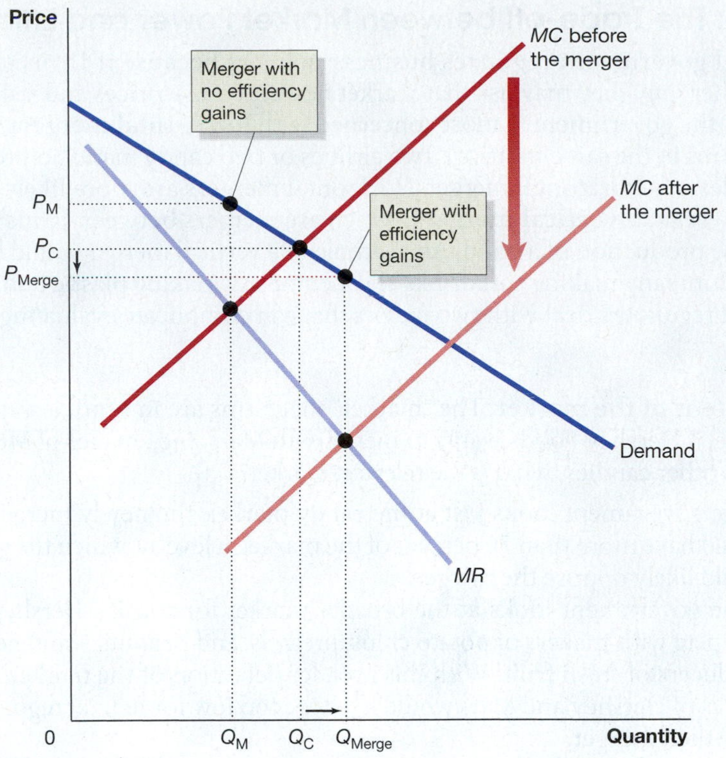

MyEconLab Animation

Figure 15.6 A Merger That Makes Consumers Better Off

This figure shows the result of all the firms in a perfectly competitive industry merging to form a monopoly. If the merger does not affect costs, the result is the same as in Figure 15.5 on page 512: Price rises from P_C to P_M, quantity falls from Q_C to Q_M, consumer surplus declines, and a loss of economic efficiency results. If, however, the monopoly has lower costs than the perfectly competitive firms, as shown by the marginal cost curve shifting to *MC* after the merger, it is possible that the price of the good will actually decline from P_C to P_{Merge} and that output will increase from Q_C to Q_{Merge} following the merger.

increases from Q_C to Q_{Merge}. We have the following seemingly paradoxical result: *The newly merged firm has a great deal of market power, but consumers are better off and economic efficiency is increased because the firm is more efficient.* Of course, sometimes a merged firm will be more efficient and have lower costs, and other times it won't. Even if a merged firm is more efficient and has lower costs, the lower costs may not offset the increased market power of the firm enough to increase consumer surplus and economic efficiency.

As you might expect, whenever large firms propose a merger, they claim that the newly merged firm will be more efficient and have lower costs. They realize that without these claims, the Department of Justice and the FTC, along with the court system, are unlikely to approve the merger. MyEconLab Concept Check

The Department of Justice and FTC Merger Guidelines

For many years after the passage of the Sherman Act in 1890, lawyers from the Department of Justice enforced the antitrust laws. The lawyers rarely considered economic arguments, such as the possibility that consumers might be made better off by a merger if economic efficiency were significantly improved. This situation began to change in 1965, when Donald Turner became the first Ph.D. economist to head the Antitrust Division of the Department of Justice. Under Turner and his successors, economic analysis shaped antitrust policy. In 1973, the Economics Section of the Antitrust Division was established and staffed with economists who evaluate the economic consequences of proposed mergers.

Economists played a major role in the development of merger guidelines by the Department of Justice and the FTC in 1982. The guidelines made it easier for firms considering a merger to understand whether the government was likely to allow the merger or to oppose it. The guidelines were modified in 2010 and have three main parts:

1. Market definition
2. Measure of concentration
3. Merger standards

Market Definition A market consists of all firms making products that consumers view as close substitutes. Economists can identify close substitutes by looking at the effect of a price increase. If the definition of a market is too narrow, a price increase will cause firms to experience a significant decline in sales—and profits—as consumers switch to buying close substitutes.

Identifying the relevant market involved in a proposed merger begins with a narrow definition of the industry. For a hypothetical merger of Hershey Foods and Mars, Inc., economists might start with the candy industry. If all firms in the candy industry increased price by 5 percent, would their profits increase or decrease? If profits would increase, the market is defined as being just these firms. If profits would decrease, economists would try a broader definition—say, by adding in potato chips and other snacks. Would a price increase of 5 percent by all firms in the broader market raise profits? If profits increase, the relevant market has been identified. If profits decrease, economists consider a broader definition. Economists continue the process until a market has been identified.

Measure of Concentration A market is *concentrated* if a relatively small number of firms have a large share of total sales in the market. A merger between firms in a market that is already highly concentrated is very likely to increase market power. A merger between firms in an industry that has a very low concentration is unlikely to increase market power and can be ignored. The guidelines use the *Herfindahl-Hirschman Index (HHI)* of concentration, which squares the market shares of each firm in the industry and adds up the values of the squares. The following are some examples of calculating HHI:

- 1 firm, with 100 percent market share (a monopoly):

$$\text{HHI} = 100^2 = 10{,}000.$$

- 2 firms, each with a 50 percent market share:

$$\text{HHI} = 50^2 + 50^2 = 5{,}000.$$

- 4 firms, with market shares of 30 percent, 30 percent, 20 percent, and 20 percent:

$$\text{HHI} = 30^2 + 30^2 + 20^2 + 20^2 = 2{,}600.$$

- 10 firms, each with a 10 percent market share:

$$\text{HHI} = 10 \times (10)^2 = 1{,}000.$$

Merger Standards Table 15.2 shows how the Department of Justice and the FTC use the HHI calculation for a market to evaluate proposed horizontal mergers according to these standards.

The merger guidelines state that increases in economic efficiency will be taken into account and can lead to approval of a merger that otherwise would be opposed, but the burden of showing that the efficiencies exist lies with the merging firms:

> The merging firms must substantiate efficiency claims so that the [Department of Justice and the FTC] can verify by reasonable means the likelihood and magnitude of each asserted efficiency. . . . Efficiency claims will not be considered if they are vague or speculative or otherwise cannot be verified by reasonable means.

MyEconLab Concept Check

Table 15.2

Federal Government Standards for Horizontal Mergers

Value of the Herfindahl-Hirschman Index (HHI) of a Market after a Merger	Amount by Which the Merger Increases the HHI	Antitrust Action by Federal Regulators
Less than 1,500	Increase doesn't matter	Merger will be allowed.
Between 1,500 and 2,500	Fewer than 100 points	Merger is unlikely to be challenged.
Between 1,500 and 2,500	More than 100 points	Merger may be challenged.
Greater than 2,500	Fewer than 100 points	Merger is unlikely to be challenged.
Greater than 2,500	Between 100 and 200 points	Merger may be challenged.
Greater than 2,500	More than 200 points	Merger is likely to be challenged.

Regulating Natural Monopolies

If a firm is a natural monopoly, competition from other firms will not play its usual role of forcing price down to the level where the company earns zero economic profit. As a result, local or state *regulatory commissions* usually set the prices for natural monopolies, such as firms selling natural gas or electricity. What price should these commissions set? Economic efficiency requires the last unit of a good or service produced to provide an additional benefit to consumers equal to the additional cost of producing it (see Chapter 11). We can measure the additional benefit consumers receive from the last unit by the price of the product, and we can measure the additional cost to the monopoly of producing the last unit by marginal cost. Therefore, to achieve economic efficiency, regulators should require that the monopoly charge a price equal to its marginal cost. There is, however, an important drawback to doing so, as illustrated in Figure 15.7, which shows the situation of a typical regulated natural monopoly.

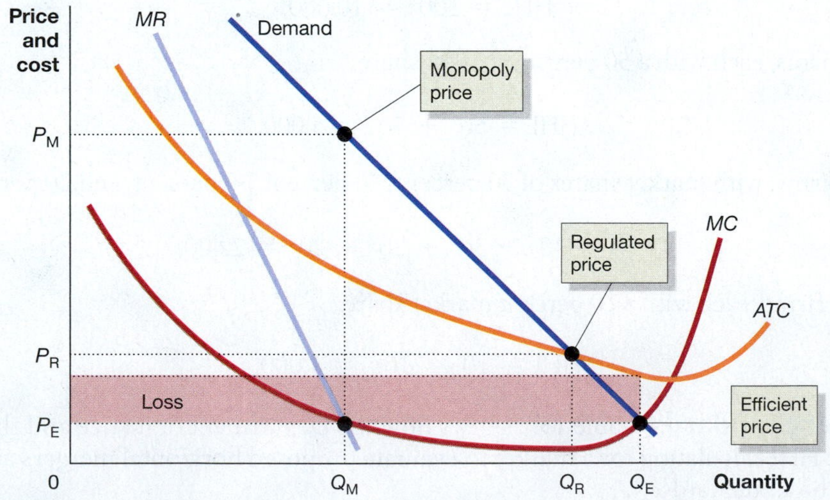

MyEconLab Animation

Figure 15.7 Regulating a Natural Monopoly

A natural monopoly that is not subject to government regulation will charge a price equal to P_M and produce Q_M. If government regulators want to achieve economic efficiency, they will set the regulated price equal to P_E, and the monopoly will produce Q_E. Unfortunately, P_E is below average total cost, and the monopoly will suffer a loss, shown by the red rectangle. Because the monopoly will not continue to produce in the long run if it suffers a loss, government regulators set a price equal to average total cost, which is P_R in the figure. The resulting production, Q_R, will be below the efficient level.

Remember that with a natural monopoly, the average total cost curve is still falling when it crosses the demand curve. If unregulated, the monopoly will charge a price equal to P_M and produce Q_M. To achieve economic efficiency, regulators should require the monopoly to charge a price equal to P_E. The monopoly will then produce Q_E. But here is the drawback: P_E is less than average total cost, so the monopoly will be suffering a loss, shown by the area of the red-shaded rectangle. In the long run, the owners of the monopoly will not continue in business if they are experiencing a loss. Realizing this, most regulators will set the regulated price, P_R, equal to the level of average total cost at which the demand curve intersects the *ATC* curve. At that price, the owners of the monopoly are able to break even on their investment by producing the quantity Q_R, although this quantity is below the efficient quantity, Q_E. MyEconLab Concept Check MyEconLab Study Plan

Solved Problem 15.5

MyEconLab Interactive Animation

What Should Your College Charge for a MOOC?

In Chapter 11, we observed that some colleges offer massive open online courses (MOOCs). We saw that the fixed cost of an online course is relatively high because instructors must develop new syllabi, exams, and teaching notes, as well as determine when and how to interact with their students. But after the course is placed online, the marginal cost of providing instruction to an additional student is low and will be constant rather than U shaped. Suppose that your college decides to offer a calculus course as a MOOC that can be taken by students anywhere in the world, whether they are actually enrolled in your college or not. The figure shows the demand and cost situation for the MOOC:

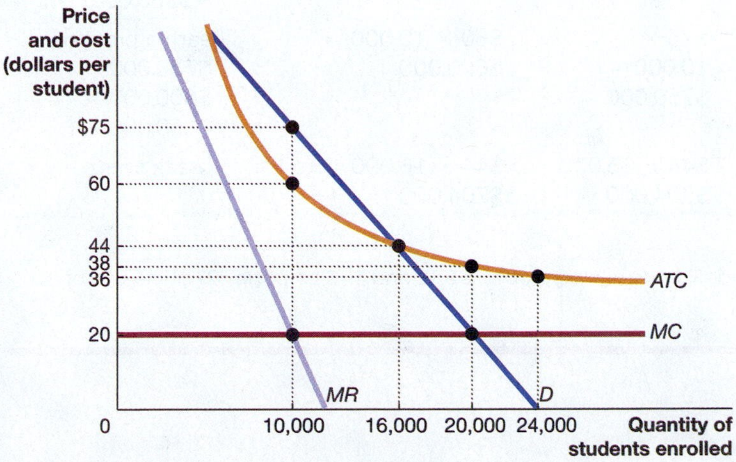

a. The faculty member who designed the course argues: "I think the course should be priced so that the maximum number of students enroll." Which price should this faculty member favor? Briefly explain.

b. An economics professor argues: "I think the course should be priced so as to achieve economic efficiency." Which price should this faculty member favor? Briefly explain.

c. The dean of the college argues: "I think the course should be priced to maximize the profit the college earns, so these funds can be used to pay some other expenses." Which price should the dean favor? Briefly explain.

d. You are a member of a student committee that is asked to recommend a price for the course and you argue: "I think the college should charge a price so that it just breaks even on the course." What price should you recommend? Briefly explain.

e. How much profit (or loss) will the college make on the course if it charges each of the prices you found in your answers to parts (a), (b), (c), and (d)?

Solving the Problem

Step 1: Review the chapter material. This problem is related to the discussion of pricing in a situation of natural monopoly, so you may want to review the section "Regulating Natural Monopolies," which begins on page 520.

Step 2: Begin your answer by noting that the situation in the figure is similar to the situation of a natural monopoly, as shown in Figure 15.7. Because the graph shows the average total cost curve for the MOOC as still falling when it crosses the demand curve, effectively this MOOC is a natural monopoly, and we can employ the analysis of prices shown in Figure 15.7 to answer the questions.

Step 3: Answer part (a) by explaining which price will maximize the number of students enrolling in the course. The graph shows that the maximum number of students to take the course will occur when the price equals 0 and the demand curve intersects the quantity axis.

Step 4: Answer part (b) by explaining which price will result in economic efficiency. Economic efficiency occurs where price equals marginal cost. In the graph, the price should be set at $20 to achieve economic efficiency.

Step 5: Answer part (c) by explaining which price will maximize the profit the college will earn from the course. To maximize profit, the college should charge a price that results in a quantity demanded at which marginal revenue equals marginal cost. In the graph, the price that maximizes profit equals $75.

Step 6: Answer part (d) by explaining which price will result in the college just breaking even on the course. To break even, the college should charge a price equal to average total cost. In the graph, at a price of $44, price is equal to average total cost, and the college just breaks even on the course.

Step 7: Answer part (e) by calculating the profit (or loss) the college will make if it charges each of the prices you found in the earlier parts of the problem. The following table shows the calculation of profit (or loss) for each price.

If the college charges this price . . .	it will earn revenue of . . .	and have a total cost equal to . . .	So, the college will . . .
0	0	the average total cost of $36 per student multiplied by the 24,000 students who enroll, or $36 × 24,000 = $864,000.	suffer a loss of 0 − $864,000 = −$864,000.
$20	$20 × 20,000 = $400,000	$38 × 20,000 = $760,000.	suffer a loss of $400,000 − $760,000 = −$360,000.
$75	$75 × 10,000 = $750,000	$60 × 10,000 = $600,000.	earn a profit of $750,000 − $600,000 = $150,000.
$44	$44 × 16,000 = $704,000	$44 × 16,000 = $704,000.	break even.

MyEconLab Study Plan

Your Turn: For more practice, do related problems 5.12 and 5.13 on page 529 at the end of this chapter.

Continued from page 499

Economics in Your Life

Can a Business Run from of Your Dorm Be a Monopoly?

At the beginning of the chapter, we asked whether the submarine sandwich business you and your roommate, Fatma, start in your dorm was a monopoly and whether you should charge high prices for the subs to increase your profit. In this chapter, we have seen that a monopoly is a firm that is the only seller of a good or service that does not have a close substitute. Even though you and Fatma would be the only sellers of submarine sandwiches on campus during the evening hours of Saturdays and Sundays, there could be other options for hungry students. For example, students could buy food from nearby off-campus restaurants, have food delivered from those restaurants, or buy from on-campus vendors that are open earlier in the day. Most goods have substitutes, and you and Fatma should realize that for many students, pizza and hamburgers from local restaurants are good substitutes for subs. High prices are likely to lead many of your customers to search for those substitutes.

Conclusion

The more intense the level of competition among firms, the better a market works. In this chapter, we have seen that, compared with perfect competition, in a monopoly, the price of a good or service is higher, output is lower, and consumer surplus and economic efficiency are reduced. Fortunately, true monopolies are rare. Even though most firms resemble monopolies in being able to charge a price above marginal cost, most markets have enough competition to keep the efficiency losses from market power low.

Visit MyEconLab for a news article and analysis related to the concepts in this chapter.

CHAPTER SUMMARY AND PROBLEMS

Key Terms

Antitrust laws, p. 515	Horizontal merger, p. 517	Natural monopoly, p. 506	Public franchise, p. 504
Collusion, p. 514	Market power, p. 513	Network externalities, p. 505	Vertical merger, p. 517
Copyright, p. 504	Monopoly, p. 500	Patent, p. 502	

15.1 Is Any Firm Ever Really a Monopoly? pages 500–502

LEARNING OBJECTIVE: Define monopoly.

Summary

A **monopoly** exists only in the rare situation in which a firm is producing a good or service for which there are no close substitutes. A narrow definition of monopoly that some economists use is that a firm has a monopoly if it can ignore the actions of all other firms. Many economists favor this broader definition of monopoly: A firm has a monopoly if no other firms are selling a substitute close enough that the firm's economic profit is competed away in the long run.

MyEconLab Visit **www.myeconlab.com** to complete these exercises online and get instant feedback.

Review Questions

1.1 What is a monopoly? Can a firm be a monopoly if close substitutes for its product exist?

1.2 If you own the only hardware store in a small town, do you have a monopoly?

Problems and Applications

1.3 The great baseball player Ty Cobb had a reputation for being very thrifty. Near the end of his life, he was interviewed by a reporter who was surprised to find that Cobb used candles, rather than electricity, to light his home. From Ty Cobb's point of view, was the local electric company a monopoly?

1.4 In a column in the *Wall Street Journal*, venture capitalist Peter Thiel described the difference between monopoly businesses and competitive ones: "Suppose you want to start a restaurant in Palo Alto that serves British food. 'No one else is doing it,' you might reason. 'We'll own the entire market." Would the only restaurant that sells British food in Palo Alto, or any other city, be considered a monopoly? What criteria would you use to determine whether the restaurant is a monopoly?

Source: Peter Thiel, "Competition Is for Losers," *Wall Street Journal*, September 12, 2014.

1.5 Harvard Business School started using case studies—descriptions of strategic problems encountered at real companies—in courses in 1912. Today, Harvard Business Publishing (HBP) sells its case studies to about 4,000 colleges worldwide. HBP is the sole publisher of Harvard Business School's case studies. What criteria would you use to determine whether HBP has a monopoly on the sale of business case studies to be used in college courses?

1.6 **(Related to the Making the Connection on page 500)** In discussing the NCAA, the late Nobel Laureate Gary Becker, an economist, wrote, "It is impossible for an outsider to look at these [NCAA] rules without concluding that their main aim is to make the NCAA an effective cartel that severely constrains competition among schools for players."

a. What is a cartel? In what ways does the NCAA act like a cartel?

b. Who gains and who loses as a result of the NCAA acting like a cartel? If you are a student who does not play intercollegiate sports but who is enrolled at a school, such as the University of Alabama or Ohio State University, with prominent sports teams, does the NCAA acting as a cartel make you better off or worse off? Briefly explain.

Source: Gary Becker, "The NCAA as a Powerful Cartel," becker-posnerlog.com, April 4, 2011.

15.2 Where Do Monopolies Come From? pages 502–507

LEARNING OBJECTIVE: Explain the four main reasons monopolies arise.

Summary

To have a monopoly, barriers to entering the market must be so high that no other firms can enter. Barriers to entry may be high enough to keep out competing firms for four main reasons: (1) A government blocks the entry of more than one firm into a market by issuing a **patent**, which is the exclusive right to make a product for 20 years, a **copyright**, which is the exclusive right to produce and sell a creation, or a *trademark*, which grants a firm legal protection against other firms using its product's name, or by giving a firm a **public franchise**, which is the right to be the only legal provider of a good or service; (2) one firm has control of a key raw material necessary to produce a good; (3) there are important *network externalities* in supplying the good or service; or

(4) economies of scale are so large that one firm has a *natural monopoly*. **Network externalities** refer to a characteristic of a product where its usefulness increases with the number of consumers who use it. A **natural monopoly** is a situation in which economies of scale are so large that one firm can supply the entire market at a lower average cost than can two or more firms.

MyEconLab Visit **www.myeconlab.com** to complete these exercises online and get instant feedback.

Review Questions

2.1 What are the four most important ways a firm becomes a monopoly?

2.2 If patents, copyrights, and trademarks reduce competition, why does the federal government grant them?

2.3 What is a public franchise? Are all public franchises natural monopolies?

2.4 What is "natural" about a natural monopoly?

Problems and Applications

2.5 The U.S. Postal Service (USPS) is a monopoly because the federal government has blocked entry into the market for delivering first-class mail. Is the USPS also a natural monopoly? How can we tell? What would happen if the law preventing competition in this market were removed?

2.6 Patents are granted for 20 years, but pharmaceutical companies can't use their patent-guaranteed monopoly powers for anywhere near this long because it takes several years to acquire approval of drugs from the Food and Drug Administration (FDA). Should the life of drug patents be extended to 20 years *after* FDA approval? What would be the costs and benefits of such an extension?

2.7 If firms incurred no cost in developing new technologies and new products, would there be any need for patents? Briefly explain.

2.8 The German company Koenig & Bauer has 90 percent of the world market for presses that print currency. Discuss the factors that would make it difficult for new companies to enter this market.

2.9 **(Related to the Making the Connection on page 503)** Why should it matter legally whether Professor Anspach is correct that Hasbro's Monopoly game closely resembles a game that had been played for decades before Charles Darrow claimed to have invented it? Does it matter economically? Briefly explain.

2.10 **(Related to the Making the Connection on page 504)** Why was De Beers worried that people might resell their old diamonds? How did De Beers attempt to convince consumers that previously owned diamonds were not good substitutes for new diamonds? How did De Beers's strategy affect the demand curve for new diamonds? How did De Beers's strategy affect its profit?

2.11 In a magazine article, a writer explained that the provision of electric power in the United States consists of two processes: the generation of electricity and the distribution of electricity. The writer argued that "power distribution is a natural monopoly.... But ... there's ... no reason why the people who generate the electricity ... should be the same people who own the power lines."

a. Why would the distribution of electric power be a natural monopoly?

b. Why would the generation of electric power *not* be a natural monopoly?

Source: Tim Worstall, "Which Should We Have: Public Utilities or Regulated Private Monopolies?" *Forbes*, March 24, 2013.

2.12 In China, the government owns many more firms than in the United States. A former Chinese government official argued that a number of government-run industries such as oil refining were natural monopolies. Is it likely that oil refining is a natural monopoly? How would you be able to tell?

Source: Shen Hong, "Former State Assets Regulator: SOE Monopolies 'Natural'," *Wall Street Journal*, January 4, 2012.

2.13 Suppose that the quantity demanded per day for a product is 90 when the price is $35. The following table shows costs for a firm with a monopoly in this market:

Quantity (per day)	Total Cost
30	$1,200
40	1,400
50	2,250
60	3,000

Briefly explain whether this firm has a natural monopoly.

2.14 As noted in this chapter, many generic versions of the diabetes drug Glucophage were introduced within the first year of Glucophage's patent expiration. The U.S. Supreme Court has ruled that patients who become ill taking generic drugs cannot sue the manufacturer of those drugs, even though "people who are hurt by a brand-name drug can sue the drug maker for damages." How might the Supreme Court's decision affect the willingness of pharmaceutical firms to invest in research and development on new drugs?

Source: David G. Savage, "Supreme Court Rules Drug Makers Can't Be Sued over Defects," *Los Angeles Times*, June 25, 2013.

15.3 How Does a Monopoly Choose Price and Output? pages 507–511

LEARNING OBJECTIVE: Explain how a monopoly chooses price and output.

Summary

Monopolists face downward-sloping demand and marginal revenue curves and, like all other firms, maximize profit by producing where marginal revenue equals marginal cost. Unlike a perfect competitor, a monopolist that earns an economic profit does not face the entry of new firms into the market. Therefore, a monopolist can earn an economic profit even in the long run.

MyEconLab Visit **www.myeconlab.com** to complete these exercises online and get instant feedback.

Review Questions

3.1 What is the relationship between a monopolist's demand curve and the market demand curve? What is the relationship between a monopolist's demand curve and its marginal revenue curve?

3.2 In what sense is a monopolist a *price maker*? Will charging the highest possible price always maximize a monopolist's profit? Briefly explain.

3.3 Draw a graph that shows a monopolist earning a profit. Be sure your graph includes the monopolist's demand, marginal revenue, average total cost, and marginal cost curves. Be sure to indicate the profit-maximizing level of output and price.

Problems and Applications

3.4 **(Related to Solved Problem 15.3 on page 510)** Ed Scahill has acquired a monopoly on the production of baseballs (don't ask how) and faces the demand and cost situation shown in the following table.

Price	Quantity (per week)	Total Revenue	Marginal Revenue	Total Cost	Marginal Cost
$20	15,000			$330,000	
19	20,000			365,000	
18	25,000			405,000	
17	30,000			450,000	
16	35,000			500,000	
15	40,000			555,000	

a. Fill in the remaining values in the table.

b. If Ed wants to maximize profit, what price should he charge, and how many baseballs should he sell? How much profit (or loss) will he make? Draw a graph to illustrate your answer. Your graph should be clearly labeled and should include Ed's demand, *ATC*, *AVC*, *AFC*, *MC*, and *MR* curves, the price he is charging, the quantity he is producing, and the area representing his profit (or loss).

c. Suppose the government imposes a tax of $50,000 per week on baseball production. Now what price should Ed charge, how many baseballs should he sell, and what will his profit (or loss) be?

d. Suppose that the government raises the tax in part (c) to $70,000. Now what price should Ed charge, how many baseballs should he sell, and what will his profit (or loss) be? Will his decision on what price to charge and how much to produce be different in the short run than in the long run? Briefly explain.

3.5 **(Related to Solved Problem 15.3 on page 510)** Use the information in Solved Problem 15.3 to answer the following questions.

a. What will Comcast do if the tax is $36.00 per month instead of $25.00? (*Hint:* Will its decision be different in the long run than in the short run?)

b. Suppose that the flat per-month tax is replaced with a tax on the firm of $25.00 per cable subscriber. Now how many subscriptions should Comcast sell if it wants to maximize profit? What price should it charge? What is its profit? (Assume that Comcast will sell only the quantities listed in the table.)

3.6 Before inexpensive pocket calculators were developed, many science and engineering students used slide rules to make numerical calculations. Slide rules are no longer produced, which means nothing prevents you from establishing a monopoly in the slide rule market. Draw a graph showing the situation your slide rule firm would be in. Be sure to include on your graph your demand, marginal revenue, average total cost, and marginal cost curves. Indicate the price you would charge and the quantity you would produce. Are you likely to make a profit or a loss? Show this area on your graph.

3.7 Does a monopolist have a supply curve? Briefly explain. (Hint: Look again at the definition of a supply curve in Chapter 3 on page 83 and consider whether this definition applies to a monopolist.)

3.8 **(Related to the Don't Let This Happen to You on page 511)** A student argues: "If a monopolist finds a way of producing a good at lower cost, he will not lower his price. Because he is a monopolist, he will keep the price and the quantity the same and just increase his profit." Do you agree? Use a graph to illustrate your answer.

3.9 When homebuilders construct a new housing development, they usually sell to a single cable television company the rights to lay cable. As a result, anyone buying a home in that development is not able to choose between competing cable companies. Some cities have begun to ban such exclusive agreements. Williams Township, Pennsylvania, decided to allow any cable company to lay cable in the utility trenches of new housing developments. The head of the township board of supervisors argued: "What I would like to see and do is give the consumers a choice. If there's no choice, then the price [of cable] is at the whim of the provider." In a situation in which the consumers in a housing development have only one cable company available, is the price really at the whim of the company? Would a company in this situation be likely to charge, say, $500 per month for basic cable services? Briefly explain.

Source: Sam Kennedy, "Williams Township May Ban Exclusive Cable Provider Pacts," (Allentown, PA) *Morning Call*, November 5, 2004.

3.10 Will a monopoly that maximizes profit also be maximizing revenue? Will it be maximizing output? Briefly explain.

15.4 Does Monopoly Reduce Economic Efficiency? pages 511–514

LEARNING OBJECTIVE: Use a graph to illustrate how a monopoly affects economic efficiency.

Summary

Compared with a perfectly competitive industry, a monopoly charges a higher price and produces a smaller quantity, which reduces consumer surplus and economic efficiency. Some loss of economic efficiency will occur whenever firms have **market power** and can charge a price greater than marginal cost. The total loss of economic efficiency in the U.S. economy due to market power is small, however, because true monopolies are very rare. In most industries, competition will keep price much closer to marginal cost than would be the case in a monopoly.

MyEconLab Visit **www.myeconlab.com** to complete these exercises online and get instant feedback.

Review Questions

4.1 Suppose that a perfectly competitive industry becomes a monopoly. Describe the effects of this change on consumer surplus, producer surplus, and deadweight loss.

4.2 Explain why market power leads to a deadweight loss. Is the total deadweight loss from market power for the economy large or small?

Problems and Applications

4.3 Review Figure 15.5 on page 512 on the inefficiency of monopoly. Will the deadweight loss due to monopoly be larger if the demand is elastic or if it is inelastic? Briefly explain.

4.4 Economist Harvey Leibenstein argued that the loss of economic efficiency in industries that are not perfectly competitive has been understated. He argued that when competition is weak, firms are under less pressure to adopt the best techniques or to hold down their costs. He referred to this effect as "x-inefficiency." If x-inefficiency causes a firm's marginal costs to rise, use a graph to show that the deadweight loss in Figure 15.5 understates the true deadweight loss caused by a monopoly.

4.5 Most cities own the water system that provides water to homes and businesses. Some cities charge a flat monthly fee, while other cities charge by the gallon. Which method of pricing is more likely to result in economic efficiency in the water market? Be sure to refer to the definition of *economic efficiency* in your answer. Why do you think the same method of pricing isn't used by all cities?

4.6 Review the concept of externalities from Chapter 5, page 148. If a market is a monopoly, will a negative externality in production always lead to production beyond the level of economic efficiency? Use a graph to illustrate your answer.

4.7 **(Related to the Chapter Opener on page 499)** Suppose a second seafood restaurant opens in Stonington, Maine. Will consumer surplus and economic efficiency necessarily increase? Briefly explain.

4.8 Suppose that the city has given Jorge a monopoly selling baseball caps at the local minor league stadium. Use the following graph to answer the questions.

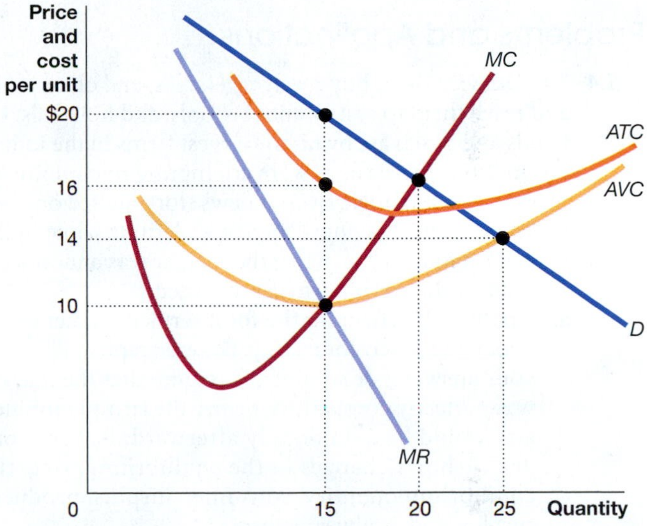

a. What quantity will Jorge produce, and what price will he charge?

b. How much profit will Jorge earn?

c. Review the definition of allocatively efficiency. If Jorge produced at the allocatively efficient level of output, what quantity would he produce?

d. How much deadweight loss does Jorge create by acting like a monopolist rather than a perfect competitor? (Assume that the marginal cost curve is linear—a straight line—between the two relevant points.)

15.5 Government Policy toward Monopoly, pages 514–522

LEARNING OBJECTIVE: Discuss government policies toward monopoly.

Summary

Because monopolies reduce consumer surplus and economic efficiency, governments often regulate them. Firms that are not monopolies have an incentive to avoid competition by **colluding**, or agreeing to charge the same price or otherwise not to compete. In the United States, **antitrust laws** are aimed at deterring monopoly, eliminating collusion, and promoting competition among firms. The Antitrust Division of the U.S. Department of Justice and the Federal Trade Commission share responsibility for enforcing the antitrust laws, including regulating mergers between firms. A **horizontal merger** is a merger between firms in the same industry. A **vertical merger** is a merger between firms at different stages of production of a good. Local governments often regulate the prices charged by natural monopolies.

MyEconLab Visit **www.myeconlab.com** to complete these exercises online and get instant feedback.

Review Questions

5.1 What is the purpose of the antitrust laws? Who is in charge of enforcing these laws?

5.2 What is the difference between a horizontal merger and a vertical merger? Which type of merger is more likely to increase the market power of a newly merged firm?

5.3 Why would it be economically efficient to require a natural monopoly to charge a price equal to marginal cost? Why do most regulatory agencies require natural monopolies to charge a price equal to average cost instead?

Problems and Applications

5.4 Food service firms buy meat, vegetables, and other foods and resell them to restaurants, schools, and hospitals. US Foods and Sysco are by far the largest firms in the industry. In 2015, these firms were attempting to combine or merge to form a single firm. A news story quoted one restaurant owner as saying: "There was definite panic in the restaurant industry ... when the merger was announced. They know they're going to get squeezed."

a. Analyze the effect on the food service market of US Foods and Sysco combining. Draw a graph to illustrate your answer. For simplicity, assume that the market was perfectly competitive before the firms combined and would be a monopoly afterward. Be sure your graph shows changes in the equilibrium price, the equilibrium quantity, consumer surplus, producer surplus, and deadweight loss.

b. Why would restaurant owners believe they would be "squeezed" by this development?

Sources: Tess Stynes, "Sysco Extends Merger Pact with U.S. Foods to May," *Wall Street Journal*, March 9, 2015; and Annie Gasparro and Jesse Newman, "Restaurants Fear Clout of a New Food Giant," *Wall Street Journal*, January 6, 2014.

5.5 Between them, Zillow and Trulia have a very large share of the market for online real estate listings. Real estate brokers who want to advertise their services next to online listings of houses for sale have few other choices. Zillow and Trulia have considered merging. The two firms argue that real estate agents have many ways to advertise their services beyond online listings, including mailing out advertising or placing ads in local newspapers. The CEO of Zillow was quoted in an article in the *Wall Street Journal* as arguing that the advertising market is "incredibly fragmented." He also said that "agents have a lot of choice in terms of where to advertise listings."

a. Wouldn't you expect the CEO of Zillow to emphasize the effectiveness of advertising on his site as opposed to other ways of advertising? Why, then, would he publicly argue that real estate agents have many other ways of advertising?

b. How would federal regulators go about evaluating a merger between Zillow and Trulia?

Source: Brent Kendall and Joe Light, "Review of Zillow–Trulia Merger Hinges on Advertising," *Wall Street Journal*, September 8, 2014.

5.6 **(Related to the Making the Connection on page 515)** Writer Mathew Yglesias disagrees with critics who claim that Amazon has a monopoly in the e-book market: "Amazon doesn't have any kind of monopoly... . One important hint ... can be found in its quarterly financial reports. That's where you find out about a company's profits."

a. What conditions would be necessary for Amazon to have a monopoly in the e-book market?

b. Do you agree that if Amazon were a monopoly, we could find evidence of that in its financial reports? Briefly explain.

Source: Matthew Yglesias, "There's One Huge Problem with Calls for Anti-Trust Action Against Amazon," vox.com, October 10, 2014.

5.7 **(Related to the Making the Connection on page 515)** After a federal court judge had found Apple guilty of conspiring with book publishers to raise e-book prices, the Department of Justice recommended that the judge order Apple not to sign agency pricing model contracts with publishers for five years. The publishers objected to the recommendation, arguing that following it would "effectively punish the [publishers] by prohibiting agreements with Apple using an agency model."

a. What is an agency pricing model?

b. Why would the Department of Justice want to keep Apple from signing agency pricing model contracts with publishers? Why would the publishers want to continue signing such contracts?

Source: Chad Bray, "Publishers Object to e-Book Plan for Apple," *Wall Street Journal*, August 7, 2013.

5.8 Draw a graph like Figure 15.6 on page 518 that shows a merger lowering costs. On your graph, show producer surplus and consumer surplus before a merger and consumer surplus and producer surplus after a merger.

5.9 Look again at the section "The Department of Justice and FTC Merger Guidelines," which begins on page 518. Evaluate the following situations.

a. A market initially has 20 firms, each with a 5 percent market share. Of the firms, 4 propose to merge, leaving a total of 17 firms in the industry. Are the Department of Justice and the Federal Trade Commission likely to oppose the merger? Briefly explain.

b. A market initially has 5 firms, each with a 20 percent market share. Of the firms, 2 propose to merge, leaving a total of 4 firms in the industry. Are the Department of Justice and the Federal Trade Commission likely to oppose the merger? Briefly explain.

5.10 The following table shows the market shares during the first three months of 2015 for companies in the U.S. personal computer (PC) market, which includes desk-based

PCs and mobile PCs, such as mini-notebooks, but not tablet computers, such as iPads:

Company	Market Share
Hewlett-Packard	26%
Dell	23
Apple	12
Lenovo	12
ASUS	7
Others	20

Use the information in the section "The Department of Justice and FTC Merger Guidelines," which begins on page 518, to predict whether the Department of Justice and the Federal Trade Commission would be likely to oppose a merger between any of the five firms listed in the table. Assume that "Others" in the table consists of four firms, each of which has a 5 percent share of the market.

Source: Juli Clover, "Apple Continues Seeing Steady Mac Sales Growth Even as U.S. PC Shipments Decline," www.macrumors.com, April 9, 2015.

5.11 Consider the natural monopoly shown in Figure 15.7 on page 520. Assume that the government regulatory agency sets the regulated price, P_R, at the level of average total cost at which the demand curve intersects the *ATC* curve. If the firm knows that it will always be able to charge a price equal to its average total cost, does it have an incentive to reduce its average cost? Briefly explain.

5.12 **(Related to Solved Problem 15.5 on page 521)** Use the following graph of a monopoly to answer the questions.

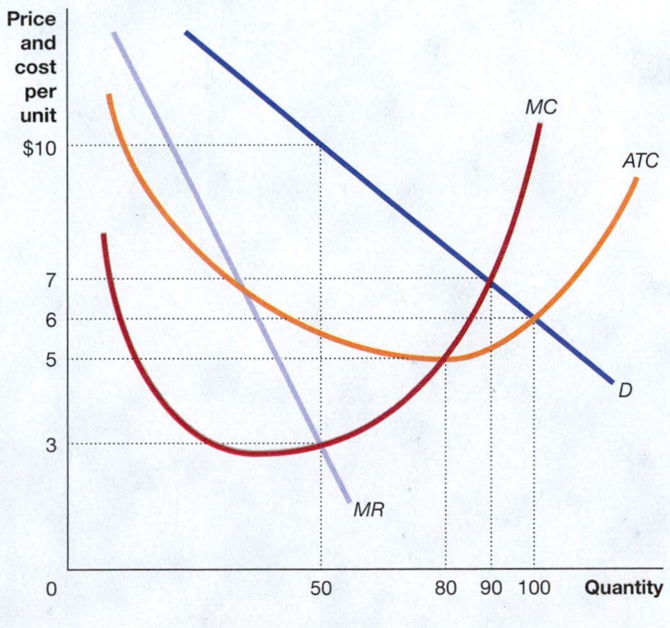

a. What quantity will the monopoly produce, and what price will the monopoly charge?
b. Suppose the monopoly is regulated. If the regulatory agency wants to achieve economic efficiency, what price should it require the monopoly to charge? How much output will the monopoly produce at this price? Will the monopoly make a profit if it charges this price? Briefly explain.

5.13 **(Related to Solved Problem 15.5 on page 521)** Use the following graph of a monopoly to answer the questions.

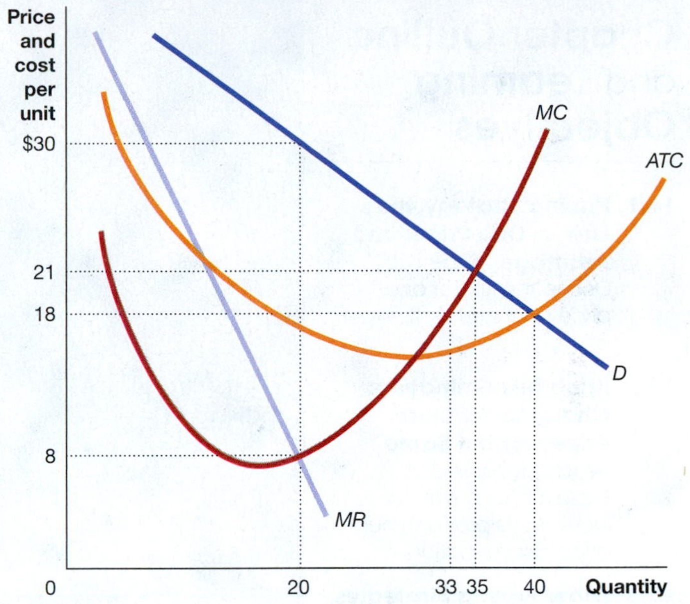

a. What quantity will the monopoly produce, and what price will the monopoly charge?
b. Suppose the government decides to regulate this monopoly and imposes a price ceiling of $18 (in other words, the monopoly can charge less than $18 but can't charge more). Now what quantity will the monopoly produce, and what price will the monopoly charge? Will every consumer who is willing to pay this price be able to buy the product? Briefly explain.

CHAPTER

16

Pricing Strategy

Chapter Outline and Learning Objectives

Walt Disney Discovers the Magic of Big Data

If you manage a business, what price should you charge for your product? As we have seen in earlier chapters, the answer seems straightforward: Charge a price that results in your selling the quantity where marginal revenue equals marginal cost. For many businesses, though, the answer is not so straightforward. Firms often face complicated pricing problems. For example, many firms charge customers different prices, based on differences in their willingness to pay for the product. The Walt Disney Company charges different prices for entry into its Magic Kingdom park in Florida, depending on your age, home address, and occupation. Children, Florida residents, and members of the military pay lower prices than do people who do not fall into those categories. How does Disney determine which price to charge which group?

Disney offers a variety of products that it needs to price correctly as it tries to maximize profit. How should it price a "vacation package" that includes a stay in a Disney resort hotel, tickets to enter the park, and meals? How should it price souvenirs in the parks? Will opening the parks very early or keeping them open very late result in people paying more for tickets? The answers to these types of questions depend on consumers' preferences. In the past few years, firms have found it easier to determine consumers' preferences by using big data. The term *big data* refers to the collection and analysis of massive amounts of data, with the goal of measuring aspects of people's behavior. For example, do people who stay in the most expensive Disney World hotels stay in the parks longer than people who stay in less expensive hotels? How much do sales of souvenirs decline when Disney increases their prices? With enough data, Disney can answer these types of questions.

Since 2013, Disney has greatly increased its ability to collect data by having visitors to its parks wear MagicBands around their wrists. Visitors use the bands to enter the park, buy souvenirs, pay for meals, and enter rides. The bands have chips that automatically record data and enter them into Disney's information technology system. The bands are an example of the "Internet of Things," which refers to the network of devices directly communicating data to a computer without a person having to enter the data. The MagicBands program and associated technology have cost Disney about $1 billion to implement, which indicates the importance the company places on gathering and analyzing data on its customers' preferences.

Disney and other firms use these methods to implement *pricing strategies* to increase their profits. In this chapter, we will study some of these pricing strategies.

Sources: Shelly Palmer, "Data Mining Disney—A Magical Experience," huffingtonpost.com, May 11, 2015; Elizabeth Miller Coyne, "The Disney Take on Big Data's Value," thenewip.net, January 13, 2015; and Brooks Barnes, "At Disney Parks, a Bracelet Meant to Build Loyalty (and Sales)," *New York Times*, January 7, 2013.

Economics in Your Life

Why So Many Prices to See a Movie?

Movie theaters vary their prices based on the ticket buyer's age and the time of day. For example, as a college student you pay one price, your grandparents pay a different price, and children in your neighborhood pay yet another price. In addition, ticket prices are lower during the day than during the evening. But if you buy popcorn at the movie theater, you pay the same price as everyone else. Why do people in certain age groups get a discount on movie admission but not on popcorn? As you read this chapter, try to answer this question. You can check your answer against the one we provide on **page 548** at the end of this chapter.

In previous chapters, we saw that entrepreneurs continually seek out economic profit. Using pricing strategies is one way firms can attempt to increase their economic profit. One of these strategies, called *price discrimination*, involves firms charging different prices for the same good or service, as Disney does when setting admission prices at Walt Disney World. In this chapter, we will see how a firm can increase its profit by charging a higher price to consumers who value the good more and a lower price to consumers who value the good less.

We will also analyze the widely used strategies of *odd pricing* and *cost-plus pricing*. Finally, we will analyze situations in which firms are able to charge consumers one price for the right to buy a good and a second price for each unit of the good purchased, a strategy economists call a *two-part tariff*.

16.1 Pricing Strategy, the Law of One Price, and Arbitrage

LEARNING OBJECTIVE: Define the law of one price and explain the role of arbitrage.

We saw in the chapter opener that sometimes firms can charge different prices for the same good. In fact, many firms rely on economic analysis to practice *price discrimination* by charging higher prices to some customers and lower prices to others. Some firms, such as Disney, practice a sophisticated form of price discrimination by using big data methods to gather and analyze data on consumers' preferences and their responsiveness to changes in prices. Managers can use the information to rapidly adjust the prices of their goods and services. This practice of rapidly adjusting prices, called *yield management*, has been particularly important to airlines and hotels. There are limits, though, to the ability of firms to charge different prices for the same product. The key limit is the possibility that in some circumstances consumers who can buy a good at a low price will resell it to consumers who would otherwise have to buy at a high price.

Arbitrage

According to the *law of one price*, identical products should sell for the same price everywhere. Let's explore why the law of one price usually holds true. Suppose that an Apple iPad sells for $499 in stores in Atlanta and for $429 in stores in San Francisco. Anyone who lives in San Francisco could buy iPads for $429 and resell them for $499 in Atlanta. They could sell them on eBay or Craigslist or ship them to someone they know in Atlanta who could sell them in local flea markets. Buying a product in one market at a low price and reselling it in another market at a high price is called *arbitrage*. The profits received from engaging in arbitrage are called *arbitrage profits*.

As people take advantage of the price difference to earn arbitrage profits, the supply of iPads in Atlanta will increase, and the price of iPads in Atlanta will decline. At the same time, the supply of iPads in San Francisco will decrease, and the price of iPads in San Francisco will rise. Eventually, the arbitrage process will eliminate most, but not all, of the price difference. Some price difference will remain because sellers must pay to list iPads on eBay or to ship them to Atlanta. The costs of carrying out a transaction—by, for example, listing products on eBay and shipping them across the country—are called **transactions costs**. The law of one price holds exactly *only if transactions costs are zero*. As we will soon see, in cases in which it is impossible to resell a product, the law of one price will not hold, and firms will be able to practice price discrimination. Apart from this important qualification, we expect that arbitrage will result in a product selling for the same price everywhere.

Transactions costs The costs in time and other resources that parties incur in the process of agreeing to and carrying out an exchange of goods or services.

MyEconLab Concept Check

Solved Problem 16.1

MyEconLab Interactive Animation

Is Arbitrage Just a Rip-off?

People are often suspicious of arbitrage. Buying something at a low price and reselling it at a high price exploits the person buying at the high price—or does it? Is this view correct? If so, do the auctions on eBay serve any useful economic purpose?

Solving the Problem

Step 1: Review the chapter material. This problem is about arbitrage, so you may want to review the section "Arbitrage," on page 532. If necessary, also review the discussion of the benefits from trade in earlier chapters (see Chapters 2 and 9).

Step 2: Use the discussion of arbitrage and the discussion in earlier chapters of the benefits from trade to answer the questions. Many of the goods on eBay have been bought at low prices and are being resold at higher prices. In fact, some people supplement their incomes by buying collectibles and other goods at garage sales and reselling them on eBay. Does eBay serve a useful economic purpose? Economists would say that it does. Consider the case of Lou, who buys collectible movie posters and resells them on eBay. Suppose Lou buys a *Jurassic World* poster at a garage sale for $30 and resells it on eBay for $60. Both the person who sold to Lou at the garage sale and the person who bought from him on eBay must have been made better off by the deals, *or they would not have made them*. Lou has performed the useful service of locating the poster and making it available for sale on eBay. In carrying out this service, Lou has incurred costs, including the opportunity cost of his time spent searching garage sales, the opportunity cost of the funds he has tied up in posters he has purchased but not yet sold, and the cost of the fees eBay charges him. It is easy to sell goods on eBay, so over time, competition among Lou and other movie poster dealers should cause the difference between the prices of posters sold at garage sales and the prices on eBay to shrink until they are equal to the dealers' costs of reselling the posters, including the opportunity cost of their time.

Your Turn: For more practice, do related problems 1.5 and 1.6 on page 550 at the end of this chapter.

MyEconLab Study Plan

Why Don't All Firms Charge the Same Price?

The law of one price may appear to be violated even where transactions costs are zero and a product can be resold. For example, different Web sites may sell what seem to be identical products for different prices. We can resolve this apparent contradiction if we look more closely at what "product" an Internet Web site—or another business—actually offers for sale.

Suppose you want to buy a Blu-ray disc of *The Avengers: Age of Ultron*. You research prices online and get the results shown in Table 16.1. Would you automatically buy from one of the last two sites listed because of their low prices? Before you answer, consider what each of these sites offers.

As we have discussed, firms differentiate the products they sell in many ways (see Chapter 13). One way is by providing faster and more reliable delivery than competitors, as Amazon.com and walmart.com have done. New Internet sellers who lack that reputation will have to differentiate their products on the basis of price, as the two fictitious firms listed in the table have done. So, the difference in the prices of products offered on Web sites does *not* violate the law of one price. A Blu-ray disc Amazon.com offers for sale is not the same product as a Blu-ray disc JustStartedinBusinessLastWednesday.com offers for sale.

MyEconLab Concept Check

MyEconLab Study Plan

Table 16.1
Which Internet Retailer Would You Buy From?

Product: *The Avengers: Age of Ultron* Blu-ray Disc		
Company	**Price**	**What does this site offer you?**
Amazon.com	$24.99	• Fast delivery to your home. • Secure packaging. • Easy payment to your credit card using a secure method that keeps your credit card number safe from computer hackers.
walmart.com	24.98	• Fast delivery to your home. • Secure packaging. • Easy payment to your credit card using a secure method that keeps your credit card number safe from computer hackers.
WaitForeverForYourOrder.com	22.50	Low price
JustStartedinBusinessLastWednesday.com	21.25	Low price

16.2 Price Discrimination: Charging Different Prices for the Same Product

LEARNING OBJECTIVE: Explain how a firm can increase its profits through price discrimination.

Price discrimination Charging different prices to different customers for the same product when the price differences are not due to differences in cost.

We saw at the beginning of this chapter that the Walt Disney Company charges different prices for the same product: admission to Disney World. Charging different prices to different customers for the same good or service when the price differences are not due to differences in cost is called **price discrimination**. But doesn't price discrimination contradict the law of one price? Why doesn't the possibility of arbitrage profits lead people to buy at the low price and resell at the high price?

The Requirements for Successful Price Discrimination

In order to successfully practice price discrimination, a firm must:

1. Possess market power.
2. Have some customers with a greater willingness to pay for the product than other customers, and be able to know which customers have a greater willingness to pay.
3. Be able to divide up—or *segment*—the market for the product so that consumers who buy the product at a low price are not able to resell it at a high price. In other words, price discrimination will not work if arbitrage is possible.

A firm selling in a perfectly competitive market cannot practice price discrimination because it can only charge the market price. For example, a farmer will be unable to sell any eggs at a price higher than the market price because consumers have many other farmers they can buy eggs from. Because most firms do not sell in perfectly competitive markets, they have market power and can set the price of the goods they sell.

Many firms may also be able to determine that some consumers have a greater willingness to pay for a product than others. However, the third requirement—that markets be segmented so that consumers buying at a low price will not be able to resell the product—can be difficult to fulfill. For example, some people really love Big Macs and would be willing to pay $10 rather than do without one. Other people would not be willing to pay a penny more than $1 for a Big Mac. Even if McDonald's could identify differences in the willingness of consumers to pay for Big Macs, it would not be able to charge them different prices. Suppose McDonald's knows that Joe is willing to pay $10,

Don't Let This Happen to You

Don't Confuse Price Discrimination with Other Types of Discrimination

Price discrimination is not the same as discrimination based on race or gender. Discriminating on the basis of arbitrary characteristics, such as race or gender, is illegal under the civil rights laws. Price discrimination is legal because it involves charging people different prices on the basis of their willingness to pay rather than on the basis of arbitrary characteristics. There is a gray area, however, when companies charge different prices on the basis of gender. For example, insurance companies usually charge women lower prices than men for automobile insurance. The courts have ruled that this is not illegal discrimination under the civil rights laws because women, on average, have better driving records than men. Because the costs of insuring men are higher than the costs of insuring women, insurance companies are allowed to charge men higher prices. Notice that this is not actually price discrimination as we have defined it here. Price discrimination involves charging different prices for the same product *where the price differences are not due to differences in cost.*

MyEconLab Study Plan

Your Turn: Test your understanding by doing related problem 2.11 on page 551 at the end of this chapter.

whereas Jill will pay only $1. If McDonald's tries to charge Joe $10, he will just have Jill buy a Big Mac for him.

An Example of Price Discrimination

Only firms that can keep consumers from reselling a product are able to practice price discrimination. Because buyers cannot resell the product, the law of one price does not hold. For example, movie theaters know that many people are willing to pay more to see a movie in the evening than during the afternoon. As a result, theaters usually charge higher prices for tickets to evening showings than for tickets to afternoon showings. They keep these markets separate by making the tickets to afternoon showings a different color or by having the time printed on them and by having a ticket taker examine the tickets. That practice makes it difficult for someone to buy a lower-priced ticket in the afternoon and use the ticket to gain admission to an evening showing.

Figure 16.1 illustrates how the owners of movie theaters use price discrimination to increase their profits. The marginal cost to the movie theater owner from another person attending a showing is very small: a little more wear on a theater seat and a few more kernels of popcorn to be swept from the floor. In previous chapters, we assumed that the marginal cost curve has a U shape. In Figure 16.1, we assume for simplicity that marginal cost is a constant $0.50, shown as a horizontal line. Panel (a) shows the demand for afternoon showings. In this segment of its market, the theater should maximize profit by selling the quantity of tickets for which marginal revenue equals marginal cost, or 450 tickets. We know from the demand curve that the theater can sell 450 tickets at a price of $7.25 per ticket. Panel (b) shows the demand for evening showings. Notice that charging $7.25 per ticket would *not* be profit maximizing in this market. At a price of $7.25, the theater sells 850 tickets, which is 225 more tickets than the profit-maximizing quantity of 625. By charging $7.25 for tickets to afternoon showings and $9.75 for tickets to evening showings, the theater has maximized profit.

Figure 16.1 also illustrates another important point about price discrimination: When firms can practice price discrimination, they will charge customers who are less sensitive to price—those whose demand for the product is *less elastic*—a higher price and charge customers who are more sensitive to price—those whose demand is *more elastic*—a lower price. In this case, the demand for tickets to evening showings is less elastic, so the price charged is higher, and the demand for tickets to afternoon showings is more elastic, so the price charged is lower. MyEconLab Concept Check

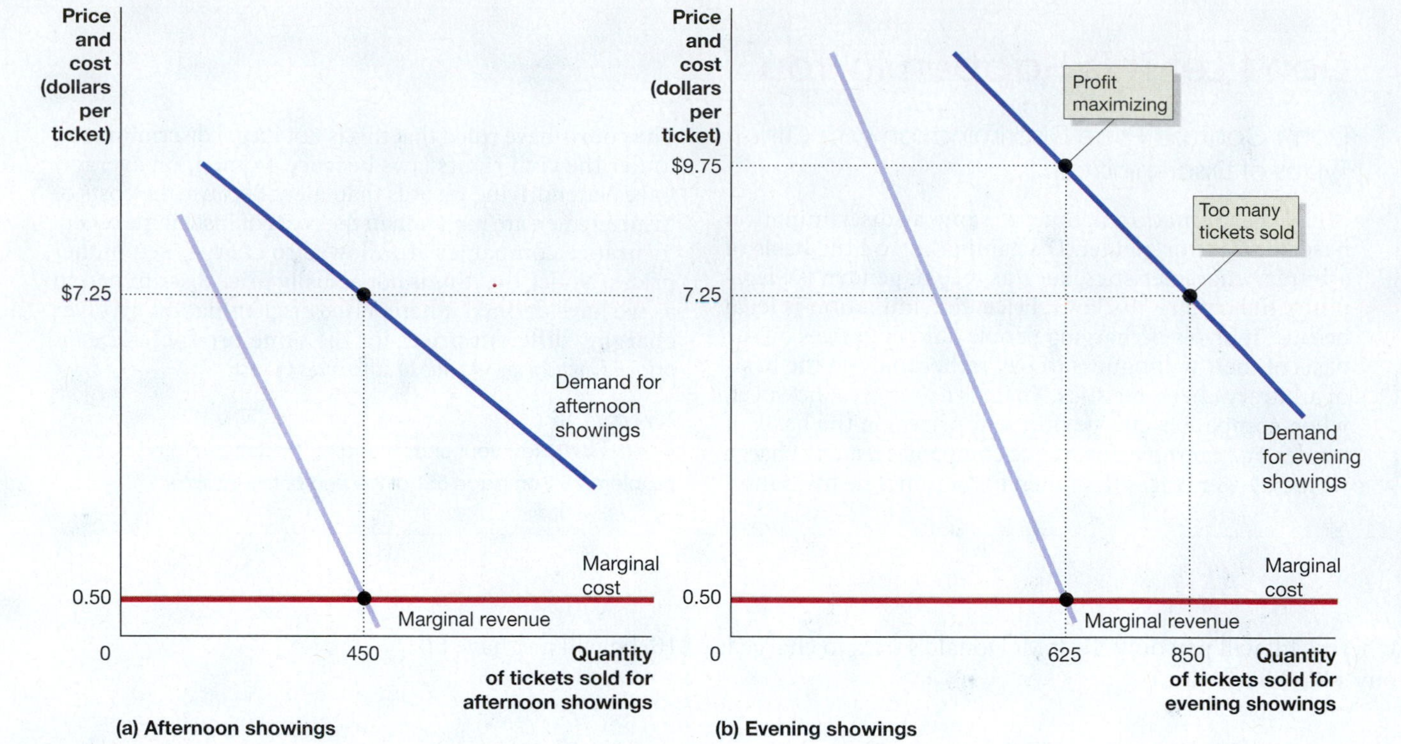

MyEconLab Animation

Figure 16.1 Price Discrimination by a Movie Theater

Fewer people want to go to the movies in the afternoon than in the evening. In panel (a), the profit-maximizing price for a ticket to an afternoon showing is $7.25. Charging this same price for evening showings would not be profit maximizing, as panel (b) shows. At a price of $7.25, the theater would sell 850 tickets to evening showings, which is more than the profit-maximizing number of 625 tickets. To maximize profit, the theater should charge $9.75 for tickets to evening showings.

Solved Problem 16.2

How Apple Uses Price Discrimination to Increase Profits

During the summer of 2015, Apple was selling MacBook Pro laptop computers with 13-inch retina displays on its Web site and in its retail stores for $1,299. But college students and faculty members could buy the same laptop from Apple for $1,249. Why would Apple charge different prices for the same laptop, depending on whether the buyer is an education customer? Draw two graphs to illustrate your answers: one for the general public and one for education customers.

Solving the Problem

Step 1: Review the chapter material. This problem is about using price discrimination to increase profits, so you may want to review the section "Price Discrimination: Charging Different Prices for the Same Product," which begins on page 534.

Step 2: Explain why charging different prices to education customers and other customers will increase Apple's profit. It makes sense for Apple to charge different prices if education customers have a different price elasticity of demand than do other customers. In that case, Apple will charge the market segment with the less elastic demand a higher price and the market segment with the more elastic demand a lower price. Because Apple is charging education customers the lower price, they must have a more elastic demand than do other customers.

Step 3: Draw a graph to illustrate your answer. Your graphs should look like the following ones, where we have chosen hypothetical quantities to illustrate the ideas. As in the case of movie theaters, you can assume for simplicity that marginal cost is constant; in the graph we assume that marginal cost is $400.

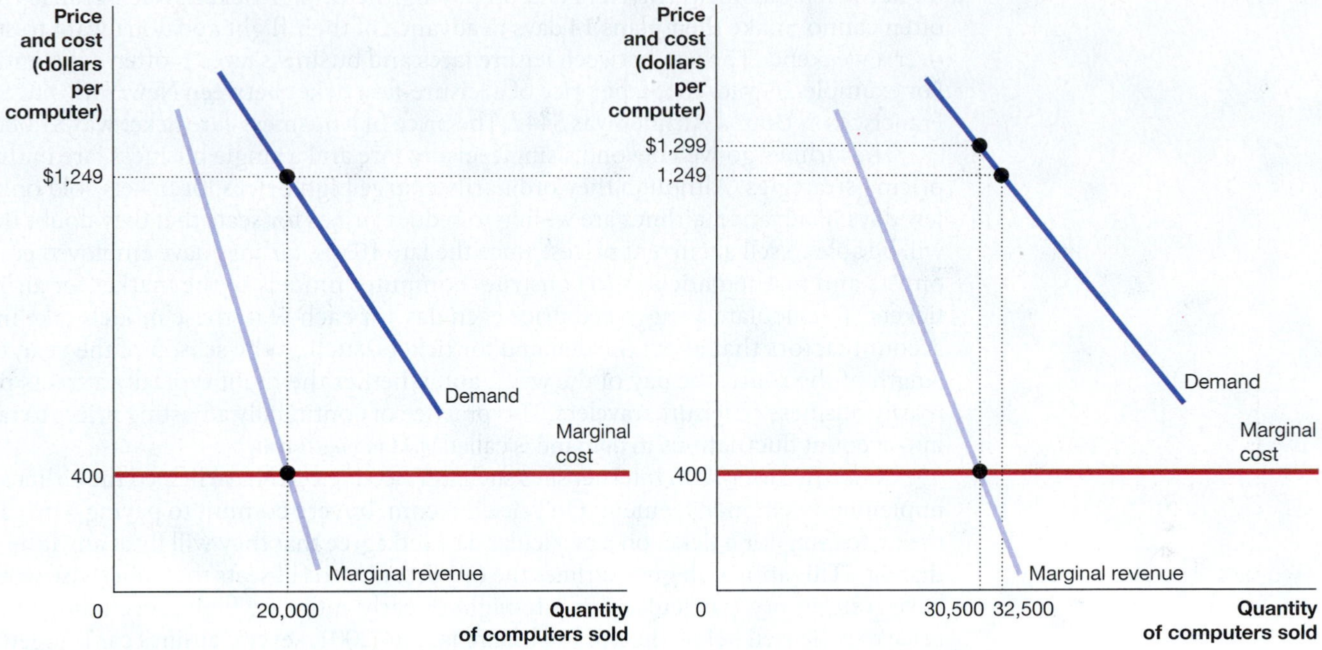

(a) Education customers

(b) The general public

Panel (a) shows that in the education customers segment of the market, marginal revenue equals marginal cost at 20,000 laptops sold. Therefore, Apple should charge a price of $1,249 to maximize profits. But if Apple also charges $1,249 in the general public segment of the market, shown in panel (b), it will sell 32,500 laptops, which is more than the profit-maximizing quantity. By charging $1,299 to the general public, Apple will sell 30,500 laptops, the profit-maximizing quantity. We have shown that Apple maximizes its profits by charging education customers a lower price than it charges the general public. Notice that although the demand curve in panel (a) is more elastic, it is also steeper. This reminds us of the important point that elasticity is different from slope (see Chapter 6).

Your Turn: For more practice, do problems 2.12 and 2.13 on page 552 at the end of this chapter.

MyEconLab Study Plan

Airlines: The Kings of Price Discrimination

Airline seats are a perishable product. Once a plane has taken off from Chicago for Los Angeles, any seat that has not been sold on that particular flight will never be sold. In addition, the marginal cost of flying one additional passenger is low. As a result, airlines have a strong incentive to manage prices to fill as many seats as possible on each flight.

Airlines divide their customers into two main categories: business travelers and leisure travelers. Business travelers often have inflexible schedules, can't commit until the last minute to travel on a particular day, and, most importantly, are not very sensitive to changes in price. The opposite is true for leisure travelers: They are flexible about when they travel, willing to buy their tickets well in advance, and sensitive to changes in price. Based on what we discussed earlier in this chapter, you can see that airlines will maximize profits by charging business travelers higher ticket prices than leisure travelers, but they need to determine who is a business traveler and who is a leisure traveler. Some airlines make this determination by requiring people who want to buy a ticket at the leisure price to buy 14 days in advance and to stay at their destination over a Saturday night. Anyone unable to meet these requirements must pay a much higher price. Business travelers end up paying the higher ticket price because they often cannot make their plans 14 days in advance of their flight and don't want to stay over a weekend. The gap between leisure fares and business fares is often substantial. For example, in mid-2015, the price of a leisure-fare ticket between New York and San Francisco on United Airlines was $442. The price of a business-fare ticket was $1,080.

The airlines go well beyond a single leisure fare and a single business fare in their pricing strategies. Although they ordinarily charge high prices for tickets sold only a few days in advance, airlines are willing to reduce prices for seats that they doubt they will be able to sell at current prices. Since the late 1980s, airlines have employed economists and mathematicians to construct computer models of the market for airline tickets. To calculate a suggested price each day for each seat, these models take into account factors that affect the demand for tickets, such as the season of the year, the length of the route, the day of the week, and whether the flight typically attracts primarily business or leisure travelers. This practice of continually adjusting prices to take into account fluctuations in demand is called *yield management*.

Since the late 1990s, Internet sites such as Priceline.com have helped the airlines to implement yield management. On Priceline.com, buyers commit to paying a price of their choosing for a ticket on a particular day and agree that they will fly at any time on that day. This approach gives airlines the opportunity to fill seats that otherwise would have gone empty, particularly on late-night or early-morning flights, even though the price may be well below the normal leisure fare. In 2001, several airlines came together to form the Internet site Orbitz, which became another means of filling seats at discount prices. In fact, the chance that you paid the same price for your airline ticket as the person sitting next to you has become quite small. Figure 16.2 shows an actual United Airlines flight from Chicago to Los Angeles. The 33 passengers on the flight paid 27 different prices for their tickets, including one passenger who used frequent flyer miles to obtain a free ticket.

MyEconLab Concept Check

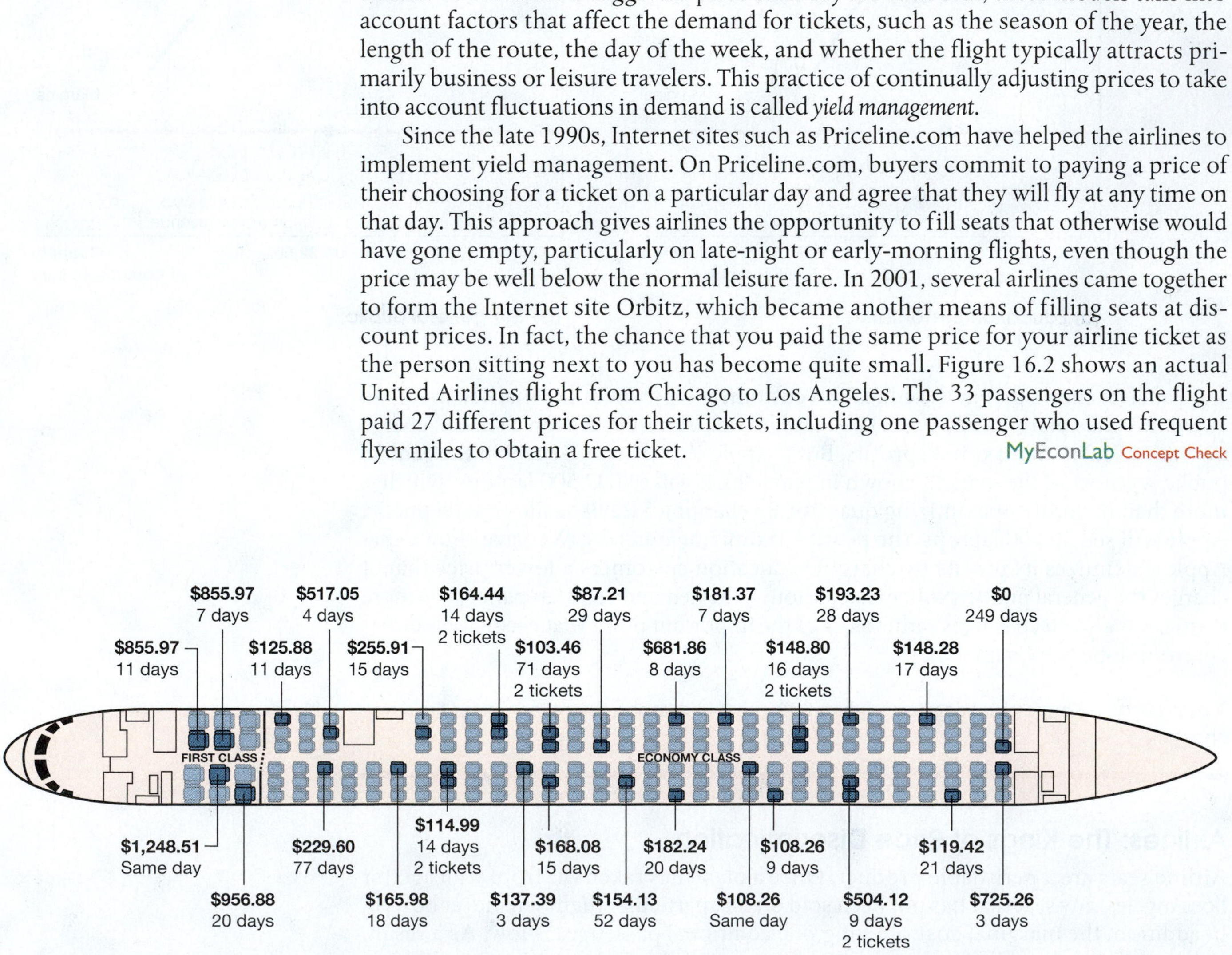

MyEconLab Animation

Figure 16.2 33 Customers and 27 Different Prices

To fill as many seats on a flight as possible, airlines charge many different ticket prices. The 33 passengers on this United Airlines flight from Chicago to Los Angeles paid 27 different prices for their tickets, including one passenger who used frequent flyer miles to obtain a free ticket. Each seat is labelled with the ticket price followed by the number of days in advance that the customer purchased the ticket.

Source: "So, How Much Did You Pay for Your Ticket," by Matthew L. Wald. *The New York Times*, April 12, 1998.

Making the Connection
MyEconLab Video

Why Is the Price of a J.Crew Jacket So Much Lower at an Outlet Mall?

To practice price discrimination, a firm must have some market power, some consumers must have greater willingness than others to pay for the firm's product, and the firm must be able to divide up—or segment—its market. Many firms, particularly clothing manufacturers, sell products in department stores or in their own retail stores and also in outlet stores. The prices for their products are lower in outlet stores than in regular stores. By dividing up the market for their products in this way, firms can increase their profits by charging higher prices to consumers with a low price elasticity of demand and lower prices to consumers with a higher price elasticity of demand.

Clothing manufacturers can segment their market into more price-sensitive consumers who would shop in outlet malls at a lower price and less price-sensitive consumers who would pay full price in regular stores.

But how do firms keep the two markets segmented? Why wouldn't all consumers buy from outlet stores at lower prices? Outlet stores are often grouped together in outlet malls. For many years, these stores sold products that had slight flaws, such as a sweater with an imperfection in the fabric, or clothes that were the previous year's style. By selling these less desirable products in outlet stores, firms such as J.Crew, Ann Taylor, and Ralph Lauren, could sell them at lower prices without reducing the willingness of less price-sensitive consumers to pay full price for their products when sold in regular stores. The more price-sensitive consumers would buy the firm's goods in outlet malls at a lower price, while the less price-sensitive consumers would pay full price in regular stores.

The ability of firms to follow this pricing strategy was limited by the amount of flawed or out-of-date merchandise they had available to sell in outlet stores. In recent years, firms have begun producing goods directly for their outlet stores. By some estimates, today more than 85 percent of goods sold in outlet stores are manufactured specifically for them. These goods are typically not as high quality as the goods the firms sell in regular stores.

Firms incur a lower cost for goods they produce for their outlet stores. But the price difference between the goods sold in regular stores and goods sold in outlet stores is only partly accounted for by the difference in production costs. Outlet malls are typically located a significant distance from major cities, which makes shopping at them less convenient. This inconvenience helps firms to maintain market segmentation because less price-sensitive consumers are unlikely to take the trouble to drive to an outlet mall rather than to shop at a more accessible mall or in a downtown store where firms can sell their products for higher prices.

Using outlet stores to price discriminate has been successful for many companies, with sales increasing faster than at conventional retail stores. But as one news story noted, firms have to carry out a balancing act to maintain their market segmentation: Products in an outlet have "to be close enough to the parent brand to [gain] some of [the parent brand's] prestige, but not close enough to devalue it."

Sources: Molly Young, "Cheap Thrills at Neiman Marcus's Cut-Price Outlet Store," *New York Times*, March 18, 2015; Richard Chang, "Outlet Malls Aren't What They Used to Be," *Sacramento Bee*, December 8, 2013; and Julie Satow, "A Magnet for Shoppers Is Getting a Makeover," *New York Times*, May 21, 2013.

Your Turn: Test your understanding by doing related problem 2.14 on page 552 at the end of this chapter.

MyEconLab Study Plan

Perfect Price Discrimination

If a firm knew every consumer's willingness to pay—and could keep consumers who bought a product at a low price from reselling it—the firm could charge every consumer a different price. In this case of *perfect price discrimination*—also known as *first-degree price discrimination*—each consumer would have to pay a price equal to the consumer's willingness to pay and, therefore, would receive no consumer surplus. To see why, remember that consumer surplus is the difference between the highest price a

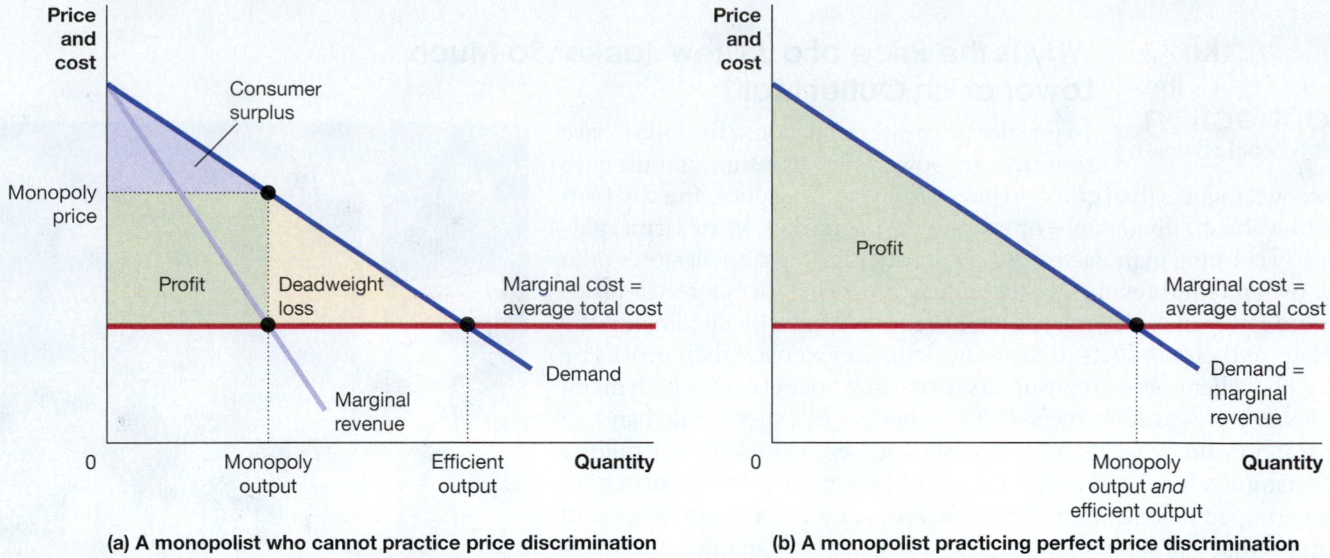

MyEconLab Animation

Figure 16.3 Perfect Price Discrimination

Panel (a) shows the case of a monopolist that cannot practice price discrimination and, therefore, can charge only a single price for its product. The graph shows that to maximize profit, the monopolist will produce the level of output where marginal revenue equals marginal cost. The resulting profit is shown by the area of the green rectangle. Given the monopoly price, the amount of consumer surplus in this market is shown by the area of the blue triangle. The economically efficient level of output occurs where price equals marginal cost. Because the monopolist stops production at a level of output where price is above marginal cost, there is a deadweight loss equal to the area of the yellow triangle. In panel (b), the monopolist is able to practice perfect price discrimination by charging a different price to each consumer. The result is to convert both the consumer surplus *and* the deadweight loss from panel (a) into profit.

consumer is willing to pay for a product and the price the consumer actually pays (see Chapter 4). But if the price the consumer pays is the maximum he or she would be willing to pay, there is no consumer surplus.

Figure 16.3 shows the effects of perfect price discrimination. To simplify the discussion, we assume that the firm is a monopoly and that it has constant marginal and average total costs. Panel (a) shows the case of a monopolist that cannot practice price discrimination and, therefore, can charge only a single price for its product (see Chapter 15). The monopolist maximizes profit by producing the level of output where marginal revenue equals marginal cost. Recall that the economically efficient level of output occurs where price is equal to marginal cost, which is the level of output in a perfectly competitive market. Because the monopolist produces where price is greater than marginal cost, it causes a loss of economic efficiency equal to the area of the deadweight loss triangle in the figure.

Panel (b) shows the situation of a monopolist practicing perfect price discrimination. Because the firm can charge each consumer the maximum each consumer is willing to pay, its marginal revenue from selling one more unit is equal to the price of that unit. Therefore, the monopolist's marginal revenue curve becomes equal to its demand curve, and the firm will continue to produce up to the point where price is equal to marginal cost. It may seem like a paradox, but the ability to practice perfect price discrimination causes the monopolist to produce the efficient level of output. By doing so, the monopolist converts the consumer surplus *and* the deadweight loss in panel (a) into profits. In both panel (a) and panel (b), the profit shown is also producer surplus.

Even though the result in panel (b) is more economically efficient than the result in panel (a), consumers clearly are worse off because the amount of consumer surplus has been reduced to zero. We probably will never see a case of perfect price discrimination in the real world because firms typically do not know how much each consumer is willing to pay and, therefore, cannot charge each consumer a different price. Still, this extreme case helps us to see the two key results of price discrimination:

1. Profits increase.
2. Consumer surplus decreases.

Perfect price discrimination improves economic efficiency. Can we also say that this will be the case if price discrimination is less than perfect? Often, less-than-perfect price discrimination will improve economic efficiency. But under certain circumstances, it may actually reduce economic efficiency, so we can't draw a general conclusion.

MyEconLab Concept Check

Price Discrimination across Time

Firms are sometimes able to engage in price discrimination over time. With this strategy, firms charge a higher price for a product when it is first introduced and a lower price later. Some consumers are *early adopters* who will pay a high price to be among the first to own certain new products. This pattern helps explain why Blu-ray players, digital cameras, and flat-screen plasma televisions all sold for very high prices when they were first introduced. After the demand of the early adopters was satisfied, the companies reduced prices to attract more price-sensitive customers. For example, the price of Blu-ray players dropped by 95 percent within five years of their introduction. Some of the price reductions over time for these products were also due to falling costs, as companies took advantage of economies of scale, but some represented price discrimination across time.

Book publishers routinely use price discrimination across time to increase profits. Hardcover editions of novels have much higher prices and are published months before paperback editions. For example, the hardcover edition of John Grisham's novel *Gray Mountain* was published in October 2014 at a price of $28.95. The paperback edition was published in August 2015 for $9.99. Although this difference in price might seem to reflect the higher costs of producing hardcover books, in fact, it does not. The marginal cost of printing another copy of the hardcover edition is about $1.50. The marginal cost of printing another copy of the paperback edition is only slightly less, about $1.25. So, the difference in price between the hardcover and paperback editions is explained primarily by differences in demand. John Grisham's most devoted fans want to read his next book at the earliest possible moment and are not very sensitive to price. Many casual readers are also interested in Grisham's books but will read something else if the price of Grisham's latest book is too high.

As Figure 16.4 shows, a publisher will maximize profit by segmenting the market—in this case, across time—and by charging a higher price to the less elastic market segment and a lower price to the more elastic segment. (This example is similar to our earlier analysis of movie tickets in Figure 16.1 on page 536.) If the publisher had skipped the hardcover and issued only the paperback version at a price of $9.99 when the book was first published in October, its revenue would have dropped by the number of readers who bought the hardcover edition multiplied by the difference in price between the hardcover and paperback editions, or $500{,}000 \times (\$28.95 - \$9.99) = \$9{,}480{,}000$.

MyEconLab Concept Check

Can Price Discrimination Be Illegal?

When discussing monopoly, we saw that Congress has passed *antitrust laws* to promote competition (see Chapter 15). Price discrimination may be illegal if its effect is to reduce competition in an industry. In 1936, Congress passed the Robinson–Patman Act, which outlawed price discrimination that reduced competition. The act also contained language that could be interpreted as making illegal *all* price discrimination not based on differences in cost. In the 1960s, the Federal Trade Commission sued Borden, Inc., under this act because Borden was selling the same evaporated milk for two different prices. Cans with the Borden label were sold for a high price, and cans the company sold to supermarkets to be repackaged as the supermarkets' private brands were sold for a much lower price. The courts ultimately ruled that Borden had not violated the law because the price differences increased, rather than reduced, competition in the market for evaporated milk. In recent years, the courts have interpreted the Robinson–Patman Act narrowly, allowing firms to use the types of price discrimination described in this chapter.

MyEconLab Concept Check

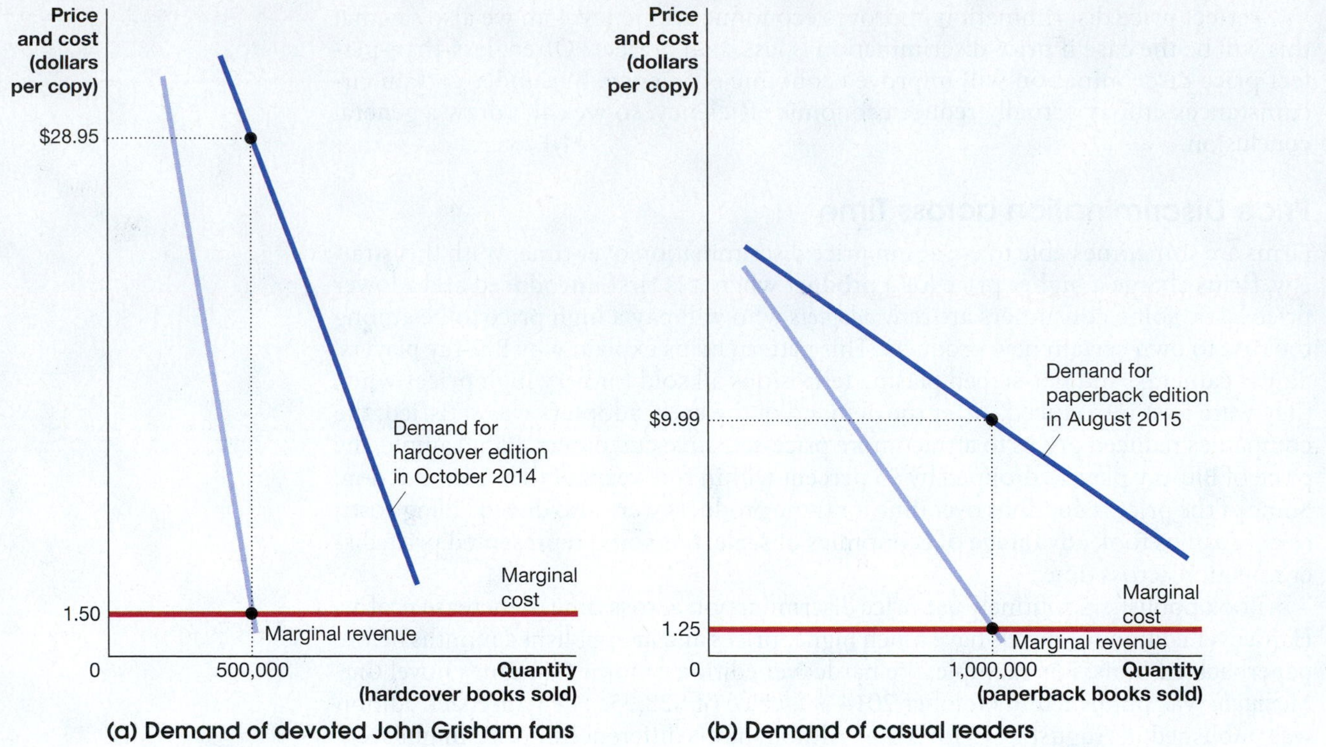

MyEconLab Animation

Figure 16.4 Price Discrimination across Time

Publishers issue most novels in hardcover editions at high prices to satisfy the demand of the novelists' most devoted fans. Later, publishers issue paperback editions at much lower prices to capture sales from casual readers. In panel (a), with a marginal cost of $1.50 per copy for a hardcover edition, the profit-maximizing level of output is 500,000 copies, which can be sold at a price of $28.95. In panel (b), the more elastic demand of casual readers and the slightly lower marginal cost result in a profit-maximizing output of 1,000,000 for the paperback edition, which can be sold at a price of $9.99.

Making the Connection
MyEconLab Video

The Internet Leaves You Open to Price Discrimination

Have you ever used Google or Pricegrabber.com to search for the best price for a book, a computer, or an airline ticket? Although the Internet can help you compare prices among different Web sites, it can also be a way for some sellers to price discriminate. When you log on to a Web site, its servers can gather important information about you, including your location—which can be determined from the address of your Internet Service Provider (ISP)—and your browsing history. If the site already has your e-mail address, it may be able to use an Internet data firm to learn facts about you, including your age, race, gender, and income.

Reporters for the *Wall Street Journal* conducted an experiment by logging on to the Web site of Staples, the office supply store, from computers in many different Zip codes. They found that the Staples Web site displayed different prices for several items based on the Zip code of the person who logged on to the site. For example, some people saw a price of $15.79 for a Swingline stapler, while other people saw a price of $14.29 for the same stapler. Similarly, some people saw a price of $28.49 for a 12-pack of Bic rollerball pens, while other people saw a price of $25.99. From the analysis in this chapter, we know that Staples was attempting to use the information it had gathered to estimate the price elasticities of demand of people shopping on its site. Those people Staples believed to have a low price elasticity of demand would see the high price for goods, and those Staples believed to have a high price elasticity of demand would see the low price. Staples managers declined to explain their pricing strategy, so the reporters did a statistical analysis of the characteristics of the Zip codes. The most important characteristic turned out to be whether a Zip code was within 20 miles of an OfficeMax or Office Depot store, which are Staples's main competitors. People living in Zip codes close to a rival store were likely to see the low price, and people in Zip codes far away from a rival store were likely to see the high price.

Is using this pricing strategy an effective way of increasing profit? In the case of Staples, the firm was able to gather only limited information on potential buyers, so it was unable to effectively price discriminate. For example, the *Wall Street Journal* reporters found that the Zip codes seeing the higher-priced stapler had lower average income than the Zip codes seeing the lower-priced stapler, even though people with lower incomes might be expected to be more sensitive to price. More generally, Web sites using personal information to price discriminate run the risk of upsetting consumers. For instance, when told of Staples's price strategy, one person who had used the firm's Web site asked: "How can they get away with that?" For a brief time, Amazon varied prices on its site depending on a shopper's buying history. One customer saw a DVD price of $26.24 when he first logged on to the site. After he deleted the "cookies" in his browser, so that he appeared to Amazon's servers to be a new customer, the price of the DVD dropped to $22.74. Widespread complaints about this pricing strategy caused Amazon to quickly drop it.

As Web sites become more sophisticated in gathering information about shoppers, firms will have a greater ability to price discriminate. Whether negative reactions from consumers will cause firms to avoid using such pricing strategies on their Web sites remains to be seen.

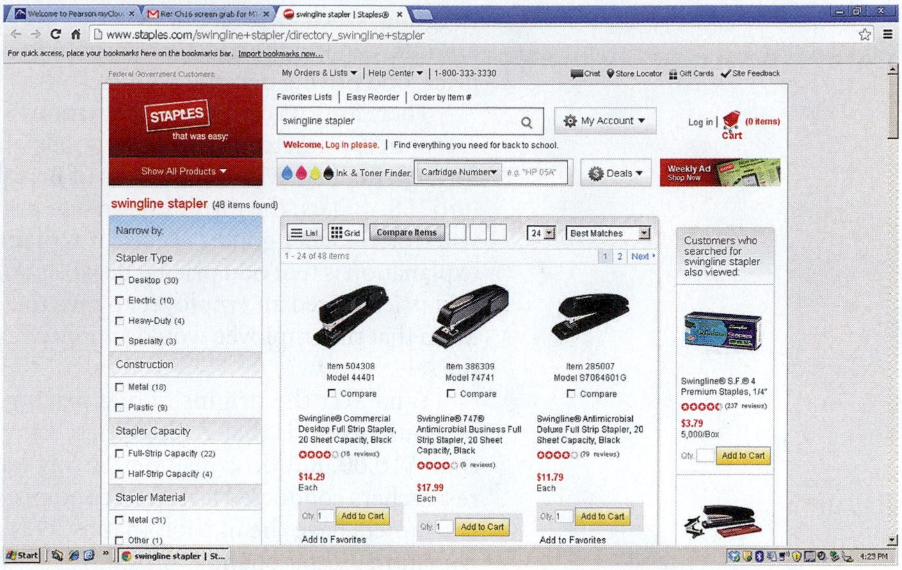

The price of this stapler may change, depending on the consumer's Zip code.

Sources: Jennifer Valentino-Devries, Jeremy Singer-Vine, and Ashkan Soltani, "Websites Vary Prices, Deals Based on Users' Information," *Wall Street Journal*, December 24, 2012; Jennifer Valentino-Devries and Jeremy Singer-Vine, "They Know What You're Shopping For," *Wall Street Journal*, December 7, 2012; and Anita Ramasastry, "Web Sites Change Prices Based on Customers' Habits," www.cnn.com, June 24, 2005.

Your Turn: Test your understanding by doing related problem 2.17 on page 553 at the end of this chapter.

MyEconLab Study Plan

16.3 Other Pricing Strategies

LEARNING OBJECTIVE: Explain how some firms increase their profits by using odd pricing, cost-plus pricing, and two-part tariffs.

In addition to price discrimination, firms use many other pricing strategies, depending on the nature of their products, the level of competition in their markets, and the characteristics of their customers. In this section, we consider three important strategies: odd pricing, cost-plus pricing, and two-part tariffs.

Odd Pricing: Why Is the Price $2.99 Instead of $3.00?

Many firms use *odd pricing*—for example, charging $4.95 instead of $5.00, or $199 instead of $200. Surveys show that 80 percent to 90 percent of the products sold in supermarkets have prices ending in "9" or "5" rather than "0." Odd pricing has a long history. In the early nineteenth century, most goods in the United States were sold in general stores and did not have fixed prices. Instead, prices were often determined by haggling, much as prices of new cars are often determined today by haggling on dealers' lots. Later in the nineteenth century, when most products began to sell for a fixed price, odd pricing became popular.

There are two common explanations for the origin of odd pricing. One explanation is that in the nineteenth century, goods imported from Great Britain had a reputation for high quality. When the prices of British goods in British currency were translated into U.S. dollars, the result was an odd price. Because customers connected odd prices with high-quality goods, even sellers of domestic goods charged odd prices. The other explanation is that odd pricing began as an attempt to guard against employee theft. An odd price forced an employee to give the customer change, which reduced the likelihood that the employee would simply pocket the customer's money without recording the sale.

Whatever the origins of odd pricing, why do firms still use it today? The most obvious answer is that an odd price, say $9.99, somehow seems significantly cheaper than $10.00. But do consumers really have this illusion? To find out, three market researchers conducted a study. Economists can estimate demand curves statistically. If consumers have the illusion that $9.99 is significantly cheaper than $10.00, they will demand a greater quantity of goods at $9.99 than the estimated demand curve predicts. The researchers surveyed consumers about their willingness to purchase six different products at a series of prices. Ten of the prices were either odd cent prices—99 cents or 95 cents—or odd dollar prices—$95 or $99. Nine of these 10 odd prices resulted in an odd-price effect, with the quantity demanded being greater than predicted using the estimated demand curve. The study provides some evidence that using odd prices makes economic sense.

Another study involved catalogs for women's clothing. With the cooperation of the clothing firm, some women were mailed catalogs with even dollar prices and other women received catalogs with prices ending in 99 cents. The women receiving the catalogs with prices ending in 99 cents bought 8 percent more clothes than the women receiving catalogs with even dollar prices.

Many firms have begun to use sales strategies that rely on insights from *behavioral economics,* which is the study of situations in which people make choices that do not appear to be economically rational (see Chapter 10). Odd pricing is an old strategy that is consistent with the modern analysis of behavioral economics. MyEconLab Concept Check

Why Do McDonald's and Other Firms Use Cost-Plus Pricing?

Many firms use *cost-plus pricing,* which involves adding a percentage *markup* to average total cost. With this pricing strategy, the firm first calculates average total cost at a particular level of production, usually equal to the firm's expected sales. The firm then applies a percentage markup, say 30 percent, to the estimated average total cost to arrive at the price. For example, if average total cost is $100 and the percentage markup is 30 percent, the price will be $130. For a firm selling multiple products, the markup is intended to cover all costs, including those that the firm cannot assign to any particular product. For example, the work performed by the employees in the accounting and finance departments at McDonald's applies to all of McDonald's products and can't be assigned directly to Big Macs or Happy Meals. MyEconLab Concept Check

Making the Connection
MyEconLab Video

Cost-Plus Pricing in the Publishing Industry

Book publishing companies incur substantial costs for editing, designing, marketing, and warehousing books. These costs are difficult to assign directly to any particular book. Most publishers arrive at a price for a book by applying a markup to their production costs, which are usually divided into plant costs and manufacturing costs. Plant costs include typesetting the manuscript and preparing graphics or artwork for printing. Manufacturing costs include the costs of printing, paper, and binding the book.

Consider the following example for a hypothetical new book by Adam Smith, *How to Succeed at Economics without Really Trying*. We will assume that the book is 250 pages long, the publisher expects to sell 5,000 copies, and plant and manufacturing costs are as given in the following table:

Plant Costs		
	Typesetting	$3,500
	Other plant costs	2,000
Manufacturing Costs		
	Printing	$5,750
	Paper	6,250
	Binding	5,000
Total Production Cost		
		$22,500

With total production cost of $22,500 and production of 5,000 books, the per-unit production cost is $22,500/5,000 = $4.50. Many publishers multiply the unit production cost number by 7 or 8 to arrive at the retail price they will charge customers in bookstores. In this case, multiplying by 7 results in a price of $31.50 for the book. The markup seems quite high, but publishers typically sell books to bookstores at a 40 percent discount. Although a customer in a bookstore will pay $31.50 for the book—or less, of course, if it is purchased from a bookseller that discounts the retail price—the publisher receives only $18.90. The difference between the $18.90 received from the bookstore and the $4.50 production cost equals the cost of editing, marketing, warehousing, paying a royalty to the author of the book, and all other costs, including the opportunity cost of the investment in the firm by its owners, plus any economic profit the owners receive.

Source: Beth Luey, *Handbook for Academic Authors*, 5th ed., New York: Cambridge University Press, 2010.

Your Turn: Test your understanding by doing related problem 3.8 on page 554 at the end of this chapter.

MyEconLab Study Plan

We have seen that firms maximize profit by producing the quantity at which marginal revenue equals marginal cost and charging a price that will cause consumers to buy that quantity. The cost-plus approach doesn't appear to maximize profit unless the cost-plus price turns out to be the same as the price that will cause the marginal revenue earned on the last unit to equal the unit's marginal cost. Economists have two views of cost-plus pricing. One is that it is simply a mistake that firms should avoid. The other view is that cost-plus pricing helps a firm come close to the profit-maximizing price when either marginal revenue or marginal cost is difficult to calculate.

Small firms often like cost-plus pricing because it is easy to use. Unfortunately, these firms can fall into the trap of mechanically applying a cost-plus pricing rule, which may result in charging prices that do not maximize profit. The most obvious problems with cost-plus pricing are that it ignores demand and focuses on average total cost rather than marginal cost. If a firm's marginal cost is significantly different from its average total cost at its current level of production, cost-plus pricing is unlikely to maximize profit.

Despite these problems, cost-plus pricing is used by some large firms that have the knowledge and resources to devise a better method of pricing if cost-plus pricing fails to maximize profit. Economists conclude that using cost-plus pricing may be the best way to determine the optimal price in two situations:

1. When marginal cost and average total cost are roughly equal
2. When a firm has difficulty estimating its demand curve

In fact, most large firms that use cost-plus pricing do not just mechanically apply a markup to their estimate of average total cost. Instead, they adjust the markup to reflect their best estimate of current demand. A large firm is likely to have a pricing policy committee that adjusts prices based on the current state of competition in the industry and the current state of the economy. If competition is strong in a weak economy, the pricing committee may decide to set price significantly below the cost-plus price.

In general, firms that take demand into account will charge lower markups on products that are more price elastic and higher markups on products that are less elastic. Supermarkets, where cost-plus pricing is widely used, have markups in the 5 to 10 percent range for products with more elastic demand, such as soft drinks and breakfast cereals, and markups in the 50 percent range for products with less elastic demand, such as fresh fruits and vegetables.

How Can Using Two-Part Tariffs Increase a Firm's Profits?

Some firms require consumers to pay an initial fee for the right to buy their product and an additional fee for each unit of the product purchased. For example, many golf and tennis clubs require members to buy an annual membership in addition to paying a fee each time they use the golf course or a tennis court. Sam's Club requires consumers to pay a membership fee before shopping at its stores. Cellphone companies sometimes charge a monthly fee and then have a per-minute charge after a certain number of minutes have been used. Economists call this pricing strategy a **two-part tariff.**

Two-part tariff A situation in which consumers pay one price (or tariff) for the right to buy as much of a related good as they want at a second price.

The Walt Disney Company is in a position to use a two-part tariff by charging consumers for admission to Walt Disney World or Disneyland and also charging them to use the rides in the parks. When Disneyland first opened, the admission price was low, but people had to purchase tickets to go on the rides. Today, you must pay a high price for admission to Disneyland or Disney World, but the rides are free once you're in the park. Figure 16.5 helps us understand which of these pricing strategies is more profitable for Disney. The numbers in the figure are simplified to make the calculations easier.

Once visitors are inside the park, Disney is in the position of a monopolist: No other firm is operating rides in Disney World. So, we can draw panel (a) in Figure 16.5 to represent the market for rides at Disney World. This graph looks like the standard monopoly graph (see Chapter 15). (Note that the marginal cost of another rider is quite low. We assume that it is a constant \$2 and equal to the average total cost.) It seems obvious—but it will turn out to be wrong!—that Disney should determine the profit-maximizing quantity of ride tickets by setting marginal revenue equal to marginal cost. In this case, the result would be 20,000 ride tickets sold per day at a price of \$26 per ride. Disney's profit from selling *ride tickets* is shown by the area of rectangle *B*. The area equals the difference between the \$26 price and the average total cost of \$2, multiplied by the 20,000 tickets sold, or $(\$26-\$2) \times 20{,}000 = \$480{,}000$. Disney also has a second source of profit from selling *admission tickets* to the park. Given the \$26 price for ride tickets, what price would Disney be able to charge for admission tickets?

Let's assume the following for simplicity: The only reason people want admission to Disney World is to go on the rides, all consumers have the same individual demand curve for rides, and Disney knows what this demand curve is. This last assumption allows Disney to practice perfect price discrimination. More realistic assumptions would make the outcome of the analysis somewhat different but would not affect the main point of how Disney uses a two-part tariff to increase its profits. With these assumptions, we can use the concept of consumer surplus to calculate the maximum total amount consumers would be willing to pay for admission. Remember that consumer surplus is equal to the area below the demand curve and above the price line, shown by the area of triangle A in panel (a). Consumers would not be willing to pay more for admission to the park than the consumer surplus they receive from the rides.

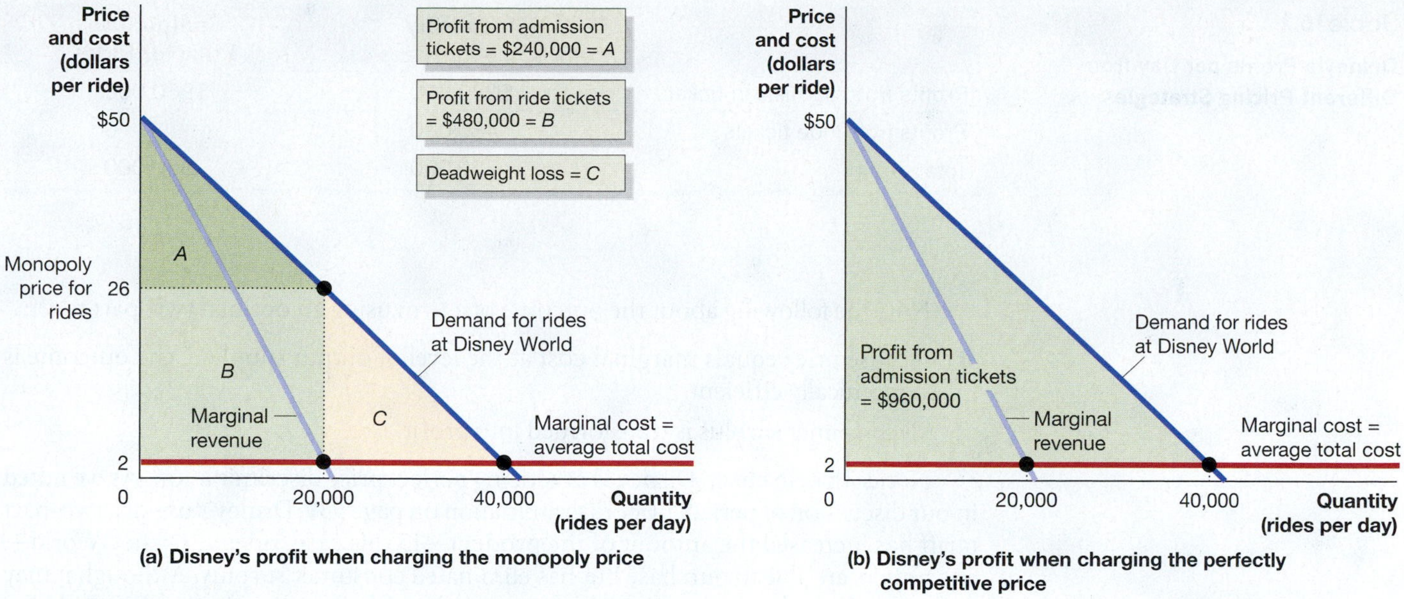

MyEconLab Animation

Figure 16.5 A Two-Part Tariff at Disney World

In panel (a), Disney charges the monopoly price of $26 per ride ticket and sells 20,000 ride tickets. Its profit from *ride tickets* is shown by the area of rectangle *B*, or $480,000. If Disney is in the position of knowing every consumer's willingness to pay, it can also charge a price for *admission tickets* that would result in the total amount paid for admission tickets being equal to total consumer surplus from the rides. Total consumer surplus from the rides equals the area of the triangle, *A*, or $240,000. So, when charging the monopoly price, Disney's total profit equals $480,000 + $240,000 or $720,000. In panel (b), Disney charges the perfectly competitive price of $2, which results in a quantity of 40,000 ride tickets sold. At the lower ride ticket price, Disney can charge a higher price for admission tickets, which will increase its total profits from operating the park to the area of the green triangle, or $960,000.

In panel (a) of Figure 16.5, the total consumer surplus when Disney charges a price of $26 per ride is $240,000. (This number is easy to calculate if you remember that the formula for the area of a triangle is $\frac{1}{2} \times$ base $\times$ height, or $\frac{1}{2} \times 20{,}000 \times \$24$.) Disney can set the price of admission tickets so that the *total* amount spent by buyers would be $240,000. In other words, Disney can set the price of admission to capture the entire consumer surplus from the rides. So, Disney's total profit from Disney World would be the $240,000 it receives from admission tickets plus the $480,000 in profit from the rides, or $720,000 per day.

Is this the most profit Disney can earn from selling admission tickets and ride tickets? The answer is "no." The key to understanding why is to notice that *the lower the price Disney charges for ride tickets, the higher the price it can charge for admission tickets.* Lower-priced ride tickets increase consumer surplus from the rides and, therefore, increase the willingness of buyers to pay a higher price for admission tickets. In panel (b) of Figure 16.5, we assume that Disney acts as it would in a perfectly competitive market and charges a price for ride tickets that is equal to marginal cost, or $2. Charging this price increases consumer surplus—*and* the maximum total amount that Disney can charge for admission tickets—from $240,000 to $960,000. (Once again, we use the formula for the area of a triangle to calculate the area of the green triangle in panel (b): $\frac{1}{2} \times 40{,}000 \times 48 = \$960{,}000$.) Disney's profits from the rides will decline to zero because it is now charging a price equal to average total cost, *but its total profit from Disney World will rise from $720,000 to $960,000 per day*. Table 16.2 summarizes this result.

What is the source of Disney's increased profit from charging a price equal to marginal cost? Disney has converted what was deadweight loss when it charged the monopoly price—the area of triangle C in panel (a)—into consumer surplus. Disney then turns this consumer surplus into profit by increasing the price of admission tickets.

Table 16.2

Disney's Profits per Day from Different Pricing Strategies

	Monopoly Price for Rides	Competitive Price for Rides
Profits from admission tickets	$240,000	$960,000
Profits from ride tickets	480,000	0
Total profit	720,000	960,000

Note the following about the outcome of a firm using an optimal two-part tariff:

1. Because price equals marginal cost at the level of output supplied, the outcome is economically efficient.
2. All consumer surplus is transformed into profit.

Notice that, in effect, Disney is practicing perfect price discrimination. As we noted in our discussion of perfect price discrimination on page 539, Disney's use of a two-part tariff has increased the amount of the product—in this case, rides at Disney World—consumers are able to purchase but has eliminated consumer surplus. Although it may seem paradoxical, consumer surplus was actually higher when consumers were being charged the monopoly price for the rides. The solution to the paradox is that although consumers pay a lower price for the rides when Disney employs a two-part tariff, the overall amount they pay to be at Disney World increases.

Disney actually does follow the profit-maximizing strategy of charging a high price for admission to the park and a very low price—zero—for the rides. It seems that Disney could increase its profits by raising the price for the rides from zero to the marginal cost of the rides. But the marginal cost is so low that it would not be worth the expense of printing ride tickets and hiring additional workers to sell the tickets and collect them at each ride. Finally, note that in practice Disney can't convert all consumer surplus into profit because (1) the demand curves of customers are not all the same, and (2) even with the help of the data it has been collecting in the past few years through the MagicBands that park visitors now wear, Disney does not know precisely what these demand curves are.

MyEconLab Study Plan

MyEconLab Concept Check

Continued from page 531

Economics in Your Life

Why So Many Prices to See a Movie?

At the beginning of the chapter, we asked you to think about what you pay for a movie ticket and what people in other age groups pay. A movie theater will try to charge different prices to different consumers, based on their willingness to pay. If you have two people of about the same age, one a student and one not, you might assume that the student has a lower income and therefore a lower willingness to pay than the nonstudent, and the movie theater would like to charge the student a lower price. The movie theater employee can ask to see a student ID to ensure that the theater is giving the discount to a student.

But why don't theaters practice price discrimination at the concession stand? It is likely that a student will also have a lower willingness to pay for popcorn, and the theater can check for a student ID at the time of purchase, but unlike with the entry ticket, the theater would have a difficult time preventing the student from giving the popcorn to a nonstudent once inside the theater. Because it is easier to limit resale in movie admissions, we often see different prices for different groups. Because it is difficult to limit resale of popcorn and other movie concessions, everyone will typically pay the same price.

Conclusion

Firms in perfectly competitive industries must sell their products at the market price. For firms in other industries—which means, of course, the vast majority of firms—pricing is an important part of the strategy used to maximize profit. We have seen in this chapter, for example, that if firms can successfully segment their customers into different groups on the basis of the customers' willingness to pay, the firms can increase their profits by charging different segments different prices.

Visit MyEconLab for a news article and analysis related to the concepts in this chapter.

CHAPTER SUMMARY AND PROBLEMS

Key Terms

Price discrimination, p. 534 | Transactions costs, p. 532 | Two-part tariff, p. 546

16.1 Pricing Strategy, the Law of One Price, and Arbitrage, pages 532–534

LEARNING OBJECTIVE: Define the law of one price and explain the role of arbitrage.

Summary

According to the *law of one price*, identical products should sell for the same price everywhere. If a product sells for different prices, it will be possible to make a profit through *arbitrage*: buying a product at a low price and reselling it at a high price. The law of one price will hold as long as arbitrage is possible. Arbitrage is sometimes blocked by high **transactions costs**, which are the costs in time and other resources incurred to carry out an exchange or because the product cannot be resold. Another apparent exception to the law of one price occurs when companies offset the higher price they charge for a product by providing superior or more reliable service to customers.

MyEconLab Visit **www.myeconlab.com** to complete these exercises online and get instant feedback.

Review Questions

1.1 What is the law of one price? What is arbitrage?

1.2 Does a product always have to sell for the same price everywhere? Briefly explain.

Problems and Applications

1.3 Economist Richard Thaler of the University of Chicago notes that most economists consider arbitrage to be one way "that markets can do their magic." Briefly explain the role arbitrage can play in helping markets to work.

Source: Richard H. Thaler, "Unless You Are Spock, Irrelevant Things Matter in Economic Behavior," *New York Times*, May 8, 2015.

1.4 Prices for many goods are higher in the city of Shenzhen on the mainland of China than in the city of Hong Kong. An article in the *Economist* notes that "individuals can arbitrage these differences through what effectively amounts to smuggling."

a. Explain what the article means when it notes that individuals can "arbitrage these price differences."

b. Ultimately, what would you expect the result to be of individuals engaging in this arbitrage? Is your answer affected by the fact that the government of China requires a visa for Shenzhen residents to visit Hong Kong and regulates the number of trips that can be made between the two cities in a given year? Briefly explain.

Source: "Restrictions on Travel to Hong Kong by Shenzhen Residents," *Economist*, April 13, 2015.

1.5 **(Related to Solved Problem 16.1 on page 533)** Suppose California has many apple trees, and the price of apples there is low. Nevada has few apple trees, and the price of apples there is high. Abner buys low-priced California apples and ships them to Nevada, where he resells them at a high price. Is Abner exploiting Nevada consumers by doing this? Is Abner likely to earn an economic profit in the long run? Briefly explain.

1.6 **(Related to Solved Problem 16.1 on page 533)** Suspicions about arbitrage have a long history. For example, Valerian of Cimiez, a Catholic bishop who lived during the fifth century, wrote: "When something is bought cheaply only so it can be retailed dearly, doing business always means cheating." What might Valerian think of eBay? Do you agree with his conclusion? Briefly explain.

Source: Michael McCormick, *The Origins of the European Economy: Communications and Commerce,* A.D. *300–900*, New York: Cambridge University Press, 2001, p. 85.

16.2 Price Discrimination: Charging Different Prices for the Same Product, pages 534–543

LEARNING OBJECTIVE: Explain how a firm can increase its profits through price discrimination.

Summary

Price discrimination occurs if a firm charges different prices for the same product when the price differences are not due to differences in cost. Three requirements must be met for a firm to successfully practice price discrimination: (1) A firm must possess market power; (2) some consumers must have a greater willingness to pay for the product than other consumers, and firms must be able to know what consumers are willing to pay; and (3) firms must be able to divide up—or segment—the market for the product so that consumers who buy the product at a low price cannot resell it at a high price. In the case of *perfect price discrimination*, each consumer pays a price equal to his or her willingness to pay.

MyEconLab Visit **www.myeconlab.com** to complete these exercises online and get instant feedback.

Review Questions

2.1 What is price discrimination? Under what circumstances can a firm successfully practice price discrimination?

2.2 In 2015, the Rock and Roll Hall of Fame and Museum charged adults $25.85 for admission. Seniors (65 years and older) and military personnel were charged $20.50, and children between 9 and 12 years old were charged $16.25. Use the admission fees to rank these groups based on their elasticities of demand from highest to lowest.

Source: www.rockhall.com.

2.3 What is yield management? Give an example of a firm using yield management to increase profits.

2.4 What is perfect price discrimination? Is it likely to ever occur? Is perfect price discrimination economically efficient? Briefly explain.

2.5 Is it possible to practice price discrimination across time? Briefly explain.

Problems and Applications

2.6 Some people—usually business travelers—have a very strong desire to fly to a particular city on a particular day, and airlines charge these travelers higher ticket prices than they charge other people, such as families who are planning vacations months in advance. Some people really like Big Macs, and other people only rarely eat Big Macs, preferring to eat other food for lunch on most days. Consider the following possible explanations of why airlines can charge different people different prices while McDonald's can't and briefly explain which explanation is correct.

1. In most cities, there are laws against charging different people different prices for food products.
2. Most people don't pay attention to prices when buying plane tickets, so the airlines can charge different prices without it being noticed.
3. People don't like hamburgers as much as they used to, so McDonald's has to keep cutting the prices it charges everyone.
4. People can't resell airline tickets, so people buying them at low price can't resell them at a high price. People can resell hamburgers more easily.

2.7 While in Shanghai, China, to teach an MBA course, Craig Richardson, an economics professor from Winston-Salem State University, asked his American students to haggle with sellers in a market where prices for the same items can vary widely. Professor Richardson explained that the same item with the same sticker price at different market stalls can have a final price that varies "by 1,500% or more, depending on the negotiating skills of the buyer."

a. Do Shanghai merchants practice price discrimination? Briefly explain.

b. Which consumers are likely to pay the highest prices for similar items in the Shanghai market?

Source: Craig J. Richardson, "An Econ Lesson in a Shanghai Market," *Wall Street Journal*, July 6, 2015.

2.8 **(Related to the Chapter Opener on page 531)** When asked what was most valuable about the big data Disney was collecting from its MagicBands program, the executive in charge of the program stated, "The biggest value comes from being able to segment customers into better, smarter segments so you know what is going on and can act on those segments." Briefly explain his reasoning.

Source: Elizabeth Miller Coyne, "The Disney Take on Big Data's Value," thenewip.net, January 13, 2015

2.9 BMW sells cars in China at a price two to three times higher than in the United States. Some people have purchased BMWs in the United States and exported them for resale in China. An article in the *Wall Street Journal* quoted a spokesperson for BMW as stating, "Vehicles exported to other countries undermine our pricing and volume positioning in the United States and other world-wide markets." The company has also tried to get the U.S. government to stop buyers from reselling cars in China because the company argues that the practice is illegal.

a. Does BMW believe that demand for its cars is more or less elastic in China than in the United States? Briefly explain.

a. If U.S. buyers were free to export to China BMWs they purchased in the United States, would you expect the prices of the cars to be same in both countries? Briefly explain.

Sources: Colum Murphy and Rose Yu, "We Don't Overcharge Our Chinese Buyers, BMW Says," *Wall Street Journal*, May 29, 2014; and Andrew Grossman, "A Profitable Trade: Illicitly Shipping BMWs to China," *Wall Street Journal*, December 2, 2013.

2.10 Online newspapers can earn revenue from subscriptions and from advertisements. The more readers who access the paper's site, the higher the advertising revenue the paper earns. To increase revenue, in 2011 the *New York Times* began offering online subscriptions for $180 per year. Anyone purchasing the subscription has unlimited access to any content on the paper's site. Other online readers are allowed to read only the front page of the newspaper and 20 stories monthly for free. Business writer Trish Gorman explained that the *Times* "had no way to know who would embrace the price increase. So the paper allowed readers to segment themselves." Briefly explain how the paper's strategy allows "readers to segment themselves." How does the strategy increase the paper's revenue?

Source: Trish Gorman, "The Price Isn't Right: What New York Times, Apple and In-N-Out Could Teach Netflix," *Forbes*, September 30, 2011.

2.11 **(Related to the Don't Let This Happen to You on page 535)** A state law in California makes it illegal for businesses to charge men and women different prices for dry cleaning, laundry, tailoring, or hair grooming. The state legislator who introduced the law did so after a dry cleaner charged her more to have her shirts dry cleaned than to have her husband's shirts dry cleaned. According to a newspaper article, the owner of the dry cleaner told the legislator that his costs for cleaning women's shirts were higher because he had to iron them by hand rather than use an automatic press. The law proved difficult to enforce, with many dry cleaners continuing to ignore it years after it was passed.

a. Was the dry cleaner practicing price discrimination, as defined in this chapter? Briefly explain.

b. Do you support laws like this one? Briefly explain.

Sources: Veronique de Turenne, "Santa Monica Sues Nine Dry Cleaners under Gender Discrimination Law," *Los Angeles Times*, May 13, 2008; and Harry Brooks, "Law Mandates Equality in Dry Cleaning, Hair Styling," *North County* (California) *Times*, October 7, 2001.

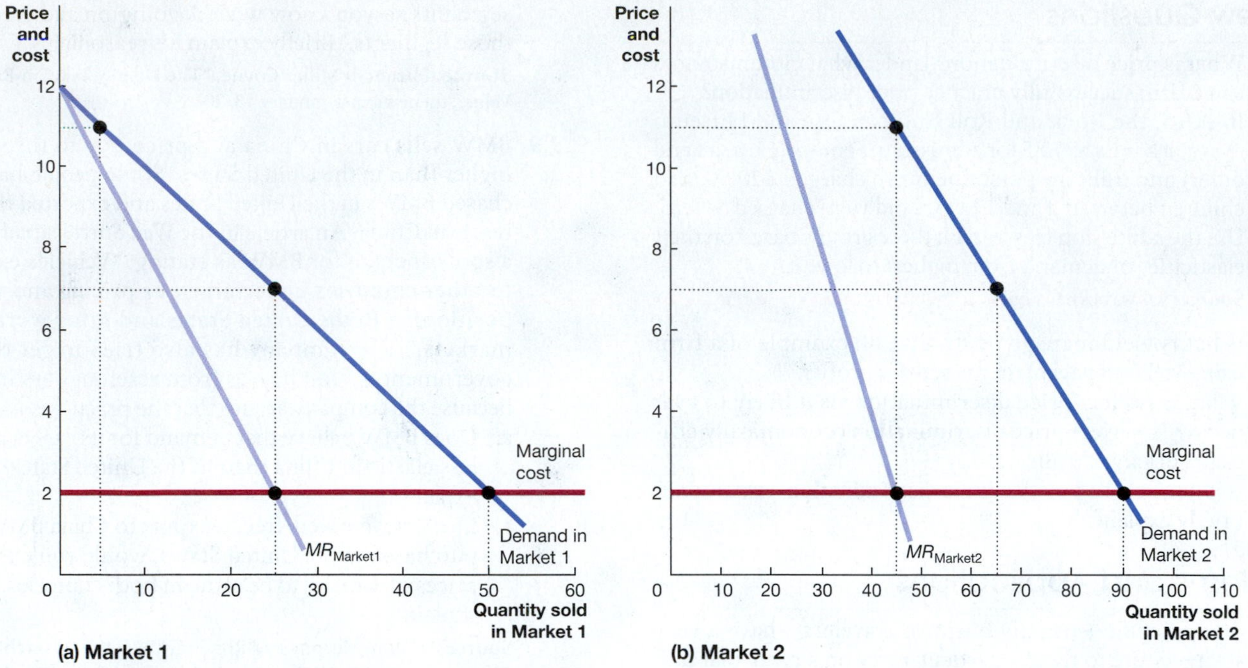

2.12 **(Related to** Solved Problem 16.2 **on page 536)** Use the graphs above to answer the questions.

a. If this firm wants to maximize profits, what price will it charge in Market 1, and what quantity will it sell?

b. If this firm wants to maximize profits, what price will it charge in Market 2, and what quantity will it sell?

2.13 **(Related to** Solved Problem 16.2 **on page 536)** In addition to discounting the price of computers purchased by students and faculty, Apple sells certain computer models only to schools and universities. According to a discussion on the Mac Rumors blog:

> Apple has quietly launched a lower cost $999 iMac for educational institutions this morning. The new low-end model is labeled "Education only" and is not available for individuals. . . . Apple, in the past, has also offered special education only models for institutions . . . [and] has adjusted the hardware down in order to fit the sub-$1000 price point.

Is Apple engaging in price discrimination in following this policy? If so, why does it prepare special models for educational institutions rather than cut the prices of existing models purchased by educational buyers? If this is not an example of price discrimination, why doesn't Apple offer these computers to the general public?

Source: "Apple Launches $999 iMac for Educational Institutions," by Arnold Kim. From www.macrumors.com, August 8, 2011. Reprinted with permission.

2.14 **(Related to the** Making the Connection **on page 539)** Jason Furman and Tim Simcoe, the chair of and a senior economist for President Barack Obama's Council of Economic Advisors, wrote, "Economists have studied [price discrimination] for many years, and while big data seems poised to revolutionize pricing practice, it has not altered the underlying principles.... Those principles suggest that [price discrimination] is often good for both firms and their customers." Furman and Simcoe describe "need-based financial aid for college students" as an example of price discrimination that is good for consumers.

a. What do Furman and Simcoe mean by "underlying principles"?

b. In what sense is need-based financial aid an example of price discrimination? Is financial aid good for both colleges and students? Briefly explain.

Source: Jason Furman and Tim Simcoe, "The Economics of Big Data and Differential Pricing," www.whitehouse.gov/blog/2015/02/06/economics-big-data-and-differential-pricing, February 6, 2015.

2.15 In 2012, some electronics firms began offering Ultra HD, often called 4K, televisions. These televisions offer a crisper picture than conventional HD televisions. Initially, these televisions had prices as high as $20,000. One electronics industry analyst was quoted in a news story as saying, "By the end of 2013, prices had fallen dramatically, with 55-inch 4K TVs priced as low as $3,500." By mid-2015, the same size 4K televisions could be purchased for $1,800. A student argues, "Sony and the other electronics firms failed to maximize profit by charging such high prices for 4K televisions in 2012. Hardly anybody can afford such prices. If they had charged $1,800 back then, they would have sold many more televisions and increased their profit." Briefly explain whether you agree with the student's analysis. Use a graph to illustrate your answer.

Sources: "Is Now the Time to Buy a 4K TV?" *Wall Street Journal,* May 11, 2014; and pricing data from bestbuy.com.

2.16 **(Related to the** Chapter Opener **on page 531)** Walt Disney World charges residents of Florida lower prices for theme park tickets than it charges non-Florida residents. For example, in 2015, an adult Florida resident was charged $201.29 for a three-day ticket. The price of the same package for a non-Florida resident was $275.00.

a. What is Disney assuming about Florida residents' willingness to pay? Why might it make this assumption?
b. How might Disney keep Florida residents from buying Walt Disney World tickets at discounted prices and reselling them to non-Florida residents at higher prices?
c. Disney offers discount tickets to students at universities located in Florida but does not offer discount tickets to students at most universities in other states. Briefly explain Disney's strategy. Would you expect the discount Disney offers to students at Florida universities to be higher or lower than the discount it offers to other residents of Florida? Briefly explain.

Source: Disney prices from allears.net, July 9, 2015.

2.17 **(Related to the Making the Connection on page 542)** Many supermarkets provide regular shoppers with "loyalty cards" that the shoppers swipe each time they check out. By swiping the card, a shopper receives reduced prices on a few goods, and the supermarket compiles information on all the shoppers' purchases. Recently, some supermarkets have switched from giving the same price reductions to all shoppers to giving shoppers differing price reductions depending on their shopping history. A manager at one company that uses this approach said, "It comes down to understanding elasticity at a household level."

a. Is the use of loyalty cards that provide the same price discounts for every shopper who uses them a form of price discrimination? Briefly explain.
b. Why would making price discounts depend on a shopper's buying history involve "elasticity at a household level"? What information from a shopper's buying history would be relevant in predicting the shopper's response to a price discount?

Source: Stephanie Clifford, "Shopper Alert: Price May Drop for You Alone," *New York Times*, August 9, 2012.

2.18 Fernando has a monopoly on sales of pizzas in the small town of North Key Largo, Florida. Use the following information on the demand for Fernando's pizzas to answer the questions.

Price	Quantity Demanded
$30	0
25	1
20	2
15	3
10	4
5	5
0	6

a. If Fernando can produce pizzas at a constant cost of $5 per pizza, how many pizzas does he produce, what price does he charge, and how much profit does he make?
b. If Fernando is able to engage in perfect price discrimination, what is his total revenue for 3 units? What is the marginal revenue of the third unit?
c. If Fernando is able to engage in perfect price discrimination, how many pizzas does he produce, and how much profit does he make?
d. Draw a graph showing producer surplus, consumer surplus, and deadweight loss if Fernando does not price discriminate. Draw a second graph showing producer surplus, consumer surplus, and deadweight loss if Fernando practices perfect price discrimination.

16.3 Other Pricing Strategies, pages 543–548

LEARNING OBJECTIVE: Explain how some firms increase their profits by using odd pricing, cost-plus pricing, and two-part tariffs.

Summary

In addition to price discrimination, firms use odd pricing, cost-plus pricing, and two-part tariffs as pricing strategies. Firms use *odd pricing*—for example, charging $1.99 rather than $2.00—because consumers tend to buy more at odd prices than would be predicted from estimated demand curves. With *cost-plus pricing*, firms set the price for a product by adding a percentage markup to average total cost. Using cost-plus pricing may be a good way to come close to the profit-maximizing price when marginal revenue or marginal cost is difficult to measure. Some firms can require consumers to pay an initial fee for the right to buy their product and an additional fee for each unit of the product purchased. Economists refer to this situation as a **two-part tariff**. Sam's Club, cellphone companies, and many golf and tennis clubs use two-part tariffs in pricing their products.

MyEconLab Visit www.myeconlab.com to complete these exercises online and get instant feedback.

Review Questions

3.1 What is odd pricing?
3.2 What is cost-plus pricing? Is using cost-plus pricing consistent with a firm maximizing profit? How does the elasticity of demand affect the percentage price markup that firms use?
3.3 Give an example of a firm using a two-part tariff as part of its pricing strategy.

Problems and Applications

3.4 One leading explanation for odd pricing is that it allows firms to trick buyers into thinking they are paying less than they really are. If this explanation is correct, in what types of markets and among what groups of consumers would you be most likely to find odd pricing? Should the government ban this practice and force companies to round up their prices to the nearest dollar? Briefly explain.

3.5 Instacart is an Internet startup that offers home delivery of groceries. It buys the groceries in regular brick-and-mortar supermarkets, marks up the prices it pays, and then charges consumers the higher prices in exchange for making home deliveries. According to an article in the *Wall Street Journal,* Instacart marks up the price of potato chips by 26 percent, but it marks up the price of eggs by only 2.5 percent. Is it likely that Instacart believes that the demand for potato chips is more elastic or less elastic than the demand for eggs? Briefly explain.

Source: Greg Bensinger and Willa Plank, "A $5.39 Bag of Chips? Doing the Math on an Instacart Order," *Wall Street Journal,* January 15, 2015.

3.6 A review of Kappo Masa, a popular restaurant in New York City, notes, "The markup that New York restaurants customarily add to retail wine and sake prices is about 150 percent. The average markup at Kappo Masa is 200 percent to 300 percent." Even 150 percent is a much larger markup than the markups restaurants use to price the meals they serve. Why do restaurants use a higher markup for wine than for food, and why might a popular restaurant mark up the price of wine more than an average restaurant does?

Source: Pete Wells, "Restaurant Review: Kappo Masa on the Upper East Side," *New York Times,* January 6, 2015.

3.7 An article in the *Wall Street Journal* gave the following explanation of how products were traditionally priced at Parker-Hannifin Corporation:

> For as long as anyone at the 89-year-old company could recall, Parker used the same simple formula to determine prices of its 800,000 parts—from heat-resistant seals for jet engines to steel valves that hoist buckets on cherry pickers. Company managers would calculate how much it cost to make and deliver each product and add a flat percentage on top, usually aiming for about 35%. Many managers liked the method because it was straightforward.

Is it likely that this system of pricing maximized the firm's profit? Briefly explain.

Source: Timothy Aeppel, "Seeking Perfect Prices, CEO Tears Up the Rules," *Wall Street Journal,* March 27, 2007.

3.8 **(Related to the Making the Connection on page 544)** Would you expect a publishing company to use a strict cost-plus pricing system for all its books? How might you find some indication about whether a publishing company actually is using cost-plus pricing for all its books?

3.9 Some professional sports teams charge fans a one-time lump sum for a personal seat license. The personal seat license allows a fan the right to buy season tickets each year. No one without a personal seat license can buy season tickets. After the original purchase from the team, the personal seat licenses usually can be bought and sold by fans—whoever owns the seat license in a given year can buy season tickets—but the team does not earn any additional revenue from this buying and selling. Suppose a new sports stadium has been built, and the team is trying to decide on the price to charge for season tickets.

a. Will the team make more profit from the combination of selling personal seat licenses and season tickets if it keeps the prices of the season tickets low or if it charges the monopoly price? Briefly explain.

b. After the first year, is the team's strategy for pricing season tickets likely to change?

c. Will it make a difference in the team's pricing strategy for season tickets if all the personal seat licenses are sold in the first year?

3.10 During the nineteenth century, the U.S. Congress encouraged railroad companies to build transcontinental railways across the Great Plains by giving them land grants. At that time, the federal government owned most of the land on the Great Plains. The land grants consisted of the land on which the railway was built and alternating sections of 1 square mile each on either side of the railway to a distance of 6 to 40 miles, depending on the location. The railroad companies were free to sell this land to farmers or anyone else who wanted to buy it. The process of selling the land took decades. Some economic historians have argued that the railroad companies charged lower prices to ship freight because they owned so much land along the tracks. Briefly explain the reasoning of these economic historians.

3.11 **(Related to the Chapter Opener on page 531)** If you visited Disneyland between 1955 and 1982, most rides would have required a ticket—in addition to the ticket necessary to enter the park. Explain why this pricing strategy earned Disney a lower profit than the current strategy of requiring visitors to purchase a ticket to enter the park but not requiring an additional ticket to be purchased for each ride.

3.12 Thomas Kinnaman, an economist at Bucknell University, has analyzed the pricing of garbage collection:

> Setting the appropriate fee for garbage collection can be tricky when there are both fixed and marginal costs of garbage collection.... A curbside price set equal to the average total cost of collection would have high garbage generators partially subsidizing the fixed costs of low garbage generators. For example, if the time that a truck idles outside a one-can household and a two-can household is the same, and the fees are set to cover the total cost of garbage collection, then the two-can household paying twice that of the one-can household has subsidized a portion of the collection costs of the one-can household.

Briefly explain how a city might solve this pricing problem by using a two-part tariff in setting the garbage collection fees it charges households.

Source: Thomas C. Kinnaman, "Examining the Justification for Residential Recycling," *Journal of Economic Perspectives,* Vol. 20, No. 4, Fall 2006, pp. 219–232.

CHAPTER

17

The Markets for Labor and Other Factors of Production

Chapter Outline and Learning Objectives

Rio Tinto Mines with Robots

When most people think of coal and iron mines, they picture workers wearing lamp helmets and carrying shovels and picks. The London-based mining company Rio Tinto is changing that perception. At Rio Tinto's large iron mines in the Pilbara region of the Australian Outback, robotic machines now carry out many traditional mining jobs. For instance, the company uses large robotic drills to dig for iron ore deposits. Employees at computer consoles 800 miles away, in the city of Perth, control the movement and operation of the drills. In the mines, the company uses machines to collect the ore. The ore is then loaded on trucks, which have no drivers and are also controlled remotely, to bring the ore to trains for shipment to the coast. The trucks, which are built in the United States by the Japanese company Komatsu, rely on sensors to safely drive in and around the mines. The company is currently using conventional trains to ship the ore to the coast, but it intends to introduce robotic trains that can be operated remotely.

Rio Tinto was able to introduce robotic machines into its mining operations because of developments in computer technology, the Global Positioning System (GPS), and robotics. The company's mining operations are another example of the "Internet of Things," in which devices directly communicate data to a computer without a person having to enter the data (see Chapter 16). Rio Tinto's incentive to adopt new robotic technology was increased by the high wages—often $100,000 or more per year—it was having to pay to attract miners and truck drivers to work in such a remote place as Pilbara.

Many companies have begun using new robotic technology to substitute capital for labor in production. For example, Kroger, the largest U.S. supermarket chain, uses body heat–detecting infrared cameras at more than 2,000 of its stores to direct workers to checkout lines. Some people see the spread of robotic technology as a boon to the economy that will lead to higher living standards, but other people fear that robots will reduce the demand for labor enough to leave some workers permanently unemployed.

Throughout this book, we have been using the model of demand and supply to analyze the markets for goods and services. We will use some of the same concepts in this chapter to analyze the markets for labor and other factors of production. As we will see, the demand and supply model can help us analyze important issues concerning the market for labor, including the effect of robotics.

Sources: Timothy Aeppel, "What Clever Robots Mean for Jobs," *Wall Street Journal*, February 24, 2015; Matthew Hall, "Forget Self-Driving Google Cars, Australia Has Self-Driving Trucks," theage.com.au, October 20, 2014; Claire Cain Miller, "Will You Lose Your Job to a Robot? Silicon Valley Is Split," *New York Times*, August 6, 2014; and Timothy Aeppel, "Be Calm, Robots Aren't About to Take Your Job, MIT Economist Says," *Wall Street Journal*, February 25, 2015.

Economics in Your Life

How Can You Convince Your Boss to Give You a Raise?

Imagine that you have worked for a local sandwich shop for over a year and are preparing to ask for a raise. You might tell the manager that you are a good employee, with a good attitude and work ethic. You might also explain that you have learned more about your job and are now able to make sandwiches more quickly, track inventory more accurately, and work the cash register more effectively than when you were first hired. Will this be enough to convince your manager to give you a raise? How can you convince your manager that you are worth a higher wage than you are currently being paid? As you read this chapter, try to answer these questions. You can check your answers against those we provide on **page 585** at the end of this chapter.

Factors of production Labor, capital, natural resources, and other inputs used to produce goods and services.

Firms use **factors of production**—such as labor, capital, and natural resources—to produce goods and services. For example, the Rio Tinto mining company uses labor (the operators of its robotic equipment), capital (driverless trucks and other robotic equipment), and natural resources (iron ore) to produce the iron the company exports from Australia to other countries around the world. In this chapter, we will explore how firms choose the profit-maximizing quantity of labor and other factors of production. The interaction between firms' demand for labor and households' supply of labor determines the equilibrium wage rate.

Because there are many different types of labor, there are many different labor markets. The equilibrium wage in the market for professional athletes in major sports leagues is much higher than the equilibrium wage in the market for college professors. We will analyze why. We will also analyze how factors such as discrimination, unions, and compensation for dangerous or unpleasant jobs help explain differences in wages. We will then look at *personnel economics,* which is concerned with how firms can use economic analysis to design their employee compensation plans. Finally, we will analyze the markets for other factors of production.

17.1 The Demand for Labor

LEARNING OBJECTIVE: Explain how firms choose the profit-maximizing quantity of labor to employ.

Derived demand The demand for a factor of production; it depends on the demand for the good the factor produces.

Until now, we have concentrated on consumer demand for final goods and services. The demand for labor is different from the demand for final goods and services because it is a *derived demand.* A **derived demand** for a factor of production depends on the demand for the good the factor produces. You demand an Apple iPhone because of the utility you receive from making phone calls, texting, using Instagram, playing games, and listening to music. Apple's demand for the labor to make iPhones is derived from the underlying consumer demand for iPhones. As a result, we can say that Apple's demand for labor depends primarily on two factors:

1. The additional iPhones Apple can produce if it hires one more worker
2. The additional revenue Apple receives from selling the additional iPhones

(In fact, Apple's suppliers, rather than Apple itself, manufacture the iPhone. For simplicity, we are assuming here that Apple does the manufacturing.)

The Marginal Revenue Product of Labor

Let's consider an example. To keep the main point clear, we'll assume that in the short run, Apple can increase production of iPhones only by increasing the quantity of labor it employs. The table in Figure 17.1 shows the relationship between the quantity of workers Apple hires, the quantity of iPhones it produces, the additional revenue from selling the additional iPhones, and the additional profit from hiring each additional worker.

For simplicity, we are keeping the scale of Apple's factory very small. We will also assume that Apple is a perfect competitor both in the market for selling smartphones and in the market for hiring labor. As a result, Apple is a *price taker* in both markets. Although this assumption is not realistic, the basic analysis would not change if we assumed that Apple can affect the price of smartphones and the wage paid to workers. Suppose that Apple can sell as many iPhones as it wants at a price of $200 and can hire as many workers as it wants at a wage of $600 per week. Remember that the additional output a firm produces as a result of hiring one more worker is called the **marginal product of labor** (see Chapter 11). In the table in Figure 17.1, we calculate the marginal product of labor as the change in total output as each additional worker is hired. Because of the *law of diminishing returns,* the marginal product of labor declines as a firm hires more workers.

Marginal product of labor The additional output a firm produces as a result of hiring one more worker.

Number of Workers	Output of iPhones per Week	Marginal Product of Labor (iPhones per week)	Product Price	Marginal Revenue Product of Labor (dollars per week)	Wage (dollars per week)	Additional Profit from Hiring One More Worker (dollars per week)
L	*Q*	*MP*	*P*	*MRP* = *P* x *MP*	*W*	*MRP* − *W*
0	0	—	$200	—	$600	—
1	6	6	200	$1,200	600	$600
2	11	5	200	1,000	600	400
3	15	4	200	800	600	200
4	18	3	200	600	600	0
5	20	2	200	400	600	−200
6	21	1	200	200	600	−400

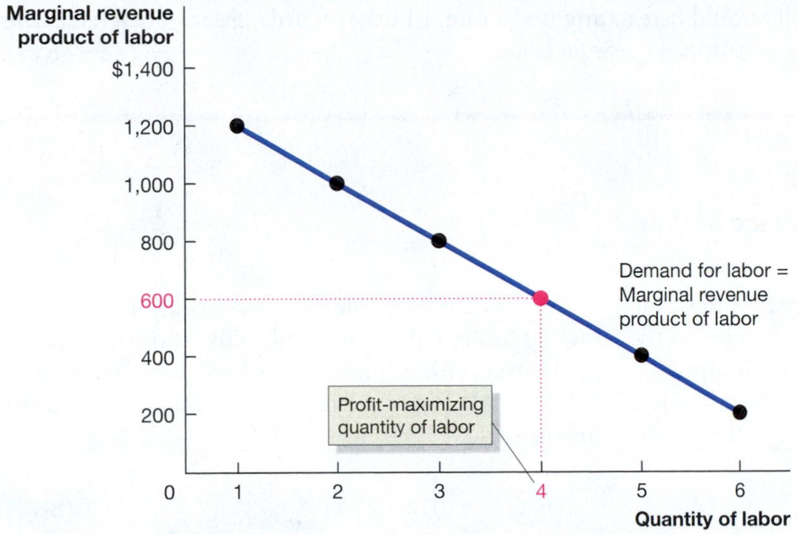

Figure 17.1

The Marginal Revenue Product of Labor and the Demand for Labor

The marginal revenue product of labor equals the marginal product of labor multiplied by the price of the good. The marginal revenue product curve slopes downward because diminishing returns cause the marginal product of labor to decline as more workers are hired. A firm maximizes profits by hiring workers up to the point where the wage equals the marginal revenue product of labor. The marginal revenue product of labor curve is the firm's demand curve for labor because it tells the firm the profit-maximizing quantity of workers to hire at each wage. For example, using the demand curve shown in this figure, if the wage is $600, the firm will hire 4 workers.

When deciding how many workers to hire, a firm is not interested in how much *output* will increase as it hires another worker but in how much *revenue* will increase as it hires another worker. In other words, what matters is how much the firm's revenue will rise when it sells the additional output it can produce by hiring one more worker. We can calculate this amount, which is called the **marginal revenue product of labor (*MRP*)**, by multiplying the additional output produced by the product price. For example, consider what happens if Apple increases the number of workers hired from 2 to 3. The table in Figure 17.1 shows that hiring the third worker allows Apple to increase its weekly output of iPhones from 11 to 15, so the marginal product of labor is 4 iPhones. The price of the iPhones is $200, so the marginal revenue product of the third worker is 4 × $200 or $800. In other words, Apple adds $800 to its revenue as a result of hiring the third worker. In the graph, we plot the values of the marginal revenue product of labor at each quantity of labor.

Marginal revenue product of labor (*MRP*) The change in a firm's revenue as a result of hiring one more worker.

To decide how many workers to hire, Apple compares the additional revenue it earns from hiring another worker to the increase in its costs from paying that worker. The difference between the additional revenue and the additional cost is the additional profit (or loss) from hiring one more worker. This additional profit is shown in the last column of the table in Figure 17.1 and is calculated by subtracting the wage from the marginal revenue product of labor. As long as the marginal revenue product of labor is greater than the wage, Apple's profits are increasing, and it should continue to hire more workers. When the marginal revenue product of labor is less than the wage, Apple's profits are falling, and it should hire fewer workers. When the marginal revenue product of labor is equal to the wage, Apple has maximized its profits by hiring the optimal number of workers. The values in the table show that Apple should hire 4 workers. If Apple hires a fifth worker, the marginal revenue product of $400 will be

Table 17.1

The Relationship between the Marginal Revenue Product of Labor and the Wage

When . . .	the firm . . .
$MRP > W$,	should hire more workers to increase profits.
$MRP < W$,	should hire fewer workers to increase profits.
$MRP = W$,	is hiring the optimal number of workers and is maximizing profits.

less than the wage of $600, and its profits will fall by $200. Table 17.1 summarizes the relationship between the marginal revenue product of labor and the wage.

We can see from Figure 17.1 that if Apple has to pay a wage of $600 per week, it should hire 4 workers. If the wage rises to $1,000, then applying the rule that profits are maximized where the marginal revenue product of labor equals the wage, Apple should hire only 2 workers. Similarly, if the wage falls to $400 per week, Apple should hire 5 workers. In fact, the marginal revenue product curve tells a firm how many workers it should hire at any wage rate. In other words, *the marginal revenue product of labor curve is the demand curve for labor.*

MyEconLab Concept Check

Solved Problem 17.1

MyEconLab Interactive Animation

Hiring Decisions by a Firm That Is a Price Maker

We have assumed that Apple can sell as many iPhones as it wants without having to cut the price. A firm in a perfectly competitive market is in this situation. These firms are *price takers.* Suppose instead that a firm has market power and is a *price maker,* so that to increase sales, it must reduce the price.

Assume that Apple faces the situation shown in the following table. Fill in the blank cells, and then determine the profit-maximizing quantity of workers for Apple to hire. Briefly explain why hiring this quantity of workers is profit maximizing.

(1) Quantity of Labor	(2) Output of iPhones per Week	(3) Marginal Product of Labor	(4) Product Price	(5) Total Revenue	(6) Marginal Revenue Product of Labor	(7) Wage	(8) Additional Profit from Hiring One Additional Worker
0	0	—	$200		—	$500	—
1	6	6	180			500	
2	11	5	160			500	
3	15	4	140			500	
4	18	3	120			500	
5	20	2	100			500	
6	21	1	80			500	

Solving the Problem

Step 1: Review the chapter material. This problem is about determining the profit-maximizing quantity of labor for a firm to hire, so you may want to review the section "The Demand for Labor," which begins on page 558.

Step 2: Fill in the blank cells in the table. As Apple hires more workers, it sells more iPhones and earns more revenue. You can calculate how revenue increases by multiplying the quantity of iPhones produced—shown in column (2)—by the price—shown in column (4). Then you can calculate the marginal revenue product of labor as the change in revenue as each additional worker is hired. (Notice that in this case, marginal revenue product is *not* calculated by multiplying the marginal product by the product price. Because Apple is a price maker, its marginal revenue from selling additional iPhones is less than the price of iPhones.) Finally, you can calculate the additional profit from hiring one more worker by subtracting the wage—shown in column (7)—from each worker's marginal revenue product.

(1) Quantity of Labor	(2) Output of iPhones per Week	(3) Marginal Product of Labor	(4) Product Price	(5) Total Revenue	(6) Marginal Revenue Product of Labor	(7) Wage	(8) Additional Profit from Hiring One Additional Worker
0	0	—	$200	$0	—	$500	—
1	6	6	180	1,080	$1,080	500	$580
2	11	5	160	1,760	680	500	180
3	15	4	140	2,100	340	500	−160
4	18	3	120	2,160	60	500	−440
5	20	2	100	2,000	−160	500	−660
6	21	1	80	1,680	−320	500	−820

Step 3: Use the information in the table to determine the profit-maximizing quantity of workers to hire. To determine the profit-maximizing quantity of workers to hire, you need to compare the marginal revenue product of labor with the wage. Column (8) makes this comparison by subtracting the wage from the marginal revenue product. As long as the values in column (8) are positive, the firm should continue to hire workers. The marginal revenue product of the second worker is $680, and the wage is $500, so column (8) shows that hiring the second worker will add $180 to Apple's profits. The marginal revenue product of the third worker is $340, and the wage is $500, so hiring the third worker would reduce Apple's profits by $160. Therefore, Apple will maximize profits by hiring 2 workers.

Your Turn: For more practice, do related problem 1.6 on page 586 at the end of this chapter.

MyEconLab Study Plan

The Market Demand Curve for Labor

We can determine the market demand curve for labor in the same way we determine the market demand curve for a good—by adding up the quantity of the good demanded by each consumer at each price (see Chapter 10). Similarly, we find the market demand curve for labor by adding up the quantity of labor demanded by each firm at each wage, holding constant all other variables that might affect the willingness of firms to hire workers.

MyEconLab Concept Check

Factors That Shift the Market Demand Curve for Labor

In constructing the demand curve for labor, we held constant all variables—except for the wage—that would affect the willingness of firms to demand labor. An increase or a decrease in the wage causes *an increase or a decrease in the quantity of labor demanded,* which we show by a movement along the demand curve. If any variable other than the wage changes, the result is *an increase or a decrease in the demand for labor,* which we show by a shift of the demand curve. The following are the five most important variables that cause the labor demand curve to shift:

1. **Increases in human capital. Human capital** represents the accumulated knowledge and skills that workers acquire from formal training and education or from life experiences. For example, a worker with a college education generally has more skills and is more productive than a worker who has only a high school diploma. If workers become more educated and are therefore able to produce more output per day, the demand for their services will increase, shifting the labor demand curve to the right.

Human capital The accumulated knowledge and skills that workers acquire from formal training and education or from life experiences.

2. **Changes in technology.** As new and better machinery and equipment are developed, workers who use them become more productive. This effect causes the labor demand curve to shift to the right over time.

3. **Changes in the price of the product.** The marginal revenue product of labor depends on the price a firm receives for its output. A higher price increases the marginal revenue product and shifts the labor demand curve to the right. A lower price shifts the labor demand curve to the left.
4. **Changes in the quantity of other inputs.** Workers are able to produce more if they have more machinery and other inputs available to them. The marginal product of labor in the United States is higher than the marginal product of labor in most other countries in large part because U.S. firms provide workers with more machinery and equipment. Over time, workers in the United States have had increasing amounts of other inputs available to them, which has increased their productivity and caused the labor demand curve to shift to the right.
5. **Changes in the number of firms in the market.** If new firms enter the market, the labor demand curve will shift to the right. If firms exit the market, the demand for labor will shift to the left. The result is similar to the effect that increasing or decreasing the number of consumers in a market has on the demand for a good.

MyEconLab Study Plan

MyEconLab Concept Check

17.2 The Supply of Labor

LEARNING OBJECTIVE: Explain how people choose the quantity of labor to supply.

Now that we have discussed the demand for labor, we can consider the supply of labor. Of the many trade-offs each of us faces in life, one of the most important is how to divide up the 24 hours in a day between labor and leisure. Every hour spent posting to Instagram, walking on the beach, or in other forms of leisure is one hour less spent working. Because in devoting an hour to leisure we give up an hour's earnings from working, the *opportunity cost* of leisure is the wage. The higher the wage we could earn working, the higher the opportunity cost of leisure. Therefore, as the wage increases, we tend to take less leisure and work more. As Figure 17.2 shows, the result is that the labor supply curve for most people is upward sloping.

Although we normally expect the labor supply curve for an individual to be upward sloping, it is possible that at very high wage levels, the labor supply curve of an individual might be *backward bending*, so that higher wages actually result in a *smaller* quantity of labor supplied, as shown in Figure 17.3. To understand why, recall the definitions of the *substitution effect* and the *income effect* (see Chapters 3 and 10). The substitution effect of a price change refers to the fact that an increase in price makes a good more expensive *relative* to other goods. In the case of a wage change, the substitution effect refers to the fact that an increase in the wage raises the opportunity cost of leisure and causes a worker to devote *more* time to working and less time to leisure.

MyEconLab Animation

Figure 17.2

The Labor Supply Curve

As the wage increases, the opportunity cost of leisure increases, causing individuals to supply a greater quantity of labor. Therefore, the labor supply curve is upward sloping.

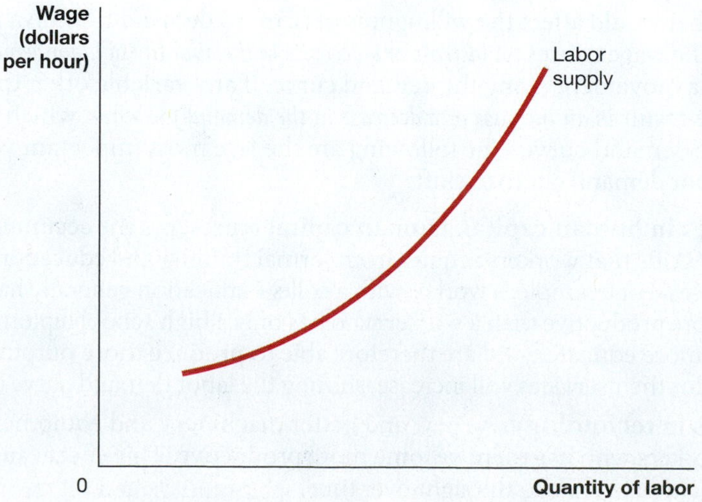

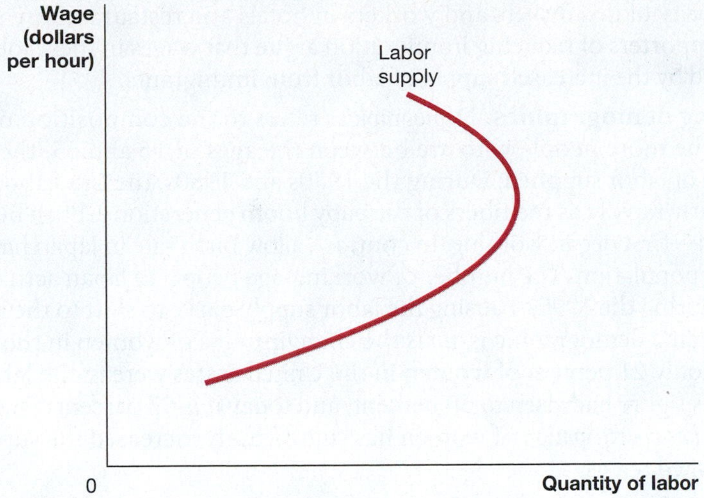

MyEconLab Animation

Figure 17.3

A Backward-Bending Labor Supply Curve

As the wage rises, a greater quantity of labor is usually supplied. As the wage rises above a certain level, the individual is able to afford more leisure even though the opportunity cost of leisure is higher. The result may be that an increase in the wage leads to a smaller quantity of labor supplied.

The income effect of a price change refers to the change in the quantity demanded of a good that results from changes in consumer purchasing power as the price changes. An increase in the wage will clearly increase a consumer's purchasing power for any given number of hours worked. For a normal good, the income effect leads to a larger quantity demanded. Because leisure is a normal good, the income effect of a wage increase will cause a worker to devote *less* time to working and more time to leisure. So, the substitution effect of a wage increase causes a worker to supply a larger quantity of labor, but the income effect causes a worker to supply a smaller quantity of labor. Whether a worker supplies more or less labor following a wage increase depends on whether the substitution effect is larger than the income effect. Figure 17.3 shows the typical case of the substitution effect being larger than the income effect at low levels of wages—so the worker supplies a larger quantity of labor as the wage rises—and the income effect being larger than the substitution effect at high levels of wages—so the worker supplies a smaller quantity of labor as the wage rises. For example, suppose an attorney has become quite successful and can charge clients very high fees. Or suppose a rock band has become very popular and receives a large payment for every concert. In these cases, there is a high opportunity cost for the lawyer to turn down another client to take a longer vacation or for the band to turn down another concert. But because their incomes are already very high, they may decide to give up additional income for more leisure. In this case, for the lawyer or the rock band, the income effect is larger than the substitution effect, and a higher wage causes them to supply *less* labor.

The Market Supply Curve of Labor

We can determine the market supply curve of labor in the same way we determine a market supply curve of a good. We find the market supply curve of a good by adding up the quantity of the good supplied by each firm at each price (see Chapter 12). Similarly, we find the market supply curve of labor by adding up the quantity of labor supplied by each worker at each wage, holding constant all other variables that might affect the willingness of workers to supply labor. MyEconLab Concept Check

Factors That Shift the Market Supply Curve of Labor

In constructing the market supply curve of labor, we hold constant all other variables that would affect the willingness of workers to supply labor, except the wage. If any of these other variables change, the market supply curve will shift. The following are the three most important variables that cause the market supply curve of labor to shift:

1. **Increasing population.** As the population grows due to the number of births exceeding the number of deaths and due to immigration, the supply curve of labor shifts to the right. The effects of immigration on labor supply are largest in the markets for unskilled workers. In some large cities in the United States, for example,

the majority of taxi drivers and workers in hotels and restaurants are immigrants. Some supporters of reducing immigration argue that wages in these jobs have been depressed by the increased supply of labor from immigrants.

2. **Changing demographics.** *Demographics* refers to the composition of the population. The more people who are between the ages of 16 and 65, the greater the quantity of labor supplied. During the 1970s and 1980s, the U.S. labor force grew particularly rapidly as members of the baby boom generation—born between 1946 and 1964—first began working. In contrast, a low birth rate in Japan has resulted in an aging population. The number of working-age people in Japan actually began to decline during the 1990s, causing the labor supply curve to shift to the left.

   A related demographic issue is the changing role of women in the labor force. In 1900, only 21 percent of women in the United States were in the labor force. By 1950, this figure had risen to 30 percent, and today it is 57 percent. This increase in the *labor force participation* of women has significantly increased the supply of labor in the United States.

3. **Changing alternatives.** The labor supply in any particular labor market depends, in part, on the opportunities available in other labor markets. For example, the problems in the financial services industry that began in 2007 reduced the opportunities for investment bankers, stockbrokers, and other financial workers. Many workers left this industry—causing the labor supply curve to shift to the left—and entered other markets, causing the labor supply curves to shift to the right in those markets. People who have lost jobs or who have low incomes are eligible for unemployment insurance and other payments from the government. The more generous these payments are, the less pressure unemployed workers have to quickly find another job. In many European countries, it is much easier than in the United States for unemployed workers to replace a larger fraction of their wage income with government payments. Many economists believe generous unemployment benefits help explain the higher unemployment rates experienced in some European countries.

MyEconLab Study Plan

MyEconLab Concept Check

17.3 Equilibrium in the Labor Market

LEARNING OBJECTIVE: Explain how equilibrium wages are determined in labor markets.

In Figure 17.4, we bring together labor demand and labor supply to determine equilibrium in the labor market. We can use demand and supply to analyze changes in the equilibrium wage and the level of employment for the entire labor market, and we can also use it to analyze markets for different types of labor, such as baseball players or college professors.

MyEconLab Animation

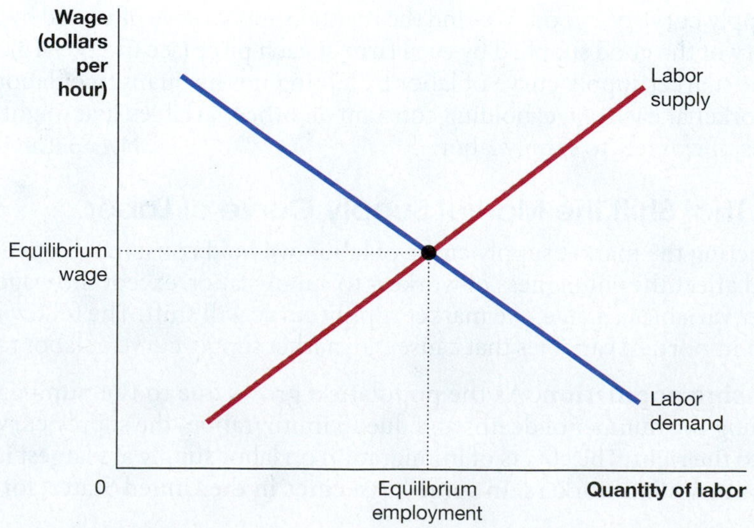

Figure 17.4

Equilibrium in the Labor Market

As in other markets, equilibrium in the labor market occurs where the demand curve for labor and the supply curve of labor intersect.

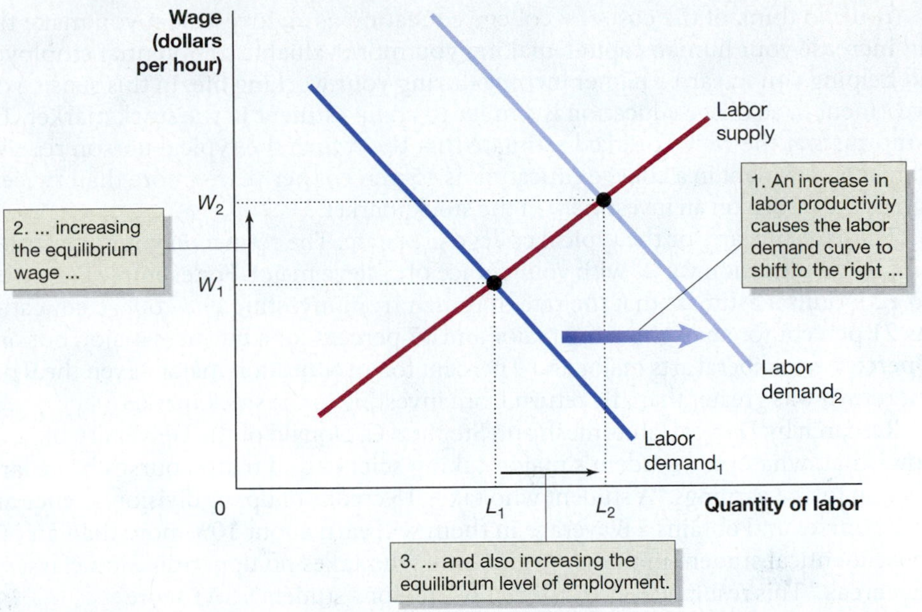

MyEconLab Animation

Figure 17.5

The Effect of an Increase in Labor Demand

Increases in labor demand will cause the equilibrium wage and the equilibrium level of employment to rise:

1. If the productivity of workers rises, the marginal revenue product increases, causing the labor demand curve to shift to the right.
2. The equilibrium wage rises from W_1 to W_2.
3. The equilibrium level of employment rises from L_1 to L_2.

The Effect on Equilibrium Wages of a Shift in Labor Demand

In many labor markets, increases over time in labor productivity will cause the demand for labor to increase. As Figure 17.5 shows, if labor supply is unchanged, an increase in labor demand will increase both the equilibrium wage and the number of workers employed.

MyEconLab Concept Check

Making the Connection

MyEconLab Video

Is Investing in a College Education a Good Idea?

You pay a cost to attend college: both the monetary cost of paying for tuition, books, and other expenses, and the nonmonetary opportunity cost of delaying your entry into the workforce. Is the cost worth it?

Most people realize the value of a college education. As the following graph shows, in 2015, full-time workers aged 25 and over with a college degree earned more per week than other workers; for example, they earned 2.5 times as much as high school dropouts. The earnings premium from a college education has persisted over time. A recent study by economists at the Federal Reserve Bank of New York estimates that over the period from 1970 to 2013, the average college graduate earned \$23,500 more per year than the average person who had only a high school degree.

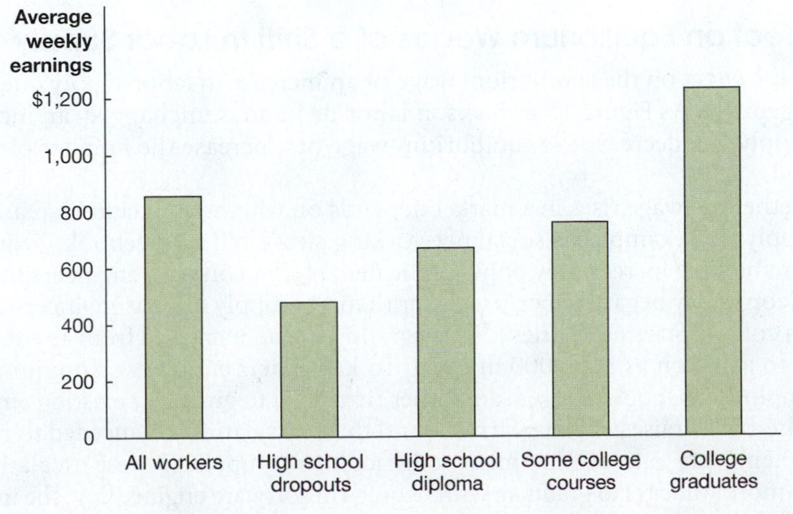

Source: U.S. Bureau of Labor Statistics, "Usual Weekly Earnings of Wage and Salary Workers, First Quarter 2015," April 21, 2015.

You can think of the cost of a college education as an investment you make that will increase your human capital, making you more valuable to potential employers and helping you to earn a higher income during your working life. In this sense, your investment in a college education is similar to an investment in the stock market. The economists at the New York Fed estimate that the return the typical person receives from an investment in a college education is 15 percent per year—more than twice as high as the return on an investment in the stock market.

These results are for the typical college graduate. The return on your investment in a college education varies with your choice of college major. For example, New York Fed economists estimate that the rate of return from investing in a college education was 21 percent for an engineering major and 17 percent for a business major, but only 12 percent for a liberal arts major and 9 percent for an education major. (Even the 9 percent return was greater than the return from investing in the stock market.)

Research by Daniel Hamermesh and Stephen G. Donald of the University of Texas shows that, whatever a student's major, taking science and math courses has a large effect on future earnings: "A student who takes 15 credits of upper-division science and math courses and obtains a B average in them will earn about 10% more than an otherwise identical student in the same major … who takes no upper-division classes in these areas." This result held even after adjusting for a student's SAT score.

In economic recessions when unemployment in the economy rises, college graduates are less likely to lose their jobs and are likely to experience smaller declines in wages than are high school graduates. Research by Joseph Altonji, Lisa Kahn, and Jamin Speer of Yale University indicates that people with certain college majors fare better during recessions than people with other college majors. For example, during years when the economy is not in recession, economics majors earn about 25 percent more than the average of all college graduates. During recessions, economics majors earn about 35 percent more than the typical college graduate, as their earnings decline by less. If graduating from college is a good idea, majoring in economics is a particularly good idea—and taking some science and math courses isn't a bad idea, either!

Sources: Joseph G. Altonji, Lisa B. Kahn, and Jamin D. Speer, "Cashier or Consultant? Entry Labor Market Conditions, Field of Study, and Career Success," forthcoming, *Journal of Labor Economics*; Claire Cain Miller, "A College Major Matters Even More in a Recession," *New York Times*, June 20, 2014; Jaison R. Abel and Richard Dietz, "Do the Benefits of College Still Outweigh the Costs?" Federal Reserve Bank of New York, *Current Issues in Economics and Finance*, Vol. 20, No. 3, 2014; and Daniel S. Hamermesh and Stephen G. Donald, "The Effect of College Curriculum on Earnings: An Affinity Identifier for Non-Ignorable Non-Response Bias," *Journal of Econometrics*, Vol. 144, No. 2, June 2008, pp. 479–491.

MyEconLab Study Plan

Your Turn: Test your understanding by doing related problem 3.3 on page 588 at the end of this chapter.

The Effect on Equilibrium Wages of a Shift in Labor Supply

What is the effect on the equilibrium wage of an increase in labor supply due to population growth? As Figure 17.6 shows, if labor demand is unchanged, an increase in labor supply will decrease the equilibrium wage but increase the number of workers employed.

Whether the wage rises in a market depends on whether demand increases faster than supply. For example, as social networking sites such as Facebook, Twitter, and Instagram became increasingly popular, the demand for software engineers in California's Silicon Valley began to increase faster than the supply of new engineers graduating from college. Starting salaries for new graduates had increased from about $80,000 in 2009 to as much as $150,000 in 2015. To keep their engineers from jumping to other employers, Google, Tagged, and other firms had to give their existing employees across-the-board raises. Startup firms found that the salaries they needed to pay were raising their costs to levels that made it difficult to compete. If these escalating salaries lead more students to graduate with degrees in software engineering, the increased labor supply could eventually bring down salaries. MyEconLab Concept Check

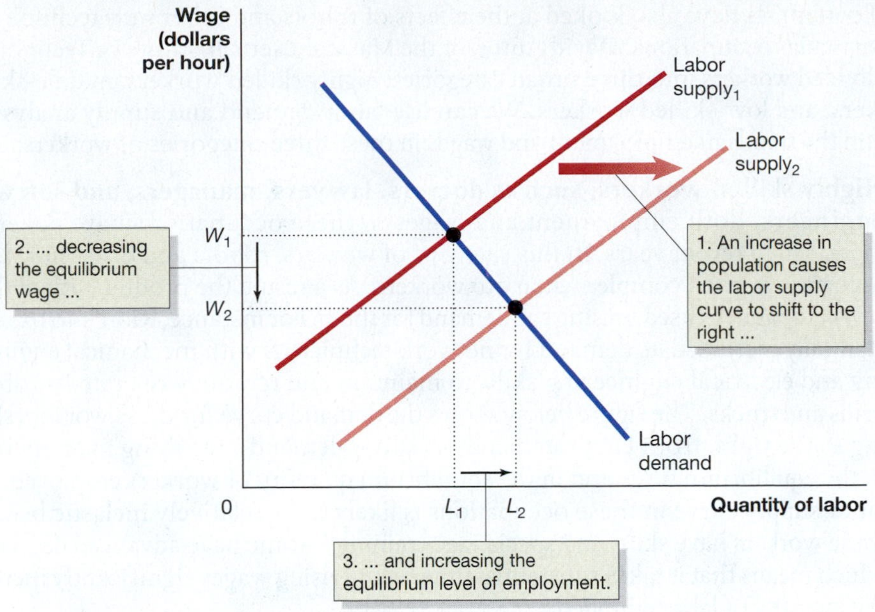

MyEconLab Animation

Figure 17.6

The Effect of an Increase in Labor Supply

Increases in labor supply will cause the equilibrium wage to fall but the equilibrium level of employment to rise:

1. As population increases, the labor supply curve shifts to the right.
2. The equilibrium wage falls from W_1 to W_2.
3. The equilibrium level of employment increases from L_1 to L_2.

Making the Connection

MyEconLab Video

Should You Fear the Effect of Robots on the Labor Market?

Will you have trouble finding a job because robots will eventually become sophisticated enough to replace people in a wide range of occupations? Economists who have studied the effects of robots are divided in their answers to this question. First, although there is no universally agreed upon definition of robots, most economists consider them to be a type of capital that performs sophisticated physical activities that previously only people performed. So the self-driving trucks Rio Tinto uses, as described in the chapter opener, are robots, while a personal computer is not.

Fears that firms will permanently reduce their demand for labor as they increase their use of capital date back at least to the late 1700s in England, when textile workers known as Luddites—after their leader Ned Ludd—smashed machinery in an attempt to save their jobs. Since that time, the term Luddite has described people who oppose increases in capital because they fear the increases will result in permanent job losses. Economists believe that these fears often stem from the "lump-of-labor" fallacy, which holds that there is only a fixed amount of work to be performed in the economy. So the more work that is performed by machines, the less work that will be available for people to perform.

However, capital is a *complement* to labor, as well as a substitute for it. For instance, although some automobile workers lost their jobs as firms began to use robots to weld car chassis, the remaining workers became more productive because they had additional capital to work with, and their productivity resulted in higher wages. In fact, most economists argue that the main reason that the wages of workers today are much higher than they were 100 years ago is that workers today are much more productive because they have more capital to work with. Higher productivity can also reduce firms' costs, leading to lower prices. Lower prices increase both the quantity of goods demanded and the demand for labor.

Will this long-run trend continue as more and more of the increases in capital involve robots and other new technologies associated with the Internet of Things? Most economists are optimistic that the long-run result of these new technologies will be higher productivity and higher wages, although some economists take a more pessimistic view. For example, Carl Benedikt Frey and Michael A. Osborne of the University of Oxford estimate that as many as 47 percent of U.S. workers could lose their current jobs to robots and other new technology. Seth Benzell of Boston University and colleagues argue that there are plausible economic models in which the benefits from the lower prices that result from the higher productivity of robots will be offset by the lower wages workers earn after losing their current jobs.

Economists have also looked at the effects of robots and other new technologies on particular occupations. David Autor, of the Massachusetts Institute of Technology, has divided workers into three broad categories: highly skilled workers, middle-skilled workers, and low-skilled workers. We can use labor demand and supply analysis to explain the trends in employment and wages in these three categories of workers:

1. **Highly skilled workers, such as doctors, lawyers, managers, and software engineers.** Both employment and wages in these occupations have generally increased in recent years. In this category of workers, robots and other new technologies are often complementary to workers. As a result, the productivity of these workers has increased, raising the demand for them. For instance, Rio Tinto has substantially increased its demand for network technicians with mechanical engineering and electrical engineering skills to maintain and remotely operate its robotic drills and trucks. The figure below shows the demand curve for these workers shifting to the right, from Labor demand$_1$ to Labor demand$_2$, resulting in an increase in the equilibrium wage and in the equilibrium quantity of workers employed. The labor supply curve in these occupations is likely to be relatively inelastic because these workers have skills and specialized training—some have advanced degrees—which means that it takes substantial time before rising wages significantly increase the quantity of labor supplied.

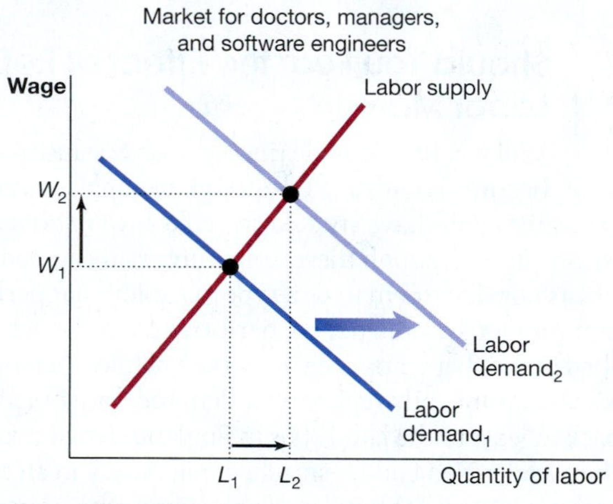

2. **Middle-skilled workers, such as salespeople, office workers, carpenters, plumbers, and factory workers.** Both employment and wages in these occupations have generally declined in recent years. In this category, robots and new technology are often substitutes for workers; for instance, the robotic truck and drill technology at Rio Tinto's mines are a substitute for the drivers and drill operators the company previously employed. The figure below shows the demand curve for these workers shifting to left, from Labor demand$_1$ to Labor demand$_2$, resulting in a decrease in the equilibrium wage and in the equilibrium quantity of workers employed.

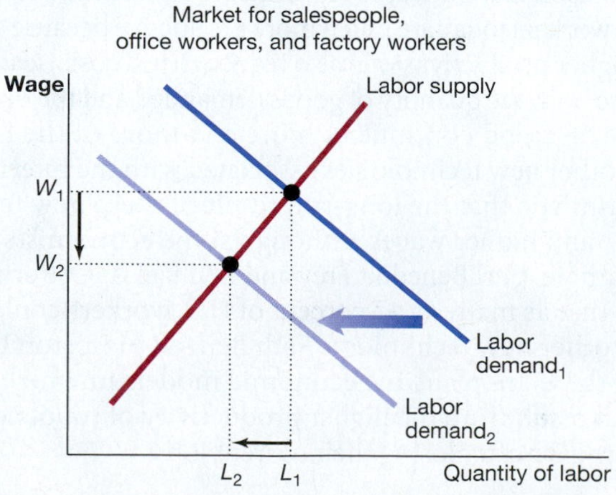

3. **Lower-skilled workers, such as food workers, health care aides, janitors, and flight attendants.** Employment has generally increased in these occupations in recent years, but wages have declined. Robots and new technology have relatively little effect on the workers in this category. For the most part, robots have not replaced servers in restaurants, home health care aides, and similar workers. Nor are the new technologies complements to the tasks—cooking, cleaning, driving trucks—these workers perform. New technologies have therefore not had a significant effect on the demand for these workers. (Although the aging of the population and rising incomes have increased demand for the services some of these workers provide, for simplicity, we will ignore this fact.) The figure below shows the labor demand curve as unchanged. However, some workers in the second category—factory workers and office workers, for example—who have lost their jobs, have shifted into the occupations in this category, causing the labor supply curve to shift to the right, from Labor supply_1 to Labor supply_2, resulting in an increase in the equilibrium quantity of workers employed, but a decrease in the equilibrium wage.

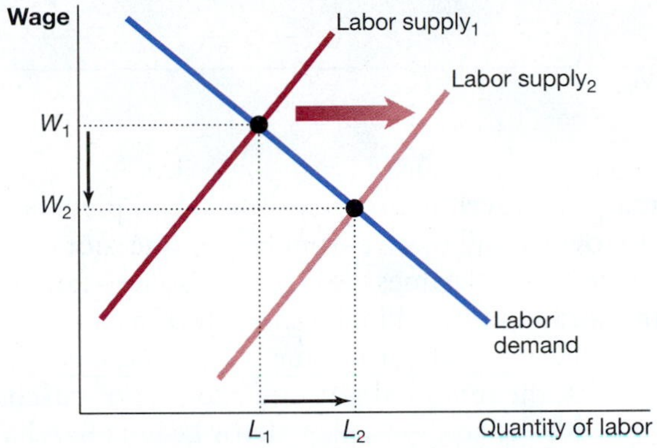

The process of workers and firms adapting to robots and other new technologies is ongoing, and economists continue to debate what the long-run consequences of these technologies will be.

Sources: Carl Benedikt Frey and Michael A. Osborne, "The Future of Employment: How Susceptible Are Jobs to Computerisation?" www.oxfordmartin.ox.ac.uk, September 17, 2013; Timothy Aeppel, "What Clever Robots Mean for Jobs," *Wall Street Journal*, February 24, 2015; Seth G. Benzell, et al., "Robots Are Us: Some Economics of Human Replacement," National Bureau of Economic Research, Working Paper 20941, February 2015; and David H. Autor, "Polanyi's Paradox and the Shape of Employment Growth," in Federal Reserve Bank of Kansas City, *Re-Evaluating Labor Market Dynamics*, 2014, pp. 129–177.

Your Turn: Test your understanding by doing related problem 3.8 on page 588 at the end of this chapter. MyEconLab Study Plan

17.4 Explaining Differences in Wages

LEARNING OBJECTIVE: Use demand and supply analysis to explain how compensating differentials, discrimination, and labor unions cause wages to differ.

A key conclusion of our discussion of the labor market is that the equilibrium wage equals the marginal revenue product of labor. The more productive workers are and the higher the price for which workers' output can be sold, the higher the wages workers will receive. We can expand on this conclusion by using the demand and supply model to analyze why wages differ. For instance, many people wonder why professional athletes are paid so much more than most other workers. Figure 17.7 shows the demand and supply curves for Major League Baseball players and the demand and supply curves for college professors.

MyEconLab Animation

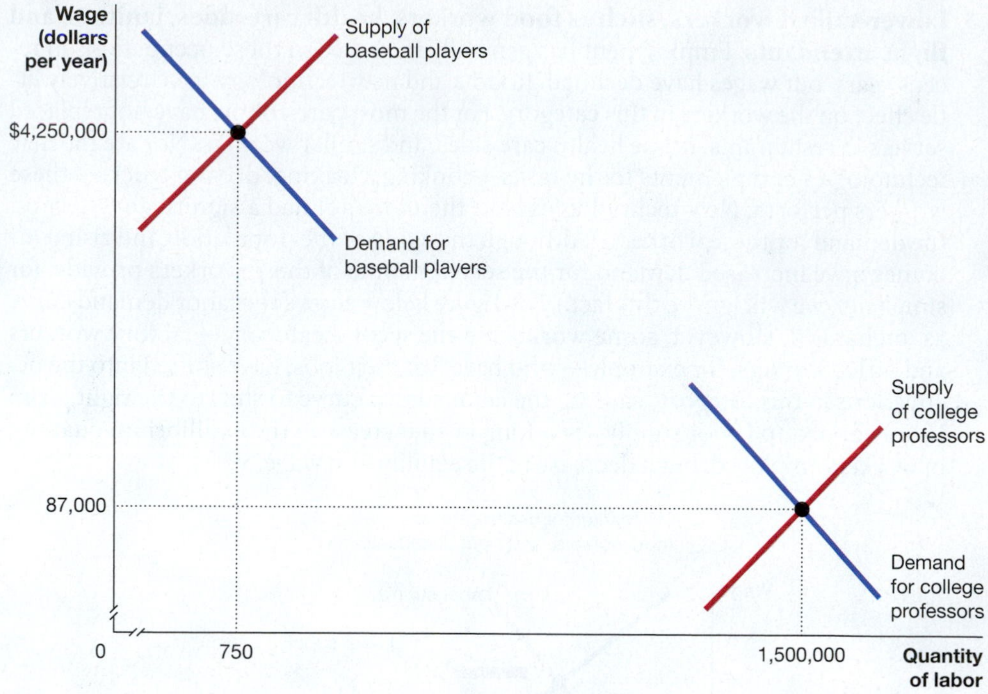

Figure 17.7

Baseball Players Are Paid More Than College Professors

The marginal revenue product of baseball players is very high, and the supply of people with the ability to play Major League Baseball is low. The result is that the 750 Major League Baseball players receive an average wage of $4,250,000. The marginal revenue product of college professors is much lower, and the supply of people with the ability to be college professors is much higher. The result is that the 1.5 million college professors in the United States receive an average wage of $87,000, far below the average wage of baseball players.

Consider the marginal revenue product of baseball players, which is the additional revenue a team owner will receive from hiring one more player. Baseball players are hired to produce baseball games that are then sold to fans, who pay admission to baseball stadiums, and to radio and television stations and to cable systems that broadcast the games. Because a Major League Baseball team can sell each baseball game for a large amount, the marginal revenue product of baseball players is high. The supply of people with the ability to play Major League Baseball is also very limited. As a result, the average annual salary of the 750 Major League Baseball players was $4,250,000 in 2015.

The marginal revenue product of college professors is much lower than for baseball players. College professors are hired to produce college educations that are sold to students and their parents. Although one year's college tuition is quite high at many colleges, hiring one more professor allows a college to admit at most a few more students. So, the marginal revenue product of a college professor is much lower than the marginal revenue product of a baseball player. There are also many more people who possess the skills to be a college professor than possess the skills to be a Major League Baseball player. As a result, the average annual salary of the country's 1.5 million college professors was about $87,000 in 2015.

We can use the analysis to answer the additional question of why the best professional athletes tend to end up in the largest cities. For example, in 2015, one of the highest-paid baseball players was Los Angeles Dodgers pitcher Zack Greinke, whose salary was $23 million. Why are the Dodgers willing to pay Zack Greinke more than the Kansas City Royals or Milwaukee Brewers, two of his previous teams, were? Greinke's marginal product—which we can think of as the extra games a team will win by employing him—should be about the same in Los Angeles as in Kansas City or Milwaukee. But his *marginal revenue product* will be higher in Los Angeles. Because the Dodgers play in the second-largest metropolitan area in the United States, the number of Dodgers fans is much larger than the number of Kansas City or Milwaukee fans, so winning additional games will result in a greater increase in attendance at Dodgers games than it would at Royals or Brewers games. It will also result in a greater increase in viewers for Dodgers games on television. Therefore, the Dodgers are able to sell the extra wins that Greinke produces for much more than the Royals or Brewers can. This difference explains why the Dodgers were willing to pay Greinke much more than the Royals or Brewers were.

Don't Let This Happen to You

Remember That Prices and Wages Are Determined at the Margin

You have probably heard some variation of the following remark: "We could live without baseball, but we can't live without the trash being hauled away. In a more rational world, trash collectors would be paid more than baseball players." This remark seems logical: The total value to society of having the trash hauled away certainly is greater than the total value of baseball games. But wages—like prices—do not depend on total value but on *marginal* value. The *additional* baseball games the Los Angeles Dodgers have won by signing Zack Greinke to a contract resulted in millions of dollars in increased revenue. The supply of people with the ability to play Major League Baseball is very limited. The supply of people with the ability to be trash collectors is much greater. If a trash-hauling firm hires another worker, the *additional* trash-hauling services it can now offer will bring in a relatively small amount of revenue. The *total* value of baseball games and the *total* value of trash hauling are not relevant in determining the relative salaries of baseball players and trash collectors.

This point is related to the *diamond and water paradox* Adam Smith noted in 1776 in his book *The Wealth of Nations*. On the one hand, water is very valuable—we literally couldn't live without it—but its price is very low. On the other hand, apart from a few industrial purposes, diamonds are used only for jewelry, yet their price is quite high. We resolve the paradox by noting that the price of water is low because the supply is very large and the additional benefit consumers receive from the last gallon purchased is low. The price of diamonds is high because the supply is very small, and the additional benefit consumers receive from the last diamond purchased is high.

MyEconLab Study Plan

Your Turn: Test your understanding by doing related problem 4.7 on page 589 at the end of this chapter.

Making the Connection
MyEconLab Video

Technology and the Earnings of "Superstars"

The gap between Zack Greinke's salary and the salary of the lowest-paid baseball players is much greater than the gap between the salaries paid during the 1950s and 1960s to top players such as Mickey Mantle and Willie Mays and the salaries of the lowest-paid players. Similarly, the gap between the $30 million Brad Pitt is paid to star in a movie and the salary paid to an actor in a minor role is much greater than the gap between the salaries paid during the 1930s and 1940s to stars such as Clark Gable and Cary Grant and the salaries paid to bit players. In fact, in most areas of sports and entertainment, the highest-paid performers—the "superstars"—now have much higher incomes relative to other members of their professions than was true a few decades ago.

Why does Zack Greinke earn more today relative to the typical baseball player than baseball stars did in the 1950s and 1960s?

The increase in the relative incomes of superstars is mainly due to technological advances. The spread of cable television has increased the number of potential viewers of Dodgers games, but many of those viewers will watch only if the Dodgers are winning. This growth in viewers increases the value to the Dodgers of winning games and, therefore, increases Greinke's marginal revenue product and the salary he can earn.

With Blu-ray discs, DVDs, Internet streaming video, and pay-per-view cable, the value to movie studios of producing a hit movie has greatly risen. Not surprisingly, movie studios have also increased their willingness to pay large salaries to stars such as Brad Pitt and Leonardo DiCaprio because they think these superstars will significantly increase the chances that a film will be successful.

This process has been going on for a long time. For instance, before the invention of the motion picture, anyone who wanted to see a play had to attend the theater and see a live performance. Limits on the number of people who could see the best actors and actresses perform created an opportunity for many more people to succeed in the acting profession, and the gap between the salaries earned by the best actors and the salaries earned by average actors was relatively small. Today, when a hit movie starring

Brad Pitt is available on DVD or streaming, millions of people will buy or rent it, and they will not be forced to spend money to see a less popular actor, as their great-great-grandparents might have been.

MyEconLab Study Plan

Your Turn: Test your understanding by doing related problems 4.10 and 4.11 on page 589 at the end of this chapter.

Differences in marginal revenue products are the most important factor in explaining differences in wages, but they are not the whole story. To provide a more complete explanation for differences in wages, we must take into account three important aspects of labor markets: compensating differentials, discrimination, and labor unions.

Compensating Differentials

Suppose Paul runs a pizza parlor and acquires a reputation for being a bad boss who yells at his workers and is generally unpleasant. Two blocks away, Brendan also runs a pizza parlor, but he is always very polite to his workers. We would expect in these circumstances that Paul will have to pay a higher wage than Brendan to attract and retain workers. Higher wages that compensate workers for unpleasant aspects of a job are called **compensating differentials.**

Compensating differentials Higher wages that compensate workers for unpleasant aspects of a job.

If working in a dynamite factory requires the same degree of training and education as working in a semiconductor factory but is much more dangerous, a larger number of workers will want to work making semiconductors rather than dynamite. As a consequence, the wages of dynamite workers will be higher than the wages of semiconductor workers. We can think of the difference in wages as being the price of risk. As each worker decides on his or her willingness to assume risk and decides how much higher the wage must be to compensate for assuming more risk, wages will adjust so that dynamite factories will pay wages that are just high enough to compensate workers who choose to work there for the extra risk they assume. Only when workers in dynamite factories have been fully compensated with higher wages for the additional risk they assume will dynamite companies be able to attract enough workers.

One surprising implication of compensating differentials is that *laws protecting the health and safety of workers may not make workers better off.* To see this point, suppose that dynamite factories pay wages of $35 per hour and semiconductor factories pay wages of $30 per hour, with the $5 difference in wages being a compensating differential for the greater risk of working in a dynamite factory. Suppose that the government passes a law regulating the manufacture of dynamite in order to improve safety in dynamite factories. As a result of this law, dynamite factories are no longer any more dangerous than semiconductor factories. Once this change occurs, the wages in dynamite factories will decline to $30 per hour, the same as in semiconductor factories. Are workers in dynamite factories any better or worse off? Before the law was passed, their wages were $35 per hour, but $5 per hour was a compensating differential for the extra risk they were exposed to. Now the extra risk has been eliminated, but their wages are only $30 per hour. The conclusion seems to be that dynamite workers are no better off as a result of the safety legislation.

This conclusion is true, though, only if the compensating differential actually does compensate workers fully for the additional risk. Nobel Laureate George Akerlof of Georgetown University and William Dickens of the Brookings Institution have argued that the psychological principle known as *cognitive dissonance* might cause workers to underestimate the true risk of their jobs. According to this principle, people prefer to think of themselves as intelligent and rational and tend to reject evidence that seems to contradict this image. Because working in a very hazardous job may seem irrational, workers in such jobs may refuse to believe that the jobs really are hazardous. Akerlof and Dickens present evidence that workers in chemical plants producing benzene and workers in nuclear power plants underestimate the hazards of their jobs. If Akerlof and Dickens are correct, the wages of these workers will not be high enough to compensate them fully for the risk they have assumed. So, in this situation, safety legislation may make workers better off.

MyEconLab Concept Check

Table 17.2

Why Do White Males Earn More Than Other Groups?

Group	Weekly Earnings
White males	$969
White females	776
Black males	731
Hispanic males	656
Black females	654
Hispanic females	580

Note: The values are median weekly earnings for full-time wage and salary workers, aged 25 and older. Persons of Hispanic origin can be of any race.

Source: U.S. Bureau of Labor Statistics, "Usual Weekly Earnings of Wage and Salary Workers, First Quarter 2015," April 21, 2015.

Discrimination

Table 17.2 shows that in the United States, white males on average earn more than other groups. One possible explanation for this fact is **economic discrimination**, in which an employer pays a person a lower wage or excludes a person from an occupation on the basis of an irrelevant characteristic such as race or gender.

Economic discrimination The practice of paying a person a lower wage or excluding a person from an occupation on the basis of an irrelevant characteristic such as race or gender.

If employers discriminated by hiring only white males for high-paying jobs or by paying white males higher wages than other groups working the same jobs, white males would have higher earnings, as Table 17.2 shows. However, excluding groups from certain jobs or paying one group more than another has been illegal in the United States since the passage of the Equal Pay Act of 1963 and the Civil Rights Act of 1964. Nevertheless, it is possible that employers are ignoring the law and practicing economic discrimination.

Most economists believe that only part of the gap between the wages of white males and the wages of other groups is due to discrimination. Instead, some of the gap is explained by three main factors:

1. Differences in education
2. Differences in experience
3. Differing preferences for jobs

MyEconLab Concept Check

Differences in Education Some of the difference between the incomes of white workers and the incomes of black workers can be explained by differences in education. Historically, African Americans and Hispanics have had less schooling than have whites. The gap has narrowed significantly over the years, but it has not completely closed. As Table 17.3 shows, a higher percentage of white students graduate on time from public high schools than do African-American or Hispanic students. Similarly, a higher percentage of the white population aged 25 and older graduates from college than is true of the African-American or Hispanic populations.

These statistics understate the true gap in education between whites and blacks and Hispanics because many black and Hispanic students receive a substandard

Table 17.3

Differences in Education among Ethnic Groups

Group	Percentage That Graduated on Time from Public High Schools	Percentage That Graduated from College
Whites	87%	36%
Hispanics	75	15
African Americans	71	22

Sources: National Center for Education Statistics, *Dropouts, Completers and Graduation Rate Reports*, Table 2, Public High School 4-year Adjusted Cohort Graduation Rate (ACGR), by Race/Ethnicity and Selected Demographics for the United States, the 50 States, and the District of Columbia: School Year 2012–13; and U.S. Census Bureau, *Educational Attainment in the United States: 2014—Detailed Tables*, Table 1, Educational Attainment of the Population 18 Years and Over, by Age, Sex, Race, and Hispanic Origin: 2014.

education in inner-city schools. Not surprisingly, studies have shown that differing levels of education can account for a significant part of the gap between the earnings of different ethnic groups. Some of the difference in educational levels may reflect past and current discrimination by governments in failing to provide equal educational opportunities.

Differences in Experience Women are much more likely than men to leave their jobs for a period of time after having a child. Women with several children will sometimes have several interruptions in their careers. Some women leave the workforce for several years until their children are of school age. As a result, on average, women with children have less workforce experience than do men of the same age. Because workers with greater experience are, on average, more productive, the difference in levels of experience helps to explain some of the difference in earnings between men and women. Providing some support for this explanation is the fact that, on average, married women earn about 25 percent less than married men, but women who have never been married—and whose careers are less likely to have been interrupted—earn only about 9 percent less than men who have never been married.

Differing Preferences for Jobs Significant differences exist between the types of jobs held by women and men:

- Women represent 90 percent or more of the people employed in some relatively low-paying jobs, such as preschool teachers, dental assistants, and childcare workers.
- Men represent more than 90 percent of the people employed in some relatively high-paying jobs, such as airline pilots, engineering managers, and electricians.

Although the overrepresentation of women in low-paying jobs and men in high-paying jobs may be due, in part, to discrimination, it is also likely to reflect differences in job preferences between men and women. For example, because many women interrupt their careers—at least briefly—when their children are born, they are more likely to take jobs where work experience is less important. More women may also be likely to take jobs, such as teaching, that allow them to be home in the afternoons when their children return from school.

Solved Problem 17.4

MyEconLab Interactive Animation

Is Passing "Comparable Worth" Legislation a Good Way to Close the Gap between Men's and Women's Pay?

As we have seen, because of either discrimination or differing preferences, certain jobs are filled primarily by men, and other jobs are filled primarily by women. On average, the "men's jobs" have higher wages than the "women's jobs." Some commentators have argued that many "men's jobs" are more highly paid than "women's jobs," despite the jobs being comparable in terms of the education and skills required and the working conditions involved. These commentators have argued that the earnings gap between men and women could be closed at least partially if the government required employers to pay the same wages for jobs that have *comparable worth*. Many economists are skeptical of these proposals because they believe allowing markets to determine wages results in a more efficient outcome.

Suppose that electricians are currently being paid a market equilibrium wage of $800 per week, and dental assistants are being paid a market equilibrium wage of $500 per week. Comparable-worth legislation is passed, and a study finds that an electrician and a dental assistant have comparable jobs, so employers will now be required to pay workers in both jobs $650 per week. Analyze the effects of this requirement on the market for electricians and on the market for dental assistants. Be sure to use demand and supply graphs.

Solving the Problem

Step 1: Review the chapter material. This problem is about economic discrimination, so you may want to review the section "Discrimination," which begins on page 573.

Step 2: Draw the graphs. When the government sets the price in a market, the result is a surplus or a shortage, depending on whether the government-mandated price is above or below the competitive market equilibrium (see Chapter 4). A wage of $650 per week is below the market wage for electricians and above the market wage for dental assistants. Therefore, we expect the requirement to result in a shortage of electricians and a surplus of dental assistants.

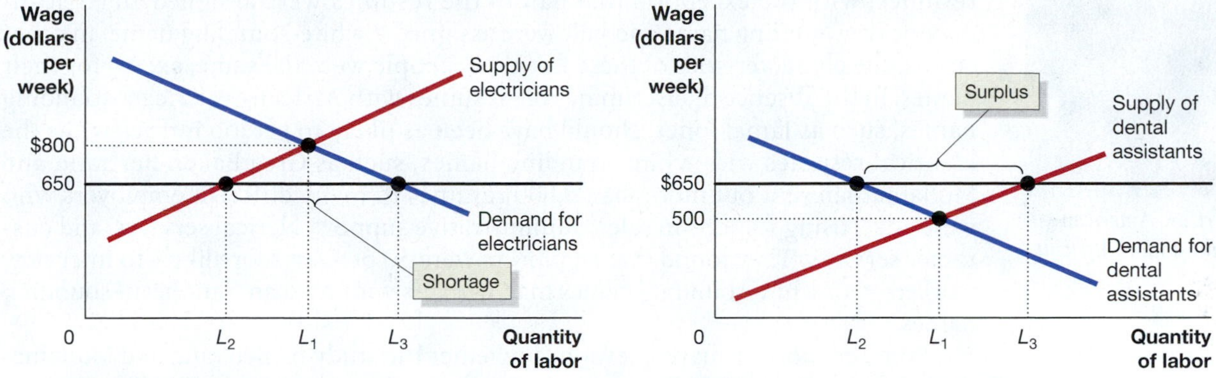

(a) Market for electricians (b) Market for dental assistants

In panel (a), without comparable-worth legislation, the equilibrium wage for electricians is $800, and the equilibrium quantity of electricians hired is L_1. Setting the wage for electricians below equilibrium at $650 reduces the quantity of labor supplied in this occupation from L_1 to L_2 but increases the quantity of labor demanded by employers from L_1 to L_3. The result is a shortage of electricians equal to $L_3 - L_2$, as shown by the bracket in the graph.

In panel (b), without comparable-worth legislation, the equilibrium wage for dental assistants is $500, and the equilibrium quantity of dental assistants hired is L_1. Setting the wage for dental assistants above equilibrium at $650 increases the quantity of labor supplied in this occupation from L_1 to L_3 but reduces the quantity of labor demanded by employers from L_1 to L_2. The result is a surplus of dental assistants equal to $L_3 - L_2$, as shown by the bracket in the graph.

Extra Credit: Most economists are skeptical of government attempts to set wages and prices, as comparable-worth legislation would require. Supporters of comparable-worth legislation, by contrast, see differences between men's and women's wages as being mainly due to discrimination and see government legislation as a solution.

Your Turn: For more practice, do related problems 4.17 and 4.18 on page 590 at the end of this chapter.

MyEconLab Study Plan

The Difficulty of Measuring Discrimination When two people are paid different wages, discrimination may be the explanation. But differences in productivity or preferences may also be an explanation. Labor economists have attempted to measure what part of differences in wages between black workers and white workers and between men and women is due to discrimination and what part is due to other factors. Unfortunately, it is difficult to precisely measure differences in productivity or in worker preferences. As a result, we can't know exactly the extent of economic discrimination in the United States today.

Making the Connection
MyEconLab Video

Does Greg Have an Easier Time Finding a Job Than Jamal?

Does having an African-American–sounding name make it more difficult to find a job?

One difficulty in accurately measuring economic discrimination is that two workers may not only differ in race and gender but also in characteristics that employers expect will affect the workers' productivity. If Worker A is hired instead of Worker B, is it because A is a white male, while B is a black female, or is it because of A's and B's other characteristics?

Marianne Bertrand of the University of Chicago and Sendhil Mullainathan of Harvard found an ingenious way of gaining insight into the extent of economic discrimination. They responded to help wanted ads in newspapers by sending identical résumés, with the exception that half of the résumés were assigned an African-American–sounding name and half were assigned a white-sounding name. In other words, the characteristics of these fictitious people were the same, except for their names. In the absence of discrimination, résumés with African-American–sounding names, such as Jamal Jones, should have been as likely to get job interviews as the identical résumés with white-sounding names, such as Greg Baker. Bertrand and Mullainathan sent out more than 5,000 résumés to many different employers who were advertising for jobs in sales, administrative support, clerical services, and customer services. They found that employers were 50 percent more likely to interview workers with white-sounding names than workers with African-American–sounding names.

Some economists have questioned whether the study by Bertrand and Mullainathan, as well as other similar studies, actually do show that employers discriminate. They argue that employers may believe that the typical white job applicant and the typical black job applicant have different characteristics, apart from those included in the résumés, that may affect their productivity. If so, the employers may be responding to these differences in productivity rather than solely to the job applicant's race. Because Bertrand and Mullainathan based their artificial résumés on actual résumés, however, the artificial résumés probably included all the characteristics that actual job applicants think are relevant. Bertrand and Mullainathan believe that the results of their experiment show that "differential treatment by race … appears to still be prominent in the U.S. labor market."

Sources: Marianne Bertrand and Sendhil Mullainathan, "Are Emily and Greg More Employable Than Lakisha and Jamal? A Field Experiment on Labor Market Discrimination," *American Economic Review*, Vol. 94, No. 4, September 2004, pp. 991–1013; and David Neumark, "Detecting Discrimination in Audit and Correspondence Studies," *Journal of Human Resources*, Vol. 47, No. 4, Fall 2012, pp. 1128–1157.

MyEconLab Study Plan

Your Turn: Test your understanding by doing related problems 4.19 and 4.20 on pages 490–491 at the end of this chapter.

Does It Pay to Discriminate? Many economists believe that in the long run, markets can undermine economic discrimination. One reason is that *employers who discriminate pay an economic penalty*. To see why, let's consider a simplified example. Suppose that men and women are equally qualified to be airline pilots and that, initially, airlines do not discriminate. In Figure 17.8, we divide the airlines into two groups: "A" airlines and "B" airlines. If neither group of airlines discriminates, we would expect them to pay an equal wage of $1,100 per week to both men and women pilots. Now suppose that "A" airlines decide to discriminate and to fire all their women pilots. This action will reduce the supply of pilots to these airlines and, as shown in panel (a), will force up the wage from $1,100 to $1,300 per week. At the same time, as women fired from the jobs with "A" airlines apply for jobs with "B" airlines, the supply of pilots to "B" airlines will increase, and the equilibrium wage will fall from $1,100 to $900 per week. All the women pilots will end up being employed at the nondiscriminating airlines and will be paid a lower wage than the men who are employed by the discriminating airlines.

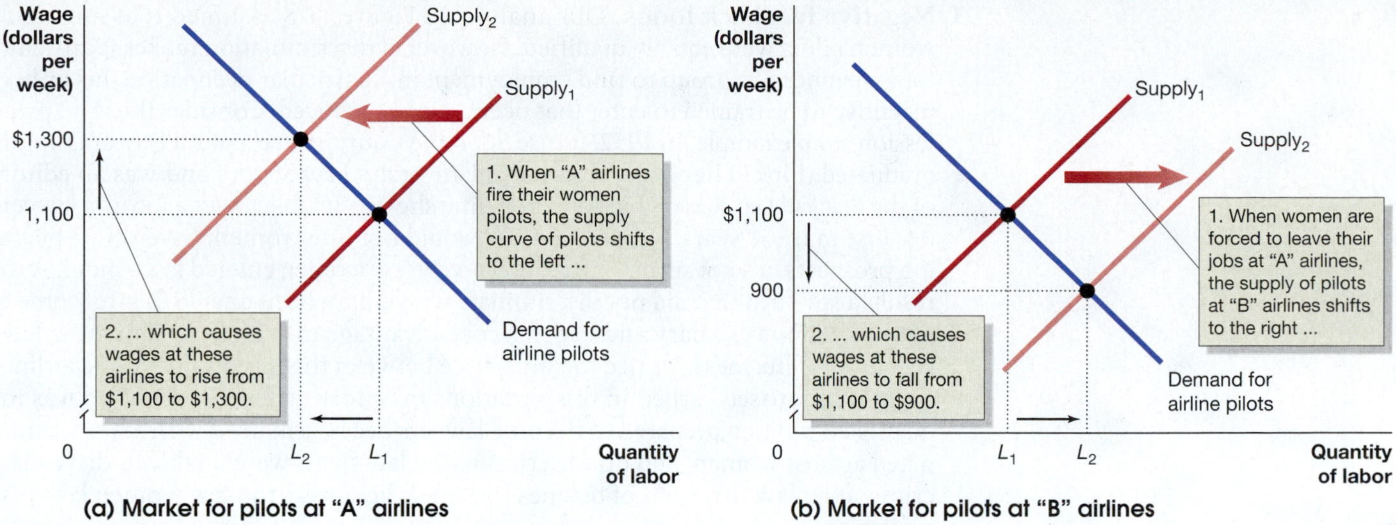

MyEconLab Animation

Figure 17.8 Discrimination and Wages

In this hypothetical example, we assume that initially neither "A" airlines nor "B" airlines discriminate. As a result, men and women pilots receive the same wage of $1,100 per week at both groups of airlines. We then assume that "A" airlines discriminate by firing all their women pilots. Panel (a) shows that discrimination reduces the supply of pilots to "A" airlines and raises the wage paid by these airlines from $1,100 to $1,300. Panel (b) shows that discrimination increases the supply of pilots to "B" airlines and lowers the wage paid by these airlines from $1,100 to $900. All the women pilots will end up being employed at the nondiscriminating airlines and will be paid a lower wage than the men who are employed by the discriminating airlines.

But this situation cannot persist for two reasons. First, male pilots employed by "B" airlines will also receive the lower wage. This lower wage gives them an incentive to quit their jobs at "B" airlines and apply at "A" airlines, which will shift the labor supply curve for "B" airlines to the left and the labor supply curve for "A" airlines to the right. Second, "A" airlines are paying $1,300 per week to hire pilots who are no more productive than the pilots being paid $900 per week by "B" airlines. As a result, "B" airlines will have lower costs and will be able to charge lower prices. Eventually, high-price "A" airlines will lose their customers to low-price "B" airlines and will be driven out of business. The market will have imposed an economic penalty on the discriminating airlines. So, discrimination will not persist, and the wages of men and women pilots will become equal.

Can we conclude from this analysis that competition in markets will eliminate all economic discrimination? Unfortunately, this optimistic conclusion is not completely accurate. We know that until the Civil Rights Act of 1964 was passed, many firms in the United States refused to hire black workers. Even though this practice had persisted for decades, nondiscriminating competitors did not drive these firms out of business. Why not? There were three important factors:

1. **Worker discrimination.** In some cases, white workers refused to work alongside black workers. As a result, some industries—such as the important cotton textile industry in the South—were all white. Because of discrimination by white workers, an entrepreneur who wanted to use low-cost black labor might need to hire an all-black workforce. Some entrepreneurs tried this approach, but because black workers had been excluded from these industries, they often lacked the skills and experience to form an effective workforce.
2. **Customer discrimination.** Some white consumers were unwilling to buy from companies in certain industries if they employed black workers. This discrimination was not a significant barrier in manufacturing industries, where customers would not know the race of the workers producing the good. It was, however, a problem for firms in industries in which workers came into direct contact with the public.

3. **Negative feedback loops.** Our analysis in Figure 17.8 assumed that men and women pilots were equally qualified. However, if discrimination makes it difficult for a member of a group to find employment in a particular occupation, his or her incentive to be trained to enter that occupation is reduced. Consider the legal profession as an example. In 1952, future Supreme Court Justice Sandra Day O'Connor graduated third in her class at Stanford University Law School and was an editor of the *Stanford Law Review*, but for some time she was unable to get a job as a lawyer because in those years, many law firms would not hire women. Given such bleak job prospects, it's not surprising that relatively few women entered law school. As a result, a law firm that did not discriminate would have been unable to hire women lawyers at a lower salary and use this cost advantage to drive discriminating law firms out of business. Notice the difference between this situation and the airline example discussed earlier. In this situation, an unfortunate feedback loop was in place: Few women prepared to become lawyers because many law firms discriminated against women, and nondiscriminating law firms were unable to drive discriminating law firms out of business because there were too few women lawyers available.

Most economists agree that the market imposes an economic penalty on firms that discriminate, but because of the factors just discussed, it may take the market a very long time to eliminate discrimination entirely. The passage of the Civil Rights Act of 1964, which outlawed hiring discrimination on the basis of race and sex, greatly sped up the process of reducing economic discrimination in the United States. MyEconLab Concept Check

Labor Unions

Labor union An organization of employees that has a legal right to bargain with employers about wages and working conditions.

Workers' wages can differ depending on whether the workers are members of **labor unions**, which are organizations of employees that have the legal right to bargain with employers about wages and working conditions. If a union is unable to reach an agreement with a company, it has the legal right to call a *strike*, which means its members refuse to work until a satisfactory agreement has been reached. As Figure 17.9 shows, a smaller fraction of the U.S. labor force is unionized than in most other high-income countries.

As Table 17.4 shows, in the United States, workers who are in unions receive higher wages than workers who are not in unions. Do union members earn more than nonunion members because they are in unions? The answer might seem to be "yes," but many union workers are in industries, such as automobile manufacturing, in which their marginal revenue products are high, so their wages would be high even if they were not unionized. Economists who have attempted to estimate statistically

Figure 17.9

The United States Is Less Unionized Than Most Other High-Income Countries

The percentage of the labor force belonging to unions is lower in the United States than in most other high-income countries.

Source: Organization for Economic Co-operation and Development.

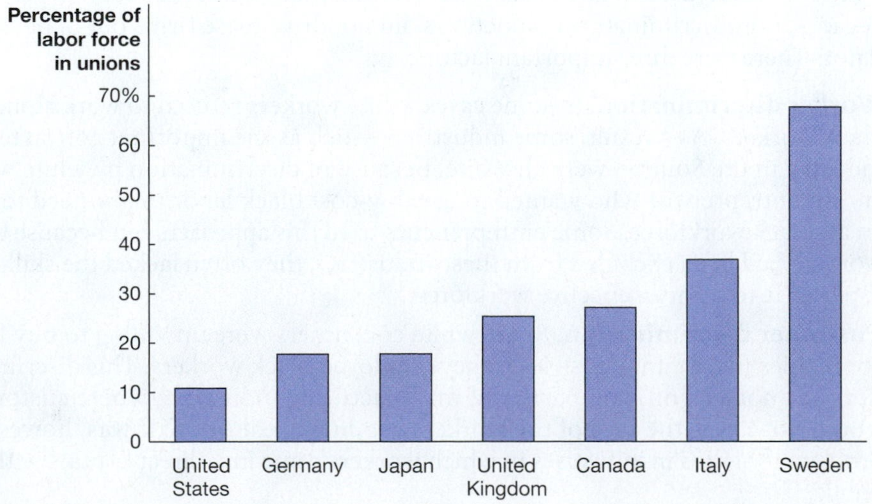

	Average Weekly Earnings
Union workers	$970
Nonunion workers	763

Note: "Union workers" includes union members as well as workers who are represented by unions but who are not members of them.

Source: U.S. Bureau of Labor Statistics, "Union Members Summary," January 23, 2015.

Table 17.4

Union Workers Earn More Than Nonunion Workers

the effect of unionization on wages have concluded that being in a union increases a worker's wages about 10 percent, holding constant other factors, such as the industry the worker is in. A related question is whether unions raise the total amount of wages received by all workers, whether unionized or not. Because the share of national income received by workers has remained roughly constant over the years, most economists do not believe that unions have raised the total amount of wages received by workers.

MyEconLab Concept Check

MyEconLab Study Plan

17.5 Personnel Economics

LEARNING OBJECTIVE: Discuss the role personnel economics can play in helping firms deal with human resources issues.

Traditionally, labor economists have focused on issues such as the effects of labor unions on wages or the determinants of changes in average wages over time. They have spent less time analyzing *human resources issues*, which address how firms hire, train, and promote workers and set their wages and benefits. In recent years, some labor economists, including Edward Lazear of Stanford University and William Neilson of the University of Tennessee, have begun exploring the application of economic analysis to human resources issues. This new focus has become known as *personnel economics*.

Personnel economics analyzes the link between differences among jobs and differences in the way workers are paid. Jobs have different skill requirements, require more or less interaction with other workers, have to be performed in more or less unpleasant environments, and so on. Firms need to design compensation policies that take into account these differences among jobs. Personnel economics also analyzes other human resources policies, such as promotions, training, and pensions. In this brief overview, we look only at compensation policies.

Personnel economics The application of economic analysis to human resources issues.

Should Workers' Pay Depend on How Much They Work or on How Much They Produce?

One issue personnel economics addresses is when workers should receive *straight-time pay*—a certain wage per hour or salary per week or month—and when they should receive *commission* or *piece-rate pay*—a wage based on how much output they produce.

Suppose that Anne owns a car dealership and is trying to decide whether to pay her salespeople a salary of $800 per week or a commission of $200 on each car they sell. Figure 17.10 compares the compensation a salesperson would receive under the two systems, according to the number of cars the salesperson sells.

With a straight salary, the salesperson receives $800 per week, no matter how many cars she sells. This outcome is shown by the horizontal line in Figure 17.10. If she receives a commission of $200 per car, her compensation will increase with every car she sells. This outcome is shown by the upward-sloping line. A salesperson who sells fewer than 4 cars per week would earn more by receiving a straight salary of $800 per week. A salesperson who sells more than 4 cars per week would be better off receiving the $200-per-car commission. We can identify two advantages Anne would receive from paying her salespeople commissions rather than salaries: She would attract and retain the most productive employees, and she would provide an incentive to her employees to sell more cars.

MyEconLab Animation

Figure 17.10

Paying Car Salespeople by Salary or by Commission

This figure compares the compensation a car salesperson receives if she is on a straight salary of $800 per week and if she receives a commission of $200 for each car she sells. With a straight salary, she receives $800 per week, no matter how many cars she sells. This outcome is shown by the horizontal line in the figure. If she receives a commission of $200 per car, her compensation will increase with every car she sells. This outcome is shown by the upward-sloping line. If she sells fewer than 4 cars per week, she would be better off with the $800 salary. If she sells more than 4 cars per week, she would be better off with the $200-per-car commission.

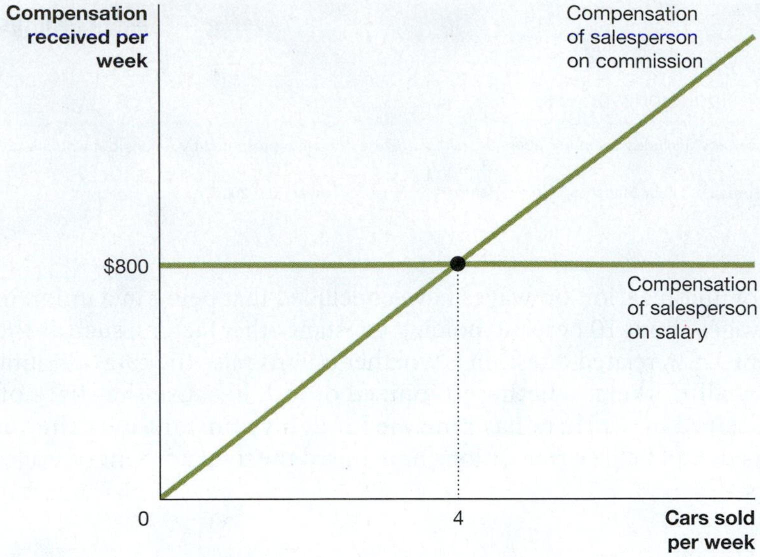

Suppose that other car dealerships are all paying salaries of $800 per week. If Anne pays her employees on commission, any of her employees who are unable to sell at least 4 cars per week can improve their pay by going to work for one of her competitors. And any salespeople at Anne's competitors who can sell more than 4 cars per week can raise their pay by quitting and coming to work for Anne. Over time, Anne will find her least productive employees leaving, while she is able to hire new employees who are more productive.

Paying a commission also increases the incentive Anne's salespeople have to sell more cars. If Anne paid a salary, her employees would receive the same amount no matter how few cars they sold. An employee on salary might decide on a particularly hot or cold day that it was less trouble to stay inside the building than to go out on the car lot to greet potential customers. An employee on commission would know that the additional effort expended on selling more cars would be rewarded with additional compensation.

MyEconLab Concept Check

Making the Connection MyEconLab Video

A Better Way to Sell Contact Lenses

A contact lens manufacturer increased its profit by taking the advice of economists to compensate its salespeople with a straight commission on sales.

Many firms rely on salespeople to sell their goods. By one estimate, firms spend about three times as much on paying their salespeople as they do on advertising. Evidence on how salespeople respond to different ways of being compensated can be difficult to obtain. This difficulty arises partly because firms are often reluctant to discuss the details of their compensation plans with people outside the firm and partly because the connection between a firm's compensation plan and its sales can be difficult to determine, given other factors that may affect a firm's sales.

Sanjog Misra of Rochester University and Harikesh Nair of Stanford University were able to overcome some of these difficulties when a large contact lens manufacturer agreed to provide them with details of the firm's compensation plan and with detailed data on compensation received and sales made by individual salespeople. The firm used its salespeople to market its contact lenses to ophthalmologists and opticians. It had no way of closely monitoring its salespeople's effort, so it needed to rely on its compensation plan to motivate them. The salespeople received a salary and could also earn a commission on sales over an assigned quarterly quota of the number of lenses sold. The commission was capped, though, so salespeople did not receive a commission on lenses sold above a ceiling amount. Firms often use ceilings to avoid paying "windfall" commissions that might result when a new product is introduced that proves very popular and causes sales increases that are not the result of increased effort by the firms' salespeople. The firm might also increase a salesperson's quota if he or she consistently exceeds it. Raising output quotas is sometimes called "ratcheting."

Misra and Nair discovered that the firm's compensation plan was inefficient. Salespeople appeared to work harder just before the end of a quarter in order to satisfy their sales quotas. They also appeared to reduce their effort once they had met their quotas. The researchers found that salespeople were often reluctant to exceed their quotas for fear the firm would increase—ratchet up—their quota in future quarters.

To reduce these inefficiencies, Misra and Nair recommended that the firm eliminate the sales quotas and compensation ceilings and move to a compensation plan that consisted of a straight commission on sales. The firm accepted the recommendation, and after implementing the new plan, sales increased by more than 20 percent, or nearly $80,000 per salesperson per quarter. The new plan succeeded in increasing effort by the sales force by increasing the compensation the salespeople received. The increase in the firm's revenue more than offset the increase in its compensation cost, resulting in a 6 percent increase in the firm's profit.

Sociologists sometimes question whether worker productivity can be increased through the use of monetary incentives. The experience of this contact lens firm provides a clear example of workers reacting favorably to the opportunity to increase work effort in exchange for higher compensation.

Source: Sanjog Misra and Harikesh S. Nair, "A Structural Model of Sales-Force Compensation Dynamics: Estimation and Field Implementation," *Quantitative Marketing and Economics*, Vol. 9, No. 3, September 2011, pp. 211–257.

Your Turn: Test your understanding by doing related problems 5.6, 5.7, and 5.8 on page 591 at the end of this chapter.

MyEconLab Study Plan

Other Considerations in Setting Compensation Systems

The discussion so far has indicated that companies will find it more profitable to use a commission or piece-rate system of compensation rather than a salary system. In fact, many firms continue to pay their workers salaries, which means they are paying their workers on the basis of how long they work rather than on the basis of how much they produce. Firms may choose a salary system for several good reasons:

- **Difficulty measuring output.** Often firms have difficulty attributing output to any particular worker. For example, an engineering firm may carry out a project using teams of workers whose individual contributions are difficult to distinguish. On assembly lines, such as those used in the automobile industry, the amount produced by each worker is determined by the speed of the line, which is set by managers rather than by workers. Managers at many firms perform such a wide variety of tasks that measuring their output would be costly, if it could be done at all.
- **Concerns about quality.** If workers are paid on the basis of the number of units produced, they may become less concerned about quality. An office assistant who is paid on the basis of the quantity of documents prepared may become careless about how many errors the documents contain. In some cases, there are ways around this problem; for example, the assistant may be required to correct the mistakes on his or her own time, without pay.
- **Worker dislike of risk.** Piece-rate or commission systems of compensation increase the risk to workers because sometimes output declines for reasons not connected to the worker's effort. For example, if there is a very snowy winter, few customers may show up at Anne's auto dealership. Through no fault of their own, her salespeople may have great difficulty selling any cars. If they are paid a salary, their income will not be affected, but if they are on commission, their incomes may drop to low levels. The flip side of this is that by paying salaries, Anne assumes a greater risk. During a snowy winter, her payroll expenses will remain high even

though her sales are low. With a commission system of compensation, her payroll expenses will decline along with her sales. But owners of firms are typically better able to bear risk than are workers. As a result, some firms may find that workers who would earn more under a commission system will prefer to receive a salary to reduce their risk. In these situations, paying a lower salary may reduce the firm's payroll expenses compared with what they would have been under a commission or piece-rate system.

Personnel economics is a relatively new field, but it holds great potential for helping firms deal more efficiently with human resources issues.

MyEconLab Study Plan

MyEconLab Concept Check

17.6 The Markets for Capital and Natural Resources

LEARNING OBJECTIVE: Show how equilibrium prices are determined in the markets for capital and natural resources.

The approach we have used to analyze the market for labor can also be used to analyze the markets for other factors of production. We have seen that the demand for labor is determined by the marginal revenue product of labor because the value to a firm of hiring another worker equals the increase in the firm's revenue from selling the additional output it can produce by hiring the worker. The demand for capital and natural resources is determined in a similar way.

The Market for Capital

Physical capital includes machines, equipment, and buildings. Firms sometimes buy capital, but we will focus on situations in which firms rent capital. A chocolate manufacturer renting a warehouse and an airline leasing a plane are examples of firms renting capital. Like the demand for labor, the demand for capital is a derived demand. When a firm is considering increasing its capital by, for example, employing another machine, the value it receives equals the increase in the firm's revenue from selling the additional output it can produce by employing the machine. The *marginal revenue product of capital* is the change in the firm's revenue as a result of employing one more unit of capital. We have seen that the marginal revenue product of labor curve is the demand curve for labor. Similarly, the marginal revenue product of capital curve is the demand curve for capital.

Firms producing capital goods face increasing marginal costs, so the supply curve of capital goods is upward sloping. Figure 17.11 shows equilibrium in the market for

MyEconLab Animation

Figure 17.11

Equilibrium in the Market for Capital

The rental price of capital is determined by demand and supply in the market for capital. In equilibrium, the rental price of capital is equal to the marginal revenue product of capital.

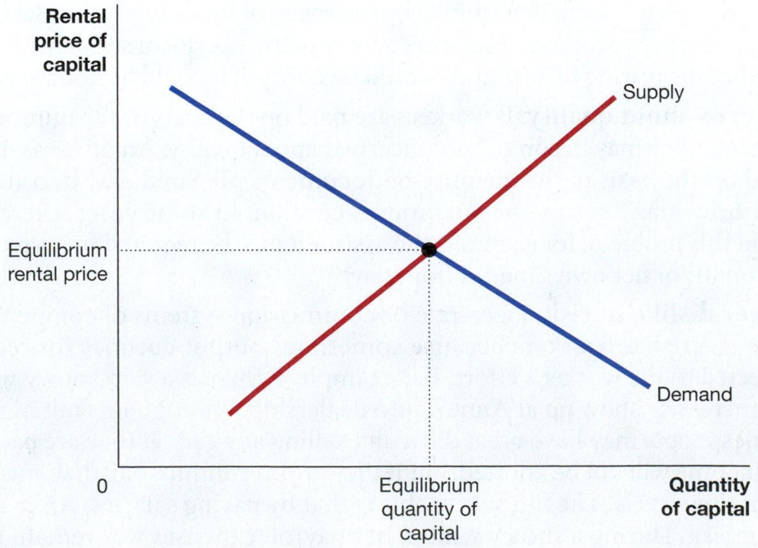

capital. In equilibrium, suppliers of capital receive a rental price equal to the marginal revenue product of capital, just as suppliers of labor receive a wage equal to the marginal revenue product of labor.

MyEconLab Concept Check

The Market for Natural Resources

The market for natural resources can be analyzed in the same way as the markets for labor and capital. When a firm is considering employing more natural resources, the value it receives equals the increase in the firm's revenue from selling the additional output it can produce by buying the natural resources. So, the demand for natural resources is also a derived demand. The *marginal revenue product of natural resources* is the change in a firm's revenue as a result of employing one more unit of natural resources, such as a barrel of oil. The marginal revenue product of natural resources curve is also the demand curve for natural resources.

Although the total quantity of most natural resources is ultimately fixed—as the humorist Will Rogers once remarked, "Buy land. They ain't making any more of it"—in many cases, the quantity supplied still responds to the price. For example, although the total quantity of oil deposits in the world is fixed, an increase in the price of oil will result in an increase in the quantity of oil supplied during a particular period. The result, as shown in panel (a) of Figure 17.12, is an upward-sloping supply curve. In some cases, however, the quantity of a natural resource that will be supplied is fixed and will not change as the price changes. The land available at a busy intersection is fixed, for example. In panel (b) of Figure 17.12, we illustrate this situation with a supply curve that is a vertical line, or perfectly inelastic. The owner of a factor of production that is in fixed supply receives an **economic rent** (or **pure rent**). In this case, the price of the factor is determined only by demand. For example, if a new

Economic rent (or pure rent) The price of a factor of production that is in fixed supply.

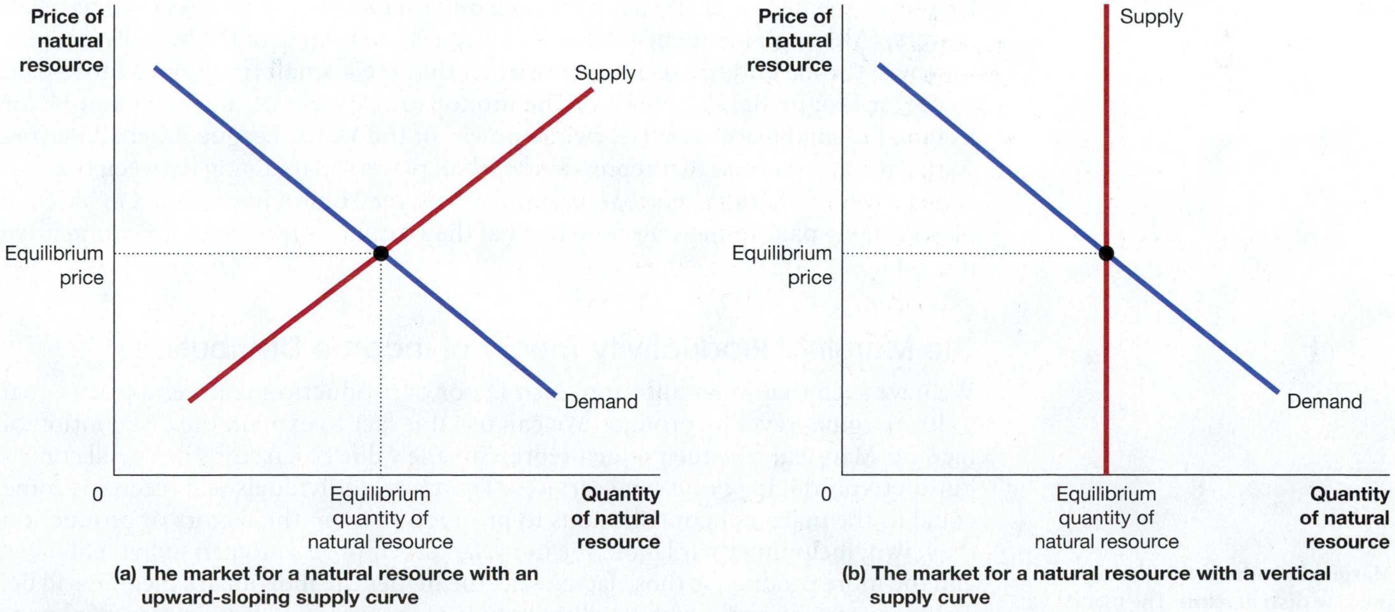

MyEconLab Animation

Figure 17.12 Equilibrium in the Market for Natural Resources

In panel (a), the supply curve of a natural resource is upward sloping. The price of the natural resource is determined by the interaction of demand and supply. In panel (b), the supply curve of the natural resource is a vertical line, indicating that the quantity supplied does not respond to changes in price. In this case, the price of the natural resource is determined only by demand. The price of a factor of production with a vertical supply curve is called an *economic rent*, or a *pure rent*.

highway diverts much of the traffic from a previously busy intersection, the demand for the land will decline, and the price of the land will fall, but the quantity of the land will not change.

MyEconLab Concept Check

Monopsony

Monopsony The situation in which a firm is sole buyer of a factor of production.

We have analyzed the case of *monopoly*, where a firm is the sole *seller* of a good or service (see Chapter 15). What happens if a firm is the sole *buyer* of a factor of production? This case, which is called **monopsony**, is comparatively rare. An example is a firm in an isolated town—perhaps a lumber mill in a small town in Washington or Oregon—that is the sole employer of labor in that location. In the nineteenth and early twentieth centuries, some coal mining firms were the sole employers in certain small towns in West Virginia, and some pineapple plantations were the sole employers on certain small islands in Hawaii. In these cases, not only would the firm own the mill, mine, or plantation, but it would also own the stores and other businesses in the town. Workers would have the choice of working for the sole employer in the town or moving to another town.

We know that a firm with a monopoly in an output market takes advantage of its market power to reduce the quantity supplied to force up the market price and increase its profits. A firm that has a monopsony in a factor market would employ a similar strategy: It would restrict the quantity of the factor demanded to force down the price of the factor and increase profit. A firm with a monopsony in a labor market will hire fewer workers and pay lower wages than would be the case in a competitive market. Because fewer workers are hired than would be hired in a competitive market, monopsony results in a deadweight loss. Monopoly and monopsony have similar effects on the economy: In both cases, a firm's market power results in a lower equilibrium quantity, a deadweight loss, and a reduction in economic efficiency compared with a competitive market.

In some cases, monopsony in labor markets is offset by worker membership in a labor union. A notable example of this is professional sports. For instance, Major League Baseball effectively has a monopsony on employing professional baseball players. (Although independent baseball leagues exist, none of the best players play for these teams, and the teams pay salaries that are a small fraction of those paid by Major League Baseball teams.) The monopsony power of the owners of Major League Baseball teams is offset by the power of the Major League Baseball Players Association, the union that represents baseball players. Bargaining between the representatives of Major League Baseball and the players' union has resulted in baseball players being paid something close to what they would be receiving in a competitive market.

MyEconLab Concept Check

The Marginal Productivity Theory of Income Distribution

Marginal productivity theory of income distribution The theory that the distribution of income is determined by the marginal productivity of the factors of production that individuals own.

We have seen that in equilibrium, each factor of production receives a price equal to its marginal revenue product. We can use this fact to explain the distribution of income. Marginal revenue product represents the value of a factor's marginal contribution to producing goods and services. Therefore, individuals will receive income equal to the marginal contributions to production from the factors of production they own, including their labor. The more factors of production an individual owns and the more productive those factors are, the higher the individual's income will be. This approach to explaining the distribution of income is called the **marginal productivity theory of income distribution**. The theory was developed by John Bates Clark, who taught at Columbia University in the late nineteenth and early twentieth centuries.

MyEconLab Concept Check

MyEconLab Study Plan

Continued from page 557

Economics in Your Life

How Can You Convince Your Boss to Give You a Raise?

At the beginning of this chapter, we asked you to imagine that you work at a local sandwich shop and that you plan to ask your manager for a raise. One way to show the manager your worth is to demonstrate how many dollars your work earns for the sandwich shop: your marginal revenue product. You could certainly suggest that as you have become better at your job and have gained new skills, you have become a more productive employee. But more importantly, you could say that your productivity results in increased revenue for the sandwich shop. By showing how your employment contributes to higher revenue and profit, you may be able to convince your manager to give you a raise.

Conclusion

In this chapter, we used the demand and supply model to explain why wages differ among workers. The demand for workers depends on their productivity and on the prices firms receive for the output the workers produce. The supply of workers to an occupation depends on the wages and working conditions offered by employers and on the skills required. The demand and supply for labor can also help us analyze issues such as economic discrimination and the effect of labor unions.

Visit MyEconLab for a news article and analysis related to the concepts in this chapter.

CHAPTER SUMMARY AND PROBLEMS

Key Terms

Compensating differentials, p. 572
Derived demand, p. 558
Economic discrimination, p. 573
Economic rent (or pure rent), p. 583
Factors of production, p. 558
Human capital, p. 561
Labor union, p. 578
Marginal product of labor, p. 558
Marginal productivity theory of income distribution, p. 584
Marginal revenue product of labor (*MRP*), p. 559
Monopsony, p. 584
Personnel economics, p. 579

17.1 The Demand for Labor, pages 558–562

LEARNING OBJECTIVE: Explain how firms choose the profit-maximizing quantity of labor to employ.

Summary

The demand for labor is a **derived demand** because it depends on consumers' demand for goods and services. The additional output produced by a firm as a result of hiring another worker is called the **marginal product of labor**. The amount by which a firm's revenue will increase as a result of hiring one more worker is called the **marginal revenue product of labor (*MRP*)**. A firm's marginal revenue product of labor curve is its demand curve for labor. Firms maximize profit by hiring workers up to the point where the wage is equal to the marginal revenue product of labor. We find the market demand curve for labor by adding up the quantity of labor demanded by each firm at each wage, holding constant all other variables that might affect the willingness of firms to hire workers. The most important variables that shift the labor demand curve are changes in human capital, technology, the price of the product, the quantity of other inputs, and the number of firms in the market. **Human capital** is the accumulated training and skills that workers possess.

MyEconLab Visit **www.myeconlab.com** to complete these exercises online and get instant feedback.

Review Questions

1.1 In what sense is the demand for labor a derived demand?

1.2 What is the difference between the marginal product of labor and the marginal revenue product of labor?

1.3 Why is the demand curve for labor downward sloping?

1.4 What are the five most important variables that cause the market demand curve for labor to shift?

Problems and Applications

1.5 Frank Gunter owns an apple orchard. He employs 87 apple pickers and pays them each $8 per hour to pick apples, which he sells for $1.60 per box. If Frank is maximizing profit, what is the marginal revenue product of the last worker he hired? What is that worker's marginal product?

1.6 **(Related to Solved Problem 17.1 on page 560)** Complete the following table for Terrell's Televisions:

Number of Workers (*L*)	Output of Televisions per Week (*Q*)	Marginal Product of Labor (television sets per week) (*MP*)	Product Price (*P*)	Marginal Revenue Product of Labor (dollars per week)	Wage (dollars per week) (*W*)	Additional Profit from Hiring One More Worker (dollars per week)
0	0		$300		$1,800	
1	8		300		1,800	
2	15		300		1,800	
3	21		300		1,800	
4	26		300		1,800	
5	30		300		1,800	
6	33		300		1,800	

a. From the information in the table, can you determine whether this firm is a price taker or a price maker? Briefly explain.

b. Use the information in the table to draw a graph like Figure 17.1 on page 559 that shows the demand for labor by this firm. Be sure to indicate the profit-maximizing quantity of labor on your graph.

1.7 State whether each of the following events will result in a movement along the market demand curve for labor in electronics factories in China or whether it will cause the market demand curve for labor to shift. If the demand curve shifts, indicate whether it will shift to the left or to the right and draw a graph to illustrate the shift.

a. The wage rate declines.

b. The price of televisions declines.

c. Several firms exit the television market in China.

d. Chinese high schools introduce new vocational courses in assembling electronic products.

1.8 Baseball writer Rany Jazayerli assessed then Kansas City Royals outfielder Jose Guillen as follows: "Guillen has negative value the way his contract stands." How could a baseball player's contract cause him to have negative value to a baseball team?

Source: Rany Jazayerli, "Radical Situations Call for Radical Solutions," www.ranyontheroyals.com, June 6, 2009.

1.9 The following comments were made by two employers regarding a proposed increase in the federal minimum wage:

> Dillon Edwards, founder of Parlor Coffee: "[The increase] should definitely be [to] more than [$8.75 an hour]. . . . It needs to be at least in double digits."
>
> Beth Fahey, owner of Creative Cakes: "If you raise the minimum wage . . . I can't raise everybody. If I do, the price of a doughnut is going to be $3 and nobody's going to buy it."

Briefly explain for which employer is the marginal revenue product of labor likely to be greater.

Source: Leslie Josephs and Adam Janofsky, "As Minimum Wages Rise, Smaller Firms Get Squeezed," *Wall Street Journal*, June 11, 2015.

17.2 The Supply of Labor, pages 562–564

LEARNING OBJECTIVE: Explain how people choose the quantity of labor to supply.

Summary

As the wage increases, the opportunity cost of leisure increases, causing individuals to supply a greater quantity of labor. Normally, the labor supply curve is upward sloping, but it is possible that at very high wage levels, the supply curve might become backward bending. This outcome occurs when someone with a high income is willing to accept a somewhat lower income in exchange for more leisure. We find the market labor supply curve by adding up the quantity of labor supplied by each worker at each wage, holding constant all other variables that might affect the willingness of workers to supply labor. The most important variables that shift the labor supply curve are increases in population, changing demographics, and changing alternatives.

MyEconLab Visit **www.myeconlab.com** to complete these exercises online and get instant feedback.

Review Questions

2.1 How can we measure the opportunity cost of leisure? What are the substitution effect and the income effect resulting from a wage change? Why is the supply curve of labor usually upward sloping?

2.2 What are the three most important variables that cause the market supply curve of labor to shift?

Problems and Applications

2.3 Daniel was earning $65 per hour and working 45 hours per week. Then Daniel's wage rose to $75 per hour, and as a result, he now works 40 hours per week. What can we conclude from this information about the income effect and the substitution effect of a wage change for Daniel?

2.4 A columnist writing in the *Wall Street Journal* argues that because "hourly wages in real terms" rose, the "price of time" also rose. What is the "price of time"? Is the columnist correct that when real hourly wages rise, the price of time increases? Briefly explain.

Source: Brett Arends, "Spend Some Time, Save Some Money," *Wall Street Journal*, May 19, 2009.

2.5 Most labor economists believe that many adult males are on a vertical section of their labor supply curves. Use the concepts of income and substitution effects to explain under what circumstances an individual's labor supply curve would be vertical.

Source: Robert Whaples, "Is There Consensus among American Labor Economists? Survey Results on Forty Propositions," *Journal of Labor Research*, Vol. 17, No. 4, Fall 1996.

2.6 Suppose that a large oil field is discovered in Michigan. By imposing a tax on the oil, the state government is able to eliminate the state income tax on wages. What is likely to be the effect on the labor supply curve in Michigan?

2.7 A columnist in the *New York Times* notes that the U.S. labor supply "in the next decade is expected to expand at less than half the pace of the 1960s, 1970s and 1980s." What explains these changing growth rates in the U.S. labor supply?

Source: Eduardo Porter, "The Payoff in Delaying Retirement," *New York Times*, March 5, 2013.

2.8 State whether each of the following events will result in a movement along the market supply curve of agricultural labor in the United States or whether it will cause the market supply curve of agricultural labor to shift. If the supply curve shifts, indicate whether it will shift to the left or to the right and draw a graph to illustrate the shift.

a. The agricultural wage rate declines.
b. Wages outside agriculture increase.
c. The law is changed to allow for unlimited immigration into the United States.

17.3 Equilibrium in the Labor Market, pages 564–569

LEARNING OBJECTIVE: Explain how equilibrium wages are determined in labor markets.

Summary

The intersection between labor supply and labor demand determines the equilibrium wage and the equilibrium level of employment. If labor supply is unchanged, an increase in labor demand will increase both the equilibrium wage and the number of workers employed. If labor demand is unchanged, an increase in labor supply will lower the equilibrium wage and increase the number of workers employed.

MyEconLab Visit **www.myeconlab.com** to complete these exercises online and get instant feedback.

Review Questions

3.1 If the labor demand curve shifts to the left and the labor supply curve remains unchanged, what will happen to the equilibrium wage and the equilibrium level of employment? Illustrate your answer with a graph.

3.2 If the labor supply curve shifts to the left and the labor demand curve remains unchanged, what will happen to the equilibrium wage and the equilibrium level of employment? Illustrate your answer with a graph.

Problems and Applications

3.3 **(Related to the Making the Connection on page 565)** Over time, the gap between the wages of workers with college degrees and the wages of workers without college degrees has been increasing. Shouldn't this gap have increased the incentive for workers to earn college degrees, thereby increasing the supply of college-educated workers and reducing the size of the gap?

3.4 An article in the *Wall Street Journal* discussed why the hotel workers' union in New York City was against a proposal for more hotels to be built in Midtown Manhattan: "The union is concerned that rapid hotel development shrinks room prices and profit margins, driving down the wages of its members." Is the union's reasoning consistent with the economic analysis in this chapter? Briefly explain.

Source: Laura Kusisto, "City, Union Seek Hotel Limit in Grand Central Area," *Wall Street Journal*, June 17, 2014.

3.5 Sean Astin, who played the hobbit Sam in *The Lord of the Rings* movies, wrote the following about an earlier film he had appeared in: "Now I was in a movie I didn't respect, making obscene amounts of money (five times what a teacher makes, and teachers do infinitely more important work)." Are salaries determined by the importance of the work being done? If not, what are salaries determined by?

Source: Sean Astin, with Joe Layden, *There and Back Again: An Actor's Tale*, New York: St. Martin's Press, 2004, p. 35.

3.6 A woman who owned a music store in New York City was quoted in an article in the *Wall Street Journal* as "bemoaning the comparative salaries of tubists and stockbrokers. 'People should be paid in terms of what they contribute to people's well being.'"

a. Briefly explain on what basis people are actually paid.
b. Is there a connection between how people are paid and what they contribute to people's well-being? Briefly explain.

Source: Corinne Ramey, "NYC's Last Classical Sheet Music Store to Close," *Wall Street Journal*, March 2, 2015.

3.7 In the year 541, an outbreak of bubonic plague hit the Byzantine Empire. Because the plague was spread by flea-infested rats that often lived on ships, ports were hit particularly hard. In some ports, more than 40 percent of the population died. The emperor, Justinian, was concerned that the wages of sailors were rising very rapidly as a result of the plague. In 544, he placed a ceiling on the wages of sailors. Use a demand and supply graph of the market for sailors to show the effect of the plague on the wages of sailors. Use the same graph to show the effect of Justinian's wage ceiling. Briefly explain what is happening in your graph.

Source: Michael McCormick, *The Origins of the European Economy: Communications and Commerce, A.D. 300–900*, New York: Cambridge University Press, 2001, p. 109.

3.8 **(Related to the Making the Connection on page 567)** During the same period that robots and other new technologies have been affecting the labor market, there has been an increase in imports to the United States of manufactured goods—including shoes, clothing, and automobiles—from countries in which workers receive lower wages. In addition, some U.S. firms have engaged in "offshoring," in which they move some operations—such as telephone helplines—to other countries where wages are lower. Are the workers most likely to lose their jobs to robots also likely to be affected by these developments? Briefly explain. How might it be possible to distinguish between the effects on the labor market from these different developments?

17.4 Explaining Differences in Wages, pages 569–579

LEARNING OBJECTIVE: Use demand and supply analysis to explain how compensating differentials, discrimination, and labor unions cause wages to differ.

Summary

The equilibrium wage is determined by the intersection of the labor demand curve and the labor supply curve. Some differences in wages are explained by **compensating differentials**, which are higher wages that compensate workers for unpleasant aspects of a job. Wages can also differ because of **economic discrimination**, which involves paying a person a lower wage or excluding a person from an occupation on the basis of irrelevant characteristics, such as race or gender. **Labor unions** are organizations of employees that have the legal right to bargain with employers about wages and working conditions. Being in a union increases a worker's wages about 10 percent, holding constant other factors, such as the industry the workers are in.

MyEconLab Visit **www.myeconlab.com** to complete these exercises online and get instant feedback.

Review Questions

4.1 What is a compensating differential? Give an example.

4.2 Define *economic discrimination*. Is the fact that one group in the population has higher earnings than other groups evidence of economic discrimination? Briefly explain.

4.3 In what sense do employers who discriminate pay an economic penalty? Is this penalty enough to eliminate discrimination? Briefly explain.

4.4 Is the fraction of U.S. workers in labor unions larger or smaller than in other countries?

Problems and Applications

4.5 Writing on the Baseball Prospectus Web site, Dan Fox argued: "What a player is really worth depends a great deal on the teams that are interested in signing him." Do you agree? Shouldn't a baseball player with a particular level of ability be worth the same to every team? Briefly explain.

Source: Dan Fox, "Schrodinger's Bat," www.baseballprospectus.com, May 17, 2007.

4.6 **(Related to the Chapter Opener on page 557)** An article in the *Wall Street Journal* on the use of driverless trucks at Rio Tinto's Australian mines observes, "The new equipment cut many driving jobs… . But the reductions will be partly offset by new types of work. The company now needs more network technicians … a hybrid of electrical and mechanical engineering that hardly existed five years ago." Is it likely that total employment at Rio Tinto's mines will have increased or decreased as a result of its use of robots? Are the *average* wages Rio Tinto pays likely to be higher or lower? Are the wages of the truck drivers who were replaced by robots likely to end up higher or lower in their new jobs? Briefly explain your answers.

Source: Timothy Aeppel, "What Clever Robots Mean for Jobs," *Wall Street Journal*, February 24, 2015.

4.7 **(Related to the Don't Let This Happen to You on page 571)** Joe Morgan is a sportscaster and former baseball player. After he stated that he thought the salaries of Major League Baseball players were justified, a baseball fan wrote the following to Rob Neyer, a sports columnist:

> Mr. Neyer,
>
> What are your feelings about Joe Morgan's comment that players are justified in being paid what they're being paid? How is it ok for A-Rod [New York Yankees infielder Alex Rodriguez] to earn $115,000 per GAME while my boss works 80 hour weeks and earns $30,000 per year?

How would you answer this fan's questions?

Source: ESPN.com, August 30, 2002.

4.8 Managers of Major League Baseball (MLB) teams have the responsibility of running their teams and making many decisions that can affect whether these teams win or lose. Yet in 2014 only 2 of the 30 MLB managers received a salary higher than the average salary paid to baseball players. Provide an economic explanation of why baseball managers are generally paid less than baseball players.

Source: John Belaska, "How Much Are MLB Managers Making in 2014?" therichest.com, March 2, 2014.

4.9 Through the 2014 season, Nick Saban's record as the head football coach at the University of Alabama was 86 wins and 17 losses. His $7 million salary is the highest received by any college football coach. One sports writer described Saban as the most underpaid college football coach. In what sense might Saban be underpaid? In your answer, be sure to refer to the difference between the marginal product of labor and the marginal revenue product of labor.

Source: Adam Kramer, "Nick Saban Is the Most Underpaid, Highest-Paid Coach in the Country," bleacherreport.com, November 12, 2013.

4.10 **(Related to the Making the Connection on page 571)** According to Alan Krueger, an economist at Princeton University, the share of concert ticket revenue received by the top 1 percent of all acts rose from 26 percent in 1982 to 56 percent in 2003. Does this information indicate that the top acts in 2003 must have been much better performers relative to other acts than was the case in 1982? If not, can you think of another explanation?

Source: Eduardo Porter, "More Than Ever, It Pays to Be the Top Executive," *New York Times*, May 25, 2007.

4.11 **(Related to the Making the Connection on page 571)** Why are there superstar basketball players but no superstar plumbers?

4.12 Sam Goldwyn, a movie producer during Hollywood's Golden Age in the 1930s and 1940s, once remarked about one of his stars: "We're overpaying him, but he's worth it."

a. In what sense did Goldwyn mean that he was overpaying this star?

b. If he was overpaying the star, why would the star have still been worth it?

4.13 Prior to the early twentieth century, a worker who was injured on the job could collect damages only by suing his employer. To sue successfully, the worker—or his family, if the worker had been killed—had to show that the injury was due to the employer's negligence, that the worker did not know the job was hazardous, and that the worker's own negligence had not contributed to the accident. These lawsuits were difficult for workers to win, and even workers who had been seriously injured on the job often were unable to collect any damages from their employers. Beginning in 1910, most states passed workers' compensation laws that required employers to purchase insurance that would compensate workers for injuries suffered on the job. A study by Price Fishback of the University of Arizona and Shawn Kantor of the University of California, Merced, shows that after the passage of workers' compensation laws, wages received by workers in the coal and lumber industries fell. Briefly explain why passage of workers' compensation laws would lead to a fall in wages in some industries.

Source: Price V. Fishback and Shawn Everett Kantor, "Did Workers Pay for the Passage of Workers' Compensation Laws?" *Quarterly Journal of Economics*, Vol. 110, No. 3, August 1995, pp. 713–742.

4.14 The following table is similar to Table 17.2 on page 573, except that it includes the earnings of Asian males and females. Does the fact that Asian males are the highest-earning group in the table affect the likelihood that economic discrimination is the best explanation for why earnings differ among the groups listed in the table? Briefly explain your argument.

Group	Weekly Earnings
Asian males	$1,129
White males	969
Asian females	881
White females	776
Black males	731
Hispanic males	656
Black females	654
Hispanic females	580

Source: U.S. Bureau of Labor Statistics, "Usual Weekly Earnings of Wage and Salary Workers, First Quarter 2015," April 21, 2015.

4.15 During the 1970s, many women changed their minds about whether they would leave the labor force after marrying and having children or whether they would be in the labor force most of their adult lives. In 1968, the National Longitudinal Survey asked a representative sample of women aged 14 to 24 whether they expected to be in the labor force at age 35. Twenty-nine percent of white women and 59 percent of black women responded that they expected to be in the labor force at that age. In fact, when these women were 35 years old, 60 percent of those who were married and 80 percent of those who were unmarried were in the labor force. In other words, many more women ended up being in the labor force than expected to be when they were of high school and college age. What effect did this fact have on the earnings of these women? Briefly explain.

Source: Claudia Goldin, *Understanding the Gender Gap: An Economic History of American Women*, New York: Oxford University Press, 1990, p. 155.

4.16 Lawrence Katz, an economist at Harvard, was quoted in a newspaper article as arguing that differences between the incomes of male physicians and female physicians "are largely explained by individual choices." He also noted that discrimination could account for part of the gap, "though it isn't clear how much."

a. What did Katz mean by "individual choices"? How can individual choices result in differences between how much men and women are paid?

b. Why is it difficult to estimate how much of the gap between what men and women are paid is due to discrimination?

Source: Josh Mitchell, "Women Notch Progress," *Wall Street Journal*, December 4, 2012.

4.17 **(Related to Solved Problem 17.4 on page 574)** Use the following graphs to answer the questions.

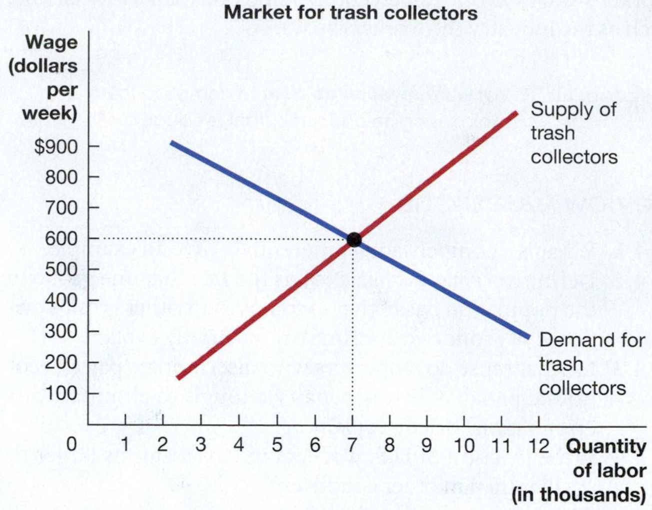

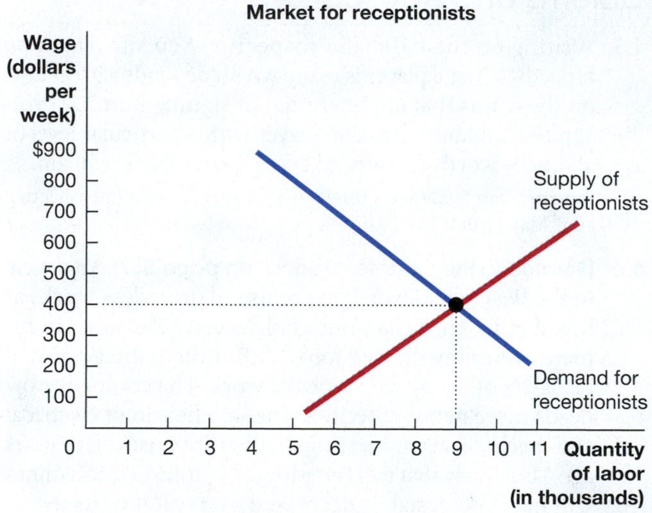

a. What is the equilibrium quantity of trash collectors hired, and what is the equilibrium wage?

b. What is the equilibrium quantity of receptionists hired, and what is the equilibrium wage?

c. Briefly discuss why trash collectors might earn a higher weekly wage than receptionists.

d. Suppose that comparable-worth legislation is passed, and the government requires that trash collectors and receptionists be paid the same wage, $500 per week. Now how many trash collectors will be hired, and how many receptionists will be hired?

4.18 **(Related to Solved Problem 17.4 on page 574)** In most universities, economics professors receive larger salaries than English professors. Suppose that the government requires that from now on, all universities must pay economics professors the same salaries as English professors. Use demand and supply graphs to analyze the effect of this requirement.

4.19 **(Related to the Making the Connection on page 576)** Why might employers be more likely to interview a job applicant with a white-sounding name than an applicant with an African-American–sounding name? Leaving aside legal penalties, will employers who follow this practice incur an economic penalty? Briefly explain.

4.20 **(Related to the Making the Connection on page 576)** An article in the *New York Times* reports that some firms request job applicants to report their SAT scores, even when the job applicant is middle-aged and took the test decades before. The article notes:

> SATs and other academic artifacts remain relevant in part because they are easy—if imperfect—metrics for hiring managers to understand… . Academic research has proved that cognitive ability can predict job performance, but there is scant evidence linking high SAT scores with employee success.

If the link between SAT scores and job performance is weak, why would firms ask job applicants to report their scores? Relate your answer to the reason firms might be more likely to interview an applicant with a white-sounding name even if the applicant's resume was identical to that of an applicant with a black-sounding name.

Source: Melissa Korn, "Job Hunting? Dig Up Those Old SAT Scores," *New York Times*, February 25, 2014.

4.21 Daniel Hamermesh is an economist at the University of Texas who has done a great deal of research on labor markets. According to an article in *Forbes*, Hamermesh writes that "below-average-looking men earn 17% less than those considered good-looking, while below-average-looking females earn 12% less than their attractive counterparts." Is this difference in earnings due to economic discrimination? Briefly explain.

Source: Susan Adams, "Does Beauty Really Pay?" *Forbes*, August 30, 2011.

17.5 Personnel Economics, pages 579–582

LEARNING OBJECTIVE: Discuss the role personnel economics can play in helping firms deal with human resources issues.

Summary

Personnel economics is the application of economic analysis to human resources issues. One insight of personnel economics is that the productivity of workers can often be increased if firms move from straight-time pay to commission or piece-rate pay.

MyEconLab Visit **www.myeconlab.com** to complete these exercises online and get instant feedback.

Review Questions

5.1 What is personnel economics?

5.2 What are the two ways that the productivity of a firm's employees may increase when a firm moves from straight-time pay to commission or piece-rate pay?

5.3 If piece-rate or commission systems of compensating workers have important advantages for firms, why don't more firms use them?

Problems and Applications

5.4 According to a study, the number of jobs in which firms used bonuses, commissions, or piece rates to tie workers' pay to their performance increased from an estimated 30 percent of all jobs in the 1970s to 40 percent in the 1990s. Why would systems that tie workers' pay to how much they produce have become increasingly popular with firms? The same study found that these pay systems were more common in higher-paid jobs than in lower-paid jobs. Briefly explain this result.

Source: Thomas Lemieux, W. Bentley MacLeod, and Daniel Parent, "Performance Pay and Wage Inequality," *Quarterly Journal of Economics*, Vol. 124, No. 1, February 2009, pp. 1–49.

5.5 Many companies that pay workers an hourly wage require some minimum level of acceptable output. Suppose a company that has been using this system decides to switch to a piece-rate system under which workers are compensated on the basis of how much output they produce. Is it likely that workers under a piece-rate system will end up choosing to produce less than the minimum output required under the hourly wage system? Briefly explain.

5.6 **(Related to the Making the Connection on page 580)** In most jobs, the harder you work, the more you earn. Some workers would rather work harder and earn more; others would rather work less hard, even though as a result they earn less. Suppose, though, that all workers at a company fall into the "work harder and earn more" group. Suppose also that the workers all have the same abilities. In these circumstances, would output per worker be the same under an hourly wage compensation system as under a piece-rate system? Briefly explain.

5.7 **(Related to the Making the Connection on page 580)** For years, the Goodyear Tire & Rubber Company compensated its sales force by paying a salesperson a salary plus a bonus, based on the number of tires he or she sold. Eventually, Goodyear made two changes to this policy: (1) The basis for the bonus was changed from the *quantity* of tires sold to the *revenue* from the tires sold; and (2) salespeople were required to get approval from corporate headquarters in Akron, Ohio, before offering to sell tires to customers at reduced prices. Explain why these changes were likely to increase Goodyear's profits.

Source: Timothy Aeppel, "Amid Weak Inflation, Firms Turn Creative to Boost Prices," *Wall Street Journal*, September 18, 2002.

5.8 **(Related to the Making the Connection on page 580)** When the contact lens firm discussed in the *Making the Connection* implemented a new compensation plan, who benefited from the change? Is it likely that there were any losers from the change? Briefly explain.

17.6 The Markets for Capital and Natural Resources, pages 582–584

LEARNING OBJECTIVE: Show how equilibrium prices are determined in the markets for capital and natural resources.

Summary

The approach used to analyze the market for labor can also be used to analyze the markets for other factors of production. In equilibrium, the price of capital is equal to the marginal revenue product of capital, and the price of natural resources is equal to the marginal revenue product of natural resources. The price received by a factor that is in fixed supply is called an **economic rent** (or a **pure rent**). A **monopsony** is a situation in which a firm is the sole buyer of a factor of production. According to the **marginal productivity theory of income distribution**, the distribution of income is determined by the marginal productivity of the factors of production individuals own.

MyEconLab Visit **www.myeconlab.com** to complete these exercises online and get instant feedback.

Review Questions

6.1 In equilibrium, what determines the price of capital? What determines the price of natural resources? What is an economic rent?

6.2 What is a monopsony?

6.3 What is the marginal productivity theory of income distribution?

Problems and Applications

6.4 Adam operates a pin factory. Suppose Adam faces the situation shown in the following table and the cost of renting a machine is $550 per week.

a. Fill in the blank cells in the table and determine the profit-maximizing number of machines for Adam to rent. Briefly explain why renting this number of machines is profit maximizing.

b. Draw Adam's demand curve for capital.

Number of Machines	Output of Pins (boxes per week)	Marginal Product of Capital	Product Price (dollars per box)	Total Revenue	Marginal Revenue Product of Capital	Rental Cost per Machine	Additional Profit from Renting One Additional Machine
0	0	____	$100		____	$550	
1	12		100			550	
2	21		100			550	
3	28		100			550	
4	34		100			550	
5	39		100			550	
6	43		100			550	

6.5 Many people have predicted, using a model like the one in panel (b) of Figure 17.12 on page 583, that the price of natural resources should rise consistently over time in comparison with the prices of other goods because the demand curve for natural resources is continually shifting to the right, while the supply curve must be shifting to the left as natural resources are used up. However, the relative prices of most natural resources have not been increasing. Draw a graph showing the demand and supply for natural resources that can explain why prices haven't risen even though demand has.

6.6 In 1879, economist Henry George published *Progress and Poverty*, which became one of the best-selling books of the nineteenth century. In this book, George argued that all existing taxes should be replaced with a single tax on land. Tax incidence refers to the actual division of the burden of a tax between buyers and sellers in a market (see Chapter 4). If land is taxed, how will the burden of the tax be divided between the sellers of land and the buyers of land? Illustrate your answer with a graph of the market for land.

6.7 The total amount of oil in the earth is not increasing. Does this mean that in the market for oil, the supply curve is perfectly inelastic? Briefly explain.

6.8 In a competitive labor market, imposing a minimum wage should reduce the equilibrium level of employment. Will this result still hold if the labor market is a monopsony? Briefly explain.

CHAPTER
18

Public Choice, Taxes, and the Distribution of Income

Chapter Outline and Learning Objectives

Should the Government Use the Tax System to Reduce Inequality?

What is the purpose of taxes? Your first answer is probably that taxes enable the government to pay for its spending. Taxes, though, also affect the decisions of individuals and firms. For instance, some people choose to live in a suburb outside of a big city in order to avoid the income tax the city may impose on their earnings. Because the United States imposes a higher tax on corporate profits than do most other countries, some U.S. firms have moved their headquarters overseas so that they will pay lower taxes.

Over the years, Congress and the president have used taxes to try to achieve certain policy objectives. As we saw when discussing the Affordable Care Act, the federal government imposes taxes intended to provide firms with an incentive to offer health insurance to their employees and individuals an incentive to enroll in a health insurance plan.

During the 2016 presidential election campaign, candidates debated whether the tax system should be used to reduce income inequality. Running for the Democratic nomination, former Secretary of State Hillary Clinton proposed increasing taxes on some high-income individuals and using the funds to finance government programs aimed at raising living standards for people with lower incomes. Republican candidates, including former Florida Governor Jeb Bush and Florida Senator Marco Rubio, argued that increasing income inequality was not the result of tax changes and that increasing taxes on individuals with high incomes was likely to reduce economic efficiency while having little effect on inequality.

The questions raised by the debate over taxes during the 2016 election campaign were not new. For example, Presidents John F. Kennedy and Ronald Reagan proposed significant cuts in income taxes that they claimed would enhance economic efficiency, while their opponents claimed that the tax cuts rewarded high-income taxpayers and increased income inequality. The design of the tax system and the criteria used to evaluate it are important issues. Has the tax code improved or reduced economic efficiency? Has the government, through its tax and other policies, had much effect on the distribution of income? We explore these questions in this chapter.

Sources: Amy Chozick, "Hillary Clinton Offers Her Vision of a 'Fairness Economy' to Close the Income Gap," *New York Times*, July 13, 2015; and Jonathan Weisman, "Reformers Try to Tackle the Tax Machine," *New York Times*, February 14, 2015.

Economics in Your Life

How Much Tax Should You Pay?

The government is ever present in your life. Just today, you likely drove on roads that the government paid to build and maintain. You may attend a public college or university, paid for, at least in part, by the government. The government gets the money to fund these expenses by taxing citizens, including you. Think of the different taxes you pay. Do you think you pay more than, less than, or just about your fair share in taxes? How do you determine what amount is your fair share? As you read this chapter, try to answer these questions. You can check your answers against those we provide on **page 622** at the end of this chapter.

We have seen that the government plays a significant role in helping the market system work efficiently by providing secure rights to private property and an independent court system to enforce contracts (see Chapter 2). We have also seen that the government itself must sometimes supply goods—known as *public goods*—that private firms will not supply (see Chapter 5). But how do governments decide which policies to adopt? In recent years, economists led by the late Nobel Laureate James Buchanan and Gordon Tullock, of George Mason University, have developed the **public choice model**, which applies economic analysis to government decision making. In this chapter, we will explore how public choice can help us understand how policymakers make decisions.

Public choice model A model that applies economic analysis to government decision making.

We will also discuss the principles that governments use to create tax policy. In particular, we will see how economists identify which taxes are most economically efficient. At the end of this chapter, we will discuss the extent to which government policy—including tax policy—affects the distribution of income.

18.1 Public Choice

LEARNING OBJECTIVE: Describe the public choice model and use it to analyze government decision making.

In earlier chapters, we focused on explaining the actions of households and firms. We have assumed that households and firms act to make themselves as well off as possible. In particular, we have assumed that households choose the goods they buy to maximize their utility and that firms choose the quantities and prices of the goods they sell to maximize profit. Because government policy plays an important role in the economy, we need to consider how government policymakers—such as senators, governors, presidents, and state legislators—arrive at their decisions. One of the key insights from the public choice model is that policymakers are no different from consumers or managers of firms: Policymakers are likely to pursue their own self-interest, even if it conflicts with the public interest. In particular, we expect that public officials will take actions that are likely to result in their being reelected.

How Do We Know the Public Interest? Models of Voting

It is possible to argue that elected officials simply represent the preferences of the voters who elect them. After all, it would seem logical that voters will not reelect a politician who fails to act in the public interest. A closer look at voting, however, makes it less clear that politicians are simply representing the views of the voters.

The Voting Paradox Many policy decisions involve multiple alternatives. Because the size of the federal budget is limited, policymakers face trade-offs. To take a simple example, suppose that there is $1 billion available in the budget, and Congress must choose whether to spend it on *only one* of three alternatives: (1) research on breast cancer, (2) subsidies for mass transit, or (3) increased border security. Assume that the votes of members of Congress will represent the preferences of their constituents. We might expect that Congress will vote for the alternative favored by a majority of the voters. In fact, though, there are circumstances in which majority voting will fail to result in a consistent decision. For example, suppose for simplicity that there are only three voters, and they have the preferences shown at the top of Table 18.1.

In the table, we show the three policy alternatives in the first column. The remaining columns show the voters' rankings of the alternatives. For example, Lena would prefer to see the money spent on cancer research. Her second choice is mass transit, and her third choice is border security. What happens if a series of votes are taken in which each pair of alternatives is considered in turn? The bottom of Table 18.1 shows the results of these votes. If the vote is between spending the money on cancer research and spending the money on mass transit, cancer research wins because Lena and David both prefer spending the money on cancer research rather than on mass transit.

Table 18.1

The Voting Paradox

Policy	Lena	David	Kathleen
Cancer research	1st	2nd	3rd
Mass transit	2nd	3rd	1st
Border security	3rd	1st	2nd

Votes	Outcome
Cancer research versus mass transit	Cancer research wins
Mass transit versus border security	Mass transit wins
Border security versus cancer research	Border security wins

So, if the votes of members of Congress represent the preferences of voters, we have a clear verdict, and the money is spent on breast cancer research. Suppose, though, that the vote is between spending the money on mass transit and spending the money on border security. Then, because Lena and Kathleen prefer spending on mass transit to spending on border security, mass transit wins. Now, finally, suppose the vote is between spending on cancer research and spending on border security. Surprisingly, border security wins because that is what David and Kathleen prefer. The outcome of this vote is surprising because if voters prefer cancer research to mass transit and mass transit to border security, we would expect that consistency in decision making would ensure that they prefer cancer research to border security. But in this example, the collective preferences of the voters turn out not to be consistent. The failure of majority voting to always result in consistent choices is called the **voting paradox**.

Voting paradox The failure of majority voting to always result in consistent choices.

This example is artificial because we assumed that there were only three alternatives, there were only three voters, and a simple majority vote determined the outcomes. In fact, though, Nobel Laureate Kenneth Arrow of Stanford University has shown mathematically that the failure of majority votes to always represent voters' preferences is a very general result. The **Arrow impossibility theorem** states that no system of voting can be devised that will consistently represent the underlying preferences of voters. This theorem suggests that there is no way through democratic voting to ensure that the preferences of voters are translated into policy choices. In fact, the Arrow impossibility theorem indicates that voting might lead to shifts in policy that may not be efficient. For instance, which of the three alternatives for spending the $1 billion Congress will actually choose would depend on the order in which the alternatives happen to be voted on, which might change from one year to the next. So, for economic issues, such as the funding of public goods, we cannot count on the political process to necessarily result in an efficient outcome. In other words, the "voting market"—as represented by elections—may often do a less efficient job of representing consumer preferences than do markets for goods and services.

Arrow impossibility theorem A mathematical theorem that holds that no system of voting can be devised that will consistently represent the underlying preferences of voters.

The Median Voter Theorem In practice, many political issues are decided by a majority vote. In those cases, what can we say about which voters' preferences the outcome is likely to represent? An important result known as the **median voter theorem** states that the outcome of a majority vote is likely to represent the preferences of the voter who is in the political middle. To take another simplified example, suppose there are five voters, and their preferences for spending on breast cancer research are shown in Figure 18.1. Their preferences range from Kathleen, who prefers to spend nothing on breast cancer research—preferring the funds to be spent on other programs or for federal spending to be reduced and taxes lowered—to Lena, who prefers to spend $6 billion.

Median voter theorem The proposition that the outcome of a majority vote is likely to represent the preferences of the voter who is in the political middle.

In this case, David is the median voter because he is in the political middle; two voters would prefer to spend less than he does, and two voters would prefer to spend more than he does. To see why the median voter's preferences are likely to prevail, consider first a vote between David's preferred outcome of spending $2 billion and a proposal to spend $6 billion. Because only Lena favors $6 billion and the other voters all prefer spending less, the proposal to spend $2 billion would win four votes to one. Similarly, consider a vote between spending $2 billion and spending $1 billion. Three voters prefer spending more than $1 billion, and only two prefer spending $1 billion or less, so

Figure 18.1

The Median Voter Theorem

The median voter theorem states that the outcome of a majority vote is likely to represent the preferences of the voter who is in the political middle. In this case, David is in the political middle because two voters want to spend more on breast cancer research than he does and two voters want to spend less. In any vote between a proposal to spend $2 billion and a proposal to spend a different amount, a proposal to spend $2 billion will win.

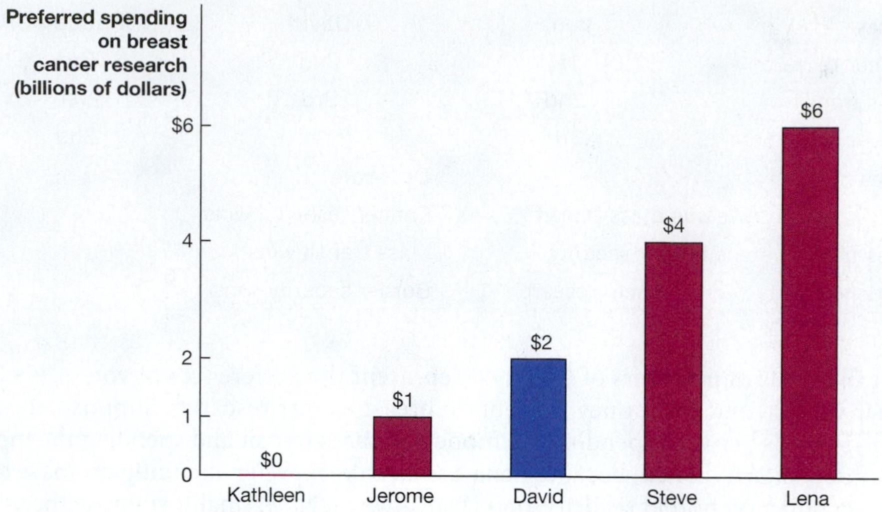

the proposal to spend $2 billion will win three votes to two. Only the proposal to spend $2 billion will have the support of a majority when paired with proposals to spend a different amount. Notice also that the amount spent as a result of the voting is less than the amount that would result from taking the simple average of the voter's preferences, which would be $2.6 billion.

One implication of the median voter theorem is that the political process tends to serve individuals whose preferences are in the middle but not those individuals whose preferences are far away from the median. There is an important contrast between the political process, which results in collective actions in which everyone is obliged to participate, and the market process, in which individuals are free to participate or not. For instance, even though Kathleen would prefer not to spend government funds on breast cancer research, once a majority has voted to spend $2 billion, Kathleen is obliged to go along with the spending—and the taxes required to fund the spending. This outcome is in contrast with the market for goods and services, where if, for instance, Kathleen disagrees with the majority of consumers who like iPads, she is under no obligation to buy one. Similarly, even though Lena and Steve might prefer to pay significantly higher taxes to fund additional spending on breast cancer research, they are obliged to go along with the lower level of spending that the majority approved. If Lena would like to have her iPad gold plated, she can choose to do so, even if the vast majority of consumers would consider such spending a waste of money. MyEconLab Concept Check

Government Failure?

The voting models we have just looked at indicate that individuals are less likely to see their preferences represented in the outcomes of government policies than in the outcomes of markets. The public choice model goes beyond this observation to question whether the self-interest of policymakers is likely to cause them to take actions that are inconsistent with the preferences of voters, even where those preferences are clear. There are several aspects of the way the political process works that might lead to this outcome.

Rent seeking Attempts by individuals and firms to use government action to make themselves better off at the expense of others.

Rent Seeking Economists usually focus on the actions of individuals and firms as they attempt to make themselves better off by interacting in markets. The public choice model shifts the focus to attempts by individuals and firms to engage in **rent seeking**, which is the use of government action to make themselves better off at the expense of others. One of the benefits of the market system is that it channels self-interested behavior in a way that benefits society as a whole. Although Apple developed the iPad to make a profit, its actions increased the well-being of millions of consumers. When Samsung introduced the Galaxy Tab to compete with the iPad, it was also motivated by the desire for profit, but it further increased consumer well-being by expanding the choice of tablets available. Rent seeking, in contrast, can benefit a few individuals or firms at the expense of all other individuals and firms. For example, U.S. sugar firms have successfully convinced Congress to impose a quota on imports of sugar (see Chapter 9). The quota has benefited the owners of U.S. sugar firms and the people who work for them but has reduced consumer surplus, hurt U.S. candy companies and their workers, and reduced economic efficiency.

Because firms can benefit from government intervention in the economy, as the sugar companies have benefited from the sugar quota, they are willing to spend money to influence government policymakers. Members of Congress, state legislators, governors, and presidents need funds to finance their election campaigns. So, these policymakers may accept campaign contributions from rent-seeking firms and may be willing to introduce *special-interest legislation* on their behalf.

Logrolling and Rational Ignorance Two other factors help explain why rent-seeking behavior can sometimes succeed. It may seem puzzling that the sugar quota has been enacted when it helps very few workers and firms. Why would members of Congress vote for the sugar quota if they do not have sugar companies in their districts? One possibility is *logrolling*, which refers to the situation where a member of Congress votes to approve a bill in exchange for favorable votes from other members on other bills. For example, a member of Congress from Texas might vote for the sugar quota, even though none of the member's constituents will benefit from it. In exchange, members of Congress from districts where sugar producers are located will vote for legislation the member of Congress from Texas would like to see passed. As Pennsylvania Senator Pat Toomey put it after his attempt to eliminate the sugar quota was voted down: "They circle the wagons, work together, protect each others' interests." This vote trading may result in a majority of Congress supporting legislation that benefits the economic interests of a few while harming the economic interests of a much larger group.

But if the majority of voters are harmed by rent-seeking legislation, how does it get passed, even given the effects of logrolling? Consider another possible explanation for the survival of the sugar quota (see Chapter 9). Although total consumer surplus declines by $3.26 billion per year because of the sugar quota, when it is spread across a population of 320 million, the loss per person is only about $10. Because the loss is so small, most people do not take it into account when deciding who to vote for, and many people are not even aware that the sugar quota exists. Other voters may be convinced to support restrictions on trade because the jobs saved by tariffs and quotas are visible and often highly publicized, while the jobs lost because of these restrictions and the reductions in consumer surplus are harder to detect. Because becoming informed on an issue may require time and effort and the economic payoff is often low, some economists argue that many voters are *rationally ignorant* of the effect of rent-seeking legislation. In this view, because voters frequently lack an economic incentive to become informed about legislation, the preferences of voters do not act as a constraint on legislators voting for rent-seeking legislation.

Regulatory Capture One way in which the government intervenes in the economy is by establishing a regulatory agency or commission that is given authority over a particular industry or type of product. For example, no firm is allowed to sell prescription drugs in the United States without first receiving authorization from the Food and Drug Administration (FDA). Ideally, regulatory agencies will make decisions in the public interest. The FDA should weigh the benefits to patients from quickly approving a new drug against the costs involved if a drug with potentially dangerous side effects is approved too rapidly. However, because the firms being regulated have a financial stake in the regulatory agency's actions, the firms have an incentive to try to influence those actions. In extreme cases, this influence may lead the agency to make decisions that are in the best interests of the firms being regulated, even if these actions are not in the public interest. In that case, the agency has been subject to *regulatory capture* by the industry being regulated. Some economists point to the Interstate Commerce Commission (ICC) as an example of regulatory capture. Although Congress has since abolished the ICC, for decades it determined the prices that railroads and long-distance trucking firms could charge to haul freight. Congress originally established the ICC to safeguard the interests of consumers, but some economists have argued that for many years the ICC operated to suppress competition, which was in the interests of the railroads and trucking firms rather than in the interests of consumers. Economists debate the extent to which regulatory capture explains the decisions of some government agencies.

The presence of externalities can lead to market failure, which is the situation where the market does not supply the economically efficient quantity of a good or service (see Chapter 5). Public choice analysis indicates that *government failure* can also occur. For the reasons we have discussed in this section, it is possible that government intervention in the economy may reduce economic efficiency rather than increase it. Economists disagree about the extent to which government failure results in serious economic inefficiency in the U.S. economy. Most economists, though, accept the basic argument of the public choice model that policymakers may have incentives to intervene in the economy in ways that do not promote efficiency and that proposals for such intervention should be evaluated with care.

MyEconLab Concept Check

Is Government Regulation Necessary?

The public choice model raises important questions about the effect of government regulation on economic efficiency. Can we conclude that Congress should abolish agencies such as the Food and Drug Administration (FDA), the Environmental Protection Agency (EPA), and the Federal Trade Commission (FTC)? In fact, most economists agree that these agencies can serve useful purposes. For instance, the EPA can help correct the effect of externalities, such as the pollution that some companies emit as they produce goods. Regulatory agencies can also improve economic efficiency in markets where consumers have difficulty obtaining the information they need to make informed purchases. For example, consumers have no easy way of detecting bacteria and other contaminants in food or determining whether prescription drugs are safe and effective. The FDA was established in the early twentieth century to monitor the nation's food supply following newspaper accounts of unsanitary practices in many meatpacking plants.

Although government regulation can clearly provide important benefits to consumers, we need to take into account the costs of regulations. Recent estimates indicate that the costs of federal regulations may be several thousand dollars per taxpayer. Economics can help policymakers devise regulations that provide benefits to consumers that exceed their costs.

MyEconLab Study Plan

MyEconLab Concept Check

18.2 The Tax System

LEARNING OBJECTIVE: Explain the tax system in the United States, including the principles that governments use to create tax policy.

Regardless of how the size of government and the types of activities it engages in are determined, government spending has to be financed. The government primarily relies on taxes to raise the revenue it needs. Some taxes, such as those on cigarettes or alcohol, are intended to discourage what society views as undesirable behavior in addition to raising revenue. These are the most widely used taxes:

- **Individual income taxes.** The federal government, most state governments, and some local governments tax the wages, salaries, and other income of households and the profits of small businesses, which are typically taxed the same as wages and salaries. The individual income tax is the largest source of revenue for the federal government. Because low-income people do not pay federal individual income taxes, in recent years nearly half of all households have paid no federal income tax.

- **Social insurance taxes.** The federal government taxes wages and salaries to raise revenue for the Social Security and Medicare programs. *Social Security* makes payments to retired workers and to disabled individuals. *Medicare* helps pay the medical expenses of people over age 65. The Social Security and Medicare taxes are often called *payroll taxes*. As the U.S. population has aged, payroll taxes have increased. By 2015, more than three-quarters of taxpayers paid a greater amount in payroll taxes than in federal individual income taxes. The federal government and state governments also tax wages and salaries to raise revenue for the unemployment insurance system, which makes payments to workers who have lost their jobs.
- **Sales taxes.** Most state and local governments tax retail sales of most products. More than half the states exempt food from the sales tax, and a few states also exempt clothing.
- **Property taxes.** Most local governments tax homes, offices, factories, and the land they are built on. In the United States, the property tax is the largest source of funds for public schools.
- **Excise taxes.** The federal government and some state governments levy excise taxes on specific goods, such as gasoline, cigarettes, and beer.

An Overview of the U.S. Tax System

Panels (a) and (b) of Figure 18.2 show the revenue sources of the federal, state, and local governments. Panel (a) shows that the federal government raises more than 75 percent of its revenue from the social insurance taxes and individual income taxes. Corporate

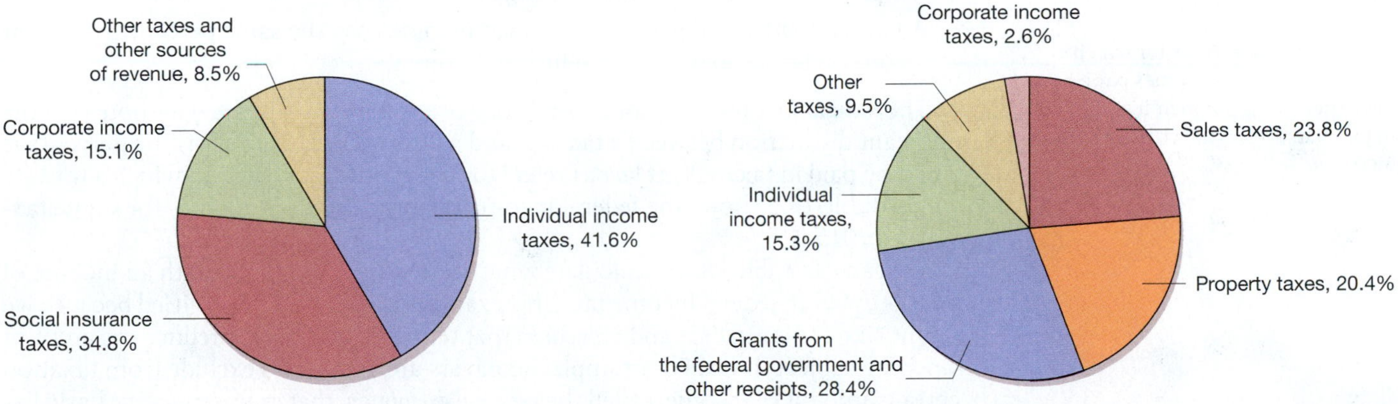

Tax	Amount (billions)	Amount per Household	Percentage of Total Tax Receipts
Individual income taxes	$1,375	$11,160	41.6%
Social insurance taxes	1,150	9,333	34.8
Corporate income taxes	497	4,036	15.1
Other taxes and sources of revenue	280	2,272	8.5
Total	$3,303	$26,801	100.0%

(a) Sources of federal government revenue, 2014

Tax	Amount (billions)	Amount per Household	Percentage of Total Tax Receipts
Grants from the federal government and other receipts	$627	$5,086	28.4%
Sales taxes	525	4,258	23.8
Property taxes	450	3,655	20.4
Individual income taxes	337	2,732	15.3
Other taxes	210	1,704	9.5
Corporate income taxes	57	465	2.6
Total	$2,206	$17,901	100.0%

(b) Sources of state and local government revenue, 2014

MyEconLab Animation

Figure 18.2 Federal, State, and Local Sources of Revenue, 2014

Individual income taxes are the most important source of revenue for the federal government, and social insurance taxes are the second most important source. State and local governments receive large transfers from the federal government, in part to help pay for federally mandated programs. Many local governments depend on property taxes to raise most of their tax revenue.

income taxes and excise taxes account for much smaller fractions of federal revenues. In 2014, federal revenues of all types amounted to more than $3.3 trillion, or $26,801 per household. Over the past 40 years, federal revenues as a share of gross domestic product (GDP—the value of all the goods and services produced in the U.S. economy) have typically remained in a fairly narrow range between 17 percent and 19 percent, with a low of 16 percent in 2009 and a high of 21 percent in 2000.

Panel (b) shows that state and local governments rely on a different mix of revenue sources than does the federal government. In the past, the largest source of revenue for state and local governments was sales taxes. State and local governments also receive large grants from the federal government, which in 2014 were their largest source of revenue. These grants are intended in part to pay for programs that the federal government requires state and local governments to carry out. These programs, often called *federal mandates,* include the *Medicaid* program, which finances health care for many low-income people, and the Temporary Assistance for Needy Families (TANF) program, which provides financial assistance to poor families. Local governments also raise substantial revenue from property taxes. Many local school districts, in particular, rely almost entirely on revenues from property taxes. MyEconLab Concept Check

Progressive and Regressive Taxes

Economists often categorize taxes on the basis of the percentage of their income that people at different income levels pay in taxes:

Regressive tax A tax for which people with lower incomes pay a higher percentage of their income in tax than do people with higher incomes.

Progressive tax A tax for which people with lower incomes pay a lower percentage of their income in tax than do people with higher incomes.

- A tax is **regressive** if people with lower incomes pay a higher percentage of their income in tax than do people with higher incomes.
- A tax is **progressive** if people with lower incomes pay a lower percentage of their income in tax than do people with higher incomes.
- A tax is *proportional* if people with lower incomes pay the same percentage of their income in tax as do people with higher incomes.

The federal income tax is an example of a progressive tax. To see why, note first the important distinction between a tax rate and a tax bracket. A *tax rate* is the percentage of income paid in taxes. A *tax bracket* refers to the income range within which a tax rate applies. Table 18.2 shows the federal income tax brackets and tax rates for single taxpayers in 2015.

We can use Table 18.2 to calculate what Matt, a single taxpayer with an income of $100,000, pays in federal income tax. This example is somewhat simplified because we are ignoring the *exemptions* and *deductions* that taxpayers can use to reduce the amount of income subject to tax. For example, taxpayers are allowed to exclude from taxation a certain amount of income, called the *personal exemption,* that represents very basic living expenses. Ignoring Matt's exemptions and deductions, he will have to make the tax payment to the federal government shown in Table 18.3. Matt's first $9,225 of income is in the 10 percent bracket, so he pays $922.50 in taxes on that part of his income. His next $28,225 of income is in the 15 percent bracket, so he pays $4,233.75. His next $53,300 of income is in the 25 percent bracket, so he pays $13,325. His last $9,250 of

Table 18.2

Federal Income Tax Brackets and Tax Rates for Single Taxpayers, 2015

Income	Tax Rate
$0–$9,225	10%
$9,226–$37,450	15
$37,451–$90,750	25
$90,751–$189,300	28
$189,301–$411,500	33
$411,501–$413,200	35
Over $413,200	39.6

Source: Internal Revenue Service.

Table 18.3

Federal Income Tax Paid on Taxable Income of $100,000

On Matt's . . .	Matt pays tax of . . .
first $9,225 of income	$922.50
next $28,225 of income	4,233.75
next $53,300 of income	13,325.00
last $9,250 of income	2,590.00
His total federal income tax payment is	$21,071.25

income is in the 28 percent bracket, so he pays $2,590, which brings his total federal income tax bill to $21,071.25.

MyEconLab Concept Check

Making the Connection

MyEconLab Video

Which Groups Pay the Most in Federal Taxes?

In the chapter opener, we mentioned the ongoing debate over whether to increase taxes on people with high incomes. To evaluate this debate, it's useful to know how much each income group pays of the total taxes collected by the federal government. The following table shows projections for 2016 by the Tax Policy Center, with taxpayers divided into quintiles from the 20 percent with the lowest income to the 20 percent with the highest income. The last row shows taxpayers whose incomes put them in the top 1 percent. Column (1) shows the percentage of total income earned by each income group. Column (2) shows the percentage of all federal taxes—including Social Security and Medicare payroll taxes—paid by each income group. Column (3) shows the average federal tax rate for each group, calculated by dividing total taxes paid by total income.

Income Category	Share of Total Income Earned (1)	Share of Total Federal Taxes Paid (2)	All Federal Taxes Paid as a Fraction of Income (average federal tax rate) (3)
Lowest 20%	4.2%	0.9%	4.3%
Second 20%	8.3	3.4	8.3
Third 20%	13.9	9.4	13.7
Fourth 20%	20.4	17.4	17.4
Highest 20%	53.2	68.7	26.3
Total	100.0%	100.0%	20.4%
Highest 1%	16.8	28.1	34.1

Note: Columns may not sum to precisely 100 percent due to rounding.

Source: Urban-Brookings Tax Policy Center, Tables T15-0050 and T15-0060, June 23, 2015.

The data in column (2) show that the 20 percent of taxpayers with the highest incomes pay 69 percent of federal taxes, which is greater than their 53 percent share of total income earned, as shown in column (1). Only taxpayers in the highest quintile pay a larger share of taxes than their share of income. Taxpayers whose incomes put them in the top 1 percent pay more than 28 percent of federal taxes. Many individuals in the lowest quintile of income, particularly those with children, receive tax credits from the federal government so that they in effect pay negative taxes. Column (3) indicates that average tax rates rise as income rises.

If we look at just the federal individual income tax considered separately from the payroll tax and other federal taxes, the results are similar. In 2016:

- Taxpayers in the top 1 percent of the income distribution were projected to earn 17 percent of all income while paying 43 percent of all federal individual income taxes
- The top 20 percent of the income distribution earned 53 percent of income while paying 86 percent of individual taxes.

- The bottom 40 percent of the income distribution earned 13 percent of income but actually paid *negative* 4 percent of federal individual income taxes when taking into account tax credits, such as the child tax credit.

We can conclude that the federal taxes are progressive. Whether the federal tax system should be made more or less progressive remains a topic of political debate.

MyEconLab Study Plan

Your Turn: Test your understanding by doing related problem 2.9 on page 626 at the end of this chapter.

Marginal and Average Income Tax Rates

Marginal tax rate The fraction of each additional dollar of income that must be paid in taxes.

Average tax rate Total tax paid divided by total income.

The fraction of each additional dollar of income that must be paid in taxes is called the **marginal tax rate**. The **average tax rate** is the total tax paid divided by total income. When a tax is progressive, as is the federal income tax, the marginal and average tax rates differ. For example, in Table 18.3, Matt had a marginal tax rate of 28 percent because that is the rate he paid on the last dollar of his income. But his average tax rate was:

$$\left(\frac{\$21{,}071.25}{\$100{,}000}\right) \times 100 = 21.1\%.$$

His average tax rate was lower than his marginal tax rate because the first $90,750 of his income was taxed at rates below his marginal rate of 28 percent.

The marginal tax rate is a better indicator than the average tax rate of how a change in a tax will affect people's willingness to work, save, and invest. For example, if Matt is considering working longer hours to raise his income, he will use his marginal tax rate to determine how much extra income he will earn after taxes. He will ignore his average tax rate because it does not represent the taxes he must pay on the *additional* income he earns. The higher the marginal tax rate, the lower the return he receives from working additional hours and the less likely he is to work those additional hours.

MyEconLab Concept Check

The Corporate Income Tax

The federal government taxes the profits earned by corporations under the *corporate income tax*. Like the individual income tax, the corporate income tax is progressive, with the lowest tax rate being 15 percent and the highest being 35 percent. Unlike the individual income tax, however, where relatively few taxpayers are taxed at the highest rate, many corporations are in the 35 percent tax bracket.

Economists debate the costs and benefits of a separate tax on corporate profits. The corporate income tax ultimately must be paid by a corporation's owners—who are its shareholders—or by its employees, in the form of lower wages, or by its customers, in the form of higher prices. Some economists argue that if the purpose of the corporate income tax is to tax the owners of corporations, it would be better to do so directly by taxing the owners' incomes rather than by taxing the owners indirectly through the corporate income tax. Individual taxpayers already pay income taxes on the dividends and capital gains they receive from owning stock in corporations. In effect, the corporate income tax "double taxes" earnings on individual shareholders' investments in corporations. An alternative policy that avoids this double taxation would be for corporations to calculate their total profits each year and send a notice to each shareholder, indicating the shareholder's portion of the profits. Shareholders would then be required to include this amount as taxable income on their personal income tax. Under another alternative policy, the federal government could continue to tax corporate income through the corporate income tax but allow individual taxpayers to receive corporate dividends and capital gains tax-free.

MyEconLab Concept Check

Table 18.4

Corporate Income Tax Rates around the World

Country	Tax in 2000	Tax in 2014
France	37%	33%
Germany	52	30
Ireland	24	13
Italy	41	31
Japan	42	36
Spain	35	30
Sweden	28	22
United Kingdom	30	21
United States	40	40

Note: The rates given include taxes at all levels of government. In the United States, the rate includes state as well as federal taxes.

Source: KPMG, *KPMG's Corporate and Indirect Tax Survey, 2014.*

International Comparison of Corporate Income Taxes

In recent years, several countries have cut corporate income taxes to increase investment spending and growth. Table 18.4 compares corporate income tax rates in several high-income countries. The tax rates given in the table include taxes at all levels of government. So, in the United States, for example, they include taxes imposed on corporate profits by state governments as well as by the federal government. The table shows that several countries, including Italy, Germany, the United Kingdom, and Ireland, significantly reduced their corporate income tax rates between 2000 and 2014. Ireland, in particular, has been successful in using lower corporate income tax rates to attract foreign corporations to locate facilities there. Lower tax rates have led Microsoft, Intel, and Dell, among other U.S. firms, to base some of their operations in Ireland. The table also shows that corporate income tax rates are higher in the United States than in other high-income countries.

The relatively high U.S. corporate tax rate has led many large U.S. firms with significant sales in foreign countries to avoid returning profits earned in those countries back to the United States. By keeping their profits overseas, these U.S. firms do not have to pay U.S. taxes on them, although the funds are also not available to be spent in the United States. As a result, many large U.S. firms pay a marginal tax rate well below the 40 percent rate indicated in Table 18.4. MyEconLab Concept Check

Evaluating Taxes

We have seen that to raise revenue, governments have available a variety of taxes. In selecting which taxes to use, governments take into account the following goals and principles:

- The goal of economic efficiency
- The ability-to-pay principle
- The horizontal-equity principle
- The benefits-received principle
- The goal of attaining social objectives

The Goal of Economic Efficiency We can briefly review the effect of taxes on economic efficiency (see Chapter 4). A government tax on an activity raises the cost of engaging in that activity, so less of the activity will occur. Figure 18.3 uses a demand and supply graph to illustrate this point for a sales tax. A sales tax increases the cost of supplying a good, which causes the supply curve to shift up by the amount of the tax. In the figure, the equilibrium price rises from P_1 to P_2, and the equilibrium quantity falls from Q_1 to Q_2. When a good is taxed, less of it is produced.

MyEconLab Animation

Figure 18.3

The Efficiency Loss from a Sales Tax

This figure reviews the discussion of the efficiency loss from a tax (see Chapter 4). A sales tax increases the cost of supplying a good, which causes the supply curve to shift up, from S_1 to S_2. Without the tax, the equilibrium price of the good is P_1, and the equilibrium quantity is Q_1. After the tax is imposed, the equilibrium price rises to P_2, and the equilibrium quantity falls to Q_2. After paying the tax, producers receive P_3. The government receives tax revenue equal to the green-shaded rectangle. Some consumer surplus and some producer surplus become tax revenue for the government, and some become deadweight loss, shown by the yellow-shaded triangle. The deadweight loss is the *excess burden* of the tax.

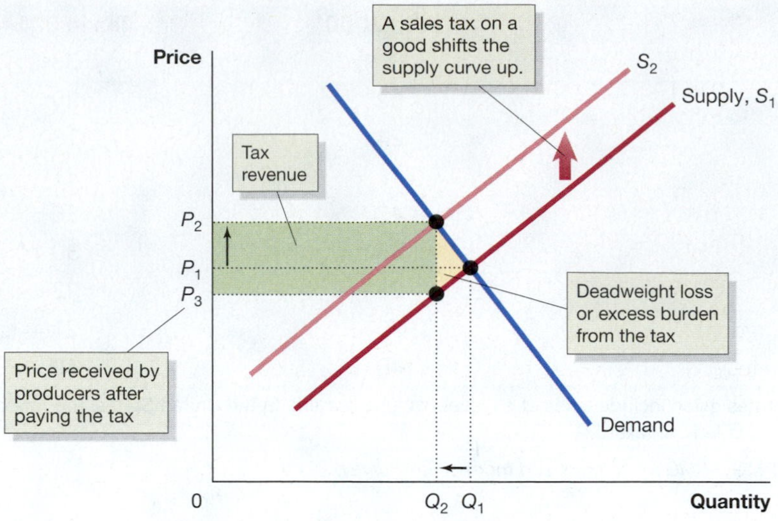

The government collects tax revenue equal to the tax per unit multiplied by the number of units sold. The green-shaded rectangle in Figure 18.3 represents the government's tax revenue. Although sellers appear to receive a higher price for the good—P_2—the price they receive after paying the tax falls to P_3. Because the price consumers pay has risen, consumer surplus has fallen. Because the price producers receive has also fallen, producer surplus has fallen. Some of the reduction in consumer surplus and producer surplus becomes tax revenue for the government. The rest of the reduction in consumer surplus and producer surplus is equal to the deadweight loss from the tax and is shown in the figure by the yellow-shaded triangle. The deadweight loss from a tax is known as the *excess burden* of the tax. The **excess burden** is a measure of the efficiency loss to the economy that results from the tax having reduced the quantity of the good produced. *A tax is efficient if it imposes a small excess burden relative to the tax revenue it raises.*

Excess burden A measure of the efficiency loss to the economy that results from a tax having reduced the quantity of a good produced; also known as the deadweight loss.

Economists believe that to improve the economic efficiency of a tax system, the government should reduce its reliance on taxes that have a high deadweight loss relative to the revenue raised. The tax on interest earned from savings is an example of a tax with a high deadweight loss because savings often come from income already taxed once. Therefore, taxing interest earned on savings from income that has already been taxed is essentially double taxation.

There are other examples of significant deadweight losses of taxation. High taxes on work can reduce the number of hours an individual works, as well as how hard the individual works or whether the individual starts a business. In each case, the reduction in the taxed activity—here, work—generates less government revenue, and individuals are worse off because the tax encourages them to change their behavior.

Taxation can have substantial effects on economic efficiency by altering incentives to work, save, or invest. A good illustration of this effect can be seen in the large differences between annual hours worked in Europe and in the United States. Europeans typically work fewer hours than do Americans. According to an analysis by Nobel Laureate Edward Prescott of Arizona State University, this difference was not always present. In the early 1970s, when European and U.S. tax rates on income were comparable, European and U.S. hours worked per employee were also comparable. Prescott finds that virtually all of the difference between labor supply in the United States and labor supply in France and Germany since that time is due to differences in their tax systems. In 2014, the top individual income tax rate in Germany was 45 percent, and in France it was 51.25 percent, as opposed to 39.6 percent in the United States.

The administrative burden of a tax represents another example of the deadweight loss of taxation. Individuals spend many hours during the year keeping records for income tax purposes, and they spend many more hours prior to April 15 preparing their tax returns. The opportunity cost of this time is billions of dollars each year and represents an administrative burden of the federal income tax. For corporations, complexity in tax planning arises in many areas. The federal government also has to devote resources to enforcing the tax laws. Although the government collects the revenue from taxation, the resources spent on administrative burdens benefit neither taxpayers nor the government.

Wouldn't tax simplification reduce the administrative burden and the deadweight loss of taxation? The answer is "yes." So why is the tax code complicated? In part, complexity arises because the political process has resulted in different types of income being taxed at different rates, requiring rules to limit taxpayers' ability to avoid taxes by shifting income from one category to another. In addition, interest groups seek to pay lower taxes, while the majority of taxpayers, who do not benefit from these "tax loopholes," find it difficult to organize a drive for a simpler tax system.

The Ability-to-Pay Principle The *ability-to-pay principle* holds that when the government raises revenue through taxes, it is fair to expect a greater share of the tax burden to be borne by people who have a greater ability to pay. To follow this principle, the government should attempt to achieve *vertical equity* by raising more taxes from people with high incomes than from people with low incomes. The federal income tax is consistent with the ability-to-pay principle. The sales tax, in contrast, is not consistent with the ability-to-pay principle because low-income people tend to spend a larger fraction of their income than do high-income people. As a result, low-income people will pay a greater fraction of their income in sales taxes than will high-income people.

The Horizontal-Equity Principle The *horizontal-equity principle* states that people in the same economic situation should be treated equally. Although this principle seems desirable, it is not easy to follow in practice because it is sometimes difficult to determine whether two people are in the same economic situation. For example, two people with the same income are not necessarily in the same economic situation. Suppose one person does not work but receives an income of $50,000 per year entirely from interest received on bonds, and another person receives an income of $50,000 per year from working at two jobs 16 hours a day. In this case, we could argue that the two people are in different economic situations and should not pay the same tax. Although policymakers and economists usually consider horizontal equity when evaluating proposals to change the tax system, it is not a principle they can easily follow.

The Benefits-Received Principle According to the *benefits-received principle*, people who receive the benefits from a government program should pay the taxes that support the program. For example, if a city operates a marina that private boat owners use, the government can raise the revenue to operate the marina by levying a tax on the boat owners. Raising the revenue through a general income tax that both boat owners and non–boat owners pay would be inconsistent with the benefits-received principle. Because the government has many programs, however, it would be impractical to identify and tax the beneficiaries of every program.

The Goal of Attaining Social Objectives Taxes are sometimes used to attain social objectives. For example, the government might want to discourage smoking and drinking alcohol. Taxing cigarettes and alcoholic beverages is one way to help achieve this objective. Taxes intended to discourage certain activities are sometimes called *sin taxes*.

MyEconLab Concept Check MyEconLab Study Plan

18.3 Tax Incidence Revisited: The Effect of Price Elasticity

LEARNING OBJECTIVE: Explain the effect of price elasticity on tax incidence.

There is an important difference between who is legally required to send a tax payment to the government and who actually bears the burden of a tax (see Chapter 4). Recall that the actual division of the burden of a tax between buyers and sellers in a market is

MyEconLab Animation

Figure 18.4

The Effect of Elasticity on Tax Incidence

When demand is more elastic than supply, consumers bear less of the burden of a tax. When supply is more elastic than demand, firms bear less of the burden of a tax. D_1 is inelastic between points A and B, and D_2 is elastic between points A and C. With demand curve D_1, a 10-cent-per-gallon tax raises the equilibrium price from \$3.00 (point A) to \$3.08 (point B), so consumers pay 8 cents of the tax, and firms pay 2 cents. With D_2, a 10-cent-per-gallon tax on gasoline raises the equilibrium price only from \$3.00 (point A) to \$3.02 (point C), so consumers pay 2 cents of the tax. Because in this case producers receive \$2.92 per gallon after paying the tax, their share of the tax is 8 cents per gallon.

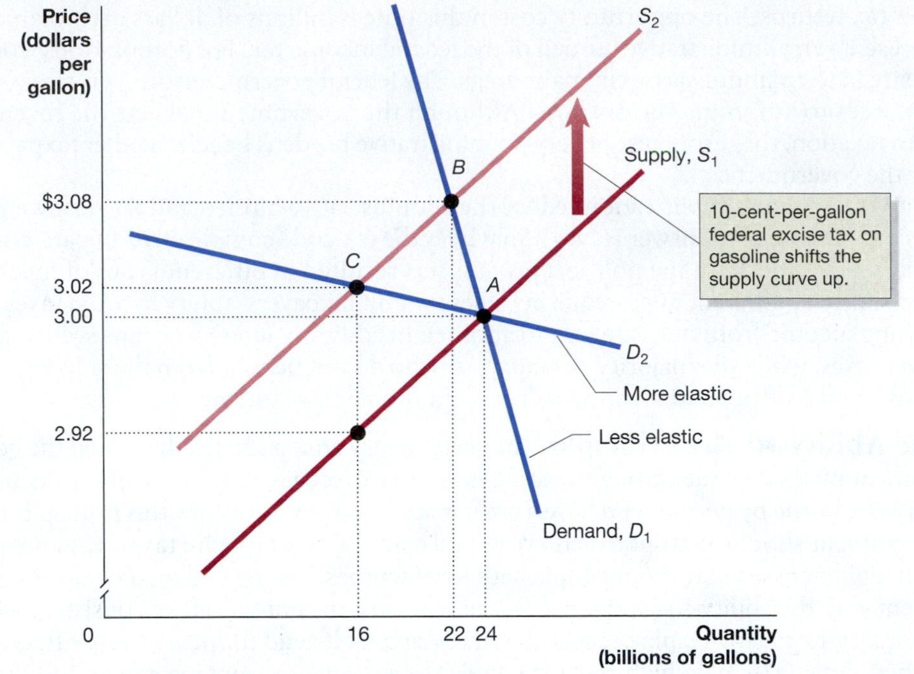

Tax incidence The actual division of the burden of a tax between buyers and sellers in a market.

known as **tax incidence**. We can go beyond the basic analysis of tax incidence by considering how the price elasticity of demand and price elasticity of supply affect how the burden of a tax is shared between consumers and firms.

If the government imposes a 10-cent-per-gallon federal excise tax on gasoline, consumers will pay the majority of the tax because the elasticity of demand for gasoline is smaller than the elasticity of supply. In fact, we can draw a general conclusion: *When the demand for a product is less elastic than the supply, consumers pay the majority of the tax on the product. When demand for a product is more elastic than the supply, firms pay the majority of the tax on the product.*

Figure 18.4 shows why this conclusion is correct: D_1 is inelastic between points A and B, and D_2 is elastic between points A and C. With demand curve D_1, the 10-cent-per-gallon tax raises the market price of gasoline from \$3.00 (point A) to \$3.08 (point B) per gallon, so consumers pay 8 cents of the tax, and firms pay 2 cents. With D_2, the market price rises only to \$3.02 (point C) per gallon, and consumers pay only 2 cents

Don't Let This Happen to You

Don't Confuse Who Pays a Tax with Who Bears the Burden of the Tax

Consider the following statement: "Of course, I bear the burden of the sales tax on everything I buy. I can show you my sales receipts with the 6 percent sales tax clearly labeled. The seller doesn't bear that tax. I do."

The statement is incorrect. To understand why it is incorrect, think about what would happen to the price of a product if the sales tax on it were eliminated. Figure 18.4 shows that the price of the product would fall because the supply curve would shift down by the amount of the tax. The equilibrium price, however, would fall by less than the amount of the tax. (If you doubt that this is true, draw the graph to convince yourself.) So, the gain from eliminating the tax would be received partly by consumers in the form of a lower price but also partly by sellers in the form of a new price that is higher than the amount they received from the old price minus the tax. Therefore, the burden from imposing a sales tax is borne partly by consumers and partly by sellers.

In determining the burden of a tax, what counts is not what is printed on the receipt for a product but how the price of a product changes as a result of the tax.

MyEconLab Study Plan

Your Turn: Test your understanding by doing related problem 3.5 on page 627 at the end of this chapter.

of the tax. With demand curve D_2, sellers of gasoline receive only $2.92 per gallon after paying the tax. So, the amount they receive per gallon after taxes falls from $3.00 to $2.92 per gallon, and they pay 8 cents of the tax.

MyEconLab Concept Check

Making the Connection

MyEconLab Video

Do Corporations Really Bear the Burden of the Federal Corporate Income Tax?

During the 2012 presidential election campaign, hecklers at an Iowa appearance by former Massachusetts Governor Mitt Romney suggested that taxes on corporations be raised. Romney responded by saying: "Corporations are people, my friend." The hecklers responded: "No, they're not!" To which Romney responded: "Of course they are. Everything corporations earn ultimately goes to people. Where do you think it goes?" Romney was correct that corporations are legal persons in the eyes of the law. But there is a larger question: Who actually pays the corporate income tax? The incidence of the corporate income tax is one of the most controversial questions in the economics of tax policy. It is straightforward to determine the incidence of the gasoline tax using demand and supply analysis. Determining the incidence of the corporate income tax is more complicated because economists disagree about how corporations respond to the tax.

Will this consumer be paying part of Apple's corporate income tax when she buys an iPad?

A study by the Congressional Budget Office stated:

> A corporation may write its check to the Internal Revenue Service for payment of the corporate income tax, but the money must come from somewhere: from reduced returns to investors in the company, lower wages to its workers, or higher prices that consumers pay for the products the company produces.

Most economists agree that some of the burden of the corporate income tax is passed on to consumers in the form of higher prices. There is also some agreement that, because the corporate income tax reduces the rates of return received by investors, it results in less investment in corporations. This reduced investment means workers have less capital available to them. When workers have less capital, their productivity and their wages both fall (see Chapter 17). In this way, some of the burden of the corporate income tax is shifted from corporations to workers in the form of lower wages. Some studies have found that workers ultimately bear as much as 90 percent of the burden of the corporate income tax in the form of lower wages. The deadweight loss or excess burden from the corporate income tax is substantial. A study by the Congressional Budget Office estimated that this excess burden could equal more than half of the revenues raised by the tax. This estimate would make the corporate income tax one of the most inefficient taxes imposed by the federal government.

As a consequence, economists have long argued for reform of the system of double taxing income earned on investments that corporations finance by issuing stock. This income is taxed once by the corporate income tax and again by the individual income tax as profits are distributed to shareholders. Not surprisingly, discussion of the corporate income tax has played an important role in the ongoing debate in Congress over reforming the U.S. tax system.

Sources: Ashley Parker, "'Corporations Are People,' Romney Tells Iowa Hecklers Angry over His Tax Policy," *New York Times*, August 11, 2011; Jennifer C. Gravelle, "Corporate Tax Incidence: A Review of Empirical Estimates and Analysis," Congressional Budget Office, Working Paper 2011-01, June 2011; and Congressional Budget Office, "The Incidence of the Corporate Income Tax," March 1996.

Your Turn: Test your understanding by doing related problem 3.6 on page 627 at the end of this chapter.

MyEconLab Study Plan

Solved Problem 18.3

MyEconLab Interactive Animation

The Effect of Price Elasticity on the Excess Burden of a Tax

Explain whether you agree with the following statement: "For a given supply curve, the excess burden of a tax will be greater when demand is less elastic than when it is more elastic." Illustrate your answer with a demand and supply graph.

Solving the Problem

Step 1: Review the chapter material. This problem is about both excess burden and tax incidence, so you may want to review the section "Evaluating Taxes," which begins on page 605, and the section "Tax Incidence Revisited: The Effect of Price Elasticity," which begins on page 607.

Step 2: Draw a graph to illustrate the relationship between tax incidence and excess burden. Figure 18.4 on page 608 is a good example of the type of graph to draw. Be sure to indicate the areas representing excess burden.

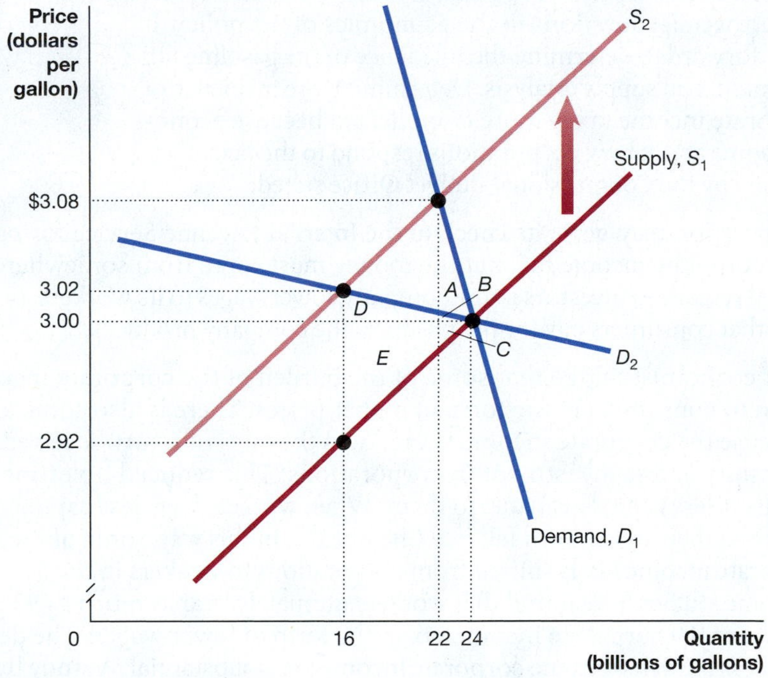

Step 3: Use the graph to evaluate the statement. As we have seen, for a given supply curve, when demand is more elastic, as with demand curve D_2, the fall in equilibrium quantity is greater than when demand is less elastic, as with demand curve D_1. The deadweight loss when demand is less elastic is shown by the area of the triangle made up of areas A, B, and C. The deadweight loss when demand is more elastic is shown by the area of the triangle made up of areas B, C, D, and E. The area of the deadweight loss is clearly larger when demand is more elastic than when it is less elastic. Recall that the excess burden of a tax is measured by the deadweight loss. Therefore, when demand is less elastic, the excess burden of a tax is *smaller* than when demand is more elastic. We can conclude that the statement is incorrect.

MyEconLab Study Plan

Your Turn: For more practice, do related problems 3.9 and 3.10 on page 627 at the end of this chapter.

Annual Income	Percentage of All Households
$0–$20,000	24%
$20,000–$40,000	22
$40,000–$75,000	22
$75,000–$100,000	9
$100,000–$200,000	16
$200,000 and above	7

Source: The numbers are estimates from Urban-Brookings Tax Policy Center, Tables T15-0044, June 23, 2015.

Table 18.5

The Distribution of Household Income in the United States, 2015

18.4 Income Distribution and Poverty

LEARNING OBJECTIVE: Discuss the distribution of income in the United States and understand the extent of income mobility.

In every country, some individuals will have very high incomes, and some individuals will have very low incomes. But how unequal is the distribution of income in the United States today? How does it compare with the distribution of income in the United States in the past or with the distribution of income in other countries today? What determines the distribution of income? And, to return to an issue raised at the beginning of this chapter, how does the tax system affect the distribution of income? These are questions we will explore in the remainder of this chapter.

Measuring the Income Distribution and Measuring Poverty

Tables 18.5 and 18.6 show that the distribution of income clearly is unequal. Table 18.5 shows that in 2015, while 24 percent of U.S. households had annual incomes less than $20,000, the top 23 percent of households had incomes greater than $100,000.

Table 18.6 divides households in the United States into five groups, from the 20 percent with the lowest incomes to the 20 percent with the highest incomes. The fraction of total income received by each of the five groups is shown for selected years. Table 18.6 reinforces the fact that income is unequally distributed in the United States. The first row shows that in 2014, the 20 percent of U.S. households with the lowest incomes received only 3.1 percent of all income, while the 20 percent with the highest incomes received 51.2 percent of all income.

Table 18.6 also shows that over time, there have been some changes in the distribution of income. There was a moderate decline in inequality between 1936 and 1980, followed by an increase in inequality during the years after 1980. We will discuss some reasons for the recent increase in income inequality later in this chapter.

Year	Lowest 20%	Second 20%	Middle 20%	Fourth 20%	Highest 20%
2014	3.1%	8.2%	14.3%	23.2%	51.2%
2000	3.6	8.9	14.8	23.0	49.8
1990	3.9	9.6	15.9	24.0	46.6
1980	4.3	10.3	16.9	24.9	43.7
1970	4.1	10.8	17.4	24.5	43.3
1960	3.2	10.6	17.6	24.7	44.0
1950	3.1	10.5	17.3	24.1	45.0
1936	4.1	9.2	14.1	20.9	51.7

Sources: Carmen DeNavas-Walt and Bernadette D. Proctor, U.S. Census Bureau, Current Population Reports, P60–252, *Income and Poverty in the United States: 2014*, Washington, DC: U.S. Government Printing Office, September 2015; U.S. Census Bureau, *Income in the United States, 2002*, P60–221, September 2003; and U.S. Census Bureau, *Historical Statistics of the United States, Colonial Times to 1970*, Washington, DC: U.S. Government Printing Office, 1975.

Table 18.6

How Has the Distribution of Income Changed over Time?

MyEconLab Animation

Figure 18.5

Poverty in the United States, 1960–2014

The poverty rate in the United States declined from 22 percent of the population in 1960 to 11 percent in 1973. Over the past 30 years, the poverty rate has fluctuated between 11 and 15 percent of the population.

Source: Carmen DeNavas-Walt and Bernadette D. Proctor, U.S. Census Bureau, Current Population Reports, P60–252, *Income and Poverty in the United States: 2014*, Washington, DC: U.S. Government Printing Office, September 2015.

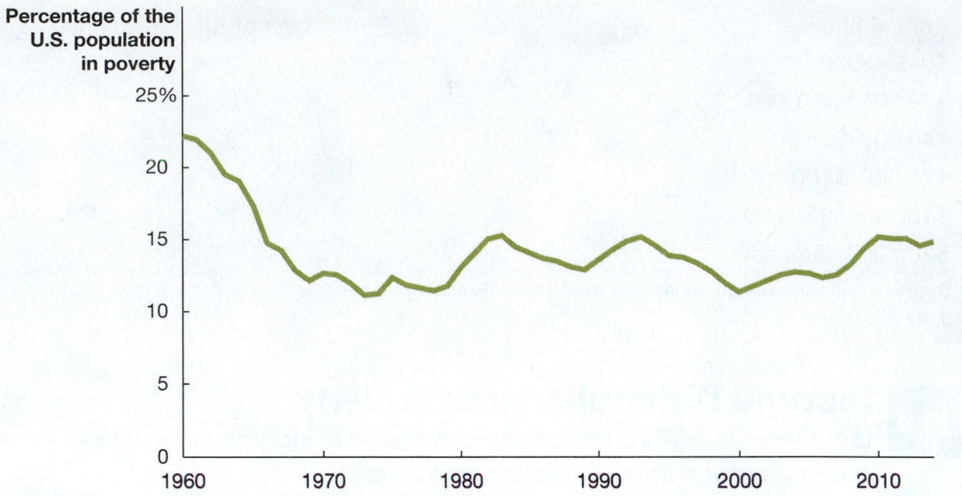

The Poverty Rate in the United States Some of the discussion of the distribution of income focuses on poverty. The federal government has a formal definition of poverty that was first developed in the early 1960s. According to this definition, a family is below the **poverty line** if its annual income is less than three times the amount necessary to purchase the minimum quantity of food required for adequate nutrition. In 2015, the poverty line was $24,250 for a family of four. Figure 18.5 shows the **poverty rate**, or the percentage of the U.S. population that was poor during each year between 1960 and 2014. Between 1960 and 1973, the poverty rate declined by half, falling from 22 percent to 11 percent of the population. In the past 40 years, however, the poverty rate has declined very little. In 2014, it was actually higher than it was in 1967.

Poverty line A level of annual income equal to three times the amount of money necessary to purchase the minimum quantity of food required for adequate nutrition.

Poverty rate The percentage of the population that is poor according to the federal government's definition.

Different groups in the population have substantially different poverty rates. Table 18.7 shows that while the overall poverty rate in 2014 was 14.8 percent, the rates among women who head a family with no husband present, among black people, and among Hispanic people were much higher. The poverty rates for white and Asian people, as well as for families headed by married couples, were below average.

MyEconLab Concept Check

Showing the Income Distribution with a Lorenz Curve

Figure 18.6 presents the distribution of income using a **Lorenz curve**, which shows the distribution of income by arraying incomes from lowest to highest on the horizontal axis and indicating the cumulative fraction of income earned by each fraction of households on the vertical axis. If the distribution of income were perfectly equal, a Lorenz curve would be a straight line because the first 20 percent of households would earn

Lorenz curve A curve that shows the distribution of income by arraying incomes from lowest to highest on the horizontal axis and indicating the cumulative fraction of income earned by each fraction of households on the vertical axis.

Table 18.7

Poverty Rates Vary across Groups, 2014

Group	Poverty Rate
Total population	14.8%
Female head of family, no husband present (all races)	30.6
Blacks	26.2
Hispanics	23.6
Asians	12.0
White, not Hispanic	10.1
Married couple families (all races)	6.2

Note: Hispanics can be of any race.

Source: Carmen DeNavas-Walt and Bernadette D. Proctor, U.S. Census Bureau, Current Population Reports, P60–252, *Income and Poverty in the United States: 2014*, Washington, DC: U.S. Government Printing Office, September 2015.

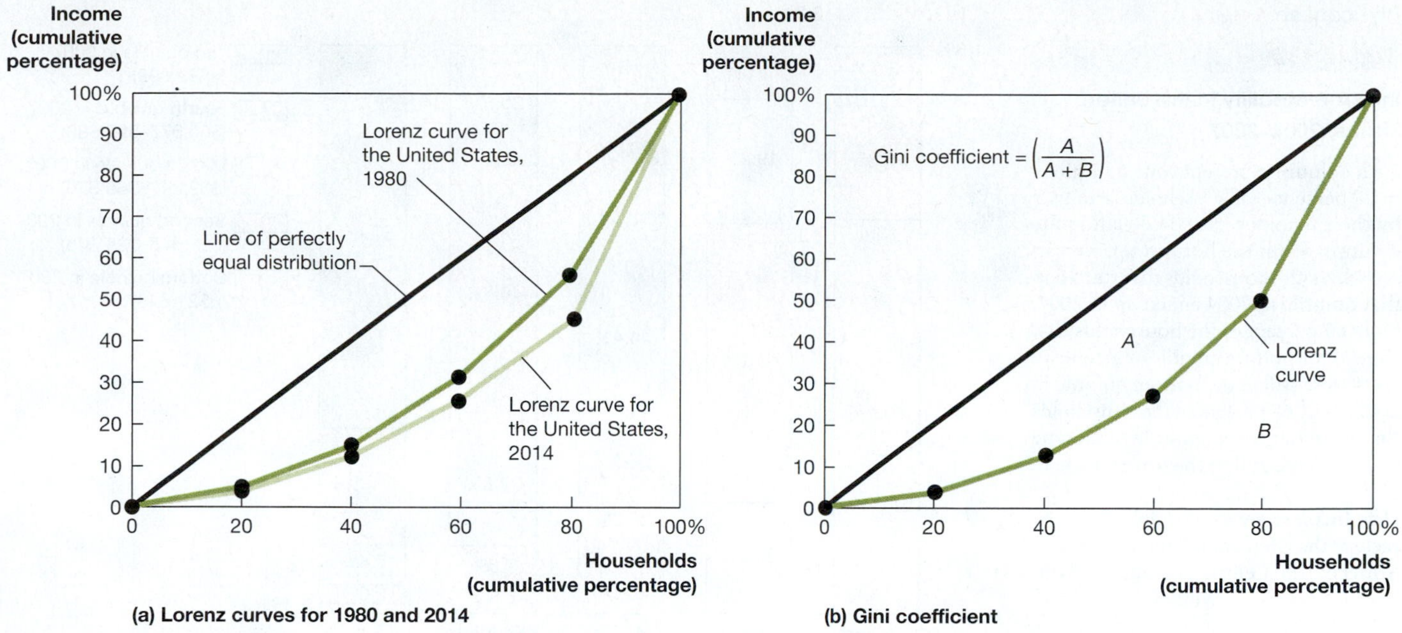

MyEconLab Animation

Figure 18.6 The Lorenz Curve and Gini Coefficient

In panel (a), the Lorenz curves show the distribution of income by arraying incomes from the lowest to the highest on the horizontal axis and indicating the cumulative fraction of income by each fraction of households on the vertical axis. The straight line represents perfect income equality. Because the Lorenz curve for 1980 is closer to the line of perfect equality than the Lorenz curve for 2014, we know that income was more equally distributed in 1980 than in 2014. In panel (b), we show the Gini coefficient, which is equal to the area between the line of perfect income equality and the Lorenz curve—area *A*—divided by the whole area below the line of perfect equality—area A plus area *B*. The closer the Gini coefficient is to 1, the more unequal the income distribution.

20 percent of total income, the first 40 percent of households would earn 40 percent of total income, and so on. Panel (a) of Figure 18.6 shows a Lorenz curve for the actual distribution of income in the United States in 1980 and another curve for the distribution of income in 2014, using the data from Table 18.6. We know that income was distributed more unequally in 2014 than in 1980 because the Lorenz curve for 2014 is farther away from the line of equal distribution than is the Lorenz curve for 1980.

Panel (b) illustrates how to calculate the *Gini coefficient*, which is one way of summarizing the information provided by a Lorenz curve. The Gini coefficient is equal to the area between the line of perfect income equality and the Lorenz curve—area A in panel (b)—divided by the whole area below the line of perfect equality—area *A* plus area *B* in panel (b). Or:

$$\text{Gini coefficient} = \left(\frac{A}{A + B}\right).$$

If the income distribution were completely *equal*, the Lorenz curve would be the same as the line of perfect income equality, area *A* would be zero, and the Gini coefficient would be zero. If the income distribution were completely *unequal*, area *B* would be zero, and the Gini coefficient would equal 1. Therefore, the greater the degree of income inequality, the greater the value of the Gini coefficient. In 1980, the Gini coefficient for the United States was 0.403. In 2014, it was 0.480, which tells us again that income inequality increased between 1980 and 2014. MyEconLab Concept Check

Problems in Measuring Poverty and the Distribution of Income

The measures of poverty and the distribution of income that we have discussed to this point may be misleading for two reasons. First, these measures are snapshots in time that do not take into account *income mobility*, which refers to changes in an individual's

MyEconLab Animation

Figure 18.7

Income Mobility in the United States, 2004–2007

Each column represents one quintile—or 20 percent—of households, arranged by their incomes in 2004. Reading the columns from the bottom up, we can see where the households that started in that quintile in 2004 ended up in 2007. Only 69 percent of the households that were in the bottom quintile of income in 2004 were still in the bottom quintile in 2007. Only 68 percent of the households that were in the top quintile of income in 2004 were still in the top quintile in 2007.

Note: Incomes are in 2007 dollars to correct for the effects of inflation.

Source: U.S. Census Bureau, "Dynamics of Economic Well-Being: Movements in the U.S. Income Distribution, 2004–2007," *Current Population Reports*, P70–124, March 2011.

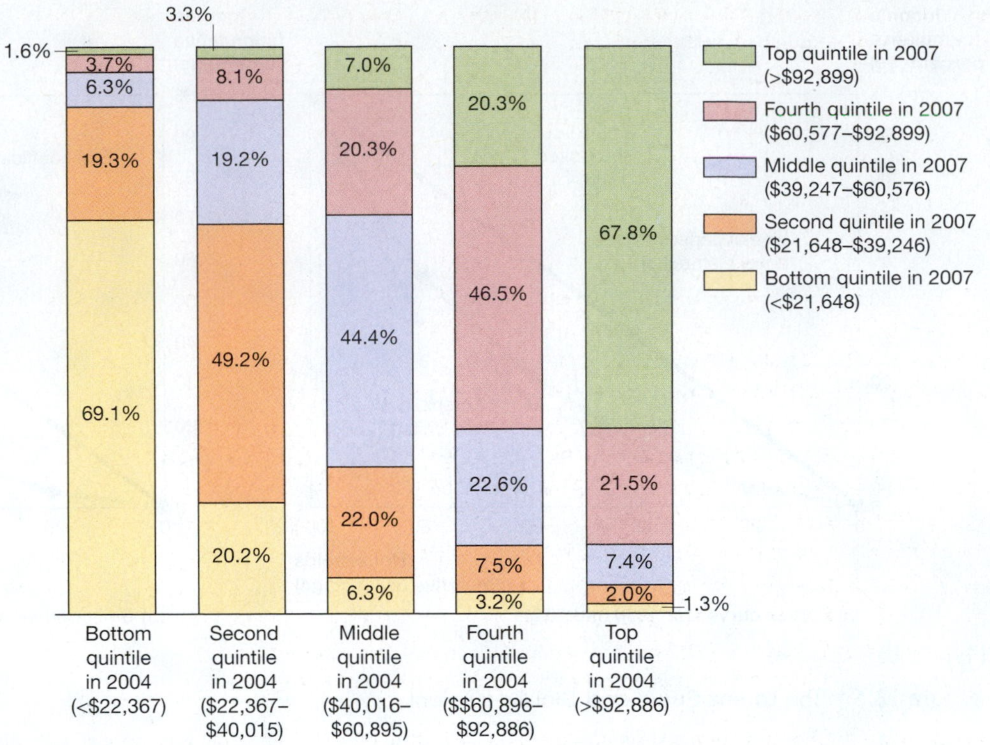

or a family's income over time. Second, they ignore the effects of government programs meant to reduce poverty.

Income Mobility in the United States We expect that most people will not remain in the same place on the income distribution their whole lives. When you graduate from college, your income will rise as you assume a new job. A family may be below the poverty line one year because the main wage earner is unemployed but may rise well above the poverty line the next year, when that wage earner finds a job. A medical student may have a very low income for several years but a very high income after graduating and establishing a medical practice. It is also true that someone might have a high income one year—perhaps from making a very profitable investment in the stock market—and have a much lower income in future years.

Statistics on income mobility are more difficult to collect than statistics on income during a particular year because they require following the same people over a number of years. A study by the U.S. Census Bureau tracked the incomes of the same households for each year from 2004 to 2007. Figure 18.7 shows the results of the study. Each column represents one quintile—or 20 percent—of households, arranged by their incomes in 2004. Reading the columns from the bottom up, we can see where the households that started in that quintile in 2004 ended up in 2007. For example, the bottom quintile (the first column) consists of households with incomes of less than $22,367 in 2004. (All values are measured in 2007 dollars to correct for the effects of inflation.) About 69 percent of these households were still in the bottom quintile in 2007. Only a small number—1.6 percent—had moved all the way to the top quintile, but more than one-quarter had moved into either the second quintile or the middle quintile. At the other end of the income distribution, of those households in the top income quintile—with incomes of $92,886 or more—in 2004, only two-thirds were still in the top quintile in 2007. Given the relatively short time period involved, this study indicates that there is significant income mobility in the United States.

The U.S. economy experienced rapid growth between 2004 and 2007, which may have increased the degree of income mobility. However, an earlier study by Peter Gottschalk of Boston College and Sheldon Danziger of the University of Michigan also provides evidence of significant income mobility. In that study, only 47 percent of people who were in the lowest 20 percent of incomes in 1968 were still in the lowest bracket in 1991. More than 25 percent had incomes in 1991 that put them in the middle- or higher-income brackets. Of those people who were in the highest-income bracket in 1968, only 42 percent were still in the highest bracket in 1991. Almost 8 percent of this group had fallen to the lowest-income bracket.

Some economists and policymakers are concerned, though, that the extent of economic mobility in the United States may have declined over time and that mobility may now be lower in the United States than in Canada and Western Europe. For example, a study by Markus Jäntti, of Stockholm University in Sweden, and colleagues found that 42 percent of U.S. males who began life in the bottom quintile of the income distribution remained there as adults. In contrast, only 25 percent of Danish males and 30 percent of British males born into the bottom quintile remained there as adults.

Finally, another study by the U.S. Census Bureau found that of people who were poor at some time during the years 2004–2006, about half were in poverty for four months or less. Of the people who were poor in January 2004, only about 23 percent remained in poverty every month through December 2006. Only 2.8 percent of the U.S. population was poor every month during those three years.

Solved Problem 18.4

MyEconLab Interactive Animation

What's the Difference between Income Mobility and Income Inequality?

An article in the *Wall Street Journal* contains the observation, "The distinction between economic mobility and income inequality … is important at a time when politicians are using the words almost interchangeably."

a. What is the difference between income inequality and economic mobility?

b. Do you agree that it is important for members of Congress and other policymakers to understand the difference? Briefly explain.

Solving the Problem

Step 1: Review the chapter material. This problem is about income mobility, so you may want to review the section "Income Mobility in the United States," which begins on page 614.

Step 2: Answer part (a) by defining income inequality and economic mobility. The income distribution shows how total income is distributed across the population. A common way of illustrating the income distribution is to show what percentage of total income is earned by different percentages of the population, as in Table 18.6 on page 611. The distribution of income typically refers to the situation *in a particular year*. Income mobility looks at how a person or family's income changes *over time*.

Step 3: Answer part (b) by discussing whether the difference between income inequality and income mobility is important for economic policymakers. The distinction between the two concepts is important for policymakers because rapid income mobility might offset income inequality if a low-income person has a high probability of rising to a higher income level over time. For instance, a person might be born into a low-income family but have risen to the middle of the income distribution or higher by the time she is in her 40s. On the other hand, high levels of income inequality combined with low levels of income mobility would be a greater cause for concern because the result would be that the typical low-income person at any particular time would have only a low probability of rising to a higher income level over time. For instance, someone who takes a low paying, entry-level job immediately after leaving school would still be in a similar position when he is in his 40s.

Source: Damian Paletta, "New Data Muddle Debate on Economic Mobility," *Wall Street Journal*, January 23, 2014.

MyEconLab Study Plan

Your Turn: For more practice, do related problem 4.12 on page 629 at the end of this chapter.

The Effect of Taxes and Transfers A second reason the conventional statistics on poverty and income distribution may be misleading is that they omit the effects of government programs. Because of government programs, there is a difference between the income people earn and the income they actually have available to spend. The data in Table 18.6 on page 611 show the distribution of income before taxes are paid. We have seen that at the federal level, taxes are progressive, meaning that people with high incomes pay a larger share of their incomes in taxes than do people with low incomes. Therefore, income remaining after taxes is more equally distributed than is income before taxes. The table also does not include income from *transfer payments* individuals receive from the government, such as Social Security payments to retired and disabled people. The Social Security system has been very effective in reducing the poverty rate among people older than 65. In 1960, 35 percent of people over age 65 in the United States had incomes below the poverty line. By 2014, only 9 percent of people over age 65 had incomes below the poverty line.

Individuals with low incomes also receive noncash benefits, such as health insurance through the Medicare program, food stamps, free school lunches, and rent subsidies. The government's Supplemental Nutrition Assistance Program, more commonly called the *food stamp program*, has been a particularly important noncash benefit. Under this program, individuals with low incomes can buy, at a discount, coupons to purchase food in supermarkets. In 2014, more than 46 million people participated in this program, at a cost to the federal government of $74 billion. Because individuals with low incomes are more likely to receive transfer payments and other benefits from the government than are individuals with high incomes, the distribution of income is more equal if we take these benefits into account.

A study by the Congressional Budget Office (CBO) analyzed the effects of federal taxes and transfer programs on the distribution of income in 2011, the most recent year for which data are available. The first column of Table 18.8 shows the ratio of the highest income quintile of households to each of the lower quintiles with income measured before taxes are paid and transfers are received. The second column shows the same ratios after household income is adjusted to take into account taxes and transfers. The table shows that taking into account taxes and transfers makes a significant difference to the income distribution, particularly with respect to the gap between the highest and lowest quintiles. Before the effects of taxes and transfers, the top quintile has about 15 times the income of the lowest quintile. Taking into account the effects of taxes and transfers, the top quintile has about 8 times the income of the lowest quintile. The CBO study looked at only the effects of federal tax and transfer policies. Taking into account the effects of state and local tax and transfer policies would likely further reduce the inequality of the income distribution.

MyEconLab Concept Check

Table 18.8

The Effect of Taxes and Transfers on the Distribution of Household Income in the United States, 2011

Quintile	Ratio of Highest Income Quintile to Other Income Quintiles *before* Taxes and Transfers	Ratio of Highest Income Quintile to Other Income Quintiles *after* Taxes and Transfers
Lowest 20%	15.1	7.8
Second 20%	7.9	4.5
Middle 20%	4.7	3.2
Fourth 20%	2.8	2.3
Highest 20%	1.0	1.0

Source: Congressional Budget Office, *The Distribution of Household Income and Federal Taxes, 2011*, November 2014.

Explaining Income Inequality

The novelists Ernest Hemingway and F. Scott Fitzgerald supposedly once had a conversation about the rich. Fitzgerald said to Hemingway: "You know, the rich are different from you and me." To which Hemingway replied: "Yes. They have more money." Although witty, Hemingway's joke doesn't help answer the question of why the rich have more money. We can consider several factors that help explain income inequality.

Differences in Returns to the Factors of Production One answer to the question of why incomes differ is given by the *marginal productivity theory of income distribution* (see Chapter 17). In equilibrium, each factor of production receives a payment equal to its marginal revenue product. The more factors of production an individual owns, the more productive those factors are, and the higher the price the output that can be produced with those factors can be sold for, the higher the individual's income will be.

The most important factor of production that most people own is their labor. Therefore, the income they earn depends on how productive they are and on the prices of the goods and services their labor helps produce. Baseball player Zack Greinke earned a salary of $23 million in 2015 because he is a very productive player, and his employer, the Los Angeles Dodgers, can sell tickets and television rights to the baseball games Greinke plays in for a high price. Individuals who help to produce goods and services that can be sold for only a low price earn lower incomes.

An individual's productivity depends in part on his or her **human capital**, which refers to the accumulated knowledge and skills that workers acquire from formal training and education or from life experiences. Human capital is not equally distributed across workers. For example, some people have degrees in software engineering that prepare them for high-paying jobs, while other people drop out of high school and are prepared only for lower-paying jobs.

Human capital The accumulated knowledge and skills that workers acquire from formal training and education or from life experiences.

Many people own other factors of production beyond just their labor. For example, many people own capital by owning stock in corporations or by owning shares in mutual funds that buy the stock of corporations. Ownership of capital is not equally distributed, and income earned from capital is more unequally distributed than income earned from labor. Some people supply entrepreneurial skills by starting and managing businesses. Their income is increased by the profits from these businesses.

The Effects of Technological Change and International Trade We saw in Table 18.6 that income inequality has increased during the past 30 years. Two factors that appear to have contributed to this increase are technological change and expanding international trade. As we saw in Chapter 17, rapid technological change, particularly the development of information technology, has led to the substitution of robots and other technology for unskilled and semi-skilled workers, including some salespeople, office workers, and factory workers. The new technologies have been complements to other workers, including professionals, managers, and software engineers, increasing their productivity. As a result, there has been a decline in the wages of many unskilled and semi-skilled workers relative to the wages of more highly skilled workers.

Economists Lawrence Katz and Claudia Goldin of Harvard University argue that over the long run, income inequality in the United States has been driven by a race between technological change, which destroys unskilled jobs and increases the returns to skilled jobs, and education, which prepares workers for skilled jobs. Rising educational attainment between 1910 and the 1970s narrowed the income distribution by reducing the relative wages of skilled workers. Educational attainment in the United States since the 1970s has increased more slowly, leading to rising relative wages of skilled workers.

Expanding international trade has put some U.S. workers, such as those in many manufacturing industries, in competition with foreign workers to a greater extent than in the past. This competition has caused the wages of some unskilled workers to decline relative to the wages of workers who do not face this competition. Some economists have also argued that the incomes of low-income workers have been depressed by competition with workers who have immigrated to the United States.

The Effects of Assortative Mating Some economists have noted an increase in assortative mating that may have increased income inequality. *Assortative mating* refers to marriages between people with similar educations. Research by Jeremy Greenwood of the University of Pennsylvania and colleagues shows that the tendency for men and women of similar educational backgrounds to marry has increased substantially since 1960. Assortative mating increases income inequality across households because, as we saw in Chapter 17, people with more years of education tend to earn higher incomes.

To take a simple example, consider two women, one with a master's degree in engineering who has an income of $125,000 per year and one who dropped out of high school and has an income of $25,000 per year; and two men, one with a master's degree and an income of $125,000 and one a high-school dropout with an income of $25,000. If the man and woman with master's degrees marry each other and the two high-school dropouts marry each other, one household will have an income of $250,000 per year, and the other will have an income of $50,000 per year. But if the two people with master's degrees each marry one of the high-school dropouts, the two households will each have incomes of $150,000. Greenwood and colleagues estimate that in 2005, if people married each other without regard to educational background, then the Gini coefficient measure of income inequality would have been reduced from 0.45 to 0.34, a reduction of almost 25 percent.

Luck Finally, like everything else in life, earning an income is subject to good and bad luck. A poor person who becomes a millionaire by winning the state lottery is an obvious example, as is a person whose earning power drastically declines as a result of a debilitating illness or accident. So, we can say that as a group, the people with high incomes are likely to have greater-than-average productivity and own greater-than-average amounts of capital. They are also likely to have experienced good luck. As a group, people with low incomes are likely to have lower-than-average productivity and own lower-than-average amounts of capital. They are also likely to have been unlucky.

MyEconLab Concept Check

Policies to Reduce Income Inequality

The factors that determine the income distribution are complex and not easily affected by government policies. Some economists and policymakers have concluded that attempts by the federal government to reduce income inequality are likely to be ineffective and may even be counterproductive if the policies slow the rate of economic growth, thereby limiting gains for lower-income workers. But as the debates during the 2016 presidential race indicated, candidates in both parties have begun to offer policies aimed at reducing income inequality.

Reducing Inequality through Taxes and Transfers As Table 18.8 on page 616 shows, federal tax and transfer programs already have a significant effect on the distribution of income. Some economists and policymakers argue that the after-tax distribution of income could be made more equal if the top marginal tax rate were to rise from the current 39.6 percent closer to the 70 percent rate that prevailed prior to 1980. (Because this rate applied to very high incomes and because the tax code contained additional deductions that have since been eliminated, many fewer people paid this top marginal rate than pay the top rate today.) Higher-income people are more likely than lower-income people to own assets, such as stocks and bonds, and the returns people receive on their financial assets often receive favorable tax treatment. For example, people who own stock in corporations receive dividend payments and earn *capital gains* if they sell the stock for a profit. Both dividends and capital gains are taxed at rates that are lower than the top marginal individual income tax rates. Raising taxes on dividends and capital gains could potentially reduce the after-tax inequality of incomes.

Other economists and policymakers are skeptical of the idea that raising taxes is an efficient way to reduce income inequality. These economists argue that higher marginal tax rates will discourage work, saving, and investment, thereby slowing economic growth and increases in incomes for all groups. Similarly, they argue that higher taxes on dividends and capital gains will reduce incentives to save and invest. They also argue that past periods of high marginal tax rates have seen higher-income people devote time and money to *tax avoidance*, which involves searching for provisions of the tax code that will allow individuals to reduce their tax payments. Resources spent on tax avoidance add to the excess burden of the tax code.

Some economists and policymakers have noted that many small business owners, as sole proprietors, pay individual income taxes on their business earnings. Reducing these rates may provide incentives to open new businesses and help provide the funds to expand existing businesses. In addition, tax simplification, which involves reducing the complexity of the tax code, would reduce the record keeping and other administrative costs, which are a particularly significant burden on small businesses. As we saw in Chapter 8, the United States has experienced a dramatic slowdown in the number of small businesses opening each year. Because unskilled workers are more likely to be hired by small businesses, policies that strengthen small businesses may help reduce income inequality.

Because of exemptions and deductions, the lower 40 percent of the income distribution does not pay the federal individual income tax. But all workers must pay the payroll taxes that fund the Social Security and Medicare programs from the first dollar they earn. Some economists and policymakers have advocated reducing the federal payroll tax to boost the after-tax incomes of lower-income workers. Others have proposed an increase in the Earned Income Tax Credit, which provides payments to low-income workers.

Reducing Inequality through Improvements in Human Capital Many economists believe that workers who acquire skills that are complementary to the new technologies being developed will be able to find jobs that pay higher wages. For example, as we saw in Chapter 17, as mining company Rio Tinto introduced robots into its iron ore mines, it increased its demand for workers with the skills to service and program the robots. President Barack Obama proposed making community colleges free for most students and starting an American Technical Training Fund to provide federal funds for training programs intended to prepare workers for jobs using new technologies.

During the 2016 presidential campaign, both Democrat Hillary Clinton and Republican Marco Rubio proposed expanding apprenticeship programs to increase the number of workers with technical training. Apprenticeship programs are typically sponsored by firms that seek workers with particular skills. These programs have long played an important part in worker training in some countries, including Germany and the United Kingdom. They have been less popular among workers and firms in the United States, and the number of workers enrolled in them has declined over the past 10 years. The recent policy proposals are an attempt to reverse that decline.

Other policymakers have focused on ensuring that workers obtain basic skills through improvements in K–12 education, particularly in low-income urban areas. Some proposals have focused on expanding preschool programs to provide low-income children with skills that can help them succeed in kindergarten and later grades. Research showing that children from single-parent households are less likely to finish high school or acquire basic skills has led some policymakers to propose programs aimed at providing support to these households.

Economists have not arrived at a consensus about what has caused the increase in income inequality or about the likely effects of the proposals that have been made to reverse the increase. Policymakers will undoubtedly continue to have a spirited debate over these policies.

MyEconLab Concept Check

Making the Connection

MyEconLab Video

Who Are the 1 Percent, and How Do They Earn Their Incomes?

In the past few years, concerns about increasing inequality have often focused on the top 1 percent of the income distribution. During 2012, the "Occupy Wall Street" movement, which held demonstrations against income inequality in New York and other cities, used the slogan "We are the 99%" to indicate what they saw as the unfair advantages the 1 percent received at the expense of the rest of the population. In 2014, the French economist Thomas Piketty's book *Capital in the Twenty-First Century* received considerable publicity due to the author's controversial analysis of income inequality and, in particular, the rise in the share of income earned by people at the top of the income distribution.

In 2015, an annual income from all sources of about $700,000 was necessary to be in the top 1 percent of all households in the United States. The share of total income earned by households in this group rose from about 9 percent in 1979 to about 17 percent in 2015. The group's share of federal individual income taxes paid increased from 18 percent to 44 percent. The debate over the reasons for the increased share of income earned by the top 1 percent mirrors the debate over the broader increase in income inequality, with some of the same potential causes being cited.

As with any other income group, the same people are not in the top 1 percent of income earners every year. Each year some people rise into the group, and some people fall out of it. Nevertheless, the typical occupations of people in the top 1 percent have been part of the debate over income inequality and have influenced the discussion about possible policy measures that Congress and the president might take to reduce it. Some policymakers and economists have argued that investment bankers and other people working for financial firms dominate the top 1 percent of income earners in the United States. However, the following figure, which reflects research by Jon Bakija of Williams College, Adam Cole of the Treasury Department, and Bradley T. Heim of Indiana University, shows that financial professionals make up fewer than 14 percent of the top 1 percent. Executives and managers of nonfinancial firms are the largest group in the top 1 percent (31 percent), with doctors and other medical professionals being the second-largest group (16 percent).

Some policymakers have proposed reducing income inequality by increasing taxes on capital gains, which represent increases in prices of assets, such as stocks or bonds. Currently, capital gains are taxed at lower rates than is wage and salary income. A Congressional Budget Office analysis of tax data, shows, however, that in 2011, less than 19 percent of the income of the top 1 percent was in the form of capital gains.

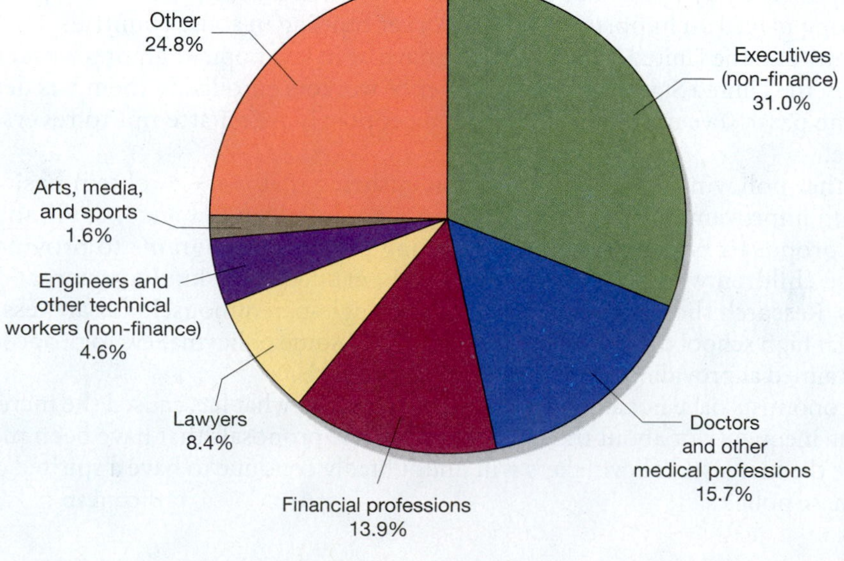

(The group earns about 22 percent of their income from other returns on their investments, such as interest paid on bonds or dividends paid on stocks.) Nearly 60 percent of their income was in the form of wages and salaries or income from operating a business. The amount of income earned by the top 1 percent from operating a business increased from 14 percent in 1979 to 27 percent in 2011, which may indicate that entrepreneurial activity has become a more important way of generating a high income, rather than a less important way, as some policymakers have argued.

Some high-income households, such as members of the Walton family (heirs to Sam Walton, founder of Walmart), earn most of their income from the return on inherited wealth. However, research by Steven Kaplan of the University of Chicago and Joshua Rauh of Stanford has shown that the currently wealthy are much *more* likely to be the first in their family to run a firm and much *less* likely to have been born into a wealthy family than was true in the 1980s.

The debate over the top 1 percent will undoubtedly continue to be a particularly contentious part of the larger debate on income inequality in the United States.

Sources: Congressional Budget Office, *The Distribution of Household Income and Federal Taxes, 2011*, November 2014; Jon Bakija, Adam Cole, and Bradley T. Heim, "Jobs and Income Growth of Top Earners and the Causes of Changing Income Inequality: Evidence from U.S. Tax Return Data," April 2012; James Piereson, "The Truth about the 'One Percent,' *Wall Street Journal*, February 18, 2014; Thomas Piketty, *Capital in the Twenty-First Century*, Cambridge, MA: Harvard University Press, 2014; and Steven N. Kaplan and Joshua Rauh, "It's the Market: The Broad-Based Rise in the Return to Top Talent," *Journal of Economic Perspectives*, Vol. 27, No. 3, Summer 2013, pp. 35–56.

Your Turn: Test your understanding by doing related problems 4.15 on page 629 at the end of this chapter.

MyEconLab Study Plan

Income Distribution and Poverty around the World

How does income inequality in the United States compare with income inequality in other countries? Table 18.9 compares for several countries the ratio of total income received by the 20 percent of the population with the highest incomes and the 20 percent with the lowest incomes. The United States has the most unequal distribution of income of any high-income country in the world, although there are some developing countries in which the distribution of income is more unequal. Of course, we have to make such comparisons with care because transfer payments are not counted in these income measures. For example, the Social Security and Medicare systems in the United States are much more generous than the corresponding systems in Japan but less generous than those in France and Germany.

Although poverty remains a problem in high-income countries, it is a much larger problem in low-income countries. The level of poverty in much of sub-Saharan Africa, in particular, is a human catastrophe. In 2015, the poverty line in the United States for a family of four was an annual income of $24,250, but economists often use a much lower threshold income of $1.25 per day when calculating the rate of poverty in poor

Table 18.9

Income Inequality around the World

Country	Ratio of Income Received by Highest 20% to Income Received by Lowest 20%
United States	16.5
Canada	13.3
China	10.0
Italy	5.7
United Kingdom	4.6
Germany	4.6
France	4.5
Sweden	3.7
Japan	3.0

Sources: The World Bank; Eurostat; and Statistics Canada.

Table 18.10

Poverty Has Declined Dramatically around the World Since 1970

	Percentage of the Population in Poverty		
Region	**1970**	**1992**	**2010**
Developing World	26.8%	11.8%	4.5%
East Asia	58.8	11.5	0.4
South Asia	20.1	10.5	1.6
Middle East and North Africa	8.4	0.5	0.5
Latin America	11.6	3.3	2.0
Sub-Saharan Africa	39.9	37.4	24.4

Note: The methods used to estimate poverty rates in 1970 are different from the methods used to estimate poverty rates for 1992 and 2010, so the results are not completely comparable.

Sources: Xavier Sala-i-Martin and Maxim Pinkovskiy, "Parametric Estimations of the World Distribution of Income," National Bureau of Economic Research, Working Paper 15433, October 2009. Copyright © 2009 by Xavier Sala-i-Martin and Maxim Pinkovskiy. Reprinted by permission; and Xavier Sala-i-Martin and Maxim Pinkovskiy, "Lights, Camera, . . . Income! Estimating Poverty Using National Accounts, Survey Means, and Lights," Federal Reserve Bank of New York Staff Reports, Staff Report No. 669, January 2015, Table X.

countries. Table 18.10 shows estimates from Maxim Pinkovskiy of the Federal Reserve Bank of New York and Xavier Sala-i-Martin of Columbia University using this measure of the poverty line. Their estimates indicate that in 1970, about 27 percent of the population of the developing world was poor. (The developing world excludes high-income countries such as the United States, Japan, Canada, and the countries of Western Europe.) By 1992, the poverty rate had declined to less than 12 percent, and by 2010 it was less than 5 percent. The greatest reduction in poverty has taken place in Asia, including China, where the majority of people were poor in 1970, while very few are today. Poverty rates remain high in sub-Saharan Africa, although even in those countries poverty has been much reduced. Why has poverty fallen more dramatically in Asia than in sub-Saharan Africa? The key explanation is that the countries of Asia have had higher rates of economic growth than have the countries of sub-Saharan Africa. Recent economic research demonstrates a positive relationship between economic growth and the incomes of lower-income people.

Continued from page 595

Economics in Your Life

How Much Tax Should You Pay?

At the beginning of this chapter, we asked you to think about where government gets the money to provide goods and services and about whether you pay your fair share of taxes. After reading this chapter, you should see that you pay taxes in many different forms. When you work, you pay both individual income taxes and social insurance taxes on your income. When you buy gasoline, you pay an excise tax, which, in part, pays for highways. When you buy goods at a local store, you pay state and local sales taxes, which the government uses to fund police, fire fighting, and other services. Whether you are paying your fair share of taxes is a normative question. The U.S. tax system is progressive, so higher-income individuals pay a larger percentage of their income in taxes than do lower-income individuals. In fact, as we saw in the *Making the Connection* on page 603, people in the lowest 40 percent of the income distribution pay no federal individual income tax at all. You may find that you will not pay much in federal income taxes in your first job after college. But as your income grows during your career, so will the percentage of your income you pay in taxes.

Conclusion

The public choice model provides insights into how government decisions are made. The decisions of policymakers will not necessarily reflect the preferences of voters. Attempts by government to intervene in the economy may increase economic efficiency, as when governments take actions to deal with externalities, but they may also lead to government failure and a reduction in economic efficiency.

A saying attributed to Benjamin Franklin is that "nothing in this world is certain but death and taxes." But which taxes? As we saw at the beginning of this chapter, politicians continue to debate whether the government should use the tax system and other programs to reduce the level of income inequality in the United States. The tax system represents a balance among the principles of economic efficiency, ability to pay, payment for benefits received, and achievement of social objectives. Those favoring government intervention to reduce inequality argue that it is unfair for some people to have much higher incomes than others. Others argue that income inequality largely reflects higher incomes resulting from greater skills and from entrepreneurial ability and that higher taxes reduce work, saving, and investment.

Many economists are skeptical of tax policy proposals intended to significantly reduce income inequality. They argue that a market system relies on individuals being willing to work hard and take risks, with the promise of high incomes if they are successful. Taking some of that income from them in the name of reducing income inequality reduces the incentives to work hard and take risks. As we saw in Chapter 1, policymakers are often faced with a trade-off between economic efficiency and equity. Ultimately, whether policies to reduce income inequality should be pursued is a normative question. Economics alone cannot decide the issue.

Visit MyEconLab for a news article and analysis related to the concepts in this chapter.

CHAPTER SUMMARY AND PROBLEMS

Key Terms

18.1 Public Choice, pages 596–600

LEARNING OBJECTIVE: Describe the public choice model and use it to analyze government decision making.

Summary

The **public choice model** applies economic analysis to government decision making. The observation that majority voting may not always result in consistent choices is called the **voting paradox**. The **Arrow impossibility theorem** states that no system of voting can be devised that will consistently represent the underlying preferences of voters. The **median voter theorem** states that the outcome of a majority vote is likely to represent the preferences of the voter who is in the political middle. Individuals and firms sometimes engage in **rent seeking**, which is the use of government action to make themselves better off at the expense of others. Although government intervention can sometimes improve economic efficiency, public choice analysis indicates that *government failure* can also occur, reducing economic efficiency.

MyEconLab Visit **www.myeconlab.com** to complete these exercises online and get instant feedback.

Review Questions

1.1 What is the public choice model?

1.2 What is the difference between the voting paradox and the Arrow impossibility theorem?

1.3 What is rent seeking, and how is it related to regulatory capture?

1.4 What is the relationship between market failure and government failure?

Problems and Applications

1.5 Will the preferences shown in the following table lead to a voting paradox? Briefly explain.

Policy	Lena	David	Kathleen
Cancer research	1st	2nd	3rd
Mass transit	2nd	1st	1st
Border security	3rd	3rd	2nd

1.6 Many political observers have noted that Republican presidential candidates tend to emphasize their conservative positions on policy issues while running for their party's nomination, and Democratic presidential candidates tend to emphasize their liberal positions on policy issues while running for their party's nomination. In the general election, though, Republican candidates tend to downplay their conservative positions and Democratic candidates tend to downplay their liberal positions. Can the median voter theorem help explain this pattern? Briefly explain.

1.7 Briefly explain whether you agree with the following argument:

> The median voter theorem will be an accurate predictor of the outcomes of elections when a majority of voters have preferences very similar to those of the median voter. When the majority of voters have preferences very different from those of the median voter, the median voter theorem will not lead to accurate predictions of the outcomes of elections.

1.8 An article in the *Economist* on the work of the late Nobel Laureate James Buchanan made the following observation: "It was important ... to understand the ways that government could fail systematically."

a. What does government failure mean in this context? How does public choice theory help us to understand how government could fail systematically?

b. The same article notes that "rent-seeking is a very useful concept to have around when thinking about policy." What is rent seeking? Why is the concept useful when thinking about policy?

Source: "Don't Hate the Player, Hate the Game," *Economist*, January 17, 2013.

1.9 An article in the *New York Times* on President Obama's unsuccessful attempt to eliminate tax benefits for college savings accounts notes, "In theory, tax reform is supposed to be built around cutting back preferences like these, in order to pay for some combination of lower tax rates and tax preferences aimed at people with lower incomes." The writer concludes that in practice, tax reform is difficult to enact. Briefly explain why it may be difficult politically to eliminate tax preference for some groups in order to improve the efficiency of the tax code by reducing general tax rates.

Source: Josh Barro, "A 'Rich' Person Is Someone Who Makes 50 Percent More Than You," *New York Times*, January 29, 2015.

1.10 An article in the *Wall Street Journal* about attempts by Congress to rewrite the tax code to make it more efficient noted that there were many provisions in the code intended to reduce the taxes paid by industries in districts of the members of Congress supporting the provisions. In total, these provisions result in tax losses of $1 trillion to the federal government. The article observed that eliminating these provisions is "virtually impossible ... [because] congressional sponsors engage in logrolling to make sure almost everything stays in year after year."

a. Briefly explain what the journalist means by "logrolling."

b. Suppose that eliminating these tax provisions would increase the federal government's tax receipts by $1 trillion, which could then be used to lower the tax rates of the individual income tax. Wouldn't such a change benefit most taxpayers? If so, is the change likely to be enacted? Briefly explain.

Source: John D. McKinnon, "Republicans Block Symbolic Step to Extend Tax Breaks," *Wall Street Journal*, December 19, 2013.

1.11 In Chapter 4, we discussed the federal government's agricultural programs. In arguing that the costs of these programs exceed their benefits, economist Vincent H. Smith stated, "The 10% to 15% of farm families that receive more than 85% of all farm subsidies—amounting to millions of dollars a year in a few cases—have annual household incomes many times as large as those of the average U.S. taxpayer." According to the U.S. Government Accountability Office, these programs cost taxpayers about $20 billion annually.

a. What is the stated purpose of the federal government's agricultural programs?

b. Are the points Smith raises consistent with the purpose of the programs? If not, what explains how the programs currently work?

Source: Vincent H. Smith, "Should Washington End Agriculture Subsidies?" *Wall Street Journal*, July 12, 2015.

1.12 The late Nobel Laureate James Buchanan, who was one of the key figures in developing the public choice model, wrote, "The relevant difference between markets and politics does not lie in the kinds of values/interests that persons pursue, but in the conditions under which they pursue their various interests." Do you agree with this statement? Are there significant ways in which the business marketplace differs from the political marketplace?

Source: James M. Buchanan, "The Constitution of Economic Policy," *American Economic Review*, Vol. 77, No. 3, June 1987, p. 246.

18.2 The Tax System, pages 600–607

LEARNING OBJECTIVE: Understand the tax system in the United States, including the principles that governments use to create tax policy.

Summary

Governments raise the funds they need through taxes. The most widely used taxes are income taxes, social insurance taxes, sales taxes, property taxes, and excise taxes. Governments take into account several important objectives when deciding which taxes to use: efficiency, ability to pay, horizontal equity, benefits received, and attaining social objectives. A **regressive tax** is a tax for which people with lower incomes pay a higher percentage of their incomes in tax than do people with higher incomes. A **progressive tax** is a tax for which people with lower incomes pay a lower percentage of their incomes in tax than do people with higher incomes. The **marginal tax rate** is the fraction of each additional dollar of income that must be paid in taxes. The **average tax rate** is the total tax paid divided by total income. When analyzing the effect of taxes on how much people are willing to work, save, or invest, economists focus on the marginal tax rate rather than the average tax rate. The **excess burden** of a tax is the efficiency loss to the economy that results from a tax having reduced the quantity of a good produced.

MyEconLab Visit **www.myeconlab.com** to complete these exercises online and get instant feedback.

Review Questions

2.1 Which type of tax raises the most revenue for the federal government? What is the largest source of revenue for state and local governments?

2.2 In 2012, Congress and President Barack Obama passed legislation raising tax rates on families earning $450,000 or more. Did this change in the law make the U.S. tax system more progressive or less progressive? Be sure to provide definitions of *progressive tax* and *regressive tax* in your answer.

2.3 What is the difference between a marginal tax rate and an average tax rate? Which is more important in determining the effect of a change in taxes on economic behavior?

2.4 Briefly discuss each of the five goals and principles governments consider when deciding which taxes to use.

Problems and Applications

2.5 An article in a Federal Reserve publication notes that "nearly all taxes create some market inefficiency in the form of deadweight loss." The article notes that when something is taxed, the result is "an outcome in which both [buyers and sellers] would gain from more production."

a. Briefly explain why taxes result in deadweight loss.

b. If buyers and sellers would gain from more production of a good or service that is taxed, why doesn't more of the good or service get produced?"

Source: Tim Sablik, "Taxing the Behemoths," Federal Reserve Bank of Richmond, *Econ Focus*, Third Quarter 2013.

2.6 The federal government imposes a tax on sales of cigarettes. The following data are from a Gallup poll:

Percentage Who Smoke, by Annual Household Income	
Income	**Percentage Who Smoke**
Less than $12,000	34%
$12,000–$35,999	28
$36,000–$59,999	22
$60,000–$89,999	16
$90,000+	13

Based on these data, would the federal cigarette tax be considered progressive or regressive? Be sure to define *progressive tax* and *regressive tax* in your answer.

Source: Lydia Saad, "Cigarette Tax Will Affect Low-Income Americans Most," *Gallup, Inc.*, April 1, 2009.

2.7 Many state governments use lotteries to raise revenue. If we think of a lottery as a type of tax, is a lottery likely to be progressive or regressive? What data would you need to determine whether the effect of a lottery is progressive or regressive?

2.8 Use the information in Table 18.2 on page 602 to calculate the total federal income tax paid, the marginal tax rate, and the average tax rate for people with the following incomes. (For simplicity, assume that these people have no exemptions or deductions from their incomes.)

a. $25,000
b. $125,000
c. $300,000

2.9 **(Related to the Making the Connection on page 603)** President Barack Obama proposed legislation that Congress failed to enact that would have included the so-called "Buffett Rule," named after billionaire Warren Buffett, who noted that he was paying a lower tax rate than his secretary. The Buffett Rule would set a new tax rate for those earning incomes of more than $1 million per year.

a. Looking at the table on page 603 for the percentage of federal taxes paid by the different income categories, is Mr. Buffett's situation of paying a lower tax rate than his secretary typical of the highest 1 percent of U.S. income earners?
b. According to an article in the *New York Times*, "[Buffett's] income comes mostly from his investments, which are taxed at the capital gains rate of 15 percent. His secretary is most likely paid a salary and bonus, which would be taxed as ordinary income, at a rate that goes as high as 35 percent." What are capital gains? Which goals and principles of evaluating taxes are relevant to considering whether the federal government should continue to tax capital gains at a lower rate than ordinary income? Briefly explain.

Source: Paul Sullivan, "'Buffett Rule' Is More Complicated Than Politics Suggest," *New York Times*, September 23, 2011.

2.10 Currently, the Social Security and Medicare programs are funded by payroll taxes rather than by the federal personal income tax. In 2015, the payroll tax for Social Security was 12.4 percent on wage, salary, and self-employment income up to $118,500. (Half of the tax is collected from employers and half from employees.) Above that income level, the tax dropped to zero. The Medicare tax was 2.9 percent on all wage, salary, and self-employment income. Some economists and policymakers have proposed eliminating the payroll tax and shifting to funding Social Security and Medicare out of the federal personal income tax. Would this proposal make the federal income tax system as a whole more progressive or less progressive? Briefly explain.

2.11 Almost all states levy sales taxes on retail products, but about half of them exempt purchases of food. In addition, virtually all services are exempt from state sales taxes. Evaluate these tax rate differences, using the goals and principles of taxation discussed on pages 605–607.

2.12 Suppose the government eliminates the income tax and replaces it with a consumption tax. With a consumption tax, individuals pay a tax on only the part of their income they spend rather than save. Think about the effect of this change on the market for automobiles. Can you necessarily tell what will happen to the price and quantity of automobiles? Briefly explain.

2.13 Use the following table to answer the questions.

Annual Income	Tax Liability
$15,000	$0
30,000	4,500
45,000	11,250
60,000	21,000
75,000	30,000

a. What is the average tax rate at each income level?
b. Based on these data, is the tax progressive or regressive? Briefly explain.
c. Is it possible based on these data to determine the marginal tax rate of someone earning $65,000 per year? Briefly explain.

18.3 Tax Incidence Revisited: The Effect of Price Elasticity, pages 607–610

LEARNING OBJECTIVE: Explain the effect of price elasticity on tax incidence.

Summary

Tax incidence is the actual division of the burden of a tax. In most cases, buyers and sellers share the burden of a tax levied on a good or service. When the elasticity of demand for a product is smaller in absolute value than the elasticity of supply, consumers pay the majority of the tax on the product. When the elasticity of demand for a product is larger in absolute value than the elasticity of supply, sellers pay the majority of the tax on the product.

Review Questions

3.1 What does *tax incidence* mean?

3.2 Briefly discuss the effect of price elasticity of supply and demand on tax incidence.

Problems and Applications

3.3 According to the 2004 *Economic Report of the President*, "The actual incidence of a tax may have little to do with the legal specification of its incidence." Briefly explain what this statement means and discuss whether you agree with it.

Source: Executive Office of the President, *Economic Report of the President, 2004*, Washington, DC: USGPO, 2004.

3.4 According to the 2004 *Economic Report of the President*, "Another crucial principle [of tax incidence] is that only people can pay taxes. Businesses and other artificial entities cannot pay taxes." Do you agree that businesses cannot pay taxes? Don't businesses pay the federal corporate income tax? Briefly explain.

Source: Executive Office of the President, *Economic Report of the President, 2004*, Washington, DC: USGPO, 2004.

3.5 **(Related to the Don't Let This Happen to You on page 608)** According to an article in the *New York Times*, some New Yorkers were deciding to buy existing condominiums (condos) rather than newly constructed condos. One reason given was that "[some buyers] seek to avoid the 1.825 percent transfer tax that buyers must pay on a brand-new condo. (In resales, the seller pays the tax.)" Analyze this reason for buying a resale rather than a new condo.

Source: Teri Karush Rogers, "Mint Condition, Low Miles," *New York Times*, May 29, 2009.

3.6 **(Related to the Making the Connection on page 609)** Business historian John Steele Gordon noted in a *Wall Street Journal* column that the first federal corporate income tax was enacted in 1909, before passage of the Sixteenth Amendment made a federal income tax constitutional. According to Gordon, Congress enacted the corporate income tax because of "the political pressure to tax the rich." Is the corporate income tax an efficient means of taxing the rich? Briefly explain.

Source: John Steele Gordon, "Top 10 Reasons to Abolish the Corporate Income Tax," *Wall Street Journal*, December 29, 2014.

3.7 According to an article in the *New York Times*, when the French government imposed a new tax on sales of beer, it estimated that the retail price of beer would rise by the equivalent of 6 cents per half pint. A spokesman for the beer industry argued that the actual increase in price would be 25 cents per half pint. Discuss the differences between the French government's and the beer industry's estimates of the price elasticity of demand for beer.

Source: Aurelien Breeden, "Beer Lovers Fear an Unequal Tax Bite in Wine Country," *New York Times*, November 26, 2012.

3.8 Governments often have multiple objectives in imposing a tax. In each part of this question, use a demand and supply graph to illustrate your answer.

a. If the government wants to minimize the excess burden from excise taxes, should these taxes be imposed on goods that have price-elastic demand or goods that have price-inelastic demand?

b. Suppose that rather than minimizing excess burden, the government is most interested in maximizing the revenue it receives from the tax. In this situation, should the government impose excise taxes on goods that have price-elastic demand or on goods that have price-inelastic demand?

c. Suppose that the government wants to discourage smoking and drinking alcohol. Will a tax be more effective in achieving this objective if the demand for these goods is price elastic or if the demand is price inelastic?

3.9 **(Related to Solved Problem 18.3 on page 610)** Use the following graph of the market for cigarettes to answer the questions.

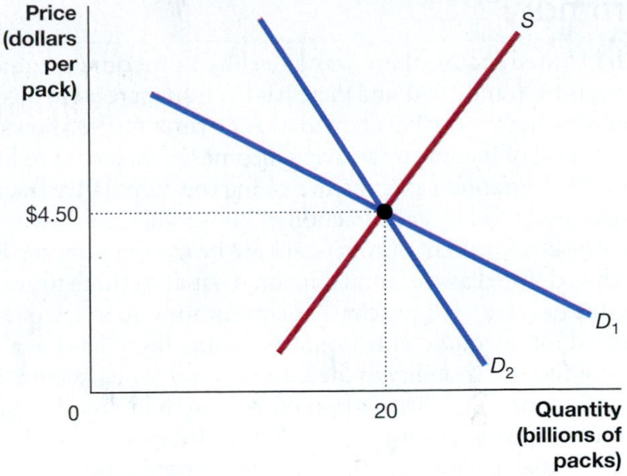

a. If the government imposes a 10-cent-per-pack tax on cigarettes, will the price consumers pay rise more if the demand curve is D_1 or if the demand curve is D_2? Briefly explain.

b. If the government imposes a 10-cent-per-pack tax on cigarettes, will the revenue the government collects be greater if the demand curve is D_1 or if the demand curve is D_2? Briefly explain.

c. If the government imposes a 10-cent-per-pack tax on cigarettes, will the excess burden from the tax be greater if the demand curve is D_1 or if the demand curve is D_2? Briefly explain.

3.10 **(Related to Solved Problem 18.3 on page 610)** Explain whether you agree with the following statement: "For a given demand curve, the excess burden of a tax will be greater when supply is less price elastic than when it is more price elastic." Illustrate your answer with a demand and supply graph.

3.11 Suppose the government decides to tax sales of pizzas. Use the following graph to answer the questions.

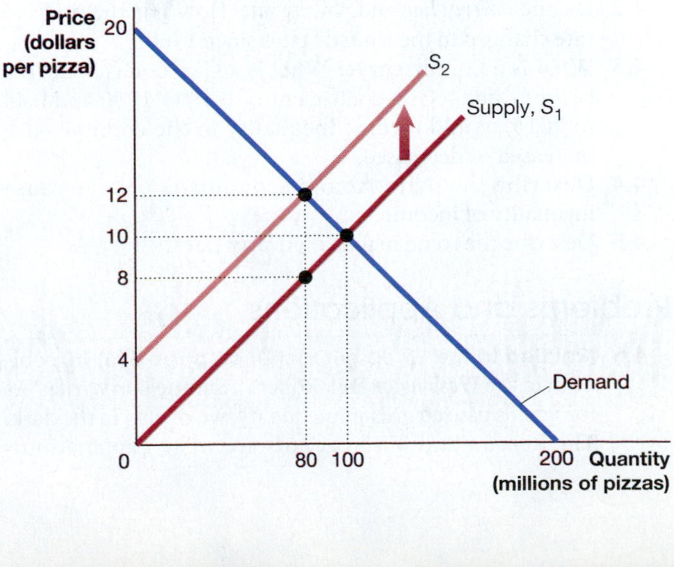

a. How much of a per unit tax did the government impose on pizzas?
b. Before the tax, what price do consumers pay for pizza? How does the price consumers pay change after the tax?
c. Before the tax, what price do sellers receive? How does the price sellers receive change after the tax?
d. Are consumers or producers bearing a greater burden of this tax? Briefly explain.

18.4 Income Distribution and Poverty, pages 611–622

LEARNING OBJECTIVE: Discuss the distribution of income in the United States and understand the extent of income mobility.

Summary

In the United States, there was a decline in income inequality between 1936 and 1980, and there has been an increase in income inequality between 1980 and today. A **Lorenz curve** shows the distribution of income by arraying incomes from lowest to highest on the horizontal axis and indicating the cumulative fraction of income earned by each fraction of households on the vertical axis. About 15 percent of Americans are below the **poverty line**, which is defined as the annual income equal to three times the amount necessary to purchase the minimum quantity of food required for adequate nutrition. Over time, there has been significant income mobility in the United States. The United States has a more unequal distribution of income than do other high-income countries. The *marginal productivity theory of income distribution* states that in equilibrium, each factor of production receives a payment equal to its marginal revenue product. The more factors of production an individual owns and the more productive those factors are, the higher the individual's income will be. **Human capital** is the accumulated knowledge and skills that workers acquire from formal training and education or from life experiences. Economists and policymakers have been debating policies to reduce income inequality. The **poverty rate**—the percentage of the population that is poor—has been declining in most countries around the world, with the important exception of Africa.

MyEconLab Visit **www.myeconlab.com** to complete these exercises online and get instant feedback.

Review Questions

4.1 Discuss the extent of income inequality in the United States. Has inequality in the distribution of income in the United States increased or decreased over time? Briefly explain.

4.2 Define *poverty line* and *poverty rate*. How has the poverty rate changed in the United States since 1960?

4.3 What is a Lorenz curve? What is a Gini coefficient? If a country had a Gini coefficient of 0.48 in 1960 and 0.44 in 2016, would income inequality in the country have increased or decreased?

4.4 Describe the main factors economists believe cause inequality of income.

4.5 Describe the trend in global poverty rates.

Problems and Applications

4.6 **(Related to the Chapter Opener on page 595)** In a column in the *Washington Post*, Robert J. Samuelson wrote: "As for what's caused greater inequality, we're also in the dark. The Reagan and Bush tax cuts are weak explanations, because gains have occurred in pretax incomes. . . . Up to a point, inequality is inevitable and desirable."
a. What are pretax incomes?
b. Do you agree with Samuelson's argument that income inequality may be inevitable and desirable? Briefly explain.

Source: Robert J. Samuelson, "The Rich and the Rest," *Washington Post*, April 18, 2007.

4.7 A column in the *New York Times* observes that the "growing trend of 'assortative mating' is a major cause of income inequality."
a. What is assortative mating?
b. How can assortative mating contribute to income inequality?
c. If assortative mating is a major cause of income inequality, what are the likely consequences for government policies intended to reduce income inequality?

Source: John Tierney, "For Couples, Time Can Upend the Laws of Attraction," *New York Times*, June 29, 2015.

4.8 Use the following Lorenz curve graph to answer the questions.

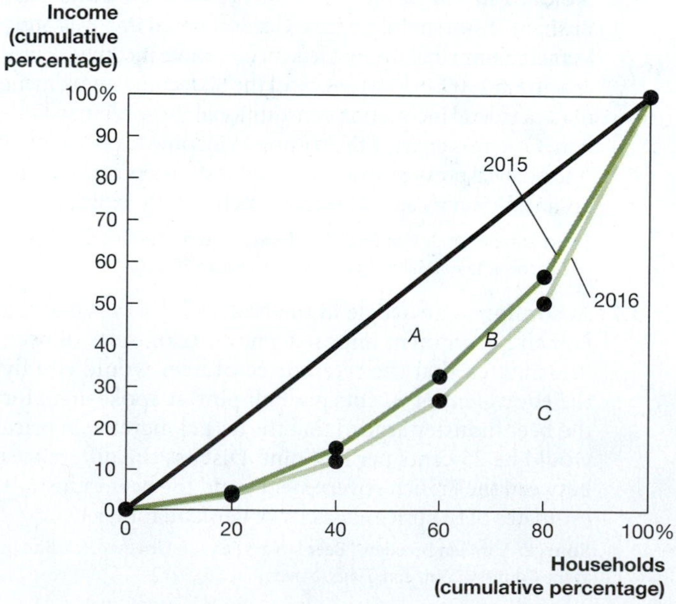

a. Did the distribution of income become more equal in 2016 than it was in 2015, or did it become less equal? Briefly explain.
b. If area A = 2,150, area B = 250, and area C = 2,600, calculate the Gini coefficient for 2015 and the Gini coefficient for 2016.

4.9 Draw a Lorenz curve showing the distribution of income for the five people in the following table.

Name	Annual Earnings
Lena	$70,000
David	60,000
Steve	50,000
Jerome	40,000
Lori	30,000

4.10 **(Related to the Chapter Opener on page 595)** An article in the *New York Times* about former Secretary of State Hillary Clinton's campaign for president noted that she proposed to "increase taxes on the wealthiest Americans to combat a widening gap between rich and poor."

a. Currently, does the effect of federal taxes make the distribution of income more or less equal? Briefly explain.

b. What are the benefits and drawbacks of using the federal income tax code to reduce income inequality?

Source: Amy Chozick, "Hillary Clinton Offers Her Vision of a 'Fairness Economy' to Close the Income Gap," *New York Times*, July 13, 2015.

4.11 An article in the *Wall Street Journal* explained that the 10 wealthiest four-year colleges in the United States accounted for one-third of the total cash and investments held by all four-year colleges. The 40 wealthiest colleges accounted for two-thirds of all the cash and investments. A blog entry for an economics course taught at the University of Michigan compared the distribution of wealth across universities with the distribution of total household income in the United States: "One interesting thing is that the Lorenz Curve [for the United States and] ... the wealth for U.S. Universities have a similar distribution."

a. Assume that the federal government imposes a tax on the 40 wealthiest four-year colleges and distributes the proceeds to the least-wealthy colleges and universities. Would the value of the Gini coefficient used to measure the wealth distribution of four-year institutions increase or decrease? Briefly explain.

b. Assume that you represent one of the 40 wealthiest U.S. universities. Offer one reason why you believe that a wealth tax on your institution would not be a good public policy.

Sources: Melissa Korn, "For U.S. Universities, the Rich Get Richer Faster," *Wall Street Journal*, April 16, 2015; and "Lorenz Curve on U.S. Universities," Economics 411: Monetary and Fiscal Theory, https://411w15.econ.lsa.umich.edu/?p=5182, April 18, 2015.

4.12 **(Related to Solved Problem 18.4 on page 615)** Evaluate the following statement: "Policies to redistribute income are desperately needed in the United States. Without such policies, the roughly 15 percent of the population that is currently poor has no hope of ever climbing above the poverty line."

4.13 Why do economists often use a lower poverty threshold for low-income countries than for high-income countries such as the United States? Is there a difference between *relative* poverty and *absolute* poverty? Briefly explain.

4.14 Suppose that a country has 20 million households. Ten million are poor households that each have labor market earnings of $20,000 per year, and 10 million are rich households that each have labor market earnings of $80,000 per year. If the government enacted a marginal tax of 10 percent on all labor market earnings above $20,000 and transferred this money to households earning $20,000, would the incomes of the poor rise by $6,000 per year? Briefly explain.

4.15 **(Related to the Making the Connection on page 620)** In an article in the *Wall Street Journal*, Edward Lazear of Stanford University was quoted as saying, "There is some good news. . . . Most of the inequality reflects an increase in returns to 'investing in skills.'" Why would it be good news if it were true that most of the income inequality in the United States reflected an increase to returns in investing in skills?

Source: Greg Ip and John D. McKinnon, "Bush Reorients Rhetoric, Acknowledges Income Gap," *Wall Street Journal*, March 26, 2007.

CHAPTER

19

GDP: Measuring Total Production and Income

Chapter Outline and Learning Objectives

Ford Motor Company Rides the Business Cycle

In the more than 100 years that the Ford Motor Company has been in business, its experiences have often mirrored those of the U.S. economy. So, it was no surprise that in 2008, with the U.S. economy suffering from its worst downturn since the 1930s, sales of Ford cars and trucks plummeted. Overall, the automobile industry, which sold 16.1 million new vehicles in 2007, saw sales tumble to 10.4 million in 2009. Although Ford was hit hard, General Motors and Chrysler, Ford's two great American rivals, were even worse off, and both declared bankruptcy. Those firms survived largely because the federal government invested more than $62 billion in them. Ford suffered heavy losses but did not require direct government aid.

In 2015, the economy was several years into its recovery from the downturn, and Ford's sales had risen by more than one-third since their low point in 2009. With these fluctuations in sales, Ford and the automobile industry as a whole were experiencing the effects of the *business cycle*, which refers to alternating periods of economic expansion and recession. Production and employment increase during expansions and decrease during recessions.

Whether the general level of economic activity is increasing is important not just to firms such as Ford but also to workers wondering whether they will be able to keep their jobs and to college students wondering whether they will be able to find jobs when they graduate. One study found that during the slow recovery from the 2007–2009 recession, only 56 percent of those students who graduated from college in the spring of 2010 had found a job a year later. The average salary of graduates who did find a job was $27,000, down from an average of $30,000 for the classes of 2006 to 2008. What's more, students who graduate during recessions will continue to earn less for as long as 15 years after they graduate. The overall state of the economy is clearly important!

Sources: Vehicle sales data are from the U.S. Bureau of Economic Analysis and the Ford Motor Company; Catherine Rampell, "Many with New College Degrees Find the Job Market Humbling," *New York Times*, May 18, 2011; and Lisa B. Kahn, "The Long-Term Labor Market Consequences of Graduating from College in a Bad Economy," *Labour Economics*, Vol. 17, No. 2, April 2010, pp. 303–316.

Economics in Your Life

What's the Best Country for You to Work In?

Suppose that Ford offers you a job after graduation in 2016. The firm has vacancies in Canada and China, and because you are fluent in Mandarin, you get to choose the country where you will work and live. Gross domestic product (GDP) is a measure of an economy's total production of goods and services, so one factor in your decision is likely to be the growth rate of GDP in each country. Based on the International Monetary Fund's forecasts for 2016, GDP would increase by 2.4 percent in Canada but by 6.8 percent in China. What effect do these two very different growth rates have on your decision to work and live in one country or the other? If China's much higher growth rate does not necessarily lead you to decide to work and live in China, why not? As you read this chapter, try to answer these questions. You can check your answers against those we provide on **page 649** at the end of this chapter.

Microeconomics The study of how households and firms make choices, how they interact in markets, and how the government attempts to influence their choices.

Macroeconomics The study of the economy as a whole, including topics such as inflation, unemployment, and economic growth.

As we saw in Chapter 1, we can divide economics into the subfields of microeconomics and macroeconomics. **Microeconomics** is the study of how households and firms make choices, how they interact in markets, and how the government attempts to influence their choices.

Macroeconomics is the study of the economy as a whole, including topics such as inflation, unemployment, and economic growth. In microeconomic analysis, economists generally study individual markets, such as the market for smartphones. In macroeconomic analysis, economists study factors that affect many markets at the same time.

In the following chapters, we will deal with many key macroeconomic issues, including:

Business cycle Alternating periods of economic expansion and economic recession.

Expansion The period of a business cycle during which total production and total employment are increasing.

Recession The period of a business cycle during which total production and total employment are decreasing.

Economic growth The ability of an economy to produce increasing quantities of goods and services.

Inflation rate The percentage increase in the price level from one year to the next.

- The **business cycle**, which refers to the alternating periods of expansion and recession that the U.S. economy has experienced since at least the early nineteenth century. A business cycle **expansion** is a period during which total production and total employment are increasing. A business cycle **recession** is a period during which total production and total employment are decreasing. We will discuss the factors that influence the business cycle and policies the government may use to reduce its effects.
- **Economic growth**, which refers to the ability of an economy to produce increasing quantities of goods and services. Economic growth is important because an economy that grows too slowly fails to raise living standards. In some countries in Africa, little economic growth has occurred in the past 50 years, and many people remain in severe poverty. Macroeconomics analyzes both what determines a country's rate of economic growth and the reasons growth rates differ so greatly across countries.
- Fluctuations in the total level of employment in an economy. In the short run, the level of employment is significantly affected by the business cycle, but in the long run, the effects of the business cycle disappear, and other factors determine the level of employment. A related question is why some economies are more successful than others at maintaining high levels of employment over time.
- Fluctuations in the **inflation rate**, which is the percentage increase in the average level of prices from one year to the next. Like employment, inflation is affected both by the business cycle and by long-run factors.
- Linkages among economies in the form of international trade and international finance.

Macroeconomic analysis provides information that consumers and firms need in order to understand current economic conditions and to help predict future conditions. A family may be reluctant to buy a house if employment in the economy is declining because some family members may be at risk of losing their jobs. Similarly, firms may be willing to invest in building new factories or to undertake major new expenditures on information technology only if they expect future sales to be strong. For example, in 2015, Ford opened two new factories in China and announced that it would spend more than $1 billion to expand an existing factory. Ford was relying on macroeconomic forecasts indicating that the Chinese economy would continue to grow rapidly and that sales of cars in the country would increase from 24 million in 2014 to 32 million in 2020. Macroeconomic analysis can also assist the federal government design policies that help the U.S. economy perform more efficiently.

In this and the following chapters, we begin our study of macroeconomics by considering how best to measure key macroeconomic variables. We start by considering measures of total production and total income in an economy.

19.1 Gross Domestic Product Measures Total Production

LEARNING OBJECTIVE: Explain how total production is measured.

"U.S. GDP Swings to Contraction in First Quarter"

"Canada GDP Posts Surprise Drop in April"

"Brazil GDP Shrinks in First Quarter"

"5 Things You Need to Know about India's GDP Growth"

"China Maintains 7% GDP Growth in Second Quarter"

These headlines are from articles that appeared in the *Wall Street Journal* during 2015. Why is GDP so often the focus of news stories? In this section, we explore what GDP is and how it is measured. We also explore why understanding GDP is important to consumers, firms, and government policymakers.

Measuring Total Production: Gross Domestic Product

Economists use **gross domestic product (GDP)** to measure total production. GDP is the market *value* of all *final* goods and services produced in a country during a period of time, typically one year. In the United States, the Bureau of Economic Analysis (BEA) in the Department of Commerce compiles the data needed to calculate GDP. The BEA issues reports on the GDP every three months. GDP is a central concept in macroeconomics, so we need to consider its definition carefully.

Gross domestic product (GDP) The market value of all final goods and services produced in a country during a period of time, typically one year.

GDP Is Measured Using Market Values, Not Quantities The word *value* is important in the definition of GDP. In microeconomics, we measure production in quantity terms: the number of cars Ford produces, the tons of wheat U.S. farmers grow, or the number of burritos Chipotle sells. When we measure total production in the economy, we can't just add together the quantities of every good and service because the result would be a meaningless jumble. Tons of wheat would be added to gallons of milk, numbers of burritos, and so on. Instead, we measure production by taking the *value*, in dollar terms, of all the goods and services produced.

GDP Includes Only the Market Value of Final Goods In measuring GDP, we include only the value of *final goods and services*. A **final good or service** is one that is purchased by its final user and is not included in the production of any other good or service. Examples of final goods are a hamburger purchased by a consumer and a computer purchased by a business. In contrast, **intermediate goods and services** become part of other goods and services. For example, Ford does not produce tires for its cars and trucks; it buys them from tire companies, such as Goodyear and Michelin. The tires are an *intermediate good*, while a Ford truck is a *final good*. In calculating GDP, we include the value of the Ford truck but not the value of the tire. If we included the value of the tire, we would be *double counting*: The value of the tire would be counted once when the tire company sold it to Ford and a second time when Ford sold the truck, with the tire installed, to a consumer.

Final good or service A good or service purchased by a final user.

Intermediate good or service A good or service that is an input into another good or service, such as a tire on a truck.

GDP Includes Only Current Production GDP includes only production that takes place during the indicated time period. For example, GDP in 2016 includes only the goods and services produced during that year. In particular, GDP does *not* include the value of used goods. If you buy a Blu-ray of *Star Wars: The Force Awakens* from Amazon.com, the purchase is included in GDP. If six months later you resell the Blu-ray on eBay, that transaction is not included in GDP. MyEconLab Concept Check

Solved Problem 19.1

MyEconLab Interactive Animation

Calculating GDP

Suppose that a very simple economy produces only four goods and services: eye examinations, pizzas, shoes, and cheese. Assume that all the cheese in this economy is used in the production of pizzas. Use the information in the following table to compute GDP for the year 2017.

Production and Price Statistics for 2017

Product	(1) Quantity	(2) Price per Unit
Eye examinations	100	$50.00
Pizzas	80	10.00
Shoes	20	100.00
Cheese	80	2.00

Solving the Problem

Step 1: **Review the chapter material.** This problem is about GDP, so you may want to review the section "Measuring Total Production: Gross Domestic Product," which begins on page 633.

Step 2: **Determine which goods and services listed in the table should be included in the calculation of GDP.** GDP is the value of all final goods and services. Therefore, we need to calculate the value of the final goods and services listed in the table. Eye examinations, pizzas, and shoes are final goods. Cheese would also be a final good if, for instance, a consumer bought it to use in a meal. However, here we are assuming that restaurants buy all the cheese to use in making pizzas, so the cheese is an intermediate good, and its value is not included in GDP.

Step 3: **Calculate the value of the three final goods and services listed in the table.** Value is equal to the quantity produced multiplied by the price per unit, so we multiply the numbers in column (1) by the numbers in column (2) to calculate the numbers in column (3).

Product	(1) Quantity	(2) Price per Unit	(3) Value
Eye examinations	100	$50	$5,000
Pizzas	80	10	800
Shoes	20	100	2,000

Step 4: **Add the value for each of the three final goods and services to find GDP.** GDP = Value of eye examinations produced + Value of pizzas produced + Value of shoes produced = $5,000 + $800 + $2,000 = $7,800.

MyEconLab Study Plan

Your Turn: For more practice, do related problem 1.11 on page 651 at the end of this chapter.

Production, Income, and the Circular-Flow Diagram

When we measure the value of total production in the economy by calculating GDP, we are at the same time measuring the value of total income. To see why the value of total production is equal to the value of total income, consider what happens to the money you spend on a single product. Suppose you buy a pair of New Balance running shoes for $149 at a Foot Locker store. *All* of that $149 must end up as someone's income. New Balance and Foot Locker will receive some of the $149 as profits, workers at New Balance will receive some as wages, the salesperson who sold you the shoes will receive some as salary, the firms that sell components to New Balance will receive some as profits, the workers for those firms will receive some as wages, and so on. Every penny must end up as someone's income. (Note, though, that any sales tax on the shoes will be collected by the store and sent to the government, without ending up as anyone's income.) Therefore, if we add up the values of every good and service sold in the economy, we must get a total that is exactly equal to the value of all the income in the economy.

The circular-flow diagram in Figure 19.1 was introduced in Chapter 2 to illustrate the interaction of firms and households in markets. We use it here to illustrate the flow of spending and money in the economy. Firms sell goods and services to three groups: domestic households, foreign firms and households, and the government. Expenditures by foreign firms and households (shown as "Rest of the World" in the diagram) on domestically produced goods and services are called *exports*. For example, American Airlines sells many tickets to passengers in Europe and Asia. As noted at the bottom of Figure 19.1, we can measure GDP by adding up the total expenditures of these groups on goods and services.

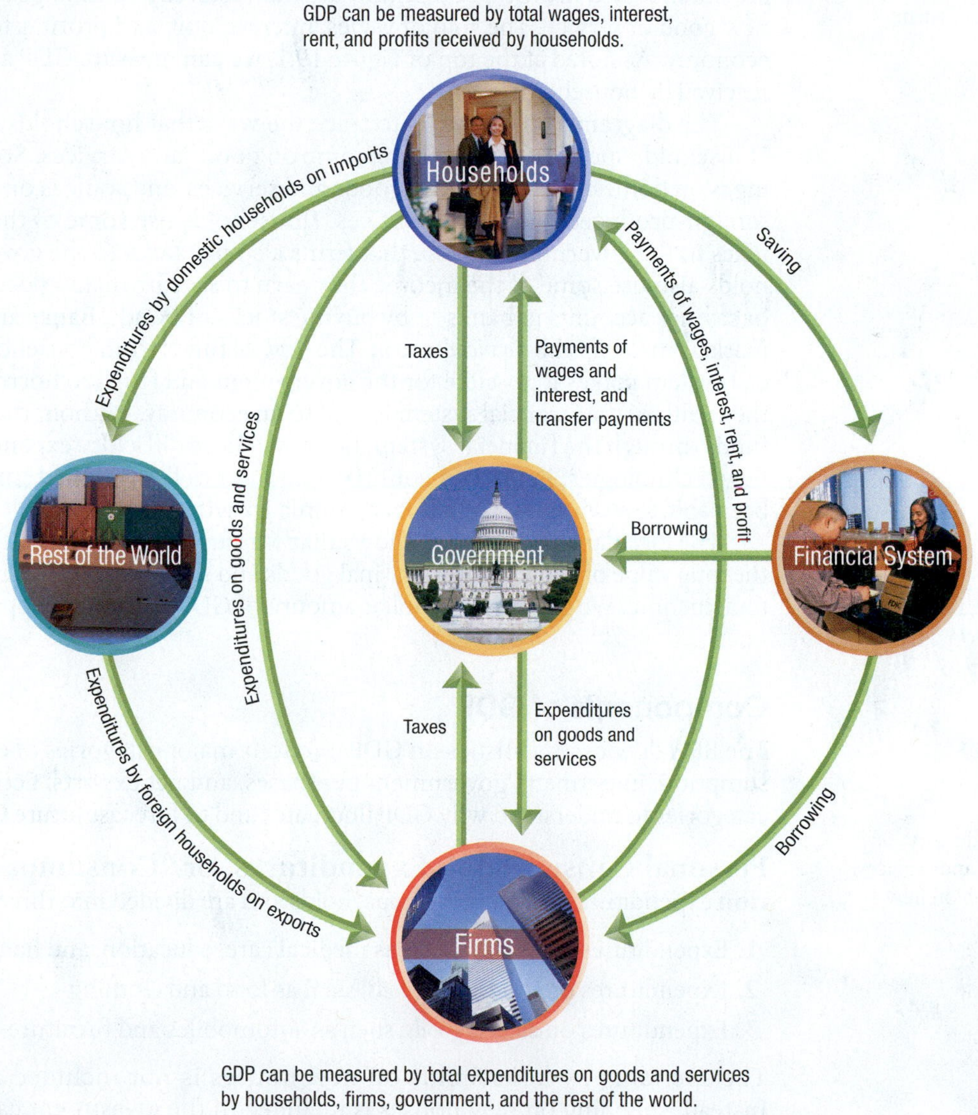

MyEconLab Animation

Figure 19.1 The Circular Flow and the Measurement of GDP

The circular-flow diagram illustrates the flow of spending and money in the economy. Firms sell goods and services to three groups: domestic households, foreign firms and households, and the government. To produce goods and services, firms use factors of production: labor, capital, natural resources, and entrepreneurship. Households supply the factors of production to firms in exchange for income in the form of wages, interest, profit, and rent. Firms make payments of wages and interest to households in exchange for hiring workers and other factors of production. The sum of wages, interest, rent, and profit is total income in the economy. We can measure GDP as the total income received by households. The diagram also shows that households use their income to purchase goods and services, pay taxes, and save for the future. Firms and the government borrow the funds that flow from households into the financial system. We can measure GDP either by calculating the total value of expenditures on final goods and services or by calculating the value of total income.

Firms use the *factors of production*—labor, capital, natural resources, and entrepreneurial ability—to produce goods and services. Households supply the factors of production to firms in exchange for income. We divide income into four categories: wages, interest, rent, and profit. Firms pay wages to households in exchange for labor services, interest for the use of capital, and rent for natural resources such as land. Profit is the income that remains after a firm has paid wages, interest, and rent. Profit is the return to entrepreneurs and other business owners for bearing the risk of producing and selling goods and services. As Figure 19.1 shows, federal, state, and local governments make payments of wages and interest to households in exchange for hiring workers and other factors of production. Governments also make *transfer payments* to households. **Transfer payments** include Social Security payments to retired and disabled people and unemployment insurance payments to unemployed workers. These payments are not included in GDP because they are not received in exchange for production of a new good or service. The sum of wages, interest, rent, and profit is total income in the economy. As noted at the top of Figure 19.1, we can measure GDP as the total income received by households.

Transfer payments Payments by the government to households for which the government does not receive a new good or service in return.

The diagram also allows us to trace the ways that households use their income. Households spend some of their income on goods and services. Some of this spending is on domestically produced goods and services, and some is on *imports*, which are foreign-produced goods and services. Households use some of their income to pay taxes to the government. (Note that firms also pay taxes to the government.) Households also use some of the income they earn to save by making deposits in checking or savings accounts in banks or by buying stocks or bonds. Banks and stock and bond markets make up the *financial system*. The flow of funds from households into the financial system makes it possible for the government and firms to borrow. As we will see, the health of the financial system is vital to an economy. Without the ability to borrow funds through the financial system, firms will have difficulty expanding and adopting new technologies. In fact, no country without a well-developed financial system has been able to sustain high levels of economic growth.

The circular-flow diagram shows that we can measure GDP either by calculating the total value of expenditures on final goods and services or by calculating the value of total income. We get the same dollar amount of GDP with either approach.

MyEconLab Concept Check

Components of GDP

The BEA divides its statistics on GDP into four major categories of expenditures: consumption, investment, government purchases, and net exports. Economists use these categories to understand why GDP fluctuates and to forecast future GDP.

Consumption Spending by households on goods and services, not including spending on new houses.

Personal Consumption Expenditures, or "Consumption"

Consumption expenditures are made by households and are divided into three categories:

1. Expenditures on *services*, such as medical care, education, and haircuts
2. Expenditures on *nondurable goods*, such as food and clothing
3. Expenditures on *durable goods*, such as automobiles and furniture

The spending by households on new houses is not included in consumption. Instead, spending on new houses is included in the investment category, which we discuss next.

Investment Spending by firms on new factories, office buildings, machinery, and additions to inventories, plus spending by households and firms on new houses.

Gross Private Domestic Investment, or "Investment"

Spending on *gross private domestic investment*, or simply **investment**, is also divided into three categories.

1. *Business fixed investment* is spending by firms on new factories, office buildings, and machinery used to produce other goods. Since 2013, this category of investment has included business spending on research and development. The BEA had previously considered such spending to be an intermediate good.

Don't Let This Happen to You

Remember What Economists Mean by *Investment*

Notice that the definition of *investment* in this chapter is narrower than in everyday use. For example, people often say they are investing in the stock market or in rare coins. As we have seen, economists reserve the word *investment* for purchases of machinery, factories, and houses. Economists don't include purchases of shares of stock or rare coins or deposits in savings accounts in the definition of investment because these activities don't result in the production of new goods. For example, a share of Twitter's stock represents part ownership of that company. When you buy a share of Twitter's stock, nothing new is produced; there is just a transfer from the seller to you of that small piece of ownership of Twitter. Similarly, buying a rare coin or putting $1,000 into a savings account does not result in an increase in production. GDP is not affected by any of these activities, so they are not included in the economic definition of investment.

MyEconLab Study Plan

Your Turn: Test your understanding by doing related problem 1.12 on page 651 at the end of this chapter.

2. *Residential investment* is spending by households and firms on new single-family and multi-unit houses.
3. *Changes in business inventories* are changes in the stocks of goods that have been produced but not yet sold. If Ford has $200 million worth of unsold cars at the beginning of the year and $350 million worth of unsold cars at the end of the year, then the firm has spent $150 million on inventory investment during the year.

Government Consumption and Gross Investment, or "Government Purchases" **Government purchases** are spending by federal, state, and local governments on goods and services, such as teachers' salaries, highways, and aircraft carriers. Again, government spending on transfer payments is not included in government purchases because it does not result in the production of new goods and services.

Government purchases Spending by federal, state, and local governments on goods and services.

Net Exports of Goods and Services, or "Net Exports" **Net exports** are equal to *exports* minus *imports*. Exports are goods and services produced in the United States and purchased by foreign firms, households, and governments. We add exports to our other categories of expenditures because otherwise we would not be including all spending on new goods and services produced in the United States. For example, if a farmer in South Dakota sells wheat to China, the value of the wheat is included in GDP because it represents production in the United States. Imports are goods and services produced in foreign countries and purchased by U.S. firms, households, and governments. We subtract imports from total expenditures because otherwise we would be including spending that does not result in production of new goods and services in the United States. For example, if U.S. consumers buy $1 billion worth of furniture manufactured in China, that spending is included in consumption expenditures. But the value of those imports is subtracted from GDP because the imports do not represent production in the United States.

Net exports Exports minus imports.

MyEconLab Concept Check

An Equation for GDP and Some Actual Values

A simple equation sums up the components of GDP:

$$Y = C + I + G + NX.$$

The equation tells us that GDP (denoted as Y) equals consumption (C) plus investment (I) plus government purchases (G) plus net exports (NX). Figure 19.2 shows the values of the components of GDP for the year 2014. The graph in the figure highlights the fact

COMPONENTS OF GDP (billions of dollars)		
Consumption		$11,930
Durable goods	$1,303	
Nondurable goods	2,666	
Services	7,962	
Investment		2,852
Business fixed investment	2,211	
Residential investment	559	
Change in business inventories	82	
Government purchases		3,175
Federal	1,219	
State and local	1,956	
Net Exports		–538
Exports	2,337	
Imports	2,875	
Total GDP		$17,419

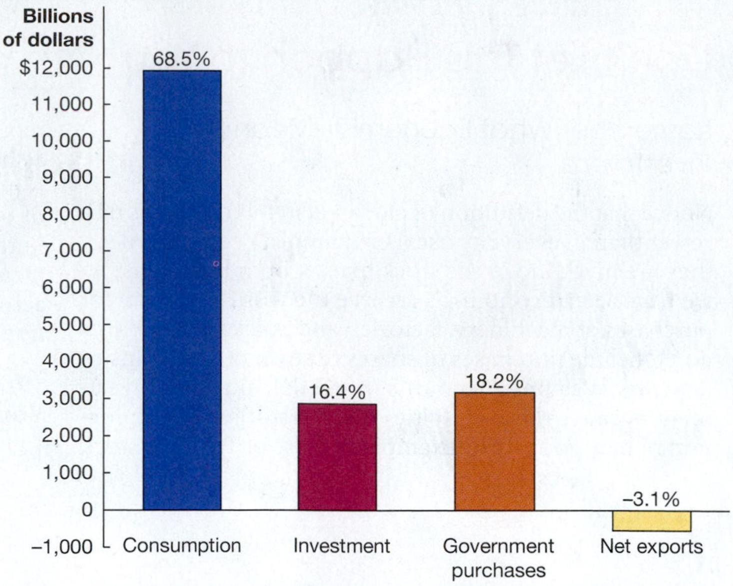

Figure 19.2 Components of GDP in 2014

Consumption accounts for a much larger percentage of GDP than any of the other components. In recent years, net exports have typically been negative, which reduces GDP. Note that the subtotals may not sum to the totals for each category because of rounding.
Source: U.S. Bureau of Economic Analysis.

that consumption is by far the largest component of GDP. The table provides a more detailed breakdown and shows several interesting points:

- Consumer spending on services is greater than the sum of spending on durable and nondurable goods. There has been a continuing trend in the United States and other high-income countries away from the production of goods and toward the production of services. As the populations of these countries have become, on average, both older and wealthier, their demand for services such as medical care and financial advice has increased faster than their demand for goods.
- Business fixed investment is the largest component of investment. As we will see in later chapters, spending by firms on new factories, computers, and machinery can fluctuate. For example, a decline in business fixed investment played an important role in the 2007–2009 recession.
- Purchases made by state and local governments are greater than purchases made by the federal government. Because basic government activities, such as education and law enforcement, occur largely at the state and local levels, state and local government spending is greater than federal government spending.
- Imports are greater than exports, so net exports are negative. We will discuss in Chapter 29 why imports have typically been larger than exports for the U.S. economy.

MyEconLab Concept Check

Making the Connection
MyEconLab Video

Adding More of Lady Gaga to GDP

The Bureau of Economic Analysis (BEA) is always researching to improve its measurement of GDP. A few years ago, the BEA changed how it accounts for spending on research and development (R&D). Prior to 2013, the BEA considered R&D by firms or the government to be an intermediate good, just as tires or batteries are considered intermediate goods in automobile manufacturing. But spending on R&D is similar to investment spending. For example, when Ford buys new machine tools—which are included in investment spending—it does so to help manufacture automobiles now and in the future. Similarly,

The cost to Lady Gaga and her record company of writing and recording her songs is now part of GDP.

when Ford spends on R&D to improve the battery in its Ford Focus electric car, it does so to help improve the car now and in the future. The BEA now counts spending on R&D as investment. In other words, the BEA shifted from not counting spending on R&D as part of GDP to counting it.

The term *research and development* brings to mind scientists working in laboratories, trying to develop new pharmaceutical drugs or improved computer chips. But just as firms and the government devote resources to R&D, movie and television studios, book authors, and musicians devote time and resources to producing new movies, television programs, books, and recordings. In past years, the BEA counted spending by firms and individuals on developing entertainment products as part of the cost of producing those products, in the same way that it counted the cost of labor and materials. So the cost of developing entertainment products was *not* included in GDP. But in 2013, the BEA changed its procedures to include those costs as part of investment and began including it in GDP. For example, prior to 2013, sales of Lady Gaga's songs on iTunes and on CDs as well as ticket sales for her concerts were included in GDP, but the cost to Lady Gaga and her record company of writing and recording her songs was not included. Now both types of spending are included in GDP.

By broadening the definition of investment spending, the BEA increased measured GDP in 2013 by about 3 percent. The BEA adjusted its historical data on GDP back to 1929, so while the levels of GDP increased, the changes in GDP from one year to the next were not greatly affected. The BEA makes changes to its calculations of GDP after consulting with government statistical agencies in other countries. The objective is to allow economists, firms, and policymakers to more accurately compare GDP in different countries. The broadening of the definition of investment was meant to increase the importance of *intellectual property (IP)*, such as software, movies, and books, in GDP. A study by the U.S. Patent and Trademark Office estimated that in the United States, IP-intensive industries, including pharmaceuticals, computers and software, telecommunications, book publishing, and radio and television broadcasting, account for about 40 million jobs and more than one-third of GDP.

As the economy changes over time, the BEA evaluates whether to adjust the way it measures GDP.

Sources: David Kestenbaum, "Lady Gaga Writing a New Song Is Like a Factory Investing in a New Machine," www.npr.org, April 25, 2013; Osagie Imasogie and Thaddeus J. Kobylarz, "Yes, Lady Gaga's Songs Contribute to GDP," *Wall Street Journal*, May 27, 2013; U.S. Bureau of Economic Analysis, "Preview of the 2013 Comprehensive Revision of the National Income and Product Accounts," *Survey of Current Business*, Vol. 93, No. 3, March 2013; and U.S. Department of Commerce, *Intellectual Property and the U.S. Economy: Industries in Focus*, March 2012.

Your Turn: Test your understanding by doing related problem 1.13 on page 651 at the end of this chapter.

MyEconLab Study Plan

Measuring GDP Using the Value-Added Method

We have seen that GDP can be calculated by adding together all expenditures on final goods and services. An alternative way of calculating GDP is the *value-added method*. **Value added** refers to the additional market value a firm gives to a product and is equal to the difference between the price for which the firm sells a good and the price it paid other firms for intermediate goods. Table 19.1 gives a hypothetical example of the value added by each firm involved in the production of a shirt offered for sale on L.L.Bean's Web site.

Value added The market value a firm adds to a product.

Suppose a cotton farmer sells $1 of raw cotton to a textile mill. If, for simplicity, we ignore any inputs the farmer may have purchased from other firms—such as cottonseed

Table 19.1
Calculating Value Added

Firm	Value of Product	Value Added		
Cotton farmer	Value of raw cotton = $1	Value added by cotton farmer	=	$1
Textile mill	Value of raw cotton woven into cotton fabric = $3	Value added by textile mill = ($3 − $1)	=	$2
Shirt company	Value of cotton fabric made into a shirt = $15	Value added by shirt company = ($15 − $3)	=	$12
L.L.Bean	Value of shirt for sale on L.L.Bean's Web site = $35	Value added by L.L.Bean = ($35 − $15)	=	$20
	Total Value Added		=	**$35**

or fertilizer—then the farmer's value added is $1. The textile mill then weaves the raw cotton into cotton fabric, which it sells to a shirt company for $3. The textile mill's value added ($2) is the difference between the price it paid for the raw cotton ($1) and the price for which it can sell the cotton fabric ($3). Similarly, the shirt company's value added is the difference between the price it paid for the cotton fabric ($3) and the price it receives for the shirt from L.L.Bean ($15). L.L.Bean's value added is the difference between the price it pays for the shirt ($15) and the price for which it can sell the shirt on its Web site ($35). Notice that *the price of the shirt on L.L.Bean's Web site is exactly equal to the sum of the value added by each firm involved in the production of the shirt.* We can calculate GDP by adding up the market value of every final good and service produced during a particular period. Or, we can arrive at the same value for GDP by adding up the value added by every firm involved in producing those final goods and services.

MyEconLab Study Plan

MyEconLab Concept Check

19.2 Does GDP Measure What We Want It to Measure?

LEARNING OBJECTIVE: Discuss whether GDP is a good measure of well-being.

Economists use GDP to measure total production in the economy. For that purpose, we would like GDP to be as comprehensive as possible, not overlooking any significant production that takes place in the economy. Most economists believe that GDP does a good—but not flawless—job of measuring production. GDP is also sometimes used as a measure of well-being. Although it is generally true that the more goods and services people have, the better off they are, we will see that GDP provides only a rough measure of well-being.

Shortcomings in GDP as a Measure of Total Production

When the BEA calculates GDP, it does not include two types of production: production in the home and production in the underground economy.

Household Production With few exceptions, the BEA does not attempt to estimate the value of goods and services that are not bought and sold in markets. If a carpenter makes and sells bookcases, the value of those bookcases will be counted in GDP. If the carpenter makes a bookcase for personal use, it will not be counted in GDP. *Household production* refers to goods and services people produce for themselves. The most important type of household production is the services a homemaker provides to the homemaker's family. If a person has been caring for children, cleaning the house, and preparing the family meals, the value of such services is not included in GDP. If the person then decides to work outside the home, enrolls the children in day care, hires a cleaning service, and begins buying the family's meals in restaurants, the value of GDP will rise by the amount paid for day care, cleaning services, and restaurant meals, even though production of these services has not actually increased.

Underground economy Buying and selling of goods and services that is concealed from the government to avoid taxes or regulations or because the goods and services are illegal.

The Underground Economy Individuals and firms sometimes conceal the buying and selling of goods and services, in which case their production isn't counted in GDP. Individuals and firms conceal what they buy and sell for three main reasons: They are dealing in illegal goods and services, such as drugs or prostitution; they want to avoid paying taxes on the income they earn; or they want to avoid government regulations. This concealed buying and selling is called the **underground economy**. Estimates of the size of the underground economy in the United States vary widely, but it is probably at most 10 percent of measured GDP, or about $1.8 trillion. The underground economy in some low-income countries, such as Zimbabwe or Peru, may be more than 50 percent of measured GDP. Recently, countries in Western Europe have decided to include estimates of spending on illegal drugs and prostitution in their measures of GDP. To this point, the BEA has decided not to follow this approach. If it did, estimates are that measured U.S. GDP would increase by about 3 percent.

Is not counting household production or production in the underground economy a serious shortcoming of GDP? Most economists would answer "no" because the most important use of GDP is to measure changes in how the economy is performing over short periods of time, such as from one year to the next. For this purpose, omitting household production and production in the underground economy doesn't matter because there is not likely to be much change in household production or the size of the underground economy from one year to the next.

We also use GDP to measure how production of goods and services grows over fairly long periods of a decade or more. For this purpose, omitting household production and production in the underground economy may be more important. For example, beginning in the 1970s, the number of women working outside the home increased dramatically. Some of the goods and services—such as childcare and restaurant meals—produced in the following years were not true additions to total production; rather, they were replacing what had been household production. MyEconLab Concept Check

Making the Connection MyEconLab Video

Why Do Many Developing Countries Have Such Large Underground Economies?

Recent estimates put the size of the underground economy at 8 percent of measured GDP in the United States and 13 percent in Western Europe. The underground economy is much larger in many developing countries—perhaps 50 percent or more of measured GDP. In developing countries, the underground economy is often referred to as the *informal sector*, as opposed to the *formal sector*, in which output of goods and services is measured. Although it might not seem to matter whether production of goods and services is measured and included in GDP or unmeasured, a large informal sector can be a sign of government policies that are retarding economic growth.

In some developing countries, more than half the workers may be in the underground economy.

Because firms in the informal sector are operating illegally, they tend to be smaller and have less capital than firms operating legally. The entrepreneurs who start firms in the informal sector may be afraid the government could someday close or confiscate their firms. Therefore, the entrepreneurs limit their investments in these firms. As a consequence, workers in these firms have less machinery and equipment to work with and so can produce fewer goods and services. Entrepreneurs in the informal sector also have to pay the costs of avoiding government authorities. For example, construction firms operating in the informal sector in Brazil have to employ lookouts who can warn workers to hide when government inspectors come around. In many countries, firms in the informal sector have to pay substantial bribes to government officials to remain in business. The informal sector is large in some developing economies because taxes are high and government regulations are extensive. For example, firms in Brazil pay 85 percent of all taxes collected, as compared with 40 percent in the United States. Not surprisingly, about half of all Brazilian workers are employed in the informal sector. According to one estimate, firms in the informal sector in Brazil can earn three times the profit of similar-sized firms in the formal sector. In Zimbabwe and Peru, the fraction of workers in the informal sector may be as high as 60 or 70 percent. One estimate puts the size of the informal sector in India at nearly 50 percent.

Many economists believe taxes in developing countries are so high because these countries are attempting to pay for government sectors that are as large relative to their economies as the government sectors of industrial economies. Including transfer payments, government spending in Brazil, for example, is 41 percent of measured GDP, compared to 36 percent in the United States. In the early twentieth century, when the United States was much poorer than it is today, government spending was only about 8 percent of GDP, so the tax burden on U.S. firms was much lower. In countries such as Brazil, bringing firms into the formal sector from the informal sector may require reductions in government spending and taxes. In most developing countries, however, voters are reluctant to see government services reduced.

Sources: "The Price Is Wrong," *Economist*, September 28, 2013; "Dynamic but Dirty," *Economist*, December 2, 2010; "Notes from the Underground," *Economist*, April 2, 2009; Mary Anastasia O'Grady, "Why Brazil's Underground Economy Grows and Grows," *Wall Street Journal*, September 10, 2004; and the International Monetary Fund.

MyEconLab Study Plan

Your Turn: Test your understanding by doing related problems 2.8 and 2.9 on page 652 at the end of this chapter.

Shortcomings of GDP as a Measure of Well-Being

The main purpose of GDP is to measure a country's total production. GDP is also frequently used, though, as a measure of well-being. For example, news stories often include tables that show for different countries the levels of GDP per person, which is usually called *GDP per capita*. GDP per capita is calculated by dividing the value of GDP for a country by the country's population. These articles imply that people in the countries with higher levels of GDP per capita are better off. Although increases in GDP often do lead to increases in the well-being of the population, it is important to be aware that GDP is not a perfect measure of well-being for several reasons.

The Value of Leisure Is Not Included in GDP If an economic consultant decides to retire, GDP will decline even though the consultant may value increased leisure more than the income he or she was earning from running a consulting firm. The consultant's well-being has increased, but GDP has decreased. In 1890, the typical American worked 60 hours per week. Today, the typical American works fewer than 40 hours per week. If Americans still worked 60-hour weeks, GDP would be much higher than it is now, but the well-being of a typical person would be lower because less time would be available for leisure activities.

GDP Is Not Adjusted for Pollution or Other Negative Effects of Production When a dry cleaner cleans and presses clothes, the value of this service is included in GDP. If the chemicals the dry cleaner uses pollute the air or water, GDP is not adjusted to compensate for the cost of the pollution. Similarly, the value of cigarettes produced is included in GDP, with no adjustment made for the cost of the lung cancer that some smokers develop.

We should note, though, that increasing GDP often leads countries to devote more resources to pollution reduction. For example, in the United States between 1970 and 2013, as GDP was steadily increasing, emissions of the six main air pollutants declined by more than 50 percent. Developing countries often have higher levels of pollution than high-income countries because the lower GDPs of the developing countries make them more reluctant to spend resources on pollution reduction. Levels of pollution in China are much higher than those in the United States, Japan, or the countries of Western Europe. According to the World Health Organization, 7 of the 10 most polluted cities in the world are in China, but as Chinese GDP continues to rise, the country is likely to devote more resources to reducing pollution.

GDP Is Not Adjusted for Changes in Crime and Other Social Problems An increase in crime reduces well-being but may actually increase GDP if it leads to greater spending on police, security guards, and alarm systems. GDP is also not adjusted for changes in divorce rates, drug addiction, or other factors that may affect people's well-being.

GDP Measures the Size of the Pie but Not How the Pie Is Divided When a country's GDP increases, the country has more goods and services, but those goods and services may be very unequally distributed. Therefore, GDP may not provide good information about the goods and services consumed by a typical person.

To summarize, we can say that a person's well-being depends on many factors that are not considered in calculating GDP. Because GDP is designed to measure total production, it should not be surprising that it does an imperfect job of measuring well-being.

MyEconLab Concept Check

19.3 Real GDP versus Nominal GDP

LEARNING OBJECTIVE: Discuss the difference between real GDP and nominal GDP.

Because GDP is measured in value terms, we have to be careful about interpreting changes over time. To see why, consider interpreting an increase in the total value of pickup truck production from $40 billion in 2016 to $44 billion in 2017. Because $44 billion is 10 percent greater than $40 billion, were 10 percent more trucks produced in 2017 than in 2016? We can draw this conclusion only if the average price of trucks did not change between 2016 and 2017. In fact, when GDP increases from one year to the next, the increase is due partly to increases in production of goods and services and partly to increases in prices. Because we are mainly interested in GDP as a measure of production, we need a way of separating the price changes from the quantity changes.

Calculating Real GDP

The BEA separates price changes from quantity changes by calculating a measure of production called *real GDP*. **Nominal GDP** is calculated by summing the current values of final goods and services. **Real GDP** is calculated by designating a particular year as the *base year* and then using the prices of goods and services in the base year to calculate the value of goods and services in all other years. For instance, if the base year is 2009, real GDP for 2017 would be calculated by using prices of goods and services from 2009. By keeping prices constant, we know that changes in real GDP represent changes in the quantity of goods and services produced in the economy.

Nominal GDP The value of final goods and services evaluated at current-year prices.

Real GDP The value of final goods and services evaluated at base-year prices.

Solved Problem 19.3

MyEconLab Interactive Animation

Calculating Real GDP

Suppose that a very simple economy produces only the following three final goods and services: eye examinations, pizzas, and shoes. Use the information in the table on the right to compute real GDP for the year 2017. Assume that the base year is 2009.

	2009		2017	
Product	Quantity	Price	Quantity	Price
Eye examinations	80	$40	100	$50
Pizzas	90	11	80	10
Shoes	15	90	20	100

Solving the Problem

Step 1: **Review the chapter material.** This problem is about calculating real GDP, so you may want to review the section, "Calculating Real GDP," which begins on this page.

Step 2: **Calculate the value of the three goods and services listed in the table, using the quantities for 2017 and the prices for 2009.** Real GDP is the value of all final goods and services, evaluated at base-year prices. In this case, the base year is 2009, and we have the price of each product in that year:

Product	2017 Quantity	2009 Price	Value
Eye examinations	100	$40	$4,000
Pizzas	80	11	880
Shoes	20	90	1,800

Step 3: Add up the values of the three products to find real GDP. Real GDP for 2017 equals the sum of:

Quantity of eye examinations in 2017 × Price of eye examinations in 2009 = $4,000
Quantity of pizzas produced in 2017 × Price of pizzas in 2009 = $880
Quantity of shoes produced in 2017 × Price of shoes in 2009 = $1,800
or, $6,680

Extra Credit: Notice that the quantities of each good produced in 2009 were irrelevant for calculating real GDP in 2017. Notice also that the value of $6,680 for real GDP in 2017 is lower than the value of $7,800 for nominal GDP in 2017 that we calculated in Solved Problem 19.1 on page 634.

MyEconLab Study Plan

Your Turn: For more practice, do related problem 3.4 on page 653 at the end of this chapter.

One drawback to calculating real GDP using base-year prices is that, over time, prices may change relative to each other. For example, the price of smartphones may fall relative to the price of milk. Because this change is not reflected in the fixed prices from the base year, the estimate of real GDP is somewhat distorted. The further away the current year is from the base year, the worse the problem becomes. To make the calculation of real GDP more accurate, in 1996, the BEA switched to using *chain-weighted prices*, and it now publishes statistics on real GDP in "chained (2009) dollars."

The details of calculating real GDP using chain-weighted prices are more complicated than we need to discuss here, but the basic idea is straightforward: Starting with the base year, the BEA takes an average of prices in that year and prices in the following year. It then uses this average to calculate real GDP in the year following the base year (currently the year 2009). For the next year—in other words, the year that is two years after the base year—the BEA calculates real GDP by taking an average of prices in that year and the previous year. In this way, prices in each year are "chained" to prices from the previous year, and the distortion from changes in relative prices is minimized.

Holding prices constant means that the *purchasing power* of a dollar remains the same from one year to the next. Ordinarily, the purchasing power of the dollar falls every year as price increases reduce the amount of goods and services that a dollar can buy. MyEconLab Concept Check

Comparing Real GDP and Nominal GDP

Real GDP holds prices constant, which makes it a better measure than nominal GDP of changes in the production of goods and services from one year to the next. In fact, growth in the economy is almost always measured as growth in real GDP. If a headline in the *Wall Street Journal* states "U.S. Economy Grew 2.3% Last Year," the article will report that real GDP increased by 2.3 percent during the previous year.

We describe real GDP as being measured in "base-year dollars." For example, nominal GDP in 2014 was $17,419 billion, and, with a base year of 2009, real GDP in 2014 was $16,086 billion in 2009 dollars. Because, on average, prices rise from one year to the next, real GDP is greater than nominal GDP in years before the base year and less than nominal GDP for years after the base year. In the base year, real GDP and nominal GDP are the same because both are calculated for the base year using the same prices and quantities. Figure 19.3 shows movements in nominal GDP and real GDP between 1990 and 2014. In the years before 2009, prices were, on average, lower than in 2009, so nominal GDP was lower than real GDP. In 2009, nominal and real GDP were equal. Since 2009, prices have been, on average, higher than in 2009, so nominal GDP is higher than real GDP. MyEconLab Concept Check

The GDP Deflator

Price level A measure of the average prices of goods and services in the economy.

Economists and policymakers are interested not just in the level of total production, as measured by real GDP, but also in the *price level*. The **price level** measures the average prices of goods and services in the economy. One of the goals of economic policy is to maintain a

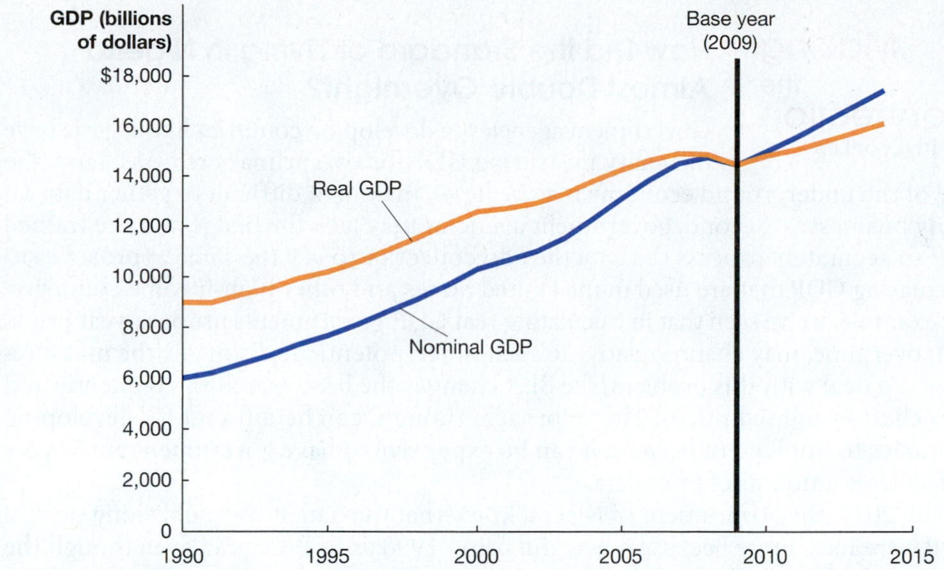

MyEconLab Real-time data

Figure 19.3

Nominal GDP and Real GDP, 1990–2014

Currently, the base year for calculating GDP is 2009. In the years before 2009, prices were, on average, lower than in 2009, so nominal GDP was lower than real GDP. In 2009, nominal and real GDP were equal. Since 2009, prices have been, on average, higher than in 2009, so nominal GDP is higher than real GDP.

Source: U.S. Bureau of Economic Analysis.

stable price level. We can use values for nominal GDP and real GDP to compute a measure of the price level called the *GDP deflator*. We calculate the **GDP deflator** using this formula:

GDP deflator A measure of the price level, calculated by dividing nominal GDP by real GDP and multiplying by 100.

$$\text{GDP deflator} = \frac{\text{Nominal GDP}}{\text{Real GDP}} \times 100.$$

To see why the GDP deflator is a measure of the price level, think about what would happen if prices of goods and services rose while production remained the same. In that case, nominal GDP would increase, but real GDP would remain constant, so the GDP deflator would increase. In reality, both prices and production usually increase each year, but the more prices increase relative to the increase in production, the more nominal GDP increases relative to real GDP, and the higher the value for the GDP deflator. Increases in the GDP deflator allow economists and policymakers to track increases in the price level over time.

Remember that in the base year (currently 2009), nominal GDP is equal to real GDP, so the value of the GDP price deflator will always be 100 in the base year. The following table gives the values for nominal and real GDP for 2013 and 2014:

	2013	2014
Nominal GDP	$16,768 billion	$17,419 billion
Real GDP	$15,710 billion	$16,086 billion

We can use the information from this table to calculate values for the GDP price deflator for 2013 and 2014:

Formula	Applied to 2013	Applied to 2014
$\text{GDP deflator} = \left(\frac{\text{Nominal GDP}}{\text{Real GDP}}\right) \times 100$	$\left(\frac{\$16{,}768 \text{ billion}}{\$15{,}710 \text{ billion}}\right) \times 100 = 106.7$	$\left(\frac{\$17{,}419 \text{ billion}}{\$16{,}086 \text{ billion}}\right) \times 100 = 108.3$

From these values for the deflator, we can calculate that the price level increased by 1.5 percent between 2013 and 2014:

$$\left(\frac{108.3 - 106.7}{106.7}\right) \times 100 = 1.5\%.$$

In the next chapter, we will see that economists and policymakers also rely on another measure of the price level, known as the consumer price index. In addition, we will discuss the strengths and weaknesses of different measures of the price level.

MyEconLab Concept Check

Making the Connection

MyEconLab Video

How Did the Standard of Living in Nigeria Almost Double Overnight?

Government agencies in developing countries like Nigeria have difficulty measuring GDP for two primary reasons: First, the size of the underground economy may be large, making it difficult to gather data on many businesses. Second, government agencies may lack the budgets or the trained staff to accurately process the data they do collect or to use the same approaches to calculating GDP that are used in the United States and other high-income countries. For example, we've seen that in calculating real GDP, governments use base-year prices that, over time, may change relative to each other, potentially distorting the measurement. To deal with this problem, the BEA changes the base year fairly frequently and uses chain-weighted prices. This approach, though, can be difficult for developing countries to implement because it can be expensive to have government employees collect large amounts of price data.

By 2010, the government of Nigeria knew that the data it was publishing on real GDP were inaccurate because it was still using 1990 as its base year, even though the economy had changed dramatically over the years. The Nigerian National Bureau of Statistics was given a larger budget and the task of both changing the real GDP base year to 2010 and gathering data on previously unrecorded output in the underground economy. As an article in the *Wall Street Journal* put it, "Nigerian number crunchers traversed the West African nation by motorcycle and speedboat, visiting Internet cafe owners, movie producers and other businesspeople to record previously uncaptured commercial activity." The number of businesses being surveyed for data increased from 85,000 to 850,000.

When the new data on GDP were released in 2014, the results were dramatic. The estimate for real GDP for 2013 was changed from $270 billion to $510 billion, an 89 percent increase. The increase was large enough for Nigeria to pass South Africa as the largest economy in Africa. As the figure below shows, the new data also gave a more accurate picture of the structure of the Nigerian economy. For instance, where previously the service sector was believed to make up less than one-third of the economy, it was shown to actually be more than half the economy. In addition, although not shown in the figure, the telecommunications sector actually makes up 9 percent of the economy, rather than the 1 percent in previous estimates, and the oil industry is only 14 percent of the economy rather than 33 percent.

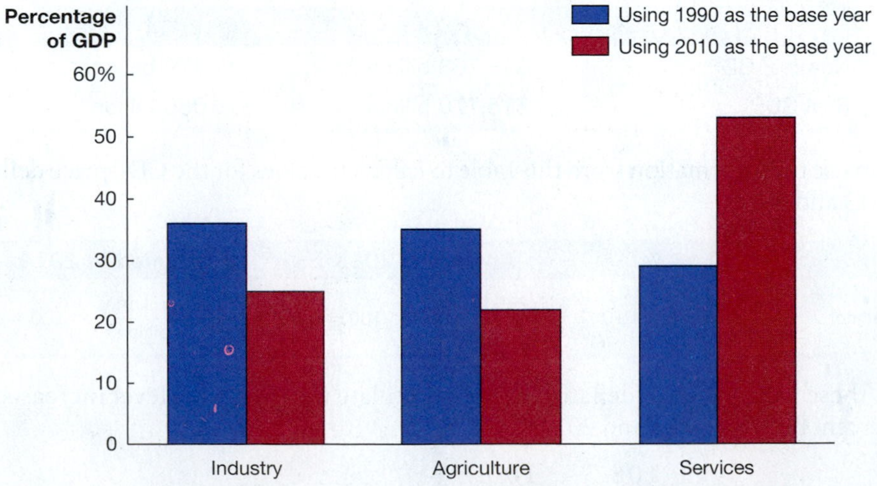

But had the standard of living of the typical Nigerian actually increased? The new estimates made it appear so, with real GDP per person increasing from $1,500 to $2,688. Of course, all that had really changed was how accurately the government was measuring real GDP. The country was producing no more goods and services on April 6, 2014, when the new GDP data were announced, than it had been the day before.

Nigeria's experience with measuring its GDP demonstrates the problems governments have in accurately constructing these statistics and how misleading it can be to rely on them as measures of a country's standard of living.

Sources: Drew Hinshaw and Patrick McGroarty, "Nigeria's Economy Surpasses South Africa's in Size," *Wall Street Journal*, April 6, 2014; Javier Blas and William Wallis, "Nigeria Almost Doubles GDP in Recalculation," *Financial Times*, April 7, 2014; and "How Nigeria's Economy Grew by 89% Overnight," *Economist*, April 7, 2014.

Your Turn: Test your understanding by doing related problem 3.10 on page 653 at the end of this chapter.

MyEconLab Study Plan

19.4 Other Measures of Total Production and Total Income

MyEconLab Study Plan

LEARNING OBJECTIVE: Describe other measures of total production and total income.

National income accounting refers to the methods the BEA uses to track total production and total income in the economy. The statistical tables containing this information are called the *National Income and Product Accounts* (*NIPA*) tables. Every quarter, the BEA releases NIPA tables containing data on several measures of total production and total income. We have already discussed GDP, which is the most important measure of total production and total income. In addition to computing GDP, the BEA computes the following four measures of production and income: gross national product, national income, personal income, and disposable personal income.

Gross National Product

We have seen that GDP is the value of final goods and services produced within the United States. *Gross national product* (*GNP*) is the value of final goods and services produced by residents of the United States, even if the production takes place *outside* the United States. U.S. firms have facilities in foreign countries, and foreign firms have facilities in the United States. Ford, for example, has assembly plants in the United Kingdom, and Toyota has assembly plants in the United States. GNP includes foreign production by U.S. firms but excludes U.S. production by foreign firms. For the United States, GNP is almost the same as GDP. For example, in 2014, GDP was $17,419 billion, and GNP was $17,631 billion, or only about 1.2 percent more than GDP.

For many years, GNP was the main measure of total production compiled by the federal government and used by economists and policymakers in the United States. However, in many countries other than the United States, a significant percentage of domestic production takes place in foreign-owned facilities. For those countries, GDP is much larger than GNP and is a more accurate measure of the level of production within the country's borders. As a result, many countries and international agencies had long preferred using GDP to using GNP. In 1991, the United States joined those countries in using GDP as its main measure of total production. MyEconLab Concept Check

National Income

In the production of goods and services, some machinery, equipment, and buildings wear out and have to be replaced. The value of this worn-out machinery, equipment, and buildings is called *depreciation*. In the NIPA tables, depreciation is called the *consumption of fixed capital*. If we subtract this value from GDP, we are left with *national income*.

Earlier in this chapter, we stressed that the value of total production is equal to the value of total income. This point is not strictly true if by "value of total production" we mean GDP and by "value of total income" we mean national income because national income will always be smaller than GDP by an amount equal to depreciation. In practice, though, the difference between the value of GDP and value of national income does not matter for most macroeconomic issues. MyEconLab Concept Check

Personal Income

Personal income is income received by households. To calculate personal income, we subtract the earnings that corporations retain rather than pay to shareholders in the form of dividends. We also add in the payments received by households from the government in the form of *transfer payments* or interest on government bonds. MyEconLab Concept Check

Disposable Personal Income

Disposable personal income is equal to personal income minus personal tax payments, such as the federal personal income tax. It is the best measure of the income households actually have available to spend.

Figure 19.4 shows the values of these measures of total production and total income for 2014 in a table and a graph. MyEconLab Concept Check

The Division of Income

Figure 19.1 on page 635 illustrates the important fact that we can measure GDP in terms of total expenditure or as the total income received by households. GDP calculated as the sum of income payments to households is sometimes called *gross domestic income*. Figure 19.5 shows the division of total income among wages, interest, rent, profit, and certain non-income items. The non-income items are included in gross domestic income because sales taxes, depreciation, and a few other items are included in the value of goods and services produced but are not directly received by households as income. *Wages* include all compensation received by employees, including fringe benefits such as health insurance. *Interest* is net interest received by households, or the difference between the interest received on savings accounts, government bonds, and other investments and the interest paid on car loans, home mortgages, and other debts. *Rent* is rent received by households. *Profits* include the profits of sole proprietorships, which are usually small businesses, and the profits of corporations. Figure 19.5 shows that the largest component of gross domestic income is wages, which are about three times as large as profits. MyEconLab Concept Check

Measure	Billions of dollars
GDP	$17,419
GNP	17,631
National income	15,077
Personal income	14,734
Disposable personal income	12,990

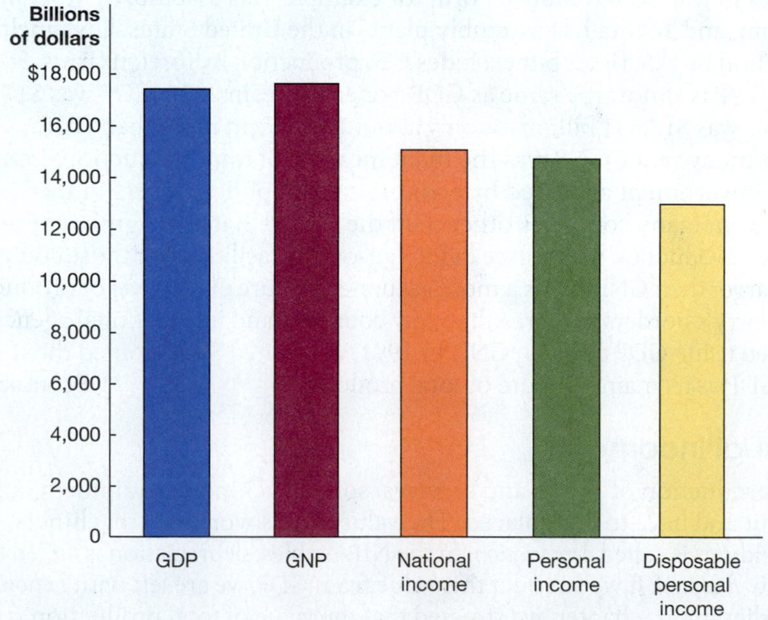

MyEconLab Real-time data

Figure 19.4 Measures of Total Production and Total Income, 2014

The most important measure of total production and total income is gross domestic product (GDP). As we will see in later chapters, for some purposes, the other measures of total production and total income shown in the figure turn out to be more useful than GDP.

Source: U.S. Bureau of Economic Analysis.

		Billions of dollars
Wages		$9,237
Interest		660
Rent		640
Profit		3,076
Profits of sole proprietors	1,380	
Profits of corporations	1,696	
Taxes, depreciation, and statistical discrepancy		3,989

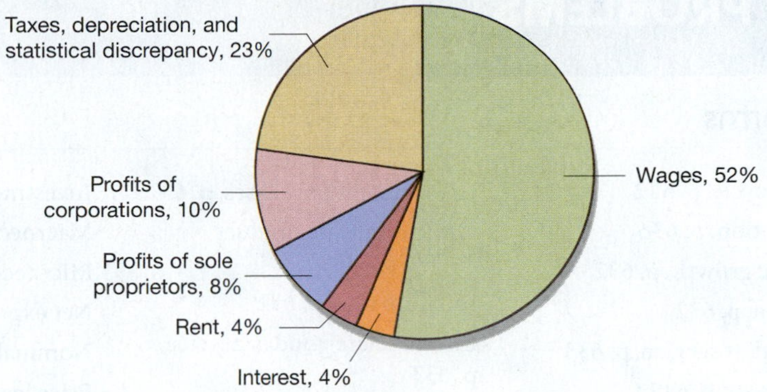

MyEconLab Animation

Figure 19.5 The Division of Income, 2014

We can measure GDP in terms of total expenditure or as the total income received by households. The largest component of income received by households is wages, which are more than three times as large as the profits received by sole proprietors and the profits received by corporations combined.

Note: The components in the figure do not sum to 100 percent because of rounding.

Source: U.S. Bureau of Economic Analysis.

Continued from page 631

Economics in Your Life

What's the Best Country for You to Work In?

At the beginning of the chapter, we posed two questions: What effect should Canada's and China's two very different growth rates have on your decision to work and live in one country or the other? And if China's much higher growth rate does not necessarily lead you to decide to work and live there, why not? This chapter has shown that although it is *generally* true that the more goods and services people have, the better off they are, GDP provides only a rough measure of well-being. GDP does not include the value of leisure; nor is it adjusted for pollution and other negative effects of production or crime and other social problems. So, in deciding where to live and work, you would need to balance China's much higher growth rate of GDP against these other considerations. You would also need to take into account that although China's *growth rate* is higher than Canada's, Canada's current *level* of real GDP is higher than China's.

Conclusion

In this chapter, we have begun the study of macroeconomics by examining an important concept: how a country's total production and income can be measured. Understanding GDP is important for understanding the business cycle and the process of long-run economic growth. In the next chapter, we discuss the issues involved in measuring two other key economic variables: the unemployment rate and the inflation rate.

Visit MyEconLab for a news article and analysis related to the concepts in this chapter.

CHAPTER SUMMARY AND PROBLEMS

Key Terms

19.1 Gross Domestic Product Measures Total Production, pages 633–640

LEARNING OBJECTIVE: Explain how total production is measured.

Summary

Economics is divided into the subfields of **microeconomics**—which studies how households and firms make choices—and **macroeconomics**—which studies the economy as a whole. An important macroeconomic topic is the **business cycle**, which refers to alternating periods of economic expansion and economic recession. An **expansion** is a period during which production and employment are increasing. A **recession** is a period during which production and employment are decreasing. Another important macroeconomic topic is **economic growth**, which refers to the ability of the economy to produce increasing quantities of goods and services. Macroeconomics also studies the **inflation rate**, or the percentage increase in the price level from one year to the next. Economists measure total production by **gross domestic product (GDP)**, which is the value of all *final goods and services* produced in an economy during a period of time. A **final good or service** is purchased by a final user. An **intermediate good or service** is an input into another good or service and is not included in GDP. When we measure the value of total production in the economy by calculating GDP, we are simultaneously measuring the value of total income. GDP is divided into four major categories of expenditures: consumption, investment, government purchases, and net exports. **Consumption** is spending by households on goods and services, not including spending on new houses. **Investment** is spending by firms on new factories, office buildings, machinery, research and development, and additions to inventories, plus spending by households and firms on new houses. **Government purchases** is spending by federal, state, and local governments on goods and services. **Net exports** are equal to exports minus imports. Government **transfer payments** are not included in GDP because they are payments to individuals for which the government does not receive a good or service in return. We can also calculate GDP by adding up the **value added** by every firm involved in producing final goods and services.

MyEconLab Visit **www.myeconlab.com** to complete these exercises online and get instant feedback.

Review Questions

1.1 Why in microeconomics do we measure production in terms of quantity, but in macroeconomics we measure production in terms of market value?

1.2 If the U.S. Bureau of Economic Analysis added up the values of every good and service sold during the year, would the total be larger, smaller, or equal to GDP? Briefly explain.

1.3 In the circular flow of income, why must the value of total production in an economy equal the value of total income?

1.4 Describe the four major components of expenditures in GDP and write the equation that represents the relationship between GDP and the four expenditure components.

1.5 What is meant by a firm's "value added"?

Problems and Applications

1.6 A student remarks, "It doesn't make sense that intermediate goods are not counted in GDP. A computer chip is an intermediate good, and without it, a laptop won't work. So, why don't we count the computer chip in GDP?" Provide an answer to the student's question.

1.7 Briefly explain whether each of the following transactions represents the purchase of a final good.

a. The purchase of flour by a bakery
b. The purchase of an aircraft carrier by the federal government
c. The purchase of French wine by a U.S. consumer
d. The purchase of a new airliner by American Airlines

1.8 An article in the *Wall Street Journal* states that a "change in … inventories subtracted 0.57 percentage point from" what would have been the increase in GDP. For this result to occur, must there have been an increase or a decrease in inventories? Briefly explain.

Source: Eric Morath and Ben Leubsdorf, "GDP Slows to Crawl in First Quarter, up 0.1%," *Wall Street Journal*, April 30, 2014.

1.9 **(Related to the Chapter Opener on page 631)** Which component of GDP will be affected by each of the following transactions involving Ford Motor Company? If you believe that none of the components of GDP will be affected by a transaction, briefly explain why.

a. You purchase a new Ford Escape hybrid from a Ford dealer.
b. You purchase a 2011 Ford Escape hybrid from a friend.
c. Ford purchases door handles for the Escape from an auto parts manufacturer in Indiana.
d. Ford produces 1,000 Escapes in a factory in Missouri and ships them to a car dealer in Shanghai, China.

e. Ford purchases new machine tools to use in its Missouri Escape factory.

f. The state of Missouri builds a new highway to help improve access to the Ford Escape plant.

1.10 Is the value of a house built in 2006 and resold in 2017 included in the GDP of 2017? Briefly explain. Would the services of the real estate agent who helped sell (or buy) the house in 2017 be counted in GDP for 2017? Briefly explain.

1.11 **(Related to Solved Problem 19.1 on page 634)** Suppose that a simple economy produces only four goods: shoes, hamburgers, shirts, and cotton. Assume that all the cotton is used in the production of shirts. Use the information in the following table to calculate nominal GDP for 2017.

Production and Price Statistics for 2017

Product	Quantity	Price
Shoes	100	$60.00
Hamburgers	100	2.00
Shirts	50	25.00
Cotton	80	0.60

1.12 **(Related to the Don't Let This Happen to You on page 637)** Briefly explain whether you agree with the following statement: "In years when people buy many shares of stock, investment will be high and, therefore, so will GDP."

1.13 **(Related to the Making the Connection on page 638)** According to Dan Sichel, an economist at Wellesley College, the amount of time a singer spends working on a record album in a recording studio is "quite analogous to a factory investing in a new machine." Do you agree? Briefly explain.

Source: David Kestenbaum, "Lady Gaga Writing a New Song Is Like a Factory Investing in a New Machine," www.npr.org, April 25, 2013.

1.14 An artist buys scrap metal from a local steel mill as a raw material for her metal sculptures. Last year, she bought $5,000 worth of the scrap metal. During the year, she produced 10 metal sculptures that she sold for $800 each to a local art store. The local art store sold all of the sculptures to local art collectors, at an average price of $1,000 each. For the 10 metal sculptures, what was the total value added by the artist, and what was the total value added by the local art store?

19.2 Does GDP Measure What We Want It to Measure? pages 640–643

LEARNING OBJECTIVE: Discuss whether GDP is a good measure of well-being.

Summary

GDP does not include household production, which refers to goods and services people produce for themselves, nor does it include production in the **underground economy**, which consists of concealed buying and selling. The underground economy in some developing countries may be more than half of measured GDP. GDP is not a perfect measure of well-being because it does not include the value of leisure, it is not adjusted for pollution or other negative effects of production, and it is not adjusted for changes in crime and other social problems.

MyEconLab Visit **www.myeconlab.com** to complete these exercises online and get instant feedback.

Review Questions

2.1 Why does the size of a country's GDP matter? How does it affect the quality of life of the country's people?

2.2 What is the underground economy? Why do some countries have larger underground economies than other countries?

2.3 Why is GDP an imperfect measure of economic well-being? What types of production does GDP not measure? If GDP included these types of production, would it still be an imperfect measure of economic well-being?

Problems and Applications

2.4 Which of the following are likely to increase measured GDP, and which are likely to reduce it?

a. The fraction of women working outside the home increases.

b. There is a sharp increase in the crime rate.

c. Higher tax rates cause some people to hide more of the income they earn.

2.5 Michael Burda of Humboldt University in Germany and Daniel Hamermesh of the University of Texas examined how workers in the United States who lost their jobs spent their time. They discovered that during the period when the workers were unemployed, the decline in the number of hours of paid work these workers did was almost the same as the increase in the number of hours these workers devoted to household production. Do Burda and Hamermesh's findings allow us to draw any conclusions about whether total production in the economy—whether that production is included in GDP or not—decreased when these workers became unemployed? Does your answer depend on whether the household production they carried out while unemployed were activities, such as childcare, that the workers had been paying other people to perform before they lost their jobs? Briefly explain.

Source: Michael Burda and Daniel S. Hamermesh, "Unemployment, Market Work, and Household Production," *Economic Letters*, Vol. 107, May 2010, pp. 131–133.

2.6 A typical U.S. worker today works fewer than 40 hours per week, while in 1890, he or she worked 60 hours per week. Does this difference in the length of work weeks matter in comparing the economic well-being of U.S. workers today with that of 1890? Or can we use the difference between real GDP per capita today and in 1890 to measure differences in economic well-being while ignoring differences in the number of hours worked per week? Briefly explain.

2.7 Economic historians Roger Ransom and Richard Sutch have estimated that African-American farmers in the U.S. South worked about 30 percent fewer hours per year after the Civil War than they had as slaves before the Civil War. If after the Civil War, African-American farmers had continued to work these additional hours, their production and income would have been higher, and U.S. GDP would have been higher. Would the farmers' well-being also have been higher as a result of working these additional hours? Does your answer affect how we should interpret changes in U.S. GDP from before the Civil War to after it? Briefly explain.

Source: Roger L. Ransom and Richard Sutch, *One Kind of Freedom: The Economic Consequences of Emancipation*, 2nd edition, New York: Cambridge University Press, 2001.

2.8 **(Related to the Making the Connection on page 641)** An article in the *New York Times* describes the much greater use of cash, as opposed to checks and credit cards, in buying and selling in China. The article describes someone bringing several bags of cash containing the equivalent of $130,000 into a car dealership to buy a new BMW. Another article notes, "Many economists believe that the rise in [use of] cash is strongly related to growth in the so-called underground economy."
a. What is the underground economy?
b. Why might buyers and sellers in the underground economy prefer to use cash?

Sources: David Barboza, "Chinese Way of Doing Business: In Cash We Trust," *New York Times*, April 30, 2013; and Bruce Bartlett, "America's Most Profitable Export Is Cash," *New York Times*, April 9, 2013.

2.9 **(Related to the Making the Connection on page 641)** An article in the *Wall Street Journal* notes that many economists believe that GDP data for India are unreliable because "the average firm employs just a handful of people and the overwhelming majority of the adult population works off the books and far from major cities."
a. What does the article mean by working "off the books"?
b. Why would the problems listed make it difficult for the Indian government to accurately measure GDP?
c. What problems can be caused for a government or for businesses in a country if the government cannot accurately measure GDP?

Source: Raymond Zhong, "Just How Bad Are India's Official GDP Numbers?" *Wall Street Journal*, August 27, 2014.

2.10 The following table shows data from the Organization for Economic Co-operation and Development (OECD) on the average number of hours employed people worked per week and on real GDP per capita for seven countries.

	Average Hours Worked	Real per Capita GDP
Germany	26.2	$41,007
Canada	32.8	$41,475
Japan	33.3	$34,929
OECD average (34 nations)	34.0	$36,074
United States	34.4	$50,429
Greece	39.6	$23,919
Korea	41.6	$32,711
Mexico	43.0	$16,022

The average German worker worked 8 fewer hours but earned $9,000 less per year than did the average worker in the United States. Can we conclude anything about the well-being of the average German worker versus the well-being of the average worker in the United States from these data? What measures besides average number of hours worked and real per capita GDP would you like to see in evaluating the well-being of workers in OECD countries?

Sources: Eric Morath, "Are Americans Working Less Than the Rest of the World?" *Wall Street Journal*, July 10, 2015; and OECD Data, https://data.oecd.org/emp/hours-worked.htm#indicator-chart.

19.3 Real GDP versus Nominal GDP, pages 643–647

LEARNING OBJECTIVE: Discuss the difference between real GDP and nominal GDP.

Summary

Nominal GDP is the value of final goods and services evaluated at current-year prices. **Real GDP** is the value of final goods and services evaluated at *base-year* prices. By keeping prices constant, we know that changes in real GDP represent changes in the quantity of goods and services produced in the economy. When the **price level**, the average prices of goods and services in the economy, is increasing, real GDP is greater than nominal GDP in years before the base year and less than nominal GDP for years after the base year. The **GDP deflator** is a measure of the price level and is calculated by dividing nominal GDP by real GDP and multiplying by 100.

MyEconLab Visit **www.myeconlab.com** to complete these exercises online and get instant feedback.

Review Questions

3.1 Why does inflation make nominal GDP a poor measure of the increase in total production from one year to the next? How does the U.S. Bureau of Economic Analysis deal with this drawback?

3.2 What is the GDP deflator, and how is it calculated?

3.3 Assuming that inflation has occurred over time, what is the relationship between nominal GDP and real GDP in each of the following situations?
a. In the years after the base year
b. In the base year
c. In the years before the base year

Problems and Applications

3.4 **(Related to Solved Problem 19.3 on page 643)** Suppose the information in the following table is for a simple economy that produces only four goods and services: shoes, hamburgers, shirts, and cotton. Assume that all the cotton is used in the production of shirts.

	2009		2016		2017	
Product	**Quantity**	**Price**	**Quantity**	**Price**	**Quantity**	**Price**
Shoes	90	$50.00	100	$60.00	100	$65.00
Hamburgers	75	2.00	100	2.00	120	2.25
Shirts	50	30.00	50	25.00	65	25.00
Cotton	100	0.80	800	0.60	120	0.70

a. Use the information in the table to calculate real GDP for 2016 and 2017, assuming that the base year is 2009.
b. What is the growth rate of real GDP during 2017?

3.5 Briefly explain whether you agree with the following statements.
a. "If nominal GDP is less than real GDP, then the price level must have fallen during the year."
b. "Whenever real GDP declines, nominal GDP must also decline."
c. "If a recession is so severe that the price level declines, then we know that both real GDP and nominal GDP must decline."
d. "Nominal GDP declined between 2008 and 2009; therefore, the GDP deflator must also have declined."

3.6 An article in the *Wall Street Journal* discussed the views of Canadian Minister of Finance Joe Oliver on the effect of falling oil prices on the Canadian economy. According to the article, Oliver argued that "lower oil prices would have a broadly neutral impact on real … gross domestic product, but have a negative effect on nominal GDP." Given this view, can we tell what Oliver must be expecting the effect of lower oil prices to be on the inflation rate? Briefly explain.

Source: Scott Hagget, "Canada Pushes Back Budget to April Due to Market Instability," *New York Times*, January 15, 2015.

3.7 The following table lists hypothetical values.

(1) Year	(2) Nominal GDP	(3) GDP Deflator (base year = 2014)	(4) Real GDP (base year = 2014)	(5) Percentage Change in Real GDP	(6) GDP Deflator (base year = 2016)	(7) Real GDP (base year = 2016)	(8) Percentage Change in Real GDP
2012	$980.00	90			81.8		
2013	1,020.00	92			83.6		
2014	1,050.00	100			90.9		
2015	1,200.00	105			95.5		
2016	1,400.00	110			100.0		

a. Fill in column (4) by calculating real GDP using the GDP deflator with a base year of 2014 from column (3). Fill in column (7) by calculating real GDP using the GDP deflator with a base year of 2016 from column (6).
b. Fill in column (5) by calculating the annual percentage change in real GDP for each year, using the values from column (4), and fill in column (8) by calculating the annual percentage change in real GDP by using the values from column (7).
c. What effect does the change in the base year used to compute real GDP have on your calculations of the percentage changes in real GDP?

3.8 According to an article in the *Economist*, "China's GDP grew by 7% in the second quarter, which was higher than had been expected." Is it likely that the article is referring to the change in nominal GDP or the change in real GDP? Briefly explain.

Source: "World This Week," *Economist*, July 15, 2015.

3.9 Use the data in the following table to calculate the GDP deflator for each year (values are in billions of dollars):

Year	Nominal GDP	Real GDP
2010	$14,964	$14,784
2011	15,518	15,021
2012	16,163	15,369
2013	16,768	15,710
2014	16,245	16,086

Which year from 2011 to 2014 saw the largest percentage increase in the price level, as measured by changes in the GDP deflator? Briefly explain.

3.10 **(Related to the Making the Connection on page 646)** An article in the *Economist* on the revisions to Nigeria's GDP commented, "The GDP revision is not mere trickery. It provides a truer picture of Nigeria's size by giving due weight to the bits of the economy, such as telecoms, banking and the Nollywood film industry, that have been growing fast in recent years."
a. What does the article mean by "giving due weight" to the sectors of the economy that have been growing quickly?
b. How did the Nigerian National Bureau of Statistics accomplish the task of giving these sectors their due weight?
c. Why does making this change in calculating GDP provide a truer picture of the size of Nigeria's economy?

Source: "Africa's New Number One," *Economist*, April 12, 2014.

19.4 Other Measures of Total Production and Total Income, pages 647–649

LEARNING OBJECTIVE: Describe other measures of total production and total income.

Summary

The most important measure of total production and total income is gross domestic product (GDP). As we will see in later chapters, for some purposes, other measures of total production and total income are actually more useful than GDP. These measures are gross national product (GNP), national income, personal income, and disposable personal income.

MyEconLab Visit **www.myeconlab.com** to complete these exercises online and get instant feedback.

Review Questions

4.1 What is the difference between GDP and GNP? Briefly explain whether the difference is important for the United States.

4.2 What are the differences between national income, personal income, and disposable personal income?

4.3 What is gross domestic income? Which component of gross domestic income is the largest?

Problems and Applications

4.4 Suppose Turkey has many of its citizens temporarily working in other countries, and many of its firms have facilities in other countries. Furthermore, relatively few citizens of foreign countries are working in Turkey, and relatively few foreign firms have facilities in Turkey. In these circumstances, which would you expect to be larger for Turkey, GDP or GNP? Briefly explain.

4.5 An article in the *Economist* on the Irish economy argues, "Irish progress, both economic and fiscal, is typically measured using GDP… . But for an economy where foreign firms are so dominant, GNP … is more relevant." Briefly explain the writer's reasoning.

Source: "Fitter, yet Fragile," *Economist*, January 5, 2013.

4.6 Suppose the amount the federal government collects in personal income taxes increases, while the level of GDP remains the same. What will happen to the values of national income, personal income, and disposable personal income?

4.7 If you were attempting to forecast the level of consumption spending by households, which measure of total production or total income might be most helpful to you in making your forecast? Briefly explain.

4.8 Briefly discuss the accuracy of the following statement: "Corporate profits are much too high: Most corporations make profits equal to 50 percent of the price of the products they sell."

Real-Time Data Exercises

D19.1 (Analyzing the components of personal consumption expenditures) Go to the Web site of the Federal Reserve Bank of St. Louis (FRED) (research.stlouisfed.org/fred2/).

a. Find the values for the most recent quarter for these four variables: (1) Personal Consumption Expenditures (PCEC); (2) Personal Consumption Expenditures: Durable Goods (PCDG): (3) Personal Consumption Expenditures: Nondurable Goods (PCND); and (4) Personal Consumption Expenditures: Services (PCESV).

b. What percentage of total household expenditures is devoted to the consumption of goods (both durable and nondurable goods)?

D19.2 (Analyzing the components of investment) Go to the Web site of the Federal Reserve Bank of St. Louis (FRED) (research.stlouisfed.org/fred2/).

a. Find the values for the most recent quarter for these three variables: (1) Gross Private Domestic Investment (GPDI); (2) Private Nonresidential Fixed Investment (PNFI); and (3) Private Residential Fixed Investment (PRFI).

b. Use these values to calculate the difference between private domestic investment and residential and nonresidential fixed private investment. What component of GDP does the value calculated represent?

D19.3 (Calculating net exports) Go to the Web site of the Federal Reserve Bank of St. Louis (FRED) (research.stlouisfed.org/fred2/).

a. Find the values for the most recent two years for Real Exports of Goods and Services (EXPGSCA) and Real Imports of Goods and Services (IMPGSCA).

b. Compute the value of net exports for each of the two most recent years.

D19.4 (Comparing GDP and GNP) Go to the Web site of the Federal Reserve Bank of St. Louis (FRED) (research.stlouisfed.org/fred2/).

a. Find the values for the most recent quarter for Gross Domestic Product (GDP) and Gross National Product (GNP).

b. Given these values, explain whether foreign production by U.S. firms exceeded U.S. production by foreign firms.

D19.5 (Analyzing the components of personal income) Go to the Web site of the Federal Reserve Bank of St. Louis (FRED) (research.stlouisfed.org/fred2/).

a. Find the values for the most recent quarter for these three variables: (1) Personal Income (PINCOME); (2) Disposable Personal Income (DPI); and (3) Personal Consumption Expenditures (PCEC).

b. Use these values to calculate the difference between personal income and disposable personal income. What does this value represent?

D19.6 (Calculating the GDP deflator and the inflation rate) Go to the Web site of the Federal Reserve Bank of St. Louis (FRED) (research.stlouisfed.org/fred2/).

a. Find the values for the most recent quarter and the values for the same quarter one year ago for nominal Gross Domestic Product (GDP) and Real Gross Domestic Product (GDPC1).

b. Use these values to calculate the GDP price deflator for the most recent quarter and the GDP price deflator for the quarter one year ago.

c. Using the two GDP price deflators, calculate the inflation rate during this year.
d. Look again at Figure 19.3 on page 645. Briefly explain why the nominal and real GDP lines intersect at the base year. What is the value of the GDP deflator in the year when the nominal and real GDP lines intersect?

D19.7 (Calculating real GDP and the real growth rate) Go to the Web site of the Federal Reserve Bank of St. Louis (FRED) (research.stlouisfed.org/fred2/).

a. Find the values for the most recent quarter and the same quarter one year ago for nominal Gross Domestic Product (GDP) and the GDP Implicit Price Deflator (GDPDEF)
b. Use these values to calculate real GDP for the most recent quarter and for the quarter one year ago.
c. Use the two real GDP values to calculate the real growth rate of the economy during this year.

CHAPTER

20

Unemployment and Inflation

Chapter Outline and Learning Objectives

Why Is JPMorgan Chase Laying Off Workers?

When we study macroeconomics, we are looking at the big picture: total production, total employment, and the price level. But the big picture is made up of millions of individual consumers, workers, and firms. Many workers lost their jobs during the severe 2007–2009 recession, and many firms suffered sharp declines in sales. The banking industry was hit particularly hard by the recession. JPMorgan Chase, headquartered in New York City, is the largest bank in the United States and employs more than 240,000 people. The bank was founded in the early twentieth century by legendary financier J.P. Morgan. The bank saw its profit decline by two-thirds from 2007 to 2008 as the U.S. financial system experienced its worst crisis since the Great Depression of the 1930s. By 2009, the U.S. unemployment rate had risen to 10 percent for only the second time since the 1930s.

By 2015, both the U.S. economy and JPMorgan were well into a recovery from the recession. But banks were still struggling for three key reasons: First, interest rates throughout the economy remained at very low levels, reducing banks' profits by narrowing the difference between the interest rates banks paid customers on checking and saving deposits and the interest rates that banks were able to charge on loans to households and firms. Second, large banks were also dealing with increased federal regulation that caused some to stop certain activities, which in the case of JPMorgan included making student loans. Finally, banks were dealing with technological change as more banking activity, including depositing checks and applying for loans, was taking place online. In May 2015, JPMorgan announced that it would lay off 5,000 employees, with each bank branch losing an average of two tellers. The three other largest U.S. banks—Bank of America, Citigroup, and Wells Fargo—were also laying off workers for similar reasons.

The national unemployment rate, which had remained stubbornly high for several years after the 2007–2009 recession ended, had finally reached more normal levels by 2015. Many economists, though, were concerned that wages were increasing only slowly and that the fraction of people who either had jobs or were actively looking for them was at the lowest level in many years.

In this chapter, we will focus on measuring changes in unemployment as well as changes in the price level, or inflation. Because both unemployment and inflation are major macroeconomic problems, it is important to understand how these variables are measured.

Sources: Emily Glazer, "J.P. Morgan Aims to Cut 5,000 Jobs," *Wall Street Journal*, May 28, 2015; Ryan Tracy, Victoria McGrane, and Justin Baer, "Fed Lifts Capital Requirements for Banks," *Wall Street Journal*, July 20, 2015; Eric Morath, "Jobs at a Crossroads: Hiring Up, Pay Flat," *Wall Street Journal*, July 2, 2015; and Rachel Louise Ensign and Lisa Beilfuss, "U.S. Bancorp Says Pressure from Low Rates Looks to Ease," *Wall Street Journal*, July 15, 2015.

Economics in Your Life

Should You Change Your Career Plans if You Graduate during a Recession?

Suppose that you are a sophomore majoring in either economics or finance. You plan to find a job in the banking industry after graduation. The economy is now in a deep recession, and the unemployment rate is the highest in your lifetime, at more than 10 percent. Sizable layoffs have occurred in the banking industry. Should you change your major? Should you still consider a job in the banking industry? As you read this chapter, try to answer these questions. You can check your answers against those we provide on **page 683** at the end of this chapter.

Unemployment and inflation are the macroeconomic problems that are most often discussed in the media and during political campaigns. For many people, the state of the economy can be summarized in just two measures: the unemployment rate and the inflation rate. In the 1960s, Arthur Okun, who was chairman of the Council of Economic Advisers during President Lyndon Johnson's administration, coined the term *misery index*, which adds together the inflation rate and the unemployment rate to give a rough measure of the state of the economy. As we will see in later chapters, although unemployment and inflation are important problems in the short run, the long-run success of an economy is best judged by its ability to generate high levels of real GDP per person. We devote this chapter to discussing how the government measures the unemployment and inflation rates. In particular, we will look closely at the statistics on unemployment and inflation that the federal government issues each month.

20.1 Measuring the Unemployment Rate, the Labor Force Participation Rate, and the Employment-Population Ratio

LEARNING OBJECTIVE: Define the unemployment rate, the labor force participation rate, and the employment-population ratio and understand how they are computed.

At 8:30 A.M. on a Friday early in each month, the U.S. Department of Labor reports its estimate of the previous month's unemployment rate. If the unemployment rate is higher or lower than expected, investors are likely to change their views on the health of the economy. The result is seen an hour later, when trading begins on the New York Stock Exchange. Good news about unemployment usually causes stock prices to rise, and bad news causes stock prices to fall. The unemployment rate can also have important political implications. In most presidential elections, the incumbent president is reelected if the unemployment rate is falling early in the election year but is defeated if the unemployment rate is rising. This relationship held true in 2012, when the unemployment rate was lower during the first six months of 2012 than it had been during the last six months of 2011, and incumbent Barack Obama was reelected.

The unemployment rate is a key macroeconomic statistic. But how does the Department of Labor prepare its estimates of the unemployment rate, and how accurate are these estimates? We will explore the answers to these questions in this section.

The Household Survey

Each month, the U.S. Bureau of the Census conducts the *Current Population Survey* (often called the *household survey*) to collect data needed to compute the unemployment rate. The bureau interviews adults in a sample of 60,000 households, chosen to represent the U.S. population, about the employment status of everyone in the household 16 years of age and older. The Department of Labor's Bureau of Labor Statistics (BLS) uses these data to calculate the monthly unemployment rate. People are considered:

Employed In government statistics, someone who currently has a job or who is temporarily away from his or her job.

Unemployed In government statistics, someone who is not currently at work but who is available for work and who has actively looked for work during the previous month.

Labor force The sum of employed and unemployed workers in the economy.

Unemployment rate The percentage of the labor force that is unemployed.

- **Employed** if they worked during the week before the survey or if they were temporarily away from their jobs because they were ill, on vacation, on strike, or for other reasons.
- **Unemployed** if they did not work in the previous week but were available for work and had actively looked for work at some time during the previous four weeks.

The **labor force** is the sum of the *employed* and the *unemployed*. The **unemployment rate** is the percentage of the labor force that is unemployed.

The BLS classifies the following groups of people who do not have a job and who are not actively looking for a job as *not in the labor force*:

- Retirees, homemakers, full-time students, and those on active military service, in prison, or in hospitals.

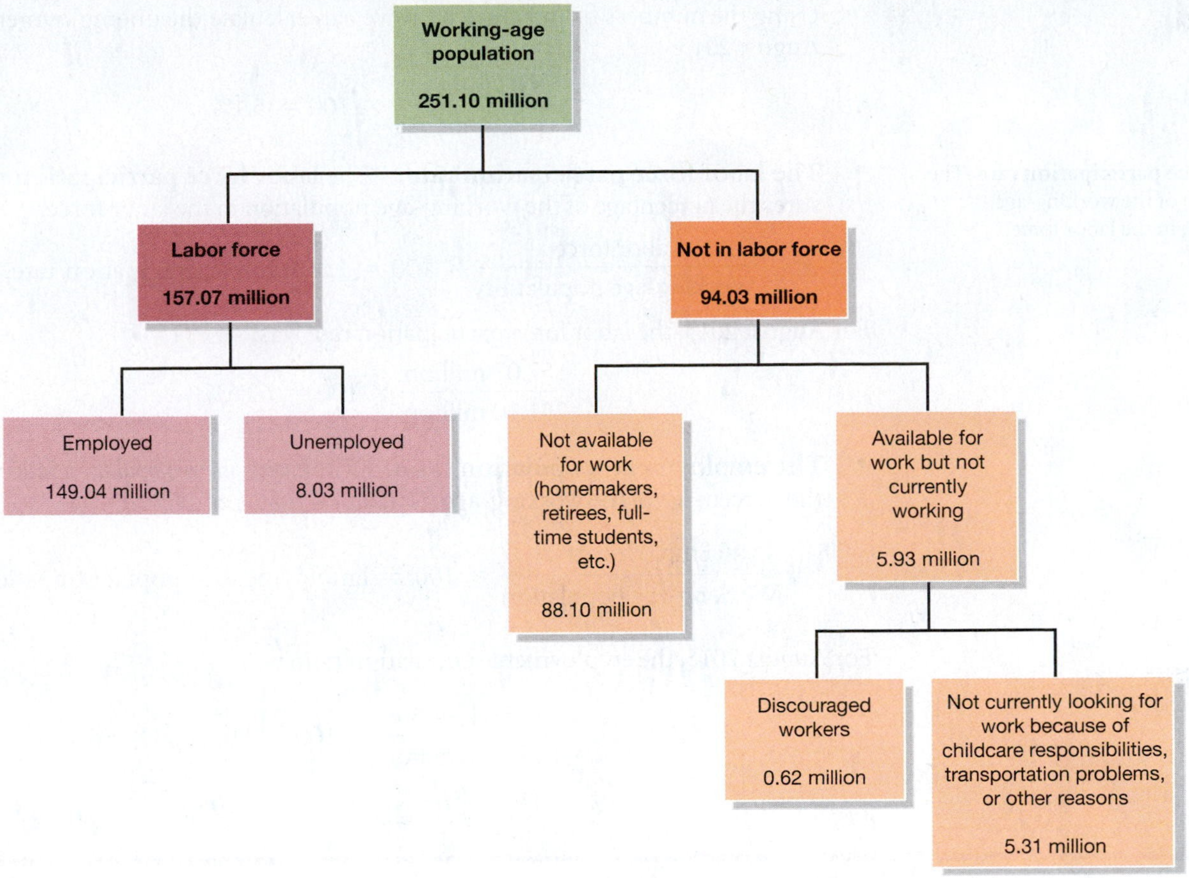

MyEconLab Animation

Figure 20.1 The Employment Status of the Civilian Working-Age Population, August 2015

In August 2015, the working-age population of the United States was 251.10 million. The working-age population is divided into those in the labor force (157.07 million) and those not in the labor force (94.03 million). The labor force is divided into the employed (149.04 million) and the unemployed (8.03 million). Those not in the labor force are divided into those not available for work (88.10 million) and those available for work but not currently working (5.93 million). Finally, those available for work but not in the labor force are divided into discouraged workers (0.62 million) and those not currently looking for work for other reasons (5.31 million).

Source: U.S. Department of Labor, Bureau of Labor Statistics, *The Employment Situation—August 2015*, September 4, 2015.

- People who are available for work and who have actively looked for a job at some point during the previous 12 months but have not looked during the previous 4 weeks. Some people are not actively looking for work for reasons such as transportation difficulties or childcare responsibilities.
- People who are available for work but have *not* actively looked for a job during the previous four weeks because they believe no jobs are available for them. These people are labeled **discouraged workers.**

Discouraged workers People who are available for work but have not looked for a job during the previous four weeks because they believe no jobs are available for them.

Figure 20.1 shows the employment status of the civilian working-age population in August 2015.

We can use the information in the figure to calculate three important macroeconomic indicators:

- **The unemployment rate.** The unemployment rate measures the percentage of the labor force that is unemployed:

$$\frac{\text{Number of unemployed}}{\text{Labor force}} \times 100 = \text{Unemployment rate.}$$

Using the numbers from Figure 20.1, we can calculate the unemployment rate for August 2015:

$$\frac{8.03\text{ million}}{157.07\text{ million}} \times 100 = 5.1\%.$$

Labor force participation rate The percentage of the working-age population in the labor force.

- **The labor force participation rate.** The **labor force participation rate** measures the percentage of the working-age population in the labor force:

$$\frac{\text{Labor force}}{\text{Working-age population}} \times 100 = \text{Labor force participation rate.}$$

For August 2015, the labor force participation rate was:

$$\frac{157.07\text{ million}}{251.10\text{ million}} \times 100 = 62.6\%.$$

- **The employment–population ratio.** The *employment–population ratio* measures the percentage of the working-age population that is employed:

$$\frac{\text{Employment}}{\text{Working-age population}} \times 100 = \text{Employment} - \text{population ratio.}$$

For August 2015, the employment–population ratio was:

$$\frac{149.04\text{ million}}{251.10\text{ million}} \times 100 = 59.3\%.$$ MyEconLab Concept Check

Solved Problem 20.1

MyEconLab Interactive Animation

What Happens if the BLS Includes the Military?

In the BLS household survey, people on active military service are not included in the totals for employment, the labor force, or the working-age population. Suppose the BLS included the military in these categories. How would the unemployment rate, the labor force participation rate, and the employment–population ratio change?

Solving the Problem

Step 1: Review the chapter material. This problem is about calculating the unemployment rate, the labor force participation rate, and the employment–population ratio, so you may want to review the section "Measuring the Unemployment Rate, the Labor Force Participation Rate, and the Employment–Population Ratio," which begins on page 658.

Step 2: Show that including people in the military decreases the measured unemployment rate. The unemployment rate is calculated as:

$$\frac{\text{Number of unemployed}}{\text{Labor force}} \times 100.$$

Including people in the military would increase the number of people counted as being in the labor force but would leave unchanged the number of people counted as unemployed. Therefore, the unemployment rate would decrease.

Step 3: Show how including people in the military would affect the measured labor force participation rate and the measured employment–population ratio. The labor force participation rate is calculated as:

$$\frac{\text{Labor force}}{\text{Working-age population}} \times 100,$$

and the employment–population ratio is calculated as:

$$\frac{\text{Employment}}{\text{Working-age population}} \times 100.$$

Including people in the military would increase the number of people in the labor force, the number of people employed, and the number of people in the working-age population, all by the same amount. The labor force participation rate and the employment–population ratio would both increase because adding the same number to both the numerator and the denominator of a fraction that is less than one increases the value of the fraction.

To help see this point, consider the following simple example. Suppose that 100,000,000 people are in the working-age population and 50,000,000 are in the labor force, not counting people in the military. Suppose that 1,000,000 people are in the military. Then, the labor force participation rate excluding the military is:

$$\frac{50{,}000{,}000}{100{,}000{,}000} \times 100 = 50\%,$$

and the labor force participation rate including the military is:

$$\frac{51{,}000{,}000}{101{,}000{,}000} \times 100 = 50.5\%.$$

A similar calculation shows that including the military would also increase the employment–population ratio.

Your Turn: For more practice, do related problem 1.8 on page 684 at the end of this chapter.

MyEconLab Study Plan

Problems with Measuring the Unemployment Rate

Although the BLS reports the unemployment rate measured to the tenth of a percentage point, it is not a perfect measure of the actual state of joblessness in the economy. One problem that the BLS confronts is distinguishing between the unemployed and people who are not in the labor force. During an economic recession, for example, an increase in discouraged workers usually occurs, as people who have had trouble finding a job stop actively looking. Because these workers are not counted as unemployed, the unemployment rate as measured by the BLS may understate the true degree of joblessness in the economy. The BLS also counts people as being employed if they hold part-time jobs even though they would prefer to hold full-time jobs. In a recession, counting as "employed" a part-time worker who wants to work full time understates the degree of joblessness in the economy and makes the employment situation appear better than it is.

Not counting discouraged workers as unemployed and counting people as employed who are working part time, although they would prefer to be working full time, has a substantial effect on the measured unemployment rate. In Figure 20.2, the red line shows the official measure of the unemployment rate. The blue line shows what the unemployment rate would be if the BLS had counted as unemployed (1) all people who were available for work but not actively looking for jobs, and (2) all people who were in part-time jobs but wanted full-time jobs. The difference between the two measures of the unemployment rate is substantial and was particularly large during the slow recovery following the 2007–2009 recession. For example, in August 2015, using the broader definition of unemployment would have increased the measured unemployment rate from 5.1 percent to 10.3 percent.

There are other measurement problems, however, that cause the measured unemployment rate to *overstate* the true extent of joblessness. These problems arise because the BLS does not verify the responses of people included in the survey. Some people who claim to be unemployed and actively looking for work may not really be actively looking. A person might claim to be actively looking for a job in order to remain eligible for government payments to the unemployed. In this case, a person who is actually not in the labor force is counted as unemployed. Other people might be employed but

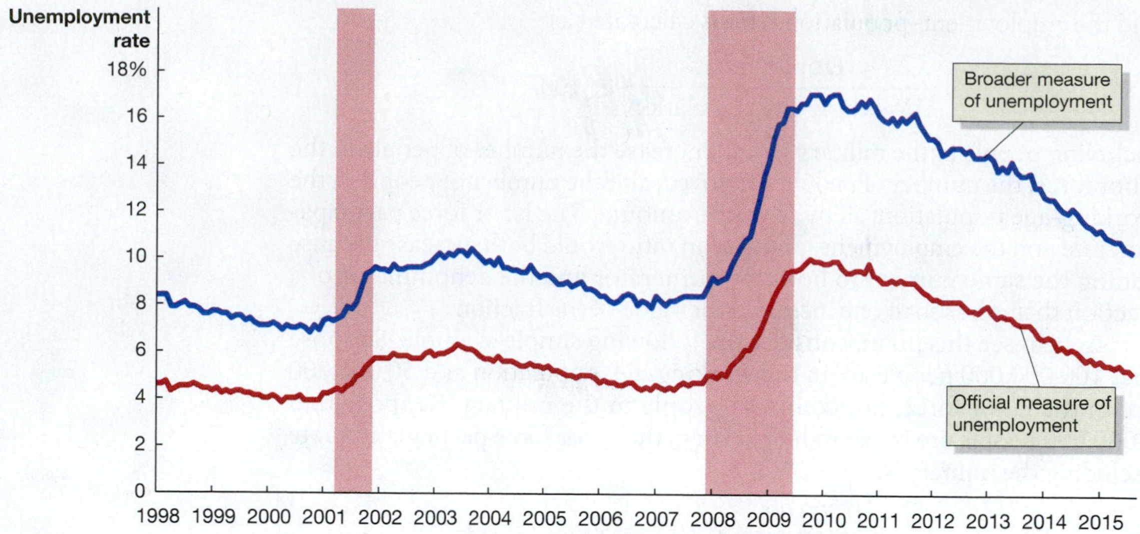

MyEconLab Real-time data

Figure 20.2 **The Official Unemployment Rate and a Broad Measure of the Unemployment Rate, 1998–2015**

The red line shows the official measure of the unemployment rate. The blue line shows what the unemployment rate would be if the BLS had counted as unemployed (1) all people who were available for work but not actively looking for jobs, and (2) all people who were in part-time jobs but wanted full-time jobs. The difference between the measures was particularly large during the 2007–2009 recession and the weak recovery that followed. Shaded areas indicate months of recession.

Note: The official measure (red line) is BLS series U-3, and the broader measure (blue line) is BLS series U-6.

Source: U.S. Bureau of Labor Statistics.

engaged in illegal activity—such as drug dealing—or might want to conceal a legitimate job to avoid paying taxes. In these cases, individuals who are actually employed are counted as unemployed. These inaccurate responses to the survey bias the unemployment rate as measured by the BLS toward overstating the true extent of joblessness. We can conclude that, although the unemployment rate provides some useful information about the employment situation in the country, it is far from an exact measure of joblessness in the economy.

MyEconLab Concept Check

Trends in Labor Force Participation

The labor force participation rate is important because it determines the amount of labor that will be available to the economy from a given population. The higher the labor force participation rate, the more labor that will be available and the higher a country's levels of GDP and GDP per person. Figure 20.3 highlights two important trends in the

MyEconLab Real-time data

Figure 20.3

Trends in the Labor Force: Participation Rates of Adult Men and Women since 1948

The labor force participation rate of adult men has declined gradually since 1948, but the labor force participation rate of adult women has increased significantly, making the overall labor force participation rate higher today than it was in 1948.

Source: U.S. Bureau of Labor Statistics.

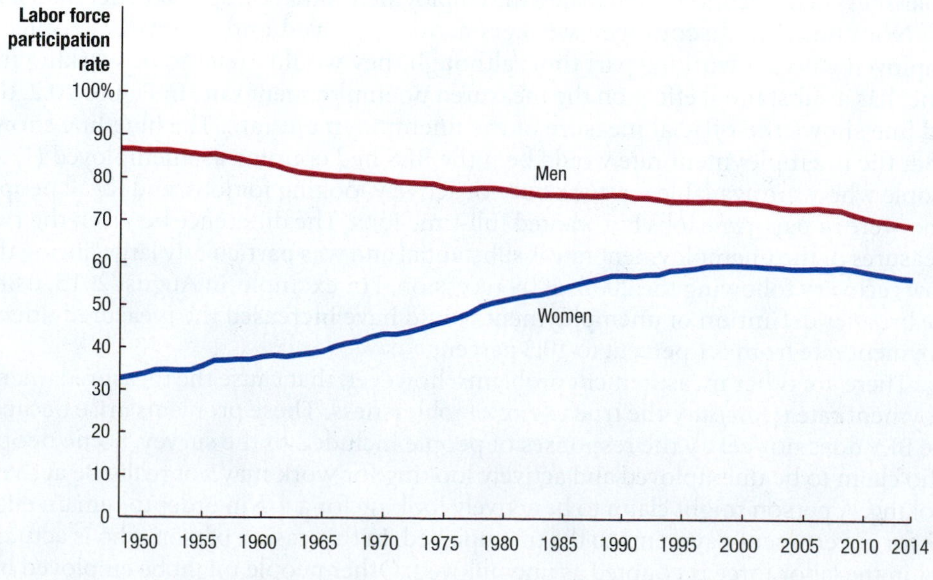

labor force participation rates of adults aged 16 years and over in the United States since 1948: the falling labor force participation rate of adult men and the rising labor force participation rate of adult women. (Note, though, that by 2014, the labor force participation rate of women had not yet fully recovered from the effects of the recession.)

The labor force participation rate of adult males fell from 87 percent in 1948 to 69 percent in 2014. Most of this decline is due to older men retiring earlier and younger men remaining in school longer. There has also been a decline in labor force participation among males who are not in school but who are too young to retire. Over the longer term, this decline in labor force participation among prime-age males appears to be partly due to Congress having made it easier for people to receive cash payments under the Social Security Disability Insurance program. In the shorter term, the decline is due to the severity of the 2007–2009 recession and the weak recovery that followed the recession.

The decline in the labor force participation rate of adult men has been more than offset by a sharp increase in the labor force participation rate of adult women, which rose from 33 percent in 1948 to 57 percent in 2014. As a result, the overall labor force participation rate rose from 59 percent in 1948 to 63 percent in 2014. The increase in the labor force participation rate of women has several causes, including changing social attitudes due in part to the women's movement, federal legislation outlawing discrimination, increasing wages for women, the typical family having fewer children, and an increase in female-headed households. MyEconLab Concept Check

Unemployment Rates for Different Groups

Different groups in the population can have very different unemployment rates. Figure 20.4 shows unemployment rates in August 2015 for different ethnic groups and for groups with different levels of education. While the overall unemployment rate was 5.1 percent, Asians had an unemployment rate of 3.5 percent, and African Americans had an unemployment rate of 9.5 percent. The unemployment rate for people over age 25 without a high school degree was 7.7 percent, while the unemployment rate for college graduates was only 2.5 percent. MyEconLab Concept Check

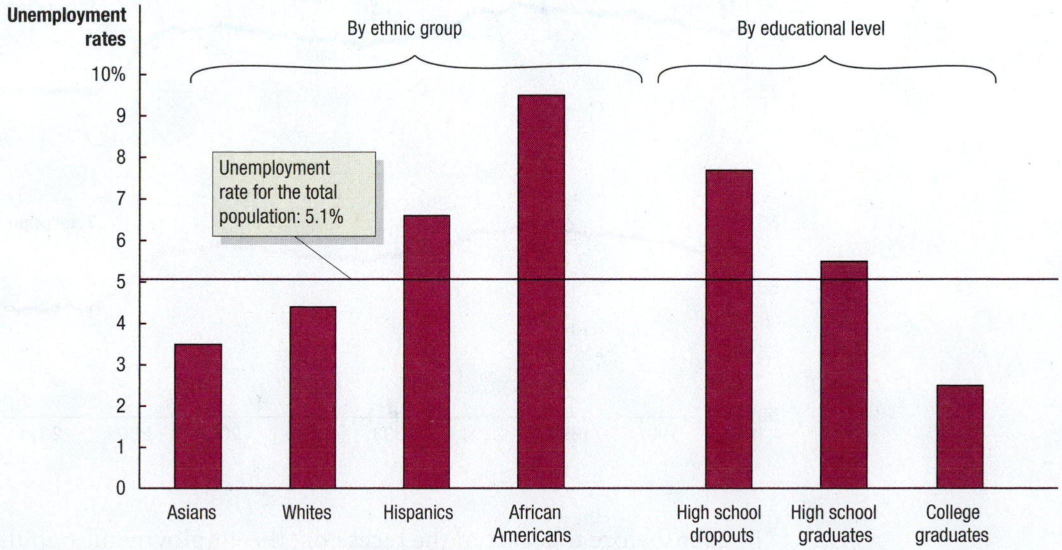

MyEconLab Real-time data

Figure 20.4 Unemployment Rates in the United States, August 2015

The unemployment rate of African Americans is the highest of the four ethnic groups shown, while the unemployment rate of Asians is the lowest. High school dropouts have an unemployment rate that is triple the unemployment rate for college graduates.

Notes: The unemployment rates for ethnic groups apply to people 16 years and older; the unemployment rates by educational attainment apply to people 25 years and older. People identified as Hispanic may be of any race.

Source: U.S. Department of Labor, Bureau of Labor Statistics, *The Employment Situation—August 2015*, September 4, 2015.

How Long Are People Typically Unemployed?

The longer a person is unemployed, the greater the hardship. During the Great Depression of the 1930s, some people were unemployed for years at a time. In the modern U.S. economy, a typical unemployed person stays unemployed for a relatively brief period of time, although that time lengthens significantly during a severe recession. For example, when the economy was expanding in early 2007, fewer than 20 percent of the unemployed had been jobless for more than six months. By the end of the 2007–2009 recession, though, half of the unemployed had been jobless for more than six months. The average period of unemployment had more than doubled from about 4 months to about 10 months. The severity of unemployment during and after the 2007–2009 recession was a sharp break with the normal U.S. experience in which the typical person who loses a job will find another one or be recalled to a previous job within a few months.

MyEconLab Concept Check

Making the Connection

Eight Million Workers Are Missing!

Although the unemployment rate is the most widely followed measure of the state of the labor market, during the recovery from the 2007–2009 recession, many economists and policymakers became concerned about the employment–population ratio. As we saw earlier, the employment–population ratio measures the percentage of the working-age population that is employed. Figure 20.2 on page 662 shows that by mid-2015, the unemployment rate had fallen from its high of 10 percent in 2009 to 5.1 percent, or to roughly normal levels. But the red line in the figure below shows that the employment–population ratio did not recover completely from its decline during the 2007–2009 recession.

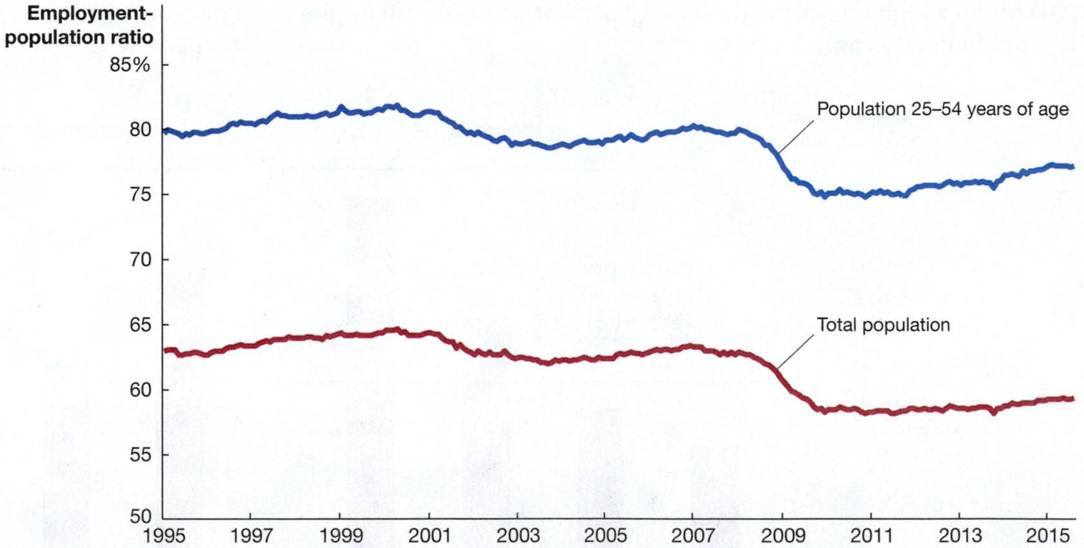

In 2006, before the start of the recession, the employment–population ratio was 63.4 percent. In August 2015, more than six years after the end of the recession, the ratio was still only 59.4 percent. If the employment–population ratio had regained its pre-recession level, an additional 8 million people would have been working in 2015 than actually were. With 8 million additional workers, GDP would have been significantly larger than it was.

Why hasn't the employment–population ratio returned to its pre-recession levels? Part of the explanation is that as the baby boom generation—people born between the years 1946 and 1964—has gotten older, the average age of the population has increased. People in their late 50s and early 60s are less likely to have jobs than are younger people. This fact is illustrated by the blue line, which shows the employment–population ratio just for people aged 25 to 54—the age range in which people are most likely to be working. The employment–population ratio for this age range declined by about 3 percentage points between 2006 and 2015, or about one-fourth less than the decline in employment–population ratio for the whole working-age population. Economists have not reached a consensus in explaining the remainder of the decline in the employment–population ratio. Some economists note that not only did many people lose their jobs during the recession, but the slow recovery from the recession meant that some people were out of work for years. Often people who have not held a job for a long period have difficulty finding a new one because their skills deteriorate and employers therefore become more reluctant to hire them. This "labor-market scarring" may help explain some of the decline in the employment–population ratio. Other economists point to the increased number of people who receive Social Security Disability Insurance. Under this program, people with disabilities receive cash payments from the federal government and receive medical benefits under the Medicaid program. Some people who might otherwise be working are being supported by disability payments instead.

Economists at the Congressional Budget Office (CBO) estimate that the Affordable Care Act, which provides subsidies to buy medical insurance and expands Medicare coverage (see Chapter 7), has resulted in a decline in employment. According to a CBO report, as a result of the act, "some people will decide not to work or to work fewer hours than would otherwise be the case—including some people who will choose to retire earlier than they would have otherwise, and some people who will work less themselves and rely more on a spouse's earnings."

Economists Jeffrey Clemens and Michael Wither of the University of California, San Diego, have analyzed the effects of the increase in the federal minimum wage from $5.15 an hour in 2007 to $7.25 an hour in 2009. They find that by making it more difficult for low-skilled workers to find jobs, the increase in the minimum wage reduced the employment–population ratio. They estimate that this effect accounts for about 14 percent of the total decline in the ratio.

Finally, as we saw in Chapter 8, new businesses are being started at lower rates than in past years and barriers to entering certain occupations have increased as some states have imposed additional licensing requirements. Difficulties in starting new businesses mean that some people who would otherwise be self-employed as small business owners may have left the labor force instead.

As we will see in later chapters, economic growth in the United States has slowed in recent years. Many economists believe that one key to increasing growth and living standards is for the government to develop policies that will help to reverse the decline in the employment–population ratio.

Sources: Josh Zumbrun, "Labor-Market Dropouts Stay on the Sidelines," *Wall Street Journal*, December 28, 2014; Doug Elmendorf, "Frequently Asked Questions about CBO's Estimates of the Labor Market Effects of the Affordable Care Act," cbo.gov, February 10, 2014; Jeffrey Clemens and Michael Wither, "The Minimum Wage and the Great Recession: Evidence of Effects on the Employment and Income Trajectories of Low-Skilled Workers," Working Paper, University of California, San Diego, November 24, 2014; Janet L. Yellen, "Labor Market Dynamics and Monetary Policy," Speech at the Federal Reserve Bank of Kansas City Economic Symposium, Jackson Hole, Wyoming, August 22, 2014; Samuel Kapon and Joseph Tracy, "A Mis-Leading Labor Market Indicator," libertystreeteconomics.nyfed.org, February 3, 2014; and U.S. Bureau of Labor Statistics.

Your Turn: Test your understanding by doing related problem 1.10 on page 685 at the end of this chapter.

MyEconLab Study Plan

The Establishment Survey: Another Measure of Employment

In addition to the household survey, the BLS uses the *establishment survey*, sometimes called the *payroll survey*, to measure total employment in the economy. This monthly survey samples about 300,000 business establishments (such as factories, stores, and offices). A small company typically operates only one establishment, but a large company may operate many establishments. The establishment survey provides

TABLE 20.1 Household and Establishment Survey Data for July and August 2015 MyEconLab Real-time data

	Household Survey			Establishment Survey		
	July	August	Change	July	August	Change
Employed	148,840,000	149,036,000	196,000	142,115,000	142,288,000	173,000
Unemployed	8,266,000	8,029,000	−237,000			
Labor force	157,106,000	157,065,000	−41,000			
Unemployment rate	5.3%	5.1%	−0.2%			

Source: U.S. Department of Labor, Bureau of Labor Statistics, *The Employment Situation—August 2015*, September 4, 2015.

information on the total number of persons who are employed and *on a company payroll*. The establishment survey has four drawbacks:

1. The survey does not provide information on the number of self-employed persons because they are not on a company payroll.
2. The survey may fail to count some persons employed at newly opened firms that are not included in the survey.
3. The survey provides no information on unemployment.
4. The values for employment that the BLS initially announces can be significantly revised as data from additional establishments become available.

Despite these drawbacks, the establishment survey has the advantage of being determined by actual payrolls rather than by unverified answers, as is the case with the household survey. As a result, many economists rely more on establishment survey data than on household survey data in analyzing current labor market conditions. Some financial analysts who forecast the future state of the economy to help forecast stock prices also rely more on establishment survey data than on household survey data.

Table 20.1 shows household survey and establishment survey data for the months of July and August 2015. Notice that the household survey, because it includes the self-employed, gives a larger total for employment than does the establishment survey. The household survey provides information on the number of persons unemployed and on the number of persons in the labor force. This information is not available in the establishment survey. Between July and August 2015, employment rose by 196,000 in the household survey, but rose by only 173,000 in the establishment survey. This discrepancy is due partly to the slightly different groups covered by the two surveys and partly to inaccuracies in the surveys. MyEconLab Concept Check

Revisions in the Establishment Survey Employment Data: How Bad Was the 2007–2009 Recession?

Economists and policymakers rely on government economic data, such as the employment data from the establishment survey, to understand the current state of the economy. Given the size of the U.S. economy, though, government agencies, such as the Bureau of Economic Analysis, the Bureau of Labor Statistics, and the Census Bureau, need considerable time to gather complete and accurate data on GDP, employment, and other macroeconomic variables. To avoid long waits in supplying data to policymakers and the general public, government agencies typically issue preliminary estimates that they revise as additional information becomes available. As we noted earlier, the data on employment from the establishment survey can be subject to particularly large revisions over time.

Figure 20.5 shows for each month from December 2007 to December 2010 the difference between the value for the change in employment as initially reported in the establishment survey and the revised value available in September 2015. The green bars show months for which the BLS revised its preliminary estimates to show that fewer jobs were lost (or more jobs were created) than originally reported, and the red bars show months for which the BLS revised its preliminary estimates to show that more jobs were lost (or fewer jobs were created). For example, the BLS initially reported that

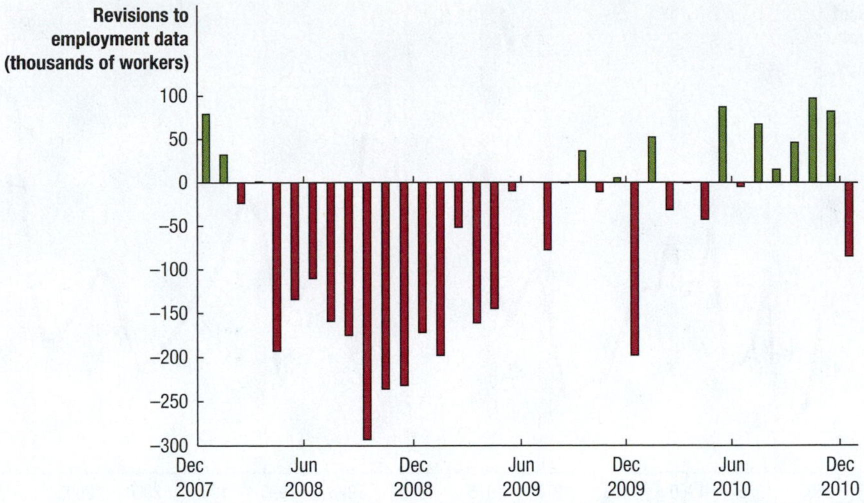

MyEconLab Animation

Figure 20.5

Revisions to Employment Changes, as Reported in the Establishment Survey, 2007–2010

Over time, the BLS revises its preliminary estimates of changes in employment. During the 2007–2009 recession, many more jobs were lost than the preliminary estimates showed. The green bars show months for which the BLS revised its preliminary estimates to show fewer jobs were lost (or more jobs were created), and the red bars show months for which the BLS revised its preliminary estimates to show more jobs were lost (or fewer jobs were created).

Source: U.S. Bureau of Labor Statistics.

employment declined by 159,000 jobs during September 2008. In fact, after additional data became available, the BLS revised its estimate to show that employment had declined by 452,000 jobs during the month—a difference of nearly 300,000 more jobs lost. As the recession deepened between April 2008 and April 2009, the BLS's initial reports underestimated the number of jobs lost by 2.3 million. In other words, the recession of 2007–2009 turned out to be much more severe than economists and policymakers realized at the time. MyEconLab Concept Check

Job Creation and Job Destruction over Time

One important fact about employment is not very well known: The U.S. economy creates and destroys millions of jobs every year. In 2014, for example, about 29.1 million jobs were created, and about 26.1 million jobs were destroyed. This degree of job creation and destruction is not surprising in a vibrant market system where new firms are constantly being started, some existing firms are expanding, some existing firms are contracting, and some firms are going out of business. The creation and destruction of jobs results from changes in consumer tastes, technological progress, and the successes and failures of entrepreneurs in responding to the opportunities and challenges of shifting consumer tastes and technological change. The large volume of job creation and job destruction helps explain why during most years, the typical person who loses a job is unemployed for a relatively brief period of time.

When the BLS announces each month the increases or decreases in the number of persons employed and unemployed, these are net *figures.* That is, the change in the number of persons employed is equal to the total number of jobs created minus the number of jobs eliminated. Take, for example, the months from September to December 2014. During that period, 7,635,000 jobs were created, and 6,526,000 jobs were eliminated, for a net increase of 1,109,000 jobs. Because the net change is so much smaller than the total job increases and decreases, the net change doesn't fully represent how dynamic the U.S. job market really is. MyEconLab Concept Check

MyEconLab Study Plan

20.2 Types of Unemployment

LEARNING OBJECTIVE: Identify the three types of unemployment.

Figure 20.6 illustrates that the unemployment rate follows the business cycle, rising during recessions and falling during expansions. Notice, though, that the unemployment rate never falls to zero. To understand why, we need to discuss the three types of unemployment:

1. Frictional unemployment
2. Structural unemployment
3. Cyclical unemployment

MyEconLab Real-time data

Figure 20.6

The Annual Unemployment Rate in the United States, 1950–2014

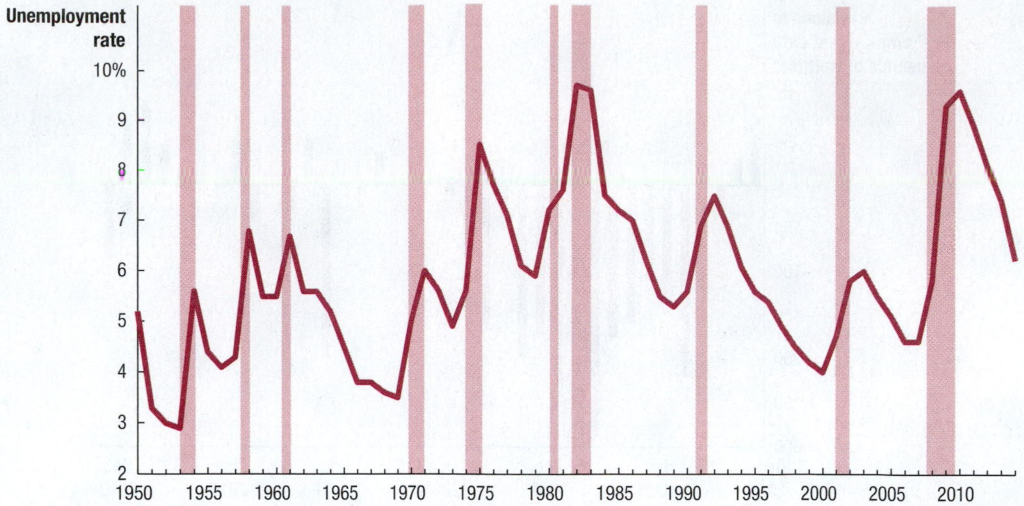

The unemployment rate rises during recessions and falls during expansions. Shaded areas indicate recessions.
Source: U.S. Bureau of Labor Statistics.

Frictional Unemployment and Job Search

Workers have different skills, interests, and abilities, and jobs have different skill requirements, working conditions, and pay levels. As a result, a new worker entering the labor force or a worker who has lost a job probably will not find an acceptable job right away. Most workers spend at least some time in *job search*, just as most firms spend time searching for a new person to fill a job opening. **Frictional unemployment** is short-term unemployment that arises from the process of matching workers with jobs. Some frictional unemployment is unavoidable. As we have seen, the U.S. economy creates and destroys millions of jobs each year. The process of job search takes time, so there will always be some workers who are frictionally unemployed because they are between jobs and in the process of searching for new ones.

Frictional unemployment Short-term unemployment that arises from the process of matching workers with jobs.

Some frictional unemployment is due to seasonal factors, such as weather or fluctuations in demand for some products or services during different times of the year. For example, stores located in beach resort areas reduce their hiring during the winter, and ski resorts reduce their hiring during the summer. Department stores increase their hiring in November and December and reduce their hiring after New Year's Day. In agricultural areas, employment increases during harvest season and declines thereafter. Construction workers in many parts of the United States experience greater unemployment during the winter than during the summer. *Seasonal unemployment* refers to unemployment due to factors such as weather, variations in tourism, and other calendar-related events. Because seasonal unemployment can make the unemployment rate seem artificially high during some months and artificially low during other months, the BLS reports two unemployment rates each month—one that is *seasonally adjusted* and one that is not seasonally adjusted. The seasonally adjusted data eliminate the effects of seasonal unemployment. Economists and policymakers rely on the seasonally adjusted data as a more accurate measure of the current state of the labor market.

Would eliminating all frictional unemployment be good for the economy? No, because some frictional unemployment actually increases economic efficiency. Frictional unemployment occurs because workers and firms take the time necessary to ensure a good match between the attributes of workers and the characteristics of jobs. By devoting time to job search, workers end up with jobs they find satisfying and in which they can be productive. Of course, having workers who are satisfied and productive is also in the best interest of firms.

MyEconLab Concept Check

Structural Unemployment

Computer-generated three-dimensional animation, which has been used in movies such as *Inside Out* and *Minions*, has become much more popular than traditional hand-drawn two-dimensional animation. As a result, many people who are highly skilled in hand-drawn animation lost their jobs at movie studios such as Walt Disney Pictures and DreamWorks. To become employed again, many of these people either became skilled in computer-generated animation or found new occupations. In the meantime, they were unemployed. Economists consider these animators *structurally unemployed*. **Structural unemployment** arises from a persistent mismatch between the job skills or attributes of workers and the requirements of jobs. While frictional unemployment is short term, structural unemployment can last for longer periods because workers need time to learn new skills. For example, employment by U.S. steel firms fell by more than half between the early 1980s and the early 2000s as a result of competition from foreign producers and technological change that substituted machines for workers. Many steelworkers found new jobs in other industries only after lengthy periods of retraining.

Structural unemployment Unemployment that arises from a persistent mismatch between the skills or attributes of workers and the requirements of jobs.

Some workers lack even basic skills, such as literacy, or have addictions to alcohol or other drugs that make it difficult for them to perform adequately the duties of almost any job. These workers may remain structurally unemployed for long periods. MyEconLab Concept Check

Cyclical Unemployment

When the economy moves into recession, many firms find their sales falling and cut back on production. As production falls, firms start laying off workers. Workers who lose their jobs because of a recession are experiencing **cyclical unemployment**. For example, Ford Motor Company laid off workers during the recession of 2007–2009. As the economy slowly recovered from the recession, Ford began rehiring those workers. The Ford workers who had been laid off from their jobs during the recession and then rehired during the following expansion had experienced cyclical unemployment. MyEconLab Concept Check

Cyclical unemployment Unemployment caused by a business cycle recession.

Full Employment

As the economy moves through the expansion phase of the business cycle, cyclical unemployment eventually drops to zero. The unemployment rate will not be zero, however, because of frictional and structural unemployment. As Figure 20.6 shows, the unemployment rate in the United States is rarely less than 4 percent. The fluctuations that we see in Figure 20.6 are mainly due to the changes in the level of cyclical unemployment. When the only remaining unemployment is structural and frictional unemployment, the economy is said to be at *full employment*.

Economists consider the sum of frictional and structural unemployment to be the normal underlying level of unemployment in the economy, or the **natural rate of unemployment**. Economists disagree on the exact value of the natural rate of unemployment, and there is good reason to believe that it doesn't remain constant over long periods of a decade or more. Currently, most economists estimate the natural rate to be between 5.0 percent and 5.5 percent. The natural rate of unemployment is also sometimes called the *full-employment rate of unemployment*. MyEconLab Concept Check

Natural rate of unemployment The normal rate of unemployment, consisting of frictional unemployment and structural unemployment.

Making the Connection MyEconLab Video

How Should We Categorize Unemployment at JPMorgan Chase?

We saw at the beginning of the chapter that JPMorgan Chase announced in 2015 that it was laying off 5,000 employees, with each bank branch losing on average two tellers. In addition, the bank was exiting certain lines of business, including making student loans. Did the layoffs at JPMorgan result in an increase in frictional unemployment, structural unemployment, or cyclical unemployment? In answering this question, we should acknowledge that dividing unemployment into these three categories is useful in understanding the sources of unemployment, but it can be difficult to apply these categories in a particular case.

Which category of unemployment do the workers laid off at JPMorgan Chase fit into?

The BLS, for instance, provides estimates of total unemployment but does not classify it as frictional, structural, or cyclical.

Despite these difficulties, we can roughly categorize the unemployment resulting from the layoffs at JPMorgan. At the time of the layoffs, the U.S. economy was expanding, and the demand for loans and other services the bank offered was increasing, so the unemployment at JPMorgan was not cyclical, and the firm was unlikely to rehire the workers it was laying off, even if the economic recovery became even stronger.

The decision to lay off bank tellers was the result of technological change. As more people deposit checks and make their loan payments online using smartphone apps, fewer people visit bank branches, so JPMorgan doesn't need as many bank tellers. Because other banks are affected by the same changes in technology, the laid-off bank tellers were likely to need to retrain for other jobs to find employment again. So, these workers were structurally unemployed.

As the largest U.S. bank, JPMorgan is subject to federal regulations that do not affect smaller banks. The bank was dropping some types of services, including making student loans, because new federal regulations had increased the costs facing the largest U.S. banks. So, if JPMorgan's employees who were providing these services were able to find employment with smaller banks not subject to the new regulations, during the time the employees were out of work they would have been frictionally unemployed.

It therefore seems likely that some of the unemployment at JPMorgan Chase in 2015 was structural and some was frictional. Given the state of the economy, none of it was likely cyclical.

Sources: Emily Glazer, "J.P. Morgan Aims to Cut 5,000 Jobs," *Wall Street Journal*, May 28, 2015; and Ryan Tracy, Victoria McGrane, and Justin Baer, "Fed Lifts Capital Requirements for Banks," *Wall Street Journal*, July 20, 2015.

MyEconLab Study Plan

Your Turn: Test your understanding by doing related problems 2.6, 2.7, and 2.8 on pages 685–686 at the end of this chapter.

20.3 Explaining Unemployment

LEARNING OBJECTIVE: Explain what factors determine the unemployment rate.

We have seen that some unemployment is a result of the business cycle. In later chapters, we will explore the causes of the business cycle, which will help us understand cyclical unemployment. In this section, we look at the factors that determine the levels of frictional and structural unemployment.

Government Policies and the Unemployment Rate

Workers search for jobs by sending out résumés, registering with Internet job sites such as Monster.com, and getting job referrals from friends and relatives. Firms fill job openings by advertising in newspapers, listing openings online, participating in job fairs, and recruiting on college campuses. Here's how government policies can aid these private employment efforts:

- Governments can help reduce the level of frictional unemployment by pursuing policies that help speed up the process of matching unemployed workers with unfilled jobs.
- Governments can help reduce structural unemployment by implementing policies that aid worker retraining. For example, the federal government's Trade Adjustment Assistance program offers training to workers who lose their jobs as a result of competition from foreign firms.

Some government policies, however, can add to the level of frictional and structural unemployment. These government policies increase the unemployment rate either by increasing the time workers devote to searching for jobs, by providing disincentives for firms to hire workers, or by keeping wages above their market level.

Unemployment Insurance and Other Payments to the Unemployed

Suppose you have been in the labor force for a few years but have just lost your job. You could probably find a low-wage job immediately if you needed to—perhaps at Walmart or McDonald's. But you might decide to search for a better, higher-paying job by sending out résumés and responding to want ads and Internet job postings. Remember that the *opportunity cost* of any activity is the highest-valued alternative that you must give up to engage in that activity. In this case, the opportunity cost of continuing to search for a job is the salary you are giving up at the job you could have taken. The longer you search, the greater your chances of finding a better, higher-paying job, but the longer you search, the more salary you have given up by not working, so the greater the opportunity cost.

In the United States and most other high-income countries, the unemployed are eligible for *unemployment insurance payments* from the government. In the United States, these payments vary by state but are generally equal to about half the average wage. The unemployed spend more time searching for jobs because they receive these payments. This additional time spent searching raises the unemployment rate. Can we conclude that the unemployment insurance program is a bad idea? Most economists would say "no." Before Congress established the unemployment insurance program at the end of the 1930s, unemployed workers suffered very large declines in their incomes, which led them to greatly reduce their spending. This reduced spending contributed to the severity of recessions. Unemployment insurance helps the unemployed maintain their income and spending, which lessens the personal hardship of being unemployed and also helps reduce the severity of recessions.

In the United States, unemployed workers are generally eligible to receive unemployment insurance payments for only six months, although this period is typically extended during recessions, as happened during and after the recession of 2007–2009. After that, the opportunity cost of continuing to search for a job rises. In many other high-income countries, such as Canada and most of the countries of Western Europe, workers are eligible to receive unemployment payments for a year or more, and the payments may equal as much as 70 percent of their previous wage. In addition, many of these countries have generous *social insurance programs* that allow unemployed adults to receive some government payments even after their eligibility for unemployment insurance has ended. In the United States, very few government programs make payments to healthy adults, with the exception of the Temporary Assistance for Needy Families program, which allows single parents to receive payments for up to five years. Although there are many reasons unemployment rates may differ across countries, most economists believe that because the opportunity cost of job search is lower in Canada and the countries of Western Europe, unemployed workers in those countries search longer for jobs and, therefore, the unemployment rates in those countries tend to be higher than in the United States. During the 2007–2009 recession, however, unemployment rates were lower in Canada and Germany than in the United States.

Minimum Wage Laws In 1938, the federal government enacted a national minimum wage law. At first, the lowest legal wage firms could pay workers was \$0.25 per hour. Over the years, Congress has gradually raised the minimum wage; in 2015, it was \$7.25 per hour. Some states and cities also have minimum wage laws. For example, in 2015, the minimum wage in California was \$9.00 per hour, and the minimum wage in San Francisco was \$12.25 per hour. If the minimum wage is set above the market wage determined by the demand and supply of labor, the quantity of labor supplied will be greater than the quantity of labor demanded. Some workers will become unemployed who would have been employed if there was no minimum wage. As a result, the unemployment rate will be higher than it would be without a minimum wage. Economists agree that the current minimum wage is above the market wage for some workers, but they disagree on the amount of unemployment that has resulted. Because teenagers generally have relatively few job-related skills, they are the group most likely to receive the minimum wage. Studies estimate that a 10 percent increase in the minimum wage reduces teenage employment by about 2 percent. Because teenagers and others receiving the minimum wage are a relatively small part of the labor force, most economists believe that, at the minimum wage's current level, it has a fairly small effect on the unemployment rate in the United States. MyEconLab Concept Check

Labor Unions

Labor unions are organizations of workers that bargain with employers for higher wages and better working conditions for their members. In unionized industries, the wage is usually above what otherwise would be the market wage. This above-market wage results in employers in unionized industries hiring fewer workers, but does it also significantly increase the overall unemployment rate in the economy? Most economists would say the answer is "no" because in the United States only about 9 percent of workers outside the government sector are unionized. Although unions remain strong in a few industries, such as airlines, automobiles, steel, and telecommunications, most industries are not unionized. The result is that most workers who can't find jobs in unionized industries because the wage is above its market level can find jobs in other industries. MyEconLab Concept Check

Efficiency Wages

Some firms pay above-market wages not because the government requires them to or because they are unionized but because they believe doing so will increase their profits. Because wages are the largest cost for many employers, paying higher wages seems like a good way for firms to *lower* profits rather than to increase them. The key to understanding this wage policy is that the level of wages can affect the level of workers' productivity. Many studies have shown that workers are motivated by higher wages to work harder. An **efficiency wage** is an above-market wage that a firm pays to motivate workers to be more productive. Can't firms ensure that workers work hard by supervising them? In some cases, they can. For example, a telemarketing firm can monitor workers electronically to ensure that they make the required number of phone calls per hour. In many business situations, however, it is much more difficult to monitor workers. Many firms must rely on workers being motivated enough to work hard. By paying an above-market wage, a firm raises the cost to workers of losing their jobs because many alternative jobs will pay only the market wage. The increase in productivity that results from paying the high wage can more than offset the extra cost of the wage, thereby lowering the firm's costs of production.

Efficiency wage An above-market wage that a firm pays to increase workers' productivity.

Because the efficiency wage is above the market wage, it results in the quantity of labor supplied being greater than the quantity of labor demanded, just as do minimum wage laws and labor unions. So, efficiency wages also contribute to economies experiencing some unemployment even when cyclical unemployment is zero. MyEconLab Concept Check

MyEconLab Study Plan

20.4 Measuring Inflation

LEARNING OBJECTIVE: Define the price level and the inflation rate and understand how they are computed.

One of the facts of economic life is that the prices of most goods and services rise over time. As a result, the cost of living continually rises. In 1914, Henry Ford began paying his workers a wage of $5 per day, which was more than twice as much as other automobile manufacturers were paying. Ford's $5-a-day wage provided his workers with a middle-class income because prices were so low. In 1914, Ford's Model T, the best-selling car in the country, sold for less than $600, the price of a man's suit was $15, the price of a ticket to a movie theater was $0.15, and the price of a box of Kellogg's Corn Flakes was $0.08. In 2015, with the cost of living being much higher than it was in 1914, the federal minimum wage law required firms to pay a wage of at least $7.25 per *hour*, more than Ford's highly paid workers earned in a day.

Knowing how the government compiles the employment and unemployment statistics is important in interpreting them. The same is true of the government's statistics on the cost of living. The **price level** measures the average prices of goods and services in the economy (see Chapter 19). The **inflation rate** is the percentage increase in the price level from one year to the next. In the last chapter, we introduced the *GDP deflator* as a measure of the price level. The GDP deflator is the broadest measure we have of the price level because it includes the price of every final good and service. But for some purposes, it is too broad. For example, if we want to know how inflation affects a typical household, the GDP price deflator may be misleading because it includes the prices of products such as large electric generators and machine tools that are part of the investment component of GDP but are not purchased by a typical household. In this chapter, we will focus on measuring the inflation rate by changes in the *consumer price index* because changes in this index come closest to measuring changes in the cost of living as experienced by a typical household. We will also briefly discuss a third measure of inflation: the *producer price index.*

Price level A measure of the average prices of goods and services in the economy.

Inflation rate The percentage increase in the price level from one year to the next.

The Consumer Price Index

To obtain prices of a representative group of goods and services, the BLS surveys 14,000 households nationwide on their spending habits. It uses the results of this survey to construct a *market basket* of 211 types of goods and services purchased by a typical urban family of four. Figure 20.7 shows the goods and services in the market basket, grouped into eight broad categories. Almost three-quarters of the market basket falls into just three categories: housing, transportation, and food. Each month, hundreds of BLS employees visit 23,000 stores in 87 cities and record prices of the goods and services in the market basket. Each price in the consumer price index is given a weight equal to the fraction of a typical family's budget spent on that good or service.

The **consumer price index (CPI)** is a measure of the average change over time in the prices a typical urban family of four pays for the goods and services they purchase. One year is chosen as the base year, and the value of the CPI is set equal to 100 for that year. In any year other than the base year, the CPI is equal to the ratio of the dollar amount necessary to buy the market basket of goods in that year divided by the dollar amount necessary to buy the market basket of goods in the base year,

Consumer price index (CPI) A measure of the average change over time in the prices a typical urban family of four pays for the goods and services they purchase.

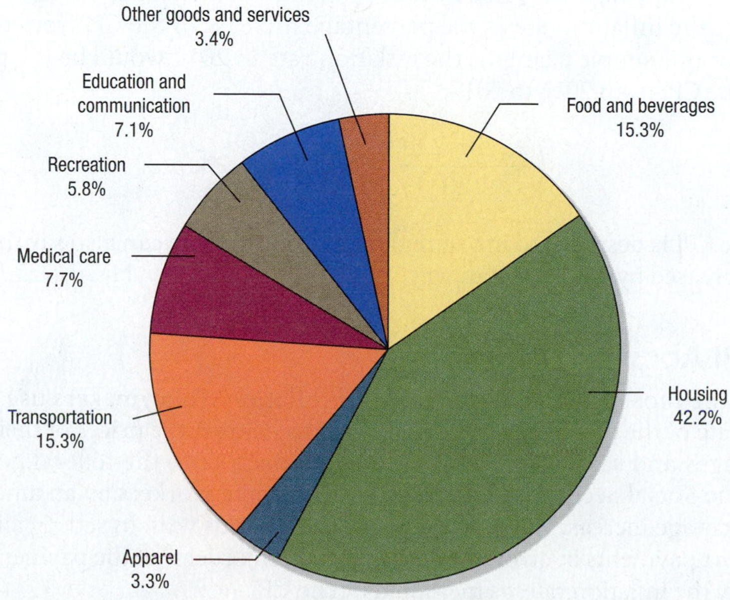

MyEconLab Animation

Figure 20.7

The CPI Market Basket, December 2014

The Bureau of Labor Statistics surveys 14,000 households on their spending habits. The results are used to construct a *market basket* of goods and services purchased by a typical urban family of four. The chart shows these goods and services, grouped into eight broad categories. The percentages represent the expenditure shares of the categories within the market basket. The categories housing, transportation, and food make up about three-quarters of the market basket.

Source: U.S. Bureau of Labor Statistics.

multiplied by 100. Because the CPI measures the cost to a typical family of buying a representative basket of goods and services, it is sometimes called the *cost-of-living index*.

A simple example can clarify how the CPI is constructed. For purposes of this example, we assume that the market basket has only three products: eye examinations, pizzas, and books:

	Base Year (1999)			2016		2017	
Product	**Quantity**	**Price**	**Expenditures**	**Price**	**Expenditures (on base-year quantities)**	**Price**	**Expenditures (on base-year quantities)**
Eye examinations	1	$50.00	$50.00	$100.00	$100.00	$85.00	$85.00
Pizzas	20	10.00	200.00	15.00	300.00	14.00	280.00
Books	20	25.00	500.00	25.00	500.00	27.50	550.00
TOTAL			$750.00		$900.00		$915.00

Suppose that during the base year, 1999, a survey determines that each month, a typical family purchases 1 eye examination, 20 pizzas, and 20 books. At 1999 prices, a family must spend $750.00 to purchase this market basket of goods and services. The CPI for every year after the base year is determined by dividing the amount necessary to purchase the market basket in that year by the amount required in the base year, then multiplying by 100. Notice that the quantities of the products purchased in 2016 and 2017 are irrelevant in calculating the CPI because *we are assuming that households buy the same market basket of products each month*. Using the numbers in the table, we can calculate the CPI for 2016 and 2017:

Formula	Applied to 2016	Applied to 2017
$\text{CPI} = \dfrac{\text{Expenditures in the current year}}{\text{Expenditures in the base year}} \times 100$	$\left(\dfrac{\$900}{\$750}\right) \times 100 = 120$	$\left(\dfrac{\$915}{\$750}\right) \times 100 = 122$

How do we interpret values such as 120 and 122? First, recognize that they are *index numbers*, which means they are not measured in dollars or any other units. *The CPI is intended to measure changes in the price level over time.* We can't use the CPI to tell us in an absolute sense how high the price level is—only how much it has changed over time. We measure the inflation rate as the percentage increase in the CPI from one year to the next. For our simple example, the inflation rate in 2017 would be the percentage change in the CPI from 2016 to 2017:

$$\left(\frac{122 - 120}{120}\right) \times 100 = 1.7\%.$$

Because the CPI is designed to measure the cost of living, we can also say that the cost of living increased by 1.7 percent during 2017. MyEconLab Concept Check

Is the CPI Accurate?

The CPI is the most widely used measure of inflation. Policymakers use the CPI to track the state of the economy. Businesses use it to help set the prices of their products and the wages and salaries of their employees. Each year, the federal government increases the Social Security payments made to retired workers by an amount equal to the percentage increase in the CPI during the previous year. In setting alimony and child support payments in divorce cases, judges often order that the payments increase each year by the inflation rate, as measured by the CPI.

Don't Let This Happen to You

Don't Miscalculate the Inflation Rate

Suppose you are given the data in the following table and are asked to calculate the inflation rate for 2014:

Year	CPI
2013	233
2014	237

It is tempting to avoid any calculations and simply report that the inflation rate in 2014 was 137 percent because 237 is a 137 percent increase from 100. But 137 percent would be the wrong answer. A value for the CPI of 237 in 2014 tells us that the price level in 2014 was 137 percent higher than in the *base year*, but the inflation rate is the percentage increase in the price level from the *previous year*, *not* the percentage increase from the base year. The correct calculation of the inflation rate for 2014 is:

$$\left(\frac{237 - 233}{233}\right) \times 100 = 1.7\%.$$

MyEconLab Study Plan

Your Turn: Test your understanding by doing related problem 4.5 and 4.6 on page 687 at the end of this chapter.

It is important that the CPI be as accurate as possible, but four biases cause changes in the CPI to overstate the true inflation rate:

1. **Substitution bias.** In constructing the CPI, the BLS assumes that each month, consumers purchase the same amount of each product in the market basket. In fact, consumers are likely to buy fewer of those products that increase most in price and more of those products that increase least in price (or fall the most in price). For instance, if apple prices rise rapidly during a particular month while orange prices fall, consumers will reduce their apple purchases and increase their orange purchases. Therefore, the prices of the market basket consumers actually buy will rise less than the prices of the market basket the BLS uses to compute the CPI.
2. **Increase in quality bias.** Over time, most products included in the CPI improve in quality: Automobiles become more durable and side air bags become standard equipment, smartphones have better processors and more memory, dishwashers use less water while getting dishes cleaner, and so on. Increases in the prices of these products partly reflect their improved quality and partly are pure inflation. The BLS attempts to make adjustments so that only the pure inflation part of price increases is included in the CPI. These adjustments are difficult to make, however, so the recorded price increases overstate the pure inflation in some products.
3. **New product bias.** For many years, the BLS updated the market basket of goods used in computing the CPI only every 10 years. So, new products introduced between updates were not included in the market basket. For example, the 1987 update took place before cellphones were introduced. Although millions of U.S. households used cellphones by the mid-1990s, they were not included in the CPI until the 1997 update. The prices of many products, such as cellphones, Blu-ray players, and 4K televisions, decrease in the years immediately after they are introduced. If the market basket is not updated frequently, these price decreases are not included in the CPI.
4. **Outlet bias.** During the mid-1990s, many consumers began to increase their purchases from discount stores such as Sam's Club and Costco. By the late 1990s, the Internet began to account for a significant fraction of sales of some products. Because the BLS continued to collect price statistics from traditional full-price retail stores, the CPI did not reflect the prices some consumers actually paid.

Most economists believe these biases cause changes in the CPI to overstate the true inflation rate by 0.5 percentage point to 1 percentage point. That is, if the CPI indicates that the inflation rate is 3 percent, it is probably between 2 percent and 2.5 percent. The BLS continues to take steps to reduce the size of the bias. For example, the BLS has reduced the size of the substitution and new product biases by updating the market basket every 2 years rather than every 10 years. The BLS has reduced the size of the outlet bias by conducting a point-of-purchase survey to track where consumers actually make their purchases. Finally, the BLS has used statistical methods to reduce the size of the quality bias. Prior to these changes, the size of the total bias in the CPI was probably greater than 1 percentage point. MyEconLab Concept Check

The Producer Price Index

Producer price index (PPI) An average of the prices received by producers of goods and services at all stages of the production process.

In addition to the GDP deflator and the CPI, the government also computes the **producer price index (PPI)**. Like the CPI, the PPI tracks the prices of a market basket of goods. But while the CPI tracks the prices of goods and services purchased by a typical household, the PPI tracks the prices firms receive for goods and services at all stages of production. The PPI includes the prices of intermediate goods, such as flour, yarn, steel, and lumber; and raw materials, such as raw cotton, coal, and crude petroleum. If the prices of these goods rise, the cost to firms of producing final goods and services will rise, which may lead firms to increase the prices of goods and services purchased by consumers. Changes in the PPI therefore can give an early warning of future movements in the CPI. MyEconLab Concept Check

MyEconLab Study Plan

20.5 Using Price Indexes to Adjust for the Effects of Inflation

LEARNING OBJECTIVE: Use price indexes to adjust for the effects of inflation.

You are likely to receive a much higher salary after graduation than your parents did 25 or more years ago, but prices 25 years ago were, on average, much lower than prices today. In other words, the purchasing power of a dollar was much higher 25 years ago because the prices of most goods and services were much lower. Price indexes such as the CPI give us a way of adjusting for the effects of inflation so that we can compare dollar values from different years.

For example, suppose your mother received a salary of $25,000 in 1989. By using the CPI, we can calculate what $25,000 in 1989 was equivalent to in 2014. The CPI is 124 for 1989 and 237 for 2014. Because 237/124 = 1.9, we know that, on average, prices were almost twice as high in 2014 as in 1989. We can use this result to inflate a salary of $25,000 received in 1989 to its value in terms of 2014 purchasing power:

$$\text{Value in 2014 dollars} = \text{Value in 1989 dollars} \times \left(\frac{\text{CPI in 2014}}{\text{CPI in 1989}}\right)$$

$$= \$25{,}000 \times \left(\frac{237}{124}\right) = \$47{,}782.$$

Our calculation shows that if you were paid a salary of $47,782 in 2014, you would be able to purchase roughly the same amount of goods and services that your mother could have purchased with a salary of $25,000 in 1989. Economic variables that are calculated in current-year prices are referred to as *nominal variables*. The calculation we have just made uses a price index to adjust a nominal variable—your mother's salary—for the effects of inflation.

For some purposes, we are interested in tracking changes in an economic variable over time rather than in seeing what its value would be in today's dollars. In that case, to correct for the effects of inflation, we can divide the nominal variable by a price index and multiply by 100 to obtain a *real variable*. The real variable will be measured in dollars of the base year for the price index. Currently, the base year for the CPI is the average of prices in the years 1982 to 1984. MyEconLab Concept Check

Solved Problem 20.5

MyEconLab Interactive Animation

What Has Been Happening with Real Wages in the United States?

In addition to data on employment, the BLS establishment survey gathers data on average hourly earnings of production workers. Production workers are all workers, except for managers and professionals. Average hourly earnings are the wages or salaries earned by these workers per hour. Economists and policymakers closely follow changes in average hourly earnings because they are a broad measure of a typical worker's income. Note, though, that in order to measure changes in the purchasing power of these wages, we have to convert the nominal values reported by the BLS to real values. Use the information in the following table to compute real average hourly earnings for each year. Compare the percentage change in nominal average hourly earnings between 2013 and 2014 with the percentage change in real average hourly earnings. Be sure to explain what the values you calculate for real average hourly earnings represent.

Year	Nominal Average Hourly Earnings	CPI (1982–1984 = 100)
2012	$19.73	230
2013	$20.14	233
2014	$20.60	237

Solving the Problem

Step 1: Review the chapter material. This problem is about using price indexes to correct for the effects of inflation, so you may want to review the section "Using Price Indexes to Adjust for the Effects of Inflation," which begins on page 676.

Step 2: Begin by defining real average hourly earnings, calculating the value of real average hourly earnings for each year, and explaining what the values you calculated represent. Nominal average hourly earnings are the number of dollars a worker receives. To calculate real average hourly earnings, we have to divide the nominal average earnings by the CPI for that year and multiply by 100. For example, real average hourly earnings for 2012 equal:

$$\left(\frac{\$19.73}{230}\right) \times 100 = \$8.59$$

The results for all three years are:

Year	Nominal Average Hourly Earnings	CPI (1982–1984 = 100)	Real Average Hourly Earnings (1982–1984 dollars)
2012	$19.73	230	$8.59
2013	$20.14	233	$8.65
2014	$20.60	237	$8.70

The base year for the CPI is the average of prices during the period 1982–1984. So, the values for the real average hourly earnings we calculated are in 1982–1984 dollars. In other words, these values for the real wage tell us that in 2013, $20.14 would buy what $8.65 would have bought in 1982–1984 and that in 2014, $20.60 would buy what $8.70 would have bought in 1982–1984.

Step 3: Complete your answer by calculating the percentage change in nominal average hourly earnings and in real average hourly earnings between 2013 and 2014. The percentage change in nominal average hourly earnings equals:

$$\left(\frac{\$20.60 - \$20.14}{\$20.14}\right) \times 100 = 2.3\%.$$

And the percentage change real average hourly earnings equals:

$$\left(\frac{\$8.70 - \$8.65}{\$8.65}\right) \times 100 = 0.6\%.$$

We can conclude that although nominal average hourly earnings increased by more than 2 percent, real average hourly earnings increased by less than 1 percent.

Extra Credit: The values we computed for the real average hourly earnings are measured in 1982–1984 dollars. Because this period is more than 30 years ago, the values are somewhat difficult to interpret. We can convert the earnings to 2014 dollars by using the method we used on page 676 to calculate your mother's salary. But for purposes of calculating the *change* in the value of real average hourly earnings over time, converting the earnings to 2014 dollars doesn't matter. The change from 2013 to 2014 would still be 0.6 percent. You can check this point by using the "mother's salary" method to calculate the real average hourly earnings for 2013 and 2014 in 2014 dollars. Then calculate the percentage change. Unless you make an arithmetic error, you should find that the answer is still 0.6 percent. Finally, keep in mind that average hourly earnings do not include employee benefits, such as employer contributions to retirement programs or the value of employer provided medical insurance. Because benefits have increased over the years relative to wages and salaries, changes in average hourly earnings can be a misleading measure of changes in the typical worker's standard of living.

MyEconLab Study Plan

Your Turn: For more practice, do related problems 5.4, 5.5, 5.6, and 5.7 on pages 688–689 at the end of this chapter.

20.6 Nominal Interest Rates versus Real Interest Rates

LEARNING OBJECTIVE: Distinguish between the nominal interest rate and the real interest rate.

The difference between nominal and real values is important when money is being borrowed and lent. The *interest rate* is the cost of borrowing funds, expressed as a percentage of the amount borrowed (see Chapter 8). If you lend someone $1,000 for one year and charge an interest rate of 6 percent, the borrower will pay back $1,060, or 6 percent more than the amount you lent. But is $1,060 received one year from now really 6 percent more than $1,000 today? If prices rise during the year, you will not be able to buy as much with $1,060 one year from now as you could with that amount today. Your true return from lending the $1,000 is equal to the percentage change in your purchasing power after taking into account the effects of inflation.

Nominal interest rate The stated interest rate on a loan.

Real interest rate The nominal interest rate minus the inflation rate.

The stated interest rate on a loan is the **nominal interest rate**. The **real interest rate** corrects the nominal interest rate for the effect of inflation on purchasing power. As a simple example, suppose that the only good you purchase is DVDs, and at the beginning of the year the price of DVDs is $10.00. With $1,000, you can purchase 100 DVDs. If you lend the $1,000 out for one year at an interest rate of 6 percent, you will receive $1,060 at the end of the year. Suppose the inflation rate during the year is 2 percent, so that the price of DVDs has risen to $10.20 by the end of the year. How has your purchasing power increased as a result of making the loan? At the beginning of the year, your $1,000 could purchase 100 DVDs. At the end of the year, your $1,060 can purchase $1,060/$10.20 = 103.92 DVDs. In other words, you can purchase almost 4 percent more DVDs. So, in this case, the real interest rate you received from lending was a little less than 4 percent (actually, 3.92 percent). For low rates of inflation, a convenient approximation for the real interest rate is:

$$\text{Real interest rate} = \text{Nominal interest rate} - \text{Inflation rate}.$$

We can calculate the real interest rate in our example using this formula as 6 percent − 2 percent = 4 percent, which is close to the actual value of 3.92 percent.

If the inflation rate during the year was 5 percent, the real interest rate would be only 1 percent. Holding the nominal interest rate constant, the higher the inflation rate, the lower the real interest rate. Notice that if the inflation rate turns out to be higher than expected, borrowers pay and lenders receive a lower real interest rate than either of them expected. For example, if both you and the person to whom you lent the $1,000 to expected the inflation rate to be 2 percent, you both expected the real interest rate on the loan to be 4 percent. If the inflation rate turns out actually to be 4 percent, the real interest rate on the loan will be 2 percent: That's bad news for you but good news for your borrower.

For the economy as a whole, we can measure the nominal interest rate as the interest rate on three-month U.S. Treasury bills. U.S. Treasury bills are short-term loans investors make to the federal government. We can use the inflation rate as measured by changes in the CPI to calculate the real interest rate on Treasury bills. Figure 20.8 shows the nominal and real interest rates for the period from 1970 through the beginning of 2015. Notice that when the inflation rate is low, as it has been during most years since the early 1990s, the gap between the nominal and real interest rates is small. When the inflation rate is high, as it was during the mid- to late 1970s, the gap between the nominal and real interest rates becomes large. In fact, a particular nominal interest rate can be associated in different periods with very different real interest rates. For example, during late 1975, the nominal interest rate was about 5.5 percent, but because the inflation rate was 7 percent, the real interest rate was −1.5 percent. In early 1987, the nominal interest rate was also 5.5 percent, but because the inflation rate was only 2 percent, the real interest rate was 3.5 percent.

This example shows that it is impossible to know whether a particular nominal interest rate is "high" or "low." It all depends on the inflation rate. *The real interest rate*

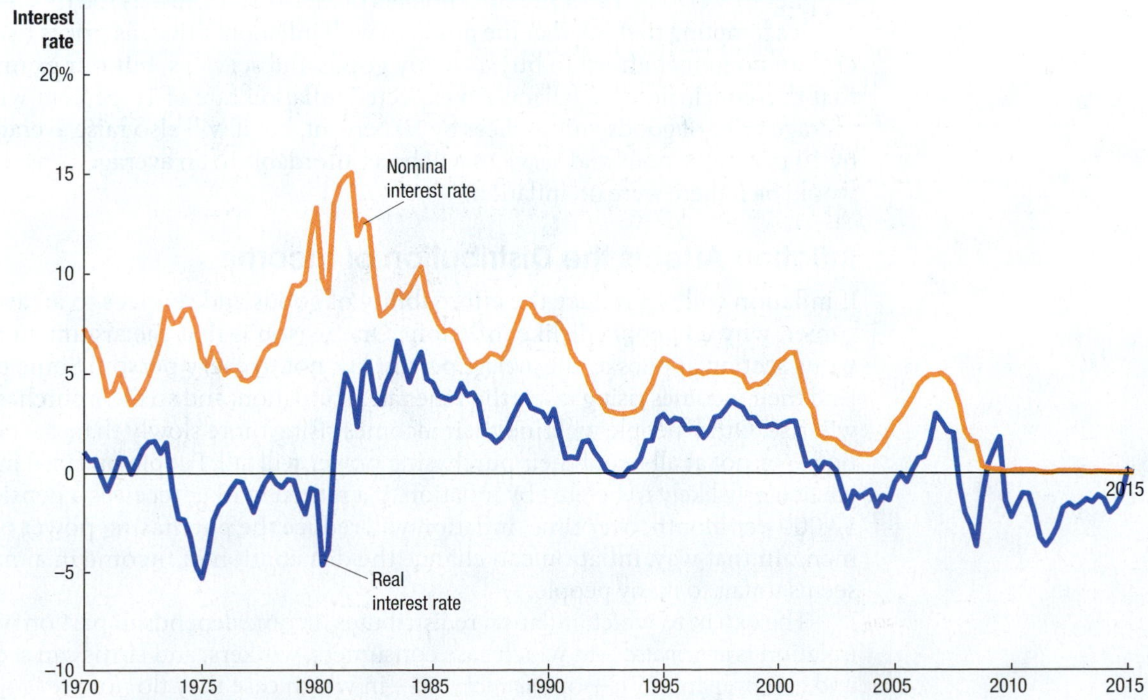

MyEconLab Real-time data

Figure 20.8 Nominal and Real Interest Rates, 1970–2015

The real interest rate is equal to the nominal interest rate minus the inflation rate. The real interest rate provides a better measure of the true cost of borrowing and the true return to lending than does the nominal interest rate. The nominal interest rate in the figure is the interest rate on three-month U.S. Treasury bills. The inflation rate is measured by the percentage change in the CPI from the same quarter during the previous year.

Source: Federal Reserve Bank of St. Louis.

provides a better measure of the true cost of borrowing and the true return from lending than does the nominal interest rate. When firms are deciding whether to borrow the funds to buy an investment good, such as a new factory, they will look at the real interest rate because it measures the true cost to the firm of borrowing.

Deflation A decline in the price level.

Is it possible for the nominal interest rate to be less than the real interest rate? Yes, but only when the inflation rate is negative. A negative inflation rate is referred to as **deflation** and occurs on the rare occasions when the price level falls. During the years shown in Figure 20.8, the inflation rate as measured by changes in the CPI was negative only during the first nine months of 2009 and three months in early 2015. MyEconLab Concept Check

MyEconLab Study Plan

20.7 Does Inflation Impose Costs on the Economy?

LEARNING OBJECTIVE: Discuss the problems that inflation causes.

Imagine waking up tomorrow morning and finding that every price in the economy has doubled. The prices of food, gasoline, clothing, laptops, houses, and haircuts have all doubled. But suppose that all wages and salaries have also doubled. Will this doubling of prices and wages matter? Think about walking into McDonald's, expecting to find a Big Mac selling for $4.50. Instead, you find it selling for $9.00. Will you turn around and walk out? Probably not, because your salary has also increased overnight from $45,000 per year to $90,000 per year. So, the purchasing power of your salary has remained the same, and you are just as likely to buy the Big Mac today as you were yesterday.

This hypothetical situation makes an important point: Nominal incomes generally increase with inflation. Remember that we can think of the $4.50 price of a Big Mac as representing either the value of the product or the value of all the income generated in producing the product (see Chapter 19). The two amounts are the same, whether the Big Mac sells for $4.50 or $9.00. When the price of the Big Mac rises from $4.50 to $9.00, that extra $4.50 ends up as income that goes to the workers at McDonald's, the firms selling supplies to McDonald's, or the stockholders of McDonald's, just as the first $4.50 did.

It's tempting to think that the problem with inflation is that, as prices rise, consumers can no longer afford to buy as many goods and services, but our example shows that this conclusion is a fallacy. An expected inflation rate of 10 percent will raise the average price of goods and services by 10 percent, but it will also raise average incomes by 10 percent. Goods and services will be as affordable to an average consumer as they would be if there were no inflation.

Inflation Affects the Distribution of Income

If inflation will not reduce the affordability of goods and services to an average consumer, why do people dislike inflation? One reason is that the argument in the previous section applies to the *average* person but not to every person. Some people will find their incomes rising faster than the rate of inflation, and so their purchasing power will rise. Other people will find their incomes rising more slowly than the rate of inflation—or not at all—and their purchasing power will fall. People on fixed incomes are particularly likely to be hurt by inflation. If a retired worker receives a pension fixed at $3,000 per month, over time, inflation will reduce the purchasing power of that payment. In that way, inflation can change the distribution of income in a manner that seems unfair to many people.

The extent to which inflation redistributes income depends in part on whether the inflation is *anticipated*—in which case consumers, workers, and firms can see it coming and can prepare for it—or *unanticipated*—in which case they do not see it coming and do not prepare for it. MyEconLab Concept Check

The Problem with Anticipated Inflation

Like many of life's problems, inflation is easier to manage if you see it coming. Suppose that everyone knows that the inflation rate for the next 10 years will be 10 percent per year. Workers know that unless their wages go up by at least 10 percent per year, the real purchasing power of their wages will fall. Businesses will be willing to increase workers' wages enough to compensate for inflation because they know that the prices of the products they sell will increase. Lenders will realize that the loans they make will be paid back with dollars that are losing 10 percent of their value each year, so they will charge higher interest rates to compensate. Borrowers will be willing to pay the higher interest rates because they also know they are paying back these loans with dollars that are losing value. So far, there don't seem to be costs to anticipated inflation.

Even when inflation is perfectly anticipated, however, some individuals and firms will experience a cost:

1. Inevitably, there will be a redistribution of income, as some people's incomes fall behind even an anticipated level of inflation.
2. Firms and consumers have to hold some paper money to facilitate their buying and selling. Anyone holding paper money will find its purchasing power decreasing each year by the rate of inflation. To avoid this cost, workers and firms will try to hold as little paper money as possible, but they will have to hold some.
3. Firms that have catalogs listing the prices of their products will have to update them more frequently. Supermarkets and other stores that mark prices on packages or on store shelves will have to devote more time and labor to changing the marked prices. The costs to firms of changing prices are called **menu costs**. At moderate rates of anticipated inflation, menu costs are relatively small, but at high rates of inflation, such as those experienced in some developing countries, menu costs can become substantial.
4. Taxes paid by investors will increase because investors are taxed on the nominal payments they receive from owning stocks and bonds or from making loans, rather than on the real payments—the nominal payments corrected for inflation. Because investors are interested in the real, after-tax return they receive when investing in firms, the higher taxes that investors pay as a result of inflation mean that firms must pay more for the funds they need to expand. MyEconLab Concept Check

Menu costs The costs to firms of changing prices.

The Problem with Unanticipated Inflation

In any high-income economy—such as the United States—households, workers, and firms routinely enter into contracts that commit them to make or receive certain payments for years in the future. For example, when firms sign wage contracts, they commit to paying a specified wage for the duration of the contract. When people buy homes, they usually borrow most of the amount they need from banks. These loans, called *mortgage loans*, commit a borrower to make a fixed monthly payment for the length of the loan. Most mortgage loans are for long periods, often as long as 30 years.

To make these long-term commitments, households, workers, and firms must forecast the rate of inflation. If a firm believes the inflation rate over the next three years will be 6 percent per year, signing a three-year contract with a union that calls for wage increases of 8 percent per year may seem reasonable because the firm may be able to raise its prices by at least the rate of inflation each year. If the firm believes that the inflation rate will be only 2 percent over the next three years, paying wage increases of 8 percent may significantly reduce its profit or even force it out of business.

When people borrow money or a bank like JPMorgan Chase lends money, they must forecast the inflation rate so they can calculate the real rate of interest on a loan. In 1980, banks were charging interest rates of 18 percent or more on mortgage loans. This rate seems very high compared to the less than 5 percent charged on such loans in 2015, but the inflation rate in 1980 was more than 13 percent and was expected to remain high. In fact, the inflation rate *declined* unexpectedly, and by 1983 it was only about 3 percent. People who borrowed money for 30 years at the high interest rates of 1980 soon found that the real interest rate on their loans was much higher than they had expected.

When the actual inflation rate turns out to be very different from the expected inflation rate, some people gain, and other people lose. This outcome seems unfair to most people because they are either winning or losing only because something unanticipated has happened. This apparently unfair redistribution is a key reason people dislike unanticipated inflation. MyEconLab Concept Check

Making the Connection
MyEconLab Video

What's So Bad about Falling Prices?

We have just discussed how inflation being higher than expected can cause problems for consumers, workers, and firms. But what if an economy begins to experience falling prices—*deflation*, rather than inflation? A falling price level might seem like good news for the economy. After all, falling prices should encourage consumers to increase their spending as goods and services become less expensive. In fact, though, deflation tends to have the opposite effect on consumers. Episodes of deflation are relatively rare, but we can draw some lessons from two important deflationary episodes: the United States during the 1930s and Japan during the 1990s. In both cases, many consumers reduced their spending in the face of falling prices, apparently because they were waiting for prices to go even lower. Waiting for prices to fall even lower was also a problem for the U.S. housing market in the late 2000s. A large run-up in housing prices took place from 2002 to 2006. When prices began to decline, many potential buyers postponed purchases in the expectation that prices would continue to fall.

The following figure shows changes in the CPI in the United States during the years between 1925 and 1940. The beginning of the Great Depression in 1929 caused the country to experience severe deflation.

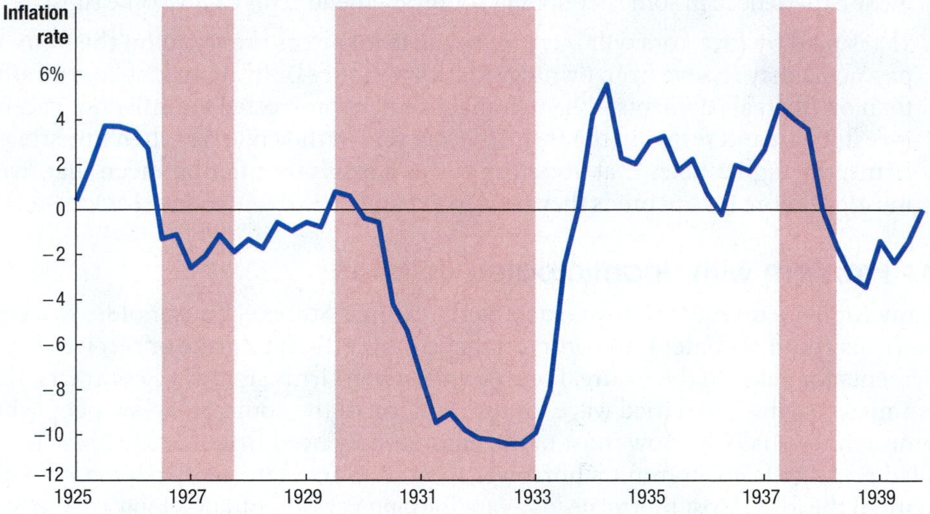

The deflation of the 1930s hurt the U.S. economy not just because it may have led some consumers to postpone purchases but also because it increased the burden on borrowers. Suppose that in 1929 you had borrowed money for five years at a nominal interest rate of 5 percent. What real interest rate would you have paid during those years? We have seen that to calculate the real interest rate, we need to subtract the inflation rate from the nominal interest rate. With deflation, the change in the price level is negative, so to calculate the real interest rate, we are in effect *adding* the change in the price level to the nominal interest rate. The following table uses the actual deflation rate in each year to calculate the resulting real interest rates on your loan:

	1929	1930	1931	1932	1933
Nominal interest rate	5%	5%	5%	5%	5%
Change in the consumer price index	0	−2.3	−9.0	−9.9	−5.1
Real interest rate	5.0	7.3	14.0	14.9	10.1

The bottom row of the table shows that although the nominal interest rate on your loan is only 5 percent, in three of the five years the real interest rate you pay is greater than 10 percent. In fact, high real interest rates inflicted serious losses on both household and business borrowers during the early 1930s and contributed to the severity of the Great Depression.

During the 2001 and 2007–2009 recessions, some policymakers and economists feared that the U.S. economy would experience deflation. Fortunately, significant deflation did not occur. If it had, those recessions would likely have been more severe than they were.

MyEconLab Concept Check

Your Turn: Test your understanding by doing related problems 7.9 and 7.10 on page 690 at the end of this chapter.

MyEconLab Study Plan

Continued from page 657

Economics in Your Life

Should You Change Your Career Plans if You Graduate during a Recession?

At the beginning of this chapter, we asked whether layoffs in the banking industry should cause you to change your major and give up your plans to pursue a career in banking. We have seen in this chapter that unemployment rates are higher and layoffs are more common in a recession than in an economic expansion. Because you are a sophomore, you will graduate a few years later, when the recession will likely have ended and the unemployment rate will have declined. You might also want to investigate whether the layoffs in the banking industry represent a permanent contraction in the size of the industry or a temporary decline caused by the recession. If the reduction of banking jobs is more likely to be permanent, then you might consider a career in another industry. If the layoffs appear to be related to the current recession, then you probably do not need to change your career plans.

Conclusion

Inflation and unemployment are key macroeconomic problems. Presidential elections are often won and lost on the basis of which candidate is able to convince the public that he or she can best deal with these problems. Many economists, however, would argue that, in the long run, maintaining high rates of growth of real GDP per person is the most important macroeconomic concern. Only when real GDP per person is increasing will a country's standard of living increase. In the next chapter, we look more closely at the important topic of economic growth.

Visit MyEconLab for a news article and analysis related to the concepts in this chapter.

CHAPTER SUMMARY AND PROBLEMS

Key Terms

Consumer price index (CPI), p. 673	Employed, p. 658	Menu costs, p. 681	Real interest rate, p. 678
Cyclical unemployment, p. 669	Frictional unemployment, p. 668	Natural rate of unemployment, p. 669	Structural unemployment, p. 669
Deflation, p. 680	Inflation rate, p. 673	Nominal interest rate, p. 678	Unemployed, p. 658
Discouraged workers, p. 659	Labor force, p. 658	Price level, p. 673	Unemployment rate, p. 658
Efficiency wage, p. 672	Labor force participation rate, p. 660	Producer price index (PPI), p. 676	

20.1 Measuring the Unemployment Rate, the Labor Force Participation Rate, and the Employment–Population Ratio, pages 658–667

LEARNING OBJECTIVE: Define the unemployment rate, the labor force participation rate, and the employment-population ratio and understand how they are computed.

Summary

The U.S. Bureau of Labor Statistics uses the results of the monthly household survey to calculate the *unemployment rate*, the *labor force participation rate*, and the *employment–population ratio*. The **labor force** is the total number of people who have jobs (the **employed**) plus the number of people who do not have jobs but are actively looking for them (the **unemployed**). The **unemployment rate** is the percentage of the labor force that is unemployed. **Discouraged workers** are people who are available for work but who are not actively looking for a job because they believe no jobs are available for them. Discouraged workers are not counted as unemployed. The **labor force participation rate** is the percentage of the working-age population in the labor force. Since 1950, the labor force participation rate of women has been rising, while the labor force participation rate of men has been falling. The employment–population ratio measures the percentage of the working-age population that is employed. Asians, whites, and college graduates have below-average unemployment rates. African Americans, Hispanics, and high school dropouts have above-average unemployment rates. Except during severe recessions, a typical unemployed person finds a new job or returns to his or her previous job within a few months. Each year, millions of jobs are created in the United States, and millions of jobs are destroyed.

MyEconLab Visit **www.myeconlab.com** to complete these exercises online and get instant feedback.

Review Questions

1.1 How is the unemployment rate measured? What are the three conditions someone needs to meet to be counted as unemployed?

1.2 What are the problems in measuring the unemployment rate? In what ways does the official BLS measure of the unemployment rate *understate* the true degree of unemployment? In what ways does the official BLS measure *overstate* the true degree of unemployment?

1.3 Which groups tend to have above-average unemployment rates, and which groups tend to have below-average unemployment rates?

1.4 What does the labor force participation rate measure? Since 1950, how have the labor force participation rates of men and women changed?

1.5 What does the employment–population ratio measure? How does an unemployed person dropping out of the labor force affect the unemployment rate? How does it affect the employment–population ratio?

1.6 What is the difference between the household survey and the establishment survey? Which survey do many economists prefer for measuring changes in employment? Why?

Problems and Applications

1.7 Fill in the blank cells in the following table of data collected in the household survey for June 2015:

Working-age population	
Employment	148,739,000
Unemployment	
Unemployment rate	5.3%
Labor force	
Labor force participation rate	62.6%
Employment–population ratio	

1.8 **(Related to Solved Problem 20.1 on page 660)** Homemakers are not included in the employment or labor force totals compiled in the BLS household survey. They are included in the working-age population totals. Suppose that homemakers were counted as employed and included in labor force statistics. How would that change affect the unemployment rate, the labor force participation rate, and the employment–population ratio?

1.9 In June 2015, the unemployment rate declined to 5.3 percent from 5.5 percent in May. The labor force participation rate also declined from May to June, from 62.9 percent to 62.6 percent. If the labor force participation rate had remained unchanged from May to June, would the unemployment rate for June have been lower than, higher than, or equal to 5.3 percent? Briefly explain.

1.10 **(Related to the Making the Connection on page 664)** In discussing the labor market during the recovery from the 2007–2009 recession, Federal Reserve Chair Janet Yellen noted that "the employment-to-population ratio has increased far less over the past several years than the unemployment rate alone would indicate, based on past experience."

a. During an economic expansion, why would we normally expect the employment–population ratio to increase as the unemployment rate falls?

b. Why didn't the employment–population ratio increase as much as might have been expected during the recovery from the 2007–2009 recession?

Source: Janet L. Yellen, "Labor Market Dynamics and Monetary Policy," Speech at the Federal Reserve Bank of Kansas City Economic Symposium, Jackson Hole, Wyoming, August 22, 2014.

1.11 In early 2015, the employment–population ratio was increasing while the labor force participation rate remained largely unchanged. Shouldn't both of these data series move in the same direction? Briefly explain how it is possible that they didn't.

1.12 An article in the *Wall Street Journal* contained the following observation: "Every month, millions of workers leave the job market because of retirement, to care for children or aging parents, to pursue more education, or out of discouragement. Millions of others jump in after graduating."

a. Are the millions of workers leaving the job market for the reasons given counted as unemployed in the BLS data? Briefly explain.

b. Will the BLS count people entering the job market after graduating from high school or college as part of the labor force even if they don't find a job right away? Briefly explain.

Source: Josh Zumbrun, "Labor-Market Dropouts Stay on the Sidelines," *Wall Street Journal*, December 28, 2014.

1.13 An article in the *Wall Street Journal* noted that over a four-month period in late 2014, employment in the state of Georgia "rose 1% even as the state's jobless rate climbed 1.2 percentage points." Briefly explain how the state's unemployment rate could have increased at the same time that employment in the state was increasing.

Source: Cameron McWhirter and Ben Leubsdorf, "Rising Jobless Rates Are a Southern Mystery," *Wall Street Journal*, October 5, 2014.

1.14 In his 2015 State of the Union address, President Barack Obama observed that "over the past five years, our businesses have created more than 11 million new jobs." Is it likely that the U.S. economy created only 11 million jobs during this time period? If not, what was President Obama referring to?

Source: Barack Obama, "Remarks by the President in State of the Union Address," whitehouse.gov, January 20, 2015.

20.2 Types of Unemployment, pages 667–670

LEARNING OBJECTIVE: Identify the three types of unemployment.

Summary

There are three types of unemployment: frictional, structural, and cyclical. **Frictional unemployment** is short-term unemployment that arises from the process of matching workers with jobs. One type of frictional unemployment is *seasonal unemployment*, which refers to unemployment due to factors such as weather, variations in tourism, and other calendar-related events. **Structural unemployment** arises from a persistent mismatch between the job skills or attributes of workers and the requirements of jobs. **Cyclical unemployment** is caused by a business cycle recession. The **natural rate of unemployment** is the normal rate of unemployment, consisting of structural unemployment and frictional unemployment. The natural rate of unemployment is also sometimes called the *full-employment rate of unemployment*.

MyEconLab Visit **www.myeconlab.com** to complete these exercises online and get instant feedback.

Review Questions

2.1 What are the three types of unemployment? Which type of unemployment do you consider most likely to result in hardship for people who are unemployed? Briefly explain.

2.2 What is the relationship between frictional unemployment and job search?

2.3 What is the natural rate of unemployment? What is the relationship between the natural rate of unemployment and full employment?

Problems and Applications

2.4 **(Related to the Chapter Opener on page 657)** Ford Motor Company employed fewer people in 2015 than it did in 1980. Is this decline in employment frictional, structural, cyclical, or some combination of these factors? What information would you need to arrive at a definite answer?

2.5 A politician makes the following argument: "The economy would operate more efficiently if frictional unemployment were eliminated. Therefore, a goal of government policy should be to reduce the frictional rate of unemployment to the lowest possible level." Briefly explain whether you agree with this argument.

2.6 **(Related to the Making the Connection on page 669)** What advice for finding a job would you give someone who is frictionally unemployed? What advice would you give someone who is structurally unemployed? What advice would you give someone who is cyclically unemployed?

2.7 (Related to the Making the Connection on page 669) The BLS estimated that there were 2.7 million job "quits" in May 2015. The BLS defines a job quit as a "voluntary separation initiated by an employee."

a. Economists distinguish three types of unemployment: frictional, structural, and cyclical. How would you classify unemployment caused by an increase in job quits?
b. Would an increase in the number of job quits suggest that it was becoming easier or more difficult for people to find jobs? Briefly explain.

Source: Bureau of Labor Statistics, "Job Openings and Labor Turnover Survey," July 7, 2015.

2.8 (Related to the Making the Connection on page 669) The headline on an article in the *New York Times* was "Unemployed in Europe Stymied by Lack of Technology Skills." Are these workers likely to be cyclically, frictionally, or structurally unemployed? Briefly explain.

Source: Liz Alderman, "Unemployed in Europe Stymied by Lack of Technology Skills," *New York Times*, January 3, 2014.

20.3 Explaining Unemployment, pages 670–672

LEARNING OBJECTIVE: Explain what factors determine the unemployment rate.

Summary

Government policies can reduce the level of frictional and structural unemployment by aiding the search for jobs and the retraining of workers. Some government policies, however, can add to the level of frictional and structural unemployment. Unemployment insurance payments can raise the unemployment rate by extending the time that unemployed workers search for jobs. Government policies have caused the unemployment rates in most other high-income countries typically to be higher than in the United States. Wages above market levels can also increase unemployment. Wages may be above market levels because of the minimum wage, labor unions, and *efficiency wages*. An **efficiency wage** is a higher-than-market wage that a firm pays to increase workers' productivity.

MyEconLab Visit **www.myeconlab.com** to complete these exercises online and get instant feedback.

Review Questions

3.1 What effect does the payment of government unemployment insurance have on the unemployment rate? On the severity of recessions?

3.2 Discuss the effect of each of the following on the unemployment rate.

a. The federal minimum wage law
b. Labor unions
c. Efficiency wages

3.3 Why has the unemployment rate in the United States typically been lower than the unemployment rates in Canada and the countries in Western Europe?

Problems and Applications

3.4 When Ségolène Royal was running unsuccessfully for president of France, she proposed that workers who lost their jobs would receive unemployment payments equal to 90 percent of their previous wages during their first year of unemployment. If this proposal had been enacted, what would the effect likely have been on the unemployment rate in France? Briefly explain.

Source: Alessandra Galloni and David Gauthier-Villars, "France's Royal Introduces Platform Ahead of Election," *Wall Street Journal*, February 12, 2007.

3.5 Jared Bernstein, an economist at the Center on Budget and Policy Priorities, has stated: "I want to see receipt of unemployment insurance … go up in recessions." If government unemployment insurance payments didn't go up, he explains, it "would be a sign that something's very wrong." What would be very wrong about government unemployment insurance payments failing to rise during a recession? What would be the consequences for the unemployed and for the economy?

Source: Jared Bernstein, "Lessons of the Great Recession: How the Safety Net Performed," *New York Times*, June 24, 2013.

3.6 Discuss the likely effect of each of the following on the unemployment rate.

a. The length of time workers are eligible to receive unemployment insurance payments doubles.
b. The minimum wage is abolished.
c. Most U.S. workers join labor unions.
d. More companies make information about job openings easily available on Internet job sites.

3.7 In 1914, Henry Ford increased the wage he paid workers in his car factory in Dearborn, Michigan, to $5 per day. This wage was more than twice as much as other car manufacturers were paying. Ford was quoted as saying, "The payment of five dollars a day for an eight-hour day was one of the finest cost-cutting moves we ever made." How can paying an above-market wage result in a firm cutting its costs?

3.8 In 2015, an article on bloomberg.com noted that Walmart, Starbucks, TJ Maxx, IKEA, Gap, and several other big retailers had announced increases in the wages they were paying newly hired workers. The same article also noted that "[labor] turnover in the retail sector has been steadily rising and now stands at 5 percent a month."

a. What do the authors mean by labor turnover?
b. Is it likely that the increase in labor turnover is connected to the increases in entry-level wages being paid by large retailers? Briefly explain.

Source: Kyle Stock and Kim Bhasin, "Why Retailers Are Suddenly Desperate to Keep Their Least-Valuable Workers," bloomberg.com, March 6, 2015.

20.4 Measuring Inflation, pages 672–676

LEARNING OBJECTIVE: Define the price level and the inflation rate and understand how they are computed.

Summary

The **price level** measures the average prices of goods and services. The **inflation rate** is equal to the percentage change in the price level from one year to the next. The federal government compiles statistics on three different measures of the price level: the consumer price index, the GDP price deflator, and the producer price index. The **consumer price index (CPI)** is a measure of the average change over time in the prices a typical urban family of four pays for the goods and services they purchase. Changes in the CPI are the best measure of changes in the cost of living as experienced by a typical household. Biases in the construction of the CPI cause changes in it to overstate the true inflation rate by 0.5 percentage point to 1 percentage point. The **producer price index (PPI)** is an average of prices received by producers of goods and services at all stages of production.

MyEconLab Visit **www.myeconlab.com** to complete these exercises online and get instant feedback.

Review Questions

4.1 Briefly describe the three major measures of the price level.

4.2 Which price index does the government use to measure changes in the cost of living?

4.3 What potential biases exist in calculating the CPI? What steps has the Bureau of Labor Statistics taken to reduce the size of the biases?

4.4 What is the difference between the CPI and the PPI?

Problems and Applications

4.5 **(Related to the Don't Let This Happen to You on page 675)** Briefly explain whether you agree with the following statement: "I don't believe the government price statistics. The CPI for 2014 was 237, but I know that the inflation rate couldn't have been as high as 137 percent in 2014."

4.6 **(Related to the Don't Let This Happen to You on page 675)** An article in the *Wall Street Journal* asks the question "How can inflation be low when everything is so expensive?" The article also notes that "the CPI shows that prices are the highest they've ever been." Is there a contradiction between a low inflation rate as measured by the CPI and the observations that prices are "the highest they've ever been" and everything is "so expensive"? Briefly explain.

Source: Josh Zumbrun, "5 Things You Always Wanted to Know about Inflation Statistics," *Wall Street Journal*, May 15, 2014.

4.7 Consider a simple economy that produces only three products: haircuts, hamburgers, and Blu-rays. Use the information in the following table to calculate the inflation rate for 2016, as measured by the CPI.

	Base Year (1999)		2015	2016
Product	Quantity	Price	Price	Price
Haircuts	2	$10.00	$11.00	$16.20
Hamburgers	10	2.00	2.45	2.40
Blu-rays	6	15.00	15.00	14.00

4.8 The Standard & Poor's/Case-Shiller Home Price Index is one of the leading indicators of housing price trends in the United States. The base year for the index is January 2000. The following table lists index numbers for April 2014 and April 2015 for five cities.

City	April 2014	April 2015
New York	174.5	179.3
Miami	183.2	198.5
Phoenix	145.4	150.4
Dallas	136.8	148.8
San Francisco	192.5	211.5

a. In which of these five cities did housing prices increase the fastest from April 2014 to April 2015? In which did they increase the slowest? Briefly explain the basis for your answers.

b. Can you determine from these numbers which city had the highest house prices in April 2015? Briefly explain.

Source: "House Price Indices," Federal Reserve Bank of St. Louis (FRED), research.stlouisfed.org/fred2/.

4.9 Suppose the CPI of a country follows the path shown in the following figure.

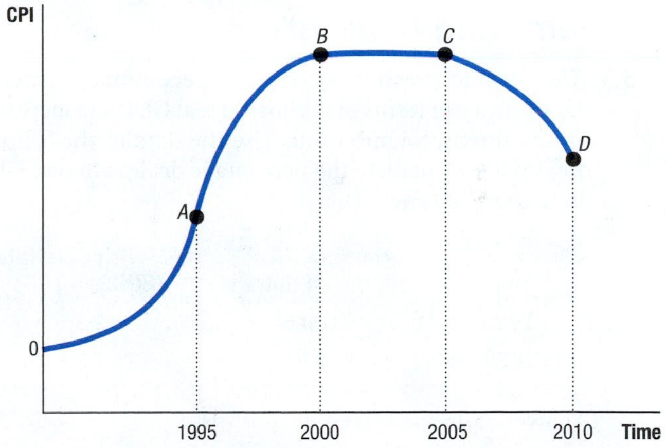

a. During which period did the country experience zero inflation?

b. During which period did the country experience an increasing rate of inflation?

c. During which period did the country experience a slowdown in inflation, although the inflation rate remained positive? (This situation is called "disinflation.")

d. During which period did the country experience deflation?

4.10 An article in the *Wall Street Journal* notes that the BLS has changed the methods it uses to calculate the CPI with the result that the measured inflation rate is lower than it would have been if the BLS had still used the old methods. The article notes, "But this is not a massive conspiracy to hide runaway inflation." What was the BLS's motivation in changing its methods of calculating the CPI?

Source: Josh Zumbrun, "5 Things You Always Wanted to Know about Inflation Statistics," *Wall Street Journal*, May 15, 2014.

4.11 In the fall of 2015, Apple introduced a new model of its iPhone. The new model had a faster processor and a better camera than the previous model but sold for the same price. How was the CPI affected by the introduction of the new model of the iPhone?

20.5 Using Price Indexes to Adjust for the Effects of Inflation, pages 676–678

LEARNING OBJECTIVE: Use price indexes to adjust for the effects of inflation.

Summary

Price indexes are designed to measure changes in the price level over time, not the absolute level of prices. To correct for the effects of inflation, we can divide a *nominal variable* by a price index and multiply by 100 to obtain a *real variable*. The real variable will be measured in dollars of the base year for the price index.

MyEconLab Visit **www.myeconlab.com** to complete these exercises online and get instant feedback.

Review Questions

5.1 What is the difference between a nominal variable and a real variable?

5.2 During a period of deflation, which is likely to increase faster: nominal average hourly earnings or real average hourly earnings? Briefly explain.

Problems and Applications

5.3 The Great Depression was the worst economic disaster in U.S. history in terms of declines in real GDP and increases in the unemployment rate. Use the data in the following table to calculate the percentage decline in real GDP between 1929 and 1933:

Year	Nominal GDP (billions of dollars)	GDP Price Deflator (2009 = 100)
1929	$104.6	9.9
1933	57.2	7.3

Source: U.S. Bureau of Economic Analysis.

5.4 **(Related to Solved Problem 20.5 on page 677)** In 1924, the famous novelist F. Scott Fitzgerald wrote an article for the *Saturday Evening Post* titled "How to Live on $36,000 a Year," in which he wondered how he and his wife had managed to spend all of that very high income without saving any of it. The CPI in 1924 was 17, and the CPI in 2014 was 237. What income would you have needed in 2014 to have had the same purchasing power that Fitzgerald's $36,000 had in 1924? Be sure to show your calculation.

Source: F. Scott Fitzgerald, "How to Live on $36,000 a Year," *Saturday Evening Post*, April 5, 1924.

5.5 **(Related to Solved Problem 20.5 on page 677)** Use the information in the following table to determine the percentage changes in the U.S. and French *real* minimum wages between 1957 and 2014. Does it matter for your answer that you have not been told the base year for the U.S. CPI or the French CPI? Was the percentage increase in the price level greater in the United States or in France during these years?

	United States		France	
Year	Minimum Wage (dollars per hour)	CPI	Minimum Wage (euros per hour)	CPI
1957	$1.00	27	€0.19	8
2014	7.25	237	9.61	106

Sources: John M. Abowd, Francis Kramarz, Thomas Lemieux, and David N. Margolis, "Minimum Wages and Youth Employment in France and the United States," in D. Blanchflower and R. Freeman, eds., *Youth Employment and Joblessness in Advanced Countries*, Chicago: University of Chicago Press, 1999, pp. 427–472 (the value for the minimum wage is given in francs; it was converted to euros at a conversion rate of 1 euro = 6.55957 francs); Insee online data bank, www.insee.fr; U.S. Department of Labor; and U.S. Bureau of Labor Statistics.

5.6 **(Related to Solved Problem 20.5 on page 677)** In an article in the *Wall Street Journal*, a professor of financial planning noted the effect of rising prices on purchasing power: "Today, $2,000 a month seems reasonable [as an income for a retired person in addition to the person's Social Security payments], but 40 years from now that's going to be three cups of coffee and a donut." Suppose that currently three cups of coffee and a donut can be purchased for $10. The CPI in 2014 was 237. What would the CPI have to be in 2054 for $2,000 to be able to purchase only three cups of coffee and a donut? Assume that the prices of coffee and donuts increase at the same rate as the CPI during these 40 years.

Source: Matthias Rieker, "Rising Use of Immediate Annuities Raises Some Concerns," *Wall Street Journal*, December 4, 2014.

5.7 **(Related to Solved Problem 20.5 on page 677)** The table on the next page shows the top 10 films of all time through July 2015, measured by box office receipts in the United States, as well as several other notable films farther down the list.

The CPI in 2015 was 238. Use this information and the data in the table to calculate the box office receipts for each film in 2015 dollars. Assume that each film generated all of its box office receipts during the year it was released. Use your results to prepare a new list of the top 10 films, based on their earnings in 2015 dollars. (Some of the films, such as the first *Star Wars* film, *Gone with the Wind*, and *Snow White and the Seven Dwarfs*, were re-released to theaters several times, so their receipts were actually earned during several different years, but we will ignore that complication.)

Source: boxofficemojo.com and the U.S. Bureau of Labor Statistics.

Rank	Film	Total Box Office Receipts	Year Released	CPI
1	*Avatar*	$760,507,625	2009	215
2	*Titanic*	658,672,302	1997	161
3	*Jurassic World*	628,700,000	2015	238
4	*Marvel's The Avengers*	623,357,910	2012	230
5	*The Dark Knight*	534,858,444	2008	215
6	*Star Wars: Episode I—The Phantom Menace*	474,544,677	1999	167
7	*Star Wars*	460,998,007	1977	61
8	*Avengers: Age of Ultron*	456,774,004	2015	238
9	*The Dark Knight Rises*	448,139,099	2012	230
10	*Shrek 2*	441,226,247	2004	189
11	*ET: The Extra-Terrestrial*	435,110,554	1982	97
79	*Jaws*	260,000,000	1975	54
161	*Gone with the Wind*	198,676,459	1939	14
183	*Snow White and the Seven Dwarfs*	184,925,486	1937	14
257	*The Sound of Music*	158,671,368	1965	32
303	*101 Dalmatians*	144,880,014	1961	30

20.6 Nominal Interest Rates versus Real Interest Rates, pages 678–680

LEARNING OBJECTIVE: Distinguish between the nominal interest rate and the real interest rate.

Summary

The stated interest rate on a loan is the **nominal interest rate.** The **real interest rate** is the nominal interest rate minus the inflation rate. Because it is corrected for the effects of inflation, the real interest rate provides a better measure of the true cost of borrowing and the true return from lending than does the nominal interest rate. The nominal interest rate is always greater than the real interest rate unless the economy experiences **deflation**, which is a decline in the price level.

MyEconLab Visit **www.myeconlab.com** to complete these exercises online and get instant feedback.

Review Questions

6.1 What is the difference between the nominal interest rate and the real interest rate?

6.2 If inflation is expected to increase, what will happen to the nominal interest rate? Briefly explain.

6.3 The chapter states that it is impossible to know whether a particular nominal interest rate is "high" or "low." Briefly explain why.

6.4 If the economy is experiencing deflation, will the nominal interest rate be higher or lower than the real interest rate?

Problems and Applications

6.5 The following appeared in a news article: "Inflation in the Lehigh Valley during the first quarter of ... [the year] was less than half the national rate. ... So, unlike much of the nation, the fear here is deflation—when prices sink so low the CPI drops below zero." Do you agree with the reporter's definition of deflation? Briefly explain.

Source: Dan Shope, "Valley's Inflation Rate Slides," (Allentown, PA) *Morning Call*, July 9, 1996.

6.6 Suppose you were borrowing money to buy a car.

a. Which of these situations would you prefer: The interest rate on your car loan is 20 percent and the inflation rate is 19 percent, or the interest rate on your car loan is 5 percent and the inflation rate is 2 percent? Briefly explain.

b. Now suppose you are JPMorgan Chase, and you are making car loans. Which situation in part (a) would you now prefer? Briefly explain.

6.7 In June 2014, the nominal interest rate on a one-year Treasury bill was 0.10 percent. From June 2014 to June 2015, the consumer price index rose from 237.3 to 237.8. If you bought the one-year Treasury bill in May 2014, calculate the real interest rate you earned over the following 12-month period. Given the results of your calculation, why were investors willing to buy Treasury bills in May 2014?

6.8 Describing the situation in England in 1920, the historian Robert Skidelsky wrote the following: "Who would not borrow at 4 percent a year, with prices going up 4 percent a *month*?" What was the real interest rate paid by borrowers in this situation? (*Hint:* What is the annual inflation rate, if the monthly inflation rate is 4 percent?)

Source: Robert Skidelsky, *John Maynard Keynes: Volume 2, The Economist as Saviour 1920–1937*, New York: The Penguin Press, 1992, p. 39.

6.9 Suppose that the only good you purchase is hamburgers, and that at the beginning of the year, the price of a hamburger is \$2.00. Suppose you lend \$1,000 for one year at an interest rate of 5 percent. At the end of the year, a hamburger costs \$2.08. What is the real rate of interest you earned on your loan?

20.7 Does Inflation Impose Costs on the Economy? pages 680–683

LEARNING OBJECTIVE: Discuss the problems that inflation causes.

Summary

Inflation does not reduce the affordability of goods and services to an average consumer, but it does impose costs on the economy. When inflation is anticipated, its main costs are that paper money loses some of its value and firms incur *menu costs*. **Menu costs** include the costs of changing prices on products and updating catalogs. When inflation is unanticipated, the actual inflation rate can turn out to be different from the expected inflation rate. As a result, income is redistributed as some people gain and some people lose.

MyEconLab Visit **www.myeconlab.com** to complete these exercises online and get instant feedback.

Review Questions

7.1 Why do nominal incomes generally increase with inflation? If nominal incomes increase with inflation, does inflation reduce the purchasing power of an average consumer? Briefly explain.

7.2 How can inflation affect the distribution of income?

7.3 Which is a greater problem: anticipated inflation or unanticipated inflation? Briefly explain.

7.4 What are menu costs? What effect has the Internet had on the size of menu costs?

7.5 What problems does deflation cause?

Problems and Applications

7.6 Suppose that the inflation rate turns out to be much higher than most people expected. In that case, would you rather have been a borrower or a lender? Briefly explain.

7.7 Suppose James and Frank both retire this year. For income during retirement, James will rely on a pension from his company that pays him a fixed $2,500 per month for as long as he lives. James hasn't saved anything for retirement. Frank has no pension but has saved a considerable amount, which he has invested in certificates of deposit (CDs) at his bank. Currently, Frank's CDs pay him interest of $2,300 per month.

a. Ten years from now, is James or Frank likely to have a higher real income? In your answer, be sure to define *real income*.

b. Now suppose that instead of being a constant amount, James's pension increases each year by the same percentage as the CPI. For example, if the CPI increases by 5 percent in the first year after James retires, then his pension in the second year equals $2,500 + ($2,500 × 0.05) = $2,625. In this case, 10 years from now, is James or Frank likely to have a higher real income?

7.8 Suppose that Apple and the investors buying the firm's bonds both expect a 2 percent inflation rate for the year. Given this expectation, suppose the nominal interest rate on the bonds is 6 percent and the real interest rate is 4 percent. Suppose that a year after the investors purchase the bonds, the inflation rate turns out to be 6 percent, rather than the 2 percent that had been expected. Who gains and who loses from the unexpectedly high inflation rate?

7.9 **(Related to the Making the Connection on page 682)** During the spring of 2015, the United Kingdom experienced a brief period of deflation. According to an article in the *Wall Street Journal*, "The U.K.'s history of sticky and hard-to-control inflation suggests that a short period of falling prices will be taken as a reprieve for consumers, not as a signal to defer purchases." Why might consumers see deflation as a "signal to defer purchases"? Shouldn't lower prices cause consumers to buy more, not less? Briefly explain.

Source: Richard Barley, "U.K. Deflation More Curiosity Than Concern," *Wall Street Journal*, May 19, 2015.

7.10 **(Related to the Making the Connection on page 682)** During the late nineteenth century in the United States, many farmers borrowed heavily to buy land. During most of the period between 1870 and the mid-1890s, the United States experienced mild deflation: The price level declined each year. Many farmers engaged in political protests during these years, and deflation was often a subject of their protests. Explain why farmers would have felt burdened by deflation.

Real-Time Data Exercises

D20.1 **(Using the CPI to measure inflation)** Go to the Web site of the Federal Reserve Bank of St. Louis (FRED) (research.stlouisfed.org/fred2/).

a. Find values for the most recent month and for the same month one year earlier for the Consumer Price Index (CPIAUCSL).

b. Use the values you found in part (a) to calculate the inflation rate for the past year.

D20.2 **(Using CPI data and Excel to calculate the inflation rate)** Go to the Web site of the Federal Reserve Bank of St. Louis (FRED) (research.stlouisfed.org/fred2/).

a. Locate the data for the Consumer Price Index (CPIAUCSL). Click on the "Download Data" link on the left of the page. Change the beginning date to six years prior to the most recent observation. You can leave the ending date as it is. Then click on the "Download Data" button to download the data and save it to your computer. Finally, open the Excel file that you just downloaded. (*Note:* You can also use another compatible spreadsheet program, such as OpenOffice's Calc.)

b. Using Excel, calculate the percentage change in CPI from a year earlier for each observation, beginning with the observation one year later than the first observation. To make this calculation, click on the blank cell next to the observation corresponding to that date and then enter the following formula (note that in Excel, the symbol for multiplication is *):

$$\text{Percentage change} = \left(\frac{CPI_t - CPI_{t-1}}{CPI_{t-1}}\right) \times 100,$$

where $t-1$ is the first observation and t is the observation one year later. Repeat this process for the remaining observations. (You can use the copy and paste functions to avoid having to retype the formula.)

c. Using your calculations from part (b), create a graph of the percentage changes from a year earlier.

d. Use your calculations from part (b) to explain which period experienced the highest inflation rate. What was the inflation rate during that period?

D20.3 (Using CPI data and Excel to calculate an alternative measure of the inflation rate) In addition to the usual CPI, the BLS also calculates a CPI that does not include the prices of food and energy. Because the prices of food and energy tend to fluctuate more than other prices, some economists believe that omitting them provides a better measure of the long-run inflation rate. Go to the Web site of the Federal Reserve Bank of St. Louis (FRED) (research.stlouisfed.org/fred2/).

a. Locate the data for the Consumer Price Index (CPIAUCSL) and the Consumer Price Index less Food and Energy (CPILFESL). Click on the "Download Data" link on the left of the page. Change the beginning date to 2006-07-01. You can leave the ending date as it is. Then click on the "Download Data" button to download the data and save it to your computer. Finally, open the Excel file that you just downloaded. (*Note:* You can also use another compatible spreadsheet program, such as OpenOffice's Calc.)

b. Using Excel, calculate the percentage change in each CPI from a year ago for each of the observations, beginning with the observation 2007-07-01. To make this calculation, click on the blank cell next to the observation corresponding to 2007-07-01, and then enter the following formula (note that in Excel, the symbol for multiplication is *):

$$\text{Percentage change} = \left(\frac{\text{CPI}_t - \text{CPI}_{t-1}}{\text{CPI}_{t-1}}\right) \times 100$$

where $t-1$ = 2007-07-01 and t = 2006-07-01. Repeat this process for the remaining observations. (You can use the copy and paste functions to avoid having to retype the formula.)

c. Using your calculations from part (b), create a graph of the percentage changes from a year ago for both indexes. Make sure both data lines are on the same graph.

d. Discuss differences between the two measures of the inflation rate. For instance, from your calculations, what was the inflation rate in June 2009 using the two CPI measures?

D20.4 (Analyzing inflation in CPI categories) Calculating inflation rates for categories of goods and services in the CPI market basket (see page 673) can provide insight into inflation in different sectors of the economy. Go to the Web site of the Federal Reserve Bank of St. Louis (FRED) (research.stlouisfed.org/fred2/).

a. Find the most recent values and values from the same month in 2010 for the following four categories of the Consumer Price Index: (1) Food and Beverages (CPIFABSL), (2) Apparel (CPIAPPSL), (3) Transportation (CPITRNSL), and (4) Medical Care (CPIMEDSL).

b. Using the data from part (a), calculate the inflation rate over the period from 2010 to the present period for each of the four CPI categories.

c. According to your calculations, which category experienced the least amount of inflation and which category experienced the most inflation?

D20.5 (Analyzing the labor force and unemployment) Go to the Web site of the Federal Reserve Bank of St. Louis (FRED) (research.stlouisfed.org/fred2/).

a. Find the most recent values for these three variables: (1) Unemployed (UNEMPLOY), (2) Civilian Labor Force (CLF16OV), and (3) Employment Level – Part-Time for Economic Reasons, Slack Work or Business Conditions (LNS12032195). Are these data reported annually, quarterly, or monthly? What units are these values reported in?

b. Using the values you found in part (a), calculate the civilian unemployment rate and the civilian unemployment rate including persons who are underemployed (part-time for economic reasons).

D20.6 (Calculating the unemployment rate for different groups) Go to the Web site of the Federal Reserve Bank of St. Louis (FRED) (research.stlouisfed.org/fred2/).

a. Find the most recent values for these four variables: (1) Unemployment Level – Men (LNS13000001), (2) Unemployment Level – Women (LNS13000002), (3) Civilian Labor Force Level – Men (LNS11000001), and (4) Civilian Labor Force Level – Women (LNS11000002). Are these data reported annually, quarterly, or monthly? What units are these values reported in?

b. Using the values you found in part (a), calculate the unemployment rate for men and the unemployment rate for women.

c. Explain why some people are considered discouraged workers. What will happen to the unemployment rate if there is an increase in discouraged workers?

D20.7 (Calculating the employment-population ratio) Go to the Web site of the Federal Reserve Bank of St. Louis (FRED) (research.stlouisfed.org/fred2/).

a. Find the most recent values for these three variables: (1) Unemployed (UNEMPLOY), (2) Civilian Employment (CE16OV), and (3) Not in Labor Force (LNS15000000).

b. Using the values you found in part (a), calculate the working-age population (in thousands) and the employment–population ratio.

c. Holding all other factors constant, what would you expect to happen to the employment–population ratio if the economy entered a recession? Briefly explain.

D20.8 (Calculating the cyclical unemployment rate) Go to the Web site of the Federal Reserve Bank of St. Louis (FRED) (research.stlouisfed.org/fred2/).

a. Find the value for the most recent month and for the same month two years earlier for the Civilian Unemployment Rate (UNRATE) and the Natural Rate of Unemployment (NROU).

b. Using the values you found in part (a), calculate the cyclical rate of unemployment.

c. Given the change in cyclical unemployment over this two-year period, what can you conclude about the state of the economy?

D20.9 (The unemployment rate and the business cycle) Go to the Web site of the Federal Reserve Bank of St. Louis (FRED) (research.stlouisfed.org/fred2/).

a. Find the most recent values for these three variables: (1) Unemployed (UNEMPLOY), Civilian Employment

(CE16OV), (2) Employment Level – Part-Time for Economic Reasons, All Industries (LNS12032194), and (3) Not in Labor Force, Searched for Work and Available (LNU05026642).

b. Using the values you found in part (a), calculate the official unemployment rate.

c. Some economists argue that the official unemployment rate understates the degree of joblessness in the economy because it uses too narrow a definition of unemployment. The BLS also calculates a broader measure of the unemployment rate, which includes people who work part time for economic reasons and people who are available for work but not actively searching. Using the data you found in part (a), calculate this broader measure of the unemployment rate.

d. How would you expect the gap between the official rate of unemployment and the broader rate to change over the course of the business cycle?

D20.10 **(Calculating the real interest rate)** Go to the Web site of the Federal Reserve Bank of St. Louis (FRED) (research.stlouisfed.org/fred2/).

a. Find the most recent values for the 3-Month Treasury Bill: Secondary Market Rate (TB3MS) and the University of Michigan Inflation Expectation (MICH).

b. Using the data you found in part (a), calculate the expected real interest rate.

c. If the actual inflation rate is greater than the expected inflation rate, how are borrowers and lenders affected?

D20.11 **(Calculating the effect of inflation on real wages)** Go to the Web site of the Federal Reserve Bank of St. Louis (FRED) (research.stlouisfed.org/fred2/).

a. Find the values for the most recent month and for the month one year earlier for the Consumer Price Index for All Urban Consumers: All Items (CPIAUCNS) and Average Hourly Earnings of Production and Nonsupervisory Employees: Total Private (AHETPI).

b. Using the data you found in part (a), calculate the average hourly real wage for each year.

c. Calculate the percentage change in the average hourly nominal wage and the average hourly real wage during this year.

d. Given your calculation in part (c), explain whether an average worker was better or worse off than a year earlier.

CHAPTER 21

Economic Growth, the Financial System, and Business Cycles

Chapter Outline and Learning Objectives

Economic Growth and the Business Cycle at Corning, Inc.

Amory Houghton founded the company that became Corning, Inc., in 1851. At first, the company manufactured basic glass products such as jars. Over time, though, the company developed a number of new products using innovative technologies. For instance, in 1921, a Corning employee invented a machine that made millions of light bulbs for Thomas Edison. In the 1970s, Corning developed fiber-optic cable that eventually became the means for carrying the electronic signals needed for modern telecommunications and the Internet. In 2007, researchers at the company developed a damage-resistant glass called Gorilla glass that is used on the screens of iPhones and many other portable electronic devices. By 2015, Corning, headquartered in Corning, New York, had more than 34,000 employees and sales of nearly $10 billion.

Corning is one of many firms responsible for the technological progress that has been the basis for the growth of the U.S. economy and the rise in U.S. living standards. Corning's experiences have mirrored two key macroeconomic facts: In the long run, the U.S. economy has experienced economic growth, and in the short run, the economy has experienced a series of business cycles. During the 2001 recession, Corning suffered a $5 billion loss as the market for fiber-optic cable collapsed as a result of the bursting of the "dot-com" stock market bubble. Similarly, the recession of 2007–2009 caused a sharp decline in the demand for durable goods, including automobiles, televisions, and computers. Because Corning supplies ceramics for automobile emissions systems, as well as display panels for televisions and computers, its sales declined and its profits fell by more than 60 percent between 2008 and 2009.

Unlike many firms, Corning did continue to earn a profit during the recession. The company managed to remain profitable due to products like Gorilla glass that continue to sell well even during recessions. The next success for Corning could be a thinner version of Gorilla glass, called Willow glass, that can be wound and shipped in rolls, which might make it possible for Apple and other firms to produce foldable smartphones and other electronic devices.

In this chapter, we provide an overview of long-run growth and the business cycle and discuss their importance for firms, consumers, and the economy as a whole.

Sources: Robin Goldwyn Blumenthal, "Corning's Latest Magic: Turning Glass into Cash," *Barron's*, June 6, 2015; Connie Guglielmo, "Working with Innovators from Thomas Edison to Steve Jobs, Corning Finds a Glass Fix," *Forbes*, September 23, 2013; and Corning, Inc., Annual Reports on corning.com.

Economics in Your Life

Do You Help the Economy More if You Spend or if You Save?

Suppose the U.S. government sends you an income tax refund. You're not sure what to do with the money, so you ask your two roommates for advice. One roommate tells you that if you want to help the economy, you should save all the money because a country's economic growth depends on the amount of saving by households. The other roommate disagrees and advises you to spend all the money because consumer spending is a major component of gross domestic product (GDP), and your spending would help increase production and create more jobs. Which of your two roommates is right? As you read this chapter, try to answer this question. You can check your answer against the one we provide on **page 722** at the end of this chapter.

A successful economy is capable of increasing production of goods and services faster than the growth in population. Attaining this level of growth is the only way that the standard of living of the average person in a country can increase. Unfortunately, some economies around the world are not growing at all or are growing very slowly. Most people in those countries live on about the same levels of income as their ancestors did decades, or even centuries, ago. In the United States and other developed countries, however, incomes and living standards are much higher today than they were 50 years ago. An important macroeconomic topic is why some countries grow much faster than others.

As we will see, one determinant of economic growth is the ability of firms to expand their operations, buy additional equipment, train workers, and adopt new technologies. To carry out these activities, firms must acquire funds from households, either directly through financial markets—such as the stock and bond markets—or indirectly through financial intermediaries—such as banks. Financial markets and financial intermediaries together comprise the *financial system*. In this chapter, we present an overview of the financial system and see how funds flow from households to firms through the *market for loanable funds*.

Business cycle Alternating periods of economic expansion and economic recession.

Since at least the early nineteenth century, the U.S. economy has experienced periods of expanding production and employment followed by periods of recession during which production and employment decline. These alternating periods of expansion and recession are called the **business cycle**. Business cycles are not uniform: Periods of expansion are not the same length, nor are periods of recession. But every period of expansion in U.S. history has been followed by a period of recession, and every period of recession has been followed by a period of expansion.

In this chapter, we begin to explore two key aspects of macroeconomics: the long-run growth that has steadily raised living standards in the United States and the short-run fluctuations of the business cycle.

21.1 Long-Run Economic Growth

LEARNING OBJECTIVE: Discuss the importance of long-run economic growth.

Most people in high-income countries such as the United States, Canada, Japan, and the countries in Western Europe expect that over time, their standard of living will improve. They expect that year after year, firms will introduce new and improved products, new prescription drugs and better surgical techniques will overcome more diseases, and their ability to afford these goods and services will increase. For most people, these are reasonable expectations.

In 1900, the United States was already enjoying the highest standard of living in the world. Yet in that year, only 3 percent of U.S. homes had electricity, only 15 percent had indoor flush toilets, and only 25 percent had running water. The lack of running water meant that before people could cook or bathe, they had to pump water from wells and haul it to their homes in buckets—on average about 10,000 gallons per year per family. Not surprisingly, water consumption averaged only about 5 gallons per person per day, compared with about 150 gallons today. The result was that people washed themselves and their clothing only infrequently. A majority of families living in cities had to use outdoor toilets, which they shared with other families. Diseases such as smallpox, typhus, dysentery, and cholera were still common. In 1900, 5,000 of the 45,000 children born in Chicago died before their first birthday. Life expectancy at birth was about 47 years, compared with 80 years in 2015. Few families had electric lights, relying instead on burning candles or burning kerosene or coal oil in lamps. Many homes were heated in the winter by burning coal, which contributed to the severe pollution that fouled the air of most large cities. In 1900, there were no modern appliances, so housework was time-consuming and physically demanding. The typical American homemaker baked a half-ton of bread per year.

The process of **long-run economic growth** brought the typical American from the standard of living of 1900 to the standard of living of today. The best measure of the standard of living is real GDP per person, which is usually called *real GDP per capita*. So, we measure long-run economic growth by increases in real GDP per capita over long periods of time, generally decades or more. We use real GDP rather than nominal GDP to adjust for changes in the price level over time. Figure 21.1 shows the growth in real GDP per capita in the United States from 1900 to 2014. The figure shows that the trend in real GDP per capita is strongly upward, although it fluctuates in the short run because of the business cycle. It is the upward trend in real GDP per capita that we focus on when discussing long-run economic growth.

Long-run economic growth The process by which rising productivity increases the average standard of living.

The values in Figure 21.1 are measured in prices of 2009, so they represent constant amounts of purchasing power. In 1900, real GDP per capita was about $6,000. More than a century later, in 2014, it had risen to about $50,010, which means that an average American in 2014 could purchase more than eight times as many goods and services as an average American in 1900. Large as it is, this increase in real GDP per capita actually understates the true increase in the standard of living of Americans in 2014 compared with 1900. Many of today's goods and services were not available in 1900. For example, if you lived in 1900 and became ill with a serious infection, you could not purchase antibiotics to treat your illness—no matter how high your income. You might have died from an illness for which even a very poor person in today's society could receive effective medical treatment. Of course, the quantity of goods and services that a person can buy is not a perfect measure of how happy or contented that person may be. A person's happiness also depends on education, health, spiritual well-being, and many other factors ignored in calculating GDP. Nevertheless, economists rely heavily on comparisons of real GDP per capita because it is the best means of comparing the performance of one economy over time or the performance of different economies at any particular time. MyEconLab Concept Check

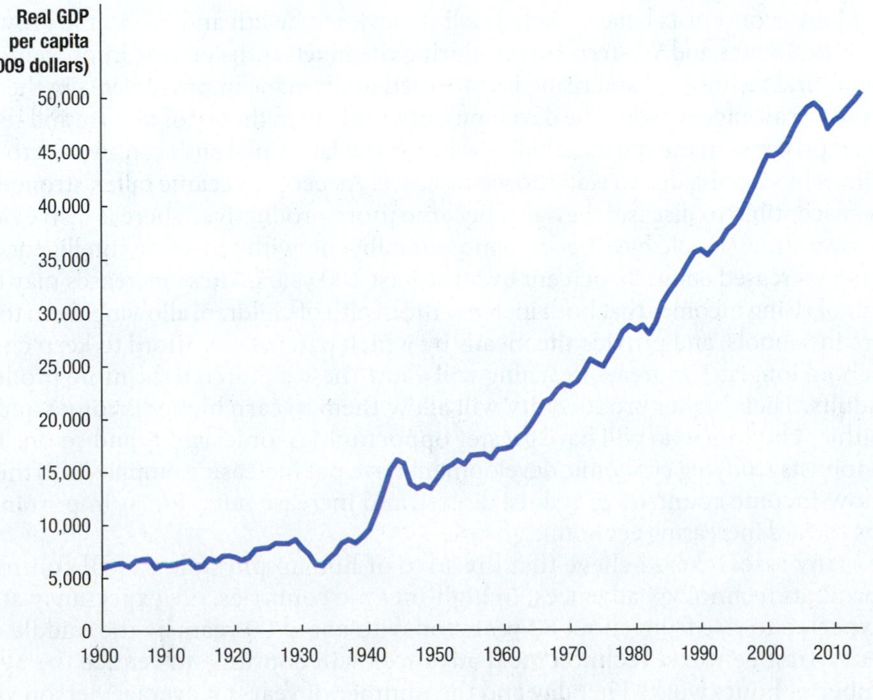

MyEconLab Real-time data

Figure 21.1

The Growth in Real GDP per Capita, 1900–2014

Measured in 2009 dollars, real GDP per capita in the United States grew from about $6,000 in 1900 to about $50,010 in 2014. An average American in 2014 could buy more than eight times as many goods and services as an average American in 1900.

Sources: Samuel H. Williamson, "What Was the U.S. GDP Then?" MeasuringWorth, July 2015; and U.S. Bureau of Economic Analysis.

Making the Connection
MyEconLab Video

The Connection between Economic Prosperity and Health

We can see the direct effect of economic growth on living standards by looking at improvements in health in high-income countries over the past 100 years. The research of the late Robert Fogel, winner of the Nobel Prize in Economics, highlights the close connection between economic growth, improvements in technology, and improvements in human physiology. One important measure of health is life expectancy at birth. As the following graph shows, in 1900, life expectancy was less than 50 years in the United States, the United Kingdom, and France. Today, life expectancy is about 80 years. Although life expectancies in the lowest-income countries remain very short, some countries that have begun to experience economic growth have seen dramatic increases in life expectancies. For example, life expectancy in India has more than doubled from 27 years in 1900 to 68 years today.

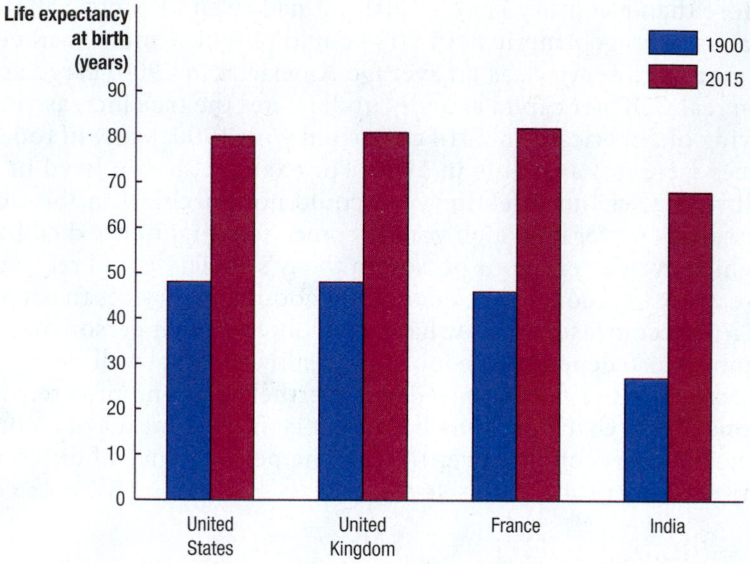

Many economists believe there is a link between health and economic growth. In the United States and Western Europe during the nineteenth century, improvements in agricultural technology and rising incomes led to dramatic improvements in the nutrition of the average person. The development of the germ theory of disease and technological progress in the purification of water in the late nineteenth century led to sharp declines in sickness due to waterborne diseases. As people became taller, stronger, and less susceptible to disease, they also became more productive. There is also evidence that over time, people have become more intelligent, with scores on intelligence tests having increased about 30 percent over the past 100 years. These increases may be the result of rising incomes that both increase the health of children, allowing them to learn more in schools, and provide the means by which parents can afford to keep children in school longer. The greater learning will allow these children to be more productive as adults. Their higher productivity will allow them to earn higher incomes and have healthier children who will have greater opportunities for learning, and so on. Today, economists studying economic development have put increasing emphasis on the need for low-income countries to reduce disease and increase nutrition as important first steps toward increasing economic growth.

Many researchers believe that the state of human physiology will continue to improve as technology advances. In high-income countries, life expectancy at birth is expected to rise from about 80 years today to about 90 years by the middle of the twenty-first century. Technological advances will continue to reduce the average number of hours worked per day and the number of years an average person spends in the paid workforce. Individuals spend about 10 hours per day sleeping, eating, and bathing. Their remaining "discretionary hours" are divided between paid work and leisure. The following graph is based on estimates by Robert Fogel that contrast how individuals in the United States will divide their time in 2040 compared with 1880 and 1995. Not only will technology and economic growth allow people in the near future to live longer lives, but a much smaller fraction of those lives will need to be spent at paid work.

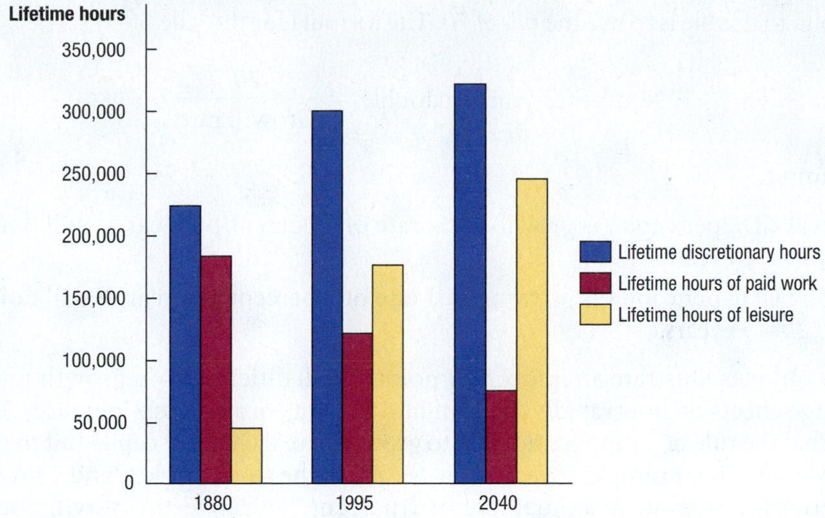

Sources: Robert William Fogel, *The Escape from Hunger and Premature Death, 1700–2100*, New York: Cambridge University Press, 2004; Alison Gopnik, "Smarter Every Year? Mystery of the Rising IQs," *Wall Street Journal*, May 27, 2015; and U.S. Central Intelligence Agency, *The 2015 World Factbook*, online version.

Your Turn: Test your understanding by doing related problem 1.7 on page 724 at the end of this chapter.

MyEconLab Study Plan

Calculating Growth Rates and the Rule of 70

The growth rate of real GDP or real GDP per capita during a particular year is equal to the percentage change from the previous year. For example, measured in 2009 prices, real GDP equaled \$15,710 billion in 2013 and rose to \$16,086 billion in 2014. We calculate the growth of real GDP in 2014 as:

$$\left(\frac{\$16{,}086 \text{ billion} - \$15{,}710 \text{ billion}}{\$15{,}710 \text{ billion}}\right) \times 100 = 2.4\%.$$

For longer periods of time, we can use the *average annual growth rate*. For example, real GDP in the United States was \$2,184 billion in 1950 and \$16,086 billion in 2014. To find the average annual growth rate during this 64-year period, we compute the annual growth rate that would result in \$2,184 billion increasing to \$16,086 billion over 64 years. In this case, the growth rate is 3.2 percent. That is, if \$2,184 billion grows at an average rate of 3.2 percent per year, after 64 years, it will have grown to \$16,086 billion.

For shorter periods of time, we get approximately the same answer by averaging the growth rate for each year. For example, real GDP in the United States grew by 2.3 percent in 2012, 2.2 percent in 2013, and 2.4 percent in 2014. So, the average annual growth rate of real GDP for the period 2012–2014 was 2.3 percent, which is the average of the three annual growth rates:

$$\frac{2.3\% + 2.2\% + 2.4\%}{3} = 2.3\%.$$

Finally, when discussing long-run economic growth, we usually shorten "average annual growth rate" to "growth rate."

We can judge how rapidly an economic variable is growing by calculating the number of years it would take to double. For example, if real GDP per capita in a country doubles, say, every 20 years, most people in the country will experience significant increases in their standard of living over the course of their lives. If real GDP per capita doubles only every 100 years, increases in the standard of living will occur too slowly to notice. One easy way to calculate approximately how many years it will take real GDP per capita to double is to use the *rule of 70*. The formula for the rule of 70 is:

$$\text{Number of years to double} = \frac{70}{\text{Growth rate}}.$$

For example:

- If real GDP per capita is growing at a rate of 5 percent per year, it will double in $70/5 = 14$ years.
- If real GDP per capita is growing at a rate of 2 percent per year, it will double in $70/2 = 35$ years.

These examples illustrate an important point: Small differences in growth rates can have large effects on how rapidly the standard of living in a country increases. Finally, notice that the rule of 70 applies not just to growth in real GDP per capita but to growth in any variable. For example, if you invest $1,000 in the stock market, and your investment grows at an average annual rate of 7 percent, your investment will double to $2,000 in 10 years. MyEconLab Concept Check

What Determines the Rate of Long-Run Growth?

Labor productivity The quantity of goods and services that can be produced by one worker or by one hour of work.

A key point in explaining long-run growth is that *increases in real GDP per capita depend on increases in labor productivity*. **Labor productivity** is the quantity of goods and services that can be produced by one worker or by one hour of work. In analyzing long-run growth, economists usually measure labor productivity as output per hour of work to avoid the effects of fluctuations in the length of the workday and in the fraction of the population employed. If the quantity of goods and services consumed by the average person is to increase, the quantity of goods and services produced per hour of work must also increase. Why in 2014 was the average American able to consume more than eight times as many goods and services as the average American in 1900? Because the average American worker in 2014 was eight times as productive as the average American worker in 1900.

If increases in labor productivity are the key to long-run economic growth, what causes labor productivity to increase? Economists believe two key factors determine labor productivity:

1. The quantity of capital per hour worked
2. The level of technology

Therefore, economic growth occurs if the quantity of capital per hour worked increases and if there is technological change.

Capital Manufactured goods that are used to produce other goods and services.

Increases in Capital per Hour Worked

Workers today in high-income countries such as the United States have more physical capital available than workers in low-income countries or workers in the high-income countries of 100 years ago. Recall that **capital** refers to manufactured goods that are used to produce other goods and services. Examples of capital are computers, factory buildings, machine tools, warehouses, and trucks. The total amount of physical capital available in a country is known as the country's *capital stock*.

As the amount of capital per hour worked increases, worker productivity increases. An accountant who records a firm's revenues and costs using Excel is more productive than an accountant who uses only pen and paper. A worker who uses a backhoe can excavate more earth than a worker who uses only a shovel.

In explaining economic growth, economists take into account not just *physical capital*, like computers and factories, but also *human capital*, which is the accumulated knowledge and skills workers acquire from education and training or from their life experiences. For example, workers with a college education generally have more skills and are more productive than workers who have only a high school degree. Increases in human capital are particularly important in stimulating economic growth.

Technological Change Economic growth depends more on *technological change* than on increases in capital per hour worked. *Technology* refers to the processes a firm uses to turn inputs into outputs of goods and services. Technological change is an increase in the quantity of output firms can produce, using a given quantity of inputs. Technological change can come from many sources. For example, a firm's managers may rearrange a factory floor or the layout of a retail store to increase production and sales. Most technological change, however, is embodied in new machinery, equipment, or software.

A very important point is that just accumulating more inputs—such as labor, capital, and natural resources—will not ensure that an economy experiences economic growth unless technological change also occurs. For example, the Soviet Union failed to maintain a high rate of economic growth, even though it continued to increase the quantity of capital available per hour worked, because it experienced relatively little technological change.

Entrepreneurs are critical for implementing technological change. Recall that an entrepreneur is someone who operates a business, bringing together the factors of production—labor, capital, and natural resources—to produce goods and services (see Chapter 2). In a market economy, entrepreneurs make the crucial decisions about whether to introduce new technology to produce better or lower-cost products. Entrepreneurs also decide whether to allocate a firm's resources to research and development that can result in new technologies. One of the difficulties centrally planned economies have in sustaining economic growth is that managers employed by the government are usually much slower to develop and adopt new technologies than are entrepreneurs in a market system.

Solved Problem 21.1

MyEconLab Interactive Animation

Where Does Productivity Come From?

A column in the *Wall Street Journal* argued that "productivity growth is a key ingredient to prosperity." What did the columnist mean by "prosperity"? What is the connection between productivity growth and prosperity?

Solving the Problem

Step 1: Review the chapter material. This problem is about what determines the rate of long-run growth, so you may want to review the section "What Determines the Rate of Long-Run Growth?" which begins on page 700.

Step 2: Answer the first question by explaining what the columnist meant by the word "prosperity" in this context. By *prosperity*, most people mean a high standard of living. In the context of economic growth, the key measure of the standard of living is real GDP per capita.

Step 3: Answer the second question by explaining the connection between productivity growth and prosperity. *Productivity* refers to the amount of goods and services produced per worker. As we have seen, per capita real GDP increases only if productivity increases. Therefore, increases in a country's standard of living—its prosperity—are tied to increases in productivity.

Source: Jon Hilsenrath, "More Disturbing Findings Emerge on U.S. Productivity Path," *Wall Street Journal*, February 12, 2015.

Your Turn: For more practice, do related problems 1.10 and 1.11 on pages 724–725 at the end of this chapter.

MyEconLab Study Plan

Property Rights Finally, an additional requirement for economic growth is that the government must provide secure rights to private property. A market system cannot function unless rights to private property are secure (see Chapter 2). In addition, the government can aid economic growth by establishing an independent court system that enforces contracts between private individuals. Many economists would also say that the government has a role in facilitating the development of an efficient financial system, as well as systems of education, transportation, and communication. Economist Richard Sylla of New York University has argued that every country that has experienced economic growth first experienced a "financial revolution." For example, before the United States was able to experience significant economic growth in the early nineteenth century, the country's banking and monetary systems were reformed under the guidance of Alexander Hamilton, who was appointed the country's first secretary of the Treasury in 1789. Without supportive government policies, long-run economic growth is unlikely to occur. MyEconLab Concept Check

Making the Connection
MyEconLab Video

Can India Sustain Its Rapid Growth?

When you have a computer problem and need technical support, the person who takes your call may well be in India. In addition to information technology, in recent years Indian firms have made gains in the global markets for steel, oil, and automobiles, among other goods.

To many people in the United States, the rapid economic rise of India has been unexpected. As the following figure shows, Indian real GDP per capita increased very slowly up to the time India became independent from England in 1947. As a result, in 1950, India was desperately poor. India's real GDP per capita in 1950 was less than $1,000 measured in 2015 dollars, or less than 7 percent of 1950 U.S. real GDP per capita. During the first 40 years of independence, India's growth rate increased but was still too slow to significantly reduce the country's poverty. Recent years tell a much different story, however. In 1991, the Indian government decided to scale back central planning, reduce regulations, and introduce market-based reforms. The result was that the growth rate doubled over the following decade. In the most recent period, growth has been even more rapid.

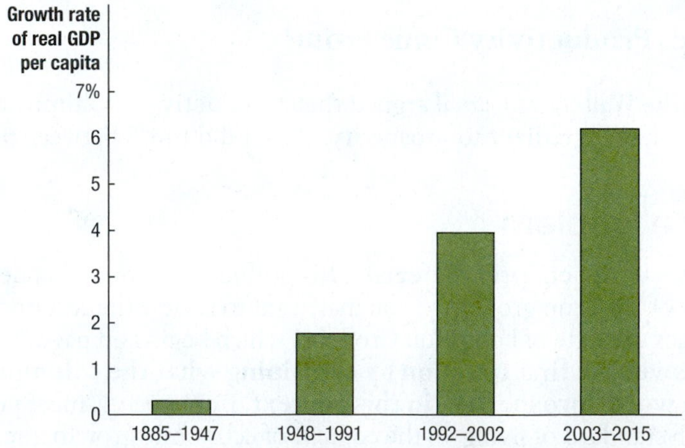

Still, India remains a very poor country. Nearly half of its population of 1.3 billion is employed in agriculture, and many can barely produce enough to feed themselves. Infant mortality rates are still at 10 times the levels in high-income countries, and about 40 percent of adult women and 20 percent of adult men are unable to read and write. The rapid economic growth that began in 1991 will have to continue in the coming decades if the average person in India is eventually to enjoy a standard of living equal to that in the United States and other high-income countries. But can India continue its rapid growth?

Some economists and policymakers worry that India's growth rates may begin to decline, leaving hundreds of millions of its people stuck in deep poverty. These economists point to several problems facing the Indian economy. The public education system has struggled to provide basic instruction, particularly in rural and poorer urban areas. India's expenditures on education rank 134th out of 173 countries, and are far below the levels in most successful developing countries. As a result, many adults lack the basic skills needed for a productive workforce. Even many high school and college graduates lack the skills to work in firms that compete in global markets. High rates of infectious disease also reduce the productivity of the workforce. Only 60 percent of urban residents have access to modern sewage systems, and fewer than one-quarter of rural residents do. In general, India has struggled to meet its infrastructure needs, as highways, bridges, and its train system—which dates from the British colonial period—have deteriorated.

India also suffers from political problems with ethnic, religious, cultural, and geographic divisions—there are 15 official languages—often making it difficult for the government to successfully implement policy reforms. Many observers believe that government corruption has increased, making it more difficult for businesses to obtain the permits necessary to operate. One estimate puts the size of the underground economy at more than 50 percent of GDP. Laws restricting the sale of agricultural land for industrial use have slowed the growth of manufacturing. Although Narendra Modi was elected prime minister in 2014 partly by promising new policies to spur economic growth, some economists and policymakers worry that the pace of market-oriented reforms has slowed over the years. They also urge the government to allow greater foreign investment in the financial and retail sectors. Greater foreign investment would allow these sectors to gain access to new technology and to increase productivity.

The economic progress India has made in the past 25 years has already lifted hundreds of millions of people out of poverty. For that progress to continue, however, many economists believe that the Indian government will need to upgrade infrastructure, improve the provision of educational and health services, and renew its commitment to the rule of law and to market-based reforms.

Sources: "Ready, Steady, Go," *Economist*, April 18, 2015; Ellen Barry, "After a Year of Outsize Expectations, Narendra Modi Adjusts His Plan for India," *New York Times*, May 25, 2015; Amartya Sen, "Why India Trails China," *New York Times*, June 19, 2013; Geeta Anand, "India Graduates Millions, but Too Few Are Fit to Hire," *Wall Street Journal*, April 5, 2011; data in graph are authors' calculations from the Maddison Project database, www.ggdc.net/maddison/maddison-project/home.htm; and International Monetary Fund, *World Economic Outlook Database*.

Your Turn: Test your understanding by doing related problems 1.13 and 1.14 on page 725 at the end of this chapter.

MyEconLab Study Plan

Potential GDP

Because economists take a long-run perspective in discussing economic growth, the concept of *potential GDP* is useful. **Potential GDP** is the level of real GDP attained when all firms are producing at *capacity*. The capacity of a firm is *not* the maximum output the firm is capable of producing. A Corning factory could operate 24 hours per day for 52 weeks per year and would be at its maximum production level. The factory's capacity, however, is measured by its production when operating on normal hours, using a normal workforce. If all firms in the economy were operating at capacity, the level of total production of final goods and services would equal potential GDP. Potential GDP increases over time as the labor force grows, new factories and office buildings are built, new machinery and equipment are installed, and technological change takes place.

Potential GDP The level of real GDP attained when all firms are producing at capacity.

From 1949 to 2015, potential GDP in the United States grew at an average annual rate of 3.2 percent. In other words, each year, on average, the capacity of the economy to produce final goods and services expanded by 3.2 percent. In any particular year, the *actual* level of real GDP increased by more or less than 3.2 percent as the economy moved through the business cycle. Figure 21.2 shows movements in actual and potential GDP for the years since 1989. The red line represents potential GDP, and the blue line represents actual real GDP. Notice that in each of the three recessions since 1989, actual real GDP has fallen below potential GDP. During the 2007–2009 recession, the

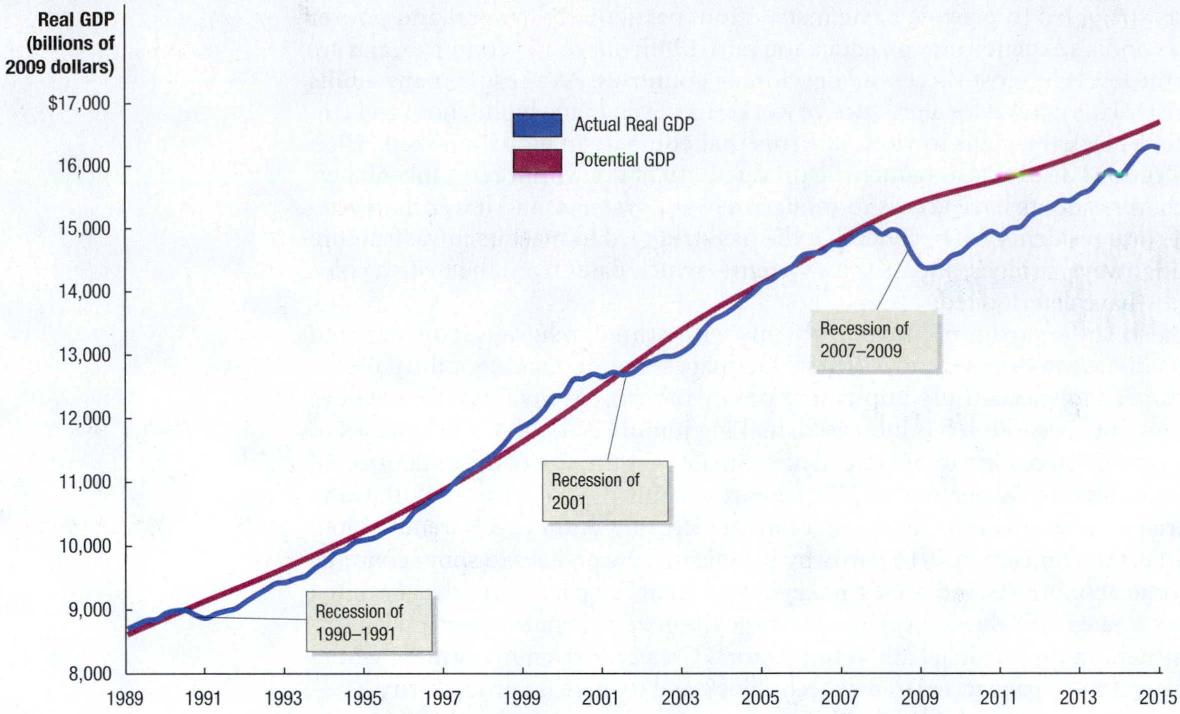

MyEconLab Real-time data

Figure 21.2 Actual and Potential GDP

Potential GDP increases every year as the labor force and the capital stock grow and technological change occurs. The red line represents potential GDP, and the blue line represents actual real GDP. During the three recessions since 1989, actual real GDP has been less than potential GDP.

Source: Federal Reserve Bank of St. Louis.

gap between actual real GDP and potential GDP was particularly large, which shows the severity of the recession.

MyEconLab Study Plan

MyEconLab Concept Check

21.2 Saving, Investment, and the Financial System

LEARNING OBJECTIVE: Discuss the role of the financial system in facilitating long-run economic growth.

The process of economic growth depends on the ability of firms to expand their operations, buy additional equipment, train workers, and adopt new technologies. Firms can finance some of these activities from *retained earnings,* which are profits that are reinvested in the firm rather than paid to the firm's owners. For many firms, retained earnings are not sufficient to finance the rapid expansion required in economies experiencing high rates of economic growth. Firms can acquire funds from households, either directly through financial markets—such as the stock and bond markets—or indirectly through financial intermediaries—such as banks. Financial markets and financial intermediaries together comprise the **financial system**. Without a well-functioning financial system, economic growth is impossible because firms will be unable to expand and adopt new technologies. As we noted earlier, no country without a well-developed financial system has been able to sustain high levels of economic growth.

Financial system The system of financial markets and financial intermediaries through which firms acquire funds from households.

An Overview of the Financial System

The financial system channels funds from savers to borrowers and channels returns on the borrowed funds back to savers. In this section, we discuss the key components of the financial system and the services they provide to households and firms.

Financial Markets In **financial markets**, such as the stock market or the bond market, firms raise funds by selling financial securities directly to savers (see Chapter 8). A *financial security* is a document—sometimes in electronic form—that states the terms under which funds pass from the buyer of the security—who is providing funds—to the seller. *Stocks* are financial securities that represent partial ownership of a firm. If you buy one share of stock in Corning, you become one of millions of owners of that firm. *Bonds* are financial securities that represent promises to repay a fixed amount of funds. When Corning sells a bond, the firm promises to pay the purchaser of the bond an interest payment each year for the term of the bond, as well as a final payment of the amount of the loan.

Financial markets Markets where financial securities, such as stocks and bonds, are bought and sold.

Financial Intermediaries **Financial intermediaries**, such as banks, mutual funds, pension funds, and insurance companies, act as go-betweens for borrowers and lenders. In effect, financial intermediaries borrow funds from savers and lend them to borrowers. When you deposit funds in your checking account, you are lending your funds to the bank. The bank may lend your funds (together with the funds of other savers) to an entrepreneur who wants to start a business. Suppose Lena wants to open a laundry. Rather than your lending money directly to Lena's Laundry, the bank acts as a go-between for you and Lena. Intermediaries pool the funds of many small savers to lend to many individual borrowers. The intermediaries pay interest to savers in exchange for the use of savers' funds and earn a profit by lending money to borrowers and charging them a higher rate of interest on the loans. For example, a bank might pay you as a depositor a 2 percent rate of interest, while it lends the money to Lena's Laundry at a 6 percent rate of interest.

Financial intermediaries Firms, such as banks, mutual funds, pension funds, and insurance companies, that borrow funds from savers and lend them to borrowers.

Banks, mutual funds, pension funds, and insurance companies also make investments in stocks and bonds on behalf of savers. For example, *mutual funds* sell shares to savers and then use the funds to buy a portfolio of stocks, bonds, mortgages, and other financial securities. Large mutual fund companies, such as Fidelity, Vanguard, and Dreyfus, offer many stock and bond funds. Some funds hold a wide range of stocks or bonds; others specialize in securities issued by a particular industry or sector, such as health care; and others invest as index funds in fixed market baskets of securities, such as shares of the Standard & Poor's 500 firms. Over the past 30 years, the role of mutual funds in the financial system has increased dramatically. Today, competition among hundreds of mutual fund firms gives investors thousands of funds from which to choose.

The Services the Financial System Provides: Risk Sharing, Liquidity, and Information In addition to matching households that have excess funds with firms that want to borrow funds, the financial system provides three key services for savers and borrowers: risk sharing, liquidity, and information. *Risk* is the chance that the value of a financial security will change relative to what you expect. For example, you may buy a share of stock in Corning at a price of $25, only to have the price fall to $5. Most individual savers are not gamblers and seek a steady return on their savings rather than erratic swings between high and low earnings. The financial system provides *risk sharing* by allowing savers to spread their money among many financial investments. For example, you can divide your money among a bank certificate of deposit, individual bonds, and a stock mutual fund.

Liquidity is the ease with which a financial security can be exchanged for money. The financial system provides the service of liquidity by offering savers markets where they can sell their holdings of financial securities. For example, savers can easily sell their holdings of the stocks and bonds issued by large corporations on the major stock and bond markets.

A third service that the financial system provides savers is the collection and communication of *information*, or facts about borrowers and expectations about returns on financial securities. For example, Lena's Laundry may want to borrow $10,000 from you. Finding out what Lena intends to do with the funds and how likely she is to pay you back may be costly and time-consuming. By depositing $10,000 in the bank, you are, in effect, allowing the bank to gather this information for you. Because banks specialize in gathering information about borrowers, they are able to do it faster and at a lower cost than can individual savers. The financial system plays an important role in communicating information. If you read a news story announcing that an automobile firm has invented a car with an engine that runs on water, how would you determine the effect of that discovery on the firm's profits? Financial markets do the job for you by incorporating information into the prices of stocks, bonds, and other financial securities. In this example, the expectation of higher future profits would boost the prices of the automobile firm's stock and bonds. MyEconLab Concept Check

The Macroeconomics of Saving and Investment

As we have seen, the funds available to firms through the financial system come from saving. When firms use funds to purchase machinery, factories, and office buildings, they are engaging in investment. In this section, we explore the macroeconomics of saving and investment. A key point we will develop is that *the total value of saving in the economy must equal the total value of investment*. *National income accounting* refers to the methods the Bureau of Economic Analysis uses to keep track of total production and total income in the economy (see Chapter 19). We can use some relationships from national income accounting to understand why total saving must equal total investment.

We begin with the relationship between gross domestic product, GDP (Y), and its components, consumption (C), investment (I), government purchases (G), and net exports (NX):

$$Y = C + I + G + NX.$$

Remember that GDP is a measure of both total production in the economy and total income.

In an *open economy*, there is interaction with other economies in terms of both trading of goods and services and borrowing and lending. All economies today are open economies, although they vary significantly in the extent of their openness. In a *closed economy*, there is no trading or borrowing and lending with other economies. For simplicity, we will develop the relationship between saving and investment for a closed economy, which allows us to focus on the most important points in a simpler framework. (See Chapter 29 for the case of an open economy.)

In a closed economy, net exports are zero, so we can rewrite the relationship between GDP and its components as:

$$Y = C + I + G.$$

The Savings Equals Investment Condition If we rearrange the equation showing the relationship between GDP and its components, we have an expression for investment in terms of the other variables:

$$I = Y - C - G.$$

This expression tells us that in a closed economy, investment spending is equal to total income minus consumption spending and minus government purchases.

We can also derive an expression for total saving. *Private saving* is equal to what households retain of their income after purchasing goods and services (C) and paying taxes (T). Households receive income for supplying the factors of production to firms. This portion of household income is equal to Y. Households also receive income from government in the form of *transfer payments* (TR), which include Social Security payments and unemployment insurance payments. We can write this expression for private saving ($S_{Private}$):

$$S_{Private} = Y + TR - C - T.$$

The government also engages in saving. *Public saving* (S_{Public}) equals the amount of tax revenue the government retains after paying for government purchases and making transfer payments to households:

$$S_{Public} = T - G - TR.$$

So, total saving in the economy (S) is equal to the sum of private saving and public saving:

$$S = S_{Private} + S_{Public},$$

or:

$$S = (Y + TR - C - T) + (T - G - TR),$$

or:

$$S = Y - C - G.$$

The right side of this expression is identical to the expression we derived earlier for investment spending. So, we can conclude that total saving must equal total investment:

$$S = I.$$

Budget Deficits and Budget Surpluses When the government spends the same amount that it collects in taxes, there is a *balanced budget*. When the government spends more than it collects in taxes, there is a *budget deficit*. In the case of a deficit, T is less than $G + TR$, which means that public saving is negative. Negative saving is also known as *dissaving*. How can public saving be negative? When the federal government runs a budget deficit, the U.S. Department of the Treasury sells Treasury bonds to borrow the money necessary to fund the gap between taxes and spending. In this case, rather than adding to the total amount of saving available to be borrowed for investment spending, the government is subtracting from it. (Notice that if households borrow more than they save, the total amount of saving will also fall.) With less saving, investment must also be lower. We can conclude that, holding constant all other factors, there is a lower level of investment spending in the economy when there is a budget deficit than when there is a balanced budget.

When the government spends less than it collects in taxes, there is a *budget surplus*. A budget surplus increases public saving and the total level of saving in the economy. A higher level of saving results in a higher level of investment spending. Therefore, holding constant all other factors, there is a higher level of investment spending in the economy when there is a budget surplus than when there is a balanced budget.

The U.S. federal government has experienced dramatic swings in the state of its budget over the past 20 years. In 1992, the federal budget deficit was $297.4 billion. The federal budget had a surplus of $189.5 billion in 2000, but a sharp decline in taxes and increase in government spending resulting from the recession of 2007–2009 led to a record budget deficit of $1.4 trillion in 2009. By 2015, the budget deficit had declined to less than $500 billion. MyEconLab Concept Check

The Market for Loanable Funds

We have seen that the value of total saving must equal the value of total investment, but we have not yet discussed how this equality is actually brought about in the financial system. We can think of the financial system as being composed of many markets through which funds flow from lenders to borrowers: the market for certificates of deposit at banks, the market for stocks, the market for bonds, the market for mutual

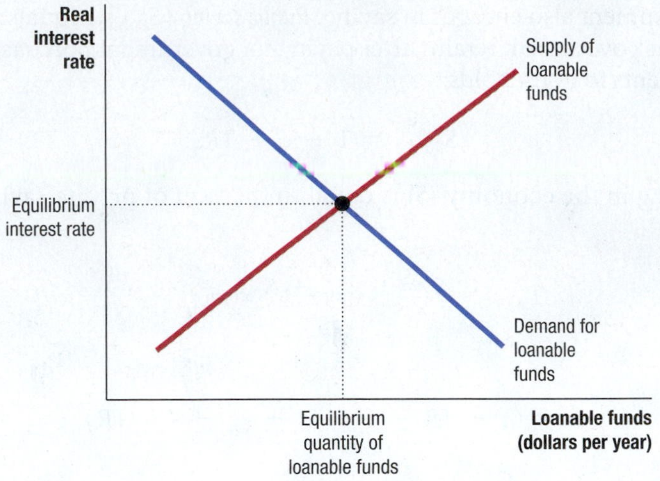

MyEconLab Animation

Figure 21.3 The Market for Loanable Funds

The demand for loanable funds is determined by the willingness of firms to borrow money to engage in new investment projects. The supply of loanable funds is determined by the willingness of households to save and by the extent of government saving or dissaving. Equilibrium in the market for loanable funds determines the real interest rate and the quantity of loanable funds exchanged.

Market for loanable funds The interaction of borrowers and lenders that determines the market interest rate and the quantity of loanable funds exchanged.

fund shares, and so on. For simplicity, we can combine these markets into a single market for *loanable funds*. In the model of the **market for loanable funds**, the interaction of borrowers and lenders determines the market interest rate and the quantity of loanable funds exchanged. As we will discuss in a later chapter, firms can also borrow from savers in other countries (see Chapter 29). For the remainder of this section, we will assume that there are no interactions between households and firms in the United States and those in other countries.

Demand and Supply in the Loanable Funds Market The demand for loanable funds is determined by the willingness of firms to borrow money to engage in new investment projects, such as building new factories or carrying out research and development of new products. In determining whether to borrow funds, firms compare the return they expect to make on an investment with the interest rate they must pay to borrow the necessary funds. For example, if Home Depot is considering opening several new stores and expects to earn a return of 12 percent on its investment, the investment will be profitable if Home Depot can borrow the funds at an interest rate of 8 percent but will not be profitable if the interest rate is 15 percent. In Figure 21.3, the demand for loanable funds is downward sloping because the lower the interest rate, the more investment projects firms can profitably undertake, and the greater the quantity of loanable funds they will demand.

The supply of loanable funds is determined by the willingness of households to save and by the extent of government saving or dissaving. When households save, they reduce the amount of goods and services they can consume and enjoy today. The willingness of households to save rather than consume their incomes today will be determined in part by the interest rate they receive when they lend their savings. The higher the interest rate, the greater the reward for saving and the larger the amount of funds households will save. Therefore, the supply curve for loanable funds in Figure 21.3 is upward sloping because the higher the interest rate, the greater the quantity of saving supplied.

Recall the distinction between the *nominal interest rate* and the *real interest rate* (see Chapter 20). The nominal interest rate is the stated interest rate on a loan. The real interest rate corrects the nominal interest rate for the effect of inflation and is equal to the nominal interest rate minus the inflation rate. Because both borrowers and lenders are concerned about the real interest rate they will receive or pay, equilibrium in the market for loanable funds determines the real interest rate rather than the nominal interest rate.

Making the Connection
MyEconLab Video

Ebenezer Scrooge: Accidental Promoter of Economic Growth?

Ebenezer Scrooge's name has become synonymous with miserliness. Before his reform at the end of Charles Dickens's *A Christmas Carol*, Scrooge is extraordinarily reluctant to spend money. Although he earns a substantial income, he lives in a cold, dark house that he refuses to heat or light adequately, and he eats a meager diet of gruel because he refuses to buy more expensive food. Throughout most of the book, Dickens portrays Scrooge's behavior in a negative way. Only at the end of the book, when the reformed Scrooge begins to spend lavishly on himself and others, does Dickens praise his behavior.

Who was better for economic growth: Scrooge the saver or Scrooge the spender?

As economist Steven Landsburg of the University of Rochester points out, however, economically speaking, it may be the pre-reform Scrooge who is more worthy of praise:

> In this whole world, there is nobody more generous than the miser—the man who could deplete the world's resources but chooses not to. The only difference between miserliness and philanthropy is that the philanthropist serves a favored few while the miser spreads his largess far and wide.

We can extend Landsburg's discussion to consider whether the actions of the pre-reform Scrooge or the actions of the post-reform Scrooge are more helpful to economic growth. Pre-reform Scrooge spends very little, investing most of his income in the financial markets. These funds became available for firms to borrow to build new factories and to carry out research and development. Post-reform Scrooge spends much more—and saves much less. Funds that he had previously saved are now spent on food for Bob Cratchit's family and on "making merry" at Christmas. In other words, the actions of post-reform Scrooge contribute to more consumption goods being produced and fewer investment goods. We can conclude that Scrooge's reform caused economic growth to slow down—if only by a little. The larger point is, of course, that savers provide the funds that are indispensable for the investment spending that economic growth requires, and the only way to save is to not consume.

Source: Steven Landsburg, "What I Like about Scrooge," *Slate*, December 9, 2004.

Your Turn: Test your understanding by doing related problems 2.14 and 2.15 on page 727 at the end of this chapter.

MyEconLab Study Plan

Explaining Movements in Saving, Investment, and Interest Rates Equilibrium in the market for loanable funds determines the quantity of loanable funds that will flow from lenders to borrowers each period. Equilibrium also determines the real interest rate that lenders will receive and that borrowers must pay. We draw the demand curve for loanable funds by holding constant all factors, other than the interest rate, that affect the willingness of borrowers to demand funds. We draw the supply curve by holding constant all factors, other than the interest rate, that affect the willingness of lenders to supply funds. A shift in either the demand curve or the supply curve will change the equilibrium interest rate and the equilibrium quantity of loanable funds.

MyEconLab Animation

Figure 21.4

An Increase in the Demand for Loanable Funds

An increase in the demand for loanable funds increases the equilibrium interest rate from i_1 to i_2 and increases the equilibrium quantity of loanable funds from L_1 to L_2. As a result, saving and investment both increase.

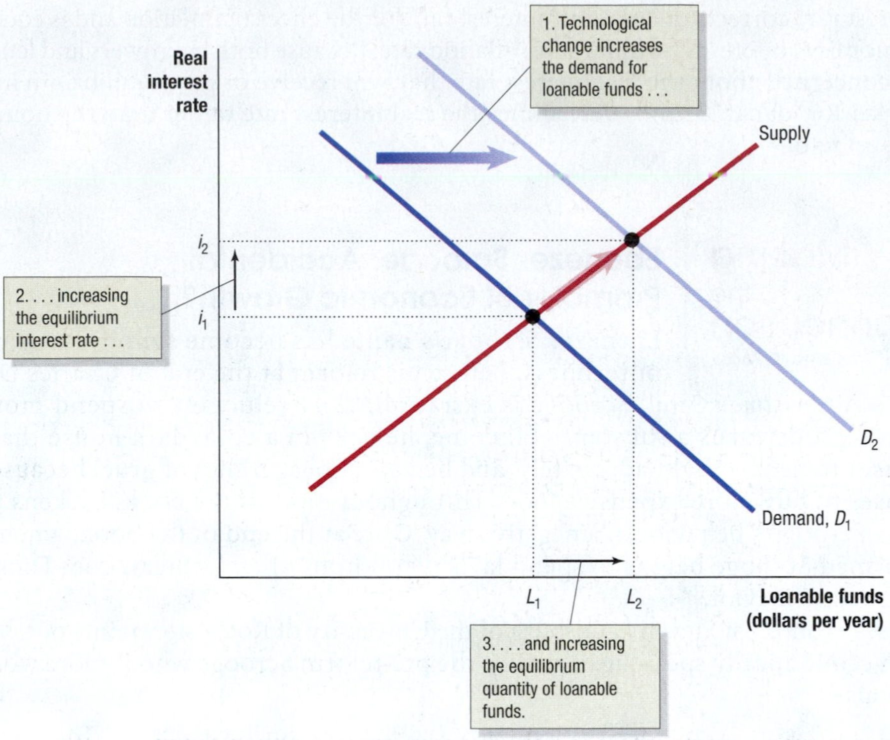

If, for example, the profitability of new investment increases due to technological change or because the government reduces corporate taxes, firms will increase their demand for loanable funds. Figure 21.4 shows the effect of an increase in demand in the market for loanable funds. As in the markets for goods and services, an increase in demand in the market for loanable funds shifts the demand curve to the right. In the new equilibrium, the interest rate increases from i_1 to i_2, and the equilibrium quantity of loanable funds increases from L_1 to L_2. Notice that an increase in the quantity of loanable funds means that both the quantity of saving by households and the quantity of investment by firms have increased. Increasing investment increases the capital stock and the quantity of capital per hour worked, helping to increase economic growth.

We can also use the market for loanable funds to examine the effect of a government budget deficit. Putting aside the effects of foreign saving, recall that if the government begins running a budget deficit, it reduces the total amount of saving in the economy. Suppose the government increases spending, which results in a budget deficit. We illustrate the effects of the budget deficit in Figure 21.5 by shifting the supply curve for loanable funds to the left. In the new equilibrium, the interest rate is higher, and the equilibrium quantity of loanable funds is lower. Running a deficit has reduced the level of total saving in the economy and, by increasing the interest rate, has also reduced the level of investment spending by firms. By borrowing to finance its budget deficit, the government will have *crowded out* some firms that would otherwise have been able to borrow to finance investment. **Crowding out** refers to a decline in private expenditures (in this case, investment spending) as a result of an increase in government purchases. In Figure 21.5, the decline in investment spending due to crowding out is shown by the movement from L_1 to L_2 on the demand for loanable funds curve. Lower investment spending means that the capital stock and the quantity of capital per hour worked will not increase as much.

Crowding out A decline in private expenditures as a result of an increase in government purchases.

A government budget surplus has the opposite effect of a deficit: A budget surplus increases the total amount of saving in the economy, shifting the supply curve for loanable funds to the right. In the new equilibrium, the interest rate will be lower, and the quantity of loanable funds will be higher. We can conclude that a budget surplus increases the level of saving and investment.

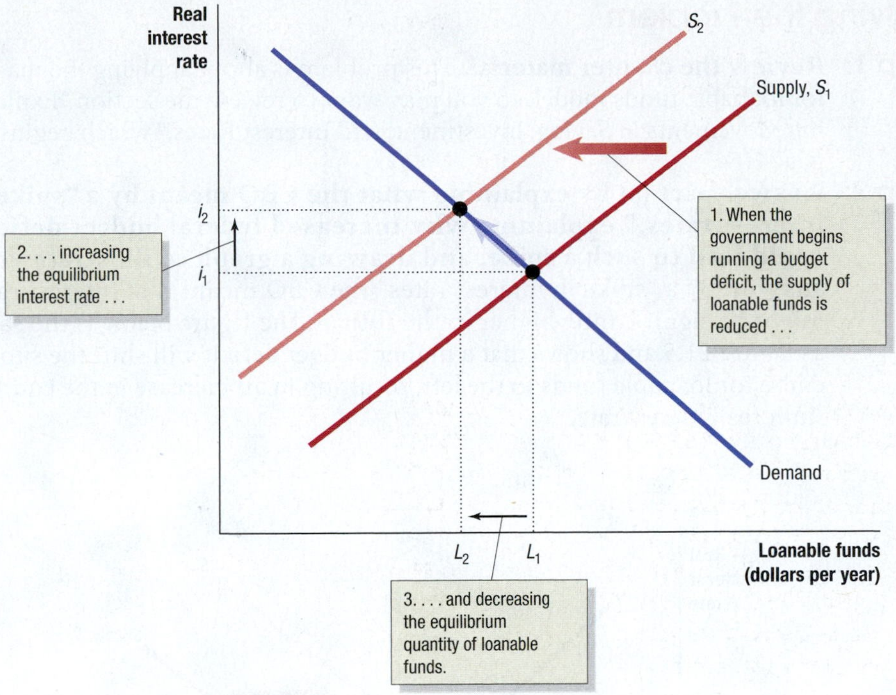

MyEconLab Animation

Figure 21.5

The Effect of a Budget Deficit on the Market for Loanable Funds

When the government begins running a budget deficit, the supply curve for loanable funds shifts to the left. The equilibrium interest rate increases from i_1 to i_2, and the equilibrium quantity of loanable funds falls from L_1 to L_2. As a result, saving and investment both decline.

In practice, however, the effect of government budget deficits and surpluses on the equilibrium interest rate is relatively small. (This finding reflects in part the importance of global saving in determining the interest rate.) For example, one study found that increasing government borrowing by an amount equal to 1 percent of GDP would increase the equilibrium real interest rate by only about 0.003 percentage point. However, this small effect on interest rates does not imply that we can ignore the effect of deficits on economic growth. Paying off government debt in the future may require higher taxes, which can depress economic growth. In 2015, many economists and policymakers were concerned that the large deficits projected for future years might be an obstacle to growth.

In addition to budget deficits, other government policies can affect the supply of loanable funds. The federal government gives special tax incentives for saving. For example, individuals can delay paying taxes on income they put into 401(k) retirement accounts until they actually retire. The delay in paying taxes increases the after-tax return to saving, so this policy encourages individuals to save.

Solved Problem 21.2

Are Future Budget Deficits a Threat to the Economy?

Congress gives the Congressional Budget Office (CBO) the responsibility of estimating the effects of federal spending and taxing policies on the economy. An *Associated Press* news story on a CBO report noted that federal budget deficits in the United States were likely to increase in future years. According to the CBO, these higher deficits might "pose a threat to the economy by crowding out business investment and threatening a spike in interest rates."

a. What did the CBO mean by a "spike in interest rates"? Why might increased federal budget deficits lead to a spike in interest rates? Illustrate your answer with a graph.

b. Is the spike in interest rates connected to crowding out? Why might crowding out be considered a threat to the economy?

Solving the Problem

Step 1: Review the chapter material. This problem is about applying the market for loanable funds model, so you may want to review the section "Explaining Movements in Saving, Investment, and Interest Rates," which begins on page 709.

Step 2: Answer part (a) by explaining what the CBO meant by a "spike in interest rates," explaining why increased federal budget deficits could lead to such a spike, and drawing a graph to illustrate your answer. By a "spike in interest rates" the CBO meant that interest rates might be significantly higher in the future. The figure below is the same as Figure 21.5 and shows that a higher budget deficit will shift the supply curve for loanable funds to the left, resulting in an increase in the equilibrium real interest rate.

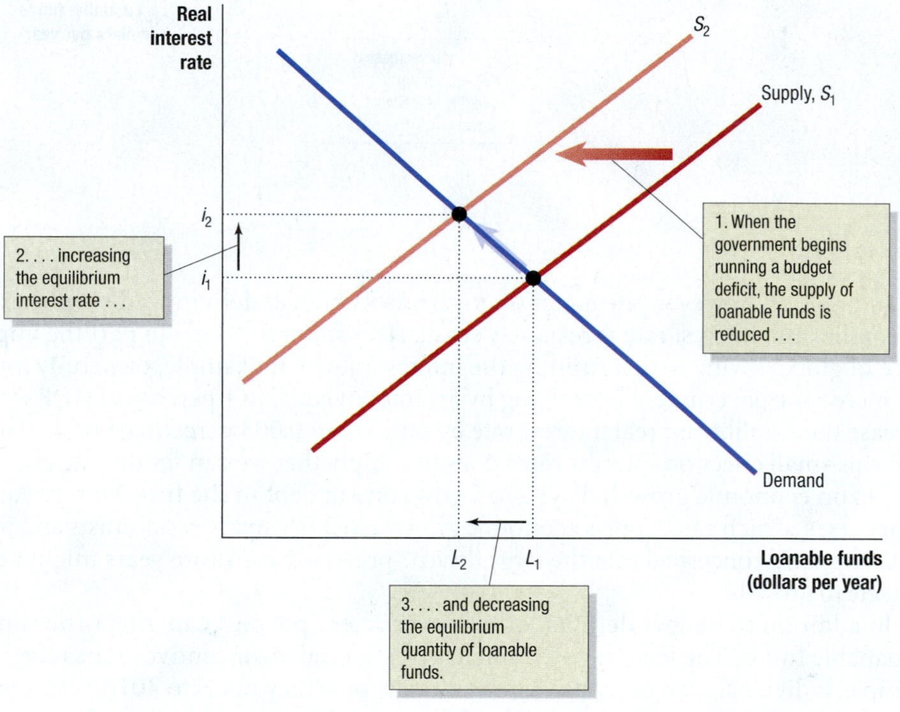

Step 3: Answer part (b) by explaining how a spike in interest rates is connected to crowding out and why crowding out might be considered a threat to the economy. A spike in interest rates is the way that higher budget deficits can cause crowding out. The higher interest rates will result in a decline in investment spending by firms. Lower investment spending can reduce economic growth. It is this possibility of higher deficits leading to slower economic growth that the CBO was referring to as a threat to the economy.

Source: Andrew Taylor, "CBO: Deficits to Drift Lower on Lower Health Costs," *Associated Press*, April 14, 2014.

MyEconLab Study Plan

Your Turn: For more practice, do related problem 2.16 on page 727 at the end of this chapter.

Table 21.1

Summary of Loanable Funds Model

An increase in ...	will shift the ...	causing ...	Graph of the effect on equilibrium in the loanable funds market
the government's budget deficit	supply of loanable funds curve to the left	the real interest rate to increase and investment to decrease.	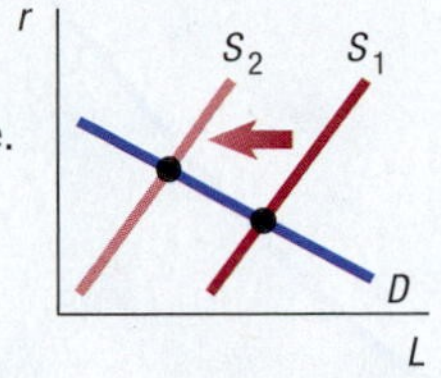
the desire of households to consume today	supply of loanable funds curve to the left	the real interest rate to increase and investment to decrease.	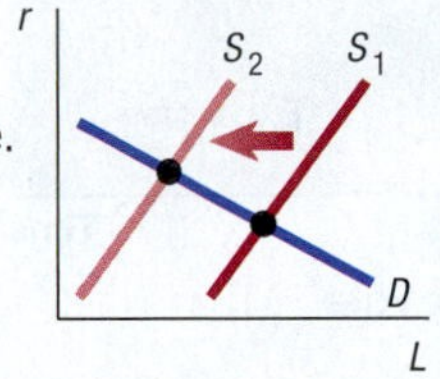
tax benefits for saving, such as 401(k) retirement accounts, which increase the incentive to save	supply of loanable funds curve to the right	the real interest rate to decrease and investment to increase.	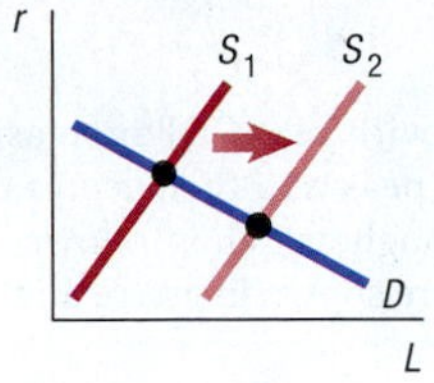
expected future profits	demand for loanable funds curve to the right	the real interest rate and the level of investment to increase.	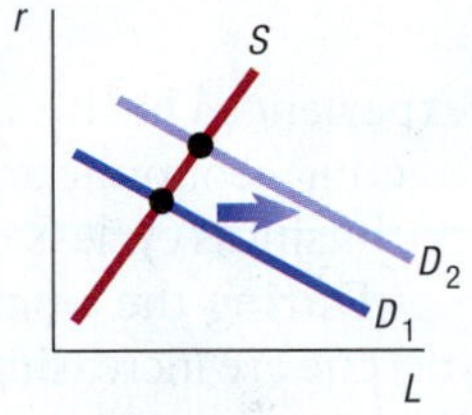
corporate taxes	demand for loanable funds curve to the left	the real interest rate and the level of investment to decrease.	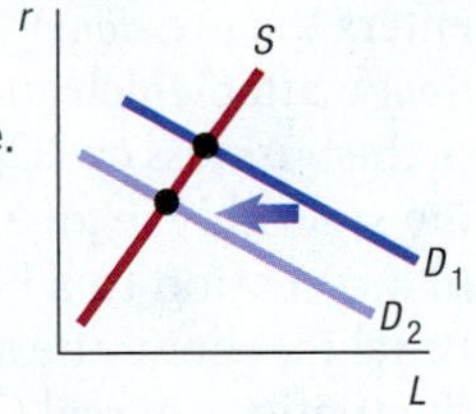

Table 21.1 summarizes the key factors that cause shifts in the demand and supply curves for loanable funds. MyEconLab Concept Check

MyEconLab Study Plan

21.3 The Business Cycle

LEARNING OBJECTIVE: Explain what happens during the business cycle.

Figure 21.1 on page 697 illustrates the tremendous increase during the past century in the standard of living of the average American. But close inspection of the figure reveals that real GDP per capita did not increase every year during this time. For example, during the first half of the 1930s, real GDP per capita *fell* for several years in a row. What accounts for these fluctuations in the long-run upward trend?

Some Basic Business Cycle Definitions

The fluctuations in real GDP *per capita* shown in Figure 21.1 reflect underlying fluctuations in real GDP. Since at least the early nineteenth century, the U.S. economy has

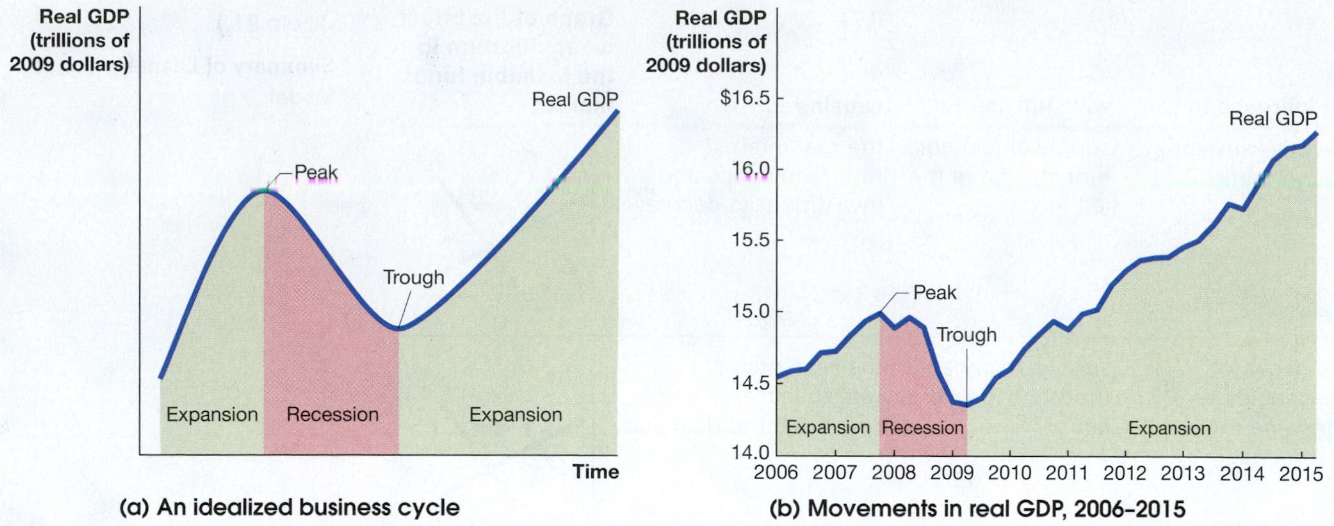

MyEconLab Real-time data

Figure 21.6 The Business Cycle

Panel (a) shows an idealized business cycle, with real GDP increasing smoothly in an expansion to a business cycle peak and then decreasing smoothly in a recession to a business cycle trough, which is followed by another expansion. The periods of expansion are shown in green, and the period of recession is shown in red. Panel (b) shows the actual movements in real GDP from 2006 to 2015. The recession that began following the business cycle peak in December 2007 was the longest and the most severe since the Great Depression of the 1930s.

experienced business cycles that consist of alternating periods of expanding and contracting economic activity. Because real GDP is our best measure of economic activity, the business cycle is usually illustrated using movements in real GDP.

During the *expansion phase* of the business cycle, production, employment, and income are increasing. The period of expansion ends with a *business cycle peak*. Following the business cycle peak, production, employment, and income decline as the economy enters the *recession phase* of the cycle. The recession comes to an end with a *business cycle trough*, after which another period of expansion begins. Figure 21.6 illustrates the phases of the business cycle. Panel (a) shows an idealized business cycle, with real GDP increasing smoothly in an expansion to a business cycle peak and then decreasing smoothly in a recession to a business cycle trough, which is followed by another expansion. Panel (b) shows the somewhat messier reality of an actual business cycle by plotting fluctuations in real GDP during the period from 2006 to 2015. The figure shows that the expansion that began in 2001 continued until a business cycle peak was reached in December 2007. The following recession was the longest and the most severe since the Great Depression of the 1930s. The severity of the recession led some economists to refer to it as the "Great Recession." The economy reached a business cycle trough in June 2009, when the next expansion began. Although real GDP grew following the business cycle trough, the growth was slower than is typical at the beginning of a business cycle expansion. MyEconLab Concept Check

How Do We Know When the Economy Is in a Recession?

The federal government produces many statistics that make it possible to monitor the economy. But the federal government does not officially decide when a recession begins or when it ends. Instead, most economists and policymakers accept the decisions of the Business Cycle Dating Committee of the National Bureau of Economic Research (NBER), a private research group located in Cambridge, Massachusetts. Although writers for newspapers and magazines often define a recession as two consecutive quarters of declining real GDP, the NBER has a broader definition: "A recession is a significant decline in activity spread across the economy, lasting more than a few months, visible in industrial production, employment, real income, and wholesale–retail trade."

Table 21.2

The U.S. Business Cycle Since 1950

Peak	Trough	Length of Recession
July 1953	May 1954	10 months
August 1957	April 1958	8 months
April 1960	February 1961	10 months
December 1969	November 1970	11 months
November 1973	March 1975	16 months
January 1980	July 1980	6 months
July 1981	November 1982	16 months
July 1990	March 1991	8 months
March 2001	November 2001	8 months
December 2007	June 2009	18 months

Source: National Bureau of Economic Research.

The NBER is fairly slow in announcing business cycle dates because gathering and analyzing economic statistics takes time. Typically, the NBER will announce that the economy is in a recession only well after the recession has begun. For instance, it did not announce that a recession had begun in December 2007 until 11 months later, at the end of November 2008. Table 21.2 lists the business cycle peaks and troughs identified by the NBER for the years since 1950. The length of each recession is the number of months from each peak to the following trough. MyEconLab Concept Check

Making the Connection

MyEconLab Video

Can a Recession Be a Good Time for a Business to Expand?

During a recession, business managers have to quickly make many decisions, such as whether to reduce production, cut prices, close stores or other facilities, or lay off workers. In addition to making decisions aimed at dealing with the immediate effects of the recession, managers have to consider how to prepare for the expansion that will follow the recession. Managers know that every recession, even one as severe as the recession of 2007–2009, will be followed by an expansion during which demand for their products is likely to increase. But it can be difficult to commit resources to future expansion when current conditions are bleak and when the end of the recession is difficult to predict.

Businesses such as VF viewed the recession of 2007–2009 as an opportunity to expand operations.

The payoff to preparing for future growth can be very large, however. For example, at the end of World War II in 1945, many economists and business managers expected that the U.S. economy would enter a severe recession. Sears and Montgomery Ward were the two largest department store chains in the country. Robert Wood, CEO of Sears, expected continuing prosperity and moved to open new stores across the country. Sewell Avery, CEO of Montgomery Ward, expected falling incomes and rising unemployment and refused to authorize any new stores and closed a number of existing ones. As a result, when strong economic growth occurred during the late 1940s, Sears rapidly gained market share at Montgomery Ward's expense.

Following the September 11, 2001, terrorist attacks in the United States, the managers of many hotels expected a prolonged period of reduced travel. They responded by laying off workers and postponing or canceling new construction. Isadore Sharp, the chairman and CEO of Four Seasons Hotels, decided that although the recession would severely hurt the hotel industry, the effects would be short-lived. He decided to finish construction of 18 hotels and begin construction of 10 more. By his own account: "We maintained or enhanced our market share in most regions, contrary to the predictions of various industry experts." In a letter to his shareholders in March 2002, he wrote: "We are well positioned for the economic recovery expected later this year."

During the severe recession of 2007–2009, managers had similar decisions to make. Based in Greensboro, North Carolina, VF Corporation is the largest apparel maker in the world. Among its brands are North Face, Timberland, and Wrangler. While many firms, such as J.Crew, Anne Klein, and Liz Claiborne, were closing stores or postponing opening new ones, Eric Wiseman, CEO of VF, pushed ahead, opening 89 stores in 2008 and 70 in 2009. One retail analyst was quoted as saying, "Unfortunately, many companies pull in the reins in a downturn, but these are often the best opportunities to grow." Similarly, Intel, the computer chip manufacturer, decided in early 2009 to proceed with a $7 billion expansion of its factories in the United States, while many rival firms were reducing their spending on new factories as computer sales declined. Paul Otellini, CEO of Intel, was quoted as saying, "I thought it was important for a company like Intel to stand up and say we have confidence." Heavy equipment manufacturer Caterpillar, Inc., announced that it would build several new facilities and expand some existing ones "to meet the expected increase in customer demand."

By 2015, the recovery from the 2007–2009 recession was well underway, although it was slower than a typical recovery. VF's decision to expand appeared to have been a good one as sales and profits continued to increase and its stock price was near an all-time high. The company continued to open new stores and was operating nearly 1,500 stores worldwide. The verdict for Caterpillar and Intel was more mixed, although both firms remained profitable. Intel's announcement in mid-2015 that technical problems would delay its latest generation of computer chips until late 2017 might represent a temporary setback, or it could indicate that it was beginning to fall behind rival chipmakers. Caterpillar was being hurt by declining prices for coal, iron ore, oil, and other commodities, which was reducing demand for equipment used for mining and oil exploration. Still, Caterpillar's CEO expected that sales would increase in the future as growth in the world economy caused a turnaround in commodity prices.

Over the long run, betting on the future of the U.S. economy has paid off for most firms.

Sources: Lisa Beilfuss, "VF Corp. Tops Expectations on Strength in Outdoor Sales," *Wall Street Journal*, July 24, 2015; Tiernan Ray, "Is Intel in Trouble?" *Barrons*, July 18, 2015; James R. Hagerty, "Caterpillar Resists Calls to Slash Spending," *Wall Street Journal*, July 23, 2015; Robert Sobel, *When Giants Stumble*, Paramus, NJ: Prentice Hall, 1999; Isadore Sharp, *Four Seasons: The Story of a Business Philosophy*, New York: Portfolio, 2009; Bob Tita, "Caterpillar to Expand Kansas Plant," *Wall Street Journal*, August 18, 2011; Rachel Dodes, "VF Dresses Up Its Operations, Bucking Recession," *Wall Street Journal*, March 31, 2009; and Don Clark, "Intel to Spend Heavily on U.S. Plants," *Wall Street Journal*, February 10, 2009.

MyEconLab Study Plan

Your Turn: Test your understanding by doing related problem 3.6 on page 728 at the end of this chapter.

What Happens during the Business Cycle?

Each business cycle is different. The lengths of the expansion and recession phases and the sectors of the economy that are most affected are rarely the same in any two cycles. But most business cycles share these characteristics:

1. As the economy nears the end of an expansion, interest rates are usually rising, and the wages of workers are usually increasing faster than prices. As a result of rising interest rates and wages, the profits of firms will be falling. Typically, toward the end of an expansion, both households and firms will have substantially increased their debts. These debts are the result of the borrowing that firms and households undertake to help finance their spending during the expansion. Rising debts can eventually lead households and firms to reduce their spending.
2. A recession will often begin with a decline in spending by firms on capital goods, such as machinery, equipment, new factories, and new office buildings, or by households on new houses and consumer durables, such as furniture and automobiles. As spending declines, firms that build houses and firms that sell capital goods and consumer durables will find their sales declining. As sales decline, firms cut back on production and begin to lay off workers. Rising unemployment and falling profits reduce income, which leads to further declines in spending.

3. As the recession continues, economic conditions eventually begin to improve. The declines in spending finally come to an end; households and firms begin to reduce their debts, thereby increasing their ability to spend; and interest rates decline, making it more likely that households and firms will borrow to finance new spending. Firms begin to increase their spending on capital goods as they anticipate the need for additional production during the next expansion. Increased spending by households on new houses and consumer durables and by businesses on capital goods will finally bring the recession to an end and begin the next expansion.

Corning, Technology, and the Business Cycle We have seen that long-run economic growth depends on the development of new technologies, such as those introduced over the years by firms like Corning. Often, though, these firms are exposed to the effects of the business cycle because new technologies are embodied in *durables*, which are goods that are expected to last for three or more years. Consumer durables include automobiles, laptops, and appliances. Producer durables include machine tools, electric generators, and commercial airplanes. *Nondurables* are goods that are expected to last for fewer than three years. Consumer nondurables include goods such as food and clothing. Durables are affected more by the business cycle than are nondurables. During a recession, workers reduce spending if they lose their jobs, fear losing their jobs, or suffer wage cuts. Because people can often continue using their existing automobiles, appliances, and smartphones, they are more likely to postpone spending on durables than spending on nondurables. Similarly, when firms experience declining sales and profits during a recession, they often cut back on purchases of producer durables.

We mentioned in our discussion of Corning at the beginning of this chapter that the firm has substantial sales to firms that produce automobiles, televisions, and computers. As a result, Corning's sales are significantly affected by the business cycle. Panel (a) of Figure 21.7 shows movements in real GDP for each quarter from the beginning of

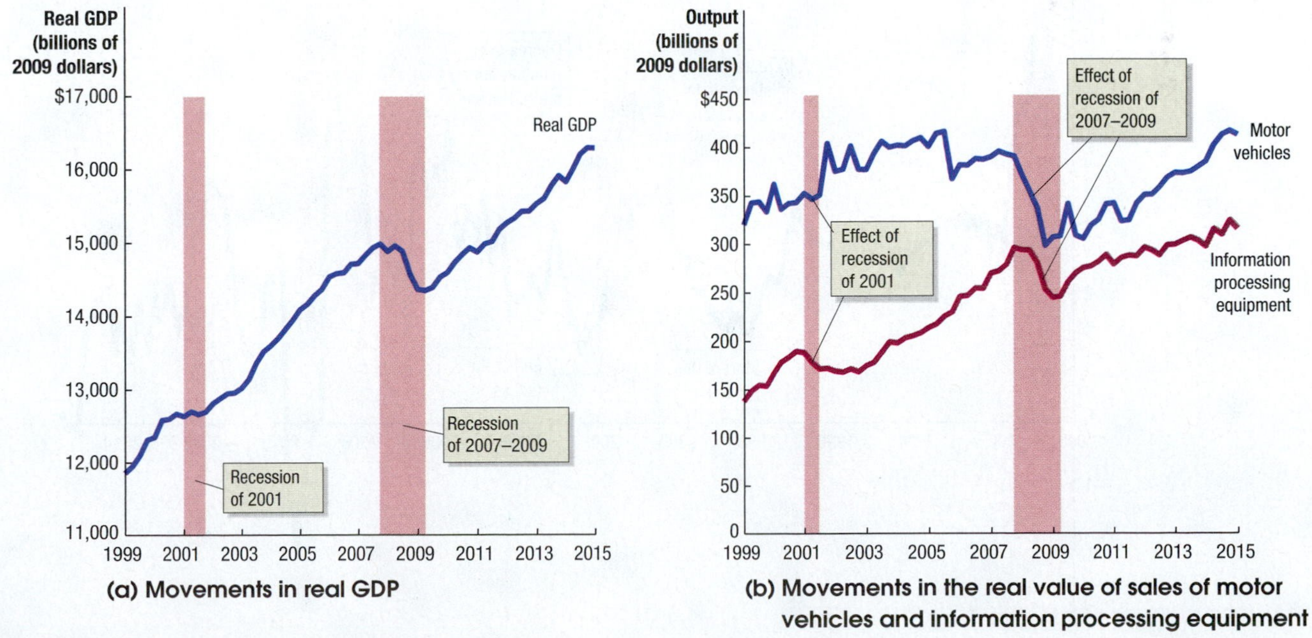

MyEconLab Real-time data

Figure 21.7 The Effect of the Business Cycle on Corning

Panel (a) shows movements in real GDP for each quarter from the beginning of 1999 through the beginning of 2015. Panel (b) shows movements in the real value of automobile production and the real value of production of information processing equipment for the same years. In panel (b), the effects of the recessions on the sales of firms that Corning sells its products to are more dramatic than the effects on the economy as a whole.

Sources: U.S. Bureau of Economic Analysis.

1999 through the beginning of 2015. We can see both the upward trend in real GDP over time and the effects of the recessions of 2001 and 2007–2009. Data for Corning's sales of individual products are not available, but panel (b) shows movements in the real value of automobile production and the real value of production of information processing equipment, such as computers. Panel (b) shows that recessions affect these industries more than they affect the economy as a whole. For example, during the 2007–2009 recession, real GDP declined by about 4 percent, while motor vehicle production declined by nearly 25 percent, and production of information processing equipment declined by 17 percent. As production declined in these industries, Corning's sales of ceramics for automobile emissions systems and display panels for computers dropped as well. As these industries recovered from the recession, so did Corning's sales.

The Effect of the Business Cycle on the Inflation Rate The *price level* measures the average prices of goods and services in the economy, and the *inflation rate* is the percentage increase in the price level from one year to the next (see Chapter 20). An important fact about the business cycle is that the inflation rate usually increases during economic expansions—particularly near the end of an expansion—and the inflation rate usually decreases during recessions. Figure 21.8 illustrates this pattern for the three recessions since 1990.

In every recession since 1950, the inflation rate has been lower during the 12 months after the recession ends than it was during the 12 months before the recession began. The average decline in the inflation rate has been about 2.5 percentage points. This result is not surprising. During a business cycle expansion, spending by businesses and

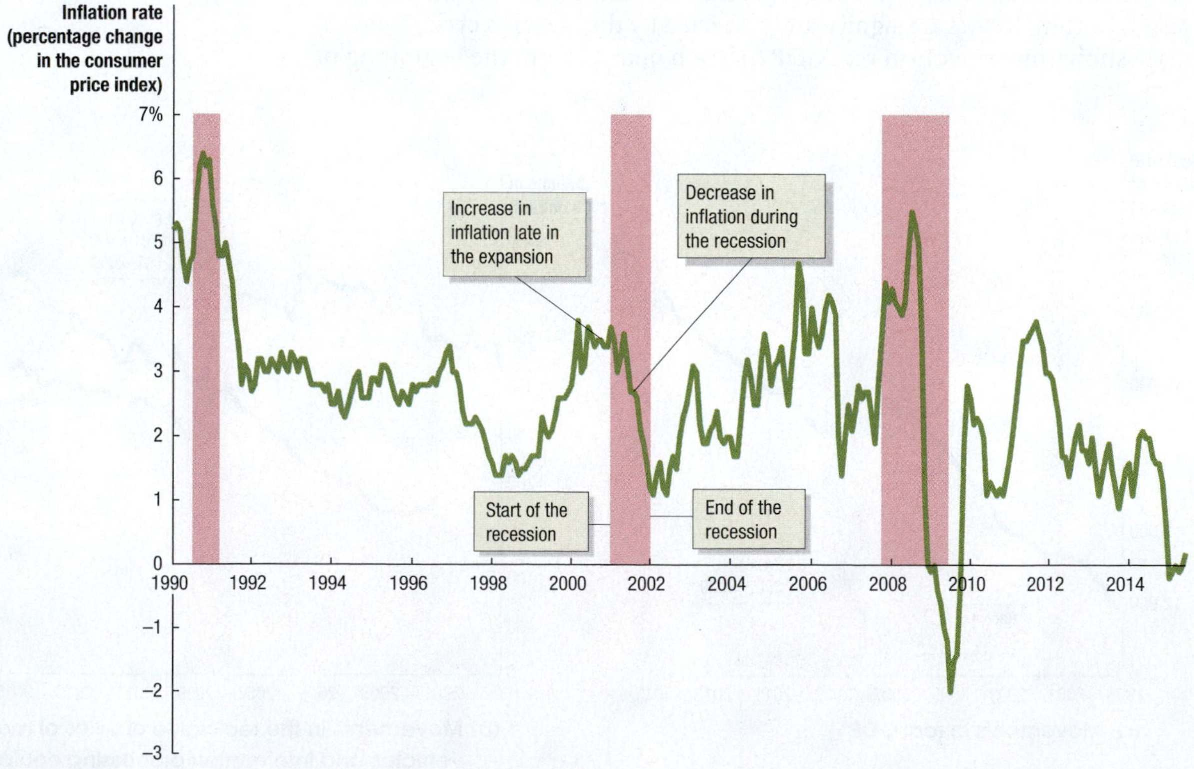

MyEconLab Real-time data

Figure 21.8 The Effect of Recessions on the Inflation Rate

Toward the end of a typical expansion, the inflation rate begins to rise. During recessions, marked by the shaded vertical bars, the inflation rate declines. By the end of a recession, the inflation rate is significantly below what it had been at the beginning of the recession.

Note: The points on the figure represent the annual inflation rate measured by the percentage change in the consumer price index from the same month during the previous year.

Source: U.S. Bureau of Labor Statistics.

households is strong, and producers of goods and services find it easier to raise prices. As spending declines during a recession, firms have a more difficult time selling their goods and services and are likely to increase prices less than they otherwise might have.

Don't Let This Happen to You

Don't Confuse the Price Level and the Inflation Rate

Do you agree with the following statement: "The consumer price index is a widely used measure of the inflation rate"? This statement may sound plausible, but it is incorrect. The consumer price index (CPI) tells us what a typical urban family of four pays for the goods and services they purchase relative to a base year, but values for the CPI do not directly measure the inflation rate (see Chapter 20). We can measure the inflation rate as the *percentage change* in the CPI from one year to the next. In macroeconomics, it is important not to confuse the level of a variable with the change in the variable. To give another example, real GDP does not measure economic growth. Economic growth is measured by the percentage change in real GDP from one year to the next.

MyEconLab Study Plan

Your Turn: Test your understanding by doing related problem 3.8 on page 728 at the end of this chapter.

The Effect of the Business Cycle on the Unemployment Rate Recessions cause the inflation rate to fall, but they cause the unemployment rate to increase. As firms see their sales decline, they begin to reduce production and lay off workers. Figure 21.9 illustrates this pattern for the three recessions since 1990. Notice in the

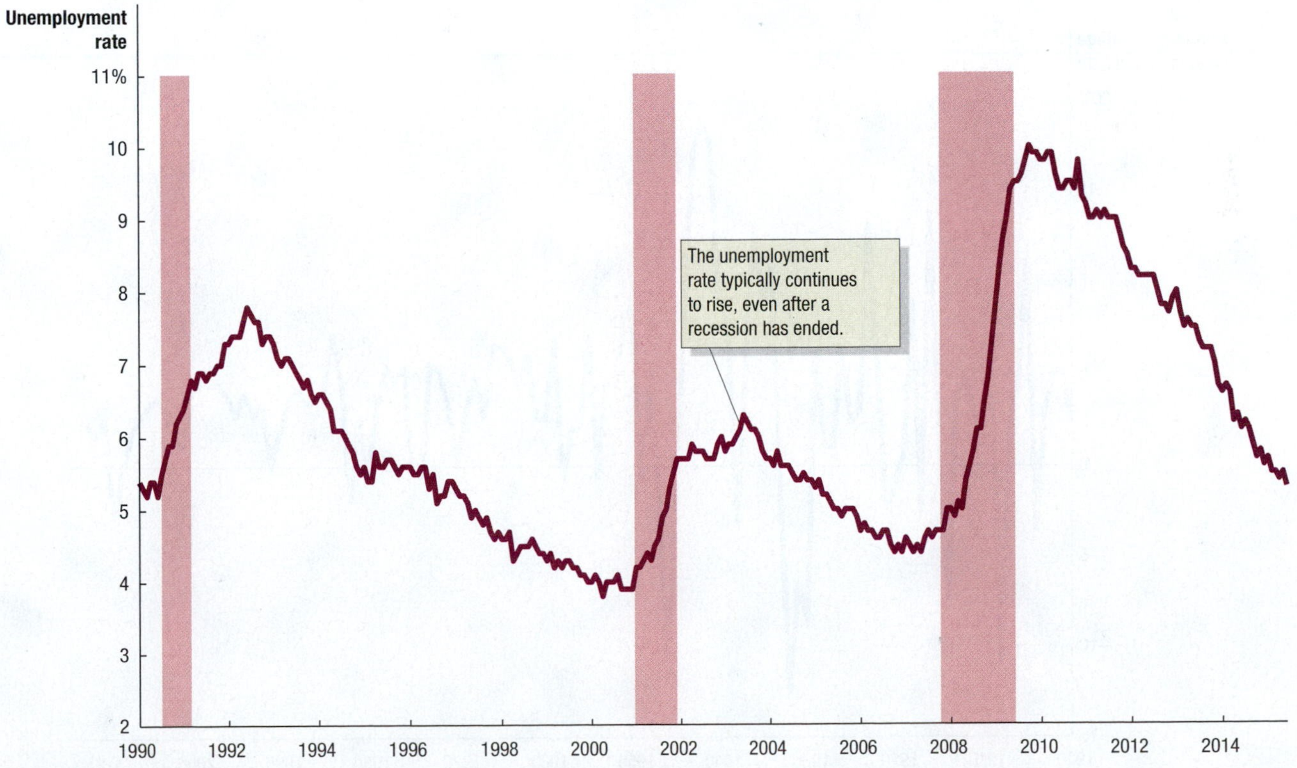

MyEconLab Real-time data

Figure 21.9 How Recessions Affect the Unemployment Rate

Unemployment rises during recessions and falls during expansions. The reluctance of firms to hire new employees during the early stages of a recovery usually causes the unemployment rate to continue to rise even after a recession has ended.

Source: U.S. Bureau of Labor Statistics.

figure that the unemployment rate continued to rise even after the recessions of 1990–1991, 2001, and 2007–2009 had ended. This lag before the unemployment rate begins to decline is typical and is due to two factors. First, even though employment begins to increase as a recession ends, it may be increasing more slowly than the increase in the labor force resulting from population growth. If employment increases slowly enough relative to the growth in the labor force, it is possible for the unemployment rate to rise. Second, some firms continue to operate well below their capacity even after a recession has ended and sales have begun to increase. As a result, at first, firms may not hire back all the workers they have laid off and may even continue for a while to lay off more workers.

During the recessions since 1950, the unemployment rate has risen on average by about 1.2 percentage points during the 12 months after a recession has begun. So, on average, more than 1 million more workers have been unemployed during the 12 months after a recession has begun than during the previous 12 months.

Is the "Great Moderation" Over? Figure 21.10, which shows the year-to-year percentage changes in real GDP since 1900, illustrates a striking change in fluctuations in real GDP beginning around 1950. Before 1950, real GDP went through much greater year-to-year fluctuations than it has since that time. Fluctuations since the mid-1980s have been particularly mild. By the early twenty-first century, some economists had begun referring to the absence of severe recessions in the United States as the *Great Moderation*. However, economists began questioning this view with the recession that began in December 2007. That recession was the longest and the most severe since the Great Depression of the 1930s and has been called the *Great Recession*.

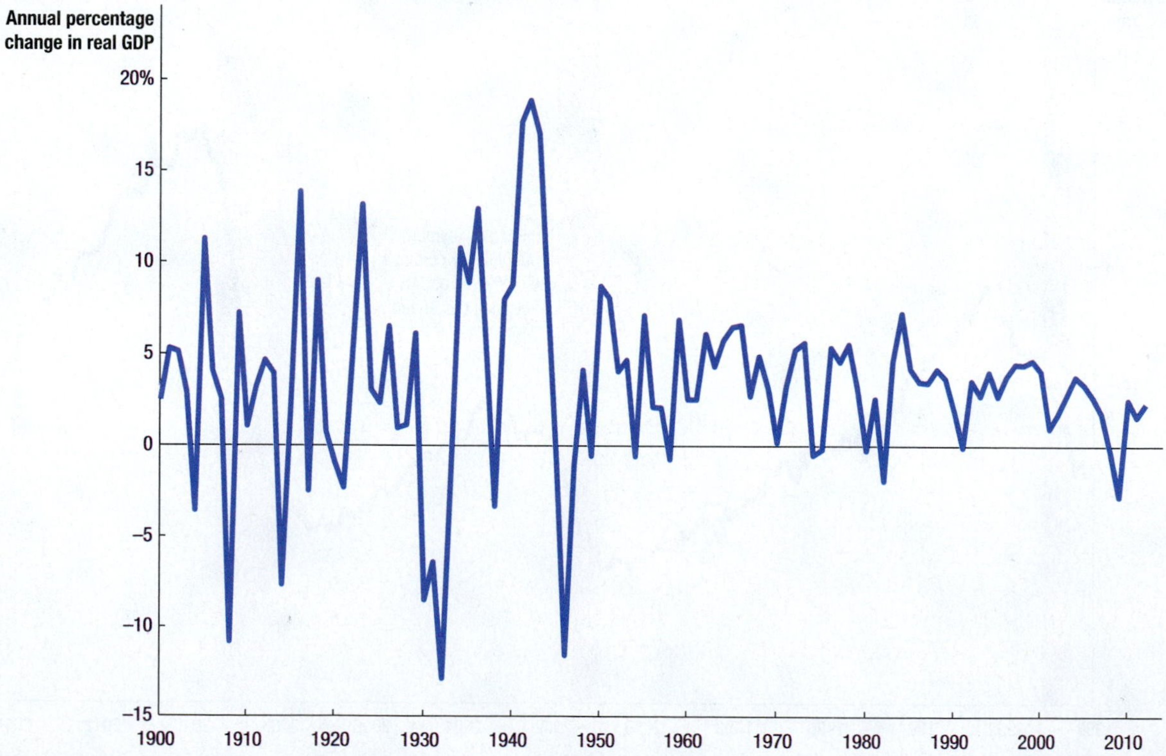

MyEconLab Real-time data

Figure 21.10 Fluctuations in Real GDP, 1900–2014

Fluctuations in real GDP were greater before 1950 than they have been since 1950.

Sources: Samuel H. Williamson, "What Was the U.S. GDP Then?" MeasuringWorth, July 2015; and U.S. Bureau of Economic Analysis.

Period	Average Length of Expansions	Average Length of Recessions
1870–1900	26 months	26 months
1900–1950	25 months	19 months
1950–2009	61 months	11 months

Table 21.3

Until 2007, the Business Cycle Had Become Milder

The percentage decline in real GDP during 2009 was the largest since 1932. Economists and policymakers remain unsure whether the Great Moderation will return even as the economy continued to expand more than six years after the end of the Great Recession.

The unusual severity of the 2007–2009 recession can be seen by comparing its length to those of other recessions. Table 21.3 shows that in the late nineteenth century, the average length of recessions was the same as the average length of expansions. During the first half of the twentieth century, the average length of expansions decreased slightly, and the average length of recessions decreased significantly. As a result, expansions were about six months longer than recessions during these years. The most striking change came after 1950, when the length of expansions greatly increased and the length of recessions decreased. After 1950, expansions were more than five times as long as recessions. In other words, in the late nineteenth century, the U.S. economy spent as much time in recession as it did in expansion. After 1950, the U.S. economy experienced long expansions interrupted by relatively short recessions.

The recession of 2007–2009 is an exception to this experience of relatively short, mild recessions. The recession lasted 18 months, the longest of the post-1950 period. Does the length and depth of the 2007–2009 recession indicate that the United States is returning to an era of severe fluctuations in real GDP? A full answer to this question will not be possible for at least several years. But in the next section, we provide some perspective on the question by considering why the period from 1950 to 2007 was one of relative macroeconomic stability.

MyEconLab Concept Check

Will the U.S. Economy Return to Stability?

Shorter recessions, longer expansions, and less severe fluctuations in real GDP have resulted in a significant improvement in the economic well-being of Americans. Economists have offered several explanations for why the U.S. economy experienced a period of relative stability from 1950 to 2007:

- **The increasing importance of services and the declining importance of goods.** As services such as medical care and investment advice have become a much larger fraction of GDP, there has been a corresponding relative decline in the production of goods. For example, at one time, manufacturing production accounted for about 40 percent of GDP, but in 2015, it accounted for about 12 percent. Manufacturing production, particularly of durable goods such as automobiles, fluctuates more than the production of services because during a recession, households will cut back more on purchases of durables than they will on purchases of services.
- **The establishment of unemployment insurance and other government transfer programs that provide funds to the unemployed.** Before the 1930s, programs such as unemployment insurance, which provides government payments to workers who lose their jobs, and Social Security, which provides government payments to retired and disabled workers, did not exist. These and other government programs make it possible for workers who lose their jobs during recessions to have higher incomes and, therefore, to spend more than

they would otherwise. This additional spending may have helped to shorten recessions.

- **Active federal government policies to stabilize the economy.** Before the Great Depression of the 1930s, the federal government did not attempt to end recessions or prolong expansions. Because the Great Depression was so severe, with the unemployment rate rising to more than 20 percent of the labor force and real GDP declining by almost 30 percent, public opinion began favoring government attempts to stabilize the economy. In the years since World War II, the federal government has actively used macroeconomic policy measures to try to end recessions and prolong expansions. Many economists believe that these government policies have played a key role in stabilizing the economy. Other economists, however, argue that active government policy has had little effect. The debate over the role of macroeconomic policy became particularly intense during and after the 2007–2009 recession (see Chapters 26 and 27).
- **The increased stability of the financial system.** The severity of the Great Depression of the 1930s was caused in part by instability in the financial system. More than 5,000 banks failed between 1929 and 1933, reducing the savings of many households and making it difficult for households and firms to obtain the credit needed to maintain their spending. In addition, a decline of more than 80 percent in stock prices greatly reduced the wealth of many households and made it difficult for firms to raise funds by selling stock. Most economists believe that the return of financial instability during the 2007–2009 recession is a key reason the recession was so severe. If the United States is to return to macroeconomic stability, stability will first have to return to the financial system.

MyEconLab Study Plan

MyEconLab Concept Check

Continued from page 695

Economics in Your Life

Do You Help the Economy More if You Spend or if You Save?

At the beginning of this chapter, we posed a question: Which of your two roommates is right—the one who argues that you would help the economy more by saving your tax refund, or the one who argues that you should spend it? In this chapter, we have seen that consumption spending promotes the production of more consumption goods and services—such as jeans and haircuts—and fewer investment goods and services—such as physical capital and research and development. Saving (or not consuming) is necessary to fund investment expenditure. So, saving your refund will help the economy over the long run. But if the economy is in a recession, spending your refund will spur more production of consumption goods. In a sense, then, both of your roommates are correct: Spending your refund will help stimulate the economy during a recession, while saving it will help the economy grow over the long run.

Conclusion

The U.S. economy remains a remarkable engine for improving the well-being of Americans. The standard of living of Americans today is much higher than it was 100 years ago. But households and firms are still subject to the ups and downs of the business cycle. In the following chapters, we will continue our analysis of this basic fact of macroeconomics: Ever-increasing long-run prosperity is achieved in the context of short-run instability.

Visit MyEconLab for a news article and analysis related to the concepts in this chapter.

CHAPTER SUMMARY AND PROBLEMS

Key Terms

Business cycle, p. 696
Capital, p. 700
Crowding out, p. 710
Financial intermediaries, p. 705
Financial markets, p. 705
Financial system, p. 704
Labor productivity, p. 700
Long-run economic growth, p. 697
Market for loanable funds, p. 708
Potential GDP, p. 703

21.1 Long-Run Economic Growth, pages 696–704

LEARNING OBJECTIVE: Discuss the importance of long-run economic growth.

Summary

The U.S. economy has experienced both *long-run economic growth* and the *business cycle*. The **business cycle** refers to alternating periods of economic expansion and economic recession. **Long-run economic growth** is the process by which rising productivity increases the standard of living of the typical person. Because of economic growth, the typical American today can buy almost eight times as much as the typical American of 1900. Long-run growth is measured by increases in real GDP per capita. Increases in real GDP per capita depend on increases in labor productivity. **Labor productivity** is the quantity of goods and services that can be produced by one worker or by one hour of work. Economists believe two key factors determine labor productivity: the quantity of capital per hour worked and the level of technology. **Capital** refers to manufactured goods that are used to produce other goods and services. *Human capital* is the accumulated knowledge and skills workers acquire from education, training, or their life experiences. Economic growth occurs if the quantity of capital per hour worked increases and if technological change occurs. Economists often discuss economic growth in terms of growth in **potential GDP**, which is the level of GDP attained when all firms are producing at capacity.

MyEconLab Visit www.myeconlab.com to complete these exercises online and get instant feedback.

Review Questions

1.1 By how much did real GDP per capita increase in the United States between 1900 and 2014? Discuss whether the increase in real GDP per capita is likely to be greater or smaller than the true increase in living standards.

1.2 What is the rule of 70? If real GDP per capita grows at a rate of 5 percent per year, how many years will it take to double?

1.3 What two key factors cause labor productivity to increase over time?

1.4 What is potential GDP? Does potential GDP remain constant over time?

Problems and Applications

1.5 Briefly discuss whether you would rather live in the United States of 1900 with an income of $1,000,000 per year or the United States of 2016 with an income of $50,000 per year. Assume that the incomes for both years are measured in 2016 dollars.

1.6 Based on what you read about economic growth in this chapter, discuss the importance of growth in GDP, particularly real GDP per capita, to the quality of life of a country's citizens.

1.7 **(Related to the Making the Connection on page 698)** Think about the relationship between economic prosperity and life expectancy. What implications does this relationship have for the size of an economy's health care sector? In particular, is this sector of the U.S. economy likely to expand or contract in coming years?

1.8 Use the following table to answer the questions.

Year	Real GDP (billions of 2009 dollars)
1990	$8,955
1991	8,948
1992	9,267
1993	9,521
1994	9,905

a. Calculate the growth rate of real GDP for each year from 1991 to 1994.

b. Calculate the average annual growth rate of real GDP for the period from 1991 to 1994.

1.9 As discussed in this chapter, real GDP per capita in the United States grew from about $6,000 in 1900 to about $50,010 in 2014, which represents an average annual growth rate of 1.9 percent. If the U.S. economy continues to grow at this rate, how many years will it take for real GDP per capita to double? If government economic policies meant to stimulate economic growth result in the annual growth rate increasing to 2.2 percent, how many years will it take for real GDP per capita to double?

1.10 **(Related to Solved Problem 21.1 on page 701)** The business consulting firm McKinsey & Company released a report on world economic growth that contained the observation "productivity needs to drive growth." Is it likely that McKinsey was referring to growth in real GDP or growth in real GDP per capita? Do you agree with this observation? Briefly explain.

Source: McKinsey Global Institute, "Global Growth: Can Productivity Save the Day in an Aging World?" January 2015.

1.11 **(Related to Solved Problem 21.1 on page 701)** An article in the *Wall Street Journal* notes that "raising productivity in the long run is the most effective way to elevate standards of living." Do you agree? Briefly explain.

Source: Greg Ip, "Politicians Should Pay Heed to Productivity Problem," *Wall Street Journal*, July 22, 2015.

1.12 An article in the *Economist* notes, "For 60 years, from 1770 to 1830, growth in British wages, adjusted for inflation, was imperceptible because productivity growth was restricted to a few industries." Not until the late nineteenth, when productivity "gains had spread across the whole economy," did a sustained increase in real wages begin. Why would you expect there to be a close relationship between productivity gains and increases in real wages?

Source: "The Onrushing Wave," *Economist*, January 18, 2014.

1.13 **(Related to the Making the Connection on page 702)** Amartya Sen, a professor of economics at Harvard University and a Nobel Laureate, has argued, "For India to match China in its range of manufacturing capacity … it needs a better-educated and healthier labor force at all levels of society." What role do education and health care play in economic growth? How has India been able to experience rapid economic growth since 1991 despite poor education and health care systems?

Source: Amartya Sen, "Why India Trails China," *New York Times*, June 19, 2013.

1.14 **(Related to the Making the Connection on page 702)** India's labor force has been gradually shifting out of the low-productivity agricultural sector into the higher-productivity service and industrial sectors.

a. Briefly explain how this shift is affecting India's real GDP per capita.
b. Is this shift likely to result in continuing increases in India's growth rate in coming decades? Briefly explain.

21.2 Saving, Investment, and the Financial System, pages 704–713

LEARNING OBJECTIVE: Discuss the role of the financial system in facilitating long-run economic growth.

Summary

Financial markets and financial intermediaries together comprise the **financial system**. A well-functioning financial system is an important determinant of economic growth. Firms acquire funds from households, either directly through financial markets—such as the stock and bond markets—or indirectly through financial intermediaries—such as banks. The funds available to firms come from *saving*. There are two categories of saving in the economy: *private saving* by households and *public saving* by the government. The value of total saving in the economy is always equal to the value of total investment spending. In the model of the **market for loanable funds**, the interaction of borrowers and lenders determines the market interest rate and the quantity of loanable funds exchanged.

MyEconLab Visit **www.myeconlab.com** to complete these exercises online and get instant feedback.

Review Questions

2.1 Why is a country's financial system important for long-run economic growth?

2.2 How does the financial system—both financial markets and financial intermediaries—provide risk sharing, liquidity, and information to savers and borrowers?

2.3 Briefly explain why the total value of saving in the economy must equal the total value of investment.

2.4 What are loanable funds? Why do businesses demand loanable funds? Why do households supply loanable funds?

Problems and Applications

2.5 Suppose you can receive an interest rate of 3 percent on a certificate of deposit at a bank that is charging borrowers 7 percent on new car loans. Why might you be unwilling to loan money directly to someone who wants to borrow from you to buy a new car, even if that person offers to pay you an interest rate higher than 3 percent?

2.6 An International Monetary Fund Factsheet makes the following observation regarding sound financial systems: "A country's financial system … provide[s] a framework … [for] supporting economic growth." Do you agree with this observation? Briefly explain.

Source: "Financial System Soundness," *International Monetary Fund Factsheet*, September 21, 2015.

2.7 Consider the following data for a closed economy:

$Y = \$11$ trillion
$C = \$8$ trillion
$I = \$2$ trillion
$TR = \$1$ trillion
$T = \$3$ trillion

Use these data to calculate the following:

a. Private saving
b. Public saving
c. Government purchases
d. The government budget deficit or budget surplus

2.8 Consider the following data for a closed economy:

$Y = \$12$ trillion
$C = \$8$ trillion
$G = \$2$ trillion
$S_{\text{Public}} = \$-0.5$ trillion
$T = \$2$ trillion

Use these data to calculate the following:

a. Private saving
b. Investment spending
c. Transfer payments
d. The government budget deficit or budget surplus

2.9 In problem 2.8, suppose that government purchases increase from \$2 trillion to \$2.5 trillion. If the values for Y and C are unchanged, what must happen to the values of S and I? Briefly explain.

2.10 Match each of the following scenarios with the appropriate graph of the market for loanable funds.

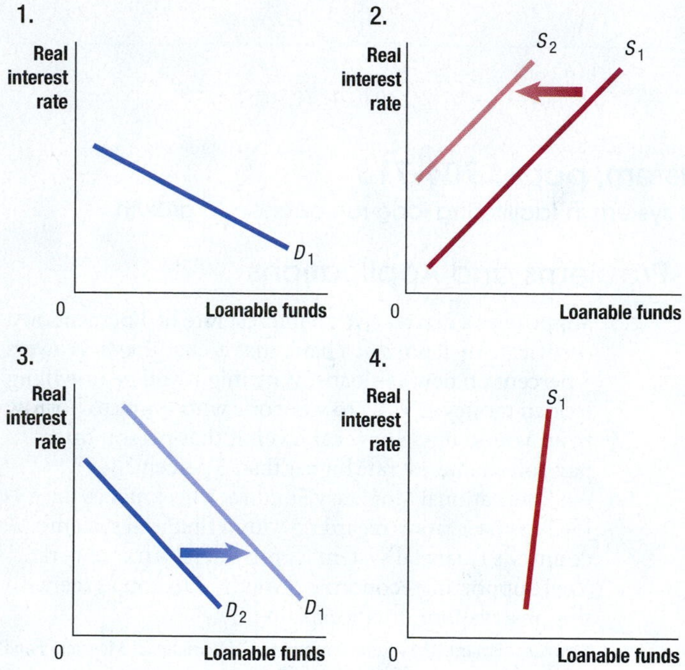

a. An increase in the real interest rate results in only a small increase in private saving by households.
b. A decrease in the real interest rate results in a substantial increase in spending on investment projects by businesses.
c. The federal government eliminates 401(k) retirement accounts.
d. The federal government reduces the tax on corporate profits. (Assume no change in the federal budget deficit or budget surplus.)

2.11 Use the following graph to answer the questions.

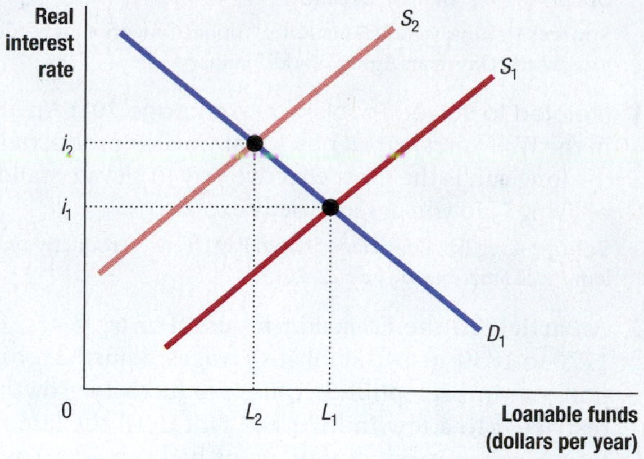

a. Does the shift from S_1 to S_2 represent an increase or a decrease in the supply of loanable funds?
b. With the shift in supply, what happens to the equilibrium quantity of loanable funds?
c. With the change in the equilibrium quantity of loanable funds, what happens to the quantity of saving? What happens to the quantity of investment?

2.12 Use the following graph to answer the questions.

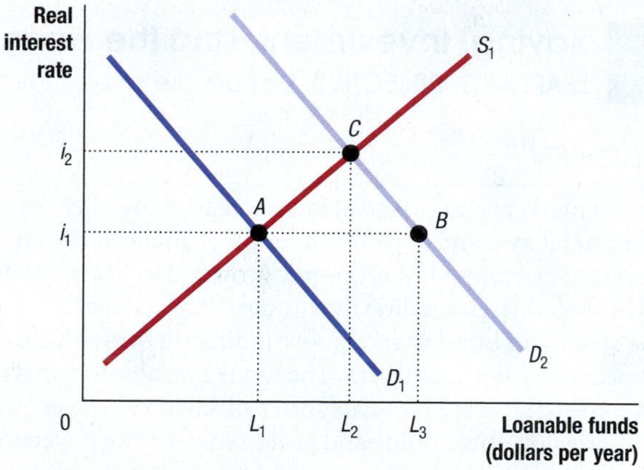

a. With the shift in the demand curve for loanable funds, what happens to the equilibrium real interest rate and the equilibrium quantity of loanable funds?
b. How can the equilibrium quantity of loanable funds increase when the real interest rate increases? Doesn't the quantity of loanable funds demanded decrease when the interest rate increases?
c. How much would the quantity of loanable funds demanded have increased if the interest rate had remained at i_1?
d. How much does the quantity of loanable funds supplied increase with the increase in the interest rate from i_1 to i_2?

2.13 Firms care about their after-tax rate of return on investment projects. In the market for loanable funds, draw a graph and explain the effect of an increase in taxes on business profits. (For simplicity, assume no change in the federal budget deficit or budget surplus.) What happens to the equilibrium real interest rate and the quantity of loanable funds? What will be the effect on the level of investment by firms and the economy's capital stock in the future?

2.14 **(Related to the Making the Connection on page 709)** A writer for the *Wall Street Journal* wrote a whimsical "Letter to Stingy American Consumers":

> Dear American Consumer:
>
> This is The *Wall Street Journal*. … The sun shined in April and you didn't spend much money. … You've been saving more too. … This saving is not like you. … Do you know the American economy is counting on you?

Economist Steven Landsburg praised Ebenezer Scrooge for choosing to save rather than spend his money, arguing that saving—not consumption—fuels economic growth. The *Wall Street Journal* letter pretends to chide the American consumer for saving rather than spending income, arguing that spending—not saving—fuels economic growth. Which argument is correct?

Source: John Hilsenrath, "Grand Central: A Letter to Stingy American Consumers," *Wall Street Journal*, June 2, 2015.

2.15 **(Related to the Making the Connection on page 709)** The *Making the Connection* claims that Ebenezer Scrooge promoted economic growth more when he was a miser and saved most of his income than when he reformed and began spending freely. Suppose, though, that after he reformed he spent most of his income buying food for the Cratchits and other poor families. Many economists believe that there is a close connection between how much very poor people eat and how much they are able to work and how productive they are while working. Does this fact affect the conclusion about whether the pre-reform or post-reform Scrooge had a more positive impact on economic growth? Briefly explain.

2.16 **(Related to Solved Problem 21.2 on page 711)** The federal government in the United States has been running large budget deficits. Suppose that Congress and the president take actions that turn the budget deficits into budget surpluses.

a. Use a market for loanable funds graph to illustrate the effect of the federal budget surpluses. What happens to the equilibrium real interest rate and the quantity of loanable funds? What happens to the level of saving and investment?

b. Now suppose that households believe that surpluses will result in Congress and the president cutting taxes in the near future in order to move from budget surpluses to balanced budgets. As a result, households increase their consumption spending in anticipation of paying lower taxes. Briefly explain how your analysis in part (a) will be affected.

2.17 Savers are taxed on the nominal interest payments they receive rather than the real interest payments. Suppose the federal government shifts from taxing nominal interest payments to taxing only real interest payments. (That is, savers will be allowed to subtract the inflation rate from the nominal interest rate they receive and only pay taxes on the resulting real interest rate.) Use a market for loanable funds graph to analyze the effects of this change in tax policy. What happens to the equilibrium real interest rate and the equilibrium quantity of loanable funds? What happens to the level of saving and investment?

21.3 The Business Cycle, pages 713–722

LEARNING OBJECTIVE: Explain what happens during the business cycle.

Summary

During the expansion phase of the business cycle, production, employment, and income are increasing. The period of expansion ends with a business cycle peak. Following the business cycle peak, production, employment, and income decline during the recession phase of the cycle. The recession comes to an end with a business cycle trough, after which another period of expansion begins. The inflation rate usually rises near the end of a business cycle expansion and then falls during a recession. The unemployment rate declines during the latter part of an expansion and increases during a recession. The unemployment rate often continues to increase even after an expansion has begun. Until the severe recession of 2007–2009, recessions had been milder and the economy had been more stable in the period since 1950. Economists debate whether the economy will return to the stability it experienced during the period of the Great Moderation.

MyEconLab Visit **www.myeconlab.com** to complete these exercises online and get instant feedback.

Review Questions

3.1 What are the names of the following events that occur during a business cycle?

a. The high point of economic activity
b. The low point of economic activity
c. The period between the high point of economic activity and the following low point
d. The period between the low point of economic activity and the following high point

3.2 Briefly describe the effect of the business cycle on the inflation rate and the unemployment rate. Why might the unemployment rate continue to rise during the early stages of an expansion?

3.3 Briefly compare the severity of recessions before and after 1950. What explanations have economists offered for the period of relative macroeconomic stability from 1950 to 2007?

Problems and Applications

3.4 **(Related to the Chapter Opener on page 695)** Briefly explain whether production of each of the following goods is likely to fluctuate more or less than real GDP does during the business cycle.

a. Ford F-150 trucks
b. McDonald's Big Macs
c. Corning's screens for 4K televisions
d. Huggies diapers
e. Boeing passenger aircraft

3.5 The National Bureau of Economic Research, a private group, is responsible for declaring when recessions begin and end in the United States. Can you think of reasons the Bureau of Economic Analysis, part of the federal government, might not want to take on this responsibility?

3.6 **(Related to the Making the Connection on page 715)** As we have seen, some firms prosper by expanding during recessions. What risks do firms take when they pursue this strategy? Are there circumstances in particular industries that might cause firms to be more cautious during a recession? Briefly explain.

3.7 An article in the *Wall Street Journal* noted that at the end of 2014, "U.S. families' debt burdens have settled at their lowest level in over a decade." Does this information indicate that the U.S. economy was close to the end of an economic expansion in late 2014? Briefly explain.

Source: Neil Shah, "Americans' Debt-Cutting Levels Off," *Wall Street Journal*, December 11, 2014.

3.8 **(Related to the Don't Let This Happen to You on page 719)** Briefly explain whether you agree with this statement: "Real GDP in 2014 was $16.1 trillion. This value is a large number. Therefore, economic growth must have been high during 2014."

3.9 **(Related to the Chapter Opener on page 695)** In its annual report for 2009, Corning noted declines in sales for most of its products. But it also said that these declines were "offset somewhat by an increase in sales of Gorilla glass, a protective cover glass that is optimized for portable display devices. Sales of Gorilla glass have continued to increase as the Company moves to capitalize on market opportunities for this product." Why might sales of Gorilla glass be less affected by the business cycle than sales of some of the firm's other products, such as screen for LCD televisions or ceramics used in automobile emission systems?

Source: Corning, Inc., "Form 10-K (Annual Report), 2010, p. 34.

3.10 Robert Samuelson, a columnist for the *Washington Post*, argues that the Great Moderation actually caused the Great Recession. During the Great Moderation, "consumers could assume more debt—and lenders could lend more freely." Why might consumers have been willing to assume more debt and banks and other lenders have been willing to make loans more freely during the Great Moderation? Why might these actions have made the severe recession of 2007–2009 more likely?

Source: Robert J. Samuelson, "Is the Economy Experiencing Another Great Moderation?" *Washington Post*, June 4, 2014.

Real-Time Data Exercises

D21.1 **(Analyzing real GDP over the business cycle)** Go to the Web site of the Federal Reserve Bank of St. Louis (FRED) (research.stlouisfed.org/fred2/).

a. Find the values for the most recent quarter for the following three variables: (1) Nominal Gross Domestic Product (GDP), (2) Real Gross Domestic Product (GDPC1), and (3) Real Potential Gross Domestic Product (GDPPOT).
b. Using the data from part (a), calculate the GDP Price Deflator for the most recent quarter.
c. Calculate for this quarter the percentage difference between real GDP and potential GDP.
d. Using Figure 21.2 on page 704, describe the relationship between real GDP and potential GDP over the past 10 years.

D21.2 **(Analyzing saving and investment)** Go to the Web site of the Federal Reserve Bank of St. Louis (FRED) (research.stlouisfed.org/fred2/).

a. Find the most recent values and the values from the same quarter three years earlier for Gross Private Saving (GPSAVE) and Gross Government Saving (GGSAVE).
b. Using the values found in part (a), calculate the value of total saving in the economy for these two periods.
c. Draw a graph to show the loanable funds market in equilibrium. Explain which curve represents total saving.
d. On the graph you drew in part (c), show the effect on the loanable funds market from the change you calculated in part (b) for total saving between the two periods.

D21.3 **(Analyzing saving and investment)** Go to the Web site of the Federal Reserve Bank of St. Louis (FRED) (research.stlouisfed.org/fred2/).

a. Find the most recent value and the value from the same quarter four years earlier for Gross Government Saving (GGSAVE).
b. Total saving in the economy is composed of private saving and government saving. What does government saving represent?
c. Using the values found in part (a), explain whether the government budget in each of the two periods is balanced, in a surplus, or in a deficit. From the first period to the most recent period, has government saving increased, decreased, or remained constant?
d. Draw a graph showing the loanable funds market in equilibrium. Use the graph to show the effect of the change in government saving that you calculated in part (c) on the loanable funds market. (Assume that the level of private saving is unchanged.) Explain what will happen to the level of investment in the economy.

CHAPTER

22

Long-Run Economic Growth: Sources and Policies

Chapter Outline and Learning Objectives

Will Economic Reforms in Mexico Boost Growth?

Founded in 1947, Flambeau, Inc., is a family firm based in Middlefield, Ohio, that makes plastic products including Duncan yo-yos, hunting decoys, and storage containers used in homes and businesses. In recent years, the company has faced strong competition from imports and has sought ways to reduce costs. The firm considered building a factory in China but chose instead to build in Saltillo, Mexico, because it was closer, and managers from the company could more easily oversee production. Flambeau President Jason Sauey explained, "It's not just about cost; it's about speed of response and quality."

Flambeau is not alone in choosing to locate plants in Mexico rather than China. More than 18,000 U.S. companies, including many Fortune 500 firms, have operations in Mexico. As Christopher Wilson, an economist at the Woodrow Wilson International Center for Scholars in Washington, observed: "Mexico has become the most competitive place to manufacture goods for the North American market." Proximity to the United States is an advantage of doing business in Mexico, rather than China or India, but investing in Mexico can be risky. Organized crime and corruption are major concerns. Coca-Cola, for example, suspended its operations in Chilpancingo because of attacks on its employees. Some local Mexican firms have been reluctant to expand because they fear attracting the attention of criminal gangs who might demand payments or government inspectors who might demand bribes.

These problems indicate that the Mexican government has failed to fully establish the rule of law, which is critical for the long-term prospects of the Mexican economy. Without the rule of law, entrepreneurs cannot fulfill their role in the market system of bringing together the factors of production—labor, capital, and natural resources—to produce goods and services. Mexican entrepreneurs also suffer from problems in the banking system that make it difficult to obtain the funding needed to finance expansion.

Although Mexico has experienced some increases in real GDP per capita during the past 30 years, its record of economic growth has been disappointing, particularly in comparison with China and other rapidly growing countries in the developing world. Being able to attain faster rates of growth would benefit people in Mexico—particularly those with low incomes—and the wider world economy.

Sources: Damien Cave, "As Ties with China Unravel, U.S. Companies Head to Mexico," *New York Times*, May 31, 2014; Matthias Rieker, "Making Yo-Yos and More," *Wall Street Journal*, July 16, 2012; Dolia Estevez, "U.S. Warns against Rising Costs of Doing Business in Mexico Due to Criminal Activity," *Forbes*, June 5, 2014; and flambeau.com.

Economics in Your Life

Would You Be Better Off without China?

For decades, China was a very poor country whose economy was growing very slowly. The government introduced economic reforms in 1978, which spurred rapid economic growth. Suppose that you could choose to live and work in a world with the Chinese economy growing very rapidly or in a world with the Chinese economy growing as slowly as it did before 1978. In which world would you choose to live? How does the current high-growth, high-export Chinese economy affect you as a consumer? How does it affect you as someone about to start a career? As you read the chapter, try to answer these questions. You can check your answers against those we provide on **page 760** at the end of this chapter.

Economic growth is not inevitable. For most of human history, no sustained increases in output per capita occurred, and, in the words of the philosopher Thomas Hobbes, the lives of most people were "poor, nasty, brutish, and short." Sustained economic growth first began with the Industrial Revolution in England in the late eighteenth century. From there, economic growth spread to the United States, Canada, and the countries of Western Europe. Following the end of World War II in 1945, rapid economic growth also began in Japan and, eventually, in several other Asian countries, but the economies of many other countries stagnated, leaving their people trapped in poverty.

Real GDP per capita is the best measure of a country's standard of living because it represents the ability of the average person to buy goods and services. Economic growth occurs when real GDP per capita increases. In this chapter, we will develop a *model of economic growth* that will help us answer important questions like these:

- Why have countries such as the United States and the United Kingdom, which had high standards of living at the beginning of the twentieth century, continued to grow rapidly?
- Why have countries such as Argentina, which at one time had relatively high standards of living, failed to keep pace?
- Why was the Soviet Union unable to sustain the rapid growth rates of its early years?
- Why are some countries that were very poor at the beginning of the twentieth century still very poor?
- Why have some countries, such as South Korea and Japan, that once were very poor now become much richer?
- What explains China's very rapid recent growth rates?

22.1 Economic Growth over Time and around the World

LEARNING OBJECTIVE: Define economic growth, calculate economic growth rates, and describe global trends in economic growth.

You live in a world that is very different from the world when your grandparents were young. You can listen to music on an iPhone that fits in your pocket; your grandparents played vinyl records on large stereo systems. You can send a text message to someone in another city, state, or country; your grandparents mailed letters that took days or weeks to arrive. More importantly, you have access to health care and medicines that have prolonged life and improved its quality. In many poorer countries, however, people endure grinding poverty and have only the bare necessities of life, just as their parents, grandparents, and great-grandparents did.

The difference between you and people in poor countries is that you live in a country that has experienced substantial economic growth. A growing economy produces both increasing quantities of goods and services and better goods and services. It is only through economic growth that living standards can increase, but through most of human history, no economic growth took place. Even today, billions of people are living in countries where economic growth is extremely slow.

Economic Growth from 1,000,000 B.C. to the Present

In 1,000,000 B.C., our ancestors survived by hunting animals and gathering edible plants. Farming was many years in the future, and production was limited to food, clothing, shelter, and simple tools. Bradford DeLong, an economist at the University of California, Berkeley, estimates that in those primitive circumstances, GDP per capita was about $145 per year in 2015 dollars, which was the minimum amount necessary to sustain life. DeLong estimates that real GDP per capita worldwide was still $145 in the year A.D. 1300. In other words, no sustained economic growth occurred between 1,000,000 B.C. and A.D. 1300. A peasant toiling on a farm in France in the year 1300 was no better off than his ancestors thousands of years before. In fact, for most of human existence, the typical person had only the bare minimum of food, clothing, and shelter necessary to sustain life. Few people survived beyond age 40, and most people suffered from debilitating illnesses.

Sustained economic growth did not begin until the **Industrial Revolution**, which started in England around the year 1750. The production of cotton cloth in factories using machinery powered by steam engines marked the beginning of the Industrial Revolution. Before that time, production of goods had relied almost exclusively on human or animal power. The use of mechanical power spread to the production of many other goods, greatly increasing the quantity of goods each worker could produce. First England and then other countries, such as the United States, France, and Germany, experienced *long-run economic growth*, with sustained increases in real GDP per capita that eventually raised living standards in those countries to the high levels of today.

Industrial Revolution The application of mechanical power to the production of goods, beginning in England around 1750.

Making the Connection
MyEconLab Video

Why Did the Industrial Revolution Begin in England?

The Industrial Revolution was a key turning point in human history. Before it, economic growth was slow and halting. After it, economic growth became rapid and sustained in a number of countries. Although historians and economists agree on the importance of the Industrial Revolution, they have not reached a consensus on why it happened in the time and place that it did. Why the eighteenth century and not the sixteenth century or the twenty-first century? Why England and not China or India or Africa or Japan?

There is always a temptation to read history backward. We know when and where the Industrial Revolution occurred; therefore, it had to happen where it did and when it did. But what was so special about England in the eighteenth century? Nobel Laureate Douglass North of Washington University in St. Louis has argued that institutions in England differed significantly from those in other countries in ways that greatly aided economic growth. North believes that the Glorious Revolution of 1688 was a key turning point. After that date, the British Parliament, rather than the king, controlled the government. The British court system also became independent of the king. As a result, the British government was credible when it committed to upholding private property rights, protecting wealth, and eliminating arbitrary increases in taxes. These institutional changes gave entrepreneurs the confidence and the incentive to make the investments necessary to use the important technological developments of the second half of the eighteenth century—particularly the spinning jenny and the water frame, which were used in the production of cotton textiles, and the steam engine, which was used in mining and in the manufacture of textiles and other products. Without the institutional changes, entrepreneurs would have been reluctant to risk their property or their wealth by starting new businesses.

The British government's guarantee of property rights set the stage for the Industrial Revolution.

Although not all economists agree with North's specific argument about the origins of the Industrial Revolution, we will see that most economists accept the idea that economic growth is not likely to occur unless a country's government provides the type of institutional framework North describes.

Sources: Douglass C. North, *Understanding the Process of Economic Change*, Princeton, NJ: Princeton University Press, 2005; and Douglass C. North and Barry R. Weingast, "Constitutions and Commitment: The Evolution of Institutions Governing Public Choice in Seventeenth-Century England," *Journal of Economic History*, Vol. 49, No. 4, December 1989, pp. 803–832.

Your Turn: Test your understanding by doing related problem 1.3 on page 762 at the end of this chapter.

MyEconLab Study Plan

MyEconLab Animation

Figure 22.1

Average Annual Growth Rates for the World Economy

World economic growth was essentially zero in the years before 1300, and it was very slow—an average of only 0.2 percent per year—between 1300 and 1800. The Industrial Revolution made possible the sustained increases in real GDP per capita that have allowed some countries to attain high standards of living.

Source: J. Bradford DeLong, "Estimates World GDP, One Million B.C.–Present," Working paper, University of California, Berkeley.

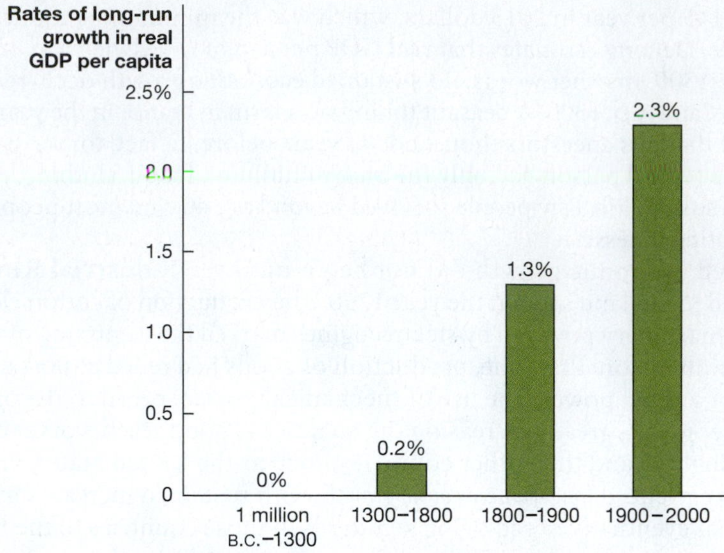

Figure 22.1 shows how growth rates of real GDP per capita for the entire world have changed over long periods. Prior to A.D. 1300, there were no sustained increases in real GDP per capita. Over the next 500 years, to 1800, there was very slow growth. Significant growth began in the nineteenth century, as a result of the Industrial Revolution. A further acceleration in growth occurred during the twentieth century, as the average growth rate increased from 1.3 percent per year to 2.3 percent per year. MyEconLab Concept Check

Small Differences in Growth Rates Are Important

The difference between 1.3 percent and 2.3 percent may seem trivial, but over long periods, small differences in growth rates can have a large effect. Suppose you have $100 in a savings account earning an interest rate of 1.3 percent, which means you will receive an interest payment of $1.30 this year. If the interest rate on the account is 2.3 percent, you will earn $2.30. The difference of an extra $1.00 interest payment seems insignificant. But if you leave the interest as well as the original $100 in your account for another year, the difference becomes greater because now the higher interest rate is applied to a larger amount—$102.30—and the lower interest rate is applied to a smaller amount—$101.30. This process, known as *compounding*, magnifies even small differences in interest rates over long periods of time. Over a period of 50 years, your $100 would grow to $312 at an interest rate of 2.3 percent but to only $191 at an interest rate of 1.3 percent.

The principle of compounding applies to economic growth rates as well as to interest rates. For example, in 1950, real GDP per capita in Argentina was $5,474 (measured in 2005 dollars), which was larger than Italy's real GDP per capita of $5,361. Over the next 64 years, the economic growth rate in Italy averaged 2.5 percent per year, while in Argentina, the growth rate was only 1.5 percent per year. Although this difference in growth rates of only 1 percentage point may seem small, in 2014, real GDP per capita in Italy had risen to $26,550, while real GDP per capita in Argentina was only $13,980. In other words, because of a relatively small difference in the growth rates of the two economies, the standard of living of a typical person in Italy went from being a little below that of a typical person in Argentina to being much higher. Here is the key point to keep in mind: *In the long run, small differences in economic growth rates result in big differences in living standards.* MyEconLab Concept Check

Why Do Growth Rates Matter?

Why should anyone care about growth rates? Growth rates matter because an economy that grows too slowly fails to raise living standards. In some countries in Africa and

Asia, very little economic growth has occurred in the past 50 years, so many people remain in severe poverty. In high-income countries, only 4 out of every 1,000 babies die before they are one year old. In the poorest countries, more than 100 out of every 1,000 babies die before they are one year old, and millions of children die annually from diseases that could be avoided by having access to clean water or that could be cured by using medicines that cost only a few dollars.

Although their problems are less dramatic, countries that experience slow growth have also missed opportunities to improve the lives of their citizens. For example, the failure of Argentina to grow as rapidly as other countries that had similar levels of GDP per capita in 1950 has left many of its people in poverty. Life expectancy in Argentina is lower than in the United States and other high-income countries, and about 50 percent more babies in Argentina die before the age of one. MyEconLab Concept Check

Don't Let This Happen to You

Don't Confuse the Average Annual Percentage Change with the Total Percentage Change

When economists talk about growth rates over a period of more than one year, the numbers are always *average annual percentage changes* and *not* total percentage changes. For example, in the United States, real GDP per capita was $14,398 in 1950 and $50,398 in 2014. The percentage change in real GDP per capita between these two years is:

$$\left(\frac{\$50{,}398 - \$14{,}398}{\$14{,}398}\right) \times 100 = 250\%.$$

However, this is *not* the growth rate between the two years. The growth rate between these two years is the rate at which $14,398 in 1950 would have to grow on average *each year* to end up as $50,398 in 2014, which is 2.0 percent.

MyEconLab Study Plan

Your Turn: Test your understanding by doing related problem 1.6 on page 763 at the end of this chapter.

"The Rich Get Richer and ... "

We can divide the world's economies into two groups:

1. The *high-income countries,* sometimes also referred to as the *industrial countries* or the *developed countries,* including Australia, Canada, Japan, New Zealand, the United States, and the countries of Western Europe
2. The lower-income countries, or *developing countries,* including most of the countries of Africa, Asia, and Latin America

In the 1980s and 1990s, a small group of countries, mostly East Asian countries such as Singapore, South Korea, and Taiwan, began to experience high rates of growth and are sometimes referred to as the *newly industrializing countries.*

Figure 22.2 shows the levels of GDP per capita around the world in 2014. GDP is measured in U.S. dollars, corrected for differences across countries in the cost of living. In 2014, GDP per capita ranged from a high of $144,400 in the Persian Gulf country of Qatar to a low of $600 in the Central African Republic. To understand why the gap between rich and poor countries exists, we need to look at what causes economies to grow. MyEconLab Concept Check

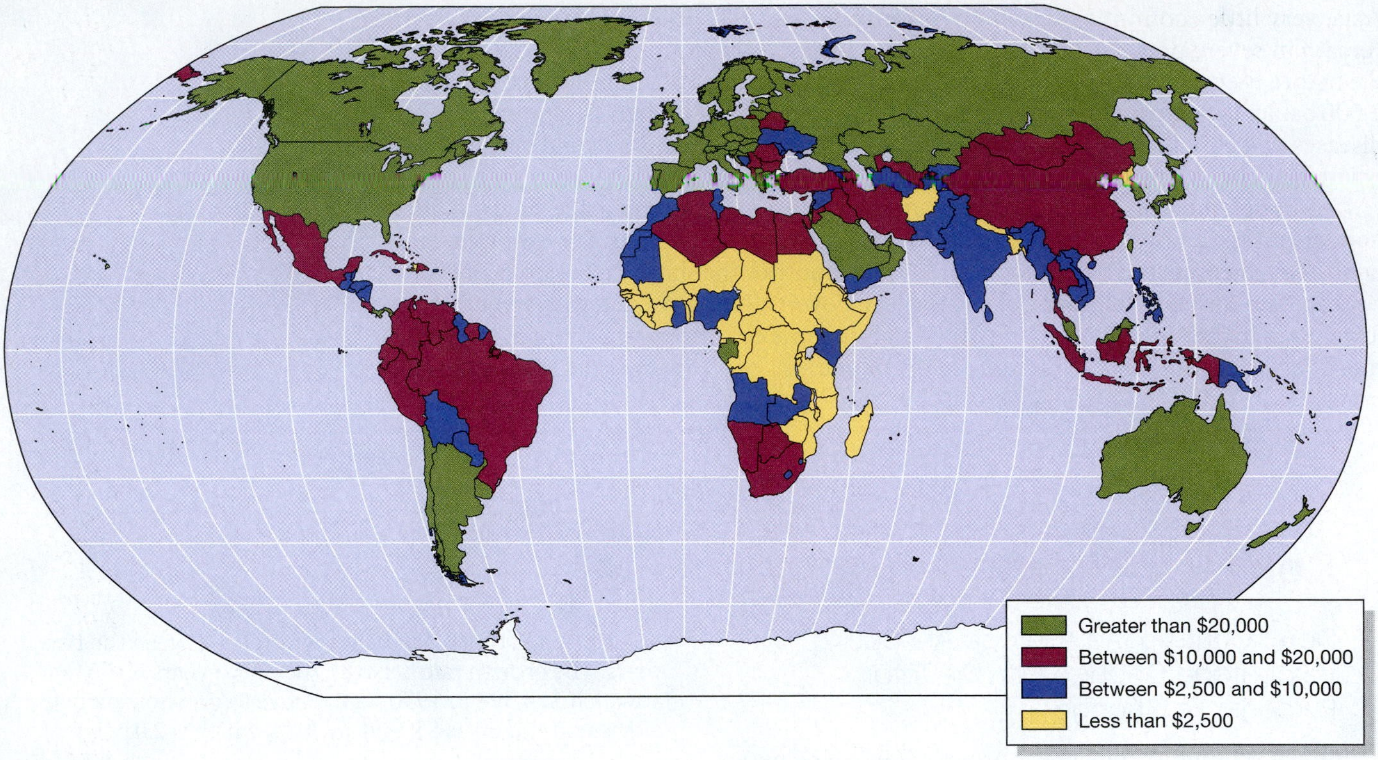

MyEconLab Animation

Figure 22.2 GDP per Capita, 2014

GDP per capita is measured in U.S. dollars, corrected for differences across countries in the cost of living.

Making the Connection

MyEconLab Video

Is Income All That Matters?

The more income you have, the more goods and services you can buy. When people are surviving on very low incomes of $2 per day or less, their ability to buy even minimal amounts of food, clothing, and housing is limited. So, most economists argue that unless the incomes of the very poor increase significantly, they will be unable to attain a higher standard of living. In some countries—primarily those colored yellow in Figure 22.2—the growth in average income has been very slow, or even negative, over a period of decades. Most economists and policymakers have concluded that the standard of living in these countries has been largely unchanged for many years.

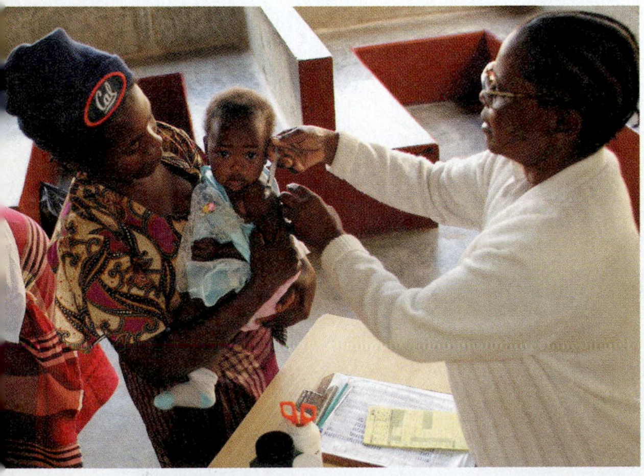

In sub-Saharan Africa and other parts of the world, increases in technology and knowledge are leading to improvements in health care and the standard of living.

Some economists argue, though, that if we look beyond income to other measures of the standard of living, we can see that even the poorest countries have made significant progress in recent decades. For example, Charles Kenny, an economist with the Center for Global Development, argues that "those countries with the lowest quality of life are making the fastest progress in improving it—across a range of measures including health, education, and civil and political liberties." For example, since 1960 deaths among children have declined, often by more than 50 percent, in nearly all countries, including most of those with the lowest incomes. Even in sub-Saharan Africa, where growth in incomes has been very slow, the percentage of children dying before age five has decreased by more than 30 percent over the past 50 years. Similarly, the percentage of people able to read and write has more than doubled in sub-Saharan Africa since 1970. Many more people now live in democracies where basic civil rights are respected than at any other time in world history. Although some countries, such as Somalia, the Democratic Republic of the Congo, Syria, and Afghanistan, have suffered from civil wars, improved political stability in many countries has reduced the likelihood of dying from violence.

What explains these improvements in health, education, democracy, and political stability? William Easterly, an economist at New York University, has found that although, at any given time, countries that have a higher income also have a higher standard of living, over time, increases in income *within a particular country* are typically not the main cause of improvements in its standard of living in terms of health, education, individual rights, political stability, and similar factors. Kenny's argument and Easterly's finding are connected: Some increases in living standards do not require significant increases in income. The key factors in raising living standards in low-income countries have been increases in technology and knowledge—such as the development of inexpensive vaccines that reduce epidemics or the use of mosquito-resistant netting that reduces the prevalence of malaria—that are inexpensive enough to be widely available. Changes in attitudes, such as placing a greater value on education, particularly for girls, or increasing support for political freedoms, have also played a role in improving conditions in low-income countries.

There are limits, of course, to how much living standards can increase if incomes stagnate. Ultimately, much higher rates of economic growth will be necessary for low-income countries to significantly close the gap in living standards with high-income countries.

Sources: Charles Kenny, *Getting Better*, New York: Basic Books, 2011; Ursula Casabonne and Charles Kenny, "The Best Things in Life Are (Nearly) Free: Technology, Knowledge, and Global Health," *World Development*, Vol. 40, No. 1, January 2012, pp. 21–35; and William Easterly, "Life during Growth," *Journal of Economic Growth*, Vol. 4, No. 3, September 1999, pp. 239–276.

Your Turn: Test your understanding by doing related problems 1.7 and 1.8 on page 763 at the end of this chapter.

MyEconLab Study Plan

22.2 What Determines How Fast Economies Grow?

LEARNING OBJECTIVE: Use the economic growth model to explain why growth rates differ across countries.

To explain changes in economic growth rates over time within countries and differences in growth rates among countries, we need to develop an *economic growth model*. An **economic growth model** explains growth rates in real GDP per capita over the long run. As we have seen, the average person can buy more goods and services only if the average worker produces more goods and services (see Chapter 21). Recall that **labor productivity** is the quantity of goods and services that can be produced by one worker or by one hour of work. Because of the importance of labor productivity in explaining economic growth, the economic growth model focuses on the causes of long-run increases in labor productivity.

Economic growth model A model that explains growth rates in real GDP per capita over the long run.

Labor productivity The quantity of goods and services that can be produced by one worker or by one hour of work.

How can a country's workers become more productive? Economists believe two key factors determine labor productivity:

1. The quantity of capital available to workers
2. The level of technology

Therefore, to explain changes in real GDP per capita, the economic growth model focuses on technological change and changes over time in the quantity of capital available to workers. Recall that **technological change** is a change in the quantity of output firms can produce using a given quantity of inputs.

Technological change A change in the quantity of output a firm can produce using a given quantity of inputs.

There are three main sources of technological change:

1. **Better machinery and equipment.** Beginning with the steam engine during the Industrial Revolution, the invention of new machinery has been an important source of rising labor productivity. Today, continuing improvements in computers, factory machine tools, electric generators, and many other machines contribute to increases in labor productivity.

Human capital The accumulated knowledge and skills that workers acquire from education and training or from their life experiences.

2. **Increases in human capital.** Capital refers to *physical capital*, including computers, factory buildings, machine tools, warehouses, and trucks. The more physical capital workers have available, the more output they can produce. **Human capital** is the accumulated knowledge and skills that workers acquire from education and training or from their life experiences. As workers increase their human capital through education or on-the-job training, their productivity also increases. The more educated workers are, the greater is their human capital.
3. **Better means of organizing and managing production.** Labor productivity increases if managers can do a better job of organizing production. For example, the *just-in-time system*, first developed by Toyota Motor Corporation, involves assembling goods from parts that arrive at the factory at exactly the time they are needed. With this system, firms need fewer workers to store and keep track of parts in the factory, so the quantity of goods produced per hour worked increases.

Note that technological change is *not* the same thing as more physical capital. New capital can *embody* technological change, as when a faster computer chip is embodied in a new computer. But simply adding more capital that is the same as existing capital is not technological change. To summarize: A country's standard of living will be higher the more capital workers have available on their jobs, the better the capital, the more human capital workers have, and the better the job managers do in organizing production.

The Per-Worker Production Function

Per-worker production function The relationship between real GDP per hour worked and capital per hour worked, holding the level of technology constant.

Often when analyzing economic growth, we look at increases in real GDP *per hour worked* and increases in capital *per hour worked*. We use measures of GDP per hour and capital per hour rather than per person, so we can analyze changes in the underlying ability of an economy to produce more goods with a given amount of labor without having to worry about changes in the fraction of the population working or in the length of the workday. We can illustrate the economic growth model using the **per-worker production function**, which is the relationship between real GDP per hour worked and capital per hour worked, *holding the level of technology constant*. For simplicity, from now on we will shorten "per-worker production function" to just "production function." Figure 22.3 shows the production function as a graph. We measure capital per hour worked along the horizontal axis and real GDP per hour worked along the vertical axis. Letting K stand for capital, L stand for labor, and Y stand for real GDP, real GDP per hour worked is Y/L, and capital per hour worked is K/L. The curve represents the production function. Notice that we do not explicitly show technological change in the

MyEconLab Animation

Figure 22.3

The Per-Worker Production Function

The per-worker production function shows the relationship between capital per hour worked and real GDP per hour worked, holding technology constant. Increases in capital per hour worked increase output per hour worked but at a diminishing rate. For example, an increase in capital per hour worked from $75 to $100 increases real GDP per hour worked from $48 to $53. An increase in capital per hour worked from $100 to $125 increases real GDP per hour worked by a smaller amount, from $53 to $57. Each additional $25 increase in capital per hour worked results in a progressively smaller increase in output per hour worked.

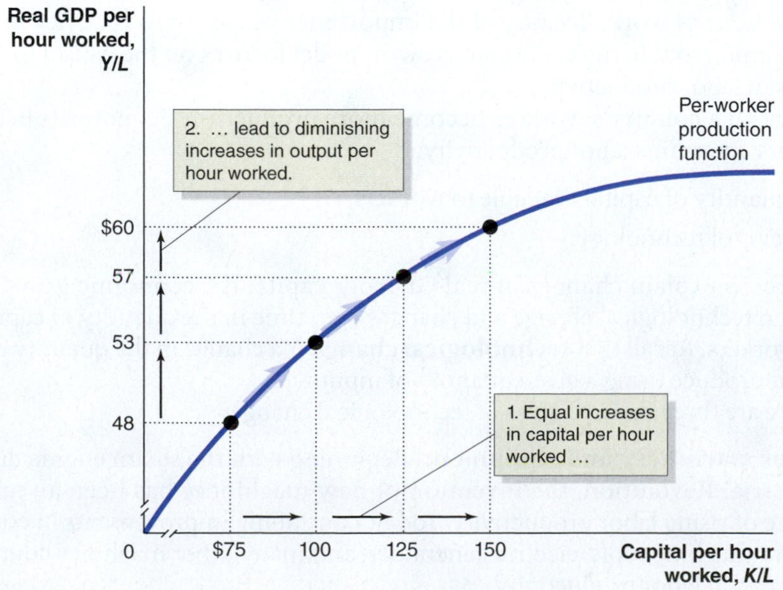

figure. We assume that as we move along the production function, the level of technology remains constant. As we will see, we can illustrate technological change using this graph by *shifting up* the curve representing the production function.

The figure shows that increases in the quantity of capital per hour worked result in movements up along the production function, increasing the quantity of output each worker produces. When *we hold technology constant,* however, equal increases in the amount of capital per hour worked lead to *diminishing* increases in output per hour worked. For example, increasing capital per hour worked from $75 to $100 increases real GDP per hour worked from $48 to $53, an increase of $5. Another $25 increase in capital per hour worked, from $100 to $125, increases real GDP per hour worked from $53 to $57, an increase of only $4. Each additional $25 increase in capital per hour worked results in progressively smaller increases in real GDP per hour worked. In fact, at very high levels of capital per hour worked, further increases in capital per hour worked will not result in any increase in real GDP per hour worked. This effect results from the *law of diminishing returns,* which states that as we add more of one input—in this case, capital—to a fixed quantity of another input—in this case, labor—output increases by smaller additional amounts.

Why are there diminishing returns to capital? Consider a simple example in which you own a copy store. At first you have 10 employees but only 1 copy machine, so each of your workers is able to produce relatively few copies per day. When you buy a second copy machine, your employees will be able to produce more copies. Adding additional copy machines will continue to increase your output—but by increasingly smaller amounts. For example, adding a twentieth copy machine to the 19 you already have will not increase the copies each worker is able to make by nearly as much as adding a second copy machine did. Eventually, adding additional copying machines will not increase your output at all. MyEconLab Concept Check

Which Is More Important for Economic Growth: More Capital or Technological Change?

Technological change helps economies avoid diminishing returns to capital. Let's consider two simple examples of the effects of technological change. First, suppose you have 10 copy machines in your copy store. Each copy machine can produce 10 copies per minute. You don't believe that adding an eleventh machine identical to the 10 you already have will significantly increase the number of copies your employees can produce in a day. Then you find out that a new copy machine has become available that produces 20 copies per minute. If you replace your existing machines with the new machines, the productivity of your workers will increase. The replacement of existing capital with more productive capital is an example of technological change.

Or suppose you realize that the layout of your store could be improved. Maybe the paper for the machines is on shelves at the back of the store, which requires your workers to spend time walking back and forth whenever the machines run out of paper. By placing the paper closer to the copy machines, you can improve the productivity of your workers. Reorganizing how production takes place so as to increase output is also an example of technological change. MyEconLab Concept Check

Technological Change: The Key to Sustaining Economic Growth

Figure 22.4 shows the effect of technological change on the production function. Technological change shifts up the production function and allows an economy to produce more real GDP per hour worked with the same quantity of capital per hour worked. For example, if the current level of technology puts the economy on Production function$_1$, then when capital per hour worked is $150, real GDP per hour worked is $60. Technological change that shifts the economy to Production function$_2$ makes it possible to produce $65 in goods and services per hour worked with the same level of capital per hour worked. Further increases in technology that shift the economy to higher production functions result in further increases in real GDP per hour worked. Because of diminishing returns to capital, continuing increases in real GDP per hour worked can be sustained only if there is technological change. Remember that a country will

MyEconLab Animation

Figure 22.4

Technological Change Increases Output per Hour Worked

Technological change shifts up the production function and allows more output per hour worked with the same amount of capital per hour worked. For example, along Production function$_1$ with \$150 in capital per hour worked, the economy can produce \$60 in real GDP per hour worked. However, an increase in technology that shifts the economy to Production function$_2$ makes it possible to produce \$65 in real GDP per hour worked with the same level of capital per hour worked.

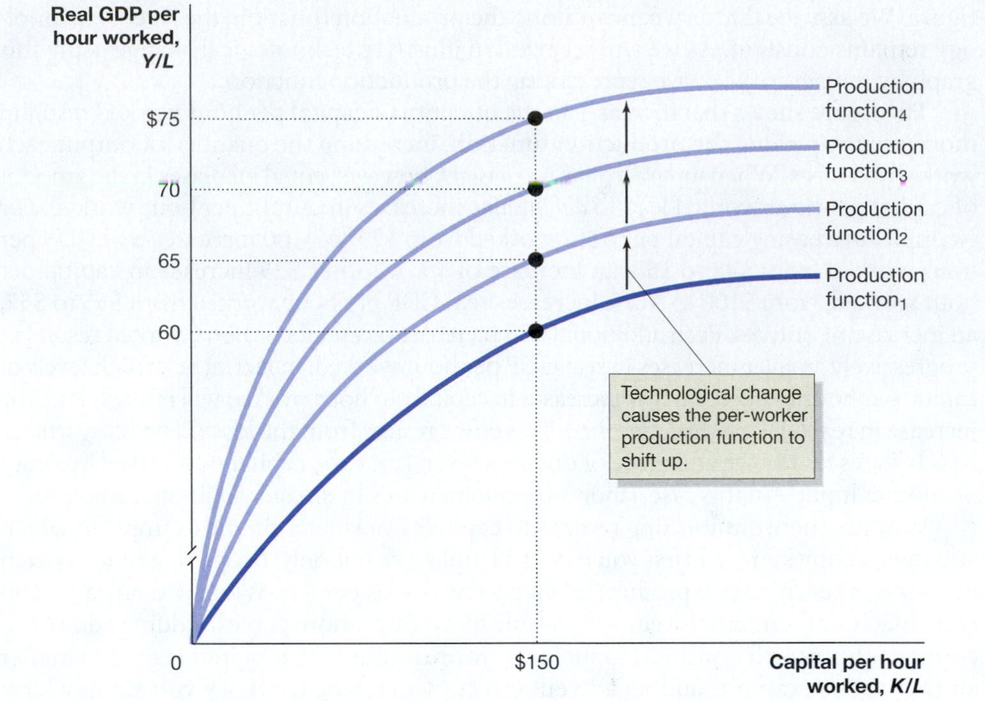

experience increases in its standard of living only if it experiences increases in real GDP per hour worked. Therefore, we can draw the following important conclusion: *In the long run, a country will experience an increasing standard of living only if it experiences continuing technological change.*

MyEconLab Concept Check

Making the Connection

MyEconLab Video

What Explains the Economic Failure of the Soviet Union?

The economic growth model can help explain one of the most striking events of the twentieth century: the economic collapse of the Soviet Union. The Soviet Union was formed from the old Russian Empire following the Russian Revolution of 1917. Under Communism, the Soviet Union was a centrally planned economy in which the government owned nearly every business and made all production and pricing decisions. In 1960, Nikita Khrushchev, the leader of the Soviet Union, addressed the United Nations in New York City. He declared to the United States and the other democracies: "We will bury you. Your grandchildren will live under Communism."

In the former Soviet Union there were frequent shortages, and unhappy consumers often had to wait in long lines to shop for groceries and other goods.

Many people at the time took Khrushchev's boast seriously. Capital per hour worked grew rapidly in the Soviet Union from 1950 through the 1980s. At first, these increases in capital per hour worked also produced rapid increases in real GDP per hour worked. Rapid increases in real GDP per hour worked during the 1950s caused some economists in the United States to predict incorrectly that the Soviet Union would someday surpass the United States economically. In fact, diminishing returns to capital meant that the additional factories the Soviet Union was building resulted in smaller and smaller increases in real GDP per hour worked.

The Soviet Union did experience some technological change—but at a rate much slower than in the United States and other high-income countries. Why did the Soviet Union fail the crucial requirement for growth: implementing new technologies? The key reason is that in a centrally planned economy, the people managing most businesses are government employees and not entrepreneurs or independent businesspeople, as is the case in market economies. Soviet managers had little incentive to adopt new ways of producing goods and services. Their pay depended on producing the quantity of output specified in the government's economic plan, not on discovering new, better, and lower-cost ways to produce goods. In addition, these managers did not have to worry about competition from either domestic or foreign firms.

Entrepreneurs and managers of firms in the United States, by contrast, are under intense competitive pressure from other firms. They must constantly search for better ways of producing the goods and services they sell. Developing and using new technologies is an important way to gain a competitive edge and earn a higher profit. The drive for profit provides an incentive for technological change that centrally planned economies are unable to duplicate. In market economies, entrepreneurs and managers who have their own money on the line make decisions about which investments to make and which technologies to adopt. Nothing concentrates the mind like having your own funds at risk.

In hindsight, it is clear that a centrally planned economy, such as the Soviet Union's, could not, over the long run, grow faster than a market economy. The Soviet Union collapsed in 1991, and contemporary Russia now has a more market-oriented system, although the government continues to play a much larger role in the economy than does the government in the United States.

Your Turn: Test your understanding by doing related problem 2.7 on page 764 at the end of this chapter.

MyEconLab Study Plan

Solved Problem 22.2

MyEconLab Interactive Animation

Using the Economic Growth Model to Analyze the Failure of the Soviet Economy

Use the economic growth model and the information in the *Making the Connection* on page 740 to analyze the economic problems the Soviet Union encountered.

Solving the Problem

Step 1: Review the chapter material. This problem is about using the economic growth model to explain the failure of the Soviet economy, so you may want to review the *Making the Connection* on page 740.

Step 2: Draw a graph like Figure 22.3 on page 738 to illustrate the economic problems of the Soviet Union. For simplicity, assume that the Soviet Union experienced no technological change.

The Soviet Union experienced rapid increases in capital per hour worked from 1950 through the 1980s, but its failure to implement new technology meant that output per hour worked grew at a slower and slower rate.

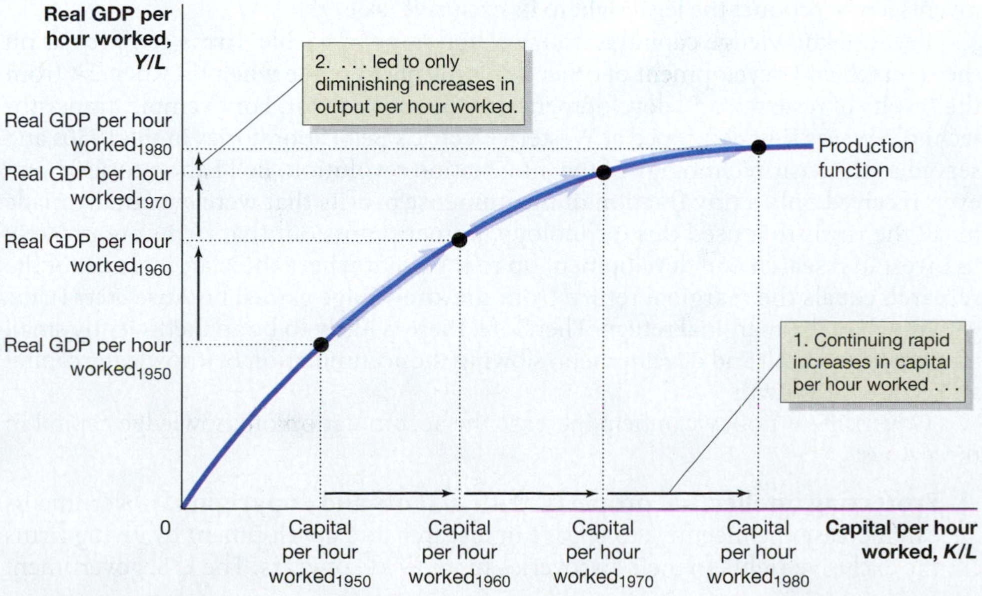

Extra Credit: The Soviet Union hoped to raise the standard of living of its citizens above that enjoyed in the United States and other high-income countries. Its strategy was to make continuous increases in the quantity of capital available to its workers. The economic growth model helps us understand the flaws in this policy for achieving economic growth.

MyEconLab Study Plan

Your Turn: For more practice, do related problems 2.8, 2.9, and 2.10 on page 764 at the end of this chapter.

New Growth Theory

New growth theory A model of long-run economic growth that emphasizes that technological change is influenced by economic incentives and so is determined by the working of the market system.

The economic growth model we have been using was first developed in the 1950s by Nobel Laureate Robert Solow of MIT. According to this model, productivity growth is the key factor in explaining long-run growth in real GDP per capita. In recent years, some economists have become dissatisfied with this model because it does not explain the factors that determine productivity growth. Paul Romer, of New York University, developed the **new growth theory** to provide a better explanation of the sources of technological change that underlie productivity growth. Romer argues that the rate of technological change is influenced by how individuals and firms respond to economic incentives. Earlier accounts of economic growth did not explain technological change or attributed it to factors such as chance scientific discoveries.

Romer argues that the accumulation of *knowledge capital* is a key determinant of economic growth. Firms add to an economy's stock of knowledge capital when they engage in research and development or otherwise contribute to technological change. We have seen that accumulation of physical capital is subject to diminishing returns: Increases in capital per hour worked lead to increases in real GDP per hour worked but at a decreasing rate. Romer argues that the same is true of knowledge capital *at the firm level*. As firms add to their stock of knowledge capital, they increase their output but at a decreasing rate. At the level of the entire economy, however, Romer argues that knowledge capital is subject to *increasing returns*. Increasing returns can exist because knowledge, once discovered, becomes available to everyone. The use of physical capital, such as a computer or machine tool, is *rival* because if one firm uses it, other firms cannot, and it is *excludable* because the firm that owns the capital can keep other firms from using it. The use of knowledge capital, such as the chemical formula for a drug that cures cancer, is nonrival, however, because one firm's using that knowledge does not prevent another firm from using it. Knowledge capital is also nonexcludable because once something like a chemical formula becomes known, it becomes widely available for other firms to use (unless, as we discuss shortly, the government gives the firm that invents a new product the legal right to its exclusive use).

Because knowledge capital is nonrival and nonexcludable, firms can *free ride* on the research and development of other firms. Firms free ride when they benefit from the results of research and development they did not pay for. For example, transistor technology was first developed at Western Electric's Bell Laboratories in the 1950s and served as the basic technology of the information revolution. Bell Laboratories, however, received only a tiny fraction of the immense profits that were eventually made by all the firms that used this technology. Romer points out that firms are unlikely to invest in research and development up to the point where the marginal cost of the research equals the marginal return from the knowledge gained because *other* firms gain much of the marginal return. Therefore, there is likely to be an inefficiently small amount of research and development, slowing the accumulation of knowledge capital and economic growth.

Government policy can help increase the accumulation of knowledge capital in three ways:

1. **Protecting intellectual property with patents and copyrights.** Governments can increase the incentive to engage in research and development by giving firms the exclusive rights to their discoveries for a period of years. The U.S. government

grants patents to companies that develop new products or new ways of making existing products. A **patent** gives a firm the exclusive legal right to a new product for a period of 20 years from the date the patent is filed with the government. For example, a pharmaceutical firm that develops a drug that cures cancer can secure a patent on the drug, keeping other firms from manufacturing the drug without permission. The profit earned during the period the patent is in force provides firms with an incentive for undertaking research and development. The patent system has drawbacks, however. In filing for a patent, a firm must disclose information about the product or process. This information enters the public record and may help competing firms develop products or processes that are similar but that do not infringe on the patent. To avoid this problem, a firm may try to keep the results of its research a *trade secret*, without patenting it. (A famous example of a trade secret is the formula for Coca-Cola.) Tension also arises between the government's objectives of providing patent protection that gives firms the incentive to engage in research and development and making sure that the knowledge gained through the research is widely available, which increases the positive effect of the knowledge on the economy. Economists debate the features of an ideal patent system.

Patent The exclusive right to produce a product for a period of 20 years from the date the patent is applied for.

2. **Supporting research and development.** The government can help increase the quantity of research and development that takes place. In the United States, the federal government conducts some research directly. For example, the National Institutes of Health conducts medical research. The forerunner of the Internet—the Advanced Research Project Agency Network (ARPANET)—was developed by the U.S. Department of Defense to improve communication among defense researchers around the country. The government also subsidizes research by providing grants and other payments to researchers in universities through the National Science Foundation and other agencies. Finally, the government provides tax benefits to firms that invest in research and development.
3. **Subsidizing education.** People with technical training carry out research and development. If firms are unable to capture all the profit from research and development, they will pay lower wages and salaries to technical workers. These lower wages and salaries reduce the incentive to workers to receive this training. If the government subsidizes education, it can increase the number of workers who have technical training. In the United States, the government subsidizes education by directly providing free education from grades kindergarten through 12 and by providing support for public colleges and universities. The government also provides student loans at reduced interest rates.

These government policies can bring the accumulation of knowledge capital closer to the optimal level. MyEconLab Concept Check

Joseph Schumpeter and Creative Destruction

The new growth theory has revived interest in the ideas of Joseph Schumpeter. Born in Austria in 1883, Schumpeter served briefly as that country's finance minister. In 1932, he became an economics professor at Harvard University. Schumpeter developed a model of growth that emphasized his view that new products unleash a "gale of creative destruction" that drives older products—and, often, the firms that produced them—out of the market. According to Schumpeter, the key to rising living standards is not small changes to existing products but, rather, new products that meet consumer wants in qualitatively better ways. For example, in the early twentieth century, the automobile displaced the horse-drawn carriage by meeting consumer demand for personal transportation in a way that was qualitatively better. In the early twenty-first century, the DVD and the DVD player displaced the VHS tape and the VCR by better meeting consumer demand for watching films at home. Downloading or streaming movies from the Internet are now in the process of displacing the DVD just as the DVD displaced the VHS tape.

To Schumpeter, the entrepreneur is central to economic growth: "The function of entrepreneurs is to reform or revolutionize the pattern of production by exploiting an invention or, more generally, an untried technological possibility for producing new commodities or producing an old one in a new way."

The profit an entrepreneur hopes to earn provides the incentive for bringing together the factors of production—labor, capital, and natural resources—to start new firms and introduce new goods and services. Successful entrepreneurs can use their profits to finance the development of new products and are better able to attract funds from investors. MyEconLab Concept Check

22.3 Economic Growth in the United States

LEARNING OBJECTIVE: Discuss fluctuations in productivity growth in the United States.

The economic growth model can help us understand the record of growth in the United States. Figure 22.5 shows average annual growth rates in real GDP per hour worked since 1800. As the United States experienced the Industrial Revolution during the nineteenth century, U.S. firms increased the quantities of capital per hour worked. New technologies such as the steam engine, the railroad, and the telegraph also became available. Together, these factors resulted in an average annual growth rate of real GDP per worker of 1.3 percent from 1800 to 1900. Real GDP *per capita* grew at a slower rate of 1.1 percent during this period. At this growth rate, real GDP per capita would double about every 63 years, which means that living standards were growing steadily but relatively slowly.

By the twentieth century, technological change had been institutionalized. Many large corporations began to set up research and development facilities to improve the quality of their products and the efficiency with which they produced them. Universities also began to conduct research that had business applications. After World War II, many corporations began to provide significant funds to universities to help pay for research. In 1950, the federal government created the National Science Foundation, whose main goal is to support university researchers. The accelerating rate of technological change led to more rapid growth rates.

MyEconLab Animation

Figure 22.5

Average Annual Growth Rates in Real GDP per Hour Worked in the United States, 1800–2014

The growth rate in the United States increased from 1800 through the mid-1970s. Then, for more than 20 years, growth slowed before increasing for a 10-year period beginning in the mid-1990s. During the past 10 years, growth has slowed again.

Note: The values for 1800–1900 are real GDP per worker. The values for 1900–2014 are real GDP per hour worked; for the period 1900–2014 they are the authors' calculations, based on the methods used in Neville Francis and Valerie A. Ramey, "The Source of Historical Economic Fluctuations: An Analysis Using Long-Run Restrictions," in Jeffrey Frankel, Richard Clarida, and Francesco Giavazzi, eds., *International Seminar in Macroeconomics*, Chicago: University of Chicago Press, 2005; the authors thank Neville Francis for kindly providing some of the data used.

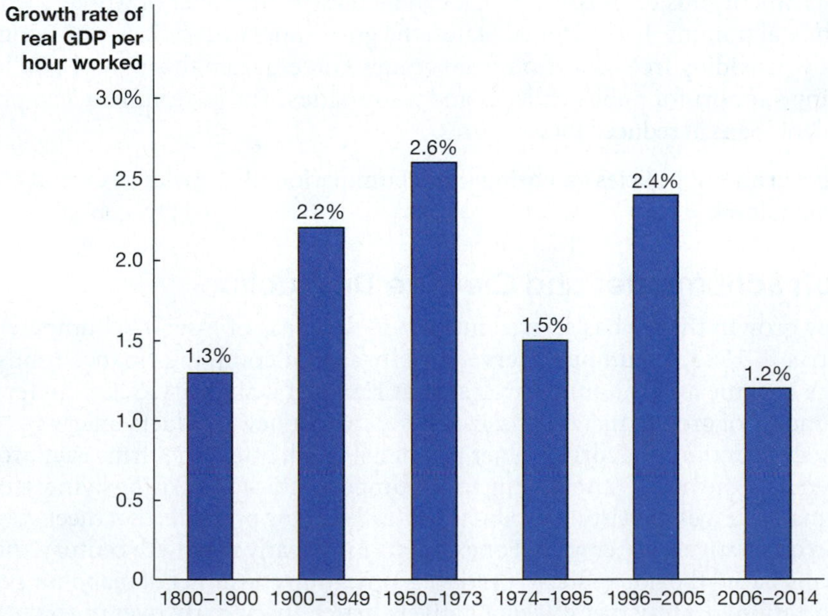

Economic Growth in the United States since 1950

Continuing technological change allowed the U.S. economy to avoid the diminishing returns to capital that stifled growth in the Soviet economy. In fact, until the 1970s, the growth rate of the U.S. economy accelerated over time. As Figure 22.5 shows, growth in the first half of the twentieth century was faster than growth during the nineteenth century, and growth in the immediate post–World War II period from 1950 to 1973 was faster yet. Then the unexpected happened: For more than 20 years, from 1974 to 1995, the growth rate of real GDP per hour worked slowed. The growth rate during these years was more than 1 percentage point per year lower than during the 1950–1973 period. Beginning in the mid-1990s, the growth rate picked up again, and many economists argued that the effects of the revolution in *information technology* (*IT*), including increased use of computers, software, cellphones, and related innovations, were causing a return to higher rates of long-run growth. But, then, beginning in 2006, growth again slowed. MyEconLab Concept Check

Is the United States Headed for a Long Period of Slow Growth?

Economists have not reached a consensus in explaining the swings in U.S. productivity growth since the mid-1970s. Broadly speaking, economists' views fall into two camps:

- **The optimistic view.** Some economists argue that although productivity has become more difficult to measure, the United States is likely to experience high rates of productivity growth in the long run, which will significantly increase the standard of living of the average person in the decades ahead.
- **The pessimistic view.** Other economists believe that productivity growth entered a long-run decline in the mid-1970s that was overcome for only a brief period of time by the initial effects of the revolution in information technology. These economists argue that future productivity growth rates are likely to remain low and, therefore, the standard of living of the average person in the United States will increase only slowly.

We can briefly discuss some of the key issues involved in this debate.

Measurement Issues Some economists argue that recent productivity growth rates may appear worse than they are because of problems in measuring output. If growth in real GDP understates the true growth rate of output, then measured productivity growth will also understate the true growth rate of productivity. After 1970, services—such as haircuts and financial advice—became a larger fraction of GDP, and goods—such as automobiles and hamburgers—became a smaller fraction. It is more difficult to measure increases in the output of services than to measure increases in the output of goods. For example, before banks began using automated teller machines (ATMs) in the 1980s, you could withdraw money only by going to a bank before closing time—which was usually 3:00 P.M. Once ATMs became available, you could withdraw money at any time of the day or night at a variety of locations. This increased convenience from ATMs does not show up in GDP. If this and similar improvements in the quality and convenience of services were included in GDP, measured output per hour worked would have grown more rapidly.

There may also be a measurement problem in accounting for improvements in the environment and in health and safety. Beginning in 1970, new laws required firms to spend billions of dollars reducing pollution, improving workplace safety, and redesigning products to improve their safety. This spending did not result in additional output that would be included in GDP—although it may have increased overall well-being. If these increases in well-being had been included in GDP, measured output per hour worked would have grown more rapidly.

All the high-income countries have experienced roughly similar movements in productivity growth rates. Because they all began producing more services and fewer goods and enacted stricter environmental regulations at about the same time, explanations of the productivity slowdown that emphasize measurement problems become more plausible.

The Role of Information Technology Some economists argue that the development of information technology (IT) caused the higher productivity growth that began in the mid-1990s. As computers became less expensive and faster, they made it possible for people and organizations to communicate and process data more efficiently. Today, a single laptop computer has more computing power than all the mainframe computers NASA used to control the *Apollo* spacecrafts that landed on the moon in the late 1960s and early 1970s.

Faster data processing has had a major effect on nearly every firm. Business record keeping, once done laboriously by hand, is now done more quickly and accurately by computers. During the 1990s, firms used the Internet to market and sell products. Smartphones, tablets, laptop computers, and wireless Internet access allow people to work at home and while traveling. These developments in IT have significantly increased labor productivity.

Despite the wonders of IT, productivity growth since 2006 has fallen to an even lower rate than during the period of slow growth from the mid-1970s to the mid-1990s. Is IT no longer a productivity booster, or are the data not capturing some of IT's benefits? What insight do the answers to these questions give us about how rapid growth will be in the coming decades?

Some economists believe that developments in IT have improved the delivery of services to both consumers and firms in ways that the GDP statistics fail to capture. For instance, receiving detailed driving directions using TomTom or a similar app is much easier than before smartphones were developed. In recent years the widespread use of apps to arrange for car rides, make short-term room rentals, locate friends, and so on have provided benefits to consumers that are not measured or are only partially measured by GDP. Similarly, a store manager can quickly check on available warehouse inventory using a dedicated smartphone or tablet app.

Economists who believe that IT is having large, but difficult to measure, effects on the economy are usually also optimistic about future growth rates. They believe that continuing advances in semiconductor technology—which underlie progress in IT—will result in substantial gains in labor productivity. The gains will come from higher productivity in the IT sector itself and in other sectors of the economy as the result of progress made possible by advances in IT. For example, ever more rapid and inexpensive computing lowers the cost and speeds the adoption of existing products, such as 3D printers, and helps innovators develop new products, which, in turn, raise productivity growth above its current levels.

Other economists doubt that the unmeasured benefits of the IT revolution are any greater than the unmeasured benefits of earlier innovations. Robert J. Gordon of Northwestern University has argued that productivity increases from the IT revolution were in fact much smaller than increases resulting from earlier innovations, such as the railroad, electrification of homes and businesses, petroleum refining, and the automobile. Moreover, Gordon and some other economists argue that most of the gains from the IT revolution occurred in the 1990s, as a result of the development of the World Wide Web, Windows 95, and computerized inventory control systems. These innovations raised labor productivity because they changed how businesses operated. By the early 2000s, the IT revolution was having a greater effect on consumer products, such as smartphones and tablets, than on labor productivity. Gordon identifies other factors, such as an aging population, declining educational achievement, and the consequences of increased regulations and higher taxes, that will lead to lower productivity growth rates. Gordon forecasts an extended period of productivity growth rates of 0.5 percent or less.

"Secular Stagnation ..." In the late 1930s, toward the end of the Great Depression, Alvin Hansen of Harvard University predicted that the U.S. economy would experience an extended period of slow growth, or *secular stagnation*. The rapid growth rates the U.S. economy experienced beginning in 1950 indicate that Hansen's analysis was incorrect. Recently, however, Lawrence Summers of Harvard, along with some other economists, has revived the term in arguing that growth rates are likely to remain low in future years. These economists do not focus on potentially slow rates of technological progress. Instead, they believe that real GDP may grow slowly because of insufficient demand for investment spending.

In Chapter 21, we saw that in the loanable funds model, the equilibrium level of saving and investment is determined at the level of the real interest rate where the quantity of loanable funds demanded equals the quantity of loanable funds supplied. Economists who forecast a future of secular stagnation believe that the demand for loanable funds may be low in coming years for three main reasons:

1. Slowing population growth in the United States will reduce the demand for housing.
2. Modern information technology firms, such as Twitter, Google, and Facebook, require much less capital than older industrial firms, such as General Motors or Whirlpool.
3. The price of capital, particularly information technology goods such as computers, has been falling relative to the prices of other goods. Accordingly, firms can meet their needs for capital with lower levels of expenditure.

As a result of these factors, the real interest rate that brings equality to the loanable funds market may be very low—possibly even negative. So, investment spending will be very low. With this component of GDP growing slowly, GDP will itself only grow slowly.

... or a Return to Faster Growth? Critics of the secular stagnation view believe that low rates of investment in recent years have resulted from the severity of the recession of 2007–2009 and the relatively slow recovery from that recession. They argue that as the economic recovery continues, the demand for investment goods will increase. In addition, they argue that economic growth in other countries may increase the demand for U.S. goods, allowing exports to increase, thereby offsetting the effects on GDP of lower production of investment goods.

The debate over future growth rates is an important one. If the optimistic forecasts are correct, then in future decades, the U.S. standard of living will be much higher than if the pessimistic forecasts are correct. A large difference in the standard of living will have an enormous effect on nearly every aspect of life in the United States, including the extent of poverty, the ability of individuals and the government to finance increasing medical costs, and the ability of the country to deal with the effects of an aging population. MyEconLab Concept Check

MyEconLab Study Plan

22.4 Why Isn't the Whole World Rich?

LEARNING OBJECTIVE: Explain economic catch-up and discuss why many poor countries have not experienced rapid economic growth.

The economic growth model tells us that economies grow when the quantity of capital per hour worked increases and when technological change occurs. This model seems to provide a good blueprint for developing countries to become rich:

1. Increase the quantity of capital per hour worked.
2. Use the best available technology.

There are economic incentives for both of these things to happen in poor countries. The profitability of using additional capital or better technology is generally greater in a developing country than in a high-income country. For example, replacing an existing computer with a new, faster computer will generally have a relatively small payoff for a firm in the United States. In contrast, installing a new computer in a Zambian firm where records have been kept by hand is likely to have an enormous payoff.

This observation leads to an important conclusion: *The economic growth model predicts that poor countries will grow faster than rich countries.* If this prediction is correct, we should observe poor countries catching up to rich countries in levels of GDP per capita (or income per capita). Has this **catch-up**—or *convergence*—actually occurred? Here we come to a paradox: If we look only at the countries that currently have high incomes, we see that the lower-income countries have been catching up to the higher-income

Catch-up The prediction that the level of GDP per capita (or income per capita) in poor countries will grow faster than in rich countries.

countries, but the developing countries as a group have not been catching up to the high-income countries as a group.

Catch-up: Sometimes but Not Always

We can construct a graph that makes it easier to see whether catch-up is happening. In Figure 22.6, the horizontal axis shows the initial level of real GDP per capita, and the vertical axis shows the rate at which real GDP per capita is growing. We can then plot points on the graph for rich and poor countries. Each point represents the combination of a country's initial level of real GDP per capita and its growth rate over the following years. The catch-up line in the figure shows the situation where the catch-up prediction holds exactly: Low-income countries should be on the upper-left section of the line because they would have low initial levels of real GDP per capita but fast growth rates. High-income countries should be in the lower-right section of the line because they would have high initial levels of real GDP per capita but slow growth rates. When we plot the actual observations for each country, the closer the points for each country are to the line, the more accurate the catch-up prediction is.

Catch-up among the High-Income Countries If we look at only the countries that currently have high incomes, we can see the catch-up predicted by the economic growth model. Figure 22.7 shows that the high-income countries that had the lowest incomes in 1960, such as Taiwan, Korea, and Hong Kong, grew the fastest between 1960 and 2011 (which is the most recent year for which comprehensive data are available). Countries that had the highest incomes in 1960, such as Switzerland, Australia, and the United States, grew the slowest.

Are the Developing Countries Catching Up to the High-Income Countries? If we expand our analysis to include every country for which statistics are available, it becomes more difficult to find the catch-up predicted by the economic growth model. Figure 22.8 does not show a consistent relationship between the level of real GDP per capita in 1960 and growth from 1960 to 2011. Some countries that had low levels of real GDP per capita in 1960, such as Niger and the Democratic Republic of the Congo, actually experienced *negative* economic growth: They had *lower* levels of real GDP per capita in 2011 than in 1960. Other countries that started with low levels of real GDP per capita, such as Malaysia and China, grew rapidly. Some middle-income countries in 1960, such as Venezuela, grew slowly between 1960 and 2011, while others, such as Ireland, grew much more rapidly. MyEconLab Concept Check

MyEconLab Animation

Figure 22.6

The Catch-up Predicted by the Economic Growth Model

According to the economic growth model, countries that start with lower levels of real GDP per capita should grow faster (points near the upper-left section of the line) than countries that start with higher levels of real GDP per capita (points near the lower-right section of the line).

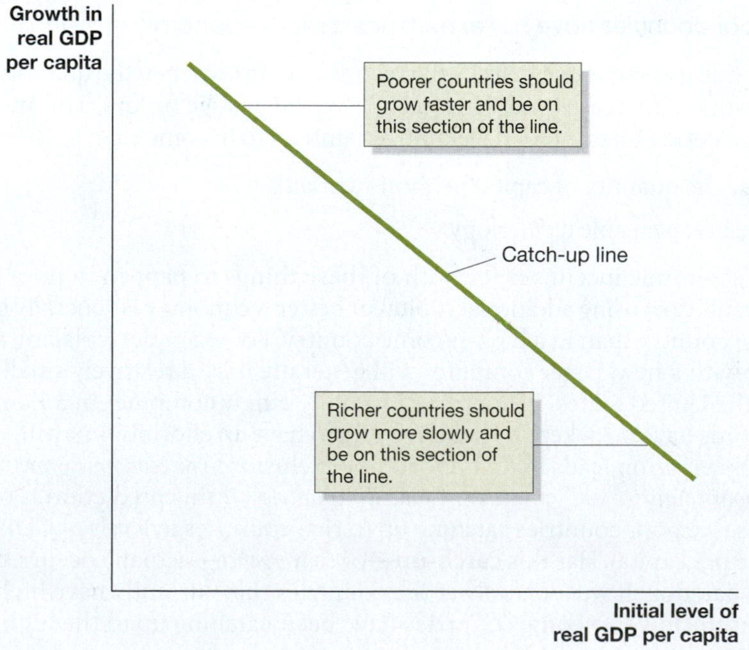

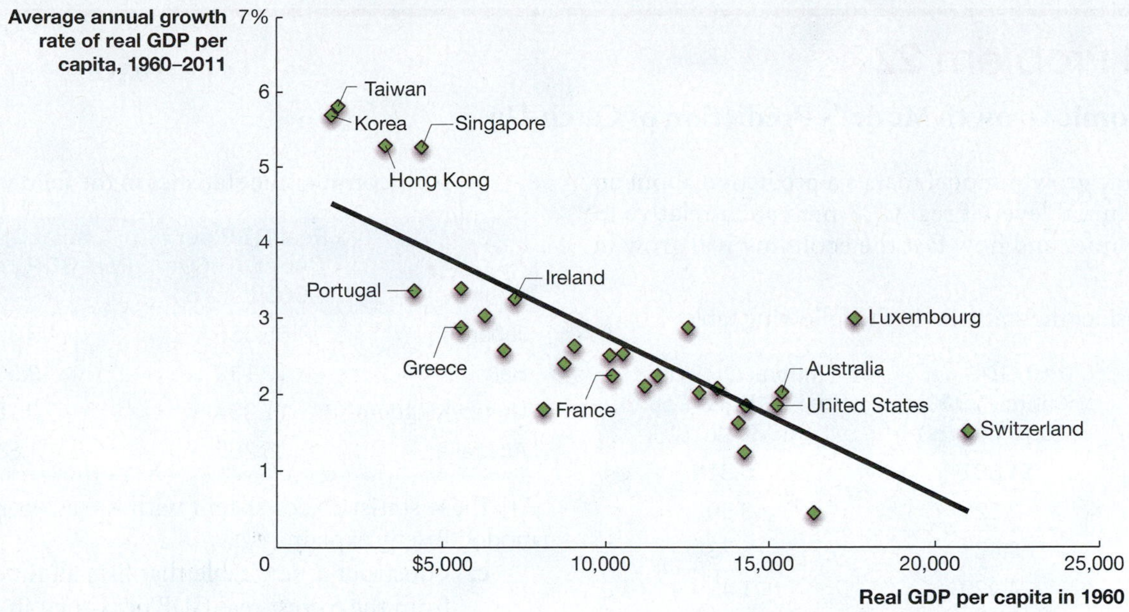

MyEconLab Animation

Figure 22.7 There Has Been Catch-up among High-Income Countries

If we look only at countries that currently have high incomes, we see that countries such as Taiwan, Korea, and Singapore that had the lowest incomes in 1960 grew the fastest between 1960 and 2011. Countries such as Switzerland and the United States that had the highest incomes in 1960 grew the slowest.

Note: Data are real GDP per capita in 2005 dollars. Each point in the figure represents one high-income country.

Source: Authors' calculations from data in *Penn World Table Version 8.1*; Robert C. Feenstra, Robert Inklaar, and Marcel P. Timmer, "The Next Generation of the Penn World Table" www.ggdc.net/pwt, April 2015.

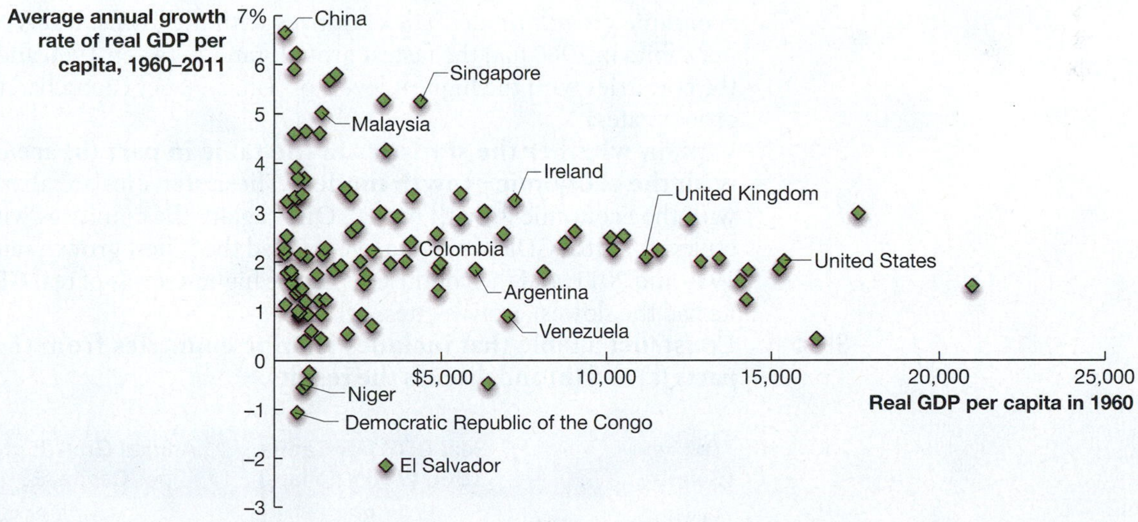

MyEconLab Animation

Figure 22.8 Most of the World Hasn't Been Catching Up

If we look at all countries for which statistics are available, we do not see the catch-up predicted by the economic growth model. Some countries that had low levels of real GDP per capita in 1960, such as Niger and the Democratic Republic of the Congo, actually experienced *negative* economic growth. Other countries that started with low levels of real GDP per capita, such as Malaysia and China, grew rapidly. Some middle-income countries in 1960, such as Venezuela, hardly grew between 1960 and 2011, while others, such as Ireland, experienced significant growth.

Note: Data are real GDP per capita in 2005 dollars. Each point in the figure represents one country.

Source: Authors' calculations from data in *Penn World Table Version 8.1*; Robert C. Feenstra, Robert Inklaar, and Marcel P. Timmer, "The Next Generation of the Penn World Table" www.ggdc.net/pwt, April 2015.

Solved Problem 22.4

MyEconLab Interactive Animation

The Economic Growth Model's Prediction of Catch-Up

The economic growth model makes a prediction about an economy's initial level of real GDP per capita relative to other economies and how fast the economy will grow in the future.

a. Consider the statistics in the following table:

Country	Real GDP per Capita, 1960 (2005 dollars)	Annual Growth in Real GDP per Capita, 1960–2011
Taiwan	$1,861	5.81%
Panama	2,120	3.50
Brazil	2,483	2.73
Costa Rica	4,920	1.42
Venezuela	7,015	0.91

Are these statistics consistent with the economic growth model? Briefly explain.

b. Now consider the statistics in the following table:

Country	Real GDP per Capita, 1960 (2005 dollars)	Annual Growth in Real GDP per Capita, 1960–2011
Japan	$5,586	3.39%
Belgium	10,132	2.50
United Kingdom	11,204	2.10
Australia	15,255	1.85

Are these statistics consistent with the economic growth model? Briefly explain.

c. Construct a new table that lists all nine countries, from the lowest real GDP per capita in 1960 to the highest, along with their growth rates. Are the statistics in your new table consistent with the economic growth model?

Solving the Problem

Step 1: Review the chapter material. This problem is about catch-up in the economic growth model, so you may want to review the section "Why Isn't the Whole World Rich?" which begins on page 747.

Step 2: Explain whether the statistics in the table in part (a) are consistent with the economic growth model. These statistics are consistent with the economic growth model. The countries with the lowest levels of real GDP per capita in 1960 had the fastest growth rates between 1960 and 2011, and the countries with the highest levels of real GDP per capita had the slowest growth rates.

Step 3: Explain whether the statistics in the table in part (b) are consistent with the economic growth model. These statistics are also consistent with the economic growth model. Once again, the countries with the lowest levels of real GDP per capita in 1960 had the fastest growth rates between 1960 and 2011, and the countries with the highest levels of real GDP per capita had the slowest growth rates.

Step 4: Construct a table that includes all nine countries from the tables in parts (a) and (b) and discuss the results.

Country	Real GDP per Capita, 1960 (2005 dollars)	Annual Growth in Real GDP per Capita, 1960–2011
Taiwan	$1,861	5.81%
Panama	2,120	3.50
Brazil	2,483	2.73
Costa Rica	4,920	1.42
Japan	5,586	3.39
Venezuela	7,015	0.91
Belgium	10,132	2.50
United Kingdom	11,204	2.10
Australia	15,255	1.85

The statistics in the new table are *not* consistent with the predictions of the economic growth model. For example, Australia and the United Kingdom had higher levels of real GDP per capita in 1960 than did Costa Rica and Venezuela. The economic growth model predicts that Australia and the United Kingdom should, therefore, have grown more slowly than Costa Rica and Venezuela. The data in the table show, however, that Australia and the United Kingdom grew faster. Similarly, Belgium grew faster than Costa Rica, even though its real GDP per capita was already much higher than Costa Rica's in 1960.

Extra Credit: The statistics in these tables confirm what we saw in Figures 22.7 and 22.8 on page 749: There has been catch-up among the high-income countries, but there has not been catch-up if we include in the analysis all the countries of the world.

Your Turn: For more practice, do related problems 4.4 and 4.5 on page 766 at the end of this chapter.

MyEconLab Study Plan

Why Haven't Most Western European Countries, Canada, and Japan Caught Up to the United States?

Figure 22.7 on page 749 indicates that there has been catch-up among the high-income countries over the past 50 years. If we look at the catch-up of other high-income countries to the United States during the most recent period, we discover a surprising fact: Over the past 25 years, other high-income countries have actually fallen further behind the United States rather than catching up to it. Figure 22.9 shows real GDP per capita in Canada, Japan, and the five largest economies in Western Europe relative to real GDP per capita in the United States. The blue bars show real GDP per capita in 1990 relative to the United States, and the red bars show real GDP per capita in 2014 relative to the United States. In each case, relative levels of real GDP per capita were lower in 2014 than they were in 1990. Each of these countries experienced significant catch-up to the United States between 1960 and 1990, but they have experienced no catch-up since 1990.

Why have other high-income countries had trouble completely closing the gap in real GDP per capita with the United States? Many economists believe there are two

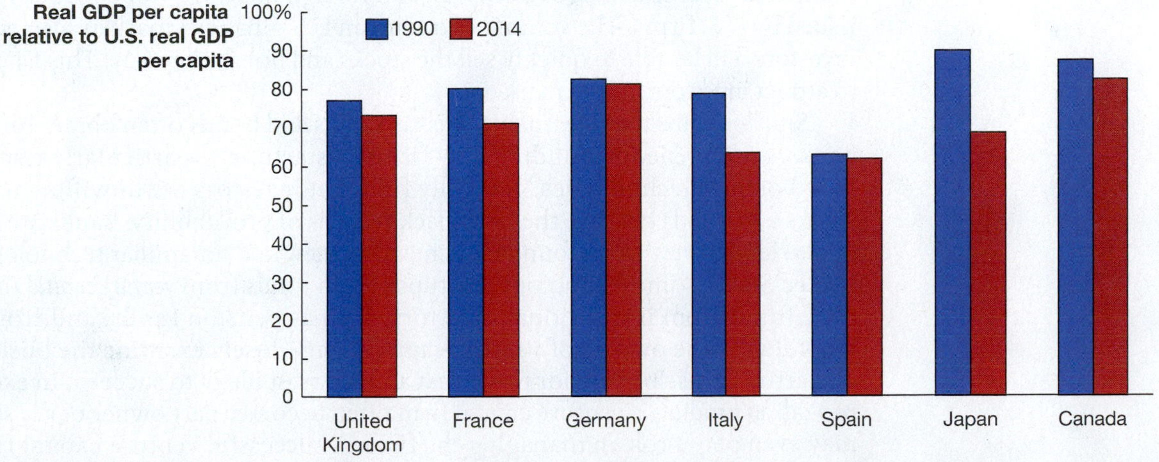

MyEconLab Real-time data

Figure 22.9 **Other High-Income Countries Have Stopped Catching Up to the United States**

The blue bars show real GDP per capita in 1990 relative to the United States, and the red bars show real GDP per capita in 2014 relative to the United States. In each case, relative levels of real GDP per capita are lower in 2014 than they were in 1990, which means that these countries have ceased catching up to the United States.

Source: Authors' calculations from data in Organization for Economic Co-operation and Development, stat.oecd.org.

main explanations: the greater flexibility of U.S. labor markets and the greater efficiency of the U.S. financial system. U.S. labor markets are more flexible than labor markets in other countries for several reasons. In many European countries, government regulations make it difficult for firms to fire workers and thereby make firms reluctant to hire workers in the first place. As a result, many younger workers have difficulty finding jobs, and once a job is found, a worker tends to remain in it even if his or her skills and preferences are not a good match for the characteristics of the job. In the United States, by contrast, government regulations are less restrictive, workers have an easier time finding jobs, and workers change jobs fairly frequently. This high rate of job mobility ensures a better match between workers' skills and preferences and the characteristics of jobs, which increases labor productivity. Many European countries also have restrictive work rules that limit the ability of firms to implement new technologies. These rules restrict the tasks firms can ask workers to perform and the number of hours they work. The rules reduce the ability of firms to use new technologies that may require workers to learn new skills, perform new tasks, or work during the night or early mornings.

Workers in the United States tend to enter the labor force earlier, retire later, and experience fewer long spells of unemployment than do workers in Europe. Unemployed workers in the United States typically receive smaller government payments for a shorter period of time than do unemployed workers in Canada and most of the countries of Western Europe. Because the opportunity cost of being unemployed is lower in those countries, the unemployment rate tends to be higher, and the fraction of the labor force that is unemployed for more than one year also tends to be higher. Studies have shown that workers who are employed for longer periods tend to have greater skills, greater productivity, and higher wages. Many economists believe that the design of the U.S. unemployment insurance program has contributed to the greater flexibility of U.S. labor markets and to higher rates of growth in labor productivity and real GDP per capita.

As we have seen, technological change is essential for rapid productivity growth. To obtain the funds needed to implement new technologies, firms turn to the financial system. It is important that funds for investment be not only available but also allocated efficiently. Large corporations can raise funds by selling stocks and bonds in financial markets. U.S. corporations benefit from the efficiency of U.S. financial markets (see Chapter 8). The level of legal protection of investors is relatively high in U.S. financial markets, which encourages both U.S. and foreign investors to buy stocks and bonds issued by U.S. firms. The volume of trading in U.S. financial markets also ensures that investors will be able to quickly sell the stocks and bonds they buy. This *liquidity* serves to attract investors to U.S. markets.

Smaller firms that are unable to issue stocks and bonds often obtain funding from banks. Entrepreneurs founding new firms—"startups"—particularly firms that are based on new technologies, generally find that investors are unwilling to buy their stocks and bonds because the firms lack records of profitability. Banks are also reluctant to lend to new firms founded to introduce new and unfamiliar technologies. In the United States, some technology startups obtain funds from *venture capital firms*, which raise funds from institutional investors, such as pension funds, and from wealthy individuals. The owners of venture capital firms closely examine the business plans of startup firms, looking for those that appear most likely to succeed. In exchange for providing funding, a venture capital firm often becomes part owner of the startup and may even play a role in managing the firm. A successful venture capital firm is able to attract investors who would not otherwise be willing to provide funds to startups because the investors lack enough information about the startup. A number of well-known U.S. high-technology firms, such as Google, relied on venture capital firms to fund their early expansion. The ability of venture capital firms to finance technology-driven startup firms may be giving the United States an advantage in bringing new products and new processes to market.

The U.S. financial system suffered severe problems between 2007 and 2009. But, over the long run, it has succeeded in efficiently allocating investment funds.

MyEconLab Concept Check

Why Don't More Low-Income Countries Experience Rapid Growth?

The economic growth model predicts that the countries that were very poor in 1960 should have grown rapidly over the next 50 years. As we have just seen, some did, but many did not. Why are many low-income countries growing so slowly? There is no single answer, but most economists point to four key factors:

1. Failure to enforce the rule of law
2. Wars and revolutions
3. Poor public education and health
4. Low rates of saving and investment

Failure to Enforce the Rule of Law In the years since 1960, increasing numbers of developing countries, including China, have abandoned centrally planned economies in favor of more market-oriented economies. For entrepreneurs in a market economy to succeed, however, the government must guarantee private **property rights** and enforce contracts. Unless entrepreneurs feel secure in their property, they will not risk starting a business. Business owners also have difficulty being successful unless they can use an independent court system to enforce contracts. The **rule of law** refers to the ability of a government to enforce the laws of the country, particularly with respect to protecting private property and enforcing contracts. The failure of many developing countries to guarantee property rights and to enforce contracts has hindered their economic growth.

Property rights The rights individuals or firms have to the exclusive use of their property, including the right to buy or sell it.

Rule of law The ability of a government to enforce the laws of the country, particularly with respect to protecting private property and enforcing contracts.

Consider, for example, the production of shoes. Suppose the owner of a shoe factory signs a contract with a leather tannery to deliver a specific quantity of leather on a particular date for a particular price. On the basis of this contract, the owner of the shoe factory signs a contract to deliver a specific quantity of shoes to a shoe wholesaler. This contract states the quantity of shoes to be delivered, the quality of the shoes, the delivery date, and the price. The owner of the leather tannery uses the contract with the shoe factory to enter into a contract with cattle ranchers for the delivery of hides. The shoe wholesaler enters into contracts to deliver shoes to retail stores, where they are sold to consumers. For the flow of goods from cattle ranchers to shoe customers to operate efficiently, each business must carry out the terms of the contract it has signed. In developed countries, such as the United States, businesses know that if they fail to carry out a contract, they may be sued in court and forced to compensate the other party for any economic damages.

Many developing countries do not have functioning, independent court systems. Even if a court system does exist, a case may not be heard for many years. In some countries, bribery of judges and political favoritism in court rulings are common. If firms cannot enforce contracts through the court system, they may insist on carrying out only face-to-face cash transactions. For example, the shoe manufacturer will wait until the leather producer brings the hides to the factory and will then buy the hides for cash. The wholesaler will wait until the shoes have been produced before making plans for sales to retail stores. Production still takes place, but it is carried out more slowly and inefficiently. With slow and inefficient production, firms have difficulty finding investors willing to provide them with the funds they need to expand.

Making the Connection
MyEconLab Video

Why Hasn't Mexico Grown as Fast as China?

Many people consider China *the* great economic growth success story. The decision by Chinese government leaders in the 1970s to turn away from a centrally planned economy and toward a market system unleashed economic growth that has lifted more than a billion people in China out of poverty. As we will discuss in Section 22.5, the Chinese economy still faces significant obstacles to maintaining high growth rates, and the Chinese Communist Party has maintained its dictatorship over the country. Despite these problems, many economists and policymakers see China as an example of the rapid growth that low-income countries can attain.

As we saw in the chapter opener, some U.S. firms have chosen in recent years to locate factories and other facilities in Mexico rather than in China because Mexico is closer to the United States and because labor costs have been increasing more rapidly in China. This trend has been good news for the Mexican economy because it has increased factory employment and given the country easier access to U.S. technology. Overall, though, the growth rates of the Mexican economy have been disappointing. The graph below compares the growth rates of real GDP per capita for the Mexican and Chinese economies over the past 35 years.

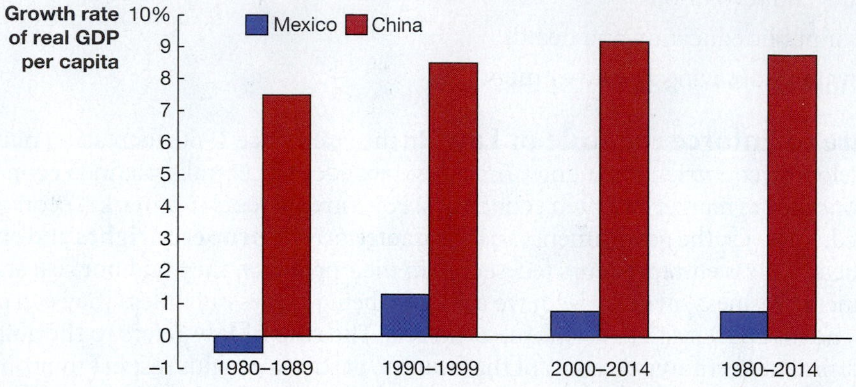

Taking the whole period between 1980 and 2014, the average annual growth rate for the Chinese economy has been 8.8 percent, while the growth rate for the Mexican economy has been a very slow 0.8 percent. In Chapter 21, we saw that if we divide a growth rate into 70, the result is approximately the number of years it will take real GDP per capita to double. When we apply that rule here, we find that it will take real GDP per capita more than 85 years to double in Mexico but only 8 years in China.

What explains the slow growth of the Mexican economy? For most of the period from the Mexican Revolution of 1910 until 2000, the Institutional Revolutionary Party (PRI) dominated the Mexican government. For decades, the party followed a policy of limiting imports and foreign investment, concentrating on building up domestic industry behind high tariff walls. The Mexican government took over, or nationalized, some businesses, including the oil industry. By the 1980s, dissatisfaction with the country's poor economic performance led the PRI, under President Miguel de la Madrid, to institute a series of reforms. The reforms, which were broadened in the 1990s, included allowing banks again to be private businesses; signing the North American Free Trade Agreement (NAFTA) with the United States and Canada, which greatly reduced tariffs on imports; and allowing foreign investment in most sectors of the economy apart from the oil industry. As the graph above shows, though, these reforms have not resulted in high rates of economic growth.

Some economic historians believe that the Spanish colonial background of the nineteenth century and earlier hobbled the Mexican economy. Unlike in the United States, in Mexico and other Spanish and Portuguese colonies, land was often concentrated in very large estates, which led to highly unequal distributions of income and may have made it difficult for a broad-based middle class capable of supporting a large manufacturing base to develop. Other countries in Latin America, though, including Chile and Uruguay, with similar colonial backgrounds have experienced much more rapid growth.

Some economists believe that the financial sector has been an important obstacle to growth. The Mexican legal system makes it difficult for banks to seize a business's assets when the business defaults on a loan. As a result, Mexican banks are reluctant to make loans to businesses. As we noted in the chapter opener, Mexico also suffers from government corruption that either makes businesses reluctant to expand or forces them to operate in the underground economy. In either case, the businesses are unable to take advantage of economies of scale and may be unwilling to make large investments in machinery or buildings. In certain areas of Mexico, criminal gangs have also disrupted business. The educational system in Mexico has failed to provide many students with the skills needed to find work at firms competing in the global marketplace. Finally, infrastructure, including poor roads and inconsistent and expensive provision of electricity—with occasional blackouts—have also hindered business expansion.

Timothy J. Kehoe of the University of Minnesota and Kim J. Ruhl of New York University note that China also suffers from institutional problems, but it has grown much faster than Mexico. China, though, began its rapid growth from very low levels of income, so that in 2014, real GDP per capita in Mexico was still more than twice the level in China. Kehoe and Ruhl argue that, as a middle-income country, Mexico has already taken advantage of many of the relatively easy ways of increasing real GDP—including moving resources out of the low-productivity agricultural sector, accumulating capital in manufacturing, and adopting modern technology. We saw in the discussion of Figure 22.9 that, probably for institutional reasons, many high-income countries have made no progress in closing the gap in real GDP per capita between themselves and the United States during the past 25 years. Mexico may now be in a similar situation of having difficulty growing fast enough to close the gap with higher-income countries. Because Mexico's institutional barriers to growth are more severe than those in European countries, the gap in real GDP per capita between the United States and Mexico may persist at a high level.

Economists and policymakers in Mexico continue to look for ways to increase growth rates. Without an increase in growth, it may be decades before millions of low-income people in Mexico are able to escape poverty.

Sources: "The 100-Year View," *Economist*, May 2, 2015; Gordon H. Hanson, "Why Isn't Mexico Rich?" *Journal of Economic Literature*, Vol. 48, No. 4, December 2010, pp. 987–1004; Timothy J. Kehoe and Kim J. Ruhl, "Why Have Economic Reforms in Mexico Not Generated Growth?" *Journal of Economic Literature*, Vol. 48, No. 4, December 2010, pp. 1004–1027; Nora Lustig, "Life Is Not Easy: Mexico's Quest for Stability and Growth," *Journal of Economic Perspectives*, Vol. 15, No. 1, Winter 2001, pp. 85–106; and Federal Reserve Bank of St. Louis.

Your Turn: Test your understanding by doing related problems 4.8 and 4.9 on page 767 at the end of this chapter.

MyEconLab Study Plan

Wars and Revolutions Many of the countries that were very poor in 1960 have experienced extended periods of war or violent changes of government during the years since. These wars have made it impossible for countries such as Afghanistan, Angola, Ethiopia, the Central African Republic, and the Democratic Republic of the Congo to accumulate capital or adopt new technologies. In fact, conducting any kind of business has been very difficult. Ending war has a positive effect on growth, as shown by the case of Mozambique, which suffered through almost two decades of civil war and declining real GDP per capita. With the end of civil war, Mozambique experienced a strong annual growth rate of 8 percent in real GDP per capita from 1990 to 2014.

Poor Public Education and Health We have seen that human capital is one of the determinants of labor productivity. Many low-income countries have weak public school systems, so many workers are unable to read and write. Few workers acquire the skills necessary to use the latest technology.

People in many low-income countries suffer from diseases that are either nonexistent or easily treated in high-income countries. For example, few people in developed countries suffer from malaria, but about 500,000 Africans die from it each year. Treatments for AIDS have greatly reduced deaths from this disease in the United States and Europe. But millions of people in low-income countries continue to die from AIDS. These countries often lack the resources, and their governments are often too ineffective, to provide even routine medical care, such as childhood vaccinations.

People who are sick work less and are less productive when they do work. Poor nutrition or exposure to certain diseases in childhood can leave people permanently weakened and can affect their intelligence as adults. Poor health has a significant negative effect on the human capital of workers in developing countries.

Low Rates of Saving and Investment To invest in factories, machinery, and computers, firms need funds. Some of the funds can come from the owners of the firm and from their friends and families, but firms in high-income countries raise most of their funds from bank loans and the sale of stocks and bonds in financial markets. In most developing countries, stock and bond markets do not exist, and often the banking system is very weak. In high-income countries, the funds that banks lend to businesses come from the savings of households. In high-income countries, many households are able to save a significant fraction of their income. In developing countries, many households barely survive on their incomes and, therefore, have little or no savings.

The low saving rates in developing countries can contribute to a *vicious cycle of poverty*. Because households have low incomes, they save very little. Because households save very little, few funds are available for firms to borrow. Lacking funds, firms do not invest in the new factories, machinery, and equipment needed for economic growth. Because the economy does not grow, household incomes remain low, as do their savings, and so on.

MyEconLab Concept Check

The Benefits of Globalization

Foreign direct investment (FDI) The purchase or building by a corporation of a facility in a foreign country.

Foreign portfolio investment The purchase by an individual or a firm of stocks or bonds issued in another country.

One way for a developing country to break out of the vicious cycle of low saving and investment and low growth is through foreign investment. **Foreign direct investment (FDI)** occurs when corporations build or purchase facilities in foreign countries. **Foreign portfolio investment** occurs when an individual or a firm buys stocks or bonds issued in another country. Foreign direct investment and foreign portfolio investment can give a low-income country access to technology and funds that otherwise would not be available. Until fairly recently, many developing countries were reluctant to take advantage of this opportunity.

From the 1940s through the 1970s, many developing countries closed themselves off from the global economy. During the 1930s and early 1940s, the global trading and financial system collapsed as a result of the Great Depression and World War II. Developing countries that relied on exporting to the high-income countries were hurt economically. Also, many countries in Africa and Asia achieved independence from the colonial powers of Europe during the 1950s and 1960s and were afraid of being dominated by them economically. As a result, many developing countries imposed high tariffs on foreign imports and strongly discouraged or even prohibited foreign investment. These policies made it difficult to break out of the vicious cycle of poverty.

Globalization The process of countries becoming more open to foreign trade and investment.

The policies of erecting high tariff barriers and avoiding foreign investment failed to produce much growth, so by the 1980s, many developing countries began to change policies. The result was **globalization**, which refers to the process of countries becoming more open to foreign trade and investment. Developing countries that are more globalized have grown faster than developing countries that are less globalized. Globalization has benefited developing countries by making it easier for them to obtain technology and investment funds.

MyEconLab Study Plan

MyEconLab Concept Check

22.5 Growth Policies

LEARNING OBJECTIVE: Discuss government policies that foster economic growth.

What can governments do to promote long-run economic growth? We have seen that even small differences in growth rates compounded over the years can lead to major differences in standards of living. Therefore, there is potentially a very high payoff to government policies that increase growth rates. We have already discussed some of these policies in this chapter. In this section, we explore additional policies.

Enhancing Property Rights and the Rule of Law

A market system cannot work well unless property rights are enforced. Entrepreneurs are unlikely to risk their own funds, and investors are unlikely to lend their funds to entrepreneurs, if property is not protected from being arbitrarily seized. We have seen that in many developing countries, the rule of law and property rights are undermined by government *corruption*. In some developing countries, it is impossible for an entrepreneur to obtain a permit to start a business without paying bribes, often to several different government officials. Is it possible for a country to reform a corrupt government bureaucracy?

Although today the United States ranks among the least corrupt countries, recent research by economists Edward Glaeser and Claudia Goldin of Harvard University has shown that in the late nineteenth and early twentieth centuries, corruption was a significant problem in the United States. The fact that political reform movements and crusading newspapers helped to reduce corruption in the United States to relatively low levels by the 1920s provides some hope for reform movements that aim to reduce corruption in developing countries today.

Property rights are unlikely to be secure in countries that are afflicted by wars and civil strife. For a number of countries, increased political stability is a necessary prerequisite to economic growth.

MyEconLab Concept Check

Making the Connection

MyEconLab Video

Will China's Standard of Living Ever Exceed That of the United States?

Some economists argue that China may have overinvested in physical capital, such as bullet trains.

In 2014, GDP per capita in the United States was more than four times higher than GDP per capita in China. However, the growth rate of real GDP per capita in the United States has averaged only 1.7 percent per year since 1980, compared to China's average growth rate of 8.8 percent per year over the same time period. If these growth rates were to continue, China's standard of living, as measured by real GDP per capita, would exceed the U.S. standard of living in the year 2036.

For China to maintain its high rates of growth in real GDP per capita, however, it would have to maintain high rates of productivity growth, which is unlikely for several reasons. First, the United States invests more in activities, such as research and development, that result in new technologies and increases in productivity. Although China has been successful in adopting existing technologies developed in the United States and other countries, it has been much less successful in developing new technologies. Second, a good part of China's growth is due to the transition from a centrally planned economy to a market economy, so China's growth rate is likely to decrease as the transition is completed. Third, China's economic growth has depended on moving workers from agriculture, where their productivity was low, to manufacturing jobs in cities, where their productivity is much higher. The large supply of low-wage agricultural workers helped to keep manufacturing wages low and provided China with a cost advantage in manufacturing goods compared with the United States and other high-income countries. China has exhausted much of its supply of low-wage agricultural workers, so manufacturing wages have begun to rise, eroding China's cost advantage. As we saw in the chapter opener, some U.S. firms have reacted to rising labor costs in China by moving factories to Mexico—or back to the United States.

Another looming problem is demographic. Because of China's low birth rate, the country will soon experience a decline in its labor force. Over the next two decades, the population of men and women between the ages of 15 and 29 will fall by roughly 100 million, or about 30 percent. China will also experience a large increase in older workers, a group that will on average be less productive and less healthy than younger workers. Given current trends, the U.S. Census Bureau projects fewer people under age 50 in China in 2030 than today, including fewer people in their 20s and early 30s, and many more people in their 60s and older. China still has potential sources for enhancing productivity, including the wider application of technology and the movement of workers into high-productivity industries, such as the manufacture of automobiles and household appliances, provided that domestic demand increases rapidly. These factors can fuel future growth, but at some point, China's demographic problems could slow growth.

Perhaps most troubling for China is the fact that the country remains autocratic, with the Communist Party refusing to allow meaningful elections and continuing to limit freedom of expression. The government has yet to establish secure property rights and the rule of law. Some observers believe that the lack of political freedom in China may ultimately lead to civil unrest, which could slow growth rates. Whether or not civil unrest eventually develops, the lack of democracy in China may already be resulting in problems that could slow growth in the near future. Large, state-owned firms, controlled by Communist Party members, continue to receive government subsidies. The result is that these firms, which typically have low productivity and are not globally competitive, receive funds that otherwise would have allowed high-productivity firms to expand.

Nouriel Roubini, an economist at New York University, argues that China's Communist Party may be repeating some of the mistakes the Soviet Communist Party committed decades ago. He argues that by employing policies that have resulted in investment spending being 50 percent of GDP, the government may have boosted short-term growth at the expense of the health of the economy in the long term. He notes:

> China is rife with overinvestment in physical capital, infrastructure, and property. To a visitor, this is evident in sleek but empty airports and bullet trains ... highways to nowhere, thousands of colossal new central and provincial government buildings, ghost towns, and brand-new aluminum smelters kept closed to prevent global prices from plunging.

Growth in China is already showing signs of slowing. Between 2010 and 2014, real GDP per capita grew at an annual rate of 6.0 percent. While still rapid, this growth rate is well below what the Chinese economy had achieved in previous decades. In early 2015, Chinese Premier Li Keqiang noted, "The downward pressure on economic growth continues to increase."

China has been engaged in an economic experiment: Can a country maintain high rates of economic growth in the long run while denying its citizens basic political rights?

Sources: Mark Magnier, "China's First-Quarter Growth Slowest in Six Years at 7%," *Wall Street Journal*, April 15, 2015; Pranab Bardhan, "The Slowing of Two Economic Giants," *New York Times*, July 14, 2013; Alex Frangos and Eric Bellman, "China Slump Ripples Globally," *Wall Street Journal*, July 15, 2013; Nicholas Eberstadt, "The Demographic Future," *Foreign Affairs*, Vol. 89, No. 6, November/December 2010, pp. 54–64; and Nouriel Roubini, "Beijing's Empty Bullet Trains," *Slate*, April 14, 2011.

MyEconLab Study Plan

Your Turn: Test your understanding by doing related problems 5.4 and 5.5 on pages 767–768 at the end of this chapter.

Improving Health and Education

Recently, many economists have become convinced that poor health is a major impediment to growth in some countries. The research of the late Nobel Laureate Robert Fogel emphasizes the important interaction between health and economic growth (see Chapter 21). As people's health improves and they become stronger and less susceptible to diseases, they also become more productive. Recent initiatives in developing countries to increase vaccinations against infectious diseases, to improve access to treated water, and to improve sanitation have begun to reduce rates of illness and death.

We discussed earlier in this chapter Paul Romer's argument that there are increasing returns to knowledge capital. Nobel Laureate Robert Lucas of the University of Chicago similarly argues that there are increasing returns to *human* capital. Lucas argues that productivity increases as the total stock of human capital increases but that these productivity increases are not completely captured by individuals as they decide how much education to purchase. Therefore, the market may produce an inefficiently low level of education and training unless the government subsidizes education. Some researchers have been unable to find evidence of increasing returns to human capital, but many economists believe that government subsidies for education have played an important role in promoting economic growth.

The rising incomes that result from economic growth can help developing countries deal with the *brain drain*, which refers to highly educated and successful individuals leaving developing countries for high-income countries. This migration occurs when successful individuals believe that economic opportunities are very limited in the domestic economy. Rapid economic growth in India and China in recent years has resulted in more entrepreneurs, engineers, and scientists deciding to remain in those countries rather than leave for the United States or other high-income countries. MyEconLab Concept Check

Policies That Promote Technological Change

One of the lessons of the economic growth model is that technological change is more important than increases in capital in explaining long-run growth. Government policies that facilitate access to technology are crucial for low-income countries. The easiest way for developing countries to gain access to technology is through foreign direct investment, where foreign firms are allowed to build new facilities or to buy domestic firms. Recent economic growth in India has been greatly aided by the Indian government's relaxation of regulations on foreign investment. Relaxing these regulations made it possible for India to gain access to the technology of Dell, Microsoft, and other multinational corporations.

In high-income countries, government policies can aid the growth of technology by subsidizing research and development. As we noted previously, in the United States, the federal government conducts some research and development on its own and also provides grants to researchers in universities. Tax breaks to firms undertaking research and development also facilitate technological change. MyEconLab Concept Check

Policies That Promote Saving and Investment

Firms turn to the loanable funds market to finance expansion and research and development (see Chapter 21). Policies that increase the incentives to save and invest will increase the equilibrium level of loanable funds and may increase the level of real GDP per capita. For instance, governments can use tax incentives to increase saving. In the United States, many workers are able to save for retirement by placing funds in 401(k) or 403(b) plans or in Individual Retirement Accounts (IRAs). Income placed in these accounts is not taxed until it is withdrawn during retirement. Because the funds are allowed to accumulate tax-free, the return is increased, which raises the incentive to save.

Governments also increase incentives for firms to engage in investment in physical capital by using *investment tax credits*. Investment tax credits allow firms to deduct from their taxes some fraction of the funds they have spent on investment. Reductions in the taxes firms pay on their profits also increase the after-tax return on investments. MyEconLab Concept Check

Is Economic Growth Good or Bad?

Although we didn't state so explicitly, in this chapter we have assumed that economic growth is desirable and that governments should undertake policies that will increase growth rates. It seems undeniable that increasing the growth rates of very low-income countries would help relieve the daily suffering that many people in those countries endure. But some people are unconvinced that, at least in the high-income countries, further economic growth is desirable.

The arguments against further economic growth reflect concern about the effects of growth on the environment or concern about the effects of the globalization process that has accompanied economic growth. In 1972, the Club of Rome published a controversial book titled *The Limits to Growth*, which predicted that economic growth would likely grind to a halt in the United States and other high-income countries because of increasing pollution and the depletion of natural resources, such as oil. Although these dire predictions have not yet come to pass, many people remain concerned that economic growth may be contributing to global warming, the destruction of rain forests, and other environmental problems.

In an earlier chapter, we discussed the opposition to globalization (see Chapter 9). We noted that some people believe that globalization has undermined the distinctive cultures of many countries, as imports of food, clothing, movies, and other goods have displaced domestically produced goods. We have seen that allowing foreign direct investment is an important way in which low-income countries can gain access to the latest technology. Some people, however, believe multinational firms behave unethically in low-income countries because they claim the firms pay very low wages and fail to follow the same safety and environmental regulations the firms are required to follow in high-income countries.

As with many other normative questions, economic analysis can contribute to the ongoing political debate over the consequences of economic growth, but it cannot settle the issue.

MyEconLab Study Plan

MyEconLab Concept Check

Continued from page 731

Economics in Your Life

Would You Be Better Off without China?

At the beginning of the chapter, we asked you to imagine that you could choose to live and work in a world with the Chinese economy growing very rapidly or in a world with the Chinese economy as it was before 1978—very poor and growing slowly. In which world would you choose to live? How does the current high-growth, high-export Chinese economy affect you as a consumer? How does it affect you as someone about to start a career?

It's impossible to walk into most stores in the United States without seeing products imported from China. Many of these products were at one time made in the United States. Imports from China replace domestically produced goods when the imports are either priced lower or have higher quality than the domestic goods they replace. Therefore, the rapid economic growth that has enabled Chinese firms to be competitive with firms in the United States has benefited you as a consumer: You have lower-priced goods and better goods available for purchase than you would if China had remained very poor. As you begin your career, there are some U.S. industries that, because of competition from Chinese firms, will have fewer jobs to offer. As we saw when discussing international trade, expanding trade changes the types of products each country makes, and, therefore, the types of jobs available, but it does not affect the total number of jobs (see Chapter 9). So, the economic rise of China will affect the mix of jobs available to you in the United States but will not make finding a job any more difficult.

Conclusion

For much of human history, most people have had to struggle to survive. Even today, a large fraction of the world's population lives in extreme poverty. The differences in living standards among countries today are a result of many decades of sharply different rates of economic growth. According to the economic growth model, increases in the quantity of capital per hour worked and increases in technology determine the growth in real GDP per hour worked and a country's standard of living. The keys to higher living standards seem straightforward:

1. Establish the rule of law.
2. Provide basic education and health care for the population.
3. Increase the amount of capital per hour worked.
4. Adopt the best technology.
5. Participate in the global economy.

However, for many countries, these policies have proved very difficult to implement.

Having discussed what determines the growth rate of economies, we will turn in the following chapters to the question of why economies experience short-run fluctuations in output, employment, and inflation.

Visit MyEconLab for a news article and analysis related to the concepts in this chapter.

CHAPTER SUMMARY AND PROBLEMS

Key Terms

Catch-up, p. 747
Economic growth model, p. 737
Foreign direct investment (FDI), p. 756
Foreign portfolio investment, p. 756
Globalization, p. 756
Human capital, p. 738
Industrial Revolution, p. 733
Labor productivity, p. 737
New growth theory, p. 742
Patent, p. 743
Per-worker production function, p. 738
Property rights, p. 753
Rule of law, p. 753
Technological change, p. 737

22.1 Economic Growth over Time and around the World, pages 732–737

LEARNING OBJECTIVE: Define economic growth, calculate economic growth rates, and describe global trends in economic growth.

Summary

For most of history, the average person survived with barely enough food. Living standards began to rise significantly only after the start of the **Industrial Revolution** in England in the 1700s, with the application of mechanical power to the production of goods. The best measure of a country's standard of living is its level of real GDP per capita. Economic growth occurs when real GDP per capita increases, thereby increasing the country's standard of living.

MyEconLab Visit **www.myeconlab.com** to complete these exercises online and get instant feedback.

Review Questions

1.1 Why does a country's economic growth rate matter?

1.2 Explain the difference between the total percentage increase in real GDP between 2005 and 2015 and the average annual growth rate in real GDP between the same years.

Problems and Applications

1.3 **(Related to the Making the Connection on page 733)** Economists Carol Shiue and Wolfgang Keller of the University of Colorado published a study of "market efficiency" in the eighteenth century in England, other European countries, and China. If the markets in a country are efficient, a product should have the same price wherever in the country it is sold, allowing for the effect of transportation costs. If prices are not the same in two areas within a country, it is possible to make a profit by buying the product where its price is low and reselling it where its price is high. This trading will drive prices to equality. Trade is most likely to occur, however, if entrepreneurs feel confident that the government will not seize their gains and the courts will enforce contracts. Therefore, in the eighteenth century, the more efficient a country's markets, the more its institutions favored long-run growth. Shiue and Keller found that in 1770, the efficiency of markets in England was significantly greater than the efficiency of markets elsewhere in Europe and in China. How does this finding relate to Douglass North's argument concerning why the Industrial Revolution occurred in England?

Source: Carol H. Shiue and Wolfgang Keller, "Markets in China and Europe on the Eve of the Industrial Revolution," *American Economic Review*, Vol. 97, No. 4, September 2007, pp. 1189–1216.

1.4 Use the data on real GDP in the following table to answer the following questions. The values are measured in each country's domestic currency. The base year for Brazil is 1995; the base year for Mexico is 2008; and the base year for Thailand is 1988.

Country	2011	2012	2013	2014
Brazil	1,192	1,213	1,247	1,248
Mexico	12,774	13,286	13,471	13,757
Thailand	4,600	4,898	5,040	5,076

a. Which country experienced the highest rate of economic growth during 2012 (that is, for which country did real GDP increase the most from 2011 to 2012)?
b. Which country experienced the highest average annual growth rate between 2012 and 2014?
c. Does it matter for your answers to parts (a) and (b) that each country's real GDP is measured in a different currency and uses a different base year? Briefly explain.

Source: International Monetary Fund, *World Economic Outlook Database*, April 2015.

1.5 Andover Bank and Lowell Bank each sell one-year certificates of deposit (CDs). The interest rates on these CDs are given in the following table for a three-year period.

Bank	2016	2017	2018
Andover Bank	5%	5%	5%
Lowell Bank	2%	6%	7%

Suppose you deposit $1,000 in a CD in each bank at the beginning of 2016. At the end of 2016, you take your $1,000 and any interest earned and invest it in a CD for the following year. You do this again at the end of 2017. At the end of 2018, will you have earned more on your Andover Bank CDs or on your Lowell Bank CDs? Briefly explain.

1.6 **(Related to the Don't Let This Happen to You on page 735)** Use the data for the United States in this table to answer the following questions.

Year	Real GDP per Capita (2009 prices)
2010	$47,719
2011	48,116
2012	48,822
2013	49,184
2014	50,010

a. What was the percentage change in real GDP per capita between 2010 and 2014?

b. What was the average annual growth rate in real GDP per capita between 2010 and 2014? (*Hint:* Remember that the average annual growth rate for relatively short periods can be approximated by averaging the growth rates for each year during the period [see Chapter 21].)

1.7 **(Related to the Making the Connection on page 736)** In his book *The White Man's Burden,* William Easterly reports:

> A vaccination campaign in southern Africa virtually eliminated measles as a killer of children. Routine childhood immunization combined with measles vaccination in seven southern African nations starting in 1996 virtually eliminated measles in those countries by 2000. A national campaign in Egypt to make parents aware of the use of oral rehydration therapy from 1982 to 1989 cut childhood deaths from diarrhea by 82 percent over that period.

a. Is it likely that real GDP per capita increased significantly in southern Africa and Egypt as a result of the near elimination of measles and the large decrease in childhood deaths from diarrhea? If these events did not increase real GDP per capita, is it still possible that they increased the standard of living in southern Africa and Egypt? Briefly explain.

b. Which seems more achievable for a developing country: the elimination of measles and childhood deaths from diarrhea or sustained increases in real GDP per capita? Briefly explain.

Source: William Easterly, *The White Man's Burden: Why the West's Efforts to Aid the Rest Have Done So Much Ill and So Little Good,* New York: The Penguin Press, 2006, p. 241.

1.8 **(Related to the Making the Connection on page 736)** Economist Charles Kenny of the Center for Global Development has argued:

> The process technologies—institutions like laws and inventory management systems—that appear central to raising incomes per capita flow less like water and more like bricks. But ideas and inventions—the importance of [education] and vaccines for DPT—really might flow more easily across borders and over distances.

If Kenny is correct, what are the implications of these facts for the ability of low-income countries to rapidly increase their rates of growth of real GDP per capita in the decades ahead? What are the implications for the ability of these countries to increase their standards of living? Briefly explain.

Source: Charles Kenny, *Getting Better,* New York: Basic Books, 2011, p. 117.

22.2 What Determines How Fast Economies Grow? pages 737–744

LEARNING OBJECTIVE: Use the economic growth model to explain why growth rates differ across countries.

Summary

An **economic growth model** explains changes in real GDP per capita in the long run. **Labor productivity** is the quantity of goods and services that can be produced by one worker or by one hour of work. Economic growth depends on increases in labor productivity. Labor productivity will increase if there is an increase in the amount of *capital* available to each worker or if there is an improvement in *technology*. **Technological change** is a change in the ability of a firm to produce a given level of output with a given quantity of inputs. There are three main sources of technological change: better machinery and equipment, increases in human capital, and better means of organizing and managing production. **Human capital** is the accumulated knowledge and skills that workers acquire from education and training or from their life experiences. We can say that an economy will have a higher standard of living the more capital it has per hour worked, the more human capital its workers have, the better its capital, and the better the job its business managers do in organizing production.

The **per-worker production function** shows the relationship between capital per hour worked and output per hour worked, holding technology constant. *Diminishing returns to capital* means that increases in the quantity of capital per hour worked will result in diminishing increases in output per hour worked. Technological change shifts up the per-worker production function, resulting in more output per hour worked at every level of capital per hour worked. The economic growth model stresses the importance of changes in capital per hour worked and technological change in explaining growth in output per hour worked. **New growth theory** is a model of long-run economic growth that emphasizes that technological change is influenced by how individuals and firms respond to economic incentives.

One way governments can promote technological change is by granting **patents**, which are exclusive rights to a product for a period of 20 years from the date the patent is filed with the government. To Joseph Schumpeter, the entrepreneur is central to the "creative destruction" by which the standard of living increases as qualitatively better products replace existing products.

MyEconLab Visit **www.myeconlab.com** to complete these exercises online and get instant feedback.

Review Questions

2.1 Using the per-worker production function graph from Figures 22.3 and 22.4 on pages 738 and 740, show the effect on real GDP per hour worked of an increase in capital per hour worked, holding technology constant. Now, again using the per-worker production function graph, show the effect on real GDP per hour worked of an increase in technology, holding constant the quantity of capital per hour worked.

2.2 What are the consequences for growth of diminishing returns to capital? How are some economies able to maintain high growth rates despite diminishing returns to capital?

2.3 What is the *new growth theory*? How does the new growth theory differ from the growth theory developed by Robert Solow?

2.4 Why are firms likely to underinvest in research and development? Briefly discuss three ways in which government policy can increase the accumulation of knowledge capital.

2.5 Why does knowledge capital experience increasing returns at the economy level while physical capital experiences decreasing returns?

Problems and Applications

2.6 Which of the following will result in a movement along China's per-worker production function, and which will result in a shift of China's per-worker production function? Briefly explain.
   a. Capital per hour worked increases from 200 yuan per hour worked to 250 yuan per hour worked.
   b. The Chinese government doubles its spending on support for university research.
   c. A reform of the Chinese school system results in more highly trained Chinese workers.

2.7 **(Related to the Making the Connection on page 740)** The *Making the Connection* emphasizes that a key difference between market economies and centrally planned economies, like that of the former Soviet Union, is as follows:

> In market economies, entrepreneurs and managers who have their own money on the line make decisions about which investments to make and which technologies to adopt. Nothing concentrates the mind like having your own funds at risk.

But in large corporations, investment decisions are often made by salaried managers who do not have their own money on the line. These managers are spending the money of the firm's shareholders rather than their own money. Why, then, do the investment decisions of salaried managers in the United States tend to be better for the long-term growth of the economy than were the decisions of salaried bureaucrats in the Soviet Union?

2.8 **(Related to Solved Problem 22.2 on page 741)** Use the following graph to answer the questions. In each case, briefly explain your answer.

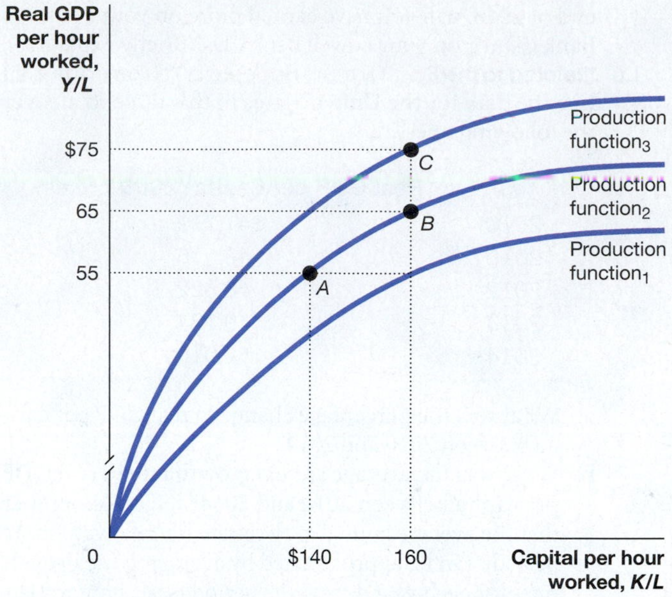

   a. True or false: The movement from point *A* to point *B* shows the effects of technological change.
   b. True or false: The economy can move from point *B* to point *C* only if there are no diminishing returns to capital.
   c. True or false: To move from point *A* to point *C*, the economy must increase the amount of capital per hour worked *and* experience technological change.

2.9 **(Related to Solved Problem 22.2 on page 741)** If the per-worker production function were shaped as shown in the following graph, what would be the implications for economic growth of a country that was accumulating increasing quantities of capital per hour worked? Briefly explain.

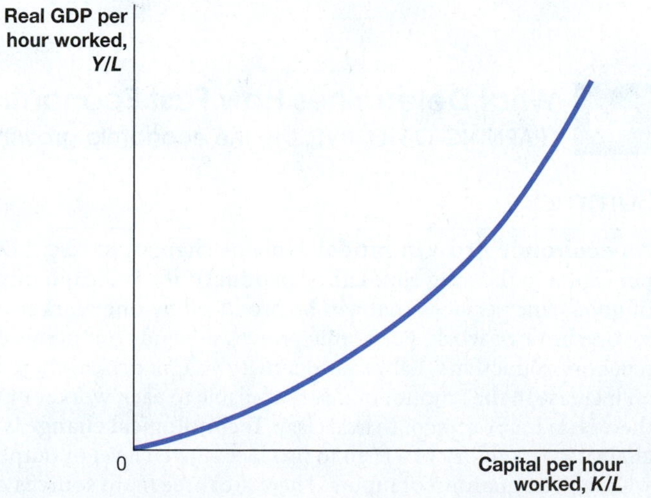

2.10 **(Related to Solved Problem 22.2 on page 741)** Shortly before the fall of the Soviet Union, the economist Gur Ofer of Hebrew University of Jerusalem wrote, "The most outstanding characteristic of Soviet growth strategy is its consistent policy of very high rates of investment, leading to a rapid growth rate of [the] capital stock." Explain why this economic growth strategy turned out to be a very poor one.

Source: Gur Ofer, "Soviet Economic Growth, 1928–1985," *Journal of Economic Literature*, Vol. 25, No. 4, December 1987, p. 1,784.

2.11 People who live in rural areas often have less access to capital and, as a result, their productivity is lower on average than the productivity of people who live in cities. An article in the *New York Times* quotes a financial analyst as arguing that "the core driver" of economic growth in China "is the simple process of urbanization."

a. What does the analyst mean by the "process of urbanization"?

b. If the analyst is correct that urbanization is the core driver of economic growth in China, would we expect that China will be able to continue to experience high rates of economic growth in the long run? Briefly explain.

Source: Neil Irwin, "China Will Keep Growing. Just Ask the Soviets," *New York Times*, October 24, 2014.

2.12 Why is the role of entrepreneurs much more important in the new growth theory than in the traditional economic growth model?

22.3 Economic Growth in the United States, pages 744–747

LEARNING OBJECTIVE: Discuss fluctuations in productivity growth in the United States.

Summary

Productivity in the United States grew rapidly from the end of World War II until the mid-1970s. Growth then slowed down for 20 years before increasing again for a decade after 1995. Growth has slowed again during the most recent period. Economists debate whether this growth slowdown will be long-lived or whether the U.S. economy will return to the faster growth rates of earlier years.

MyEconLab Visit **www.myeconlab.com** to complete these exercises online and get instant feedback.

Review Questions

3.1 Describe the record of productivity growth in the United States from 1800 to the present.

3.2 Briefly describe the debate among economists over how high U.S. productivity growth rates are likely to be in the future.

Problems and Applications

3.3 Figure 22.5 on page 744 shows growth rates in real GDP per hour worked in the United States for various periods from 1800 onward. How might the growth rates in the figure be different if they were calculated for real GDP *per capita* instead of per hour worked? (*Hint:* How do you think the number of hours worked per person has changed in the United States since 1800?)

3.4 A column in the *Wall Street Journal* considers two observations about the U.S. economy: "We live in an era of accelerating technological progress. ..." and "In the years since the recession ... the economy has been growing very slowly." The writer concludes that "Both statements can't be completely correct." Do you agree with this conclusion? Briefly explain.

Source: Josh Zumbrun, "Goldman Sachs and J.P. Morgan Can't Agree Why the Economy's Productivity Has Slumped," *Wall Street Journal*, June 16, 2015.

3.5 Economist Robert Gordon of Northwestern University has argued:

> My interpretation of the [information] revolution is that it is increasingly burdened by diminishing returns. The push to ever smaller devices runs up against the fixed size of the human finger that must enter information on the device. Most of the innovations since 2000 have been directed to consumer enjoyment rather than business productivity, including video games, DVD players, and iPods. iPhones are nice, but the ability to reschedule business meetings and look up corporate documents while on the road already existed by 2003.

If Gordon's observations about the information revolution are correct, what are the implications for future labor productivity growth rates in the United States?

Source: Robert J. Gordon, "Revisiting U.S. Productivity Growth over the Past Century with a View of the Future," National Bureau of Economic Research, Working Paper 15834, March 2010.

3.6 Some economists argue that the apparent slowdown in productivity growth in the United States in recent years is a measurement problem resulting from the failure of GDP to capture the effects of many recent innovations, such as cloud computing. James Manyika, head of technology at McKinsey & Company, argues that for many of these innovations, "we have all these benefits but we're not paying for them."

a. Before the arrival of the Internet, people looking for facts, such as the population of France or the salary of the president of the United States, had to go to the library to look them up. Now people can find that information in a few seconds with a Google search. Are the benefits to you of being able to do a Google search included in GDP? Briefly explain.

b. Does your answer to part (a) indicate that the slowdown in U.S. productivity growth in recent years is just a measurement problem? What other information would you need to arrive at a definite answer?

Source: Timothy Aeppel, "Silicon Valley Doesn't Believe U.S. Productivity Is Down," *Wall Street Journal*, July 16, 2015.

22.4 Why Isn't the Whole World Rich? pages 747–756

LEARNING OBJECTIVE: Explain economic catch-up and discuss why many poor countries have not experienced rapid economic growth.

Summary

The economic growth model predicts that poor countries will grow faster than rich countries, resulting in **catch-up**. In recent decades, some poor countries have grown faster than rich countries, but many have not. Some poor countries have not experienced rapid growth for four main reasons: wars and revolutions, poor public education and health, failure to enforce the rule of law, and low rates of saving and investment. The **rule of law** refers to the ability of a government to enforce the laws of the country, particularly with respect to protecting **property rights** and enforcing contracts. **Globalization** has aided countries that have opened their economies to foreign trade and investment. **Foreign direct investment (FDI)** is the purchase or building by a corporation of a facility in a foreign country. **Foreign portfolio investment** is the purchase by an individual or firm of stocks or bonds issued in another country.

MyEconLab Visit **www.myeconlab.com** to complete these exercises online and get instant feedback.

Review Questions

4.1 Why does the economic growth model predict that poor countries should catch up to rich countries in real GDP per capita? Have poor countries been catching up to rich countries?

4.2 What are the main reasons many poor countries have experienced slow growth?

4.3 What does *globalization* mean? How have developing countries benefited from globalization?

Problems and Applications

4.4 **(Related to Solved Problem 22.4 on page 750)** Briefly explain whether the statistics in the following table are consistent with the economic growth model's predictions of catch-up.

Country	Real GDP per Capita, 1960 (2005 dollars)	Growth in Real GDP per Capita, 1960–2011
China	$331	6.66%
Uganda	657	1.37
Madagascar	1,051	−0.23
Ireland	7,223	3.25
United States	15,398	2.02

Source: Authors' calculations from data in *Penn World Table Version 8.1*; Robert C. Feenstra, Robert Inklaar, and Marcel P. Timmer, "The Next Generation of the Penn World Table" www.ggdc.net/pwt, April 2015.

4.5 **(Related to Solved Problem 22.4 on page 750)** In the following graph, each dot represents a particular country's initial level of real GDP per capita and its growth rate of real GDP per capita.

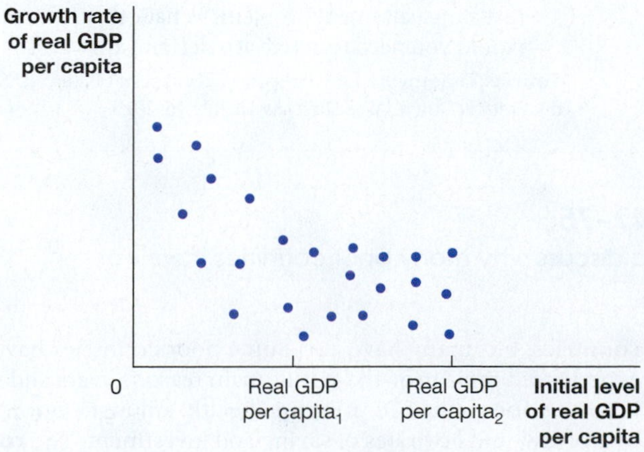

a. For the range of initial GDP per capita from 0 to Real GDP per capita$_2$, does the figure support the economic growth model's prediction of catch-up? Briefly explain.

b. For the range of initial GDP per capita from 0 to Real GDP per capita$_1$, does the figure support the catch-up prediction? Briefly explain.

c. For the range from initial Real GDP per capita$_1$ to Real GDP per capita$_2$, does the figure support the catch-up prediction? Briefly explain.

4.6 Refer to Figures 22.7–22.9 on pages 749 and 751. The lines in the following three graphs show the average relationship between the initial level of real GDP per capita and the growth rate of real GDP per capita for three groups of countries over a given time period. Match each group of countries with the graph that best depicts the relationship between the initial level of real GDP per capita and the growth rate of real GDP per capita for that group.

1.

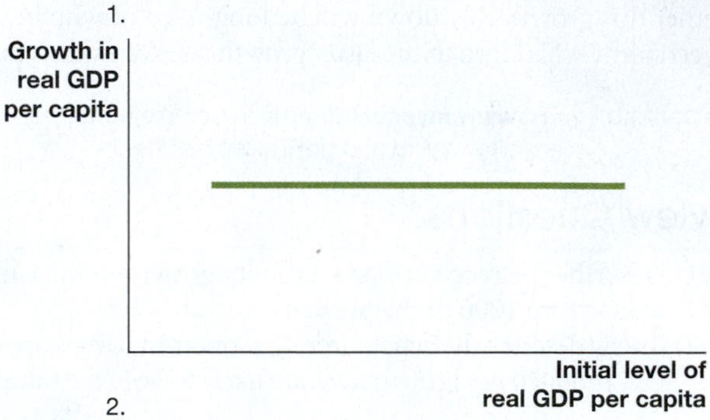

2.

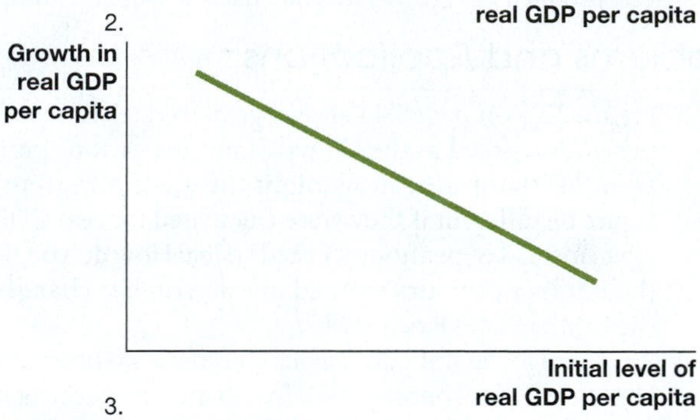

3.

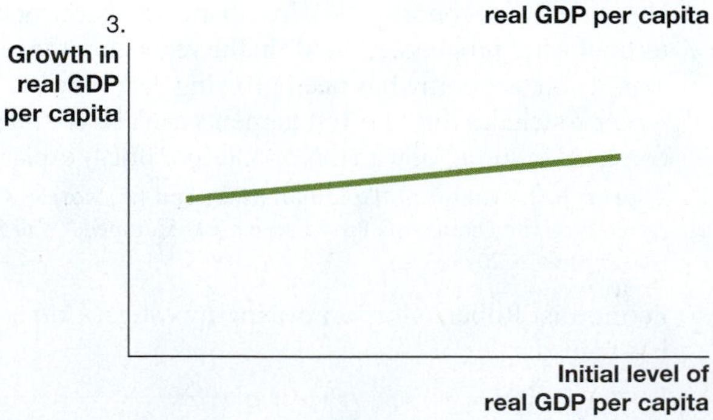

a. All countries for which statistics are available, 1960–2011

b. United States, Western Europe, Canada, and Japan, 1990–2014

c. Current high-income countries, 1960–2011

4.7 An article in the *New York Times* notes that since 2001 Italy has had the lowest rate of growth in labor productivity among European countries that use the euro common currency. The article quoted Italy's economy minister as saying, "The real tragedy for Italy is falling productivity." At the time the minister made these remarks, the unemployment rate in Italy was greater than 12 percent—more than twice the rate in Germany, the United Kingdom, or the United States. Despite the high unemployment rate, why might Italy's economy minister call low productivity growth rates "the real tragedy"?

Source: Reuters, "Italy Economy Minister Warns Deflation Would Be 'Disaster,'" *New York Times*, May 31, 2014.

4.8 **(Related to the** Making the Connection **on page 753)** A study by the McKinsey Global Institute reported that labor productivity increased at an average annual rate of 5.8 percent between 1999 and 2013 in Mexico's large companies, but it fell at an average annual rate of 6.5 percent over the same period for its smaller firms, such as family-owned stores and bakeries. Briefly explain why productivity growth would be much higher for Mexico's largest companies than for its smaller companies.

Source: Anthony Harrup, "Two Economies Explain Mexico's Productivity Quandary," *Wall Street Journal*, March 27, 2014.

4.9 **(Related to the** Making the Connection **on page 753)** In 2014, real GDP per capita in Mexico increased by 0.9 percent. A Mexican economist was quoted in an article in the *Wall Street Journal* as saying, "It's clearly insufficient if we want to significantly reduce poverty and move Mexico toward a middle-class country."

a. Given that growth rate, how long would it take the standard of living of the average person in Mexico to double?
b. Why isn't the Mexican economy growing more rapidly?

Source: Juan Montes, "Mexican Economy Expanded Modestly in 2014," *Wall Street Journal*, February 20, 2015.

4.10 In 2015, President Barack Obama was quoted in an article in the *Wall Street Journal* as warning against "rising anti-globalization sentiment," which the president called "a big mistake."

a. What did President Obama mean by "anti-globalization sentiment"?
b. Why might he have considered such sentiment to be a big mistake for the U.S. economy?
c. Is there an argument to be made that globalization hurts rather than helps the U.S. economy? Briefly explain.

Source: Gerald F. Seib, "Obama Presses Case for Asia Trade Deal, Warns Failure Would Benefit China," *Wall Street Journal*, April 27, 2015.

4.11 A columnist in the *New York Times* observes that "many analysts agree that economic reform, of which integration into the global economy was a key element, has lifted millions of people out of poverty in India." What does "integration into the global economy" mean? How might integration into the global economy reduce poverty in India?

Source: Vivek Dehejia, "Has Globalization Helped India's Poor?" *New York Times*, October 7, 2011.

4.12 The Roman Empire lasted from 27 B.C. to A.D. 476. The empire was wealthy enough to build such monuments as the Roman Coliseum. Roman engineering skill was at a level high enough that aqueducts built during the empire to carry water long distances remained in use for hundreds of years. Yet, although the empire experienced some periods of growth in real GDP per capita, these periods did not last, and there is little evidence that growth would have been sustained even if the empire had survived. Why didn't the Roman Empire experience sustained economic growth? What would the world be like today if it had? (*Note:* There are no definite answers to these questions; they are intended to get you to think about the preconditions for economic growth. Looking beyond this problem, if you are interested in the macroeconomics of the Roman economy, see Peter Temin, *The Roman Market Economy*, Princeton: Princeton University Press, 2013, Chapters 9–11.)

22.5 Growth Policies, pages 756–761

LEARNING OBJECTIVE: Discuss government policies that foster economic growth.

Summary

Governments can attempt to increase economic growth through policies that enhance property rights and the rule of law, improve health and education, subsidize research and development, and provide incentives for saving and investment. Whether continued economic growth is desirable is a normative question that cannot be settled by economic analysis.

MyEconLab Visit **www.myeconlab.com** to complete these exercises online and get instant feedback.

Review Questions

5.1 Briefly describe three government policies that can increase economic growth.

5.2 Can economic analysis arrive at the conclusion that economic growth will always improve economic well-being? Briefly explain.

Problems and Applications

5.3 **(Related to the** Chapter Opener **on page 731)** An article on the Mexican economy in the *Economist* notes, "A huge, unproductive informal sector and general lawlessness also drag the economy down." If these factors were the main barriers to more rapid economic growth in Mexico, would that be good news or bad news for the Mexican government's attempts to increase its economy's growth rate? Briefly explain.

Source: "The 100-Year View," *Economist*, May 2, 2015.

5.4 **(Related to the** Making the Connection **on page 757)** In China, why may a lower birth rate lead to slower growth in real GDP per capita? Why might high levels of spending on investment in China lead to high rates of growth in the short run but not in the long run?

5.5 **(Related to the Making the Connection on page 757)** Pranab Bardhan, an economist at the University of California, Berkeley, argues: "China may be close to exhausting the possibilities of technological catch-up with the West, particularly in manufacturing."
a. What does Bardhan mean by "technological catch-up"?
b. If Bardhan is correct, what problems might the Chinese economy encounter in the future?
c. Briefly discuss the similarities and differences between the Chinese economy today and the Soviet economy in the 1980s.

Source: Pranab Bardhan, "The Slowing of Two Economic Giants," *New York Times*, July 14, 2013.

5.6 Briefly explain which of the following policies are likely to increase the rate of economic growth in the United States.
a. Congress passes an investment tax credit, which reduces a firm's taxes if it installs new machinery and equipment.
b. Congress passes a law that allows taxpayers to reduce their income taxes by the amount of state sales taxes they pay.
c. Congress provides more funds for low-interest loans to college students.

5.7 In an interview on PBS about economic development in Africa, economist George Ayettey stated that of the 54 African countries, only 8 had a free press. For Africa's economic development, Ayittey argued strongly for the establishment of a free press. Why would a free press be vital for the enhancement of property rights and the rule of law? How could a free press help reduce corruption?

Source: George Ayittey, *Border Jumpers*, Anchor Interview Transcript, WideAngle, PBS.org, July 24, 2005.

5.8 More people in high-income countries than in low-income countries tend to believe that rapid rates of economic growth are not desirable. Recall the concept of a "normal good" (see Chapter 3). Does this concept provide insight into why some people in high-income countries might be more concerned with certain consequences of rapid economic growth than are people in low-income countries?

Real-Time Data Exercises

D22.1 **(Analyzing labor productivity)** Using data from the St. Louis Federal Reserve (FRED) (research.stlouisfed.org/fred2/), analyze the relationship between labor productivity in the manufacturing sector and in the non-farm business sector as a whole.
a. Download data since 1987 on output per hour of all persons in the manufacturing sector (OPHMFG) and in the non-farm business sector (OPHNFB).
b. Which has increased more since 1987, labor productivity in manufacturing or in the non-farm business sector?
c. The manufacturing sector has been shrinking relative to the size of the economy in the United States and other advanced economies. What do your results imply about future labor productivity growth in advanced economies?

D22.2 **(Comparing labor productivity across countries)** Using data from the St. Louis Federal Reserve (FRED) (research.stlouisfed.org/fred2/), analyze differences in labor productivity among China, India, and the United States.
a. From 1952 to the present, chart the following series on the same graph: real GDP per worker for China (RGDPL2CNA627NUPN), real GDP per worker for India (RGDPLWINA627NUPN), and real GDP per worker for the United States (RGDPLWUSA627NUPN). To chart the series on the same graph follow these steps: (1) On the page for real GDP per worker for China, click on the "Edit graph" link under the graph; (2) on the bottom of the next page, click on the "Add Data Series" link; (3) search for the other two series and click on them to add them to your graph.
b. Calculate the relative productivity of workers in China and the United States by dividing U.S. labor productivity by China's labor productivity. Describe the change in this measure of relative productivity since 1952.
c. Repeat part (b) for the United States and India.

D22.3 **(The U.S. economy in a world context)** The U.S. Central Intelligence Agency's World Factbook (https://www.cia.gov/library/publications/the-world-factbook/) offers many comparative tables of world data. Go to this site and find the following:
a. The countries with the highest and lowest real GDPs
b. The countries with the highest and lowest per capita real GDPs, adjusted for purchasing power
c. The countries with the most equal and least equal income distributions
d. The countries with the highest and lowest real GDP growth rates
e. The rank of the United States in these categories

CHAPTER 23

Aggregate Expenditure and Output in the Short Run

Chapter Outline and Learning Objectives

Fluctuating Demand Helps—and Hurts—Intel and Other Firms

Robert Noyce and Gordon Moore founded Intel in 1968. Today, the company is the world's largest semiconductor manufacturer and a major supplier of the microprocessors and memory chips that power desktop and laptop computers sold by Dell, Apple, Lenovo, Hewlett-Packard, and other computer manufacturers.

To this point, Intel's success has depended on the health of the computer market. As a result, the firm faces two problems: First, in the past few years, sales of computers have declined because many consumers and some businesses have switched to using tablets and smartphones to access the Internet. Second, Intel is vulnerable to the swings of the business cycle because sales of computers rise during economic expansions and fall during recessions. Intel was particularly hurt by the 2007–2009 recession. During the last quarter of 2008, Intel's revenues fell 90 percent, and the firm laid off 6,000 workers. Conditions improved for the firm beginning in 2010, as the U.S. economy recovered from the recession, although the firm was still struggling to reduce its dependence on selling chips to computer manufacturers. In 2015, Intel decided to lay off several hundred employees because businesses were only slowly increasing spending on computers and other information processing equipment.

The recovery from the 2007–2009 recession was by some measures the weakest since the end of World War II in 1945. By 2015, though, some industries were prospering. For example, sales of automobiles reached pre-recession levels. However, other industries still struggled. A weak recovery in spending by businesses on factories, office buildings, and other structures was bad news for some firms, including steelmakers. Worthington Industries, an Ohio-based steelmaker, announced that it would lay off 555 employees in 2015. Other U.S. steel companies also suffered from sluggish domestic and foreign demand. "Clearly, this is a rough patch," said Christopher Plummer, president and CEO of Metal Strategies.

These firms were dealing with changes in total spending, or *aggregate expenditure*. In this chapter, we will explore how changes in aggregate expenditure affect the level of total production in the economy.

Sources: Don Clark and Angela Chen, "Intel President Renée James to Leave as Others Also Depart," *Wall Street Journal*, July 2, 2015; Dan Gearino, "Worthington Industries to lay off 555 nationwide, including 80 in Fairfield County," *Columbus Dispatch*, March 25, 2015; John Carney, "Raising the Roof on Home Sales," *Wall Street Journal*, June 29, 2015; and Don Clark, "The Lawmaker: How Gordon Moore Predicted the Digital Revolution," *Wall Street Journal*, April 17, 2015.

Economics in Your Life

When Consumer Confidence Falls, Is Your Job at Risk?

Suppose that while attending college, you work part time at a company that manufactures door handles that it sells to automobile companies. One morning, you read in a news story online that consumer confidence in the economy has fallen, and, as a result, many households expect their future income to be well below their current income. Should you be concerned about losing your job? What factors should you consider in deciding how likely your company is to lay you off? As you read this chapter, try to answer these questions. You can check your answers against those we provide on **page 805** at the end of this chapter.

In Chapter 22, we discussed the determinants of long-run growth in the economy. We now turn to exploring the causes of the business cycle. We begin by examining the effect of changes in total spending on real gross domestic product (GDP).

Aggregate expenditure (AE) Total spending in the economy: the sum of consumption, planned investment, government purchases, and net exports.

During some years, total spending in the economy, or **aggregate expenditure (AE)**, and total production of goods and services increase by the same amount. In this case, most firms will sell about as much as they expected to sell, and they probably will not increase or decrease production or the number of workers they hire. During other years, total spending in the economy increases more than the production of goods and services. In those years, firms will increase production and hire more workers. But there are times, such as 2008 and early 2009, when total spending does not increase as much as total production. As a result, firms cut back on production and lay off workers, and the economy moves into a recession. In this chapter, we will explore why changes in total spending play such an important role in the economy.

23.1 The Aggregate Expenditure Model

LEARNING OBJECTIVE: Understand how macroeconomic equilibrium is determined in the aggregate expenditure model.

The business cycle involves the interaction of many economic variables. A simple model called the *aggregate expenditure model* can help us understand the relationships among some of these variables. Recall that GDP is the value of all the final goods and services produced in an economy during a particular year. Real GDP corrects nominal GDP for the effects of inflation. The **aggregate expenditure model** focuses on the short-run relationship between total spending and real GDP. An important assumption of the model is that the price level is constant. In Chapter 24, we will develop a more complete model of the business cycle that relaxes the assumption of constant prices.

Aggregate expenditure model A macroeconomic model that focuses on the short-run relationship between total spending and real GDP, assuming that the price level is constant.

The key idea of the aggregate expenditure model is that *in any particular year, the level of GDP is determined mainly by the level of aggregate expenditure.* To understand the relationship between aggregate expenditure and real GDP, we need to look more closely at the components of aggregate expenditure.

Aggregate Expenditure

Economists first began to study the relationship between changes in aggregate expenditure and changes in GDP during the Great Depression of the 1930s. The United States, the United Kingdom, and other industrial countries suffered declines in real GDP of 20 percent or more during the early 1930s. In 1936, the English economist John Maynard Keynes published a book, *The General Theory of Employment, Interest, and Money*, that systematically analyzed the relationship between changes in aggregate expenditure and changes in GDP. Keynes identified four components of aggregate expenditure that together equal GDP (these are the same four components we discussed in Chapter 19):

- ***Consumption (C).*** Spending by households on goods and services, such as automobiles and haircuts.
- ***Planned investment (I).*** Planned spending by firms on capital goods, such as factories, office buildings, and machine tools, and on research and development, and spending by households and firms on new houses.
- ***Government purchases (G).*** Spending by local, state, and federal governments on goods and services, such as aircraft carriers, bridges, and the salaries of FBI agents.
- ***Net exports (NX).*** Spending by foreign firms and households on goods and services produced in the United States minus spending by U.S. firms and households on goods and services produced in other countries.

So, we can write:

$$\text{Aggregate expenditure} = \text{Consumption} + \text{Planned investment} + \text{Government purchases} + \text{Net exports},$$

or:

$$AE = C + I + G + NX.$$

Governments around the world gather statistics on aggregate expenditure on the basis of these four components. And economists and business analysts usually explain changes in GDP in terms of changes in these four components of spending. MyEconLab Concept Check

The Difference between Planned Investment and Actual Investment

Before considering further the relationship between aggregate expenditure and GDP, we need to consider an important distinction: Notice that *planned* investment spending, rather than actual investment spending, is a component of aggregate expenditure. You might wonder how the amount that businesses plan to spend on investment can be different from the amount they actually spend. We can begin resolving this puzzle by remembering that goods that have been produced but have not yet been sold are referred to as **inventories**. Changes in inventories are included as part of investment spending, along with spending on machinery, equipment, office buildings, and factories. We assume that the amount businesses plan to spend on machinery and office buildings is equal to the amount they actually spend, but the amount businesses plan to spend on inventories may be different from the amount they actually spend.

Inventories Goods that have been produced but not yet sold.

For example, Doubleday Publishing may print 1.5 million copies of the latest John Grisham novel, expecting to sell them all. If Doubleday does sell all 1.5 million, its inventories will be unchanged, but if it sells only 1.2 million, it will have an unplanned increase in inventories. In other words, changes in inventories depend on sales of goods, which firms cannot always forecast with perfect accuracy.

For the economy as a whole, we can say that actual investment spending will be greater than planned investment spending when there is an unplanned increase in inventories. Actual investment spending will be less than planned investment spending when there is an unplanned decrease in inventories. *Therefore, actual investment will equal planned investment only when there is no unplanned change in inventories.* In this chapter, we will use I to represent planned investment. We will also assume that the government data on investment spending compiled by the U.S. Bureau of Economic Analysis represents planned investment spending. This assumption is a simplification, however, because the government collects data on actual investment spending, which equals planned investment spending only when unplanned changes in inventories are zero. MyEconLab Concept Check

Macroeconomic Equilibrium

Macroeconomic equilibrium is similar to microeconomic equilibrium. In microeconomics, equilibrium in the apple market occurs when the quantity of apples demanded equals the quantity of apples supplied. When the apple market is in equilibrium, the quantity of apples produced and sold will not change unless the demand for apples or the supply of apples changes. For the economy as a whole, macroeconomic equilibrium occurs when total spending, or aggregate expenditure, equals total production, or GDP:

$$\text{Aggregate expenditure} = \text{GDP}.$$

As we have seen, over the *long run*, real GDP in the United States increases, and the standard of living rises (see Chapter 22). In this chapter, we are interested in understanding why GDP fluctuates in the *short run*. To simplify the analysis of macroeconomic equilibrium, we assume that the economy is not growing. In Chapter 24, we will discuss the more realistic case of macroeconomic equilibrium in a growing economy. If we assume that the economy is not growing, then equilibrium GDP will not change unless aggregate expenditure changes. MyEconLab Concept Check

Adjustments to Macroeconomic Equilibrium

The apple market isn't always in equilibrium because sometimes the quantity of apples demanded is greater than the quantity supplied, and sometimes the quantity supplied is greater than the quantity demanded. The same outcome holds for the economy as a whole. Sometimes the economy is in macroeconomic equilibrium, and sometimes it isn't. When aggregate expenditure is greater than GDP, the total amount of spending in the economy is greater than the total amount of production. With spending being greater than production, many businesses will sell more goods and services than they had expected to sell. For example, the manager of a Home Depot store might like to keep 50 refrigerators in stock to give customers the opportunity to see a variety of different sizes and models. If sales are unexpectedly high, the store may have only 20 refrigerators in stock. In that case, the store will have an unplanned decrease in inventories: Its inventory of refrigerators will decline by 30.

How will the store manager react when more refrigerators are sold than expected? The manager is likely to order more refrigerators. If other stores selling refrigerators are experiencing similar sales increases and are also increasing their orders, then Whirlpool, KitchenAid, and other refrigerator manufacturers will significantly increase their production. These manufacturers may also increase the number of workers they hire. If the increase in sales is affecting not just refrigerators but also other appliances, automobiles, furniture, and other goods and services, then GDP and total employment will begin to increase. In summary, *when aggregate expenditure is greater than GDP, inventories will decline, and GDP and total employment will increase.*

Now suppose that aggregate expenditure is less than GDP. With spending being less than production, many businesses will sell fewer goods and services than they had expected to sell, so their inventories will increase. For example, the manager of the Home Depot store who wants 50 refrigerators in stock may find that because of slow sales, the store has 75 refrigerators, so the store manager will cut back on orders for new refrigerators. If other stores also cut back on their orders, General Electric and Whirlpool will reduce production and lay off workers.

If the decrease in sales is affecting not just refrigerators but also many other goods and services, GDP and total employment will begin to decrease. Falling sales followed by reductions in production and employment occurred at many firms during 2008. In summary, *when aggregate expenditure is less than GDP, inventories will increase, and GDP and total employment will decrease.*

Only when aggregate expenditure equals GDP will firms sell what they expected to sell. In that case, their inventories will be unchanged, and they will not have an incentive to increase or decrease production. The economy will be in macroeconomic equilibrium. Table 23.1 summarizes the relationship between aggregate expenditure and GDP.

Increases and decreases in aggregate expenditure cause the year-to-year changes we see in GDP. Economists devote considerable time and energy to forecasting what will happen to each component of aggregate expenditure. If economists forecast that

Table 23.1

The Relationship between Aggregate Expenditure and GDP

If . . .	then . . .	and . . .
aggregate expenditure is *equal* to GDP	inventories are *unchanged*	the economy is in *macroeconomic equilibrium.*
aggregate expenditure is *less* than GDP	inventories *rise*	GDP and employment *decrease.*
aggregate expenditure is *greater* than GDP	inventories *fall*	GDP and employment *increase.*

aggregate expenditure will decline in the future, that is equivalent to forecasting that GDP will decline and that the economy will enter a recession. Firms, policymakers, and individuals closely watch these forecasts because changes in GDP can have dramatic consequences. When GDP is increasing, so are wages, profits, and job opportunities. Declining GDP can be bad news for workers, firms, and job seekers.

When economists forecast that aggregate expenditure is likely to decline and that the economy is headed for a recession, the federal government may implement *macroeconomic policies* in an attempt to head off the decrease in expenditure and keep the economy from falling into recession. We will discuss these macroeconomic policies in Chapters 26 and 27.

MyEconLab Concept Check

MyEconLab Study Plan

23.2 Determining the Level of Aggregate Expenditure in the Economy

LEARNING OBJECTIVE: Discuss the determinants of the four components of aggregate expenditure and define marginal propensity to consume and marginal propensity to save.

To better understand how macroeconomic equilibrium is determined in the aggregate expenditure model, we look more closely at the components of aggregate expenditure. Table 23.2 lists the four components of aggregate expenditure for 2014. The components are measured in *real* terms, which means that their values are corrected for inflation by being measured in billions of 2009 dollars. Consumption is clearly the largest component of aggregate expenditure. Investment and government purchases are of roughly similar size. Net exports was negative because in 2014, as in most years since the early 1970s, the United States imported more goods and services than it exported. Next, we consider the variables that determine each of the four components of aggregate expenditure.

Consumption

Figure 23.1 shows movements in real consumption from 1979 through the second quarter of 2015. Notice that consumption follows a smooth, upward trend. Only during periods of recession does the growth in consumption decline.

Here are the five most important variables that determine the level of consumption:

1. Current disposable income
2. Household wealth
3. Expected future income
4. The price level
5. The interest rate

Next we discuss how changes in each of these variables affect consumption.

Current Disposable Income The most important determinant of consumption is the current disposable income of households. Recall that disposable income is the income remaining to households after they have paid the personal income tax and received government *transfer payments*, such as Social Security payments (see Chapter 19). For most households, the higher their disposable income, the more they spend, and the lower their income, the less they spend. Macroeconomic consumption

MyEconLab Real-time data

Table 23.2

Components of Real Aggregate Expenditure, 2014

Expenditure Category	Real Expenditure (billions of 2009 dollars)
Consumption	$10,876
Planned investment	2,718
Government purchases	2,838
Net exports	−443

Source: U.S. Bureau of Economic Analysis.

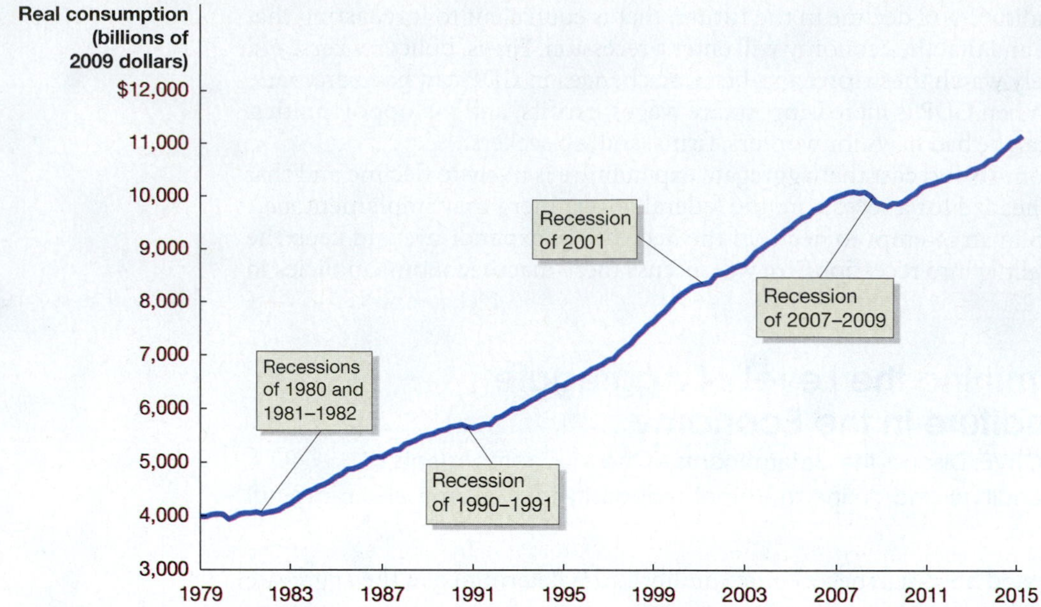

MyEconLab Real-time data

Figure 23.1 Real Consumption, 1979–2015

Consumption follows a smooth, upward trend, interrupted only infrequently by brief recessions.

Note: The values are quarterly data seasonally adjusted at an annual rate.

Source: U.S. Bureau of Economic Analysis.

is the total of all the consumption of U.S. households. We would expect consumption to increase when the current disposable income of households increases and to decrease when the current disposable income of households decreases. As we have seen, total income in the United States expands during most years. Only during recessions, which happen infrequently, does total income decline. The main reason for the general upward trend in consumption shown in Figure 23.1 is that disposable income has followed a similar upward trend.

Household Wealth Consumption depends in part on the wealth of households. A household's *wealth* is the value of its *assets* minus the value of its *liabilities*. Recall that an asset is anything of value owned by a person or a firm, and a liability is anything owed by a person or a firm (see Chapter 8). A household's assets include its home, stock and bond holdings, and bank accounts. A household's liabilities include any loans that it owes. A household with $10 million in wealth is likely to spend more than a household with $10,000 in wealth, even if both households have the same disposable income. Therefore, when the wealth of households increases, consumption should increase, and when the wealth of households decreases, consumption should decrease. Shares of stock are an important category of household wealth. When stock prices increase, household wealth will increase, and so should consumption. For example, a family whose stock holdings increase in value from $30,000 to $100,000 may be willing to spend a larger fraction of its income because it is less concerned with adding to its savings. A decline in stock prices should lead to a decline in consumption. Economists who have studied the determinants of consumption have concluded that permanent increases in wealth have a larger impact than temporary increases. One estimate of the effect of changes in wealth on consumption spending indicates that, for every permanent $1 increase in household wealth, consumption spending will increase by between 4 and 5 cents per year.

Expected Future Income Consumption depends in part on expected future income. Most people prefer to keep their consumption fairly stable from year to year, even if their income fluctuates significantly. Some salespeople, for example, earn most of their income from commissions, which are fixed percentages of the prices of the products they sell. A salesperson might have a high income in some years and a much lower income in other years. Most people in this situation keep their consumption steady and do not increase it during good years and then drastically cut it back during slower years. If we looked only at the current income of someone in this situation, we might have difficulty estimating the person's current consumption. Instead, we need to take into account the person's expected future income. We can conclude that current income explains current consumption well *but only when current income is not unusually high or unusually low compared with expected future income.*

The Price Level Recall that the *price level* measures the average prices of goods and services in the economy (see Chapter 20). Changes in the price level affect consumption. It is tempting to think that an increase in prices will reduce consumption by making goods and services less affordable. In fact, the effect of an increase in the price of *one* product on the quantity demanded of that product is different from the effect of an increase in the price level on *total* spending by households on goods and services. Changes in the price level affect consumption mainly through their effect on household wealth. An increase in the price level will result in a decrease in the *real* value of household wealth. For example, if you have $2,000 in a checking account, the higher the price level, the fewer goods and services you can buy with your money. Therefore, as the price level rises, the real value of your wealth declines, and so will your consumption, at least a little. Conversely, if the price level falls—which happens rarely in the United States—the real value of your $2,000 increases, and your consumption will also increase.

The Interest Rate Finally, consumption depends on the interest rate. When the interest rate is high, the reward for saving is increased, and households are likely to save more and spend less. Recall the distinction between the *nominal interest rate* and the *real interest rate* (see Chapter 20):

- The nominal interest rate is the stated interest rate on a loan or a financial investment such as a bond.
- The real interest rate corrects the nominal interest rate for the effect of inflation and is equal to the nominal interest rate minus the inflation rate.

Because households are concerned with the payments they will make or receive after the effects of inflation are taken into account, consumption spending depends on the real interest rate.

We have seen that consumption spending is divided into three categories:

1. Spending on *services,* such as medical care, education, and haircuts
2. Spending on *nondurable goods,* such as food and clothing
3. Spending on *durable goods,* such as automobiles and furniture

Spending on durable goods is most likely to be affected by changes in the interest rate because a high real interest rate increases the cost of spending financed by borrowing. The monthly payment on a four-year car loan will be higher if the real interest rate on the loan is 6 percent than if it is 4 percent.

The Consumption Function Panel (a) in Figure 23.2 illustrates the relationship between consumption and disposable income during the years 1960 to 2014. In panel (b), we draw a straight line through the points representing consumption and disposable income. The fact that most of the points lie almost on the line shows the close relationship between consumption and disposable income. Because changes in consumption depend on changes in disposable income, we can say that *consumption is a function of disposable income.* The relationship between consumption spending and disposable income illustrated in panel (b) of Figure 23.2 is called the **consumption function.**

Consumption function The relationship between consumption spending and disposable income.

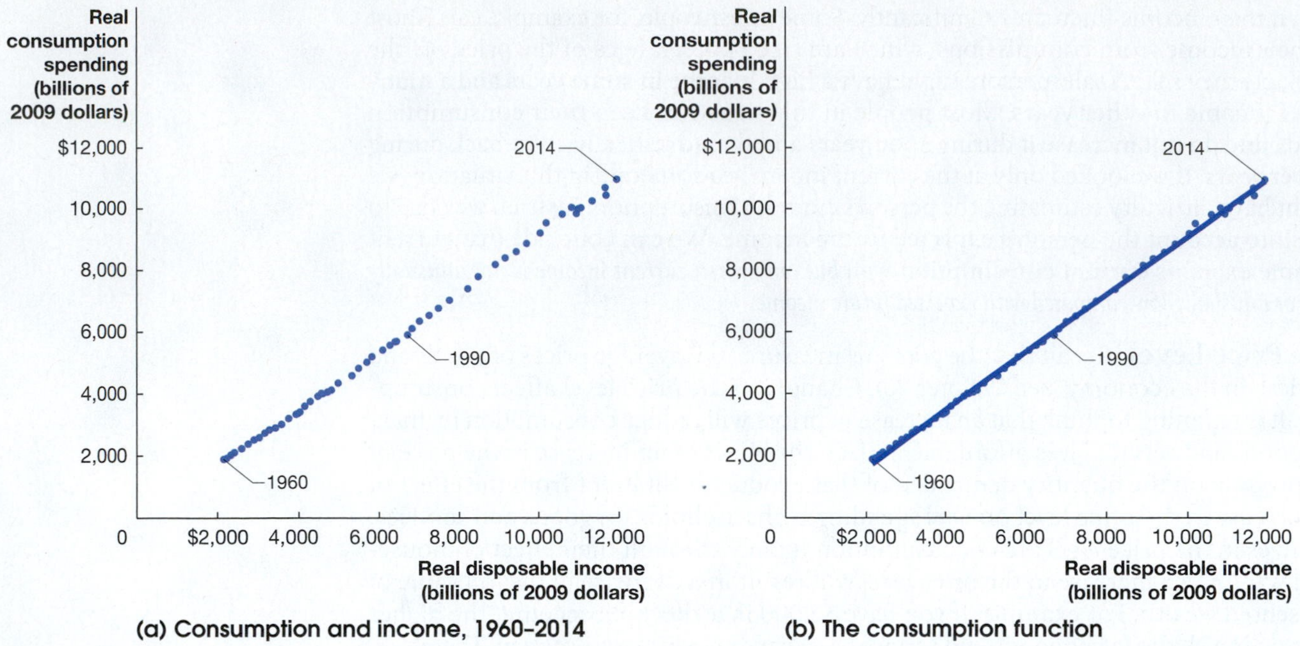

MyEconLab Real-time data

Figure 23.2 The Relationship between Consumption and Income, 1960–2014

Panel (a) shows the relationship between consumption and income. The points represent combinations of real consumption spending and real disposable income for the years 1960 to 2014. In panel (b), we draw a straight line through the points from panel (a). The line, which represents the relationship between consumption and disposable income, is called the *consumption function*. The slope of the consumption function is the marginal propensity to consume.

Source: U.S. Bureau of Economic Analysis.

Marginal propensity to consume (*MPC*) The slope of the consumption function: The amount by which consumption spending changes when disposable income changes.

The slope of the consumption function, which is equal to the change in consumption divided by the change in disposable income, is called the **marginal propensity to consume (*MPC*)**. Using the Greek letter delta, Δ, to represent "change in," *C* to represent consumption spending, and *YD* to represent disposable income, we can write the expression for the *MPC* as follows:

$$MPC = \frac{\text{Change in consumption}}{\text{Change in disposable income}} = \frac{\Delta C}{\Delta YD}.$$

For example, between 2013 and 2014, consumption spending increased by $285 billion, while disposable income increased by $313 billion. The marginal propensity to consume was, therefore:

$$\frac{\Delta C}{\Delta YD} = \frac{\$285 \text{ billion}}{\$313 \text{ billion}} = 0.91.$$

The value for the *MPC* tells us that households in 2014 spent 91 percent of the increase in their disposable income.

We can also use the *MPC* to determine how much consumption will change as income changes. To see this relationship, we rewrite the expression for the *MPC*:

$$\text{Change in consumption} = \text{Change in disposable income} \times MPC.$$

For example, with an *MPC* of 0.91, a $10 billion increase in disposable income will increase consumption by $10 billion × 0.91, or $9.1 billion. MyEconLab Concept Check

The Relationship between Consumption and National Income

We have seen that consumption spending by households depends on disposable income. We now shift our focus slightly to the similar relationship that exists between consumption spending and GDP. We make this shift because we are interested in using the aggregate expenditure model to explain changes in real GDP rather than changes in disposable income. The first step in examining the relationship between consumption and GDP is to recall that the differences between GDP and national income are small and can be ignored without affecting our analysis (see Chapter 19). In fact, in this and the following chapters, we will use the terms *GDP* and *national income* interchangeably. Also recall that disposable income is equal to national income plus government transfer payments minus taxes. Taxes minus government transfer payments are called *net taxes.* So, we can write the following:

$$\text{Disposable income} = \text{National income} - \text{Net taxes}.$$

We can rearrange the equation like this:

$$\text{National income} = \text{GDP} = \text{Disposable income} + \text{Net taxes}.$$

The table in Figure 23.3 shows hypothetical values for national income (or GDP), net taxes, disposable income, and consumption spending. Notice that national income and disposable income differ by a constant amount, which is equal to net taxes of $1,000 billion. In reality, net taxes are not a constant amount because they are affected by changes in income. As income rises, net taxes rise because some taxes, such as the personal income tax, increase and some government transfer payments, such as government payments to unemployed workers, fall. Nothing important is affected in our analysis, however, by our simplifying assumption that net taxes are constant.

National Income or GDP (billions of dollars)	Net Taxes (billions of dollars)	Disposable Income (billions of dollars)	Consumption (billions of dollars)	Change in National Income (billions of dollars)	Change in Disposable Income (billions of dollars)
$1,000	$1,000	$0	$750	—	—
3,000	1,000	2,000	2,250	$2,000	$2,000
5,000	1,000	4,000	3,750	2,000	2,000
7,000	1,000	6,000	5,250	2,000	2,000
9,000	1,000	8,000	6,750	2,000	2,000
11,000	1,000	10,000	8,250	2,000	2,000
13,000	1,000	12,000	9,750	2,000	2,000

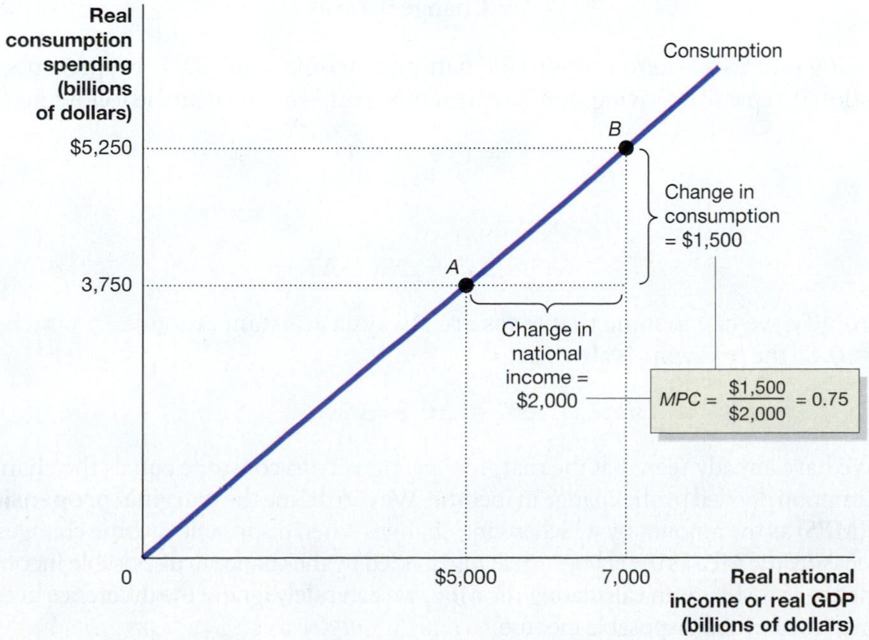

MyEconLab Animation

Figure 23.3

The Relationship between Consumption and National Income

Because national income differs from disposable income only by net taxes—which, for simplicity, we assume are constant—we can graph the consumption function using national income rather than disposable income. We can also calculate the *MPC*, which is the slope of the consumption function, using either the change in national income or the change in disposable income and always get the same value. The slope of the consumption function between points *A* and *B* is equal to the change in consumption—$1,500 billion—divided by the change in national income—$2,000 billion—or 0.75.

The graph in Figure 23.3 shows a line representing the relationship between consumption and national income. The line is very similar to the consumption function shown in panel (b) of Figure 23.2. We defined the marginal propensity to consume (*MPC*) as the change in consumption divided by the change in disposable income, which is the slope of the consumption function. In fact, notice that if we calculate the slope of the line in Figure 23.3 between points *A* and *B*, we get a result that will not change whether we use the values for national income or the values for disposable income. Using the values for national income:

$$\frac{\Delta C}{\Delta Y} = \frac{\$5{,}250 \text{ billion} - \$3{,}750 \text{ billion}}{\$7{,}000 \text{ billion} - \$5{,}000 \text{ billion}} = 0.75.$$

Using the corresponding values for disposable income from the table:

$$\frac{\Delta C}{\Delta YD} = \frac{\$5{,}250 \text{ billion} - \$3{,}750 \text{ billion}}{\$6{,}000 \text{ billion} - \$4{,}000 \text{ billion}} = 0.75.$$

It should not be surprising that we get the same result in either case. National income and disposable income differ by a constant amount, so changes in the two numbers always give us the same value, as shown in the last two columns of the table in Figure 23.3. Therefore, we can graph the consumption function using national income rather than using disposable income. We can also calculate the *MPC* using either the change in national income or the change in disposable income and always get the same value.

MyEconLab Concept Check

Income, Consumption, and Saving

To complete our discussion of consumption, we can look briefly at the relationships among income, consumption, and saving. Households spend their income, save it, or use it to pay taxes. For the economy as a whole, we can write the following:

National income = Consumption + Saving + Taxes.

When national income increases, there must be some combination of an increase in consumption, an increase in saving, and an increase in taxes:

Change in national income = Change in consumption + Change in saving + Change in taxes.

Using symbols, where *Y* represents national income (and GDP), *C* represents consumption, *S* represents saving, and *T* represents taxes, we can write the following:

$$Y = C + S + T$$

and:

$$\Delta Y = \Delta C + \Delta S + \Delta T.$$

To simplify, we can assume that taxes are always a constant amount, in which case $\Delta T = 0$, so the following is also true:

$$\Delta Y = \Delta C + \Delta S.$$

Marginal propensity to save (*MPS*) The amount by which saving changes when disposable income changes.

We have already seen that the marginal propensity to consume equals the change in consumption divided by the change in income. We can define the **marginal propensity to save (*MPS*)** as the amount by which saving changes when disposable income changes. We can measure the *MPS* as the change in saving divided by the change in disposable income. In calculating the *MPS*, as in calculating the *MPC*, we can safely ignore the difference between national income and disposable income.

If we divide the previous equation by the change in income, ΔY, we get an equation that shows the relationship between the marginal propensity to consume and the marginal propensity to save:

$$\frac{\Delta Y}{\Delta Y} = \frac{\Delta C}{\Delta Y} + \frac{\Delta S}{\Delta Y},$$

or:

$$1 = MPC + MPS.$$

This equation tells us that when taxes are constant, the marginal propensity to consume plus the marginal propensity to save must always equal 1. They must add up to 1 because part of any increase in income is consumed, and whatever remains must be saved. MyEconLab Concept Check

Solved Problem 23.2

Calculating the Marginal Propensity to Consume and the Marginal Propensity to Save

Fill in the blank cells in the following table. For simplicity, assume that taxes are zero. Show that the *MPC* plus the *MPS* equals 1.

National Income and Real GDP (*Y*)	Consumption (*C*)	Saving (*S*)	Marginal Propensity to Consume (*MPC*)	Marginal Propensity to Save (*MPS*)
$9,000	$8,000			
10,000	8,600			
11,000	9,200			
12,000	9,800			
13,000	10,400			

Solving the Problem

Step 1: Review the chapter material. This problem is about the relationship among income, consumption, and saving, so you may want to review the section "Income, Consumption, and Saving," which begins on page 780.

Step 2: Fill in the table. We know that $Y = C + S + T$. With taxes equal to zero, this equation becomes $Y = C + S$. We can use this equation to fill in the "Saving" column. We can use the equations for the *MPC* and the *MPS* to fill in the other two columns:

$$MPC = \frac{\Delta C}{\Delta Y}$$

$$MPS = \frac{\Delta S}{\Delta Y}$$

For example, to calculate the value of the *MPC* in the second row, we have:

$$MPC = \frac{\Delta C}{\Delta Y} = \frac{\$8{,}600 - \$8{,}000}{\$10{,}000 - \$9{,}000} = \frac{\$600}{\$1{,}000} = 0.6.$$

To calculate the value of the *MPS* in the second row, we have:

$$MPS = \frac{\Delta S}{\Delta Y} = \frac{\$1{,}400 - \$1{,}000}{\$10{,}000 - \$9{,}000} = \frac{\$400}{\$1{,}000} = 0.4.$$

National Income and Real GDP (*Y*)	Consumption (*C*)	Saving (*S*)	Marginal Propensity to Consume (*MPC*)	Marginal Propensity to Save (*MPS*)
$9,000	$8,000	$1,000	—	—
10,000	8,600	1,400	0.6	0.4
11,000	9,200	1,800	0.6	0.4
12,000	9,800	2,200	0.6	0.4
13,000	10,400	2,600	0.6	0.4

Step 3: Show that the *MPC* plus the *MPS* equals 1. At every level of national income, the *MPC* is 0.6 and the *MPS* is 0.4. Therefore, the *MPC* plus the *MPS* is always equal to 1.

Your Turn: For more practice, do related problem 2.10 on page 807 at the end of this chapter.

Planned Investment

Figure 23.4 shows movements in real investment spending from 1979 through the second quarter of 2015. Notice that, unlike consumption, investment does not follow a smooth, upward trend. Investment declined significantly during the recessions of 1980, 1981–1982, 1990–1991, 2001, and 2007–2009.

These are the four most important variables that determine the level of investment:

1. Expectations of future profitability
2. The interest rate
3. Taxes
4. Cash flow

Expectations of Future Profitability Investment goods, such as factories, office buildings, and machinery and equipment, are long-lived. A firm is unlikely to build a new factory unless it is optimistic that the demand for its product will remain strong for at least several years. When the economy moves into a recession, many firms postpone buying investment goods even if the demand for their own product is strong

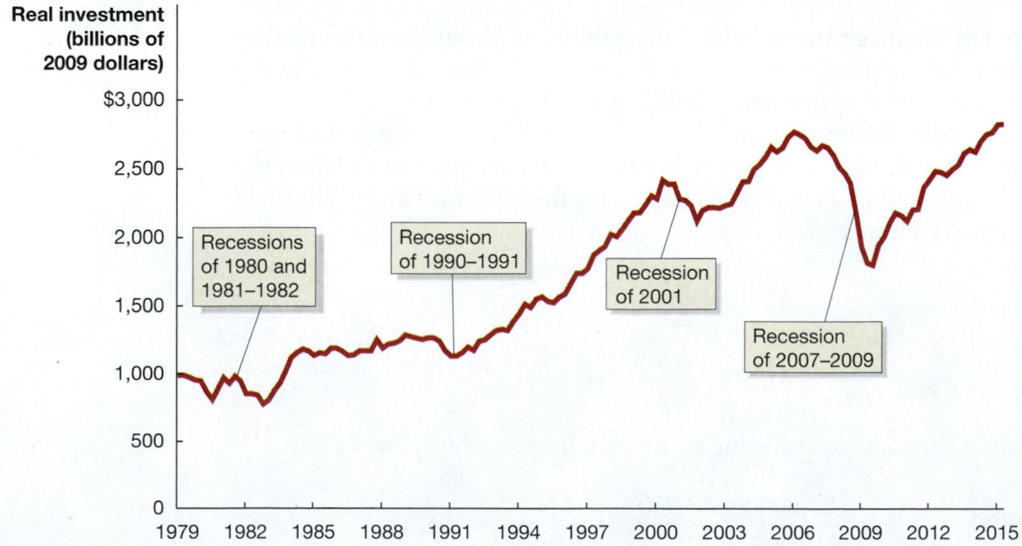

MyEconLab Real-time data

Figure 23.4 Real Investment, 1979–2015

Investment is subject to larger changes than is consumption. Investment declined significantly during the recessions of 1980, 1981–1982, 1990–1991, 2001, and 2007–2009.

Note: The values are quarterly data, seasonally adjusted at an annual rate.

Source: U.S. Bureau of Economic Analysis.

because they are afraid that the recession may become worse. During an expansion, some firms may become optimistic and begin to increase spending on investment goods even before the demand for their own product has increased. The key point is that *the optimism or pessimism of firms is an important determinant of investment spending*.

Residential construction is included in investment spending. Since 1990, residential construction has averaged about 30 percent of total investment spending. But the swings in residential construction have been quite substantial, ranging from a high of 36 percent of investment spending at the height of the housing boom in 2005 down to 18 percent in 2011. The sharp decline in spending on residential construction beginning in 2006 helped to cause the 2007–2009 recession and contributed to its severity.

The Interest Rate Some business investment is financed by borrowing, as firms issue corporate bonds or receive loans from banks. Households also borrow to finance most of their spending on new homes. The higher the interest rate, the more expensive it is for firms and households to borrow. Because households and firms are interested in the cost of borrowing after taking into account the effects of inflation, investment spending depends on the real interest rate. Therefore, holding constant the other factors that affect investment spending, there is an inverse relationship between the real interest rate and investment spending: *A higher real interest rate results in less investment spending, and a lower real interest rate results in more investment spending*. The ability of households to borrow money at very low real interest rates helps explain the rapid increase in spending on residential construction from 2002 to 2006.

Taxes Taxes affect the level of investment spending. Firms focus on the profits that remain after they have paid taxes. The federal government imposes a *corporate income tax* on the profits corporations earn, including profits from the new buildings, equipment, and other investment goods they purchase. A reduction in the corporate income tax increases the after-tax profitability of investment spending. An increase in the corporate income tax decreases the after-tax profitability of investment spending. *Investment tax incentives* increase investment spending. An investment tax incentive provides firms with a tax reduction when they buy new investment goods.

Cash Flow Most firms do not borrow to finance spending on new factories, machinery, and equipment. Instead, they use their own funds. **Cash flow** is the difference between the cash revenues received by a firm and the cash spending by the firm. Neither noncash receipts nor noncash spending is included in cash flow. For example, tax laws allow firms to count the depreciation of worn-out or obsolete machinery and equipment as a cost, even if new machinery and equipment have not actually been purchased. Because this is noncash spending, firms do not include it when calculating cash flow. The largest contributor to cash flow is profit. The more profitable a firm is, the greater its cash flow and the greater its ability to finance investment. During periods of recession, many firms experience reduced profits, which in turn reduces their ability to finance spending on new factories or machinery and equipment.

Cash flow The difference between the cash revenues received by a firm and the cash spending by the firm.

Making the Connection
MyEconLab Video

Is Student Loan Debt Causing Fewer Young People to Buy Houses?

Although our discussion in this section has concentrated on the components of investment that represent spending by businesses, household purchases of new homes are an important part of investment spending. As the graph on the next page shows, spending on residential construction rose rapidly in the period just before the recession of 2007–2009, declined dramatically during the recession, and recovered only slowly thereafter. The slow recovery in spending on residential construction is one reason the recovery from the recession was weaker than most recoveries.

Some economists believe that one factor holding back recovery in the housing market was low home-buying rates among younger households. In 2014, homeownership rates among people younger than 35 were the lowest they have been in the United States in at least 25 years. Do high levels of student debt explain why young people are buying fewer homes? If you have a college degree, you are likely to earn more than

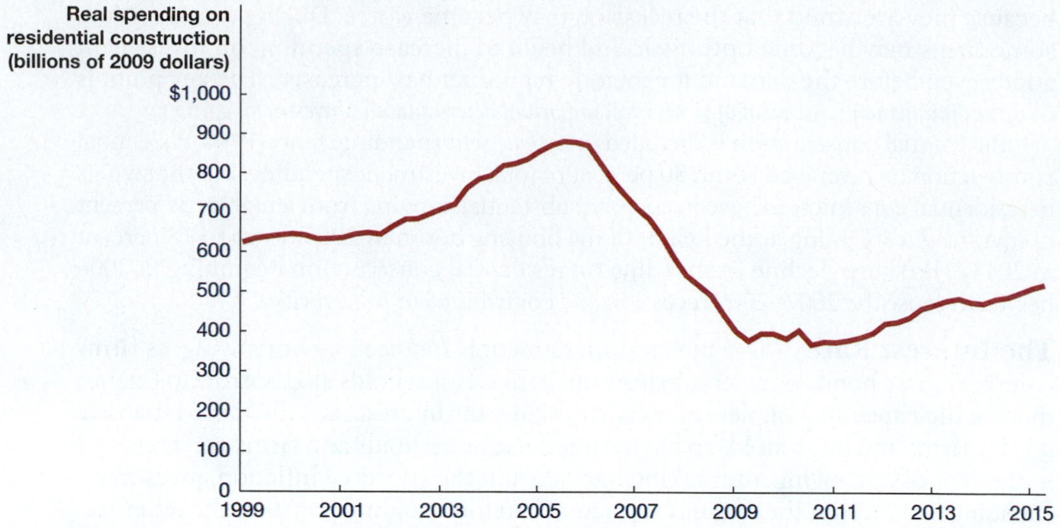

people without a college degree. So, many people consider student debt taken on to earn a degree to be a good investment. For the class of 2014, the average student debt per borrower was a record $33,000. Total student debt in 2014 was $1.1 trillion, more than the amount that all Americans owe on credit cards or automobile loans, and twice the level of student debt in 2007. Does increasing student debt explain the decline in home purchases among younger households? Economists differ in their answers to this question because other factors may be affecting homeownership rates.

Harvard economist and former Obama administration economic adviser Larry Summers argues that many college graduates have trouble accumulating the funds for a down payment on a house because they are making student loan payments. He also argues that these payments have led young college graduates to delay forming families, thereby reducing their need to move from an apartment to a house. One survey indicates that 45 percent of college graduates under age 24 are living at home or with another family member. Some economists point to rising delinquency rates on student loans as a factor that makes it difficult for some young college graduates to qualify for a mortgage loan necessary to buy a house.

Other economists are skeptical of a link between student debt and a reduced demand for housing by young college graduates. Economists who have carried out statistical studies of the link have arrived at mixed results. In testifying before Congress, Federal Reserve Chair Janet Yellen remarked of the connection between students' debt and the demand for housing that "I don't know of clear evidence of it."

Some economists believe that new government lending guidelines may be playing a role. When deciding whether to grant a mortgage loan, banks and other lenders have interpreted the guidelines to mean that they must give greater consideration to how much debt graduates have. As a result, fewer young college graduates qualify for mortgage loans. Finally, some economists argue that the weak recovery of the U.S. labor market from the recession of 2007–2009 is the key reason that young college graduates have been buying fewer houses. With unemployment rates remaining high and wages growing slowly, many young people have difficulty affording homes, even if they have limited or no student debt. As the recovery became stronger in 2015, these economists expected that younger people would be increasing their demand for housing.

Sources: Mitchell E. Daniels, "How Student Debt Harms the Economy," *Wall Street Journal*, January 27, 2015; Zeppo Mitchell, "Larry Summers: Student Debt Is Slowing the U.S. Housing Recovery," *Wall Street Journal*, May 21, 2014; Josh Mitchell, "Student Debt Takes a Toll on Some Home Buyers," *Wall Street Journal*, June 20, 2014; Susan Dynarski, "Remember the Problems with Mortgage Defaults? They're Coming Back with Student Loans," *New York Times*, June 12, 2014; Meta Brown, et al., "Measuring Student Debt and Its Performance," Federal Reserve Bank of New York, Staff Report No. 668, April 2014; and U.S. Bureau of Economic Analysis.

MyEconLab Study Plan

Your Turn: Test your understanding by doing related problem 2.11 on page 807 at the end of this chapter.

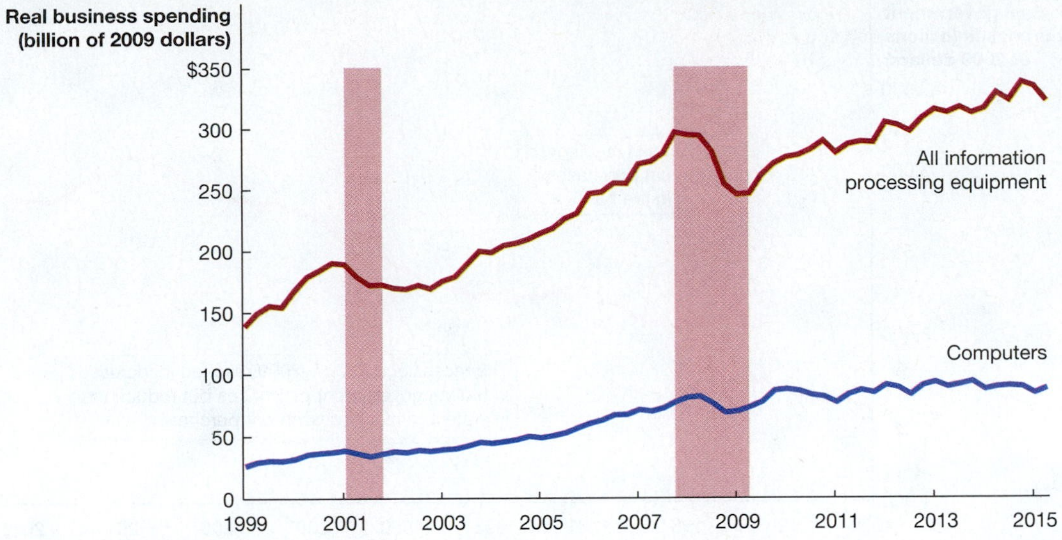

MyEconLab Animation

Figure 23.5 Spending on Information Processing Equipment, 1999–2015

Business spending on information processing equipment, particularly computers, has grown only slowly since the end of the recession of 2007–2009.

Source: U.S. Bureau of Economic Analysis.

The Surprisingly Slow Growth of Business Spending on Information Processing Equipment In recent years, most businesses have increased their use of information technology in a variety of ways, including expanding their presence on the Internet, especially by using social networking apps such as Twitter, Instagram, and Facebook; designing company apps; and providing employees with tablets and smartphones. As Figure 23.5 shows, though, the focus of many businesses on information technology is not reflected in spending on information processing equipment. The blue line shows spending on computers, printers, and related equipment, while the red line shows spending on all information processing equipment, which in addition to computers, includes photocopiers, fax machines, and other office equipment. In 2015, total spending on information processing equipment had grown by less than 10 percent from its levels at the beginning of the recession in 2007. Spending on computers was also growing slowly and in 2015 was barely above 2010 levels.

A key reason for this slow growth in spending on information technology equipment is that over time, the frontier of developments in information technology has shifted away from equipment—particularly computers and servers—and toward software, such as apps used on smartphones and tablets. This shift has been bad news for firms like Intel, whose sales of processors are heavily dependent on sales of computers. Intel has had only mixed success in reducing its dependence on sales to computer manufacturers by shifting toward making components for tablets, smartwatches, and smartphones, including a modem chip for Apple's iPhone.

Government Purchases

Total government purchases include all spending by federal, local, and state governments for goods and services. Recall that government purchases do not include transfer payments, such as Social Security payments by the federal government or pension payments by local governments to retired police officers and firefighters, because the government does not receive a good or service in return (see Chapter 19).

Figure 23.6 shows levels of real government purchases from 1979 through the second quarter of 2015. Government purchases grew steadily for most of this period,

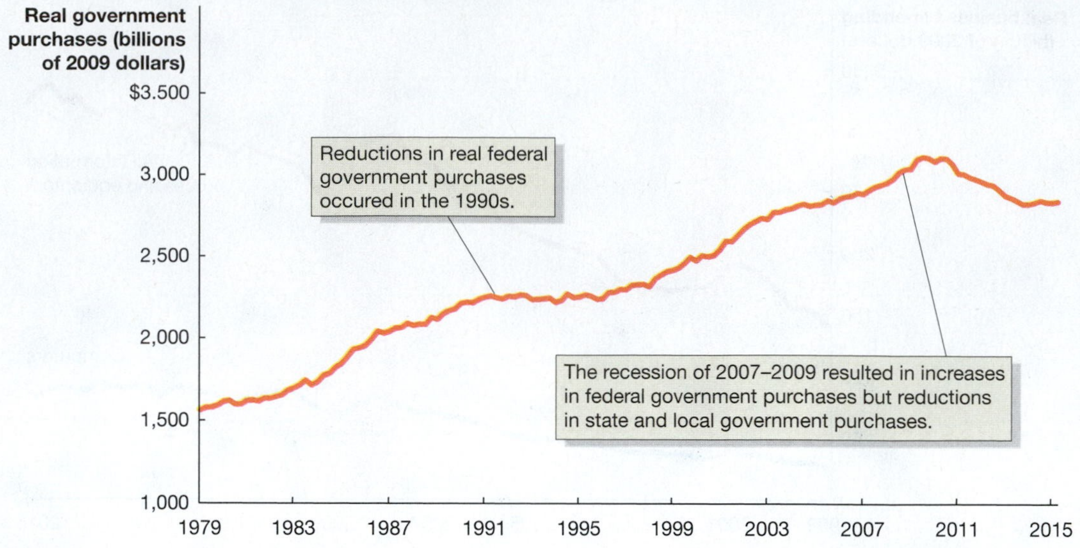

MyEconLab Real-time data

Figure 23.6 Real Government Purchases, 1979–2015

Government purchases grew steadily for most of the 1979–2015 period, with the exception of the early 1990s, when concern about the federal budget deficit caused real government purchases to fall for three years, beginning in 1992, and the period following the recession of 2007–2009 when many state and local governments reduced spending.

Note: The values are quarterly data, seasonally adjusted at an annual rate.

Source: U.S. Bureau of Economic Analysis.

with the exception of the early 1990s and the period following the end of the recession of 2007–2009. During the early 1990s, Congress and Presidents George H. W. Bush and Bill Clinton enacted a series of spending reductions after they became concerned that spending by the federal government was growing much faster than tax receipts. As a result, real government purchases declined for three years beginning in 1992. Contributing to the slow growth of government purchases during the 1990s was the end of the Cold War between the United States and the Soviet Union in 1989. Real federal government spending on national defense declined by 24 percent from 1990 to 1998, before rising by 60 percent between 1998 and 2010 in response to the war on terrorism and the wars in Iraq and Afghanistan. As those wars wound down, defense spending declined by 18 percent between 2010 and 2015. Total federal government purchases increased in 2009 and 2010, as President Barack Obama and Congress attempted to offset declining consumption and investment spending during the recession. Federal government purchases then declined beginning in 2011 and continuing through 2015. The recession and the slow recovery resulted in declining tax revenues to state and local governments. As a result, real state and local government purchases declined between 2009 and 2013, before increasing, along with tax revenues, beginning in 2014. MyEconLab Concept Check

Net Exports

Net exports equal exports minus imports. We can calculate net exports by taking the value of spending by foreign firms and households on goods and services produced in the United States and *subtracting* the value of spending by U.S. firms and households on goods and services produced in other countries. Figure 23.7 illustrates movements in real net exports from 1979 through the second quarter of 2015. During nearly all these years, the United States imported more goods and services than it exported, so net exports were negative. Net exports usually increase when the U.S. economy is in a recession—although they fell during the 2001 recession—and fall when the U.S. economy is in an expansion.

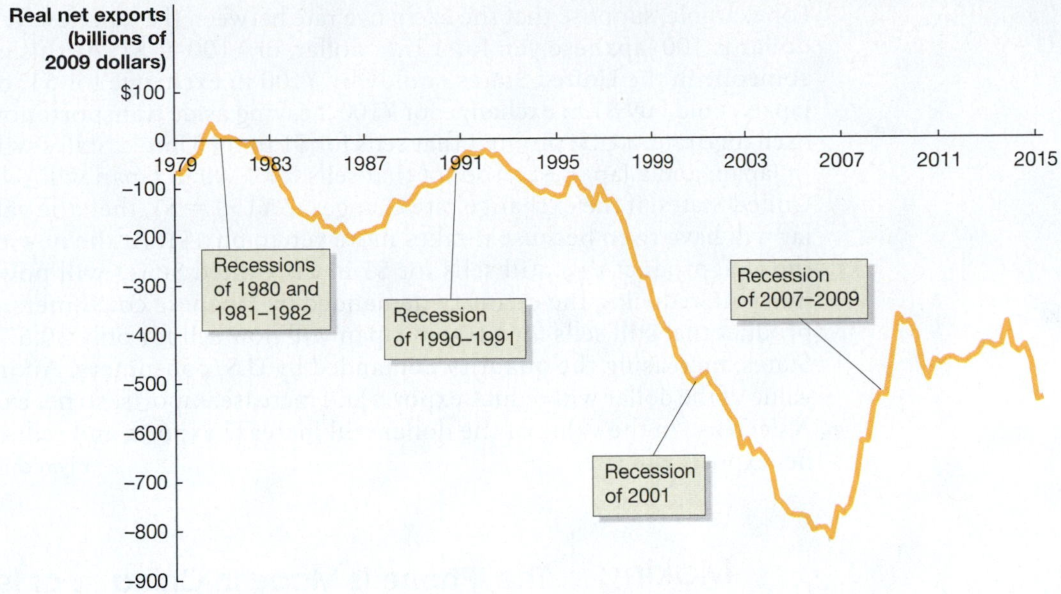

MyEconLab Real-time data

Figure 23.7 Real Net Exports, 1979–2015

Net exports were negative in most years between 1979 and 2015. Net exports have usually increased when the U.S. economy is in a recession and decreased when the U.S. economy is in an expansion, although they fell during the 2001 recession.

Note: The values are quarterly data, seasonally adjusted at an annual rate.

Source: U.S. Bureau of Economic Analysis.

The following are the three most important variables that determine the level of net exports:

1. The price level in the United States relative to the price levels in other countries
2. The growth rate of GDP in the United States relative to the growth rates of GDP in other countries
3. The exchange rate between the dollar and other currencies

The Price Level in the United States Relative to the Price Levels in Other Countries If inflation in the United States is lower than inflation in other countries, prices of U.S. products increase more slowly than the prices of products in other countries. This slower increase in the U.S. price level increases the demand for U.S. products relative to the demand for foreign products. So, U.S. exports increase and U.S. imports decrease, which increases net exports. The reverse happens during periods when the inflation rate in the United States is higher than the inflation rates in other countries: U.S. exports decrease and U.S. imports increase, which decreases net exports.

The Growth Rate of GDP in the United States Relative to the Growth Rates of GDP in Other Countries As GDP increases in the United States, the incomes of households rise, leading them to increase their purchases of goods and services. Some of the additional goods and services purchased with rising incomes are produced in the United States, but some are imported. When incomes rise faster in the United States than in other countries, U.S. consumers' purchases of foreign goods and services increase faster than foreign consumers' purchases of U.S. goods and services. As a result, net exports fall. When incomes in the United States rise more slowly than incomes in other countries, net exports rise.

The Exchange Rate between the Dollar and Other Currencies As the value of the U.S. dollar rises, the foreign currency price of U.S. products sold in other countries rises, and the dollar price of foreign products sold in the United States falls.

For example, suppose that the exchange rate between the Japanese yen and the U.S. dollar is 100 Japanese yen for 1 U.S. dollar, or ¥100 = $1. At this exchange rate, someone in the United States could buy ¥100 in exchange for $1, or someone in Japan could buy $1 in exchange for ¥100. Leaving aside transportation costs, at this exchange rate, a U.S. product that sells for $1 in the United States will sell for ¥100 in Japan, and a Japanese product that sells for ¥100 in Japan will sell for $1 in the United States. If the exchange rate changes to ¥150 = $1, then the value of the dollar will have risen because it takes more yen to buy $1. At the new exchange rate, the U.S. product that still sells for $1 in the United States will now sell for ¥150 in Japan, reducing the quantity demanded by Japanese consumers. The Japanese product that still sells for ¥100 in Japan will now sell for only $0.67 in the United States, increasing the quantity demanded by U.S. consumers. An increase in the value of the dollar will reduce exports and increase imports, so net exports will fall. A decrease in the value of the dollar will increase exports and reduce imports, so net exports will rise.

MyEconLab Concept Check

Making the Connection

MyEconLab Video

The iPhone Is Made in China ... or Is It?

The box says iPhones are made in China, but are they?

Designers and software engineers at Apple in Cupertino, California, designed the iPhone. However, the iPhone is sold in a box labeled "Made in China." The price of the iPhone when it is shipped from a factory in China is about $275. (The retail price is higher because Apple adds a markup, as do Best Buy and other stores that sell the iPhone.) So if you buy an iPhone, the purchase enters the GDP statistics as a $275 import to the United States from China. Recently, economists have begun to question whether the standard way of keeping track of imports and exports accurately reflects how modern businesses operate.

Recall from Chapter 2 that the iPhone contains components that are produced by a number of firms, based in several different countries, including the United States. Apple uses this *global supply chain* to take advantage of both lower production costs in other countries and the ability of different firms to use their engineering and manufacturing skills to produce the iPhone's many components. Apple arranges for these firms to ship the components to factories in China for final assembly. These Chinese factories are owned by Foxconn, a firm based in Taiwan. So, only final assembly of the iPhone takes place in China; no Chinese firm makes any of the iPhone's components.

How much of the price of the iPhone is accounted for by the value of final assembly? According to a study by economists Yuqing Xing and Neal Detert of the Asian Development Bank, less than 4 percent. In fact, they note that the value of the iPhone components China imports from U.S. firms is greater than the value of assembling the iPhones in Chinese factories. As measured in the GDP statistics, in 2015 the United States imported more than $20 billion worth of iPhones from China. In fact, most of that $20 billion represents the value of the iPhone's components, none of which are made in China.

The current system of accounting for imports and exports in the GDP statistics dates to a time when most products were produced entirely within one country. So a good the United States imported from France or Japan would have been produced completely in that country. As large firms have increasingly relied on global supply chains, the statistics on imports and exports have failed to keep up. As Pascal Lamy of the World Trade Organization put it: "The concept of country of origin for manufactured goods has gradually become obsolete." In other words, "trade statistics can mislead as much as inform," as economists Kenneth Kraemer of the University of

California, Irvine, Greg Linden of the University of California, Berkeley, and Jason Dedrick of Syracuse University put it. The U.S. Bureau of Economic Analysis and the government statistical agencies in other countries are all aware of the flaws that have developed in accounting for imports and exports. But the complexity of global supply chains makes it difficult to develop more accurate measures of imports and exports.

Sources: Izabella Kaminska, "iPhone6, the GDP Effect," ftalphaville.ft.com, September 2, 2014; Phil Izzo, "Who Gets Credit for iPhone Trade," *Wall Street Journal*, March 17, 2012; Kenneth L. Kraemer, Greg Linden, and Jason Dedrick, "Capturing Value in Global Networks: Apple's iPad and iPhone," University of California, Irvine, Working paper, July 2011; Yuqing Xing and Neal Detert, "How the iPhone Widens the United States Trade Deficit with the People's Republic of China," ADBI Working Paper Series, No. 257, May 2011; and Andrew Batson, "Not Really, 'Made in China,'" *Wall Street Journal*, December 15, 2010.

Your Turn: Test your understanding by doing related problems 2.13 and 2.14 on page 808 at the end of this chapter.

MyEconLab Study Plan

23.3 Graphing Macroeconomic Equilibrium

LEARNING OBJECTIVE: Use a 45°-line diagram to illustrate macroeconomic equilibrium.

Having examined the components of aggregate expenditure, we can now look more closely at macroeconomic equilibrium. We saw earlier in the chapter that macroeconomic equilibrium occurs when GDP is equal to aggregate expenditure. We can use a graph called the 45°-*line diagram* to illustrate macroeconomic equilibrium. (The 45°-line diagram is also sometimes called the *Keynesian cross* because it is based on the analysis of John Maynard Keynes.) To become familiar with this diagram, consider Figure 23.8, which is a 45°-line diagram that shows the relationship between the quantity of Pepsi sold (on the vertical axis) and the quantity of Pepsi produced (on the horizontal axis).

The line on the diagram forms an angle of 45° with the horizontal axis. The line represents all the points that are equal distances from both axes. So, points such as

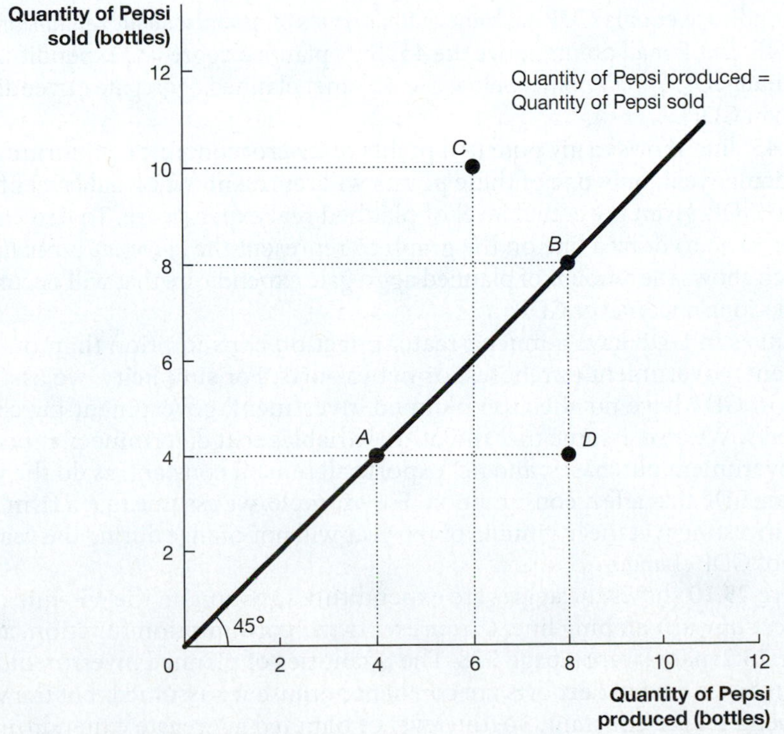

MyEconLab Animation

Figure 23.8

An Example of a 45°-Line Diagram

The 45° line shows all the points that are equal distances from both axes. Points such as *A* and *B*, at which the quantity produced equals the quantity sold, are on the 45° line. Points such as *C*, at which the quantity sold is greater than the quantity produced, lie above the line. Points such as *D*, at which the quantity sold is less than the quantity produced, lie below the line.

MyEconLab Animation

Figure 23.9

The Relationship between Planned Aggregate Expenditure and GDP on a 45°-Line Diagram

Every point of macroeconomic equilibrium is on the 45° line, where planned aggregate expenditure equals GDP. At points above the line, planned aggregate expenditure is greater than GDP. At points below the line, planned aggregate expenditure is less than GDP.

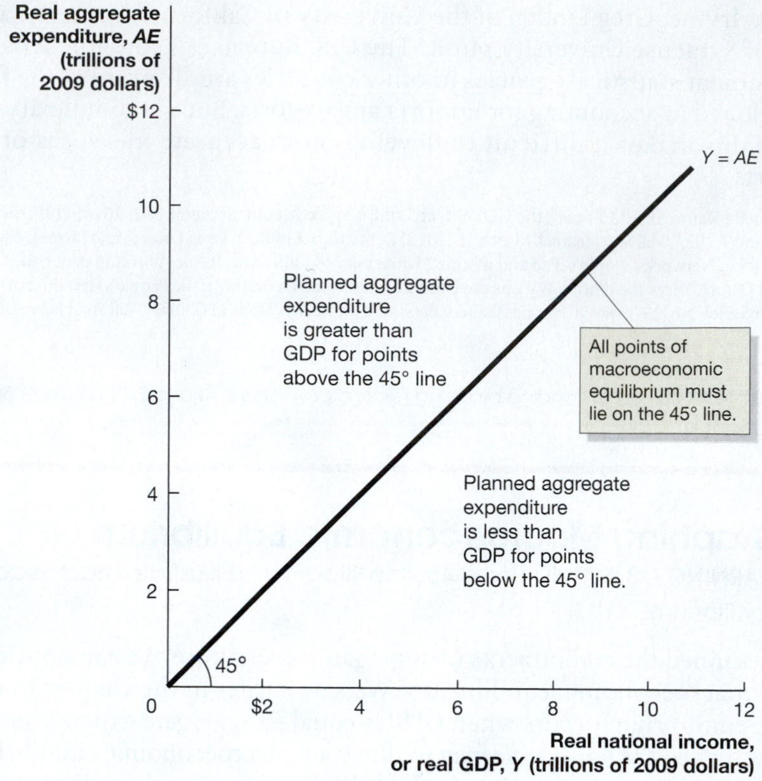

A and B, where the number of bottles of Pepsi produced equals the number of bottles sold, are on the 45° line. Points such as C, where the quantity sold is greater than the quantity produced, lie above the line. Points such as D, where the quantity sold is less than the quantity produced, lie below the line.

Figure 23.9 is similar to Figure 23.8 except that it measures real national income, or real GDP (*Y*), on the horizontal axis and planned real aggregate expenditure (*AE*) on the vertical axis. Because macroeconomic equilibrium occurs where planned aggregate expenditure equals GDP, *we know that all points of macroeconomic equilibrium must lie along the 45° line.* For all points above the 45° line, planned aggregate expenditure will be greater than GDP. For all points below the 45° line, planned aggregate expenditure will be less than GDP.

The 45° line shows many potential points of macroeconomic equilibrium. During any particular year, only one of these points will represent the actual level of equilibrium real GDP, given the actual level of planned real expenditure. To determine this point, we need to draw a line on the graph to represent the *aggregate expenditure function,* which shows the amount of planned aggregate expenditure that will occur at every level of national income, or GDP.

Changes in GDP have a much greater effect on consumption than on planned investment, government purchases, or net exports. For simplicity, we assume that changes in GDP have no effect on planned investment, government purchases, or net exports. We also assume that the other variables that determine planned investment, government purchases, and net exports all remain constant, as do the variables other than GDP that affect consumption. For example, we assume that a firm's level of planned investment at the beginning of the year will not change during the year, even if the level of GDP changes.

Figure 23.10 shows the aggregate expenditure function on the 45°-line diagram. The lowest upward-sloping line, C, represents the consumption function, as shown in Figure 23.2, panel (b), on page 778. The quantities of planned investment, government purchases, and net exports are constant because we assumed that the variables they depend on are constant. So, the level of planned aggregate expenditure at any

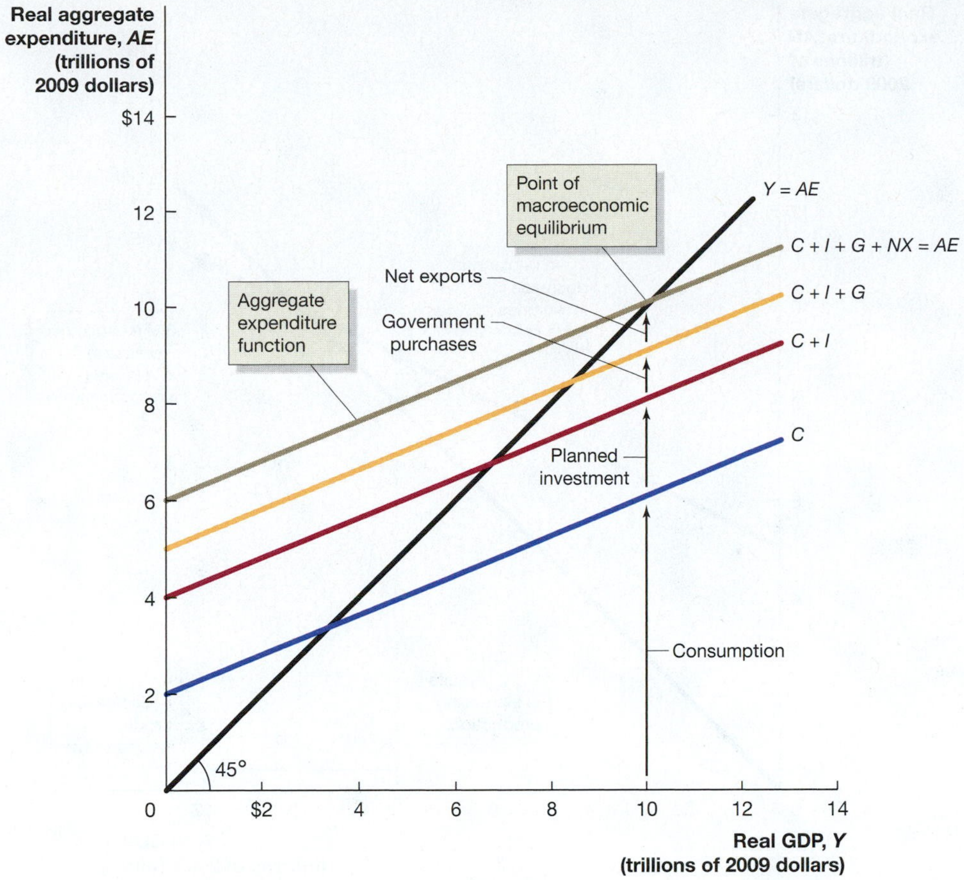

MyEconLab Animation

Figure 23.10

Macroeconomic Equilibrium on the 45°-Line Diagram

Macroeconomic equilibrium occurs where the aggregate expenditure (*AE*) line crosses the 45° line. The lowest upward-sloping line, *C*, represents the consumption function. The quantities of planned investment, government purchases, and net exports are constant because we assumed that the variables they depend on are constant. So, the total of planned aggregate expenditure at any level of GDP is the amount of consumption at that level of GDP plus the sum of the constant amounts of planned investment, government purchases, and net exports. We successively add each component of spending to the consumption function line to arrive at the gray line representing aggregate expenditure.

level of GDP is the amount of consumption spending at that level of GDP plus the sum of the constant amounts of planned investment, government purchases, and net exports. In Figure 23.10, we add each component of spending successively to the consumption function line to arrive at the line representing planned aggregate expenditure (*AE*). The $C + I$ line is higher than the *C* line by the constant amount of planned investment; the $C + I + G$ line is higher than the $C + I$ line by the constant amount of government purchases; and the $C + I + G + NX$ line is higher than the $C + I + G$ line by the constant amount of *NX*. (In many years, however, *NX* is negative, which would cause the $C + I + G + NX$ line to be *below* the $C + I + G$ line.) The $C + I + G + NX$ line shows all four components of expenditure and is the aggregate expenditure (*AE*) function. At the point where the *AE* line crosses the 45° line, planned aggregate expenditure is equal to GDP, and the economy is in macroeconomic equilibrium.

Figure 23.11 makes the relationship between planned aggregate expenditure and GDP clearer by showing only the 45° line and the *AE* line. The figure shows that the *AE* line intersects the 45° line at a level of real GDP of $10 trillion. Therefore, $10 trillion represents the equilibrium level of real GDP. To see why, consider the situation if real GDP were only $8 trillion. By moving vertically from $8 trillion on the horizontal axis up to the *AE* line, we see that planned aggregate expenditure will be greater than $8 trillion at this level of real GDP. Whenever total spending is greater than total production, firms' inventories will fall. The fall in inventories is equal to the vertical distance between the *AE* line, which shows the level of total spending, and the 45° line, which shows the $8 trillion of total production. Unplanned declines in inventories lead firms to increase their production. As real GDP increases from $8 trillion, so will total income and, therefore, consumption. The economy will move up the *AE* line as consumption increases. The gap between total spending and total production will fall, but as long as the *AE* line is above the 45° line, inventories will continue to decline, and firms will

MyEconLab Animation

Figure 23.11

Macroeconomic Equilibrium

Macroeconomic equilibrium occurs where the *AE* line crosses the 45° line, which occurs at GDP of $10 trillion. If GDP is less than $10 trillion, the corresponding point on the *AE* line is above the 45° line, planned aggregate expenditure is greater than total production, firms will experience an unplanned decrease in inventories, and GDP will increase. If GDP is greater than $10 trillion, the corresponding point on the *AE* line is below the 45° line, planned aggregate expenditure is less than total production, firms will experience an unplanned increase in inventories, and GDP will decrease.

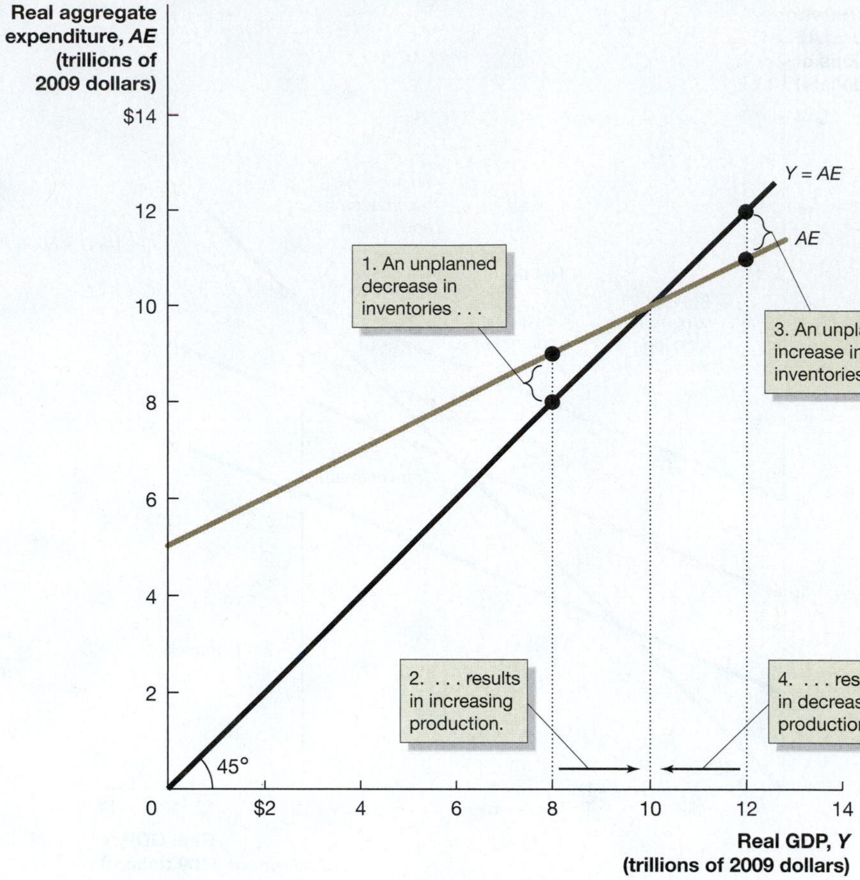

continue to expand production. When real GDP rises to $10 trillion, inventories stop falling, and the economy will be in macroeconomic equilibrium.

As Figure 23.11 shows, if GDP is initially $12 trillion, planned aggregate expenditure will be less than GDP, and firms will experience an unplanned increase in inventories. Rising inventories lead firms to decrease production. As GDP falls from $12 trillion, consumption will also fall, which causes the economy to move down the *AE* line. The gap between planned aggregate expenditure and GDP will fall, but as long as the *AE* line is below the 45° line, inventories will continue to rise, and firms will continue to cut production. When GDP falls to $10 trillion, inventories will stop rising, and the economy will be in macroeconomic equilibrium.

Showing a Recession on the 45°-Line Diagram

Notice that *macroeconomic equilibrium can occur at any point on the 45° line*. Ideally, equilibrium will occur at *potential GDP*. At potential GDP, firms will be operating at their normal level of capacity, and the economy will be at the *natural rate of unemployment*. As we have seen, at the natural rate of unemployment, the economy will be at *full employment*: Everyone in the labor force who wants a job will have one, except the structurally and frictionally unemployed (see Chapter 20). However, for equilibrium to occur at potential GDP, planned aggregate expenditure must be high enough. As Figure 23.12 shows, if there is insufficient total spending, equilibrium will occur at a lower level of real GDP. In this situation, many firms will be operating below their normal capacity, and the unemployment rate will be above the natural rate of unemployment.

Suppose that the level of potential GDP is $10 trillion. As Figure 23.12 shows, when GDP is $10 trillion, planned aggregate expenditure is below $10 trillion, perhaps because firms have become pessimistic about their future profitability and have reduced their investment spending. The shortfall in planned aggregate expenditure

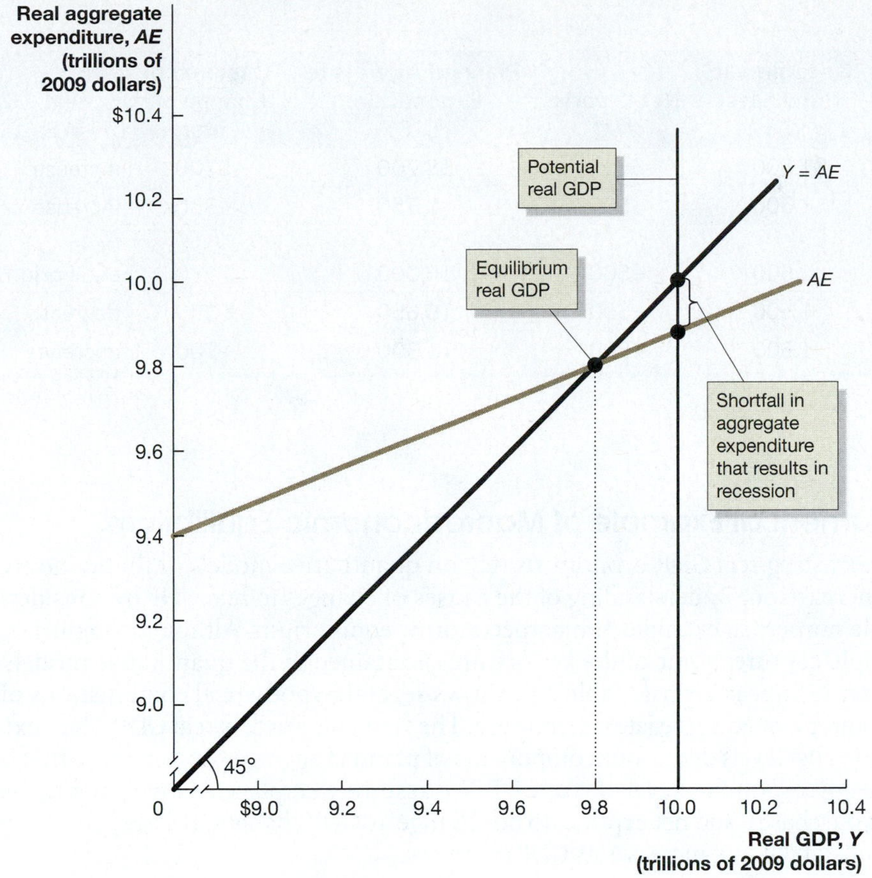

MyEconLab Animation

Figure 23.12

Showing a Recession on the 45°-Line Diagram

When the aggregate expenditure line intersects the 45° line at a level of GDP below potential GDP, the economy is in recession. The figure shows that potential GDP is $10 trillion, but because planned aggregate expenditure is too low, the equilibrium level of GDP is only $9.8 trillion, where the *AE* line intersects the 45° line. As a result, some firms will be operating below their normal capacity, and unemployment will be above the natural rate of unemployment. We can measure the shortfall in planned aggregate expenditure as the vertical distance between the *AE* line and the 45° line at the level of potential GDP.

that leads to the recession can be measured as the vertical distance between the *AE* line and the 45° line at the level of potential GDP. The shortfall in planned aggregate expenditure is exactly equal to the unplanned increase in inventories that would occur if the economy were initially at a level of GDP of $10 trillion. The unplanned increase in inventories measures the amount by which current planned aggregate expenditure is too low for the current level of production to be the equilibrium level. Put another way, if any of the four components of aggregate expenditure increased by this amount, the *AE* line would shift upward and intersect the 45° line at GDP of $10 trillion, and the economy would be in macroeconomic equilibrium at full employment.

Figure 23.12 shows that macroeconomic equilibrium will occur when real GDP is $9.8 trillion. Because real GDP is 2 percent below potential GDP of $10 trillion, many firms will be operating below their normal capacity, and the unemployment rate will be well above the natural rate of unemployment. The economy will remain at this level of real GDP until there is an increase in one or more of the components of aggregate expenditure. MyEconLab Concept Check

The Important Role of Inventories

Whenever planned aggregate expenditure is less than real GDP, some firms will experience unplanned increases in inventories. If firms do not cut back their production promptly when spending declines, they will accumulate inventories. If firms accumulate excess inventories, then even if spending quickly returns to its normal level, firms will have to sell their excess inventories before they can return to producing at normal levels. For example, more than half of the sharp 5.4 percent annual rate of decline in real GDP during the first quarter of 2009 resulted from firms cutting production as they sold off unintended accumulations of inventories. MyEconLab Concept Check

Table 23.3 Macroeconomic Equilibrium

Real GDP (*Y*)	Consumption (*C*)	Planned Investment (*I*)	Government Purchases (*G*)	Net Exports (*NX*)	Planned Aggregate Expenditure (*AE*)	Unplanned Change in Inventories	Real GDP Will . . .
$8,000	$6,200	$1,500	$1,500	−$500	$8,700	−$700	increase
9,000	6,850	1,500	1,500	−500	9,350	−350	increase
10,000	7,500	1,500	1,500	−500	10,000	0	be in equilibrium
11,000	8,150	1,500	1,500	−500	10,650	+350	decrease
12,000	8,800	1,500	1,500	−500	11,300	+700	decrease

Note: The values are in billions of 2009 dollars.

A Numerical Example of Macroeconomic Equilibrium

In forecasting real GDP, economists rely on quantitative models of the economy. We can increase our understanding of the causes of changes in real GDP by considering a simple numerical example of macroeconomic equilibrium. Although simplified, this example captures some of the key features contained in the quantitative models that economic forecasters use. Table 23.3 shows several hypothetical combinations of real GDP and planned aggregate expenditure. The first column lists real GDP. The next four columns list levels of the four components of planned aggregate expenditure that occur at the corresponding level of real GDP. We assume that planned investment, government purchases, and net exports do not change as GDP changes. Because consumption depends on GDP, it increases as GDP increases.

Don't Let This Happen to You

Don't Confuse Aggregate Expenditure with Consumption Spending

Macroeconomic equilibrium occurs where planned aggregate expenditure equals GDP. But remember that planned aggregate expenditure equals the sum of consumption spending, planned investment spending, government purchases, and net exports, *not* consumption spending alone. If GDP were equal to consumption, the economy would not be in equilibrium. Planned investment plus government purchases plus net exports will always be a positive number. Therefore, if consumption were equal to GDP, aggregate expenditure would have to be greater than GDP. In that case, inventories would be decreasing, and GDP would be *increasing*; GDP would not be in equilibrium.

Test your understanding of macroeconomic equilibrium with this problem:

Question: Do you agree with the following argument?

> This chapter says macroeconomic equilibrium occurs where planned aggregate expenditure equals GDP. GDP is equal to national income. So, at equilibrium, planned aggregate expenditure must equal national income. But we know that consumers do not spend all of their income: They save at least some and use some to pay taxes. Therefore, aggregate expenditure will never equal national income, and the basic macroeconomic story is incorrect.

Answer: Remember that national income equals GDP (disregarding depreciation, as we have done throughout this chapter). So, it is correct to say that in macroeconomic equilibrium, planned aggregate expenditure must equal national income. But the last sentence of the argument is incorrect because it assumes that aggregate expenditure is the same as consumption spending. Because of saving and taxes, consumption spending is always much less than national income, but in equilibrium, the sum of consumption spending, planned investment spending, government purchases, and net exports does, in fact, equal GDP and national income. So, the argument is incorrect because it confuses consumption spending with aggregate expenditure.

MyEconLab Study Plan

Your Turn: Test your understanding by doing related problem 3.11 on page 809 at the end of this chapter.

In the first row of the table, GDP of \$8,000 billion (or \$8 trillion) results in consumption of \$6,200 billion. Adding consumption, planned investment, government purchases, and net exports across the row gives planned aggregate expenditure of \$8,700 billion, which is shown in the sixth column. Because planned aggregate expenditure is greater than GDP, inventories will fall by \$700 billion. This unplanned decline in inventories will lead firms to increase production, and GDP will increase. GDP will continue to increase until it reaches \$10,000 billion. At that level of GDP, planned aggregate expenditure is also \$10,000 billion, unplanned changes in inventories are zero, and the economy is in macroeconomic equilibrium.

In the last row, GDP of \$12,000 billion results in consumption of \$8,800 billion and planned aggregate expenditure of \$11,300 billion. Because planned aggregate expenditure is less than GDP, inventories will increase by \$700 billion. This unplanned increase in inventories will lead firms to decrease production, and GDP will decrease. GDP will continue to decrease until it reaches \$10,000 billion, unplanned changes in inventories are zero, and the economy is in macroeconomic equilibrium.

Only when real GDP equals \$10,000 billion will the economy be in macroeconomic equilibrium. At other levels of real GDP, planned aggregate expenditure will be higher or lower than GDP, and the economy will be expanding or contracting. MyEconLab Concept Check

Solved Problem 23.3

MyEconLab Interactive Animation

Determining Macroeconomic Equilibrium

Fill in the blank cells in the following table and determine the equilibrium level of real GDP.

Real GDP (*Y*)	Consumption (*C*)	Planned Investment (*I*)	Government Purchases (*G*)	Net Exports (*NX*)	Planned Aggregate Expenditure (*AE*)	Unplanned Change in Inventories
\$8,000	\$6,200	\$1,675	\$1,675	−\$500		
9,000	6,850	1,675	1,675	−500		
10,000	7,500	1,675	1,675	−500		
11,000	8,150	1,675	1,675	−500		
12,000	8,800	1,675	1,675	−500		

Solving the Problem

Step 1: Review the chapter material. This problem is about determining macroeconomic equilibrium, so you may want to review the section "A Numerical Example of Macroeconomic Equilibrium," which begins on page 794.

Step 2: Fill in the missing values in the table. We can calculate the missing values in the last two columns by using two equations:

$$\text{Planned aggregate expenditure } (AE) = \text{Consumption } (C) + \text{Planned investment } (I) + \text{Government purchases } (G) + \text{Net exports } (NX)$$

and:

$$\text{Unplanned change in inventories} = \text{Real GDP } (Y) - \text{Planned aggregate expenditure } (AE).$$

For example, to fill in the first row, we have $AE = \$6{,}200$ billion + \$1,675 billion + \$1,675 billion + (−\$500 billion) = \$9,050 billion, and unplanned change in inventories = \$8,000 billion − \$9,050 billion = −\$1,050 billion.

Real GDP (*Y*)	Consumption (*C*)	Planned Investment (*I*)	Government Purchases (*G*)	Net Exports (*NX*)	Planned Aggregate Expenditure (*AE*)	Unplanned Change in Inventories
$8,000	$6,200	$1,675	$1,675	−$500	$9,050	−1,050
9,000	6,850	1,675	1,675	−500	9,700	−700
10,000	7,500	1,675	1,675	−500	10,350	−350
11,000	8,150	1,675	1,675	−500	11,000	0
12,000	8,800	1,675	1,675	−500	11,650	350

Step 3: **Determine the equilibrium level of real GDP.** Once you fill in the table, you should see that equilibrium real GDP must be $11,000 billion because only at that level is real GDP equal to planned aggregate expenditure.

MyEconLab Study Plan

Your Turn: For more practice, do related problem 3.12 on page 809 at the end of this chapter.

23.4 The Multiplier Effect

LEARNING OBJECTIVE: Describe the multiplier effect and use the multiplier formula to calculate changes in equilibrium GDP.

So far, we have seen that aggregate expenditure determines real GDP in the short run, and we have seen how the economy adjusts if it is not in equilibrium. We have also seen that whenever aggregate expenditure changes, there will be a new level of equilibrium real GDP. In this section, we will look more closely at the effects of a change in aggregate expenditure on equilibrium real GDP. We begin the discussion with Figure 23.13, which illustrates the effect of an increase in planned investment spending. We assume that the economy starts in equilibrium at point *A*, at which real GDP is $9.6 trillion. Firms then become more optimistic about the future profitability of investment and increase spending on factories, machinery, and equipment by $100 billion. This increase in investment spending shifts the *AE* line up by

MyEconLab Animation

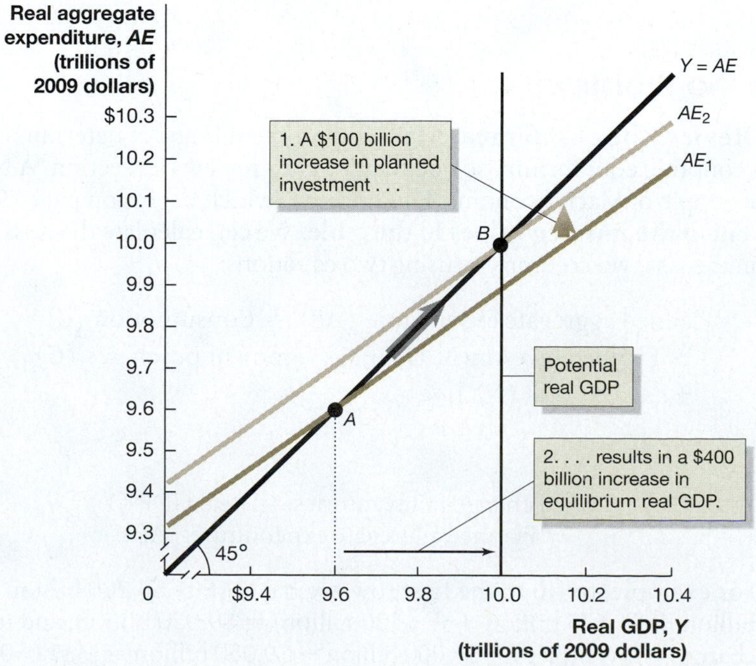

Figure 23.13

The Multiplier Effect

The economy begins at point *A*, at which equilibrium real GDP is $9.6 trillion. A $100 billion increase in planned investment shifts up aggregate expenditure from AE_1 to AE_2. The new equilibrium is at point *B*, where real GDP is $10.0 trillion, which is potential real GDP. Because of the multiplier effect, a $100 billion increase in investment results in a $400 billion increase in equilibrium real GDP.

\$100 billion, from AE_1 to AE_2. The new equilibrium occurs at point *B*, at which real GDP is \$10.0 trillion, which equals potential real GDP.

Notice that the initial \$100 billion increase in planned investment spending results in a \$400 billion increase in equilibrium real GDP. The increase in planned investment spending has had a *multiplied effect* on equilibrium real GDP. It is not only investment spending that will have this multiplied effect; any increase in *autonomous expenditure* will shift up the aggregate expenditure function and lead to a multiplied increase in equilibrium GDP. **Autonomous expenditure** does not depend on the level of GDP. In the aggregate expenditure model we have been using, planned investment spending, government spending, and net exports are all autonomous expenditures. Consumption has both an autonomous component, which does not depend on the level of GDP, and a nonautonomous—or *induced*—component, which does depend on the level of GDP. For example, if households decide to spend more of their incomes—and save less—at every level of income, there will be an autonomous increase in consumption spending, and the aggregate expenditure function will shift up. If, however, real GDP increases and households increase their consumption spending, as indicated by the consumption function, there will be a movement up along the aggregate expenditure function, and the increase in consumption spending will be nonautonomous.

Autonomous expenditure An expenditure that does not depend on the level of GDP.

The ratio of the increase in equilibrium real GDP to the increase in autonomous expenditure is called the **multiplier**. The series of induced increases in consumption spending that results from an initial increase in autonomous expenditure is called the **multiplier effect**. The multiplier effect occurs because an initial increase in autonomous expenditure sets off a series of increases in real GDP.

Multiplier The increase in equilibrium real GDP divided by the increase in autonomous expenditure.

Multiplier effect The process by which an increase in autonomous expenditure leads to a larger increase in real GDP.

We can look more closely at the multiplier effect. Suppose the whole \$100 billion increase in investment spending shown in Figure 23.13 consists of firms building additional factories and office buildings. Initially, this additional spending will cause the construction of factories and office buildings to increase by \$100 billion, so GDP will also increase by \$100 billion. Remember that increases in production result in equal increases in national income. So, this increase in real GDP of \$100 billion is also an increase in national income of \$100 billion. In this example, the income is received as wages and salaries by the employees of the construction firms, as profit by the owners of the firms, and so on. After receiving this additional income, these workers, managers, and owners will increase their consumption of cars, appliances, furniture, and many other products. If the marginal propensity to consume (*MPC*) is 0.75, we know the increase in consumption spending will be \$75 billion. This additional \$75 billion in spending will cause the firms making the cars, appliances, and other products to increase production by \$75 billion, so GDP will rise by \$75 billion. This increase in GDP means national income has also increased by another \$75 billion. This increased income will be received by the owners and employees of the firms producing the cars, appliances, and other products. These workers, managers, and owners in turn will increase their consumption spending, and the process of increasing production, income, and consumption will continue.

Eventually, the total increase in consumption will be \$300 billion. (We will soon show how we determined this value.) The \$300 billion increase in consumption combined with the initial \$100 billion increase in investment spending will result in a total change in equilibrium GDP of \$400 billion. Table 23.4 summarizes how changes in GDP and spending caused by the initial \$100 billion increase in investment will result in equilibrium GDP rising by \$400 billion. We can think of the multiplier effect occurring in rounds of spending. In round 1, there is an increase of \$100 billion in autonomous expenditure—the \$100 billion in planned investment spending in our example—which causes GDP to rise by \$100 billion. In round 2, induced expenditure rises by \$75 billion (which equals the \$100 billion increase in real GDP in round 1 multiplied by the *MPC*). The \$75 billion in induced expenditure in round 2 causes a \$75 billion increase in real GDP, which leads to a \$56 billion increase in induced expenditure in round 3, and so on. The final column adds up the total increases in expenditure, which equal the total increase in GDP. In each round, the additional induced

Table 23.4

The Multiplier Effect in Action

	Additional Autonomous Expenditure (investment)	Additional Induced Expenditure (consumption)	Total Additional Expenditure = Total Additional GDP
Round 1	$100 billion	$0	$100 billion
Round 2	0	75 billion	175 billion
Round 3	0	56 billion	231 billion
Round 4	0	42 billion	273 billion
Round 5	0	32 billion	305 billion
.	.	.	.
.	.	.	.
.	.	.	.
Round 10	0	8 billion	377 billion
.	.	.	.
.	.	.	.
.	.	.	.
Round 15	0	2 billion	395 billion
.	.	.	.
.	.	.	.
.	.	.	.
Round 19	0	1 billion	398 billion
.	.	.	.
.	.	.	.
.	.	.	.
Round *n*	0	0	400 billion

expenditure becomes smaller because the *MPC* is less than 1. By round 10, additional induced expenditure is only $8 billion, and the total increase in GDP from the beginning of the process is $377 billion. By round 19, the process is almost complete: Additional induced expenditure is only about $1 billion, and the total increase in GDP is $398 billion. Eventually, the process will be finished, although we cannot say precisely how many spending rounds it will take, so we simply label the last round *n* rather than give it a specific number.

We can calculate the value of the multiplier in our example by dividing the increase in equilibrium real GDP by the increase in autonomous expenditure:

$$\frac{\Delta Y}{\Delta I} = \frac{\text{Change in real GDP}}{\text{Change in investment spending}} = \frac{\$400 \text{ billion}}{\$100 \text{ billion}} = 4.$$

With a multiplier of 4, each increase in autonomous expenditure of $1 will result in an increase in equilibrium GDP of $4.

Making the Connection MyEconLab Video

The Multiplier in Reverse: The Great Depression of the 1930s

An increase in autonomous expenditure causes an increase in equilibrium real GDP, but the reverse is also true: A decrease in autonomous expenditure causes a decrease in real GDP. Many Americans became aware of this fact in the 1930s, when reductions in autonomous expenditure were magnified by the multiplier into the largest decline in real GDP in U.S. history.

In August 1929, the economy reached a business cycle peak, and a downturn in production began. In October, the stock market crashed, destroying billions of dollars of wealth and increasing pessimism among households and firms. Both consumption spending and planned investment spending declined. The passage by the U.S. Congress of the Smoot-Hawley Tariff Act in June 1930 helped set off a trade war that reduced exports. A series of banking crises that began in the fall of 1930 limited the ability of households and firms to finance consumption and investment. As aggregate expenditure declined, many firms experienced declining sales and began to lay off workers. Falling levels of production and income induced further declines in consumption spending, which led to further cutbacks in production and employment, leading to further declines in income, and so on, in a downward spiral. The following table shows the severity of the economic downturn by contrasting the business cycle peak of 1929 with the business cycle trough of 1933:

The multiplier effect contributed to the very high levels of unemployment during the Great Depression.

Year	Consumption	Investment	Exports	Real GDP	Unemployment Rate
1929	$781 billion	$124 billion	$41 billion	$1,057 billion	2.9%
1933	$638 billion	$27 billion	$22 billion	$778 billion	20.9%

Note: The values are in 2009 dollars.

Sources: U.S. Bureau of Economic Analysis; and David R. Weir, "A Century of U.S. Unemployment, 1890–1990," in Roger L. Ransom, Richard Sutch, and Susan B. Carter, eds., *Research in Economic History*, Vol. 14, San Diego, CA: JAI Press, 1992, Table D3, pp. 341–343.

We can use a 45°-line diagram to illustrate the multiplier effect working in reverse during these years. The economy was at potential real GDP in 1929, before the declines in aggregate expenditure began. Declining consumption, planned investment, and net exports shifted the aggregate expenditure function down from AE_{1929} to AE_{1933}, reducing equilibrium real GDP from $1,057 billion in 1929 to $778 billion in 1933. The depth and length of this economic downturn led to its being labeled the Great Depression.

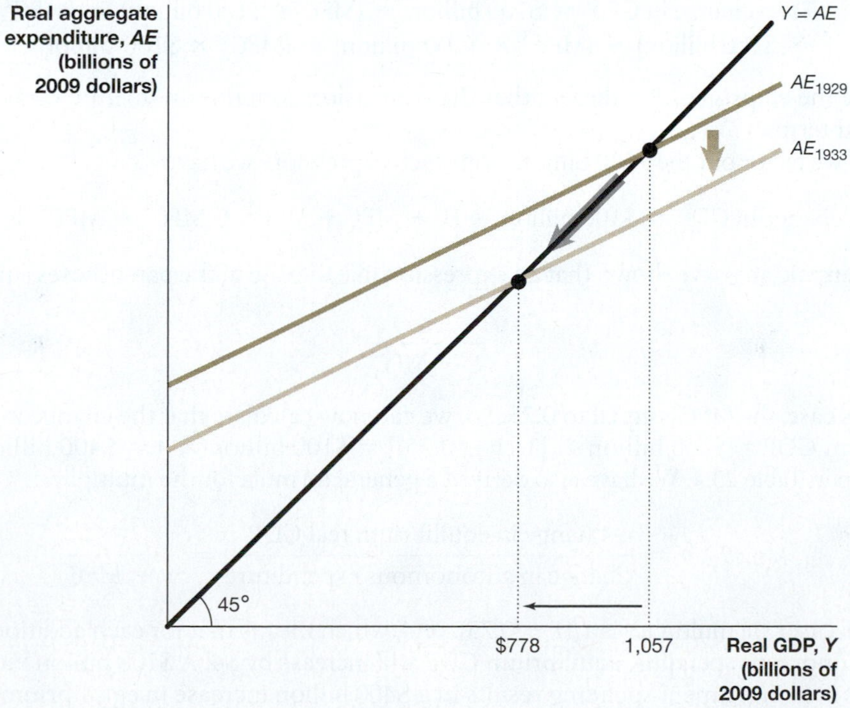

The severity of the Great Depression forced thousands of firms to declare bankruptcy. Even firms that survived experienced sharp declines in sales. By 1933, production at U.S. Steel had declined 90 percent, and production at General Motors had declined more than 75 percent. High rates of unemployment forced many families into poverty and a daily struggle for survival. Recovery from the business cycle trough in 1933 was slow. Real GDP did not regain its 1929 level until 1936, and a growing labor force meant that the unemployment rate did not return to its 1929 level until 1942, after the United States entered World War II.

MyEconLab Study Plan

Your Turn: Test your understanding by doing related problem 4.6 on page 810 at the end of this chapter.

A Formula for the Multiplier

Table 23.4 on page 798 shows that during the multiplier process, each round of increases in consumption is smaller than in the previous round, so eventually, the increases will come to an end, and we will have a new macroeconomic equilibrium. But how do we know that when we add all the increases in GDP, the total will be \$400 billion? We can verify this result by first writing out the total change in equilibrium GDP:

The total change in equilibrium real GDP equals the initial increase in planned investment spending $= 100$ billion

Plus the first induced increase in consumption $= MPC \times \$100$ billion

Plus the second induced increase in consumption $= MPC \times (MPC \times \$100 \text{ billion}) = MPC^2 \times \$100$ billion

Plus the third induced increase in consumption $= MPC \times (MPC^2 \times \$100 \text{ billion}) = MPC^3 \times \$100$ billion

Plus the fourth induced increase in consumption $= MPC \times (MPC^3 \times \$100 \text{ billion}) = MPC^4 \times \$100$ billion

and so on ...

Or:

$$\text{Total change in GDP} = \$100 \text{ billion} + (MPC \times \$100 \text{ billion}) + (MPC^2 \times \$100 \text{ billion}) + (MPC^3 \times \$100 \text{ billion}) + (MPC^4 \times \$100 \text{ billion}) + \dots$$

where the ellipsis (...) indicates that the expression contains an infinite number of similar terms.

If we factor out the \$100 billion from each expression, we have:

$$\text{Total change in GDP} = \$100 \text{ billion} \times (1 + MPC + MPC^2 + MPC^3 + MPC^4 + \dots)$$

Mathematicians have shown that an expression like the one in the parentheses sums to:

$$\frac{1}{1 - MPC}.$$

In this case, the *MPC* is equal to 0.75. So, we can now calculate that the change in equilibrium GDP $= \$100$ billion $\times [1/(1 - 0.75)] = \$100$ billion $\times 4 = \$400$ billion, as shown in Table 23.4. We have also derived a general formula for the multiplier:

$$\text{Multiplier} = \frac{\text{Change in equilibrium real GDP}}{\text{Change in autonomous expenditure}} = \frac{1}{1 - MPC}.$$

In this case, the multiplier is $1/(1 - 0.75)$, or 4, which means that for each additional \$1 of autonomous spending, equilibrium GDP will increase by \$4. A \$100 billion increase in planned investment spending results in a \$400 billion increase in equilibrium GDP.

Notice that the value of the multiplier depends on the value of the *MPC*. In particular, the larger the value of the *MPC*, the larger the value of the multiplier. For example, if the *MPC* were 0.9 instead of 0.75, the value of the multiplier would increase from 4 to $1/(1 - 0.9) = 10$.

MyEconLab Concept Check

Summarizing the Multiplier Effect

You should note four key points about the multiplier effect:

1. The multiplier effect occurs both when autonomous expenditure increases and when it decreases. For example, with an *MPC* of 0.75, a *decrease* in planned investment of $100 billion will lead to a *decrease* in equilibrium income of $400 billion.
2. The multiplier effect makes the economy more sensitive to changes in autonomous expenditure than it would otherwise be. Between the fourth quarter of 2005 and the second quarter of 2009, spending on residential construction declined by 57 percent. This decline in investment set off a series of declines in production, income, and spending so that firms such as automobile dealerships and clothing stores, which are far removed from the housing industry, also experienced declines in sales. Because of the multiplier effect, a decline in spending and production in one sector of the economy can lead to declines in spending and production in many other sectors of the economy.
3. The larger the *MPC*, the larger the value of the multiplier. With an *MPC* of 0.75, the multiplier is 4, but with an *MPC* of 0.50, the multiplier is only 2. This direct relationship between the value of the *MPC* and the value of the multiplier holds true because the larger the *MPC*, the larger the change in consumption that takes place after each change in income during the multiplier process.
4. The formula for the multiplier, $1/(1 - MPC)$, is oversimplified because it ignores some real-world complications, such as the effect that increases in GDP have on imports, inflation, interest rates, and individual income taxes. These effects combine to cause the simple formula to overstate the true value of the multiplier. Beginning in Chapter 24, we will start to take into account these real-world complications.

MyEconLab Concept Check

Solved Problem 23.4

MyEconLab Interactive Animation

Using the Multiplier Formula

Use the information in the table to answer the following questions:

Real GDP (*Y*)	Consumption (*C*)	Planned Investment (*I*)	Government Purchases (*G*)	Net Exports (*NX*)
$8,000	$6,900	$1,000	$1,000	−$500
9,000	7,700	1,000	1,000	−500
10,000	8,500	1,000	1,000	−500
11,000	9,300	1,000	1,000	−500
12,000	10,100	1,000	1,000	−500

Note: The values are in billions of 2009 dollars.

a. What is the equilibrium level of real GDP?

b. What is the *MPC*?

c. Suppose government purchases increase by $200 billion. What will be the new equilibrium level of real GDP? Use the multiplier formula to determine your answer.

Solving the Problem

Step 1: Review the chapter material. This problem is about the multiplier process, so you may want to review the section "The Multiplier Effect," which begins on page 796.

Step 2: Answer part (a) by determining equilibrium real GDP. Just as in Solved Problem 23.2 on page 781, we can find macroeconomic equilibrium by calculating the level of planned aggregate expenditure for each level of real GDP:

Real GDP (*Y*)	Consumption (*C*)	Planned Investment (*I*)	Government Purchases (*G*)	Net Exports (*NX*)	Planned Aggregate Expenditure (*AE*)
$8,000	$6,900	$1,000	$1,000	−$500	$8,400
9,000	7,700	1,000	1,000	−500	9,200
10,000	8,500	1,000	1,000	−500	10,000
11,000	9,300	1,000	1,000	−500	10,800
12,000	10,100	1,000	1,000	−500	11,600

We can see that macroeconomic equilibrium will occur when real GDP equals $10,000 billion.

Step 3: Answer part (b) by calculating the *MPC*.

$$MPC = \frac{\Delta C}{\Delta Y}.$$

In this case:

$$MPC = \frac{\$800 \text{ billion}}{\$1{,}000 \text{ billion}} = 0.8.$$

Step 4: Answer part (c) by using the multiplier formula to calculate the new equilibrium level of real GDP. We could find the new level of equilibrium real GDP by constructing a new table with government purchases increased from $1,000 to $1,200. But the multiplier allows us to calculate the answer directly. In this case:

$$\text{Multiplier} = \frac{1}{1 - MPC} = \frac{1}{1 - 0.8} = 5.$$

So:

$$\text{Change in equilibrium real GDP} = \text{Change in autonomous expenditure} \times 5.$$

Or:

$$\text{Change in equilibrium real GDP} = \$200 \text{ billion} \times 5 = \$1{,}000 \text{ billion}.$$

Therefore:

$$\text{New level of equilibrium GDP} = \$10{,}000 \text{ billion} + \$1{,}000 \text{ billion} = \$11{,}000 \text{ billion}.$$

MyEconLab Study Plan

Your Turn: For more practice, do related problem 4.7 on page 810 at the end of this chapter.

The Paradox of Thrift

We have seen that an increase in saving can increase the rate of economic growth in the long run by providing funds for investment (see Chapters 20 and 21). But in the short run, if households save more of their income and spend less of it, aggregate expenditure and real GDP will decline. In discussing the aggregate expenditure model, John Maynard Keynes argued that if many households decide at the same time to increase their saving and reduce their spending, they may make themselves worse off by causing aggregate expenditure to fall, thereby pushing the economy into a recession. The lower incomes in the recession might mean that total saving does not increase, despite the attempts by many individuals to increase their own saving. Keynes called this outcome the *paradox of thrift* because what appears to be something favorable to the long-run performance of the economy might be counterproductive in the short run.

Households saved very little of their income in the mid-2000s but increased their saving markedly in late 2008 and 2009. The personal saving rate is saving by households as a percentage of disposable personal income. By mid-2009, the personal saving rate had increased to 6 percent. Some economists argued that this increase in saving contributed to the recession and weak recovery by reducing consumption spending. Other economists are skeptical of the reasoning behind the paradox of thrift. An increase in saving, by increasing the supply of loanable funds, should lower the real interest rate and increase the level of investment spending (see Chapter 21). This increase in investment spending might offset some or all of the decline in consumption spending attributable to increased saving. Economists continue to debate the short-run effects of an increase in saving. MyEconLab Concept Check

MyEconLab Study Plan

23.5 The Aggregate Demand Curve

LEARNING OBJECTIVE: Understand the relationship between the aggregate demand curve and aggregate expenditure.

When demand for a product increases, firms usually respond by increasing production, but they are also likely to increase prices. Similarly, when demand falls, production falls, but prices may also fall. We would expect, then, that an increase or a decrease in aggregate expenditure would affect not just real GDP but also the *price level*. Will a change in the price level, in turn, affect the components of aggregate expenditure? In fact, as we will see, increases in the price level cause aggregate expenditure to fall, and decreases in the price level cause aggregate expenditure to rise. There are three main reasons for this inverse relationship between changes in the price level and changes in aggregate expenditure. We discussed the first two reasons in Section 23.2 when considering the factors that determine consumption and net exports:

1. A rising price level decreases consumption by decreasing the real value of household wealth; a falling price level has the reverse effect.
2. If the price level in the United States rises relative to the price levels in other countries, U.S. exports will become relatively more expensive, and foreign imports will become relatively less expensive, causing net exports to fall. A falling price level in the United States has the reverse effect.
3. When prices rise, firms and households need more money to finance buying and selling. If the central bank (the Federal Reserve in the United States) does not increase the money supply, the result will be an increase in the interest rate. In Chapter 25, we will analyze in more detail why the interest rate increases. As we discussed in Section 23.2, at a higher interest rate, investment spending falls as firms borrow less money to build new factories or to install new machinery and equipment and households borrow less money to buy new houses. A falling price level has the reverse effect: Other things being equal, interest rates will fall, and investment spending will rise.

We can now incorporate the effect of a change in the price level into the basic aggregate expenditure model, in which equilibrium real GDP is determined by the intersection of the aggregate expenditure (*AE*) line and the 45° line. Remember that we measure the price level as an index number with a value of 100 in the base year. If the price level rises from, say, 100 to 103, consumption, planned investment, and net exports will all fall, causing the *AE* line to shift down in the 45°-line diagram. The *AE* line shifts down because with higher prices, less spending will occur in the economy at every level of GDP. Panel (a) of Figure 23.14 shows that the downward shift of the *AE* line results in a lower level of equilibrium real GDP.

If the price level falls from, say, 100 to 97, then investment, consumption, and net exports will all rise. As panel (b) of Figure 23.14 shows, the *AE* line will shift up, which will cause equilibrium real GDP to increase.

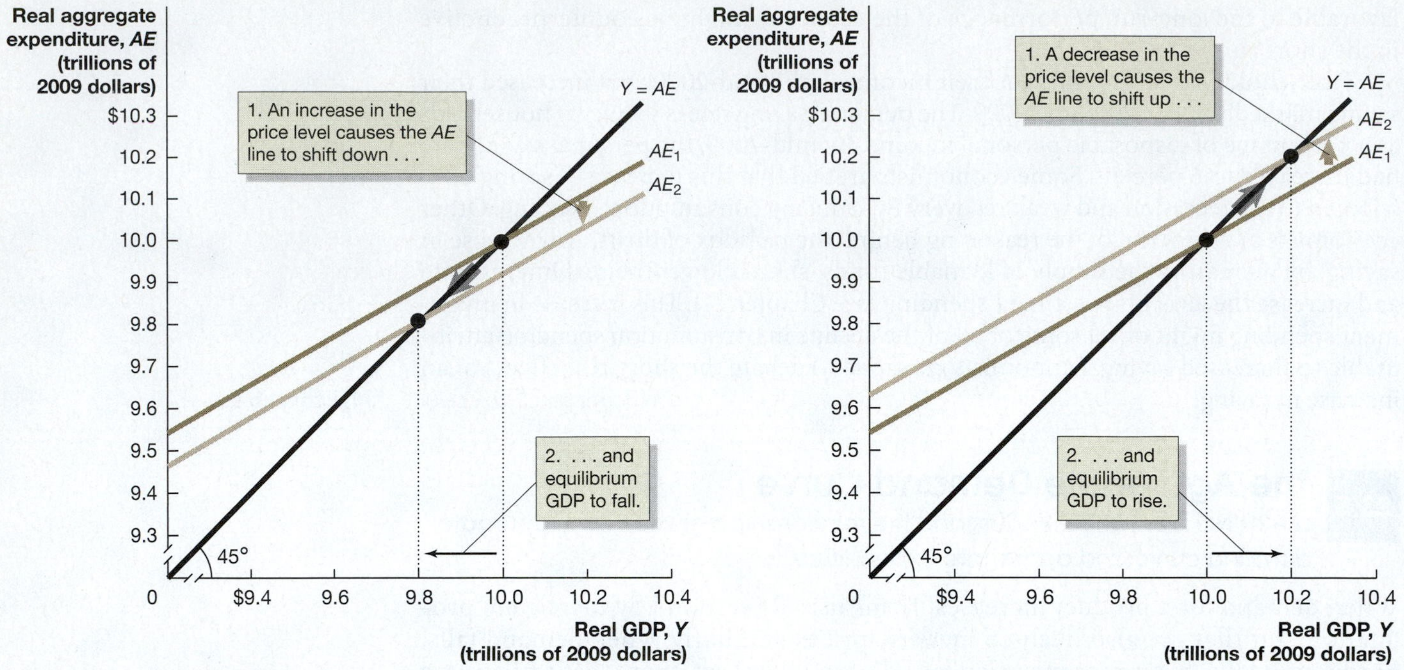

(a) The effect of a higher price level on real GDP **(b) The effect of a lower price level on real GDP**

MyEconLab Animation

Figure 23.14 The Effect of a Change in the Price Level on Real GDP

In panel (a), an increase in the price level results in declining consumption, planned investment, and net exports and causes the aggregate expenditure line to shift down from AE_1 to AE_2. As a result, equilibrium real GDP declines from \$10.0 trillion to \$9.8 trillion.

In panel (b), a decrease in the price level results in rising consumption, planned investment, and net exports and causes the aggregate expenditure line to shift up from AE_1 to AE_2. As a result, equilibrium real GDP increases from \$10.0 trillion to \$10.2 trillion.

Aggregate demand (*AD*) curve A curve that shows the relationship between the price level and the level of planned aggregate expenditure in the economy, holding constant all other factors that affect aggregate expenditure.

MyEconLab Study Plan

Figure 23.15 summarizes the effect of changes in the price level on real GDP. The table shows the combinations of price level and real GDP from Figure 23.14. The graph plots the numbers from the table. In the graph, the price level is measured on the vertical axis, and real GDP is measured on the horizontal axis. The relationship shown in Figure 23.15 between the price level and the level of planned aggregate expenditure is known as the **aggregate demand (*AD*) curve**. MyEconLab Concept Check

MyEconLab Animation

Figure 23.15

The Aggregate Demand Curve

The aggregate demand (*AD*) curve shows the relationship between the price level and the level of planned aggregate expenditure in the economy. When the price level is 97, real GDP is \$10.2 trillion. An increase in the price level to 100 causes consumption, investment, and net exports to fall, which reduces real GDP to \$10.0 trillion.

Price level	Equilibrium real GDP
97	\$10.2 trillion
100	10.0 trillion
103	9.8 trillion

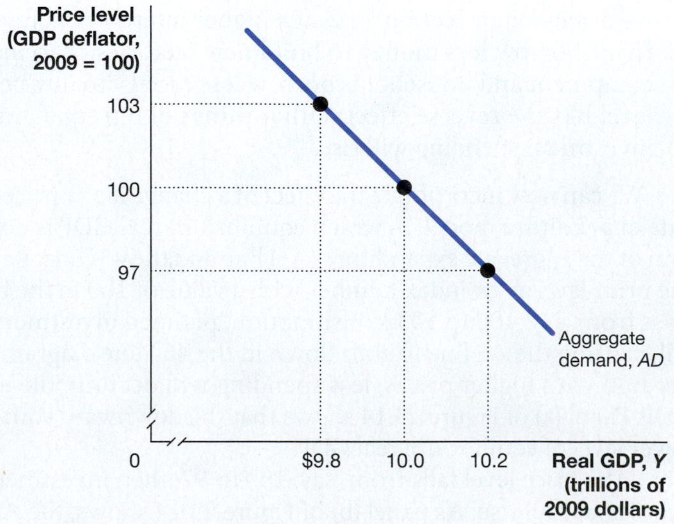

Continued from page 771

Economics in Your Life

When Consumer Confidence Falls, Is Your Job at Risk?

At the beginning of this chapter, we asked you to suppose that you work part time for a company that manufacturers door handles for automobiles. You have learned that consumer confidence in the economy has fallen and that many households expect their future income to be well below their current income. Should you be concerned about losing your job? We have seen in this chapter that if consumers expect their future income to decline, they will cut their consumption spending, and consumption spending is more than two-thirds of aggregate expenditure. So, if the decline in consumer confidence is correctly forecasting a decline in consumption spending, then aggregate expenditure and GDP will also likely decline. In deciding how likely your company is to lay you off, you should consider the following factors: If the economy moves into a recession, spending on automobiles by households and firms is likely to fall, which could reduce your firm's sales and possibly cost you a job. Before you panic, though, keep in mind that surveys of consumer confidence do not have a good track record in predicting recessions, so you may not have to move back in with your parents after all.

Conclusion

In this chapter, we examined a key macroeconomic idea: In the short run, the level of GDP is determined mainly by the level of aggregate expenditure. When economists forecast changes in GDP, they do so by forecasting changes in the four components of aggregate expenditure. We constructed an aggregate demand curve by taking into account how changes in the price level affect aggregate expenditure.

But our story is incomplete. In Chapter 24, we will analyze the *aggregate supply curve*. Then we will use the aggregate demand curve and the aggregate supply curve to show how equilibrium real GDP and the equilibrium price level are simultaneously determined.

We also need to discuss the roles that the financial system and government policy play in determining real GDP and the price level in the short run. We will cover these important topics in the following chapters.

Visit MyEconLab for a news article and analysis related to the concepts in this chapter.

CHAPTER SUMMARY AND PROBLEMS

Key Terms

Aggregate demand (*AD*) curve, p. 804
Aggregate expenditure (*AE*), p. 772
Aggregate expenditure model, p. 772
Autonomous expenditure, p. 797
Cash flow, p. 783
Consumption function, p. 777
Inventories, p. 773
Marginal propensity to consume (*MPC*), p. 778
Marginal propensity to save (*MPS*), p. 780
Multiplier, p. 797
Multiplier effect, p. 797

23.1 The Aggregate Expenditure Model, pages 772–775

LEARNING OBJECTIVE: Understand how macroeconomic equilibrium is determined in the aggregate expenditure model.

Summary

Aggregate expenditure (*AE*) is the total amount of spending in the economy. The **aggregate expenditure model** focuses on the relationship between total spending and real GDP in the short run, assuming that the price level is constant. In any particular year, the level of GDP is determined by the level of total spending, or aggregate expenditure, in the economy. The four components of aggregate expenditure are consumption (*C*), planned investment (*I*), government purchases (*G*), and net exports (*NX*). When aggregate expenditure is greater than GDP, there is an unplanned decrease in **inventories**, which are goods that have been produced but not yet sold, and GDP and total employment will increase. When aggregate expenditure is less than GDP, there is an unplanned increase in inventories, and GDP and total employment will decline. When aggregate expenditure is equal to GDP, firms will sell what they expected to sell, production and employment will be unchanged, and the economy will be in macroeconomic equilibrium.

MyEconLab Visit **www.myeconlab.com** to complete these exercises online and get instant feedback.

Review Questions

1.1 What is the key idea in the aggregate expenditure macroeconomic model?

1.2 What are inventories? What usually happens to inventories at the beginning of a recession? At the beginning of an expansion?

1.3 Which of the following does the aggregate expenditure model seek to explain: long-run economic growth, the business cycle, inflation, or cyclical unemployment?

Problems and Applications

1.4 Into which category of aggregate expenditure would each of the following transactions fall?

a. The Jones family buys a new car.
b. The San Diego Unified School District buys 12 new school buses.
c. The Jones family buys a newly constructed house from the Garcia Construction Co.
d. Joe Jones orders a Burberry coat from an online site in the United Kingdom.
e. Prudential insurance company purchases 250 new iPads from Apple.

1.5 Assume that Intel sells $1 billion of computer chips to Dell, Inc., for use in Dell's personal computers. How does this transaction affect aggregate expenditure?

1.6 In reporting on real GDP growth in the second quarter of 2015, an article in the *Wall Street Journal* noted that the 2.3 percent annual growth rate "would have been stronger if it hadn't been for companies drawing down inventories."

a. If companies are "drawing down inventories," is aggregate expenditure likely to have been larger or smaller than GDP?
b. Assume that the reduction in inventories was unplanned. What would you expect to happen to production in the future following an unplanned reduction in inventories?

Source: Justin Lahart, "Consumers Priming U.S. Pump," *Wall Street Journal*, July 30, 2015.

1.7 In the third quarter of 2015, business inventories in the United States increased by $62 billion. Can we tell from this information whether aggregate expenditure was higher or lower than GDP during the third quarter of 2015? If not, what other information do we need?

Source: Bureau of Economic Analysis.

1.8 An article in the *Wall Street Journal* stated that in China, "carmakers continue to grapple with ... rising inventories." Why might carmakers in China find that their inventories are unexpectedly rising? How are these carmakers likely to react to the increase in inventories?

Source: Colum Murphy, "China's Automobile Sales to Slow Further in 2015," *Wall Street Journal*, January 12, 2015.

1.9 According to an article in the *Wall Street Journal*, in late 2014, the Japanese economy experienced a large increase in business inventories. The article noted, "The large buildup of inventories is a reflection that the ... drop in demand was bigger than expected." Does it matter that Japanese firms didn't expect the drop in demand? Won't a decline in demand always lead to an increase in firms' holdings of inventories? Briefly explain.

Source: Eleanor Warnock, "Rising Inventories Hamper Japan Recovery," *Wall Street Journal*, September 30, 2014.

23.2 Determining the Level of Aggregate Expenditure in the Economy, pages 775–789

LEARNING OBJECTIVE: Discuss the determinants of the four components of aggregate expenditure and define marginal propensity to consume and marginal propensity to save.

Summary

The five determinants of consumption are current disposable income, household wealth, expected future income, the price level, and the interest rate. The **consumption function** is the relationship between consumption and disposable income. The **marginal propensity to consume (*MPC*)** is the change in consumption divided by the change in disposable income. The **marginal propensity to save (*MPS*)** is the change in saving divided by the change in disposable income. The determinants of planned investment are expectations of future profitability, the real interest rate, taxes, and **cash flow**, which is the difference between the cash revenues received by a firm and the cash spending by the firm. Government purchases include spending by the federal government and by local and state governments for goods and services. Government purchases do not include *transfer payments*, such as Social Security payments by the federal government or pension payments by local governments to retired police officers and firefighters. The three determinants of net exports are changes in the price level in the United States relative to changes in the price levels in other countries, the growth rate of GDP in the United States relative to the growth rates of GDP in other countries, and the exchange rate between the dollar and other currencies.

MyEconLab Visit **www.myeconlab.com** to complete these exercises online and get instant feedback.

Review Questions

2.1 In the aggregate expenditure model, why is it important to know the factors that determine consumption spending, investment spending, government purchases, and net exports?

2.2 What are the five main determinants of consumption spending? Which of these is the most important? How would a rise in stock prices or housing prices affect consumption spending?

2.3 Compare what happened to real investment between 1979 and the second quarter of 2015 with what happened to real consumption during that period.

2.4 What are the four main determinants of investment? How would a change in interest rates affect investment?

2.5 What are the three main determinants of net exports? How would an increase in the growth rate of GDP in the BRIC nations (Brazil, Russia, India, and China) affect U.S. net exports?

Problems and Applications

2.6 **(Related to the Chapter Opener on page 771)** Suppose a major U.S. appliance manufacturer is forecasting demand for its products during the next year. How will the forecast be affected by each of the following?

a. A survey shows a sharp rise in consumer confidence that income growth will be increasing.

b. Real interest rates are expected to increase.

c. The value of the U.S. dollar is expected to increase versus foreign currencies.

d. Planned investment spending in the economy is expected to decrease.

2.7 Draw the consumption function and label each axis. Show the effect of an increase in income on consumption spending. Does the change in income cause a movement along the consumption function or a shift of the consumption function? How would an increase in expected future income or an increase in household wealth affect the consumption function? Would these increases cause a movement along the consumption function or a shift of the consumption function? Briefly explain.

2.8 An economics student raises the following objection: "The textbook said that a higher interest rate lowers investment, but this doesn't make sense. I know that if I can get a higher interest rate, I am certainly going to invest more in my savings account." Briefly explain whether you agree with this reasoning.

2.9 Unemployed workers receive unemployment insurance payments from the government. Does the existence of unemployment insurance make it likely that consumption will fluctuate more or less over the business cycle than it would in the absence of unemployment insurance? Briefly explain.

2.10 **(Related to Solved Problem 23.2 on page 781)** Fill in the blank cells in the following table. Assume for simplicity that taxes are zero. Also assume that the values represent billions of 2009 dollars.

National Income and Real GDP (*Y*)	Consumption (*C*)	Saving (*S*)	Marginal Propensity to Consume (*MPC*)	Marginal Propensity to Save (*MPS*)
$9,000	$8,000			
10,000	8,750			
11,000	9,500			
12,000	10,250			
13,000	11,000			

2.11 **(Related to the Making the Connection on page 783)** In an opinion column in the *Wall Street Journal*, Purdue University President Mitchell Daniels wrote that "today's 20- and 30-year-olds are delaying marriage and delaying childbearing, both unhelpful trends from an economic and social standpoint." Why might young people be delaying marriage and childbearing? Why would this trend be unhelpful from an economic point of view? Is the trend possibly connected with the slow recovery from the 2007–2009 recession? Briefly explain.

Source: Mitchell E, Daniels, "How Student Debt Harms the Economy," *Wall Street Journal*, January 27, 2015.

2.12 **(Related to the Chapter Opener on page 771)** An article in the *Wall Street Journal* on changes in Intel's sales noted, "Intel sells its chips to customers in U.S. dollars, but many PC makers that buy those chips sell their products in local currencies." In these circumstances, would an increase in the value of the dollar relative to foreign currencies be likely to help or hurt Intel's sales? Briefly explain.

Source: Tess Stynes, "Intel Earnings: What to Watch," *Wall Street Journal*, July 15, 2015.

2.13 **(Related to the Making the Connection on page 788)** Briefly explain which of the following statement is correct.

a. The iPhone is made in China, using Chinese-made parts.
b. The iPhone is made in the United States, using U.S.-made parts.
c. The iPhone is made in the United States, using Chinese-made parts.
d. The iPhone is made China, using parts that are all made outside China.

What relevance does your answer have to how the Bureau of Economic Analysis calculates data on U.S. imports?

2.14 **(Related to the Making the Connection on page 788)** In a speech to a conference of government trade officials, Angel Gurría, secretary general of the Organization for Economic Co-operation and Development, made the following observation: "As goods and services cross borders several times at different stages of processing, conventional trade statistics may not tell the whole story."

a. What does Gurría mean by "conventional trade statistics"?
b. Why might conventional trade statistics no longer be as reliable as they once were?
c. What difficulties might the problems with trade statistics cause for policymakers?

Source: Angel Gurría, "Understanding Global Value Chains," Speech delivered at the G20 trade ministers conference in Puerto Vallarta, Mexico, April 19, 2012, www.oecd.org/about/secretary-general/g20understandingglobalvaluechains.htm.

23.3 Graphing Macroeconomic Equilibrium, pages 789–796

LEARNING OBJECTIVE: Use a 45°-line diagram to illustrate macroeconomic equilibrium.

Summary

The 45°-line diagram shows all the points where aggregate expenditure equals real GDP. On the 45°-line diagram, macroeconomic equilibrium occurs where the line representing the aggregate expenditure function crosses the 45° line. The economy is in recession when the aggregate expenditure line intersects the 45° line at a level of GDP that is below potential GDP. Numerically, macroeconomic equilibrium occurs when:

Consumption + Planned investment + Government purchases + Net exports = GDP.

MyEconLab Visit **www.myeconlab.com** to complete these exercises online and get instant feedback.

Review Questions

3.1 What is the meaning of the 45° line in the 45°-line diagram?

3.2 Use a 45°-line diagram to illustrate macroeconomic equilibrium. Make sure your diagram shows the aggregate expenditure function and the level of equilibrium real GDP and that your axes are properly labeled.

3.3 What does the slope of the aggregate expenditure line equal? How is the slope of the aggregate expenditure line related to the slope of the consumption function?

3.4 What is likely to happen if firms accumulate large amounts of unplanned inventory at the beginning of a recession?

3.5 What is the difference between aggregate expenditure and consumption spending?

Problems and Applications

3.6 At point A in the following graph, is planned aggregate expenditure greater than, equal to, or less than GDP? What about at point B? At point C? For points A and C, indicate the vertical distance that measures the unintended change in inventories.

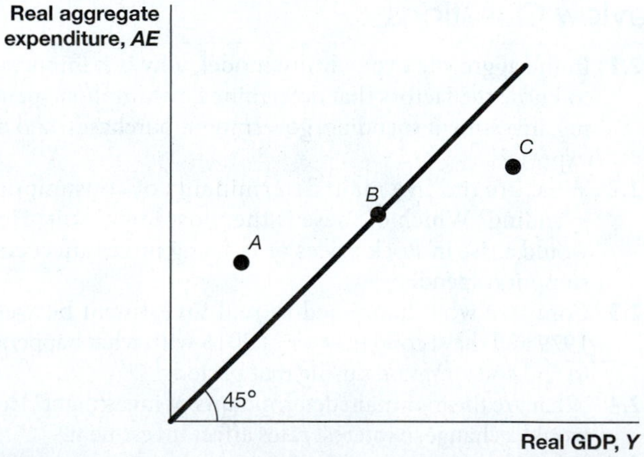

3.7 Suppose we drop the assumption that net exports do not depend on real GDP. Draw a graph with the value of net exports on the vertical axis and the value of real GDP on the horizontal axis. Now, add a line representing the relationship between net exports and real GDP. Does your net exports line have a positive or negative slope? Briefly explain.

3.8 A Federal Reserve publication notes that "the shedding of unwanted inventories often accounts for a large portion of the decline in gross domestic product (GDP) during economic recessions." What does the author mean be "shedding of unwanted inventories"? What makes the inventories unwanted? Why would shedding inventories lead to a decline in GDP?

Source: Jeremy M. Piger, "Is the Business Cycle Still an Inventory Cycle?" *Economic Synopses*, Federal Reserve Bank of St. Louis, No. 2, 2005.

3.9 An article on bloomberg.com about the Japanese economy noted, "Whether the 2.4 percent annualized gain in gross domestic product reported Wednesday can be maintained depends on consumers stepping in to buy the products that companies are piling up in warehouses."

a. Did business inventories in Japan increase or decrease during this period? Briefly explain.

b. What would happen if consumers do not buy the products that companies are piling up? Illustrate your answer with a 45°-line diagram.

Source: Keiko Ujikane and Toru Fujioka, "Japan's Economy Grows as Investment Gains, Inventories Rise," bloomberg.com, May 20, 2015.

3.10 Consider the table in the next column, which shows the change in inventories for each quarter from the first quarter of 2007 (2007:I) through the fourth quarter of 2010 (2010:IV) measured in billions of 2009 dollars. Provide a macroeconomic explanation for this pattern. (*Hint:* When did the recession during this period begin and end?)

Accompanies problem 3.10.

Year	Quarter	Change in Inventories
2007	I	$19.6
	II	49.4
	III	50.2
	IV	23.0
2008	I	−20.2
	II	−26.4
	III	−20.7
	IV	−67.4
2009	I	−144.5
	II	−190.1
	III	−206.1
	IV	−49.6
2010	I	9.8
	II	48.8
	III	116.2
	IV	58.1

3.11 (Related to the Don't Let This Happen to You on page 794) Briefly explain whether you agree with the following argument: "The equilibrium level of GDP is determined by the level of aggregate expenditure. Therefore, GDP will decline only if households decide to spend less on goods and services."

3.12 (Related to Solved Problem 23.3 on page 795) Fill in the blank cells in the table below. Assume that the value of the *MPC* does not change as real GDP changes. Also assume that the values represent billions of 2009 dollars.

a. What is the value of the *MPC*?

b. What is the value of equilibrium real GDP?

Accompanies problem 3.12.

Real GDP (*Y*)	Consumption (*C*)	Planned Investment (*I*)	Government Purchases (*G*)	Net Exports (*NX*)	Planned Aggregate Expenditure (*AE*)	Unplanned Change in Inventories
$9,000	$7,600	$1,200	$1,200	−$400		
10,000	8,400	1,200	1,200	−400		
11,000		1,200	1,200	−400		
12,000		1,200	1,200	−400		
13,000		1,200	1,200	−400		

23.4 The Multiplier Effect, pages 796–803

LEARNING OBJECTIVE: Describe the multiplier effect and use the multiplier formula to calculate changes in equilibrium GDP.

Summary

Autonomous expenditure is expenditure that does not depend on the level of GDP. An autonomous change is a change in expenditure not caused by a change in income. An *induced change* is a change in aggregate expenditure caused by a change in income. An autonomous change in expenditure will cause rounds of induced changes in expenditure. Therefore, an autonomous change in expenditure will have a *multiplier effect* on equilibrium GDP. The **multiplier effect** is the process by which an increase in autonomous expenditure leads to a larger increase in real GDP. The **multiplier** is the ratio of the change in equilibrium GDP to the change in autonomous expenditure. The formula for the multiplier is:

$$\frac{1}{1 - MPC}.$$

Because of the paradox of thrift, an attempt by many individuals to increase their saving may lead to a reduction in aggregate expenditure and a recession.

Review Questions

4.1 The following graph contains two aggregate expenditure functions. Consider a movement from point A to point B and a movement from point B to point C. Which movement shows a change in *autonomous* expenditure? Which movement shows a change in *induced* expenditure? Briefly explain your answers.

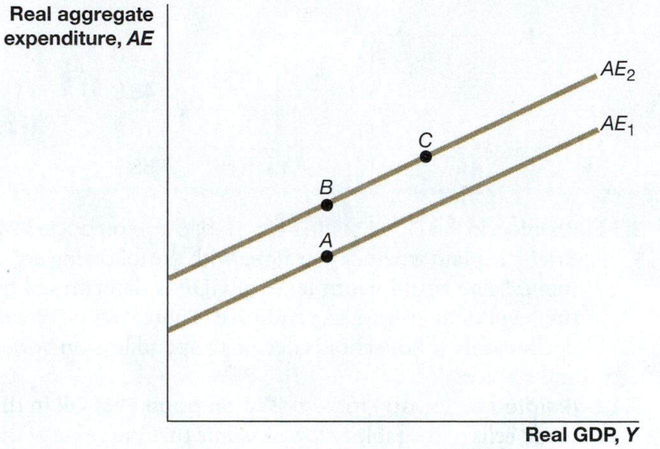

4.2 What is the multiplier effect? Use a 45°-line diagram to illustrate the multiplier effect of a decrease in government purchases.

4.3 What is the formula for the multiplier? Explain why this formula is considered to be too simple.

Problems and Applications

4.4 In Figure 23.13 on page 796, the economy is initially in equilibrium at point A. Aggregate expenditure and real GDP both equal $9.6 trillion. The increase in investment of $100 billion increases aggregate expenditure to $9.7 trillion. If real GDP increases to $9.7 trillion, will the economy be in equilibrium? Briefly explain. What happens to aggregate expenditure when real GDP increases to $9.7 trillion?

4.5 An opinion column in the *New York Times* quotes an economist's analysis of the effect of government infrastructure spending on new bridges and highways in the United States: "The investment multiplier would give a further kick to the U.S. economy."

a. What does the economist mean by the "investment multiplier"?
b. Briefly explain what the economist means by saying that the investment multiplier would "give a further kick to the U.S. economy."

Source: Thomas L. Friedman, "Why 2014 Is a Big Deal," *New York Times*, December 13, 2014.

4.6 **(Related to the Making the Connection on page 798)** If the multiplier had a value of 4 in 1929, how large must the change in autonomous expenditure have been to have caused the decline in real GDP between 1929 and 1933 shown in the table on page 799 ? If the multiplier had a value of 2, how large must the change in autonomous expenditure have been?

4.7 **(Related to Solved Problem 23.4 on page 801)** Use the information in the following table to answer the questions. Assume that the values represent billions of 2009 dollars.

Real GDP (*Y*)	Consumption (*C*)	Planned Investment (*I*)	Government Purchases (*G*)	Net Exports (*NX*)
$8,000	$7,300	$1,000	$1,000	−$500
9,000	7,900	1,000	1,000	−500
10,000	8,500	1,000	1,000	−500
11,000	9,100	1,000	1,000	−500
12,000	9,700	1,000	1,000	−500

a. What is the equilibrium level of real GDP?
b. What is the *MPC*?
c. Suppose net exports increase by $400 billion. What will be the new equilibrium level of real GDP? Use the multiplier formula to determine your answer.

4.8 An article published in an economics journal found the following: "For the poorest households, the marginal propensity to consume was close to 70%. For the richest households, the *MPC* was only 35%." Assume that the macroeconomy can be divided into three sections. Section A consists of the poorest households, Section B consists of the richest households, and Section C consists of all other households.

a. Compute the value of the multiplier for Section A.
b. Compute the value of the multiplier for Section B.
c. Assume that there was an increase in planned investment of $4 billion. Compute the change in equilibrium real GDP if the *MPC* for the economy was 70 percent (or 0.70). Compute the change in equilibrium real GDP if the *MPC* for the economy was 35 percent (or 0.35).

Source: Atif Mian and Amir Sufi, "Who Spends Extra Cash?" *House of Debt*, April 13, 2014.

4.9 Explain whether each of the following would cause the value of the multiplier to be larger or smaller.

a. An increase in real GDP increases imports.
b. An increase in real GDP increases interest rates.
c. An increase in real GDP increases the marginal propensity to consume.
d. An increase in real GDP causes the average tax rate paid by households to decrease.
e. An increase in real GDP increases the price level.

4.10 Suppose the rate of growth of the economies in the BRIC nations (Brazil, Russia, India, and China) slows down, causing U.S. net exports to fall by $75 billion. If the *MPC* is 0.8, what will be the change in equilibrium U.S. GDP?

4.11 Would a larger multiplier lead to longer and more severe recessions or shorter and less severe recessions? Briefly explain.

4.12 A study by the management consulting company McKinsey & Company recommended that the U.S. increase spending on infrastructure, such as bridges and highways, by between \$150 and \$180 billion per year. The study estimated that the result would be an increase in GDP of between \$270 billion and \$320 billion per year. What is the implied value of the multiplier if the McKinsey study's estimate of the effect of infrastructure spending on GDP is correct?

Source: David Harrison, "Nation's Crumbling Roads Put a Dent in Drivers' Wallets," *Wall Street Journal*, July 31, 2015.

4.13 Use the following graph to answer the questions.

a. What is the value of equilibrium real GDP?
b. What is the value of the *MPC*?
c. What is the value of the multiplier?
d. What is the value of unplanned changes in inventories when real GDP has each of the following values?
   i. \$10 trillion
   ii. \$12 trillion
   iii. \$14 trillion

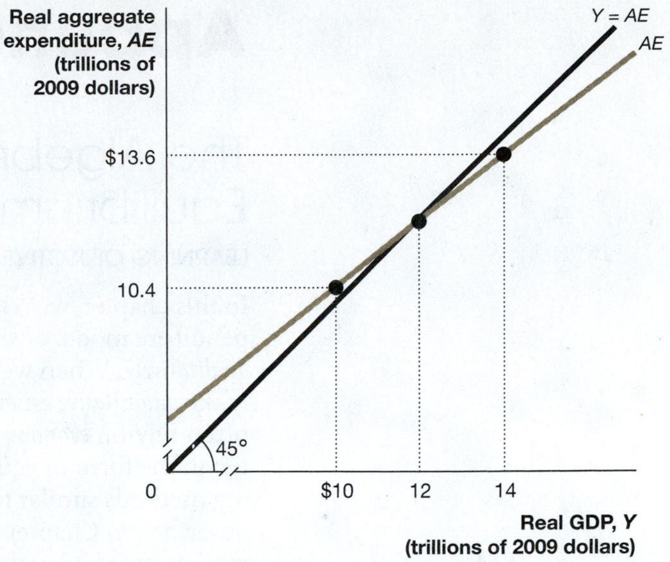

23.5 The Aggregate Demand Curve, pages 803–804

LEARNING OBJECTIVE: Understand the relationship between the aggregate demand curve and aggregate expenditure.

Summary

Increases in the price level cause a reduction in consumption, investment, and net exports. This causes the aggregate expenditure function to shift down on the 45°-line diagram, leading to a lower equilibrium real GDP. A decrease in the price level leads to a higher equilibrium real GDP. The **aggregate demand (*AD*) curve** shows the relationship between the price level and the level of aggregate expenditure, holding constant all factors other than the price level that affect aggregate expenditure.

MyEconLab Visit **www.myeconlab.com** to complete these exercises online and get instant feedback.

Review Questions

5.1 Explain the difference between aggregate expenditure and aggregate demand.

5.2 Explain which components of aggregate expenditure are affected by a change in the price level.

5.3 Does a change in the price level cause a movement along the aggregate expenditure line or a shift of the aggregate expenditure line? Does a change in the price level cause a movement along the aggregate demand curve or a shift of the aggregate demand curve?

Problems and Applications

5.4 Explain why the aggregate expenditure line is upward sloping, while the aggregate demand curve is downward sloping.

5.5 Explain whether you agree with the following statement: "The reason the aggregate demand curve slopes downward is that when the price level is higher, people cannot afford to buy as many goods and services."

5.6 Suppose that exports become more sensitive to changes in the price level in the United States. That is, when the price level in the United States rises, exports decline by more than they previously did. Will this change make the aggregate demand curve steeper or less steep? Briefly explain.

Real-Time Data Exercises

D23.1 (Calculating the multiplier effect) Using data from the Federal Reserve Bank of St. Louis (FRED) (research.stlouisfed.org/fred2/), analyze the effect of a decline in exports on GDP.

a. Download data since 1990 on Real Exports of Goods and Services (EXPGSC1).
b. What was the dollar value of the decline in real exports between the second quarter of 2008 and the first quarter of 2009? If the multiplier is 2, holding everything else constant, what was the effect of this decline in exports on real GDP?

Appendix

The Algebra of Macroeconomic Equilibrium

LEARNING OBJECTIVE: Apply the algebra of macroeconomic equilibrium.

In this chapter, we relied primarily on graphs and tables to illustrate the aggregate expenditure model of short-run real GDP. Graphs help us understand economic change *qualitatively*. When we write an economic model using equations, we make it easier to make *quantitative estimates*. When economists forecast future movements in GDP, they often rely on *econometric models*. An econometric model is an economic model written in the form of equations, where each equation has been statistically estimated using methods similar to the methods used in estimating demand curves that we briefly described in Chapter 3. We can use equations to represent the aggregate expenditure model described in this chapter.

The following equations are based on the example shown in Table 23.3 on page 794. Y stands for real GDP, and the numbers (with the exception of the *MPC*) represent billions of dollars.

1. $C = 1{,}000 + 0.65Y$	Consumption function
2. $I = 1{,}500$	Planned investment function
3. $G = 1{,}500$	Government purchases function
4. $NX = -500$	Net export function
5. $Y = C + I + G + NX$	Equilibrium condition

The first equation is the consumption function. The *MPC* is 0.65, and 1,000 is autonomous consumption, which is the level of consumption that does not depend on income. If we think of the consumption function as a line on the 45°-line diagram, 1,000 would be the intercept, and 0.65 would be the slope. The "functions" for the other three components of planned aggregate expenditure are very simple because we have assumed that these components are not affected by GDP and, therefore, are constant. Economists who use this type of model to forecast GDP would, of course, use more realistic investment, government, and net export functions. The *parameters* of the functions—such as the value of autonomous consumption and the value of the *MPC* in the consumption function—would be estimated statistically, using data on the values of each variable over a period of years.

In this model, GDP is in equilibrium when it equals planned aggregate expenditure. Equation 5—the equilibrium condition—shows us how to calculate equilibrium in the model: We need to substitute equations 1 through 4 into equation 5. Doing so gives us the following:

$$Y = 1{,}000 + 0.65Y + 1{,}500 + 1{,}500 - 500.$$

We need to solve this expression for Y to find equilibrium GDP. The first step is to subtract $0.65Y$ from both sides of the equation:

$$Y - 0.65Y = 1{,}000 + 1{,}500 + 1{,}500 - 500.$$

Then, we solve for Y:

$$0.35Y = 3{,}500.$$

Or:

$$Y = \frac{3{,}500}{0.35} = 10{,}000.$$

To make this result more general, we can replace particular values with general values represented by letters:

1. $C = \overline{C} + MPC(Y)$	Consumption function
2. $I = \overline{I}$	Planned investment function
3. $G = \overline{G}$	Government purchases function
4. $NX = \overline{NX}$	Net export function
5. $Y = C + I + G + NX$	Equilibrium condition

The letters with bars over them represent fixed, or autonomous, values. So, for example, $\overline{C}$ represents autonomous consumption, which had a value of 1,000 in our original example. Now, solving for equilibrium, we get:

$$Y = \overline{C} + MPC(Y) + \overline{I} + \overline{G} + \overline{NX},$$

or:

$$Y - MPC(Y) = \overline{C} + \overline{I} + \overline{G} + \overline{NX},$$

or:

$$Y(1 - MPC) = \overline{C} + \overline{I} + \overline{G} + \overline{NX},$$

or:

$$Y = \frac{\overline{C} + \overline{I} + \overline{G} + \overline{NX}}{1 - MPC}.$$

Remember that $1/(1 - MPC)$ is the multiplier, and all four variables in the numerator of the equation represent autonomous expenditure. Therefore, an alternative expression for equilibrium GDP is:

Equilibrium GDP = Autonomous expenditure × Multiplier.

MyEconLab Concept Check

23A The Algebra of Macroeconomic Equilibrium, pages 812–813

LEARNING OBJECTIVE: Apply the algebra of macroeconomic equilibrium.

MyEconLab Visit **www.myeconlab.com** to complete these exercises online and get instant feedback.

Review Questions

23A.1 Write a general expression for the aggregate expenditure function. If you think of the aggregate expenditure function as a line on the 45°-line diagram, what would be the intercept and what would be the slope, using the general values represented by letters?

23A.2 Find equilibrium GDP using the following macroeconomic model (where the numbers, with the exception of the *MPC*, represent billions of dollars).

1. $C = 1{,}500 + 0.75Y$	Consumption function
2. $I = 1{,}250$	Planned investment function
3. $G = 1{,}250$	Government purchases function
4. $NX = -250$	Net export function
5. $Y = C + I + G + NX$	Equilibrium condition

23A.3 For the macroeconomic model in problem 23A.2, write the aggregate expenditure function. For GDP of $16,000, what is the value of aggregate expenditure, and what is the value of the unintended change in inventories? For GDP of $12,000, what is the value of aggregate expenditure, and what is the value of the unintended change in inventories?

23A.4 Suppose that autonomous consumption is 500, government purchases are 1,000, planned investment spending is 1,250, net exports are −250, and the *MPC* is 0.8. What is equilibrium GDP?

CHAPTER

24

Aggregate Demand and Aggregate Supply Analysis

Chapter Outline and Learning Objectives

The Fortunes of Delta Airlines Follow the Business Cycle

An infestation of insects that threatened cotton fields in Southern states led B. R. Coad and Collett E. Woolman to form a crop-dusting business, the Huff Daland Dusters, in 1924. By 1930 the company was renamed the Delta Air Corporation and offered airmail and passenger service. Delta Air Lines has grown into the world's largest airline, flying over 170 million passengers to more than 300 destinations worldwide in 2015 and earning revenue of more than $40 billion.

Despite Delta's long-run success, its fortunes and the fortunes of the other U.S. airlines are dependent on the ups and downs of the business cycle. As a *Wall Street Journal* article put it: "Year after year, domestic revenue came in at 0.73% of GDP." That relationship is good news during economic expansions, when GDP is increasing, but it's bad news during recessions, when GDP is falling. During the severe 2007–2009 recession, Delta both sold fewer passenger tickets and had to cut the prices of the tickets it did sell. The result was a $1.2 billion loss in 2009.

By 2015, with GDP steadily growing during the economic expansion, Delta was earning a record profit as both the number of passengers flown and ticket prices were increasing. Delta was also benefiting from falling jet fuel prices as increased output from U.S. shale oil fields led to a worldwide decline in oil prices. Many business analysts consider Delta to be the best managed of the four large U.S. airlines—the other three being Southwest, American Airlines, and United. Still, Delta management was taking steps to reduce the problems the airline would experience when—inevitably—the next recession occurred. Domestically, Delta was attempting to reduce costs by "upgauging," or adding seats to existing planes and replacing small planes with larger planes. Internationally, Delta continued a strategy of buying partial ownership of foreign airlines. In 2015, it purchased part of China Eastern Airlines. Under terms of the deal, the two airlines would list each other's flights on their reservation systems and share some facilities at Chinese airports. By expanding overseas, Delta was not only participating in rapidly growing markets but also insulating itself to some extent from the fluctuations of the U.S. business cycle.

To better understand how the business cycle affects Delta Air Lines and other firms, we need to explore the effects that recessions and expansions have on production, employment, and prices.

Sources: Susan Carey, "Delta Air Lines to Buy China Eastern Stake for $450 Million," *Wall Street Journal*, July 27, 2015; Bob McAdoo and Scott Buck, "American Airlines Shares Have Over 70% Upside," barrons.com, July 27, 2015; Susan Carey, "Airline Industry Sees Pain Extending Beyond the Recession," *Wall Street Journal*, August 17, 2009; and Delta Air Lines, "Earnings Releases," various dates.

Economics in Your Life

Is an Employer Likely to Cut Your Pay during a Recession?

Suppose that you have worked as a barista for a local coffeehouse for two years. From on-the-job training and experience, you have honed your coffee-making skills and mastered the perfect latte. Then the economy moves into a recession, and sales at the coffeehouse decline. Is the owner of the coffeehouse likely to cut the prices of lattes and other drinks? Suppose the owner asks to meet with you to discuss your wages for next year. Is the owner likely to cut your pay? As you read this chapter, try to answer these questions. You can check your answers against those we provide on **page 843** at the end of this chapter.

We have seen that the U.S. economy has experienced a long-run upward trend in real GDP. These increases in real GDP have raised the standard of living in the United States to a level much higher today than it was 100 years ago. In the short run, however, real GDP fluctuates around this long-run upward trend because of the business cycle. Fluctuations in GDP lead to fluctuations in employment. These fluctuations in real GDP and employment are the most visible and dramatic part of the business cycle. During recessions, we are more likely to see factories close, small businesses declare bankruptcy, and workers lose their jobs. During expansions, we are more likely to see new businesses open and new jobs created. In addition to these changes in output and employment, the business cycle causes changes in wages and prices. Some firms react to a decline in sales by cutting back on production, but they may also cut the prices they charge and the wages they pay. Other firms respond to a recession by raising prices and workers' wages by less than they otherwise would have.

In this chapter, we expand our discussion of the business cycle by developing the aggregate demand and aggregate supply model. This model will help us analyze the effects of recessions and expansions on production, employment, and prices.

24.1 Aggregate Demand

LEARNING OBJECTIVE: Identify the determinants of aggregate demand and distinguish between a movement along the aggregate demand curve and a shift of the curve.

Aggregate demand and aggregate supply model A model that explains short-run fluctuations in real GDP and the price level.

Aggregate demand (*AD*) curve A curve that shows the relationship between the price level and the quantity of real GDP demanded by households, firms, and the government.

Short-run aggregate supply (*SRAS*) curve A curve that shows the relationship in the short run between the price level and the quantity of real GDP supplied by firms.

To understand what happens during the business cycle, we need an explanation of why real GDP, the unemployment rate, and the inflation rate fluctuate. We have already seen that fluctuations in the unemployment rate are caused mainly by fluctuations in real GDP. In this chapter, we use the **aggregate demand and aggregate supply model** to explain short-run fluctuations in real GDP and the price level. As Figure 24.1 shows, real GDP and the price level in this model are determined in the short run by the intersection of the *aggregate demand curve* and the *aggregate supply curve*. Fluctuations in real GDP and the price level are caused by shifts in the aggregate demand curve or in the aggregate supply curve.

The **aggregate demand (*AD*) curve** shows the relationship between the price level and the quantity of real GDP demanded by households, firms, and the government. The **short-run aggregate supply (*SRAS*) curve** shows the relationship in the short run between the price level and the quantity of real GDP supplied by firms. The aggregate demand and short-run aggregate supply curves in Figure 24.1 look similar to the individual market demand and supply curves we studied in Chapter 3. However, because these curves apply to the whole economy, rather than to just a single market, the aggregate demand and aggregate supply model is very different from the model of demand and supply in individual markets. Because we are dealing with the economy as a whole, we need *macroeconomic* explanations of why the aggregate demand curve is downward sloping, why the short-run aggregate supply curve is upward sloping, and why the curves shift. We begin by explaining why the aggregate demand curve is downward sloping.

Why Is the Aggregate Demand Curve Downward Sloping?

We have seen that GDP has four components:

- Consumption (*C*)
- Investment (*I*)
- Government purchases (*G*)
- Net exports (*NX*)

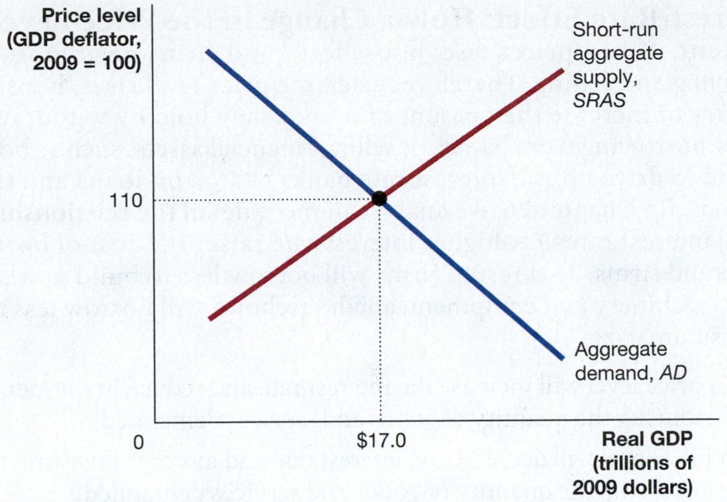

MyEconLab Animation

Figure 24.1 Aggregate Demand and Aggregate Supply

In the short run, real GDP and the price level are determined by the intersection of the aggregate demand curve and the short-run aggregate supply curve. In the figure, real GDP is measured on the horizontal axis, and the price level is measured on the vertical axis by the GDP deflator. In this example, the equilibrium real GDP is $17.0 trillion, and the equilibrium price level is 110.

If we let Y stand for GDP, we have the following relationship:

$$Y = C + I + G + NX.$$

The aggregate demand curve is downward sloping because a fall in the price level increases the quantity of real GDP demanded. To understand why, we need to look at how changes in the price level affect each component of aggregate demand. We begin with the assumption that government purchases are determined by the policy decisions of lawmakers and are not affected by changes in the price level. We can then consider the effect of changes in the price level on the three other components: consumption, investment, and net exports.

The Wealth Effect: How a Change in the Price Level Affects Consumption Current income is the most important variable determining consumption by households. As income rises, consumption will rise, and as income falls, consumption will fall. But consumption also depends on household wealth, which is the difference between the value of a household's assets and the value of its debts. Consider two households, both with incomes of $80,000 per year. The first household has wealth of $5 million, and the second household has wealth of $50,000. The first household is likely to spend more of its income than the second household. So, as total household wealth rises, consumption will rise. Some household wealth is held in cash or other *nominal assets* that lose value as the price level rises and gain value as the price level falls. For instance, if you have $10,000 in cash, a 10 percent increase in the price level will reduce the purchasing power of that cash by 10 percent. When the price level rises, the *real value* of household wealth declines, and so will consumption, thereby reducing the demand for goods and services. When the price level falls, the real value of household wealth rises, and so will consumption and the demand for goods and services. The effect of the price level on consumption is called the *wealth effect*, and it is one reason the aggregate demand curve is downward sloping.

The Interest-Rate Effect: How a Change in the Price Level Affects Investment When prices rise, households and firms need more money to finance buying and selling. Therefore, when the price level rises, households and firms will try to increase the amount of money they hold by withdrawing funds from banks, borrowing from banks, or selling financial assets, such as bonds. These actions tend to drive up the interest rate banks charge on loans and the interest rate on bonds. (In Chapter 26, we analyze in more detail the relationship between money and interest rates.) A higher interest rate raises the cost of borrowing for households and firms. As a result, firms will borrow less to build new factories or install new machinery and equipment, and households will borrow less to buy new houses. To summarize:

- A higher price level will increase the interest rate and reduce investment spending, thereby reducing the quantity of goods and services demanded.
- A lower price level will decrease the interest rate and increase investment spending, thereby increasing the quantity of goods and services demanded.

To a smaller extent, consumption will also fall when the interest rate rises as households borrow less to finance spending on automobiles, furniture, and other durable goods.

The effect of the price level on investment and consumption is known as the *interest-rate effect*, and it is a second reason the aggregate demand curve is downward sloping.

The International-Trade Effect: How a Change in the Price Level Affects Net Exports *Net exports* equals spending by foreign households and firms on goods and services produced in the United States minus spending by U.S. households and firms on goods and services produced in other countries. If the price level in the United States rises relative to the price levels in other countries, U.S. exports will become relatively more expensive, and foreign imports will become relatively less expensive. Some consumers in foreign countries will shift from buying U.S. products to buying domestic products, and some U.S. consumers will also shift from buying U.S. products to buying imported products. U.S. exports will fall and U.S. imports will rise, causing net exports to fall, thereby reducing the quantity of goods and services demanded. A lower price level in the United States relative to other countries has the reverse effect, causing net exports to rise, thereby increasing the quantity of goods and services demanded. The effect of the price level on net exports is known as the *international-trade effect*, and it is a third reason the aggregate demand curve is downward sloping. MyEconLab Concept Check

Shifts of the Aggregate Demand Curve versus Movements along It

An important point to remember is that the aggregate demand curve tells us the relationship between the price level and the quantity of real GDP demanded, *holding everything else constant*. If the price level changes but other variables that affect the willingness of households, firms, and the government to spend are unchanged, the result is a movement up or down a stationary aggregate demand curve. If any variable other than the price level changes, the aggregate demand curve will shift. For example, if government purchases increase and the price level remains unchanged, the aggregate demand curve will shift to the right at every price level. Or, if firms become pessimistic about the future profitability of investment and cut back spending on factories and machinery, the aggregate demand curve will shift to the left. MyEconLab Concept Check

The Variables That Shift the Aggregate Demand Curve

The variables that cause the aggregate demand curve to shift fall into three categories:

1. Changes in government policies
2. Changes in the expectations of households and firms
3. Changes in foreign variables

Changes in Government Policies As we will discuss further in Chapters 26 and 27, the federal government uses monetary policy and fiscal policy to shift the aggregate demand curve. **Monetary policy** is the actions the Federal Reserve—the nation's central bank—takes to manage the money supply and interest rates and to ensure the flow of funds from lenders to borrowers. The Federal Reserve takes these actions to achieve macroeconomic policy objectives, such as high employment, price stability, high rates of economic growth, and stability of the financial system. For example, the Federal Reserve can lower the cost to firms and households of borrowing by taking actions that reduce interest rates. Lower borrowing costs increase consumption and investment spending, which shifts the aggregate demand curve to the right. Higher interest rates shift the aggregate demand curve to the left.

Monetary policy The actions the Federal Reserve takes to manage the money supply and interest rates to achieve macroeconomic policy objectives.

Fiscal policy is the changes in federal taxes and purchases that are intended to achieve macroeconomic policy objectives. Because government purchases are one component of aggregate demand:

Fiscal policy Changes in federal taxes and purchases that are intended to achieve macroeconomic policy objectives.

- An increase in *government purchases* shifts the aggregate demand curve to the right, and a decrease in government purchases shifts the aggregate demand curve to the left.
- An increase in *personal income taxes* reduces the amount of spendable income available to households, which reduces consumption spending and shifts the aggregate demand curve to the left. A decrease in personal income taxes shifts the aggregate demand curve to the right.
- An increase in *business taxes* reduces the profitability of investment spending and shifts the aggregate demand curve to the left. A decrease in business taxes shifts the aggregate demand curve to the right.

Changes in the Expectations of Households and Firms If households become more optimistic about their future incomes, they are likely to increase their current consumption. This increased consumption will shift the aggregate demand curve to the right. If households become more pessimistic about their future incomes, the aggregate demand curve will shift to the left. Similarly, if firms become more optimistic about the future profitability of investment spending, the aggregate demand curve will shift to the right. If firms become more pessimistic, the aggregate demand curve will shift to the left.

Don't Let This Happen to You

Understand Why the Aggregate Demand Curve Is Downward Sloping

The aggregate demand curve and the demand curve for a single product are both downward sloping—but for different reasons. When we draw a demand curve for a single product, such as apples, we know that it will slope downward because as the price of apples rises, apples become more expensive relative to other products—such as oranges—and consumers will buy fewer apples and more of the other products. In other words, consumers substitute other products for apples. When the overall price level rises, the prices of all domestically produced goods and services are rising, so consumers have no other domestic products to which they can switch. The aggregate demand curve slopes downward because a higher price level:

- Reduces the real value of household wealth, which decreases consumption
- Raises interest rates, which decreases investment and consumption
- Makes U.S. exports more expensive and foreign imports less expensive, which decreases net exports

MyEconLab Study Plan

Your Turn: Test your understanding by doing related problem 1.8 on pages 844–845 at the end of this chapter.

Changes in Foreign Variables If households and firms in other countries buy fewer U.S. goods or if households and firms in the United States buy more foreign goods, net exports will fall, and the aggregate demand curve will shift to the left. When real GDP increases, so does the income available for consumers to spend. If real GDP in the United States increases faster than real GDP in other countries, U.S. imports will increase faster than U.S. exports, and net exports will fall. Net exports will also fall if the *exchange rate* between the dollar and foreign currencies rises because the price in foreign currency of U.S. products sold in other countries will rise, and the dollar price of foreign products sold in the United States will fall. For example, if the current exchange rate between the dollar and the euro is $1 = €1 then:

- A $20 Blu-ray disc exported from the United States to France will cost €20 in France.
- A €50 bottle of wine exported from France will cost $50 in the United States.

But if the exchange rate rises to $1 = €1.50 then:

- The disc's price will rise from €20 to €30 in France, causing its sales to decline.
- The price of the French wine will fall from $50 to $33.33 per bottle in the United States, causing its sales to increase.

As a result, U.S. exports will fall, U.S. imports will rise, and the aggregate demand curve will shift to the left.

An increase in net exports at every price level will shift the aggregate demand curve to the right. Net exports will increase if real GDP grows more slowly in the United States than in other countries or if the value of the dollar falls against other currencies. A change in net exports that results from a change in the price level in the United States will result in a movement along the aggregate demand curve, *not* a shift of the aggregate demand curve.

MyEconLab Concept Check

Solved Problem 24.1

MyEconLab Interactive Animation

Movements along the Aggregate Demand Curve versus Shifts of the Aggregate Demand Curve

Germany, along with 18 other countries in Europe, uses the euro as its currency. According to an article in the *Wall Street Journal*, in 2014 German net exports rose to "€217 billion ($246 billion), shattering the previous record of €195.3 billion set in 2007." The story quoted an economist working for a German bank as saying, "I think that due to the weaker euro we should get stronger exports."

a. At the time this article was written, what was the exchange rate between the U.S. dollar and the euro?

b. What does the economist mean by a "weaker euro"?

c. Why would a weaker euro cause an increase in German net exports?

d. Briefly explain whether a weaker euro will cause a shift in the aggregate demand curve of the German economy or a movement along the aggregate demand curve. Illustrate your answer with a graph.

Solving the Problem

Step 1: Review the chapter material. This problem is about understanding the difference between movements along an aggregate demand curve and shifts of an aggregate demand curve, so you may want to review the section "Shifts of the Aggregate Demand Curve versus Movements along It," and the section "The Variables that Shift the Aggregate Demand Curve," which both begin on page 818.

Step 2: Answer part (a) by calculating the exchange rate between the euro and the U.S. dollar at the time the article was written. If €217 billion was the equivalent of \$246 billion at the time the article was written, then the exchange rate must have been \$246 billion/€217 billion = \$1.13 dollars per euro, or \$1 = €0.88.

Step 3: Answer part (b) by explaining what the economist meant by a "weaker euro." A weaker euro means an exchange rate such that a dollar (or a unit of another foreign currency) would buy more euros, or, equivalently, a euro would buy fewer dollars (or units of another foreign currency).

Step 4: Answer part (c) by explaining why a weaker euro would cause an increase in German net exports. If it takes fewer dollars to buy German goods priced in euros, then U.S. consumers will buy more of them, increasing German exports. If it takes more euros to buy U.S. goods priced in dollars, then German consumers will buy fewer of them, decreasing German imports. We can apply similar reasoning to the products of other countries outside the eurozone. So we would expect that a weaker euro will result in an increase in German net exports.

Step 5: Answer part (d) by explaining whether a weaker euro would cause a shift in the aggregate demand curve for the German economy or a movement along it and by drawing a graph to illustrate your answer. Only changes in the price level in Germany will cause a movement along the aggregate demand curve for the German economy. Although a decline in the value of the euro affects the prices of exports from Germany and imports to Germany, it doesn't directly affect the price level in Germany. By increasing German net exports, the weaker euro will cause the aggregate demand curve for the German economy to shift to the right at every price level, as shown in the following graph:

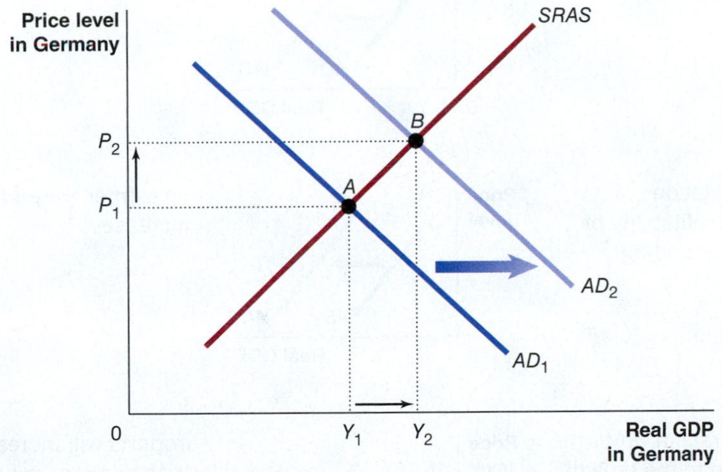

Source: Todd Buell and Bertrand Benoit, "Germany Enjoys Record Year for Trade," *Wall Street Journal*, February 9, 2015.

Your Turn: For more practice, do related problems 1.9 and 1.10 on page 845 at the end of this chapter.

MyEconLab Study Plan

Table 24.1 summarizes the most important variables that cause the aggregate demand curve to shift. The table shows the shift in the aggregate demand curve that results from an increase in each of the variables. A *decrease* in these variables will cause the aggregate demand curve to shift in the opposite direction.

Table 24.1

Variables That Shift the Aggregate Demand Curve

<table>
<tr><th>An increase in . . .</th><th>shifts the aggregate demand curve . . .</th><th>because . . .</th></tr>
<tr><td>interest rates</td><td>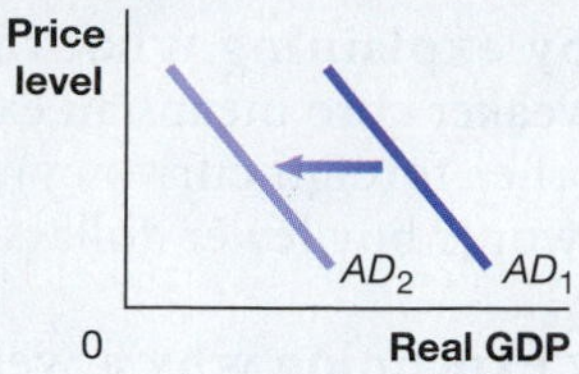</td><td>higher interest rates raise the cost to households and firms of borrowing, reducing consumption and investment spending.</td></tr>
<tr><td>government purchases</td><td>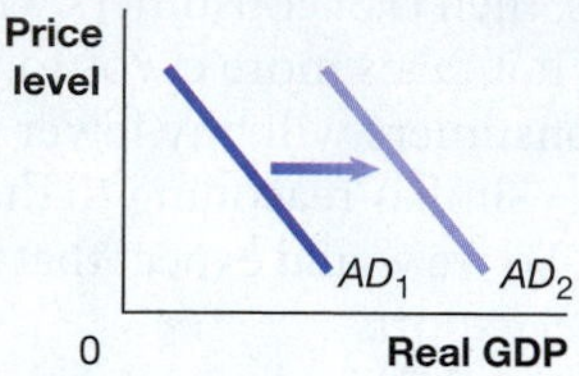</td><td>government purchases are a component of aggregate demand.</td></tr>
<tr><td>personal income taxes or business taxes</td><td>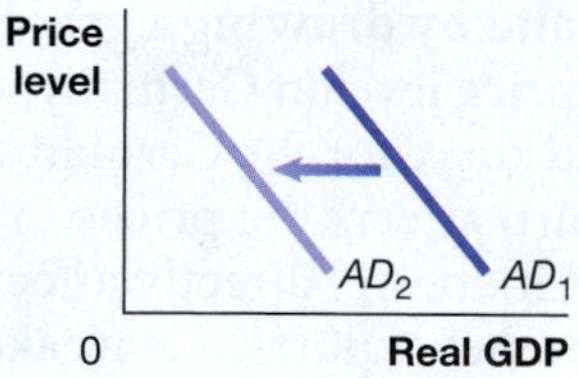</td><td>consumption spending falls when personal taxes rise, and investment falls when business taxes rise.</td></tr>
<tr><td>households' expectations of their future incomes</td><td>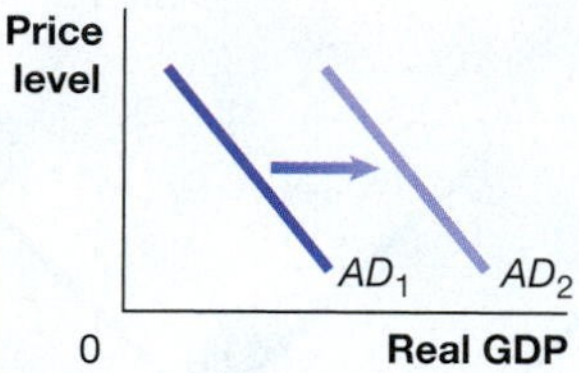</td><td>consumption spending increases.</td></tr>
<tr><td>firms' expectations of the future profitability of investment spending</td><td>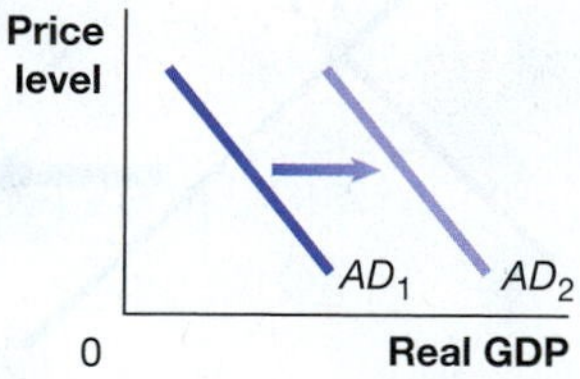</td><td>investment spending increases.</td></tr>
<tr><td>the growth rate of domestic GDP relative to the growth rate of foreign GDP</td><td>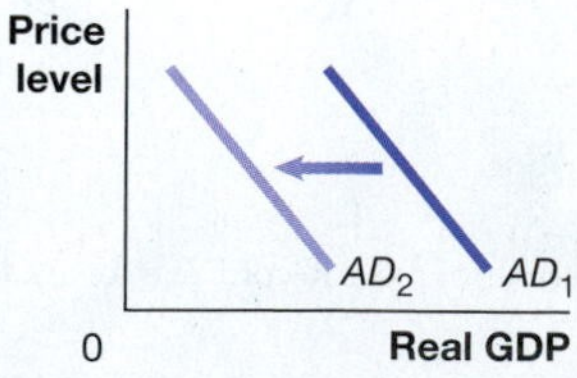</td><td>imports will increase faster than exports, reducing net exports.</td></tr>
<tr><td>the exchange rate (the value of the dollar) relative to foreign currencies</td><td>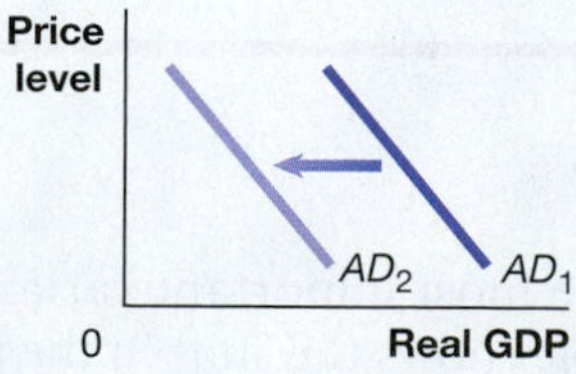</td><td>imports will rise and exports will fall, reducing net exports.</td></tr>
</table>

Making the Connection

MyEconLab Video

Which Components of Aggregate Demand Changed the Most during the 2007–2009 Recession?

The recession of 2007–2009 was the longest and most severe since the Great Depression of the 1930s. We can better understand what happened during the 2007–2009 recession by looking at changes over time in the components of aggregate demand. In the following graphs, we show changes in the three components of aggregate demand that had the largest movements between the first quarter of 2005 and the second quarter of 2015: consumption, residential investment spending on new homes and apartments, and net exports. The shaded area represents the 2007–2009 recession. We know that potential GDP, or the level of GDP when all firms are producing at capacity, grows over time. So, economists are often interested in measuring changes in the components of aggregate demand *relative to potential GDP*, which is what we have done in these graphs.

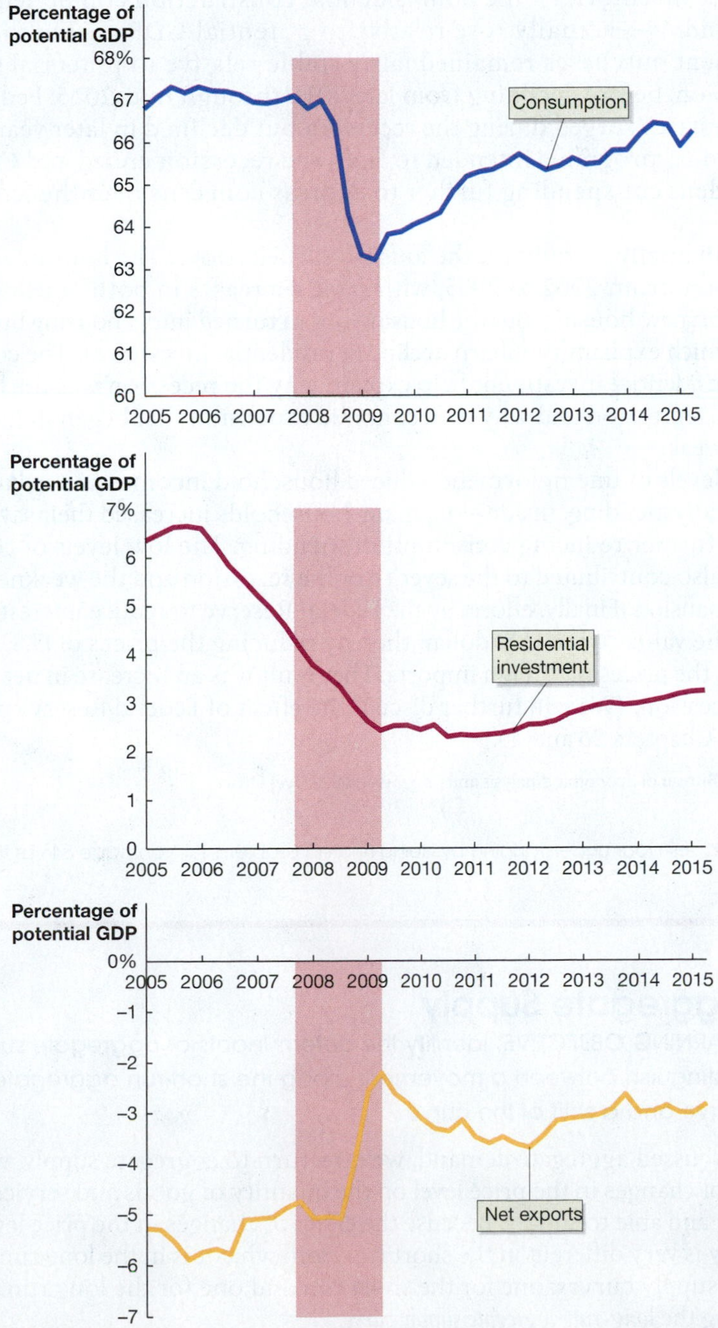

MyEconLab Real-time data

The graphs illustrate a number of facts about the 2007–2009 recession:

- In the two years before the beginning of the recession, spending on residential investment had already declined significantly relative to potential GDP.
- For the first two years following the end of the recession, spending on residential investment did not increase relative to potential GDP. Beginning in late 2011, spending on residential investment began to increase slowly, but in mid-2015, it was still far below its 2005–2006 level.
- Consumption, which usually remains relatively stable during a recession, declined significantly relative to potential GDP during the recession and had still not quite regained its 2007 level six years after the recession had ended.
- Net exports increased during the recession. (Because net exports was negative throughout this period, it increased by becoming a smaller negative number.)

Although not shown in the graphs, business fixed investment and changes in business inventories—the nonresidential construction components of investment spending—actually rose relative to potential GDP during the recession. Government purchases remained fairly stable relative to potential GDP during the recession, before declining from late 2010 through mid-2015. Federal government purchases surged during the recession but declined in later years as temporary spending programs intended to fight the recession ended and Congress and the president cut spending further to address concerns over the federal budget deficit.

We can briefly account for the four facts listed above. The housing sector underwent a boom from 2002 to 2005, with rapid increases in both housing prices and spending on new housing. But the housing boom turned into a housing bust beginning in 2006, which explains the sharp decline in residential investment. The continued low levels of residential investment help explain why the recession was the longest since the Great Depression and why the economic expansion that began in June 2009 was relatively weak.

High levels of unemployment reduced household incomes and led to declines in consumption spending. In addition, many households increased their saving and paid off debts, further reducing consumption spending. The low levels of consumption spending also contributed to the severity of the recession and the weakness of the following expansion. Finally, efforts by the Federal Reserve to reduce interest rates helped to lower the value of the U.S. dollar, thereby reducing the prices of U.S. exports and increasing the prices of foreign imports. The result was an increase in net exports during the recession. (We will further discuss the effect of Federal Reserve policy on net exports in Chapters 26 and 29.)

Sources: U.S. Bureau of Economic Analysis and Congressional Budget Office.

MyEconLab Study Plan

Your Turn: Test your understanding by doing related problem 1.11 on page 845 at the end of this chapter.

24.2 Aggregate Supply

LEARNING OBJECTIVE: Identify the determinants of aggregate supply and distinguish between a movement along the short-run aggregate supply curve and a shift of the curve.

Having discussed aggregate demand, we now turn to aggregate supply, which shows the effect of changes in the price level on the quantity of goods and services that firms are willing and able to supply. Because the effect of changes in the price level on aggregate supply is very different in the short run from what it is in the long run, we use two aggregate supply curves: one for the short run and one for the long run. We start by considering the *long-run aggregate supply curve*.

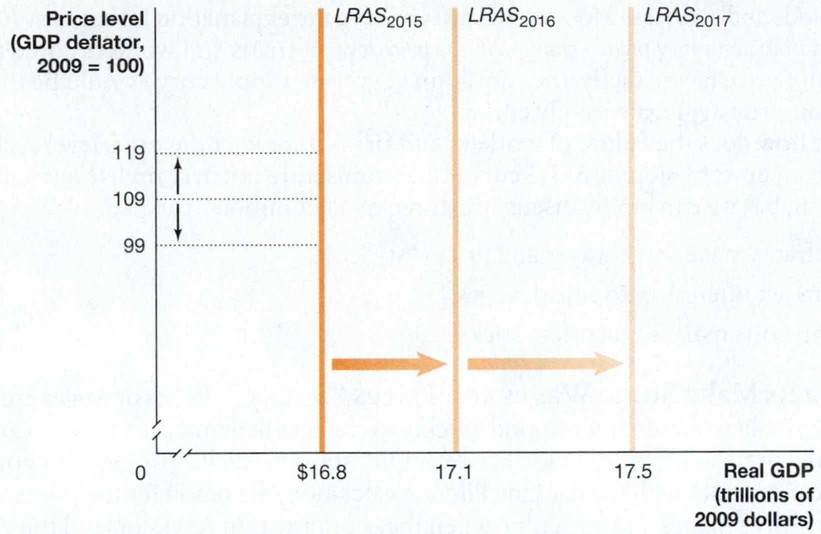

MyEconLab Animation

Figure 24.2

The Long-Run Aggregate Supply Curve

Changes in the price level do not affect the level of aggregate supply in the long run. Therefore, the long-run aggregate supply (*LRAS*) curve is a vertical line at the potential level of real GDP. For instance, the price level was 109 in 2015, and potential GDP was \$16.8 trillion. If the price level had been 119, or if it had been 99, long-run aggregate supply would still have been a constant \$16.8 trillion. Each year, the long-run aggregate supply curve shifts to the right, as the number of workers in the economy increases, more machinery and equipment are accumulated, and technological change occurs.

The Long-Run Aggregate Supply Curve

In the long run, the level of real GDP is determined by the number of workers, the *capital stock*—including factories, office buildings, and machinery and equipment—and the available technology (see Chapter 22). Because changes in the price level do not affect the number of workers, the capital stock, or technology, *in the long run, changes in the price level do not affect the level of real GDP*. Remember that the level of real GDP in the long run is called *potential GDP*, or *full-employment GDP*. At potential GDP, firms will operate at their normal level of capacity, and everyone who wants a job will have one, except the structurally and frictionally unemployed. There is no reason for this normal level of capacity to change just because the price level has changed. The **long-run aggregate supply (*LRAS*) curve** shows the relationship in the long run between the price level and the quantity of real GDP supplied. As Figure 24.2 shows, in 2015, the price level was 109, and potential GDP was \$16.8 trillion. If the price level had been 119, or if it had been 99, long-run aggregate supply would still have been a constant \$16.8 trillion. Therefore, the *LRAS* curve is a vertical line.

Long-run aggregate supply (*LRAS*) curve A curve that shows the relationship in the long run between the price level and the quantity of real GDP supplied.

Figure 24.2 also shows that the long-run aggregate supply curve shifts to the right each year. This shift occurs because potential GDP increases each year, as (1) the number of workers in the economy increases, (2) the economy accumulates more machinery and equipment, and (3) technological change occurs. Figure 24.2 shows potential GDP increasing from \$16.8 trillion in 2015 to \$17.1 trillion in 2016 and to \$17.5 trillion in 2017.

MyEconLab Concept Check

The Short-Run Aggregate Supply Curve

While the *LRAS* curve is vertical, the *SRAS* curve is upward sloping because, over the short run, as the price level increases, the quantity of goods and services firms are willing to supply will increase. Firms supply more goods and services as the price level increases for two key reasons:

1. As prices of final goods and services rise, prices of inputs—such as the wages of workers or the price of natural resources—rise more slowly. Profits rise when the prices of goods and services firms sell rise more rapidly than the prices they pay for inputs. Therefore, a higher price level leads to higher profits and increases the willingness of firms to supply more goods and services.
2. As the price level rises, some firms are slow to adjust their prices. A firm that is slow to raise its prices when the price level is increasing may find its sales increasing and, therefore, will increase production.

Why do some firms adjust prices more slowly than others, and why might the wages of workers and the prices of other inputs change more slowly than the prices of final goods and services? Most economists believe the explanation is that *some firms and workers fail to accurately predict changes in the price level*. If firms and workers could predict the future price level exactly, the short-run aggregate supply curve would be the same as the long-run aggregate supply curve.

But how does the failure of workers and firms to predict the price level accurately result in an upward-sloping *SRAS* curve? Economists are not in complete agreement on this point, but we can briefly discuss the three most common explanations:

1. Contracts make some wages and prices "sticky."
2. Firms are often slow to adjust wages.
3. Menu costs make some prices sticky.

Contracts Make Some Wages and Prices "Sticky" Prices or wages are said to be "sticky" when they do not respond quickly to changes in demand or supply. Contracts can make wages or prices sticky. For example, suppose Delta Air Lines negotiates a three-year contract with the Air Line Pilots Association, the union for the pilots who fly the company's planes, during a time when the economy is in recession and the number of passenger tickets being sold is falling. Suppose that after the union signs the contract, the economy begins to expand rapidly, and the number of tickets sold increases, so that Delta can raise ticket prices. Delta will find that flying more passengers will be profitable because the prices it charges are rising, while the wages it pays its pilots are fixed by contract. Or a steel mill might sign a multiyear contract to buy coal, which is used in making steel, at a time when the demand for steel is falling. If demand for steel and steel prices begin to rise rapidly, producing additional steel will be profitable because coal prices will remain fixed by contract. In both of these cases, rising prices lead to higher output. If these examples are representative of enough firms in the economy, a rising price level should lead to a greater quantity of goods and services supplied. In other words, the short-run aggregate supply curve will be upward sloping.

Notice, though, that if the pilots working for Delta or the managers of the coal companies had accurately predicted what would happen to prices, this prediction would have been reflected in the contracts, and Delta and the steel mill would not have earned greater profits when prices rose. In that case, rising prices would not have led to higher output.

Firms Are Often Slow to Adjust Wages We just noted that the wages of many union workers remain fixed by contract for several years. Many nonunion workers have their wages or salaries adjusted only once a year. Suppose you accept a job at a management consulting firm in June, at a salary of $45,000 per year. The firm probably will not adjust your salary until the following June, even if the prices it can charge for its services later in the year are higher or lower than the firm had expected them to be when it hired you. If firms are slow to adjust wages, a rise in the price level will increase the profitability of hiring more workers and producing more output. A fall in the price level will decrease the profitability of hiring more workers and producing more output. Once again, we have an explanation for why the short-run aggregate supply curve slopes upward.

Firms are often slower to *cut* wages than to increase them. Cutting wages can have a negative effect on the morale and productivity of workers and can also cause some of a firm's best workers to quit and look for jobs elsewhere.

Making the Connection

MyEconLab Video

How Sticky Are Wages?

When we discussed the model of demand and supply in Chapter 3, we assumed that if the demand curve or supply curve for a product shifted, the price would adjust quickly from the old equilibrium to the new equilibrium. As we have just discussed, though, many economists argue that at least some wages and prices are sticky and do *not* adjust quickly to changes in demand or supply. Other economists argue that stickiness in wages and prices is not widespread enough to be important in macroeconomic analysis. In other words, these economists believe that the aggregate supply curve may be vertical in the short run, as well as in the long run.

Recently, a number of economists have examined the evidence for wage stickiness. Each month, the Bureau of Labor Statistics (BLS) collects data on average hourly earnings for all workers and for various subcategories of workers, such as workers in manufacturing. Using these data is not the best way to measure wage stickiness, though, because each of the BLS categories contains many workers. As a result, the average hourly earnings data the BLS reports represent the average change in wages but do not show how many workers received wage increases, wage decreases, or unchanged wages or how large those changes may have been. To better understand how frequently employers change wages, economists have looked instead at data on individual workers.

Separate studies of data on individual workers have arrived at similar results. One important result from these studies is that during a recession, firms are much more likely to reduce wages offered to newly hired workers than to reduce wages paid to current workers in the same job. For example, Mary C. Daly, Bart Hobijn, and Timothy Ni of the Federal Reserve Bank of San Francisco have shown that rather than cut wages during a recession, many firms reduce the *raises* they give workers, with more workers having their wages frozen, sometimes for long periods. Recall that the nominal wage is the number of dollars a firm pays a worker, while the real wage is the nominal wage divided by a price index. If a firm freezes a worker's nominal wage, the worker's real wage will gradually decline over time because of inflation. Most workers appear to be less upset if their real wage falls because of inflation than if it falls because of a cut in their nominal wage.

Daly, Hobijn, and Ni have used census data on individual workers to calculate the percentage of workers who each month were paid the same wage as they received in the same month during the previous year. The following figure shows these data for the years from 1997 through 2014. (The shaded areas are periods of recession.) Note that the percentage of workers with unchanged wages increases dramatically during recessions and the following months as the unemployment rate rises. The persistence of high rates of workers with frozen wages several years after the end of the 2007–2009 recession is an indication of how slowly the labor market recovered and how low the inflation rate has been since the recession. Other researchers using data for other countries have also found that firms are reluctant to cut nominal wages during recessions but instead freeze workers' nominal wages and allow inflation to gradually reduce real wages.

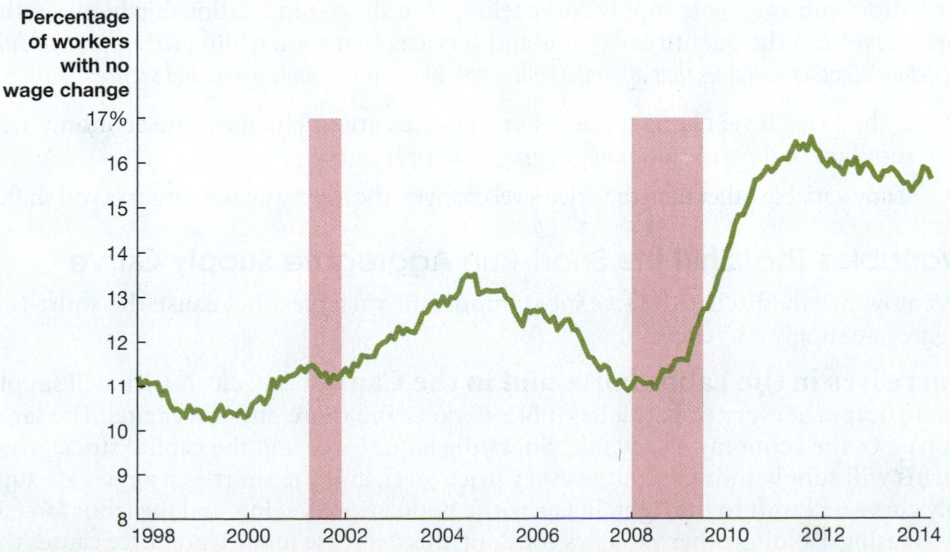

During recessions, why do firms often freeze nominal wages—frequently for extended periods—while they also lay off workers? Many economists believe that the main reason is that wage cuts upset workers. As a consequence, the productivity of workers who receive wage cuts may fall, and some workers may quit to find new jobs, either immediately or once the economy improves and the unemployment rate falls.

As Truman Bewley, an economist at Yale, puts it, "The advantage of layoffs over pay reductions was that they 'get misery out of the door.'"

Sources: Mary C. Daly, Bart Hobijn, and Timothy Ni, "The Path of Wage Growth and Unemployment," *Federal Reserve Bank of San Francisco Economic Letter*, July 15, 2013; Anabela Carneiro, Paulo Guimarães, and Pedro Portugal, "Real Wages and the Business Cycle: Accounting for Worker, Firm, and Job Title Heterogeneity," *American Economic Review: Macroeconomics*, Vol. 4, No. 2, April 2012, pp. 133–152; Hervé Le Bihan, Jérémi Montornès, and Thomas Heckel, "Sticky Wages: Evidence from Quarterly Microeconomic Data," *American Economic Review: Macroeconomics*, Vol. 4, No. 3, July 2012, pp. 1–32; Alessandro Barattieri, Susanto Basu, and Peter Gottschalk, "Some Evidence on the Importance of Sticky Wages," National Bureau of Economic Research, Working Paper 16130, June 2010; William T. Dickens et al., "How Wages Change: Micro Evidence from the International Wage Flexibility Project," *Journal of Economic Perspectives*, Vol. 21, No. 2, Spring 2007, pp. 195–214; and data from Federal Reserve Bank of San Francisco, "Nominal Wage Rigidity Data Releases."

MyEconLab Study Plan

Your Turn: Test your understanding by doing related problems 2.12 and 2.13 on pages 846–847 at the end of this chapter.

Menu Costs Make Some Prices Sticky Firms base their prices today partly on what they expect future prices to be. For instance, if you own a restaurant, you will determine the prices printed on your menu based on what you expect the demand to be for the meals you sell and what you expect to pay for labor, rent, ingredients, and other inputs. Similarly, many firms list the prices of their products on their Web sites. If demand for their products or their production costs are higher or lower than the firms had expected, they may want to charge prices that are different from the ones in their menus or on their Web sites. Changing prices would be costly, however, because it would require printing new menus or entering new prices on their Web sites. The costs to firms of changing prices are called **menu costs**. To see why menu costs can lead to an upward-sloping short-run aggregate supply curve, consider the effect of an unexpected increase in the price level. In this case, firms will want to increase the prices they charge. Some firms, however, may not be willing to increase prices because of menu costs. Because their prices are now lower relative to competitors, these firms will find their sales increasing, which will cause them to increase output. Once again, a higher price level leads to a larger quantity of goods and services supplied.

Menu costs The costs to firms of changing prices.

MyEconLab Concept Check

Shifts of the Short-Run Aggregate Supply Curve versus Movements along It

Keep in mind the difference between a shift in a curve and a movement along a curve. The short-run aggregate supply curve tells us the short-run relationship between the price level and the quantity of goods and services firms are willing to supply, *holding constant all other variables that affect the willingness of firms to supply goods and services*:

- If the price level changes but other variables are unchanged, the economy will move up or down a stationary aggregate supply curve.
- If any variable other than the price level changes, the aggregate supply curve will shift.

MyEconLab Concept Check

Variables That Shift the Short-Run Aggregate Supply Curve

We now briefly discuss the five most important variables that cause the short-run aggregate supply curve to shift.

Increases in the Labor Force and in the Capital Stock A firm will supply more output at every price if it has more workers and more physical capital. The same is true of the economy as a whole. So, as the labor force and the capital stock grow, firms will supply more output at every price level, and the short-run aggregate supply curve will shift to the right. In Japan, the population is aging, and the labor force is decreasing. Holding other variables constant, this decrease in the labor force causes the short-run aggregate supply curve in Japan to shift to the left.

Technological Change As positive technological change takes place, the productivity of workers and machinery increases, which means firms can produce more goods and services with the same amount of labor and machinery. This increase in productivity reduces the firms' costs of production and allows them to produce more output at every price level. As a result, the short-run aggregate supply curve shifts to the right.

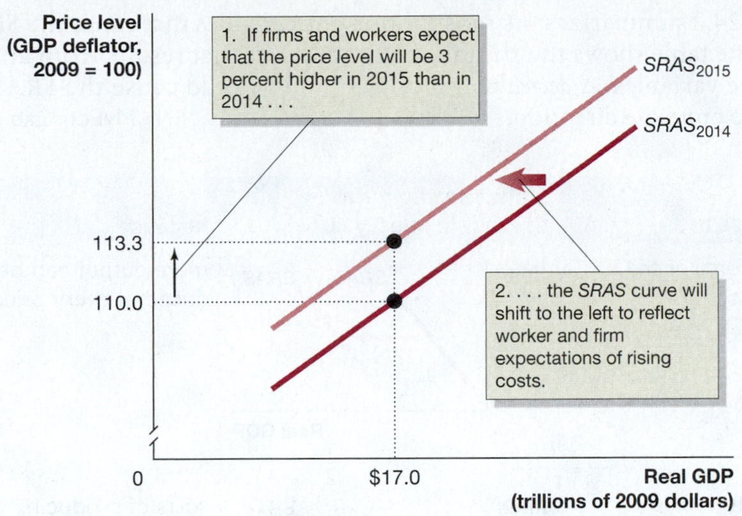

MyEconLab Animation

Figure 24.3

How Expectations of the Future Price Level Affect the Short-Run Aggregate Supply Curve

The *SRAS* curve shifts to reflect worker and firm expectations of future prices.

1. If workers and firms expect that the price level will rise by 3 percent, from 110.0 to 113.3, they will adjust their wages and prices by that amount.
2. Holding constant all other variables that affect aggregate supply, the short-run aggregate supply curve will shift to the left.

If workers and firms expect that the price level will be lower in the future, the short-run aggregate supply curve will shift to the right.

Expected Changes in the Future Price Level If workers and firms believe that the price level is going to increase by 3 percent during the next year, they will try to adjust their wages and prices accordingly. For instance, if a labor union believes there will be 3 percent inflation next year, it knows that wages must rise 3 percent to preserve the purchasing power of those wages. Similar adjustments by other workers and firms will result in costs increasing throughout the economy by 3 percent. The result, shown in Figure 24.3, is that the short-run aggregate supply curve will shift to the left, so that any level of real GDP is now associated with a price level that is 3 percent higher. In general, *if workers and firms expect the price level to increase by a certain percentage, the SRAS curve will shift by an equivalent amount,* holding constant all other variables that affect the *SRAS* curve.

Adjustments of Workers and Firms to Errors in Past Expectations about the Price Level Workers and firms sometimes make incorrect predictions about the price level. As time passes, they will attempt to compensate for these errors. Suppose that the Air Line Pilots Association signs a contract with Delta that provides for only small wage increases because the company and the union both expect only small increases in the price level. If increases in the price level turn out to be unexpectedly large, the union will take this into account when negotiating the next contract. The higher wages Delta pilots receive under the new contract will increase the company's costs and result in its needing to receive higher prices to produce the same level of output. If workers and firms across the economy are adjusting to the price level being higher than expected, the *SRAS* curve will shift to the left. If they are adjusting to the price level being lower than expected, the *SRAS* curve will shift to the right.

Unexpected Changes in the Price of an Important Natural Resource An unexpected event that causes the short-run aggregate supply curve to shift is called a **supply shock**. Supply shocks are often caused by unexpected increases or decreases in the prices of important natural resources that cause firms' costs to be different from what they had expected. Oil prices can be particularly volatile. Some firms use oil in the production process. Other firms use products, such as plastics, that are made from oil. If oil prices rise unexpectedly, the costs of production will rise for these firms. Some utilities also burn oil to generate electricity, so electricity prices will rise. Rising oil prices lead to rising gasoline prices, which raise transportation costs for many firms. Because firms face rising costs, they will supply the same level of output only if they receive higher prices, and the short-run aggregate supply curve will shift to the left.

Supply shock An unexpected event that causes the short-run aggregate supply curve to shift.

The U.S. economy has experienced at least some inflation every year since the 1930s, so workers and firms always expect next year's price level to be higher than this year's price level. Holding everything else constant, expectations of a higher price level will cause the *SRAS* curve to shift to the left. But everything else is not constant because every year, the U.S. labor force and the U.S. capital stock expand and changes in technology occur, and these factors cause the *SRAS* curve to shift to the right. Whether in any particular year the *SRAS* curve shifts to the left or to the right depends on how large an effect these variables have during that year.

Table 24.2 summarizes the most important variables that cause the *SRAS* curve to shift. The table shows the shift in the *SRAS* curve that results from an *increase* in each of the variables. A *decrease* in these variables would cause the *SRAS* curve to shift in the opposite direction.

MyEconLab Study Plan

MyEconLab Concept Check

Table 24.2

Variables That Shift the Short-Run Aggregate Supply Curve

An increase in . . .	shifts the short-run aggregate supply curve . . .	because . . .
the labor force or the capital stock	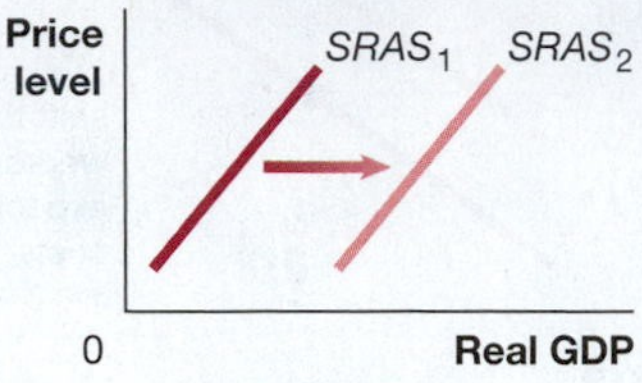	more output can be produced at every price level.
productivity	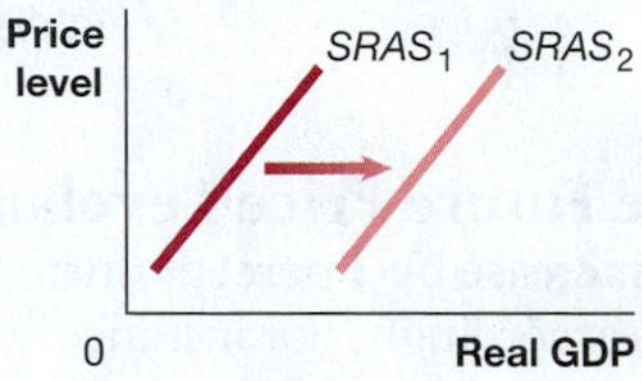	costs of producing output fall.
the expected future price level	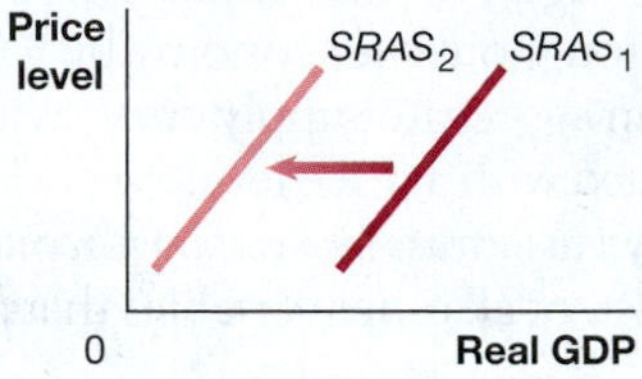	workers and firms increase wages and prices.
workers and firms adjusting to having previously underestimated the price level	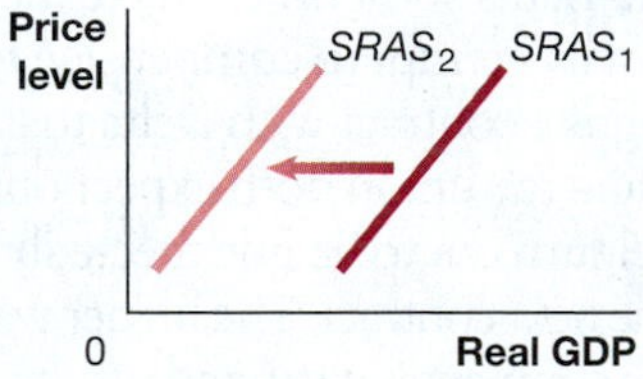	workers and firms increase wages and prices.
the expected price of an important natural resource	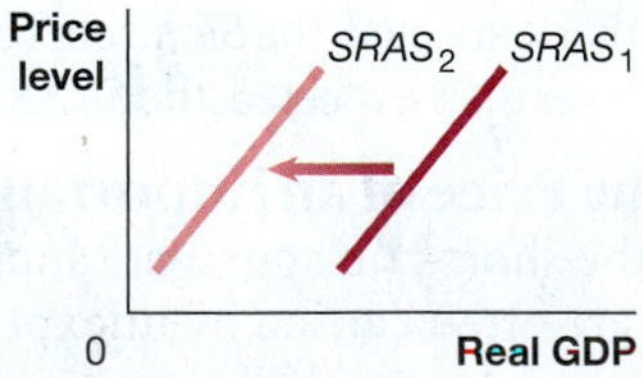	costs of producing output rise.

24.3 Macroeconomic Equilibrium in the Long Run and the Short Run

LEARNING OBJECTIVE: Use the aggregate demand and aggregate supply model to illustrate the difference between short-run and long-run macroeconomic equilibrium.

Now that we have discussed the components of the aggregate demand and aggregate supply model, we can use it to analyze changes in real GDP and the price level. In Figure 24.4, we bring the aggregate demand curve, the short-run aggregate supply curve, and the long-run aggregate supply curve together in one graph, to show the *long-run macroeconomic equilibrium* for the economy. In the figure, equilibrium occurs at real GDP of $17.0 trillion

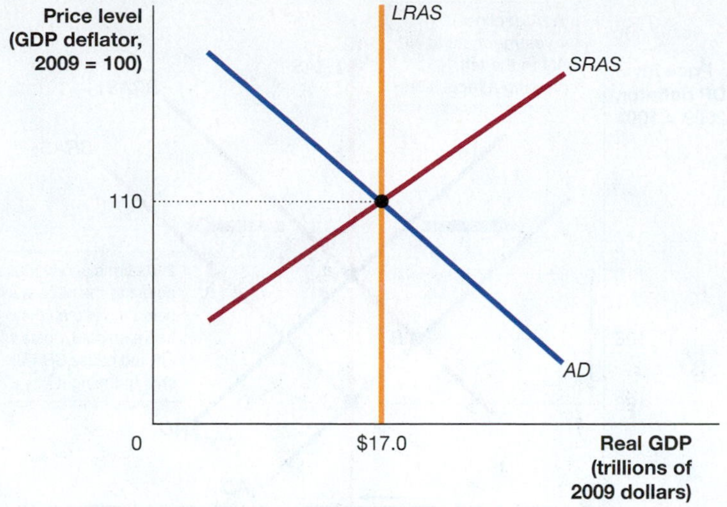

MyEconLab Animation

Figure 24.4

Long-Run Macroeconomic Equilibrium

In long-run macroeconomic equilibrium, the *AD* and *SRAS* curves intersect at a point on the *LRAS* curve. In this case, equilibrium occurs at real GDP of \$17.0 trillion and a price level of 110.

and a price level of 110. Notice that in long-run equilibrium, the short-run aggregate supply curve and the aggregate demand curve intersect at a point on the long-run aggregate supply curve. Because equilibrium occurs at a point along the long-run aggregate supply curve, we know the economy is at potential GDP: Firms will be operating at their normal level of capacity, and everyone who wants a job will have one, except the structurally and frictionally unemployed. We know, however, that the economy is often not in long-run macroeconomic equilibrium. In the following section, we discuss the economic forces that can push the economy away from long-run equilibrium.

Recessions, Expansions, and Supply Shocks

Because the full analysis of the aggregate demand and aggregate supply model can be complicated, we begin with a simplified case, using two assumptions:

1. The economy has not been experiencing any inflation. The price level is currently 110, and workers and firms expect it to remain at 110 in the future.
2. The economy is not experiencing any long-run growth. Potential GDP is \$17.0 trillion and will remain at that level in the future.

These assumptions are simplifications because in reality, the U.S. economy has experienced at least some inflation every year since the 1930s, and potential GDP also increases every year. However, the assumptions allow us to understand more easily the key ideas of the aggregate demand and aggregate supply model. In this section, we examine the short-run and long-run effects of recessions, expansions, and supply shocks.

Recession

The Short-Run Effect of a Decline in Aggregate Demand Suppose that rising interest rates cause firms to reduce spending on factories and equipment and cause households to reduce spending on new homes. The decline in investment that results will shift the aggregate demand curve to the left, from AD_1 to AD_2, as shown in Figure 24.5. The economy moves from point A to a new *short-run macroeconomic equilibrium,* where the AD_2 curve intersects the $SRAS_1$ curve at point B. In the new short-run equilibrium, real GDP has declined from \$17.0 trillion to \$16.8 trillion and is below its potential level. This lower level of GDP will result in declining profits for many firms and layoffs for some workers: The economy will be in recession.

Adjustment Back to Potential GDP in the Long Run We know that a recession will eventually end because there are forces at work that push the economy back to potential GDP in the long run. Figure 24.5 shows how the economy moves from recession back to potential GDP. The shift from AD_1 to AD_2 initially leads to a short-run equilibrium, with the price level having fallen from 110 to 108 (point *B*). Workers and firms will begin to adjust to the price level being lower than they had expected it to be. Workers will be

MyEconLab Animation

Figure 24.5

The Short-Run and Long-Run Effects of a Decrease in Aggregate Demand

In the short run, a decrease in aggregate demand causes a recession. In the long run, it causes only a decline in the price level.

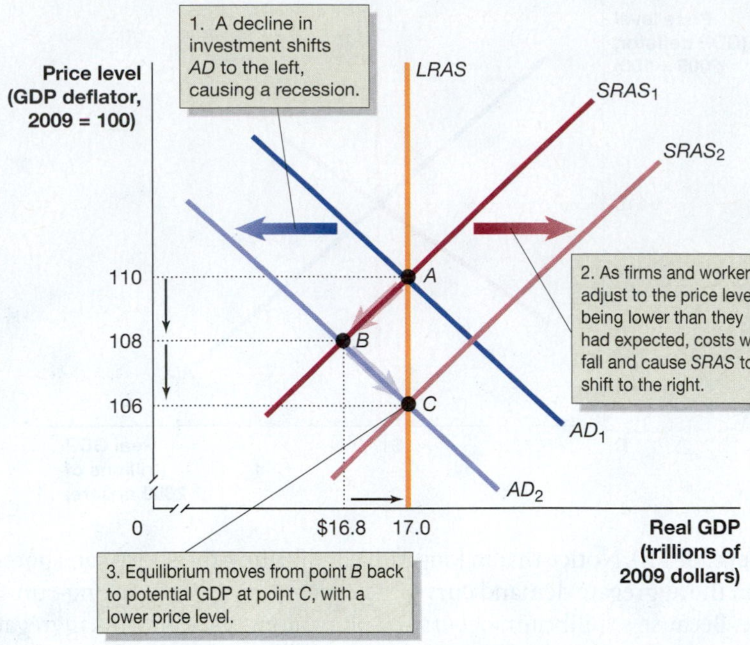

willing to accept lower wages—because each dollar of wages is able to buy more goods and services—and firms will be willing to accept lower prices. In addition, the unemployment resulting from the recession will make workers more willing to accept lower wages, and the decline in demand will make firms more willing to accept lower prices. As a result, the *SRAS* curve will shift to the right, from $SRAS_1$ to $SRAS_2$. At this point, the economy will be back in long-run equilibrium (point *C*). The shift from $SRAS_1$ to $SRAS_2$ will not happen instantly. It may take the economy several years to return to potential GDP. The important conclusion is that a decline in aggregate demand causes a recession in the short run, but in the long run it causes only a decline in the price level.

Economists refer to the process of adjustment back to potential GDP just described as an *automatic mechanism* because it occurs without any actions by the government. An alternative to waiting for the automatic mechanism to end a recession is for the government to use monetary policy or fiscal policy to shift the *AD* curve to the right and restore potential GDP more quickly. We will discuss monetary policy and fiscal policy in Chapters 26 and 27. Economists debate whether it is better to wait for the automatic mechanism to end recessions or to use monetary policy and fiscal policy.

Making the Connection

MyEconLab Video

Does It Matter What Causes a Decline in Aggregate Demand?

We have seen that GDP has four components and that a decrease in any of them can cause the aggregate demand curve to shift to the left, leading to a recession. In practice, most recessions in the United States since World War II have begun with a decline in residential construction. Edward Leamer of the University of California, Los Angeles, has gone so far as to argue that "housing *is* the business cycle," meaning that declines in residential construction are the most important reason for the declines in aggregate demand that lead to recessions. The shaded periods in the graph on the next page represent recessions. The graph shows that spending on residential construction has declined prior to every recession since 1955.

The collapse in spending on housing added to the severity of the 2007–2009 recession.

The graph also highlights a fact that we noted earlier in this chapter: The decline in residential construction during the 2007–2009 recession was particularly severe. Spending on residential construction declined by almost 60 percent from the fourth quarter of 2005 to the third quarter of 2010. Largely because of these problems in the housing sector, the decline in real GDP during the recession of 2007–2009 was larger than during any other recession since the Great Depression of the 1930s.

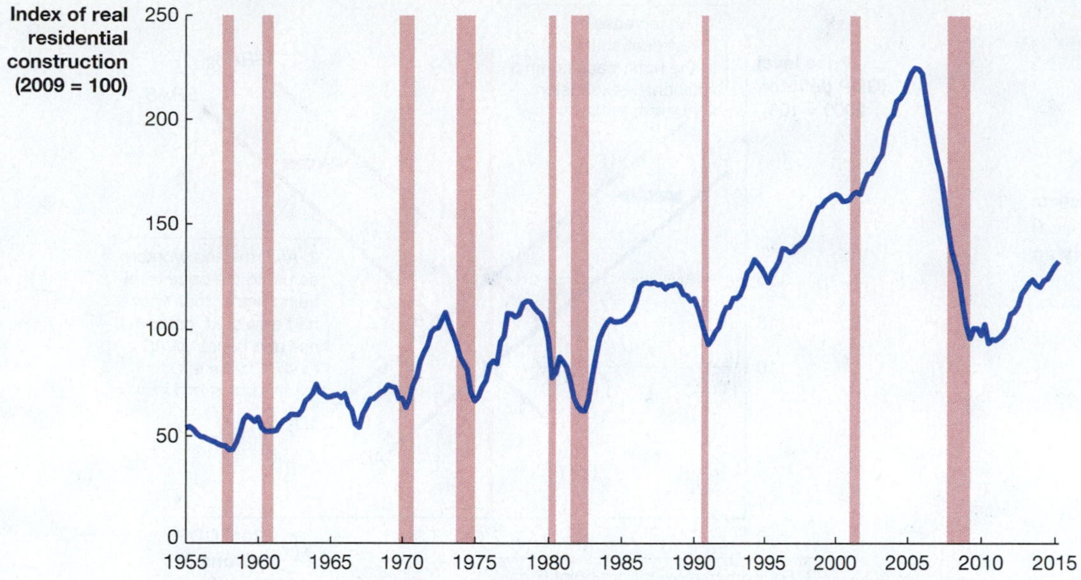

What typically causes declines in spending on residential construction? Late in a business cycle expansion, the inflation rate and interest rates start to increase (see Chapter 21). Higher interest rates often result from monetary policy actions as the Federal Reserve tries to slow down the economy and reduce the rate of inflation (see Chapter 26). Higher interest rates reduce consumer demand for new houses by increasing the cost of loans.

But the collapse in residential construction prior to and during the recession of 2007–2009 was due more to the deflating of the "housing bubble" of 2002–2005 and to the financial crisis that began in 2007 than to higher interest rates. We will discuss both the housing bubble and the financial crisis later in this chapter. At this point, we can note that research by Carmen M. Reinhart and Kenneth S. Rogoff of Harvard University shows that declines in aggregate demand that result from financial crises tend to be larger and longer-lasting than declines due to other factors. So, the experience of 2007–2009 indicates that, in fact, the source of the decline in aggregate demand can be important in determining the severity of a recession.

Sources: Edward E. Leamer, "Housing *Is* the Business Cycle," in *Housing, Housing Finance, and Monetary Policy*, Federal Reserve Bank of Kansas City, August 2007; Carmen M. Reinhart and Kenneth S. Rogoff, "The Aftermath of Financial Crises," *American Economic Review*, Vol. 99, No. 2, May 2009, pp. 466–472; and U.S. Bureau of Economic Analysis.

Your Turn: Test your understanding by doing related problem 3.6 on page 848 at the end of this chapter.

MyEconLab Study Plan

Expansion

The Short-Run Effect of an Increase in Aggregate Demand Suppose that instead of becoming pessimistic, many firms become optimistic about the future profitability of new investment, as happened during the information technology and telecommunications booms of the late 1990s. The resulting increase in investment will shift the *AD* curve to the right, as shown in Figure 24.6. Equilibrium moves from point *A* to point *B*. Real GDP rises from $17.0 trillion to $17.3 trillion, and the price level rises from 110 to 113. Real GDP will be above potential GDP: Firms are operating beyond their normal level of capacity, and some workers who would ordinarily be structurally or frictionally unemployed or who would not be in the labor force are employed.

MyEconLab Animation

Figure 24.6

The Short-Run and Long-Run Effects of an Increase in Aggregate Demand

In the short run, an increase in aggregate demand causes an increase in real GDP. In the long run, it causes only an increase in the price level.

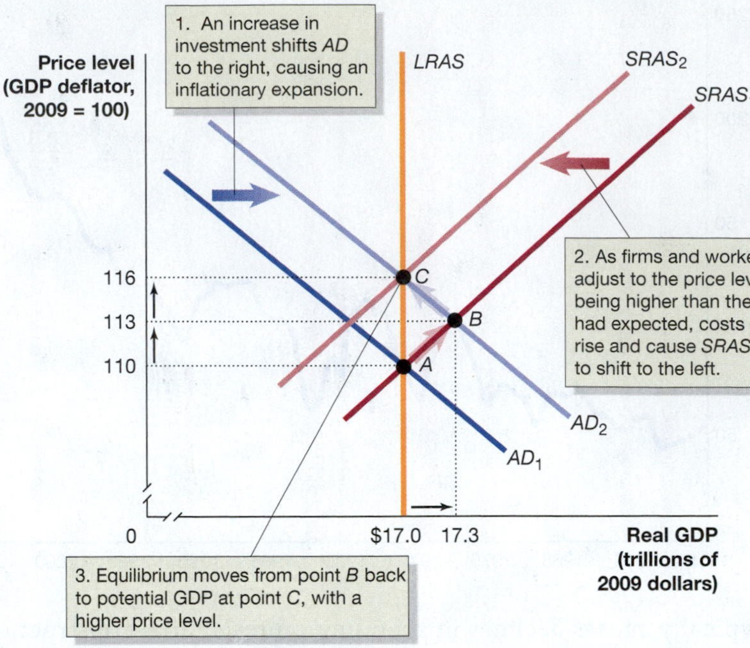

Adjustment Back to Potential GDP in the Long Run Just as an automatic mechanism brings the economy back to potential GDP from a recession, an automatic mechanism brings the economy back from a short-run equilibrium beyond potential GDP. Figure 24.6 illustrates this mechanism. The shift from AD_1 to AD_2 initially leads to a short-run equilibrium, with the price level rising from 110 to 113 (point *B*). Workers and firms will begin to adjust to the price level being higher than they had expected. Workers will push for higher wages—because each dollar of wages is able to buy fewer goods and services—and firms will charge higher prices. In addition, the low levels of unemployment resulting from the expansion will make it easier for workers to negotiate for higher wages, and the increase in demand will make it easier for firms to receive higher prices. As a result, the *SRAS* curve will shift to the left, from $SRAS_1$ to $SRAS_2$. At this point, the economy will be back in long-run equilibrium. Once again, the shift from $SRAS_1$ to $SRAS_2$ will not happen instantly. The process of returning to potential GDP may stretch out for more than a year.

Supply Shock

The Short-Run Effect of a Supply Shock Suppose oil prices increase substantially. This supply shock will increase many firms' costs and cause the *SRAS* curve to shift to the left, as shown in panel (a) of Figure 24.7. Notice that the price level is higher in the new short-run equilibrium (112 rather than 110), but real GDP is lower ($16.7 trillion rather than $17.0 trillion). This unpleasant combination of inflation and recession is called **stagflation**.

Stagflation A combination of inflation and recession, usually resulting from a supply shock.

Adjustment Back to Potential GDP in the Long Run A recession caused by a supply shock increases unemployment and reduces output. Workers will eventually be willing to accept lower wages, and firms will be willing to accept lower prices. In panel (b) of Figure 24.7, the short-run aggregate supply curve shifts from $SRAS_2$ to $SRAS_1$, moving equilibrium from point *B* back to point *A*. Real GDP is back to potential GDP at the original price level. It may take several years for this process to be completed. An alternative would be to use monetary and fiscal policy to shift the aggregate demand curve to the right. Using policy in this way would bring real GDP back to potential GDP more quickly but would result in a permanently higher price level.

MyEconLab Concept Check

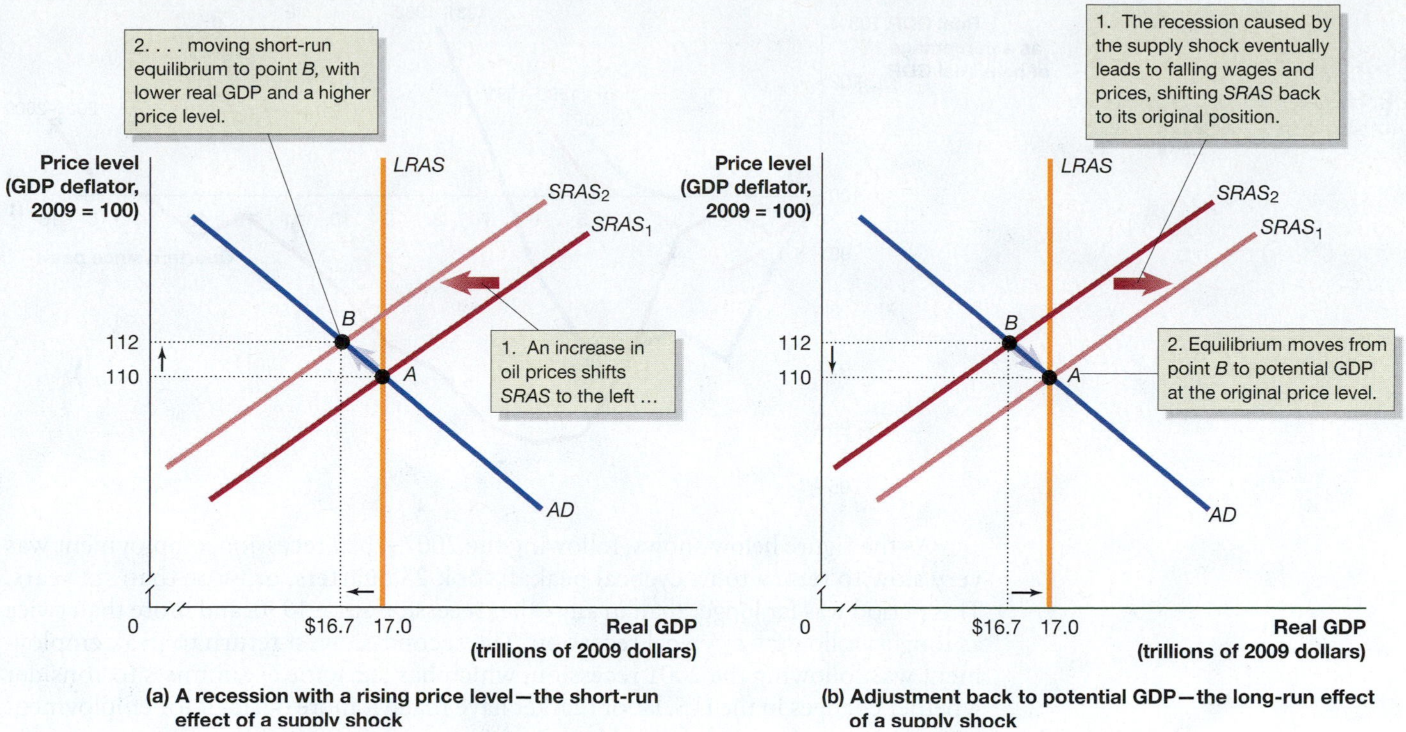

MyEconLab Animation

Figure 24.7 The Short-Run and Long-Run Effects of a Supply Shock

Panel (a) shows that a supply shock, such as a large increase in oil prices, will cause a recession and a higher price level in the short run. The recession caused by the supply shock increases unemployment and reduces output. Panel (b) shows that rising unemployment and falling output result in workers being willing to accept lower wages and firms being willing to accept lower prices. The short-run aggregate supply curve shifts from $SRAS_2$ to $SRAS_1$. Equilibrium moves from point *B* back to potential GDP and the original price level at point *A*.

Making the Connection

MyEconLab Video

How Long Is the Long Run in Macroeconomics?

Once a recession starts, how long does it take for real GDP and employment to return to the levels they had achieved at the business cycle peak? On average, in the recessions since 1950, it has taken six quarters, or about a year and a half, for real GDP to return to its cyclical peak. During the same period, it has taken employment on average about 9.5 quarters, or nearly two and a half years, to return to its cycle peak. But these averages disguise great variation across recessions.

The figure at the top of the next page shows the recessions of 1981–1982, 1990–1991, 2001, and 2007–2009. The value of real GDP at the business cycle peak is set equal to 100. Therefore, values less than 100 represent levels of real GDP below the level at the business cycle peak. The horizontal axis shows the number of quarters since the business cycle peak. The severity of the 2007–2009 recession can be seen clearly in the figure. Real GDP reached a cyclical peak in the fourth quarter of 2007. Real GDP didn't return to this level until the second quarter of 2011, which was 14 quarters, or *three and a half years,* after the recession began. That was far longer than in any other recession since 1950. Some economists describe the 1981–1982 recession as a V-shaped recession because although the decline in real GDP was large, real GDP returned to its cyclical peak relatively quickly. The 2007–2009 recession, in contrast, was a U-shaped recession because it took an extended period for real GDP to return to its cyclical peak.

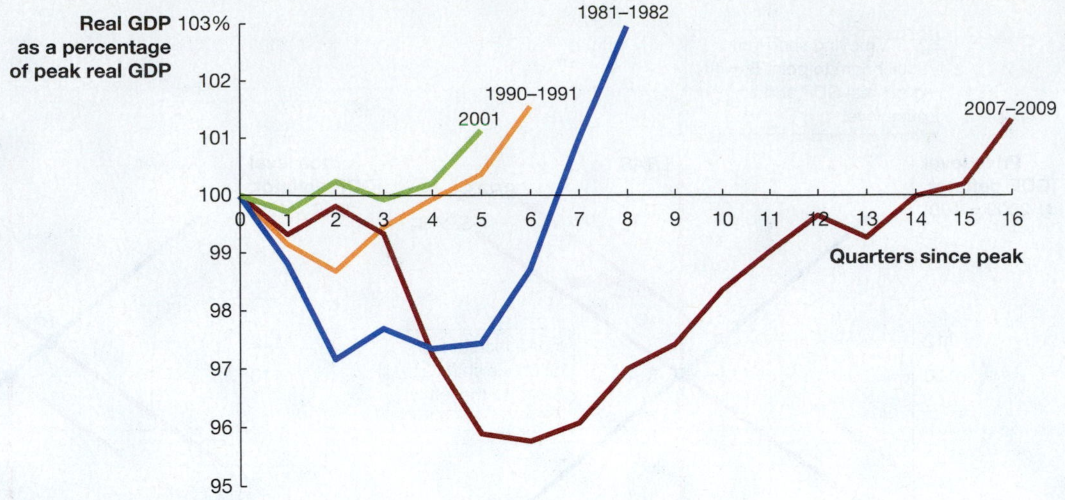

As the figure below shows, following the 2007–2009 recession, employment was very slow to return to its cyclical peak: It took 25 quarters, or more than six years. This period was far longer than in any other recession since 1950, and more than twice as long as following a typical recession. The second-slowest return to peak employment was following the 2001 recession, which has led some economists to consider whether changes in the U.S. labor market have made it more difficult for employment to return to normal levels following a recession.

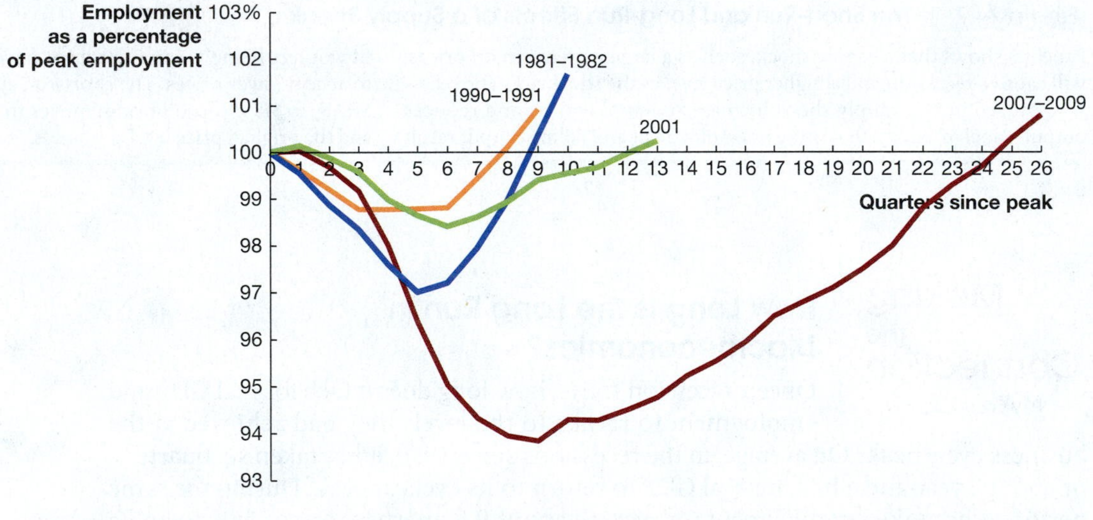

The severity of the 2007–2009 recession took most economists and policymakers by surprise because they did not predict that the decline in housing prices that began in 2006 would eventually lead to a major financial crisis in 2008. Even as the recession was ending in 2009, members of President Obama's economic staff, economists at the Federal Reserve, and economists at the Congressional Budget Office all expected that the economy would return to normal levels of real GDP and employment far sooner than it did.

In Chapters 26 and 27, we will discuss the disagreements among economists and policymakers over why the U.S. economy took so long to return to potential GDP and full employment following the 2007–2009 recession.

Sources: Board of Governors of the Federal Reserve System, "Economic Projections of Federal Reserve Board Members and Federal Reserve Bank Presidents," various dates; Congressional Budget Office, "Data Underlying Selected Economic Figures, Real Gross Domestic Product," various dates; Christina Romer and Jared Bernstein, "The Job Impact of the American Recovery and Reinvestment Plan," January 9, 2009; U.S. Bureau of Economic Analysis; U.S. Bureau of Labor Statistics; and National Bureau of Economic Research.

MyEconLab Study Plan **Your Turn:** Test your understanding by doing related problem 3.9 on page 848 at the end of this chapter.

24.4 A Dynamic Aggregate Demand and Aggregate Supply Model*

LEARNING OBJECTIVE: Use the dynamic aggregate demand and aggregate supply model to analyze macroeconomic conditions.

The basic aggregate demand and aggregate supply model used so far in this chapter provides important insights into how short-run macroeconomic equilibrium is determined. Unfortunately, the model also provides some misleading results. For instance, it incorrectly predicts that a recession caused by the aggregate demand curve shifting to the left will result in a lower price level, which has not happened over an entire year since the 1930s. The difficulty with the basic model arises because we assumed that (1) the economy does not experience continuing inflation and (2) the economy does not experience long-run growth. We can develop a more useful aggregate demand and aggregate supply model by dropping these assumptions. The result will be a model that takes into account that the economy is not *static*, with an unchanging level of potential GDP and no continuing inflation, but *dynamic*, with potential GDP that grows over time and inflation that continues every year. We can create a *dynamic aggregate demand and aggregate supply model* by making changes to the basic model that incorporate the following important macroeconomic facts:

- Potential GDP increases continually, shifting the long-run aggregate supply curve to the right.
- During most years, the aggregate demand curve shifts to the right.
- Except during periods when workers and firms expect high rates of inflation, the short-run aggregate supply curve shifts to the right.

Figure 24.8 illustrates how incorporating these macroeconomic facts changes the basic aggregate demand and aggregate supply model. We start with $SRAS_1$ and AD_1 intersecting at point *A*, at a price level of 110 and real GDP of $17.0 trillion. Because this intersection occurs at a point on $LRAS_1$, we know the economy is in long-run equilibrium. We show the long-run aggregate supply curve shifting to the right, from $LRAS_1$ to $LRAS_2$, because during the year, potential GDP increases as the U.S. labor force and the U.S. capital stock increase and technological progress occurs. The short-run aggregate supply curve shifts from $SRAS_1$ to $SRAS_2$ because the same variables that cause the long-run aggregate supply curve to shift to the right will also increase the quantity of goods and services that firms are willing to supply in the short run. Finally, the aggregate demand curve shifts to the right, from AD_1 to AD_2. The aggregate demand curve shifts for several reasons: As the population grows and incomes rise, consumption will increase over time. As the economy grows, firms will expand capacity, and new firms will be formed, increasing investment. An expanding population and an expanding economy require increased government services, such as more police officers and teachers, so government purchases will increase.

The new equilibrium in Figure 24.8 occurs at point *B*, where AD_2 intersects $SRAS_2$ on $LRAS_2$. In the new equilibrium, the price level remains at 110, while real GDP increases to $17.4 trillion. Notice that there has been no inflation because the price level is unchanged, at 110. There has been no inflation because aggregate demand and aggregate supply shifted to the right by exactly as much as long-run aggregate supply. In fact, though, we wouldn't expect that all three curves will typically shift by the same amount. For instance, the *SRAS* curve is also affected by workers' and firms' expectations of future changes in the price level and by supply shocks. These variables can partially or completely offset the normal tendency of the *SRAS* curve to shift to the right over the course of a year. We also know that changes in the expenditures of consumers, firms, and the government may result in the *AD* curve shifting to the right by more or less than the *SRAS* and *LRAS* curves. In fact, as we will see shortly, *changes in the price level and in real GDP in the short run are determined by how much the* SRAS *and* AD *curves shift.*

*This section may be omitted without loss of continuity.

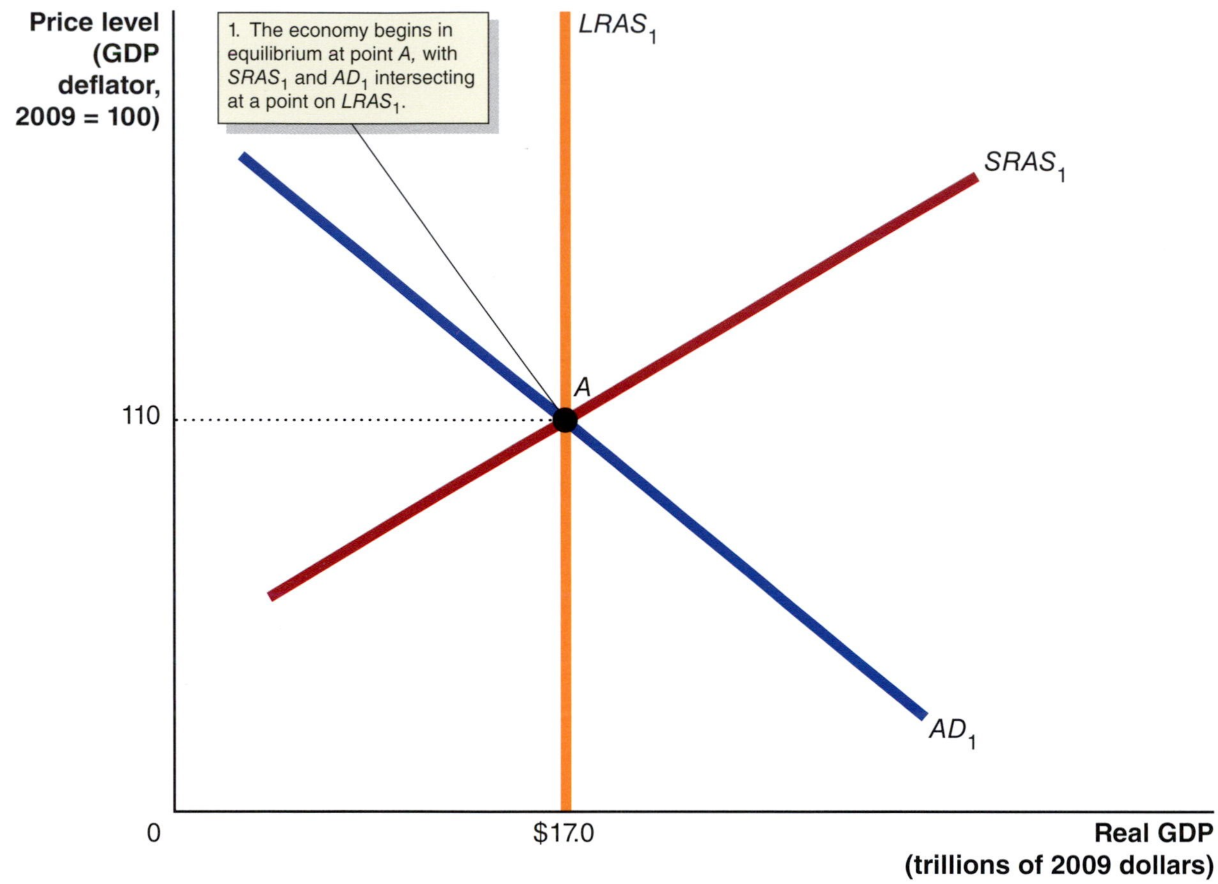

MyEconLab Animation

Figure 24.8 A Dynamic Aggregate Demand and Aggregate Supply Model

We start with the basic aggregate demand and aggregate supply model.

What Is the Usual Cause of Inflation?

The dynamic aggregate demand and aggregate supply model provides a more accurate explanation of the source of most inflation. If total spending in the economy grows faster than total production, prices rise. Figure 24.9 illustrates this point by showing that if the *AD* curve shifts to the right by more than the *LRAS* curve, inflation results because equilibrium occurs at a higher price level, point *B*. In the new equilibrium, the *SRAS* curve has shifted to the right by less than the *LRAS* curve because the anticipated increase in prices offsets some of the effect of the technological change and increases in the labor force and capital stock that occur during the year. Although inflation generally results from total spending growing faster than total production, a shift to the left of the short-run aggregate supply curve can also cause an increase in the price level, as we noted in Section 24.3 when discussing supply shocks.

As we saw in Figure 24.8, if aggregate demand increases by the same amount as short-run and long-run aggregate supply, the price level will not change. In this case, the economy experiences economic growth without inflation.

The Recession of 2007–2009

We can use the dynamic aggregate demand and aggregate supply model to analyze the recession of 2007–2009. The recession began in December 2007, with the end of the

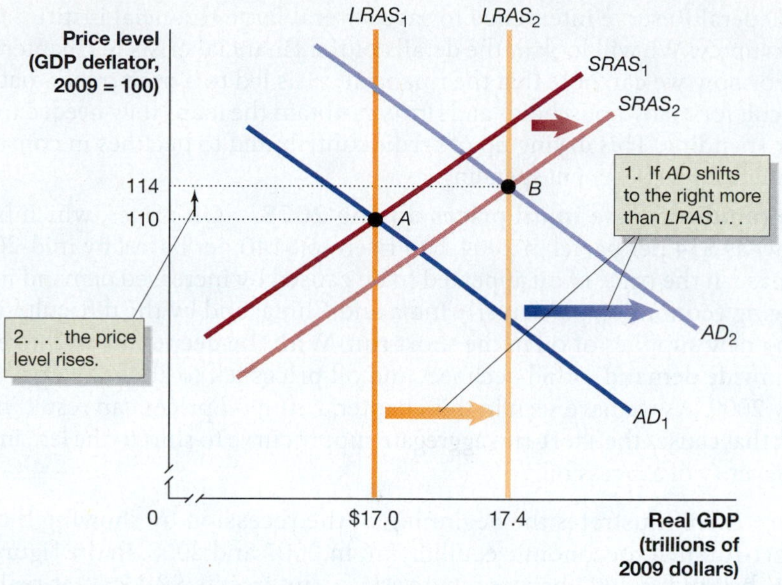

MyEconLab Animation

Figure 24.9 Using Dynamic Aggregate Demand and Aggregate Supply to Understand Inflation

The most common cause of inflation is total spending increasing faster than total production.

1. The economy begins at point *A*, with real GDP of \$17.0 trillion and a price level of 110. An increase in full-employment real GDP from \$17.0 trillion to \$17.4 trillion causes long-run aggregate supply to shift to the right from $LRAS_1$ to $LRAS_2$. Aggregate demand shifts to the right from AD_1 to AD_2.
2. Because *AD* shifts to the right by more than the *LRAS* curve, the price level in the new equilibrium rises from 110 to 114.

economic expansion that started in November 2001. Several factors combined to cause the recession:

- **The end of the housing bubble.** The figure in the *Making the Connection* on page 833 shows that spending on residential construction increased rapidly from 2002 to 2005, before declining more than 60 percent between the end of 2005 and the beginning of 2010. The increase in spending on housing through 2005 was partly the result of actions the Federal Reserve had taken to lower interest rates during and after the recession of 2001. As interest rates on mortgage loans declined, more consumers began to buy new homes. But by 2005, it was clear that a speculative bubble was partly responsible for the rapidly rising prices of both newly built and existing homes. A bubble occurs when people become less concerned with the underlying value of an asset—either a physical asset, such as a house, or a financial asset, such as a stock—and focus instead on expectations of the price of the asset increasing. In some areas of the country, such as California, Arizona, and Florida, many homes were purchased by investors who intended to resell them for higher prices than they paid for them and did not intend to live in them. Some popular television programs explored ways that people could "flip" houses by buying and quickly reselling them. Speculative bubbles eventually end, and the housing bubble started to deflate in 2006. Both new home sales and housing prices began to decline. The growth of aggregate demand slowed as spending on residential construction—a component of investment spending—fell.
- **The financial crisis.** Problems in the housing market were bad news for workers and firms involved with residential construction. In addition, falling housing prices led to an increased number of borrowers defaulting on their mortgage loans. These defaults caused banks and some other financial institutions to suffer heavy losses. Beginning in the spring of 2008, the U.S. Department of the Treasury and

the Federal Reserve intervened to save several large financial institutions from bankruptcy. We will look at the details of the financial crisis in Chapters 25 and 26. For now we can note that the financial crisis led to a *credit crunch* that made it difficult for many households and firms to obtain the loans they needed to finance their spending. This drying up of credit contributed to declines in consumption spending and investment spending.

- **The rapid increase in oil prices during 2008.** Oil prices, which had been as low as $34 per barrel in 2004, had risen to $140 per barrel by mid-2008. The increase in the price of oil appeared to be caused by increased demand in rapidly growing economies, particularly India and China, and by the difficulty in developing new supplies of oil in the short run. With the deepening of the recession, worldwide demand for oil declined, and oil prices fell to about $40 per barrel in early 2009. As we have seen in this chapter, rising oil prices can result in a *supply shock* that causes the short-run aggregate supply curve to shift to the left, increasing the severity of a recession.

Figure 24.10 illustrates the beginning of the recession by showing the economy's short-run macroeconomic equilibrium in 2007 and 2008. In the figure, short-run equilibrium for 2007 occurs where AD_{2007} intersects $SRAS_{2007}$ at real GDP of $14.87 trillion and a price level of 97.3. Real GDP in 2007 was below potential GDP of $14.95 trillion, shown by $LRAS_{2007}$. During 2008, aggregate demand shifted to the

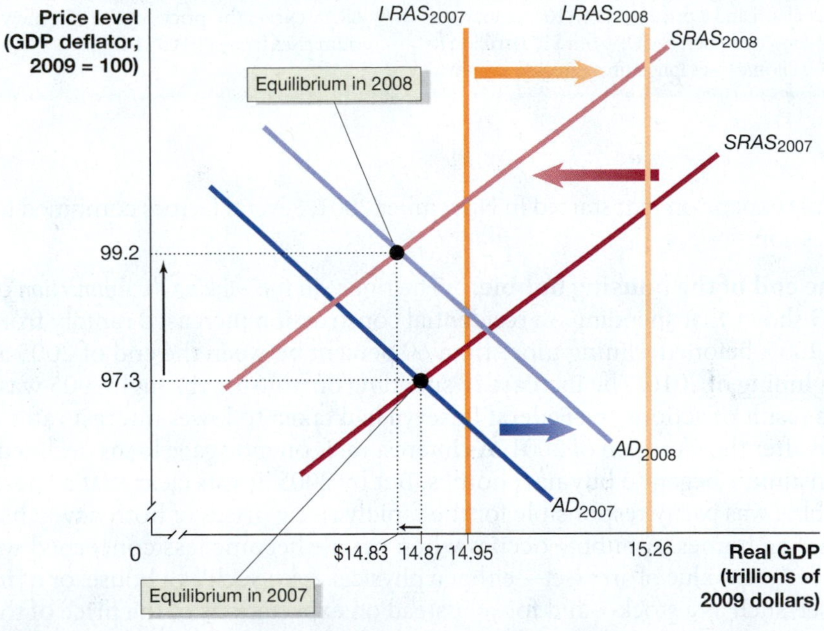

MyEconLab Animation

Figure 24.10 The Beginning of the Recession of 2007–2009

Between 2007 and 2008, the *AD* curve shifted to the right but not by nearly enough to offset the shift to the right of the *LRAS* curve, which represented the increase in potential GDP from $14.95 trillion to $15.26 trillion. Because of a sharp increase in oil prices, short-run aggregate supply shifted to the left, from $SRAS_{2007}$ to $SRAS_{2008}$. Real GDP decreased from $14.87 trillion in 2007 to $14.83 trillion in 2008, which was far below the potential GDP, shown by $LRAS_{2008}$. Because the increase in aggregate demand was small, the price level increased only from 97.3 in 2007 to 99.2 in 2008, so the inflation rate for 2008 was only 2.0 percent.

right, from AD_{2007} to AD_{2008}. Aggregate demand increased by less than potential GDP because of the negative effects of the bursting of the housing bubble and the financial crisis on consumption spending and investment spending. The supply shock from higher oil prices caused short-run aggregate supply to shift to the left, from $SRAS_{2007}$ to $SRAS_{2008}$.

Short-run equilibrium for 2008 occurred at real GDP of $14.83 trillion and a price level of 99.2. A large gap opened between short-run equilibrium real GDP and potential GDP. Not surprisingly, unemployment rose from 4.6 percent in 2007 to 5.8 percent in 2008. The price level increased only from 97.3 to 99.2, so the inflation rate was a low 2.0 percent.

The recession persisted into 2009, as potential GDP increased to $15.50 trillion, while real GDP fell to $14.42 trillion. (The situation in 2009 is not shown in Figure 24.10.) The increased gap between real GDP and potential GDP caused the unemployment rate to soar to 9.3 percent—the highest unemployment rate since the recession of 1981–1982 and the second highest since the Great Depression of the 1930s. Although the recession ended in June 2009, real GDP grew only slowly during 2010 and 2011, leaving the unemployment rate above 8.5 percent.

The severity of the recession of 2007–2009 resulted in some of the most dramatic changes in government economic policy since the Great Depression. We will explore these new policies in Chapters 26 and 27. MyEconLab Concept Check

Solved Problem 24.4

MyEconLab Interactive Animation

Showing the Oil Shock of 1974–1975 on a Dynamic Aggregate Demand and Aggregate Supply Graph

The 1974–1975 recession clearly illustrates how a supply shock affects the economy. Following the Arab–Israeli War of 1973, the Organization of the Petroleum Exporting Countries (OPEC) took actions that increased the price of a barrel of oil from less than $3 to more than $10. Use this information and the statistics in the following table to draw a dynamic aggregate demand and aggregate supply graph showing macroeconomic equilibrium for 1974 and 1975. Assume that the aggregate demand curve did not shift between 1974 and 1975. Provide a brief explanation of your graph.

	Actual Real GDP	Potential GDP	Price Level
1974	$5.40 trillion	$5.43 trillion	28.7
1975	$5.39 trillion	$5.63 trillion	31.4

Sources: U.S. Bureau of Economic Analysis; and Federal Reserve Bank of St. Louis.

Solving the Problem

Step 1: Review the chapter material. This problem is about applying the dynamic aggregate demand and aggregate supply model, so you may want to review the section "A Dynamic Aggregate Demand and Aggregate Supply Model," which begins on page 837.

Step 2: Use the information in the table to draw the graph. You need to draw five curves: *SRAS* and *LRAS* for both 1974 and 1975 and *AD*, which is the same for both years. You know that the two *LRAS* curves will be vertical lines at the values given for potential GDP in the table. Because of the large supply shock, you know that the *SRAS* curve shifted to the left. The problem asks you to assume that the *AD* curve did not shift. Your graph should look like the following:

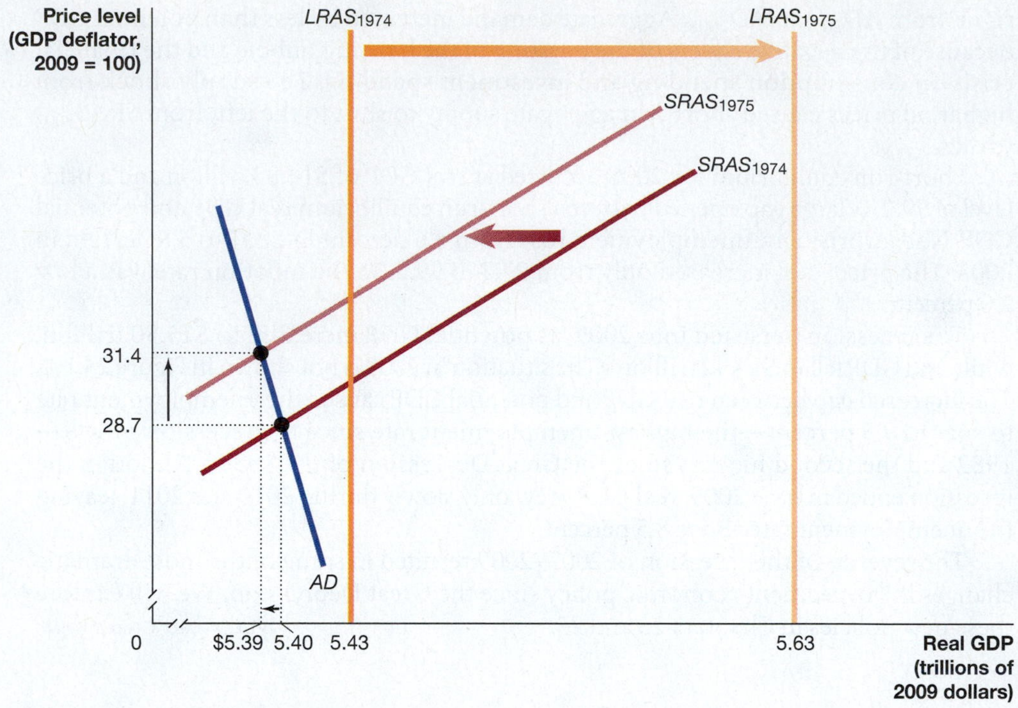

Step 3: Explain your graph. $LRAS_{1974}$ and $LRAS_{1975}$ are at the levels of potential GDP for each year. Macroeconomic equilibrium for 1974 occurs where the *AD* curve intersects the $SRAS_{1974}$ curve, with real GDP of $5.40 trillion and a price level of 28.7. Macroeconomic equilibrium for 1975 occurs where the *AD* curve intersects the $SRAS_{1975}$ curve, with real GDP of $5.39 trillion and a price level of 31.4.

Extra Credit: As a result of the supply shock, equilibrium real GDP moved from just below potential GDP in 1974 (the recession actually began right at the end of 1973) to well below potential GDP in 1975. With real GDP in 1975 about 4.3 percent below its potential level, the unemployment rate soared from 5.6 percent in 1974 to 8.5 percent in 1975.

MyEconLab Study Plan

Your Turn: For more practice, do related problems 4.5 and 4.6 on page 849 at the end of this chapter.

Continued from page 815

Economics in Your Life

Is an Employer Likely to Cut Your Pay during a Recession?

At the beginning of this chapter, we asked you to consider whether during a recession your employer is likely to reduce your pay and cut the prices of the products he or she sells. We have seen that even during a recession, the price level rarely falls. In fact, in the United States, the GDP deflator has not fallen for an entire year since the 1930s. Although some firms reduced prices during the recession of 2007–2009, most firms did not. So, the owner of the coffeehouse where you work will probably not cut the price of lattes unless sales have declined drastically. We also saw that most firms are more reluctant to cut wages than to increase them because wage cuts can lower worker morale and productivity. Because the recession of 2007–2009 was particularly severe, some firms did cut wages. But given that you are a highly skilled barista, your employer is unlikely to cut your wages for fear that you might quit and work for a competitor.

Conclusion

Chapter 3 demonstrated the power of the microeconomic model of demand and supply in explaining how the prices and quantities of individual products are determined. This chapter showed that we need a different model to explain the behavior of the whole economy. We saw that the macroeconomic model of aggregate demand and aggregate supply explains fluctuations in real GDP and the price level.

Fluctuations in real GDP, employment, and the price level have led the federal government to implement macroeconomic policies. We will explore these policies in later chapters after first considering the role money plays in the economy.

Visit MyEconLab for a news article and analysis related to the concepts in this chapter.

CHAPTER SUMMARY AND PROBLEMS

Key Terms

Aggregate demand (*AD*) curve, p. 816
Aggregate demand and aggregate supply model, p. 816
Fiscal policy, p. 819
Long-run aggregate supply (*LRAS*) curve, p. 825
Menu costs, p. 828
Monetary policy, p. 819
Short-run aggregate supply (*SRAS*) curve, p. 816
Stagflation, p. 834
Supply shock, p. 829

24.1 Aggregate Demand, pages 816–824

LEARNING OBJECTIVE: Identify the determinants of aggregate demand and distinguish between a movement along the aggregate demand curve and a shift of the curve.

Summary

The **aggregate demand and aggregate supply model** enables us to explain short-run fluctuations in real GDP and the price level. The **aggregate demand (*AD*) curve** shows the relationship between the price level and the level of planned aggregate expenditures by households, firms, and the government. The **short-run aggregate supply (*SRAS*) curve** shows the relationship in the short run between the price level and the quantity of real GDP supplied by firms. The long-run aggregate supply curve shows the relationship in the long run between the price level and the quantity of real GDP supplied. The four components of aggregate demand are consumption (*C*), investment (*I*), government purchases (*G*), and net exports (*NX*). The aggregate demand curve is downward sloping because a decline in the price level causes consumption, investment, and net exports to increase. If the price level changes but all else remains constant, the result is a movement up or down a stationary aggregate demand curve. If any variable other than the price level changes, the aggregate demand curve will shift. The variables that cause the aggregate demand curve to shift are divided into three categories: changes in government policies, changes in the expectations of households and firms, and changes in foreign variables. For example, **monetary policy** involves the actions the Federal Reserve takes to manage the money supply and interest rates to pursue macroeconomic policy objectives. When the Federal Reserve takes actions to change interest rates, consumption and investment spending will change, shifting the aggregate demand curve. **Fiscal policy** involves changes in the federal government's taxes and purchases that are intended to achieve macroeconomic policy objectives. Changes in federal taxes and purchases shift the aggregate demand curve.

MyEconLab Visit **www.myeconlab.com** to complete these exercises online and get instant feedback.

Review Questions

1.1 What relationship does the aggregate demand curve show? What relationship does the aggregate supply curve show?

1.2 Explain the three reasons the aggregate demand curve slopes downward.

1.3 What are the differences between the *AD* curve and the demand curve for an individual product, such as apples?

1.4 What variables cause the *AD* curve to shift? For each variable, identify whether an increase in that variable will cause the *AD* curve to shift to the right or to the left and also indicate which component(s) of GDP—consumption, investment, government purchases, or net exports—will change.

Problems and Applications

1.5 Explain how each of the following events would affect the aggregate demand curve.
a. An increase in the price level
b. An increase in government purchases
c. Higher state income taxes
d. Higher interest rates
e. Faster income growth in other countries
f. A higher exchange rate between the dollar and foreign currencies

1.6 From August 2009 to August 2015, the Standard & Poor's Index of 500 stock prices more than doubled, while the consumer price index increased by just over 10 percent. Briefly explain what effect, if any, these changes had on the aggregate demand curve.

1.7 Consider the two aggregate demand curves in the following graph. What would cause a movement from point *A* to point *B* on AD_1? What would cause a movement from point *A* to point *C*?

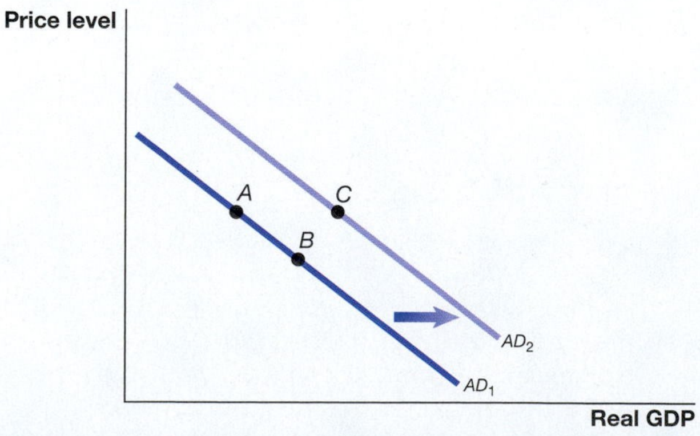

1.8 **(Related to the Don't Let This Happen to You on page 819)** An economics student makes the following statement: "It's easy to understand why the aggregate demand curve is downward sloping: When the price level increases, consumers substitute into less expensive products, which decreases total spending in the economy." Briefly explain whether you agree.

1.9 **(Related to Solved Problem 24.1 on page 820)** Explain whether each of the following will cause a shift of the *AD* curve or a movement along the *AD* curve.
a. Firms become more optimistic and increase their spending on machinery and equipment.
b. The federal government increases taxes in an attempt to reduce a budget deficit.
c. The U.S. economy experiences 4 percent inflation.

1.10 **(Related to Solved Problem 24.1 on page 820)** A reporter for the *Wall Street Journal* wrote, "A strong dollar and weak growth overseas portend downward pressure on U.S. exports."
a. What does the reporter mean by a "strong dollar"?
b. What does the reporter mean by "weak growth overseas"?
c. Briefly explain why the combination of a strong dollar and weak growth overseas might result in lower U.S. exports.
d. Will the result of a strong dollar be a movement along the U.S. aggregate demand curve or a shift of the aggregate demand curve? Briefly explain.

Source: Jon Hilsenrath, "Rising Dollar and Falling Oil Could Be Recipe for a U.S. Asset Boom," *Wall Street Journal*, December 11, 2014.

1.11 **(Related to the Making the Connection on page 823)** If real GDP in the United States declined by more during the 2007–2009 recession than did real GDP in Canada, China, and other trading partners of the United States, would the effect be to increase or decrease U.S. net exports? Briefly explain.

24.2 Aggregate Supply, pages 824–830

LEARNING OBJECTIVE: Identify the determinants of aggregate supply and distinguish between a movement along the short-run aggregate supply curve and a shift of the curve.

Summary

The **long-run aggregate supply (*LRAS*) curve** is a vertical line because in the long run, real GDP is always at its potential level and is unaffected by the price level. The short-run aggregate supply curve slopes upward because workers and firms fail to predict accurately the future price level. The three main explanations of why this failure results in an upward-sloping aggregate supply curve are that (1) contracts make wages and prices "sticky," (2) businesses often adjust wages slowly, and (3) menu costs make some prices sticky. **Menu costs** are the costs to firms of changing prices. If the price level changes but all else remains constant, the result is a movement up or down a stationary aggregate supply curve. If any other variable that affects the willingness of firms to supply goods and services changes, the aggregate supply curve will shift. The aggregate supply curve shifts as a result of increases in the labor force and capital stock, technological change, expected increases or decreases in the future price level, adjustments of workers and firms to errors in past expectations about the price level, and unexpected increases or decreases in the price of an important raw material. A **supply shock** is an unexpected event that causes the short-run aggregate supply curve to shift.

MyEconLab Visit **www.myeconlab.com** to complete these exercises online and get instant feedback.

Review Questions

2.1 Explain why the long-run aggregate supply curve is vertical.

2.2 What variables cause the long-run aggregate supply curve to shift? For each variable, identify whether an increase in that variable will cause the long-run aggregate supply curve to shift to the right or to the left.

2.3 Why does the short-run aggregate supply curve slope upward?

2.4 What variables cause the short-run aggregate supply curve to shift? For each variable, identify whether an increase in that variable will cause the short-run aggregate supply curve to shift to the right or to the left.

Problems and Applications

2.5 Explain how each of the following events would affect the long-run aggregate supply curve.
a. A higher price level
b. An increase in the labor force
c. An increase in the quantity of capital goods
d. Technological change

2.6 A student was asked to draw an aggregate demand and aggregate supply graph to illustrate the effect of an increase in aggregate supply. The student drew the following graph:

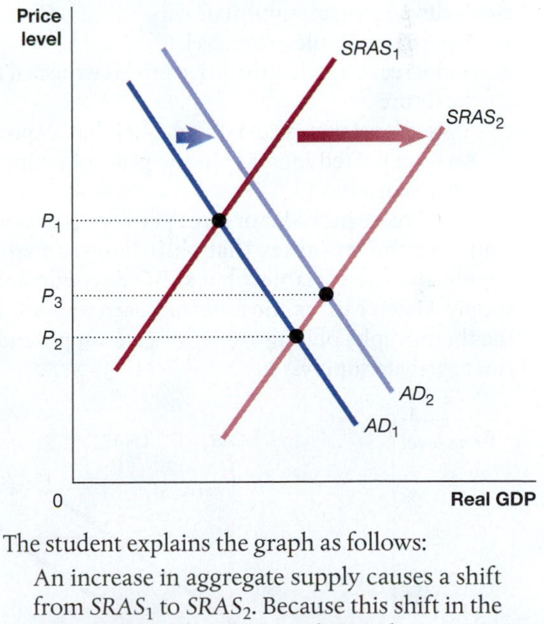

The student explains the graph as follows:

> An increase in aggregate supply causes a shift from $SRAS_1$ to $SRAS_2$. Because this shift in the aggregate supply curve results in a lower price level, consumption, investment, and net exports will increase. This change causes the aggregate demand curve to shift to the right, from AD_1 to AD_2. We know that real GDP will increase, but we can't be sure whether the price level will rise or fall because that depends on whether the

aggregate supply curve or the aggregate demand curve has shifted farther to the right. I assume that aggregate supply shifts out farther than aggregate demand, so I show the final price level, P_3, as being lower than the initial price level, P_1.

Explain whether you agree with the student's analysis. Be careful to explain exactly what—if anything—you find wrong with this analysis.

2.7 Consider the short-run aggregate supply curves in the following graph. What would cause a movement from point *A* to point *B* on $SRAS_1$? What would cause a movement from point *A* to point *C*?

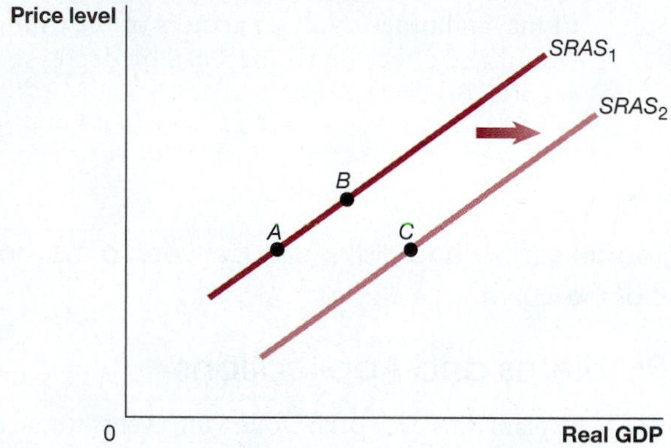

2.8 An article in the *Economist* noted that "the economy's potential to supply goods and services [is] determined by such things as the labour force and capital stock, as well as inflation expectations." Do you agree with this list of the determinants of potential GDP? Briefly explain.

Source: "Money's Muddled Message," *Economist*, March 19, 2009.

2.9 Explain how each of the following events would affect the short-run aggregate supply curve.

a. An increase in the price level
b. An increase in what the price level is expected to be in the future
c. A price level that is currently higher than expected
d. An unexpected increase in the price of an important raw material
e. An increase in the labor force participation rate

2.10 Consider the variables that shift long-run aggregate supply and the variables that shift short-run aggregate supply. Match each of the following scenarios with one of the three graphs of long-run aggregate supply and short-run aggregate supply.

1.

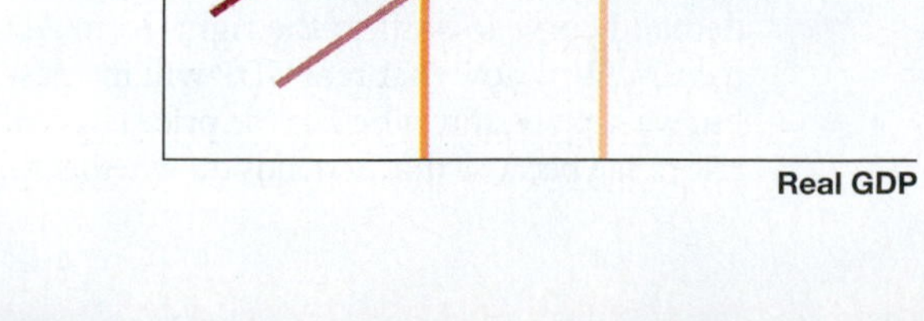

2.

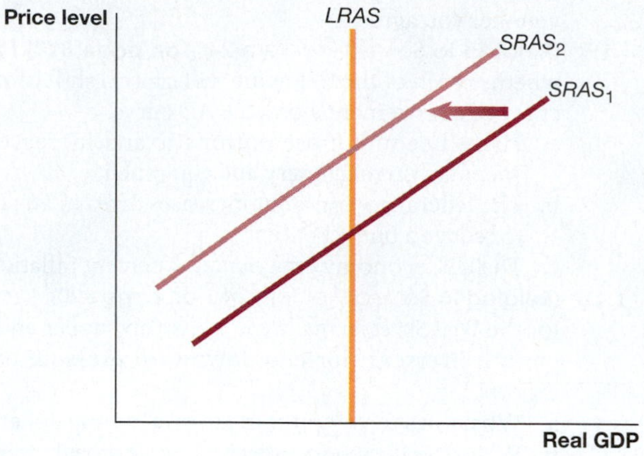

3.

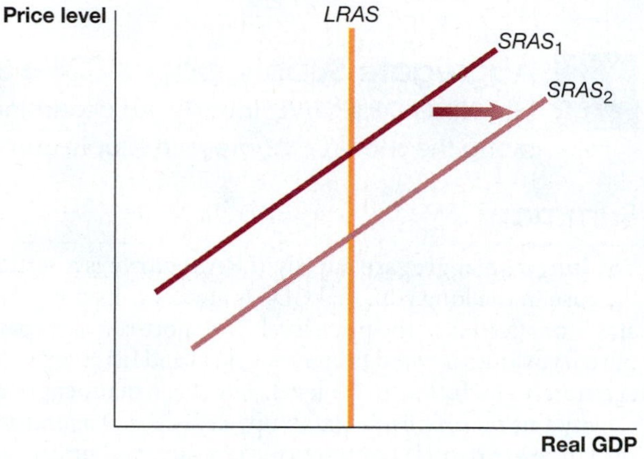

a. The expected future price level decreases.
b. Workers and firms adjust to having previously underestimated the price level
c. A positive technological change occurs.

2.11 The American Trucking Association anticipates a shortage of truck drivers in coming years as the number of retirees exceeds the number of new drivers who enter the profession. The number of train boxcars is also expected to fall by over 40 percent in coming years because federal regulations limit boxcars to 50 years of service and many currently in use will reach that limit by 2020. Lumber and paper producers that depend on boxcars for their shipments fear that they will have to depend more on trucks for transportation, which will cost as much as 20 percent more than shipping by rail. Is the reduction in the number of trucks and boxcars likely to affect the short-run aggregate supply curve? Is it likely to affect the long-run aggregate supply curve? Briefly explain.

Sources: Lindsay Ellis and Laura Stevens, "International Paper Focuses on Improving Shipment Planning," *Wall Street Journal*, July 30, 2015; and Bob Tita, "Why Railroads Can't Keep Enough Boxcars in Service," *Wall Street Journal*, June 21, 2015.

2.12 **(Related to the Making the Connection on page 826)** Economists Mary Daly, Bart Hobijn, and Timothy Ni of the Federal Reserve Bank of San Francisco argue that "employers hesitate to reduce wages and workers are reluctant to accept wage cuts, even during recessions." If a firm faces declining sales during a recession, why might the firm's managers decide to lay off some workers and freeze the wages of other workers rather than cut workers' nominal wages?

Source: Mary C. Daly, Bart Hobijn, and Timothy Ni, "The Path of Wage Growth and Unemployment," *Federal Reserve Bank of San Francisco Economic Letter*, July 15, 2013.

2.13 **(Related to the** Making the Connection **on page 826)** An article in the *Economist* discussing the 2007–2009 recession states that "employers found it difficult to reduce the cash value of the wages paid to their staff. (Foisting a pay cut on your entire workforce hardly boosts morale.)"

a. During a recession, couldn't firms reduce their labor costs by the same, or possibly more, if they laid off fewer workers while cutting wages? Why did few firms use this approach?

b. What does the article mean by firms reducing the "cash value" of workers' wages? Is it possible for firms to reduce workers' wages over time without reducing their cash value? Briefly explain.

Source: "Careful Now," *Economist*, April 11, 2015.

2.14 What are menu costs? If menu costs were eliminated, would the short-run aggregate supply curve be a vertical line? Briefly explain.

24.3 Macroeconomic Equilibrium in the Long Run and the Short Run, pages 830–836

LEARNING OBJECTIVE: Use the aggregate demand and aggregate supply model to illustrate the difference between short-run and long-run macroeconomic equilibrium.

Summary

In long-run macroeconomic equilibrium, the aggregate demand and short-run aggregate supply curves intersect at a point *on* the long-run aggregate supply curve. In short-run macroeconomic equilibrium, the aggregate demand and short-run aggregate supply curves often intersect at a point *off* the long-run aggregate supply curve. An automatic mechanism drives the economy to long-run equilibrium. If short-run equilibrium occurs at a point below potential GDP, wages and prices will fall, and the short-run aggregate supply curve will shift to the right until potential GDP is restored. If short-run equilibrium occurs at a point beyond potential GDP, wages and prices will rise, and the short-run aggregate supply curve will shift to the left until potential GDP is restored. Real GDP can be temporarily above or below its potential level, either because of shifts in the aggregate demand curve or because supply shocks lead to shifts in the short-run aggregate supply curve. **Stagflation** is a combination of inflation and recession, usually resulting from a supply shock.

MyEconLab Visit **www.myeconlab.com** to complete these exercises online and get instant feedback.

Review Questions

3.1 Describe the relationship of the *AD*, *SRAS*, and *LRAS* curves when the economy is in long-run macroeconomic equilibrium.

3.2 Why might a supply shock lead to stagflation?

3.3 Suppose the economy enters a recession. If government policymakers—Congress, the president, and members of the Federal Reserve—do not take any policy actions in response to the recession, which of the alternatives listed below is the likely result? Be sure to carefully explain why you chose the answer you did.

1. The unemployment rate will rise and remain higher even in the long run, and real GDP will drop below potential GDP and remain lower than potential GDP in the long run.
2. The unemployment rate will rise in the short run but return to the natural rate of unemployment in the long run, and real GDP will drop below potential GDP in the short run but return to potential GDP in the long run.
3. The unemployment rate will rise and remain higher even in the long run, and real GDP will drop below potential GDP in the short run but return to potential GDP in the long run.
4. The unemployment rate will rise in the short run but return to the natural rate of unemployment in the long run, and real GDP will drop below potential GDP in the short run and remain lower than potential GDP in the long run.

Problems and Applications

3.4 An article in the *Economist* noted that in the first half of 2015, the value of Canadian oil exports declined and that "energy firms, which account for around a third of capital spending, are expected to slash investment by nearly 40% this year." As a result, real GDP in Canada declined during the first six months of 2015.

a. Use a basic aggregate demand and aggregate supply graph (with *LRAS* constant) to illustrate this situation.

b. On your graph show the adjustment back to long-run equilibrium.

Source: "A Rough Ride," *Economist*, July 11, 2015.

3.5 Draw a basic aggregate demand and aggregate supply graph (with *LRAS* constant) that shows the economy in long-run equilibrium.

a. Assume that there is a large increase in demand for U.S. exports. Show the resulting short-run equilibrium on your graph. In this short-run equilibrium, is the unemployment rate likely to be higher or lower than it was before the increase in exports? Briefly explain. Explain how the economy adjusts back to long-run equilibrium. When the economy has adjusted back to long-run equilibrium, how have the values of each of the following changed relative to what they were before the increase in exports:

   i. Real GDP
   ii. The price level
   iii. The unemployment rate

b. Assume that there is an unexpected increase in the price of oil. Show the resulting short-run equilibrium on your

graph. Explain how the economy adjusts back to long-run equilibrium. In this short-run equilibrium, is the unemployment rate likely to be higher or lower than it was before the unexpected increase in the price of oil? Briefly explain. When the economy has adjusted back to long-run equilibrium, how have the values of each of the following changed relative to what they were before the unexpected increase in the price of oil:
i. Real GDP
ii. The price level
iii. The unemployment rate

3.6 **(Related to the Making the Connection on page 832)** Edward Leamer of the University of California, Los Angeles, has argued that "housing *is* the business cycle." Why would spending on housing be likely to fluctuate more than spending by households on consumer durables, such as automobiles or furniture, or spending by firms on plant and equipment?

Source: Edward E. Leamer, "Housing *Is* the Business Cycle," in *Housing, Housing Finance, and Monetary Policy*, Federal Reserve Bank of Kansas City, August 2007.

3.7 Consider the data in the following table for 1969 and 1970 (where the values for real GDP and potential GDP are in 2009 dollars):

Year	Actual Real GDP	Potential GDP	Unemployment Rate
1969	$4.71 trillion	$4.57 trillion	3.5%
1970	$4.72 trillion	$4.74 trillion	4.9%

Sources: U.S. Bureau of Labor Statistics; and Federal Reserve Bank of St. Louis.

a. In 1969, actual real GDP was greater than potential GDP. Briefly explain how this is possible.
b. Even though real GDP in 1970 was slightly greater than real GDP in 1969, the unemployment rate increased substantially from 1969 to 1970. Why did this increase in unemployment occur?
c. Was the inflation rate in 1970 likely to have been higher or lower than the inflation rate in 1969? Does your answer depend on whether the recession that began in December 1969 was caused by a change in a component of aggregate demand or by a supply shock?

3.8 Use the graph below to answer the following questions.

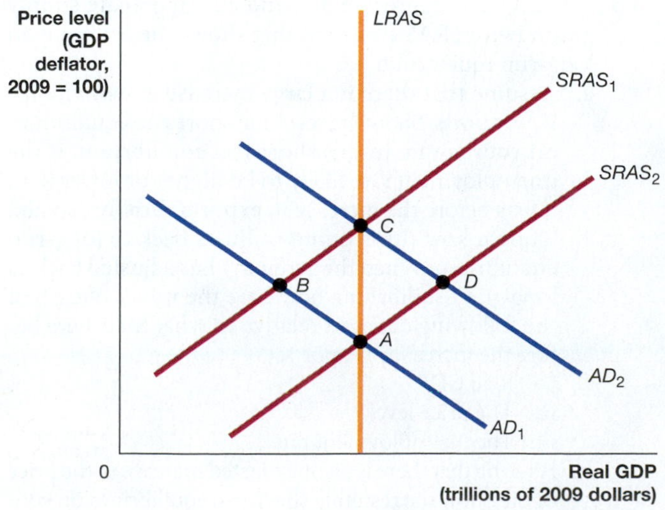

a. Which of the points *A*, *B*, *C*, or *D* can represent a long-run equilibrium?
b. Suppose that initially the economy is at point *A*. If aggregate demand increases from AD_1 to AD_2, which point represents short-run equilibrium? Which point represents the eventual long-run equilibrium? Briefly explain how the economy adjusts from the short-run equilibrium to the long-run equilibrium.

3.9 **(Related to the Making the Connection on page 835)** In early 2009, Christina Romer, who was then the chair of the Council of Economic Advisers, and Jared Bernstein, who was then an economic adviser to Vice President Joseph Biden, forecast how long they expected it would take for real GDP to return to potential GDP, assuming that Congress passed fiscal policy legislation proposed by President Obama:

> It should be understood that all of the estimates presented in this memo are subject to significant margins of error. There is the obvious uncertainty that comes from modeling a hypothetical package rather than the final legislation passed by the Congress. But there is the more fundamental uncertainty that comes with any estimate of the effects of a program. Our estimates of economic relationships ... are derived from historical experience and so will not apply exactly in any given episode. Furthermore, the uncertainty is surely higher than normal now because the current recession is unusual both in its fundamental causes and its severity.

Why would the causes of a recession and its severity affect the accuracy of forecasts of when the economy would return to potential GDP?

Source: Christina Romer and Jared Bernstein, *The Job Impact of the American Recovery and Reinvestment Plan*, January 9, 2009, p. 2.

3.10 The following graphs show either aggregate demand or short-run aggregate supply shifting to the right or to the left.

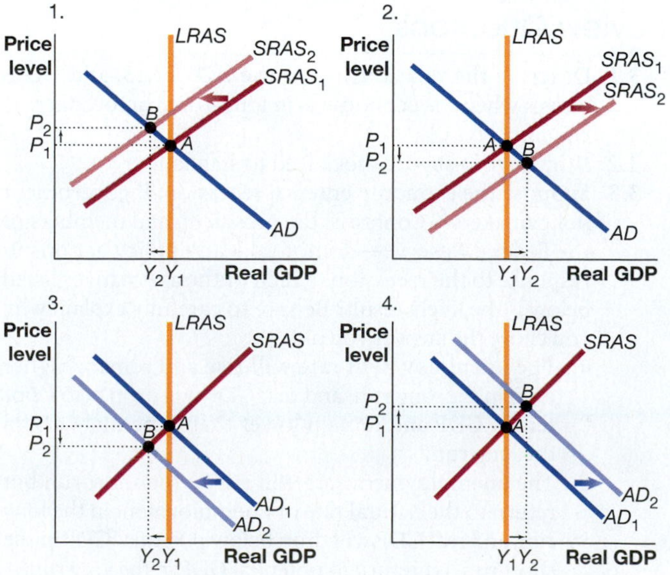

a. Match the following scenarios to the appropriate graph.
   i. An increase in the expected price level
   ii. An increase in households' expectations of their future income
   iii. A decrease in the price of an important natural resource
   iv. A decrease in firms' expectations of the future profitability of investment spending

b. Match one or more of the four graphs to each of the following scenarios:
   i. The economy experiences a recession
   ii. The economy experiences short-term inflation
   iii. The economy experiences stagflation

24.4 A Dynamic Aggregate Demand and Aggregate Supply Model, pages 837–842

LEARNING OBJECTIVE: Use the dynamic aggregate demand and aggregate supply model to analyze macroeconomic conditions.

Summary

To make the aggregate demand and aggregate supply model more realistic, we need to make it *dynamic* by incorporating three facts that were left out of the basic model: (1) Potential GDP increases continually, shifting the long-run aggregate supply curve to the right; (2) during most years, aggregate demand shifts to the right; and (3) except during periods when workers and firms expect high rates of inflation, the aggregate supply curve shifts to the right. The dynamic aggregate demand and aggregate supply model allows us to analyze macroeconomic conditions, including the beginning of the 2007–2009 recession.

MyEconLab Visit **www.myeconlab.com** to complete these exercises online and get instant feedback.

Review Questions

4.1 What are the key differences between the basic aggregate demand and aggregate supply model and the dynamic aggregate demand and aggregate supply model?

4.2 In the dynamic aggregate demand and aggregate supply model, what is the result of aggregate demand increasing more than potential GDP increases? What is the result of aggregate demand increasing less than potential GDP increases?

4.3 Briefly discuss the factors that caused the recession of 2007–2009.

Problems and Applications

4.4 Draw a dynamic aggregate demand and aggregate supply graph showing the economy moving from potential GDP in 2017 to potential GDP in 2018, with no inflation. Your graph should contain the *AD*, *SRAS*, and *LRAS* curves for both 2017 and 2018 and should indicate the short-run macroeconomic equilibrium for each year and the directions in which the curves have shifted. Identify what must happen to have growth during 2018 without inflation.

4.5 **(Related to Solved Problem 24.4 on page 841)** Consider the information in the following table for the first two years of the Great Depression (where the values for real GDP and potential GDP are in 2009 dollars):

Year	Actual Real GDP	Potential GDP	Price Level
1929	$1,056.6 billion	$1,006.3 billion	10.6
1930	$966.7 billion	$1,094.1 billion	10.2

Sources: U.S. Bureau of Labor Statistics; and Federal Reserve Bank of St. Louis.

a. The table shows that something happened during 1929–1930 that has not happened during the recessions of the past 50 years. What is it?

b. Draw a dynamic aggregate demand and aggregate supply graph to illustrate what happened during these years. Your graph should contain the *AD*, *SRAS*, and *LRAS* curves for both 1929 and 1930 and should indicate the short-run macroeconomic equilibrium for each year and the directions in which the curves shifted.

4.6 **(Related to Solved Problem 24.4 on page 841)** An article in the *New York Times* in early 2015 stated that economists at the Federal Reserve were forecasting that "real GDP would expand at a faster pace than potential output in 2015" and that the inflation rate during 2015 would be about 1 percent.

a. Fill in the blank cells in the table with estimates that are consistent with these forecasts.

	2015	2016
Real GDP	$16.5 trillion	
Potential GDP	$16.8 trillion	$17.1 trillion
GDP deflator	119.2	

b. Draw a dynamic aggregate demand and aggregate supply graph to illustrate your answer to part a.

Source: Reuters, "Factbox: Fed Staff Forecasts from FOMC Minutes," *New York Times*, April 8, 2015.

4.7 In the following graph, suppose that the economy moves from point A in year 1 to point B in year 2. Using the graph, briefly explain your answer to each of the questions.

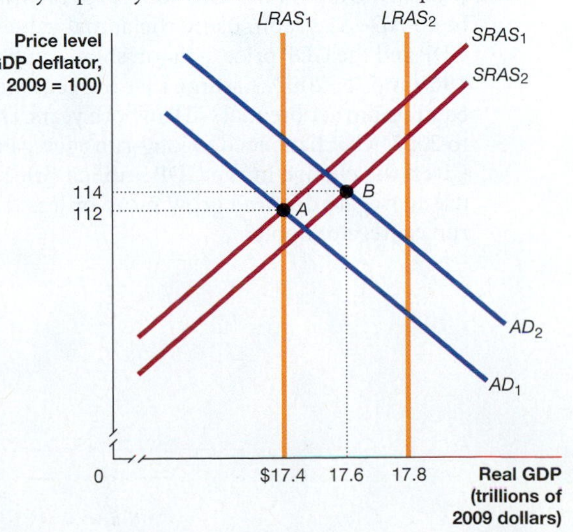

a. What is the growth rate in potential GDP from year 1 to year 2?
b. Is the unemployment rate in year 2 higher or lower than in year 1?
c. What is the inflation rate in year 2?
d. What is the growth rate of real GDP in year 2?

4.8 Explain whether you agree with the following statement:

> The dynamic aggregate demand and aggregate supply model predicts that a recession caused by a decline in *AD* will cause the inflation rate to fall. I know that the 2007–2009 recession was caused by a fall in *AD*, but the inflation rate was not lower as a result of the recession. The prices of most products were definitely higher in 2008 than they were in 2007, so the inflation rate could not have fallen.

4.9 In a speech in late 2011, President Barack Obama argued, "Probably the single greatest cause of the financial crisis and this brutal recession has been the housing bubble that burst four years ago." What did the president mean by the "housing bubble"? How can a housing bubble bring on a recession?

Source: Laura Meckler, "Obama Says Plan Will Cut Mortgage Payments for Millions," *Wall Street Journal*, October 24, 2011.

4.10 **(Related to the Chapter Opener on page 815)** Jet fuel is the largest operating cost for Delta Air Lines. In 2015, Delta's CEO Richard Anderson announced that the firm was likely to save more than $2 billion during the year because of lower fuel prices. Are firms like airlines that have costs that are dependent on raw material prices likely to be more or less affected by the business cycle than firms like automobile companies whose costs are not as dependent on raw material prices? Briefly explain.

Source: Paul R. La Monica, "Delta Air Lines Is Saving $2 Billion on Fuel," money.cnn.com, January 20, 2015.

Real-Time Data Exercises

D24.1 **(Showing movements in equilibrium real GDP and the price level)** Go to the Web site of the Federal Reserve Bank of St. Louis (FRED) (research.stlouisfed.org/fred2/) and find data on real GDP (GDPCA) and the GDP price deflator (USAGDPDEFAISMEI) for 1960, 1973, 1975, and 2007.

a. In an *AD–AS* graph, using the actual values for real GDP and the GDP price deflator, show equilibrium for 1960 and for 2007. Assume that the economy was at equilibrium at potential GDP in both years. From 1960 to 2007, what happened to long-run aggregate supply? Given the change in the GDP implicit price deflator, did aggregate demand grow more or less than long-run aggregate supply?
b. In an *AD–AS* graph, using the actual values for real GDP and the GDP price deflator, show equilibrium for 1973 and for 1975. Assume that the economy was in equilibrium at potential GDP in 1973 but in only a short-run equilibrium in 1975. Given the changes in real GDP and the GDP implicit price deflator, briefly explain what happened to short-run aggregate supply from 1973 to 1975.

D24.2 **(The effects of a positive supply shock)** Using data from the St. Louis Federal Reserve (research.stlouisfed.org/fred2/) FRED database, examine the experience of the U.S. economy during the 1990s. The U.S. economy experienced a positive supply shock with the spread of information communication technology and the Internet after 1995.

a. Download monthly data on the Personal Consumption Expenditure Price Index (PCEPI) from 1981 to the present. Calculate the inflation rate from 1982 to 2007 as the percentage change in the PCEPI from the same month in the previous year.
b. Calculate the average inflation rate from 1982 through 1994 and the average inflation rate from 1995 through 2007.
c. Are your calculations consistent with a positive supply shock after 1994? Briefly explain.

D24.3 **(Comparing business cycles across countries)** During the 2007–2009 period, the economies of the United Kingdom and the United States experienced similar problems. High oil prices and a housing bubble affected both economies. The financial crisis in the United States also affected investment in the United Kingdom, both by limiting credit and by increasing risk premiums. Using data from the St. Louis Federal Reserve (research.stlouisfed.org/fred2/) FRED database, examine the behavior of the U.K. economy since 2007.

a. Download quarterly data for real GDP (GBRRGDPQDSNAQ) and the GDP deflator (GBRGDPDEFQISMEI) for the United Kingdom from 2006 to the present. Calculate the growth rate of real GDP as the percentage change from the same quarter in the previous year and calculate the inflation rate as the percentage change in the GDP deflator from the same quarter in the previous year. Download data on the unemployment rate (GBRURHARMMDSMEI) for the same time period. For the frequency of the unemployment rate data, select quarterly, to match the frequency of the real GDP and GDP deflator data.
b. Download the three data series from 2007 to the present in the same graph. What do the data indicate about how similar the experience of the United Kingdom was to that of the United States during those years?

Appendix

Macroeconomic Schools of Thought

LEARNING OBJECTIVE: Compare macroeconomic schools of thought.

Macroeconomics became a separate field of economics in 1936, with the publication of John Maynard Keynes's book *The General Theory of Employment, Interest, and Money*. Keynes, an economist at the University of Cambridge in England, was attempting to explain the devastating Great Depression of the 1930s. Real GDP in the United States declined more than 25 percent between 1929 and 1933 and did not return to its potential level until the United States entered World War II in 1941 (see Chapter 23). The unemployment rate soared above 20 percent by 1933 and did not return to its 1929 level until 1942. Keynes developed a version of the aggregate demand and aggregate supply model to explain these facts. The widespread acceptance of Keynes's model during the 1930s and 1940s became known as the **Keynesian revolution**.

Keynesian revolution The name given to the widespread acceptance during the 1930s and 1940s of John Maynard Keynes's macroeconomic model.

In fact, using the aggregate demand and aggregate supply model remains the most widely accepted approach to analyzing macroeconomic issues. Because the model has been modified significantly from Keynes's day, many economists who use the model today refer to themselves as *new Keynesians*. The new Keynesians emphasize the importance of the stickiness of wages and prices in explaining fluctuations in real GDP. A significant number of economists, however, dispute whether using the aggregate demand and aggregate supply model, as we have discussed it in this chapter, is the best way to analyze macroeconomic issues. These alternative *schools of thought* use models that differ significantly from the standard aggregate demand and aggregate supply model. We can briefly consider four major alternative models:

1. The monetarist model
2. The new classical model
3. The real business cycle model
4. The Austrian model

The Monetarist Model

The monetarist model—also known as the neo-quantity theory of money model—was developed beginning in the 1940s by Milton Friedman, an economist at the University of Chicago who was awarded the Nobel Prize in Economics in 1976. Friedman argued that the Keynesian approach overstates the amount of macroeconomic instability in the economy. In particular, he argued that the economy will ordinarily be at potential GDP. In the book *A Monetary History of the United States: 1867–1960*, written with Anna Jacobson Schwartz, Friedman argued that most fluctuations in real output are caused by fluctuations in the money supply rather than by fluctuations in consumption spending or investment spending. Friedman and Schwartz argued that the severity of the Great Depression was caused by the Federal Reserve allowing the quantity of money in the economy to fall by more than 25 percent between 1929 and 1933.

In the United States, the Federal Reserve is responsible for managing the quantity of money. As we will discuss further in Chapter 26, the Federal Reserve has typically focused more on controlling interest rates than on controlling the money supply. Friedman argued that the Federal Reserve should change its practices and adopt a **monetary growth rule**, which is a plan for increasing the quantity of money at a fixed rate. He believed that adopting a monetary growth rule would reduce fluctuations in real GDP, employment, and inflation.

Monetary growth rule A plan for increasing the quantity of money at a fixed rate that does not respond to changes in economic conditions.

Friedman's ideas, which are referred to as **monetarism**, attracted significant support during the 1970s and early 1980s, when the U.S. economy experienced high rates of unemployment and inflation. The support for monetarism declined during the late 1980s and 1990s, when the unemployment and inflation rates were relatively low. In Chapter 25, we will discuss the *quantity theory of money*, which underlies the monetarist model.

Monetarism The macroeconomic theories of Milton Friedman and his followers, particularly the idea that the quantity of money should be increased at a constant rate.

The New Classical Model

The new classical model was developed in the mid-1970s by a group of economists including Nobel Laureate Robert Lucas of the University of Chicago, Nobel Laureate Thomas Sargent of New York University, and Robert Barro of Harvard University. Some of the views held by the new classical macroeconomists are similar to those held by economists before the Great Depression. Keynes referred to the economists before the Great Depression as *classical economists*. Like the classical economists, the new classical macroeconomists believe that the economy normally will be at potential GDP. They also believe that wages and prices adjust quickly to changes in demand and supply. Put another way, they believe the stickiness in wages and prices emphasized by the new Keynesians is unimportant.

Lucas argues that workers and firms have *rational expectations*, meaning that they form their expectations of the future values of economic variables, such as the inflation rate, by making use of all available information, including information on changes in the quantity of money and other factors that might affect aggregate demand. Fluctuations in output and employment occur if households and firms form incorrect expectations of the inflation rate. If the actual inflation rate is lower than the expected inflation rate, the actual real wage will be higher than the expected real wage. Higher real wages will lead to a recession because firms will hire fewer workers and cut back on production. As workers and firms adjust their expectations to the lower inflation rate, the real wage will decline, and employment and production will expand, bringing the economy out of recession. The ideas of Lucas and his followers are referred to as the **new classical macroeconomics**. Supporters of the new classical model agree with supporters of the monetarist model that the Federal Reserve should adopt a monetary growth rule. They argue that a monetary growth rule will make it easier for workers and firms to accurately forecast the price level, thereby reducing fluctuations in real GDP.

New classical macroeconomics The macroeconomic theories of Robert Lucas and others, particularly the idea that workers and firms have rational expectations.

The Real Business Cycle Model

In the 1980s, some economists, including Nobel Laureates Finn Kydland of the University of California, Santa Barbara, and Edward Prescott of Arizona State University, argued that Lucas was correct in assuming that workers and firms formed their expectations rationally and that wages and prices adjust quickly to supply and demand but was wrong about the source of fluctuations in real GDP. They argued that fluctuations in real GDP are caused by temporary shocks to productivity and not by inaccurate forecasts of the price level. These shocks can be negative, such as a decline in the availability of oil or other raw materials, or positive, such as technological change that makes it possible to produce more output with the same quantity of inputs.

According to this school of thought, shifts in the aggregate demand curve have no effect on real GDP because the short-run aggregate supply curve is vertical. (Other schools of thought believe that the short-run aggregate supply curve is upward sloping and that only the *long-run* aggregate supply curve is vertical.) Fluctuations in real GDP occur when a negative productivity shock causes the short-run aggregate supply curve to shift to the left—reducing real GDP—or a positive productivity shock causes the short-run aggregate supply curve to shift to the right—increasing real GDP. Because this model focuses on "real" factors—productivity shocks—rather than changes in the quantity of money to explain fluctuations in real GDP, it is known as the **real business cycle model**.

Real business cycle model A macroeconomic model that focuses on real, rather than monetary, causes of the business cycle.

The Austrian Model

The *Austrian school* of economics began in the late nineteenth century with the writings of Carl Menger, an economist at the University of Vienna. Important later contributors to this school of thought were Ludwig von Mises, who spent the later years of his career at New York University, and Friedrich von Hayek, who spent most of his career at the London School of Economics. The Austrian school is best known for arguing the superiority of the market system over government economic planning. Hayek, in particular, emphasized that only the price system operating through markets could make use of the dispersed information available to households and firms to bring about an efficient allocation of resources.

During the 1930s, Hayek developed a theory of the business cycle that emphasized the problems arising from central banks forcing interest rates to very low levels. Low interest rates cause businesses to spend more on factories, machinery, office buildings, and other types of capital. Initially, the surge in investment spending will produce an economic expansion, but the additional capital goods eventually produce more output than firms can sell for a profit. Businesses suffer losses, reduce output, and lay off workers, resulting in a recession. The lower the central bank drives interest rates, the greater the increase in investment spending, the larger the economic expansion, and the deeper the eventual recession.

For a time in the early 1930s, Hayek's theory of the business cycle attracted significant interest from economists, particularly in the United Kingdom. After the publication of Keynes's *General Theory* in 1936, interest in Hayek's theory declined, and today only a relatively few economists belong to the Austrian school. In the past few years, however, Austrian economists have argued that the events of the 2007–2009 recession fit their model well: The Federal Reserve lowered interest rates to fight the 2001 recession, and the low interest rates sparked a surge in capital spending—in this case, spending on houses rather than on factories or office buildings. Eventually, the excessive investment in housing ended with a housing bust and a severe recession.

Making the Connection

Karl Marx: Capitalism's Severest Critic

The schools of macroeconomic thought we have discussed in this appendix are considered part of mainstream economic theory because of their acceptance of the market system as the best means of raising living standards in the long run. One quite influential critic of mainstream economic theory was Karl Marx. Marx was born in Trier, Germany, in 1818. After graduating from the University of Berlin in 1841, he began a career as a political journalist and agitator. His political activities caused him to be expelled first from Germany and then from France and Belgium. In 1849, he moved to London, where he spent the remainder of his life.

In 1867, Marx published the first volume of his greatest work, *Das Kapital*. Marx read closely the most prominent mainstream economists, including Adam Smith, David Ricardo, and John Stuart Mill. But Marx believed that he understood how market systems would evolve in the long run much better than those earlier authors. He argued that the market system would eventually be replaced by a Communist economy, in which the workers would control production. He believed in the *labor theory of value*, which attributed all the value of a good or service to the labor embodied in it. According to Marx, the owners of businesses—capitalists—did not earn profits by contributing anything of value to the production of goods or services. Instead, they earned profits because their "monopoly of the means of production"—their ownership of factories and machinery—allowed them to exploit workers by paying them wages that were much lower than the value of workers' contributions to production.

Karl Marx predicted that a final economic crisis would lead to the collapse of the market system.

Marx argued that the wages of workers would be driven to levels that allowed only bare survival. He also argued that small firms would eventually be driven out of business by larger firms, forcing owners of small firms into the working class. Control of production would ultimately be concentrated in the hands of a few firms, which would have difficulty selling the goods they produced to the impoverished masses. A final economic crisis would lead the working classes to rise up, seize control of the economy, and establish Communism. Marx died in 1883, without having provided a detailed explanation of how the Communist economy would operate.

Marx had relatively little influence on mainstream thinking in the United States, but several political parties in Europe were guided by his ideas. In 1917, the Bolshevik

Party seized control of Russia and established the Soviet Union, the first Communist state. Although the Soviet Union was a vicious dictatorship under Vladimir Lenin and his successor, Joseph Stalin, its prestige rose when it avoided the macroeconomic difficulties that plagued the market economies during the 1930s. By the late 1940s, Communist parties had also come to power in China and the countries of Eastern Europe. Poor economic performance contributed to the eventual collapse of the Soviet Union and its replacement by a market system, although one with significant government intervention in the economy. The Communist Party remains in power in China, but the economy is evolving toward a market system. Today, only North Korea and Cuba have economies that claim to be based on the ideas of Karl Marx.

Key Terms

CHAPTER

25

Money, Banks, and the Federal Reserve System

Chapter Outline and Learning Objectives

Can Greece Function without Banks?

How often do you use a bank? If you are like most people, you withdraw cash from an ATM a couple of times per week and occasionally deposit checks. You may have visited a bank to apply for a student loan or a car loan. If you own your own business, you will have had many more interactions with banks. For example, you may have taken out a long-term loan to finance expanding your business.

Individuals and businesses in most countries would consider it difficult to function without banks. But that's the situation people in Greece faced in 2015. In 2001, Greece and most other European countries abandoned their individual currencies in favor of the euro. (Greece's currency had been the drachma.) Following the 2007–2009 financial crisis, the Greek government had trouble paying interest on the bonds it had issued. Many people feared that Greece might leave the euro and resume using the drachma. If that happened, the drachma might be worth less than the euro, which gave people in Greece an incentive to hold as many euros as they could. In 2015, Greece appeared to be in danger of defaulting on its debts. People responded by withdrawing large amounts of euros from Greek banks. To keep the banks from losing all their funds, the Greek government decided to close the banks for three weeks and limit withdrawals from ATM machines to 60 euros (about $66) per day.

Closing the banks dealt a heavy blow to the Greek economy. With the banks closed, many businesses insisted on being paid in cash. Consumers had trouble finding cash, though, because many ATMs had been emptied of currency. Some stores began accepting promises to pay later from customers who had no cash. Nikos Manisoitis & Son is a Greek firm that imports spices, pasta, and other products. The owner complained: "We feel like hostages. We can't move our money from the banks, and we fear that we are about to lose everything." Some importers loaded suitcases with euros and flew to other countries to pay their suppliers.

As we saw in Chapter 21, a country needs a well-functioning financial system if its economy is to prosper and grow. Greece's situation in the summer of 2015 shows what can happen when a country's banking system breaks down. In this chapter, we will study the role banks play in the financial system. We will also discuss the link between changes in the money supply and the inflation rate, as well as provide an overview of the operations of the Federal Reserve, which is the central bank of the United States.

Sources: Suzanne Daley, "Greeks Spend in Droves, Afraid of Losing Savings to a Bailout," *New York Times*, July 8, 2015; Liz Alderman, "Greek Economy under Siege, with Fears That the Worst Is Coming," *New York Times*, July 9, 2015; and "When Banks Die," *Economist*, July 5, 2015.

Economics in Your Life

What if Money Became Increasingly Valuable?

Most people are used to the fact that as prices rise each year, the purchasing power of money falls. You will be able to buy fewer goods and services with $1,000 one year from now, and you will be able to buy even fewer goods and services the year after that. In fact, with an inflation rate of just 3 percent, in 25 years, $1,000 will buy only what $475 can buy today. Suppose that you could live in an economy where the purchasing power of money *rose* each year? What would be the advantages and disadvantages of living in such an economy? As you read this chapter, try to answer these questions. You can check your answers against those we provide **on page** 885 at the end of this chapter.

In this chapter, we will explore the role of money in the economy. We will see how the banking system creates money and what policy tools the Federal Reserve uses to manage the quantity of money in the United States. We will also examine the crisis in the banking system during and after the 2007–2009 recession. At the end of this chapter, we will explore the link between changes in the quantity of money and changes in the price level. What you learn in this chapter will serve as an important foundation for understanding monetary policy and fiscal policy, which we study in Chapters 26 through 28.

25.1 What Is Money, and Why Do We Need It?

LEARNING OBJECTIVE: Define money and discuss the four functions of money.

Money Assets that people are generally willing to accept in exchange for goods and services or for payment of debts.

Asset Anything of value owned by a person or a firm.

Could an economy function without money? There are historical examples of economies in which people traded goods for other goods rather than use money. For example, on the American frontier during colonial times, very little money was available, so a farmer might have traded a plow for a cow. Most economies, though, use money. The economic definition of **money** is any asset that people are generally willing to accept in exchange for goods and services or for payment of debts. Recall that an **asset** is anything of value owned by a person or a firm (see Chapter 8). There are many possible kinds of money: In West Africa, at one time, cowrie shells served as money. During World War II, prisoners of war used cigarettes as money.

Barter and the Invention of Money

To understand the importance of money, let's consider further the situation in economies that do not use money. Economies where goods and services are traded directly for other goods and services are called *barter economies*. Barter economies have a major shortcoming. To illustrate this shortcoming, consider a farmer on the American frontier in colonial days. Suppose the farmer needed a cow and proposed trading a spare plow to a neighbor for one of the neighbor's cows. If the neighbor did not want the plow, the trade would not happen. For a barter trade to take place between two people, each person must want what the other one has. Economists refer to this requirement as a *double coincidence of wants*. The farmer who wants the cow might eventually be able to obtain one if he first trades with some other neighbor for something the neighbor with the cow wants. However, it may take several trades before the farmer is ultimately able to trade for what the neighbor with the cow wants. Locating several trading partners and making several intermediate trades can take considerable time and energy.

Commodity money A good used as money that also has value independent of its use as money.

To avoid the problems with barter, societies have an incentive to identify a product that most people will accept in exchange for what they have to trade. For example, in colonial times, animal skins were very useful in making clothing. The first governor of Tennessee actually received a salary of 1,000 deerskins per year, and the state's secretary of the Treasury received 450 otter skins per year. A good used as money that also has value independent of its use as money is called a **commodity money**. Historically, once a good became widely accepted as money, even people who did not have an immediate use for it would be willing to accept it. A colonial farmer—or the governor of Tennessee—might not want a deerskin, but as long as he knew he could use the deerskin to buy other goods and services, he would be willing to accept it in exchange for what he had to sell.

Trading goods and services is much easier when money becomes available. People only need to sell what they have for money and then use the money to buy what they want. If the colonial family could find someone to buy their plow, they could use the money to buy the cow they wanted. The family with the cow would accept the money because they knew they could use it to buy what they wanted. When money is available, families are more likely to specialize and less likely to produce everything or nearly everything they need themselves.

Most people in modern economies are highly specialized. They do only one thing—work as a nurse, an accountant, or an engineer—and use the money they earn to buy everything else they need. As we discussed in Chapter 2, people become much more productive by specializing because they can pursue their *comparative advantage*. The high income levels in modern economies are based on the specialization that money makes possible. We can now answer the question, "Why do we need money?" *By making exchange easier, money allows people to specialize and become more productive.* MyEconLab Concept Check

The Functions of Money

Anything used as money—whether a deerskin, a cowrie seashell, cigarettes, or a dollar bill—must serve four key functions in the economy:

1. It must act as a medium of exchange.
2. It must serve as a unit of account.
3. It must serve as a store of value.
4. It must offer a standard of deferred payment.

Medium of Exchange Money serves as a medium of exchange when sellers are willing to accept it in exchange for goods or services. When the local supermarket accepts your $5 bill in exchange for bread and milk, the $5 bill is serving as a medium of exchange. With a medium of exchange, people can sell goods and services for money and use the money to buy what they want. An economy is more efficient when people accept a single good as a medium of exchange.

Unit of Account In a barter system, each good has many prices. A cow may be worth 2 plows, 20 bushels of wheat, or 6 axes. Once a single good is used as money, each good has a single price rather than many prices. This function of money gives buyers and sellers a *unit of account*, a way of measuring value in the economy in terms of money. Because the U.S. economy uses dollars as money, each good has a price in terms of dollars.

Store of Value Money allows people to easily store value: If you do not use all your dollars to buy goods and services today, you can hold the rest to use in the future. Money is not the only store of value, however. Any asset—shares of Facebook stock, Treasury bonds, real estate, or Renoir paintings, for example—represents a store of value. Financial assets, such as stocks and bonds, offer an important benefit relative to holding money because they pay a higher rate of interest or may increase in value in the future. Other assets also have advantages relative to money because they provide services. A house, for example, offers you a place to sleep.

Why, then, do people hold any money? The answer has to do with *liquidity*, or the ease with which people can convert an asset into the medium of exchange. Because money is the medium of exchange, it is the most liquid asset. If you want to buy something and you need to sell an asset to do so, you are likely to incur a cost. For example, if you want to buy a car and need to sell bonds or stocks to do so, you will need to pay a commission to your broker. To avoid such costs, people are willing to hold some of their wealth in the form of money, even though other assets offer a greater return as stores of value.

Standard of Deferred Payment Money is useful because it can serve as a standard of deferred payment in borrowing and lending. It can facilitate exchange at a *given point in time* by providing a medium of exchange and unit of account. Money can facilitate exchange *over time* by providing a store of value and a standard of deferred payment. For example, a computer manufacturer may buy hard drives from another firm in exchange for the promise of making payment in 60 days.

How important is it that money be a reliable store of value and standard of deferred payment? People care about how much food, clothing, and other goods and services their dollars will buy. The value of money depends on its *purchasing power*, which refers to its ability to buy goods and services. Inflation causes a decline in purchasing power because with rising prices, a given amount of money can purchase fewer goods and services. When inflation reaches very high levels, money is no longer a reliable store of value or standard of deferred payment. MyEconLab Concept Check

What Can Serve as Money?

Having a medium of exchange helps to make transactions easier, which allows the economy to work more efficiently. The next question to consider is: What can serve as money? That is, which assets can be used as the medium of exchange? We saw earlier that an asset must, at a minimum, be generally accepted as payment to serve as money. In practical terms, however, it must be even more.

These five criteria make an asset suitable for use as a medium of exchange:

1. The asset must be *acceptable* to (that is, usable by) most people.
2. It should be of *standardized quality* so that any two units are identical.
3. It should be *durable* so that value is not lost by its quickly wearing out.
4. It should be *valuable* relative to its weight so that amounts large enough to be useful in trade can be easily transported.
5. It should be *divisible* so that it can be used in purchases of both low-priced and high-priced goods.

Dollar bills meet all these criteria. What determines the acceptability of dollar bills as a medium of exchange? Basically, it is through self-fulfilling expectations: You value something as money only if you believe that others will accept it from you as payment. A society's willingness to use paper dollars as money is what makes them an acceptable medium of exchange.

Commodity Money Commodity money has value independent of its use as money. Gold, for example, was a common form of money in the nineteenth and early twentieth centuries because it was a medium of exchange, a unit of account, a store of value, and a standard of deferred payment. But commodity money has a significant problem: Its value depends on its purity. Therefore, someone who wanted to cheat could mix a low-value metal, like iron, with a precious metal, like gold or silver. Another problem with using gold as money was that the money supply was difficult to control because it depended partly on unpredictable discoveries of new gold fields.

Fiat Money It can be inefficient for an economy to rely on only gold or other precious metals for its money supply. What if you had to transport bars of gold to settle your transactions? Not only would doing so be difficult and costly, but you would run the risk of being robbed. To get around this problem, private institutions or governments began to store gold and issue paper certificates that could be redeemed for gold. In modern economies, paper currency is generally issued by a *central bank*, which is an agency of the government that regulates the money supply. The **Federal Reserve** is the central bank of the United States. Today, no government in the world issues paper currency that can be redeemed for gold. Paper currency has no value unless it is used as money, and it is therefore not a commodity money. Instead, paper currency is a **fiat money**, which has no value except as money. If paper currency has no value except as money, why do consumers and firms use it?

Federal Reserve The central bank of the United States.

Fiat money Money, such as paper currency, that is authorized by a central bank or governmental body and that does not have to be exchanged by the central bank for gold or some other commodity money.

If you look at the top of a U.S. dollar bill, you will see the words "Federal Reserve Note" because it is issued by the Federal Reserve. Because U.S. dollars are fiat money, the Federal Reserve is not required to give you gold or silver for your dollar bills. Federal Reserve currency is *legal tender* in the United States, which means the federal government requires that it be accepted in payment of debts and requires that cash or checks denominated in dollars be used in payment of taxes. Despite being legal tender, dollar bills would not be a good medium of exchange and could not serve as money if people didn't usually accept them. The key to this acceptance is that *households and firms have confidence that if they accept paper dollars in exchange for goods and services, the dollars will not lose much value during the time they hold them.* Without this confidence, dollar bills would not serve as a medium of exchange. MyEconLab Concept Check

Making the Connection
MyEconLab Video

Apple Didn't Want My Cash!

The law doesn't stop Apple from requiring customers to use a credit card rather than cash, but the company decided to lift its ban on paying for iPads with cash after bad publicity.

If Federal Reserve Notes are legal tender, doesn't that mean that everyone in the United States, including every business, has to accept paper money? The answer to this question is "no," as a woman in California found out when she went to an Apple store in Palo Alto and tried to buy an iPad using $600 in currency. The store refused to sell her the iPad for cash. At that time, the iPad had just been released, and Apple did not want to sell large numbers to people who were buying them to resell on eBay, Craigslist, or elsewhere. So, a customer wanting to buy an iPad had to pay with either a credit card or a debit card, which would make it easier for Apple to keep track of anyone attempting to buy more than the limit of two per customer.

Because Federal Reserve Notes are legal tender, creditors must accept them in payment of debts, and the government will accept them in payment of taxes. However, as this incident demonstrates, firms do not have to accept cash as payment for goods and services. As the U.S. Treasury Department explains on its Web site:

> There is ... no Federal statute mandating that a private business, a person or an organization must accept currency or coins as payment for goods and/or services. ... For example, a bus line may prohibit payment of fares in pennies or dollar bills. In addition, movie theaters, convenience stores and gas stations may refuse to accept large denomination currency (usually notes above $20) as a matter of policy.

The woman who tried to buy an iPad for cash was disabled and on a limited income, so the incident led to negative publicity for Apple. As a result, Apple decided to lift its ban on paying for iPads with cash, provided that the customer was willing to set up an Apple account at the time of purchase. In addition, Apple presented a free iPad to the customer who was originally turned down when she tried to pay with cash.

Sources: Michael Winter, "Apple Ends No-Cash Policy and California Woman Gets Free iPad," www.usatoday.com, May 20, 2010; and U.S. Treasury, "FAQs: Currency," www.treasury.gov/resource-center/faqs/Currency/Pages/edu_faq_currency_index2.aspx.

Your Turn: Test your understanding by doing related problem 1.9 on page 887 at the end of this chapter.

MyEconLab Study Plan

25.2 How Is Money Measured in the United States Today?

LEARNING OBJECTIVE: Discuss the definitions of the money supply used in the United States today.

People are interested in the money supply because, as we will see, changes in the money supply can affect other economic variables, including employment, gross domestic product (GDP), and inflation. If the only function of money was to serve as a medium of exchange, then a narrow definition of the money supply should include only currency, checking account deposits, and traveler's checks because households and firms can easily use these assets to buy goods and services. A broader definition of the money supply would include other assets that can be used as a medium of exchange even though they are not as liquid as currency or checking account deposits. For example, you can't directly buy goods or services with funds in a bank savings account, but it is easy to withdraw funds from your savings account and then use these funds to buy goods and services.

Congress gave the Federal Reserve the responsibility of regulating the money supply and the task of determining how to measure it. The Federal Reserve's measures of the money supply have changed several times over the decades. Currently, the Federal Reserve publishes data on two measures of the money supply: *M1* and *M2*. These measures, sometimes called *monetary aggregates,* are important to understand, so we devote the following sections to discussing them.

M1: A Narrow Definition of the Money Supply

M1 The narrow definition of the money supply: the sum of currency in circulation, checking account deposits in banks, and holdings of traveler's checks.

Figure 25.1 illustrates the definitions of the money supply. The narrow definition of the money supply, **M1**, includes the following:

1. *Currency*, which is all the paper money and coins held by households and firms (not including currency held by banks)
2. The value of all checking account deposits in banks
3. The value of traveler's checks (Because this last category is so small—typically less than $4 billion—relative to the other two categories, we will ignore it in our discussion of the money supply.)

Although currency has almost as large a value as checking account deposits, checking account deposits are used much more often than currency to make payments. More than 80 percent of all expenditures on goods and services are made with checks rather than with currency. In fact, the total amount of currency in circulation—$1.3 trillion in July 2015—is a misleading number. This amount is more than $4,000 per person—adult or child—in the United States. If this sounds like an unrealistically large amount of currency to be held per person, it is. Economists estimate that more than 60 percent of U.S. currency is actually outside the borders of the United States. More than three-quarters of U.S. paper currency is in denominations of $100 or larger—too large to be used for routine buying and selling within the United States.

Who holds these dollars outside the United States? Foreign banks and foreign governments hold some U.S. currency, but most is held by households and firms in countries where there is not much confidence in the local currency or where the underground economy is large. When inflation rates are very high, many households and firms do not want to hold their domestic currency because it is losing its value too rapidly. The value of the U.S. dollar will be much more stable than their domestic currency. If enough people are willing to accept dollars as well as—or instead of—domestic currency, dollars become a second currency for the country. When inflation soared in the African country of Zimbabwe to the point where it took 15 *billion* Zimbabwean dollars

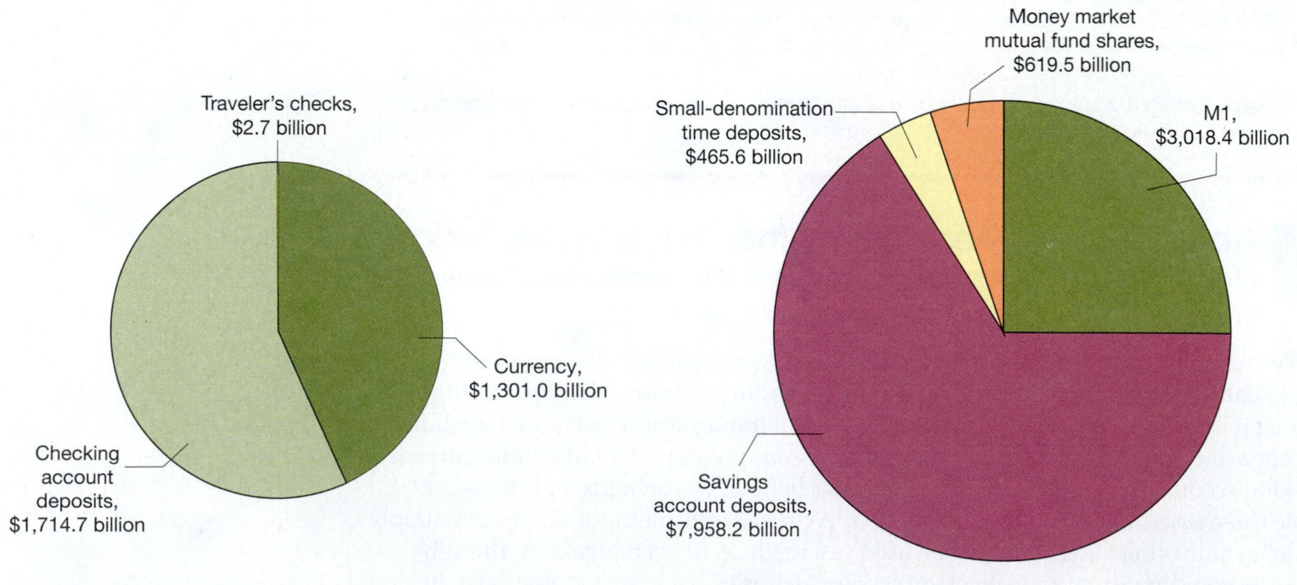

(a) M1 = $3,018.4 billion

(b) M2 = $12,061.7 billion

MyEconLab Real-time data

Figure 25.1 Measuring the Money Supply

The Federal Reserve uses two different measures of the money supply: M1 and M2. Panel (a) shows the assets in M1. Panel (b) shows M2, which includes the assets in M1, as well as money market mutual fund shares, small-denomination time deposits, and savings account deposits.

Source: Board of Governors of the Federal Reserve System, "Federal Reserve Statistical Release, H.6," July 30, 2015.

to buy a can of Coca-Cola, the government went so far as to adopt the U.S. dollar as the country's official currency. MyEconLab Concept Check

M2: A Broad Definition of Money

Before 1980, U.S. law prohibited banks from paying interest on checking account deposits. Households and firms held checking account deposits primarily to buy goods and services. M1 was, therefore, very close to the function of money as a medium of exchange. Almost all currency, checking account deposits, and traveler's checks were held with the intention of buying and selling, not with the intention of storing value. In 1980, the law was changed to allow banks to pay interest on certain types of checking accounts. This change reduced the difference between checking accounts and savings accounts, although people are still not allowed to write checks against their savings account balances.

After 1980, economists began to pay closer attention to a broader definition of the money supply, **M2**. As panel (b) of Figure 25.1 shows, M2 includes everything that is in M1, plus savings account deposits, small-denomination time deposits—such as certificates of deposit (CDs)—balances in money market deposit accounts in banks, and noninstitutional money market fund shares. Small-denomination time deposits are similar to savings accounts, but the deposits are for a fixed period of time—usually from six months to several years—and withdrawals before that time are subject to a penalty. Mutual fund companies sell shares to investors and use the funds raised to buy financial assets such as stocks and bonds. Some of these mutual funds, such as Vanguard's Treasury Money Market Fund or Fidelity's Cash Reserves Fund, are called *money market mutual funds* because they invest in very short-term bonds, such as U.S. Treasury bills. The balances individual investors hold in these funds are included in M2. Each week, the Federal Reserve publishes statistics on M1 and M2. In the discussion that follows, we will use the M1 definition of the money supply because it corresponds most closely to money as a medium of exchange.

M2 A broader definition of the money supply: It includes M1 plus savings account deposits, small-denomination time deposits, balances in money market deposit accounts in banks, and noninstitutional money market fund shares.

There are two key points to keep in mind about the money supply:

1. The narrowest definition of the money supply consists of *both* currency and checking account deposits.
2. Because balances in checking account deposits are included in the money supply, banks play an important role in the way the money supply increases and decreases. We will discuss this second point further in the next section. MyEconLab Concept Check

Don't Let This Happen to You

Don't Confuse Money with Income or Wealth

According to *Forbes*, in 2015, Bill Gates's wealth of $79 billion made him the richest person in the world. He also has a very large income, but how much money does he have? Your *wealth* is equal to the value of your assets minus the value of any debts you have. Your *income* is equal to your earnings during the year. Bill Gates's earnings as chairman of Microsoft and from his investments are very large. But his *money* is just equal to what he has in currency and checking accounts. Only a small proportion of Gates's $79 billion in wealth is likely to be in currency or checking accounts. Most of his wealth is invested in stocks and bonds and other financial assets that are not included in the definition of money.

In everyday conversation, we often describe someone who is wealthy or who has a high income as "having a lot of money." But when economists use the word *money*, they are usually referring to currency plus checking account deposits. It is important to keep straight the differences between wealth, income, and money.

Just as money and income are not the same for a person, they are not the same for the whole economy. National income in the United States was equal to $15.1 trillion in 2014. The money supply in 2014 was $2.8 trillion (using the M1 measure). There is no reason why national income in a country should be equal to the country's money supply, nor will an increase in a country's money supply necessarily increase the country's national income.

Source: "The World's Billionaires," *Forbes*, March 2, 2015.

MyEconLab Study Plan

Your Turn: Test your understanding by doing related problems 2.5 and 2.6 on page 887 at the end of this chapter.

Solved Problem 25.2

MyEconLab Interactive Animation

The Definitions of M1 and M2

Suppose you decide to withdraw $2,000 from your checking account and put the money into a bank certification of deposit (CD). Briefly explain how this action will affect M1 and M2.

Solving the Problem

Step 1: Review the chapter material. This problem is about the definitions of the money supply, so you may want to review the section "How Is Money Measured in the United States Today?" which begins on page 861.

Step 2: Use the definitions of M1 and M2 to answer the problem. Funds in checking accounts are included in both M1 and M2. Funds in CDs are included only in M2. It is tempting to answer this problem by saying that shifting $2,000 from a checking account to a CD reduces M1 by $2,000 and increases M2 by $2,000, but the $2,000 in your checking account was already counted in M2. So, the correct answer is that your action reduces M1 by $2,000 but leaves M2 unchanged.

MyEconLab Study Plan

Your Turn: For more practice, do related problems 2.7 and 2.8 on page 887 at the end of this chapter.

What about Credit Cards and Debit Cards?

Many people buy goods and services with credit cards, yet credit cards are not included in either definition of the money supply. The reason is that when you buy something with a credit card, you are in effect taking out a loan from the bank that issued the credit card. The transaction is complete only when you pay your credit card bill at the end of the month—often with a check or an electronic transfer from your checking account. In contrast, with a debit card, the funds to make the purchase are taken directly from your checking account. In either case, the cards themselves do not represent money. MyEconLab Concept Check

Making the Connection

MyEconLab Video

Are Bitcoins Money?

Bitcoins are created by computer calculations, not by central banks.

Typically, when we think of "money," we think of currency issued by a government. But we have just seen that currency represents only a small part of the money supply of the United States, whether measured as M1 or M2. The non-currency components of M1 or M2, although not issued by the government, are familiar financial assets such as checking or savings accounts. Some households and firms have shifted away from M1 or M2 to finance their buying and selling of goods and services and are instead using e-money, or digital funds. The best-known form of e-money is PayPal, which until 2015 was owned by eBay, the online auction site. An individual or a firm can set up a PayPal account by transferring funds from a checking account or credit card. As long as a seller is willing to accept funds from a buyer's PayPal (or other e-money) account, e-money functions like conventional government-issued money.

Recently, journalists, economists, and policymakers have been debating the merits of bitcoin, a new form of e-money. Unlike PayPal and other similar services for transferring money electronically, bitcoin is not owned by a firm but is instead the product of a decentralized system of linked computers. Bitcoin was founded in 2009 by "Satoshi Nakamoto," which is likely an assumed name taken by bitcoin's founder or founders. Bitcoins are produced by people performing the complicated calculations necessary to ensure that online purchases made with bitcoins are legitimate—that is, that someone doesn't try to spend the same bitcoin multiple times. People who successfully complete these calculations are awarded a fixed amount of bitcoins—typically 25. This process of bitcoin "mining" will continue until a maximum of 21 million bitcoins has been produced—a total expected to be reached in 2030.

Because people can buy and sell bitcoins in exchange for dollars and other currencies on Web sites, some people refer to it as a "cryptocurrency." You can buy bitcoins and store them in a "digital wallet" on a smartphone. You can then buy something in a store that accepts bitcoins by scanning a bar code with your phone. A number of Web sites, such as BitPay, which is based in Atlanta, allow merchants to process purchases made with bitcoins in a manner similar to the way they process credit card payments.

Why would buyers and sellers prefer to use bitcoins rather than cash or a credit card? The popularity of bitcoins with some buyers may be due to its being a new and fashionable way to make purchases, and because of the convenience of using a smartphone to make a purchase. In addition, some people are afraid that because central banks in most countries greatly increased the money supply during and after the recession of 2007–2009, the result will eventually be high rates of inflation. These people hope that because the total amount of bitcoins is limited, inflation will not undermine their value. Finally, when you buy something with a credit card, the credit card company has a permanent record of your transaction. Bitcoin transactions are more private because no such record of your transaction exists.

Some retailers prefer bitcoins to credit card purchases because the retailers pay only about 1 percent of the sale in processing costs, as opposed to about 3 percent for a credit card purchase. In addition, a bitcoin sale is final, just as if the purchase were made with cash, unlike credit card sales, where the buyer can dispute the purchase even months after it was made.

Despite these possible benefits to using bitcoin, by 2015, it had not yet been widely adopted. The introduction of Apple Pay and Google Wallet provided consumers with a way to use their smartphones linked to a credit card to make payments, which undercut one of bitcoin's advantages. Some firms also questioned whether the software underlying bitcoin was capable of dealing with a large number of transactions, which would be a barrier to the cryptocurrency being widely used. The most popular online bitcoin exchange, Japan-based Mt. Gox, collapsed, further reducing confidence in the cryptocurrency. At the time of the firm's collapse, the CEO said that software problems had allowed hackers to withdraw more than $500 million worth of bitcoins investors had stored on the exchange. The Japanese police later arrested the CEO.

Some policymakers are concerned that investors on exchanges might manipulate the prices of bitcoins and other virtual currencies. The value of bitcoins in exchange for dollars rose from $5 per bitcoin in June 2012 to $266 per bitcoin in April 2013, before falling to $94 per bitcoin in July 2013 and then rising to $287 in July 2015. Whether these swings in value represented underlying movements in demand and supply for bitcoins or manipulation of their values was not clear.

Should the Federal Reserve include bitcoins and other virtual or cryptocurrencies in its measures of the money supply? So far, the volume of transactions in these currencies has been small, which makes the question of little practical importance. At this point, the Federal Reserve treats virtual currencies as being the equivalent of credit or debit cards, rather than currency or checking account balances, and does not include them in M1 or M2.

Sources: Paul Vigna, "Bitcoiners Decamp to Bretton Woods, Assess the Future of Bitcoin," *Wall Street Journal*, July 30, 2015; Takashi Mochizuki, "Japanese Police Arrest Mark Karpelès of Collapsed Bitcoin Exchange Mt. Gox," *Wall Street Journal*, August 1, 2015; Lingling Wei, "Fed Studying Risks at Online Payment Providers," *Wall Street Journal*, June 3, 2013; and "How Does Bitcoin Work?" *Economist*, April 11, 2013.

Your Turn: Test your understanding by doing related problem 2.11 on page 888 at the end of this chapter.

MyEconLab Study Plan

25.3 How Do Banks Create Money?

LEARNING OBJECTIVE: Explain how banks create money.

We have seen that the most important component of the money supply is checking accounts in banks. To understand the role money plays in the economy, we need to look more closely at how banks operate. Banks are profit-making private businesses, just like department stores and supermarkets. Some banks are quite small, with just a few branches, and do business in a limited area. Others are among the largest corporations in the United States, with thousands of branches spread across many states. Banks play an important role in the economy by accepting deposits and making loans. By taking these actions, banks fulfill a key function in the *money supply process* by which central banks control the money supply.

Bank Balance Sheets

To understand how banks create money, we need to briefly examine a typical bank balance sheet. On a balance sheet, a firm's assets are listed on the left, and its liabilities and stockholders' equity are listed on the right (see Chapter 8). Assets are the value of anything owned by the firm, liabilities are the value of anything the firm owes, and stockholders' equity is the difference between the total value of assets and the total value of liabilities. Stockholders' equity represents the value of the firm if it were closed, all its assets were sold, and all its liabilities were paid off. A corporation's stockholders' equity is also called its *net worth*. A bank's stockholders' equity or net worth is also called its *capital*.

Figure 25.2 shows a typical balance sheet for a large bank. The key assets on a bank's balance sheet are its *reserves*, loans, and holdings of securities, such as U.S. Treasury bills. **Reserves** are deposits that a bank has retained rather than loaned out or invested. Banks keep reserves either physically within the bank, as *vault cash*, or on deposit with the Federal Reserve. Banks are required by law to keep as reserves 10 percent of their checking account deposits above a threshold level, which in 2015 was $103.6 million. These reserves are called **required reserves**. The minimum fraction of deposits that banks are required to keep as reserves is called the **required reserve ratio**. We can abbreviate the required reserve ratio as *RR*. Any reserves that banks hold above the legal requirement are called **excess reserves**. The balance sheet in Figure 25.2 shows that loans are a typical bank's largest asset.

Reserves Deposits that a bank keeps as cash in its vault or on deposit with the Federal Reserve.

Required reserves Reserves that a bank is legally required to hold, based on its checking account deposits.

Required reserve ratio The minimum fraction of deposits banks are required by law to keep as reserves.

Excess reserves Reserves that banks hold over the legal requirement.

Banks make *consumer loans* to households and *commercial loans* to firms. A loan is an asset to a bank because it represents a promise by the person taking out the loan to make certain specified payments to the bank. A bank's reserves and its holdings of securities are also assets because they are things of value the bank owns.

Figure 25.2

The Balance Sheet of a Typical Large Bank

The entries on a bank's balance sheet of greatest economic importance are its reserves, loans, and deposits. Notice that the difference between the value of this bank's total assets and its total liabilities is equal to its stockholders' equity. As a consequence, the left side of the balance sheet always equals the right side.
Note: Some entries have been combined to simplify the balance sheet.

Assets (in billions)		Liabilities and Stockholders' Equity (in billions)	
Reserves	$135	Deposits	$1,000
Loans	900	Short-term borrowing	400
Securities	700	Long-term debt	360
Buildings and equipment	15	Other liabilities	275
Other assets	550	Total liabilities	$2,035
		Stockholders' equity	265
Total assets	$2,300	Total liabilities and stockholders' equity	$2,300

Making the Connection
MyEconLab Video

Would You Borrow from an Online Peer-to-Peer Lender?

The basic business of banks is taking in deposits from savers and using those funds to make loans to households and firms. Banks often require *collateral* before making a loan, which means that if the borrower stops making payments on the loan, the bank can seize the asset the borrower pledged as collateral. For example, if you take out a loan to buy a car and stop making payments on the loan, the bank can repossess your car and sell it to get its money back.

In addition to collateral, banks rely on a borrower's *credit score* in deciding whether to make a loan. The best-known credit score is compiled by the FICO company, which rates borrowers on a scale of 350 to 850, with higher scores meaning the borrower is less likely to default. Credit scores are determined by a variety of factors, including whether the borrower has been on time with payments on other loans and on credit cards; how long the borrower has lived at his current residence; how long the borrower has held her current job; and how much other debt the borrower has. Borrowers with high scores are called *prime borrowers,* and borrowers with low scores are called *subprime borrowers.* A bank will typically charge a prime borrower a lower interest rate than it will charge a subprime borrower. The higher interest rate on a *subprime loan* compensates the bank for the greater risk that the borrower will default. Lenders differ in the minimum score they use to consider someone a prime borrower, but it is typically around 650.

Some people with low credit scores who can't get a bank loan turn to peer-to-peer lending to borrow the funds to meet needs such as buying furniture.

During the housing bubble of the early 2000s, many banks and other lenders made mortgage loans to subprime borrowers buying houses. High default rates on these mortgages following the bursting of the housing bubble in 2006 contributed to the 2007–2009 financial crisis and led policymakers to tighten regulations on banks granting subprime loans. Some consumer advocates also criticize these loans because they believe that the high interest rates exploit borrowers. To avoid both the new regulations and the criticism, many banks have cut back on subprime loans, particularly subprime *personal loans,* which are made to individuals who do not provide collateral for the loan. In past years, after getting a job, many new college graduates would take out a personal loan from a bank to buy the furniture or small appliances needed to set up an apartment. You may have a low credit score if you were late with a couple of credit card payments, have only a short work history, and have just moved into a new apartment. A bank may then consider you a subprime borrower and be unwilling to lend you money.

You could borrow on your credit card by taking a cash advance, but the interest rate is likely to be high—typically more than 20 percent. When banks cut back on subprime personal loans, it left a hole in the financial system. In the past few years, some new businesses have developed to fill that hole. For example, Lending Club and FreedomPlus facilitate peer-to-peer lending on the Internet. These businesses gather information about a borrower, determine the interest rate on the loan, and then post the loan online. Individual investors can then choose to fund the loan. Some loans are funded by a single investor, while others are funded by several investors. The loans can be as short as a few weeks or as long as several years and can have interest rates from 7 percent to more than 20 percent, with the typical interest rate being around 14 percent. Peer-to-peer lending firms are part of the "sharing economy," which also includes the car ride firm Uber and short-term apartment rental firm Airbnb. In the case of peer-to-peer lending, it's money that is being shared.

By 2015, peer-to-peer lending sites were making $10 billion worth of loans. While this amount has been growing rapidly, it still far less than the trillions of dollars in loans of all types made by banks. It remains to be seen whether the peer-to-peer lending sites will end up becoming a major source of credit to households and firms.

Sources: Ianthe Jeanne Dugan and Telis Demos, "New Lenders Spring Up to Cater to Subprime Sector," *Wall Street Journal,* March 5, 2014; and "From the People, for the People," *Economist,* May 9, 2015.

Your Turn: Test your understanding by doing related problems 3.7 and 3.8 on pages 888–889 at the end of this chapter.

MyEconLab Study Plan

Deposits are a typical bank's largest liability. Deposits include checking accounts, savings accounts, and CDs. Deposits are liabilities to banks because they are owed to the households or firms that have deposited the funds. If you deposit $100 in your checking account, the bank owes you the $100, and you can ask for it back at any time. So, your checking account is an asset to you, and it is a liability to the bank. Banks also borrow short term from other banks and from the Federal Reserve and borrow long term by selling bonds to investors. These *borrowings* are also liabilities. MyEconLab Concept Check

Using T-Accounts to Show How a Bank Can Create Money

It is easier to show how banks create money by using a T-account than by using a balance sheet. A T-account is a stripped-down version of a balance sheet that shows only how a transaction *changes* a bank's balance sheet. Suppose you deposit $1,000 in currency into an account at Bank of America. This transaction raises the total deposits at Bank of America by $1,000 and also raises its reserves by $1,000. We show this result on the following T-account:

Assets		Liabilities	
Reserves	+$1,000	Deposits	+$1,000

Your deposit of $1,000 into your checking account increases Bank of America's assets and liabilities by the same amount.

Remember that because the total value of all the entries on the right side of a balance sheet must always be equal to the total value of all the entries on the left side of a balance sheet, any transaction that increases (or decreases) one side of the balance sheet must also increase (or decrease) the other side of the balance sheet. In this case, the T-account shows that we increased both sides of the balance sheet by $1,000.

Initially, this transaction does not increase the money supply. The currency component of the money supply declines by $1,000 because the $1,000 you deposited is no longer in circulation and, therefore, is not counted in the money supply. But the decrease in currency is offset by a $1,000 increase in the checking account deposit component of the money supply.

This initial change is not the end of the story, however. Banks are required to keep 10 percent of deposits as reserves. Because the Federal Reserve pays banks only a low rate of interest on their reserves, banks have an incentive to loan out or buy securities with the other 90 percent. Suppose, for simplicity, that initially Bank of America holds no excess reserves. In that case, Bank of America can keep $100 of your deposit as required reserves and loan out the other $900, which represents its excess reserves. Assume that Bank of America loans out the $900 to someone to buy a very inexpensive used car. Bank of America could give the $900 to the borrower in currency, but usually banks make loans by increasing the borrower's checking account. We can show this transaction with another T-account:

Assets		Liabilities	
Reserves	+$1,000	Deposits	+$1,000
Loans	+$900	Deposits	+$900

1. By loaning out $900 in excess reserves . . .

2. . . . Bank of America has increased the money supply by $900.

Notice that *by making this $900 loan, Bank of America has increased the money supply by $900.* The initial $1,000 in currency you deposited into your checking account has been turned into $1,900 in checking account deposits—a net increase in the money supply of $900.

But the story does not end here. The person who took out the $900 loan did so to buy a used car. To keep things simple, let's suppose he buys the car for exactly $900 and pays by writing a check on his account at Bank of America. The seller of the used car will now deposit the check in her bank. That bank may also be a branch of Bank of America, but in most cities, there are many banks, so let's assume that the seller of the car has her account at a branch of PNC Bank. Once she deposits the check, PNC Bank will send it to Bank of America to *clear* the check and collect the $900. We show the result in the following T-accounts:

Bank of America

Assets		Liabilities	
Reserves	+$100	Deposits	+$1,000
Loans	+$900		

1. When the $900 check that was deposited in a PNC account arrives to be cleared, the increase in Bank of America's reserves (shown in the previous T-account) falls by $900 to $100 . . .

2. . . . and the increase in Bank of America's deposits falls by $900 to $1,000.

PNC Bank

Assets		Liabilities	
Reserves	+$900	Deposits	+$900

After the check drawn on the account at Bank of America clears, PNC's reserves and deposits both increase by $900.

After the car buyer's check clears, Bank of America has lost $900 in deposits—the amount loaned to the car buyer—and $900 in reserves—the amount it had to pay PNC when PNC sent Bank of America the car buyer's check. PNC has an increase in checking account deposits of $900—the deposit of the car seller—and an increase in reserves of $900—the amount it received from Bank of America.

PNC has 100 percent reserves against this new $900 deposit, but it needs only 10 percent reserves. The bank has an incentive to keep $90 as reserves and to loan out the other $810, which are excess reserves. If PNC does this, we can show the change in its balance sheet by using another T-account:

PNC Bank

Assets		Liabilities	
Reserves	+$900	Deposits	+$900
Loans	+$810	Deposits	+$810

By making an $810 loan, PNC has increased both its loans and its deposits by $810.

In loaning out the $810 in excess reserves, PNC creates a new checking account deposit of $810. The initial deposit of $1,000 in currency into Bank of America has now resulted in the creation of $\$1{,}000 + \$900 + \$810 = \$2{,}710$ in checking account deposits. The money supply has increased by $\$2{,}710 - \$1{,}000 = \$1{,}710$.

The process is still not finished. The person who borrows the $810 will spend it by writing a check against his account. Whoever receives the $810 will deposit it in her bank, which could be a Bank of America branch or a PNC branch or a branch of some other bank. That new bank—if it's not PNC—will send the check to PNC and will receive $810 in new reserves. That new bank will have an incentive to loan out 90 percent of these reserves—keeping 10 percent to meet the legal requirement—and the process will go on. At each stage, the additional loans being made and the additional deposits being created are shrinking by 10 percent, because each bank has to keep that amount as required reserves. We can use a table to show the total increase in checking account deposits started by your initial deposit of $1,000. The dots in the table represent additional rounds in the money supply process: MyEconLab Concept Check

Bank	Increase in Checking Account Deposits
Bank of America	$1,000
PNC	+ 900 (= 0.9 × $1,000)
Third Bank	+ 810 (= 0.9 × $900)
Fourth Bank	+ 729 (= 0.9 × $810)
•	+ •
•	+ •
•	+ •
Total change in checking account deposits	= $10,000

The Simple Deposit Multiplier

Simple deposit multiplier The ratio of the amount of deposits created by banks to the amount of new reserves.

Your initial deposit of $1,000 increased the reserves of the banking system by $1,000 and led to a total increase in checking account deposits of $10,000. The ratio of the amount of deposits created by banks to the amount of new reserves is called the **simple deposit multiplier**. In this case, the simple deposit multiplier is equal to $10,000/$1,000 = 10. Why 10? How do we know that your initial $1,000 deposit ultimately leads to a total increase in deposits of $10,000?

There are two ways to answer this question. First, each bank in the money supply process is keeping reserves equal to 10 percent of its deposits. For the banking system as a whole, the total increase in reserves is $1,000—the amount of your original currency deposit. Therefore, the system as a whole will end up with $10,000 in deposits because $1,000 is 10 percent of $10,000.

A second way to answer the question is by deriving an expression for the simple deposit multiplier. The total increase in deposits equals:

$$\$1{,}000 + [0.9 \times \$1{,}000] + [(0.9 \times 0.9) \times \$1{,}000] + [(0.9 \times 0.9 \times 0.9) \times \$1{,}000] + \ldots$$

or:

$$\$1{,}000 + [0.9 \times \$1{,}000] + [0.9^2 \times \$1{,}000] + [0.9^3 \times \$1{,}000] + \ldots$$

or:

$$\$1{,}000 \times (1 + 0.9 + 0.9^2 + 0.9^3 + \ldots).$$

The rules of algebra tell us that an expression like the one in the parentheses sums to:

$$\frac{1}{1 - 0.9}.$$

Simplifying further, we have:

$$\frac{1}{0.10} = 10.$$

So:

$$\text{Total increase in deposits} = \$1{,}000 \times 10 = \$10{,}000.$$

Don't Let This Happen to You

Don't Confuse Assets and Liabilities

Consider the following reasoning: "How can checking account deposits be a liability to a bank? After all, they are something of value that is in the bank. Therefore, checking account deposits should be counted as a bank *asset* rather than as a bank liability."

This statement is incorrect. The balance in a checking account represents something the bank *owes* to the owner of the account. Therefore, it is a liability to the bank, although it is an asset to the owner of the account. Similarly, your car loan is a liability to you—because it is a debt you owe to the bank—but it is an asset to the bank.

MyEconLab Study Plan

Your Turn: Test your understanding by doing related problem 3.11 on page 889 at the end of this chapter.

Note that 10 is equal to 1 divided by the required reserve ratio, *RR*, which in this case is 10 percent, or 0.10. So, we have another way of expressing the simple deposit multiplier:

$$\text{Simple deposit multiplier} = \frac{1}{RR}.$$

This formula makes it clear that the higher the required reserve ratio, the smaller the simple deposit multiplier. With a required reserve ratio of 10 percent, the simple deposit multiplier is 10. If the required reserve ratio were 20 percent, the simple deposit multiplier would fall to 1/0.20, or 5.

We can use this formula to calculate the total increase in checking account deposits from an increase in bank reserves due to, for instance, currency being deposited in a bank:

$$\text{Change in checking account deposits} = \text{Change in bank reserves} \times \frac{1}{RR}.$$

For example, if \$100,000 in currency is deposited in a bank and the required reserve ratio is 10 percent, then:

$$\text{Change in checking account deposits} = \$100{,}000 \times \frac{1}{0.10}$$
$$= \$100{,}000 \times 10 = \$1{,}000{,}000.$$

MyEconLab Concept Check

Solved Problem 25.3

MyEconLab Interactive Animation

Showing How Banks Create Money

Suppose you deposit \$5,000 in currency into your checking account at a branch of PNC Bank, which we will assume has no excess reserves at the time you make your deposit. Also assume that the required reserve ratio is 0.10.

a. Use a T-account to show the initial effect of this transaction on PNC's balance sheet.

b. Suppose that PNC makes the maximum loan it can from the funds you deposited. Use a T-account to show the initial effect on PNC's balance sheet from granting the loan. Also include in this T-account the transaction from part (a).

c. Now suppose that whoever took out the loan in part (b) writes a check for this amount and that the person receiving the check deposits it in Bank of America. Show the effect of these transactions on the balance sheets of PNC Bank and Bank of America *after the check has cleared.* On the T-account for PNC Bank, include the transactions from parts (a) and (b).

d. What is the maximum increase in checking account deposits that can result from your \$5,000 deposit? What is the maximum increase in the money supply that can result from your deposit? Explain.

Solving the Problem

Step 1: Review the chapter material. This problem is about how banks create checking account deposits, so you may want to review the section "Using T-Accounts to Show How a Bank Can Create Money," which begins on page 868.

Step 2: Answer part (a) by using a T-account to show the effect of the deposit. Keeping in mind that T-accounts show only the changes in a balance sheet that result from the relevant transaction and that assets are on the left side of the account and liabilities are on the right side, we have:

PNC Bank

Assets		Liabilities	
Reserves	+$5,000	Deposits	+$5,000

Because the bank now has your $5,000 in currency in its vault, its reserves (and, therefore, its assets) have risen by $5,000. This transaction also increases your checking account balance by $5,000. Because the bank owes you this money, the bank's liabilities have also risen by $5,000.

Step 3: Answer part (b) by using a T-account to show the effect of the loan. The problem tells you to assume that PNC Bank currently has no excess reserves and that the required reserve ratio is 10 percent. This requirement means that if the bank's checking account deposits go up by $5,000, the bank must keep $500 as reserves and can loan out the remaining $4,500. Remembering that new loans usually take the form of setting up or increasing a checking account for the borrower, we have:

PNC Bank

Assets		Liabilities	
Reserves	+$5,000	Deposits	+$5,000
Loans	+$4,500	Deposits	+$4,500

The first line of the T-account shows the transaction from part (a). The second line shows that PNC has loaned out $4,500 by increasing the checking account of the borrower by $4,500. The loan is an asset to PNC because it represents the borrower's promise to make certain payments spelled out in the loan agreement.

Step 4: Answer part (c) by using T-accounts for PNC and Bank of America to show the effect of the check clearing. We now show the effect of the borrower having spent the $4,500 he received as a loan from PNC. The person who received the $4,500 check deposits it in her account at Bank of America. We need two T-accounts to show this activity:

PNC Bank

Assets		Liabilities	
Reserves	+$500	Deposits	+$5,000
Loans	+$4,500		

Bank of America

Assets		Liabilities	
Reserves	+$4,500	Deposits	+$4,500

Look first at the T-account for PNC. Once Bank of America sends the check written by the borrower to PNC, PNC loses $4,500 in reserves, and Bank of America gains $4,500 in reserves. The $4,500 is also deducted from the account of the borrower. PNC is now satisfied with the result. It received a $5,000 deposit in currency from you. When that money was sitting in the bank vault, it wasn't earning any interest for PNC. Now $4,500 of the $5,000 has been loaned out and is earning interest. These interest payments allow PNC to cover its costs, which it has to do to remain in business.

Bank of America now has an increase in deposits of $4,500, resulting from the check being deposited, and an increase in reserves of $4,500. Bank of America is in the same situation as PNC was in part (a): It has excess reserves as a result of this transaction and a strong incentive to lend them out.

Step 5: Answer part (d) by using the simple deposit multiplier formula to calculate the maximum increase in checking account deposits and the maximum increase in the money supply. The simple deposit multiplier expression is (remember that *RR* is the required reserve ratio):

$$\text{Change in checking account deposits} = \text{Change in bank reserves} \times \frac{1}{RR}.$$

In this case, bank reserves rose by $5,000 as a result of your initial deposit, and the required reserve ratio is 0.10, so:

$$\text{Change in checking account deposits} = \$5{,}000 \times \frac{1}{0.10}$$

$$= \$5{,}000 \times 10 = \$50{,}000.$$

Because checking account deposits are part of the money supply, it is tempting to say that the money supply has also increased by $50,000. Remember, though, that your $5,000 in currency was counted as part of the money supply while you had it, but it is not counted when it is sitting in a bank vault. Therefore:

$$\text{Increase in checking account deposits} - \text{Decline in currency in circulation} = \text{Change in the money supply.}$$

Or,

$$\$50{,}000 - \$5{,}000 = \$45{,}000.$$

Your Turn: For more practice, do related problem 3.12 on page 889 at the end of the chapter.

MyEconLab Study Plan

The Simple Deposit Multiplier versus the Real-World Deposit Multiplier

The story we have just told of the money supply process has been simplified in two ways. First, we assumed that banks do not keep any excess reserves. That is, we assumed that when you deposited $1,000 in currency into your checking account at Bank of America, it loaned out $900, keeping only the $100 in required reserves. In fact, banks often keep some excess reserves to guard against the possibility that many depositors may simultaneously make withdrawals from their accounts. Since the financial crisis that began in 2007, banks have kept substantial excess reserves. The more excess reserves banks keep, the smaller the deposit multiplier. Imagine an extreme case in which Bank of America kept your entire $1,000 as reserves, loaning out none of it. In this case, the process we described earlier—loans leading to the creation of new deposits, leading to the making of additional loans, and so on—will not take place. The $1,000 increase in reserves will lead to just a $1,000 increase in deposits, and the deposit multiplier will be $1,000/$1,000 = 1, not 10.

Second, we assumed that the whole amount of every check is deposited in a bank; no one takes any of it out as currency. In reality, households and firms keep roughly constant the amount of currency they hold relative to the value of their checking account balances. So, we would expect to see people increasing the amount of currency they hold as the balances in their checking accounts rise. Once again, think of the extreme case. Suppose that when Bank of America makes the initial $900 loan to the borrower who wants to buy a used car, the seller of the car cashes the check instead of depositing it. In that case, PNC does not receive any new reserves and does not make any new loans. Once again, the $1,000 increase in your checking account at Bank of America is the only increase in deposits, and the deposit multiplier is 1.

The effect of these two simplifications is to reduce the real-world deposit multiplier to about 1.6 during normal times. So, a $1 increase in the reserves of the banking system typically results in about a $1.60 increase in deposits. Following the financial crisis of 2007–2009, the surge in bank holdings of excess reserves reduced the multiplier to less than 1.

Although the story of the deposit multiplier can be complicated, the key point to bear in mind is that the most important part of the money supply is the checking account balance component. When banks make loans, they increase checking account balances, and the money supply expands. Banks make new loans whenever they gain reserves. The whole process can also work in reverse: If banks lose reserves, they reduce their outstanding loans and deposits, and the money supply contracts.

We can summarize these important conclusions:

1. When banks gain reserves, they make new loans, and the money supply expands.
2. When banks lose reserves, they reduce their loans, and the money supply contracts.

MyEconLab Study Plan

MyEconLab Concept Check

25.4 The Federal Reserve System

LEARNING OBJECTIVE: Compare the three policy tools the Federal Reserve uses to manage the money supply.

Many people are surprised to learn that banks do not keep locked away in their vaults all the funds that are deposited in checking accounts. The United States, like nearly all other countries, has a **fractional reserve banking system**, which means that banks keep less than 100 percent of deposits as reserves. When people deposit money in a bank, the bank loans most of the money to someone else. What happens if depositors want their money back? Depositors withdrawing money would seem to be a problem because banks have loaned out most of the money and can't easily get it back.

Fractional reserve banking system A banking system in which banks keep less than 100 percent of deposits as reserves.

In practice, withdrawals are usually not a problem for banks. On a typical day, about as much money is deposited as is withdrawn. If a small amount more is withdrawn than deposited, banks can cover the difference from their excess reserves or by borrowing from other banks. Sometimes depositors lose confidence in a bank when they question the value of the bank's underlying assets, particularly its loans. Often, the reason for a loss of confidence is bad news about the loans the bank has made, whether the news is accurate or not. When many depositors simultaneously decide to withdraw their money from a bank, there is a **bank run**. If many banks experience runs at the same time, the result is a **bank panic**. It is possible for one bank to handle a run by borrowing from other banks, but if many banks simultaneously experience runs, the banking system may be in trouble.

Bank run A situation in which many depositors simultaneously decide to withdraw money from a bank.

Bank panic A situation in which many banks experience runs at the same time.

A central bank, like the Federal Reserve in the United States, can help stop a bank panic by acting as a *lender of last resort*. In acting as a lender of last resort, a central bank makes loans to banks that cannot borrow funds elsewhere. The banks can use these loans to pay off depositors. When the panic ends and the depositors put their money back in their accounts, the banks can repay the loans to the central bank.

The Establishment of the Federal Reserve System

Bank panics lead to severe disruptions in business activity because households and firms have trouble gaining access to their accounts and may be unable to borrow money. As we saw in the chapter opener, in 2015, bank runs in Greece prompted the

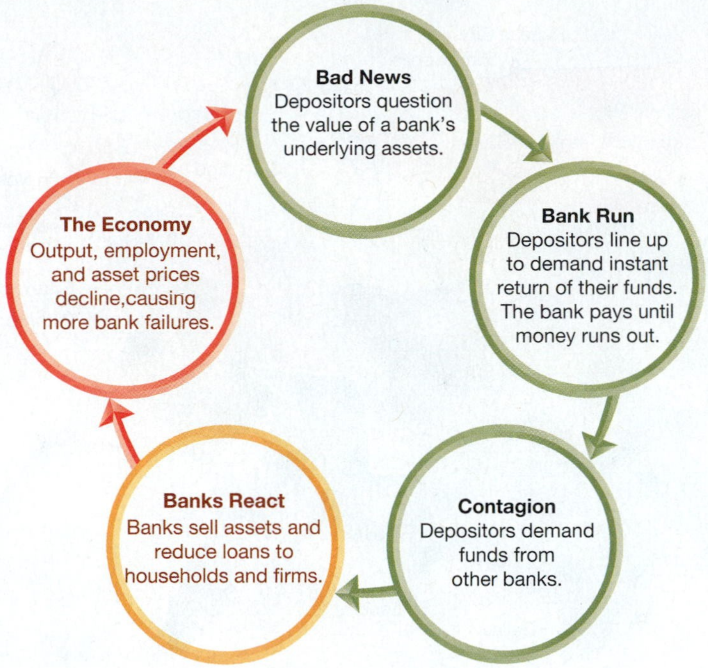

MyEconLab Animation

Figure 25.3

The Feedback Loop during a Bank Panic

Bank runs can cause good banks, as well as bad banks, to fail. Bank failures are costly because they reduce the ability of households and firms to get loans. Once a panic starts, falling incomes, employment, and asset prices can cause more bank failures. This feedback loop means that a panic can continue unless the government intervenes.

government to order banks closed for three weeks, which led to disruptions in the Greek economy, with declines in output and employment. In the United States, each bank panic in the late nineteenth and early twentieth centuries was accompanied by a recession. Figure 25.3 shows how a feedback loop during a bank run can lead to a recession. With the intention of putting an end to bank panics, in 1913, Congress passed the Federal Reserve Act, which set up the Federal Reserve System—often referred to as "the Fed." The system began operation in 1914, with the authority to make loans to banks. The loans the Fed makes to banks are called **discount loans**, and the interest rate it charges on the loans is called the **discount rate**. When a bank receives a loan from the Fed, its reserves increase by the amount of the loan.

Discount loans Loans the Federal Reserve makes to banks.

Discount rate The interest rate the Federal Reserve charges on discount loans.

The Fed's first test as a lender of last resort came in the early years of the Great Depression of the 1930s, when many banks were hit by bank runs as depositors pulled funds out of checking and savings accounts. Although the Fed had been established to act as a lender of last resort, Fed officials declined to make loans to many banks because the officials were worried that banks experiencing runs had made bad loans and other investments. The Fed believed that making loans to banks that were in financial trouble because of bad investments might reduce the incentive bank managers had to be careful in their investment decisions. Partly due to the Fed's unwillingness to act as a lender of last resort, more than 5,000 banks failed during the early 1930s. Today, many economists are critical of the Fed's decisions in the early 1930s because they believe these decisions increased the severity of the Great Depression. In 1934, Congress established the Federal Deposit Insurance Corporation (FDIC) to insure deposits in most banks up to a limit, which is currently $250,000 per deposit. If the bank you have your checking account in goes out of business, the FDIC will refund your money after a wait of at most two days. Deposit insurance has greatly reduced bank runs because it has reassured all but the largest depositors that their deposits are safe, even if their bank goes out of business. During the financial crisis of 2007–2009, some banks experienced runs when depositors with funds exceeding the deposit insurance limit feared that they would suffer losses if their banks failed.

In setting up the Federal Reserve System, Congress divided the country into 12 Federal Reserve districts, as shown in Figure 25.4. Each district has its own Federal Reserve Bank, which provides services to banks in that district. The real power of the Fed, however, lies in Washington, DC, with the Board of Governors. The seven members of the Board of Governors are appointed by the president of the United States to 14-year,

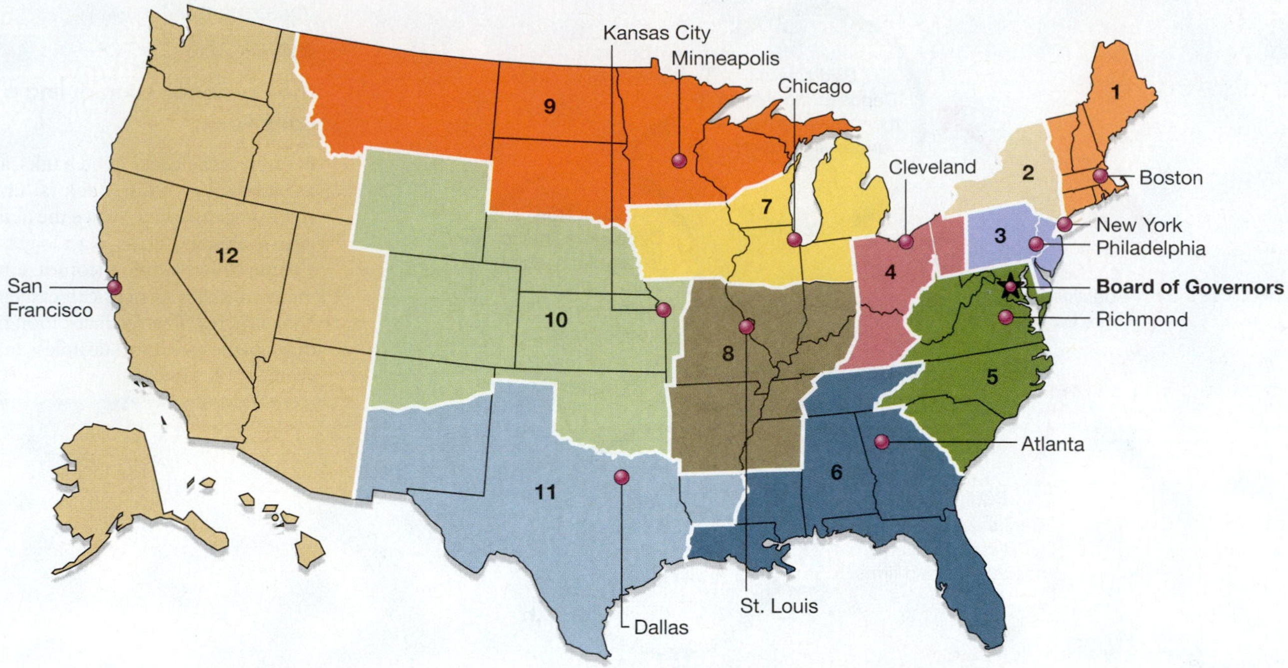

Board of Governors
Responsible for overseeing the Federal Reserve System. Seven members are appointed by the president and serve 14-year, nonrenewable terms. One member is appointed chair and serves a 4-year, renewable term.

Federal Open Market Committee (FOMC)
Responsible for open market operations. Twelve members, consisting of the 7 members of the Board of Governors, the president of the Federal Reserve Bank of New York, and 4 presidents of the other 11 district banks, who serve rotating 1-year terms. The chair of the Board of Governors also serves as chair of the FOMC.

MyEconLab Animation

Figure 25.4 The Federal Reserve System

The United States is divided into 12 Federal Reserve districts, each of which has a Federal Reserve Bank. The real power within the Federal Reserve System, however, lies in Washington, DC, with the Board of Governors, which consists of 7 members appointed by the president. The 12-member Federal Open Market Committee carries out monetary policy.

Source: Board of Governors of the Federal Reserve System.

nonrenewable terms. One member of the Board of Governors is appointed chair and serves a 4-year, renewable term. In addition to acting as a lender of last resort to banks, the Fed acts as a bankers' bank, providing services such as check clearing to banks, and has the responsibility of managing the U.S. money supply. MyEconLab Concept Check

How the Federal Reserve Manages the Money Supply

Monetary policy The actions the Federal Reserve takes to manage the money supply and interest rates to pursue macroeconomic policy objectives.

Although Congress established the Fed primarily to stop bank panics by acting as a lender of last resort, today the Fed is also responsible for managing the money supply. As we will discuss in more detail in Chapter 26, managing the money supply is part of **monetary policy**, which the Fed undertakes to pursue macroeconomic policy objectives. To manage the money supply, the Fed uses three *monetary policy tools*:

1. Open market operations
2. Discount policy
3. Reserve requirements

Remember that the most important component of the money supply is checking account deposits. Not surprisingly, all three of the Fed's policy tools are aimed at affecting the reserves of banks as a means of changing the volume of checking account deposits.

Open Market Operations Eight times per year, the **Federal Open Market Committee (FOMC)** meets in Washington, DC, to discuss monetary policy. The committee has 12 voting members:

Federal Open Market Committee (FOMC) The Federal Reserve committee responsible for open market operations and managing the money supply in the United States.

- The 7 members of the Federal Reserve's Board of Governors.
- The president of the Federal Reserve Bank of New York.
- The presidents of 4 of the other 11 Federal Reserve Banks. These 4 presidents serve one-year rotating terms as voting members of the FOMC.

All 12 Federal Reserve Bank presidents attend meetings and participate in discussions. The chair of the Board of Governors also serves as the chair of the FOMC.

The U.S. Treasury borrows money by selling bills, notes, and bonds. Remember that the *maturity* of a financial asset is the period of time until the purchaser receives payment of the face value or principal. Usually, bonds have face values of $1,000. Treasury bills have maturities of 1 year or less, Treasury notes have maturities of 2 years to 10 years, and Treasury bonds have maturities of 30 years. To control the size of the money supply, the Fed buys and sells Treasury securities in a process called **open market operations**.

Open market operations The buying and selling of Treasury securities by the Federal Reserve in order to control the money supply.

To increase the money supply, the FOMC directs the *trading desk*, located at the Federal Reserve Bank of New York, to carry out an *open market purchase* by buying U.S. Treasury securities—most frequently bills, but sometimes notes or bonds—from banks. The Fed pays for the Treasury bills by depositing the funds in the reserve accounts banks maintain with the Fed.

Suppose that the Fed engages in an open market purchase of $10 million. We can illustrate the results with two T-accounts: one for the Fed and one for the banking system. The banking system's T-account is based on the banking system's balance sheet, which simply adds together all the assets and liabilities of all the commercial banks in the United States. As a result of the open market purchase, the banking system's holdings of Treasury bills fall by $10 million and its reserves increase by $10 million:

Banking System

Assets		Liabilities	
Treasury bills	–$10 million		
Reserves	+$10 million		

The Fed's holdings of Treasury bills increase by $10 million, and the value of the banking system's reserve balances—which are a liability to the Fed—also increase by $10 million:

Federal Reserve

Assets		Liabilities	
Treasury bills	+$10 million	Reserves	+$10 million

This increase in reserves starts the process of expanding loans and checking account deposits that increases the money supply.

To decrease the money supply, the FOMC directs the trading desk to carry out an *open market sale* by selling Treasury securities. When the buyers of the Treasury securities pay for them with checks, the banking system's reserves fall. This decrease in reserves starts a contraction of loans and checking account deposits that reduces the money supply.

There are three reasons the Fed conducts monetary policy principally through open market operations:

1. Because the Fed initiates open market operations, it completely controls their volume, which means the Fed can carry out both large and small open market operations.

2. Open market operations are easily reversible. For example, if the Fed believes that previous open market purchases have caused the money supply to increase too rapidly, it can engage in open market sales.
3. The Fed can implement its open market operations quickly, with no administrative delay or required changes in regulations.

Many other central banks, including the European Central Bank and the Bank of Japan, also use open market operations to conduct monetary policy.

The Federal Reserve is responsible for putting the paper currency of the United States into circulation. (The currency is actually printed by the U.S. Treasury.) Recall that if you look at the top of a dollar bill, you see the words "Federal Reserve Note." When the Fed takes actions to increase the money supply, commentators sometimes say that it is "printing more money." The main way the Fed increases the money supply, however, is not by printing more currency but by buying Treasury securities. Similarly, to reduce the money supply, the Fed doesn't set fire to stacks of paper currency. Instead, it sells Treasury securities. We will spend more time discussing the Fed's management of the money supply in Chapter 26 when we discuss monetary policy.

Discount Policy As we have seen, when a bank borrows money from the Fed by taking out a discount loan, the interest rate the bank pays is called the discount rate. By lowering the discount rate, the Fed can encourage banks to take additional loans and thereby increase their reserves. With more reserves, banks will make more loans to households and firms, which will increase checking account deposits and the money supply. Raising the discount rate will have the reverse effect.

Reserve Requirements When the Fed reduces the required reserve ratio, it converts required reserves into excess reserves. For example, suppose a bank has $100 million in checking account deposits, and the required reserve ratio is 10 percent. The bank will be required to hold $10 million as reserves. If the Fed reduces the required reserve ratio to 8 percent, the bank will need to hold only $8 million as reserves. The Fed can thereby convert $2 million worth of reserves from required reserves to excess reserves. This $2 million is then available for the bank to lend out. If the Fed *raises* the required reserve ratio from 10 percent to 12 percent, it will have the reverse effect.

The Fed rarely changes reserve requirements because doing so can disrupt banks' operations by forcing them to significantly change their holdings of loans, bonds, and other securities. Also, because the Fed pays banks only a low interest rate on reserves, the use of reserve requirements to manage the money supply effectively places a tax on banks' deposit-taking and lending activities, which can be costly for the economy. The Fed relies instead on open market operations as its main tool for managing the money supply.

MyEconLab Concept Check

The "Shadow Banking System" and the Financial Crisis of 2007–2009

The banks we have been discussing in this chapter are *commercial banks,* whose most important economic role is to accept funds from depositors and lend those funds to borrowers. Large firms can sell stocks and bonds on financial markets, but investors are typically unwilling to buy stocks and bonds from small and medium-sized firms because they lack sufficient information about the financial health of smaller firms (see Chapter 8). So, smaller firms—and households—have traditionally relied on bank loans for their credit needs. In the past 25 years, however, two important developments have occurred in the financial system: (1) Banks have begun to resell many of their loans rather than keeping them until borrowers pay them off, and (2) financial firms other than commercial banks have become important sources of credit to businesses.

Securitization Comes to Banking Traditionally, when a bank made a *residential mortgage loan* to a household to buy a home or made a commercial loan to a business, the bank would keep the loan and collect the payments until the borrower paid off the loan. A financial asset—such as a loan or a stock or a bond—is considered

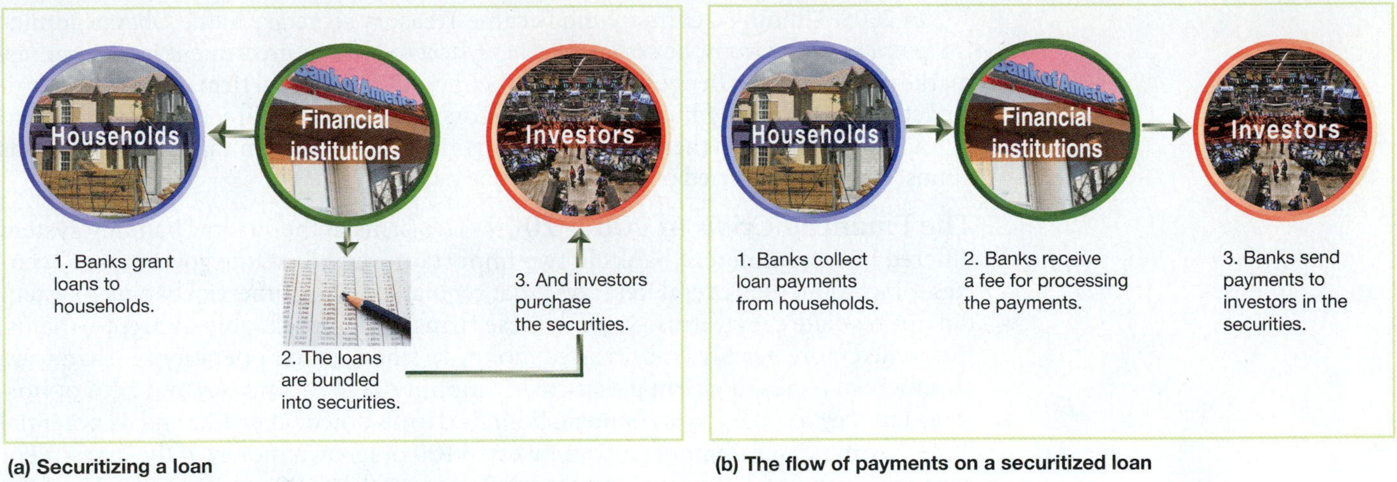

MyEconLab Animation

Figure 25.5 The Process of Securitization

Panel (a) shows how in the securitization process banks grant loans to households and bundle the loans into securities that are then sold to investors. Panel (b) shows that banks collect payments on the original loans and, after taking a fee, send the payments to the investors who bought the securities.

a **security** if it can be bought and sold in a *financial market*. Shares of stock issued by the Coca-Cola Company are an example of a security because they can be bought and sold on the New York Stock Exchange. When a financial asset is first sold, the sale takes place in the *primary market*. If an investor resells the asset, the sale takes place in the *secondary market*. Prior to 1970, most loans were not securities because they could not be resold—there was no secondary market for them. After 1970, residential mortgages and then other loans, including car loans and commercial loans, began to be *securitized*. The process of **securitization** creates a secondary market in which loans that have been bundled together can be bought and sold in financial markets, just as corporate or government bonds are. Figure 25.5 outlines the securitization process. We will discuss the process of securitization further in Chapter 26 when we consider monetary policy.

Security A financial asset—such as a stock or a bond—that can be bought and sold in a financial market.

Securitization The process of transforming loans or other financial assets into securities.

The Shadow Banking System In addition to the changes resulting from securitization, the financial system was transformed in the 1990s and 2000s by the increasing importance of *nonbank financial firms*. Investment banks, such as Goldman Sachs and Morgan Stanley, differ from commercial banks in that they do not accept deposits, and they rarely lend directly to households. Instead, investment banks traditionally concentrated on providing advice to firms issuing stocks and bonds or considering mergers with other firms. In the late 1990s, investment banks expanded their buying of mortgages, bundling large numbers of them together as bonds known as *mortgage-backed securities*, and reselling them to investors. Mortgage-backed securities proved very popular with investors because they often paid higher interest rates than other securities that seemed to have comparable default risk.

Money market mutual funds have also increased their importance in the financial system over time. These funds sell shares to investors and use the money to buy short-term securities such as Treasury bills and commercial paper issued by corporations. Commercial paper represents short-term borrowing corporations use to fund their day-to-day operations. Many corporations that previously met such needs by borrowing from banks began instead to sell commercial paper to money market mutual funds.

Hedge funds raise money from wealthy investors and use sophisticated investment strategies that often involve significant risk. By the mid-2000s, hedge funds had become an important source of demand for securitized loans and an important source of loans to other financial firms.

In 2008, Timothy Geithner, who became Treasury secretary in the Obama administration, used the term the *shadow banking system* to refer to investment banks, money market mutual funds, hedge funds, and other nonbank financial firms engaged in similar activities. By raising money from investors and lending it directly or indirectly to firms and households, these firms were carrying out a function that at one time was almost exclusively carried out by commercial banks.

The Financial Crisis of 2007–2009 The firms in the shadow banking system differed from commercial banks in two important ways: First, the government agencies—including the Federal Reserve—that regulated the commercial banking system did not regulate these firms. Second, these firms were more highly *leveraged*—that is, they relied more heavily on borrowed money to finance their operations—than were commercial banks. If a firm uses a small amount of its own money and a lot of borrowed money to make an investment, both the firm's potential profits and its potential losses are increased. Suppose a firm invests $100 of its own money. If the investment earns a return of $3, the firm has earned 3 percent ($3/$100) on its funds. But if the firm's investment consists of $10 of its own money and $90 it has borrowed, a profit of $3 becomes a return of 30 percent ($3/$10) on the firm's $10 investment. If the investment loses $2, however, the firm's return is −20 percent (−$2/$10). Leveraged investments have a potential for both large gains and large losses.

As mentioned earlier, commercial banks rarely experienced runs after Congress established federal deposit insurance in the 1930s. However, beginning in 2007, some firms in the shadow banking system experienced runs. As we will discuss further in Chapter 26, the underlying cause of the financial crisis of 2007–2009 was problems in the U.S. housing market. As housing prices began to fall, a significant number of borrowers defaulted on their mortgages, which caused mortgage-backed securities to lose value. Financial firms that had invested in these securities, including both commercial banks and many firms in the shadow banking system, suffered losses. The more leveraged the firm, the larger the losses. Although deposit insurance helped commercial banks avoid runs, investment banks and other financial firms that had borrowed short term and invested the funds long term were in trouble. As lenders refused to renew their short-term loans, many of these firms had to sell their holdings of securities in an attempt to raise cash. But as the prices of the securities continued to fall, the losses to these firms increased.

In the spring of 2008, the investment bank Bear Stearns was saved from bankruptcy only when the Federal Reserve arranged for it to be acquired by JPMorgan Chase. In the fall of 2008, the Federal Reserve and the U.S. Treasury decided not to take action to save the investment bank Lehman Brothers, which failed. The failure of Lehman Brothers echoed throughout the financial system, setting off a panic. The process of securitization—apart from government-guaranteed residential mortgages—ground to a halt. The well-publicized difficulties of a money market mutual fund that had suffered losses on loans to Lehman Brothers led to a wave of withdrawals from these funds. In turn, the funds were no longer able to fulfill their role as buyers of corporate commercial paper. As banks and other financial firms sold assets and cut back on lending to shore up their financial positions, the flow of funds from savers to borrowers was disrupted. The resulting *credit crunch* significantly worsened the recession that had begun in December 2007.

The Fed's Response The Fed, in combination with the U.S. Treasury, took vigorous action to deal with the financial crisis. We will discuss the Fed's actions further in Chapter 26, but for now, we can mention several particularly important policy actions:

- In the fall of 2008, under the Troubled Asset Relief Program (TARP), the Fed and Treasury began attempting to stabilize the commercial banking system by providing funds to banks in exchange for stock. Taking partial ownership of private commercial banks was an unprecedented move by the federal government.
- The Fed also modified its discount policy by setting up several new "lending facilities." These lending facilities made it possible for the Fed to grant discount loans to financial firms—such as investment banks—that had not previously been eligible.

- The Fed addressed problems in the commercial paper market by directly buying commercial paper for the first time since the 1930s.

Although the recession continued into 2009, the extraordinary actions of the Treasury and Fed stabilized the financial system. It took several years, however, for the flow of funds from savers to borrowers to return to normal levels, and economists and policymakers continue to debate the wisdom of some of the Fed's actions. MyEconLab Concept Check

25.5 The Quantity Theory of Money

LEARNING OBJECTIVE: Explain the quantity theory of money and use it to explain how high rates of inflation occur.

People have been aware of the connection between increases in the money supply and inflation for centuries. In the sixteenth century, the Spanish conquered Mexico and Peru and shipped large quantities of gold and silver from those countries back to Spain. The gold and silver were minted into coins and spent across Europe to further the political ambitions of the Spanish kings. Prices in Europe rose steadily during these years, and many observers discussed the relationship between this inflation and the flow of gold and silver into Europe from the Americas.

Connecting Money and Prices: The Quantity Equation

In the early twentieth century, Irving Fisher, an economist at Yale University, formalized the connection between money and prices by using the *quantity equation*:

$$M \times V = P \times Y.$$

The quantity equation states that the money supply (*M*) multiplied by the *velocity of money* (*V*) equals the price level (*P*) multiplied by real output (*Y*). Fisher defined the **velocity of money**, often called simply "velocity," as the average number of times each dollar of the money supply is used to purchase goods and services included in GDP. Rewriting the original equation by dividing both sides by M, we have the equation for velocity:

Velocity of money The average number of times each dollar in the money supply is used to purchase goods and services included in GDP.

$$V = \frac{P \times Y}{M}.$$

If we use M1 to measure the money supply, the GDP price deflator to measure the price level, and real GDP to measure real output, the value for velocity for 2014 was:

$$V = \frac{1.09 \times \$16.0 \text{ trillion}}{\$2.8 \text{ trillion}} = 6.2.$$

This result tells us that, during 2014, each dollar of M1 was on average spent about six times on goods or services included in GDP.

Because velocity is defined to be equal to $(P \times Y)/M$, we know that the quantity equation must always hold true: The left side of the equation *must* be equal to the right side. A theory is a statement about the world that might possibly be false. Therefore, the quantity equation is not a theory. Irving Fisher turned the quantity equation into the **quantity theory of money** by arguing that velocity was constant. He argued that the average number of times a dollar is spent depends on factors that do not change often, such as how often people get paid, how often they do their grocery shopping, and how often businesses mail bills. Because this assertion may be true or false, the quantity theory of money is, in fact, a theory. MyEconLab Concept Check

Quantity theory of money A theory about the connection between money and prices that assumes that the velocity of money is constant.

The Quantity Theory Explanation of Inflation

The quantity equation gives us a way of showing the relationship between changes in the money supply and changes in the price level, or inflation. To see this relationship more clearly, we can use a handy mathematical rule that states that an equation in which variables are multiplied together is equal to an equation in which the *growth rates* of these variables are *added* together. So, we can transform the quantity equation from:

$$M \times V = P \times Y$$

to:

Growth rate of the money supply + Growth rate of velocity =
Growth rate of the price level (or the inflation rate) + Growth rate of real output.

This way of writing the quantity equation is more useful for investigating the effect of changes in the money supply on the inflation rate. Remember that the growth rate for any variable is the percentage change in the variable from one year to the next. The growth rate of the price level is the inflation rate, so we can rewrite the quantity equation to help understand the factors that determine inflation:

Inflation rate = Growth rate of the money supply +
Growth rate of velocity − Growth rate of real output.

If Irving Fisher was correct that velocity is constant, then the growth rate of velocity will be zero. For example, if velocity is always equal to six, then its percentage change from one year to the next will always be zero. This assumption allows us to rewrite the equation one last time:

Inflation rate = Growth rate of the money supply − Growth rate of real output.

This equation leads to the following predictions:

1. If the money supply grows at a faster rate than real GDP, there will be inflation.
2. If the money supply grows at a slower rate than real GDP, there will be deflation. (Recall that *deflation* is a decline in the price level.)
3. If the money supply grows at the same rate as real GDP, the price level will be stable, and there will be neither inflation nor deflation.

It turns out that Irving Fisher was wrong in asserting that the velocity of money is constant. From year to year, there can be significant fluctuations in velocity. As a result, the predictions of inflation based on the quantity theory of money do not hold every year, but most economists agree that the quantity theory provides useful insight into the long-run relationship between the money supply and inflation: *In the long run, inflation results from the money supply growing at a faster rate than real GDP.* MyEconLab Concept Check

How Accurate Are Forecasts of Inflation Based on the Quantity Theory?

Note that the accuracy of the quantity theory depends on whether the key assumption that velocity is constant is correct. If velocity is not constant, there may not be a tight link between increases in the money supply and increases in the price level. For example, an increase in the quantity of money might be offset by a decline in velocity, leaving the price level unaffected. Because velocity can move erratically in the short run, we would not expect the quantity equation to provide good forecasts of inflation in the short run. Over the long run, however, there is a strong link between changes in the money supply and inflation. Panel (a) of Figure 25.6 shows by decade the relationship in the United States between the growth of the M2 measure of the money supply and the inflation rate. (We use M2 here because data on M2 are available for a longer period of time than are data for M1.) Because of variations in the rate of growth of real GDP and in velocity, there is not an exact relationship between the growth rate of M2 and the inflation rate. But there is a clear pattern that decades with higher growth rates in the money supply were also decades with higher inflation rates. In other words, most of the variation in inflation rates across decades can be explained by variation in the rates of growth of the money supply.

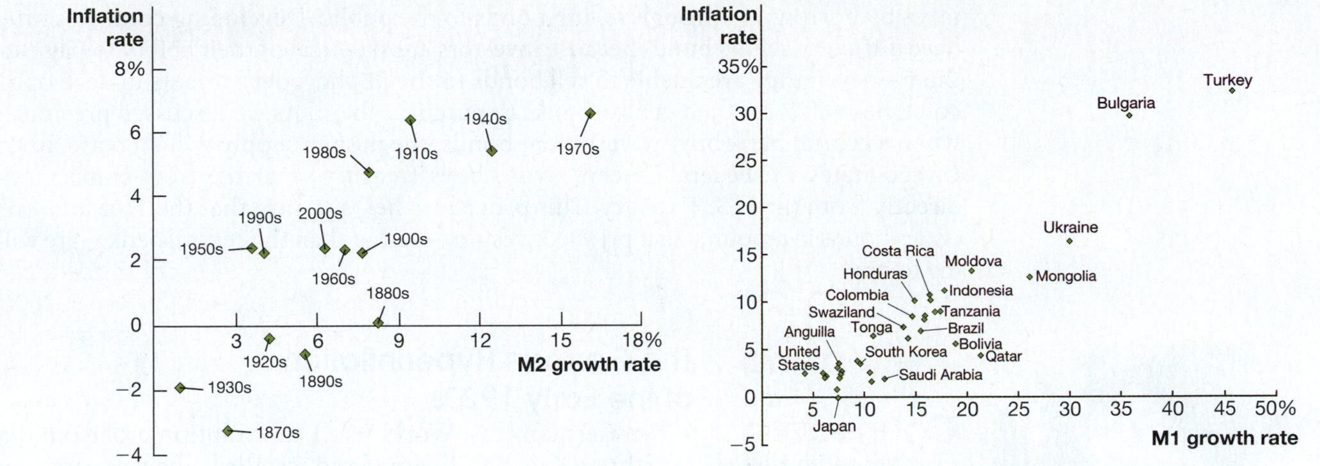

a) Inflation and money supply growth in the United States, 1870s–2000s

(b) Inflation and money supply growth in 56 countries, 1995–2011

MyEconLab Animation

Figure 25.6 The Relationship between Money Growth and Inflation over Time and around the World

Panel (a) shows that, by and large, the rate of inflation in the United States has been highest during the decades in which the money supply has increased most rapidly, and the rate of inflation has been lowest during the decades in which the money supply has increased least rapidly. Panel (b) shows the relationship between money supply growth and inflation for 56 countries between 1995 and 2011. There is not an exact relationship between money supply growth and inflation, but countries such as Bulgaria, Turkey, and Ukraine that had high rates of money supply growth had high inflation rates, and countries such as the United States and Japan had low rates of money supply growth and low inflation rates.

Sources: Panel (a): For the 1870s to the 1960s, Milton Friedman and Anna J. Schwartz, *Monetary Trends in the United States and United Kingdom: Their Relation to Income, Prices, and Interest Rates, 1867–1975*, Chicago: University of Chicago Press, 1982, Table 4.8; and for the 1970s to the 2000s, Federal Reserve Board of Governors and U.S. Bureau of Economic Analysis; Panel (b): International Monetary Fund, *International Monetary Statistics.*

Panel (b) provides further evidence consistent with the quantity theory by looking at rates of growth of the money supply and rates of inflation across 56 countries for the years 1995–2011. Although there is not an exact relationship between rates of growth of the money supply and rates of inflation across countries, panel (b) shows that countries where the money supply grew rapidly tended to have high inflation rates, while countries where the money supply grew more slowly tended to have much lower inflation rates. Not included in panel (b) are data for Zimbabwe, which may be the most extreme case of inflation in recent years. In some years since 1995, the money supply in Zimbabwe grew by more than 7,500 percent. The result was an accelerating rate of inflation that eventually reached 15 billion percent during 2008. Zimbabwe was suffering from *hyperinflation*—that is, a rate of inflation that exceeds 50 percent per month.

MyEconLab Concept Check

High Rates of Inflation

The quantity theory can help us understand the reasons for very high rates of inflation. Hyperinflation is caused by central banks increasing the money supply at a rate far in excess of the growth rate of real GDP. A high rate of inflation causes money to lose its value so rapidly that households and firms avoid holding it. If, as happened in Zimbabwe, the inflation rate becomes high enough, people stop using paper currency, so it no longer serves the important functions of money discussed earlier in this chapter. Economies suffering from high inflation usually also suffer from very slow growth, if not severe recession.

Given the dire consequences that follow from high inflation, why do governments cause it by expanding the money supply so rapidly? The main reason is that governments often want to spend more than they are able to raise through taxes. Developed countries, such as the United States, can usually bridge gaps between spending and taxes by borrowing through selling bonds to the public. Developing countries often have difficulty selling bonds because investors are skeptical of their ability to pay back the money. If they are unable to sell bonds to the public, governments in developing countries will force their central banks to purchase them. As we discussed previously, when a central bank buys government bonds, the money supply will increase. In the United States, the Federal Reserve always buys Treasury securities from banks, never directly from the U.S. Treasury. This procedure helps ensure that the Treasury only issues bonds in amounts that private investors—rather than the central bank—are willing to buy.

MyEconLab Concept Check

During the German hyperinflation of the 1920s, paper currency became so worthless that people used it to light their stoves.

Making the Connection
MyEconLab Video

The German Hyperinflation of the Early 1920s

When Germany lost World War I, a revolution broke out that overthrew Kaiser Wilhelm II and installed a new government known as the Weimar Republic. In the peace treaty of 1919, the Allies—the United States, Great Britain, France, and Italy—imposed payments called *reparations* on the new German government. The reparations were meant as compensation to the Allies for the damage Germany had caused during the war. It was very difficult for the German government to use tax revenue to cover both its normal spending and the reparations.

The German government decided to pay for the difference between its spending and its tax revenues by selling bonds to the central bank, the Reichsbank. After a few years, the German government fell far behind in its reparations payments. In January 1923, the French government sent troops into the German industrial area known as the Ruhr to try to collect the payments directly. German workers in the Ruhr went on strike, and the German government decided to support them by paying their salaries. The government raised the funds by selling additional bonds to the Reichsbank, thereby further increasing the money supply.

The inflationary increase in the money supply was very large: The total number of marks—the German currency—in circulation rose from 115 million in January 1922 to 1.3 billion in January 1923 and then to 497 billion *billion*, or 497,000,000,000,000,000,000, in December 1923. Just as the quantity theory predicts, the result was a staggeringly high rate of inflation. The German price index that stood at 100 in 1914 and 1,440 in January 1922 had risen to 126,160,000,000,000 in December 1923. The German mark became worthless. The German government ended the hyperinflation by (1) negotiating a new agreement with the Allies that reduced its reparations payments, (2) reducing other government expenditures and raising taxes to balance its budget, and (3) replacing the existing mark with a new mark. Each new mark was worth 1 trillion old marks. The German central bank was also limited to issuing a total of 3.2 billion new marks.

These steps were enough to bring the hyperinflation to an end—but not before the savings of anyone holding the old marks had been wiped out. Most middle-income Germans were extremely resentful of this outcome. Many historians believe that the hyperinflation greatly reduced the allegiance of many Germans to the Weimar Republic and may have helped pave the way for Adolph Hitler and the Nazis to seize power 10 years later.

Sources: Thomas Sargent, "The Ends of Four Big Inflations," *Rational Expectations and Inflation*, 3rd ed., Princeton, NJ: Princeton University Press, 2013; and John Parke Young, *European Currency and Finance*, Washington, DC: Government Printing Office, 1925.

MyEconLab Study Plan

Your Turn: Test your understanding by doing related problem 5.10 on page 891 at the end of this chapter.

Continued from page 857

Economics in Your Life

What if Money Became Increasingly Valuable?

At the beginning of this chapter, we asked you to consider whether you would like to live in an economy in which the purchasing power of money rises every year. The first thing to consider when thinking about the advantages and disadvantages of this situation is that the only way for the purchasing power of money to increase is for the price level to fall; in other words, *deflation* must occur. Because the price level in the United States hasn't fallen for an entire year since the 1930s, most people alive today have experienced only rising price levels—and declining purchasing power of money. Would replacing rising prices with falling prices necessarily be a good thing? It might be tempting to say "yes," because if you have a job, your salary will buy more goods and services each year. But, in fact, just as a rising price level results in most wages and salaries rising each year, a falling price level is likely to mean falling wages and salaries each year. So, it is likely that, on average, people would not see the purchasing power of their incomes increase, even if the purchasing power of any currency they held increased. There can also be a significant downside to deflation, particularly if the transition from inflation to deflation happens suddenly. Recall that the real interest rate is equal to the nominal interest rate minus the inflation rate. If an economy experiences deflation, then the real interest rate will be greater than the nominal interest rate. A rising real interest rate can be bad news for anyone who has borrowed, including homeowners who may have substantial mortgage loans. So, you are probably better off living in an economy experiencing mild inflation than one experiencing deflation.

Conclusion

Money plays a key role in the functioning of an economy by facilitating trade in goods and services and by making specialization possible. Without specialization, no advanced economy can prosper. Households and firms, banks, and the central bank (the Federal Reserve in the United States) are participants in the process of creating the money supply. In Chapter 26, we will discuss how the Federal Reserve uses monetary policy to promote its economic objectives.

Visit MyEconLab for a news article and analysis related to the concepts of this chapter.

CHAPTER SUMMARY AND PROBLEMS

Key Terms

25.1 What Is Money, and Why Do We Need It? pages 858–861

LEARNING OBJECTIVE: Define money and discuss the four functions of money.

Summary

A *barter economy* is an economy that does not use money and in which people trade goods and services directly for other goods and services. Barter trade occurs only if there is a *double coincidence of wants*, where both parties to the trade want what the other one has. Because barter is inefficient, there is strong incentive to use **money**, which is any **asset** that people are generally willing to accept in exchange for goods or services or in payment of debts. An *asset* is anything of value owned by a person or a firm. A **commodity money** is a good used as money that also has value independent of its use as money. Money has four functions: It is a medium of exchange, a unit of account, a store of value, and a standard of deferred payment. At one time, governments issued gold coins and paper currency that were convertible into gold. Today, no government in the world issues paper currency that can be redeemed for gold. Instead, paper currency is **fiat money**, which has no value except as money.

MyEconLab Visit **www.myeconlab.com** to complete these exercises online and get instant feedback.

Review Questions

1.1 A baseball fan with a Mike Trout baseball card wants to trade it for a Miguel Cabrera baseball card, but everyone the fan knows who has a Cabrera card doesn't want a Trout card. What do economists call the problem this fan is having?

1.2 What is the difference between commodity money and fiat money?

1.3 What are the four functions of money? Can something be considered money if it does not fulfill all four functions?

1.4 Why do businesses accept paper currency when they know that, unlike a gold coin, the paper the currency is printed on is worth very little?

Problems and Applications

1.5 The English economist William Stanley Jevons described a world tour during the 1880s by a French singer, Mademoiselle Zélie. One stop on the tour was a theater in the Society Islands, part of French Polynesia in the South Pacific. She performed for her usual fee, which was one-third of the receipts. This turned out to be 3 pigs, 23 turkeys, 44 chickens, 5,000 coconuts, and "considerable quantities of bananas, lemons, and oranges." She estimated that all of this would have had a value in France of 4,000 francs. According to Jevons, "as Mademoiselle could not consume any considerable portion of the receipts herself, it became necessary in the meantime to feed the pigs and poultry with the fruit." Do the goods Mademoiselle Zélie received as payment fulfill the four functions of money described in this chapter? Briefly explain.

Source: W. Stanley Jevons, *Money and the Mechanism of Exchange*, New York: D. Appleton and Company, 1889, pp. 1–2.

1.6 **(Related to the Chapter Opener on page 857)** An article in the *New York Times* in 2015 noted, "A rising number of Greeks in rural areas are swapping goods and services in cashless transactions since the government shut down banks on June 28 for three weeks." If Greeks were able to swap goods and services for other goods and services, did it matter that currency was not available because the banks had been closed? Briefly explain.

Source: Lefteris Karagiannopoulos, "Hay for Cheese? Barter Booms in Cash-Squeezed Rural Greece," *New York Times*, July 29, 2015.

1.7 In the late 1940s, the Communists under Mao Zedong were defeating the government of China in a civil war. The paper currency issued by the Chinese government was losing much of its value, and most businesses refused to accept it. At the same time, there was a paper shortage in Japan. During these years, Japan was still under military occupation by the United States, following its defeat in World War II. Some of the U.S. troops in Japan realized that they could use dollars to buy up vast amounts of paper currency in China, ship it to Japan to be recycled into paper, and make a substantial profit. Under these circumstances, was the Chinese paper currency a commodity money or a fiat money? Briefly explain.

1.8 According to Peter Heather, a historian at King's College London, during the time of the Roman Empire, the German tribes east of the Rhine River (the area the Romans called Germania) produced no coins of their own but used Roman coins instead:

Although no coinage was produced in Germania, Roman coins were in plentiful circulation and could easily have provided a medium of exchange (already in the first century, Tacitus tells us, Germani of the Rhine region were using good-quality Roman silver coins for this purpose).

a. What is a medium of exchange?
b. What does the author mean when he writes that Roman coins could have provided the German tribes with a medium of exchange?
c. Why would any member of a German tribe have been willing to accept a Roman coin from another member of the tribe in exchange for goods or services when the tribes were not part of the Roman Empire and were not governed by Roman law?

Source: Peter Heather, *The Fall of the Roman Empire: A New History of Rome and the Barbarians*, New York: Oxford University Press, 2006, p. 89.

1.9 **(Related to the Making the Connection on page 861)** Suppose that Congress passes a new law that requires all firms to accept paper currency in exchange for whatever they are selling. Briefly discuss who would gain and who would lose from this legislation.

1.10 On January 1, 2002, Germany officially adopted the euro as its currency, and the deutsche mark stopped being legal tender. According to an article in the *Wall Street Journal*, even 10 years later many Germans continued using the deutsche mark, and many stores in Germany continued to accept it. Briefly explain how it is possible for people to continue to use a currency when the government that issued it has replaced it with another currency.

Source: Vanessa Fuhrmans, "Who Needs the Euro When You Can Pay with Deutsche Marks?" *Wall Street Journal*, July 18, 2012.

25.2 How Is Money Measured in the United States Today? pages 861–865

LEARNING OBJECTIVE: Discuss the definitions of the money supply used in the United States today.

Summary

The narrowest definition of the money supply in the United States today is **M1**, which includes currency, checking account balances, and traveler's checks. A broader definition of the money supply is **M2**, which includes everything that is in M1, plus savings accounts, small-denomination time deposits (such as certificates of deposit [CDs]), money market deposit accounts in banks, and noninstitutional money market fund shares.

MyEconLab Visit **www.myeconlab.com** to complete these exercises online and get instant feedback.

Review Questions

2.1 What is the main difference between the M1 and M2 definitions of the money supply?

2.2 Why does the Federal Reserve use two definitions of the money supply rather than one?

2.3 Distinguish among money, income, and wealth. Which one of the three does the central bank of a country control?

Problems and Applications

2.4 Briefly explain whether each of the following is counted in M1.

a. The coins in your pocket
b. The funds in your checking account
c. The funds in your savings account
d. The traveler's checks that you have left over from a trip
e. Your Citibank Platinum MasterCard

2.5 **(Related to the Don't Let This Happen to You on page 863)** Briefly explain whether you agree with the following statement: "I recently read that more than half of the money the government prints is actually held by people in foreign countries. If that's true, then the United States is less than half as wealthy as government statistics indicate."

2.6 **(Related to the Don't Let This Happen to You on page 863)** An article in the *New York Times* contains the statement: "Income is only one way of measuring wealth." Do you agree that income is a way of measuring wealth?

Source: Sam Roberts, "As the Data Show, There's a Reason the Wall Street Protesters Chose New York," *New York Times*, October 25, 2011.

2.7 **(Related to Solved Problem 25.2 on page 864)** Suppose you decide to withdraw $100 in currency from your checking account. What is the effect on M1? Ignore any actions the bank may take as a result of your having withdrawn the $100.

2.8 **(Related to Solved Problem 25.2 on page 864)** Suppose you withdraw $1,000 from a money market mutual fund and deposit the funds in your bank checking account. Briefly explain how this action will affect M1 and M2.

2.9 Based on a Survey of Consumer Payment Choice, researchers from the Federal Reserve Bank of Boston estimated that the average consumer, 18 years of age and older, held about $340 in currency. However, as noted in the chapter, there is actually about $4,000 of currency for every person in the United States.

a. How can the amount of U.S. currency in circulation be so much higher than the amount held by the U.S. population?
b. What does the difference in part (a) imply about the measures of the money supply of the United States?

Source: Kevin Foster, Scott Schuh, and Hanbing Zhang, "The 2010 Survey of Consumer Payment Choice," Federal Reserve Bank of Boston Research Data Report, No. 13-2, November 2013.

2.10 Friedrich Schneider, an economist at the Johannes Kepler University of Linz in Austria, made the following observation about China: "The average Chinese trusts neither the Chinese banks nor the Communist Party."

a. If Schneider is correct, how might businesses and consumers prefer to carry out transactions?

b. The Chinese government has refused to print currency in denominations higher than the 100-renminbi note, which is the equivalent of about $16. The United States prints $100 bills, and all other countries print currency in denominations that are at least that high. Given your answer to part (a), why might the Chinese government be reluctant to print currency in high denominations?

Source: David Barboza, "Chinese Way of Doing Business: In Cash We Trust," *New York Times*, April 30, 2013.

2.11 **(Related to the Making the Connection on page 864)** In 2015, some business startups were offering the service of transferring money in the form of bitcoins among individuals and businesses in developing countries. At the same time, an article in the *Wall Street Journal* noted that in the United States, "Most ordinary consumers remain wary of using an unproven, six-year-old digital currency that many associate with illicit drugs, extreme price fluctuations and security risks." Why might using bitcoins be more attractive to individuals and firms in developing countries than to individuals and firms in the United States?

Source: Michael J. Casey and Paul Vigna, "Interest in Bitcoin Grows on Wall Street," *Wall Street Journal*, March 29, 2015.

2.12 The U.S. penny is made primarily of zinc. There have been several times in recent years when zinc prices have been high, and it has cost the U.S. Treasury more than one cent to manufacture a penny. There are currently about 1.4 billion pennies in circulation. Economist François Velde of the Federal Reserve Bank of Chicago has proposed making the current penny worth 5 cents. If the U.S. Treasury adopted Velde's proposal, what would be the effect on the value of M1? Is this change likely to have much effect on the economy? (*Hint:* According to the information given in this chapter, what is the current value of M1?)

Source: Austan Goolsbee, "Now That a Penny Isn't Worth Much, It's Time to Make It Worth 5 Cents," *New York Times*, February 1, 2007.

25.3 How Do Banks Create Money? pages 865–874

LEARNING OBJECTIVE: Explain how banks create money.

Summary

On a bank's balance sheet, *reserves* and loans are assets, and deposits are liabilities. **Reserves** are deposits that the bank has retained rather than loaned out or invested. **Required reserves** are reserves that banks are legally required to hold. The fraction of deposits that banks are required to keep as reserves is called the **required reserve ratio**. Any reserves banks hold over the legal requirement are called **excess reserves**. When a bank accepts a deposit, it keeps only a fraction of the funds as reserves and loans out the remainder. In making a loan, a bank increases the checking account balance of the borrower. When the borrower uses a check to buy something with the funds the bank has loaned, the seller deposits the check in his or her bank. The seller's bank keeps part of the deposit as reserves and loans out the remainder. This process continues until no banks have excess reserves. In this way, the process of banks making new loans increases the volume of checking account balances and the money supply. This money creation process can be illustrated with T-accounts, which are stripped-down versions of balance sheets that show only how a transaction changes a bank's balance sheet. The **simple deposit multiplier** is the ratio of the change in deposits to the change in reserves. An expression for the simple deposit multiplier is $1/RR$.

MyEconLab Visit **www.myeconlab.com** to complete these exercises online and get instant feedback.

Review Questions

3.1 What are the largest asset and the largest liability of a typical bank?

3.2 Suppose you decide to withdraw $100 in cash from your checking account. Draw a T-account showing the effect of this transaction on your bank's balance sheet.

3.3 What does it mean to say that banks "create money"?

3.4 Give the formula for the simple deposit multiplier. If the required reserve ratio is 20 percent, what is the maximum increase in checking account deposits that will result from an increase in bank reserves of $20,000? Is this maximum increase likely to occur? Briefly explain.

Problems and Applications

3.5 Following the financial crisis of 2007–2009, Congress passed the Wall Street Reform and Consumer Protection Act, also known as the Dodd-Frank Act. The act increased regulation of the banking system, and from 2010 to 2015 only one new bank opened in the United States. According to an article in the *Wall Street Journal*, "Lawmakers are concerned about the dearth of new banks because small banks make the majority of farm and small-business loans." Why might farms and small-businesses be more likely to rely on banks for funding than would large corporations?

Source: Ryan Tracy, "A Local Bank in Amish Country Flourishes amid Dearth of Small Lenders," *Wall Street Journal*, March 29, 2015.

3.6 The following is from an article on community banks: "Their commercial-lending businesses, funded by their stable deposit bases, make them steady earners." What is commercial lending? In what sense are loans "funded" by deposits?

Source: Karen Richardson, "Clean Books Bolster Traditional Lenders," *Wall Street Journal*, April 30, 2007.

3.7 **(Related to the Making the Connection on page 866)** In a newspaper column, author Delia Ephron described a conversation with a friend who had a large balance on her credit card with an interest rate of 18 percent per year. The friend was worried about paying off the debt. Ephron was earning only 0.4 percent interest on her bank certificate of deposit (CD). She considered withdrawing the money from her CD and loaning it to her friend so her friend could pay off her credit card balance: "So I was thinking that all of us earning 0.4 percent could instead loan money to our friends at 0.5 percent. … [M]y friend would get out of debt [and] I would earn $5 a month instead of $4." Why don't more people use their savings to make loans rather than keeping the funds in bank accounts that earn very low rates of interest?

Source: Delia Ephron, "Banks Taketh, but Don't Giveth," *New York Times*, January 27, 2012.

3.8 **(Related to the Making the Connection on page 866)** An economist commented on the situation a bank faces when making personal loans to subprime borrowers: "You have to be alert to the trade-off between serving consumers and being viewed as taking advantage of them." If banks charge subprime borrowers a higher interest on loans than they charge prime borrowers, are the banks taking advantage of the subprime borrowers? Briefly explain.

Source: Ianthe Jeanne Dugan and Telis Demos, "New Lenders Spring Up to Cater to Subprime Sector," *Wall Street Journal*, March 5, 2014.

3.9 Suppose that Deja owns a McDonald's franchise. She decides to move her restaurant's checking account to Wells Fargo, which causes the changes shown on the following T-account. If the required reserve ratio is 0.10, or 10 percent, and Wells Fargo currently has no excess reserves, what is the maximum loan Wells Fargo can make as result of this transaction?

Wells Fargo

Assets		Liabilities	
Reserves	+$100,000	Deposits	+$100,000

3.10 Consider the following simplified balance sheet for a bank:

Assets		Liabilities	
Reserves	$10,000	Deposits	$70,000
Loans	$66,000	Stockholders' equity	$6,000

a. If the required reserve ratio is 0.10, or 10 percent, how much in excess reserves does the bank hold?

b. What is the maximum amount by which the bank can expand its loans?

c. If the bank makes the loans in part (b), show the *immediate* effect on the bank's balance sheet.

3.11 **(Related to the Don't Let This Happen to You on page 871)** Briefly explain whether you agree with the following statement: "Assets are things of value that people own. Liabilities are debts. Therefore, a bank will always consider a checking account deposit to be an asset and a car loan to be a liability."

3.12 **(Related to Solved Problem 25.3 on page 871)** Suppose you deposit $2,000 in currency into your checking account at a branch of Bank of America, which we will assume has no excess reserves at the time you make your deposit. Also assume that the required reserve ratio is 0.20, or 20 percent.

a. Use a T-account to show the initial effect of this transaction on Bank of America's balance sheet.

b. Suppose that Bank of America makes the maximum loan it can from the funds you deposited. Using a T-account, show the initial effect of granting the loan on Bank of America's balance sheet. Also include on this T-account the transaction from part (a).

c. Now suppose that whoever took out the loan in part (b) writes a check for this amount and that the person receiving the check deposits it in a branch of Citibank. Show the effect of these transactions on the balance sheets of Bank of America and Citibank after the check has been cleared. (On the T-account for Bank of America, include the transactions from parts (a) and (b).)

d. What is the maximum increase in checking account deposits that can result from your $2,000 deposit? What is the maximum increase in the money supply? Briefly explain.

25.4 The Federal Reserve System, pages 874–881

LEARNING OBJECTIVE: Compare the three policy tools the Federal Reserve uses to manage the money supply.

Summary

The United States has a **fractional reserve banking system** in which banks keep less than 100 percent of deposits as reserves. In a **bank run**, many depositors decide simultaneously to withdraw money from a bank. In a **bank panic**, many banks experience runs at the same time. The **Federal Reserve System** ("the Fed") is the central bank of the United States. It was originally established in 1913 to stop bank panics. The recession of 2007–2009 put renewed emphasis on the Fed's goal of financial market stability. **Monetary policy** refers to the actions the Federal Reserve takes to manage the money supply and interest rates to pursue macroeconomic policy objectives. The Fed's three monetary policy tools are open market operations, discount policy, and reserve requirements. **Open market operations** are the buying and selling of Treasury securities by the Federal Reserve. The loans the Fed makes to banks are called **discount loans**, and the interest rate the Fed charges on discount loans is the **discount rate**. The **Federal Open Market Committee (FOMC)** meets in Washington, DC, eight times per year to discuss monetary policy. In the past 20 years, a "shadow banking system" has developed. During the financial crisis of 2007–2009, the existence of the shadow banking system complicated the Fed's policy response. A **security** is a financial asset—such as a stock or a bond—that can be bought and sold in a financial market. The process of **securitization** creates a secondary market in which loans that have been bundled together can be bought and sold in financial markets just as corporate or government bonds are.

MyEconLab Visit **www.myeconlab.com** to complete these exercises online and get instant feedback.

Review Questions

4.1 Why did Congress decide to establish the Federal Reserve System in 1913?

4.2 What policy tools does the Fed use to control the money supply? Which tool is the most important?

4.3 Why does an open market purchase of Treasury securities by the Federal Reserve increase bank reserves? Why does an open market sale of Treasury securities by the Federal Reserve decrease bank reserves?

4.4 What is the "shadow banking system"? Why were the financial firms of the shadow banking system more vulnerable than commercial banks to bank runs?

Problems and Applications

4.5 In an article in the *Wall Street Journal*, Kevin Brady, a member of Congress from Texas, stated, "To get Congress to pass the Federal Reserve Act [in 1913, President Woodrow] Wilson had to retain the support of ... northeastern lawmakers while convincing southern and western Democrats that legislation would not ... create a [single] central bank. Wilson's ingenious solution was federalism." Explain what Congressman Brady meant when he stated that Woodrow Wilson used "federalism" to convince Congress to pass the Federal Reserve Act.

Source: Kevin Brady, "How the Fed's East Coast Tilt Warps Monetary Policy," *Wall Street Journal*, June 4, 2015.

4.6 Suppose that the Federal Reserve makes a $10 million discount loan to First National Bank (FNB) by increasing FNB's account at the Fed.

a. Use a T-account to show the effect of this transaction on FNB's balance sheet. Remember that the funds a bank has on deposit at the Fed count as part of its reserves.

b. Assume that before receiving the discount loan, FNB has no excess reserves. What is the maximum amount of this $10 million that FNB can lend out?

c. What is the maximum total increase in the money supply that can result from the Fed's discount loan? Assume that the required reserve ratio is 10 percent.

4.7 An article in the *New York Times* states that "the Bank of Japan, the central bank ... is creating money on a vast scale by buying government bonds." How can a central bank "create money" by buying bonds? Doesn't the government create money by printing currency? Briefly explain.

Source: Jonathan Soble, "Japan's Economy Expands, but Less Than Expected," *New York Times*, February 15, 2015.

4.8 Suppose that the Federal Reserve engages in an open market sale of $25 million in U.S. Treasury bills to banks. In the T-accounts for the Fed and for the banking system shown here, fill in the missing information.

Federal Reserve

Assets		Liabilities	
________	−$25 million	Reserves	−$25 million

Banking System

Assets		Liabilities	
Treasury bills	+$25 million		
________	−$25 million		

4.9 In a speech delivered in June 2008, Timothy Geithner, then president of the Federal Reserve Bank of New York and later U.S. Treasury secretary, said:

> The structure of the financial system changed fundamentally during the boom. ... [The] non-bank financial system grew to be very large. ... [The] institutions in this parallel financial system [are] vulnerable to a classic type of run, but without the protections such as deposit insurance that the banking system has in place to reduce such risks.

a. What did Geithner mean by the "nonbank financial system"?

b. What is a "classic type of run," and why were institutions in the nonbank financial system vulnerable to such a run?

c. Why would deposit insurance provide the banking system with protection against runs?

Source: Timothy F. Geithner, "Reducing Systemic Risk in a Dynamic Financial System," Remarks at the Economic Club of New York, June 9, 2008.

4.10 An article in the *Wall Street Journal* on the shadow banking system contained the following observation: "If investors rush to the exits en masse, acting as a herd, asset prices could plummet and markets could face funding problems." Why might people who have invested in a money market mutual fund, for example, be more likely to "rush to the exits" if they heard bad news about the fund's investments than would bank depositors if they received bad news about their bank's investments?

Source: Ian Talley, "IMF Warns (Again) of Growing Shadow-Banking Risks," *Wall Street Journal*, April 8, 2015.

4.11 An article in the *Wall Street Journal* reported in 2015 that the People's Bank of China, which is the central bank of China, "is freeing up cash by reducing the amount that banks must keep in reserve." What monetary policy tool was the People's Bank of China using? In what sense did this policy change "free up cash"? What was the People's Bank of China hoping the result of this policy action would be?

Source: Lingling Wei, "China Central Bank Checks Europe Playbook on Credit," *Wall Street Journal*, April 19, 2015.

25.5 The Quantity Theory of Money, pages 881–884

LEARNING OBJECTIVE: Explain the quantity theory of money and use it to explain how high rates of inflation occur.

Summary

The *quantity equation*, which relates the money supply to the price level, is $M \times V = P \times Y$, where M is the money supply, V is the *velocity of money*, P is the price level, and Y is real output. The **velocity of money** is the average number of times each dollar in the money supply is spent during the year. Economist Irving Fisher developed the **quantity theory of money**, which assumes that the velocity of money is constant. If the quantity theory of money is correct, the inflation rate should equal the rate of growth of the money supply minus the rate of growth of real output. Although the quantity theory of money is not literally correct because the velocity of money is not constant, it is true that in the long run, inflation results from the money supply growing faster than real GDP. When governments attempt to raise revenue by selling large quantities of bonds to the central bank, the money supply will increase rapidly, resulting in high rates of inflation.

MyEconLab Visit **www.myeconlab.com** to complete these exercises online and get instant feedback.

Review Questions

5.1 What is the quantity theory of money? What explanation does the quantity theory provide for inflation?

5.2 Is the quantity theory of money better able to explain the inflation rate in the long run or in the short run? Briefly explain.

5.3 What is hyperinflation? Why do governments sometimes allow it to occur?

Problems and Applications

5.4 If the money supply is growing at a rate of 6 percent per year, real GDP is growing at a rate of 3 percent per year, and velocity is constant, what will the inflation rate be? If velocity is increasing 1 percent per year instead of remaining constant, what will the inflation rate be?

5.5 If velocity does not change when the money supply of a country increases, will nominal GDP definitely increase? Will real GDP definitely increase? Briefly explain.

5.6 During the years from 2010 to 2014, the average annual growth rate of M1 was 12.7 percent, while the inflation rate as measured by the GDP deflator averaged 1.8 percent. Are these values consistent with the quantity equation? If you would need additional information to answer, state what the information is. Are the values consistent with the quantity theory of money? Briefly explain.

Source: Data from the Federal Reserve Bank of St. Louis.

5.7 In an article in the *American Free Press*, Professor Peter Spencer of York University in England is quoted as saying: "This printing of money 'will keep the [deflation] wolf from the door.'" In the same article, Ambrose Evans-Pritchard, a writer for the London-based newspaper *The Telegraph*, is quoted as saying, "Deflation has … insidious traits. It causes shoppers to hold back. Once this psychology gains a grip, it can gradually set off a self-feeding spiral that is hard to stop."

a. What is price deflation?

b. What does Professor Spencer mean by the statement, "This printing of money 'will keep the [deflation] wolf from the door'"?

c. Why would deflation cause "shoppers to hold back," and what does Evans-Pritchard mean when he says, "Once this psychology gains a grip, it can gradually set off a self-feeding spiral that is hard to stop"?

Source: Doug French, "We Should Celebrate Price Deflation," *American Free Press*, November 17, 2008.

5.8 During the Civil War, the Confederate States of America printed large amounts of its own currency—Confederate dollars—to fund the war. By the end of the war, the Confederate government had printed nearly 1.5 billion paper dollars. How would such a large quantity of Confederate dollars have affected the value of the Confederate currency? With the war drawing to an end, would Southerners have been as willing to use and accept Confederate dollars? How else could they have bought and sold goods?

Source: Federal Reserve Bank of Richmond, "Textual Transcript of Confederate Currency."

5.9 An article in the *Economist* notes that the government of Venezuela running a large budget deficit "caused the money supply almost to quadruple in two years and led to the world's highest inflation rate, of over 60% a year."

a. Why would running a large budget deficit cause the money supply in Venezuela to increase so rapidly?

b. If the money supply increased by 150 percent per year (or 300 percent over two years) while the inflation rate was 60 percent, what must have happened to velocity in Venezuela during this period?

Source: "Of Oil and Coconut Water," *Economist*, September 20, 2014.

5.10 **(Related to the Making the Connection on page 884)** During the German hyperinflation of the 1920s, many households and firms in Germany were hurt economically. Do you think any groups in Germany benefited from the hyperinflation? Briefly explain.

Real-Time Data Exercises

D25.1 **(The components of M1)** Go to the Web site of the Federal Reserve Bank of St. Louis (FRED) (research.stlouisfed.org/fred2/) and find the most recent values for the following four variables: (1) M1 Money Stock (M1), (2) the Currency Component of M1 (CURRENCY), (3) Total Checkable Deposits (TCD), and (4) Travelers Checks Outstanding (WTCSL). Which of the components of M1 is the largest? Which is the smallest?

D25.2 **(Calculating M1 from data on M2)** Go to the Web site of the Federal Reserve Bank of St. Louis (FRED) (research.stlouisfed.org/fred2/) and find the most recent values for the following four variables: (1) M2 Money Stock (M2), (2) the Total Savings Deposits at all Depository Institutions (SAVINGS), (3) Retail Money Funds (WRMFSL), and (4) Small Time Deposits – Total (WSMTIME).

a. Using these data, calculate the value of M1.
b. What are Retail Money Funds? What percentage of M2 are they?
c. If households were to shift funds from savings accounts to checking accounts, what would happen to the values of M1 and M2?

D25.3 **(The relationship between M1 and M2)** Go to the Web site of the Federal Reserve Bank of St. Louis (FRED) (research.stlouisfed.org/fred2/) and find the most recent monthly values and values from the same month 5 years and 10 years earlier for the M1 Money Stock (M1SL) and the M2 Money Stock (M2SL).
a. Using these data, calculate M1 as a proportion of M2 for each of the years.
b. Explain whether this proportion has increased, decreased, or remained the same over time. Can you think of an explanation for any changes you observe?

D25.4 **(The equation of exchange)** Go to the Web site of the Federal Reserve Bank of St. Louis (FRED) (research.stlouisfed.org/fred2/) and find the most recent values and values for the same quarter in 1985 for the following three variables: (1) Nominal Gross Domestic Product (GDP), (2) the Velocity of M1 Money Stock (M1V), and (3) the Velocity of M2 Money Stock (M2V).
a. Using these data, calculate M1 and M2 for both periods.
b. Describe how M1 velocity and M2 velocity differ in the two quarters.

D25.5 **(Applying the equation of exchange)** Go to the Web site of the Federal Reserve Bank of St. Louis (FRED) (research.stlouisfed.org/fred2/) and find the most recent values and values from the same quarter 10 years earlier for the following three variables: (1) Real Gross Domestic Product (GDPC1), (2) the GDP Price Deflator (GDPDEF), and (3) the M2 Money Stock (M2SL).
a. Using these data, calculate the average annual rate of change in both real GDP and M2 over this 10-year period.
b. If we assume that velocity was constant during this period, what was the average annual inflation rate?
c. Using the GDP Price Deflator data, calculate the average annual inflation rate over this 10-year period.
d. Use your answers to parts (b) and (c) to discuss what must have happened to velocity during this period.

D25.6 **(Applying the equation of exchange)** Go to the Web site of the Federal Reserve Bank of St. Louis (FRED) (research.stlouisfed.org/fred2/) and find the most recent value for Real Gross Domestic Product (GDPC1) and the value from the same quarter eight years in the future for Real Potential Gross Domestic Product (GDPPOT).
a. Using these data, calculate the average annual rate of growth in real GDP over this eight-year period, assuming that real GDP equals potential GDP in the quarter that is eight years in the future.
b. If the velocity of money is constant during this eight-year period, what will the growth rate of M1 have to be if the annual inflation rate averages 2 percent? Briefly explain.
c. Suppose that M1 grows at this rate, but the actual inflation over this period averages more than 2 percent. What can you conclude about velocity during this period?

CHAPTER

26

Monetary Policy

Chapter Outline and Learning Objectives

Why Would a Bank Pay a Negative Interest Rate?

In 2015, some banks in Europe were in an unusual—and unwelcome—situation: They were receiving negative nominal interest rates on loans. That is, the banks had to make interest payments to borrowers rather than receive interest payments from borrowers. One borrower in Spain boasted, "I'm going to frame my bank statement, which shows that Bankinter is paying me interest on my mortgage. That's financial history." Why would a bank pay someone to borrow money? The answer is that the interest rates on these loans were not fixed but were instead adjusted based on changes in short-term interest rates that depend on the actions of central banks in Europe. When some of these interest rates became negative, banks had to automatically make the interest rates on some of their mortgage loans negative as well.

Central banks, including the U.S. Federal Reserve, had driven interest rates to historically low levels as they tried to pull their economies out of the severe worldwide recession of 2007–2009. In conducting monetary policy, the Fed often concentrates on the federal funds rate, which is the interest rate that banks charge each other on short-term loans. In December 2008, the Fed reduced its target for the federal funds rate to almost zero, and kept it there for nearly seven years.

In the fall of 2015, many businesspeople, policymakers, and economists were focused on predicting when Fed Chair Janet Yellen would raise the target for the federal funds rate and by how much. Does this focus indicate that the Fed chair is more important to the U.S. economy than the president of the United States? Most economists would answer "yes." The president can take actions that affect the economy, but needs the approval of Congress before enacting most polices. In contrast, the structure of the Fed gives the chair substantial control over monetary policy. As a result, the Fed chair can often have greater influence over the economy than the president.

European banks paying negative interest rates on loans is a striking example of how central bank policy can affect businesses. Homebuilders like Toll Brothers and car dealers like Ford that sell durable goods are also directly affected by changes in interest rates because their customers frequently borrow money to buy these goods. Other businesses will be affected indirectly because changes in interest rates cause changes in aggregate demand. Not surprisingly, many businesses watch the Fed carefully for signs of whether interest rates are likely to rise or fall.

In this chapter, we will study the Federal Reserve and how monetary policy affects GDP, employment, and inflation.

Sources: Patricia Kowsmann and Jeannette Neumann, "Tumbling Interest Rates in Europe Leave Some Banks Owing Money on Loans to Borrowers," *Wall Street Journal*, April 13, 2015; and Min Zeng, "Government Bond Yields Turn Negative," *Wall Street Journal*, January 14, 2015.

Economics in Your Life

Should You Buy a House during a Recession?

Think ahead a few years to when you might be married and maybe even (gasp!) have children. You decide to leave behind years of renting apartments and buy a house, but then you read a *Wall Street Journal* article that states that a majority of economists predict a recession is likely to begin soon. What should you do? Would it be a good time or a bad time to buy a house? As you read this chapter, try to answer these questions. You can check your answers against those we provide on **page 929** at the end of this chapter.

In Chapter 25, we saw that banks play an important role in providing credit to households and firms and in creating money in the form of checking account deposits. We also saw that Congress established the Federal Reserve to stabilize the financial system and that the Fed is responsible for managing the money supply. In this chapter, we will discuss the Fed's main policy goals. We will also explore how the Federal Reserve decides which *monetary policy* actions to take to achieve its goals.

26.1 What Is Monetary Policy?

LEARNING OBJECTIVE: Define monetary policy and describe the Federal Reserve's monetary policy goals.

In 1913, Congress passed the Federal Reserve Act, creating the Federal Reserve System (the Fed). The main responsibility of the Fed was to make discount loans to banks to prevent the bank panics we discussed in Chapter 25. As a result of the Great Depression of the 1930s, Congress amended the Federal Reserve Act to give the Federal Reserve's Board of Governors broader responsibility to act "so as to promote effectively the goals of maximum employment, stable prices, and moderate long-term interest rates."

Since World War II, the Federal Reserve has carried out an active *monetary policy*. **Monetary policy** is the actions the Fed takes to manage the money supply and interest rates to achieve its macroeconomic policy goals.

Monetary policy The actions the Federal Reserve takes to manage the money supply and interest rates to achieve macroeconomic policy goals.

The Goals of Monetary Policy

The Fed has four main *monetary policy goals* that are intended to promote a well-functioning economy:

1. Price stability
2. High employment
3. Stability of financial markets and institutions
4. Economic growth

We briefly consider each of these goals.

Price Stability Rising prices reduce the usefulness of money as a medium of exchange and a store of value. Especially after inflation rose dramatically and unexpectedly during the 1970s, policymakers in most industrial countries have had price stability as a key policy goal. Figure 26.1 shows that from the early 1950s until 1968, the inflation rate in the United States remained below 4 percent per year. Inflation rose above 10 percent for several years in the late 1970s and early 1980s. After 1992, the inflation rate has usually been below 4 percent. The 2007–2009 recession caused several months of deflation—a falling price level—during early 2009, and the slowness of the recovery from the recession resulted in three months of deflation during early 2015.

The inflation rates during the years 1979–1981 were the highest the United States has ever experienced during peacetime. When Paul Volcker became chairman of the Federal Reserve's Board of Governors in August 1979, he made fighting inflation his top policy goal. Later Fed chairs continued to focus on inflation, arguing that if inflation is low over the long run, the price system will do a better job of efficiently allocating resources, and the Fed will have the flexibility it needs to increase aggregate demand to fight recessions. Although the severity of the 2007–2009 recession led the Fed to adopt extraordinary policy measures that we will discuss later in this chapter, price stability remains a key policy goal of the Fed.

High Employment In addition to price stability, high employment (or a low rate of unemployment) is an important monetary policy goal. Unemployed workers and

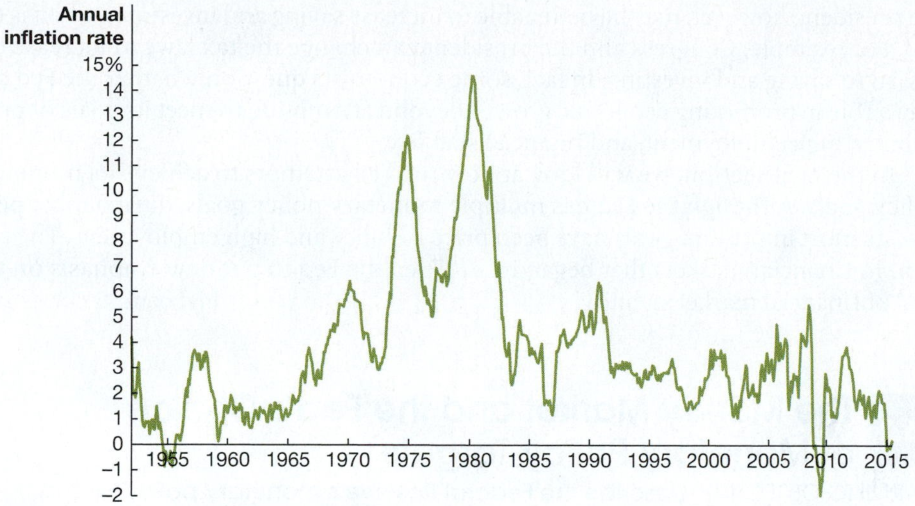

MyEconLab Real-time data

Figure 26.1

The Inflation Rate, January 1952–June 2015

For most of the 1950s and 1960s, the inflation rate in the United States was 4 percent or less. During the 1970s, the inflation rate increased, peaking during 1979–1981, when it averaged more than 10 percent. After 1992, the inflation rate was usually less than 4 percent, until increases in oil prices pushed it above 5 percent during the summer of 2008. The effects of the recession caused several months of deflation—a falling price level—during early 2009, and the slowness of the recovery caused three months of deflation in early 2015.

Note: The inflation rate is measured as the percentage change in the consumer price index from the same month in the previous year.

Source: Federal Reserve Bank of St. Louis.

underused factories and office buildings reduce GDP below its potential level. Unemployment can cause workers who lack jobs to suffer financial distress and lower self-esteem. The goal of high employment extends beyond the Fed to other branches of the federal government. At the end of World War II, Congress passed the Employment Act of 1946, which stated that it was the "responsibility of the Federal Government ... to foster and promote ... conditions under which there will be afforded useful employment, for those able, willing, and seeking to work, and to promote maximum employment, production, and purchasing power." Because price stability and high employment are explicitly mentioned in the Employment Act, it is sometimes said that the Fed has a *dual mandate* to attain these two goals.

Stability of Financial Markets and Institutions Firms often need to borrow funds as they design, develop, produce, and market their products. Savers look to financial investments to increase the value of their savings as they prepare to buy homes, pay for the educations of their children, and provide for their retirement. The Fed promotes the stability of financial markets and institutions so that an efficient flow of funds from savers to borrowers will occur. As we saw in Chapter 25, the financial crisis of 2007–2009 brought the issue of stability in financial markets to the forefront.

The financial crisis was similar to the banking crises that led Congress to create the Federal Reserve System in 1913. A key difference is that while earlier banking crises affected commercial banks, the events of 2007–2009 also affected investment banks and other financial firms in the *shadow banking system*. Investment banks, money market mutual funds, and other financial firms can be subject to *liquidity problems* because they often borrow short term—sometimes as short as overnight—and invest the funds in long-term securities. Just as commercial banks can experience a crisis if depositors begin to withdraw funds, investment banks and other financial firms can experience a crisis if investors stop providing them with short-term loans. In 2008, the Fed took several steps to ease the liquidity problems of these financial firms because the Fed believed these problems were increasing the severity of the recession. In Section 26.6, we will discuss in more detail the new policies the Fed enacted to help deal with the financial crisis.

Economic Growth We discussed in Chapters 21 and 22 the importance of economic growth to raising living standards. Policymakers aim to encourage *stable* economic growth, which allows households and firms to plan accurately and encourages firms to engage in the investment that is needed to sustain growth. Policy can spur economic growth by providing incentives for saving to ensure a large pool of investment funds, as well as by providing direct incentives for business investment. Congress and the president, however, may be better able to increase saving and investment than is the Fed. For example, Congress and the president can change the tax laws to increase the return to saving and investing. In fact, some economists question whether the Fed can play a role in promoting economic growth beyond attempting to meet its goals of price stability, high employment, and financial stability.

In the next section, we will look at how the Fed attempts to achieve its monetary policy goals. Although the Fed has multiple monetary policy goals, during most periods, its most important goals have been price stability and high employment. The turmoil in financial markets that began in 2007 led the Fed to put new emphasis on the goal of financial market stability.

MyEconLab Study Plan

MyEconLab Concept Check

26.2 The Money Market and the Fed's Choice of Monetary Policy Targets

LEARNING OBJECTIVE: Describe the Federal Reserve's monetary policy targets and explain how expansionary and contractionary monetary policies affect the interest rate.

The Fed uses its policy tools to achieve its monetary policy goals. Recall that the Fed's policy tools are open market operations, discount policy—making discount loans to banks and changing the discount rate it charges on those loans—and changes in reserve requirements. At times, the Fed encounters conflicts among its policy goals. For example, as we will discuss later in this chapter, the Fed can raise interest rates to reduce the inflation rate. But higher interest rates typically reduce household and firm spending, which may result in slower growth and higher unemployment. So, a policy that is intended to achieve one monetary policy goal, such as reducing inflation, may make it more difficult to achieve another policy goal, such as high employment.

Monetary Policy Targets

The Fed tries to keep both the unemployment and inflation rates low, but it can't affect either of these economic variables directly. The Fed cannot tell firms how many people to employ or what prices to charge for their products. Instead, the Fed uses variables, called *monetary policy targets*, that it can affect directly and that, in turn, affect variables, such as real GDP, employment, and the price level, that are closely related to the Fed's policy goals. The two main monetary policy targets are the money supply and the interest rate. As we will see, the Fed typically uses the interest rate as its policy target.

Bear in mind that while the Fed has typically used the money supply and the interest rate as its targets, these targets were not central to the Fed's policy decisions during the recession of 2007–2009. As we will discuss in Section 26.6, because U.S. financial markets suffered a degree of disruption not seen since the Great Depression of the 1930s, the Fed was forced to develop new policy tools. However, it is still important to have a good grasp of how the Fed carries out policy during normal times.

MyEconLab Concept Check

The Demand for Money

The Fed's two monetary policy targets are related. To understand this relationship, we first need to examine the *money market*, which brings together the demand and supply for money. Figure 26.2 shows the demand curve for money. The interest rate is on the vertical axis, and the quantity of money is on the horizontal axis. Here we are using the M1 definition of money, which equals currency plus checking account deposits. Notice that the demand curve for money is downward sloping.

To understand why the demand curve for money is downward sloping, consider that households and firms have a choice between holding money and holding other

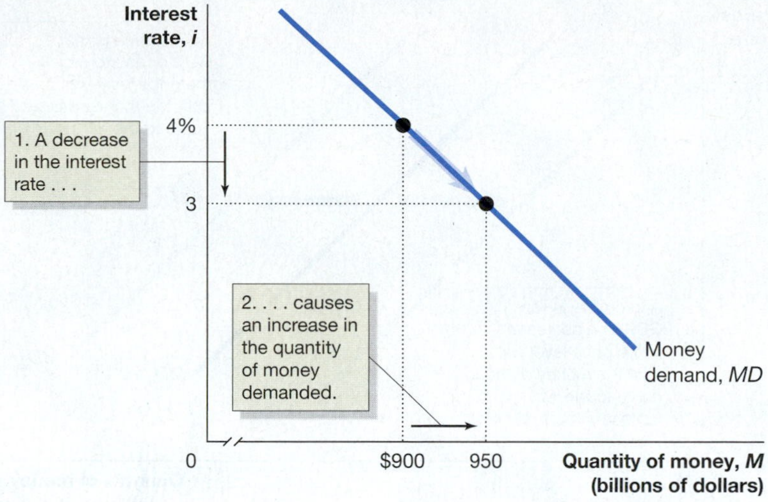

MyEconLab Animation

Figure 26.2

The Demand for Money

The money demand curve slopes downward because a lower interest rate causes households and firms to switch from financial assets such as U.S. Treasury bills to money. All other things being equal, a fall in the interest rate from 4 percent to 3 percent will increase the quantity of money demanded from $900 billion to $950 billion. An increase in the interest rate will decrease the quantity of money demanded.

financial assets, such as U.S. Treasury bills. In making the choice, households and firms take into account that:

- Money has one particularly desirable characteristic: You can use it to buy goods, services, or financial assets.
- Money also has one undesirable characteristic: It earns either a zero interest rate or a very low interest rate.

The currency in your wallet earns no interest, and the money in your checking account earns either no interest or very little interest. Alternatives to money, such as U.S. Treasury bills, pay interest but have to be sold if you want to use the funds to buy something. When interest rates rise on financial assets such as U.S. Treasury bills, the amount of interest that households and firms lose by holding money increases. When interest rates fall, the amount of interest households and firms lose by holding money decreases. Remember that *opportunity cost* is what you have to forgo to engage in an activity. The interest rate is the opportunity cost of holding money.

We now have an explanation for why the demand curve for money slopes downward: When interest rates on Treasury bills and other financial assets are low, the opportunity cost of holding money is low, so the quantity of money demanded by households and firms will be high; when interest rates are high, the opportunity cost of holding money will be high, so the quantity of money demanded will be low. In Figure 26.2, a decrease in the interest rate from 4 percent to 3 percent causes the quantity of money demanded by households and firms to rise from $900 billion to $950 billion. MyEconLab Concept Check

Shifts in the Money Demand Curve

We saw in Chapter 3 that the demand curve for a good is drawn holding constant all variables, other than the price, that affect the willingness of consumers to buy the good. Changes in variables other than the price cause the demand curve to shift. Similarly, the demand curve for money is drawn holding constant all variables, other than the interest rate, that affect the willingness of households and firms to hold money. Changes in variables other than the interest rate cause the demand curve to shift. The two most important variables that cause the money demand curve to shift are real GDP and the price level.

Figure 26.3 illustrates shifts in the money demand curve. An increase in real GDP means that the amount of buying and selling of goods and services will increase. This additional buying and selling increases the demand for money as a medium of exchange, so the quantity of money households and firms want to hold increases at each interest rate, shifting the money demand curve to the right. A decrease in real GDP

MyEconLab Animation

Figure 26.3

Shifts in the Money Demand Curve

Changes in real GDP or the price level cause the money demand curve to shift. An increase in real GDP or an increase in the price level will cause the money demand curve to shift to the right from MD_1 to MD_2. A decrease in real GDP or a decrease in the price level will cause the money demand curve to shift to the left from MD_1 to MD_3.

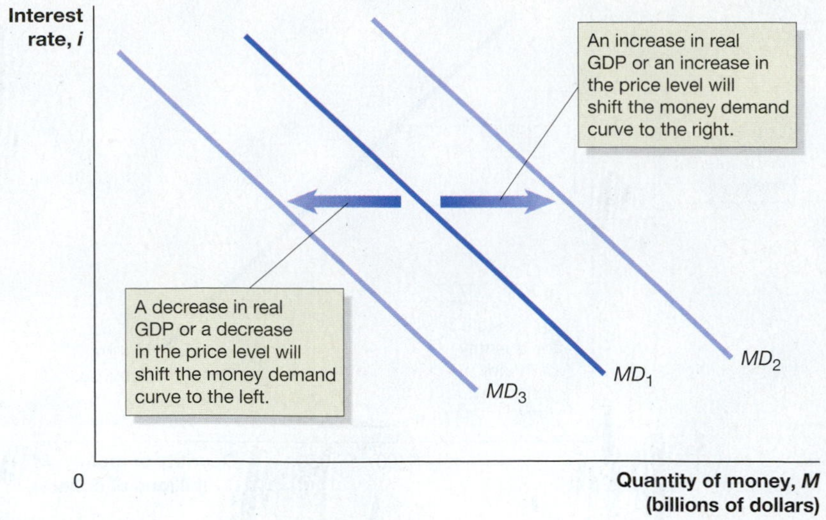

decreases the quantity of money demanded at each interest rate, shifting the money demand curve to the left. A higher price level increases the quantity of money required for a given amount of buying and selling. Eighty years ago, for example, when the price level was much lower and someone could purchase a new car for $500 and a salary of $30 per week was typical for someone in the middle class, the quantity of money demanded by households and firms was much lower than today, even adjusting for the effect of the lower real GDP and smaller population of those years. An increase in the price level increases the quantity of money demanded at each interest rate, shifting the money demand curve to the right. A decrease in the price level decreases the quantity of money demanded at each interest rate, shifting the money demand curve to the left.

MyEconLab Concept Check

How the Fed Manages the Money Supply: A Quick Review

Having discussed money demand, we now turn to money supply. In Chapter 25, we saw how the Federal Reserve manages the money supply. Eight times per year, the Federal Open Market Committee (FOMC) meets in Washington, DC. If the FOMC decides to increase the money supply, it orders the trading desk at the Federal Reserve Bank of New York to purchase U.S. Treasury securities. The sellers of these Treasury securities deposit the funds they receive from the Fed in banks, which increases bank reserves. Typically, banks loan out most of these reserves, which creates new checking account deposits and expands the money supply. If the FOMC decides to decrease the money supply, it orders the trading desk to sell Treasury securities, which decreases bank reserves and contracts the money supply.

MyEconLab Concept Check

Equilibrium in the Money Market

In Figure 26.4, we include both the money demand and money supply curves. We can use this figure to see how the Fed affects both the money supply and the interest rate. For simplicity, we assume that the Federal Reserve is able to completely control the money supply. With this assumption, the money supply curve is a vertical line, and changes in the interest rate have no effect on the quantity of money supplied. Just as with other markets, equilibrium in the *money market* occurs where the money demand curve crosses the money supply curve. If the Fed increases the money supply, the money supply curve will shift to the right, and the equilibrium interest rate will fall. In Figure 26.4, when the Fed increases the money supply from $900 billion to $950 billion, the money supply curve shifts to the right from MS_1 to MS_2, and the equilibrium interest rate falls from 4 percent to 3 percent.

In the money market, the adjustment from one equilibrium to another equilibrium is different from the adjustment in the market for a good. In Figure 26.4, the money

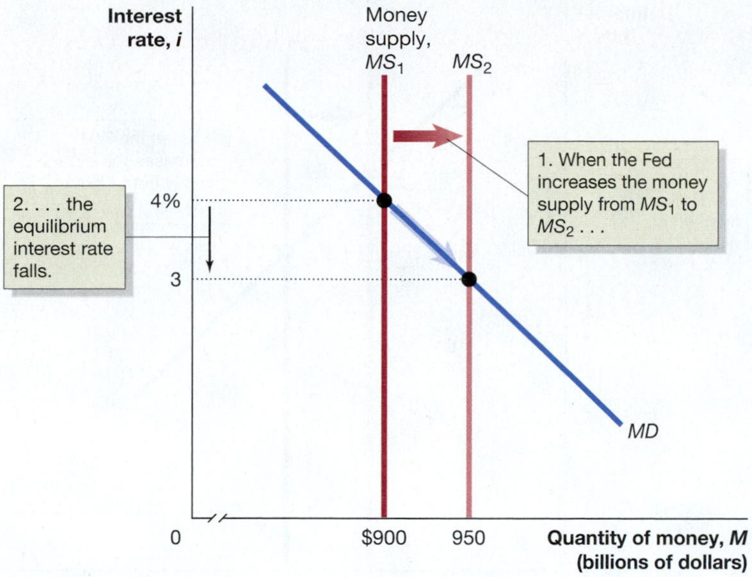

MyEconLab Animation

Figure 26.4

The Effect on the Interest Rate When the Fed Increases the Money Supply

When the Fed increases the money supply, households and firms will initially hold more money than they want, relative to other financial assets. Households and firms use the money they don't want to hold to buy Treasury bills and make deposits in interest-paying bank accounts. This increase in demand allows banks and sellers of Treasury bills and similar securities to offer lower interest rates. Eventually, interest rates will fall enough that households and firms will be willing to hold the additional money the Fed has created. In the figure, an increase in the money supply from \$900 billion to \$950 billion causes the money supply curve to shift to the right, from MS_1 to MS_2, and causes the equilibrium interest rate to fall from 4 percent to 3 percent.

market is initially in equilibrium, with an interest rate of 4 percent and a money supply of \$900 billion. When the Fed increases the money supply by \$50 billion, households and firms have more money than they want to hold at an interest rate of 4 percent. What do households and firms do with the extra \$50 billion? They are most likely to use the money to buy short-term financial assets, such as Treasury bills, or to deposit the money in interest-paying bank accounts, such as certificates of deposit. This increase in demand for interest-paying bank accounts and short-term financial assets allows banks to offer lower interest rates on certificates of deposit, and it allows sellers of Treasury bills and similar assets to also offer lower interest rates. As the interest rates on certificates of deposit, Treasury bills, and other short-term assets fall, the opportunity cost of holding money also falls. The result is a movement down the money demand curve. Eventually the interest rate falls enough that households and firms are willing to hold the additional \$50 billion worth of money the Fed has created, and the money market will be back in equilibrium. To summarize: *When the Fed increases the money supply, the short-term interest rate must fall until it reaches a level at which households and firms are willing to hold the additional money.*

Figure 26.5 shows what happens when the Fed decreases the money supply. The money market is initially in equilibrium, at an interest rate of 4 percent and a money supply of \$900 billion. If the Fed decreases the money supply to \$850 billion, households and firms will be holding less money than they would like, relative to other financial assets, at an interest rate of 4 percent. To increase their money holdings, they will sell Treasury bills and other short-term financial assets and withdraw funds from certificates of deposit and other interest-paying bank accounts. Banks will have to offer higher interest rates to retain depositors, and sellers of Treasury bills and similar securities will have to offer higher interest rates to find buyers. Rising short-term interest rates increase the opportunity cost of holding money, causing a movement up the money demand curve. Equilibrium is restored at an interest rate of 5 percent.

MyEconLab Concept Check

A Tale of Two Interest Rates

In Chapter 21, we discussed the loanable funds model of the interest rate. In that model, the equilibrium interest rate is determined by the demand and supply for loanable funds. So, we have two models of the interest rate:

1. The loanable funds model is concerned with the *long-term real rate of interest,* which is the interest rate that is most relevant when savers consider purchasing a long-term financial security such as a corporate bond. It is also the rate of interest that is most

MyEconLab Animation

Figure 26.5

The Effect on the Interest Rate When the Fed Decreases the Money Supply

When the Fed decreases the money supply, households and firms will initially hold less money than they want, relative to other financial assets. Households and firms will sell Treasury bills and other financial assets and withdraw money from interest-paying bank accounts. These actions will increase interest rates. Interest rates will rise to the point at which households and firms will be willing to hold the smaller amount of money that results from the Fed's actions. In the figure, a reduction in the money supply from \$900 billion to \$850 billion causes the money supply curve to shift to the left, from MS_1 to MS_2, and causes the equilibrium interest rate to rise from 4 percent to 5 percent.

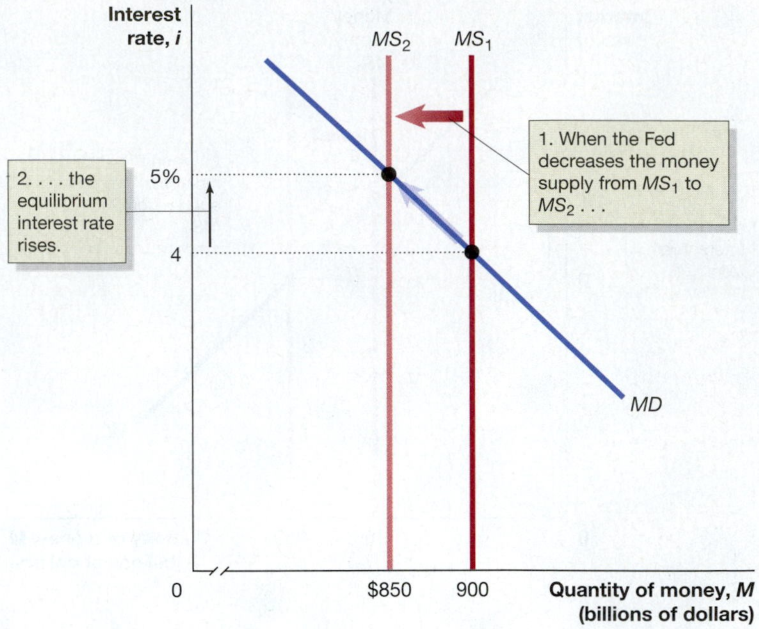

relevant to firms that are borrowing to finance long-term investment projects such as new factories or office buildings, or to households that are taking out mortgage loans to buy new homes.

2. The money market model is concerned with the *short-term nominal rate of interest.* When analyzing monetary policy, economists focus on the short-term nominal interest rate because it is the interest rate most affected by increases and decreases in the money supply.

Often—but not always—there is a close connection between movements in the short-term nominal interest rate and movements in the long-term real interest rate. So, when the Fed takes actions to increase the short-term nominal interest rate, usually the long-term real interest rate also increases. In other words, as we will discuss in the next section, when the interest rate on Treasury bills rises, the real interest rate on mortgage loans usually also rises, although sometimes only after a delay. MyEconLab Concept Check

Choosing a Monetary Policy Target

As we have seen, the Fed uses monetary policy targets to affect economic variables, such as real GDP or the price level, that are closely related to the Fed's policy goals. The Fed can use either the money supply or the interest rate as its monetary policy target. As Figure 26.5 shows, the Fed is capable of affecting both. The Fed has generally focused on the interest rate rather than on the money supply. In 1980, Congress began allowing banks to pay interest on checking accounts. At the same time, money market mutual funds were becoming more popular with small savers as a way to earn higher interest rates than banks offered. As a result of these developments, some economists argued that the Fed should focus less on M1 than on M2. They argued that the relationship between M2 and inflation and changes in GDP was more stable than the relationship between M1 and these variables. But even the relationship between M2 and other key economic variables broke down in the early 1990s. In July 1993, then Fed Chairman Alan Greenspan informed the U.S. Congress that the Fed would cease using M1 or M2 targets to guide the conduct of monetary policy. The Fed has correspondingly increased its reliance on interest rate targets.

There are many different interest rates in the economy. For purposes of monetary policy, the Fed has targeted the interest rate known as the *federal funds rate.* In the next section, we will discuss the federal funds rate before examining how targeting the interest rate can help the Fed achieve its monetary policy goals. MyEconLab Concept Check

The Importance of the Federal Funds Rate

Recall that every bank must keep 10 percent of its checking account deposits above a certain threshold amount as reserves, either as currency held in the bank or as deposits with the Fed (see Chapter 25). The Fed pays banks only a low interest rate on their reserve deposits, so banks normally have an incentive to invest reserves above the 10 percent minimum rather than leave these funds with the Fed. During the financial crisis, bank reserves soared as banks attempted to meet an increase in deposit withdrawals and as they became reluctant to lend to any borrowers except those with flawless credit histories. Banks continued to hold large reserve deposits for several years following the end of the financial crisis. These conditions were very unusual, however. In normal times, banks keep few excess reserves, and when they need additional reserves, they borrow in the *federal funds market* from banks that have reserves available. The **federal funds rate** is the interest rate banks charge each other on loans in the federal funds market. The loans are usually very short term, often just overnight.

Federal funds rate The interest rate banks charge each other for overnight loans.

Despite the name, the Fed does not actually set the federal funds rate. Instead, the rate is determined by the demand for and supply of reserves. Because the Fed can increase and decrease the supply of bank reserves through open market operations, it can set a *target* for the federal funds rate and usually come very close to hitting it. The FOMC announces a target for the federal funds rate after each meeting. In Figure 26.6, the orange line shows the Fed's targets for the federal funds rate since 2000. The jagged green line represents the actual federal funds rate on a weekly basis. The figure shows the rapid declines in the target for the federal funds rate beginning in September 2007, as the Fed responded to the start of the financial crisis. In December 2008, the Fed announced a range of 0 to 0.25 percent as its target. The actual federal funds rate fluctuated between 0.06 and 0.23 percent. These very low federal funds rates reflect the severity of the financial crisis.

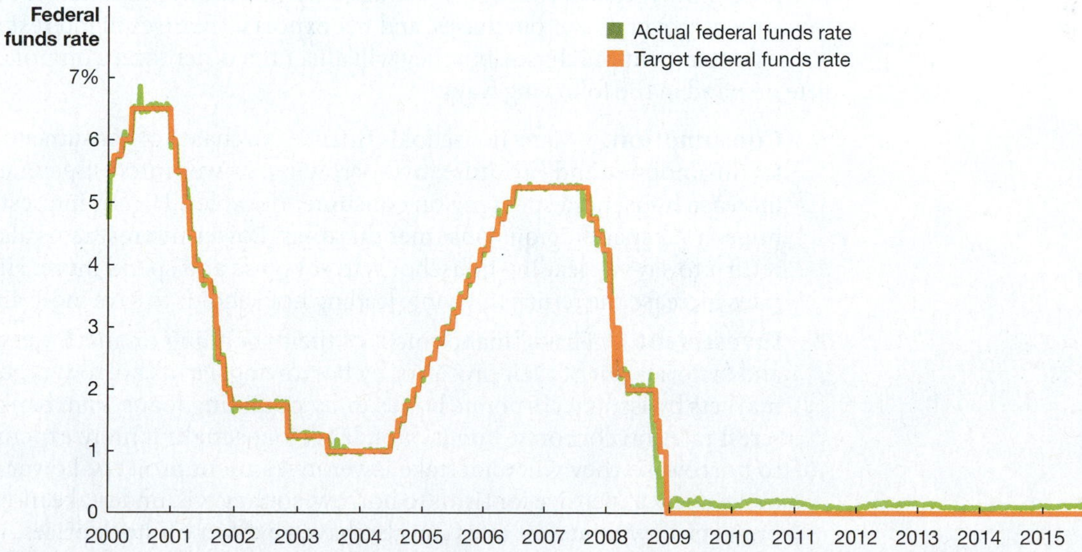

MyEconLab Real-time data

Figure 26.6 Federal Funds Rate Targeting, January 2000–October 2015

The Fed does not set the federal funds rate. However, the Fed's ability to increase or decrease bank reserves quickly through open market operations keeps the actual federal funds rate close to the Fed's target rate. The orange line is the Fed's target for the federal funds rate, and the jagged green line represents the actual value for the federal funds rate on a weekly basis.

Note: The federal funds target for the period after December 2008 was 0 to 0.25 percent through October 2015.

Source: Board of Governors of the Federal Reserve System.

Because only banks can borrow or lend in the federal funds market, the federal funds rate is not directly relevant for households and firms. However, changes in the federal funds rate usually result in changes in interest rates on both short-term financial assets, such as Treasury bills, and long-term financial assets, such as corporate bonds and mortgages. A change in the federal funds rate has a greater effect on short-term interest rates than on long-term interest rates, and its effect on long-term interest rates may occur only after a lag in time. Although a majority of economists support the Fed's choice of the interest rate as its monetary policy target, some economists believe the Fed should concentrate on the money supply instead. We will discuss these views in Section 26.5.

MyEconLab Study Plan

MyEconLab Concept Check

26.3 Monetary Policy and Economic Activity

LEARNING OBJECTIVE: Use aggregate demand and aggregate supply graphs to show the effects of monetary policy on real GDP and the price level.

The Fed uses the federal funds rate as a monetary policy target because it controls this interest rate through open market operations and because it believes that changes in the federal funds rate will ultimately affect economic variables that are related to its monetary policy goals. It is important to consider again the distinction between the nominal interest rate and the real interest rate. Recall that we calculate the real interest rate by subtracting the inflation rate from the nominal interest rate. Ultimately, the ability of the Fed to use monetary policy to affect economic variables such as real GDP depends on its ability to affect long-term real interest rates, such as the real interest rates on mortgages and corporate bonds. Because the federal funds rate is a short-term nominal interest rate, the Fed sometimes has difficulty affecting long-term real interest rates. Nevertheless, for purposes of the following discussion, we will assume that the Fed is able to use open market operations to affect long-term real interest rates.

How Interest Rates Affect Aggregate Demand

Changes in interest rates affect *aggregate demand*, which is the total level of spending in the economy. Recall that aggregate demand has four components: consumption, investment, government purchases, and net exports. Changes in interest rates will not affect government purchases, but they will affect the other three components of aggregate demand in the following ways:

- **Consumption.** Many households finance purchases of consumer durables, such as automobiles and furniture, by borrowing. Lower interest payments on loans increase household spending on consumer durables. Higher interest rates reduce household spending on consumer durables. Lower interest rates also reduce the return to saving, leading households to save less and spend more. Higher interest rates increase the return to saving, leading households to save more and spend less.
- **Investment.** Firms finance most of their spending on machinery, equipment, and factories out of their profits or by borrowing. Firms borrow either in financial markets by issuing corporate bonds or by obtaining loans from banks. Higher interest rates on corporate bonds or on bank loans make it more expensive for firms to borrow, so they will undertake fewer investment projects. Lower interest rates make it less expensive for firms to borrow, so they will undertake more investment projects. Lower interest rates can also have an effect on stock prices, which can increase firms' investment spending. As interest rates decline, stocks become a more attractive investment relative to bonds. The increase in demand for stocks raises their prices. By issuing additional shares of stock, firms can acquire the funds they need to buy new factories and equipment, so investment increases.

  Spending by households on new homes is also part of investment. When interest rates on mortgage loans rise, the cost of buying new homes rises, and fewer new homes will be purchased. When interest rates on mortgage loans fall, more new homes will be purchased.

- **Net exports.** Recall that net exports is equal to spending by foreign households and firms on goods and services produced in the United States minus spending by U.S. households and firms on goods and services produced in other countries. The value of net exports depends partly on the exchange rate between the U.S. dollar and foreign currencies. When the value of the dollar rises, households and firms in other countries will pay more for goods and services produced in the United States, but U.S. households and firms will pay less for goods and services produced in other countries. As a result, the United States will export less and import more, so net exports will fall. When the value of the dollar falls, net exports will rise. If interest rates in the United States rise relative to interest rates in other countries, investing in U.S. financial assets will become more desirable, causing foreign investors to increase their demand for dollars, which will increase the value of the dollar. As the value of the dollar increases, net exports will fall. If interest rates in the United States decline relative to interest rates in other countries, the value of the dollar will fall, and net exports will rise. MyEconLab Concept Check

The Effects of Monetary Policy on Real GDP and the Price Level

In Chapter 24, we developed the *aggregate demand and aggregate supply model* to explain fluctuations in real GDP and the price level. In the basic version of the model, we assume that there is no economic growth, so the long-run aggregate supply curve does not shift. In panel (a) of Figure 26.7, we assume that short-run equilibrium is at point A, where the aggregate demand (AD_1) curve intersects the short-run aggregate supply (*SRAS*) curve. Real GDP is below potential GDP, as shown by the *LRAS* curve, so the economy is in a recession, with some firms operating below normal capacity and some workers having been laid off. To reach its goal of high employment, the Fed carries out

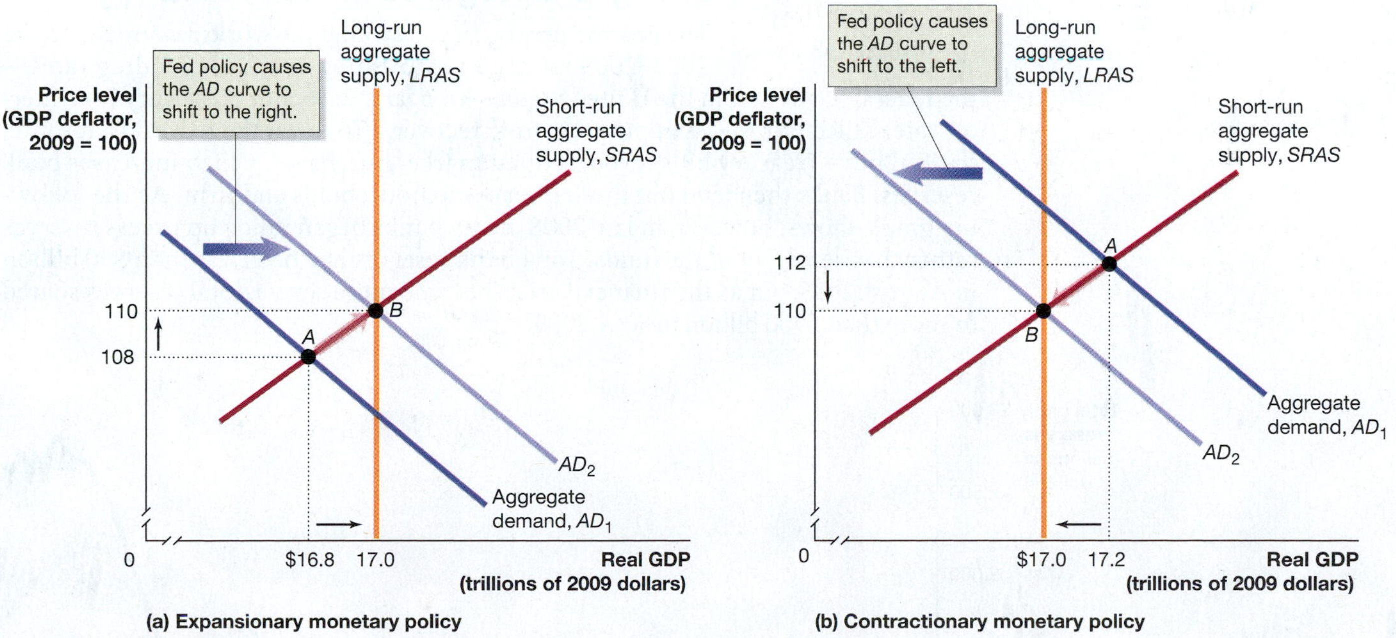

MyEconLab Animation

Figure 26.7 Monetary Policy

In panel (a), short-run equilibrium is at point A, with real GDP of $16.8 trillion and a price level of 108. An expansionary monetary policy causes aggregate demand to shift to the right, from AD_1 to AD_2, increasing real GDP from $16.8 trillion to $17.0 trillion and the price level from 108 to 110 (point B). With real GDP back at its potential level, the Fed can meet its goal of high employment. In panel (b), short-run equilibrium is at point A, with real GDP at $17.2 trillion and the price level at 112. Because real GDP is greater than potential GDP, the economy experiences rising wages and prices. A contractionary monetary policy causes aggregate demand to shift to the left, from AD_1 to AD_2, causing real GDP to decrease from $17.2 trillion to $17.0 trillion and the price level to decrease from 112 to 110 (point B). With real GDP back at its potential level, the Fed can meet its goal of price stability.

Expansionary monetary policy The Federal Reserve's policy of decreasing interest rates to increase real GDP.

an **expansionary monetary policy** by increasing the money supply and decreasing interest rates. Lower interest rates cause an increase in consumption, investment, and net exports, which shifts the aggregate demand curve to the right, from AD_1 to AD_2. Real GDP increases from \$16.8 trillion to potential GDP of \$17.0 trillion, and the price level rises from 108 to 110 (point *B*). The policy successfully returns real GDP to its potential level. Rising production leads to increasing employment, allowing the Fed to achieve its goal of high employment.

In panel (b) of Figure 26.7, short-run equilibrium is at point A, with real GDP of \$17.2 trillion, which is above potential GDP of \$17.0 trillion. With some firms producing beyond their normal capacity and the unemployment rate being very low, wages and prices are increasing. To reach its goal of price stability, the Fed needs to carry out a **contractionary monetary policy** by decreasing the money supply and increasing interest rates. Higher interest rates cause a decrease in consumption, investment, and net exports, which shifts the aggregate demand curve from AD_1 to AD_2. Real GDP decreases from \$17.2 trillion to \$17.0 trillion, and the price level falls from 112 to 110 (point *B*). Why would the Fed want to intentionally cause real GDP to decline? Because in the long run, real GDP cannot continue to remain above potential GDP. Attempting to keep real GDP above potential GDP would result in rising inflation. As aggregate demand declines and real GDP returns to its potential level, upward pressure on wages and prices will be reduced, allowing the Fed to achieve its goal of price stability.

Contractionary monetary policy The Federal Reserve's policy of increasing interest rates to reduce inflation.

We can conclude that the Fed can use monetary policy to affect the price level and, in the short run, the level of real GDP, allowing it to attain its policy goals of high employment and price stability.

MyEconLab Concept Check

Making the Connection
MyEconLab Video

Too Low for Zero: Central Banks, Quantitative Easing, and Negative Interest Rates

The Fed and central banks around the world responded to the 2007–2009 recession by pushing overnight lending rates—the federal funds rate in the United States—to nearly zero. But these very low interest rates failed to result in rapid economic recovery. To lower the federal funds rate, the Fed buys Treasury bills through open market purchases, which increases bank reserves. Banks then lend out these reserves to households and firm. As the following graph shows, however, in late 2008, many banks began piling up excess reserves rather than lending out the funds. Total bank reserves had been less than \$50 billion in August 2008, but as the financial crisis became more severe, total reserves soared to more than \$900 billion by May 2009.

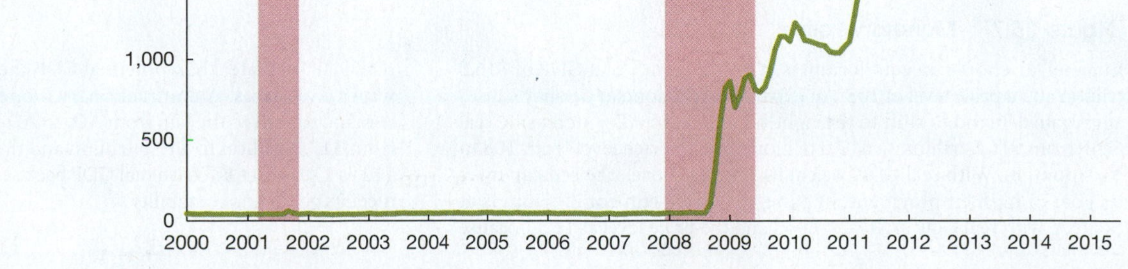

The increase in bank reserves was partly due to the Fed having received authorization from Congress in October 2008 to start paying interest of 0.25 percent on bank reserves held as deposits at the Fed. Primarily, though, the increase in reserves occurred because banks were reluctant to make loans at low interest rates to households and firms whose financial positions had been damaged by the recession. Some economists argued that the Fed was facing a situation known as a *liquidity trap*, in which short-term interest rates are pushed to zero, leaving the central bank unable to lower them further. Liquidity traps may also have occurred in the United States during the 1930s and in Japan during the 1990s.

To try to spur economic recovery, the Fed, the European Central Bank, the Bank of Japan, and other central banks turned to a policy of *quantitative easing* (*QE*), which involves buying securities beyond the short-term government securities that are usually involved in open market operations. The Fed began purchasing 10-year U.S. Treasury notes to push their interest rates lower. Interest rates on home mortgage loans typically move closely with interest rates on 10-year Treasury notes. The Fed also purchased certain *mortgage-backed securities*. The Fed's objective was to keep interest rates on mortgages low and to keep funds flowing into the mortgage market to help stimulate demand for housing.

The Fed's first round of QE began in November 2008. Because the U.S. economy recovered more slowly than expected, the Fed engaged in two additional rounds of QE before ending the program in October 2014. The use of QE by the Fed and other central banks, combined with very low inflation rates and the slow recovery from the 2007–2009 recession, led to historically low interest rates in most countries. The graph below shows interest rates on 10-year U.S. Treasury notes and on the corresponding German government bonds.

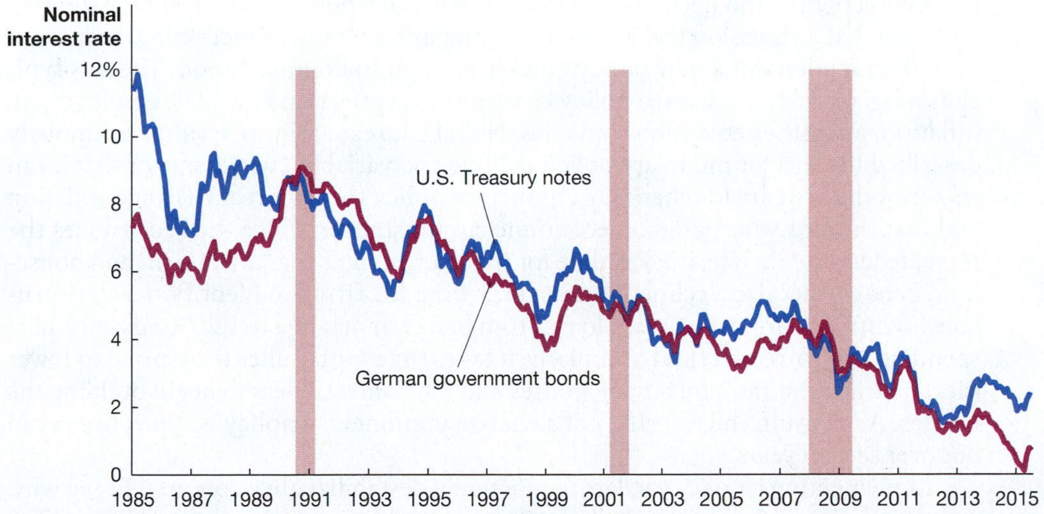

Nominal interest rates on government bonds were so low that real interest rates were nearly zero or even negative. For example, in April 2015, the nominal interest rate on 10-year German government bonds was 0.12%, while the inflation rate in Germany was 0.5%. Even more remarkable, in early 2015, the German government sold 5-year bonds with a *nominal* interest rate of −0.08%. This negative interest rate meant that investors were willing to pay the German government to keep their money for five years. Why would an investor accept a negative interest rate? With interest rates on many corporate bonds and on bank deposits being at very low levels, investors did not believe that the interest rates were sufficiently high to compensate for the default risk on those bonds and deposits. So, investors were willing to receive a negative nominal interest rate from the German government because they believed there was no chance that the government would default. As we saw in the chapter opener, some banks tie the interest rates they charge on loans to the interest rates on government bonds. The result of determining loan interest rates in this way was that banks like the Spanish bank Bankinter had to make interest payments *to* borrowers.

Economists remain divided over whether central banks had succeeded in using QE to expand the growth of employment and output. Economists who were skeptical of QE pointed to negative nominal interest rates as an example of the distortions in the financial system that had resulted from these policies. Later in this chapter, we will consider other new programs the Fed put in place to deal with the recession of 2007–2009 and the slow recovery that followed, as its traditional focus on lowering the federal funds rate to stimulate the economy proved ineffective.

Sources: Emese Bartha and Ben Edwards, "Germany Sells Five-Year Debt at Negative Yield for First Time on Record," *Wall Street Journal*, February 25, 2015; and data from the Federal Reserve Bank of St. Louis and the Organization for Economic Co-operation and Development.

MyEconLab Study Plan

Your Turn: Test your understanding by doing related problems 3.9 and 3.10 on page 932 at the end of this chapter.

Can the Fed Eliminate Recessions?

Panel (a) of Figure 26.7 on page 905 shows a completely successful expansionary monetary policy that shifts the *AD* curve to bring real GDP back to potential GDP. In practice, this ideal is very difficult for the Fed to achieve, as the length and severity of the 2007–2009 recession illustrates. In practice, the best the Fed can do is keep recessions shorter and milder than they would otherwise be.

If the Fed is to succeed in offsetting the effects of the business cycle, it needs to quickly recognize the need for a change in monetary policy. If the Fed is late in recognizing that a recession has begun or that the inflation rate is increasing, it may not be able to implement a new policy quickly enough to do much good. There is typically a *lag*, or delay, between a policy change and its effect on real GDP, employment, inflation, and other economic variables. Nobel Laureate Milton Friedman famously described the lags for monetary policy as "long and variable," which means that it can take months or years for changes in monetary policy to affect real GDP and inflation and that the lags vary based on economic circumstances. Once the Fed reduces the target federal funds rate, it takes time for the interest rates that affect firm and household behavior to also decline. Then it takes time for firms to identify newly profitable investment projects, obtain loans from banks or arrange to sell bonds, and start spending the borrowed funds. Similarly, it takes time for families to respond to lower mortgage interest rates by buying houses and for homebuilders to begin building the houses. As a result, the full effect of a change in monetary policy is typically spread out over several years.

Implementing a policy too late may actually destabilize the economy. To see why, consider Figure 26.8. The straight line represents the long-run growth trend in real GDP in the United States. On average, real GDP grows about 3 percent per year. The actual path of real GDP differs from the underlying trend because of the business cycle, which is shown by the red curved line. As we saw in Chapter 21, the actual business cycle is more irregular than the stylized cycle shown here.

Suppose that a recession begins in August 2018. Because it takes months for economic statistics to be gathered by the Commerce Department, the Census Bureau, the Bureau of Labor Statistics, and the Fed itself, there is a lag before the Fed recognizes that a recession has begun. Finally, in June 2019, the FOMC concludes that the economy is in recession and begins an expansionary monetary policy. As it turns out, June 2019 is actually the trough of the recession, meaning that the recession has already ended, and an expansion has begun. In these circumstances, the Fed's expansionary policy is not needed to end the recession. The increase in aggregate demand caused by the Fed's lowering interest rates is likely to push the economy beyond potential GDP and cause

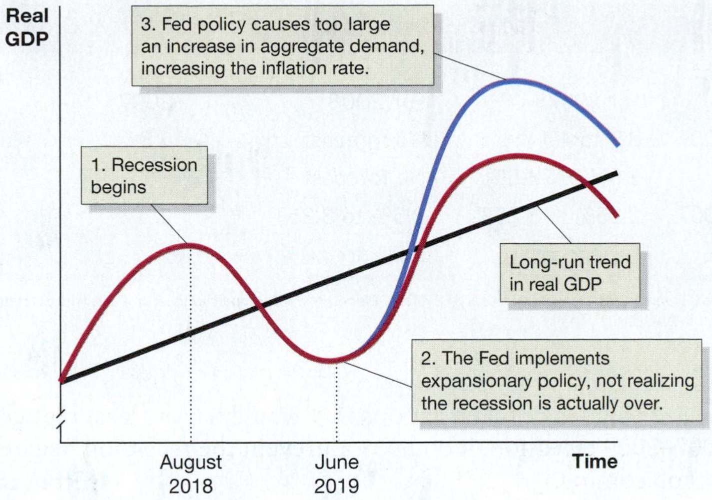

MyEconLab Animation

Figure 26.8

The Effect of a Poorly Timed Monetary Policy on the Economy

The upward-sloping straight line represents the long-run growth trend in real GDP. The curved red line represents the path real GDP takes because of the business cycle. If the Fed is too late in implementing a change in monetary policy, real GDP will follow the curved blue line. The Fed's expansionary monetary policy results in too great an increase in aggregate demand during the next expansion, which causes an increase in the inflation rate.

a significant acceleration in inflation. Real GDP ends up following the path indicated by the blue curved line. The Fed has inadvertently engaged in a *procyclical policy*, which increases the severity of the business cycle, as opposed to a *countercyclical policy*, which is meant to reduce the severity of the business cycle and which is what the Fed intends to use. As we saw in Chapter 21, the typical recession since 1950 has lasted less than one year, which increases the likelihood that the Fed may accidentally engage in a procyclical policy. Making this mistake is, of course, less likely in a long and severe recession such as the recession of 2007–2009.

MyEconLab Concept Check

Fed Forecasts

Because it can take a long time for a change in monetary policy to affect real GDP, the Fed tries to set policy according to what it forecasts the state of the economy will be in the future, when the policy change actually affects the economy. For example, when the Fed considered raising its target for the federal funds rate in 2015, the lag associated with monetary policy meant that the full effect of the rate increase on the economy would be spread out over several years. In making that increase, the Fed was thinking about the economy's future performance.

For the Fed to succeed in reducing the severity of business cycles, it must often act before a recession or an acceleration of inflation shows up in the economic data. So, good policy requires good economic forecasts based on models that describe accurately how the economy functions. Unfortunately, economic forecasts and models can be unreliable because changes in aggregate demand and short-run aggregate supply can be unpredictable. For example, the forecasts of most economists at the end of 2006 and the beginning of 2007 did not anticipate the severity of the recession that began in December 2007. Only after financial market conditions began to deteriorate rapidly did economists significantly reduce their forecasts of GDP growth in 2008 and 2009.

Table 26.1 summarizes the Fed's estimates for the growth rate of real GDP for 2007 and 2008 given in its *Monetary Policy Report to Congress*. To keep a recession from starting in 2007, the Fed would have had to change policy before 2007. However, in February 2006, the Fed expected the economy to grow by 3 percent to 4 percent in 2007, so it had little reason to change policy. Similarly, the Fed could have changed policy in an attempt to keep the economy growing in 2008, but it would have had to change policy before 2008, and as late as July 2007, the Fed still expected the economy to grow by 2.5 percent to 3.0 percent in 2008. In fact, real GDP increased by only 1.8 percent in 2007, and it declined by 0.3 percent in 2008. We can conclude that,

Table 26.1

Fed Forecasts of Real GDP Growth during 2007 and 2008

	Forecast Growth Rate		Actual Growth Rate	
Date forecast was made	For 2007	For 2008	2007	2008
February 2006	3% to 4%	No forecast	1.8%	−0.3%
May 2006	2.5% to 3.25%	No forecast		
February 2007	2.25% to 3.25%	2.5% to 3.25%		
July 2007	No forecast	2.5% to 3.0%		

Sources: Board of Governors of the Federal Reserve System, *Monetary Policy Report to the Congress*, various dates; and U.S. Bureau of Economic Analysis.

although the Fed could have taken actions that would have at least reduced the severity of the 2007–2009 recession, it could not prevent the recession because it did not see the recession coming.

MyEconLab Concept Check

Making the Connection

MyEconLab Video

Trying to Hit a Moving Target: Making Policy with "Real-Time Data"

The Fed relies on macroeconomic data to formulate monetary policy. One key piece of economic data is GDP, which is calculated quarterly by the Bureau of Economic Analysis (BEA). Unfortunately for Fed policymakers, the GDP data the BEA provides are frequently revised, and the revisions can be large enough that the actual state of the economy can be different from what it at first appeared to be.

The BEA's *advance estimate* of a quarter's GDP is not released until about a month after the quarter has ended. This delay can be a problem for policymakers because it means that they will not receive an estimate of GDP for the period from January through March, for instance, until the end of April. Presenting even more difficulty is the fact that the advance estimate will be subject to a number of revisions. The second estimate of a quarter's GDP is released about two months after the end of the quarter. The third estimate is released about three months after the end of the quarter. Although the BEA used to refer to the third estimate as the "final estimate," in fact, it continues to revise its estimates through the years. The BEA releases its first annual, second annual, and third annual estimates one, two, and three years after the third estimate. And that is not the end: Benchmark revisions occur in later years.

Why are there so many estimates? Because GDP is such a comprehensive measure of output in the economy, it is very time-consuming to collect the necessary data. To provide the advance estimate, the BEA relies on surveys conducted by the Commerce Department of retail sales and manufacturing shipments, as well as data from trade organizations, estimates of government spending, and so on. As time passes, these organizations gather additional data, and the BEA is able to refine its estimates.

Do these revisions to the GDP estimates matter? Sometimes they do, as the following example indicates. At the beginning of 2008, some economists believed that the U.S. economy might be in a recession. The effects of the continuing decline in housing prices were being felt in the financial system, and the unemployment rate was increasing. Members of the Fed's Open Market Committee remained cautiously optimistic, however, forecasting that real GDP would increase about 1.7 percent during the year. The BEA's advance estimate of the first quarter's GDP seemed to confirm that this forecast of slow growth might be accurate by showing an increase in real GDP of 0.6 percent at an annual rate. As the following graph shows, though, that estimate of real GDP growth was revised a number of times over the years, mostly downward.

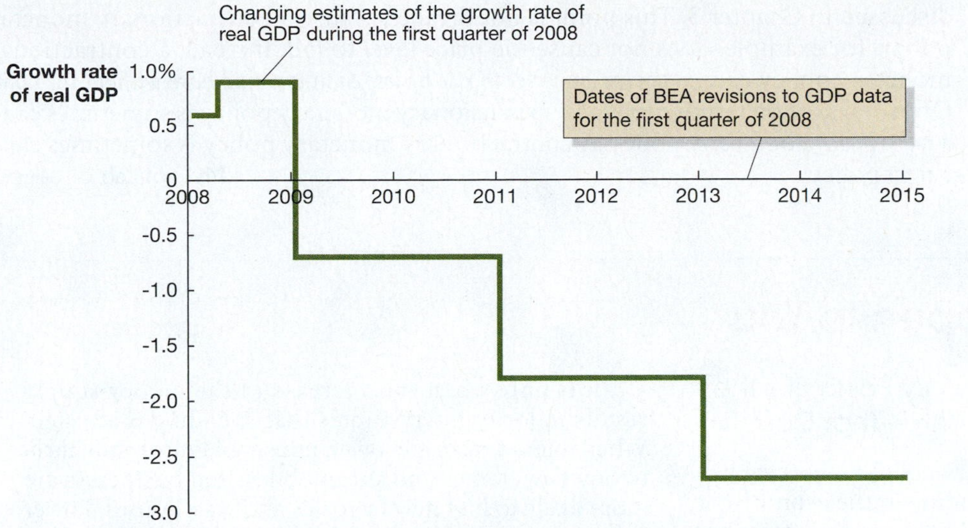

Currently, BEA data indicate that real GDP actually declined by 2.7 percent at an annual rate during the first quarter of 2008. This swing of more than 3 percentage points is a large difference, which changes the picture of what happened during the first quarter of 2008 from one of an economy experiencing slow growth to one of an economy suffering a sharp downturn as it fell into the worst recession since the Great Depression of the 1930s. The National Bureau of Economic Research has since determined that December 2007 was the beginning of the recession of 2007–2009.

This example shows that in addition to the other problems the Federal Reserve encounters in successfully conducting monetary policy, it must make decisions using data that may be subject to substantial revisions.

Sources: Federal Reserve Bank of Philadelphia, "Historical Data Files for the Real-Time Data Set," August 7, 2015; Board of Governors of the Federal Reserve System, "Minutes of the Federal Open Market Committee January 29–30, 2008," February 20, 2008; and Bruce T. Grimm and Teresa Weadock, "Gross Domestic Product: Revisions and Source Data," *Survey of Current Business*, Vol. 86, No. 2, February 2006, pp. 11–15.

Your Turn: Test your understanding by doing related problems 3.11 and 3.12 on page 932 at the end of this chapter.

MyEconLab Study Plan

A Summary of How Monetary Policy Works

Table 26.2 compares the steps involved in expansionary and contractionary monetary policies. We need to note an important qualification to this summary. At every point, we should add the phrase "relative to what would have happened without the policy." The table isolates the effect of monetary policy, *holding constant all other factors affecting the variables involved*. In other words, we are invoking the *ceteris paribus* condition,

Table 26.2 Expansionary and Contractionary Monetary Policies

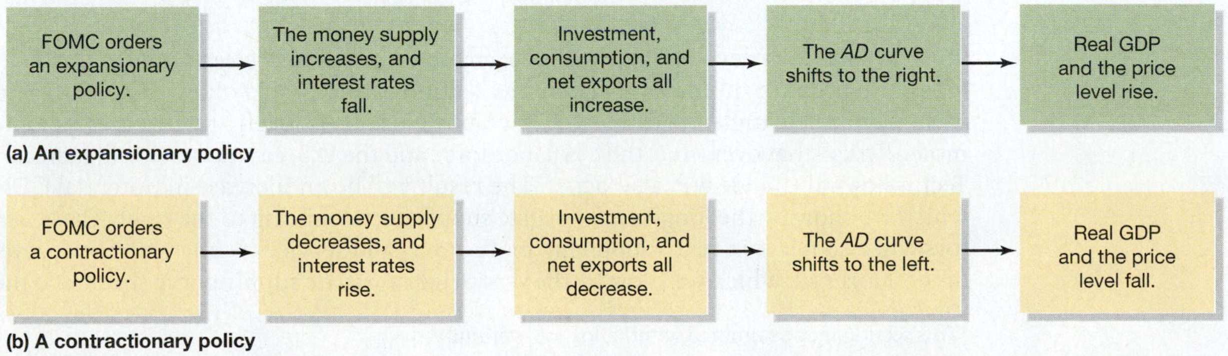

discussed in Chapter 3. This point is important because a contractionary monetary policy, for example, does not cause the price level to fall; instead, a contractionary monetary policy causes the price level *to rise by less than it would have without the policy*. One final note on terminology: An expansionary monetary policy is sometimes called a *loose* policy, or an *easy* policy. A contractionary monetary policy is sometimes called a *tight* policy.

MyEconLab Concept Check

Don't Let This Happen to You

Remember That with Monetary Policy, It's the Interest Rates—Not the Money—That Counts

It is tempting to think of monetary policy as working like this: If the Fed wants more spending in the economy, it increases the money supply, and people spend more because they now have more money. If the Fed wants less spending in the economy, it decreases the money supply, and people spend less because they now have less money. In fact, that is *not* how monetary policy works. Remember the important difference between money and income: The Fed increases the money supply by buying Treasury bills. The sellers of the Treasury bills have just exchanged one asset—Treasury bills—for another asset—a check from the Fed; the sellers have *not* increased their income. Even though the money supply is now larger, no one's income has increased, so no one's spending should be affected.

It is only when this increase in the money supply results in lower interest rates that spending is affected. When interest rates are lower, households are more likely to buy new homes and automobiles, and businesses are more likely to buy new factories and warehouses. Lower interest rates also lead to a lower value of the dollar, which lowers the prices of exports and raises the prices of imports, thereby increasing net exports. It isn't the increase in the money supply that has brought about this additional spending, *it's the lower interest rates*. To understand how monetary policy works, and to interpret news reports about the Fed's actions, remember that it is the change in interest rates, not the change in the money supply, that is most important.

MyEconLab Study Plan

Your Turn: Test your understanding by doing related problem 3.13 on page 933 at the end of this chapter.

MyEconLab Study Plan

26.4 Monetary Policy in the Dynamic Aggregate Demand and Aggregate Supply Model*

LEARNING OBJECTIVE: Use the dynamic aggregate demand and aggregate supply model to analyze monetary policy.

The overview of monetary policy we just finished contains a key idea: The Fed can use monetary policy to affect aggregate demand, thereby changing the price level and the level of real GDP. The discussion of monetary policy illustrated by Figure 26.7 on page 905 is simplified, however, because it ignores two important facts about the economy:

1. The economy experiences continuing inflation, with the price level rising every year.
2. The economy experiences long-run growth, with the *LRAS* curve shifting to the right every year.

In Chapter 24, we developed a *dynamic aggregate demand and aggregate supply model* that takes into account these two facts. In this section, we use the dynamic model to gain a more complete understanding of monetary policy. Let's briefly review the dynamic model. Recall that over time, the U.S. labor force and the U.S. capital stock will increase. Technological change will also occur. The result will be an increase in potential GDP, which we show by the long-run aggregate supply curve shifting to the right. These factors will also result in firms supplying more goods and services at any given price level in the short run, which we show by the short-run aggregate supply curve shifting to the

*This section may be omitted without loss of continuity.

right. During most years, the aggregate demand curve will also shift to the right, indicating that aggregate expenditure will be higher at every price level. Aggregate expenditure usually increases for these key reasons:

- As population grows and incomes rise, consumption will increase over time.
- As the economy grows, firms expand capacity, and new firms are established, increasing investment spending.
- An expanding population and an expanding economy require increased government services, such as more police officers and teachers, so government purchases will expand.

The Effects of Monetary Policy on Real GDP and the Price Level: A More Complete Account

During certain periods, *AD* does not increase enough during the year to keep real GDP at potential GDP. This slow growth in aggregate demand may be due to households and firms becoming pessimistic about the future state of the economy, leading them to cut back their spending on consumer durables, houses, and factories. As we have seen, the collapse of the housing bubble and the resulting financial crisis had a negative effect on aggregate demand during the 2007–2009 recession. There are other reasons why aggregate demand might grow slowly: The federal government could decide to balance the budget by cutting back its purchases and raising taxes, or recessions in other countries might cause a decline in U.S. exports. In the hypothetical situation shown in Figure 26.9, in the first year, equilibrium is at point A, with potential GDP of \$17.0 trillion and a price level of 110. In the second year, *LRAS* increases to \$17.4 trillion, but *AD* increases only to $AD_{2(\text{without policy})}$, which is not enough to keep real GDP at potential GDP. If the Fed does not intervene, the new short-run equilibrium will occur at \$17.3 trillion (point *B*). The \$100 billion gap between this level of real GDP and potential GDP at $LRAS_2$ means that some firms are operating at less than their normal capacity. Incomes and profits will fall, firms will begin to lay off workers, and the unemployment rate will rise.

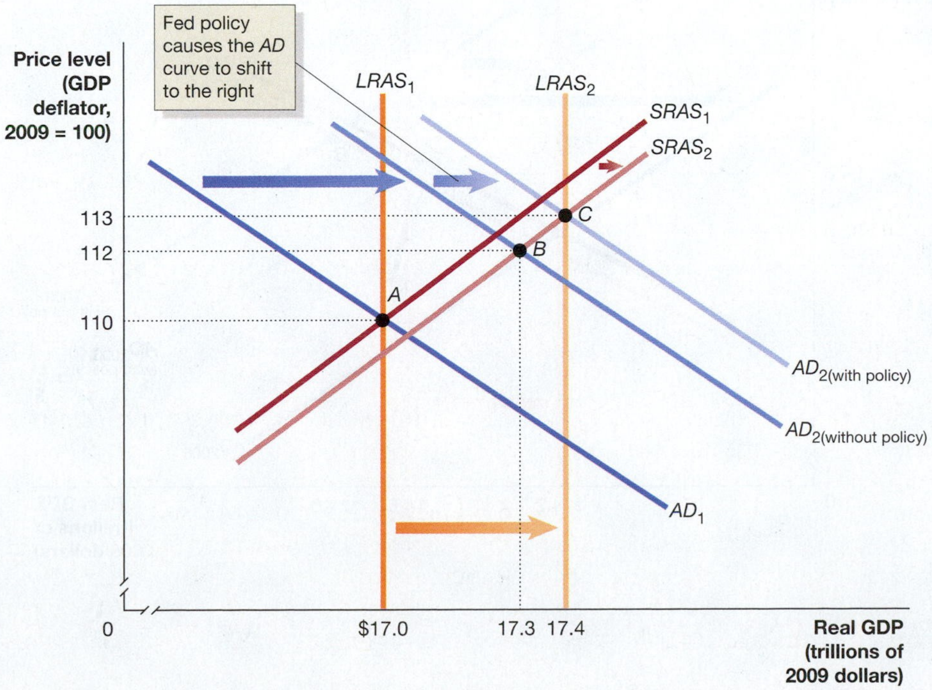

MyEconLab Animation

Figure 26.9

An Expansionary Monetary Policy

Initially, equilibrium is at point *A*, with real GDP of \$17.0 trillion and a price level of 110. Without monetary policy, aggregate demand will shift from AD_1 to $AD_{2(\text{without policy})}$, which is not enough to keep the economy at full employment because long-run aggregate supply has shifted from $LRAS_1$ to $LRAS_2$. Short-run equilibrium is at point *B*, with real GDP of \$17.3 trillion and a price level of 112. By lowering interest rates, the Fed increases investment, consumption, and net exports sufficiently to shift aggregate demand to $AD_{2(\text{with policy})}$. Equilibrium will be at point *C*, with real GDP of \$17.4 trillion, which is its full employment level, and a price level of 113. The price level is higher than it would have been if the Fed had not acted to increase spending in the economy.

Economists at the Federal Reserve closely monitor the economy and continually update forecasts of future levels of real GDP and prices. When these economists anticipate that aggregate demand is not growing fast enough to allow the economy to remain at full employment, they present their findings to the FOMC, which decides whether circumstances require a change in monetary policy. For example, suppose that the FOMC meets and considers a forecast from the staff indicating that during the following year, a gap of $100 billion will open between equilibrium real GDP and potential GDP. In other words, the macroeconomic equilibrium illustrated by point *B* in Figure 26.9 will occur. The FOMC may then decide to carry out an expansionary monetary policy to lower interest rates to stimulate aggregate demand. The figure shows the results of a successful attempt to do this: *AD* has shifted to the right, and equilibrium occurs at potential GDP (point *C*). The Fed will have successfully headed off the falling incomes and rising unemployment that otherwise would have occurred. Bear in mind that we are illustrating a perfectly executed monetary policy that keeps the economy at potential GDP, which is difficult to achieve in practice for reasons discussed in the previous section.

Notice in Figure 26.9 that the expansionary monetary policy caused the inflation rate to be higher than it would have been. Without the expansionary policy, the price level would have risen from 110 to 112, so the inflation rate for the year would have been 1.8 percent. By shifting the aggregate demand curve, the expansionary policy caused the price level to increase from 112 to 113, raising the inflation rate from 1.8 percent to 2.7 percent. MyEconLab Concept Check

Using Monetary Policy to Fight Inflation

In addition to using an expansionary monetary policy to reduce the severity of recessions, the Fed can use a contractionary monetary policy to keep aggregate demand from expanding so rapidly that the inflation rate begins to increase. Figure 26.10 shows the situation during 2005 and 2006, when the Fed faced this possibility. During 2005,

MyEconLab Animation

Figure 26.10

A Contractionary Monetary Policy in 2006

In 2005, equilibrium is at point *A*, with real GDP equal to potential GDP of $14.2 trillion and a price level of 92.0. From 2005 to 2006, potential GDP increased from $14.2 trillion to $14.6 trillion, as long-run aggregate supply increased from $LRAS_{2005}$ to $LRAS_{2006}$. The Fed raised interest rates because it believed the housing boom was causing aggregate demand to increase too rapidly. Without the increase in interest rates, aggregate demand would have shifted from AD_{2005} to $AD_{2006(\text{without policy})}$, and the new short-run equilibrium would have occurred at point *B*. Real GDP would have been $14.8 trillion—$200 billion greater than potential GDP—and the price level would have been 96.1. The increase in interest rates resulted in aggregate demand increasing only to $AD_{2006(\text{with policy})}$. Equilibrium occurred at point *C*, with real GDP of $14.6 trillion, which was equal to potential GDP, and the price level rose only to 94.8.

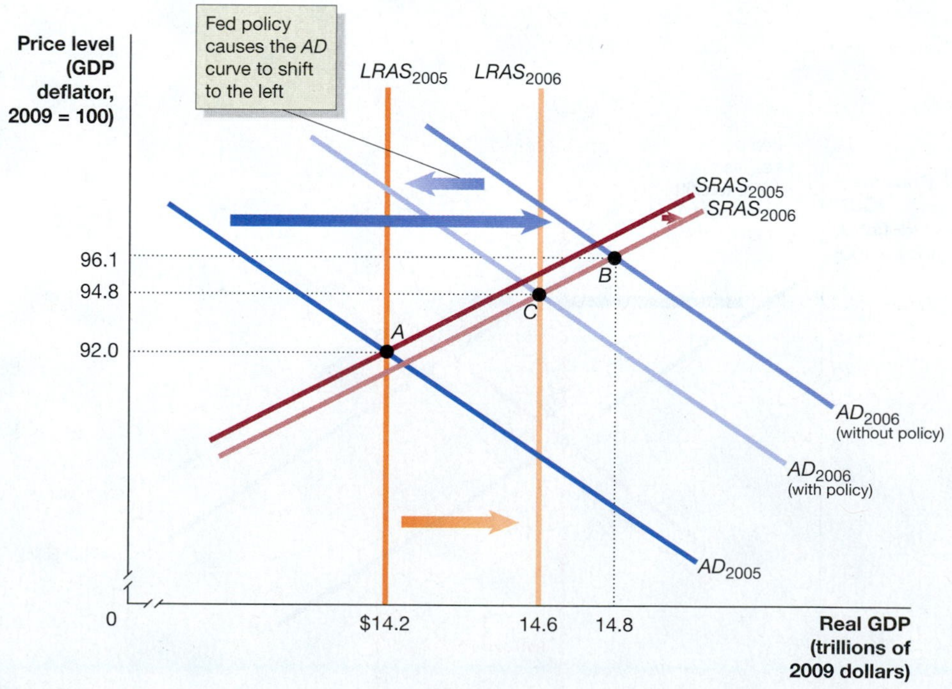

real GDP was equal to potential GDP, but Fed Chair Alan Greenspan and other members of the FOMC were concerned that the continuing boom in the housing market might lead aggregate demand to increase so rapidly that the inflation rate would begin to accelerate. The Fed had been gradually increasing the target for the federal funds rate since mid-2004.

When Ben Bernanke was appointed Fed chair in early 2006, he advocated continued increases in the target for the federal funds rate to slow the growth in aggregate demand. By June 2006, the target for the federal funds rate had been raised to 5.25 percent, from the low target rate of 1 percent that had prevailed from June 2003 to May 2004. The FOMC issues a statement after each meeting that summarizes the committee's views on the current state of the economy and gives some indication of how monetary policy might change in the near future. After its meeting on June 29, 2006, the FOMC included the following remarks in its statement:

> The Federal Open Market Committee decided today to raise its target for the federal funds rate ... to 5-1/4 percent. Recent indicators suggest that economic growth is moderating from its quite strong pace earlier this year, partly reflecting a gradual cooling of the housing market and the lagged effects of increases in ... interest rates. ... Although the moderation in the growth of aggregate demand should help to limit inflation pressures over time, the Committee judges that some inflation risks remain.

The committee kept the target for the federal funds rate constant at 5.25 percent until September 2007, when concern about problems in financial markets led it to cut the target to 4.75 percent. Although it is impossible to know exactly what would have happened during 2006 without the Fed's policy change, Figure 26.10 presents a plausible scenario. The figure shows that without the Fed's actions to increase interest rates, aggregate demand would have shifted farther to the right, and equilibrium would have occurred at a level of real GDP that was beyond the potential level. The price level would have risen from 92.0 in 2005 to 96.1 in 2006, meaning that the inflation rate would have been 4.5 percent. Because the Fed kept aggregate demand from increasing as much as it otherwise would have, short-run equilibrium occurred at potential GDP, and the price level in 2006 rose to only 94.8, keeping the inflation rate at 3.0 percent. MyEconLab Concept Check

Solved Problem 26.4

MyEconLab Interactive Animation

The Effects of Monetary Policy

The hypothetical information in the following table shows what the values for real GDP and the price level will be in 2019 if the Fed does *not* use monetary policy:

Year	Potential GDP	Real GDP	Price Level
2018	$17.9 trillion	$17.9 trillion	114
2019	18.3 trillion	18.1 trillion	116

a. If the Fed wants to keep real GDP at its potential level in 2019, should it use an expansionary policy or a contractionary policy? Should the trading desk buy Treasury bills or sell them?

b. Suppose the Fed's policy is successful in keeping real GDP at its potential level in 2019. State whether each of the following will be higher or lower than if the Fed had taken no action:

i. Real GDP

ii. Potential GDP

iii. The inflation rate

iv. The unemployment rate

c. Draw an aggregate demand and aggregate supply graph to illustrate your answer. Be sure that your graph contains *LRAS* curves for 2018 and 2019; *SRAS* curves for 2018 and 2019; *AD* curves for 2018 and for 2019, with and without monetary policy action; and equilibrium real GDP and the price level in 2019, with and without policy.

Solving the Problem

Step 1: Review the chapter material. This problem is about the effects of monetary policy on real GDP and the price level, so you may want to review the section "The Effects of Monetary Policy on Real GDP and the Price Level: A More Complete Account," which begins on page 913.

Step 2: Answer the questions in part (a) by explaining how the Fed can keep real GDP at its potential level. The information in the table tells us that without monetary policy, the economy will be below potential GDP in 2019. To keep real GDP at its potential level, the Fed must undertake an expansionary policy. To carry out an expansionary policy, the trading desk needs to buy Treasury bills. Buying Treasury bills will increase reserves in the banking system. Banks will increase their loans, which will increase the money supply and lower the interest rate.

Step 3: Answer part (b) by explaining the effect of the Fed's policy. If the Fed's policy is successful, real GDP in 2019 will increase from $18.1 trillion, as given in the table, to its potential level of $18.3 trillion. Potential GDP is not affected by monetary policy, so its value will not change. Because the level of real GDP will be higher, the unemployment rate will be lower than it would have been without policy. The expansionary monetary policy shifts the *AD* curve to the right, so short-run equilibrium will move up the short-run aggregate supply (*SRAS*) curve, and the price level will be higher.

Step 4: Answer part (c) by drawing the graph. Your graph should look similar to Figure 26.9.

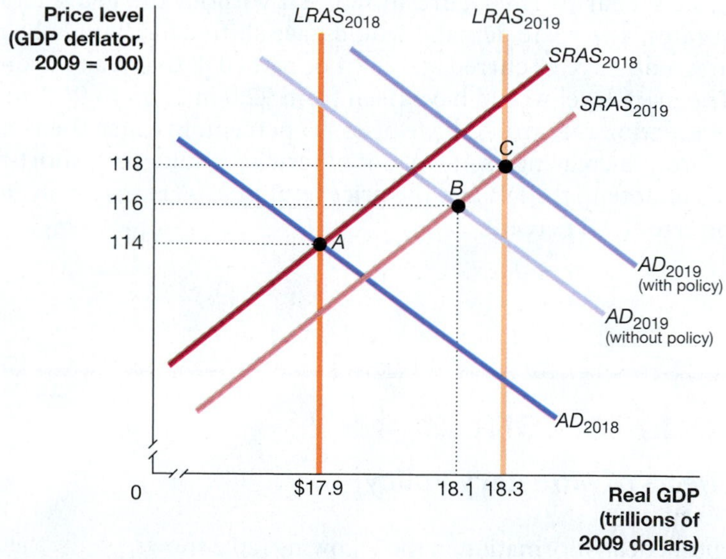

Equilibrium in 2018 is at point *A*, with the *AD* and *SRAS* curves intersecting along the *LRAS* curve. Real GDP is at its potential level of $17.9 trillion, and the price level is 114. Without monetary policy, the *AD* curve shifts to $AD_{2019(\text{without policy})}$, and short-run equilibrium is at point *B*. Because potential GDP has increased from $17.9 trillion to $18.3 trillion, real GDP of $18.1 trillion is below the potential level. The price level has increased from 114 to 116. With policy, the *AD* curve shifts to $AD_{2019(\text{with policy})}$, and equilibrium is at point *C*. Real GDP is at its potential level of $18.3 trillion. We don't have enough information to be sure of the new equilibrium price level. We do know that it will be higher than 116. The graph shows the price level rising to 118. Therefore, without the Fed's expansionary policy, the inflation rate in 2019 would have been about 1.8 percent. With policy, it will be about 3.5 percent.

Extra Credit: Bear in mind that, in reality, the Fed is unable to use monetary policy to keep real GDP exactly at its potential level, as this problem suggests.

Your Turn: For more practice, do related problems 4.4 and 4.5 on pages 933–934 at the end of this chapter.

MyEconLab Study Plan

26.5 A Closer Look at the Fed's Setting of Monetary Policy Targets

LEARNING OBJECTIVE: Describe the Fed's setting of monetary policy targets.

We have seen that in carrying out monetary policy, the Fed changes its target for the federal funds rate depending on the state of the economy. Is the Fed's approach correct? During times when the economy is not experiencing a financial crisis, is using the federal funds rate as a target the best way to conduct monetary policy? If the Fed targets the federal funds rate, how should it decide what the target level should be? In this section, we consider these important issues concerning the Fed's targeting policy.

Should the Fed Target the Money Supply?

Some economists have argued that rather than use an interest rate as its monetary policy target, the Fed should use the money supply. Many of the economists who make this argument belong to a school of thought known as *monetarism*. The leader of the monetarist school was Milton Friedman, who was skeptical that the Fed would be able to correctly time changes in monetary policy.

Friedman and his followers favored replacing *monetary policy* with a *monetary growth rule*. Ordinarily, we expect monetary policy to respond to changing economic conditions: When the economy is in recession, the Fed reduces interest rates, and when inflation is increasing, the Fed raises interest rates. A monetary growth rule, in contrast, is a plan for increasing the money supply at a constant rate that does not change in response to economic conditions. Friedman and his followers proposed a monetary growth rule of increasing the money supply every year at a rate equal to the long-run annual growth rate of real GDP, which has been about 3 percent since 1950. If the Fed adopted this monetary growth rule, it would stick to it through changing economic conditions.

But what happens under a monetary growth rule if the economy moves into recession? Shouldn't the Fed abandon the rule to drive down interest rates? Friedman argued that the Fed should stick to the rule even during recessions because he believed that active monetary policy destabilizes the economy by increasing the number of recessions and their severity. By keeping the money supply growing at a constant rate, Friedman argued, the Fed would greatly increase economic stability.

During the 1970s, some economists and politicians pressured the Federal Reserve to adopt a monetary growth rule. Most of that pressure has disappeared in recent years because the fairly close relationship between movements in the money supply and movements in real GDP and the price level that existed before 1980 has become much weaker. Since 1980, the growth rate of M1 has been unstable. In some years, M1 has grown more than 10 percent, while in other years, it has actually fallen. Yet despite these wide fluctuations in the growth of M1, growth in real GDP has been fairly stable, and inflation has remained low during most years. MyEconLab Concept Check

Why Doesn't the Fed Target Both the Money Supply and the Interest Rate?

Most economists believe that the interest rate is the best monetary policy target. But as we have just seen, other economists believe the Fed should target the money supply. Why doesn't the Fed satisfy both groups by targeting both the money supply and the interest rate? The simple answer is that the Fed can't target both at the same time. To see why, look at Figure 26.11, which shows the money market.

MyEconLab Animation

Figure 26.11

The Fed Can't Target Both the Money Supply and the Interest Rate

The Fed is forced to choose between using either the interest rate or the money supply as its monetary policy target. In this figure, the Fed can set a target of $900 billion for the money supply or a target of 5 percent for the interest rate, but the Fed can't hit both targets because it can achieve only combinations of the interest rate and the money supply that represent equilibrium in the money market.

Source: Federal Reserve Bank of St. Louis.

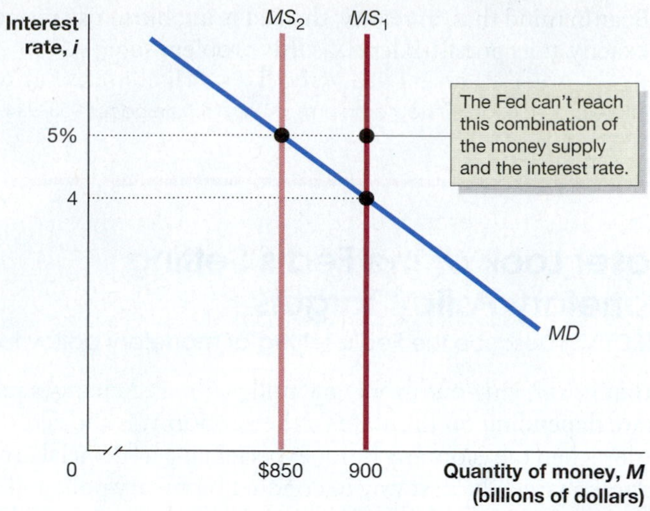

Remember that the Fed controls the money supply, but it does not control money demand. Money demand is determined by decisions of households and firms as they weigh the trade-off between the convenience of money and its low interest rate compared with other financial assets. Suppose the Fed is targeting the interest rate and decides, given conditions in the economy, that the interest rate should be 5 percent. Or, suppose the Fed is targeting the money supply and decides that the money supply should be $900 billion. Figure 26.11 shows that the Fed can bring about an interest rate of 5 percent or a money supply of $900 billion, but it can't bring about both. The point representing an interest rate of 5 percent and a money supply of $900 billion is not on the money demand curve, so it can't represent an equilibrium in the money market. The Fed can only attain combinations of the interest rate and the money supply that represent equilibrium. Therefore, the Fed has to choose between targeting an interest rate and targeting the money supply. For most of the period since World War II, the Fed has chosen the federal funds rate as its target. MyEconLab Concept Check

The Taylor Rule

Taylor rule A rule developed by John Taylor that links the Fed's target for the federal funds rate to economic variables.

How does the Fed choose a target for the federal funds rate? The discussions at the meetings of the FOMC can be complex, and they take into account many economic variables. John Taylor of Stanford University has analyzed Fed decision making and developed the **Taylor rule** to explain federal funds rate targeting. The Taylor rule begins with an estimate of the value of the equilibrium real federal funds rate, which is the federal funds rate—adjusted for inflation—that would be consistent with real GDP being equal to potential GDP in the long run. Taylor believes this rate to be 2 percent. According to the Taylor rule, the Fed should set the target for the federal funds rate so that it is equal to the sum of the inflation rate, the equilibrium real federal funds rate, and two additional terms. The first of these additional terms is the *inflation gap*—the difference between current inflation and a target rate; the second is the *output gap*—the percentage difference between real GDP and potential GDP. The inflation gap and output gap are each given "weights" that reflect their influence on the federal funds target rate. With weights of 1/2 for both gaps, we have the following Taylor rule:

$$\text{Federal funds target rate} = \text{Current inflation rate} + \text{Equilibrium real federal funds rate} + [(1/2) \times \text{Inflation gap}] + [(1/2) \times \text{Output gap}].$$

The Taylor rule includes expressions for the inflation gap and the output gap because the Fed is concerned about both inflation and fluctuations in real GDP. Taylor demonstrated that if the equilibrium real federal funds rate is 2 percent and the target rate of inflation is 2 percent, the preceding equation does a good job of explaining changes in the Fed's target for the federal funds rate during most years. Consider an example in which the current inflation rate is 1 percent, and real GDP is 1 percent below potential GDP. In that case, the inflation gap equals 1 percent − 2 percent = −1 percent, and the output gap is also −1 percent. Inserting these values in the Taylor rule, we can calculate the predicted value for the federal funds target rate:

$$\text{Federal funds target rate} = 1\% + 2\% + [(1/2) \times -1\%] + [(1/2) \times -1\%] = 2\%$$

The Taylor rule accurately predicted changes in the federal funds target during the period of Alan Greenspan's leadership of the Federal Reserve from 1987 to 2006. For the period of the late 1970s and early 1980s, when Paul Volcker was chairman of the Federal Reserve, the Taylor rule predicts a federal funds rate target *lower* than the actual target the Fed used. In other words, Chairman Volcker kept the federal funds rate at an unusually high level to bring down the very high inflation rates of the late 1970s and early 1980s. In contrast, using data from the chairmanship of Arthur Burns from 1970 to 1978, the Taylor rule predicts a federal funds rate target *higher* than the actual target. Chairman Burns kept the federal funds rate at an unusually low level during these years, which helps to explain why the inflation rate grew worse. During the mid-2000s, the actual federal funds rate was also lower than the predicted federal funds rate. Some economists, including Taylor, argue that these low targets for the federal funds rate contributed to the excessive increase in spending on housing that we will discuss in the next section.

Taylor has proposed that the Fed adopt an explicit rule to guide its monetary policy actions. The Fed would not be constrained to mechanically following the exact Taylor rule given earlier, but whatever rule the Fed adopted, it would have to publically justify deviating from the rule, if a majority of the FOMC came to believe that was necessary. Representative Kevin Brady, Chairman of the Congressional Joint Economic Committee, has introduced the Sound Dollar Act, one provision of which incorporates Taylor's proposal. Former Fed Chair Ben Bernanke and most current members of the FOMC are against the proposal because they believe it might limit the Fed's ability to pursue innovative policies in a financial crisis. They also note that the Taylor rule does not account for changes over time in the equilibrium real interest rate, or for changes the FOMC might want to make in the target inflation rate. MyEconLab Concept Check

Solved Problem 26.5

MyEconLab Interactive Animation

Applying the Taylor Rule

An article in the *Wall Street Journal* discussed the views of John Williams, the president of the Federal Reserve Bank of San Francisco, about the Taylor rule. According to the article, Williams argued that if the Fed had attempted to follow the Taylor rule during the recession of 2007–2009, it would have had to do "something not easily done, and that would have been for the Fed to have pushed short-term rates deeply into negative territory."

a. What does it mean for an interest rate to be negative?
b. Use the equation for the Taylor rule to show how the federal funds rate target might be negative. Assume that the equilibrium real federal funds rate and the target rate of inflation are both 2 percent and the current inflation rate is 0 percent.

Solving the Problem

Step 1: Review the chapter material. This problem is about using the Taylor rule to evaluate monetary policy, so you may want to review the section "The Taylor Rule," which begins on page 918.

Step 2: Answer part (a) by explaining what it means for an interest rate to be negative. We expect interest rates to be positive, which results in the borrower paying the lender back more than the amount of the funds borrowed. As we saw in the chapter opener and discussed further in the *Making the*

Connection on page 906, with a negative interest rate, the borrower would pay the lender back less than the amount of the funds borrowed. Note that Williams is referring to a negative *nominal* interest rate, which is very rare. A negative *real* interest rate that results from the inflation rate being higher than the nominal interest rate occurs more frequently.

Step 3: Answer part (b) by constructing an example where the target federal funds rate might be negative. This is the equation for the Taylor rule:

$$\begin{aligned}\text{Federal funds target rate} = {} & \text{Current inflation rate} \\ & + \text{Equilibrium real federal funds rate} \\ & + [(1/2) \times \text{Inflation gap}] \\ & + [(1/2) \times \text{Output gap}].\end{aligned}$$

If we substitute the values given in the problem, we have:

$$\begin{aligned}\text{Federal funds rate target} = {} & 0\% + 2\% + [(1/2) \times (0\% - 2)] \\ & + [(1/2) \times \text{output gap}],\end{aligned}$$

or:

$$\text{Federal funds taget rate target} = 1\% + [(1/2) \times \text{output gap}].$$

So, for the federal funds rate target to be negative, the output gap will have to be larger (in absolute value) than -2%. For example, if the output gap is -4%, then:

$$\text{Federal funds rate target} = 1\% + [(1/2) \times (-4)] = -1\%$$

In fact, the output gap rose above -6 percent during the recession. So, Williams is correct that following the Taylor rule exactly would have required the federal funds rate to be negative, which means that banks would have to have been willing to pay interest when lending to other banks in the federal funds market rather than receive interest. This outcome is very unlikely.

Extra Credit: The inability of the Fed to push the federal funds rate to negative values is sometimes called the *zero lower bound* to monetary policy.

Source: Michael S. Derby and Benjamin Fritz, "Fed's Williams Says Summer Rate Rise Possible if Data Supports Action," *Wall Street Journal*, May 1, 2015.

MyEconLab Study Plan

Your Turn: For more practice, do related problems 5.5, 5.6, and 5.7 on pages 934–935 at the end of this chapter.

Inflation Targeting

Inflation targeting A framework for conducting monetary policy that involves the central bank announcing its target level of inflation.

Many economists and central bankers believe that *inflation targeting* provides a useful framework for carrying out monetary policy. With **inflation targeting**, a central bank publicly sets an explicit target for the inflation rate over a period of time, and the government and the public then judge the performance of the central bank on the basis of its success in hitting the target.

Beginning in the 1980s, inflation targeting was adopted by a number of central banks around the world, including the Bank of England and, after its founding in the late 1990s, the European Central Bank. After many years of not having an explicit inflation target, the Fed announced in 2012 that it would attempt to maintain an average inflation rate of 2 percent per year.

With inflation targeting, the Fed can still respond to periods of recession or other economic problems without following an inflexible rule. An inflation target allows monetary policy to focus on inflation and inflation forecasts except during times of severe recession. Arguments supporting the Fed's use of an explicit inflation target focus on the following points. First, announcing explicit targets for inflation draws the public's attention to what the Fed can actually achieve in practice. Most economists believe that over the long run, monetary policy has a greater effect on inflation than on the growth of real GDP. Second, announcing an inflation target provides an anchor for inflationary expectations. If households, firms, and participants in financial markets believe that the Fed will hit an annual inflation target of 2 percent, then they will expect that if inflation is temporarily lower or higher, it will eventually return to the target rate. Third, inflation targets promote accountability for the Fed by providing a yardstick against which its performance can be measured.

Some economists and policymakers were critical of the Fed's decision to adopt an explicit inflation target. Opponents make several arguments. First, rigid numerical targets for inflation diminish the flexibility of monetary policy to address other policy goals. Second, because monetary policy affects inflation with a lag, inflation targeting requires that the Fed use forecasts of future inflation, which may turn out to be inaccurate. Third, holding the Fed accountable only for a goal of low inflation may make it more difficult for elected officials to monitor the Fed's support for good economic policy overall. Finally, inflation targets may increase uncertainty over whether the Fed will take prompt action to return the economy to full employment following a recession.

Economists and policymakers continue to debate whether inflation targets improve economic policy. MyEconLab Concept Check

Making the Connection
MyEconLab Video

Should the Fed Worry about the Prices of Food and Gasoline?

Surveys show that many people in the United States are skeptical about whether changes in the consumer price index (CPI) are a good measure of inflation. The CPI measures the price level based on a market basket that contains 211 goods and services, including shirts, refrigerators, textbooks, and doctor visits. But many people think of inflation in terms of increases in the prices of the goods they buy most frequently—particularly food and gasoline.

Not only does the Fed not concentrate on changes in the prices of food and gasoline, it actually prefers to *exclude* food and gasoline prices when measuring inflation. Fed policymakers refer to these adjusted measures of inflation as "core" inflation. Why does the Fed ignore the prices that many people think are the most important? The key reason is that monetary policy affects the economy with a lag of many months. As a result, Fed policymakers don't want to react to every movement—up or down—in prices. The green line in the graph shows the CPI calculated using prices for all 211 goods and services in the consumer market basket. The red line shows the CPI calculated by leaving out the prices of food and energy, such as gasoline and natural gas used in heating homes.

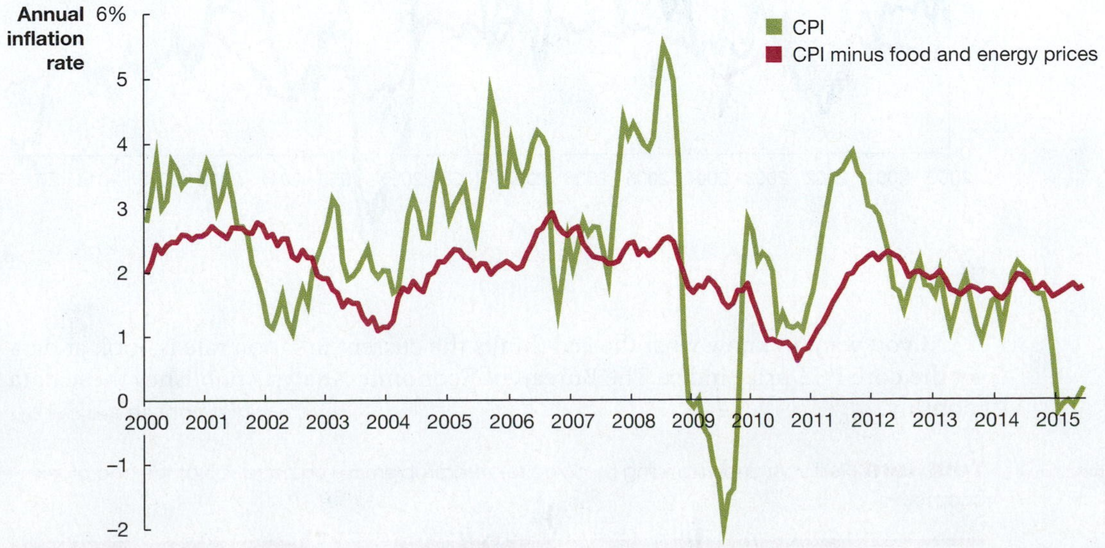

As the graph shows, food and energy prices are much more volatile than are the prices of all the goods in the CPI. For instance, during the recession of 2007–2009, the inflation rate measured by the CPI was negative—deflation occurred—during nine months. When changes in food and energy prices are excluded, by contrast, the inflation rate is positive in every month. This pattern repeated in early 2015, when falling energy prices caused the CPI to decline for several months.

Why are food and energy prices so volatile? Food prices can be volatile because weather-related problems such as too little or too much rain can lead to large fluctuations in supply. Energy prices can fluctuate when political unrest in the Middle East or other energy-producing regions disrupts supply or when the Organization of the Petroleum Exporting Countries (OPEC) oil cartel attempts to increase prices. Because the factors that cause volatility in food and energy prices tend not to persist for more than a few months, they don't have a long-lasting effect on the overall rate of inflation. As Fed Chair Janet Yellen has put it, Fed policymakers "pay attention to core inflation and similar measures because, in light of the volatility of food and energy prices, core inflation has been a better forecaster of overall inflation." In other words, to reach its goal of price stability, the Fed has to concentrate on the underlying inflation rate and avoid being distracted by temporary increases in food or energy prices—however painful the typical consumer may find those increases to be.

The Fed's preferred measure of inflation is the core *personal consumption expenditures (PCE) price index*, which excludes food and energy prices. The PCE price index is a measure of the price level that is similar to the GDP deflator, except it includes only the prices of goods from the consumption category of GDP. The PCE price index includes the prices of more goods and services than the CPI, so it is a broader measure of inflation.

The following graph shows movements in the CPI, the PCE price index, and the core PCE price index from January 2000 through July 2015. Although the three measures of inflation move roughly together, the core PCE price index has been more stable than the other two. Note in particular that in early 2009, when the CPI and the PCE price index were indicating that the economy was experiencing deflation, the core PCE price index was still showing inflation rates above 1 percent. The core PCE price index also showed more stability in late 2014 and early 2015, a period of rapid declines in oil prices.

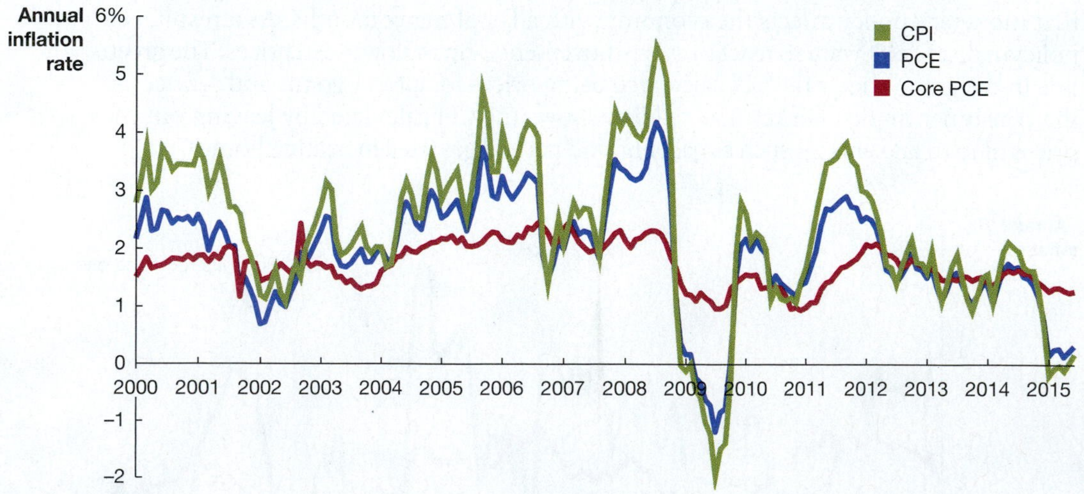

If you want to know what the Fed thinks the current inflation rate is, look at data on the core PCE price index. The Bureau of Economic Analysis publishes these data monthly.

MyEconLab Real-time data

MyEconLab Study Plan

Your Turn: Test your understanding by doing related problem 5.9 on page 935 at the end of this chapter.

26.6 Fed Policies during the 2007–2009 Recession

LEARNING OBJECTIVE: Describe the policies the Federal Reserve used during the 2007–2009 recession.

As we have seen, the Fed's traditional response to a recession is to lower the target for the federal funds rate. The severity of the recession of 2007–2009, particularly the problems in financial markets during those years, complicated the Fed's job. By December 2008, the Fed had effectively lowered the target for the federal funds rate to zero, but the zero interest rate alone did not result in a sufficient increase in aggregate demand to end the recession. In this section, we will discuss some of the additional policy measures the Fed took during the 2007–2009 recession. Some of these measures were used for the first time in the Fed's history.

The Inflation and Deflation of the Housing Market Bubble

To understand the 2007–2009 recession and the financial crisis that accompanied it, we need to start by considering the housing market. The Fed lowered the target for the federal funds rate during the 2001 recession to stimulate demand for housing. The policy was successful, and most builders, such as Toll Brothers, experienced several years of high demand. By 2005, however, many economists argued that a "bubble" had formed in the housing market. As we discussed in Chapter 8, the price of any asset reflects the returns the owner of the asset expects to receive. For example, the price of a share of stock reflects the profitability of the firm issuing the stock because the owner of a share of stock has a claim on the firm's profits.

Many economists believe, however, that sometimes a *stock market bubble* can form when the prices of stocks rise above levels that can be justified by the profitability of the firms issuing the stocks. Stock market bubbles end when enough investors decide stocks are overvalued and begin to sell. Why would an investor be willing to pay more for stocks than would be justified by their underlying value? There are two main explanations:

1. The investor may be caught up in the enthusiasm of the moment and, by failing to gather sufficient information, may overestimate the true value of the stocks.
2. The investor may expect to profit from buying stocks at inflated prices if the investor can sell them at even higher prices before the bubble bursts.

The price of a house should reflect the value of the housing services it provides. We can use the rents charged for comparable houses in an area to measure the value of housing services. We would expect, then, that housing prices and rents would increase at roughly the same rate. If prices of single-family homes rise significantly relative to rents for single-family homes, it is likely that the housing market is experiencing a bubble. As Figure 26.12 shows, housing prices and housing rents generally

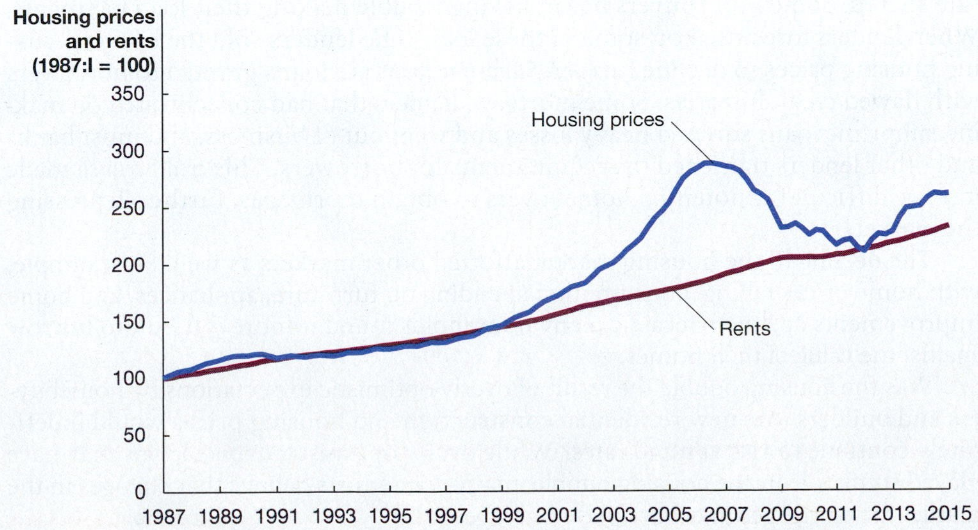

MyEconLab Real-time data

Figure 26.12

Housing Prices and Housing Rents, 1987–2015

Typically, housing prices increase at about the same rate as housing rents. But during the housing bubble, housing prices increased far more than did rents.

Note: For both series, the values for the first quarter of 1987 (1987:I) are set equal to 100.

Source: Federal Reserve Bank of St. Louis.

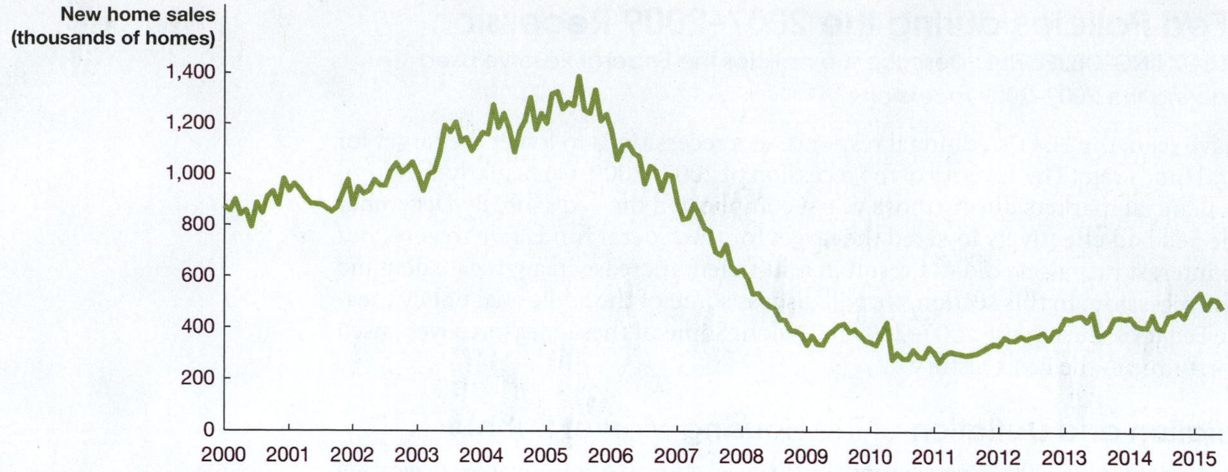

MyEconLab Real-time data

Figure 26.13 The Housing Bubble

Sales of new homes in the United States went on a roller-coaster ride, rising by 60 percent between January 2000 and July 2005 before falling by 80 percent between July 2005 and May 2010.

Note: The data are seasonally adjusted at an annual rate.
Source: U.S. Bureau of the Census.

increase at about the same rate, but between January 2000 and May 2006, housing prices nearly doubled, while rents increased by less than 25 percent. This large divergence between housing prices and rents is evidence of a bubble. In addition, in some cities, there was an increase in the number of buyers who did not intend to live in the houses they purchased but were using them as investments. Like stock investors during a stock market bubble, these housing investors were expecting to make a profit by selling houses at higher prices than they had paid for them, and they were not concerned about whether the prices of the houses were above the value of the housing services provided.

During 2006 and 2007, the air was rapidly escaping from the housing bubble. Figure 26.13 shows new home sales for each month from January 2000 through June 2015. New home sales rose by 60 percent between January 2000 and July 2005 and then fell by 80 percent between July 2005 and May 2010. Sales then began to gradually increase but were still at low levels well into 2015. Sales of existing homes followed a similar pattern. Prices of new and existing homes in most markets also began to decline beginning in 2006, and the inventory of unsold homes offered for sale soared. Some homebuyers began having trouble making their loan payments. When lenders foreclosed on some of these loans, the lenders sold the homes, causing housing prices to decline further. *Subprime loans* are loans granted to borrowers with flawed credit histories. Some mortgage lenders that had concentrated on making subprime loans suffered heavy losses and went out of business, and most banks and other lenders tightened the requirements for borrowers. This *credit crunch* made it more difficult for potential homebuyers to obtain mortgages, further depressing the market.

The decline in the housing market affected other markets as well. For example, with home prices falling, consumption spending on furniture, appliances, and home improvements declined because many households found it more difficult to borrow against the value of their homes.

Was the housing bubble the result of overly optimistic expectations by homebuyers and builders that new residential construction and housing prices would indefinitely continue to rise at rapid rates? While overly optimistic expectations may have played some role in the housing bubble, many economists believe that changes in the market for mortgages may have played a bigger role. MyEconLab Concept Check

The Changing Mortgage Market

Until the 1970s, the commercial banks and savings and loans that granted mortgages kept the loans until the borrowers paid them off. As we saw in Chapter 25, a financial asset such as a mortgage is a security only if it can be resold in a secondary market. Many members of Congress believed that home ownership could be increased by creating a secondary market in mortgages. If banks and savings and loans could resell mortgages, then individual investors would in effect be able to provide funds for mortgages. The process would work like this: If a bank or savings and loan granted a mortgage and then resold the mortgage to an investor, the bank could use the funds received from the investor to grant another mortgage. In this way, banks and savings and loans could grant more mortgage loans because they would no longer depend only on deposits for the funds needed to make the loans. One barrier to creating a secondary market in mortgages was that most investors were unwilling to buy mortgages because they were afraid of losing money if the borrower stopped making payments, or *defaulted*, on the loan.

To reassure investors, Congress used two *government-sponsored enterprises* (*GSEs*): the Federal National Mortgage Association ("Fannie Mae") and the Federal Home Loan Mortgage Corporation ("Freddie Mac"). These two institutions stand between investors and banks that grant mortgages. Fannie Mae and Freddie Mac sell bonds to investors and use the funds to purchase mortgages from banks. By the 1990s, a large secondary market existed in mortgages, with funds flowing from investors through Fannie Mae and Freddie Mac to banks and, ultimately, to individuals and families borrowing money to buy houses. MyEconLab Concept Check

The Role of Investment Banks

By the 2000s, further changes had taken place in the mortgage market. First, investment banks became significant participants in the secondary market for mortgages. As we have seen, investment banks, such as Goldman Sachs and Morgan Stanley, differ from commercial banks in that they do not take in deposits and rarely lend directly to households. Instead, investment banks concentrate on providing advice to firms issuing stocks and bonds or considering mergers with other firms. Investment banks began buying mortgages, bundling large numbers of them together as bonds called *mortgage-backed securities,* and reselling them to investors. Mortgage-backed securities proved very popular with investors because they often paid higher interest rates than other securities that investors believed had comparable default risk.

Second, by the height of the housing bubble in 2005 and early 2006, lenders had greatly loosened the standards for obtaining a mortgage loan. Traditionally, only borrowers with good credit histories and who were willing to make a down payment equal to at least 20 percent of the value of the house they were buying would be able to receive a mortgage. By 2005, however, lenders were issuing many mortgages to subprime borrowers with flawed credit histories. In addition, "Alt-A" borrowers—who stated but did not document their incomes—and borrowers who made very small down payments found it easier to get loans. Lenders also created new types of *adjustable-rate mortgages* that allowed borrowers to pay a very low interest rate for the first few years of the mortgage and then pay a higher rate in later years. The chance that the borrowers using these nontraditional mortgages would default was higher than for borrowers using traditional mortgages. Why would borrowers take out mortgages if it might be difficult for them to make the payments, and why would lenders grant these mortgages? Both borrowers and lenders were anticipating that housing prices would continue to rise, which would reduce the chance that borrowers would default on the mortgages and would also make it easier for borrowers to convert to more traditional mortgages in the future.

Unfortunately, the decline in housing prices led to rising defaults among subprime and Alt-A borrowers, borrowers with adjustable-rate mortgages, and borrowers who had made only small down payments. When borrowers began defaulting on mortgages, the values of many mortgage-backed securities declined sharply. Investors feared that if they purchased these securities, they would not receive the promised payments because the payments on the securities depended on borrowers making their mortgage payments, which an increasing number of borrowers were failing to do. Many commercial and investment banks owned these mortgage-backed securities, so the decline in the value of the securities caused these banks to suffer heavy losses. By mid-2007, the decline in the value of mortgage-backed securities and the large losses suffered by commercial and investment banks began to concern investors and policymakers. Many investors refused to buy mortgage-backed securities, and some investors would buy only bonds issued by the U.S. Treasury. MyEconLab Concept Check

Making the Connection
MyEconLab Video

The Wonderful World of Leverage

Traditionally, most people taking out a mortgage made a down payment equal to 20 percent of the price of the house and borrowed the remaining 80 percent. During the housing boom, however, many people purchased houses with down payments of 5 percent or less. These borrowers were highly *leveraged*, which means that their investment in their house was made mostly with borrowed money.

Making a very small down payment on a home mortgage leaves a buyer vulnerable to falling house prices.

To see how leverage works in the housing market, consider the following example: Suppose you buy a $200,000 house on January 1, 2018. On January 1, 2019, the price of the house—if you decide to sell it—has risen to $220,000. What return have you earned on your investment in the house? The answer depends on how much you invested when you bought the house. For example, if you paid $200,000 in cash for the house, your return on that $200,000 investment is the $20,000 increase in the price of the house divided by your $200,000 investment, or 10 percent. Suppose that rather than paying cash, you made a down payment of 20 percent, or $40,000, and borrowed the rest by taking out a mortgage loan of $160,000. Now the return on your investment in the house is the $20,000 increase in the price of the house divided by your $40,000 investment, or 50 percent. If the down payment is less than 20 percent, your return on investment will be higher. The second column in the following table shows how the return on your investment increases as your down payment decreases:

	Return on your investment as a result of . . .	
Down Payment	a 10 percent increase in the price of your house.	a 10 percent decrease in the price of your house.
100%	10%	−10%
20	50	−50
10	100	−100
5	200	−200

An investment financed at least partly by borrowing is called a *leveraged investment*. As this example shows, the larger the fraction of an investment financed by borrowing, the greater the degree of leverage in the investment, and the greater the potential return. But as the third column in the table shows, the reverse is also true: The greater the leverage, the greater the potential loss. To see why, suppose once again that you buy a house for $200,000, except that in this case, after one year, the price of the house falls to $180,000. If you paid $200,000 in cash for the house—so your leverage was zero—the $20,000 decline in the price of the house represents a loss of 10 percent of your investment. But if you made a down payment of only $10,000 and borrowed the remaining $190,000, then the $20,000 decline in the price of the house represents a loss of 200 percent of your investment. In fact, the house is now worth $10,000 less than the amount of your mortgage loan. The *equity* in your house is the difference between the market price of the house and the amount you owe on a loan. If the amount you owe is greater than the price of the house, you have *negative equity*. A homeowner who has negative equity is also said to be "upside down" or "underwater" on his or her mortgage.

When the housing bubble burst and housing prices started to fall, many people found that they had negative equity. In that situation, some people defaulted on their loans, sometimes by simply moving out and abandoning their homes. Leverage had contributed to the housing boom and bust and the severity of the 2007–2009 recession.

Your Turn: Test your understanding by doing related problem 6.9 on page 936 at the end of this chapter.

MyEconLab Study Plan

The Fed and the Treasury Department Respond

Because the problems in financial markets resulting from the bursting of the housing bubble were so severe, the Fed entered into an unusual partnership with the U.S. Treasury Department to develop suitable policies. Fed Chairman Ben Bernanke and U.S. Treasury Secretaries Henry Paulson (in the Bush administration) and Timothy Geithner (in the Obama administration) responded to the crisis by intervening in financial markets in unprecedented ways.

Initial Fed and Treasury Actions The financial crisis significantly worsened following the bankruptcy of the investment bank Lehman Brothers on September 15, 2008. So it is useful to look at the actions taken by the Fed and the Treasury before and after that date. Table 26.3 shows four key actions the Fed and Treasury took to deal with problems in the financial system before the bankruptcy of Lehman Brothers.

Table 26.3

Treasury and Fed Actions at the Beginning of the Financial Crisis

Date	Action	Goal
March 2008	Although the Fed traditionally made discount loans only to commercial banks, the Fed announced it would temporarily make discount loans to *primary dealers*—firms that participate in regular open market transactions with the Fed.	Provide short-term funds to these dealers, some of which are investment banks, so they would not have to raise funds by selling securities, which might further reduce the prices of these securities.
March 2008	The Fed announced that it would loan up to $200 billion of Treasury securities in exchange for mortgage-backed securities.	Make it possible for primary dealers that owned mortgage-backed securities that were difficult or impossible to sell to have access to Treasury securities that they could use as collateral for short-term loans.
March 2008	The Fed and the Treasury helped JPMorgan Chase acquire the investment bank Bear Stearns, which was close to failing.	Avoid a financial panic that the Fed and the Treasury believed would result from Bear Stearns's failure. Its failure might have caused many investors and financial firms to stop making loans to other investment banks.
September 2008	The Treasury moved to have the federal government take control of Fannie Mae and Freddie Mac. Although the federal government sponsored Fannie Mae and Freddie Mac, they were actually private businesses. The firms were placed under the supervision of the Federal Housing Finance Agency.	Avoid further devastating a weak housing market. The Treasury believed that the bankruptcy of Fannie Mae and Freddie Mac would have caused a collapse in confidence in mortgage-backed securities.

Responses to the Failure of Lehman Brothers Some economists and policymakers criticized the decision by the Fed and the Treasury to help arrange the sale of Bear Stearns to JPMorgan Chase. Their main concern was with the *moral hazard problem*, which is the possibility that managers of financial firms such as Bear Stearns might make riskier investments if they believe that the federal government will save them from bankruptcy. The Treasury and the Fed acted to save Bear Stearns because they believed that the failure of a large financial firm could have wider economic repercussions. As we discussed in Chapter 25, when a financial firm sells off its holdings of bonds and other assets, it causes their prices to fall, which in turn can undermine the financial position of other firms that also own these assets. In September 2008, when the investment bank Lehman Brothers was near bankruptcy, the Fed and the Treasury had to weigh the moral hazard problem against the possibility that the failure of Lehman Brothers would lead to further declines in asset prices and endanger the financial positions of other firms. Chairman Ben Bernanke and other Fed officials were also concerned that they lacked the legal authority to make loans to Lehman Brothers. They believed that the Federal Reserve Act prohibited making loans to a firm that was insolvent, meaning that the value of the firm's assets—such as its holdings of mortgage securities—was less than the value of its liabilities—such as the loans it had received from other financial firms.

The Fed and the Treasury decided to allow Lehman Brothers to go bankrupt, which it did on September 15. The adverse reaction in financial markets was stronger than the Fed and the Treasury had expected, and just two days later, the Fed agreed to provide an $85 billion loan to the American International Group (AIG)—the largest insurance company in the United States—in exchange for the federal government receiving an 80 percent ownership stake, effectively giving the government control of the company.

One important result of the failure of Lehman Brothers was the heavy losses suffered by Reserve Primary Fund, a money market mutual fund that had made short-term loans to Lehman Brothers. The problems at Reserve led many investors to withdraw their funds from it and other money market funds. These withdrawals reduced the ability of the money market funds to purchase commercial paper from corporations. Because in recent years corporations had become dependent on selling commercial paper to finance their operations, the Treasury and the Fed moved to stabilize this market and ensure that the flow of funds from investors to corporations continued. The Treasury announced a plan to temporarily provide insurance for deposits in money market mutual funds, similar to the existing insurance on bank deposits. The Fed announced that for a limited time, it would lend directly to corporations by purchasing three-month commercial paper issued by nonfinancial corporations.

Finally, in October 2008, Congress passed the *Troubled Asset Relief Program (TARP)*, under which the Treasury attempted to stabilize the commercial banking system by providing funds to banks in exchange for stock. Taking partial ownership positions in private commercial banks was an unprecedented action for the federal government.

Many of the Treasury's and the Fed's new approaches to policy were controversial because they involved partial government ownership of financial firms, implicit guarantees to large financial firms that they would not be allowed to go bankrupt, and unprecedented intervention in financial markets. Although the approaches were new, they were intended to achieve the traditional macroeconomic policy goals of high employment, price stability, and stability of financial markets. What remains to be seen is whether these new approaches represent a permanent increase in federal government involvement in U.S. financial markets or whether policy will eventually return to more traditional approaches.

MyEconLab Study Plan

MyEconLab Concept Check

Continued from page 895

Economics in Your Life

Should You Buy a House during a Recession?

At the beginning of this chapter, we asked whether it is a good idea to buy a house during a recession. Buying a house is the largest purchase you are likely to make in your lifetime, so you need to carefully consider a number of factors, including the price of the house relative to comparable houses in the neighborhood; whether house prices in the neighborhood have been rising or falling; and the location of the house relative to stores, work, and good schools. Also important is the interest rate you will have to pay on the mortgage loan you would need in order to buy the house. As we have seen in this chapter, during a recession, the Fed often takes actions to lower interest rates. So, mortgage rates are typically lower during a recession than at other times. You may want to take advantage of low interest rates to buy a house during a recession. But recessions are also times of rising unemployment, and you would not want to make a commitment to borrow a lot of money for 15 or more years if you were in danger of losing your job. We can conclude that if your job seems secure, buying a house during a recession may be a good idea.

Conclusion

Monetary policy is one way governments pursue goals for inflation, employment, and financial stability. The chair of the Federal Reserve may have a greater ability than the president of the United States to affect the U.S. economy. Congress and the president, however, also use their power over spending and taxes to try to stabilize the economy. In Chapter 27, we will discuss how *fiscal policy*—changes in government spending and taxes—affect the economy.

Visit MyEconLab for a news article and analysis related to the concepts of this chapter.

CHAPTER SUMMARY AND PROBLEMS

Key Terms

Contractionary monetary policy, p. 906
Expansionary monetary policy, p. 906
Federal funds rate, p. 903
Inflation targeting, p. 920
Monetary policy, p. 896
Taylor rule, p. 918

26.1 What Is Monetary Policy? pages 896–898

LEARNING OBJECTIVE: Define monetary policy and describe the Federal Reserve's monetary policy goals.

Summary

Monetary policy is the actions the Fed takes to manage the money supply and interest rates to achieve its macroeconomic policy goals. The Fed has four *monetary policy goals* that are intended to promote a well-functioning economy: price stability, high employment, stability of financial markets and institutions, and economic growth.

MyEconLab Visit **www.myeconlab.com** to complete these exercises online and get instant feedback.

Review Questions

1.1 When Congress established the Federal Reserve in 1913, what was its main responsibility? When did Congress broaden the Fed's responsibilities?

1.2 What are the Fed's four monetary policy goals?

1.3 In what sense does the Fed have a "dual mandate"?

1.4 How can investment banks be subject to liquidity problems?

Problems and Applications

1.5 What is a bank panic? Why are policymakers more concerned about bank failures than failures of restaurants or clothing stores?

1.6 An article in the *Wall Street Journal* quoted a Federal Reserve economist as referring to "the Fed's existing dual mandate to achieve maximum sustainable employment in the context of price stability."

a. Does "maximum sustainable employment" mean a zero percent unemployment rate? Briefly explain.

b. Does "price stability" mean a zero percent inflation rate? Briefly explain.

Source: Pedro Nicolaci Da Costa, "Fed Should Make Bond Buys a Regular Policy Tool, a Boston Fed Paper Finds," *Wall Street Journal*, April 23, 2015.

1.7 A former Federal Reserve official argued that at the Fed, "the objectives of price stability and low long-term interest rates are essentially the same objective." Briefly explain his reasoning.

Source: William Poole, "Understanding the Fed," *Federal Reserve Bank of St. Louis Review*, Vol. 89, No. 1, January/February 2007, p. 4.

1.8 In the summer of 2015, many economists and policymakers expected that the Federal Reserve would increase its target for the federal funds rate by the end of the year. Some economists argued, though, that it would be better for the Fed to leave its target unchanged. At the time, the unemployment rate was 5.3 percent, close to full employment, but the inflation rate was below the Fed's target of 2 percent. What policy goal would the Fed promote if it did *not* increase its target for the federal funds rate? Briefly explain.

Source: Min Zeng, "Inflation Expectations Fall, Making Rate Hike 'More Difficult to Justify,'" *Wall Street Journal*, August 6, 2015.

26.2 The Money Market and the Fed's Choice of Monetary Policy Targets, pages 898–904

LEARNING OBJECTIVE: Describe the Federal Reserve's monetary policy targets and explain how expansionary and contractionary monetary policies affect the interest rate.

Summary

The Fed's *monetary policy targets* are economic variables that it can affect directly and that in turn affect variables such as real GDP and the price level that are closely related to the Fed's policy goals. The two main monetary policy targets are the money supply and the interest rate. The Fed has most often chosen to use the interest rate as its monetary policy target. The Federal Open Market Committee announces a target for the **federal funds rate** after each meeting. The federal funds rate is the interest rate banks charge each other for overnight loans. To lower the interest rate, the Fed increases the money supply. To raise the interest rate, the Fed decreases the money supply. In a graphical analysis of the money market, when the money supply curve shifts to the right, the result is a movement down the money demand curve and a new equilibrium at a lower interest rate. When the money supply curve shifts to the left, the result is a movement up the money demand curve and a new equilibrium at a higher interest rate.

MyEconLab Visit **www.myeconlab.com** to complete these exercises online and get instant feedback.

Review Questions

2.1 What is a monetary policy target? Why does the Fed use policy targets?

2.2 What do economists mean by the *demand for money*? What is the advantage of holding money? What is the disadvantage? Why does an increase in the interest rate decrease the quantity of money demanded?

2.3 Draw a demand and supply graph showing equilibrium in the money market. Suppose the Fed wants to lower the equilibrium interest rate. Show on the graph how the Fed would accomplish this objective.

2.4 What is the federal funds rate? What role does it play in monetary policy?

Problems and Applications

2.5 In the following graph of the money market, what could cause the money supply curve to shift from MS_1 to MS_2? What could cause the money demand curve to shift from MD_1 to MD_2?

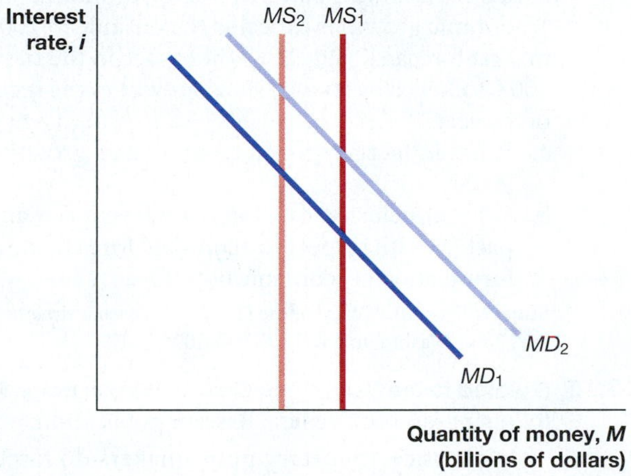

2.6 In 2015, one article in the *Wall Street Journal* discussed the possibility of "a September quarter-point increase in the Fed's range for overnight target rates," while another article noted, "the U.S. central bank's discount rate ... has been set at 0.75% since February 2010."

a. What is the name of the Fed's "target rate"?
b. Briefly explain who borrows money and who lends money at this "target rate."
c. What is the discount rate, and how is it different from the "target rate"?

Sources: Justin Lahart, "Jobs Give Fed Green Light; Inflation Sets Speed Limit," *Wall Street Journal*, August 7, 2015; and Ben Leubsdorf, "Five Regional Fed Banks Asked to Raise Discount Rate," *Wall Street Journal*, July 14, 2015.

2.7 In response to problems in financial markets and a slowing economy, the Federal Open Market Committee (FOMC) began lowering its target for the federal funds rate from 5.25 percent in September 2007. Over the next year, the FOMC cut its federal funds rate target in a series of steps. Economist Price Fishback of the University of Arizona observed, "The Fed has been pouring more money into the banking system by cutting the target federal funds rate to 0 to 0.25 percent in December 2008." What is the relationship between the federal funds rate falling and the money supply increasing? How does lowering the target for the federal funds rate "pour money" into the banking system?

Source: Price Fishback, "The Financial Meltdown Now and Then," freakonomics.com, May 12, 2009.

2.8 An article in the *New York Times* in 1993 stated the following about Fed Chairman Alan Greenspan's decision to no longer announce targets for the money supply: "Since the late 1970's, the Federal Reserve has made many of its most important decisions by setting a specific target for growth in the money supply ... and often adjusted interest rates to meet them." If the Fed would no longer have a specific target for the money supply, what was it targeting? Why did the Fed give up targeting the money supply?

Source: Steven Greenhouse, "Fed Abandons Policy Tied to Money Supply," *New York Times*, July 23, 1993.

26.3 Monetary Policy and Economic Activity, pages 904–912

LEARNING OBJECTIVE: Use aggregate demand and aggregate supply graphs to show the effects of monetary policy on real GDP and the price level.

Summary

An **expansionary monetary policy** lowers interest rates to increase consumption, investment, and net exports. This increase in aggregate demand increases real GDP and the price level. An expansionary monetary policy can help the Fed achieve its goal of high employment. A **contractionary monetary policy** raises interest rates to decrease consumption, investment, and net exports. This decrease in aggregate demand reduces both real GDP and the inflation rate below what they would be in the absence of policy. A contractionary monetary policy can help the Fed achieve its goal of price stability.

MyEconLab Visit **www.myeconlab.com** to complete these exercises online and get instant feedback.

Review Questions

3.1 Briefly discuss how an increase in interest rates affects each component of aggregate demand.

3.2 If the Fed believes the economy is headed for a recession, what actions should it take? If the Fed believes the inflation rate is about to sharply increase, what actions should it take?

3.3 What is quantitative easing? Why have central banks used this policy?

Problems and Applications

3.4 A student says the following: "I understand why the Fed uses expansionary policy, but I don't understand why it would ever use contractionary policy. Why would the government ever want the economy to contract?" Briefly answer the student's question.

3.5 In explaining why monetary policy did not pull Japan out of a recession in the early 2000s, an official at the Bank of Japan was quoted as saying that despite "major increases in the money supply," the money "stay[ed] in banks." Explain what the official meant by saying that the money stayed in banks. Why would that be a problem? Where does the money go if an expansionary monetary policy is successful?

Source: James Brooke, "Critics Say Koizumi's Economic Medicine Is a Weak Tea," *New York Times*, February 27, 2002.

3.6 An article in the *Wall Street Journal* discussing the Federal Reserve's monetary policy included the following observation: "Fed officials have been signaling since last year that they expected to raise rates in 2015 ... pushing up the value of the currency and contributing to the economic slowdown officials now confront."

a. What does "pushing up the value of the currency" mean?

b. Why would the Fed's increasing U.S. interest rates cause the value of the currency to increase?

c. Why would an increase in the value of the currency contribute to a slowdown in the growth of the U.S. economy?

Source: Jon Hilsenrath, "Fed's Rate Decisions Hang on Dollar, Growth Concerns," *Wall Street Journal*, April 22, 2015.

3.7 According to an article in the *Wall Street Journal*, "Brazil's economy grew just 2.3% in 2013, compared with 7.5% in 2010. The country also has struggled with persistently high inflation, which has forced its central bank to raise interest rates."

a. Why would the Brazilian central bank have been "forced" to raise interest rates because of rising inflation?

b. Could the increase in interest rates be connected to the slowing rate of economic growth? Briefly explain.

Source: Emily Glazer and Luciana Magalhaes, "Brazil's Debt-Laden Firms Try to Stay Afloat," *Wall Street Journal*, March 18, 2014.

3.8 William McChesney Martin, who was Federal Reserve chairman from 1951 to 1970, was once quoted as saying, "The role of the Federal Reserve is to remove the punchbowl just as the party gets going." What did he mean?

3.9 **(Related to the Making the Connection on page 908)** An article in the *Wall Street Journal* in 2015 reported that the interest rate on five-year German government bonds had become negative: "The negative yield means investors are effectively paying the German state for holding its debt." The article quoted an investment analyst as saying: "The negative yield is not scaring investors away."

a. What caused the interest rate on German government bonds to become negative?

b. Why are investors willing to buy bonds with a negative interest rate?

Source: Emese Bartha and Ben Edwards, "Germany Sells Five-Year Debt at Negative Yield for First Time on Record," *Wall Street Journal*, February 25, 2015.

3.10 **(Related to the Making the Connection on page 908)** An article in the *Wall Street Journal* notes that before the financial crisis of 2007–2009, the Fed "managed just one short-term interest rate and expected that to be enough to meet its goals for inflation and unemployment."

a. What short-term interest rate is the article referring to? How would the Fed expect controlling that one interest rate would allow it to meet its goals for inflation and unemployment?

b. The article also notes that after the financial crisis, "the Fed is working through a broader spectrum of interest rates." What does "a broader spectrum of interest rates" mean? How is the Fed able to affect a broader spectrum of interest rates?

Source: Jon Hilsenrath, "Easy-Money Era a Long Game for Fed," *Wall Street Journal*, March 17, 2013.

3.11 **(Related to the Making the Connection on page 910)** Each year, the president's Council of Economic Advisers prepares and sends to Congress *The Economic Report of the President*. The report published in February 2008 contained the following summary of the economic situation: "Economic growth is expected to continue in 2008. Most market forecasts suggest a slower pace in the first half of 2008, followed by strengthened growth in the second half of the year."

a. What in fact happened to economic growth during 2008?

b. What conclusion can you draw from your answer to part (a) with respect to economic forecasting and the formulation of economic policy?

Source: Executive Office of the President, *Economic Report of the President*, 2008, Washington, DC: USGPO, 2008, p. 17.

3.12 **(Related to the Making the Connection on page 910)** The following is from a Federal Reserve publication:

> In practice, monetary policymakers do not have up-to-the-minute, reliable information about the state of the economy and prices. Information is limited because of lags in the publication of data. Also, policymakers have less-than-perfect understanding of the way the economy works, including the knowledge of when and to what extent policy actions will affect aggregate demand. The operation of the economy changes over time, and with it the response of the economy to policy measures. These limitations add to uncertainties in the policy process and make determining the appropriate setting of monetary policy ... more difficult.

If the Fed itself admits that there are many obstacles in the way of effective monetary policy, why does it still engage in active monetary policy rather than use a monetary growth rule, as suggested by Milton Friedman and his followers?

Source: Board of Governors of the Federal Reserve System, *The Federal Reserve System: Purposes and Functions*, Washington, DC, 1994.

3.13 **(Related to the Don't Let This Happen to You on page 912)** Briefly explain whether you agree with the following statement: "The Fed has an easy job. Say it wants to increase real GDP by $200 billion. All it has to do is increase the money supply by that amount."

3.14 **(Related to the Chapter Opener on page 895)** An investment blog said about Fed Chair Janet Yellen, "She is arguably the world's most powerful woman, and perhaps the most powerful person in the world. Can you name anybody with more might?" Do you agree with this assessment? Briefly explain.

Source: Barbara Friedberg, "Fed Chief Janet Yellen: The Most Powerful Woman in the World," blog.personalcapital.com, September 17, 2014.

26.4 Monetary Policy in the Dynamic Aggregate Demand and Aggregate Supply Model, pages 912–917

LEARNING OBJECTIVE: Use the dynamic aggregate demand and aggregate supply model to analyze monetary policy.

Summary

We can use the *dynamic aggregate demand and aggregate supply model* introduced in Chapter 24 to look more closely at expansionary and contractionary monetary policies. The dynamic aggregate demand and aggregate supply model takes into account that (1) the economy experiences continuing inflation, with the price level rising every year, and (2) the economy experiences long-run growth, with the *LRAS* curve shifting to the right every year. In the dynamic model, an expansionary monetary policy tries to ensure that the aggregate demand curve will shift far enough to the right to bring about macroeconomic equilibrium with real GDP equal to potential GDP. A contractionary monetary policy attempts to offset movements in aggregate demand that would cause macroeconomic equilibrium to occur at a level of real GDP that is greater than potential GDP.

MyEconLab Visit **www.myeconlab.com** to complete these exercises online and get instant feedback.

Review Questions

4.1 What are the key differences between how we illustrate an expansionary monetary policy in the basic aggregate demand and aggregate supply model and in the dynamic aggregate demand and aggregate supply model?

4.2 What are the key differences between how we illustrate a contractionary monetary policy in the basic aggregate demand and aggregate supply model and in the dynamic aggregate demand and aggregate supply model?

Problems and Applications

4.3 Explain whether you agree with this argument:

> If the Fed actually ever carried out a contractionary monetary policy, the price level would fall. Because the price level has not fallen in the United States over an entire year since the 1930s, we can conclude that the Fed has not carried out a contractionary policy since the 1930s.

4.4 **(Related to Solved Problem 26.4 on page 915)** Use the graph to answer the following questions.

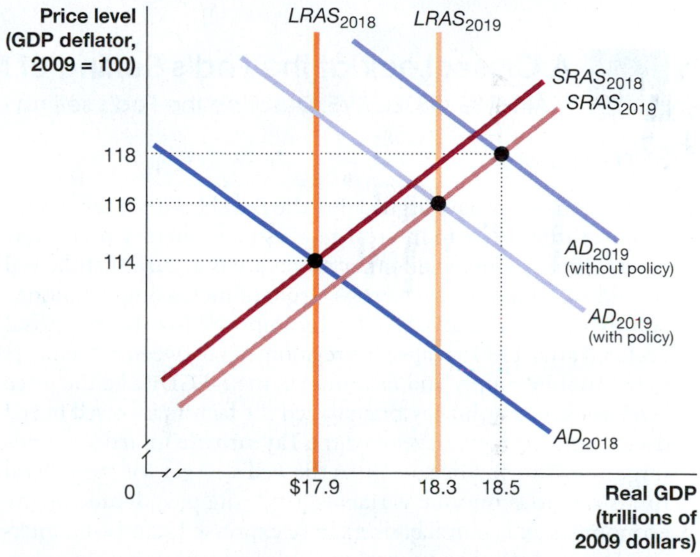

a. If the Fed does not take any policy action, what will be the level of real GDP and the price level in 2019?

b. If the Fed wants to keep real GDP at its potential level in 2019, should it use an expansionary policy or a contractionary policy? Should the trading desk be buying Treasury bills or selling them?

c. If the Fed takes no policy action, what will be the inflation rate in 2019? If the Fed uses monetary policy to keep real GDP at its potential level, what will be the inflation rate in 2019?

4.5 **(Related to Solved Problem 26.4 on page 915)** The hypothetical information in the following table shows what the situation will be in 2019 if the Fed does *not* use monetary policy.

Year	Potential GDP	Real GDP	Price Level
2018	$17.9 trillion	$17.9 trillion	110.0
2019	18.3 trillion	18.2 trillion	112.0

a. If the Fed wants to keep real GDP at its potential level in 2019, should it use an expansionary policy or a contractionary policy? Should the trading desk be buying T-bills or selling them?

b. If the Fed's policy is successful in keeping real GDP at its potential level in 2019, state whether each of the following will be higher, lower, or the same as it would have been if the Fed had taken no action:
   i. Real GDP
   ii. Potential GDP
   iii. The inflation rate
   iv. The unemployment rate

c. Draw an aggregate demand and aggregate supply graph to illustrate the effects of the Fed's policy. Be sure that your graph contains *LRAS* curves for 2018 and 2019; *SRAS* curves for 2018 and 2019; *AD* curves for 2018 and 2019, with and without monetary policy action; and equilibrium real GDP and the price level in 2019, with and without policy.

4.6 According to an article in the *Wall Street Journal*, the Reserve Bank of India lowered its key policy interest rate in 2015, "citing weakness in parts of the economy as well as favorable inflation figures." The article notes that the central bank lists constraints to further interest rate cuts, including the "risk that inflation could flare again."

a. Use the dynamic aggregate demand and aggregate supply model to show where the Reserve Bank of India expected real GDP to be in 2015 without the interest rate cut, and indicate what the central bank is trying to achieve with the interest rate cut. Assume, for simplicity, that real GDP in India in 2014 equaled potential GDP.

b. Is there a connection between India experiencing slow growth in output at the same time that it experienced a lower inflation rate? Briefly explain.

Source: Gabriele Parussini, "India Cuts Key Interest Rate for Second Time This Year," *Wall Street Journal*, March 4, 2015.

26.5 A Closer Look at the Fed's Setting of Monetary Policy Targets, pages 917–922

LEARNING OBJECTIVE: Describe the Fed's setting of monetary policy targets.

Summary

Some economists have argued that the Fed should use the money supply, rather than an interest rate, as its monetary policy target. Milton Friedman and other monetarists argued that the Fed should adopt a monetary growth rule of increasing the money supply every year at a fixed rate. Support for this proposal declined after 1980 because the relationship between movements in the money supply and movements in real GDP and the price level weakened. John Taylor analyzed the factors involved in Fed decision making and developed the **Taylor rule** for federal funds targeting. The Taylor rule links the Fed's target for the federal funds rate to economic variables. Over the past decade, many economists and central bankers have expressed significant interest in using **inflation targeting**, under which monetary policy is conducted to commit the central bank to achieving a publicly announced inflation target. In 2012, the Fed joined a number of foreign central banks in adopting inflation targeting. The Fed's performance in the 1980s, 1990s, and early 2000s generally received high marks from economists.

MyEconLab Visit **www.myeconlab.com** to complete these exercises online and get instant feedback.

Review Questions

5.1 What is a *monetary rule*, as opposed to a *monetary policy*? What monetary rule would Milton Friedman have liked the Fed to follow? Why has support for a monetary rule of the kind Friedman advocated declined since 1980?

5.2 For more than 20 years, the Fed has used the federal funds rate as its monetary policy target. Why doesn't the Fed target the money supply at the same time?

5.3 What is the Taylor rule? What is its purpose?

Problems and Applications

5.4 In an interview, Paul Volcker, chairman of the Federal Reserve's Board of Governors from 1979 to 1987, was asked about the Fed's use of monetary policy to reduce the rate of inflation. Volcker replied:

> The Federal Reserve had been attempting to deal with … inflation for some time. … By the time I became chairman … we adopted an approach of … saying, We'll take the emphasis off of interest rates and put the emphasis on the growth in the money supply, which is at the root cause of inflation … we will stop the money supply from increasing as rapidly as it was … and interest rates went up a lot. … We said … we'll take whatever consequences that means for the interest rate because that will enable us to get inflation under control.

Explain why the Fed, while Paul Volcker was chairman, did not target both the growth of the money supply and interest rates.

Source: "Paul Volcker Interview," http://www.pbs.org/fmc/interviews/volcker.htm.

5.5 **(Related to Solved Problem 26.5 on page 919)** Suppose that the equilibrium real federal funds rate is 2 percent and the target rate of inflation is 2 percent. Use the following information and the Taylor rule to calculate the federal funds rate target:

Current inflation rate = 4 percent
Potential GDP = 17.0 trillion
Real GDP = 17.17 trillion

5.6 **(Related to Solved Problem 26.5 on page 919)** In discussing the Taylor rule, John Taylor wrote, "I realize that there are differences of opinion about what is the best rule to guide policy and that some at the Fed (including Janet Yellen) now prefer a rule with a higher coefficient [on the output gap]."

a. If Fed policy were guided by a Taylor rule with a coefficient of 1, rather than 0.5, on the output gap, would the federal funds rate be higher or lower during a recession? Briefly explain.

b. Why might economists and policymakers disagree over the best rule to guide monetary policy?

Source: John Taylor, "Cross-Checking 'Checking in on the Taylor Rule,'" www.economicsone.com, July 16, 2013.

5.7 **(Related to Solved Problem 26.5 on page 919)** Two economists at the Federal Reserve Bank of Cleveland note that "estimates of potential GDP are very fluid, [which] suggests there is considerable error in our current measure." They conclude that "this lack of precision should be recognized when policy recommendations are made using a Taylor-type rule." Briefly explain their reasoning.

Source: Charles Carlstrom and Timothy Stehulak, "Mutable Economic Laws and Calculating Unemployment and Output Gaps—An Application to Taylor Rules," Federal Reserve Bank of Cleveland, June 6, 2015.

5.8 While serving as the president of the Federal Reserve Bank of St. Louis, William Poole stated, "Although my own preference is for zero inflation properly managed, I believe that a central bank consensus on some other numerical goal of reasonably low inflation is more important than the exact number." Briefly explain why the economy might benefit from an explicit inflation target even if the target chosen is not a zero rate of inflation.

Source: William Poole, "Understanding the Fed," *Federal Reserve Bank of St. Louis Review*, Vol. 89, No. 1, January/February 2007, p. 4.

5.9 **(Related to the Making the Connection on page 921)** October 2015 was the forty-second consecutive month that the rate of inflation as measured by the personal consumption expenditures (PCE) price index was below the Federal Reserve's target of 2 percent.

a. Briefly explain why using the consumer price index (CPI) might yield a rate of inflation different from that found using the PCE price index.

b. Explain how the choice of the price index the Federal Reserve uses to measure inflation can affect monetary policy.

Source: Zeppo Mitchell, "Inflation Misses Fed 2% Target for 38th Straight Month," *Wall Street Journal*, August 3, 2015.

26.6 Fed Policies during the 2007–2009 Recession, pages 923–928

LEARNING OBJECTIVE: Describe the policies the Federal Reserve used during the 2007–2009 recession.

Summary

A housing bubble that began to deflate in 2006 helped cause the recession of 2007–2009 and an accompanying financial crisis. In response, the Federal Reserve instituted a variety of policy actions. In a series of steps, it cut the target for the federal funds rate from 5.25 percent in September 2007 to effectively zero in December 2008. The decline in the housing market caused wider problems in the financial system, as defaults on home mortgages rose and the value of mortgage-backed securities declined. The Fed and the U.S. Treasury Department implemented a series of new policies to provide liquidity and restore confidence. The Fed expanded the types of firms eligible for discount loans and began lending directly to corporations by purchasing commercial paper. Under the *Troubled Asset Relief Program*, the Treasury provided financial support to banks and other financial firms in exchange for part ownership. The Treasury also moved to have the federal government take control of Fannie Mae and Freddie Mac, government-sponsored firms that play a key role in the mortgage market. The failure of the investment bank Lehman Brothers in September 2008 led to a deepening of the financial crisis and provided the motivation for some of the new policies. Ultimately, the new policies stabilized the financial system, but their long-term effects remain the subject of debate.

MyEconLab Visit **www.myeconlab.com** to complete these exercises online and get instant feedback.

Review Questions

6.1 What is a mortgage? What were the important developments in the mortgage market during the years after 1970?

6.2 Beginning in 2008, the Federal Reserve and the U.S. Treasury Department responded to the financial crisis by intervening in financial markets in unprecedented ways. Briefly summarize the actions of the Fed and the Treasury.

Problems and Applications

6.3 A newspaper article in the fall of 2007 stated, "The luxury-home builder Hovnanian Enterprises reported its fourth consecutive quarterly loss on Thursday, citing continuing problems of credit availability and high inventory." Why was Hovnanian suffering losses? What does the article mean by "credit availability"? How would problems of credit availability affect a homebuilder such as Hovnanian Enterprises?

Source: "New Loss for Home Builder," Associated Press, September 7, 2007.

6.4 An article in a Federal Reserve publication observes that "20 or 30 years ago, local financial institutions were the only option for some borrowers. Today, borrowers have access to national (and even international) sources of mortgage finance." What caused this change in the sources of mortgage finance? What would be the likely consequence of this change for the interest rates borrowers have to pay on mortgages? Briefly explain.

Source: Daniel J. McDonald and Daniel L. Thornton, "A Primer on the Mortgage Market and Mortgage Finance," *Federal Reserve Bank of St. Louis Review*, January/February 2008, pp. 31–45.

6.5 The Federal Reserve releases transcripts of its Federal Open Market Committee (FOMC) meetings only after a five-year lag in order to preserve the confidentiality of the discussions. When the transcripts of the FOMC's 2008 meetings were released, one member of the Board of Governors was quoted as saying in an April 2008 meeting, "I think it is very possible that we will look back and say, particularly after the Bear Stearns episode, that we have turned the corner in terms of the financial disruption." Did this member's analysis turn out to be correct? Briefly explain why his prediction may have seemed reasonable at the time.

Source: Jon Hilsenrath, "New View into Fed's Response to Crisis," *Wall Street Journal*, February 21, 2014.

6.6 In late 2012, the U.S. Treasury sold the last of the stock it had purchased in the insurance company AIG. The Treasury earned a profit on the $22.7 billion it had invested in AIG in 2008. An article in *Wall Street Journal* noted, "This step in AIG's turnaround, which essentially closes the book on one of the most controversial bailouts of the financial crisis, seemed nearly unattainable in 2008, when the insurer's imminent collapse sent shockwaves through the global economy."

a. Why did the federal government bail out AIG?
b. Why was the government bailout controversial?
c. Does the fact the federal government earned a profit on its investment in AIG mean that economists and policymakers who opposed the bailout were necessarily wrong? Briefly explain.

Source: Jeffrey Sparshott and Erik Holm, "End of a Bailout: U.S. Sells Last AIG Shares," *Wall Street Journal*, December 11, 2012.

6.7 Recall that *securitization* is the process of turning a loan, such as a mortgage, into a bond that can be bought and sold in secondary markets. An article in the *Economist* notes:

> That securitization caused more subprime mortgages to be written is not in doubt. By offering access to a much deeper pool of capital, securitization helped to bring down the cost of mortgages and made home-ownership more affordable for borrowers with poor credit histories.

What is a "subprime mortgage"? What is a "deeper pool of capital"? Why would securitization give mortgage borrowers access to a deeper pool of capital? Would a subprime borrower be likely to pay a higher or a lower interest rate than a borrower with a better credit history? Under what circumstances might a lender prefer to loan money to a borrower with a poor credit history rather than to a borrower with a good credit history? Briefly explain.

Source: "Ruptured Credit," *Economist*, May 15, 2008.

6.8 In 2015, Richard Fuld, the last CEO of Lehman Brothers, gave a talk in which, according to an article in the *Wall Street Journal*, "He outlined what he called the 'perfect storm' of events that led to the financial crisis, saying 'it all started with the government' and policies that subsidized cheap loans for people to buy homes in order to help them chase the American dream."

a. Briefly outline the events that led to the financial crisis. Do you agree with Fuld that the events constitute a "perfect storm"—that is, a series of unfortunate events happening at the same time in a way that would have been difficult to anticipate?
b. Which government policies mentioned in the chapter could be said to be subsidizing cheap loans? What does Fuld mean by saying that these policies were intended to help people "chase the American dream"?

Source: Maureen Farrell, "Lehman's Fuld Says It Wasn't His Fault," *Wall Street Journal*, May 28, 2015.

6.9 **(Related to the Making the Connection on page 926)** Suppose you buy a house for $150,000. One year later, the market price of the house has risen to $165,000. What is the return on your investment in the house if you made a down payment of 20 percent and took out a mortgage loan for the other 80 percent? What if you made a down payment of 5 percent and borrowed the other 95 percent? Be sure to show your calculations in your answer.

Real-Time Data Exercises

D26.1 **(Following news of FOMC meetings)** Go to www.federalreserve.gov, the Web site for the Federal Reserve Board of Governors, and read the most recent Federal Open Market Committee (FOMC) press release. At the Web site, select "Monetary Policy" at the top of the screen and then select "Federal Open Market Committee" on the far left of the screen. Select "Meeting calendars and information." Finally, scroll down and select Statement for the date of the most recent FOMC meeting. Answer the following questions on the basis of the FOMC press release.

a. Did the FOMC change the target for the federal funds rate? If so, what was the change?
b. On balance, in its statement, does the FOMC appear to be more concerned about slow economic growth or high inflation?
c. Did the FOMC change the interest rate paid on bank reserves?
d. Did the Fed announce any other monetary policy actions?

D26.2 **(Movements in the federal funds rate relative to the target)** Go to the Web site of the Federal Reserve Bank of St. Louis (FRED) (research.stlouisfed.org/fred2) and download and graph the data series for the effective federal funds rate (DFF), the upper limit of the target range for the federal funds rate (DFEDTARU), and the lower limit for the target range (DFEDTARL). Plot on the same graph values for all three data series from December 16, 2008, to the most recent day available. Over this period, has the Fed been able to keep the effective federal funds rate within the target range? Briefly explain.

D26.3 (Comparing different measures of the inflation rate) Go to the Web site of the Federal Reserve Bank of St. Louis (FRED) (research.stlouisfed.org/fred2/) and find the most recent values and values from the same month one year before for the following three measures of the price level: (1) the Consumer Price Index for All Urban Consumers: All Items (CPIAUCSL), (2) the Personal Consumption Expenditures: Chain-type Price Index (PCEPI), and (3) the Personal Consumption Expenditures excluding food and energy (chain-type price index) (DPCCRG3A086NBEA).

a. Using these data, calculate the inflation rate over this year as measured by each of the three price indexes.
b. Which of the three measures of inflation was highest during this year? Which measure was lowest? Why do the measures of inflation differ?

CHAPTER

27

Fiscal Policy

Chapter Outline and Learning Objectives

Does Government Spending Create Jobs?

The Golden Gate Bridge is an international symbol of San Francisco. The bridge spans the entrance to San Francisco Bay from the Pacific Ocean. Construction of the bridge began in 1933, and the bridge was open to traffic in 1937. Doyle Drive is a 1.6-mile stretch of U.S. Highway 101 and the main approach to the bridge from the San Francisco side. Doyle Drive was in desperate need of reconstruction, but for many years the city of San Francisco and the state of California had failed to provide the funding. In early 2009, President Barack Obama and Congress enacted the American Recovery and Reinvestment Act (ARRA, often referred to as the "stimulus bill") in an attempt to increase aggregate demand during the recession of 2007–2009. The ARRA is an example of *discretionary fiscal policy* aimed at increasing real GDP and employment. Some of the funds from the act were allocated to the Doyle Drive project. San Francisco Mayor Gavin Newsom welcomed the news: "This project is shovel ready and a signature example of how the federal stimulus can close the funding gap, stimulate the economy, improve transportation, and create jobs in San Francisco."

The Doyle Drive project was designed by the Flatiron Corporation, and construction was carried out by Kiewit Construction, headquartered in Omaha, Nebraska. Kiewit hired hundreds of workers for the project, which was completed in July 2015. The project to rebuild Doyle Drive is an example of increased government spending resulting in increased employment. Or is it? A majority of economists agree that a temporary increase in government spending can lead to increased employment during a recession. But some economists argue that fiscal policy actions like ARRA shift employment from one group of workers to another but do not increase total employment. The argument over the effect of government spending on employment continued years after the end of the recession of 2007–2009.

When the federal government spends more than it collects in taxes, the result is a federal budget deficit. Following the recession, the federal government ran the largest peacetime deficits in history. During 2011 and 2012, Congress and President Obama enacted cuts in federal spending, increases in taxes, and limits on future spending increases to try to reduce the budget deficit. In 2015, Congress and the president somewhat loosened the limits on federal spending while continuing to debate whether additional spending was necessary to help the economy finally make it back to potential GDP.

In this chapter, we will examine discretionary fiscal policy, the federal budget deficit, and the debate over their effects.

Sources: David R. Baker, "Presidio Parkway, the New Doyle Drive, Is Now Open," sfgate.com, July 13, 2015; Metropolitan Transit Commission, "Speaker Pelosi and Mayor Newsom Announce Doyle Drive Project Is Shovel Ready," February 28, 2009; Jonathan Weisman, "Republicans Aim to Hamper Obama's Policies with Spending Bills," *New York Times*, July 7, 2015; and http://goldengatebridge.org.

Economics in Your Life

What Would You Do with an Extra $500?

Suppose that the federal government announces that it will immediately mail you, and everyone else in the economy, a $500 tax rebate. In addition, you expect that in future years, your taxes will also decrease by $500. How will you respond to this increase in your disposable income? What effect will this tax rebate likely have on equilibrium real GDP in the short run? As you read this chapter, try to answer these questions. You can check your answers against those we provide on **page 971** at the end of this chapter.

In Chapter 26, we discussed how the Federal Reserve uses monetary policy to pursue macroeconomic policy goals, including price stability and high employment. In this chapter, we will explore how the government uses *fiscal policy*, which involves changes in taxes and government purchases, to achieve similar policy goals. As we have seen, in the short run, the price level and the levels of real GDP and total employment in the economy depend on aggregate demand and short-run aggregate supply. In the long run, the levels of real GDP and employment depend on long-run aggregate supply. The government can affect the levels of both aggregate demand and aggregate supply through fiscal policy. We will discuss how Congress and the president decide which fiscal policy actions to take to achieve their goals. We will also discuss the debates among economists and policymakers over the effectiveness of fiscal policy.

27.1 What Is Fiscal Policy?

LEARNING OBJECTIVE: Define fiscal policy.

Since the end of World War II, the federal government has been committed under the Employment Act of 1946 to intervening in the economy "to promote maximum employment, production, and purchasing power." As we saw in Chapter 26, the Federal Reserve's Federal Open Market Committee meets eight times per year to decide whether to change monetary policy. Less frequently, Congress and the president also make changes in taxes and government purchases to achieve macroeconomic policy goals, such as high employment, price stability, and high rates of economic growth. Changes in federal taxes and purchases that are intended to achieve macroeconomic policy goals are called **fiscal policy**.

Fiscal policy Changes in federal taxes and purchases that are intended to achieve macroeconomic policy goals.

What Fiscal Policy Is and What It Isn't

In the United States, federal, state, and local governments all have responsibility for taxing and spending. Economists typically use the term *fiscal policy* to refer only to the actions of the federal government. State and local governments sometimes change their taxing and spending policies to aid their local economies, but these are not fiscal policy actions because they are not intended to affect the national economy. The federal government makes many decisions about taxes and spending, but not all of these decisions are fiscal policy actions because they are not intended to achieve macroeconomic policy goals. For example, a decision to cut the taxes of people who buy hybrid cars is an environmental policy action, not a fiscal policy action. Similarly, the spending increases to fund the war on terrorism and the wars in Iraq and Afghanistan were part of defense and homeland security policy, not fiscal policy. MyEconLab Concept Check

Automatic Stabilizers versus Discretionary Fiscal Policy

There is an important distinction between *automatic stabilizers* and *discretionary fiscal policy*. Government spending and taxes that automatically increase or decrease along with the business cycle are called **automatic stabilizers**. The word *automatic* in this case refers to the fact that changes in these types of spending and taxes happen without actions by the government. For example, when the economy is expanding and employment is increasing, government spending on unemployment insurance payments to workers who have lost their jobs will automatically decrease. During a recession, as employment declines, this type of spending will automatically increase. Similarly, when the economy is expanding and incomes are rising, the amount the government collects in taxes will increase as people pay additional taxes on their higher incomes. When the economy is in a recession, the amount the government collects in taxes will fall.

Automatic stabilizers Government spending and taxes that automatically increase or decrease along with the business cycle.

With discretionary fiscal policy, the government takes actions to change spending or taxes. The tax cuts and spending increases in the American Recovery and Reinvestment Act (ARRA) that Congress and the president enacted in 2009, as mentioned in the chapter opener, are examples of discretionary fiscal policy actions. MyEconLab Concept Check

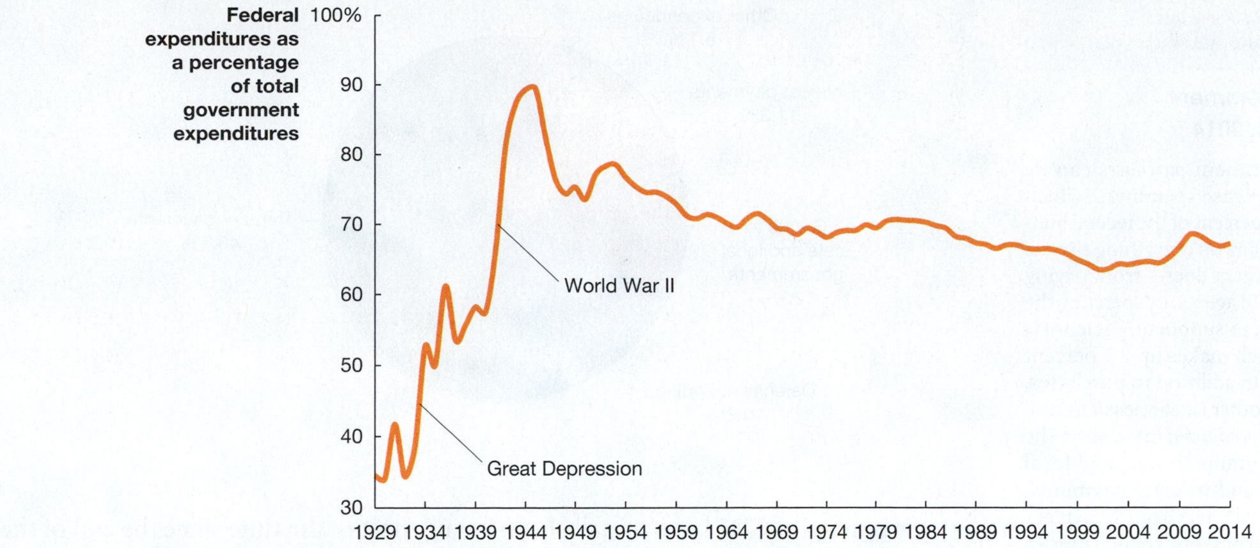

MyEconLab Real-time data

Figure 27.1 The Federal Government's Share of Total Government Expenditures, 1929–2014

Until the Great Depression of the 1930s, the majority of government spending in the United States occurred at the state and local levels. Since World War II, the federal government's share of total government expenditures has been between two-thirds and three-quarters.

Source: U.S. Bureau of Economic Analysis.

An Overview of Government Spending and Taxes

To provide a context for discussing fiscal policy, it is important to understand the big picture of government taxing and spending. Before the Great Depression of the 1930s, the majority of government spending in the United States took place at the state and local levels. As Figure 27.1 shows, the size of the federal government expanded significantly during the crisis of the Great Depression. Since World War II, the federal government's share of total government expenditures has been between two-thirds and three-quarters.

Economists often measure government spending relative to the size of the economy by calculating government spending as a percentage of GDP. Remember that there is a difference between federal government *purchases* and federal government *expenditures*. When the federal government purchases an aircraft carrier or the services of an FBI agent, it receives a good or service in return. Federal government expenditures include purchases plus federal government spending—such as Social Security payments—that does not involve purchases. As Figure 27.2 shows, federal government *purchases*

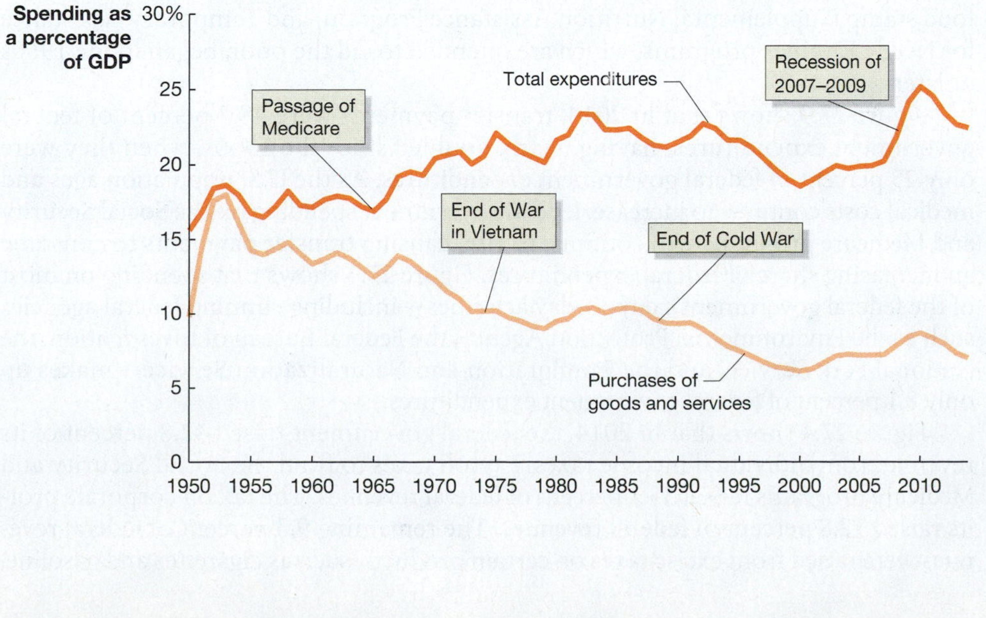

MyEconLab Real-time data

Figure 27.2

Federal Purchases and Federal Expenditures as a Percentage of GDP, 1950–2014

As a fraction of GDP, the federal government's *purchases* of goods and services have been declining since the Korean War in the early 1950s. Total *expenditures* by the federal government—including transfer payments—as a fraction of GDP slowly rose from 1950 through the early 1990s and fell from 1992 to 2001, before rising again. The recession of 2007–2009 and the slow recovery that followed led to a surge in federal government expenditures, causing them to rise to their highest level as a percentage of GDP since the end of World War II in 1945.

Source: U.S. Bureau of Economic Analysis.

MyEconLab Real-time data

Figure 27.3

Federal Government Expenditures, 2014

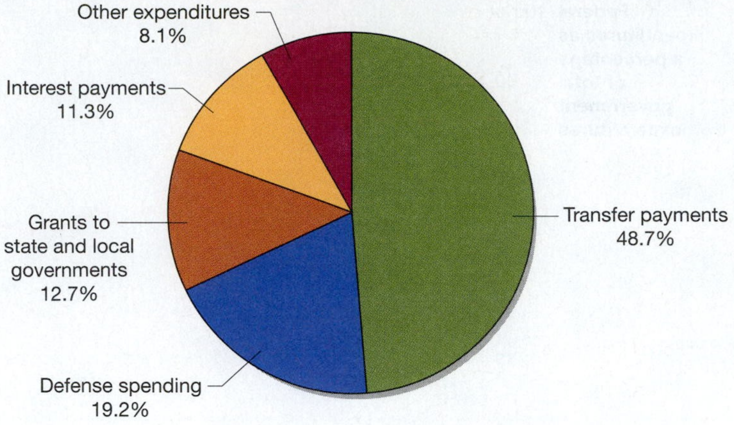

Federal government *purchases* can be divided into defense spending—which makes up 19.2 percent of the federal budget—and spending on everything else the federal government does—from paying the salaries of FBI agents, to operating the national parks, to supporting scientific research—which makes up 8.1 percent of the budget. In addition to purchases, there are three other categories of federal government *expenditures*: interest on the national debt, grants to state and local governments, and transfer payments. Transfer payments rose from 25 percent of federal government expenditures in the 1960s to 48.7 percent in 2014.

Source: U.S. Bureau of Economic Analysis.

as a percentage of GDP have actually been falling most of the time since the end of the Korean War in the early 1950s. Total federal *expenditures* as a percentage of GDP rose from 1950 to the early 1990s and then fell from 1992 to 2000, before rising again. The decline in expenditures between 1992 and 2001 was partly the result of the end of the Cold War between the Soviet Union and the United States, which allowed for a substantial reduction in defense spending. Real federal government spending on national defense declined by almost 25 percent between 1990 and 1998, before rising by more than 60 percent between 1998 and 2010 in response to the war on terrorism and the wars in Iraq and Afghanistan and then declining more than 15 percent by 2014 as those wars wound down. The recession of 2007–2009 and the slow recovery that followed led to a surge in federal government expenditures, which in 2011 rose to their highest level as a percentage of GDP since the end of World War II in 1945 before declining again in the following years as a result of limits on spending enacted by Congress and the president.

In addition to purchases, there are three other categories of federal government expenditures: *interest on the national debt*, *grants to state and local governments*, and *transfer payments*. Interest on the national debt represents payments to holders of the bonds the federal government has issued to borrow money. Grants to state and local governments are payments made by the federal government to support government activity at the state and local levels. For example, to help reduce crime, Congress implemented a program of grants to local governments to hire more police officers. The largest and fastest-growing category of federal expenditures is transfer payments. Some of these programs, such as Social Security and unemployment insurance, began in the 1930s. Others, such as Medicare, which finances health care for the elderly, or the food stamp (Supplemental Nutrition Assistance Program) and Temporary Assistance for Needy Families programs, which are intended to aid the poor, began in the 1960s or later.

Figure 27.3 shows that in 2014, transfer payments were 48.7 percent of federal government expenditures, having nearly doubled since the 1960s, when they were only 25 percent of federal government expenditures. As the U.S. population ages and medical costs continue to increase, federal government spending on the Social Security and Medicare programs will continue to rise, causing transfer payments to consume an increasing share of federal expenditures. Figure 27.3 shows that spending on most of the federal government's day-to-day activities—including running federal agencies such as the Environmental Protection Agency, the Federal Bureau of Investigation, the National Park Service, and the Immigration and Naturalization Service—makes up only 8.1 percent of federal government expenditures.

Figure 27.4 shows that in 2014, the federal government raised 42.8 percent of its revenue from individual income taxes. Payroll taxes to fund the Social Security and Medicare programs raised 35.1 percent of federal revenues. The tax on corporate profits raised 12.8 percent of federal revenues. The remaining 9.3 percent of federal revenues were raised from excise taxes on certain products, such as cigarettes and gasoline,

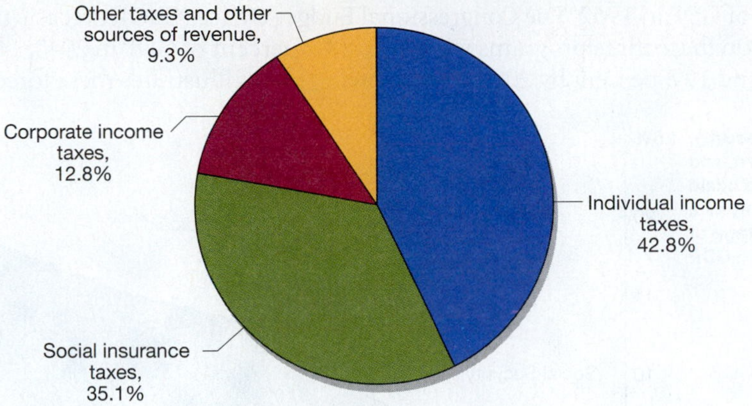

MyEconLab Real-time data

Figure 27.4

Federal Government Revenue, 2014

In 2014, individual income taxes raised 42.8 percent of the federal government's revenues. Corporate income taxes raised 12.8 percent of revenue. Payroll taxes to fund the Social Security and Medicare programs raised 35.1 percent of revenue. The remaining 9.3 percent of revenues were raised from excise taxes, tariffs on imports, and other sources.

Source: U.S. Bureau of Economic Analysis.

from tariffs on goods imported from other countries, from payments by the Federal Reserve from its profits on its security holdings, and from other sources, such as payments by companies that cut timber on federal lands. MyEconLab Concept Check

Making the Connection
MyEconLab Video

Is Spending on Social Security and Medicare a Fiscal Time Bomb?

The federal government established Social Security in 1935 to provide payments to retired workers. The program began as a "pay-as-you-go" system, meaning that payments to current retirees were made with taxes collected from current workers. In the early years of the program, many workers were paying into the system, and there were relatively few retirees. For example, in 1940, more than 35 million workers were paying into the system, and only 222,000 people were receiving benefits—a ratio of more than 150 workers to each retiree. In those early years, most retirees received far more in benefits than they had paid in taxes. The first beneficiary was a legal secretary named Ida May Fuller. She worked for three years after the program began and paid total taxes of only $24.75. During her retirement, she collected $22,888.92 in benefits.

The Social Security and Medicare programs have been very successful in reducing poverty among older Americans, but in recent years, the ability of the federal government to finance current promises has been called into doubt. After World War II, the United States experienced a "baby boom," as birthrates rose and remained high through the early 1960s. Falling birthrates after 1965 have caused long-run problems for the Social Security system because the number of workers per retiree has continually declined. Currently, there are only 2.8 workers per retiree, and that ratio could decline to 2 workers per retiree by 2035. Congress has attempted to deal with this problem by gradually raising the age to receive full benefits from 65 to 67 and by increasing payroll taxes. Social Security and Medicare are financed from a payroll tax on individuals' wages and self-employment income. Workers and firms are each liable for half the tax. In 1940, the payroll tax rate was 2 percent; in 2015, it was 15.3 percent. Beginning in 2013, individuals earning more than $200,000 in either wages or self-employment income have paid two additional Medicare taxes: an additional 0.9 percent tax on their wages and an additional 3.8 percent tax on their investment income.

The federal government established the Medicare program in 1965 to provide health care coverage to people age 65 and over. The long-term financial situation for Medicare is an even greater cause for concern than is Social Security. As Americans live longer and as new—and expensive—medical procedures are developed, the projected expenditures under the Medicare program will eventually far outstrip projected tax revenues. The federal government also faces increasing expenditures under the Medicaid program, which is administered by state governments and provides health care coverage to low-income people. In 2015, federal spending on Social Security, Medicare, and Medicaid equaled 10.1 percent of GDP. Spending on these three programs was less than

3 percent of GDP in 1962. The Congressional Budget Office (CBO) forecasts that federal spending on these three programs will rise to 14.2 percent of GDP in 2040, 16.2 percent by 2060, and 19.8 percent by 2090. The following graph illustrates these forecasts.

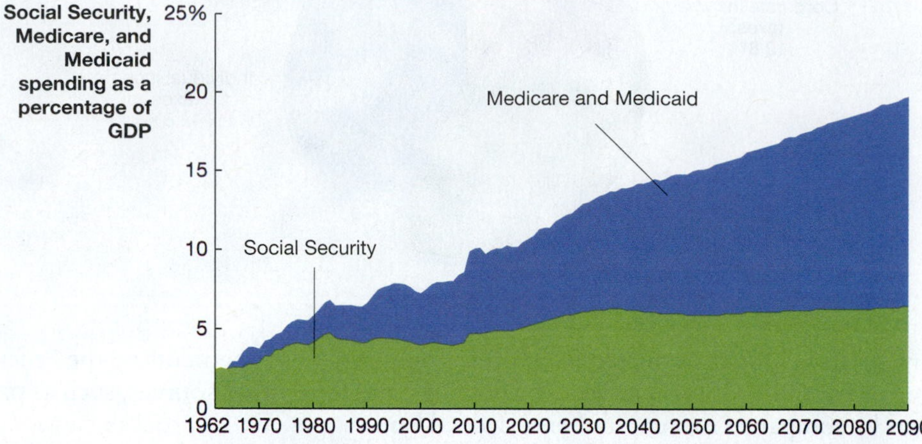

Note: The area labeled "Medicare and Medicaid" also includes federal spending on the Children's Health Insurance Program (CHIP) and federal subsidies to health care exchanges.

Over the past 40 years, the federal government has spent an average of about 21.5 percent of GDP on *all programs* combined—from buying aircraft carriers to paying the salaries of FBI agents to making Social Security and Medicare payments. So, if current trends continue, the federal government will eventually be spending, as a fraction of GDP, nearly as much on these three programs as it currently does on all programs combined.

The Board of Trustees of the Social Security Administration forecasts that through 2090, the gap between the benefits projected to be paid under the Social Security and Medicare programs and projected tax revenues is a staggering $49 *trillion*, or more than two and half times the value of GDP in 2015. If current projections are accurate, policymakers are faced with the choice of significantly restraining spending on these programs, greatly increasing taxes on households and firms, or implementing some combination of spending restraints and tax increases. The alternatives are all unpleasant. A report from the CBO concluded: "Even if taxation reached levels that were unprecedented in the United States, current spending policies could become financially unsustainable."

A lively political debate has taken place over the future of the Social Security and Medicare programs. Some policymakers have proposed increasing taxes to fund future benefit payments. The tax increases needed, however, could be as much as 50 percent higher than current rates, and tax increases of that magnitude could discourage work effort, entrepreneurship, and investment, thereby slowing economic growth. There have also been proposals to slow the rate of growth of future benefits, while guaranteeing benefits to current recipients. While this strategy would avoid the need to raise taxes significantly, it would also require younger workers to save more for their retirements. Some economists and policymakers have argued for slower benefit growth for higher-income workers while leaving future benefits unchanged for lower-income workers. Whatever changes are ultimately made in the Medicare and Social Security programs, the outcome of this policy debate will have important effects on the futures of today's college students.

Sources: Congressional Budget Office, "Supplemental Data for CBO's 2015 Long-Term Budget Outlook," June 2015; Congressional Budget Office, "Baseline Projections of Mandatory Outlays," January 2015; Board of Trustees, Federal Old-Age and Survivors Insurance and Federal Disability Insurance Trust Funds, "The 2015 Annual Report of the Board of Trustees of the Federal Old-Age and Survivors Insurance and Disability Insurance Trust Funds," July 22, 2015; and the Social Security Administration Web site (www.ssa.gov).

MyEconLab Study Plan

Your Turn: Test your understanding by doing related problem 1.7 on page 972 at the end of this chapter.

27.2 The Effects of Fiscal Policy on Real GDP and the Price Level

LEARNING OBJECTIVE: Explain how fiscal policy affects aggregate demand and how the government can use fiscal policy to stabilize the economy.

The federal government uses macroeconomic policies to offset the effects of the business cycle on the economy. We saw in Chapter 26 that the Federal Reserve carries out monetary policy through changes in interest rates and the money supply. Congress and the president carry out fiscal policy through changes in government purchases and taxes. Because changes in government purchases and taxes lead to changes in aggregate demand, they can affect the level of real GDP, employment, and the price level. When the economy is in a recession, *increases* in government purchases or *decreases* in taxes will increase aggregate demand. As we saw in Chapter 24, the inflation rate may increase when real GDP is beyond potential GDP. Decreases in government purchases or increase in taxes can slow the growth of aggregate demand and reduce the inflation rate.

Expansionary and Contractionary Fiscal Policy

Expansionary fiscal policy involves increasing government purchases or decreasing taxes. An increase in government purchases will increase aggregate demand directly because government purchases are a component of aggregate demand. A cut in taxes has an indirect effect on aggregate demand. Remember that the income households have available to spend after they have paid their taxes is called *disposable income* (see Chapter 19). Cutting the individual income tax will increase household disposable income and consumption spending. Cutting taxes on business income can increase aggregate demand by increasing investment spending.

Figure 27.5 shows the results of an expansionary fiscal policy, using the basic aggregate demand and aggregate supply model. In this model, there is no economic

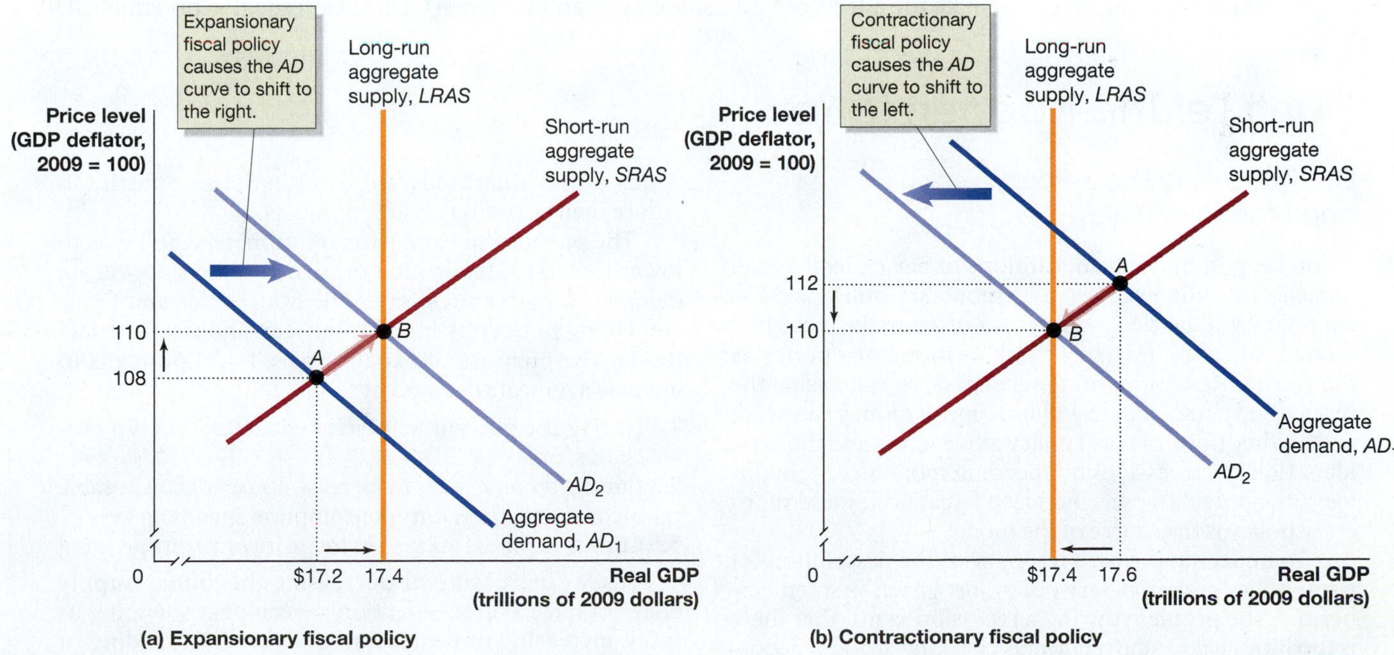

MyEconLab Animation

Figure 27.5 Fiscal Policy

In panel (a), short-run equilibrium is at point A, with real GDP of $17.2 trillion and a price level of 108. Real GDP is below potential GDP, so the economy is in a recession. An expansionary fiscal policy will cause aggregate demand to shift to the right, from AD_1 to AD_2, increasing real GDP from $17.2 trillion to $17.4 trillion and the price level from 108 to 110 (point *B*).

In panel (b), the economy begins at point A, with real GDP at $17.6 trillion and the price level at 112. Because real GDP is greater than potential GDP, the economy will experience rising wages and prices. A contractionary fiscal policy will cause aggregate demand to shift to the left, from AD_1 to AD_2, decreasing real GDP from $17.6 trillion to $17.4 trillion and the price level from 112 to 110 (point *B*).

growth, so the long-run aggregate supply (*LRAS*) curve does not shift. Notice that this figure is very similar to Figure 26.7 on page 905, which shows the effects of an expansionary monetary policy. The goal of both expansionary monetary policy and expansionary fiscal policy is to increase aggregate demand relative to what it would have been without the policy.

In panel (a) of Figure 27.5, we assume that short-run equilibrium occurs at point *A*, where the aggregate demand (AD_1) curve intersects the short-run aggregate supply (*SRAS*) curve. Real GDP is below potential GDP, so the economy is in a recession, with some firms operating below normal capacity and some workers having been laid off. To bring real GDP back to potential GDP, Congress and the president increase government purchases or cut taxes, which will shift the aggregate demand curve to the right, from AD_1 to AD_2. Real GDP increases from $17.2 trillion to potential GDP of $17.4 trillion, and the price level rises from 108 to 110 (point *B*). The policy has successfully returned real GDP to its potential level. Rising production will lead to increasing employment, reducing the unemployment rate.

Contractionary fiscal policy involves decreasing government purchases or increasing taxes. Policymakers use contractionary fiscal policy to reduce increases in aggregate demand that seem likely to lead to inflation. In panel (b) of Figure 27.5, short-run equilibrium occurs at point A, with real GDP of $17.6 trillion, which is above potential GDP of $17.4 trillion. With some firms producing beyond their normal capacity and the unemployment rate very low, wages and prices will be increasing. To bring real GDP back to potential GDP, Congress and the president decrease government purchases or increase taxes, which will shift the aggregate demand curve to the left, from AD_1 to AD_2. Real GDP falls from $17.6 trillion to $17.4 trillion, and the price level falls from 112 to 110 (point *B*).

We can conclude that Congress and the president can attempt to stabilize the economy by using fiscal policy to affect the price level and the level of real GDP. Of course, in practice it is extremely difficult for Congress and the president to use fiscal policy to eliminate the effects of the business cycle and keep real GDP always equal to potential GDP.

MyEconLab Concept Check

Don't Let This Happen to You

Don't Confuse Fiscal Policy and Monetary Policy

If you keep in mind the definitions of *money*, *income*, and *spending*, the difference between monetary policy and fiscal policy will be clearer. Students often make these two related mistakes: (1) They think of monetary policy as the Federal Reserve fighting recessions by increasing the money supply so people will have more money to spend; and (2) they think of fiscal policy as Congress and the president fighting recessions by spending more money. In this view, the only difference between fiscal policy and monetary policy is the source of the money.

To understand what's wrong with the descriptions of fiscal policy and monetary policy just given, first remember that the problem during a recession is not that there is too little *money*—currency plus checking account deposits—but too little *spending*. There may be too little spending for a number of reasons. For example, households may cut back on their spending on cars and houses because they are pessimistic about the future. Firms may reduce their spending because they have lowered their estimates of the future profitability of new machinery and factories. Or major trading partners of the United States—such as Japan and Canada—may be suffering from recessions, which cause households and firms in those countries to reduce their spending on U.S. products.

The purpose of expansionary monetary policy is to lower interest rates, which in turn increases aggregate demand. When interest rates fall, households and firms are willing to borrow more to buy cars, houses, and factories. The purpose of expansionary fiscal policy is to increase aggregate demand by:

1. Having the government directly increase its own purchases, or
2. Cutting income taxes to increase household disposable income and, therefore, consumption spending, or
3. Cutting business taxes to increase investment spending

Just as increasing or decreasing the money supply does not have a direct effect on government spending or taxes, increasing or decreasing government spending or taxes does not have a direct effect on the money supply. Fiscal policy and monetary policy have the same goals, but they attempt to reach those goals in different ways.

MyEconLab Study Plan

Your Turn: Test your understanding by doing related problem 2.6 on page 973 at the end of this chapter.

Table 27.1

Countercyclical Fiscal Policy

Problem	Type of Policy Required	Actions by Congress and the President	Result
Recession	Expansionary	Increase government purchases or cut taxes	Real GDP and the price level rise.
Rising inflation	Contractionary	Decrease government purchases or raise taxes	Real GDP and the price level fall.

A Summary of How Fiscal Policy Affects Aggregate Demand

Table 27.1 summarizes how fiscal policy affects aggregate demand. Just as we did with monetary policy, we must add a very important qualification to this summary of fiscal policy: The table isolates the effect of fiscal policy *by holding constant monetary policy and all other factors affecting the variables involved*. In other words, we are again invoking the *ceteris paribus* condition we discussed in Chapter 3. This point is important because, for example, in the actual economy, a contractionary fiscal policy does not cause the price level to fall. A contractionary fiscal policy causes the price level *to rise by less than it would have without the policy.*

MyEconLab Concept Check

MyEconLab Study Plan

27.3 Fiscal Policy in the Dynamic Aggregate Demand and Aggregate Supply Model*

LEARNING OBJECTIVE: Use the dynamic aggregate demand and aggregate supply model to analyze fiscal policy.

The overview of fiscal policy we just finished contains a key idea: Congress and the president can use fiscal policy to affect aggregate demand, thereby changing the price level and the level of real GDP. The discussion of expansionary and contractionary fiscal policy illustrated by Figure 27.5 on page 945 is simplified, however, because it ignores two important facts about the economy: (1) The economy experiences continuing inflation, with the price level rising every year, and (2) the economy experiences long-run growth, with the *LRAS* curve shifting to the right every year. In Chapter 24, we developed a *dynamic aggregate demand and aggregate supply model* that took these two facts into account. In this section, we use the dynamic model to gain a more complete understanding of fiscal policy.

To briefly review the dynamic model, recall that over time, potential GDP increases, which we show by shifting the *LRAS* curve to the right. The factors that cause the *LRAS* curve to shift also cause firms to supply more goods and services at any given price level in the short run, which we show by shifting the *SRAS* curve to the right. Finally, during most years, the aggregate demand curve also shifts to the right, indicating that aggregate expenditure is higher at every price level.

Figure 27.6 shows the results of an expansionary fiscal policy using the dynamic aggregate demand and aggregate supply model. Notice that this figure is very similar to Figure 26.9 on page 913, which showed the effects of an expansionary monetary policy. The goal of both expansionary monetary policy and expansionary fiscal policy is to increase aggregate demand relative to what it would have been without the policy.

In the hypothetical situation shown in Figure 27.6, equilibrium is initially at point A, with real GDP equal to potential GDP of $17.0 trillion and the price level equal to 110. In the second year, *LRAS* increases to $17.4 trillion, but aggregate demand increases only from AD_1 to $AD_{2\text{(without policy)}}$, which is not enough to keep real GDP equal to potential GDP. Let's assume that the Fed does not react to the situation with an expansionary monetary policy. In that case, short-run equilibrium will occur at point *B*, with real GDP of $17.3 trillion and a price level of 113. The $100 billion gap between real GDP and potential GDP means that some firms are operating at less than their full capacity. Incomes and profits will be falling, firms will begin to lay off workers, and the unemployment rate will increase.

*This section may be omitted without loss of continuity.

MyEconLab Animation

Figure 27.6

An Expansionary Fiscal Policy in the Dynamic Model

Equilibrium is initially at point *A*, with real GDP equal to potential GDP of $17.0 trillion and the price level equal to 110. Without an expansionary policy, aggregate demand will shift from AD_1 to $AD_{2(\text{without policy})}$, which is not enough to keep real GDP equal to potential GDP because long-run aggregate supply has shifted from $LRAS_1$ to $LRAS_2$. The new short-run equilibrium is at point *B*, with real GDP of $17.3 trillion and a price level of 113. Increasing government purchases or cutting taxes will shift aggregate demand to $AD_{2(\text{with policy})}$. Equilibrium will be at point *C*, with real GDP of $17.4 trillion, which is its potential level, and a price level of 115. The price level is higher than it would have been without an expansionary fiscal policy.

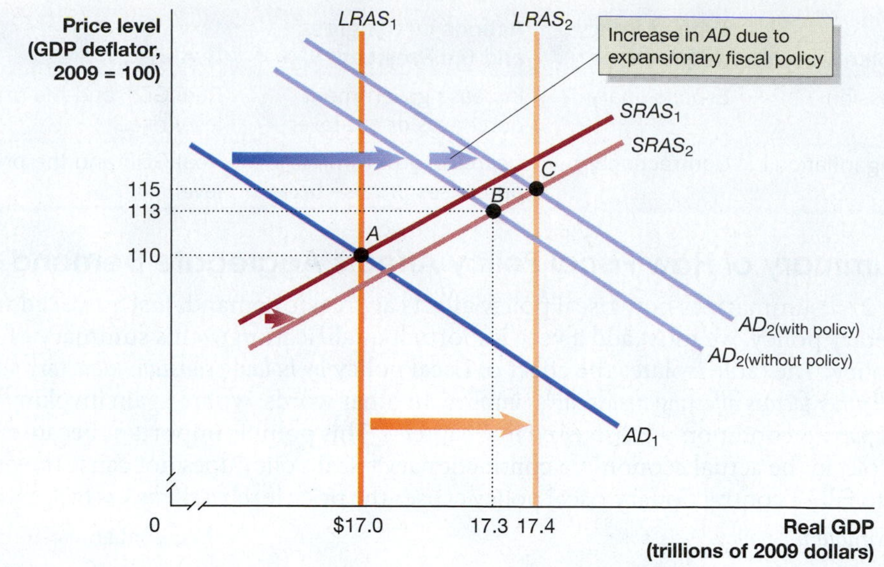

Increasing government purchases or cutting taxes can shift aggregate demand to $AD_{2(\text{with policy})}$. Equilibrium will be at point *C*, with real GDP of $17.4 trillion, which is its potential level, and a price level of 115. The price level is higher than it would have been without an expansionary fiscal policy.

Contractionary fiscal policy involves decreasing government purchases or increasing taxes. Policymakers use contractionary fiscal policy to reduce increases in aggregate demand that seem likely to lead to inflation. In Figure 27.7, equilibrium is initially at point *A*, with real GDP equal to potential GDP of $17.0 trillion and the price level equal to 110. Once again, *LRAS* increases to $17.4 trillion in the second year. In this scenario, the shift in aggregate demand to $AD_{2(\text{without policy})}$ results in a short-run macroeconomic equilibrium at point *B*, with real GDP of $17.5 trillion, which is greater than potential GDP. If we assume that the Fed does not respond to the situation with a contractionary monetary policy, the economy will experience a rising inflation rate. Decreasing government purchases or increasing taxes can keep real GDP from moving beyond its potential level. The result, shown in Figure 27.7, is that in the new equilibrium at point *C*, the inflation rate is 2.7 percent rather than 4.5 percent. MyEconLab Concept Check

MyEconLab Study Plan

MyEconLab Animation

Figure 27.7

A Contractionary Fiscal Policy in the Dynamic Model

Equilibrium is initially at point *A*, with real GDP equal to potential GDP of $17.0 trillion and the price level equal to 110. Without a contractionary policy, aggregate demand will shift from AD_1 to $AD_{2(\text{without policy})}$, which results in a short-run equilibrium at point *B*, with real GDP of $17.5 trillion, which is greater than potential GDP, and a price level of 115. Decreasing government purchases or increasing taxes can shift aggregate demand to $AD_{2(\text{with policy})}$. Equilibrium will be at point *C*, with real GDP of $17.4 trillion, which is its potential level, and a price level of 113. The inflation rate will be 2.7 percent, as opposed to the 4.5 percent it would have been without the contractionary fiscal policy.

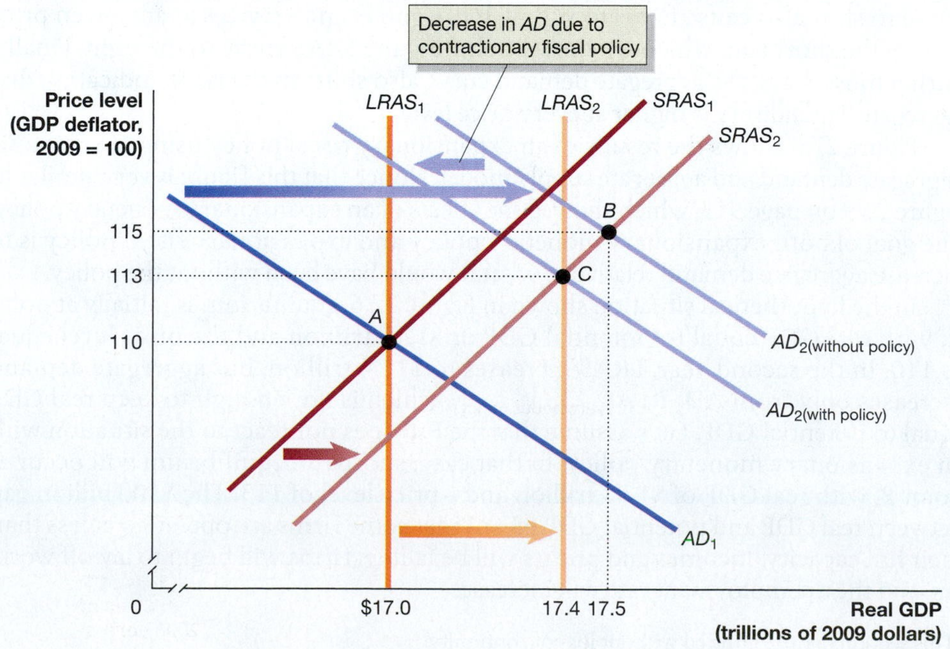

27.4 The Government Purchases and Tax Multipliers

LEARNING OBJECTIVE: Explain how the government purchases and tax multipliers work.

We saw in the chapter opener that Congress and the president authorized spending to rebuild Doyle Drive in San Francisco in order to increase aggregate demand during the recession of 2007–2009. Suppose that Congress and the president decide to spend $100 billion on rebuilding Doyle Drive and similar projects. (The total increase in federal spending under the American Recovery and Reinvestment Act (ARRA) of 2009 was actually about $500 *billion*, including the $83 million in ARRA funds contributed to the project to reconstruct Doyle Drive.) How much will equilibrium real GDP increase as a result of this increase in government purchases? We might expect real GDP to increase by more than $100 billion because the initial increase in aggregate demand should lead to additional increases in income and spending. For example, to reconstruct Doyle Drive, the California Department of Transportation hired Kiewit, a private construction firm. Kiewit and its subcontractors, in turn, hired workers for the project. The firms that carried out the many other projects authorized under the ARRA also hired new workers. Workers who were formerly unemployed are likely to increase their spending on cars, furniture, appliances, and other products. Sellers of these products will increase their production and hire more workers, and so on. At each step, real GDP and income will rise, thereby increasing consumption spending and aggregate demand.

Economists refer to the initial increase in government purchases as *autonomous* because it is a result of a decision by the government and is not directly caused by changes in the level of real GDP. The increases in consumption spending that result from the initial autonomous increase in government purchases are *induced* because they are caused by the initial increase in autonomous spending. Economists call the series of induced increases in consumption spending that results from an initial increase in autonomous expenditures the **multiplier effect**.

Multiplier effect The series of induced increases in consumption spending that results from an initial increase in autonomous expenditures.

Figure 27.8 illustrates how an increase in government purchases affects the aggregate demand curve. The initial increase causes the aggregate demand curve to shift to the right because total spending in the economy is now higher at every price level. The shift to the right from AD_1 to the dashed AD curve represents the effect of the initial increase of $100 billion in government purchases. Because this initial increase in government purchases raises incomes and leads to further increases in consumption spending, the aggregate demand curve will ultimately shift from AD_1 all the way to AD_2.

To better understand the multiplier effect, let's start with a simplified analysis in which we assume that the price level is constant. In other words, initially we will ignore

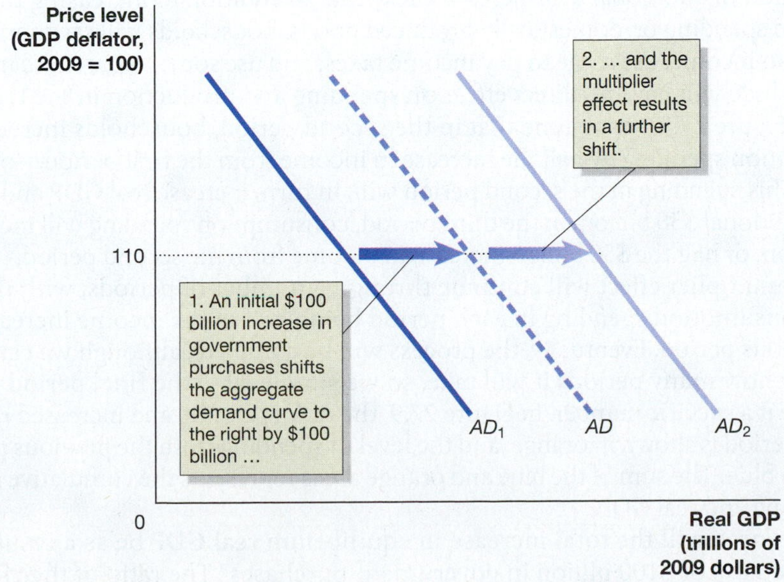

MyEconLab Animation

Figure 27.8

The Multiplier Effect and Aggregate Demand

An initial increase in government purchases of $100 billion causes the aggregate demand curve to shift to the right, from AD_1 to the dashed AD curve, and represents the effect of the initial increase of $100 billion in government purchases. Because this initial increase raises incomes and leads to further increases in consumption spending, the aggregate demand curve will ultimately shift further to the right, to AD_2.

Period	Additional Spending This Period	Cumulative Increase in Spending and Real GDP
1	$100 billion in government purchases	$100 billion
2	$50 billion in consumption spending	$150 billion
3	$25 billion in consumption spending	$175 billion
4	$12.5 billion in consumption spending	$187.5 billion
⋮	⋮	⋮
n	0	$200 billion

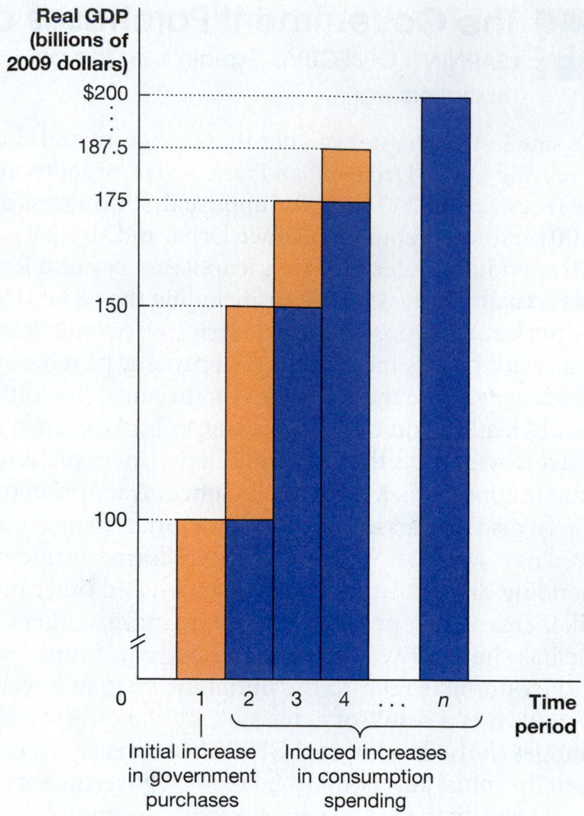

MyEconLab Animation

Figure 27.9 The Multiplier Effect of an Increase in Government Purchases

Following an initial increase in government purchases, spending and real GDP increase over a number of periods due to the multiplier effect. The new spending and increased real GDP in each period is shown in orange, and the level of spending from the previous period is shown in blue. The sum of the blue and orange areas represents the cumulative increase in spending and real GDP. In total, equilibrium real GDP will increase by $200 billion as a result of an initial increase of $100 billion in government purchases.

the effect of an upward-sloping *SRAS* curve. Figure 27.9 shows how spending and real GDP increase over a number of periods, beginning with the initial increase in government purchases in the first period, which raises real GDP and total income in the economy by $100 billion. How much additional consumption spending will result from $100 billion in additional income? We know that in addition to increasing their consumption spending on domestically produced goods, households will save some of the increase in income, use some to pay income taxes, and use some to purchase imported goods, which will have no direct effect on spending and production in the U.S. economy. In Figure 27.9, we assume that in the second period, households increase their consumption spending by half the increase in income from the first period—or by $50 billion. This spending in the second period will, in turn, increase real GDP and income by an additional $50 billion. In the third period, consumption spending will increase by $25 billion, or half the $50 billion increase in income from the second period.

The multiplier effect will continue through a number of periods, with the additional consumption spending in each period being half of the income increase from the previous period. Eventually, the process will be complete, although we cannot say precisely how many periods it will take, so we simply label the final period *n* rather than give it a specific number. In Figure 27.9, the new spending and increased real GDP in each period is shown in orange, and the level of spending from the previous period is shown in blue. The sum of the blue and orange areas represents the cumulative increase in spending and real GDP.

How large will the total increase in equilibrium real GDP be as a result of the initial increase of $100 billion in government purchases? The ratio of the change in equilibrium real GDP to the initial change in government purchases is called the *government purchases multiplier*:

$$\text{Government purchases multiplier} = \frac{\text{Change in equilibrium real GDP}}{\text{Change in government purchases}}.$$

If, for example, the government purchases multiplier has a value of 2, an increase in government purchases of $100 billion should increase equilibrium real GDP by 2 × $100 billion = $200 billion. We show this result in Figure 27.9 by having the cumulative increase in real GDP equal $200 billion.

Tax cuts also have a multiplier effect because they increase the disposable income of households. When household disposable income rises, so will consumption spending. These increases in consumption spending will set off further increases in real GDP and income, just as increases in government purchases do. Suppose we consider a change in taxes of a specific amount—say, a tax cut of $100 billion—with the tax *rate* remaining unchanged. The expression for this tax multiplier is:

$$\text{Tax multiplier} = \frac{\text{Change in equilibrium real GDP}}{\text{Change in taxes}}.$$

The tax multiplier is a negative number because changes in taxes and changes in real GDP move in opposite directions: An increase in taxes reduces disposable income, consumption, and real GDP, and a decrease in taxes raises disposable income, consumption, and real GDP. For example, if the tax multiplier is −1.6, a $100 billion *cut* in taxes will increase real GDP by −1.6 × (−$100 billion) = $160 billion. We would expect the tax multiplier to be smaller in absolute value than the government purchases multiplier. To see why, think about the difference between a $100 billion increase in government purchases and a $100 billion decrease in taxes. The whole of the $100 billion in government purchases results in an increase in aggregate demand. But households will save rather than spend some portion of a $100 billion decrease in taxes, and they will spend some portion on imported goods. The fraction of the tax cut that households save or spend on imports will not increase aggregate demand. Therefore, the first period of the multiplier process will involve a smaller increase in aggregate demand than occurs when there is an increase in government purchases, and the total increase in equilibrium real GDP will be smaller.

The Effect of Changes in the Tax Rate

A change in the tax *rate* has a more complicated effect on equilibrium real GDP than does a tax cut of a fixed amount. To begin with, the value of the tax rate affects the size of the multiplier effect. The higher the tax rate, the smaller the multiplier effect. To see why, think about the size of the additional spending increases that take place in each period following an increase in government purchases. The higher the tax rate, the smaller the amount of any increase in income that households have available to spend, which reduces the size of the multiplier effect. So, a cut in the tax rate affects equilibrium real GDP through two channels: (1) A cut in the tax rate increases the disposable income of households, which leads them to increase their consumption spending, and (2) a cut in the tax rate increases the size of the multiplier effect. MyEconLab Concept Check

Taking into Account the Effects of Aggregate Supply

To this point, as we discussed the multiplier effect, we assumed that the price level was constant. We know, though, that because the *SRAS* curve is upward sloping, when the *AD* curve shifts to the right, the price level will rise. As a result of the rise in the price level, equilibrium real GDP will not increase by the full amount that the multiplier effect indicates. Figure 27.10 illustrates how an upward-sloping *SRAS* curve affects the size of the multiplier. To keep the graph relatively simple, we assume that the *SRAS* and *LRAS* curves do not shift. Short-run equilibrium is initially at point A, with real GDP

MyEconLab Animation

Figure 27.10

The Multiplier Effect and Aggregate Supply

Short-run equilibrium is initially at point *A*. An increase in government purchases causes the aggregate demand curve to shift to the right, from AD_1 to the dashed *AD* curve. The multiplier effect results in the aggregate demand curve shifting further to the right, to AD_2 (point *B*). Because of the upward-sloping supply curve, the shift in aggregate demand results in a higher price level. In the new equilibrium at point *C*, both real GDP and the price level have increased. The increase in real GDP is less than that indicated by the multiplier effect with a constant price level.

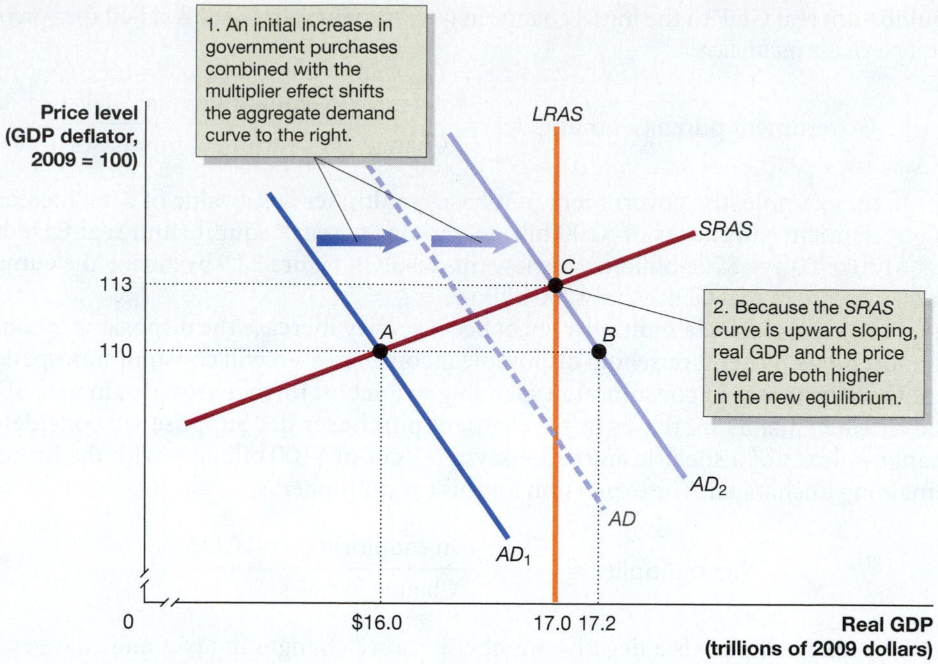

below its potential level. An increase in government purchases shifts the aggregate demand curve from AD_1 to the dashed *AD* curve. Just as in Figure 27.8, the multiplier effect causes a further shift in the aggregate demand curve to AD_2. If the price level remained constant, real GDP would increase from $16.0 trillion at point *A* to $17.2 trillion at point *B*. However, because the *SRAS* curve is upward sloping, the price level rises from 110 to 113, reducing the total quantity of goods and services demanded in the economy. The new equilibrium occurs at point *C*, with real GDP having risen to $17.0 trillion, or by $200 billion less than if the price level had remained unchanged. We can conclude that the actual change in real GDP resulting from an increase in government purchases or a cut in taxes will be less than that indicated by the simple multiplier effect with a constant price level. MyEconLab Concept Check

The Multipliers Work in Both Directions

Increases in government purchases and cuts in taxes have a positive multiplier effect on equilibrium real GDP. Decreases in government purchases and increases in taxes also have a multiplier effect on equilibrium real GDP, but in this case, the effect is negative. An increase in taxes will reduce household disposable income and consumption. As households buy fewer cars, furniture, refrigerators, and other goods, the firms that sell these goods will cut back their production and begin laying off workers. Falling incomes will lead to further reductions in consumption. A reduction in government spending on defense would set off a similar process of decreases in real GDP and income. The reduction would affect defense contractors first because they sell directly to the government, and then it would spread to other firms.

We look more closely at the government purchases multiplier and the tax multiplier in the appendix to this chapter. MyEconLab Concept Check

Solved Problem 27.4

MyEconLab Interactive Animation

Fiscal Policy Multipliers

Briefly explain whether you agree with the following statement: "Real GDP is currently $17.2 trillion, and potential GDP is $17.4 trillion. If Congress and the president would increase government purchases by $200 billion or cut taxes by $200 billion, the economy could be brought to equilibrium at potential GDP."

Solving the Problem

Step 1: Review the chapter material. This problem is about the multiplier process, so you may want to review the section "The Government Purchases and Tax Multipliers," which begins on page 949.

Step 2: Explain how the necessary increase in purchases or cut in taxes is less than $200 billion because of the multiplier effect. The statement is incorrect because it does not consider the multiplier effect. Because of the multiplier effect, an increase in government purchases or a decrease in taxes of less than $200 billion is necessary to increase equilibrium real GDP by $200 billion. For instance, assume that the government purchases multiplier is 2 and the tax multiplier is −1.6. We can then calculate the necessary increase in government purchases as follows:

$$\text{Government puchases multipiler} = \frac{\text{Change in equilibrium real GDP}}{\text{Change in government purchases}}$$

$$2 = \frac{\$200 \text{ billon}}{\text{Change in government purchases}}$$

$$\text{Change in government purchases} = \frac{\$200 \text{ billon}}{2} = \$100 \text{ billon.}$$

And the necessary change in taxes:

$$\text{Tax multipler} = \frac{\text{Change in equilibrium real GDP}}{\text{Change in taxes}}$$

$$-1.6 = \frac{\$200 \text{ billon}}{\text{Change in taxes}}$$

$$\text{Change in taxes} = \frac{\$200 \text{ billion}}{-1.6} = -\$125 \text{ billion.}$$

Your Turn: For more practice, do related problems 4.6 and 4.7 on page 975 at the end of this chapter.

MyEconLab Study Plan

27.5 The Limits to Using Fiscal Policy to Stabilize the Economy

LEARNING OBJECTIVE: Discuss the difficulties that can arise in implementing fiscal policy.

Poorly timed fiscal policy, like poorly timed monetary policy, can do more harm than good. As we discussed in Chapter 26, it takes time for policymakers to collect statistics and identify changes in the economy. If the government decides to increase spending or cut taxes to fight a recession that is about to end, the effect may be to increase the inflation rate. Similarly, cutting spending or raising taxes to slow down an economy that has actually already moved into a recession can increase the length and depth of the recession.

Getting the timing right can be more difficult with fiscal policy than with monetary policy for two main reasons. Control over monetary policy is concentrated in the hands of the Federal Open Market Committee, which can change monetary policy at any of its meetings. By contrast, the president and a majority of the 535 members of Congress have to agree on changes in fiscal policy. The delays caused by the legislative process can be very long. For example, in 1962, President John F. Kennedy concluded that the U.S. economy was operating below potential GDP and proposed a tax cut to stimulate aggregate demand. Congress eventually agreed to the tax cut—but not until 1964. The events of 2001 and 2009 show, though, that it is sometimes possible to authorize changes in fiscal policy relatively quickly. When George W. Bush came into office in January 2001, the economy was on the verge of a recession, and he immediately proposed a tax cut. Congress passed the tax cut, and the president signed it into law in early June 2001. Similarly, Barack Obama proposed a stimulus package as soon as he came into office in January 2009, and Congress had passed the proposal by February.

Even after a change in fiscal policy has been approved, it takes time to implement it. Suppose Congress and the president agree to increase aggregate demand by spending $30 billion more on constructing subway systems in several cities. It will probably take at least several months to prepare detailed plans for the construction. Local governments will then ask for bids from private construction companies. Once the winning bidders have been selected, they will usually need several months to begin the project. Only then will significant amounts of spending actually take place. This delay may push the spending beyond the end of the recession that the spending was intended to fight. Delays of this type are less of a concern during long and severe recessions, such as that of 2007–2009.

Making the Connection
MyEconLab Video

Why Was the Recession of 2007–2009 So Severe?

As this stock trader knows, the financial crisis made the recession of 2007–2009 more severe and long-lasting than many other recessions.

Even some economists who are normally skeptical of fiscal policy believed that the severity of the 2007–2009 recession required Congress and the president to increase spending and cut taxes to increase aggregate demand. As we saw in Chapters 25 and 26, the recession was accompanied by a financial crisis. The U.S. economy had not experienced a significant financial crisis since the Great Depression of the 1930s. Both the Great Depression and the recession of 2007–2009 were severe. Do recessions accompanied by financial crises tend to be more severe than recessions that do not involve financial crises?

In an attempt to answer this question, Carmen Reinhart and Kenneth Rogoff of Harvard University have gathered data on recessions and financial crises in a number of countries. The table at the top of the next page shows the average change in key economic variables during the period following a financial crisis for a number of countries, including the United States during the Great Depression and European and Asian countries in the post–World War II era. The table shows that for these countries, on average, the recessions following financial crises were quite severe:

- Unemployment rates increased by 7 percentage points—for example, from 5 percent to 12 percent—and continued increasing for nearly five years after a crisis had begun.
- Real GDP per capita also declined sharply, and the average length of a recession following a financial crisis has been nearly two years.
- Adjusted for inflation, stock prices declined by more than half, and housing prices declined by more than one-third.
- Government debt soared by 86 percent. The increased government debt was partly the result of increased government spending, including spending to bail out failed financial institutions. But most of the increased debt was due to government budget deficits resulting from sharp declines in tax revenues as wages and profits fell during the recession. (We discuss government budget deficits and government debt in Section 27.6.)

Economic Variable	Average Change	Average Duration of Change	Number of Countries
Unemployment rate	+7 percentage points	4.8 years	14
Real GDP per capita	−9.3%	1.9 years	14
Real stock prices	−55.9%	3.4 years	22
Real house prices	−35.5%	6 years	21
Real government debt	+86%	3 years	13

The following table shows some key indicators for the 2007–2009 U.S. recession compared with other U.S. recessions of the post–World War II period:

	Duration	Decline in Real GDP	Peak Unemployment Rate
Average for postwar recessions	10.4 months	−1.7%	7.6%
Recession of 2007–2009	18 months	−4.2%	10.0%

Consistent with Reinhart and Rogoff's findings that recessions following financial panics tend to be unusually severe, the 2007–2009 recession was the worst in the United States since the Great Depression of the 1930s. The recession lasted nearly twice as long as the average of earlier postwar recessions, GDP declined by more than twice the average, and the peak unemployment rate was about one-third higher than the average.

While some economists argue that better monetary or fiscal policies might have shortened the recession and made it less severe, most economists agree that the financial panic plays a key role in explaining the severity of the 2007–2009 recession.

Note: In the second table, the duration of recessions is based on National Bureau of Economic Research business cycle dates, the decline in real GDP is measured as the simple percentage change from the quarter of the cyclical peak to the quarter of the cyclical trough, and the peak unemployment rate is the highest unemployment rate in any month following the cyclical peak.

Sources: The first table is adapted from data in Carmen M. Reinhart and Kenneth S. Rogoff, *This Time Is Different: Eight Centuries of Financial Folly*, Princeton, NJ: Princeton University Press, 2009, Figures 14.1–14.5; and the second table uses data from the U.S. Bureau of Economic Analysis and National Bureau of Economic Research.

Your Turn: Test your understanding by doing related problem 5.6 on page 976 at the end of this chapter.

MyEconLab Study Plan

Does Government Spending Reduce Private Spending?

In addition to the timing issue, using increases in government purchases to increase aggregate demand presents another potential problem. We have been assuming that when the federal government increases its purchases by $30 billion, the multiplier effect will cause the increase in aggregate demand to be greater than $30 billion. However, the size of the multiplier effect may be limited if the increase in government purchases causes one of the nongovernment, or private, components of aggregate expenditures—consumption, investment, or net exports—to fall. A decline in private expenditures as a result of an increase in government purchases is called **crowding out**.

MyEconLab Concept Check

Crowding out A decline in private expenditures as a result of an increase in government purchases.

Crowding Out in the Short Run

Consider the case of a temporary increase in government purchases. Suppose the federal government decides to fight a recession by spending $30 billion more this year on subway construction. When the $30 billion has been spent, the program will end, and government purchases will drop back to their previous level. As the spending takes place, income and real GDP will increase. These increases in income and real GDP will cause households and firms to increase their demand for currency and checking

MyEconLab Animation

Figure 27.11

An Expansionary Fiscal Policy Increases Interest Rates

An increase in government purchases will increase the demand for money from Money demand_1 to Money demand_2 as real GDP and income rise. With the supply of money constant, at $950 billion, the result is an increase in the equilibrium interest rate from 3 percent to 5 percent, which crowds out some consumption, investment, and net exports.

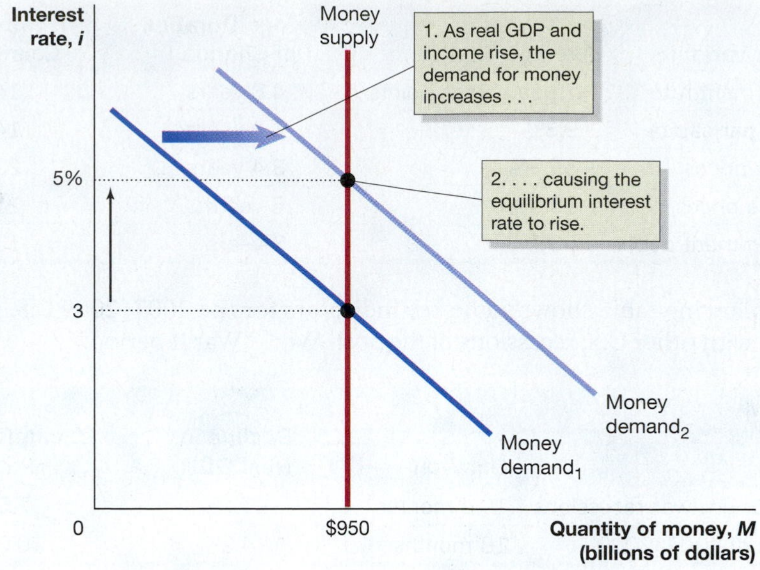

account balances to accommodate the increased buying and selling. Figure 27.11 shows the result, using the money market graph introduced in Chapter 26.

At higher levels of real GDP and income, households and firms demand more money at every interest rate. When the demand for money increases, the equilibrium interest rate will rise. Higher interest rates will result in a decline in each component of private expenditures. Consumption spending and investment spending will decline because households will borrow less to buy houses, cars, furniture, and appliances, and firms will borrow less to buy factories, warehouses, and machine tools. Net exports will also decline because higher interest rates in the United States will attract foreign investors. German, Japanese, and Canadian investors will want to exchange the currencies of their countries for U.S. dollars to invest in U.S. Treasury bills and other U.S. financial assets. This increased demand for U.S. dollars will cause an increase in the exchange rate between the dollar and other currencies. When the dollar increases in value, the prices of U.S. products in foreign countries rise—causing a reduction in U.S. exports—and the prices of foreign products in the United States fall—causing an increase in U.S. imports. Falling exports and rising imports mean that net exports are falling.

The greater the sensitivity of consumption, investment, and net exports to changes in interest rates, the more crowding out will occur. In a deep recession, many firms may be pessimistic about the future and have so much excess capacity that investment spending will fall to very low levels and will be unlikely to fall much further, even if interest rates rise. In this case, crowding out is unlikely to be a problem. If the economy is close to potential GDP, however, and firms are optimistic about the future, an increase in interest rates may result in a significant decline in investment spending.

Figure 27.12 shows that crowding out may reduce the effectiveness of an expansionary fiscal policy. Short-run equilibrium is initially at point A, with real GDP at $17.2 trillion. Real GDP is below potential GDP, so the economy is in a recession. Suppose that Congress and the president decide to increase government purchases to increase real GDP to potential GDP. In the absence of crowding out, the increase in government purchases will shift the aggregate demand curve to $AD_{2(\text{no crowding out})}$, and equilibrium will be at point *B*, with real GDP equal to potential GDP of $17.4 trillion. But the higher interest rate resulting from the increased government purchases will reduce consumption, investment, and net exports, causing the aggregate demand curve to shift back to $AD_{2(\text{crowding out})}$. The result is a new short-run equilibrium at point *C*, with real GDP of $17.3 trillion, which is $100 billion short of potential GDP. (Note that the price level increase shown in Figure 27.10 on page 952 also contributes to reducing the effect of an increase in government purchases on equilibrium real GDP.) MyEconLab Concept Check

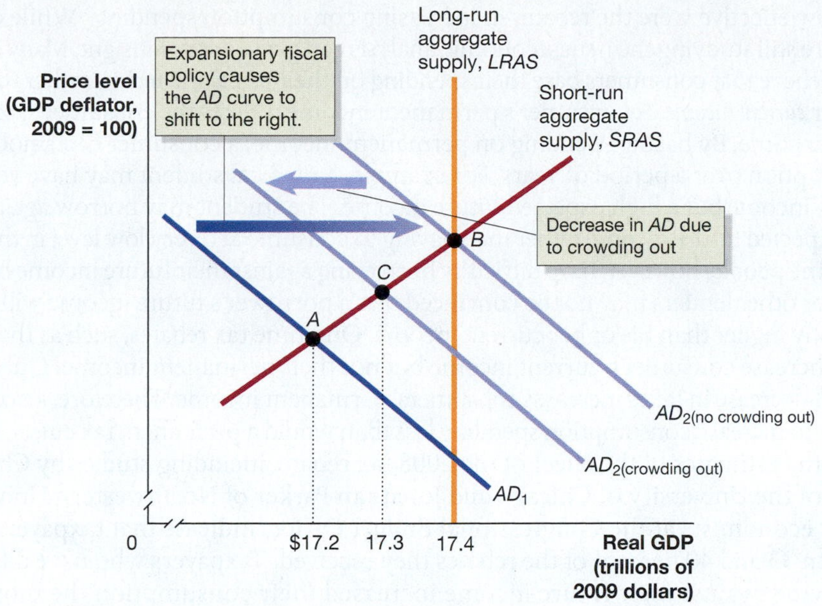

MyEconLab Animation

Figure 27.12

The Effect of Crowding Out in the Short Run

Equilibrium is initially at point *A*, with real GDP of $17.2 trillion below potential GDP, so the economy is in a recession. In the absence of crowding out, an increase in government purchases will shift aggregate demand to $AD_{2(\text{no crowding out})}$, and equilibrium is at potential GDP of $17.4 trillion (point *B*). But the higher interest rate resulting from the increased government purchases will reduce consumption, investment, and net exports, causing aggregate demand to shift to $AD_{2(\text{no crowding out})}$. The result is a new short-run equilibrium at point *C*, with real GDP of $17.3 trillion, which is $100 billion short of potential GDP.

Crowding Out in the Long Run

Most economists agree that in the short run, an increase in government purchases results in partial, but not complete, crowding out. What is the long-run effect of a *permanent* increase in government spending? In this case, most economists agree that the result is complete crowding out. In the long run, the decline in investment, consumption, and net exports exactly offsets the increase in government purchases, and aggregate demand remains unchanged. Recall that *in the long run, real GDP returns to potential GDP* (see Chapter 24). Suppose that real GDP currently equals potential GDP and that government spending is 35 percent of GDP. In that case, private expenditures—the sum of consumption, investment, and net exports—will make up the other 65 percent of GDP. If government spending is increased permanently to 37 percent of GDP, in the long run, private expenditures must fall to 63 percent of GDP. There has been complete crowding out: Private expenditures have fallen by the same amount that government spending has increased. If government spending is taking a larger share of GDP, then private spending must take a smaller share.

An expansionary fiscal policy does not have to cause complete crowding out in the short run. If real GDP is below potential GDP, it is possible for both government purchases and private expenditures to increase. But in the long run, any permanent increase in government spending must come at the expense of private expenditures. Keep in mind, however, that it may take several—possibly many—years to arrive at this long-run outcome.

MyEconLab Concept Check

Fiscal Policy in Action: Did the Stimulus Package of 2009 Succeed?

As we have seen, Congress and the president can increase government purchases and cut taxes to increase aggregate demand either to avoid a recession or to shorten the length or severity of a recession that is already under way. The recession of 2007–2009 occurred during the end of the presidency of George W. Bush and the beginning of the presidency of Barack Obama. Both presidents used fiscal policy to fight the recession.

In 2008, economists advising President Bush believed that the housing crisis, the resulting credit crunch, and rising oil prices were pushing the economy into a recession. (As we now know, a recession had actually already begun in December 2007.) These economists proposed cutting taxes to increase household disposable income, which would increase consumption spending and aggregate demand. Congress enacted a tax cut that took the form of *rebates* of taxes that households had already paid. Rebate checks totaling $95 billion were sent to taxpayers between April and July 2008.

How effective were the rebates in increasing consumption spending? While economists are still studying the issue, economic analysis can give us some insight. Many economists believe that consumers base their spending on their *permanent income* rather than just on their *current income*. A consumer's permanent income reflects the consumer's expected future income. By basing spending on permanent income, a consumer can smooth out consumption over a period of years. For example, a medical student may have very low current income but a high expected future income. The student may borrow against this high expected future income rather than having to consume at a very low level in the present. Some people, however, have difficulty borrowing against their future income because banks or other lenders may not be convinced that a borrower's future income will be significantly higher than his or her current income. One-time tax rebates, such as the one in 2008, increase consumers' current income but not their permanent income. Only a permanent decrease in taxes increases consumers' permanent income. Therefore, a tax rebate is likely to increase consumption spending less than would a permanent tax cut.

Some estimates of the effect of the 2008 tax rebate, including studies by Christian Broda of the University of Chicago and Jonathan Parker of Northwestern University, and by economists at the Congressional Budget Office, indicate that taxpayers spent between 33 and 40 percent of the rebates they received. Taxpayers who have difficulty borrowing against their future income increased their consumption the most. The 2008 tax rebates totaled $95 billion, so consumers may have increased their spending by about $35 billion.

American Recovery and Reinvestment Act of 2009 Although the tax rebates helped to increase aggregate demand, we saw in Chapter 26 that the recession worsened in September 2008, following the bankruptcy of the Lehman Brothers investment bank and the deepening of the financial crisis. President Obama took office in January 2009, pledging to pursue an expansionary fiscal policy. Congress responded in February by passing the American Recovery and Reinvestment Act of 2009, an $840 billion package of spending increases and tax cuts that was by far the largest fiscal policy action in U.S. history. The "stimulus package," as it came to be known, is difficult to summarize, but Figure 27.13 provides some highlights.

About two-thirds of the stimulus package took the form of increases in government expenditures, and one-third took the form of tax cuts. Panel (a) shows the major

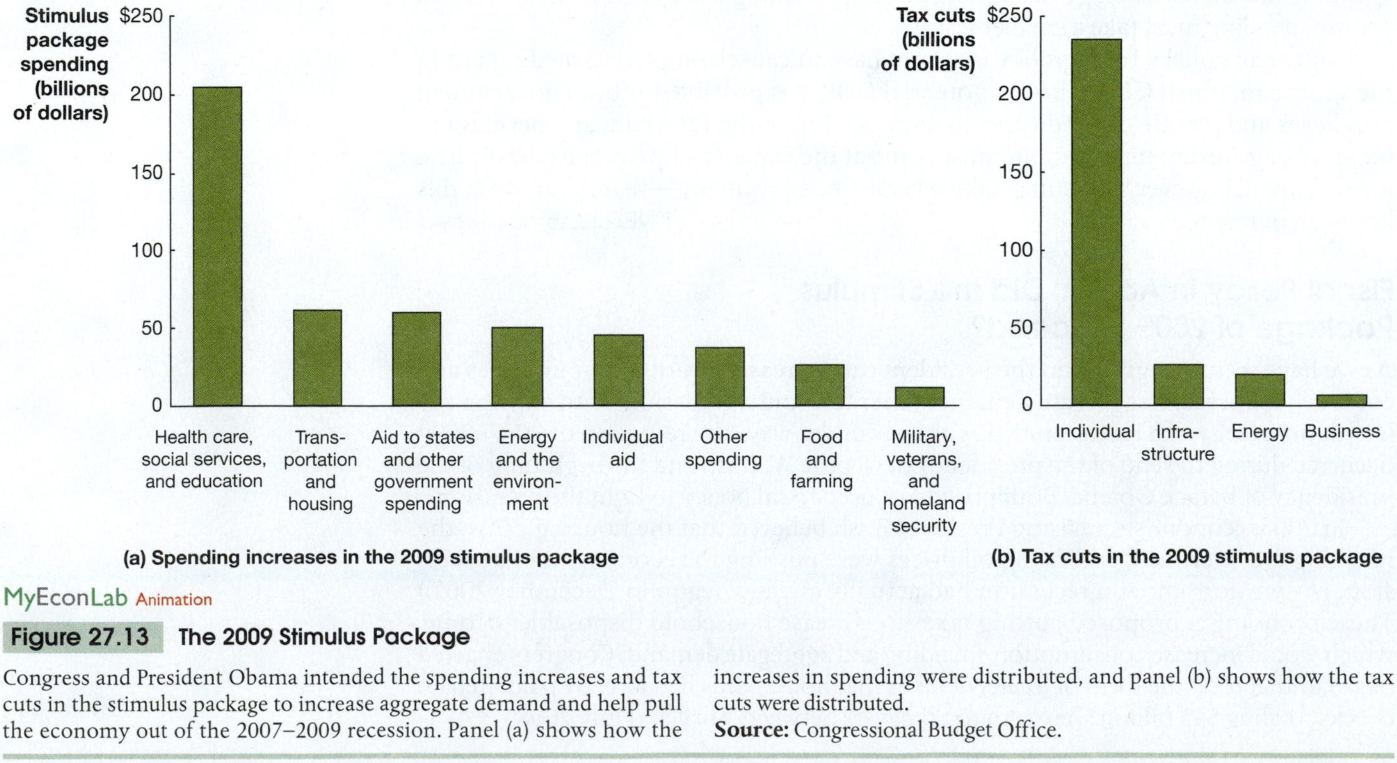

MyEconLab Animation

Figure 27.13 The 2009 Stimulus Package

Congress and President Obama intended the spending increases and tax cuts in the stimulus package to increase aggregate demand and help pull the economy out of the 2007–2009 recession. Panel (a) shows how the increases in spending were distributed, and panel (b) shows how the tax cuts were distributed.

Source: Congressional Budget Office.

categories of spending increases. The largest category—health care, social services, and education—included funds for biomedical research and grants to state governments to help fund Medicare spending, as well as funds for many other programs. The energy category included funds for research into alternative energy sources as well as modernization of the electric grid. Transportation and housing included substantial spending on infrastructure projects, such as repairing and expanding highways, bridges, and airports. The spending to reconstruct Doyle Drive in San Francisco, as mentioned in the chapter opener, is an example of the infrastructure spending included in the act. Individual aid included spending on extended unemployment insurance payments. Panel (b) shows the major categories of tax cuts. The largest category was individual tax cuts, which included a $400 reduction in payroll taxes for workers earning up to $75,000 per year and a tax credit of up to $2,500 for tuition and other college expenses.

Congress and the president intended the changes to federal expenditures and taxes from the stimulus package to be temporary. Figure 27.14 shows the effect of the stimulus package on federal government expenditures and revenue over time. Panel (a) shows that the effect on federal government expenditures was greatest during 2010 and declined sharply during 2011. Panel (b) shows that the effect on federal government revenue was greatest during 2010 and had declined to almost zero by early 2011.

How Can We Measure the Effectiveness of the Stimulus Package? At the time the stimulus package was passed, economists working for the Obama administration estimated that the increase in aggregate demand resulting from the package would increase real GDP by 3.5 percent by the end of 2010 and increase employment by 3.5 million. In fact, between the beginning of 2009 and the end of 2010, real GDP increased by 4.0 percent, while employment declined by 3.3 million. Do these results indicate that the stimulus package was successful in increasing GDP but not employment? We have to be careful in drawing that conclusion. To judge the effectiveness of the stimulus package, we have to measure its effects on real GDP and employment, *holding constant all other factors affecting real GDP and employment.* In other words, the actual movements in real GDP and employment are a mixture of the effects of the stimulus package and the effects of other factors, such as the Federal Reserve's monetary policy

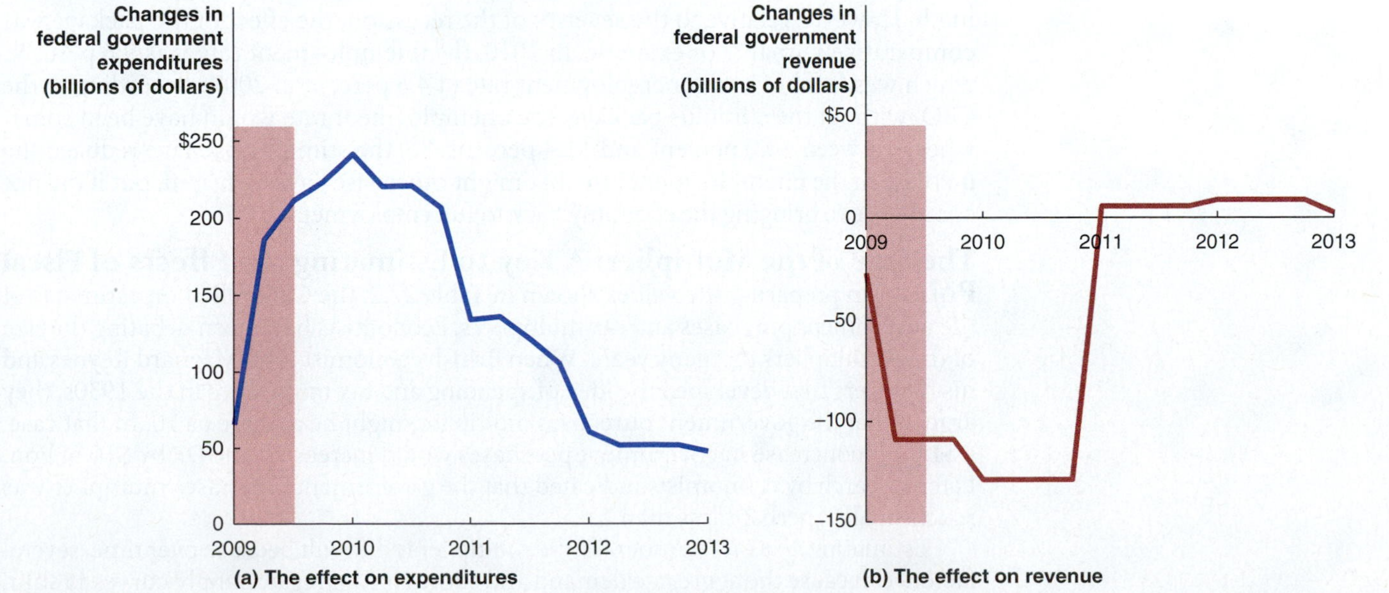

MyEconLab Animation

Figure 27.14 The Effect of the Stimulus Package on Federal Expenditures and Revenue

Congress and President Obama intended the spending increases and tax cuts in the stimulus package to be temporary. Panel (a) shows that the effect of the stimulus package on federal expenditures was greatest during 2010 and declined in the following years. Panel (b) shows that the effect on federal government revenue was greatest during 2010 and had declined to almost zero by early 2011.
Source: Federal Reserve Bank of St. Louis.

Table 27.2

CBO Estimates of the Effects of the Stimulus Package

Year	Change in Real GDP	Change in the Unemployment Rate	Change in Employment (millions of people)
2009	0.4% to 1.8%	−0.1% to −0.5%	0.3 to 1.3
2010	0.7% to 4.1%	−0.4% to −1.8%	0.9 to 4.7
2011	0.4% to 2.3%	−0.2% to −1.4%	0.6 to 3.6
2012	0.1% to 0.8%	−0.1% to −0.6%	0.2 to 1.3
2013	0.1% to 0.4%	0% to −0.3%	0.1 to 0.5
2014	0% to 0.2%	0% to −0.2%	0.1 to 0.3

Source: Congressional Budget Office, "Estimated Impact of the American Recovery and Reinvestment Act on Employment and Economic Output in 2014," February 2015.

and the typical changes in real GDP and employment during a business cycle that occur independently of government policy. Isolating the effects of the stimulus package from the effects of these other factors is very difficult and explains why economists differ in their views on the effectiveness of the stimulus package.

Table 27.2 shows estimates from economists at the CBO of the effectiveness of the stimulus package. The CBO is a nonpartisan organization, and many economists believe its estimates are reasonable. But because the estimates depend on particular assumptions about the size of the government purchases and tax multipliers, some economists believe that the CBO estimates are too high, while other economists believe the estimates are too low. To reflect the uncertainty in its calculation, the CBO provides a range of estimates. For example, in the absence of the stimulus package, the CBO estimates that in 2010 between 0.9 million and 4.7 million *fewer* people would have been employed than actually were, and the unemployment rate would have been between 0.4 percent and 1.8 percentage points *higher* than it actually was. By 2014, the effects of the stimulus package were small because several years had passed since most of the temporary spending increases and tax cuts had ended and because the economy had gradually moved back toward potential GDP.

If the CBO's estimates of the effects of the stimulus package are accurate, then this fiscal policy action reduced the severity of the recession of 2007–2009 and its aftermath. However, relative to the severity of the recession, the effect of the package was comparatively small. For example, in 2010, the unemployment rate was 9.6 percent, which was far above the unemployment rate of 4.6 percent in 2007. According to the CBO, without the stimulus package, the unemployment rate would have been somewhere between 10.0 percent and 11.4 percent. So, the stimulus package reduced the increase in the unemployment rate that might otherwise have occurred, but it did not come close to bringing the economy back to full employment.

The Size of the Multiplier: A Key to Estimating the Effects of Fiscal Policy In preparing the values shown in Table 27.2, the CBO relied on estimates of the government purchases and tax multipliers. Economists have been debating the size of these multipliers for many years. When British economist John Maynard Keynes and his followers first developed the idea of spending and tax multipliers in the 1930s, they argued that the government purchases multiplier might be as large as 10. In that case, a $1 billion increase in government purchases would increase real GDP by $10 billion. Later research by economists indicated that the government purchases multiplier was much smaller, perhaps less than 2.

Estimating an exact number for the multiplier is difficult because over time, several factors can cause the aggregate demand and short-run aggregate supply curves to shift, leading to a change in equilibrium real GDP. It can be challenging to isolate the effect of an increase in government purchases on equilibrium GDP. Before the stimulus package was proposed to Congress in 2009, economists in the Obama administration estimated the package's effect on GDP by using an average of multiplier estimates from the Federal Reserve and from a private macroeconomic forecasting firm. Their estimate that the government purchases multiplier was 1.57 means that a $1 billion increase in government purchases would increase equilibrium real GDP by $1.57 billion.

Because of the difficulty of estimating the size of the multiplier, some economists argue that the value economists in the Obama administration used was too high, while others argue that it was too low. Robert Barro of Harvard University maintains that increases in government spending during wartime are so large relative to other changes in aggregate demand that data from periods of war are best suited to estimating the size of the multiplier. Using such data, Barro estimated that the government purchases multiplier is only 0.8. Lawrence Christiano, Martin Eichenbaum, and Sergio Rebelo of Northwestern University argue, on the other hand, that the multiplier is likely to be larger when, as during 2009, short-term interest rates are near zero. They estimate that for these periods, the government purchases multiplier could be as large as 3.7.

As Table 27.3 shows, economists' estimates of the size of the multiplier vary widely. The uncertainty about the size of the multiplier indicates the difficulty that economists have in arriving at a firm estimate of the effects of fiscal policy. MyEconLab Concept Check

Table 27.3

Estimates of the Size of the Multiplier

Economist Making the Estimate	Type of Multiplier	Size of Multiplier
Congressional Budget Office	Government purchases	0.5–2.5
Lawrence Christiano, Martin Eichenbaum, and Sergio Rebelo, Northwestern University	Government purchases	1.05 when short-term interest rates are not zero; 3.7 when short-term interest rates are expected to be zero for at least five quarters
Tommaso Monacelli, Roberto Perotti, and Antonella Trigari, Universita Bocconi	Government purchases	1.2 after one year; 1.5 after two years
Ethan Ilzetzki, London School of Economics, Enrique G. Mendoza, University of Pennsylvania, and Carlos A. Vegh, University of Maryland	Government purchases	0.8
Valerie Ramey, University of California, San Diego	Military expenditure	0.6–1.1
Robert J. Barro, Harvard University, and Charles J. Redlick, Bain Capital, LLC	Military expenditure	0.4–0.5 after one year; 0.6–0.7 after two years
John Cogan and John Taylor, Stanford University, and Tobias Cwik and Volker Wieland, Goethe University	A permanent increase in government expenditures	0.4
Christina Romer, University of California, Berkeley, and Jared Bernstein, chief economist and economic policy adviser to Vice President Joseph Biden	A permanent increase in government expenditures	1.6
Christina Romer (prior to serving as chair of the Council of Economic Advisers) and David Romer, University of California, Berkeley	Tax	2–3
Congressional Budget Office	Tax	0.3–1.5 for a two-year tax cut for lower- and middle-income people; 0.1–0.6 for a one-year tax cut for higher-income people
Robert J. Barro, Harvard University, and Charles J. Redlick, Bain Capital, LLC	Tax	1.1

Note: The sources of these estimates are given on the Credits page in the back of the book.

Making the Connection

MyEconLab Video

Do We Depend Too Much on the Fed?

Should macroeconomic policy rely less on Fed Chair Yellen and her colleagues?

We have seen that the recovery from the Great Recession of 2007–2009 was slower than many economists had expected. As Fed Chair Janet Yellen noted in a speech in 2014, "Five years after the end of the recession, the labor market has yet to fully recover." The $840 billion American Recovery and Reinvestment Act (ARRA) of 2009 was by far the largest fiscal policy action in U.S. history. However, the figure below shows that in 2015, real GDP had not yet returned to potential GDP. The gap between potential GDP and real GDP, which had been as large as 7 percent during the worst of the recession, was still nearly 3 percent—unusually high so far into an economic recovery. The U.S. economy was still operating well below capacity, producing fewer goods and services and creating fewer jobs than it would have at potential GDP.

As Table 27.2 on page 960 showed, by 2011, most of the effects of ARRA on real GDP and employment had already occurred. If macroeconomic policy were to help bring the economy back to potential GDP, it appeared that it would therefore be up to the Federal Reserve. As we saw in Chapter 26, the Fed used innovative policies, including multiple rounds of quantitative easing (QE), in an attempt to increase aggregate demand. With the Fed having ended the last round of QE in October 2014, some economists and policymakers argued that fiscal policy actions were necessary to expand production and employment. Reports of crumbling bridges and railroad accidents led some policymakers to argue that increased infrastructure spending on highways, bridges, and railroad lines would provide both a short-term boost to aggregate demand and longer-term gains to productivity and economic growth. In 2015, President Obama proposed $478 billion in additional infrastructure spending to be paid for by a new tax on the foreign earnings of U.S. corporations. However, not all economists are convinced of the effectiveness of infrastructure spending, particularly if members of Congress direct the spending to projects in their states or districts that might not produce large benefits relative to their costs.

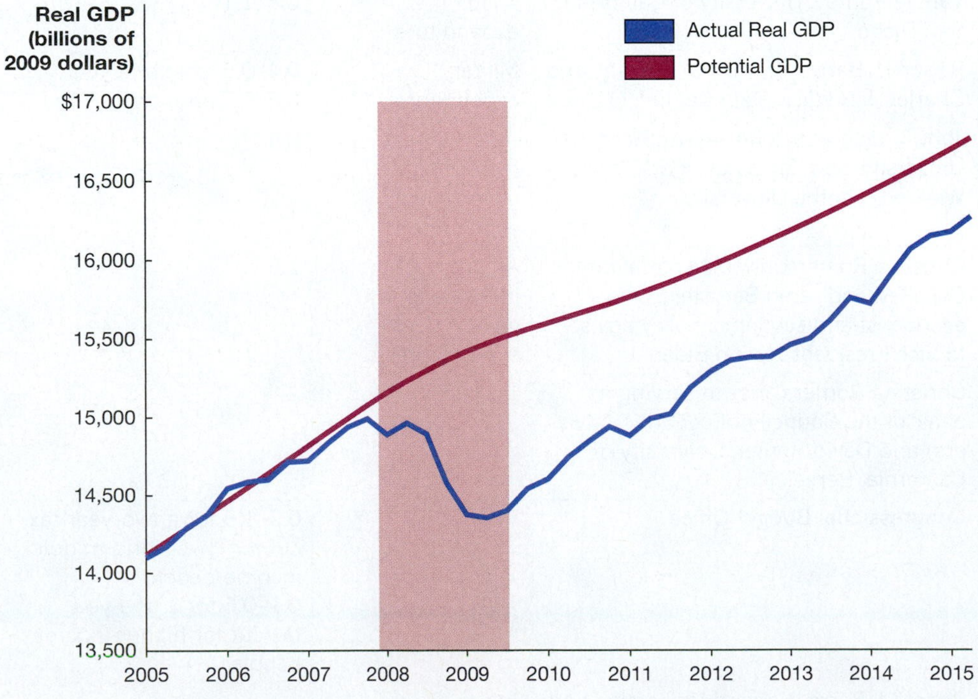

Supporters of infrastructure projects argue that long-term spending might convince businesses that aggregate demand increases would be maintained over a period of years, providing them with the confidence to expand production and employment. Supporters of tax reform to increase economic growth propose lowering tax rates on businesses to spur investment in new innovations and shifting toward consumption-based taxes to spur saving. Some economists argue that trade policy, although not traditionally fiscal policy, could be used to increase the efficiency of the economy and spur exports, while immigration policy could attract high-skilled immigrants, which would increase long-run growth.

The slow recovery from the Great Recession inspired a wide-ranging debate over the use of monetary and fiscal policies to manage the economy.

Sources: Michael D. Shear, "Obama Proposes Tax for Upgrade of Infrastructure," *New York Times*, February 2, 2015; R. Glenn Hubbard, "Stop Depending on the Fed," politico.com, August 20, 2014; Martin S. Feldstein, "Saving the Fed from Itself," *New York Times*, December 8, 2013; Mark Magnier, "Benefits of Infrastructure Spending Not So Clear-Cut, Economists Say," *Wall Street Journal*, February 1, 2015; and Janet L. Yellen, "Labor Market Dynamics and Monetary Policy," Talk delivered at the Federal Reserve Bank of Kansas City Economic Symposium, Jackson Hole, Wyoming, August 22, 2014.

Your Turn: Test your understanding by doing related problem 5.8 on page 976 at the end of this chapter.

MyEconLab Study Plan

27.6 Deficits, Surpluses, and Federal Government Debt

LEARNING OBJECTIVE: Define federal budget deficit and federal government debt and explain how the federal budget can serve as an automatic stabilizer.

The federal government's budget shows the relationship between its expenditures and its tax revenue. If the federal government's expenditures are greater than its tax revenue, a **budget deficit** results. If the federal government's expenditures are less than its tax revenue, a **budget surplus** results. As with many other macroeconomic variables, it is useful to consider the size of the surplus or deficit relative to the size of the overall economy. Figure 27.15 shows that, as a percentage of GDP, the largest deficits of the twentieth century came during World Wars I and II. During major wars, higher taxes only partially offset massive increases in government expenditures, leaving large budget deficits. Figure 27.15 also shows that during recessions, government spending increases and tax revenues fall, increasing the budget deficit. In 1970, the federal government entered a long period of continuous budget deficits. From 1970 through 1997, the federal government's budget was in deficit every year. From 1998 through 2001, there were four years of budget surpluses. The recessions of 2001 and 2007–2009, tax cuts, and increased government spending on homeland security and the wars in Iraq and Afghanistan helped keep the budget in deficit in the years after 2001.

Budget deficit The situation in which the government's expenditures are greater than its tax revenue.

Budget surplus The situation in which the government's expenditures are less than its tax revenue.

Figure 27.15 also shows the effects on the federal budget deficit of the Obama administration's $840 billion stimulus package and the severity of the 2007–2009 recession.

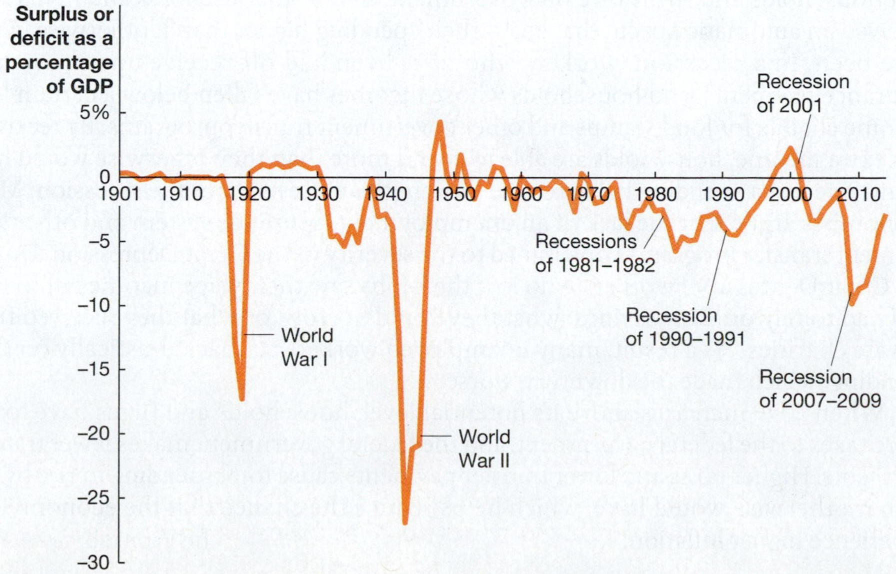

MyEconLab Real-time data

Figure 27.15

The Federal Budget Deficit, 1901–2015

During wars, government spending increases far more than tax revenues, increasing the budget deficit. The budget deficit also increases during recessions, as government spending increases and tax revenues fall.

Note: The value for 2015 is an estimate prepared by the Congressional Budget Office in March 2015.

Sources: *Budget of the United States Government, Fiscal Year 2003, Historical Tables*, Washington, DC: U.S. Government Printing Office, 2002; U.S. Bureau of Economic Analysis; and Congressional Budget Office.

From 2009 through 2011, the federal budget deficit was greater than 8 percent of GDP, which was the first time in the history of the country that the deficit had been this large except during major wars. The economic recovery combined with tax increases and reductions in federal spending lowered the deficit to less than 3 percent of GDP in 2015.

How the Federal Budget Can Serve as an Automatic Stabilizer

Discretionary fiscal policy can increase the federal budget deficit during recessions by increasing spending or cutting taxes to increase aggregate demand. For example, as we have just seen, the Obama administration's spending increases and tax cuts significantly increased the federal budget deficit during 2009 and 2010. In many milder recessions, though, no significant fiscal policy actions are taken. In fact, most of the increase in the federal budget deficit during a typical recession takes place without Congress and the president taking any action but is instead due to the effects of the *automatic stabilizers* we mentioned earlier in this chapter.

Deficits occur automatically during recessions for two reasons: First, during a recession, wages and profits fall, causing government tax revenues to fall. Second, the government automatically increases its spending on transfer payments when the economy moves into a recession. The federal government's contributions to the unemployment insurance program will increase as unemployment rises. Spending will also increase on programs to aid low-income people, such as the food stamp, Temporary Assistance for Needy Families, and Medicaid programs. These spending increases take place without Congress and the president taking any action. Existing laws already specify who is eligible for unemployment insurance and these other programs. As the number of eligible persons increases during a recession, so does government spending on these programs.

Because budget deficits automatically increase during recessions and decrease during expansions, economists often look at the *cyclically adjusted budget deficit or surplus*, which can provide a more accurate measure of the effects on the economy of the government's spending and tax policies than can the actual budget deficit or surplus. The **cyclically adjusted budget deficit or surplus** measures what the deficit or surplus would be if real GDP were at potential GDP. For example, the federal budget deficit in 2014 was 2.7 percent of GDP. The CBO estimates that if real GDP had been at its potential level, the deficit would have been about 1.6 percent of GDP, with the remaining 1.1 percent representing the increase in the deficit due to the effects of automatic stabilizers. When the federal government runs an expansionary fiscal policy, the result is a cyclically adjusted budget deficit. When the federal government runs a contractionary fiscal policy, the result is a cyclically adjusted budget surplus.

Cyclically adjusted budget deficit or surplus The deficit or surplus in the federal government's budget if the economy were at potential GDP.

Automatic budget surpluses and deficits can help to stabilize the economy. When the economy moves into a recession, wages and profits fall, reducing the taxes that households and firms owe the government. In effect, households and firms have received an automatic tax cut that keeps their spending higher than it otherwise would have been. In a recession, workers who have been laid off receive unemployment insurance payments, and households whose incomes have fallen below a certain level become eligible for food stamps and other government transfer programs. By receiving this extra income, households are able to spend more than they otherwise would have spent. The extra spending helps reduce the length and severity of the recession. Many economists argue that the lack of an unemployment insurance system and other government transfer programs contributed to the severity of the Great Depression. During the Great Depression, workers who lost their jobs saw their wage income fall to zero and had to rely on their savings, what they could borrow, or what they received from private charities. As a result, many unemployed workers cut back drastically on their spending, which made the downturn worse.

When GDP increases above its potential level, households and firms have to pay more taxes to the federal government, and the federal government makes fewer transfer payments. Higher taxes and lower transfer payments cause total spending to rise by less than it otherwise would have, which helps reduce the chance that the economy will experience higher inflation.

MyEconLab Concept Check

Making the Connection
MyEconLab Video

Did Fiscal Policy Fail during the Great Depression?

Although government spending increased during the Great Depression, the cyclically adjusted budget was in surplus most years.

Modern macroeconomic analysis began during the 1930s, with the publication of *The General Theory of Employment, Interest, and Money* by John Maynard Keynes. One conclusion many economists drew from Keynes's book was that an expansionary fiscal policy would be necessary to pull the United States out of the Great Depression. When Franklin D. Roosevelt became president in 1933, federal government expenditures increased as part of his New Deal program, and there was a federal budget deficit during each remaining year of the decade, except for 1937. The U.S. economy recovered very slowly, however, and did not reach potential GDP again until the outbreak of World War II in 1941.

Some economists and policymakers at the time argued that because the economy recovered slowly despite increases in government spending, fiscal policy had been ineffective. During the debate over President Obama's stimulus package, the argument that fiscal policy had failed during the New Deal was raised again. Economic historians have noted, however, that despite the increases in government spending, Congress and the president had not, in fact, implemented an expansionary fiscal policy during the 1930s. In separate studies, economists E. Cary Brown of MIT and Larry Peppers of Washington and Lee University argued that there was a cyclically adjusted budget deficit during only one year of the 1930s, and that one deficit was small. The following table provides data supporting their arguments. (All variables in the table are nominal rather than real.) The second column shows federal government expenditures increasing from 1933 to 1936, falling in 1937, and then increasing in 1938 and 1939. The third column shows a similar pattern, with the federal budget being in deficit each year after 1933 except for 1937. The fourth column, however, shows that in each year after 1933, the federal government ran a cyclically adjusted budget *surplus*. Because the level of income was so low and the unemployment rate was so high during these years, tax collections were far below what they would have been if the economy had been at potential GDP. As the fifth column shows, in 1933 and again from 1937 to 1939, the cyclically adjusted surpluses were large relative to GDP.

Year	Federal Government Expenditures (billions of dollars)	Actual Federal Budget Deficit or Surplus (billions of dollars)	Cyclically Adjusted Budget Deficit or Surplus (billions of dollars)	Cyclically Adjusted Budget Deficit or Surplus as a Percentage of GDP
1929	$2.6	$1.0	$1.24	1.20%
1930	2.7	0.2	0.81	0.89
1931	4.0	−2.1	−0.41	−0.54
1932	3.0	−1.3	0.50	0.85
1933	3.4	−0.9	1.06	1.88
1934	5.5	−2.2	0.09	0.14
1935	5.6	−1.9	0.54	0.74
1936	7.8	−3.2	0.47	0.56
1937	6.4	0.2	2.55	2.77
1938	7.3	−1.3	2.47	2.87
1939	8.4	−2.1	2.00	2.17

Although President Roosevelt proposed many new government spending programs, he had also promised during the 1932 presidential election campaign to balance the federal budget. He achieved a balanced budget only in 1937, but his reluctance to allow the actual budget deficit to grow too large helps explain why the cyclically adjusted budget remained in surplus. Many economists today would agree with

E. Cary Brown's conclusion: "Fiscal policy, then, seems to have been an unsuccessful recovery device in the 'thirties—not because it did not work, but because it was not tried."

Sources: E. Cary Brown, "Fiscal Policy in the 'Thirties: A Reappraisal," *American Economic Review*, Vol. 46, No. 5, December 1956, pp. 857–879; Larry Peppers, "Full Employment Surplus Analysis and Structural Changes," *Explorations in Economic History*, Vol. 10, Winter 1973, pp. 197–210; and U.S. Bureau of Economic Analysis.

MyEconLab Study Plan

Your Turn: Test your understanding by doing related problem 6.7 on page 977 at the end of this chapter.

Should the Federal Budget Always Be Balanced?

Although many economists believe that it is a good idea for the federal government to have a balanced budget when real GDP is at potential GDP, few economists believe that the federal government should attempt to balance its budget every year. To see why economists take this view, consider what the federal government would have to do to keep the budget balanced during a recession, when the budget automatically moves into deficit. To bring the budget back into balance, the government would have to raise taxes or cut spending, but these actions would reduce aggregate demand, thereby making the recession worse. Similarly, when GDP increases above its potential level, the budget automatically moves into surplus. To eliminate this surplus, the government would have to cut taxes or increase government spending. But these actions would increase aggregate demand, thereby pushing GDP further beyond potential GDP and increasing the risk of higher inflation. To balance the budget every year, the government might have to take actions that would destabilize the economy.

Solved Problem 27.6

MyEconLab Interactive Animation

The Greek Government Confronts a Budget Deficit

According to an article in the *Wall Street Journal*, in 2015, some economists believed that the Greek economy might be about to enter a recession. The article noted, "Renewed recession in Greece ... could force the government to impose further spending cuts and tax hikes to avoid a renewed budget deficit."

a. Why would the Greek economy entering a recession lead to the Greek government having a budget deficit?

b. If the Greek government, in reaction to the budget deficit, takes the steps the article indicates, what would be the likely effect on the Greek economy?

Solving the Problem

Step 1: **Review the chapter material.** This problem is about the effects of a government attempting to balance its budget during a recession, so you may want to review the sections "How the Federal Budget Can Serve as an Automatic Stabilizer" and "Should the Federal Budget Always Be Balanced?" which are on pages 964 and 966.

Step 2: **Answer part (a) by explaining why a government's budget will automatically run a deficit during a recession.** Deficits occur automatically during recessions because falling wages and profits cause government tax revenues to fall and because government spending on transfer payments, such as unemployment insurance payments, increases.

Step 3: **Answer part (b) by explaining the likely effect on the Greek economy if the Greek government were to cut spending and increase taxes.** We have seen that reductions in government spending and increases in taxes will reduce aggregate demand. A reduction in aggregate demand will likely reduce real GDP and employment, making the recession in Greece worse.

Source: Nektaria Stamouli and Stelios Bouras, "Greek Economy Risks Slipping Back Into Recession, Say Analysts," *Wall Street Journal*, April 6, 2015.

MyEconLab Study Plan

Your Turn: For more practice, do related problem 6.9 on page 977 at the end of this chapter.

Some economists argue that the federal government should normally run a deficit, even at potential GDP. When the federal budget is in deficit, the U.S. Treasury sells bonds to investors to raise the funds necessary to pay the government's bills. Borrowing to pay the bills is a bad policy for a household, a firm, or the government when the bills are for current expenses, but it is not a bad policy if the bills are for long-lived capital goods. For instance, most families pay for a new home by taking out a 15- to 30-year mortgage. Because houses last many years, it makes sense to pay for a house out of the income the family makes over a long period of time rather than out of the income they receive in the year they bought the house. Businesses often borrow the funds to buy machinery, equipment, and factories by selling 30-year corporate bonds. Because these capital goods generate profits for the businesses over many years, it makes sense to pay for them over a period of years as well. By similar reasoning, when the federal government contributes to the building of a new highway, bridge, or subway, it may want to borrow funds by selling Treasury bonds. The alternative is to pay for these long-lived capital goods out of the tax revenues received in the year the goods were purchased. But that means that the taxpayers in that year have to bear the whole burden of paying for the projects, even though taxpayers for many years in the future will be enjoying the benefits. MyEconLab Concept Check

The Federal Government Debt

Every time the federal government runs a budget deficit, the Treasury must borrow funds from investors by selling Treasury securities. For simplicity, we will refer to all Treasury securities as "bonds." When the federal government runs a budget surplus, the Treasury pays off some existing bonds. Figure 27.15 on page 963 shows that there are many more years of federal budget deficits than years of federal budget surpluses. As a result, the total number of Treasury bonds outstanding has grown over the years. The total value of U.S. Treasury bonds outstanding is called the *federal government debt* or, sometimes, the *national debt*. Each year the federal budget is in deficit, the federal government debt grows. Each year the federal budget is in surplus, the debt shrinks.

Figure 27.16 shows federal government debt as a percentage of GDP in the years from 1901 to 2015. The ratio of debt to GDP increased during World Wars I and II and the Great Depression, reflecting the large government budget deficits of those years. After the end of World War II, GDP grew faster than the debt until the early 1980s, which caused the ratio of debt to GDP to fall. The large budget deficits of the 1980s and early 1990s sent the debt-to-GDP ratio climbing. The budget surpluses of 1998 to 2001 caused the debt-to-GDP ratio to fall, but it rose again with the return of deficits beginning in 2002. The large deficits beginning in 2008 caused the ratio to rise above 100 percent of GDP for the first time since 1947.

MyEconLab Concept Check

Is Government Debt a Problem?

Debt can be a problem for a government for the same reasons it can be a problem for a household or a business. If a family has difficulty making the monthly mortgage payment, it will have to cut back spending on other goods and services. If the family is unable to make the payments, it will have to *default* on the loan and will probably lose its house. The federal government is not in danger of defaulting on its debt. Ultimately, the government can raise the funds it needs through taxes to make the interest payments on the debt. If the debt becomes very large relative to the economy, however, the government may have to raise taxes to high levels or cut back on other types of spending to make the interest payments on the debt. Interest payments are currently about 11 percent of total federal expenditures. At this level, tax increases or significant cutbacks in other types of federal spending are not required.

In the long run, a debt that increases in size relative to GDP, as happened after 2008, can pose a problem. As we discussed previously, crowding out of investment spending may occur if increasing debt drives up interest rates. Lower investment spending means a lower capital stock in the long run and a reduced capacity of the economy to produce goods and services. This effect is somewhat offset if some of the government debt was incurred to finance improvements in *infrastructure*, such as bridges, highways, and ports; to finance education; or to finance research and development. Improvements in infrastructure, a better-educated labor force, and additional research and development can add to the productive capacity of the economy. MyEconLab Concept Check

MyEconLab Study Plan

MyEconLab Real-time data

Figure 27.16

The Federal Government Debt, 1901–2015

The federal government debt increases whenever the federal government runs a budget deficit. The large deficits incurred during World Wars I and II, the Great Depression, and the 1980s and early 1990s increased the ratio of debt to GDP. The large deficits after 2008 caused the ratio to spike up to its highest level since 1947.

Note: The value for 2015 is an estimate prepared by the Congressional Budget Office in March 2015.

Sources: U.S. Bureau of the Census, *Historical Statistics of the United States, Colonial Times to 1970*, Washington, DC: U.S. Government Printing Office, 1975; *Budget of the United States Government, Fiscal Year 2003*, Historical Printing Office, 2002; Federal Reserve Bank of St. Louis; and Congressional Budget Office.

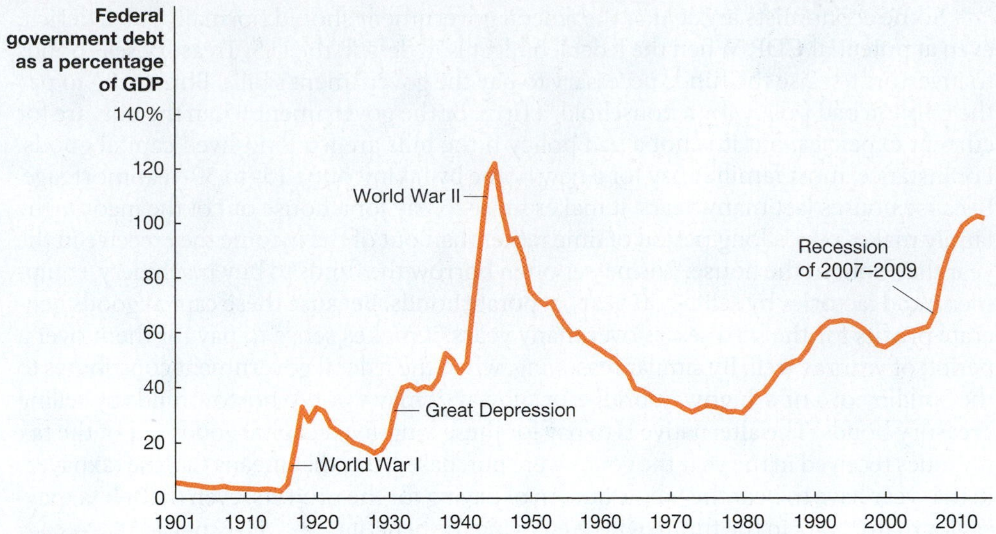

27.7 The Effects of Fiscal Policy in the Long Run

LEARNING OBJECTIVE: Discuss the effects of fiscal policy in the long run.

Some fiscal policy actions are intended to meet the short-run goal of stabilizing the economy. Other fiscal policy actions are intended to have long-run effects by expanding the productive capacity of the economy and increasing the rate of economic growth. Because these policy actions primarily affect aggregate supply rather than aggregate demand, they are sometimes called *supply-side economics*. Most fiscal policy actions that attempt to increase aggregate supply do so by changing taxes to increase the incentives to work, save, invest, and start a business.

The Long-Run Effects of Tax Policy

Tax wedge The difference between the pretax and posttax return to an economic activity.

The difference between the pretax and posttax return to an economic activity is called the **tax wedge**. It is determined by the *marginal tax rate*, which is the fraction of each additional dollar of income that must be paid in taxes. For example, the U.S. federal income tax has several tax brackets, which are the income ranges within which a tax rate applies. In 2015, for a single taxpayer, the tax rate was 10 percent on the first $9,225 earned during a year. The tax rate rose for higher income brackets, until it reached 39.6 percent on income earned above $413,200. Suppose you are paid a wage of $20 per hour. If your marginal income tax rate is 25 percent, then your posttax wage is $15, and the tax wedge is $5. When discussing the model of demand and supply in Chapter 3, we saw that increasing the price of a good or service increases the quantity supplied. So, we would expect that reducing the tax wedge by cutting the marginal tax rate on income would result in a larger quantity of labor supplied because the posttax wage would be higher. Similarly, we saw in Chapter 21 that a reduction in the income tax rate would increase the posttax return to saving, causing an increase in the supply of loanable funds, a lower equilibrium interest rate, and an increase in investment spending. In general, economists believe that the smaller the tax wedge for any economic activity—such as working, saving, investing, or starting a business—the more of that economic activity that will occur. When workers, savers, investors, or entrepreneurs change their actions as a result of a tax change, economists say that there has been a *behavioral response* to the tax change.

We can look briefly at the effects on aggregate supply of cutting each of the following taxes:

- **Individual income tax.** As we have seen, reducing the marginal tax rates on individual income will reduce the tax wedge workers face, thereby increasing the quantity of labor supplied. Many small businesses are *sole proprietorships*, whose profits are taxed at the individual income tax rates. Therefore, cutting the individual income tax rates also raises the return to entrepreneurship, encouraging the opening of new businesses. Most households are taxed on their returns from saving at the individual income tax rates. Reducing marginal income tax rates, therefore, also increases the return to saving.

- **Corporate income tax.** The federal government taxes the profits corporations earn under the corporate income tax. In 2015, most corporations faced a marginal corporate tax rate of 35 percent. Cutting the marginal corporate income tax rate would encourage investment spending by increasing the return corporations receive from new investments in equipment, factories, and office buildings. Because innovations are often embodied in new investment goods, cutting the corporate income tax can potentially increase the pace of technological change.
- **Taxes on dividends and capital gains.** Corporations distribute some of their profits to shareholders in the form of payments known as *dividends.* Shareholders also may benefit from higher corporate profits by receiving *capital gains.* A capital gain is the increase in the price of an asset, such as a share of stock. Rising profits usually result in rising stock prices and capital gains to shareholders. Individuals pay taxes on both dividends and capital gains (although the tax on capital gains can be postponed if the stock is not sold). As a result, the same earnings are, in effect, taxed twice: once when a corporation pays the corporate income tax on its profits and a second time when individual investors receive the profits in the form of dividends or capital gains. Economists debate the costs and benefits of a separate tax on corporate profits. With the corporate income tax remaining in place, one way to reduce the "double taxation" problem is to reduce the tax rates on dividends and capital gains. These rates were reduced in 2003 before being increased in 2013. Generally, the marginal tax rates on dividends and capital gains are still below the top marginal tax rate on individual income. Lowering the tax rates on dividends and capital gains increases the supply of loanable funds from households to firms, increasing saving and investment and lowering the equilibrium real interest rate.

Tax Simplification

In addition to the potential gains from cutting individual taxes, there are also gains from tax simplification. The complexity of the tax code, which is 3,000 pages long, has created a whole industry of tax preparation services, such as H&R Block. The Internal Revenue Service estimates that taxpayers spend more than 6.4 billion hours each year filling out their tax forms, or about 45 hours per tax return. Households and firms have to deal with more than 480 tax forms to file their federal taxes and spend more than $10 billion per year to hire accountants to help fill out the forms. It is not surprising that there are more H&R Block offices around the country than Starbucks coffeehouses.

If the tax code were greatly simplified, the economic resources currently used by the tax preparation industry would be available to produce other goods and services. In addition to wasting resources, the complexity of the tax code may also distort the decisions households and firms make. For example, the tax rate on dividends has clearly affected whether corporations pay dividends. When Congress passed a reduction in the tax on dividends in 2003, many firms—including Microsoft—began paying dividends for the first time. A simplified tax code would increase economic efficiency by reducing the number of decisions households and firms make solely to reduce their tax payments.

MyEconLab Concept Check

The Economic Effect of Tax Reform

We can analyze the economic effects of tax reduction and simplification by using the aggregate demand and aggregate supply model. Figure 27.17 shows that without tax changes, the long-run aggregate supply curve will shift from $LRAS_1$ to $LRAS_2$. This shift represents the increases in the labor force and the capital stock and the technological change that would occur even without tax reduction and simplification. To focus on the effect of tax changes on aggregate supply, we will ignore any shifts in the short-run aggregate supply curve, and we will assume that the aggregate demand curve remains unchanged, at AD_1. In this case, equilibrium moves from point A to point B, with real GDP increasing from Y_1 to Y_2 and the price level decreasing from P_1 to P_2.

MyEconLab Animation

Figure 27.17

The Supply-Side Effects of a Tax Change

The initial equilibrium is at point A. With no tax change, the long-run aggregate supply curve shifts to the right, from $LRAS_1$ to $LRAS_2$. Equilibrium moves to point B, with the price level falling from P_1 to P_2 and real GDP increasing from Y_1 to Y_2. With tax reductions and simplifications, the long-run aggregate supply curve shifts further to the right, to $LRAS_3$, and equilibrium moves to point C, with the price level falling to P_3 and real GDP increasing to Y_3.

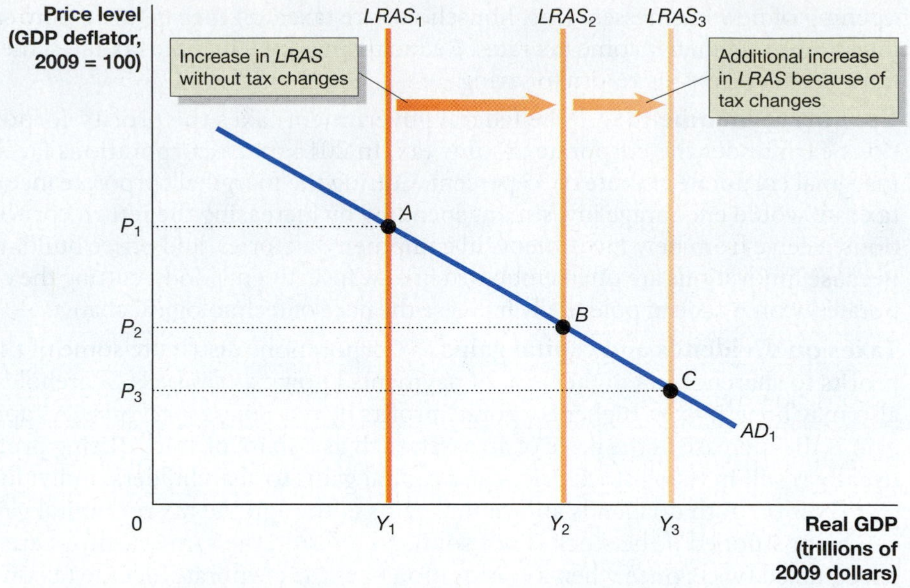

If tax reduction and simplification are effective, the economy will experience increases in labor supply, saving, investment, and the formation of new firms. Economic efficiency will also be improved. Together these factors will result in an increase in the quantity of real GDP supplied at every price level. We show the effects of the tax changes in Figure 27.17 by a shift in the long-run aggregate supply curve to $LRAS_3$. With aggregate demand remaining unchanged, equilibrium moves from point A to point C (rather than to point B, which is the equilibrium without tax changes), with real GDP increasing from Y_1 to Y_3 and the price level decreasing from P_1 to P_3. Notice that compared with the equilibrium without tax changes (point B), the equilibrium with tax changes (point C) occurs at a lower price level and a higher level of real GDP. We can conclude that the tax changes have benefited the economy by increasing output and employment while at the same time reducing the price level.

Clearly, our analysis is unrealistic because we have ignored the changes that will occur in aggregate demand and short-run aggregate supply. How would a more realistic analysis differ from the simplified one in Figure 27.17? The change in real GDP would be the same because in the long run, real GDP is equal to its potential level, which is represented by the *long-run aggregate supply* curve. The outcome for the price level would be different, however, because we would expect both the aggregate demand curve and the short-run aggregate supply curve to shift to the right. The most likely outcome is that the price level would end up higher in the new equilibrium than in the original equilibrium. However, because the position of the long-run aggregate supply curve is further to the right as a result of the tax changes, the increase in the price level will be smaller; that is, the price level at point C is likely to be lower than P_2, even if it is higher than P_3, although—as we will discuss in the next section—not all economists would agree. We can conclude that a successful policy of tax reductions and simplifications will benefit the economy by increasing output and employment and, at the same time, may result in smaller increases in the price level.

MyEconLab Concept Check

How Large Are Supply-Side Effects?

Most economists would agree that there are supply-side effects to reducing taxes: Decreasing marginal income tax rates will increase the quantity of labor supplied, cutting the corporate income tax will increase investment spending, and so on. The magnitude of the effects is the subject of considerable debate, however. For example, some economists argue that the increase in the quantity of labor supplied following a tax cut will be limited because many people work a number of hours set by their employers and lack the opportunity to work additional hours. Similarly, some economists believe that tax changes have only a small effect on saving and investment. In this view, saving and investment are affected much more by changes in income or changes in expectations of the future profitability of new investment due to technological change or improving macroeconomic conditions than they are by changes in taxes.

Economists who are skeptical of the magnitude of supply-side effects believe that tax cuts have their greatest effect on aggregate demand rather than on aggregate supply. In their view, focusing on the effect of tax cuts on aggregate demand, while ignoring any effect on aggregate supply, yields accurate forecasts of future movements in real GDP and the price level, which indicates that the supply-side effects must be small. If tax changes have only small effects on aggregate supply, they are unlikely to reduce the size of price increases to the extent shown in Figure 27.17.

Ultimately, the debate over the size of the supply-side effects of tax policy can be resolved only through careful study of the effects of differences in tax rates on labor supply and on saving and investment decisions. Some recent studies have arrived at conflicting conclusions, however. For example, a study by Nobel Laureate Edward Prescott of Arizona State University concludes that the differences between the United States and Europe with respect to the average number of hours worked per week and the average number of weeks worked per year are due to differences in tax rates. The lower marginal tax rates in the United States compared with Europe increase the return to working for U.S. workers and result in a larger quantity of labor supplied. But another study by Alberto Alesina and Edward Glaeser of Harvard University and Bruce Sacerdote of Dartmouth College argues that the more restrictive labor market regulations in Europe explain the shorter work weeks and longer vacations of European workers and that differences in tax rates have only a small effect.

As in other areas of economics, differences among economists in their estimates of the supply-side effects of tax changes may narrow over time as they conduct more studies.

MyEconLab Concept Check MyEconLab Study Plan

Continued from page 939

Economics in Your Life

What Would You Do with an Extra $500?

At the beginning of the chapter, we asked how you would respond to a $500 tax rebate and what effect this tax rebate would likely have on equilibrium real GDP in the short run. This chapter has shown that tax cuts increase disposable income and, therefore, consumption spending. So, you will likely respond to a permanent $500 increase in your disposable income by increasing your spending. How much your spending increases depends in part on your overall financial situation. As mentioned in the chapter, people who are able to borrow usually try to smooth out their spending over time and don't increase spending much in response to a one-time increase in their income. But if you are a student struggling to get by on a low income and you are unable to borrow against the higher income you expect to earn in the future, you may well spend most of the rebate. This chapter has also shown that tax cuts have a multiplier effect on the economy. That is, an increase in consumption spending sets off further increases in real GDP and income. So, if the economy is not already at potential GDP, this tax rebate will likely increase equilibrium real GDP in the short run.

Conclusion

In this chapter, we have seen how the federal government uses changes in government purchases and taxes to achieve its economic policy goals. We have seen that economists debate the effectiveness of discretionary fiscal policy actions intended to stabilize the economy. Congress and the president share responsibility for economic policy with the Federal Reserve. In the next chapter, we will discuss further some of the challenges that the Federal Reserve faces as it carries out monetary policy. In the following chapters, we will look more closely at the international economy, including how monetary and fiscal policy are affected by the linkages between economies.

Visit MyEconLab for a news article and analysis related to the concepts in this chapter.

CHAPTER SUMMARY AND PROBLEMS

Key Terms

Automatic stabilizers, p. 940	Crowding out, p. 955	Fiscal policy, p. 940	Tax wedge, p. 968
Budget deficit, p. 963	Cyclically adjusted budget deficit or surplus, p. 964	Multiplier effect, p. 949	
Budget surplus, p. 963			

27.1 What Is Fiscal Policy? pages 940–944

LEARNING OBJECTIVE: Define fiscal policy.

Summary

Fiscal policy involves changes in federal taxes and purchases that are intended to achieve macroeconomic policy goals. **Automatic stabilizers** are government spending and taxes that automatically increase or decrease along with the business cycle. Since World War II, the federal government's share of total government expenditures has been between two-thirds and three-quarters. Federal government *expenditures* as a percentage of GDP rose from 1950 to the early 1990s, fell between 1992 and 2001, and then rose once again. Federal government *purchases* have declined as a percentage of GDP since the end of the Korean War in the early 1950s. The largest component of federal expenditures is transfer payments. The largest sources of federal government revenue are individual income taxes, followed by social insurance taxes, which are used to fund the Social Security and Medicare systems.

MyEconLab Visit **www.myeconlab.com** to complete these exercises online and get instant feedback.

Review Questions

1.1 What is fiscal policy? Who is responsible for fiscal policy?

1.2 Economist Mark Thoma wrote, "One of the difficulties in using fiscal policy to combat recessions is getting Congress to agree on what measures to implement. … Automatic stabilizers bypass this difficulty by doing exactly what their name implies." What are automatic stabilizers? Name two examples of automatic stabilizers and explain how they can reduce the severity of a recession.

Source: Mark Thoma, "The Importance of Automatic Stabilizers to the Economy," cbsnews.com, January 25, 2010.

1.3 What is the difference between federal purchases and federal expenditures? Are federal purchases higher today as a percentage of GDP than they were in 1960? Are federal expenditures as a percentage of GDP higher?

Problems and Applications

1.4 In 2009, Congress and the president enacted "cash for clunkers" legislation that paid up to $4,500 to people buying new cars if they traded in an older, low-gas-mileage car. Was this legislation an example of fiscal policy? Does your answer depend on what goals Congress and the president had in mind when they enacted the legislation?

Source: Justin Lahart, "Trade-in Program Tunes Up Economic Engine," *Wall Street Journal*, August 4, 2009.

1.5 Briefly explain whether each of the following is (1) an example of a discretionary fiscal policy, (2) an example of an automatic stabilizer, or (3) not an example of fiscal policy.

a. The federal government increases spending on rebuilding the New Jersey shore following a hurricane.
b. The Federal Reserve sells Treasury securities.
c. The total amount the federal government spends on unemployment insurance decreases during an expansion.
d. The revenue the federal government collects from the individual income tax declines during a recession.
e. The federal government changes the required fuel efficiency for new cars.
f. Congress and the president enact a temporary cut in payroll taxes.
g. During a recession, California voters approve additional spending on a statewide high-speed rail system.

1.6 The federal government collected less in total individual income taxes in 1983 than in 1982. Can we conclude that Congress and the president cut individual income tax rates in 1983? Briefly explain.

1.7 **(Related to the Making the Connection on page 943)** According to a Congressional Budget Office (CBO) report:

> During the next decade alone, the number of people age 65 or older is expected to rise by more than one-third, and the share of the population age 65 or older is projected to grow from the current 15 percent to 21 percent in 2040.

Why is the over-65 population increasing so rapidly? What are the implications of this increase for future federal spending on Social Security and Medicare as a percentage of GDP? What choices do policymakers face in dealing with this issue?

Source: Congressional Budget Office, "The 2015 Long-Term Budget Outlook," June 2015, p. 21.

27.2 The Effects of Fiscal Policy on Real GDP and the Price Level, pages 945–947

LEARNING OBJECTIVE: Explain how fiscal policy affects aggregate demand and how the government can use fiscal policy to stabilize the economy.

Summary

To fight recessions, Congress and the president can increase government purchases or cut taxes. This expansionary policy increases aggregate demand, raising the level of real GDP and the price level. To fight rising inflation, Congress and the president can decrease government purchases or raise taxes. This contractionary policy reduces aggregate demand relative to what it would otherwise be, thereby reducing the inflation rate.

MyEconLab Visit **www.myeconlab.com** to complete these exercises online and get instant feedback.

Review Questions

2.1 What is an expansionary fiscal policy? What is a contractionary fiscal policy?

2.2 If Congress and the president decide that an expansionary fiscal policy is necessary, what changes should they make in government spending or taxes? What changes should they make if they decide that a contractionary fiscal policy is necessary?

Problems and Applications

2.3 Briefly explain whether you agree with the following statements: "An expansionary fiscal policy involves an increase in government purchases or an increase in taxes. A contractionary fiscal policy involves a decrease in government purchases or a decrease in taxes."

2.4 Identify each of the following as (1) part of an expansionary fiscal policy, (2) part of a contractionary fiscal policy, or (3) not part of fiscal policy.

a. The corporate income tax rate is increased.
b. Defense spending is increased.
c. The Federal Reserve lowers the target for the federal funds rate.
d. Families are allowed to deduct all their expenses for day care from their federal income taxes.
e. The individual income tax rate is decreased.

2.5. Use an aggregate demand and aggregate supply graph to illustrate the situation where equilibrium initially occurs with real GDP equal to potential GDP and then the aggregate demand curve shifts to the left. What actions can Congress and the president take to move real GDP back to potential GDP? Show the results of these actions on your graph. Assume that the *LRAS* curve doesn't shift.

2.6. **(Related to the Don't Let This Happen to You on page 946)** Is it possible for Congress and the president to carry out an expansionary fiscal policy if the money supply does not increase? Briefly explain.

2.7 A political commentator argues: "Congress and the president are more likely to enact an expansionary fiscal policy than a contractionary fiscal policy because expansionary policies are popular and contractionary policies are unpopular." Briefly explain whether you agree.

2.8 **(Related to the Chapter Opener on page 939)** In 2015, in proposing a $478 billion increase in federal spending on infrastructure, President Obama argued that the spending would increase total employment in the United States.

a. Will increases in federal spending always increase real GDP and employment in the short run? Briefly explain.
b. Are there circumstances in which the federal government would not want to increase its spending even if the result was to increase real GDP and employment in the short run? What was President Obama assuming about the state of the economy in 2015?

Source: Michael D. Shear, "Obama Proposes Tax for Upgrade of Infrastructure," *New York Times*, February 2, 2015.

27.3 Fiscal Policy in the Dynamic Aggregate Demand and Aggregate Supply Model, pages 947–948

LEARNING OBJECTIVE: Use the dynamic aggregate demand and aggregate supply model to analyze fiscal policy.

Summary

We can use the *dynamic aggregate demand and aggregate supply model* to look more closely at expansionary and contractionary fiscal policies. This model takes into account that (1) the economy experiences continuing inflation, with the price level rising every year, and (2) the economy experiences long-run growth, with the *LRAS* curve shifting to the right every year. In the dynamic model, an expansionary fiscal policy tries to ensure that the aggregate demand curve will shift far enough to the right to bring about macroeconomic equilibrium with real GDP equal to potential GDP. A contractionary fiscal policy attempts to offset movements in aggregate demand that would cause macroeconomic equilibrium to occur at a level of real GDP that is greater than potential GDP.

MyEconLab Visit **www.myeconlab.com** to complete these exercises online and get instant feedback.

Review Questions

3.1 What are the key differences between how we illustrate an expansionary fiscal policy in the basic aggregate demand and aggregate supply model and in the dynamic aggregate demand and aggregate supply model?

3.2 What are the key differences between how we illustrate a contractionary fiscal policy in the basic aggregate demand and aggregate supply model and in the dynamic aggregate demand and aggregate supply model?

Problems and Applications

3.3 A report from the Congressional Budget Office (CBO) notes, "Potential GDP is CBO's estimate of the maximum sustainable output of the economy." In early 2015, the CBO estimated that the gap between real GDP and potential GDP would fall from 2.9 percent in 2014 to zero in 2017. In 2014, real GDP was $16.3 trillion, and the CBO's estimate of potential GDP was $16.8 trillion. The CBO forecast that potential GDP would increase to $17.5 trillion.

a. Why does the CBO include the word "sustainable" in its definition of potential GDP?

b. Draw an aggregate demand and aggregate supply graph to illustrate the macroeconomic situation in 2014 and in 2017 (you do not have to show on your graph the situation in 2015 or 2016). Be sure that your graph contains *LRAS* curves for 2014 and 2017, *SRAS* curves for 2014 and 2017, and *AD* curves for 2014 and 2017, and that it shows equilibrium real GDP and the price levels for both years.

Sources: Congressional Budget Office, "The 2015 Long-Term Budget Outlook," June 2015, p. 36; and Congressional Budget Office, "The Budget and Economic Outlook: 2015 to 2025," January 2015.

3.4 Use the graph to answer the following questions.

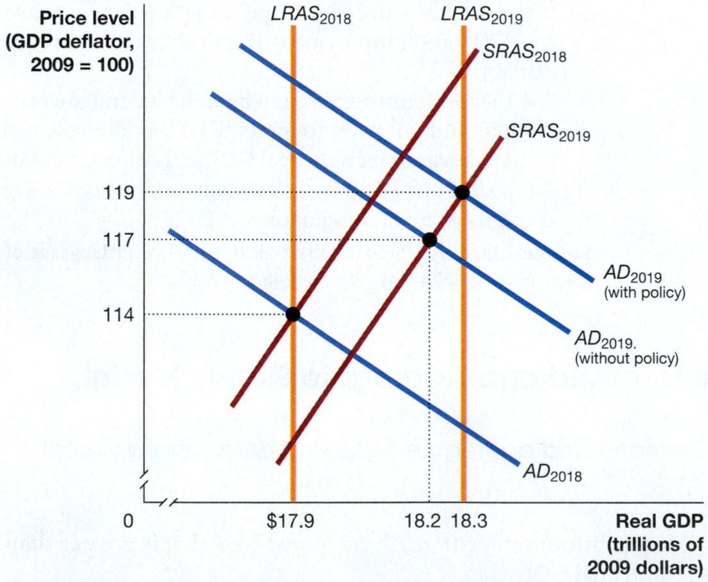

a. If the government takes no policy actions, what will be the values of real GDP and the price level in 2019?

b. What actions can the government take to bring real GDP to its potential level in 2019?

c. If the government takes no policy actions, what will the inflation rate be in 2019? If the government uses fiscal policy to keep real GDP at its potential level, what will the inflation rate be in 2019?

3.5 The hypothetical information in the following table shows what the situation will be in 2019 if Congress and the president do *not* use fiscal policy:

Year	Potential GDP	Real GDP	Price Level
2018	$17.9 trillion	$17.9 trillion	113.7
2019	$18.3 trillion	$17.9 trillion	115.9

a. If Congress and the president want to keep real GDP at its potential level in 2019, should they use an expansionary policy or a contractionary policy? In your answer, be sure to explain whether Congress and the president should increase or decrease government purchases and taxes.

b. If Congress and the president are successful in keeping real GDP at its potential level in 2019, state whether each of the following will be higher, lower, or the same as it would have been if they had taken no action:

i. Real GDP
ii. Potential GDP
iii. The inflation rate
iv. The unemployment rate

c. Draw an aggregate demand and aggregate supply graph to illustrate your answer. Be sure that your graph contains *LRAS* curves for 2018 and 2019; *SRAS* curves for 2018 and 2019; *AD* curves for 2018 and 2019, with and without fiscal policy action; and equilibrium real GDP and the price level in 2019, with and without fiscal policy.

3.6 Use a dynamic aggregate demand and aggregate supply graph to illustrate the change in macroeconomic equilibrium from 2019 to 2020, assuming that the economy experiences deflation during 2020. In order for deflation to take place in 2020, does the economy also have to be experiencing a recession? Briefly explain.

27.4 The Government Purchases and Tax Multipliers, pages 949–953

LEARNING OBJECTIVE: Explain how the government purchases and tax multipliers work.

Summary

Because of the **multiplier effect**, an increase in government purchases or a cut in taxes will have a multiplied effect on equilibrium real GDP. The *government purchases multiplier* is equal to the change in equilibrium real GDP divided by the change in government purchases. The *tax multiplier* is equal to the change in equilibrium real GDP divided by the change in taxes. Increases in government purchases and cuts in taxes have a positive multiplier effect on equilibrium real GDP. Decreases in government purchases and increases in taxes have a negative multiplier effect on equilibrium real GDP.

MyEconLab Visit **www.myeconlab.com** to complete these exercises online and get instant feedback.

Review Questions

4.1 Why can a $1 increase in government purchases lead to more than a $1 increase in income and spending?

4.2 Define *government purchases multiplier* and *tax multiplier*.

4.3 Why does a higher income tax rate reduce the multiplier effect?

Problems and Applications

4.4 **(Related to the Chapter Opener on page 939)** Another infrastructure project in northern California funded in part by ARRA funds involved expanding the Caldecott Tunnel between the cities of Oakland and Orinda. A spokesperson for the California state agency in charge of the project mentioned that the Caldecott Tunnel project would have a "ripple effect" on employment. What did the spokesperson mean by a ripple effect?

Source: Zusha Elinson, "Caldecott Tunnel Edges Forward, Tribute to Stimulus Bill," *New York Times*, September 10, 2011.

4.5 In *The General Theory of Employment, Interest, and Money*, John Maynard Keynes wrote:

> If the Treasury were to fill old bottles with banknotes, bury them at suitable depths in disused coal mines which are then filled up to the surface with town rubbish, and leave it to private enterprise ... to dig the notes up again ... there need be no more unemployment and, with the help of the repercussions, the real income of the community ... would probably become a good deal greater than it is.

Which important macroeconomic effect is Keynes discussing here? What does he mean by "repercussions"? Why does he appear unconcerned about whether government spending is wasteful?

Source: John Maynard Keynes, *The General Theory of Employment, Interest and Money*, New York: Harcourt Brace, 1936, p. 128.

4.6 **(Related to Solved Problem 27.4 on page 952)** Suppose that real GDP is currently $17.1 trillion, potential GDP is $17.4 trillion, the government purchases multiplier is 2, and the tax multiplier is −1.6.

a. Holding other factors constant, by how much will government purchases need to be increased to bring the economy to equilibrium at potential GDP?

b. Holding other factors constant, by how much will taxes have to be cut to bring the economy to equilibrium at potential GDP?

c. Construct an example of a *combination* of increased government spending and tax cuts that will bring the economy to equilibrium at potential GDP.

4.7 **(Related to Solved Problem 27.4 on page 952)** Briefly explain whether you agree with the following statement:

> Real GDP is currently $17.7 trillion, and potential GDP is $17.4 trillion. If Congress and the president would decrease government purchases by $300 billion or increase taxes by $300 billion, the economy could be brought to equilibrium at potential GDP.

4.8 A Federal Reserve publication argues that the size of the multiplier "depends on the type of fiscal policy changes in question and the environment in which they are implemented."

a. What does the author mean by "the type of fiscal policy changes in question"? Why does the type of policy matter for the size of the multiplier?

b. What does the author mean by "the environment in which they are implemented"? Would the size of the multiplier be affected by how close real GDP is to potential GDP? Briefly explain.

Source: Daniel J. Wilson, "Government Spending: An Economic Boost?" *Federal Reserve Bank of San Francisco Economic Letter*, February 6, 2012.

4.9 If the short-run aggregate supply (*SRAS*) curve were a horizontal line at the current price level, what would be the effect on the size of the government purchases and tax multipliers? Briefly explain.

27.5 The Limits to Using Fiscal Policy to Stabilize the Economy, pages 953–963

LEARNING OBJECTIVE: Discuss the difficulties that can arise in implementing fiscal policy.

Summary

Poorly timed fiscal policy can do more harm than good. Getting the timing right with fiscal policy can be difficult because a president obtaining approval from Congress for a new fiscal policy can be a very long process, and it can take months for an increase in authorized spending to actually take place. Because an increase in government purchases may lead to a higher interest rate, it may result in a decline in consumption, investment, and net exports. A decline in private expenditures as a result of an increase in government purchases is called **crowding out**. Crowding out may cause an expansionary fiscal policy to fail to meet its goal of keeping real GDP at potential GDP.

MyEconLab Visit **www.myeconlab.com** to complete these exercises online and get instant feedback.

Review Questions

5.1 Which can be changed more quickly: monetary policy or fiscal policy? Briefly explain.

5.2 What is meant by "crowding out"? Explain the difference between crowding out in the short run and in the long run.

Problems and Applications

5.3 Some economists argue that because increases in government spending crowd out private spending, increased government spending will reduce the long-run growth rate of real GDP.

a. Is this outcome most likely to occur if the private spending being crowded out is consumption spending, investment spending, or net exports? Briefly explain.

b. In terms of its effect on the long-run growth rate of real GDP, would it matter if the additional government spending involves (i) increased spending on highways and bridges or (ii) increased spending on national parks? Briefly explain.

5.4 According to a study by Kanishka Misra of the University of Michigan and Paolo Surico of the London Business School, "Almost half of American families did not adjust their consumption following receipt of the … 2008 tax rebate." Don't we expect that people will increase their consumption if their disposable income increases? Was there anything about the form of the 2008 tax cut that made it more likely that people would not respond by increasing their consumption spending? Briefly explain.

Source: Kanishka Misra and Paolo Surico, "Consumption, Income Changes, and Heterogeneity: Evidence from Two Fiscal Stimulus Programs," *American Economic Journal: Macroeconomics*, Vol. 6, No. 4, October 2014, pp. 84–106.

5.5 We saw that in calculating the stimulus package's effect on real GDP, economists in the Obama administration estimated that the government purchases multiplier has a value of 1.57. John F. Cogan, Tobias Cwik, John B. Taylor, and Volker Wieland argue that the value is only 0.4.

a. Briefly explain how the government purchases multiplier can have a value of less than 1.

b. Why does an estimate of the size of the multiplier matter in evaluating the effects of an expansionary fiscal policy?

Source: John Cogan, Tobias Cwik, John Taylor, and Volker Wieland, "New Keynesian versus Old Keynesian Government Spending Multipliers," *Journal of Economic Dynamics and Control*, Vol. 34, No. 3, March 2010, pp. 281–295.

5.6 **(Related to the Making the Connection on page 954)** Why would a recession accompanied by a financial crisis be more severe than a recession that did not involve a financial crisis? Were the large budget deficits in 2009 and 2010 primarily the result of the stimulus package of 2009? Briefly explain.

5.7 Suppose that at the same time Congress and the president pursue an expansionary fiscal policy, the Federal Reserve pursues an expansionary monetary policy. How might an expansionary monetary policy affect the extent of crowding out in the short run?

5.8 **(Related to the Making the Connection on page 962)** A report from the International Monetary Fund in late 2014 contained the following observations: "Five years after the global financial crisis, the economic recovery continues but remains weak.… Given … the current environment of low government borrowing costs … might this be a good time to increase public infrastructure investment?"

a. What does the report mean by "low government borrowing costs"? Why would low government borrowing costs be relevant to whether a government increases infrastructure investment?

b. The report also notes, "In advanced economies an increase in infrastructure investment … is one of the few remaining policy levers available to support growth." What does the report mean by a "policy lever"? Why would the authors of the report consider infrastructure one of the few remaining policy levers?

Source: International Monetary Fund, "World Economic Outlook: Legacies, Clouds, Uncertainties," October 2014, pp. 75–76.

27.6 Deficits, Surpluses, and Federal Government Debt, pages 963–968

LEARNING OBJECTIVE: Define federal budget deficit and federal government debt and explain how the federal budget can serve as an automatic stabilizer.

Summary

A **budget deficit** occurs when the federal government's expenditures are greater than its tax revenues. A **budget surplus** occurs when the federal government's expenditures are less than its tax revenues. A budget deficit automatically increases during recessions and decreases during expansions. The automatic movements in the federal budget help to stabilize the economy by cushioning the fall in spending during recessions and restraining the increase in spending during expansions. The **cyclically adjusted budget deficit or surplus** measures what the deficit or surplus would be if the economy were at potential GDP. The federal government debt (or national debt) is the value of outstanding bonds issued by the U.S. Treasury. The national debt is a problem if interest payments on it require taxes to be raised substantially or require other federal expenditures to be cut.

MyEconLab Visit **www.myeconlab.com** to complete these exercises online and get instant feedback.

Review Questions

6.1 In what ways does the federal budget serve as an automatic stabilizer for the economy?

6.2 What is the cyclically adjusted budget deficit or surplus? Suppose that real GDP is currently at potential GDP, and the federal budget is balanced. If the economy moves into a recession, what will happen to the federal budget?

6.3 Why do few economists believe it would be a good idea to balance the federal budget every year?

6.4 What is the difference between the federal budget deficit and federal government debt?

Problems and Applications

6.5 *Wall Street Journal* writers Josh Zumbrun and Nick Timiraos published answers to several of their readers' questions regarding the federal government's debt. Two of the questions were:

a. Why is government debt different from mine?

b. How important is it to pay off this debt?

Write a brief response to each of these questions.

Source: Josh Zumbrun and Nick Timiraos, "Q&A: What the $18 Trillion National Debt Means for the U.S. Economy," *Wall Street Journal*, February 1, 2015.

6.6 In a column in the *Financial Times*, the prime minister and the finance minister of the Netherlands argue that the European Union, an organization of 28 countries in Europe, should appoint "a commissioner for budgetary discipline." They believe that "the new commissioner should be given clear powers to set requirements for the budgetary policy of countries that run excessive deficits." What is an "excessive" budget deficit? Does judging whether a deficit is excessive depend in part on whether the country is in a recession? How can budgetary policies be used to reduce a budget deficit?

Source: Mark Rutte and Jan Kees de Jager, "Expulsion from the Eurozone Has to Be the Final Penalty," *Financial Times*, September 7, 2011.

6.7 **(Related to the Making the Connection on page 965)** The following is from a message by President Herbert Hoover to Congress, dated May 5, 1932:

> I need not recount that the revenues of the Government as estimated for the next fiscal year show a decrease of about $1,700,000,000 below the fiscal year 1929, and inexorably require a broader basis of taxation and a drastic reduction of expenditures in order to balance the Budget. Nothing is more necessary at this time than balancing the Budget.

Do you think President Hoover was correct in saying that, in 1932, nothing was more necessary than balancing the federal government's budget? Explain.

Source: Herbert Hoover, "Special Message to the Congress on Budgetary Legislation," in *Public Papers of the Presidents of the United States: Herbert Hoover, 1932–1933*, 1977, p. 194.

6.8 In February 2013, the Congressional Budget Office (CBO) forecast that the federal budget deficit for fiscal year 2013 would be approximately $850 billion. In May 2013, the CBO revised down its forecast of the budget deficit to $642 billion. The CBO stated that a major reason for the downward revision was "factors related mainly to the strengthening economy."

a. Why would a "strengthening economy" lead to a downward revision of the projected budget deficit?

b. Suppose that Congress and the president were committed to balancing the budget each year. Does what happened during 2013 provide any insight into difficulties they might run into in trying to balance the budget every year?

Source: Susan Davis, "CBO Drops 2013 Deficit Estimate to $642 Billion," usatoday.com, May 15, 2013.

6.9 **(Related to Solved Problem 27.6 on page 966)** An article in the *Wall Street Journal* in 2015 noted that an official of the European Union was forecasting that "Greece faces two years of recession amid sharp budget cuts." What typically happens to a government's budget deficit during a recession? Do governments typical respond with budget cuts as the Greek government did? Briefly explain.

Source: Gabriele Steinhauser and Andrea Thomas, "Greece Faces Two-Year Recession amid Bailout Cuts," *Wall Street Journal*, August 12, 2015.

6.10 In 2015, an article in the *Wall Street Journal* noted that "Prime Minister Shinzo Abe is expected to unveil a plan to balance Japan's budget in five years ... as a step toward reducing the country's debt burden, according to government officials." What is the connection between the government's budget deficit and its debt? If the debt is a "burden," briefly explain what it is a burden on.

Source: Tatsuo Ito, "Japan Government Takes On Its Deficit-Ridden Finances," *Wall Street Journal*, June 17, 2015.

6.11 A political columnist wrote the following:

> Today ... the main purpose [of governments issuing bonds] is to let craven politicians launch projects they know the public, at the moment, would rather not fully finance. The tab for these projects will not come due, probably, until after the politicians have long since departed for greener (excuse the expression) pastures.

Do you agree with this commentator's explanation for why some government spending is financed through tax receipts and other government spending is financed through borrowing, by issuing bonds? Briefly explain.

Source: Paul Carpenter, "The Bond Issue Won't Be Repaid by Park Tolls," (Allentown, PA) *Morning Call*, May 26, 2002.

27.7 The Effects of Fiscal Policy in the Long Run, pages 968–971

LEARNING OBJECTIVE: Discuss the effects of fiscal policy in the long run.

Summary

Some fiscal policy actions are intended to have long-run effects by expanding the productive capacity of the economy and increasing the rate of economic growth. Because these policy actions primarily affect aggregate supply rather than aggregate demand, they are sometimes called *supply-side economics*. The difference between the pretax and posttax return to an economic activity is called the **tax wedge**. Economists believe that the smaller the tax wedge for any economic activity—such as working, saving, investing, or starting a business—the more of that economic activity will occur. Economists debate the size of the supply-side effects of tax changes.

MyEconLab Visit **www.myeconlab.com** to complete these exercises online and get instant feedback.

Review Questions

7.1 What is meant by "supply-side economics"?
7.2 What is the "tax wedge"?

Problems and Applications

7.3 It seems that both households and businesses would benefit if the federal income tax were simpler and tax forms were easier to fill out. Why then have the tax laws become increasingly complicated?

7.4 Some economists and policymakers have argued in favor of a "flat tax." A flat tax would replace the current individual income tax system, with its many tax brackets, exemptions, and deductions, with a new system containing a single tax rate and few, or perhaps no, deductions and exemptions. Suppose a political candidate hired you to develop two arguments in favor of a flat tax. What two arguments would you advance? Alternatively, if you were hired to develop two arguments against a flat tax, what two arguments would you advance?

7.5 Suppose that an increase in marginal tax rates on individual income affects both aggregate demand and aggregate supply. Briefly describe the effect of the tax increase on equilibrium real GDP and the equilibrium price level. Will the changes in equilibrium real GDP and the price level be larger or smaller than they would be if the tax increase affected only aggregate demand? Briefly explain.

7.6 Writing in the *Wall Street Journal*, Martin Feldstein, an economist at Harvard University, argues that "behavioral responses" of taxpayers to the cuts in marginal tax rates enacted in 1986 resulted in "an enormous rise in the taxes paid, particularly by those who experienced the greatest reductions in marginal tax rates." How is it possible for cuts in marginal tax rates to result in an increase in total taxes collected? What does Feldstein mean by a "behavioral response" to tax cuts?

Source: Martin Feldstein, "The Tax Reform Evidence from 1986," *Wall Street Journal*, October 24, 2011.

Real-Time Data Exercises

D27.1 **(Comparing macroeconomic conditions in different countries)** The International Monetary Fund (IMF) publishes *The World Economic Outlook*. Go to www.imf.org and look at the most recent version available. The IMF measures the output gap as the difference between real GDP and potential GDP as a percentage of potential GDP. A negative value for the output gap means that real GDP is below potential GDP. Look at the data on the output gap for Japan, the United Kingdom, and the United States for 2013 to 2018 (the values for the later years will be forecasts).

a. Which country had the largest output gap (in absolute value) in 2013? Which country had the smallest output gap?
b. Discuss what fiscal policies the governments of these countries could use to bring the output gaps to zero.
c. Describe at least two problems that these countries would have in implementing your suggested policies.

D27.2 **(Comparing the actual and cyclically adjusted budget deficits in the United States)** The Congressional Budget Office (CBO) provides data on the actual and cyclically adjusted budget deficits. You can find data for the years 1965–2014 at https://www.cbo.gov/sites/default/files/114th-congress-2015-2016/reports/49892/49892-breakout-AppendixD.pdf.

a. The CBO calls the budget deficit or surplus "Deficit or Surplus with Automatic Stabilizers," and calls the cyclically adjusted deficit or surplus the "Deficit or Surplus without Automatic Stabilizers." Briefly explain why the CBO uses these labels.
b. For the years 2000-2014, enter the data from the columns "Deficit or Surplus with Automatic Stabilizers," and "Deficit or Surplus without Automatic Stabilizers" into an Excel spreadsheet. Use the data to graph the budget deficit or surplus and the cyclically adjusted deficit or surplus for these years.
c. Calculate the average surplus or deficit and the average cyclically adjusted surplus or deficit for these years. Which was larger? Briefly explain your result.

D27.3 **(Comparing budget deficits in different countries)** The International Monetary Fund (IMF) publishes *The World Economic Outlook*. Go to www.imf.org and find the IMF data for the cyclically adjusted budget deficit as a percentage of potential GDP (which the IMF calls "General Government Structural Balance") for Brazil, China, France, and Germany from 2000 to 2018 (the values for the later years will be forecasts). Use the series for the cyclically adjusted budget deficit that is measured as a percentage of potential GDP.

a. Download the data and plot them in a graph. Which country relied the most on discretionary fiscal policy in response to the financial crisis of 2008 and 2009? Briefly explain how you are able to tell.
b. From 2013 to 2018, which of these four countries is expected to have the most expansionary fiscal policy? Briefly explain.

Appendix

A Closer Look at the Multiplier

LEARNING OBJECTIVE: Apply the multiplier formula.

In this chapter, we saw that changes in government purchases and changes in taxes have a multiplied effect on equilibrium real GDP. In this appendix, we will build a simple economic model of the multiplier effect. When economists forecast the effect of a change in spending or taxes, they often rely on *econometric models*. These are economic models written in the form of equations, where each equation has been statistically estimated, using methods similar to those used in estimating demand curves, as briefly described in Chapter 3.

An Expression for Equilibrium Real GDP

We can write a set of equations that includes the key macroeconomic relationships we have studied in this and previous chapters. It is important to note that in this model, we will be assuming that the price level is constant. We know that this assumption is unrealistic because an upward-sloping *SRAS* curve means that when the aggregate demand curve shifts, the price level will change. Nevertheless, our model will be approximately correct when changes in the price level are small. It also serves as an introduction to more complicated models that take into account changes in the price level. For simplicity, we start with three assumptions: (1) Taxes, T, do not depend on the level of real GDP, Y; (2) there are no government transfer payments to households; and (3) we have a closed economy, with no imports or exports. The numbers (with the exception of the *MPC*) represent billions of dollars:

(1) $C = 1{,}000 + 0.75(Y - T)$	Consumption function
(2) $I = 1{,}500$	Planned investment function
(3) $G = 1{,}500$	Government purchases function
(4) $T = 1{,}000$	Tax function
(5) $Y = C + I + G$	Equilibrium condition

The first equation is the consumption function. The marginal propensity to consume, or *MPC*, is 0.75, and 1,000 is the level of autonomous consumption, which is the level of consumption that does not depend on income. We assume that consumption depends on disposable income, which is $Y - T$. The functions for planned investment spending, government spending, and taxes are very simple because we have assumed that these variables are not affected by GDP and, therefore, are constant. Economists who use this type of model to forecast GDP would, of course, use more realistic planned investment, government purchases, and tax functions.

Equation (5)—the equilibrium condition—states that equilibrium GDP equals the sum of consumption, planned investment spending, and government purchases. To calculate a value for equilibrium real GDP, we need to substitute equations (1) through (4) into equation (5). This substitution gives us the following:

$$
\begin{aligned}
Y &= 1{,}000 + 0.75(Y - 1{,}000) + 1{,}500 + 1{,}500 \\
&= 1{,}000 + 0.75Y - 750 + 1{,}500 + 1{,}500.
\end{aligned}
$$

We need to solve this equation for Y to find equilibrium GDP. The first step is to subtract $0.75Y$ from both sides of the equation:

$$Y - 0.75Y = 1{,}000 - 750 + 1{,}500 + 1{,}500.$$

Then, we solve for Y:

$$0.25Y = 3{,}250,$$

or:

$$Y = \frac{3{,}250}{0.25} = 13{,}000.$$

To make this result more general, we can replace particular values with general values represented by letters:

$C = \overline{C} + MPC(Y - T)$	Consumption function
$I = \overline{I}$	Planned investment function
$G = \overline{G}$	Government purchases function
$T = \overline{T}$	Tax function
$Y = C + T + G$	Equilibrium condition

The letters with bars above them represent fixed, or *autonomous*, values that do not depend on the values of other variables. So, $\overline{C}$ represents autonomous consumption, which had a value of 1,000 in our original example. Now, solving for equilibrium, we get:

$$Y = \overline{C} + MPC(Y - \overline{T}) + \overline{I} + \overline{G}$$

or:

$$Y - MPC(Y) = \overline{C} - (MPC \times \overline{T}) + \overline{I} + \overline{G}$$

or:

$$Y(1 - MPC) = \overline{C} - (MPC \times \overline{T}) + \overline{I} + \overline{G}$$

or:

$$Y = \frac{\overline{C} - (MPC \times \overline{T}) + \overline{I} + \overline{G}}{1 - MPC}.$$

MyEconLab Concept Check

A Formula for the Government Purchases Multiplier

To find a formula for the government purchases multiplier, we need to rewrite the last equation for changes in each variable rather than levels. Letting Δ stand for the change in a variable, we have:

$$\Delta Y = \frac{\Delta\overline{C} - (MPC \times \Delta\overline{T}) + \Delta\overline{I} + \Delta\overline{G}}{1 - MPC}.$$

We can find a formula for the government purchases multiplier, which is the ratio of the change in equilibrium real GDP to the change in government purchases. If we hold constant changes in autonomous consumption spending, planned investment spending, and taxes, then from the previous equation we have the following:

$$\Delta Y = \frac{\Delta G}{1 - MPC}.$$

So, we have:

$$\text{Government purchases multiplier} = \frac{\Delta Y}{\Delta G} = \frac{1}{1 - MPC}.$$

For an *MPC* of 0.75, the government purchases multiplier will be:

$$\frac{1}{1 - 0.75} = 4.$$

A government purchases multiplier of 4 means that an increase in government spending of \$10 billion will increase equilibrium real GDP by 4 × \$10 billion = \$40 billion.

MyEconLab Concept Check

A Formula for the Tax Multiplier

We can also find a formula for the tax multiplier. We start again with this equation:

$$\Delta Y = \frac{\Delta \bar{C} - (MPC \times \Delta \bar{T}) + \Delta \bar{I} + \Delta \bar{G}}{1 - MPC}.$$

Now we hold constant the values of autonomous consumption spending, planned investment spending, and government purchases, but we allow the value of taxes to change:

$$\Delta Y = \frac{-MPC \times \Delta T}{1 - MPC}.$$

So, we have:

$$\text{The tax multiplier} = \frac{\Delta Y}{\Delta T} = \frac{-MPC}{1 - MPC}.$$

For an *MPC* of 0.75, the tax multiplier will be:

$$\frac{-0.75}{1 - 0.75} = -3.$$

The tax multiplier is a negative number because an increase in taxes causes a decrease in equilibrium real GDP, and a decrease in taxes causes an increase in equilibrium real GDP. A tax multiplier of -3 means that a decrease in taxes of \$10 billion will increase equilibrium real GDP by $-3 \times -\$10$ billion $= \$30$ billion. Earlier in this chapter, we discussed the economic reasons for the tax multiplier being smaller than the government spending multiplier.

MyEconLab Concept Check

The "Balanced Budget" Multiplier

What will be the effect of equal increases (or decreases) in government purchases and taxes on equilibrium real GDP? At first, it might appear that the tax increase would exactly offset the government purchases increase, leaving real GDP unchanged. But we have just seen that the government purchases multiplier is larger (in absolute value) than the tax multiplier. We can use our formulas for the government purchases multiplier and the tax multiplier to calculate the net effect of increasing government purchases by \$10 billion at the same time that taxes are increased by \$10 billion:

$$\text{Increase in real GDP from the increase in government purchases} = \$10 \text{ billion} \times \frac{1}{1 - MPC}.$$

$$\text{Decrease in real GDP from the increase in taxes} = \$10 \text{ billion} \times \frac{-MPC}{1 - MPC}.$$

So, the combined effect equals:

$$\$10 \text{ billion} \times \left[\left(\frac{1}{1 - MPC}\right) + \left(\frac{-MPC}{1 - MPC}\right)\right],$$

or:

$$\$10 \text{ billion} \times \left(\frac{1 - MPC}{1 - MPC}\right) = \$10 \text{ billion}.$$

The balanced budget multiplier is, therefore, equal to $(1-MPC)/(1-MPC)$, or 1. Equal dollar increases and decreases in government purchases and in taxes lead to the same dollar increase in real GDP in the short run.

MyEconLab Concept Check

The Effects of Changes in Tax Rates on the Multiplier

We now consider the effect of a change in the tax *rate*, as opposed to a change in a fixed amount of taxes. Changing the tax rate actually changes the value of the multiplier. To see this, suppose that the tax rate is 20 percent, or 0.2. In that case, an increase in household income of \$10 billion will increase *disposable income* by only \$8 billion [or 10 billion × (1 − 0.2) In general, an increase in income can be multiplied by (1 − *t*) to find the increase in disposable income, where *t* is the tax rate. So, we can rewrite the consumption function as:

$$C = \overline{C} + MPC(1 - t)Y.$$

We can use this expression for the consumption function to find an expression for the government purchases multiplier, using the same method we used previously:

$$\text{Government purchases multiplier} = \frac{\Delta Y}{\Delta G} = \frac{1}{1 - MPC(1 - t)}.$$

We can see the effect of changing the tax rate on the size of the multiplier by trying some values. First, assume that $MPC = 0.75$ and $t = 0.2$. Then:

$$\text{Government purchases multiplier} = \frac{\Delta Y}{\Delta G} = \frac{1}{1 - 0.75(1 - 0.2)} = \frac{1}{1 - 0.6} = 2.5$$

This value is smaller than the multiplier of 4 that we calculated by assuming that there was only a fixed amount of taxes (which is the same as assuming that the marginal tax *rate* was zero). This multiplier is smaller because spending in each period is now reduced by the amount of taxes households must pay on any additional income they earn. We can calculate the multiplier for an *MPC* of 0.75 and a lower tax rate of 0.1:

$$\text{Government purchases multiplier} = \frac{\Delta Y}{\Delta G} = \frac{1}{1 - 0.75(1 - 0.1)} = \frac{1}{1 - 0.675} = 3.1.$$

Cutting the tax rate from 20 percent to 10 percent increased the value of the multiplier from 2.5 to 3.1.

MyEconLab Concept Check

The Multiplier in an Open Economy

Up to now, we have assumed that the economy is closed, with no imports or exports. We can consider the case of an open economy by including net exports in our analysis. Recall that net exports equal exports minus imports. Exports are determined primarily by factors—such as the exchange value of the dollar and the levels of real GDP in other countries—that we do not include in our model. So, we will assume that exports are fixed, or autonomous:

$$\text{Exports} = \overline{\text{Exports}}.$$

Imports will increase as real GDP increases because households will spend some portion of an increase in income on imports. We can define the *marginal propensity to import* (*MPI*) as the fraction of an increase in income that is spent on imports. So, our expression for imports is:

$$\text{Imports} = MPI \times Y.$$

We can substitute our expressions for exports and imports into the expression we derived earlier for equilibrium real GDP:

$$Y = \overline{C} + MPC(1 - t)Y + \overline{I} + \overline{G} + [\overline{\text{Exports}} - (MPI \times Y)],$$

where the expression $[\overline{\text{Exports}} - (MPI \times Y)]$ represents net exports. We can now find an expression for the government purchases multiplier by using the same method we used previously:

$$\text{Government purchases multiplier} = \frac{\Delta Y}{\Delta G} = \frac{1}{1 - [MPC(1 - t) - MPI]}.$$

We can see the effect of changing the value of the marginal propensity to import on the size of the multiplier by trying some values of key variables. First, assume that $MPC = 0.75$, $t = 0.2$, and $MPI = 0.1$. Then:

$$\text{Government purchases multiplier} = \frac{\Delta Y}{\Delta G} = \frac{1}{1 - (0.75(1 - 0.2) - 0.1)} = \frac{1}{1 - 0.5} = 2.$$

This value is smaller than the multiplier of 2.5 that we calculated by assuming that there were no exports or imports (which is the same as assuming that the marginal propensity to import is zero). This multiplier is smaller because spending in each period is now reduced by the amount of imports households buy with any additional income they earn. We can calculate the multiplier with $MPC = 0.75$, $t = 0.2$, and a higher MPI of 0.2:

$$\text{Government purchases multiplier} = \frac{\Delta Y}{\Delta G} = \frac{1}{1 - (0.75(1 - 0.2) - 0.2)} = \frac{1}{1 - 0.4} = 1.7.$$

Increasing the marginal propensity to import from 0.1 to 0.2 decreases the value of the multiplier from 2 to 1.7. We can conclude that countries with a higher marginal propensity to import will have smaller multipliers than countries with a lower marginal propensity to import.

Bear in mind that the multiplier is a short-run effect that assumes that real GDP is less than potential GDP. In the long run, real GDP equals potential GDP, so an increase in government purchases causes a decline in the nongovernment components of real GDP but leaves the level of real GDP unchanged.

The analysis in this appendix is simplified compared to what would be carried out by an economist forecasting the effects of changes in government purchases or changes in taxes on equilibrium real GDP in the short run. In particular, our assumption that the price level is constant is unrealistic. However, looking more closely at the determinants of the multiplier has helped us see some important macroeconomic relationships more clearly.

MyEconLab Concept Check

27A A Closer Look at the Multiplier, pages 979–983

LEARNING OBJECTIVE: Apply the multiplier formula.

MyEconLab Visit **www.myeconlab.com** to complete these exercises online and get instant feedback.

Problem and Applications

27A.1 Assuming a fixed amount of taxes and a closed economy, calculate the value of the government purchases multiplier, the tax multiplier, and the balanced budget multiplier if the marginal propensity to consume equals 0.6.

27A.2 Calculate the value of the government purchases multiplier if the marginal propensity to consume equals 0.8, the tax rate equals 0.25, and the marginal propensity to import equals 0.2.

27A.3 Use a graph to show the change in the aggregate demand curve resulting from an increase in government purchases if the government purchases multiplier equals 2. On the same graph, show the change in the aggregate demand curve resulting from an increase in government purchases if the government purchases multiplier equals 4.

27A.4 Using your understanding of multipliers, explain why an increase in the tax rate would decrease the size of the government purchases multiplier. Similarly, explain why a decrease in the marginal propensity to import would increase the size of the government purchases multiplier.

27A.5 In 2012, the ratio of imports to GDP was 14 percent in Japan and 83 percent in Belgium. On the basis of this information, can you draw any conclusions about the relative sizes of the government purchases multiplier in each country?

CHAPTER

28

Inflation, Unemployment, and Federal Reserve Policy

Chapter Outline and Learning Objectives

Why Does Goodyear Worry about Monetary Policy?

The Federal Reserve's dual mandate of price stability and high employment can present the Federal Open Market Committee (FOMC) with difficult decisions. For example, in mid-2015, although the unemployment rate had fallen from a high of 10.0 percent in October 2009 to 5.1 percent, the inflation rate had been well below the Fed's target of 2 percent for more than three years. Investors, as well as many households and firms, anticipated that Federal Reserve Chair Janet Yellen and her colleagues on the FOMC would finally increase the target for the federal funds rate. The federal funds rate had remained effectively at zero since December 2008, which represented a period of very low interest rates longer than any other in U.S. history. The labor market seemed healthy enough to withstand higher interest rates, but higher rates could slow growth and move inflation further below the Fed's target. The Fed was also concerned that higher interest rates would increase the exchange rate between the U.S. dollar and other currencies, making U.S. exports more expensive.

Many businesses—especially those that depend on sales of durable goods that are typically purchased with borrowed funds—closely follow monetary policy because the Fed's actions to increase and decrease interest rates affect their sales. Among these businesses is the Goodyear Tire & Rubber Company. Founded in 1898 in Akron, Ohio, Goodyear employs more than 65,000 people and had sales of more than $18 billion in 2015. As the recession of 2007–2009 devastated the U.S. automobile market, sales of Goodyear tires plummeted, and the firm laid off thousands of workers. As the economy began to recover, in part because of the Fed's monetary policies, car and truck sales expanded, and Goodyear's fortunes improved. After a combined loss of $668 million from 2008 to 2010, Goodyear's profits in 2014 were $2.4 billion.

Interest rates affect Goodyear through their effect on car and truck sales but also through their effect on the exchange rate. As investors anticipated the Fed's raising the target for the federal funds rate, other U.S. interest rates rose, making financial investments in the United State more attractive to foreign investors. The result was a rising exchange rate and a decline in the dollar value of Goodyear's foreign sales.

The strong dollar also meant that the dollar prices of imports to the United States were falling, which would likely contribute to the inflation rate remaining below the Fed's target rate of 2 percent. In 2015, as the Fed prepared to increase its target for the federal funds rate, Yellen and her colleagues were attempting to achieve their dual mandate by reaching their targets for both the unemployment rate and the inflation rate.

Sources: Jeff Bennett, "Goodyear's Profit Drops on Currency Fluctuations," *Wall Street Journal*, July 29, 2015; Jon Hilsenrath, "Grand Central: Fed Doesn't Demand Wage Growth Before Increasing Interest Rate," *Wall Street Journal*, August 3, 2015; and Goodyear Tire & Rubber Company, *Annual Reports*, various years.

Economics in Your Life

Are There Benefits to Delaying a Job Search?

During a recession, your friend is laid off from her entry-level job as a computer analyst. You call her, but she does not seem very upset. "Our state offers workers up to 99 weeks of unemployment compensation. I have almost two years before I have to find a new job. With my education and job experience, I should be able to find a new job by then without much trouble." Your friend did well in school, but you are not sure that waiting to find a new job is a good idea. What advice would you give someone who has decided to wait so long to look for a new job? As you read the chapter, try to answer this question. You can check your answer against the one we provide on **page 1009** at the end of this chapter.

An important consideration for the Federal Reserve as it carries out monetary policy is that in the short run, there can be a trade-off between unemployment and inflation: Lower unemployment rates can result in higher inflation rates. In the long run, however, this trade-off disappears, and the unemployment rate is independent of the inflation rate. In this chapter, we will explore the relationship between inflation and unemployment in both the short run and the long run, and we will discuss what this relationship means for monetary policy. We will also provide an overview of how monetary policy has evolved over the years and conclude with a discussion of the debate over Fed policy during and after the 2007–2009 recession.

28.1 The Discovery of the Short-Run Trade-Off between Unemployment and Inflation

LEARNING OBJECTIVE: Describe the Phillips curve and the nature of the short-run trade-off between unemployment and inflation.

During most of the Fed's history, unemployment and inflation have been the two great macroeconomic problems it has contended with. When aggregate demand increases, unemployment usually falls, and inflation rises. When aggregate demand decreases, unemployment usually rises, and inflation falls. As a result, there is a *short-run trade-off* between unemployment and inflation: Higher unemployment is usually accompanied by lower inflation, and lower unemployment is usually accompanied by higher inflation. As we will see later in this chapter, this trade-off exists in the short run—a period that may be as long as several years—but disappears in the long run.

Although today the short-run trade-off between unemployment and inflation plays a role in the Fed's monetary policy decisions, this trade-off was not widely recognized until the late 1950s. In 1957, New Zealand economist A. W. Phillips plotted data on the unemployment rate and the inflation rate in Great Britain and drew a curve showing their average relationship. Since that time, a graph showing the short-run relationship between the unemployment rate and the inflation rate has been called a **Phillips curve**. (Phillips actually measured inflation by the percentage change in wages rather than by the percentage change in prices. Because wages and prices usually move together, this difference is not important to our discussion.) Figure 28.1 shows a graph similar to the one Phillips prepared. Each point on the Phillips curve represents a possible combination of the unemployment rate and the inflation rate that might be observed in a given year. Point A represents a year in which the inflation rate is 4 percent and the unemployment rate is 5 percent, and point *B* represents a year in which the inflation rate

Phillips curve A graph showing the short-run relationship between the unemployment rate and the inflation rate.

MyEconLab Animation

Figure 28.1

The Phillips Curve

A. W. Phillips was the first economist to show that there is usually an inverse relationship between unemployment and inflation. Here we can see this relationship at work: In the year represented by point *A*, the inflation rate is 4 percent and the unemployment rate is 5 percent. In the year represented by point *B*, the inflation rate is 2 percent and the unemployment rate is 6 percent.

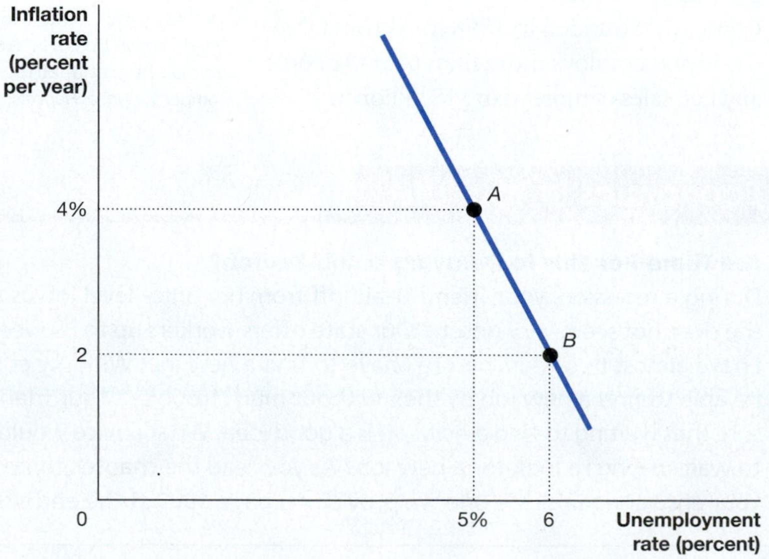

is 2 percent and the unemployment rate is 6 percent. Phillips documented that there is usually an *inverse relationship* between unemployment and inflation. During years when the unemployment rate is low, the inflation rate tends to be high, and during years when the unemployment rate is high, the inflation rate tends to be low.

Explaining the Phillips Curve with Aggregate Demand and Aggregate Supply Curves

The inverse relationship between unemployment and inflation that Phillips discovered is consistent with the aggregate demand and aggregate supply analysis we developed in Chapter 24. Figure 28.2 shows why this inverse relationship exists.

Panel (a) shows the aggregate demand and aggregate supply (*AD–AS*) model, and panel (b) shows the Phillips curve. For simplicity, in panel (a), we are using the basic *AD–AS* model, and we are assuming that the long-run aggregate supply curve and the short-run aggregate supply curve do not shift. To take a hypothetical example, assume that the economy in 2017 is at point A, with real GDP of $17.0 trillion and a price level of 110.0. If there is weak growth in aggregate demand during 2018, short-run equilibrium is at point *B*, with real GDP of $17.3 trillion and a price level of 112.2. The inflation rate is 2 percent, and the unemployment rate is 6 percent, which corresponds to point *B* on the Phillips curve in panel (b). If there is strong growth in aggregate demand during 2018, short-run equilibrium is at point *C*, with real GDP of $17.6 trillion and a price level of 114.4. Strong aggregate demand growth results in a higher inflation rate of 4 percent but a lower unemployment rate of 5 percent. This combination of higher inflation and lower unemployment is shown as point *C* on the Phillips curve in panel (b).

To summarize, the *AD–AS* model indicates that slow growth in aggregate demand leads to both higher unemployment and lower inflation. This result explains why

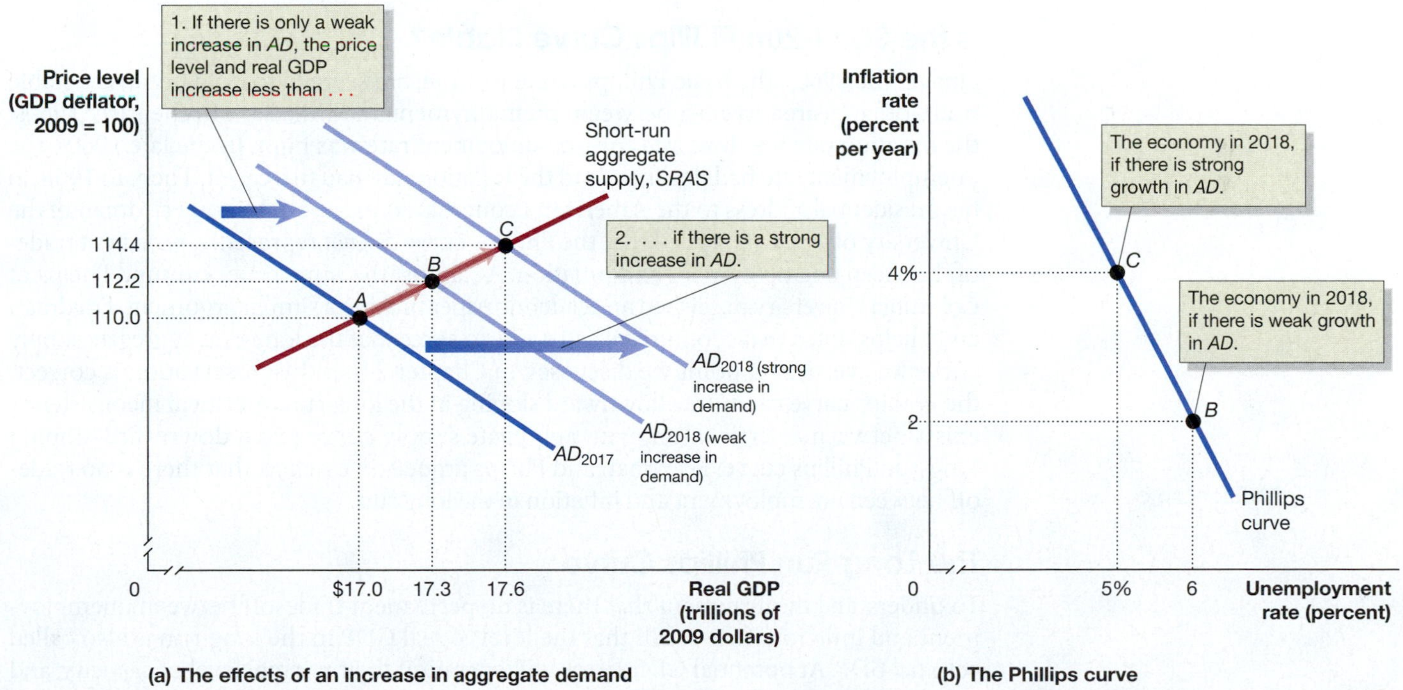

MyEconLab Animation

Figure 28.2 Using Aggregate Demand and Aggregate Supply to Explain the Phillips Curve

In panel (a), short-run equilibrium in 2017 is at point A, with real GDP of $17.0 trillion and a price level of 110.0. If there is weak growth in aggregate demand during 2016, short-run equilibrium is at point B, with real GDP of $17.3 trillion and a price level of 112.2. The inflation rate is 2 percent, and the unemployment rate is 6 percent, which corresponds to point B on the Phillips curve in panel (b). If there is strong growth in aggregate demand during 2018, short-run equilibrium is at point C, with real GDP of $17.6 trillion and a price level of 114.4. Strong aggregate demand growth results in a higher inflation rate of 4 percent but a lower unemployment rate of 5 percent. This combination of higher inflation and lower unemployment is shown as point C on the Phillips curve in panel (b).

there is a short-run trade-off between unemployment and inflation, as shown by the downward-sloping Phillips curve. The *AD–AS* model and the Phillips curve provide different ways of illustrating the same macroeconomic events. The Phillips curve has an advantage over the *AD–AS* model, however, when we want to explicitly analyze *changes* in the inflation and unemployment rates. MyEconLab Concept Check

Is the Phillips Curve a Policy Menu?

Structural relationship A relationship that depends on the basic behavior of consumers and firms and that remains unchanged over long periods.

During the 1960s, some economists argued that the Phillips curve represented a *structural relationship* in the economy. A **structural relationship** depends on the basic behavior of consumers and firms and that remains unchanged over long periods. Structural relationships are useful in formulating economic policy because policymakers can anticipate that these relationships are constant—that is, the relationships will not change as a result of changes in policy.

If the Phillips curve were a structural relationship, it would present policymakers with a reliable menu of combinations of unemployment and inflation. Potentially, policymakers could use expansionary monetary and fiscal policies to choose a point on the curve that had lower unemployment and higher inflation. They could also use contractionary monetary and fiscal policies to choose a point that had lower inflation and higher unemployment. Because many economists and policymakers in the 1960s viewed the Phillips curve as a structural relationship, they believed it represented a *permanent trade-off between unemployment and inflation*. As long as policymakers were willing to accept a permanently higher inflation rate, they would be able to keep the unemployment rate permanently lower. Similarly, a permanently lower inflation rate could be achieved at the cost of a permanently higher unemployment rate. As we discuss in the next section, however, economists came to realize that the Phillips curve did *not*, in fact, represent a permanent trade-off between unemployment and inflation.

MyEconLab Concept Check

Is the Short-Run Phillips Curve Stable?

During the 1960s, the basic Phillips curve relationship seemed to hold because a stable trade-off appeared to exist between unemployment and inflation. In the early 1960s, the inflation rate was low, and the unemployment rate was high. In the late 1960s, the unemployment rate had declined, and the inflation rate had increased. Then, in 1968, in his presidential address to the American Economic Association, Milton Friedman of the University of Chicago argued that the Phillips curve did *not* represent a *permanent* trade-off between unemployment and inflation. At almost the same time, Edmund Phelps of Columbia University published an academic paper making a similar argument. Friedman and Phelps noted that economists had come to agree that the long-run aggregate supply curve was vertical (a point we discussed in Chapter 24). If this observation is correct, the Phillips curve cannot be downward sloping in the long run. A critical inconsistency exists between a vertical long-run aggregate supply curve and a downward-sloping long-run Phillips curve. Friedman and Phelps argued, in essence, that there is no trade-off between unemployment and inflation in the long run.

MyEconLab Concept Check

The Long-Run Phillips Curve

To understand the argument that there is no permanent trade-off between unemployment and inflation, first recall that the level of real GDP in the long run is also called *potential GDP*. At potential GDP, firms will operate at their normal level of capacity, and everyone who wants a job will have one, except the structurally and frictionally unemployed. Friedman defined the **natural rate of unemployment** as the unemployment rate that exists when the economy is at potential GDP. The actual unemployment rate will fluctuate in the short run but will always come back to the natural rate in the long run. In the same way, the actual level of real GDP will fluctuate in the short run but will always come back to potential GDP in the long run.

Natural rate of unemployment The unemployment rate that exists when the economy is at potential GDP.

In the long run, a higher or lower price level has no effect on real GDP because real GDP is always at potential GDP in the long run. In the same way, in the long run, a higher or lower inflation rate will have no effect on the unemployment rate because

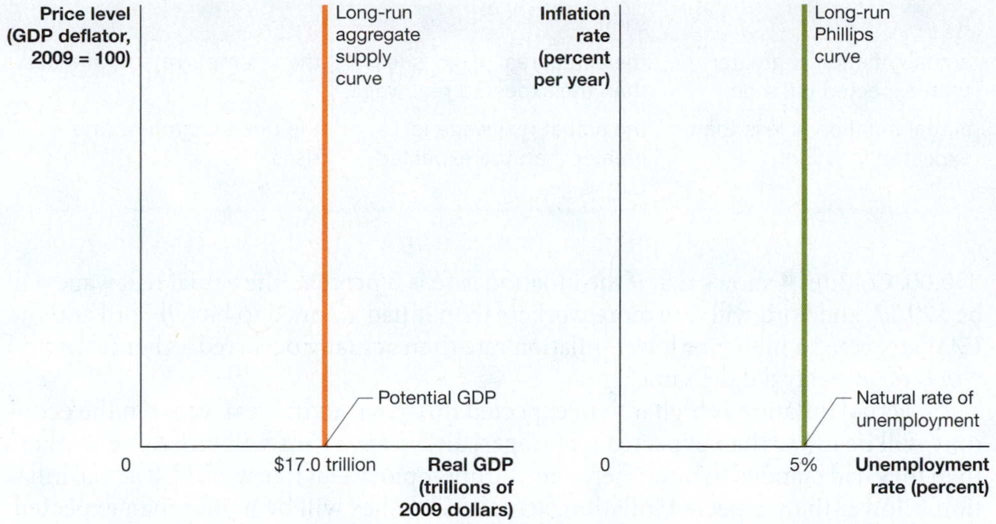

MyEconLab Animation

Figure 28.3

A Vertical Long-Run Aggregate Supply Curve Means a Vertical Long-Run Phillips Curve

Milton Friedman and Edmund Phelps argued that there is no trade-off between unemployment and inflation in the long run. If real GDP automatically returns to its potential level in the long run, the unemployment rate must return to the natural rate of unemployment in the long run. In this figure, we assume that potential GDP is $17.0 trillion and the natural rate of unemployment is 5 percent.

the unemployment rate is always equal to the natural rate in the long run. Figure 28.3 illustrates Friedman's conclusion that the long-run aggregate supply curve is a vertical line at the potential real GDP, and *the long-run Phillips curve is a vertical line at the natural rate of unemployment.* MyEconLab Concept Check

The Role of Expectations of Future Inflation

If the long-run Phillips curve is a vertical line, *no trade-off exists between unemployment and inflation in the long run.* This conclusion seemed to contradict the experience of the 1950s and 1960s, which showed a stable trade-off between unemployment and inflation. Friedman argued that the statistics from those years actually showed only a short-run trade-off between inflation and unemployment.

Friedman argued that the short-run trade-off existed only because workers and firms sometimes expected the inflation rate to be either higher or lower than it turned out to be. Differences between the expected inflation rate and the actual inflation rate could lead the unemployment rate to rise above or fall below the natural rate. To see why, consider a simple case of Ford negotiating a wage contract with the United Auto Workers (UAW) union. Remember that both Ford and the UAW are interested in the real wage, which is the nominal wage corrected for inflation. Column 1 of Table 28.1 shows Ford and the UAW agreeing on a wage of $34.65 per hour to be paid during 2018. Column 2 shows the situation if both Ford and the UAW expect that the price level will increase from 110.0 in 2017 to 115.5 in 2018, so the inflation rate will be 5 percent. We can calculate the real wage Ford expects to pay and the UAW expects to receive as follows:

$$\text{Real wage} = \frac{\text{Nominal wage}}{\text{Price level}} \times 100 = \frac{\$34.65}{115.5} \times 100 = \$30.00.$$

But suppose that the actual inflation rate turns out to be higher or lower than the expected inflation rate of 5 percent. Column 3 shows that if the price level (P) rises only to 112.2 in 2018, the inflation rate will be 2 percent, and the actual real wage will be $30.88, which is higher than Ford and the UAW had expected. With a higher real wage, Ford will hire fewer workers than it had planned to at the expected real wage of

Table 28.1

The Effect of Unexpected Price Level Changes on the Real Wage

Nominal Wage	Expected Real Wage	Actual Real Wage With 2% Inflation	Actual Real Wage With 8% Inflation
	Expected P_{2018} = 115.5	Actual P_{2018} = 112.2	Actual P_{2018} = 118.8
	Expected inflation = 5%	Actual inflation = 2%	Actual inflation = 8%
$34.65	$\frac{\$34.65}{115.5} \times 100 = \$30.00$	$\frac{\$34.65}{112.2} \times 100 = \$30.88$	$\frac{\$34.65}{118.8} \times 100 = \$29.17$

Table 28.2

The Basis for the Short-Run Phillips Curve

If ...	then ...	and ...
actual inflation is greater than expected inflation,	the actual real wage is less than the expected real wage,	the unemployment rate falls.
actual inflation is less than expected inflation,	the actual real wage is greater than the expected real wage,	the unemployment rate rises.

$30.00. Column 4 shows that if the inflation rate is 8 percent, the actual real wage will be $29.17, and Ford will hire more workers than it had planned to hire. If Ford and the UAW expected a higher or lower inflation rate than actually occurred, other firms and workers probably did the same.

If actual inflation is higher than expected inflation, actual real wages in the economy will be lower than expected real wages, and many firms will hire more workers than they had planned to hire. Therefore, the unemployment rate will fall. If actual inflation is lower than expected inflation, actual real wages will be higher than expected, many firms will hire fewer workers than they had planned to hire, and the unemployment rate will rise. Table 28.2 summarizes this argument.

Friedman and Phelps concluded that *an increase in the inflation rate increases employment (and decreases unemployment) only if the increase in the inflation rate is unexpected.* Friedman argued that in 1968, the unemployment rate was 3.6 percent rather than 5 percent only because the inflation rate of 4 percent was above the 1 percent to 2 percent inflation that workers and firms had expected: "There is always a temporary trade-off between inflation and unemployment; there is no permanent trade-off. The temporary trade-off comes not from inflation per se, but from unanticipated inflation." MyEconLab Concept Check

Making the Connection MyEconLab Video

Do Workers Understand Inflation?

A higher inflation rate can lead to lower unemployment if *both* workers and firms mistakenly expect the inflation rate to be lower than it turns out to be. But this same result might be due to firms forecasting inflation more accurately than workers do or because firms understand better the effects of inflation. Some large firms employ economists to help them gather and analyze information that is useful in forecasting inflation. Many firms also have human resources or employee compensation departments that gather data on wages competing firms pay and analyze trends in compensation. Workers generally rely on much less systematic information about wages and prices. Workers also often fail to realize a fact we discussed in Chapter 20: *Expected inflation increases the value of total production and the value of total income by the same amount.* Therefore, although not all wages will rise as prices rise, inflation will increase average wages in the economy at the same time that it increases average prices.

Will prices rise faster than his wage?

Nobel Laureate Robert Shiller of Yale University conducted a survey on inflation and discovered that, although most economists believe an increase in inflation will lead quickly to an increase in wages, a majority of the general public thinks otherwise. As part of the survey, Shiller asked how "the effect of general inflation on wages or salary relates to your own experience and your own job." The most popular response was: "The price increase will create extra profits for my employer, who can now sell output for more; there will be no effect on my pay. My employer will see no reason to raise my pay."

Shiller also asked the following question:

> Imagine that next year the inflation rate unexpectedly doubles. How long would it probably take, in these times, before your income is increased enough so that you can afford the same things as you do today? In other words, how long will it be before a full inflation correction in your income has taken place?

Eighty-one percent of the public answered either that it would take several years for the purchasing power of their income to be restored or that it would never be restored.

If workers fail to understand that rising inflation leads over time to comparable increases in wages, then when inflation increases, firms, in the short run, can increase wages by less than inflation without needing to worry about workers quitting or their morale falling. As a result, a higher inflation rate will lead in the short run to lower real wages and lower unemployment. In other words, we have an explanation for a downward-sloping short-run Phillips curve.

Source: Robert J. Shiller, "Why Do People Dislike Inflation?" in *Reducing Inflation: Motivation and Strategy* by Christina D. Romer and David H. Romer, eds., Chicago: University of Chicago Press, 1997.

Your Turn: Test your understanding by doing related problems 1.11 and 1.12 on page 1011 at the end of this chapter.

MyEconLab Study Plan

28.2 The Short-Run and Long-Run Phillips Curves

LEARNING OBJECTIVE: Explain the relationship between the short-run and long-run Phillips curves.

If there is both a short-run Phillips curve and a long-run Phillips curve, how are the two curves related? We can begin answering this question with the help of Figure 28.4, which represents macroeconomic conditions in the United States during the 1960s. In the late 1960s, workers and firms were still expecting the inflation rate to be about 1.5 percent, as it had been from 1960 to 1965. Expansionary monetary and fiscal policies, however, had moved the short-run equilibrium up the short-run Phillips curve to an inflation rate of 4.5 percent and an unemployment rate of 3.5 percent. This very low unemployment rate was possible only because the real wage rate was unexpectedly low.

Once workers and firms began to expect that the inflation rate would continue to be about 4.5 percent, they changed their behavior. Firms knew that only nominal wage increases of more than 4.5 percent would increase real wages. Workers realized that unless they received a nominal wage increase of at least 4.5 percent, their real wage would be falling. Higher expected inflation rates had an effect throughout the economy. For example, when banks make loans, they are interested in the *real interest rate* on the loan (see Chapter 25). The real interest rate is the nominal interest rate minus the expected inflation rate. Banks will charge a nominal interest rate of 4.5 percent to receive a real interest rate of 3 percent on home mortgage loans when they expect the inflation rate to be 1.5 percent. If banks revise their expectations of the inflation rate to 4.5 percent, they will increase the nominal interest rate they charge on mortgage loans to 7.5 percent.

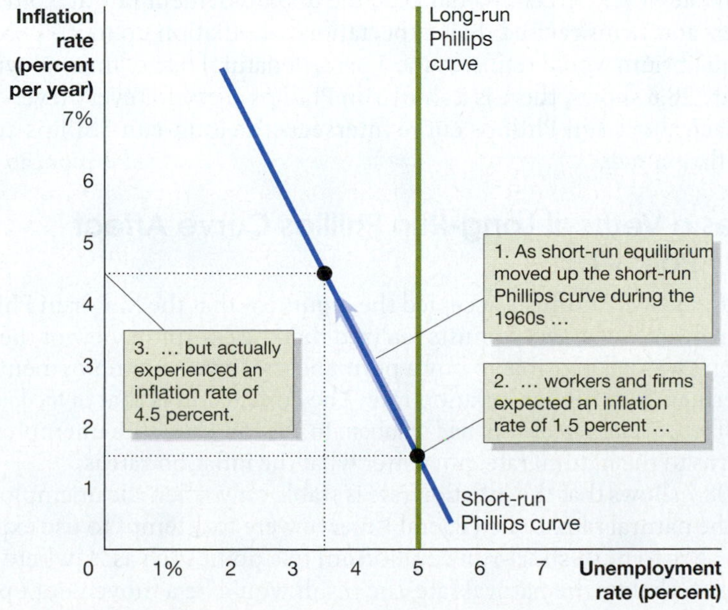

MyEconLab Animation

Figure 28.4

The Short-Run Phillips Curve of the 1960s and the Long-Run Phillips Curve

In the late 1960s, U.S. workers and firms were expecting the 1.5 percent inflation rates of the recent past to continue. However, expansionary monetary and fiscal policies moved short-run equilibrium up the short-run Phillips curve to an inflation rate of 4.5 percent and an unemployment rate of 3.5 percent.

MyEconLab Animation

Figure 28.5

Expectations and the Short-Run Phillips Curve

By the end of the 1960s, workers and firms had revised their expectations of inflation from 1.5 percent to 4.5 percent. As a result, the short-run Phillips curve shifted up, which made the short-run trade-off between unemployment and inflation worse.

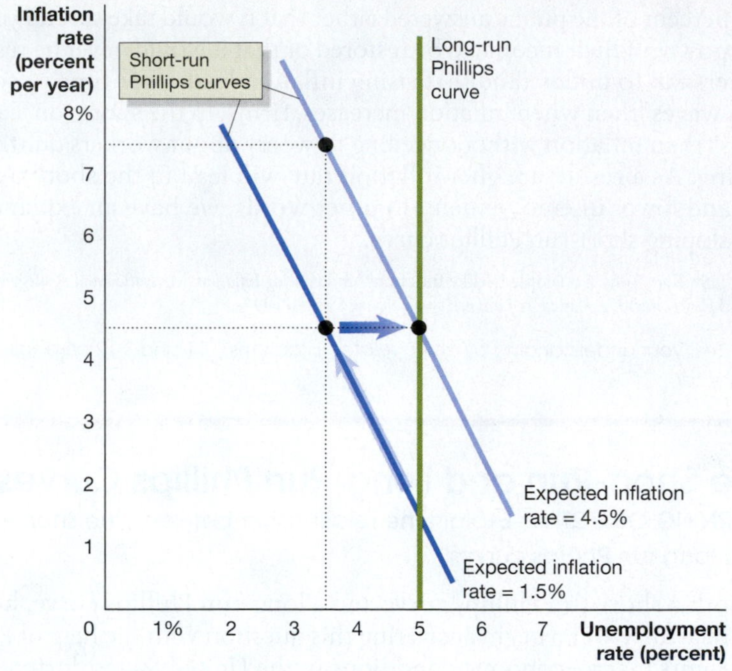

Shifts in the Short-Run Phillips Curve

A new, higher expected inflation rate can become *embedded* in the economy, meaning that workers, firms, consumers, and the government all take the inflation rate into account when making decisions. The short-run trade-off between unemployment and inflation now takes place from this higher, less favorable level, as shown in Figure 28.5.

As long as workers and firms expected the inflation rate to be 1.5 percent, the short-run trade-off between unemployment and inflation was the more favorable one shown by the lower Phillips curve. Along this Phillips curve, an inflation rate of 4.5 percent was enough to drive down the unemployment rate to 3.5 percent. Once workers and firms adjusted their expectations to an inflation rate of 4.5 percent, the short-run trade-off deteriorated to the one shown by the higher Phillips curve. At this higher expected inflation rate, the real wage rose, causing some workers to lose their jobs, and equilibrium returned to the natural rate of unemployment of 5 percent—but now with an inflation rate of 4.5 percent rather than 1.5 percent. On the higher short-run Phillips curve, an inflation rate of 7.5 percent would be necessary to reduce the unemployment rate to 3.5 percent. An inflation rate of 7.5 percent would keep the unemployment rate at 3.5 percent only until workers and firms revised their expectations of inflation up to 7.5 percent. In the long run, equilibrium would return to the 5 percent natural rate of unemployment.

As Figure 28.6 shows, there is a short-run Phillips curve for every level of expected inflation. Each short-run Phillips curve intersects the long-run Phillips curve at the expected inflation rate.

MyEconLab Concept Check

How Does a Vertical Long-Run Phillips Curve Affect Monetary Policy?

By the 1970s, most economists accepted the argument that the long-run Phillips curve is vertical. In other words, economists realized that the common view of the 1960s had been wrong: It was *not* possible to buy a permanently lower unemployment rate at the cost of a permanently higher inflation rate. The conclusion is that *in the long run, there is no trade-off between unemployment and inflation*. In the long run, the unemployment rate always returns to the natural rate, no matter what the inflation rate is.

Figure 28.7 shows that the inflation rate is stable only when the unemployment rate is equal to the natural rate. If the Federal Reserve were to attempt to use expansionary monetary policy to push short-run equilibrium to a point such as A, where the unemployment rate is below the natural rate, the result would be a movement up the short-run Phillips curve with increasing inflation. If short-run equilibrium remained below

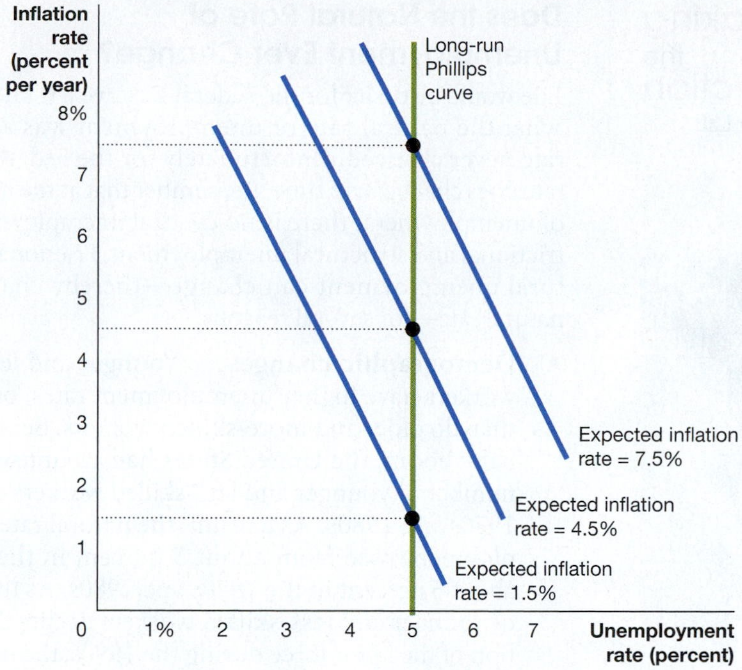

MyEconLab Animation

Figure 28.6

A Short-Run Phillips Curve for Every Expected Inflation Rate

There is a different short-run Phillips curve for every expected inflation rate. Each short-run Phillips curve intersects the long-run Phillips curve at the expected inflation rate.

the natural rate long enough, the short-run Phillips curve would shift up as workers and firms adjusted to the new, higher inflation rate. During the 1960s and 1970s, the short-run Phillips curve did shift up, presenting policymakers with a more unfavorable short-run trade-off between unemployment and inflation.

If the Federal Reserve used contractionary policy to push short-run equilibrium to a point such as *B*, where the unemployment rate is above the natural rate, the inflation rate would decrease. If short-run equilibrium remained above the natural rate long enough, the short-run Phillips curve would shift down as workers and firms adjusted to the new, lower inflation rate. Only at a point such as *C*, where the unemployment rate is equal to the natural rate, will the inflation rate be stable. Because the inflation rate has no tendency to increase or decrease when the unemployment rate equals the natural rate, the natural rate of unemployment is sometimes called the **nonaccelerating inflation rate of unemployment (NAIRU)**. We can conclude that *in the long run, the Federal Reserve can affect the inflation rate but not the unemployment rate.* MyEconLab Concept Check

Nonaccelerating inflation rate of unemployment (NAIRU) The unemployment rate at which the inflation rate has no tendency to increase or decrease.

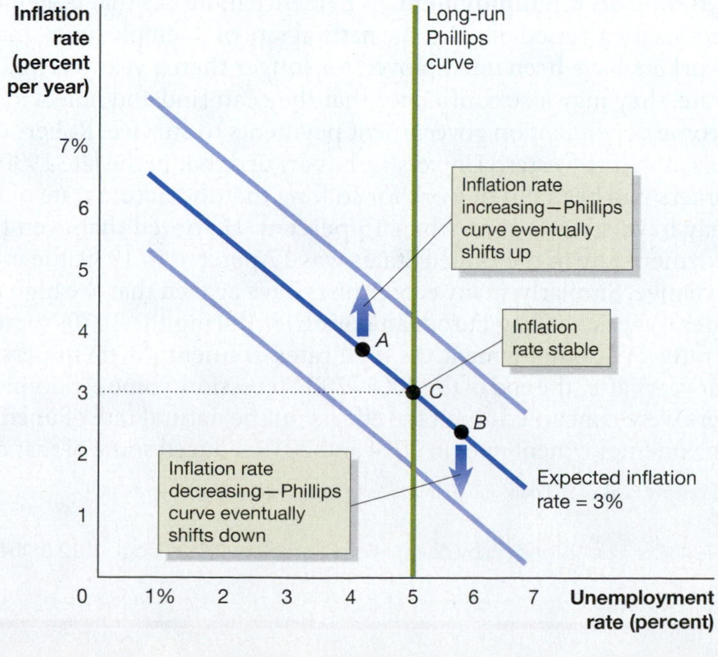

MyEconLab Animation

Figure 28.7

The Inflation Rate and the Natural Rate of Unemployment in the Long Run

The inflation rate is stable only if the unemployment rate equals the natural rate of unemployment (point *C*). If the unemployment rate is below the natural rate (point *A*), the inflation rate increases, and, eventually, the short-run Phillips curve shifts up. If the unemployment rate is above the natural rate (point *B*), the inflation rate decreases, and, eventually, the short-run Phillips curve shifts down.

Making the Connection
MyEconLab Video

Does the Natural Rate of Unemployment Ever Change?

An increase in the number of younger and less-skilled workers in an economy can make the natural rate of unemployment increase.

Life would be easier for the Federal Reserve if it knew exactly what the natural rate of unemployment was and if that rate never changed. Unfortunately for the Fed, the natural rate does change over time. Remember that at the natural rate of unemployment, there is no cyclical unemployment, only frictional and structural unemployment. Frictional or structural unemployment can change—thereby changing the natural rate—for several reasons:

- **Demographic changes.** Younger and less-skilled workers have higher unemployment rates, on average, than do older and more-skilled workers. Because of the baby boom, the United States had an unusually large number of younger and less-skilled workers during the 1970s and 1980s. As a result, the natural rate of unemployment rose from about 5 percent in the 1960s to about 6 percent in the 1970s and 1980s. As the number of younger and less-skilled workers declined as a fraction of the labor force during the 1990s, the natural rate returned to about 5 percent.
- **Labor market institutions.** Labor market institutions such as the unemployment insurance system, unions, and legal barriers to firing workers can increase the unemployment rate (see Chapter 20). Because many European countries have generous unemployment insurance systems, strong unions, and restrictive policies on firing workers, the natural rate of unemployment in most of these countries has been well above the rate in the United States. During and after the recession of 2007–2009, some economists believed that many workers in the United States had become less mobile because of the bursting of the housing bubble. These economists argued that because workers either were unable to sell their homes or were unwilling to do so because they did not want to sell for a low price, they were less likely to move from a geographic area of high unemployment to one of lower unemployment. Economists at JPMorgan Chase estimated that this lack of mobility might have temporarily increased the natural rate of unemployment from about 5 percent to about 6 percent. Economists at the Congressional Budget Office estimated that the increase in the natural rate had been somewhat smaller—from 5.0 percent to 5.5 percent.
- **Past high rates of unemployment.** Evidence indicates that if high unemployment persists for a period of years, the natural rate of unemployment may increase. When workers have been unemployed for longer than a year or two, their skills deteriorate, they may lose confidence that they can find and hold a job, and they may become dependent on government payments to survive. Robert Gordon, an economist at Northwestern University, has argued that in the late 1930s, so many U.S. workers had been out of work for so long that the natural rate of unemployment may have risen to more than 15 percent. He noted that even though the unemployment rate in the United States was 17 percent in 1939, the inflation rate did not change. Similarly, many economists have argued that the high unemployment rates experienced by European countries during the 1970s increased their natural rates of unemployment. As high rates of unemployment persisted more than four years after the end of the 2007–2009 recession, some economists and policymakers were concerned about the effects on the natural rate of unemployment. Declining unemployment rates in 2014 and 2015 reduced some of that concern.

Sources: Federal Reserve Bank of St. Louis; and "Damage Assessment," *Economist*, May 14, 2009.

MyEconLab Study Plan

Your Turn: Test your understanding by doing related problem 2.8 on page 1012 at the end of this chapter.

Solved Problem 28.2

MyEconLab Interactive Animation

Changing Views of the Phillips Curve

Writing in a Federal Reserve publication, Bennett McCallum, an economist at Carnegie Mellon University, argues that during the 1970s, the Fed was "acting under the influence of 1960s academic ideas that posited the existence of a long-run and exploitable Phillips-type tradeoff between inflation and unemployment rates." What does McCallum mean by a "long-run and exploitable Phillips-type tradeoff"? How would the Fed have attempted to exploit this long-run trade-off? What would be the consequences for the inflation rate?

Solving the Problem

Step 1: Review the chapter material. This problem is about the relationship between the short-run and long-run Phillips curves, so you may want to review the section "The Short-Run and Long-Run Phillips Curves," which begins on page 991.

Step 2: Explain what a "long-run exploitable Phillips-type tradeoff" means. A "long-run exploitable Phillips-type tradeoff" means a Phillips curve that in the long run is downward sloping rather than vertical. An "exploitable" trade-off is one that the Fed could take advantage of to *permanently* reduce unemployment, at the expense of higher inflation, or to permanently reduce inflation, at the expense of higher unemployment.

Step 3: Explain how the inflation rate will accelerate if the Fed tries to exploit a long-run trade-off between unemployment and inflation. As we have seen, during the 1960s, the Fed conducted expansionary monetary policies to move up what it thought was a stationary short-run Phillips curve. By the late 1960s, these policies resulted in very low unemployment rates. In the long run, there is no stable trade-off between unemployment and inflation. Attempting to permanently keep the unemployment rate at very low levels leads to a rising inflation rate, which is what happened in the late 1960s and early 1970s.

Source: Bennett T. McCallum, "Recent Developments in Monetary Policy Analysis: The Roles of Theory and Evidence," *Federal Reserve Bank of Richmond Economic Quarterly*, Winter 2002, p. 73.

Your Turn: For more practice, do related problem 2.12 on page 1013 at the end of this chapter.

MyEconLab Study Plan

28.3 Expectations of the Inflation Rate and Monetary Policy

LEARNING OBJECTIVE: Discuss how expectations of the inflation rate affect monetary policy.

How quickly does short-run equilibrium adjust from a point that is on the short-run Phillips curve but not on the long-run Phillips curve back to a point that is on the long-run Phillips curve? It depends on how quickly workers and firms adjust their expectations of future inflation to changes in current inflation. The experience in the United States over the past 60 years indicates that how quickly workers and firms adjust their expectations of inflation depends on how high the inflation rate is. There are three possibilities:

- **Low inflation.** When the inflation rate is low, as it was during most of the 1950s, the early 1960s, the 1990s, and the 2000s, workers and firms tend to ignore it. For example, if the inflation rate is low, a restaurant may not want to pay for printing new menus that would show slightly higher prices.
- **Moderate but stable inflation.** For the four-year period from 1968 to 1971, the inflation rate in the United States stayed in the narrow range between 4 percent and 5 percent. This rate was high enough that workers and firms could not ignore

it without seeing their real wages and profits decline. It was also likely that the next year's inflation rate would be very close to the current year's inflation rate. In fact, workers and firms during the 1960s acted as if they expected changes in the inflation rate during one year to continue into the following year. People are said to have *adaptive expectations* of inflation if they assume that future rates of inflation will follow the pattern of rates of inflation in the recent past.

- **High and unstable inflation.** Inflation rates above 5 percent during peacetime have been rare in U.S. history, but the inflation rate was above 5 percent every year from 1973 through 1982. Not only was the inflation rate high during those years, it was also unstable—rising from 6 percent in 1973 to 11 percent in 1974, before falling below 6 percent in 1976 and rising again to 13.5 percent in 1980. In the mid-1970s, Nobel Laureates Robert Lucas of the University of Chicago and Thomas Sargent of New York University argued that the gains to accurately forecast inflation had dramatically increased. Workers and firms that failed to correctly anticipate the fluctuations in inflation during these years could experience substantial declines in real wages and profits. Therefore, Lucas and Sargent argued, people should use all available information when forming their expectations of future inflation. Expectations formed by using all available information about an economic variable are called **rational expectations**.

Rational expectations Expectations formed by using all available information about an economic variable.

The Implications of Rational Expectations for Monetary Policy

Lucas and Sargent pointed out an important consequence of rational expectations: An expansionary monetary policy would not work. In other words, there might not be a trade-off between unemployment and inflation, even in the short run. By the mid-1970s, most economists had accepted the idea that an expansionary monetary policy could cause the actual inflation rate to be higher than the expected inflation rate. This gap between actual and expected inflation would cause the actual real wage to fall below the expected real wage, pushing the unemployment rate below the natural rate. Short-run equilibrium would move up the short-run Phillips curve.

Lucas and Sargent argued that this explanation of the Phillips curve assumed that workers and firms either ignored inflation or used adaptive expectations in making their forecasts of inflation. If workers and firms have rational expectations, they will use all available information, *including knowledge of the effects of Federal Reserve policy*. If workers and firms know that an expansionary monetary policy will raise the inflation rate, they should use this information in their forecasts of inflation. If they do, an expansionary monetary policy will not cause the actual inflation rate to be above the expected inflation rate. Instead, the actual inflation rate will equal the expected inflation rate, the actual real wage will equal the expected real wage, and the unemployment rate will not fall below the natural rate.

Figure 28.8 illustrates this argument. Suppose that equilibrium is initially at point *A*, where the short-run Phillips curve intersects the long-run Phillips curve. The actual and expected inflation rates are both equal to 1.5 percent, and the unemployment rate equals the natural rate of 5 percent. Now suppose the Fed engages in an expansionary monetary policy. If workers ignore inflation or if they form their expectations adaptively, the expansionary monetary policy will cause the actual inflation rate to be higher than the expected inflation rate, and short-run equilibrium will move from point *A* on the short-run Phillips curve to point *B*. The inflation rate will rise to 4.5 percent, and the unemployment rate will fall to 3.5 percent. The decline in unemployment will be only temporary because workers and firms will eventually adjust to the fact that the actual inflation rate is 4.5 percent, not the 1.5 percent they had expected. The short-run Phillips curve will shift up, and the unemployment rate will return to 5 percent at point *C*.

Lucas and Sargent argued that if workers and firms have rational expectations, they will realize that the Fed's expansionary policy will result in an inflation rate of 4.5 percent. Therefore, as soon as the Fed announces its new policy, workers and firms

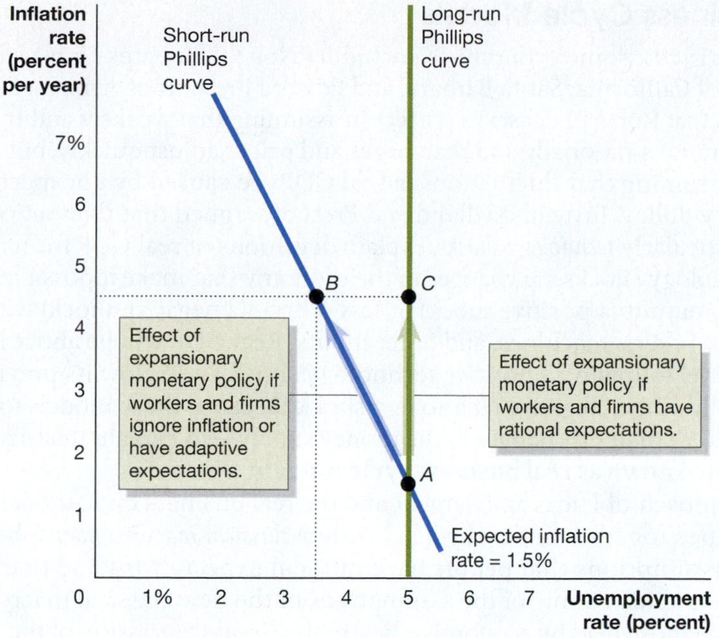

MyEconLab Animation

Figure 28.8

Rational Expectations and the Phillips Curve

If workers and firms ignore inflation, or if they have adaptive expectations, an expansionary monetary policy will cause short-run equilibrium to move from point *A* on the short-run Phillips curve to point *B*; inflation will rise, and unemployment will fall. If workers and firms have rational expectations, an expansionary monetary policy will cause the short-run equilibrium to move up the long-run Phillips curve from point *A* to point *C*. Inflation will still rise, but there will be no change in unemployment.

should adjust their expectations of inflation from 1.5 percent to 4.5 percent. There will be no temporary decrease in the real wage, leading to a temporary increase in employment and real GDP. Instead, short-run equilibrium will move immediately from point A to point C on the long-run Phillips curve. The unemployment rate will never drop below 5 percent, and the *short-run* Phillips curve will be vertical. MyEconLab Concept Check

Is the Short-Run Phillips Curve Really Vertical?

The claim by Lucas and Sargent that the short-run Phillips curve is vertical and that an expansionary monetary policy cannot reduce the unemployment rate below the natural rate surprised many economists. An obvious objection to the argument of Lucas and Sargent was that the 1950s and 1960s seemed to show that there was a short-run trade-off between unemployment and inflation and that, therefore, the short-run Phillips curve was downward sloping and not vertical. Lucas and Sargent argued that the apparent short-run trade-off was actually the result of *unexpected* changes in monetary policy. During those years, the Fed did not announce changes in policy, so workers, firms, and financial markets had to *guess* when the Fed had begun using a new policy. In that case, an expansionary monetary policy might cause the unemployment rate to fall because workers and firms would be taken by surprise, and their expectations of inflation would be too low. Lucas and Sargent argued that a policy that was announced ahead of time would not cause a change in unemployment.

Many economists have remained skeptical of the argument that the short-run Phillips curve is vertical. The two main objections raised are that (1) workers and firms may not have rational expectations, and (2) the rapid adjustment of wages and prices needed for the short-run Phillips curve to be vertical will not actually take place. Many economists doubt that people are able to use information about the Fed's monetary policy to make reliable forecasts of the inflation rate. If workers and firms do not know what effect an expansionary monetary policy will have on the inflation rate, the actual real wage may still end up being lower than the expected real wage. Also, firms may have contracts with their workers and suppliers that keep wages and prices from adjusting quickly. If wages and prices adjust slowly, then even if workers and firms have rational expectations, an expansionary monetary policy may still be able to reduce the unemployment rate in the short run. MyEconLab Concept Check

Real Business Cycle Models

During the 1980s, some economists, including Nobel Laureates Finn Kydland of the University of California, Santa Barbara, and Edward Prescott of Arizona State University, argued that Robert Lucas was correct in assuming that workers and firms formed their expectations rationally and that wages and prices adjust quickly, but that he was wrong in assuming that fluctuations in real GDP are caused by unexpected changes in monetary policy. Instead, Kydland and Prescott argued that fluctuations in "real" factors, particularly *technology shocks*, explain deviations of real GDP from its potential level. Technology shocks are changes to the economy that make it possible to produce either more output (a positive shock) or less output (a negative shock) with the same number of workers, machines, and other inputs. Real GDP will be above its previous potential level following a positive technology shock and below its previous potential level following a negative technology shock. Because these models focus on real factors—rather than on changes in the money supply—to explain fluctuations in real GDP, they are known as **real business cycle models**.

Real business cycle models Models that focus on real rather than monetary explanations of fluctuations in real GDP.

The approach of Lucas and Sargent and the real business cycle models are sometimes grouped together under the label *the new classical macroeconomics* because they share the assumptions that people have rational expectations and that wages and prices adjust rapidly. Some of the assumptions of the new classical macroeconomics are similar to those held by economists before the Great Depression of the 1930s. John Maynard Keynes, in his 1936 book *The General Theory of Employment, Interest, and Money*, referred to these earlier economists as "classical economists." Like the classical economists, the new classical macroeconomists believe that the economy will normally be at its potential level.

Economists who find the assumptions of rational expectations and rapid adjustment of wages and prices appealing are likely to accept the real business cycle model approach. Other economists are skeptical of these models because the models explain recessions as being caused by negative technology shocks. Negative technology shocks are uncommon and, apart from the oil price increases of the 1970s, real business cycle theorists have had difficulty identifying shocks that would have been large enough to cause recessions. Some economists have begun to develop real business cycle models that allow for the possibility that changes in monetary policy may affect the level of real GDP. If real business cycle models continue to develop along these lines, they may eventually converge with the models the Fed uses.

MyEconLab Study Plan

MyEconLab Concept Check

28.4 Federal Reserve Policy from the 1970s to the Present

LEARNING OBJECTIVE: Use a Phillips curve graph to show how the Federal Reserve can permanently lower the inflation rate.

We have already seen that the high inflation rates of the late 1960s and early 1970s were due in part to the Federal Reserve's attempts to keep the unemployment rate below the natural rate. By the mid-1970s, the Fed also had to deal with the inflationary effect of oil price increases resulting from actions by the Organization of the Petroleum Exporting Countries (OPEC). By the late 1970s, as the Fed attempted to deal with the problem of high and worsening inflation rates, it received conflicting policy advice. Many economists argued that the inflation rate could be reduced only at the cost of a temporary increase in the unemployment rate. Followers of the Lucas–Sargent rational expectations approach, however, argued that a painless reduction in the inflation rate was possible. Before analyzing the actual policies the Fed used, we can look at why the oil price increases of the mid-1970s made the inflation rate worse.

The Effect of a Supply Shock on the Phillips Curve

As we saw in Chapter 24, the increases in oil prices in 1974 caused the short-run aggregate supply curve to shift to the left. This shift is shown in panel (a) of Figure 28.9. (For simplicity, in this panel, we use the basic rather than the dynamic *AD–AS* model.)

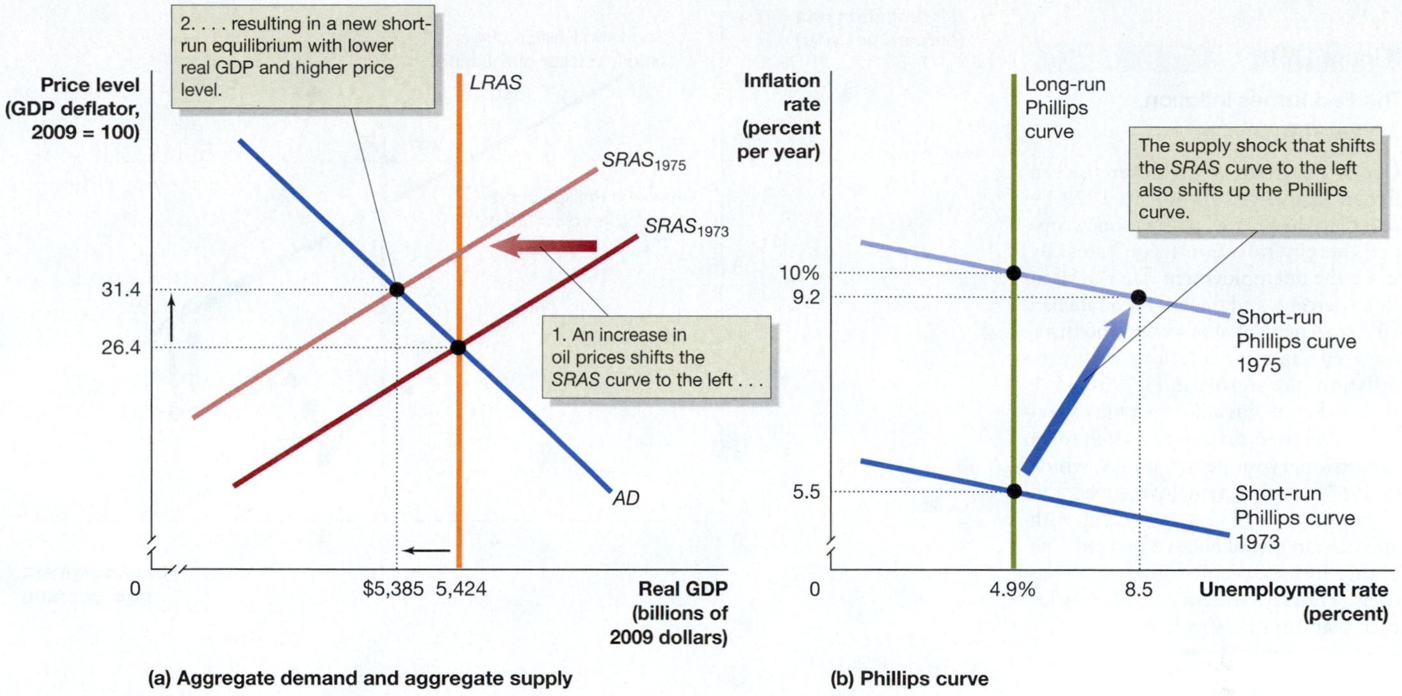

MyEconLab Animation

Figure 28.9 A Supply Shock Shifts the *SRAS* Curve and the Short-Run Phillips Curve

When actions by OPEC increased the price of a barrel of oil from less than $3 to more than $10, panel (a) shows that the *SRAS* curve shifted to the left. Between 1973 and 1975, real GDP declined from $5,424 billion to $5,385 billion, and the price level rose from 26.4 to 31.4. Panel (b) shows that the supply shock shifted up the Phillips curve. In 1973, the U.S. economy had an inflation rate of 5.5 percent and an unemployment rate of 4.9 percent. By 1975, the inflation rate had risen to about 9.2 percent and the unemployment rate to about 8.5 percent.

The result was an increase in the price level from 26.4 to 31.4 and a decrease in real GDP from $5,424 billion to $5,385 billion. On a Phillips curve graph—panel (b) of Figure 28.9—we can shift the short-run Phillips curve up to show that the inflation rate and unemployment rate both increased: from an unemployment rate of 4.9 percent and an inflation rate of about 5.5 percent in 1973 to an unemployment rate of 8.5 percent and an inflation rate of about 9.2 percent in 1975.

This combination of rising unemployment and rising inflation placed the Federal Reserve in a difficult position. If the Fed used an expansionary monetary policy to fight the high unemployment rate, the *AD* curve would shift to the right, and short-run equilibrium would move up the short-run Phillips curve. Real GDP would increase, and the unemployment rate would fall—but at the cost of higher inflation. If the Fed used a contractionary monetary policy to fight the high inflation rate, the *AD* curve would shift to the left, and short-run equilibrium would move down the short-run Phillips curve. As a result, real GDP would fall, and the inflation rate would be reduced—but at the cost of higher unemployment. In the end, the Fed chose to fight high unemployment with an expansionary monetary policy, even though that decision worsened the inflation rate.

MyEconLab Concept Check

Paul Volcker and Disinflation

By the late 1970s, the Federal Reserve had gone through two decades of continually increasing the rate of growth of the money supply. In August 1979, President Jimmy Carter appointed Paul Volcker as chairman of the Federal Reserve. Along with most other economists, Volcker was convinced that high inflation rates were damaging the economy. To reduce inflation, Volcker began reducing the annual growth rate of the money supply. This contractionary monetary policy raised interest rates, causing a

MyEconLab Animation

Figure 28.10

The Fed Tames Inflation, 1979–1989

Under Chairman Paul Volcker, the Fed began fighting inflation in 1979 by reducing the growth of the money supply, thereby raising interest rates. By 1982, the unemployment rate had risen to 10 percent, and the inflation rate had fallen to 6 percent. As workers and firms lowered their expectations of future inflation, the short-run Phillips curve shifted down. This adjustment in expectations allowed the Fed to switch to an expansionary monetary policy, which by 1987 brought unemployment back to the natural rate of unemployment, with an inflation rate of about 4 percent. The orange line shows the actual combinations of unemployment and inflation for each year from 1979 to 1989.

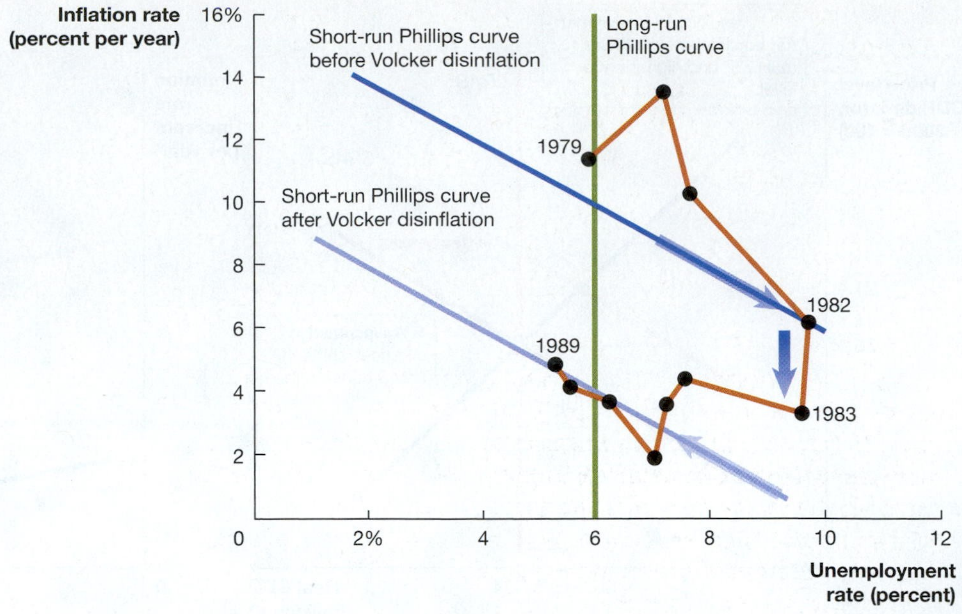

decline in aggregate demand. Figure 28.10 uses the Phillips curve model to analyze the movements in unemployment and inflation from 1979 to 1989.

The Fed's contractionary monetary policy moved short-run equilibrium down the short-run Phillips curve, lowering the inflation rate from 11 percent in 1979 to 6 percent in 1982—but at a cost of raising the unemployment rate from 6 percent to 10 percent. As workers and firms lowered their expectations of future inflation, the short-run Phillips curve shifted down, improving the short-run trade-off between unemployment and inflation. This adjustment in expectations allowed the Fed to switch to an expansionary monetary policy. By 1987, equilibrium was back to the natural rate of unemployment, which during these years was about 6 percent. The orange line in Figure 28.10 shows the actual combinations of unemployment and inflation for each year from 1979 to 1989.

Disinflation A significant reduction in the inflation rate.

Under Volcker's leadership, the Fed had reduced the inflation rate from more than 10 percent to less than 5 percent. The inflation rate has generally remained below 5 percent ever since. A significant reduction in the inflation rate is called **disinflation**. In fact, this episode is often called the "Volcker disinflation." The disinflation had come at a very high price, however. From September 1982 through June 1983, the unemployment rate was above 10 percent for the first time since the end of the Great Depression of the 1930s.

Some economists argue that the Volcker disinflation provides evidence against the view that workers and firms have rational expectations. Newspapers and television widely publicized Volcker's announcement in October 1979 that he planned to use a contractionary monetary policy to bring down the inflation rate. If workers and firms had rational expectations, we might expect that they would have quickly reduced their expectations of future inflation. There should have been a smooth movement down the long-run Phillips curve. As we have seen, however, there was a movement down the existing short-run Phillips curve, and only after several years of high unemployment did the short-run Phillips curve shift down. Apparently, workers and firms had adaptive expectations—changing their expectations of future inflation only after the current inflation rate had fallen.

Robert Lucas and Thomas Sargent argue, however, that a less painful disinflation would have occurred if workers and firms had *believed* Volcker's announcement that he was fighting inflation. The problem was that previous Fed chairmen had made similar

Don't Let This Happen to You

Don't Confuse Disinflation with Deflation

Disinflation refers to a decline in the *inflation rate*. *Deflation* refers to a decline in the *price level*. Paul Volcker and the Federal Reserve brought about a substantial disinflation in the United States during the years between 1979 and 1983. The inflation rate fell from more than 11 percent in 1979 to less than 5 percent in 1984. Yet even in 1984, there was no deflation: The price level was still rising—but at a slower rate.

The last period of significant deflation in the United States was in the early 1930s, during the Great Depression. The following table shows the consumer price index for each of those years.

Year	Consumer Price Index	Deflation Rate
1929	17.1	—
1930	16.7	−2.3%
1931	15.2	−9.0
1932	13.7	−9.9
1933	13.0	−5.1

Because the price level fell each year from 1929 to 1933, there was deflation.

MyEconLab Study Plan

Your Turn: Test your understanding by doing related problem 4.5 on page 1014 at the end of this chapter.

promises throughout the 1970s, but the inflation rate had continued to increase. By 1979, the credibility of the Fed was at a low point. Some support for Lucas's and Sargent's argument comes from surveys of business economists at the time, which showed that they also reduced their forecasts of future inflation only slowly, even though they were well aware of Volcker's announcement of a new policy.

MyEconLab Concept Check

Solved Problem 28.4

MyEconLab Interactive Animation

Using Monetary Policy to Lower the Inflation Rate

Consider the following hypothetical situation: The unemployment rate is currently at the natural rate of 5 percent, the actual inflation rate is 6 percent, and, because it has remained at 6 percent for several years, workers and firms expect the inflation rate to remain at 6 percent in the future. The Federal Reserve decides to reduce the inflation rate permanently to 2 percent. How can the Fed use monetary policy to achieve this objective? Be sure to use a Phillips curve graph in your answer.

Solving the Problem

Step 1: Review the chapter material. This problem is about using a Phillips curve graph to show how the Fed can fight inflation, so you may want to review the section "Paul Volcker and Disinflation," which begins on page 999.

Step 2: Explain how the Fed can use monetary policy to reduce the inflation rate. To reduce the inflation rate significantly, the Fed will have to raise the target for the federal funds rate. Higher interest rates will reduce aggregate demand, raise unemployment, and move equilibrium down the short-run Phillips curve.

Step 3: Illustrate your argument with a Phillips curve graph. How much the unemployment rate would have to rise to drive the inflation rate down from 6 percent to 2 percent depends on the steepness of the short-run Phillips curve. In drawing this graph, we have assumed that the unemployment rate would have to rise from 5 percent to 7 percent.

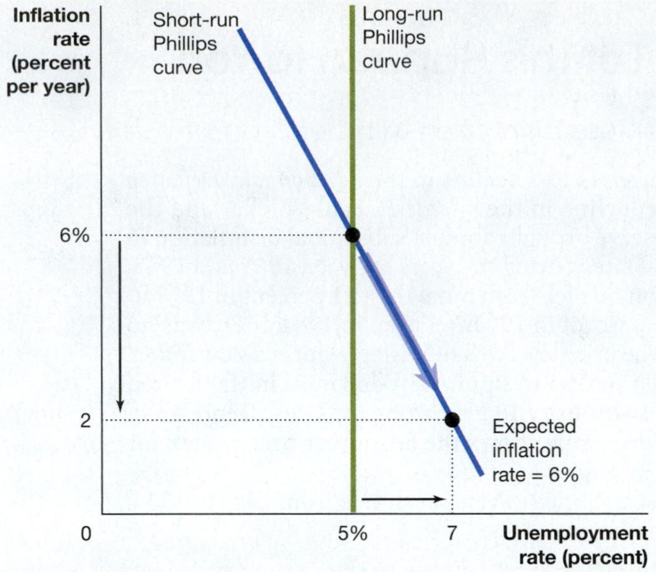

Step 4: Show on your graph how the Fed can achieve a permanent reduction in the inflation rate from 6 percent to 2 percent. For the decline in the inflation rate to be permanent, the expected inflation rate has to decline from 6 percent to 2 percent. We can show this decline on the graph:

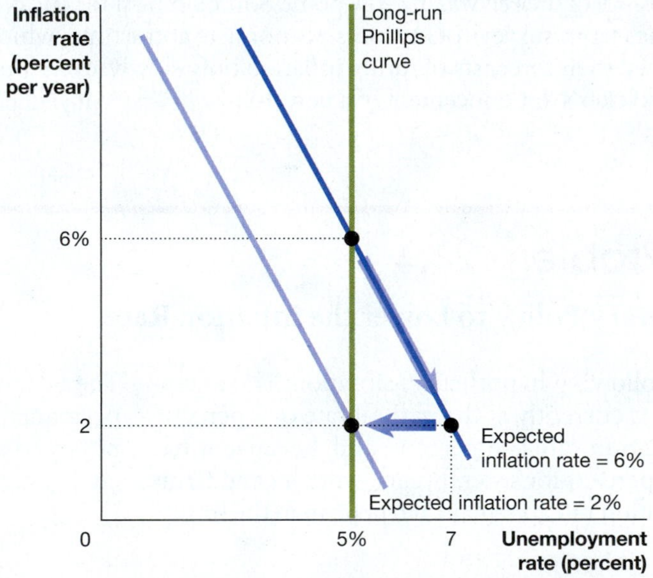

Once the short-run Phillips curve has shifted down, the Fed can use an expansionary monetary policy to push equilibrium back to the natural rate of unemployment. This policy is similar to the one carried out by the Fed after Paul Volcker became chairman in 1979. The downside to these policies of disinflation is that they lead to significant short-term increases in unemployment.

Extra Credit: A follower of the new classical macroeconomics approach would have a more optimistic view of the consequences of using monetary policy to lower the inflation rate from 6 percent to 2 percent. According to new classical approach, the Fed's policy announcement should cause people to immediately revise downward their expectations of future inflation from 6 percent to 2 percent. Short-run equilibrium would move directly down the long-run Phillips curve from an inflation rate of 6 percent to an inflation rate of 2 percent, while keeping the unemployment rate constant at 5 percent. For the reasons discussed in this chapter, many economists are skeptical that disinflation can be brought about so painlessly.

MyEconLab Study Plan

Your Turn: For more practice, do related problem 4.7 on page 1014 at the end of this chapter.

Alan Greenspan, Ben Bernanke, Janet Yellen, and the Crisis in Monetary Policy

President Ronald Reagan appointed Alan Greenspan to succeed Paul Volcker as Fed chairman in 1987. Greenspan served for more than 18 years. When he stepped down in January 2006, President George W. Bush appointed Ben Bernanke to take his place. In January 2013, President Barack Obama appointed Janet Yellen to take Bernanke's place. Greenspan, Bernanke, and Yellen shared Volcker's determination to keep the inflation rate low. Table 28.3 shows that the average annual inflation rate was lower during Greenspan's and Bernanke's terms, and the initial months of Yellen's term, than it had been during the terms of their three most immediate predecessors. Under Greenspan's leadership of the Fed, inflation was reduced nearly to the low levels experienced during the term of Chairman William McChesney Martin in the 1950s and 1960s. Greenspan's term was marked by only two short and mild recessions, in 1990–1991 and 2001. When Greenspan left office in 2006, he was widely applauded by economists, policymakers, and the media.

Following the severe recession of 2007-2009, some critics questioned whether decisions the Fed made under Greenspan's leadership might have played a role in bringing on the financial crisis that led to the recession. We will discuss those arguments after briefly reviewing two other developments in monetary policy during the past 20 years:

- **Deemphasizing the money supply.** Greenspan's term was notable for the Fed's continued movement away from using the money supply as a monetary policy target. We saw in Chapter 25 that during the 1980s and 1990s, the close relationship between growth in the money supply and inflation broke down. Before 1987, the Fed would announce annual targets for the growth rates of M1 and M2. In February 1987, near the end of Paul Volcker's term, the Fed announced that it would no longer set targets for M1. In July 1993, Alan Greenspan announced that the Fed also would no longer set targets for M2. Instead, the Federal Open Market Committee (FOMC) has relied on setting targets for the federal funds rate to meet its dual mandate of price stability and high employment.
- **Emphasizing Fed credibility.** The Fed learned an important lesson during the 1970s: Workers, firms, and investors in stock and bond markets have to view Fed announcements as credible if monetary policy is to be effective. As inflation worsened throughout the late 1960s and the 1970s, the Fed announced repeatedly that it would take actions to reduce inflation. In fact, policies either were not implemented or were ineffective, and inflation rose. These repeated failures to follow through on announced policies had greatly reduced the Fed's credibility by the time Paul Volcker took office in August 1979. The contractionary monetary policy that the Fed announced in October 1979 had less effect on the expectations of workers, firms, and investors than it would have had if the Fed's credibility had been greater. It took a severe recession to convince people that this time, the inflation rate really was coming down. Only then were workers willing to accept lower nominal wage increases, banks willing to accept lower interest rates on mortgage loans, and investors willing to accept lower interest rates on bonds.

Table 28.3

The Record of Fed Chairs and Inflation

Federal Reserve Chairman	Term	Average Annual Inflation Rate during Term
William McChesney Martin	April 1951 to January 1970	2.2%
Arthur Burns	February 1970 to March 1978	6.5
G. William Miller	March 1978 to August 1979	9.1
Paul Volcker	August 1979 to August 1987	6.2
Alan Greenspan	August 1987 to January 2006	3.1
Ben Bernanke	January 2006 to January 2014	2.2
Janet Yellen	January 2014 to October 2015*	0.9

*** The value for Janet Yellen is computed for just these initial months of her term.**

Sources: U.S. Bureau of Labor Statistics; and Federal Reserve Board of Governors.

Over the past 25 years, the Fed has taken steps to enhance its credibility. Most importantly, whenever a change in Fed policy has been announced, the change has actually taken place. In addition, Greenspan revised the previous Fed policy of keeping secret the target for the federal funds rate. Since February 1994, any change in the target rate has been announced at the conclusion of the FOMC meeting at which the change is made. In addition, the minutes of the FOMC meetings are now made public after a brief delay. In February 2000, the Fed began making its intentions for future policy clearer by stating at the end of each FOMC meeting whether it considered the economy in the future to be at greater risk of higher inflation or of recession. In 2011, Ben Bernanke began holding press conferences following some FOMC meetings, which was the first time a Fed chair had done so.

The Decision to Intervene in the Failure of Long-Term Capital Management Greenspan's ability to help guide the economy through a long period of economic stability and his moves to enhance Fed credibility were widely applauded. However, two actions by the Fed during Greenspan's term have been identified as possibly contributing to the financial crisis that increased the length and severity of the 2007–2009 recession. One was the decision during 1998 to help save the hedge fund Long-Term Capital Management (LTCM). Hedge funds raise money, typically from wealthy investors, and use sophisticated investment strategies that often involve significant risk. Hedge funds generally rely heavily on borrowing in order to leverage their investments, thereby increasing potential returns. LTCM included as partners Robert Merton and Myron Scholes, who had both been awarded the Nobel Prize in Economics.

In the spring of 1998, LTCM suffered heavy losses on several of its investments, partly because the Russian government announced it would no longer make payments on some of its bonds, causing their value to sharply decline. Other financial firms that had loaned money to LTCM feared that the hedge fund would go bankrupt and began to push for repayment of their loans. We have seen that a run on a financial firm can cause widespread problems in the financial system. If LTCM had been forced to quickly sell all of its investments, the prices of the securities it owned would have declined, causing problems for other financial firms that held the same securities (see Chapter 25). The Fed was concerned that a sudden failure of LTCM might lead to failures of other financial firms. With the support of Alan Greenspan, William McDonough, president of the Federal Reserve Bank of New York, held a meeting between the management of LTCM and the financial firms to which LTCM owed money. The firms were persuaded to give LTCM enough time to slowly sell off—or "unwind"—its investments to keep the prices of those investments from falling too rapidly and to avoid a financial panic.

The Fed's actions succeeded in avoiding wider damage from LTCM's failure, but some critics argued that the Fed's intervention had negative consequences in the long run because it allowed the owners of LTCM and the firms that had loaned LTCM money to avoid the full consequences of LTCM's failed investments. These critics argued that the Fed's intervention set the stage for other firms—particularly highly leveraged investment banks and hedge funds—to take on excessive risk, with the expectation that the Fed would intervene on their behalf should they suffer heavy losses on the investments.

Although some critics see the Fed's actions in the case of LTCM as encouraging the excessive risk taking that helped result in the financial crisis of 2007–2009, other observers doubt that the Fed's actions had much effect on the behavior of managers of financial firms.

The Decision to Keep the Target for the Federal Funds Rate at 1 Percent from June 2003 to June 2004 In response to the popping of the dot-com stock bubble in the spring of 2000, the beginning of a recession in March 2001, and the terrorist attacks of September 11, 2001, the Fed successively lowered the target for the federal funds rate. The target rate was cut in a series of steps from 6.5 percent in May 2000 to 1 percent in June 2003. The target remained at 1 percent until the Fed raised it to 1.25 percent in June 2004. Some economists and policymakers have criticized the Fed's decision to continue cutting the target for the federal funds rate for more than 18 months after the end of the recession in November 2001 and to keep the rate at 1 percent for another year. At the time, the FOMC argued that although the recession of 2001 was mild, the very low inflation rates of late 2001 and 2002 raised the possibility that the U.S. economy could slip into a period of deflation. As we have seen, deflation can damage the economy by raising real interest rates and by causing consumers to postpone purchases, based on the expectation that future prices will be lower than current prices (see Chapter 26).

Critics argued, though, that by keeping interest rates low for an extended period, the Fed helped to fuel the housing bubble that eventually deflated beginning in 2006, with disastrous results for the economy. We have seen that the origins of the housing bubble are complex and that contributing factors included the increase in securitization of mortgages, the willingness of banks and other lenders to give loans to subprime and Alt-A borrowers, and the widespread use of adjustable-rate mortgages that allowed borrowers to qualify for larger loans than would have been possible using conventional mortgages. Economists will continue to debate whether the Fed's policy of keeping the target for the federal funds rate very low for an extended period caused the housing bubble. MyEconLab Concept Check

Making the Connection
MyEconLab Video

Should the Fed Attempt to Guide the Expectations of Investors?

In testifying before Congress in 2015, Federal Reserve Chair Janet Yellen discussed how the Fed has been using "forward guidance" as a monetary policy tool since 2008. Forward guidance refers to central banks telling the public what future monetary policy will be. As Yellen put it, "The FOMC is . . . providing forward guidance that offers information about our policy outlook and expectations for the future path of the federal funds rate."

Federal Reserve Chair Janet Yellen testified before Congress in 2015 and explained the monetary policy tool of "forward guidance."

The Fed targets the federal funds rate and can control its value. But the Fed has less control over long-term interest rates, such as the interest rates on mortgage loans or corporate bonds, that have a direct effect on household and firm spending. The level of long-term interest rates depends partly on the expectations of households, firms, and investors of future short-term interest rates. For example, when investors believe that the federal funds rate will be low in future years, the interest rate on 10-year U.S. Treasury notes will usually also be low. The interest rate on 10-year Treasury notes plays an important role in the financial system because changes in it are typically reflected in other long-term interest rates, particularly the interest rate on mortgage loans. Beginning in 2008, the Fed used forward guidance to help keep the interest rate on 10-year Treasury notes low. As the figure below shows, this key interest rate generally remained at very low levels during and following the recession.

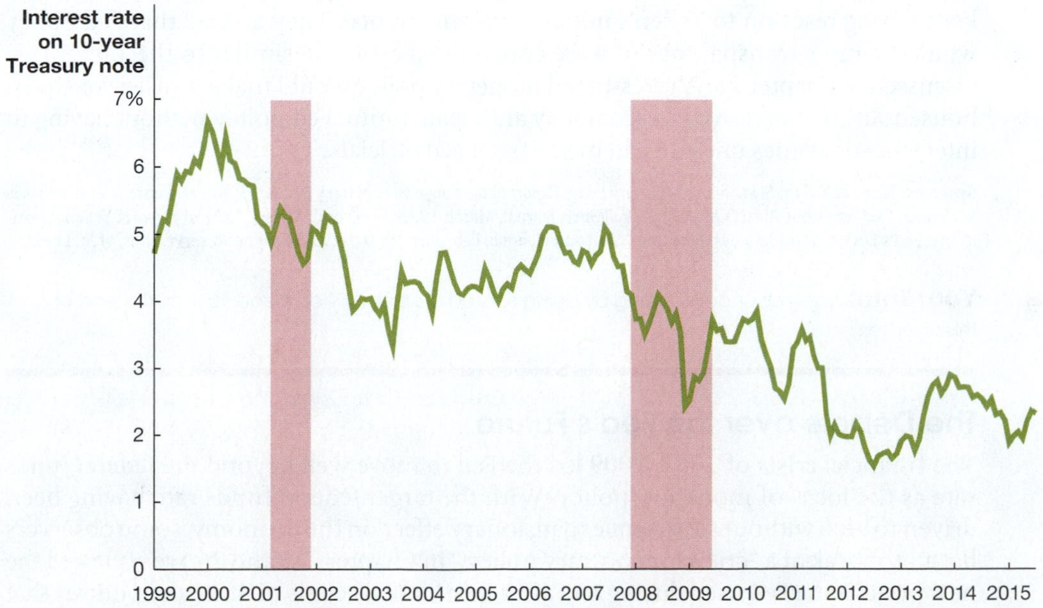

After becoming Fed chair in 2013, Yellen quickly learned how sensitive investors are to any hint from the Fed that interest rate policy might change. At a press conference after her first FOMC meeting, some of her remarks seemed to indicate that the Fed might raise its target for the federal funds rate earlier than investors had anticipated. The result shown in the graph below was a quick upward spike in the interest rate on the 10-year Treasury note.

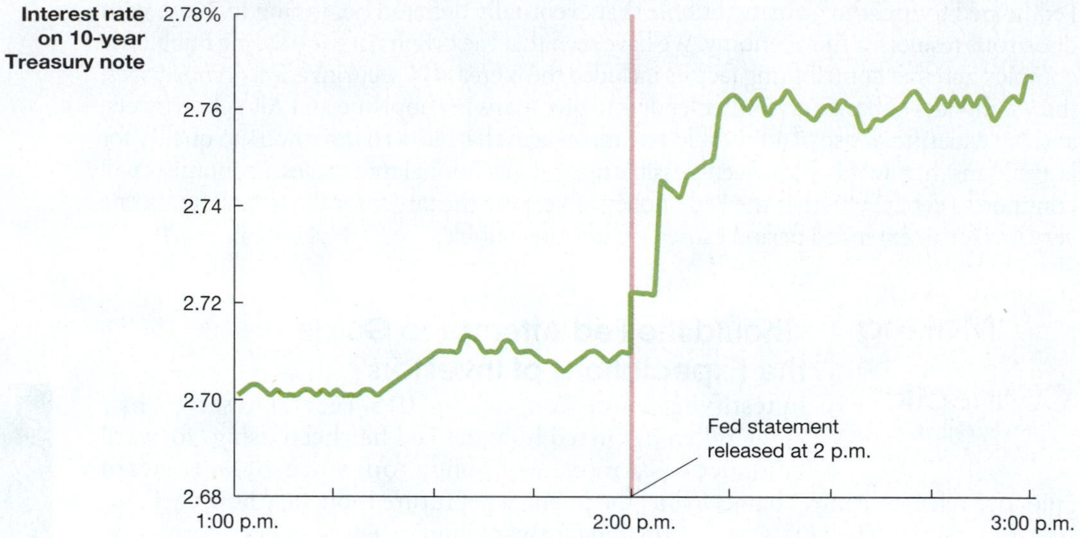

Eventually, Yellen and other Fed officials were able to reassure investors that Fed policy had not abruptly changed, and the interest rate on the 10-year Treasury declined. Still, as Yellen put it, "We will try as hard as we can not to be a source of instability here."

Many economists credited the Fed's policy of forward guidance, in combination with its policy of quantitative easing (discussed in Chapter 26), with aiding the recovery from the 2007–2009 recession by keeping long-term interest rates low. Some economists, though, were concerned that forward guidance was contributing to a prolonged period of abnormally low interest rates. Such low interest rates could lead to distortions in the financial system and the wider economy by, for instance, leading to speculative bubbles in stocks or other financial assets as investors borrowed at low interest rates to buy these assets. Some economists were also troubled by the effect that stray remarks by Fed officials can have on financial markets—as shown by the bond market's strong reaction to Yellen's initial press conference. They argued that Fed policy would be more transparent if it were constrained by a rule similar to the Taylor rule discussed in Chapter 26. A rules-based monetary policy would make it easier for firms, households, and investors to accurately anticipate future Fed policy without having to interpret sometimes unclear statements from Fed officials.

Sources: Janet L. Yellen, *Semiannual Monetary Policy Report to the Congress*, February 25, 2015; Jon Hilsenrath and Victoria McGrane, "Yellen Debut Rattles Markets," *Wall Street Journal*, March 19, 2014; David Wessel, "Ahead of Janet Yellen's Testimony, Fed's Forward Guidance Is Working," *Wall Street Journal*, February 10, 2014; and Federal Reserve Bank of St. Louis.

MyEconLab Study Plan

Your Turn: Test your understanding by doing related problem 4.9 on page 1015 at the end of this chapter.

The Debate over the Fed's Future

The financial crisis of 2007–2009 led the Fed to move well beyond the federal funds rate as the focus of monetary policy. With the target federal funds rate having been driven to zero without sufficient expansionary effect on the economy, some observers began to speak of a "crisis in monetary policy." In Chapters 25 and 26, we reviewed the new policies the Fed used during and after the financial crisis. Like many policies that represent a sharp break with the past, the Fed's actions had both supporters and critics. While most economists and policymakers gave the Fed credit for keeping the financial crisis from leading to a downturn as severe as the Great Depression of the 1930s, some argued that the Fed had overstepped its authority as determined by the Federal Reserve Act. In this section, we review some of the changes to Fed operations contained in the Wall Street Reform and Consumer Protection Act (Dodd-Frank Act), which Congress passed in 2010, and also discuss current proposals in Congress for additional changes.

Changes under the Dodd-Frank Act Traditionally, the Fed had made discount loans only to commercial banks. Under Section 13(3) of the Federal Reserve Act, though, the Fed had the legal authority in "unusual and exigent circumstances" to make loans to "any individual, partnership, or corporation." During the financial crisis, the Fed invoked this authority to make loans to investment banks, provide funds for JPMorgan Chase's purchase of the failing investment bank Bear Stearns, provide funds to the AIG insurance company, and buy commercial paper issued by nonfinancial firms.

Some members of Congress were critical of these actions because they saw them as going too far beyond the Fed's mandate and were concerned that the Fed would make similar loans as a routine part of monetary policy. As a result, a provision of the Dodd-Frank Act revised Section 13(3) of the Federal Reserve Act to restrict the Fed's ability to make loans except to commercial banks. In particular, the Fed is no longer allowed to make loans "for the purpose of assisting a single and specific company avoid bankruptcy." During the crisis, the Fed took action to save Bear Stearns and AIG under what is called the **too-big-to-fail policy**, which holds that the federal government should not allow large financial firms to fail, for fear of damaging the financial system. As we saw in Chapter 26, however, some economists believe that this policy increases moral hazard because managers of financial firms may make riskier investments if they believe that the federal government will save them from bankruptcy. These provisions of the Dodd-Frank Act make it much more difficult for the Fed to use a too-big-to-fail policy.

Too-big-to-fail policy A policy under which the federal government does not allow large financial firms to fail, for fear of damaging the financial system.

Some economists are critical of these restrictions on the Fed's ability to lend freely in a crisis. They argue that the failure of the Lehman Brothers investment bank in September 2008 shows the damage to the financial system that can occur as the result of the failure of a single large financial firm.

Proposals for Further Changes to the Fed In 2015, several proposals in Congress were intended to change the Fed's operations or structure. There were competing bills, and it was unclear which, if any, of them might be enacted into law, but these were the key changes being considered:

- **Require the Fed to adopt a formal policy rule.** As we noted in Chapter 26, the Sound Dollar Act incorporated a provision that would require the Fed to adopt a policy rule like the Taylor rule. Although the FOMC would be able to deviate from the rule in a crisis, it would be required to state the reasons for the deviation. The purpose of the rule is to reduce the discretion of the FOMC to pursue policies, such as those pursued prior to Paul Volcker becoming Fed chair in 1979, that might result in high inflation rates. It would also avoid prolonged periods of very low targets for the federal funds rate, such as occurred in 2003–2004 and again after 2011. In both these cases, the Taylor rule indicated a higher target for the federal funds rate than the Fed actually implemented. A rules-based policy also makes it easier for businesses, households, and investors to anticipate future Fed actions. Critics of this proposal argued that it would further reduce the ability of the Fed to respond rapidly to a financial crisis.
- **Make price stability the Fed's sole policy goal.** For many years, the Fed has interpreted the Federal Reserve Act as giving it a *dual mandate* of price stability and high employment. Because, as we have seen, in the long run the Fed can affect the price level but not the level of real GDP or employment, some policymakers and

economists believe that the Fed should have the single goal of price stability. Critics of this proposal believe it would handicap the Fed in responding to declines in output and employment during recessions.

- **Changes to the Fed's structure.** Members of Congress proposed various changes to the Fed's structure. One relatively minor change would make all 12 Federal Reserve District Bank presidents voting members of the FOMC. Recall from Chapter 25 that under the current procedure, the president of the Federal Reserve Bank of New York is always a voting member of the FOMC, while 4 of the other 11 District Bank presidents rotate through one-year terms as voting members. Another proposal was to add two new Federal Reserve Districts and realign the boundaries of the current districts to reflect the changes in the distribution of the U.S. population since the Fed's founding in 1914. Finally, some members of Congress proposed that the president of the United States directly appoint the presidents of the Federal Reserve District Banks. Currently, the presidents are elected by the boards of directors of the District Banks, subject to the approval of the Fed's Board of Governors.
- **Audit the Fed's monetary policy actions.** The General Accountability Office (GAO) audits—or reviews—the Fed's finances, as it does the finances of other federal agencies. Congress has not given the GAO the authority to audit the Fed's monetary policy actions, although the Dodd-Frank Act changed the law to allow the GAO to audit other Fed activities, such as loans made to a single firm—like the loans provided to Bear Stearns during the financial crisis. Senator Rand Paul of Kentucky proposed that the GAO's authority be extended so that it can audit and provide public evaluations of the Fed's monetary policy actions. Fed officials and many economists were critical of this proposal because they believed the audits might be used by Congress to pressure the Fed into avoiding monetary policy actions that were in the best interest of the economy, but that might be politically unpopular.

A key point in the debate over changes to the Fed's structure and operations is concern over undermining the Fed's ability to carry out monetary policy without regard to possible political pressure from Congress or the president. The main reason to keep the Fed—or any country's central bank—independent of the rest of the government is to avoid inflation. Whenever a government is spending more than it is collecting in taxes, it must borrow the difference by selling bonds. The governments of many developing countries have difficulty finding anyone other than their central bank to buy their bonds. The more bonds the central bank buys, the faster the money supply grows, and the higher the inflation rate will be. Even in developed countries, governments that control their central banks may be tempted to sell bonds to the central bank rather than to the public.

Another fear is that a government that controls the central bank may use that control to further its political interests. It is difficult in any democratic country for a government to be reelected at a time of high unemployment. In the United States, for example, a president who had control over the Fed might be tempted to increase the money supply and drive down interest rates to increase production and employment just before running for reelection, even if doing so led in the long run to higher inflation and accompanying economic costs.

We might expect that the more independent a country's central bank is, the lower the inflation rate in the country, and the less independent a country's central bank, the higher the inflation rate. In a classic study, Alberto Alesina and Lawrence Summers, who were both economists at Harvard University at the time, tested this idea by comparing the degree of central bank independence and the inflation rate for 16 high-income countries during the years 1955–1988. Figure 28.11 shows the results.

Countries with highly independent central banks, such as the United States, Switzerland, and Germany, had lower inflation rates than countries whose central banks had little independence, such as New Zealand, Italy, and Spain. In the following

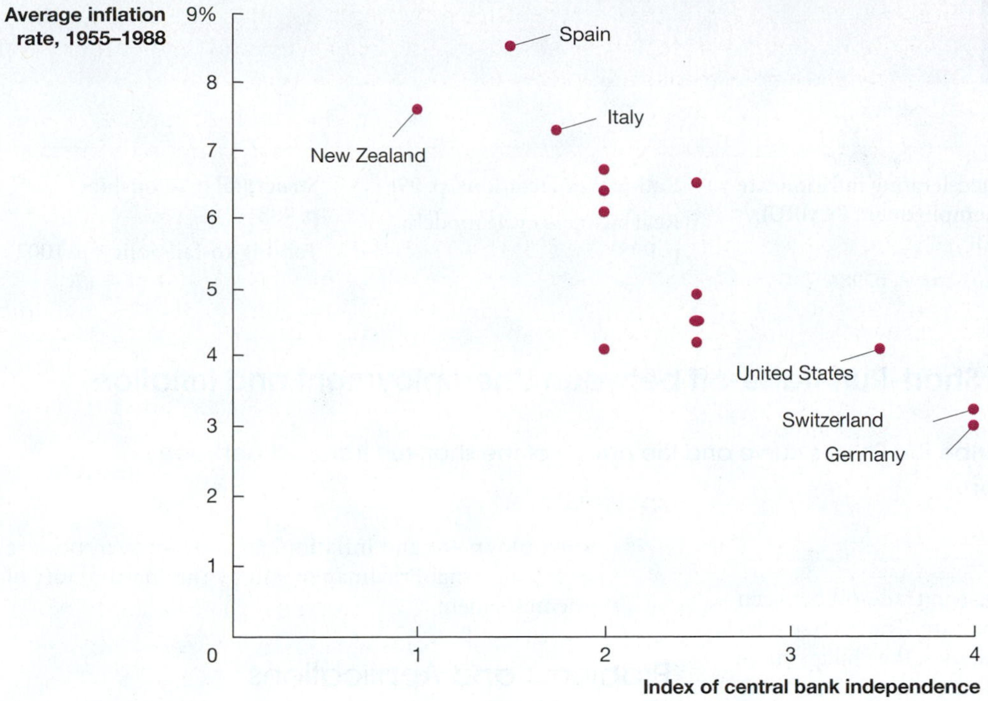

MyEconLab Animation

Figure 28.11

The More Independent the Central Bank, the Lower the Inflation Rate

For 16 high-income countries, the greater the degree of central bank independence from the rest of the government, the lower the inflation rate. Central bank independence is measured by an index ranging from 1 (minimum independence) to 4 (maximum independence). During these years, Germany had a high index of independence of 4 and a low average inflation rate of just over 3 percent. New Zealand had a low index of independence of 1 and a high average inflation rate of over 7 percent.

Source: "Central Bank Independence and Macroeconomic Performance: Some Comparative Evidence" by Alberto Alesina and Lawrence H. Summer from the Journal of Money, Credit and Banking, Vol. 25, No. 2, May 1993. Copyright © 1993 by the Ohio State University. Reprinted by permission.

years, New Zealand and Canada granted their banks more independence, at least partly to better fight inflation.

It remains to be seen which, if any, of the proposals for changing the Fed's structure and operations will be enacted by Congress and whether such changes will have a significant effect on the Fed's ability to carry out monetary policy free of political pressure.

MyEconLab Concept Check

MyEconLab Study Plan

Continued from page 985

Economics in Your Life

Are There Benefits to Delaying a Job Search?

At the beginning of the chapter, we posed this question: What advice would you give someone who has decided to wait a considerable time to look for a new job? As we discussed in the chapter, evidence shows that many of those who are unemployed for longer than a year or two find it more difficult to find new employment than if they searched for a new job soon after they were laid off. The longer workers are unemployed, especially in a high-technology field, the more their skills deteriorate. By delaying her job search, your friend risks being unemployed for longer than she expects if her skills deteriorate. Eventually, she may have to be retrained or take additional courses in a different field in order to find a job. Tell your friend to start her job search right away!

Conclusion

The workings of the economy are complex. The attempts by the Federal Reserve to keep unemployment near the natural rate while also keeping the inflation rate low have not always been successful. Economists continue to debate the best approaches for the Fed to use.

Visit MyEconLab for a news article and analysis related to the concepts in this chapter.

CHAPTER SUMMARY AND PROBLEMS

Key Terms

Disinflation, p. 1000
Natural rate of unemployment, p. 988
Nonaccelerating inflation rate of unemployment (NAIRU), p. 993
Phillips curve, p. 986
Rational expectations, p. 996
Real business cycle models, p. 998
Structural relationship, p. 988
Too-big-to-fail policy, p. 1007

28.1 The Discovery of the Short-Run Trade-off between Unemployment and Inflation, pages 986–991

LEARNING OBJECTIVE: Describe the Phillips curve and the nature of the short-run trade-off between unemployment and inflation.

Summary

The **Phillips curve** illustrates the short-run trade-off between the unemployment rate and the inflation rate. The inverse relationship between unemployment and inflation the Phillips curve shows is consistent with the aggregate demand and aggregate supply (*AD–AS*) model. The *AD–AS* model indicates that slow growth in aggregate demand leads to both higher unemployment and lower inflation, and rapid growth in aggregate demand leads to both lower unemployment and higher inflation. This relationship explains why there is a short-run trade-off between unemployment and inflation. Many economists initially believed that the Phillips curve was a **structural relationship** that depended on the basic behavior of consumers and firms and that remained unchanged over time. If the Phillips curve were a stable relationship, it would present policymakers with a menu of combinations of unemployment and inflation from which they could choose. Milton Friedman argued that there is a **natural rate of unemployment**, which is the unemployment rate that exists when real GDP equals potential GDP. Because in the long run unemployment always returns to the natural rate, there is no trade-off between unemployment and inflation in the long run, and the long-run Phillips curve is a vertical line at the natural rate of unemployment.

MyEconLab Visit **www.myeconlab.com** to complete these exercises online and get instant feedback.

Review Questions

1.1 What is the Phillips curve? Draw a graph of a short-run Phillips curve.

1.2 What actions should the Fed take if it wants to move from a point on the short-run Phillips curve representing high unemployment and low inflation to a point representing lower unemployment and higher inflation?

1.3 Why did economists during the early 1960s think of the Phillips curve as a "policy menu"? Were they correct to think of it in this way? Briefly explain.

1.4 Why did Milton Friedman argue that the Phillips curve did not represent a permanent trade-off between unemployment and inflation? In your answer, be sure to explain what Friedman meant by the "natural rate of unemployment."

Problems and Applications

1.5 Use these two graphs to answer the following questions.

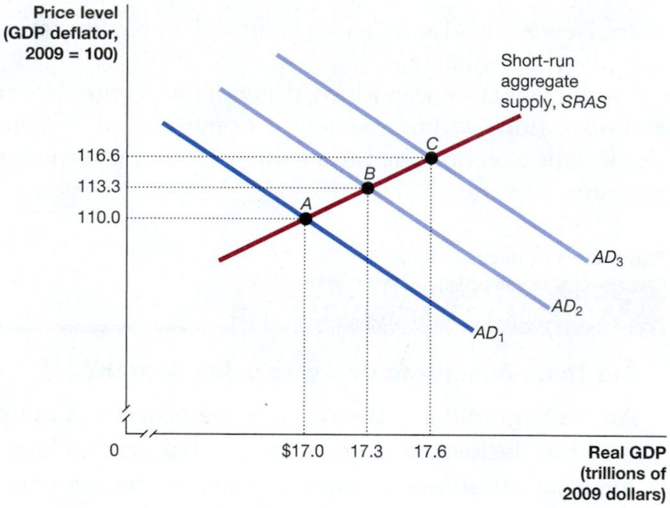

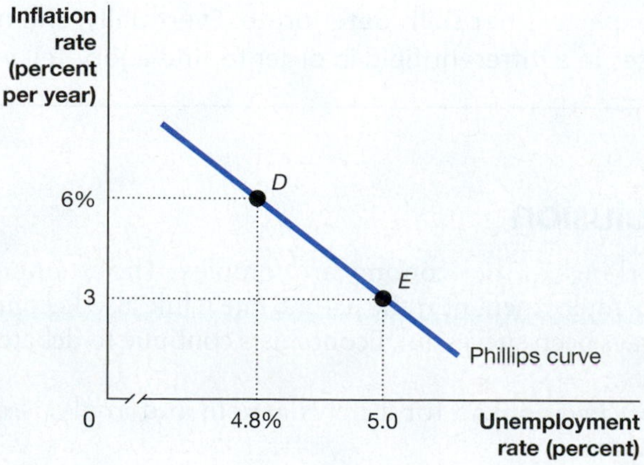

a. Briefly explain which point on the Phillips curve graph best represents the same economic situation as point *B* on the aggregate demand and aggregate supply graph.
b. Briefly explain which point on the Phillips curve graph best represents the same economic situation as point *C* on the aggregate demand and aggregate supply graph.

1.6 Given that the Phillips curve is derived from the aggregate demand and aggregate supply model, why do we use the Phillips curve analysis? What benefits does the Phillips curve analysis offer compared to the aggregate demand and aggregate supply model?

1.7 In macroeconomics courses in the 1960s and early 1970s, some economists argued that one of the U.S. political parties was willing to have higher unemployment in order to achieve lower inflation and that the other major political party was willing to have higher inflation in order to achieve lower unemployment. Why might such views of the trade-off between inflation and unemployment have existed in the 1960s? Why are such views rare today?

1.8 The text discussed how if Ford and the UAW fail to accurately forecast the inflation rate, the real wage will be different than the company and the union expected. Why, then, do the company and the union sign long-term contracts rather than negotiate a new contract each year?

1.9 General Juan Perón, the former dictator of Argentina, once said of the labor market in his country: "Prices have gone up the elevator, and wages have had to use the stairs." In this situation, what was happening to real wages in Argentina? Was unemployment likely to have been relatively high or relatively low?

Source: Robert J. Shiller, "Why Do People Dislike Inflation?" in Christina D. Romer and David H. Romer, eds., *Reducing Inflation: Motivation and Strategy*, Chicago: University of Chicago Press, 1997.

1.10 An article in the *Wall Street Journal* has the headline "Don't Look Now, but Market Inflation Expectations Are Falling." If inflation turns out to be lower than households and firms had previously expected, will the actual real wage end up being higher or lower than the expected real wage? Will employment in the short run end up being higher or lower? Briefly explain.

Source: Jon Hilsenrath, "Don't Look Now, but Market Inflation Expectations Are Falling," *Wall Street Journal*, August 10, 2015.

1.11 **(Related to the Making the Connection on page 990)** Robert Shiller asked a sample of the general public and a sample of economists the following question: "Do you agree that preventing high inflation is an important national priority, as important as preventing drug abuse or preventing deterioration in the quality of our schools?" Fifty-two percent of the general public, but only 18 percent of economists, fully agreed. Why does the general public believe inflation is a bigger problem than economists do?

1.12 **(Related to the Making the Connection on page 990)** When Robert Shiller asked a sample of the general public what they thought caused inflation, the most frequent answer he received was "corporate greed." Do you agree that greed causes inflation? Briefly explain.

1.13 **(Related to the Chapter Opener on page 985)** In its 2014 *Annual Report*, Goodyear noted, "The increasing strength of the U.S. dollar created unfavorable foreign currency translation for many of our businesses around the world."
a. What did the company mean by the "increasing strength of the U.S. dollar"?
b. What did it mean by an "unfavorable foreign currency translation"?
c. During this period was Fed policy attempting to reach a point on the short-run Phillips curve representing higher unemployment and lower inflation, or a point representing higher inflation and lower unemployment? Briefly explain.
d. What connection is there between Fed policy and this statement in Goodyear's annual report?

Source: Goodyear Tire & Rubber Company, *2014 Annual Report*, p. 3.

28.2 The Short-Run and Long-Run Phillips Curves, pages 991–995

LEARNING OBJECTIVE: Explain the relationship between the short-run and long-run Phillips curves.

Summary

There is a short-run trade-off between unemployment and inflation only if the actual inflation rate differs from the inflation rate that workers and firms had expected. There is a different short-run Phillips curve for every expected inflation rate. Each short-run Phillips curve intersects the long-run Phillips curve at the expected inflation rate. With a vertical long-run Phillips curve, it is not possible for policymakers to buy a permanently lower unemployment rate at the cost of a permanently higher inflation rate. If the Federal Reserve attempts to keep the unemployment rate below the natural rate, the inflation rate will increase. Eventually, the expected inflation rate will also increase, which causes the short-run Phillips curve to shift up and pushes the unemployment rate back to the natural rate. The reverse happens if the Fed attempts to keep the unemployment rate above the natural rate. In the long run, the Federal Reserve can affect the inflation rate but not the unemployment rate. The **nonaccelerating inflation rate of unemployment (NAIRU)** is the unemployment rate at which the inflation rate has no tendency to increase or decrease.

MyEconLab Visit **www.myeconlab.com** to complete these exercises online and get instant feedback.

Review Questions

2.1 Suppose that the expected inflation rate increases from 4 percent to 6 percent. What will happen to the short-run Phillips curve?

2.2 What is the relationship between the short-run Phillips curve and the long-run Phillips curve?

2.3 Why is it inconsistent to believe that the long-run aggregate supply curve is vertical and the long-run Phillips curve is downward sloping?

Problems and Applications

2.4 Use the following information to draw a graph showing the short-run and long-run Phillips curves:

Natural rate of unemployment = 5 percent
Current rate of unemployment = 4 percent
Expected inflation rate = 4 percent
Current inflation rate = 6 percent

Be sure your graph shows the point where the short-run and long-run Phillips curves intersect.

2.5 Consider the long-run Phillips curve and the short-run Phillips curve in this graph. What would cause a movement from point *A* to point *B*? What would cause a movement from point *A* to point *C*?

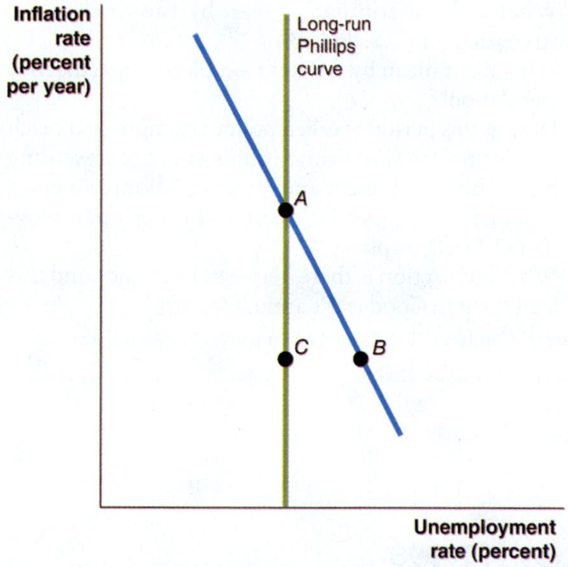

2.6 In 1968, Herbert Stein, who would later serve on President Nixon's Council of Economic Advisers, wrote: "Some who would opt for avoiding inflation would say that in the long run such a policy would cost little, if any, additional unemployment." Was Stein correct? Did most economists in 1968 agree with him? Briefly explain.

Source: Herbert Stein, *The Fiscal Revolution in America*, Chicago: University of Chicago Press, 1969, p. 382.

2.7 In the next column are four graphs and four economic scenarios, each of which would cause either a movement along the short-run or long-run Phillips curve or a shift in the short-run or long-run Phillips curve. Match each scenario with the appropriate graph.

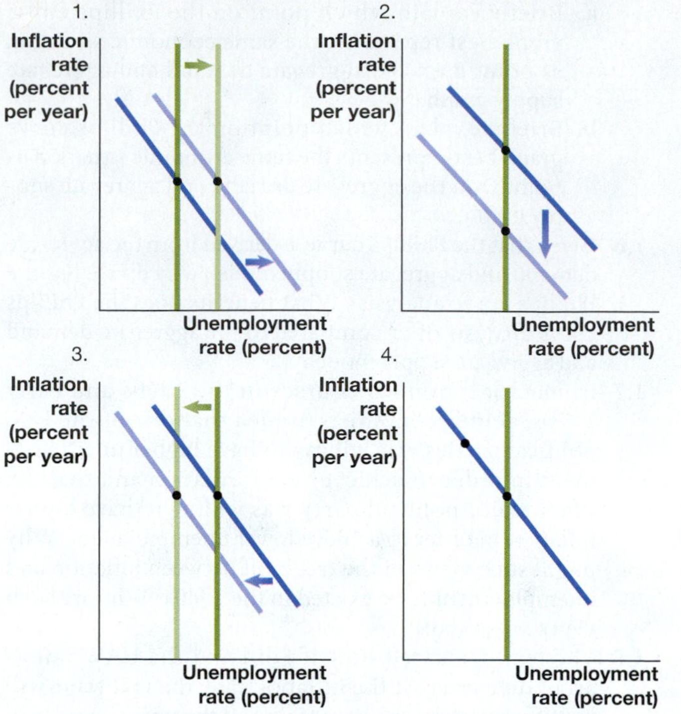

a. The proportion of younger and less-skilled workers in the labor force decreases.
b. The Fed carries out an expansionary monetary policy.
c. Congress enacts significant new legal barriers to firing workers.
d. Workers and firms lower the inflation rate they expect.

2.8 **(Related to the Making the Connection on page 994)** In 2015, an article in a publication of the Federal Reserve Bank of San Francisco noted, "FOMC participants have steadily lowered their estimates of the natural rate of unemployment . . . over the past several years." The article also noted that "a lower natural rate of unemployment also implies a lower target policy rate."

a. Why might members of the FOMC have believed that the natural rate of unemployment was lower in 2015 than it had been several years earlier?
b. What does the article mean by the Fed's "target policy rate"?
c. Why would a lower estimate of the natural rate of unemployment lead the Fed to lower its target policy rate?

Source: Mary C. Daly, Fernanda Nechio, and Benjamin Pyle, "Finding Normal: Natural Rates and Policy Prescriptions," *FRBSF Economic Letter*, July 6, 2015.

2.9 Over time, the Federal Reserve Board of Governors has changed its estimate of the nonaccelerating inflation rate of unemployment (NAIRU). The following are the board's NAIRU estimates for selected years.

Year	NAIRU (percent)
1970	6.0
1980	6.4
1990	5.6
2000	5.1
2008	4.8

a. Why would the board change its estimate of the NAIRU over time?
b. Suppose that the board simply kept its estimate fixed at 5.5 percent. What would have been the consequences for monetary policy during a period when the actual NAIRU was higher? What would have been the consequences for monetary policy during a period when the actual NAIRU was lower?

Source: Board of Governors of the Federal Reserve System.

2.10 In congressional testimony, former Federal Reserve Chairman Ben Bernanke said:

> Another significant factor influencing medium-term trends in inflation is the public's expectations of inflation. These expectations have an important bearing on whether transitory influences on prices, such as changes in energy costs, become embedded in wage and price decisions and so leave a lasting imprint on the rate of inflation.

What did Bernanke mean when he said that the public's expectations of inflation could "become embedded in wage and price decisions"? What would be the effect on the short-run Phillips curve of the public coming to expect a higher inflation rate?

Source: "Testimony of Chairman Ben S. Bernanke before the Joint Economic Committee, U.S. Congress," March 28, 2007.

2.11 In early 2015, an article in the *Economist* noted that it was possible that in the United States, "the NAIRU may already have been reached and inflation will start accelerating; the Fed should act soon."

a. What is the NAIRU?
b. If this evaluation of the economic situation is correct, what action should the Fed take?
c. If the Fed fails to act, what is likely to happen to the short-run Phillips curve over time? Briefly explain.

Source: "Jobs Matter, Not the Dollar," *Economist*, March 25, 2015.

2.12 **(Related to Solved Problem 28.2 on page 995)** In a speech in September 1975, Fed Chairman Arthur Burns said the following:

> There is no longer a meaningful trade-off between unemployment and inflation. In the current environment, a rapidly rising level of consumer prices will not lead to the creation of new jobs. . . . Highly expansionary monetary and fiscal policies might, for a short time, provide some additional thrust to economic activity. But inflation would inevitably accelerate—a development that would create even more difficult economic problems than we have encountered over the past year.

How do Burns's views in this speech compare with the views at the Fed in the late 1960s? Why do you think he specifically says that "in the current environment" there is no trade-off between unemployment and inflation?

Source: Arthur F. Burns, "The Real Issues of Inflation and Unemployment," in Federal Reserve Bank of New York, *Federal Reserve Readings on Inflation*, February 1975.

28.3 Expectations of the Inflation Rate and Monetary Policy, pages 995–998

LEARNING OBJECTIVE: Discuss how expectations of the inflation rate affect monetary policy.

Summary

When the inflation rate is moderate and stable, workers and firms tend to have *adaptive expectations*. That is, they form their expectations under the assumption that future inflation rates will follow the pattern of inflation rates in the recent past. Robert Lucas and Thomas Sargent argued that during the high and unstable inflation rates of the mid- to late 1970s, workers and firms would have *rational expectations*. **Rational expectations** are formed by using all the available information about an economic variable, including the effect of the policy being used by the Federal Reserve. Lucas and Sargent argued that if people have rational expectations, expansionary monetary policy will not work if workers and firms anticipate the policy. If workers and firms know that an expansionary monetary policy is going to raise the inflation rate, the actual inflation rate will be the same as the expected inflation rate. Therefore, the unemployment rate won't fall. Many economists remain skeptical of Lucas's and Sargent's argument. **Real business cycle models** focus on "real" factors—technology shocks—rather than changes in monetary policy to explain fluctuations in real GDP.

MyEconLab Visit www.myeconlab.com to complete these exercises online and get instant feedback.

Review Questions

3.1 Why do workers, firms, banks, and investors in financial markets care about the future rate of inflation? How do they form their expectations of future inflation? Do current conditions in the economy have any effect on how they form their expectations? Briefly explain.

3.2 What does it mean to say that workers and firms have rational expectations?

3.3 Why did Robert Lucas and Thomas Sargent argue that the Phillips curve might be vertical in the short run? What difference would it make for monetary policy if they were right?

Problems and Applications

3.4 During a time when the inflation rate is increasing each year for a number of years, are adaptive expectations or rational expectations likely to give the more accurate forecasts? Briefly explain.

3.5 An article in the *Economist* states that, "Robert Lucas . . . showed how incorporating expectations into macroeconomic models muddled the framework economists prior to the 'rational expectations revolution' thought they saw so clearly." What economic framework did economists change as a result of Lucas's arguments? Do all economists agree with Lucas's main conclusions about whether monetary policy is effective? Briefly explain.

Source: "How to Know What Causes What," *Economist*, October 10, 2011.

3.6 In an article in *Forbes*, Paul Roderick Gregory, an economist at the University of Houston, commented on the use of monetary policy to fight a recession: "Those who devise stimulus programs must know in advance the extent to which households and businesses will correctly anticipate the policy. A policy that has been used x times in the past is unlikely to have a stimulative effect because it will be easily anticipated." Does Gregory believe that households and businesses have adaptive expectations or rational expectations regarding monetary policy? Briefly explain.

Source: Paul Roderick Gregory, "Thomas Sargent, Rational Expectations And The Keynesian Consensus," *Forbes*, October 11, 2011.

3.7 If both the short-run and long-run Phillips curves are vertical, what will be the effect on the inflation rate and the unemployment rate of an expansionary monetary policy? Use a Phillips curve graph to illustrate your answer.

3.8 An article in the *Economist* observes that "a sudden unanticipated spurt of inflation could lead to rapid economic growth."

a. Briefly explain the reasoning behind this statement.

b. Does it matter whether a spurt of inflation is unanticipated? Might different economists provide different answers to this question? Briefly explain.

Source: "How We Got Here," *Economist*, January 21, 2013.

28.4 Federal Reserve Policy from the 1970s to the Present, pages 998–1009

LEARNING OBJECTIVE: Use a Phillips curve graph to show how the Federal Reserve can permanently lower the inflation rate.

Summary

Inflation worsened through the 1970s. Paul Volcker became Fed chairman in 1979, and, under his leadership, the Fed used contractionary monetary policy to reduce inflation. A significant reduction in the inflation rate is called **disinflation**. This contractionary monetary policy pushed short-run equilibrium down the short-run Phillips curve. As workers and firms lowered their expectations of future inflation, the short-run Phillips curve shifted down, improving the short-run trade-off between unemployment and inflation. This change in expectations allowed the Fed to switch to an expansionary monetary policy to bring the unemployment rate back to the natural rate. During Alan Greenspan's term as Fed chairman, inflation remained low, and the credibility of the Fed increased. In recent years, some economists have argued that monetary policy decisions during Greenspan's term may have contributed to the problems the financial system experienced during the 2007–2009 recession. The Fed's actions during and after the financial crisis, including its use of a **too-big-to-fail policy**, led some economists and policymakers to believe that reforms were needed in the Fed's structure and operations. However, other economists and policymakers fear that reducing the Fed's independence may undermine good policy.

MyEconLab Visit **www.myeconlab.com** to complete these exercises online and get instant feedback.

Review Questions

4.1 What was the "Volcker disinflation"? What happened to the unemployment rate during the period of the Volcker disinflation?

4.2 What changes did the Dodd-Frank Act make in the Fed's operations? List three key proposals for changes in the Fed's operations or structure.

4.3 Why do most economists believe that it is important for a country's central bank to be independent of the rest of the country's central government?

Problems and Applications

4.4 An article in the *New York Times* in 2015 quoted Minneapolis Fed President Narayana Kocherlakota as stating that "disinflation is worrisome." Most economists applaud the "Volcker disinflation" of the 1980s. Why might disinflation have been a good thing in the 1980s but worrisome in 2015?

Source: Reuters, "Fed's Kocherlakota Sees Risk of U.S. Disinflation," *New York Times*, April 14, 2015.

4.5 **(Related to the** Don't Let This Happen to You **on page 1001)** Look again at the table on prices during the early 1930s on page 1001. Was there disinflation during 1933? Briefly explain.

4.6 Suppose the current inflation rate and the expected inflation rate are both 4 percent. The current unemployment rate and the natural rate of unemployment are both 5 percent. Use a Phillips curve graph to show the effect of a supply shock. If the Federal Reserve keeps monetary policy unchanged, what will happen eventually to the unemployment rate? Show this change on your Phillips curve graph.

4.7 **(Related to** Solved Problem 28.4 **on page 1001)** Suppose the inflation rate has been 15 percent for the past four years. The unemployment rate is currently at the natural rate of unemployment of 5 percent. The Federal Reserve decides that it wants to permanently reduce the inflation rate to 5 percent. How can the Fed use monetary policy to achieve this objective? Be sure to use a Phillips curve graph in your answer.

4.8 While many economists and policymakers supported the Fed's decision to maintain the federal funds rate at a near-zero level for over six years, Charles Schwab, the founder and chairman of a discount brokerage firm that bears his name, argued that the economy was harmed by keeping interest rates low for an extended period of time:

> U.S. households lost billions in interest income during the Fed's near-zero interest rate experiment. . . . Because they are often

reliant on income from savings, seniors were hit the hardest. . . . Seniors make up 13% of the U.S. population and spend about $1.2 trillion annually. . . . This makes for a potent multiplier effect.

a. What type of spending was Schwab expecting would have increased if the Fed had raised interest rate earlier than it did?
b. Would higher interest rates have had an effect on other types of spending? Briefly explain.
c. Which of the types of spending that you discussed in answering parts (a) and (b) does the Fed appear to believe has the more "potent multiplier effect"? Briefly explain.

Source: Charles R. Schwab, "Raise Interest Rates, Make Grandma Smile," *Wall Street Journal*, November 19, 2014.

4.9 **(Related to the Making the Connection on page 1005)** In an opinion column in the *New York Times*, economist Justin Wolfers of the University of Michigan noted, "Over recent years, policy makers have also worked to lower long-term interest rates by shaping expectations about future monetary policy decisions."

a. What does the Fed call such an attempt to shape expectations of future policy decisions?
b. Briefly explain how this approach works.

Source: Justin Wolfers, "The Fed Has Not Stopped Trying to Stimulate the Economy," *New York Times*, October 29, 2014.

4.10 Robert Lucas said, "In practice, it is much more painful to put a modern economy through a deflation than the monetary theory we have would lead us to expect. I take this to mean that we have 'price stickiness.'"

a. What does Lucas mean by "the monetary theory we have"?
b. What events may have led Lucas to conclude that it is more painful to reduce the inflation rate than theory would predict?
c. Why does he conclude that the U.S. economy apparently has "price stickiness"?

Source: Paul A. Samuelson and William A. Barnett, eds., *Inside the Economist's Mind: Conversations with Eminent Economists*, Malden, MA: Blackwell Publishing, 2007.

4.11 An opinion column in the *Wall Street Journal* notes, "In a democracy, the tradeoff for a central bank's independence is accountability to the nation's elected leadership."

a. Why would a country want to grant its central bank more independence than it grants, say, its department of agriculture or department of education?
b. In the United States, how is the Fed held accountable to the nation's elected leadership?

Source: David Wessel, "Explaining 'Audit the Fed,'" *Wall Street Journal*, February 17, 2015.

4.12 In an opinion column in the *Wall Street Journal*, Stanford University economist John Taylor, originator of the Taylor rule, argued, "As I see it, the broader evidence in the United States and in many other countries . . . is that a rules-based policy has worked and that discretion—constrained or otherwise—has not."

a. What does Taylor mean by a "rules-based policy"?
b. How can we tell whether a monetary policy has worked?
c. Why have many Fed officials been opposed to adopting a rules-based policy?

Source: John B. Taylor, "Taylor on Bernanke: Monetary Rules Work Better Than 'Constrained Discretion,'" *Wall Street Journal*, May 2, 2015.

Real-Time Data Exercises

D28.1 **(Testing the Phillips curve)** Go to the Web site of the Federal Reserve Bank of St. Louis (FRED) (research.stlouisfed.org/fred2) and download annual unemployment data (UNRATE) for 1962 to the present. (To convert the data from a monthly frequency to an annual frequency, click on "Graph" and "Frequency.") Next, download the annual inflation rate measured using the consumer price index, or CPI (CPIAUCSL). (Once you have converted the data from a monthly frequency to an annual frequency, you can find the inflation rate by clicking on "Units" and selecting "Percent Change from Year Ago.") Plot both series on the same graph. Briefly explain whether for each of the following periods, the relationship between the annual unemployment rate and the annual inflation rate is consistent with a movement along the short-run Phillips curve or with a shift in the Phillips curve.

a. 1966–1969
b. 1973–1975
c. 1992–1994
d. 2000–2002

D28.2 **(Comparing actual inflation and expected inflation)** Go to the Web site of the Federal Reserve Bank of St. Louis (FRED) (research.stlouisfed.org/fred2) and download monthly data on the inflation rate expected by consumers as measured by the University of Michigan's survey (MICH) for 1978 to the present. Next, download the monthly inflation rate measured using the consumer price index, or CPI (CPIAUCSL), for the same period. (You can find the inflation rate by clicking on "Units" and selecting "Percent Change from Year Ago.") Plot both series on the same graph. During which periods did consumers do a good job of forecasting the inflation rate? During which periods did they do a poor job? Do consumers' expectations of the inflation rate tend to be more volatile or less volatile than the actual inflation rate?

CHAPTER
29

Macroeconomics in an Open Economy

Chapter Outline and Learning Objectives

IBM Sings the Dollar Blues

The company that became the International Business Machines Corporation (IBM) was founded in New York City in 1911. For decades, under the leadership of CEOs Tom Watson, Sr., and his son Tom Watson, Jr., IBM was best known for manufacturing large computer systems used by corporations. As business computing made the transition from mainframes to desktop computers, IBM established a new standard with its personal computers powered by Intel chips and using an operating system developed by Microsoft. In 2015, IBM was well into another transition, away from manufacturing hardware and toward selling cloud-based computing software services. As CEO Virginia Rometty put it, "We've reinvented this company one more time." Today, IBM has more than 375,000 employees, $90 billion in revenue, and $20 billion in profits.

Most people think of IBM as a giant of U.S. business. However, as the company name indicates, IBM is an international company with offices throughout Europe, Latin America, Africa, and Asia. In 2014, more than two-thirds of IBM's revenue was earned outside the United States. As a result, the company's profits are affected by fluctuations in the value of the dollar in exchange for other currencies. In some years, converting revenue from foreign currencies yields fewer dollars than in other years. For example, in 2014, IBM's global revenue was nearly $2 billion lower when measured in terms of dollars than when measured in local currencies—pounds in Great Britain, euros in Germany, yen in Japan. Why the discrepancy? The value of the dollar had increased relative to most other currencies. So, converting pounds, euros, and yen into dollars yielded fewer dollars for IBM. As an article in the *Wall Street Journal* put it, "The company . . . has run into a stiff headwind from the rising value of the dollar."

As we saw in Chapter 26, one reason for the increasing value of the U.S. dollar in 2015 was rising U.S. interest rates. Higher interest rates made financial investments in the United States more attractive to foreign investors, which increased the demand for U.S. dollars and the exchange rate between the dollar and other currencies. In this chapter and the next, we will look more closely at how exchange rates are determined and at other important issues involving the international financial system.

Sources: Don Clark, "IBM Pumps $4 Billion into Cloud and Mobile Initiatives," *Wall Street Journal*, February 26, 2015; Steve Lohr, "IBM Revenue Falls 13% Despite Big Gains in New Fields," *New York Times*, July 20, 2015; and International Business Machines Corporation, *2014 IBM Annual Report*, February 24, 2015.

Economics in Your Life

The South Korean Central Bank and Your Car Loan

Suppose that you are shopping for a new car, which you plan to finance with a loan from a local bank. While reading an article in the *Wall Street Journal* on your smartphone one morning, you see this headline: "The Bank of Korea, South Korea's central bank, announces it will sell its large holdings of U.S. Treasury bonds." Will the Bank of Korea's decision to sell its U.S. Treasury bonds affect the interest rate you pay on your car loan? As you read this chapter, try to answer this question. You can check your answer against the one we provide on **page 1037** at the end of this chapter.

In Chapter 9, we looked at the basics of international trade. In this chapter, we look more closely at the linkages among countries at the macroeconomic level. Countries are linked by trade in goods and services and by flows of financial investment. We will see how policymakers in all countries take these linkages into account when conducting monetary policy and fiscal policy.

29.1 The Balance of Payments: Linking the United States to the International Economy

LEARNING OBJECTIVE: Explain how the balance of payments is calculated.

Open economy An economy that has interactions in trade or finance with other countries.

Closed economy An economy that has no interactions in trade or finance with other countries.

Balance of payments The record of a country's trade with other countries in goods, services, and assets.

Today, consumers, firms, and investors routinely interact with consumers, firms, and investors in other economies. A consumer in France may use computer software produced in the United States, watch a television manufactured in South Korea, and wear a sweater made in Italy. A U.S. firm like IBM may sell its products in dozens of countries around the world. An investor in London may sell a U.S. Treasury bill to an investor in Mexico City. Nearly all economies are **open economies** and have extensive interactions in trade or finance with other countries. Open economies interact by trading goods and services and by making investments in each other's economies. A **closed economy** has no interactions in trade or finance with other countries. No economy today is completely closed, although a few countries, such as North Korea, have very limited economic interactions with other countries.

A good way to understand the interactions between one economy and other economies is through the **balance of payments**, which is a record of a country's trade with other countries in goods, services, and assets. Just as the U.S. Bureau of Economic Analysis is responsible for collecting data on the gross domestic product (GDP), it is also responsible for collecting data on the balance of payments. Table 29.1 shows the balance of payments for the United States in 2014. Notice that the table contains three "accounts": the *current account*, the *financial account*, and the *capital account*.

The Current Account

Current account The part of the balance of payments that records a country's net exports, net income on investments, and net transfers.

The **current account** records *current*, or short-term, flows of funds into and out of a country. The current account for the United States includes: (1) exports and imports of goods and services (recall that the difference between exports and imports of goods and services is called *net exports*); (2) income received by U.S. residents from investments in other countries and income paid on investments in the United States owned by residents of other countries (the difference between investment income received and investment income paid is called *net income on investments*); and (3) the difference between transfers made to residents of other countries and transfers received by U.S. residents from other countries (called *net transfers*). If you make a donation to a charity caring for orphans in Afghanistan, it will be included in net transfers. Any payments received by U.S. residents are positive numbers in the current account, and any payments made by U.S. residents are negative numbers in the current account.

Balance of trade The difference between the value of the goods a country exports and the value of the goods a country imports.

The Balance of Trade Part of the current account is the **balance of trade**, which is the difference between the value of the goods a country exports and the value of the goods the country imports. The balance of trade is the largest item in the current account and is a topic that politicians and the media often discuss. If a country exports more goods than it imports, it has a *trade surplus*. If a country exports less than it imports, it has a *trade deficit*. In 2014, the United States had a trade deficit of $741 billion. In the same year, Japan had a trade deficit of $121 billion, and China had a trade surplus of $369 billion. Figure 29.1 on page 1020 shows imports and exports of goods between the United States and its trading partners and between Japan and its trading partners. The data show that the United States ran a trade deficit in 2014 with all its major trading partners and with every region of the world apart from Latin America (except Mexico) and Africa. Japan ran trade surpluses with the United States, Asia (except China), and Latin America, and it ran trade deficits with the other regions. (Note that exports from

MyEconLab Real-time data

Table 29.1

The U.S. Balance of Payments, 2014 (billions of dollars)

Current Account		
Exports of goods	$1,633	
Imports of goods	−2,374	
Balance of trade		−741
Exports of services	711	
Imports of services	−477	
Balance of services		234
Income received on investments	823	
Income payments on investments	−585	
Net income on investments		238
Net transfers		−120
Balance on current account		**−389**
Financial Account		
Increase in foreign holdings of assets in the United States	1,031	
Increase in U.S. holdings of assets in foreign countries	−792	
Balance on financial account		**239**
Balance on Capital Account		**0**
Statistical discrepancy		**150**
Balance of payments		**0**

The sum of the balance of trade and the balance of services equals net exports.

Note: Subtotals may not sum to totals because of rounding.

Source: U.S. Bureau of Economic Analysis, "U.S. International Transactions," June 18, 2015.

the United States to Japan in panel (a) of Figure 29.1 should equal imports by Japan from the United States in panel (b). These two numbers are different because international trade statistics are not measured exactly.)

Net Exports Equals the Sum of the Balance of Trade and the Balance of Services Recall that *net exports* is a component of aggregate expenditure. Net exports is not explicitly shown in Table 29.1, but we can calculate it by adding the balance of trade and the balance of services. The *balance of services* is the difference between the value of the services a country exports and the value of the services the country imports. Notice that, technically, net exports is *not* equal to the current account balance because this account also includes net income on investments and net transfers. Because these other two items are relatively small, though, it is often a convenient simplification to think of net exports as being equal to the current account balance. MyEconLab Concept Check

The Financial Account

The **financial account** records purchases of assets a country has made abroad and foreign purchases of assets in the country. The financial account records long-term flows of funds into and out of a country. There is a *capital outflow* from the United States when an investor in the United States buys a bond issued by a foreign company or government or when a U.S. firm builds a factory in another country. There is a *capital inflow* into the United States when a foreign investor buys a bond issued by a U.S. firm or by the government or when a foreign firm builds a factory in the United States. Notice that we are using the word *capital* here to apply not just to physical assets, such as factories, but also to financial assets, such as shares of stock. When firms build or buy facilities in

Financial account The part of the balance of payments that records purchases of assets a country has made abroad and foreign purchases of assets in the country.

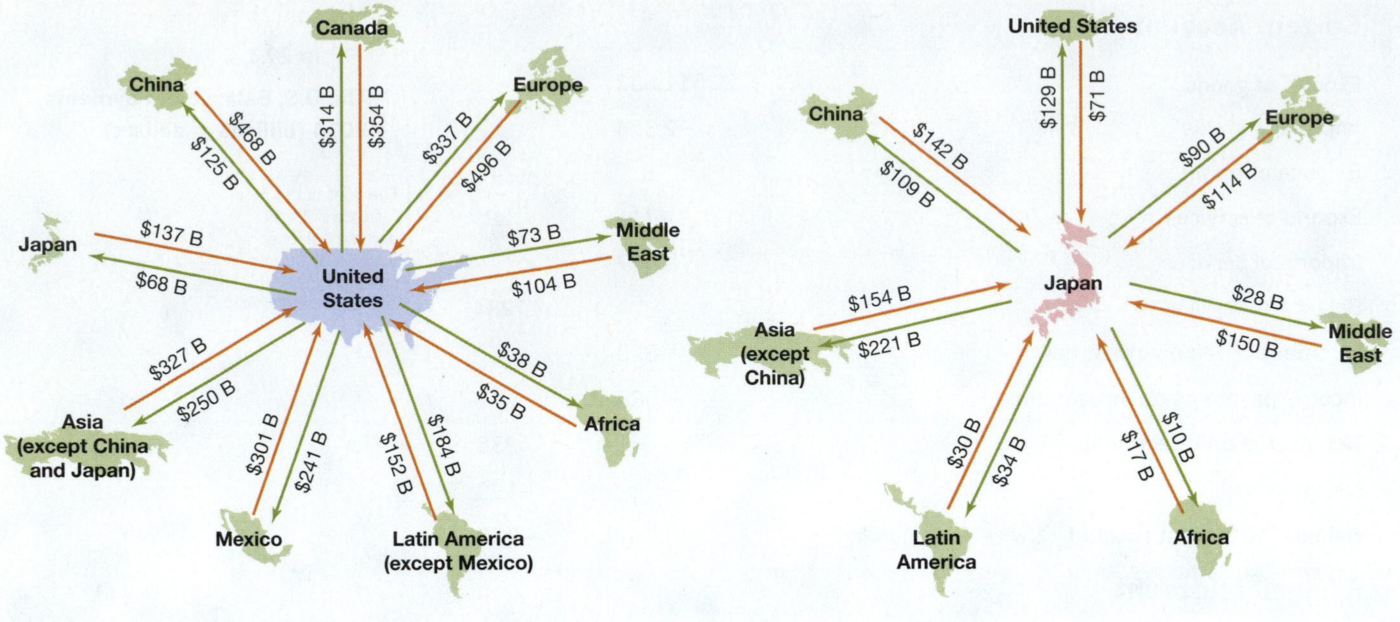

(a) Trade flows for the United States (in billions of dollars) **(b) Trade flows for Japan (in billions of dollars)**

MyEconLab Animation

Figure 29.1 Trade Flows for the United States and Japan, 2014

Panel (a) shows that in 2014, the United States ran a trade deficit with all its major trading partners and with every region of the world except for Latin America and Africa. Panel (b) shows that Japan ran trade deficits with China, Latin America, Europe, Africa, and the Middle East, and it ran trade surpluses with the United States and Asia. In each panel, the green arrows represent exports from the United States or Japan, and the red arrows represent imports.

Note: Japanese data are converted from yen to dollars at the average 2014 exchange rate of 105.7 yen per dollar.

Sources: U.S. Bureau of Economic Analysis, "U.S. International Transactions," June 18, 2015; and Japanese Ministry of Finance, *Trade Statistics of Japan.*

foreign countries, they are engaging in *foreign direct investment*. When investors buy stock or bonds issued in another country, they are engaging in *foreign portfolio investment*.

Net foreign investment The difference between capital outflows from a country and capital inflows, also equal to net foreign direct investment plus net foreign portfolio investment.

Another way of thinking of the balance on the financial account is as a measure of *net capital flows*, or the difference between capital inflows and capital outflows. (Here we are omitting a few transactions included in the capital account, as discussed in the next section.) A concept closely related to net capital flows is **net foreign investment**, which is equal to capital outflows minus capital inflows. Net capital flows and net foreign investment are always equal but have opposite signs: When net capital flows are positive, net foreign investment is negative, and when net capital flows are negative, net foreign investment is positive. Net foreign investment is also equal to net foreign direct investment plus net foreign portfolio investment. In Section 29.3, we will use the relationship between the balance on the financial account and net foreign investment to understand an important aspect of the international economic system. MyEconLab Concept Check

The Capital Account

Capital account The part of the balance of payments that records relatively minor transactions, such as migrants' transfers and sales and purchases of nonproduced, nonfinancial assets.

A third, less important, part of the balance of payments is called the *capital account*. The **capital account** records relatively minor transactions, such as migrants' transfers—which consist of goods and financial assets people take with them when they leave or enter a country—and sales and purchases of nonproduced, nonfinancial assets. A nonproduced, nonfinancial asset is a copyright, patent, trademark, or right to natural resources. The definitions of the financial account and the capital account are often misunderstood because the capital account prior to 1999 recorded all the transactions now included in both the financial account and the capital account. In other words, capital account transactions went from being a very important part of the balance of payments to being a relatively unimportant part. Because the balance on what is now called the capital account is so small—only $45 million in 2014, which we rounded to zero in Table 29.1—for simplicity we will ignore it in the remainder of this chapter.

MyEconLab Concept Check

Why Is the Balance of Payments Always Zero?

The sum of the current account balance, the financial account balance, and the capital account balance equals the balance of payments. Table 29.1 on page 1019 shows that the balance of payments for the United States in 2014 was zero. It's not just by chance that this balance was zero; *the balance of payments is always zero*. Notice that the current account balance in 2014 was −$389 billion. The balance on the financial account (which has the opposite sign to the balance on the current account) was $239 billion. To make the balance on the current account equal to the balance on the financial account, the balance of payments includes an entry called the *statistical discrepancy*. (Remember that we are ignoring the balance on the capital account. If we included it, we would say that the statistical discrepancy takes on a value equal to the difference between the current account balance and the sum of the balance on the financial account and the balance on the capital account.)

Why does the U.S. Department of Commerce include the statistical discrepancy entry to force the balance of payments to equal zero? If the sum of the current account balance and the financial account balance does not equal zero, some imports or exports of goods and services or some capital inflows or capital outflows were not measured accurately.

To better understand why the balance of payments must equal zero every year, consider the following: In 2014, the United States spent $389 billion more on goods, services, and other items in the current account than it received. What happened to that $389 billion? We know that every dollar of that $389 billion was used by foreign individuals or firms to invest in the United States or was added to foreign holdings of dollars. We know this because logically there is nowhere else for the dollars to go: If the dollars weren't spent on U.S. goods and services—and we know they weren't because if they had been, they would have shown up in the current account—they must have been spent on investments in the United States or not spent at all. Dollars that aren't spent are added to foreign holdings of dollars. Changes in foreign holdings of dollars are called *official reserve transactions*. Foreign investment in the United States and additions to foreign holdings of dollars both show up as positive entries in the U.S. financial

Don't Let This Happen to You

Don't Confuse the Balance of Trade, the Current Account Balance, and the Balance of Payments

The terminology of international economics can be tricky. Remember that the *balance of trade* includes only trade in goods; it does not include services. This observation is important because the United States, for example, usually imports more *goods* than it exports, but it usually exports more *services* than it imports. As a result, the U.S. trade deficit is almost always larger than the current account deficit. The *current account balance* includes the balance of trade, the balance of services, net investment income, and net transfers. Net investment income and net transfers are much smaller than the balance of trade and the balance of services.

Even though the *balance of payments* is equal to the sum of the current account balance and the financial account balance—and must equal zero—you may sometimes see references to a balance of payments "surplus" or "deficit." These references have two explanations. The first is that the person making the reference has confused the balance of payments with either the balance of trade or the current account balance. This mistake is very common. The second explanation is that the person is not including official reserve transactions in the financial account. If we separate changes in U.S. holdings of foreign currencies and changes in foreign holdings of U.S. dollars from other financial account entries, the current account balance and the financial account balance do not have to sum to zero, and there can be a balance of payments surplus or deficit. These distinctions may sound complicated—and they are! But don't worry. Knowing how official reserve transactions are accounted for is not crucial to understanding the basic ideas behind the balance of payments.

MyEconLab Study Plan

Your Turn: Test your understanding by doing related problem 1.6 on pages 1038–1039 at the end of this chapter.

account. Therefore, a current account deficit must be exactly offset by a financial account surplus, leaving the balance of payments equal to zero. Similarly, a country that runs a current account surplus, such as China, must run a financial account deficit of exactly the same size. If a country's current account surplus is not exactly equal to its financial account deficit, or if a country's current account deficit is not exactly equal to its financial account surplus, some transactions must not have been accounted for. The statistical discrepancy is included in the balance of payments to compensate for these uncounted transactions.

MyEconLab Concept Check

Solved Problem 29.1

MyEconLab Interactive Animation

Understanding the Arithmetic of the Balance of Payments

Test your understanding of the relationship between the current account and the financial account by evaluating the following assertion by a political commentator:

> The industrial countries are committing economic suicide. Every year, they invest more and more in emerging countries, such as South Korea. Every year, more U.S., Japanese, and European manufacturing firms move their factories to emerging countries. With extensive new factories and low wages, emerging countries now export far more to the industrial countries than they import.

Solving the Problem

Step 1: Review the chapter material. This problem is about the relationship between the current account and the financial account, so you may want to review the section "Why Is the Balance of Payments Always Zero?" which begins on page 1021.

Step 2: Explain the errors in the commentator's argument. The argument sounds plausible. It would be easy to find statements similar to this one in recent books and articles by well-known political commentators. But the argument contains an important error: The commentator has failed to understand the relationship between the current account and the financial account. The commentator asserts that emerging countries are receiving large capital inflows from industrial countries. In other words, emerging countries are running financial account surpluses. The commentator also asserts that emerging countries are exporting more than they are importing. In other words, they are running current account surpluses. As we have seen in this section, it is impossible to run a current account surplus *and* a financial account surplus simultaneously. A country that runs a current account surplus *must* run a financial account deficit and vice versa.

Extra Credit: Most emerging economies that have received large inflows of foreign investment during the past two decades, such as South Korea, Thailand, and Malaysia, have run current account deficits: They import more goods and services than they export. Emerging economies that run current account surpluses, such as Singapore, also run financial account deficits: They invest more abroad than other countries invest in them.

The point here is not obvious; if it was, it wouldn't confuse so many intelligent politicians, journalists, and political commentators. Unless you understand the relationship between the current account and the financial account, you won't be able to understand a key aspect of the international economy.

MyEconLab Study Plan

Your Turn: For more practice, do related problems 1.7, 1.8, and 1.9 on page 1039 at the end of this chapter.

29.2 The Foreign Exchange Market and Exchange Rates

LEARNING OBJECTIVE: Explain how exchange rates are determined and how changes in exchange rates affect the prices of imports and exports.

A firm that operates entirely within the United States will price its products in dollars and will use dollars to pay its suppliers' bills, wages and salaries to its workers, interest to its bondholders, and dividends to its shareholders. A multinational corporation such as IBM, in contrast, may sell its products in many different countries and receive payments in many different currencies. Its suppliers and workers may also be spread around the world and may have to be paid in local currencies. In addition to exchanging currencies, corporations may also use the international financial system to borrow in a foreign currency. For example, during a period of rapid expansion in East Asian countries such as Thailand and South Korea during the late 1990s, many large firms received dollar loans from foreign banks. When firms make extensive use of foreign currencies, they must deal with fluctuations in the exchange rate.

The **nominal exchange rate** is the value of one country's currency in terms of another country's currency. Economists also calculate the *real exchange rate*, which corrects the nominal exchange rate for changes in prices of goods and services. We discuss the real exchange rate later in this section. The nominal exchange rate determines how many units of a foreign currency you can purchase with $1. For example, the exchange rate between the U.S. dollar and the Japanese yen can be expressed as ¥100 = $1. (This exchange rate can also be expressed as how many U.S. dollars are required to buy 1 Japanese yen: $0.01 = ¥1.) The market for foreign exchange is very active, with the equivalent of more than $4 trillion worth of currency being traded each day. The exchange rates that result from this trading are reported on a number of online sites devoted to economic news and in the business or financial sections of most newspapers.

Nominal exchange rate The value of one country's currency in terms of another country's currency.

Banks and other financial institutions around the world employ currency traders, who are linked together by computer. Rather than exchange large amounts of paper currency, they buy and sell deposits in banks. For example, a bank buying or selling dollars will actually be buying or selling dollar bank deposits. Dollar bank deposits exist not just in banks in the United States but also in banks around the world. Suppose that the Crédit Agricole bank in France wants to sell U.S. dollars and buy Japanese yen. The bank may exchange U.S. dollar deposits that it owns for Japanese yen deposits owned by the Deutsche Bank in Germany. Businesses and individuals usually obtain foreign currency from banks in their own country.

Making the Connection
MyEconLab Video

Exchange Rate Listings

You can find the exchange rates between the dollar and other major currencies on many online sites, such as wsj.com, Bloomberg.com, or finance.yahoo.com, as well as in the financial pages of most newspapers. The exchange rates in the following table are for August 14, 2015. The euro is the common currency used by 19 European countries, including France, Germany, and Italy, but not the United Kingdom.

Exchange Rate between the U.S. Dollar and the Indicated Currency

Currency	Units of Foreign Currency per U.S. Dollar	U.S. Dollars per Unit of Foreign Currency
Canadian dollar	1.31	0.763
Japanese yen	124.32	0.008
Mexican peso	16.37	0.061
British pound	0.64	1.56
Euro	0.90	1.11

Notice that the expression for the exchange rate stated as units of foreign currency per U.S. dollar is the *reciprocal* of the exchange rate stated as U.S. dollars per unit of foreign currency. So, the exchange rate between the U.S. dollar and the British pound can be stated as either 0.64 British pounds per U.S. dollar or 1/0.64 = 1.56 U.S. dollars per British pound.

Banks are the most active participants in the market for foreign exchange. Typically, banks buy currency for slightly less than the amount for which they sell it. This spread between the buying and selling prices allows banks to cover their costs from currency trading. Therefore, when most businesses and individuals buy foreign currency from a bank, they receive fewer units of foreign currency per dollar than would be indicated by the exchange rate shown on online business sites or printed in the newspaper.

Source: *Wall Street Journal*, August 14, 2015.

MyEconLab Study Plan

Your Turn: Test your understanding by doing related problem 2.5 on pages 1039–1040 at the end of this chapter.

The market exchange rate is determined by the interaction of demand and supply, just as other prices are. There are three sources of foreign currency demand for the U.S. dollar:

1. Foreign firms and households that want to buy goods and services produced in the United States.
2. Foreign firms and households that want to invest in the United States either through foreign direct investment—buying or building factories or other facilities in the United States—or through foreign portfolio investment—buying stocks and bonds issued in the United States.
3. Currency traders who believe that the value of the dollar in the future will be greater than its value today.

Equilibrium in the Market for Foreign Exchange

Figure 29.2 shows the demand and supply of U.S. dollars for Japanese yen. Notice that as we move up the vertical axis, the value of the dollar increases relative to the value of the yen. When the exchange rate is ¥150 = $1, the dollar is worth 1.5 times as much relative to the yen as when the exchange rate is ¥100 = $1. Consider, first, the demand curve for dollars in exchange for yen. The demand curve has the normal downward slope. When the value of the dollar is high, the quantity of dollars demanded will be low. A Japanese investor will be more likely to buy a $1,000 bond issued by the U.S.

MyEconLab Animation

Figure 29.2

Equilibrium in the Foreign Exchange Market

When the exchange rate is ¥150 to the dollar, the exchange rate is above its equilibrium level, and there will be a surplus of dollars. When the exchange rate is ¥100 to the dollar, it is below its equilibrium level, and there will be a shortage of dollars. At an exchange rate of ¥120 to the dollar, the foreign exchange market is in equilibrium.

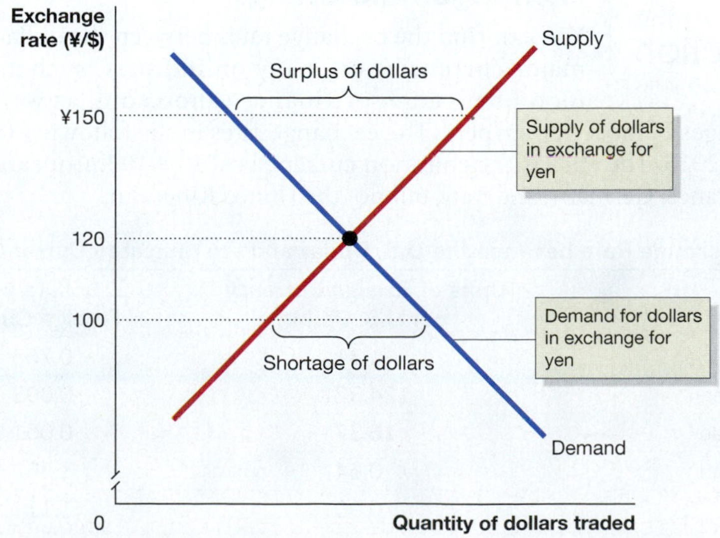

Treasury when the exchange rate is ¥100 = $1 and the investor pays only ¥100,000 to buy $1,000 than when the exchange rate is ¥150 = $1 and the investor must pay ¥150,000. Similarly, a Japanese firm is more likely to buy $150 million worth of microchips from Intel Corporation when the exchange rate is ¥100 = $1 and the microchips can be purchased for ¥15 billion than when the exchange rate is ¥150 = $1 and the microchips cost ¥22.5 billion.

Now consider the supply curve for dollars in exchange for yen. The supply curve has the normal upward slope. When the value of the dollar is high, the quantity of dollars supplied in exchange for yen will be high. A U.S. investor will be more likely to buy a ¥200,000 bond issued by the Japanese government when the exchange rate is ¥200 = $1 and he needs to pay only $1,000 to buy ¥200,000 than when the exchange rate is ¥100 = $1 and he must pay $2,000. The owner of a U.S. electronics store is more likely to buy ¥20 million worth of television sets from the Sony Corporation when the exchange rate is ¥200 = $1 and she needs to pay only $100,000 to purchase the televisions than when the exchange rate is ¥100 = $1 and she must pay $200,000.

As in any other market, equilibrium occurs in the foreign exchange market where the quantity supplied equals the quantity demanded. In Figure 29.2, ¥120 = $1 is the equilibrium exchange rate. At exchange rates above ¥120 = $1, there will be a surplus of dollars and downward pressure on the exchange rate. The surplus and the downward pressure will not be eliminated until the exchange rate falls to ¥120 = $1. If the exchange rate is below ¥120 = $1, there will be a shortage of dollars and upward pressure on the exchange rate. The shortage and the upward pressure will not be eliminated until the exchange rate rises to ¥120 = $1. Surpluses and shortages in the foreign exchange market are eliminated very quickly because the volume of trading in major currencies such as the dollar and the yen is large, and currency traders are linked together by computer.

Currency appreciation occurs when the market value of a country's currency increases relative to the value of another country's currency. **Currency depreciation** occurs when the market value of a country's currency decreases relative to the value of another country's currency.

MyEconLab Concept Check

Currency appreciation An increase in the market value of one currency relative to another currency.

Currency depreciation A decrease in the market value of one currency relative to another currency.

How Do Shifts in Demand and Supply Affect the Exchange Rate?

Shifts in the demand and supply curves cause the equilibrium exchange rate to change. Three main factors cause the demand and supply curves in the foreign exchange market to shift:

1. Changes in the demand for U.S.-produced goods and services and changes in the demand for foreign-produced goods and services
2. Changes in the desire to invest in the United States and changes in the desire to invest in foreign countries
3. Changes in the expectations of currency traders about the likely future value of the dollar and the likely future value of foreign currencies

Shifts in the Demand for Foreign Exchange Consider how the three factors just listed will affect the demand for U.S. dollars in exchange for Japanese yen. During an economic expansion in Japan, the incomes of Japanese households will rise, and the demand by Japanese consumers and firms for U.S. goods will increase. At any given exchange rate, the demand for U.S. dollars will increase, and the demand curve will shift to the right. Similarly, if interest rates in the United States rise, the desirability of investing in U.S. financial assets will increase, and the demand curve for dollars will also shift to the right. **Speculators** are currency traders who buy and sell foreign exchange in an attempt to profit from changes in exchange rates. If a speculator becomes convinced that the value of the dollar is going to rise relative to the value of the yen, the speculator will sell yen and buy dollars. If the current exchange rate is ¥120 = $1, and the speculator is convinced that it will soon rise to ¥140 = $1, the speculator could sell

Speculators Currency traders who buy and sell foreign exchange in an attempt to profit from changes in exchange rates.

¥600,000,000 and receive \$5,000,000 (= ¥600,000,000/¥120) in return. If the speculator is correct and the value of the dollar rises against the yen to ¥140 = \$1, the speculator will be able to exchange \$5,000,000 for ¥700,000,000 (= \$5,000,000 × ¥140) for a profit of ¥100,000,000.

To summarize, the demand curve for dollars shifts to the right when incomes in Japan rise, when interest rates in the United States rise, or when speculators decide that the value of the dollar will rise relative to the value of the yen.

During a recession in Japan, Japanese incomes will fall, reducing the demand for U.S.-produced goods and services and shifting the demand curve for dollars to the left. Similarly, if interest rates in the United States fall, the desirability of investing in U.S. financial assets will decrease, and the demand curve for dollars will shift to the left. Finally, if speculators become convinced that the future value of the dollar will be lower than its current value, the demand for dollars will fall, and the demand curve will shift to the left.

Shifts in the Supply of Foreign Exchange The factors that affect the supply curve for dollars are similar to those that affect the demand curve for dollars. An economic expansion in the United States increases the incomes of Americans and increases their demand for goods and services, including goods and services made in Japan. As U.S. consumers and firms increase their spending on Japanese products, they must supply dollars in exchange for yen, which causes the supply curve for dollars to shift to the right. Similarly, an increase in interest rates in Japan will make financial investments in Japan more attractive to U.S. investors. These higher Japanese interest rates will cause the supply curve for dollars to shift to the right, as U.S. investors exchange dollars for yen. Finally, if speculators become convinced that the future value of the yen will be higher relative to the dollar than it is today, the supply curve for dollars will shift to the right as traders attempt to exchange dollars for yen.

A recession in the United States will decrease the demand for Japanese products and cause the supply curve for dollars to shift to the left. Similarly, a decrease in interest rates in Japan will make financial investments in Japan less attractive and cause the supply curve for dollars to shift to the left. If traders become convinced that the future value of the yen will be lower relative to the dollar, the supply curve will also shift to the left.

Adjustment to a New Equilibrium The factors that affect the demand and supply for currencies are constantly changing. Whether the exchange rate increases or decreases depends on the direction and size of the shifts in the demand curve and supply curve. For example, as Figure 29.3 shows, if the demand curve for dollars in

MyEconLab Animation

Figure 29.3

Shifts in the Demand and Supply Curve Resulting in a Higher Exchange Rate

Holding other factors constant, an increase in the supply of dollars will decrease the equilibrium exchange rate. An increase in the demand for dollars will increase the equilibrium exchange rate. In the case shown in this figure, both the demand curve and the supply curve have shifted to the right. Because the demand curve has shifted to the right by more than the supply curve, the equilibrium exchange rate has increased from ¥120 to \$1 at point *A* to ¥130 to \$1 at point *B*.

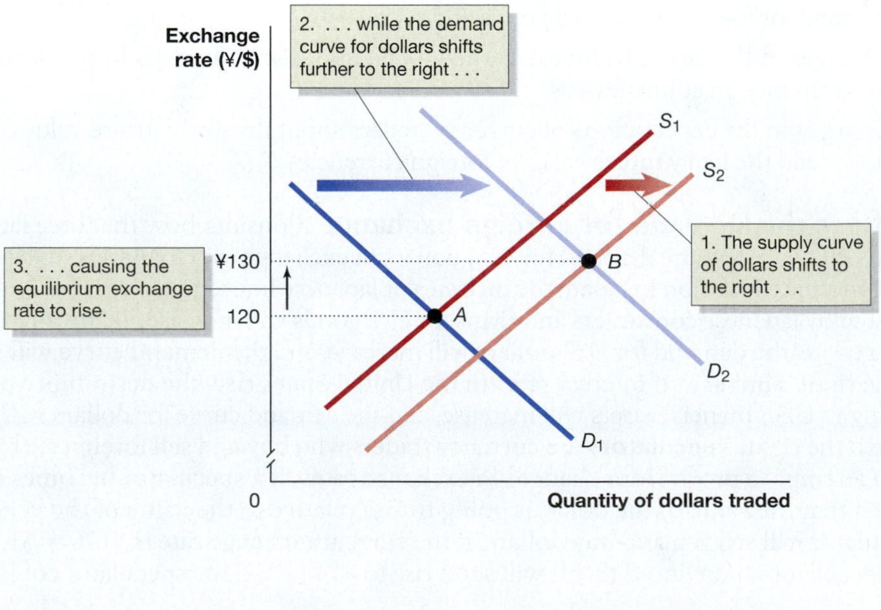

exchange for Japanese yen shifts to the right by more than the supply curve shifts, the equilibrium exchange rate will increase. MyEconLab Concept Check

Some Exchange Rates Are Not Determined by the Market

To this point, we have assumed that exchange rates are determined by the market. This assumption is a good one for many currencies, including the U.S. dollar, the euro, the Japanese yen, and the British pound. Some currencies, however, have *fixed exchange rates* that do not change over long periods. For example, for more than 10 years, the value of the Chinese yuan was fixed against the U.S. dollar at a rate of 8.28 yuan to the dollar. As we will discuss in more detail in Chapter 30, a country's central bank has to intervene in the foreign exchange market to buy and sell its currency if it wishes to keep the exchange rate fixed. MyEconLab Concept Check

How Movements in the Exchange Rate Affect Exports and Imports

When the market value of the dollar increases, the foreign currency price of U.S. exports rises, and the dollar price of foreign imports falls. Suppose that initially the market exchange rate between the U.S. dollar and the euro is \$1 = €1. In that case, a Blu-ray disc that has a price of \$20 in the United States will have a price of €20 in France. A bottle of French wine that has a price of €50 in France will have a price of \$50 in the United States. Now suppose the market exchange rate between the U.S. dollar and the euro changes to \$1.20 = €1. Because it now takes more dollars to buy a euro, the dollar has *depreciated* against the euro, and the euro has *appreciated* against the dollar. The depreciation of the dollar has decreased the euro price of the Blu-ray disc from €20 to \$20/(1.20 dollars/euro) = €16.67. The dollar price of the French wine has risen from \$50 to €50 × 1.20 dollars/euro = \$60. As a result, we would expect more Blu-ray discs to be sold in France and less French wine to be sold in the United States.

To generalize, we can conclude:

1. A depreciation in the domestic currency will increase exports and decrease imports, thereby increasing net exports. If real GDP is currently below potential GDP, then, holding all other factors constant, a depreciation in the domestic currency should increase net exports, aggregate demand, and real GDP.
2. An appreciation in the domestic currency should have the opposite effect: Exports should fall, and imports should rise, which will reduce net exports, aggregate demand, and real GDP. MyEconLab Concept Check

Making the Connection MyEconLab Video

Is a Strong Currency Good for a Country?

News stories often refer to a country as having a "strong" currency when the currency's value has been rising relative to other countries' currencies. Should a country want a strong currency? "Strong" certainly seems better than "weak," so most people would answer "yes" to that question. During late 2014 and 2015, as investors anticipated that the Federal Reserve would take action to increase U.S. interest rates, the value of the dollar increased, as shown in the graph on the next page. The graph shows the *trade-weighted exchange rate* for the U.S. dollar, which is an index number similar to the consumer price index (CPI). Just as the CPI weights individual prices by the share the product takes up in a household's budget, the trade-weighted exchange rate for the U.S. dollar weights each individual exchange rate by the share of that country's trade with the United States.

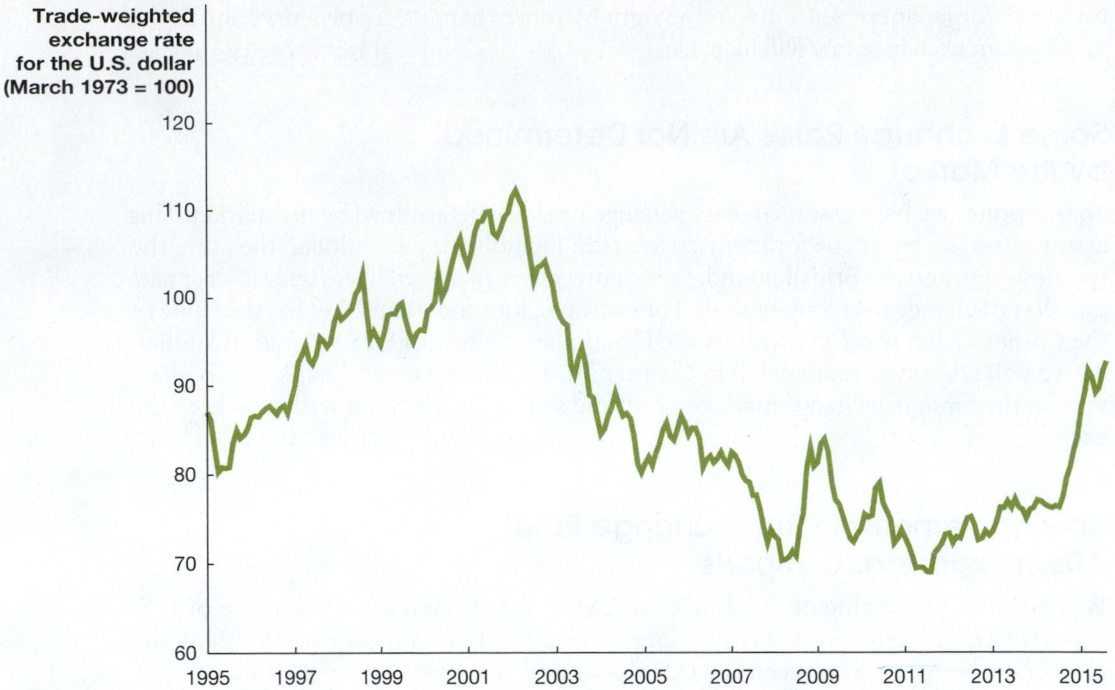

In June 2015, President Barack Obama attended a meeting of the Group of 7, an organization of high-income countries. He was initially quoted as saying at that meeting that a strong dollar was a problem for the United States. There was a public outcry, and the president later denied he had made the statement. But clearly, not everyone in a country benefits from a strong currency. Firms that are exporters generally don't benefit. As one headline in the *Wall Street Journal* put it, "Strong Dollar Squeezes U.S. Firms." The CEO of Caterpillar, the U.S.-based heavy equipment manufacturer, was quoted as saying, "The rising dollar will not be good for U.S. manufacturing and the U.S. economy." A strong dollar increases the foreign currency price of U.S. exports, so to buy U.S.-produced goods, European consumers have to pay more euros, Canadian consumers have to pay more Canadian dollars, and Japanese consumers have to pay more yen. The result is a decline in profits for U.S. exporters. As we saw in the chapter opener, IBM experienced a lower profit in 2014 due to the strong dollar. U.S. firms facing competition from foreign imports can also be hurt by a strong dollar as the dollar prices of foreign imports are reduced.

Although a strong dollar can be bad news for U.S. exporters like Caterpillar and IBM, it can actually be *good* news for U.S. consumers. Between the beginning of 2014 and the middle of 2015, the average price of goods imported into the United States dropped by over 9 percent. U.S. consumers benefited from lower prices of imported goods from cars to clothing to electronics.

If many U.S. firms were hurt by the strong value of the dollar in 2014 and 2015, while U.S. consumers were helped, the reverse was true in Japan, where the value of the yen was falling. The Bank of Japan was pursuing an expansionary monetary policy that had driven Japanese interest rates to low levels. Investors reacted by selling yen and buying U.S. dollars and other currencies, driving down the value of the yen. The value of the yen declined by more than 30 percent in exchange for the U.S. dollar. Five Japanese automobile companies were able to report record profits as the prices of the cars they were exporting fell in terms of dollars and other foreign currencies. But because Japan relies heavily on imports of food, oil, and other important goods, consumers suffered as yen prices of foreign imports soared. As one Japanese politician put it, the Japanese government, by allowing the value of the yen to decline, had shown "little concern for . . . ordinary households."

We can conclude that neither a "strong" currency nor a "weak" currency is all good or all bad for a country's businesses and households. Swings in exchange rates create both winners and losers.

Sources: James Ramage, "Dollar Retreats as Investors Cash in on Jobs-Report Gains," *Wall Street Journal*, June 8, 2015; Paul Ziobro, Josh Mitchell, and Theo Francis, "Strong Dollar Squeezes U.S. Firms," *Wall Street Journal*, January 27, 2015; Mitsuru Obe, "Falling Yen Stirs Debate in Japan," *Wall Street Journal*, December 7, 2014; and data from the Federal Reserve Bank of St. Louis and the U.S. Bureau of Economic Analysis.

Your Turn: Test your understanding by doing related problem 2.6 on page 1040 at the end of this chapter.

MyEconLab Study Plan

Don't Let This Happen to You

Don't Confuse What Happens When a Currency Appreciates with What Happens When It Depreciates

One of the most confusing aspects of exchange rates is that they can be expressed in two ways. We can express the exchange rate between the dollar and the yen either as how many yen can be purchased with $1 or as how many dollars can be purchased with ¥1. That is, we can express the exchange rate as ¥100 = $1 or as $0.01 = ¥1.

When a currency appreciates, it increases in value relative to another currency. When it depreciates, it decreases in value relative to another currency. If the exchange rate changes from ¥100 = $1 to ¥120 = $1, the dollar has appreciated and the yen has depreciated because it now takes more yen to buy $1. If the exchange rate changes from $0.010 = ¥1 to $0.015 = ¥1, however, the dollar has depreciated and the yen has appreciated because it now takes more dollars to buy ¥1. This situation can appear somewhat confusing because the exchange rate seems to have "increased" in both cases. To determine which currency has appreciated and which has depreciated, it is important to remember that an appreciation of the domestic currency means that it now takes *more* units of the foreign currency to buy one unit of the domestic currency. A depreciation of the domestic currency means it takes *fewer* units of the foreign currency to buy one unit of the domestic currency. This observation holds no matter which way we express the exchange rate.

MyEconLab Study Plan

Your Turn: Test your understanding by doing related problem 2.7 on page 1040 at the end of the chapter.

Solved Problem 29.2

MyEconLab Interactive Animation

Subaru Benefits from a Weak Yen

Today, most Japanese automobile companies have manufacturing plants in the United States. Honda, for example, exports from Japan only 21 percent of the cars it sells in the United States. Fuji Heavy Industries, whose main car brand is Subaru, is an exception in still producing most of its cars in Japan. An article in the *Wall Street Journal* observed that for Fuji Heavy Industries, "the plunging yen has turned a problem—a shortage of production in the U.S.—into an unexpected boon."

a. What does the article mean by a "plunging yen"?

b. Why would a plunging yen be a boon for Fuji Heavy Industries?

c. Briefly explain whether a plunging yen would help or hurt Honda.

Solving the Problem

Step 1: Review the chapter material. This problem is about changes in the value of a currency, so you may want to review the section "How Movements in the Exchange Rate Affect Exports and Imports" on page 1027.

Step 2: Answer part (a) by explaining what the article means by a "plunging yen." In this case, a plunging yen means a yen that is worth less in exchange for the U.S. dollar. With a plunging yen, a larger number of yen would be needed to exchange for one U.S. dollar.

Step 3: Answer part (b) by explaining how a plunging yen will affect Fuji Heavy Industries. When Fuji Heavy Industries manufactures cars in Japan, it pays its production costs—including the salaries of its assembly-line workers and payments to its suppliers—with yen. With a falling value of the yen, the dollar price of cars Fuji sells in the United States decreases. As a result,

Fuji will gain sales from other companies, particularly those that produce their cars in the United States. If Fuji produced its cars in the United States, it would *not* have gained this advantage.

Step 4: Answer part (c) by explaining whether a plunging yen will help or hurt Honda. Because most of the cars Honda sells in the United States are also produced here, most of the company's production costs and also most of the revenue it earns are in dollars. So, Honda will not be directly affected by fluctuations in the yen–dollar exchange rate. Honda will, though, likely lose some sales to Fuji as the dollar prices of Subarus declines.

Extra Credit: Managers at Honda, Toyota, and Nissan are aware that when the value of the yen declines against the dollar, they would be better off producing in Japan the cars they planned to sell in the United States. But, unlike the managers of Fuji, the managers of these firms decided that moving production to the United States would allow them to plan better and to stabilize their profits because their sales would no longer be affected as much by fluctuations in the exchange rate.

Source: Yoko Kubota, "Subaru Rides a Weaker Yen into the U.S.," *Wall Street Journal*, November 15, 2014.

MyEconLab Study Plan

Your Turn: For more practice, do related problem 2.10 on page 1040 at the end of this chapter.

The Real Exchange Rate

Real exchange rate The price of domestic goods in terms of foreign goods.

We have seen that an important factor in determining the level of a country's exports to and imports from another country is the relative prices of each country's goods. The relative prices of two countries' goods are determined by two factors: the relative price levels in the two countries and the nominal exchange rate between the two countries' currencies. Economists combine these two factors in the **real exchange rate**, which is the price of domestic goods in terms of foreign goods. Recall that the price level is a measure of the average prices of goods and services in an economy. We can calculate the real exchange rate between two currencies as:

$$\text{Real exchange rate} = \text{Norminal exchange rate} \times \left(\frac{\text{Domestic price level}}{\text{Foreign price level}}\right).$$

Notice that both changes in the nominal exchange rate and changes in the relative price levels cause movements in the real exchange rate. Suppose that the exchange rate between the U.S. dollar and the British pound is $\$1 = £1$, the price level in the United States is 100, and the price level in the United Kingdom is also 100. Then the real exchange rate between the dollar and the pound is:

$$\text{Real exchange rate} = 1\text{ pound/dollar} \times \left(\frac{100}{100}\right) = 1.00.$$

Now suppose that the nominal exchange rate increases to 1.1 pounds per dollar, while the price level in the United States rises to 105 and the price level in the United Kingdom remains 100. In this case, the real exchange rate will be:

$$\text{Real exchange rate} = 1.1\text{ pound/dollar} \times \left(\frac{105}{100}\right) = 1.15.$$

The increase in the real exchange rate from 1.00 to 1.15 tells us that the prices of U.S. goods and services are now 15 percent higher relative to British goods and services.

Real exchange rates are reported as index numbers, with one year chosen as the base year. As with the consumer price index, the main value of the real exchange rate is in tracking changes over time—in this case, changes in the relative prices of domestic goods in terms of foreign goods.

MyEconLab Study Plan

MyEconLab Concept Check

29.3 The International Sector and National Saving and Investment

LEARNING OBJECTIVE: Define and apply the saving and investment equation.

Having studied what determines the exchange rate, we are now ready to explore further the linkages between the U.S. economy and foreign economies. Until 1970, U.S. imports and exports were usually 4 percent to 5 percent of GDP (see Figure 9.1 in Chapter 9). Imports and exports are now three times as large a fraction of U.S. GDP. Imports have also consistently been larger than exports, meaning that net exports have been negative.

Net Exports Equal Net Foreign Investment

If your spending is greater than your income, what can you do? You can sell some assets—maybe those 20 shares of stock in IBM your grandparents gave you—or you can borrow money. A firm can be in the same situation: If a firm's costs are greater than its revenues, it has to make up the difference by selling assets or by borrowing. A country is in the same situation when it imports more than it exports: The country must finance the difference by selling assets—such as land, office buildings, or factories—to foreigners or by borrowing from foreigners.

In other words, for any country, a current account deficit must be exactly offset by a financial account surplus. When a country sells more assets to foreigners than it buys from foreigners, or when it borrows more from foreigners than it lends to foreigners—as it must if it is running a current account deficit—the country experiences a net capital inflow and a financial account surplus. Remember that net exports is roughly equal to the current account balance. Remember also that the financial account balance is roughly equal to net capital flows, which are in turn equal to net foreign investment but with the opposite sign. To review these two points, look again at Table 29.1 on page 1019, which shows that the current account balance is determined mainly by the balance of trade and the balance of services, and the financial account is equal to net capital flows. Also, remember the definition of net foreign investment.

When imports are greater than exports, net exports are negative, and there will be a net capital inflow as people in the United States sell assets and borrow to pay for the surplus of imports over exports. Therefore, net capital flows will be equal to net exports (but with the opposite sign), and net foreign investment will also be equal to net exports (with the same sign). Because net exports are usually negative for the United States, in most years, the United States must be a net borrower from abroad, and U.S. net foreign investment will be negative.

We can summarize this discussion with the following equations:

$$\text{Current account balance} + \text{Financial account balance} = 0$$

or:

$$\text{Current account balance} = -\text{Financial account balance}$$

or:

$$\text{Net exports} = \text{Net foreign investment.}$$

The last equation tells us, once again, that countries such as the United States that import more than they export must borrow more from abroad than they lend abroad: If net exports are negative, net foreign investment will also be negative by the same amount. Countries such as China that export more than they import must lend abroad more than they borrow from abroad: If net exports are positive, net foreign investment will also be positive by the same amount. MyEconLab Concept Check

Domestic Saving, Domestic Investment, and Net Foreign Investment

We can think of the total saving in any economy as equal to saving by the private sector plus saving by the government sector, which we call *public saving* (see Chapter 21, Section 21.2). When the government runs a budget surplus by spending less than it receives in taxes, public saving is positive. When the government runs a budget deficit, public saving is negative. Negative saving is also known as *dissaving*. We can write the following expression for the level of saving in the economy:

$$\text{National saving} = \text{Private saving} + \text{Public saving}$$

or:

$$S = S_{private} + S_{public}.$$

Private saving is equal to what households have left of their income after spending on consumption goods and paying taxes (for simplicity, we assume that transfer payments are zero):

$$\text{Private saving} = \text{National income} - \text{Consumption} - \text{Taxes}$$

or:

$$S_{private} = Y - C - T.$$

Public saving is equal to the difference between government spending and taxes:

$$\text{Government saving} = \text{Taxes} - \text{Government spending}$$

or:

$$S_{public} = T - G.$$

Finally, remember the basic macroeconomic equation for GDP or national income:

$$Y = C + I + G + NX.$$

We can use this last equation, our definitions of private and public saving, and the fact that net exports equal net foreign investment to arrive at an important relationship, called the **saving and investment equation**:

Saving and investment equation An equation that shows that national saving is equal to domestic investment plus net foreign investment.

$$\text{National saving} = \text{Domestic investment} + \text{Net foreign investment}$$

or:

$$S = I + NFI.$$

This equation is an *identity* because it must always be true, given the definitions we have used.

The saving and investment equation tells us that a country's saving will be invested either domestically or overseas. If you save $1,000 and use the funds to buy a bond issued by IBM, IBM may use the $1,000 to partially pay for a cloud computing facility in the United States (*I*) or for a software consulting office in China (*NFI*).

Solved Problem 29.3

MyEconLab Interactive Animation

Arriving at the Saving and Investment Equation

Use the definitions of private and public saving, the equation for GDP or national income, and the fact that net exports (*NX*) must equal net foreign investment (*NFI*) to arrive at the saving and investment equation.

Solving the Problem

Step 1: Review the chapter material. This problem is about the saving and investment equation, so you may want to review the section "Domestic Saving, Domestic Investment, and Net Foreign Investment," which begins on page 1031.

Step 2: Derive an expression for national saving (*S*) in terms of national income (*Y*), consumption (*C*), and government purchases (*G*). We can bring together the four equations we need:

1. $S_{private} = Y - C - T$
2. $S_{public} = T - G$

3. $Y = C + I + G + NX$
4. $NX = NFI$

Because national saving (S) appears in the saving and investment equation, we need to find an equation for it in terms of the other variables. Adding equation (1) plus equation (2) yields national saving:

$$S = S_{\text{private}} + S_{\text{public}} = (Y - C - T) + (T - G) = Y - C - G.$$

Step 3: Use the result from step 2 to derive an expression for national saving in terms of investment (I) and net exports (NX). Because GDP (Y) does not appear in the saving and investment equation, we need to substitute the expression for it given in equation (3):

$$S = (C + I + G + NX) - C - G$$

and simplify:

$$S = I + NX.$$

Step 4: Use the results of steps 2 and 3 to derive the saving and investment equation. Finally, substitute net foreign investment for net exports:

$$S = I + NFI.$$

Your Turn: For more practice, do related problem 3.8 on page 1041 at the end of this chapter.

MyEconLab Study Plan

A country such as the United States that has negative net foreign investment must be saving less than it is investing domestically. To understand why, rewrite the saving and investment equation by moving domestic investment to the left side:

$$S - I = NFI.$$

If net foreign investment is negative—as it is for the United States nearly every year—domestic investment (I) must be greater than national saving (S).

In most years, the level of saving in Japan has been well above domestic investment. The result has been high levels of Japanese net foreign investment. For example, Japanese automobile companies Toyota, Honda, and Nissan have all constructed factories in the United States. Sony purchased the Columbia Pictures film studio. Japan has made many similar investments in countries around the world, which has sometimes caused resentment in those countries. There were some protests in the United States in the 1980s, for example, when Japanese investors purchased the Pebble Beach golf course in California and the Rockefeller Center complex in New York City. (Both were eventually purchased by U.S. investors.)

Japan typically needs a high level of net exports to help offset a low level of domestic investment. When exports of a product begin to decline and imports begin to increase, governments are often tempted to impose tariffs or quotas to reduce imports. (See Chapter 9 to review tariffs and quotas and their negative effects on the economy.) In fact, some Japanese firms have been urging the Japanese government to impose trade restrictions on imports from China. MyEconLab Concept Check

MyEconLab Study Plan

29.4 The Effect of a Government Budget Deficit on Investment

LEARNING OBJECTIVE: Explain the effect of a government budget deficit on investment in an open economy.

The link we have just developed among saving, investment, and net foreign investment can help us understand some of the effects of changes in a government's budget deficit. When the government runs a budget deficit, national saving will decline unless private saving increases by the amount of the budget deficit, which is unlikely. As the saving and investment equation ($S = I + NFI$) shows, the result of a decline in national saving must be a decline in either domestic investment or net foreign investment. The algebra is clear, but why, economically, does an increase in the government budget deficit cause a fall in domestic investment or net foreign investment?

To understand the answer to this question, remember that if the federal government runs a budget deficit, the U.S. Treasury must raise an amount equal to the deficit by selling bonds. To attract investors, the Treasury may have to raise the interest rates on its bonds. As interest rates on Treasury bonds rise, other interest rates, including those on corporate bonds and bank loans, will also rise. Higher interest rates will discourage some firms from borrowing funds to build new factories or to buy new equipment or computers. Higher interest rates on financial assets in the United States will attract foreign investors. Investors in Canada, Japan, or China will have to buy U.S. dollars to be able to purchase bonds in the United States. This greater demand for dollars will increase their value relative to foreign currencies. As the value of the dollar rises, exports from the United States will fall, and imports to the United States will rise. Net exports and, therefore, net foreign investment will fall.

When a government budget deficit leads to a decline in net exports, the result is sometimes called the *twin deficits*, which refers to the possibility that a government budget deficit will also lead to a current account deficit. The twin deficits idea first became widely discussed in the United States during the early 1980s, when the federal government ran a large budget deficit that resulted in high interest rates, a high exchange value of the dollar, and a large current account deficit.

Figure 29.4 shows that in the early 1980s, the United States had large federal budget deficits and large current account deficits. The figure also shows, however, that the twin deficits idea does not consistently match the experience of the United States after 1990. The large federal budget deficits of the early 1990s occurred at a time of relatively small current account deficits, and the budget surpluses of the late 1990s occurred at a time of then-record current account deficits. Both the current account deficit and the federal budget deficit increased in the early 2000s, but the federal budget deficit declined in the mid-2000s much more than did the current account deficit. Beginning in 2008, the federal budget deficit soared and then sharply declined, while the current account deficit declined.

The experience of other countries also shows only mixed support for the twin deficits idea. Germany ran large budget deficits and large current account deficits during the early 1990s, but both Canada and Italy ran large budget deficits during the 1980s

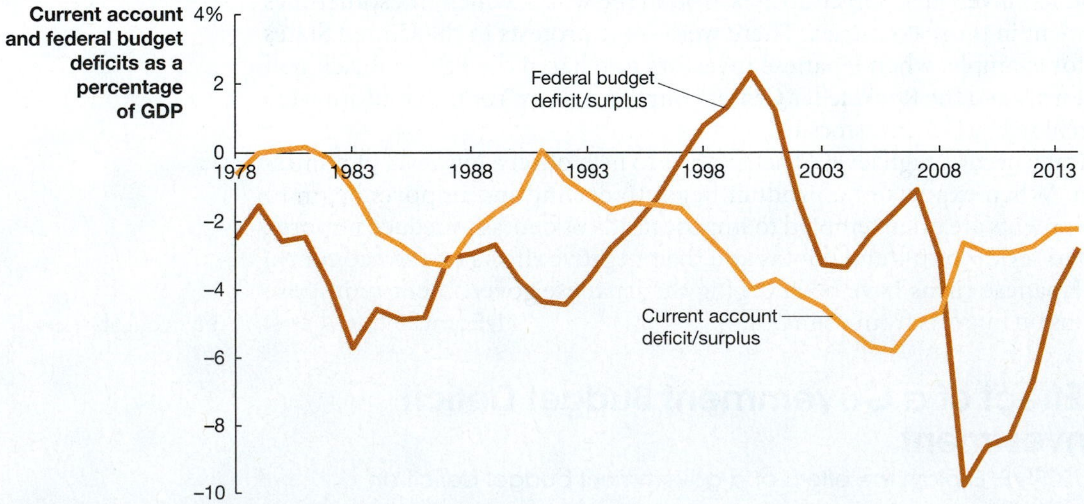

MyEconLab Real-time data

Figure 29.4 The Twin Deficits, 1978–2014

During the early 1980s, large federal budget deficits occurred at the same time as large current account deficits, but twin deficits did not occur in most other periods during these years.

Source: U.S. Bureau of Economic Analysis.

without running current account deficits. The saving and investment equation shows that an increase in the government budget deficit will not lead to an increase in the current account deficit, provided that either private saving increases or domestic investment declines. According to the twin deficits idea, when the federal government ran budget surpluses in the late 1990s, the current account should also have been in surplus, or at least the current account deficit should have been small. In fact, the increase in national saving due to the budget surpluses was more than offset by a sharp decline in private saving, and the United States ran very large current account deficits. MyEconLab Concept Check

Making the Connection

MyEconLab Video

Why Is the United States Called the "World's Largest Debtor"?

The following graph shows the current account balance as a percentage of GDP for the United States for the period 1960–2014. The United States has had a current account deficit every year since 1982, with the exception of 1991. Between 1960 and 1975, the United States ran a current account deficit in only five years. Many economists believe that the current account deficits of the 1980s were closely related to the federal budget deficits of those years. High interest rates attracted foreign investors to U.S. bonds, which raised the exchange rate between the dollar and foreign currencies. The high exchange rate reduced U.S. exports and increased imports, leading to current account deficits.

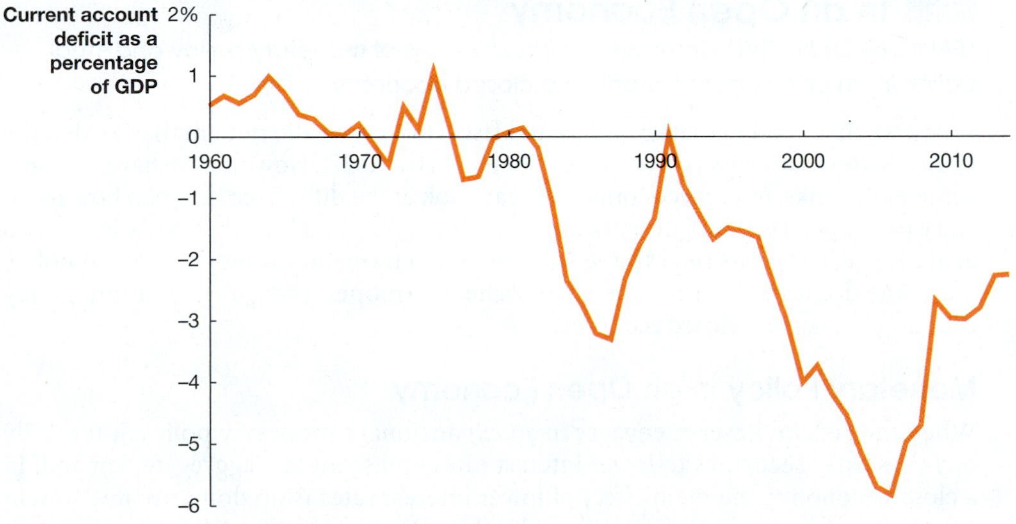

MyEconLab Real-time data

Source: Federal Reserve Bank of St Louis.

As the federal budget deficit narrowed in the mid-1990s and disappeared in the late 1990s, the foreign exchange value of the dollar remained high—and large current account deficits continued—because foreign investors persisted in investing in the United States, despite low interest rates. In the late 1990s, a number of countries around the world, such as South Korea, Indonesia, Brazil, and Russia, suffered severe economic problems. In a process known as a *flight to quality*, many investors sold their investments in those countries and bought investments in the United States. In addition, the strong performance of the U.S. stock market through the spring of 2000 attracted many investors. Finally, the sharp decline in private saving in the United States that began during the late 1990s also contributed to the U.S. current account deficit. The fall in the value of the dollar after 2008 helped reduce the size of the current account deficit. In late 2014 and 2015, though, the deficit was increasing along with the value of the dollar.

Are persistent current account deficits a problem for the United States? Current account deficits result in U.S. net foreign investment being negative. Each year, foreign investors accumulate many more U.S. assets—such as stocks, bonds, and factories—than U.S. investors accumulate foreign assets. In 1986, for the first time since the nineteenth century, the value of foreign-owned assets in the United States became larger than the value of U.S.-owned assets abroad. At the end of 2014, foreign investors owned about $7 trillion more of U.S. assets than U.S. investors owned of foreign assets, which is why the United States is sometimes called "the world's largest debtor." But the continued willingness of foreign investors to buy U.S. stocks and bonds and of foreign companies to build factories in the United States can be seen as a vote of confidence in the strength of the U.S. economy and the buying power of U.S. consumers. When private saving rates declined in the United States to historically low levels in the mid-2000s, only the continued flow of funds from foreign investors made it possible for the United States to maintain the high levels of domestic investment required for economic growth. Beginning in 2009, private saving rates increased, but public saving turned sharply negative between 2009 and 2012 as the federal budget deficit soared. Even though public saving has been less negative in the past few years, domestic investment in the United States remains reliant on funds from foreign investors.

Source: Elena L. Nguyen, "The U.S. Net International Investment Position at the End of the First Quarter of 2015, Year 2014, and Annual Revisions," *Survey of Current Business*, July 2015, pp. 1–10.

MyEconLab Study Plan

Your Turn: Test your understanding by doing related problem 4.7 on page 1042 at the end of this chapter.

29.5 Monetary Policy and Fiscal Policy in an Open Economy

LEARNING OBJECTIVE: Compare the effectiveness of monetary policy and fiscal policy in an open economy and in a closed economy.

When we discussed monetary policy and fiscal policy, we did not emphasize that the United States is an open economy (see Chapters 26 and 27). Now that we have explored some of the links among economies, we can look at the difference between how monetary policy and fiscal policy work in an open economy and how they work in a closed economy. Economists refer to the ways in which monetary policy and fiscal policy affect the domestic economy as *policy channels*. An open economy has more policy channels than does a closed economy.

Monetary Policy in an Open Economy

When the Federal Reserve engages in an expansionary monetary policy, it typically buys Treasury securities to lower interest rates and stimulate aggregate demand. In a closed economy, the main effect of lower interest rates is on domestic investment spending and purchases of consumer durables. In an open economy, lower interest rates will also affect the exchange rate between the dollar and foreign currencies. Lower interest rates will cause some investors in the United States and abroad to switch from investing in U.S. financial assets to investing in foreign financial assets. The result is a lower demand for the dollar relative to foreign currencies and a decline in the dollar's value. A lower exchange rate will decrease the prices of U.S. products in foreign markets and increase the prices of foreign products in the United States. As a result, net exports will increase. This additional policy channel will increase the ability of an expansionary monetary policy to affect aggregate demand.

When the Fed wants to reduce aggregate demand to reduce inflation, it engages in a contractionary monetary policy. The Fed sells Treasury securities to increase interest rates and reduce aggregate demand. In a closed economy, the main effect is once again on domestic investment spending and purchases of consumer durables. In an open economy, higher interest rates will lead to a higher foreign exchange value of the dollar. The prices of U.S. products in foreign markets will increase, and the prices of foreign products in the United States will fall. As a result, net exports will fall. The contractionary policy will have a larger effect on aggregate demand, and therefore it will be more effective in slowing the growth in economic activity. To summarize: *Monetary policy has a greater effect on aggregate demand in an open economy than in a closed economy.* MyEconLab Concept Check

Fiscal Policy in an Open Economy

To engage in an expansionary fiscal policy, the federal government increases its purchases or cuts taxes. Increases in government purchases directly increase aggregate demand. Tax cuts increase aggregate demand by increasing household disposable income and business income, which results in increased consumption spending and investment spending. An expansionary fiscal policy may result in higher interest rates. In a closed economy, the main effect of higher interest rates is to reduce domestic investment spending and purchases of consumer durables. In an open economy, higher interest rates will also lead to an increase in the foreign exchange value of the dollar and a decrease in net exports. Therefore, in an open economy, an expansionary fiscal policy may be less effective because the *crowding out effect* may be larger. In a closed economy, only consumption and investment are crowded out by an expansionary fiscal policy. In an open economy, net exports may also be crowded out.

The government can fight inflation by using a contractionary fiscal policy to slow the growth of aggregate demand. A contractionary fiscal policy cuts government purchases or raises taxes to reduce household disposable income and consumption spending. It also reduces the federal budget deficit (or increases the budget surplus), which may lower interest rates. Lower interest rates will increase domestic investment and purchases of consumer durables, thereby offsetting some of the reduction in government spending and increases in taxes. In an open economy, lower interest rates will also reduce the foreign exchange value of the dollar and increase net exports. Therefore, in an open economy, a contractionary fiscal policy will have a smaller effect on aggregate demand and therefore will be less effective in slowing an economy. In summary: *Fiscal policy has a smaller effect on aggregate demand in an open economy than in a closed economy.* MyEconLab Concept Check

MyEconLab Study Plan

Continued from page 1017

Economics in Your Life

The South Korean Central Bank and Your Car Loan

At the beginning of this chapter, we posed this question: Will the Bank of Korea's decision to sell its U.S. Treasury bonds affect the interest rate you pay on your car loan? To sell its holdings of Treasury bonds, South Korea's central bank may have to offer them at a lower price. When the prices of bonds fall, the interest rates on them rise. As the interest rates on U.S. Treasury bonds increase, the interest rates on corporate bonds and bank loans, including car loans, may also increase. So, the decision of the Bank of Korea has the potential to increase the interest rate you pay on your car loan. In practice, the interest rate on your car loan is likely to be affected only if the Bank of Korea sells a very large number of bonds and if investors consider it likely that other foreign central banks may soon do the same thing. The basic point is important, however: Economies are interdependent, and interest rates in the United States are not determined entirely by the actions of people in the United States.

Conclusion

At one time, U.S. policymakers—and economics textbooks—ignored the linkages between the United States and other economies. In the modern world, these linkages have become increasingly important, and economists and policymakers must take them into account when analyzing the economy. In Chapter 30, we will discuss further how the international financial system operates.

Visit MyEconLab for a news article and analysis related to the concepts in this chapter.

CHAPTER SUMMARY AND PROBLEMS

Key Terms

Balance of payments, p. 1018
Balance of trade, p. 1018
Capital account, p. 1020
Closed economy, p. 1018
Currency appreciation, p. 1025
Currency depreciation, p. 1025
Current account, p. 1018
Financial account, p. 1019
Net foreign investment, p. 1020
Nominal exchange rate, p. 1023
Open economy, p. 1018
Real exchange rate, p. 1030
Saving and investment equation, p. 1032
Speculators, p. 1025

29.1 The Balance of Payments: Linking the United States to the International Economy, pages 1018–1022

LEARNING OBJECTIVE: Explain how the balance of payments is calculated.

Summary

Nearly all economies are **open economies** that trade with and invest in other economies. A **closed economy** has no transactions in trade or finance with other economies. The **balance of payments** is the record of a country's trade with other countries in goods, services, and assets. The **current account** records a country's net exports, net investment income, and net transfers. The **financial account** shows investments a country has made abroad and foreign investments received by the country. The **balance of trade** is the difference between the value of the goods a country exports and the value of the goods a country imports. **Net foreign investment** is the difference between capital outflows from a country and capital inflows. The **capital account** is a part of the balance of payments that records relatively minor transactions. Apart from measurement errors, the sum of the current account and the financial account must equal zero. Therefore, the balance of payments must also equal zero.

MyEconLab Visit **www.myeconlab.com** to complete these exercises online and get instant feedback.

Review Questions

1.1 What is the relationship among the current account, the financial account, and the balance of payments?

1.2 What is the difference between net exports and the current account balance?

1.3 The late economist Herbert Stein described the accounts that comprise a country's balance of payments:

> A country is more likely to have a deficit in its current account the higher its price level, the higher its gross [domestic] product, the higher its interest rates, the lower its barriers to imports, and the more attractive its investment opportunities—all compared with conditions in other countries—and the higher its exchange rate. The effects of a change in one of these factors on the current account balance cannot be predicted without considering the effect on the other causal factors.

a. Briefly describe the transactions included in a country's current account.

b. Briefly explain why, compared to other countries, a country is more likely to have a deficit in its current account, holding other factors constant, if it has each of the following:

i. A higher price level
ii. An increase in interest rates
iii. Lower barriers to imports
iv. More attractive investment opportunities

Source: Herbert Stein, "Balance of Payments," *Library of Economics and Liberty*, http://www.econlib.org.

Problems and Applications

1.4 In 2014, France had a current account deficit of €19.5 billion (approximately $25.9 billion). Did France experience a net capital outflow or a net capital inflow during 2014? Briefly explain.

Source: Banque de France, "France's Balance of Payments," https://www.banque-france.fr/en/economics-statistics/stats-infos/frances-balance-of-payments.html.

1.5 Use the information in the following table to solve for the value of the statistical discrepancy and prepare a balance of payments account, like the one shown in Table 29.1 on page 1019. Assume that the balance on the capital account is zero.

Increase in foreign holdings of assets in the United States	$1,181
Exports of goods	856
Imports of services	−256
Statistical discrepancy	?
Net transfers	−60
Exports of services	325
Income received on investments	392
Imports of goods	−1,108
Increase in U.S. holdings of assets in foreign countries	−1,040
Income payments on investments	−315

1.6 **(Related to the Don't Let This Happen to You on page 1021)** In 2014, Germany had a balance of trade surplus of €217 billion and a current account surplus of €215 billion.

Explain how Germany's current account surplus could be smaller than its trade surplus. In 2014, what would we expect Germany's balance on the financial account to have been? Briefly explain.

Source: Statistisches Bundesamt.

1.7 **(Related to Solved Problem 29.1 on page 1022)** A news article notes, "China recorded a current-account surplus of $76.6 billion in the second quarter but that was offset by a deficit of the same amount on its capital and financial account." Is this outcome surprising? Briefly explain.

Source: Grace Zhu, "China's Current-Account Surplus at $76.6 bln: SAFE," marketwatch.com, August 7, 2015.

1.8 **(Related to Solved Problem 29.1 on page 1022)** An article in the *Wall Street Journal* about China's balance of payments contained the following observations: "A country's balance of payments still has to add up to zero. If foreign investors wish to acquire assets denominated in yuan, the necessary implication is that China will have to run a trade deficit."

a. Do you agree that the balance of payments must add up to zero?

b. If China were to have a deficit in its balance of trade of −100 billion yuan, must it have a surplus in its financial account of +100 billion yuan? Briefly explain.

Source: Andrew Colquhoun, "The Yuan Isn't Ready to Be a Global Reserve Currency," *Wall Street Journal*, August 12, 2015.

1.9 **(Related to Solved Problem 29.1 on page 1022)** An article in the *New York Times* has the headline "U.S. Trade Deficit Widened Over Summer." The first sentence in the article is, "The current-account trade deficit widened slightly in the July–September quarter." The statement that the "trade deficit for goods and services" declined during this period appears later in the article. Is this article's headline consistent with the two statements in the article? Briefly explain.

Source: Associated Press, "U.S. Trade Deficit Widened Over Summer," *New York Times*, December 17, 2014.

1.10 An article in the *Wall Street Journal* refers to "debt-strapped emerging markets already struggling with current-account deficits." Why might we expect that countries running current account deficits might also have substantial foreign debts?

Source: Anjani Trivedi, "Emerging Markets Suffer Largest Outflow in Seven Years," *Wall Street Journal*, June 12, 2015.

29.2 The Foreign Exchange Market and Exchange Rates, pages 1023–1030

LEARNING OBJECTIVE: Explain how exchange rates are determined and how changes in exchange rates affect the prices of imports and exports.

Summary

The **nominal exchange rate** is the value of one country's currency in terms of another country's currency. The exchange rate is determined in the foreign exchange market by the demand and supply of a country's currency. Changes in the exchange rate are caused by shifts in demand or supply. The three main sets of factors that cause the demand and supply curves in the foreign exchange market to shift are: (1) changes in the demand for U.S.-produced goods and services and changes in the demand for foreign-produced goods and services; (2) changes in the desire to invest in the United States and changes in the desire to invest in foreign countries; and (3) changes in the expectations of currency traders—particularly **speculators**—concerning the likely future value of the dollar and the likely future values of foreign currencies. **Currency appreciation** occurs when a currency's market value increases relative to another currency. **Currency depreciation** occurs when a currency's market value decreases relative to another currency. The **real exchange rate** is the price of domestic goods in terms of foreign goods. The real exchange rate is calculated by multiplying the nominal exchange rate by the ratio of the domestic price level to the foreign price level.

MyEconLab Visit **www.myeconlab.com** to complete these exercises online and get instant feedback.

Review Questions

2.1 If the exchange rate between the Japanese yen and the U.S. dollar expressed in terms of yen per dollar is ¥125 = $1, what is the exchange rate when expressed in terms of dollars per yen?

2.2 Suppose that the current exchange rate between the dollar and the euro is €0.80 = $1. If the exchange rate changes to €0.85 = $1, has the euro appreciated or depreciated against the dollar? Briefly explain.

2.3 Why do foreign households and foreign firms demand U.S. dollars in exchange for foreign currency? Why do U.S. households and firms supply U.S. dollars in exchange for foreign currency?

2.4 What are the three main sets of factors that cause the supply and demand curves in the foreign exchange market to shift?

Problems and Applications

2.5 **(Related to the Making the Connection on page 1023)** On January 1, 2002, there were 15 member countries in the European Union. Twelve of those countries eliminated their own individual currencies and began using a new common currency, the euro. For a three-year period from January 1, 1999, through December 31, 2001, these 12 countries priced goods and services in terms of both their own currencies and the euro. During that period, the values of their currencies were fixed against each other and against the euro. So during that time, the dollar had an exchange rate against each of these currencies and against the euro. The following table shows the fixed exchange rates of four European currencies against the euro and their exchange rates against the U.S. dollar on March 2, 2001. Use the information in the table on the next page to calculate the exchange rate between the dollar and the euro (in euros per dollar) on March 2, 2001.

Currency	Units per Euro (fixed)	Units per U.S. Dollar (as of March 2, 2001)
German mark	1.9558	2.0938
French franc	6.5596	7.0223
Italian lira	1,936.2700	2,072.8700
Portuguese escudo	200.4820	214.6300

2.6 **(Related to the Making the Connection on page 1027)** Paul De Grauwe, an economist at the London School of Economics, wrote in the *Economist* that the quantitative easing policies of the European Central Bank "will contribute to a further weakening of the euro vis-à-vis other currencies such as the dollar, the pound and the yuan, thereby increasing exports and boosting inflation."

a. What does De Grauwe mean by "a weakening of the euro"?

b. What is quantitative easing, and why should it lead to a weakening of the euro?

c. If you ran a business in France that exports to the United States and Japan, would this development help you? If you were a consumer in France, would this development help you? Briefly explain.

Source: Paul De Grauwe, "The Sad Consequences of the Fear of QE," *Economist*, January 21, 2015.

2.7 **(Related to the Don't Let This Happen to You on page 1029)** If we know the exchange rate between Country A's currency and Country B's currency and we know the exchange rate between Country B's currency and Country C's currency, then we can compute the exchange rate between Country A's currency and Country C's currency.

a. Suppose the exchange rate between the Japanese yen and the U.S. dollar is currently ¥95 = $1 and the exchange rate between the British pound and the U.S. dollar is £0.64 = $1. What is the exchange rate between the yen and the pound?

b. Suppose the exchange rate between the yen and the dollar changes to ¥100 = $1 and the exchange rate between the pound and the dollar changes to £0.55 = $1. Has the dollar appreciated or depreciated against the yen? Has the dollar appreciated or depreciated against the pound? Has the yen appreciated or depreciated against the pound?

2.8 Graph the demand and supply of U.S. dollars for euros and label each axis. Show graphically and explain the effect on the demand and supply of dollars and the resulting change in the exchange rate of euros for U.S. dollars if the European Central Bank takes action to increase interest rates.

Source: Jon Hilsenrath, "Rising Dollar and Falling Oil Could Be Recipe for a U.S. Asset Boom," *Wall Street Journal*, December 11, 2014.

2.9 Use the graph to answer the following questions.

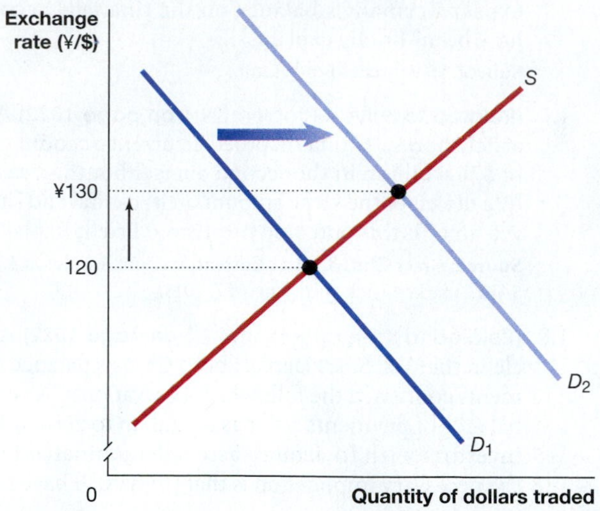

a. Briefly explain whether the dollar appreciated or depreciated against the yen.

b. Which of the following events could have caused the shift in demand shown in the graph?

i. Interest rates in the United States declined.

ii. Income rose in Japan.

iii. Speculators began to believe the value of the dollar would be higher in the future.

2.10 **(Related to Solved Problem 29.2 on page 1029)** An article in the *Wall Street Journal* notes, "For every one yen rise in the value of the dollar, Fuji Heavy's full-year operating profit increases by ¥9.7 billion, the company says." Would Honda's profits be likely to increase as much as a result of a rise in the value of the dollar versus the yen? Briefly explain.

Source: Yoko Kubota, "Subaru Rides a Weaker Yen into the U.S.," *Wall Street Journal*, November 15, 2014.

2.11 According to an article in the *Wall Street Journal*, in 2014, "The Australian dollar tumbled after muted inflation data scotched investors' expectations that the central bank would raise interest rates."

a. Why would the inflation rate being lower than expected make it less likely that the Australian central bank would raise interest rates?

b. Why would the fact that it was less likely that the Australian central bank was going to raise interest rates cause the value of the Australian dollar to fall?

Source: James Ramage, "Australian Dollar Tumbles after Data Scotches Rate-Increase Expectations," *Wall Street Journal*, April 23, 2014.

2.12 **(Related to the Chapter Opener on page 1017)** In preparing their financial statements, U.S. firms with sales in foreign currencies have to engage in "foreign currency translations"; that is, they have to convert foreign currency values into U.S. dollars. In its *2014 Annual Report*, IBM made the following statement: "As with all companies with a similar global business profile, with the dollar strengthening, the company also expects that currency will have a significant translation impact on its profit growth."

a. What does the report mean by "the dollar strengthening"?
b. As a U.S.-based company, doesn't IBM benefit when the U.S. dollar is stronger? Briefly explain.

Source: International Business Machines Corporation, *2014 IBM Annual Report*, February 24, 2015, p. 64.

2.13 In the summer of 2015, the exchange rate of China's currency, the yuan, declined against other currencies. The lower value for the yuan was expected to have a negative effect on firms such as Apple and Yum Brands (owners of KFC and Pizza Hut) that have stores or restaurants in China. But the lower value of the yuan was expected to benefit Foxconn, a firm based in Taiwan that assembles iPhones in China. Briefly explain how the decline in the value of the yuan would have a negative effect on firms, such as Apple and Yum, but would benefit other firms, such as Foxconn, that also operate in China.

Source: Lorraine Luk and Eva Dou, "Devalued Yuan Set to Take Bite Out of Apple, Give Boost to Chinese Rivals," *Wall Street Journal*, August 11, 2015.

29.3 The International Sector and National Saving and Investment, pages 1031–1033

LEARNING OBJECTIVE: Define and apply the saving and investment equation.

Summary

A current account deficit must be exactly offset by a financial account surplus. The financial account is equal to net capital flows, which is equal to net foreign investment but with the opposite sign. Because the current account balance is roughly equal to net exports, we can conclude that net exports will equal net foreign investment. National saving is equal to private saving plus government saving. Private saving is equal to national income minus consumption and minus taxes. Government saving is the difference between taxes and government spending. GDP (or national income) is equal to the sum of investment, consumption, government spending, and net exports. We can use this fact, our definitions of private and government saving, and the fact that net exports equal net foreign investment to arrive at an important relationship known as the **saving and investment equation**: $S = I + NFI$.

MyEconLab Visit www.myeconlab.com to complete these exercises online and get instant feedback.

Review Questions

3.1 Explain the relationship between net exports and net foreign investment.

3.2 What is the saving and investment equation? If national saving declines, what will happen to domestic investment and net foreign investment?

3.3 If a country saves more than it invests domestically, what must be true of its net foreign investment?

Problems and Applications

3.4 Writing in the *New York Times*, Simon Johnson, an economist at MIT, makes the argument that people outside the United States may at some point decide to "save less (in which case they may hold onto their existing United States government debt but not want to buy so much of new issues)." What does saving by people outside the United States have to do with sales of U.S. government debt? Does the level of domestic investment occurring in foreign countries matter for your answer? Briefly explain.

Source: Simon Johnson, "The Real Fiscal Risks in the United States," *New York Times*, December 6, 2012.

3.5 In 2014, domestic investment in Japan was 21.7 percent of GDP, and Japanese national saving was 22.4 percent of GDP. What percentage of GDP was Japanese net foreign investment?

3.6 In 2014, France's net foreign investment was negative. Which was larger in France in 2014: national saving or domestic investment? Briefly explain.

3.7 Briefly explain whether you agree with the following statement: "Because in 2014 national saving was a larger percentage of GDP in the United States than in the United Kingdom, domestic investment must also have been a larger percentage of GDP in the United States than in the United Kingdom."

3.8 **(Related to Solved Problem 29.3 on page 1032)** Look again at Solved Problem 29.3, where the saving and investment equation $S = I + NX$ is derived. In deriving this equation, we assumed that national income was equal to Y. But Y only includes income *earned* by households. In the modern U.S. economy, households receive substantial transfer payments—such as Social Security payments and unemployment insurance payments—from the government. Suppose that we define national income as being equal to $Y + TR$, where TR equals government transfer payments, and we also define government spending as being equal to $G + TR$. Show that after making these adjustments, we end up with the same saving and investment equation.

3.9 Use the saving and investment equation to explain why the United States experienced large current account deficits in the late 1990s.

3.10 Former congressman and presidential candidate Richard Gephardt once proposed that tariffs be imposed on imports from countries with which the United States has a trade deficit. If this proposal were enacted and if it were to succeed in reducing the U.S. current account deficit to zero, what would be the likely effect on domestic investment spending within the United States? Assume that no other federal government economic policy is changed. (*Hint:* Use the saving and investment equation to answer this question.)

29.4 The Effect of a Government Budget Deficit on Investment, pages 1033–1036

LEARNING OBJECTIVE: Explain the effect of a government budget deficit on investment in an open economy.

Summary

When the government runs a budget deficit, national saving will decline unless private saving increases by the full amount of the budget deficit, which is unlikely. As the saving and investment equation ($S = I + NFI$) shows, the result of a decline in national saving must be a decline in either domestic investment or net foreign investment.

MyEconLab Visit **www.myeconlab.com** to complete these exercises online and get instant feedback.

Review Questions

4.1 What happens to national saving when the government runs a budget surplus? What is the twin deficits idea? Did it hold for the United States in the 1990s? Briefly explain.

4.2 Why were the early and mid-1980s particularly difficult times for U.S. exporters?

4.3 Why is the United States sometimes called the "world's largest debtor"?

Problems and Applications

4.4 An investment analyst recommended that investors "gravitate toward the stronger currencies and countries that are running current-account and fiscal surpluses," such as South Korea and Taiwan.

a. Holding all other factors constant, would we expect a country that is running a government budget surplus to have a currency that is increasing in value or decreasing in value? Briefly explain.

b. Holding all other factors constant, would we expect a country that has a currency that is increasing in value to have an increasing or decreasing current account surplus? Briefly explain.

c. Is the combination of economic characteristics this analyst has identified likely to be commonly found among countries? Briefly explain.

Source: Paul J. Lim, "Suddenly, BRIC Markets Are on a Shakier Foundation," *New York Times*, January 9, 2015.

4.5 According to an article in the *Economist*, "countries with persistent current-account deficits tend to have higher real interest rates than surplus countries." What do high interest rates have to do with current account deficits?

Source: "Carry on Trading," *Economist*, August 10, 2013.

4.6 Section 29.4 states: "The budget surpluses of the late 1990s occurred at a time of then-record current account deficits." Holding everything else constant, what would the likely effect have been on domestic investment in the United States during those years if the current account had been balanced instead of being in deficit?

4.7 **(Related to the Making the Connection on page 1035)** Why might "the continued willingness of foreign investors to buy U.S. stocks and bonds and foreign companies to build factories in the United States" result in the United States running a current account deficit?

4.8 An article in GulfNews.com noted that in September 2012, the Indian government of Prime Minister Manmohan Singh made "urgently needed reforms to reduce the fiscal deficit and attract foreign investment to help the current account deficit and growth."

a. Could there be a connection between India's fiscal (budget) deficit and its current account deficit? Briefly explain.

b. How would attracting foreign investment help the current account deficit and (economic) growth?

c. The article further notes that the Reserve Bank of India (the central bank) stated. "Financing the CAD [current account deficit] with increasingly risky and volatile flows increases the economy's vulnerability to sudden shifts in risk appetite and liquidity preference, potentially threatening macroeconomic and exchange rate stability." What does India's central bank mean by "risky and volatile flows" that finance the current account deficit? How could those flows threaten India's macroeconomic stability?

Source: "India's Central Bank Lowers Interest Rate," gulfnews.com, January 29, 2013.

29.5 Monetary Policy and Fiscal Policy in an Open Economy, pages 1036–1037

LEARNING OBJECTIVE: Compare the effectiveness of monetary policy and fiscal policy in an open economy and in a closed economy.

Summary

When the Federal Reserve engages in an expansionary monetary policy, it buys government bonds to lower interest rates and increase aggregate demand. In a closed economy, the main effect of lower interest rates is on domestic investment spending and purchases of consumer durables. In an open economy, lower interest rates will also cause an increase in net exports. When the Fed wants to slow the rate of economic growth to reduce inflation, it engages in a contractionary monetary policy by selling government bonds to increase interest rates and reduce aggregate demand. In a closed economy, the main effect is once again on domestic investment and purchases of consumer durables. In an open economy, higher interest rates will also reduce net exports. We can conclude that monetary policy has a greater impact on aggregate demand in an open economy than in a closed economy. To engage in an expansionary fiscal policy, the government increases government spending or cuts taxes. An expansionary fiscal policy can lead to higher interest rates. In a closed economy, the main effect of higher interest rates is on domestic investment spending and spending on consumer durables. In an open economy, higher interest rates will also reduce net exports. A contractionary fiscal policy will reduce the budget deficit and may lower interest rates. In a closed economy, lower interest rates increase domestic investment and spending on consumer durables. In an open economy, lower interest rates also increase net exports. We can conclude that fiscal policy has a smaller effect on aggregate demand in an open economy than in a closed economy.

MyEconLab Visit **www.myeconlab.com** to complete these exercises online and get instant feedback.

Review Questions

5.1 What is meant by a *policy channel*?

5.2 Why does monetary policy have a greater effect on aggregate demand in an open economy than in a closed economy?

5.3 Why does fiscal policy have a smaller effect on aggregate demand in an open economy than in a closed economy?

Problems and Applications

5.4 An article in the *Economist* quotes the finance minister of Peru as saying, "We are one of the most open economies of Latin America." What did he mean by Peru being an "open economy"? Is fiscal policy in Peru likely to be more or less effective than it would be in a less open economy? Briefly explain.

Source: "Hold on Tight," *Economist*, February 2, 2013.

5.5 Suppose that Federal Reserve policy leads to higher interest rates in the United States.
   a. How will this policy affect real GDP in the short run if the United States is a closed economy?
   b. How will this policy affect real GDP in the short run if the United States is an open economy?
   c. How will your answer to part (b) change if interest rates also rise in the countries that are the major trading partners of the United States?

5.6 An economist remarks, "In the 1960s, using fiscal policy would have been a better way to stabilize the economy, but I believe that monetary policy is better today." What has changed about the U.S. economy that might have led the economist to this conclusion?

5.7 Suppose the federal government increases spending without also increasing taxes. In the short run, how will this action affect real GDP and the price level in a closed economy? How will the effects of this action differ in an open economy?

Real-Time Data Exercises

D29.1 **(Exchange rate movements)** Go to the Web site of the Federal Reserve Bank of St. Louis (FRED) (research.stlouisfed.org/fred2/) and download the most recent value and the value from the same month one year earlier from FRED for the U.S./Euro Foreign Exchange Rate (EXUSEU).
   a. Using these values, compute the percentage change in the euro's value.
   b. Explain whether the dollar appreciated or depreciated against the euro.

D29.2 **(Exchange rate movements)** Go to the Web site of the Federal Reserve Bank of St. Louis (FRED) (research.stlouisfed.org/fred2/) and download and plot the U.S. dollar–euro exchange rate (EXUSEU), the U.S. dollar–yen exchange rate (EXJPUS), and the U.S. dollar–Canadian dollar exchange rate (EXCAUS) for the period from 2001 to the present. Answer the following questions on the basis of your graphs.
   a. In what year did the euro reach its highest value?
   b. During the financial crisis of 2007–2009, did the yen appreciate or depreciate against the dollar? Briefly explain.
   c. Against which currency did the U.S. dollar depreciate the most during this period?

D29.3 **(Exchange rate movements)** One way to gauge the general value of one currency relative to other currencies is to calculate the *trade-weighted exchange rate*, which is an index number similar to the consumer price index. The trade-weighted exchange rate for the U.S. dollar weights each individual exchange rate by the share of that country's trade with the United States. Go to the Web site of the Federal Reserve Bank of St. Louis (FRED) (research.stlouisfed.org/fred2/) and download monthly data on the trade-weighted exchange rate for the U.S. dollar against major currencies (TWEXMMTH) from 1973 to the present.
   a. What has been the long-term trend in the exchange value of the dollar? What effect should changes in the exchange rate during this period have had on U.S. net exports? Briefly explain.
   b. What has been the trend in the exchange value of the dollar over the past year? What effect should changes in the exchange rate during the past year have had on U.S. net exports? Briefly explain.

D29.4 **(Exchange rates and exports)** Go to the Web site of the Federal Reserve Bank of St. Louis (FRED) (research.stlouisfed.org/fred2/) and find the most recent values for the Japan/U.S. Foreign Exchange Rate (DEXJPUS) and the U.S. Exports of Goods to Japan (EXPJP) and the values for one year earlier. Given the change in the exchange rate between the two periods, is the change in U.S. exports to Japan consistent with what the analysis in this chapter would predict? Briefly explain.

D29.5 **(Exchange rates and imports)** Go to the Web site of the Federal Reserve Bank of St. Louis (FRED) (research.stlouisfed.org/fred2/) and find the most recent values from FRED for the Japan/U.S. Foreign Exchange Rate (DEXJPUS) and the U.S. Imports of Goods from Japan (IMPJP) and the values for one year earlier. Given the change in the exchange rate between the two periods, is the change in U.S. imports from Japan consistent with what the analysis in this chapter would predict? Briefly explain.

CHAPTER 30

The International Financial System

Chapter Outline and Learning Objectives

Bayer Uses a Weak Euro to Increase Sales

Most people in the United States know the German firm Bayer mainly from its aspirin, which is sold in bottles with labels that display the firm's name in a distinctive cross. Although the chemical formula for aspirin had been known for decades, it was only in 1899 that Bayer began marketing aspirin as a pain reliever. Because no other effective over-the-counter pain relievers were available until the 1950s, Bayer aspirin was probably the most profitable medication ever sold.

Today, Bayer sells a variety of products, including prescription and over-the-counter pharmaceuticals and agricultural products. Bayer's acquisition of Merck & Company's over-the-counter unit in 2014 added brand names such as Coppertone, Dr. Scholl's, and Claritin to its product line. In addition to exports, Bayer has affiliates in North America, Latin and South America, Europe and Asia that manufacture and sell its products. As a result, it receives revenue in many different currencies. As the exchange rate of each of the currencies changes relative to the euro, the value of Bayer's sales and profits change.

German manufacturers benefited from the introduction of the euro, the common currency of 19 members of the European Union. Because of the euro, Bayer and other German firms don't have to worry about fluctuations in exchange rates within most of Europe. Before the adoption of the euro, countries such as France, Italy, and Spain were able to bring about declines in the exchange values of their currencies, which made the output of their companies' products more competitive with those of Germany. These countries can no longer pursue this strategy in competing with Germany. When Bayer and other German companies export outside Europe, they still must deal with fluctuations in the value of the euro. When the value of the euro increases, as it did during 2012 and 2013, the prices of goods exported from Germany increase, and Bayer's sales can be hurt. But when the value of the euro falls, as it did during 2014 and 2015, it's good news for Bayer and other German exporters. For example, in the second quarter of 2015, Bayer's profits rose nearly 20 percent as a result of the lower value of the euro.

In this chapter, we will look more closely at the international financial system and at what determines fluctuations in exchange rates.

Sources: Bryce Hoffman, "Bayer CEO Focuses On Company's Strengths," *Forbes*, April 4, 2015; Christopher Alessi, "Bayer Profit Rises on Healthy Currency Effects," *Wall Street Journal*, July 29, 2015; Peter Loftus, "Bayer Bulks Up Its Medicine Chest With Merck Brands," *Wall Street Journal*, May 7, 2014; and American Chemical Society, "Molecule of the Week: Aspirin," June 4, 2012.

Economics in Your Life

Exchange Rate Risk Can Affect Your Savings

Suppose that you decide to accept a job in Japan. You plan to work there for the next 10 years, build up some savings, and then return to the United States. As you prepare for your move, you read that economists expect the average productivity of Japanese firms to grow faster than the average productivity of U.S. firms over the next 10 years. If economists are correct, all else being equal, will the savings that you accumulate (in yen) be worth more or less in U.S. dollars than it would have been worth without the relative gains in Japanese productivity? As you read this chapter, try to answer this question. You can check your answer against the one we provide on **page 1061** at the end of this chapter.

A key fact about the international economy is that exchange rates among the major currencies fluctuate. These fluctuations have important consequences for firms, consumers, and governments. In Chapter 29, we discussed the basics of how exchange rates are determined. We also looked at the relationship between a country's imports and exports, and at capital flows into and out of a country. In this chapter, we will look further at the international financial system and at the role central banks play in the system.

30.1 Exchange Rate Systems

LEARNING OBJECTIVE: Describe how different exchange rate systems operate.

Floating currency The outcome of a country allowing its currency's exchange rate to be determined by demand and supply.

Exchange rate system An agreement among countries about how exchange rates should be determined.

Managed float exchange rate system The current exchange rate system, under which the value of most currencies is determined by demand and supply, with occasional government intervention.

Fixed exchange rate system A system under which countries agree to keep the exchange rates among their currencies fixed for long periods.

A country's exchange rate can be determined in several ways. Some countries simply allow the exchange rate to be determined by demand and supply, just as other prices are. A country that allows demand and supply to determine the value of its currency is said to have a **floating currency**. Some countries attempt to keep the exchange rate between their currency and another currency constant. For example, China kept the exchange rate constant between its currency, the yuan, and the U.S. dollar, from 1994 until 2005, when it began allowing greater exchange rate flexibility. When countries can agree on how exchange rates should be determined, economists say that there is an **exchange rate system**. Currently, many countries, including the United States, allow their currencies to float most of the time, although they occasionally intervene to buy and sell their currency or other currencies to affect exchange rates. In other words, many countries attempt to *manage* the float of their currencies. As a result, the current exchange rate system is a **managed float exchange rate system**.

Historically, the two most important alternatives to the managed float exchange rate system were the *gold standard* and the *Bretton Woods system*. These were both **fixed exchange rate systems**, in which exchange rates remained constant for long periods. Under the gold standard, a country's currency consisted of gold coins and paper currency that the government was committed to redeem for gold. The gold standard was a fixed exchange rate system that lasted from the nineteenth century until the 1930s.

Under the gold standard, exchange rates were determined by the relative amounts of gold in each country's currency, and the size of a country's money supply was determined by the amount of gold available. To rapidly expand its money supply during a war or an economic depression, a country would need to leave the gold standard. By the mid-1930s, in response to the Great Depression, the United States and most other countries had abandoned the gold standard. Although during the following decades there were occasional discussions about restoring the gold standard, there was no serious attempt to do so.

A conference held in Bretton Woods, New Hampshire, in 1944 set up an exchange rate system in which the United States pledged to buy or sell gold at a fixed price of $35 per ounce. The central banks of all other members of the new Bretton Woods system pledged to buy and sell their currencies at a fixed rate against the dollar. By fixing their exchange rates against the dollar, these countries were fixing the exchange rates among their currencies as well. Unlike under the gold standard, neither the United States nor any other country was willing to redeem its paper currency for gold domestically. The United States would redeem dollars for gold only if they were presented by a foreign central bank. Fixed exchange rate regimes can run into difficulties because exchange rates are not free to adjust quickly to changes in demand and supply for currencies. As we will see in the next section, central banks often encounter problems if they are required to keep an exchange rate fixed over a period of years. By the early 1970s, the difficulty of keeping exchange rates fixed led to the end of the Bretton Woods system. The appendix to this chapter contains additional discussion of the gold standard and the Bretton Woods system.

MyEconLab Study Plan

MyEconLab Concept Check

Don't Let This Happen to You

Remember That Modern Currencies Are Fiat Money

Although the United States has not been on the gold standard since 1933, many people still believe that somehow gold continues to "back" U.S. currency. The U.S. Department of the Treasury still owns billions of dollars' worth of gold bars, most of which are stored at the Fort Knox Bullion Depository in Kentucky. (Even more gold is stored in a basement of the Federal Reserve Bank of New York, which holds about one-quarter of the world's monetary gold supply—almost 10 percent of all the gold ever mined. This gold, however, is entirely owned by foreign governments and international agencies.) The gold in Fort Knox no longer has any connection to the amount of paper money issued by the Federal Reserve. U.S. currency—like the currencies of other countries—is *fiat money*, which means it has no value except as money (see Chapter 25). The link between gold and money that existed for centuries has been broken in modern economies.

MyEconLab Study Plan

Your Turn: Test your understanding by doing related problem 1.3 on page 1062 at the end of this chapter.

30.2 The Current Exchange Rate System

LEARNING OBJECTIVE: Discuss the three key features of the current exchange rate system.

The current exchange rate system has three important features:

1. The United States allows the dollar to float against other major currencies.
2. Nineteen countries in Europe have adopted a single currency, the **euro**.
3. Some developing countries have attempted to keep their currencies' exchange rates fixed against the dollar or another major currency.

Euro The common currency of many European countries.

We begin our discussion of the current exchange rate system by looking at the changing value of the dollar over time. In discussing the value of the dollar, we can look further at what determines exchange rates in the short run and in the long run.

The Floating Dollar

Since 1973, the value of the U.S. dollar has fluctuated widely against other major currencies. Panel (a) of Figure 30.1 shows the exchange rate between the U.S.

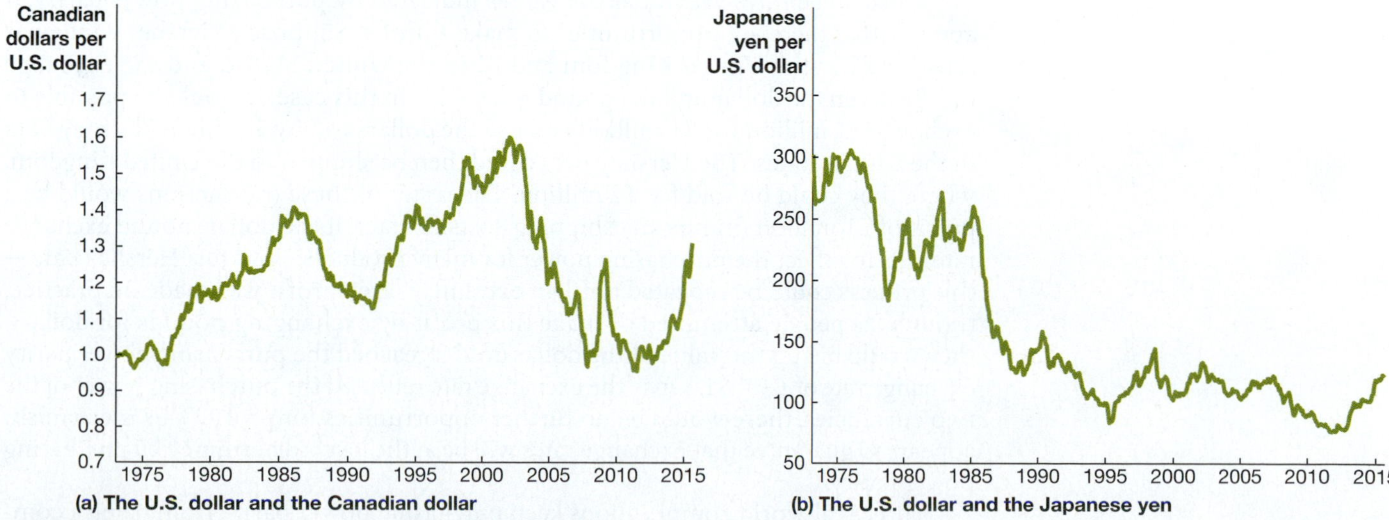

MyEconLab Real-time data

Figure 30.1 Canadian Dollar–U.S. Dollar and Yen–U.S. Dollar Exchange Rates, 1973–2015

Panel (a) shows that from the end of the Bretton Woods system in 1973 through August 2015, the U.S. dollar gained more than 30 percent in value against the Canadian dollar. Panel (b) shows that during the same period, the U.S. dollar lost almost 60 percent of its value against the Japanese yen.

Source: Federal Reserve Bank of St Louis.

dollar and the Canadian dollar between January 1973 and August 2015, and panel (b) shows the exchange rate between the U.S. dollar and the Japanese yen for the same period. Remember that the dollar increases in value when it takes more units of foreign currency to buy \$1, and it falls in value when it takes fewer units of foreign currency to buy \$1. From January 1973 to August 2015, the U.S. dollar lost nearly 60 percent in value against the yen, while it gained more than 30 percent in value against the Canadian dollar. Both exchange rates fluctuated substantially during those years. MyEconLab Concept Check

What Determines Exchange Rates in the Long Run?

Over the past 40 years, why has the value of the U.S. dollar fallen substantially against the Japanese yen but risen against the Canadian dollar? In the short run, the two most important causes of exchange rate movements are changes in interest rates—which cause investors to change their views of which countries' financial investments will yield the highest returns—and changes in investors' expectations about the future values of currencies. Over the long run, other factors are also important in explaining movements in exchange rates.

Purchasing power parity The theory that in the long run exchange rates move to equalize the purchasing powers of different currencies.

The Theory of Purchasing Power Parity It seems reasonable that, in the long run, exchange rates should be at a level that makes it possible to buy the same amount of goods and services with the equivalent amount of any country's currency. In other words, the purchasing power of every country's currency should be the same. The idea that in the long run exchange rates move to equalize the purchasing power of different currencies is called the theory of **purchasing power parity**.

Consider a simple example: Suppose that a Hershey candy bar has a price of \$1 in the United States and £1 in the United Kingdom and that the exchange rate is £1 = \$1. In that case, at least with respect to candy bars, the dollar and the pound have equivalent purchasing power. If the price of a Hershey bar increases to £2 in the United Kingdom but stays at \$1 in the United States, the exchange rate will have to change to £2 per \$1 in order for the pound to maintain its relative purchasing power. As long as the exchange rate adjusts to reflect purchasing power, it will be possible to buy a Hershey bar for \$1 in the United States or to exchange \$1 for £2 and buy the candy bar in the United Kingdom.

If exchange rates are not at the values indicated by purchasing power parity, it appears that there are opportunities to make a profit. Suppose a Hershey candy bar sells for £2 in the United Kingdom and \$1 in the United States, and the exchange rate between the dollar and the pound is £1 = \$1. In this case, it would be possible to exchange £1 million for \$1 million and use the dollars to buy 1 million Hershey bars in the United States. The Hershey bars could then be shipped to the United Kingdom, where they could be sold for £2 million. The result of these transactions would be a profit of £1 million (minus any shipping costs). In fact, if the dollar–pound exchange rate fails to reflect the purchasing power for many products—not just Hershey bars—this process could be repeated until an extremely large profit was made. In practice, though, as people attempted to make this profit by exchanging pounds for dollars, they would bid up the value of the dollar until it reached the purchasing power parity exchange rate of £2 = \$1. Once the exchange rate reflected the purchasing power of the two currencies, there would be no further opportunities for profit. This mechanism appears to guarantee that exchange rates will be at the levels determined by purchasing power parity.

Three real-world complications keep purchasing power parity from being a complete explanation of exchange rates, even in the long run:

1. **Not all products can be traded internationally.** Where goods are traded internationally, profits can be made whenever exchange rates do not reflect their purchasing power parity values. However, more than half of all goods and services produced in the United States and most other countries are not traded

internationally. When goods are not traded internationally, their prices will not be the same in every country. Suppose that the exchange rate is £1 for $1, but the price for having a cavity filled by a dentist is twice as high in the United States as it is in the United Kingdom. In this case, there is no way to buy up the low-priced British service and resell it in the United States. Because many goods and services are not traded internationally, exchange rates will not reflect exactly the relative purchasing powers of currencies.

2. **Products and consumer preferences are different across countries.** We expect the same product to sell for the same price around the world, but if a product is similar but not identical to another product, their prices might be different. For example, a 3-ounce Hershey candy bar may sell for a different price in the United States than does a 3-ounce Cadbury candy bar in the United Kingdom. Prices of the same product may also differ across countries if consumer preferences differ. If consumers in the United Kingdom like candy bars more than do consumers in the United States, a Hershey candy bar may sell for more in the United Kingdom than in the United States.
3. **Countries impose barriers to trade.** Most countries, including the United States, impose *tariffs* and *quotas* on imported goods. A **tariff** is a tax imposed by a government on imports. A **quota** is a government-imposed numerical limit on the quantity of a good that can be imported. For example, the United States has a quota on imports of sugar. As a result, the price of sugar in the United States is much higher than the price of sugar in other countries. Because of the quota, there is no legal way to buy up the cheap foreign sugar and resell it in the United States.

Tariff A tax imposed by a government on imports.

Quota A numerical limit that a government imposes on the quantity of a good that can be imported into the country.

Making the Connection
MyEconLab Video

The Big Mac Theory of Exchange Rates

In a lighthearted attempt to test the accuracy of the theory of purchasing power parity, the *Economist* regularly compares the prices of Big Macs in different countries. If purchasing power parity holds, you should be able to take the dollars required to buy a Big Mac in the United States and exchange it for the amount of foreign currency needed to buy a Big Mac in any other country. The following table is from July 2015, when Big Macs were selling for an average price of $4.79 in the United States. The "implied exchange rate" shows what the exchange rate would be if purchasing power parity held for Big Macs. For example, a Big Mac sold for 49 pesos in Mexico and $4.79 in the United States, so for purchasing power parity to hold, the exchange rate should have been 49 pesos/$4.79, or 10.23 pesos = $1. The actual exchange rate in July 2015 was 15.74 pesos = $1. So, on Big Mac purchasing power parity grounds, the Mexican peso was *undervalued* against the dollar by 35 percent: ([10.23 − 15.74]/15.74) × 100 = −35%). That is, if Big Mac purchasing power parity held, it would have taken 35 percent fewer Mexican pesos to buy a dollar than it actually did.

Is the price of a Big Mac in Mexico City the same as the price of a Big Mac in New York?

Could you take advantage of this difference between the purchasing power parity exchange rate and the actual exchange rate to become fabulously wealthy by buying up low-priced Big Macs in Mexico City and reselling them at a higher price in New York? Unfortunately, the low-priced Mexican Big Macs would be a soggy mess by the time you got them to New York. The fact that Big Mac prices are not the same around the world illustrates one reason purchasing power parity does not hold exactly: Many goods are not traded internationally.

Country	Big Mac Price	Implied Exchange Rate	Actual Exchange Rate
Mexico	49 pesos	10.23 pesos per dollar	15.74 pesos per dollar
Japan	370 yen	77.24 yen per dollar	123.94 yen per dollar
United Kingdom	2.89 pounds	0.60 pound per dollar	0.64 pound per dollar
Switzerland	6.5 Swiss francs	1.36 Swiss francs per dollar	0.95 Swiss francs per dollar
Indonesia	30,500 rupiahs	6,367 rupiahs per dollar	13,345 rupiahs per dollar
Canada	5.85 Canadian dollars	1.22 Canadian dollars per U.S. dollar	1.29 Canadian dollars per U.S. dollar
China	17 yuan	3.55 yuan per dollar	6.21 yuan per dollar

Source: "The Big Mac Index," *Economist*, July 16, 2015.

MyEconLab Study Plan

Your Turn: Test your understanding by doing related problem 2.10 on page 1063 at the end of this chapter.

Solved Problem 30.2

MyEconLab Interactive Animation

Calculating Purchasing Power Parity Exchange Rates Using Big Macs

Fill in the missing cells in the following table. Remember that the implied exchange rate shows what the exchange rate would be if purchasing power parity held for Big Macs. Assume that the Big Mac is selling for $4.79 in the United States. Explain whether the U.S. dollar is overvalued or undervalued relative to each currency and predict what will happen in the future to each exchange rate if the actual rate moves toward the purchasing power parity exchange rate. Finally, calculate the implied exchange rate between the Polish zloty and the Brazilian real (the plural of *real* is *reais*) and explain which currency is undervalued in terms of Big Mac purchasing power parity.

Country	Big Mac Price	Implied Exchange Rate	Actual Exchange Rate
Brazil	13.5 reais		3.15 reais per dollar
Poland	9.6 zlotys		3.77 zlotys per dollar
South Korea	4,300 won		1,143.5 won per dollar
Sweden	43.7 kronor		8.52 kronor per dollar

Solving the Problem

Step 1: Review the chapter material. This problem is about the theory of purchasing power parity as illustrated by prices of Big Macs, so you may want to review the section "The Theory of Purchasing Power Parity," which begins on page 1048, and the *Making the Connection,* "The Big Mac Theory of Exchange Rates" on page 1049.

Step 2: Fill in the table. To calculate the purchasing power parity exchange rate, divide the foreign currency price of a Big Mac by the U.S. price. For example, the implied exchange rate between the Brazilian real and the U.S. dollar is 13.5 reais/$4.79, or 2.82 reais per dollar.

Country	Big Mac Price	Implied Exchange Rate	Actual Exchange Rate
Brazil	13.5 reais	2.82 reais per dollar	3.15 reais per dollar
Poland	9.6 zlotys	2.00 zlotys per dollar	3.77 zlotys per dollar
South Korea	4,300 won	897.7 won per dollar	1,143.5 won per dollar
Sweden	43.7 kronor	9.12 kronor per dollar	8.52 kronor per dollar

Step 3: **Explain whether the U.S. dollar is overvalued or undervalued against the other currencies.** The dollar is overvalued if the actual exchange rate is greater than the implied exchange rate, and it is undervalued if the actual exchange rate is less than the implied exchange rate. In this case, the dollar is overvalued against the real, the zloty, and the won, but it is undervalued against the krona. So, we would predict that in the future the value of the dollar should rise against the krona but fall against the real, the zloty, and the won.

Step 4: **Calculate the implied exchange rate between the zloty and the real.** The implied exchange rate between the zloty and the real is 9.6 zlotys/13.5 reais, or 0.71 zlotys per real. We can calculate the actual exchange rate by taking the ratio of zlotys per dollar to reais per dollar: 3.77 zlotys/3.15 reais, or 1.20 zlotys per real. Therefore, the zloty is undervalued relative to the real because our Big Mac purchasing power parity calculation tells us that it should take fewer zlotys to buy a real than it actually does.

Source: "The Big Mac Index," *Economist*, July 16, 2015.

Your Turn: For more practice, do related problem 2.11 on page 1063 at the end of this chapter.

MyEconLab Study Plan

The Four Determinants of Exchange Rates in the Long Run We can take into account the shortcomings of the theory of purchasing power parity to develop a more complete explanation of how exchange rates are determined in the long run. There are four main determinants of exchange rates in the long run:

1. **Relative price levels.** The purchasing power parity theory is correct in arguing that, in the long run, the most important determinant of exchange rates between two countries' currencies is their relative price levels. If prices of goods and services rise faster in Canada than in the United States, the value of the Canadian dollar has to decline to maintain demand for Canadian products. Over the past 40 years, the price level in Canada has risen somewhat faster than the price level in the United States, while the price level in Japan has risen more slowly. These facts help explain why the U.S. dollar has increased in value against the Canadian dollar while losing value against the Japanese yen.
2. **Relative rates of productivity growth.** When the productivity of a firm increases, the firm is able to produce more goods and services using fewer workers, machines, or other inputs. The firm's costs of production fall, and usually so do the prices of its products. If the average productivity of Japanese firms increases faster than the average productivity of U.S. firms, Japanese products will have relatively lower prices than U.S. products, which increases the quantity demanded of Japanese products relative to U.S. products. As a result, the value of the yen should rise against the dollar. For most of the period from the early 1970s to the early 1990s, Japanese productivity increased faster than U.S. productivity, which contributed to the fall in the value of the dollar versus the yen. However, between 1992 and 2015, U.S. productivity increased faster than Japanese productivity, which explains why the value of the dollar stopped its rapid decline against the yen in the early 1990s.
3. **Preferences for domestic and foreign goods.** If consumers in Canada increase their preferences for U.S. products, the demand for U.S. dollars will increase relative to the demand for Canadian dollars, and the U.S. dollar will increase in value relative to the Canadian dollar. During the 1970s and 1980s, many U.S. consumers increased their preferences for Japanese products, particularly automobiles and consumer electronics. This greater preference for Japanese products helped to increase the value of the yen relative to the dollar.
4. **Tariffs and quotas.** The U.S. sugar quota forces firms such as Hershey Foods Corporation to buy expensive U.S. sugar rather than less expensive foreign sugar. The quota increases the demand for dollars relative to the currencies of foreign sugar

producers and, therefore, leads to a higher exchange rate. Changes in tariffs and quotas have not been a significant factor, though, in explaining trends in the U.S. dollar–Canadian dollar or U.S. dollar–yen exchange rates.

Because these four factors change over time, the value of one country's currency can increase or decrease by substantial amounts in the long run. These changes in exchange rates can create uncertainty for firms. A decline in the value of a country's currency lowers the foreign currency prices of the country's exports and increases the prices of imports. An increase in the value of a country's currency has the reverse effect. Firms can be both helped and hurt by exchange rate fluctuations. MyEconLab Concept Check

The Euro

A second key aspect of the current exchange rate system is that most countries in Western Europe have adopted a single currency. After World War II, many of these countries wanted to more closely integrate their economies. In 1957, Belgium, France, West Germany, Italy, Luxembourg, and the Netherlands signed the Treaty of Rome, which established the European Economic Community, often called the European Common Market. Tariffs and quotas on products being shipped within the European Common Market were greatly reduced. Over the years, Britain, Sweden, Denmark, Finland, Austria, Greece, Ireland, Spain, and Portugal joined the European Economic Community, which was renamed the European Union (EU) in 1991. By 2015, 28 countries were members of the EU.

EU members decided to move to a common currency beginning in 1999. Three of the 15 countries that were then members of the EU—the United Kingdom, Denmark, and Sweden—decided to retain their domestic currencies. The move to a common currency took place in several stages. On January 1, 1999, the exchange rates of the 12 participating countries were permanently fixed against each other and against the common currency, the *euro*. At first, the euro was a pure *unit of account*. No euro currency was actually in circulation, although firms began quoting prices in both domestic currency

MyEconLab Animation

Figure 30.2

Countries Adopting the Euro

The 19 member countries of the European Union (EU) that have adopted the euro as their common currency as of the end of 2015 are shaded with red hash marks. The members of the EU that have not adopted the euro are colored tan. Countries in white are not members of the EU.

and in euros. On January 1, 2002, euro coins and paper currency were introduced, and on June 1, 2002, the old domestic currencies were withdrawn from circulation. Figure 30.2 shows the 19 countries in the EU that had adopted the euro as of the end of 2015. These countries are sometimes called the *eurozone*.

A new European Central Bank (ECB) was also established. Although the central banks of the member countries continue to exist, the ECB has assumed responsibility for monetary policy and for issuing currency. The ECB is run by a governing council that consists of a six-member executive board—appointed by the participating governments—and the governors of the central banks of the 19 member countries that have adopted the euro. The ECB represents a unique experiment in allowing a multinational organization to control the domestic monetary policies of independent countries.

MyEconLab Concept Check

Making the Connection
MyEconLab Video

Greece and Germany: Diverse Economies, Common Currency

Most of Europe experienced relative economic stability from the introduction of the euro in 2002 to the beginning of the global economic downturn in 2007. With low interest rates, low inflation rates, and expanding employment and production, the advantages of having a common currency seemed obvious. Firms no longer had to worry about exchange rate instability when selling within Europe, and the cost of doing business was reduced because, for example, it was no longer necessary for a French firm to exchange francs for marks to do business in Germany.

By 2008, however, some economists and policymakers questioned whether the euro was making the effects of the global recession worse. The countries using the euro cannot pursue independent monetary policies because the ECB determines those policies from its headquarters in Frankfurt, Germany. Countries that were particularly hard hit by the recession—for example, Spain, where the unemployment rate had more than doubled to 18 percent by 2009 and was 22 percent in mid-2015—were unable to pursue a more expansionary policy than the ECB was willing to implement for the eurozone as a whole. Similarly, countries could not attempt to revive their exports by allowing their currencies to depreciate because (1) many of their exports were to other eurozone countries, and (2) the value of the euro was determined by factors affecting the eurozone as a whole.

In 2010, a *sovereign debt* crisis developed when investors began to believe that a number of European governments, particularly those of Greece, Ireland, Spain, Portugal, and Italy, would have difficulty making interest payments on their bonds—or sovereign debt. The International Monetary Fund and the European Union put together aid packages to keep the countries from defaulting. In exchange for the aid, these countries were required to adopt *austerity programs*—cutting government spending and raising taxes—even though doing so sparked protests from unions, students, and other groups. The controversy was greatest over Greece, which had large debts and a high unemployment rate, and where political resistance to multiple rounds of austerity made it uncertain whether the country would remain in the eurozone.

Did the euro contribute to the slow recovery from the 2007–2009 financial crisis? The figure below shows the average unemployment rate for the eurozone countries for the period 2007–2014 compared with the unemployment rates for the United States, the United Kingdom, and Iceland. The eurozone was still suffering from high unemployment rates more than seven years after the beginning of the financial crisis. The German economy, however, performed very well during and after the financial crisis, with its unemployment rate in 2014 being below what it had been in 2007. In fact, German firms, including Bayer, benefited from the euro because if the country had retained the deutsche mark as its currency, the deutsche mark would likely have increased in value during 2014 and 2015. The euro decreased in value during that period, thereby increasing German exports more than would have happened without the common currency. As the blue line shows, the unemployment rate in the eurozone looks significantly worse if Germany is left out.

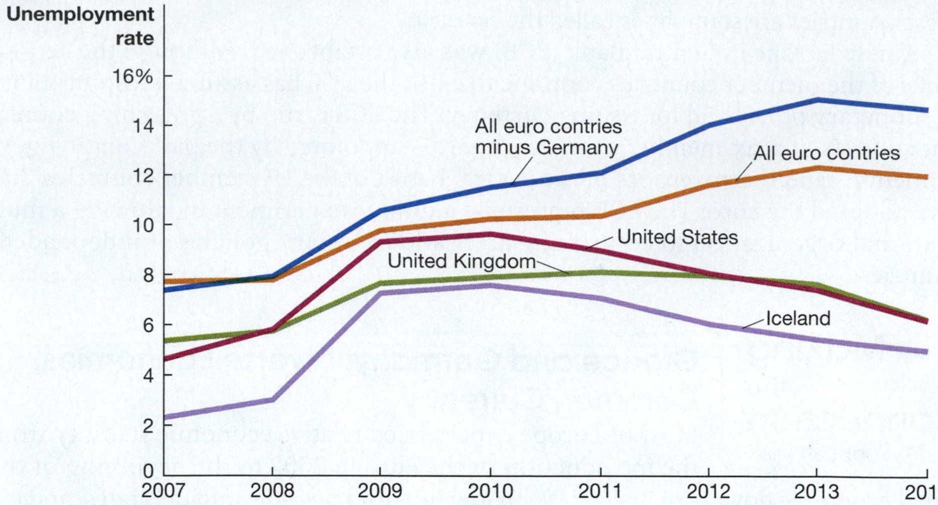

The United Kingdom, Iceland, and the United States all use their own currencies and all recovered more quickly from the financial crisis and recession than did most of the countries using the euro. The United Kingdom is a member of the European Union but continues to use the pound as its currency. Iceland is not a member of the European Union and does not use the euro. The situation in Iceland is particularly interesting because no country was more severely affected by the global financial crisis. Although it is a small country, its banks aggressively made loans around the world in the years leading up to the crisis. By 2007, Icelandic banks had made loans equal to nine times the country's GDP. When many borrowers defaulted on those loans, the government of Iceland took over the banks and assumed their debt of about $100 billion—or more than $300,000 for each citizen of Iceland. Iceland's krona, the British pound, and the U.S. dollar all depreciated against the euro in the period immediately following the financial crisis, which was good news for these countries because it helped them increase exports, but it was bad news for countries using the euro, many of which faced declining exports outside Europe.

The crisis over Greece highlighted another key problem facing the euro: the lack of coordinated government spending policies. The eurozone is a *monetary union*—the member countries all use the same currency and follow a joint monetary policy—but not a *fiscal union*—the member countries pursue independent fiscal policies. Although we don't usually think of countries in these terms, the states of the United States, the provinces of Canada, and the prefectures of Japan represent both monetary unions and fiscal unions. If during a recession Nevada suffers a particularly sharp decline in production and employment, the federal government provides support to the economy of Nevada through unemployment insurance and other transfer programs. Greece, by contrast, must fund such payments largely from its own revenues. The resulting large government budget deficits contributed to the sovereign debt crisis discussed earlier.

Some economists and policymakers wonder whether a monetary union of such diverse economies can survive in the absence of further fiscal integration. However, the political support for further fiscal integration of the eurozone countries seemed lacking. In 2015, the ultimate fate of Europe's great economic experiment of having independent countries use a single currency was very much in doubt.

Note: Data for the figure are from the International Monetary Fund. The unemployment rate for the euro countries is for all members of the eurozone as of 2008, weighted by their shares in total employment in 2007.

Sources: Nektaria Stamouli, "Greece Wants European Parliament Involved in Overseeing Bailout," *Wall Street Journal*, August 19, 2015; "A Third Bail-out Gets the Green Light," *Economist*, August 15, 2015; and Terence Roth, "Everything You Need to Know about European Political Union," *Economist*, July 27, 2015.

MyEconLab Study Plan

Your Turn: Test your understanding by doing related problems 2.12 and 2.13 on page 1064 at the end of this chapter.

Pegging against the Dollar

A final key feature of the current exchange rate system is that some developing countries have attempted to keep their exchange rates fixed against the dollar or another major currency. Having a fixed exchange rate can provide important advantages for a country that has extensive trade with another country. When the exchange rate is fixed, business planning becomes much easier. For instance, if the South Korean won increases in value relative to the dollar, Korean car manufacturer Hyundai may have to raise the dollar price of cars it exports to the United States, thereby reducing sales. If the exchange rate between the Korean won and the dollar is fixed, Hyundai's planning is much easier.

In the 1980s and 1990s, an additional reason developed for having fixed exchange rates. During those decades, the flow of foreign investment funds to developing countries, particularly those in East Asia, increased substantially. It became possible for firms in countries such as Korea, Thailand, Malaysia, and Indonesia to borrow dollars directly from foreign investors or indirectly from foreign banks. For example, a Thai firm might borrow U.S. dollars from a Japanese bank. If the Thai firm wants to build a new factory in Thailand with the borrowed dollars, it has to exchange the dollars for the equivalent amount of Thai currency, the baht. When the factory opens and production begins, the Thai firm will be earning the additional baht it needs to exchange for dollars to make the interest payments on the loan. A problem arises if the value of the baht falls against the dollar. Suppose that the exchange rate is 25 baht per dollar when the firm takes out the loan. A Thai firm making an interest payment of $100,000 per month on a dollar loan could buy the necessary dollars for 2.5 million baht. But if the value of the baht declines to 50 baht to the dollar, it would take 5 million baht to buy the dollars necessary to make the interest payment. These increased payments might be a crushing burden for the Thai firm. The government of Thailand would have a strong incentive to avoid this problem by keeping the exchange rate between the baht and the dollar fixed.

Finally, in the 1980s and 1990s, some countries feared the inflationary consequences of a floating exchange rate. When the value of a currency falls, the prices of imports rise. If imports are a significant fraction of the goods consumers buy, a fall in the value of the currency may significantly increase the inflation rate. During the 1990s, an important part of Brazil's and Argentina's anti-inflation policies was a fixed exchange rate against the dollar. (As we will see, there are difficulties with following a fixed exchange rate policy, and ultimately, both Brazil and Argentina abandoned fixed exchange rates.)

The East Asian Exchange Rate Crisis of the Late 1990s When a country keeps its currency's exchange rate fixed against another country's currency, it is **pegging** its currency. It is not necessary for both countries involved in a peg to agree to it. When a developing country has pegged the value of its currency against the dollar, the responsibility for maintaining the peg has been entirely with the developing country.

Pegging A policy by which a country keeps fixed the exchange rate between its currency and another country's currency.

Countries attempting to maintain a peg can run into problems, however. When the government fixes the price of a good or service, the result can be persistent surpluses or shortages (see Chapter 4). Figure 30.3 shows the exchange rate between the dollar and the Thai baht. The figure is drawn from the Thai point of view, so we measure the exchange rate on the vertical axis as dollars per baht. The figure represents the situation in the 1990s, when the government of Thailand pegged the exchange rate between the dollar and the baht above the equilibrium exchange rate, as determined by demand and supply. A currency pegged at a value above the market equilibrium exchange rate is said to be *overvalued*. A currency pegged at a value below the market equilibrium exchange rate is said to be *undervalued*.

Pegging both made it easier for Thai firms to export products to the United States and protected Thai firms that had taken out dollar loans. The pegged exchange rate was 25.19 baht to the dollar, or about $0.04 to the baht. By 1997, this exchange rate was well above the market equilibrium exchange rate of 35 baht to the dollar, or about $0.03

Figure 30.3

By 1997, the Thai Baht Was Overvalued against the Dollar

The government of Thailand pegged the value of the baht against the dollar to make it easier for Thai firms to export to the United States and to protect Thai firms that had taken out dollar loans. The pegged exchange rate of $0.04 per baht was well above the equilibrium exchange rate of $0.03 per baht. In the example in this figure, the overvalued exchange rate created a surplus of 70 million baht, which the Thai central bank had to purchase with dollars.

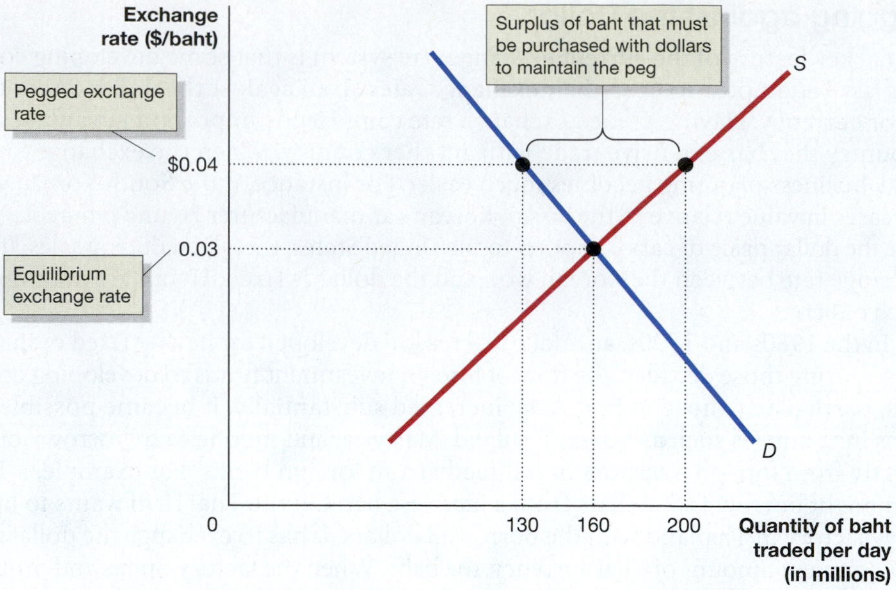

to the baht. The result was a surplus of baht on the foreign exchange market. To keep the exchange rate at the pegged level, the Thai central bank, the Bank of Thailand, had to buy these baht with dollars. In doing so, the Bank gradually used up its holdings of dollars, or its *dollar reserves*. To continue supporting the pegged exchange rate, the Bank borrowed additional dollar reserves from the International Monetary Fund (IMF). The Bank of Thailand also raised interest rates to attract more foreign investors to investments in Thailand, thereby increasing the demand for the baht. The Bank of Thailand took these actions even though allowing the value of the baht to decline against the dollar would have helped Thai firms exporting to the United States by reducing the dollar prices of their goods. The Thai government was afraid of the negative consequences of abandoning the peg even though the peg had led to the baht being overvalued.

Although higher domestic interest rates helped attract foreign investors, they made it more difficult for Thai firms and households to borrow the funds they needed to finance their spending. As a consequence, domestic investment and consumption declined, pushing the Thai economy into recession. International investors realized that there were limits to how high the Bank of Thailand would be willing to push interest rates and how many dollar loans the IMF would be willing to extend to Thailand. These investors began to speculate against the baht by exchanging baht for dollars at the official, pegged exchange rate. If, as they expected, Thailand were forced to abandon the peg, they would be able to buy back the baht at a much lower exchange rate, making a substantial profit. Because these actions by investors make it more difficult to maintain a fixed exchange rate, they are called *destabilizing speculation*. Figure 30.4 shows the results of this destabilizing speculation. The decreased demand for baht shifted the demand curve for baht from D_1 to D_2, increasing the quantity of baht the Bank of Thailand needed to buy in exchange for dollars.

Foreign investors also began to sell off their investments in Thailand and exchange their holdings of baht for dollars. This *capital flight* forced the Bank of Thailand to run through its dollar reserves. Dollar loans from the IMF temporarily allowed Thailand to defend the pegged exchange rate. Finally, on July 2, 1997, Thailand abandoned its pegged exchange rate against the dollar and allowed the baht to float. Thai firms that had borrowed dollars were now faced with interest payments that were much higher than they had planned. Many firms were forced into bankruptcy, and the Thai economy plunged into a deep recession.

Many currency traders became convinced that other East Asian countries, such as South Korea, Indonesia, and Malaysia, would have to follow Thailand and abandon their pegged exchange rates. The result was a wave of speculative selling of these countries'

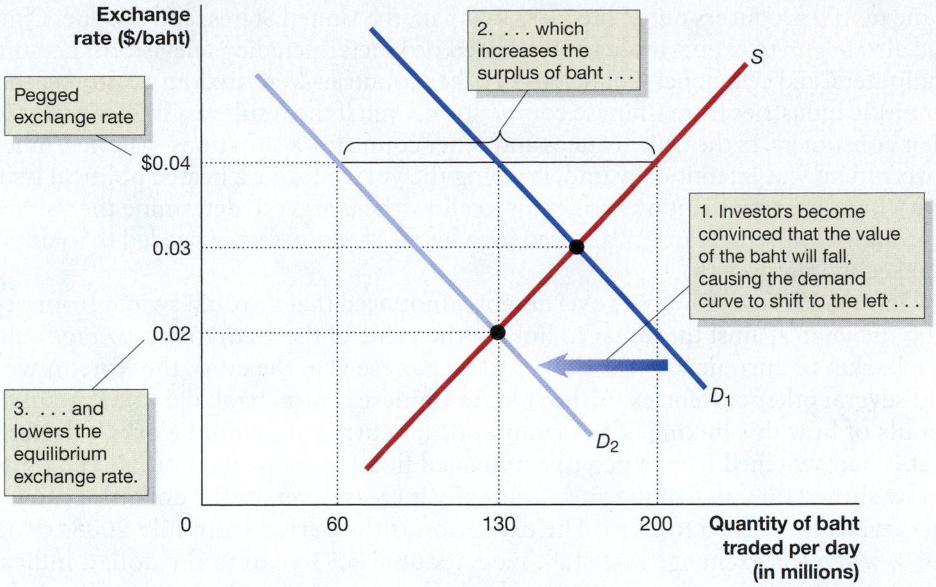

MyEconLab Animation

Figure 30.4

Destabilizing Speculation against the Thai Baht

In 1997, the pegged exchange rate of \$0.04 = 1 baht was above the equilibrium exchange rate of \$0.03 = 1 baht. As investors became convinced that Thailand would have to abandon its pegged exchange rate against the dollar and allow the value of the baht to fall, they decreased their demand for baht, causing the demand curve to shift from D_1 to D_2. The new equilibrium exchange rate became \$0.02 = 1 baht. To defend the pegged exchange rate, the Bank of Thailand had to increase the quantity of baht it purchased in exchange for dollars from 70 million to 140 million per day. The *destabilizing speculation* by investors caused Thailand to abandon its pegged exchange rate in July 1997.

currencies. These waves of selling—sometimes called *speculative attacks*—were difficult for countries to fight off. Even if a country's currency was not initially overvalued at the pegged exchange rate, the speculative attacks would cause a large reduction in the demand for the country's currency. The demand curve for the currency would shift to the left, which would force the country's central bank to quickly exhaust its dollar reserves. Within a few months, South Korea, Indonesia, the Philippines, and Malaysia abandoned their pegged currencies. All these countries also plunged into recession.

The Decline in Pegging Following the disastrous events experienced by the East Asian countries, the number of countries with pegged exchange rates declined sharply. Most countries that continue to use pegged exchange rates are small and trade primarily with a single, much larger, country. For instance, several Caribbean countries continue to peg against the dollar, and several former French colonies in Africa that formerly pegged against the French franc now peg against the euro. Overall, the trend has been toward replacing pegged exchange rates with managed floating exchange rates.

MyEconLab Concept Check

Making the Connection
MyEconLab Video

The Chinese Yuan: The World's Most Controversial Currency

In 1978, China began to move away from central planning and toward a market system. The result was a sharp acceleration in economic growth. Real GDP per capita grew at a rate of 6.5 percent per year between 1979 and 1995 and at the even more rapid rate of 8.8 percent per year between 1996 and 2014. An important part of Chinese economic policy was the decision in 1994 to peg the value of the Chinese currency, the yuan, to the dollar at a fixed rate of 8.28 yuan to the dollar. Pegging against the dollar ensured that Chinese exporters would face stable dollar prices for the goods they sold in the United States. By the early 2000s, many economists and policymakers argued that the yuan was undervalued against the dollar—possibly significantly undervalued. Some policymakers claimed that the undervaluation of the yuan gave Chinese firms an unfair advantage in competing with U.S. firms.

To support the undervalued exchange rate, the Chinese central bank had to buy large amounts of dollars with yuan. By 2005, the Chinese government had accumulated more than \$700 billion, a good portion of which it had used to buy U.S. Treasury bonds. By this time, China was coming under pressure from its trading partners to allow the yuan to increase in value. Chinese exports of textile products were driving some textile producers out of business in Japan, the United States, and Europe. China had also begun to export more sophisticated products, including televisions, personal computers, and cellphones. Politicians in other countries were anxious to protect their domestic industries from Chinese competition, even if the result was higher prices for their consumers. In the United States and other countries, accusations that the Chinese government was intentionally undervaluing the yuan became a heated political issue. The Chinese government was reluctant to allow the market to determine the value of the yuan, however, because it believed high levels of exports were needed to maintain rapid economic growth.

In July 2005, the Chinese government announced that it would switch from pegging the yuan against the dollar to linking the value of the yuan to the average value of a basket of currencies—the dollar, the Japanese yen, the euro, the Korean won, and several other currencies. Although the Chinese central bank did not explain the details of how this linking of the yuan to other currencies would work, it declared that it had switched from a peg to a managed floating exchange rate. As the figure below shows, the value of the yuan gradually increased versus the dollar for most of the period from 2005 to 2015. The exception is the period from July 2008 to May 2010, when the exchange rate stabilized at about 6.83 yuan to the dollar, indicating that China had apparently returned to a "hard peg." This change in policy led to renewed criticism from policymakers in the United States. In mid-2010, President Barack Obama argued that "market-determined exchange rates are essential to global economic activity." In the face of this criticism, the Chinese central bank allowed the yuan to resume its slow increase in value versus the dollar. (Note that the figure shows the number of yuan per dollar, so an increase represents a *depreciation* of the yuan relative to the dollar and a decrease represents an *appreciation* of the yuan relative to the dollar.)

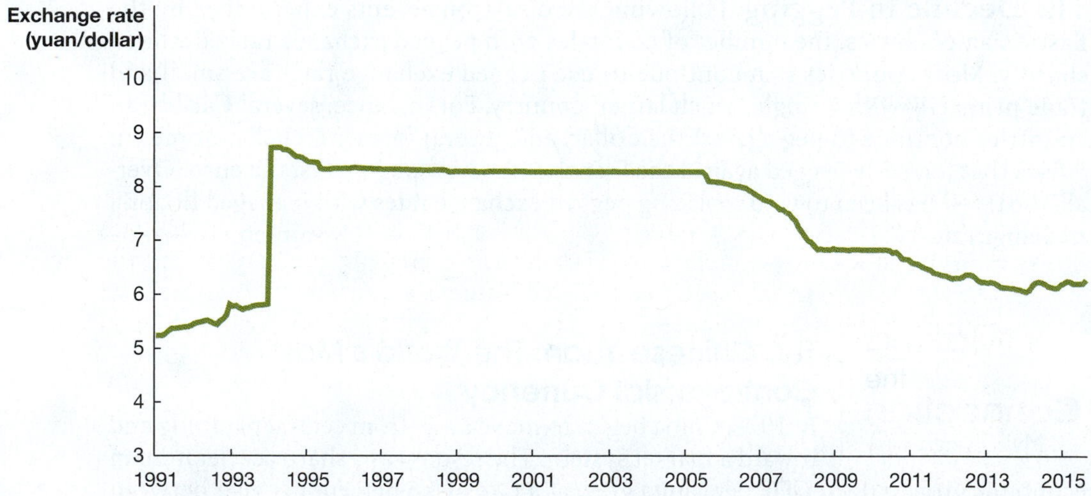

In 2015, the Chinese government was concerned that the growth rate of real GDP had slowed to about 7 percent, the lowest rate in more than 6 years. On August 11 of that year, the yuan was once again in the news when the Chinese central bank made a surprise announcement that it would buy dollars with yuan in order to reduce its value by about 3 percent, the largest one-day decline in the currency since 1994. The Chinese central bank again stated that it would allow the market to play a greater role in determining the value of the yuan. Many policymakers and economists were skeptical that the central bank truly intended to relax its control over the currency. And once again, politicians in the United States and elsewhere were critical of what they considered to be an attempt by the Chinese government to manipulate the value of yuan to gain an unfair advantage over its trading partners.

As long as the Chinese central bank continues to override the market to control the value of the yuan, controversy over Chinese exchange rate policies is likely to continue.

Sources: "Yuan Thing after Another," *Economist*, August 15, 2015; Lingling Wei, "China Moves to Devalue Yuan," *Wall Street Journal*, August 11, 2015; Greg Ip, "Why China's Yuan 'Reform' Merits Skepticism," *Wall Street Journal*, August 19, 2015; and Federal Reserve Bank of St. Louis.

Your Turn: Test your understanding by doing related problems 2.19 and 2.20 on page 1064 at the end of this chapter.

MyEconLab Study Plan

30.3 International Capital Markets

LEARNING OBJECTIVE: Discuss the growth of international capital markets.

One important reason exchange rates fluctuate is that investors seek out the best investments they can find anywhere in the world. For instance, if Chinese investors increase their demand for U.S. Treasury bills, the demand for dollars will increase, and the value of the dollar will rise. But if interest rates in the United States decline, foreign investors may sell U.S. investments, and the value of the dollar will fall.

Shares of stock and long-term debt, including corporate and government bonds and bank loans, are bought and sold on *capital markets*. Before 1980, most U.S. corporations raised funds only in U.S. stock and bond markets or from U.S. banks. And U.S. investors rarely invested in foreign capital markets. In the 1980s and 1990s, European governments removed many restrictions on foreign investments in their financial markets. It became possible for U.S. and other foreign investors to freely invest in Europe and for European investors to freely invest in foreign markets. Improvements in communications and computer technology made it possible for U.S. investors to receive better and more timely information about foreign firms and for foreign investors to receive better information about U.S. firms. The growth in economies around the world also increased the savings available to be invested.

Although at one time the U.S. capital market was larger than all other capital markets combined, that is no longer the case. Today, there are large capital markets in Europe and Japan, and there are smaller markets in Latin America and East Asia. The three most important international financial centers today are New York, London, and Tokyo. Each day, the *Wall Street Journal* provides data not just on the Dow Jones Industrial Average and the Standard & Poor's 500 stock indexes of U.S. stocks, but also on foreign stock indexes such as the Nikkei 225 average of Japanese stocks, the FTSE 100 index of stocks on the London Stock Exchange, and the Hang Seng Index of stocks traded on the Hong Kong stock exchange. By 2015, corporations, banks, and governments were raising more than $1 trillion in funds on global financial markets each year.

Beginning in the 1990s, the flow of foreign funds into U.S. stocks and bonds—or *portfolio investments*—increased substantially. As Figure 30.5 shows, foreign purchases of stocks and bonds issued by corporations and bonds issued by the federal government increased dramatically between 1995 and 2007. In 2014, foreign purchases of U.S. corporate stocks and bonds, while still substantial, had declined, partly because of low interest rates in the United States. Growth in China, India, and some European countries also attracted both U.S. and foreign investors to securities issued in those countries. The fact that the United States continued to run large current account deficits resulted in a continuing foreign demand for U.S. government bonds. The current account deficits led to an accumulation of dollars by foreign central banks and foreign investors who used the dollars to purchase U.S. government bonds.

Figure 30.6 shows the distribution in June 2015 of foreign holdings of U.S. stocks and bonds by country. Japan and China together hold almost one-quarter of foreign-owned U.S. securities. The large holdings in the Cayman Islands and Luxembourg are the result of investors taking advantage of the favorable tax treatment of investment income available in those countries.

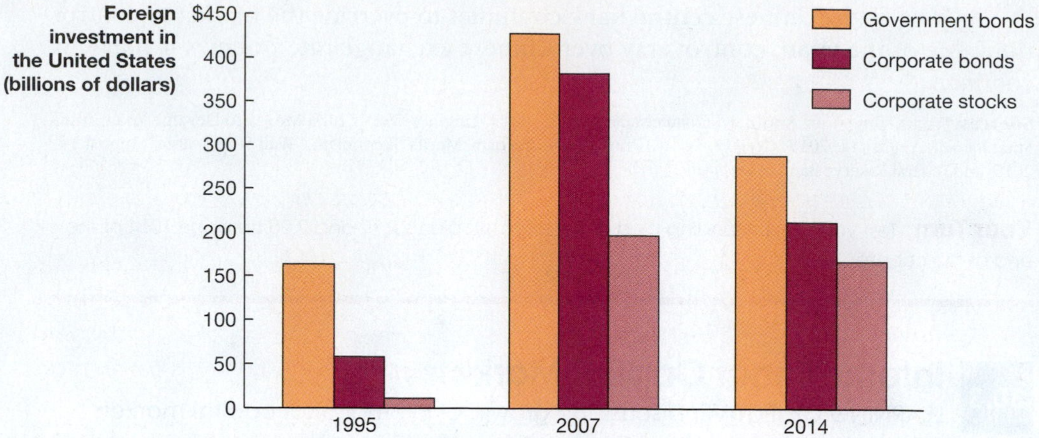

MyEconLab Animation

Figure 30.5 Growth of Foreign Portfolio Investment in the United States

Between 1995 and 2007, there was a large increase in foreign purchases of stocks and bonds issued by U.S. corporations and of bonds issued by the federal government. In 2014, partly because of low interest rates in the United States, foreign purchases of U.S. corporate stocks and bonds had declined. Foreign purchases of U.S. government bonds remained high.

Sources: International Monetary Fund, *International Capital Markets*, August 2001; and Board of Governors of the Federal Reserve System.

The globalization of financial markets has helped increase growth and efficiency in the world economy. It is now possible for the savings of households around the world to be channeled to the best investments available. It is also possible for firms in nearly every country to tap the savings of foreign households to gain the funds needed for expansion. No longer are firms forced to rely only on the savings of domestic households to finance investment.

But the globalization of financial markets also has a downside, as the events of 2007–2009 showed. Because financial securities issued in one country are held by investors and firms in many other countries, if those securities decline in value, the financial pain will be widely distributed. For example, the sharp decline in the value of mortgage-backed securities issued in the United States hurt not only U.S. investors and financial firms but investors and financial firms in many other countries as well.

MyEconLab Study Plan

MyEconLab Concept Check

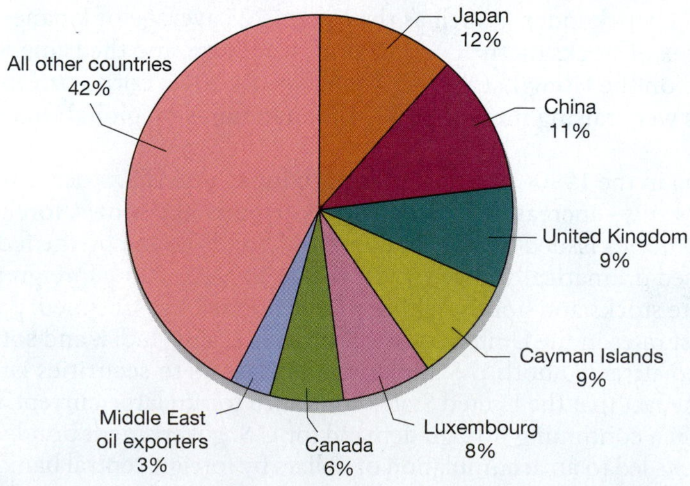

MyEconLab Animation

Figure 30.6 The Distribution of Foreign Holdings of U.S. Stocks and Bonds by Country, June 2015

Investors in China and Japan own almost one-quarter of foreign-owned U.S. stocks and bonds.

Source: U.S. Department of the Treasury.

Continued from page 1045

Economics in Your Life

Exchange Rate Risk Can Affect Your Savings

At the beginning of this chapter, we posed this question: If economists are correct about the relative rates of average productivity growth between Japan and the United States in the next decade, then, all else being equal, will the savings that you accumulate (in yen) be worth more or less in U.S. dollars than the savings would have been worth without the relative gains in Japanese productivity? We saw in this chapter that when the average productivity of firms in one country increases faster than the average productivity of firms in another country, the value of the faster-growing country's currency should—all else being equal—rise against the slower-growing country's currency. But the savings that you accumulate in yen while you are in Japan are likely to be worth more in U.S. dollars than they would have been worth without the gains in Japanese productivity.

Conclusion

Fluctuations in exchange rates continue to cause difficulties for firms and governments. From the gold standard to the Bretton Woods system to currency pegging, governments have attempted to find a workable system of fixed exchange rates. Fixing exchange rates runs into the same problems as fixing any other price: As demand and supply shift, surpluses and shortages will occur unless the price adjusts. Nineteen countries in Europe are attempting to avoid this problem by using a single currency. Economists are looking closely at the results of that experiment.

Visit MyEconLab for a news article and analysis related to the concepts in this chapter.

CHAPTER SUMMARY AND PROBLEMS

Key Terms

Euro, p. 1047
Exchange rate system, p. 1046
Fixed exchange rate system, p. 1046
Floating currency, p. 1046
Managed float exchange rate system, p. 1046
Pegging, p. 1055
Purchasing power parity, p. 1048
Quota, p. 1049
Tariff, p. 1049

30.1 Exchange Rate Systems, pages 1046–1047

LEARNING OBJECTIVE: Describe how different exchange rate systems operate.

Summary

When countries agree on how exchange rates should be determined, economists say that there is an **exchange rate system**. A **floating currency** is the outcome of a country allowing its currency's exchange rate to be determined by demand and supply. The current exchange rate system is a **managed float exchange rate system**, under which the value of most currencies is determined by demand and supply, with occasional government intervention. A **fixed exchange rate system** is a system under which countries agree to keep the exchange rates among their currencies fixed. Under the gold standard, the exchange rate between two currencies was automatically determined by the quantity of gold in each currency. By the end of the Great Depression of the 1930s, every country had abandoned the gold standard. Under the Bretton Woods system, which was in place between 1944 and the early 1970s, the United States agreed to exchange dollars for gold at a price of $35 per ounce. The central banks of all other members of the system pledged to buy and sell their currencies at a fixed rate against the dollar.

MyEconLab Visit **www.myeconlab.com** to complete these exercises online and get instant feedback.

Review Questions

1.1 What is an exchange rate system? What is the difference between a fixed exchange rate system and a managed float exchange rate system?

1.2 How were exchange rates determined under the gold standard? How did the Bretton Woods system differ from the gold standard?

Problems and Applications

1.3 **(Related to the Don't Let This Happen to You on page 1047)** Briefly explain whether you agree with the following statement: "The Federal Reserve is limited in its ability to issue paper currency by the amount of gold the federal government has in Fort Knox. To issue more paper currency, the government first has to buy more gold."

1.4 An article in the *Atlantic* referred to a poll of economists that found no support for the United States to readopt the gold standard:

> It prevents the central bank from fighting recessions by outsourcing monetary policy decisions to how much gold we have—which, in turn, depends on our trade balance and on how much of the shiny rock we can dig up. When we peg the dollar to gold we have to raise interest rates when gold is scarce, regardless of the state of the economy.

Why does the writer state that a gold standard would prevent "the central bank from fighting recessions"?

Source: Matthew O'Brien, "Why the Gold Standard Is the World's Worst Economic Idea, in 2 Charts," *Atlantic*, August 26, 2012.

1.5 The United States and most other countries abandoned the gold standard during the 1930s. Why would the 1930s have been a particularly difficult time for countries to have remained on the gold standard? (*Hint:* Think about the macroeconomic events of the 1930s and about the possible problems with carrying out an expansionary monetary policy while remaining on the gold standard.)

1.6 After World War II, why might countries have preferred the Bretton Woods system to reestablishing the gold standard? In your answer, be sure to note the important ways in which the Bretton Woods system differed from the gold standard.

30.2 The Current Exchange Rate System, pages 1047–1059

LEARNING OBJECTIVE: Discuss the three key features of the current exchange rate system.

Summary

The current exchange rate system has three key features: (1) The U.S. dollar floats against other major currencies, (2) most countries in Western Europe have adopted a common currency, and (3) some developing countries have fixed their currencies' exchange rates against the dollar or against another major currency. Since 1973, the value of the U.S. dollar has fluctuated widely against other major currencies. The theory of **purchasing power parity** states that in the long run, exchange rates move to equalize the purchasing power of different currencies. This theory helps to explain some of the long-run movements in the value of the U.S. dollar relative to other currencies. Purchasing power parity does not provide a complete explanation of movements in exchange rates for several reasons, including the existence of *tariffs* and *quotas*. A **tariff** is a tax imposed by a government on imports. A **quota** is a government-imposed limit on the quantity of a good that can be imported. Currently, 19 European Union member countries use a common currency known as the **euro**. The experience of the countries using the euro will provide economists with information about the costs and benefits to countries of using the same currency.

When a country keeps its currency's exchange rate fixed against another country's currency, it is **pegging** its currency. Pegging can result in problems similar to the difficulties countries encountered with fixed exchange rates under the Bretton Woods system. If investors become convinced that a country pegging its exchange rate will eventually allow the exchange rate to decline to a lower level, the demand curve for the currency will shift to the left. This destabilizing speculation makes it difficult for a central bank to maintain a fixed exchange rate.

MyEconLab Visit **www.myeconlab.com** to complete these exercises online and get instant feedback.

Review Questions

2.1 What is the theory of purchasing power parity? Does the theory give a complete explanation for movements in exchange rates in the long run? Briefly explain.

2.2 Briefly describe the four determinants of exchange rates in the long run.

2.3 Which European countries currently use the euro as their currency? Why did these countries agree to replace their previous currencies with the euro?

2.4 What does it mean when one currency is "pegged" against another currency? Why do countries peg their currencies? What problems can result from pegging?

Problems and Applications

2.5 An article in the *Toronto Star* discussed the Canadian teams that play in the National Hockey League, the National Basketball Association, Major League Baseball, and Major League Soccer. The article noted, "Under their collective agreements players get paid in U.S. dollars. The majority of [team] revenue, however, is in Canadian currency." Are Canadian professional sports teams better off when the Canadian dollar increases in value relative to the U.S. dollar or when it decreases in value? Briefly explain.

Source: Josh Rubin, "MLSE, Blue Jays Deal with Dollar Dive," thestar.com, January 25, 2015.

2.6 An article in the *Economist* discussed the situation facing the U.S. economy in mid-2015: "The combination of weaker-than-expected CPI inflation and some dovish comments in the minutes of the Federal Reserve's July meeting have caused the dollar ... to fall. Inflation continues to languish close to zero due to cheap oil and the effect of a strengthening dollar." By "dovish comments," the article meant that some members of the Fed's Federal Open Market Committee did not believe that the target for the federal funds rate should be raised in the coming months.

a. If investors come to believe that the Fed might not be increasing interest rates, why would the value of the dollar decline?

b. What does "the strengthening of the dollar" mean? Why would a strengthening of the dollar reduce the inflation rate in the United States?

Source: "Fed Leaders Begin to Recognise that September Is Too Soon to Hike Rates," *Economist*, August 20, 2015.

2.7 Consider this statement:

> It takes more than 120 yen to buy 1 U.S. dollar and more than 1.5 dollars to buy 1 British pound. These values show that the United States must be a much wealthier country than Japan and that the United Kingdom must be wealthier than the United States.

Do you agree with this reasoning? Briefly explain.

2.8 According to the theory of purchasing power parity, if the inflation rate in Australia is higher than the inflation rate in New Zealand, what should happen to the exchange rate between the Australian dollar and the New Zealand dollar? Briefly explain.

2.9 In December 2014, you needed 30 percent more pesos to buy one U.S. dollar than you had needed in December 2004. Over the same time period, the consumer price index in Mexico increased 49.5 percent, and the consumer price index in the United States increased 23.3 percent. Are these data consistent with the theory of purchasing power parity? Briefly explain.

2.10 **(Related to the Making the Connection on page 1049)** Look again at the table on page 1050 that shows the prices of Big Macs and the implied and actual exchange rates. Indicate whether the U.S. dollar is overvalued or undervalued against each currency.

2.11 **(Related to Solved Problem 30.2 on page 1050)** Fill in the missing values in the following table. Assume that the Big Mac is selling for $4.79 in the United States. Explain whether the U.S. dollar is overvalued or undervalued relative to each of the other currencies and predict what will happen in the future to each exchange rate if the actual exchange rate moves toward the purchasing power parity exchange rate. Finally, calculate the implied exchange rate between the Russian ruble and the New Zealand dollar and explain which currency is overvalued in terms of Big Mac purchasing power parity.

Country	Big Mac Price	Implied Exchange Rate	Actual Exchange Rate
Chile	2,100 pesos		642.45 pesos per dollar
Israel	17.5 shekels		3.78 shekels per dollar
Russia	107 rubles		56.82 rubles per dollar
New Zealand	5.9 New Zealand dollars		1.51 New Zealand dollars per U.S. dollar

Source: "The Big Mac Index," *Economist*, July 16, 2015.

2.12 **(Related to the Making the Connection on page 1053)** Britain decided not to join other European Union countries in using the euro as its currency. One British opponent of adopting the euro argued, "It comes down to economics. We just don't believe that it's possible to manage the entire economy of Europe with just one interest rate policy. How do you alleviate recession in Germany and curb inflation in Ireland?"

a. What interest rate policy would be used to alleviate recession in Germany?
b. What interest rate policy would be used to curb inflation in Ireland?
c. What does adopting the euro have to do with interest rate policy?

Source: Alan Cowell, "Nuanced Conflict over Euro in Britain," *New York Times*, June 22, 2001.

2.13 **(Related to the Making the Connection on page 1053)** An article in *USA Today* argues, "Ironically, the euro's fall—and the benefit for German exports—is largely the result of eurozone policies that Germany has taken the lead in opposing . . . [including] easier money policies by the European Central Bank."

a. How does the "euro's fall" benefit German exports?
b. How is the euro's fall related to policies of the European Central Bank?

Source: Mihret Yohannes, "Germany Benefits from Weak Euro Policies It Deplores," usatoday.com, March 4, 2015.

2.14 In January 2007, before the financial crisis, the exchange rate was $1.30 per euro. In July 2008, during the financial crisis, the exchange rate was $1.58 per euro. Was this change in the dollar–euro exchange rate good news or bad news for U.S. firms exporting goods and services to Europe? Was it good news or bad news for European consumers buying goods and services imported from the United States? Briefly explain.

2.15 Although it is a member of the European Community, Denmark is not part of the eurozone; it has its own currency, the krone. Because the krone is pegged to the euro, Denmark's central bank is obliged to maintain the value of the krone within 2.25 percent either above or below the value of the euro. To maintain the peg with the euro, in 2015 the Danish central bank was forced to offer negative interest rates on deposits of krone that it held. Was the Danish central bank's action in response to an increase or a decrease in the value of the euro? Briefly explain.

Source: Charles Duxbury and Josie Cox, "Denmark Cuts Rates Again to Protect Currency Peg," *Wall Street Journal*, February 5, 2015.

2.16 **(Related to the Chapter Opener on page 1045)** The German firm Bayer reported that its pharmaceutical group experienced a 21 percent increase in profit for the second quarter of 2015. The firm stated that the increase was partly the result of "favorable currency effects."

a. Briefly explain what the firm means by "favorable currency effects."
b. How would favorable currency effects increase Bayer's profit?
c. Would these effects still have raised Bayer's profit if all of the firm's production and all of its sales were within Europe? Briefly explain.

Source: Christopher Alessi, "Bayer Profit Rises on Healthy Currency Effects," *Wall Street Journal*, July 29, 2015.

2.17 Use the graph to answer the following questions.

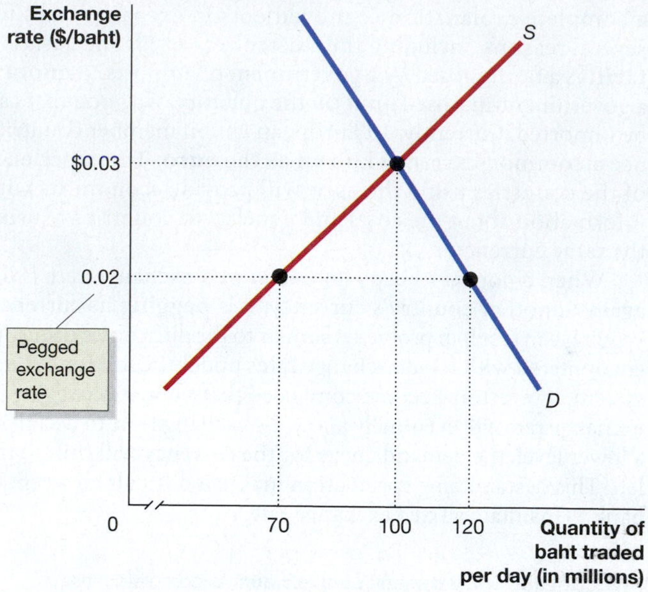

a. According to the graph, is there a surplus or a shortage of baht in exchange for U.S. dollars? Briefly explain.
b. To maintain the pegged exchange rate, will the Thai central bank need to buy baht in exchange for dollars or sell baht in exchange for dollars? How many baht will the Thai central bank need to buy or sell?

2.18 The *Economist* observed, "In Argentina, many loans were taken out in dollars: this had catastrophic consequences for borrowers once the peg collapsed." What does the article mean when it says that Argentina's "peg collapsed"? Why was this collapse catastrophic for borrowers in Argentina who had taken out dollar loans?

Source: "Spoilt for Choice," *Economist*, June 3, 2002.

2.19 **(Related to the Making the Connection on page 1057)** Graph the demand and supply of Chinese yuan for U.S. dollars and label each axis. To maintain a pegged exchange rate, the Chinese central bank can use yuan to buy U.S. dollars. Indicate whether the Chinese central bank would typically be interested in pegging the exchange rate above or below the market equilibrium exchange rate, and show on the graph the quantity of yuan the Chinese central bank would have to supply each trading period.

2.20 **(Related to the Making the Connection on page 1057)** In August 2015, after the Chinese central bank moved to decrease the value of the yuan in exchange for the dollar, a column in the *Wall Street Journal* offered this opinion: "China's trading partners are right to suspect that the real purpose of the so-called reform is a competitive devaluation that boosts exports and growth at the rest of the world's expense."

a. What does the writer mean by a "competitive devaluation"?
b. How would such a devaluation boost Chinese exports and growth?
c. Why would a boost in Chinese exports and growth come at the rest of the world's expense?

Source: Greg Ip, "Why China's Yuan 'Reform' Merits Skepticism," *Wall Street Journal*, August 19, 2015.

30.3 International Capital Markets, pages 1059–1060

LEARNING OBJECTIVE: Discuss the growth of international capital markets.

Summary

A key reason exchange rates fluctuate is that investors seek out the best investments they can find anywhere in the world. Since 1980, the markets for stocks and bonds have become global. Foreign purchases of U.S. corporate bonds and stocks and U.S. government bonds have increased greatly in the period since 1995. As a result of the globalization of capital markets, firms around the world are no longer forced to rely only on the savings of domestic households for funds.

MyEconLab Visit **www.myeconlab.com** to complete these exercises online and get instant feedback.

Review Questions

3.1 What were the main factors behind the globalization of capital markets in the 1980s and 1990s?

3.2 Briefly describe the pattern of foreign investments in U.S. securities between 1995 and 2014.

Problems and Applications

3.3 Why are foreign investors more likely to invest in U.S. government bonds than in U.S. corporate stocks and bonds?

3.4 The text states that "the globalization of financial markets has helped increase growth and efficiency in the world economy." Briefly explain which aspects of globalization help to increase growth in the world economy.

3.5 The global financial crisis of 2007–2009 led some economists and policymakers to suggest the reinstitution of capital controls—or limits on the flow of foreign exchange and financial investments across countries—which existed in many European countries prior to the 1960s. Why would a financial crisis lead policymakers to reconsider using capital controls? What problems might result from reinstituting capital controls?

Real-Time Data Exercises

D30.1 (Big Mac prices and purchasing power parity) Go to the Web site of the Federal Reserve Bank of St. Louis Federal Reserve (FRED) (research.stlouisfed.org/fred2/) and find the most recent values for the Japan/U.S. Foreign Exchange Rate (DEXJPUS), China/U.S. Foreign Exchange Rate (DEXCHUS), and the Mexico/U.S. Foreign Exchange Rate (DEXMXUS).

a. Explain whether the exchange rates are quoted as U.S. dollars per unit of foreign currency or units of foreign currency per U.S. dollar.

b. Suppose a Big Mac sells for 300 yen in Japan, 14 yuan in China, and 34 pesos in Mexico. What is the price of a Big Mac in each country in terms of U.S. dollars?

c. Are your results from part (b) consistent with the theory of purchasing power parity? Briefly explain.

d. Assuming no transportation costs and a no-cost means of preserving Big Macs while they are being transported, explain in which county you would want to purchase a Big Mac and in which country you would want to sell the same Big Mac in order to make the highest profit possible.

D30.2 (Explaining movements in the yuan-dollar exchange rate) Go to the Web site of the Federal Reserve Bank of St. Louis (FRED) (research.stlouisfed.org/fred2/) and find the values for the China/U.S. Foreign Exchange Rate (DEXCHUS) from 1981 to the most recent date available.

a. Compared with its value in 1981, has the yuan appreciated or depreciated against the U.S. dollar? Briefly explain.

b. Summarize the movements in the yuan–dollar exchange rate during these years and explain why the pattern occurred.

D30.3 (Analyzing global capital flows) The U.S. Treasury publishes data on capital flows. Treasury International Capital Flows can be found at www.treasury.gov/resource-center/data-chart-center/tic/Pages/index.aspx. Go to "Monthly Transactions in Long-Term Securities."

a. Look at recent net purchases of long-term securities. How has the volume of purchases changed over the past five years?

b. Now look at gross purchases of long-term securities. Which countries hold the most U.S. securities? How have foreign holdings of U.S. securities changed over time?

Appendix

The Gold Standard and the Bretton Woods System

LEARNING OBJECTIVE: Explain the gold standard and the Bretton Woods system.

It is easier to understand the current exchange rate system by considering further two earlier systems—the gold standard and the Bretton Woods system—that together lasted from the early nineteenth century through the early 1970s.

The Gold Standard

As we saw in this chapter, under the gold standard, the currency of a country consisted of gold coins and paper currency that people could redeem for gold. Great Britain adopted the gold standard in 1816, but as late as 1870, only a few nations had followed. In the late nineteenth century, however, Great Britain's share of world trade had increased, as had its overseas investments. The dominant position of Great Britain in the world economy motivated other countries to adopt the gold standard. By 1913, every country in Europe, except Spain and Bulgaria, and most countries in the Western Hemisphere had adopted the gold standard.

Under the gold standard, the exchange rate between two currencies was automatically determined by the quantity of gold in each currency. If there was 1/5 ounce of gold in a U.S. dollar and 1 ounce of gold in a British pound, the price of gold in the United States would be \$5 per ounce, and the price of gold in Britain would be £1 per ounce. The exchange rate would therefore be \$5 = £1. MyEconLab Concept Check

The End of the Gold Standard

From a modern point of view, the greatest drawback to the gold standard was that the central bank lacked control of the money supply. The size of a country's money supply depended on its gold supply, which could be greatly affected by chance discoveries of gold or by technological change in gold mining. For example, the gold discoveries in California in 1849 and Alaska in the 1890s caused rapid increases in the U.S. money supply. Because the central bank cannot determine how much gold will be discovered, it lacks the control of the money supply necessary to pursue an active monetary policy. During wartime, countries usually went off the gold standard to allow their central banks to expand the money supply as rapidly as was necessary to pay for the war. Britain left the gold standard at the beginning of World War I in 1914 and did not resume redeeming its paper currency for gold until 1925.

When the Great Depression began in 1929, governments came under pressure to leave the gold standard to allow their central banks to pursue active monetary policies. In 1931, Great Britain became the first major country to abandon the gold standard. A number of other countries also went off the gold standard that year. The United States remained on the gold standard until 1933, and a few countries, including France, Italy, and Belgium, stayed on even longer. By the late 1930s, the gold standard had collapsed.

The earlier a country abandoned the gold standard, the easier time it had fighting the Depression with expansionary monetary policies. The countries that abandoned the gold standard by 1932 suffered an average decline in production of only 3 percent between 1929 and 1934. The countries that stayed on the gold standard until 1933 or later suffered an average decline of more than 30 percent. The devastating economic performance of the countries that stayed on the gold standard the longest during the 1930s is the key reason no attempt was made to bring back the gold standard in later years. MyEconLab Concept Check

The Bretton Woods System

In addition to the collapse of the gold standard, the global economy suffered during the 1930s from tariff wars. The United States had started the tariff wars in June 1930 by enacting the Smoot-Hawley Tariff Act, which raised the average U.S. tariff rate to more than 50 percent. Many other countries raised tariffs during the next few years, leading to a collapse in world trade.

As World War II was coming to an end, economists and government officials in the United States and Europe concluded that they needed to restore the international economic system to avoid another depression. In 1947, the United States and most other major countries, apart from the Soviet Union, began participating in the General Agreement on Tariffs and Trade (GATT), under which they worked to reduce trade barriers. The GATT was very successful in sponsoring rounds of negotiations among countries, which led to sharp declines in tariffs. U.S. tariffs dropped from an average rate of more than 50 percent in the early 1930s to an average rate of less than 2 percent in 2015. In 1995, the GATT was replaced by the World Trade Organization (WTO), which has similar objectives.

The effort to develop a new exchange rate system to replace the gold standard was more complicated than establishing the GATT. A conference held in Bretton Woods, New Hampshire, in 1944 set up a system in which the United States pledged to buy or sell gold at a fixed price of $35 per ounce. The central banks of all other members of the new **Bretton Woods system** pledged to buy and sell their currencies at a fixed rate against the dollar. By fixing their exchange rates against the dollar, these countries were fixing the exchange rates among their currencies as well. Unlike under the gold standard, neither the United States nor any other country was willing to redeem its paper currency for gold domestically. The United States would redeem dollars for gold only if they were presented by a foreign central bank. The United States continued the prohibition, first enacted in the early 1930s, against private citizens owning gold, except in the form of jewelry or rare coins. The prohibition was not lifted until the 1970s, when it again became possible for Americans to own gold as an investment.

Bretton Woods system An exchange rate system that lasted from 1944 to 1973, under which countries pledged to buy and sell their currencies at a fixed rate against the dollar.

Under the Bretton Woods system, central banks were committed to selling dollars in exchange for their own currencies. This commitment required them to hold *dollar reserves*. If a central bank ran out of dollar reserves, it could borrow them from the newly created **International Monetary Fund (IMF)**. In addition to providing loans to central banks that were short of dollar reserves, the IMF would oversee the operation of the system and approve adjustments to the agreed-on fixed exchange rates.

International Monetary Fund (IMF) An international organization that provides foreign currency loans to central banks and oversees the operation of the international monetary system.

Under the Bretton Woods system, a fixed exchange rate was called a *par exchange rate*. If the par exchange rate was not the same as the exchange rate that would have been determined in the market, the result would be a surplus or a shortage. For example, Figure 30A.1 shows the exchange rate between the dollar and the British pound. The figure is drawn from the British point of view, so we measure the exchange rate on the vertical axis as dollars per pound. In this case, the par exchange rate between the dollar and the pound is above the equilibrium exchange rate, as determined by demand and supply.

At the par exchange rate of $4 per pound, the quantity of pounds demanded by people who want to buy British goods and services or who want to invest in British assets is smaller than the quantity of pounds supplied by people who would like to exchange them for dollars. As a result, the Bank of England must use dollars to buy the surplus of £1 million per day. Only at an exchange rate of $2.80 per pound would the surplus be eliminated. If the par exchange rate was below the equilibrium exchange rate, there would be a shortage of domestic currency in the foreign exchange market.

A persistent shortage or surplus of a currency under the Bretton Woods system was seen as evidence of a *fundamental disequilibrium* in a country's exchange rate. After consulting with the IMF, countries in this position were allowed to adjust their exchange rates. In the early years of the Bretton Woods system, many countries found that their currencies were *overvalued* versus the dollar, meaning that their par exchange rates were too high. A reduction in a fixed exchange rate is a **devaluation**. An increase in a fixed exchange rate is a **revaluation**. In 1949, there was a devaluation of several currencies,

Devaluation A reduction in a fixed exchange rate.

Revaluation An increase in a fixed exchange rate.

MyEconLab Animation

Figure 30A.1

A Fixed Exchange Rate above Equilibrium Results in a Surplus of Pounds

Under the Bretton Woods system, if the par exchange rate was above equilibrium, the result would be a surplus of domestic currency in the foreign exchange market. If the par exchange rate was below equilibrium, the result would be a shortage of domestic currency. In the figure, the par exchange rate between the pound and the dollar is \$4 = £1, while the equilibrium exchange rate is \$2.80 = £1. This gap forces the Bank of England to buy £1 million per day in exchange for dollars.

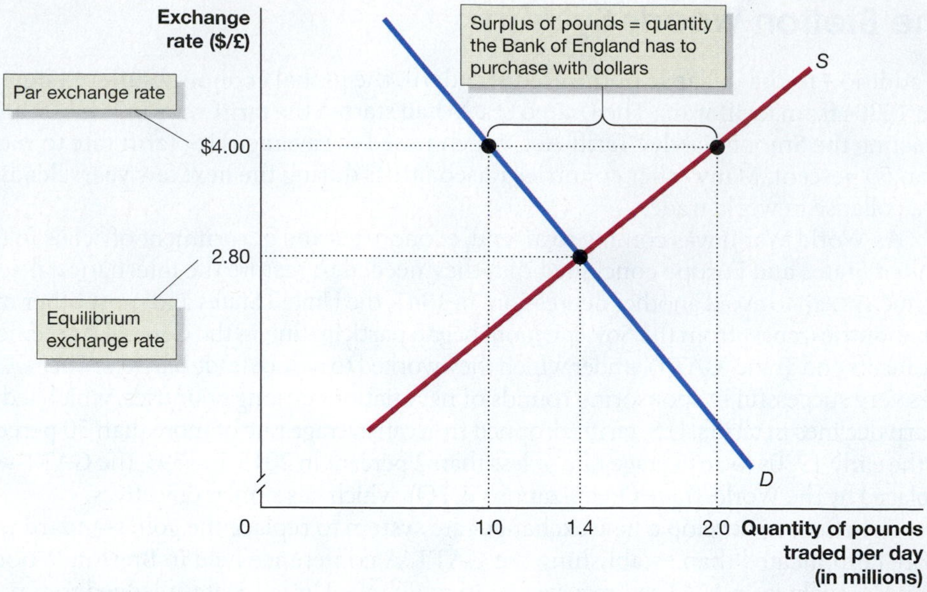

including the British pound, reflecting the fact that those currencies had been overvalued against the dollar. MyEconLab Concept Check

The Collapse of the Bretton Woods System

By the late 1960s, the Bretton Woods system faced two severe problems. The first was that after 1963, the total number of dollars held by foreign central banks was larger than the gold reserves of the United States. In practice, most central banks—with the Bank of France being the main exception—rarely redeemed dollars for gold. But the basis of the system was a credible promise by the United States to redeem dollars for gold if called upon to do so. By the late 1960s, as the gap between the dollars held by foreign central banks and the gold reserves of the United States grew larger and larger, other countries began to doubt the U.S. promise to redeem dollars for gold.

The second problem the Bretton Woods system faced was that some countries with undervalued currencies, particularly West Germany, were unwilling to revalue their currencies. Governments resisted revaluation because it would have increased the prices of their countries' exports. Many German firms put pressure on the government not to endanger their sales in the U.S. market by raising the exchange rate of the deutsche mark against the dollar. Figure 30A.2 shows the situation the German government faced in 1971. The figure takes the German point of view, so the exchange rate is expressed in terms of dollars per deutsche mark.

Under the Bretton Woods system, the Bundesbank, the German central bank, was required to buy and sell deutsche marks for dollars at a rate of \$0.27 per deutsche mark. The equilibrium that would have prevailed in the foreign exchange market if the Bundesbank had not intervened was about \$0.35 per deutsche mark. Because the par exchange rate was below the equilibrium exchange rate, the quantity of deutsche marks demanded by people wanting to buy German goods and services or wanting to invest in German assets was greater than the quantity of deutsche marks supplied by people who wanted to exchange them for dollars. To maintain the exchange rate at \$0.27 per deutsche mark, the Bundesbank had to buy dollars and sell deutsche marks. The number of deutsche marks supplied by the Bundesbank was equal to the shortage of deutsche marks at the par exchange rate.

By selling deutsche marks and buying dollars to defend the par exchange rate, the Bundesbank was increasing the West German money supply, risking an increase in the inflation rate. Because Germany had suffered a devastating hyperinflation during the 1920s, the fear of inflation was greater in Germany than in any other industrial country. No German government could survive politically if it allowed a significant increase in

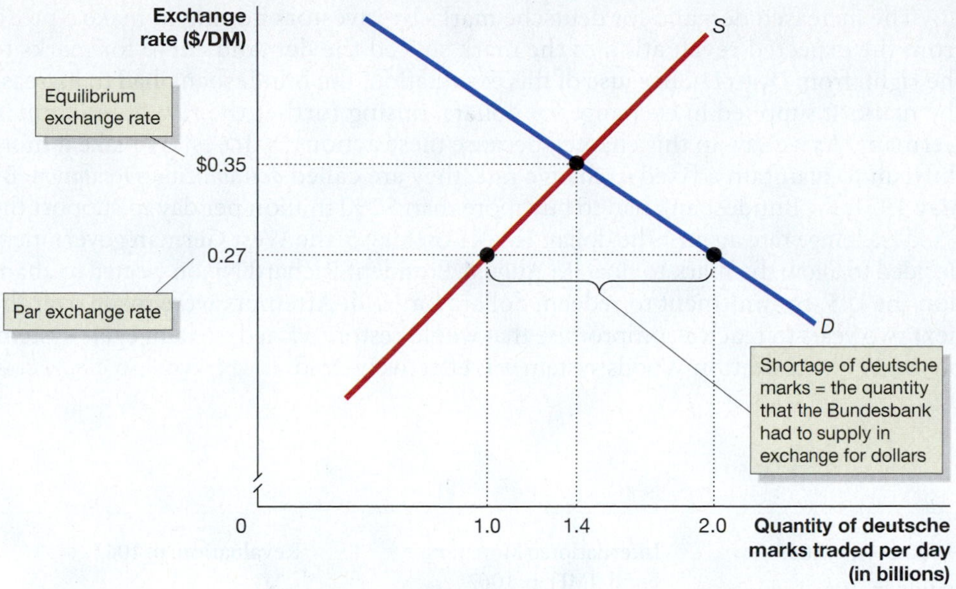

MyEconLab Animation

Figure 30A.2

West Germany's Undervalued Exchange Rate

The Bundesbank, the German central bank, was committed under the Bretton Woods system to defending a par exchange rate of $0.27 per deutsche mark (DM). Because this exchange rate was lower than what the equilibrium market exchange rate would have been, there was a shortage of DMs in the foreign exchange market. The Bundesbank had to supply DMs equal to the shortage in exchange for dollars. The shortage in the figure is equal to 1 billion DMs per day.

inflation. Knowing this fact, many investors in Germany and elsewhere became convinced that, eventually, the German government would have to allow a revaluation of the mark.

During the 1960s, most European countries, including Germany, relaxed their **capital controls**, which are limits on the flow of foreign exchange and financial investment across countries. The loosening of capital controls made it easier for investors to speculate on changes in exchange rates. For instance, an investor in the United States could sell $1 million and receive about 3.7 million deutsche marks at the par exchange rate of $0.27 per deutsche mark. If the exchange rate rose to $0.35 per deutsche mark, the investor could then exchange deutsche marks for dollars, receiving $1.3 million at the new exchange rate: a return of 30 percent on an initial $1 million investment. The more convinced investors became that Germany would have to allow a revaluation, the more dollars they exchanged for deutsche marks. Figure 30A.3 shows the results.

Capital controls Limits on the flow of foreign exchange and financial investment across countries.

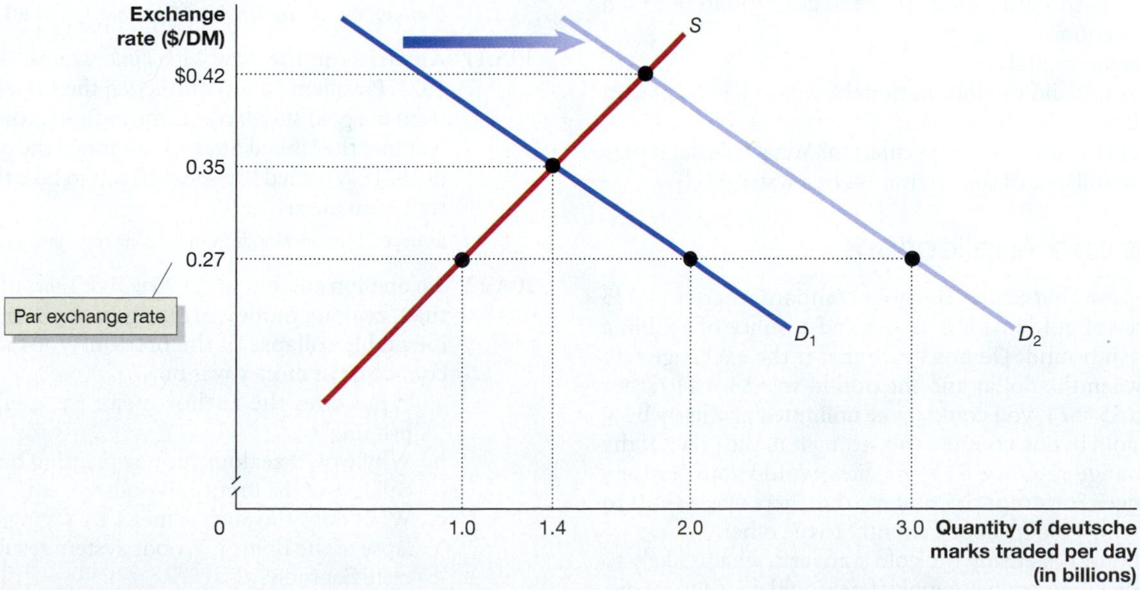

MyEconLab Animation

Figure 30A.3 Destabilizing Speculation against the Deutsche Mark, 1971

In 1971, the par exchange rate of $0.27 = 1 deutsche mark was below the equilibrium exchange rate of $0.35 = 1 deutsche mark. As investors became convinced that West Germany would have to revalue the deutsche mark, they increased their demand for marks, shifting the demand curve from D_1 to D_2. The new equilibrium exchange rate became $0.42 = 1 deutsche mark. This increase in demand raised the quantity of marks the Bundesbank had to supply in exchange for dollars to defend the par exchange rate from 1 billion deutsche marks to 2 billion deutsche marks per day.

The increased demand for deutsche marks by investors hoping to make a profit from the expected revaluation of the mark shifted the demand curve for marks to the right, from D_1 to D_2. Because of this expectation, the Bundesbank had to increase the marks it supplied in exchange for dollars, raising further the risk of inflation in Germany. As we saw in this chapter, because these actions by investors make it more difficult to maintain a fixed exchange rate, they are called *destabilizing speculation*. By May 1971, the Bundesbank had to buy more than $250 million per day to support the fixed exchange rate against the dollar. Finally, on May 5, the West German government decided to allow the mark to float. In August, President Richard Nixon elected to abandon the U.S. commitment to redeem dollars for gold. Attempts were made over the next two years to reach a compromise that would restore a fixed exchange rate system, but by 1973, the Bretton Woods system was effectively dead.

MyEconLab Study Plan

MyEconLab Concept Check

Key Terms

Bretton Woods system, p. 1067
Capital controls, p. 1069
Devaluation, p. 1067
International Monetary Fund (IMF), p. 1067
Revaluation, p. 1067

30.A The Gold Standard and the Bretton Woods System, pages 1066–1070

LEARNING OBJECTIVE: Explain the gold standard and the Bretton Woods system.

MyEconLab Visit **www.myeconlab.com** to complete these exercises online and get instant feedback.

Review Questions

30A.1 What determined the exchange rates among currencies under the gold standard? Why did the gold standard collapse?

30A.2 Briefly describe how the Bretton Woods system operated.

30A.3 What is the difference between a devaluation and a revaluation?

30A.4 What are capital controls?

30A.5 What role did the International Monetary Fund play in the Bretton Woods system?

30A.6 What is destabilizing speculation? What role did it play in the collapse of the Bretton Woods system?

Problems and Applications

30A.7 Suppose that under the gold standard, there was 1/5 ounce of gold in a U.S. dollar and 1 ounce of gold in a British pound. Demonstrate that if the exchange rate between the dollar and the pound was $4 = £1 rather than $5 = £1, you could make unlimited profits by buying gold in one country and selling it in the other. If the exchange rate was $6 = £1, how would your strategy change? For simplicity, assume that there was no cost to shipping gold from one country to the other.

30A.8 If a country is using the gold standard, what is likely to happen to its money supply if new gold deposits are discovered in the country, as happened in the United States with the gold discoveries in California in 1849? Is this change in the money supply desirable? Briefly explain.

30A.9 An article in the *Economist* observes, "When the Depression [of the 1930s] struck, this gold standard became a noose around the necks of struggling economies." In what sense was the gold standard a "noose around the necks of struggling economies" during the 1930s?

Source: "A Brief Post on Competitive Devaluation," *Economist*, October 31, 2011.

30A.10 An article in the *Economist* observed that there were "some perturbing parallels between the gold standard and the euro." What parallels are there between the gold standard and the euro? What would make these parallels perturbing?

Source: "Perturbing Parallels," *Economist*, July 5, 2013.

30A.11 An article in the *New York Times* states, "On Aug. 15, 1971, President Nixon unhitched the value of the dollar from the gold standard." Is the author of this article correct that the United States abandoned the gold standard in 1971? What led President Nixon to take the action described in the article?

Source: "Bretton Woods System" *New York Times*, August 20, 2015.

30A.12 An opinion column in the *New York Times* offers the view that "zealous money printing in the 1960s led to the inevitable collapse of the Bretton Woods system (and complete fiat money was born)."

a. What does the author mean by "zealous money printing"?
b. Why would zealous money printing have led to the collapse of the Bretton Woods system?
c. What does the author mean by saying that the collapse of the Bretton Woods system resulted in "complete fiat money"?

Source: Mark Spitznagel, "The Myth of Black Swan Market Events," *New York Times*, February 13, 2015.

30A.13 One economist has argued that the East Asian exchange rate crisis of the late 1990s was due to "the simple failure of governments to remember the lessons from the breakdown of the Bretton Woods System." What are these lessons? In what sense did the East Asian governments fail to learn these lessons?

Source: Thomas D. Willett, "Crying for Argentina," *Milken Institute Review*, Second Quarter 2002.

30A.14 Economists Michael Bordo of Rutgers University and Angela Redish of the University of British Columbia have argued that the "Bretton Woods system functioned for a number of years but beginning in the late 1960s, in the face of inflationary US monetary policy it became a slow moving train wreck." Why would inflationary U.S. monetary policy cause problems for the Bretton Woods system?

Source: Michael Bordo and Angela Redish, "Putting the 'System' in the International Monetary System," www.voxeu.org, June 20, 2013.

30A.15 An article in the *Economist* notes that after the end of the Bretton Woods system, "the Europeans did not like leaving their currencies to the whims of the markets." What does it mean for a country to leave its currency to the "whims of the markets"? What problems might a country experience as a result? What exchange rate system did most European countries ultimately adopt?

Source: "Forty Years On," *Economist*, August 13, 2011.

Real-Time Data Exercise

D30A.1 **(Gold prices and the gold standard)** Go to the Web site of the Federal Reserve Bank of St. Louis (FRED) (research.stlouisfed.org/fred2/) and find the Gold Fixing Price 10:30 A.M. (London time) in the London Bullion Market in U.S. Dollars (GOLDAMGBD228NLBM) from 1968 to the most recent available date.

a. What explains the relative stability of the price of gold from 1968 to 1971?

b. What implications do the movements in gold prices since 1971 have for an attempt by the United States and other countries to reestablish a gold standard?

GLOSSARY

A

Absolute advantage The ability of an individual, a firm, or a country to produce more of a good or service than competitors, using the same amount of resources.

Accounting profit A firm's net income, measured as revenue minus operating expenses and taxes paid.

Adverse selection The situation in which one party to a transaction takes advantage of knowing more than the other party to the transaction.

Aggregate demand (*AD*) curve A curve that shows the relationship between the price level and the level of planned aggregate expenditure in the economy, holding constant all other factors that affect aggregate expenditure.

Aggregate demand and aggregate supply model A model that explains short-run fluctuations in real GDP and the price level.

Aggregate expenditure (*AE*) Total spending in the economy: the sum of consumption, planned investment, government purchases, and net exports.

Aggregate expenditure model A macroeconomic model that focuses on the short-run relationship between total spending and real GDP, assuming that the price level is constant.

Allocative efficiency A state of the economy in which production is in accordance with consumer preferences; in particular, every good or service is produced up to the point where the last unit provides a marginal benefit to society equal to the marginal cost of producing it.

Antitrust laws Laws aimed at eliminating collusion and promoting competition among firms.

Arrow impossibility theorem A mathematical theorem that holds that no system of voting can be devised that will consistently represent the underlying preferences of voters.

Asset Anything of value owned by a person or a firm.

Asymmetric information A situation in which one party to an economic transaction has less information than the other party.

Autarky A situation in which a country does not trade with other countries.

Automatic stabilizers Government spending and taxes that automatically increase or decrease along with the business cycle.

Autonomous expenditure An expenditure that does not depend on the level of GDP.

Average fixed cost Fixed cost divided by the quantity of output produced.

Average product of labor The total output produced by a firm divided by the quantity of workers.

Average revenue (*AR*) Total revenue divided by the quantity of the product sold.

Average tax rate Total tax paid divided by total income.

Average total cost Total cost divided by the quantity of output produced.

Average variable cost Variable cost divided by the quantity of output produced.

B

Balance of payments The record of a country's trade with other countries in goods, services, and assets.

Balance of trade The difference between the value of the goods a country exports and the value of the goods a country imports.

Balance sheet A financial statement that sums up a firm's financial position on a particular day, usually the end of a quarter or year.

Bank panic A situation in which many banks experience runs at the same time.

Bank run A situation in which many depositors simultaneously decide to withdraw money from a bank.

Barrier to entry Anything that keeps new firms from entering an industry in which firms are earning economic profits.

Behavioral economics The study of situations in which people make choices that do not appear to be economically rational.

Black market A market in which buying and selling take place at prices that violate government price regulations.

Bond A financial security that represents a promise to repay a fixed amount of funds.

Brand management The actions of a firm intended to maintain the differentiation of a product over time.

Bretton Woods system An exchange rate system that lasted from 1944 to 1973, under which countries pledged to buy and sell their currencies at a fixed rate against the dollar.

Budget constraint The limited amount of income available to consumers to spend on goods and services.

Budget deficit The situation in which the government's expenditures are greater than its tax revenue.

Budget surplus The situation in which the government's expenditures are less than its tax revenue.

Business cycle Alternating periods of economic expansion and economic recession.

Business strategy Actions that a firm takes to achieve a goal, such as maximizing profits.

C

Capital account The part of the balance of payments that records relatively minor transactions, such as migrants' transfers and sales and purchases of nonproduced, nonfinancial assets.

Capital controls Limits on the flow of foreign exchange and financial investment across countries.

Capital Manufactured goods that are used to produce other goods and services.

Cartel A group of firms that collude by agreeing to restrict output to increase prices and profits.

Cash flow The difference between the cash revenues received by a firm and the cash spending by the firm.

Catch-up The prediction that the level of GDP per capita (or income per capita) in poor countries will grow faster than in rich countries.

Centrally planned economy An economy in which the government decides how economic resources will be allocated.

Ceteris paribus ("all else equal") condition The requirement that when analyzing the relationship between two variables—such as price and quantity demanded—other variables must be held constant.

Circular-flow diagram A model that illustrates how participants in markets are linked.

Closed economy An economy that has no interactions in trade or finance with other countries.

Coase theorem The argument of economist Ronald Coase that if transactions costs are low, private bargaining will result in an efficient solution to the problem of externalities.

Collusion An agreement among firms to charge the same price or otherwise not to compete.

Command-and-control approach A policy that involves the government imposing quantitative limits on the amount of pollution firms are allowed to emit or requiring firms to install specific pollution control devices.

Commodity money A good used as money that also has value independent of its use as money.

Common resource A good that is rival but not excludable.

Comparative advantage The ability of an individual, a firm, or a country to produce a good or service at a lower opportunity cost than competitors.

Compensating differentials Higher wages that compensate workers for unpleasant aspects of a job.

Competitive market equilibrium A market equilibrium with many buyers and sellers.

Complements Goods and services that are used together.

Constant returns to scale The situation in which a firm's long-run average costs remain unchanged as it increases output.

Consumer price index (CPI) A measure of the average change over time in the prices a typical urban family of four pays for the goods and services they purchase.

Consumer surplus The difference between the highest price a consumer is willing to pay for a good or service and the actual price the consumer pays.

Consumption Spending by households on goods and services, not including spending on new houses.

Consumption function The relationship between consumption spending and disposable income.

Contractionary monetary policy The Federal Reserve's policy of increasing interest rates to reduce inflation.

Cooperative equilibrium An equilibrium in a game in which players cooperate to increase their mutual payoff.

Copyright A government-granted exclusive right to produce and sell a creation.

Corporate governance The way in which a corporation is structured and the effect that structure has on the corporation's behavior.

Corporation A legal form of business that provides owners with protection from losing more than their investment should the business fail.

Coupon payment An interest payment on a bond.

Cross-price elasticity of demand The percentage change in the quantity demanded of one good divided by the percentage change in the price of another good.

Crowding out A decline in private expenditures as a result of an increase in government purchases.

Currency appreciation An increase in the market value of one currency relative to another currency.

Currency depreciation A decrease in the market value of one currency relative to another currency.

Current account The part of the balance of payments that records a country's net exports, net income on investments, and net transfers.

Cyclically adjusted budget deficit or surplus The deficit or surplus in the federal government's budget if the economy were at potential GDP.

Cyclical unemployment Unemployment caused by a business cycle recession.

D

Deadweight loss The reduction in economic surplus resulting from a market not being in competitive equilibrium.

Deflation A decline in the price level.

Demand curve A curve that shows the relationship between the price of a product and the quantity of the product demanded.

Demand schedule A table that shows the relationship between the price of a product and the quantity of the product demanded.

Demographics The characteristics of a population with respect to age, race, and gender.

Derived demand The demand for a factor of production; it depends on the demand for the good the factor produces.

Devaluation A reduction in a fixed exchange rate.

Direct finance A flow of funds from savers to firms through financial markets, such as the New York Stock Exchange.

Discount loans Loans the Federal Reserve makes to banks.

Discount rate The interest rate the Federal Reserve charges on discount loans.

Discouraged workers People who are available for work but have not looked for a job during the previous four weeks because they believe no jobs are available for them.

Diseconomies of scale The situation in which a firm's long-run average costs rise as the firm increases output.

Disinflation A significant reduction in the inflation rate.

Dividends Payments by a corporation to its shareholders.

Dominant strategy A strategy that is the best for a firm, no matter what strategies other firms use.

Dumping Selling a product for a price below its cost of production.

E

Economic discrimination The practice of paying a person a lower wage or excluding a person from an occupation on the basis of an irrelevant characteristic such as race or gender.

Economic efficiency A market outcome in which the marginal benefit to consumers of the last unit produced is equal to its marginal cost of production and in which the sum of consumer surplus and producer surplus is at a maximum.

Economic growth model A model that explains growth rates in real GDP per capita over the long run.

Economic growth The ability of an economy to produce increasing quantities of goods and services.

Economic loss The situation in which a firm's total revenue is less than its total cost, including all implicit costs.

Economic model A simplified version of reality used to analyze real-world economic situations.

Economic profit A firm's revenues minus all of its implicit and explicit costs.

Economic rent (or **pure rent**) The price of a factor of production that is in fixed supply.

Economics The study of the choices people make to attain their goals, given their scarce resources.

Economic surplus The sum of consumer surplus and producer surplus.

Economic variable Something measurable that can have different values, such as the incomes of doctors.

Economies of scale The situation when a firm's long-run average costs fall as it increases the quantity of output it produces.

Efficiency wage An above-market wage that a firm pays to increase workers' productivity.

Elastic demand Demand is elastic when the percentage

change in the quantity demanded is *greater* than the percentage change in price, so the price elasticity is *greater* than 1 in absolute value.

Elasticity A measure of how much one economic variable responds to changes in another economic variable.

Employed In government statistics, someone who currently has a job or who is temporarily away from his or her job.

Endowment effect The tendency of people to be unwilling to sell a good they already own even if they are offered a price that is greater than the price they would be willing to pay to buy the good if they didn't already own it.

Entrepreneur Someone who operates a business, bringing together the factors of production—labor, capital, and natural resources—to produce goods and services.

Equity The fair distribution of economic benefits.

Euro The common currency of many European countries.

Excess burden A measure of the efficiency loss to the economy that results from a tax having reduced the quantity of a good produced; also known as the deadweight loss.

Excess reserves Reserves that banks hold over the legal requirement.

Exchange rate system An agreement among countries about how exchange rates should be determined.

Excludability The situation in which anyone who does not pay for a good cannot consume it.

Expansionary monetary policy The Federal Reserve's policy of decreasing interest rates to increase real GDP.

Expansion The period of a business cycle during which total production and total employment are increasing.

Expansion path A curve that shows a firm's cost-minimizing combination of inputs for every level of output.

Explicit cost A cost that involves spending money.

Exports Goods and services produced domestically but sold in other countries.

External economies Reductions in a firm's costs that result from an increase in the size of an industry.

Externality A benefit or cost that affects someone who is not directly involved in the production or consumption of a good or service.

F

Factor market A market for the factors of production, such as labor, capital, natural resources, and entrepreneurial ability.

Factors of production Labor, capital, natural resources, and other inputs used to make goods and services.

Federal funds rate The interest rate banks charge each other for overnight loans.

Federal Open Market Committee (FOMC) The Federal Reserve committee responsible for open market operations and managing the money supply in the United States.

Federal Reserve The central bank of the United States.

Fee-for-service A system under which doctors and hospitals receive a payment for each service they provide.

Fiat money Money, such as paper currency, that is authorized by a central bank or governmental body and that does not have to be exchanged by the central bank for gold or some other commodity money.

Final good or service A good or service purchased by a final user.

Financial account The part of the balance of payments that records purchases of assets a country has made abroad and foreign purchases of assets in the country.

Financial intermediaries Firms, such as banks, mutual funds, pension funds, and insurance companies, that borrow funds from savers and lend them to borrowers.

Financial markets Markets where financial securities, such as stocks and bonds, are bought and sold.

Financial system The system of financial markets and financial intermediaries through which firms acquire funds from households.

Fiscal policy Changes in federal taxes and purchases that are intended to achieve macroeconomic policy goals.

Fiscal policy Changes in federal taxes and purchases that are intended to achieve macroeconomic policy objectives.

Fixed costs Costs that remain constant as output changes.

Fixed exchange rate system A system under which countries agree to keep the exchange rates among their currencies fixed for long periods.

Floating currency The outcome of a country allowing its currency's exchange rate to be determined by demand and supply.

Foreign direct investment (FDI) The purchase or building by a corporation of a facility in a foreign country.

Foreign portfolio investment The purchase by an individual or a firm of stocks or bonds issued in another country.

Fractional reserve banking system A banking system in which banks keep less than 100 percent of deposits as reserves.

Free market A market with few government restrictions on how a good or service can be produced or sold or on how a factor of production can be employed.

Free riding Benefiting from a good without paying for it.

Free trade Trade between countries that is without government restrictions.

Frictional unemployment Short-term unemployment that arises from the process of matching workers with jobs.

G

Game theory The study of how people make decisions in situations in which attaining their goals depends on their interactions with others; in economics, the study of the decisions of firms in industries where the profits of a firm depend on its interactions with other firms.

GDP deflator A measure of the price level, calculated by dividing nominal GDP by real GDP and multiplying by 100.

Globalization The process of countries becoming more open to foreign trade and investment.

Government purchases Spending by federal, state, and local governments on goods and services.

Gross domestic product (GDP) The market value of all final goods and services produced in a country during a period of time, typically one year.

H

Health care Goods and services, such as prescription drugs, consultations with a doctor, and surgeries, that are intended to maintain or improve a person's health.

Health insurance A contract under which a buyer agrees to make payments, or *premiums*, in exchange for the provider's agreeing to pay some or all of the buyer's medical bills.

Horizontal merger A merger between firms in the same industry.

Human capital The accumulated knowledge and skills that workers acquire from formal training and education or from life experiences.

I

Implicit cost A nonmonetary opportunity cost.

Imports Goods and services bought domestically but produced in other countries.

Income effect The change in the quantity demanded of a good that results from the effect of a change in price on consumer purchasing power, holding all other factors constant.

Income elasticity of demand A measure of the responsiveness of the quantity demanded to changes in income, measured by the percentage change in the quantity demanded divided by the percentage change in income.

Income statement A financial statement that shows a firm's revenues, costs, and profit over a period of time.

Indifference curve A curve that shows the combinations of consumption bundles that give the consumer the same utility.

Indirect finance A flow of funds from savers to borrowers through financial intermediaries such as banks. Intermediaries raise funds from savers to lend to firms (and other borrowers).

Industrial Revolution The application of mechanical power to the production of goods, beginning in England around 1750.

Inelastic demand Demand is inelastic when the percentage change in quantity demanded is *less* than the percentage change in price, so the price elasticity is *less* than 1 in absolute value.

Inferior good A good for which the demand increases as income falls and decreases as income rises.

Inflation rate The percentage increase in the price level from one year to the next.

Inflation targeting A framework for conducting monetary policy that involves the central bank announcing its target level of inflation.

Interest rate The cost of borrowing funds, usually expressed as a percentage of the amount borrowed.

Intermediate good or service A good or service that is an input into another good or service, such as a tire on a truck.

International Monetary Fund (IMF) An international organization that provides foreign currency loans to central banks and oversees the operation of the international monetary system.

Inventories Goods that have been produced but not yet sold.

Investment Spending by firms on new factories, office buildings, machinery, and additions to inventories, plus spending by households and firms on new houses.

Isocost line All the combinations of two inputs, such as capital and labor, that have the same total cost.

Isoquant A curve that shows all the combinations of two inputs, such as capital and labor, that will produce the same level of output.

K

Keynesian revolution The name given to the widespread acceptance during the 1930s and 1940s of John Maynard Keynes's macroeconomic model.

L

Labor force participation rate The percentage of the working-age population in the labor force.

Labor force The sum of employed and unemployed workers in the economy.

Labor productivity The quantity of goods and services that can be produced by one worker or by one hour of work.

Labor productivity The quantity of goods and services that can be produced by one worker or by one hour of work.

Labor union An organization of employees that has a legal right to bargain with employers about wages and working conditions.

Law of demand A rule that states that, holding everything else constant, when the price of a product falls, the quantity demanded of the product will increase, and when the price of a product rises, the quantity demanded of the product will decrease.

Law of diminishing marginal utility The principle that consumers experience diminishing additional satisfaction as they consume more of a good or service during a given period of time.

Law of diminishing returns The principle that, at some point, adding more of a variable input, such as labor, to the same amount of a fixed input, such as capital, will cause the marginal product of the variable input to decline.

Law of supply A rule that states that, holding everything else constant, increases in price cause increases in the quantity supplied, and decreases in price cause decreases in the quantity supplied.

Liability Anything owed by a person or a firm.

Limited liability A legal provision that shields owners of a corporation from losing more than they have invested in the firm.

Long-run aggregate supply (*LRAS*) curve A curve that shows the relationship in the long run between the price level and the quantity of real GDP supplied.

Long-run average cost curve A curve that shows the lowest cost at which a firm is able to produce a given quantity of output in the long run, when no inputs are fixed.

Long-run competitive equilibrium The situation in which the entry and exit of firms has resulted in the typical firm breaking even.

Long-run economic growth The process by which rising productivity increases the average standard of living.

Long-run supply curve A curve that shows the relationship in the long run between market price and the quantity supplied.

Long run The period of time in which a firm can vary all its inputs, adopt new technology, and increase or decrease the size of its physical plant.

Lorenz curve A curve that shows the distribution of income by arraying incomes from lowest to highest on the horizontal axis and indicating the cumulative fraction of income earned by each fraction of households on the vertical axis.

M

M1 The narrow definition of the money supply: the sum of currency in circulation, checking account deposits in banks, and holdings of traveler's checks.

M2 A broader definition of the money supply: It includes M1 plus savings account deposits, small-denomination time deposits, balances in money market deposit accounts in banks, and noninstitutional money market fund shares.

Macroeconomics The study of the economy as a whole, including topics such as inflation, unemployment, and economic growth.

Macroeconomics The study of the economy as a whole, including topics such as inflation, unemployment, and economic growth.

Managed float exchange rate system The current exchange rate system, under which the value of most currencies is determined by demand and supply, with occasional government intervention.

Marginal analysis Analysis that involves comparing marginal benefits and marginal costs.

Marginal benefit The additional benefit to a consumer from consuming one more unit of a good or service.

Marginal cost The additional cost to a firm of producing one more unit of a good or service.

Marginal productivity theory of income distribution The theory that the distribution of income is determined by the marginal productivity of the factors of production that individuals own.

Marginal product of labor The additional output a firm produces as a result of hiring one more worker.

Marginal propensity to consume (*MPC*) The slope of the consumption function: The amount by which consumption spending changes when disposable income changes.

Marginal propensity to save (*MPS*) The amount by which saving changes when disposable income changes.

Marginal rate of substitution (*MRS*) The rate at which a consumer would be willing to trade off one good for another.

Marginal rate of technical substitution (*MRTS*) The rate at which a firm is able to substitute one input for another while keeping the level of output constant.

Marginal revenue (*MR*) The change in total revenue from selling one more unit of a product.

Marginal revenue product of labor (*MRP*) The change in a firm's revenue as a result of hiring one more worker.

Marginal tax rate The fraction of each additional dollar of income that must be paid in taxes.

Marginal utility (*MU*) The change in total utility a person receives from consuming one additional unit of a good or service.

Market A group of buyers and sellers of a good or service and the institution or arrangement by which they come together to trade.

Market-based reforms Changes in the market for health care that would make it more like the markets for other goods and services.

Market demand The demand by all the consumers of a given good or service.

Market economy An economy in which the decisions of households and firms interacting in markets allocate economic resources.

Market equilibrium A situation in which quantity demanded equals quantity supplied.

Market failure A situation in which the market fails to produce the efficient level of output.

Market for loanable funds The interaction of borrowers and lenders that determines the market interest rate and the quantity of loanable funds exchanged.

Marketing All the activities necessary for a firm to sell a product to a consumer.

Market power The ability of a firm to charge a price greater than marginal cost.

Median voter theorem The proposition that the outcome of a majority vote is likely to represent the preferences of the voter who is in the political middle.

Menu costs The costs to firms of changing prices.

Microeconomics The study of how households and firms make choices, how they interact in markets, and how the government attempts to influence their choices.

Minimum efficient scale The level of output at which all economies of scale are exhausted.

Mixed economy An economy in which most economic decisions result from the interaction of buyers and sellers in markets but in which the government plays a significant role in the allocation of resources.

Monetarism The macroeconomic theories of Milton Friedman and his followers, particularly the idea that the quantity of money should be increased at a constant rate.

Monetary growth rule A plan for increasing the quantity of money at a fixed rate that does not respond to changes in economic conditions.

Monetary policy The actions the Federal Reserve takes to manage the money supply and interest rates to achieve macroeconomic policy goals.

Monetary policy The actions the Federal Reserve takes to manage the money supply and interest rates to pursue macroeconomic policy objectives.

Money Assets that people are generally willing to accept in exchange for goods and services or for payment of debts.

Monopolistic competition A market structure in which barriers to entry are low and many firms compete by selling similar, but not identical, products.

Monopoly A firm that is the only seller of a good or service that does not have a close substitute.

Monopsony The situation in which a firm is sole buyer of a factor of production.

Moral hazard The actions people take after they have entered into a transaction that make the other party to the transaction worse off.

Multiplier effect The process by which an increase in autonomous expenditure leads to a larger increase in real GDP.

Multiplier The increase in equilibrium real GDP divided by the increase in autonomous expenditure.

N

Nash equilibrium A situation in which each firm chooses the best strategy, given the strategies chosen by other firms.

Natural monopoly A situation in which economies of scale are so large that one firm can supply the entire market at a lower average total cost than can two or more firms.

Natural rate of unemployment The normal rate of unemployment, consisting of frictional unemployment and structural unemployment.

Net exports Exports minus imports.

Net foreign investment The difference between capital outflows from a country and capital inflows, also equal to net foreign direct investment plus net foreign portfolio investment.

Network externality A situation in which the usefulness of a product increases with the number of consumers who use it.

New classical macroeconomics The macroeconomic theories of Robert Lucas and others, particularly the idea that workers and firms have rational expectations.

New growth theory A model of long-run economic growth that emphasizes that technological change is influenced by economic incentives and so is determined by the working of the market system.

Nominal exchange rate The value of one country's currency in terms of another country's currency.

Nominal GDP The value of final goods and services evaluated at current-year prices.

Nominal interest rate The stated interest rate on a loan.

Nonaccelerating inflation rate of unemployment (NAIRU) The unemployment rate at which the inflation rate has no tendency to increase or decrease.

Noncooperative equilibrium An equilibrium in a game in which players do not cooperate but pursue their own self-interest.

Normal good A good for which the demand increases as income rises and decreases as income falls.

Normative analysis Analysis concerned with what ought to be.

O

Oligopoly A market structure in which a small number of interdependent firms compete.

Open economy An economy that has interactions in trade or finance with other countries.

Open market operations The buying and selling of Treasury securities by the Federal Reserve in order to control the money supply.

Opportunity cost The highest-valued alternative that must be given up to engage in an activity.

P

Partnership A firm owned jointly by two or more persons and not organized as a corporation.

Patent The exclusive right to a product for a period of 20 years from the date the patent application is filed with the government.

Patent The exclusive right to produce a product for a period of 20 years from the date the patent is applied for.

Patient Protection and Affordable Care Act (ACA) Health care reform legislation passed by Congress and signed by President Barack Obama in 2010.

Payoff matrix A table that shows the payoffs that each firm earns from every combination of strategies by the firms.

Pegging A policy by which a country keeps fixed the exchange rate between its currency and another country's currency.

Per-worker production function The relationship between real GDP per hour worked and capital per hour worked, holding the level of technology constant.

Perfectly competitive market A market that meets the conditions of having (1) many buyers and sellers, (2) all firms selling identical products, and (3) no barriers to new firms entering the market.

Perfectly elastic demand The case where the quantity demanded is infinitely responsive to price and the price elasticity of demand equals infinity.

Perfectly inelastic demand The case where the quantity demanded is completely unresponsive to price and the price elasticity of demand equals zero.

Personnel economics The application of economic analysis to human resources issues.

Phillips curve A graph showing the short-run relationship between the unemployment rate and the inflation rate.

Pigovian taxes and subsidies Government taxes and subsidies intended to bring about an efficient level of output in the presence of externalities.

Positive analysis Analysis concerned with what is.

Potential GDP The level of real GDP attained when all firms are producing at capacity.

Poverty line A level of annual income equal to three times the amount of money necessary to purchase the minimum quantity of food required for adequate nutrition.

Poverty rate The percentage of the population that is poor according to the federal government's definition.

Present value The value in today's dollars of funds to be paid or received in the future.

Price ceiling A legally determined maximum price that sellers may charge.

Price discrimination Charging different prices to different customers for the same product when the price differences are not due to differences in cost.

Price elasticity of demand The responsiveness of the quantity demanded to a change in price, measured by dividing the percentage change in the quantity demanded of a product by the percentage change in the product's price.

Price elasticity of supply The responsiveness of the quantity supplied to a change in price, measured by dividing the percentage change in the quantity supplied of a product by the percentage change in the product's price.

Price floor A legally determined minimum price that sellers may receive.

Price leadership A form of implicit collusion in which one firm in an oligopoly announces a price change and the other firms in the industry match the change.

Price level A measure of the average prices of goods and services in the economy.

Price taker A buyer or seller that is unable to affect the market price.

Principal–agent problem A problem caused by agents pursuing their own interests rather than the interests of the principals who hired them.

Prisoner's dilemma A game in which pursuing dominant strategies results in noncooperation that leaves everyone worse off.

Private benefit The benefit received by the consumer of a good or service.

Private cost The cost borne by the producer of a good or service.

Private good A good that is both rival and excludable.

Producer price index (PPI) An average of the prices received by producers of goods and services at all stages of the production process.

Producer surplus The difference between the lowest price a firm would be willing to accept for a good or service and the price it actually receives.

Production function The relationship between the inputs employed by a firm and the maximum output it can produce with those inputs.

Production possibilities frontier (*PPF*) A curve showing the maximum attainable combinations of two goods that can be produced with available resources and current technology.

Productive efficiency A situation in which a good or service is produced at the lowest possible cost.

Product market A market for goods—such as computers—or services—such as medical treatment.

Productive efficiency The situation in which a good or service is produced at the lowest possible cost.

Profit Total revenue minus total cost.

Progressive tax A tax for which people with lower incomes pay a lower percentage of their income in tax than do people with higher incomes.

Property rights The rights individuals or firms have to the exclusive use of their property, including the right to buy or sell it.

Protectionism The use of trade barriers to shield domestic firms from foreign competition.

Public choice model A model that applies economic analysis to government decision making.

Public franchise A government designation that a firm is the only legal provider of a good or service.

Public good A good that is both nonrival and nonexcludable.

Purchasing power parity The theory that in the long run exchange rates move to equalize the purchasing powers of different currencies.

Q

Quantity demanded The amount of a good or service that a consumer is willing and able to purchase at a given price.

Quantity supplied The amount of a good or service that a firm is willing and able to supply at a given price.

Quantity theory of money A theory about the connection between money and prices that assumes that the velocity of money is constant.

Quota A numerical limit a government imposes on the quantity of a good that can be imported into the country.

R

Rational expectations Expectations formed by using all available information about an economic variable.

Real business cycle model A macroeconomic model that focuses on real, rather than monetary, causes of the business cycle.

Real business cycle models Models that focus on real rather than monetary explanations of fluctuations in real GDP.

Real exchange rate The price of domestic goods in terms of foreign goods.

Real GDP The value of final goods and services evaluated at base-year prices.

Real interest rate The nominal interest rate minus the inflation rate.

Recession The period of a business cycle during which total production and total employment are decreasing.

Regressive tax A tax for which people with lower incomes pay a higher percentage of their income in tax than do people with higher incomes.

Rent seeking Attempts by individuals and firms to use government action to make themselves better off at the expense of others.

Required reserve ratio The minimum fraction of deposits banks are required by law to keep as reserves.

Required reserves Reserves that a bank is legally required to hold, based on its checking account deposits.

Reserves Deposits that a bank keeps as cash in its vault or on deposit with the Federal Reserve.

Revaluation An increase in a fixed exchange rate.

Rivalry The situation that occurs when one person's consumption of a unit of a good means no one else can consume it.

Rule of law The ability of a government to enforce the laws of the country, particularly with respect to protecting private property and enforcing contracts.

S

Saving and investment equation An equation that shows that national saving is equal to domestic investment plus net foreign investment.

Scarcity A situation in which unlimited wants exceed the limited resources available to fulfill those wants.

Securitization The process of transforming loans or other financial assets into securities.

Security A financial asset—such as a stock or a bond—that can be bought and sold in a financial market.

Separation of ownership from control A situation in which the top management, rather than the shareholders, controls day-to-day operations.

Short-run aggregate supply (*SRAS*) curve A curve that shows the relationship in the short run between the price level and the quantity of real GDP supplied by firms.

Shortage A situation in which the quantity demanded is greater than the quantity supplied.

Short run The period of time during which at least one of a firm's inputs is fixed.

Shutdown point The minimum point on a firm's average variable cost curve; if the price falls below this point, the firm shuts down production in the short run.

Simple deposit multiplier The ratio of the amount of deposits created by banks to the amount of new reserves.

Single-payer health care system A system, such as the one in Canada, in which the government provides health insurance to all of the country's residents.

Social benefit The total benefit from consuming a good or service, including both the private benefit and any external benefit.

Social cost The total cost of producing a good or service, including both the private cost and any external cost.

Socialized medicine A health care system under which the government owns most of the hospitals and employs most of the doctors.

Sole proprietorship A firm owned by a single individual and not organized as a corporation.

Speculators Currency traders who buy and sell foreign exchange in an attempt to profit from changes in exchange rates.

Stagflation A combination of inflation and recession, usually resulting from a supply shock.

Stock A financial security that represents partial ownership of a firm.

Stockholders' equity The difference between the value of a corporation's assets and the value of its liabilities; also known as *net worth*.

Structural relationship A relationship that depends on the basic behavior of consumers and firms and that remains unchanged over long periods.

Structural unemployment Unemployment that arises from a persistent mismatch between the skills or attributes of workers and the requirements of jobs.

Substitutes Goods and services that can be used for the same purpose.

Substitution effect The change in the quantity demanded of a good that results from a change in price making the good more or less expensive relative to other goods, holding constant the effect of the price change on consumer purchasing power.

Sunk cost A cost that has already been paid and cannot be recovered.

Supply curve A curve that shows the relationship between the price of a product and the quantity of the product supplied.

Supply schedule A table that shows the relationship between the price of a product and the quantity of the product supplied.

Supply shock An unexpected event that causes the short-run aggregate supply curve to shift.

Surplus A situation in which the quantity supplied is greater than the quantity demanded.

T

Tariff A tax imposed by a government on imports.

Tax incidence The actual division of the burden of a tax between buyers and sellers in a market.

Tax wedge The difference between the pretax and posttax return to an economic activity.

Taylor rule A rule developed by John Taylor that links the Fed's target for the federal funds rate to economic variables.

Technological change A change in the ability of a firm to produce a given level of output with a given quantity of inputs.

Technological change A positive or negative change in the ability of a firm to produce a given level of output with a given quantity of inputs.

Technology The processes a firm uses to turn inputs into outputs of goods and services.

Terms of trade The ratio at which a country can trade its exports for imports from other countries.

Too-big-to-fail policy A policy under which the federal government does not allow large financial firms to fail, for fear of damaging the financial system.

Total cost The cost of all the inputs a firm uses in production.

Total revenue The total amount of funds a seller receives from selling a good or service, calculated by multiplying price per unit by the number of units sold.

Trade The act of buying and selling.

Trade-off The idea that, because of scarcity, producing more of one good or service means producing less of another good or service.

Tragedy of the commons The tendency for a common resource to be overused.

Transactions costs The costs in time and other resources that parties incur in the process of agreeing to and carrying out an exchange of goods or services.

Transactions costs The costs in time and other resources that parties incur in the process of agreeing to and carrying out an exchange of goods or services.

Transfer payments Payments by the government to households for which the government does not receive a new good or service in return.

Two-part tariff A situation in which consumers pay one price (or tariff) for the right to buy as much of a related good as they want at a second price.

U

Underground economy Buying and selling of goods and services that is concealed from the government to avoid taxes or regulations or because the goods and services are illegal.

Unemployed In government statistics, someone who is not currently at work but who is available for work and who has actively looked for work during the previous month.

Unemployment rate The percentage of the labor force that is unemployed.

Unit-elastic demand Demand is unit elastic when the percentage change in quantity demanded is *equal to* the percentage change in price, so the price elasticity is equal to 1 in absolute value.

Utility The enjoyment or satisfaction people receive from consuming goods and services.

V

Value added The market value a firm adds to a product.

Variable costs Costs that change as output changes.

Velocity of money The average number of times each dollar in the money supply is used to purchase goods and services included in GDP.

Vertical merger A merger between firms at different stages of production of a good.

Voluntary exchange A situation that occurs in markets when both the buyer and the seller of a product are made better off by the transaction.

Voluntary export restraint (VER) An agreement negotiated between two countries that places a numerical limit on the quantity of a good that can be imported by one country from the other country.

Voting paradox The failure of majority voting to always result in consistent choices.

W

Wall Street Reform and Consumer Protection Act (Dodd-Frank Act) Legislation passed during 2010 that was intended to reform regulation of the financial system.

World Trade Organization (WTO) An international organization that oversees international trade agreements.

COMPANY INDEX

SUBJECT INDEX

Key terms and the page on which they are defined appear in **boldface**.

CREDITS

Photo

Front matter, *page vii(t),* Courtesy of Glenn Hubbard; page *vii(b),* Courtesy of Tony O'Brien

Chapter 1, *page 2,* Phanie/Alamy Stock Photo; *page 9,* Chris Grosser/Southcreek Global/ZUMApress.com/Alamy Stock Photo; *page 16,* Paul Bradbur/Caiaimage/OJO+/Getty Images

Chapter 2, *page 40,* Michael Short/Bloomberg/Getty Images; *page 53,* Rolf Bruderer/Glow Images; *page 55B,* Mikael Damkier/Shutterstock; *page 55L,* Elena Elisseeva/Shutterstock; *page 55R,* Stockbroker/MBI/Alamy Stock Photo; *page 55T,* JupiterImages/Getty Images; *page 58,* Qilai Shen/Bloomberg/Getty Images; *page 61,* Photos 12/Alamy Stock Photo

Chapter 3, *page 72,* Xinhua/Alamy Stock Photo; *page 77,* Maxim Shemetov/Reuters; *page 78,* Tim Boyle/Getty Images; *page 81,* Peter Horree/Alamy Stock Photo

Chapter 4, *page 108,* Symphonie/The Image Bank/Getty Images; *page 124,* Silke Woweries/Corbis

Chapter 5, *page 146,* De Visu/Shutterstock; *page 157,* Jason Hetherington/The Image Bank/Getty Images

Chapter 6, *page 182,* Bloomberg/Getty Images; *page 197,* Oleksiy Maksymenko Photography/Alamy Stock Photo

Chapter 7, *page 216,* Bill Aron/PhotoEdit, Inc.

Chapter 8, *page 250,* Anil Kumar/Alamy Stock Photo; *page 261,* Wang Lei/CHINE NOUVELLE/SIPA/Newscom

Chapter 9, *page 284,* Pablo Martinez Monsivais/AP Images; *page 288,* Boston Globe/Getty Images; *page 302,* i4images rm/Alamy Stock Photo; *page 307,* Lucenet Patrice/Oredia/Alamy Stock Photo

Chapter 10, *page 318,* Mark Lennihan/AP Images; *page 330,* Giles Angel/Alamy Stock Photo; *page 336,* photopitu/Fotolia; *page 339,* Jay Paul/The New York Times/Redux Pictures; *page 341,* Bebeto Matthews/AP Images

Chapter 11, *page 364,* Thomas Imo/Alamy Stock Photo; *page 366,* BRIAN KERSEY/UPI/Newscom; *page 368,* Damon Higgins/Corbis; *page 373,* Ria Novosti/Alamy Stock Photo; *page 383,* CSU Archives/Everett Collection Inc/Alamy Stock Photo; *page 400,* Mark LoMoglio/Icon Sportswire CCX/Newscom

Chapter 12, *page 406,* Alan Hopps/Moment Open/Getty Images; *page 429,* Alex Segre/Alamy Stock Photo

Chapter 13, *page 442,* Glen Martin/Getty Images; *page 452,* Craig Warga/Bloomberg/Getty Images; *page 457,* Fred Prouser/Reuters; *page 459,* studiomode/Alamy Stock Photo

Chapter 14, *page 470,* Felix Choo/Alamy Stock Photo; *page 475,* Mel Evans/AP Images; *page 481,* Alamy; *page 490,* Damian Dovarganes/AP Images

Chapter 15, *page 498,* Katja Heinemann/Robert Harding World Imagery; *page 501,* Robert Willett/Raleigh News & Observer/TNS/Tribune Content Agency LLC/Alamy Stock Photo; *page 503,* John Mutrux/MCT/Newscom; *page 505,* Gregory Wrona/Alamy Stock Photo; *page 516,* Pixellover RM 9/Alamy Stock Photo

Chapter 16, *page 530,* Charles Ridgway/Alamy Stock Photo; *page 539,* M. Timothy O'Keefe/Alamy Stock Photo

Chapter 17, *page 556,* Amy Coopes/AFP/Getty Images; *page 571,* Rob Carmell/CSM/Newscom; *page 576,* Ronnie Kaufman/Larry Hirshowitz/Blend Images/Alamy Stock Photo; *page 580,* Peathegee Inc/Blend Images/Getty Images

Chapter 18, *page 594,* Daniel Acker/Bloomberg/Getty Images; *page 609,* Amy Sussman/Corbis

Chapter 19, *page 630,* Regina H. Boone/Detroit Free Press/TNS/Tribune Content Agency LLC/Alamy Stock Photo; *page 635B,* Mikael Damkier/Shutterstock; *page 635C,* Yoshio Tomii/SuperStock; *page 635L,* Eric Gevaert/Shutterstock; *page 635R,* Bill Aron/PhotoEdit, Inc.; *page 635T,* JupiterImages/Getty Images; *page 639,* Herve Coste/MAXPPP/Newscom; *page 641,* Nureldin Abdallah Mohamed/Reuters

Chapter 20, *page 656,* Eduardo Munoz/Reuters; *page 669,* Andrew Burton/Reuters/Landov

Chapter 21, *page 694,* Steve Marcus/Reuters/Landov; *page 709,* Everett Collection; *page 715,* Bradley C. Bower/Bloomberg/Getty Images

Chapter 22, *page 730,* Sollina Images/Blend Images/Getty Images; *page 733,* Franck Iren/Author's Image Ltd/Alamy Stock Photo; *page 736,* Grant Neuenburg/Corbis; *page 740,* Peter Turnley/Corbis; *page 757,* Claro Cortes IV/Corbis

Chapter 23, *page 770,* Hon Siu Keung/EyePress/Newscom; *page 788,* Kin Cheung/AP Images; *page 799,* Everett Collection/SuperStock

Chapter 24, *page 814,* Steve Allen/Allen Creative/Alamy Stock Photo; *page 832,* Kimberly White/Corbis; *page 853,* Lebrecht Music and Arts Photo Library/Alamy Stock Photo

Chapter 25, *page 856,* Laurence Geai/SIPA/Newscom; *page 861,* Bloomberg/Getty Images; *page 864,* Bloomberg/Getty Images; *page 867,* Air Images/Shutterstock; *page 879,* Lynne Sladky/AP Images; *page 879,* Ezio Petersen/UPI/Landov; *page 879,* Eightfish/Alamy; *page 879,* Dietmar Plewka/imagebroker/Alamy; *page 884,* Bettmann/Corbis

Chapter 26, *page 894,* PHILIPPE DESMAZES/AFP/Getty Images; *page 926,* Rebecca Cook/Reuters/Corbis

Chapter 27, *page 938,* Bob Kreisel/Alamy Stock Photo; *page 954,* Richard Drew/AP Images; *page 962,* Bao Dandan/Xinhua/Alamy Stock Photo; *page 965,* AP Images

Chapter 28, *page 984,* Bloomberg/Getty Images; *page 990,* Paul Bradbury/OJO+/ Getty Images; *page 994,* Lynne Sladky/AP Images; *page 1005,* Ron Sachs/ZUMA Press/Newscom

Chapter 29, *page 1016,* Du Gang/ ZUMA Press/Newscom

Chapter 30, *page 1044,* Kristoffer Tripplaar/Alamy Stock Photo; *page 1049,* Bloomberg/Getty Images

Text

Chapter 1 *page 22,* John Hechinger, "FBI Presses Banks to Boost Security as Robberies Rise," *Wall Street Journal,* October 8, 2002.

page 27, © 2011 City Maps Inc.

Chapter 5 *page 151,* Ronald H. Coase, "The Problem of Social Cost," *Journal of Law and Economics,* Vol. 3, October, 1960, pp. 1–44.

Chapter 6 *page 192,* Table 6.2, *"Estimated Real-World Price Elasticities of Demand,"* Kelly D. Brownell and Thomas R. Frieden, "Ounces of Prevention—The Public Policy Case for Taxes on Sugared Beverages," *New England Journal of Medicine,* April 30, 2009; Sheila M. Olmstead and Robert N. Stavins, "Comparing Price and Non-Price Approaches to Urban Water Conservation," Resources for the Future, Discussion paper 08-22, June 2008; Jonathan E. Hughes, Christopher R. Knittel, and Daniel Sperling, "Evidence of a Shift in the Short-Run Price Elasticity of Gasoline Demand," *Energy Journal,* Vol. 29, No. 1, January 2008; Robert P. Trost, Frederick Joutz, David Shin, and Bruce McDonwell, "Using Shrinkage Estimators to Obtain Regional Short-Run and Long-Run Price Elasticities of Residential Natural Gas Demand in the U.S.," George Washington University Working Paper, March 13, 2009; Lesley Chiou, "Empirical Analysis of Competition between Wal-Mart and Other Retail Channels," *Journal of Economics and Management Strategy,* Vol. 18, No. 2, Summer 2009; Judith Chevalier and Austan Goolsbee, "Price Competition Online: Amazon versus Barnes and Noble," *Quantitative Marketing and Economics,* Vol. 1, No. 2, June 2003; Henry Saffer and Frank Chaloupka, "The Demand for Illicit Drugs," *Economic Inquiry,* Vol. 37, No. 3, July 1999; "Response to Increases in Cigarette Prices by Race/ Ethnicity, Income, and Age Groups—United States, 1976–1993," *Morbidity and Mortality Weekly Report,* July 31, 1998; James Wetzel and George Hoffer, "Consumer Demand for Automobiles: A Disaggregated Market Approach," *Journal of Consumer Research,* Vol. 9, No. 2, September 1982; Jerry A. Hausman, "The Price Elasticity of Demand for Breakfast Cereal," in Timothy F. Bresnahan and Robert J. Gordon, eds., *The Economics of New Goods,* Chicago: University of Chicago Press, 1997; Christopher J. Ruhm, et al., "What U.S. Data Should Be Used to Measure the Price Elasticity of Demand for Alcohol," *Journal of Health Economics,* Vol. 31, No. 16, December 2012; Susan Dynarski, Jonathan Gruber, and Danielle Li, "Cheaper By the Dozen: Using Sibling Discounts at Catholic Schools to Estimate the Price Elasticity of Private School Attendance," NBER Working Paper 15461, October 2009; and U.S. Department of Agriculture, Economic Research Service.

Chapter 8 *pages 267–268,* Michael Lewis, "The End," *Portfolio,* December 2008.

Chapter 10 *page 334,* Steffen Andersen, et al., "Stakes Matter in Ultimatum Game," *American Economic Review,* Vol. 101, No. 7, December 2011, pp. 3427–3439.

page 335, Gary Becker and Kevin M. Murphy, *Social Economics,* Cambridge: Harvard University Press, 2000, p. 9.

Chapter 12 *page 427,* Sharon M. Oster, *Modern Competitive Analysis,* Third Edition, New York: Oxford University Press, 1999.

Chapter 13 *page 457,* Peter F. Drucker, *Management: Tasks, Responsibilities, Practices,* New York: Harper & Row, 1974, pages 63–64.

Chapter 15 *page 514,* Joseph Schumpeter, *Capitalism, Socialism, and Democracy,* New York: Harper and Row, 1942, p. 84.

page 519, U.S. Department of Justice, *Horizontal Merger Guidelines Issued by the U.S. Department of Justice and the Federal Trade Commission, April 8, 1997,* updated June 25, 2015.

Chapter 18 *page 618,* Jeremy Greenwood, Nezih Guner, Georgi Kocharkov, and Cezar Santos, "Marry Your Like: Assortative Mating and Income Inequality," *American Economic Review,* Vol. 104, No. 5, May 2014, pp. 348–53.

Chapter 19 *page 632,* Christina Rogers, "Ford Trims Production in China on Select Models to Avoid Price Cuts," *Wall Street Journal,* May 21, 2015.

Chapter 21 *page 702,* Richard Sylla, "Financial Systems and Economic Modernization," *Journal of Economic History,* Vol. 62. No. 2, June 2002.

Chapter 22 *pages 743–744,* Joseph Schumpeter, *Socialism, and Democracy,* New York: Harper, 1962 (originally published 1942), p. 13.

page 746, Robert J. Gordon, "Is U.S. Economic Growth Over? Innovation Confronts Six Headwinds," NBER Working Paper 18315, August 2012.

page 757, Edward Glaeser and Claudia Goldin, eds., *Corruption and Reform: Lessons from America's History,* Chicago, IL: University of Chicago Press, 2006.

Chapter 28 *pages 988–989,* Milton Friedman, "The Role of Monetary Policy," *American Economic Review,* Vol. 58, No. 1, March 1968, 1–17.